Financial
Reporting
Handbook
2013

Financial Reporting Handbook 2013

Incorporating all the Standards
as at 1 December 2012

Technical Editor
Claire Locke

ISBN 1-11845-234

Published in Australia by John Wiley & Sons Australia, Ltd, Milton, Queensland 4064

Typeset and edited by Institute of Chartered Accountants Australia, Sydney, New South Wales 2000
Proofreaders: Lee Regidor, Steven Schwarz
Desktop Publishers: Steven Schwarz, Claire Schwarz
Project Manager: Claire Schwarz
Publications Team Leader: Samantha Skinner

Printed in Australia by Ligare Book Printer, Riverwood, Sydney 2012

Foreword

The *Financial Reporting Handbook 2013* from the Institute of Chartered Accountants Australia (the Institute) is an essential reference tool designed to meet the demands of today's dynamic economic environment.

Developed for Chartered Accountants, accountancy students and other professionals in Australian business, the handbook is an essential guide to Australian Accounting Standards.

The handbook comprises the Australian Accounting Standards and Interpretations issued by the Australian Accounting Standards Board (AASB) applicable at 30 June 2013 as issued up to 1 December 2012, together with the professional and ethical Standards most relevant to financial reporting.

This edition will provide you with all the new, amended and compiled Standards and Interpretations applicable for the 2013 reporting season, as well as commentary on the Standards and the future of financial reporting, including the AASB's Reduced Disclosure Regime. Also included in this edition are the new Standards applicable from 2013 – AASB 10 *Consolidated Financial Statements*, AASB 11 *Joint Arrangements*, AASB 12 *Disclosure of Interests in Other Entities*, AASB 13 *Fair Value Measurement* and AASB 119 *Employee Benefits*, and AASB 9 *Financial Instruments* applicable from 1 January 2015.

A companion volume to this handbook is the Institute's *Auditing, Assurance and Ethics Handbook 2013*, bringing together all of the new and revised Australian Auditing Standards in Clarity format, Guidance Statements and professional and ethical Standards issued as at 1 December 2012.

Together, these handbooks are part of the suite of products and services available to Institute members and the student and business community.

I am confident you will find the *Financial Reporting Handbook 2013* a valuable addition to your reference material.

Tim Gullifer FCA
President
Institute of Chartered Accountants Australia
1 January 2013

About the Technical Editor

Claire Locke, BA(Hons) (Dunelm), FCA is a member of the Leadership and Quality team at the Institute of Chartered Accountants Australia, and a sessional lecturer in the Masters of Accounting program at Macquarie University, specialising in financial reporting. Additionally, Claire presents seminars on financial reporting issues to a range of accounting firms throughout Australia. Claire's background is in the audit and training divisions of accounting firms in Australia and the United Kingdom.

Contents

About the Technical Editor   vi

About the Institute of Chartered Accountants Australia   xii

Introduction   xiii

Reduced Disclosure Regime   xvi

Statements of Accounting Concepts

SAC 1   Definition of the Reporting Entity   1

SAC 2   Objective of General Purpose Financial Reporting   10

Accounting Standards (AASBs)

Framework for the Preparation and Presentation of Financial Statements   19

AASB 1   First-time Adoption of Australian Accounting Standards   40

AASB 2   Share-based Payment   69

AASB 3   Business Combinations   119

AASB 4   Insurance Contracts   158

AASB 5   Non-current Assets Held for Sale and Discontinued Operations   180

AASB 6   Exploration for and Evaluation of Mineral Resources   198

AASB 7   Financial Instruments: Disclosures   209

AASB 8   Operating Segments   246

AASB 9   Financial Instruments   259

AASB 10   Consolidated Financial Statements   309

AASB 11   Joint Arrangements   340

AASB 12   Disclosure of Interests in Other Entities   364

AASB 13   Fair Value Measurement   380

AASB 101   Presentation of Financial Statements   412

AASB 102   Inventories   444

AASB 107   Statement of Cash Flows   459

AASB 108   Accounting Policies, Changes in Accounting Estimates and Errors   481

AASB 110   Events after the Reporting Period   495

AASB 111   Construction Contracts   504

AASB 112   Income Taxes   516

AASB 116   Property, Plant and Equipment   561

AASB 117   Leases   581

AASB 118   Revenue   598

AASB 119   Employee Benefits (Compiled November 2010:
                 applicable 30 June 2013)   616

AASB 119   Employee Benefits (Revised September 2011:
                 applicable to periods beginning from 1 January 2013)   664

AASB 120   Accounting for Government Grants and Disclosure
                 of Government Assistance   698

AASB 121   The Effects of Changes in Foreign Exchange Rates   708

AASB 123   Borrowing Costs   725

AASB 124   Related Party Disclosures   734

Accounting Standards (AASBs) *(cont.)*

AASB 127	Consolidated and Separate Financial Statements (Compiled September 2011: applicable 30 June 2013)	754
AASB 127	Separate Financial Statements (Revised August 2011: applicable to periods beginning from 1 January 2013)	776
AASB 128	Investments in Associates (Compiled September 2011: applicable 30 June 2013)	783
AASB 128	Investments in Associates and Joint Ventures (Revised August 2011: applicable to periods beginning from 1 January 2013)	797
AASB 129	Financial Reporting in Hyperinflationary Economies	808
AASB 131	Interests in Joint Ventures	818
AASB 132	Financial Instruments: Presentation	833
AASB 133	Earnings per Share	885
AASB 134	Interim Financial Reporting	923
AASB 136	Impairment of Assets	947
AASB 137	Provisions, Contingent Liabilities and Contingent Assets	1005
AASB 138	Intangible Assets	1030
AASB 139	Financial Instruments: Recognition and Measurement	1059
AASB 140	Investment Property	1145
AASB 141	Agriculture	1164
AASB 1004	Contributions	1177
AASB 1023	General Insurance Contracts	1202
AASB 1031	Materiality	1238
AASB 1038	Life Insurance Contracts	1244
AASB 1039	Concise Financial Reports	1278
AASB 1048	Interpretation of Standards	1285
AASB 1049	Whole of Government and General Government Sector Financial Reporting	1294
AASB 1050	Administered Items	1370
AASB 1051	Land Under Roads	1381
AASB 1052	Disaggregated Disclosures	1392
AASB 1053	Application of Tiers of Australian Accounting Standards	1402
AASB 1054	Australian Additional Disclosures	1428
AASB 2010-2	Amendments to Australian Accounting Standards arising from Reduced Disclosure Requirements	1436
AASB 2010-7	Amendments to Australian Accounting Standards arising from AASB 9 (December 2010) [AASB 1, 3, 4, 5, 7, 101, 102, 108, 112, 118, 120, 121, 127, 128, 131, 132, 136, 137, 139, 1023 & 1038 and Interpretations 2, 5, 10, 12, 19 & 127]	1460
AASB 2011-2	Amendments to Australian Accounting Standards arising from the Trans-Tasman Convergence Project – Reduced Disclosure Requirements [AASB 101 & AASB 1054]	1498
AASB 2011-4	Amendments to Australian Accounting Standards to Remove Individual Key Management Personnel Disclosure Requirements [AASB 124]	1502

Contents

Accounting Standards (AASBs) *(cont.)*

AASB 2011-6 Amendments to Australian Accounting Standards
– Extending Relief from Consolidation, the Equity Method
and Proportionate Consolidation – Reduced Disclosure
Requirements [AASB 127, AASB 128 & AASB 131] 1507

AASB 2011-7 Amendments to Australian Accounting Standards
arising from the Consolidation and Joint Arrangements Standards
[AASB 1, 2, 3, 5, 7, 101, 107, 112, 118, 121, 124, 132, 133, 136,
138, 139, 1023 & 1038 and Interpretations 5, 9, 16 & 17] 1516

AASB 2011-8 Amendments to Australian Accounting Standards
arising from AASB 13 [AASB 1, 2, 3, 4, 5, 7, 9, 101, 102, 108,
110, 116, 117, 118, 119, 120, 121, 128, 131, 132, 133, 134, 136,
138, 139, 140, 141, 1004, 1023 & 1038 and Interpretations 2, 4,
12, 13, 14, 17, 19, 131 & 132] 1536

AASB 2011-10 Amendments to Australian Accounting Standards
arising from AASB 119 (September 2011) [AASB 1, AASB 8,
AASB 101, AASB 124, AASB 134, AASB 1049
& AASB 2011-8, and Interpretation 14] 1569

AASB 2011-11 Amendments to AASB 119 (September 2011)
arising from Reduced Disclosure Requirements 1579

AASB 2011-12 Amendments to Australian Accounting Standards
arising from Interpretation 20 1583

AASB 2012-1 Amendments to Australian Accounting Standards
– Fair Value Measurement – Reduced Disclosure Requirements
[AASB 3, AASB 7, AASB 13, AASB 140 and AASB 141] 1586

AASB 2012-2 Amendments to Australian Accounting Standards
– Disclosures – Offsetting Financial Assets and Financial
Liabilities [AASB 7 and AASB 132] 1590

AASB 2012-3 Amendments to Australian Accounting Standards
– Offsetting Financial Assets and Financial Liabilities [AASB 132] 1597

AASB 2012-4 Amendments to Australian Accounting Standards
– Government Loans [AASB 1] 1602

AASB 2012-5 Amendments to Australian Accounting Standards
arising from Annual Improvements 2009 – 2011 Cycle
[AASB 1, AASB 101, AASB 116, AASB 132 & AASB 134
and Interpretation 2] 1606

AASB 2012-7 Amendments to Australian Accounting Standards
arising from Reduced Disclosure Requirements
[AASB 7, AASB 12, AASB 101 and AASB 127] 1615

Accounting Standards (AAS)

AAS 25 Financial Reporting by Superannuation Plans 1620

Interpretations

Interpretation 1 Changes in Existing Decommissioning, Restoration
and Similar Liabilities 1662

Interpretation 2 Members' Shares in Co-operative Entities and Similar Instruments 1675

Interpretation 4 Determining whether an Arrangement contains a Lease 1688

Interpretation 5 Rights to Interests arising from Decommissioning, Restoration
and Environmental Rehabilitation Funds 1704

Interpretations *(cont.)*

Interpretation 6	Liabilities arising from Participating in a Specific Market – Waste Electrical and Electronic Equipment	1714
Interpretation 7	Applying the Restatement Approach under AASB 129 Financial Reporting in Hyperinflationary Economies	1720
Interpretation 9	Reassessment of Embedded Derivatives	1732
Interpretation 10	Interim Financial Reporting and Impairment	1741
Interpretation 12	Service Concession Arrangements	1746
Interpretation 13	Customer Loyalty Programmes	1778
Interpretation 14	AASB 119 – The Limit on a Defined Benefit Asset, Minimum Funding Requirements and their Interaction	1789
Interpretation 15	Agreements for the Construction of Real Estate	1806
Interpretation 16	Hedges of a Net Investment in a Foreign Operation	1822
Interpretation 17	Distributions of Non-cash Assets to Owners	1840
Interpretation 18	Transfers of Assets from Customers	1855
Interpretation 19	Extinguishing Financial Liabilities with Equity Instruments	1866
Interpretation 20	Stripping Costs in the Production Phase of a Surface Mine	1875
Interpretation 107	Introduction of the Euro	1884
Interpretation 110	Government Assistance – No Specific Relation to Operating Activities	1888
Interpretation 112	Consolidation – Special Purpose Entities	1891
Interpretation 113	Jointly Controlled Entities – Non-Monetary Contributions by Venturers	1897
Interpretation 115	Operating Leases – Incentives	1901
Interpretation 125	Income Taxes – Changes in the Tax Status of an Entity or its Shareholders	1905
Interpretation 127	Evaluating the Substance of Transactions Involving the Legal Form of a Lease	1908
Interpretation 129	Service Concession Arrangements: Disclosures	1916
Interpretation 131	Revenue – Barter Transactions Involving Advertising Services	1920
Interpretation 132	Intangible Assets – Web Site Costs	1924
Interpretation 1003	Australian Petroleum Resource Rent Tax	1931
Interpretation 1019	The Superannuation Contributions Surcharge	1936
Interpretation 1030	Depreciation of Long-Lived Physical Assets: Condition-Based Depreciation and Related Methods	1940
Interpretation 1031	Accounting for the Goods and Services Tax (GST)	1945
Interpretation 1038	Contributions by Owners Made to Wholly-Owned Public Sector Entities	1949
Interpretation 1039	Substantive Enactment of Major Tax Bills in Australia	1961
Interpretation 1042	Subscriber Acquisition Costs in the Telecommunications Industry	1965
Interpretation 1047	Professional Indemnity Claims Liabilities in Medical Defence Organisations	1971
Interpretation 1052	Tax Consolidation Accounting	1978
Interpretation 1055	Accounting for Road Earthworks	2000

Contents

Professional Standards

APES 110	Code of Ethics for Professional Accountants	2005
APES 205	Conformity with Accounting Standards	2102
APES 315	Compilation of Financial Information	2107

Material for Members of the Institute of Chartered Accountants Australia

This section has been removed from and can be accessed from the online *Members' handbook* at charteredaccountants.com.au/Members/Members-Handbook.

About the Institute of Chartered Accountants Australia

The Institute is the professional body for Chartered Accountants in Australia and members operating throughout the world.

Representing more than 70,000 current and future professionals and business leaders, the Institute has a pivotal role in upholding financial integrity in society. Members strive to uphold the profession's commitment to ethics and quality in everything they do, alongside an unwavering dedication to act in the public interest.

Chartered Accountants hold diverse positions across the business community, as well as in professional services, government, not-for-profit, education and academia. The leadership and business acumen of members underpin the Institute's deep knowledge base in a broad range of policy areas impacting the Australian economy and domestic and international capital markets.

The Institute of Chartered Accountants Australia was established by Royal Charter in 1928 and today has around 60,000 members and more than 12,000 talented graduates working and undertaking the Chartered Accountants Program.

The Institute is a founding member of the Global Accounting Alliance (GAA), which is an international coalition of accounting bodies and an 800,000-strong network of professionals and leaders worldwide.

charteredaccountants.com.au

For Institute enquiries

National Customer Service Centre
Ph: 1300 137 322 within Australia
         +61 2 9290 5660 if overseas
Fax: +61 2 9262 4841
Email: service@charteredaccountants.com.au

Operating Hours
8:30am – 6.00pm AEST/AEDST
Monday to Friday (excluding national public holidays)

Introduction

What are Accounting Standards?

Accounting Standards are the 'rules of the road' that govern the way in which financial statements are prepared, with the objective of achieving relevant, reliable and comparable financial statements.

How are Accounting Standards established?

Accounting Standards in Australia are referred to as AASB Standards (AASBs) made by the Australian Accounting Standards Board. With the globalisation of business a driving factor, the Board makes Standards by adopting the content and wording of the International Financial Reporting Standards (IFRS) as set by the International Accounting Standards Board (IASB) in London. IFRSs are amended only to add any Australian legislative requirements or specific requirements for not-for-profit accounting issues, before being issued as AASBs.

What about US adoption of IFRS?

Together with the US Financial Accounting Standards Board (FASB), the IASB has been working towards the convergence of the IASB and FASB Accounting Standards. This program took a major step forward in November 2007, with the announcement by the US Securities and Exchange Commission (SEC) of the removal for non-US companies reporting under IFRS of the requirement to reconcile their financial statements to US GAAP. Even more promising was the issue in November 2008 of the SEC's proposed 'Roadmap' detailing the milestones on the way to the adoption of IFRSs by all US companies. Although the SEC had been expected to make a final decision on adoption by 2011, no decision has yet been made and is now not anticipated in the near future. In July 2012 the SEC's final staff report on IFRSs was issued, summarising the workplan for US incorporation of IFRS into the financial reporting system for US issuers. However, this report did not confirm when, or in fact whether, the US would adopt IFRS.

What are the changes for 2013?

Although many Accounting Standards have changed for 30 June 2013 the impact is relatively minor, reflecting the period of stability we are currently enjoying before the significant changes of 2013–2015.

*   The presentation and disclosure of the statement of profit and loss and other comprehensive income is amended in AASB 101 and throughout the Accounting Standards. Entities are now required to group items presented in other comprehensive income (OCI) on the basis of whether they are potentially reclassifiable to profit and loss or not. Entities are also required to show tax associated with items presented before tax separately for each of these two groups of OCI items.

*   Whole of government reporting (AASB 1049) has been amended in relation to the ABS GFS Manual. There are additional changes resulting from minor improvements to AASB 1049.

*   AASB 112 *Income taxes* now contains a rebuttable presumption that recovery of the carrying amount of an investment property measured at fair value will be through sale. This amendment also incorporates into AASB 112 the requirements of Interpretation 121 *Income Taxes – Recovery of Revalued Non-Depreciable Assets*; consequently the AASB has withdrawn Interpretation 121.

What are the major changes in the foreseeable future?

As an outcome of the convergence project, we are facing a suite of new Standards, revising the treatment of group accounting, a revised AASB 9 *Financial Instruments* covering both financial assets and financial liabilities, and a new Standard, clarifying the definition of fair value. Although these Standards are not applicable until 2013–2015, they are available for early adoption now. In any event, entities will need to disclose the impact of these changes in their financial statement note on Standards issued but not yet adopted. These new Standards and other significant upcoming changes are explained below.

- Wholesale revision to accounting for financial instruments is a step closer, with a revised AASB 9 *Financial Instruments* (December 2010) incorporating revised requirements for the classification and measurement of financial assets and financial liabilities. Mandatory application of this Standard has been delayed to 2015 from its original application date of 2013.

- A suite of Standards (AASBs 10, 11, 12, 127, 128 and 2011-7) revising accounting requirements for consolidation, joint ventures and off balance sheet arrangements is applicable from 1 January 2013, with early adoption permitted by for-profit entities, provided the whole suite of Standards is adopted at the same time. Significant changes include a new definition of 'control' that will expand the number and type of entities that are consolidated, a redefinition of which entities qualify as joint ventures and the removal of the option to account for joint ventures using proportional consolidation.

- Fair value guidance is now included in a single Standard AASB 13 *Fair Value Measurement*, defining fair value and providing guidance on how to determine and disclose fair value measurements from 1 January 2013. AASB 13 does not change the requirements regarding which items should be measured or disclosed at fair value.

- The 'corridor method' of deferring gains and losses when accounting for defined benefit plans has been eliminated from AASB 119 *Employee Benefits* from 1 January 2013. Instead, all actuarial gains and losses are to be included immediately in other comprehensive income.

Another noteworthy change is the removal from AASB 1024 of individual key management personnel disclosure requirements. These disclosures were required by the Australian-specific paragraphs applying to disclosing entities and have been removed from AASB 124 from 1 July 2013. Additionally, offsetting financial asset and financial liabilities requirements have been amended in AASB 7 (1 July 2013) and AASB 132 (1 July 2014).

Important information on compilations

The AASB is now issuing amendments to Standards by means of amending Standards, and periodically issuing compiled versions of the Standards incorporating amendments to date.

30 June 2013 year ends

The Standards in this handbook reflect the Standards and Interpretations as compiled and issued by the AASB as at 1 December 2012 and mandatorily applicable for 30 June 2013 year ends. Entities early-adopting any amendments with later application dates will need to refer to the amending Standards not yet compiled (included in this handbook for your convenience).

Also included in this handbook is the suite of Standards revising the treatment of group accounting, revised AASB 9, AASB 13, AASB 119 and AASB 1053. Although these Standards are not applicable until 2013–2015, they are available for early adoption now.

Alternative year ends

Financial reporting is currently undergoing a period of change with multiple amendments to Accounting Standards and Interpretations – these amendments have a variety of application dates. As a result, the version of a Standard that was applicable for the 30 June 2012 year end may be different to that applicable for the 31 December 2012 year end, and different again to the version printed in this handbook, being the version mandatorily applicable for 30 June 2013.

To assist you to identify the correct version for your reporting period, in this handbook the commentary from the Institute at the front of each individual Standard lists all amendments to that Standard and highlights any amendments yet to be compiled into the Standard.

To access the compiled version of a Standard or Interpretation applicable for year ends other than 30 June 2013, refer to the Institute's web-based handbook at charteredaccountants.com.au (login required) or the AASB website at www.aasb.gov.au. The AASB has a search tool to assist you to identify the correct version of a Standard or an Interpretation for a particular reporting period.

Claire Locke, FCA
Technical Specialist
Institute of Chartered Accountants Australia

Kerry Hicks, FCA
Head of Reporting
Institute of Chartered Accountants Australia

December 2012

Reduced Disclosure Regime

The AASB in June 2010 issued its Accounting Standards implementing the reduced disclosure regime (RDR). The Standards apply to reporting periods beginning on or after 1 July 2013, with early adoption permitted from 30 June 2010.

Under these Standards, Tier 1 (publicly accountable entities), apply full IFRS as adopted in Australia. All other preparers of general purpose financial statements fall into Tier 2 and are able to apply IFRS recognition, measurement and presentation requirements with substantially reduced disclosures. The AASB has left the reporting entity regime unchanged at this point so non-reporting entities can continue to prepare special purpose financial statements.

The two new RDR Standards are:

- AASB 1053 *Application of Tiers of Australian Accounting Standards*
- AASB 2010-2 *Amendment to Australian Accounting Standards arising from Reduced Disclosure Requirements*

AASB 1053 implements the two-tier arrangements, while AASB 2010-2 makes amendments to many of the existing AASB Standards and Interpretations to introduce the RDR requirements into these pronouncements. Since these Standards were issued, a number of other amending Standards have been issued to apply RDR requirements to amended or new accounting Standards, such as the group accounting suite of Standards.

The use of RDR contained in AASB 1053 is an option for Tier 2 entities producing general purpose reports, and it must be applied in its entirety. Tier 2 entities are all those reporting entities that are not publicly accountable. Public accountability refers to entities which trade securities in a public market or hold assets in a fiduciary capacity. Typical 'non-publicly accountable' entities likely to benefit from the RDR include:

- unlisted public companies
- not-for-profit private sector entities
- public sector entities other than federal, state, territory and local governments.

Tier 2 entities that take advantage of RDR are required to follow the same recognition and measurement requirements as under the full suite of IFRS/AASB Standards; the major saving is in halving the number of disclosures. This reduction in disclosures means Tier 2 entities will not be able to claim IFRS compliance, and instead will make a statement of compliance with RDR. Another important consideration for entities adopting RDR is that the requirement to prepare true and fair financial statements remains. Entities will need to consider whether they need to present additional disclosures above and beyond those required by RDR.

The AASB's review of special purpose financial statements (SPFSs) is now at Stage 2 of the differential reporting project. The AASB had proposed requiring all entities whose accounts are publicly available and/or comply with Australian Accounting Standards to prepare general purpose financial statements, effectively removing the ability of these entities to prepare SPFSs. The AASB is now conducting further research into the potential impact of this proposal.

Most significantly reduced under RDR are the disclosures resulting from the following Accounting Standards:

AASB 3 *Business Combinations*

Disclosures no longer required include information about the nature and effect of business combinations during the year.

AASB 7 *Financial Instruments: Disclosures*

For most Tier 2 entities, this will be the area of the most significant reduction in disclosures. Reduced AASB 7 disclosures include:

- detailed disclosure of financial assets and liabilities at fair value through profit and loss are no longer required
- simplified collateral disclosures
- simplified disclosure of defaults and breaches

- significantly reduced fair value disclosures
- removal of the requirement to disclose the nature and extent of risks which included qualitative and quantitative disclosures relating to credit risk, liquidity risk and market risk, including sensitivity analysis.

AASB 101 *Presentation of Financial Statements*

Reductions in disclosures required include:

- removal of the requirement for a third statement of financial position requirements where there is a retrospective accounting policy change or restatement
- removal of capital management disclosures
- removal of the requirement to disclose the amount of income tax relating to each component of other comprehensive income
- removal of details about franking and franking credits, and about commitments
- removal of details about capital and other commitments, including lease commitments
- removal of details of audit and non fees and other auditor details
- the statement of IFRS compliance has been replaced with an RDR compliance statement.

AASB 107 *Statement of Cash Flows*

Disclosures no longer required under RDR include:

- a reconciliation of cash flows arising from operating activities to profit or loss for entities that use the direct method to present cash flows from operating activities
- information relating to cash flows on obtaining and losing control of subsidiaries.

AASB 108 *Accounting Policies, Changes in Accounting Estimates and Errors*

The disclosures relating to new or amended Accounting Standards issued but not yet applied are not required under RDR.

AASB 111 *Construction Contracts*

The disclosures relating to contracts in progress at the end of the reporting period are reduced under RDR.

AASB 123 *Borrowing Costs*

Disclosure of the capitalisation rate(s) on borrowing costs capitalised are not required.

AASB 124 *Related Party Disclosures*

Disclosures reduced or no longer required under RDR include:

- information about parent entities incorporated outside Australia
- detailed disclosures about key management personnel remuneration.

AASB 127 *Consolidated and Separate Financial Statements*

Disclosure of significant investments is no longer required under RDR.

AASB 128 *Investments in Associates*

The summarised financial information about associates has been eliminated.

AASB 136 *Impairment of Assets*

Most of the detailed disclosures relating to impairment of assets are not required under RDR.

RDR suite of Standards

The AASB has launched a special section of the its website to act as a portal for updates regarding all aspects of RDR, including compiled RDR versions Standards for early adopters.

At the time of printing (December 2012) the AASB has not yet released the RDR versions of Standards applicable for 30 June 2013 year ends. We anticipate these Standards will be available on the AASB website March/April 2013.

In this handbook you will find AASB 1053, implementing the two-tier arrangement, and the Standards introducing the RDR requirements throughout the Standards: AASB 2010-2, AASB 2011-2, AASB 2011-6, AASB 2011-11, AASB 2012-1 and AASB 2012-7.

SAC 1
Definition of the Reporting Entity

(August 1990)

Prepared by the Public Sector Accounting Standards Board of the Australian Accounting Research Foundation and by the Accounting Standards Review Board.

Issued by the Australian Accounting Research Foundation on behalf of the Australian Society of Certified Practising Accountants and The Institute of Chartered Accountants in Australia and by the Accounting Standards Review Board.

Note from the Institute of Chartered Accountants Australia

This note, prepared by the technical editors, is not part of Statement of Accounting Concepts SAC 1.

Historical development

August 1990: SAC 1 'Definition of the Reporting Entity' was issued by the Australian Accounting Research Foundation (AARF).

November 1990: SAC 1, together with SACs 2, 3 and 4 was made mandatory for the members of the Australian accounting professional bodies (the Institute of Chartered Accountants Australia and CPA Australia) by virtue of the jointly issued Miscellaneous Professional Statement APS 1 'Conformity with Statements of Accounting Concepts and Accounting Standards'.

July 1993: The Australian professional bodies announced that the mandatory status of the Statements of Accounting Concepts including SAC 1 would be withdrawn from APS 1. The revised APS 1 'Conformity with Accounting Standards' was issued in December 2003. Since that time the role of SAC 1 has been as a source of guidance in respect of the meaning and characteristics of a reporting entity.

2005: SAC 1 continues as part of Australian GAAP for 2005 onward because the IASB conceptual document and its Australian equivalents (the IASB Framework and the AASB Framework) provide limited guidance in respect of the reporting entity concept.

Note: Proposed changes to the financial reporting regime will substantially change the application of the reporting entity concept. Until, or if, these proposals are adopted the reporting entity concept remains applicable.

Contents

Paragraphs

Citation   1

Application and Operative Date   2

Introduction   3–5

Definitions   6

Discussion

General Purpose Financial Reporting   7–9

The Reporting Entity Concept   10–18

Identification of Whether Dependent Users Exist   19

     Separation of management from economic interest   20

     Economic or political importance/influence   21

     Financial characteristics   22

Implications of Application of the Reporting Entity Concept

     Implications of the criterion for identification of a reporting entity   23–28

     Groups of entities as reporting entities   29–32

     Implications of the reporting entity concept for current practice   33

Implications of the Reporting Entity Concept for Differential Reporting   34–37

Accounting Concepts

Discussion and Definitions   38–39

Concept of the Reporting Entity   40

     Preparation of general purpose financial reports   41

Citation

1   This Statement may be cited as Statement of Accounting Concepts SAC 1 'Definition of the Reporting Entity'.

Application and Operative Date

2   This Statement applies to each reporting entity in relation to its first reporting period that ends on or after 31 August 1990, and in relation to subsequent reporting periods.

Introduction

3   The purpose of this Statement is to define and explain the concept of a reporting entity and to establish a benchmark for the minimum required quality of financial reporting for such an entity.[1] This Statement outlines the circumstances in which an entity or economic entity should be identified as a reporting entity. It also outlines the criterion for determining, for financial reporting purposes, the boundaries of a reporting entity.

4   In relation to the benchmark for the minimum required quality of financial reporting, this Statement specifies that reporting entities shall prepare general purpose financial reports and that these are reports which comply with Statements of Accounting Concepts and Accounting Standards.

5   This Statement does not consider techniques of accounting for and the method of presentation of financial information about a reporting entity. Such considerations are included in Accounting Standards.

---

1   In the Discussion section of this Statement, the term 'entity' should be read as referring also to an economic entity, except where the narrower meaning of the term is specified.

Definitions

6   For the purposes of this Statement:

'**control**' means the capacity of an entity to dominate decision-making, directly or indirectly, in relation to the financial and operating policies of another entity so as to enable that other entity to operate with it in achieving the objectives of the controlling entity;

'**economic entity**' means a group of entities comprising a controlling entity and one or more controlled entities operating together to achieve objectives consistent with those of the controlling entity;

'**entity**' means any legal, administrative, or fiduciary arrangement, organisational structure or other party (including a person) having the capacity to deploy scarce resources in order to achieve objectives; and

'**general purpose financial report**' means a financial report intended to meet the information needs common to users who are unable to command the preparation of reports tailored so as to satisfy, specifically, all of their information needs.

Discussion

General Purpose Financial Reporting

7   Statement of Accounting Concepts SAC 2 'Objective of General Purpose Financial Reporting' states that general purpose financial reports are prepared to provide users with information about the reporting entity which is useful for making and evaluating decisions about the allocation of scarce resources (hereinafter 'resources'). When general purpose financial reports meet this objective they will also be a means by which managements and governing bodies discharge their accountability to those users. If Statements of Accounting Concepts and Accounting Standards are to be effective in ensuring adequate disclosure of information to users of general purpose financial reports, it is necessary that all those entities which should report, do report. In addition, if the regulation of general purpose financial reporting is to be developed on a rational and efficient basis, it is equally important that those entities for which there is no justification to report are not required to report.

8   Financial reports which meet the objective of general purpose financial reporting are general purpose financial reports. General purpose financial reports should be prepared when there exists, in relation to an entity, users whose information needs have common elements, and those users cannot command the preparation of information to satisfy their individual information needs. Such reports will provide users with appropriate information for making decisions relating to the efficient allocation of resources.

9   Efficient allocation of resources is facilitated by ensuring that general purpose financial reports contain information of at least the minimum required quality. Accordingly, general purpose financial reports should be prepared in accordance with Statements of Accounting Concepts and Accounting Standards.

The Reporting Entity Concept

10   A number of alternative concepts of the reporting entity are implicit in existing legislation and regulations which specify the entities which should prepare general purpose financial reports. These concepts include the legal entity concept, which has been employed in legislation in the private sector, and a broad concept based on accountability of elected representatives and appointed officials, which has been employed in the public sector. In the private sector it has been common for entities to be required to report whenever they have had legal status (for example, companies have been so obliged). In the public sector the accent on accountability has seen widespread application of the fund concept of reporting, which implies a concern with reporting the results of individual funds. In other cases, the concept based on accountability of elected representatives and appointed officials has led to entities which have such representatives and/or officials preparing general purpose financial reports.

11   The concepts referred to in paragraph 10 do not give adequate consideration to user needs in identifying the reporting entity. In the private sector it is possible that users exist in respect of reporting entities which are not legal entities and for which legislation requiring the preparation of general purpose financial reports does not exist, for example, partnerships, most trusts, and associations. Similarly, in the public sector it is possible that users exist in respect of entities other than the fund or the electoral entity, for example, in respect of individual statutory authorities, departments and governments. If accounting concepts, developed within a framework which identifies users' information needs as primary, are to satisfy the objective of general purpose financial reporting, those concepts must be related to users' information needs.

12   This Statement adopts a concept of the reporting entity which is tied to the information needs of users and the nature of general purpose financial reports. The concept requires that individual reporting entities be identified by reference to the existence of users who are dependent on general purpose financial reports for information for making and evaluating resource allocation decisions. This means that a class of entity defined under another concept, such as the legal or fund concepts (for example, proprietary companies or special and general purpose funds), may include some entities which should be identified as reporting entities, by virtue of the existence of users dependent on general purpose financial reports prepared by the entity, and other entities which should not be so identified.

13   It should therefore be noted that the concept of the reporting entity adopted by this Statement is not dependent on the sector – public or private – within which the entity operates, the purpose for which the entity was created – business or non-business/profit or not-for-profit – or the manner in which the entity is constituted – legal or other. It is a concept which is tied to the objective of general purpose financial reporting and, as noted in paragraph 12, is a concept which requires all entities with users dependent on general purpose financial reports for information to prepare such reports.

14   The concept of the reporting entity and the identification of the boundaries of a reporting entity are related. For example:

   (a)   if the concept of the reporting entity adopted was based on a class of legal entity (such as a company), this would imply identification of the boundaries of the entity by reference to legal considerations, which would mean that only entities of that legal class could be aggregated to form a reporting entity; and

   (b)   if the fund concept of the reporting entity was adopted, this would imply identification of the boundaries of the reporting entity by reference to the functional uses for which resources were designated and deployed. This would (unless more than one concept of the reporting entity was adopted) render illogical and inoperative the concept of aggregating separate funds to recognise the existence of a reporting entity.

15   However, the concept of the reporting entity established by this Statement is one linked to the information needs of users of general purpose financial reports in making and evaluating resource allocation decisions. The provision of information for these purposes is the criterion used to determine the boundaries of a particular reporting entity.

16   The disclosure of the resources that an entity has the capacity to deploy, and the results of their deployment, will assist users to determine the performance and financial position of the entity. Such information will assist users in making resource allocation decisions and is necessary for the evaluation of past decisions. For these purposes, information about all resources able to be deployed by a reporting entity is relevant, whatever the legal or administrative structure established to manage those resources. Thus, where an entity controls other entities, there should be disclosed information regarding the resources of controlled entities as well as the resources of the controlling entity because all of these resources may be deployed by the controlling entity for its own advantage.

17   Accordingly, while in some instances a reporting entity will comprise an individual entity, in other instances a reporting entity will comprise a group of entities, some of which individually may be reporting entities. One of the entities within the group will control the other entities so that they operate together to achieve objectives consistent with those

of the controlling entity. The group, which may be termed an economic entity, will be a reporting entity where there exist users dependent on general purpose financial reports for making and evaluating resource allocation decisions regarding the collective operation of the group of entities. Whether one entity has the capacity to control other entities, and therefore whether an economic entity exists, will depend on an evaluation of the circumstances of the particular entities. In determining whether control exists, the factors to be considered include the following: extent and implications of financial dependence, capacity to appoint or remove managements or governing bodies, and power to direct operations.

18 For the purposes of this Statement, an individual would normally constitute an entity as defined in paragraph 6. However, it should be noted that individuals with the capacity to deploy resources, but not in order to achieve their own objectives, will not meet the definition of an economic entity, for example: a trustee whose relationship with a trust does not extend beyond the normal responsibilities of a trustee, and a liquidator of an entity.

Identification of Whether Dependent Users Exist

19 For the purposes of this Statement, the identification of an entity as a reporting entity is linked to the information needs of users of general purpose financial reports. In many instances, it will be readily apparent whether, in relation to an entity, there exist users who are dependent on general purpose financial reports as a basis for making and evaluating resource allocation decisions. For those entities in respect of which it is not readily apparent whether such dependent users exist, the factors outlined in paragraphs 20 to 22 are identified as the primary factors to be considered in determining whether a reporting entity exists. These factors are indicative only, and are not the only factors that will be relevant in determining whether, in a particular circumstance, an entity is a reporting entity.

Separation of management from economic interest

20 The greater the spread of ownership/membership and the greater the extent of the separation between management and owners/members or others with an economic interest in the entity, the more likely it is that there will exist users dependent on general purpose financial reports as a basis for making and evaluating resource allocation decisions.

Economic or political importance/influence

21 Economic or political importance/influence refers to the ability of an entity to make a significant impact on the welfare of external parties. The greater the economic or political importance of an entity, the more likely it is that there will exist users dependent on general purpose financial reports as a basis for making and evaluating resource allocation decisions. Reporting entities identified on the basis of this factor are likely to include organisations which enjoy dominant positions in markets and those which are concerned with balancing the interests of significant groups, for example, employer/employee associations and public sector entities which have regulatory powers.

Financial characteristics

22 Financial characteristics that should be considered include the size (for example, value of sales or assets, or number of employees or customers) or indebtedness of an entity. In the case of non-business entities in particular, the amount of resources provided or allocated by governments or other parties to the activities conducted by the entities should be considered. The larger the size or the greater the indebtedness or resources allocated, the more likely it is that there will exist users dependent on general purpose financial reports as a basis for making and evaluating resource allocation decisions.

Implications of Application of the Reporting Entity Concept

Implications of the criterion for identification of a reporting entity

23 As the concept of the reporting entity reflected in this Statement is related to the information needs of users, it is evident that the creation of a company, statutory authority or other organisational structure does not of itself mean that the entity or organisation will

qualify as a reporting entity. Judgement will be required in determining whether an entity satisfies the criterion for being so classified.

24   For entities which operate in the public sector, the implications of the factors listed in paragraphs 20 to 22 are that most government departments and statutory authorities will be reporting entities. This arises by virtue of the separation between the parties with an economic interest in the activities undertaken in the sector and the parties responsible for the management of those activities. (Management is elected by the parties which have an economic interest in the activities, that is, members of the public, or is appointed by others who have been so elected.) It is fundamental that those who manage resources on behalf of others should account for their performance to those who have provided the resources. Thus, in the public sector, the practical use of the factors listed in paragraphs 20 to 22 will be to identify entities which are not reporting entities. For example, medical centres established and controlled by a hospital may not be considered to be reporting entities where, individually, the amount of resources allocated to each is very low relative to the total resource allocation to the hospital and, because of that and other factors, there do not exist users dependent on general purpose financial reports relating to each centre. In such circumstances, information about the medical centres controlled by the hospital would be incorporated into the general purpose financial report of the hospital. This does not mean that the hospital will not require financial information from each of the centres for making resource allocation decisions. Rather, the implication is that financial reports prepared for this purpose by the centres would not be in the nature of general purpose financial reports, but instead would be in the nature of special purpose financial reports.

25   An implication of applying the reporting entity concept in the public sector is that a government as a whole, whether at the Federal, State, Territorial or local government level, would be identified as a reporting entity because it is reasonable to expect that users will require general purpose financial reports to facilitate their decision-making in relation to the resource allocations made by, and the accountability of, those governments. At a lower level of reporting, a number of individual statutory authorities and departments (and the entities they control) may also be defined as individual reporting entities because of their economic or political significance and/or their financial characteristics (for example, resources controlled and level of indebtedness). In some cases, these factors may also identify a ministerial portfolio as a reporting entity.

26   In the private sector, the factors listed in paragraphs 20 to 22 will identify as reporting entities all entities in which there is significant separation of ownership/membership and management, for example public companies and listed trusts. In contrast, entities in which the members and management are an identical group, as would be the case for most sole traders, partnerships and exempt proprietary companies, would usually not be identified as reporting entities on the basis of this factor. However, there will exist circumstances in which entities such as these ought to be regarded as reporting entities. For example, an entity which undertakes the raising of debt or equity funds from the public will become a reporting entity because there will exist potential resource providers who require general purpose financial reports as a basis for making resource allocation decisions. For similar reasons, undertaking to sell an entity may result in the identification of the entity as a reporting entity. Also, the size and/or economic significance of some entities to their suppliers, clients or employees or to the public may dictate that those entities are reporting entities even though the members manage the entity. Examples of this would be professional partnerships which service a very large number of customers or clients and which enjoy a special status in the community, and exempt proprietary companies which attract a special public interest because of their financial characteristics.

27   There will exist some entities which will not be regarded as reporting entities, but which form part of an economic entity which is a reporting entity. This would be the case, for example, where a company is a wholly-owned subsidiary of another entity in the economic entity, and the size and other economic characteristics of the company are such that there do not exist users dependent on general purpose financial reports as a source of information for making and evaluating resource allocation decisions about the wholly-owned company. Instead, users are interested in information about the collective operation of the company and the other entities comprising the economic entity. Similarly, a segment of an economic entity is unlikely to be regarded as a reporting entity because

information about a segment is usually directed at improving the knowledge of users of the general purpose financial reports for the whole reporting entity, rather than catering for the needs of those users interested only in information about that segment.

28   Classification as a reporting entity may not be constant from one reporting period to the next. For example, a partnership or company established for the conduct of a family business may not, under normal circumstances, qualify as a reporting entity. However, where one or more partners or owners become distanced from the business or are in dispute with other participants, or where new non-family shareholders are admitted to the company, users dependent on general purpose financial reports may exist in respect of the financial reports for the periods during which disputations or non-family shareholdings occur. As such, the partnership or company would meet the conditions for classification as a reporting entity in respect of one or more reporting periods.

Groups of entities as reporting entities

29   The concept of control as the basis for identifying an economic entity has important implications. In the public sector, the entities making up the budget sector (that is, those entities which are heavily reliant on the budget for resources) may individually be identified as reporting entities. Because they are controlled by a government, those entities together with that government and the other entities that the government controls would, as an economic entity, meet the definition of a reporting entity. In preparing a general purpose financial report for this reporting entity, that is, for the government as a whole, it may be desirable to report detailed information regarding the operation of particular segments of the government as a whole, for example, the budget sector. This Statement does not, however, require the preparation of a separate general purpose financial report relating to the group of entities comprising the budget sector because, without their controlling entity (the government as a whole), they do not form an economic entity.

30   In the private sector, it has been common practice for groups of entities to be recognised as an economic entity only where the entities making up the group are established in the same legal form (for example, all are companies). An implication of the concept of control is that an economic entity may comprise entities which are established in a form different from that of the controlling entity, and such entities may be parts of, or a combination of, entities recognised for other purposes.

31   Because an economic entity, as defined in this Statement, comprises only the controlling entity and controlled entities, those entities which are significantly influenced, but not controlled, by a member of the economic entity do not form part of the economic entity. (Entities which are significantly influenced are termed associated entities.) This means that in preparing the general purpose financial report for the economic entity, additional information about an investment in an associated entity may be reported, possibly in a supplementary form, but it would not be reported on the basis of the associated entity forming part of the economic entity.

32   The focus on user needs as the basis for determining the existence of a reporting entity implies that the fact that an economic entity (for example, a corporate group or a government) may be a reporting entity does not affect whether the controlling entity or any of the controlled entities are reporting entities in their own right.

Implications of the reporting entity concept for current practice

33   It is likely that application of this Statement will result in substantial changes to current practice. For example, it will result in some partnerships, trusts, government departments, statutory authorities and other organisations that currently do not prepare general purpose financial reports being identified as reporting entities which therefore ought to prepare such reports in accordance with Statements of Accounting Concepts and Accounting Standards. Similarly, it will result in a government as a whole being identified as a reporting entity which therefore ought to prepare general purpose financial reports. Other entities, for example some private companies, which currently prepare general purpose financial reports may not meet the criterion for identification as reporting entities. This Statement would not, therefore, require such entities to prepare general purpose financial reports. In this regard, however, it should be noted that the fact that this Statement may not require a particular entity to prepare general purpose financial reports does not preclude

other parties, for example, regulatory authorities and financial institutions, from imposing a requirement on that entity to prepare general purpose financial reports.

Implications of the Reporting Entity Concept for Differential Reporting

34   Statements of Accounting Concepts and Accounting Standards are applicable to all entities which prepare general purpose financial reports. It is sometimes proposed that certain entities should be permitted to depart from all or certain of these Statements and Standards in the preparation of their financial reports. This notion is referred to as differential applicability of Statements of Accounting Concepts and Accounting Standards, or differential reporting.

35   Bases that have been proposed for identifying the entities which should be permitted to depart from these Statements and Standards are:

(a)   the size of the entity – that is, entities classed as small in relation to certain size benchmarks, based on any combination of turnover, assets and number of employees, would be permitted to depart;

(b)   ownership characteristics – for example, privately-owned entities would be permitted to depart, whereas publicly-owned entities would not be permitted to depart; and

(c)   a combination of size and ownership characteristics – for example, privately-owned entities which are classed as small would be permitted to depart from the Statements and Standards.

36   In this Statement the need to prepare general purpose financial reports is linked to the existence of users dependent on those reports as a basis for making and evaluating resource allocation decisions. The existence of users dependent on general purpose financial reports is not determined by either the size or the ownership characteristics of an entity. Accordingly, the bases outlined in paragraph 35 are not supported by this Statement. However, the reporting entity concept enunciated herein embodies a concept of differential reporting in that certain entities will not be identified as reporting entities and thus would not be required to prepare general purpose financial reports or comply with Statements of Accounting Concepts and Accounting Standards in the preparation of other financial reports. The entities which need not prepare general purpose financial reports are those in respect of which it is reasonable to expect that users dependent upon information contained in general purpose financial reports for making and evaluating resource allocation decisions do not exist.

37   As paragraphs 24 to 28 outline, it is likely that some types of entities will be identified as reporting entities by this Statement, while others will not. Accordingly, in most instances the following private sector entities are unlikely to be required by this Statement to prepare general purpose financial reports: sole traders, partnerships, privately-owned companies and trusts other than those where funds are subscribed by the public. There may be some instances when it is considered necessary or desirable that a general purpose financial report about an entity in these categories be prepared, for example when a privately-owned company intends to raise funds from the public. In these circumstances the report is required to comply with all Statements of Accounting Concepts and Accounting Standards. In the public sector, although most government departments and statutory authorities are likely to be required to prepare general purpose financial reports, the financial characteristics of some authorities and government agencies will mean that they will not be required by this Statement to prepare such reports. Types of entities which always would be identified as reporting entities and types of entities that are or are not likely to be identified as reporting entities are indicated in Professional Statement APS 1 'Conformity with Statements of Accounting Concepts and Accounting Standards', issued by the Australian Society of Certified Practising Accountants and The Institute of Chartered Accountants in Australia.

Accounting Concepts

Discussion and Definitions

38   The following concepts shall be interpreted in the context of paragraphs 1 to 37 of this Statement.

39   Paragraph 6 (definitions) shall be read as forming part of the accounting concepts set out in this Statement.

Concept of the Reporting Entity

40   Reporting entities are all entities (including economic entities) in respect of which it is reasonable to expect the existence of users dependent on general purpose financial reports for information which will be useful to them for making and evaluating decisions about the allocation of scarce resources.

Preparation of general purpose financial reports

41   Reporting entities shall prepare general purpose financial reports. Such reports shall be prepared in accordance with Statements of Accounting Concepts and Accounting Standards.

SAC 2

Objective of General Purpose Financial Reporting

(August 1990)

Prepared by the Public Sector Accounting Standards Board of the Australian Accounting Research Foundation and by the Accounting Standards Review Board.

Issued by the Australian Accounting Research Foundation on behalf of the Australian Society of Certified Practising Accountants and The Institute of Chartered Accountants in Australia and by the Accounting Standards Review Board.

Note from the Institute of Chartered Accountants Australia

This note, prepared by the technical editors, is not part of Statement of Accounting Concepts SAC 2.

Historical development

August 1990: SAC 2 'Objective of General Purpose Financial Reporting' was issued by the Australian Accounting Research Foundation (AARF).

November 1990: SAC 2, together with SACs 1, 3 and 4, was made mandatory for the members of the Australian accounting professional bodies (the Institute of Chartered Accountants Australia and CPA Australia) by virtue of the jointly issued Miscellaneous Professional Statement APS 1 'Conformity with Statements of Accounting Concepts and Accounting Standards'.

July 1993: The Australian professional bodies announced that the mandatory status of the Statements of Accounting Concepts including SAC 2 would be withdrawn from APS 1. The revised APS 1 'Conformity with Accounting Standards' was issued in December 2003. Since that time the role of SAC 2 has been as a source of guidance in respect of the role and information disclosures of general-purpose financial reports.

2005: SAC 2 continues as part of Australian GAAP for 2005 because the IASB conceptual document and its Australian equivalents (the IASB Framework and the AASB Framework) provide limited guidance in respect of general-purpose financial reports.

Note: Proposed changes to the financial reporting regime will substantially change the application of the reporting entity concept. Until, or if, these proposals are adopted the reporting entity concept remains applicable.

Contents

Paragraphs

Citation 1
Application and Operative Date 2
Introduction 3–4
Definitions 5
Discussion
Scope and Applicability 6–10
Purpose of General Purpose Financial Reporting 11–15
Users of General Purpose Financial Reports 16
    Resource providers 17
    Recipients of goods and services 18
    Parties performing a review or oversight function 19
    Managements and governing bodies 20
Purposes for which User Groups Require Financial Information
    Resource providers 21
    Recipients of goods and services 22–24
    Parties performing a review or oversight function 25
Objective of General Purpose Financial Reporting 26–27
Types of Information Relevant to Users' Needs 28
    Performance 29–31
    Financial position 32–37
    Financing and investing 38
    Compliance 39–40
Accounting Concepts
Discussion and Definitions 41–42
Objective of General Purpose Financial Reporting 43
    Accountability 44
    Information disclosures 45

Citation

1   This Statement may be cited as Statement of Accounting Concepts SAC 2 'Objective of General Purpose Financial Reporting'.

Application and Operative Date

2   This Statement applies to each reporting entity in relation to its first reporting period that ends on or after 31 August 1990, and in relation to subsequent reporting periods.

Introduction

3   The purpose of this Statement is to establish the objective of general purpose financial reporting by reporting entities in the private and public sectors. The Statement identifies the users of general purpose financial reports, the common information needs of such users and the broad types of information, consistent with those needs, that general purpose financial reports should provide.

4   Although the specification of an objective will have implications for the type of information to be included in general purpose financial reports and for the manner in which such information is to be communicated to users, this Statement contains no conclusions regarding the particular qualities that information should possess to meet this

objective, the number, nature and form of the financial statements to be prepared, and the nature and measurement of the elements of such statements. These matters are the subject of other Statements of Accounting Concepts.

Definitions

5   For the purposes of this Statement:

'accountability' means the responsibility to provide information to enable users to make informed judgements about the performance, financial position, financing and investing, and compliance of the reporting entity;

'compliance' means adherence to those statutory requirements, regulations, rules, ordinances, directives or other externally-imposed requirements in respect of which non-compliance may have, or may have had, a financial effect on the reporting entity;

'financial position' means the economic condition of a reporting entity, having regard to its control over resources, financial structure, capacity for adaptation and solvency;

'financing and investing' means those activities of a reporting entity that relate to the financing of its operations and the investment of its resources;

'general purpose financial report' means a financial report intended to meet the information needs common to users who are unable to command the preparation of reports tailored so as to satisfy, specifically, all of their information needs;

'performance' means the proficiency of a reporting entity in acquiring resources economically and using those resources efficiently and effectively in achieving specified objectives; and

'reporting entity' means an entity (including an economic entity) in respect of which it is reasonable to expect the existence of users dependent on general purpose financial reports for information which will be useful to them for making and evaluating decisions about the allocation of scarce resources.

Discussion

Scope and Applicability

6   The objective specified in this Statement applies to general purpose financial reporting by all reporting entities.

7   General purpose financial reporting focuses on providing information to meet the common information needs of users who are unable to command the preparation of reports tailored to their particular information needs. These users must rely on the information communicated to them by the reporting entity.

8   Some users have specialised needs and will possess the authority to obtain the information to meet those needs. Examples of such users are taxation authorities, central banks and grants commissions. Although such users may make use of the information contained in general purpose financial reports, because they have the authority to command the information they require they do not need to rely on information provided to other groups. Special purpose financial reports directed at the needs of such users are beyond the scope of this Statement.

9   This Statement encompasses general purpose financial reporting by business and non-business reporting entities in the public and private sectors. It covers general purpose financial reporting by all types of reporting entities, whether legal, administrative or economic entities, and therefore encompasses all types of government entities, including government departments, statutory authorities, and, as a whole, Federal, State, Territorial and local governments; investor-owned entities, including companies and unit trusts; mutual co-operative entities, including building societies and credit unions; human service entities, including churches, foundations, professional associations and charities; superannuation plans; partnerships; and sole proprietorships.

10   Financial reporting encompasses the provision of financial statements and related financial and other information. Financial reports, comprising financial statements, notes,

supplementary schedules and explanatory material intended to be read with the financial statements, are the principal means of communicating financial information about a reporting entity to users. However, other information can best be provided, or can only be provided, outside financial reports. Financial reports are not the only source of relevant information about a reporting entity, and users of financial reports may need to consult other sources to satisfy their information needs. This Statement does not attempt to draw a clear distinction between financial reports and financial reporting, nor does it attempt to define the boundaries of general purpose financial reporting. Distinctions will be made and boundaries drawn, as required, in other Statements of Accounting Concepts and in Accounting Standards.

Purpose of General Purpose Financial Reporting

11   General purpose financial reporting is not an end in itself, but is a means of communicating relevant and reliable information about a reporting entity to users. The objective specified in this Statement derives from the information needs of those identified as the users of general purpose financial reports. Those needs depend, in turn, on the activities of reporting entities and the decisions users make about them.

12   Reporting entities control resources and influence members of the community through providing goods and services, levying prices, charges, rates and taxes, and acquiring and investing resources. The community interest is best served if scarce resources controlled by reporting entities are allocated to those entities which will use them in the most efficient and effective manner in providing goods and services. Efficient use of resources raises output, has desirable macroeconomic effects by enhancing employment and the standard of living, and enables social policy objectives to be achieved at the lowest cost. Members of the community make resource allocation decisions in respect of reporting entities – that is, they make reasoned choices among alternative uses of scarce resources. For example, investors decide whether to invest in an entity; creditors decide whether to lend resources to an entity; governments and parliaments decide, on behalf of constituents, whether to fund particular programmes for delivery by an entity; taxpayers decide who should represent them in government; donors decide whether to donate resources to an entity; individuals decide whether to contribute to a superannuation plan; employees decide whether to sell their services to a particular entity; owners/members of reporting entities decide whether they should contribute resources to the entity and who should manage the entity on their behalf; and ratepayers decide whether they should support the particular programmes of their local government and who should represent them on the local government council.

13   Efficient allocation of scarce resources will be enhanced if those who make resource allocation decisions, such as those groups identified above, have the appropriate financial information on which to base their decisions. General purpose financial reporting aims to provide this information.

14   General purpose financial reporting also provides a mechanism to enable managements and governing bodies to discharge their accountability. Managements and governing bodies are account-able to those who provide resources to the entity for planning and controlling the operations of the entity. In a broader sense, because of the influence reporting entities exert on members of the community at both the microeconomic and macroeconomic levels, they are accountable to the public at large. General purpose financial reporting provides a means by which this responsibility can be discharged.

15   Although the subsequent discussion of users and their information needs at times distinguishes between business and non-business entities, the common objective specified in this Statement reflects the inherent similarities between the two types of entities. While business entities seek to earn profits or desired rates of return and non-business entities pursue primarily non-financial objectives, both types of entities provide goods and services to the community and use scarce resources in the process; both obtain these resources from external sources and are accountable to the providers of the resources or their representatives; both control stocks of resources; both incur obligations; and both must be financially viable to meet their operating objectives.

Users of General Purpose Financial Reports

16   Many individuals and organisations base resource allocation decisions on their relationship with and knowledge about reporting entities and are therefore potentially interested in the information provided in general purpose financial reports. The following three categories of user groups are identified as the primary users of general purpose financial reports, and those whose common information needs should dictate the type of information to be disclosed by such reports: resource providers, recipients of goods and services, and parties performing a review or oversight function.

Resource providers

17   Providers of resources include those who may be compensated either directly or indirectly for the resources they provide. The former category includes employees, lenders, creditors, suppliers and, in the case of business entities, investors and contributors. The latter category includes donors, members of non-business entities such as clubs, societies and professional bodies, and, in the case of public sector bodies, parliament, taxpayers and ratepayers.

Recipients of goods and services

18   Recipients of goods and services are those who consume or otherwise benefit from the goods and services provided by the reporting entity. This category comprises customers and beneficiaries. In many non-business entities recipients of goods and services include resource providers, for example, ratepayers, taxpayers and members of professional associations.

Parties performing a review or oversight function

19   Certain parties, including parliaments, governments, regulatory agencies, analysts, labour unions, employer groups, media and special interest community groups, perform oversight or review services on behalf of the community. Members of this group tend to have indirect or derived interests in general purpose financial reports since they advise or represent those who have direct interests.

Managements and governing bodies

20   Managements and governing bodies are another category of user interested in the information provided in general purpose financial reports. However, managements and governing bodies need, in addition to the information contained in general purpose financial reports, management accounting and other information to carry out their planning and control responsibilities. Since this type of reporting has to be tailored to meet the specialised needs of these users, and since they will have the ability to determine the form and content of any such reports, this reporting is in the nature of special purpose financial reporting and is therefore beyond the scope of this Statement.

Purposes for which User Groups Require Financial Information

Resource providers

21   Providers of resources want to know whether the reporting entity is achieving the objectives which formed the reason for the provision of resources in the past and is operating economically and efficiently and using resources as prescribed. In the case of investor-owned business entities, investors and other resource providers will want to know whether the entity is operating profitably and generating favourable cash flows in the process, since their decisions relate to amounts, timing and uncertainties of expected cash flows. In the case of public sector entities and non-business entities in the private sector, taxpayers (and ratepayers) and contributors, respectively, want to know whether the entity is delivering the services expected of it, that is, whether it is achieving its objectives, and is doing so economically and efficiently. Other providers of resources to public sector entities and non-business entities in the private sector, for example, employees, suppliers, creditors and lenders, will principally be interested in the entity's ability to generate cash flows for timely payment of the entity's obligations to them. However, they will be indirectly concerned about the extent to which the entity is achieving its objectives since the ability of the entity to generate future cash flows will depend on its performance in this regard. Information provided in general purpose financial reports to enable resource providers to make these assessments will assist them in determining whether continued

support of the entity's activities is warranted and in predicting the level of resources necessary to support those activities.

Recipients of goods and services

22   Recipients of goods and services may want to assess the ability of the reporting entity to continue to provide goods and services in the future, the likely level at which the goods and services will be provided and the likely cost of the goods and services. In this regard, as with resource providers, they want to know whether the entity is achieving its objectives and is operating economically and efficiently in the provision of the goods and services.

23   In the case of business entities, the focus of this user group is on the ability of the entity to generate favourable cash flows, since only by obtaining sufficient cash to pay for the resources it uses and to meet its other obligations will the entity be able to continue to provide the goods and services in the future. Assessments by these users will affect their decisions to seek alternative suppliers of the goods and services.

24   In the case of non-business entities, and to an extent public sector business entities, the focus of this user group is on the extent to which the entity is using resources in their interests. Assessments made by this category of users in relation to public sector entities may influence their voting preferences and representations made to parliamentary and other representatives, and may lead to the continuation, expansion, contraction or even cessation of the entity's activities. Assessments made by this category of users in relation to private sector non-business entities may influence their voting preferences concerning the existing management or governing body of the entity and their decisions as to whether to continue to obtain the goods and services provided by the entity.

Parties performing a review or oversight function

25   Parties performing review or oversight services of interest to members of the community want to know whether the reporting entity has been operating in the interests of such members. Like resource providers and recipients of goods and services, they want to know whether the entity is achieving its objectives and is operating economically and efficiently in carrying out its operations. Assessments by these users of the extent to which the entity is operating satisfactorily in these respects will influence the decisions they make about the activities of the entities and, in respect of the advice they give to their constituents, will affect the decisions of those constituents. These users may have specific guidelines against which to assess the operations of the entity, and some may be able to demand special purpose financial reports to enable them to carry out this function.

Objective of General Purpose Financial Reporting

26   In view of the information needs of the users of general purpose financial reports identified in the preceding paragraphs, the position adopted in this Statement is that the objective of general purpose financial reporting is to provide information to users that is useful for making and evaluating decisions about the allocation of scarce resources.

27   When general purpose financial reports meet this objective they will also be the means by which managements and governing bodies discharge their accountability to the users of the reports. The provision of information for accountability purposes is an important function of the process of general purpose financial reporting, particularly in relation to public sector entities and non-business entities in the private sector. However, the rendering of accountability by reporting entities through general purpose financial reporting is encompassed by the broader objective of providing information useful for making and evaluating decisions about the allocation of scarce resources, since users will ultimately require the information for resource allocation decisions.

Types of Information Relevant to Users' Needs

28   The particular information users require for making and evaluating resource allocation decisions will overlap since all users will be interested, to varying degrees, in assessing whether the reporting entity is achieving its objectives and is operating economically and efficiently in the process, in assessing the ability of the entity to continue to provide goods and services in the future, and in confirming that resources have been used for the

purposes intended. General purpose financial reports can provide information useful for these purposes by disclosing information about the performance, financial position, and financing and investing of the reporting entity, including information about compliance. The information useful for these purposes may be both historical and prospective in nature. Paragraphs 29 to 40 provide examples of information that users may require for making and evaluating decisions about the allocation of scarce resources.

Performance

29   Aspects of the performance of a reporting entity can be measured in financial and non-financial terms. Disclosure of the revenues generated by the entity during the reporting period and the expenses incurred in generating this revenue, together with the assets, liabilities and equity of the entity at the end of the reporting period, will provide users with information to assist them to assess the financial performance of the entity over the reporting period. The information will be useful in determining the cost of providing goods and services and the change in the entity's control over resources during the reporting period. In relation to business entities, users will be able to evaluate the change in the entity's control over resources by reference to the resources or funds employed by the entity in achieving the change. In terms of the purposes for which users require information, as identified in paragraphs 21 to 25, this information is relevant to the users of general purpose financial reports of business entities in predicting both the capacity of the entity to generate cash from its existing resource base and the effectiveness with which it would employ additional resources. In relation to non-business entities, the information is useful in assessing the resources necessary to enable the entity to continue to provide services in the future and the likely cost of those services.

30   Non-financial measures of performance may also be relevant to users for the purposes identified, particularly in relation to non-business entities. The absence of a profit or rate of return objective for these entities means that financial measures of performance are unlikely to be sufficient to assess fully the extent to which those entities have achieved their objectives, which typically include social as well as financial dimensions. The extent to which non-financial performance measures can be considered to fall within the scope of general purpose financial reporting will be the subject of a separate Statement of Accounting Concepts.

31   In the public sector, information about government policies that affect a reporting entity's operations may be relevant to assessments of performance. For example, it may be relevant that an entity is subject to a government policy of break-even pricing or a stipulated target rate of return on assets.

Financial position

32   Disclosure of information about the financial position of the reporting entity involves disclosure of information about its control over resources, financial structure, capacity for adaptation and solvency.

33   The disclosure of information about the resources over which the entity has control, that is, disclosure of its assets, is relevant to users for making and evaluating decisions about the allocation of scarce resources. In terms of the purposes for which users require information, as identified in paragraphs 21 to 25, the information is useful in predicting the ability of the entity to continue to meet its objectives, whether these relate to the generation of positive cash flows in the future or the continued provision of goods and services.

34   The disclosure of information about the financial structure of the entity, that is, the sources, types and time patterns of finance, whether debt or equity, and the types of assets used by the entity, is relevant to users for making and evaluating decisions about the allocation of scarce resources. In particular, it is useful in predicting the future distribution of cash flows among providers of resources and the ability of the entity to attract resources in the future, and in assessing the extent to which restrictions and limitations on the uses to which the entity's resources can be put will affect the ability of the entity to meet its objectives.

35   The disclosure of information about the capacity of the reporting entity to modify the composition of the resources under its control is relevant to making and evaluating

decisions about the allocation of scarce resources. Such modification may be required by changes in the environment within which the entity operates or in response to directives from controlling bodies. In this respect, disclosure of information on the location, realisable value and current state of repair of the entity's assets would be relevant to users, as would disclosure of any restrictions that may have been imposed on the entity regarding its use of the assets.

36   Information about the solvency of the entity, that is, information about the availability of assets to meet financial commitments as they fall due, is relevant for making and evaluating decisions about the allocation of scarce resources. This information, such as disclosure of the liquidity of the entity's assets and the availability of cash from sources external to the entity, is useful in predicting the ability of the entity to meet its financial commitments as they fall due and, therefore, in predicting the ability of the entity to continue to provide goods and services in the future.

37   In the public sector, the ability of an entity to continue to provide goods and services in the future will, in addition to the dimensions of financial position outlined in paragraph 32, be influenced by government policy objectives.

Financing and investing

38   Information about financing and investing, for example, disclosure of the sources and applications of funds during the reporting period, is relevant for making and evaluating decisions about the allocation of scarce resources. This information indicates the way in which the reporting entity has financed its operations and invested its resources during the reporting period. It is useful to users in confirming that resources have been used for the purposes intended and, as an input to assessing the solvency of the entity and analysing the change in the entity's financial position, it is useful in assessing the ability of the reporting entity to continue to provide goods and services in the future and in assessing whether the reporting entity is achieving its objectives.

Compliance

39   Information about compliance is relevant to making and evaluating decisions about the allocation of scarce resources because knowledge of non-compliance with externally-imposed requirements governing the reporting entity's operations may affect users' assessments of the reporting entity's performance, financial position, or financing and investing. For example, information about compliance with the following types of externally-imposed requirements may be relevant to users: conditions imposed by borrowing agreements, licencing agreements and grant arrangements; memorandum and articles of association and/or enabling legislation; spending mandates and borrowing limits; equal employment opportunity legislation; occupational health and safety legislation; environmental protection legislation; requirements to provide particular types or levels of service under a government grant programme or specific government directive; and requirements to observe specified tendering procedures for significant expenditures. Users should be able to presume that, in the absence of disclosures to the contrary, the reporting entity has complied with all externally-imposed requirements in respect of which non-compliance is relevant to assessments of the reporting entity's performance, financial position, or financing and investing. Information about compliance is relevant to users irrespective of the sector in which the reporting entity operates or whether the reporting entity is of a business or non-business nature.

40   The concept of compliance appropriate for general purpose financial reporting depends substantially on the types of information which are identified as being encompassed by general purpose financial reporting. If general purpose financial reports include non-financial information about an entity's performance, information about non-financial dimensions of compliance would be relevant to users. Because the boundaries of general purpose financial reporting will continue to evolve, the concept of compliance currently adopted in this Statement is consistent with the boundaries of general purpose financial reporting reflected in the current reporting practices of most reporting entities. Accordingly, the definition of compliance included in this Statement refers to adherence to externally-imposed requirements in respect of which non-compliance may have, or may have had, a financial effect on the reporting entity. As such, reporting about compliance as defined in paragraph 5 would entail disclosure of the nature and probable financial effect of any

non-compliance by the reporting entity with externally-imposed requirements which has occurred and which is relevant to assessments of the reporting entity's performance, financial position, or financing and investing.

Accounting Concepts

Discussion and Definitions

41   The following concepts shall be interpreted in the context of paragraphs 1 to 40 of this Statement.

42   Paragraph 5 (definitions) shall be read as forming part of the accounting concepts set out in this Statement.

Objective of General Purpose Financial Reporting

43   General purpose financial reports shall provide information useful to users for making and evaluating decisions about the allocation of scarce resources.

Accountability

44   Managements and governing bodies shall present general purpose financial reports in a manner which assists in discharging their accountability.

Information disclosures

45   General purpose financial reports shall disclose information relevant to the assessment of performance, financial position, and financing and investing, including information about compliance.

AASB Framework
Framework for the Preparation and Presentation of Financial Statements

(Compiled September 2009)

Note from the Institute of Chartered Accountants Australia

This note, prepared by the technical editors, is not part of the AASB Framework.

Historical development

July 2004: The AASB Framework is the Australian equivalent of the IASB Framework. It was issued in July 2004 as an Australian guidance document to accompany the 2005 platform of Australian equivalents of International Financial Reporting Standards.

24 September 2007: AASB 2007-8 'Amendments to Australian Accounting Standards' amends the Framework, changing the term 'general purpose financial reports' to 'general purpose financial statements'. This Standard is applicable to annual reporting periods beginning on or after 1 January 2009.

13 December 2007: AASB 2007-10 'Further Amendments to Australian Accounting Standards arising from AASB 101' amends the Framework, replacing the term 'financial report' with 'financial statements'. This Standard is applicable to annual reporting periods beginning on or after 1 January 2009.

11 September 2009: The AASB Framework was reissued by the AASB, compiled to include the AASB 2007-8 and 2007-10 amendments.

The IASB is working on a project to revise the conceptual framework, with resulting changes also being adopted by the AASB version of the Framework. For up to date information refer to the AASB website at www.aasb.gov.au.

AASB Framework compared to IASB Framework

Additions

Paragraph	Description
Aus 1.1	Clarifies that the concepts in the AASB Framework are not set out as mandatory requirements for preparers of general purpose financial statements.
Aus 1.2	The application date of the AASB Framework (i.e. periods beginning 1 January 2005).
Aus 1.3	Prohibits the early application of the AASB Framework.
Aus 1.4	Explains which Statements of Accounting Concepts have been superseded by the AASB Framework (i.e. SAC 3 'Qualitative Characteristics of Financial Information' and SAC 4 'Recognition of the Elements of Financial Statements').
Aus 1.5	Clarifies that SAC 3 and SAC 4 remain applicable until the AASB Framework applies.
Aus 14.1	Reference to more detailed discussion of the stewardship function in SAC 2 'Objective of General Purpose Financial Reporting'.
Aus 15.1	In respect of not-for-profit entities, the ownership groups are more interested in the ability of the entity to achieve its non-financial objectives but this ability may in turn depend on the entity's financial position and financial performance.
Aus 49.1	Explains how assets provide the means for not-for-profit entities in the public or private sector to achieve their objectives by providing goods and services.
Aus 54.1	Explains how the provision of goods and services by not-for-profit entities may not result in net cash flows.

Aus 54.2	Explains how assets such as monuments and museums benefit not-for-profit entities by enabling them to meet their objectives of providing goods and services to beneficiaries.
Deletions	
Paragraph	*Description*
1(c)	One of the purposes of the IASB Framework is to assist national Standard-setting bodies in developing national Standards. Not relevant to Australia given its policy of international convergence of accounting Standards.

Contents

Compilation Details

Comparison with IASB Framework

Framework for the Preparation and Presentation of Financial Statements

	Paragraphs
Application	Aus1.1 – Aus1.5
Introduction	
Purpose and Status	1 – 4
Scope	5 – 8
Users and Their Information Needs	9 – 11
The Objective of Financial Reports	12 – Aus14.1
Financial Position, Financial Performance and Cash Flows	15 – 20
Note and Supplementary Schedules	21
Underlying Assumptions	
Accrual Basis	22
Going Concern	23
Qualitative Characteristics of Financial Reports	24
Understandability	25
Relevance	26 – 28
Materiality	29 – 30
Reliability	31 – 32
Faithful Representation	33 – 34
Substance Over Form	35
Neutrality	36
Prudence	37
Completeness	38
Comparability	39 – 42
Constraints on Relevant and Reliable Information	
Timeliness	43
Balance between Benefit and Cost	44
Balance between Qualitative Characteristics	45
True and Fair View/Fair Presentation	46
The Elements of Financial Statements	47 – 48
Financial Position	49 – 52
Assets	53 – 59
Liabilities	60 – 64
Equity	65 – 68
Performance	69 – 73
Income	74 – 77
Expenses	78 – 80
Capital Maintenance Adjustments	81

	Paragraphs
Recognition of the Elements of Financial Statements	82 – 84
The Probability of Future Economic Benefit	85
Reliability of Measurement	86 – 88
Recognition of Assets	89 – 90
Recognition of Liabilities	91
Recognition of Income	92 – 93
Recognition of Expenses	94 – 98
Measurement of the Elements of Financial Statements	99 – 101
Concepts of Capital and Capital Maintenance	
Concepts of Capital	102 – 103
Concepts of Capital Maintenance and the Determination of Profit	104 – 110

Compilation Details

Framework for the Preparation and Presentation of Financial Statements as amended

This compiled Framework applies to annual reporting periods beginning on or after 1 January 2009. It takes into account amendments up to and including 13 December 2007 and was prepared on 11 September 2009 by the staff of the Australian Accounting Standards Board (AASB).

This compilation is not a separate Framework issued by the AASB. Instead, it is a representation of the Framework (July 2004) as amended by Accounting Standards, which are listed in the Table below.

Table of Pronouncements

Pronouncement	Date made	Application date *(annual reporting periods … on or after …)*	Application, saving or transitional provisions
Framework	15 Jul 2004	*(beginning)* 1 Jan 2005	
AASB 2007-8	24 Sep 2007	*(beginning)* 1 Jan 2009	see (a) below
AASB 2007-10	13 Dec 2007	*(beginning)* 1 Jan 2009	see (a) below

(a)   Entities may elect to apply this Standard to annual reporting periods beginning on or after 1 January 2005 but before 1 January 2009, provided that AASB 101 *Presentation of Financial Statements* (September 2007) is also applied to such periods.

Table of Amendments

Paragraph affected	How affected	By … [paragraph]
Aus1.1	amended	AASB 2007-8 [7]
Aus1.6	deleted	AASB 2007-10 [10]
6-7	amended	AASB 2007-10 [11]
21	amended	AASB 2007-10 [12]
23	amended	AASB 2007-10 [12]
88	amended	AASB 2007-10 [13]

General Terminology Amendments

References to 'financial report(s)' that were amended to 'financial statements' by AASB 2007-10, paragraph 14, are not shown in the above Table of Amendments.

Comparison with IASB Framework

The AASB *Framework* and the IASB *Framework*

This *Framework for the Preparation and Presentation of Financial Statements* incorporates the *Framework for the Preparation and Presentation of Financial Statements* as issued by the International Accounting Standards Board (IASB). Paragraphs that have been added to this Framework (and do not appear in the text of the IASB *Framework*) are identified with the prefix "Aus", followed by the number of the relevant IASB paragraph and decimal numbering.

Framework

The Australian Accounting Standards Board issued the *Framework for the Preparation and Presentation of Financial Statements* on 15 July 2004.

This compiled version of the *Framework* applies to annual reporting periods beginning on or after 1 January 2009. It incorporates relevant amendments contained in AASB Standards made by the AASB up to and including 13 December 2007 (see Compilation Details).

Framework for the Preparation and Presentation of Financial Statements

Application

Aus1.1   The concepts in this *Framework* are not set out as requirements for the purpose of preparing general purpose financial statements. This is consistent with the:

(a)   purpose of Statements of Accounting Concepts set out in Policy Statement 5 *The Nature and Purpose of Statements of Accounting Concepts*;

(b)   non-mandatory status of Statements of Accounting Concepts under Professional Statement APS 1 *Conformity with Accounting Standards*; and

(c)   *Australian Securities and Investments Commission Act 2001*, section 227(1).

Aus1.2   This *Framework* applies to periods beginning on or after 1 January 2005.
[Note: For application dates of paragraphs changed or added by an amending Standard, see Compilation Details.]

Aus1.3   This *Framework* shall not be applied to annual reporting periods beginning before 1 January 2005.

Aus1.4   When applicable, this *Framework* supersedes:

(a)   Statement of Accounting Concepts SAC 3 *Qualitative Characteristics of Financial Information* as issued in August 1990; and

(b)   Statement of Accounting Concepts SAC 4 *Definition and Recognition of the Elements of Financial Statements* as issued in March 1995.

Aus1.5   SAC 3 and SAC 4 remain applicable until superseded by this *Framework*.

Introduction

Purpose and Status

1   This *Framework* sets out the concepts that underlie the preparation and presentation of financial statements for external users. The purpose of the *Framework* is to:

(a)   assist the AASB in the development of future Australian Accounting Standards and in its review of existing Australian Accounting Standards, including evaluating proposed International Accounting Standards Board pronouncements;

(b)   assist the AASB in promoting harmonisation of regulations, accounting standards and procedures relating to the presentation of financial statements by providing a basis for reducing the number of alternative accounting treatments permitted by Australian Accounting Standards;

(c)   [deleted by the AASB];

(d)   assist preparers of financial statements in applying Australian Accounting Standards and in dealing with topics that have yet to form the subject of an Australian Accounting Standard;

(e)   assist auditors in forming an opinion as to whether financial statements conform with Australian Accounting Standards;

(f)   assist users of financial statements in interpreting the information contained in financial statements prepared in conformity with Australian Accounting Standards; and

(g)   provide those who are interested in the work of the AASB with information about its approach to the formulation of Australian Accounting Standards.

2   This *Framework* is not an Australian Accounting Standard and hence does not define standards for any particular measurement or disclosure issue. Nothing in this *Framework* overrides any specific Australian Accounting Standard.

3   The AASB recognises that in a limited number of cases there may be a conflict between the *Framework* and an Australian Accounting Standard. In those cases where there is a conflict, the requirements of the Australian Accounting Standard prevail over those of the *Framework*. As, however, the AASB will be guided by the *Framework* in the development of future Standards and in its review of existing Standards, the number of cases of conflict between the *Framework* and Australian Accounting Standards will diminish through time.

4   The *Framework* will be revised from time to time on the basis of the Board's experience of working with it.

Scope

5   The *Framework* deals with:

(a)   the objective of financial statements;

(b)   the qualitative characteristics that determine the usefulness of information in financial statements;

(c)   the definition, recognition and measurement of the elements from which financial statements are constructed; and

(d)   concepts of capital and capital maintenance.

6   The *Framework* is concerned with general purpose financial statements (hereafter referred to as 'financial statements') including consolidated financial statements. Such financial statements are prepared and presented at least annually and are directed toward the common information needs of a wide range of users. Some of these users may require, and have the power to obtain, information in addition to that contained in the financial statements. Many users, however, have to rely on the financial statements as their major source of financial information and such financial statements should, therefore, be prepared and presented with their needs in view. Special purpose financial reports, for example, prospectuses and computations prepared for taxation purposes, are outside the scope of this *Framework*. Nevertheless, the *Framework* may be applied in the preparation of such special purpose reports where their requirements permit.

7   Financial statements form part of the process of financial reporting. A complete set of financial statements normally includes a balance sheet, an income statement, a statement of cash flows and a statement of changes in equity, and those notes and other statements and explanatory material that are an integral part of the financial statements. They may also include supplementary schedules and information based on or derived from, and expected to be read with, such statements. Such schedules and supplementary information may deal, for example, with financial information about industrial and geographical segments and disclosures about the effects of changing prices. Financial statements do not, however, include such items as reports by directors, statements by the chairman, discussion and analysis by management and similar items that may be included in an annual or interim report.

8   The *Framework* applies to the financial statements of all commercial, industrial and business reporting entities, whether in the public or the private sectors. The term "reporting entity" is defined in SAC 1 *Definition of the Reporting Entity*.

Users and Their Information Needs

9   The users of financial statements include present and potential investors, employees, lenders, suppliers and other trade creditors, customers, governments and their agencies and the public. They use financial statements in order to satisfy some of their different needs for information, including the following.

(a)   *Investors* The providers of risk capital and their advisers are concerned with the risk inherent in, and return provided by, their investments. They need information to help them determine whether they should buy, hold or sell. Shareholders are also interested in information which enables them to assess the ability of the entity to pay dividends.

(b)   *Employees* Employees and their representative groups are interested in information about the stability and profitability of their employers. They are also interested in information which enables them to assess the ability of the entity to provide remuneration, retirement benefits and employment opportunities.

(c)   *Lenders* Lenders are interested in information that enables them to determine whether their loans, and the interest attaching to them, will be paid when due.

(d)   *Suppliers and other trade creditors* Suppliers and other creditors are interested in information that enables them to determine whether amounts owing to them will be paid when due. Trade creditors are likely to be interested in an entity over a shorter period than lenders unless they are dependent upon the continuation of the entity as a major customer.

(e)   *Customers* Customers have an interest in information about the continuance of an entity, especially when they have a long-term involvement with, or are dependent on, the entity.

(f)   *Governments and their agencies* Governments and their agencies are interested in the allocation of resources and, therefore, the activities of entities. They also require information in order to regulate the activities of entities, determine taxation policies and as the basis for national income and similar statistics.

(g)   *Public* Entities affect members of the public in a variety of ways. For example, entities may make a substantial contribution to the local economy in many ways including the number of people they employ and their patronage of local suppliers. Financial statements may assist the public by providing information about the trends and recent developments in the prosperity of the entity and the range of its activities.

10   While all of the information needs of these users cannot be met by financial statements, there are needs which are common to all users. As investors are providers of risk capital to the entity, the provision of financial statements that meet their needs will also meet most of the needs of other users that financial statements can satisfy.

11   The management of an entity has the primary responsibility for the preparation and presentation of the financial statements of the entity. Management is also interested in the information contained in the financial statements even though it has access to additional management and financial information that helps it carry out its planning, decision-making and control responsibilities. Management has the ability to determine the form and content of such additional information in order to meet its own needs. The reporting of such information, however, is beyond the scope of this *Framework*. Nevertheless, published financial statements are based on the information used by management about the financial position, financial performance and cash flows of the entity.

The Objective of Financial Statements

12   The objective of financial statements is to provide information about the financial position, financial performance and cash flows of an entity that is useful to a wide range of users in making economic decisions.

13   Financial statements prepared for this purpose meet the common needs of most users. However, financial statements do not provide all the information that users may need to make economic decisions since they largely portray the financial effects of past events and do not necessarily provide non-financial information.

14   Financial statements also show the results of the stewardship of management, or the accountability of management for the resources entrusted to it. Those users who wish to assess the stewardship or accountability of management do so in order that they may make economic decisions; these decisions may include, for example, whether to hold or sell their investment in the entity or whether to reappoint or replace the management.

Aus14.1   A more detailed discussion is provided in SAC 2 *Objective of General Purpose Financial Reporting*.

Financial Position, Financial Performance and Cash Flows

15   The economic decisions that are taken by users of financial statements require an evaluation of the ability of an entity to generate cash and cash equivalents and of the timing and certainty of their generation. This ability ultimately determines, for example, the capacity of an entity to pay its employees and suppliers, meet interest payments, repay loans and make distributions to its owners. Users are better able to evaluate this ability to generate cash and cash equivalents if they are provided with information that focuses on the financial position, financial performance and cash flows of an entity.

Aus15.1   In respect of not-for-profit entities, ownership groups and contributors of donations are generally not concerned with obtaining a financial return but are usually more interested in the ability of an entity to achieve its non-financial objectives, which in turn may depend upon the entity's financial position and financial performance.

16   The financial position of an entity is affected by the economic resources it controls, its financial structure, its liquidity and solvency, and its capacity to adapt to changes in the environment in which it operates. Information about the economic resources controlled by the entity and its capacity in the past to modify these resources is useful in predicting the ability of the entity to generate cash and cash equivalents in the future[1]. Information about financial structure is useful in predicting future borrowing needs and how future profits and cash flows will be distributed among those with an interest in the entity; it is also useful in predicting how successful the entity is likely to be in raising further finance. Information about liquidity and solvency is useful in predicting the ability of the entity to meet its financial commitments as they fall due. Liquidity refers to the availability of cash in the near future after taking account of financial commitments over this period. Solvency refers to the availability of cash over the longer term to meet financial commitments as they fall due.

17   Information about the performance of an entity, in particular its profitability, is required in order to assess potential changes in the economic resources that it is likely to control in the future. Information about variability of performance is important in this respect. Information about performance is useful in predicting the capacity of the entity to generate cash flows from its existing resource base. It is also useful in forming judgements about the effectiveness with which the entity might employ additional resources.

18   Information concerning cash movements of an entity is useful in order to assess its investing, financing and operating activities during the reporting period. This information is useful in providing the user with a basis to assess the ability of the entity to generate cash and cash equivalents and the needs of the entity to utilise those cash flows[2].

19   Information about financial position is primarily provided in a balance sheet. Information about performance is primarily provided in an income statement. Information about cash

---

1   For not-for-profit users, also see paragraph AUS15.1

2   For not-for-profit users, also see paragraph AUS15.1

movements is provided in the cash flow statement. Information about movements in an entity's equity during the period is provided in the statement of changes in equity.

20   The component parts of the financial statements interrelate because they reflect different aspects of the same transactions or other events. Although each statement provides information that is different from the others, none is likely to serve only a single purpose or provide all the information necessary for particular needs of users. For example, an income statement provides an incomplete picture of performance unless it is used in conjunction with the balance sheet, cash flow statement and the statement of changes in equity.

Notes and Supplementary Schedules

21   The financial statements also contain notes and supplementary schedules and other information. For example, they may contain additional information that is relevant to the needs of users about the items in the balance sheet and income statement. They may include disclosures about the risks and uncertainties affecting the entity and any resources and obligations not recognised in the balance sheet (such as mineral reserves). Information about geographical and industry segments and the effect on the entity of changing prices may also be provided in the form of supplementary information.

Underlying Assumptions

Accrual Basis

22   In order to meet their objectives, financial statements are prepared on the accrual basis of accounting. Under this basis, the effects of transactions and other events are recognised when they occur (and not as cash or its equivalent is received or paid) and they are recorded in the accounting records and reported in the financial statements of the periods to which they relate. Financial statements prepared on the accrual basis inform users not only of past transactions involving the payment and receipt of cash but also of obligations to pay cash in the future and of resources that represent cash to be received in the future. Hence, they provide the type of information about past transactions and other events that is most useful to users in making economic decisions.

Going Concern

23   The financial statements are normally prepared on the assumption that an entity is a going concern and will continue in operation for the foreseeable future. Hence, it is assumed that the entity has neither the intention nor the need to liquidate or curtail materially the scale of its operations; if such an intention or need exists, the financial statements may have to be prepared on a different basis and, if so, the basis used is disclosed.

Qualitative Characteristics of Financial Statements

24   Qualitative characteristics are the attributes that make the information provided in financial statements useful to users. The four principal qualitative characteristics are understandability, relevance, reliability and comparability.

Understandability

25   An essential quality of the information provided in financial statements is that it is readily understandable by users. For this purpose, users are assumed to have a reasonable knowledge of business and economic activities and accounting and a willingness to study the information with reasonable diligence. However, information about complex matters that should be included in the financial statements, because of its relevance to the economic decision-making needs of users, should not be excluded merely on the grounds that it may be too difficult for certain users to understand.

Relevance

26   To be useful, information must be relevant to the decision-making needs of users. Information has the quality of relevance when it influences the economic decisions of users by helping them evaluate past, present or future events or confirming, or correcting, their past evaluations.

27   The predictive and confirmatory roles of information are interrelated. For example, information about the current level and structure of asset holdings has value to users when they endeavour to predict the ability of the entity to take advantage of opportunities and its ability to react to adverse situations. The same information plays a confirmatory role in respect of past predictions about, for example, the way in which the entity would be structured or the outcome of planned operations.

28   Information about financial position and past performance is frequently used as the basis for predicting future financial position and performance and other matters in which users are directly interested, such as dividend and wage payments, security price movements and the ability of the entity to meet its commitments as they fall due. To have predictive value, information need not be in the form of an explicit forecast. The ability to make predictions from financial statements is enhanced, however, by the manner in which information on past transactions and events is displayed. For example, the predictive value of the income statement is enhanced if unusual and infrequent items of income or expense are separately disclosed.

Materiality

29   The relevance of information is affected by its nature and materiality. In some cases, the nature of information alone is sufficient to determine its relevance. For example, the reporting of a new segment may affect the assessment of the risks and opportunities facing the entity irrespective of the materiality of the results achieved by the new segment in the reporting period. In other cases, both the nature and materiality are important, for example, the amounts of inventories held in each of the main categories that are appropriate to the business.

30   Information is material if its omission or misstatement could influence the economic decisions of users taken on the basis of the financial statements. Materiality depends on the size of the item or error judged in the particular circumstances of its omission or misstatement. Thus, materiality provides a threshold or cut-off point rather than being a primary qualitative characteristic which information must have if it is to be useful.

Reliability

31   To be useful, information must also be reliable. Information has the quality of reliability when it is free from material error and bias and can be depended upon by users to represent faithfully that which it either purports to represent or could reasonably be expected to represent.

32   Information may be relevant but so unreliable in nature or representation that its recognition may be potentially misleading. For example, if the validity and amount of a claim for damages under a legal action are disputed, it may be inappropriate for the entity to recognise the full amount of the claim in the balance sheet, although it may be appropriate to disclose the amount and circumstances of the claim.

Faithful Representation

33   To be reliable, information must represent faithfully the transactions and other events it either purports to represent or could reasonably be expected to represent. Thus, for example, a balance sheet should represent faithfully the transactions and other events that result in assets, liabilities and equity of the entity at the reporting date which meet the recognition criteria.

34   Most financial information is subject to some risk of being less than a faithful representation of that which it purports to portray. This is not due to bias, but rather to inherent difficulties either in identifying the transactions and other events to be measured or in devising and applying measurement and presentation techniques that can convey messages that correspond with those transactions and events. In certain cases, the measurement of the financial effects of items could be so uncertain that entities generally would not recognise them in the financial statements; for example, although most entities generate goodwill internally over time, it is usually difficult to identify or measure that goodwill reliably. In other cases, however, it may be relevant to recognise items and to disclose the risk of error surrounding their recognition and measurement.

Substance Over Form

35   If information is to represent faithfully the transactions and other events that it purports to represent, it is necessary that they are accounted for and presented in accordance with their substance and economic reality and not merely their legal form. The substance of transactions or other events is not always consistent with that which is apparent from their legal or contrived form. For example, an entity may dispose of an asset to another party in such a way that the documentation purports to pass legal ownership to that party; nevertheless, agreements may exist that ensure that the entity continues to enjoy the future economic benefits embodied in the asset. In such circumstances, the reporting of a sale would not represent faithfully the transaction entered into (if indeed there was a transaction).

Neutrality

36   To be reliable, the information contained in financial statements must be neutral, that is, free from bias. Financial statements are not neutral if, by the selection or presentation of information, they influence the making of a decision or judgement in order to achieve a predetermined result or outcome.

Prudence

37   The preparers of financial statements do, however, have to contend with the uncertainties that inevitably surround many events and circumstances, such as the collectability of doubtful receivables, the probable useful life of plant and equipment and the number of warranty claims that may occur. Such uncertainties are recognised by the disclosure of their nature and extent and by the exercise of prudence in the preparation of the financial statements. Prudence is the inclusion of a degree of caution in the exercise of the judgements needed in making the estimates required under conditions of uncertainty, such that assets or income are not overstated and liabilities or expenses are not understated. However, the exercise of prudence does not allow, for example, the creation of hidden reserves or excessive provisions, the deliberate understatement of assets or income, or the deliberate overstatement of liabilities or expenses, because the financial statements would not be neutral and, therefore, not have the quality of reliability.

Completeness

38   To be reliable, the information in financial statements must be complete within the bounds of materiality and cost. An omission can cause information to be false or misleading and thus unreliable and deficient in terms of its relevance.

Comparability

39   Users must be able to compare the financial statements of an entity through time in order to identify trends in its financial position and performance. Users must also be able to compare the financial statements of different entities in order to evaluate their relative financial position, financial performance and cash flows. Hence, the measurement and display of the financial effect of like transactions and other events must be carried out in a consistent way throughout an entity and over time for that entity and in a consistent way for different entities.

40   An important implication of the qualitative characteristic of comparability is that users be informed of the accounting policies employed in the preparation of the financial statements, any changes in those policies and the effects of such changes. Users need to be able to identify differences between the accounting policies for like transactions and other events used by the same entity from period to period and by different entities. Compliance with Australian Accounting Standards, including the disclosure of the accounting policies used by the entity, helps to achieve comparability.

41   The need for comparability should not be confused with mere uniformity and should not be allowed to become an impediment to the introduction of improved accounting standards. It is not appropriate for an entity to continue accounting in the same manner for a transaction or other event if the policy adopted is not in keeping with the qualitative characteristics of relevance and reliability. It is also inappropriate for an entity to leave its accounting policies unchanged when more relevant and reliable alternatives exist.

42   Because users wish to compare the financial position, financial performance and cash flows of an entity over time, it is important that the financial statements show corresponding information for the preceding periods.

Constraints on Relevant and Reliable Information

Timeliness

43   If there is undue delay in the reporting of information it may lose its relevance. Management may need to balance the relative merits of timely reporting and the provision of reliable information. To provide information on a timely basis it may often be necessary to report before all aspects of a transaction or other event are known, thus impairing reliability. Conversely, if reporting is delayed until all aspects are known, the information may be highly reliable but of little use to users who have had to make decisions in the interim. In achieving a balance between relevance and reliability, the overriding consideration is how best to satisfy the economic decision-making needs of users.

Balance between Benefit and Cost

44   The balance between benefit and cost is a pervasive constraint rather than a qualitative characteristic. The benefits derived from information should exceed the cost of providing it. The evaluation of benefits and costs is, however, substantially a judgemental process. Furthermore, the costs do not necessarily fall on those users who enjoy the benefits. Benefits may also be enjoyed by users other than those for whom the information is prepared; for example, the provision of further information to lenders may reduce the borrowing costs of an entity. For these reasons, it is difficult to apply a cost-benefit test in any particular case. Nevertheless, standard-setters in particular, as well as the preparers and users of financial statements, should be aware of this constraint.

Balance between Qualitative Characteristics

45   In practice, a balancing, or trade-off, between qualitative characteristics is often necessary. Generally, the aim is to achieve an appropriate balance among the characteristics in order to meet the objective of financial statements. The relative importance of the characteristics in different cases is a matter of professional judgement.

True and Fair View/Fair Presentation

46   Financial statements are frequently described as showing a true and fair view of, or as presenting fairly, the financial position, financial performance and cash flows of an entity. Although this *Framework* does not deal directly with such concepts, the application of the principal qualitative characteristics and of appropriate accounting standards normally results in financial statements that convey what is generally understood as a true and fair view of, or as presenting fairly such information.

The Elements of Financial Statements

47   Financial statements portray the financial effects of transactions and other events by grouping them into broad classes according to their economic characteristics. These broad classes are termed the elements of financial statements. The elements directly related to the measurement of financial position in the balance sheet are assets, liabilities and equity. The elements directly related to the measurement of performance in the income statement are income and expenses. The cash flow statement usually reflects income statement elements and changes in balance sheet elements; accordingly, this *Framework* identifies no elements that are unique to this statement.

48   The presentation of these elements in the balance sheet and the income statement involves a process of sub-classification. For example, assets and liabilities may be classified by their nature or function in the business of the entity in order to display information in the manner most useful to users for purposes of making economic decisions.

Financial Position

49   The elements directly related to the measurement of financial position are assets, liabilities and equity. These are defined as follows:

(a)   An asset is a resource controlled by the entity as a result of past events and from which future economic benefits are expected to flow to the entity.

AASB Framework   **Institute of Chartered Accountants Australia**

(b)   A liability is a present obligation of the entity arising from past events, the settlement of which is expected to result in an outflow from the entity of resources embodying economic benefits.

(c)   Equity is the residual interest in the assets of the entity after deducting all its liabilities.

Aus49.1   In respect of not-for-profit entities in the public or private sector, in pursuing their objectives, goods and services are provided that have the capacity to satisfy human wants and needs. Assets provide a means for entities to achieve their objectives. Future economic benefits or service potential is the essence of assets. Future economic benefits is synonymous with the notion of service potential, and is used in this *Framework* as a reference also to service potential. Future economic benefits can be described as the scarce capacity to provide benefits to the entities that use them, and is common to all assets irrespective of their physical or other form.

50   The definitions of an asset and a liability identify their essential features but do not attempt to specify the criteria that need to be met before they are recognised in the balance sheet. Thus, the definitions embrace items that are not recognised as assets or liabilities in the balance sheet because they do not satisfy the criteria for recognition discussed in paragraphs 82 to 98. In particular, the expectation that future economic benefits will flow to or from an entity must be sufficiently certain to meet the probability criterion in paragraph 83 before an asset or liability is recognised.

51   In assessing whether an item meets the definition of an asset, liability or equity, attention needs to be given to its underlying substance and economic reality and not merely its legal form. Thus, for example, in the case of finance leases, the substance and economic reality are that the lessee acquires the economic benefits of the use of the leased asset for the major part of its useful life in return for entering into an obligation to pay for that right an amount approximating to the fair value of the asset and the related finance charge. Hence, the finance lease gives rise to items that satisfy the definition of an asset and a liability and are recognised as such in the lessee's balance sheet.

52   Balance sheets drawn up in accordance with current Australian Accounting Standards may include items that do not satisfy the definitions of an asset or liability and are not shown as part of equity. The definitions set out in paragraph 49 will, however, underlie future reviews of existing Australian Accounting Standards and the formulation of further Standards.

Assets

53   The future economic benefit embodied in an asset is the potential to contribute, directly or indirectly, to the flow of cash and cash equivalents to the entity. The potential may be a productive one that is part of the operating activities of the entity. It may also take the form of convertibility into cash or cash equivalents or a capability to reduce cash outflows, such as when an alternative manufacturing process lowers the costs of production.

54   An entity usually employs its assets to produce goods or services capable of satisfying the wants or needs of customers; because these goods or services can satisfy these wants or needs, customers are prepared to pay for them and hence contribute to the cash flow of the entity. Cash itself renders a service to the entity because of its command over other resources.

Aus54.1   In respect of not-for-profit entities, whether in the public or private sector, the future economic benefits are also used to provide goods and services in accordance with the entities' objectives. However, since the entities do not have the generation of profit as a principal objective, the provision of goods and services may not result in net cash inflows to the entities as the recipients of the goods and services may not transfer cash or other benefits to the entities in exchange.

Aus54.2   In respect of not-for-profit entities, the fact that they do not charge, or do not charge fully, their beneficiaries or customers for the goods and services they provide does not deprive those outputs of utility or value; nor does it preclude the entities from benefiting from the assets used to provide the goods and services. For example, assets such as monuments, museums, cathedrals and historical treasures provide needed or desired services to beneficiaries, typically at little or no direct cost to the beneficiaries. These assets benefit the entities by enabling them to meet their objectives of providing needed services to beneficiaries.

55   The future economic benefits embodied in an asset may flow to the entity in a number of ways. For example, an asset may be:

(a)   used singly or in combination with other assets in the production of goods or services to be sold by the entity;

(b)   exchanged for other assets;

(c)   used to settle a liability; or

(d)   distributed to the owners of the entity.

56   Many assets, for example, property, plant and equipment, have a physical form. However, physical form is not essential to the existence of an asset; hence patents and copyrights, for example, are assets if future economic benefits are expected to flow from them to the entity and if they are controlled by the entity.

57   Many assets, for example, receivables and property, are associated with legal rights, including the right of ownership. In determining the existence of an asset, the right of ownership is not essential; thus, for example, property held on a lease is an asset if the entity controls the benefits which are expected to flow from the property. Although the capacity of an entity to control benefits is usually the result of legal rights, an item may nonetheless satisfy the definition of an asset even when there is no legal control. For example, know-how obtained from a development activity may meet the definition of an asset when, by keeping that know-how secret, an entity controls the benefits that are expected to flow from it.

58   The assets of an entity result from past transactions or other past events. Entities normally obtain assets by purchasing or producing them, but other transactions or events may generate assets. Examples include property received by an entity from government as part of a program to encourage economic growth in an area, and the discovery of mineral deposits. Transactions or events expected to occur in the future do not, in themselves, give rise to assets. Hence, for example, an intention to purchase inventory does not, of itself, meet the definition of an asset.

59   There is a close association between incurring expenditure and generating assets but the two do not necessarily coincide. Hence, when an entity incurs expenditure, this may provide evidence that future economic benefits were sought but is not conclusive proof that an item satisfying the definition of an asset has been obtained. Similarly the absence of a related expenditure does not preclude an item from satisfying the definition of an asset and thus becoming a candidate for recognition in the balance sheet. For example, items that have been donated to the entity may satisfy the definition of an asset.

Liabilities

60   An essential characteristic of a liability is that the entity has a present obligation. An obligation is a duty or responsibility to act or perform in a certain way. Obligations may be legally enforceable as a consequence of a binding contract or statutory requirement. This is normally the case, for example, with amounts payable for goods and services received. Obligations also arise, however, from normal business practice, custom and a desire to maintain good business relations or act in an equitable manner. If, for example, an entity decides as a matter of policy to rectify faults in its products even when these become apparent after the warranty period has expired, the amounts that are expected to be expended in respect of goods already sold are liabilities.

61   A distinction needs to be drawn between a present obligation and a future commitment. A decision by the management of an entity to acquire assets in the future does not, of itself, give rise to a present obligation. An obligation normally arises only when the asset is delivered or the entity enters into an irrevocable agreement to acquire the asset. In the latter case, the irrevocable nature of the agreement means that the economic consequences of failing to honour the obligation, for example, because of the existence of a substantial penalty, leave the entity with little, if any, discretion to avoid the outflow of resources to another party.

AASB

62 The settlement of a present obligation usually involves the entity giving up resources embodying economic benefits in order to satisfy the claim of the other party. Settlement of a present obligation may occur in a number of ways, for example, by:

(a) payment of cash;

(b) transfer of other assets;

(c) provision of services;

(d) replacement of that obligation with another obligation; or

(e) conversion of the obligation to equity.

An obligation may also be extinguished by other means, such as a creditor waiving or forfeiting its rights.

63 Liabilities result from past transactions or other past events. Thus, for example, the acquisition of goods and the use of services give rise to trade payables (unless paid for in advance or on delivery), and the receipt of a bank loan results in an obligation to repay the loan. An entity may also recognise future rebates based on annual purchases by customers as liabilities; in this case, the sale of the goods in the past is the transaction that gives rise to the liability.

64 Some liabilities can be measured only by using a substantial degree of estimation. Some entities describe these liabilities as provisions. In some countries, such provisions are not regarded as liabilities because the concept of a liability is defined narrowly so as to include only amounts that can be established without the need to make estimates. The definition of a liability in paragraph 49 follows a broader approach. Thus, when a provision involves a present obligation and satisfies the rest of the definition, it is a liability even if the amount has to be estimated. Examples include provisions for payments to be made under existing warranties and provisions to cover pension obligations.

Equity

65 Although equity is defined in paragraph 49 as a residual, it may be sub-classified in the balance sheet. For example, in a corporate entity, funds contributed by shareholders, retained earnings, reserves representing appropriations of retained earnings and reserves representing capital maintenance adjustments may be shown separately. Such classifications can be relevant to the decision-making needs of the users of financial statements when they indicate legal or other restrictions on the ability of the entity to distribute or otherwise apply its equity. They may also reflect the fact that parties with ownership interests in an entity have differing rights in relation to the receipt of dividends or the repayment of contributed equity.

66 The creation of reserves is sometimes required by statute or other law in order to give the entity and its creditors an added measure of protection from the effects of losses. Other reserves may be established if national tax law grants exemptions from, or reductions in, taxation liabilities when transfers to such reserves are made. The existence and size of these legal, statutory and tax reserves is information that can be relevant to the decision-making needs of users. Transfers to such reserves are appropriations of retained earnings rather than expenses.

67 The amount at which equity is shown in the balance sheet is dependent on the measurement of assets and liabilities. Normally, the aggregate amount of equity only by coincidence corresponds with the aggregate market value of the shares of the entity or the sum that could be raised by disposing of either the net assets on a piecemeal basis or the entity as a whole on a going concern basis.

68 Commercial, industrial and business activities are often undertaken by means of entities such as sole proprietorships, partnerships, trusts and various types of government business undertakings. The legal and regulatory framework for such entities is often different from that applying to corporate entities. For example, there may be few, if any, restrictions on the distribution to owners or other beneficiaries of amounts included in equity. Nevertheless, the definition of equity and the other aspects of this *Framework* that deal with equity are appropriate for such entities.

Performance

69   Profit is frequently used as a measure of performance or as the basis for other measures, such as return on investment or earnings per share. The elements directly related to the measurement of profit are income and expenses. The recognition and measurement of income and expenses, and hence profit, depends in part on the concepts of capital and capital maintenance used by the entity in preparing its financial statements. These concepts are discussed in paragraphs 102 to 110.

70   The elements of income and expenses are defined as follows.

(a)   Income is increases in economic benefits during the accounting period in the form of inflows or enhancements of assets or decreases of liabilities that result in increases in equity, other than those relating to contributions from equity participants.

(b)   Expenses are decreases in economic benefits during the accounting period in the form of outflows or depletions of assets or incurrences of liabilities that result in decreases in equity, other than those relating to distributions to equity participants.

71   The definitions of income and expenses identify their essential features but do not attempt to specify the criteria that would need to be met before they are recognised in the income statement. Criteria for the recognition of income and expenses are discussed in paragraphs 82 to 98.

72   Income and expenses may be presented in the income statement in different ways so as to provide information that is relevant for economic decision-making. For example, it is common practice to distinguish between those items of income and expenses that arise in the course of the ordinary activities of the entity and those that do not. This distinction is made on the basis that the source of an item is relevant in evaluating the ability of the entity to generate cash and cash equivalents in the future[3]. For example, incidental activities such as the disposal of a long-term investment are unlikely to recur on a regular basis. When distinguishing between items in this way, consideration needs to be given to the nature of the entity and its operations. Items that arise from the ordinary activities of one entity may be unusual in respect of another.

73   Distinguishing between items of income and expense and combining them in different ways also permits several measures of entity performance to be displayed. These have differing degrees of inclusiveness. For example, the income statement could display gross margin, profit or loss before taxation, and profit or loss.

Income

74   The definition of income encompasses both revenue and gains. Revenue arises in the course of the ordinary activities of an entity and is referred to by a variety of different names including sales, fees, interest, dividends, royalties and rent.

75   Gains represent other items that meet the definition of income and may, or may not, arise in the course of the ordinary activities of an entity. Gains represent increases in economic benefits and as such are no different in nature from revenue. Hence, they are not regarded as constituting a separate element in this *Framework*.

76   Gains include, for example, those arising on the disposal of non-current assets. The definition of income also includes unrealised gains; for example, those arising on the revaluation of marketable securities and those resulting from increases in the carrying amount of long-term assets. When gains are recognised in the income statement, they are usually displayed separately because knowledge of them is useful for the purpose of making economic decisions. Gains are often reported net of related expenses.

77   Various kinds of assets may be received or enhanced by income. Examples include cash, receivables and goods and services received in exchange for goods and services supplied. Income may also result from the settlement of liabilities. For example, an entity may provide goods and services to a lender in settlement of an obligation to repay an outstanding loan.

---

3   For not-for-profit users, also see paragraph AUS15.1

Expenses

78   The definition of expenses encompasses losses as well as those expenses that arise in the course of the ordinary activities of the entity. Expenses that arise in the course of the ordinary activities of the entity include, for example, cost of sales, wages and depreciation. They usually take the form of an outflow or depletion of assets such as cash and cash equivalents, inventory, property, plant and equipment.

79   Losses represent other items that meet the definition of expenses and may, or may not, arise in the course of the ordinary activities of the entity. Losses represent decreases in economic benefits and as such they are no different in nature from other expenses. Hence, they are not regarded as a separate element in this *Framework*.

80   Losses include, for example, those resulting from disasters such as fire and flood, as well as those arising on the disposal of non-current assets. The definition of expenses also includes unrealised losses, for example, those arising from the effects of increases in the rate of exchange for a foreign currency in respect of the borrowings of an entity in that currency. When losses are recognised in the income statement, they are usually displayed separately because knowledge of them is useful for the purpose of making economic decisions. Losses are often reported net of related income.

Capital Maintenance Adjustments

81   The revaluation or restatement of assets and liabilities gives rise to increases or decreases in equity. While these increases or decreases meet the definition of income and expenses, they are not included in the income statement under certain concepts of capital maintenance. Instead these items are included in equity as capital maintenance adjustments or revaluation reserves. These concepts of capital maintenance are discussed in paragraphs 102 to 110 of this *Framework*.

Recognition of the Elements of Financial Statements

82   Recognition is the process of incorporating in the balance sheet or income statement an item that meets the definition of an element and satisfies the criteria for recognition set out in paragraph 83. It involves the depiction of the item in words and by a monetary amount and the inclusion of that amount in the balance sheet or income statement totals. Items that satisfy the recognition criteria should be recognised in the balance sheet or income statement. The failure to recognise such items is not rectified by disclosure of the accounting policies used nor by notes or explanatory material.

83   An item that meets the definition of an element should be recognised if:

    (a)   it is probable that any future economic benefit associated with the item will flow to or from the entity; and

    (b)   the item has a cost or value that can be measured with reliability.

84   In assessing whether an item meets these criteria, and therefore qualifies for recognition in the financial statements, regard needs to be given to the materiality considerations discussed in paragraphs 29 and 30. The interrelationship between the elements means that an item that meets the definition and recognition criteria for a particular element, for example, an asset, automatically requires the recognition of another element, for example, income or a liability.

The Probability of Future Economic Benefit

85   The concept of probability is used in the recognition criteria to refer to the degree of uncertainty that the future economic benefits associated with the item will flow to or from the entity. The concept is in keeping with the uncertainty that characterises the environment in which an entity operates. Assessments of the degree of uncertainty attaching to the flow of future economic benefits are made on the basis of the evidence available when the financial statements are prepared. For example, when it is probable that a receivable owed by an entity will be paid, it is then justifiable, in the absence of any evidence to the contrary, to recognise the receivable as an asset. For a large population of receivables, however, some degree of non-payment is normally considered probable; hence an expense representing the expected reduction in economic benefits is recognised.

Reliability of Measurement

86   The second criterion for the recognition of an item is that it possesses a cost or value that
can be measured with reliability, as discussed in paragraphs 31 to 38 of this *Framework*.
In many cases, cost or value must be estimated. The use of reasonable estimates is an
essential part of the preparation of financial statements and does not undermine their
reliability. When, however, a reasonable estimate cannot be made the item is not recognised
in the balance sheet or income statement. For example, the expected proceeds from a
lawsuit may meet the definitions of both an asset and income as well as the probability
criterion for recognition. However, if it is not possible for the claim to be measured reliably,
it should not be recognised as an asset or as income. The existence of the claim, however,
would be disclosed in the notes, explanatory material or supplementary schedules.

87   An item that, at a particular point in time, fails to meet the recognition criteria in
paragraph 83, may qualify for recognition at a later date as a result of subsequent
circumstances or events.

88   An item that possesses the essential characteristics of an element but fails to meet the
criteria for recognition may nonetheless warrant disclosure in the notes, explanatory
material or in supplementary schedules. This is appropriate when knowledge of the
item is considered to be relevant to the evaluation of the financial position, financial
performance and cash flows of an entity by the users of financial statements.

Recognition of Assets

89   An asset is recognised in the balance sheet when it is probable that the future economic
benefits will flow to the entity and the asset has a cost or value that can be measured
reliably.

90   An asset is not recognised in the balance sheet when expenditure has been incurred for
which it is considered improbable that economic benefits will flow to the entity beyond
the current accounting period. Instead, such a transaction results in the recognition of an
expense in the income statement. This treatment does not imply either that the intention of
management in incurring expenditure was other than to generate future economic benefits
for the entity or that management was misguided. The only implication is that the degree
of certainty that economic benefits will flow to the entity beyond the current accounting
period is insufficient to warrant the recognition of an asset.

Recognition of Liabilities

91   A liability is recognised in the balance sheet when it is probable that an outflow of resources
embodying economic benefits will result from the settlement of a present obligation and
the amount at which the settlement will take place can be measured reliably. In practice,
obligations under contracts that are equally proportionately unperformed (for example,
liabilities for inventory ordered but not yet received) are generally not recognised as
liabilities in the financial statements. However, such obligations may meet the definition
of liabilities and, provided the recognition criteria are met in the particular circumstances,
may qualify for recognition. In such circumstances, recognition of liabilities entails
recognition of related assets or expenses.

Recognition of Income

92   Income is recognised in the income statement when an increase in future economic
benefits related to an increase in an asset or a decrease of a liability has arisen that can be
measured reliably. This means, in effect, that recognition of income occurs simultaneously
with the recognition of increases in assets or decreases in liabilities (for example, the net
increase in assets arising on a sale of goods or services or the decrease in liabilities arising
from the waiver of a debt payable).

93   The procedures normally adopted in practice for recognising income, for example, the
requirement that revenue should be earned, are applications of the recognition criteria
in this *Framework*. Such procedures are generally directed at restricting the recognition
as income to those items that can be measured reliably and have a sufficient degree of
certainty.

Recognition of Expenses

94   Expenses are recognised in the income statement when a decrease in future economic benefits related to a decrease in an asset or an increase of a liability has arisen that can be measured reliably. This means, in effect, that recognition of expenses occurs simultaneously with the recognition of an increase in liabilities or a decrease in assets (for example, the accrual of employee entitlements or the depreciation of equipment).

95   Expenses are recognised in the income statement on the basis of a direct association between the costs incurred and the earning of specific items of income. This process, commonly referred to as the matching of costs with revenues, involves the simultaneous or combined recognition of revenues and expenses that result directly and jointly from the same transactions or other events. For example, the various components of expense making up the cost of goods sold are recognised at the same time as the income derived from the sale of the goods. However, the application of the matching concept under this Framework does not allow the recognition of items in the balance sheet which do not meet the definition of assets or liabilities.

96   When economic benefits are expected to arise over several accounting periods and the association with income can only be broadly or indirectly determined, expenses are recognised in the income statement on the basis of systematic and rational allocation procedures. This is often necessary in recognising the expenses associated with the using up of assets such as property, plant, equipment, goodwill, patents and trademarks. In such cases, the expense is referred to as depreciation or amortisation. These allocation procedures are intended to recognise expenses in the accounting periods in which the economic benefits associated with these items are consumed or expire.

97   An expense is recognised immediately in the income statement when an expenditure produces no future economic benefits or when, and to the extent that, future economic benefits do not qualify, or cease to qualify, for recognition in the balance sheet as an asset.

98   An expense is also recognised in the income statement in those cases when a liability is incurred without the recognition of an asset, as when a liability under a product warranty arises.

Measurement of the Elements of Financial Statements

99   Measurement is the process of determining the monetary amounts at which the elements of the financial statements are to be recognised and carried in the balance sheet and income statement. This involves the selection of the particular basis of measurement.

100   A number of different measurement bases are employed to different degrees and in varying combinations in financial statements, including the following.

    (a)   *Historical cost* Assets are recorded at the amount of cash or cash equivalents paid or the fair value of the consideration given to acquire them at the time of their acquisition. Liabilities are recorded at the amount of proceeds received in exchange for the obligation, or in some circumstances (for example, income taxes), at the amounts of cash or cash equivalents expected to be paid to satisfy the liability in the normal course of business.

    (b)   *Current cost* Assets are carried at the amount of cash or cash equivalents that would have to be paid if the same or an equivalent asset was acquired currently. Liabilities are carried at the undiscounted amount of cash or cash equivalents that would be required to settle the obligation currently.

    (c)   *Realisable (settlement) value* Assets are carried at the amount of cash or cash equivalents that could currently be obtained by selling the asset in an orderly disposal. Liabilities are carried at their settlement values; that is, the undiscounted amounts of cash or cash equivalents expected to be paid to satisfy the liabilities in the normal course of business.

    (d)   *Present value* Assets are carried at the present discounted value of the future net cash inflows that the item is expected to generate in the normal course of business. Liabilities are carried at the present discounted value of the future net cash outflows that are expected to be required to settle the liabilities in the normal course of business.

101   The measurement basis most commonly adopted by entities in preparing their financial
statements is historical cost. This is usually combined with other measurement bases.
For example, inventories are usually carried at the lower of cost and net realisable value,
marketable securities may be carried at market value and pension liabilities are carried at
their present value. Furthermore, some entities use the current cost basis as a response to
the inability of the historical cost accounting model to deal with the effects of changing
prices of non-monetary assets.

Concepts of Capital and Capital Maintenance

Concepts of Capital

102   A financial concept of capital is adopted by most entities in preparing their financial
statements. Under a financial concept of capital, such as invested money or invested
purchasing power, capital is synonymous with the net assets or equity of the entity.
Under a physical concept of capital, such as operating capability, capital is regarded as
the productive capacity of the entity based on, for example, units of output per day.

103   The selection of the appropriate concept of capital by an entity should be based on the
needs of the users of its financial statements. Thus, a financial concept of capital should be
adopted if the users of financial statements are primarily concerned with the maintenance
of nominal invested capital or the purchasing power of invested capital. If, however, the
main concern of users is with the operating capability of the entity, a physical concept of
capital should be used. The concept chosen indicates the goal to be attained in determining
profit, even though there may be some measurement difficulties in making the concept
operational.

Concepts of Capital Maintenance and the Determination of Profit

104   The concepts of capital in paragraph 102 give rise to the following concepts of capital
maintenance.

(a)   *Financial capital maintenance* Under this concept, a profit is earned only if the
financial (or money) amount of the net assets at the end of the period exceeds
the financial (or money) amount of net assets at the beginning of the period, after
excluding any distributions to, and contributions from, owners during the period.
Financial capital maintenance can be measured in either nominal monetary units
or units of constant purchasing power.

(b)   *Physical capital maintenance* Under this concept, a profit is earned only if the
physical productive capacity (or operating capability) of the entity (or the resources
or funds needed to achieve that capacity) at the end of the period exceeds the
physical productive capacity at the beginning of the period, after excluding any
distributions to, and contributions from, owners during the period.

105   The concept of capital maintenance is concerned with how an entity defines the capital
that it seeks to maintain. It provides the linkage between the concepts of capital and the
concepts of profit because it provides the point of reference by which profit is measured.
It is a prerequisite for distinguishing between an entity's return on capital and its return
of capital. Only inflows of assets in excess of amounts needed to maintain capital may
be regarded as profit and therefore as a return on capital. Hence, profit is the residual
amount that remains after expenses (including capital maintenance adjustments, where
appropriate) have been deducted from income. If expenses exceed income, the residual
amount is a net loss.

106   The physical capital maintenance concept requires the adoption of the current cost basis
of measurement. The financial capital maintenance concept, however, does not require
the use of a particular basis of measurement. Selection of the basis under this concept is
dependent on the type of financial capital that the entity is seeking to maintain.

107   The principal difference between the two concepts of capital maintenance is the treatment
of the effects of changes in the prices of assets and liabilities of the entity. In general
terms, an entity has maintained its capital if it has as much capital at the end of the period
as it had at the beginning of the period. Any amount over and above that required to
maintain the capital at the beginning of the period is profit.

108 Under the concept of financial capital maintenance where capital is defined in terms of nominal monetary units, profit represents the increase in nominal money capital over the period. Thus, increases in the prices of assets held over the period, conventionally referred to as holding gains, are, conceptually, profits. They may not be recognised as such, however, until the assets are disposed of in an exchange transaction. When the concept of financial capital maintenance is defined in terms of constant purchasing power units, profit represents the increase in invested purchasing power over the period. Thus, only that part of the increase in the prices of assets that exceeds the increase in the general level of prices is regarded as profit. The rest of the increase is treated as a capital maintenance adjustment and, hence, as part of equity.

109 Under the concept of physical capital maintenance when capital is defined in terms of the physical productive capacity, profit represents the increase in that capital over the period. All price changes affecting the assets and liabilities of the entity are viewed as changes in the measurement of the physical productive capacity of the entity. Hence, they are treated as capital maintenance adjustments that are part of equity and not as profit.

110 The selection of the measurement bases and concept of capital maintenance will determine the accounting model used in the preparation of the financial statements. Different accounting models exhibit different degrees of relevance and reliability and, as in other areas, management must seek a balance between relevance and reliability. This Framework is applicable to a range of accounting models and provides guidance on preparing and presenting the financial statements constructed under the chosen model. At the present time, it is not the intention of the AASB to prescribe a particular model other than in exceptional circumstances, such as for those entities reporting in the currency of a hyperinflationary economy. This intention will, however, be reviewed in the light of world developments.

AASB 1
First-time Adoption of Australian Accounting Standards
(Compiled June 2012)

Note from the Institute of Chartered Accountants Australia

This note, prepared by the technical editors, is not part of Accounting Standard AASB 1.

Historical development

15 July 2004: AASB 1 'First-Time Adoption of Australian equivalents to International Financial Reporting Standards' is the Australian equivalent of IFRS 1 of the same name. It was made by the AASB on 15 July 2004 as part of the AASB's program to adopt International Financial Reporting Standards by 2005.

9 December 2004: AASB 2004-1 'Amendments to Australian Accounting Standards' adds paragraph 36B (and preceding heading), and is applicable to annual reporting periods beginning on or after 1 January 2005.

22 December 2004: AASB 2004-2 'Amendments to Australian Accounting Standards' adds paragraphs 13(k), 13(l), and 25G (and preceding heading), and is applicable to annual reporting periods beginning on or after 1 January 2005.

22 December 2004: AASB 2004-3 'Amendments to Australian Accounting Standards' amends paragraphs 13(c), 20, and 20A as a consequence of the reissue of AASB 119 'Employee Benefits' (December 2004). Paragraph IG18 is also amended. The amendments apply to annual reporting periods beginning on or after 1 January 2006, and on or after 1 January 2005 for entities that choose to early-adopt AASB 119 and AASB 2004-3.

9 June 2005: AASB 2005-4 'Amendments to Australian Accounting Standards' amends paragraphs 25A, 25A(a) to 25A(e), 43A, IG56(d)(iii), and IG56(d)(iv). The amendments apply to annual reporting periods beginning on or after 1 January 2006. Entities that choose to early-adopt the amendments in AASB 2005-4 in respect of AASB 139 to apply to annual reporting periods beginning on or after 1 January 2005 must also apply the amendments made to AASB 1 by AASB 2005-4.

9 June 2005: AASB 2005-5 'Amendments to Australian Accounting Standards' adds paragraphs 25F (and preceding heading), IG204 (and preceding heading), IG205 and IG example 202 and amends paragraphs 12, 13(i), 13(j), and 13(k). The amendments apply to annual reporting periods beginning on or after 1 January 2006. If an entity applies UIG Interpretation 4 'Determining whether an Arrangement contains a Lease', the amendments and added paragraph 25F may be applied to annual reporting periods beginning on or after 1 January 2005.

30 June 2005: AASB 2005-8 'Amendments to Australian Accounting Standards' amends paragraphs Aus25D.1, 36A(c), and 36B (and preceding heading). The amendments apply to annual reporting periods ending on or after 31 December 2005, and entities may early-adopt for annual reporting periods beginning on or after 1 January 2005.

5 September 2005: AASB 2005-10 'Amendments to Australian Accounting Standards' adds paragraph 36C and amends paragraph 36A(a). The amendments are applicable to annual reporting periods beginning on or after 1 January 2007, although entities may choose to early-adopt this Standard for annual reporting periods beginning on or after 1 January 2005.

21 March 2006: AASB 2006-2 'Amendments to Australian Accounting Standards' adds paragraph Aus3.2. The amendment is applicable to annual reporting periods ending on or after 20 June 2006. Entities may choose to early-adopt for annual reporting periods beginning on or after 1 January 2005.

The AASB decided at its meeting on 6 April 2006 to delete all the Australian paragraphs in the Implementation Guidance accompanying, but not part of, AASB 1. The following paragraphs were deleted: AIG10.1, AIG Example A1, AIG10.2, AIG25.1, AIG 29.1, AIG 62.1, AIG 62.2, AIG 100.1, AIG 100.2, AIG 100.3, Example A100.

AASB

15 February 2007: AASB 2007-2a 'Amendments to Australian Accounting Standards' amends paragraphs 25E and Appendix A. The amendment is applicable to annual reporting periods ending on or after 28 February 2007. Entities may elect to early-adopt for annual reporting periods beginning on or after 1 January 2005.

15 February 2007: AASB 2007-2b 'Amendments to Australian Accounting Standards' amends paragraphs 9, 12, 13(k), 13(l), 25F and 25H and adds paragraph 13(m). The amendment is applicable to annual reporting periods beginning on or after 1 January 2008. Entities may elect to early-adopt to annual reporting periods beginning on or after 1 January 2005, provided that Interpretation 12 'Service Concession Arrangements' is also applied.

30 April 2007: AASB 2007-4 'Amendments to Australian Accounting Standards' amends paragraphs 9, 10, 12, 13(i), 20A, 25, 25F, 26, 35, 36, 36A, 45, B2(c) and B2(g) of Appendix B. It deletes paragraphs AUS25D.1, AUS34B.1 and AUS36.1 and adds paragraphs 34B and B2(i) of Appendix B. The amendment is applicable to annual reporting periods beginning on or after 1 July 2007. Entities may elect to early-adopt for annual reporting periods beginning on or after 1 January 2005.

14 June 2007: AASB 2007-6 'Amendments to Australian Accounting Standards' was issued by the AASB. This Standard is applicable to annual reporting periods beginning on or after 1 January 2009.

28 June 2007: AASB 2007-7 'Amendments to Australian Accounting Standards' amends paragraphs 12, and 34A. This amendment is applicable to annual reporting periods beginning on or after 1 July 2007. Entities may elect to early-adopt for annual reporting periods beginning on or after 1 January 2005.

24 September 2007: AASB 2007-8 'Amendments to Australian Accounting Standards arising from AASB 101' amends AASB 1 to align with revised AASB 101. This Standard is applicable to annual reporting periods beginning on or after 1 January 2009.

13 December 2007: AASB 2007-10 'Further Amendments to Australian Accounting Standards arising from AASB 101' amends AASB 1, primarily replacing the term 'financial report' with 'financial statements'. This Standard is applicable to annual reporting periods beginning on or after 1 January 2009.

6 March 2008: AASB 2008-3 'Amendments to Australian Accounting Standards arising from AASB 3 and AASB 127' amends AASB 1 for the issue of AASB 3 Revised. This Standard is applicable to annual reporting periods beginning on or after 1 July 2009.

24 July 2008: AASB 2008-6 'Further Amendments to Australian Accounting Standards arising from the Annual Improvements Project' amends AASB 1 and AASB 5 to include requirements relating to a sale plan involving the loss of control of a subsidiary. This Standard is applicable to annual reporting periods beginning on or after 1 July 2009.

25 July 2008: AASB 2008-7 'Amendments to Australian Accounting Standards – Cost of an Investment in a Subsidiary, Jointly Controlled Entity or Associate' amends AASB 1 to allow first-time adopters, in their separate financial statements, to use a deemed cost option for determining the cost of an investment in a subsidiary, jointly controlled entity or associate. This Standard is applicable to annual reporting periods beginning on or after 1 January 2009.

22 April 2009: AASB 2009-1 'Amendments to Australian Accounting Standards' adds a footnote clarifying that notwithstanding paragraph IG23 of this Standard, a not-for-profit public sector entity may choose to expense borrowing costs. This Standard is applicable to periods beginning on or after 1 January 2009 that end on or after 30 April 2009.

21 May 2009: AASB 1 'First-time Adoption of Australian Accounting Standards' was reissued by the AASB, applicable to annual reporting periods beginning on or after 1 July 2009. This Standard can be applied early.

25 June 2009: AASB 2009-6 'Amendments to Australian Accounting Standards' amends AASB 1 'First-time Adoption of Australian Equivalents to International Financial Reporting Standards' for editorial corrections made by the International Accounting Standards Board (IASB) to its Standards and Interpretations (IFRSs) and as a consequence of issuing revised AASB 101 'Presentation of Financial Statements' (September 2007). This Standard is applicable to annual reporting periods beginning on or after 1 January 2009 that end on or after 30 June 2009. These amendments do not impact on AASB 1 'First-time Adoption of Australian Accounting Standards'.

24 September 2009: AASB 2009-9 'Amendments to Australian Accounting Standards' amends AASB 1 'First-time Adoption of Australian Accounting Standards' to include additional exemptions for first time adopters. This Standard applies to annual reporting periods beginning on or after 1 January 2010 and can be applied early.

5 October 2009: Erratum makes further terminology-related and editorial changes resulting from AASB 2009-6 to AASB 1 'First-time Adoption of Australian Equivalents to International Financial Reporting Standards'. This erratum applies to annual reporting periods beginning on or after 1 January 2009 that end on or after 30 June 2009. These amendments do not impact on AASB 1 'First-time Adoption of Australian Accounting Standards'.

12 October 2009: AASB 1 'First-time Adoption of Australian Equivalents to International Financial Reporting Standards' was reissued by the AASB, applicable to annual reporting periods beginning on or after 1 January 2009 but before 1 July 2009 that end on or after 30 June 2009. This version of AASB 1 has been compiled for the amending Standards applying to annual reporting periods beginning on or after 1 January 2009.

7 December 2009: AASB 2009-11 'Amendments to Australian Accounting Standards arising from AASB 9' amends AASB 1 to give effect to consequential changes arising from the issuance of AASB 9. This Standard is applicable to annual reporting periods beginning on or after 1 January 2013 with early adoption permitted from annual reporting periods ending on or after 31 December 2009 that begin before 1 January 2013 provided AASB 9 is also applied for the same period. The application date of AASB 2009-11 has been amended to 1 January 2015 by AASB 2012-6. **These amendments have been superseded by AASB 2010-7 and are not included in this compiled Standard.**

21 December 2009: AASB 2009-13 'Amendments to Australian Accounting Standards arising from Interpretation 19' amends AASB 1 consequential to the issuance of Interpretation 19. This Standard is applicable to annual reporting periods beginning on or after 1 July 2010 with early adoption permitted.

3 February 2010: AASB 2010-1 'Amendments to Australian Accounting Standards – Limited Exemption from Comparative AASB 7 Disclosures for First-time Adopters' amends AASB 1 to give limited exemption from comparative AASB 7 disclosures for first-time adopters. This Standard is applicable to annual reporting periods beginning on or after 1 July 2010 with early adoption permitted.

1 March 2010: AASB 1 was reissued by the AASB, compiled to include the AASB 2009-9, AASB 2009-13 and AASB 2010-1 amendments and applies to annual reporting periods beginning on or after 1 July 2010 but before 1 January 2013.

23 June 2010: AASB 2010-4 'Further Amendments to Australian Accounting Standards arising from the Annual Improvements Project' amends AASB 1 accounting policy changes in the year of adoption, revaluation basis as deemed cost, and use of deemed cost for operations subject to rate regulation. This Standard is applicable to annual reporting periods beginning on or after 1 January 2011, with early adoption permitted for annual reporting periods beginning on or after 1 January 2005 but before 1 January 2011.

27 October 2010: AASB 2010-5 'Further Amendments to Australian Accounting Standards' makes editorial amendments to AASB 1. This Standard is applicable to annual reporting periods beginning on or after 1 January 2011.

8 November 2010: AASB 2010-6 'Amendments to Australian Accounting Standards – Disclosure on Transfers of Financial Assets' adds and amends disclosure requirements about transfers of financial assets. This Standard is applicable to annual reporting periods beginning on or after 1 July 2011.

31 December 2010: AASB 2010-9: 'Amendments to Australian Accounting Standards – Severe Hyperinflation and Removal of Fixed Dates for First-time Adopters' amends AASB 1 to provide relief for first-time adopters of Australian Accounting Standards from having to reconstruct transactions relating to hyperinflation that occurred before their date of transition to Australian Accounting Standards. This Standard applies to annual reporting periods beginning on or after 1 July 2011 with early adoption permitted.

1 March 2011: AASB 2010-7 'Amendments to Australian Accounting Standards arising from AASB 9 (December 2010)' as compiled amends AASB 1 to give effect to consequential changes arising from the reissue of AASB 9 in December 2010 and supersedes AASB 2009-11 which related to the previous version of AASB 9. This Standard applies to annual reporting periods beginning on or after 1 January 2013 and can be adopted early. The application date of AASB 2010-7 has been amended to 1 January 2015 by AASB 2012-6. **These amendments are not included in this compiled Standard.**

11 May 2011: AASB 2011-1 'Amendments to Australian Accounting Standards arising from the Trans-Tasman Convergence Project' amends AASB 1 as a result of the Trans-Tasman project to more closely align IFRSs as applied through Australian and New Zealand Standards. AASB 2011-1 deletes Australian specific disclosure requirements. Where appropriate these disclosures are now included in AASB 1054 'Australian Additional Requirements'. These Standards apply to annual reporting periods beginning on or after 1 July 2011 with early adoption permitted.

29 August 2011: AASB 2011-7 'Amendments to Australian Accounting Standards arising from the Consolidation and Joint Arrangements Standards' amends AASB 1 to give effect to many consequential changes arising from the issue of AASB 10, 11, 12, 127 and 128. This Standard applies to annual reporting periods beginning on or after 1 January 2013 and can be adopted early by for-profit entities. **These amendments are not included in this compiled Standard.**

2 September 2011: AASB 2011-8 'Amendments to Australian Accounting Standards arising from AASB 13' amends AASB 1 to give effect to a consequential change in the definition of fair value arising from the issue of AASB 13. This Standard applies to annual reporting periods beginning on or after 1 January 2013 and can be adopted early. **These amendments are not included in this compiled Standard.**

5 September 2011: AASB 2011-9 'Amendments to Australian Accounting Standards – Presentation of Items of Other Comprehensive income' amends the presentation of items in other comprehensive income. This Standard applies to annual reporting periods beginning on or after 1 July 2012 and can be adopted early.

5 September 2011: AASB 2011-10 'Amendments to Australian Accounting Standards arising from AASB 119 (September 2011)' amends AASB 1 to give effect to a consequential change arising from the issue of AASB 119. This Standard applies to annual reporting periods beginning on or after 1 January 2013 and can be adopted early. **These amendments are not included in this compiled Standard.**

23 September 2011: AASB 1 was reissued by the AASB, compiled to include the AASB 2010-4, 2010-5, 2010-6, 2010-9 and AASB 2011-1 amendments and applies to annual reporting periods ending on or after 1 July 2011 but before 1 July 2012.

20 June 2012: AASB 1 was reissued by the AASB, compiled to include the AASB 2011-9 amendments and applies to annual reporting periods beginning on or after 1 July 2012 but before 1 January 2013.

29 June 2012: AASB 2012-4 'Amendments to Australian Accounting Standards – Government' amends AASB 1 in relation to the transitional provisions for government loans. This Standard applies to annual reporting periods beginning on or after 1 January 2013 and can be applied early. **These amendments are not included in this compiled Standard.**

29 June 2012: AASB 2012-5 'Amendments to Australian Accounting Standards arising from Annual Improvements 2009–2011 Cycle' amends AASB 1 in relation to repeated application of AASB 1 and borrowing costs. This Standard applies to annual reporting periods beginning on or after 1 January 2013 and can be applied early. **These amendments are not included in this compiled Standard.**

References

Interpretation 9 *Reassessment of Embedded Derivatives*, Interpretation 11 AASB 2 – *Group and Treasury Share Transactions*, and Interpretation 12 *Service Concession Arrangements*, apply to AASB 1.

IFRIC items not taken onto the agenda: *No. 53 Impracticability Exception and Transition Date Exchange Rate* issued in October 2004 and IFRS 1-2 *Accounting for costs included in self constructed assets on transition* apply to AASB 1.

AASB 1 compared to IFRS 1

Additions

Paragraph	Description
Aus 1.1	Which entities AASB 1 applies to (i.e. reporting entities and general purpose financial statements).
Aus 1.2	The application date of AASB 1 (i.e. annual reporting periods beginning 1 July 2009).
Aus 1.3	Allows early application of AASB 1.

Aus 1.4	Makes the requirements of AASB 1 subject to AASB 1031 'Materiality'.
Aus 1.5	Specifies this Standard supersedes the previous version of AASB 1.
Aus 3.2	Clarifies how not-for-profit entities that have previously not complied with the GAAP can satisfy the requirements of paragraph 3.

Deletion

| *Paragraph* | *Description* |
| 40 | Withdrawal of IFRS 1 (2003). |

Contents

Compilation Details

Comparison with IFRS 1

Accounting Standard
AASB 1 First-time Adoption of Australian Accounting Standards

	Paragraphs
Objective	1
Application	Aus1.1 – Aus1.5
Scope	2 – 5
Recognition and measurement	
Opening Australian-Accounting-Standards statement of financial position	6
Accounting policies	7 – 12
Exceptions to the retrospective application of other Australian Accounting Standards	13
Estimates	14 – 17
Exemptions from other Australian Accounting Standards	18 – 19
Presentation and disclosure	20
Comparative information	21
Non-Australian-Accounting-Standards comparative information and historical summaries	22
Explanation of transition to Australian Accounting Standards	23
Reconciliations	24 – 28
Designation of financial assets or financial liabilities	29
Use of fair value as deemed cost	30
Use of deemed cost for investments in subsidiaries, jointly controlled entities and associates	31
Use of deemed cost for oil and gas assets	31A
Use of deemed cost for operations subject to rate regulation	31B
Use of deemed cost after severe hyperinflation	31C
Interim financial reports	32 – 33
Effective date	34 – 39K

Appendices:

A. Defined terms

B. Exceptions to the retrospective application of other Australian Accounting Standards

C. Exemptions for business combinations

D. Exemptions from other Australian Accounting Standards

E. Short-term exemptions from Australian Accounting Standards

Deleted IFRS 1 Text

Implementation Guidance
(available on the AASB website)

Basis for Conclusions on IFRS 1
(available on the AASB website)

Table of Concordance for IFRS 1
(available on the AASB website)

Australian Accounting Standard AASB 1 *First-time Adoption of Australian Accounting Standards* (as amended) is set out in paragraphs 1 – 39K and Appendices A – E. All the paragraphs have equal authority. Paragraphs in **bold type** state the main principles. AASB 1 is to be read in the context of other Australian Accounting Standards, including AASB 1048 *Interpretation of Standards*, which identifies the Australian Accounting Interpretations. In the absence of explicit guidance, AASB 108 *Accounting Policies, Changes in Accounting Estimates and Errors* provides a basis for selecting and applying accounting policies.

Compilation Details

Accounting Standard AASB 1 *First-time Adoption of Australian Accounting Standards* as amended

This compiled Standard applies to annual reporting periods beginning on or after 1 July 2012 but before 1 January 2013. It takes into account amendments up to and including 5 September 2011 and was prepared on 20 June 2012 by the staff of the Australian Accounting Standards Board (AASB).

This compilation is not a separate Accounting Standard made by the AASB. Instead, it is a representation of AASB 1 (May 2009) as amended by other Accounting Standards, which are listed in the Table below.

Table of Standards

Standard	Date made	Application date *(annual reporting periods ... on or after ...)*	Application, saving or transitional provisions
AASB 1	21 May 2009	*(beginning)* 1 July 2009	see (a) below
AASB 2009-9	24 Sep 2009	*(beginning)* 1 Jan 2010	see (b) below
AASB 2009-11	7 Dec 2009	*(beginning)* 1 Jan 2013	not compiled*
AASB 2009-13	21 Dec 2009	*(beginning)* 1 Jul 2010	see (c) below
AASB 2010-1	3 Feb 2010	*(beginning)* 1 Jul 2010	see (d) below
AASB 2010-4	23 Jun 2010	*(beginning)* 1 Jan 2011	see (e) below
AASB 2010-2	30 Jun 2010	*(beginning)* 1 Jul 2013	not compiled*
AASB 2010-5	27 Oct 2010	*(beginning)* 1 Jan 2011	see (e) below
AASB 2010-6	8 Nov 2010	*(beginning)* 1 Jul 2011	see (f) below
AASB 2010-7	6 Dec 2010	*(beginning)* 1 Jan 2013	not compiled*
AASB 2010-9	31 Dec 2010	*(beginning)* 1 Jul 2011	see (f) below
AASB 2010-10	31 Dec 2010	*(beginning)* 1 Jan 2013	not compiled*
AASB 2011-1	11 May 2011	*(beginning)* 1 Jul 2011	see (g) below
AASB 2011-7	29 Aug 2011	*(beginning)* 1 Jan 2013	not compiled*
AASB 2011-8	2 Sep 2011	*(beginning)* 1 Jan 2013	not compiled*
AASB 2011-9	5 Sep 2011	*(beginning)* 1 Jul 2012	see (h) below
AASB 2011-10	5 Sep 2011	*(beginning)* 1 Jan 2013	not compiled*
AASB 2011-12	14 Nov 2011	*(beginning)* 1 Jan 2013	not compiled*

*   The amendments made by this Standard are not included in this compilation, which presents the principal Standard as applicable to annual reporting periods beginning on or after 1 July 2012 but before 1 January 2013.

(a)   Entities may elect to apply this Standard to annual reporting periods beginning on or after 1 January 2005 but before 1 July 2009.

(b)   Entities may elect to apply this Standard to annual reporting periods beginning on or after 1 January 2005 but before 1 January 2010.

(c)   Entities may elect to apply this Standard to annual reporting periods beginning on or after 1 January 2005 but before 1 July 2010, provided that Interpretation 19 *Extinguishing Financial Liabilities with Equity Instruments* is also applied to such periods.

(d) Entities may elect to apply this Standard to annual reporting periods beginning on or after 1 January 2005 but before 1 July 2010.

(e) Entities may elect to apply this Standard to annual reporting periods beginning on or after 1 January 2005 but before 1 January 2011.

(f) Entities may elect to apply this Standard to annual reporting periods beginning on or after 1 January 2005 but before 1 July 2011.

(g) Entities may elect to apply this Standard, or its amendments to individual pronouncements, to annual reporting periods beginning on or after 1 January 2005 but before 1 July 2011, provided that AASB 1054 *Australian Additional Disclosures* is, or its relevant individual disclosure requirements are, also applied to such periods.

(h) Entities may elect to apply this Standard to annual reporting periods beginning on or after 1 January 2005 but before 1 July 2012.

Table of Amendments

Paragraph affected	How affected	By ... [paragraph]
Aus3.1	deleted	AASB 2011-1 [8]
21	amended	AASB 2011-9 [11]
27	amended	AASB 2010-4 [8]
27A	added	AASB 2010-4 [8]
31A (and preceding heading)	added	AASB 2009-9 [6]
31B (and preceding heading)	added	AASB 2010-4 [8]
31C (and preceding heading)	added	AASB 2010-9 [6]
32	amended	AASB 2010-4 [8]
39A	added	AASB 2009-9 [7]
39C	added renumbered as 39D added	AASB 2010-1 [6] AASB 2010-5 [10] AASB 2010-5 [11]
39E	added	AASB 2010-4 [8]
39F	added	AASB 2010-6 [5]
39H	added	AASB 2010-9 [10]
39K	added	AASB 2011-9 [11]
A, definition of 'IFRSs'	amended	AASB 2010-5 [12]
B2	amended	AASB 2010-9 [7]
C4	amended	AASB 2010-5 [13]
D1	amended amended amended amended	AASB 2009-9 [8] AASB 2010-4 [9] AASB 2010-5 [14] AASB 2010-9 [8]
D5 (preceding heading)	amended	AASB 2009-9 [8]
D8	amended	AASB 2010-4 [9]
D8A	added	AASB 2009-9 [8]
D8B	added	AASB 2010-4 [9]
D9A	added	AASB 2009-9 [8]
D15	amended	AASB 2010-5 [15]
D20	amended	AASB 2010-9 [8]
D21A	added	AASB 2009-9 [8]
D25 (and preceding heading)	added	AASB 2009-13 [5]
D26-D30 (and preceding heading)	added	AASB 2010-9 [9]
E3 (and preceding heading)	added	AASB 2010-1 [7]
E4	added	AASB 2010-6 [6]

Comparison with IFRS 1

AASB 1 *First-time Adoption of Australian Accounting Standards* as amended incorporates IFRS 1 *First-time Adoption of International Financial Reporting Standards* as issued and amended by the International Accounting Standards Board (IASB). Paragraphs that have been added to this Standard (and do not appear in the text of IFRS 1) are identified with the prefix "Aus", followed by the number of the preceding IASB paragraph and decimal numbering. Paragraphs that apply only to not-for-profit entities begin by identifying their limited applicability.

Entities that comply with AASB 1 as amended will simultaneously be in compliance with IFRS 1 as amended, with the exception of not-for-profit public sector entities applying paragraph Aus3.2.

Accounting Standard AASB 1

The Australian Accounting Standards Board made Accounting Standard AASB 1 *First-time Adoption of Australian Accounting Standards* under section 334 of the *Corporations Act 2001* on 21 May 2009.

This compiled version of AASB 1 applies to annual reporting periods beginning on or after 1 July 2012 but before 1 January 2013. It incorporates relevant amendments contained in other AASB Standards made by the AASB up to and including 5 September 2011 (see Compilation Details).

Accounting Standard AASB 1

First-time Adoption of Australian Accounting Standards

Objective

1   The objective of this Standard is to ensure that an entity's *first Australian-Accounting-Standards financial statements*, and its interim financial reports for part of the period covered by those financial statements, contain high quality information that:

(a)   is transparent for users and comparable over all periods presented;

(b)   provides a suitable starting point for accounting in accordance with Australian Accounting Standards[1]; and

(c)   can be generated at a cost that does not exceed the benefits.

Application

Aus1.1   This Standard applies to:

(a)   each entity that is required to prepare financial reports in accordance with Part 2M.3 of the Corporations Act and that is a reporting entity;

(b)   general purpose financial statements of each other reporting entity; and

(c)   financial statements that are, or are held out to be, general purpose financial statements.

Aus1.2   This Standard applies to annual reporting periods beginning on or after 1 July 2009. [Note: For application dates of paragraphs changed or added by an amending Standard, see Compilation Details.]

Aus1.3   This Standard may be applied to annual reporting periods beginning on or after 1 January 2005 but before 1 July 2009. If an entity applies this Standard to an annual reporting period beginning before 1 July 2009, it shall disclose that fact.

Aus1.4   The requirements specified in this Standard apply to the financial statements where information resulting from their application is material in accordance with AASB 1031 *Materiality*.

---

1   The term 'Australian Accounting Standards' refers to Standards (including Interpretations) made by the AASB that apply to any reporting period beginning on or after 1 January 2005.

Aus1.5   When applied or operative, this Standard supersedes AASB 1 *First-time Adoption of Australian Equivalents to International Financial Reporting Standards* issued in July 2004, as amended.

Scope

2   An entity shall apply this Standard in:

   (a)   its first Australian-Accounting-Standards financial statements; and

   (b)   each interim financial report, if any, that it presents in accordance with AASB 134 *Interim Financial Reporting* for part of the period covered by its first Australian-Accounting-Standards financial statements.

3   An entity's first Australian-Accounting-Standards financial statements are the first annual financial statements in which the entity adopts Australian Accounting Standards, by an explicit and unreserved statement in those financial statements of compliance with Australian Accounting Standards. Financial statements in accordance with Australian Accounting Standards are an entity's first Australian-Accounting-Standards financial statements if, for example, the entity:

   (a)   presented its most recent previous financial statements:

      (i)   in accordance with national requirements that are not consistent with Australian Accounting Standards or *International Financial Reporting Standards (IFRSs)* in all respects;

      (ii)   in conformity with Australian Accounting Standards or IFRSs in all respects, except that the financial statements did not contain an explicit and unreserved statement that they complied with Australian Accounting Standards or IFRSs;

      (iii)   containing an explicit statement of compliance with some, but not all, Australian Accounting Standards or IFRSs;

      (iv)   in accordance with national requirements inconsistent with Australian Accounting Standards or IFRSs, using some individual Australian Accounting Standards or IFRSs to account for items for which national requirements did not exist; or

      (v)   in accordance with national requirements, with a reconciliation of some amounts to the amounts determined in accordance with Australian Accounting Standards or IFRSs;

   (b)   prepared financial statements in accordance with Australian Accounting Standards or IFRSs for internal use only, without making them available to the entity's owners or any other external users;

   (c)   prepared a reporting package in accordance with Australian Accounting Standards or IFRSs for consolidation purposes without preparing a complete set of financial statements as defined in AASB 101 *Presentation of Financial Statements* (as revised in 2007); or

   (d)   did not present financial statements for previous periods.

Aus3.1   [Deleted by the AASB]

Aus3.2   In rare circumstances, a not-for-profit public sector entity may experience extreme difficulties in complying with the requirements of certain Australian Accounting Standards due to information deficiencies that have caused the entity to state non-compliance with *previous GAAP*. In these cases, the conditions specified in paragraph 3 for the application of this Standard are taken to be satisfied provided the entity:

   (a)   discloses in its first Australian-Accounting-Standards financial statements:

      (i)   an explanation of information deficiencies and its strategy for rectifying those deficiencies; and

      (ii)   the Australian Accounting Standards that have not been complied with; and (b)　　makes an explicit and unreserved statement of compliance with other Australian Accounting Standards for which there are no information deficiencies.

4　This Standard applies when an entity first adopts Australian Accounting Standards. It does not apply when, for example, an entity:

　　　　(a)　　stops presenting financial statements in accordance with national requirements, having previously presented them as well as another set of financial statements that contained an explicit and unreserved statement of compliance with Australian Accounting Standards or IFRSs;

　　　　(b)　　presented financial statements in the previous year in accordance with national requirements and those financial statements contained an explicit and unreserved statement of compliance with Australian Accounting Standards or IFRSs; or

　　　　(c)　　presented financial statements in the previous year that contained an explicit and unreserved statement of compliance with Australian Accounting Standards or IFRSs, even if the auditors qualified their audit report on those financial statements.

5　This Standard does not apply to changes in accounting policies made by an entity that already applies Australian Accounting Standards. Such changes are the subject of:

　　　　(a)　　requirements on changes in accounting policies in AASB 108 *Accounting Policies, Changes in Accounting Estimates and Errors*; and

　　　　(b)　　specific transitional requirements in other Australian Accounting Standards.

Recognition and measurement

Opening Australian-Accounting-Standards statement of financial position

6　An entity shall prepare and present an *opening Australian-Accounting-Standards statement of financial position* at the *date of transition to Australian Accounting Standards*. This is the starting point for its accounting in accordance with Australian Accounting Standards.

Accounting policies

7　**An entity shall use the same accounting policies in its opening Australian-Accounting-Standards statement of financial position and throughout all periods presented in its first Australian-Accounting-Standards financial statements. Those accounting policies shall comply with each Australian Accounting Standard effective at the end of its *first Australian-Accounting-Standards reporting period*, except as specified in paragraphs 13-19 and Appendices B-E.**

8　An entity shall not apply different versions of Australian Accounting Standards that were effective at earlier dates. An entity may apply a new Standard that is not yet mandatory if that Standard permits early application.

> **Example: Consistent application of latest version of Australian Accounting Standards**
>
> **Background**
>
> The end of entity A's first Australian-Accounting-Standards reporting period is 31 December 20X5. Entity A decides to present comparative information in those financial statements for one year only (see paragraph 21). Therefore, its date of transition to Australian Accounting Standards is the beginning of business on 1 January 20X4 (or, equivalently, close of business on 31 December 20X3). Entity A presented financial statements in accordance with its previous GAAP annually to 31 December each year up to, and including, 31 December 20X4.
>
> **Application of requirements**
>
> Entity A is required to apply the Australian Accounting Standards effective for periods ending on 31 December 20X5 in:
>
> (a) preparing and presenting its opening Australian-Accounting-Standards statement of financial position at 1 January 20X4; and
>
> (b) preparing and presenting its statement of financial position for 31 December 20X5 (including comparative amounts for 20X4), statement of comprehensive income, statement of changes in equity and statement of cash flows for the year to 31 December 20X5 (including comparative amounts for 20X4) and disclosures (including comparative information for 20X4).
>
> If a new Standard is not yet mandatory but permits early application, entity A is permitted, but not required, to apply that Standard in its first Australian-Accounting-Standards financial statements.

9   The transitional provisions in other Australian Accounting Standards apply to changes in accounting policies made by an entity that already uses Australian Accounting Standards; they do not apply to a *first-time adopter*'s transition to Australian Accounting Standards, except as specified in Appendices B-E.

10   Except as described in paragraphs 13-19 and Appendices B-E, an entity shall, in its opening Australian-Accounting-Standards statement of financial position:

   (a)   recognise all assets and liabilities whose recognition is required by Australian Accounting Standards;

   (b)   not recognise items as assets or liabilities if Australian Accounting Standards do not permit such recognition;

   (c)   reclassify items that it recognised in accordance with previous GAAP as one type of asset, liability or component of equity, but are a different type of asset, liability or component of equity in accordance with Australian Accounting Standards; and

   (d)   apply Australian Accounting Standards in measuring all recognised assets and liabilities.

11   The accounting policies that an entity uses in its opening Australian-Accounting-Standards statement of financial position may differ from those that it used for the same date using its previous GAAP. The resulting adjustments arise from events and transactions before the date of transition to Australian Accounting Standards. Therefore, an entity shall recognise those adjustments directly in retained earnings (or, if appropriate, another category of equity) at the date of transition to Australian Accounting Standards.

12   This Standard establishes two categories of exceptions to the principle that an entity's opening Australian-Accounting-Standards statement of financial position shall comply with each Australian Accounting Standard:

   (a)   paragraphs 14-17 and Appendix B prohibit retrospective application of some aspects of other Australian Accounting Standards.

   (b)   Appendices C-E grant exemptions from some requirements of other Australian Accounting Standards.

Exceptions to the retrospective application of other Australian Accounting Standards

13   This Standard prohibits retrospective application of some aspects of other Australian Accounting Standards. These exceptions are set out in paragraphs 14-17 and Appendix B.

Estimates

14   **An entity's estimates in accordance with Australian Accounting Standards at the date of transition to Australian Accounting Standards shall be consistent with estimates made for the same date in accordance with previous GAAP (after adjustments to reflect any difference in accounting policies), unless there is objective evidence that those estimates were in error.**

15   An entity may receive information after the date of transition to Australian Accounting Standards about estimates that it had made under previous GAAP. In accordance with paragraph 14, an entity shall treat the receipt of that information in the same way as non-adjusting events after the reporting period in accordance with AASB 110 *Events after the Reporting Period*. For example, assume that an entity's date of transition to Australian Accounting Standards is 1 January 20X4 and new information on 15 July 20X4 requires the revision of an estimate made in accordance with previous GAAP at 31 December 20X3. The entity shall not reflect that new information in its opening Australian-Accounting-Standards statement of financial position (unless the estimates need adjustment for any differences in accounting policies or there is objective evidence that the estimates were in error). Instead, the entity shall reflect that new information in profit or loss (or, if appropriate, other comprehensive income) for the year ended 31 December 20X4.

16   An entity may need to make estimates in accordance with Australian Accounting Standards at the date of transition to Australian Accounting Standards that were not required at that date under previous GAAP. To achieve consistency with AASB 110, those estimates in accordance with Australian Accounting Standards shall reflect conditions that existed at the date of transition to Australian Accounting Standards. In particular, estimates at the date of transition to Australian Accounting Standards of market prices, interest rates or foreign exchange rates shall reflect market conditions at that date.

17   Paragraphs 14-16 apply to the opening Australian-Accounting-Standards statement of financial position. They also apply to a comparative period presented in an entity's first Australian-Accounting-Standards financial statements, in which case the references to the date of transition to Australian Accounting Standards are replaced by references to the end of that comparative period.

Exemptions from other Australian Accounting Standards

18   An entity may elect to use one or more of the exemptions contained in Appendices C-E. An entity shall not apply these exemptions by analogy to other items.

19   Some exemptions in Appendices C-E refer to *fair value*. In determining fair values in accordance with this Standard, an entity shall apply the definition of fair value in Appendix A and any more specific guidance in other Australian Accounting Standards on the determination of fair values for the asset or liability in question. Those fair values shall reflect conditions that existed at the date for which they were determined.

Presentation and disclosure

20   This Standard does not provide exemptions from the presentation and disclosure requirements in other Australian Accounting Standards.

Comparative information

21   To comply with AASB 101, an entity's first Australian-Accounting-Standards financial statements shall include at least three statements of financial position, two statements of profit or loss and other comprehensive income, two separate statements of profit or loss (if presented), two statements of cash flows and two statements of changes in equity and related notes, including comparative information.

Non-Australian-Accounting-Standards comparative information and historical summaries

22   Some entities present historical summaries of selected data for periods before the first period for which they present full comparative information in accordance with Australian Accounting Standards. This Standard does not require such summaries to comply with the recognition and measurement requirements of Australian Accounting Standards.

Furthermore, some entities present comparative information in accordance with previous GAAP as well as the comparative information required by AASB 101. In any financial statements containing historical summaries or comparative information in accordance with previous GAAP, an entity shall:

(a) label the previous GAAP information prominently as not being prepared in accordance with Australian Accounting Standards; and

(b) disclose the nature of the main adjustments that would make it comply with Australian Accounting Standards. An entity need not quantify those adjustments.

Explanation of transition to Australian Accounting Standards

23 **An entity shall explain how the transition from previous GAAP to Australian Accounting Standards affected its reported financial position, financial performance and cash flows.**

Reconciliations

24 To comply with paragraph 23, an entity's first Australian-Accounting-Standards financial statements shall include:

(a) reconciliations of its equity reported in accordance with previous GAAP to its equity in accordance with Australian Accounting Standards for both of the following dates:

(i) the date of transition to Australian Accounting Standards; and

(ii) the end of the latest period presented in the entity's most recent annual financial statements in accordance with previous GAAP.

(b) a reconciliation to its total comprehensive income in accordance with Australian Accounting Standards for the latest period in the entity's most recent annual financial statements. The starting point for that reconciliation shall be total comprehensive income in accordance with previous GAAP for the same period or, if an entity did not report such a total, profit or loss under previous GAAP.

(c) if the entity recognised or reversed any impairment losses for the first time in preparing its opening Australian-Accounting-Standards statement of financial position, the disclosures that AASB 136 *Impairment of Assets* would have required if the entity had recognised those impairment losses or reversals in the period beginning with the date of transition to Australian Accounting Standards.

25 The reconciliations required by paragraph 24(a) and (b) shall give sufficient detail to enable users to understand the material adjustments to the statement of financial position and statement of comprehensive income. If an entity presented a statement of cash flows under its previous GAAP, it shall also explain the material adjustments to the statement of cash flows.

26 If an entity becomes aware of errors made under previous GAAP, the reconciliations required by paragraph 24(a) and (b) shall distinguish the correction of those errors from changes in accounting policies.

27 AASB 108 does not apply to the changes in accounting policies an entity makes when it adopts Australian Accounting Standards or to changes in those policies until after it presents its first Australian-Accounting-Standards financial statements. Therefore, AASB 108's requirements about changes in accounting policies do not apply in an entity's first Australian-Accounting-Standards financial statements.

27A If during the period covered by its first Australian-Accounting-Standards financial statements an entity changes its accounting policies or its use of the exemptions contained in this Standard, it shall explain the changes between its first Australian-Accounting-Standards interim financial report and its first Australian-Accounting-Standards financial statements, in accordance with paragraph 23, and it shall update the reconciliations required by paragraph 24(a) and (b).

28 If an entity did not present financial statements for previous periods, its first Australian-Accounting-Standards financial statements shall disclose that fact.

Designation of financial assets or financial liabilities

29   An entity is permitted to designate a previously recognised financial asset or financial liability as a financial asset or financial liability at fair value through profit or loss or a financial asset as available for sale in accordance with paragraph D19. The entity shall disclose the fair value of financial assets or financial liabilities designated into each category at the date of designation and their classification and carrying amount in the previous financial statements.

Use of fair value as deemed cost

30   If an entity uses fair value in its opening Australian-Accounting-Standards statement of financial position as *deemed cost* for an item of property, plant and equipment, an investment property or an intangible asset (see paragraphs D5 and D7), the entity's first Australian-Accounting-Standards financial statements shall disclose, for each line item in the opening Australian-Accounting-Standards statement of financial position:

    (a)   the aggregate of those fair values; and

    (b)   the aggregate adjustment to the carrying amounts reported under previous GAAP.

Use of deemed cost for investments in subsidiaries, jointly controlled entities and associates

31   Similarly, if an entity uses a deemed cost in its opening Australian-Accounting-Standards statement of financial position for an investment in a subsidiary, jointly controlled entity or associate in its separate financial statements (see paragraph D15), the entity's first Australian-Accounting-Standards separate financial statements shall disclose:

    (a)   the aggregate deemed cost of those investments for which deemed cost is their previous GAAP carrying amount;

    (b)   the aggregate deemed cost of those investments for which deemed cost is fair value; and

    (c)   the aggregate adjustment to the carrying amounts reported under previous GAAP.

Use of deemed cost for oil and gas assets

31A   If an entity uses the exemption in paragraph D8A(b) for oil and gas assets, it shall disclose that fact and the basis on which carrying amounts determined under previous GAAP were allocated.

Use of deemed cost for operations subject to rate regulation

31B   If an entity uses the exemption in paragraph D8B for operations subject to rate regulation, it shall disclose that fact and the basis on which carrying amounts were determined under previous GAAP.

Use of deemed cost after severe hyperinflation

31C   If an entity elects to measure assets and liabilities at fair value and to use that fair value as the deemed cost in its opening Australian-Accounting-Standards statement of financial position because of severe hyperinflation (see paragraphs D26-D30), the entity's first Australian-Accounting-Standards financial statements shall disclose an explanation of how, and why, the entity had, and then ceased to have, a functional currency that has both of the following characteristics:

    (a)   a reliable general price index is not available to all entities with transactions and balances in the currency.

    (b)   exchangeability between the currency and a relatively stable foreign currency does not exist.

Interim financial reports

32   To comply with paragraph 23, if an entity presents an interim financial report in accordance with AASB 134 for part of the period covered by its first Australian-Accounting-Standards financial statements, the entity shall satisfy the following requirements in addition to the requirements of AASB 134:

(a) Each such interim financial report shall, if the entity presented an interim financial report for the comparable interim period of the immediately preceding financial year, include:

 (i) a reconciliation of its equity in accordance with previous GAAP at the end of that comparable interim period to its equity under Australian Accounting Standards at that date; and

 (ii) a reconciliation to its total comprehensive income in accordance with Australian Accounting Standards for that comparable interim period (current and year to date). The starting point for that reconciliation shall be total comprehensive income in accordance with previous GAAP for that period or, if an entity did not report such a total, profit or loss in accordance with previous GAAP.

(b) In addition to the reconciliations required by (a), an entity's first interim financial report in accordance with AASB 134 for part of the period covered by its first Australian-Accounting-Standards financial statements shall include the reconciliations described in paragraph 24(a) and (b) (supplemented by the details required by paragraphs 25 and 26) or a cross reference to another published document that includes these reconciliations.

(c) If an entity changes its accounting policies or its use of the exemptions contained in this Standard, it shall explain the changes in each such interim financial report in accordance with paragraph 23 and update the reconciliations required by (a) and (b).

33 AASB 134 requires minimum disclosures, which are based on the assumption that users of the interim financial report also have access to the most recent annual financial statements. However, AASB 134 also requires an entity to disclose 'any events or transactions that are material to an understanding of the current interim period'. Therefore, if a first-time adopter did not, in its most recent annual financial statements in accordance with previous GAAP, disclose information material to an understanding of the current interim period, its interim financial report shall disclose that information or include a cross-reference to another published document that includes it.

Effective date

34 An entity shall apply this Standard if its first Australian-Accounting-Standards financial statements are for an annual reporting period beginning on or after 1 July 2009. Earlier application is permitted.

35 AASB 2007-6 *Amendments to Australian Accounting Standards arising from AASB 123* amended paragraphs of the previous version of this Standard that correspond with paragraphs D1(n) and D23 in this version. An entity shall apply the amendments for annual reporting periods beginning on or after 1 July 2009. If an entity applies AASB 123 *Borrowing Costs* (as revised in 2007) for an earlier period, those amendments shall be applied for that earlier period.

36 AASB 2008-3 *Amendments to Australian Accounting Standards arising from AASB 3* and AASB 127 amended paragraphs of the previous version of this Standard that correspond with paragraphs 19, C1 and C4(f) and (g) in this version. If an entity applies AASB 3 *Business Combinations* (revised 2008) for an earlier period, the amendments shall also be applied for that earlier period.

37 AASB 2008-3 amended paragraphs of the previous version of this Standard that correspond with paragraphs B1 and B7 in this version. If an entity applies AASB 127 *Consolidated and Separate Financial Statements* (amended 2008) for an earlier period, the amendments shall be applied for that earlier period.

38 AASB 2008-7 *Amendments to Australian Accounting Standards – Cost of an Investment in a Subsidiary, Jointly Controlled Entity or Associate*, issued in July 2008, added paragraphs to the previous version of this Standard that correspond with paragraphs 31, D1(g), D14 and D15 in this version. An entity shall apply those paragraphs for annual reporting periods beginning on or after 1 July 2009. Earlier application is permitted. If an entity applies the paragraphs for an earlier period, it shall disclose that fact.

39   The paragraph of the previous version of this Standard that corresponds with paragraph B7 in this version was amended by AASB 2008-6 *Further Amendments to Australian Accounting Standards arising from the Annual Improvements Project* issued in July 2008. An entity shall apply those amendments for annual reporting periods beginning on or after 1 July 2009. If an entity applies AASB 127 (amended 2008) for an earlier period, the amendments shall be applied for that earlier period.

39A   AASB 2009-9 *Amendments to Australian Accounting Standards – Additional Exemptions for First-time Adopters*, issued in September 2009, added paragraphs 31A, D8A, D9A and D21A and amended paragraph D1(c), (d) and (l). An entity shall apply those amendments for annual reporting periods beginning on or after 1 January 2010. Earlier application is permitted. If an entity applies the amendments for an earlier period it shall disclose that fact.

39C   AASB 2009-13 *Amendments to Australian Accounting Standards arising from Interpretation 19*, issued in December 2009, added paragraph D25. An entity shall apply that amendment when it applies Interpretation 19 *Extinguishing Financial Liabilities with Equity Instruments* as identified in AASB 1048 *Interpretation of Standards*.

39D   AASB 2010-1 *Amendments to Australian Accounting Standards – Limited Exemption from Comparative AASB 7 Disclosures for First-time Adopters*, issued in February 2010, added paragraph E3. An entity shall apply that amendment for annual reporting periods beginning on or after 1 July 2010. Earlier application is permitted. If an entity applies the amendment for an earlier period, it shall disclose that fact.

39E   AASB 2010-4 *Further Amendments to Australian Accounting Standards arising from the Annual Improvements Project* issued in June 2010 added paragraphs 27A, 31B and D8B and amended paragraphs 27, 32, D1(c) and D8. An entity shall apply those amendments for annual reporting periods beginning on or after 1 January 2011. Earlier application is permitted. If an entity applies the amendments for an earlier period it shall disclose that fact. Entities that adopted Australian Accounting Standards in periods before the effective date of AASB 1 or applied AASB 1 in a previous period are permitted to apply the amendment to paragraph D8 retrospectively in the first annual reporting period after the amendment is effective. An entity applying paragraph D8 retrospectively shall disclose that fact.

39F   AASB 2010-6 *Amendments to Australian Accounting Standards – Disclosures on Transfers of Financial Assets*, issued in November 2010, added paragraph E4. An entity shall apply that amendment for annual reporting periods beginning on or after 1 July 2011. Earlier application is permitted. If an entity applies the amendment for an earlier period, it shall disclose that fact.

39H   AASB 2010-9 *Amendments to Australian Accounting Standards – Severe Hyperinflation and Removal of Fixed Dates for First-time Adopters*, issued in December 2010, amended paragraphs B2, D1 and D20 and added paragraphs 31C and D26-D30. An entity shall apply those amendments for annual reporting periods beginning on or after 1 July 2011. Earlier application is permitted.

39K   AASB 2011-9 *Amendments to Australian Accounting Standards – Presentation of Items of Other Comprehensive Income*, issued in September 2011, amended paragraph 21. An entity shall apply that amendment when it applies AASB 101 as amended in September 2011.

Withdrawal of IFRS 1 (issued 2003)

39   [Deleted by the AASB]

Appendix A

Defined Terms

This appendix is an integral part of AASB 1.

date of transition to Australian Accounting Standards	The beginning of the earliest period for which an entity presents full comparative information under Australian Accounting Standards in its **first Australian-Accounting-Standards financial statements**.
deemed cost	An amount used as a surrogate for cost or depreciated cost at a given date. Subsequent depreciation or amortisation assumes that the entity had initially recognised the asset or liability at the given date and that its cost was equal to the deemed cost.
fair value	The amount for which an asset could be exchanged, or a liability settled, between knowledgeable, willing parties in an arm's length transaction.
first Australian-Accounting-Standards financial statements	The first annual financial statements in which an entity adopts Australian Accounting Standards, by an explicit and unreserved statement of compliance with Australian Accounting Standards.
first Australian-Accounting-Standards reporting period	The latest reporting period covered by an entity's **first Australian-Accounting-Standards financial statements**.
first-time adopter	An entity that presents its **first Australian-Accounting-Standards financial statements**.
International Financial Reporting Standards (IFRSs)	Standards and Interpretations issued by the International Accounting Standards Board (IASB). They comprise:

(a)   International Financial Reporting Standards;

(b)   International Accounting Standards;

(c)   IFRIC Interpretations; and

(d)   SIC Interpretations.[1]

opening Australian-Accounting-Standards statement of financial position	**An entity's statement of financial position at the date of transition to Australian Accounting Standards.**
previous GAAP	The basis of accounting that a **first-time adopter** used immediately before adopting Australian Accounting Standards.

---

1   Definition of IFRSs amended after the name changes introduced by the revised Constitution of the IFRS Foundation in 2010.

Appendix B

Exceptions to the Retrospective Application of Other Australian Accounting Standards

This appendix is an integral part of AASB 1.

B1   An entity shall apply the following exceptions:

   (a)   derecognition of financial assets and financial liabilities (paragraphs B2 and B3);

   (b)   hedge accounting (paragraphs B4-B6); and

   (c)   non-controlling interests (paragraph B7).

Derecognition of financial assets and financial liabilities

B2   Except as permitted by paragraph B3, a first-time adopter shall apply the derecognition requirements in AASB 139 *Financial Instruments: Recognition and Measurement* prospectively for transactions occurring on or after the date of transition to Australian Accounting Standards. For example, if a first-time adopter derecognised non-derivative financial assets or non-derivative financial liabilities in accordance with its previous GAAP as a result of a transaction that occurred before the date of transition to Australian Accounting Standards, it shall not recognise those assets and liabilities in accordance with Australian Accounting Standards (unless they qualify for recognition as a result of a later transaction or event).

B3   Notwithstanding paragraph B2, an entity may apply the derecognition requirements in AASB 139 retrospectively from a date of the entity's choosing, provided that the information needed to apply AASB 139 to financial assets and financial liabilities derecognised as a result of past transactions was obtained at the time of initially accounting for those transactions.

Hedge accounting

B4   As required by AASB 139, at the date of transition to Australian Accounting Standards, an entity shall:

   (a)   measure all derivatives at fair value; and

   (b)   eliminate all deferred losses and gains arising on derivatives that were reported in accordance with previous GAAP as if they were assets or liabilities.

B5   An entity shall not reflect in its opening Australian-Accounting-Standards statement of financial position a hedging relationship of a type that does not qualify for hedge accounting in accordance with AASB 139 (for example, many hedging relationships where the hedging instrument is a cash instrument or written option; where the hedged item is a net position; or where the hedge covers interest risk in a held-to-maturity investment). However, if an entity designated a net position as a hedged item in accordance with previous GAAP, it may designate an individual item within that net position as a hedged item in accordance with Australian Accounting Standards, provided that it does so no later than the date of transition to Australian Accounting Standards.

B6   If, before the date of transition to Australian Accounting Standards, an entity had designated a transaction as a hedge but the hedge does not meet the conditions for hedge accounting in AASB 139, the entity shall apply paragraphs 91 and 101 of AASB 139 to discontinue hedge accounting. Transactions entered into before the date of transition to Australian Accounting Standards shall not be retrospectively designated as hedges.

Non-controlling interests

B7   A first-time adopter shall apply the following requirements of AASB 127 *Consolidated and Separate Financial Statements* (as amended in 2008) prospectively from the date of transition to Australian Accounting Standards:

(a)   the requirement in paragraph 28 that total comprehensive income is attributed to the owners of the parent and to the non-controlling interests even if this results in the non-controlling interests having a deficit balance;

(b)   the requirements in paragraphs 30 and 31 for accounting for changes in the parent's ownership interest in a subsidiary that do not result in a loss of control; and

(c)   the requirements in paragraphs 34-37 for accounting for a loss of control over a subsidiary, and the related requirements of paragraph 8A of AASB 5 *Non-current Assets Held for Sale and Discontinued Operations*.

However, if a first-time adopter elects to apply AASB 3 *Business Combinations* (as revised in 2008) retrospectively to past business combinations, it also shall apply AASB 127 (as amended in 2008) in accordance with paragraph C1 of this Standard.

Appendix C

Exemptions for Business Combinations

This appendix is an integral part of AASB 1. An entity shall apply the following requirements to business combinations that the entity recognised before the date of transition to Australian Accounting Standards.

C1   A first-time adopter may elect not to apply AASB 3 *Business Combinations* (as revised in 2008) retrospectively to past business combinations (business combinations that occurred before the date of transition to Australian Accounting Standards). However, if a first-time adopter restates any business combination to comply with AASB 3 (as revised in 2008), it shall restate all later business combinations and shall also apply AASB 127 *Consolidated and Separate Financial Statements* (as amended in 2008) from that same date. For example, if a first-time adopter elects to restate a business combination that occurred on 30 June 20X6, it shall restate all business combinations that occurred between 30 June 20X6 and the date of transition to Australian Accounting Standards, and it shall also apply AASB 127 (amended 2008) from 30 June 20X6.

C2   An entity need not apply AASB 121 *The Effects of Changes in Foreign Exchange Rates* retrospectively to fair value adjustments and goodwill arising in business combinations that occurred before the date of transition to Australian Accounting Standards. If the entity does not apply AASB 121 retrospectively to those fair value adjustments and goodwill, it shall treat them as assets and liabilities of the entity rather than as assets and liabilities of the acquiree. Therefore, those goodwill and fair value adjustments either are already expressed in the entity's functional currency or are non-monetary foreign currency items, which are reported using the exchange rate applied in accordance with previous GAAP.

C3   An entity may apply AASB 121 retrospectively to fair value adjustments and goodwill arising in either:

(a)   all business combinations that occurred before the date of transition to Australian Accounting Standards; or

(b)   all business combinations that the entity elects to restate to comply with AASB 3, as permitted by paragraph C1 above.

C4   If a first-time adopter does not apply AASB 3 retrospectively to a past business combination, this has the following consequences for that business combination:

(a)   The first-time adopter shall keep the same classification (as an acquisition by the legal acquirer, a reverse acquisition by the legal acquiree, or a uniting of interests) as in its previous GAAP financial statements.

(b)   The first-time adopter shall recognise all its assets and liabilities at the date of transition to Australian Accounting Standards that were acquired or assumed in a past business combination, other than:

(i)   some financial assets and financial liabilities derecognised in accordance with previous GAAP (see paragraph B2); and

(ii)   assets, including goodwill, and liabilities that were not recognised in the acquirer's consolidated statement of financial position in accordance with previous GAAP and also would not qualify for recognition in accordance with Australian Accounting Standards in the separate statement of financial position of the acquiree (see (f)-(i) below).

The first-time adopter shall recognise any resulting change by adjusting retained earnings (or, if appropriate, another category of equity), unless the change results from the recognition of an intangible asset that was previously subsumed within goodwill (see (g)(i) below).

(c)   The first-time adopter shall exclude from its opening Australian-Accounting-Standards statement of financial position any item recognised in accordance with previous GAAP that does not qualify for recognition as an asset or liability under Australian Accounting Standards. The first-time adopter shall account for the resulting change as follows:

(i)   the first-time adopter may have classified a past business combination as an acquisition and recognised as an intangible asset an item that does not qualify for recognition as an asset in accordance with AASB 138 *Intangible Assets*. It shall reclassify that item (and, if any, the related deferred tax and non-controlling interests) as part of goodwill (unless it deducted goodwill directly from equity in accordance with previous GAAP, see (g)(i) and (i) below).

(ii)   the first-time adopter shall recognise all other resulting changes in retained earnings.[1]

(d)   Australian Accounting Standards require subsequent measurement of some assets and liabilities on a basis that is not based on original cost, such as fair value. The first-time adopter shall measure these assets and liabilities on that basis in its opening Australian-Accounting-Standards statement of financial position, even if they were acquired or assumed in a past business combination. It shall recognise any resulting change in the carrying amount by adjusting retained earnings (or, if appropriate, another category of equity), rather than goodwill.

(e)   Immediately after the business combination, the carrying amount in accordance with previous GAAP of assets acquired and liabilities assumed in that business combination shall be their deemed cost in accordance with Australian Accounting Standards at that date. If Australian Accounting Standards require a cost-based measurement of those assets and liabilities at a later date, that deemed cost shall be the basis for cost-based depreciation or amortisation from the date of the business combination.

(f)   If an asset acquired, or liability assumed, in a past business combination was not recognised in accordance with previous GAAP, it does not have a deemed cost of zero in the opening Australian-Accounting-Standards statement of financial position. Instead, the acquirer shall recognise and measure it in its consolidated statement of financial position on the basis that Australian Accounting Standards would require in the statement of financial position of the acquiree. To illustrate: if the acquirer had not, in accordance with its previous GAAP, capitalised finance leases acquired in a past business combination, it shall capitalise those leases in its consolidated financial statements, as AASB 117 *Leases* would require the acquiree to do in its Australian-Accounting-Standards statement of financial position. Similarly, if the acquirer had not, in accordance with its previous GAAP, recognised a contingent liability that still exists at the date of transition to Australian Accounting Standards,

---

1   Such changes include reclassifications from or to intangible assets if goodwill was not recognised in accordance with previous GAAP as an asset. This arises if, in accordance with previous GAAP, the entity (a) deducted goodwill directly from equity or (b) did not treat the business combination as an acquisition.

the acquirer shall recognise that contingent liability at that date unless AASB 137 *Provisions, Contingent Liabilities and Contingent Assets* would prohibit its recognition in the financial statements of the acquiree. Conversely, if an asset or liability was subsumed in goodwill in accordance with previous GAAP but would have been recognised separately under AASB 3, that asset or liability remains in goodwill unless Australian Accounting Standards would require its recognition in the financial statements of the acquiree.

(g) The carrying amount of goodwill in the opening Australian-Accounting-Standards statement of financial position shall be its carrying amount in accordance with previous GAAP at the date of transition to Australian Accounting Standards, after the following two adjustments:

    (i) If required by (c)(i) above, the first-time adopter shall increase the carrying amount of goodwill when it reclassifies an item that it recognised as an intangible asset in accordance with previous GAAP. Similarly, if (f) above requires the first-time adopter to recognise an intangible asset that was subsumed in recognised goodwill in accordance with previous GAAP, the first-time adopter shall decrease the carrying amount of goodwill accordingly (and, if applicable, adjust deferred tax and non-controlling interests).

    (ii) Regardless of whether there is any indication that the goodwill may be impaired, the first-time adopter shall apply AASB 136 *Impairment of Assets* in testing the goodwill for impairment at the date of transition to Australian Accounting Standards and in recognising any resulting impairment loss in retained earnings (or, if so required by AASB 136, in revaluation surplus). The impairment test shall be based on conditions at the date of transition to Australian Accounting Standards.

(h) No other adjustments shall be made to the carrying amount of goodwill at the date of transition to Australian Accounting Standards. For example, the first-time adopter shall not restate the carrying amount of goodwill:

    (i) to exclude in-process research and development acquired in that business combination (unless the related intangible asset would qualify for recognition in accordance with AASB 138 in the statement of financial position of the acquiree);

    (ii) to adjust previous amortisation of goodwill;

    (iii) to reverse adjustments to goodwill that AASB 3 would not permit, but were made in accordance with previous GAAP because of adjustments to assets and liabilities between the date of the business combination and the date of transition to Australian Accounting Standards.

(i) If the first-time adopter recognised goodwill in accordance with previous GAAP as a deduction from equity:

    (i) it shall not recognise that goodwill in its opening Australian-Accounting-Standards statement of financial position. Furthermore, it shall not reclassify that goodwill to profit or loss if it disposes of the subsidiary or if the investment in the subsidiary becomes impaired.

    (ii) adjustments resulting from the subsequent resolution of a contingency affecting the purchase consideration shall be recognised in retained earnings.

(j) In accordance with its previous GAAP, the first-time adopter may not have consolidated a subsidiary acquired in a past business combination (for example, because the parent did not regard it as a subsidiary in accordance with previous GAAP or did not prepare consolidated financial statements). The first-time adopter shall adjust the carrying amounts of the subsidiary's assets and liabilities to the amounts that Australian Accounting Standards would require in the subsidiary's statement of financial position. The deemed cost of goodwill equals the difference at the date of transition to Australian Accounting Standards between:

    (i) the parent's interest in those adjusted carrying amounts; and

    (ii) the cost in the parent's separate financial statements of its investment in the subsidiary.

(k)   The measurement of non-controlling interests and deferred tax follows from the measurement of other assets and liabilities. Therefore, the above adjustments to recognised assets and liabilities affect non-controlling interests and deferred tax.

C5   The exemption for past business combinations also applies to past acquisitions of investments in associates and of interests in joint ventures. Furthermore, the date selected for paragraph C1 applies equally for all such acquisitions.

Appendix D

Exemptions from Other Australian Accounting Standards

This appendix is an integral part of AASB 1.

D1   An entity may elect to use one or more of the following exemptions:

     (a)   share-based payment transactions (paragraphs D2 and D3);

     (b)   insurance contracts (paragraph D4);

     (c)   deemed cost (paragraphs D5-D8B);

     (d)   leases (paragraphs D9 and D9A);

     (e)   employee benefits (paragraphs D10 and D11);

     (f)   cumulative translation differences (paragraphs D12 and D13);

     (g)   investments in subsidiaries, jointly controlled entities and associates (paragraphs D14 and D15);

     (h)   assets and liabilities of subsidiaries, associates and joint ventures (paragraphs D16 and D17);

     (i)   compound financial instruments (paragraph D18);

     (j)   designation of previously recognised financial instruments (paragraph D19);

     (k)   fair value measurement of financial assets or financial liabilities at initial recognition (paragraph D20);

     (l)   decommissioning liabilities included in the cost of property, plant and equipment (paragraphs D21 and D21A);

     (m)   financial assets or intangible assets accounted for in accordance with Interpretation 12 *Service Concession Arrangements* as identified in AASB 1048 *Interpretation of Standards* (paragraph D22);

     (n)   borrowing costs (paragraph D23);

     (o)   transfers of assets from customers (paragraph D24);

     (p)   extinguishing financial liabilities with equity instruments (paragraph D25); and

     (q)   severe hyperinflation (paragraphs D26-D30).

An entity shall not apply these exemptions by analogy to other items.

Share-based payment transactions

D2   A first-time adopter is encouraged, but not required, to apply AASB 2 *Share-based Payment* to equity instruments that were granted on or before 7 November 2002. A first-time adopter is also encouraged, but not required, to apply AASB 2 to equity instruments that were granted after 7 November 2002 and vested before the later of (a) the date of transition to Australian Accounting Standards and (b) 1 January 2005. However, if a first-time adopter elects to apply AASB 2 to such equity instruments, it may do so only if the entity has disclosed publicly the fair value of those equity instruments, determined at the measurement date, as defined in AASB 2. For all grants of equity instruments to which AASB 2 has not been applied (e.g. equity instruments granted on or before 7 November 2002), a first-time adopter shall nevertheless disclose the information required by paragraphs 44 and 45 of AASB 2. If a first-time adopter modifies the terms or conditions of a grant of equity instruments to which AASB 2 has not been applied, the entity is not required to apply paragraphs 26-29 of AASB 2 if the modification occurred before the date of transition to Australian Accounting Standards.

D3   A first-time adopter is encouraged, but not required, to apply AASB 2 to liabilities arising from share-based payment transactions that were settled before the date of transition to Australian Accounting Standards. A first-time adopter is also encouraged, but not required, to apply AASB 2 to liabilities that were settled before 1 January 2005. For liabilities to which AASB 2 is applied, a first-time adopter is not required to restate comparative information to the extent that the information relates to a period or date that is earlier than 7 November 2002.

Insurance contracts

D4   A first-time adopter may apply the transitional provisions in AASB 4 *Insurance Contracts*, AASB 1023 *General Insurance Contracts* and AASB 1038 *Life Insurance Contracts*. AASB 4 restricts changes in accounting policies for insurance contracts, including changes made by a first-time adopter.

Deemed cost

D5   An entity may elect to measure an item of property, plant and equipment at the date of transition to Australian Accounting Standards at its fair value and use that fair value as its deemed cost at that date.

D6   A first-time adopter may elect to use a previous GAAP revaluation of an item of property, plant and equipment at, or before, the date of transition to Australian Accounting Standards as deemed cost at the date of the revaluation, if the revaluation was, at the date of the revaluation, broadly comparable to:

(a)   fair value; or

(b)   cost or depreciated cost in accordance with Australian Accounting Standards, adjusted to reflect, for example, changes in a general or specific price index.

D7   The elections in paragraphs D5 and D6 are also available for:

(a)   investment property, if an entity elects to use the cost model in AASB 140 *Investment Property*; and

(b)   intangible assets that meet:

(i)   the recognition criteria in AASB 138 *Intangible Assets* (including reliable measurement of original cost); and

(ii)   the criteria in AASB 138 for revaluation (including the existence of an active market).

An entity shall not use these elections for other assets or for liabilities.

D8   A first-time adopter may have established a deemed cost in accordance with previous GAAP for some or all of its assets and liabilities by measuring them at their fair value at one particular date because of an event such as a privatisation or initial public offering.

(a)   If the measurement date is *at or before* the date of transition to Australian Accounting Standards, the entity may use such event-driven fair value measurements as deemed cost for Australian Accounting Standards at the date of that measurement.

(b)   If the measurement date is *after* the date of transition to Australian Accounting Standards, but during the period covered by the first Australian-Accounting-Standards financial statements, the event-driven fair value measurements may be used as deemed cost when the event occurs. An entity shall recognise the resulting adjustments directly in retained earnings (or if appropriate, another category of equity) at the measurement date. At the date of transition to Australian Accounting Standards, the entity shall either establish the deemed cost by applying the criteria in paragraphs D5-D7 or measure assets and liabilities in accordance with the other requirements in this Standard.

D8A Under some national accounting requirements exploration and development costs for oil and gas properties in the development or production phases are accounted for in cost centres that include all properties in a large geographical area. A first-time adopter using such accounting under previous GAAP may elect to measure oil and gas assets at the date of transition to Australian Accounting Standards on the following basis:

(a) exploration and evaluation assets at the amount determined under the entity's previous GAAP; and

(b) assets in the development or production phases at the amount determined for the cost centre under the entity's previous GAAP. The entity shall allocate this amount to the cost centre's underlying assets pro rata using reserve volumes or reserve values as of that date.

The entity shall test exploration and evaluation assets and assets in the development and production phases for impairment at the date of transition to Australian Accounting Standards in accordance with AASB 6 *Exploration for and Evaluation of Mineral Resources* or AASB 136 respectively and, if necessary, reduce the amount determined in accordance with (a) or (b) above. For the purposes of this paragraph, oil and gas assets comprise only those assets used in the exploration, evaluation, development or production of oil and gas.

D8B Some entities hold items of property, plant and equipment or intangible assets that are used, or were previously used, in operations subject to rate regulation. The carrying amount of such items might include amounts that were determined under previous GAAP but do not qualify for capitalisation in accordance with Australian Accounting Standards. If this is the case, a first-time adopter may elect to use the previous GAAP carrying amount of such an item at the date of transition to Australian Accounting Standards as deemed cost. If an entity applies this exemption to an item, it need not apply it to all items. At the date of transition to Australian Accounting Standards, an entity shall test for impairment in accordance with AASB 136 each item for which this exemption is used. For the purposes of this paragraph, operations are subject to rate regulation if they provide goods or services to customers at prices (i.e. rates) established by an authorised body empowered to establish rates that bind the customers and that are designed to recover the specific costs the entity incurs in providing the regulated goods or services and to earn a specified return. The specified return could be a minimum or range and need not be a fixed or guaranteed return.

Leases

D9 A first-time adopter may apply the transitional provisions in Interpretation 4 *Determining whether an Arrangement contains a Lease* as identified in AASB 1048. Therefore, a first-time adopter may determine whether an arrangement existing at the date of transition to Australian Accounting Standards contains a lease on the basis of facts and circumstances existing at that date.

D9A If a first-time adopter made the same determination of whether an arrangement contained a lease in accordance with previous GAAP as that required by Interpretation 4 (as identified in AASB 1048) but at a date other than that required by Interpretation 4, the first-time adopter need not reassess that determination when it adopts Australian Accounting Standards. For an entity to have made the same determination of whether the arrangement contained a lease in accordance with previous GAAP, that determination would have to have given the same outcome as that resulting from applying AASB 117 *Leases* and Interpretation 4.

Employee benefits

D10 In accordance with AASB 119 *Employee Benefits*, an entity may elect to use a 'corridor' approach that leaves some actuarial gains and losses unrecognised. Retrospective application of this approach requires an entity to split the cumulative actuarial gains and losses from the inception of the plan until the date of transition to Australian Accounting Standards into a recognised portion and an unrecognised portion. However, a first-time adopter may elect to recognise all cumulative actuarial gains and losses at the date of transition to Australian Accounting Standards, even if it uses the corridor approach for later actuarial gains and losses. If a first-time adopter uses this election, it shall apply it to all plans.

D11 An entity may disclose the amounts required by paragraph 120A(p) of AASB 119 as the amounts are determined for each accounting period prospectively from the date of transition to Australian Accounting Standards.

Cumulative translation differences

D12 AASB 121 *The Effects of Changes in Foreign Exchange Rates* requires an entity:

(a) to recognise some translation differences in other comprehensive income and accumulate these in a separate component of equity; and

(b) on disposal of a foreign operation, to reclassify the cumulative translation difference for that foreign operation (including, if applicable, gains and losses on related hedges) from equity to profit or loss as part of the gain or loss on disposal.

D13 However, a first-time adopter need not comply with these requirements for cumulative translation differences that existed at the date of transition to Australian Accounting Standards. If a first-time adopter uses this exemption:

(a) the cumulative translation differences for all foreign operations are deemed to be zero at the date of transition to Australian Accounting Standards; and

(b) the gain or loss on a subsequent disposal of any foreign operation shall exclude translation differences that arose before the date of transition to Australian Accounting Standards and shall include later translation differences.

Investments in subsidiaries, jointly controlled entities and associates

D14 When an entity prepares separate financial statements, AASB 127 *Consolidated and Separate Financial Statements* (as amended in 2008) requires it to account for its investments in subsidiaries, jointly controlled entities and associates either:

(a) at cost; or

(b) in accordance with AASB 139 *Financial Instruments: Recognition and Measurement*.

D15 If a first-time adopter measures such an investment at cost in accordance with AASB 127, it shall measure that investment at one of the following amounts in its separate opening Australian-Accounting-Standards statement of financial position:

(a) cost determined in accordance with AASB 127; or

(b) deemed cost. The deemed cost of such an investment shall be its:

(i) fair value (determined in accordance with AASB 139) at the entity's date of transition to Australian Accounting Standards in its separate financial statements; or

(ii) previous GAAP carrying amount at that date.

A first-time adopter may choose either (i) or (ii) above to measure its investment in each subsidiary, jointly controlled entity or associate that it elects to measure using a deemed cost.

Assets and liabilities of subsidiaries, associates and joint ventures

D16 If a subsidiary becomes a first-time adopter later than its parent, the subsidiary shall, in its financial statements, measure its assets and liabilities at either:

(a) the carrying amounts that would be included in the parent's consolidated financial statements, based on the parent's date of transition to Australian Accounting Standards, if no adjustments were made for consolidation procedures and for the effects of the business combination in which the parent acquired the subsidiary; or

(b) the carrying amounts required by the rest of this Standard, based on the subsidiary's date of transition to Australian Accounting Standards. These carrying amounts could differ from those described in (a):

(i) when the exemptions in this Standard result in measurements that depend on the date of transition to Australian Accounting Standards.

(ii) when the accounting policies used in the subsidiary's financial statements differ from those in the consolidated financial statements. For example, the subsidiary may use as its accounting policy the cost model in AASB 116 *Property, Plant and Equipment*, whereas the group may use the revaluation model.

A similar election is available to an associate or joint venture that becomes a first-time adopter later than an entity that has significant influence or joint control over it.

D17 However, if an entity becomes a first-time adopter later than its subsidiary (or associate or joint venture) the entity shall, in its consolidated financial statements, measure the assets and liabilities of the subsidiary (or associate or joint venture) at the same carrying amounts as in the financial statements of the subsidiary (or associate or joint venture), after adjusting for consolidation and equity accounting adjustments and for the effects of the business combination in which the entity acquired the subsidiary. Similarly, if a parent becomes a first-time adopter for its separate financial statements earlier or later than for its consolidated financial statements, it shall measure its assets and liabilities at the same amounts in both financial statements, except for consolidation adjustments.

Compound financial instruments

D18 AASB 132 *Financial Instruments: Presentation* requires an entity to split a compound financial instrument at inception into separate liability and equity components. If the liability component is no longer outstanding, retrospective application of AASB 132 involves separating two portions of equity. The first portion is in retained earnings and represents the cumulative interest accreted on the liability component. The other portion represents the original equity component. However, in accordance with this Standard, a first-time adopter need not separate these two portions if the liability component is no longer outstanding at the date of transition to Australian Accounting Standards.

Designation of previously recognised financial instruments

D19 AASB 139 permits a financial asset to be designated on initial recognition as available for sale or a financial instrument (provided it meets certain criteria) to be designated as a financial asset or financial liability at fair value through profit or loss. Despite this requirement exceptions apply in the following circumstances:

(a) an entity is permitted to make an available-for-sale designation at the date of transition to Australian Accounting Standards.

(b) an entity is permitted to designate, at the date of transition to Australian Accounting Standards, any financial asset or financial liability as at fair value through profit or loss provided the asset or liability meets the criteria in paragraph 9(b)(i), 9(b)(ii) or 11A of AASB 139 at that date.

Fair value measurement of financial assets or financial liabilities at initial recognition

D20 Notwithstanding the requirements of paragraphs 7 and 9, an entity may apply the requirements in the last sentence of AASB 139 paragraph AG76 and in paragraph AG76A prospectively to transactions entered into on or after the date of transition to Australian Accounting Standards.

Decommissioning liabilities included in the cost of property, plant and equipment

D21 Interpretation 1 *Changes in Existing Decommissioning, Restoration and Similar Liabilities* as identified in AASB 1048 requires specified changes in a decommissioning, restoration or similar liability to be added to or deducted from the cost of the asset to which it relates; the adjusted depreciable amount of the asset is then depreciated prospectively over its remaining useful life. A first-time adopter need not comply with these requirements for changes in such liabilities that occurred before the date of transition to Australian Accounting Standards. If a first-time adopter uses this exemption, it shall:

(a) measure the liability as at the date of transition to Australian Accounting Standards in accordance with AASB 137 *Provisions, Contingent Liabilities and Contingent Assets*;

(b) to the extent that the liability is within the scope of Interpretation 1, estimate the amount that would have been included in the cost of the related asset when the liability first arose, by discounting the liability to that date using its best estimate of the historical risk-adjusted discount rate(s) that would have applied for that liability over the intervening period; and

(c) calculate the accumulated depreciation on that amount, as at the date of transition to Australian Accounting Standards, on the basis of the current estimate of the useful life of the asset, using the depreciation policy adopted by the entity in accordance with Australian Accounting Standards.

D21A An entity that uses the exemption in paragraph D8A(b) (for oil and gas assets in the development or production phases accounted for in cost centres that include all properties in a large geographical area under previous GAAP) shall, instead of applying paragraph D21 or Interpretation 1 (as identified in AASB 1048):

(a) measure decommissioning, restoration and similar liabilities as at the date of transition to Australian Accounting Standards in accordance with AASB 137; and

(b) recognise directly in retained earnings any difference between that amount and the carrying amount of those liabilities at the date of transition to Australian Accounting Standards determined under the entity's previous GAAP.

Financial assets or intangible assets accounted for in accordance with Interpretation 12

D22 A first-time adopter may apply the transitional provisions in Interpretation 12 *Service Concession Arrangements* as identified in AASB 1048.

Borrowing costs

D23 A first-time adopter may apply the transitional provisions set out in paragraphs 27 and 28 of AASB 123 *Borrowing Costs*, as revised in 2007. In those paragraphs references to the application date shall be interpreted as 1 January 2009 or the date of transition to Australian Accounting Standards, whichever is later.

Transfers of assets from customers

D24 A first-time adopter may apply the transitional provisions set out in paragraph Aus21.2 of Interpretation 18 *Transfers of Assets from Customers* as identified in AASB 1048. In that paragraph, reference to the application date shall be interpreted as 1 July 2009 or the date of transition to Australian Accounting Standards, whichever is later. In addition, a first-time adopter may designate any date before the date of transition to Australian Accounting Standards and apply Interpretation 18 to all transfers of assets from customers received on or after that date.

Extinguishing financial liabilities with equity instruments

D25 A first-time adopter may apply the transitional provisions in Interpretation 19 *Extinguishing Financial Liabilities with Equity Instruments* as identified in AASB 1048.

Severe hyperinflation

D26 If an entity has a functional currency that was, or is, the currency of a hyperinflationary economy, it shall determine whether it was subject to severe hyperinflation before the date of transition to Australian Accounting Standards. This applies to entities that are adopting Australian Accounting Standards for the first time, as well as entities that have previously applied Australian Accounting Standards.

D27   The currency of a hyperinflationary economy is subject to severe hyperinflation if it has both of the following characteristics:

(a)   a reliable general price index is not available to all entities with transactions and balances in the currency.

(b)   exchangeability between the currency and a relatively stable foreign currency does not exist.

D28   The functional currency of an entity ceases to be subject to severe hyperinflation on the functional currency normalisation date. That is the date when the functional currency no longer has either, or both, of the characteristics in paragraph D27, or when there is a change in the entity's functional currency to a currency that is not subject to severe hyperinflation.

D29   When an entity's date of transition to Australian Accounting Standards is on, or after, the functional currency normalisation date, the entity may elect to measure all assets and liabilities held before the functional currency normalisation date at fair value on the date of transition to Australian Accounting Standards. The entity may use that fair value as the deemed cost of those assets and liabilities in the opening Australian-Accounting-Standards statement of financial position.

D30   When the functional currency normalisation date falls within a 12-month comparative period, the comparative period may be less than 12 months, provided that a complete set of financial statements (as required by paragraph 10 of AASB 101) is provided for that shorter period.

Appendix E

Short-term Exemptions from Australian Accounting Standards

This appendix is an integral part of AASB 1.

Disclosures about financial instruments

E3   A first-time adopter may apply the transition provisions in paragraph 44G of AASB 7.[1]

E4   A first-time adopter may apply the transitional provisions in paragraph 44M of AASB 7.[2]

Deleted IFRS 1 Text

Deleted IFRS 1 text is not part of AASB 1.

Paragraph 40

This IFRS supersedes IFRS 1 (issued in 2003 and amended at May 2008).

---

1   Paragraph E3 was added as a consequence of AASB 2010-1 *Amendments to Australian Accounting Standards – Limited Exemption from Comparative AASB 7 Disclosures for First-time Adopters* issued in February 2010. To avoid the potential use of hindsight and to ensure that first-time adopters are not disadvantaged as compared with current Australian Accounting Standards preparers, the AASB decided that first-time adopters should be permitted to use the same transition provisions permitted for existing preparers of financial statements prepared in accordance with Australian Accounting Standards that are included in AASB 2009-2 *Amendments to Australian Accounting Standards – Improving Disclosures about Financial Instruments.*

2   Paragraph E4 was added as a consequence of AASB 2010-6 *Amendments to Australian Accounting Standards – Disclosures on Transfers of Financial Assets* issued in November 2010. To avoid the potential use of hindsight and to ensure that first-time adopters are not disadvantaged as compared with current Australian-Accounting-Standards financial statements preparers, the Board decided that first-time adopters should be permitted to use the same transition provisions permitted for existing preparers of financial statements prepared in accordance with Australian Accounting Standards that are included in AASB 2010-6 *Amendments to Australian Accounting Standards – Disclosures on Transfers of Financial Assets.*

AASB 2
Share-based Payment

(Compiled December 2009)

Note from the Institute of Chartered Accountants Australia

This note, prepared by the technical editors, is not part of Accounting Standard AASB 2.

Historical development

15 July 2004: AASB 2 'Share-based Payment' is the Australian equivalent of IFRS 2 of the same name. It was made by the AASB on 15 July 2004 as part of the AASB's program to adopt International Financial Reporting Standards by 2005.

15 February 2007: AASB 2007-1 'Amendments to Australian Accounting Standards' adds paragraphs Aus52.1 and 53-59, and is applicable to annual reporting periods beginning on or after 1 March 2007. Entities may elect to early-adopt it to annual reporting periods beginning on or after 1 January 2005 but before 1 March 2007. If an entity applies AASB Interpretation 11 'AASB 2 – Group and Treasury Share Transactions' to such an annual reporting period, this Standard shall also be applied to that period.

30 April 2007: AASB 2007-4 'Amendments to Australian Accounting Standards' amends paragraph IG12 and is applicable to annual reporting periods beginning on or after 1 July 2007. Entities may elect to early-adopt it to annual reporting periods beginning on or after 1 January 2005.

28 June 2007: AASB 2007-7 'Amendments to Australian Accounting Standards' amends paragraph IG8 and is applicable to annual reporting periods beginning on or after 1 July 2007. Entities may elect to early-adopt it to annual reporting periods beginning on or after 1 January 2005.

13 December 2007: AASB 2007-10 'Further Amendments to Australian Accounting Standards arising from AASB 101' amends AASB 2, replacing the term 'financial report' with 'financial statements'. This Standard is applicable to annual reporting periods beginning on or after 1 January 2009.

7 February 2008: 2008-1 'Amendments to Australian Accounting Standard – Share-based Payments: Vesting Conditions and Cancellations' amends AASB 2 to clarify that vesting conditions comprise service conditions and performance conditions only and that other features of a share-based payment transaction are not vesting conditions. This Standard is applicable to annual reporting periods beginning on or after 1 January 2009.

6 March 2008: AASB 2008-3 'Amendments to Australian Accounting Standards arising from AASB 3 and AASB 127' amends AASB 2 for the issue of AASB 3 Revised. This Standard is applicable to annual reporting periods beginning on or after 1 July 2009.

21 May 2009: AASB 2009-4 'Amendments to Australian Accounting Standards arising from the Annual Improvements Project' amends the scope of AASB 2. This Standard is applicable to annual reporting periods beginning on or after 1 July 2009 and may be adopted early.

25 June 2009: AASB 2009-6 'Amendments to Australian Accounting Standards' amends AASB 2 for editorial corrections made by the International Accounting Standards Board (IASB) to its Standards and Interpretations (IFRSs) and as a consequence of issuing revised AASB 101 'Presentation of Financial Statements' (September 2007). This Standard is applicable to annual reporting periods beginning on or after 1 January 2009 that end on or after 30 June 2009.

24 July 2009: AASB 2009-8 'Amendments to Australian Accounting Standards – Group Cash-settled Share-based Payment Transactions' amends AASB 2 to include group cash or equity-settled-share-based payment transactions. This Standard applies to annual reporting periods beginning on or after 1 January 2010 and can be applied early.

19 October 2009: AASB 2 was reissued by the AASB, compiled to include the AASB 2007-10, AASB 2008-1, AASB 2008-3, AASB 2009-4 and AASB 2009-6 amendments. This compiled Standard applies to annual reporting periods beginning on or after 1 July 2009 but before 1 January 2010.

Early application is permitted. On the same date the AASB reissued the version of AASB 2 applicable to annual reporting periods beginning on or after 1 January 2009 but before 1 July 2009. This version of AASB 2 has been compiled for the amending Standards applying to annual reporting periods beginning on or after 1 January 2009.

4 December 2009: AASB 2 was reissued by the AASB, compiled to include the AASB 2009-8 amendments and applies to annual reporting periods beginning on or after 1 January 2010.

29 August 2011: AASB 2011-7 'Amendments to Australian Accounting Standards arising from the Consolidation and Joint Arrangements Standards' amends AASB 2 to give effect to many consequential changes arising from the issue of AASB 10, 11, 12, 127 and 128. This Standard applies to annual reporting periods beginning on or after 1 January 2013 and can be adopted early by for-profit entities. **These amendments are not included in this compiled Standard.**

5 September 2011: AASB 2011-8 'Amendments to Australian Accounting Standards arising from AASB 13' amends AASB 2 to give effect to a consequential change in the definition of fair value arising from the issue of AASB 13. This Standard applies to annual reporting periods beginning on or after 1 January 2013 and can be adopted early. **These amendments are not included in this compiled Standard**.

References

The AASB items not taken onto the agenda: *Employee Share Loan Plans* applies to AASB 2.

IFRIC items not taken onto the agenda: IFRS 2-1 'Employee share loan plans', IFRS 2-2 'Scope of IFRS 2 – Share plans with cash alternatives at the discretion of entity', IFRS 2-3 'Share plans with cash alternatives at the discretion of employees – grant date and vesting periods', IFRS 2-4 'Fair value measurement of post-vesting transfer restrictions', IFRS 2-5 'Incremental fair value to employees as a result of unexpected capital restructurings', IFRS 2-6 'Employee benefit trusts in the separate financial statements of the sponsor' apply, IFRS 2-13 'Transactions in which the manner of settlement is contingent on future events' and IFRS 2-15 'Share-based payment awards settled net of tax withholdings' apply to AASB 2.

AASB 2 compared to IFRS 2

Additions

Paragraph	Description
Aus 1.1	Which entities AASB 2 applies to (i.e. reporting entities and general purpose financial reports).
Aus 1.2	The application date of AASB 2 (i.e. annual reporting periods beginning 1 January 2005).
Aus 1.3	Prohibits early application of AASB 2.
Aus 1.4	Makes the requirements of AASB 2 subject to AASB 1031 'Materiality'.
Aus 1.5	Notice of the new Standard published on 22 July 2004.
Aus 52.1	States the transitional provisions in the following paragraphs are not to be applied by entities that have previously applied this Standard.

Deletion

Paragraph	Description
60	Effective date of IFRS 2.
62	Effective date of amendments to IFRS 2.

Contents

Compilation Details

Comparison with IFRS 2

Accounting Standard
AASB 2 Share-based Payment

	Paragraphs
Objective	1
Application	Aus1.1 – Aus1.5
Scope	2 – 6
Recognition	7 – 9
Equity-settled Share-based Payment Transactions	
Overview	10 – 13A
Transactions in which services are received	14 – 15
Transactions measured by reference to the fair value of the equity instruments granted	
Determining the fair value of equity instruments granted	16 – 18
Treatment of vesting conditions	19 – 21
Treatment of non-vesting conditions	21A
Treatment of a reload feature	22
After vesting date	23
If the fair value of the equity instruments cannot be estimated reliably	24 – 25
Modifications to the terms and conditions on which equity instruments were granted, including cancellations and settlements	26 – 29
Cash-settled Share-based Payment Transactions	30 – 33
Share-based Payment Transactions with Cash Alternatives	34
Share-based payment transactions in which the terms of the arrangement provide the counterparty with a choice of settlement	35 – 40
Share-based payment transactions in which the terms of the arrangement provide the entity with a choice of settlement	41 – 43
Share-based Payment Transactions among Group Entities	43A – 43D
Disclosures	44 – 52
Transitional Provisions	Aus52.1 – 59
Effective Date	61 – 63
Withdrawal of Interpretations	64

Appendices:

A Defined Terms

B Application Guidance

Implementation Guidance

Basis for Conclusions on IFRS 2
(available on the AASB website)

Australian Accounting Standard AASB 2 *Share-based Payment* (as amended) is set out in paragraphs 1 – 64 and Appendices A – B. All the paragraphs have equal authority. Paragraphs in **bold type** state the main principles. Terms defined in this Standard are in *italics* the first time they appear in the Standard. AASB 2 is to be read in the context of other Australian Accounting Standards, including AASB 1048 *Interpretation and Application of Standards*, which identifies the Australian Accounting Interpretations. In the absence of explicit guidance, AASB 108 *Accounting Policies, Changes in Accounting Estimates and Errors* provides a basis for selecting and applying accounting policies.

Compilation Details

Accounting Standard AASB 2 *Share-based Payment* as amended

This compiled Standard applies to annual reporting periods beginning on or after 1 January 2010. It takes into account amendments up to and including 24 July 2009 and was prepared on 4 December 2009 by the staff of the Australian Accounting Standards Board (AASB).

This compilation is not a separate Accounting Standard made by the AASB. Instead, it is a representation of AASB 2 (July 2004) as amended by other Accounting Standards, which are listed in the Table below.

Table of Standards

Standard	Date made	Application date *(annual reporting periods ... on or after ...)*	Application, saving or transitional provisions
AASB 2	15 Jul 2004	*(beginning)* 1 Jan 2005	
AASB 2007-1	15 Feb 2007	*(beginning)* 1 Mar 2007	see (a) below
AASB 2007-4	30 Apr 2007	*(beginning)* 1 Jul 2007	see (b) below
AASB 2007-7	28 Jun 2007	*(beginning)* 1 Jul 2007	see (b) below
AASB 2007-8	24 Sep 2007	*(beginning)* 1 Jan 2009	see (c) below
AASB 2007-10	13 Dec 2007	*(beginning)* 1 Jan 2009	see (c) below
AASB 2008-1	7 Feb 2008	*(beginning)* 1 Jan 2009	see (d) below
AASB 2008-3	6 Mar 2008	*(beginning)* 1 Jul 2009	see (e) below
AASB 2009-4	21 May 2009	*(beginning)* 1 Jul 2009	see (f) below
AASB 2009-6	25 Jun 2009	*(beginning)* 1 Jan 2009 and *(ending)* 30 Jun 2009	see (g) below
AASB 2009-8	24 Jul 2009	*(beginning)* 1 Jan 2010	see (h) below

(a)   Entities may elect to apply this Standard to annual reporting periods beginning on or after 1 January 2005 but before 1 March 2007. If an entity applies AASB Interpretation 11 *AASB 2 – Group and Treasury Share Transactions* to such an annual reporting period, this Standard shall also be applied to that period.

(b)   Entities may elect to apply this Standard to annual reporting periods beginning on or after 1 January 2005 but before 1 July 2007.

(c)   Entities may elect to apply this Standard to annual reporting periods beginning on or after 1 January 2005 but before 1 January 2009, provided that AASB 101 *Presentation of Financial Statements* (September 2007) is also applied to such periods.

(d)   Entities may elect to apply this Standard to annual reporting periods beginning on or after 1 January 2005 but before 1 January 2009.

(e)   Entities may elect to apply this Standard to annual reporting periods beginning on or after 30 June 2007 but before 1 July 2009, provided that AASB 3 *Business Combinations* (March 2008) and AASB 127 *Consolidated and Separate Financial Statements* (March 2008) are also applied to such periods.

(f)   Entities may elect to apply this Standard, or its amendments to individual pronouncements, to annual reporting periods beginning on or after 1 January 2005 but before 1 July 2009.

(g)   Entities may elect to apply this Standard to annual reporting periods beginning on or after 1 January 2005 but before 1 January 2009, provided that AASB 101 *Presentation of Financial Statements* (September 2007) is also applied to such periods, and to annual reporting periods beginning on or after 1 January 2009 that end before 30 June 2009.

(h)   Entities may elect to apply this Standard to annual reporting periods beginning on or after 1 January 2005 but before 1 January 2010.

Table of Amendments to Standard

Paragraph affected	How affected	By ... [paragraph]
Aus1.1	amended	AASB 2007-8 [7, 8]
Aus1.4	amended	AASB 2007-8 [8]
2	amended	AASB 2009-8 [7]
3	deleted	AASB 2009-8 [7]
3A	added	AASB 2009-8 [7]
5	amended	AASB 2008-3 [15]
	amended	AASB 2009-4 [7]
13A	added	AASB 2009-8 [8]
21A (and preceding heading)	added	AASB 2008-1 [5]
24	amended	AASB 2007-8 [6]
28	amended	AASB 2008-1 [6, 7]
28A	added	AASB 2008-1 [8]
30	amended	AASB 2007-8 [6]
33	amended	AASB 2007-8 [6]
43A-43D (and preceding heading)	added	AASB 2009-8 [9]
44	amended	AASB 2007-10 [28]
46	amended	AASB 2007-10 [28]
50	amended	AASB 2007-10 [28]
Aus52.1	added	AASB 2007-1 [5]
53-59	added	AASB 2007-1 [5]
60 (preceding heading)	amended	AASB 2009-4 [8]
61	note added	AASB 2008-3 [16]
	added	AASB 2009-4 [9]
62	note added	AASB 2008-1 [9]
63	added	AASB 2009-8 [10]
64 (and preceding heading)	added	AASB 2009-8 [11]
Appendix A, definition of 'cash-settled share-based payment transaction'	amended	AASB 2009-8 [12]
Appendix A, definition of 'equity-settled share-based payment transaction'	amended	AASB 2009-8 [12]
Appendix A, definition of 'share-based payment arrangement'	amended	AASB 2009-8 [12]
Appendix A, definition of 'share-based payment transaction'	amended	AASB 2009-8 [12]
Appendix A, definition of 'vest'	amended	AASB 2008-1 [10]
Appendix A, definition of 'vesting conditions'	amended	AASB 2008-1 [10]
Appendix B, B45-B61 (and preceding heading and subheadings)	added	AASB 2009-8 [13]

Table of Amendments to Implementation Guidance

Paragraph affected	How affected	By ... [paragraph]
IG4A (and preceding heading)	added	AASB 2008-1 [11]
IG5 (and preceding heading)	amended	AASB 2009-8 [14]
IG5A-IG5D (and preceding heading and Example 1)	added	AASB 2009-8 [15]
IG6 (preceding heading)	added	AASB 2009-8 [16]
IG8	amended	AASB 2007-7 [8]

Paragraph affected	How affected	By ... [paragraph]
IG8 (following heading)	deleted	AASB 2009-8 [17]
IG9 (preceding heading)	amended	AASB 2009-8 [18]
IG11 (Example 1)	renumbered and footnote deleted	AASB 2009-8 [19]
IG12	amended amended	AASB 2007-4 [18] AASB 2009-8 [20]
IG14 (Example 6)	amended	AASB 2009-6 [28]
IG15 (Example 9)	amended	AASB 2007-8 [6]
IG15A	added	AASB 2008-1 [12]
IG17 (Example 11)	amended amended	AASB 2007-10 [28] AASB 2009-6 [28]
IG18 (preceding heading)	amended	AASB 2009-8 [18]
IG19	amended	AASB 2007-8 [6]
IG20 (preceding heading)	amended	AASB 2009-8 [18]
IG22A (and preceding heading and Example 14)	added	AASB 2009-8 [21]
IG23	amended	AASB 2009-6 [28]
IG24 (and preceding heading)	added	AASB 2008-1 [13]

Comparison with IFRS 2

AASB 2 and IFRS 2

AASB 2 *Share-based Payment* as amended incorporates IFRS 2 *Share-based Payment* as issued and amended by the International Accounting Standards Board (IASB). Paragraphs that have been added to this Standard (and do not appear in the text of IFRS 2) are identified with the prefix "Aus", followed by the number of the preceding IASB paragraph and decimal numbering.

Compliance with IFRS 2

Entities that comply with AASB 2 as amended will simultaneously be in compliance with IFRS 2 as amended.

Accounting Standard AASB 2

The Australian Accounting Standards Board made Accounting Standard AASB 2 *Share-based Payment* under section 334 of the *Corporations Act 2001* on 15 July 2004.

This compiled version of AASB 2 applies to annual reporting periods beginning on or after 1 January 2010. It incorporates relevant amendments contained in other AASB Standards made by the AASB up to and including 24 July 2009 (see Compilation Details).

Accounting Standard AASB 2

Share-based Payment

Objective

1　　The objective of this Standard is to specify the financial reporting by an entity when it undertakes a *share-based payment transaction*. In particular, it requires an entity to reflect in its profit or loss and financial position the effects of share-based payment transactions, including expenses associated with transactions in which *share options* are granted to employees.

Application

Aus1.1	This Standard applies to:

(a)	each entity that is required to prepare financial reports in accordance with Part 2M.3 of the Corporations Act and that is a reporting entity;

(b)	general purpose financial statements of each other reporting entity; and

(c)	financial statements that are, or are held out to be, general purpose financial statements.

Aus1.2	This Standard applies to annual reporting periods beginning on or after 1 January 2005.

[Note: For application dates of paragraphs changed or added by an amending Standard, see Compilation Details.]

Aus1.3	This Standard shall not be applied to annual reporting periods beginning before 1 January 2005.

Aus1.4	The requirements specified in this Standard apply to the financial statements where information resulting from their application is material in accordance with AASB 1031 *Materiality*.

Aus1.5	Notice of this Standard was published in the *Commonwealth of Australia Gazette* No S 294, 22 July 2004.

Scope

2	An entity shall apply this Standard in accounting for all share-based payment transactions, whether or not the entity can identify specifically some or all of the goods or services received, including:

(a)	*equity-settled share-based payment transactions*;

(b)	*cash-settled share-based payment transactions*; and

(c)	transactions in which the entity receives or acquires goods or services and the terms of the arrangement provide either the entity or the supplier of those goods or services with a choice of whether the entity settles the transaction in cash (or other assets) or by issuing equity instruments,

except as noted in paragraphs 3A-6. In the absence of specifically identifiable goods or services, other circumstances may indicate that goods or services have been (or will be) received, in which case this Standard applies.

3	[Deleted by the IASB]

3A	A share-based payment transaction may be settled by another group entity (or a shareholder of any group entity) on behalf of the entity receiving or acquiring the goods or services. Paragraph 2 also applies to an entity that:

(a)	receives goods or services when another entity in the same group (or a shareholder of any group entity) has the obligation to settle the share-based payment transaction; or

(b)	has an obligation to settle a share-based payment transaction when another entity in the same group receives the goods or services,

unless the transaction is clearly for a purpose other than payment for goods or services supplied to the entity receiving them.

4	For the purposes of this Standard, a transaction with an employee (or other party) in his/her capacity as a holder of equity instruments of the entity is not a share-based payment transaction. For example, if an entity grants all holders of a particular class of its equity instruments the right to acquire additional equity instruments of the entity at a price that is less than the *fair value* of those equity instruments, and an employee receives such a right because he/she is a holder of equity instruments of that particular class, the granting or exercise of that right is not subject to the requirements of this Standard.

5   As noted in paragraph 2, this Standard applies to share-based payment transactions in which an entity acquires or receives goods or services. Goods includes inventories, consumables, property, plant and equipment, intangible assets and other non-financial assets. However, an entity shall not apply this Standard to transactions in which the entity acquires goods as part of the net assets acquired in a business combination as defined by AASB 3 *Business Combinations* (as revised in 2008), in a combination of entities or businesses under common control as described in paragraphs B1-B4 of AASB 3, or the contribution of a business on the formation of a joint venture as defined by AASB 131 *Interests in Joint Ventures*. Hence, equity instruments issued in a business combination in exchange for control of the acquiree are not within the scope of this Standard. However, equity instruments granted to employees of the acquiree in their capacity as employees (e.g. in return for continued service) are within the scope of this Standard. Similarly, the cancellation, replacement or other modification of *share-based payment arrangements* because of a business combination or other equity restructuring shall be accounted for in accordance with this Standard. AASB 3 provides guidance on determining whether equity instruments issued in a business combination are part of the consideration transferred in exchange for control of the acquiree (and therefore within the scope of AASB 3) or are in return for continued service to be recognised in the post-combination period (and therefore within the scope of this Standard).

6   This Standard does not apply to share-based payment transactions in which the entity receives or acquires goods or services under a contract within the scope of paragraphs 8-10 of AASB 132 *Financial Instruments: Presentation* or paragraphs 5-7 of AASB 139 *Financial Instruments: Recognition and Measurement*.

Recognition

7   **An entity shall recognise the goods or services received or acquired in a share-based payment transaction when it obtains the goods or as the services are received. The entity shall recognise a corresponding increase in equity if the goods or services were received in an equity-settled share-based payment transaction, or a liability if the goods or services were acquired in a cash-settled share-based payment transaction.**

8   **When the goods or services received or acquired in a share-based payment transaction do not qualify for recognition as assets, they shall be recognised as expenses.**

9   Typically, an expense arises from the consumption of goods or services. For example, services are typically consumed immediately, in which case an expense is recognised as the counterparty renders service. Goods might be consumed over a period of time or, in the case of inventories, sold at a later date, in which case an expense is recognised when the goods are consumed or sold. However, sometimes it is necessary to recognise an expense before the goods or services are consumed or sold, because they do not qualify for recognition as assets. For example, an entity might acquire goods as part of the research phase of a project to develop a new product. Although those goods have not been consumed, they might not qualify for recognition as assets under the applicable Standard.

Equity-settled Share-based Payment Transactions

Overview

10   **For equity-settled share-based payment transactions, the entity shall measure the goods or services received, and the corresponding increase in equity, directly, at the fair value of the goods or services received, unless that fair value cannot be estimated reliably. If the entity cannot estimate reliably the fair value of the goods or services received, the entity shall measure their value, and the corresponding increase in equity, indirectly, by reference to[1] the fair value of the *equity instruments granted*.**

---

1   This Standard uses the phrase 'by reference to' rather than 'at', because the transaction is ultimately measured by multiplying the fair value of the equity instruments granted, measured at the date specified in paragraph 11 or 13 (whichever is applicable), by the number of equity instruments that vest, as explained in paragraph 19.

AASB

11   To apply the requirements of paragraph 10 to transactions with *employees and others providing similar services²*, the entity shall measure the fair value of the services received by reference to the fair value of the equity instruments granted, because typically it is not possible to estimate reliably the fair value of the services received, as explained in paragraph 12. The fair value of those equity instruments shall be measured at *grant date*.

12   Typically, shares, share options or other equity instruments are granted to employees as part of their remuneration package, in addition to a cash salary and other employment benefits. Usually, it is not possible to measure directly the services received for particular components of the employee's remuneration package. It might also not be possible to measure the fair value of the total remuneration package independently, without measuring directly the fair value of the equity instruments granted. Furthermore, shares or share options are sometimes granted as part of a bonus arrangement, rather than as a part of basic remuneration, for example, as an incentive to the employees to remain in the entity's employ or to reward them for their efforts in improving the entity's performance. By granting shares or share options, in addition to other remuneration, the entity is paying additional remuneration to obtain additional benefits. Estimating the fair value of those additional benefits is likely to be difficult. Because of the difficulty of measuring directly the fair value of the services received, the entity shall measure the fair value of the employee services received by reference to the fair value of the equity instruments granted.

13   To apply the requirements of paragraph 10 to transactions with parties other than employees, there shall be a rebuttable presumption that the fair value of the goods or services received can be estimated reliably. That fair value shall be measured at the date the entity obtains the goods or the counterparty renders service. In rare cases, if the entity rebuts this presumption because it cannot estimate reliably the fair value of the goods or services received, the entity shall measure the goods or services received, and the corresponding increase in equity, indirectly, by reference to the fair value of the equity instruments granted, measured at the date the entity obtains the goods or the counterparty renders service.

13A   In particular, if the identifiable consideration received (if any) by the entity appears to be less than the fair value of the equity instruments granted or liability incurred, typically this situation indicates that other consideration (i.e. unidentifiable goods or services) has been (or will be) received by the entity. The entity shall measure the identifiable goods or services received in accordance with this Standard. The entity shall measure the unidentifiable goods or services received (or to be received) as the difference between the fair value of the share-based payment and the fair value of any identifiable goods or services received (or to be received). The entity shall measure the unidentifiable goods or services received at the grant date. However, for cash-settled transactions, the liability shall be remeasured at the end of each reporting period until it is settled in accordance with paragraphs 30-33.

Transactions in which services are received

14   If the equity instruments granted *vest* immediately, the counterparty is not required to complete a specified period of service before becoming unconditionally entitled to those equity instruments. In the absence of evidence to the contrary, the entity shall presume that services rendered by the counterparty as consideration for the equity instruments have been received. In this case, on grant date the entity shall recognise the services received in full, with a corresponding increase in equity.

15   If the equity instruments granted do not vest until the counterparty completes a specified period of service, the entity shall presume that the services to be rendered by the counterparty as consideration for those equity instruments will be received in the future, during the *vesting period*. The entity shall account for those services as they are rendered by the counterparty during the vesting period, with a corresponding increase in equity. For example:

   (a)   if an employee is granted share options conditional upon completing three years' service, then the entity shall presume that the services to be rendered by the

---

2   In the remainder of this Standard, all references to employees also include others providing similar services.

employee as consideration for the share options will be received in the future, over that three-year vesting period; or

(b) if an employee is granted share options conditional upon the achievement of a performance condition and remaining in the entity's employ until that performance condition is satisfied, and the length of the vesting period varies depending on when that performance condition is satisfied, the entity shall presume that the services to be rendered by the employee as consideration for the share options will be received in the future, over the expected vesting period. The entity shall estimate the length of the expected vesting period at grant date, based on the most likely outcome of the performance condition. If the performance condition is a *market condition*, the estimate of the length of the expected vesting period shall be consistent with the assumptions used in estimating the fair value of the options granted, and shall not be subsequently revised. If the performance condition is not a market condition, the entity shall revise its estimate of the length of the vesting period, if necessary, if subsequent information indicates that the length of the vesting period differs from previous estimates.

Transactions measured by reference to the fair value of the equity instruments granted

Determining the fair value of equity instruments granted

16   For transactions measured by reference to the fair value of the equity instruments granted, an entity shall measure the fair value of equity instruments granted at the *measurement date*, based on market prices if available, taking into account the terms and conditions upon which those equity instruments were granted (subject to the requirements of paragraphs 19-22).

17   If market prices are not available, the entity shall estimate the fair value of the equity instruments granted using a valuation technique to estimate what the price of those equity instruments would have been on the measurement date in an arm's length transaction between knowledgeable, willing parties. The valuation technique shall be consistent with generally accepted valuation methodologies for pricing financial instruments, and shall incorporate all factors and assumptions that knowledgeable, willing market participants would consider in setting the price (subject to the requirements of paragraphs 19-22).

18   Appendix B contains further guidance on the measurement of the fair value of shares and share options, focusing on the specific terms and conditions that are common features of a grant of shares or share options to employees.

Treatment of vesting conditions

19   A grant of equity instruments might be conditional upon satisfying specified *vesting conditions*. For example, a grant of shares or share options to an employee is typically conditional on the employee remaining in the entity's employ for a specified period of time. There might be performance conditions that must be satisfied, such as the entity achieving a specified growth in profit or a specified increase in the entity's share price. Vesting conditions, other than market conditions, shall not be taken into account when estimating the fair value of the shares or share options at the measurement date. Instead, vesting conditions shall be taken into account by adjusting the number of equity instruments included in the measurement of the transaction amount so that, ultimately, the amount recognised for goods or services received as consideration for the equity instruments granted shall be based on the number of equity instruments that eventually vest. Hence, on a cumulative basis, no amount is recognised for goods or services received if the equity instruments granted do not vest because of failure to satisfy a vesting condition, for example, the counterparty fails to complete a specified service period, or a performance condition is not satisfied, subject to the requirements of paragraph 21.

20   To apply the requirements of paragraph 19, the entity shall recognise an amount for the goods or services received during the vesting period based on the best available estimate of the number of equity instruments expected to vest and shall revise that estimate, if necessary, if subsequent information indicates that the number of equity instruments expected to vest differs from previous estimates. On vesting date, the entity shall revise

the estimate to equal the number of equity instruments that ultimately vested, subject to the requirements of paragraph 21.

21 Market conditions, such as a target share price upon which vesting (or exercisability) is conditioned, shall be taken into account when estimating the fair value of the equity instruments granted. Therefore, for grants of equity instruments with market conditions, the entity shall recognise the goods or services received from a counterparty who satisfies all other vesting conditions (e.g. services received from an employee who remains in service for the specified period of service), irrespective of whether that market condition is satisfied.

Treatment of non-vesting conditions

21A Similarly, an entity shall take into account all non-vesting conditions when estimating the fair value of the equity instruments granted. Therefore, for grants of equity instruments with non-vesting conditions, the entity shall recognise the goods or services received from a counterparty that satisfies all vesting conditions that are not market conditions (e.g. services received from an employee who remains in service for the specified period of service), irrespective of whether those non-vesting conditions are satisfied.

Treatment of a reload feature

22 For options with a *reload feature*, the reload feature shall not be taken into account when estimating the fair value of options granted at the measurement date. Instead, a *reload option* shall be accounted for as a new option grant, if and when a reload option is subsequently granted.

After vesting date

23 Having recognised the goods or services received in accordance with paragraphs 10-22, and a corresponding increase in equity, the entity shall make no subsequent adjustment to total equity after vesting date. For example, the entity shall not subsequently reverse the amount recognised for services received from an employee if the vested equity instruments are later forfeited or, in the case of share options, the options are not exercised. However, this requirement does not preclude the entity from recognising a transfer within equity, that is, a transfer from one component of equity to another.

If the fair value of the equity instruments cannot be estimated reliably

24 The requirements in paragraphs 16-23 apply when the entity is required to measure a share-based payment transaction by reference to the fair value of the equity instruments granted. In rare cases, the entity may be unable to estimate reliably the fair value of the equity instruments granted at the measurement date, in accordance with the requirements in paragraphs 16-22. In these rare cases only, the entity shall instead:

(a) measure the equity instruments at their *intrinsic value*, initially at the date the entity obtains the goods or the counterparty renders service and subsequently at the end of each reporting period and at the date of final settlement, with any change in intrinsic value recognised in profit or loss. For a grant of share options, the share-based payment arrangement is finally settled when the options are exercised, are forfeited (e.g. upon cessation of employment) or lapse (e.g. at the end of the option's life); and

(b) recognise the goods or services received based on the number of equity instruments that ultimately vest or (where applicable) are ultimately exercised. To apply this requirement to share options, for example, the entity shall recognise the goods or services received during the vesting period, if any, in accordance with paragraphs 14 and 15, except that the requirements in paragraph 15(b) concerning a market condition do not apply. The amount recognised for goods or services received during the vesting period shall be based on the number of share options expected to vest. The entity shall revise that estimate, if necessary, if subsequent information indicates that the number of share options expected to vest differs from previous estimates. On vesting date, the entity shall revise the estimate to equal the number of equity instruments that ultimately vested. After vesting date, the entity shall reverse the amount recognised for goods or services received if the share options are later forfeited, or lapse at the end of the share option's life.

25   If an entity applies paragraph 24, it is not necessary to apply paragraphs 26-29, because any modifications to the terms and conditions on which the equity instruments were granted will be taken into account when applying the intrinsic value method set out in paragraph 24. However, if an entity settles a grant of equity instruments to which paragraph 24 has been applied:

(a)   if the settlement occurs during the vesting period, the entity shall account for the settlement as an acceleration of vesting, and shall therefore recognise immediately the amount that would otherwise have been recognised for services received over the remainder of the vesting period; and

(b)   any payment made on settlement shall be accounted for as the repurchase of equity instruments, that is, as a deduction from equity, except to the extent that the payment exceeds the intrinsic value of the equity instruments, measured at the repurchase date. Any such excess shall be recognised as an expense.

Modifications to the terms and conditions on which equity instruments were granted, including cancellations and settlements

26   An entity might modify the terms and conditions on which the equity instruments were granted. For example, it might reduce the exercise price of options granted to employees (i.e. reprice the options), which increases the fair value of those options. The requirements in paragraphs 27-29 to account for the effects of modifications are expressed in the context of share-based payment transactions with employees. However, the requirements shall also be applied to share-based payment transactions with parties other than employees that are measured by reference to the fair value of the equity instruments granted. In the latter case, any references in paragraphs 27-29 to grant date shall instead refer to the date the entity obtains the goods or the counterparty renders service.

27   The entity shall recognise, as a minimum, the services received measured at the grant date fair value of the equity instruments granted, unless those equity instruments do not vest because of failure to satisfy a vesting condition (other than a market condition) that was specified at grant date. This applies irrespective of any modifications to the terms and conditions on which the equity instruments were granted, or a cancellation or settlement of that grant of equity instruments. In addition, the entity shall recognise the effects of modifications that increase the total fair value of the share-based payment arrangement or are otherwise beneficial to the employee. Guidance on applying this requirement is given in Appendix B.

28   If a grant of equity instruments is cancelled or settled during the vesting period (other than a grant cancelled by forfeiture when the vesting conditions are not satisfied):

(a)   the entity shall account for the cancellation or settlement as an acceleration of vesting, and shall therefore recognise immediately the amount that otherwise would have been recognised for services received over the remainder of the vesting period;

(b)   any payment made to the employee on the cancellation or settlement of the grant shall be accounted for as the repurchase of an equity interest, that is, as a deduction from equity, except to the extent that the payment exceeds the fair value of the equity instruments granted, measured at the repurchase date. Any such excess shall be recognised as an expense. However, if the share-based payment arrangement included liability components, the entity shall remeasure the fair value of the liability at the date of cancellation or settlement. Any payment made to settle the liability component shall be accounted for as an extinguishment of the liability; and

(c)   if new equity instruments are granted to the employee and, on the date when those new equity instruments are granted, the entity identifies the new equity instruments granted as replacement equity instruments for the cancelled equity instruments, the entity shall account for the granting of replacement equity instruments in the same way as a modification of the original grant of equity instruments, in accordance with paragraph 27 and the guidance in Appendix B. The incremental fair value granted is the difference between the fair value of the replacement equity instruments and the net fair value of the cancelled equity instruments, at the date the replacement equity instruments are granted. The net fair value of the cancelled equity instruments is their fair value, immediately before the cancellation, less the amount of any payment made to the employee on cancellation of the equity instruments that is accounted for as a deduction from equity in accordance with (b) above. If the entity does not identify new equity instruments granted as replacement equity instruments for the cancelled equity instruments, the entity shall account for those new equity instruments as a new grant of equity instruments.

28A If an entity or counterparty can choose whether to meet a non-vesting condition, the entity shall treat the entity's or counterparty's failure to meet that non-vesting condition during the vesting period as a cancellation.

29 If an entity repurchases vested equity instruments, the payment made to the employee shall be accounted for as a deduction from equity, except to the extent that the payment exceeds the fair value of the equity instruments repurchased, measured at the repurchase date. Any such excess shall be recognised as an expense.

Cash-settled Share-based Payment Transactions

30 **For cash-settled share-based payment transactions, the entity shall measure the goods or services acquired and the liability incurred at the fair value of the liability. Until the liability is settled, the entity shall remeasure the fair value of the liability at the end of each reporting period and at the date of settlement, with any changes in fair value recognised in profit or loss for the period.**

31 For example, an entity might grant share appreciation rights to employees as part of their remuneration package, whereby the employees will become entitled to a future cash payment (rather than an equity instrument), based on the increase in the entity's share price from a specified level over a specified period of time. Or an entity might grant to its employees a right to receive a future cash payment by granting to them a right to shares (including shares to be issued upon the exercise of share options) that are redeemable, either mandatorily (e.g. upon cessation of employment) or at the employee's option.

32 The entity shall recognise the services received, and a liability to pay for those services, as the employees render service. For example, some share appreciation rights vest immediately, and the employees are therefore not required to complete a specified period of service to become entitled to the cash payment. In the absence of evidence to the contrary, the entity shall presume that the services rendered by the employees in exchange for the share appreciation rights have been received. Thus, the entity shall recognise immediately the services received and a liability to pay for them. If the share appreciation rights do not vest until the employees have completed a specified period of service, the entity shall recognise the services received, and a liability to pay for them, as the employees render service during that period.

33 The liability shall be measured, initially and at the end of each reporting period until settled, at the fair value of the share appreciation rights, by applying an option pricing model, taking into account the terms and conditions on which the share appreciation rights were granted, and the extent to which the employees have rendered service to date.

Share-based Payment Transactions with Cash Alternatives

34 **For share-based payment transactions in which the terms of the arrangement provide either the entity or the counterparty with the choice of whether the entity settles the transaction in cash (or other assets) or by issuing equity instruments, the entity shall account for that transaction, or the components of that transaction, as a cash-settled share-based payment transaction if, and to the extent that, the entity has incurred a liability to settle in cash or other assets, or as an equity-settled share-based payment transaction if, and to the extent that, no such liability has been incurred.**

Share-based payment transactions in which the terms of the arrangement provide the counterparty with a choice of settlement

35   If an entity has granted the counterparty the right to choose whether a share-based payment transaction is settled in cash[3] or by issuing equity instruments, the entity has granted a compound financial instrument, which includes a debt component (i.e. the counterparty's right to demand payment in cash) and an equity component (i.e. the counterparty's right to demand settlement in equity instruments rather than in cash). For transactions with parties other than employees, in which the fair value of the goods or services received is measured directly, the entity shall measure the equity component of the compound financial instrument as the difference between the fair value of the goods or services received and the fair value of the debt component, at the date when the goods or services are received.

36   For other transactions, including transactions with employees, the entity shall measure the fair value of the compound financial instrument at the measurement date, taking into account the terms and conditions on which the rights to cash or equity instruments were granted.

37   To apply paragraph 36, the entity shall first measure the fair value of the debt component, and then measure the fair value of the equity component – taking into account that the counterparty must forfeit the right to receive cash in order to receive the equity instrument. The fair value of the compound financial instrument is the sum of the fair values of the two components. However, share-based payment transactions in which the counterparty has the choice of settlement are often structured so that the fair value of one settlement alternative is the same as the other. For example, the counterparty might have the choice of receiving share options or cash-settled share appreciation rights. In such cases, the fair value of the equity component is zero, and hence the fair value of the compound financial instrument is the same as the fair value of the debt component. Conversely, if the fair values of the settlement alternatives differ, the fair value of the equity component usually will be greater than zero, in which case the fair value of the compound financial instrument will be greater than the fair value of the debt component.

38   The entity shall account separately for the goods or services received or acquired in respect of each component of the compound financial instrument. For the debt component, the entity shall recognise the goods or services acquired, and a liability to pay for those goods or services, as the counterparty supplies goods or renders service, in accordance with the requirements applying to cash-settled share-based payment transactions (paragraphs 30-33). For the equity component (if any), the entity shall recognise the goods or services received, and an increase in equity, as the counterparty supplies goods or renders service, in accordance with the requirements applying to equity-settled share-based payment transactions (paragraphs 10-29).

39   At the date of settlement, the entity shall remeasure the liability to its fair value. If the entity issues equity instruments on settlement rather than paying cash, the liability shall be transferred direct to equity, as the consideration for the equity instruments issued.

40   If the entity pays in cash on settlement rather than issuing equity instruments, that payment shall be applied to settle the liability in full. Any equity component previously recognised shall remain within equity. By electing to receive cash on settlement, the counterparty forfeited the right to receive equity instruments. However, this requirement does not preclude the entity from recognising a transfer within equity, that is, a transfer from one component of equity to another.

---

3   In paragraphs 35 to 43, all references to cash also include other assets of the entity.

AASB 2   **Institute of Chartered Accountants Australia**

Share-based payment transactions in which the terms of the arrangement provide the entity with a choice of settlement

41   For a share-based payment transaction in which the terms of the arrangement provide an entity with the choice of whether to settle in cash or by issuing equity instruments, the entity shall determine whether it has a present obligation to settle in cash and account for the share-based payment transaction accordingly. The entity has a present obligation to settle in cash if the choice of settlement in equity instruments has no commercial substance (e.g. because the entity is legally prohibited from issuing shares), or the entity has a past practice or a stated policy of settling in cash, or generally settles in cash whenever the counterparty asks for cash settlement.

42   If the entity has a present obligation to settle in cash, it shall account for the transaction in accordance with the requirements applying to cash-settled share-based payment transactions, in paragraphs 30-33.

43   If no such obligation exists, the entity shall account for the transaction in accordance with the requirements applying to equity-settled share-based payment transactions, in paragraphs 10-29. Upon settlement:

(a)   if the entity elects to settle in cash, the cash payment shall be accounted for as the repurchase of an equity interest, that is, as a deduction from equity, except as noted in (c) below;

(b)   if the entity elects to settle by issuing equity instruments, no further accounting is required (other than a transfer from one component of equity to another, if necessary), except as noted in (c) below; and

(c)   if the entity elects the settlement alternative with the higher fair value, as at the date of settlement, the entity shall recognise an additional expense for the excess value given, that is, the difference between the cash paid and the fair value of the equity instruments that would otherwise have been issued, or the difference between the fair value of the equity instruments issued and the amount of cash that would otherwise have been paid, whichever is applicable.

Share-based Payment Transactions among Group Entities

43A   For share-based payment transactions among group entities, in its separate or individual financial statements, the entity receiving the goods or services shall measure the goods or services received as either an equity-settled or a cash-settled share-based payment transaction by assessing:

(a)   the nature of the awards granted; and

(b)   its own rights and obligations.

The amount recognised by the entity receiving the goods or services may differ from the amount recognised by the consolidated group or by another group entity settling the share-based payment transaction.

43B   The entity receiving the goods or services shall measure the goods or services received as an equity-settled share-based payment transaction when:

(a)   the awards granted are its own equity instruments; or

(b)   the entity has no obligation to settle the share-based payment transaction.

The entity shall subsequently remeasure such an equity-settled share-based payment transaction only for changes in non-market vesting conditions in accordance with paragraphs 19-21. In all other circumstances, the entity receiving the goods or services shall measure the goods or services received as a cash-settled share-based payment transaction.

43C   The entity settling a share-based payment transaction when another entity in the group receives the goods or services shall recognise the transaction as an equity-settled share-based payment transaction only if it is settled in the entity's own equity instruments. Otherwise, the transaction shall be recognised as a cash-settled share-based payment transaction.

43D   Some group transactions involve repayment arrangements that require one group entity to pay another group entity for the provision of the share-based payments to the suppliers of goods or services. In such cases, the entity that receives the goods or services shall account for the share-based payment transaction in accordance with paragraph 43B regardless of intragroup repayment arrangements.

Disclosures

44   An entity shall disclose information that enables users of the financial statements to understand the nature and extent of share-based payment arrangements that existed during the period.

45   To give effect to the principle in paragraph 44, the entity shall disclose at least the following:

    (a)   a description of each type of share-based payment arrangement that existed at any time during the period, including the general terms and conditions of each arrangement, such as vesting requirements, the maximum term of options granted, and the method of settlement (e.g. whether in cash or equity). An entity with substantially similar types of share-based payment arrangements may aggregate this information, unless separate disclosure of each arrangement is necessary to satisfy the principle in paragraph 44;

    (b)   the number and weighted average exercise prices of share options for each of the following groups of options:

        (i)   outstanding at the beginning of the period;

        (ii)   granted during the period;

        (iii)   forfeited during the period;

        (iv)   exercised during the period;

        (v)   expired during the period;

        (vi)   outstanding at the end of the period; and

        (vii)   exercisable at the end of the period;

    (c)   for share options exercised during the period, the weighted average share price at the date of exercise. If options were exercised on a regular basis throughout the period, the entity may instead disclose the weighted average share price during the period; and

    (d)   for share options outstanding at the end of the period, the range of exercise prices and weighted average remaining contractual life. If the range of exercise prices is wide, the outstanding options shall be divided into ranges that are meaningful for assessing the number and timing of additional shares that may be issued and the cash that may be received upon exercise of those options.

46   An entity shall disclose information that enables users of the financial statements to understand how the fair value of the goods or services received, or the fair value of the equity instruments granted, during the period was determined.

47   If the entity has measured the fair value of goods or services received as consideration for equity instruments of the entity indirectly, by reference to the fair value of the equity instruments granted, to give effect to the principle in paragraph 46, the entity shall disclose at least the following:

    (a)   for share options granted during the period, the weighted average fair value of those options at the measurement date and information on how that fair value was measured, including:

        (i)   the option pricing model used and the inputs to that model, including the weighted average share price, exercise price, expected volatility, option life, expected dividends, the risk-free interest rate and any other inputs to the model, including the method used and the assumptions made to incorporate the effects of expected early exercise;

AASB

      (ii)   how expected volatility was determined, including an explanation of the extent to which expected volatility was based on historical volatility; and

      (iii)   whether and how any other features of the option grant were incorporated into the measurement of fair value, such as a market condition;

  (b)   for other equity instruments granted during the period (i.e. other than share options), the number and weighted average fair value of those equity instruments at the measurement date, and information on how that fair value was measured, including:

      (i)   if fair value was not measured on the basis of an observable market price, how it was determined;

      (ii)   whether and how expected dividends were incorporated into the measurement of fair value; and

      (iii)   whether and how any other features of the equity instruments granted were incorporated into the measurement of fair value; and

  (c)   for share-based payment arrangements that were modified during the period:

      (i)   an explanation of those modifications;

      (ii)   the incremental fair value granted (as a result of those modifications); and

      (iii)   information on how the incremental fair value granted was measured, consistently with the requirements set out in (a) and (b) above, where applicable.

48   If the entity has measured directly the fair value of goods or services received during the period, the entity shall disclose how that fair value was determined, for example, whether fair value was measured at a market price for those goods or services.

49   If the entity has rebutted the presumption in paragraph 13, it shall disclose that fact, and give an explanation of why the presumption was rebutted.

50   An entity shall disclose information that enables users of the financial statements to understand the effect of share-based payment transactions on the entity's profit or loss for the period and on its financial position.

51   To give effect to the principle in paragraph 50, the entity shall disclose at least the following:

  (a)   the total expense recognised for the period arising from share-based payment transactions in which the goods or services received did not qualify for recognition as assets and hence were recognised immediately as an expense, including separate disclosure of that portion of the total expense that arises from transactions accounted for as equity-settled share-based payment transactions; and

  (b)   for liabilities arising from share-based payment transactions:

      (i)   the total carrying amount at the end of the period; and

      (ii)   the total intrinsic value at the end of the period of liabilities for which the counterparty's right to cash or other assets had vested by the end of the period (e.g. vested share appreciation rights).

52   If the information required to be disclosed by this Standard does not satisfy the principles in paragraphs 44, 46 and 50, the entity shall disclose such additional information as is necessary to satisfy them.

Transitional Provisions

Aus52.1   The following transitional paragraphs shall not be applied by entities that have previously applied this Standard, unless required to do so by another Australian equivalent to IFRSs.

53   For equity-settled share-based payment transactions, the entity shall apply this Standard to grants of shares, share options or other equity instruments that were granted after 7 November 2002 and had not yet vested at the application date of this Standard.

54   The entity is encouraged, but not required, to apply this Standard to other grants of equity instruments if the entity has disclosed publicly the fair value of those equity instruments, determined at the measurement date.

55   For all grants of equity instruments to which this Standard is applied, the entity shall restate comparative information and, where applicable, adjust the opening balance of retained earnings for the earliest period presented.

56   For all grants of equity instruments to which this Standard has not been applied (e.g. equity instruments granted on or before 7 November 2002), the entity shall nevertheless disclose the information required by paragraphs 44 and 45.

57   If, after the Standard becomes applicable, an entity modifies the terms or conditions of a grant of equity instruments to which this Standard has not been applied, the entity shall nevertheless apply paragraphs 26-29 to account for any such modifications.

58   For liabilities arising from share-based payment transactions existing at the application date of this Standard, the entity shall apply the Standard retrospectively. For these liabilities, the entity shall restate comparative information, including adjusting the opening balance of retained earnings in the earliest period presented for which comparative information has been restated, except that the entity is not required to restate comparative information to the extent that the information relates to a period or date that is earlier than 7 November 2002.

59   The entity is encouraged, but not required, to apply retrospectively the Standard to other liabilities arising from share-based payment transactions, for example, to liabilities that were settled during a period for which comparative information is presented.

Effective Date

60   [Deleted by the AASB]

61   AASB 2008-3 *Amendments to Australian Accounting Standards Arising from AASB 3 and AASB 127* and AASB 2009-4 *Amendments to Australian Accounting Standards arising from the Annual Improvements Project*, issued in May 2009, amended paragraph 5. An entity shall apply those amendments for annual reporting periods beginning on or after 1 July 2009. Earlier application is permitted. If an entity applies AASB 3 (revised 2008) for an earlier period, the amendments shall also be applied for that earlier period.

62   [Deleted by the AASB]

63   An entity shall apply the following amendments made by AASB 2009-8 *Amendments to Australian Accounting Standards – Group Cash-settled Share-based Payment Transactions* issued in July 2009 retrospectively, subject to the transitional provisions in paragraphs 53-59, in accordance with AASB 108 *Accounting Policies, Changes in Accounting Estimates and Errors* for annual reporting periods beginning on or after 1 January 2010:

(a)   the amendment of paragraph 2, the deletion of paragraph 3 and the addition of paragraphs 3A and 43A-43D and of paragraphs B45, B47, B50, B54, B56-B58 and B60 in Appendix B in respect of the accounting for transactions among group entities.

(b)   the revised definitions in Appendix A of the following terms:

•   cash-settled share-based payment transaction;

•   equity-settled share-based payment transaction;

•   share-based payment arrangement; and

•   share-based payment transaction.

If the information necessary for retrospective application is not available, an entity shall reflect in its separate or individual financial statements the amounts previously recognised in the group's consolidated financial statements. Earlier application is permitted. If an entity applies the amendments for a period beginning on or after 1 January 2005 but before 1 January 2010, it shall disclose that fact.

Withdrawal of Interpretations

64 AASB 2009-8 *Amendments to Australian Accounting Standards – Group Cash-settled Share-based Payment Transactions* issued in July 2009 supersedes Interpretation 8 *Scope of AASB 2* and Interpretation 11 *AASB 2 – Group and Treasury Share Transactions.* The amendments made by that document incorporated the previous requirements set out in Interpretation 8 and Interpretation 11 as follows:

(a) amended paragraph 2 and added paragraph 13A in respect of the accounting for transactions in which the entity cannot identify specifically some or all of the goods or services received. Those requirements were effective for annual reporting periods beginning on or after 1 May 2006.

(b) added paragraphs B46, B48, B49, B51-B53, B55, B59 and B61 in Appendix B in respect of the accounting for transactions among group entities. Those requirements were effective for annual reporting periods beginning on or after 1 March 2007.

Those requirements were applied retrospectively in accordance with the requirements of AASB 108, subject to the transitional provisions of AASB 2.

Appendix A
Defined Terms

This appendix is an integral part of AASB 2.

cash-settled share-based payment transaction	A **share-based payment transaction** in which the entity acquires goods or services by incurring a liability to transfer cash or other assets to the supplier of those goods or services for amounts that are based on the price (or value) of **equity instruments** (including shares or **share options**) of the entity or another group entity.
employees and others providing similar services	Individuals who render personal services to the entity and either (a) the individuals are regarded as employees for legal or tax purposes, (b) the individuals work for the entity under its direction in the same way as individuals who are regarded as employees for legal or tax purposes, or (c) the services rendered are similar to those rendered by employees. For example, the term encompasses all management personnel, that is, those persons having authority and responsibility for planning, directing and controlling the activities of the entity, including non-executive directors.
equity instrument	A contract that evidences a residual interest in the assets of an entity after deducting all of its liabilities[1].
equity instrument granted	The right (conditional or unconditional) to an **equity instrument** of the entity conferred by the entity on another party, under a **share-based payment arrangement**.
equity-settled share-based payment transaction	A **share-based payment transaction** in which the entity:
	(a) receives goods or services as consideration for its own **equity instruments** (including shares or **share options**); or
	(b) receives goods or services but has no obligation to settle the transaction with the supplier.
fair value	The amount for which an asset could be exchanged, a liability settled, or an **equity instrument granted** could be exchanged, between knowledgeable, willing parties in an arm's length transaction.

---

1 The *Framework for the Preparation and Presentation of Financial Statements* defines a liability as a present obligation of the entity arising from past events, the settlement of which is expected to result in an outflow from the entity of resources embodying economic benefits (i.e. an outflow of cash or other assets of the entity).

grant date	The date at which the entity and another party (including an employee) agree to a **share-based payment arrangement**, being when the entity and the counterparty have a shared understanding of the terms and conditions of the arrangement. At grant date the entity confers on the counterparty the right to cash, other assets, or **equity instruments** of the entity, provided the specified **vesting conditions**, if any, are met. If that agreement is subject to an approval process (for example, by shareholders), grant date is the date when that approval is obtained.
intrinsic value	The difference between the **fair value** of the shares to which the counterparty has the (conditional or unconditional) right to subscribe or which it has the right to receive, and the price (if any) the counterparty is (or will be) required to pay for those shares. For example, a **share option** with an exercise price of CU15[2], on a share with a **fair value** of CU20, has an intrinsic value of CU5.
market condition	A condition upon which the exercise price, vesting or exercisability of an **equity instrument** depends that is related to the market price of the entity's **equity instruments**, such as attaining a specified share price or a specified amount of **intrinsic value** of a **share option**, or achieving a specified target that is based on the market price of the entity's **equity instruments** relative to an index of market prices of **equity instruments** of other entities.
measurement date	The date at which the **fair value** of the **equity instruments granted** is measured for the purposes of this Standard. For transactions with **employees and others providing similar services**, the measurement date is **grant date**. For transactions with parties other than employees (and those providing similar services), the measurement date is the date the entity obtains the goods or the counterparty renders service.
reload feature	A feature that provides for an automatic grant of additional **share options** whenever the option holder exercises previously granted options using the entity's shares, rather than cash, to satisfy the exercise price.
reload option	A new **share option** granted when a share is used to satisfy the exercise price of a previous **share option**.
share-based payment arrangement	An agreement between the entity (or another group[3] entity or any shareholder of any group entity) and another party (including an employee) that entitles the other party to receive:

    (a)   cash or other assets of the entity for amounts that are based on the price (or value) of **equity instruments** (including shares or **share options**) of the entity or another group entity; or

    (b)   **equity instruments** (including shares or **share options**) of the entity, or another group entity,

provided the specified **vesting conditions**, if any, are met.

share-based payment transaction	A transaction in which the entity:

    (a)   receives goods or services from the supplier of those goods or services (including an employee) in a **share-based payment arrangement**; or

    (b)   incurs an obligation to settle the transaction with the supplier in a **share-based payment arrangement** when another group entity receives those goods or services.

---

2   In this appendix, monetary amounts are denominated in 'currency units' (CU).

3   A 'group' is defined in paragraph 4 of AASB 127 *Consolidated and Separate Financial Statements* as 'a parent and all its subsidiaries' from the perspective of the reporting entity's ultimate parent.

share option	A contract that gives the holder the right, but not the obligation, to subscribe to the entity's shares at a fixed or determinable price for a specified period of time.
vest	To become an entitlement. Under a **share-based payment arrangement**, a counterparty's right to receive cash, other assets or **equity instruments** of the entity vests when the counterparty's entitlement is no longer conditional on the satisfaction of any **vesting conditions**.
vesting conditions	The conditions that determine whether the entity receives the services that entitle the counterparty to receive cash, other assets or **equity instruments** of the entity, under a **share-based payment arrangement**. Vesting conditions are either service conditions or performance conditions. Service conditions require the counterparty to complete a specified period of service. Performance conditions require the counterparty to complete a specified period of service and specified performance targets to be met (such as a specified increase in the entity's profit over a specified period of time). A performance condition might include a **market condition**.
vesting period	The period during which all the specified **vesting conditions** of a **share-based payment arrangement** are to be satisfied.

Appendix B

Application Guidance

This appendix is an integral part of AASB 2.

Estimating the fair value of equity instruments granted

B1   Paragraphs B2-B41 of this appendix discuss measurement of the fair value of shares and share options granted, focusing on the specific terms and conditions that are common features of a grant of shares or share options to employees. Therefore, it is not exhaustive. Furthermore, because the valuation issues discussed below focus on shares and share options granted to employees, it is assumed that the fair value of the shares or share options is measured at grant date. However, many of the valuation issues discussed below (e.g. determining expected volatility) also apply in the context of estimating the fair value of shares or share options granted to parties other than employees at the date the entity obtains the goods or the counterparty renders service.

Shares

B2   For shares granted to employees, the fair value of the shares shall be measured at the market price of the entity's shares (or an estimated market price, if the entity's shares are not publicly traded), adjusted to take into account the terms and conditions upon which the shares were granted (except for vesting conditions that are excluded from the measurement of fair value in accordance with paragraphs 19-21).

B3   For example, if the employee is not entitled to receive dividends during the vesting period, this factor shall be taken into account when estimating the fair value of the shares granted. Similarly, if the shares are subject to restrictions on transfer after vesting date, that factor shall be taken into account, but only to the extent that the post-vesting restrictions affect the price that a knowledgeable, willing market participant would pay for that share. For example, if the shares are actively traded in a deep and liquid market, post-vesting transfer restrictions may have little, if any, effect on the price that a knowledgeable, willing market participant would pay for those shares. Restrictions on transfer or other restrictions that exist during the vesting period shall not be taken into account when estimating the grant date fair value of the shares granted, because those restrictions stem from the existence of vesting conditions, which are accounted for in accordance with paragraphs 19-21.

Share options

B4   For share options granted to employees, in many cases market prices are not available, because the options granted are subject to terms and conditions that do not apply to traded options. If traded options with similar terms and conditions do not exist, the fair value of the options granted shall be estimated by applying an option pricing model.

B5   The entity shall consider factors that knowledgeable, willing market participants would consider in selecting the option pricing model to apply. For example, many employee options have long lives, are usually exercisable during the period between vesting date and the end of the options' life, and are often exercised early. These factors should be considered when estimating the grant date fair value of the options. For many entities, this might preclude the use of the Black-Scholes-Merton formula, which does not allow for the possibility of exercise before the end of the option's life and may not adequately reflect the effects of expected early exercise. It also does not allow for the possibility that expected volatility and other model inputs might vary over the option's life. However, for share options with relatively short contractual lives, or that must be exercised within a short period of time after vesting date, the factors identified above may not apply. In these instances, the Black-Scholes-Merton formula may produce a value that is substantially the same as a more flexible option pricing model.

B6   All option pricing models take into account, as a minimum, the following factors:
(a)   the exercise price of the option;
(b)   the life of the option;
(c)   the current price of the underlying shares;
(d)   the expected volatility of the share price;
(e)   the dividends expected on the shares (if appropriate); and
(f)   the risk-free interest rate for the life of the option.

B7   Other factors that knowledgeable, willing market participants would consider in setting the price shall also be taken into account (except for vesting conditions and reload features that are excluded from the measurement of fair value in accordance with paragraphs 19-22).

B8   For example, a share option granted to an employee typically cannot be exercised during specified periods (e.g. during the vesting period or during periods specified by securities regulators). This factor shall be taken into account if the option pricing model applied would otherwise assume that the option could be exercised at any time during its life. However, if an entity uses an option pricing model that values options that can be exercised only at the end of the options' life, no adjustment is required for the inability to exercise them during the vesting period (or other periods during the options' life), because the model assumes that the options cannot be exercised during those periods.

B9   Similarly, another factor common to employee share options is the possibility of early exercise of the option, for example, because the option is not freely transferable, or because the employee must exercise all vested options upon cessation of employment. The effects of expected early exercise shall be taken into account, as discussed in paragraphs B16-B21.

B10   Factors that a knowledgeable, willing market participant would not consider in setting the price of a share option (or other equity instrument) shall not be taken into account when estimating the fair value of share options (or other equity instruments) granted. For example, for share options granted to employees, factors that affect the value of the option from the individual employee's perspective only are not relevant to estimating the price that would be set by a knowledgeable, willing market participant.

Inputs to option pricing models

B11   In estimating the expected volatility of and dividends on the underlying shares, the objective is to approximate the expectations that would be reflected in a current market or negotiated exchange price for the option. Similarly, when estimating the effects of early exercise of employee share options, the objective is to approximate the expectations that an outside party with access to detailed information about employees' exercise behaviour would develop based on information available at the grant date.

B12   Often, there is likely to be a range of reasonable expectations about future volatility, dividends and exercise behaviour. If so, an expected value should be calculated, by weighting each amount within the range by its associated probability of occurrence.

B13   Expectations about the future are generally based on experience, modified if the future is reasonably expected to differ from the past. In some circumstances, identifiable factors may indicate that unadjusted historical experience is a relatively poor predictor of future experience. For example, if an entity with two distinctly different lines of business disposes of the one that was significantly less risky than the other, historical volatility may not be the best information on which to base reasonable expectations for the future.

B14   In other circumstances, historical information may not be available. For example, a newly listed entity will have little, if any, historical data on the volatility of its share price. Unlisted and newly listed entities are discussed further below.

B15   In summary, an entity should not simply base estimates of volatility, exercise behaviour and dividends on historical information without considering the extent to which the past experience is expected to be reasonably predictive of future experience.

Expected early exercise

B16   Employees often exercise share options early, for a variety of reasons. For example, employee share options are typically non-transferable. This often causes employees to exercise their share options early, because that is the only way for the employees to liquidate their position. Also, employees who cease employment are usually required to exercise any vested options within a short period of time, otherwise the share options are forfeited. This factor also causes the early exercise of employee share options. Other factors causing early exercise are risk aversion and lack of wealth diversification.

B17   The means by which the effects of expected early exercise are taken into account depends upon the type of option pricing model applied. For example, expected early exercise could be taken into account by using an estimate of the option's expected life (which, for an employee share option, is the period of time from grant date to the date on which the option is expected to be exercised) as an input into an option pricing model (e.g. the Black-Scholes-Merton formula). Alternatively, expected early exercise could be modelled in a binomial or similar option pricing model that uses contractual life as an input.

B18   Factors to consider in estimating early exercise include:

    (a)   the length of the vesting period, because the share option typically cannot be exercised until the end of the vesting period. Hence, determining the valuation implications of expected early exercise is based on the assumption that the options will vest. The implications of vesting conditions are discussed in paragraphs 19-21;

    (b)   the average length of time similar options have remained outstanding in the past;

    (c)   the price of the underlying shares. Experience may indicate that the employees tend to exercise options when the share price reaches a specified level above the exercise price;

(d)   the employee's level within the organisation. For example, experience might indicate that higher-level employees tend to exercise options later than lower-level employees (discussed further in paragraph B21); and

(e)   expected volatility of the underlying shares. On average, employees might tend to exercise options on highly volatile shares earlier than on shares with low volatility.

B19   As noted in paragraph B17, the effects of early exercise could be taken into account by using an estimate of the option's expected life as an input into an option pricing model. When estimating the expected life of share options granted to a group of employees, the entity could base that estimate on an appropriately weighted average expected life for the entire employee group or on appropriately weighted average lives for subgroups of employees within the group, based on more detailed data about employees' exercise behaviour (discussed further below).

B20   Separating an option grant into groups for employees with relatively homogeneous exercise behaviour is likely to be important. Option value is not a linear function of option term; value increases at a decreasing rate as the term lengthens. For example, if all other assumptions are equal, although a two-year option is worth more than a one-year option, it is not worth twice as much. That means that calculating estimated option value on the basis of a single weighted average life that includes widely differing individual lives would overstate the total fair value of the share options granted. Separating options granted into several groups, each of which has a relatively narrow range of lives included in its weighted average life, reduces that overstatement.

B21   Similar considerations apply when using a binomial or similar model. For example, the experience of an entity that grants options broadly to all levels of employees might indicate that top-level executives tend to hold their options longer than middle-management employees hold theirs and that lower-level employees tend to exercise their options earlier than any other group. In addition, employees who are encouraged or required to hold a minimum amount of their employer's equity instruments, including options, might on average exercise options later than employees not subject to that provision. In those situations, separating options by groups of recipients with relatively homogeneous exercise behaviour will result in a more accurate estimate of the total fair value of the share options granted.

Expected volatility

B22   Expected volatility is a measure of the amount by which a price is expected to fluctuate during a period. The measure of volatility used in option pricing models is the annualised standard deviation of the continuously compounded rates of return on the share over a period of time. Volatility is typically expressed in annualised terms that are comparable regardless of the time period used in the calculation, for example, daily, weekly or monthly price observations.

B23   The rate of return (which may be positive or negative) on a share for a period measures how much a shareholder has benefited from dividends and appreciation (or depreciation) of the share price.

B24   The expected annualised volatility of a share is the range within which the continuously-compounded annual rate of return is expected to fall approximately two-thirds of the time. For example, to say that a share with an expected continuously-compounded rate of return of 12 per cent has a volatility of 30 per cent means that the probability that the rate of return on the share for one year will be between –18 per cent (12% – 30%) and 42 per cent (12% + 30%) is approximately two-thirds. If the share price is CU100 at the beginning of the year and no dividends are paid, the year-end share price would be expected to be between CU83.53 (CU100 × $e^{-0.18}$) and CU152.20 (CU100 × $e^{0.42}$) approximately two-thirds of the time.

B25 Factors to consider in estimating expected volatility include:

(a) implied volatility from traded share options on the entity's shares, or other traded instruments of the entity that include option features (such as convertible debt), if any;

(b) the historical volatility of the share price over the most recent period that is generally commensurate with the expected term of the option (taking into account the remaining contractual life of the option and the effects of expected early exercise);

(c) the length of time an entity's shares have been publicly traded. A newly listed entity might have a high historical volatility, compared with similar entities that have been listed longer. Further guidance for newly listed entities is given below;

(d) the tendency of volatility to revert to its mean, that is, its long-term average level, and other factors indicating that expected future volatility might differ from past volatility. For example, if an entity's share price was extraordinarily volatile for some identifiable period of time because of a failed takeover bid or a major restructuring, that period could be disregarded in computing historical average annual volatility; and

(e) appropriate and regular intervals for price observations. The price observations should be consistent from period to period. For example, an entity might use the closing price for each week or the highest price for the week, but it should not use the closing price for some weeks and the highest price for other weeks. Also, the price observations should be expressed in the same currency as the exercise price.

Newly listed entities

B26 As noted in paragraph B25, an entity should consider historical volatility of the share price over the most recent period that is generally commensurate with the expected option term. If a newly listed entity does not have sufficient information on historical volatility, it should nevertheless compute historical volatility for the longest period for which trading activity is available. It could also consider the historical volatility of similar entities following a comparable period in their lives. For example, an entity that has been listed for only one year and grants options with an average expected life of five years might consider the pattern and level of historical volatility of entities in the same industry for the first six years in which the shares of those entities were publicly traded.

Unlisted entities

B27 An unlisted entity will not have historical information to consider when estimating expected volatility. Some factors to consider instead are set out below.

B28 In some cases, an unlisted entity that regularly issues options or shares to employees (or other parties) might have set up an internal market for its shares. The volatility of those share prices could be considered when estimating expected volatility.

B29 Alternatively, the entity could consider the historical or implied volatility of similar listed entities, for which share price or option price information is available, to use when estimating expected volatility. This would be appropriate if the entity has based the value of its shares on the share prices of similar listed entities.

B30 If the entity has not based its estimate of the value of its shares on the share prices of similar listed entities, and has instead used another valuation methodology to value its shares, the entity could derive an estimate of expected volatility consistent with that valuation methodology. For example, the entity might value its shares on a net asset or earnings basis. It could consider the expected volatility of those net asset values or earnings.

Expected dividends

B31   Whether expected dividends should be taken into account when measuring the fair value of shares or options granted depends on whether the counterparty is entitled to dividends or dividend equivalents.

B32   For example, if employees were granted options and are entitled to dividends on the underlying shares or dividend equivalents (which might be paid in cash or applied to reduce the exercise price) between grant date and exercise date, the options granted should be valued as if no dividends will be paid on the underlying shares, that is, the input for expected dividends should be zero.

B33   Similarly, when the grant date fair value of shares granted to employees is estimated, no adjustment is required for expected dividends if the employee is entitled to receive dividends paid during the vesting period.

B34   Conversely, if the employees are not entitled to dividends or dividend equivalents during the vesting period (or before exercise, in the case of an option), the grant date valuation of the rights to shares or options should take expected dividends into account. That is to say, when the fair value of an option grant is estimated, expected dividends should be included in the application of an option pricing model. When the fair value of a share grant is estimated, that valuation should be reduced by the present value of dividends expected to be paid during the vesting period.

B35   Option pricing models generally call for expected dividend yield. However, the models may be modified to use an expected dividend amount rather than a yield. An entity may use either its expected yield or its expected payments. If the entity uses the latter, it should consider its historical pattern of increases in dividends. For example, if an entity's policy has generally been to increase dividends by approximately 3 per cent per year, its estimated option value should not assume a fixed dividend amount throughout the option's life unless there is evidence that supports that assumption.

B36   Generally, the assumption about expected dividends should be based on publicly available information. An entity that does not pay dividends and has no plans to do so should assume an expected dividend yield of zero. However, an emerging entity with no history of paying dividends might expect to begin paying dividends during the expected lives of its employee share options. Those entities could use an average of their past dividend yield (zero) and the mean dividend yield of an appropriately comparable peer group.

Risk-free interest rate

B37   Typically, the risk-free interest rate is the implied yield currently available on zero-coupon government issues of the country in whose currency the exercise price is expressed, with a remaining term equal to the expected term of the option being valued (based on the option's remaining contractual life and taking into account the effects of expected early exercise). It may be necessary to use an appropriate substitute, if no such government issues exist or circumstances indicate that the implied yield on zero-coupon government issues is not representative of the risk-free interest rate (for example, in high inflation economies). Also, an appropriate substitute should be used if market participants would typically determine the risk-free interest rate by using that substitute, rather than the implied yield of zero-coupon government issues, when estimating the fair value of an option with a life equal to the expected term of the option being valued.

Capital structure effects

B38   Typically, third parties, not the entity, write traded share options. When these share options are exercised, the writer delivers shares to the option holder. Those shares are acquired from existing shareholders. Hence the exercise of traded share options has no dilutive effect.

B39   In contrast, if share options are written by the entity, new shares are issued when those share options are exercised (either actually issued or issued in substance, if shares previously repurchased and held in treasury are used). Given that the shares will be issued at the exercise price rather than the current market price at the date of exercise, this actual or potential dilution might reduce the share price, so that the option holder does not make as large a gain on exercise as on exercising an otherwise similar traded option that does not dilute the share price.

B40 Whether this has a significant effect on the value of the share options granted depends on various factors, such as the number of new shares that will be issued on exercise of the options compared with the number of shares already issued. Also, if the market already expects that the option grant will take place, the market may have already factored the potential dilution into the share price at the date of grant.

B41 However, the entity should consider whether the possible dilutive effect of the future exercise of the share options granted might have an impact on their estimated fair value at grant date. Option pricing models can be adapted to take into account this potential dilutive effect.

Modifications to equity-settled share-based payment arrangements

B42 Paragraph 27 requires that, irrespective of any modifications to the terms and conditions on which the equity instruments were granted, or a cancellation or settlement of that grant of equity instruments, the entity should recognise, as a minimum, the services received measured at the grant date fair value of the equity instruments granted, unless those equity instruments do not vest because of failure to satisfy a vesting condition (other than a market condition) that was specified at grant date. In addition, the entity should recognise the effects of modifications that increase the total fair value of the share-based payment arrangement or are otherwise beneficial to the employee.

B43 To apply the requirements of paragraph 27:

(a) if the modification increases the fair value of the equity instruments granted (e.g. by reducing the exercise price), measured immediately before and after the modification, the entity shall include the incremental fair value granted in the measurement of the amount recognised for services received as consideration for the equity instruments granted. The incremental fair value granted is the difference between the fair value of the modified equity instrument and that of the original equity instrument, both estimated as at the date of the modification. If the modification occurs during the vesting period, the incremental fair value granted is included in the measurement of the amount recognised for services received over the period from the modification date until the date when the modified equity instruments vest, in addition to the amount based on the grant date fair value of the original equity instruments, which is recognised over the remainder of the original vesting period. If the modification occurs after vesting date, the incremental fair value granted is recognised immediately, or over the vesting period if the employee is required to complete an additional period of service before becoming unconditionally entitled to those modified equity instruments;

(b) similarly, if the modification increases the number of equity instruments granted, the entity shall include the fair value of the additional equity instruments granted, measured at the date of the modification, in the measurement of the amount recognised for services received as consideration for the equity instruments granted, consistently with the requirements in (a) above. For example, if the modification occurs during the vesting period, the fair value of the additional equity instruments granted is included in the measurement of the amount recognised for services received over the period from the modification date until the date when the additional equity instruments vest, in addition to the amount based on the grant date fair value of the equity instruments originally granted, which is recognised over the remainder of the original vesting period; and

(c) if the entity modifies the vesting conditions in a manner that is beneficial to the employee, for example, by reducing the vesting period or by modifying or eliminating a performance condition (other than a market condition, changes to which are accounted for in accordance with (a) above), the entity shall take the modified vesting conditions into account when applying the requirements of paragraphs 19-21.

B44   Furthermore, if the entity modifies the terms or conditions of the equity instruments granted in a manner that reduces the total fair value of the share-based payment arrangement, or is not otherwise beneficial to the employee, the entity shall nevertheless continue to account for the services received as consideration for the equity instruments granted as if that modification had not occurred (other than a cancellation of some or all the equity instruments granted, which shall be accounted for in accordance with paragraph 28). For example:

    (a)   if the modification reduces the fair value of the equity instruments granted, measured immediately before and after the modification, the entity shall not take into account that decrease in fair value and shall continue to measure the amount recognised for services received as consideration for the equity instruments based on the grant date fair value of the equity instruments granted;

    (b)   if the modification reduces the number of equity instruments granted to an employee, that reduction shall be accounted for as a cancellation of that portion of the grant, in accordance with the requirements of paragraph 28; and

    (c)   if the entity modifies the vesting conditions in a manner that is not beneficial to the employee, for example, by increasing the vesting period or by modifying or adding a performance condition (other than a market condition, changes to which are accounted for in accordance with (a) above), the entity shall not take the modified vesting conditions into account when applying the requirements of paragraphs 19-21.

Share-based payment transactions among group entities (2009 amendments)

B45   Paragraphs 43A-43C address the accounting for share-based payment transactions among group entities in each entity's separate or individual financial statements. Paragraphs B46-B61 discuss how to apply the requirements in paragraphs 43A-43C. As noted in paragraph 43D, share-based payment transactions among group entities may take place for a variety of reasons depending on facts and circumstances. Therefore, this discussion is not exhaustive and assumes that when the entity receiving the goods or services has no obligation to settle the transaction, the transaction is a parent's equity contribution to the subsidiary, regardless of any intragroup repayment arrangements.

B46   Although the discussion below focuses on transactions with employees, it also applies to similar share-based payment transactions with suppliers of goods or services other than employees. An arrangement between a parent and its subsidiary may require the subsidiary to pay the parent for the provision of the equity instruments to the employees. The discussion below does not address how to account for such an intragroup payment arrangement.

B47   Four issues are commonly encountered in share-based payment transactions among group entities. For convenience, the examples below discuss the issues in terms of a parent and its subsidiary.

Share-based payment arrangements involving an entity's own equity instruments

B48   The first issue is whether the following transactions involving an entity's own equity instruments should be accounted for as equity-settled or as cash-settled in accordance with the requirements of this Standard:

    (a)   an entity grants to its employees rights to equity instruments of the entity (e.g. share options), and either chooses or is required to buy equity instruments (i.e. treasury shares) from another party, to satisfy its obligations to its employees; and

(b)   an entity's employees are granted rights to equity instruments of the entity (e.g. share options), either by the entity itself or by its shareholders, and the shareholders of the entity provide the equity instruments needed.

B49   The entity shall account for share-based payment transactions in which it receives services as consideration for its own equity instruments as equity-settled. This applies regardless of whether the entity chooses or is required to buy those equity instruments from another party to satisfy its obligations to its employees under the share-based payment arrangement. It also applies regardless of whether:

(a)   the employee's rights to the entity's equity instruments were granted by the entity itself or by its shareholder(s); or

(b)   the share-based payment arrangement was settled by the entity itself or by its shareholder(s).

B50   If the shareholder has an obligation to settle the transaction with its investee's employees, it provides equity instruments of its investee rather than its own. Therefore, if its investee is in the same group as the shareholder, in accordance with paragraph 43C, the shareholder shall measure its obligation in accordance with the requirements applicable to cash-settled share-based payment transactions in the shareholder's separate financial statements and those applicable to equity-settled share-based payment transactions in the shareholder's consolidated financial statements.

Share-based payment arrangements involving equity instruments of the parent

B51   The second issue concerns share-based payment transactions between two or more entities within the same group involving an equity instrument of another group entity. For example, employees of a subsidiary are granted rights to equity instruments of its parent as consideration for the services provided to the subsidiary.

B52   Therefore, the second issue concerns the following share-based payment arrangements:

(a)   a parent grants rights to its equity instruments directly to the employees of its subsidiary: the parent (not the subsidiary) has the obligation to provide the employees of the subsidiary with the equity instruments; and

(b)   a subsidiary grants rights to equity instruments of its parent to its employees: the subsidiary has the obligation to provide its employees with the equity instruments.

A parent grants rights to its equity instruments to the employees of its subsidiary (paragraph B52(a))

B53   The subsidiary does not have an obligation to provide its parent's equity instruments to the subsidiary's employees. Therefore, in accordance with paragraph 43B, the subsidiary shall measure the services received from its employees in accordance with the requirements applicable to equity-settled share-based payment transactions, and recognise a corresponding increase in equity as a contribution from the parent.

B54   The parent has an obligation to settle the transaction with the subsidiary's employees by providing the parent's own equity instruments. Therefore, in accordance with paragraph 43C, the parent shall measure its obligation in accordance with the requirements applicable to equity-settled share-based payment transactions.

A subsidiary grants rights to equity instruments of its parent to its employees (paragraph B52(b))

B55   Because the subsidiary does not meet either of the conditions in paragraph 43B, it shall account for the transaction with its employees as cash-settled. This requirement applies irrespective of how the subsidiary obtains the equity instruments to satisfy its obligations to its employees.

Share-based payment arrangements involving cash-settled payments to employees

B56   The third issue is how an entity that receives goods or services from its suppliers (including employees) should account for share-based arrangements that are cash-settled when the entity itself does not have any obligation to make the required payments to its suppliers. For example, consider the following arrangements in which the parent (not the entity itself) has an obligation to make the required cash payments to the employees of the entity:

(a)   the employees of the entity will receive cash payments that are linked to the price of its equity instruments.

(b)   the employees of the entity will receive cash payments that are linked to the price of its parent's equity instruments.

B57   The subsidiary does not have an obligation to settle the transaction with its employees. Therefore, the subsidiary shall account for the transaction with its employees as equity-settled, and recognise a corresponding increase in equity as a contribution from its parent. The subsidiary shall remeasure the cost of the transaction subsequently for any changes resulting from non-market vesting conditions not being met in accordance with paragraphs 19-21. This differs from the measurement of the transaction as cash-settled in the consolidated financial statements of the group.

B58   Because the parent has an obligation to settle the transaction with the employees, and the consideration is cash, the parent (and the consolidated group) shall measure its obligation in accordance with the requirements applicable to cash-settled share-based payment transactions in paragraph 43C.

Transfer of employees between group entities

B59   The fourth issue relates to group share-based payment arrangements that involve employees of more than one group entity. For example, a parent might grant rights to its equity instruments to the employees of its subsidiaries, conditional upon the completion of continuing service with the group for a specified period. An employee of one subsidiary might transfer employment to another subsidiary during the specified vesting period without the employee's rights to equity instruments of the parent under the original share-based payment arrangement being affected. If the subsidiaries have no obligation to settle the share-based payment transaction with their employees, they account for it as an equity-settled transaction. Each subsidiary shall measure the services received from the employee by reference to the fair value of the equity instruments at the date the rights to those equity instruments were originally granted by the parent as defined in Appendix A, and the proportion of the vesting period the employee served with each subsidiary.

B60   If the subsidiary has an obligation to settle the transaction with its employees in its parent's equity instruments, it accounts for the transaction as cash-settled. Each subsidiary shall measure the services received on the basis of grant date fair value of the equity instruments for the proportion of the vesting period the employee served with each subsidiary. In addition, each subsidiary shall recognise any change in the fair value of the equity instruments during the employee's service period with each subsidiary.

B61   Such an employee, after transferring between group entities, may fail to satisfy a vesting condition other than a market condition as defined in Appendix A, e.g. the employee leaves the group before completing the service period. In this case, because the vesting condition is service to the group, each subsidiary shall adjust the amount previously recognised in respect of the services received from the employee in accordance with the principles in paragraph 19. Hence, if the rights to the equity instruments granted by the parent do not vest because of an employee's failure to meet a vesting condition other than a market condition, no amount is recognised on a cumulative basis for the services received from that employee in the financial statements of any group entity.

Implementation Guidance
AASB 2 Share-based Payment

Contents

Paragraphs

Definition of grant date	IG1 – IG4
Definition of vesting conditions	IG4A
Transactions with parties other than employees	IG5 – IG7
Transitional arrangements	IG8
Equity-settled share-based payment transactions	IG9 – IG17
Cash-settled share-based payment transactions	IG18 – IG19
Share-based payment arrangements with cash alternatives	IG20 – IG22
Share-based payment transactions among group entities	IG22A
Illustrative disclosures	IG23
Summary of conditions for a counterparty to receive an equity instrument granted and of accounting treatments	IG24

Implementation Guidance
AASB 2 Share-based Payment

This guidance accompanies, but is not part of, AASB 2.

Definition of grant date

IG1   AASB 2 defines grant date as the date at which the entity and the employee (or other party providing similar services) agree to a share-based payment arrangement, being when the entity and the counterparty have a shared understanding of the terms and conditions of the arrangement. At grant date the entity confers on the counterparty the right to cash, other assets, or equity instruments of the entity, provided the specified vesting conditions, if any, are met. If that agreement is subject to an approval process (for example, by shareholders), grant date is the date when that approval is obtained.

IG2   As noted above, grant date is when both parties agree to a share-based payment arrangement. The word 'agree' is used in its usual sense, which means that there must be both an offer and acceptance of that offer. Hence, the date at which one party makes an offer to another party is not grant date. The date of grant is when that other party accepts the offer. In some instances, the counterparty explicitly agrees to the arrangement, for example, by signing a contract. In other instances, agreement might be implicit, for example, for many share-based payment arrangements with employees, the employees' agreement is evidenced by their commencing to render services.

IG3   Furthermore, for both parties to have agreed to the share-based payment arrangement, both parties must have a shared understanding of the terms and conditions of the arrangement. Therefore, if some of the terms and conditions of the arrangement are agreed on one date, with the remainder of the terms and conditions agreed on a later date, then grant date is on that later date, when all of the terms and conditions have been agreed. For example, if an entity agrees to issue share options to an employee, but the exercise price of the options will be set by a compensation committee that meets in three months' time, grant date is when the exercise price is set by the compensation committee.

IG4   In some cases, grant date might occur after the employees to whom the equity instruments were granted have begun rendering services. For example, if a grant of equity instruments is subject to shareholder approval, grant date might occur some months after the employees have begun rendering services in respect of that grant. The Standard requires the entity to recognise the services when received. In this situation, the entity should estimate the grant date fair value of the equity instruments (e.g. by estimating the fair value of the equity instruments at the end of the reporting period), for the purposes of recognising the services received during the period between service commencement date and grant date. Once the date of grant has been established, the entity should revise the earlier estimate so that the amounts recognised for services received in respect of the grant are ultimately based on the grant date fair value of the equity instruments.

Definition of vesting conditions

IG4A   AASB 2 defines vesting conditions as the conditions that determine whether the entity receives the services that entitle the counterparty to receive cash, other assets or equity instruments of the entity under a share-based payment arrangement. The following flowchart illustrates the evaluation of whether a condition is a service or performance condition or a non-vesting condition.

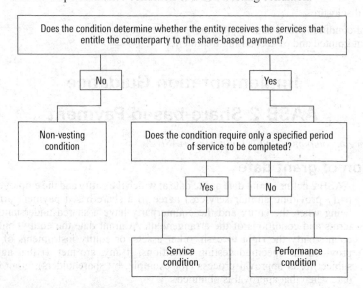

Transactions with parties other than employees

IG5   For transactions with parties other than employees (and others providing similar services) that are measured by reference to the fair value of the equity instruments granted, paragraph 13 of AASB 2 includes a rebuttable presumption that the fair value of the goods or services received can be estimated reliably. In these situations, paragraph 13 of AASB 2 requires the entity to measure that fair value at the date the entity obtains the goods or the counterparty renders service.

Transaction in which the entity cannot identify specifically some or all of the goods or services received

IG5A   In some cases, however, it might be difficult to demonstrate that goods or services have been (or will be) received. For example, an entity may grant shares to a charitable organisation for nil consideration. It is usually not possible to identify the specific goods or services received in return for such a transaction. A similar situation might arise in transactions with other parties.

IG5B   Paragraph 11 of AASB 2 requires transactions in which share-based payments are made to employees to be measured by reference to the fair value of the share-based payments at grant date.[1] Hence, the entity is not required to measure directly the fair value of the employee services received.

IG5C It should be noted that the phrase 'the fair value of the share-based payment' refers to the fair value of the particular share-based payment concerned. For example, an entity might be required by government legislation to issue some portion of its shares to nationals of a particular country that may be transferred only to other nationals of that country. Such a transfer restriction may affect the fair value of the shares concerned, and therefore those shares may have a fair value that is less than the fair value of otherwise identical shares that do not carry such restrictions. In this situation, the phrase 'the fair value of the share-based payment' would refer to the fair value of the restricted shares, not the fair value of other, unrestricted shares.

IG5D Paragraph 13A of AASB 2 specifies how such transactions should be measured. The following example illustrates how the entity should apply the requirements of the Standard to a transaction in which the entity cannot identify specifically some or all of the goods or services received.

IG Example 1
Share-based payment transaction in which the entity cannot identify specifically some or all of the goods or services received

Background

An entity granted shares with a total fair value of CU100,000[a] to parties other than employees who are from a particular section of the community (historically disadvantaged individuals), as a means of enhancing its image as a good corporate citizen. The economic benefits derived from enhancing its corporate image could take a variety of forms, such as increasing its customer base, attracting or retaining employees, or improving or maintaining its ability to tender successfully for business contracts.

The entity cannot identify the specific consideration received. For example, no cash was received and no service conditions were imposed. Therefore, the identifiable consideration (nil) is less than the fair value of the equity instruments granted (CU100,000).

Application of requirements

Although the entity cannot identify the specific goods or services received, the circumstances indicate that goods or services have been (or will be) received, and therefore AASB 2 applies.

In this situation, because the entity cannot identify the specific goods or services received, the rebuttable presumption in paragraph 13 of AASB 2, that the fair value of the goods or services received can be estimated reliably, does not apply. The entity should instead measure the goods or services received by reference to the fair value of the equity instruments granted.

[a] In this example, and in all other examples in this guidance, monetary amounts are denominated in 'currency units (CU)'.

Measurement date for transactions with parties other than employees

IG6 If the goods or services are received on more than one date, the entity should measure the fair value of the equity instruments granted on each date when goods or services are received. The entity should apply that fair value when measuring the goods or services received on that date.

IG7 However, an approximation could be used in some cases. For example, if an entity received services continuously during a three-month period, and its share price did not change significantly during that period, the entity could use the average share price during the three-month period when estimating the fair value of the equity instruments granted.

Transitional arrangements

IG8 In paragraph 54 of AASB 2, the entity is encouraged, but not required, to apply the requirements of the Standard to other grants of equity instruments (i.e. grants other than those specified in paragraph 53 of the Standard), if the entity has disclosed publicly the fair value of those equity instruments, measured at the measurement

---

1 In AASB 2, all references to employees include others providing similar services.

date. For example, such equity instruments include equity instruments for which the entity has disclosed in the notes to its financial statements the information required in the US by SFAS 123 *Accounting for Stock-based Compensation*.

Equity-settled share-based payment transactions

IG9   For equity-settled transactions measured by reference to the fair value of the equity instruments granted, paragraph 19 of AASB 2 states that vesting conditions, other than market conditions[2], are not taken into account when estimating the fair value of the shares or share options at the measurement date (i.e. grant date, for transactions with employees and others providing similar services). Instead, vesting conditions are taken into account by adjusting the number of equity instruments included in the measurement of the transaction amount so that, ultimately, the amount recognised for goods or services received as consideration for the equity instruments granted is based on the number of equity instruments that eventually vest. Hence, on a cumulative basis, no amount is recognised for goods or services received if the equity instruments granted do not vest because of failure to satisfy a vesting condition, for example, the counterparty fails to complete a specified service period, or a performance condition is not satisfied. This accounting method is known as the modified grant date method, because the number of equity instruments included in the determination of the transaction amount is adjusted to reflect the outcome of the vesting conditions, but no adjustment is made to the fair value of those equity instruments. That fair value is estimated at grant date (for transactions with employees and others providing similar services) and not subsequently revised. Hence, neither increases nor decreases in the fair value of the equity instruments after grant date are taken into account when determining the transaction amount (other than in the context of measuring the incremental fair value transferred if a grant of equity instruments is subsequently modified).

IG10   To apply these requirements, paragraph 20 of AASB 2 requires the entity to recognise the goods or services received during the vesting period based on the best available estimate of the number of equity instruments expected to vest and to revise that estimate, if necessary, if subsequent information indicates that the number of equity instruments expected to vest differs from previous estimates. On vesting date, the entity revises the estimate to equal the number of equity instruments that ultimately vested (subject to the requirements of paragraph 21 concerning market conditions).

IG11   In the examples below, the share options granted all vest at the same time, at the end of a specified period. In some situations, share options or other equity instruments granted might vest in instalments over the vesting period. For example, suppose an employee is granted 100 share options, which will vest in instalments of 25 share options at the end of each year over the next four years. To apply the requirements of the Standard, the entity should treat each instalment as a separate share option grant, because each instalment has a different vesting period, and hence the fair value of each instalment will differ (because the length of the vesting period affects, for example, the likely timing of cash flows arising from the exercise of the options).

---

2   In the remainder of this paragraph, the discussion of vesting conditions excludes market conditions, which are subject to the requirements of paragraph 21, AASB 2. In paragraphs B56-B62 the term 'share-based payment awards' refers to vested or unvested share-based payment transactions.

IG Example 1A

Background

An entity grants 100 share options to each of its 500 employees. Each grant is conditional upon the employee working for the entity over the next three years. The entity estimates that the fair value of each share option is CU15.

On the basis of a weighted average probability, the entity estimates that 20 per cent of employees will leave during the three-year period and therefore forfeit their rights to the share options.

Application of requirements

Scenario 1

If everything turns out exactly as expected, the entity recognises the following amounts during the vesting period, for services received as consideration for the share options.

Year	Calculation	Remuneration expense for period CU	Cumulative remuneration expense CU
1	50,000 options × 80% × CU15 × 1/3 years	200,000	200,000
2	(50,000 options × 80% × CU15 × 2/3 years) – CU200,000	200,000	400,000
3	(50,000 options × 80% × CU15) – CU400,000	200,000	600,000

Scenario 2

During year 1, 20 employees leave. The entity revises its estimate of total employee departures over the three-year period from 20 per cent (100 employees) to 15 per cent (75 employees). During year 2, a further 22 employees leave. The entity revises its estimate of total employee departures over the three-year period from 15 per cent to 12 per cent (60 employees). During year 3, a further 15 employees leave. Hence, a total of 57 employees forfeited their rights to the share options during the three-year period, and a total of 44,300 share options (443 employees × 100 options per employee) vested at the end of year 3.

Year	Calculation	Remuneration expense for period CU	Cumulative remuneration expense CU
1	50,000 options × 85% × CU15 × 1/3 years	212,500	212,500
2	(50,000 options × 88% × CU15 × 2/3 years) – CU212,500	227,500	440,000
3	(44,300 options × CU15) – CU440,000	224,500	664,500

IG12   In Example 1A, the share options were granted conditionally upon the employees completing a specified service period. In some cases, a share option or share grant might also be conditional upon the achievement of a specified performance target. Examples 2, 3 and 4 illustrate the application of the Standard to share option or share grants with performance conditions (other than market conditions, which are discussed in paragraph IG13 and illustrated in Examples 5 and 6). In Example 2, the length of the vesting period varies, depending on when the performance condition is satisfied. Paragraph 15 of the Standard requires the entity to estimate the length of the expected vesting period, based on the most likely outcome of the performance condition, and to revise that estimate, if necessary, if subsequent information indicates that the length of the vesting period is likely to differ from previous estimates.

IG Example 2

Grant with a performance condition, in which the length of the vesting period varies

Background

At the beginning of year 1, the entity grants 100 shares each to 500 employees, conditional upon the employee remaining in the entity's employ during the vesting period. The shares will vest at the end of year 1 if the entity's earnings increase by more than 18 per cent; at the end of year 2 if the entity's earnings increase by more than an average of 13 per cent per year over the two-year period; and at the end of year 3 if the entity's earnings increase by more than an average of 10 per cent per year over the three-year period. The shares have a fair value of CU30 per share at the start of year 1, which equals the share price at grant date. No dividends are expected to be paid over the three-year period.

By the end of year 1, the entity's earnings have increased by 14 per cent, and 30 employees have left. The entity expects that earnings will continue to increase at a similar rate in year 2, and therefore expects that the shares will vest at the end of year 2. The entity expects, on the basis of a weighted average probability, that a further 30 employees will leave during year 2, and therefore expects that 440 employees will vest in 100 shares each at the end of year 2.

By the end of year 2, the entity's earnings have increased by only 10 per cent and therefore the shares do not vest at the end of year 2. 28 employees have left during the year. The entity expects that a further 25 employees will leave during year 3, and that the entity's earnings will increase by at least 6 per cent, thereby achieving the average of 10 per cent per year.

By the end of year 3, 23 employees have left and the entity's earnings had increased by 8 per cent, resulting in an average increase of 10.67 per cent per year. Therefore, 419 employees received 100 shares at the end of year 3.

Application of requirements

Year	Calculation	Remuneration expense for period CU	Cumulative remuneration expense CU
1	440 employees × 100 shares × CU30 × 1/2 years	660,000	660,000
2	(417 employees × 100 shares × CU30 × 2/3 years) – CU660,000	174,000	834,000
3	(419 employees × 100 shares × CU30) – CU834,000	423,000	1,257,000

IG Example 3

Grant with a performance condition, in which the number of equity instruments varies

Background

At the beginning of year 1, Entity A grants share options to each of its 100 employees working in the sales department. The share options will vest at the end of year 3, provided that the employees remain in the entity's employ, and provided that the volume of sales of a particular product increases by at least an average of 5 per cent per year. If the volume of sales of the product increases by an average of between 5 per cent and 10 per cent per year, each employee will receive 100 share options. If the volume of sales increases by an average of between 10 per cent and 15 per cent each year, each employee will receive 200 share options. If the volume of sales increases by an average of 15 per cent or more, each employee will receive 300 share options.

On grant date, Entity A estimates that the share options have a fair value of CU20 per option. Entity A also estimates that the volume of sales of the product will increase by an average of between 10 per cent and 15 per cent per year, and therefore expects that, for each employee who remains in service until the end of year 3, 200 share options will vest. The entity also estimates, on the basis of a weighted average probability, that 20 per cent of employees will leave before the end of year 3.

continued

AASB 2   **Institute of Chartered Accountants Australia**

By the end of year 1, seven employees have left and the entity still expects that a total of 20 employees will leave by the end of year 3. Hence, the entity expects that 80 employees will remain in service for the three-year period. Product sales have increased by 12 per cent and the entity expects this rate of increase to continue over the next 2 years.

By the end of year 2, a further five employees have left, bringing the total to 12 to date. The entity now expects only three more employees will leave during year 3, and therefore expects a total of 15 employees will have left during the three-year period, and hence 85 employees are expected to remain. Product sales have increased by 18 per cent, resulting in an average of 15 per cent over the two years to date. The entity now expects that sales will average 15 per cent or more over the three-year period, and hence expects each sales employee to receive 300 share options at the end of year 3.

By the end of year 3, a further two employees have left. Hence, 14 employees have left during the three-year period, and 86 employees remain. The entity's sales have increased by an average of 16 per cent over the three years. Therefore, each of the 86 employees receives 300 share options.

Application of requirements

Year	Calculation	Remuneration expense for period CU	Cumulative remuneration expense CU
1	80 employees × 200 options × CU20 × 1/3 years	106,667	106,667
2	(85 employees × 300 options × CU20 × 2/3 years) – CU106,667	233,333	340,000
3	(86 employees × 300 options × CU20) – CU340,000	176,000	516,000

IG Example 4
Grant with a performance condition, in which the exercise price varies

Background

At the beginning of year 1, an entity grants to a senior executive 10,000 share options, conditional upon the executive remaining in the entity's employ until the end of year 3. The exercise price is CU40. However, the exercise price drops to CU30 if the entity's earnings increase by at least an average of 10 per cent per year over the three-year period.

On grant date, the entity estimates that the fair value of the share options, with an exercise price of CU30, is CU16 per option. If the exercise price is CU40, the entity estimates that the share options have a fair value of CU12 per option.

During year 1, the entity's earnings increased by 12 per cent, and the entity expects that earnings will continue to increase at this rate over the next two years. The entity therefore expects that the earnings target will be achieved, and hence the share options will have an exercise price of CU30.

During year 2, the entity's earnings increased by 13 per cent, and the entity continues to expect that the earnings target will be achieved.

During year 3, the entity's earnings increased by only 3 per cent, and therefore the earnings target was not achieved. The executive completes three years' service, and therefore satisfies the service condition. Because the earnings target was not achieved, the 10,000 vested share options have an exercise price of CU40.

Application of requirements

Because the exercise price varies depending on the outcome of a performance condition that is not a market condition, the effect of that performance condition (i.e. the possibility that the exercise price might be CU40 and the possibility that the exercise price might be CU30) is not taken into account when estimating the fair value of the share options at grant date. Instead, the entity estimates the fair value of the share options at grant date under each scenario (i.e. exercise price of CU40 and exercise price of CU30) and ultimately revises the transaction amount to reflect the outcome of that performance condition, as illustrated below.

Year	Calculation	Remuneration expense for period CU	Cumulative remuneration expense CU
1	10,000 options × CU16 × 1/3 years	53,333	53,333
2	(10,000 options × CU16 × 2/3 years) – CU53,333	53,334	106,667
3	(10,000 options × CU12) – CU106,667	13,333	120,000

IG13   Paragraph 21 of the Standard requires market conditions, such as a target share price upon which vesting (or exercisability) is conditional, to be taken into account when estimating the fair value of the equity instruments granted. Therefore, for grants of equity instruments with market conditions, the entity recognises the goods or services received from a counterparty who satisfies all other vesting conditions (e.g. services received from an employee who remains in service for the specified period of service), irrespective of whether that market condition is satisfied. Example 5 illustrates these requirements.

IG Example 5
Grant with a market condition

Background

At the beginning of year 1, an entity grants to a senior executive 10,000 share options, conditional upon the executive remaining in the entity's employ until the end of year 3. However, the share options cannot be exercised unless the share price has increased from CU50 at the beginning of year 1 to above CU65 at the end of year 3. If the share price is above CU65 at the end of year 3, the share options can be exercised at any time during the next seven years, that is, by the end of year 10.

The entity applies a binomial option pricing model, which takes into account the possibility that the share price will exceed CU65 at the end of year 3 (and hence the share options become exercisable) and the possibility that the share price will not exceed CU65 at the end of year 3 (and hence the options will be forfeited). It estimates the fair value of the share options with this market condition to be CU24 per option.

Application of requirements

Because paragraph 21 of the Standard requires the entity to recognise the services received from a counterparty who satisfies all other vesting conditions (e.g. services received from an employee who remains in service for the specified service period), irrespective of whether that market condition is satisfied, it makes no difference whether the share price target is achieved. The possibility that the share price target might not be achieved has already been taken into account when estimating the fair value of the share options at grant date. Therefore, if the entity expects the executive to complete the three-year service period, and the executive does so, the entity recognises the following amounts in years 1, 2 and 3.

Year	Calculation	Remuneration expense for period CU	Cumulative remuneration expense CU
1	10,000 options × CU24 × 1/3 years	80,000	80,000
2	(10,000 options × CU24 × 2/3 years) – CU80,000	80,000	160,000
3	(10,000 options × CU24) – CU160,000	80,000	240,000

As noted above, these amounts are recognised irrespective of the outcome of the market condition. However, if the executive left during year 2 (or year 3), the amount recognised during year 1 (and year 2) would be reversed in year 2 (or year 3). This is because the service condition, in contrast to the market condition, was not taken into account when estimating the fair value of the share options at grant date. Instead, the service condition is taken into account by adjusting the transaction amount to be based on the number of equity instruments that ultimately vest, in accordance with paragraphs 19 and 20 of the Standard.

IG14   In Example 5, the outcome of the market condition did not change the length of the vesting period. However, if the length of the vesting period varies depending on when a performance condition is satisfied, paragraph 15 of the Standard requires the entity to presume that the services to be rendered by the employees as consideration for the equity instruments granted will be received in the future, over the expected vesting period. The entity is required to estimate the length of the expected vesting period at grant date, based on the most likely outcome of the performance condition. If the performance condition is a market condition, the estimate of the length of the expected vesting period must be consistent with the assumptions used in estimating the fair value of the share options granted, and is not subsequently revised. Example 6 illustrates these requirements.

IG Example 6

Grant with a market condition, in which the length of the vesting period varies

Background

At the beginning of year 1, an entity grants 10,000 share options with a ten-year life to each of ten senior executives. The share options will vest and become exercisable immediately if and when the entity's share price increases from CU50 to CU70, provided that the executive remains in service until the share price target is achieved.

The entity applies a binomial option pricing model, which takes into account the possibility that the share price target will be achieved during the ten-year life of the options, and the possibility that the target will not be achieved. The entity estimates that the fair value of the share options at grant date is CU25 per option. From the option pricing model, the entity determines that the mode of the distribution of possible vesting dates is five years. In other words, of all the possible outcomes, the most likely outcome of the market condition is that the share price target will be achieved at the end of year 5. Therefore, the entity estimates that the expected vesting period is five years. The entity also estimates that two executives will have left by the end of year 5, and therefore expects that 80,000 share options (10,000 share options x 8 executives) will vest at the end of year 5.

Throughout years 1–4, the entity continues to estimate that a total of two executives will leave by the end of year 5. However, in total three executives leave, one in each of years 3, 4 and 5. The share price target is achieved at the end of year 6. Another executive leaves during year 6, before the share price target is achieved.

Application of requirements

Paragraph 15 of the Standard requires the entity to recognise the services received over the expected vesting period, as estimated at grant date, and also requires the entity not to revise that estimate. Therefore, the entity recognises the services received from the executives over years 1–5. Hence, the transaction amount is ultimately based on 70,000 share options (10,000 share options × 7 executives who remain in service at the end of year 5). Although another executive left during year 6, no adjustment is made, because the executive had already completed the expected vesting period of five years. Therefore, the entity recognises the following amounts in years 1 to 5.

Year	Calculation	Remuneration expense for period CU	Cumulative remuneration expense CU
1	80,000 options × CU25 × 1/5 years	400,000	400,000
2	(80,000 options × CU25 × 2/5 years) – CU400,000	400,000	800,000
3	(80,000 options × CU25 × 3/5 years) – CU800,000	400,000	1,200,000
4	(80,000 options × CU25 × 4/5 years) – CU1,200,000	400,000	1,600,000
5	(70,000 options × CU25) – CU1,600,000	150,000	1,750,000

IG15   Paragraphs 26-29 and B42-B44 of the Standard set out requirements that apply if a share option is repriced (or the entity otherwise modifies the terms or conditions of a share-based payment arrangement). Examples 7 to 9 illustrate some of these requirements.

IG Example 7

Grant of share options that are subsequently repriced

Background

At the beginning of year 1, an entity grants 100 share options to each of its 500 employees. Each grant is conditional upon the employee remaining in service over the next three years. The entity estimates that the fair value of each option is CU15. On the basis of a weighted average probability, the entity estimates that 100 employees will leave during the three-year period and therefore forfeit their rights to the share options.

Suppose that 40 employees leave during year 1. Also suppose that by the end of year 1, the entity's share price has dropped, and the entity reprices its share options, and that the repriced share options vest at the end of year 3. The entity estimates that a further 70 employees will leave during years 2 and 3, and hence the total expected employee departures over the three-year vesting period is 110 employees. During year 2, a further 35 employees leave, and the entity estimates that a further 30 employees will leave during year 3, to bring the total expected employee departures over the three-year vesting period to 105 employees. During year 3, a total of 28 employees leave, and hence a total of 103 employees ceased employment during the vesting period. For the remaining 397 employees, the share options vested at the end of year 3.

The entity estimates that, at the date of repricing, the fair value of each of the original share options granted (i.e. before taking into account the repricing) is CU5 and that the fair value of each repriced share option is CU8.

Application of requirements

Paragraph 27 of the Standard requires the entity to recognise the effects of modifications that increase the total fair value of the share-based payment arrangement or are otherwise beneficial to the employee. If the modification increases the fair value of the equity instruments granted (e.g. by reducing the exercise price), measured immediately before and after the modification, paragraph B43(a) of Appendix B requires the entity to include the incremental fair value granted (i.e. the difference between the fair value of the modified equity instrument and that of the original equity instrument, both estimated as at the date of the modification) in the measurement of the amount recognised for services received as consideration for the equity instruments granted. If the modification occurs during the vesting period, the incremental fair value granted is included in the measurement of the amount recognised for services received over the period from the modification date until the date when the modified equity instruments vest, in addition to the amount based on the grant date fair value of the original equity instruments, which is recognised over the remainder of the original vesting period.

The incremental value is CU3 per share option (CU8 – CU5). This amount is recognised over the remaining two years of the vesting period, along with remuneration expense based on the original option value of CU15.

The amounts recognised in years 1 – 3 are as follows.

Year	Calculation	Remuneration expense for period CU	Cumulative remuneration expense CU
1	(500 – 110) employees ×100 options × CU15 × 1/3 years	195,000	195,000
2	[(500 – 105) employees × 100 options × (CU15 × 2/3 years + CU3 × 1/2 years)] – CU195,000	259,250	454,250
3	[(500 – 103) employees × 100 options × (CU15 + CU3)] – CU454,250	260,350	714,600

IG Example 8
Grant of share options with a vesting condition that is subsequently modified

Background

At the beginning of year 1, the entity grants 1,000 share options to each member of its sales team, conditional upon the employee's remaining in the entity's employ for three years, and the team selling more than 50,000 units of a particular product over the three-year period. The fair value of the share options is CU15 per option at the date of grant.

During year 2, the entity increases the sales target to 100,000 units. By the end of year 3, the entity has sold 55,000 units, and the share options are forfeited. Twelve members of the sales team have remained in service for the three-year period.

Application of requirements

Paragraph 20 of the Standard requires, for a performance condition that is not a market condition, the entity to recognise the services received during the vesting period based on the best available estimate of the number of equity instruments expected to vest and to revise that estimate, if necessary, if subsequent information indicates that the number of equity instruments expected to vest differs from previous estimates. On vesting date, the entity revises the estimate to equal the number of equity instruments that ultimately vested. However, paragraph 27 of the Standard requires, irrespective of any modifications to the terms and conditions on which the equity instruments were granted, or a cancellation or settlement of that grant of equity instruments, the entity to recognise, as a minimum, the services received, measured at the grant date fair value of the equity instruments granted, unless those equity instruments do not vest because of failure to satisfy a vesting condition (other than a market condition) that was specified at grant date. Furthermore, paragraph B44(c) of Appendix B specifies that, if the entity modifies the vesting conditions in a manner that is not beneficial to the employee, the entity does not take the modified vesting conditions into account when applying the requirements of paragraphs 19 to 21 of the Standard.

Therefore, because the modification to the performance condition made it less likely that the share options will vest, which was not beneficial to the employee, the entity takes no account of the modified performance condition when recognising the services received. Instead, it continues to recognise the services received over the three-year period based on the original vesting conditions. Hence, it ultimately recognises cumulative remuneration expense of CU180,000 over the three-year period (12 employees × 1,000 options × CU15).

The same result would have occurred if, instead of modifying the performance target, the entity had increased the number of years of service required for the share options to vest from three years to ten years. Because such a modification would make it less likely that the options will vest, which would not be beneficial to the employees, the entity would take no account of the modified service condition when recognising the services received. Instead, it would recognise the services received from the twelve employees who remained in service over the original three-year vesting period.

AASB

IG Example 9

Grant of shares, with a cash alternative subsequently added

Background

At the beginning of year 1, the entity grants 10,000 shares with a fair value of CU33 per share to a senior executive, conditional upon the completion of three years' service. By the end of year 2, the share price has dropped to CU25 per share. At that date, the entity adds a cash alternative to the grant, whereby the executive can choose whether to receive 10,000 shares or cash equal to the value of 10,000 shares on vesting date. The share price is CU22 on vesting date.

Application of requirements

Paragraph 27 of the Standard requires, irrespective of any modifications to the terms and conditions on which the equity instruments were granted, or a cancellation or settlement of that grant of equity instruments, the entity to recognise, as a minimum, the services received measured at the grant date fair value of the equity instruments granted, unless those equity instruments do not vest because of failure to satisfy a vesting condition (other than a market condition) that was specified at grant date. Therefore, the entity recognises the services received over the three-year period, based on the grant date fair value of the shares.

Furthermore, the addition of the cash alternative at the end of year 2 creates an obligation to settle in cash. In accordance with the requirements for cash-settled share-based payment transactions (paragraphs 30-33 of the Standard), the entity recognises the liability to settle in cash at the modification date, based on the fair value of the shares at the modification date and the extent to which the specified services have been received. Furthermore, the entity remeasures the fair value of the liability at the end of each reporting period and at the date of settlement, with any changes in fair value recognised in profit or loss for the period. Therefore, the entity recognises the following amounts.

Year	Calculation	Expense CU	Equity CU	Liability CU
1	Remuneration expense for year: 10,000 shares × CU33 × 1/3 years	110,000	110,000	
2	Remuneration expense for year: (10,000 shares × CU33 × 2/3 years) – CU110,000	110,000	110,000	
	Reclassify equity to liabilities: 10,000 shares × CU25 × 2/3 years		(166,667)	166,667
3	Remuneration expense for year: (10,000 shares × CU33) – CU220,000	110,000	26,667	83,333*
	Adjust liability to closing fair value: (CU166,667 + CU83,333) – (CU22 × 10,000 shares)	(30,000)		(30,000)
	Total	300,000	80,000	220,000

* Allocated between liabilities and equity to bring in the final third of the liability based on the fair value of the shares as at the date of the modification.

IG15A   If a share-based payment has a non-vesting condition that the counterparty can choose not to meet and the counterparty does not meet that non-vesting condition during the vesting period, paragraph 28A of the Standard requires that event to be treated as a cancellation. Example 9A illustrates the accounting for this type of event.

IG Example 9A

Share-based payment with vesting and non-vesting conditions when the counterparty can choose whether the non-vesting condition is met

Background

An entity grants an employee the opportunity to participate in a plan in which the employee obtains share options if he agrees to save 25 per cent of his monthly salary of CU400 for a three-year period. The monthly payments are made by deduction from the employee's salary. The employee may use the accumulated savings to exercise his options at the end of three years, or take a refund of his contributions at any point during the three-year period. The estimated annual expense for the share-based payment arrangement is CU120.

After 18 months, the employee stops paying contributions to the plan and takes a refund of contributions paid to date of CU1,800.

continued

Application of requirements

There are three components to this plan: paid salary, salary deduction paid to the savings plan and share-based payment. The entity recognises an expense in respect of each component and a corresponding increase in liability or equity as appropriate. The requirement to pay contributions to the plan is a non-vesting condition, which the employee chooses not to meet in the second year. Therefore, in accordance with paragraphs 28(b) and 28A of the Standard, the repayment of contributions is treated as an extinguishment of the liability and the cessation of contributions in year 2 is treated as a cancellation.

Year 1	Expense CU	Cash CU	Liability CU	Equity CU
Paid salary (75% × 400 × 12)	3,600	(3,600)		
Salary deduction paid to the savings plan (25% × 400 × 12)	1,200		(1,200)	
Share-based payment	120			(120)
Total	4,920	(3,600)	(1,200)	(120)
Year 2				
Paid salary (75% × 400 × 6 + 100% × 400 × 6)	4,200	(4,200)		
Salary deduction paid to the savings plan (25% × 400 × 6)	600		(600)	
Refund of contributions to the employee		(1,800)	1,800	
Share-based payment (acceleration of remaining expense) (120 × 3 – 120)	240			(240)
Total	5,040	(6,000)	1,200	(240)

IG16   Paragraph 24 of the Standard requires that, in rare cases only, in which the Standard requires the entity to measure an equity-settled share-based payment transaction by reference to the fair value of the equity instruments granted, but the entity is unable to estimate reliably that fair value at the specified measurement date (e.g. grant date, for transactions with employees), the entity shall instead measure the transaction using an intrinsic value measurement method. Paragraph 24 also contains requirements on how to apply this method. The following example illustrates these requirements.

IG Example 10

Grant of share options that is accounted for by applying the intrinsic value method

Background

At the beginning of year 1, an entity grants 1,000 share options to 50 employees. The share options will vest at the end of year 3, provided the employees remain in service until then. The share options have a life of 10 years. The exercise price is CU60 and the entity's share price is also CU60 at the date of grant.

At the date of grant, the entity concludes that it cannot estimate reliably the fair value of the share options granted.

At the end of year 1, three employees have ceased employment and the entity estimates that a further seven employees will leave during years 2 and 3. Hence, the entity estimates that 80 per cent of the share options will vest.

Two employees leave during year 2, and the entity revises its estimate of the number of share options that it expects will vest to 86 per cent.

Two employees leave during year 3. Hence, 43,000 share options vested at the end of year 3.

The entity's share price during years 1 – 10, and the number of share options exercised during years 4 – 10, are set out below. Share options that were exercised during a particular year were all exercised at the end of that year.

continued

Year		Share price at year-end	Number of share options exercised at year-end
1		63	0
2		65	0
3		75	0
4		88	6,000
5		100	8,000
6		90	5,000
7		96	9,000
8		105	8,000
9		108	5,000
10		115	2,000

Application of requirements

In accordance with paragraph 24 of the Standard, the entity recognises the following amounts in years 1 – 10.

Year	Calculation	Expense for period CU	Cumulative expense CU
1	50,000 options × 80% × (CU63 – CU60) × 1/3 years	40,000	40,000
2	[50,000 options × 86% × (CU65 – CU60) × 2/3 years] – CU40,000	103,333	143,333
3	[43,000 options × (CU75 – CU60)] – CU143,333	501,667	645,000
4	[37,000 outstanding options × (CU88 – CU75)] + [6,000 exercised options × (CU88 – CU75)]	559,000	1,204,000
5	[29,000 outstanding options × (CU100 – CU88)] + [8,000 exercised options × (CU100 – CU88)]	444,000	1,648,000
6	[24,000 outstanding options × (CU90 – CU100)] + [5,000 exercised options × (CU90 – CU100)]	(290,000)	1,358,000
7	[15,000 outstanding options × (CU96 – CU90)] + [9,000 exercised options × (CU96 – CU90)]	144,000	1,502,000
8	[7,000 outstanding options × (CU105 – CU96)] + [8,000 exercised options × (CU105 – CU96)]	135,000	1,637,000
9	[2,000 outstanding options × (CU108 – CU105)] + [5,000 exercised options × (CU108 – CU105)]	21,000	1,658,000
10	2,000 exercised options × (CU115 – CU108)	14,000	1,672,000

IG17   There are many different types of employee share and share option plans. The following example illustrates the application of AASB 2 to one particular type of plan – an employee share purchase plan. Typically, an employee share purchase plan provides employees with the opportunity to purchase the entity's shares at a discounted price. The terms and conditions under which employee share purchase plans operate differ from country to country. That is to say, not only are there many different types of employee share and share options plans, there are also many different types of employee share purchase plans. Therefore, the following example illustrates the application of AASB 2 to one specific employee share purchase plan.

IG Example 11

Employee share purchase plan

Background

An entity offers all its 1,000 employees the opportunity to participate in an employee share purchase plan. The employees have two weeks to decide whether to accept the offer. Under the terms of the plan, the employees are entitled to purchase a maximum of 100 shares each. The purchase price will be 20 per cent less than the market price of the entity's shares at the date the offer is accepted, and the purchase price must be paid immediately upon acceptance of the offer. All shares purchased must be held in trust for the employees, and cannot be sold for five years. The employee is not permitted to withdraw from the plan during that period. For example, if the employee ceases employment during the five-year period, the shares must nevertheless remain in the plan until the end of the five-year period. Any dividends paid during the five-year period will be held in trust for the employees until the end of the five-year period.

In total, 800 employees accept the offer and each employee purchases, on average, 80 shares, that is, the employees purchase a total of 64,000 shares. The weighted average market price of the shares at the purchase date is CU30 per share, and the weighted average purchase price is CU24 per share.

Application of requirements

For transactions with employees, AASB 2 requires the transaction amount to be measured by reference to the fair value of the equity instruments granted (AASB 2, paragraph 11). To apply this requirement, it is necessary first to determine the type of equity instrument granted to the employees. Although the plan is described as an employee share purchase plan (ESPP), some ESPPs include option features and are therefore, in effect, share option plans. For example, an ESPP might include a 'lookback feature', whereby the employee is able to purchase shares at a discount, and choose whether the discount is applied to the entity's share price at the date of grant or its share price at the date of purchase. Or an ESPP might specify the purchase price, and then allow the employees a significant period of time to decide whether to participate in the plan.

Another example of an option feature is an ESPP that permits the participating employees to cancel their participation before or at the end of a specified period and obtain a refund of amounts previously paid into the plan.

However, in this example, the plan includes no option features. The discount is applied to the share price at the purchase date, and the employees are not permitted to withdraw from the plan.

Another factor to consider is the effect of post-vesting transfer restrictions, if any. Paragraph B3 of AASB 2 states that, if shares are subject to restrictions on transfer after vesting date, that factor should be taken into account when estimating the fair value of those shares, but only to the extent that the post vesting restrictions affect the price that a knowledgeable, willing market participant would pay for that share. For example, if the shares are actively traded in a deep and liquid market, post-vesting transfer restrictions may have little, if any, effect on the price that a knowledgeable, willing market participant would pay for those shares.

In this example, the shares are vested when purchased, but cannot be sold for five years after the date of purchase. Therefore, the entity should consider the valuation effect of the five-year post-vesting transfer restriction. This entails using a valuation technique to estimate what the price of the restricted share would have been on the purchase date in an arm's length transaction between knowledgeable, willing parties. Suppose that, in this example, the entity estimates that the fair value of each restricted share is CU28. In this case, the fair value of the equity instruments granted is CU4 per share (being the fair value of the restricted share of CU28 less the purchase price of CU24). Because 64,000 shares were purchased, the total fair value of the equity instruments granted is CU256,000.

In this example, there is no vesting period. Therefore, in accordance with paragraph 14 of AASB 2, the entity should recognise an expense of CU256,000 immediately.

However, in some cases, the expense relating to an ESPP might not be material. AASB 108 *Accounting Policies, Changes in Accounting Policies and Errors* states that the accounting policies in Standards need not be applied when the effect of applying them is immaterial (AASB 108, paragraph 8). AASB 108 also states that an omission or misstatement of an item is material if it could, individually or collectively, influence the economic decisions that users make on the basis of the financial statements. Materiality depends on the size and nature of the omission or misstatement judged in the surrounding circumstances. The size or nature of the item, or a combination of both, could be the determining factor (AASB 108, paragraph 5). Therefore, in this example, the entity should consider whether the expense of CU256,000 is material.

Cash-settled share-based payment transactions

IG18   Paragraphs 30-33 of the Standard set out requirements for transactions in which an entity acquires goods or services by incurring liabilities to the supplier of those goods or services in amounts based on the price of the entity's shares or other equity instruments. The entity is required to recognise initially the goods or services acquired, and a liability to pay for those goods or services, when the entity obtains the goods or as the services are rendered, measured at the fair value of the liability. Thereafter, until the liability is settled, the entity is required to recognise changes in the fair value of the liability.

IG19   For example, an entity might grant share appreciation rights to employees as part of their remuneration package, whereby the employees will become entitled to a future cash payment (rather than an equity instrument), based on the increase in the entity's share price from a specified level over a specified period of time. If the share appreciation rights do not vest until the employees have completed a specified period of service, the entity recognises the services received, and a liability to pay for them, as the employees render service during that period. The liability is measured, initially and at the end of each reporting period until settled, at the fair value of the share appreciation rights, by applying an option pricing model, and the extent to which the employees have rendered service to date. Changes in fair value are recognised in profit or loss. Therefore, if the amount recognised for the services received was included in the carrying amount of an asset recognised in the entity's statement of financial position (e.g. inventory), the carrying amount of that asset is not adjusted for the effects of the liability remeasurement. Example 12 illustrates these requirements.

IG Example 12

Background

An entity grants 100 cash share appreciation rights (SARs) to each of its 500 employees, on condition that the employees remain in its employ for the next three years.

During year 1, 35 employees leave. The entity estimates that a further 60 will leave during years 2 and 3. During year 2, 40 employees leave and the entity estimates that a further 25 will leave during year 3. During year 3, 22 employees leave. At the end of year 3, 150 employees exercise their SARs, another 140 employees exercise their SARs at the end of year 4 and the remaining 113 employees exercise their SARs at the end of year 5.

The entity estimates the fair value of the SARs at the end of each year in which a liability exists as shown below. At the end of year 3, all SARs held by the remaining employees vest. The intrinsic values of the SARs at the date of exercise (which equal the cash paid out) at the end of years 3, 4 and 5 are also shown below.

Year		Fair value	Intrinsic value
1		CU14.40	
2		CU15.50	
3		CU18.20	CU15.00
4		CU21.40	CU20.00
5			CU25.00

continued

Application of requirements

Year	Calculation		Expense CU	Liability CU
1	(500 – 95) employees × 100 SARs × CU14.40 × 1/3 years		194,400	194,400
2	(500 – 100) employees × 100 SARs × CU15.50 × 2/3 years – CU194,400		218,933	413,333
3	(500 – 97 – 150) employees × 100 SARs × CU18.20 – CU413,333	47,127		460,460
	+ 150 employees × 100 SARs × CU15.00	225,000		
	Total		272,127	
4	(253 – 140) employees × 100 SARs × CU21.40 – CU460,460	(218,640)		241,820
	+ 140 employees × 100 SARs × CU20.00	280,000		
	Total		61,360	
5	0 employees × 100 SARs × CU25.00 – CU241,820	(241,820)		0
	+ 113 employees × 100 SARs × CU25.00	282,500		
	Total		40,680	
	Total		787,500	

Share-based payment arrangements with cash alternatives

IG20   Some employee share-based payment arrangements permit the employee to choose whether to receive cash or equity instruments. In this situation, a compound financial instrument has been granted, that is, a financial instrument with debt and equity components. Paragraph 37 of the Standard requires the entity to estimate the fair value of the compound financial instrument at grant date, by first measuring the fair value of the debt component, and then measuring the fair value of the equity component – taking into account that the employee must forfeit the right to receive cash to receive the equity instrument.

IG21   Typically, share-based payment arrangements with cash alternatives are structured so that the fair value of one settlement alternative is the same as the other. For example, the employee might have the choice of receiving share options or cash share appreciation rights. In such cases, the fair value of the equity component will be zero, and hence the fair value of the compound financial instrument will be the same as the fair value of the debt component. However, if the fair values of the settlement alternatives differ, usually the fair value of the equity component will be greater than zero, in which case the fair value of the compound financial instrument will be greater than the fair value of the debt component.

IG22   Paragraph 38 of the Standard requires the entity to account separately for the services received in respect of each component of the compound financial instrument. For the debt component, the entity recognises the services received, and a liability to pay for those services, as the counterparty renders service, in accordance with the requirements applying to cash-settled share-based payment transactions. For the equity component (if any), the entity recognises the services received, and an increase in equity, as the counterparty renders service, in accordance with the requirements applying to equity-settled share-based payment transactions. Example 13 illustrates these requirements.

IG Example 13

Background

An entity grants to an employee the right to choose either 1,000 phantom shares, that is, a right to a cash payment equal to the value of 1,000 shares, or 1,200 shares. The grant is conditional upon the completion of three years' service. If the employee chooses the share alternative, the shares must be held for three years after vesting date.

At grant date, the entity's share price is CU50 per share. At the end of years 1, 2 and 3, the share price is CU52, CU55 and CU60 respectively. The entity does not expect to pay dividends in the next three years. After taking into account the effects of the post-vesting transfer restrictions, the entity estimates that the grant date fair value of the share alternative is CU48 per share.

At the end of year 3, the employee chooses:

Scenario 1: The cash alternative

Scenario 2: The equity alternative

Application of requirements

The fair value of the equity alternative is CU57,600 (1,200 shares × CU48). The fair value of the cash alternative is CU50,000 (1,000 phantom shares × CU50). Therefore, the fair value of the equity component of the compound instrument is CU7,600 (CU57,600 − CU50,000).

The entity recognises the following amounts.

Year	Calculation	Expense CU	Equity CU	Liability CU
1	Liability component: (1,000 × CU52 × 1/3 years)	17,333		17,333
	Equity component: (CU7,600 × 1/3 years)	2,533	2,533	
2	Liability component: (1,000 × CU55 × 2/3 years) − CU17,333	19,333		19,333
	Equity component: (CU7,600 × 1/3 years)	2,533	2,533	
3	Liability component: (1,000 × CU60) − CU36,666	23,334		23,334
	Equity component: (CU7,600 × 1/3 years)	2,534	2,534	
End Year 3	Scenario 1: cash of CU60,000 paid			(60,000)
	Scenario 1 totals	67,600	7,600	0
	Scenario 2: 1,200 shares issued		60,000	(60,000)
	Scenario 2 totals	67,600	67,600	0

Share-based payment transactions among group entities

IG22A   Paragraphs 43A and 43B of AASB 2 specify the accounting requirements for share-based payment transactions among group entities in the separate or individual financial statements of the entity receiving the goods or services. Example 14 illustrates the journal entries in the separate or individual financial statements for a group transaction in which a parent grants rights to its equity instruments to the employees of its subsidiary.

IG Example 14

Share-based payment transactions in which a parent grants rights to its equity instruments to the employees of its subsidiary

Background

A parent grants 200 share options to each of 100 employees of its subsidiary, conditional upon the completion of two years' service with the subsidiary. The fair value of the share options on grant date is CU30 each. At grant date, the subsidiary estimates that 80 per cent of the employees will complete the two-year service period. This estimate does not change during the vesting period. At the end of the vesting period, 81 employees complete the required two years of service. The parent does not require the subsidiary to pay for the shares needed to settle the grant of share options.

Application of requirements

As required by paragraph B53 of the Standard, over the two-year vesting period, the subsidiary measures the services received from the employees in accordance with the requirements applicable to equity-settled share-based payment transactions. Thus, the subsidiary measures the services received from the employees on the basis of the fair value of the share options at grant date. An increase in equity is recognised as a contribution from the parent in the separate or individual financial statements of the subsidiary.

The journal entries recorded by the subsidiary for each of the two years are as follows:

Year 1

Dr Remuneration expense

$(200 \times 100 \times CU30 \times 0.8/2)$ CU240,000

Cr Equity (Contribution from the parent)   CU240,000

Year 2

Dr Remuneration expense

$(200 \times 100 \times CU30 \times 0.81 - 240,000)$ CU246,000

Cr Equity (Contribution from the parent)   CU246,000

Illustrative disclosures

IG23   The following example illustrates the disclosure requirements in paragraphs 44-52 of the Standard[3].

Extract from the Notes to the Financial Statements of Company Z for the year ended 31 December 20X5.

Share-based Payment

During the period ended 31 December 20X5, the Company had four share-based payment arrangements, which are described below.

Type of arrangement	Senior management share option plan	General employee share option plan	Executive share plan	Senior management share appreciation cash plan
Date of grant	1 January 20X4	1 January 20X5	1 January 20X5	1 July 20X5
Number granted	50,000	75,000	50,000	25,000
Contractual life	10 years	10 years	N/A	10 years
Vesting conditions	1.5 years' service and achievement of a share price target, which was achieved	Three years' service	Three years' service and achievement of a target growth in earnings per share	Three years' service and achievement of a target increase in market share

continued

---

3   Note that the illustrative example is not intended to be a template or model and is therefore not exhaustive. For example, it does not illustrate the disclosure requirements in paragraphs 47(c), 48 and 49 of AASB 2.

The estimated fair value of each share option granted in the general employee share option plan is CU23.60. This was calculated by applying a binomial option pricing model. The model inputs were the share price at grant date of CU50, exercise price of CU50, expected volatility of 30 per cent, no expected dividends, contractual life of ten years, and a risk-free interest rate of 5 per cent. To allow for the effects of early exercise, it was assumed that the employees would exercise the options after vesting date when the share price was twice the exercise price. Historical volatility was 40 per cent, which includes the early years of the Company's life; the Company expects the volatility of its share price to reduce as it matures.

The estimated fair value of each share granted in the executive share plan is CU50.00, which is equal to the share price at the date of grant.

Further details of the two share option plans are as follows.

	20X4		20X5	
	Number of options	Weighted average exercise price	Number of options	Weighted average exercise price
Outstanding at start of year	0	–	45,000	CU40
Granted	50,000	CU40	75,000	CU50
Forfeited	(5,000)	CU40	(8,000)	CU46
Exercised	0	–	(4,000)	CU40
Outstanding at end of year	45,000	CU40	108,000	CU46
Exercisable at end of year	0	CU40	38,000	CU40

The weighted average share price at the date of exercise for share options exercised during the period was CU52. The options outstanding at 31 December 20X5 had an exercise price of CU40 or CU50, and a weighted average remaining contractual life of 8.64 years.

	20X4 CU	20X5 CU
Expense arising from share-based payment transactions	495,000	1,105,867
Expense arising from share and share option plans	495,000	1,007,000
Closing balance of liability for cash share appreciation plan	–	98,867
Expense arising from increase in fair value of liability for cash share appreciation plan	–	9,200

Summary of conditions for a counterparty to receive an equity instrument granted and of accounting treatments

IG24   The table below categorises, with examples, the various conditions that determine whether a counterparty receives an equity instrument granted and the accounting treatment of share-based payments with those conditions.

Summary of conditions that determine whether a counterparty receives an equity instrument granted						
Vesting Conditions				**Non-Vesting Conditions**		
Service conditions	**Performance conditions**			Neither the entity nor the counterparty can choose whether the condition is met	Counterparty can choose whether to meet the condition	Entity can choose whether to meet the condition
	Performance conditions that are market conditions	Other performance conditions				
Example conditions	Requirement to remain in service for three years	Target based on the market price of the entity's equity instruments	Target based on a successful initial public offering with a specified service requirement	Target based on a commodity index	Paying contributions towards the exercise price of a share-based payment	Continuation of the plan by the entity
Include in grant-date fair value?	No	Yes	No	Yes	Yes	Yes [a]
Accounting treatment if the condition is not met after the grant date and during the vesting period	Forfeiture. The entity revises the expense to reflect the best available estimate of the number of equity instruments expected to vest. (paragraph 19)	No change to accounting. The entity continues to recognise the expense over the remainder of the vesting period. (paragraph 21)	Forfeiture. The entity revises the expense to reflect the best available estimate of the number of equity instruments expected to vest. (paragraph 19)	No change to accounting. The entity continues to recognise the expense over the remainder of the vesting period. (paragraph 21A)	Cancellation. The entity recognises immediately the amount of the expense that would otherwise have been recognised over the remainder of the vesting period. (paragraph 28A)	Cancellation. The entity recognises immediately the amount of the expense that would otherwise have been recognised over the remainder of the vesting period. (paragraph 28A)

(a)   In the calculation of the fair value of the share-based payment, the probability of continuation of the plan by the entity is assumed to be 100 per cent.

AASB 3
Business Combinations
(Compiled November 2010)

Note from the Institute of Chartered Accountants Australia

This note, prepared by the technical editors, is not part of Accounting Standard AASB 3.

Historical development

15 July 2004: AASB 3 'Business Combinations' is the Australian equivalent of IFRS 3 of the same name. It was made by the AASB on 15 July 2004 as part of the AASB's program to adopt International Financial Reporting Standards by 2005.

22 June 2005: AASB 2005-6 'Amendments to Australian Accounting Standards' adds the heading following paragraph 9, and amends paragraphs 2, 3(b), 10 to 13 inclusive, 52(b)(ii), and 57. The Standard deletes paragraphs Aus3.1, Aus3.2, and Aus56.1. These amendments are applicable to annual reporting periods beginning on or after 1 January 2006, with early adoption permitted for annual reporting periods beginning on or after 1 January 2005.

30 April 2007: AASB 2007-4 'Amendments to Australian Accounting Standards' amends paragraphs 4, 49 and B8 and is applicable to annual reporting periods beginning on or after 1 July 2007. Entities may elect to early-adopt it to annual reporting periods beginning on or after 1 January 2005.

13 December 2007: AASB 2007-10 'Further Amendments to Australian Accounting Standards arising from AASB 101' amends AASB 3, replacing the term 'financial report' with 'financial statements'. This Standard is applicable to annual reporting periods beginning on or after 1 January 2009.

13 December 2007: AASB 2007-9 'Amendments to Australian Accounting Standards arising from the review of AAS 27, AAS 29 and AAS 31' was issued by the AASB. This Standard is applicable to annual reporting periods beginning on or after 1 July 2008 with early adoption permitted.

6 March 2008: AASB 3 'Business Combinations' was issued by the AASB superseding the previous version of the Standard, applicable to annual reporting periods beginning on 1 July 2009.

AASB 3 (revised) is applicable prospectively to business combinations for which the acquisition date is on or after the beginning of the first annual reporting periods beginning on or after 1 July 2009. Early adoption is permitted only for for-profit entities for annual reporting periods beginning on or after 30 June 2007 but before 1 July 2009. Application to not-for-profit entities is dealt with by AASB 2008-11, referred to below.

Key changes in revised AASB 3 include providing a choice to measure a non-controlling interest at fair value or at its proportionate share of the acquired entity's net assets. The Standard also requires that costs of acquisition are expensed, and liabilities recognised for contingent payments are measured at fair value at the acquisition date, and any subsequent changes to the fair value are included in the income statement, rather than against goodwill on the balance sheet.

7 November 2008: AASB 3 was reissued by the AASB, compiled to include the AASB 2007-9 amendments.

December 2008: AASB 2008-11 'Amendments to Australian Accounting Standard – Business Combinations Among Not-for-Profit Entities [AASB 3]' confirms that revised AASB 3 must be applied by not-for-profit entities, other than where there is common control.

20 October 2009: AASB 3 revised was reissued by the AASB, compiled to include the AASB 2008-11 amendments. On the same date the previous version of AASB 3 was reissued by the AASB, applicable to annual reporting periods beginning on or after 1 January 2009 but before 1 July 2009. This version of AASB 3 has been compiled for the amending Standards applying to annual reporting periods beginning on or after 1 January 2009.

---

7 December 2009: AASB 2009-11 'Amendments to Australian Accounting Standards arising from AASB 9' amends AASB 3 to give effect to consequential changes arising from the issuance of AASB 9. This Standard is applicable to annual reporting periods beginning on or after 1 January 2013 with early adoption permitted from annual reporting periods ending on or after 31 December 2009 that begin before 1 January 2013 provided AASB 9 is also applied for the same period. The application date of AASB 2009-11 has been amended to 1 January 2015 by AASB 2012-6. **These amendments have been superseded by AASB 2010-7 and are not included in this compiled Standard.**

2 June 2010: AASB 2010-3 'Amendments to Australian Accounting Standards arising from the Annual Improvements Project' amends AASB 3 in relation to measurement of non-controlling interests, unreplaced and voluntarily replaced, and share-based payment awards. This Standard is applicable to annual reporting periods beginning on or after 1 July 2010 with early adoption permitted.

7 September 2010: AASB 3 was reissued by the AASB, compiled to include the AASB 2010-3 amendments and applies to annual reporting periods beginning on or after 1 July 2010 but before 1 January 2013.

27 October 2010: AASB 2010-5 'Further Amendments to Australian Accounting Standards' makes editorial amendments to AASB 3. This Standard is applicable to annual reporting periods beginning on or after 1 January 2011.

26 November 2010: AASB 3 was reissued by the AASB, compiled to include the AASB 2010-5 amendments and applies to annual reporting periods ending on or after 1 January 2011 but before 1 January 2013.

1 March 2011: AASB 2010-7 'Amendments to Australian Accounting Standards arising from AASB 9 (December 2010)' as compiled amends AASB 3 to give effect to consequential changes arising from the reissue of AASB 9 in December 2010 and supersedes AASB 2009-11 which related to the previous version of AASB 9. This Standard applies to annual reporting periods beginning on or after 1 January 2013 and can be adopted early. The application date of AASB 2010-7 has been amended to 1 January 2015 by AASB 2012-6. **These amendments are not included in this compiled Standard.**

29 August 2011: AASB 2011-7 'Amendments to Australian Accounting Standards arising from the Consolidation and Joint Arrangements Standards' amends AASB 3 to give effect to many consequential changes arising from the issue of AASB 10, 11, 12, 127 and 128. This Standard applies to annual reporting periods beginning on or after 1 January 2013 and can be adopted early by for-profit entities. **These amendments are not included in this compiled Standard.**

2 September 2011: AASB 2011-8 'Amendments to Australian Accounting Standards arising from AASB 13' amends AASB 3 to give effect to a consequential change in the definition of fair value arising from the issue of AASB 13. This Standard applies to annual reporting periods beginning on or after 1 January 2013 and can be adopted early. **These amendments are not included in this compiled Standard.**

21 March 2012: AASB 2012-1 'Amendments to Australian Accounting Standards – Fair Value Measurement – Reduced Disclosure Requirements' amends AASB 3 to establish and amend reduced disclosure requirements arising from AASB 13 'Fair Value Measurement'. **These amendments are not included in this compiled Standard.**

Reference

Interpretation 9 *Reassessment of Embedded Derivatives* and Interpretation 17 *Distributions of Non-cash Assets to Owners* apply to AASB 3.

IFRS 3R-1 *Customer-related intangible assets*, IFRS 3R-2 *Acquisition related costs in a business combination*, IFRS 3R-3 *Earlier application of revised IFRS 3*, IFRS 3R-4 *Measurement of NCI* and IFRS 3R-5 *Unreplaced and voluntarily replaced share-based payment awards*, apply to AASB 3.

AASB

AASB 3 compared to IFRS 3

Additions

Paragraph	Description
Aus 1.1	Which entities AASB 3 applies to (i.e. reporting entities and general purpose financial statements).
Aus 1.2	The application date of AASB 3 (i.e. annual reporting periods beginning 1 July 2009).
Aus 1.3	Permits early application of AASB 3 for for-profit entities only from 30 June 2007.
Aus 1.4	Makes the requirements of AASB 3 subject to AASB 1031 'Materiality'.
Aus 1.5	Explains which Australian Standards have been superseded by AASB 3.
Aus 1.6	Explains the paragraphs to be applied to the transfer of assets and liabilities within local government.
Aus 2.1	Clarifies that a restructure of administrative arrangements per AASB 1004 'Contributions' is outside the scope.
Aus 63.1 to Aus 63.9	Contain the requirements for a local government restructure.
App AusB68	Transitional provisions.

Deletions

Paragraph	Description
64	Effective date of IFRS 3.
68	Withdrawal of IFRS 3 (2004) deleted.
App B68	Transitional provisions of IFRS 3.

Contents

Compilation Details

Comparison with IFRS 3

Accounting Standard
AASB 3 Business Combinations

	Paragraphs
Objective	1
Application	Aus1.1 – Aus1.6
Scope	2 – Aus2.1
Identifying a business combination	3
The acquisition method	4 – 5
Identifying the acquirer	6 – 7
Determining the acquisition date	8 – 9
Recognising and measuring the identifiable assets acquired, the liabilities assumed and any non-controlling interest in the acquiree	
Recognition principle	10
Recognition conditions	11 – 14
Classifying or designating identifiable assets acquired and liabilities assumed in a business combination	15 – 17
Measurement principle	18 – 20
Exception to the recognition or measurement principles	21
Exception to the recognition principle	
Contingent liabilities	22 – 23
Exceptions to both the recognition and measurement principles	
Income taxes	24 – 25
Employee benefits	26
Indemnification assets	27 – 28
Exceptions to the measurement principle	
Reacquired rights	29
Share-based payment transactions	30
Assets held for sale	31
Recognising and measuring goodwill or a gain from a bargain purchase	32 – 33
Bargain purchases	34 – 36
Consideration transferred	37 – 38
Contingent consideration	39 – 40
Additional guidance for applying the acquisition method to particular types of business combinations	
A business combination achieved in stages	41 – 42
A business combination achieved without the transfer of consideration	43 – 44
Measurement period	45 – 50
Determining what is part of the business combination transaction	51 – 52
Acquisition-related costs	53
Subsequent measurement and accounting	54
Reacquired rights	55

Paragraphs

Contingent liabilities   56
Indemnification assets   57
Contingent consideration   58
Disclosures   59 – 63
Restructures of local governments   Aus63.1 – Aus63.9
Effective date and transition
    Effective date   64B – 64C
    Transition   65 – 66
       Income taxes   67

Appendices:
A. Defined Terms
B. Application Guidance

Deleted IFRS 3 Text

Illustrative Examples
(available on the AASB website)

Basis for Conclusions on AASB 2008-11

Basis for Conclusions on IFRS 3
(available on the AASB website)

Australian Accounting Standard AASB 3 *Business Combinations* (as amended) is set out in paragraphs 1 – 67 and Appendices A – B. All the paragraphs have equal authority. Paragraphs in **bold type** state the main principles. Terms defined in this Standard are in *italics* the first time they appear in the Standard. AASB 3 is to be read in the context of other Australian Accounting Standards, including AASB 1048 *Interpretation of Standards*, which identifies the Australian Accounting Interpretations. In the absence of explicit guidance, AASB 108 *Accounting Policies, Changes in Accounting Estimates and Errors* provides a basis for selecting and applying accounting policies.

Compilation Details

Accounting Standard AASB 3 *Business Combinations* as amended

This compiled Standard applies to annual reporting periods beginning on or after 1 January 2011 but before 1 January 2013. It takes into account amendments up to and including 27 October 2010 and was prepared on 26 November 2010 by the staff of the Australian Accounting Standards Board (AASB).

This compilation is not a separate Accounting Standard made by the AASB. Instead, it is a representation of AASB 3 (March 2008) as amended by other Accounting Standards, which are listed in the Table below.

Table of Standards

Standard	Date made	Application date *(annual reporting periods ... on or after ...)*	Application, saving or transitional provisions
AASB 3	6 Mar 2008	*(beginning)* 1 Jul 2009	see (a) below
AASB 2008-11	13 Nov 2008	*(beginning)* 1 Jul 2009	see (b) below
AASB 2009-11	7 Dec 2009	*(beginning)* 1 Jan 2013	not compiled*
AASB 2010-3	23 Jun 2010	*(beginning)* 1 Jul 2010	see (c) below
AASB 2010-2	30 Jun 2010	*(beginning)* 1 Jul 2013	not compiled*
AASB 2010-5	27 Oct 2010	*(beginning)* 1 Jan 2011	see (d) below

*   The amendments made by this Standard are not included in this compilation, which presents the principal Standard as applicable to annual reporting periods beginning on or after 1 January 2011 but before 1 January 2013.

(a)   For-profit entities may elect to apply this Standard to annual reporting periods beginning on or after 30 June 2007 but before 1 July 2009, provided that AASB 127 *Consolidated and Separate Financial Statements* (March 2008) is also applied to such periods.

(b)   Entities may elect to apply this Standard to annual reporting periods beginning on or after 30 June 2007 but before 1 July 2009, provided that AASB 127 *Consolidated and Separate Financial Statements* (March 2008) is also applied to such periods.

(c)   Entities may elect to apply this Standard to annual reporting periods beginning on or after 30 June 2007 but before 1 July 2010.

(d)   Entities may elect to apply this Standard to annual reporting periods beginning on or after 30 June 2007 but before 1 January 2011.

Table of Amendments

Paragraph affected	How affected	By ... [paragraph]
Aus1.3	amended	AASB 2008-11 [5]
Aus1.5	amended	AASB 2008-11 [6]
Aus1.6	added	AASB 2008-11 [7]
19	amended	AASB 2010-3 [6]
30 (and preceding heading)	amended	AASB 2010-3 [6]
Aus63.1-Aus63.9 (and preceding heading)	added	AASB 2008-11 [8]
64B-64C	added	AASB 2010-3 [6]
65A-65E	added	AASB 2010-3 [6]
B56	amended	AASB 2010-3 [7]
B62A (and preceding heading)	added	AASB 2010-3 [7]
B62B	added amended	AASB 2010-3 [7] AASB 2010-5 [16]

Basis for Conclusions on AASB 2008-11

The Basis for Conclusions accompanying AASB 2008-11 *Amendments to Australian Accounting Standard – Business Combinations Among Not-for-Profit Entities* is attached to this compiled Standard.

Comparison with IFRS 3

AASB 3 and IFRS 3

AASB 3 *Business Combinations* as amended incorporates IFRS 3 *Business Combinations* as issued and amended by the International Accounting Standards Board (IASB). Paragraphs that have been added to this Standard (and do not appear in the text of IFRS 3) are identified with the prefix "Aus", followed by the number of the preceding IASB paragraph and decimal numbering.

Compliance with IFRS 3

For-profit entities that comply with AASB 3 as amended will simultaneously be in compliance with IFRS 3 as amended.

Not-for-profit entities using the added "Aus" paragraphs in the Standard that specifically apply to not-for-profit entities may not be simultaneously complying with IFRS 3. Whether a not-for-profit entity will be in compliance with IFRS 3 will depend on whether the "Aus" paragraphs provide additional guidance for not-for-profit entities or contain requirements that are inconsistent with the corresponding IASB Standard and will be applied by the not-for-profit entity.

Accounting Standard AASB 3

The Australian Accounting Standards Board made Accounting Standard AASB 3 *Business Combinations* under section 334 of the *Corporations Act 2001* on 6 March 2008.

This compiled version of AASB 3 applies to annual reporting periods beginning on or after 1 January 2011 but before 1 January 2013. It incorporates relevant amendments contained in other AASB Standards made by the AASB up to and including 27 October 2010 (see Compilation Details).

Accounting Standard AASB 3

Business Combinations

Objective

1. The objective of this Standard is to improve the relevance, reliability and comparability of the information that a reporting entity provides in its financial statements about a *business combination* and its effects. To accomplish that, this Standard establishes principles and requirements for how the *acquirer*:

   (a) recognises and measures in its financial statements the *identifiable* assets acquired, the liabilities assumed and any *non-controlling interest* in the *acquiree*;

   (b) recognises and measures the *goodwill* acquired in the business combination or a gain from a bargain purchase; and

   (c) determines what information to disclose to enable users of the financial statements to evaluate the nature and financial effects of the business combination.

Application

Aus1.1 **This Standard applies to:**

   (a) **each entity that is required to prepare financial reports in accordance with Part 2M.3 of the Corporations Act and that is a reporting entity;**

   (b) **general purpose financial statements of each other reporting entity; and**

   (c) **financial statements that are, or are held out to be, general purpose financial statements.**

Aus1.2 **This Standard applies prospectively to business combinations for which the acquisition date is on or after the beginning of the first annual reporting period beginning on or after 1 July 2009.**

   [Note: For application dates of paragraphs changed or added by an amending Standard, see Compilation Details.]

Aus1.3   This Standard may be applied from the beginning of an annual reporting
            period that begins on or after 30 June 2007 but before 1 July 2009. If an entity
            applies this Standard to an annual reporting period beginning before 1 July
            2009, it shall disclose that fact and apply AASB 127 *Consolidated and Separate
            Financial Statements* (as amended in March 2008) at the same time.

Aus1.4   The requirements specified in this Standard apply to the financial report
            where information resulting from their application is material in accordance
            with AASB 1031 *Materiality*.

Aus1.5   When applied or operative, this Standard supersedes:

            (a)   AASB 3 *Business Combinations* (July 2004, as amended);

            (b)   Interpretation 1001 *Consolidated Financial Reports in relation to Pre-Date-
                   of-Transition Dual Listed Company Arrangements* issued in July 2005;

            (c)   Interpretation 1002 *Post-Date-of-Transition Stapling Arrangements* issued
                   in December 2005; and

            (d)   Interpretation 1013 *Consolidated Financial Reports in relation to Pre-Date-
                   of-Transition Stapling Arrangements* issued in April 2005.

Aus1.6   Where assets and liabilities are transferred to a local government from another
            local government at no cost, or for nominal consideration, pursuant to legislation,
            ministerial directive or other externally imposed requirement, paragraphs Aus63.1
            to Aus63.9 shall be applied.

Scope

2   This Standard applies to a transaction or other event that meets the definition of a business
       combination. This Standard does not apply to:

       (a)   the formation of a joint venture.

       (b)   the acquisition of an asset or a group of assets that does not constitute a *business*.
              In such cases the acquirer shall identify and recognise the individual identifiable
              assets acquired (including those assets that meet the definition of, and recognition
              criteria for, *intangible assets* in AASB 138 *Intangible Assets*) and liabilities
              assumed. The cost of the group shall be allocated to the individual identifiable
              assets and liabilities on the basis of their relative *fair values* at the date of purchase.
              Such a transaction or event does not give rise to goodwill.

       (c)   a combination of entities or businesses under common control (paragraphs B1-B4
              provide related application guidance).

Aus 2.1   A restructure of administrative arrangements, as defined in Appendix A of
             AASB 1004 *Contributions*, is outside the scope of this Standard. AASB 1004
             specifies requirements for restructures of administrative arrangements.[1]

Identifying a business combination

3   An entity shall determine whether a transaction or other event is a business
       combination by applying the definition in this Standard, which requires that the
       assets acquired and liabilities assumed constitute a business. If the assets acquired
       are not a business, the reporting entity shall account for the transaction or other
       event as an asset acquisition. Paragraphs B5-B12 provide guidance on identifying a
       business combination and the definition of a business.

The acquisition method

4   An entity shall account for each business combination by applying the acquisition
       method.

5   Applying the acquisition method requires:

       (a)   identifying the acquirer;

       (b)   determining the *acquisition date*;

---

1   The definition of, and requirements for, a restructure of administrative arrangements are included in the
       version of AASB 1004 issued in December 2007.

AASB 3   **Institute of Chartered Accountants Australia**

(c)   recognising and measuring the identifiable assets acquired, the liabilities assumed and any non-controlling interest in the acquiree; and

(d)   recognising and measuring goodwill or a gain from a bargain purchase.

Identifying the acquirer

6   **For each business combination, one of the combining entities shall be identified as the acquirer.**

7   The guidance in AASB 127 shall be used to identify the acquirer – the entity that obtains *control* of the acquiree. If a business combination has occurred but applying the guidance in AASB 127 does not clearly indicate which of the combining entities is the acquirer, the factors in paragraphs B14-B18 shall be considered in making that determination.

Determining the acquisition date

8   **The acquirer shall identify the acquisition date, which is the date on which it obtains control of the acquiree.**

9   The date on which the acquirer obtains control of the acquiree is generally the date on which the acquirer legally transfers the consideration, acquires the assets and assumes the liabilities of the acquiree – the closing date. However, the acquirer might obtain control on a date that is either earlier or later than the closing date. For example, the acquisition date precedes the closing date if a written agreement provides that the acquirer obtains control of the acquiree on a date before the closing date. An acquirer shall consider all pertinent facts and circumstances in identifying the acquisition date.

Recognising and measuring the identifiable assets acquired, the liabilities assumed and any non-controlling interest in the acquiree

Recognition principle

10   **As of the acquisition date, the acquirer shall recognise, separately from goodwill, the identifiable assets acquired, the liabilities assumed and any non-controlling interest in the acquiree. Recognition of identifiable assets acquired and liabilities assumed is subject to the conditions specified in paragraphs 11 and 12.**

Recognition conditions

11   To qualify for recognition as part of applying the acquisition method, the identifiable assets acquired and liabilities assumed must meet the definitions of assets and liabilities in the *Framework for the Preparation and Presentation of Financial Statements* at the acquisition date. For example, costs the acquirer expects but is not obliged to incur in the future to effect its plan to exit an activity of an acquiree or to terminate the employment of or relocate an acquiree's employees are not liabilities at the acquisition date. Therefore, the acquirer does not recognise those costs as part of applying the acquisition method. Instead, the acquirer recognises those costs in its post-combination financial statements in accordance with other Australian Accounting Standards.

12   In addition, to qualify for recognition as part of applying the acquisition method, the identifiable assets acquired and liabilities assumed must be part of what the acquirer and the acquiree (or its former *owners*) exchanged in the business combination transaction rather than the result of separate transactions. The acquirer shall apply the guidance in paragraphs 51-53 to determine which assets acquired or liabilities assumed are part of the exchange for the acquiree and which, if any, are the result of separate transactions to be accounted for in accordance with their nature and the applicable Australian Accounting Standards.

13   The acquirer's application of the recognition principle and conditions may result in recognising some assets and liabilities that the acquiree had not previously recognised as assets and liabilities in its financial statements. For example, the acquirer recognises the acquired identifiable intangible assets, such as a brand name, a patent or a customer relationship, that the acquiree did not recognise as assets in its financial statements because it developed them internally and charged the related costs to expense.

14   Paragraphs B28-B40 provide guidance on recognising operating leases and intangible assets. Paragraphs 22-28 specify the types of identifiable assets and liabilities that include items for which this Standard provides limited exceptions to the recognition principle and conditions.

Classifying or designating identifiable assets acquired and liabilities assumed in a business combination

15   **At the acquisition date, the acquirer shall classify or designate the identifiable assets acquired and liabilities assumed as necessary to apply other Australian Accounting Standards subsequently. The acquirer shall make those classifications or designations on the basis of the contractual terms, economic conditions, its operating or accounting policies and other pertinent conditions as they exist at the acquisition date.**

16   In some situations, Australian Accounting Standards provide for different accounting depending on how an entity classifies or designates a particular asset or liability. Examples of classifications or designations that the acquirer shall make on the basis of the pertinent conditions as they exist at the acquisition date include but are not limited to:

   (a)   classification of particular financial assets and liabilities as a financial asset or liability at fair value through profit or loss, or as a financial asset available for sale or held to maturity, in accordance with AASB 139 *Financial Instruments: Recognition and Measurement*;

   (b)   designation of a derivative instrument as a hedging instrument in accordance with AASB 139; and

   (c)   assessment of whether an embedded derivative should be separated from the host contract in accordance with AASB 139 (which is a matter of 'classification' as this Standard uses that term).

17   This Standard provides two exceptions to the principle in paragraph 15:

   (a)   classification of a lease contract as either an operating lease or a finance lease in accordance with AASB 117 *Leases*; and

   (b)   classification of a contract as an insurance contract in accordance with AASB 4 *Insurance Contracts*.

   The acquirer shall classify those contracts on the basis of the contractual terms and other factors at the inception of the contract (or, if the terms of the contract have been modified in a manner that would change its classification, at the date of that modification, which might be the acquisition date).

Measurement principle

18   **The acquirer shall measure the identifiable assets acquired and the liabilities assumed at their acquisition-date fair values.**

19   For each business combination, the acquirer shall measure at the acquisition date components of non-controlling interests in the acquiree that are present ownership interests and entitle their holders to a proportionate share of the entity's net assets in the event of liquidation at either:

   (a)   fair value; or

   (b)   the present ownership instruments' proportionate share in the recognised amounts of the acquiree's identifiable net assets.

   All other components of non-controlling interests shall be measured at their acquisition-date fair values, unless another measurement basis is required by Australian Accounting Standards.

20   Paragraphs B41-B45 provide guidance on measuring the fair value of particular identifiable assets and a non-controlling interest in an acquiree. Paragraphs 24-31 specify the types of identifiable assets and liabilities that include items for which this Standard provides limited exceptions to the measurement principle.

Exceptions to the recognition or measurement principles

21 This Standard provides limited exceptions to its recognition and measurement principles. Paragraphs 22-31 specify both the particular items for which exceptions are provided and the nature of those exceptions. The acquirer shall account for those items by applying the requirements in paragraphs 22-31, which will result in some items being:

(a) recognised either by applying recognition conditions in addition to those in paragraphs 11 and 12 or by applying the requirements of other Australian Accounting Standards, with results that differ from applying the recognition principle and conditions.

(b) measured at an amount other than their acquisition-date fair values.

Exception to the recognition principle

Contingent liabilities

22 AASB 137 *Provisions, Contingent Liabilities and Contingent Assets* defines a contingent liability as:

(a) a possible obligation that arises from past events and whose existence will be confirmed only by the occurrence or non-occurrence of one or more uncertain future events not wholly within the control of the entity; or

(b) a present obligation that arises from past events but is not recognised because:

(i) it is not probable that an outflow of resources embodying economic benefits will be required to settle the obligation; or

(ii) the amount of the obligation cannot be measured with sufficient reliability.

23 The requirements in AASB 137 do not apply in determining which contingent liabilities to recognise as of the acquisition date. Instead, the acquirer shall recognise as of the acquisition date a contingent liability assumed in a business combination if it is a present obligation that arises from past events and its fair value can be measured reliably. Therefore, contrary to AASB 137, the acquirer recognises a contingent liability assumed in a business combination at the acquisition date even if it is not probable that an outflow of resources embodying economic benefits will be required to settle the obligation. Paragraph 56 provides guidance on the subsequent accounting for contingent liabilities.

Exceptions to both the recognition and measurement principles

Income taxes

24 The acquirer shall recognise and measure a deferred tax asset or liability arising from the assets acquired and liabilities assumed in a business combination in accordance with AASB 112 *Income Taxes*.

25 The acquirer shall account for the potential tax effects of temporary differences and carryforwards of an acquiree that exist at the acquisition date or arise as a result of the acquisition in accordance with AASB 112.

Employee benefits

26 The acquirer shall recognise and measure a liability (or asset, if any) related to the acquiree's employee benefit arrangements in accordance with AASB 119 *Employee Benefits*.

Indemnification assets

27 The seller in a business combination may contractually indemnify the acquirer for the outcome of a contingency or uncertainty related to all or part of a specific asset or liability. For example, the seller may indemnify the acquirer against losses above a specified amount on a liability arising from a particular contingency; in other words, the seller will guarantee that the acquirer's liability will not exceed a specified amount. As a result, the acquirer obtains an indemnification asset. The acquirer shall recognise an indemnification asset at the same time that it recognises the indemnified item measured on the same basis as the indemnified item, subject to the need for a valuation allowance for uncollectible amounts. Therefore, if the indemnification relates to an asset or a liability

that is recognised at the acquisition date and measured at its acquisition-date fair value, the acquirer shall recognise the indemnification asset at the acquisition date measured at its acquisition-date fair value. For an indemnification asset measured at fair value, the effects of uncertainty about future cash flows because of collectibility considerations are included in the fair value measure and a separate valuation allowance is not necessary (paragraph B41 provides related application guidance).

28   In some circumstances, the indemnification may relate to an asset or a liability that is an exception to the recognition or measurement principles. For example, an indemnification may relate to a contingent liability that is not recognised at the acquisition date because its fair value is not reliably measurable at that date. Alternatively, an indemnification may relate to an asset or a liability, for example, one that results from an employee benefit, that is measured on a basis other than acquisition-date fair value. In those circumstances, the indemnification asset shall be recognised and measured using assumptions consistent with those used to measure the indemnified item, subject to management's assessment of the collectibility of the indemnification asset and any contractual limitations on the indemnified amount. Paragraph 57 provides guidance on the subsequent accounting for an indemnification asset.

Exceptions to the measurement principle

Reacquired rights

29   The acquirer shall measure the value of a reacquired right recognised as an intangible asset on the basis of the remaining contractual term of the related contract regardless of whether market participants would consider potential contractual renewals in determining its fair value. Paragraphs B35 and B36 provide related application guidance.

Share-based payment transactions

30   The acquirer shall measure a liability or an equity instrument related to share-based payment transactions of the acquiree or the replacement of an acquiree's share-based payment transactions with share-based payment transactions of the acquirer in accordance with the method in AASB 2 Share-based Payment at the acquisition date. (This Standard refers to the result of that method as the 'market-based measure' of the share-based payment transaction.)

Assets held for sale

31   The acquirer shall measure an acquired non-current asset (or disposal group) that is classified as held for sale at the acquisition date in accordance with AASB 5 *Non-current Assets Held for Sale and Discontinued Operations* at fair value less costs to sell in accordance with paragraphs 15-18 of that Standard.

Recognising and measuring goodwill or a gain from a bargain purchase

32   **The acquirer shall recognise goodwill as of the acquisition date measured as the excess of (a) over (b) below:**

    (a)   the aggregate of:

        (i)   the consideration transferred measured in accordance with this Standard, which generally requires acquisition-date fair value (see paragraph 37);

        (ii)   the amount of any non-controlling interest in the acquiree measured in accordance with this Standard; and

        (iii)   in a business combination achieved in stages (see paragraphs 41 and 42), the acquisition-date fair value of the acquirer's previously held *equity interest* in the acquiree.

    (b)   the net of the acquisition-date amounts of the identifiable assets acquired and the liabilities assumed measured in accordance with this Standard.

33   In a business combination in which the acquirer and the acquiree (or its former owners) exchange only equity interests, the acquisition-date fair value of the acquiree's equity interests may be more reliably measurable than the acquisition-date fair value of the acquirer's equity interests. If so, the acquirer shall determine the amount of goodwill by using the acquisition-date fair value of the acquiree's equity interests instead of the

acquisition-date fair value of the equity interests transferred. To determine the amount of goodwill in a business combination in which no consideration is transferred, the acquirer shall use the acquisition-date fair value of the acquirer's interest in the acquiree determined using a valuation technique in place of the acquisition-date fair value of the consideration transferred (paragraph 32(a)(i)). Paragraphs B46-B49 provide related application guidance.

Bargain purchases

34 Occasionally, an acquirer will make a bargain purchase, which is a business combination in which the amount in paragraph 32(b) exceeds the aggregate of the amounts specified in paragraph 32(a). If that excess remains after applying the requirements in paragraph 36, the acquirer shall recognise the resulting gain in profit or loss on the acquisition date. The gain shall be attributed to the acquirer.

35 A bargain purchase might happen, for example, in a business combination that is a forced sale in which the seller is acting under compulsion. However, the recognition or measurement exceptions for particular items discussed in paragraphs 22-31 may also result in recognising a gain (or change the amount of a recognised gain) on a bargain purchase.

36 Before recognising a gain on a bargain purchase, the acquirer shall reassess whether it has correctly identified all of the assets acquired and all of the liabilities assumed and shall recognise any additional assets or liabilities that are identified in that review. The acquirer shall then review the procedures used to measure the amounts this Standard requires to be recognised at the acquisition date for all of the following:

(a) the identifiable assets acquired and liabilities assumed;

(b) the non-controlling interest in the acquiree, if any;

(c) for a business combination achieved in stages, the acquirer's previously held equity interest in the acquiree; and

(d) the consideration transferred.

The objective of the review is to ensure that the measurements appropriately reflect consideration of all available information as of the acquisition date.

Consideration transferred

37 The consideration transferred in a business combination shall be measured at fair value, which shall be calculated as the sum of the acquisition-date fair values of the assets transferred by the acquirer, the liabilities incurred by the acquirer to former owners of the acquiree and the equity interests issued by the acquirer. (However, any portion of the acquirer's share-based payment awards exchanged for awards held by the acquiree's employees that is included in consideration transferred in the business combination shall be measured in accordance with paragraph 30 rather than at fair value.) Examples of potential forms of consideration include cash, other assets, a business or a subsidiary of the acquirer, *contingent consideration*, ordinary or preference equity instruments, options, warrants and member interests of *mutual entities*.

38 The consideration transferred may include assets or liabilities of the acquirer that have carrying amounts that differ from their fair values at the acquisition date (for example, non-monetary assets or a business of the acquirer). If so, the acquirer shall remeasure the transferred assets or liabilities to their fair values as of the acquisition date and recognise the resulting gains or losses, if any, in profit or loss. However, sometimes the transferred assets or liabilities remain within the combined entity after the business combination (for example, because the assets or liabilities were transferred to the acquiree rather than to its former owners), and the acquirer therefore retains control of them. In that situation, the acquirer shall measure those assets and liabilities at their carrying amounts immediately before the acquisition date and shall not recognise a gain or loss in profit or loss on assets or liabilities it controls both before and after the business combination.

Contingent consideration

39 The consideration the acquirer transfers in exchange for the acquiree includes any asset or liability resulting from a contingent consideration arrangement (see paragraph 37).

The acquirer shall recognise the acquisition-date fair value of contingent consideration as part of the consideration transferred in exchange for the acquiree.

40   The acquirer shall classify an obligation to pay contingent consideration as a liability or as equity on the basis of the definitions of an equity instrument and a financial liability in paragraph 11 of AASB 132 *Financial Instruments: Presentation*, or other applicable Australian Accounting Standards. The acquirer shall classify as an asset a right to the return of previously transferred consideration if specified conditions are met. Paragraph 58 provides guidance on the subsequent accounting for contingent consideration.

Additional guidance for applying the acquisition method to particular types of business combinations

A business combination achieved in stages

41   An acquirer sometimes obtains control of an acquiree in which it held an equity interest immediately before the acquisition date. For example, on 31 December 20X1, Entity A holds a 35 per cent non-controlling equity interest in Entity B. On that date, Entity A purchases an additional 40 per cent interest in Entity B, which gives it control of Entity B. This Standard refers to such a transaction as a business combination achieved in stages, sometimes also referred to as a step acquisition.

42   In a business combination achieved in stages, the acquirer shall remeasure its previously held equity interest in the acquiree at its acquisition-date fair value and recognise the resulting gain or loss, if any, in profit or loss. In prior reporting periods, the acquirer may have recognised changes in the value of its equity interest in the acquiree in other comprehensive income (for example, because the investment was classified as available for sale). If so, the amount that was recognised in other comprehensive income shall be recognised on the same basis as would be required if the acquirer had disposed directly of the previously held equity interest.

A business combination achieved without the transfer of consideration

43   An acquirer sometimes obtains control of an acquiree without transferring consideration. The acquisition method of accounting for a business combination applies to those combinations. Such circumstances include:

(a)   The acquiree repurchases a sufficient number of its own shares for an existing investor (the acquirer) to obtain control.

(b)   Minority veto rights lapse that previously kept the acquirer from controlling an acquiree in which the acquirer held the majority voting rights.

(c)   The acquirer and acquiree agree to combine their businesses by contract alone. The acquirer transfers no consideration in exchange for control of an acquiree and holds no equity interests in the acquiree, either on the acquisition date or previously. Examples of business combinations achieved by contract alone include bringing two businesses together in a stapling arrangement or forming a dual listed corporation.

44   In a business combination achieved by contract alone, the acquirer shall attribute to the owners of the acquiree the amount of the acquiree's net assets recognised in accordance with this Standard. In other words, the equity interests in the acquiree held by parties other than the acquirer are a non-controlling interest in the acquirer's post-combination financial statements even if the result is that all of the equity interests in the acquiree are attributed to the non-controlling interest.

Measurement period

45   If the initial accounting for a business combination is incomplete by the end of the reporting period in which the combination occurs, the acquirer shall report in its financial statements provisional amounts for the items for which the accounting is incomplete. During the measurement period, the acquirer shall retrospectively adjust the provisional amounts recognised at the acquisition date to reflect new information obtained about facts and circumstances that existed as of the acquisition date and, if known, would have affected the measurement of the amounts recognised as of that

AASB

date. During the measurement period, the acquirer shall also recognise additional assets or liabilities if new information is obtained about facts and circumstances that existed as of the acquisition date and, if known, would have resulted in the recognition of those assets and liabilities as of that date. The measurement period ends as soon as the acquirer receives the information it was seeking about facts and circumstances that existed as of the acquisition date or learns that more information is not obtainable. However, the measurement period shall not exceed one year from the acquisition date.

46   The measurement period is the period after the acquisition date during which the acquirer may adjust the provisional amounts recognised for a business combination. The measurement period provides the acquirer with a reasonable time to obtain the information necessary to identify and measure the following as of the acquisition date in accordance with the requirements of this Standard:

(a)   the identifiable assets acquired, liabilities assumed and any non-controlling interest in the acquiree;

(b)   the consideration transferred for the acquiree (or the other amount used in measuring goodwill);

(c)   in a business combination achieved in stages, the equity interest in the acquiree previously held by the acquirer; and

(d)   the resulting goodwill or gain on a bargain purchase.

47   The acquirer shall consider all pertinent factors in determining whether information obtained after the acquisition date should result in an adjustment to the provisional amounts recognised or whether that information results from events that occurred after the acquisition date. Pertinent factors include the date when additional information is obtained and whether the acquirer can identify a reason for a change to provisional amounts. Information that is obtained shortly after the acquisition date is more likely to reflect circumstances that existed at the acquisition date than is information obtained several months later. For example, unless an intervening event that changed its fair value can be identified, the sale of an asset to a third party shortly after the acquisition date for an amount that differs significantly from its provisional fair value determined at that date is likely to indicate an error in the provisional amount.

48   The acquirer recognises an increase (decrease) in the provisional amount recognised for an identifiable asset (liability) by means of a decrease (increase) in goodwill. However, new information obtained during the measurement period may sometimes result in an adjustment to the provisional amount of more than one asset or liability. For example, the acquirer might have assumed a liability to pay damages related to an accident in one of the acquiree's facilities, part or all of which are covered by the acquiree's liability insurance policy. If the acquirer obtains new information during the measurement period about the acquisition-date fair value of that liability, the adjustment to goodwill resulting from a change to the provisional amount recognised for the liability would be offset (in whole or in part) by a corresponding adjustment to goodwill resulting from a change to the provisional amount recognised for the claim receivable from the insurer.

49   During the measurement period, the acquirer shall recognise adjustments to the provisional amounts as if the accounting for the business combination had been completed at the acquisition date. Thus, the acquirer shall revise comparative information for prior periods presented in financial statements as needed, including making any change in depreciation, amortisation or other income effects recognised in completing the initial accounting.

50   After the measurement period ends, the acquirer shall revise the accounting for a business combination only to correct an error in accordance with AASB 108 *Accounting Policies, Changes in Accounting Estimates and Errors*.

Determining what is part of the business combination transaction

51   The acquirer and the acquiree may have a pre-existing relationship or other arrangement before negotiations for the business combination began, or they may enter into an arrangement during the negotiations that is separate from the business combination. In either situation, the acquirer shall identify any amounts that are

not part of what the acquirer and the acquiree (or its former owners) exchanged in the business combination, i.e. amounts that are not part of the exchange for the acquiree. The acquirer shall recognise as part of applying the acquisition method only the consideration transferred for the acquiree and the assets acquired and liabilities assumed in the exchange for the acquiree. Separate transactions shall be accounted for in accordance with the relevant Australian Accounting Standards.

52   A transaction entered into by or on behalf of the acquirer or primarily for the benefit of the acquirer or the combined entity, rather than primarily for the benefit of the acquiree (or its former owners) before the combination, is likely to be a separate transaction. The following are examples of separate transactions that are not to be included in applying the acquisition method:

(a)   a transaction that in effect settles pre-existing relationships between the acquirer and acquiree;

(b)   a transaction that remunerates employees or former owners of the acquiree for future services; and

(c)   a transaction that reimburses the acquiree or its former owners for paying the acquirer's acquisition-related costs.

Paragraphs B50-B62 provide related application guidance.

Acquisition-related costs

53   Acquisition-related costs are costs the acquirer incurs to effect a business combination. Those costs include finder's fees; advisory, legal, accounting, valuation and other professional or consulting fees; general administrative costs, including the costs of maintaining an internal acquisitions department; and costs of registering and issuing debt and equity securities. The acquirer shall account for acquisition-related costs as expenses in the periods in which the costs are incurred and the services are received, with one exception. The costs to issue debt or equity securities shall be recognised in accordance with AASB 132 and AASB 139.

Subsequent measurement and accounting

54   In general, an acquirer shall subsequently measure and account for assets acquired, liabilities assumed or incurred and equity instruments issued in a business combination in accordance with other applicable Australian Accounting Standards for those items, depending on their nature. However, this Standard provides guidance on subsequently measuring and accounting for the following assets acquired, liabilities assumed or incurred and equity instruments issued in a business combination:

(a)   reacquired rights;

(b)   contingent liabilities recognised as of the acquisition date;

(c)   indemnification assets; and

(d)   contingent consideration.

Paragraph B63 provides related application guidance.

Reacquired rights

55   A reacquired right recognised as an intangible asset shall be amortised over the remaining contractual period of the contract in which the right was granted. An acquirer that subsequently sells a reacquired right to a third party shall include the carrying amount of the intangible asset in determining the gain or loss on the sale.

Contingent liabilities

56   After initial recognition and until the liability is settled, cancelled or expires, the acquirer shall measure a contingent liability recognised in a business combination at the higher of:

(a)   the amount that would be recognised in accordance with AASB 137; and

(b)   the amount initially recognised less, if appropriate, cumulative amortisation recognised in accordance with AASB 118 *Revenue*.

This requirement does not apply to contracts accounted for in accordance with AASB 139.

Indemnification assets

57   At the end of each subsequent reporting period, the acquirer shall measure an indemnification asset that was recognised at the acquisition date on the same basis as the indemnified liability or asset, subject to any contractual limitations on its amount and, for an indemnification asset that is not subsequently measured at its fair value, management's assessment of the collectibility of the indemnification asset. The acquirer shall derecognise the indemnification asset only when it collects the asset, sells it or otherwise loses the right to it.

Contingent consideration

58   Some changes in the fair value of contingent consideration that the acquirer recognises after the acquisition date may be the result of additional information that the acquirer obtained after that date about facts and circumstances that existed at the acquisition date. Such changes are measurement period adjustments in accordance with paragraphs 45-49. However, changes resulting from events after the acquisition date, such as meeting an earnings target, reaching a specified share price or reaching a milestone on a research and development project, are not measurement period adjustments. The acquirer shall account for changes in the fair value of contingent consideration that are not measurement period adjustments as follows:

(a)   Contingent consideration classified as equity shall not be remeasured and its subsequent settlement shall be accounted for within equity.

(b)   Contingent consideration classified as an asset or a liability that:

(i)   is a financial instrument and is within the scope of AASB 139 shall be measured at fair value, with any resulting gain or loss recognised either in profit or loss or in other comprehensive income in accordance with that Standard.

(ii)   is not within the scope of AASB 139 shall be accounted for in accordance with AASB 137 or other Australian Accounting Standards as appropriate.

Disclosures

59   The acquirer shall disclose information that enables users of its financial statements to evaluate the nature and financial effect of a business combination that occurs either:

(a)   during the current reporting period; or

(b)   after the end of the reporting period but before the financial statements are authorised for issue.

60   To meet the objective in paragraph 59, the acquirer shall disclose the information specified in paragraphs B64-B66.

61   The acquirer shall disclose information that enables users of its financial statements to evaluate the financial effects of adjustments recognised in the current reporting period that relate to business combinations that occurred in the period or previous reporting periods.

62   To meet the objective in paragraph 61, the acquirer shall disclose the information specified in paragraph B67.

63   If the specific disclosures required by this and other Australian Accounting Standards do not meet the objectives set out in paragraphs 59 and 61, the acquirer shall disclose whatever additional information is necessary to meet those objectives.

Restructures of local governments

Aus63.1   Where assets and liabilities are transferred to a local government from another local government at no cost, or for nominal consideration, pursuant to legislation, ministerial directive or other externally imposed requirement, the transferee local government shall recognise assets and liabilities and any gain or loss.

Aus63.2   Assets transferred to a local government from another local government at no cost, or for nominal consideration, by virtue of legislation, ministerial directive

or other externally imposed requirement shall be recognised initially either at the amounts at which the assets were recognised by the transferor local government as at the date of the transfer, or at their fair values.

Aus63.3   A restructure of local governments involves the transfer of assets and liabilities of a local government to another local government, at no cost or for nominal consideration, by virtue of legislation, ministerial directive or other externally imposed requirement. This gives rise to assets and liabilities and a gain or loss of the transferee local government. A restructure of local governments may take the form of a new local government being constituted and other local governments being abolished as a result of a State government's policy to effectively amalgamate a number of local governments.

Aus63.4   A restructure of local governments involves a change in the resources controlled by the local governments involved in the restructure. The transferor local government will decrease its assets by the carrying amount of the assets transferred. The transferred assets will usually be recognised by the transferee at their carrying amounts in the books of the transferor at the time of the transfer. Such amounts provide a practical basis for recognising the transfer of assets, particularly when many assets are involved, as is usually the case in a restructure of local governments. However, the recognition of transferred assets at fair value is permitted by this Standard.

Aus63.5   The restructures of local governments referred to in paragraphs Aus63.3 and Aus63.4 do not involve transfers between the local government and its ownership group but give rise to a gain or loss that is recognised in the statement of comprehensive income.

Aus63.6   **Assets and liabilities transferred during the reporting period and recognised in accordance with paragraph Aus63.1 shall be disclosed separately, by class, by way of note or otherwise, and the transferor local government shall be identified.**

Aus63.7   **Any gain or loss recognised in accordance with paragraph Aus63.1 shall be separately disclosed in the statement of comprehensive income.**

Aus63.8   The disclosures required by paragraph Aus63.6 will assist users to identify the assets and liabilities recognised as a result of a restructure separately from other assets and liabilities and to identify the transferor local government. In addition, the disclosures required by paragraph Aus63.7 will assist users to identify separately the gain or loss which results from a restructure of local governments.

Aus63.9   Local governments are not required to apply paragraphs 59 to 63 and the related Appendix B Application Guidance paragraphs of this Standard when disclosing information about restructures of local governments.

Effective date and transition
Effective date

64   [Deleted by the AASB]

64B   AASB 2010-3 *Amendments to Australian Accounting Standards arising from the Annual Improvements Project* issued in June 2010 amended paragraphs 19, 30 and B56 and added paragraphs B62A and B62B. An entity shall apply those amendments for annual reporting periods beginning on or after 1 July 2010. Earlier application is permitted. If an entity applies the amendments for an earlier period it shall disclose that fact. Application shall be prospective from the date when the entity first applied this Standard.

64C   Paragraphs 65A-65E were added by AASB 2010-3 issued in June 2010. An entity shall apply those amendments for annual reporting periods beginning on or after 1 July 2010. Earlier application is permitted. If an entity applies the amendments for an earlier period it shall disclose that fact. The amendments shall be applied to contingent consideration balances arising from business combinations with an acquisition date prior to the application of this Standard, as issued in 2008.

Transition

65 Assets and liabilities that arose from business combinations whose acquisition dates preceded the application of this Standard shall not be adjusted upon application of this Standard.

65A Contingent consideration balances arising from business combinations whose acquisition dates preceded the date when an entity first applied this Standard as issued in 2008 shall not be adjusted upon first application of this Standard. Paragraphs 65B-65E shall be applied in the subsequent accounting for those balances. Paragraphs 65B-65E shall not apply to the accounting for contingent consideration balances arising from business combinations with acquisition dates on or after the date when the entity first applied this Standard as issued in 2008. In paragraphs 65B-65E business combination refers exclusively to business combinations whose acquisition date preceded the application of this Standard as issued in 2008.

65B If a business combination agreement provides for an adjustment to the cost of the combination contingent on future events, the acquirer shall include the amount of that adjustment in the cost of the combination at the acquisition date if the adjustment is probable and can be measured reliably.

65C A business combination agreement may allow for adjustments to the cost of the combination that are contingent on one or more future events. The adjustment might, for example, be contingent on a specified level of profit being maintained or achieved in future periods, or on the market price of the instruments issued being maintained. It is usually possible to estimate the amount of any such adjustment at the time of initially accounting for the combination without impairing the reliability of the information, even though some uncertainty exists. If the future events do not occur or the estimate needs to be revised, the cost of the business combination shall be adjusted accordingly.

65D However, when a business combination agreement provides for such an adjustment, that adjustment is not included in the cost of the combination at the time of initially accounting for the combination if it either is not probable or cannot be measured reliably. If that adjustment subsequently becomes probable and can be measured reliably, the additional consideration shall be treated as an adjustment to the cost of the combination.

65E In some circumstances, the acquirer may be required to make a subsequent payment to the seller as compensation for a reduction in the value of the assets given, equity instruments issued or liabilities incurred or assumed by the acquirer in exchange for control of the acquiree. This is the case, for example, when the acquirer guarantees the market price of equity or debt instruments issued as part of the cost of the business combination and is required to issue additional equity or debt instruments to restore the originally determined cost. In such cases, no increase in the cost of the business combination is recognised. In the case of equity instruments, the fair value of the additional payment is offset by an equal reduction in the value attributed to the instruments initially issued. In the case of debt instruments, the additional payment is regarded as a reduction in the premium or an increase in the discount on the initial issue.

66 An entity, such as a mutual entity, that has not yet applied AASB 3 and had one or more business combinations that were accounted for using the purchase method shall apply the transition provisions in paragraphs AusB68 and B69.

Income taxes

67 For business combinations in which the acquisition date was before this Standard is applied, the acquirer shall apply the requirements of paragraph 68 of AASB 112, as amended by AASB 2008-3 *Amendments to Australian Accounting Standards arising from AASB 3 and AASB 127*, prospectively. That is to say, the acquirer shall not adjust the accounting for prior business combinations for previously recognised changes in recognised deferred tax assets. However, from the date when this Standard is applied, the acquirer shall recognise, as an adjustment to profit or loss (or, if AASB 112 requires, outside profit or loss), changes in recognised deferred tax assets.

Withdrawal of IFRS 3 (2004)

68 [Deleted by the AASB]

Appendix A
Defined Terms

This appendix is an integral part of AASB 3.

acquiree	The business or businesses that the **acquirer** obtains control of in a **business combination**.
acquirer	The entity that obtains control of the **acquiree**.
acquisition date	The date on which the **acquirer** obtains control of the **acquiree**.
business	An integrated set of activities and assets that is capable of being conducted and managed for the purpose of providing a return in the form of dividends, lower costs or other economic benefits directly to investors or other owners, members or participants.
business combination	A transaction or other event in which an **acquirer** obtains control of one or more **businesses**. Transactions sometimes referred to as 'true mergers' or 'mergers of equals' are also **business combinations** as that term is used in this Standard.
contingent consideration	Usually, an obligation of the **acquirer** to transfer additional assets or **equity interests** to the former owners of an **acquiree** as part of the exchange for **control** of the **acquiree** if specified future events occur or conditions are met. However, contingent consideration also may give the **acquirer** the right to the return of previously transferred consideration if specified conditions are met.
control	The power to govern the financial and operating policies of an entity so as to obtain benefits from its activities.
equity interests	For the purposes of this Standard, *equity interests* is used broadly to mean ownership interests of investor-owned entities and owner, member or participant interests of **mutual entities**.
fair value	The amount for which an asset could be exchanged, or a liability settled, between knowledgeable, willing parties in an arm's length transaction.
goodwill	An asset representing the future economic benefits arising from other assets acquired in a **business combination** that are not individually identified and separately recognised.
identifiable	An asset is *identifiable* if it either:

(a)   is separable, i.e. capable of being separated or divided from the entity and sold, transferred, licensed, rented or exchanged, either individually or together with a related contract, identifiable asset or liability, regardless of whether the entity intends to do so; or

(b)   arises from contractual or other legal rights, regardless of whether those rights are transferable or separable from the entity or from other rights and obligations.

intangible asset	An **identifiable** non-monetary asset without physical substance.

mutual entity	An entity, other than an investor-owned entity, that provides dividends, lower costs or other economic benefits directly to its **owners**, members or participants. For example, a mutual insurance company, a credit union and a co-operative entity are all mutual entities.
non-controlling interest	The equity in a subsidiary not attributable, directly or indirectly, to a parent.
owners	For the purposes of this Standard, *owners* is used broadly to include holders of **equity interests** of investor-owned entities and owners or members of, or participants in, **mutual entities**.

Appendix B

Application Guidance

This appendix is an integral part of AASB 3.

Business combinations of entities under common control (application of paragraph 2(c))

B1 This Standard does not apply to a business combination of entities or businesses under common control. A business combination involving entities or businesses under common control is a business combination in which all of the combining entities or businesses are ultimately controlled by the same party or parties both before and after the business combination, and that control is not transitory.

B2 A group of individuals shall be regarded as controlling an entity when, as a result of contractual arrangements, they collectively have the power to govern its financial and operating policies so as to obtain benefits from its activities. Therefore, a business combination is outside the scope of this Standard when the same group of individuals has, as a result of contractual arrangements, ultimate collective power to govern the financial and operating policies of each of the combining entities so as to obtain benefits from their activities, and that ultimate collective power is not transitory.

B3 An entity may be controlled by an individual or by a group of individuals acting together under a contractual arrangement, and that individual or group of individuals may not be subject to the financial reporting requirements of Australian Accounting Standards. Therefore, it is not necessary for combining entities to be included as part of the same consolidated financial statements for a business combination to be regarded as one involving entities under common control.

B4 The extent of non-controlling interests in each of the combining entities before and after the business combination is not relevant to determining whether the combination involves entities under common control. Similarly, the fact that one of the combining entities is a subsidiary that has been excluded from the consolidated financial statements is not relevant to determining whether a combination involves entities under common control.

Identifying a business combination (application of paragraph 3)

B5 This Standard defines a business combination as a transaction or other event in which an acquirer obtains control of one or more businesses. An acquirer might obtain control of an acquiree in a variety of ways, for example:

(a) by transferring cash, cash equivalents or other assets (including net assets that constitute a business);

(b) by incurring liabilities;

(c) by issuing equity interests;

(d)   by providing more than one type of consideration; or

(e)   without transferring consideration, including by contract alone (see paragraph 43).

B6   A business combination may be structured in a variety of ways for legal, taxation or other reasons, which include but are not limited to:

(a)   one or more businesses become subsidiaries of an acquirer or the net assets of one or more businesses are legally merged into the acquirer;

(b)   one combining entity transfers its net assets, or its owners transfer their equity interests, to another combining entity or its owners;

(c)   all of the combining entities transfer their net assets, or the owners of those entities transfer their equity interests, to a newly formed entity (sometimes eferred to as a roll-up or put-together transaction); or

(d)   a group of former owners of one of the combining entities obtains control of the combined entity.

Definition of a business (application of paragraph 3)

B7   A business consists of inputs and processes applied to those inputs that have the ability to create outputs. Although businesses usually have outputs, outputs are not required for an integrated set to qualify as a business. The three elements of a business are defined as follows:

(a)   **Input:** Any economic resource that creates, or has the ability to create, outputs when one or more processes are applied to it. Examples include non-current assets (including intangible assets or rights to use non-current assets), intellectual property, the ability to obtain access to necessary materials or rights and employees.

(b)   **Process:** Any system, standard, protocol, convention or rule that when applied to an input or inputs, creates or has the ability to create outputs. Examples include strategic management processes, operational processes and resource management processes. These processes typically are documented, but an organised workforce having the necessary skills and experience following rules and conventions may provide the necessary processes that are capable of being applied to inputs to create outputs. (Accounting, billing, payroll and other administrative systems typically are not processes used to create outputs.)

(c)   **Output:** The result of inputs and processes applied to those inputs that provide or have the ability to provide a return in the form of dividends, lower costs or other economic benefits directly to investors or other owners, members or participants.

B8   To be capable of being conducted and managed for the purposes defined, an integrated set of activities and assets requires two essential elements – inputs and processes applied to those inputs, which together are or will be used to create outputs. However, a business need not include all of the inputs or processes that the seller used in operating that business if market participants are capable of acquiring the business and continuing to produce outputs, for example, by integrating the business with their own inputs and processes.

B9   The nature of the elements of a business varies by industry and by the structure of an entity's operations (activities), including the entity's stage of development. Established businesses often have many different types of inputs, processes and outputs, whereas new businesses often have few inputs and processes and sometimes only a single output (product). Nearly all businesses also have liabilities, but a business need not have liabilities.

B10   An integrated set of activities and assets in the development stage might not have outputs. If not, the acquirer should consider other factors to determine whether the set is a business. Those factors include, but are not limited to, whether the set:

(a)   has begun planned principal activities;

(b)   has employees, intellectual property and other inputs and processes that could be applied to those inputs;

(c)   is pursuing a plan to produce outputs; and

(d)   will be able to obtain access to customers that will purchase the outputs.

Not all of those factors need to be present for a particular integrated set of activities and assets in the development stage to qualify as a business.

B11   Determining whether a particular set of assets and activities is a business should be based on whether the integrated set is capable of being conducted and managed as a business by a market participant. Thus, in evaluating whether a particular set is a business, it is not relevant whether a seller operated the set as a business or whether the acquirer intends to operate the set as a business.

B12   In the absence of evidence to the contrary, a particular set of assets and activities in which goodwill is present shall be presumed to be a business. However, a business need not have goodwill.

Identifying the acquirer (application of paragraphs 6 and 7)

B13   The guidance in AASB 127 *Consolidated and Separate Financial Statements* shall be used to identify the acquirer – the entity that obtains control of the acquiree. If a business combination has occurred but applying the guidance in AASB 127 does not clearly indicate which of the combining entities is the acquirer, the factors in paragraphs B14-B18 shall be considered in making that determination.

B14   In a business combination effected primarily by transferring cash or other assets or by incurring liabilities, the acquirer is usually the entity that transfers the cash or other assets or incurs the liabilities.

B15   In a business combination effected primarily by exchanging equity interests, the acquirer is usually the entity that issues its equity interests. However, in some business combinations, commonly called 'reverse acquisitions', the issuing entity is the acquiree. Paragraphs B19-B27 provide guidance on accounting for reverse acquisitions. Other pertinent facts and circumstances shall also be considered in identifying the acquirer in a business combination effected by exchanging equity interests, including:

(a)   *the relative voting rights in the combined entity after the business combination* – The acquirer is usually the combining entity whose owners as a group retain or receive the largest portion of the voting rights in the combined entity. In determining which group of owners retains or receives the largest portion of the voting rights, an entity shall consider the existence of any unusual or special voting arrangements and options, warrants or convertible securities.

(b)   *the existence of a large minority voting interest in the combined entity if no other owner or organised group of owners has a significant voting interest* – The acquirer is usually the combining entity whose single owner or organised group of owners holds the largest minority voting interest in the combined entity.

(c)   *the composition of the governing body of the combined entity* – The acquirer is usually the combining entity whose owners have the ability to elect or appoint or to remove a majority of the members of the governing body of the combined entity.

(d)   *the composition of the senior management of the combined entity* – The acquirer is usually the combining entity whose (former) management dominates the management of the combined entity.

(e)   *the terms of the exchange of equity interests* – The acquirer is usually the combining entity that pays a premium over the pre-combination fair value of the equity interests of the other combining entity or entities.

B16   The acquirer is usually the combining entity whose relative size (measured in, for example, assets, revenues or profit) is significantly greater than that of the other combining entity or entities.

B17   In a business combination involving more than two entities, determining the acquirer shall include a consideration of, among other things, which of the combining entities initiated the combination, as well as the relative size of the combining entities.

B18   A new entity formed to effect a business combination is not necessarily the acquirer. If a new entity is formed to issue equity interests to effect a business combination, one of the combining entities that existed before the business combination shall be identified as the acquirer by applying the guidance in paragraphs B13-B17. In contrast, a new entity that transfers cash or other assets or incurs liabilities as consideration may be the acquirer.

Reverse acquisitions

B19   A reverse acquisition occurs when the entity that issues securities (the legal acquirer) is identified as the acquiree for accounting purposes on the basis of the guidance in paragraphs B13-B18. The entity whose equity interests are acquired (the legal acquiree) must be the acquirer for accounting purposes for the transaction to be considered a reverse acquisition. For example, reverse acquisitions sometimes occur when a private operating entity wants to become a public entity but does not want to register its equity shares. To accomplish that, the private entity will arrange for a public entity to acquire its equity interests in exchange for the equity interests of the public entity. In this example, the public entity is the **legal acquirer** because it issued its equity interests, and the private entity is the **legal acquiree** because its equity interests were acquired. However, application of the guidance in paragraphs B13-B18 results in identifying:

   (a)   the public entity as the **acquiree** for accounting purposes (the accounting acquiree); and

   (b)   the private entity as the **acquirer** for accounting purposes (the accounting acquirer).

       The accounting acquiree must meet the definition of a business for the transaction to be accounted for as a reverse acquisition, and all of the recognition and measurement principles in this Standard, including the requirement to recognise goodwill, apply.

Measuring the consideration transferred

B20   In a reverse acquisition, the accounting acquirer usually issues no consideration for the acquiree. Instead, the accounting acquiree usually issues its equity shares to the owners of the accounting acquirer. Accordingly, the acquisition-date fair value of the consideration transferred by the accounting acquirer for its interest in the accounting acquiree is based on the number of equity interests the legal subsidiary would have had to issue to give the owners of the legal parent the same percentage equity interest in the combined entity that results from the reverse acquisition. The fair value of the number of equity interests calculated in that way can be used as the fair value of consideration transferred in exchange for the acquiree.

Preparation and presentation of consolidated financial statements

B21   Consolidated financial statements prepared following a reverse acquisition are issued under the name of the legal parent (accounting acquiree) but described in the notes as a continuation of the financial statements of the legal subsidiary (accounting acquirer), with one adjustment, which is to adjust retroactively the accounting acquirer's legal capital to reflect the legal capital of the accounting acquiree. That adjustment is required to reflect the capital of the legal parent (the accounting acquiree). Comparative information presented in those consolidated financial statements also is retroactively adjusted to reflect the legal capital of the legal parent (accounting acquiree).

B22   Because the consolidated financial statements represent the continuation of the financial statements of the legal subsidiary except for its capital structure, the consolidated financial statements reflect:

   (a)   the assets and liabilities of the legal subsidiary (the accounting acquirer) recognised and measured at their pre-combination carrying amounts.

   (b)   the assets and liabilities of the legal parent (the accounting acquiree) recognised and measured in accordance with this Standard.

   (c)   the retained earnings and other equity balances of the legal subsidiary (accounting acquirer) before the business combination.

   (d)   the amount recognised as issued equity interests in the consolidated financial statements determined by adding the issued equity interest of the legal subsidiary (the accounting acquirer) outstanding immediately before the business combination to the fair value of the legal parent (accounting acquiree) determined in accordance with this Standard. However, the equity structure (i.e. the number and type of equity interests issued) reflects the equity structure of the legal parent (the accounting acquiree), including the equity interests the legal parent issued to effect the combination. Accordingly, the equity structure of the legal subsidiary (the accounting acquirer) is restated using the exchange ratio established in the acquisition agreement to reflect the number of shares of the legal parent (the accounting acquiree) issued in the reverse acquisition.

(e) the non-controlling interest's proportionate share of the legal subsidiary's (accounting acquirer's) pre-combination carrying amounts of retained earnings and other equity interests as discussed in paragraphs B23 and B24.

Non-controlling interest

B23 In a reverse acquisition, some of the owners of the legal acquiree (the accounting acquirer) might not exchange their equity interests for equity interests of the legal parent (the accounting acquiree). Those owners are treated as a non-controlling interest in the consolidated financial statements after the reverse acquisition. That is because the owners of the legal acquiree that do not exchange their equity interests for equity interests of the legal acquirer have an interest in only the results and net assets of the legal acquiree – not in the results and net assets of the combined entity. Conversely, even though the legal acquirer is the acquiree for accounting purposes, the owners of the legal acquirer have an interest in the results and net assets of the combined entity.

B24 The assets and liabilities of the legal acquiree are measured and recognised in the consolidated financial statements at their pre-combination carrying amounts (see paragraph B22(a)). Therefore, in a reverse acquisition the non-controlling interest reflects the non-controlling shareholders' proportionate interest in the pre-combination carrying amounts of the legal acquiree's net assets even if the non-controlling interests in other acquisitions are measured at their fair value at the acquisition date.

Earnings per share

B25 As noted in paragraph B22(d), the equity structure in the consolidated financial statements following a reverse acquisition reflects the equity structure of the legal acquirer (the accounting acquiree), including the equity interests issued by the legal acquirer to effect the business combination.

B26 In calculating the weighted average number of ordinary shares outstanding (the denominator of the earnings per share calculation) during the period in which the reverse acquisition occurs:

(a) the number of ordinary shares outstanding from the beginning of that period to the acquisition date shall be computed on the basis of the weighted average number of ordinary shares of the legal acquiree (accounting acquirer) outstanding during the period multiplied by the exchange ratio established in the merger agreement; and

(b) the number of ordinary shares outstanding from the acquisition date to the end of that period shall be the actual number of ordinary shares of the legal acquirer (the accounting acquiree) outstanding during that period.

B27 The basic earnings per share for each comparative period before the acquisition date presented in the consolidated financial statements following a reverse acquisition shall be calculated by dividing:

(a) the profit or loss of the legal acquiree attributable to ordinary shareholders in each of those periods by

(b) the legal acquiree's historical weighted average number of ordinary shares outstanding multiplied by the exchange ratio established in the acquisition agreement.

Recognising particular assets acquired and liabilities assumed (application of paragraphs 10-13)

Operating leases

B28   The acquirer shall recognise no assets or liabilities related to an operating lease in which the acquiree is the lessee except as required by paragraphs B29 and B30.

B29   The acquirer shall determine whether the terms of each operating lease in which the acquiree is the lessee are favourable or unfavourable. The acquirer shall recognise an intangible asset if the terms of an operating lease are favourable relative to market terms and a liability if the terms are unfavourable relative to market terms. Paragraph B42 provides guidance on measuring the acquisition-date fair value of assets subject to operating leases in which the acquiree is the lessor.

B30   An identifiable intangible asset may be associated with an operating lease, which may be evidenced by market participants' willingness to pay a price for the lease even if it is at market terms. For example, a lease of gates at an airport or of retail space in a prime shopping area might provide entry into a market or other future economic benefits that qualify as identifiable intangible assets, for example, as a customer relationship. In that situation, the acquirer shall recognise the associated identifiable intangible asset(s) in accordance with paragraph B31.

Intangible assets

B31   The acquirer shall recognise, separately from goodwill, the identifiable intangible assets acquired in a business combination. An intangible asset is identifiable if it meets either the separability criterion or the contractual-legal criterion.

B32   An intangible asset that meets the contractual-legal criterion is identifiable even if the asset is not transferable or separable from the acquiree or from other rights and obligations. For example:

(a)   an acquiree leases a manufacturing facility under an operating lease that has terms that are favourable relative to market terms. The lease terms explicitly prohibit transfer of the lease (through either sale or sublease). The amount by which the lease terms are favourable compared with the terms of current market transactions for the same or similar items is an intangible asset that meets the contractual-legal criterion for recognition separately from goodwill, even though the acquirer cannot sell or otherwise transfer the lease contract.

(b)   an acquiree owns and operates a nuclear power plant. The licence to operate that power plant is an intangible asset that meets the contractual-legal criterion for recognition separately from goodwill, even if the acquirer cannot sell or transfer it separately from the acquired power plant. An acquirer may recognise the fair value of the operating licence and the fair value of the power plant as a single asset for financial reporting purposes if the useful lives of those assets are similar.

(c)   an acquiree owns a technology patent. It has licensed that patent to others for their exclusive use outside the domestic market, receiving a specified percentage of future foreign revenue in exchange. Both the technology patent and the related licence agreement meet the contractual-legal criterion for recognition separately from goodwill even if selling or exchanging the patent and the related licence agreement separately from one another would not be practical.

B33   The separability criterion means that an acquired intangible asset is capable of being separated or divided from the acquiree and sold, transferred, licensed, rented or exchanged, either individually or together with a related contract, identifiable asset or liability. An intangible asset that the acquirer would be able to sell, license or otherwise exchange for something else of value meets the separability criterion even if the acquirer does not intend to sell, license or otherwise exchange it. An acquired intangible asset meets the separability criterion if there is evidence of exchange transactions for that type of asset or an asset of a similar type, even if those transactions are infrequent and regardless of whether the acquirer is involved in them. For example, customer and subscriber lists are frequently licensed and thus meet the separability criterion. Even if an acquiree believes its customer lists have characteristics different from other customer lists, the fact that customer lists are frequently licensed generally means that the acquired customer list meets the separability criterion. However, a customer list acquired in a business combination would not meet the separability criterion if the terms of confidentiality or other agreements prohibit an entity from selling, leasing or otherwise exchanging information about its customers.

B34 An intangible asset that is not individually separable from the acquiree or combined entity meets the separability criterion if it is separable in combination with a related contract, identifiable asset or liability. For example:

(a) market participants exchange deposit liabilities and related depositor relationship intangible assets in observable exchange transactions. Therefore, the acquirer should recognise the depositor relationship intangible asset separately from goodwill.

(b) an acquiree owns a registered trademark and documented but unpatented technical expertise used to manufacture the trademarked product. To transfer ownership of a trademark, the owner is also required to transfer everything else necessary for the new owner to produce a product or service indistinguishable from that produced by the former owner. Because the unpatented technical expertise must be separated from the acquiree or combined entity and sold if the related trademark is sold, it meets the separability criterion.

Reacquired rights

B35 As part of a business combination, an acquirer may reacquire a right that it had previously granted to the acquiree to use one or more of the acquirer's recognised or unrecognised assets. Examples of such rights include a right to use the acquirer's trade name under a franchise agreement or a right to use the acquirer's technology under a technology licensing agreement. A reacquired right is an identifiable intangible asset that the acquirer recognises separately from goodwill. Paragraph 29 provides guidance on measuring a reacquired right and paragraph 55 provides guidance on the subsequent accounting for a reacquired right.

B36 If the terms of the contract giving rise to a reacquired right are favourable or unfavourable relative to the terms of current market transactions for the same or similar items, the acquirer shall recognise a settlement gain or loss. Paragraph B52 provides guidance for measuring that settlement gain or loss.

Assembled workforce and other items that are not identifiable

B37 The acquirer subsumes into goodwill the value of an acquired intangible asset that is not identifiable as of the acquisition date. For example, an acquirer may attribute value to the existence of an assembled workforce, which is an existing collection of employees that permits the acquirer to continue to operate an acquired business from the acquisition date. An assembled workforce does not represent the intellectual capital of the skilled workforce – the (often specialised) knowledge and experience that employees of an acquiree bring to their jobs. Because the assembled workforce is not an identifiable asset to be recognised separately from goodwill, any value attributed to it is subsumed into goodwill.

B38 The acquirer also subsumes into goodwill any value attributed to items that do not qualify as assets at the acquisition date. For example, the acquirer might attribute value to potential contracts the acquiree is negotiating with prospective new customers at the acquisition date. Because those potential contracts are not themselves assets at the acquisition date, the acquirer does not recognise them separately from goodwill. The acquirer should not subsequently reclassify the value of those contracts from goodwill for events that occur after the acquisition date. However, the acquirer should assess the facts and circumstances surrounding events occurring shortly after the acquisition to determine whether a separately recognisable intangible asset existed at the acquisition date.

B39 After initial recognition, an acquirer accounts for intangible assets acquired in a business combination in accordance with the provisions of AASB 138 *Intangible Assets*. However, as described in paragraph 3 of AASB 138, the accounting for some acquired intangible assets after initial recognition is prescribed by other Australian Accounting Standards.

B40   The identifiability criteria determine whether an intangible asset is recognised separately from goodwill. However, the criteria neither provide guidance for measuring the fair value of an intangible asset nor restrict the assumptions used in estimating the fair value of an intangible asset. For example, the acquirer would take into account assumptions that market participants would consider, such as expectations of future contract renewals, in measuring fair value. It is not necessary for the renewals themselves to meet the identifiability criteria. (However, see paragraph 29, which establishes an exception to the fair value measurement principle for reacquired rights recognised in a business combination.) Paragraphs 36 and 37 of AASB 138 provide guidance for determining whether intangible assets should be combined into a single unit of account with other intangible or tangible assets.

Measuring the fair value of particular identifiable assets and a non-controlling interest in an acquiree (application of paragraphs 18 and 19)

Assets with uncertain cash flows (valuation allowances)

B41   The acquirer shall not recognise a separate valuation allowance as of the acquisition date for assets acquired in a business combination that are measured at their acquisition-date fair values because the effects of uncertainty about future cash flows are included in the fair value measure. For example, because this Standard requires the acquirer to measure acquired receivables, including loans, at their acquisition-date fair values, the acquirer does not recognise a separate valuation allowance for the contractual cash flows that are deemed to be uncollectible at that date.

Assets subject to operating leases in which the acquiree is the lessor

B42   In measuring the acquisition-date fair value of an asset such as a building or a patent that is subject to an operating lease in which the acquiree is the lessor, the acquirer shall take into account the terms of the lease. In other words, the acquirer does not recognise a separate asset or liability if the terms of an operating lease are either favourable or unfavourable when compared with market terms as paragraph B29 requires for leases in which the acquiree is the lessee.

Assets that the acquirer intends not to use or to use in a way that is different from the way other market participants would use them

B43   For competitive or other reasons, the acquirer may intend not to use an acquired asset, for example, a research and development intangible asset, or it may intend to use the asset in a way that is different from the way in which other market participants would use it. Nevertheless, the acquirer shall measure the asset at fair value determined in accordance with its use by other market participants.

Non-controlling interest in an acquiree

B44   This Standard allows the acquirer to measure a non-controlling interest in the acquiree at its fair value at the acquisition date. Sometimes an acquirer will be able to measure the acquisition-date fair value of a non-controlling interest on the basis of active market prices for the equity shares not held by the acquirer. In other situations, however, an active market price for the equity shares will not be available. In those situations, the acquirer would measure the fair value of the non-controlling interest using other valuation techniques.

B45   The fair values of the acquirer's interest in the acquiree and the non-controlling interest on a per-share basis might differ. The main difference is likely to be the inclusion of a control premium in the per-share fair value of the acquirer's interest in the acquiree or, conversely, the inclusion of a discount for lack of control (also referred to as a minority discount) in the per-share fair value of the non-controlling interest.

Measuring goodwill or a gain from a bargain purchase

Measuring the acquisition-date fair value of the acquirer's interest in the acquiree using valuation techniques (application of paragraph 33)

B46 In a business combination achieved without the transfer of consideration, the acquirer must substitute the acquisition-date fair value of its interest in the acquiree for the acquisition-date fair value of the consideration transferred to measure goodwill or a gain on a bargain purchase (see paragraphs 32-34). The acquirer should measure the acquisition-date fair value of its interest in the acquiree using one or more valuation techniques that are appropriate in the circumstances and for which sufficient data are available. If more than one valuation technique is used, the acquirer should evaluate the results of the techniques, considering the relevance and reliability of the inputs used and the extent of the available data.

Special considerations in applying the acquisition method to combinations of mutual entities (application of paragraph 33)

B47 When two mutual entities combine, the fair value of the equity or member interests in the acquiree (or the fair value of the acquiree) may be more reliably measurable than the fair value of the member interests transferred by the acquirer. In that situation, paragraph 33 requires the acquirer to determine the amount of goodwill by using the acquisition-date fair value of the acquiree's equity interests instead of the acquisition-date fair value of the acquirer's equity interests transferred as consideration. In addition, the acquirer in a combination of mutual entities shall recognise the acquiree's net assets as a direct addition to capital or equity in its statement of financial position, not as an addition to retained earnings, which is consistent with the way in which other types of entities apply the acquisition method.

B48 Although they are similar in many ways to other businesses, mutual entities have distinct characteristics that arise primarily because their members are both customers and owners. Members of mutual entities generally expect to receive benefits for their membership, often in the form of reduced fees charged for goods and services or patronage dividends. The portion of patronage dividends allocated to each member is often based on the amount of business the member did with the mutual entity during the year.

B49 A fair value measurement of a mutual entity should include the assumptions that market participants would make about future member benefits as well as any other relevant assumptions market participants would make about the mutual entity. For example, an estimated cash flow model may be used to determine the fair value of a mutual entity. The cash flows used as inputs to the model should be based on the expected cash flows of the mutual entity, which are likely to reflect reductions for member benefits, such as reduced fees charged for goods and services.

Determining what is part of the business combination transaction (application of paragraphs 51 and 52)

B50 The acquirer should consider the following factors, which are neither mutually exclusive nor individually conclusive, to determine whether a transaction is part of the exchange for the acquiree or whether the transaction is separate from the business combination:

    (a)   **the reasons for the transaction** – Understanding the reasons why the parties to the combination (the acquirer and the acquiree and their owners, directors and managers – and their agents) entered into a particular transaction or arrangement may provide insight into whether it is part of the consideration transferred and the assets acquired or liabilities assumed. For example, if a transaction is arranged primarily for the benefit of the acquirer or the combined entity rather than primarily for the benefit of the acquiree or its former owners before the combination, that portion of the transaction price paid (and any related assets or liabilities) is less likely to be part of the exchange for the acquiree. Accordingly, the acquirer would account for that portion separately from the business combination.

    (b)   **who initiated the transaction** – Understanding who initiated the transaction may also provide insight into whether it is part of the exchange for the acquiree.

For example, a transaction or other event that is initiated by the acquirer may be entered into for the purpose of providing future economic benefits to the acquirer or combined entity with little or no benefit received by the acquiree or its former owners before the combination. On the other hand, a transaction or arrangement initiated by the acquiree or its former owners is less likely to be for the benefit of the acquirer or the combined entity and more likely to be part of the business combination transaction.

(c)   **the timing of the transaction** – The timing of the transaction may also provide insight into whether it is part of the exchange for the acquiree. For example, a transaction between the acquirer and the acquiree that takes place during the negotiations of the terms of a business combination may have been entered into in contemplation of the business combination to provide future economic benefits to the acquirer or the combined entity. If so, the acquiree or its former owners before the business combination are likely to receive little or no benefit from the transaction except for benefits they receive as part of the combined entity.

Effective settlement of a pre-existing relationship between the acquirer and acquiree in a business combination (application of paragraph 52(a))

B51   The acquirer and acquiree may have a relationship that existed before they contemplated the business combination, referred to here as a 'pre-existing relationship'. A pre-existing relationship between the acquirer and acquiree may be contractual (for example, vendor and customer or licensor and licensee) or non-contractual (for example, plaintiff and defendant).

B52   If the business combination in effect settles a pre-existing relationship, the acquirer recognises a gain or loss, measured as follows:

(a)   for a pre-existing non-contractual relationship (such as a lawsuit), fair value.

(b)   for a pre-existing contractual relationship, the lesser of (i) and (ii):

   (i)   the amount by which the contract is favourable or unfavourable from the perspective of the acquirer when compared with terms for current market transactions for the same or similar items. (An unfavourable contract is a contract that is unfavourable in terms of current market terms. It is not necessarily an onerous contract in which the unavoidable costs of meeting the obligations under the contract exceed the economic benefits expected to be received under it.)

   (ii)   the amount of any stated settlement provisions in the contract available to the counterparty to whom the contract is unfavourable.

   If (ii) is less than (i), the difference is included as part of the business combination accounting.

The amount of gain or loss recognised may depend in part on whether the acquirer had previously recognised a related asset or liability, and the reported gain or loss therefore may differ from the amount calculated by applying the above requirements.

B53   A pre-existing relationship may be a contract that the acquirer recognises as a reacquired right. If the contract includes terms that are favourable or unfavourable when compared with pricing for current market transactions for the same or similar items, the acquirer recognises, separately from the business combination, a gain or loss for the effective settlement of the contract, measured in accordance with paragraph B52.

Arrangements for contingent payments to employees or selling shareholders (application of paragraph 52(b))

B54   Whether arrangements for contingent payments to employees or selling shareholders are contingent consideration in the business combination or are separate transactions depends on the nature of the arrangements. Understanding the reasons why the acquisition agreement includes a provision for contingent payments, who initiated the arrangement and when the parties entered into the arrangement may be helpful in assessing the nature of the arrangement.

B55 If it is not clear whether an arrangement for payments to employees or selling shareholders is part of the exchange for the acquiree or is a transaction separate from the business combination, the acquirer should consider the following indicators:

(a) *Continuing employment* – The terms of continuing employment by the selling shareholders who become key employees may be an indicator of the substance of a contingent consideration arrangement. The relevant terms of continuing employment may be included in an employment agreement, acquisition agreement or some other document. A contingent consideration arrangement in which the payments are automatically forfeited if employment terminates is remuneration for post-combination services. Arrangements in which the contingent payments are not affected by employment termination may indicate that the contingent payments are additional consideration rather than remuneration.

(b) *Duration of continuing employment* – If the period of required employment coincides with or is longer than the contingent payment period, that fact may indicate that the contingent payments are, in substance, remuneration.

(c) *Level of remuneration* – Situations in which employee remuneration other than the contingent payments is at a reasonable level in comparison with that of other key employees in the combined entity may indicate that the contingent payments are additional consideration rather than remuneration.

(d) *Incremental payments to employees* – If selling shareholders who do not become employees receive lower contingent payments on a per-share basis than the selling shareholders who become employees of the combined entity, that fact may indicate that the incremental amount of contingent payments to the selling shareholders who become employees is remuneration.

(e) *Number of shares owned* – The relative number of shares owned by the selling shareholders who remain as key employees may be an indicator of the substance of the contingent consideration arrangement. For example, if the selling shareholders who owned substantially all of the shares in the acquiree continue as key employees, that fact may indicate that the arrangement is, in substance, a profit-sharing arrangement intended to provide remuneration for post-combination services. Alternatively, if selling shareholders who continue as key employees owned only a small number of shares of the acquiree and all selling shareholders receive the same amount of contingent consideration on a per-share basis, that fact may indicate that the contingent payments are additional consideration. The pre-acquisition ownership interests held by parties related to selling shareholders who continue as key employees, such as family members, should also be considered.

(f) *Linkage to the valuation* – If the initial consideration transferred at the acquisition date is based on the low end of a range established in the valuation of the acquiree and the contingent formula relates to that valuation approach, that fact may suggest that the contingent payments are additional consideration. Alternatively, if the contingent payment formula is consistent with prior profit-sharing arrangements, that fact may suggest that the substance of the arrangement is to provide remuneration.

(g) *Formula for determining consideration* – The formula used to determine the contingent payment may be helpful in assessing the substance of the arrangement. For example, if a contingent payment is determined on the basis of a multiple of earnings, that might suggest that the obligation is contingent consideration in the business combination and that the formula is intended to establish or verify the fair value of the acquiree. In contrast, a contingent payment that is a specified percentage of earnings might suggest that the obligation to employees is a profit-sharing arrangement to remunerate employees for services rendered.

(h) *Other agreements and issues* – The terms of other arrangements with selling shareholders (such as agreements not to compete, executory contracts, consulting contracts and property lease agreements) and the income tax treatment of contingent payments may indicate that contingent payments are attributable to something other than consideration for the acquiree. For example, in connection with the acquisition, the acquirer might enter into a property lease arrangement with a significant selling shareholder. If the lease payments specified in the lease contract are significantly below market, some or all of the contingent payments to the lessor (the selling shareholder) required by a separate arrangement for contingent payments might be, in substance, payments for the use of the leased property that the acquirer should recognise separately in its post-combination financial statements. In contrast, if the lease contract specifies lease payments that are consistent with market terms for the leased property, the arrangement for contingent payments to the selling shareholder may be contingent consideration in the business combination.

Acquirer share-based payment awards exchanged for awards held by the acquiree's employees (application of paragraph 52(b))

B56   An acquirer may exchange its share-based payment awards[1] (replacement awards) for awards held by employees of the acquiree. Exchanges of share options or other share-based payment awards in conjunction with a business combination are accounted for as modifications of share-based payment awards in accordance with AASB 2 *Share-based Payment*. If the acquirer replaces the acquiree awards, either all or a portion of the market-based measure of the acquirer's replacement awards shall be included in measuring the consideration transferred in the business combination. Paragraphs B57-B62 provide guidance on how to allocate the market-based measure. However, in situations in which acquiree awards would expire as a consequence of a business combination and if the acquirer replaces those awards when it is not obliged to do so, all of the market-based measure of the replacement awards shall be recognised as remuneration cost in the post-combination financial statements in accordance with AASB 2. That is to say, none of the market-based measure of those awards shall be included in measuring the consideration transferred in the business combination. The cquirer is obliged to replace the acquiree awards if the acquiree or its employees have the ability to enforce replacement. For example, for the purposes of applying this guidance, the acquirer is obliged to replace the acquiree's awards if replacement is required by:

(a)   the terms of the acquisition agreement;

(b)   the terms of the acquiree's awards; or

(c)   applicable laws or regulations.

B57   To determine the portion of a replacement award that is part of the consideration transferred for the acquiree and the portion that is remuneration for post-combination service, the acquirer shall measure both the replacement awards granted by the acquirer and the acquiree awards as of the acquisition date in accordance with AASB 2. The portion of the market-based measure of the replacement award that is part of the consideration transferred in exchange for the acquiree equals the portion of the acquiree award that is attributable to pre-combination service.

B58   The portion of the replacement award attributable to pre-combination service is the market-based measure of the acquiree award multiplied by the ratio of the portion of the vesting period completed to the greater of the total vesting period or the original vesting period of the acquiree award. The vesting period is the period during which all the specified vesting conditions are to be satisfied. Vesting conditions are defined in AASB 2.

B59   The portion of a non-vested replacement award attributable to post-combination service, and therefore recognised as remuneration cost in the post-combination financial statements, equals the total market-based measure of the replacement award less the amount attributed to pre-combination service. Therefore, the acquirer attributes any excess of the market-based measure of the replacement award over the market-based measure of the acquiree award to post-combination service and recognises that excess as remuneration cost in the post-combination financial statements. The acquirer shall attribute a portion of a replacement award to post-combination service if it requires post-combination service, regardless of whether employees had rendered all of the service required for their acquiree awards to vest before the acquisition date.

---

1   In paragraphs B56-B62 the term 'share-based payment awards' refers to vested or unvested share-based payment transactions.

B60 The portion of a non-vested replacement award attributable to pre-combination service, as well as the portion attributable to post-combination service, shall reflect the best available estimate of the number of replacement awards expected to vest. For example, if the market-based measure of the portion of a replacement award attributed to pre-combination service is CU100 and the acquirer expects that only 95 er cent of the award will vest, the amount included in consideration transferred in the business combination is CU95. Changes in the estimated number of replacement awards expected to vest are reflected in remuneration cost for the periods in which the changes or forfeitures occur not as adjustments to the consideration transferred in the business combination. Similarly, the effects of other events, such as modifications or the ultimate outcome of awards with performance conditions, that occur after the acquisition date are accounted for in accordance with AASB 2 in determining remuneration cost for the period in which an event occurs.

B61 The same requirements for determining the portions of a replacement award attributable to pre-combination and post-combination service apply regardless of whether a replacement award is classified as a liability or as an equity instrument in accordance with the provisions of AASB 2. All changes in the market-based measure of awards classified as liabilities after the acquisition date and the related income tax effects are recognised in the acquirer's post-combination financial statements in the period(s) in which the changes occur.

B62 The income tax effects of replacement awards of share-based payments shall be recognised in accordance with the provisions of AASB 112 *Income Taxes*.

Equity-settled share-based payment transactions of the acquiree

B62A The acquiree may have outstanding share-based payment transactions that the acquirer does not exchange for its share-based payment transactions. If vested, those acquiree share-based payment transactions are part of the non-controlling interest in the acquiree and are measured at their market-based measure. If unvested, they are measured at their market-based measure as if the acquisition date were the grant date in accordance with paragraphs 19 and 30.

B62B The market-based measure of unvested share-based payment transactions is allocated to the non-controlling interest on the basis of the ratio of the portion of the vesting period completed to the greater of the total vesting period and the original vesting period of the share-based payment transaction. The balance is allocated to post-combination service.

Other Australian Accounting Standards that provide guidance on subsequent measurement and accounting (application of paragraph 54)

B63 Examples of other Australian Accounting Standards that provide guidance on subsequently measuring and accounting for assets acquired and liabilities assumed or incurred in a business combination include:

(a) AASB 138 prescribes the accounting for identifiable intangible assets acquired in a business combination. The acquirer measures goodwill at the amount recognised at the acquisition date less any accumulated impairment losses. AASB 136 *Impairment of Assets* prescribes the accounting for impairment losses.

(b) AASB 4 *Insurance Contracts* provides guidance on the subsequent accounting for an insurance contract acquired in a business combination.

(c) AASB 112 prescribes the subsequent accounting for deferred tax assets (including unrecognised deferred tax assets) and liabilities acquired in a business combination.

(d) AASB 2 provides guidance on subsequent measurement and accounting for the portion of replacement share-based payment awards issued by an acquirer that is attributable to employees' future services.

(e) AASB 127 (as amended in March 2008) provides guidance on accounting for changes in a parent's ownership interest in a subsidiary after control is obtained.

Disclosures (application of paragraphs 59 and 61)

B64   To meet the objective in paragraph 59, the acquirer shall disclose the following information for each business combination that occurs during the reporting period:

(a)   the name and a description of the acquiree.

(b)   the acquisition date.

(c)   the percentage of voting equity interests acquired.

(d)   the primary reasons for the business combination and a description of how the acquirer obtained control of the acquiree.

(e)   a qualitative description of the factors that make up the goodwill recognised, such as expected synergies from combining operations of the acquiree and the acquirer, intangible assets that do not qualify for separate recognition or other factors.

(f)   the acquisition-date fair value of the total consideration transferred and the acquisition-date fair value of each major class of consideration, such as:

    (i)   cash;

    (ii)   other tangible or intangible assets, including a business or subsidiary of the acquirer;

    (iii)   liabilities incurred, for example, a liability for contingent consideration; and

    (iv)   equity interests of the acquirer, including the number of instruments or interests issued or issuable and the method of determining the fair value of those instruments or interests.

(g)   for contingent consideration arrangements and indemnification assets:

    (i)   the amount recognised as of the acquisition date;

    (ii)   a description of the arrangement and the basis for determining the amount of the payment; and

    (iii)   an estimate of the range of outcomes (undiscounted) or, if a range cannot be estimated, that fact and the reasons why a range cannot be estimated. If the maximum amount of the payment is unlimited, the acquirer shall disclose that fact.

(h)   for acquired receivables:

    (i)   the fair value of the receivables;

    (ii)   the gross contractual amounts receivable; and

    (iii)   the best estimate at the acquisition date of the contractual cash flows not expected to be collected.

The disclosures shall be provided by major class of receivable, such as loans, direct finance leases and any other class of receivables.

(i)   the amounts recognised as of the acquisition date for each major class of assets acquired and liabilities assumed.

(j)   for each contingent liability recognised in accordance with paragraph 23, the information required in paragraph 85 of AASB 137 *Provisions, Contingent Liabilities and Contingent Assets*. If a contingent liability is not recognised because its fair value cannot be measured reliably, the acquirer shall disclose:

    (i)   the information required by paragraph 86 of AASB 137; and

    (ii)   the reasons why the liability cannot be measured reliably.

(k)   the total amount of goodwill that is expected to be deductible for tax purposes.

(l)   for transactions that are recognised separately from the acquisition of assets and assumption of liabilities in the business combination in accordance with paragraph 51:

    (i)   a description of each transaction;

    (ii)   how the acquirer accounted for each transaction;

AASB

    (iii)   the amounts recognised for each transaction and the line item in the financial statements in which each amount is recognised; and

    (iv)   if the transaction is the effective settlement of a pre-existing relationship, the method used to determine the settlement amount.

(m)   the disclosure of separately recognised transactions required by (l) shall include the amount of acquisition-related costs and, separately, the amount of those costs recognised as an expense and the line item or items in the statement of comprehensive income in which those expenses are recognised. The amount of any issue costs not recognised as an expense and how they were recognised shall also be disclosed.

(n)   in a bargain purchase (see paragraphs 34-36):

    (i)   the amount of any gain recognised in accordance with paragraph 34 and the line item in the statement of comprehensive income in which the gain is recognised; and

    (ii)   a description of the reasons why the transaction resulted in a gain.

(o)   for each business combination in which the acquirer holds less than 100 per cent of the equity interests in the acquiree at the acquisition date:

    (i)   the amount of the non-controlling interest in the acquiree recognised at the acquisition date and the measurement basis for that amount; and

    (ii)   for each non-controlling interest in an acquiree measured at fair value, the valuation techniques and key model inputs used for determining that value.

(p)   in a business combination achieved in stages:

    (i)   the acquisition-date fair value of the equity interest in the acquiree held by the acquirer immediately before the acquisition date; and

    (ii)   the amount of any gain or loss recognised as a result of remeasuring to fair value the equity interest in the acquiree held by the acquirer before the business combination (see paragraph 42) and the line item in the statement of comprehensive income in which that gain or loss is recognised.

(q)   the following information:

    (i)   the amounts of revenue and profit or loss of the acquiree since the acquisition date included in the consolidated statement of comprehensive income for the reporting period; and

    (ii)   the revenue and profit or loss of the combined entity for the current reporting period as though the acquisition date for all business combinations that occurred during the year had been as of the beginning of the annual reporting period.

If disclosure of any of the information required by this subparagraph is impracticable, the acquirer shall disclose that fact and explain why the disclosure is impracticable. This Standard uses the term 'impracticable' with the same meaning as in AASB 108 *Accounting Policies, Changes in Accounting Estimates and Errors*.

B65   For individually immaterial business combinations occurring during the reporting period that are material collectively, the acquirer shall disclose in aggregate the information required by paragraph B64(e)-(q).

B66   If the acquisition date of a business combination is after the end of the reporting period but before the financial statements are authorised for issue, the acquirer shall disclose the information required by paragraph B64 unless the initial accounting for the business combination is incomplete at the time the financial statements are authorised for issue. In that situation, the acquirer shall describe which disclosures could not be made and the reasons why they cannot be made.

B67   To meet the objective in paragraph 61, the acquirer shall disclose the following information for each material business combination or in the aggregate for individually immaterial business combinations that are material collectively:

(a)   if the initial accounting for a business combination is incomplete (see paragraph 45) for particular assets, liabilities, non-controlling interests or items of consideration and the amounts recognised in the financial statements for the business combination thus have been determined only provisionally:

    (i)   the reasons why the initial accounting for the business combination is incomplete;

    (ii)   the assets, liabilities, equity interests or items of consideration for which the initial accounting is incomplete; and

    (iii)   the nature and amount of any measurement period adjustments recognised during the reporting period in accordance with paragraph 49.

(b)   for each reporting period after the acquisition date until the entity collects, sells or otherwise loses the right to a contingent consideration asset, or until the entity settles a contingent consideration liability or the liability is cancelled or expires:

    (i)   any changes in the recognised amounts, including any differences arising upon settlement;

    (ii)   any changes in the range of outcomes (undiscounted) and the reasons for those changes; and

    (iii)   the valuation techniques and key model inputs used to measure contingent consideration.

(c)   for contingent liabilities recognised in a business combination, the acquirer shall disclose the information required by paragraphs 84 and 85 of AASB 137 for each class of provision.

(d)   a reconciliation of the carrying amount of goodwill at the beginning and end of the reporting period showing separately:

    (i)   the gross amount and accumulated impairment losses at the beginning of the reporting period.

    (ii)   additional goodwill recognised during the reporting period, except goodwill included in a disposal group that, on acquisition, meets the criteria to be classified as held for sale in accordance with AASB 5 *Non-current Assets Held for Sale and Discontinued Operations*.

    (iii)   adjustments resulting from the subsequent recognition of deferred tax assets during the reporting period in accordance with paragraph 67.

    (iv)   goodwill included in a disposal group classified as held for sale in accordance with AASB 5 and goodwill derecognised during the reporting period without having previously been included in a disposal group classified as held for sale.

    (v)   impairment losses recognised during the reporting period in accordance with AASB 136. (AASB 136 requires disclosure of information about the recoverable amount and impairment of goodwill in addition to this requirement.)

    (vi)   net exchange rate differences arising during the reporting period in accordance with AASB 121 *The Effects of Changes in Foreign Exchange Rates*.

    (vii)   any other changes in the carrying amount during the reporting period.

    (viii) the gross amount and accumulated impairment losses at the end of the reporting period.

(e)   the amount and an explanation of any gain or loss recognised in the current reporting period that both:

    (i)   relates to the identifiable assets acquired or liabilities assumed in a business combination that was effected in the current or previous reporting period; and

    (ii)   is of such a size, nature or incidence that disclosure is relevant to understanding the combined entity's financial statements.

Transitional provisions for business combinations involving only mutual entities or by contract alone (application of paragraph 66)

AASB

B68 [Deleted by the AASB]

AusB68 Paragraph Aus1.2 provides that this Standard applies prospectively to business combinations for which the acquisition date is on or after the beginning of the first annual reporting period beginning on or after 1 July 2009. Paragraph Aus1.3 allows earlier application by for-profit entities only. However, an entity shall apply this Standard only at the beginning of an annual reporting period that begins on or after 30 June 2007. If an entity applies this Standard before its effective date, the entity shall disclose that fact and shall apply AASB 127 (as amended in March 2008) at the same time.

B69 The requirement to apply this Standard prospectively has the following effect for a business combination involving only mutual entities or by contract alone if the acquisition date for that business combination is before the application of this Standard:

(a) *Classification* – An entity shall continue to classify the prior business combination in accordance with the entity's previous accounting policies for such combinations.

(b) *Previously recognised goodwill* – At the beginning of the first annual period in which this Standard is applied, the carrying amount of goodwill arising from the prior business combination shall be its carrying amount at that date in accordance with the entity's previous accounting policies. In determining that amount, the entity shall eliminate the carrying amount of any accumulated amortisation of that goodwill and the corresponding decrease in goodwill. No other adjustments shall be made to the carrying amount of goodwill.

(c) *Goodwill previously recognised as a deduction from equity* – The entity's previous accounting policies may have resulted in goodwill arising from the prior business combination being recognised as a deduction from equity. In that situation the entity shall not recognise that goodwill as an asset at the beginning of the first annual period in which this Standard is applied. Furthermore, the entity shall not recognise in profit or loss any part of that goodwill when it disposes of all or part of the business to which that goodwill relates or when a cash-generating unit to which the goodwill relates becomes impaired.

(d) *Subsequent accounting for goodwill* – From the beginning of the first annual period in which this Standard is applied, an entity shall discontinue amortising goodwill arising from the prior business combination and shall test goodwill for impairment in accordance with AASB 136.

(e) *Previously recognised negative goodwill* – An entity that accounted for the prior business combination by applying the purchase method may have recognised a deferred credit for an excess of its interest in the net fair value of the acquiree's identifiable assets and liabilities over the cost of that interest (sometimes called negative goodwill). If so, the entity shall derecognise the carrying amount of that deferred credit at the beginning of the first annual period in which this Standard is applied with a corresponding adjustment to the opening balance of retained earnings at that date.

Deleted IFRS 3 Text

Deleted IFRS 3 text is not part of AASB 3.

Paragraph 64

This IFRS shall be applied prospectively to business combinations for which the acquisition date is on or after the beginning of the first annual reporting period beginning on or after 1 July 2009. Earlier application is permitted. However, this IFRS shall be applied only at the beginning of an annual reporting period that begins on or after 30 June 2007. If an entity applies this IFRS before 1 July 2009, it shall disclose that fact and apply IAS 27 (as amended in 2008) at the same time.

Paragraph 68

This IFRS supersedes IFRS 3 *Business Combinations* (as issued in 2004).

Paragraph B68

Paragraph 64 provides that this IFRS applies prospectively to business combinations for which the acquisition date is on or after the beginning of the first annual reporting period beginning on or after 1 July 2009. Earlier application is permitted. However, an entity shall apply this IFRS only at the beginning of an annual reporting period that begins on or after 30 June 2007. If an entity applies this IFRS before its effective date, the entity shall disclose that fact and shall apply IAS 27 (as amended in 2008) at the same time.

Basis for Conclusions on AASB 2008-11

This Basis for Conclusions accompanies, but is not part of, AASB 3. The Basis for Conclusions was originally published with AASB 2008-11 Amendments to Australian Accounting Standard – Business Combinations Among Not-for-Profit Entities.

Background

BC1   This Basis for Conclusions summarises the Australian Accounting Standards Board's (AASB) decisions in reaching the conclusions in this Standard. Individual Board members gave greater weight to some factors than to others.

Significant Issues

BC2   The AASB issued a revised AASB 3 *Business Combinations* in March 2008. At that time, the Board decided that the requirements of AASB 3 (March 2008) should only be available for early adoption by for-profit entities, until further work was undertaken on the implications of applying the requirements of AASB 3 (March 2008) to not-for-profit entities. Accordingly, the Board included in the Preface to AASB 3 (March 2008) the following statement:

> Prior to the mandatory application date of this Standard, being 1 July 2009, the AASB will consider its suitability for combinations among not-for-profit entities. In doing so, the AASB will have regard to the criteria being developed for judging when IFRSs should be modified for application by not-for-profit entities. Those criteria will assist in clarifying whether this Standard should be amended to include an additional scope exclusion or other amendments and, if so, the extent of that exclusion or other amendments in an Australian not-for-profit context. In light of this, not-for-profit entities cannot adopt this Standard prior to the mandatory application date.

BC3   As part of its subsequent deliberations, the Board noted the view of some that the difficulties in applying the acquisition method when a business combination does not involve consideration (including the difficulties of identifying an acquirer), which is often the case in business combinations among not-for-profit entities, means that the principles in AASB 3 (March 2008) are inappropriate for such combinations. However, the Board decided that, in principle, there is no conceptual basis for accounting for business combinations among not-for-profit entities differently from other analogous types of business combinations.

BC4 In particular, the Board noted that the types of difficulties noted in paragraph BC3 are also issues that may be encountered in business combinations of for-profit entities (such as combinations by contract alone). Therefore, consistent with transaction-neutral principles, the Board did not consider that there was sufficient reason to justify a different accounting treatment for business combinations among not-for-profit entities.

BC5 The Board observed that the motivations for business combinations among not-for-profit entities, such as to provide their beneficiaries with a broader range of, or access to, services and cost savings through economies of scale, are similar to those for business combinations among other entities. The Board noted a possible alternative to the acquisition method in AASB 3 for business combinations among not-for-profit entities might be the 'fresh start' method, especially where it is difficult to identify the acquirer. The fresh start method assumes that none of the combining entities survives the business combination as an independent reporting entity. Rather, the business combination is viewed as a transfer of the net assets of the combining entities to a new entity that assumes control over them. The Board noted the potential significant costs and practical difficulties that a fresh start alternative would impose, and therefore concluded that the potential advantages of using the fresh start method for some business combinations among not-for-profit entities would be outweighed by the disadvantages.

BC6 However, the Board noted that the accounting for business combinations may differ depending on whether entities, such as local governments or universities, are commonly controlled. In that regard, the Board confirmed that further work should be undertaken on its longer-term 'control in the public sector' project, which should include consideration of whether local governments or universities within a jurisdiction are subject to common control.

BC7 In the interim, the Board decided to maintain the status quo in respect of accounting for restructures of local governments by substantially incorporating the requirements originally transferred from AAS 27 *Financial Reporting by Local Governments* to superseded AASB 3 (as amended in December 2007 by AASB 2007-9 *Amendments to Australian Accounting Standards arising from the Review of AASs 27, 29 and 31*) into revised AASB 3 (March 2008, as amended). The Board noted that the relief carried forward from AAS 27 might be impacted by the progress it makes on its 'control in the public sector' project.

BC8 The Board noted that this approach to restructures of local governments, consistent with its general approach to the short-term review of AASs 27, 29 and 31, is pragmatic and a consequence of the past requirements in AAS 27.

BC9 The Board also considered the amendments made by the New Zealand Financial Reporting Standards Board to revised NZ IFRS 3 *Business Combinations* (March 2008) in the context of business combinations among not-for-profit entities, including definitions of public benefit entities, business and equity interests. In making its decision, the Board considered the work undertaken to date on Invitation to Comment ITC 14 *Not-for-Profit Entity Definition and Guidance*, which sought input on using the definition and guidance from NZ IAS 1 *Presentation of Financial Statements* in Australia. The Board suspended further work on ITC 14 until the development of guidelines that can be used for modifying IFRSs for application by not-for-profit entities. In light of this, the Board decided that no further changes should be made to AASB 3 (March 2008, as amended) in respect of not-for-profit entities.

AASB 4
Insurance Contracts

(Compiled November 2010)

Note from the Institute of Chartered Accountants Australia

This note, prepared by the technical editors, is not part of the Accounting Standard AASB 4.

Historical development

July 2004: AASB 4 'Insurance Contracts' is the Australian equivalent of IFRS 4 of the same name. It was made by the AASB on 15 July 2004 as part of the AASB's program to adopt International Financial Reporting Standards (IFRSs) by 2005.

The AASB has adopted the requirements of IFRS 4 across three Standards, namely AASB 4, AASB 1023 'General Insurance Contracts' and AASB 1038 'Life Insurance Contracts'.

5 September 2005: AASB 2005-10 'Amendments to Australian Accounting Standards' adds paragraphs 35(d), 39(a), and amends paragraphs 2(b), 3, 38, and 39. These amendments are applicable to annual reporting periods beginning on or after 1 January 2007, with early adoption permitted for annual reporting periods beginning on or after 1 January 2005.

6 September 2005: AASB 2005-9 'Amendments to Australian Accounting Standards' adds paragraph 41A and Appendix A, and amends paragraphs 4(d), B18(g), and B19(f). These amendments are applicable to annual reporting periods beginning on or after 1 January 2006, with early adoption permitted for annual reporting periods beginning on or after 1 January 2005.

30 April 2007: AASB 2007-4 'Amendments to Australian Accounting Standards' amends paragraphs 3, 4, 17, 31, 33, 35, B7 and B18, and IG 2, 3 and 5 is applicable to annual reporting periods beginning on or after 1 July 2007. Entities may elect to early-adopt it to annual reporting periods beginning on or after 1 January 2005.

28 June 2007: AASB 2007-7 'Amendments to Australian Accounting Standards' Implementation Guidance paragraphs IGI-IG71 and is applicable to annual reporting periods beginning on or after 1 July 2007. Entities may elect to early-adopt it to annual reporting periods beginning on or after 1 January 2005.

24 September 2007: AASB 2007-8 'Amendments to Australian Accounting Standards' was issued by the AASB. This Standard is applicable to annual reporting periods beginning on or after 1 January 2009.

13 December 2007: AASB 2007-10 'Further Amendments to Australian Accounting Standards arising from AASB 101' amends AASB 4, replacing the term 'financial report' with 'financial statements'. This Standard is applicable to annual reporting periods beginning on or after 1 January 2009.

6 March 2008: AASB 2008-3 'Amendments to Australian Accounting Standards arising from AASB 3 and AASB 127' amends AASB 4 for the issue of AASB 3 Revised. This Standard is applicable to annual reporting periods beginning on or after 1 July 2009.

22 April 2009: AASB 2009-2 'Amendments to Australian Accounting Standards – Improving Disclosures about Financial Instruments' amends AASB 4 consequentially to the AASB 7 amendments requiring enhanced disclosures about fair value measurements and liquidity risk. This Standard is applicable to annual reporting periods beginning on or after 1 January 2009 that end on or after 30 April 2009.

23 October 2009: AASB 4 was reissued by the AASB, compiled to include the AASB 2007-8, AASB 2007-10, AASB 2008-3 and AASB 2009-2 amendments and applies to annual reporting periods beginning on or after 1 July 2009. Early application is permitted.

On the same date the AASB reissued the version of AASB 4 applicable to annual reporting periods beginning on or after 1 January 2009 but before 1 July 2009. This version of AASB 4 has been compiled for the amending Standards applying to annual reporting periods beginning on or after 1 January 2009. This Standard can be accessed from the AASB website at www.aasb.gov.au.

---

7 December 2009: AASB 2009-11 'Amendments to Australian Accounting Standards arising from AASB 9' amends AASB 4 to give effect to consequential changes arising from the issuance of AASB 9. This Standard is applicable to annual reporting periods beginning on or after 1 January 2013 with early adoption permitted from annual reporting periods ending on or after 31 December 2009 that begin before 1 January 2013 provided AASB 9 is also applied for the same period. The application date of AASB 2009-11 has been amended to 1 January 2015 by AASB 2012-6. **These amendments have been superseded by AASB 2010-7 and are not included in this compiled Standard.**

27 October 2010: AASB 2010-5 'Further Amendments to Australian Accounting Standards' makes editorial amendments to AASB 4. This Standard is applicable to annual reporting periods beginning on or after 1 January 2011.

26 November 2010: AASB 4 was reissued by the AASB, compiled to include the AASB 2009-12 and AASB 2010-5 amendments and applies to annual reporting periods ending on or after 1 January 2011.

1 March 2011: AASB 2010-7 'Amendments to Australian Accounting Standards arising from AASB 9 (December 2010)' as compiled amends AASB 4 to give effect to consequential changes arising from the reissue of AASB 9 in December 2010 and supersedes AASB 2009-11 which related to the previous version of AASB 9. This Standard applies to annual reporting periods beginning on or after 1 January 2013 and can be adopted early. The application date of AASB 2010-7 has been amended to 1 January 2015 by AASB 2012-6. **These amendments are not included in this compiled Standard.**

2 September 2011: AASB 2011-8 'Amendments to Australian Accounting Standards arising from AASB 13' amends AASB 4 to give effect to a consequential change in the definition of fair value arising from the issue of AASB 13. This Standard applies to annual reporting periods beginning on or after 1 January 2013 and can be adopted early. **These amendments are not included in this compiled Standard.**

Reference

IFRIC items not taken onto the agenda: IFRS 4-1 *Discretionary participation features in insurance contracts or forward liabilities* and IFRS 4-2 *Scope issue for REITS* apply to AASB 4.

AASB 4 compared to IFRS 4

Additions

Paragraph	Description
Aus 1.1	Which entities AASB 4 applies to (i.e. reporting entities and general purpose financial reports).
Aus 1.2	The application date of AASB 4 (i.e. annual reporting periods beginning 1 January 2005).
Aus 1.3	Prohibits early application of AASB 4.
Aus 1.4	Makes the requirements of AASB 4 subject to AASB 1031 'Materiality'.
Aus 1.5	Notice of the new Standard published on 22 July 2004.
Aus 3.1	Clarifies this Standard does not apply to contracts covered by AASB 1023 and 1038
Aus 6.1	Clarifies that AASB 4 applies to fixed fee service contracts where the level of service depends on an uncertain future event (e.g. roadside assistance contracts).
Appendix	Additional Australian defined terms for 'general insurance contract' and 'life insurance contract'.

Deletions

Paragraph	Description
41	Effective date of IFRS 4.

Contents

Compilation Details
Comparison with IFRS 4
Accounting Standard
AASB 4 Insurance Contracts

	Paragraphs
Objective	1
Application	Aus1.1 – Aus1.5
Scope	2 – Aus6.1
Embedded derivatives	7 – 9
Unbundling of deposit components	10 – 12
Recognition and Measurement	
Temporary exemption from some other Australian Accounting Standards	13 – 14
Liability adequacy test	15 – 19
Impairment of reinsurance assets	20
Changes in accounting policies	21 – 23
Current market interest rates	24
Continuation of existing practices	25
Prudence	26
Future investment margins	27 – 29
Shadow accounting	30
Insurance contracts acquired in a business combination or portfolio transfer	31 – 33
Discretionary participation features	
Discretionary participation features in insurance contracts	34
Discretionary participation features in financial instruments	35
Disclosure	
Explanation of recognised amounts	36 – 37
Nature and extent of risks arising from insurance contracts	38 – 39A
Effective Date and Transition	40
Disclosure	42 – 44
Redesignation of financial assets	45

Appendices:
A. Defined terms
B. Definition of an insurance contract

Implementation Guidance on IFRS 4
(available on the AASB website)

Basis for conclusions on IFRS 4
(available on the AASB website)

Australian Accounting Standard AASB 4 *Insurance Contracts* (as amended) is set out in paragraphs 1 – 45 and Appendices A – B. All the paragraphs have equal authority. Paragraphs in **bold type** state the main principles. Terms defined in this Standard are in *italics* the first time they appear in the Standard. AASB 4 is to be read in the context of other Australian Accounting Standards, including AASB 1048 *Interpretation of Standards*, which identifies the Australian Accounting Interpretations. In the absence of explicit guidance, AASB 108 *Accounting Policies, Changes in Accounting Estimates and Errors* provides a basis for selecting and applying accounting policies.

Compilation Details

Accounting Standard AASB 4 *Insurance Contracts* as amended

This compiled Standard applies to annual reporting periods beginning on or after 1 January 2011. It takes into account amendments up to and including 27 October 2010 and was prepared on 26 November 2010 by the staff of the Australian Accounting Standards Board (AASB).

This compilation is not a separate Accounting Standard made by the AASB. Instead, it is a representation of AASB 4 (July 2004) as amended by other Accounting Standards, which are listed in the Table below.

Table of Standards

Standard	Date made	Application date *(annual reporting periods ... on or after ...)*	Application, saving or transitional provisions
AASB 4	15 Jul 2004	*(beginning)* 1 Jan 2005	
AASB 2005-9	6 Sep 2005	*(beginning)* 1 Jan 2006	see (a) below
AASB 2005-10	5 Sep 2005	*(beginning)* 1 Jan 2007	see (b) below
AASB 2007-4	30 Apr 2007	*(beginning)* 1 Jul 2007	see (c) below
AASB 2007-7	28 Jun 2007	*(beginning)* 1 Jul 2007	see (c) below
AASB 2007-8	24 Sep 2007	*(beginning)* 1 Jan 2009	see (d) below
AASB 2007-10	13 Dec 2007	*(beginning)* 1 Jan 2009	see (d) below
AASB 2008-3	6 Mar 2008	*(beginning)* 1 Jul 2009	see (e) below
AASB 2009-2	22 Apr 2009	*(beginning)* 1 Jan 2009 and *(ending)* 30 Apr 2009	see (f) below
AASB 2010-5	27 Oct 2010	*(beginning)* 1 Jan 2011	see (g) below

(a) Entities may elect to apply this Standard to annual reporting periods beginning on or after 1 January 2005 but before 1 January 2006.

(b) Entities may elect to apply this Standard to annual reporting periods beginning on or after 1 January 2005 but before 1 January 2007.

(c) Entities may elect to apply this Standard to annual reporting periods beginning on or after 1 January 2005 but before 1 July 2007.

(d) Entities may elect to apply this Standard to annual reporting periods beginning on or after 1 January 2005 but before 1 January 2009, provided that AASB 101 *Presentation of Financial Statements* (September 2007) is also applied to such periods.

(e) Entities may elect to apply this Standard to annual reporting periods beginning on or after 30 June 2007 but before 1 July 2009, provided that AASB 3 *Business Combinations* (March 2008) and AASB 127 *Consolidated and Separate Financial Statements* (March 2008) are also applied to such periods.

(f) Entities may elect to apply this Standard to annual reporting periods beginning on or after 1 January 2005 but before 1 January 2009 and to annual reporting periods beginning on or after 1 January 2009 that end before 30 April 2009.

(g) Entities may elect to apply this Standard to annual reporting periods beginning on or after 1 January 2005 but before 1 January 2011.

Table of Amendments to Standard

Paragraph affected	How affected	By ... [paragraph]
2	amended	AASB 2005-10 [36]
3	amended	AASB 2005-10 [37]
	amended	AASB 2007-4 [20]
Aus3.1	added	AASB 2010-5 [17]
4	amended	AASB 2005-9 [7, 25]
	amended	AASB 2007-4 [20]
Aus4.1–Aus4.2	deleted	AASB 2010-5 [17]

Paragraph affected	How affected	By ... [paragraph]
14	amended	AASB 2007-8 [6]
15	amended	AASB 2007-8 [6]
17	amended	AASB 2007-4 [20]
30	amended	AASB 2007-8 [20]
31	amended	AASB 2007-4 [20]
33	amended	AASB 2007-4 [20]
34	amended	AASB 2008-3 [8]
35	amended amended	AASB 2005-10 [38] AASB 2007-4 [20]
37	amended	AASB 2007-8 [6]
38 (and preceding heading)	amended	AASB 2005-10 [39]
39	amended amended amended	AASB 2005-10 [39] AASB 2007-8 [6] AASB 2009-2 [7]
39A	added amended	AASB 2005-10 [40] AASB 2007-8 [20]
40	amended	AASB 2010-5 [18]
41A	note added	AASB 2005-9 [8]
41B	note added	AASB 2007-8 [21]
Appendix A	amended	AASB 2005-9 [9]
B7	amended	AASB 2007-4 [20]
B18	amended amended amended	AASB 2005-9 [10] AASB 2005-9 [25] AASB 2007-4 [20]
B19	amended	AASB 2005-9 [11]

Table of Amendments to Implementation Guidance

Paragraph affected	How affected	By ... [paragraph]
IG1-IG71 (all)	deleted	AASB 2007-7 [9]
IG Example 2	amended	AASB 2007-4 [20]
IG Example 3	amended	AASB 2007-4 [20]
IG Example 5	amended	AASB 2007-4 [20]

General Terminology Amendments

References to 'financial report(s)' were amended to 'financial statements' by AASB 2007-8 and AASB 2007-10, except in relation to specific Corporations Act references. These amendments are not shown in the above Tables of Amendments.

Comparison with IFRS 4

AASB 4 and IFRS 4

AASB 4 *Insurance Contracts* as amended incorporates IFRS 4 *Insurance Contracts* as issued and amended by the International Accounting Standards Board (IASB). Paragraphs that have been added to this Standard (and do not appear in the text of IFRS 4) are identified with the prefix "Aus", followed by the number of the preceding IASB paragraph and decimal numbering.

Compliance with IFRS 4

Entities that comply with AASB 4 as amended will simultaneously be in compliance with IFRS 4 as amended.

Accounting Standard AASB 4

The Australian Accounting Standards Board made Accounting Standard AASB 4 *Insurance Contracts* under section 334 of the *Corporations Act 2001* on 15 July 2004.

This compiled version of AASB 4 applies to annual reporting periods beginning on or after 1 January 2011. It incorporates relevant amendments contained in other AASB Standards made by the AASB up to and including 27 October 2010 (see Compilation Details).

Accounting Standard AASB 4

Insurance Contracts

Objective

1   The objective of this Standard, in conjunction with AASB 1023 *General Insurance Contracts* and AASB 1038 *Life Insurance Contracts*, is to specify the financial reporting for *insurance contracts* by any entity that issues such contracts (described in this Standard as an *insurer*) until the AASB and IASB complete the second phase of the insurance project. In particular, this Standard requires:

   (a)   limited improvements to accounting by insurers for insurance contracts; and

   (b)   disclosure that identifies and explains the amounts in an insurer's financial statements arising from insurance contracts and helps users of those financial statements understand the amount, timing and uncertainty of future cash flows from insurance contracts.

Application

Aus1.1   **This Standard applies to:**

   (a)   each entity that is required to prepare financial reports in accordance with Part 2M.3 of the Corporations Act and that is a reporting entity;

   (b)   general purpose financial statements of each other reporting entity; and

   (c)   financial statements that are, or are held out to be, general purpose financial statements.

Aus1.2   **This Standard applies to annual reporting periods beginning on or after 1 January 2005.**

   [Note: For application dates of paragraphs changed or added by an amending Standard, see Compilation Details.]

Aus1.3   **This Standard shall not be applied to annual reporting periods beginning before 1 January 2005.**

Aus1.4   **The requirements specified in this Standard apply to the financial statements where information resulting from their application is material in accordance with AASB 1031** *Materiality***.**

Aus1.5   Notice of this Standard was published in the *Commonwealth of Australia Gazette* No S 294, 22 July 2004.

Scope

2   An entity shall apply this Standard to:

  (a)   insurance contracts (including *reinsurance contracts*) that it issues and reinsurance contracts that it holds; and

  (b)   financial instruments that it issues with a *discretionary participation feature* (see paragraph 35). AASB 7 *Financial Instruments: Disclosures* requires disclosure about financial instruments, including financial instruments that contain such features.

3   This Standard does not address other aspects of accounting by insurers, such as accounting for financial assets held by insurers and financial liabilities issued by insurers (see AASB 132 *Financial Instruments: Presentation*, AASB 139 *Financial Instruments: Recognition and Measurement* and AASB 7), except in the transitional provisions in paragraph 45.

Aus3.1   An entity shall not apply this Standard to:

  (a)   *general insurance contracts* (see AASB 1023 *General Insurance Contracts*), except for fixed-fee service contracts that meet the definition of an insurance contract under this Standard; and

  (b)   *life insurance contracts* (see AASB 1038 Life *Insurance Contracts*).

4   An entity shall not apply this Standard to:

  (a)   product warranties issued directly by a manufacturer, dealer or retailer (see AASB 118 *Revenue* and AASB 137 *Provisions, Contingent Liabilities and Contingent Assets*);

  (b)   employers' assets and liabilities under employee benefit plans (see AASB 119 *Employee Benefits* and AASB 2 *Share-based Payment*) and retirement benefit obligations reported by defined benefit retirement plans (see AAS 25 *Financial Reporting by Superannuation Plans*);

  (c)   contractual rights or contractual obligations that are contingent on the future use of, or right to use, a non-financial item (for example, some licence fees, royalties, contingent lease payments and similar items), as well as a lessee's residual value guarantee embedded in a finance lease (see AASB 117 *Leases*, AASB 118 *Revenue* and AASB 138 *Intangible Assets*);

  (d)   *financial guarantee contracts* unless the issuer has previously asserted explicitly that it regards such contracts as insurance contracts and has used accounting applicable to insurance contracts, in which case the issuer may elect to apply either AASB 139, AASB 132 and AASB 7 or AASB 1023 to such financial guarantee contracts. The issuer may make that election contract by contract, but the election for each contract is irrevocable;

  (e)   contingent consideration payable or receivable in a business combination (see AASB 3 *Business Combinations*); and

  (f)   *direct insurance contracts* that the entity holds (i.e. direct insurance contracts in which the entity is the *policyholder*). However, a *cedant* shall apply this Standard to reinsurance contracts that it holds.

5   For ease of reference, this Standard describes any entity that issues an insurance contract as an insurer, whether or not the issuer is regarded as an insurer for legal or supervisory purposes.

6   A reinsurance contract is a type of insurance contract. Accordingly, all references in this Standard to insurance contracts also apply to reinsurance contracts.

Aus6.1   This Standard applies to fixed-fee service contracts, described in paragraphs B6 and B7, which meet the definition of an insurance contract under this Standard.

Embedded derivatives

7   AASB 139 requires an entity to separate some embedded derivatives from their host contract, measure them at fair value and include changes in their *fair value* in profit or loss. AASB 139 applies to derivatives embedded in an insurance contract unless the embedded derivative is itself an insurance contract.

8   As an exception to the requirement in AASB 139, an insurer need not separate, and measure at fair value, a policyholder's option to surrender an insurance contract for a fixed amount (or for an amount based on a fixed amount and an interest rate), even if the exercise price differs from the carrying amount of the host *insurance liability*. However, the requirement in AASB 139 does apply to a put option or cash surrender option embedded in an insurance contract if the surrender value varies in response to the change in a financial variable (such as an equity or commodity price or index), or a non-financial variable that is not specific to a party to the contract. Furthermore, that requirement also applies if the holder's ability to exercise a put option or cash surrender option is triggered by a change in such a variable (for example, a put option that can be exercised if a stock market index reaches a specified level).

9   Paragraph 8 applies equally to options to surrender a financial instrument containing a discretionary participation feature.

Unbundling of deposit components

10   Some insurance contracts contain both an insurance component and a *deposit component*. In some cases, an insurer is required or permitted to *unbundle* those components:

  (a)   unbundling is required if both the following conditions are met:

   (i)   the insurer can measure the deposit component (including any embedded surrender options) separately (i.e. without considering the insurance component); and

   (ii)   the insurer's accounting policies do not otherwise require it to recognise all obligations and rights arising from the deposit component;

  (b)   unbundling is permitted, but not required, if the insurer can measure the deposit component separately as in (a)(i) but its accounting policies require it to recognise all obligations and rights arising from the deposit component, regardless of the basis used to measure those rights and obligations; and

  (c)   unbundling is prohibited if an insurer cannot measure the deposit component separately as in (a)(i).

11   The following is an example of a case when an insurer's accounting policies do not require it to recognise all obligations arising from a deposit component. A cedant receives compensation for losses from a *reinsurer*, but the contract obliges the cedant to repay the compensation in future years. That obligation arises from a deposit component. If the cedant's accounting policies would otherwise permit it to recognise the compensation as income without recognising the resulting obligation, unbundling is required.

12   To unbundle a contract, an insurer shall:

  (a)   apply this Standard to the insurance component; and

  (b)   apply AASB 139 to the deposit component.

Recognition and Measurement

Temporary exemption from some other Australian Accounting Standards

13   Paragraphs 10-12 of AASB 108 *Accounting Policies, Changes in Accounting Estimates and Errors* specify criteria for an entity to use in developing an accounting policy if no Standard applies specifically to an item. However, this Standard exempts an insurer from applying those criteria to its accounting policies for:

  (a)   insurance contracts that it issues (including related acquisition costs and related intangible assets, such as those described in paragraphs 31 and 32); and

  (b)   reinsurance contracts that it holds.

14   Nevertheless, this Standard does not exempt an insurer from some implications of the criteria in paragraphs 10-12 of AASB 108. Specifically, an insurer:

    (a)   shall not recognise as a liability any provisions for possible future claims, if those claims arise under insurance contracts that are not in existence at the end of the reporting period (such as catastrophe provisions and equalisation provisions);

    (b)   shall carry out the *liability adequacy* test described in paragraphs 15-19;

    (c)   shall remove an insurance liability (or a part of an insurance liability) from its statement of financial position when, and only when, it is extinguished – that is, when the obligation specified in the contract is discharged or cancelled or expires;

    (d)   shall not offset:

        (i)   *reinsurance assets* against the related insurance liabilities; or

        (ii)   income or expense from reinsurance contracts against the expense or income from the related insurance contracts; and

    (e)   shall consider whether its reinsurance assets are impaired (see paragraph 20).

Liability adequacy test

15   **An insurer shall assess at the end of each reporting period whether its recognised insurance liabilities are adequate, using current estimates of future cash flows under its insurance contracts. If that assessment shows that the carrying amount of its insurance liabilities (less related deferred acquisition costs and related intangible assets, such as those discussed in paragraphs 31 and 32) is inadequate in the light of the estimated future cash flows, the entire deficiency shall be recognised in profit or loss.**

16   If an insurer applies a liability adequacy test that meets specified minimum requirements, this Standard imposes no further requirements. The minimum requirements are the following:

    (a)   the test considers current estimates of all contractual cash flows, and of related cash flows such as claims handling costs, as well as cash flows resulting from embedded options and guarantees; and

    (b)   if the test shows that the liability is inadequate, the entire deficiency is recognised in profit or loss.

17   If an insurer's accounting policies do not require a liability adequacy test that meets the minimum requirements of paragraph 16, the insurer shall:

    (a)   determine the carrying amount of the relevant insurance liabilities[1] less the carrying amount of:

        (i)   any related deferred acquisition costs; and

        (ii)   any related intangible assets, such as those acquired in a business combination or portfolio transfer (see paragraphs 31 and 32). However, related reinsurance assets are not considered because an insurer accounts for them separately (see paragraph 20).

    (b)   determine whether the amount described in (a) is less than the carrying amount that would be required if the relevant insurance liabilities were within the scope of AASB 137. If it is less, the insurer shall recognise the entire difference in profit or loss and decrease the carrying amount of the related deferred acquisition costs or related intangible assets or increase the carrying amount of the relevant insurance liabilities.

18   If an insurer's liability adequacy test meets the minimum requirements of paragraph 16, the test is applied at the level of aggregation specified in that test. If its liability adequacy test does not meet those minimum requirements, the comparison described in paragraph 17

---

1   The relevant insurance liabilities are those insurance liabilities (and related deferred acquisition costs and related intangible assets) for which the insurer's accounting policies do not require a liability adequacy test that meets the minimum requirements of paragraph 16.

shall be made at the level of a portfolio of contracts that are subject to broadly similar risks and managed together as a single portfolio.

19   The amount described in paragraph 17(b) (i.e. the result of applying AASB 137) shall reflect future investment margins (see paragraphs 27 29) if, and only if, the amount described in paragraph 17(a) also reflects those margins.

Impairment of reinsurance assets

20   If a cedant's reinsurance asset is impaired, the cedant shall reduce its carrying amount accordingly and recognise that impairment loss in profit or loss. A reinsurance asset is impaired if, and only if:

(a)   there is objective evidence, as a result of an event that occurred after initial recognition of the reinsurance asset, that the cedant may not receive all amounts due to it under the terms of the contract; and

(b)   that event has a reliably measurable impact on the amounts that the cedant will receive from the reinsurer.

Changes in accounting policies

21   Paragraphs 22-30 apply both to changes made by an insurer that already applies IFRSs and to changes made by an insurer adopting Australian equivalents to IFRSs for the first time.

22   **An insurer may change its accounting policies for insurance contracts if, and only if, the change makes the financial statements more relevant to the economic decision-making needs of users and no less reliable, or more reliable and no less relevant to those needs. An insurer shall judge relevance and reliability by the criteria in AASB 108.**

23   To justify changing its accounting policies for insurance contracts, an insurer shall show that the change brings its financial statements closer to meeting the criteria in AASB 108, but the change need not achieve full compliance with those criteria. The following specific issues are discussed below:

(a)   current interest rates (paragraph 24);

(b)   continuation of existing practices (paragraph 25);

(c)   prudence (paragraph 26);

(d)   future investment margins (paragraphs 27-29); and

(e)   shadow accounting (paragraph 30).

Current market interest rates

24   An insurer is permitted, but not required, to change its accounting policies so that it remeasures designated insurance liabilities[2] to reflect current market interest rates and recognises changes in those liabilities in profit or loss. At that time, it may also introduce accounting policies that require other current estimates and assumptions for the designated liabilities. The election in this paragraph permits an insurer to change its accounting policies for designated liabilities, without applying those policies consistently to all similar liabilities as AASB 108 would otherwise require. If an insurer designates liabilities for this election, it shall continue to apply current market interest rates (and, if applicable, the other current estimates and assumptions) consistently in all periods to all these liabilities until they are extinguished.

Continuation of existing practices

25   An insurer may continue the following practices, but the introduction of any of them does not satisfy paragraph 22:

(a)   measuring insurance liabilities on an undiscounted basis;

(b)   measuring contractual rights to future investment management fees at an amount that exceeds their fair value as implied by a comparison with current fees charged by other market participants for similar services. It is likely that the fair value

---

2   In this paragraph, insurance liabilities include related deferred acquisition costs and related intangible assets, such as those discussed in paragraphs 31 and 32.

at inception of those contractual rights equals the origination costs paid, unless future investment management fees and related costs are out of line with market comparables; and

(c) using non-uniform accounting policies for the insurance contracts (and related deferred acquisition costs and related intangible assets, if any) of subsidiaries, except as permitted by paragraph 24. If those accounting policies are not uniform, an insurer may change them if the change does not make the accounting policies more diverse and also satisfies the other requirements in this Standard.

Prudence

26   An insurer need not change its accounting policies for insurance contracts to eliminate excessive prudence. However, if an insurer already measures its insurance contracts with sufficient prudence, it shall not introduce additional prudence.

Future investment margins

27   An insurer need not change its accounting policies for insurance contracts to eliminate future investment margins. However, there is a rebuttable presumption that an insurer's financial statements will become less relevant and reliable if it introduces an accounting policy that reflects future investment margins in the measurement of insurance contracts, unless those margins affect the contractual payments. Two examples of accounting policies that reflect those margins are:

(a) using a discount rate that reflects the estimated return on the insurer's assets; or

(b) projecting the returns on those assets at an estimated rate of return, discounting those projected returns at a different rate and including the result in the measurement of the liability.

28   An insurer may overcome the rebuttable presumption described in paragraph 27 if, and only if, the other components of a change in accounting policies increase the relevance and reliability of its financial statements sufficiently to outweigh the decrease in relevance and reliability caused by the inclusion of future investment margins. For example, suppose that an insurer's existing accounting policies for insurance contracts involve excessively prudent assumptions set at inception and a discount rate prescribed by a regulator without direct reference to market conditions, and ignore some embedded options and guarantees. The insurer might make its financial statements more relevant and no less reliable by switching to a comprehensive investor-oriented basis of accounting that is widely used and involves:

(a) current estimates and assumptions;

(b) a reasonable (but not excessively prudent) adjustment to reflect risk and uncertainty;

(c) measurements that reflect both the intrinsic value and time value of embedded options and guarantees; and

(d) a current market discount rate, even if that discount rate reflects the estimated return on the insurer's assets.

29   In some measurement approaches, the discount rate is used to determine the present value of a future profit margin. That profit margin is then attributed to different periods using a formula. In those approaches, the discount rate affects the measurement of the liability only indirectly. In particular, the use of a less appropriate discount rate has a limited or no effect on the measurement of the liability at inception. However, in other approaches, the discount rate determines the measurement of the liability directly. In the latter case, because the introduction of an asset-based discount rate has a more significant effect, it is highly unlikely that an insurer could overcome the rebuttable presumption described in paragraph 27.

Shadow accounting

30   In some accounting models, realised gains or losses on an insurer's assets have a direct effect on the measurement of some or all of (a) its insurance liabilities, (b) related deferred acquisition costs and (c) related intangible assets, such as those described in paragraphs 31 and 32. An insurer is permitted, but not required, to change its accounting policies so that a recognised but unrealised gain or loss on an asset affects those measurements in the same way that a realised gain or loss does. The related adjustment to the insurance

liability (or deferred acquisition costs or intangible assets) shall be recognised in other comprehensive income if, and only if, the unrealised gains or losses are recognised in other comprehensive income. This practice is sometimes described as 'shadow accounting'.

Insurance contracts acquired in a business combination or portfolio transfer

31   To comply with AASB 3, an insurer shall, at the acquisition date, measure at fair value the insurance liabilities assumed and *insurance assets* acquired in a business combination. However, an insurer is permitted, but not required, to use an expanded presentation that splits the fair value of acquired insurance contracts into two components:

(a)   a liability measured in accordance with the insurer's accounting policies for insurance contracts that it issues; and

(b)   an intangible asset, representing the difference between (i) the fair value of the contractual insurance rights acquired and insurance obligations assumed and (ii) the amount described in (a). The subsequent measurement of this asset shall be consistent with the measurement of the related insurance liability.

32   An insurer acquiring a portfolio of insurance contracts may use the expanded presentation described in paragraph 31.

33   The intangible assets described in paragraphs 31 and 32 are excluded from the scope of AASB 136 *Impairment of Assets* and from the scope of AASB 138 in respect of recognition and measurement. However, AASB 136 and AASB 138 apply to customer lists and customer relationships reflecting the expectation of future contracts that are not part of the contractual insurance rights and contractual insurance obligations that existed at the date of a business combination or portfolio transfer.

Discretionary participation features

Discretionary participation features in insurance contracts

34   Some insurance contracts contain a discretionary participation feature as well as a *guaranteed element*. The issuer of such a contract:

(a)   may, but need not, recognise the guaranteed element separately from the discretionary participation feature. If the issuer does not recognise them separately, it shall classify the whole contract as a liability. If the issuer classifies them separately, it shall classify the guaranteed element as a liability;

(b)   shall, if it recognises the discretionary participation feature separately from the guaranteed element, classify that feature as either a liability or a separate component of equity. This Standard does not specify how the issuer determines whether that feature is a liability or equity. The issuer may split that feature into liability and equity components and shall use a consistent accounting policy for that split. The issuer shall not classify that feature as an intermediate category that is neither liability nor equity;

(c)   may recognise all premiums received as revenue without separating any portion that relates to the equity component. The resulting changes in the guaranteed element and in the portion of the discretionary participation feature classified as a liability shall be recognised in profit or loss. If part or all of the discretionary participation feature is classified in equity, a portion of profit or loss may be attributable to that feature (in the same way that a portion may be attributable to non-controlling interests). The issuer shall recognise the portion of profit or loss attributable to any equity component of a discretionary participation feature as an allocation of profit or loss, not as expense or income (see AASB 101 *Presentation of Financial Statements*);

(d)   shall, if the contract contains an embedded derivative within the scope of AASB 139, apply AASB 139 to that embedded derivative; and

(e)   shall, in all respects not described in paragraphs 14-20 and 34(a)(d), continue its existing accounting policies for such contracts, unless it changes those accounting policies in a way that complies with paragraphs 21-30.

Discretionary participation features in financial instruments

35   The requirements in paragraph 34 also apply to a financial instrument that contains a discretionary participation feature. In addition:

(a)   if the issuer classifies the entire discretionary participation feature as a liability, it shall apply the liability adequacy test in paragraphs 15-19 to the whole contract (i.e. both the guaranteed element and the discretionary participation feature). The issuer need not determine the amount that would result from applying AASB 139 to the guaranteed element;

(b)   if the issuer classifies part or all of that feature as a separate component of equity, the liability recognised for the whole contract shall not be less than the amount that would result from applying AASB 139 to the guaranteed element. That amount shall include the intrinsic value of an option to surrender the contract, but need not include its time value if paragraph 9 exempts that option from measurement at fair value. The issuer need not disclose the amount that would result from applying AASB 139 to the guaranteed element, nor need it present that amount separately. Furthermore, the issuer need not determine that amount if the total liability recognised is clearly higher; and

(c)   although these contracts are financial instruments, the issuer may continue to recognise the premiums for those contracts as revenue and recognise as an expense the resulting increase in the carrying amount of the liability; and

(d)   although these contracts are financial instruments, an issuer applying paragraph 20(b) of AASB 7 to contracts with a discretionary participation feature shall disclose the total interest expense recognised in profit or loss, but need not calculate such interest expense using the effective interest method.

Disclosure

Explanation of recognised amounts

36   **An insurer shall disclose information that identifies and explains the amounts in its financial statements arising from insurance contracts.**

37   To comply with paragraph 36, an insurer shall disclose:

(a)   its accounting policies for insurance contracts and related assets, liabilities, income and expense;

(b)   the recognised assets, liabilities, income and expense (and, if it presents its statement of cash flows using the direct method, cash flows) arising from insurance contracts. Furthermore, if the insurer is a cedant, it shall disclose:

(i)   gains and losses recognised in profit or loss on buying reinsurance; and

(ii)   if the cedant defers and amortises gains and losses arising on buying reinsurance, the amortisation for the period and the amounts remaining unamortised at the beginning and end of the period;

(c)   the process used to determine the assumptions that have the greatest effect on the measurement of the recognised amounts described in (b). When practicable, an insurer shall also give quantified disclosure of those assumptions;

(d)   the effect of changes in assumptions used to measure insurance assets and insurance liabilities, showing separately the effect of each change that has a material effect on the financial statements; and

(e)   reconciliations of changes in insurance liabilities, reinsurance assets and, if any, related deferred acquisition costs.

Nature and extent of risks arising from insurance contracts

38   **An insurer shall disclose information that enables users of its financial statements to evaluate the nature and extent of risks arising from insurance contracts.**

39   To comply with paragraph 38, an insurer shall disclose:

(a)   its objectives, policies and processes for managing risks arising from insurance contracts and the methods used to manage those risks;

(b)   [deleted by the IASB];

(c)   information about *insurance risk* (both before and after risk mitigation by reinsurance), including information about:

   (i)   sensitivity to insurance risk (see paragraph 39A);

   (ii)   concentrations of insurance risk, including a description of how management determines concentrations and a description of the shared characteristics that identifies each concentration (e.g. type of *insured event*, geographical area, or currency); and

   (iii)   actual claims compared with previous estimates (i.e. claims development). The disclosure about claims development shall go back to the period when the earliest material claim arose for which there is still uncertainty about the amount and timing of the claims payments, but need not go back more than ten years. An insurer need not disclose this information for claims for which uncertainty about the amount and timing of claims payments is typically resolved within one year;

(d)   information about credit risk, liquidity risk and market risk that paragraphs 31-42 of AASB 7 would require if the insurance contracts were within the scope of AASB 7. However:

   (i)   an insurer need not provide the maturity analyses required by paragraphs 39(a) and (b) of AASB 7 if it discloses information about the estimated timing of the net cash outflows resulting from recognised insurance liabilities instead. This may take the form of an analysis, by estimated timing, of the amounts recognised in the statement of financial position; and

   (ii)   if an insurer uses an alternative method to manage sensitivity to market conditions, such as an embedded value analysis, it may use that sensitivity analysis to meet the requirement in paragraph 40(a) of AASB 7. Such an insurer shall also provide the disclosures required by paragraph 41 of AASB 7; and

(e)   information about exposures to market risk arising from embedded derivatives contained in a host insurance contract if the insurer is not required to, and does not, measure the embedded derivatives at fair value.

39A   To comply with paragraph 39(c)(i), an insurer shall disclose either (a) or (b) as follows:

(a)   a sensitivity analysis that shows how profit or loss and equity would have been affected if changes in the relevant risk variable that were reasonably possible at the end of the reporting period had occurred; the methods and assumptions used in preparing the sensitivity analysis; and any changes from the previous period in the methods and assumptions used. However, if an insurer uses an alternative method to manage sensitivity to market conditions, such as an embedded value analysis, it may meet this requirement by disclosing that alternative sensitivity analysis and the disclosures required by paragraph 41 of AASB 7; and

(b)   qualitative information about sensitivity, and information about those terms and conditions of insurance contracts that have a material effect on the amount, timing and uncertainty of the insurer's future cash flows.

Effective Date and Transition

40   The transitional provisions in paragraphs 42-45 apply both to an entity that is already applying IFRSs when it first applies this Standard and to an entity that applies Australian equivalents to IFRSs for the first time (a first-time adopter).

41   [Deleted by the AASB]

41A   [Deleted by the AASB]

41B   [Deleted by the AASB]

Disclosure

42   An entity need not apply the disclosure requirements in this Standard to comparative information that relates to annual periods beginning before 1 January 2005, except for the disclosures required by paragraph 37(a) and (b) about accounting policies, and recognised assets, liabilities, income and expense and cash flows.

43   Where an entity applies the disclosure requirements in this Standard to comparative information that relates to annual periods beginning before 1 January 2005, if it is impracticable to apply a particular requirement of paragraphs 10-35 to comparative information that relates to annual periods beginning before 1 January 2005, an entity shall disclose that fact. Applying the liability adequacy test (paragraphs 15-19) to such comparative information might sometimes be impracticable, but it is highly unlikely to be impracticable to apply other requirements of paragraphs 10-35 to such comparative information. AASB 108 explains the term 'impracticable'.

44   In applying paragraph 39(c)(iii), an entity need not disclose information about claims development that occurred earlier than five years before the end of the first annual reporting period in which it applies this Standard. Furthermore, if it is impracticable, when an entity first applies this Standard, to prepare information about claims development that occurred before the beginning of the earliest period for which an entity presents full comparative information that complies with this Standard, the entity shall disclose that fact.

Redesignation of financial assets

45   When an insurer changes its accounting policies for insurance liabilities, it is permitted, but not required, to reclassify some or all of its financial assets as 'at fair value through profit or loss'. This reclassification is permitted if an insurer changes accounting policies when it first applies this Standard and if it makes a subsequent policy change permitted by paragraph 22. The reclassification is a change in accounting policy and AASB 108 applies.

Appendix A

Defined Terms

This appendix is an integral part of AASB 4.

cedant	The **policyholder** under a **reinsurance contract**.
deposit component	A contractual component that is not accounted for as a derivative under AASB 139 and would be within the scope of AASB 139 if it were a separate instrument.
direct insurance contract	An **insurance contract** that is not a **reinsurance contract**
discretionary participation feature	A contractual right to receive, as a supplement to **guaranteed benefits**, additional benefits:

(a)   that are likely to be a significant portion of the total contractual benefits;

(b)   whose amount or timing is contractually at the discretion of the issuer; and

(c)   that are contractually based on:

   (i)   the performance of a specified pool of contracts or a specified type of contract;

   (ii)   realised and/or unrealised investment returns on a specified pool of assets held by the issuer; or

   (iii)   the profit or loss of the company, fund or other entity that issues the contract.

fair value	The amount for which an asset could be exchanged, or a liability settled, between knowledgeable, willing parties in an arm's length transaction.
financial guarantee contract	A contract that requires the issuer to make specified payments to reimburse the holder for a loss it incurs because a specified debtor fails to make payment when due in accordance with the original or modified terms of a debt instrument.
financial risk	The risk of a possible future change in one or more of a specified interest rate, financial instrument price, commodity price, foreign exchange rate, index of prices or rates, credit rating or credit index or other variable, provided in the case of a non-financial variable that the variable is not specific to a party to the contract.
guaranteed benefits	Payments or other benefits to which a particular **policyholder** or investor has an unconditional right that is not subject to the contractual discretion of the issuer.
guaranteed element	An obligation to pay **guaranteed benefits**, included in a contract that contains a **discretionary participation feature**.
insurance asset	An **insurer's** net contractual rights under an **insurance contract**.
insurance contract	A contract under which one party (the **insurer**) accepts significant **insurance risk** from another party (the **policyholder**) by agreeing to compensate the policyholder if a specified uncertain future event (the **insured event**) adversely affects the **policyholder**. (See Appendix B for guidance on this definition.)
insurance liability	An **insurer's** net contractual obligations under an **insurance contract**.
insurance risk	Risk, other than **financial risk**, transferred from the holder of a contract to the issuer.
insured event	An uncertain future event that is covered by an **insurance contract** and creates **insurance risk**.
insurer	The party that has an obligation under an **insurance contract** to compensate a **policyholder** if an **insured event** occurs.
liability adequacy test	An assessment of whether the carrying amount of an **insurance liability** needs to be increased (or the carrying amount of related deferred acquisition costs or related intangible assets decreased), based on a review of future cash flows.
policyholder	A party that has a right to compensation under an **insurance contract** if an **insured event** occurs.
reinsurance assets	A **cedant's** net contractual rights under a **reinsurance contract**.
reinsurance contract	An **insurance contract** issued by one **insurer** (the **reinsurer**) to compensate another **insurer** (the **cedant**) for losses on one or more contracts issued by the **cedant**.
reinsurer	The party that has an obligation under a **reinsurance contract** to compensate a **cedant** if an **insured event** occurs.
unbundle	Account for the components of a contract as if they were separate contracts.

Additional Australian Defined Terms

general insurance contract An **insurance contract** that is not a **life insurance contract**.

life insurance contract An **insurance contract**, or a financial instrument with a **discretionary participation feature**, regulated under the *Life Insurance Act 1995*, and similar contracts issued by entities operating outside Australia.

Appendix B
Definition of an Insurance Contract

This appendix is an integral part of AASB 4.

B1   This appendix gives guidance on the definition of an insurance contract in Appendix A. It addresses the following issues:

(a)   the term 'uncertain future event' (paragraphs B2-B4);

(b)   payments in kind (paragraphs B5-B7);

(c)   insurance risk and other risks (paragraphs B8-B17);

(d)   examples of insurance contracts (paragraphs B18-B21);

(e)   significant insurance risk (paragraphs B22-B28); and

(f)   changes in the level of insurance risk (paragraphs B29 and B30).

Uncertain future event

B2   Uncertainty (or risk) is the essence of an insurance contract. Accordingly, at least one of the following is uncertain at the inception of an insurance contract:

(a)   whether an insured event will occur;

(b)   when it will occur; or

(c)   how much the insurer will need to pay if it occurs.

B3   In some insurance contracts, the insured event is the discovery of a loss during the term of the contract, even if the loss arises from an event that occurred before the inception of the contract. In other insurance contracts, the insured event is an event that occurs during the term of the contract, even if the resulting loss is discovered after the end of the contract term.

B4   Some insurance contracts cover events that have already occurred, but whose financial effect is still uncertain. An example is a reinsurance contract that covers the direct insurer against adverse development of claims already reported by policyholders. In such contracts, the insured event is the discovery of the ultimate cost of those claims.

Payments in kind

B5   Some insurance contracts require or permit payments to be made in kind. An example is when the insurer replaces a stolen article directly, instead of reimbursing the policyholder. Another example is when an insurer uses its own hospitals and medical staff to provide medical services covered by the contracts.

B6   Some fixed-fee service contracts in which the level of service depends on an uncertain event meet the definition of an insurance contract in this Standard but are not regulated as insurance contracts in some countries. One example is a maintenance contract in which the service provider agrees to repair specified equipment after a malfunction. The fixed service fee is based on the expected number of malfunctions, but it is uncertain whether a particular machine will break down. The malfunction of the equipment adversely affects its owner and the contract compensates the owner (in kind, rather than cash). Another example is a contract for car breakdown services in which the provider agrees, for a fixed annual fee, to provide roadside assistance or tow the car to a nearby garage.

The latter contract could meet the definition of an insurance contract even if the provider does not agree to carry out repairs or replace parts.

B7   Applying the Standard to the contracts described in paragraph B6 is likely to be no more burdensome than applying the Standard that would be applicable if such contracts were outside the scope of this Standard.

(a)   There are unlikely to be material liabilities for malfunctions and breakdowns that have already occurred.

(b)   If AASB 118 *Revenue* applied, the service provider would recognise revenue by reference to the stage of completion (and subject to other specified criteria). That approach is also acceptable under this Standard, which permits the service provider (i) to continue it's existing accounting policies for these contracts unless they involve practices prohibited by paragraph 14 and (ii) to improve its accounting policies if so permitted by paragraphs 22-30.

(c)   The service provider considers whether the cost of meeting its contractual obligation to provide services exceeds the revenue received in advance. To do this, it applies the liability adequacy test described in paragraphs 15-19 of this Standard. If this Standard did not apply to these contracts, the service provider would apply AASB 137 to determine whether the contracts are onerous.

(d)   For these contracts, the disclosure requirements in this Standard are unlikely to add significantly to disclosures required by other Australian Accounting Standards.

Distinction between insurance risk and other risks

B8   The definition of an insurance contract refers to insurance risk, which this Standard defines as risk, other than *financial risk*, transferred from the holder of a contract to the issuer. A contract that exposes the issuer to financial risk without significant insurance risk is not an insurance contract.

B9   The definition of financial risk in Appendix A includes a list of financial and non-financial variables. That list includes non-financial variables that are not specific to a party to the contract, such as an index of earthquake losses in a particular region or an index of temperatures in a particular city. It excludes non-financial variables that are specific to a party to the contract, such as the occurrence or non-occurrence of a fire that damages or destroys an asset of that party. Furthermore, the risk of changes in the fair value of a non-financial asset is not a financial risk if the fair value reflects not only changes in market prices for such assets (a financial variable) but also the condition of a specific non-financial asset held by a party to a contract (a non-financial variable). For example, if a guarantee of the residual value of a specific car exposes the guarantor to the risk of changes in the car's physical condition, that risk is insurance risk, not financial risk.

B10   Some contracts expose the issuer to financial risk, in addition to significant insurance risk. For example, many life insurance contracts both guarantee a minimum rate of return to policyholders (creating financial risk) and promise death benefits that at some times significantly exceed the policyholder's account balance (creating insurance risk in the form of mortality risk). Such contracts are insurance contracts.

B11   Under some contracts, an insured event triggers the payment of an amount linked to a price index. Such contracts are insurance contracts, provided the payment that is contingent on the insured event can be significant. For example, a life-contingent annuity linked to a cost-of-living index transfers insurance risk because payment is triggered by an uncertain event - the survival of the annuitant. The link to the price index is an embedded derivative, but it also transfers insurance risk. If the resulting transfer of insurance risk is significant, the embedded derivative meets the definition of an insurance contract, in which case it need not be separated and measured at fair value (see paragraph 7 of this Standard).

B12   The definition of insurance risk refers to risk that the insurer accepts from the policyholder. In other words, insurance risk is a pre-existing risk transferred from the policyholder to the insurer. Thus, a new risk created by the contract is not insurance risk.

B13   The definition of an insurance contract refers to an adverse effect on the policyholder.

The definition does not limit the payment by the insurer to an amount equal to the financial impact of the adverse event. For example, the definition does not exclude 'new-for-old' coverage that pays the policyholder sufficient to permit replacement of a damaged old asset by a new asset. Similarly, the definition does not limit payment under a term life insurance contract to the financial loss suffered by the deceased's dependants, nor does it preclude the payment of predetermined amounts to quantify the loss caused by death or an accident.

B14   Some contracts require a payment if a specified uncertain event occurs, but do not require an adverse effect on the policyholder as a precondition for payment. Such a contract is not an insurance contract even if the holder uses the contract to mitigate an underlying risk exposure. For example, if the holder uses a derivative to hedge an underlying non-financial variable that is correlated with cash flows from an asset of the entity, the derivative is not an insurance contract because payment is not conditional on whether the holder is adversely affected by a reduction in the cash flows from the asset. Conversely, the definition of an insurance contract refers to an uncertain event for which an adverse effect on the policyholder is a contractual precondition for payment. This contractual precondition does not require the insurer to investigate whether the event actually caused an adverse effect, but permits the insurer to deny payment if it is not satisfied that the event caused an adverse effect.

B15   Lapse or persistency risk (i.e. the risk that the counterparty will cancel the contract earlier or later than the issuer had expected in pricing the contract) is not insurance risk because the payment to the counterparty is not contingent on an uncertain future event that adversely affects the counterparty. Similarly, expense risk (i.e. the risk of unexpected increases in the administrative costs associated with the servicing of a contract, rather than in costs associated with insured events) is not insurance risk because an unexpected increase in expenses does not adversely affect the counterparty.

B16   Therefore, a contract that exposes the issuer to lapse risk, persistency risk or expense risk is not an insurance contract unless it also exposes the issuer to insurance risk. However, if the issuer of that contract mitigates that risk by using a second contract to transfer part of that risk to another party, the second contract exposes that other party to insurance risk.

B17   An insurer can accept significant insurance risk from the policyholder only if the insurer is an entity separate from the policyholder. In the case of a mutual insurer, the mutual accepts risk from each policyholder and pools that risk. Although policyholders bear that pooled risk collectively in their capacity as owners, the mutual has still accepted the risk that is the essence of an insurance contract.

Examples of insurance contracts

B18   The following are examples of contracts that are insurance contracts, if the transfer of insurance risk is significant:

(a)   insurance against theft or damage to property;

(b)   insurance against product liability, professional liability, civil liability or legal expenses;

(c)   life insurance and prepaid funeral plans (although death is certain, it is uncertain when death will occur or, for some types of life insurance, whether death will occur within the period covered by the insurance);

(d)   life-contingent annuities and pensions (i.e. contracts that provide compensation for the uncertain future event—the survival of the annuitant or pensioner—to assist the annuitant or pensioner in maintaining a given standard of living, which would otherwise be adversely affected by his or her survival);

(e)   disability and medical cover;

(f)   surety bonds, fidelity bonds, performance bonds and bid bonds (i.e. contracts that provide compensation if another party fails to perform a contractual obligation, for example an obligation to construct a building);

(g)   credit insurance that provides for specified payments to be made to reimburse the holder for a loss it incurs because a specified debtor fails to make payment when due under the original or modified terms of a debt instrument. These contracts could have various legal forms, such as that of a guarantee, some types of letter of credit, a credit derivative default contract or an insurance contract. However, although these contracts meet the definition of an insurance contract, they also meet the definition of a financial guarantee contract in AASB 139 and are within the scope of AASB 132 and AASB 139, not this Standard (see paragraph 4(d)). Nevertheless, if an issuer of financial guarantee contracts has previously asserted explicitly that it regards such contracts as insurance contracts and has used accounting applicable to insurance contracts, the issuer may elect to apply either AASB 139 and AASB 132[1] or AASB 1023 to such financial guarantee contracts;

(h) product warranties. Product warranties issued by another party for goods sold by a manufacturer, dealer or retailer are within the scope of this Standard. However, product warranties issued directly by a manufacturer, dealer or retailer are outside its scope, because they are within the scope of AASB 118 and AASB 137;

(i) title insurance (i.e. insurance against the discovery of defects in title to land that were not apparent when the insurance contract was written). In this case, the insured event is the discovery of a defect in the title, not the defect itself;

(j) travel assistance (i.e. compensation in cash or in kind to policyholders for losses suffered while they are travelling). Paragraphs B6 and B7 discuss some contracts of this kind;

(k) catastrophe bonds that provide for reduced payments of principal, interest or both if a specified event adversely affects the issuer of the bond (unless the specified event does not create significant insurance risk, for example if the event is a change in an interest rate or foreign exchange rate);

(l) insurance swaps and other contracts that require a payment based on changes in climatic, geological or other physical variables that are specific to a party to the contract; and

(m) reinsurance contracts.

B19 The following are examples of items that are not insurance contracts:

(a) investment contracts that have the legal form of an insurance contract but do not expose the insurer to significant insurance risk, for example life insurance contracts in which the insurer bears no significant mortality risk (such contracts are non-insurance financial instruments or service contracts, see paragraphs B20 and B21);

(b) contracts that have the legal form of insurance, but pass all significant insurance risk back to the policyholder through non-cancellable and enforceable mechanisms that adjust future payments by the policyholder as a direct result of insured losses, for example some financial reinsurance contracts or some group contracts (such contracts are normally noninsurance financial instruments or service contracts, see paragraphs B20 and B21);

(c) self-insurance, in other words retaining a risk that could have been covered by insurance (there is no insurance contract because there is no agreement with another party);

(d) contracts (such as gambling contracts) that require a payment if a specified uncertain future event occurs, but do not require, as a contractual precondition for payment, that the event adversely affects the policyholder. However, this does not preclude the specification of a predetermined payout to quantify the loss caused by a specified event such as death or an accident (see also paragraph B13);

(e) derivatives that expose one party to financial risk but not insurance risk, because they require that party to make payment based solely on changes in one or more of a specified interest rate, financial instrument price, commodity price, foreign exchange rate, index of prices or rates, credit rating or credit index or other variable, provided in the case of a non-financial variable that the variable is not specific to a party to the contract (see AASB 139);

---

1 When an entity applies AASB 7, the reference to AASB 132 is replaced by a reference to AASB 7.

(f)   a credit-related guarantee (or letter of credit, credit derivative default contract or credit insurance contract) that requires payments even if the holder has not incurred a loss on the failure of the debtor to make payments when due (see AASB 139);

(g)   contracts that require a payment based on a climatic, geological or other physical variable that is not specific to a party to the contract (commonly described as weather derivatives); and

(h)   catastrophe bonds that provide for reduced payments of principal, interest or both, based on a climatic, geological or other physical variable that is not specific to a party to the contract.

B20   If the contracts described in paragraph B19 create financial assets or financial liabilities, they are within the scope of AASB 139. Among other things, this means that the parties to the contract use what is sometimes called deposit accounting, which involves the following:

(a)   one party recognises the consideration received as a financial liability, rather than as revenue; and

(b)   the other party recognises the consideration paid as a financial asset, rather than as an expense.

B21   If the contracts described in paragraph B19 do not create financial assets or financial liabilities, AASB 118 applies. Under AASB 118, revenue associated with a transaction involving the rendering of services is recognised by reference to the stage of completion of the transaction if the outcome of the transaction can be estimated reliably.

Significant insurance risk

B22   A contract is an insurance contract only if it transfers significant insurance risk. Paragraphs B8-B21 discuss insurance risk. The following paragraphs discuss the assessment of whether insurance risk is significant.

B23   Insurance risk is significant if, and only if, an insured event could cause an insurer to pay significant additional benefits in any scenario, excluding scenarios that lack commercial substance (i.e. have no discernible effect on the economics of the transaction). If significant additional benefits would be payable in scenarios that have commercial substance, the condition in the previous sentence may be met even if the insured event is extremely unlikely or even if the expected (i.e. probability-weighted) present value of contingent cash flows is a small proportion of the expected present value of all the remaining contractual cash flows.

B24   The additional benefits described in paragraph B23 refer to amounts that exceed those that would be payable if no insured event occurred (excluding scenarios that lack commercial substance). Those additional amounts include claims handling and claims assessment costs, but exclude:

(a)   the loss of the ability to charge the policyholder for future services. For example, in an investment-linked life insurance contract, the death of the policyholder means that the insurer can no longer perform investment management services and collect a fee for doing so. However, this economic loss for the insurer does not reflect insurance risk, just as a mutual fund manager does not take on insurance risk in relation to the possible death of the client. Therefore, the potential loss of future investment management fees is not relevant in assessing how much insurance risk is transferred by a contract;

(b)   waiver on death of charges that would be made on cancellation or surrender. Because the contract brought those charges into existence, the waiver of these charges does not compensate the policyholder for a pre-existing risk. Hence, they are not relevant in assessing how much insurance risk is transferred by a contract;

(c)   a payment conditional on an event that does not cause a significant loss to the holder of the contract. For example, consider a contract that requires the issuer to pay one million currency units if an asset suffers physical damage causing an insignificant economic loss of one currency unit to the holder. In this contract, the holder transfers to the insurer the insignificant risk of losing one currency unit.

AASB

At the same time, the contract creates non-insurance risk that the issuer will need to pay 999,999 currency units if the specified event occurs. Because the issuer does not accept significant insurance risk from the holder, this contract is not an insurance contract; and

(d) possible reinsurance recoveries. The insurer accounts for these separately.

B25 An insurer shall assess the significance of insurance risk contract by contract, rather than by reference to materiality to the financial statements.[2] Thus, insurance risk may be significant even if there is a minimal probability of material losses for a whole book of contracts. This contract-by-contract assessment makes it easier to classify a contract as an insurance contract. However, if a relatively homogeneous book of small contracts is known to consist of contracts that all transfer insurance risk, an insurer need not examine each contract within that book to identify a few non-derivative contracts that transfer insignificant insurance risk.

B26 It follows from paragraphs B23-B25 that if a contract pays a death benefit exceeding the amount payable on survival, the contract is an insurance contract unless the additional death benefit is insignificant (judged by reference to the contract rather than to an entire book of contracts). As noted in paragraph B24(b), the waiver on death of cancellation or surrender charges is not included in this assessment if this waiver does not compensate the policyholder for a pre-existing risk. Similarly, an annuity contract that pays out regular sums for the rest of a policyholder's life is an insurance contract, unless the aggregate life-contingent payments are insignificant.

B27 Paragraph B23 refers to additional benefits. These additional benefits could include a requirement to pay benefits earlier if the insured event occurs earlier and the payment is not adjusted for the time value of money. An example is whole life insurance for a fixed amount (in other words, insurance that provides a fixed death benefit whenever the policyholder dies, with no expiry date for the cover). It is certain that the policyholder will die, but the date of death is uncertain. The insurer will suffer a loss on those individual contracts for which policyholders die early, even if there is no overall loss on the whole book of contracts.

B28 If an insurance contract is unbundled into a deposit component and an insurance component, the significance of insurance risk transfer is assessed by reference to the insurance component. The significance of insurance risk transferred by an embedded derivative is assessed by reference to the embedded derivative.

Changes in the level of insurance risk

B29 Some contracts do not transfer any insurance risk to the issuer at inception, although they do transfer insurance risk at a later time. For example, consider a contract that provides a specified investment return and includes an option for the policyholder to use the proceeds of the investment on maturity to buy a life-contingent annuity at the current annuity rates charged by the insurer to other new annuitants when the policyholder exercises the option. The contract transfers no insurance risk to the issuer until the option is exercised, because the insurer remains free to price the annuity on a basis that reflects the insurance risk transferred to the insurer at that time. However, if the contract specifies the annuity rates (or a basis for setting the annuity rates), the contract transfers insurance risk to the issuer at inception.

B30 A contract that qualifies as an insurance contract remains an insurance contract until all rights and obligations are extinguished or expire.

---

2   For this purpose, contracts entered into simultaneously with a single counterparty (or contracts that are otherwise interdependent) form a single contract.

AASB 5
Non-current Assets Held for Sale and Discontinued Operations

(Compiled June 2012)

Note from the Institute of Chartered Accountants Australia

This note, prepared by the technical editors, is not part of Accounting Standard AASB 5.

Historical development

July 2004: AASB 5 'Non-Current Assets Held for Sale and Discontinued Operations' is the Australian equivalent of IFRS 5 of the same name. It was made by the AASB on 15 July 2004 as part of the AASB's program to adopt International Financial Reporting Standards by 2005.

26 February 2007: AASB 2007-3 'Amendments to Australian Accounting Standards' was issued by the AASB. This Standard is applicable to annual reporting periods beginning on or after 1 January 2009.

30 April 2007: AASB 2007-4 'Amendments to Australian Accounting Standards' amends paragraph 28 and adds paragraphs Aus42.1 and 43 and is applicable to annual reporting periods beginning on or after 1 January 2009. Entities may elect to early-adopt it to annual reporting periods beginning on or after 1 January 2005.

28 June 2007: AASB 7-7 'Amendments to Australian Accounting Standards' amends paragraph 43 and is applicable to annual reporting periods beginning on or after 1 January 2007. Entities may elect to early-adopt it to annual reporting periods beginning on or after 1 January 2005.

24 September 2007: AASB 2007-8 'Amendments to Australian Accounting Standards' was issued by the AASB. This Standard is applicable to annual reporting periods beginning on or after 1 January 2009.

13 December 2007: AASB 2007-9 'Amendments to Australian Accounting Standards arising from the Review of AAS 27, AAS 29 and AAS 31' was issued by the AASB. This Standard is applicable to annual reporting periods beginning on or after 1 July 2008, with early adoption permitted.

13 December 2007: AASB 2007-10 'Further Amendments to Australian Accounting Standards arising from AASB 101' amends AASB 5, replacing the term 'financial report' with 'financial statements'. This Standard is applicable to annual reporting periods beginning on or after 1 January 2009.

6 March 2008: AASB 2008-3 'Amendments to Australian Accounting Standards arising from AASB 3 and AASB 127' amends AASB 5 for the issue of AASB 3 Revised. This Standard is applicable to annual reporting periods beginning on or after 1 July 2009.

24 July 2008: AASB 2008-5 'Amendments to Australian Accounting Standards arising from the Annual Improvements Project' amends AASB 5 in relation to point-of-sale costs. This Standard is applicable to annual reporting periods beginning on or after 1 January 2009.

24 July 2008: AASB 2008-6 'Further Amendments to Australian Accounting Standards arising from the Annual Improvements Project' amends AASB 1 and AASB 5 to include requirements relating to a sale plan involving the loss of control of a subsidiary. This Standard is applicable to annual reporting periods beginning on or after 1 July 2009.

7 November 2008: AASB 5 was reissued by the AASB, compiled to include the AASB 2007-9 amendments.

18 December 2008: AASB 2008-13 'Amendments to Australian Accounting Standards arising from AASB Interpretation 17 – Distributions of non-cash assets to owners' amends AASB 5 in respect of the classification, presentation and measurement of non-current assets held for distribution to owners in their capacity as owners. This Standard is applicable prospectively to annual reporting periods beginning on or after 1 July 2009. Retrospective application is not permitted.

AASB

21 May 2009: AASB 2009-5 'Amendments to Australian Accounting Standards' is the annual improvements Standard, amending AASB 5 in relation to the disclosure of non-current assets (or disposal groups) classified as held for sale or discontinued operations. This Standard applies to annual reporting periods beginning on or after 1 January 2010 and may be applied early.

25 June 2009: AASB 2009-6 'Amendments to Australian Accounting Standards' amends AASB 5 for editorial corrections made by the International Accounting Standards Board (IASB) to its Standards and Interpretations (IFRSs) and as a consequence of issuing revised AASB 101 'Presentation of Financial Statements' (September 2007). This Standard is applicable to annual reporting periods beginning on or after 1 January 2009 that end on or after 30 June 2009.

25 June 2009: AASB 2009-7 'Amendments to Australian Accounting Standards' amends AASB 5 arising from editorial corrections by the AASB and by the International Accounting Standards Board (IASB). This Standard is applicable to annual reporting periods beginning on or after 1 July 2009.

27 October 2009: AASB 5 was reissued by the AASB, compiled to include the AASB 2007-3, AASB 2007-8, AASB 2007-10, AASB 2008-3, AASB 2008-5, AASB 2008-6, AASB 2008-13, AASB 2009-6 and AASB 2009-7 amendments and applies to annual reporting periods beginning on or after 1 July 2009 but before 1 January 2010. Early application is permitted.

On the same date the AASB reissued the version of AASB 5 applicable to annual reporting periods beginning on or after 1 January 2009 but before 1 July 2009. This version of AASB 5 has been compiled for the amending Standards applying to annual reporting periods beginning on or after 1 January 2009.

4 December 2009: AASB 5 was reissued by the AASB, compiled to include the AASB 2009-5 amendments and applies to annual reporting periods beginning on or after 1 January 2010.

7 December 2009: AASB 2009-11 'Amendments to Australian Accounting Standards arising from AASB 9' amends AASB 5 to give effect to consequential changes arising from the issuance of AASB 9. This Standard is applicable to annual reporting periods beginning on or after 1 January 2013 with early adoption permitted from annual reporting periods ending on or after 31 December 2009 that begin before 1 January 2013 provided AASB 9 is also applied for the same period. The application date of AASB 2009-11 has been amended to 1 January 2015 by AASB 2012-6. **These amendments have been superseded by AASB 2010-7 and are not included in this compiled Standard.**

15 December 2009: AASB 2009-12 'Amendments to Australian Accounting Standards' amends AASB 5 for editorial corrections. This Standard is applicable to annual reporting periods beginning on or after 1 January 2011 with early adoption permitted.

27 October 2010: AASB 2010-5 'Further Amendments to Australian Accounting Standards' makes editorial amendments to AASB 5. This Standard is applicable to annual reporting periods beginning on or after 1 January 2011.

1 March 2011: AASB 2010-7 'Amendments to Australian Accounting Standards arising from AASB 9 (December 2010)' as compiled amends AASB 5 to give effect to consequential changes arising from the reissue of AASB 9 in December 2010 and supersedes AASB 2009-11 which related to the previous version of AASB 9. This Standard applies to annual reporting periods beginning on or after 1 January 2013 and can be adopted early. The application date of AASB 2010-7 has been amended to 1 January 2015 by AASB 2012-6. **These amendments are not included in this compiled Standard.**

11 May 2011: AASB 2011-1 'Amendments to Australian Accounting Standards arising from the Trans-Tasman Convergence Project' amends AASB 5 as a result of the Trans-Tasman project, to more closely align IFRSs as applied through Australian and New Zealand Standards. AASB 2011-1 deletes Australian specific disclosure requirements. Where appropriate these disclosures are now included in AASB 1054 'Australian Additional Requirements'. These Standards apply to annual reporting periods beginning on or after 1 July 2011 with early adoption permitted.

29 August 2011: AASB 2011-7 'Amendments to Australian Accounting Standards arising from the Consolidation and Joint Arrangements Standards' amends AASB 5 to give effect to many consequential changes arising from the issue of AASB 10, 11, 12, 127 and 128. This Standard applies to annual reporting periods beginning on or after 1 January 2013 and can be adopted early by for-profit entities. **These amendments are not included in this compiled Standard.**

2 September 2011: AASB 2011-8 'Amendments to Australian Accounting Standards arising from AASB 13' amends AASB 5 to give effect to a consequential change in the definition of fair value arising from the issue of AASB 13. This Standard applies to annual reporting periods beginning on or after 1 January 2013 and can be adopted early. **These amendments are not included in this compiled Standard.**

5 September 2011: AASB 2011-9 'Amendments to Australian Accounting Standards – Presentation of Items of Other Comprehensive income' amends the presentation of items in other comprehensive income. This Standard applies to annual reporting periods beginning on or after 1 July 2012 and can be adopted early.

23 September 2011: AASB 5 was reissued by the AASB, compiled to include the AASB 2009-12, AASB 2010-5 and AASB 2011-1 amendments and applies to annual reporting periods ending on or after 1 July 2011 but before 1 July 2012.

20 June 2012: AASB 5 was reissued by the AASB, compiled to include the AASB 2011-9 amendments and applies to annual reporting periods beginning on or after 1 July 2012 but before 1 January 2013.

Reference

IFRIC items not taken onto the agenda: IFRS 5-1 *Plan to sell the controlling interest in a subsidiary*, IFRS 5-2 *Disclosures*, IFRS 5-3 *Write-down of disposal group* and IFRS 5-4 *Reversal of disposal group impairment losses relating to goodwill* apply to AASB 5.

AASB 5 compared to IFRS 5

Additions

Paragraph	Description
Aus 1.1	Which entities AASB 5 applies to (i.e. reporting entities and general purpose financial statements).
Aus 1.2	The application date of AASB 5 (i.e. annual reporting periods beginning 1 January 2005).
Aus 1.3	Prohibits early application of AASB 5.
Aus 1.4	Makes the requirements of AASB 5 subject to AASB 1031 'Materiality'.
Aus 1.5	Explains which Australian Standards have been superseded by AASB 5.
Aus 1.6	Clarifies that the superseded Australian Standards remain in force until AASB 5 applies.
Aus 1.7	Notice of the new Standard published on 22 July 2004.
Aus 2.1	The requirements in AASB 5 do not apply to the restructuring of administrative arrangements or administrative activities of government departments.
Aus 2.2	Clarifies that the disclosure requirements for restructuring of administrative arrangements between government departments are set out in AAS 29 'Financial Reporting by Government Departments'.
Aus 2.3	Explains how a discontinuance of an administrative activity of a government department may constitute a discontinued operation from the point of view of the government.
Aus 2.4	Clarifies that AASB 5 rather than AAS 27 'Financial Reporting by Local Governments' applies to a restructuring that results in a discontinued operation of the transferor local government.
Aus 42.1	Transitional paragraph is not to be applied by entities that have previously applied AASB 5.
Aus 44B.1	Application of AASB 2008-3 amendments.

Deletions

Paragraph	*Description*
44, 44A, 44B	Effective date of IFRS 5.
45	Reference to superseded IAS 35 'Discontinued Operations'.

Contents

Compilation Details

Comparison with IFRS 5

Accounting Standard
AASB 5 Non-current Assets Held for Sale and Discontinued Operations

	Paragraphs
Objective	1
Application	Aus1.1 – Aus1.7
Scope	2 – 5B
Classification of Non-current Assets (or Disposal Groups) as Held for Sale or as Held for Distribution to Owners	6 – 12A
Non-current assets that are to be abandoned	13 – 14
Measurement of Non-current Assets (or Disposal Groups) Classified as Held for Sale	
Measurement of a non-current asset (or disposal group)	15 – 19
Recognition of impairment losses and reversals	20 – 25
Changes to a plan of sale	26 – 29
Presentation and Disclosure	30
Presenting discontinued operations	31 – 36A
Gains or losses relating to continuing operations	37
Presentation of a non-current asset or disposal group classified as held for sale	38 – 40
Additional disclosures	41 – 42
Transitional Provisions	Aus42.1 – 43
Effective Date	Aus44B.1 – 44I

Appendices:

A. Defined Terms

B. Application Supplement

Implementation Guidance on IFRS 5
(available on the AASB website)

Basis for Conclusions on IFRS 5
(available on the AASB website)

Australian Accounting Standard AASB 5 *Non-current Assets Held for Sale and Discontinued Operations* (as amended) is set out in paragraphs 1 – 44I and in Appendices A – B. All the paragraphs have equal authority. Paragraphs in **bold type** state the main principles. Terms defined in this Standard are in *italics* the first time they appear in the Standard. AASB 5 is to be read in the context of other Australian Accounting Standards, including AASB 1048 *Interpretation of Standards*, which identifies the Australian Accounting Interpretations. In the absence of explicit guidance, AASB 108 *Accounting Policies, Changes in Accounting Estimates and Errors* provides a basis for selecting and applying accounting policies.

Compilation Details

Accounting Standard AASB 5 *Non-current Assets Held for Sale and Discontinued Operations* as amended

This compiled Standard applies to annual reporting periods beginning on or after 1 July 2012 but before 1 January 2013. It takes into account amendments up to and including 5 September 2011 and was prepared on 20 June 2012 by the staff of the Australian Accounting Standards Board (AASB).

This compilation is not a separate Accounting Standard made by the AASB. Instead, it is a representation of AASB 5 (July 2004) as amended by other Accounting Standards, which are listed in the Table below.

Table of Standards

Standard	Date made	Application date *(annual reporting periods ... on or after ...)*	Application, saving or transitional provisions
AASB 5	15 Jul 2004	*(beginning)* 1 Jan 2005	
AASB 2007-3	26 Feb 2007	*(beginning)* 1 Jan 2009	see (a) below
AASB 2007-4	30 Apr 2007	*(beginning)* 1 Jul 2007	see (b) below
AASB 2007-7	28 Jun 2007	*(beginning)* 1 Jul 2007	see (b) below
AASB 2007-8	24 Sep 2007	*(beginning)* 1 Jan 2009	see (c) below
AASB 2007-9	13 Dec 2007	*(beginning)* 1 Jul 2008	see (d) below
AASB 2007-10	13 Dec 2007	*(beginning)* 1 Jan 2009	see (c) below
AASB 2008-3	6 Mar 2008	*(beginning)* 1 Jul 2009	see (e) below
AASB 2008-5	24 Jul 2008	*(beginning)* 1 Jan 2009	see (f) below
AASB 2008-6	24 Jul 2008	*(beginning)* 1 Jul 2009	see (g) below
AASB 2008-13	18 Dec 2008	*(beginning)* 1 Jul 2009	see (h) below
AASB 2009-5	21 May 2009	*(beginning)* 1 Jan 2010	see (i) below
AASB 2009-6	25 Jun 2009	*(beginning)* 1 Jan 2009 and *(ending)* 30 Jun 2009	see (j) below
AASB 2009-7	25 Jun 2009	*(beginning)* 1 Jul 2009	see (k) below
AASB 2009-11	7 Dec 2009	*(beginning)* 1 Jan 2013	not compiled*
AASB 2009-12	15 Dec 2009	*(beginning)* 1 Jan 2011	see (l) below
AASB 2010-2	30 Jun 2010	*(beginning)* 1 Jul 2013	not compiled*
AASB 2010-5	27 Oct 2010	*(beginning)* 1 Jan 2011	see (l) below
AASB 2010-7	6 Dec 2010	*(beginning)* 1 Jan 2013	not compiled*
AASB 2011-1	11 May 2011	*(beginning)* 1 Jul 2011	see (m) below
AASB 2011-7	29 Aug 2011	*(beginning)* 1 Jan 2013	not compiled*
AASB 2011-8	2 Sep 2011	*(beginning)* 1 Jan 2013	not compiled*
AASB 2011-9	5 Sep 2011	*(beginning)* 1 Jul 2012	see (n) below

*   The amendments made by this Standard are not included in this compilation, which presents the principal Standard as applicable to annual reporting periods beginning on or after 1 July 2012 but before 1 January 2013.

(a)   Entities may elect to apply this Standard to annual reporting periods beginning on or after 1 January 2005 but before 1 January 2009, provided that AASB 8 *Operating Segments* is also applied to such periods.

(b)   Entities may elect to apply this Standard to annual reporting periods beginning on or after 1 January 2005 but before 1 July 2007.

(c)   Entities may elect to apply this Standard to annual reporting periods beginning on or after 1 January 2005 but before 1 January 2009, provided that AASB 101 *Presentation of Financial Statements* (September 2007) is also applied to such periods.

(d)   Entities may elect to apply this Standard to annual reporting periods beginning on or after 1 January 2005 but before 1 July 2008, provided that the Standards and Interpretation listed in paragraph 6 of AASB 2007-9 are also applied to such periods.

(e)   Entities may elect to apply this Standard to annual reporting periods beginning on or after 30 June 2007 but before 1 July 2009, provided that AASB 3 *Business Combinations* (March 2008) and AASB 127 *Consolidated and Separate Financial Statements* (March 2008) are also applied to such periods.

(f)   Paragraph 11 of this Standard specifies application provisions. Entities may elect to apply this Standard, or its amendments to individual Standards, to annual reporting periods beginning on or after 1 January 2005 but before 1 January 2009.

(g)   Entities may elect to apply this Standard to annual reporting periods beginning on or after 1 January 2005 but before 1 July 2009, provided that AASB 127 *Consolidated and Separate Financial Statements* (March 2008) is also applied to such periods.

(h)   Entities may elect to apply this Standard to annual reporting periods beginning on or after 1 January 2005 but before 1 July 2009, provided that AASB Interpretation 17 *Distributions of Non-cash Assets to Owners* is also applied to such periods.

(i)   Entities may elect to apply this Standard, or its amendments to individual Standards, to annual reporting periods beginning on or after 1 January 2005 but before 1 January 2010.

(j)   Entities may elect to apply this Standard to annual reporting periods beginning on or after 1 January 2005 but before 1 January 2009, provided that AASB 101 *Presentation of Financial Statements* (September 2007) is also applied to such periods, and to annual reporting periods beginning on or after 1 January 2009 that end before 30 June 2009.

(k)   Entities may elect to apply this Standard to annual reporting periods beginning before 1 July 2009 that end on or after 1 July 2008.

(l)   Entities may elect to apply this Standard to annual reporting periods beginning on or after 1 January 2005 but before 1 January 2011.

(m)   Entities may elect to apply this Standard, or its amendments to individual pronouncements, to annual reporting periods beginning on or after 1 January 2005 but before 1 July 2011, provided that AASB 1054 *Australian Additional Disclosures* is, or its relevant individual disclosure requirements are, also applied to such periods.

(n)   Entities may elect to apply this Standard to annual reporting periods beginning on or after 1 January 2005 but before 1 July 2012.

Table of Amendments

Paragraph affected	How affected	By ... [paragraph]
1	amended	AASB 2007-8 [6]
Aus1.1	amended	AASB 2007-8 [7, 8]
Aus1.4	amended	AASB 2007-8 [8]
Aus1.8	amended	AASB 2007-8 [8]
	deleted	AASB 2011-1 [9]
2 (footnote)	amended	AASB 2007-8 [6]
	amended	AASB 2010-5 [19]
Aus2.1-Aus2.4	amended	AASB 2007-9 [11]
5	amended	AASB 2008-5 [10]
5A	added	AASB 2008-13 [5]
	amended	AASB 2009-7 [7]
5B	added	AASB 2009-5 [8]
6 (preceding heading)	amended	AASB 2008-13 [6]
8	amended	AASB 2008-13 [7]
8A	added	AASB 2008-6 [9]
12	amended	AASB 2007-8 [6]
	amended	AASB 2007-10 [35, 36]
	amended	AASB 2009-12 [9]
12A	added	AASB 2008-13 [8]
15A	added	AASB 2008-13 [9]

Paragraph affected	How affected	By ... [paragraph]
28	amended	AASB 2007-4 [22]
	amended	AASB 2007-8 [23]
30	amended	AASB 2007-10 [36]
33	amended	AASB 2007-8 [6]
	amended	AASB 2008-3 [17]
33A	added	AASB 2007-8 [24]
	amended	AASB 2011-9 [12]
34	amended	AASB 2007-8 [6]
	amended	AASB 2007-10 [36]
36A	added	AASB 2008-6 [9]
38	amended	AASB 2007-8 [6, 25]
40	amended	AASB 2007-8 [6]
41	amended	AASB 2007-3 [7]
	amended	AASB 2007-8 [6]
Aus42.1	added	AASB 2007-4 [21]
43	added	AASB 2007-4 [21]
	amended	AASB 2007-7 [10]
44A	note added	AASB 2007-8 [26]
44B	note added	AASB 2008-3 [18]
Aus44B.1 (and preceding heading)	added	AASB 2008-3 [19]
	amended	AASB 2008-6 [10]
44C	added	AASB 2008-6 [11]
44D	amended	AASB 2009-7 [8]
Aus44D	added	AASB 2008-13 [10]
	renumbered as 44D	AASB 2009-7 [8]
44E	added	AASB 2009-5 [8]
44I	added	AASB 2011-9 [12]
Appendix A, definition of 'current asset'	amended	AASB 2007-8 [27]
	amended	AASB 2009-6 [30]

Comparison with IFRS 5

AASB 5 and IFRS 5

AASB 5 *Non-current Assets Held for Sale and Discontinued Operations* as amended incorporates IFRS 5 *Non-current Assets Held for Sale and Discontinued Operations* as issued and amended by the International Accounting Standards Board (IASB). Paragraphs that have been added to this Standard (and do not appear in the text of IFRS 5) are identified with the prefix "Aus", followed by the number of the preceding IASB paragraph and decimal numbering.

Compliance with IFRS 5

Entities that comply with AASB 5 as amended will simultaneously be in compliance with IFRS 5 as amended, except for government controlled entities that restructure administrative arrangements or administered activities.

Accounting Standard AASB 5

The Australian Accounting Standards Board made Accounting Standard AASB 5 *Non current Assets Held for Sale and Discontinued Operations* under section 334 of the *Corporations Act 2001* on 15 July 2004.

This compiled version of AASB 5 applies to annual reporting periods beginning on or after 1 July 2012 but before 1 January 2013. It incorporates relevant amendments contained in other AASB Standards made by the AASB up to and including 5 September 2011 (see Compilation Details).

Accounting Standard AASB 5

Non-current Assets Held for Sale and Discontinued Operations

Objective

1   The objective of this Standard is to specify the accounting for assets held for sale, and the presentation and disclosure of *discontinued operations*. In particular, the Standard requires:

(a)   assets that meet the criteria to be classified as held for sale to be measured at the lower of carrying amount and *fair value* less *costs to sell*, and depreciation on such assets to cease; and

(b)   assets that meet the criteria to be classified as held for sale to be presented separately in the statement of financial position and the results of discontinued operations to be presented separately in the statement of comprehensive income.

Application

Aus1.1   **This Standard applies to:**

(a)   **each entity that is required to prepare financial reports in accordance with Part 2M.3 of the Corporations Act and that is a reporting entity;**

(b)   **general purpose financial statements of each other reporting entity; and**

(c)   **financial statements that are, or are held out to be, general purpose financial statements.**

Aus1.2   **This Standard applies to annual reporting periods beginning on or after 1 January 2005.**
[Note: For application dates of paragraphs changed or added by an amending Standard, see Compilation Details.]

Aus1.3   **This Standard shall not be applied to annual reporting periods beginning before 1 January 2005.**

Aus1.4   **The requirements specified in this Standard apply to the financial statements where information resulting from their application is material in accordance with AASB 1031 *Materiality*.**

Aus1.5   **When applicable, this Standard supersedes AASB 1042 *Discontinuing Operations* as notified in the *Commonwealth of Australia Gazette* No S 456, 22 August 2000.**

Aus1.6   AASB 1042 remains applicable until superseded by this Standard.

Aus1.7   Notice of this Standard was published in the *Commonwealth of Australia Gazette* No S 294, 22 July 2004.

Scope

2   The classification and presentation requirements of this Standard apply to all recognised *non-current assets*[1] and to all *disposal groups* of an entity. The measurement requirements of this Standard apply to all recognised non-current assets and disposal groups (as set out in paragraph 4), except for those assets listed in paragraph 5 which shall continue to be measured in accordance with the Standard noted.

Aus2.1   **The requirements in this Standard do not apply to:**

(a)   **the restructuring of administrative arrangements; and**

(b)   **the restructuring of administered activities of government departments.**

---

1   For assets classified according to a liquidity presentation, non-current assets are assets that include amounts expected to be recovered more than twelve months after the reporting period. Paragraph 3 applies to the classification of such assets.

Aus2.2	AASB 1004 *Contributions* includes requirements for the disclosure of assets, liabilities and items of equity resulting from the restructuring of administrative arrangements.

Aus2.2   AASB 1004 *Contributions* includes requirements for the disclosure of assets, liabilities and items of equity resulting from the restructuring of administrative arrangements.

Aus2.3   An administered activity of a government department does not give rise to income and expenses of the department reporting the administered activity (see AASB 1050 *Administered Items*) and therefore, from the point of view of the department, the discontinuance of an administered activity does not give rise to a discontinued operation. However, if a government were to discontinue an activity that one of its departments had disclosed as an administered activity, from the point of view of that government the discontinuance may constitute a discontinued operation.

Aus2.4   Although AASB 3 *Business Combinations* contains requirements relating to the restructuring of local governments, these requirements only apply to the local government receiving assets or liabilities as a result of the restructuring. This Standard applies to the local government transferring assets and liabilities where the restructuring results in a discontinued operation of the transferor local government.

3   Assets classified as non-current in accordance with AASB 101 *Presentation of Financial Statements* shall not be reclassified as *current assets* until they meet the criteria to be classified as held for sale in accordance with this Standard. Assets of a class that an entity would normally regard as non-current that are acquired exclusively with a view to resale shall not be classified as current unless they meet the criteria to be classified as held for sale in accordance with this Standard.

4   Sometimes an entity disposes of a group of assets, possibly with some directly associated liabilities, together in a single transaction. Such a disposal group may be a group of *cash-generating units*, a single cash-generating unit, or part of a cash-generating unit[2]. The group may include any assets and any liabilities of the entity, including current assets, current liabilities and assets excluded by paragraph 5 from the measurement requirements of this Standard. If a non-current asset within the scope of the measurement requirements of this Standard is part of a disposal group, the measurement requirements of this Standard apply to the group as a whole, so that the group is measured at the lower of its carrying amount and fair value less costs to sell. The requirements for measuring the individual assets and liabilities within the disposal group are set out in paragraphs 18, 19 and 23.

5   The measurement provisions of this Standard[3] do not apply to the following assets, which are covered by the Australian Accounting Standards listed, either as individual assets or as part of a disposal group:

(a)   deferred tax assets (AASB 112 *Income Taxes*);

(b)   assets arising from employee benefits (AASB 119 *Employee Benefits*);

(c)   financial assets within the scope of AASB 139 *Financial Instruments: Recognition and Measurement*;

(d)   non-current assets that are accounted for in accordance with the fair value model in AASB 140 *Investment Property*;

(e)   non-current assets that are measured at fair value less costs to sell in accordance with AASB 141 *Agriculture;* and

(f)   contractual rights under insurance contracts as defined in AASB 4 *Insurance Contracts*.

5A   The classification, presentation and measurement requirements in this Standard applicable to a non-current asset (or disposal group) that is classified as held for sale apply also to a non-current asset (or disposal group) that is classified as held for distribution to owners acting in their capacity as owners (held for distribution to owners).

---

2   However, once the cash flows from an asset or group of assets are expected to arise principally from sale rather than continuing use, they become less dependent on cash flows arising from other assets, and a disposal group that was part of a cash-generating unit becomes a separate cash-generating unit.

3   Other than paragraphs 18 and 19, which require the assets in question to be measured in accordance with other applicable Australian Accounting Standards.

5B   This Standard specifies the disclosures required in respect of non-current assets (or disposal groups) classified as held for sale or discontinued operations. Disclosures in other Standards do not apply to such assets (or disposal groups) unless those Standards require:

(a)   specific disclosures in respect of non-current assets (or disposal groups) classified as held for sale or discontinued operations; or

(b)   disclosures about measurement of assets and liabilities within a disposal group that are not within the scope of the measurement requirement of AASB 5 and such disclosures are not already provided in the other notes to the financial statements.

Additional disclosures about non-current assets (or disposal groups) classified as held for sale or discontinued operations may be necessary to comply with the general requirements of AASB 101, in particular paragraphs 15 and 125 of that Standard.

Classification of Non-current Assets (or Disposal Groups) as Held for Sale or as Held for Distribution to Owners

6   **An entity shall classify a non-current asset (or disposal group) as held for sale if its carrying amount will be recovered principally through a sale transaction rather than through continuing use.**

7   For this to be the case, the asset (or disposal group) must be available for immediate sale in its present condition subject only to terms that are usual and customary for sales of such assets (or disposal groups) and its sale must be *highly probable*.

8   For the sale to be highly probable, the appropriate level of management must be committed to a plan to sell the asset (or disposal group), and an active program to locate a buyer and complete the plan must have been initiated. Further, the asset (or disposal group) must be actively marketed for sale at a price that is reasonable in relation to its current fair value. In addition, the sale should be expected to qualify for recognition as a completed sale within one year from the date of classification, except as permitted by paragraph 9, and actions required to complete the plan should indicate that it is unlikely that significant changes to the plan will be made or that the plan will be withdrawn. The probability of shareholders' approval (if required in the jurisdiction) should be considered as part of the assessment of whether the sale is highly probable.

8A   An entity that is committed to a sale plan involving loss of control of a subsidiary shall classify all the assets and liabilities of that subsidiary as held for sale when the criteria set out in paragraphs 6-8 are met, regardless of whether the entity will retain a non-controlling interest in its former subsidiary after the sale.

9   Events or circumstances may extend the period to complete the sale beyond one year. An extension of the period required to complete a sale does not preclude an asset (or disposal group) from being classified as held for sale if the delay is caused by events or circumstances beyond the entity's control and there is sufficient evidence that the entity remains committed to its plan to sell the asset (or disposal group). This will be the case when the criteria in Appendix B are met.

10   Sale transactions include exchanges of non-current assets for other non-current assets when the exchange has commercial substance in accordance with AASB 116 *Property, Plant and Equipment*.

11   When an entity acquires a non-current asset (or disposal group) exclusively with a view to its subsequent disposal, it shall classify the non-current asset (or disposal group) as held for sale at the acquisition date only if the one-year requirement in paragraph 8 is met (except as permitted by paragraph 9) and it is highly probable that any other criteria in paragraphs 7 and 8 that are not met at that date will be met within a short period following the acquisition (usually within three months).

12   If the criteria in paragraphs 7 and 8 are met after the reporting period, an entity shall not classify a non-current asset (or disposal group) as held for sale in those financial statements when issued. However, when those criteria are met after the reporting period but before the authorisation of the financial statements for issue, the entity shall disclose the information specified in paragraph 41(a), (b) and (d) in the notes.

12A A non-current asset (or disposal group) is classified as held for distribution to owners when the entity is committed to distribute the asset (or disposal group) to the owners. For this to be the case, the assets must be available for immediate distribution in their present condition and the distribution must be highly probable. For the distribution to be highly probable, actions to complete the distribution must have been initiated and should be expected to be completed within one year from the date of classification. Actions required to complete the distribution should indicate that it is unlikely that significant changes to the distribution will be made or that the distribution will be withdrawn. The probability of shareholders' approval (if required in the jurisdiction) should be considered as part of the assessment of whether the distribution is highly probable.

Non-current assets that are to be abandoned

13 An entity shall not classify as held for sale a non-current asset (or disposal group) that is to be abandoned. This is because its carrying amount will be recovered principally through continuing use. However, if the disposal group to be abandoned meets the criteria in paragraph 32(a)-(c), the entity shall present the results and cash flows of the disposal group as discontinued operations in accordance with paragraphs 33 and 34 at the date on which it ceases to be used. Non-current assets (or disposal groups) to be abandoned include non-current assets (or disposal groups) that are to be used to the end of their economic life and non-current assets (or disposal groups) that are to be closed rather than sold.

14 An entity shall not account for a non-current asset that has been temporarily taken out of use as if it had been abandoned.

Measurement of Non-current Assets (or Disposal Groups) Classified as Held for Sale

Measurement of a non-current asset (or disposal group)

15 **An entity shall measure a non-current asset (or disposal group) classified as held for sale at the lower of its carrying amount and fair value less costs to sell.**

15A **An entity shall measure a non-current asset (or disposal group) classified as held for distribution to owners at the lower of its carrying amount and fair value less costs to distribute[4].**

16 If a newly acquired asset (or disposal group) meets the criteria to be classified as held for sale (see paragraph 11), applying paragraph 15 will result in the asset (or disposal group) being measured on initial recognition at the lower of its carrying amount had it not been so classified (for example, cost) and fair value less costs to sell. Hence, if the asset (or disposal group) is acquired as part of a business combination, it shall be measured at fair value less costs to sell.

17 When the sale is expected to occur beyond one year, the entity shall measure the costs to sell at their present value. Any increase in the present value of the costs to sell that arises from the passage of time shall be presented in profit or loss as a financing cost.

18 Immediately before the initial classification of the asset (or disposal group) as held for sale, the carrying amounts of the asset (or all the assets and liabilities in the group) shall be measured in accordance with applicable Australian Accounting Standards.

19 On subsequent remeasurement of a disposal group, the carrying amounts of any assets and liabilities that are not within the scope of the measurement requirements of this Standard, but are included in a disposal group classified as held for sale, shall be remeasured in accordance with applicable Australian Accounting Standards before the fair value less costs to sell of the disposal group is remeasured.

Recognition of impairment losses and reversals

20 An entity shall recognise an impairment loss for any initial or subsequent write-down of the asset (or disposal group) to fair value less costs to sell, to the extent that it has not been recognised in accordance with paragraph 19.

---

4 Costs to distribute are the incremental costs directly attributable to the distribution, excluding finance costs and income tax expense.

21 An entity shall recognise a gain for any subsequent increase in fair value less costs to sell of an asset, but not in excess of the cumulative impairment loss that has been recognised either in accordance with this Standard or previously in accordance with AASB 136 *Impairment of Assets*.

22 An entity shall recognise a gain for any subsequent increase in fair value less costs to sell of a disposal group:

(a) to the extent that it has not been recognised in accordance with paragraph 19; but

(b) not in excess of the cumulative impairment loss that has been recognised, either in accordance with this Standard or previously in accordance with AASB 136, on the non-current assets that are within the scope of the measurement requirements of this Standard.

23 The impairment loss (or any subsequent gain) recognised for a disposal group shall reduce (or increase) the carrying amount of the non-current assets in the group that are within the scope of the measurement requirements of this Standard, in the order of allocation set out in paragraphs 104(a) and (b) and 122 of AASB 136.

24 A gain or loss not previously recognised by the date of the sale of a non-current asset (or disposal group) shall be recognised at the date of derecognition. Requirements relating to derecognition are set out in:

(a) paragraphs 67-72 of AASB 116 for property, plant and equipment; and

(b) paragraphs 112-117 of AASB 138 *Intangible Assets* for intangible assets.

25 An entity shall not depreciate (or amortise) a non-current asset while it is classified as held for sale or while it is part of a disposal group classified as held for sale. Interest and other expenses attributable to the liabilities of a disposal group classified as held for sale shall continue to be recognised.

Changes to a plan of sale

26 If an entity has classified an asset (or disposal group) as held for sale, but the criteria in paragraphs 7-9 are no longer met, the entity shall cease to classify the asset (or disposal group) as held for sale.

27 The entity shall measure a non-current asset that ceases to be classified as held for sale (or ceases to be included in a disposal group classified as held for sale) at the lower of:

(a) its carrying amount before the asset (or disposal group) was classified as held for sale, adjusted for any depreciation, amortisation or revaluations that would have been recognised had the asset (or disposal group) not been classified as held for sale; and

(b) its *recoverable amount* at the date of the subsequent decision not to sell.[5]

28 The entity shall include any required adjustment to the carrying amount of a non-current asset that ceases to be classified as held for sale in profit or loss[6] from continuing operations in the period in which the criteria in paragraphs 7-9 are no longer met. The entity shall present that adjustment in the same caption in the statement of comprehensive income used to present a gain or loss, if any, recognised in accordance with paragraph 37.

29 If an entity removes an individual asset or liability from a disposal group classified as held for sale, the remaining assets and liabilities of the disposal group to be sold shall continue to be measured as a group only if the group meets the criteria in paragraphs 7-9. Otherwise, the remaining non-current assets of the group that individually meet the criteria to be classified as held for sale shall be measured individually at the lower of their carrying amounts and fair values less costs to sell at that date. Any non-current assets that do not meet the criteria shall cease to be classified as held for sale in accordance with paragraph 26.

---

5   If the non-current asset is part of a cash-generating unit, its recoverable amount is the carrying amount that would have been recognised after the allocation of any impairment loss arising on that cash-generating unit in accordance with AASB 136.

6   Unless the asset is property, plant and equipment or an intangible asset that had been revalued in accordance with AASB 116 or AASB 138 before classification as held for sale, in which case the adjustment shall be treated as a revaluation increase or decrease.

Presentation and Disclosure

30   **An entity shall present and disclose information that enables users of the financial statements to evaluate the financial effects of discontinued operations and disposals of non-current assets (or disposal groups).**

Presenting discontinued operations

31   A *component of an entity* comprises operations and cash flows that can be clearly distinguished, operationally and for financial reporting purposes, from the rest of the entity. In other words, a component of an entity will have been a cash-generating unit or a group of cash-generating units while being held for use.

32   A discontinued operation is a component of an entity that either has been disposed of, or is classified as held for sale, and:

    (a)   represents a separate major line of business or geographical area of operations;

    (b)   is part of a single co-ordinated plan to dispose of a separate major line of business or geographical area of operations; or

    (c)   is a subsidiary acquired exclusively with a view to resale.

33   An entity shall disclose:

    (a)   a single amount in the statement of comprehensive income comprising the total of:

       (i)   the post-tax profit or loss of discontinued operations; and

       (ii)   the post-tax gain or loss recognised on the measurement to fair value less costs to sell or on the disposal of the assets or disposal group(s) constituting the discontinued operation;

    (b)   an analysis of the single amount in (a) into:

       (i)   the revenue, expenses and pre-tax profit or loss of discontinued operations;

       (ii)   the related income tax expense as required by paragraph 81(h) of AASB 112;

       (iii)   the gain or loss recognised on the measurement to fair value less costs to sell or on the disposal of the assets or disposal group(s) constituting the discontinued operation; and

       (iv)   the related income tax expense as required by paragraph 81(h) of AASB 112.

      The analysis may be presented in the notes or in the statement of comprehensive income. If it is presented in the statement of comprehensive income it shall be presented in a section identified as relating to discontinued operations, that is, separately from continuing operations. The analysis is not required for disposal groups that are newly acquired subsidiaries that meet the criteria to be classified as held for sale on acquisition (see paragraph 11).

    (c)   the net cash flows attributable to the operating, investing and financing activities of discontinued operations. These disclosures may be presented either in the notes or in the financial statements. These disclosures are not required for disposal groups that are newly acquired subsidiaries that meet the criteria to be classified as held for sale on acquisition (see paragraph 11).

    (d)   the amount of income from continuing operations and from discontinued operations attributable to owners of the parent. These disclosures may be presented either in the notes or in the statement of comprehensive income

33A   If an entity presents the items of profit or loss in a separate statement as described in paragraph 10A of AASB 101 (as amended in 2011), a section identified as relating to discontinued operations is presented in that statement.

34   An entity shall re-present the disclosures in paragraph 33 for prior periods presented in the financial statements so that the disclosures relate to all operations that have been discontinued by the end of the reporting period for the latest period presented.

35   Adjustments in the current period to amounts previously presented in discontinued operations that are directly related to the disposal of a discontinued operation in a prior

period shall be classified separately in discontinued operations. The nature and amount of such adjustments shall be disclosed. Examples of circumstances in which these adjustments may arise include the following:

(a)   the resolution of uncertainties that arise from the terms of the disposal transaction, such as the resolution of purchase price adjustments and indemnification issues with the purchaser;

(b)   the resolution of uncertainties that arise from and are directly related to the operations of the component before its disposal, such as environmental and product warranty obligations retained by the seller; and

(c)   the settlement of employee benefit plan obligations, provided that the settlement is directly related to the disposal transaction.

36   If an entity ceases to classify a component of an entity as held for sale, the results of operations of the component previously presented in discontinued operations in accordance with paragraphs 33-35 shall be reclassified and included in income from continuing operations for all periods presented. The amounts for prior periods shall be described as having been re-presented.

36A   An entity that is committed to a sale plan involving loss of control of a subsidiary shall disclose the information required in paragraphs 33-36 when the subsidiary is a disposal group that meets the definition of a discontinued operation in accordance with paragraph 32.

Gains or losses relating to continuing operations

37   Any gain or loss on the remeasurement of a non-current asset (or disposal group) classified as held for sale that does not meet the definition of a discontinued operation shall be included in profit or loss from continuing operations.

Presentation of a non-current asset or disposal group classified as held for sale

38   An entity shall present a non-current asset classified as held for sale and the assets of a disposal group classified as held for sale separately from other assets in the statement of financial position. The liabilities of a disposal group classified as held for sale shall be presented separately from other liabilities in the statement of financial position. Those assets and liabilities shall not be offset and presented as a single amount. The major classes of assets and liabilities classified as held for sale shall be separately disclosed either in the statement of financial position or in the notes, except as permitted by paragraph 39. An entity shall present separately any cumulative income or expense recognised in other comprehensive income relating to a non-current asset (or disposal group) classified as held for sale.

39   If the disposal group is a newly acquired subsidiary that meets the criteria to be classified as held for sale on acquisition (see paragraph 11), disclosure of the major classes of assets and liabilities is not required.

40   An entity shall not reclassify or re-present amounts presented for non-current assets or for the assets and liabilities of disposal groups classified as held for sale in the statements of financial position for prior periods to reflect the classification in the statement of financial position for the latest period presented.

Additional disclosures

41   An entity shall disclose the following information in the notes in the period in which a non-current asset (or disposal group) has been either classified as held for sale or sold:

(a)   a description of the non-current asset (or disposal group);

(b)   a description of the facts and circumstances of the sale, or leading to the expected disposal, and the expected manner and timing of that disposal;

(c)   the gain or loss recognised in accordance with paragraphs 20-22 and, if not separately presented in the statement of comprehensive income, the caption in the statement of comprehensive income that includes that gain or loss; and

(d)   if applicable, the reportable segment in which the non-current asset (or disposal group) is presented in accordance with AASB 8 *Operating Segments*.

42 If either paragraph 26 or paragraph 29 applies, an entity shall disclose, in the period of the decision to change the plan to sell the non-current asset (or disposal group), a description of the facts and circumstances leading to the decision and the effect of the decision on the results of operations for the period and any prior periods presented.

Transitional Provisions

Aus42.1 The following transitional paragraph shall not be applied by entities that have previously applied this Standard, unless required to do so by another Australian equivalent to IFRSs.

43 The Standard shall be applied prospectively to non-current assets (or disposal groups) that meet the criteria to be classified as held for sale and operations that meet the criteria to be classified as discontinued after the application date of the Standard. An entity may apply the requirements of the Standard to all non-current assets (or disposal groups) that meet the criteria to be classified as held for sale and operations that meet the criteria to be classified as discontinued after any date before the application date of the Standard, provided the valuations and other information needed to apply the Standard were obtained at the time those criteria were originally met.

Effective Date

44 [Deleted by the AASB]

44A [Deleted by the AASB]

44B [Deleted by the AASB]

Aus44B.1 AASB 2008-3 *Amendments to Australian Accounting Standards arising from AASB 3 and AASB 127* added the disclosures required by paragraph 33(d). The amendment shall be applied retrospectively.

44C Paragraphs 8A and 36A were added by AASB 2008-6 *Further Amendments to Australian Accounting Standards arising from the Annual Improvements Project* issued in July 2008. An entity shall apply those amendments for annual reporting periods beginning on or after 1 July 2009. Earlier application is permitted. However, an entity shall not apply the amendments for annual reporting periods beginning before 1 July 2009 unless it also applies AASB 127 *Consolidated and Separate Financial Statements* (as amended in 2008). If an entity applies the amendments before 1 July 2009 it shall disclose that fact. An entity shall apply the amendments prospectively from the date at which it first applied AASB 5, subject to the transitional provisions in paragraph 45 of AASB 127 (as amended in 2008).

44D Paragraphs 5A, 12A and 15A were added and paragraph 8 was amended by AASB 2008-13 *Amendments to Australian Accounting Standards arising from AASB Interpretation 17 - Distributions of Non-cash Assets to Owners* in December 2008. Those amendments shall be applied prospectively to non-current assets (or disposal groups) that are classified as held for distribution to owners in annual reporting periods beginning on or after 1 July 2009. Retrospective application is not permitted. Earlier application is permitted. If an entity applies the amendments for a period beginning on or after 1 January 2005 but before 1 July 2009 it shall disclose that fact and also apply AASB 3 (March 2008, as amended), AASB 127 *Consolidated and Separate Financial Statements* (as amended in July 2008) and AASB Interpretation 17 *Distributions of Non-cash Assets to Owners*.

44E Paragraph 5B was added by AASB 2009-5 *Further Amendments to Australian Accounting Standards arising from the Annual Improvements Project* issued in May 2009. An entity shall apply that amendment prospectively for annual reporting periods beginning on or after 1 January 2010. Earlier application is permitted. If an entity applies the amendment for an earlier period it shall disclose that fact.

44I AASB 2011-9 *Amendments to Australian Accounting Standards – Presentation of Items of Other Comprehensive Income*, issued in September 2011, amended paragraph 33A. An entity shall apply that amendment when it applies AASB 101 as amended in September 2011.

Withdrawal of IAS 35

45 [Deleted by the AASB]

Appendix A

Defined Terms

This appendix is an integral part of AASB 5.

cash-generating unit	The smallest identifiable group of assets that generates cash inflows that are largely independent of the cash inflows from other assets or groups of assets.
component of an entity	Operations and cash flows that can be clearly distinguished, operationally and for financial reporting purposes, from the rest of the entity.
costs to sell	The incremental costs directly attributable to the disposal of an asset (or **disposal group**), excluding finance costs and income tax expense.
current asset	An entity shall classify an asset as current when:

(a)   it expects to realise the asset, or intends to sell or consume it, in its normal operating cycle;

(b)   it holds the asset primarily for the purpose of trading;

(c)   it expects to realise the asset within twelve months after the reporting period; or

(d)   the asset is cash or a cash equivalent (as defined in AASB 7) unless the asset is restricted from being exchanged or used to settle a liability for at least twelve months after the reporting period.

discontinued operation	A **component of an entity** that either has been disposed of or is classified as held for sale and:

(a)   represents a separate major line of business or geographical area of operations;

(b)   is part of a single co-ordinated plan to dispose of a separate major line of business or geographical area of operations; or

(c)   is a subsidiary acquired exclusively with a view to resale.

disposal group	A group of assets to be disposed of, by sale or otherwise, together as a group in a single transaction, and liabilities directly associated with those assets that will be transferred in the transaction. The group includes goodwill acquired in a business combination if the group is a **cash-generating unit** to which goodwill has been allocated in accordance with the requirements of paragraphs 80-87 of AASB 136 *Impairment of Assets* or if it is an operation within such a cash-generating unit.
fair value	The amount for which an asset could be exchanged, or a liability settled, between knowledgeable, willing parties in an arm's length transaction.
firm purchase commitment	An agreement with an unrelated party, binding on both parties and usually legally enforceable, that (a) specifies all significant terms, including the price and timing of the transactions, and (b) includes a disincentive for non-performance that is sufficiently large to make performance **highly probable**.
highly probable	Significantly more likely than **probable**.
non-current asset	An asset that does not meet the definition of a **current asset**.
probable	More likely than not.

recoverable amount	The higher of an asset's **fair value** less **costs to sell** and its **value in use**.
value in use[1]	The present value of estimated future cash flows expected to arise from the continuing use of an asset and from its disposal at the end of its useful life.

Appendix B

Application Supplement

This appendix is an integral part of AASB 5.

Extension of the period required to complete a sale

B1   As noted in paragraph 9, an extension of the period required to complete a sale does not preclude an asset (or disposal group) from being classified as held for sale if the delay is caused by events or circumstances beyond the entity's control and there is sufficient evidence that the entity remains committed to its plan to sell the asset (or disposal group). An exception to the one-year requirement in paragraph 8 shall therefore apply in the following situations in which such events or circumstances arise:

(a)   at the date an entity commits itself to a plan to sell a non-current asset (or disposal group) it reasonably expects that others (not a buyer) will impose conditions on the transfer of the asset (or disposal group) that will extend the period required to complete the sale, and:

  (i)   actions necessary to respond to those conditions cannot be initiated until after a *firm purchase commitment* is obtained; and

  (ii)   a firm purchase commitment is highly probable within one year;

(b)   an entity obtains a firm purchase commitment and, as a result, a buyer or others unexpectedly impose conditions on the transfer of a non-current asset (or disposal group) previously classified as held for sale that will extend the period required to complete the sale, and:

  (i)   timely actions necessary to respond to the conditions have been taken; and

  (ii)   a favourable resolution of the delaying factors is expected;

(c)   during the initial one-year period, circumstances arise that were previously considered unlikely and, as a result, a non-current asset (or disposal group) previously classified as held for sale is not sold by the end of that period, and:

  (i)   during the initial one-year period the entity took action necessary to respond to the change in circumstances;

  (ii)   the non-current asset (or disposal group) is being actively marketed at a price that is reasonable, given the change in circumstances; and

  (iii) the criteria in paragraphs 7 and 8 are met.

---

1   Not for profit entities should refer to AASB 136 *Impairment of Assets* when the future economic benefits of an asset are not primarily dependent on the asset's ability to generate net cash inflows.

AASB 6
Exploration for and Evaluation of Mineral Resources
(Compiled October 2009)

Note from the Institute of Chartered Accountants Australia

This note, prepared by the technical editors, is not part of Accounting Standard AASB 6.

Historical development

December 2004: AASB 6 'Exploration for and Evaluation of Mineral Resources' is the Australian equivalent of IFRS 6 of the same name. It was made by the AASB on 9 December 2004 as part of the AASB's program to adopt International Financial Reporting Standards by 2005.

The Standard grandfathers 'area of interest' accounting to continue for exploration and evaluation costs and while impairment testing is required, the factors to be considered align closely with the requirements of the previous AASB 1022 'Accounting for the Extractive Industries'. AASB 6 is narrower in scope than AASB 1022, applying only to exploration and evaluation of mineral resources and not other phases of extractive industry activity that will now be regulated by other Australian equivalents to IFRS.

26 February 2007: AASB 2007-3 'Amendments to Australian Accounting Standards' was issued by the AASB. This Standard is applicable to annual reporting periods beginning on or after 1 January 2009.

30 April 2007: AASB 2007-4 'Amendments to Australian Accounting Standards' amends paragraph 9 and is applicable to annual reporting periods beginning on or after 1 January 2007. Entities may elect to early-adopt it to annual reporting periods beginning on or after 1 January 2005.

24 September 2007: AASB 2007-8 'Amendments to Australian Accounting Standards' amends AASB 6, changing the term 'general purpose financial reports' to 'general purpose financial statements'. This Standard is applicable to annual reporting periods beginning on or after 1 January 2009.

13 December 2007: AASB 2007-10 'Further Amendments to Australian Accounting Standards arising from AASB 101' amends AASB 6, replacing the term 'financial report' with 'financial statements'. This Standard is applicable to annual reporting periods beginning on or after 1 January 2009.

30 October 2009: AASB 6 was reissued by the AASB, compiled to include the AASB 2007-3, AASB 2007-8 and AASB 2007-10 amendments and applies to annual reporting periods beginning on or after 1 January 2009. Early application is permitted.

Reference

IFRIC items not taken onto the agenda: IFRS 6-1 *Application of the 'full-cost' method* applies to AASB 6.

AASB 6 compared to IFRS 6

Additions

Paragraph	Description
Aus 2.1	Which entities AASB 6 applies to (i.e. reporting entities and general purpose financial statements).
Aus 2.2	The application date of AASB 6 (i.e. annual reporting periods beginning 1 January 2005).
Aus 2.3	Prohibits early application of AASB 6.
Aus 2.4	Makes the requirements of AASB 6 subject to AASB 1031 'Materiality'.
Aus 2.5	Explains which Australian Standards have been superseded by AASB 6.

Aus 2.6	Clarifies that the superseded Australian Standards remain in force until AASB 6 applies.
Aus 2.7	Notice of the new Standard published on 13 December 2004.
Aus 7.1	The area of interest approach must be applied when accounting for exploration and evaluation costs. For each area of interest the relevant expenditures must be either expensed as incurred or capitalised in accordance with paragraph 7.2
Aus 7.2	Recognition requirements for an exploration and evaluation asset in relation to an area of interest which maintain the previous Australian requirements in AASB 1022 'Accounting for the Extractive Industries' (i.e. current rights to tenure and either costs expected to be recoverable or not at a stage to make a proper assessment of recoverability).
Aus 7.3	Discussion of the meaning of an area of interest including the observation that in most cases it will comprise a single mine or deposit or a separate oil or gas field.
Aus 9.1	Clarifies that direct and indirect costs associated with exploration and evaluation activities must be allocated to each area of interest (including the costs of outside contractors) for the purpose of expense/asset recognition.
Aus 9.2	Clarifies that the costs of acquiring lease or other rights to tenure in an area of interest are included if they form part of the exploration and evaluation activities.
Aus 9.3	Depreciation of equipment used in exploration and evaluation activities is an example of an indirect cost included in the recognition of exploration and evaluation assets.
Aus 9.4	General and administrative costs are only allocated to the cost of an exploration and evaluation asset if directly related to the operational activities of the relevant area of interest. Examples of general and administrative costs that must be expensed as incurred are directors' fees and share registry expenses.
Aus 13.1	If an entity changes its accounting policy for exploration and evaluation expenditures it must nonetheless continue to comply with paragraphs Aus 7.1 and Aus 7.2.
Aus 22.1	The level identified by the entity for impairment testing of exploration and evaluation assets shall no larger than the relevant area of interest.
Aus 24.1	If an entity recognises any exploration and evaluation assets, then it must disclose an explanation that recoverability is dependent on successful development and commercial exploitation or through sale.
Aus 27.1	The fact that an entity is applying the Australian equivalent to IFRS 6 must be disclosed for annual reporting periods beginning 1 January 2006.
Appendix A	Additional Australian defined terms for 'area of interest and 'economically recoverable reserves'.

Deletions

Paragraph	*Description*
26	Effective date of IFRS 6.

AASB

Contents

Compilation Details

Comparison with IFRS 6

Accounting Standard
AASB 6 Exploration for and Evaluation of Mineral Resources

	Paragraphs
Objective	1 – 2
Application	Aus2.1 – Aus2.7
Scope	3 – 5
Recognition of Exploration and Evaluation Assets	
Temporary exemption from AASB 108 paragraphs 11 and 12	6 – 7
Treatment of exploration and evaluation expenditures	Aus7.1 – Aus7.3
Measurement of Exploration and Evaluation Assets	
Measurement at recognition	8
Elements of cost of exploration and evaluation assets	9 – 11
Measurement after recognition	12
Changes in accounting policies	13 – 14
Presentation	
Classification of exploration and evaluation assets	15 – 16
Reclassification of exploration and evaluation assets	17
Impairment	
Recognition and measurement	18 – 20
Specifying the level at which exploration and evaluation assets are assessed for impairment	21 – Aus22.1
Disclosure	23 – 25
Transitional Provisions	27 – Aus27.1

Appendices:

A. Defined terms

B. Amendments to other Australian Accounting Standards

Basis for conclusions on IFRS 6
(available on the AASB website)

Australian Accounting Standard AASB 6 *Exploration for and Evaluation of Mineral Resources* (as amended) is set out in paragraphs 1 – Aus27.1 and Appendix A. All the paragraphs have equal authority. Paragraphs in **bold type** state the main principles. Terms defined in this Standard are in *italics* the first time they appear in the Standard. AASB 6 is to be read in the context of other Australian Accounting Standards, including AASB 1048 *Interpretation and Application of Standards*, which identifies the Australian Accounting Interpretations. In the absence of explicit guidance, AASB 108 *Accounting Policies, Changes in Accounting Estimates and Errors* provides a basis for selecting and applying accounting policies.

Compilation Details

Accounting Standard AASB 6 *Exploration for and Evaluation of Mineral Resources* as amended

This compiled Standard applies to annual reporting periods beginning on or after 1 January 2009. It takes into account amendments up to and including 13 December 2007 and was prepared on 30 October 2009 by the staff of the Australian Accounting Standards Board (AASB).

This compilation is not a separate Accounting Standard made by the AASB. Instead, it is a representation of AASB 6 (December 2004) as amended by other Accounting Standards, which are listed in the Table below.

Table of Standards

Standard	Date made	Application date *(annual reporting periods ... on or after ...)*	Application, saving or transitional provisions
AASB 6	9 Dec 2004	*(beginning)* 1 Jan 2005	
AASB 2007-3	26 Feb 2007	*(beginning)* 1 Jan 2009	see (a) below
AASB 2007-4	30 Apr 2007	*(beginning)* 1 Jul 2007	see (b) below
AASB 2007-8	24 Sep 2007	*(beginning)* 1 Jan 2009	see (c) below
AASB 2007-10	13 Dec 2007	*(beginning)* 1 Jan 2009	see (c) below

(a) Entities may elect to apply this Standard to annual reporting periods beginning on or after 1 January 2005 but before 1 January 2009, provided that AASB 8 *Operating Segments* is also applied to such periods.

(b) Entities may elect to apply this Standard to annual reporting periods beginning on or after 1 January 2005 but before 1 July 2007.

(c) Entities may elect to apply this Standard to annual reporting periods beginning on or after 1 January 2005 but before 1 January 2009, provided that AASB 101 *Presentation of Financial Statements* (September 2007) is also applied to such periods.

Table of Amendments

Paragraph affected	How affected	By ... [paragraph]
Aus7.2	amended	AASB 2007-8 [6]
9	amended	AASB 2007-4 [23]
21	amended	AASB 2007-3 [8]

General Terminology Amendments

References to 'financial report(s)' were amended to 'financial statements' by AASB 2007-8 and AASB 2007-10, except in relation to specific Corporations Act references. These amendments are not shown in the above Table of Amendments.

Comparison with IFRS 6

AASB 6 and IFRS 6

AASB 6 *Exploration for and Evaluation of Mineral Resources* as amended incorporates IFRS 6 *Exploration for and Evaluation of Mineral Resources* as issued and amended by the International Accounting Standards Board (IASB). Paragraphs that have been added to this Standard (and do not appear in the text of IFRS 6) are identified with the prefix "Aus", followed by the number of the preceding IASB paragraph and decimal numbering.

Compliance with IFRS 6

Entities that comply with AASB 6 as amended will simultaneously be in compliance with IFRS 6 as amended.

Accounting Standard AASB 6

The Australian Accounting Standards Board made Accounting Standard AASB 6 *Exploration for and Evaluation of Mineral Resources* under section 334 of the *Corporations Act 2001* on 9 December 2004.

This compiled version of AASB 6 applies to annual reporting periods beginning on or after 1 January 2009. It incorporates relevant amendments contained in other AASB Standards made by the AASB up to and including 13 December 2007 (see Compilation Details).

Accounting Standard AASB 6
Exploration for and Evaluation of Mineral Resources

Objective

1   The objective of this Standard is to specify the financial reporting for the *exploration for and evaluation of mineral resources*.

2   In particular, the Standard requires:

    (a)   limited improvements to existing accounting practices for *exploration and evaluation expenditures*;

    (b)   entities that recognise *exploration and evaluation* assets to assess such assets for impairment in accordance with this Standard and measure any impairment in accordance with AASB 136 *Impairment of Assets*; and

    (c)   disclosures that identify and explain the amounts in the entity's financial statements arising from the exploration for and evaluation of mineral resources and help users of those financial statements understand the amount, timing and certainty of future cash flows from any exploration and evaluation assets recognised.

Application

Aus2.1   **This Standard applies to:**

    (a)   **each entity that is required to prepare financial reports in accordance with Part 2M.3 of the Corporations Act and that is a reporting entity;**

    (b)   **general purpose financial statements of each other reporting entity; and**

    (c)   **financial statements that are, or are held out to be, general purpose financial statements.**

Aus2.2   **This Standard applies to annual reporting periods beginning on or after 1 January 2005.**
    [Note: For application dates of paragraphs changed or added by an amending Standard, see Compilation Details.]

Aus2.3   **This Standard shall not be applied to annual reporting periods beginning before 1 January 2005.**

Aus2.4   **The requirements specified in this Standard apply to the financial statements where information resulting from their application is material in accordance with AASB 1031 *Materiality*.**

Aus2.5   **When applicable, this Standard supersedes:**

    (a)   **AASB 1022 *Accounting for Extractive Industries* as notified in the *Commonwealth of Australia Gazette*, No S 338, 30 October 1989; and**

    (b)   **AAS 7 *Accounting for the Extractive Industries* issued in November 1989.**

Aus2.6   AASB 1022 and AAS 7 remain applicable until superseded by this Standard.

Aus2.7   Notice of this Standard was published in the *Commonwealth of Australia Gazette* No S 507, 13 December 2004.

Scope

3   An entity shall apply the Standard to exploration and evaluation expenditures that it incurs.

4   The Standard does not address other aspects of accounting by entities engaged in the exploration for and evaluation of mineral resources.

5   An entity shall not apply the Standard to expenditures incurred:

   (a)   before the exploration for and evaluation of mineral resources, such as expenditures incurred before the entity has obtained the legal rights to explore a specific area; and

   (b)   after the technical feasibility and commercial viability of extracting a mineral resource are demonstrable.

Recognition of Exploration and Evaluation Assets

Temporary exemption from AASB 108 paragraphs 11 and 12

6   When developing its accounting policies, an entity recognising exploration and evaluation assets shall apply paragraph 10 of AASB 108 *Accounting Policies, Changes in Accounting Estimates and Errors* and paragraphs Aus7.1 and Aus7.2 below.

7   Paragraphs 11 and 12 of AASB 108 specify sources of authoritative requirements and guidance that management is required to consider in developing an accounting policy for an item if no Standard applies specifically to that item. Subject to paragraphs 9 and 10 below, this Standard exempts an entity from applying those paragraphs to its accounting policies for the recognition and measurement of exploration and evaluation assets.

Treatment of exploration and evaluation expenditures

Aus7.1   An entity's accounting policy for the treatment of its exploration and evaluation expenditures shall be in accordance with the following requirements. For each *area of interest*, expenditures incurred in the exploration for and evaluation of mineral resources shall be:

   (a)   expensed as incurred; or

   (b)   partially or fully capitalised, and recognised as an exploration and evaluation asset if the requirements of paragraph Aus7.2 are satisfied.

   An entity shall make this decision separately for each area of interest.

Aus7.2   An exploration and evaluation asset shall only be recognised in relation to an area of interest if the following conditions are satisfied:

   (a)   the rights to tenure of the area of interest are current; and

   (b)   at least one of the following conditions is also met:

      (i)   the exploration and evaluation expenditures are expected to be recouped through successful development and exploitation of the area of interest, or alternatively, by its sale; and

      (ii)   exploration and evaluation activities in the area of interest have not at the end of the reporting period reached a stage which permits a reasonable assessment of the existence or otherwise of *economically recoverable reserves*, and active and significant operations in, or in relation to, the area of interest are continuing.

Aus7.3   An area of interest refers to an individual geological area whereby the presence of a mineral deposit or an oil or natural gas field is considered favourable or has been proved to exist. It is common for an area of interest to contract in size progressively, as exploration and evaluation lead towards the identification of a mineral deposit or an oil or natural gas field, which may prove to contain economically recoverable reserves. When this happens during the exploration for and evaluation of mineral resources, exploration and evaluation expenditures are still included in the cost of the exploration and evaluation asset notwithstanding that the size of the area of interest may contract as the exploration and evaluation operations progress. In most cases, an area of interest will comprise a single mine or deposit or a separate oil or gas field.

Measurement of Exploration and Evaluation Assets

Measurement at recognition

8   **Exploration and evaluation assets shall be measured at cost at recognition.**

Elements of cost of exploration and evaluation assets

9   An entity shall determine an accounting policy specifying which expenditures are recognised as exploration and evaluation assets and apply the policy consistently. In making this determination, an entity considers the degree to which the expenditure can be associated with finding specific mineral resources. The following are examples of expenditures that might be included in the initial measurement of exploration and evaluation assets (the list is not exhaustive):

(a)   acquisition of rights to explore;

(b)   topographical, geological, geochemical and geophysical studies;

(c)   exploratory drilling;

(d)   trenching;

(e)   sampling; and

(f)   activities in relation to evaluating the technical feasibility and commercial viability of extracting a mineral resource.

Aus9.1   In accordance with paragraph 9, where an entity recognises exploration and evaluation assets, direct and indirect costs associated with the exploration for and evaluation of mineral resources and which specifically relate to an area of interest are allocated to that area of interest. In making this allocation, no distinction is drawn between costs incurred within the entity and the cost of services performed by outside contractors or consultants on behalf of the entity.

Aus9.2   The costs of acquiring leases or other rights of tenure in the area of interest are included in the cost of the exploration and evaluation asset if they are acquired as part of the exploration for and evaluation of mineral resources.

Aus9.3   Indirect costs that are included in the cost of an exploration and evaluation asset include, among other things, charges for depreciation of equipment used in exploration and evaluation activities.

Aus9.4   General and administrative costs are allocated to, and included in, the cost of an exploration and evaluation asset, but only to the extent that those costs can be related directly to operational activities in the area of interest to which the exploration and evaluation asset relates. In all other cases, these costs are expensed as incurred. For example, general and administrative costs such as directors' fees, secretarial and share registry expenses, and salaries and other expenses of general management are recognised as expenses when incurred since they are only indirectly related to operational activities.

10   Expenditures related to the development of mineral resources shall not be recognised as exploration and evaluation assets. The *Framework for the Preparation and Presentation of Financial Statements* and AASB 138 *Intangible Assets* provide guidance on the recognition of assets arising from development.

11   In accordance with AASB 137 *Provisions, Contingent Liabilities and Contingent Assets* an entity recognises any obligations for removal and restoration that are incurred during a particular period as a consequence of having undertaken the exploration for and evaluation of mineral resources.

Measurement after recognition

12   After recognition, an entity shall apply either the cost model or the revaluation model to the exploration and evaluation assets. If the revaluation model is applied (either the

model in AASB 116 *Property, Plant and Equipment* or the model in AASB 138), it shall be consistent with the classification of the assets (see paragraph 15).

Changes in accounting policies

13 **An entity may change its accounting policies for exploration and evaluation expenditures if the change makes the financial statements more relevant to the economic decision-making needs of users and no less reliable, or more reliable and no less relevant to those needs. An entity shall judge relevance and reliability using the criteria in AASB 108.**

Aus13.1 Notwithstanding paragraph 13, any change in an entity's accounting policy for exploration and evaluation expenditures shall also remain in accordance with paragraphs Aus7.1 and Aus7.2.

14 To justify changing its accounting policies for exploration and evaluation expenditures, an entity shall demonstrate that the change brings its financial statements closer to meeting the criteria in AASB 108, but the change need not achieve full compliance with those criteria.

Presentation

Classification of exploration and evaluation assets

15 An entity shall classify exploration and evaluation assets as tangible or intangible according to the nature of the assets acquired and apply the classification consistently.

16 Some exploration and evaluation assets are treated as intangible (e.g. drilling rights), whereas others are tangible (e.g. vehicles and drilling rigs). To the extent that a tangible asset is consumed in developing an intangible asset, the amount reflecting that consumption is part of the cost of the intangible asset. However, using a tangible asset to develop an intangible asset does not change a tangible asset into an intangible asset.

Reclassification of exploration and evaluation assets

17 An exploration and evaluation asset shall no longer be classified as such when the technical feasibility and commercial viability of extracting a mineral resource are demonstrable. Exploration and evaluation assets shall be assessed for impairment, and any impairment loss recognised, before reclassification.

Impairment

Recognition and measurement

18 **Exploration and evaluation assets shall be assessed for impairment when facts and circumstances suggest that the carrying amount of an exploration and evaluation asset may exceed its recoverable amount. When facts and circumstances suggest that the carrying amount exceeds the recoverable amount, an entity shall measure, present and disclose any resulting impairment loss in accordance with AASB 136, except as provided by paragraph 21 below.**

19 For the purposes of exploration and evaluation assets only, paragraph 20 of this Standard shall be applied rather than paragraphs 8 17 of AASB 136 when identifying an exploration and evaluation asset that may be impaired. Paragraph 20 uses the term 'assets' but applies equally to separate exploration and evaluation assets or a cash-generating unit.

20 One or more of the following facts and circumstances indicate that an entity should test exploration and evaluation assets for impairment (the list is not exhaustive):

(a) the period for which the entity has the right to explore in the specific area has expired during the period or will expire in the near future, and is not expected to be renewed;

(b) substantive expenditure on further exploration for and evaluation of mineral resources in the specific area is neither budgeted nor planned;

(c) exploration for and evaluation of mineral resources in the specific area have not led to the discovery of commercially viable quantities of mineral resources and the entity has decided to discontinue such activities in the specific area;

(d)   sufficient data exist to indicate that, although a development in the specific area is likely to proceed, the carrying amount of the exploration and evaluation asset is unlikely to be recovered in full from successful development or by sale.

In any such case, or similar cases, the entity shall perform an impairment test in accordance with AASB 136. Any impairment loss is recognised as an expense in accordance with AASB 136.

Specifying the level at which exploration and evaluation assets are assessed for impairment

21   **An entity shall determine an accounting policy for allocating exploration and evaluation assets to cash-generating units or groups of cash-generating units for the purpose of assessing such assets for impairment. Each cash-generating unit or group of units to which an exploration and evaluation asset is allocated shall not be larger than an operating segment determined in accordance with AASB 8 *Operating Segments*.**

22   The level identified by the entity for the purposes of testing exploration and evaluation assets for impairment may comprise one or more cash-generating units.

Aus22.1   Notwithstanding paragraphs 21 and 22, the level identified by the entity for the purposes of testing exploration and evaluation assets for impairment shall be no larger than the area of interest to which the exploration and evaluation asset relates.

Disclosure

23   **An entity shall disclose information that identifies and explains the amounts recognised in its financial statements arising from the exploration for and evaluation of mineral resources.**

24   To comply with paragraph 23, an entity shall disclose:

(a)   its accounting policies for exploration and evaluation expenditures including the recognition of exploration and evaluation assets; and

(b)   the amounts of assets, liabilities, income and expense and operating and investing cash flows arising from the exploration for and evaluation of mineral resources.

Aus24.1   In addition to the disclosure required by paragraph 24(b), an entity that recognises exploration and evaluation assets for any of its areas of interest shall, in disclosing the amounts of those assets, provide an explanation that recoverability of the carrying amount of the exploration and evaluation assets is dependent on successful development and commercial exploitation, or alternatively, sale of the respective areas of interest.

25   An entity shall treat exploration and evaluation assets as a separate class of assets and make the disclosures required by either AASB 116 or AASB 138 consistent with how the assets are classified.

Effective date of IFRS 6

26   [Deleted by the AASB]

Transitional Provisions

27   If it is impracticable to apply a particular requirement of paragraph 18 to comparative information that relates to annual reporting periods beginning before 1 January 2005, an entity shall disclose that fact. AASB 108 explains the term 'impracticable'.

Aus27.1   For annual reporting periods beginning before 1 January 2006, an entity applying the Standard shall disclose the fact that it is applying the Standard, being the Australian equivalent to IFRS 6.

Appendix A
Defined Terms

This appendix is an integral part of AASB 6.

exploration and evaluation assets	**Exploration and evaluation expenditures** recognised as assets in accordance with the entity's accounting policy.
exploration and evaluation expenditures	Expenditures incurred by an entity in connection with the **exploration for and evaluation of mineral resources** before the technical feasibility and commercial viability of extracting a mineral resource are demonstrable.
exploration for and evaluation of mineral resources	The search for mineral resources, including minerals, oil, natural gas and similar non-regenerative resources after the entity has obtained legal rights to explore in a specific area, as well as the determination of the technical feasibility and commercial viability of extracting the mineral resource.

Additional Australian Defined Terms

area of interest	An individual geological area which is considered to constitute a favourable environment for the presence of a mineral deposit or an oil or natural gas field, or has been proved to contain such a deposit or field.
economically recoverable reserves	The estimated quantity of product in an **area of interest** that can be expected to be profitably extracted, processed and sold under current and foreseeable economic conditions.

Appendix B
Amendments to Other Australian Accounting Standards

The following amendments are made by AASB 2004-1 Amendments to Australian Accounting Standards. In this appendix, new text is underlined and deleted text is struck through.

B1   In AASB 1 *First-time Adoption of Australian Equivalents to International Financial Reporting Standards*, a heading and paragraph 36B are added as follows:

Exemption from the requirement to provide comparative disclosures for AASB 6

36B   In its first Australian-equivalents-to-IFRSs financial report, an entity that adopts Australian equivalents to IFRSs before 1 January 2006 need not present the disclosures required by AASB 6 *Exploration for and Evaluation of Mineral Resources* for comparative periods.

B2   In AASB 116 *Property, Plant and Equipment*, paragraph 3 is amended to read as follows:

3.   This Standard does not apply to:

(a)   property, plant and equipment classified as held for sale in accordance with AASB 5 *Non-current Assets Held for Sale and Discontinued Operations*;

(b)   biological assets related to agricultural activity (see AASB 141 *Agriculture*); ~~or~~

(c)   the recognition and measurement of exploration and evaluation assets (see AASB 6 *Exploration for and Evaluation of Mineral Resources*); or

(de)   mineral rights and mineral reserves such as oil, natural gas and similar non-regenerative resources.

However, this Standard applies to property, plant and equipment used to develop or maintain the assets described in (b) and -(ed).

B3   In AASB 138 *Intangible Assets*, paragraph 2 is amended to read as follows:

2.   **This Standard shall be applied in accounting for intangible assets, except:**

     (a)   **intangible assets that are within the scope of another Australian Accounting Standard;**

     (b)   **financial assets, as defined in AASB 139 *Financial Instruments: Recognition and Measurement*;**

     (c)   **the recognition and measurement of exploration and evaluation assets (see AASB 6 *Exploration for and Evaluation of Mineral Resources*); and**

     (dc)   **mineral rights and expenditure on the exploration for, or development and extraction of; minerals, oil, natural gas and similar non-regenerative resources.**

AASB 7
Financial Instruments: Disclosures

(Compiled June 2012)

Note from the Institute of Chartered Accountants Australia

This note, prepared by the technical editors, is not part of Accounting Standard AASB 7.

Historical development

31 August 2005: AASB 7 'Financial Instruments: Disclosures' is the Australian equivalent of IFRS 7 of the same name. It was issued by the AASB on 31 August 2005 as part of the AASB's program to adopt International Financial Reporting Standards by 2005. The Standard was issued to replace both AASB 130 'Disclosures in the Financial Statements of Banks and Similar Financial Institutions' and the disclosure requirements contained in paragraphs 51 to 95 of AASB 132 'Financial Instruments: Disclosure and Presentation'.

Note that the Standard applies to annual reporting periods beginning on or after 1 January 2007, with early adoption permitted for annual reporting periods beginning on or after 1 January 2005.

30 April 2007: AASB 2007-4 'Amendments to Australian Accounting Standards' amends paragraphs B26 and D1 and is applicable to annual reporting periods beginning on or after 1 July 2007. Entities may elect to early-adopt it to annual reporting periods beginning on or after 1 January 2005.

24 September 2007: AASB 2007-8 'Amendments to Australian Accounting Standards' was issued by the AASB. This Standard is applicable to annual reporting periods beginning on or after 1 January 2009.

13 December 2007: AASB 2007-10 'Further Amendments to Australian Accounting Standards arising from AASB 101' amends AASB 7, replacing the term 'financial report' with 'financial statements'. This Standard is applicable to annual reporting periods beginning on or after 1 January 2009.

5 March 2008: AASB 2008-2 'Amendments to Australian Accounting Standards – Puttable Financial Instruments and Obligations arising on Liquidation' classifies as equity instruments certain puttable financial instruments. This Standard is applicable to annual reporting periods beginning on or after 1 January 2009.

6 March 2008: AASB 2008-3 'Amendments to Australian Accounting Standards arising from AASB 3 and AASB 127' amends AASB 7 for the issue of AASB 3 Revised. This Standard is applicable to annual reporting periods beginning on or after 1 July 2009.

24 July 2008: AASB 2008-5 'Amendments to Australian Accounting Standards arising from the Annual Improvements Project' amends AASB 7 in relation to presentation of finance costs. This Standard is applicable to annual reporting periods beginning on or after 1 January 2009.

22 October 2008: AASB 2008-10 'Amendments to Australian Accounting Standards – Reclassification of Financial Assets' was issued by the AASB. The amendment aligns the disclosures in AASB 7 with the amendments to AASB 139, which permit an entity to reclassify some financial assets, in certain circumstances. This Standard is applicable from 1 July 2008. Early adoption is not permitted.

7 November 2008: AASB 7 was reissued by the AASB, compiled to include the AASB 2008-10 amendments.

18 December 2008: AASB 2008-12 'Amendments to Australian Accounting Standards – Reclassification of Financial Assets – Effective Date and Transition' was issued by the AASB, clarifying the amendments in AASB 2008-10 are applicable on or after 1 July 2008.

22 April 2009: AASB 2009-2 'Amendments to Australian Accounting Standards – Improving Disclosures about Financial Instruments' amends AASB 7 to require enhanced disclosures about fair value measurements and liquidity risk. This Standard is applicable to annual reporting periods beginning on or after 1 January 2009 that end on or after 30 April 2009.

---

25 June 2009: AASB 2009-6 'Amendments to Australian Accounting Standards' amends AASB 7 for editorial corrections made by the International Accounting Standards Board (IASB) to its Standards and Interpretations (IFRSs) and as a consequence of issuing revised AASB 101 *Presentation of Financial Statements* (September 2007). This Standard is applicable to annual reporting periods beginning on or after 1 January 2009 that end on or after 30 June 2009.

25 June 2009: AASB 2009-7 'Amendments to Australian Accounting Standards' amends AASB 7 arising from editorial corrections by the AASB and by the International Accounting Standards Board (IASB). This Standard is applicable to annual reporting periods beginning on or after 1 July 2009.

30 October 2009: AASB 7 was reissued by the AASB, compiled to include the AASB 2007-8, AASB 2007-10, AASB 2008-2, AASB 2008-3, AASB 2008-5, AASB 2009-2, AASB 2009-6 and AASB 2009-7 amendments and applies to annual reporting periods beginning on or after 1 July 2009. Early application is permitted only for annual reporting periods ending on or after 1 July 2008.

7 December 2009: AASB 2009-11 'Amendments to Australian Accounting Standards arising from AASB 9' amends AASB 7 to give effect to consequential changes arising from the issuance of AASB 9. This Standard is applicable to annual reporting periods beginning on or after 1 January 2013 with early adoption permitted from annual reporting periods ending on or after 31 December 2009 that begin before 1 January 2013 provided AASB 9 is also applied for the same period. The application date of AASB 2009-11 has been amended to 1 January 2015 by AASB 2012-6. **These amendments have been superseded by AASB 2010-7 and are not included in this compiled Standard.**

3 February 2010: AASB 2010-1 'Amendments to Australian Accounting Standards – Limited Exemption from Comparative AASB 7 Disclosures for First-time Adopters' amends AASB 7 to give limited exemption from comparative AASB 7 disclosures for first-time adopters. This Standard is applicable to annual reporting periods beginning on or after 1 July 2010 with early adoption permitted.

2 June 2010: AASB 2010-3 'Amendments to Australian Accounting Standards arising from the Annual Improvements Project' amends AASB 7 in relation to transition requirements for contingent consideration from a business combination that occurred before the effective date of the revised AASB 3 (2008). This Standard is applicable to annual reporting periods beginning on or after 1 July 2010 with early adoption permitted.

23 June 2010: AASB 2010-4 'Further Amendments to Australian Accounting Standards arising from the Annual Improvements Project' amends AASB 7 to clarify disclosures. This Standard is applicable to annual reporting periods beginning on or after 1 January 2011, with early adoption permitted for annual reporting periods beginning on or after 1 January 2005 but before 1 January 2011.

7 September 2010: AASB 7 was reissued by the AASB, compiled to include the AASB 2010-1 and AASB 1010-3 amendments and applies to annual reporting periods beginning on or after 1 July 2010 but before 1 January 2011.

8 November 2010: AASB 2010-6 'Amendments to Australian Accounting Standards – Disclosure on Transfers of Financial Assets' adds and amends disclosure requirements about transfers of financial assets. This Standard is applicable to annual reporting periods beginning on or after 1 July 2011.

1 March 2011: AASB 2010-7 'Amendments to Australian Accounting Standards arising from AASB 9 (December 2010)' as compiled amends AASB 7 to give effect to consequential changes arising from the reissue of AASB 9 in December 2010, and supersedes AASB 2009-11 which related to the previous version of AASB 9. This Standard applies to annual reporting periods beginning on or after 1 January 2013 and can be adopted early. The application date of AASB 2010-7 has been amended to 1 January 2015 by AASB 2012-6. **These amendments are not included in this compiled Standard.**

29 August 2011: AASB 2011-7 'Amendments to Australian Accounting Standards arising from the Consolidation and Joint Arrangements Standards' amends AASB 7 to give effect to many consequential changes arising from the issue of AASB 10, 11, 12, 127 and 128. This Standard applies to annual reporting periods beginning on or after 1 January 2013 and can be adopted early by for-profit entities. **These amendments are not included in this compiled Standard.**

2 September 2011: AASB 2011-8 'Amendments to Australian Accounting Standards arising from AASB 13' amends AASB 7 to give effect to a consequential change in the definition of fair value arising from the issue of AASB 13. This Standard applies to annual reporting periods beginning on or after 1 January 2013 and can be adopted early. **These amendments are not included in this compiled Standard.**

5 September 2011: AASB 2011-9 'Amendments to Australian Accounting Standards – Presentation of Items of Other Comprehensive income' amends the presentation of items in other comprehensive income. This Standard applies to annual reporting periods beginning on or after 1 July 2012 and can be adopted early.

23 September 2011: AASB 7 was reissued by the AASB, compiled to include the AASB 2010-4 and AASB 2010-6 amendments and applies to annual reporting periods ending on or after 1 July 2011 but before 1 July 2012.

21 March 2012: AASB 2012-1 'Amendments to Australian Accounting Standards – Fair Value Measurement – Reduced Disclosure Requirements' amends AASB 7 to establish and amend reduced disclosure requirements arising from AASB 13 'Fair Value Measurement'. **These amendments are not included in this compiled Standard.**

20 June 2012: AASB 7 was reissued by the AASB, compiled to include the AASB 2011-9 amendments and applies to annual reporting periods beginning on or after 1 July 2012 but before 1 January 2013.

29 June 2012: AASB 2012-2 'Amendments to Australian Accounting Standards – Disclosures – Offsetting Financial Assets and Financial Liabilities' extends AASB 7 disclosures in relation to the effect of netting arrangements and applies to reporting periods beginning on or after 1 January 2013. **These amendments are not included in this compiled Standard.**

10 September 2012: AASB 2012-7 'Amendments to Australian Accounting Standards arising from Reduced Disclosure Requirements' amends AASB 7 in relation to reduced disclosure requirements and applies to annual reporting periods beginning on or after 1 July 2013. **These amendments are not included in this compiled Standard.**

References

Interpretation 12 *Service Concession Arrangements* applies to AASB 7.

IFRIC items not taken onto the agenda: IFRS 7-1 *Presentation of 'net finance costs' on the face of the income statement* applies to AASB 7.

AASB 7 compared to IFRS 7

Additions

Paragraph	Description
Aus 2.1	Which entities AASB 7 applies to (i.e. reporting entities and general purpose financial statements).
Aus 2.2	The application date of AASB 7 (i.e. annual reporting periods beginning 1 January 2007).
Aus 2.3	Permits early application of AASB 7 for annual reporting periods beginning on or after 1 January 2005.
Aus 2.4	Makes the requirements of AASB 7 subject to AASB 1031 'Materiality'.
Aus 2.5	Explains which Australian Standards have been superseded by AASB 7 (i.e. AASB 130 and paragraphs 51 to 95 of AASB 132).
Aus 2.6	Clarifies that the superseded Australian Standards remain in force until AASB 7 applies.
Aus 2.7	Notes that the Standard will be registed on the Federal Register of Legislative Instruments.
Aus 2.8	Requires that notwithstanding paragraph Aus 2.3, an entity shall apply the Standard as amended by Appendix D if an entity applies the Standard to annual reporting periods beginning before 1 January 2006 and does not apply AASB 139 as amended by AASB 2005-4.

Deletions

Paragraph	Description
43	Effective date of IFRS 7.
44	Effective date of IFRS 7.
45	Withdrawal of IAS 30.

Contents

Compilation Details

Comparison with IFRS 7

Accounting Standard
AASB 7 Financial Instruments: Disclosures

	Paragraphs
Objective	1 – 2
Application	Aus2.1 – Aus2.8
Scope	3 – 5
Classes of Financial Instruments and Level of Disclosure	6
Significance of Financial Instruments for Financial Position and Performance	7
Statement of financial position	
Categories of financial assets and financial liabilities	8
Financial assets or financial liabilities at fair value through profit or loss	9 – 11
Reclassification	12 – 12A
Derecognition	13
Collateral	14 – 15
Allowance account for credit losses	16
Compound financial instruments with multiple embedded derivatives	17
Defaults and breaches	18 – 19
Statement of comprehensive income	
Items of income, expense, gains or losses	20
Other disclosures	
Accounting policies	21
Hedge accounting	22 – 24
Fair value	25 – 30
Nature and Extent of Risks Arising from Financial Instruments	31 – 32
Qualitative disclosures	33
Quantitative disclosures	34 – 35
Credit risk	36
Financial assets that are either past due or impaired	37
Collateral and other credit enhancements obtained	38
Liquidity risk	39
Market risk	
Sensitivity analysis	40 – 41
Other market risk disclosures	42
Effective Date and Transition	44B – 44K
Transfers of financial assets	42A – 42C
Transferred financial assets that are not derecognised in their entirety	42D
Transferred financial assets that are derecognised in their entirety	42E – 42G
Supplementary information	42H
Effective Date and Transition	44B – 44Q

Appendices:

A. Defined terms

B. Application guidance

C. Amendments to other Australian Accounting Standards

D. Amendments to AASB 7 if AASB 2005-4 *Amendments to Australian Accounting Standards* (relating to the fair value option) has not been applied

Deleted IFRS 7 Text

Implementation Guidance on IFRS 7
(available on the AASB website)

Basis for Conclusions on IFRS 7
(available on the AASB website)

Australian Accounting Standard AASB 7 *Financial Instruments: Disclosures* (as amended) is set out in paragraphs 1 – 44Q and Appendices A, B and D. All the paragraphs have equal authority. Paragraphs in **bold type** state the main principles. Terms defined in this Standard are in *italics* the first time they appear in the Standard. AASB 7 is to be read in the context of other Australian Accounting Standards, including AASB 1048 *Interpretation of Standards*, which identifies the Australian Accounting Interpretations. In the absence of explicit guidance, AASB 108 *Accounting Policies, Changes in Accounting Estimates and Errors* provides a basis for selecting and applying accounting policies.

Compilation Details

Accounting Standard AASB 7 *Financial Instruments: Disclosures* as amended

This compiled Standard applies to annual reporting periods beginning on or after 1 July 2012 but before 1 January 2013. It takes into account amendments up to and including 5 September 2011 and was prepared on 20 June 2012 by the staff of the Australian Accounting Standards Board (AASB).

This compilation is not a separate Accounting Standard made by the AASB. Instead, it is a representation of AASB 7 (August 2005) as amended by other Accounting Standards, which are listed in the Table below.

Table of Standards

Standard	Date made	Application date *(annual reporting periods ... on or after ...)*	Application, saving or transitional provisions
AASB 7	31 Aug 2005	*(beginning)* 1 Jan 2007	see (a) below
AASB 2007-4	30 Apr 2007	*(beginning)* 1 Jul 2007	see (b) below
AASB 2007-8	24 Sep 2007	*(beginning)* 1 Jan 2009	see (c) below
AASB 2007-10	13 Dec 2007	*(beginning)* 1 Jan 2009	see (c) below
AASB 2008-2	5 Mar 2008	*(beginning)* 1 Jan 2009	see (d) below
AASB 2008-3	6 Mar 2008	*(beginning)* 1 Jul 2009	see (e) below
AASB 2008-5	24 Jul 2008	*(beginning)* 1 Jan 2009	see (f) below
AASB 2008-10	22 Oct 2008	*(ending)* 1 Jul 2008	see (g) below
AASB 2008-12	18 Dec 2008	*(ending)* 1 Jul 2008	see (g) below
AASB 2009-2	22 Apr 2009	*(beginning)* 1 Jan 2009 and *(ending)* 30 Apr 2009	see (h) below

Standard	Date made	Application date *(annual reporting periods ... on or after ...)*	Application, saving or transitional provisions
AASB 2009-6	25 Jun 2009	*(beginning)* 1 Jan 2009 and *(ending)* 30 Jun 2009	see (i) below
AASB 2009-7	25 Jun 2009	*(beginning)* 1 Jul 2009	see (j) below
AASB 2009-11	7 Dec 2009	*(beginning)* 1 Jan 2013	not compiled*
AASB 2010-1	3 Feb 2010	*(beginning)* 1 Jul 2010	see (k) below
AASB 2010-3	23 Jun 2010	*(beginning)* 1 Jul 2010	see (k) below
AASB 2010-4	23 Jun 2010	*(beginning)* 1 Jan 2011	see (l) below
AASB 2010-2	30 Jun 2010	*(beginning)* 1 Jul 2013	not compiled*
AASB 2010-6	8 Nov 2010	*(beginning)* 1 Jul 2011	see (m) below
AASB 2010-7	6 Dec 2010	*(beginning)* 1 Jan 2013	not compiled*
AASB 2011-7	29 Aug 2011	*(beginning)* 1 Jan 2013	not compiled*
AASB 2011-8	2 Sep 2011	*(beginning)* 1 Jan 2013	not compiled*
AASB 2011-9	5 Sep 2011	*(beginning)* 1 Jul 2012	see (n) below
AASB 2012-1	21 Mar 2012	*(beginning)* 1 Jul 2013	not compiled*

* The amendments made by this Standard are not included in this compilation, which presents the principal Standard as applicable to annual reporting periods beginning on or after 1 July 2012 but before 1 January 2013.

(a) Entities may elect to apply this Standard to annual reporting periods beginning on or after 1 January 2005 but before 1 January 2007.

(b) Entities may elect to apply this Standard to annual reporting periods beginning on or after 1 January 2005 but before 1 July 2007.

(c) Entities may elect to apply this Standard to annual reporting periods beginning on or after 1 January 2005 but before 1 January 2009, provided that AASB 101 *Presentation of Financial Statements* (September 2007) is also applied to such periods.

(d) Entities may elect to apply this Standard to annual reporting periods beginning on or after 1 January 2005 but before 1 January 2009.

(e) Entities may elect to apply this Standard to annual reporting periods beginning on or after 30 June 2007 but before 1 July 2009, provided that AASB 3 *Business Combinations* (March 2008) and AASB 127 *Consolidated and Separate Financial Statements* (March 2008) are also applied to such periods.

(f) Entities may elect to apply this Standard, or its amendments to individual Standards, to annual reporting periods beginning on or after 1 January 2005 but before 1 January 2009.

(g) Entities are not permitted to apply this Standard to earlier annual reporting periods.

(h) Entities may elect to apply this Standard to annual reporting periods beginning on or after 1 January 2005 but before 1 January 2009 and to annual reporting periods beginning on or after 1 January 2009 that end before 30 April 2009.

(i) Entities may elect to apply this Standard to annual reporting periods beginning on or after 1 January 2005 but before 1 January 2009, provided that AASB 101 Presentation of Financial Statements (September 2007) is also applied to such periods, and to annual reporting periods beginning on or after 1 January 2009 that end before 30 June 2009.

(j) Entities may elect to apply this Standard to annual reporting periods beginning before 1 July 2009 that end on or after 1 July 2008.

(k) Entities may elect to apply this Standard to annual reporting periods beginning on or after 1 January 2005 but before 1 July 2010.

(l) Entities may elect to apply this Standard to annual reporting periods beginning on or after 1 January 2005 but before 1 January 2011.

(m) Entities may elect to apply this Standard to annual reporting periods beginning on or after 1 January 2005 but before 1 July 2011.

(n) Entities may elect to apply this Standard to annual reporting periods beginning on or after 1 January 2005 but before 1 July 2012.

Table of Amendments

Paragraph affected	How affected	By ... [paragraph]
1	amended	AASB 2007-10 [38]
Aus2.1	amended	AASB 2007-8 [7, 8]
Aus2.4	amended	AASB 2007-8 [8]
3	amended	AASB 2008-2 [6]
	amended	AASB 2008-5 [12]
	amended	AASB 2008-3 [20]
6	amended	AASB 2007-8 [6]
7	amended	AASB 2007-10 [38]
8 (and preceding heading)	amended	AASB 2007-8 [6]
12	amended	AASB 2008-10 [9]
12A	added	AASB 2008-10 [10]
13 (and preceding heading)	deleted	AASB 2010-6 [7]
18	amended	AASB 2007-10 [39]
20 (and preceding heading)	amended	AASB 2007-8 [28, 29]
21	amended	AASB 2007-8 [30]
23	amended	AASB 2007-8 [31]
26	amended	AASB 2007-8 [6]
27	amended	AASB 2007-8 [32]
	amended	AASB 2007-10 [38]
	amended	AASB 2009-2 [8]
27A	added	AASB 2009-2 [8]
27B	added	AASB 2009-2 [8]
	amended	AASB 2011-9 [13]
30	amended	AASB 2007-10 [38]
31	amended	AASB 2007-10 [38]
32A	added	AASB 2010-4 [10]
34	amended	AASB 2010-4 [10]
36-38	amended	AASB 2010-4 [10]
39	amended	AASB 2009-2 [9]
42A-42H (and preceding headings)	added	AASB 2010-6 [7]
43 (preceding heading)	amended	AASB 2007-4 [24]
	amended	AASB 2009-2 [10]
44A	note added	AASB 2007-8 [33]
44B	note added	AASB 2008-3 [21]
	paragraph added (in place of note)	AASB 2010-3 [8]
44C	note added	AASB 2008-2 [7]
44D	added	AASB 2008-5 [13]
Aus44E	added	AASB 2008-12 [4]
	renumbered as 44E and amended	AASB 2009-7 [9]
Aus44F	added	AASB 2008-12 [4]
	renumbered as 44F and amended	AASB 2009-7 [10]
44G	added	AASB 2009-2 [10]
	amended	AASB 2010-1 [8]
44K	added	AASB 2010-3 [8]

Paragraph affected	How affected	By ... [paragraph]
44L	added	AASB 2010-4 [10]
44M	added	AASB 2010-6 [8]
44Q	added	AASB 2011-9 [13]
Appendix A, definition of 'liquidity risk'	amended	AASB 2009-2 [11]
Appendix A, list of terms defined in AASB 132 or AASB 139	amended	AASB 2009-6 [31]
B3	amended	AASB 2007-10 [40]
B5	amended amended	AASB 2007-8 [34] AASB 2007-10 [38]
B10A	added	AASB 2009-2 [12]
B11 (and preceding heading)	amended	AASB 2009-2 [12]
B11A-B11F	added	AASB 2009-2 [12]
B12-B13	deleted	AASB 2009-2 [12]
B14	amended deleted	AASB 2007-8 [6, 35] AASB 2009-2 [12]
B15-B16	deleted	AASB 2009-2 [12]
B22	amended	AASB 2007-8 [6]
B26	amended	AASB 2007-4 [24]
B29-B39 (and preceding headings)	added	AASB 2010-6 [9]
D1	amended	AASB 2007-4 [24]

General Terminology Amendments

References to 'reporting date' were amended to 'end of the reporting period' by AASB 2007-8. These amendments are not shown in the above Table of Amendments.

Comparison with IFRS 7

AASB 7 and IFRS 7

AASB 7 *Financial Instruments: Disclosures* as amended incorporates IFRS 7 *Financial Instruments: Disclosures* as issued and amended by the International Accounting Standards Board (IASB). Paragraphs that have been added to this Standard (and do not appear in the text of IFRS 7) are identified with the prefix "Aus", followed by the number of the preceding IASB paragraph and decimal numbering.

Compliance with IFRS 7

Entities that comply with AASB 7 as amended will simultaneously be in compliance with IFRS 7 as amended.

Accounting Standard AASB 7

The Australian Accounting Standards Board made Accounting Standard AASB 7 *Financial Instruments: Disclosures* under section 334 of the *Corporations Act 2001* on 31 August 2005.

This compiled version of AASB 7 applies to annual reporting periods beginning on or after 1 July 2012 but before 1 January 2013. It incorporates relevant amendments contained in other AASB Standards made by the AASB up to and including 5 September 2011 (see Compilation Details).

Accounting Standard AASB 7

Financial Instruments: Disclosures

Objective

1   The objective of this Standard is to require entities to provide disclosures in their financial statements that enable users to evaluate:

(a)   the significance of financial instruments for the entity's financial position and performance; and

(b)   the nature and extent of risks arising from financial instruments to which the entity is exposed during the period and at the end of the reporting period, and how the entity manages those risks.

2   The principles in this Standard complement the principles for recognising, measuring and presenting financial assets and financial liabilities in AASB 132 *Financial Instruments: Presentation* and AASB 139 *Financial Instruments: Recognition and Measurement.*

Application

Aus2.1   **This Standard applies to:**

(a)   **each entity that is required to prepare financial reports in accordance with Part 2M.3 of the Corporations Act and that is a reporting entity;**

(b)   **general purpose financial statements of each other reporting entity; and**

(c)   **financial statements that are, or are held out to be, general purpose financial statements.**

Aus2.2   **This Standard applies to annual reporting periods beginning on or after 1 January 2007.**

[Note: For application dates of paragraphs changed or added by an amending Standard, see Compilation Details.]

Aus2.3   **This Standard may be applied to annual reporting periods beginning on or after 1 January 2005 but before 1 January 2007. An entity that is required to prepare financial reports in accordance with Part 2M.3 of the Corporations Act may apply this Standard to such annual reporting periods, when an election has been made in accordance with subsection 334(5) of the Corporations Act. When an entity applies this Standard to such an annual reporting period, it shall disclose that fact.**

Aus2.4   **The requirements specified in this Standard apply to the financial statements where information resulting from their application is material in accordance with AASB 1031 *Materiality.***

Aus2.5   **When applied or operative, this Standard supersedes:**

(a)   **AASB 130 *Disclosures in the Financial Statements of Banks and Similar Financial Institutions* as notified in the *Commonwealth of Australia Gazette* No S 204, 22 July 2004; and**

(b)   **paragraphs 51-95 of AASB 132 *Financial Instruments: Disclosure and Presentation* as notified in the *Commonwealth of Australia Gazette* No S 204, 22 July 2004.**

Aus2.6   Both AASB 130 and the disclosure requirements of AASB 132 remain applicable until superseded by this Standard.

Aus2.7   This Standard will be registered on the Federal Register of Legislative Instruments in accordance with the *Legislative Instruments Act 2003.*

Aus2.8   Notwithstanding paragraph Aus2.3, if an entity applies this Standard to annual reporting periods beginning before 1 January 2006 and it does not apply AASB 139 as amended by AASB 2005-4 it shall for that period apply this Standard as amended by Appendix D to this Standard.

Scope

3   This Standard shall be applied by all entities to all types of financial instruments, except:

(a)   those interests in subsidiaries, associates or joint ventures that are accounted for in accordance with AASB 127 *Consolidated and Separate Financial Statements*, AASB 128 *Investments in Associates* or AASB 131 *Interests in Joint Ventures*. However, in some cases, AASB 127, AASB 128 or AASB 131 permits an entity to account for an interest in a subsidiary, associate or joint venture using AASB 139; in those cases, entities shall apply the requirements of this Standard. Entities shall also apply this Standard to all derivatives linked to interests in subsidiaries, associates or joint ventures unless the derivative meets the definition of an equity instrument in AASB 132;

(b)   employers' rights and obligations arising from employee benefit plans, to which AASB 119 *Employee Benefits* applies;

(c)   [deleted by the IASB]

(d)   insurance contracts as defined in AASB 4 *Insurance Contracts*. However, this Standard applies to derivatives that are embedded in insurance contracts if AASB 139 *Financial Instruments: Measurement and Recognition* requires the entity to account for them separately. Moreover, an issuer shall apply this Standard to *financial guarantee contracts* if the issuer applies AASB 139 in recognising and measuring the contracts, but shall apply AASB 1023 *General Insurance Contracts* if the issuer elects, in accordance with paragraph 2.2(f) of AASB 1023, to apply AASB 1023 in recognising and measuring them;

(e)   financial instruments, contracts and obligations under share-based payment transactions to which AASB 2 *Share-based Payment* applies, except that this Standard applies to contracts within the scope of paragraphs 5-7 of AASB 139; and

(f)   instruments that are required to be classified as equity instruments in accordance with paragraphs 16A and 16B or paragraphs 16C and 16D of AASB 132.

4   This Standard applies to recognised and unrecognised financial instruments. Recognised financial instruments include financial assets and financial liabilities that are within the scope of AASB 139. Unrecognised financial instruments include some financial instruments that, although outside the scope of AASB 139, are within the scope of this Standard (such as some loan commitments).

5   This Standard applies to contracts to buy or sell a non-financial item that are within the scope of AASB 139 (see paragraphs 5-7 of AASB 139).

Classes of Financial Instruments and Level of Disclosure

6   When this Standard requires disclosures by class of financial instrument, an entity shall group financial instruments into classes that are appropriate to the nature of the information disclosed and that take into account the characteristics of those financial instruments. An entity shall provide sufficient information to permit reconciliation to the line items presented in the statement of financial position.

Significance of Financial Instruments for Financial Position and Performance

7   An entity shall disclose information that enables users of its financial statements to evaluate the significance of financial instruments for its financial position and performance.

Statement of financial position

Categories of financial assets and financial liabilities

8   The carrying amounts of each of the following categories, as defined in AASB 139, shall be disclosed either in the statement of financial position or in the notes:

(a)   financial assets at fair value through profit or loss, showing separately (i) those designated as such upon initial recognition and (ii) those classified as held for trading in accordance with AASB 139;

(b)   held-to-maturity investments;

(c)   loans and receivables;

(d)   available-for-sale financial assets;

(e)   financial liabilities at fair value through profit or loss, showing separately (i) those designated as such upon initial recognition and (ii) those classified as held for trading in accordance with AASB 139; and

(f)   financial liabilities measured at amortised cost.

Financial assets or financial liabilities at fair value through profit or loss

9   If the entity has designated a loan or receivable (or group of loans or receivables) as at fair value through profit or loss, it shall disclose:

(a)   the maximum exposure to *credit risk* (see paragraph 36(a)) of the loan or receivable (or group of loans or receivables) at the end of the reporting period;

(b)   the amount by which any related credit derivatives or similar instruments mitigate that maximum exposure to credit risk;

(c)   the amount of change, during the period and cumulatively, in the fair value of the loan or receivable (or group of loans or receivables) that is attributable to changes in the credit risk of the financial asset determined either:

(i)   as the amount of change in its fair value that is not attributable to changes in market conditions that give rise to *market risk*; or

(ii)   using an alternative method the entity believes more faithfully represents the amount of change in its fair value that is attributable to changes in the credit risk of the asset.

Changes in market conditions that give rise to market risk include changes in an observed (benchmark) interest rate, commodity price, foreign exchange rate or index of prices or rates; and

(d)   the amount of the change in the fair value of any related credit derivatives or similar instruments that has occurred during the period and cumulatively since the loan or receivable was designated.

10   If the entity has designated a financial liability as at fair value through profit or loss in accordance with paragraph 9 of AASB 139, it shall disclose:

(a)   the amount of change, during the period and cumulatively, in the fair value of the financial liability that is attributable to changes in the credit risk of that liability determined either:

(i)   as the amount of change in its fair value that is not attributable to changes in market conditions that give rise to market risk (see Appendix B, paragraph B4); or

(ii)   using an alternative method the entity believes more faithfully represents the amount of change in its fair value that is attributable to changes in the credit risk of the liability.

Changes in market conditions that give rise to market risk include changes in a benchmark interest rate, the price of another entity's financial instrument, a commodity price, a foreign exchange rate or an index of prices or rates. For contracts that include a unit-linking feature, changes in market conditions include changes in the performance of the related internal or external investment fund; and

(b)   the difference between the financial liability's carrying amount and the amount the entity would be contractually required to pay at maturity to the holder of the obligation.

11   The entity shall disclose:

(a)   the methods used to comply with the requirements in paragraphs 9(c) and 10(a); and

(b)   if the entity believes that the disclosure it has given to comply with the requirements in paragraph 9(c) or 10(a) does not faithfully represent the change in the fair value of the financial asset or financial liability attributable to changes in its credit risk, the reasons for reaching this conclusion and the factors it believes are relevant.

Reclassification

12   If the entity has reclassified a financial asset (in accordance with paragraphs 51-54 of AASB 139) as one measured:

(a)   at cost or amortised cost, rather than at fair value; or

(b)   at fair value, rather than at cost or amortised cost,

it shall disclose the amount reclassified into and out of each category and the reason for that reclassification.

12A   If the entity has reclassified a financial asset out of the fair value through profit or loss category in accordance with paragraph 50B or 50D of AASB 139 or out of the available-for-sale category in accordance with paragraph 50E of AASB 139, it shall disclose:

(a)   the amount reclassified into and out of each category;

(b)   for each reporting period until derecognition, the carrying amounts and fair values of all financial assets that have been reclassified in the current and previous reporting periods;

(c)   if a financial asset was reclassified in accordance with paragraph 50B, the rare situation, and the facts and circumstances indicating that the situation was rare;

(d)   for the reporting period when the financial asset was reclassified, the fair value gain or loss on the financial asset recognised in profit or loss or other comprehensive income in that reporting period and in the previous reporting period;

(e)   for each reporting period following the reclassification (including the reporting period in which the financial asset was reclassified) until derecognition of the financial asset, the fair value gain or loss that would have been recognised in profit or loss or other comprehensive income if the financial asset had not been reclassified, and the gain, loss, income and expense recognised in profit or loss; and

(f)   the effective interest rate and estimated amounts of cash flows the entity expects to recover, as at the date of reclassification of the financial asset.

13   [Deleted by the IASB]

Collateral

14   An entity shall disclose:

(a)   the carrying amount of financial assets it has pledged as collateral for liabilities or contingent liabilities, including amounts that have been reclassified in accordance with paragraph 37(a) of AASB 139; and

(b)   the terms and conditions relating to its pledge.

15   When an entity holds collateral (of financial or non-financial assets) and is permitted to sell or repledge the collateral in the absence of default by the owner of the collateral, it shall disclose:

(a)   the fair value of the collateral held;

(b)   the fair value of any such collateral sold or repledged, and whether the entity has an obligation to return it; and

(c)   the terms and conditions associated with its use of the collateral.

Allowance account for credit losses

16   When financial assets are impaired by credit losses and the entity records the impairment in a separate account (e.g. an allowance account used to record individual impairments or a similar account used to record a collective impairment of assets) rather than directly reducing the carrying amount of the asset, it shall disclose a reconciliation of changes in that account during the period for each class of financial assets.

Compound financial instruments with multiple embedded derivatives

17   If an entity has issued an instrument that contains both a liability and an equity component (see paragraph 28 of AASB 132) and the instrument has multiple embedded derivatives whose values are interdependent (such as a callable convertible debt instrument), it shall disclose the existence of those features.

Defaults and breaches

18   For *loans payable* recognised at the end of the reporting period, an entity shall disclose:

(a)   details of any defaults during the period of principal, interest, sinking fund, or redemption terms of those loans payable;

(b)   the carrying amount of the loans payable in default at the end of the reporting period; and

(c)   whether the default was remedied, or the terms of the loans payable were renegotiated, before the financial statements were authorised for issue.

19   If, during the period, there were breaches of loan agreement terms other than those described in paragraph 18, an entity shall disclose the same information as required by paragraph 18 if those breaches permitted the lender to demand accelerated repayment (unless the breaches were remedied, or the terms of the loan were renegotiated, on or before the end of the reporting period).

Statement of comprehensive income

Items of income, expense, gains or losses

20   An entity shall disclose the following items of income, expense, gains or losses either in the statement of comprehensive income or in the notes:

(a)   net gains or net losses on:

(i)   financial assets or financial liabilities at fair value through profit or loss, showing separately those on financial assets or financial liabilities designated as such upon initial recognition, and those on financial assets or financial liabilities that are classified as held for trading in accordance with AASB 139;

(ii)   available-for-sale financial assets, showing separately the amount of gain or loss recognised in other comprehensive income during the period and the amount reclassified from equity to profit or loss for the period;

(iii)   held-to-maturity investments;

(iv)   loans and receivables; and

(v)   financial liabilities measured at amortised cost;

(b)   total interest income and total interest expense (calculated using the effective interest method) for financial assets or financial liabilities that are not at fair value through profit or loss;

(c)   fee income and expense (other than amounts included in determining the effective interest rate) arising from:

(i)   financial assets or financial liabilities that are not at fair value through profit or loss; and

(ii)   trust and other fiduciary activities that result in the holding or investing of assets on behalf of individuals, trusts, retirement benefit plans, and other institutions;

> (d)   interest income on impaired financial assets accrued in accordance with paragraph AG93 of AASB 139; and
>
> (e)   the amount of any impairment loss for each class of financial asset.

Other disclosures

Accounting policies

21   In accordance with paragraph 117 of AASB 101 *Presentation of Financial Statements* (as revised in 2007), an entity discloses, in the summary of significant accounting policies, the measurement basis (or bases) used in preparing the financial statements and the other accounting policies used that are relevant to an understanding of the financial statements.

Hedge accounting

22   An entity shall disclose the following separately for each type of hedge described in AASB 139 (i.e. fair value hedges, cash flow hedges, and hedges of net investments in foreign operations):

    (a)   a description of each type of hedge;

    (b)   a description of the financial instruments designated as hedging instruments and their fair values at the end of the reporting period; and

    (c)   the nature of the risks being hedged.

23   For cash flow hedges, an entity shall disclose:

    (a)   the periods when the cash flows are expected to occur and when they are expected to affect profit or loss;

    (b)   a description of any forecast transaction for which hedge accounting had previously been used, but which is no longer expected to occur;

    (c)   the amount that was recognised in other comprehensive income during the period;

    (d)   the amount that was reclassified from equity to profit or loss for the period, showing the amount included in each line item in the statement of comprehensive income; and

    (e)   the amount that was removed from equity during the period and included in the initial cost or other carrying amount of a non-financial asset or non-financial liability whose acquisition or incurrence was a hedged highly probable forecast transaction.

24   An entity shall disclose separately:

    (a)   in fair value hedges, gains or losses:

        (i)   on the hedging instrument; and

        (ii)   on the hedged item attributable to the hedged risk;

    (b)   the ineffectiveness recognised in profit or loss that arises from cash flow hedges; and

    (c)   the ineffectiveness recognised in profit or loss that arises from hedges of net investments in foreign operations.

Fair value

25   Except as set out in paragraph 29, for each class of financial assets and financial liabilities (see paragraph 6), an entity shall disclose the fair value of that class of assets and liabilities in a way that permits it to be compared with its carrying amount.

26   In disclosing fair values, an entity shall group financial assets and financial liabilities into classes, but shall offset them only to the extent that their carrying amounts are offset in the statement of financial position.

27   An entity shall disclose for each class of financial instruments the methods and, when a valuation technique is used, the assumptions applied in determining fair values of each class of financial assets or financial liabilities. For example, if applicable, an entity discloses information about the assumptions relating to prepayment rates, rates of estimated credit losses, and interest rates or discount rates. If there has been a change in valuation technique, the entity shall disclose that change and the reasons for making it.

27A   To make the disclosures required by paragraph 27B an entity shall classify fair value measurements using a fair value hierarchy that reflects the significance of the inputs used in making the measurements. The fair value hierarchy shall have the following levels:

(a)   quoted prices (unadjusted) in active markets for identical assets or liabilities (Level 1);

(b)   inputs other than quoted prices included within Level 1 that are observable for the asset or liability, either directly (i.e. as prices) or indirectly (i.e. derived from prices) (Level 2); and

(c)   inputs for the asset or liability that are not based on observable market data (unobservable inputs) (Level 3).

The level in the fair value hierarchy within which the fair value measurement is categorised in its entirety shall be determined on the basis of the lowest level input that is significant to the fair value measurement in its entirety. For this purpose, the significance of an input is assessed against the fair value measurement in its entirety. If a fair value measurement uses observable inputs that require significant adjustment based on unobservable inputs, that measurement is a Level 3 measurement. Assessing the significance of a particular input to the fair value measurement in its entirety requires judgement, considering factors specific to the asset or liability.

27B   For fair value measurements recognised in the statement of financial position an entity shall disclose for each class of financial instruments:

(a)   the level in the fair value hierarchy into which the fair value measurements are categorised in their entirety, segregating fair value measurements in accordance with the levels defined in paragraph 27A.

(b)   any significant transfers between Level 1 and Level 2 of the fair value hierarchy and the reasons for those transfers. Transfers into each level shall be disclosed and discussed separately from transfers out of each level. For this purpose, significance shall be judged with respect to profit or loss, and total assets or total liabilities.

(c)   for fair value measurements in Level 3 of the fair value hierarchy, a reconciliation from the beginning balances to the ending balances, disclosing separately changes during the period attributable to the following:

   (i)   total gains or losses for the period recognised in profit or loss, and a description of where they are presented in the statement(s) of profit or loss and other comprehensive income;

   (ii)   total gains or losses recognised in other comprehensive income;

   (iii)   purchases, sales, issues and settlements (each type of movement disclosed separately); and

   (iv)   transfers into or out of Level 3 (e.g. transfers attributable to changes in the observability of market data) and the reasons for those transfers. For significant transfers, transfers into Level 3 shall be disclosed and discussed separately from transfers out of Level 3.

(d)   the amount of total gains or losses for the period in (c)(i) above included in profit or loss that are attributable to gains or losses relating to those assets and liabilities held at the end of the reporting period and a description of where those gains or losses are presented in the statement(s) of profit or loss and other comprehensive income.

(e)   for fair value measurements in Level 3, if changing one or more of the inputs to reasonably possible alternative assumptions would change fair value significantly, the entity shall state that fact and disclose the effect of those changes. The entity shall disclose how the effect of a change to a reasonably possible alternative assumption was calculated. For this purpose, significance shall be judged with respect to profit or loss, and total assets or total liabilities, or, when changes in fair value are recognised in other comprehensive income, total equity.

An entity shall present the quantitative disclosures required by this paragraph in tabular format unless another format is more appropriate.

28   If the market for a financial instrument is not active, an entity establishes its fair value using a valuation technique (see paragraphs AG74-AG79 of AASB 139). Nevertheless, the best evidence of fair value at initial recognition is the transaction price (i.e. the fair value of the consideration given or received), unless conditions described in paragraph AG76 of AASB 139 are met. It follows that there could be a difference between the fair value at initial recognition and the amount that would be determined at that date using the valuation technique. If such a difference exists, an entity shall disclose, by class of financial instrument:

(a)   its accounting policy for recognising that difference in profit or loss to reflect a change in factors (including time) that market participants would consider in setting a price (see paragraph AG76A of AASB 139); and

(b)   the aggregate difference yet to be recognised in profit or loss at the beginning and end of the period and a reconciliation of changes in the balance of this difference.

29   Disclosures of fair value are not required:

(a)   when the carrying amount is a reasonable approximation of fair value, for example, for financial instruments such as short-term trade receivables and payables;

(b)   for an investment in equity instruments that do not have a quoted market price in an active market, or derivatives linked to such equity instruments, that is measured at cost in accordance with AASB 139 because its fair value cannot be measured reliably; or

(c)   for a contract containing a discretionary participation feature (as described in AASB 4) if the fair value of that feature cannot be measured reliably.

30   In the cases described in paragraph 29(b) and (c), an entity shall disclose information to help users of the financial statements make their own judgements about the extent of possible differences between the carrying amount of those financial assets or financial liabilities and their fair value, including:

(a)   the fact that fair value information has not been disclosed for these instruments because their fair value cannot be measured reliably;

(b)   a description of the financial instruments, their carrying amount, and an explanation of why fair value cannot be measured reliably;

(c)   information about the market for the instruments;

(d)   information about whether and how the entity intends to dispose of the financial instruments; and

(e)   if financial instruments whose fair value previously could not be reliably measured are derecognised, that fact, their carrying amount at the time of derecognition, and the amount of gain or loss recognised.

Nature and Extent of Risks Arising from Financial Instruments

31   An entity shall disclose information that enables users of its financial statements to evaluate the nature and extent of risks arising from financial instruments to which the entity is exposed at the end of the reporting period.

32   The disclosures required by paragraphs 33-42 focus on the risks that arise from financial instruments and how they have been managed. These risks typically include, but are not limited to, credit risk, *liquidity risk* and market risk.

32A   Providing qualitative disclosures in the context of quantitative disclosures enables users to link related disclosures and hence form an overall picture of the nature and extent of risks arising from financial instruments. The interaction between qualitative and quantitative disclosures contributes to disclosure of information in a way that better enables users to evaluate an entity's exposure to risks.

Qualitative disclosures

33   For each type of risk arising from financial instruments, an entity shall disclose:

    (a)   the exposures to risk and how they arise;

    (b)   its objectives, policies and processes for managing the risk and the methods used to measure the risk; and

    (c)   any changes in (a) or (b) from the previous period.

Quantitative disclosures

34   For each type of risk arising from financial instruments, an entity shall disclose:

    (a)   summary quantitative data about its exposure to that risk at the end of the reporting period. This disclosure shall be based on the information provided internally to key management personnel of the entity (as defined in AASB 124 *Related Party Disclosures*), for example the entity's board of directors or chief executive officer;

    (b)   the disclosures required by paragraphs 36-42, to the extent not provided in accordance with (a); and

    (c)   concentrations of risk if not apparent from the disclosures made in accordance with (a) and (b).

35   If the quantitative data disclosed as at the end of the reporting period are unrepresentative of an entity's exposure to risk during the period, an entity shall provide further information that is representative.

Credit risk

36   An entity shall disclose by class of financial instrument:

    (a)   the amount that best represents its maximum exposure to credit risk at the end of the reporting period without taking account of any collateral held or other credit enhancements (e.g. netting agreements that do not qualify for offset in accordance with AASB 132); this disclosure is not required for financial instruments whose carrying amount best represents the maximum exposure to credit risk;

    (b)   a description of collateral held as security and of other credit enhancements, and their financial effect (e.g. a quantification of the extent to which collateral and other credit enhancements mitigate credit risk) in respect of the amount that best represents the maximum exposure to credit risk (whether disclosed in accordance with (a) or represented by the carrying amount of a financial instrument); and

    (c)   information about the credit quality of financial assets that are neither *past due* nor impaired.

    (d)   [deleted by the IASB]

Financial assets that are either past due or impaired

37   An entity shall disclose by class of financial asset:

    (a)   an analysis of the age of financial assets that are past due as at the end of the reporting period but not impaired; and

    (b)   an analysis of financial assets that are individually determined to be impaired as at the end of the reporting period, including the factors the entity considered in determining that they are impaired.

    (c)   [deleted by the IASB]

Collateral and other credit enhancements obtained

38   When an entity obtains financial or non-financial assets during the period by taking possession of collateral it holds as security or calling on other credit enhancements (e.g. guarantees), and such assets meet the recognition criteria in other Australian Accounting Standards, an entity shall disclose for such assets held at the reporting date:

    (a)   the nature and carrying amount of the assets; and

    (b)   when the assets are not readily convertible into cash, its policies for disposing of such assets or for using them in its operations.

Liquidity risk

39   An entity shall disclose:

(a)   a maturity analysis for non-derivative financial liabilities (including issued financial guarantee contracts) that shows the remaining contractual maturities.

(b)   a maturity analysis for derivative financial liabilities. The maturity analysis shall include the remaining contractual maturities for those derivative financial liabilities for which contractual maturities are essential for an understanding of the timing of the cash flows (see paragraph B11B).

(c)   a description of how it manages the liquidity risk inherent in (a) and (b).

Market risk

Sensitivity analysis

40   Unless an entity complies with paragraph 41, it shall disclose:

(a)   a sensitivity analysis for each type of market risk to which the entity is exposed at the end of the reporting period, showing how profit or loss and equity would have been affected by changes in the relevant risk variable that were reasonably possible at that date;

(b)   the methods and assumptions used in preparing the sensitivity analysis; and

(c)   changes from the previous period in the methods and assumptions used, and the reasons for such changes.

41   If an entity prepares a sensitivity analysis, such as value-at-risk, that reflects interdependencies between risk variables (e.g. interest rates and exchange rates) and uses it to manage financial risks, it may use that sensitivity analysis in place of the analysis specified in paragraph 40. The entity shall also disclose:

(a)   an explanation of the method used in preparing such a sensitivity analysis, and of the main parameters and assumptions underlying the data provided; and

(b)   an explanation of the objective of the method used and of limitations that may result in the information not fully reflecting the fair value of the assets and liabilities involved.

Other market risk disclosures

42   When the sensitivity analyses disclosed in accordance with paragraph 40 or 41 are unrepresentative of a risk inherent in a financial instrument (e.g. because the year-end exposure does not reflect the exposure during the year), the entity shall disclose that fact and the reason it believes the sensitivity analyses are unrepresentative.

Transfers of financial assets

42A   The disclosure requirements in paragraphs 42B-42H relating to transfers of financial assets supplement the other disclosure requirements of this Standard. An entity shall present the disclosures required by paragraphs 42B-42H in a single note in its financial statements. An entity shall provide the required disclosures for all transferred financial assets that are not derecognised and for any continuing involvement in a transferred asset, existing at the reporting date, irrespective of when the related transfer transaction occurred. For the purposes of applying the disclosure requirements in those paragraphs, an entity transfers all or a part of a financial asset (the transferred financial asset), if, and only if, it either:

(a)   transfers the contractual rights to receive the cash flows of that financial asset; or

(b)   retains the contractual rights to receive the cash flows of that financial asset, but assumes a contractual obligation to pay the cash flows to one or more recipients in an arrangement.

42B   An entity shall disclose information that enables users of its financial statements:

(a)   to understand the relationship between transferred financial assets that are not derecognised in their entirety and the associated liabilities; and

(b)   to evaluate the nature of, and risks associated with, the entity's continuing involvement in derecognised financial assets.

42C   For the purposes of applying the disclosure requirements in paragraphs 42E-42H, an entity has continuing involvement in a transferred financial asset if, as part of the transfer, the entity retains any of the contractual rights or obligations inherent in the transferred financial asset or obtains any new contractual rights or obligations relating to the transferred financial asset. For the purposes of applying the disclosure requirements in paragraphs 42E-42H, the following do not constitute continuing involvement:

(a)   normal representations and warranties relating to fraudulent transfer and concepts of reasonableness, good faith and fair dealings that could invalidate a transfer as a result of legal action;

(b)   forward, option and other contracts to reacquire the transferred financial asset for which the contract price (or exercise price) is the fair value of the transferred financial asset; or

(c)   an arrangement whereby an entity retains the contractual rights to receive the cash flows of a financial asset but assumes a contractual obligation to pay the cash flows to one or more entities and the conditions in paragraph 19(a)-(c) of AASB 139 are met.

Transferred financial assets that are not derecognised in their entirety

42D   An entity may have transferred financial assets in such a way that part or all of the transferred financial assets do not qualify for derecognition. To meet the objectives set out in paragraph 42B(a), the entity shall disclose at each reporting date for each class of transferred financial assets that are not derecognised in their entirety:

(a)   the nature of the transferred assets.

(b)   the nature of the risks and rewards of ownership to which the entity is exposed.

(c)   a description of the nature of the relationship between the transferred assets and the associated liabilities, including restrictions arising from the transfer on the reporting entity's use of the transferred assets.

(d)   when the counterparty (counterparties) to the associated liabilities has (have) recourse only to the transferred assets, a schedule that sets out the fair value of the transferred assets, the fair value of the associated liabilities and the net position (the difference between the fair value of the transferred assets and the associated liabilities).

(e)   when the entity continues to recognise all of the transferred assets, the carrying amounts of the transferred assets and the associated liabilities.

(f)   when the entity continues to recognise the assets to the extent of its continuing involvement (see paragraphs 20(c)(ii) and 30 of AASB 139), the total carrying amount of the original assets before the transfer, the carrying amount of the assets that the entity continues to recognise, and the carrying amount of the associated liabilities.

Transferred financial assets that are derecognised in their entirety

42E   To meet the objectives set out in paragraph 42B(b), when an entity derecognises transferred financial assets in their entirety (see paragraph 20(a) and (c)(i) of AASB 139) but has continuing involvement in them, the entity shall disclose, as a minimum, for each type of continuing involvement at each reporting date:

(a)   the carrying amount of the assets and liabilities that are recognised in the entity's statement of financial position and represent the entity's continuing involvement in the derecognised financial assets, and the line items in which the carrying amount of those assets and liabilities are recognised.

(b)   the fair value of the assets and liabilities that represent the entity's continuing involvement in the derecognised financial assets.

(c)   the amount that best represents the entity's maximum exposure to loss from its continuing involvement in the derecognised financial assets, and information showing how the maximum exposure to loss is determined.

(d) the undiscounted cash outflows that would or may be required to repurchase derecognised financial assets (e.g. the strike price in an option agreement) or other amounts payable to the transferee in respect of the transferred assets. If the cash outflow is variable then the amount disclosed should be based on the conditions that exist at each reporting date.

(e) a maturity analysis of the undiscounted cash outflows that would or may be required to repurchase the derecognised financial assets or other amounts payable to the transferee in respect of the transferred assets, showing the remaining contractual maturities of the entity's continuing involvement.

(f) qualitative information that explains and supports the quantitative disclosures required in (a)-(e).

42F An entity may aggregate the information required by paragraph 42E in respect of a particular asset if the entity has more than one type of continuing involvement in that derecognised financial asset, and report it under one type of continuing involvement.

42G In addition, an entity shall disclose for each type of continuing involvement:

(a) the gain or loss recognised at the date of transfer of the assets.

(b) income and expenses recognised, both in the reporting period and cumulatively, from the entity's continuing involvement in the derecognised financial assets (e.g. fair value changes in derivative instruments).

(c) if the total amount of proceeds from transfer activity (that qualifies for derecognition) in a reporting period is not evenly distributed throughout the reporting period (e.g. if a substantial proportion of the total amount of transfer activity takes place in the closing days of a reporting period):

    (i) when the greatest transfer activity took place within that reporting period (e.g. the last five days before the end of the reporting period),

    (ii) the amount (e.g. related gains or losses) recognised from transfer activity in that part of the reporting period, and

    (iii) the total amount of proceeds from transfer activity in that part of the reporting period. An entity shall provide this information for each period for which a statement of comprehensive income is presented.

Supplementary information

42H An entity shall disclose any additional information that it considers necessary to meet the disclosure objectives in paragraph 42B.

Effective Date and Transition

43 [Deleted by the AASB]

44 [Deleted by the AASB]

44A [Deleted by the AASB]

44B AASB 2008-3 *Amendments to Australian Accounting Standards arising from AASB 3 and AASB 127* deleted paragraph 3(c). An entity shall apply that amendment for annual reporting periods beginning on or after 1 July 2009. If an entity applies AASB 3 (revised 2008) for an earlier period, the amendment shall also be applied for that earlier period. However, the amendment does not apply to contingent consideration that arose from a business combination for which the acquisition date preceded the application of AASB 3 (revised 2008). Instead, an entity shall account for such consideration in accordance with paragraphs 65A-65E of AASB 3 (as amended in 2010).

44C [Deleted by the AASB]

44D Paragraph 3(a) was amended by AASB 2008-5 *Amendments to Australian Accounting Standards arising from the Annual Improvements Project* issued in July 2008. An entity shall apply that amendment for annual reporting periods beginning on or after 1 January 2009. Earlier application is permitted. If an entity applies the amendment for an earlier period it shall disclose that fact and apply for that earlier period the amendments to paragraph 1 of AASB 128, paragraph 1 of AASB 131 and paragraph 4 of AASB 132 issued in July 2008. An entity is permitted to apply the amendment prospectively.

44E AASB 2008-10 *Amendments to Australian Accounting Standards – Reclassification of Financial Assets*, issued in October 2008, amended paragraph 12 and added paragraph 12A. An entity shall apply those amendments on or after 1 July 2008.

44F AASB 2008-12 *Amendments to Australian Accounting Standards – Reclassification of Financial Assets – Effective Date and Transition*, issued in December 2008, added paragraph 44E. An entity shall apply that amendment on or after 1 July 2008.

44G AASB 2009-2 *Amendments to Australian Accounting Standards – Improving Disclosures about Financial Instruments*, issued in April 2009, amended paragraphs 27, 39 and B11 and added paragraphs 27A, 27B, B10A and B11A-B11F. An entity shall apply those amendments for annual reporting periods beginning on or after 1 January 2009 that end on or after 30 April 2009. An entity need not provide the disclosures required by the amendments for:

(a) any annual or interim period, including any statement of financial position, presented within an annual comparative period ending before 31 December 2009, or

(b) any statement of financial position as at the beginning of the earliest comparative period as at a date before 31 December 2009.

Earlier application is permitted. If an entity applies the amendments for an earlier period, it shall disclose that fact.[1]

44K Paragraph 44B was added by AASB 2010-3 *Amendments to Australian Accounting Standards arising from the Annual Improvements Project* issued in June 2010. An entity shall apply the last two sentences of paragraph 44B for annual reporting periods beginning on or after 1 July 2010. Earlier application is permitted.

44L AASB 2010-4 *Further Amendments to Australian Accounting Standards arising from the Annual Improvements Project* issued in June 2010 added paragraph 32A and amended paragraphs 34 and 36-38. An entity shall apply those amendments for annual reporting periods beginning on or after 1 January 2011. Earlier application is permitted. If an entity applies the amendments for an earlier period it shall disclose that fact.

44M AASB 2010-6 *Amendments to Australian Accounting Standards – Disclosures on Transfers of Financial Assets*, issued in November 2010, deleted paragraph 13 and added paragraphs 42A-42H and B29-B39. An entity shall apply those amendments for annual reporting periods beginning on or after 1 July 2011. Earlier application is permitted. If an entity applies the amendments from an earlier date, it shall disclose that fact. An entity need not provide the disclosures required by those amendments for any period presented that begins before the date of initial application of the amendments.

44Q AASB 2011-9 *Amendments to Australian Accounting Standards – Presentation of Items of Other Comprehensive Income*, issued in September 2011, amended paragraph 27B. An entity shall apply that amendment when it applies AASB 101 as amended in September 2011.

Withdrawal of IAS 30

45 [Deleted by the AASB]

---

1 Paragraph 44G was amended as a consequence of AASB 2010-1 *Amendments to Australian Accounting Standards – Limited Exemption from Comparative AASB 7 Disclosures for First-time Adopters* issued in February 2010. The AASB amended paragraph 44G to clarify its conclusions and intended transition for AASB 2009-2 *Amendments to Australian Accounting Standards – Improving Disclosures about Financial Instruments*.

Appendix A
Defined Terms

This appendix is an integral part of AASB 7.

credit risk	The risk that one party to a financial instrument will cause a financial loss for the other party by failing to discharge an obligation.
currency risk	The risk that the fair value or future cash flows of a financial instrument will fluctuate because of changes in foreign exchange rates.
interest rate risk	The risk that the fair value or future cash flows of a financial instrument will fluctuate because of changes in market interest rates.
liquidity risk	The risk that an entity will encounter difficulty in meeting obligations associated with financial liabilities that are settled by delivering cash or another financial asset.
loans payable	Loans payable are financial liabilities, other than short-term trade payables on normal credit terms.
market risk	The risk that the fair value or future cash flows of a financial instrument will fluctuate because of changes in market prices. Market risk comprises three types of risk: **currency risk**, **interest rate risk** and **other price risk**.
other price risk	The risk that the fair value or future cash flows of a financial instrument will fluctuate because of changes in market prices (other than those arising from **interest rate risk** or **currency risk**), whether those changes are caused by factors specific to the individual financial instrument or its issuer, or factors affecting all similar financial instruments traded in the market.
past due	A financial asset is past due when a counterparty has failed to make a payment when contractually due.

The following terms are defined in paragraph 11 of AASB 132 or paragraph 9 of AASB 139 and are used in this Standard with the meaning specified in AASB 132 and AASB 139:

(a)   amortised cost of a financial asset or financial liability;

(b)   available-for-sale financial assets;

(c)   derecognition;

(d)   derivative;

(e)   effective interest method;

(f)   equity instrument;

(g)   fair value;

(h)   financial asset;

(i)   financial asset or financial liability at fair value through profit or loss;

(j)   financial asset or financial liability held for trading;

(k)   financial guarantee contract;

(l)   financial instrument;

(m)   financial liability;

(n)   forecast transaction;

(o)   hedging instrument;

(p)   held-to-maturity instruments;

(q)   loans and receivables; and

(r)   regular way purchase or sale.

Appendix B

Application Guidance

This appendix is an integral part of AASB 7.

Classes of Financial Instruments and Level of Disclosure (paragraph 6)

B1 Paragraph 6 requires an entity to group financial instruments into classes that are appropriate to the nature of the information disclosed and that take into account the characteristics of those financial instruments. The classes described in paragraph 6 are determined by the entity and are, thus, distinct from the categories of financial instruments specified in AASB 139 (which determine how financial instruments are measured and where changes in fair value are recognised).

B2 In determining classes of financial instrument, an entity shall, at a minimum:

(a) distinguish instruments measured at amortised cost from those measured at fair value; and

(b) treat as a separate class or classes those financial instruments outside the scope of this Standard.

B3 An entity decides, in the light of its circumstances, how much detail it provides to satisfy the requirements of this Standard, how much emphasis it places on different aspects of the requirements and how it aggregates information to display the overall picture without combining information with different characteristics. It is necessary to strike a balance between overburdening financial statements with excessive detail that may not assist users of financial statements and obscuring important information as a result of too much aggregation. For example, an entity shall not obscure important information by including it among a large amount of insignificant detail. Similarly, an entity shall not disclose information that is so aggregated that it obscures important differences between individual transactions or associated risks.

Significance of Financial Instruments for Financial Position and Performance

Financial liabilities at fair value through profit or loss (paragraphs 10 and 11)

B4 If an entity designates a financial liability as at fair value through profit or loss, paragraph 10(a) requires it to disclose the amount of change in the fair value of the financial liability that is attributable to changes in the liability's credit risk. Paragraph 10(a)(i) permits an entity to determine this amount as the amount of change in the liability's fair value that is not attributable to changes in market conditions that give rise to market risk. If the only relevant changes in market conditions for a liability are changes in an observed (benchmark) interest rate, this amount can be estimated as follows:

(a) first, the entity computes the liability's internal rate of return at the start of the period using the observed market price of the liability and the liability's contractual cash flows at the start of the period. It deducts from this rate of return the observed (benchmark) interest rate at the start of the period, to arrive at an instrument-specific component of the internal rate of return;

(b) next, the entity calculates the present value of the cash flows associated with the liability using the liability's contractual cash flows at the end of the period and a discount rate equal to the sum of (i) the observed (benchmark) interest rate at the end of the period and (ii) the instrument-specific component of the internal rate of return as determined in (a); and

(c) the difference between the observed market price of the liability at the end of the period and the amount determined in (b) is the change in fair value that is not attributable to changes in the observed (benchmark) interest rate. This is the amount to be disclosed.

This example assumes that changes in fair value arising from factors other than changes in the instrument's credit risk or changes in interest rates are not significant. If the instrument in the example contains an embedded derivative, the change in fair value of the embedded derivative is excluded in determining the amount to be disclosed in accordance with paragraph 10(a).

Other disclosure – accounting policies (paragraph 21)

B5   Paragraph 21 requires disclosure of the measurement basis (or bases) used in preparing the financial statements and the other accounting policies used that are relevant to an understanding of the financial statements. For financial instruments, such disclosure may include:

(a)   for financial assets or financial liabilities designated as at fair value through profit or loss:

   (i)   the nature of the financial assets or financial liabilities the entity has designated as at fair value through profit or loss;

   (ii)   the criteria for so designating such financial assets or financial liabilities on initial recognition; and

   (iii)   how the entity has satisfied the conditions in paragraph 9, 11A or 12 of AASB 139 for such designation. For instruments designated in accordance with paragraph (b)(i) of the definition of a financial asset or financial liability at fair value through profit or loss in AASB 139, that disclosure includes a narrative description of the circumstances underlying the measurement or recognition inconsistency that would otherwise arise. For instruments designated in accordance with paragraph (b)(ii) of the definition of a financial asset or financial liability at fair value through profit or loss in AASB 139, that disclosure includes a narrative description of how designation at fair value through profit or loss is consistent with the entity's documented risk management or investment strategy;

(b)   the criteria for designating financial assets as available for sale;

(c)   whether regular way purchases and sales of financial assets are accounted for at trade date or at settlement date (see paragraph 38 of AASB 139);

(d)   when an allowance account is used to reduce the carrying amount of financial assets impaired by credit losses:

   (i)   the criteria for determining when the carrying amount of impaired financial assets is reduced directly (or, in the case of a reversal of a write-down, increased directly) and when the allowance account is used; and

   (ii)   the criteria for writing off amounts charged to the allowance account against the carrying amount of impaired financial assets (see paragraph 16);

(e)   how net gains or net losses on each category of financial instrument are determined (see paragraph 20(a)), for example, whether the net gains or net losses on items at fair value through profit or loss include interest or dividend income;

(f)   the criteria the entity uses to determine that there is objective evidence that an impairment loss has occurred (see paragraph 20(e)); and

(g)   when the terms of financial assets that would otherwise be past due or impaired have been renegotiated, the accounting policy for financial assets that are the subject of renegotiated terms (see paragraph 36(d)).

Paragraph 122 of AASB 101 (as revised in 2007) also requires entities to disclose, in the summary of significant accounting policies or other notes, the judgments, apart from those involving estimations, that management has made in the process of applying the entity's accounting policies and that have the most significant effect on the amounts recognised in the financial statements.

Nature and Extent of Risks Arising from Financial Instruments (paragraphs 31-42)

B6   [Deleted by the AASB]

Quantitative disclosures (paragraph 34)

B7   Paragraph 34(a) requires disclosures of summary quantitative data about an entity's exposure to risks based on the information provided internally to key management personnel of the entity. When an entity uses several methods to manage a risk exposure, the entity shall disclose information using the method or methods that provide the most relevant and reliable information. AASB 108 *Accounting Policies, Changes in Accounting Estimates and Errors* discusses relevance and reliability.

B8   Paragraph 34(c) requires disclosures about concentrations of risk. Concentrations of risk arise from financial instruments that have similar characteristics and are affected similarly by changes in economic or other conditions. The identification of concentrations of risk requires judgement taking into account the circumstances of the entity. Disclosure of concentrations of risk shall include:

(a)   a description of how management determines concentrations;

(b)   a description of the shared characteristic that identifies each concentration (e.g. counterparty, geographical area, currency or market); and

(c)   the amount of the risk exposure associated with all financial instruments sharing that characteristic.

Maximum credit risk exposure (paragraph 36(a))

B9   Paragraph 36(a) requires disclosure of the amount that best represents the entity's maximum exposure to credit risk. For a financial asset, this is typically the gross carrying amount, net of:

(a)   any amounts offset in accordance with AASB 132; and

(b)   any impairment losses recognised in accordance with AASB 139.

B10   Activities that give rise to credit risk and the associated maximum exposure to credit risk include, but are not limited to:

(a)   granting loans and receivables to customers and placing deposits with other entities. In these cases, the maximum exposure to credit risk is the carrying amount of the related financial assets;

(b)   entering into derivative contracts, for example, foreign exchange contracts, interest rate swaps and credit derivatives. When the resulting asset is measured at fair value, the maximum exposure to credit risk at the end of the reporting period will equal the carrying amount;

(c)   granting financial guarantees. In this case, the maximum exposure to credit risk is the maximum amount the entity could have to pay if the guarantee is called on, which may be significantly greater than the amount recognised as a liability; and

(d)   making a loan commitment that is irrevocable over the life of the facility or is revocable only in response to a material adverse change. If the issuer cannot settle the loan commitment net in cash or another financial instrument, the maximum credit exposure is the full amount of the commitment. This is because it is uncertain whether the amount of any undrawn portion may be drawn upon in the future. This may be significantly greater than the amount recognised as a liability.

Quantitative liquidity risk disclosures (paragraphs 34(a) and 39(a) and (b))

B10A In accordance with paragraph 34(a) an entity discloses summary quantitative data about its exposure to liquidity risk on the basis of the information provided internally to key management personnel. An entity shall explain how those data are determined. If the outflows of cash (or another financial asset) included in those data could either:

(a)   occur significantly earlier than indicated in the data, or

(b)   be for significantly different amounts from those indicated in the data (e.g. for a derivative that is included in the data on a net settlement basis but for which the counterparty has the option to require gross settlement),

the entity shall state that fact and provide quantitative information that enables users of its financial statements to evaluate the extent of this risk unless that information is included in the contractual maturity analyses required by paragraph 39(a) or (b).

B11   In preparing the maturity analyses required by paragraphs 39(a) and (b), an entity uses its judgement to determine an appropriate number of time bands. For example, an entity might determine that the following time bands are appropriate:

(a)   not later than one month;

(b)   later than one month and not later than three months;

(c)   later than three months and not later than one year; and

(d)   later than one year and not later than five years.

B11A   In complying with paragraphs 39(a) and (b), an entity shall not separate an embedded derivative from a hybrid (combined) financial instrument. For such an instrument, an entity shall apply paragraph 39(a).

B11B   Paragraph 39(b) requires an entity to disclose a quantitative maturity analysis for derivative financial liabilities that shows remaining contractual maturities if the contractual maturities are essential for an understanding of the timing of the cash flows. For example, this would be the case for:

(a)   an interest rate swap with a remaining maturity of five years in a cash flow hedge of a variable rate financial asset or liability.

(b)   all loan commitments.

B11C   Paragraphs 39(a) and (b) requires an entity to disclose maturity analyses for financial liabilities that show the remaining contractual maturities for some financial liabilities. In this disclosure:

(a)   when a counterparty has a choice of when an amount is paid, the liability is allocated to the earliest period in which the entity can be required to pay. For example, financial liabilities that an entity can be required to repay on demand (e.g. demand deposits) are included in the earliest time band.

(b)   when an entity is committed to make amounts available in instalments, each instalment is allocated to the earliest period in which the entity can be required to pay. For example, an undrawn loan commitment is included in the time band containing the earliest date it can be drawn down.

(c)   for issued financial guarantee contracts the maximum amount of the guarantee is allocated to the earliest period in which the guarantee could be called.

B11D   The contractual amounts disclosed in the maturity analyses as required by paragraphs 39(a) and (b) are the contractual undiscounted cash flows, for example:

(a)   gross finance lease obligations (before deducting finance charges);

(b)   prices specified in forward agreements to purchase financial assets for cash;

(c)   net amounts for pay-floating/receive-fixed interest rate swaps for which net cash flows are exchanged;

(d)   contractual amounts to be exchanged in a derivative financial instrument (e.g. a currency swap) for which gross cash flows are exchanged; and

(e)   gross loan commitments.

Such undiscounted cash flows differ from the amount included in the statement of financial position because the amount in that statement is based on discounted cash flows. When the amount payable is not fixed, the amount disclosed is determined by reference to the conditions existing at the end of the reporting period. For example, when the amount payable varies with changes in an index, the amount disclosed may be based on the level of the index at the end of the period.

B11E Paragraph 39(c) requires an entity to describe how it manages the liquidity risk inherent in the items disclosed in the quantitative disclosures required in paragraphs 39(a) and (b). An entity shall disclose a maturity analysis of financial assets it holds for managing liquidity risk (e.g. financial assets that are readily saleable or expected to generate cash inflows to meet cash outflows on financial liabilities), if that information is necessary to enable users of its financial statements to evaluate the nature and extent of liquidity risk.

B11F Other factors that an entity might consider in providing the disclosure required in paragraph 39(c) include, but are not limited to, whether the entity:

(a) has committed borrowing facilities (e.g. commercial paper facilities) or other lines of credit (e.g. stand-by credit facilities) that it can access to meet liquidity needs;

(b) holds deposits at central banks to meet liquidity needs;

(c) has very diverse funding sources;

(d) has significant concentrations of liquidity risk in either its assets or its funding sources;

(e) has internal control processes and contingency plans for managing liquidity risk;

(f) has instruments that include accelerated repayment terms (e.g. on the downgrade of the entity's credit rating);

(g) has instruments that could require the posting of collateral (e.g. margin calls for derivatives);

(h) has instruments that allow the entity to choose whether it settles its financial liabilities by delivering cash (or another financial asset) or by delivering its own shares; or

(i) has instruments that are subject to master netting agreements.

B12-B16 [Deleted by the IASB]

Market risk – sensitivity analysis (paragraphs 40 and 41)

B17 Paragraph 40(a) requires a sensitivity analysis for each type of market risk to which the entity is exposed. In accordance with paragraph B3, an entity decides how it aggregates information to display the overall picture without combining information with different characteristics about exposures to risks from significantly different economic environments. For example:

(a) an entity that trades financial instruments might disclose this information separately for financial instruments held for trading and those not held for trading; and

(b) an entity would not aggregate its exposure to market risks from areas of hyperinflation with its exposure to the same market risks from areas of very low inflation.

If an entity has exposure to only one type of market risk in only one economic environment, it would not show disaggregated information.

B18 Paragraph 40(a) requires the sensitivity analysis to show the effect on profit or loss and equity of reasonably possible changes in the relevant risk variable (e.g. prevailing market interest rates, currency rates, equity prices or commodity prices). For this purpose:

(a) entities are not required to determine what the profit or loss for the period would have been if relevant risk variables had been different. Instead, entities disclose the effect on profit or loss and equity at the end of the reporting period assuming that a reasonably possible change in the relevant risk variable had occurred at the end of the reporting period and had been applied to the risk exposures in existence at that date. For example, if an entity has a floating rate liability at the end of the year, the entity would disclose the effect on profit or loss (i.e. interest expense) for the current year if interest rates had varied by reasonably possible amounts; and

(b) entities are not required to disclose the effect on profit or loss and equity for each change within a range of reasonably possible changes of the relevant risk variable. Disclosure of the effects of the changes at the limits of the reasonably possible range would be sufficient.

AASB

B19　In determining what a reasonably possible change in the relevant risk variable is, an entity should consider:

(a)　the economic environments in which it operates. A reasonably possible change should not include remote or 'worst case' scenarios or 'stress tests'. Moreover, if the rate of change in the underlying risk variable is stable, the entity need not alter the chosen reasonably possible change in the risk variable. For xample, assume that interest rates are 5 per cent and an entity determines that a fluctuation in interest rates of ±50 basis points is reasonably possible. It would disclose the effect on profit or loss and equity if interest rates were to change to 4.5 per cent or 5.5 per cent. In the next period, interest rates have increased to 5.5 per cent. The entity continues to believe that interest rates may fluctuate by ±50 basis points (i.e. that the rate of change in interest rates is stable). The entity would disclose the effect on profit or loss and equity if interest rates were to change to 5 per cent or 6 per cent. The entity would not be required to revise its assessment that interest rates might reasonably fluctuate by ±50 basis points, unless there is evidence that interest rates have become significantly more volatile; and

(b)　the time frame over which it is making the assessment. The sensitivity analysis shall show the effects of changes that are considered to be reasonably possible over the period until the entity will next present these disclosures, which is usually its next annual reporting period.

B20　Paragraph 41 permits an entity to use a sensitivity analysis that reflects interdependencies between risk variables, such as a value-at-risk methodology, if it uses this analysis to manage its exposure to financial risks. This applies even if such a methodology measures only the potential for loss and does not measure the potential for gain. Such an entity might comply with paragraph 41(a) by disclosing the type of value-at-risk model used (e.g. whether the model relies on Monte Carlo simulations), an explanation about how the model works and the main assumptions (e.g. the holding period and confidence level). Entities might also disclose the historical observation period and weightings applied to observations within that period, an explanation of how options are dealt with in the calculations, and which volatilities and correlations (or, alternatively, Monte Carlo probability distribution simulations) are used.

B21　An entity shall provide sensitivity analyses for the whole of its business, but may provide different types of sensitivity analysis for different classes of financial instruments.

Interest rate risk

B22　*Interest rate risk* arises on interest-bearing financial instruments recognised in the statement of financial position (e.g. loans and receivables and debt instruments issued) and on some financial instruments not recognised in the statement of financial position (e.g. some loan commitments).

Currency risk

B23　*Currency risk* (or foreign exchange risk) arises on financial instruments that are denominated in a foreign currency, that is in a currency other than the functional currency in which they are measured. For the purpose of this Standard, currency risk does not arise from financial instruments that are non-monetary items or from financial instruments denominated in the functional currency.

B24　A sensitivity analysis is disclosed for each currency to which an entity has significant exposure.

Other price risk

B25　*Other price risk* arises on financial instruments because of changes in, for example, commodity prices or equity prices. To comply with paragraph 40, an entity might disclose the effect of a decrease in a specified stock market index, commodity price, or other risk variable. For example, if an entity gives residual value guarantees that are financial instruments, the entity discloses an increase or decrease in the value of the assets to which the guarantee applies.

B26　Two examples of financial instruments that give rise to equity price risk are (a) a holding of equities in another entity and (b) an investment in a trust that in turn holds investments in equity instruments. Other examples include forward contracts and options to buy or sell specified quantities of an equity instrument and swaps that are indexed to equity prices. The fair values of such financial instruments are affected by changes in the market price of the underlying equity instruments.

B27   In accordance with paragraph 40(a), the sensitivity of profit or loss (that arises, e.g. from instruments classified as at fair value through profit or loss and impairments of available-for-sale financial assets) is disclosed separately from the sensitivity of equity (that arises, e.g. from instruments classified as available for sale).

B28   Financial instruments that an entity classifies as equity instruments are not remeasured. Neither profit or loss nor equity will be affected by the equity price risk of those instruments. Accordingly, no sensitivity analysis is required.

Continuing involvement (paragraph 42C)

B29   The assessment of continuing involvement in a transferred financial asset for the purposes of the disclosure requirements in paragraphs 42E-42H is made at the level of the reporting entity. For example, if a subsidiary transfers to an unrelated third party a financial asset in which the parent of the subsidiary has continuing involvement, the subsidiary does not include the parent's involvement in the assessment of whether it has continuing involvement in the transferred asset in its stand-alone financial statements (i.e. when the subsidiary is the reporting entity). However, a parent would include its continuing involvement (or that of another member of the group) in a financial asset transferred by its subsidiary in determining whether it has continuing involvement in the transferred asset in its consolidated financial statements (i.e. when the reporting entity is the group).

B30   An entity does not have a continuing involvement in a transferred financial asset if, as part of the transfer, it neither retains any of the contractual rights or obligations inherent in the transferred financial asset nor acquires any new contractual rights or obligations relating to the transferred financial asset. An entity does not have continuing involvement in a transferred financial asset if it has neither an interest in the future performance of the transferred financial asset nor a responsibility under any circumstances to make payments in respect of the transferred financial asset in the future.

B31   Continuing involvement in a transferred financial asset may result from contractual provisions in the transfer agreement or in a separate agreement with the transferee or a third party entered into in connection with the transfer.

Transferred financial assets that are not derecognised in their entirety

B32   Paragraph 42D requires disclosures when part or all of the transferred financial assets do not qualify for derecognition. Those disclosures are required at each reporting date at which the entity continues to recognise the transferred financial assets, regardless of when the transfers occurred.

Types of continuing involvement (paragraphs 42E–42H)

B33   Paragraphs 42E-42H require qualitative and quantitative disclosures for each type of continuing involvement in derecognised financial assets. An entity shall aggregate its continuing involvement into types that are representative of the entity's exposure to risks. For example, an entity may aggregate its continuing involvement by type of financial instrument (e.g. guarantees or call options) or by type of transfer (e.g. factoring of receivables, securitisations and securities lending).

Maturity analysis for undiscounted cash outflows to repurchase transferred assets (paragraph 42E(e))

B34   Paragraph 42E(e) requires an entity to disclose a maturity analysis of the undiscounted cash outflows to repurchase derecognised financial assets or other amounts payable to the transferee in respect of the derecognised financial assets, showing the remaining contractual maturities of the entity's continuing involvement. This analysis distinguishes cash flows that are required to be paid (e.g. forward contracts), cash flows that the entity may be required to pay (e.g. written put options) and cash flows that the entity might choose to pay (e.g. purchased call options).

B35   An entity shall use its judgement to determine an appropriate number of time bands in preparing the maturity analysis required by paragraph 42E(e). For example, an entity might determine that the following maturity time bands are appropriate:

(a)   not later than one month;

(b)   later than one month and not later than three months;

(c)   later than three months and not later than six months;

(d)   later than six months and not later than one year;

(e)   later than one year and not later than three years;

(f)   later than three years and not later than five years; and

(g)   more than five years.

B36   If there is a range of possible maturities, the cash flows are included on the basis of the earliest date on which the entity can be required or is permitted to pay.

Qualitative information (paragraph 42E(f))

B37   The qualitative information required by paragraph 42E(f) includes a description of the derecognised financial assets and the nature and purpose of the continuing involvement retained after transferring those assets. It also includes a description of the risks to which an entity is exposed, including:

(a)   a description of how the entity manages the risk inherent in its continuing involvement in the derecognised financial assets.

(b)   whether the entity is required to bear losses before other parties, and the ranking and amounts of losses borne by parties whose interests rank lower than the entity's interest in the asset (i.e. its continuing involvement in the asset).

(c)   a description of any triggers associated with obligations to provide financial support or to repurchase a transferred financial asset.

Gain or loss on derecognition (paragraph 42G(a))

B38   Paragraph 42G(a) requires an entity to disclose the gain or loss on derecognition relating to financial assets in which the entity has continuing involvement. The entity shall disclose if a gain or loss on derecognition arose because the fair values of the components of the previously recognised asset (i.e. the interest in the asset derecognised and the interest retained by the entity) were different from the fair value of the previously recognised asset as a whole. In that situation, the entity also shall disclose whether the fair value measurements included significant inputs that were not based on observable market data, as described in paragraph 27A.

Supplementary information (paragraph 42H)

B39   The disclosures required in paragraphs 42D–42G may not be sufficient to meet the disclosure objectives in paragraph 42B. If this is the case, the entity shall disclose whatever additional information is necessary to meet the disclosure objectives. The entity shall decide, in the light of its circumstances, how much additional information it needs to provide to satisfy the information needs of users and how much emphasis it places on different aspects of the additional information. It is necessary to strike a balance between burdening financial statements with excessive detail that may not assist users of financial statements and obscuring information as a result of too much aggregation.

Appendix C

Amendments to other Australian Accounting Standards

This appendix is for information purposes.

The following amendments are made by AASB 2005-10 *Amendments to Australian Accounting Standards*. The amendments in this appendix are to be applied for annual periods beginning on or after 1 January 2007. If an entity applies the Standard for an earlier period, these amendments would be applied for that earlier period. In this appendix, new text is underlined and deleted text is struck through.

C1   In Australian Accounting Standards and Interpretations, references to AASB 132 *Financial Instruments: Disclosure and Presentation* are replaced by references to AASB 132 *Financial Instruments: Presentation*, unless otherwise stated below.

C2   AASB 132 *Financial Instruments: Disclosure and Presentation* is amended as described below.

The title is amended to 'AASB 132 *Financial Instruments: Presentation*'.

Paragraph 1 is deleted and paragraphs 2-4(a) are amended as follows:

2.   ~~This Standard contains requirements for the presentation of financial instruments and identifies the information that should be disclosed about them. The presentation requirements apply~~ The objective of this Standard is to establish principles for presenting financial instruments as liabilities or equity and for offsetting financial assets and financial liabilities. It applies to the classification of financial instruments, from the perspective of the issuer, into financial assets, financial liabilities and equity instruments; the classification of related interest, dividends, losses and gains; and the circumstances in which financial assets and financial liabilities should be offset. ~~The Standard requires disclosure of information about factors that affect the amount, timing and certainty of an entity's future cash flows relating to financial instruments and the accounting policies applied to those instruments. This Standard also requires disclosure of information about the nature and extent of an entity's use of financial instruments, the business purposes they serve, the risks associated with them, and management's policies for controlling those risks.~~

3.   The principles in this Standard complement the principles for recognising and measuring financial assets and financial liabilities in AASB 139 *Financial Instruments: Recognition and Measurement*, and for disclosing information about them in AASB 7 *Financial Instruments: Disclosures*.

Scope

4.   **This Standard shall be applied by all entities to all types of financial instruments except:**

(a)   **those interests in subsidiaries, associates and joint ventures that are accounted for in accordance with ~~under~~ AASB 127 *Consolidated and Separate Financial Statements*, AASB 128 *Investments in Associates* or AASB 131 *Interests in Joint Ventures*. However, in some cases, AASB 127, AASB 128 or AASB 131 permits an entity to account for ~~entities shall apply this Standard to~~ an interest in a subsidiary, associate or joint venture ~~that according to AASB 127, AASB 128 or AASB 131 is accounted for under~~ using AASB 139 ~~*Financial Instruments: Recognition and Measurement*~~; in those ~~In these~~ cases, entities shall apply the disclosure requirements in AASB 127, AASB 128 ~~and~~ or AASB 131 in addition to those in this Standard. Entities shall also apply this Standard to all derivatives ~~on~~ linked to interests in subsidiaries, associates or joint ventures.**

AASB

Paragraphs 5 and 7 are deleted.

The second sentence of paragraph 40 is amended as follows:

40.   ... In addition to the requirements of this Standard, disclosure of interest and dividends is subject to the requirements of AASB 101 and <u>AASB 7</u>. ~~AASB 130 Disclosures in the Financial Statements of Banks and Similar Financial Institutions.~~ ...

The last sentence of paragraph 47 is amended as follows:

47.   ... When an entity has a right of set-off, but does not intend to settle net or to realise the asset and settle the liability simultaneously, the effect of the right on the entity's credit risk exposure is disclosed in accordance with paragraph ~~76~~ <u>36</u> of AASB 7.

The last sentence of paragraph 50 is amended as follows:

50.   ... When financial assets and financial liabilities subject to a master netting arrangement are not offset, the effect of the arrangement on an entity's exposure to credit risk is disclosed in accordance with paragraph ~~76~~ <u>36</u> of AASB 7.

Paragraphs 51-95 are deleted.

In the Appendix (Application Guidance), paragraphs AG24 and AG40 and the last sentence of paragraph AG39 are deleted.

C3   AASB 101 *Presentation of Financial Statements* is amended as described below.

Paragraph 4 is deleted.

In paragraph 56, 'AASB 132' is replaced by 'AASB 7 *Financial Instruments: Disclosures*', and in paragraphs 105(d)(ii) and 124, 'AASB 132' is replaced by 'AASB 7'.

The last sentence of paragraph 71(b) is amended as follows:

71(b)   ... For example, a ~~bank~~ <u>financial institution may</u> amend~~s~~ the above descriptions to <u>provide information that is relevant to the operations of a financial institution</u> ~~apply the more specific requirements in AASB 130~~.

The fourth sentence of paragraph 84 is amended as follows:

84.   ... For example, a ~~bank~~ <u>financial institution may</u> amend~~s~~ the descriptions to <u>provide information that is relevant to the operations of a financial institution.</u> ~~apply the more specific requirements in AASB 130.~~

C4   AASB 114 *Segment Reporting* is amended as described below.

In paragraphs 27(a) and (b), 31, 32, 46 and 74, the phrase 'the board of directors and [to] [the] chief executive officer' is replaced by 'key management personnel'.

In paragraphs 27(b), 30 and 32 the phrase 'the directors and management' is replaced by 'key management personnel'.

The first sentence of paragraph 27 is amended as follows:

27.   **An entity's internal organisational and management structure and its system of internal financial reporting to <u>key management personnel (e.g. the board of directors and the chief executive officer)</u> shall normally be the basis for identifying the predominant source and nature of risks and differing rates of return facing the entity and, therefore, for determining which reporting format is primary and which is secondary, except as provided in subparagraphs (a) and (b) below: ...**

The third sentence of paragraph 28 is amended as follows:

28.   ... Therefore, except in rare circumstances, an entity will report segment information in its financial report on the same basis as it reports internally to <u>key management personnel</u> ~~top management~~. ...

The first sentence of paragraph 33 is amended as follows:

33.   Under this Standard, most entities will identify their business and geographical segments as the organisational units for which information is reported to <u>key management personnel</u> ~~the board of directors (particularly the supervisory non-~~

~~management directors, if any) and to the chief executive officer (~~, or the senior operating decision maker, which in some cases may be a group of ~~several~~ people,) for the purpose of evaluating each unit's past performance and for making decisions about future allocations of resources. ...

C5   In paragraph 31 of AASB 117 *Leases*, 'AASB 132 *Financial Instruments: Disclosure and Presentation*' is replaced by 'AASB 7 *Financial Instruments: Disclosures*', and in paragraphs 35, 47 and 56, 'AASB 132' is replaced by 'AASB 7'.

C6   In paragraph 72 of AASB 133 *Earnings per Share*, 'AASB 132' is replaced by 'AASB 7 *Financial Instruments: Disclosures*'.

C7   AASB 139 *Financial Instruments: Recognition and Measurement* is amended as described below.

Paragraph 1 is amended as follows:

1.   The objective of this Standard is to establish principles for recognising and measuring financial assets, financial liabilities and some contracts to buy or sell non-financial items. Requirements for presenting ~~and disclosing~~ information about financial instruments are ~~set out~~ in AASB 132 *Financial Instruments: ~~Disclosure and Presentation~~*. Requirements for disclosing information about financial instruments are in AASB 7 *Financial Instruments: Disclosures.*

In paragraph 45, 'AASB 132' is replaced by 'AASB 7'.

Paragraph 48 is amended as follows:

48.   In determining the fair value of a financial asset or a financial liability for the purpose of applying this Standard, ~~or~~ AASB 132 or AASB 7, an entity shall apply paragraphs AG69-AG82 of Appendix A.

C8   AASB 139 *Financial Instruments: Recognition and Measurement* is amended as described below.

In paragraph 9, the definition of a financial asset or financial liability at fair value through profit or loss is amended as follows:

9.   ... In ~~AASB 132, paragraphs 66, 94 and AG40~~ AASB 7, paragraphs 9-11 and B4 require the entity to provide disclosures about financial assets and financial liabilities it has designated as at fair value through profit or loss, ...

C9   In AASB 1 *First-time Adoption of Australian Equivalents to International Financial Reporting Standards*, paragraph 36A is amended, and a heading and paragraph 36C are added as follows:

36A   In its first Australian-equivalents-to-IFRSs financial report, an entity that adopts Australian equivalents to IFRSs before 1 January 2006 shall present at least one year of comparative information, but this comparative information need not comply with AASB 132, AASB 139, AASB 4, AASB 1023 ~~and~~ or AASB 1038. An entity that chooses to present comparative information that does not comply with AASB 132, AASB 139, AASB 4, AASB 1023 ~~and~~ or AASB 1038 in its first year of transition shall:

(a)   apply the recognition and measurement requirements of its previous GAAP in the comparative information ~~to~~ for financial instruments within the scope of AASB 132 and AASB 139 and ~~to~~ for insurance contracts within the scope of AASB 4, AASB 1023 and AASB 1038;

...

In the case of an entity that chooses to present comparative information that does not comply with AASB 132, AASB 139, AASB 4, AASB 1023 and AASB 1038, references to the 'date of transition to Australian equivalents to IFRSs' shall mean, in the case of those Standards only, the beginning of the first Australian-equivalents-to-IFRSs reporting period. Such entities are required to comply with paragraph 15(c) of AASB 101 to provide additional disclosures when compliance with the specific requirements in Australian-equivalents-to-IFRSs is insufficient to enable users to understand the impact of particular transactions, other events and conditions on the entity's financial position and financial performance.

AASB

Exemption from the requirement to provide comparative disclosures for AASB 7

36C An entity that adopts Australian-equivalents-to-IFRSs before 1 January 2006 and chooses to adopt AASB 7 *Financial Instruments: Disclosures* in its first Australian-equivalents-to-IFRSs financial report need not present the comparative disclosures required by AASB 7 in that financial report.

C10 AASB 4 *Insurance Contracts* is amended as described below.

Paragraph 2(b) is amended as follows:

2(b) financial instruments that it issues with a *discretionary participation feature* (see paragraph 35). ~~AASB 132 *Financial Instruments: Disclosure and Presentation*~~ AASB 7 *Financial Instruments: Disclosures* requires disclosure about financial instruments, including financial instruments that contain such features.

Paragraph 35(d) is added as follows:

35(d) although these contracts are financial instruments, an issuer applying paragraph 19(b) of AASB 7 to contracts with a discretionary participation feature shall disclose the total interest expense recognised in profit or loss, but need not calculate such interest expense using the effective interest method.

After paragraph 37, the heading and paragraphs 38 and 39 are amended and paragraph 39A is added as follows:

~~Amount, timing and uncertainty of cash flows~~ Nature and extent of risks arising from insurance contracts

38 An insurer shall disclose information that ~~helps~~ enables users of its financial report to ~~understand~~ evaluate the ~~amount, timing and uncertainty of future cash flows~~ nature and extent of risks arising from insurance contracts.

39 To comply with paragraph 38, an insurer shall disclose:

(a) its objectives, policies and processes for ~~in~~ managing risks arising from insurance contracts and the methods used to manage ~~and its policies for mitigating~~ those risks;

(b) ~~those terms and conditions of insurance contracts that have a material effect on the amount, timing and uncertainty of the insurer's future cash flows.~~ [Deleted by the IASB];

(c) information about *insurance risk* (both before and after risk mitigation by reinsurance), including information about:

(i) ~~the~~ sensitivity to insurance risk (see paragraph 39A) ~~of profit or loss and equity to changes in variables that have a material effect on them~~;

(ii) concentrations of insurance risk, including a description of how management determines concentrations and a description of the shared characteristic that identifies each concentration (e.g. type of insured event, geographical area, or currency); and

(iii) actual claims compared with previous estimates (i.e. claims development). The disclosure about claims development shall go back to the period when the earliest material claim arose for which there is still uncertainty about the amount and timing of the claims payments, but need not go back more than ten years. An insurer need not disclose this information for claims for which uncertainty about the amount and timing of claims payments is typically resolved within one year;

    (d)   ~~the~~ information about ~~interest rate risk and~~ credit risk, liquidity risk and market risk that ~~AASB 132~~ paragraphs 31-42 of AASB 7 would require if the insurance contracts were within the scope of ~~AASB 132~~ AASB 7. However:

        (i)   an insurer need not provide the maturity analysis required by paragraph 39(a) of AASB 7 if it discloses information about the estimated timing of the net cash outflows resulting from recognised insurance liabilities instead. This may take the form of an analysis, by estimated timing, of the amounts recognised in the balance sheet;

        (ii)   if an insurer uses an alternative method to manage sensitivity to market conditions, such as an embedded value analysis, it may use that sensitivity analysis to meet the requirement in paragraph 40(a) of AASB 7. Such an insurer shall also provide the disclosures required by paragraph 41 of AASB 7; and

    (e)   information about exposures to ~~interest rate risk or~~ market risk ~~under~~ arising from embedded derivatives contained in a host insurance contract if the insurer is not required to, and does not, measure the embedded derivatives at fair value.

39A   To comply with paragraph 39(c)(i), an insurer shall disclose either (a) or (b) as follows:

    (a)   a sensitivity analysis that shows how profit or loss and equity would have been affected had changes in the relevant risk variable that were reasonably possible at the reporting date occurred; the methods and assumptions used in preparing the sensitivity analysis; and any changes from the previous period in the methods and assumptions used. However, if an insurer uses an alternative method to manage sensitivity to market conditions, such as an embedded value analysis, it may meet this requirement by disclosing that alternative sensitivity analysis and the disclosures required by paragraph 41 of AASB 7; and

    (b)   qualitative information about sensitivity, and information about those terms and conditions of insurance contracts that have a material effect on the amount, timing and uncertainty of the insurer's future cash flows.

Appendix D

Amendments to AASB 7 if AASB 2005-4
Amendments to Australian Accounting Standards
(relating to the fair value option)
has not been applied

This Appendix is an integral part of AASB 7.

In June 2005 the AASB amended AASB 139 *Financial Instruments: Recognition and Measurement* by the issue of AASB 2005-4 *Amendments to Australian Accounting Standards* in order to replicate the IASB's Amendments to IAS 39 *Financial Instruments: Recognition and Measurement*. The amendments to AASB 139 by AASB 2005-4 apply to annual periods beginning on or after 1 January 2006. If an entity applies AASB 7 for annual periods beginning before 1 January 2006 and it does not apply AASB 139 as amended by AASB 2005-4, it shall use AASB 7 for that period amended as follows. In the amended paragraphs, new text is underlined and deleted text is struck through.

D1   The heading above paragraph 9 and paragraph 11 are amended as follows, and paragraph 9 is deleted.

Financial ~~assets or financial~~ liabilities at fair value through profit or loss

11   The entity shall disclose:

(a)   the methods used to comply with the requirements in ~~paragraphs 9(c) and~~ paragraph 10(a); and

(b)   if the entity believes that the disclosure it has given to comply with the requirements in ~~paragraphs 9(c) or~~ paragraph 10(a) does not faithfully represent the change in the fair value of the ~~financial asset or~~ financial liability attributable to changes in its credit risk, the reasons for reaching this conclusion and the factors it believes are relevant.

Paragraph B5(a) is amended as follows:

(a)   the criteria for designating, on initial recognition, ~~for~~ financial assets or financial liabilities ~~designated~~ as at fair value through profit or loss:~~;~~

(i)   ~~the nature of the financial assets or financial liabilities the entity has designated as at fair value through profit or loss;~~

(ii)   ~~the criteria for so designating such financial assets or financial liabilities on initial recognition; and~~

(iii) ~~how the entity has satisfied the conditions in paragraph 9, 11A or 12 of IAS 39 for such designation. For instruments designated in accordance with paragraph (b)(i) of the definition of a financial asset or financial liability at fair value through profit or loss in IAS 39, that disclosure includes a narrative description of the circumstances underlying the measurement or recognition inconsistency that would otherwise arise. For instruments designated in accordance with paragraph (b)(ii) of the definition of a financial asset or financial liability at fair value through profit or loss in IAS 39, that disclosure includes a narrative description of how designation at fair value through profit or loss is consistent with the entity's documented risk management or investment strategy;~~

Deleted IFRS 7 Text

Deleted IFRS 7 text is not part of AASB 7.

Paragraph 44A

IAS 1(as revised in 2007) amended the terminology used throughout IFRSs. In addition it amended paragraphs 20, 21, 23(c) and (d), 27(c) and B5 of Appendix B. An entity shall apply those amendments for annual periods beginning on or after 1 January 2009. If an entity applies IAS 1 (revised 2007) for an earlier period, the amendments shall be applied for that earlier period.

Paragraph 44C

An entity shall apply the amendment in paragraph 3 for annual periods beginning on or after 1 January 2009. If an entity applies *Puttable Financial Instruments and Obligations Arising on Liquidation* (Amendments to IAS 32 and IAS 1), issued in February 2008, for an earlier period, the amendment in paragraph 3 shall be applied for that earlier period.

AASB 8
Operating Segments
(Compiled February 2010)

Note from the Institute of Chartered Accountants Australia

This note, prepared by the technical editors, is not part of Accounting Standard AASB 8.

Historical development

24 February 2007: AASB 8 'Operating Segments' is the Australian equivalent of IFRS 8 of the same name. The Standard was issued to replace AASB 114 'Segment Reporting'. Note that the Standard applies to annual reporting periods on or after 1 January 2009, with earlier adoption permitted.

24 September 2007: AASB 2007-8 'Amendments to Australian Accounting Standards arising from AASB 101' amends AASB 8 to align with revised AASB 101. This Standard is applicable to annual reporting periods beginning on or after 1 January 2009.

13 December 2007: AASB 2007-9 'Amendments to Australian Accounting Standards arising from the Review of AAS 27, AAS 29 and AAS 31' was issued by the AASB. This Standard is applicable to annual reporting periods beginning on or after 1 July 2008, with early adoption permitted.

21 May 2009: AASB 2009-5 'Amendments to Australian Accounting Standards' is the annual improvements Standard, amending AASB 8 in relation to the disclosure of information about segment assets. This Standard applies to annual reporting periods beginning on or after 1 January 2010 and may be applied early.

30 October 2009: AASB 8 was reissued by the AASB, compiled to include the AASB 2007-8 and AASB 2007-9 amendments and applies to annual reporting periods beginning on or after 1 January 2009 but before 1 January 2010. Early application is permitted.

4 December 2009: AASB 8 was reissued by the AASB, compiled to include the AASB 2009-5 amendments and applies to annual reporting periods beginning on or after 1 January 2010.

15 December 2009: AASB 2009-12 'Amendments to Australian Accounting Standards' amends AASB 8 in relation to operating segment disclosures for government. This Standard is applicable to annual reporting periods beginning on or after 1 January 2011 with early adoption permitted.

23 February 2010: AASB 8 was reissued by the AASB, compiled to include the AASB 2009-12 amendments and applies to annual reporting periods ending on or after 1 January 2011.

5 September 2011: AASB 2011-10 'Amendments to Australian Accounting Standards arising from AASB 119 (September 2011)' amends AASB 8 to give effect to a consequential change arising from the issue of AASB 119. This Standard applies to annual reporting periods beginning on or after 1 January 2013 and can be adopted early. **These amendments are not included in this compiled Standard.**

Reference

IFRIC items not taken onto the agenda: IFRS 8-1 *Interaction with transition requirements* of *IFRS 8* applies to AASB 8.

AASB 8 compared to IFRS 8

Additions

Paragraph	Description
Aus 2.1	Which entities AASB 8 applies to (i.e. reporting entities and general purpose financial statements of entities that are listed or similar).
Aus 2.2	The application date of AASB 8 (i.e. annual reporting periods beginning 1 January 2009).

Aus 2.3	Permits early application of AASB 8 for annual reporting periods beginning on or after 1 January 2005.
Aus 2.4	Makes the requirements of AASB 8 subject to AASB 1031 'Materiality'.
Aus 2.5	Explains which Australian Standards have been superseded by AASB 8 (i.e. AASB 114).

Deletions

Paragraph	*Description*
2	Application of IFRS 8.
35	Effective date of IFRS 8.
36A	Effective date of amended IFRS 8.
37	Withdrawal of IAS 14.

Contents

Compilation Details

Comparison with IFRS 8

Accounting Standard
AASB 8 Operating Segments

	Paragraphs
Core Principle	1
Scope	Aus 2.1 – 4
Operating Segments	5 – 10
Reportable Segments	11 – 19
Aggregation criteria	12
Quantitative thresholds	13 – 19
Disclosure	20 – 24
General information	22
Information about profit or loss, assets and liabilities	23 – 24
Measurement	25 – 30
Reconciliations	28
Restatement of previously reported information	29 – 30
Entity-wide Disclosures	31 – 34
Information about products and services	32
Information about geographical areas	33
Information about major customers	34
Transition and Effective Date	35A – 36B

Appendix:

A. Defined Term

Deleted IFRS 8 Text

Implementation Guidance on IFRS 8
(available on the AASB website)

Basis for Conclusions on IFRS 8
(available on the AASB website)

Australian Accounting Standard AASB 8 *Operating Segments* (as amended) is set out in paragraphs 1 – 36B and Appendix A. All the paragraphs have equal authority. Paragraphs in **bold** type state the main principles. Terms defined in this Standard are in *italics* the first time they appear in the Standard. AASB 8 is to be read in the context of other Australian Accounting Standards, including AASB 1048 *Interpretation and Application of Standards*, which identifies the Australian Interpretations. In the absence of explicit guidance, AASB 108 *Accounting Policies, Changes in Accounting Estimates and Errors* provides a basis for selecting and applying accounting policies.

Compilation Details

Accounting Standard AASB 8 *Operating Segments* as amended

This compiled Standard applies to annual reporting periods beginning on or after 1 January 2011. It takes into account amendments up to and including 15 December 2009 and was prepared on 23 February 2010 by the staff of the Australian Accounting Standards Board (AASB).

This compilation is not a separate Accounting Standard made by the AASB. Instead, it is a representation of AASB 8 (February 2007) as amended by other Accounting Standards, which are listed in the Table below.

Table of Standards

Standard	Date made	Application date *(annual reporting periods ... on or after ...)*	Application, saving or transitional provisions
AASB 8	26 Feb 2007	*(beginning)* 1 Jan 2009	see (a) below
AASB 2007-8	24 Sep 2007	*(beginning)* 1 Jan 2009	see (b) below
AASB 2007-9	13 Dec 2007	*(beginning)* 1 Jul 2008	see (c) below
AASB 2009-5	21 May 2009	*(beginning)* 1 Jan 2010	see (d) below
AASB 2009-12	15 Dec 2009	*(beginning)* 1 Jan 2011	see (e) below

(a) Entities may elect to apply this Standard to annual reporting periods beginning on or after 1 January 2005 but before 1 January 2009.

(b) Entities may elect to apply this Standard to annual reporting periods beginning on or after 1 January 2005 but before 1 January 2009, provided that AASB 101 *Presentation of Financial Statements* (September 2007) is also applied to such periods.

(c) Entities may elect to apply this Standard to annual reporting periods beginning on or after 1 January 2005 but before 1 July 2008, provided that the Standards and Interpretation listed in paragraph 6 of AASB 2007-9 are also applied to such periods.

(d) Entities may elect to apply this Standard, or its amendments to individual Standards, to annual reporting periods beginning on or after 1 January 2005 but before 1 January 2010.

(e) Entities may elect to apply this Standard to annual reporting periods beginning on or after 1 January 2005 but before 1 January 2011.

Table of Amendments

Paragraph affected	How affected	By ... [paragraph]
Aus2.1	amended	AASB 2007-8 [7, 8]
	amended	AASB 2007-9 [12]
Aus2.4	amended	AASB 2007-8 [8]
21	amended	AASB 2007-8 [6, 36]
23	amended	AASB 2007-8 [36]
	amended	AASB 2009-5 [9]
24 (footnote)	amended	AASB 2007-8 [6]
33 (footnote)	amended	AASB 2007-8 [6]
34	amended	AASB 2009-12 [10]
35A	added	AASB 2009-5 [10]
36	amended	AASB 2009-5 [9]
36A	note added	AASB 2007-8 [37]
36B	added	AASB 2009-12 [10]

Comparison with IFRS 8

AASB 8 and IFRS 8

AASB 8 *Operating Segments* as amended incorporates IFRS 8 *Operating Segments* as issued and amended by the International Accounting Standards Board (IASB). Paragraphs that have been added to this Standard (and do not appear in the text of IFRS 8) are identified with the prefix "Aus", followed by the number of the preceding IASB paragraph and decimal numbering. IFRS 8 text that has been deleted from this Standard (and does not affect IFRS compliance) is listed in a separate section after the Standard.

Compliance with IFRS 8

Entities that comply with AASB 8 as amended will simultaneously be in compliance with IFRS 8 as amended.

Accounting Standard AASB 8

The Australian Accounting Standards Board made Accounting Standard AASB 8 *Operating Segments* under section 334 of the *Corporations Act 2001* on 26 February 2007.

This compiled version of AASB 8 applies to annual reporting periods beginning on or after 1 January 2011. It incorporates relevant amendments contained in other AASB Standards made by the AASB up to and including 15 December 2009 (see Compilation Details).

Accounting Standard AASB 8

Operating Segments

Core Principle

1   **An entity shall disclose information to enable users of its financial statements to evaluate the nature and financial effects of the business activities in which it engages and the economic environments in which it operates.**

Scope

2   [Deleted by the AASB]

Aus2.1   This Standard applies to:

 (a)   each for-profit entity that is required to prepare financial reports in accordance with Part 2M.3 of the Corporations Act and that is a reporting entity;

 (b)   general purpose financial statements of each other for-profit reporting entity other than for-profit government departments; and

 (c)   financial statements of a for-profit entity other than for-profit government departments that are, or are held out to be, general purpose financial statements;

 in respect of:

 (d)   the separate or individual financial statements of an entity:

   (i)   whose debt or equity instruments are traded in a public market (a domestic or foreign stock exchange or an over-the-counter market, including local and regional markets); or

   (ii)   that files, or is in the process of filing, its financial statements with a securities commission or other regulatory organisation for the purpose of issuing any class of instruments in a public market; and

 (e)   the consolidated financial statements of a group with a parent:

   (i)   whose debt or equity instruments are traded in a public market (a domestic or foreign stock exchange or an over-the-counter market, including local and regional markets); or

        (ii)   that files, or is in the process of filing, the consolidated financial statements with a securities commission or other regulatory organisation for the purpose of issuing any class of instruments in a public market;

Aus2.2   This Standard applies to annual reporting periods beginning on or after 1 January 2009.

             [Note: For application dates of paragraphs changed or added by an amending Standard, see Compilation Details.]

Aus2.3   This Standard may be applied to annual reporting periods beginning on or after 1 January 2005 but before 1 January 2009. When an entity applies this Standard to an annual reporting period beginning before 1 January 2009, it shall disclose that fact.

Aus2.4   The requirements specified in this Standard apply to the financial statements where information resulting from their application is material in accordance with AASB 1031 *Materiality*.

Aus2.5   When applicable, this Standard supersedes AASB 114 *Segment Reporting* as made on 15 July 2004 and amended to 5 September 2005.

3   If an entity that is not required to apply this Standard chooses to disclose information about segments that does not comply with this Standard, it shall not describe the information as segment information.

4   If a financial report contains both the consolidated financial statements of a parent that is within the scope of this Standard as well as the parent's separate financial statements, segment information is required only in the consolidated financial statements.

Operating Segments

5   An *operating segment* is a component of an entity:

    (a)   that engages in business activities from which it may earn revenues and incur expenses (including revenues and expenses relating to transactions with other components of the same entity);

    (b)   whose operating results are regularly reviewed by the entity's chief operating decision maker to make decisions about resources to be allocated to the segment and assess its performance; and

    (c)   for which discrete financial information is available.

An operating segment may engage in business activities for which it has yet to earn revenues, for example, start-up operations may be operating segments before earning revenues.

6   Not every part of an entity is necessarily an operating segment or part of an operating segment. For example, a corporate headquarters or some functional departments may not earn revenues or may earn revenues that are only incidental to the activities of the entity and would not be operating segments. For the purposes of this Standard, an entity's post-employment benefit plans are not operating segments.

7   The term 'chief operating decision maker' identifies a function, not necessarily a manager with a specific title. That function is to allocate resources to and assess the performance of the operating segments of an entity. Often the chief operating decision maker of an entity is its chief executive officer or chief operating officer but, for example, it may be a group of executive directors or others.

8   For many entities, the three characteristics of operating segments described in paragraph 5 clearly identify its operating segments. However, an entity may produce reports in which its business activities are presented in a variety of ways. If the chief operating decision maker uses more than one set of segment information, other factors may identify a single set of components as constituting an entity's operating segments, including the nature of the business activities of each component, the existence of managers responsible for them, and information presented to the board of directors.

9   Generally, an operating segment has a segment manager who is directly accountable to and maintains regular contact with the chief operating decision maker to discuss operating activities, financial results, forecasts, or plans for the segment. The term 'segment manager' identifies a function, not necessarily a manager with a specific title. The chief operating decision maker also may be the segment manager for some operating segments. A single manager may be the segment manager for more than one operating segment. If the characteristics in paragraph 5 apply to more than one set of components of an organisation but there is only one set for which segment managers are held responsible, that set of components constitutes the operating segments.

10   The characteristics in paragraph 5 may apply to two or more overlapping sets of components for which managers are held responsible. That structure is sometimes referred to as a matrix form of organisation. For example, in some entities, some managers are responsible for different product and service lines worldwide, whereas other managers are responsible for specific geographical areas. The chief operating decision maker regularly reviews the operating results of both sets of components, and financial information is available for both. In that situation, the entity shall determine which set of components constitutes the operating segments by reference to the core principle.

Reportable Segments

11   An entity shall report separately information about each operating segment that:

(a)   has been identified in accordance with paragraphs 5-10 or results from aggregating two or more of those segments in accordance with paragraph 12; and

(b)   exceeds the quantitative thresholds in paragraph 13.

Paragraphs 14-19 specify other situations in which separate information about an operating segment shall be reported.

Aggregation criteria

12   Operating segments often exhibit similar long-term financial performance if they have similar economic characteristics. For example, similar long-term average gross margins for two operating segments would be expected if their economic characteristics were similar. Two or more operating segments may be aggregated into a single operating segment if aggregation is consistent with the core principle of this Standard, the segments have similar economic characteristics, and the segments are similar in each of the following respects:

(a)   the nature of the products and services;

(b)   the nature of the production processes;

(c)   the type or class of customer for their products and services;

(d)   the methods used to distribute their products or provide their services; and

(e)   if applicable, the nature of the regulatory environment, for example, banking, insurance or public utilities.

Quantitative thresholds

13   An entity shall report separately information about an operating segment that meets any of the following quantitative thresholds:

(a)   its reported revenue, including both sales to external customers and intersegment sales or transfers, is 10 per cent or more of the combined revenue, internal and external, of all operating segments;

(b)   the absolute amount of its reported profit or loss is 10 per cent or more of the greater, in absolute amount, of (i) the combined reported profit of all operating segments that did not report a loss and (ii) the combined reported loss of all operating segments that reported a loss;

(c)   its assets are 10 per cent or more of the combined assets of all operating segments.

Operating segments that do not meet any of the quantitative thresholds may be considered reportable, and separately disclosed, if management believes that information about the segment would be useful to users of the financial statements.

14 An entity may combine information about operating segments that do not meet the quantitative thresholds with information about other operating segments that do not meet the quantitative thresholds to produce a reportable segment only if the operating segments have similar economic characteristics and share a majority of the aggregation criteria listed in paragraph 12.

15 If the total external revenue reported by operating segments constitutes less than 75 per cent of the entity's revenue, additional operating segments shall be identified as reportable segments (even if they do not meet the criteria in paragraph 13) until at least 75 per cent of the entity's revenue is included in reportable segments.

16 Information about other business activities and operating segments that are not reportable shall be combined and disclosed in an 'all other segments' category separately from other reconciling items in the reconciliations required by paragraph 28. The sources of the revenue included in the 'all other segments' category shall be described.

17 If management judges that an operating segment identified as a reportable segment in the immediately preceding period is of continuing significance, information about that segment shall continue to be reported separately in the current period even if it no longer meets the criteria for reportability in paragraph 13.

18 If an operating segment is identified as a reportable segment in the current period in accordance with the quantitative thresholds, segment data for a prior period presented for comparative purposes shall be restated to reflect the newly reportable segment as a separate segment, even if that segment did not satisfy the criteria for reportability in paragraph 13 in the prior period, unless the necessary information is not available and the cost to develop it would be excessive.

19 There may be a practical limit to the number of reportable segments that an entity separately discloses beyond which segment information may become too detailed. Although no precise limit has been determined, as the number of segments that are reportable in accordance with paragraphs 13-18 increases above ten, the entity should consider whether a practical limit has been reached.

Disclosure

20 An entity shall disclose information to enable users of its financial statements to evaluate the nature and financial effects of the business activities in which it engages and the economic environments in which it operates.

21 To give effect to the principle in paragraph 20, an entity shall disclose the following for each period for which a statement of comprehensive income is presented:

(a) general information as described in paragraph 22;

(b) information about reported segment profit or loss, including specified revenues and expenses included in reported segment profit or loss, segment assets, segment liabilities and the basis of measurement, as described in paragraphs 23-27; and

(c) reconciliations of the totals of segment revenues, reported segment profit or loss, segment assets, segment liabilities and other material segment items to corresponding entity amounts as described in paragraph 28.

Reconciliations of the amounts in the statement of financial position for reportable segments to the amounts in the entity's statement of financial position are required for each date at which a statement of financial position is presented. Information for prior periods shall be restated as described in paragraphs 29 and 30.

General information

22 An entity shall disclose the following general information:

(a) factors used to identify the entity's reportable segments, including the basis of organisation (for example, whether management has chosen to organise the entity around differences in products and services, geographical areas, regulatory environments, or a combination of factors and whether operating segments have been aggregated); and

(b)   types of products and services from which each reportable segment derives its revenues.

Information about profit or loss, assets and liabilities

23   An entity shall report a measure of profit or loss for each reportable segment. An entity shall report a measure of total assets and liabilities for each reportable segment if such amounts are regularly provided to the chief operating decision maker. An entity shall also disclose the following about each reportable segment if the specified amounts are included in the measure of segment profit or loss reviewed by the chief operating decision maker, or are otherwise regularly provided to the chief operating decision maker, even if not included in that measure of segment profit or loss:

(a)   revenues from external customers;

(b)   revenues from transactions with other operating segments of the same entity;

(c)   interest revenue;

(d)   interest expense;

(e)   depreciation and amortisation;

(f)   material items of income and expense disclosed in accordance with paragraph 97 of AASB 101 *Presentation of Financial Statements* (as revised in 2007);

(g)   the entity's interest in the profit or loss of associates and joint ventures accounted for by the equity method;

(h)   income tax expense or income; and

(i)   material non-cash items other than depreciation and amortisation.

An entity shall report interest revenue separately from interest expense for each reportable segment unless a majority of the segment's revenues are from interest and the chief operating decision maker relies primarily on net interest revenue to assess the performance of the segment and make decisions about resources to be allocated to the segment. In that situation, an entity may report that segment's interest revenue net of its interest expense and disclose that it has done so.

24   An entity shall disclose the following about each reportable segment if the specified amounts are included in the measure of segment assets reviewed by the chief operating decision maker or are otherwise regularly provided to the chief operating decision maker, even if not included in the measure of segment assets:

(a)   the amount of investment in associates and joint ventures accounted for by the equity method; and

(b)   the amounts of additions to non-current assets[1] other than financial instruments, deferred tax assets, post-employment benefit assets (see AASB 119 *Employee Benefits* paragraphs 54-58) and rights arising under insurance contracts.

Measurement

25   The amount of each segment item reported shall be the measure reported to the chief operating decision maker for the purposes of making decisions about allocating resources to the segment and assessing its performance. Adjustments and eliminations made in preparing an entity's financial statements and allocations of revenues, expenses, and gains or losses shall be included in determining reported segment profit or loss only if they are included in the measure of the segment's profit or loss that is used by the chief operating decision maker. Similarly, only those assets and liabilities that are included in the measures of the segment's assets and segment's liabilities that are used by the chief operating decision maker shall be reported for that segment. If amounts are allocated to

---

1   For assets classified according to a liquidity presentation, non-current assets are assets that include amounts expected to be recovered more than twelve months after the reporting period.

reported segment profit or loss, assets or liabilities, those amounts shall be allocated on a reasonable basis.

26   If the chief operating decision maker uses only one measure of an operating segment's profit or loss, the segment's assets or the segment's liabilities in assessing segment performance and deciding how to allocate resources, segment profit or loss, assets and liabilities shall be reported at those measures. If the chief operating decision maker uses more than one measure of an operating segment's profit or loss, the segment's assets or the segment's liabilities, the reported measures shall be those that management believes are determined in accordance with the measurement principles most consistent with those used in measuring the corresponding amounts in the entity's financial statements.

27   An entity shall provide an explanation of the measurements of segment profit or loss, segment assets and segment liabilities for each reportable segment. At a minimum, an entity shall disclose the following:

(a)   the basis of accounting for any transactions between reportable segments;

(b)   the nature of any differences between the measurements of the reportable segments' profits or losses and the entity's profit or loss before income tax expense or income and discontinued operations (if not apparent from the reconciliations described in paragraph 28). Those differences could include accounting policies and policies for allocation of centrally incurred costs that are necessary for an understanding of the reported segment information;

(c)   the nature of any differences between the measurements of the reportable segments' assets and the entity's assets (if not apparent from the reconciliations described in paragraph 28). Those differences could include accounting policies and policies for allocation of jointly used assets that are necessary for understanding of the reported segment information;

(d)   the nature of any differences between the measurements of the reportable segments' liabilities and the entity's liabilities (if not apparent from the reconciliations described in paragraph 28). Those differences could include accounting policies and policies for allocation of jointly utilised liabilities that are necessary for an understanding of the reported segment information;

(e)   the nature of any changes from prior periods in the measurement methods used to determine reported segment profit or loss and the effect, if any, of those changes on the measure of segment profit or loss; and

(f)   the nature and effect of any asymmetrical allocations to reportable segments. For example, an entity might allocate depreciation expense to a segment without allocating the related depreciable assets to that segment.

Reconciliations

28   An entity shall provide reconciliations of all of the following:

(a)   the total of the reportable segments' revenues to the entity's revenue;

(b)   the total of the reportable segments' measures of profit or loss to the entity's profit or loss before tax expense (tax income) and discontinued operations. However, if an entity allocates to reportable segments items such as tax expense (tax income), the entity may reconcile the total of the segments' measures of profit or loss to the entity's profit or loss after those items;

(c)   the total of the reportable segments' assets to the entity's assets;

(d)   the total of the reportable segments' liabilities to the entity's liabilities if segment liabilities are reported in accordance with paragraph 23; and

(e)   the total of the reportable segments' amounts for every other material item of information disclosed to the corresponding amount for the entity.

All material reconciling items shall be separately identified and described. For example, the amount of each material adjustment needed to reconcile reportable segment profit or loss to the entity's profit or loss arising from different accounting policies shall be separately identified and described.

Restatement of previously reported information

29   If an entity changes the structure of its internal organisation in a manner that causes
the composition of its reportable segments to change, the corresponding information for
earlier periods, including interim periods, shall be restated unless the information is not
available and the cost to develop it would be excessive. The determination of whether
the information is not available and the cost to develop it would be excessive shall be
made for each individual item of disclosure. Following a change in the composition of
its reportable segments, an entity shall disclose whether it has restated the corresponding
items of segment information for earlier periods.

30   If an entity has changed the structure of its internal organisation in a manner that causes
the composition of its reportable segments to change and if segment information for
earlier periods, including interim periods, is not restated to reflect the change, the entity
shall disclose in the year in which the change occurs segment information for the current
period on both the old basis and the new basis of segmentation, unless the necessary
information is not available and the cost to develop it would be excessive.

Entity-wide Disclosures

31   Paragraphs 32-34 apply to all entities subject to this Standard including those entities that
have a single reportable segment. Some entities' business activities are not organised on
the basis of differences in related products and services or differences in geographical
areas of operations. Such an entity's reportable segments may report revenues from
a broad range of essentially different products and services, or more than one of its
reportable segments may provide essentially the same products and services. Similarly,
an entity's reportable segments may hold assets in different geographical areas and
report revenues from customers in different geographical areas, or more than one of its
reportable segments may operate in the same geographical area. Information required
by paragraphs 32-34 shall be provided only if it is not provided as part of the reportable
segment information required by this Standard.

Information about products and services

32   An entity shall report the revenues from external customers for each product and service,
or each group of similar products and services, unless the necessary information is not
available and the cost to develop it would be excessive, in which case that fact shall be
disclosed. The amounts of revenues reported shall be based on the financial information
used to produce the entity's financial statements.

Information about geographical areas

33   An entity shall report the following geographical information, unless the necessary
information is not available and the cost to develop it would be excessive:

(a)   revenues from external customers (i) attributed to the entity's country of domicile
and (ii) attributed to all foreign countries in total from which the entity derives
revenues. If revenues from external customers attributed to an individual foreign
country are material, those revenues shall be disclosed separately. An entity shall
disclose the basis for attributing revenues from external customers to individual
countries; and

(b)   non-current assets[2] other than financial instruments, deferred tax assets, post-
employment benefit assets, and rights arising under insurance contracts (i) located
in the entity's country of domicile and (ii) located in all foreign countries in total in
which the entity holds assets. If assets in an individual foreign country are material,
those assets shall be disclosed separately.

The amounts reported shall be based on the financial information that is used to produce
the entity's financial statements. If the necessary information is not available and the cost
to develop it would be excessive, that fact shall be disclosed. An entity may provide,
in addition to the information required by this paragraph, subtotals of geographical
information about groups of countries.

---

2   For assets classified according to a liquidity presentation, non-current assets are assets that include amounts
expected to be recovered more than twelve months after the reporting period.

AASB

Information about major customers

34   An entity shall provide information about the extent of its reliance on its major customers. If revenues from transactions with a single external customer amount to 10 per cent or more of an entity's revenues, the entity shall disclose that fact, the total amount of revenues from each such customer, and the identity of the segment or segments reporting the revenues. The entity need not disclose the identity of a major customer or the amount of revenues that each segment reports from that customer. For the purposes of this Standard, a group of entities known to a reporting entity to be under common control shall be considered a single customer. However, judgement is required to assess whether a government (including government agencies and similar bodies whether local, national or international) and entities known to the reporting entity to be under the control of that government are considered a single customer. In assessing this, the reporting entity shall consider the extent of economic integration between those entities.

Transition and Effective Date

35   [Deleted by the AASB]

35A   Paragraph 23 was amended by AASB 2009-5 *Further Amendments to Australian Accounting Standards arising from the Annual Improvements Project* issued in May 2009. An entity shall apply that amendment for annual reporting periods beginning on or after 1 January 2010. Earlier application is permitted. If an entity applies the amendment for an earlier period it shall disclose that fact.

36   Segment information for prior years that is reported as comparative information for the initial year of application (including application of the amendment to paragraph 23 made in May 2009) shall be restated to conform to the requirements of this Standard, unless the necessary information is not available and the cost to develop it would be excessive.

36A   [Deleted by the AASB]

36B   AASB 2009-12 *Amendments to Australian Accounting Standards* amended paragraph 34 for annual reporting periods beginning on or after 1 January 2011. If an entity applies AASB 124 (revised 2009) for an earlier period, it shall apply the amendment to paragraph 34 for that earlier period.

Withdrawal of IAS 14

37   [Deleted by the AASB]

Appendix A
Defined Term

This appendix is an integral part of AASB 8.

operating segment   An operating segment is a component of an entity:

(a)   that engages in business activities from which it may earn revenues and incur expenses (including revenues and expenses relating to transactions with other components of the same entity);

(b)   whose operating results are regularly reviewed by the entity's chief operating decision maker to make decisions about resources to be allocated to the segment and assess its performance; and

(c)   for which discrete financial information is available.

Deleted IFRS 8 Text

Deleted IFRS 8 text is not part of AASB 8.

Paragraph 2

This IFRS shall apply to:

(a)   the separate or individual financial statements of an entity:

   (i)   whose debt or equity instruments are traded in a public market (a domestic or foreign stock exchange or an over-the-counter market, including local and regional markets), or

   (ii)   that files, or is in the process of filing, its financial statements with a securities commission or other regulatory organisation for the purpose of issuing any class of instruments in a public market; and

(b)   the consolidated financial statements of a group with a parent:

   (i)   whose debt or equity instruments are traded in a public market (a domestic or foreign stock exchange or an over-the-counter market, including local and regional markets), or

   (ii)   that files, or is in the process of filing, the consolidated financial statements with a securities commission or other regulatory organisation for the purpose of issuing any class of instruments in a public market.

Paragraph 35

An entity shall apply this IFRS in its annual financial statements for periods beginning on or after 1 January 2009. Earlier application is permitted. If an entity applies this IFRS in its financial statements for a period before 1 January 2009, it shall disclose that fact.

Paragraph 36A

IAS 1 (as revised in 2007) amended the terminology used throughout IFRSs. In addition it amended paragraph 23(f). An entity shall apply those amendments for annual periods beginning on or after 1 January 2009. If an entity applies IAS 1 (revised 2007) for an earlier period, the amendments shall be applied for that earlier period.

Paragraph 37

This IFRS supersedes IAS 14 *Segment Reporting*.

AASB 9
Financial Instruments

(Compiled September 2012)

Note from the Institute of Chartered Accountants Australia

This note, prepared by the technical editors, is not part of Accounting Standard AASB 9.

Historical development

7 December 2009: AASB 9 was issued to replace AASB 139 as it applies to financial assets. AASB 9 includes requirements for the classification and measurement of financial assets resulting from the first part of Phase 1 of the IASB's project to replace IAS 39 (AASB 139).

This Standard is applicable to annual reporting periods beginning on or after 1 January 2013. This Standard may be adopted early.

6 December 2010: AASB 9 was reissued by the AASB, revised to reflect the IASB's completion of phase 1 of its project to replace IAS 39. AASB 9 (December 2010) applies to annual reporting periods beginning on or after 1 January 2013 and may be adopted early.

29 August 2011: AASB 2011-7 'Amendments to Australian Accounting Standards arising from the Consolidation and Joint Arrangements Standards' amends AASB 9 to give effect to many consequential changes arising from the issue of AASB 10, 11, 12, 127 and 128. This Standard applies to annual reporting periods beginning on or after 1 January 2013 and can be adopted early by for-profit entities. These amendments were incorporated into AASB 2012-6 and are included in this compiled Standard.

2 September 2011: AASB 2011-8 'Amendments to Australian Accounting Standards arising from AASB 13' amends AASB 9 to give effect to a consequential change in the definition of fair value arising from the issue of AASB 13. This Standard applies to annual reporting periods beginning on or after 1 January 2013 and can be adopted early.

10 September 2012: AASB 2012-6 'Amendments to Australian Accounting Standards – Mandatory Effective Date of AASB 9 and Transition Disclosures' amends the mandatory effective date of AASB 9 to annual reporting periods beginning on or after 1 January 2015 instead of 1 January 2013.

24 September 2012: AASB 9 was reissued by the AASB, compiled to include the AASB 2011-8 and AASB 2012-6 amendments and applies to annual reporting periods beginning on or after 1 January 2015.

Note: Educational material supporting the implementation of IFRS 13 is being developed by IFRS Foundation staff. This is expected to be published in December 2012. To access this publication refer to the IFAC website at www.ifac.org.

Reference

Interpretation 10 *Interim Financial Reporting and Impairment* and Interpretation 12 *Service Concession Arrangement,* apply to AASB 9.

AASB 9 compared to IFRS 9

Additions

Paragraph	Description
Aus 1.2	Which entities AASB 9 applies to (i.e. reporting entities and general purpose financial statements).
Aus 1.3	The application date of AASB 9 (i.e. annual reporting periods beginning 1 January 2015).
Aus 1.4	Allows early application of AASB 9.

Aus 1.5	If the date of application is not at the beginning of a reporting period, this must be disclosed.
Aus 1.6	Makes the requirements of AASB 9 subject to AASB 1031 'Materiality'.
Aus 1.7	Supercedes AASB 9 issued in December 2009.
Aus 1.8	Supersedes Interpretation 9 'Reassessment of Embedded Derivates'.

Deletions

Paragraph	*Description*
7.1.1	Application date of IFRS 9.
7.3.1	Supersedes IFRIC 9.
7.3.2	Supersedes IFRS 9 issued in 2009.

Contents

Compilation Details

Comparison with IFRS 9

Accounting Standard
AASB 9 Financial Instruments

	Paragraphs
Objective and application	1.1 – Aus1.8
Scope	2.1
Recognition and derecognition	
Initial recognition	3.1.1
Regular way purchase or sale of financial assets	3.1.2
Derecognition of financial assets	3.2.1 – 3.2.9
Transfers that qualify for derecognition	3.2.10 – 3.2.14
Transfers that do not qualify for derecognition	3.2.15
Continuing involvement in transferred assets	3.2.16 – 3.2.21
All transfers	3.2.22 – 3.2.23
Derecognition of financial liabilities	3.3.1 – 3.3.4
Classification	
Classification of financial assets	4.1.1 – 4.1.4
Option to designate a financial asset at fair value through profit or loss	4.1.5 – 4.1.6
Classification of financial liabilities	4.2.1
Option to designate a financial liability at fair value through profit or loss	4.2.2 – 4.2.3
Embedded derivatives	4.3.1
Hybrid contracts with financial asset hosts	4.3.2
Other hybrid contracts	4.3.3 – 4.3.7
Reclassification	4.4.1 – 4.4.3
Measurement	
Initial measurement	5.1.1 – 5.1.2
Subsequent measurement of financial assets	5.2.1 – 5.2.3
Subsequent measurement of financial liabilities	5.3.1 – 5.3.2
Reclassification of financial assets	5.6.1 – 5.6.3
Gains and losses	5.7.1 – 5.7.4
Investments in equity instruments	5.7.5 – 5.7.6
Liabilities designated as at fair value through profit or loss	5.7.7 – 5.7.9
Effective date and transition	
Effective date	7.1.2 – 7.1.3
Transition	7.2.1 – 7.2.15
Entities that have applied early AASB 9 issued in 2009	7.2.16

Appendices:

A. Defined Terms

B. Application Guidance

Deleted IFRS 9 Text

Implementation Guidance on IFRS 9
(available on the AASB website)

Basis for Conclusions on IFRS 9
(available on the AASB website)

> Australian Accounting Standard AASB 9 *Financial Instruments* (as amended) is set out in paragraphs 1.1 –
> 7.2.16 and Appendices A and B. All the paragraphs have equal authority. Paragraphs in **bold type** state the main
> principles. AASB 9 is to be read in the context of other Australian Accounting Standards, including AASB 1048
> *Interpretation of Standards*, which identifies the Australian Accounting Interpretations. In the absence of explicit
> guidance, AASB 108 *Accounting Policies, Changes in Accounting Estimates and Errors* provides a basis for
> selecting and applying accounting policies.

Compilation Details

Accounting Standard AASB 9 *Financial Instruments* as amended

This compiled Standard applies to annual reporting periods beginning on or after 1 January 2015.
It takes into account amendments up to and including 10 September 2012 and was prepared on
24 September 2012 by the staff of the Australian Accounting Standards Board (AASB).

This compilation is not a separate Accounting Standard made by the AASB. Instead, it is a
representation of AASB 9 (December 2010) as amended by other Accounting Standards, which
are listed in the Table below.

Table of Standards

Standard	Date made	Application date (*annual reporting periods ... on or after ...*)	Application, saving or transitional provisions
AASB 9	6 Dec 2010	*(beginning)* 1 Jan 2015	see (a) below
AASB 2011-8	2 Sep 2011	*(beginning)* 1 Jan 2013	see (b) below
AASB 2012-6	10 Sep 2012	*(beginning)* 1 Jan 2013	see (b) below

(a)   AASB 9 applies to annual reporting periods beginning on or after 1 January 2015 (instead of 1 January
2013) as a result of amendments made by AASB 2012-6 *Amendments to Australian Accounting Standards –
Mandatory Effective Date of AASB 9 and Transition Disclosures*.

(b)   Entities may elect to apply the amendments to AASB 9 in this Standard as set out in paragraphs Aus1.3 and
Aus1.4 of AASB 9.

Table of Amendments

Paragraph affected	How affected	By ... [paragraph]
Aus1.3	amended	AASB 2012-6 [13]
Aus1.7	amended	AASB 2012-6 [13]
3.2.1	amended	AASB 2012-6 [14]
3.2.14	amended	AASB 2012-6 [15]
4.3.7	amended	AASB 2012-6 [15]
5.1.1	amended	AASB 2012-6 [15]
5.1.1A	added	AASB 2012-6 [15]

Paragraph affected	How affected	By ... [paragraph]
5.2.1	amended	AASB 2012-6 [15]
5.4.1-5.4.3 and preceding heading	deleted	AASB 2012-6 [15]
5.6.2	amended	AASB 2012-6 [15]
7.1.2	added	AASB 2012-6 [14]
7.1.3	added	AASB 2012-6 [15]
7.2.5	amended	AASB 2012-6 [15]
7.2.10	amended	AASB 2012-6 [13]
7.2.11-7.2.12	amended	AASB 2012-6 [15]
7.2.14	amended	AASB 2012-6 [13]
Appendix A, definition of 'fair value'	amended	AASB 2011-8 [12]
B3.2.1-B3.2.3	amended	AASB 2012-6 [14]
B3.2.11	amended	AASB 2012-6 [15]
B3.2.17	amended	AASB 2012-6 [15]
B4.3.12	amended	AASB 2012-6 [14]
B5.1.1	amended	AASB 2012-6 [15]
B5.1.2A	added	AASB 2012-6 [15]
B5.2.2A	added	AASB 2012-6 [15]
B5.4.1-B5.4.13 and preceding headings	deleted	AASB 2012-6 [15]
B5.4.14 and preceding heading	amended	AASB 2012-6 [15]
B5.4.16	amended	AASB 2012-6 [15]
B5.7.15	amended	AASB 2012-6 [14]
B5.7.19	amended	AASB 2012-6 [13]
B5.7.20	amended	AASB 2012-6 [15]

Comparison with IFRS 9

AASB 9 and IFRS 9

AASB 9 *Financial Instruments* as amended incorporates IFRS 9 *Financial Instruments* as issued and amended by the International Accounting Standards Board (IASB). Paragraphs that have been added to this Standard (and do not appear in the text of IFRS 9) are identified with the prefix "Aus", followed by the number of the preceding IASB paragraph and decimal numbering. Paragraphs that apply only to not-for-profit entities begin by identifying their limited applicability.

Compliance with IFRS 9

Entities that comply with AASB 9 as amended will simultaneously be in compliance with IFRS 9 as amended.

Accounting Standard AASB 9

The Australian Accounting Standards Board made Accounting Standard AASB 9 *Financial Instruments* under section 334 of the *Corporations Act 2001* on 6 December 2010.

This compiled version of AASB 9 applies to annual reporting periods beginning on or after 1 January 2015. It incorporates relevant amendments contained in other AASB Standards made by the AASB up to and including 10 September 2012 (see Compilation Details).

Accounting Standard AASB 9

Financial Instruments

Chapter 1 Objective and application

1.1   The objective of this Standard is to establish principles for the financial reporting of *financial assets* and *financial liabilities* that will present relevant and useful information to users of financial statements for their assessment of the amounts, timing and uncertainty of an entity's future cash flows.

Aus1.2   This Standard applies to:

    (a)   **each entity that is required to prepare financial reports in accordance with Part 2M.3 of the Corporations Act and that is a reporting entity;**

    (b)   **general purpose financial statements of each other reporting entity; and**

    (c)   **financial statements that are, or are held out to be, general purpose financial statements.**

Aus1.3   **This Standard applies to annual reporting periods beginning on or after 1 January 2015. Earlier application is permitted. However, if an entity elects to apply this Standard early and has not already applied AASB 9** *Financial Instruments* **issued in December 2009 (as amended), it must apply all of the requirements in this Standard at the same time (but see also paragraph Aus1.7 of this Standard). If an entity applies this Standard in its financial statements for a period beginning before 1 January 2015, it shall disclose that fact and at the same time apply the amendments in AASB 2010-7** *Amendments to Australian Accounting Standards arising from AASB 9 (December 2010)* **(as amended).**

Aus1.4   **This Standard may be applied from:**

    (a)   **any date between the issue of this Standard and 31 December 2010, for entities initially applying this Standard before 1 January 2011; or**

    (b)   **the beginning of the first reporting period in which the entity adopts this Standard, for entities initially applying this Standard on or after 1 January 2011.**

Aus1.5   **If the date of initial application is not at the beginning of a reporting period, the entity shall disclose that fact and the reasons for using that date of initial application.**

Aus1.6   **The requirements specified in this Standard apply to the financial statements where information resulting from their application is material in accordance with AASB 1031** *Materiality*.

Aus1.7   When applied or operative, this Standard supersedes AASB 9 issued in December 2009 (as amended). However, for annual reporting periods beginning before 1 January 2015, an entity may elect to apply AASB 9 issued in December 2009 (as amended) instead of applying this Standard.

Aus1.8   When applied or operative, this Standard supersedes Interpretation 9 *Reassessment of Embedded Derivatives*, as identified in AASB 1048 *Interpretation of Standards*. The requirements added to AASB 9 in December 2010 incorporate the requirements previously set out in paragraphs 5 and 7 of Interpretation 9. As a consequential amendment, AASB 1 *First-time Adoption of Australian Accounting Standards* incorporates the requirements previously set out in paragraph 8 of Interpretation 9.

Chapter 2 Scope

2.1   An entity shall apply this Standard to all items within the scope of AASB 139 *Financial Instruments: Recognition and Measurement*.

Chapter 3 Recognition and derecognition

3.1 Initial recognition

3.1.1 An entity shall recognise a financial asset or a financial liability in its statement of financial position when, and only when, the entity becomes party to the contractual provisions of the instrument (see paragraphs B3.1.1 and B3.1.2). When an entity first recognises a financial asset, it shall classify it in accordance with paragraphs 4.1.1-4.1.5 and measure it in accordance with paragraphs 5.1.1 and 5.1.2. When an entity first recognises a financial liability, it shall classify it in accordance with paragraphs 4.2.1 and 4.2.2 and measure it in accordance with paragraph 5.1.1.

Regular way purchase or sale of financial assets

3.1.2 A *regular way purchase or sale* of financial assets shall be recognised and derecognised, as applicable, using trade date accounting or settlement date accounting (see paragraphs B3.1.3-B3.1.6).

3.2 Derecognition of financial assets

3.2.1 In consolidated financial statements, paragraphs 3.2.2-3.2.9, B3.1.1, B3.1.2 and B3.2.1-B3.2.17 are applied at a consolidated level. Hence, an entity first consolidates all subsidiaries in accordance with AASB 10 *Consolidated Financial Statements* and then applies those paragraphs to the resulting group.

3.2.2 Before evaluating whether, and to what extent, *derecognition* is appropriate under paragraphs 3.2.3-3.2.9, an entity determines whether those paragraphs should be applied to a part of a financial asset (or a part of a group of similar financial assets) or a financial asset (or a group of similar financial assets) in its entirety, as follows.

    (a)   Paragraphs 3.2.3-3.2.9 are applied to a part of a financial asset (or a part of a group of similar financial assets) if, and only if, the part being considered for derecognition meets one of the following three conditions.

        (i)   The part comprises only specifically identified cash flows from a financial asset (or a group of similar financial assets). For example, when an entity enters into an interest rate strip whereby the counterparty obtains the right to the interest cash flows, but not the principal cash flows from a debt instrument, paragraphs 3.2.3-3.2.9 are applied to the interest cash flows.

        (ii)   The part comprises only a fully proportionate (pro rata) share of the cash flows from a financial asset (or a group of similar financial assets). For example, when an entity enters into an arrangement whereby the counterparty obtains the rights to a 90 per cent share of all cash flows of a debt instrument, paragraphs 3.2.3-3.2.9 are applied to 90 per cent of those cash flows. If there is more than one counterparty, each counterparty is not required to have a proportionate share of the cash flows provided that the transferring entity has a fully proportionate share.

        (iii)   The part comprises only a fully proportionate (pro rata) share of specifically identified cash flows from a financial asset (or a group of similar financial assets). For example, when an entity enters into an arrangement whereby the counterparty obtains the rights to a 90 per cent share of interest cash flows from a financial asset, paragraphs 3.2.3-3.2.9 are applied to 90 per cent of those interest cash flows. If there is more than one counterparty, each counterparty is not required to have a proportionate share of the specifically identified cash flows provided that the transferring entity has a fully proportionate share.

    (b)   In all other cases, paragraphs 3.2.3-3.2.9 are applied to the financial asset in its entirety (or to the group of similar financial assets in their entirety). For example, when an entity transfers (i) the rights to the first or the last 90 per cent of cash collections from a financial asset (or a group of financial assets), or (ii) the rights to 90 per cent of the cash flows from a group of receivables, but provides a guarantee to compensate the buyer for any credit losses up to 8 per cent of the principal amount of the receivables, paragraphs 3.2.3-3.2.9 are applied to the financial asset (or a group of similar financial assets) in its entirety.

In paragraphs 3.2.3-3.2.12, the term 'financial asset' refers to either a part of a financial asset (or a part of a group of similar financial assets) as identified in (a) above or, otherwise, a financial asset (or a group of similar financial assets) in its entirety.

3.2.3   An entity shall derecognise a financial asset when, and only when:

(a)   the contractual rights to the cash flows from the financial asset expire, or

(b)   it transfers the financial asset as set out in paragraphs 3.2.4 and 3.2.5 and the transfer qualifies for derecognition in accordance with paragraph 3.2.6.

(See paragraph 3.1.2 for regular way sales of financial assets.)

3.2.4   An entity transfers a financial asset if, and only if, it either:

(a)   transfers the contractual rights to receive the cash flows of the financial asset; or

(b)   retains the contractual rights to receive the cash flows of the financial asset, but assumes a contractual obligation to pay the cash flows to one or more recipients in an arrangement that meets the conditions in paragraph 3.2.5.

3.2.5   When an entity retains the contractual rights to receive the cash flows of a financial asset (the 'original asset'), but assumes a contractual obligation to pay those cash flows to one or more entities (the 'eventual recipients'), the entity treats the transaction as a transfer of a financial asset if, and only if, all of the following three conditions are met.

(a)   The entity has no obligation to pay amounts to the eventual recipients unless it collects equivalent amounts from the original asset. Short-term advances by the entity with the right of full recovery of the amount lent plus accrued interest at market rates do not violate this condition.

(b)   The entity is prohibited by the terms of the transfer contract from selling or pledging the original asset other than as security to the eventual recipients for the obligation to pay them cash flows.

(c)   The entity has an obligation to remit any cash flows it collects on behalf of the eventual recipients without material delay. In addition, the entity is not entitled to reinvest such cash flows, except for investments in cash or cash equivalents (as defined in AASB 107 *Statement of Cash Flows*) during the short settlement period from the collection date to the date of required remittance to the eventual recipients, and interest earned on such investments is passed to the eventual recipients.

3.2.6   When an entity transfers a financial asset (see paragraph 3.2.4), it shall evaluate the extent to which it retains the risks and rewards of ownership of the financial asset. In this case:

(a)   if the entity transfers substantially all the risks and rewards of ownership of the financial asset, the entity shall derecognise the financial asset and recognise separately as assets or liabilities any rights and obligations created or retained in the transfer.

(b)   if the entity retains substantially all the risks and rewards of ownership of the financial asset, the entity shall continue to recognise the financial asset.

(c)   if the entity neither transfers nor retains substantially all the risks and rewards of ownership of the financial asset, the entity shall determine whether it has retained control of the financial asset. In this case:

(i)   if the entity has not retained control, it shall derecognise the financial asset and recognise separately as assets or liabilities any rights and obligations created or retained in the transfer.

AASB

> (ii) if the entity has retained control, it shall continue to recognise the financial asset to the extent of its continuing involvement in the financial asset (see paragraph 3.2.16).

3.2.7 The transfer of risks and rewards (see paragraph 3.2.6) is evaluated by comparing the entity's exposure, before and after the transfer, with the variability in the amounts and timing of the net cash flows of the transferred asset. An entity has retained substantially all the risks and rewards of ownership of a financial asset if its exposure to the variability in the present value of the future net cash flows from the financial asset does not change significantly as a result of the transfer (eg because the entity has sold a financial asset subject to an agreement to buy it back at a fixed price or the sale price plus a lender's return). An entity has transferred substantially all the risks and rewards of ownership of a financial asset if its exposure to such variability is no longer significant in relation to the total variability in the present value of the future net cash flows associated with the financial asset (eg because the entity has sold a financial asset subject only to an option to buy it back at its *fair value* at the time of repurchase or has transferred a fully proportionate share of the cash flows from a larger financial asset in an arrangement, such as a loan sub-participation, that meets the conditions in paragraph 3.2.5).

3.2.8 Often it will be obvious whether the entity has transferred or retained substantially all risks and rewards of ownership and there will be no need to perform any computations. In other cases, it will be necessary to compute and compare the entity's exposure to the variability in the present value of the future net cash flows before and after the transfer. The computation and comparison are made using as the discount rate an appropriate current market interest rate. All reasonably possible variability in net cash flows is considered, with greater weight being given to those outcomes that are more likely to occur.

3.2.9 Whether the entity has retained control (see paragraph 3.2.6(c)) of the transferred asset depends on the transferee's ability to sell the asset. If the transferee has the practical ability to sell the asset in its entirety to an unrelated third party and is able to exercise that ability unilaterally and without needing to impose additional restrictions on the transfer, the entity has not retained control. In all other cases, the entity has retained control.

Transfers that qualify for derecognition

3.2.10 If an entity transfers a financial asset in a transfer that qualifies for derecognition in its entirety and retains the right to service the financial asset for a fee, it shall recognise either a servicing asset or a servicing liability for that servicing contract. If the fee to be received is not expected to compensate the entity adequately for performing the servicing, a servicing liability for the servicing obligation shall be recognised at its fair value. If the fee to be received is expected to be more than adequate compensation for the servicing, a servicing asset shall be recognised for the servicing right at an amount determined on the basis of an allocation of the carrying amount of the larger financial asset in accordance with paragraph 3.2.13.

3.2.11 If, as a result of a transfer, a financial asset is derecognised in its entirety but the transfer results in the entity obtaining a new financial asset or assuming a new financial liability, or a servicing liability, the entity shall recognise the new financial asset, financial liability or servicing liability at fair value.

3.2.12 On derecognition of a financial asset in its entirety, the difference between:

(a) the carrying amount (measured at the date of derecognition); and

(b) the consideration received (including any new asset obtained less any new liability assumed);

shall be recognised in profit or loss.

3.2.13 If the transferred asset is part of a larger financial asset (eg when an entity transfers interest cash flows that are part of a debt instrument, see paragraph 3.2.2(a)) and the part transferred qualifies for derecognition in its entirety, the previous carrying amount of the larger financial asset shall be allocated between the part that continues to be recognised and the part that is derecognised, on the basis of the relative fair values of those parts on the date of the transfer. For this purpose, a

retained servicing asset shall be treated as a part that continues to be recognised. The difference between:

(a)   the carrying amount (measured at the date of derecognition) allocated to the part derecognised; and

(b)   the consideration received for the part derecognised (including any new asset obtained less any new liability assumed);

shall be recognised in profit or loss.

3.2.14 When an entity allocates the previous carrying amount of a larger financial asset between the part that continues to be recognised and the part that is derecognised, the fair value of the part that continues to be recognised needs to be measured. When the entity has a history of selling parts similar to the part that continues to be recognised or other market transactions exist for such parts, recent prices of actual transactions provide the best estimate of its fair value. When there are no price quotes or recent market transactions to support the fair value of the part that continues to be recognised, the best estimate of the fair value is the difference between the fair value of the larger financial asset as a whole and the consideration received from the transferee for the part that is derecognised.

Transfers that do not qualify for derecognition

3.2.15 **If a transfer does not result in derecognition because the entity has retained substantially all the risks and rewards of ownership of the transferred asset, the entity shall continue to recognise the transferred asset in its entirety and shall recognise a financial liability for the consideration received. In subsequent periods, the entity shall recognise any income on the transferred asset and any expense incurred on the financial liability.**

Continuing involvement in transferred assets

3.2.16 **If an entity neither transfers nor retains substantially all the risks and rewards of ownership of a transferred asset, and retains control of the transferred asset, the entity continues to recognise the transferred asset to the extent of its continuing involvement. The extent of the entity's continuing involvement in the transferred asset is the extent to which it is exposed to changes in the value of the transferred asset. For example:**

(a)   **When the entity's continuing involvement takes the form of guaranteeing the transferred asset, the extent of the entity's continuing involvement is the lower of (i) the amount of the asset and (ii) the maximum amount of the consideration received that the entity could be required to repay ('the guarantee amount').**

(b)   **When the entity's continuing involvement takes the form of a written or purchased option (or both) on the transferred asset, the extent of the entity's continuing involvement is the amount of the transferred asset that the entity may repurchase. However, in the case of a written put option on an asset that is measured at fair value, the extent of the entity's continuing involvement is limited to the lower of the fair value of the transferred asset and the option exercise price (see paragraph B3.2.13).**

(c)   **When the entity's continuing involvement takes the form of a cash settled option or similar provision on the transferred asset, the extent of the entity's continuing involvement is measured in the same way as that which results from non-cash settled options as set out in (b) above.**

3.2.17 **When an entity continues to recognise an asset to the extent of its continuing involvement, the entity also recognises an associated liability. Despite the other measurement requirements in this Standard, the transferred asset and the associated liability are measured on a basis that reflects the rights and obligations that the entity has retained. The associated liability is measured in such a way that the net carrying amount of the transferred asset and the associated liability is:**

(a)   **the *amortised cost* of the rights and obligations retained by the entity, if the transferred asset is measured at amortised cost, or**

(b)   equal to the fair value of the rights and obligations retained by the entity when measured on a stand-alone basis, if the transferred asset is measured at fair value.

3.2.18 The entity shall continue to recognise any income arising on the transferred asset to the extent of its continuing involvement and shall recognise any expense incurred on the associated liability.

3.2.19 For the purpose of subsequent measurement, recognised changes in the fair value of the transferred asset and the associated liability are accounted for consistently with each other in accordance with paragraph 5.7.1, and shall not be offset.

3.2.20 If an entity's continuing involvement is in only a part of a financial asset (eg when an entity retains an option to repurchase part of a transferred asset, or retains a residual interest that does not result in the retention of substantially all the risks and rewards of ownership and the entity retains control), the entity allocates the previous carrying amount of the financial asset between the part it continues to recognise under continuing involvement, and the part it no longer recognises on the basis of the relative fair values of those parts on the date of the transfer. For this purpose, the requirements of paragraph 3.2.14 apply. The difference between:

(a)   the carrying amount (measured at the date of derecognition) allocated to the part that is no longer recognised; and

(b)   the consideration received for the part no longer recognised;

shall be recognised in profit or loss.

3.2.21 If the transferred asset is measured at amortised cost, the option in this Standard to designate a financial liability as at fair value through profit or loss is not applicable to the associated liability.

All transfers

3.2.22 If a transferred asset continues to be recognised, the asset and the associated liability shall not be offset. Similarly, the entity shall not offset any income arising from the transferred asset with any expense incurred on the associated liability (see AASB 132 *Financial Instruments: Presentation* paragraph 42).

3.2.23 If a transferor provides non-cash collateral (such as debt or equity instruments) to the transferee, the accounting for the collateral by the transferor and the transferee depends on whether the transferee has the right to sell or repledge the collateral and on whether the transferor has defaulted. The transferor and transferee shall account for the collateral as follows:

(a)   If the transferee has the right by contract or custom to sell or repledge the collateral, then the transferor shall reclassify that asset in its statement of financial position (eg as a loaned asset, pledged equity instruments or repurchase receivable) separately from other assets.

(b)   If the transferee sells collateral pledged to it, it shall recognise the proceeds from the sale and a liability measured at fair value for its obligation to return the collateral.

(c)   If the transferor defaults under the terms of the contract and is no longer entitled to redeem the collateral, it shall derecognise the collateral, and the transferee shall recognise the collateral as its asset initially measured at fair value or, if it has already sold the collateral, derecognise its obligation to return the collateral.

(d)   Except as provided in (c), the transferor shall continue to carry the collateral as its asset, and the transferee shall not recognise the collateral as an asset.

3.3 Derecognition of financial liabilities

3.3.1 An entity shall remove a financial liability (or a part of a financial liability) from its statement of financial position when, and only when, it is extinguished — ie when the obligation specified in the contract is discharged or cancelled or expires.

3.3.2 **An exchange between an existing borrower and lender of debt instruments with substantially different terms shall be accounted for as an extinguishment of the original financial liability and the recognition of a new financial liability. Similarly, a substantial modification of the terms of an existing financial liability or a part of it (whether or not attributable to the financial difficulty of the debtor) shall be accounted for as an extinguishment of the original financial liability and the recognition of a new financial liability.**

3.3.3 **The difference between the carrying amount of a financial liability (or part of a financial liability) extinguished or transferred to another party and the consideration paid, including any non-cash assets transferred or liabilities assumed, shall be recognised in profit or loss.**

3.3.4 If an entity repurchases a part of a financial liability, the entity shall allocate the previous carrying amount of the financial liability between the part that continues to be recognised and the part that is derecognised based on the relative fair values of those parts on the date of the repurchase. The difference between (a) the carrying amount allocated to the part derecognised and (b) the consideration paid, including any non-cash assets transferred or liabilities assumed, for the part derecognised shall be recognised in profit or loss.

Chapter 4 Classification

4.1 Classification of financial assets

4.1.1 **Unless paragraph 4.1.5 applies, an entity shall classify financial assets as subsequently measured at either amortised cost or fair value on the basis of both:**

(a) **the entity's business model for managing the financial assets; and**

(b) **the contractual cash flow characteristics of the financial asset.**

4.1.2 **A financial asset shall be measured at amortised cost if both of the following conditions are met:**

(a) **The asset is held within a business model whose objective is to hold assets in order to collect contractual cash flows.**

(b) **The contractual terms of the financial asset give rise on specified dates to cash flows that are solely payments of principal and interest on the principal amount outstanding.**

Paragraphs B4.1.1-B4.1.26 provide guidance on how to apply these conditions.

4.1.3 **For the purpose of applying paragraph 4.1.2(b), interest is consideration for the time value of money and for the credit risk associated with the principal amount outstanding during a particular period of time.**

4.1.4 **A financial asset shall be measured at fair value unless it is measured at amortised cost in accordance with paragraph 4.1.2.**

Option to designate a financial asset at fair value through profit or loss

4.1.5 **Despite paragraphs 4.1.1-4.1.4, an entity may, at initial recognition, irrevocably designate a financial asset as measured at fair value through profit or loss if doing so eliminates or significantly reduces a measurement or recognition inconsistency (sometimes referred to as an 'accounting mismatch') that would otherwise arise from measuring assets or liabilities or recognising the gains and losses on them on different bases (see paragraphs B4.1.29-B4.1.32).**

4.1.6 AASB 7 *Financial Instruments: Disclosures* requires the entity to provide disclosures about financial assets it has designated as at fair value through profit or loss.

4.2 Classification of financial liabilities

4.2.1 **An entity shall classify all financial liabilities as subsequently measured at amortised cost using the effective interest method, except for:**

(a) *financial liabilities at fair value through profit or loss*. **Such liabilities, including** *derivatives* **that are liabilities, shall be subsequently measured at fair value.**

(b) financial liabilities that arise when a transfer of a financial asset does not qualify for derecognition or when the continuing involvement approach applies. Paragraphs 3.2.15 and 3.2.17 apply to the measurement of such financial liabilities.

(c) *financial guarantee contracts* as defined in Appendix A. After initial recognition, an issuer of such a contract shall (unless paragraph 4.2.1(a) or (b) applies) subsequently measure it at the higher of:

    (i) the amount determined in accordance with AASB 137 *Provisions, Contingent Liabilities and Contingent Assets*; and

    (ii) the amount initially recognised (see paragraph 5.1.1) less, when appropriate, cumulative amortisation recognised in accordance with AASB 118 *Revenue*.

(d) commitments to provide a loan at a below-market interest rate. After initial recognition, an issuer of such a commitment shall (unless paragraph 4.2.1(a) applies) subsequently measure it at the higher of:

    (i) the amount determined in accordance with AASB 137; and

    (ii) the amount initially recognised (see paragraph 5.1.1) less, when appropriate, cumulative amortisation recognised in accordance with AASB 118.

Option to designate a financial liability at fair value through profit or loss

4.2.2 An entity may, at initial recognition, irrevocably designate a financial liability as measured at fair value through profit or loss when permitted by paragraph 4.3.5, or when doing so results in more relevant information, because either:

(a) it eliminates or significantly reduces a measurement or recognition inconsistency (sometimes referred to as 'an accounting mismatch') that would otherwise arise from measuring assets or liabilities or recognising the gains and losses on them on different bases; or

(b) a group of financial liabilities or financial assets and financial liabilities is managed and its performance is evaluated on a fair value basis, in accordance with a documented risk management or investment strategy, and information about the group is provided internally on that basis to the entity's key management personnel (as defined in AASB 124 *Related Party Disclosures*), for example the entity's board of directors and chief executive officer.

4.2.3 AASB 7 requires the entity to provide disclosures about financial liabilities it has designated as at fair value through profit or loss.

4.3 Embedded derivatives

4.3.1 An embedded derivative is a component of a hybrid contract that also includes a non-derivative host – with the effect that some of the cash flows of the combined instrument vary in a way similar to a stand-alone derivative. An embedded derivative causes some or all of the cash flows that otherwise would be required by the contract to be modified according to a specified interest rate, financial instrument price, commodity price, foreign exchange rate, index of prices or rates, credit rating or credit index, or other variable, provided in the case of a non-financial variable that the variable is not specific to a party to the contract. A derivative that is attached to a *financial instrument* but is contractually transferable independently of that instrument, or has a different counterparty, is not an embedded derivative, but a separate financial instrument.

Hybrid contracts with financial asset hosts

4.3.2 If a hybrid contract contains a host that is an asset within the scope of this Standard, an entity shall apply the requirements in paragraphs 4.1.1-4.1.5 to the entire hybrid contract.

Other hybrid contracts

4.3.3 If a hybrid contract contains a host that is not an asset within the scope of this Standard, an embedded derivative shall be separated from the host and accounted for as a derivative under this Standard if, and only if:

(a)   the economic characteristics and risks of the embedded derivative are not closely related to the economic characteristics and risks of the host (see paragraphs B4.3.5 and B4.3.8);

(b)   a separate instrument with the same terms as the embedded derivative would meet the definition of a derivative; and

(c)   the hybrid contract is not measured at fair value with changes in fair value recognised in profit or loss (ie a derivative that is embedded in a financial liability at fair value through profit or loss is not separated).

4.3.4 If an embedded derivative is separated, the host contract shall be accounted for in accordance with the appropriate Standard. This Standard does not address whether an embedded derivative shall be presented separately in the statement of financial position.

4.3.5 Despite paragraphs 4.3.3 and 4.3.4, if a contract contains one or more embedded derivatives and the host is not an asset within the scope of this Standard, an entity may designate the entire hybrid contract as at fair value through profit or loss unless:

(a)   the embedded derivative(s) do(es) not significantly modify the cash flows that otherwise would be required by the contract; or

(b)   it is clear with little or no analysis when a similar hybrid instrument is first considered that separation of the embedded derivative(s) is prohibited, such as a prepayment option embedded in a loan that permits the holder to prepay the loan for approximately its amortised cost.

4.3.6 If an entity is required by this Standard to separate an embedded derivative from its host, but is unable to measure the embedded derivative separately either at acquisition or at the end of a subsequent financial reporting period, it shall designate the entire hybrid contract as at fair value through profit or loss.

4.3.7 If an entity is unable to measure reliably the fair value of an embedded derivative on the basis of its terms and conditions, the fair value of the embedded derivative is the difference between the fair value of the hybrid contract and the fair value of the host. If the entity is unable to measure the fair value of the embedded derivative using this method, paragraph 4.3.6 applies and the hybrid contract is designated as at fair value through profit or loss.

4.4 Reclassification

4.4.1 When, and only when, an entity changes its business model for managing financial assets it shall reclassify all affected financial assets in accordance with paragraphs 4.1.1-4.1.4.

4.4.2 An entity shall not reclassify any financial liability.

4.4.3 The following changes in circumstances are not reclassifications for the purposes of paragraphs 4.4.1 and 4.4.2:

(a)   A derivative that was previously a designated and effective *hedging instrument* in a cash flow hedge or net investment hedge no longer qualifies as such.

(b)   A derivative becomes a designated and effective hedging instrument in a cash flow hedge or net investment hedge.

Chapter 5 Measurement

5.1 Initial measurement

5.1.1 At initial recognition, an entity shall measure a financial asset or financial liability at its fair value plus or minus, in the case of a financial asset or financial liability not at fair value through profit or loss, transaction costs that are directly attributable to the acquisition or issue of the financial asset or financial liability.

5.1.1A However, if the fair value of the financial asset or financial liability at initial recognition differs from the transaction price, an entity shall apply paragraph B5.1.2A.

5.1.2 When an entity uses settlement date accounting for an asset that is subsequently measured at amortised cost, the asset is recognised initially at its fair value on the trade date (see paragraphs B3.1.3-B3.1.6).

5.2 Subsequent measurement of financial assets

5.2.1 After initial recognition, an entity shall measure a financial asset in accordance with paragraphs 4.1.1-4.1.5 at fair value or amortised cost (see paragraphs 9 and AG5-AG8 of AASB 139).

5.2.2 An entity shall apply the impairment requirements in paragraphs 58-65 and AG84-AG93 of AASB 139 to financial assets measured at amortised cost.

5.2.3 An entity shall apply the hedge accounting requirements in paragraphs 89-102 of AASB 139 to a financial asset that is designated as a *hedged item* (see paragraphs 78-84 and AG98-AG101 of AASB 139).

5.3 Subsequent measurement of financial liabilities

5.3.1 After initial recognition, an entity shall measure a financial liability in accordance with paragraphs 4.2.1-4.2.2 (see paragraphs 5.4.1-5.4.3 and B5.4.1-B5.4.17 and paragraphs 9 and AG5-AG8 of AASB 139).

5.3.2 An entity shall apply the hedge accounting requirements in paragraphs 89-102 of AASB 139 to a financial liability that is designated as a hedged item (see paragraphs 78-84 and AG98-AG101 of AASB 139).

5.4.1-5.4.3   [Deleted by the IASB]

5.5 Amortised cost measurement – *not used*

5.6 Reclassification of financial assets

5.6.1 If an entity reclassifies financial assets in accordance with paragraph 4.4.1, it shall apply the reclassification prospectively from the *reclassification date*. The entity shall not restate any previously recognised gains, losses or interest.

5.6.2 If, in accordance with paragraph 4.4.1, an entity reclassifies a financial asset so that it is measured at fair value, its fair value is measured at the reclassification date. Any gain or loss arising from a difference between the previous carrying amount and fair value is recognised in profit or loss.

5.6.3 If, in accordance with paragraph 4.4.1, an entity reclassifies a financial asset so that it is measured at amortised cost, its fair value at the reclassification date becomes its new carrying amount.

5.7 Gains and losses

5.7.1 A gain or loss on a financial asset or financial liability that is measured at fair value shall be recognised in profit or loss unless:

(a)   it is part of a hedging relationship (see paragraphs 89-102 of AASB 139);

(b)   it is an investment in an *equity instrument* and the entity has elected to present gains and losses on that investment in other comprehensive income in accordance with paragraph 5.7.5; or

(c)   it is a financial liability designated as at fair value through profit or loss and the entity is required to present the effects of changes in the liability's *credit risk* in other comprehensive income in accordance with paragraph 5.7.7.

5.7.2 A gain or loss on a financial asset that is measured at amortised cost and is not part of a hedging relationship (see paragraphs 89-102 of AASB 139) shall be recognised in profit or loss when the financial asset is derecognised, impaired or reclassified in accordance with paragraph 5.6.2, and through the amortisation process. A gain or loss on a financial liability that is measured at amortised cost and is not part of a hedging relationship (see paragraphs 89-102 of AASB 139) shall be recognised in profit or loss when the financial liability is derecognised and through the amortisation process.

5.7.3 A gain or loss on financial assets or financial liabilities that are hedged items (see paragraphs 78-84 and AG98-AG101 of AASB 139) shall be recognised in accordance with paragraphs 89-102 of AASB 139.

5.7.4 If an entity recognises financial assets using settlement date accounting (see paragraph 3.1.2 and paragraphs B3.1.3 and B3.1.6), any change in the fair value of the asset to be received during the period between the trade date and the settlement date is not recognised for assets measured at amortised cost (other than impairment losses). For assets measured at fair value, however, the change in fair value shall be recognised in profit or loss or in other comprehensive income, as appropriate under paragraph 5.7.1.

Investments in equity instruments

5.7.5 At initial recognition, an entity may make an irrevocable election to present in other comprehensive income subsequent changes in the fair value of an investment in an equity instrument within the scope of this Standard that is not *held for trading*.

5.7.6 If an entity makes the election in paragraph 5.7.5, it shall recognise in profit or loss dividends from that investment when the entity's right to receive payment of the dividend is established in accordance with AASB 118.

Liabilities designated as at fair value through profit or loss

5.7.7 An entity shall present a gain or loss on a financial liability designated as at fair value through profit or loss as follows:

(a) the amount of change in the fair value of the financial liability that is attributable to changes in the credit risk of that liability shall be presented in other comprehensive income (see paragraphs B5.7.13-B5.7.20); and

(b) the remaining amount of change in the fair value of the liability shall be presented in profit or loss;

unless the treatment of the effects of changes in the liability's credit risk described in (a) would create or enlarge an accounting mismatch in profit or loss (in which case paragraph 5.7.8 applies). Paragraphs B5.7.5-B5.7.7 and B5.7.10-B5.7.12 provide guidance on determining whether an accounting mismatch would be created or enlarged.

5.7.8 If the requirements in paragraph 5.7.7 would create or enlarge an accounting mismatch in profit or loss, an entity shall present all gains or losses on that liability (including the effects of changes in the credit risk of that liability) in profit or loss.

5.7.9 Despite the requirements in paragraphs 5.7.7 and 5.7.8, an entity shall present in profit or loss all gains and losses on loan commitments and financial guarantee contracts that are designated as at fair value through profit or loss.

Chapter 6 Hedge accounting – *not used*

Chapter 7 Effective date and transition

7.1 Effective Date

7.1.1 [Deleted by the AASB]

7.1.2 AASB 2011-7 *Amendments to Australian Accounting Standards arising from the Consolidation and Joint Arrangements Standards*, issued in August 2011, amended paragraphs 3.2.1, B3.2.1-B3.2.3, B4.3.12(c) and B5.7.15. An entity shall apply those amendments when it applies AASB 10 and AASB 11 *Joint Arrangements*.

7.1.3 AASB 2011-8 *Amendments to Australian Accounting Standards arising from AASB 13*, issued in September 2011, amended paragraphs 3.2.14, 4.3.7, 5.1.1, 5.2.1, 5.6.2, 7.2.5, 7.2.11 and 7.2.12, amended the definition of fair value in Appendix A, amended paragraphs B3.2.11, B3.2.17, B5.1.1, B5.4.14, B5.4.16 and B5.7.20, deleted paragraphs 5.4.1–5.4.3 and B5.4.1-B5.4.13, and added paragraphs 5.1.1A, B5.1.2A and B5.2.2A. An entity shall apply those amendments when it applies AASB 13 *Fair Value Measurement*.

7.2 Transition

7.2.1 An entity shall apply this Standard retrospectively, in accordance with AASB 108 *Accounting Policies, Changes in Accounting Estimates and Errors*, except as specified in paragraphs 7.2.4-7.2.15. This Standard shall not be applied to items that have already been derecognised at the date of initial application.

7.2.2 For the purposes of the transition provisions in paragraphs 7.2.1 and 7.2.3-7.2.16, the date of initial application is the date when an entity first applies the requirements of this Standard. The date of initial application may be:

(a) any date between the issue of this Standard and 31 December 2010, for entities initially applying this Standard before 1 January 2011; or

(b) the beginning of the first reporting period in which the entity adopts this Standard, for entities initially applying this Standard on or after 1 January 2011.

7.2.3 If the date of initial application is not at the beginning of a reporting period, the entity shall disclose that fact and the reasons for using that date of initial application.

7.2.4 At the date of initial application, an entity shall assess whether a financial asset meets the condition in paragraph 4.1.2(a) on the basis of the facts and circumstances that exist at the date of initial application. The resulting classification shall be applied retrospectively irrespective of the entity's business model in prior reporting periods.

7.2.5 If an entity measures a hybrid contract at fair value in accordance with paragraph 4.1.4 or paragraph 4.1.5 but the fair value of the hybrid contract had not been measured in comparative reporting periods, the fair value of the hybrid contract in the comparative reporting periods shall be the sum of the fair values of the components (ie the non-derivative host and the embedded derivative) at the end of each comparative reporting period.

7.2.6 At the date of initial application, an entity shall recognise any difference between the fair value of the entire hybrid contract at the date of initial application and the sum of the fair values of the components of the hybrid contract at the date of initial application:

(a) in the opening retained earnings of the reporting period of initial application if the entity initially applies this Standard at the beginning of a reporting period; or

(b) in profit or loss if the entity initially applies this Standard during a reporting period.

7.2.7 At the date of initial application, an entity may designate:

(a) a financial asset as measured at fair value through profit or loss in accordance with paragraph 4.1.5; or

(b) an investment in an equity instrument as at fair value through other comprehensive income in accordance with paragraph 5.7.5.

Such designation shall be made on the basis of the facts and circumstances that exist at the date of initial application. That classification shall be applied retrospectively.

7.2.8 At the date of initial application, an entity:

(a) shall revoke its previous designation of a financial asset as measured at fair value through profit or loss if that financial asset does not meet the condition in paragraph 4.1.5.

(b) may revoke its previous designation of a financial asset as measured at fair value through profit or loss if that financial asset meets the condition in paragraph 4.1.5.

Such revocation shall be made on the basis of the facts and circumstances that exist at the date of initial application. That classification shall be applied retrospectively.

7.2.9 At the date of initial application, an entity:

(a) may designate a financial liability as measured at fair value through profit or loss in accordance with paragraph 4.2.2(a).

(b)   shall revoke its previous designation of a financial liability as measured at fair value through profit or loss if such designation was made at initial recognition in accordance with the condition now in paragraph 4.2.2(a) and such designation does not satisfy that condition at the date of initial application.

(c)   may revoke its previous designation of a financial liability as measured at fair value through profit or loss if such designation was made at initial recognition in accordance with the condition now in paragraph 4.2.2(a) and such designation satisfies that condition at the date of initial application.

Such designation and revocation shall be made on the basis of the facts and circumstances that exist at the date of initial application. That classification shall be applied retrospectively.

7.2.10 If it is impracticable (as defined in AASB 108) for an entity to apply retrospectively the effective interest method or the impairment requirements in paragraphs 58-65 and AG84-AG93 of AASB 139, the entity shall treat the fair value of the financial asset or financial liability at the end of each comparative period as its amortised cost if the entity restates prior periods. If it is impracticable (as defined in AASB 108) for an entity to apply retrospectively the effective interest method or the impairment requirements in paragraphs 58-65 and AG84-AG93 of AASB 139, the fair value of the financial asset or financial liability at the date of initial application shall be treated as the new amortised cost of that financial asset or financial liability at the date of initial application of this Standard.

7.2.11 If an entity previously accounted for an investment in an equity instrument that does not have a quoted price in an active market for an identical instrument (ie a Level 1 input) (or a derivative asset that is linked to and must be settled by delivery of such an equity instrument) at cost in accordance with AASB 139, it shall measure that instrument at fair value at the date of initial application. Any difference between the previous carrying amount and fair value shall be recognised in the opening retained earnings of the reporting period that includes the date of initial application.

7.2.12 If an entity previously accounted for a derivative liability that is linked to and must be settled by delivery of an equity instrument that does not have a quoted price in an active market for an identical instrument (ie a Level 1 input) at cost in accordance with AASB 139, it shall measure that derivative liability at fair value at the date of initial application. Any difference between the previous carrying amount and fair value shall be recognised in the opening retained earnings of the reporting period that includes the date of initial application.

7.2.13 At the date of initial application, an entity shall determine whether the treatment in paragraph 5.7.7 would create or enlarge an accounting mismatch in profit or loss on the basis of the facts and circumstances that exist at the date of initial application. This Standard shall be applied retrospectively on the basis of that determination.

7.2.14 Despite the requirement in paragraph 7.2.1, an entity that adopts the classification and measurement requirements of this Standard for reporting periods:

(a)   beginning before 1 January 2012 need not restate prior periods and is not required to provide the disclosures set out in paragraphs 44S-44W of AASB 7;

(b)   beginning on or after 1 January 2012 and before 1 January 2013 shall elect either to provide the disclosures set out in paragraphs 44S-44W of AASB 7 or to restate prior periods; and

(c)   beginning on or after 1 January 2013 shall provide the disclosures set out in paragraphs 44S-44W of AASB 7. The entity need not restate prior periods.

If an entity does not restate prior periods, the entity shall recognise any difference between the previous carrying amount and the carrying amount at the beginning of the annual reporting period that includes the date of initial application in the opening retained earnings (or other component of equity, as appropriate) of the annual reporting period that includes the date of initial application. However, if an entity restates prior periods, the restated financial statements must reflect all of the requirements in this Standard.

7.2.15 If an entity prepares interim financial reports in accordance with AASB 134 *Interim Financial Reporting* the entity need not apply the requirements in this Standard to interim periods prior to the date of initial application if it is impracticable (as defined in AASB 108).

Entities that have applied early AASB 9 issued in 2009

7.2.16 An entity shall apply the transition requirements in paragraphs 7.2.1-7.2.15 at the relevant date of initial application. In other words, an entity shall apply paragraphs 7.2.4-7.2.11 if it applies AASB 9 (issued in 2009) or, not having done so, when it applies AASB 9 (December 2010) in its entirety. An entity is not permitted to apply those paragraphs more than once.

7.3 Withdrawal of IFRIC 9 and IFRS 9 (2009)

7.3.1 [Deleted by the AASB]

7.3.2 [Deleted by the AASB]

Appendix A
Defined Terms

This appendix is an integral part of AASB 9.

Derecognition	The removal of a previously recognised financial asset or financial liability from an entity's statement of financial position.
derivative	A financial instrument or other contract within the scope of this Standard (see paragraph 2.1) with all three of the following characteristics.

(a) Its value changes in response to the change in a specified interest rate, financial instrument price, commodity price, foreign exchange rate, index of prices or rates, credit rating or credit index, or other variable, provided in the case of a non-financial variable that the variable is not specific to a party to the contract (sometimes called the 'underlying').

(b) It requires no initial net investment or an initial net investment that is smaller than would be required for other types of contracts that would be expected to have a similar response to changes in market factors.

(c) It is settled at a future date.

fair value	*Fair value* is the price that would be received to sell an asset or paid to transfer a liability in an orderly transaction between market participants at the measurement date. (See AASB 13.)
financial guarantee contract	A contract that requires the issuer to make specified payments to reimburse the holder for a loss it incurs because a specified debtor fails to make payment when due in accordance with the original or modified terms of a debt instrument.
financial liability at fair value through profit or loss	A financial liability that meets either of the following conditions.

(a) It meets the definition of held for trading.

(b) Upon initial recognition it is designated by the entity as at fair value through profit or loss in accordance with paragraph 4.2.2 or 4.3.5.

held for trading	A financial asset or financial liability that:

    (a)   is acquired or incurred principally for the purpose of selling or repurchasing it in the near term;

    (b)   on initial recognition is part of a portfolio of identified financial instruments that are managed together and for which there is evidence of a recent actual pattern of short-term profit-taking; or

    (c)   is a derivative (except for a derivative that is a financial guarantee contract or a designated and effective hedging instrument).

reclassification date	The first day of the first reporting period following the change in business model that results in an entity reclassifying financial assets.
regular way purchase or sale	A purchase or sale of a financial asset under a contract whose terms require delivery of the asset within the time frame established generally by regulation or convention in the marketplace concerned.

The following terms are defined in paragraph 11 of AASB 132, paragraph 9 of AASB 139 or Appendix A of AASB 7 and are used in this Standard with the meanings specified in AASB 132, AASB 139 or AASB 7:

(a)   amortised cost of a financial asset or financial liability

(b)   credit risk

(c)   effective interest method

(d)   equity instrument

(e)   financial asset

(f)   financial instrument

(g)   financial liability

(h)   hedged item

(i)   hedging instrument

(j)   transaction costs.

Appendix B
Application Guidance

This appendix is an integral part of AASB 9.

Recognition and derecognition (chapter 3)

Initial recognition (section 3.1)

B3.1.1   As a consequence of the principle in paragraph 3.1.1, an entity recognises all of its contractual rights and obligations under derivatives in its statement of financial position as assets and liabilities, respectively, except for derivatives that prevent a transfer of financial assets from being accounted for as a sale (see paragraph B3.2.14). If a transfer of a financial asset does not qualify for derecognition, the transferee does not recognise the transferred asset as its asset (see paragraph B3.2.15).

B3.1.2   The following are examples of applying the principle in paragraph 3.1.1:

    (a)   Unconditional receivables and payables are recognised as assets or liabilities when the entity becomes a party to the contract and, as a consequence, has a legal right to receive or a legal obligation to pay cash.

    (b)   Assets to be acquired and liabilities to be incurred as a result of a firm commitment to purchase or sell goods or services are generally not recognised until at least one of the parties has performed under the agreement.

For example, an entity that receives a firm order does not generally recognise an asset (and the entity that places the order does not recognise a liability) at the time of the commitment but, rather, delays recognition until the ordered goods or services have been shipped, delivered or rendered. If a firm commitment to buy or sell non-financial items is within the scope of this Standard in accordance with paragraphs 5-7 of AASB 139, its net fair value is recognised as an asset or liability on the commitment date (see (c) below). In addition, if a previously unrecognised firm commitment is designated as a hedged item in a fair value hedge, any change in the net fair value attributable to the hedged risk is recognised as an asset or liability after the inception of the hedge (see paragraphs 93 and 94 of AASB 139).

(c)   A forward contract that is within the scope of this Standard (see paragraph 2.1) is recognised as an asset or a liability on the commitment date, rather than on the date on which settlement takes place. When an entity becomes a party to a forward contract, the fair values of the right and obligation are often equal, so that the net fair value of the forward is zero. If the net fair value of the right and obligation is not zero, the contract is recognised as an asset or liability.

(d)   Option contracts that are within the scope of this Standard (see paragraph 2.1) are recognised as assets or liabilities when the holder or writer becomes a party to the contract.

(e)   Planned future transactions, no matter how likely, are not assets and liabilities because the entity has not become a party to a contract.

Regular way purchase or sale of financial assets

B3.1.3   A regular way purchase or sale of financial assets is recognised using either trade date accounting or settlement date accounting as described in paragraphs B3.1.5 and B3.1.6. An entity shall apply the same method consistently for all purchases and sales of financial assets that are classified in the same way in accordance with this Standard. For this purpose assets that are mandatorily measured at fair value through profit or loss form a separate classification from assets designated as measured at fair value through profit or loss. In addition, investments in equity instruments accounted for using the option provided in paragraph 5.7.5 form a separate classification.

B3.1.4   A contract that requires or permits net settlement of the change in the value of the contract is not a regular way contract. Instead, such a contract is accounted for as a derivative in the period between the trade date and the settlement date.

B3.1.5   The trade date is the date that an entity commits itself to purchase or sell an asset. Trade date accounting refers to (a) the recognition of an asset to be received and the liability to pay for it on the trade date, and (b) derecognition of an asset that is sold, recognition of any gain or loss on disposal and the recognition of a receivable from the buyer for payment on the trade date. Generally, interest does not start to accrue on the asset and corresponding liability until the settlement date when title passes.

B3.1.6   The settlement date is the date that an asset is delivered to or by an entity. Settlement date accounting refers to (a) the recognition of an asset on the day it is received by the entity, and (b) the derecognition of an asset and recognition of any gain or loss on disposal on the day that it is delivered by the entity. When settlement date accounting is applied an entity accounts for any change in the fair value of the asset to be received during the period between the trade date and the settlement date in the same way as it accounts for the acquired asset. In other words, the change in value is not recognised for assets measured at amortised cost; it is recognised in profit or loss for assets classified as financial assets measured at fair value through profit or loss; and it is recognised in other comprehensive income for investments in equity instruments accounted for in accordance with paragraph 5.7.5.

Derecognition of financial assets (section 3.2)

B3.2.1   The following flow chart illustrates the evaluation of whether and to what extent a financial asset is derecognised.

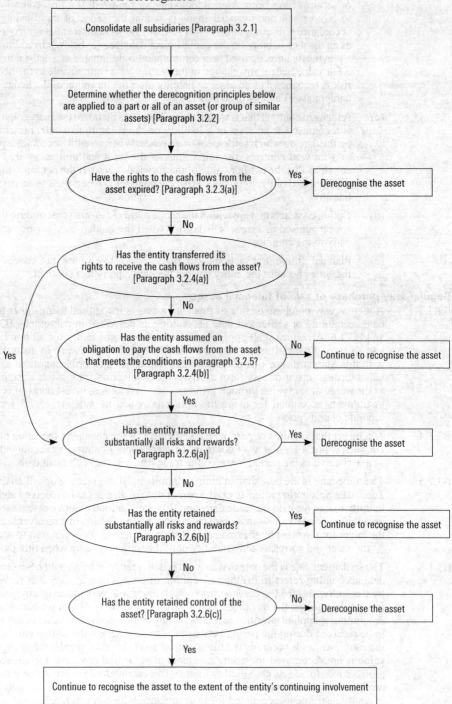

Arrangements under which an entity retains the contractual rights to receive the cash flows of a financial asset, but assumes a contractual obligation to pay the cash flows to one or more recipients (paragraph 3.2.4(b))

B3.2.2   The situation described in paragraph 3.2.4(b) (when an entity retains the contractual rights to receive the cash flows of the financial asset, but assumes a contractual obligation to pay the cash flows to one or more recipients) occurs, for example, if the entity is a trust, and issues to investors beneficial interests in the underlying financial assets that it owns and provides servicing of those financial assets. In that case, the financial assets qualify for derecognition if the conditions in paragraphs 3.2.5 and 3.2.6 are met.

B3.2.3   In applying paragraph 3.2.5, the entity could be, for example, the originator of the financial asset, or it could be a group that includes a subsidiary that has acquired the financial asset and passes on cash flows to unrelated third party investors.

Evaluation of the transfer of risks and rewards of ownership (paragraph 3.2.6)

B3.2.4   Examples of when an entity has transferred substantially all the risks and rewards of ownership are:

    (a)   an unconditional sale of a financial asset;

    (b)   a sale of a financial asset together with an option to repurchase the financial asset at its fair value at the time of repurchase; and

    (c)   a sale of a financial asset together with a put or call option that is deeply out of the money (ie an option that is so far out of the money it is highly unlikely to go into the money before expiry).

B3.2.5   Examples of when an entity has retained substantially all the risks and rewards of ownership are:

    (a)   a sale and repurchase transaction where the repurchase price is a fixed price or the sale price plus a lender's return;

    (b)   a securities lending agreement;

    (c)   a sale of a financial asset together with a total return swap that transfers the market risk exposure back to the entity;

    (d)   a sale of a financial asset together with a deep in-the-money put or call option (ie an option that is so far in the money that it is highly unlikely to go out of the money before expiry); and

    (e)   a sale of short-term receivables in which the entity guarantees to compensate the transferee for credit losses that are likely to occur.

B3.2.6   If an entity determines that as a result of the transfer, it has transferred substantially all the risks and rewards of ownership of the transferred asset, it does not recognise the transferred asset again in a future period, unless it reacquires the transferred asset in a new transaction.

Evaluation of the transfer of control

B3.2.7   An entity has not retained control of a transferred asset if the transferee has the practical ability to sell the transferred asset. An entity has retained control of a transferred asset if the transferee does not have the practical ability to sell the transferred asset. A transferee has the practical ability to sell the transferred asset if it is traded in an active market because the transferee could repurchase the transferred asset in the market if it needs to return the asset to the entity. For example, a transferee may have the practical ability to sell a transferred asset if the transferred asset is subject to an option that allows the entity to repurchase it, but the transferee can readily obtain the transferred asset in the market if the option is exercised. A transferee does not have the practical ability to sell the transferred asset if the entity retains such an option and the transferee cannot readily obtain the transferred asset in the market if the entity exercises its option.

B3.2.8   The transferee has the practical ability to sell the transferred asset only if the transferee can sell the transferred asset in its entirety to an unrelated third party and is able to exercise that ability unilaterally and without imposing additional restrictions on the transfer. The critical question is what the transferee is able to do in practice, not what contractual rights the transferee has concerning what it can do with the transferred asset or what contractual prohibitions exist. In particular:

(a)   a contractual right to dispose of the transferred asset has little practical effect if there is no market for the transferred asset, and

(b)   an ability to dispose of the transferred asset has little practical effect if it cannot be exercised freely. For that reason:

    (i)   the transferee's ability to dispose of the transferred asset must be independent of the actions of others (ie it must be a unilateral ability), and

    (ii)   the transferee must be able to dispose of the transferred asset without needing to attach restrictive conditions or 'strings' to the transfer (eg conditions about how a loan asset is serviced or an option giving the transferee the right to repurchase the asset).

B3.2.9   That the transferee is unlikely to sell the transferred asset does not, of itself, mean that the transferor has retained control of the transferred asset. However, if a put option or guarantee constrains the transferee from selling the transferred asset, then the transferor has retained control of the transferred asset. For example, if a put option or guarantee is sufficiently valuable it constrains the transferee from selling the transferred asset because the transferee would, in practice, not sell the transferred asset to a third party without attaching a similar option or other restrictive conditions. Instead, the transferee would hold the transferred asset so as to obtain payments under the guarantee or put option. Under these circumstances the transferor has retained control of the transferred asset.

Transfers that qualify for derecognition

B3.2.10   An entity may retain the right to a part of the interest payments on transferred assets as compensation for servicing those assets. The part of the interest payments that the entity would give up upon termination or transfer of the servicing contract is allocated to the servicing asset or servicing liability. The part of the interest payments that the entity would not give up is an interest-only strip receivable. For example, if the entity would not give up any interest upon termination or transfer of the servicing contract, the entire interest spread is an interest-only strip receivable. For the purposes of applying paragraph 3.2.13, the fair values of the servicing asset and interest-only strip receivable are used to allocate the carrying amount of the receivable between the part of the asset that is derecognised and the part that continues to be recognised. If there is no servicing fee specified or the fee to be received is not expected to compensate the entity adequately for performing the servicing, a liability for the servicing obligation is recognised at fair value.

B3.2.11   When measuring the fair values of the part that continues to be recognised and the part that is derecognised for the purposes of applying paragraph 3.2.13, an entity applies the fair value measurement requirements in AASB 13 in addition to paragraph 3.2.14.

Transfers that do not qualify for derecognition

B3.2.12   The following is an application of the principle outlined in paragraph 3.2.15. If a guarantee provided by the entity for default losses on the transferred asset prevents a transferred asset from being derecognised because the entity has retained substantially all the risks and rewards of ownership of the transferred asset, the transferred asset continues to be recognised in its entirety and the consideration received is recognised as a liability.

Continuing involvement in transferred assets

B3.2.13   The following are examples of how an entity measures a transferred asset and the associated liability under paragraph 3.2.16.

All assets

(a) If a guarantee provided by an entity to pay for default losses on a transferred asset prevents the transferred asset from being derecognised to the extent of the continuing involvement, the transferred asset at the date of the transfer is measured at the lower of (i) the carrying amount of the asset and (ii) the maximum amount of the consideration received in the transfer that the entity could be required to repay ('the guarantee amount'). The associated liability is initially measured at the guarantee amount plus the fair value of the guarantee (which is normally the consideration received for the guarantee). Subsequently, the initial fair value of the guarantee is recognised in profit or loss on a time proportion basis (see AASB 118) and the carrying value of the asset is reduced by any impairment losses.

Assets measured at amortised cost

(b) If a put option obligation written by an entity or call option right held by an entity prevents a transferred asset from being derecognised and the entity measures the transferred asset at amortised cost, the associated liability is measured at its cost (ie the consideration received) adjusted for the amortisation of any difference between that cost and the amortised cost of the transferred asset at the expiration date of the option. For example, assume that the amortised cost and carrying amount of the asset on the date of the transfer is CU98 and that the consideration received is CU95. The amortised cost of the asset on the option exercise date will be CU100. The initial carrying amount of the associated liability is CU95 and the difference between CU95 and CU100 is recognised in profit or loss using the effective interest method. If the option is exercised, any difference between the carrying amount of the associated liability and the exercise price is recognised in profit or loss.

Assets measured at fair value

(c) If a call option right retained by an entity prevents a transferred asset from being derecognised and the entity measures the transferred asset at fair value, the asset continues to be measured at its fair value. The associated liability is measured at (i) the option exercise price less the time value of the option if the option is in or at the money, or (ii) the fair value of the transferred asset less the time value of the option if the option is out of the money. The adjustment to the measurement of the associated liability ensures that the net carrying amount of the asset and the associated liability is the fair value of the call option right. For example, if the fair value of the underlying asset is CU80, the option exercise price is CU95 and the time value of the option is CU5, the carrying amount of the associated liability is CU75 (CU80 – CU5) and the carrying amount of the transferred asset is CU80 (ie its fair value).

(d) If a put option written by an entity prevents a transferred asset from being derecognised and the entity measures the transferred asset at fair value, the associated liability is measured at the option exercise price plus the time value of the option. The measurement of the asset at fair value is limited to the lower of the fair value and the option exercise price because the entity has no right to increases in the fair value of the transferred asset above the exercise price of the option. This ensures that the net carrying amount of the asset and the associated liability is the fair value of the put option obligation. For example, if the fair value of the underlying asset is CU120, the option exercise price is CU100 and the time value of the option is CU5, the carrying amount of the associated liability is CU105 (CU100 + CU5) and the carrying amount of the asset is CU100 (in this case the option exercise price).

(e) If a collar, in the form of a purchased call and written put, prevents a transferred asset from being derecognised and the entity measures the asset at fair value, it continues to measure the asset at fair value. The associated liability is measured at (i) the sum of the call exercise price and fair value of the put option less the time value of the call option, if the call option is in or at the money, or (ii) the sum of the fair value of the asset and the fair value of the put option less the time value of the call option if the call option is out of the money. The adjustment to the associated liability ensures that the net carrying amount of the asset and the associated liability is the fair value of the options held and written by the entity. For example, assume an entity transfers a financial asset that is measured at fair value while simultaneously purchasing a call with an exercise price of CU120 and writing a put with an exercise price of CU80. Assume also that the fair value of the asset is CU100 at the date of the transfer. The time value of the put and call are CU1 and CU5 respectively. In this case, the entity recognises an asset of CU100 (the fair value of the asset) and a liability of CU96 [(CU100 + CU1) – CU5]. This gives a net asset value of CU4, which is the fair value of the options held and written by the entity.

All transfers

B3.2.14   To the extent that a transfer of a financial asset does not qualify for derecognition, the transferor's contractual rights or obligations related to the transfer are not accounted for separately as derivatives if recognising both the derivative and either the transferred asset or the liability arising from the transfer would result in recognising the same rights or obligations twice. For example, a call option retained by the transferor may prevent a transfer of financial assets from being accounted for as a sale. In that case, the call option is not separately recognised as a derivative asset.

B3.2.15   To the extent that a transfer of a financial asset does not qualify for derecognition, the transferee does not recognise the transferred asset as its asset. The transferee derecognises the cash or other consideration paid and recognises a receivable from the transferor. If the transferor has both a right and an obligation to reacquire control of the entire transferred asset for a fixed amount (such as under a repurchase agreement), the transferee may measure its receivable at amortised cost if it meets the criteria in paragraph 4.1.2.

Examples

B3.2.16   The following examples illustrate the application of the derecognition principles of this Standard.

(a)   *Repurchase agreements and securities lending.* If a financial asset is sold under an agreement to repurchase it at a fixed price or at the sale price plus a lender's return or if it is loaned under an agreement to return it to the transferor, it is not derecognised because the transferor retains substantially all the risks and rewards of ownership. If the transferee obtains the right to sell or pledge the asset, the transferor reclassifies the asset in its statement of financial position, for example, as a loaned asset or repurchase receivable.

(b)   *Repurchase agreements and securities lending – assets that are substantially the same.* If a financial asset is sold under an agreement to repurchase the same or substantially the same asset at a fixed price or at the sale price plus a lender's return or if a financial asset is borrowed or loaned under an agreement to return the same or substantially the same asset to the transferor, it is not derecognised because the transferor retains substantially all the risks and rewards of ownership.

(c)   *Repurchase agreements and securities lending – right of substitution.* If a repurchase agreement at a fixed repurchase price or a price equal to the sale price plus a lender's return, or a similar securities lending transaction, provides the transferee with a right to substitute assets that are similar and of equal fair value to the transferred asset at the repurchase date, the asset sold or lent under a repurchase or securities lending transaction is not derecognised because the transferor retains substantially all the risks and rewards of ownership.

(d)   *Repurchase right of first refusal at fair value.* If an entity sells a financial asset and retains only a right of first refusal to repurchase the transferred asset at fair value if the transferee subsequently sells it, the entity derecognises the asset because it has transferred substantially all the risks and rewards of ownership.

(e)   *Wash sale transaction.* The repurchase of a financial asset shortly after it has been sold is sometimes referred to as a wash sale. Such a repurchase does not preclude derecognition provided that the original transaction met the derecognition requirements. However, if an agreement to sell a financial asset is entered into concurrently with an agreement to repurchase the same asset at a fixed price or the sale price plus a lender's return, then the asset is not derecognised.

(f)   *Put options and call options that are deeply in the money.* If a transferred financial asset can be called back by the transferor and the call option is deeply in the money, the transfer does not qualify for derecognition because the transferor has retained substantially all the risks and rewards of ownership. Similarly, if the financial asset can be put back by the transferee and the put option is deeply in the money, the transfer does not qualify for derecognition because the transferor has retained substantially all the risks and rewards of ownership.

(g)   *Put options and call options that are deeply out of the money.* A financial asset that is transferred subject only to a deep out-of-the-money put option held by the transferee or a deep out-of-the-money call option held by the transferor is derecognised. This is because the transferor has transferred substantially all the risks and rewards of ownership.

(h)   *Readily obtainable assets subject to a call option that is neither deeply in the money nor deeply out of the money.* If an entity holds a call option on an asset that is readily obtainable in the market and the option is neither deeply in the money nor deeply out of the money, the asset is derecognised. This is because the entity (i) has neither retained nor transferred substantially all the risks and rewards of ownership, and (ii) has not retained control. However, if the asset is not readily obtainable in the market, derecognition is precluded to the extent of the amount of the asset that is subject to the call option because the entity has retained control of the asset.

(i)   *A not readily obtainable asset subject to a put option written by an entity that is neither deeply in the money nor deeply out of the money.* If an entity transfers a financial asset that is not readily obtainable in the market, and writes a put option that is not deeply out of the money, the entity neither retains nor transfers substantially all the risks and rewards of ownership because of the written put option. The entity retains control of the asset if the put option is sufficiently valuable to prevent the transferee from selling the asset, in which case the asset continues to be recognised to the extent of the transferor's continuing involvement (see paragraph B3.2.9). The entity transfers control of the asset if the put option is not sufficiently valuable to prevent the transferee from selling the asset, in which case the asset is derecognised.

(j)   *Assets subject to a fair value put or call option or a forward repurchase agreement.* A transfer of a financial asset that is subject only to a put or call option or a forward repurchase agreement that has an exercise or repurchase price equal to the fair value of the financial asset at the time of repurchase results in derecognition because of the transfer of substantially all the risks and rewards of ownership.

(k)   *Cash-settled call or put options.* An entity evaluates the transfer of a financial asset that is subject to a put or call option or a forward repurchase agreement that will be settled net in cash to determine whether it has retained or transferred substantially all the risks and rewards of ownership. If the entity has not retained substantially all the risks and rewards of ownership of the transferred asset, it determines whether it has retained control of the transferred asset. That the put or the call or the forward repurchase agreement is settled net in cash does not automatically mean that the entity has transferred control (see paragraphs B3.2.9 and (g), (h) and (i) above).

(l)   *Removal of accounts provision.* A removal of accounts provision is an unconditional repurchase (call) option that gives an entity the right to reclaim assets transferred subject to some restrictions. Provided that such an option results in the entity neither retaining nor transferring substantially all the risks and rewards of ownership, it precludes derecognition only to the extent of the amount subject to repurchase (assuming that the transferee cannot sell the assets). For example, if the carrying amount and proceeds from the transfer of loan assets are CU100,000 and any individual loan could be called back but the aggregate amount of loans that could be repurchased could not exceed CU10,000, CU90,000 of the loans would qualify for derecognition.

(m)   *Clean-up calls.* An entity, which may be a transferor, that services transferred assets may hold a clean-up call to purchase remaining transferred assets when the amount of outstanding assets falls to a specified level at which the cost of servicing those assets becomes burdensome in relation to the benefits of servicing. Provided that such a clean-up call results in the entity neither retaining nor transferring substantially all the risks and rewards of ownership and the transferee cannot sell the assets, it precludes derecognition only to the extent of the amount of the assets that is subject to the call option.

(n)   *Subordinated retained interests and credit guarantees.* An entity may provide the transferee with credit enhancement by subordinating some or all of its interest retained in the transferred asset. Alternatively, an entity may provide the transferee with credit enhancement in the form of a credit guarantee that could be unlimited or limited to a specified amount. If the entity retains substantially all the risks and rewards of ownership of the transferred asset, the asset continues to be recognised in its entirety. If the entity retains some, but not substantially all, of the risks and rewards of ownership and has retained control, derecognition is precluded to the extent of the amount of cash or other assets that the entity could be required to pay.

(o)   *Total return swaps.* An entity may sell a financial asset to a transferee and enter into a total return swap with the transferee, whereby all of the interest payment cash flows from the underlying asset are remitted to the entity in exchange for a fixed payment or variable rate payment and any increases or declines in the fair value of the underlying asset are absorbed by the entity. In such a case, derecognition of all of the asset is prohibited.

(p)   *Interest rate swaps.* An entity may transfer to a transferee a fixed rate financial asset and enter into an interest rate swap with the transferee to receive a fixed interest rate and pay a variable interest rate based on a notional amount that is equal to the principal amount of the transferred financial asset. The interest rate swap does not preclude derecognition of the transferred asset provided the payments on the swap are not conditional on payments being made on the transferred asset.

(q)   *Amortising interest rate swaps.* An entity may transfer to a transferee a fixed rate financial asset that is paid off over time, and enter into an amortising interest rate swap with the transferee to receive a fixed interest rate and pay a variable interest rate based on a notional amount. If the notional amount of the swap amortises so that it equals the principal amount of the transferred financial asset outstanding at any point in time, the swap would generally result in the entity retaining substantial prepayment risk, in which case the entity either continues to recognise all of the transferred asset or continues to recognise the transferred asset to the extent of its continuing involvement. Conversely, if the amortisation of the notional amount of the swap is not linked to the principal amount outstanding of the transferred asset, such a swap would not result in the entity retaining prepayment risk on the asset. Hence, it would not preclude derecognition of the transferred asset provided the payments on the swap are not conditional on interest payments being made on the transferred asset and the swap does not result in the entity retaining any other significant risks and rewards of ownership on the transferred asset.

B3.2.17   This paragraph illustrates the application of the continuing involvement approach when the entity's continuing involvement is in a part of a financial asset.

Assume an entity has a portfolio of prepayable loans whose coupon and effective interest rate is 10 per cent and whose principal amount and amortised cost is CU10,000. It enters into a transaction in which, in return for a payment of CU9,115, the transferee obtains the right to CU9,000 of any collections of principal plus interest thereon at 9.5 per cent. The entity retains rights to CU1,000 of any collections of principal plus interest thereon at 10 per cent, plus the excess spread of 0.5 per cent on the remaining CU9,000 of principal. Collections from prepayments are allocated between the entity and the transferee proportionately in the ratio of 1:9, but any defaults are deducted from the entity's interest of CU1,000 until that interest is exhausted. The fair value of the loans at the date of the transaction is CU10,100 and the fair value of the excess spread of 0.5 per cent is CU40.

The entity determines that it has transferred some significant risks and rewards of ownership (for example, significant prepayment risk) but has also retained some significant risks and rewards of ownership (because of its subordinated retained interest) and has retained control. It therefore applies the continuing involvement approach.

To apply this Standard, the entity analyses the transaction as (a) a retention of a fully proportionate retained interest of CU1,000, plus (b) the subordination of that retained interest to provide credit enhancement to the transferee for credit losses.

The entity calculates that CU9,090 (90 per cent × CU10,100) of the consideration received of CU9,115 represents the consideration for a fully proportionate 90 per cent share. The remainder of the consideration received (CU25) represents consideration received for subordinating its retained interest to provide credit enhancement to the transferee for credit losses. In addition, the excess spread of 0.5 per cent represents consideration received for the credit enhancement. Accordingly, the total consideration received for the credit enhancement is CU65 (CU25 + CU40).

The entity calculates the gain or loss on the sale of the 90 per cent share of cash flows. Assuming that separate fair values of the 90 per cent part transferred and the 10 per cent part retained are not available at the date of the transfer, the entity allocates the carrying amount of the asset in accordance with paragraph 3.2.14 as follows:

	Fair value	Percentage	Allocated carrying amount
Portion transferred	9,090	90%	9,000
Portion retained	1,010	10%	1,000
Total	**10,100**		**10,000**

The entity computes its gain or loss on the sale of the 90 per cent share of the cash flows by deducting the allocated carrying amount of the portion transferred from the consideration received, ie CU90 (CU9,090 − CU9,000). The carrying amount of the portion retained by the entity is CU1,000.

In addition, the entity recognises the continuing involvement that results from the subordination of its retained interest for credit losses. Accordingly, it recognises an asset of CU1,000 (the maximum amount of the cash flows it would not receive under the subordination), and an associated liability of CU1,065 (which is the maximum amount of the cash flows it would not receive under the subordination, ie CU1,000 plus the fair value of the subordination of CU65).

continued

The entity uses all of the above information to account for the transaction as follows:

	Debit	Credit
Original asset	–	9,000
Asset recognised for subordination or the residual interest	1,000	–
Asset for the consideration received in the form of excess spread	40	–
Profit or loss (gain on transfer)	–	90
Liability	–	1,065
Cash received	9,115	–
Total	**10,155**	**10,155**

Immediately following the transaction, the carrying amount of the asset is CU2,040 comprising CU1,000, representing the allocated cost of the portion retained, and CU1,040, representing the entity's additional continuing involvement from the subordination of its retained interest for credit losses (which includes the excess spread of CU40).

In subsequent periods, the entity recognises the consideration received for the credit enhancement (CU65) on a time proportion basis, accrues interest on the recognised asset using the effective interest method and recognises any credit impairment on the recognised assets. As an example of the latter, assume that in the following year there is a credit impairment loss on the underlying loans of CU300. The entity reduces its recognised asset by CU600 (CU300 relating to its retained interest and CU300 relating to the additional continuing involvement that arises from the subordination of its retained interest for credit losses), and reduces its recognised liability by CU300. The net result is a charge to profit or loss for credit impairment of CU300.

Derecognition of financial liabilities (section 3.3)

B3.3.1   A financial liability (or part of it) is extinguished when the debtor either:

(a)   discharges the liability (or part of it) by paying the creditor, normally with cash, other financial assets, goods or services; or

(b)   is legally released from primary responsibility for the liability (or part of it) either by process of law or by the creditor. (If the debtor has given a guarantee this condition may still be met.)

B3.3.2   If an issuer of a debt instrument repurchases that instrument, the debt is extinguished even if the issuer is a market maker in that instrument or intends to resell it in the near term.

B3.3.3   Payment to a third party, including a trust (sometimes called 'in-substance defeasance'), does not, by itself, relieve the debtor of its primary obligation to the creditor, in the absence of legal release.

B3.3.4   If a debtor pays a third party to assume an obligation and notifies its creditor that the third party has assumed its debt obligation, the debtor does not derecognise the debt obligation unless the condition in paragraph B3.3.1(b) is met. If the debtor pays a third party to assume an obligation and obtains a legal release from its creditor, the debtor has extinguished the debt. However, if the debtor agrees to make payments on the debt to the third party or direct to its original creditor, the debtor recognises a new debt obligation to the third party.

B3.3.5   Although legal release, whether judicially or by the creditor, results in derecognition of a liability, the entity may recognise a new liability if the derecognition criteria in paragraphs 3.2.1-3.2.23 are not met for the financial assets transferred. If those criteria are not met, the transferred assets are not derecognised, and the entity recognises a new liability relating to the transferred assets.

B3.3.6   For the purpose of paragraph 3.3.2, the terms are substantially different if the discounted present value of the cash flows under the new terms, including any fees paid net of any fees received and discounted using the original effective interest rate, is at least 10 per cent different from the discounted present value of the remaining cash flows of the original financial liability. If an exchange of debt instruments or modification of terms is accounted for as an extinguishment, any costs or fees incurred are recognised as part of the gain or loss on the extinguishment. If the exchange or modification is not accounted for as an extinguishment, any costs or fees incurred adjust the carrying amount of the liability and are amortised over the remaining term of the modified liability.

B3.3.7   In some cases, a creditor releases a debtor from its present obligation to make payments, but the debtor assumes a guarantee obligation to pay if the party assuming primary responsibility defaults. In these circumstances the debtor:

(a)   recognises a new financial liability based on the fair value of its obligation for the guarantee, and

(b)   recognises a gain or loss based on the difference between (i) any proceeds paid and (ii) the carrying amount of the original financial liability less the fair value of the new financial liability.

Classification (chapter 4)

Classification of financial assets (section 4.1)

The entity's business model for managing financial assets

B4.1.1   Paragraph 4.1.1(a) requires an entity to classify financial assets as subsequently measured at amortised cost or fair value on the basis of the entity's business model for managing the financial assets. An entity assesses whether its financial assets meet this condition on the basis of the objective of the business model as determined by the entity's key management personnel (as defined in AASB 124).

B4.1.2   The entity's business model does not depend on management's intentions for an individual instrument. Accordingly, this condition is not an instrument-by-instrument approach to classification and should be determined on a higher level of aggregation. However, a single entity may have more than one business model for managing its financial instruments. Therefore, classification need not be determined at the reporting entity level. For example, an entity may hold a portfolio of investments that it manages in order to collect contractual cash flows and another portfolio of investments that it manages in order to trade to realise fair value changes.

B4.1.3   Although the objective of an entity's business model may be to hold financial assets in order to collect contractual cash flows, the entity need not hold all of those instruments until maturity. Thus an entity's business model can be to hold financial assets to collect contractual cash flows even when sales of financial assets occur. For example, the entity may sell a financial asset if:

(a)   the financial asset no longer meets the entity's investment policy (eg the credit rating of the asset declines below that required by the entity's investment policy);

(b)   an insurer adjusts its investment portfolio to reflect a change in expected duration (ie the expected timing of payouts); or

(c)   an entity needs to fund capital expenditures.

However, if more than an infrequent number of sales are made out of a portfolio, the entity needs to assess whether and how such sales are consistent with an objective of collecting contractual cash flows.

B4.1.4   The following are examples of when the objective of an entity's business model may be to hold financial assets to collect the contractual cash flows. This list of examples is not exhaustive.

Example	Analysis
Example 1 An entity holds investments to collect their contractual cash flows but would sell an investment in particular circumstances.	Although an entity may consider, among other information, the financial assets' fair values from a liquidity perspective (ie the cash amount that would be realised if the entity needs to sell assets), the entity's objective is to hold the financial assets and collect the contractual cash flows. Some sales would not contradict that objective.
Example 2 An entity's business model is to purchase portfolios of financial assets, such as loans. Those portfolios may or may not include financial assets with incurred credit losses. If payment on the loans is not made on a timely basis, the entity attempts to extract the contractual cash flows through various means – for example, by making contact with the debtor by mail, telephone or other methods. In some cases, the entity enters into interest rate swaps to change the interest rate on particular financial assets in a portfolio from a floating interest rate to a fixed interest rate.	The objective of the entity's business model is to hold the financial assets and collect the contractual cash flows. The entity does not purchase the portfolio to make a profit by selling them. The same analysis would apply even if the entity does not expect to receive all of the contractual cash flows (eg some of the financial assets have incurred credit losses). Moreover, the fact that the entity has entered into derivatives to modify the cash flows of the portfolio does not in itself change the entity's business model. If the portfolio is not managed on a fair value basis, the objective of the business model could be to hold the assets to collect the contractual cash flows.
Example 3 An entity has a business model with the objective of originating loans to customers and subsequently to sell those loans to a securitisation vehicle. The securitisation vehicle issues instruments to investors. The originating entity controls the securitisation vehicle and thus consolidates it. The securitisation vehicle collects the contractual cash flows from the loans and passes them on to its investors. It is assumed for the purposes of this example that the loans continue to be recognised in the consolidated statement of financial position because they are not derecognised by the securitisation vehicle.	The consolidated group originated the loans with the objective of holding them to collect the contractual cash flows. However, the originating entity has an objective of realising cash flows on the loan portfolio by selling the loans to the securitisation vehicle, so for the purposes of its separate financial statements it would not be considered to be managing this portfolio in order to collect the contractual cash flows.

B4.1.5   One business model in which the objective is not to hold instruments to collect the contractual cash flows is if an entity manages the performance of a portfolio of financial assets with the objective of realising cash flows through the sale of the assets. For example, if an entity actively manages a portfolio of assets in order to realise fair value changes arising from changes in credit spreads and yield curves, its business model is not to hold those assets to collect the contractual cash flows. The entity's objective results in active buying and selling and the entity is managing the instruments to realise fair value gains rather than to collect the contractual cash flows.

B4.1.6   A portfolio of financial assets that is managed and whose performance is evaluated on a fair value basis (as described in paragraph 4.2.2(b)) is not held to collect contractual cash flows. Also, a portfolio of financial assets that meets the definition of held for trading is not held to collect contractual cash flows. Such portfolios of instruments must be measured at fair value through profit or loss.

Contractual cash flows that are solely payments of principal and interest on the principal amount outstanding

B4.1.7   Paragraph 4.1.1 requires an entity (unless paragraph 4.1.5 applies) to classify a financial asset as subsequently measured at amortised cost or fair value on the basis of the contractual cash flow characteristics of the financial asset that is in a group of financial assets managed for the collection of the contractual cash flows.

B4.1.8   An entity shall assess whether contractual cash flows are solely payments of principal and interest on the principal amount outstanding for the currency in which the financial asset is denominated (see also paragraph B5.7.2).

B4.1.9   Leverage is a contractual cash flow characteristic of some financial assets. Leverage increases the variability of the contractual cash flows with the result that they do not have the economic characteristics of interest. Stand-alone option, forward and swap contracts are examples of financial assets that include leverage. Thus such contracts do not meet the condition in paragraph 4.1.2(b) and cannot be subsequently measured at amortised cost.

B4.1.10   Contractual provisions that permit the issuer (ie the debtor) to prepay a debt instrument (eg a loan or a bond) or permit the holder (ie the creditor) to put a debt instrument back to the issuer before maturity result in contractual cash flows that are solely payments of principal and interest on the principal amount outstanding only if:

     (a)   the provision is not contingent on future events, other than to protect:

         (i)   the holder against the credit deterioration of the issuer (eg defaults, credit downgrades or loan covenant violations), or a change in control of the issuer; or

         (ii)   the holder or issuer against changes in relevant taxation or law; and

     (b)   the prepayment amount substantially represents unpaid amounts of principal and interest on the principal amount outstanding, which may include reasonable additional compensation for the early termination of the contract.

B4.1.11   Contractual provisions that permit the issuer or holder to extend the contractual term of a debt instrument (ie an extension option) result in contractual cash flows that are solely payments of principal and interest on the principal amount outstanding only if:

     (a)   the provision is not contingent on future events, other than to protect:

         (i)   the holder against the credit deterioration of the issuer (eg defaults, credit downgrades or loan covenant violations) or a change in control of the issuer; or

         (ii)   the holder or issuer against changes in relevant taxation or law; and

     (b)   the terms of the extension option result in contractual cash flows during the extension period that are solely payments of principal and interest on the principal amount outstanding.

B4.1.12   A contractual term that changes the timing or amount of payments of principal or interest does not result in contractual cash flows that are solely principal and interest on the principal amount outstanding unless it:

     (a)   is a variable interest rate that is consideration for the time value of money and the credit risk (which may be determined at initial recognition only, and so may be fixed) associated with the principal amount outstanding; and

     (b)   if the contractual term is a prepayment option, meets the conditions in paragraph B4.1.10; or

     (c)   if the contractual term is an extension option, meets the conditions in paragraph B4.1.11.

B4.1.13   The following examples illustrate contractual cash flows that are solely payments of principal and interest on the principal amount outstanding. This list of examples is not exhaustive.

Instrument	Analysis
Instrument A Instrument A is a bond with a stated maturity date. Payments of principal and interest on the principal amount outstanding are linked to an inflation index of the currency in which the instrument is issued. The inflation link is not leveraged and the principal is protected.	The contractual cash flows are solely payments of principal and interest on the principal amount outstanding. Linking payments of principal and interest on the principal amount outstanding to an unleveraged inflation index resets the time value of money to a current level. In other words, the interest rate on the instrument reflects 'real' interest. Thus, the interest amounts are consideration for the time value of money on the principal amount outstanding. However, if the interest payments were indexed to another variable such as the debtor's performance (eg the debtor's net income) or an equity index, the contractual cash flows are not payments of principal and interest on the principal amount outstanding. That is because the interest payments are not consideration for the time value of money and for credit risk associated with the principal amount outstanding. There is variability in the contractual interest payments that is inconsistent with market interest rates.
Instrument B Instrument B is a variable interest rate instrument with a stated maturity date that permits the borrower to choose the market interest rate on an ongoing basis. For example, at each interest rate reset date, the borrower can choose to pay three-month LIBOR for a three-month term or one-month LIBOR for a one-month term.	The contractual cash flows are solely payments of principal and interest on the principal amount outstanding as long as the interest paid over the life of the instrument reflects consideration for the time value of money and for the credit risk associated with the instrument. The fact that the LIBOR interest rate is reset during the life of the instrument does not in itself disqualify the instrument. However, if the borrower is able to choose to pay one-month LIBOR for three months and that one-month LIBOR is not reset each month, the contractual cash flows are not payments of principal and interest. The same analysis would apply if the borrower is able to choose between the lender's published one-month variable interest rate and the lender's published three-month variable interest rate. However, if the instrument has a contractual interest rate that is based on a term that exceeds the instrument's remaining life, its contractual cash flows are not payments of principal and interest on the principal amount outstanding. For example, a constant maturity bond with a five-year term that pays a variable rate that is reset periodically but always reflects a five-year maturity does not result in contractual cash flows that are payments of principal and interest on the principal amount outstanding. That is because the interest payable in each period is disconnected from the term of the instrument (except at origination).

Instrument	Analysis
Instrument C Instrument C is a bond with a stated maturity date and pays a variable market interest rate. That variable interest rate is capped.	The contractual cash flows of both: (a)　an instrument that has a fixed interest rate; and (b)　an instrument that has a variable interest rate; are payments of principal and interest on the principal amount outstanding as long as the interest reflects consideration for the time value of money and for the credit risk associated with the instrument during the term of the instrument. Therefore, an instrument that is a combination of (a) and (b) (eg a bond with an interest rate cap) can have cash flows that are solely payments of principal and interest on the principal amount outstanding. Such a feature may reduce cash flow variability by setting a limit on a variable interest rate (eg an interest rate cap or floor) or increase the cash flow variability because a fixed rate becomes variable.
Instrument D Instrument D is a full recourse loan and is secured by collateral.	The fact that a full recourse loan is collateralised does not in itself affect the analysis of whether the contractual cash flows are solely payments of principal and interest on the principal amount outstanding.

B4.1.14　The following examples illustrate contractual cash flows that are not payments of principal and interest on the principal amount outstanding. This list of examples is not exhaustive.

Instrument	Analysis
Instrument E Instrument E is a bond that is convertible into equity instruments of the issuer.	The holder would analyse the convertible bond in its entirety. The contractual cash flows are not payments of principal and interest on the principal amount outstanding because the interest rate does not reflect only consideration for the time value of money and the credit risk. The return is also linked to the value of the equity of the issuer.
Instrument F Instrument F is a loan that pays an inverse floating interest rate (ie the interest rate has an inverse relationship to market interest rates). continued...	The contractual cash flows are not solely payments of principal and interest on the principal amount outstanding. The interest amounts are not consideration for the time value of money on the principal amount outstanding.

Instrument G	
Instrument G is a perpetual instrument but the issuer may call the instrument at any point and pay the holder the par amount plus accrued interest due. Instrument G pays a market interest rate but payment of interest cannot be made unless the issuer is able to remain solvent immediately afterwards. Deferred interest does not accrue additional interest.	The contractual cash flows are not payments of principal and interest on the principal amount outstanding. That is because the issuer may be required to defer interest payments and additional interest does not accrue on those deferred interest amounts. As a result, interest amounts are not consideration for the time value of money on the principal amount outstanding. If interest accrued on the deferred amounts, the contractual cash flows could be payments of principal and interest on the principal amount outstanding. The fact that Instrument G is perpetual does not in itself mean that the contractual cash flows are not payments of principal and interest on the principal amount outstanding. In effect, a perpetual instrument has continuous (multiple) extension options. Such options may result in contractual cash flows that are payments of principal and interest on the principal amount outstanding if interest payments are mandatory and must be paid in perpetuity. Also, the fact that Instrument G is callable does not mean that the contractual cash flows are not payments of principal and interest on the principal amount outstanding unless it is callable at an amount that does not substantially reflect payment of outstanding principal and interest on that principal. Even if the callable amount includes an amount that compensates the holder for the early termination of the instrument, the contractual cash flows could be payments of principal and interest on the principal amount outstanding.

B4.1.15   In some cases a financial asset may have contractual cash flows that are described as principal and interest but those cash flows do not represent the payment of principal and interest on the principal amount outstanding as described in paragraphs 4.1.2(b) and 4.1.3 of this Standard.

B4.1.16   This may be the case if the financial asset represents an investment in particular assets or cash flows and hence the contractual cash flows are not solely payments of principal and interest on the principal amount outstanding. For example, the contractual cash flows may include payment for factors other than consideration for the time value of money and for the credit risk associated with the principal amount outstanding during a particular period of time. As a result, the instrument would not satisfy the condition in paragraph 4.1.2(b). This could be the case when a creditor's claim is limited to specified assets of the debtor or the cash flows from specified assets (for example, a 'non-recourse' financial asset).

B4.1.17   However, the fact that a financial asset is non-recourse does not in itself necessarily preclude the financial asset from meeting the condition in paragraph 4.1.2(b). In such situations, the creditor is required to assess ('look through to') the particular underlying assets or cash flows to determine whether the contractual cash flows of the financial asset being classified are payments of principal and interest on the principal amount outstanding. If the terms of the financial asset give rise to any other cash flows or limit the cash flows in a manner inconsistent with payments representing principal and interest, the financial asset does not meet the condition in paragraph 4.1.2(b). Whether the underlying assets are financial assets or non-financial assets does not in itself affect this assessment.

B4.1.18   If a contractual cash flow characteristic is not genuine, it does not affect the classification of a financial asset. A cash flow characteristic is not genuine if it

AASB

affects the instrument's contractual cash flows only on the occurrence of an event that is extremely rare, highly abnormal and very unlikely to occur.

B4.1.19 In almost every lending transaction the creditor's instrument is ranked relative to the instruments of the debtor's other creditors. An instrument that is subordinated to other instruments may have contractual cash flows that are payments of principal and interest on the principal amount outstanding if the debtor's non-payment is a breach of contract and the holder has a contractual right to unpaid amounts of principal and interest on the principal amount outstanding even in the event of the debtor's bankruptcy. For example, a trade receivable that ranks its creditor as a general creditor would qualify as having payments of principal and interest on the principal amount outstanding. This is the case even if the debtor issued loans that are collateralised, which in the event of bankruptcy would give that loan holder priority over the claims of the general creditor in respect of the collateral but does not affect the contractual right of the general creditor to unpaid principal and other amounts due.

Contractually linked instruments

B4.1.20 In some types of transactions, an entity may prioritise payments to the holders of financial assets using multiple contractually linked instruments that create concentrations of credit risk (tranches). Each tranche has a subordination ranking that specifies the order in which any cash flows generated by the issuer are allocated to the tranche. In such situations, the holders of a tranche have the right to payments of principal and interest on the principal amount outstanding only if the issuer generates sufficient cash flows to satisfy higher-ranking tranches.

B4.1.21 In such transactions, a tranche has cash flow characteristics that are payments of principal and interest on the principal amount outstanding only if:

(a) the contractual terms of the tranche being assessed for classification (without looking through to the underlying pool of financial instruments) give rise to cash flows that are solely payments of principal and interest on the principal amount outstanding (eg the interest rate on the tranche is not linked to a commodity index);

(b) the underlying pool of financial instruments has the cash flow characteristics set out in paragraphs B4.1.23 and B4.1.24; and

(c) the exposure to credit risk in the underlying pool of financial instruments inherent in the tranche is equal to or lower than the exposure to credit risk of the underlying pool of financial instruments (for example, this condition would be met if the underlying pool of instruments were to lose 50 per cent as a result of credit losses and under all circumstances the tranche would lose 50 per cent or less).

B4.1.22 An entity must look through until it can identify the underlying pool of instruments that are creating (rather than passing through) the cash flows. This is the underlying pool of financial instruments.

B4.1.23 The underlying pool must contain one or more instruments that have contractual cash flows that are solely payments of principal and interest on the principal amount outstanding.

B4.1.24 The underlying pool of instruments may also include instruments that:

(a) reduce the cash flow variability of the instruments in paragraph B4.1.23 and, when combined with the instruments in paragraph B4.1.23, result in cash flows that are solely payments of principal and interest on the principal amount outstanding (eg an interest rate cap or floor or a contract that reduces the credit risk on some or all of the instruments in paragraph B4.1.23); or

(b)   align the cash flows of the tranches with the cash flows of the pool of underlying instruments in paragraph B4.1.23 to address differences in and only in:

(i)   whether the interest rate is fixed or floating;

(ii)   the currency in which the cash flows are denominated, including inflation in that currency; or

(iii)   the timing of the cash flows.

B4.1.25   If any instrument in the pool does not meet the conditions in either paragraph B4.1.23 or paragraph B4.1.24, the condition in paragraph B4.1.21(b) is not met.

B4.1.26   If the holder cannot assess the conditions in paragraph B4.1.21 at initial recognition, the tranche must be measured at fair value. If the underlying pool of instruments can change after initial recognition in such a way that the pool may not meet the conditions in paragraphs B4.1.23 and B4.1.24, the tranche does not meet the conditions in paragraph B4.1.21 and must be measured at fair value.

Option to designate a financial asset or financial liability as at fair value through profit or loss (sections 4.1 and 4.2)

B4.1.27   Subject to the conditions in paragraphs 4.1.5 and 4.2.2, this Standard allows an entity to designate a financial asset, a financial liability, or a group of financial instruments (financial assets, financial liabilities or both) as at fair value through profit or loss provided that doing so results in more relevant information.

B4.1.28   The decision of an entity to designate a financial asset or financial liability as at fair value through profit or loss is similar to an accounting policy choice (although, unlike an accounting policy choice, it is not required to be applied consistently to all similar transactions). When an entity has such a choice, paragraph 14(b) of AASB 108 requires the chosen policy to result in the financial statements providing reliable and more relevant information about the effects of transactions, other events and conditions on the entity's financial position, financial performance or cash flows. For example, in the case of designation of a financial liability as at fair value through profit or loss, paragraph 4.2.2 sets out the two circumstances when the requirement for more relevant information will be met. Accordingly, to choose such designation in accordance with paragraph 4.2.2, the entity needs to demonstrate that it falls within one (or both) of these two circumstances.

Designation eliminates or significantly reduces an accounting mismatch

B4.1.29   Measurement of a financial asset or financial liability and classification of recognised changes in its value are determined by the item's classification and whether the item is part of a designated hedging relationship. Those requirements can create a measurement or recognition inconsistency (sometimes referred to as an 'accounting mismatch') when, for example, in the absence of designation as at fair value through profit or loss, a financial asset would be classified as subsequently measured at fair value and a liability the entity considers related would be subsequently measured at amortised cost (with changes in fair value not recognised). In such circumstances, an entity may conclude that its financial statements would provide more relevant information if both the asset and the liability were measured as at fair value through profit or loss.

B4.1.30   The following examples show when this condition could be met. In all cases, an entity may use this condition to designate financial assets or financial liabilities as at fair value through profit or loss only if it meets the principle in paragraph 4.1.5 or 4.2.2(a).

(a)   An entity has liabilities under insurance contracts whose measurement incorporates current information (as permitted by AASB 4 *Insurance Contracts*, paragraph 24), and financial assets it considers related that would otherwise be measured at amortised cost.

(b)   An entity has financial assets, financial liabilities or both that share a risk, such as interest rate risk, that gives rise to opposite changes in fair value that tend to offset each other. However, only some of the instruments would be measured at fair value through profit or loss (ie are derivatives, or are classified as held for trading). It may also be the case that the requirements for hedge accounting are not met, for example because the requirements for effectiveness in paragraph 88 of AASB 139 are not met.

(c) An entity has financial assets, financial liabilities or both that share a risk, such as interest rate risk, that gives rise to opposite changes in fair value that tend to offset each other and the entity does not qualify for hedge accounting because none of the instruments is a derivative. Furthermore, in the absence of hedge accounting there is a significant inconsistency in the recognition of gains and losses. For example, the entity has financed a specified group of loans by issuing traded bonds whose changes in fair value tend to offset each other. If, in addition, the entity regularly buys and sells the bonds but rarely, if ever, buys and sells the loans, reporting both the loans and the bonds at fair value through profit or loss eliminates the inconsistency in the timing of recognition of gains and losses that would otherwise result from measuring them both at amortised cost and recognising a gain or loss each time a bond is repurchased.

B4.1.31 In cases such as those described in the preceding paragraph, to designate, at initial recognition, the financial assets and financial liabilities not otherwise so measured as at fair value through profit or loss may eliminate or significantly reduce the measurement or recognition inconsistency and produce more relevant information. For practical purposes, the entity need not enter into all of the assets and liabilities giving rise to the measurement or recognition inconsistency at exactly the same time. A reasonable delay is permitted provided that each transaction is designated as at fair value through profit or loss at its initial recognition and, at that time, any remaining transactions are expected to occur.

B4.1.32 It would not be acceptable to designate only some of the financial assets and financial liabilities giving rise to the inconsistency as at fair value through profit or loss if to do so would not eliminate or significantly reduce the inconsistency and would therefore not result in more relevant information. However, it would be acceptable to designate only some of a number of similar financial assets or similar financial liabilities if doing so achieves a significant reduction (and possibly a greater reduction than other allowable designations) in the inconsistency. For example, assume an entity has a number of similar financial liabilities that sum to CU100 and a number of similar financial assets that sum to CU50 but are measured on a different basis. The entity may significantly reduce the measurement inconsistency by designating at initial recognition all of the assets but only some of the liabilities (for example, individual liabilities with a combined total of CU45) as at fair value through profit or loss. However, because designation as at fair value through profit or loss can be applied only to the whole of a financial instrument, the entity in this example must designate one or more liabilities in their entirety. It could not designate either a component of a liability (eg changes in value attributable to only one risk, such as changes in a benchmark interest rate) or a proportion (ie percentage) of a liability.

A group of financial liabilities or financial assets and financial liabilities is managed and its performance is evaluated on a fair value basis

B4.1.33 An entity may manage and evaluate the performance of a group of financial liabilities or financial assets and financial liabilities in such a way that measuring that group at fair value through profit or loss results in more relevant information. The focus in this instance is on the way the entity manages and evaluates performance, rather than on the nature of its financial instruments.

B4.1.34 For example, an entity may use this condition to designate financial liabilities as at fair value through profit or loss if it meets the principle in paragraph 4.2.2(b) and the entity has financial assets and financial liabilities that share one or more risks and those risks are managed and evaluated on a fair value basis in accordance with a documented policy of asset and liability management. An example could be an entity that has issued 'structured products' containing multiple embedded derivatives and manages the resulting risks on a fair value basis using a mix of derivative and non-derivative financial instruments.

B4.1.35   As noted above, this condition relies on the way the entity manages and evaluates performance of the group of financial instruments under consideration. Accordingly, (subject to the requirement of designation at initial recognition) an entity that designates financial liabilities as at fair value through profit or loss on the basis of this condition shall so designate all eligible financial liabilities that are managed and evaluated together.

B4.1.36   Documentation of the entity's strategy need not be extensive but should be sufficient to demonstrate compliance with paragraph 4.2.2(b). Such documentation is not required for each individual item, but may be on a portfolio basis. For example, if the performance management system for a department – as approved by the entity's key management personnel – clearly demonstrates that its performance is evaluated on a total return basis, no further documentation is required to demonstrate compliance with paragraph 4.2.2(b).

Embedded derivatives (section 4.3)

B4.3.1   When an entity becomes a party to a hybrid contract with a host that is not an asset within the scope of this Standard, paragraph 4.3.3 requires the entity to identify any embedded derivative, assess whether it is required to be separated from the host contract and, for those that are required to be separated, measure the derivatives at fair value at initial recognition and subsequently.

B4.3.2   If a host contract has no stated or predetermined maturity and represents a residual interest in the net assets of an entity, then its economic characteristics and risks are those of an equity instrument, and an embedded derivative would need to possess equity characteristics related to the same entity to be regarded as closely related. If the host contract is not an equity instrument and meets the definition of a financial instrument, then its economic characteristics and risks are those of a debt instrument.

B4.3.3   An embedded non-option derivative (such as an embedded forward or swap) is separated from its host contract on the basis of its stated or implied substantive terms, so as to result in it having a fair value of zero at initial recognition. An embedded option-based derivative (such as an embedded put, call, cap, floor or swaption) is separated from its host contract on the basis of the stated terms of the option feature. The initial carrying amount of the host instrument is the residual amount after separating the embedded derivative.

B4.3.4   Generally, multiple embedded derivatives in a single hybrid contract are treated as a single compound embedded derivative. However, embedded derivatives that are classified as equity (see AASB 132) are accounted for separately from those classified as assets or liabilities. In addition, if a hybrid contract has more than one embedded derivative and those derivatives relate to different risk exposures and are readily separable and independent of each other, they are accounted for separately from each other.

B4.3.5   The economic characteristics and risks of an embedded derivative are not closely related to the host contract (paragraph 4.3.3(a)) in the following examples. In these examples, assuming the conditions in paragraph 4.3.3(b) and (c) are met, an entity accounts for the embedded derivative separately from the host contract.

(a)   A put option embedded in an instrument that enables the holder to require the issuer to reacquire the instrument for an amount of cash or other assets that varies on the basis of the change in an equity or commodity price or index is not closely related to a host debt instrument.

(b)   An option or automatic provision to extend the remaining term to maturity of a debt instrument is not closely related to the host debt instrument unless there is a concurrent adjustment to the approximate current market rate of interest at the time of the extension. If an entity issues a debt instrument and the holder of that debt instrument writes a call option on the debt instrument to a third party, the issuer regards the call option as extending the term to maturity of the debt instrument provided the issuer can be required to participate in or facilitate the remarketing of the debt instrument as a result of the call option being exercised.

(c) Equity-indexed interest or principal payments embedded in a host debt instrument or insurance contract – by which the amount of interest or principal is indexed to the value of equity instruments – are not closely related to the host instrument because the risks inherent in the host and the embedded derivative are dissimilar.

(d) Commodity-indexed interest or principal payments embedded in a host debt instrument or insurance contract – by which the amount of interest or principal is indexed to the price of a commodity (such as gold) – are not closely related to the host instrument because the risks inherent in the host and the embedded derivative are dissimilar.

(e) A call, put, or prepayment option embedded in a host debt contract or host insurance contract is not closely related to the host contract unless:

(i) the option's exercise price is approximately equal on each exercise date to the amortised cost of the host debt instrument or the carrying amount of the host insurance contract; or

(ii) the exercise price of a prepayment option reimburses the lender for an amount up to the approximate present value of lost interest for the remaining term of the host contract. Lost interest is the product of the principal amount prepaid multiplied by the interest rate differential. The interest rate differential is the excess of the effective interest rate of the host contract over the effective interest rate the entity would receive at the prepayment date if it reinvested the principal amount prepaid in a similar contract for the remaining term of the host contract.

The assessment of whether the call or put option is closely related to the host debt contract is made before separating the equity element of a convertible debt instrument in accordance with AASB 132.

(f) Credit derivatives that are embedded in a host debt instrument and allow one party (the 'beneficiary') to transfer the credit risk of a particular reference asset, which it may not own, to another party (the 'guarantor') are not closely related to the host debt instrument. Such credit derivatives allow the guarantor to assume the credit risk associated with the reference asset without directly owning it.

B4.3.6 An example of a hybrid contract is a financial instrument that gives the holder a right to put the financial instrument back to the issuer in exchange for an amount of cash or other financial assets that varies on the basis of the change in an equity or commodity index that may increase or decrease (a 'puttable instrument'). Unless the issuer on initial recognition designates the puttable instrument as a financial liability at fair value through profit or loss, it is required to separate an embedded derivative (ie the indexed principal payment) under paragraph 4.3.3 because the host contract is a debt instrument under paragraph B4.3.2 and the indexed principal payment is not closely related to a host debt instrument under paragraph B4.3.5(a). Because the principal payment can increase and decrease, the embedded derivative is a non-option derivative whose value is indexed to the underlying variable.

B4.3.7 In the case of a puttable instrument that can be put back at any time for cash equal to a proportionate share of the net asset value of an entity (such as units of an open-ended mutual fund or some unit-linked investment products), the effect of separating an embedded derivative and accounting for each component is to measure the hybrid contract at the redemption amount that is payable at the end of the reporting period if the holder exercised its right to put the instrument back to the issuer.

B4.3.8   The economic characteristics and risks of an embedded derivative are closely related to the economic characteristics and risks of the host contract in the following examples. In these examples, an entity does not account for the embedded derivative separately from the host contract.

(a)   An embedded derivative in which the underlying is an interest rate or interest rate index that can change the amount of interest that would otherwise be paid or received on an interest-bearing host debt contract or insurance contract is closely related to the host contract unless the hybrid contract can be settled in such a way that the holder would not recover substantially all of its recognised investment or the embedded derivative could at least double the holder's initial rate of return on the host contract and could result in a rate of return that is at least twice what the market return would be for a contract with the same terms as the host contract.

(b)   An embedded floor or cap on the interest rate on a debt contract or insurance contract is closely related to the host contract, provided the cap is at or above the market rate of interest and the floor is at or below the market rate of interest when the contract is issued, and the cap or floor is not leveraged in relation to the host contract. Similarly, provisions included in a contract to purchase or sell an asset (eg a commodity) that establish a cap and a floor on the price to be paid or received for the asset are closely related to the host contract if both the cap and floor were out of the money at inception and are not leveraged.

(c)   An embedded foreign currency derivative that provides a stream of principal or interest payments that are denominated in a foreign currency and is embedded in a host debt instrument (eg a dual currency bond) is closely related to the host debt instrument. Such a derivative is not separated from the host instrument because AASB 121 *The Effects of Changes in Foreign Exchange Rates* requires foreign currency gains and losses on monetary items to be recognised in profit or loss.

(d)   An embedded foreign currency derivative in a host contract that is an insurance contract or not a financial instrument (such as a contract for the purchase or sale of a non-financial item where the price is denominated in a foreign currency) is closely related to the host contract provided it is not leveraged, does not contain an option feature, and requires payments denominated in one of the following currencies:

      (i)   the functional currency of any substantial party to that contract;

      (ii)   the currency in which the price of the related good or service that is acquired or delivered is routinely denominated in commercial transactions around the world (such as the US dollar for crude oil transactions); or

      (iii)   a currency that is commonly used in contracts to purchase or sell non-financial items in the economic environment in which the transaction takes place (eg a relatively stable and liquid currency that is commonly used in local business transactions or external trade).

(e)   An embedded prepayment option in an interest-only or principal-only strip is closely related to the host contract provided the host contract (i) initially resulted from separating the right to receive contractual cash flows of a financial instrument that, in and of itself, did not contain an embedded derivative, and (ii) does not contain any terms not present in the original host debt contract.

(f)   An embedded derivative in a host lease contract is closely related to the host contract if the embedded derivative is (i) an inflation-related index such as an index of lease payments to a consumer price index (provided that the lease is not leveraged and the index relates to inflation in the entity's own economic environment), (ii) contingent rentals based on related sales or (iii) contingent rentals based on variable interest rates.

(g)   A unit-linking feature embedded in a host financial instrument or host insurance contract is closely related to the host instrument or host contract if the unit-denominated payments are measured at current unit values that reflect the fair values of the assets of the fund. A unit-linking feature is a contractual term that requires payments denominated in units of an internal or external investment fund.

(h)   A derivative embedded in an insurance contract is closely related to the host insurance contract if the embedded derivative and host insurance contract are so interdependent that an entity cannot measure the embedded derivative separately (ie without considering the host contract).

Instruments containing embedded derivatives

B4.3.9   As noted in paragraph B4.3.1, when an entity becomes a party to a hybrid contract with a host that is not an asset within the scope of this Standard and with one or more embedded derivatives, paragraph 4.3.3 requires the entity to identify any such embedded derivative, assess whether it is required to be separated from the host contract and, for those that are required to be separated, measure the derivatives at fair value at initial recognition and subsequently. These requirements can be more complex, or result in less reliable measures, than measuring the entire instrument at fair value through profit or loss. For that reason this Standard permits the entire hybrid contract to be designated as at fair value through profit or loss.

B4.3.10   Such designation may be used whether paragraph 4.3.3 requires the embedded derivatives to be separated from the host contract or prohibits such separation. However, paragraph 4.3.5 would not justify designating the hybrid contract as at fair value through profit or loss in the cases set out in paragraph 4.3.5(a) and (b) because doing so would not reduce complexity or increase reliability.

Reassessment of embedded derivatives

B4.3.11   In accordance with paragraph 4.3.3, an entity shall assess whether an embedded derivative is required to be separated from the host contract and accounted for as a derivative when the entity first becomes a party to the contract. Subsequent reassessment is prohibited unless there is a change in the terms of the contract that significantly modifies the cash flows that otherwise would be required under the contract, in which case reassessment is required. An entity determines whether a modification to cash flows is significant by considering the extent to which the expected future cash flows associated with the embedded derivative, the host contract or both have changed and whether the change is significant relative to the previously expected cash flows on the contract.

B4.3.12   Paragraph B4.3.11 does not apply to embedded derivatives in contracts acquired in:

(a)   a business combination (as defined in AASB 3 *Business Combinations*);

(b)   a combination of entities or businesses under common control as described in paragraphs B1-B4 of AASB 3; or

(c)   the formation of a joint venture as defined in AASB 11 *Joint Arrangements*

or their possible reassessment at the date of acquisition.[1]

Reclassification of financial assets (section 4.4)

B4.4.1   Paragraph 4.4.1 requires an entity to reclassify financial assets if the objective of the entity's business model for managing those financial assets changes. Such changes are expected to be very infrequent. Such changes must be determined by the entity's senior management as a result of external or internal changes and must be significant to the entity's operations and demonstrable to external parties. Examples of a change in business model include the following:

(a)   An entity has a portfolio of commercial loans that it holds to sell in the short-term. The entity acquires a company that manages commercial loans and

---

1   AASB 3 addresses the acquisition of contracts with embedded derivatives in a business combination.

has a business model that holds the loans in order to collect the contractual cash flows. The portfolio of commercial loans is no longer for sale, and the portfolio is now managed together with the acquired commercial loans and all are held to collect the contractual cash flows.

(b)   A financial services firm decides to shut down its retail mortgage business. That business no longer accepts new business and the financial services firm is actively marketing its mortgage loan portfolio for sale.

B4.4.2   A change in the objective of the entity's business model must be effected before the reclassification date. For example, if a financial services firm decides on 15 February to shut down its retail mortgage business and hence must reclassify all affected financial assets on 1 April (ie the first day of the entity's next reporting period), the entity must not accept new retail mortgage business or otherwise engage in activities consistent with its former business model after 15 February.

B4.4.3   The following are not changes in business model:

(a)   A change in intention related to particular financial assets (even in circumstances of significant changes in market conditions).

(b)   The temporary disappearance of a particular market for financial assets.

(c)   A transfer of financial assets between parts of the entity with different business models.

Measurement (chapter 5)

Initial measurement (section 5.1)

B5.1.1   The fair value of a financial instrument at initial recognition is normally the transaction price (ie the fair value of the consideration given or received, see also paragraph B5.1.2A and AASB 13). However, if part of the consideration given or received is for something other than the financial instrument, an entity shall measure the fair value of the financial instrument. For example, the fair value of a long-term loan or receivable that carries no interest can be measured as the present value of all future cash receipts discounted using the prevailing market rate(s) of interest for a similar instrument (similar as to currency, term, type of interest rate and other factors) with a similar credit rating. Any additional amount lent is an expense or a reduction of income unless it qualifies for recognition as some other type of asset.

B5.1.2   If an entity originates a loan that bears an off-market interest rate (eg 5 per cent when the market rate for similar loans is 8 per cent), and receives an upfront fee as compensation, the entity recognises the loan at its fair value, ie net of the fee it receives.

B5.1.2A   The best evidence of the fair value of a financial instrument at initial recognition is normally the transaction price (ie the fair value of the consideration given or received, see also AASB 13). If an entity determines that the fair value at initial recognition differs from the transaction price as mentioned in paragraph 5.1.1A, the entity shall account for that instrument at that date as follows:

(a)   at the measurement required by paragraph 5.1.1 if that fair value is evidenced by a quoted price in an active market for an identical asset or liability (ie a Level 1 input) or based on a valuation technique that uses only data from observable markets. An entity shall recognise the difference between the fair value at initial recognition and the transaction price as a gain or loss.

(b)   in all other cases, at the measurement required by paragraph 5.1.1, adjusted to defer the difference between the fair value at initial recognition and the transaction price. After initial recognition, the entity shall recognise that deferred difference as a gain or loss only to the extent that it arises from a change in a factor (including time) that market participants would take into account when pricing the asset or liability.

Subsequent measurement of financial assets (section 5.2)

B5.2.1 If a financial instrument that was previously recognised as a financial asset is measured at fair value and its fair value decreases below zero, it is a financial liability measured in accordance with paragraph 4.2.1. However, hybrid contracts with hosts that are assets within the scope of this Standard are always measured in accordance with paragraph 4.3.2.

B5.2.2 The following example illustrates the accounting for transaction costs on the initial and subsequent measurement of a financial asset measured at fair value with changes through other comprehensive income in accordance with paragraph 5.7.5. An entity acquires an asset for CU100 plus a purchase commission of CU2. Initially, the entity recognises the asset at CU102. The reporting period ends one day later, when the quoted market price of the asset is CU100. If the asset were sold, a commission of CU3 would be paid. On that date, the entity measures the asset at CU100 (without regard to the possible commission on sale) and recognises a loss of CU2 in other comprehensive income.

B5.2.2A The subsequent measurement of a financial asset or financial liability and the subsequent recognition of gains and losses described in paragraph B5.1.2A shall be consistent with the requirements of this Standard.

B5.4.1-B5.4.13 [Deleted by the IASB]

Investments in equity instruments and contracts on those investments

B5.4.14 All investments in equity instruments and contracts on those instruments must be measured at fair value. However, in limited circumstances, cost may be an appropriate estimate of fair value. That may be the case if insufficient more recent information is available to measure fair value, or if there is a wide range of possible fair value measurements and cost represents the best estimate of fair value within that range.

B5.4.15 Indicators that cost might not be representative of fair value include:

(a) a significant change in the performance of the investee compared with budgets, plans or milestones.

(b) changes in expectation that the investee's technical product milestones will be achieved.

(c) a significant change in the market for the investee's equity or its products or potential products.

(d) a significant change in the global economy or the economic environment in which the investee operates.

(e) a significant change in the performance of comparable entities, or in the valuations implied by the overall market.

(f) internal matters of the investee such as fraud, commercial disputes, litigation, changes in management or strategy.

(g) evidence from external transactions in the investee's equity, either by the investee (such as a fresh issue of equity), or by transfers of equity instruments between third parties.

B5.4.16 The list in paragraph B5.4.15 is not exhaustive. An entity shall use all information about the performance and operations of the investee that becomes available after the date of initial recognition. To the extent that any such relevant factors exist, they may indicate that cost might not be representative of fair value. In such cases, the entity must measure fair value.

B5.4.17 Cost is never the best estimate of fair value for investments in quoted equity instruments (or contracts on quoted equity instruments).

Gains and losses (section 5.7)

B5.7.1   Paragraph 5.7.5 permits an entity to make an irrevocable election to present in other comprehensive income changes in the fair value of an investment in an equity instrument that is not held for trading. This election is made on an instrument-by-instrument (ie share-by-share) basis. Amounts presented in other comprehensive income shall not be subsequently transferred to profit or loss. However, the entity may transfer the cumulative gain or loss within equity. Dividends on such investments are recognised in profit or loss in accordance with AASB 118 unless the dividend clearly represents a recovery of part of the cost of the investment.

B5.7.2   An entity applies AASB 121 to financial assets and financial liabilities that are monetary items in accordance with AASB 121 and denominated in a foreign currency. AASB 121 requires any foreign exchange gains and losses on monetary assets and monetary liabilities to be recognised in profit or loss. An exception is a monetary item that is designated as a hedging instrument in either a cash flow hedge (see paragraphs 95-101 of AASB 139) or a hedge of a net investment (see paragraph 102 of AASB 139).

B5.7.3   Paragraph 5.7.5 permits an entity to make an irrevocable election to present in other comprehensive income changes in the fair value of an investment in an equity instrument that is not held for trading. Such an investment is not a monetary item. Accordingly, the gain or loss that is presented in other comprehensive income in accordance with paragraph 5.7.5 includes any related foreign exchange component.

B5.7.4   If there is a hedging relationship between a non-derivative monetary asset and a non-derivative monetary liability, changes in the foreign currency component of those financial instruments are presented in profit or loss.

Liabilities designated as at fair value through profit or loss

B5.7.5   When an entity designates a financial liability as at fair value through profit or loss, it must determine whether presenting in other comprehensive income the effects of changes in the liability's credit risk would create or enlarge an accounting mismatch in profit or loss. An accounting mismatch would be created or enlarged if presenting the effects of changes in the liability's credit risk in other comprehensive income would result in a greater mismatch in profit or loss than if those amounts were presented in profit or loss.

B5.7.6   To make that determination, an entity must assess whether it expects that the effects of changes in the liability's credit risk will be offset in profit or loss by a change in the fair value of another financial instrument measured at fair value through profit or loss. Such an expectation must be based on an economic relationship between the characteristics of the liability and the characteristics of the other financial instrument.

B5.7.7   That determination is made at initial recognition and is not reassessed. For practical purposes the entity need not enter into all of the assets and liabilities giving rise to an accounting mismatch at exactly the same time. A reasonable delay is permitted provided that any remaining transactions are expected to occur. An entity must apply consistently its methodology for determining whether presenting in other comprehensive income the effects of changes in the liability's credit risk would create or enlarge an accounting mismatch in profit or loss. However, an entity may use different methodologies when there are different economic relationships between the characteristics of the liabilities designated as at fair value through profit or loss and the characteristics of the other financial instruments. AASB 7 requires an entity to provide qualitative disclosures in the notes to the financial statements about its methodology for making that determination.

B5.7.8   If such a mismatch would be created or enlarged, the entity is required to present all changes in fair value (including the effects of changes in the credit risk of the liability) in profit or loss. If such a mismatch would not be created or enlarged, the entity is required to present the effects of changes in the liability's credit risk in other comprehensive income.

B5.7.9 Amounts presented in other comprehensive income shall not be subsequently transferred to profit or loss. However, the entity may transfer the cumulative gain or loss within equity.

B5.7.10 The following example describes a situation in which an accounting mismatch would be created in profit or loss if the effects of changes in the credit risk of the liability were presented in other comprehensive income. A mortgage bank provides loans to customers and funds those loans by selling bonds with matching characteristics (eg amount outstanding, repayment profile, term and currency) in the market. The contractual terms of the loan permit the mortgage customer to prepay its loan (ie satisfy its obligation to the bank) by buying the corresponding bond at fair value in the market and delivering that bond to the mortgage bank. As a result of that contractual prepayment right, if the credit quality of the bond worsens (and, thus, the fair value of the mortgage bank's liability decreases), the fair value of the mortgage bank's loan asset also decreases. The change in the fair value of the asset reflects the mortgage customer's contractual right to prepay the mortgage loan by buying the underlying bond at fair value (which, in this example, has decreased) and delivering the bond to the mortgage bank. Therefore, the effects of changes in the credit risk of the liability (the bond) will be offset in profit or loss by a corresponding change in the fair value of a financial asset (the loan). If the effects of changes in the liability's credit risk were presented in other comprehensive income there would be an accounting mismatch in profit or loss. Therefore, the mortgage bank is required to present all changes in fair value of the liability (including the effects of changes in the liability's credit risk) in profit or loss.

B5.7.11 In the example in paragraph B5.7.10, there is a contractual linkage between the effects of changes in the credit risk of the liability and changes in the fair value of the financial asset (ie as a result of the mortgage customer's contractual right to prepay the loan by buying the bond at fair value and delivering the bond to the mortgage bank). However, an accounting mismatch may also occur in the absence of a contractual linkage.

B5.7.12 For the purposes of applying the requirements in paragraphs 5.7.7 and 5.7.8, an accounting mismatch is not caused solely by the measurement method that an entity uses to determine the effects of changes in a liability's credit risk. An accounting mismatch in profit or loss would arise only when the effects of changes in the liability's credit risk (as defined in AASB 7) are expected to be offset by changes in the fair value of another financial instrument. A mismatch that arises solely as a result of the measurement method (ie because an entity does not isolate changes in a liability's credit risk from some other changes in its fair value) does not affect the determination required by paragraphs 5.7.7 and 5.7.8. For example, an entity may not isolate changes in a liability's credit risk from changes in liquidity risk. If the entity presents the combined effect of both factors in other comprehensive income, a mismatch may occur because changes in liquidity risk may be included in the fair value measurement of the entity's financial assets and the entire fair value change of those assets is presented in profit or loss. However, such a mismatch is caused by measurement imprecision, not the offsetting relationship described in paragraph B5.7.6 and, therefore, does not affect the determination required by paragraphs 5.7.7 and 5.7.8.

The meaning of 'credit risk'

B5.7.13 AASB 7 defines credit risk as 'the risk that one party to a financial instrument will cause a financial loss for the other party by failing to discharge an obligation'. The requirement in paragraph 5.7.7(a) relates to the risk that the issuer will fail to perform on that particular liability. It does not necessarily relate to the creditworthiness of the issuer. For example, if an entity issues a collateralised liability and a non-collateralised liability that are otherwise identical, the credit risk of those two liabilities will be different, even though they are issued by the same entity. The credit risk on the collateralised liability will be less than the credit risk of the non-collateralised liability. The credit risk for a collateralised liability may be close to zero.

B5.7.14   For the purposes of applying the requirement in paragraph 5.7.7(a), credit risk is different from asset-specific performance risk. Asset-specific performance risk is not related to the risk that an entity will fail to discharge a particular obligation but rather it is related to the risk that a single asset or a group of assets will perform poorly (or not at all).

B5.7.15   The following are examples of asset-specific performance risk:

(a)   A liability with a unit-linking feature whereby the amount due to investors is contractually determined on the basis of the performance of specified assets. The effect of that unit-linking feature on the fair value of the liability is asset-specific performance risk, not credit risk.

(b)   A liability issued by a structured entity with the following characteristics. The entity is legally isolated so the assets in the entity are ring-fenced solely for the benefit of its investors, even in the event of bankruptcy. The entity enters into no other transactions and the assets in the entity cannot be hypothecated. Amounts are due to the entity's investors only if the ring-fenced assets generate cash flows. Thus, changes in the fair value of the liability primarily reflect changes in the fair value of the assets. The effect of the performance of the assets on the fair value of the liability is asset-specific performance risk, not credit risk.

Determining the effects of changes in credit risk

B5.7.16   For the purposes of applying the requirement in paragraph 5.7.7(a), an entity shall determine the amount of change in the fair value of the financial liability that is attributable to changes in the credit risk of that liability either:

(a)   as the amount of change in its fair value that is not attributable to changes in market conditions that give rise to market risk (see paragraphs B5.7.17 and B5.7.18); or

(b)   using an alternative method the entity believes more faithfully represents the amount of change in the liability's fair value that is attributable to changes in its credit risk.

B5.7.17   Changes in market conditions that give rise to market risk include changes in a benchmark interest rate, the price of another entity's financial instrument, a commodity price, a foreign exchange rate or an index of prices or rates.

B5.7.18   If the only significant relevant changes in market conditions for a liability are changes in an observed (benchmark) interest rate, the amount in paragraph B5.7.16(a) can be estimated as follows:

(a)   First, the entity computes the liability's internal rate of return at the start of the period using the fair value of the liability and the liability's contractual cash flows at the start of the period. It deducts from this rate of return the observed (benchmark) interest rate at the start of the period, to arrive at an instrument-specific component of the internal rate of return.

(b)   Next, the entity calculates the present value of the cash flows associated with the liability using the liability's contractual cash flows at the end of the period and a discount rate equal to the sum of (i) the observed (benchmark) interest rate at the end of the period and (ii) the instrument-specific component of the internal rate of return as determined in (a).

(c)   The difference between the fair value of the liability at the end of the period and the amount determined in (b) is the change in fair value that is not attributable to changes in the observed (benchmark) interest rate. This is the amount to be presented in other comprehensive income in accordance with paragraph 5.7.7(a).

AASB

B5.7.19   The example in paragraph B5.7.18 assumes that changes in fair value arising from factors other than changes in the instrument's credit risk or changes in observed (benchmark) interest rates are not significant. This method would not be appropriate if changes in fair value arising from other factors are significant. In those cases, an entity is required to use an alternative method that more faithfully measures the effects of changes in the liability's credit risk (see paragraph B5.7.16(b)). For example, if the instrument in the example contains an embedded derivative, the change in fair value of the embedded derivative is excluded in determining the amount to be presented in other comprehensive income in accordance with paragraph 5.7.7(a).

B5.7.20   As with all fair value measurements, an entity's measurement method for determining the portion of the change in the liability's fair value that is attributable to changes in its credit risk must make maximum use of relevant observable inputs and minimum use of unobservable inputs.

Effective date and transition (chapter 7)

Transition (section 7.2)

Financial assets held for trading

B7.2.1   At the date of initial application of this Standard, an entity must determine whether the objective of the entity's business model for managing any of its financial assets meets the condition in paragraph 4.1.2(a) or if a financial asset is eligible for the election in paragraph 5.7.5. For that purpose, an entity shall determine whether financial assets meet the definition of held for trading as if the entity had acquired the assets at the date of initial application.

Definitions (Appendix A)

Derivatives

BA.1   Typical examples of derivatives are futures and forward, swap and option contracts. A derivative usually has a notional amount, which is an amount of currency, a number of shares, a number of units of weight or volume or other units specified in the contract. However, a derivative instrument does not require the holder or writer to invest or receive the notional amount at the inception of the contract. Alternatively, a derivative could require a fixed payment or payment of an amount that can change (but not proportionally with a change in the underlying) as a result of some future event that is unrelated to a notional amount. For example, a contract may require a fixed payment of CU1,000 if six-month LIBOR increases by 100 basis points. Such a contract is a derivative even though a notional amount is not specified.

BA.2   The definition of a derivative in this Standard includes contracts that are settled gross by delivery of the underlying item (eg a forward contract to purchase a fixed rate debt instrument). An entity may have a contract to buy or sell a non-financial item that can be settled net in cash or another financial instrument or by exchanging financial instruments (eg a contract to buy or sell a commodity at a fixed price at a future date). Such a contract is within the scope of this Standard unless it was entered into and continues to be held for the purpose of delivery of a non-financial item in accordance with the entity's expected purchase, sale or usage requirements (see paragraphs 5-7 of AASB 139).

BA.3   One of the defining characteristics of a derivative is that it has an initial net investment that is smaller than would be required for other types of contracts that would be expected to have a similar response to changes in market factors. An option contract meets that definition because the premium is less than the investment that would be required to obtain the underlying financial instrument to which the option is linked. A currency swap that requires an initial exchange of different currencies of equal fair values meets the definition because it has a zero initial net investment.

BA.4   A regular way purchase or sale gives rise to a fixed price commitment between trade date and settlement date that meets the definition of a derivative. However, because of the short duration of the commitment it is not recognised as a derivative financial instrument. Rather, this Standard provides for special accounting for such regular way contracts (see paragraphs 3.1.2 and B3.1.3-B3.1.6).

BA.5   The definition of a derivative refers to non-financial variables that are not specific to a party to the contract. These include an index of earthquake losses in a particular region and an index of temperatures in a particular city. Non-financial variables specific to a party to the contract include the occurrence or non-occurrence of a fire that damages or destroys an asset of a party to the contract. A change in the fair value of a non-financial asset is specific to the owner if the fair value reflects not only changes in market prices for such assets (a financial variable) but also the condition of the specific non-financial asset held (a non-financial variable). For example, if a guarantee of the residual value of a specific car exposes the guarantor to the risk of changes in the car's physical condition, the change in that residual value is specific to the owner of the car.

Financial assets and liabilities held for trading

BA.6   Trading generally reflects active and frequent buying and selling, and financial instruments held for trading generally are used with the objective of generating a profit from short-term fluctuations in price or dealer's margin.

BA.7   Financial liabilities held for trading include:

         (a)   derivative liabilities that are not accounted for as hedging instruments;

         (b)   obligations to deliver financial assets borrowed by a short seller (ie an entity that sells financial assets it has borrowed and does not yet own);

         (c)   financial liabilities that are incurred with an intention to repurchase them in the near term (eg a quoted debt instrument that the issuer may buy back in the near term depending on changes in its fair value); and

         (d)   financial liabilities that are part of a portfolio of identified financial instruments that are managed together and for which there is evidence of a recent pattern of short-term profit-taking.

BA.8   The fact that a liability is used to fund trading activities does not in itself make that liability one that is held for trading.

Deleted IFRS 9 Text

Deleted IFRS 9 text is not part of AASB 9.

Paragraph 7.1.1

An entity shall apply this IFRS for annual periods beginning on or after 1 January 2013. Earlier application is permitted. However, if an entity elects to apply this IFRS early and has not already applied IFRS 9 issued in 2009, it must apply all of the requirements in this IFRS at the same time (but see also paragraph 7.3.2). If an entity applies this IFRS in its financial statements for a period beginning before 1 January 2013, it shall disclose that fact and at the same time apply the amendments in Appendix C.

Paragraph 7.3.1

This IFRS supersedes IFRIC 9 *Reassessment of Embedded Derivatives.* The requirements added to IFRS 9 in October 2010 incorporated the requirements previously set out in paragraphs 5 and 7 of IFRIC 9. As a consequential amendment, IFRS 1 *First-time Adoption of International Financial Reporting Standards* incorporated the requirements previously set out in paragraph 8 of IFRIC 9.

Paragraph 7.3.2

This IFRS supersedes IFRS 9 issued in 2009. However, for annual periods beginning before 1 January 2013, an entity may elect to apply IFRS 9 issued in 2009 instead of applying this IFRS.

AASB 10
Consolidated Financial Statements

(Issued August 2011)

Note from the Institute of Chartered Accountants Australia

This note, prepared by the technical editors, is not part of Accounting Standard AASB 10.

Historical development

29 August 2011: AASB 10 'Consolidated Financial Statements' is the Australian equivalent of IFRS 10 of the same name, and was issued as part of the suite of Standards revising accounting requirements for consolidation, joint ventures and off balance sheet arrangements. AASB 10 contains a revised definition of 'control' to apply to all entities and for some entities will expand the number and types of entities that are consolidated.

This Standard applies to annual reporting periods beginning on or after 1 January 2013 and can be adopted early by for-profit entities.

AASB 10 compared to IFRS 10

Additions

Paragraph	Description
Aus3.1	Which entities AASB 10 applies to (i.e. reporting entities and general purpose financial statements).
Aus3.2	The application date (i.e. annual reporting periods beginning on or after 1 January 2013).
Aus3.3	Permits early application by for-profit entities, but not by not-for-profit entities.
Aus 3.4	Makes the requirement of AASB 10 subject to AASB 1031 'Materiality'.
Aus3.5	Explains which Australian Standards have been superseded by AASB 10.
Aus4.1	Clarifies when a not-for-profit parent need not present consolidated financial statements.
Aus4.2	Clarifies when the ultimate Australian parent shall present consolidated financial statements.

Deletions

Paragraph	Description
C1	Effective date of IFRS 10.
C8	IFRS 10 supersedes the requirements on consolidated financial statements in IAS 27.
C9	IFRS 10 supersedes SIC-12.

Contents

Preface

Comparison with IFRS 10

**Introduction to IFRS 10
(available on the AASB website)**

**Accounting Standard
AASB 10 Consolidated Financial Statements**

	Paragraphs
Objective	1
Meeting the objective	2 – 3
Application	Aus3.1 – Aus3.5
Scope	4 – Aus4.2
Control	5 – 9
Power	10 – 14
Returns	15 – 16
Link between power and returns	17 – 18
Accounting requirements	19 – 21
Non-controlling interests	22 – 24
Loss of control	25 – 26

Appendices:

A. Defined Terms	
B. Application Guidance	B1
Assessing control	B2 – B4
Purpose and design of an investee	B5 – B8
Power	B9 – B54
Exposure, or rights, to variable returns from an investee	B55 – B57
Link between power and returns	B58 – B72
Relationship with other parties	B73 – B75
Control of specified assets	B76 – B79
Continuous assessment	B80 – B85
Accounting requirements	
Consolidation procedures	B86
Uniform accounting policies	B87
Measurement	B88
Potential voting rights	B89 – B91
Reporting date	B92 – B93
Non-controlling interests	B94 – B96
Loss of control	B97 – B99
C. Effective Date and Transition	
Transition	C2 – C6
References to AASB 9	C7

AASB

Australian Application Guidance

Deleted IFRS 10 Text
Basis for Conclusions on Paragraph Aus4.1
(see Basis for Conclusions on AASB 2011-5)

Basis for Conclusions on IFRS 10
(available on the AASB website)

> Australian Accounting Standard AASB 10 *Consolidated Financial Statements* is set out in paragraphs 1 – 26 and Appendices A – C. All the paragraphs have equal authority. Paragraphs in **bold type** state the main principles. Terms defined in Appendix A are in *italics* the first time they appear in the Standard. AASB 10 is to be read in the context of other Australian Accounting Standards, including AASB 1048 *Interpretation of Standards*, which identifies the Australian Accounting Interpretations. In the absence of explicit guidance, AASB 108 *Accounting Policies, Changes in Accounting Estimates and Errors* provides a basis for selecting and applying accounting policies.

Preface

Introduction

The Australian Accounting Standards Board (AASB) makes Australian Accounting Standards, including Interpretations, to be applied by:

(a)   entities required by the *Corporations Act 2001* to prepare financial reports;

(b)   governments in preparing financial statements for the whole of government and the General Government Sector (GGS); and

(c)   entities in the private or public for-profit or not-for-profit sectors that are reporting entities or that prepare general purpose financial statements.

AASB 1053 *Application of Tiers of Australian Accounting Standards* establishes a differential reporting framework consisting of two tiers of reporting requirements for preparing general purpose financial statements:

(a)   Tier 1: Australian Accounting Standards; and

(b)   Tier 2: Australian Accounting Standards – Reduced Disclosure Requirements.

Tier 1 requirements incorporate International Financial Reporting Standards (IFRSs), including Interpretations, issued by the International Accounting Standards Board (IASB), with the addition of paragraphs on the applicability of each Standard in the Australian environment.

Publicly accountable for-profit private sector entities are required to adopt Tier 1 requirements, and therefore are required to comply with IFRSs. Furthermore, other for-profit private sector entities complying with Tier 1 requirements will simultaneously comply with IFRSs. Some other entities complying with Tier 1 requirements will also simultaneously comply with IFRSs.

Tier 2 requirements comprise the recognition, measurement and presentation requirements of Tier 1 but substantially reduced disclosure requirements in comparison to Tier 1.

Australian Accounting Standards also include requirements that are specific to Australian entities. These requirements may be located in Australian Accounting Standards that incorporate IFRSs or in other Australian Accounting Standards. In most instances, these requirements are either restricted to the not-for-profit or public sectors or include additional disclosures that address domestic, regulatory or other issues. These requirements do not prevent publicly accountable for-profit private sector entities from complying with IFRSs. In developing requirements for public sector entities, the AASB considers the requirements of International Public Sector Accounting Standards (IPSASs), as issued by the International Public Sector Accounting Standards Board (IPSASB) of the International Federation of Accountants.

Differences between this Standard and superseded requirements under AASB 127 and Interpretation 112

Differences between this Standard and the superseded requirements under AASB 127 *Consolidated and Separate Financial Statements* and Interpretation 112 *Consolidation – Special Purpose Entities* are the same as the differences between IFRS 10 *Consolidated Financial Statements* and the superseded requirements under IAS 27 *Consolidated and Separate Financial Statements* and Interpretation SIC-12 *Consolidation – Special Purpose Entities*. The main differences are summarised in the project summary and feedback statement in relation to IFRS 10 and IFRS 12 *Disclosure of Interests in Other Entities*, which is available on the IASB's website at www.ifrs.org.

Implications for not-for-profit entities

This Standard applies to both for-profit and not-for-profit entities. However, prior to the 1 January 2013 mandatory application date of this Standard, the AASB will consider whether this Standard should be modified for application by not-for-profit entities having regard to its *Process for Modifying IFRSs for PBE/NFP*. In light of this, not-for-profit entities are not permitted to apply this Standard prior to the mandatory application date.

Comparison with IFRS 10

AASB 10 *Consolidated Financial Statements* incorporates IFRS 10 *Consolidated Financial Statements* issued by the International Accounting Standards Board (IASB). Paragraphs that have been added to this Standard (and do not appear in the text of IFRS 10) are identified with the prefix "Aus", followed by the number of the preceding IASB paragraph and decimal numbering.

For-profit entities that comply with AASB 10 will simultaneously be in compliance with IFRS 10.

Not-for-profit entities using the added "Aus" paragraphs in the Standard that specifically apply to not-for-profit entities may not be simultaneously complying with IFRS 10.

Accounting Standard AASB 10

The Australian Accounting Standards Board makes Accounting Standard AASB 10 *Consolidated Financial Statements* under section 334 of the *Corporations Act 2001*.

Dated 29 August 2011

Kevin M. Stevenson
Chair – AASB

Accounting Standard AASB 10

Consolidated Financial Statements

Objective

1   The objective of this Standard is to establish principles for the presentation and preparation of consolidated financial statements when an entity controls one or more other entities.

Meeting the objective

2   To meet the objective in paragraph 1, this Standard:

    (a)   requires an entity (the *parent*) that controls one or more other entities (*subsidiaries*) to present consolidated financial statements;

    (b)   defines the principle of *control*, and establishes control as the basis for consolidation;

    (c)   sets out how to apply the principle of control to identify whether an investor controls an investee and therefore must consolidate the investee; and

    (d)   sets out the accounting requirements for the preparation of consolidated financial statements.

3   This Standard does not deal with the accounting requirements for business combinations and their effect on consolidation, including goodwill arising on a business combination (see AASB 3 *Business Combinations*).

Application

Aus3.1 This Standard applies to:

    (a) each entity that is required to prepare financial reports in accordance with Part 2M.3 of the Corporations Act and that is a reporting entity;

    (b) general purpose financial statements of each other reporting entity; and

    (c) financial statements that are, or are held out to be, general purpose financial statements.

Aus3.2 This Standard applies to annual reporting periods beginning on or after 1 January 2013.

Aus3.3 This Standard may be applied by for-profit entities, but not by not-for-profit entities, to annual reporting periods beginning on or after 1 January 2005 but before 1 January 2013. If a for-profit entity applies this Standard to such an annual reporting period, it shall disclose that fact and apply AASB 11 *Joint Arrangements*, AASB 12 *Disclosure of Interests in Other Entities*, AASB 127 *Separate Financial Statements* (August 2011) and AASB 128 *Investments in Associates and Joint Ventures* (August 2011), at the same time.

Aus3.4 The requirements specified in this Standard apply to the financial statements where information resulting from their application is material in accordance with AASB 1031 *Materiality*.

Aus3.5 When applied or operative, this Standard supersedes:

    (a) the requirements relating to consolidated financial statements in AASB 127 *Consolidated and Separate Financial Statements* (March 2008, as amended); and

    (b) Interpretation 112 *Consolidation – Special Purpose Entities* (December 2004, as amended).

Scope

4 An entity that is a parent shall present consolidated financial statements. This Standard applies to all entities, except as follows:

    (a) a parent need not present consolidated financial statements if it meets all the following conditions:

        (i) it is a wholly-owned subsidiary or is a partially-owned subsidiary of another entity and all its other owners, including those not otherwise entitled to vote, have been informed about, and do not object to, the parent not presenting consolidated financial statements;

        (ii) its debt or equity instruments are not traded in a public market (a domestic or foreign stock exchange or an over-the-counter market, including local and regional markets);

        (iii) it did not file, nor is it in the process of filing, its financial statements with a securities commission or other regulatory organisation for the purpose of issuing any class of instruments in a public market; and

        (iv) its ultimate or any intermediate parent produces consolidated financial statements that are available for public use and comply with International Financial Reporting Standards (IFRSs).

    (b) post-employment benefit plans or other long-term employee benefit plans to which AASB 119 *Employee Benefits* applies.

Aus4.1 Notwithstanding paragraph 4(a)(iv), a parent that meets the criteria in paragraphs 4(a)(i), 4(a)(ii) and 4(a)(iii) need not present consolidated financial statements if its ultimate or any intermediate parent produces consolidated financial statements available for public use and the parent and its ultimate or intermediate parent are both not-for-profit entities complying with Australian Accounting Standards.

Aus4.2   Notwithstanding paragraphs 4 and Aus4.1, the ultimate Australian parent shall present consolidated financial statements that consolidate its investments in subsidiaries in accordance with this Standard when either the parent or the group is a reporting entity or both the parent and the group are reporting entities.

Control

5   **An investor, regardless of the nature of its involvement with an entity (the investee), shall determine whether it is a parent by assessing whether it controls the investee.**

6   **An investor controls an investee when it is exposed, or has rights, to variable returns from its involvement with the investee and has the ability to affect those returns through its power over the investee.**

7   **Thus, an investor controls an investee if and only if the investor has all the following:**

   (a)   power over the investee (see paragraphs 10–14);

   (b)   exposure, or rights, to variable returns from its involvement with the investee (see paragraphs 15 and 16); and

   (c)   the ability to use its power over the investee to affect the amount of the investor's returns (see paragraphs 17 and 18).

8   An investor shall consider all facts and circumstances when assessing whether it controls an investee. The investor shall reassess whether it controls an investee if facts and circumstances indicate that there are changes to one or more of the three elements of control listed in paragraph 7 (see paragraphs B80–B85).

9   Two or more investors collectively control an investee when they must act together to direct the relevant activities. In such cases, because no investor can direct the activities without the co-operation of the others, no investor individually controls the investee. Each investor would account for its interest in the investee in accordance with the relevant Standards, such as AASB 11 *Joint Arrangements*, AASB 128 *Investments in Associates and Joint Ventures* or AASB 9 *Financial Instruments*.

Power

10   An investor has power over an investee when the investor has existing rights that give it the current ability to direct the *relevant activities*, ie the activities that significantly affect the investee's returns.

11   Power arises from rights. Sometimes assessing power is straightforward, such as when power over an investee is obtained directly and solely from the voting rights granted by equity instruments such as shares, and can be assessed by considering the voting rights from those shareholdings. In other cases, the assessment will be more complex and require more than one factor to be considered, for example when power results from one or more contractual arrangements.

12   An investor with the current ability to direct the relevant activities has power even if its rights to direct have yet to be exercised. Evidence that the investor has been directing relevant activities can help determine whether the investor has power, but such evidence is not, in itself, conclusive in determining whether the investor has power over an investee.

13   If two or more investors each have existing rights that give them the unilateral ability to direct different relevant activities, the investor that has the current ability to direct the activities that most significantly affect the returns of the investee has power over the investee.

14   An investor can have power over an investee even if other entities have existing rights that give them the current ability to participate in the direction of the relevant activities, for example when another entity has *significant influence*. However, an investor that holds only protective rights does not have power over an investee (see paragraphs B26–B28), and consequently does not control the investee.

Returns

15   An investor is exposed, or has rights, to variable returns from its involvement with the investee when the investor's returns from its involvement have the potential to vary as a

result of the investee's performance. The investor's returns can be only positive, only negative or both positive and negative.

16 Although only one investor can control an investee, more than one party can share in the returns of an investee. For example, holders of non-controlling interests can share in the profits or distributions of an investee.

Link between power and returns

17 An investor controls an investee if the investor not only has power over the investee and exposure or rights to variable returns from its involvement with the investee, but also has the ability to use its power to affect the investor's returns from its involvement with the investee.

18 Thus, an investor with decision-making rights shall determine whether it is a principal or an agent. An investor that is an agent in accordance with paragraphs B58–B72 does not control an investee when it exercises decision-making rights delegated to it.

Accounting requirements

19 A parent shall prepare consolidated financial statements using uniform accounting policies for like transactions and other events in similar circumstances.

20 Consolidation of an investee shall begin from the date the investor obtains control of the investee and cease when the investor loses control of the investee.

21 Paragraphs B86–B93 set out guidance for the preparation of consolidated financial statements.

Non-controlling interests

22 A parent shall present non-controlling interests in the consolidated statement of financial position within equity, separately from the equity of the owners of the parent.

23 Changes in a parent's ownership interest in a subsidiary that do not result in the parent losing control of the subsidiary are equity transactions (ie transactions with owners in their capacity as owners).

24 Paragraphs B94–B96 set out guidance for the accounting for non-controlling interests in consolidated financial statements.

Loss of control

25 If a parent loses control of a subsidiary, the parent:

(a) derecognises the assets and liabilities of the former subsidiary from the consolidated statement of financial position.

(b) recognises any investment retained in the former subsidiary at its fair value when control is lost and subsequently accounts for it and for any amounts owed by or to the former subsidiary in accordance with relevant Standards. That fair value shall be regarded as the fair value on initial recognition of a financial asset in accordance with AASB 9 or, when appropriate, the cost on initial recognition of an investment in an associate or joint venture.

(c) recognises the gain or loss associated with the loss of control attributable to the former controlling interest.

26 Paragraphs B97–B99 set out guidance for the accounting for the loss of control.

AASB

Appendix A
Defined Terms

This appendix is an integral part of AASB 10.

consolidated financial statements	The financial statements of a **group** in which the assets, liabilities, equity, income, expenses and cash flows of the **parent** and its **subsidiaries** are presented as those of a single economic entity.
control of an investee	An investor controls an investee when the investor is exposed, or has rights, to variable returns from its involvement with the investee and has the ability to affect those returns through its power over the investee.
decision maker	An entity with decision-making rights that is either a principal or an agent for other parties.
group	A **parent** and its **subsidiaries**.
non-controlling interest	Equity in a **subsidiary** not attributable, directly or indirectly, to a **parent**.
parent	An entity that **controls** one or more entities.
power	Existing rights that give the current ability to direct the **relevant activities**.
protective rights	Rights designed to protect the interest of the party holding those rights without giving that party power over the entity to which those rights relate.
relevant activities	For the purpose of this Standard, relevant activities are activities of the investee that significantly affect the investee's returns.
removal rights	Rights to deprive the decision maker of its decision-making authority.
subsidiary	An entity that is controlled by another entity.

The following terms are defined in AASB 11, AASB 12 *Disclosure of Interests in Other Entities*, AASB 128 (August 2011) or AASB 124 *Related Party Disclosures* and are used in this Standard with the meanings specified in those Standards:

*   associate
*   interest in another entity
*   joint venture
*   key management personnel
*   related party
*   significant influence.

Appendix B

Application Guidance

This appendix is an integral part of AASB 10. It describes the application of paragraphs 1–26 and has the same authority as the other parts of the Standard.

B1 The examples in this appendix portray hypothetical situations. Although some aspects of the examples may be present in actual fact patterns, all facts and circumstances of a particular fact pattern would need to be evaluated when applying AASB 10.

Assessing control

B2 To determine whether it controls an investee an investor shall assess whether it has all the following:

    (a)   power over the investee;

    (b)   exposure, or rights, to variable returns from its involvement with the investee; and

    (c)   the ability to use its power over the investee to affect the amount of the investor's returns.

B3 Consideration of the following factors may assist in making that determination:

    (a)   the purpose and design of the investee (see paragraphs B5–B8);

    (b)   what the relevant activities are and how decisions about those activities are made (see paragraphs B11–B13);

    (c)   whether the rights of the investor give it the current ability to direct the relevant activities (see paragraphs B14–B54);

    (d)   whether the investor is exposed, or has rights, to variable returns from its involvement with the investee (see paragraphs B55–B57); and

    (e)   whether the investor has the ability to use its power over the investee to affect the amount of the investor's returns (see paragraphs B58–B72).

B4 When assessing control of an investee, an investor shall consider the nature of its relationship with other parties (see paragraphs B73–B75).

Purpose and design of an investee

B5 When assessing control of an investee, an investor shall consider the purpose and design of the investee in order to identify the relevant activities, how decisions about the relevant activities are made, who has the current ability to direct those activities and who receives returns from those activities.

B6 When an investee's purpose and design are considered, it may be clear that an investee is controlled by means of equity instruments that give the holder proportionate voting rights, such as ordinary shares in the investee. In this case, in the absence of any additional arrangements that alter decision-making, the assessment of control focuses on which party, if any, is able to exercise voting rights sufficient to determine the investee's operating and financing policies (see paragraphs B34–B50). In the most straightforward case, the investor that holds a majority of those voting rights, in the absence of any other factors, controls the investee.

B7 To determine whether an investor controls an investee in more complex cases, it may be necessary to consider some or all of the other factors in paragraph B3.

B8 An investee may be designed so that voting rights are not the dominant factor in deciding who controls the investee, such as when any voting rights relate to administrative tasks only and the relevant activities are directed by means of contractual arrangements. In such cases, an investor's consideration of the purpose and design of the investee shall also include consideration of the risks to which the investee was designed to be exposed, the risks it was designed to pass on to the parties involved with the investee and whether the investor is exposed to some or all of those risks. Consideration of the risks includes not only the downside risk, but also the potential for upside.

Power

B9   To have power over an investee, an investor must have existing rights that give it the current ability to direct the relevant activities. For the purpose of assessing power, only substantive rights and rights that are not protective shall be considered (see paragraphs B22–B28).

B10   The determination about whether an investor has power depends on the relevant activities, the way decisions about the relevant activities are made and the rights the investor and other parties have in relation to the investee.

Relevant activities and direction of relevant activities

B11   For many investees, a range of operating and financing activities significantly affect their returns. Examples of activities that, depending on the circumstances, can be relevant activities include, but are not limited to:

(a)   selling and purchasing of goods or services;

(b)   managing financial assets during their life (including upon default);

(c)   selecting, acquiring or disposing of assets;

(d)   researching and developing new products or processes; and

(e)   determining a funding structure or obtaining funding.

B12   Examples of decisions about relevant activities include but are not limited to:

(a)   establishing operating and capital decisions of the investee, including budgets; and

(b)   appointing and remunerating an investee's key management personnel or service providers and terminating their services or employment.

B13   In some situations, activities both before and after a particular set of circumstances arises or event occurs may be relevant activities. When two or more investors have the current ability to direct relevant activities and those activities occur at different times, the investors shall determine which investor is able to direct the activities that most significantly affect those returns consistently with the treatment of concurrent decision-making rights (see paragraph 13). The investors shall reconsider this assessment over time if relevant facts or circumstances change.

Application examples

Example 1

Two investors form an investee to develop and market a medical product. One investor is responsible for developing and obtaining regulatory approval of the medical product—that responsibility includes having the unilateral ability to make all decisions relating to the development of the product and to obtaining regulatory approval. Once the regulator has approved the product, the other investor will manufacture and market it—this investor has the unilateral ability to make all decisions about the manufacture and marketing of the project. If all the activities—developing and obtaining regulatory approval as well as manufacturing and marketing of the medical product—are relevant activities, each investor needs to determine whether it is able to direct the activities that most significantly affect the investee's returns. Accordingly, each investor needs to consider whether developing and obtaining regulatory approval or the manufacturing and marketing of the medical product is the activity that most significantly affects the investee's returns and whether it is able to direct that activity. In determining which investor has power, the investors would consider:

(a)   the purpose and design of the investee;

(b)   the factors that determine the profit margin, revenue and value of the investee as well as the value of the medical product;

(c)   the effect on the investee's returns resulting from each investor's decision-making authority with respect to the factors in (b); and

(d)   the investors' exposure to variability of returns.

In this particular example, the investors would also consider:

(e)   the uncertainty of, and effort required in, obtaining regulatory approval (considering the investor's record of successfully developing and obtaining regulatory approval of medical products); and

(f)   which investor controls the medical product once the development phase is successful.

continued

> **Example 2**
>
> An investment vehicle (the investee) is created and financed with a debt instrument held by an investor (the debt investor) and equity instruments held by a number of other investors. The equity tranche is designed to absorb the first losses and to receive any residual return from the investee. One of the equity investors who holds 30 per cent of the equity is also the asset manager. The investee uses its proceeds to purchase a portfolio of financial assets, exposing the investee to the credit risk associated with the possible default of principal and interest payments of the assets. The transaction is marketed to the debt investor as an investment with minimal exposure to the credit risk associated with the possible default of the assets in the portfolio because of the nature of these assets and because the equity tranche is designed to absorb the first losses of the investee. The returns of the investee are significantly affected by the management of the investee's asset portfolio, which includes decisions about the selection, acquisition and disposal of the assets within portfolio guidelines and the management upon default of any portfolio assets. All those activities are managed by the asset manager until defaults reach a specified proportion of the portfolio value (ie when the value of the portfolio is such that the equity tranche of the investee has been consumed). From that time, a third-party trustee manages the assets according to the instructions of the debt investor. Managing the investee's asset portfolio is the relevant activity of the investee. The asset manager has the ability to direct the relevant activities until defaulted assets reach the specified proportion of the portfolio value; the debt investor has the ability to direct the relevant activities when the value of defaulted assets surpasses that specified proportion of the portfolio value. The asset manager and the debt investor each need to determine whether they are able to direct the activities that most significantly affect the investee's returns, including considering the purpose and design of the investee as well as each party's exposure to variability of returns.

Rights that give an investor power over an investee

B14 Power arises from rights. To have power over an investee, an investor must have existing rights that give the investor the current ability to direct the relevant activities. The rights that may give an investor power can differ between investees.

B15 Examples of rights that, either individually or in combination, can give an investor power include but are not limited to:

(a) rights in the form of voting rights (or potential voting rights) of an investee (see paragraphs B34–B50);

(b) rights to appoint, reassign or remove members of an investee's key management personnel who have the ability to direct the relevant activities;

(c) rights to appoint or remove another entity that directs the relevant activities;

(d) rights to direct the investee to enter into, or veto any changes to, transactions for the benefit of the investor; and

(e) other rights (such as decision-making rights specified in a management contract) that give the holder the ability to direct the relevant activities.

B16 Generally, when an investee has a range of operating and financing activities that significantly affect the investee's returns and when substantive decision-making with respect to these activities is required continuously, it will be voting or similar rights that give an investor power, either individually or in combination with other arrangements.

B17 When voting rights cannot have a significant effect on an investee's returns, such as when voting rights relate to administrative tasks only and contractual arrangements determine the direction of the relevant activities, the investor needs to assess those contractual arrangements in order to determine whether it has rights sufficient to give it power over the investee. To determine whether an investor has rights sufficient to give it power, the investor shall consider the purpose and design of the investee (see paragraphs B5–B8) and the requirements in paragraphs B51–B54 together with paragraphs B18–B20.

B18 In some circumstances it may be difficult to determine whether an investor's rights are sufficient to give it power over an investee. In such cases, to enable the assessment of power to be made, the investor shall consider evidence of whether it has the practical ability to direct the relevant activities unilaterally. Consideration is given, but is not limited to, the following, which, when considered together with its rights and the indicators in paragraphs B19 and B20, may provide evidence that the investor's rights are sufficient to give it power over the investee:

(a)   The investor can, without having the contractual right to do so, appoint or approve the investee's key management personnel who have the ability to direct the relevant activities.

(b)   The investor can, without having the contractual right to do so, direct the investee to enter into, or can veto any changes to, significant transactions for the benefit of the investor.

(c)   The investor can dominate either the nominations process for electing members of the investee's governing body or the obtaining of proxies from other holders of voting rights.

(d)   The investee's key management personnel are related parties of the investor (for example, the chief executive officer of the investee and the chief executive officer of the investor are the same person).

(e)   The majority of the members of the investee's governing body are related parties of the investor.

B19   Sometimes there will be indications that the investor has a special relationship with the investee, which suggests that the investor has more than a passive interest in the investee. The existence of any individual indicator, or a particular combination of indicators, does not necessarily mean that the power criterion is met. However, having more than a passive interest in the investee may indicate that the investor has other related rights sufficient to give it power or provide evidence of existing power over an investee. For example, the following suggests that the investor has more than a passive interest in the investee and, in combination with other rights, may indicate power:

(a)   The investee's key management personnel who have the ability to direct the relevant activities are current or previous employees of the investor.

(b)   The investee's operations are dependent on the investor, such as in the following situations:

(i)   The investee depends on the investor to fund a significant portion of its operations.

(ii)   The investor guarantees a significant portion of the investee's obligations.

(iii) The investee depends on the investor for critical services, technology, supplies or raw materials.

(iv)   The investor controls assets such as licences or trademarks that are critical to the investee's operations.

(v)   The investee depends on the investor for key management personnel, such as when the investor's personnel have specialised knowledge of the investee's operations.

(c)   A significant portion of the investee's activities either involve or are conducted on behalf of the investor.

(d)   The investor's exposure, or rights, to returns from its involvement with the investee is disproportionately greater than its voting or other similar rights. For example, there may be a situation in which an investor is entitled, or exposed, to more than half of the returns of the investee but holds less than half of the voting rights of the investee.

B20   The greater an investor's exposure, or rights, to variability of returns from its involvement with an investee, the greater is the incentive for the investor to obtain rights sufficient to give it power. Therefore, having a large exposure to variability of returns is an indicator that the investor may have power. However, the extent of the investor's exposure does not, in itself, determine whether an investor has power over the investee.

B21   When the factors set out in paragraph B18 and the indicators set out in paragraphs B19 and B20 are considered together with an investor's rights, greater weight shall be given to the evidence of power described in paragraph B18.

Substantive rights

B22 An investor, in assessing whether it has power, considers only substantive rights relating to an investee (held by the investor and others). For a right to be substantive, the holder must have the practical ability to exercise that right.

B23 Determining whether rights are substantive requires judgement, taking into account all facts and circumstances. Factors to consider in making that determination include but are not limited to:

    (a) Whether there are any barriers (economic or otherwise) that prevent the holder (or holders) from exercising the rights. Examples of such barriers include but are not limited to:

        (i) financial penalties and incentives that would prevent (or deter) the holder from exercising its rights.

        (ii) an exercise or conversion price that creates a financial barrier that would prevent (or deter) the holder from exercising its rights.

        (iii) terms and conditions that make it unlikely that the rights would be exercised, for example, conditions that narrowly limit the timing of their exercise.

        (iv) the absence of an explicit, reasonable mechanism in the founding documents of an investee or in applicable laws or regulations that would allow the holder to exercise its rights.

        (v) the inability of the holder of the rights to obtain the information necessary to exercise its rights.

        (vi) operational barriers or incentives that would prevent (or deter) the holder from exercising its rights (e.g. the absence of other managers willing or able to provide specialised services or provide the services and take on other interests held by the incumbent manager).

        (vii) legal or regulatory requirements that prevent the holder from exercising its rights (e.g. where a foreign investor is prohibited from exercising its rights).

    (b) When the exercise of rights requires the agreement of more than one party, or when the rights are held by more than one party, whether a mechanism is in place that provides those parties with the practical ability to exercise their rights collectively if they choose to do so. The lack of such a mechanism is an indicator that the rights may not be substantive. The more parties that are required to agree to exercise the rights, the less likely it is that those rights are substantive. However, a board of directors whose members are independent of the decision maker may serve as a mechanism for numerous investors to act collectively in exercising their rights. Therefore, removal rights exercisable by an independent board of directors are more likely to be substantive than if the same rights were exercisable individually by a large number of investors.

    (c) Whether the party or parties that hold the rights would benefit from the exercise of those rights. For example, the holder of potential voting rights in an investee (see paragraphs B47–B50) shall consider the exercise or conversion price of the instrument. The terms and conditions of potential voting rights are more likely to be substantive when the instrument is in the money or the investor would benefit for other reasons (e.g. by realising synergies between the investor and the investee) from the exercise or conversion of the instrument.

B24 To be substantive, rights also need to be exercisable when decisions about the direction of the relevant activities need to be made. Usually, to be substantive, the rights need to be currently exercisable. However, sometimes rights can be substantive, even though the rights are not currently exercisable.

Application examples
Example 3
The investee has annual shareholder meetings at which decisions to direct the relevant activities are made. The next scheduled shareholders' meeting is in eight months. However, shareholders that individually or collectively hold at least 5 per cent of the voting rights can call a special meeting to change the existing policies over the relevant activities, but a requirement to give notice to the other shareholders means that such a meeting cannot be held for at least 30 days. Policies over the relevant activities can be changed only at special or scheduled shareholders' meetings. This includes the approval of material sales of assets as well as the making or disposing of significant investments.
The above fact pattern applies to examples 3A–3D described below. Each example is considered in isolation.
Example 3A
An investor holds a majority of the voting rights in the investee. The investor's voting rights are substantive because the investor is able to make decisions about the direction of the relevant activities when they need to be made. The fact that it takes 30 days before the investor can exercise its voting rights does not stop the investor from having the current ability to direct the relevant activities from the moment the investor acquires the shareholding.
Example 3B
An investor is party to a forward contract to acquire the majority of shares in the investee. The forward contract's settlement date is in 25 days. The existing shareholders are unable to change the existing policies over the relevant activities because a special meeting cannot be held for at least 30 days, at which point the forward contract will have been settled. Thus, the investor has rights that are essentially equivalent to the majority shareholder in example 3A above (ie the investor holding the forward contract can make decisions about the direction of the relevant activities when they need to be made). The investor's forward contract is a substantive right that gives the investor the current ability to direct the relevant activities even before the forward contract is settled.
Example 3C
An investor holds a substantive option to acquire the majority of shares in the investee that is exercisable in 25 days and is deeply in the money. The same conclusion would be reached as in example 3B.
Example 3D
An investor is party to a forward contract to acquire the majority of shares in the investee, with no other related rights over the investee. The forward contract's settlement date is in six months. In contrast to the examples above, the investor does not have the current ability to direct the relevant activities. The existing shareholders have the current ability to direct the relevant activities because they can change the existing policies over the relevant activities before the forward contract is settled.

B25 Substantive rights exercisable by other parties can prevent an investor from controlling the investee to which those rights relate. Such substantive rights do not require the holders to have the ability to initiate decisions. As long as the rights are not merely protective (see paragraphs B26–B28), substantive rights held by other parties may prevent the investor from controlling the investee even if the rights give the holders only the current ability to approve or block decisions that relate to the relevant activities.

Protective rights

B26 In evaluating whether rights give an investor power over an investee, the investor shall assess whether its rights, and rights held by others, are protective rights. Protective rights relate to fundamental changes to the activities of an investee or apply in exceptional circumstances. However, not all rights that apply in exceptional circumstances or are contingent on events are protective (see paragraphs B13 and B53).

B27 Because protective rights are designed to protect the interests of their holder without giving that party power over the investee to which those rights relate, an investor that holds only protective rights cannot have power or prevent another party from having power over an investee (see paragraph 14).

B28 Examples of protective rights include but are not limited to:

    (a)   a lender's right to restrict a borrower from undertaking activities that could significantly change the credit risk of the borrower to the detriment of the lender.

(b)   the right of a party holding a non-controlling interest in an investee to approve capital expenditure greater than that required in the ordinary course of business, or to approve the issue of equity or debt instruments.

(c)   the right of a lender to seize the assets of a borrower if the borrower fails to meet specified loan repayment conditions.

Franchises

B29   A franchise agreement for which the investee is the franchisee often gives the franchisor rights that are designed to protect the franchise brand. Franchise agreements typically give franchisors some decision-making rights with respect to the operations of the franchisee.

B30   Generally, franchisors' rights do not restrict the ability of parties other than the franchisor to make decisions that have a significant effect on the franchisee's returns. Nor do the rights of the franchisor in franchise agreements necessarily give the franchisor the current ability to direct the activities that significantly affect the franchisee's returns.

B31   It is necessary to distinguish between having the current ability to make decisions that significantly affect the franchisee's returns and having the ability to make decisions that protect the franchise brand. The franchisor does not have power over the franchisee if other parties have existing rights that give them the current ability to direct the relevant activities of the franchisee.

B32   By entering into the franchise agreement the franchisee has made a unilateral decision to operate its business in accordance with the terms of the franchise agreement, but for its own account.

B33   Control over such fundamental decisions as the legal form of the franchisee and its funding structure may be determined by parties other than the franchisor and may significantly affect the returns of the franchisee. The lower the level of financial support provided by the franchisor and the lower the franchisor's exposure to variability of returns from the franchisee the more likely it is that the franchisor has only protective rights.

Voting rights

B34   Often an investor has the current ability, through voting or similar rights, to direct the relevant activities. An investor considers the requirements in this section (paragraphs B35–B50) if the relevant activities of an investee are directed through voting rights.

Power with a majority of the voting rights

B35   An investor that holds more than half of the voting rights of an investee has power in the following situations, unless paragraph B36 or paragraph B37 applies:

(a)   the relevant activities are directed by a vote of the holder of the majority of the voting rights, or

(b)   a majority of the members of the governing body that directs the relevant activities are appointed by a vote of the holder of the majority of the voting rights.

Majority of the voting rights but no power

B36   For an investor that holds more than half of the voting rights of an investee, to have power over an investee, the investor's voting rights must be substantive, in accordance with paragraphs B22–B25, and must provide the investor with the current ability to direct the relevant activities, which often will be through determining operating and financing policies. If another entity has existing rights that provide that entity with the right to direct the relevant activities and that entity is not an agent of the investor, the investor does not have power over the investee.

B37   An investor does not have power over an investee, even though the investor holds the majority of the voting rights in the investee, when those voting rights are not substantive. For example, an investor that has more than half of the voting rights in an investee cannot have power if the relevant activities are subject to direction by a government, court, administrator, receiver, liquidator or regulator.

Power without a majority of the voting rights

B38 An investor can have power even if it holds less than a majority of the voting rights of an investee. An investor can have power with less than a majority of the voting rights of an investee, for example, through:

 (a) a contractual arrangement between the investor and other vote holders (see paragraph B39);

 (b) rights arising from other contractual arrangements (see paragraph B40);

 (c) the investor's voting rights (see paragraphs B41–B45);

 (d) potential voting rights (see paragraphs B47–B50); or

 (e) a combination of (a)–(d).

Contractual arrangement with other vote holders

B39 A contractual arrangement between an investor and other vote holders can give the investor the right to exercise voting rights sufficient to give the investor power, even if the investor does not have voting rights sufficient to give it power without the contractual arrangement. However, a contractual arrangement might ensure that the investor can direct enough other vote holders on how to vote to enable the investor to make decisions about the relevant activities.

Rights from other contractual arrangements

B40 Other decision-making rights, in combination with voting rights, can give an investor the current ability to direct the relevant activities. For example, the rights specified in a contractual arrangement in combination with voting rights may be sufficient to give an investor the current ability to direct the manufacturing processes of an investee or to direct other operating or financing activities of an investee that significantly affect the investee's returns. However, in the absence of any other rights, economic dependence of an investee on the investor (such as relations of a supplier with its main customer) does not lead to the investor having power over the investee.

The investor's voting rights

B41 An investor with less than a majority of the voting rights has rights that are sufficient to give it power when the investor has the practical ability to direct the relevant activities unilaterally.

B42 When assessing whether an investor's voting rights are sufficient to give it power, an investor considers all facts and circumstances, including:

 (a) the size of the investor's holding of voting rights relative to the size and dispersion of holdings of the other vote holders, noting that:

  (i) the more voting rights an investor holds, the more likely the investor is to have existing rights that give it the current ability to direct the relevant activities;

  (ii) the more voting rights an investor holds relative to other vote holders, the more likely the investor is to have existing rights that give it the current ability to direct the relevant activities;

  (iii) the more parties that would need to act together to outvote the investor, the more likely the investor is to have existing rights that give it the current ability to direct the relevant activities;

 (b) potential voting rights held by the investor, other vote holders or other parties (see paragraphs B47–B50);

 (c) rights arising from other contractual arrangements (see paragraph B40); and

 (d) any additional facts and circumstances that indicate the investor has, or does not have, the current ability to direct the relevant activities at the time that decisions need to be made, including voting patterns at previous shareholders' meetings.

B43 When the direction of relevant activities is determined by majority vote and an investor holds significantly more voting rights than any other vote holder or organised group of vote holders, and the other shareholdings are widely dispersed, it may be clear, after considering the factors listed in paragraph 42(a)–(c) alone, that the investor has power over the investee.

Application examples
Example 4
An investor acquires 48 per cent of the voting rights of an investee. The remaining voting rights are held by thousands of shareholders, none individually holding more than 1 per cent of the voting rights. None of the shareholders has any arrangements to consult any of the others or make collective decisions. When assessing the proportion of voting rights to acquire, on the basis of the relative size of the other shareholdings, the investor determined that a 48 per cent interest would be sufficient to give it control. In this case, on the basis of the absolute size of its holding and the relative size of the other shareholdings, the investor concludes that it has a sufficiently dominant voting interest to meet the power criterion without the need to consider any other evidence of power.
Example 5
Investor A holds 40 per cent of the voting rights of an investee and twelve other investors each hold 5 per cent of the voting rights of the investee. A shareholder agreement grants investor A the right to appoint, remove and set the remuneration of management responsible for directing the relevant activities. To change the agreement, a two-thirds majority vote of the shareholders is required. In this case, investor A concludes that the absolute size of the investor's holding and the relative size of the other shareholdings alone are not conclusive in determining whether the investor has rights sufficient to give it power. However, investor A determines that its contractual right to appoint, remove and set the remuneration of management is sufficient to conclude that it has power over the investee. The fact that investor A might not have exercised this right or the likelihood of investor A exercising its right to select, appoint or remove management shall not be considered when assessing whether investor A has power.

B44   In other situations, it may be clear after considering the factors listed in paragraph B42(a)–(c) alone that an investor does not have power.

Application example
Example 6
Investor A holds 45 per cent of the voting rights of an investee. Two other investors each hold 26 per cent of the voting rights of the investee. The remaining voting rights are held by three other shareholders, each holding 1 per cent. There are no other arrangements that affect decision-making. In this case, the size of investor A's voting interest and its size relative to the other shareholdings are sufficient to conclude that investor A does not have power. Only two other investors would need to co-operate to be able to prevent investor A from directing the relevant activities of the investee.

B45   However, the factors listed in paragraph B42(a)–(c) alone may not be conclusive. If an investor, having considered those factors, is unclear whether it has power, it shall consider additional facts and circumstances, such as whether other shareholders are passive in nature as demonstrated by voting patterns at previous shareholders' meetings. This includes the assessment of the factors set out in paragraph B18 and the indicators in paragraphs B19 and B20. The fewer voting rights the investor holds, and the fewer parties that would need to act together to outvote the investor, the more reliance would be placed on the additional facts and circumstances to assess whether the investor's rights are sufficient to give it power. When the facts and circumstances in paragraphs B18–B20 are considered together with the investor's rights, greater weight shall be given to the evidence of power in paragraph B18 than to the indicators of power in paragraphs B19 and B20.

Application examples
Example 7
An investor holds 45 per cent of the voting rights of an investee. Eleven other shareholders each hold 5 per cent of the voting rights of the investee. None of the shareholders has contractual arrangements to consult any of the others or make collective decisions. In this case, the absolute size of the investor's holding and the relative size of the other shareholdings alone are not conclusive in determining whether the investor has rights sufficient to give it power over the investee. Additional facts and circumstances that may provide evidence that the investor has, or does not have, power shall be considered.
continued

Example 8

An investor holds 35 per cent of the voting rights of an investee. Three other shareholders each hold 5 per cent of the voting rights of the investee. The remaining voting rights are held by numerous other shareholders, none individually holding more than 1 per cent of the voting rights. None of the shareholders has arrangements to consult any of the others or make collective decisions. Decisions about the relevant activities of the investee require the approval of a majority of votes cast at relevant shareholders' meetings—75 per cent of the voting rights of the investee have been cast at recent relevant shareholders' meetings. In this case, the active participation of the other shareholders at recent shareholders' meetings indicates that the investor would not have the practical ability to direct the relevant activities unilaterally, regardless of whether the investor has directed the relevant activities because a sufficient number of other shareholders voted in the same way as the investor.

B46   If it is not clear, having considered the factors listed in paragraph B42(a)–(d), that the investor has power, the investor does not control the investee.

Potential voting rights

B47   When assessing control, an investor considers its potential voting rights as well as potential voting rights held by other parties, to determine whether it has power. Potential voting rights are rights to obtain voting rights of an investee, such as those arising from convertible instruments or options, including forward contracts. Those potential voting rights are considered only if the rights are substantive (see paragraphs B22–B25).

B48   When considering potential voting rights, an investor shall consider the purpose and design of the instrument, as well as the purpose and design of any other involvement the investor has with the investee. This includes an assessment of the various terms and conditions of the instrument as well as the investor's apparent expectations, motives and reasons for agreeing to those terms and conditions.

B49   If the investor also has voting or other decision-making rights relating to the investee's activities, the investor assesses whether those rights, in combination with potential voting rights, give the investor power.

B50   Substantive potential voting rights alone, or in combination with other rights, can give an investor the current ability to direct the relevant activities. For example, this is likely to be the case when an investor holds 40 per cent of the voting rights of an investee and, in accordance with paragraph B23, holds substantive rights arising from options to acquire a further 20 per cent of the voting rights.

Application examples

Example 9

Investor A holds 70 per cent of the voting rights of an investee. Investor B has 30 per cent of the voting rights of the investee as well as an option to acquire half of investor A's voting rights. The option is exercisable for the next two years at a fixed price that is deeply out of the money (and is expected to remain so for that two-year period). Investor A has been exercising its votes and is actively directing the relevant activities of the investee. In such a case, investor A is likely to meet the power criterion because it appears to have the current ability to direct the relevant activities. Although investor B has currently exercisable options to purchase additional voting rights (that, if exercised, would give it a majority of the voting rights in the investee), the terms and conditions associated with those options are such that the options are not considered substantive.

Example 10

Investor A and two other investors each hold a third of the voting rights of an investee. The investee's business activity is closely related to investor A. In addition to its equity instruments, investor A also holds debt instruments that are convertible into ordinary shares of the investee at any time for a fixed price that is out of the money (but not deeply out of the money). If the debt were converted, investor A would hold 60 per cent of the voting rights of the investee. Investor A would benefit from realising synergies if the debt instruments were converted into ordinary shares. Investor A has power over the investee because it holds voting rights of the investee together with substantive potential voting rights that give it the current ability to direct the relevant activities.

Power when voting or similar rights do not have a significant effect on the investee's returns

B51   In assessing the purpose and design of an investee (see paragraphs B5–B8), an investor shall consider the involvement and decisions made at the investee's inception as part of its design and evaluate whether the transaction terms and features of the involvement provide the investor with rights that are sufficient to give it power. Being involved in the design of an investee alone is not sufficient to give an investor control. However, involvement in the design may indicate that the investor had the opportunity to obtain rights that are sufficient to give it power over the investee.

B52 In addition, an investor shall consider contractual arrangements such as call rights, put rights and liquidation rights established at the investee's inception. When these contractual arrangements involve activities that are closely related to the investee, then these activities are, in substance, an integral part of the investee's overall activities, even though they may occur outside the legal boundaries of the investee. Therefore, explicit or implicit decision-making rights embedded in contractual arrangements that are closely related to the investee need to be considered as relevant activities when determining power over the investee.

B53 For some investees, relevant activities occur only when particular circumstances arise or events occur. The investee may be designed so that the direction of its activities and its returns are predetermined unless and until those particular circumstances arise or events occur. In this case, only the decisions about the investee's activities when those circumstances or events occur can significantly affect its returns and thus be relevant activities. The circumstances or events need not have occurred for an investor with the ability to make those decisions to have power. The fact that the right to make decisions is contingent on circumstances arising or an event occurring does not, in itself, make those rights protective.

Application examples

Example 11

An investee's only business activity, as specified in its founding documents, is to purchase receivables and service them on a day-to- day basis for its investors. The servicing on a day-to-day basis includes the collection and passing on of principal and interest payments as they fall due. Upon default of a receivable the investee automatically puts the receivable to an investor as agreed separately in a put agreement between the investor and the investee. The only relevant activity is managing the receivables upon default because it is the only activity that can significantly affect the investee's returns. Managing the receivables before default is not a relevant activity because it does not require substantive decisions to be made that could significantly affect the investee's returns – the activities before default are predetermined and amount only to collecting cash flows as they fall due and passing them on to investors. Therefore, only the investor's right to manage the assets upon default should be considered when assessing the overall activities of the investee that significantly affect the investee's returns. In this example, the design of the investee ensures that the investor has decision-making authority over the activities that significantly affect the returns at the only time that such decision-making authority is required. The terms of the put agreement are integral to the overall transaction and the establishment of the investee. Therefore, the terms of the put agreement together with the founding documents of the investee lead to the conclusion that the investor has power over the investee even though the investor takes ownership of the receivables only upon default and manages the defaulted receivables outside the legal boundaries of the investee.

Example 12

The only assets of an investee are receivables. When the purpose and design of the investee are considered, it is determined that the only relevant activity is managing the receivables upon default. The party that has the ability to manage the defaulting receivables has power over the investee, irrespective of whether any of the borrowers have defaulted.

B54 An investor may have an explicit or implicit commitment to ensure that an investee continues to operate as designed. Such a commitment may increase the investor's exposure to variability of returns and thus increase the incentive for the investor to obtain rights sufficient to give it power. Therefore a commitment to ensure that an investee operates as designed may be an indicator that the investor has power, but does not, by itself, give an investor power, nor does it prevent another party from having power.

Exposure, or rights, to variable returns from an investee

B55 When assessing whether an investor has control of an investee, the investor determines whether it is exposed, or has rights, to variable returns from its involvement with the investee.

B56   Variable returns are returns that are not fixed and have the potential to vary as a result of the performance of an investee. Variable returns can be only positive, only negative or both positive and negative (see paragraph 15). An investor assesses whether returns from an investee are variable and how variable those returns are on the basis of the substance of the arrangement and regardless of the legal form of the returns. For example, an investor can hold a bond with fixed interest payments. The fixed interest payments are variable returns for the purpose of this Standard because they are subject to default risk and they expose the investor to the credit risk of the issuer of the bond. The amount of variability (ie how variable those returns are) depends on the credit risk of the bond. Similarly, fixed performance fees for managing an investee's assets are variable returns because they expose the investor to the performance risk of the investee. The amount of variability depends on the investee's ability to generate sufficient income to pay the fee.

B57   Examples of returns include:

     (a)   dividends, other distributions of economic benefits from an investee (e.g. interest from debt securities issued by the investee) and changes in the value of the investor's investment in that investee.

     (b)   remuneration for servicing an investee's assets or liabilities, fees and exposure to loss from providing credit or liquidity support, residual interests in the investee's assets and liabilities on liquidation of that investee, tax benefits, and access to future liquidity that an investor has from its involvement with an investee.

     (c)   returns that are not available to other interest holders. For example, an investor might use its assets in combination with the assets of the investee, such as combining operating functions to achieve economies of scale, cost savings, sourcing scarce products, gaining access to proprietary knowledge or limiting some operations or assets, to enhance the value of the investor's other assets.

Link between power and returns

Delegated power

B58   When an investor with decision-making rights (a decision maker) assesses whether it controls an investee, it shall determine whether it is a principal or an agent. An investor shall also determine whether another entity with decision-making rights is acting as an agent for the investor. An agent is a party primarily engaged to act on behalf and for the benefit of another party or parties (the principal(s)) and therefore does not control the investee when it exercises its decision-making authority (see paragraphs 17 and 18). Thus, sometimes a principal's power may be held and exercisable by an agent, but on behalf of the principal. A decision maker is not an agent simply because other parties can benefit from the decisions that it makes.

B59   An investor may delegate its decision-making authority to an agent on some specific issues or on all relevant activities. When assessing whether it controls an investee, the investor shall treat the decision-making rights delegated to its agent as held by the investor directly. In situations where there is more than one principal, each of the principals shall assess whether it has power over the investee by considering the requirements in paragraphs B5–B54. Paragraphs B60–B72 provide guidance on determining whether a decision maker is an agent or a principal.

B60   A decision maker shall consider the overall relationship between itself, the investee being managed and other parties involved with the investee, in particular all the factors below, in determining whether it is an agent:

     (a)   the scope of its decision-making authority over the investee (paragraphs B62 and B63).

     (b)   the rights held by other parties (paragraphs B64–B67).

     (c)   the remuneration to which it is entitled in accordance with the remuneration agreement(s) (paragraphs B68–B70).

     (d)   the decision maker's exposure to variability of returns from other interests that it holds in the investee (paragraphs B71 and B72).

Different weightings shall be applied to each of the factors on the basis of particular facts and circumstances.

B61 Determining whether a decision maker is an agent requires an evaluation of all the factors listed in paragraph B60 unless a single party holds substantive rights to remove the decision maker (removal rights) and can remove the decision maker without cause (see paragraph B65).

The scope of the decision-making authority

B62 The scope of a decision maker's decision-making authority is evaluated by considering:

(a) the activities that are permitted according to the decision-making agreement(s) and specified by law, and

(b) the discretion that the decision maker has when making decisions about those activities.

B63 A decision maker shall consider the purpose and design of the investee, the risks to which the investee was designed to be exposed, the risks it was designed to pass on to the parties involved and the level of involvement the decision maker had in the design of an investee. For example, if a decision maker is significantly involved in the design of the investee (including in determining the scope of decision-making authority), that involvement may indicate that the decision maker had the opportunity and incentive to obtain rights that result in the decision maker having the ability to direct the relevant activities.

Rights held by other parties

B64 Substantive rights held by other parties may affect the decision maker's ability to direct the relevant activities of an investee. Substantive removal or other rights may indicate that the decision maker is an agent.

B65 When a single party holds substantive removal rights and can remove the decision maker without cause, this, in isolation, is sufficient to conclude that the decision maker is an agent. If more than one party holds such rights (and no individual party can remove the decision maker without the agreement of other parties) those rights are not, in isolation, conclusive in determining that a decision maker acts primarily on behalf and for the benefit of others. In addition, the greater the number of parties required to act together to exercise rights to remove a decision maker and the greater the magnitude of, and variability associated with, the decision maker's other economic interests (ie remuneration and other interests), the less the weighting that shall be placed on this factor.

B66 Substantive rights held by other parties that restrict a decision maker's discretion shall be considered in a similar manner to removal rights when evaluating whether the decision maker is an agent. For example, a decision maker that is required to obtain approval from a small number of other parties for its actions is generally an agent. (See paragraphs B22–B25 for additional guidance on rights and whether they are substantive.)

B67 Consideration of the rights held by other parties shall include an assessment of any rights exercisable by an investee's board of directors (or other governing body) and their effect on the decision-making authority (see paragraph B23(b)).

Remuneration

B68 The greater the magnitude of, and variability associated with, the decision maker's remuneration relative to the returns expected from the activities of the investee, the more likely the decision maker is a principal.

B69 In determining whether it is a principal or an agent the decision maker shall also consider whether the following conditions exist:

(a) The remuneration of the decision maker is commensurate with the services provided.

(b) The remuneration agreement includes only terms, conditions or amounts that are customarily present in arrangements for similar services and level of skills negotiated on an arm's length basis.

B70 A decision maker cannot be an agent unless the conditions set out in paragraph B69(a) and (b) are present. However, meeting those conditions in isolation is not sufficient to conclude that a decision maker is an agent.

Exposure to variability of returns from other interests

B71   A decision maker that holds other interests in an investee (e.g. investments in the investee or provides guarantees with respect to the performance of the investee), shall consider its exposure to variability of returns from those interests in assessing whether it is an agent. Holding other interests in an investee indicates that the decision maker may be a principal.

B72   In evaluating its exposure to variability of returns from other interests in the investee a decision maker shall consider the following:

    (a)   the greater the magnitude of, and variability associated with, its economic interests, considering its remuneration and other interests in aggregate, the more likely the decision maker is a principal.

    (b)   whether its exposure to variability of returns is different from that of the other investors and, if so, whether this might influence its actions. For example, this might be the case when a decision maker holds subordinated interests in, or provides other forms of credit enhancement to, an investee.

The decision maker shall evaluate its exposure relative to the total variability of returns of the investee. This evaluation is made primarily on the basis of returns expected from the activities of the investee but shall not ignore the decision maker's maximum exposure to variability of returns of the investee through other interests that the decision maker holds.

Application examples

Example 13

A decision maker (fund manager) establishes, markets and manages a publicly traded, regulated fund according to narrowly defined parameters set out in the investment mandate as required by its local laws and regulations. The fund was marketed to investors as an investment in a diversified portfolio of equity securities of publicly traded entities. Within the defined parameters, the fund manager has discretion about the assets in which to invest. The fund manager has made a 10 per cent pro rata investment in the fund and receives a market-based fee for its services equal to 1 per cent of the net asset value of the fund. The fees are commensurate with the services provided. The fund manager does not have any obligation to fund losses beyond its 10 per cent investment. The fund is not required to establish, and has not established, an independent board of directors. The investors do not hold any substantive rights that would affect the decision-making authority of the fund manager, but can redeem their interests within particular limits set by the fund. Although operating within the parameters set out in the investment mandate and in accordance with the regulatory requirements, the fund manager has decision-making rights that give it the current ability to direct the relevant activities of the fund—the investors do not hold substantive rights that could affect the fund manager's decision-making authority.

The fund manager receives a market-based fee for its services that is commensurate with the services provided and has also made a pro rata investment in the fund. The remuneration and its investment expose the fund manager to variability of returns from the activities of the fund without creating exposure that is of such significance that it indicates that the fund manager is a principal.

In this example, consideration of the fund manager's exposure to variability of returns from the fund together with its decision-making authority within restricted parameters indicates that the fund manager is an agent. Thus, the fund manager concludes that it does not control the fund.

Example 14

A decision maker establishes, markets and manages a fund that provides investment opportunities to a number of investors. The decision maker (fund manager) must make decisions in the best interests of all investors and in accordance with the fund's governing agreements. Nonetheless, the fund manager has wide decision-making discretion. The fund manager receives a market-based fee for its services equal to 1 per cent of assets under management and 20 per cent of all the fund's profits if a specified profit level is achieved. The fees are commensurate with the services provided.

Although it must make decisions in the best interests of all investors, the fund manager has extensive decision-making authority to direct the relevant activities of the fund. The fund manager is paid fixed and performance-related fees that are commensurate with the services provided. In addition, the remuneration aligns the interests of the fund manager with those of the other investors to increase the value of the fund, without creating exposure to variability of returns from the activities of the fund that is of such significance that the remuneration, when considered in isolation, indicates that the fund manager is a principal.

The above fact pattern and analysis applies to examples 14A–14C described below. Each example is considered in isolation.

continued

AASB

Application examples

Example 14A

The fund manager also has a 2 per cent investment in the fund that aligns its interests with those of the other investors. The fund manager does not have any obligation to fund losses beyond its 2 per cent investment. The investors can remove the fund manager by a simple majority vote, but only for breach of contract.

The fund manager's 2 per cent investment increases its exposure to variability of returns from the activities of the fund without creating exposure that is of such significance that it indicates that the fund manager is a principal. The other investors' rights to remove the fund manager are considered to be protective rights because they are exercisable only for breach of contract. In this example, although the fund manager has extensive decision-making authority and is exposed to variability of returns from its interest and remuneration, the fund manager's exposure indicates that the fund manager is an agent. Thus, the fund manager concludes that it does not control the fund.

Example 14B

The fund manager has a more substantial pro rata investment in the fund, but does not have any obligation to fund losses beyond that investment. The investors can remove the fund manager by a simple majority vote, but only for breach of contract.

In this example, the other investors' rights to remove the fund manager are considered to be protective rights because they are exercisable only for breach of contract. Although the fund manager is paid fixed and performance-related fees that are commensurate with the services provided, the combination of the fund manager's investment together with its remuneration could create exposure to variability of returns from the activities of the fund that is of such significance that it indicates that the fund manager is a principal. The greater the magnitude of, and variability associated with, the fund manager's economic interests (considering its remuneration and other interests in aggregate), the more emphasis the fund manager would place on those economic interests in the analysis, and the more likely the fund manager is a principal.

For example, having considered its remuneration and the other factors, the fund manager might consider a 20 per cent investment to be sufficient to conclude that it controls the fund. However, in different circumstances (ie if the remuneration or other factors are different), control may arise when the level of investment is different.

Example 14C

The fund manager has a 20 per cent pro rata investment in the fund, but does not have any obligation to fund losses beyond its 20 per cent investment. The fund has a board of directors, all of whose members are independent of the fund manager and are appointed by the other investors. The board appoints the fund manager annually. If the board decided not to renew the fund manager's contract, the services performed by the fund manager could be performed by other managers in the industry.

Although the fund manager is paid fixed and performance-related fees that are commensurate with the services provided, the combination of the fund manager's 20 per cent investment together with its remuneration creates exposure to variability of returns from the activities of the fund that is of such significance that it indicates that the fund manager is a principal. However, the investors have substantive rights to remove the fund manager—the board of directors provides a mechanism to ensure that the investors can remove the fund manager if they decide to do so.

In this example, the fund manager places greater emphasis on the substantive removal rights in the analysis. Thus, although the fund manager has extensive decision-making authority and is exposed to variability of returns of the fund from its remuneration and investment, the substantive rights held by the other investors indicate that the fund manager is an agent. Thus, the fund manager concludes that it does not control the fund.

continued

Application examples

Example 15

An investee is created to purchase a portfolio of fixed rate asset-backed securities, funded by fixed rate debt instruments and equity instruments. The equity instruments are designed to provide first loss protection to the debt investors and receive any residual returns of the investee. The transaction was marketed to potential debt investors as an investment in a portfolio of asset-backed securities with exposure to the credit risk associated with the possible default of the issuers of the asset-backed securities in the portfolio and to the interest rate risk associated with the management of the portfolio. On formation, the equity instruments represent 10 per cent of the value of the assets purchased. A decision maker (the asset manager) manages the active asset portfolio by making investment decisions within the parameters set out in the investee's prospectus. For those services, the asset manager receives a market-based fixed fee (ie 1 per cent of assets under management) and performance-related fees (ie 10 per cent of profits) if the investee's profits exceed a specified level. The fees are commensurate with the services provided. The sset manager holds 35 per cent of the equity in the investee.

The remaining 65 per cent of the equity, and all the debt instruments, are held by a large number of widely dispersed unrelated third party investors. The asset manager can be removed, without cause, by a simple majority decision of the other investors.

The asset manager is paid fixed and performance-related fees that are commensurate with the services provided. The remuneration aligns the interests of the fund manager with those of the other investors to increase the value of the fund. The asset manager has exposure to variability of returns from the activities of the fund because it holds 35 per cent of the equity and from its remuneration. Although operating within the parameters set out in the investee's prospectus, the asset manager has the current ability to make investment decisions that significantly affect the investee's returns—the removal rights held by the other investors receive little weighting in the analysis because those rights are held by a large number of widely dispersed investors. In this example, the asset manager places greater emphasis on its exposure to variability of returns of the fund from its equity interest, which is subordinate to the debt instruments. Holding 35 per cent of the equity creates subordinated exposure to losses and rights to returns of the investee, which are of such significance that it indicates that the asset manager is a principal. Thus, the asset manager concludes that it controls the investee.

Example 16

A decision maker (the sponsor) sponsors a multi-seller conduit, which issues short-term debt instruments to unrelated third party investors. The transaction was marketed to potential investors as an investment in a portfolio of highly rated medium-term assets with minimal exposure to the credit risk associated with the possible default by the issuers of the assets in the portfolio. Various transferors sell high quality medium-term asset portfolios to the conduit. Each transferor services the portfolio of assets that it sells to the conduit and manages receivables on default for a market-based servicing fee. Each transferor also provides first loss protection against credit losses from its asset portfolio through over-collateralisation of the assets transferred to the conduit. The sponsor establishes the terms of the conduit and manages the operations of the conduit for a market-based fee. The fee is commensurate with the services provided. The sponsor approves the sellers permitted to sell to the conduit, approves the assets to be purchased by the conduit and makes decisions about the funding of the conduit. The sponsor must act in the best interests of all investors.

The sponsor is entitled to any residual return of the conduit and also provides credit enhancement and liquidity facilities to the conduit. The credit enhancement provided by the sponsor absorbs losses of up to 5 per cent of all of the conduit's assets, after losses are absorbed by the transferors. The liquidity facilities are not advanced against defaulted assets. The investors do not hold substantive rights that could affect the decision-making authority of the sponsor.

Even though the sponsor is paid a market-based fee for its services that is commensurate with the services provided, the sponsor has exposure to variability of returns from the activities of the conduit because of its rights to any residual returns of the conduit and the provision of credit enhancement and liquidity facilities (ie the conduit is exposed to liquidity risk by using short-term debt instruments to fund medium-term assets).

Even though each of the transferors has decision-making rights that affect the value of the assets of the conduit, the sponsor has extensive decision-making authority that gives it the current ability to direct the activities that most significantly affect the conduit's returns (ie the sponsor established the terms of the conduit, has the right to make decisions about the assets (approving the assets purchased and the transferors of those assets) and the funding of the conduit (for which new investment must be found on a regular basis)). The right to residual returns of the conduit and the provision of credit enhancement and liquidity facilities expose the sponsor to variability of returns from the activities of the conduit that is different from that of the other investors. Accordingly, that exposure indicates that the sponsor is a principal and thus the sponsor concludes that it controls the conduit. The sponsor's obligation to act in the best interest of all investors does not prevent the sponsor from being a principal.

Relationship with other parties

B73 When assessing control, an investor shall consider the nature of its relationship with other parties and whether those other parties are acting on the investor's behalf (ie they are 'de facto agents'). The determination of whether other parties are acting as de facto agents requires judgement, considering not only the nature of the relationship but also how those parties interact with each other and the investor.

B74 Such a relationship need not involve a contractual arrangement. A party is a de facto agent when the investor has, or those that direct the activities of the investor have, the ability to direct that party to act on the investor's behalf. In these circumstances, the investor shall consider its de facto agent's decision-making rights and its indirect exposure, or rights, to variable returns through the de facto agent together with its own when assessing control of an investee.

B75 The following are examples of such other parties that, by the nature of their relationship, might act as de facto agents for the investor:

    (a)   the investor's related parties.

    (b)   a party that received its interest in the investee as a contribution or loan from the investor.

    (c)   a party that has agreed not to sell, transfer or encumber its interests in the investee without the investor's prior approval (except for situations in which the investor and the other party have the right of prior approval and the rights are based on mutually agreed terms by willing independent parties).

    (d)   a party that cannot finance its operations without subordinated financial support from the investor.

    (e)   an investee for which the majority of the members of its governing body or for which its key management personnel are the same as those of the investor.

    (f)   a party that has a close business relationship with the investor, such as the relationship between a professional service provider and one of its significant clients.

Control of specified assets

B76 An investor shall consider whether it treats a portion of an investee as a deemed separate entity and, if so, whether it controls the deemed separate entity.

B77 An investor shall treat a portion of an investee as a deemed separate entity if and only if the following condition is satisfied:

    Specified assets of the investee (and related credit enhancements, if any) are the only source of payment for specified liabilities of, or specified other interests in, the investee. Parties other than those with the specified liability do not have rights or obligations related to the specified assets or to residual cash flows from those assets. In substance, none of the returns from the specified assets can be used by the remaining investee and none of the liabilities of the deemed separate entity are payable from the assets of the remaining investee. Thus, in substance, all the assets, liabilities and equity of that deemed separate entity are ring-fenced from the overall investee. Such a deemed separate entity is often called a 'silo'.

B78 When the condition in paragraph B77 is satisfied, an investor shall identify the activities that significantly affect the returns of the deemed separate entity and how those activities are directed in order to assess whether it has power over that portion of the investee. When assessing control of the deemed separate entity, the investor shall also consider whether it has exposure or rights to variable returns from its involvement with that deemed separate entity and the ability to use its power over that portion of the investee to affect the amount of the investor's returns.

B79 If the investor controls the deemed separate entity, the investor shall consolidate that portion of the investee. In that case, other parties exclude that portion of the investee when assessing control of, and in consolidating, the investee.

Continuous assessment

B80   An investor shall reassess whether it controls an investee if facts and circumstances indicate that there are changes to one or more of the three elements of control listed in paragraph 7.

B81   If there is a change in how power over an investee can be exercised, that change must be reflected in how an investor assesses its power over an investee. For example, changes to decision-making rights can mean that the relevant activities are no longer directed through voting rights, but instead other agreements, such as contracts, give another party or parties the current ability to direct the relevant activities.

B82   An event can cause an investor to gain or lose power over an investee without the investor being involved in that event. For example, an investor can gain power over an investee because decision-making rights held by another party or parties that previously prevented the investor from controlling an investee have elapsed.

B83   An investor also considers changes affecting its exposure, or rights, to variable returns from its involvement with an investee. For example, an investor that has power over an investee can lose control of an investee if the investor ceases to be entitled to receive returns or to be exposed to obligations, because the investor would fail to satisfy paragraph 7(b) (e.g. if a contract to receive performance-related fees is terminated).

B84   An investor shall consider whether its assessment that it acts as an agent or a principal has changed. Changes in the overall relationship between the investor and other parties can mean that an investor no longer acts as an agent, even though it has previously acted as an agent, and vice versa. For example, if changes to the rights of the investor, or of other parties, occur, the investor shall reconsider its status as a principal or an agent.

B85   An investor's initial assessment of control or its status as a principal or an agent would not change simply because of a change in market conditions (e.g. a change in the investee's returns driven by market conditions), unless the change in market conditions changes one or more of the three elements of control listed in paragraph 7 or changes the overall relationship between a principal and an agent.

Accounting requirements

Consolidation procedures

B86   Consolidated financial statements:

     (a)   combine like items of assets, liabilities, equity, income, expenses and cash flows of the parent with those of its subsidiaries.

     (b)   offset (eliminate) the carrying amount of the parent's investment in each subsidiary and the parent's portion of equity of each subsidiary (AASB 3 explains how to account for any related goodwill).

     (c)   eliminate in full intragroup assets and liabilities, equity, income, expenses and cash flows relating to transactions between entities of the group (profits or losses resulting from intragroup transactions that are recognised in assets, such as inventory and fixed assets, are eliminated in full). Intragroup losses may indicate an impairment that requires recognition in the consolidated financial statements. AASB 112 *Income Taxes* applies to temporary differences that arise from the elimination of profits and losses resulting from intragroup transactions.

Uniform accounting policies

B87   If a member of the group uses accounting policies other than those adopted in the consolidated financial statements for like transactions and events in similar circumstances, appropriate adjustments are made to that group member's financial statements in preparing the consolidated financial statements to ensure conformity with the group's accounting policies.

Measurement

B88 An entity includes the income and expenses of a subsidiary in the consolidated financial statements from the date it gains control until the date when the entity ceases to control the subsidiary. Income and expenses of the subsidiary are based on the amounts of the assets and liabilities recognised in the consolidated financial statements at the acquisition date. For example, depreciation expense recognised in the consolidated statement of comprehensive income after the acquisition date is based on the fair values of the related depreciable assets recognised in the consolidated financial statements at the acquisition date.

Potential voting rights

B89 When potential voting rights, or other derivatives containing potential voting rights, exist, the proportion of profit or loss and changes in equity allocated to the parent and non-controlling interests in preparing consolidated financial statements is determined solely on the basis of existing ownership interests and does not reflect the possible exercise or conversion of potential voting rights and other derivatives, unless paragraph B90 applies.

B90 In some circumstances an entity has, in substance, an existing ownership interest as a result of a transaction that currently gives the entity access to the returns associated with an ownership interest. In such circumstances, the proportion allocated to the parent and non-controlling interests in preparing consolidated financial statements is determined by taking into account the eventual exercise of those potential voting rights and other derivatives that currently give the entity access to the returns.

B91 AASB9 does not apply to interests in subsidiaries that are consolidated. When instruments containing potential voting rights in substance currently give access to the returns associated with an ownership interest in a subsidiary, the instruments are not subject to the requirements of AASB 9. In all other cases, instruments containing potential voting rights in a subsidiary are accounted for in accordance with AASB 9.

Reporting date

B92 The financial statements of the parent and its subsidiaries used in the preparation of the consolidated financial statements shall have the same reporting date. When the end of the reporting period of the parent is different from that of a subsidiary, the subsidiary prepares, for consolidation purposes, additional financial information as of the same date as the financial statements of the parent to enable the parent to consolidate the financial information of the subsidiary, unless it is impracticable to do so.

B93 If it is impracticable to do so, the parent shall consolidate the financial information of the subsidiary using the most recent financial statements of the subsidiary adjusted for the effects of significant transactions or events that occur between the date of those financial statements and the date of the consolidated financial statements. In any case, the difference between the date of the subsidiary's financial statements and that of the consolidated financial statements shall be no more than three months, and the length of the reporting periods and any difference between the dates of the financial statements shall be the same from period to period.

Non-controlling interests

B94 An entity shall attribute the profit or loss and each component of other comprehensive income to the owners of the parent and to the non-controlling interests. The entity shall also attribute total comprehensive income to the owners of the parent and to the non-controlling interests even if this results in the non-controlling interests having a deficit balance.

B95 If a subsidiary has outstanding cumulative preference shares that are classified as equity and are held by non-controlling interests, the entity shall compute its share of profit or loss after adjusting for the dividends on such shares, whether or not such dividends have been declared.

Changes in the proportion held by non-controlling interests

B96   When the proportion of the equity held by non-controlling interests changes, an entity shall adjust the carrying amounts of the controlling and non-controlling interests to reflect the changes in their relative interests in the subsidiary. The entity shall recognise directly in equity any difference between the amount by which the non-controlling interests are adjusted and the fair value of the consideration paid or received, and attribute it to the owners of the parent.

Loss of control

B97   A parent might lose control of a subsidiary in two or more arrangements (transactions). However, sometimes circumstances indicate that the multiple arrangements should be accounted for as a single transaction. In determining whether to account for the arrangements as a single transaction, a parent shall consider all the terms and conditions of the arrangements and their economic effects. One or more of the following indicate that the parent should account for the multiple arrangements as a single transaction:

(a)   They are entered into at the same time or in contemplation of each other.

(b)   They form a single transaction designed to achieve an overall commercial effect.

(c)   The occurrence of one arrangement is dependent on the occurrence of at least one other arrangement.

(d)   One arrangement considered on its own is not economically justified, but it is economically justified when considered together with other arrangements. An example is when a disposal of shares is priced below market and is compensated for by a subsequent disposal priced above market.

B98   If a parent loses control of a subsidiary, it shall:

(a)   derecognise:

    (i)   the assets (including any goodwill) and liabilities of the subsidiary at their carrying amounts at the date when control is lost; and

    (ii)   the carrying amount of any non-controlling interests in the former subsidiary at the date when control is lost (including any components of other comprehensive income attributable to them).

(b)   recognise:

    (i)   the fair value of the consideration received, if any, from the transaction, event or circumstances that resulted in the loss of control;

    (ii)   if the transaction, event or circumstances that resulted in the loss of control involves a distribution of shares of the subsidiary to owners in their capacity as owners, that distribution; and

    (iii)   any investment retained in the former subsidiary at its fair value at the date when control is lost.

(c)   reclassify to profit or loss, or transfer directly to retained earnings if required by other Standards, the amounts recognised in other comprehensive income in relation to the subsidiary on the basis described in paragraph B99.

(d)   recognise any resulting difference as a gain or loss in profit or loss attributable to the parent.

B99   If a parent loses control of a subsidiary, the parent shall account for all amounts previously recognised in other comprehensive income in relation to that subsidiary on the same basis as would be required if the parent had directly disposed of the related assets or liabilities. Therefore, if a gain or loss previously recognised in other comprehensive income would be reclassified to profit or loss on the disposal of the related assets or liabilities, the parent shall reclassify the gain or loss from equity to profit or loss (as a reclassification adjustment) when it loses control of the subsidiary. If a revaluation surplus previously recognised in other comprehensive income would be transferred directly to retained earnings on the disposal of the asset, the parent shall transfer the revaluation surplus directly to retained earnings when it loses control of the subsidiary.

Appendix C

Effective Date and Transition

This appendix is an integral part of AASB 10 and has the same authority as the other parts of the Standard.

Effective date

C1   [Deleted by the AASB – see paragraphs Aus3.2 and Aus3.3]

Transition

C2   An entity shall apply this Standard retrospectively, in accordance with AASB 108 *Accounting Policies, Changes in Accounting Estimates and Errors*, except as specified in paragraphs C3–C6.

C3   When applying this Standard for the first time, an entity is not required to make adjustments to the accounting for its involvement with either:

(a)   entities that were previously consolidated in accordance with AASB 127 *Consolidated and Separate Financial Statements* and Interpretation 112 *Consolidation – Special Purpose Entities* and, in accordance with this Standard, continue to be consolidated; or

(b)   entities that were previously unconsolidated in accordance with AASB 127 and Interpretation 112 and, in accordance with this Standard, continue not to be consolidated.

C4   When application of this Standard for the first time results in an investor consolidating an investee that was not consolidated in accordance with AASB 127 and Interpretation 112 the investor shall:

(a)   if the investee is a business (as defined in AASB 3), measure the assets, liabilities and non-controlling interests in that previously unconsolidated investee on the date of initial application as if that investee had been consolidated (and thus applied acquisition accounting in accordance with AASB 3) from the date when the investor obtained control of that investee on the basis of the requirements of this Standard.

(b)   if the investee is not a business (as defined in AASB 3), measure the assets, liabilities and non-controlling interests in that previously unconsolidated investee on the date of initial application as if that investee had been consolidated (applying the acquisition method as described in AASB 3 without recognising any goodwill for the investee) from the date when the investor obtained control of that investee on the basis of the requirements of this Standard. Any difference between the amount of assets, liabilities and non-controlling interests recognised and the previous carrying amount of the investor's involvement with the investee shall be recognised as a corresponding adjustment to the opening balance of equity.

(c)   if measuring an investee's assets, liabilities and non-controlling interest in accordance with (a) or (b) is impracticable (as defined in AASB 108), the investor shall:

(i)   if the investee is a business, apply the requirements of AASB 3. The deemed acquisition date shall be the beginning of the earliest period for which application of AASB 3 is practicable, which may be the current period.

(ii)   if the investee is not a business, apply the acquisition method as described in AASB 3 without recognising any goodwill for the investee as of the deemed acquisition date. The deemed acquisition date shall be the beginning of the earliest period for which the application of this paragraph is practicable, which may be the current period.

The investor shall recognise any difference between the amount of assets, liabilities and non-controlling interests recognised at the deemed acquisition date and any previously recognised amounts from its involvement as an adjustment to equity for that period. In addition, the investor shall provide comparative information and disclosures in accordance with AASB 108.

C5   When application of this Standard for the first time results in an investor no longer consolidating an investee that was consolidated in accordance with AASB 127 (as amended in 2008) and Interpretation 112, the investor shall measure its retained interest in the investee on the date of initial application at the amount at which it would have been measured if the requirements of this Standard had been effective when the investor became involved with, or lost control of, the investee. If measurement of the retained interest is impracticable (as defined in AASB 108), the investor shall apply the requirements of this Standard for accounting for a loss of control at the beginning of the earliest period for which application of this Standard is practicable, which may be the current period. The investor shall recognise any difference between the previously recognised amount of the assets, liabilities and non-controlling interest and the carrying amount of the investor's involvement with the investee as an adjustment to equity for that period. In addition, the investor shall provide comparative information and disclosures in accordance with AASB 108.

C6   Paragraphs 23, 25, B94 and B96–B99 were amendments to AASB 127 made in 2008 that were carried forward into AASB 10. Except when an entity applies paragraph C3, the entity shall apply the requirements in those paragraphs as follows:

(a)   An entity shall not restate any profit or loss attribution for reporting periods before it applied the amendment in paragraph B94 for the first time.

(b)   The requirements in paragraphs 23 and B96 for accounting for changes in ownership interests in a subsidiary after control is obtained do not apply to changes that occurred before an entity applied these amendments for the first time.

(c)   An entity shall not restate the carrying amount of an investment in a former subsidiary if control was lost before it applied the amendments in paragraphs 25 and B97–B99 for the first time. In addition, an entity shall not recalculate any gain or loss on the loss of control of a subsidiary that occurred before the amendments in paragraphs 25 and B97–B99 were applied for the first time.

References to AASB 9

C7   If an entity applies this Standard but does not yet apply AASB 9, any reference in this Standard to AASB 9 shall be read as a reference to AASB 139 *Financial Instruments: Recognition and Measurement*.

Withdrawal of other IFRSs

C8   [Deleted by the AASB – see paragraph Aus3.5(a)]

C9   [Deleted by the AASB – see paragraph Aus3.5(b)]

Australian Application Guidance

This guidance accompanies, but is not part of, AASB 10.

Exemption from Presenting Consolidated Financial Statements

AG1   The following table summarises the circumstances in which the exemption from presenting consolidated financial statements set out in paragraphs 4-Aus4.2 of this Standard may be available to a parent entity. The exemption is available only if the requirements of those paragraphs are satisfied. For example, the exemption is not available to a parent entity if it is a disclosing entity.

Same type of entity		
Ultimate or Intermediate Parent	FP	NFP
Parent	FP	NFP
Exemption for the parent	Available*	Available

Different type of entity		
Ultimate or Intermediate Parent	FP	NFP
Parent	NFP	FP
Exemption for the parent	Available*	Not available^

FP = for-profit entity

NFP = not-for-profit entity

*   The exemption would not be available by reference to the intermediate parent when it is a for-profit public sector entity unable to claim compliance with IFRSs – see paragraph Aus16.2 of AASB 101 *Presentation of Financial Statements*.

^   When the parent entity's NFP ultimate or intermediate parent is able to claim compliance with IFRSs, the exemption is available.

Deleted IFRS 10 Text

Deleted IFRS 10 text is not part of AASB 10.

Paragraph C1

An entity shall apply this IFRS for annual periods beginning on or after 1 January 2013. Earlier application is permitted. If an entity applies this IFRS earlier, it shall disclose that fact and apply IFRS 11, IFRS 12, IAS 27 Separate Financial Statements and IAS 28 (as amended in 2011) at the same time.

Paragraph C8

This IFRS supersedes the requirements relating to consolidated financial statements in IAS 27 (as amended in 2008).

Paragraph C9

This IFRS also supersedes SIC-12 *Consolidation – Special Purpose Entities*.

AASB 11
Joint Arrangements

(Issued August 2011)

Note from the Institute of Chartered Accountants Australia

This note, prepared by the technical editors, is not part of Accounting Standard AASB 11.

Historical development

29 August 2011: AASB 11 'Joint Arrangements' is the Australian equivalent of IFRS 11 of the same name, and was issued as part of the suite of Standards revising accounting requirements for consolidation, joint ventures and off balance sheet arrangements.

This Standard applies to annual reporting periods beginning on or after 1 January 2013 and can be adopted early by for-profit entities, provided revised AASB 10, AASB 12, AASB 127 and AASB 128 are adopted at the same time.

AASB 11 compared to IFRS 11

Additions

Paragraph	Description
Aus2.1	Which entities AASB 11 applies to (i.e. reporting entities and general purpose financial statements).
Aus2.2	The application date (i.e. annual reporting periods beginning on or after 1 January 2013).
Aus2.3	Permits early application by for-profit entities, but not by not-for-profit entities.
Aus2.4	Makes the requirement of AASB 11 subject to AASB 1031 'Materiality'.
Aus2.5	Explains which Australian Standards have been superseded by AASB 11.

Deletions

Paragraph	Description
C1	Effective date of IFRS 11.
C15	IFRS 11 supersedes the requirements on consolidated financial statements in IAS 31 and SIC-13.

Contents

Preface

Comparison with IFRS 11

Introduction to IFRS 11
(available on the AASB website)

Accounting Standard
AASB 11 Joint Arrangements

	Paragraphs
Objective	1
Meeting the objective	2
Application	Aus2.1 – Aus2.5
Scope	3
Joint arrangements	4 – 6
Joint control	7 – 13
Types of joint arrangement	14 – 19
Financial statements of parties to a joint arrangement	
Joint operations	20 – 23
Joint ventures	24 – 25
Separate financial statements	26 – 27

Appendices:

A. Defined Terms	
B. Application Guidance B1	
Joint arrangements	
Contractual arrangement	B2 – B4
Joint control	B5 – B11
Types of joint arrangement	B12 – B14
Classification of a joint arrangement	B15 – B33
Financial statements of parties to a joint arrangement	
Accounting for sales or contributions of assets to a joint operation	B34 – B35
Accounting for purchases of assets from a joint operation	B36 – B37
C. Effective Date and Transition	
Transition	
Joint ventures – transition from proportionate consolidation to the equity method	C2 – C6
Joint operations – transition from the equity method to accounting for assets and liabilities	C7 – C11
Transition provisions in an entity's separate financial statements	C12 – C13
References to AASB 9	C14

Illustrative Examples

Deleted IFRS 11 Text

Basis for Conclusions on IFRS 11
(available on the AASB website)

Australian Accounting Standard AASB 11 *Joint Arrangements* is set out in paragraphs 1 – 27 and Appendices A – C. All the paragraphs have equal authority. Paragraphs in **bold type** state the main principles. Terms defined in Appendix A are in *italics* the first time they appear in the Standard. AASB 11 is to be read in the context of other Australian Accounting Standards, including AASB 1048 *Interpretation of Standards*, which identifies the Australian Accounting Interpretations. In the absence of explicit guidance, AASB 108 *Accounting Policies, Changes in Accounting Estimates and Errors* provides a basis for selecting and applying accounting policies.

Preface

Introduction

The Australian Accounting Standards Board (AASB) makes Australian Accounting Standards, including Interpretations, to be applied by:

(a)   entities required by the *Corporations Act 2001* to prepare financial reports;

(b)   governments in preparing financial statements for the whole of government and the General Government Sector (GGS); and

(c)   entities in the private or public for-profit or not-for-profit sectors that are reporting entities or that prepare general purpose financial statements.

AASB 1053 *Application of Tiers of Australian Accounting Standards* establishes a differential reporting framework consisting of two tiers of reporting requirements for preparing general purpose financial statements:

(a)   Tier 1: Australian Accounting Standards; and

(b)   Tier 2: Australian Accounting Standards – Reduced Disclosure Requirements.

Tier 1 requirements incorporate International Financial Reporting Standards (IFRSs), including Interpretations, issued by the International Accounting Standards Board (IASB), with the addition of paragraphs on the applicability of each Standard in the Australian environment.

Publicly accountable for-profit private sector entities are required to adopt Tier 1 requirements, and therefore are required to comply with IFRSs. Furthermore, other for-profit private sector entities complying with Tier 1 requirements will simultaneously comply with IFRSs. Some other entities complying with Tier 1 requirements will also simultaneously comply with IFRSs.

Tier 2 requirements comprise the recognition, measurement and presentation requirements of Tier 1 but substantially reduced disclosure requirements in comparison to Tier 1.

Australian Accounting Standards also include requirements that are specific to Australian entities. These requirements may be located in Australian Accounting Standards that incorporate IFRSs or in other Australian Accounting Standards. In most instances, these requirements are either restricted to the not-for-profit or public sectors or include additional disclosures that address domestic, regulatory or other issues. These requirements do not prevent publicly accountable for-profit private sector entities from complying with IFRSs. In developing requirements for public sector entities, the AASB considers the requirements of International Public Sector Accounting Standards (IPSASs), as issued by the International Public Sector Accounting Standards Board (IPSASB) of the International Federation of Accountants.

Differences between this Standard and superseded requirements under AASB 131

Differences between this Standard and the superseded AASB 131 *Interests in Joint Ventures* are the same as the differences between IFRS 11 *Joint Arrangements* and the superseded requirements under IAS 31 *Joint Arrangements*. The main differences are summarised in the project summary and feedback statement on the IASB's website in relation to IFRS 11, which is available on the IASB's website at www.ifrs.org.

Implications for not-for-profit entities

This Standard applies to both for-profit and not-for-profit entities. However, prior to the 1 January 2013 mandatory application date of this Standard, the AASB will consider whether this Standard should be modified for application by not-for-profit entities having regard to its *Process for Modifying IFRSs for PBE/NFP*. In light of this, not-for-profit entities are not permitted to apply this Standard prior to the mandatory application date.

Comparison with IFRS 11

AASB 11 *Joint Arrangements* incorporates IFRS 11 *Joint Arrangements* issued by the International Accounting Standards Board (IASB). Paragraphs that have been added to this Standard (and do not appear in the text of IFRS 11) are identified with the prefix "Aus", followed by the number of the preceding IASB paragraph and decimal numbering.

Entities that comply with AASB 11 will simultaneously be in compliance with IFRS 11.

Accounting Standard AASB 11

The Australian Accounting Standards Board makes Accounting Standard AASB 11 *Joint Arrangements* under section 334 of the *Corporations Act 2001*.

Dated 29 August 2011

Kevin M. Stevenson
Chair – AASB

Accounting Standard AASB 11
Joint Arrangements

Objective

1   The objective of this Standard is to establish principles for financial reporting by entities that have an interest in arrangements that are controlled jointly (i.e. *joint arrangements*).

Meeting the objective

2   To meet the objective in paragraph 1, this Standard defines *joint control* and requires an entity that is a *party to a joint arrangement* to determine the type of joint arrangement in which it is involved by assessing its rights and obligations and to account for those rights and obligations in accordance with that type of joint arrangement.

Application

Aus2.1   This Standard applies to:

(a)   each entity that is required to prepare financial reports in accordance with Part 2M.3 of the Corporations Act and that is a reporting entity;

(b)   general purpose financial statements of each other reporting entity; and

(c)   financial statements that are, or are held out to be, general purpose financial statements.

Aus2.2   This Standard applies to annual reporting periods beginning on or after 1 January 2013.

Aus2.3   This Standard may be applied by for-profit entities, but not by not-for-profit entities, to annual reporting periods beginning on or after 1 January 2005 but before 1 January 2013. If a for-profit entity applies this Standard to such an annual reporting period, it shall disclose that fact and apply AASB 10 *Consolidated Financial Statements*, AASB 12 *Disclosure of Interests in Other Entities*, AASB 127 *Separate Financial Statements* (August 2011) and AASB 128 *Investments in Associates and Joint Ventures* (August 2011), at the same time.

Aus2.4   The requirements specified in this Standard apply to the financial statements where information resulting from their application is material in accordance with AASB 1031 *Materiality*.

Aus2.5   When applied or operative, this Standard supersedes:

(a)   AASB 131 *Interests in Joint Ventures* (July 2004, as amended); and

(b)   Interpretation 113 *Jointly Controlled Entities – Non-Monetary Contributions by Venturers* (July 2004, as amended).

Scope

3   This Standard shall be applied by all entities that are a party to a joint arrangement.

Joint arrangements

4   A joint arrangement is an arrangement of which two or more parties have joint control.

5   A joint arrangement has the following characteristics:

      (a)   The parties are bound by a contractual arrangement (see paragraphs B2–B4).

      (b)   The contractual arrangement gives two or more of those parties joint control of the arrangement (see paragraphs 7–13).

6   A joint arrangement is either a *joint operation* or a *joint venture*.

Joint control

7   Joint control is the contractually agreed sharing of control of an arrangement, which exists only when decisions about the relevant activities require the unanimous consent of the parties sharing control.

8   An entity that is a party to an arrangement shall assess whether the contractual arrangement gives all the parties, or a group of the parties, control of the arrangement collectively. All the parties, or a group of the parties, control the arrangement collectively when they must act together to direct the activities that significantly affect the returns of the arrangement (i.e. the relevant activities).

9   Once it has been determined that all the parties, or a group of the parties, control the arrangement collectively, joint control exists only when decisions about the relevant activities require the unanimous consent of the parties that control the arrangement collectively.

10   In a joint arrangement, no single party controls the arrangement on its own. A party with joint control of an arrangement can prevent any of the other parties, or a group of the parties, from controlling the arrangement.

11   An arrangement can be a joint arrangement even though not all of its parties have joint control of the arrangement. This Standard distinguishes between parties that have joint control of a joint arrangement (*joint operators* or *joint venturers*) and parties that participate in, but do not have joint control of, a joint arrangement.

12   An entity will need to apply judgement when assessing whether all the parties, or a group of the parties, have joint control of an arrangement. An entity shall make this assessment by considering all facts and circumstances (see paragraphs B5–B11).

13   If facts and circumstances change, an entity shall reassess whether it still has joint control of the arrangement.

Types of joint arrangement

14   An entity shall determine the type of joint arrangement in which it is involved. The classification of a joint arrangement as a joint operation or a joint venture depends upon the rights and obligations of the parties to the arrangement.

15   A joint operation is a joint arrangement whereby the parties that have joint control of the arrangement have rights to the assets, and obligations for the liabilities, relating to the arrangement. Those parties are called joint operators.

16   A joint venture is a joint arrangement whereby the parties that have joint control of the arrangement have rights to the net assets of the arrangement. Those parties are called joint venturers.

17   An entity applies judgement when assessing whether a joint arrangement is a joint operation or a joint venture. An entity shall determine the type of joint arrangement in which it is involved by considering its rights and obligations arising from the arrangement. An entity assesses its rights and obligations by considering the structure and legal form of the arrangement, the terms agreed by the parties in the contractual arrangement and, when relevant, other facts and circumstances (see paragraphs B12–B33).

18 Sometimes the parties are bound by a framework agreement that sets up the general contractual terms for undertaking one or more activities. The framework agreement might set out that the parties establish different joint arrangements to deal with specific activities that form part of the agreement. Even though those joint arrangements are related to the same framework agreement, their type might be different if the parties' rights and obligations differ when undertaking the different activities dealt with in the framework agreement. Consequently, joint operations and joint ventures can coexist when the parties undertake different activities that form part of the same framework agreement.

19 If facts and circumstances change, an entity shall reassess whether the type of joint arrangement in which it is involved has changed.

Financial statements of parties to a joint arrangement

Joint operations

20 A joint operator shall recognise in relation to its interest in a joint operation:

(a) its assets, including its share of any assets held jointly;

(b) its liabilities, including its share of any liabilities incurred jointly;

(c) its revenue from the sale of its share of the output arising from the joint operation;

(d) its share of the revenue from the sale of the output by the joint operation; and

(e) its expenses, including its share of any expenses incurred jointly.

21 A joint operator shall account for the assets, liabilities, revenues and expenses relating to its interest in a joint operation in accordance with the Standards applicable to the particular assets, liabilities, revenues and expenses.

22 The accounting for transactions such as the sale, contribution or purchase of assets between an entity and a joint operation in which it is a joint operator is specified in paragraphs B34–B37.

23 A party that participates in, but does not have joint control of, a joint operation shall also account for its interest in the arrangement in accordance with paragraphs 20–22 if that party has rights to the assets, and obligations for the liabilities, relating to the joint operation. If a party that participates in, but does not have joint control of, a joint operation does not have rights to the assets, and obligations for the liabilities, relating to that joint operation, it shall account for its interest in the joint operation in accordance with the Standards applicable to that interest.

Joint ventures

24 A joint venturer shall recognise its interest in a joint venture as an investment and shall account for that investment using the equity method in accordance with AASB 128 *Investments in Associates and Joint Ventures* unless the entity is exempted from applying the equity method as specified in that Standard.

25 A party that participates in, but does not have joint control of, a joint venture shall account for its interest in the arrangement in accordance with AASB 9 *Financial Instruments*, unless it has significant influence over the joint venture, in which case it shall account for it in accordance with AASB 128 (August 2011).

Separate financial statements

26 In its separate financial statements, a joint operator or joint venturer shall account for its interest in:

(a) a joint operation in accordance with paragraphs 20–22;

(b) a joint venture in accordance with paragraph 10 of AASB 127 *Separate Financial Statements*.

27   In its separate financial statements, a party that participates in, but does not have joint control of, a joint arrangement shall account for its interest in:

(a)   a joint operation in accordance with paragraph 23;

(b)   a joint venture in accordance with AASB 9, unless the entity has significant influence over the joint venture, in which case it shall apply paragraph 10 of AASB 127 (August 2011).

Appendix A
Defined Terms

This appendix is an integral part of AASB 11.

joint arrangement	An arrangement of which two or more parties have **joint control**.
joint control	The contractually agreed sharing of control of an arrangement, which exists only when decisions about the relevant activities require the unanimous consent of the parties sharing control.
joint operation	A **joint arrangement** whereby the parties that have **joint control** of the arrangement have rights to the assets, and obligations for the liabilities, relating to the arrangement.
joint operator	A party to a **joint operation** that has **joint control** of that joint operation.
joint venture	A **joint arrangement** whereby the parties that have joint control of the arrangement have rights to the net assets of the arrangement.
joint venturer	A party to a **joint venture** that has **joint control** of that joint venture.
party to a joint arrangement	An entity that participates in a **joint arrangement**, regardless of whether that entity has **joint control** of the arrangement.
separate vehicle	A separately identifiable financial structure, including separate legal entities or entities recognised by statute, regardless of whether those entities have a legal personality.

The following terms are defined in AASB 127 (August 2011), AASB 128 (August 2011) or AASB 10 *Consolidated Financial Statements* and are used in this Standard with the meanings specified in those Standards:

- control of an investee
- equity method
- power
- protective rights
- relevant activities
- separate financial statements
- significant influence.

Appendix B

Application Guidance

This appendix is an integral part of AASB 11. It describes the application of paragraphs 1–27 and has the same authority as the other parts of the Standard.

B1   The examples in this appendix portray hypothetical situations. Although some aspects of the examples may be present in actual fact patterns, all relevant facts and circumstances of a particular fact pattern would need to be evaluated when applying AASB 11.

Joint arrangements

Contractual arrangement (paragraph 5)

B2   Contractual arrangements can be evidenced in several ways. An enforceable contractual arrangement is often, but not always, in writing, usually in the form of a contract or documented discussions between the parties. Statutory mechanisms can also create enforceable arrangements, either on their own or in conjunction with contracts between the parties.

B3   When joint arrangements are structured through a *separate vehicle* (see paragraphs B19–B33), the contractual arrangement, or some aspects of the contractual arrangement, will in some cases be incorporated in the articles, charter or by-laws of the separate vehicle.

B4   The contractual arrangement sets out the terms upon which the parties participate in the activity that is the subject of the arrangement. The contractual arrangement generally deals with such matters as:

(a)   the purpose, activity and duration of the joint arrangement.

(b)   how the members of the board of directors, or equivalent governing body, of the joint arrangement, are appointed.

(c)   the decision-making process: the matters requiring decisions from the parties, the voting rights of the parties and the required level of support for those matters. The decision-making process reflected in the contractual arrangement establishes joint control of the arrangement (see paragraphs B5–B11).

(d)   the capital or other contributions required of the parties.

(e)   how the parties share assets, liabilities, revenues, expenses or profit or loss relating to the joint arrangement.

Joint control (paragraphs 7–13)

B5   In assessing whether an entity has joint control of an arrangement, an entity shall assess first whether all the parties, or a group of the parties, control the arrangement. AASB 10 defines control and shall be used to determine whether all the parties, or a group of the parties, are exposed, or have rights, to variable returns from their involvement with the arrangement and have the ability to affect those returns through their power over the arrangement. When all the parties, or a group of the parties, considered collectively, are able to direct the activities that significantly affect the returns of the arrangement (i.e. the relevant activities), the parties control the arrangement collectively.

B6   After concluding that all the parties, or a group of the parties, control the arrangement collectively, an entity shall assess whether it has joint control of the arrangement. Joint control exists only when decisions about the relevant activities require the unanimous consent of the parties that collectively control the arrangement. Assessing whether the arrangement is jointly controlled by all of its parties or by a group of the parties, or controlled by one of its parties alone, can require judgement.

B7   Sometimes the decision-making process that is agreed upon by the parties in their contractual arrangement implicitly leads to joint control. For example, assume two parties establish an arrangement in which each has 50 per cent of the voting rights and the contractual arrangement between them specifies that at least 51 per cent of the voting rights are required to make decisions about the relevant activities. In this case, the parties have implicitly agreed that they have joint control of the arrangement because decisions about the relevant activities cannot be made without both parties agreeing.

B8   In other circumstances, the contractual arrangement requires a minimum proportion of the voting rights to make decisions about the relevant activities. When that minimum required proportion of the voting rights can be achieved by more than one combination of the parties agreeing together, that arrangement is not a joint arrangement unless the contractual arrangement specifies which parties (or combination of parties) are required to agree unanimously to decisions about the relevant activities of the arrangement.

Application examples

Example 1

Assume that three parties establish an arrangement: A has 50 per cent of the voting rights in the arrangement, B has 30 per cent and C has 20 per cent. The contractual arrangement between A, B and C specifies that at least 75 per cent of the voting rights are required to make decisions about the relevant activities of the arrangement. Even though A can block any decision, it does not control the arrangement because it needs the agreement of B. The terms of their contractual arrangement requiring at least 75 per cent of the voting rights to make decisions about the relevant activities imply that A and B have joint control of the arrangement because decisions about the relevant activities of the arrangement cannot be made without both A and B agreeing.

Example 2

Assume an arrangement has three parties: A has 50 per cent of the voting rights in the arrangement and B and C each have 25 per cent. The contractual arrangement between A, B and C specifies that at least 75 per cent of the voting rights are required to make decisions about the relevant activities of the arrangement. Even though A can block any decision, it does not control the arrangement because it needs the agreement of either B or C. In this example, A, B and C collectively control the arrangement. However, there is more than one combination of parties that can agree to reach 75 per cent of the voting rights (i.e. either A and B or A and C). In such a situation, to be a joint arrangement the contractual arrangement between the parties would need to specify which combination of the parties is required to agree unanimously to decisions about the relevant activities of the arrangement.

Example 3

Assume an arrangement in which A and B each have 35 per cent of the voting rights in the arrangement with the remaining 30 per cent being widely dispersed. Decisions about the relevant activities require approval by a majority of the voting rights. A and B have joint control of the arrangement only if the contractual arrangement specifies that decisions about the relevant activities of the arrangement require both A and B agreeing.

B9   The requirement for unanimous consent means that any party with joint control of the arrangement can prevent any of the other parties, or a group of the parties, from making unilateral decisions (about the relevant activities) without its consent. If the requirement for unanimous consent relates only to decisions that give a party protective rights and not to decisions about the relevant activities of an arrangement, that party is not a party with joint control of the arrangement.

B10   A contractual arrangement might include clauses on the resolution of disputes, such as arbitration. These provisions may allow for decisions to be made in the absence of unanimous consent among the parties that have joint control. The existence of such provisions does not prevent the arrangement from being jointly controlled and, consequently, from being a joint arrangement.

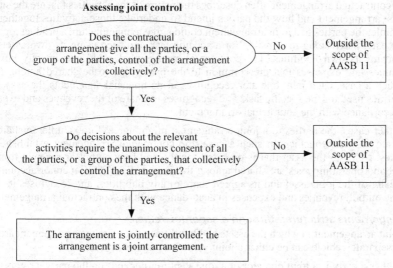

Assessing joint control

B11 When an arrangement is outside the scope of AASB 11, an entity accounts for its interest in the arrangement in accordance with relevant Standards, such as AASB 10, AASB 128 (August 2011) or AASB 9.

Types of joint arrangement (paragraphs 14–19)

B12 Joint arrangements are established for a variety of purposes (e.g. as a way for parties to share costs and risks, or as a way to provide the parties with access to new technology or new markets), and can be established using different structures and legal forms.

B13 Some arrangements do not require the activity that is the subject of the arrangement to be undertaken in a separate vehicle. However, other arrangements involve the establishment of a separate vehicle.

B14 The classification of joint arrangements required by this Standard depends upon the parties' rights and obligations arising from the arrangement in the normal course of business. This Standard classifies joint arrangements as either joint operations or joint ventures. When an entity has rights to the assets, and obligations for the liabilities, relating to the arrangement, the arrangement is a joint operation. When an entity has rights to the net assets of the arrangement, the arrangement is a joint venture. Paragraphs B16–B33 set out the assessment an entity carries out to determine whether it has an interest in a joint operation or an interest in a joint venture.

Classification of a joint arrangement

B15 As stated in paragraph B14, the classification of joint arrangements requires the parties to assess their rights and obligations arising from the arrangement. When making that assessment, an entity shall consider the following:

(a) the structure of the joint arrangement (see paragraphs B16–B21).

(b) when the joint arrangement is structured through a separate vehicle:

 (i) the legal form of the separate vehicle (see paragraphs B22–B24);

 (ii) the terms of the contractual arrangement (see paragraphs B25–B28); and

 (iii) when relevant, other facts and circumstances (see paragraphs B29–B33).

Structure of the joint arrangement

Joint arrangements not structured through a separate vehicle

B16 A joint arrangement that is not structured through a separate vehicle is a joint operation. In such cases, the contractual arrangement establishes the parties' rights to the assets, and obligations for the liabilities, relating to the arrangement, and the parties' rights to the corresponding revenues and obligations for the corresponding expenses.

B17   The contractual arrangement often describes the nature of the activities that are the subject of the arrangement and how the parties intend to undertake those activities together. For example, the parties to a joint arrangement could agree to manufacture a product together, with each party being responsible for a specific task and each using its own assets and incurring its own liabilities. The contractual arrangement could also specify how the revenues and expenses that are common to the parties are to be shared among them. In such a case, each joint operator recognises in its financial statements the assets and liabilities used for the specific task, and recognises its share of the revenues and expenses in accordance with the contractual arrangement.

B18   In other cases, the parties to a joint arrangement might agree, for example, to share and operate an asset together. In such a case, the contractual arrangement establishes the parties' rights to the asset that is operated jointly, and how output or revenue from the asset and operating costs are shared among the parties. Each joint operator accounts for its share of the joint asset and its agreed share of any liabilities, and recognises its share of the output, revenues and expenses in accordance with the contractual arrangement.

Joint arrangements structured through a separate vehicle

B19   A joint arrangement in which the assets and liabilities relating to the arrangement are held in a separate vehicle can be either a joint venture or a joint operation.

B20   Whether a party is a joint operator or a joint venturer depends on the party's rights to the assets, and obligations for the liabilities, relating to the arrangement that are held in the separate vehicle.

B21   As stated in paragraph B15, when the parties have structured a joint arrangement in a separate vehicle, the parties need to assess whether the legal form of the separate vehicle, the terms of the contractual arrangement and, when relevant, any other facts and circumstances give them:

    (a)   rights to the assets, and obligations for the liabilities, relating to the arrangement (i.e. the arrangement is a joint operation); or

    (b)   rights to the net assets of the arrangement (i.e. the arrangement is a joint venture).

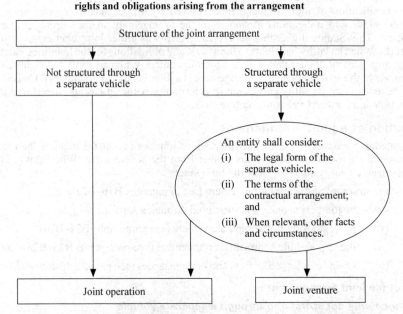

Classification of a joint arrangement: assessment of the parties' rights and obligations arising from the arrangement

The legal form of the separate vehicle

B22   The legal form of the separate vehicle is relevant when assessing the type of joint arrangement. The legal form assists in the initial assessment of the parties' rights to the assets and obligations for the liabilities held in the separate vehicle, such as whether the parties have interests in the assets held in the separate vehicle and whether they are liable for the liabilities held in the separate vehicle.

B23 For example, the parties might conduct the joint arrangement through a separate vehicle, whose legal form causes the separate vehicle to be considered in its own right (i.e. the assets and liabilities held in the separate vehicle are the assets and liabilities of the separate vehicle and not the assets and liabilities of the parties). In such a case, the assessment of the rights and obligations conferred upon the parties by the legal form of the separate vehicle indicates that the arrangement is a joint venture. However, the terms agreed by the parties in their contractual arrangement (see paragraphs B25–B28) and, when relevant, other facts and circumstances (see paragraphs B29–B33) can override the assessment of the rights and obligations conferred upon the parties by the legal form of the separate vehicle.

B24 The assessment of the rights and obligations conferred upon the parties by the legal form of the separate vehicle is sufficient to conclude that the arrangement is a joint operation only if the parties conduct the joint arrangement in a separate vehicle whose legal form does not confer separation between the parties and the separate vehicle (i.e. the assets and liabilities held in the separate vehicle are the parties' assets and liabilities).

Assessing the terms of the contractual arrangement

B25 In many cases, the rights and obligations agreed to by the parties in their contractual arrangements are consistent, or do not conflict, with the rights and obligations conferred on the parties by the legal form of the separate vehicle in which the arrangement has been structured.

B26 In other cases, the parties use the contractual arrangement to reverse or modify the rights and obligations conferred by the legal form of the separate vehicle in which the arrangement has been structured.

Application example
Example 4
Assume that two parties structure a joint arrangement in an incorporated entity. Each party has a 50 per cent ownership interest in the incorporated entity. The incorporation enables the separation of the entity from its owners and as a consequence the assets and liabilities held in the entity are the assets and liabilities of the incorporated entity. In such a case, the assessment of the rights and obligations conferred upon the parties by the legal form of the separate vehicle indicates that the parties have rights to the net assets of the arrangement.
However, the parties modify the features of the corporation through their contractual arrangement so that each has an interest in the assets of the incorporated entity and each is liable for the liabilities of the incorporated entity in a specified proportion. Such contractual modifications to the features of a corporation can cause an arrangement to be a joint operation.

B27 The following table compares common terms in contractual arrangements of parties to a joint operation and common terms in contractual arrangements of parties to a joint venture. The examples of the contractual terms provided in the following table are not exhaustive.

Assessing the terms of the contractual arrangement		
	Joint operation	**Joint venture**
The terms of the contractual arrangement	The contractual arrangement provides the parties to the joint arrangement with rights to the assets, and obligations for the liabilities, relating to the arrangement.	The contractual arrangement provides the parties to the joint arrangement with rights to the net assets of the arrangement (i.e. it is the separate vehicle, not the parties, that has rights to the assets, and obligations for the liabilities, relating to the arrangement).
		continued

Assessing the terms of the contractual arrangement		
	Joint operation	**Joint venture**
Rights to assets	The contractual arrangement establishes that the parties to the joint arrangement share all interests (e.g. rights, title or ownership) in the assets relating to the arrangement in a specified proportion (e.g. in proportion to the parties' ownership interest in the arrangement or in proportion to the activity carried out through the arrangement that is directly attributed to them).	The contractual arrangement establishes that the assets brought into the arrangement or subsequently acquired by the joint arrangement are the arrangement's assets. The parties have no interests (i.e. no rights, title or ownership) in the assets of the arrangement.
Obligations for liabilities	The contractual arrangement establishes that the parties to the joint arrangement share all liabilities, obligations, costs and expenses in a specified proportion (e.g. in proportion to the parties' ownership interest in the arrangement or in proportion to the activity carried out through the arrangement that is directly attributed to them).	The contractual arrangement establishes that the joint arrangement is liable for the debts and obligations of the arrangement.
		The contractual arrangement establishes that the parties to the joint arrangement are liable to the arrangement only to the extent of their respective investments in the arrangement or to their respective obligations to contribute any unpaid or additional capital to the arrangement, or both.
	The contractual arrangement establishes that the parties to the joint arrangement are liable for claims raised by third parties.	The contractual arrangement states that creditors of the joint arrangement do not have rights of recourse against any party with respect to debts or obligations of the arrangement.
Revenues, expenses, profit or loss	The contractual arrangement establishes the allocation of revenues and expenses on the basis of the relative performance of each party to the joint arrangement. For example, the contractual arrangement might establish that revenues and expenses are allocated on the basis of the capacity that each party uses in a plant operated jointly, which could differ from their ownership interest in the joint arrangement. In other instances, the parties might have agreed to share the profit or loss relating to the arrangement on the basis of a specified proportion such as the parties' ownership interest in the arrangement. This would not prevent the arrangement from being a joint operation if the parties have rights to the assets, and obligations for the liabilities, relating to the arrangement.	The contractual arrangement establishes each party's share in the profit or loss relating to the activities of the arrangement.
Guarantees	The parties to joint arrangements are often required to provide guarantees to third parties that, for example, receive a service from, or provide financing to, the joint arrangement. The provision of such guarantees, or the commitment by the parties to provide them, does not, by itself, determine that the joint arrangement is a joint operation. The feature that determines whether the joint arrangement is a joint operation or a joint venture is whether the parties have obligations for the liabilities relating to the arrangement (for some of which the parties might or might not have provided a guarantee).		

B28   When the contractual arrangement specifies that the parties have rights to the assets, and obligations for the liabilities, relating to the arrangement, they are parties to a joint operation and do not need to consider other facts and circumstances (paragraphs B29–B33) for the purposes of classifying the joint arrangement.

Assessing other facts and circumstances

B29 When the terms of the contractual arrangement do not specify that the parties have rights to the assets, and obligations for the liabilities, relating to the arrangement, the parties shall consider other facts and circumstances to assess whether the arrangement is a joint operation or a joint venture.

B30 A joint arrangement might be structured in a separate vehicle whose legal form confers separation between the parties and the separate vehicle. The contractual terms agreed among the parties might not specify the parties' rights to the assets and obligations for the liabilities, yet consideration of other facts and circumstances can lead to such an arrangement being classified as a joint operation. This will be the case when other facts and circumstances give the parties rights to the assets, and obligations for the liabilities, relating to the arrangement.

B31 When the activities of an arrangement are primarily designed for the provision of output to the parties, this indicates that the parties have rights to substantially all the economic benefits of the assets of the arrangement. The parties to such arrangements often ensure their access to the outputs provided by the arrangement by preventing the arrangement from selling output to third parties.

B32 The effect of an arrangement with such a design and purpose is that the liabilities incurred by the arrangement are, in substance, satisfied by the cash flows received from the parties through their purchases of the output. When the parties are substantially the only source of cash flows contributing to the continuity of the operations of the arrangement, this indicates that the parties have an obligation for the liabilities relating to the arrangement.

Application example

Example 5

Assume that two parties structure a joint arrangement in an incorporated entity (entity C) in which each party has a 50 per cent ownership interest. The purpose of the arrangement is to manufacture materials required by the parties for their own, individual manufacturing processes. The arrangement ensures that the parties operate the facility that produces the materials to the quantity and quality specifications of the parties.

The legal form of entity C (an incorporated entity) through which the activities are conducted initially indicates that the assets and liabilities held in entity C are the assets and liabilities of entity C. The contractual arrangement between the parties does not specify that the parties have rights to the assets or obligations for the liabilities of entity C. Accordingly, the legal form of entity C and the terms of the contractual arrangement indicate that the arrangement is a joint venture.

However, the parties also consider the following aspects of the arrangement:

- The parties agreed to purchase all the output produced by entity C in a ratio of 50:50. Entity C cannot sell any of the output to third parties, unless this is approved by the two parties to the arrangement. Because the purpose of the arrangement is to provide the parties with output they require, such sales to third parties are expected to be uncommon and not material.

- The price of the output sold to the parties is set by both parties at a level that is designed to cover the costs of production and administrative expenses incurred by entity C. On the basis of this operating model, the arrangement is intended to operate at a break-even level.

From the fact pattern above, the following facts and circumstances are relevant:

- The obligation of the parties to purchase all the output produced by entity C reflects the exclusive dependence of entity C upon the parties for the generation of cash flows and, thus, the parties have an obligation to fund the settlement of the liabilities of entity C.

- The fact that the parties have rights to all the output produced by entity C means that the parties are consuming, and therefore have rights to, all the economic benefits of the assets of entity C.

These facts and circumstances indicate that the arrangement is a joint operation. The conclusion about the classification of the joint arrangement in these circumstances would not change if, instead of the parties using their share of the output themselves in a subsequent manufacturing process, the parties sold their share of the output to third parties.

If the parties changed the terms of the contractual arrangement so that the arrangement was able to sell output to third parties, this would result in entity C assuming demand, inventory and credit risks. In that scenario, such a change in the facts and circumstances would require reassessment of the classification of the joint arrangement. Such facts and circumstances would indicate that the arrangement is a joint venture.

B33   The following flow chart reflects the assessment an entity follows to classify an
      arrangement when the joint arrangement is structured through a separate vehicle:

Classification of a joint arrangement structured through a separate vehicle

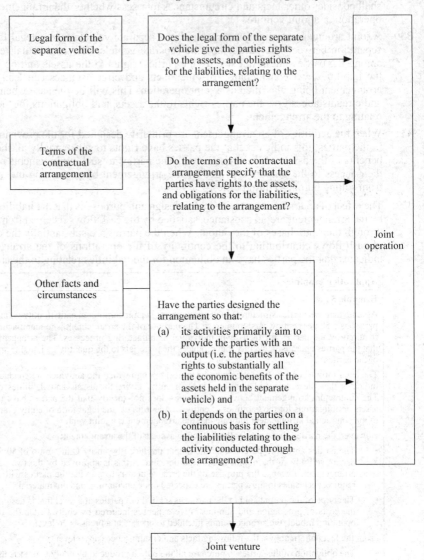

Financial statements of parties to a joint arrangement (paragraph 22)

Accounting for sales or contributions of assets to a joint operation

B34   When an entity enters into a transaction with a joint operation in which it is a joint
      operator, such as a sale or contribution of assets, it is conducting the transaction with
      the other parties to the joint operation and, as such, the joint operator shall recognise
      gains and losses resulting from such a transaction only to the extent of the other parties'
      interests in the joint operation.

B35   When such transactions provide evidence of a reduction in the net realisable value of the
      assets to be sold or contributed to the joint operation, or of an impairment loss of those
      assets, those losses shall be recognised fully by the joint operator.

Accounting for purchases of assets from a joint operation

B36 When an entity enters into a transaction with a joint operation in which it is a joint operator, such as a purchase of assets, it shall not recognise its share of the gains and losses until it resells those assets to a third party.

B37 When such transactions provide evidence of a reduction in the net realisable value of the assets to be purchased or of an impairment loss of those assets, a joint operator shall recognise its share of those losses.

Appendix C

Effective Date and Transition

This appendix is an integral part of AASB 11 and has the same authority as the other parts of the Standard.

Effective date

C1 [Deleted by the AASB – see paragraphs Aus2.2 and Aus2.3]

Transition

Joint ventures – transition from proportionate consolidation to the equity method

C2 When changing from proportionate consolidation to the equity method, an entity shall recognise its investment in the joint venture as at the beginning of the earliest period presented. That initial investment shall be measured as the aggregate of the carrying amounts of the assets and liabilities that the entity had previously proportionately consolidated, including any goodwill arising from acquisition. If the goodwill previously belonged to a larger cash-generating unit, or to a group of cash-generating units, the entity shall allocate goodwill to the joint venture on the basis of the relative carrying amounts of the joint venture and the cash-generating unit or group of cash-generating units to which it belonged.

C3 The opening balance of the investment determined in accordance with paragraph C2 is regarded as the deemed cost of the investment at initial recognition. An entity shall apply paragraphs 40–43 of AASB 128 (August 2011) to the opening balance of the investment to assess whether the investment is impaired and shall recognise any impairment loss as an adjustment to retained earnings at the beginning of the earliest period presented. The initial recognition exception in paragraphs 15 and 24 of AASB 112 *Income Taxes* does not apply when the entity recognises an investment in a joint venture resulting from applying the transition requirements for joint ventures that had previously been proportionately consolidated.

C4 If aggregating all previously proportionately consolidated assets and liabilities results in negative net assets, an entity shall assess whether it has legal or constructive obligations in relation to the negative net assets and, if so, the entity shall recognise the corresponding liability. If the entity concludes that it does not have legal or constructive obligations in relation to the negative net assets, it shall not recognise the corresponding liability but it shall adjust retained earnings at the beginning of the earliest period presented. The entity shall disclose this fact, along with its cumulative unrecognised share of losses of its joint ventures as at the beginning of the earliest period presented and at the date at which this Standard is first applied.

C5 An entity shall disclose a breakdown of the assets and liabilities that have been aggregated into the single line investment balance as at the beginning of the earliest period presented. That disclosure shall be prepared in an aggregated manner for all joint ventures for which an entity applies the transition requirements referred to in paragraphs C2–C6.

C6 After initial recognition, an entity shall account for its investment in the joint venture using the equity method in accordance with AASB 128 (August 2011).

Joint operations – transition from the equity method to accounting for assets and liabilities

C7   When changing from the equity method to accounting for assets and liabilities in respect of its interest in a joint operation, an entity shall, at the beginning of the earliest period presented, derecognise the investment that was previously accounted for using the equity method and any other items that formed part of the entity's net investment in the arrangement in accordance with paragraph 38 of AASB 128 (August 2011) and recognise its share of each of the assets and the liabilities in respect of its interest in the joint operation, including any goodwill that might have formed part of the carrying amount of the investment.

C8   An entity shall determine its interest in the assets and liabilities relating to the joint operation on the basis of its rights and obligations in a specified proportion in accordance with the contractual arrangement. An entity measures the initial carrying amounts of the assets and liabilities by disaggregating them from the carrying amount of the investment at the beginning of the earliest period presented on the basis of the information used by the entity in applying the equity method.

C9   Any difference arising from the investment previously accounted for using the equity method together with any other items that formed part of the entity's net investment in the arrangement in accordance with paragraph 38 of AASB 128 (August 2011), and the net amount of the assets and liabilities, including any goodwill, recognised shall be:

(a)   offset against any goodwill relating to the investment with any remaining difference adjusted against retained earnings at the beginning of the earliest period presented, if the net amount of the assets and liabilities, including any goodwill, recognised is higher than the investment (and any other items that formed part of the entity's net investment) derecognised.

(b)   adjusted against retained earnings at the beginning of the earliest period presented, if the net amount of the assets and liabilities, including any goodwill, recognised is lower than the investment (and any other items that formed part of the entity's net investment) derecognised.

C10   An entity changing from the equity method to accounting for assets and liabilities shall provide a reconciliation between the investment derecognised, and the assets and liabilities recognised, together with any remaining difference adjusted against retained earnings, at the beginning of the earliest period presented.

C11   The initial recognition exception in paragraphs 15 and 24 of AASB 112 does not apply when the entity recognises assets and liabilities relating to its interest in a joint operation.

Transition provisions in an entity's separate financial statements

C12   An entity that, in accordance with paragraph 10 of AASB 127, was previously accounting in its separate financial statements for its interest in a joint operation as an investment at cost or in accordance with AASB 9 shall:

(a)   derecognise the investment and recognise the assets and the liabilities in respect of its interest in the joint operation at the amounts determined in accordance with paragraphs C7–C9.

(b)   provide a reconciliation between the investment derecognised, and the assets and liabilities recognised, together with any remaining difference adjusted in retained earnings, at the beginning of the earliest period presented.

C13   The initial recognition exception in paragraphs 15 and 24 of AASB 112 does not apply when the entity recognises assets and liabilities relating to its interest in a joint operation in its separate financial statements resulting from applying the transition requirements for joint operations referred to in paragraph C12.

References to AASB 9

C14   If an entity applies this Standard but does not yet apply AASB 9, any reference to AASB 9 shall be read as a reference to AASB 139 *Financial Instruments: Recognition and Measurement*.

Withdrawal of other IFRSs

C15 [Deleted by the AASB – see paragraph Aus2.5]

Illustrative Examples

Contents

		Paragraphs
1	Construction services	IE2 – IE8
2	Shopping centre operated jointly	IE9 – IE13
3	Joint manufacturing and distribution of a product	IE14 – IE28
4	Bank operated jointly	IE29 – IE33
5	Oil and gas exploration, development and production activities	IE34 – IE43
6	Liquefied natural gas arrangement	IE44 – IE52

Illustrative Examples

These examples accompany, but are not part of, AASB 11. They illustrate aspects of AASB 11 but are not intended to provide interpretative guidance.

IE1 These examples portray hypothetical situations illustrating the judgements that might be used when applying AASB 11 in different situations. Although some aspects of the examples may be present in actual fact patterns, all relevant facts and circumstances of a particular fact pattern would need to be evaluated when applying AASB 11.

Example 1 – Construction services

IE2 A and B (the parties) are two companies whose businesses are the provision of many types of public and private construction services. They set up a contractual arrangement to work together for the purpose of fulfilling a contract with a government for the design and construction of a road between two cities. The contractual arrangement determines the participation shares of A and B and establishes joint control of the arrangement, the subject matter of which is the delivery of the road.

IE3 The parties set up a separate vehicle (entity Z) through which to conduct the arrangement. Entity Z, on behalf of A and B, enters into the contract with the government. In addition, the assets and liabilities relating to the arrangement are held in entity Z. The main feature of entity Z's legal form is that the parties, not entity Z, have rights to the assets, and obligations for the liabilities, of the entity.

IE4 The contractual arrangement between A and B additionally establishes that:

(a) the rights to all the assets needed to undertake the activities of the arrangement are shared by the parties on the basis of their participation shares in the arrangement;

(b) the parties have several and joint responsibility for all operating and financial obligations relating to the activities of the arrangement on the basis of their participation shares in the arrangement; and

(c) the profit or loss resulting from the activities of the arrangement is shared by A and B on the basis of their participation shares in the arrangement.

IE5 For the purposes of co-ordinating and overseeing the activities, A and B appoint an operator, who will be an employee of one of the parties. After a specified time, the role of the operator will rotate to an employee of the other party. A and B agree that the activities will be executed by the operator's employees on a 'no gain or loss' basis.

IE6 In accordance with the terms specified in the contract with the government, entity Z invoices the construction services to the government on behalf of the parties.

Analysis

IE7   The joint arrangement is carried out through a separate vehicle whose legal form does not confer separation between the parties and the separate vehicle (i.e. the assets and liabilities held in entity Z are the parties' assets and liabilities). This is reinforced by the terms agreed by the parties in their contractual arrangement, which state that A and B have rights to the assets, and obligations for the liabilities, relating to the arrangement that is conducted through entity Z. The joint arrangement is a joint operation.

IE8   A and B each recognise in their financial statements their share of the assets (e.g. property, plant and equipment, accounts receivable) and their share of any liabilities resulting from the arrangement (e.g. accounts payable to third parties) on the basis of their agreed participation share. Each also recognises its share of the revenue and expenses resulting from the construction services provided to the government through entity Z.

Example 2 – Shopping centre operated jointly

IE9   Two real estate companies (the parties) set up a separate vehicle (entity X) for the purpose of acquiring and operating a shopping centre. The contractual arrangement between the parties establishes joint control of the activities that are conducted in entity X. The main feature of entity X's legal form is that the entity, not the parties, has rights to the assets, and obligations for the liabilities, relating to the arrangement. These activities include the rental of the retail units, managing the car park, maintaining the centre and its equipment, such as lifts, and building the reputation and customer base for the centre as a whole.

IE10 The terms of the contractual arrangement are such that:

(a)   entity X owns the shopping centre. The contractual arrangement does not specify that the parties have rights to the shopping centre.

(b)   the parties are not liable in respect of the debts, liabilities or obligations of entity X. If entity X is unable to pay any of its debts or other liabilities or to discharge its obligations to third parties, the liability of each party to any third party will be limited to the unpaid amount of that party's capital contribution.

(c)   the parties have the right to sell or pledge their interests in entity X.

(d)   each party receives a share of the income from operating the shopping centre (which is the rental income net of the operating costs) in accordance with its interest in entity X.

Analysis

IE11 The joint arrangement is carried out through a separate vehicle whose legal form causes the separate vehicle to be considered in its own right (i.e. the assets and liabilities held in the separate vehicle are the assets and liabilities of the separate vehicle and not the assets and liabilities of the parties). In addition, the terms of the contractual arrangement do not specify that the parties have rights to the assets, or obligations for the liabilities, relating to the arrangement. Instead, the terms of the contractual arrangement establish that the parties have rights to the net assets of entity X.

IE12 On the basis of the description above, there are no other facts and circumstances that indicate that the parties have rights to substantially all the economic benefits of the assets relating to the arrangement, and that the parties have an obligation for the liabilities relating to the arrangement. The joint arrangement is a joint venture.

IE13 The parties recognise their rights to the net assets of entity X as investments and account for them using the equity method.

Example 3 – Joint manufacturing and distribution of a product

IE14 Companies A and B (the parties) have set up a strategic and operating agreement (the framework agreement) in which they have agreed the terms according to which they will conduct the manufacturing and distribution of a product (product P) in different markets.

IE15 The parties have agreed to conduct manufacturing and distribution activities by establishing joint arrangements, as described below:

(a) Manufacturing activity: the parties have agreed to undertake the manufacturing activity through a joint arrangement (the manufacturing arrangement). The manufacturing arrangement is structured in a separate vehicle (entity M) whose legal form causes it to be considered in its own right (i.e. the assets and liabilities held in entity M are the assets and liabilities of entity M and not the assets and liabilities of the parties). In accordance with the framework agreement, the parties have committed themselves to purchasing the whole production of product P manufactured by the manufacturing arrangement in accordance with their ownership interests in entity M. The parties subsequently sell product P to another arrangement, jointly controlled by the two parties themselves, that has been established exclusively for the distribution of product P as described below. Neither the framework agreement nor the contractual arrangement between A and B dealing with the manufacturing activity specifies that the parties have rights to the assets, and obligations for the liabilities, relating to the manufacturing activity.

(b) Distribution activity: the parties have agreed to undertake the distribution activity through a joint arrangement (the distribution arrangement). The parties have structured the distribution arrangement in a separate vehicle (entity D) whose legal form causes it to be considered in its own right (i.e. the assets and liabilities held in entity D are the assets and liabilities of entity D and not the assets and liabilities of the parties). In accordance with the framework agreement, the distribution arrangement orders its requirements for product P from the parties according to the needs of the different markets where the distribution arrangement sells the product. Neither the framework agreement nor the contractual arrangement between A and B dealing with the distribution activity specifies that the parties have rights to the assets, and obligations for the liabilities, relating to the distribution activity.

IE16 In addition, the framework agreement establishes:

(a) that the manufacturing arrangement will produce product P to meet the requirements for product P that the distribution arrangement places on the parties;

(b) the commercial terms relating to the sale of product P by the manufacturing arrangement to the parties. The manufacturing arrangement will sell product P to the parties at a price agreed by A and B that covers all production costs incurred. Subsequently, the parties sell the product to the distribution arrangement at a price agreed by A and B.

(c) that any cash shortages that the manufacturing arrangement may incur will be financed by the parties in accordance with their ownership interests in entity M.

Analysis

IE17 The framework agreement sets up the terms under which parties A and B conduct the manufacturing and distribution of product P. These activities are undertaken through joint arrangements whose purpose is either the manufacturing or the distribution of product P.

IE18 The parties carry out the manufacturing arrangement through entity M whose legal form confers separation between the parties and the entity. In addition, neither the framework agreement nor the contractual arrangement dealing with the manufacturing activity specifies that the parties have rights to the assets, and obligations for the liabilities, relating to the manufacturing activity. However, when considering the following facts and circumstances the parties have concluded that the manufacturing arrangement is a joint operation:

(a) The parties have committed themselves to purchasing the whole production of product P manufactured by the manufacturing arrangement. Consequently, A and B have rights to substantially all the economic benefits of the assets of the manufacturing arrangement.

(b) The manufacturing arrangement manufactures product P to meet the quantity and quality needs of the parties so that they can fulfil the demand for product P of the distribution arrangement. The exclusive dependence of the manufacturing arrangement upon the parties for the generation of cash flows and the parties' commitments to provide funds when the manufacturing arrangement incurs any cash shortages indicate that the parties have an obligation for the liabilities of the manufacturing arrangement, because those liabilities will be settled through the parties' purchases of product P or by the parties' direct provision of funds.

IE19   The parties carry out the distribution activities through entity D, whose legal form confers separation between the parties and the entity. In addition, neither the framework agreement nor the contractual arrangement dealing with the distribution activity specifies that the parties have rights to the assets, and obligations for the liabilities, relating to the distribution activity.

IE20   There are no other facts and circumstances that indicate that the parties have rights to substantially all the economic benefits of the assets relating to the distribution arrangement or that the parties have an obligation for the liabilities relating to that arrangement. The distribution arrangement is a joint venture.

IE21   A and B each recognise in their financial statements their share of the assets (e.g. property, plant and equipment, cash) and their share of any liabilities resulting from the manufacturing arrangement (e.g. accounts payable to third parties) on the basis of their ownership interest in entity M. Each party also recognises its share of the expenses resulting from the manufacture of product P incurred by the manufacturing arrangement and its share of the revenues relating to the sales of product P to the distribution arrangement.

IE22   The parties recognise their rights to the net assets of the distribution arrangement as investments and account for them using the equity method.

Variation

IE23   Assume that the parties agree that the manufacturing arrangement described above is responsible not only for manufacturing product P, but also for its distribution to third-party customers.

IE24   The parties also agree to set up a distribution arrangement like the one described above to distribute product P exclusively to assist in widening the distribution of product P in additional specific markets.

IE25   The manufacturing arrangement also sells product P directly to the distribution arrangement. No fixed proportion of the production of the manufacturing arrangement is committed to be purchased by, or to be reserved to, the distribution arrangement.

Analysis

IE26   The variation has affected neither the legal form of the separate vehicle in which the manufacturing activity is conducted nor the contractual terms relating to the parties' rights to the assets, and obligations for the liabilities, relating to the manufacturing activity. However, it causes the manufacturing arrangement to be a self-financed arrangement because it is able to undertake trade on its own behalf, distributing product P to third-party customers and, consequently, assuming demand, inventory and credit risks. Even though the manufacturing arrangement might also sell product P to the distribution arrangement, in this scenario the manufacturing arrangement is not dependent on the parties to be able to carry out its activities on a continuous basis. In this case, the manufacturing arrangement is a joint venture.

IE27   The variation has no effect on the classification of the distribution arrangement as a joint venture.

IE28   The parties recognise their rights to the net assets of the manufacturing arrangement and their rights to the net assets of the distribution arrangement as investments and account for them using the equity method.

Example 4 – Bank operated jointly

IE29   Banks A and B (the parties) agreed to combine their corporate, investment banking, asset management and services activities by establishing a separate vehicle (bank C). Both parties expect the arrangement to benefit them in different ways. Bank A believes that the arrangement could enable it to achieve its strategic plans to increase its size, offering an opportunity to exploit its full potential for organic growth through an enlarged offering of products and services. Bank B expects the arrangement to reinforce its offering in financial savings and market products.

IE30 The main feature of bank C's legal form is that it causes the separate vehicle to be considered in its own right (i.e. the assets and liabilities held in the separate vehicle are the assets and liabilities of the separate vehicle and not the assets and liabilities of the parties). Banks A and B each have a 40 per cent ownership interest in bank C, with the remaining 20 per cent being listed and widely held. The shareholders' agreement between bank A and bank B establishes joint control of the activities of bank C.

IE31 In addition, bank A and bank B entered into an irrevocable agreement under which, even in the event of a dispute, both banks agree to provide the necessary funds in equal amount and, if required, jointly and severally, to ensure that bank C complies with the applicable legislation and banking regulations, and honours any commitments made to the banking authorities. This commitment represents the assumption by each party of 50 per cent of any funds needed to ensure that bank C complies with legislation and banking regulations.

Analysis

IE32 The joint arrangement is carried out through a separate vehicle whose legal form confers separation between the parties and the separate vehicle. The terms of the contractual arrangement do not specify that the parties have rights to the assets, or obligations for the liabilities, of bank C, but it establishes that the parties have rights to the net assets of bank C. The commitment by the parties to provide support if bank C is not able to comply with the applicable legislation and banking regulations is not by itself a determinant that the parties have an obligation for the liabilities of bank C. There are no other facts and circumstances that indicate that the parties have rights to substantially all the economic benefits of the assets of bank C and that the parties have an obligation for the liabilities of bank C. The joint arrangement is a joint venture.

IE33 Both banks A and B recognise their rights to the net assets of bank C as investments and account for them using the equity method.

Example 5 – Oil and gas exploration, development and production activities

IE34 Companies A and B (the parties) set up a separate vehicle (entity H) and a Joint Operating Agreement (JOA) to undertake oil and gas exploration, development and production activities in country O. The main feature of entity H's legal form is that it causes the separate vehicle to be considered in its own right (i.e. the assets and liabilities held in the separate vehicle are the assets and liabilities of the separate vehicle and not the assets and liabilities of the parties).

IE35 Country O has granted entity H permits for the oil and gas exploration, development and production activities to be undertaken in a specific assigned block of land (fields).

IE36 The shareholders' agreement and JOA agreed by the parties establish their rights and obligations relating to those activities. The main terms of those agreements are summarised below.

Shareholders' agreement

IE37 The board of entity H consists of a director from each party. Each party has a 50 per cent shareholding in entity H. The unanimous consent of the directors is required for any resolution to be passed.

Joint Operating Agreement (JOA)

IE38 The JOA establishes an Operating Committee. This Committee consists of one representative from each party. Each party has a 50 per cent participating interest in the Operating Committee.

IE39 The Operating Committee approves the budgets and work programmes relating to the activities, which also require the unanimous consent of the representatives of each party. One of the parties is appointed as operator and is responsible for managing and conducting the approved work programmes.

IE40   The JOA specifies that the rights and obligations arising from the exploration, development and production activities shall be shared among the parties in proportion to each party's shareholding in entity H. In particular, the JOA establishes that the parties share:

(a)   the rights and the obligations arising from the exploration and development permits granted to entity H (e.g. the permits, rehabilitation liabilities, any royalties and taxes payable);

(b)   the production obtained; and

(c)   all costs associated with all work programmes.

IE41   The costs incurred in relation to all the work programmes are covered by cash calls on the parties. If either party fails to satisfy its monetary obligations, the other is required to contribute to entity H the amount in default. The amount in default is regarded as a debt owed by the defaulting party to the other party.

Analysis

IE42   The parties carry out the joint arrangement through a separate vehicle whose legal form confers separation between the parties and the separate vehicle. The parties have been able to reverse the initial assessment of their rights and obligations arising from the legal form of the separate vehicle in which the arrangement is conducted. They have done this by agreeing terms in the JOA that entitle them to rights to the assets (e.g. exploration and development permits, production, and any other assets arising from the activities) and obligations for the liabilities (e.g. all costs and obligations arising from the work programmes) that are held in entity H. The joint arrangement is a joint operation.

IE43   Both company A and company B recognise in their financial statements their own share of the assets and of any liabilities resulting from the arrangement on the basis of their agreed participating interest. On that basis, each party also recognises its share of the revenue (from the sale of their share of the production) and its share of the expenses.

Example 6 – Liquefied natural gas arrangement

IE44   Company A owns an undeveloped gas field that contains substantial gas resources. Company A determines that the gas field will be economically viable only if the gas is sold to customers in overseas markets. To do so, a liquefied natural gas (LNG) facility must be built to liquefy the gas so that it can be transported by ship to the overseas markets.

IE45   Company A enters into a joint arrangement with company B in order to develop and operate the gas field and the LNG facility. Under that arrangement, companies A and B (the parties) agree to contribute the gas field and cash, respectively, to a new separate vehicle, entity C. In exchange for those contributions, the parties each take a 50 per cent ownership interest in entity C. The main feature of entity C's legal form is that it causes the separate vehicle to be considered in its own right (i.e. the assets and liabilities held in the separate vehicle are the assets and liabilities of the separate vehicle and not the assets and liabilities of the parties).

IE46   The contractual arrangement between the parties specifies that:

(a)   companies A and B must each appoint two members to the board of entity C. The board of directors must unanimously agree the strategy and investments made by entity C.

(b)   day-to-day management of the gas field and LNG facility, including development and construction activities, will be undertaken by the staff of company B in accordance with the directions jointly agreed by the parties. Entity C will reimburse B for the costs it incurs in managing the gas field and LNG facility.

(c)   entity C is liable for taxes and royalties on the production and sale of LNG as well as for other liabilities incurred in the ordinary course of business, such as accounts payable, site restoration and decommissioning liabilities.

(d)   companies A and B have equal shares in the profit from the activities carried out in the arrangement and, as such, are entitled to equal shares of any dividends distributed by entity C.

IE47   The contractual arrangement does not specify that either party has rights to the assets, or obligations for the liabilities, of entity C.

IE48   The board of entity C decides to enter into a financing arrangement with a syndicate of lenders to help fund the development of the gas field and construction of the LNG facility. The estimated total cost of the development and construction is CU1,000 million.[1]

IE49   The lending syndicate provides entity C with a CU700 million loan. The arrangement specifies that the syndicate has recourse to companies A and B only if entity C defaults on the loan arrangement during the development of the field and construction of the LNG facility. The lending syndicate agrees that it will not have recourse to companies A and B once the LNG facility is in production because it has assessed that the cash inflows that entity C should generate from LNG sales will be sufficient to meet the loan repayments. Although at this time the lenders have no recourse to companies A and B, the syndicate maintains protection against default by entity C by taking a lien on the LNG facility.

Analysis

IE50   The joint arrangement is carried out through a separate vehicle whose legal form confers separation between the parties and the separate vehicle. The terms of the contractual arrangement do not specify that the parties have rights to the assets, or obligations for the liabilities, of entity C, but they establish that the parties have rights to the net assets of entity C. The recourse nature of the financing arrangement during the development of the gas field and construction of the LNG facility (i.e. companies A and B providing separate guarantees during this phase) does not, by itself, impose on the parties an obligation for the liabilities of entity C (i.e. the loan is a liability of entity C). Companies A and B have separate liabilities, which are their guarantees to repay that loan if entity C defaults during the development and construction phase.

IE51   There are no other facts and circumstances that indicate that the parties have rights to substantially all the economic benefits of the assets of entity C and that the parties have an obligation for the liabilities of entity C. The joint arrangement is a joint venture.

IE52   The parties recognise their rights to the net assets of entity C as investments and account for them using the equity method.

Deleted IFRS 11 Text

Deleted IFRS 11 text is not part of AASB 11.

Paragraph C1
An entity shall apply this IFRS for annual periods beginning on or after 1 January 2013. Earlier application is permitted. If an entity applies this IFRS earlier, it shall disclose that fact and apply IFRS 10, IFRS 12 *Disclosure of Interests in Other Entities*, IAS 27 (as amended in 2011) and IAS 28 (as amended in 2011) at the same time.

Paragraph C15
This IFRS supersedes the following IFRSs:

(a)   IAS 31 *Interests in Joint Ventures*; and

(b)   SIC-13 *Jointly Controlled Entities – Non-Monetary Contributions by Venturers*.

---

1   In this example monetary amounts are denominated in 'currency units (CU)'.

AASB 12
Disclosure of Interests in Other Entities

(Issued August 2011)

Note from the Institute of Chartered Accountants Australia

This note, prepared by the technical editors, is not part of Accounting Standard AASB 12.

Historical development

29 August 2011: AASB 12 'Disclosure of Interests in Other Entities' is the Australian equivalent of IFRS 12 of the same name and was issued as part of the suite of standards revising accounting requirements for consolidation, joint ventures and off balance sheet arrangements.

This Standard applies to annual reporting periods beginning on or after 1 January 2013 and can be adopted early by for-profit entities, provided revised AASB 10, AASB 11, AASB 127 and AASB 128 are adopted at the same time.

10 September 2012: AASB 2012-7 'Amendments to Australian Accounting Standards arising from Reduced Disclosure Requirements' amends AASB 12 in relation to reduced disclosure requirements and applies to annual reporting periods beginning on or after 1 July 2013. **These amendments are not included in this compiled Standard.**

AASB 12 compared to IFRS 12

Additions

Paragraph	Description
Aus4.1	Which entities AASB 12 applies to (i.e. reporting entities and general purpose financial statements).
Aus4.2	The application date (i.e. annual reporting periods beginning on or after 1 January 2013).
Aus4.3	Permits early application by for-profit entities, but not by not-for-profit entities.
Aus4.4	Encourages for-profit entities to provide the information required by AASB 12 earlier than annual reporting periods beginning on or after 1 January 2013.
Aus4.5	Makes the requirement of AASB 12 subject to AASB 1031 'Materiality'.

Deletions

Paragraph	Description
C1	Effective date of IFRS 12.
C2	Encourages entities to provide information required by IFRS 12 earlier than annual reporting periods beginning on or after 1 January 2013.

Contents

Preface

Comparison with IFRS 12

**Introduction to IFRS 12
(available on the AASB website)**

**Accounting Standard
AASB 12 Disclosure of Interests in Other Entities**

	Paragraphs
Objective	1
Meeting the objective	2 – 4
Application	Aus4.1 – Aus4.5
Scope	5 – 6
Significant judgements and assumptions	7 – 9
Interests in subsidiaries	10 – 11
The interest that non-controlling interests have in the group's activities and cash flows	12
The nature and extent of significant restrictions	13
Nature of the risks associated with the entity's interests in consolidated structured entities	14 – 17
Consequences of changes in a parent's ownership interest in a subsidiary that do not result in a loss of control	18
Consequences of losing control of a subsidiary during the reporting period	19
Interests in joint arrangements and associates	20
Nature, extent and financial effects of an entity's interests in joint arrangements and associates	21 – 22
Risks associated with an entity's interests in joint ventures and associates	23
Interests in unconsolidated structured entities	24 – 25
Nature of interests	26 – 28
Nature of risks	29 – 31

Appendices:

A. Defined terms	
B. Application guidance	B1
Aggregation	B2 – B6
Interests in other entities	B7 – B9
Summarised financial information for subsidiaries, joint ventures and associates	B10 – B17
Commitments for joint ventures	B18 – B20
Interests in unconsolidated structured entities	
Structured entities	B21 – B24
Nature of risks from interests in unconsolidated structured entities	B25 – B26
C. Effective date and transition	
References to AASB 9	C3

Deleted IFRS 12 Text

Basis for Conclusions on IFRS 12
(available on the AASB website)

Australian Accounting Standard AASB 12 *Disclosure of Interests in Other Entities* is set out in paragraphs 1 – 31 and Appendices A – C. All the paragraphs have equal authority. Paragraphs in **bold type** state the main principles. Terms defined in Appendix A are in *italics* the first time they appear in the Standard. AASB 12 is to be read in the context of other Australian Accounting Standards, including AASB 1048 *Interpretation of Standards*, which identifies the Australian Accounting Interpretations. In the absence of explicit guidance, AASB 108 *Accounting Policies, Changes in Accounting Estimates and Errors* provides a basis for selecting and applying accounting policies.

Preface

Introduction

The Australian Accounting Standards Board (AASB) makes Australian Accounting Standards, including Interpretations, to be applied by:

(a)   entities required by the *Corporations Act 2001* to prepare financial reports;

(b)   governments in preparing financial statements for the whole of government and the General Government Sector (GGS); and

(c)   entities in the private or public for-profit or not-for-profit sectors that are reporting entities or that prepare general purpose financial statements.

AASB 1053 *Application of Tiers of Australian Accounting Standards* establishes a differential reporting framework consisting of two tiers of reporting requirements for preparing general purpose financial statements:

(a)   Tier 1: Australian Accounting Standards; and

(b)   Tier 2: Australian Accounting Standards – Reduced Disclosure Requirements.

Tier 1 requirements incorporate International Financial Reporting Standards (IFRSs), including Interpretations, issued by the International Accounting Standards Board (IASB), with the addition of paragraphs on the applicability of each Standard in the Australian environment.

Publicly accountable private sector for-profit entities are required to adopt Tier 1 requirements, and therefore are required to comply with IFRSs. Furthermore, other private sector for-profit entities complying with Tier 1 requirements will simultaneously comply with IFRSs. Many other entities complying with Tier 1 requirements will also simultaneously comply with IFRSs.

Tier 2 requirements comprise the recognition, measurement and presentation requirements of Tier 1 and substantially reduced disclosures corresponding to those requirements.

Australian Accounting Standards also include requirements that are specific to Australian entities. These requirements may be located in Australian Accounting Standards that incorporate IFRSs or in other Australian Accounting Standards. In most instances, these requirements are either restricted to the not-for-profit or public sectors or include additional disclosures that address domestic, regulatory or other issues. These requirements do not change the requirement for publicly accountable private sector for-profit entities to comply with IFRSs. In developing requirements for public sector entities, the AASB considers the requirements of International Public Sector Accounting Standards (IPSASs), as issued by the International Public Sector Accounting Standards Board (IPSASB) of the International Federation of Accountants.

Differences between this Standard and AASB 127 and AASB 131

Differences between this Standard and the superseded requirements under AASB 127 *Consolidated and Separate Financial Statements* and AASB 131 *Interests in Joint Ventures* are the same as the differences between IFRS 12 *Disclosure of Interests in Other Entities* and the superseded requirements under IAS 27 *Consolidated and Separate Financial Statements* and IAS 31 *Interests in Joint Ventures*. The main differences are summarised in the project summary and feedback statements on the IASB's website in relation to IFRS 10 *Consolidated Financial Statements*, IFRS 12, and IFRS 11 *Joint Arrangements*.

Implications for not-for-profit entities

Prior to the mandatory application date of this Standard, being 1 January 2013, the AASB will consider its suitability for not-for-profit entities. In doing so, the AASB will consider whether this Standard should be modified for application by not-for-profit entities in an Australian not-for-profit context having regard to its *Process for Modifying IFRSs for PBE/NFP*. In light of this, not-for-profit entities cannot adopt this Standard prior to the mandatory application date.

Reduced disclosure requirements

Disclosure requirements under Tier 2 will be determined through a separate due process with subsequent amendments being made to this Standard through an Amending Standard.

Comparison with IFRS 12

AASB 12 *Disclosure of Interests in Other Entities* incorporates IFRS 12 *Disclosure of Interests in Other Entities* issued by the International Accounting Standards Board (IASB). Paragraphs that have been added to this Standard (and do not appear in the text of IFRS 12) are identified with the prefix "Aus", followed by the number of the preceding IASB paragraph and decimal numbering.

Entities that comply with AASB 12 will simultaneously be in compliance with IFRS 12.

Accounting Standard AASB 12

The Australian Accounting Standards Board makes Accounting Standard AASB 12 *Disclosure of Interests in Other Entities* under section 334 of the *Corporations Act 2001*.

Kevin M. Stevenson
Dated 29 August 2011   Chair – AASB

Accounting Standard AASB 12

Disclosure of Interests in Other Entities

Objective

1   The objective of this Standard is to require an entity to disclose information that enables users of its financial statements to evaluate:

(a)   the nature of, and risks associated with, its *interests in other entities*; and

(b)   the effects of those interests on its financial position, financial performance and cash flows.

Meeting the objective

2   To meet the objective in paragraph 1, an entity shall disclose:

(a)   the significant judgements and assumptions it has made in determining the nature of its interest in another entity or arrangement, and in determining the type of joint arrangement in which it has an interest (paragraphs 7–9); and

(b)   information about its interests in:

(i)   subsidiaries (paragraphs 10–19);

(ii)   joint arrangements and associates (paragraphs 20–23); and

(iii)   *structured entities* that are not controlled by the entity (unconsolidated structured entities) (paragraphs 24–31).

3   If the disclosures required by this Standard, together with disclosures required by other Standards, do not meet the objective in paragraph 1, an entity shall disclose whatever additional information is necessary to meet that objective.

4   An entity shall consider the level of detail necessary to satisfy the disclosure objective and how much emphasis to place on each of the requirements in this Standard. It shall aggregate or disaggregate disclosures so that useful information is not obscured by either the inclusion of a large amount of insignificant detail or the aggregation of items that have different characteristics (see paragraphs B2–B6).

Application

Aus4.1   **This Standard applies to:**

     (a)   **each entity that is required to prepare financial reports in accordance with Part 2M.3 of the Corporations Act and that is a reporting entity;**

     (b)   **general purpose financial statements of each other reporting entity; and**

     (c)   **financial statements that are, or are held out to be, general purpose financial statements.**

Aus4.2   **This Standard applies to annual reporting periods beginning on or after 1 January 2013.**

Aus4.3   **This Standard may be applied by for-profit entities, but not by not-for-profit entities, to annual reporting periods beginning on or after 1 January 2005 but before 1 January 2013. If a for-profit entity applies this Standard to such an annual reporting period, it shall disclose that fact and apply AASB 10** *Consolidated Financial Statements*, **AASB 11** *Joint Arrangements*, **AASB 127** *Separate Financial Statements* **(as amended in 2011) and AASB 128** *Investments in Associates and Joint Ventures* **(as amended in 2011), at the same time.**

Aus4.4   **A for-profit entity is encouraged to provide information required by this Standard earlier than annual periods beginning on or after 1 January 2013. Providing some of the disclosures required by this Standard does not compel the entity to comply with all the requirements of this Standard or to apply AASB 10, AASB 11, AASB 127 (as amended in 2011) and AASB 128 (as amended in 2011) early.**

Aus4.5   **The requirements specified in this Standard apply to the financial statements where information resulting from their application is material in accordance with AASB 1031** *Materiality*.

Scope

5   This Standard shall be applied by an entity that has an interest in any of the following:

     (a)   subsidiaries

     (b)   joint arrangements (i.e. joint operations or joint ventures)

     (c)   associates

     (d)   unconsolidated structured entities.

6   This Standard does not apply to:

     (a)   post-employment benefit plans or other long-term employee benefit plans to which AASB 119 *Employee Benefits* applies.

     (b)   an entity's separate financial statements to which AASB 127 *Separate Financial Statements* applies. However, if an entity has interests in unconsolidated structured entities and prepares separate financial statements as its only financial statements, it shall apply the requirements in paragraphs 24–31 when preparing those separate financial statements.

     (c)   an interest held by an entity that participates in, but does not have joint control of, a joint arrangement unless that interest results in significant influence over the arrangement or is an interest in a structured entity.

    (d)   an interest in another entity that is accounted for in accordance with AASB 9 *Financial Instruments*. However, an entity shall apply this Standard:

        (i)   when that interest is an interest in an associate or a joint venture that, in accordance with AASB 128 *Investments in Associates and Joint Ventures*, is measured at fair value through profit or loss; or

        (ii)   when that interest is an interest in an unconsolidated structured entity.

Significant judgements and assumptions

7   **An entity shall disclose information about significant judgements and assumptions it has made (and changes to those judgements and assumptions) in determining:**

    (a)   that it has control of another entity, i.e. an investee as described in paragraphs 5 and 6 of AASB 10 *Consolidated Financial Statements*;

    (b)   that it has joint control of an arrangement or significant influence over another entity; and

    (c)   the type of joint arrangement (i.e. joint operation or joint venture) when the arrangement has been structured through a separate vehicle.

8   The significant judgements and assumptions disclosed in accordance with paragraph 7 include those made by the entity when changes in facts and circumstances are such that the conclusion about whether it has control, joint control or significant influence changes during the reporting period.

9   To comply with paragraph 7, an entity shall disclose, for example, significant judgements and assumptions made in determining that:

    (a)   it does not control another entity even though it holds more than half of the voting rights of the other entity.

    (b)   it controls another entity even though it holds less than half of the voting rights of the other entity.

    (c)   it is an agent or a principal (see paragraphs 58–72 of AASB 10).

    (d)   it does not have significant influence even though it holds 20 per cent or more of the voting rights of another entity.

    (e)   it has significant influence even though it holds less than 20 per cent of the voting rights of another entity.

Interests in subsidiaries

10   **An entity shall disclose information that enables users of its consolidated financial statements**

    (a)   to understand:

        (i)   the composition of the group; and

        (ii)   the interest that non-controlling interests have in the group's activities and cash flows (paragraph 12); and

    (b)   to evaluate:

        (i)   the nature and extent of significant restrictions on its ability to access or use assets, and settle liabilities, of the group (paragraph 13);

        (ii)   the nature of, and changes in, the risks associated with its interests in consolidated structured entities (paragraphs 14–17);

        (iii)   the consequences of changes in its ownership interest in a subsidiary that do not result in a loss of control (paragraph 18); and

        (iv)   the consequences of losing control of a subsidiary during the reporting period (paragraph 19).

11   When the financial statements of a subsidiary used in the preparation of consolidated financial statements are as of a date or for a period that is different from that of the

consolidated financial statements (see paragraphs B92 and B93 of AASB 10), an entity shall disclose:

(a)   the date of the end of the reporting period of the financial statements of that subsidiary; and

(b)   the reason for using a different date or period.

The interest that non-controlling interests have in the group's activities and cash flows

12   An entity shall disclose for each of its subsidiaries that have non-controlling interests that are material to the reporting entity:

(a)   the name of the subsidiary.

(b)   the principal place of business (and country of incorporation if different from the principal place of business) of the subsidiary.

(c)   the proportion of ownership interests held by non-controlling interests.

(d)   the proportion of voting rights held by non-controlling interests, if different from the proportion of ownership interests held.

(e)   the profit or loss allocated to non-controlling interests of the subsidiary during the reporting period.

(f)   accumulated non-controlling interests of the subsidiary at the end of the reporting period.

(g)   summarised financial information about the subsidiary (see paragraph B10).

The nature and extent of significant restrictions

13   An entity shall disclose:

(a)   significant restrictions (e.g. statutory, contractual and regulatory restrictions) on its ability to access or use the assets and settle the liabilities of the group, such as:

(i)   those that restrict the ability of a parent or its subsidiaries to transfer cash or other assets to (or from) other entities within the group.

(ii)   guarantees or other requirements that may restrict dividends and other capital distributions being paid, or loans and advances being made or repaid, to (or from) other entities within the group.

(b)   the nature and extent to which protective rights of non-controlling interests can significantly restrict the entity's ability to access or use the assets and settle the liabilities of the group (such as when a parent is obliged to settle liabilities of a subsidiary before settling its own liabilities, or approval of non-controlling interests is required either to access the assets or to settle the liabilities of a subsidiary).

(c)   the carrying amounts in the consolidated financial statements of the assets and liabilities to which those restrictions apply.

Nature of the risks associated with an entity's interests in consolidated structured entities

14   An entity shall disclose the terms of any contractual arrangements that could require the parent or its subsidiaries to provide financial support to a consolidated structured entity, including events or circumstances that could expose the reporting entity to a loss (e.g. liquidity arrangements or credit rating triggers associated with obligations to purchase assets of the structured entity or provide financial support).

15   If during the reporting period a parent or any of its subsidiaries has, without having a contractual obligation to do so, provided financial or other support to a consolidated structured entity (e.g. purchasing assets of or instruments issued by the structured entity), the entity shall disclose:

(a)   the type and amount of support provided, including situations in which the parent or its subsidiaries assisted the structured entity in obtaining financial support; and

(b)   the reasons for providing the support.

16   If during the reporting period a parent or any of its subsidiaries has, without having a contractual obligation to do so, provided financial or other support to a previously unconsolidated structured entity and that provision of support resulted in the entity controlling the structured entity, the entity shall disclose an explanation of the relevant factors in reaching that decision.

17   An entity shall disclose any current intentions to provide financial or other support to a consolidated structured entity, including intentions to assist the structured entity in obtaining financial support.

Consequences of changes in a parent's ownership interest in a subsidiary that do not result in a loss of control

18   An entity shall present a schedule that shows the effects on the equity attributable to owners of the parent of any changes in its ownership interest in a subsidiary that do not result in a loss of control.

Consequences of losing control of a subsidiary during the reporting period

19   An entity shall disclose the gain or loss, if any, calculated in accordance with paragraph 25 of AASB 10, and:

     (a)   the portion of that gain or loss attributable to measuring any investment retained in the former subsidiary at its fair value at the date when control is lost; and

     (b)   the line item(s) in profit or loss in which the gain or loss is recognised (if not presented separately).

Interests in joint arrangements and associates

20   **An entity shall disclose information that enables users of its financial statements to evaluate:**

     (a)   **the nature, extent and financial effects of its interests in joint arrangements and associates, including the nature and effects of its contractual relationship with the other investors with joint control of, or significant influence over, joint arrangements and associates (paragraphs 21 and 22); and**

     (b)   **the nature of, and changes in, the risks associated with its interests in joint ventures and associates (paragraph 23).**

Nature, extent and financial effects of an entity's interests in joint arrangements and associates

21   An entity shall disclose:

     (a)   for each joint arrangement and associate that is material to the reporting entity:

         (i)   the name of the joint arrangement or associate.

         (ii)   the nature of the entity's relationship with the joint arrangement or associate (by, for example, describing the nature of the activities of the joint arrangement or associate and whether they are strategic to the entity's activities).

         (iii)   the principal place of business (and country of incorporation, if applicable and different from the principal place of business) of the joint arrangement or associate.

         (iv)   the proportion of ownership interest or participating share held by the entity and, if different, the proportion of voting rights held (if applicable).

     (b)   for each joint venture and associate that is material to the reporting entity:

         (i)   whether the investment in the joint venture or associate is measured using the equity method or at fair value.

         (ii)   summarised financial information about the joint venture or associate as specified in paragraphs B12 and B13.

        (iii)   if the joint venture or associate is accounted for using the equity method, the fair value of its investment in the joint venture or associate, if there is a quoted market price for the investment.

    (c)   financial information as specified in paragraph B16 about the entity's investments in joint ventures and associates that are not individually material:

        (i)   in aggregate for all individually immaterial joint ventures and, separately,

        (ii)   in aggregate for all individually immaterial associates.

22   An entity shall also disclose:

    (a)   the nature and extent of any significant restrictions (e.g. resulting from borrowing arrangements, regulatory requirements or contractual arrangements between investors with joint control of or significant influence over a joint venture or an associate) on the ability of joint ventures or associates to transfer funds to the entity in the form of cash dividends, or to repay loans or advances made by the entity.

    (b)   when the financial statements of a joint venture or associate used in applying the equity method are as of a date or for a period that is different from that of the entity:

        (i)   the date of the end of the reporting period of the financial statements of that joint venture or associate; and

        (ii)   the reason for using a different date or period.

    (c)   the unrecognised share of losses of a joint venture or associate, both for the reporting period and cumulatively, if the entity has stopped recognising its share of losses of the joint venture or associate when applying the equity method.

Risks associated with an entity's interests in joint ventures and associates

23   An entity shall disclose:

    (a)   commitments that it has relating to its joint ventures separately from the amount of other commitments as specified in paragraphs B18–B20.

    (b)   in accordance with AASB 137 *Provisions, Contingent Liabilities and Contingent Assets*, unless the probability of loss is remote, contingent liabilities incurred relating to its interests in joint ventures or associates (including its share of contingent liabilities incurred jointly with other investors with joint control of, or significant influence over, the joint ventures or associates), separately from the amount of other contingent liabilities.

Interests in unconsolidated structured entities

24   **An entity shall disclose information that enables users of its financial statements:**

    (a)   **to understand the nature and extent of its interests in unconsolidated structured entities (paragraphs 26–28); and**

    (b)   **to evaluate the nature of, and changes in, the risks associated with its interests in unconsolidated structured entities (paragraphs 29–31).**

25   The information required by paragraph 24(b) includes information about an entity's exposure to risk from involvement that it had with unconsolidated structured entities in previous periods (e.g. sponsoring the structured entity), even if the entity no longer has any contractual involvement with the structured entity at the reporting date.

Nature of interests

26   An entity shall disclose qualitative and quantitative information about its interests in unconsolidated structured entities, including, but not limited to, the nature, purpose, size and activities of the structured entity and how the structured entity is financed.

27   If an entity has sponsored an unconsolidated structured entity for which it does not provide information required by paragraph 29 (e.g. because it does not have an interest in the entity at the reporting date), the entity shall disclose:

    (a)   how it has determined which structured entities it has sponsored;

 (b) *income from those structured entities* during the reporting period, including a description of the types of income presented; and

 (c) the carrying amount (at the time of transfer) of all assets transferred to those structured entities during the reporting period.

28 An entity shall present the information in paragraph 27(b) and (c) in tabular format, unless another format is more appropriate, and classify its sponsoring activities into relevant categories (see paragraphs B2 B6).

Nature of risks

29 An entity shall disclose in tabular format, unless another format is more appropriate, a summary of:

 (a) the carrying amounts of the assets and liabilities recognised in its financial statements relating to its interests in unconsolidated structured entities.

 (b) the line items in the statement of financial position in which those assets and liabilities are recognised.

 (c) the amount that best represents the entity's maximum exposure to loss from its interests in unconsolidated structured entities, including how the maximum exposure to loss is determined. If an entity cannot quantify its maximum exposure to loss from its interests in unconsolidated structured entities it shall disclose that fact and the reasons.

 (d) a comparison of the carrying amounts of the assets and liabilities of the entity that relate to its interests in unconsolidated structured entities and the entity's maximum exposure to loss from those entities.

30 If during the reporting period an entity has, without having a contractual obligation to do so, provided financial or other support to an unconsolidated structured entity in which it previously had or currently has an interest (for example, purchasing assets of or instruments issued by the structured entity), the entity shall disclose:

 (a) the type and amount of support provided, including situations in which the entity assisted the structured entity in obtaining financial support; and

 (b) the reasons for providing the support.

31 An entity shall disclose any current intentions to provide financial or other support to an unconsolidated structured entity, including intentions to assist the structured entity in obtaining financial support.

Appendix A
Defined Terms

This appendix is an integral part of the Standard.

income from a structured entity	For the purpose of this Standard, income from a **structured entity** includes, but is not limited to, recurring and non-recurring fees, interest, dividends, gains or losses on the remeasurement or derecognition of interests in structured entities and gains or losses from the transfer of assets and liabilities to the structured entity.
interest in another entity	For the purpose of this Standard, an interest in another entity refers to contractual and non-contractual involvement that exposes an entity to variability of returns from the performance of the other entity. An interest in another entity can be evidenced by, but is not limited to, the holding of equity or debt instruments as well as other forms of involvement such as the provision of funding, liquidity support, credit enhancement and guarantees. It includes the means by which an entity has control or joint control of, or significant influence over, another entity. An entity does not necessarily have an interest in another entity solely because of a typical customer supplier relationship.
	Paragraphs B7–B9 provide further information about interests in other entities.
	Paragraphs B55–B57 of AASB 10 explain variability of returns.
structured entity	An entity that has been designed so that voting or similar rights are not the dominant factor in deciding who controls the entity, such as when any voting rights relate to administrative tasks only and the relevant activities are directed by means of contractual arrangements.
	Paragraphs B22–B24 provide further information about structured entities.

The following terms are defined in AASB 127 (August 2011), AASB 128 (August 2011), AASB 10 and AASB 11 *Joint Arrangements* and are used in this Standard with the meanings specified in those Standards:

- associate
- consolidated financial statements
- control of an entity
- equity method
- group
- joint arrangement
- joint control
- joint operation
- joint venture
- non-controlling interest
- parent
- protective rights
- relevant activities
- separate financial statements
- separate vehicle
- significant influence
- subsidiary.

Appendix B
Application Guidance

This appendix is an integral part of the Standard. It describes the application of paragraphs 1–31 and has the same authority as the other parts of the Standard.

B1 The examples in this appendix portray hypothetical situations. Although some aspects of the examples may be present in actual fact patterns, all relevant facts and circumstances of a particular fact pattern would need to be evaluated when applying AASB 12.

Aggregation (paragraph 4)

B2 An entity shall decide, in the light of its circumstances, how much detail it provides to satisfy the information needs of users, how much emphasis it places on different aspects of the requirements and how it aggregates the information. It is necessary to strike a balance between burdening financial statements with excessive detail that may not assist users of financial statements and obscuring information as a result of too much aggregation.

B3 An entity may aggregate the disclosures required by this Standard for interests in similar entities if aggregation is consistent with the disclosure objective and the requirement in paragraph B4, and does not obscure the information provided. An entity shall disclose how it has aggregated its interests in similar entities.

B4 An entity shall present information separately for interests in:

(a) subsidiaries;

(b) joint ventures;

(c) joint operations;

(d) associates; and

(e) unconsolidated structured entities.

B5 In determining whether to aggregate information, an entity shall consider quantitative and qualitative information about the different risk and return characteristics of each entity it is considering for aggregation and the significance of each such entity to the reporting entity. The entity shall present the disclosures in a manner that clearly explains to users of financial statements the nature and extent of its interests in those other entities.

B6 Examples of aggregation levels within the classes of entities set out in paragraph B4 that might be appropriate are:

(a) nature of activities (e.g. a research and development entity, a revolving credit card securitisation entity).

(b) industry classification.

(c) geography (e.g. country or region).

Interests in other entities

B7 An interest in another entity refers to contractual and non-contractual involvement that exposes the reporting entity to variability of returns from the performance of the other entity. Consideration of the purpose and design of the other entity may help the reporting entity when assessing whether it has an interest in that entity and, therefore, whether it is required to provide the disclosures in this Standard. That assessment shall include consideration of the risks that the other entity was designed to create and the risks the other entity was designed to pass on to the reporting entity and other parties.

B8 A reporting entity is typically exposed to variability of returns from the performance of another entity by holding instruments (such as equity or debt instruments issued by the other entity) or having another involvement that absorbs variability. For example, assume a structured entity holds a loan portfolio. The structured entity obtains a credit default swap from another entity (the reporting entity) to protect itself from the default of interest and principal payments on the loans. The reporting entity has involvement that exposes it to variability of returns from the performance of the structured entity because the credit default swap absorbs variability of returns of the structured entity.

B9   Some instruments are designed to transfer risk from a reporting entity to another entity. Such instruments create variability of returns for the other entity but do not typically expose the reporting entity to variability of returns from the performance of the other entity. For example, assume a structured entity is established to provide investment opportunities for investors who wish to have exposure to entity Z's credit risk (entity Z is unrelated to any party involved in the arrangement). The structured entity obtains funding by issuing to those investors notes that are linked to entity Z's credit risk (credit-linked notes) and uses the proceeds to invest in a portfolio of risk-free financial assets. The structured entity obtains exposure to entity Z's credit risk by entering into a credit default swap (CDS) with a swap counterparty. The CDS passes entity Z's credit risk to the structured entity in return for a fee paid by the swap counterparty. The investors in the structured entity receive a higher return that reflects both the structured entity's return from its asset portfolio and the CDS fee. The swap counterparty does not have involvement with the structured entity that exposes it to variability of returns from the performance of the structured entity because the CDS transfers variability to the structured entity, rather than absorbing variability of returns of the structured entity.

Summarised financial information for subsidiaries, joint ventures and associates (paragraphs 12 and 21)

B10   For each subsidiary that has non-controlling interests that are material to the reporting entity, an entity shall disclose:

(a)   dividends paid to non-controlling interests.

(b)   summarised financial information about the assets, liabilities, profit or loss and cash flows of the subsidiary that enables users to understand the interest that non-controlling interests have in the group's activities and cash flows. That information might include but is not limited to, for example, current assets, non-current assets, current liabilities, non-current liabilities, revenue, profit or loss and total comprehensive income.

B11   The summarised financial information required by paragraph B10(b) shall be the amounts before inter-company eliminations.

B12   For each joint venture and associate that is material to the reporting entity, an entity shall disclose:

(a)   dividends received from the joint venture or associate.

(b)   summarised financial information for the joint venture or associate (see paragraphs B14 and B15) including, but not necessarily limited to:

(i)   current assets.

(ii)   non-current assets.

(iii)   current liabilities.

(iv)   non-current liabilities.

(v)   revenue.

(vi)   profit or loss from continuing operations.

(vii)   post-tax profit or loss from discontinued operations.

(viii) other comprehensive income.

(ix)   total comprehensive income.

B13   In addition to the summarised financial information required by paragraph B12, an entity shall disclose for each joint venture that is material to the reporting entity the amount of:

(a)   cash and cash equivalents included in paragraph B12(b)(i).

(b)   current financial liabilities (excluding trade and other payables and provisions) included in paragraph B12(b)(iii).

(c)   non-current financial liabilities (excluding trade and other payables and provisions) included in paragraph B12(b)(iv).

(d)   depreciation and amortisation.

(e)   interest income.

(f)   interest expense.

(g)   income tax expense or income.

B14   The summarised financial information presented in accordance with paragraphs B12 and B13 shall be the amounts included in the Australian-Accounting-Standards financial statements of the joint venture or associate (and not the entity's share of those amounts). If the entity accounts for its interest in the joint venture or associate using the equity method:

     (a)   the amounts included in the Australian-Accounting-Standards financial statements of the joint venture or associate shall be adjusted to reflect adjustments made by the entity when using the equity method, such as fair value adjustments made at the time of acquisition and adjustments for differences in accounting policies.

     (b)   the entity shall provide a reconciliation of the summarised financial information presented to the carrying amount of its interest in the joint venture or associate.

B15   An entity may present the summarised financial information required by paragraphs B12 and B13 on the basis of the joint venture's or associate's financial statements if:

     (a)   the entity measures its interest in the joint venture or associate at fair value in accordance with AASB 128 (as amended in 2011); and

     (b)   the joint venture or associate does not prepare Australian-Accounting-Standards financial statements and preparation on that basis would be impracticable or cause undue cost.

In that case, the entity shall disclose the basis on which the summarised financial information has been prepared.

B16   An entity shall disclose, in aggregate, the carrying amount of its interests in all individually immaterial joint ventures or associates that are accounted for using the equity method. An entity shall also disclose separately the aggregate amount of its share of those joint ventures' or associates':

     (a)   profit or loss from continuing operations.

     (b)   post-tax profit or loss from discontinued operations.

     (c)   other comprehensive income.

     (d)   total comprehensive income.

An entity provides the disclosures separately for joint ventures and associates.

B17   When an entity's interest in a subsidiary, a joint venture or an associate (or a portion of its interest in a joint venture or an associate) is classified as held for sale in accordance with AASB 5 *Non-current Assets Held for Sale and Discontinued Operations*, the entity is not required to disclose summarised financial information for that subsidiary, joint venture or associate in accordance with paragraphs B10–B16.

Commitments for joint ventures (paragraph 23(a))

B18   An entity shall disclose total commitments it has made but not recognised at the reporting date (including its share of commitments made jointly with other investors with joint control of a joint venture) relating to its interests in joint ventures. Commitments are those that may give rise to a future outflow of cash or other resources.

B19   Unrecognised commitments that may give rise to a future outflow of cash or other resources include:

     (a)   unrecognised commitments to contribute funding or resources as a result of, for example:

         (i)   the constitution or acquisition agreements of a joint venture (that, for example, require an entity to contribute funds over a specific period).

         (ii)   capital-intensive projects undertaken by a joint venture.

       (iii)   unconditional purchase obligations, comprising procurement of equipment, inventory or services that an entity is committed to purchasing from, or on behalf of, a joint venture.

       (iv)   unrecognised commitments to provide loans or other financial support to a joint venture.

       (v)   unrecognised commitments to contribute resources to a joint venture, such as assets or services.

       (vi)   other non-cancellable unrecognised commitments relating to a joint venture.

    (b)   unrecognised commitments to acquire another party's ownership interest (or a portion of that ownership interest) in a joint venture if a particular event occurs or does not occur in the future.

B20   The requirements and examples in paragraphs B18 and B19 illustrate some of the types of disclosure required by paragraph 18 of AASB 124 *Related Party Disclosures*.

Interests in unconsolidated structured entities (paragraphs 24–31)

Structured entities

B21   A structured entity is an entity that has been designed so that voting or similar rights are not the dominant factor in deciding who controls the entity, such as when any voting rights relate to administrative tasks only and the relevant activities are directed by means of contractual arrangements.

B22   A structured entity often has some or all of the following features or attributes:

    (a)   restricted activities.

    (b)   a narrow and well-defined objective, such as to effect a tax-efficient lease, carry out research and development activities, provide a source of capital or funding to an entity or provide investment opportunities for investors by passing on risks and rewards associated with the assets of the structured entity to investors.

    (c)   insufficient equity to permit the structured entity to finance its activities without subordinated financial support.

    (d)   financing in the form of multiple contractually linked instruments to investors that create concentrations of credit or other risks (tranches).

B23   Examples of entities that are regarded as structured entities include, but are not limited to:

    (a)   securitisation vehicles.

    (b)   asset-backed financings.

    (c)   some investment funds.

B24   An entity that is controlled by voting rights is not a structured entity simply because, for example, it receives funding from third parties following a restructuring.

Nature of risks from interests in unconsolidated structured entities (paragraphs 29–31)

B25   In addition to the information required by paragraphs 29–31, an entity shall disclose additional information that is necessary to meet the disclosure objective in paragraph 24(b).

B26   Examples of additional information that, depending on the circumstances, might be relevant to an assessment of the risks to which an entity is exposed when it has an interest in an unconsolidated structured entity are:

    (a)   the terms of an arrangement that could require the entity to provide financial support to an unconsolidated structured entity (e.g. liquidity arrangements or credit rating triggers associated with obligations to purchase assets of the structured entity or provide financial support), including:

(i) a description of events or circumstances that could expose the reporting entity to a loss.

(ii) whether there are any terms that would limit the obligation.

(iii) whether there are any other parties that provide financial support and, if so, how the reporting entity's obligation ranks with those of other parties.

(b) losses incurred by the entity during the reporting period relating to its interests in unconsolidated structured entities.

(c) the types of income the entity received during the reporting period from its interests in unconsolidated structured entities.

(d) whether the entity is required to absorb losses of an unconsolidated structured entity before other parties, the maximum limit of such losses for the entity, and (if relevant) the ranking and amounts of potential losses borne by parties whose interests rank lower than the entity's interest in the unconsolidated structured entity.

(e) information about any liquidity arrangements, guarantees or other commitments with third parties that may affect the fair value or risk of the entity's interests in unconsolidated structured entities.

(f) any difficulties an unconsolidated structured entity has experienced in financing its activities during the reporting period.

(g) in relation to the funding of an unconsolidated structured entity, the forms of funding (e.g. commercial paper or medium-term notes) and their weighted-average life. That information might include maturity analyses of the assets and funding of an unconsolidated structured entity if the structured entity has longer-term assets funded by shorter-term funding.

Appendix C
Effective Date and Transition

This appendix is an integral part of the Standard and has the same authority as the other parts of the Standard.

Effective date and transition

C1 [Deleted by the AASB – see paragraphs Aus4.2 and Aus4.3]

C2 [Deleted by the AASB – see paragraph Aus4.4]

References to AASB 9

C3 If an entity applies this IFRS but does not yet apply AASB 9, any reference to AASB 9 shall be read as a reference to AASB 139 *Financial Instruments: Recognition and Measurement*.

Deleted IFRS 12 Text

Deleted IFRS 12 text is not part of AASB 12.

Paragraph C1
An entity shall apply this IFRS for annual periods beginning on or after 1 January 2013. Earlier application is permitted.

Paragraph C2
An entity is encouraged to provide information required by this IFRS earlier than annual periods beginning on or after 1 January 2013. Providing some of the disclosures required by this IFRS does not compel the entity to comply with all the requirements of this IFRS or to apply IFRS 10, IFRS 11, IAS 27 (as amended in 2011) and IAS 28 (as amended in 2011) early.

AASB 13
Fair Value Measurement

(Issued September 2011)

Note from the Institute of Chartered Accountants Australia

This note, prepared by the technical editors, is not part of Accounting Standard AASB 13.

Historical development

2 September 2011: AASB 13 'Fair Value Measurement' is the Australian equivalent of IFRS 13 of the same name, and represents the completion of the IASB project to align the IFRS and US GAAP fair value requirements (with some minor exceptions). AASB 13 specifies how 'fair value' should be used when its use is required or permitted by IFRS as a measurement technique.

This Standard applies to annual reporting periods beginning on or after 1 January 2013 and can be adopted early.

21 March 2012: AASB 2012-1 'Amendments to Australian Accounting Standards – Fair Value Measurement – Reduced Disclosure Requirements' amends AASB 13 to establish and amend reduced disclosure requirements. **These amendments are not included in this compiled Standard.**

AASB 13 compared to IFRS 13

Additions

Paragraph	Description
Aus4.1	Which entities AASB 13 applies to (i.e. reporting entities and general purpose financial statements).
Aus4.2	The application date (i.e. annual reporting periods beginning on or after 1 January 2013).
Aus4.3	Permits early application.
Aus4.4	Makes the requirement of AASB 13 subject to AASB 1031 'Materiality'.

Deletions

Paragraph	Description
7(b)	Exempts retirement benefit plan investments measured at fair value in accordance with IAS 26 from presenting the disclosures required by IAS 13.
C1	Effective date of IFRS 13.

Contents

Preface

Comparison with IFRS 13

Introduction to IFRS 13
(available on the AASB website)

Accounting Standard
AASB 13 Fair Value Measurement

	Paragraphs
Objective	1 – 4
Application	Aus4.1 – Aus4.4
Scope	5 – 8
Measurement	
Definition of fair value	9 – 10
The asset or liability	11 – 14
The transaction	15 – 21
Market participants	22 – 23
The price	24 – 26
Application to non-financial assets	
Highest and best use for non-financial assets	27 – 30
Valuation premise for non-financial assets	31 – 33
Application to liabilities and an entity's own equity instruments	
General principles	34 – 36
Liabilities and equity instruments held by other parties as assets	37 – 39
Liabilities and equity instruments not held by other parties as assets	40 – 41
Non-performance risk	42 – 44
Restriction preventing the transfer of a liability or an entity's own equity instrument	45 – 46
Financial liability with a demand feature	47
Application to financial assets and financial liabilities with offsetting positions in market risks or counterparty credit risk	48 – 52
Exposure to market risks	53 – 55
Exposure to the credit risk of a particular counterparty	56
Fair value at initial recognition	57 – 60
Valuation techniques	61 – 66
Inputs to valuation techniques	
General principles	67 – 69
Inputs based on bid and ask prices	70 – 71
Fair value hierarchy	72 – 75
Level 1 inputs	76 – 80
Level 2 inputs	81 – 85
Level 3 inputs	86 – 90
Disclosure	91 – 99

Appendices:

A. Defined Terms

B. Application Guidance

C. Effective Date and Transition

Deleted IFRS 13 Text

Illustrative Examples
(available on the AASB website)

Basis for Conclusions on IFRS 13
(available on the AASB website)

> Australian Accounting Standard AASB 13 *Fair Value Measurement* is set out in paragraphs 1 – 99 and Appendices A – C. All the paragraphs have equal authority. Paragraphs in **bold type** state the main principles. Terms defined in Appendix A are in *italics* the first time they appear in the Standard. AASB 13 is to be read in the context of other Australian Accounting Standards, including AASB 1048 *Interpretation of Standards*, which identifies the Australian Accounting Interpretations. In the absence of explicit guidance, AASB 108 *Accounting Policies, Changes in Accounting Estimates and Errors* provides a basis for selecting and applying accounting policies.

Preface

Introduction

The Australian Accounting Standards Board (AASB) makes Australian Accounting Standards, including Interpretations, to be applied by:

(a)   entities required by the *Corporations Act 2001* to prepare financial reports;

(b)   governments in preparing financial statements for the whole of government and the General Government Sector (GGS); and

(c)   entities in the private or public for-profit or not-for-profit sectors that are reporting entities or that prepare general purpose financial statements.

AASB 1053 *Application of Tiers of Australian Accounting Standards* establishes a differential reporting framework consisting of two tiers of reporting requirements for preparing general purpose financial statements:

(a)   Tier 1: Australian Accounting Standards; and

(b)   Tier 2: Australian Accounting Standards – Reduced Disclosure Requirements.

Tier 1 requirements incorporate International Financial Reporting Standards (IFRSs), including Interpretations, issued by the International Accounting Standards Board (IASB), with the addition of paragraphs on the applicability of each Standard in the Australian environment.

Publicly accountable for-profit private sector entities are required to adopt Tier 1 requirements, and therefore are required to comply with IFRSs. Furthermore, other for-profit private sector entities complying with Tier 1 requirements will simultaneously comply with IFRSs. Some other entities complying with Tier 1 requirements will also simultaneously comply with IFRSs.

Tier 2 requirements comprise the recognition, measurement and presentation requirements of Tier 1 but substantially reduced disclosure requirements in comparison with Tier 1.

Australian Accounting Standards also include requirements that are specific to Australian entities. These requirements may be located in Australian Accounting Standards that incorporate IFRSs or in other Australian Accounting Standards. In most instances, these requirements are either restricted to the not-for-profit or public sectors or include additional disclosures that address domestic, regulatory or other issues. These requirements do not prevent publicly accountable for-profit private sector entities from complying with IFRSs. In developing requirements for public sector entities, the AASB considers the requirements of International Public Sector Accounting Standards (IPSASs), as issued by the International Public Sector Accounting Standards Board (IPSASB) of the International Federation of Accountants.

Reduced disclosure requirements

Disclosure requirements under Tier 2 will be determined through a separate due process with amendments being made subsequently to this Standard as required.

Comparison with IFRS 13

AASB 13 *Fair Value Measurement* incorporates IFRS 13 *Fair Value Measurement* issued by the International Accounting Standards Board (IASB). Paragraphs that have been added to this Standard (and do not appear in the text of IFRS 13) are identified with the prefix "Aus", followed by the number of the preceding IASB paragraph and decimal numbering.

Entities that comply with AASB 13 will simultaneously be in compliance with IFRS 13.

Accounting Standard AASB 13

The Australian Accounting Standards Board makes Accounting Standard AASB 13 *Fair Value Measurement* under section 334 of the *Corporations Act 2001*.

Kevin M. Stevenson
Chair – AASB

Dated 2 September 2011

Accounting Standard AASB 13
Fair Value Measurement

Objective

1   This Standard:

  (a)   defines *fair value*;

  (b)   sets out in a single Standard a framework for measuring fair value; and

  (c)   requires disclosures about fair value measurements.

2   Fair value is a market-based measurement, not an entity-specific measurement. For some assets and liabilities, observable market transactions or market information might be available. For other assets and liabilities, observable market transactions and market information might not be available. However, the objective of a fair value measurement in both cases is the same – to estimate the price at which an *orderly transaction* to sell the asset or to transfer the liability would take place between *market participants* at the measurement date under current market conditions (i.e. an *exit price* at the measurement date from the perspective of a market participant that holds the asset or owes the liability).

3   When a price for an identical asset or liability is not observable, an entity measures fair value using another valuation technique that maximises the use of relevant *observable inputs* and minimises the use of *unobservable inputs*. Because fair value is a market-based measurement, it is measured using the assumptions that market participants would use when pricing the asset or liability, including assumptions about risk. As a result, an entity's intention to hold an asset or to settle or otherwise fulfil a liability is not relevant when measuring fair value.

4   The definition of fair value focuses on assets and liabilities because they are a primary subject of accounting measurement. In addition, this Standard shall be applied to an entity's own equity instruments measured at fair value.

Application

Aus4.1   This Standard applies to:

  (a)   each entity that is required to prepare financial reports in accordance with Part 2M.3 of the Corporations Act and that is a reporting entity;

  (b)   general purpose financial statements of each other reporting entity; and

  (c)   financial statements that are, or are held out to be, general purpose financial statements.

Aus4.2   **This Standard applies to annual reporting periods beginning on or after 1 January 2013.**

Aus4.3   **This Standard may be applied to annual reporting periods beginning on or after 1 January 2005 but before 1 January 2013. If an entity applies this Standard to such an annual reporting period, it shall disclose that fact.**

Aus4.4   **The requirements specified in this Standard apply to the financial statements where information resulting from their application is material in accordance with AASB 1031 *Materiality*.**

Scope

5   **This Standard applies when another Standard requires or permits fair value measurements or disclosures about fair value measurements (and measurements, such as fair value less costs to sell, based on fair value or disclosures about those measurements), except as specified in paragraphs 6 and 7.**

6   The measurement and disclosure requirements of this Standard do not apply to the following:

    (a)   share-based payment transactions within the scope of AASB 2 *Share-based Payment*;

    (b)   leasing transactions within the scope of AASB 117 *Leases*; and

    (c)   measurements that have some similarities to fair value but are not fair value, such as net realisable value in AASB 102 *Inventories* or value in use in AASB 136 *Impairment of Assets*.

7   The disclosures required by this Standard are not required for the following:

    (a)   plan assets measured at fair value in accordance with AASB 119 *Employee Benefits*; and

    (b)   [deleted by the AASB]

    (c)   assets for which recoverable amount is fair value less costs of disposal in accordance with AASB 136.

8   The fair value measurement framework described in this Standard applies to both initial and subsequent measurement if fair value is required or permitted by other Australian Accounting Standards.

Measurement

Definition of fair value

9   **This Standard defines fair value as the price that would be received to sell an asset or paid to transfer a liability in an orderly transaction between market participants at the measurement date.**

10   Paragraph B2 describes the overall fair value measurement approach.

The asset or liability

11   **A fair value measurement is for a particular asset or liability. Therefore, when measuring fair value an entity shall take into account the characteristics of the asset or liability if market participants would take those characteristics into account when pricing the asset or liability at the measurement date. Such characteristics include, for example, the following:**

    (a)   **the condition and location of the asset; and**

    (b)   **restrictions, if any, on the sale or use of the asset.**

12   The effect on the measurement arising from a particular characteristic will differ depending on how that characteristic would be taken into account by market participants.

13   The asset or liability measured at fair value might be either of the following:

    (a)   a stand-alone asset or liability (e.g. a financial instrument or a non-financial asset); or

    (b)   a group of assets, a group of liabilities or a group of assets and liabilities (e.g. a cash-generating unit or a business).

AASB

14   Whether the asset or liability is a stand-alone asset or liability, a group of assets, a group of liabilities or a group of assets and liabilities for recognition or disclosure purposes depends on its *unit of account*. The unit of account for the asset or liability shall be determined in accordance with the Standard that requires or permits the fair value measurement, except as provided in this Standard.

The transaction

15   A fair value measurement assumes that the asset or liability is exchanged in an orderly transaction between market participants to sell the asset or transfer the liability at the measurement date under current market conditions.

16   A fair value measurement assumes that the transaction to sell the asset or transfer the liability takes place either:

    (a)   in the *principal market* for the asset or liability; or

    (b)   in the absence of a principal market, in the *most advantageous market* for the asset or liability.

17   An entity need not undertake an exhaustive search of all possible markets to identify the principal market or, in the absence of a principal market, the most advantageous market, but it shall take into account all information that is reasonably available. In the absence of evidence to the contrary, the market in which the entity would normally enter into a transaction to sell the asset or to transfer the liability is presumed to be the principal market or, in the absence of a principal market, the most advantageous market.

18   If there is a principal market for the asset or liability, the fair value measurement shall represent the price in that market (whether that price is directly observable or estimated using another valuation technique), even if the price in a different market is potentially more advantageous at the measurement date.

19   The entity must have access to the principal (or most advantageous) market at the measurement date. Because different entities (and businesses within those entities) with different activities may have access to different markets, the principal (or most advantageous) market for the same asset or liability might be different for different entities (and businesses within those entities). Therefore, the principal (or most advantageous) market (and thus, market participants) shall be considered from the perspective of the entity, thereby allowing for differences between and among entities with different activities.

20   Although an entity must be able to access the market, the entity does not need to be able to sell the particular asset or transfer the particular liability on the measurement date to be able to measure fair value on the basis of the price in that market.

21   Even when there is no observable market to provide pricing information about the sale of an asset or the transfer of a liability at the measurement date, a fair value measurement shall assume that a transaction takes place at that date, considered from the perspective of a market participant that holds the asset or owes the liability. That assumed transaction establishes a basis for estimating the price to sell the asset or to transfer the liability.

Market participants

22   An entity shall measure the fair value of an asset or a liability using the assumptions that market participants would use when pricing the asset or liability, assuming that market participants act in their economic best interest.

23   In developing those assumptions, an entity need not identify specific market participants. Rather, the entity shall identify characteristics that distinguish market participants generally, considering factors specific to all the following:

    (a)   the asset or liability;

    (b)   the principal (or most advantageous) market for the asset or liability; and

    (c)   market participants with whom the entity would enter into a transaction in that market.

The price

24   **Fair value is the price that would be received to sell an asset or paid to transfer a liability in an orderly transaction in the principal (or most advantageous) market at the measurement date under current market conditions (i.e. an exit price) regardless of whether that price is directly observable or estimated using another valuation technique.**

25   The price in the principal (or most advantageous) market used to measure the fair value of the asset or liability shall not be adjusted for *transaction costs*. Transaction costs shall be accounted for in accordance with other Australian Accounting Standards. Transaction costs are not a characteristic of an asset or a liability; rather, they are specific to a transaction and will differ depending on how an entity enters into a transaction for the asset or liability.

26   Transaction costs do not include *transport costs*. If location is a characteristic of the asset (as might be the case, for example, for a commodity), the price in the principal (or most advantageous) market shall be adjusted for the costs, if any, that would be incurred to transport the asset from its current location to that market.

Application to non-financial assets

Highest and best use for non-financial assets

27   **A fair value measurement of a non-financial asset takes into account a market participant's ability to generate economic benefits by using the asset in its *highest and best* use or by selling it to another market participant that would use the asset in its highest and best use.**

28   The highest and best use of a non-financial asset takes into account the use of the asset that is physically possible, legally permissible and financially feasible, as follows:

(a)   A use that is physically possible takes into account the physical characteristics of the asset that market participants would take into account when pricing the asset (e.g. the location or size of a property).

(b)   A use that is legally permissible takes into account any legal restrictions on the use of the asset that market participants would take into account when pricing the asset (e.g. the zoning regulations applicable to a property).

(c)   A use that is financially feasible takes into account whether a use of the asset that is physically possible and legally permissible generates adequate income or cash flows (taking into account the costs of converting the asset to that use) to produce an investment return that market participants would require from an investment in that asset put to that use.

29   Highest and best use is determined from the perspective of market participants, even if the entity intends a different use. However, an entity's current use of a non-financial asset is presumed to be its highest and best use unless market or other factors suggest that a different use by market participants would maximise the value of the asset.

30   To protect its competitive position, or for other reasons, an entity may intend not to use an acquired non-financial asset actively or it may intend not to use the asset according to its highest and best use. For example, that might be the case for an acquired intangible asset that the entity plans to use defensively by preventing others from using it. Nevertheless, the entity shall measure the fair value of a non-financial asset assuming its highest and best use by market participants.

Valuation premise for non-financial assets

31   The highest and best use of a non-financial asset establishes the valuation premise used to measure the fair value of the asset, as follows:

(a)   The highest and best use of a non-financial asset might provide maximum value to market participants through its use in combination with other assets as a group (as installed or otherwise configured for use) or in combination with other assets and liabilities (e.g. a business).

(i) If the highest and best use of the asset is to use the asset in combination with other assets or with other assets and liabilities, the fair value of the asset is the price that would be received in a current transaction to sell the asset assuming that the asset would be used with other assets or with other assets and liabilities and that those assets and liabilities (i.e. its complementary assets and the associated liabilities) would be available to market participants.

(ii) Liabilities associated with the asset and with the complementary assets include liabilities that fund working capital, but do not include liabilities used to fund assets other than those within the group of assets.

(iii) Assumptions about the highest and best use of a non-financial asset shall be consistent for all the assets (for which highest and best use is relevant) of the group of assets or the group of assets and liabilities within which the asset would be used.

(b) The highest and best use of a non-financial asset might provide maximum value to market participants on a stand-alone basis. If the highest and best use of the asset is to use it on a stand-alone basis, the fair value of the asset is the price that would be received in a current transaction to sell the asset to market participants that would use the asset on a stand-alone basis.

32 The fair value measurement of a non-financial asset assumes that the asset is sold consistently with the unit of account specified in other Australian Accounting Standards (which may be an individual asset). That is the case even when that fair value measurement assumes that the highest and best use of the asset is to use it in combination with other assets or with other assets and liabilities because a fair value measurement assumes that the market participant already holds the complementary assets and the associated liabilities.

33 Paragraph B3 describes the application of the valuation premise concept for non-financial assets.

Application to liabilities and an entity's own equity instruments

General principles

34 **A fair value measurement assumes that a financial or non-financial liability or an entity's own equity instrument (e.g. equity interests issued as consideration in a business combination) is transferred to a market participant at the measurement date. The transfer of a liability or an entity's own equity instrument assumes the following:**

(a) **A liability would remain outstanding and the market participant transferee would be required to fulfil the obligation. The liability would not be settled with the counterparty or otherwise extinguished on the measurement date.**

(b) **An entity's own equity instrument would remain outstanding and the market participant transferee would take on the rights and responsibilities associated with the instrument. The instrument would not be cancelled or otherwise extinguished on the measurement date.**

35 Even when there is no observable market to provide pricing information about the transfer of a liability or an entity's own equity instrument (e.g. because contractual or other legal restrictions prevent the transfer of such items), there might be an observable market for such items if they are held by other parties as assets (e.g. a corporate bond or a call option on an entity's shares).

36 In all cases, an entity shall maximise the use of relevant observable inputs and minimise the use of unobservable inputs to meet the objective of a fair value measurement, which is to estimate the price at which an orderly transaction to transfer the liability or equity instrument would take place between market participants at the measurement date under current market conditions.

Liabilities and equity instruments held by other parties as assets

37   **When a quoted price for the transfer of an identical or a similar liability or entity's own equity instrument is not available and the identical item is held by another party as an asset, an entity shall measure the fair value of the liability or equity instrument from the perspective of a market participant that holds the identical item as an asset at the measurement date.**

38   In such cases, an entity shall measure the fair value of the liability or equity instrument as follows:

     (a)   using the quoted price in an *active market* for the identical item held by another party as an asset, if that price is available.

     (b)   if that price is not available, using other observable inputs, such as the quoted price in a market that is not active for the identical item held by another party as an asset.

     (c)   if the observable prices in (a) and (b) are not available, using another valuation technique, such as:

         (i)   an *income approach* (e.g. a present value technique that takes into account the future cash flows that a market participant would expect to receive from holding the liability or equity instrument as an asset; see paragraphs B10 and B11).

         (ii)   a *market approach* (e.g. using quoted prices for similar liabilities or equity instruments held by other parties as assets; see paragraphs B5–B7).

39   An entity shall adjust the quoted price of a liability or an entity's own equity instrument held by another party as an asset only if there are factors specific to the asset that are not applicable to the fair value measurement of the liability or equity instrument. An entity shall ensure that the price of the asset does not reflect the effect of a restriction preventing the sale of that asset. Some factors that may indicate that the quoted price of the asset should be adjusted include the following:

     (a)   The quoted price for the asset relates to a similar (but not identical) liability or equity instrument held by another party as an asset. For example, the liability or equity instrument may have a particular characteristic (e.g. the credit quality of the issuer) that is different from that reflected in the fair value of the similar liability or equity instrument held as an asset.

     (b)   The unit of account for the asset is not the same as for the liability or equity instrument. For example, for liabilities, in some cases the price for an asset reflects a combined price for a package comprising both the amounts due from the issuer and a third-party credit enhancement. If the unit of account for the liability is not for the combined package, the objective is to measure the fair value of the issuer's liability, not the fair value of the combined package. Thus, in such cases, the entity would adjust the observed price for the asset to exclude the effect of the third-party credit enhancement.

Liabilities and equity instruments not held by other parties as assets

40   **When a quoted price for the transfer of an identical or a similar liability or entity's own equity instrument is not available and the identical item is not held by another party as an asset, an entity shall measure the fair value of the liability or equity instrument using a valuation technique from the perspective of a market participant that owes the liability or has issued the claim on equity.**

41   For example, when applying a present value technique an entity might take into account either of the following:

     (a)   the future cash outflows that a market participant would expect to incur in fulfilling the obligation, including the compensation that a market participant would require for taking on the obligation (see paragraphs B31–B33).

     (b)   the amount that a market participant would receive to enter into or issue an identical liability or equity instrument, using the assumptions that market participants would use when pricing the identical item (e.g. having the same credit characteristics) in the principal (or most advantageous) market for issuing a liability or an equity instrument with the same contractual terms.

Non-performance risk

42　The fair value of a liability reflects the effect of *non-performance risk*. Non-performance risk includes, but may not be limited to, an entity's own credit risk (as defined in AASB 7 *Financial Instruments: Disclosures*). Non-performance risk is assumed to be the same before and after the transfer of the liability.

43　When measuring the fair value of a liability, an entity shall take into account the effect of its credit risk (credit standing) and any other factors that might influence the likelihood that the obligation will or will not be fulfilled. That effect may differ depending on the liability, for example:

(a)　whether the liability is an obligation to deliver cash (a financial liability) or an obligation to deliver goods or services (a non-financial liability).

(b)　the terms of credit enhancements related to the liability, if any.

44　The fair value of a liability reflects the effect of non-performance risk on the basis of its unit of account. The issuer of a liability issued with an inseparable third-party credit enhancement that is accounted for separately from the liability shall not include the effect of the credit enhancement (e.g. a third-party guarantee of debt) in the fair value measurement of the liability. If the credit enhancement is accounted for separately from the liability, the issuer would take into account its own credit standing and not that of the third party guarantor when measuring the fair value of the liability.

Restriction preventing the transfer of a liability or an entity's own equity instrument

45　When measuring the fair value of a liability or an entity's own equity instrument, an entity shall not include a separate input or an adjustment to other *inputs* relating to the existence of a restriction that prevents the transfer of the item. The effect of a restriction that prevents the transfer of a liability or an entity's own equity instrument is either implicitly or explicitly included in the other inputs to the fair value measurement.

46　For example, at the transaction date, both the creditor and the obligor accepted the transaction price for the liability with full knowledge that the obligation includes a restriction that prevents its transfer. As a result of the restriction being included in the transaction price, a separate input or an adjustment to an existing input is not required at the transaction date to reflect the effect of the restriction on transfer. Similarly, a separate input or an adjustment to an existing input is not required at subsequent measurement dates to reflect the effect of the restriction on transfer.

Financial liability with a demand feature

47　The fair value of a financial liability with a demand feature (e.g. a demand deposit) is not less than the amount payable on demand, discounted from the first date that the amount could be required to be paid.

Application to financial assets and financial liabilities with offsetting positions in market risks or counterparty credit risk

48　An entity that holds a group of financial assets and financial liabilities is exposed to market risks (as defined in AASB 7) and to the credit risk (as defined in AASB 7) of each of the counterparties. If the entity manages that group of financial assets and financial liabilities on the basis of its net exposure to either market risks or credit risk, the entity is permitted to apply an exception to this Standard for measuring fair value. That exception permits an entity to measure the fair value of a group of financial assets and financial liabilities on the basis of the price that would be received to sell a net long position (i.e. an asset) for a particular risk exposure or to transfer a net short position (i.e. a liability) for a particular risk exposure in an orderly transaction between market participants at the measurement date under current market conditions. Accordingly, an entity shall measure the fair value of the group of financial assets and financial liabilities consistently with how market participants would price the net risk exposure at the measurement date.

49　An entity is permitted to use the exception in paragraph 48 only if the entity does all the following:

(a)　manages the group of financial assets and financial liabilities on the basis of the entity's net exposure to a particular market risk (or risks) or to the credit risk of a particular counterparty in accordance with the entity's documented risk management or investment strategy;

(b)   provides information on that basis about the group of financial assets and financial liabilities to the entity's key management personnel, as defined in AASB 124 *Related Party Disclosures*; and

(c)   is required or has elected to measure those financial assets and financial liabilities at fair value in the statement of financial position at the end of each reporting period.

50   The exception in paragraph 48 does not pertain to financial statement presentation. In some cases the basis for the presentation of financial instruments in the statement of financial position differs from the basis for the measurement of financial instruments, for example, if a Standard does not require or permit financial instruments to be presented on a net basis. In such cases an entity may need to allocate the portfolio-level adjustments (see paragraphs 53–56) to the individual assets or liabilities that make up the group of financial assets and financial liabilities managed on the basis of the entity's net risk exposure. An entity shall perform such allocations on a reasonable and consistent basis using a methodology appropriate in the circumstances.

51   An entity shall make an accounting policy decision in accordance with AASB 108 *Accounting Policies, Changes in Accounting Estimates and Errors* to use the exception in paragraph 48. An entity that uses the exception shall apply that accounting policy, including its policy for allocating bid-ask adjustments (see paragraphs 53–55) and credit adjustments (see paragraph 56), if applicable, consistently from period to period for a particular portfolio.

52   The exception in paragraph 48 applies only to financial assets and financial liabilities within the scope of AASB 139 *Financial Instruments: Recognition and Measurement* or AASB 9 *Financial Instruments*.

Exposure to market risks

53   When using the exception in paragraph 48 to measure the fair value of a group of financial assets and financial liabilities managed on the basis of the entity's net exposure to a particular market risk (or risks), the entity shall apply the price within the bid-ask spread that is most representative of fair value in the circumstances to the entity's net exposure to those market risks (see paragraphs 70 and 71).

54   When using the exception in paragraph 48, an entity shall ensure that the market risk (or risks) to which the entity is exposed within that group of financial assets and financial liabilities is substantially the same. For example, an entity would not combine the interest rate risk associated with a financial asset with the commodity price risk associated with a financial liability because doing so would not mitigate the entity's exposure to interest rate risk or commodity price risk. When using the exception in paragraph 48, any basis risk resulting from the market risk parameters not being identical shall be taken into account in the fair value measurement of the financial assets and financial liabilities within the group.

55   Similarly, the duration of the entity's exposure to a particular market risk (or risks) arising from the financial assets and financial liabilities shall be substantially the same. For example, an entity that uses a 12 month futures contract against the cash flows associated with 12 months' worth of interest rate risk exposure on a five-year financial instrument within a group made up of only those financial assets and financial liabilities measures the fair value of the exposure to 12 month interest rate risk on a net basis and the remaining interest rate risk exposure (i.e. years 2–5) on a gross basis.

Exposure to the credit risk of a particular counterparty

56   When using the exception in paragraph 48 to measure the fair value of a group of financial assets and financial liabilities entered into with a particular counterparty, the entity shall include the effect of the entity's net exposure to the credit risk of that counterparty or the counterparty's net exposure to the credit risk of the entity in the fair value measurement when market participants would take into account any existing arrangements that mitigate credit risk exposure in the event of default (e.g. a master netting agreement with the

counterparty or an agreement that requires the exchange of collateral on the basis of each party's net exposure to the credit risk of the other party). The fair value measurement shall reflect market participants' expectations about the likelihood that such an arrangement would be legally enforceable in the event of default.

Fair value at initial recognition

57   When an asset is acquired or a liability is assumed in an exchange transaction for that asset or liability, the transaction price is the price paid to acquire the asset or received to assume the liability (an *entry price*). In contrast, the fair value of the asset or liability is the price that would be received to sell the asset or paid to transfer the liability (an exit price). Entities do not necessarily sell assets at the prices paid to acquire them. Similarly, entities do not necessarily transfer liabilities at the prices received to assume them.

58   In many cases the transaction price will equal the fair value (e.g. that might be the case when on the transaction date the transaction to buy an asset takes place in the market in which the asset would be sold).

59   When determining whether fair value at initial recognition equals the transaction price, an entity shall take into account factors specific to the transaction and to the asset or liability. Paragraph B4 describes situations in which the transaction price might not represent the fair value of an asset or a liability at initial recognition.

60   If another Standard requires or permits an entity to measure an asset or a liability initially at fair value and the transaction price differs from fair value, the entity shall recognise the resulting gain or loss in profit or loss unless that Standard specifies otherwise.

Valuation techniques

61   **An entity shall use valuation techniques that are appropriate in the circumstances and for which sufficient data are available to measure fair value, maximising the use of relevant observable inputs and minimising the use of unobservable inputs.**

62   The objective of using a valuation technique is to estimate the price at which an orderly transaction to sell the asset or to transfer the liability would take place between market participants at the measurement date under current market conditions. Three widely used valuation techniques are the market approach, the *cost approach* and the income approach. The main aspects of those approaches are summarised in paragraphs B5–B11. An entity shall use valuation techniques consistent with one or more of those approaches to measure fair value.

63   In some cases a single valuation technique will be appropriate (e.g. when valuing an asset or a liability using quoted prices in an active market for identical assets or liabilities). In other cases, multiple valuation techniques will be appropriate (e.g. that might be the case when valuing a cash-generating unit). If multiple valuation techniques are used to measure fair value, the results (i.e. respective indications of fair value) shall be evaluated considering the reasonableness of the range of values indicated by those results. A fair value measurement is the point within that range that is most representative of fair value in the circumstances.

64   If the transaction price is fair value at initial recognition and a valuation technique that uses unobservable inputs will be used to measure fair value in subsequent periods, the valuation technique shall be calibrated so that at initial recognition the result of the valuation technique equals the transaction price. Calibration ensures that the valuation technique reflects current market conditions, and it helps an entity to determine whether an adjustment to the valuation technique is necessary (e.g. there might be a characteristic of the asset or liability that is not captured by the valuation technique). After initial recognition, when measuring fair value using a valuation technique or techniques that use unobservable inputs, an entity shall ensure that those valuation techniques reflect observable market data (e.g. the price for a similar asset or liability) at the measurement date.

65   Valuation techniques used to measure fair value shall be applied consistently. However, a change in a valuation technique or its application (e.g. a change in its weighting when multiple valuation techniques are used or a change in an adjustment applied to a valuation

technique) is appropriate if the change results in a measurement that is equally or more representative of fair value in the circumstances. That might be the case if, for example, any of the following events take place:

(a)   new markets develop;

(b)   new information becomes available;

(c)   information previously used is no longer available;

(d)   valuation techniques improve; or

(e)   market conditions change.

66   Revisions resulting from a change in the valuation technique or its application shall be accounted for as a change in accounting estimate in accordance with AASB 108. However, the disclosures in AASB 108 for a change in accounting estimate are not required for revisions resulting from a change in a valuation technique or its application.

Inputs to valuation techniques

General principles

67   **Valuation techniques used to measure fair value shall maximise the use of relevant observable inputs and minimise the use of unobservable inputs.**

68   Examples of markets in which inputs might be observable for some assets and liabilities (e.g. financial instruments) include exchange markets, dealer markets, brokered markets and principal-to-principal markets (see paragraph B34).

69   An entity shall select inputs that are consistent with the characteristics of the asset or liability that market participants would take into account in a transaction for the asset or liability (see paragraphs 11 and 12). In some cases those characteristics result in the application of an adjustment, such as a premium or discount (e.g. a control premium or non-controlling interest discount). However, a fair value measurement shall not incorporate a premium or discount that is inconsistent with the unit of account in the Standard that requires or permits the fair value measurement (see paragraphs 13 and 14). Premiums or discounts that reflect size as a characteristic of the entity's holding (specifically, a blockage factor that adjusts the quoted price of an asset or a liability because the market's normal daily trading volume is not sufficient to absorb the quantity held by the entity, as described in paragraph 80) rather than as a characteristic of the asset or liability (e.g. a control premium when measuring the fair value of a controlling interest) are not permitted in a fair value measurement. In all cases, if there is a quoted price in an active market (i.e. a *Level 1 input*) for an asset or a liability, an entity shall use that price without adjustment when measuring fair value, except as specified in paragraph 79.

Inputs based on bid and ask prices

70   If an asset or a liability measured at fair value has a bid price and an ask price (e.g. an input from a dealer market), the price within the bid-ask spread that is most representative of fair value in the circumstances shall be used to measure fair value regardless of where the input is categorised within the fair value hierarchy (i.e. Level 1, 2 or 3; see paragraphs 72–90). The use of bid prices for asset positions and ask prices for liability positions is permitted, but is not required.

71   This Standard does not preclude the use of mid-market pricing or other pricing conventions that are used by market participants as a practical expedient for fair value measurements within a bid-ask spread.

Fair value hierarchy

72   To increase consistency and comparability in fair value measurements and related disclosures, this Standard establishes a fair value hierarchy that categorises into three levels (see paragraphs 76–90) the inputs to valuation techniques used to measure fair value. The fair value hierarchy gives the highest priority to quoted prices (unadjusted) in active markets for identical assets or liabilities (Level 1 inputs) and the lowest priority to unobservable inputs (*Level 3 inputs*).

73   In some cases, the inputs used to measure the fair value of an asset or a liability might be categorised within different levels of the fair value hierarchy. In those cases, the fair value measurement is categorised in its entirety in the same level of the fair value hierarchy as the lowest level input that is significant to the entire measurement. Assessing the significance of a particular input to the entire measurement requires judgement, taking into account factors specific to the asset or liability. Adjustments to arrive at measurements based on fair value, such as costs to sell when measuring fair value less costs to sell, shall not be taken into account when determining the level of the fair value hierarchy within which a fair value measurement is categorised.

74   The availability of relevant inputs and their relative subjectivity might affect the selection of appropriate valuation techniques (see paragraph 61). However, the fair value hierarchy prioritises the inputs to valuation techniques, not the valuation techniques used to measure fair value. For example, a fair value measurement developed using a present value technique might be categorised within Level 2 or Level 3, depending on the inputs that are significant to the entire measurement and the level of the fair value hierarchy within which those inputs are categorised.

75   If an observable input requires an adjustment using an unobservable input and that adjustment results in a significantly higher or lower fair value measurement, the resulting measurement would be categorised within Level 3 of the fair value hierarchy. For example, if a market participant would take into account the effect of a restriction on the sale of an asset when estimating the price for the asset, an entity would adjust the quoted price to reflect the effect of that restriction. If that quoted price is a *Level 2 input* and the adjustment is an unobservable input that is significant to the entire measurement, the measurement would be categorised within Level 3 of the fair value hierarchy.

Level 1 inputs

76   Level 1 inputs are quoted prices (unadjusted) in active markets for identical assets or liabilities that the entity can access at the measurement date.

77   A quoted price in an active market provides the most reliable evidence of fair value and shall be used without adjustment to measure fair value whenever available, except as specified in paragraph 79.

78   A Level 1 input will be available for many financial assets and financial liabilities, some of which might be exchanged in multiple active markets (e.g. on different exchanges). Therefore, the emphasis within Level 1 is on determining both of the following:

(a)   the principal market for the asset or liability or, in the absence of a principal market, the most advantageous market for the asset or liability; and

(b)   whether the entity can enter into a transaction for the asset or liability at the price in that market at the measurement date.

79   An entity shall not make an adjustment to a Level 1 input except in the following circumstances:

(a)   when an entity holds a large number of similar (but not identical) assets or liabilities (e.g. debt securities) that are measured at fair value and a quoted price in an active market is available but not readily accessible for each of those assets or liabilities individually (i.e. given the large number of similar assets or liabilities held by the entity, it would be difficult to obtain pricing information for each individual asset or liability at the measurement date). In that case, as a practical expedient, an entity may measure fair value using an alternative pricing method that does not rely exclusively on quoted prices (e.g. matrix pricing). However, the use of an alternative pricing method results in a fair value measurement categorised within a lower level of the fair value hierarchy.

(b)   when a quoted price in an active market does not represent fair value at the measurement date. That might be the case if, for example, significant events (such as transactions in a principal-to-principal market, trades in a brokered market or announcements) take place after the close of a market but before the measurement date. An entity shall establish and consistently apply a policy for identifying those events that might affect fair value measurements. However, if the quoted price is adjusted for new information, the adjustment results in a fair value measurement categorised within a lower level of the fair value hierarchy.

(c)   when measuring the fair value of a liability or an entity's own equity instrument using the quoted price for the identical item traded as an asset in an active market and that price needs to be adjusted for factors specific to the item or the asset (see paragraph 39). If no adjustment to the quoted price of the asset is required, the result is a fair value measurement categorised within Level 1 of the fair value hierarchy. However, any adjustment to the quoted price of the asset results in a fair value measurement categorised within a lower level of the fair value hierarchy.

80   If an entity holds a position in a single asset or liability (including a position comprising a large number of identical assets or liabilities, such as a holding of financial instruments) and the asset or liability is traded in an active market, the fair value of the asset or liability shall be measured within Level 1 as the product of the quoted price for the individual asset or liability and the quantity held by the entity. That is the case even if a market's normal daily trading volume is not sufficient to absorb the quantity held and placing orders to sell the position in a single transaction might affect the quoted price.

Level 2 inputs

81   Level 2 inputs are inputs other than quoted prices included within Level 1 that are observable for the asset or liability, either directly or indirectly.

82   If the asset or liability has a specified (contractual) term, a Level 2 input must be observable for substantially the full term of the asset or liability. Level 2 inputs include the following:

(a)   quoted prices for similar assets or liabilities in active markets.

(b)   quoted prices for identical or similar assets or liabilities in markets that are not active.

(c)   inputs other than quoted prices that are observable for the asset or liability, for example:

(i)   interest rates and yield curves observable at commonly quoted intervals;

(ii)   implied volatilities; and

(iii)   credit spreads.

(d)   *market-corroborated inputs*.

83   Adjustments to Level 2 inputs will vary depending on factors specific to the asset or liability. Those factors include the following:

(a)   the condition or location of the asset;

(b)   the extent to which inputs relate to items that are comparable to the asset or liability (including those factors described in paragraph 39); and

(c)   the volume or level of activity in the markets within which the inputs are observed.

84   An adjustment to a Level 2 input that is significant to the entire measurement might result in a fair value measurement categorised within Level 3 of the fair value hierarchy if the adjustment uses significant unobservable inputs.

85   Paragraph B35 describes the use of Level 2 inputs for particular assets and liabilities.

Level 3 inputs

86   Level 3 inputs are unobservable inputs for the asset or liability.

87   Unobservable inputs shall be used to measure fair value to the extent that relevant observable inputs are not available, thereby allowing for situations in which there is little, if any, market activity for the asset or liability at the measurement date. However, the fair value measurement objective remains the same, i.e. an exit price at the measurement date from the perspective of a market participant that holds the asset or owes the liability. Therefore, unobservable inputs shall reflect the assumptions that market participants would use when pricing the asset or liability, including assumptions about risk.

88   Assumptions about risk include the risk inherent in a particular valuation technique used to measure fair value (such as a pricing model) and the risk inherent in the inputs to the valuation technique. A measurement that does not include an adjustment for risk would

not represent a fair value measurement if market participants would include one when pricing the asset or liability. For example, it might be necessary to include a risk adjustment when there is significant measurement uncertainty (e.g. when there has been a significant decrease in the volume or level of activity when compared with normal market activity for the asset or liability, or similar assets or liabilities, and the entity has determined that the transaction price or quoted price does not represent fair value, as described in paragraphs B37–B47).

89 An entity shall develop unobservable inputs using the best information available in the circumstances, which might include the entity's own data. In developing unobservable inputs, an entity may begin with its own data, but it shall adjust those data if reasonably available information indicates that other market participants would use different data or there is something particular to the entity that is not available to other market participants (e.g. an entity-specific synergy). An entity need not undertake exhaustive efforts to obtain information about market participant assumptions. However, an entity shall take into account all information about market participant assumptions that is reasonably available. Unobservable inputs developed in the manner described above are considered market participant assumptions and meet the objective of a fair value measurement.

90 Paragraph B36 describes the use of Level 3 inputs for particular assets and liabilities.

Disclosure

91 **An entity shall disclose information that helps users of its financial statements assess both of the following:**

 (a) **for assets and liabilities that are measured at fair value on a recurring or non-recurring basis in the statement of financial position after initial recognition, the valuation techniques and inputs used to develop those measurements.**

 (b) **for recurring fair value measurements using significant unobservable inputs (Level 3), the effect of the measurements on profit or loss or other comprehensive income for the period.**

92 To meet the objectives in paragraph 91, an entity shall consider all the following:

 (a) the level of detail necessary to satisfy the disclosure requirements;

 (b) how much emphasis to place on each of the various requirements;

 (c) how much aggregation or disaggregation to undertake; and

 (d) whether users of financial statements need additional information to evaluate the quantitative information disclosed.

If the disclosures provided in accordance with this Standard and other Australian Accounting Standards are insufficient to meet the objectives in paragraph 91, an entity shall disclose additional information necessary to meet those objectives.

93 To meet the objectives in paragraph 91, an entity shall disclose, at a minimum, the following information for each class of assets and liabilities (see paragraph 94 for information on determining appropriate classes of assets and liabilities) measured at fair value (including measurements based on fair value within the scope of this Standard) in the statement of financial position after initial recognition:

 (a) for recurring and non-recurring fair value measurements, the fair value measurement at the end of the reporting period, and for non-recurring fair value measurements, the reasons for the measurement. Recurring fair value measurements of assets or liabilities are those that other Australian Accounting Standards require or permit in the statement of financial position at the end of each reporting period. Non-recurring fair value measurements of assets or liabilities are those that other Australian Accounting Standards require or permit in the statement of financial position in particular circumstances (e.g. when an entity measures an asset held for sale at fair value less costs to sell in accordance with AASB 5 *Non-current Assets Held for Sale and Discontinued Operations* because the asset's fair value less costs to sell is lower than its carrying amount).

(b)   for recurring and non-recurring fair value measurements, the level of the fair value hierarchy within which the fair value measurements are categorised in their entirety (Level 1, 2 or 3).

(c)   for assets and liabilities held at the end of the reporting period that are measured at fair value on a recurring basis, the amounts of any transfers between Level 1 and Level 2 of the fair value hierarchy, the reasons for those transfers and the entity's policy for determining when transfers between levels are deemed to have occurred (see paragraph 95). Transfers into each level shall be disclosed and discussed separately from transfers out of each level.

(d)   for recurring and non-recurring fair value measurements categorised within Level 2 and Level 3 of the fair value hierarchy, a description of the valuation technique(s) and the inputs used in the fair value measurement. If there has been a change in valuation technique (e.g. changing from a market approach to an income approach or the use of an additional valuation technique), the entity shall disclose that change and the reason(s) for making it. For fair value measurements categorised within Level 3 of the fair value hierarchy, an entity shall provide quantitative information about the significant unobservable inputs used in the fair value measurement. An entity is not required to create quantitative information to comply with this disclosure requirement if quantitative unobservable inputs are not developed by the entity when measuring fair value (e.g. when an entity uses prices from prior transactions or third-party pricing information without adjustment). However, when providing this disclosure an entity cannot ignore quantitative unobservable inputs that are significant to the fair value measurement and are reasonably available to the entity.

(e)   for recurring fair value measurements categorised within Level 3 of the fair value hierarchy, a reconciliation from the opening balances to the closing balances, disclosing separately changes during the period attributable to the following:

    (i)   total gains or losses for the period recognised in profit or loss, and the line item(s) in profit or loss in which those gains or losses are recognised.

    (ii)   total gains or losses for the period recognised in other comprehensive income, and the line item(s) in other comprehensive income in which those gains or losses are recognised.

    (iii)   purchases, sales, issues and settlements (each of those types of changes disclosed separately).

    (iv)   the amounts of any transfers into or out of Level 3 of the fair value hierarchy, the reasons for those transfers and the entity's policy for determining when transfers between levels are deemed to have occurred (see paragraph 95). Transfers into Level 3 shall be disclosed and discussed separately from transfers out of Level 3.

(f)   for recurring fair value measurements categorised within Level 3 of the fair value hierarchy, the amount of the total gains or losses for the period in (e)(i) included in profit or loss that is attributable to the change in unrealised gains or losses relating to those assets and liabilities held at the end of the reporting period, and the line item(s) in profit or loss in which those unrealised gains or losses are recognised.

(g)   for recurring and non-recurring fair value measurements categorised within Level 3 of the fair value hierarchy, a description of the valuation processes used by the entity (including, for example, how an entity decides its valuation policies and procedures and analyses changes in fair value measurements from period to period).

(h)   for recurring fair value measurements categorised within Level 3 of the fair value hierarchy:

    (i)   for all such measurements, a narrative description of the sensitivity of the fair value measurement to changes in unobservable inputs if a change in those inputs to a different amount might result in a significantly higher or lower fair value measurement. If there are interrelationships between those inputs and other unobservable inputs used in the fair value measurement, an entity shall also provide a description of those interrelationships and of how they might magnify or mitigate the effect of changes in the unobservable inputs on the fair value measurement. To comply with that disclosure requirement, the narrative description of the sensitivity to changes in unobservable inputs shall include, at a minimum, the unobservable inputs disclosed when complying with (d).

(ii) for financial assets and financial liabilities, if changing one or more of the unobservable inputs to reflect reasonably possible alternative assumptions would change fair value significantly, an entity shall state that fact and disclose the effect of those changes. The entity shall disclose how the effect of a change to reflect a reasonably possible alternative assumption was calculated. For that purpose, significance shall be judged with respect to profit or loss, and total assets or total liabilities, or, when changes in fair value are recognised in other comprehensive income, total equity.

(i) for recurring and non-recurring fair value measurements, if the highest and best use of a non-financial asset differs from its current use, an entity shall disclose that fact and why the non-financial asset is being used in a manner that differs from its highest and best use.

94 An entity shall determine appropriate classes of assets and liabilities on the basis of the following:

(a) the nature, characteristics and risks of the asset or liability; and

(b) the level of the fair value hierarchy within which the fair value measurement is categorised.

The number of classes may need to be greater for fair value measurements categorised within Level 3 of the fair value hierarchy because those measurements have a greater degree of uncertainty and subjectivity. Determining appropriate classes of assets and liabilities for which disclosures about fair value measurements should be provided requires judgement. A class of assets and liabilities will often require greater disaggregation than the line items presented in the statement of financial position. However, an entity shall provide information sufficient to permit reconciliation to the line items presented in the statement of financial position. If another Standard specifies the class for an asset or a liability, an entity may use that class in providing the disclosures required in this Standard if that class meets the requirements in this paragraph.

95 An entity shall disclose and consistently follow its policy for determining when transfers between levels of the fair value hierarchy are deemed to have occurred in accordance with paragraph 93(c) and (e)(iv). The policy about the timing of recognising transfers shall be the same for transfers into the levels as for transfers out of the levels. Examples of policies for determining the timing of transfers include the following:

(a) the date of the event or change in circumstances that caused the transfer.

(b) the beginning of the reporting period.

(c) the end of the reporting period.

96 If an entity makes an accounting policy decision to use the exception in paragraph 48, it shall disclose that fact.

97 For each class of assets and liabilities not measured at fair value in the statement of financial position but for which the fair value is disclosed, an entity shall disclose the information required by paragraph 93(b), (d) and (i). However, an entity is not required to provide the quantitative disclosures about significant unobservable inputs used in fair value measurements categorised within Level 3 of the fair value hierarchy required by paragraph 93(d). For such assets and liabilities, an entity does not need to provide the other disclosures required by this Standard.

98 For a liability measured at fair value and issued with an inseparable third-party credit enhancement, an issuer shall disclose the existence of that credit enhancement and whether it is reflected in the fair value measurement of the liability.

99 An entity shall present the quantitative disclosures required by this Standard in a tabular format unless another format is more appropriate.

Appendix A
Defined Terms

This appendix is an integral part of AASB 13.

active market	A market in which transactions for the asset or liability take place with sufficient frequency and volume to provide pricing information on an ongoing basis.
cost approach	A valuation technique that reflects the amount that would be required currently to replace the service capacity of an asset (often referred to as current replacement cost).
entry price	The price paid to acquire an asset or received to assume a liability in an exchange transaction.
exit price	The price that would be received to sell an asset or paid to transfer a liability.
expected cash flow	The probability-weighted average (i.e. mean of the distribution) of possible future cash flows.
fair value	The price that would be received to sell an asset or paid to transfer a liability in an orderly transaction between market participants at the measurement date.
highest and best use	The use of a non-financial asset by market participants that would maximise the value of the asset or the group of assets and liabilities (e.g. a business) within which the asset would be used.
income approach	Valuation techniques that convert future amounts (e.g. cash flows or income and expenses) to a single current (i.e. discounted) amount. The fair value measurement is determined on the basis of the value indicated by current market expectations about those future amounts.
inputs	The assumptions that market participants would use when pricing the asset or liability, including assumptions about risk, such as the following:

    (a)   the risk inherent in a particular valuation technique used to measure fair value (such as a pricing model); and

    (b)   the risk inherent in the inputs to the valuation technique.

Inputs may be observable or unobservable.

Level 1 inputs	Quoted prices (unadjusted) in active markets for identical assets or liabilities that the entity can access at the measurement date.
Level 2 inputs	Inputs other than quoted prices included within Level 1 that are observable for the asset or liability, either directly or indirectly.
Level 3 inputs	Unobservable inputs for the asset or liability.
market approach	A valuation technique that uses prices and other relevant information generated by market transactions involving identical or comparable (i.e. similar) assets, liabilities or a group of assets and liabilities, such as a business.
market-corroborated inputs	Inputs that are derived principally from or corroborated by observable market data by correlation or other means.

market participants	Buyers and sellers in the principal (or most advantageous) market for the asset or liability that have all of the following characteristics:

(a)   They are independent of each other, i.e. they are not related parties as defined in AASB 124, although the price in a related party transaction may be used as an input to a fair value measurement if the entity has evidence that the transaction was entered into at market terms.

(b)   They are knowledgeable, having a reasonable understanding about the asset or liability and the transaction using all available information, including information that might be obtained through due diligence efforts that are usual and customary.

(c)   They are able to enter into a transaction for the asset or liability.

(d)   They are willing to enter into a transaction for the asset or liability, i.e. they are motivated but not forced or otherwise compelled to do so.

most advantageous market   The market that maximises the amount that would be received to sell the asset or minimises the amount that would be paid to transfer the liability, after taking into account transaction costs and transport costs.

non-performance risk   The risk that an entity will not fulfil an obligation. Non-performance risk includes, but may not be limited to, the entity's own credit risk.

observable inputs   Inputs that are developed using market data, such as publicly available information about actual events or transactions, and that reflect the assumptions that market participants would use when pricing the asset or liability.

orderly transaction   A transaction that assumes exposure to the market for a period before the measurement date to allow for marketing activities that are usual and customary for transactions involving such assets or liabilities; it is not a forced transaction (e.g. a forced liquidation or distress sale).

principal market   The market with the greatest volume and level of activity for the asset or liability.

risk premium   Compensation sought by risk-averse market participants for bearing the uncertainty inherent in the cash flows of an asset or a liability. Also referred to as a 'risk adjustment'.

transaction costs   The costs to sell an asset or transfer a liability in the principal (or most advantageous) market for the asset or liability that are directly attributable to the disposal of the asset or the transfer of the liability and meet both of the following criteria:

(a)   They result directly from and are essential to that transaction.

(b)   They would not have been incurred by the entity had the decision to sell the asset or transfer the liability not been made (similar to costs to sell, as defined in AASB 5).

transport costs   The costs that would be incurred to transport an asset from its current location to its principal (or most advantageous) market.

unit of account   The level at which an asset or a liability is aggregated or disaggregated in a Standard for recognition purposes.

unobservable inputs   Inputs for which market data are not available and that are developed using the best information available about the assumptions that market participants would use when pricing the asset or liability.

Appendix B

Application Guidance

This appendix is an integral part of AASB 13. It describes the application of paragraphs 1–99 and has the same authority as the other parts of the Standard.

B1   The judgements applied in different valuation situations may be different. This appendix describes the judgements that might apply when an entity measures fair value in different valuation situations.

The fair value measurement approach

B2   The objective of a fair value measurement is to estimate the price at which an orderly transaction to sell the asset or to transfer the liability would take place between market participants at the measurement date under current market conditions. A fair value measurement requires an entity to determine all the following:

   (a)   the particular asset or liability that is the subject of the measurement (consistently with its unit of account).

   (b)   for a non-financial asset, the valuation premise that is appropriate for the measurement (consistently with its highest and best use).

   (c)   the principal (or most advantageous) market for the asset or liability.

   (d)   the valuation technique(s) appropriate for the measurement, considering the availability of data with which to develop inputs that represent the assumptions that market participants would use when pricing the asset or liability and the level of the fair value hierarchy within which the inputs are categorised.

Valuation premise for non-financial assets (paragraphs 31–33)

B3   When measuring the fair value of a non-financial asset used in combination with other assets as a group (as installed or otherwise configured for use) or in combination with other assets and liabilities (e.g. a business), the effect of the valuation premise depends on the circumstances. For example:

   (a)   the fair value of the asset might be the same whether the asset is used on a stand-alone basis or in combination with other assets or with other assets and liabilities. That might be the case if the asset is a business that market participants would continue to operate. In that case, the transaction would involve valuing the business in its entirety. The use of the assets as a group in an ongoing business would generate synergies that would be available to market participants (i.e. market participant synergies that, therefore, should affect the fair value of the asset on either a stand-alone basis or in combination with other assets or with other assets and liabilities).

   (b)   an asset's use in combination with other assets or with other assets and liabilities might be incorporated into the fair value measurement through adjustments to the value of the asset used on a stand-alone basis. That might be the case if the asset is a machine and the fair value measurement is determined using an observed price for a similar machine (not installed or otherwise configured for use), adjusted for transport and installation costs so that the fair value measurement reflects the current condition and location of the machine (installed and configured for use).

   (c)   an asset's use in combination with other assets or with other assets and liabilities might be incorporated into the fair value measurement through the market participant assumptions used to measure the fair value of the asset. For example, if the asset is work in progress inventory that is unique and market participants would convert the inventory into finished goods, the fair value of the inventory would assume that market participants have acquired or would acquire any specialised machinery necessary to convert the inventory into finished goods.

(d)   an asset's use in combination with other assets or with other assets and liabilities might be incorporated into the valuation technique used to measure the fair value of the asset. That might be the case when using the multi-period excess earnings method to measure the fair value of an intangible asset because that valuation technique specifically takes into account the contribution of any complementary assets and the associated liabilities in the group in which such an intangible asset would be used.

(e)   in more limited situations, when an entity uses an asset within a group of assets, the entity might measure the asset at an amount that approximates its fair value when allocating the fair value of the asset group to the individual assets of the group. That might be the case if the valuation involves real property and the fair value of improved property (i.e. an asset group) is allocated to its component assets (such as land and improvements).

Fair value at initial recognition (paragraphs 57–60)

B4   When determining whether fair value at initial recognition equals the transaction price, an entity shall take into account factors specific to the transaction and to the asset or liability. For example, the transaction price might not represent the fair value of an asset or a liability at initial recognition if any of the following conditions exist:

(a)   The transaction is between related parties, although the price in a related party transaction may be used as an input into a fair value measurement if the entity has evidence that the transaction was entered into at market terms.

(b)   The transaction takes place under duress or the seller is forced to accept the price in the transaction. For example, that might be the case if the seller is experiencing financial difficulty.

(c)   The unit of account represented by the transaction price is different from the unit of account for the asset or liability measured at fair value. For example, that might be the case if the asset or liability measured at fair value is only one of the elements in the transaction (e.g. in a business combination), the transaction includes unstated rights and privileges that are measured separately in accordance with another Standard, or the transaction price includes transaction costs.

(d)   The market in which the transaction takes place is different from the principal market (or most advantageous market). For example, those markets might be different if the entity is a dealer that enters into transactions with customers in the retail market, but the principal (or most advantageous) market for the exit transaction is with other dealers in the dealer market.

Valuation techniques (paragraphs 61–66)

Market approach

B5   The market approach uses prices and other relevant information generated by market transactions involving identical or comparable (i.e. similar) assets, liabilities or a group of assets and liabilities, such as a business.

B6   For example, valuation techniques consistent with the market approach often use market multiples derived from a set of comparables. Multiples might be in ranges with a different multiple for each comparable. The selection of the appropriate multiple within the range requires judgement, considering qualitative and quantitative factors specific to the measurement.

B7   Valuation techniques consistent with the market approach include matrix pricing. Matrix pricing is a mathematical technique used principally to value some types of financial instruments, such as debt securities, without relying exclusively on quoted prices for the specific securities, but rather relying on the securities' relationship to other benchmark quoted securities.

Cost approach

B8   The cost approach reflects the amount that would be required currently to replace the service capacity of an asset (often referred to as current replacement cost).

B9   From the perspective of a market participant seller, the price that would be received for the asset is based on the cost to a market participant buyer to acquire or construct a substitute asset of comparable utility, adjusted for obsolescence. That is because a market participant buyer would not pay more for an asset than the amount for which it could replace the service capacity of that asset. Obsolescence encompasses physical deterioration, functional (technological) obsolescence and economic (external) obsolescence and is broader than depreciation for financial reporting purposes (an allocation of historical cost) or tax purposes (using specified service lives). In many cases the current replacement cost method is used to measure the fair value of tangible assets that are used in combination with other assets or with other assets and liabilities.

Income approach

B10   The income approach converts future amounts (e.g. cash flows or income and expenses) to a single current (i.e. discounted) amount. When the income approach is used, the fair value measurement reflects current market expectations about those future amounts.

B11   Those valuation techniques include, for example, the following:

(a)   present value techniques (see paragraphs B12–B30);

(b)   option pricing models, such as the Black-Scholes-Merton formula or a binomial model (i.e. a lattice model), that incorporate present value techniques and reflect both the time value and the intrinsic value of an option; and

(c)   the multi-period excess earnings method, which is used to measure the fair value of some intangible assets.

Present value techniques

B12   Paragraphs B13–B30 describe the use of present value techniques to measure fair value. Those paragraphs focus on a discount rate adjustment technique and an *expected cash flow* (expected present value) technique. Those paragraphs neither prescribe the use of a single specific present value technique nor limit the use of present value techniques to measure fair value to the techniques discussed. The present value technique used to measure fair value will depend on facts and circumstances specific to the asset or liability being measured (e.g. whether prices for comparable assets or liabilities can be observed in the market) and the availability of sufficient data.

The components of a present value measurement

B13   Present value (i.e. an application of the income approach) is a tool used to link future amounts (e.g. cash flows or values) to a present amount using a discount rate. A fair value measurement of an asset or a liability using a present value technique captures all the following elements from the perspective of market participants at the measurement date:

(a)   an estimate of future cash flows for the asset or liability being measured.

(b)   expectations about possible variations in the amount and timing of the cash flows representing the uncertainty inherent in the cash flows.

(c)   the time value of money, represented by the rate on risk-free monetary assets that have maturity dates or durations that coincide with the period covered by the cash flows and pose neither uncertainty in timing nor risk of default to the holder (i.e. a risk-free interest rate).

(d)   the price for bearing the uncertainty inherent in the cash flows (i.e. a risk premium).

(e)   other factors that market participants would take into account in the circumstances.

(f)   for a liability, the non-performance risk relating to that liability, including the entity's (i.e. the obligor's) own credit risk.

General principles

B14 Present value techniques differ in how they capture the elements in paragraph B13. However, all the following general principles govern the application of any present value technique used to measure fair value:

(a) Cash flows and discount rates should reflect assumptions that market participants would use when pricing the asset or liability.

(b) Cash flows and discount rates should take into account only the factors attributable to the asset or liability being measured.

(c) To avoid double-counting or omitting the effects of risk factors, discount rates should reflect assumptions that are consistent with those inherent in the cash flows. For example, a discount rate that reflects the uncertainty in expectations about future defaults is appropriate if using contractual cash flows of a loan (i.e. a discount rate adjustment technique). That same rate should not be used if using expected (i.e. probability-weighted) cash flows (i.e. an expected present value technique) because the expected cash flows already reflect assumptions about the uncertainty in future defaults; instead, a discount rate that is commensurate with the risk inherent in the expected cash flows should be used.

(d) Assumptions about cash flows and discount rates should be internally consistent. For example, nominal cash flows, which include the effect of inflation, should be discounted at a rate that includes the effect of inflation. The nominal risk-free interest rate includes the effect of inflation. Real cash flows, which exclude the effect of inflation, should be discounted at a rate that excludes the effect of inflation. Similarly, after-tax cash flows should be discounted using an after-tax discount rate. Pre-tax cash flows should be discounted at a rate consistent with those cash flows.

(e) Discount rates should be consistent with the underlying economic factors of the currency in which the cash flows are denominated.

Risk and uncertainty

B15 A fair value measurement using present value techniques is made under conditions of uncertainty because the cash flows used are estimates rather than known amounts. In many cases both the amount and timing of the cash flows are uncertain. Even contractually fixed amounts, such as the payments on a loan, are uncertain if there is risk of default.

B16 Market participants generally seek compensation (i.e. a risk premium) for bearing the uncertainty inherent in the cash flows of an asset or a liability. A fair value measurement should include a risk premium reflecting the amount that market participants would demand as compensation for the uncertainty inherent in the cash flows. Otherwise, the measurement would not faithfully represent fair value. In some cases determining the appropriate risk premium might be difficult. However, the degree of difficulty alone is not a sufficient reason to exclude a risk premium.

B17 Present value techniques differ in how they adjust for risk and in the type of cash flows they use. For example:

(a) The discount rate adjustment technique (see paragraphs B18–B22) uses a risk-adjusted discount rate and contractual, promised or most likely cash flows.

(b) Method 1 of the expected present value technique (see paragraph B25) uses risk-adjusted expected cash flows and a risk-free rate.

(c) Method 2 of the expected present value technique (see paragraph B26) uses expected cash flows that are not risk-adjusted and a discount rate adjusted to include the risk premium that market participants require. That rate is different from the rate used in the discount rate adjustment technique.

Discount rate adjustment technique

B18 The discount rate adjustment technique uses a single set of cash flows from the range of possible estimated amounts, whether contractual or promised (as is the case for a bond) or most likely cash flows. In all cases, those cash flows are conditional upon the occurrence of specified events (e.g. contractual or promised cash flows for a bond are conditional on the event of no default by the debtor). The discount rate used in the discount rate adjustment technique is derived from observed rates of return for comparable assets or liabilities that are traded in the market. Accordingly, the contractual, promised or most likely cash flows are discounted at an observed or estimated market rate for such conditional cash flows (i.e. a market rate of return).

B19　The discount rate adjustment technique requires an analysis of market data for comparable assets or liabilities. Comparability is established by considering the nature of the cash flows (e.g. whether the cash flows are contractual or non-contractual and are likely to respond similarly to changes in economic conditions), as well as other factors (e.g. credit standing, collateral, duration, restrictive covenants and liquidity). Alternatively, if a single comparable asset or liability does not fairly reflect the risk inherent in the cash flows of the asset or liability being measured, it may be possible to derive a discount rate using data for several comparable assets or liabilities in conjunction with the risk-free yield curve (i.e. using a 'build-up' approach).

B20　To illustrate a build-up approach, assume that Asset A is a contractual right to receive CU800[1] in one year (i.e. there is no timing uncertainty). There is an established market for comparable assets, and information about those assets, including price information, is available. Of those comparable assets:

(a)　Asset B is a contractual right to receive CU1,200 in one year and has a market price of CU1,083. Thus, the implied annual rate of return (i.e. a one-year market rate of return) is 10.8 per cent [(CU1,200/CU1,083) – 1].

(b)　Asset C is a contractual right to receive CU700 in two years and has a market price of CU566. Thus, the implied annual rate of return (i.e. a two-year market rate of return) is 11.2 per cent [(CU700/CU566)$^{0.5}$ – 1].

(c)　All three assets are comparable with respect to risk (i.e. dispersion of possible pay-offs and credit).

B21　On the basis of the timing of the contractual payments to be received for Asset A relative to the timing for Asset B and Asset C (i.e. one year for Asset B versus two years for Asset C), Asset B is deemed more comparable to Asset A. Using the contractual payment to be received for Asset A (CU800) and the one-year market rate derived from Asset B (10.8 per cent), the fair value of Asset A is CU722 (CU800/1.108). Alternatively, in the absence of available market information for Asset B, the one-year market rate could be derived from Asset C using the build-up approach. In that case the two-year market rate indicated by Asset C (11.2 per cent) would be adjusted to a one-year market rate using the term structure of the risk-free yield curve. Additional information and analysis might be required to determine whether the risk premiums for one-year and two-year assets are the same. If it is determined that the risk premiums for one-year and two-year assets are not the same, the two-year market rate of return would be further adjusted for that effect.

B22　When the discount rate adjustment technique is applied to fixed receipts or payments, the adjustment for risk inherent in the cash flows of the asset or liability being measured is included in the discount rate. In some applications of the discount rate adjustment technique to cash flows that are not fixed receipts or payments, an adjustment to the cash flows may be necessary to achieve comparability with the observed asset or liability from which the discount rate is derived.

Expected present value technique

B23　The expected present value technique uses as a starting point a set of cash flows that represents the probability-weighted average of all possible future cash flows (i.e. the expected cash flows). The resulting estimate is identical to expected value, which, in statistical terms, is the weighted average of a discrete random variable's possible values with the respective probabilities as the weights. Because all possible cash flows are probability-weighted, the resulting expected cash flow is not conditional upon the occurrence of any specified event (unlike the cash flows used in the discount rate adjustment technique).

1　In this Standard monetary amounts are denominated in 'currency units (CU)'.

B24 In making an investment decision, risk-averse market participants would take into account the risk that the actual cash flows may differ from the expected cash flows. Portfolio theory distinguishes between two types of risk:

(a) unsystematic (diversifiable) risk, which is the risk specific to a particular asset or liability.

(b) systematic (non-diversifiable) risk, which is the common risk shared by an asset or a liability with the other items in a diversified portfolio.

Portfolio theory holds that in a market in equilibrium, market participants will be compensated only for bearing the systematic risk inherent in the cash flows. (In markets that are inefficient or out of equilibrium, other forms of return or compensation might be available.)

B25 Method 1 of the expected present value technique adjusts the expected cash flows of an asset for systematic (i.e. market) risk by subtracting a cash risk premium (i.e. risk-adjusted expected cash flows). Those risk-adjusted expected cash flows represent a certainty-equivalent cash flow, which is discounted at a risk-free interest rate. A certainty-equivalent cash flow refers to an expected cash flow (as defined), adjusted for risk so that a market participant is indifferent to trading a certain cash flow for an expected cash flow. For example, if a market participant was willing to trade an expected cash flow of CU1,200 for a certain cash flow of CU1,000, the CU1,000 is the certainty equivalent of the CU1,200 (i.e. the CU200 would represent the cash risk premium). In that case the market participant would be indifferent as to the asset held.

B26 In contrast, Method 2 of the expected present value technique adjusts for systematic (i.e. market) risk by applying a risk premium to the risk-free interest rate. Accordingly, the expected cash flows are discounted at a rate that corresponds to an expected rate associated with probability-weighted cash flows (i.e. an expected rate of return). Models used for pricing risky assets, such as the capital asset pricing model, can be used to estimate the expected rate of return. Because the discount rate used in the discount rate adjustment technique is a rate of return relating to conditional cash flows, it is likely to be higher than the discount rate used in Method 2 of the expected present value technique, which is an expected rate of return relating to expected or probability-weighted cash flows.

B27 To illustrate Methods 1 and 2, assume that an asset has expected cash flows of CU780 in one year determined on the basis of the possible cash flows and probabilities shown below. The applicable risk-free interest rate for cash flows with a one-year horizon is 5 per cent, and the systematic risk premium for an asset with the same risk profile is 3 per cent.

Possible cash flows	Probability	Probability-weighted cash flows
CU500	15%	CU75
CU800	60%	CU480
CU900	25%	CU225
Expected cash flows		CU780

B28 In this simple illustration, the expected cash flows (CU780) represent the probability-weighted average of the three possible outcomes. In more realistic situations, there could be many possible outcomes. However, to apply the expected present value technique, it is not always necessary to take into account distributions of all possible cash flows using complex models and techniques. Rather, it might be possible to develop a limited number of discrete scenarios and probabilities that capture the array of possible cash flows. For example, an entity might use realised cash flows for some relevant past period, adjusted for changes in circumstances occurring subsequently (e.g. changes in external factors, including economic or market conditions, industry trends and competition as well as changes in internal factors affecting the entity more specifically), taking into account the assumptions of market participants.

B29 In theory, the present value (i.e. the fair value) of the asset's cash flows is the same whether determined using Method 1 or Method 2, as follows:

(a) Using Method 1, the expected cash flows are adjusted for systematic (i.e. market) risk. In the absence of market data directly indicating the amount of the risk adjustment, such adjustment could be derived from an asset pricing model using the concept of certainty equivalents. For example, the risk adjustment (i.e. the cash risk premium of CU22) could be determined using the systematic risk premium of 3 per cent (CU780 − [CU780 × (1.05/1.08)]), which results in risk-adjusted expected cash flows of CU758 (CU780 − CU22). The CU758 is the certainty equivalent of CU780 and is discounted at the risk-free interest rate (5 per cent). The present value (i.e. the fair value) of the asset is CU722 (CU758/1.05).

(b) Using Method 2, the expected cash flows are not adjusted for systematic (i.e. market) risk. Rather, the adjustment for that risk is included in the discount rate. Thus, the expected cash flows are discounted at an expected rate of return of 8 per cent (i.e. the 5 per cent risk-free interest rate plus the 3 per cent systematic risk premium). The present value (i.e. the fair value) of the asset is CU722 (CU780/1.08).

B30 When using an expected present value technique to measure fair value, either Method 1 or Method 2 could be used. The selection of Method 1 or Method 2 will depend on facts and circumstances specific to the asset or liability being measured, the extent to which sufficient data are available and the judgements applied.

Applying present value techniques to liabilities and an entity's own equity instruments not held by other parties as assets (paragraphs 40 and 41)

B31 When using a present value technique to measure the fair value of a liability that is not held by another party as an asset (e.g. a decommissioning liability), an entity shall, among other things, estimate the future cash outflows that market participants would expect to incur in fulfilling the obligation. Those future cash outflows shall include market participants' expectations about the costs of fulfilling the obligation and the compensation that a market participant would require for taking on the obligation. Such compensation includes the return that a market participant would require for the following:

(a) undertaking the activity (i.e. the value of fulfilling the obligation; e.g. by using resources that could be used for other activities); and

(b) assuming the risk associated with the obligation (i.e. a *risk premium* that reflects the risk that the actual cash outflows might differ from the expected cash outflows; see paragraph B33).

B32 For example, a non-financial liability does not contain a contractual rate of return and there is no observable market yield for that liability. In some cases the components of the return that market participants would require will be indistinguishable from one another (e.g. when using the price a third party contractor would charge on a fixed fee basis). In other cases an entity needs to estimate those components separately (e.g. when using the price a third party contractor would charge on a cost plus basis because the contractor in that case would not bear the risk of future changes in costs).

B33 An entity can include a risk premium in the fair value measurement of a liability or an entity's own equity instrument that is not held by another party as an asset in one of the following ways:

(a) by adjusting the cash flows (i.e. as an increase in the amount of cash outflows); or

(b) by adjusting the rate used to discount the future cash flows to their present values (i.e. as a reduction in the discount rate).

An entity shall ensure that it does not double-count or omit adjustments for risk. For example, if the estimated cash flows are increased to take into account the compensation for assuming the risk associated with the obligation, the discount rate should not be adjusted to reflect that risk.

Inputs to valuation techniques (paragraphs 67–71)

B34 Examples of markets in which inputs might be observable for some assets and liabilities (e.g. financial instruments) include the following:

(a) *Exchange markets*. In an exchange market, closing prices are both readily available and generally representative of fair value. An example of such a market is the London Stock Exchange.

(b) *Dealer markets*. In a dealer market, dealers stand ready to trade (either buy or sell for their own account), thereby providing liquidity by using their capital to hold an inventory of the items for which they make a market. Typically bid and ask prices (representing the price at which the dealer is willing to buy and the price at which the dealer is willing to sell, respectively) are more readily available than closing prices. Over-the-counter markets (for which prices are publicly reported) are dealer markets. Dealer markets also exist for some other assets and liabilities, including some financial instruments, commodities and physical assets (e.g. used equipment).

(c) *Brokered markets*. In a brokered market, brokers attempt to match buyers with sellers but do not stand ready to trade for their own account. In other words, brokers do not use their own capital to hold an inventory of the items for which they make a market. The broker knows the prices bid and asked by the respective parties, but each party is typically unaware of another party's price requirements. Prices of completed transactions are sometimes available. Brokered markets include electronic communication networks, in which buy and sell orders are matched, and commercial and residential real estate markets.

(d) *Principal-to-principal markets*. In a principal-to-principal market, transactions, both originations and resales, are negotiated independently with no intermediary. Little information about those transactions may be made available publicly.

Fair value hierarchy (paragraphs 72–90)

Level 2 inputs (paragraphs 81–85)

B35 Examples of Level 2 inputs for particular assets and liabilities include the following:

(a) *Receive-fixed, pay-variable interest rate swap based on the London Interbank Offered Rate (LIBOR) swap rate*. A Level 2 input would be the LIBOR swap rate if that rate is observable at commonly quoted intervals for substantially the full term of the swap.

(b) *Receive-fixed, pay-variable interest rate swap based on a yield curve denominated in a foreign currency*. A Level 2 input would be the swap rate based on a yield curve denominated in a foreign currency that is observable at commonly quoted intervals for substantially the full term of the swap. That would be the case if the term of the swap is 10 years and that rate is observable at commonly quoted intervals for 9 years, provided that any reasonable extrapolation of the yield curve for year 10 would not be significant to the fair value measurement of the swap in its entirety.

(c) *Receive-fixed, pay-variable interest rate swap based on a specific bank's prime rate*. A Level 2 input would be the bank's prime rate derived through extrapolation if the extrapolated values are corroborated by observable market data, for example, by correlation with an interest rate that is observable over substantially the full term of the swap.

(d) *Three-year option on exchange-traded shares*. A Level 2 input would be the implied volatility for the shares derived through extrapolation to year 3 if both of the following conditions exist:

(i) Prices for one-year and two-year options on the shares are observable.

(ii) The extrapolated implied volatility of a three-year option is corroborated by observable market data for substantially the full term of the option.

In that case the implied volatility could be derived by extrapolating from the implied volatility of the one-year and two-year options on the shares and corroborated by the implied volatility for three-year options on comparable entities' shares, provided that correlation with the one-year and two-year implied volatilities is established.

(e)   *Licensing arrangement.* For a licensing arrangement that is acquired in a business combination and was recently negotiated with an unrelated party by the acquired entity (the party to the licensing arrangement), a Level 2 input would be the royalty rate in the contract with the unrelated party at inception of the arrangement.

(f)   *Finished goods inventory at a retail outlet.* For finished goods inventory that is acquired in a business combination, a Level 2 input would be either a price to customers in a retail market or a price to retailers in a wholesale market, adjusted for differences between the condition and location of the inventory item and the comparable (i.e. similar) inventory items so that the fair value measurement reflects the price that would be received in a transaction to sell the inventory to another retailer that would complete the requisite selling efforts. Conceptually, the fair value measurement will be the same, whether adjustments are made to a retail price (downward) or to a wholesale price (upward). Generally, the price that requires the least amount of subjective adjustments should be used for the fair value measurement.

(g)   *Building held and used.* A Level 2 input would be the price per square metre for the building (a valuation multiple) derived from observable market data, e.g. multiples derived from prices in observed transactions involving comparable (i.e. similar) buildings in similar locations.

(h)   *Cash-generating unit.* A Level 2 input would be a valuation multiple (e.g. a multiple of earnings or revenue or a similar performance measure) derived from observable market data, e.g. multiples derived from prices in observed transactions involving comparable (i.e. similar) businesses, taking into account operational, market, financial and non-financial factors.

Level 3 inputs (paragraphs 86–90)

B36   Examples of Level 3 inputs for particular assets and liabilities include the following:

(a)   *Long-dated currency swap.* A Level 3 input would be an interest rate in a specified currency that is not observable and cannot be corroborated by observable market data at commonly quoted intervals or otherwise for substantially the full term of the currency swap. The interest rates in a currency swap are the swap rates calculated from the respective countries' yield curves.

(b)   *Three-year option on exchange-traded shares.* A Level 3 input would be historical volatility, i.e. the volatility for the shares derived from the shares' historical prices. Historical volatility typically does not represent current market participants' expectations about future volatility, even if it is the only information available to price an option.

(c)   *Interest rate swap.* A Level 3 input would be an adjustment to a mid-market consensus (non-binding) price for the swap developed using data that are not directly observable and cannot otherwise be corroborated by observable market data.

(d)   *Decommissioning liability assumed in a business combination.* A Level 3 input would be a current estimate using the entity's own data about the future cash outflows to be paid to fulfil the obligation (including market participants' expectations about the costs of fulfilling the obligation and the compensation that a market participant would require for taking on the obligation to dismantle the asset) if there is no reasonably available information that indicates that market participants would use different assumptions. That Level 3 input would be used in a present value technique together with other inputs, e.g. a current risk-free interest rate or a credit-adjusted risk-free rate if the effect of the entity's credit standing on the fair value of the liability is reflected in the discount rate rather than in the estimate of future cash outflows.

(e) *Cash-generating unit*. A Level 3 input would be a financial forecast (e.g. of cash flows or profit or loss) developed using the entity's own data if there is no reasonably available information that indicates that market participants would use different assumptions.

Measuring fair value when the volume or level of activity for an asset or a liability has significantly decreased

B37 The fair value of an asset or a liability might be affected when there has been a significant decrease in the volume or level of activity for that asset or liability in relation to normal market activity for the asset or liability (or similar assets or liabilities). To determine whether, on the basis of the evidence available, there has been a significant decrease in the volume or level of activity for the asset or liability, an entity shall evaluate the significance and relevance of factors such as the following:

(a) There are few recent transactions.

(b) Price quotations are not developed using current information.

(c) Price quotations vary substantially either over time or among market-makers (e.g. some brokered markets).

(d) Indices that previously were highly correlated with the fair values of the asset or liability are demonstrably uncorrelated with recent indications of fair value for that asset or liability.

(e) There is a significant increase in implied liquidity risk premiums, yields or performance indicators (such as delinquency rates or loss severities) for observed transactions or quoted prices when compared with the entity's estimate of expected cash flows, taking into account all available market data about credit and other non-performance risk for the asset or liability.

(f) There is a wide bid-ask spread or significant increase in the bid-ask spread.

(g) There is a significant decline in the activity of, or there is an absence of, a market for new issues (i.e. a primary market) for the asset or liability or similar assets or liabilities.

(h) Little information is publicly available (e.g. for transactions that take place in a principal-to-principal market).

B38 If an entity concludes that there has been a significant decrease in the volume or level of activity for the asset or liability in relation to normal market activity for the asset or liability (or similar assets or liabilities), further analysis of the transactions or quoted prices is needed. A decrease in the volume or level of activity on its own may not indicate that a transaction price or quoted price does not represent fair value or that a transaction in that market is not orderly. However, if an entity determines that a transaction or quoted price does not represent fair value (e.g. there may be transactions that are not orderly), an adjustment to the transactions or quoted prices will be necessary if the entity uses those prices as a basis for measuring fair value and that adjustment may be significant to the fair value measurement in its entirety. Adjustments also may be necessary in other circumstances (e.g. when a price for a similar asset requires significant adjustment to make it comparable to the asset being measured or when the price is stale).

B39 This Standard does not prescribe a methodology for making significant adjustments to transactions or quoted prices. See paragraphs 61–66 and B5–B11 for a discussion of the use of valuation techniques when measuring fair value. Regardless of the valuation technique used, an entity shall include appropriate risk adjustments, including a risk premium reflecting the amount that market participants would demand as compensation for the uncertainty inherent in the cash flows of an asset or a liability (see paragraph B17). Otherwise, the measurement does not faithfully represent fair value. In some cases determining the appropriate risk adjustment might be difficult. However, the degree of difficulty alone is not a sufficient basis on which to exclude a risk adjustment. The risk adjustment shall be reflective of an orderly transaction between market participants at the measurement date under current market conditions.

B40   If there has been a significant decrease in the volume or level of activity for the asset or liability, a change in valuation technique or the use of multiple valuation techniques may be appropriate (e.g. the use of a market approach and a present value technique). When weighting indications of fair value resulting from the use of multiple valuation techniques, an entity shall consider the reasonableness of the range of fair value measurements. The objective is to determine the point within the range that is most representative of fair value under current market conditions. A wide range of fair value measurements may be an indication that further analysis is needed.

B41   Even when there has been a significant decrease in the volume or level of activity for the asset or liability, the objective of a fair value measurement remains the same. Fair value is the price that would be received to sell an asset or paid to transfer a liability in an orderly transaction (i.e. not a forced liquidation or distress sale) between market participants at the measurement date under current market conditions.

B42   Estimating the price at which market participants would be willing to enter into a transaction at the measurement date under current market conditions if there has been a significant decrease in the volume or level of activity for the asset or liability depends on the facts and circumstances at the measurement date and requires judgement. An entity's intention to hold the asset or to settle or otherwise fulfil the liability is not relevant when measuring fair value because fair value is a market-based measurement, not an entity-specific measurement.

Identifying transactions that are not orderly

B43   The determination of whether a transaction is orderly (or is not orderly) is more difficult if there has been a significant decrease in the volume or level of activity for the asset or liability in relation to normal market activity for the asset or liability (or similar assets or liabilities). In such circumstances it is not appropriate to conclude that all transactions in that market are not orderly (i.e. forced liquidations or distress sales). Circumstances that may indicate that a transaction is not orderly include the following:

(a)   There was not adequate exposure to the market for a period before the measurement date to allow for marketing activities that are usual and customary for transactions involving such assets or liabilities under current market conditions.

(b)   There was a usual and customary marketing period, but the seller marketed the asset or liability to a single market participant.

(c)   The seller is in or near bankruptcy or receivership (i.e. the seller is distressed).

(d)   The seller was required to sell to meet regulatory or legal requirements (i.e. the seller was forced).

(e)   The transaction price is an outlier when compared with other recent transactions for the same or a similar asset or liability.

An entity shall evaluate the circumstances to determine whether, on the weight of the evidence available, the transaction is orderly.

B44   An entity shall consider all the following when measuring fair value or estimating market risk premiums:

(a)   If the evidence indicates that a transaction is not orderly, an entity shall place little, if any, weight (compared with other indications of fair value) on that transaction price.

(b)   If the evidence indicates that a transaction is orderly, an entity shall take into account that transaction price. The amount of weight placed on that transaction price when compared with other indications of fair value will depend on the facts and circumstances, such as the following:

(i)   the volume of the transaction.

(ii)   the comparability of the transaction to the asset or liability being measured.

(iii)   the proximity of the transaction to the measurement date.

(c)   If an entity does not have sufficient information to conclude whether a transaction is orderly, it shall take into account the transaction price. However, that transaction price may not represent fair value (i.e. the transaction price is not necessarily the sole or primary basis for measuring fair value or estimating market risk premiums). When an entity does not have sufficient information to conclude whether particular transactions are orderly, the entity shall place less weight on those transactions when compared with other transactions that are known to be orderly.

An entity need not undertake exhaustive efforts to determine whether a transaction is orderly, but it shall not ignore information that is reasonably available. When an entity is a party to a transaction, it is presumed to have sufficient information to conclude whether the transaction is orderly.

Using quoted prices provided by third parties

B45   This Standard does not preclude the use of quoted prices provided by third parties, such as pricing services or brokers, if an entity has determined that the quoted prices provided by those parties are developed in accordance with this Standard.

B46   If there has been a significant decrease in the volume or level of activity for the asset or liability, an entity shall evaluate whether the quoted prices provided by third parties are developed using current information that reflects orderly transactions or a valuation technique that reflects market participant assumptions (including assumptions about risk). In weighting a quoted price as an input to a fair value measurement, an entity places less weight (when compared with other indications of fair value that reflect the results of transactions) on quotes that do not reflect the result of transactions.

B47   Furthermore, the nature of a quote (e.g. whether the quote is an indicative price or a binding offer) shall be taken into account when weighting the available evidence, with more weight given to quotes provided by third parties that represent binding offers.

Appendix C
Effective Date and Transition

This appendix is an integral part of AASB 13 and has the same authority as the other parts of the Standard.

C1   [Deleted by the AASB – see paragraphs Aus4.2 and Aus4.3]

C2   This Standard shall be applied prospectively as of the beginning of the annual reporting period in which it is initially applied.

C3   The disclosure requirements of this Standard need not be applied in comparative information provided for periods before initial application of this Standard.

Deleted IFRS 13 Text

Deleted IFRS 13 text is not part of AASB 13.

Paragraph 7(b)
The disclosures required by this IFRS are not required for the following:

(a)   …

(b)   retirement benefit plan investments measured at fair value in accordance with IAS 26 *Accounting and Reporting by Retirement Benefit Plans*;

(c)   …

Paragraph C1
An entity shall apply this IFRS for annual periods beginning on or after 1 January 2013. Earlier application is permitted. If an entity applies this IFRS for an earlier period, it shall disclose that fact.

AASB 101
Presentation of Financial Statements

(Compiled June 2012)

Note from the Institute of Chartered Accountants Australia

This note, prepared by the technical editors, is not part of Accounting Standard AASB 101.

Historical development

15 July 2004: AASB 101 'Presentation of Financial Statements' is the Australian equivalent of IAS 1 of the same name. It was made by the AASB on 15 July 2004 as part of the AASB's program to adopt International Financial Reporting Standards by 2005.

4 October 2006: AASB 101 is amended as a result of the AASB's decision to have the same requirements as IAS 1 in AASB 101 in respect of for-profit entities. Many of the disclosures from previous GAAP and all of the guidance from previous GAAP are not contained in the amended version.

14 June 2007: AASB 2007-6 'Amendments to Australian Accounting Standards' was issued by the AASB. This Standard is applicable to annual reporting periods beginning on or after 1 January 2009.

July 2007: Erratum amends paragraph 110. This amendment is applicable to annual reporting periods beginning on or after 1 July 2007.

24 September 2007: AASB 101 'Presentation of Financial Statements' is reissued by the AASB, superseding the August 2007 version of the Standard.

AASB 101 (revised) is applicable to annual reporting periods beginning on or after 1 January 2009 and can be adopted early to reporting periods from 1 January 2005. The major change with the issue of the revised Standard is the requirement to present owner-related changes in equity separately from non-owner changes in equity, resulting in a new statement of comprehensive income as well as change in the format of income statement and statement of changes in equity.

Additionally the terminology in the Standard has changed, with 'balance sheet' being replaced with 'statement of financial position' and the 'financial report' being replaced with 'financial statement'.

13 December 2007: AASB 2007-9 'Amendments to Australian Accounting Standards arising from the Review of AAS 27, AAS 29 and AAS 31' was issued by the AASB. This Standard is applicable to annual reporting periods beginning on or after 1 July 2008, with early adoption permitted.

5 March 2008: AASB 2008-2 'Amendments to Australian Accounting Standards – Puttable Financial Instruments and Obligations arising on Liquidation' classifies as equity instruments certain puttable financial instruments. This Standard is applicable to annual reporting periods beginning on or after 1 January 2009.

6 March 2008: AASB 2008-3 'Amendments to Australian Accounting Standards arising from AASB 3 and AASB 127' amends AASB 101 for the issue of AASB 3 Revised. This Standard is applicable to annual reporting periods beginning on or after 1 July 2009.

24 July 2008: AASB 2008-5 'Amendments to Australian Accounting Standards arising from the Annual Improvements Project' amends AASB 101 in relation to the classification of derivatives. This Standard is applicable to annual reporting periods beginning on or after 1 January 2009.

21 May 2009: AASB 2009-5 'Amendments to Australian Accounting Standards' is the annual improvements Standard, amending AASB 101 in relation to the current/non-current classification of convertible instruments. This Standard applies to annual reporting periods beginning on or after 1 January 2010 and may be applied early.

25 June 2009: AASB 2009-6 'Amendments to Australian Accounting Standards' amends AASB 101 for editorial corrections made by the International Accounting Standards Board (IASB) to its Standards and Interpretations (IFRSs) and as a consequence of issuing revised AASB 101 'Presentation of Financial Statements'. This Standard is applicable to annual reporting periods beginning on or after 1 January 2009 that end on or after 30 June 2009.

---

19 October 2009: AASB 101 revised was reissued by the AASB, compiled to include the AASB 2007-9, AASB 2008-2, AASB 2008-3, AASB 2008-5 and AASB 2009-6 amendments and applies to annual reporting periods beginning on or after 1 July 2009 but before 1 January 2010.

1 December 2009: AASB 101 was reissued by the AASB, compiled to include the AASB 2009-5 amendments and applies to annual reporting periods beginning on or after 1 January 2010.

7 December 2009: AASB 2009-11 'Amendments to Australian Accounting Standards arising from AASB 9' amends AASB 101 to give effect to consequential changes arising from the issuance of AASB 9. This Standard is applicable to annual reporting periods beginning on or after 1 January 2013 with early adoption permitted from annual reporting periods ending on or after 31 December 2009 that begin before 1 January 2013 provided AASB 9 is also applied for the same period. The application date of AASB 2009-11 has been amended to 1 January 2015 by AASB 2012-6. **These amendments have been superseded by AASB 2010-5 and are not included in this compiled Standard.**

23 June 2010: AASB 2010-4 'Further Amendments to Australian Accounting Standards arising from the Annual Improvements Project' amends AASB 101 to clarify the Statement of Changes in Equity. This Standard is applicable to annual reporting periods beginning on or after 1 January 2011, with early adoption permitted for annual reporting periods beginning on or after 1 January 2005 but before 1 January 2011.

27 October 2010: AASB 2010-5 'Further Amendments to Australian Accounting Standards' makes editorial amendments to AASB 101. In paragraphs Aus 138 (d), (e) and (f), the references to paragraphs Aus 126.2 (a), (b) and (c) are amended to parapraphs 138.2 (a), (b) and (c). This Standard is applicable to annual reporting periods beginning on or after 1 January 2011.

1 March 2011: AASB 2010-7 'Amendments to Australian Accounting Standards arising from AASB 9 (December 2010)' as compiled amends AASB 101 to give effect to consequential changes arising from the re-issue of AASB 9 in December 2010, and supersedes AASB 2009-11 which related to the previous version of AASB 9. This Standard applies to annual reporting periods beginning on or after 1 January 2013 and can be adopted early. The application date of AASB 2010-7 has been amended to 1 January 2015 by AASB 2012-6. **These amendments are not included in this compiled Standard.**

11 May 2011: AASB 2011-1 'Amendments to Australian Accounting Standards arising from the Trans-Tasman Convergence Project' amends AASB 101 as a result of the Trans-Tasman project, to more closely align IFRSs as applied through Australian and New Zealand Standards. AASB 2011-1 deletes Australian specific disclosure requirements. Where appropriate these disclosures are now included in AASB 1054 'Australian Additional Requirements'. These Standards apply to annual reporting periods beginning on or after 1 July 2011 with early adoption permitted.

29 August 2011: AASB 2011-7 'Amendments to Australian Accounting Standards arising from the Consolidation and Joint Arrangements Standards' amends AASB 101 to give effect to many consequential changes arising from the issue of AASB 10, 11, 12, 127 and 128. This Standard applies to annual reporting periods beginning on or after 1 January 2013 and can be adopted early by for-profit entities. **These amendments are not included in this compiled Standard.**

2 September 2011: AASB 2011-8 'Amendments to Australian Accounting Standards arising from AASB 13' amends AASB 101 to give effect to a consequential change in the definition of fair value arising from the issue of AASB 13. This Standard applies to annual reporting periods beginning on or after 1 January 2013 and can be adopted early. **These amendments are not included this compiled Standard.**

5 September 2011: AASB 2011-9 'Amendments to Australian Accounting Standards – Presentation of Items of Other Comprehensive income' amends the presentation of items in other comprehensive income. This Standard applies to annual reporting periods beginning on or after 1 July 2012 and can be adopted early.

5 September 2011: AASB 2011-10 'Amendments to Australian Accounting Standards arising from AASB 119 (September 2011)' amends AASB 101 to give effect to a consequential change arising from the issue of AASB 119. This Standard applies to annual reporting periods beginning on or after 1 January 2013 and can be adopted early. **These amendments are not included in this compiled Standard.**

23 September 2011: AASB 101 was reissued by the AASB, compiled to include the AASB 2010-4, AASB 2010-5 and AASB 2011-1 amendments and applies to annual reporting periods ending on or after 1 July 2011 but before 1 July 2012.

20 June 2012: AASB 101 was reissued by the AASB, compiled to include the AASB 2011-9 amendments and applies to annual reporting periods beginning on or after 1 July 2012 but before 1 January 2013.

29 June 2012: AASB 2012-5 'Amendments to Australian Accounting Standards arising from Annual Improvements 2009–2011 Cycle' amends AASB 101 to clarify the requirements for comparative information. This Standard applies to annual reporting periods beginning on or after 1 January 2013 and can be applied early. **These amendments are not included in this compiled Standard.**

10 September 2012: AASB 2012-7 'Amendments to Australian Accounting Standards arising from Reduced Disclosure Requirements' amends AASB 101 in relation to reduced disclosure requirements and applies to annual reporting periods beginning on or after 1 July 2013. **These amendments are not included in this compiled Standard**

References

Interpretation 1 *Changes in Existing Decommissioning Restoration and Similar Liabilities,* Interpretation 19 *Extinguishing Financial Liabilities with Equity Instruments*, Interpretation 14 *AASB 119 – The Limit on a Defined Benefit Asset, Minimum Funding Requirements and their Interaction,* Interpretation 115 *Operating Leases – Incentives,* Interpretation 129 *Service Concession Arrangements: Disclosures,* and Interpretation 132 *Intangible Assets – Web Site Costs* apply to AASB 101.

IFRIC items not taken onto the agenda: No. 1 *Operating and Ordinary Activities Classification of Interests and Penalties,* IAS 1-1 *Normal operating cycle,* IAS 1-2 *Comparatives. for prospectuses,* IAS 1-3 *Whether the liability component of a convertible instrument should be classified as current or non-current,* IAS 1-4 IAS 1 *Presentation of Financial Statements/IAS 39 Financial Instruments: recognition and measurement – Current or non-current presentation of derivatives classified as 'held for trading' under IAS 39,* IAS 1-5 IAS 1 *Financial Statement Presentation – Going concern disclosure,* IAS 1-6 IAS 1 *Presentation of Financial Statements – Current/non-current classification of a callable term loan,* IAS 1-7 IAS 1 *Presentation of Financial Statements – Current/non-current classification of a callable term loan* and IAS 1-11 IAS 1 *Presentation of Financial Statements* and IAS 12 *Income Taxes – Presentation of payments on non-income taxes* apply to AASB 101.

AASB Staff Article – Changes made to AASB 101 'Presentation of Financial Statements' in October 2006.

AASB 101 compared to IAS 1

Additions

Paragraph	Description
Aus 1.1	Which entities AASB 101 applies to, (i.e. reporting entities and general purpose financial statements).
Aus 1.2	The application date of AASB 101, (i.e. annual reporting periods beginning 1 January 2009).
Aus 1.3	Allows early application of AASB 101.
Aus 1.4	Makes the requirements of AASB 101 subject to AASB 1031 'Materiality'.
Aus 1.5	Explains which Australian Standards have been superseded by AASB 101.
Aus 1.6	Paragraphs 134–136 apply to reporting entities preparing financial reports in accordance with the *Corporations Act 2001*.
Aus 1.7	A not-for-profit entity need not present the disclosures required by paragraphs 134-136.
Aus 7.2	Additional definitions.

Aus 16.2 to Aus 16.3	Clarifies whether entities should report compliance with IFRSs.
Aus 19.1	Clarifies that certain entities are not permitted to depart from Standards.
Aus139A.1	Explains application of amendments arising from AASB 2008-3.

Deletions

Paragraph	Description
2	Requirement to prepare financial reports in accordance with IFRSs.
17	First sentence – fair presentation under IFRSs.
139	Application date of IAS 1 and amendments.
140	Reference to superseded IAS 1.

Contents

Compilation Details

Comparison with IAS 1

Accounting Standard
AASB 101 Presentation of Financial Statements

	Paragraphs
Objective	1
Application	Aus1.1 – Aus1.7
Scope	3 – 6
Definitions	7 – 8A
Financial Statements	
Purpose of Financial Statements	9
Complete Set of Financial Statements	10 – 14
General Features	
Fair Presentation and Compliance with IFRSs	15 – 24
Going Concern	25 – 26
Accrual Basis of Accounting	27 – 28
Materiality and Aggregation	29 – 31
Offsetting	32 – 35
Frequency of Reporting	36 – 37
Comparative Information	38 – 44
Consistency of Presentation	45 – 46
Structure and Content	
Introduction	47 – 48
Identification of the Financial Statements	49 – 53
Statement of Financial Position	
Information to be Presented in the Statement of Financial Position	54 – 59
Current/Non-current Distinction	60 – 65
Current Assets	66 – 68
Current Liabilities	69 – 76
Information to be Presented either in the Statement of Financial Position or in the Notes	77 – 80A
Statement of Profit or Loss and Other Comprehensive Income	81A – 81B
Information to be Presented in the Profit or Loss Section or the Statement of Profit or Loss	82
Information to be Presented in the Other Comprehensive Income Section	82A – 87
Profit or Loss for the Period	88 – 89
Other Comprehensive Income for the Period	90 – 96
Information to be Presented in the Statement(s) of Profit or Loss and Other Comprehensive Income or in the Notes	97 – 105
Statement of Changes in Equity	
Information to be Presented in the Statement of Changes in Equity	106
Information to be Presented in the Statement of Changes in Equity or in the Notes	106A – 110

	Paragraphs
Statement of Cash Flows	111
Notes	
Structure	112 – 116
Disclosure of Accounting Policies	117 – 124
Sources of Estimation Uncertainty	125 – 133
Capital	134 – 136
Puttable Financial Instruments Classified as Equity	136A
Other Disclosures	137 – 138
Transition and Effective Date	Aus139A.1 – 139J

Deleted IAS 1 Text

Basis for Conclusions on IAS 1
(available on the AASB website)

Implementation Guidance on IAS 1
(available on the AASB website)

Table of Concordance for IAS1
(available on the AASB website)

Australian Accounting Standard AASB 101 *Presentation of Financial Statements* (as amended) is set out in paragraphs 1 – 139J. All the paragraphs have equal authority. Paragraphs in **bold type** state the main principles. Terms defined in this Standard are in *italics* the first time they appear in the Standard. AASB 101 is to be read in the context of other Australian Accounting Standards, including AASB 1048 *Interpretation of Standards, which identifies the Australian Accounting Interpretations*. In the absence of explicit guidance, AASB 108 *Accounting Policies, Changes in Accounting Estimates and Errors* provides a basis for selecting and applying accounting policies.

Compilation Details

Accounting Standard AASB 101 *Presentation of Financial Statements* as amended

This compiled Standard applies to annual reporting periods beginning on or after 1 July 2012 but before 1 January 2013. It takes into account amendments up to and including 5 September 2011 and was prepared on 20 June 2012 by the staff of the Australian Accounting Standards Board (AASB).

This compilation is not a separate Accounting Standard made by the AASB. Instead, it is a representation of AASB 101 (September 2007) as amended by other Accounting Standards, which are listed in the Table below.

Table of Standards

Standard	Date made	Application date *(annual reporting periods ... on or after ...)*	Application, saving or transitional provisions
AASB 101	24 Sep 2007	*(beginning)* 1 Jan 2009	see (a) below
AASB 2007-9	13 Dec 2007	*(beginning)* 1 Jul 2008	see (b) below
AASB 2008-2	5 Mar 2008	*(beginning)* 1 Jan 2009	see (a) below
AASB 2008-3	6 Mar 2008	*(beginning)* 1 Jul 2009	see (c) below
AASB 2008-5	24 Jul 2008	*(beginning)* 1 Jan 2009	see (d) below
AASB 2009-5	21 May 2009	*(beginning)* 1 Jan 2010	see (e) below
AASB 2009-6	25 Jun 2009	*(beginning)* 1 Jan 2009 and *(ending)* 30 Jun 2009	see (f) below

Standard	Date made	Application date *(annual reporting periods ... on or after ...)*	Application, saving or transitional provisions
AASB 2009-11	7 Dec 2009	*(beginning)* 1 Jan 2013	not compiled*
AASB 2010-4	23 Jun 2010	*(beginning)* 1 Jan 2011	see (g) below
AASB 2010-2	30 Jun 2010	*(beginning)* 1 Jul 2013	not compiled*
AASB 2010-5	27 Oct 2010	*(beginning)* 1 Jan 2011	see (g) below
AASB 2010-7	6 Dec 2010	*(beginning)* 1 Jan 2013	not compiled*
AASB 2011-1	11 May 2011	*(beginning)* 1 Jul 2011	see (h) below
AASB 2011-2	11 May 2011	*(beginning)* 1 Jul 2013	not compiled*
AASB 2011-7	29 Aug 2011	*(beginning)* 1 Jan 2013	not compiled*
AASB 2011-8	2 Sep 2011	*(beginning)* 1 Jan 2013	not compiled*
AASB 2011-9	5 Sep 2011	*(beginning)* 1 Jul 2012	see (i) below
AASB 2011-10	5 Sep 2011	*(beginning)* 1 Jan 2013	not compiled*

*   The amendments made by this Standard are not included in this compilation, which presents the principal Standard as applicable to annual reporting periods beginning on or after 1 July 2012 but before 1 January 2013.

(a)   Entities may elect to apply this Standard to annual reporting periods beginning on or after 1 January 2005 but before 1 January 2009.

(b)   Entities may elect to apply this Standard to annual reporting periods beginning on or after 1 January 2005 but before 1 July 2008, provided that the Standards and Interpretation listed in paragraph 6 of AASB 2007-9 are also applied to such periods.

(c)   Entities may elect to apply this Standard to annual reporting periods beginning on or after 30 June 2007 but before 1 July 2009, provided that AASB 3 *Business Combinations* (March 2008) and AASB 127 *Consolidated and Separate Financial Statements* (March 2008) are also applied to such periods.

(d)   Entities may elect to apply this Standard, or its amendments to individual Standards, to annual reporting periods beginning on or after 1 January 2005 but before 1 January 2009.

(e)   Entities may elect to apply this Standard, or its amendments to individual Standards, to annual reporting periods beginning on or after 1 January 2005 but before 1 January 2010.

(f)   Entities may elect to apply this Standard to annual reporting periods beginning on or after 1 January 2005 but before 1 January 2009, provided that AASB 101 *Presentation of Financial Statements* (September 2007) is also applied to such periods, and to annual reporting periods beginning on or after 1 January 2009 that end before 30 June 2009.

(g)   Entities may elect to apply this Standard to annual reporting periods beginning on or after 1 January 2005 but before 1 January 2011.

(h)   Entities may elect to apply this Standard, or its amendments to individual pronouncements, to annual reporting periods beginning on or after 1 January 2005 but before 1 July 2011, provided that AASB 1054 *Australian Additional Disclosures* is, or its relevant individual disclosure requirements are, also applied to such periods.

(i)   Entities may elect to apply this Standard to annual reporting periods beginning on or after 1 January 2005 but before 1 July 2012.

Table of Amendments

Paragraph affected	How affected	By ... [paragraph]
7	amended	AASB 2010-5 [20]
	amended	AASB 2011-9 [14]
Aus7.1	deleted	AASB 2011-1 [10]
Aus7.2	added	AASB 2008-3 [22]
8A	added	AASB 2008-2 [8]
10	amended	AASB 2011-9 [15]
10A	added	AASB 2011-9 [15]
12	deleted	AASB 2011-9 [15]
Aus15.1-Aus15.4	deleted	AASB 2011-1 [10]
Aus16.1	deleted	AASB 2011-1 [10]

Paragraph affected	How affected	By ... [paragraph]
Aus16.2	amended	AASB 2007-9 [14]
17	amended	AASB 2011-1 [11]
19	added	AASB 2011-1 [12]
Aus19.1	added	AASB 2011-1 [12]
20-22	added	AASB 2011-1 [12]
Aus50.1	deleted	AASB 2011-1 [10]
54	amended	AASB 2008-3 [8]
68	amended	AASB 2008-5 [14]
69	amended	AASB 2009-5 [11]
71	amended	AASB 2008-5 [14]
73	amended	AASB 2009-6 [32]
80A	added	AASB 2008-2 [9]
81 (preceding heading)	amended	AASB 2011-9 [16]
81	deleted	AASB 2011-9 [16]
81A-81B	added	AASB 2011-9 [16]
82 (and preceding heading)	amended	AASB 2011-9 [16]
82A (and preceding heading)	added	AASB 2011-9 [16]
83	amended	AASB 2009-6 [33]
	amended	AASB 2008-3 [8]
	deleted	AASB 2011-9 [16]
84	deleted	AASB 2011-9 [16]
85-87	amended	AASB 2011-9 [17]
90-91	amended	AASB 2011-9 [17]
94	amended	AASB 2011-9 [17]
97 (preceding heading)	amended	AASB 2011-9 [17]
100	amended	AASB 2011-9 [17]
106 (preceding heading)	added	AASB 2010-4 [11]
106	amended	AASB 2008-3 [23]
	amended	AASB 2010-4 [11]
106A (and preceding heading)	added	AASB 2010-4 [11]
107	amended	AASB 2010-4 [11]
115	amended	AASB 2011-9 [17]
136A (and preceding heading)	added	AASB 2008-2 [10]
138	amended	AASB 2008-2 [11]
Aus138.1	deleted	AASB 2011-1 [10]
Aus138.2	amended	AASB 2010-5 [21]
	deleted	AASB 2011-1 [10]
Aus138.3-Aus138.6	deleted	AASB 2011-1 [10]
139A	note added	AASB 2008-3 [24]
Aus139A.1	added	AASB 2008-3 [25]
139B	note added	AASB 2008-2 [12]
139C	added	AASB 2008-5 [15]
139D	added	AASB 2009-5 [12]
139F	added	AASB 2010-4 [11]
139J	added	AASB 2011-9 [17]

The Australian Implementation Guidance was deleted as a consequence of the deletion of paragraphs Aus138.3-Aus138.5, to which the guidance related.

Comparison with IAS 1

AASB 101 and IAS 1

AASB 101 *Presentation of Financial Statements* as amended incorporates IAS 1 *Presentation of Financial Statements* as issued and amended by the International Accounting Standards Board (IASB). Paragraphs that have been added to this Standard (and do not appear in the text of IAS 1) are identified with the prefix "Aus", followed by the number of the preceding IASB paragraph and decimal numbering. IAS 1 text that has been deleted from this Standard (and does not affect IFRS compliance) is listed in a separate section after the Standard.

Compliance with IAS 1

For-profit entities that comply with AASB 101 as amended will simultaneously be in compliance with IAS 1 as amended.

Not-for-profit entities using the added "Aus" paragraphs in the Standard that specifically apply to not-for-profit entities may not be simultaneously complying with IAS 1. Whether a not-for-profit entity will be in compliance with IAS 1 will depend on whether the "Aus" paragraphs provide additional guidance for not-for-profit entities or contain requirements that are inconsistent with the corresponding IASB Standard and will be applied by the not-for-profit entity.

Accounting Standard AASB 101

The Australian Accounting Standards Board made Accounting Standard AASB 101 *Presentation of Financial Statements* under section 334 of the *Corporations Act 2001* on 24 September 2007.

This compiled version of AASB 101 applies to annual reporting periods beginning on or after 1 July 2012 but before 1 January 2013. It incorporates relevant amendments contained in other AASB Standards made by the AASB up to and including 5 September 2011 (see Compilation Details).

Accounting Standard AASB 101

Presentation of Financial Statements

Objective

1   This Standard prescribes the basis for presentation of general purpose financial statements to ensure comparability both with the entity's financial statements of previous periods and with the financial statements of other entities. It sets out overall requirements for the presentation of financial statements, guidelines for their structure and minimum requirements for their content.

Application

Aus1.1   **This Standard applies to:**

   (a)   **each *entity* that is required to prepare financial reports in accordance with Part 2M.3 of the Corporations Act;**

   (b)   **general purpose financial statements of each reporting entity; and**

   (c)   **financial statements that are, or are held out to be, general purpose financial statements.**

Aus1.2   **This Standard applies to *annual reporting periods* beginning on or after 1 January 2009.**
           [Note: For application dates of paragraphs changed or added by an amending Standard, see Compilation Details.]

Aus1.3   **This Standard may be applied to annual reporting periods beginning on or after 1 January 2005 but before 1 January 2009. If an entity adopts this Standard for an earlier period, it shall disclose that fact.**

Aus1.4   **The requirements specified in this Standard apply to the financial statements where information resulting from their application is *material* in accordance with AASB 1031 *Materiality*.**

Aus1.5   When applicable, this Standard supersedes AASB 101 *Presentation of Financial Statements* as made on 4 October 2006 and amended to 14 June 2007.

Aus1.6   Notwithstanding paragraph Aus1.1(a), the application of paragraphs 134-136 is limited to each entity that is required to prepare financial reports in accordance with Part 2M.3 of the Corporations Act and that is a reporting entity.

Aus1.7   Notwithstanding paragraphs Aus1.1 and Aus1.6, a not-for-profit entity need not present the disclosures required by paragraphs 134-136.

Scope

2   [Deleted by the AASB]

3   Other Australian Accounting Standards set out the recognition, measurement and disclosure requirements for specific transactions and other events.

4   This Standard does not apply to the structure and content of condensed interim financial statements prepared in accordance with AASB 134 *Interim Financial Reporting*. However, paragraphs 15–35 apply to such financial statements. This Standard applies equally to all entities, including those that present consolidated financial statements and those that present separate financial statements as defined in AASB 127 *Consolidated and Separate Financial Statements*.

5   This Standard uses terminology that is suitable for profit-oriented entities, including public sector business entities. If entities with not-for-profit activities in the private sector or the public sector apply this Standard, they may need to amend the descriptions used for particular line items in the financial statements and for the financial statements themselves.

6   Similarly, entities that do not have equity as defined in AASB 132 *Financial Instruments: Presentation* (e.g. some mutual funds) and entities whose share capital is not equity (e.g. some co-operative entities) may need to adapt the financial statement presentation of members' or unitholders' interests.

Definitions

7   **The following terms are used in this Standard with the meanings specified:**

General purpose financial statements **(referred to as 'financial statements') are those intended to meet the needs of users who are not in a position to require an entity to prepare reports tailored to their particular information needs.**

Impracticable **– Applying a requirement is impracticable when the entity cannot apply it after making every reasonable effort to do so.**

International Financial Reporting Standards (IFRSs) **are Standards and Interpretations issued by the International Accounting Standards Board (IASB). They comprise:**

    (a)   International Financial Reporting Standards;

    (b)   International Accounting Standards;

    (c)   IFRIC Interpretations; and

    (d)   SIC Interpretations.[1]

Material **– Omissions or misstatements of items are material if they could, individually or collectively, influence the economic decisions that users make on the basis of the financial statements. Materiality depends on the size and nature of the omission or misstatement judged in the surrounding circumstances. The size or nature of the item, or a combination of both, could be the determining factor.**

Assessing whether an omission or misstatement could influence economic decisions of users, and so be material, requires consideration of the characteristics of those users.

---

1   Definition of IFRSs amended after the name changes introduced by the revised Constitution of the IFRS Foundation in 2010.

The *Framework for the Preparation and Presentation of Financial Statements* states in paragraph 25 that 'users are assumed to have a reasonable knowledge of business and economic activities and accounting and a willingness to study the information with reasonable diligence'. Therefore, the assessment needs to take into account how users with such attributes could reasonably be expected to be influenced in making economic decisions.

Notes **contain information in addition to that presented in the statement of financial position, statement(s) of profit or loss and other comprehensive income, separate income statement (if presented), statement of changes in equity and statement of cash flows. Notes provide narrative descriptions or disaggregations of items presented in those statements and information about items that do not qualify for recognition in those statements.**

Other comprehensive income **comprises items of income and expense (including reclassification adjustments) that are not recognised in profit or loss as required or permitted by other Australian Accounting Standards.**

The components of other comprehensive income include:

(a)   changes in revaluation surplus (see AASB 116 *Property, Plant and Equipment* and AASB 138 *Intangible Assets*);

(b)   actuarial gains and losses on defined benefit plans recognised in accordance with paragraph 93A of AASB 119 *Employee Benefits*;

(c)   gains and losses arising from translating the financial statements of a foreign operation (see AASB 121 *The Effects of Changes in Foreign Exchange Rates*);

(d)   gains and losses on remeasuring available-for-sale financial assets (see AASB 139 *Financial Instruments: Recognition and Measurement*); and

(e)   the effective portion of gains and losses on hedging instruments in a cash flow hedge (see AASB 139).

Owners **are holders of instruments classified as equity.**

Profit or loss **is the total of income less expenses, excluding the components of other comprehensive income.**

Reclassification adjustments **are amounts reclassified to profit or loss in the current period that were recognised in other comprehensive income in the current or previous periods.**

Total comprehensive income **is the change in equity during a period resulting from transactions and other events, other than those changes resulting from transactions with owners in their capacity as owners.**

Total comprehensive income comprises all components of 'profit or loss' and of 'other comprehensive income'.

Aus7.1   [Deleted by the AASB]

Aus7.2   **In respect of public sector entities,** *local governments, governments* **and most, if not all,** *government departments* **are** *reporting entities*:

reporting entity **means an entity in respect of which it is reasonable to expect the existence of users who rely on the entity's general purpose financial statement for information that will be useful to them for making and evaluating decisions about the allocation of resources. A reporting entity can be a single entity or a group comprising a parent and all of its subsidiaries.**

government **means the Australian Government, the Government of the Australian Capital Territory, New South Wales, the Northern Territory, Queensland, South Australia, Tasmania, Victoria or Western Australia.**

government department **means a government controlled entity, created pursuant to administrative arrangements or otherwise designated as a government department by the government which controls it.**

local government **means an entity comprising all entities controlled by a governing body elected or appointed pursuant to a Local Government Act or similar legislation.**

8   Although this Standard uses the terms 'other comprehensive income', 'profit or loss' and 'total comprehensive income', an entity may use other terms to describe the totals as long as the meaning is clear. For example, an entity may use the term 'net income' to describe profit or loss.

8A   The following terms are described in AASB 132 and are used in this Standard with the meaning specified in AASB 132:

    (a)   puttable financial instrument classified as an equity instrument (described in paragraphs 16A and 16B of AASB 132); and

    (b)   an instrument that imposes on the entity an obligation to deliver to another party a pro rata share of the net assets of the entity only on liquidation and is classified as an equity instrument (described in paragraphs 16C and 16D of AASB 132).

Financial Statements

Purpose of Financial Statements

9   Financial statements are a structured representation of the financial position and financial performance of an entity. The objective of financial statements is to provide information about the financial position, financial performance and cash flows of an entity that is useful to a wide range of users in making economic decisions. Financial statements also show the results of the management's stewardship of the resources entrusted to it. To meet this objective, financial statements provide information about an entity's:

    (a)   assets;

    (b)   liabilities;

    (c)   equity;

    (d)   income and expenses, including gains and losses;

    (e)   contributions by and distributions to owners in their capacity as owners; and

    (f)   cash flows.

This information, along with other information in the notes, assists users of financial statements in predicting the entity's future cash flows and, in particular, their timing and certainty.

Complete Set of Financial Statements

10   **A complete set of financial statements comprises:**

    (a)   a statement of financial position as at the end of the period;

    (b)   a statement of profit or loss and other comprehensive income for the period;

    (c)   a statement of changes in equity for the period;

    (d)   a statement of cash flows for the period;

    (e)   notes, comprising a summary of significant accounting policies and other explanatory information; and

    (f)   a statement of financial position as at the beginning of the earliest comparative period when an entity applies an accounting policy retrospectively or makes a retrospective restatement of items in its financial statements, or when it reclassifies items in its financial statements.

An entity may use titles for the statements other than those used in this Standard. For example, an entity may use the title 'statement of comprehensive income' instead of 'statement of profit or loss and other comprehensive income'.

10A   **An entity may present a single statement of profit or loss and other comprehensive income, with profit or loss and other comprehensive income presented in two sections. The sections shall be presented together, with the profit or loss section presented first followed directly by the other comprehensive income section. An entity may present the profit or loss section in a separate statement of profit or loss. If so, the separate statement of profit or loss shall immediately precede the statement presenting comprehensive income, which shall begin with profit or loss.**

11   **An entity shall present with equal prominence all of the financial statements in a complete set of financial statements.**

12   [Deleted by the IASB]

13   Many entities present, outside the financial statements, a financial review by management that describes and explains the main features of the entity's financial performance and financial position, and the principal uncertainties it faces. Such a report may include a review of:

     (a)   the main factors and influences determining financial performance, including changes in the environment in which the entity operates, the entity's response to those changes and their effect, and the entity's policy for investment to maintain and enhance financial performance, including its dividend policy;

     (b)   the entity's sources of funding and its targeted ratio of liabilities to equity; and

     (c)   the entity's resources not recognised in the statement of financial position in accordance with IFRSs.

14   Many entities also present, outside the financial statements, reports and statements such as environmental reports and value added statements, particularly in industries in which environmental factors are significant and when employees are regarded as an important user group. Reports and statements presented outside financial statements are outside the scope of IFRSs.

General Features

Fair Presentation and Compliance with IFRSs

15   **Financial statements shall present fairly the financial position, financial performance and cash flows of an entity. Fair presentation requires the faithful representation of the effects of transactions, other events and conditions in accordance with the definitions and recognition criteria for assets, liabilities, income and expenses set out in the *Framework*. The application of IFRSs, with additional disclosure when necessary, is presumed to result in financial statements that achieve a fair presentation.**

16   **An entity whose financial statements comply with IFRSs shall make an explicit and unreserved statement of such compliance in the notes. An entity shall not describe financial statements as complying with IFRSs unless they comply with all the requirements of IFRSs.**

Aus16.1   [Deleted by the AASB]

Aus16.2   Compliance with Australian Accounting Standards by for-profit entities will not necessarily lead to compliance with IFRSs. This circumstance arises when the entity is a for-profit government department to which particular Standards apply, such as AASB 1004 *Contributions*, and to which Aus paragraphs in various other Australian Accounting Standards apply, and the entity applies a requirement that is inconsistent with an IFRS requirement.

Aus16.3   Not-for-profit entities need not comply with the paragraph 16 requirement to make an explicit and unreserved statement of compliance with IFRSs.

17   In virtually all circumstances, an entity achieves a fair presentation by compliance with Australian Accounting Standards. A fair presentation also requires an entity:

     (a)   to select and apply accounting policies in accordance with AASB 108 *Accounting Policies, Changes in Accounting Estimates and Errors*. AASB 108 sets out a hierarchy of authoritative guidance that management considers in the absence of an Australian Accounting Standard that specifically applies to an item;

     (b)   to present information, including accounting policies, in a manner that provides relevant, reliable, comparable and understandable information; and

     (c)   to provide additional disclosures when compliance with the specific requirements in Australian Accounting Standards is insufficient to enable users to understand the impact of particular transactions, other events and conditions on the entity's financial position and financial performance.

18   An entity cannot rectify inappropriate accounting policies either by disclosure of the accounting policies used or by notes or explanatory material.

19   In the extremely rare circumstances in which management concludes that compliance with a requirement in an Australian Accounting Standard would be so misleading that it would conflict with the objective of financial statements set out in the *Framework*, the entity shall depart from that requirement in the manner set out in paragraph 20 if the relevant regulatory framework requires, or otherwise does not prohibit, such a departure.

Aus19.1   In relation to paragraph 19, the following shall not depart from a requirement in an Australian Accounting Standard:

(a)   entities required to prepare financial reports under Part 2M.3 of the Corporations Act;

(b)   private and public sector not-for-profit entities; and

(c)   entities applying Australian Accounting Standards – Reduced Disclosure Requirements.

20   When an entity departs from a requirement of an Australian Accounting Standard in accordance with paragraph 19, it shall disclose:

(a)   that management has concluded that the financial statements present fairly the entity's financial position, financial performance and cash flows;

(b)   that it has complied with Australian Accounting Standards, except that it has departed from a particular requirement to achieve a fair presentation;

(c)   the title of the Australian Accounting Standard from which the entity has departed, the nature of the departure, including the treatment that the Australian Accounting Standard would require, the reason why that treatment would be so misleading in the circumstances that it would conflict with the objective of financial statements set out in the *Framework*, and the treatment adopted; and

(d)   for each period presented, the financial effect of the departure on each item in the financial statements that would have been reported in complying with the requirement.

21   When an entity has departed from a requirement of an Australian Accounting Standard in a prior period, and that departure affects the amounts recognised in the financial statements for the current period, it shall make the disclosures set out in paragraph 20(c) and (d).

22   Paragraph 21 applies, for example, when an entity departed in a prior period from a requirement in an Australian Accounting Standard for the measurement of assets or liabilities and that departure affects the measurement of changes in assets and liabilities recognised in the current period's financial statements.

23   In the extremely rare circumstances in which management concludes that compliance with a requirement in an Australian Accounting Standard would be so misleading that it would conflict with the objective of financial statements set out in the *Framework*, but the relevant regulatory framework prohibits departure from the requirement, the entity shall, to the maximum extent possible, reduce the perceived misleading aspects of compliance by disclosing:

(a)   the title of the Australian Accounting Standard in question, the nature of the requirement, and the reason why management has concluded that complying with that requirement is so misleading in the circumstances that it conflicts with the objective of financial statements set out in the *Framework*; and

(b)   for each period presented, the adjustments to each item in the financial statements that management has concluded would be necessary to achieve a fair presentation.

24   For the purpose of paragraphs 19-23, an item of information would conflict with the objective of financial statements when it does not represent faithfully the transactions, other events and conditions that it either purports to represent or could reasonably be

expected to represent and, consequently, it would be likely to influence economic decisions made by users of financial statements. When assessing whether complying with a specific requirement in an Australian Accounting Standard would be so misleading that it would conflict with the objective of financial statements set out in the *Framework*, management considers:

(a) why the objective of financial statements is not achieved in the particular circumstances; and

(b) how the entity's circumstances differ from those of other entities that comply with the requirement. If other entities in similar circumstances comply with the requirement, there is a rebuttable presumption that the entity's compliance with the requirement would not be so misleading that it would conflict with the objective of financial statements set out in the *Framework*.

Going Concern

25 **When preparing financial statements, management shall make an assessment of an entity's ability to continue as a going concern. An entity shall prepare financial statements on a going concern basis unless management either intends to liquidate the entity or to cease trading, or has no realistic alternative but to do so. When management is aware, in making its assessment, of material uncertainties related to events or conditions that may cast significant doubt upon the entity's ability to continue as a going concern, the entity shall disclose those uncertainties. When an entity does not prepare financial statements on a going concern basis, it shall disclose that fact, together with the basis on which it prepared the financial statements and the reason why the entity is not regarded as a going concern.**

26 In assessing whether the going concern assumption is appropriate, management takes into account all available information about the future, which is at least, but is not limited to, twelve months from the end of the reporting period. The degree of consideration depends on the facts in each case. When an entity has a history of profitable operations and ready access to financial resources, the entity may reach a conclusion that the going concern basis of accounting is appropriate without detailed analysis. In other cases, management may need to consider a wide range of factors relating to current and expected profitability, debt repayment schedules and potential sources of replacement financing before it can satisfy itself that the going concern basis is appropriate.

Accrual Basis of Accounting

27 **An entity shall prepare its financial statements, except for cash flow information, using the accrual basis of accounting.**

28 When the accrual basis of accounting is used, an entity recognises items as assets, liabilities, equity, income and expenses (the elements of financial statements) when they satisfy the definitions and recognition criteria for those elements in the *Framework*.

Materiality and Aggregation

29 **An entity shall present separately each material class of similar items. An entity shall present separately items of a dissimilar nature or function unless they are immaterial.**

30 Financial statements result from processing large numbers of transactions or other events that are aggregated into classes according to their nature or function. The final stage in the process of aggregation and classification is the presentation of condensed and classified data, which form line items in the financial statements. If a line item is not individually material, it is aggregated with other items either in those statements or in the notes. An item that is not sufficiently material to warrant separate presentation in those statements may warrant separate presentation in the notes.

31 An entity need not provide a specific disclosure required by an Australian Accounting Standard if the information is not material.

Offsetting

32 **An entity shall not offset assets and liabilities or income and expenses, unless required or permitted by an Australian Accounting Standard.**

33   An entity reports separately both assets and liabilities, and income and expenses. Offsetting in the statements of comprehensive income or financial position or in the separate income statement (if presented), except when offsetting reflects the substance of the transaction or other event, detracts from the ability of users both to understand the transactions, other events and conditions that have occurred and to assess the entity's future cash flows. Measuring assets net of valuation allowances — for example, obsolescence allowances on inventories and doubtful debts allowances on receivables — is not offsetting.

34   AASB 118 *Revenue* defines revenue and requires an entity to measure it at the fair value of the consideration received or receivable, taking into account the amount of any trade discounts and volume rebates the entity allows. An entity undertakes, in the course of its ordinary activities, other transactions that do not generate revenue but are incidental to the main revenue-generating activities. An entity presents the results of such transactions, when this presentation reflects the substance of the transaction or other event, by netting any income with related expenses arising on the same transaction. For example:

(a)   an entity presents gains and losses on the disposal of non-current assets, including investments and operating assets, by deducting from the proceeds on disposal the carrying amount of the asset and related selling expenses; and

(b)   an entity may net expenditure related to a provision that is recognised in accordance with AASB 137 *Provisions, Contingent Liabilities and Contingent Assets* and reimbursed under a contractual arrangement with a third party (for example, a supplier's warranty agreement) against the related reimbursement.

35   In addition, an entity presents on a net basis gains and losses arising from a group of similar transactions, for example, foreign exchange gains and losses or gains and losses arising on financial instruments held for trading. However, an entity presents such gains and losses separately if they are material.

Frequency of Reporting

36   An entity shall present a complete set of financial statements (including comparative information) at least annually. When an entity changes the end of its reporting period and presents financial statements for a period longer or shorter than one year, an entity shall disclose, in addition to the period covered by the financial statements:

(a)   the reason for using a longer or shorter period; and

(b)   the fact that amounts presented in the financial statements are not entirely comparable.

37   Normally, an entity consistently prepares financial statements for a one-year period. However, for practical reasons, some entities prefer to report, for example, for a 52-week period. This Standard does not preclude this practice.

Comparative Information

38   Except when Australian Accounting Standards permit or require otherwise, an entity shall disclose comparative information in respect of the previous period for all amounts reported in the current period's financial statements. An entity shall include comparative information for narrative and descriptive information when it is relevant to an understanding of the current period's financial statements.

39   An entity disclosing comparative information shall present, as a minimum, two statements of financial position, two of each of the other statements, and related notes. When an entity applies an accounting policy retrospectively or makes a retrospective restatement of items in its financial statements or when it reclassifies items in its financial statements, it shall present, as a minimum, three statements of financial position, two of each of the other statements, and related notes. An entity presents statements of financial position as at:

(a)   the end of the current period;

(b)   the end of the previous period (which is the same as the beginning of the current period); and

(c)   the beginning of the earliest comparative period.

40   In some cases, narrative information provided in the financial statements for the previous period(s) continues to be relevant in the current period. For example, an entity discloses in the current period details of a legal dispute whose outcome was uncertain at the end of the immediately preceding reporting period and that is yet to be resolved. Users benefit from information that the uncertainty existed at the end of the immediately preceding reporting period, and about the steps that have been taken during the period to resolve the uncertainty.

41   **When the entity changes the presentation or classification of items in its financial statements, the entity shall reclassify comparative amounts unless reclassification is impracticable. When the entity reclassifies comparative amounts, the entity shall disclose:**

   (a)   **the nature of the reclassification;**

   (b)   **the amount of each item or class of items that is reclassified; and**

   (c)   **the reason for the reclassification.**

42   **When it is impracticable to reclassify comparative amounts, an entity shall disclose:**

   (a)   **the reason for not reclassifying the amounts; and**

   (b)   **the nature of the adjustments that would have been made if the amounts had been reclassified.**

43   Enhancing the inter-period comparability of information assists users in making economic decisions, especially by allowing the assessment of trends in financial information for predictive purposes. In some circumstances, it is impracticable to reclassify comparative information for a particular prior period to achieve comparability with the current period. For example, an entity may not have collected data in the prior period(s) in a way that allows reclassification, and it may be impracticable to recreate the information.

44   AASB 108 sets out the adjustments to comparative information required when an entity changes an accounting policy or corrects an error.

Consistency of Presentation

45   **An entity shall retain the presentation and classification of items in the financial statements from one period to the next unless:**

   (a)   **it is apparent, following a significant change in the nature of the entity's operations or a review of its financial statements, that another presentation or classification would be more appropriate having regard to the criteria for the selection and application of accounting policies in AASB 108; or**

   (b)   **an Australian Accounting Standard requires a change in presentation.**

46   For example, a significant acquisition or disposal, or a review of the presentation of the financial statements, might suggest that the financial statements need to be presented differently. An entity changes the presentation of its financial statements only if the changed presentation provides information that is reliable and more relevant to users of the financial statements and the revised structure is likely to continue, so that comparability is not impaired. When making such changes in presentation, an entity reclassifies its comparative information in accordance with paragraphs 41 and 42.

Structure and Content

Introduction

47   This Standard requires particular disclosures in the statement of financial position or of comprehensive income, in the separate income statement (if presented), or in the statement of changes in equity and requires disclosure of other line items either in those statements or in the notes. AASB 107 *Statement of Cash Flows* sets out requirements for the presentation of cash flow information.

48   This Standard sometimes uses the term 'disclosure' in a broad sense, encompassing items presented in the financial statements . Disclosures are also required by other Australian Accounting Standards. Unless specified to the contrary elsewhere in this Standard or in another Australian Accounting Standard, such disclosures may be made in the financial statements.

Identification of the Financial Statements

49 **An entity shall clearly identify the financial statements and distinguish them from other information in the same published document.**

50 Australian Accounting Standards apply only to financial statements, and not necessarily to other information presented in an annual report, a regulatory filing, or another document. Therefore, it is important that users can distinguish information that is prepared using Australian Accounting Standards from other information that may be useful to users but is not the subject of those requirements.

51 **An entity shall clearly identify each financial statement and the notes. In addition, an entity shall display the following information prominently, and repeat it when necessary for the information presented to be understandable:**

   (a) **the name of the reporting entity or other means of identification, and any change in that information from the end of the preceding reporting period;**

   (b) **whether the financial statements are of the individual entity or a group of entities;**

   (c) **the date of the end of the reporting period or the period covered by the set of financial statements or notes;**

   (d) **the presentation currency, as defined in AASB 121; and**

   (e) **the level of rounding used in presenting amounts in the financial statements.**

52 An entity meets the requirements in paragraph 51 by presenting appropriate headings for pages, statements, notes, columns and the like. Judgement is required in determining the best way of presenting such information. For example, when an entity presents the financial statements electronically, separate pages are not always used; an entity then presents the above items to ensure that the information included in the financial statements can be understood.

53 An entity often makes financial statements more understandable by presenting information in thousands or millions of units of the presentation currency. This is acceptable as long as the entity discloses the level of rounding and does not omit material information.

Statement of Financial Position

Information to be Presented in the Statement of Financial Position

54 **As a minimum, the statement of financial position shall include line items that present the following amounts:**

   (a) **property, plant and equipment;**

   (b) **investment property;**

   (c) **intangible assets;**

   (d) **financial assets (excluding amounts shown under (e), (h) and (i));**

   (e) **investments accounted for using the equity method;**

   (f) **biological assets;**

   (g) **inventories;**

   (h) **trade and other receivables;**

   (i) **cash and cash equivalents;**

   (j) **the total of assets classified as held for sale and assets included in disposal groups classified as held for sale in accordance with AASB 5 *Non-current Assets Held for Sale and Discontinued Operations*;**

   (k) **trade and other payables;**

   (l) **provisions;**

   (m) **financial liabilities (excluding amounts shown under (k) and (l));**

   (n) **liabilities and assets for current tax, as defined in AASB 112 *Income Taxes*;**

   (o) **deferred tax liabilities and deferred tax assets, as defined in AASB 112;**

(p)   liabilities included in disposal groups classified as held for sale in accordance with AASB 5;

(q)   non-controlling interests, presented within equity; and

(r)   issued capital and reserves attributable to owners of the parent.

55   An entity shall present additional line items, headings and subtotals in the statement of financial position when such presentation is relevant to an understanding of the entity's financial position.

56   When an entity presents current and non-current assets, and current and non-current liabilities, as separate classifications in its statement of financial position, it shall not classify deferred tax assets (liabilities) as current assets (liabilities).

57   This Standard does not prescribe the order or format in which an entity presents items. Paragraph 54 simply lists items that are sufficiently different in nature or function to warrant separate presentation in the statement of financial position. In addition:

(a)   line items are included when the size, nature or function of an item or aggregation of similar items is such that separate presentation is relevant to an understanding of the entity's financial position; and

(b)   the descriptions used and the ordering of items or aggregation of similar items may be amended according to the nature of the entity and its transactions, to provide information that is relevant to an understanding of the entity's financial position. For example, a financial institution may amend the above descriptions to provide information that is relevant to the operations of a financial institution.

58   An entity makes the judgement about whether to present additional items separately on the basis of an assessment of:

(a)   the nature and liquidity of assets;

(b)   the function of assets within the entity; and

(c)   the amounts, nature and timing of liabilities.

59   The use of different measurement bases for different classes of assets suggests that their nature or function differs and, therefore, that an entity presents them as separate line items. For example, different classes of property, plant and equipment can be carried at cost or at revalued amounts in accordance with AASB 116.

Current/Non-current Distinction

60   An entity shall present current and non-current assets, and current and non-current liabilities, as separate classifications in its statement of financial position in accordance with paragraphs 66–76 except when a presentation based on liquidity provides information that is reliable and more relevant. When that exception applies, an entity shall present all assets and liabilities in order of liquidity.

61   Whichever method of presentation is adopted, an entity shall disclose the amount expected to be recovered or settled after more than twelve months for each asset and liability line item that combines amounts expected to be recovered or settled:

(a)   no more than twelve months after the reporting period, and

(b)   more than twelve months after the reporting period.

62   When an entity supplies goods or services within a clearly identifiable operating cycle, separate classification of current and non-current assets and liabilities in the statement of financial position provides useful information by distinguishing the net assets that are continuously circulating as working capital from those used in the entity's long-term operations. It also highlights assets that are expected to be realised within the current operating cycle, and liabilities that are due for settlement within the same period.

63   For some entities, such as financial institutions, a presentation of assets and liabilities in increasing or decreasing order of liquidity provides information that is reliable and more relevant than a current/non-current presentation because the entity does not supply goods or services within a clearly identifiable operating cycle.

64   In applying paragraph 60, an entity is permitted to present some of its assets and liabilities using a current/non-current classification and others in order of liquidity when this provides information that is reliable and more relevant. The need for a mixed basis of presentation might arise when an entity has diverse operations.

65   Information about expected dates of realisation of assets and liabilities is useful in assessing the liquidity and solvency of an entity. AASB 7 *Financial Instruments: Disclosures* requires disclosure of the maturity dates of financial assets and financial liabilities. Financial assets include trade and other receivables, and financial liabilities include trade and other payables. Information on the expected date of recovery of non-monetary assets such as inventories and expected date of settlement for liabilities such as provisions is also useful, whether assets and liabilities are classified as current or as non-current. For example, an entity discloses the amount of inventories that are expected to be recovered more than twelve months after the reporting period.

Current Assets

66   **An entity shall classify an asset as current when:**

(a)   **it expects to realise the asset, or intends to sell or consume it, in its normal operating cycle;**

(b)   **it holds the asset primarily for the purpose of trading;**

(c)   **it expects to realise the asset within twelve months after the reporting period; or**

(d)   **the asset is cash or a cash equivalent (as defined in AASB 107) unless the asset is restricted from being exchanged or used to settle a liability for at least twelve months after the reporting period.**

An entity shall classify all other assets as non-current.

67   This Standard uses the term 'non-current' to include tangible, intangible and financial assets of a long-term nature. It does not prohibit the use of alternative descriptions as long as the meaning is clear.

68   The operating cycle of an entity is the time between the acquisition of assets for processing and their realisation in cash or cash equivalents. When the entity's normal operating cycle is not clearly identifiable, it is assumed to be twelve months. Current assets include assets (such as inventories and trade receivables) that are sold, consumed or realised as part of the normal operating cycle even when they are not expected to be realised within twelve months after the reporting period. Current assets also include assets held primarily for the purpose of trading (examples include some financial assets classified as held for trading in accordance with AASB 139) and the current portion of non-current financial assets.

Current Liabilities

69   **An entity shall classify a liability as current when:**

(a)   **it expects to settle the liability in its normal operating cycle;**

(b)   **it holds the liability primarily for the purpose of trading;**

(c)   **the liability is due to be settled within twelve months after the reporting period; or**

(d)   **it does not have an unconditional right to defer settlement of the liability for at least twelve months after the reporting period (see paragraph 73). Terms of a liability that could, at the option of the counterparty, result in its settlement by the issue of equity instruments do not affect its classification.**

An entity shall classify all other liabilities as non-current.

70   Some current liabilities, such as trade payables and some accruals for employee and other operating costs, are part of the working capital used in the entity's normal operating cycle. An entity classifies such operating items as current liabilities even if they are due to be settled more than twelve months after the reporting period. The same normal operating cycle applies to the classification of an entity's assets and liabilities. When the entity's normal operating cycle is not clearly identifiable, it is assumed to be twelve months.

71   Other current liabilities are not settled as part of the normal operating cycle, but are due for settlement within twelve months after the reporting period or held primarily for the purpose of trading. Examples are some financial liabilities classified as held for trading in accordance with AASB 139, bank overdrafts, and the current portion of non-current financial liabilities, dividends payable, income taxes and other non-trade payables. Financial liabilities that provide financing on a long-term basis (i.e. are not part of the working capital used in the entity's normal operating cycle) and are not due for settlement within twelve months after the reporting period are non-current liabilities, subject to paragraphs 74 and 75.

72   An entity classifies its financial liabilities as current when they are due to be settled within twelve months after the reporting period, even if:

(a)   the original term was for a period longer than twelve months; and

(b)   an agreement to refinance, or to reschedule payments, on a long-term basis is completed after the reporting period and before the financial statements are authorised for issue.

73   If an entity expects, and has the discretion, to refinance or roll over an obligation for at least twelve months after the reporting period under an existing loan facility, it classifies the obligation as non-current, even if it would otherwise be due within a shorter period. However, when refinancing or rolling over the obligation is not at the discretion of the entity (for example, there is no arrangement for refinancing), the entity does not consider the potential to refinance the obligation and classifies the obligation as current.

74   When an entity breaches a provision of a long-term loan arrangement on or before the end of the reporting period with the effect that the liability becomes payable on demand, it classifies the liability as current, even if the lender agreed, after the reporting period and before the authorisation of the financial statements for issue, not to demand payment as a consequence of the breach. An entity classifies the liability as current because, at the end of the reporting period, it does not have an unconditional right to defer its settlement for at least twelve months after that date.

75   However, an entity classifies the liability as non-current if the lender agreed by the end of the reporting period to provide a period of grace ending at least twelve months after the reporting period, within which the entity can rectify the breach and during which the lender cannot demand immediate repayment.

76   In respect of loans classified as current liabilities, if the following events occur between the end of the reporting period and the date the financial statements are authorised for issue, those events are disclosed as non-adjusting events in accordance with AASB 110 *Events after the Reporting Period*:

(a)   refinancing on a long-term basis;

(b)   rectification of a breach of a long-term loan arrangement; and

(c)   the granting by the lender of a period of grace to rectify a breach of a long-term loan arrangement ending at least twelve months after the reporting period.

Information to be Presented either in the Statement of Financial Position or in the Notes

77   **An entity shall disclose, either in the statement of financial position or in the notes, further subclassifications of the line items presented, classified in a manner appropriate to the entity's operations.**

78   The detail provided in subclassifications depends on the requirements of Australian Accounting Standards and on the size, nature and function of the amounts involved. An entity also uses the factors set out in paragraph 58 to decide the basis of subclassification. The disclosures vary for each item, for example:

(a)   items of property, plant and equipment are disaggregated into classes in accordance with AASB 116;

(b)   receivables are disaggregated into amounts receivable from trade customers, receivables from related parties, prepayments and other amounts;

(c)   inventories are disaggregated, in accordance with AASB 102 *Inventories*, into classifications such as merchandise, production supplies, materials, work in progress and finished goods;

(d)   provisions are disaggregated into provisions for employee benefits and other items; and

(e)   equity capital and reserves are disaggregated into various classes, such as paid-in capital, share premium and reserves.

79   **An entity shall disclose the following, either in the statement of financial position or the statement of changes in equity, or in the notes:**

    (a)   for each class of share capital:

        (i)   the number of shares authorised;

        (ii)   the number of shares issued and fully paid, and issued but not fully paid;

        (iii)   par value per share, or that the shares have no par value;

        (iv)   a reconciliation of the number of shares outstanding at the beginning and at the end of the period;

        (v)   the rights, preferences and restrictions attaching to that class including restrictions on the distribution of dividends and the repayment of capital;

        (vi)   shares in the entity held by the entity or by its subsidiaries or associates; and

        (vii)   shares reserved for issue under options and contracts for the sale of shares, including terms and amounts; and

    (b)   a description of the nature and purpose of each reserve within equity.

80   **An entity without share capital, such as a partnership or trust, shall disclose information equivalent to that required by paragraph 79(a), showing changes during the period in each category of equity interest, and the rights, preferences and restrictions attaching to each category of equity interest.**

80A   **If an entity has reclassified:**

    (a)   a puttable financial instrument classified as an equity instrument; or

    (b)   an instrument that imposes on the entity an obligation to deliver to another party a pro rata share of the net assets of the entity only on liquidation and is classified as an equity instrument;

    between financial liabilities and equity, it shall disclose the amount reclassified into and out of each category (financial liabilities or equity), and the timing and reason for that reclassification.

Statement of Profit or Loss and Other Comprehensive Income

81   [Deleted by the IASB]

81A   **The statement of profit or loss and other comprehensive income (statement of comprehensive income) shall present, in addition to the profit or loss and other comprehensive income sections:**

    (a)   profit or loss;

    (b)   total other comprehensive income;

    (c)   comprehensive income for the period, being the total of profit or loss and other comprehensive income.

If an entity presents a separate statement of profit or loss it does not present the profit or loss section in the statement presenting comprehensive income.

81B   An entity shall present the following items, in addition to the profit or loss and other comprehensive income sections, as allocation of profit or loss and other comprehensive income for the period:

(a)   profit or loss for the period attributable to:

(i)   non-controlling interests, and

(ii)   owners of the parent.

(b)   comprehensive income for the period attributable to:

(i)   non-controlling interests, and

(ii)   owners of the parent.

If an entity presents profit or loss in a separate statement it shall present (a) in that statement.

Information to be Presented in the Profit or Loss Section or the Statement of Profit or Loss

82   In addition to items required by other Australian Accounting Standards, the profit or loss section or the statement of profit or loss shall include line items that present the following amounts for the period:

(a)   revenue;

(b)   finance costs;

(c)   share of the profit or loss of associates and joint ventures accounted for using the equity method;

(d)   tax expense;

(e)   [deleted by the IASB]

(ea)   a single amount for the total of discontinued operations (see AASB 5).

(f)-(i) [deleted by the IASB]

Information to be Presented in the Other Comprehensive Income Section

82A   The other comprehensive income section shall present line items for amounts of other comprehensive income in the period, classified by nature (including share of the other comprehensive income of associates and joint ventures accounted for using the equity method) and grouped into those that, in accordance with other Australian Accounting Standards:

(a)   will not be reclassified subsequently to profit or loss; and

(b)   will be reclassified subsequently to profit or loss when specific conditions are met.

83   [Deleted by the IASB]

84   [Deleted by the IASB]

85   An entity shall present additional line items, headings and subtotals in the statement(s) presenting profit or loss and other comprehensive income when such presentation is relevant to an understanding of the entity's financial performance.

86   Because the effects of an entity's various activities, transactions and other events differ in frequency, potential for gain or loss and predictability, disclosing the components of financial performance assists users in understanding the financial performance achieved and in making projections of future financial performance. An entity includes additional line items in the statement(s) presenting profit or loss and other comprehensive income and it amends the descriptions used and the ordering of items when this is necessary to explain the elements of financial performance. An entity considers factors including materiality and the nature and function of the items of income and expense. For example, a financial institution may amend the descriptions to provide information that is relevant to the operations of a financial institution. An entity does not offset income and expense items unless the criteria in paragraph 32 are met.

AASB

87   **An entity shall not present any items of income or expense as extraordinary items, in the statement(s) presenting profit or loss and other comprehensive income, or in the notes.**

Profit or Loss for the Period

88   **An entity shall recognise all items of income and expense in a period in profit or loss unless an Australian Accounting Standard requires or permits otherwise.**

89   Some Australian Accounting Standards specify circumstances when an entity recognises particular items outside profit or loss in the current period. AASB 108 specifies two such circumstances: the correction of errors and the effect of changes in accounting policies. Other Australian Accounting Standards require or permit components of other comprehensive income that meet the *Framework's* definition of income or expense to be excluded from profit or loss (see paragraph 7).

Other Comprehensive Income for the Period

90   **An entity shall disclose the amount of income tax relating to each item of other comprehensive income, including reclassification adjustments, either in the statement of profit or loss and other comprehensive income or in the notes.**

91   An entity may present items of other comprehensive income either:

    (a)   net of related tax effects; or

    (b)   before related tax effects with one amount shown for the aggregate amount of income tax relating to those items.

    If an entity elects alternative (b), it shall allocate the tax between the items that might be reclassified subsequently to the profit or loss section and those that will not be reclassified subsequently to the profit or loss section.

92   **An entity shall disclose reclassification adjustments relating to components of other comprehensive income.**

93   Other Australian Accounting Standards specify whether and when amounts previously recognised in other comprehensive income are reclassified to profit or loss. Such reclassifications are referred to in this Standard as reclassification adjustments. A reclassification adjustment is included with the related component of other comprehensive income in the period that the adjustment is reclassified to profit or loss. For example, gains realised on the disposal of available-for-sale financial assets are included in profit or loss of the current period. These amounts may have been recognised in other comprehensive income as unrealised gains in the current or previous periods. Those unrealised gains must be deducted from other comprehensive income in the period in which the realised gains are reclassified to profit or loss to avoid including them in total comprehensive income twice.

94   An entity may present reclassification adjustments in the statement of comprehensive income or in the notes. An entity presenting reclassification adjustments in the notes presents the components of other comprehensive income after any related reclassification adjustments.

95   Reclassification adjustments arise, for example, on disposal of a foreign operation (see AASB 121), on derecognition of available-for-sale financial assets (see AASB 139) and when a hedged forecast transaction affects profit or loss (see paragraph 100 of AASB 139 in relation to cash flow hedges).

96   Reclassification adjustments do not arise on changes in revaluation surplus recognised in accordance with AASB 116 or AASB 138 or actuarial gains and losses on defined benefit plans recognised in accordance with paragraph 93A of AASB 119. These components are recognised in other comprehensive income and are not reclassified to profit or loss in subsequent periods. Changes in revaluation surplus may be transferred to retained earnings in subsequent periods as the asset is used or when it is derecognised (see AASB 116 and AASB 138). Actuarial gains and losses are reported in retained earnings in the period that they are recognised as other comprehensive income (see AASB 119).

Information to be Presented in the Statement(s) of Profit or Loss and Other Comprehensive Income or in the Notes

97   **When items of income or expense are material, an entity shall disclose their nature and amount separately.**

98   Circumstances that would give rise to the separate disclosure of items of income and expense include:

(a)   write-downs of inventories to net realisable value or of property, plant and equipment to recoverable amount, as well as reversals of such write-downs;

(b)   restructurings of the activities of an entity and reversals of any provisions for the costs of restructuring;

(c)   disposals of items of property, plant and equipment;

(d)   disposals of investments;

(e)   discontinued operations;

(f)   litigation settlements; and

(g)   other reversals of provisions.

99   **An entity shall present an analysis of expenses recognised in profit or loss using a classification based on either their nature or their function within the entity, whichever provides information that is reliable and more relevant.**

100   Entities are encouraged to present the analysis in paragraph 99 in the statement(s) presenting profit or loss and other comprehensive income.

101   Expenses are subclassified to highlight components of financial performance that may differ in terms of frequency, potential for gain or loss and predictability. This analysis is provided in one of two forms.

102   The first form of analysis is the 'nature of expense' method. An entity aggregates expenses within profit or loss according to their nature (for example, depreciation, purchases of materials, transport costs, employee benefits and advertising costs), and does not reallocate them among functions within the entity. This method may be simple to apply because no allocations of expenses to functional classifications are necessary. An example of a classification using the nature of expense method is as follows:

Revenue		X
Other income		X
Changes in inventories of finished goods and work in progress	X	
Raw materials and consumables used	X	
Employee benefits expense	X	
Depreciation and amortisation expense	X	
Other expenses	X	
Total expenses		(X)
Profit before tax		X

103   The second form of analysis is the 'function of expense' or 'cost of sales' method and classifies expenses according to their function as part of cost of sales or, for example, the costs of distribution or administrative activities. At a minimum, an entity discloses its cost of sales under this method separately from other expenses. This method can provide more relevant information to users than the classification of expenses by nature, but allocating costs to functions may require arbitrary allocations and involve considerable judgement. An example of a classification using the function of expense method is as follows:

Revenue	X
Cost of sales	(X)
Gross profit	X
Other income	X
Distribution costs	(X)
Administrative expenses	(X)
Other expenses	(X)
Profit before tax	X

104   **An entity classifying expenses by function shall disclose additional information on the nature of expenses, including depreciation and amortisation expense and employee benefits expense.**

105   The choice between the function of expense method and the nature of expense method depends on historical and industry factors and the nature of the entity. Both methods provide an indication of those costs that might vary, directly or indirectly, with the level of sales or production of the entity. Because each method of presentation has merit for different types of entities, this Standard requires management to select the presentation that is reliable and more relevant. However, because information on the nature of expenses is useful in predicting future cash flows, additional disclosure is required when the function of expense classification is used. In paragraph 104, 'employee benefits' has the same meaning as in AASB 119.

Statement of Changes in Equity

Information to be Presented in the Statement of Changes in Equity

106   **An entity shall present a statement of changes in equity as required by paragraph 10. The statement of changes in equity includes the following information:**

     (a)   **total comprehensive income for the period, showing separately the total amounts attributable to owners of the parent and to non-controlling interests;**

     (b)   **for each component of equity, the effects of retrospective application or retrospective restatement recognised in accordance with AASB 108; and**

     (c)   [deleted by the IASB]

     (d)   **for each component of equity, a reconciliation between the carrying amount at the beginning and the end of the period, separately disclosing changes resulting from:**

         (i)   **profit or loss;**

         (ii)   **other comprehensive income; and**

         (iii)   **transactions with owners in their capacity as owners, showing separately contributions by and distributions to owners and changes in ownership interests in subsidiaries that do not result in a loss of control.**

Information to be Presented in the Statement of Changes in Equity or in the Notes

106A   **For each component of equity an entity shall present, either in the statement of changes in equity or in the notes, an analysis of other comprehensive income by item (see paragraph 106(d)(ii)).**

107   **An entity shall present, either in the statement of changes in equity or in the notes, the amount of dividends recognised as distributions to owners during the period, and the related amount of dividends per share.**

108   In paragraph 106, the components of equity include, for example, each class of contributed equity, the accumulated balance of each class of other comprehensive income and retained earnings.

109   Changes in an entity's equity between the beginning and the end of the reporting period reflect the increase or decrease in its net assets during the period. Except for changes resulting from transactions with owners in their capacity as owners (such as equity contributions, reacquisitions of the entity's own equity instruments and dividends) and transaction costs directly related to such transactions, the overall change in equity during a period represents the total amount of income and expense, including gains and losses, generated by the entity's activities during that period.

110   AASB 108 requires retrospective adjustments to effect changes in accounting policies, to the extent practicable, except when the transition provisions in another Australian Accounting Standard require otherwise. AASB 108 also requires restatements to correct errors to be made retrospectively, to the extent practicable. Retrospective adjustments and retrospective restatements are not changes in equity but they are adjustments to the opening balance of retained earnings, except when an Australian Accounting Standard requires retrospective adjustment of another component of equity. Paragraph 106(b) requires disclosure in the statement of changes in equity of the total adjustment to each component of equity resulting, from changes in accounting policies and separately, from corrections of errors. These adjustments are disclosed for each prior period and the beginning of the period.

Statement of Cash Flows

111   Cash flow information provides users of financial statements with a basis to assess the ability of the entity to generate cash and cash equivalents and the needs of the entity to utilise those cash flows. AASB 107 sets out requirements for the presentation and disclosure of cash flow information.

Notes

Structure

112   **The notes shall:**

(a)   **present information about the basis of preparation of the financial statements and the specific accounting policies used in accordance with paragraphs 117-124;**

(b)   **disclose the information required by Australian Accounting Standards that is not presented elsewhere in the financial statements; and**

(c)   **provide information that is not presented elsewhere in the financial statements, but is relevant to an understanding of any of them.**

113   **An entity shall, as far as practicable, present notes in a systematic manner. An entity shall cross-reference each item in the statements of financial position and of comprehensive income, in the separate income statement (if presented), and in the statements of changes in equity and of cash flows to any related information in the notes.**

114   An entity normally presents notes in the following order, to assist users to understand the financial statements and to compare them with financial statements of other entities:

(a)   statement of compliance with Australian Accounting Standards (see paragraph 16);

(b)   summary of significant accounting policies applied (see paragraph 117);

(c)   supporting information for items presented in the statements of financial position and of comprehensive income, in the separate income statement (if presented), and in the statements of changes in equity and of cash flows, in the order in which each statement and each line item is presented; and

(d)   other disclosures, including:

(i)   contingent liabilities (see AASB 137) and unrecognised contractual commitments; and

(ii)   non-financial disclosures, e.g. the entity's financial risk management objectives and policies (see AASB 7).

AASB

115   In some circumstances, it may be necessary or desirable to vary the order of specific items within the notes. For example, an entity may combine information on changes in fair value recognised in profit or loss with information on maturities of financial instruments, although the former disclosures relate to the statement(s) presenting profit or loss and other comprehensive income and the latter relate to the statement of financial position. Nevertheless, an entity retains a systematic structure for the notes as far as practicable.

116   An entity may present notes providing information about the basis of preparation of the financial statements and specific accounting policies as a separate section of the financial statements.

Disclosure of Accounting Policies

117   An entity shall disclose in the summary of significant accounting policies:

     (a)   the measurement basis (or bases) used in preparing the financial statements; and

     (b)   the other accounting policies used that are relevant to an understanding of the financial statements.

118   It is important for an entity to inform users of the measurement basis or bases used in the financial statements (for example, historical cost, current cost, net realisable value, fair value or recoverable amount) because the basis on which an entity prepares the financial statements significantly affects users' analysis. When an entity uses more than one measurement basis in the financial statements, for example when particular classes of assets are revalued, it is sufficient to provide an indication of the categories of assets and liabilities to which each measurement basis is applied.

119   In deciding whether a particular accounting policy should be disclosed, management considers whether disclosure would assist users in understanding how transactions, other events and conditions are reflected in reported financial performance and financial position. Disclosure of particular accounting policies is especially useful to users when those policies are selected from alternatives allowed in Australian Accounting Standards. An example is disclosure of whether a venturer recognises its interest in a jointly controlled entity using proportionate consolidation or the equity method (see AASB 131 *Interests in Joint Ventures*). Some Australian Accounting Standards specifically require disclosure of particular accounting policies, including choices made by management between different policies they allow. For example, AASB 116 requires disclosure of the measurement bases used for classes of property, plant and equipment.

120   Each entity considers the nature of its operations and the policies that the users of its financial statements would expect to be disclosed for that type of entity. For example, users would expect an entity subject to income taxes to disclose its accounting policies for income taxes, including those applicable to deferred tax liabilities and assets. When an entity has significant foreign operations or transactions in foreign currencies users would expect disclosure of accounting policies for the recognition of foreign exchange gains and losses.

121   An accounting policy may be significant because of the nature of the entity's operations even if amounts for current and prior periods are not material. It is also appropriate to disclose each significant accounting policy that is not specifically required by Australian Accounting Standards but the entity selects and applies in accordance with AASB 108.

122   An entity shall disclose, in the summary of significant accounting policies or other notes, the judgements, apart from those involving estimations (see paragraph 125), that management has made in the process of applying the entity's accounting policies and that have the most significant effect on the amounts recognised in the financial statements.

123   In the process of applying the entity's accounting policies, management makes various judgements, apart from those involving estimations, that can significantly affect the amounts

it recognises in the financial statements. For example, management makes judgements in determining:

(a)   whether financial assets are held-to-maturity investments;

(b)   when substantially all the significant risks and rewards of ownership of financial assets and lease assets are transferred to other entities;

(c)   whether, in substance, particular sales of goods are financing arrangements and therefore do not give rise to revenue; and

(d)   whether the substance of the relationship between the entity and a special purpose entity indicates that the entity controls the special purpose entity.

124   Some of the disclosures made in accordance with paragraph 122 are required by other Australian Accounting Standards. For example, AASB 127 requires an entity to disclose the reasons why the entity's ownership interest does not constitute control, in respect of an investee that is not a subsidiary even though more than half of its voting or potential voting power is owned directly or indirectly through subsidiaries. AASB 140 *Investment Property* requires disclosure of the criteria developed by the entity to distinguish investment property from owner-occupied property and from property held for sale in the ordinary course of business, when classification of the property is difficult.

Sources of Estimation Uncertainty

125   **An entity shall disclose information about the assumptions it makes about the future, and other major sources of estimation uncertainty at the end of the reporting period, that have a significant risk of resulting in a material adjustment to the carrying amounts of assets and liabilities within the next financial year. In respect of those assets and liabilities, the notes shall include details of:**

(a)   **their nature; and**

(b)   **their carrying amount as at the end of the reporting period.**

126   Determining the carrying amounts of some assets and liabilities requires estimation of the effects of uncertain future events on those assets and liabilities at the end of the reporting period. For example, in the absence of recently observed market prices, future-oriented estimates are necessary to measure the recoverable amount of classes of property, plant and equipment, the effect of technological obsolescence on inventories, provisions subject to the future outcome of litigation in progress, and long-term employee benefit liabilities such as pension obligations. These estimates involve assumptions about such items as the risk adjustment to cash flows or discount rates, future changes in salaries and future changes in prices affecting other costs.

127   The assumptions and other sources of estimation uncertainty disclosed in accordance with paragraph 125 relate to the estimates that require management's most difficult, subjective or complex judgements. As the number of variables and assumptions affecting the possible future resolution of the uncertainties increases, those judgements become more subjective and complex, and the potential for a consequential material adjustment to the carrying amounts of assets and liabilities normally increases accordingly.

128   The disclosures in paragraph 125 are not required for assets and liabilities with a significant risk that their carrying amounts might change materially within the next financial year if, at the end of the reporting period, they are measured at fair value based on recently observed market prices. Such fair values might change materially within the next financial year but these changes would not arise from assumptions or other sources of estimation uncertainty at the end of the reporting period.

129   An entity presents the disclosures in paragraph 125 in a manner that helps users of financial statements to understand the judgements that management makes about the future and about other sources of estimation uncertainty. The nature and extent of the information provided vary according to the nature of the assumption and other circumstances. Examples of the types of disclosures an entity makes are:

(a)   the nature of the assumption or other estimation uncertainty;

(b)   the sensitivity of carrying amounts to the methods, assumptions and estimates underlying their calculation, including the reasons for the sensitivity;

(c) the expected resolution of an uncertainty and the range of reasonably possible outcomes within the next financial year in respect of the carrying amounts of the assets and liabilities affected; and

(d) an explanation of changes made to past assumptions concerning those assets and liabilities, if the uncertainty remains unresolved.

130 This Standard does not require an entity to disclose budget information or forecasts in making the disclosures in paragraph 125.

131 Sometimes it is impracticable to disclose the extent of the possible effects of an assumption or another source of estimation uncertainty at the end of the reporting period. In such cases, the entity discloses that it is reasonably possible, on the basis of existing knowledge, that outcomes within the next financial year that are different from the assumption could require a material adjustment to the carrying amount of the asset or liability affected. In all cases, the entity discloses the nature and carrying amount of the specific asset or liability (or class of assets or liabilities) affected by the assumption.

132 The disclosures in paragraph 122 of particular judgements that management made in the process of applying the entity's accounting policies do not relate to the disclosures of sources of estimation uncertainty in paragraph 125.

133 Other Australian Accounting Standards require the disclosure of some of the assumptions that would otherwise be required in accordance with paragraph 125. For example, AASB 137 requires disclosure, in specified circumstances, of major assumptions concerning future events affecting classes of provisions. AASB 7 requires disclosure of significant assumptions the entity uses in estimating the fair values of financial assets and financial liabilities that are carried at fair value. AASB 116 requires disclosure of significant assumptions that the entity uses in estimating the fair values of revalued items of property, plant and equipment.

Capital

134 **An entity shall disclose information that enables users of its financial statements to evaluate the entity's objectives, policies and processes for managing capital.**

135 To comply with paragraph 134, the entity discloses the following:

(a) qualitative information about its objectives, policies and processes for managing capital, including:

(i) a description of what it manages as capital;

(ii) when an entity is subject to externally imposed capital requirements, the nature of those requirements and how those requirements are incorporated into the management of capital; and

(iii) how it is meeting its objectives for managing capital;

(b) summary quantitative data about what it manages as capital. Some entities regard some financial liabilities (e.g. some forms of subordinated debt) as part of capital. Other entities regard capital as excluding some components of equity (e.g. components arising from cash flow hedges);

(c) any changes in (a) and (b) from the previous period;

(d) whether during the period it complied with any externally imposed capital requirements to which it is subject; and

(e) when the entity has not complied with such externally imposed capital requirements, the consequences of such non-compliance.

The entity bases these disclosures on the information provided internally to key management personnel.

136 An entity may manage capital in a number of ways and be subject to a number of different capital requirements. For example, a conglomerate may include entities that undertake insurance activities and banking activities and those entities may operate in several jurisdictions. When an aggregate disclosure of capital requirements and how capital is managed would not provide useful information or distorts a financial statement

user's understanding of an entity's capital resources, the entity shall disclose separate information for each capital requirement to which the entity is subject.

Puttable Financial Instruments Classified as Equity

136A　For puttable financial instruments classified as equity instruments, an entity shall disclose (to the extent not disclosed elsewhere):

(a)　summary quantitative data about the amount classified as equity;

(b)　its objectives, policies and processes for managing its obligation to repurchase or redeem the instruments when required to do so by the instrument holders, including any changes from the previous period;

(c)　the expected cash outflow on redemption or repurchase of that class of financial instruments; and

(d)　information about how the expected cash outflow on redemption or repurchase was determined.

Other Disclosures

137　An entity shall disclose in the notes:

(a)　the amount of dividends proposed or declared before the financial statements were authorised for issue but not recognised as a distribution to owners during the period, and the related amount per share; and

(b)　the amount of any cumulative preference dividends not recognised.

138　An entity shall disclose the following, if not disclosed elsewhere in information published with the financial statements:

(a)　the domicile and legal form of the entity, its country of incorporation and the address of its registered office (or principal place of business, if different from the registered office);

(b)　a description of the nature of the entity's operations and its principal activities;

(c)　the name of the parent and the ultimate parent of the group; and

(d)　if it is a limited life entity, information regarding the length of its life.

Transition and Effective Date

139　[Deleted by the AASB]

139A　[Deleted by the AASB]

Aus139A.1　AASB 2008-3 *Amendments to Australian Accounting Standards arising from AASB 3 and AASB 127* amended paragraph 106. The amendment shall be applied retrospectively.

139B　[Deleted by the AASB]

139C　Paragraphs 68 and 71 were amended by AASB 2008-5 *Amendments to Australian Accounting Standards arising from the Annual Improvements Project* issued in July 2008. An entity shall apply those amendments for annual reporting periods beginning on or after 1 January 2009. Earlier application is permitted. If an entity applies the amendments for an earlier period it shall disclose that fact.

139D　Paragraph 69 was amended by AASB 2009-5 *Further Amendments to Australian Accounting Standards arising from the Annual Improvements Project* issued in May 2009. An entity shall apply that amendment for annual reporting periods beginning on or after 1 January 2010. Earlier application is permitted. If an entity applies the amendment for an earlier period it shall disclose that fact.

139F　Paragraphs 106 and 107 were amended and paragraph 106A was added by AASB 2010-4 *Further Amendments to Australian Accounting Standards arising from the Annual Improvements Project* issued in June 2010. An entity shall apply those amendments for annual reporting periods beginning on or after 1 January 2011. Earlier application is permitted.

139J   AASB 2011-9 *Amendments to Australian Accounting Standards – Presentation of Items of Other Comprehensive Income*, issued in September 2011, amended paragraphs 7, 10, 82, 85-87, 90, 91, 94, 100 and 115, added paragraphs 10A, 81A-81B and 82A, and deleted paragraphs 12, 81, 83 and 84. An entity shall apply those amendments for annual reporting periods beginning on or after 1 July 2012. Earlier application is permitted. If an entity applies the amendments for an earlier period it shall disclose that fact.

Withdrawal of IAS 1 (Revised 2003)

140   [Deleted by the AASB]

Deleted IAS 1 Text

Deleted IAS 1 text is not part of AASB 101.

Paragraph 2

An entity shall apply this Standard in preparing and presenting general purpose financial statements in accordance with International Financial Reporting Standards (IFRSs).

Paragraph 139

An entity shall apply this Standard for annual periods beginning on or after 1 January 2009. Earlier application is permitted. If an entity adopts this Standard for an earlier period, it shall disclose that fact.

Paragraph 139A

IAS 27 (as amended in 2008) amended paragraph 106. An entity shall apply that amendment for annual periods beginning on or after 1 July 2009. If an entity applies IAS 27 (amended 2008) for an earlier period, the amendment shall be applied for that earlier period. The amendment shall be applied retrospectively.

Paragraph 139B

Puttable Financial Instruments and Obligations Arising on Liquidation (Amendments to IAS 32 and IAS 1), issued in February 2008, amended paragraph 138 and inserted paragraphs 8A, 80A and 136A. An entity shall apply those amendments for annual periods beginning on or after 1 January 2009. Earlier application is permitted. If an entity applies the amendments for an earlier period, it shall disclose that fact and apply the related amendments to IAS 32, IAS 39, IFRS 7 and IFRIC 2 *Members' Shares in Co-operative Entities and Similar Instruments* at the same time.

Paragraph 140

This Standard supersedes IAS 1 *Presentation of Financial Statements* revised in 2003, as amended in 2005.

AASB 102
Inventories

(Compiled November 2009)

Note from the Institute of Chartered Accountants Australia

This note, prepared by the technical editors, is not part of Accounting Standard AASB 102.

Historical development

July 2004: AASB 102 'Inventories' is the Australian equivalent of IAS 2 of the same name. It was made by the AASB on 15 July 2004 as part of the AASB's program to adopt International Financial Reporting Standards by 2005.

26 February 2007: AASB 2007-3 'Amendments to Australian Accounting Standards' was issued by the AASB. This Standard is applicable to annual reporting periods beginning on or after 1 January 2009.

30 April 2007: AASB 2007-4 'Amendments to Australian Accounting Standards' amends paragraph 2 and is applicable to annual reporting periods beginning on or after 1 July 2007. Entities may elect to early-adopt it to annual reporting periods beginning on or after 1 January 2005.

30 April 2007: AASB 2007-5 'Amendments to Australian Accounting Standards' amends paragraphs Aus9.1, Aus34.1 and Aus36.1 and adds paragraphs Aus9.2 and Aus42.1-Aus42.2 and is applicable to annual reporting periods beginning on or after 1 July 2007. Entities may elect to early-adopt it to annual reporting periods beginning on or after 1 January 2005.

13 December 2007: AASB 2007-10 'Further Amendments to Australian Accounting Standards arising from AASB 101' amends AASB 102, replacing the term 'financial report' with 'financial statements'. This Standard is applicable to annual reporting periods beginning on or after 1 January 2009.

24 July 2008: AASB 2008-5 'Amendments to Australian Accounting Standards arising from the Annual Improvements Project' amends AASB 102 in relation to agricultural produce. This Standard is applicable to annual reporting periods beginning on or after 1 January 2009.

25 June 2009: AASB 2009-6 'Amendments to Australian Accounting Standards' amends AASB 102 for editorial corrections made by the International Accounting Standards Board (IASB) to its Standards and Interpretations (IFRSs) and as a consequence of issuing revised AASB 101 'Presentation of Financial Statements'. This Standard is applicable to annual reporting periods beginning on or after 1 January 2009 that end on or after 30 June 2009.

26 October 2009: AASB 102 was reissued by the AASB, compiled to include the AASB 2007-3, AASB 2007-10 and AASB 2009-6 amendments and applies to annual reporting periods beginning on or after 1 January 2009 that end on or after 30 June 2009. Early application is permitted.

7 December 2009: AASB 2009-11 'Amendments to Australian Accounting Standards arising from AASB 9' amends AASB 102 to give effect to consequential changes arising from the issuance of AASB 9. This Standard is applicable to annual reporting periods beginning on or after 1 January 2013 with early adoption permitted from annual reporting periods ending on or after 31 December 2009 that begin before 1 January 2013 provided AASB 9 is also applied for the same period. The application date of AASB 2009-11 has been amended to 1 January 2015 by AASB 2012-6. **These amendments have been superseded by AASB 2010-7 and are not included in this compiled Standard.**

1 March 2011: AASB 2010-7 'Amendments to Australian Accounting Standards arising from AASB 9 (December 2010)' as compiled amends AASB 102 to give effect to consequential changes arising from the reissue of AASB 9 in December 2010 and supersedes AASB 2009-11 which related to the previous version of AASB 9. This Standard applies to annual reporting periods beginning on or after 1 January 2013 and can be adopted early. The application date of AASB 2010-7 has been amended to 1 January 2015 by AASB 2012-6. **These amendments are not included in this compiled Standard.**

---

5 September 2011: AASB 2011-8 'Amendments to Australian Accounting Standards arising from AASB 13' amends AASB 102 to give effect to a consequential change in the definition of fair value arising from the issue of AASB 13. This Standard applies to annual reporting periods beginning on or after 1 January 2013 and can be adopted early. **These amendments are not included in this compiled Standard.**

References

Interpretation 132 *Intangible Assets – Web Site Costs* and Interpretation 1031 *Accounting for the Goods and Services Tax (GST)* apply to AASB 102.

Note that Rejection Statement – *Issues not added to the UIG Agenda: Inventory Rebates and Settlement Discounts* applies to AASB 102.

IFRIC items not taken onto the agenda: No. 2 *Cash Discounts* issued in August 2002, No. 3 *Discounts and Rebates* issued in November 2004 and No. 4 *Consumption of Inventories by a service organisation* issued in March 2004 apply to AASB 102.

AASB 102 compared to IAS 2

Additions

Paragraph	Description
Aus 1.1	Which entities AASB 102 applies to.
Aus 1.2	The application date of AASB 102 (i.e. annual periods beginning 1 January 2005).
Aus 1.3	Prohibits early application of AASB 102.
Aus 1.4	Makes the requirements of AASB 102 subject to AASB 1031 'Materiality'.
Aus 1.5	Explains which Standards have been superseded by AASB 102.
Aus 1.6	Clarifies that the superseded Standards apply until AASB 102 applies.
Aus 1.7	Notice of Standard published as required on 22 July 2004.
Aus 2.1	Excludes certain inventories of not-for-profit entities.
Aus 6.1	Sets out the not-for-profit definitions of 'not-for-profit entity', 'current replacement cost' and 'inventories held for distribution'.
Aus 8.1	Explanation of why current replacement cost rather than net realisable value is appropriate for inventories held for distribution by not-for-profit entities.
Aus 8.2	Clarifies that measurement of replacement cost by not-for-profit entities must reflect obsolescence or impairment.
Aus 9.1	Measurement rule for inventories held for distribution by not-for-profit entities.
Aus 9.2	Includes guidance for not-for-profit entities.
Aus 10.1	Deemed cost of inventories acquired by not-for-profit entities at no or nominal consideration is replacement cost.
Aus 34.1	Expense recognition rules for inventories held for distribution by not-for-profit entities.
Aus 36.1	Required inventory disclosures in respect of not-for-profit entities.
Aus 42.1	Transitional rules for not-for-profit entities.
Aus 42.2	Guidance on the treatment of adjustments arising from paragraph 42.1

Deletions

Paragraph	Description
40	Effective date of IAS 2 not relevant to Australia.
41	Reference to superseded IAS 2.
42	Reference to superseded SIC 1 'Consistency – Different Cost Formulas for Inventories'.

Contents

Compilation Details

Comparison with IAS 2

**Accounting Standard
AASB 102 Inventories**

Paragraphs

Objective   1
Application   Aus1.1 – Aus1.7
Scope   2 – 5
Definitions   6 – Aus8.2
Measurement of Inventories   9 – Aus9.2
Cost of Inventories   10 – Aus10.1
   Costs of Purchase   11
   Costs of Conversion   12 – 14
   Other Costs   15 – 18
   Cost of Inventories of a Service Provider   19
   Cost of Agricultural Produce Harvested from Biological Assets   20
   Techniques for the Measurement of Cost   21 – 22
Cost Formulas   23 – 27
Net Realisable Value   28 – 33
Recognition as an Expense   34 – 35
Disclosure   36 – 39
Transition   Aus42.1 – Aus42.2

Basis for Conclusions on AASB 2007-5

Basis for Conclusions on IAS 2
(available on the AASB website)

Australian Accounting Standard AASB 102 *Inventories* (as amended) is set out in paragraphs 1 – Aus42.2. All the paragraphs have equal authority. Terms defined in this Standard are in *italics* the first time they appear in the Standard. AASB 102 is to be read in the context of other Australian Accounting Standards, including AASB 1048 *Interpretation and Application of Standards*, which identifies the Australian Accounting Interpretations. In the absence of explicit guidance, AASB 108 *Accounting Policies, Changes in Accounting Estimates and Errors* provides a basis for selecting and applying accounting policies.

Compilation Details

Accounting Standard AASB 102 *Inventories* as amended

This compiled Standard applies to annual reporting periods beginning on or after 1 January 2009 that end on or after 30 June 2009. It takes into account amendments up to and including 25 June 2009 and was prepared on 2 November 2009 by the staff of the Australian Accounting Standards Board (AASB).

This compilation is not a separate Accounting Standard made by the AASB. Instead, it is a representation of AASB 102 (July 2004) as amended by other Accounting Standards, which are listed in the Table below.

Table of Standards

Standard	Date made	Application date *(annual reporting periods … on or after …)*	Application, saving or transitional provisions
AASB 102	15 Jul 2004	*(beginning)* 1 Jan 2005	
AASB 2007-3	26 Feb 2007	*(beginning)* 1 Jan 2009	see (a) below
AASB 2007-4	30 Apr 2007	*(beginning)* 1 Jul 2007	see (b) below
AASB 2007-5	25 May 2007	*(beginning)* 1 Jul 2007	see (b) below
AASB 2007-8	24 Sep 2007	*(beginning)* 1 Jan 2009	see (c) below
AASB 2007-10	13 Dec 2007	*(beginning)* 1 Jan 2009	see (c) below
AASB 2008-5	24 Jul 2008	*(beginning)* 1 Jan 2009	see (d) below
AASB 2009-6	25 Jun 2009	*(beginning)* 1 Jan 2009 and *(ending)* 30 Jun 2009	see (e) below

(a) Entities may elect to apply this Standard to annual reporting periods beginning on or after 1 January 2005 but before 1 January 2009, provided that AASB 8 *Operating Segments* is also applied to such periods.

(b) Entities may elect to apply this Standard to annual reporting periods beginning on or after 1 January 2005 but before 1 July 2007.

(c) Entities may elect to apply this Standard to annual reporting periods beginning on or after 1 January 2005 but before 1 January 2009, provided that AASB 101 *Presentation of Financial Statements* (September 2007) is also applied to such periods.

(d) Paragraph 17 of this Standard specifies application provisions. Entities may elect to apply this Standard, or its amendments to individual Standards, to annual reporting periods beginning on or after 1 January 2005 but before 1 January 2009.

(e) Entities may elect to apply this Standard to annual reporting periods beginning on or after 1 January 2005 but before 1 January 2009, provided that AASB 101 *Presentation of Financial Statements* (September 2007) is also applied to such periods, and to annual reporting periods beginning on or after 1 January 2009 that end before 30 June 2009.

Table of Amendments

Paragraph affected	How affected	By … [paragraph]
2	amended	AASB 2007-4 [25]
Aus6.1	amended	AASB 2007-8 [6]
	amended	AASB 2009-6 [34]
Aus9.1	amended	AASB 2007-5 [5]
Aus9.2	added	AASB 2007-5 [6]
20	amended	AASB 2008-5 [16]
26	amended	AASB 2007-3 [9]
29	amended	AASB 2007-3 [9]
Aus34.1	amended	AASB 2007-5 [7]
Aus36.1	amended	AASB 2007-5 [8]
Aus42.1-Aus42.2 (and preceding heading)	added	AASB 2007-5 [9]

General Terminology Amendments

References to 'financial report(s)' were amended to 'financial statements' by AASB 2007-8 and AASB 2007-10, except in relation to specific Corporations Act references. These amendments are not shown in the above Table of Amendments.

Basis for Conclusions on AASB 2007-5

The Basis for Conclusions accompanying AASB 2007-5 *Amendments to Australian Accounting Standard – Inventories Held for Distribution by Not-for-Profit Entities* is attached to this compiled Standard.

Comparison with IAS 2

AASB 102 and IAS 2

AASB 102 *Inventories* as amended incorporates IAS 2 *Inventories* as issued and amended by the International Accounting Standards Board (IASB). Paragraphs that have been added to this Standard (and do not appear in the text of IAS 2) are identified with the prefix "Aus", followed by the number of the preceding IASB paragraph and decimal numbering. Paragraphs that apply only to not-for-profit entities begin by identifying their limited applicability.

Compliance with IAS 2

For-profit entities that comply with AASB 102 as amended will simultaneously be in compliance with IAS 2 as amended.

Not-for-profit entities using the added "Aus" paragraphs in the Standard that specifically apply to not-for-profit entities may not be simultaneously complying with IAS 2. Whether a not-for-profit entity will be in compliance with IAS 2 will depend on whether the "Aus" paragraphs provide additional guidance for not-for-profit entities or contain requirements that are inconsistent with the corresponding IASB Standard and will be applied by the not-for-profit entity.

Accounting Standard AASB 102

The Australian Accounting Standards Board made Accounting Standard AASB 102 *Inventories* under section 334 of the *Corporations Act 2001* on 15 July 2004.

This compiled version of AASB 102 applies to annual reporting periods beginning on or after 1 January 2009 that end on or after 30 June 2009. It incorporates relevant amendments contained in other AASB Standards made by the AASB up to and including 25 June 2009 (see Compilation Details).

Accounting Standard AASB 102

Inventories

Objective

1   The objective of this Standard is to prescribe the accounting treatment for *inventories*. A primary issue in accounting for inventories is the amount of cost to be recognised as an asset and carried forward until the related revenues are recognised. This Standard provides guidance on the determination of cost and its subsequent recognition as an expense, including any write-down to *net realisable value*. It also provides guidance on the cost formulas that are used to assign costs to inventories.

Application

Aus1.1   **This Standard applies to:**

    (a)   each entity that is required to prepare financial reports in accordance with Part 2M.3 of the Corporations Act and that is a reporting entity;

    (b)   general purpose financial statements of each other reporting entity; and

    (c)   financial statements that are, or are held out to be, general purpose financial statements.

Aus1.2   **This Standard applies to annual reporting periods beginning on or after 1 January 2005.**

[Note: For application dates of paragraphs changed or added by an amending Standard, see Compilation Details.]

Aus1.3   **This Standard shall not be applied to annual reporting periods beginning before 1 January 2005.**

Aus1.4   The requirements specified in this Standard apply to the financial statements where information resulting from their application is material in accordance with AASB 1031 *Materiality*.

Aus1.5   When applicable, this Standard supersedes:

(a)   AASB 1019 *Inventories* as notified in the *Commonwealth of Australia Gazette* No S 132, 26 March 1998; and

(b)   AAS 2 *Inventories* as issued in March 1998.

Aus1.6   Both AASB 1019 and AAS 2 remain applicable until superseded by this Standard.

Aus1.7   Notice of this Standard was published in the *Commonwealth of Australia Gazette* No S 294, 22 July 2004.

Scope

2   This Standard applies to all inventories, except:

(a)   work in progress arising under construction contracts, including directly related service contracts (see AASB 111 *Construction Contracts*);

(b)   financial instruments (see AASB 132 *Financial Instruments: Presentation* and AASB 139 *Financial Instruments: Recognition and Measurement*); and

(c)   biological assets related to agricultural activity and agricultural produce at the point of harvest (see AASB 141 *Agriculture*).

Aus2.1   Notwithstanding paragraph 2, in respect of *not-for-profit entities*, this Standard does not apply to work in progress of services to be provided for no or nominal consideration directly in return from the recipients.

3   This Standard does not apply to the measurement of inventories held by:

(a)   producers of agricultural and forest products, agricultural produce after harvest, and minerals and mineral products, to the extent that they are measured at net realisable value in accordance with well-established practices in those industries. When such inventories are measured at net realisable value, changes in that value are recognised in profit or loss in the period of the change; and

(b)   commodity broker-traders who measure their inventories at fair value less costs to sell. When such inventories are measured at fair value less costs to sell, changes in fair value less costs to sell are recognised in profit or loss in the period of the change.

4   The inventories referred to in paragraph 3(a) are measured at net realisable value at certain stages of production. This occurs, for example, when agricultural crops have been harvested or minerals have been extracted and sale is assured under a forward contract or a government guarantee, or when an active market exists and there is a negligible risk of failure to sell. These inventories are excluded from only the measurement requirements of this Standard.

5   Broker-traders are those who buy or sell commodities for others or on their own account. The inventories referred to in paragraph 3(b) are principally acquired with the purpose of selling in the near future and generating a profit from fluctuations in price or broker-traders' margin. When these inventories are measured at fair value less costs to sell, they are excluded from only the measurement requirements of this Standard.

Definitions

6   The following terms are used in this Standard with the meanings specified.

Fair value is the amount for which an asset could be exchanged, or a liability settled, between knowledgeable, willing parties in an arm's length transaction.

Inventories are assets:

(a)   held for sale in the ordinary course of business;

(b)   in the process of production for such sale; or

(c)   in the form of materials or supplies to be consumed in the production process or in the rendering of services.

Net realisable value is the estimated selling price in the ordinary course of business less the estimated costs of completion and the estimated costs necessary to make the sale.

Aus6.1   The following terms are also used in this Standard with the meanings specified.

A *not-for-profit entity* is an entity whose principal objective is not the generation of profit. A not-for-profit entity can be a single entity or a group of entities comprising the parent entity and each of the entities that it controls.

In respect of not-for-profit entities, *current replacement cost* is the cost the entity would incur to acquire the asset at the end of the reporting period.

In respect of not-for-profit entities, *inventories held for distribution* are assets:

(a)   held for distribution at no or nominal consideration in the ordinary course of operations;

(b)   in the process of production for distribution at no or nominal consideration in the ordinary course of operations; or

(c)   in the form of materials or supplies to be consumed in the production process or in the rendering of services at no or nominal consideration.[1]

7   Net realisable value refers to the net amount that an entity expects to realise from the sale of inventory in the ordinary course of business. Fair value reflects the amount for which the same inventory could be exchanged between knowledgeable and willing buyers and sellers in the marketplace. The former is an entity-specific value; the latter is not. Net realisable value for inventories may not equal fair value less costs to sell.

8   Inventories encompass goods purchased and held for resale including, for example, merchandise purchased by a retailer and held for resale, or land and other property held for resale. Inventories also encompass finished goods produced, or work in progress being produced, by the entity and include materials and supplies awaiting use in the production process. In the case of a service provider, inventories include the costs of the service, as described in paragraph 19, for which the entity has not yet recognised the related revenue (see AASB 118 *Revenue*).

Aus8.1   A not-for-profit entity may hold inventories whose future economic benefits or service potential are not directly related to their ability to generate net cash inflows. These types of inventories may arise when an entity has determined to distribute certain goods at no charge or for a nominal amount. In these cases, the future economic benefits or service potential of the inventory for financial reporting purposes is reflected by the amount the entity would need to pay to acquire the economic benefits or service potential if this was necessary to achieve the objectives of the entity. Where the economic benefits or service potential cannot be acquired in the market, an estimate of replacement cost will need to be made.

---

1   Paragraphs 10 to 18 and 20 to 27 in this Standard apply to both inventories (as defined in paragraph 6) and inventories held for distribution (as defined in paragraph Aus6.1).

If the purpose for which the inventory is held changes, then the inventory is valued using the provisions of paragraph 9.

Aus8.2   The replacement cost that an entity would be prepared to incur in respect of an item of inventory would reflect any obsolescence or any other impairment.

Measurement of Inventories

9   Inventories shall be measured at the lower of cost and net realisable value.

Aus9.1   Notwithstanding paragraph 9, each not-for-profit entity shall measure _inventories held for distribution_ at cost, adjusted when applicable for any loss of service potential.

Aus9.2   Not-for-profit entities would need to use judgment in determining the factors relevant to the circumstances in assessing whether there is a loss of service potential for inventories held for distribution. For many inventories held for distribution, a loss of service potential would be identified and measured based on the existence of a _current replacement cost_ that is lower than the original acquisition cost or other subsequent carrying amount. For other inventories held for distribution, a loss of service potential might be identified and measured based on a loss of operating capacity due to obsolescence. Different bases for determining whether there has been a loss of service potential and the measurement of that loss may apply to different inventories held for distribution within the same entity.

Cost of Inventories

10   The cost of inventories shall comprise all costs of purchase, costs of conversion and other costs incurred in bringing the inventories to their present location and condition.

Aus10.1   Notwithstanding paragraph 10, in respect of not-for-profit entities, where inventories are acquired at no cost, or for nominal consideration, the cost shall be the current replacement cost as at the date of acquisition.

Costs of Purchase

11   The costs of purchase of inventories comprise the purchase price, import duties and other taxes (other than those subsequently recoverable by the entity from the taxing authorities), and transport, handling and other costs directly attributable to the acquisition of finished goods, materials and services. Trade discounts, rebates and other similar items are deducted in determining the costs of purchase.

Costs of Conversion

12   The costs of conversion of inventories include costs directly related to the units of production, such as direct labour. They also include a systematic allocation of fixed and variable production overheads that are incurred in converting materials into finished goods. Fixed production overheads are those indirect costs of production that remain relatively constant regardless of the volume of production, such as depreciation and maintenance of factory buildings and equipment, and the cost of factory management and administration. Variable production overheads are those indirect costs of production that vary directly, or nearly directly, with the volume of production, such as indirect materials and indirect labour.

13   The allocation of fixed production overheads to the costs of conversion is based on the normal capacity of the production facilities. Normal capacity is the production expected to be achieved on average over a number of periods or seasons under normal circumstances, taking into account the loss of capacity resulting from planned maintenance. The actual level of production may be used if it approximates normal capacity. The amount of fixed overhead allocated to each unit of production is not increased as a consequence of low production or idle plant. Unallocated overheads are recognised as an expense in the period in which they are incurred. In periods of abnormally high production, the amount of fixed overhead allocated to each unit of production is decreased so that inventories are not measured above cost. Variable production overheads are allocated to each unit of production on the basis of the actual use of the production facilities.

14   A production process may result in more than one product being produced simultaneously. This is the case, for example, when joint products are produced or when there is a main product and a by-product. When the costs of conversion of each product are not separately identifiable, they are allocated between the products on a rational and consistent basis. The allocation may be based, for example, on the relative sales value of each product either at the stage in the production process when the products become separately identifiable, or at the completion of production. Most by-products, by their nature, are immaterial. When this is the case, they are often measured at net realisable value and this value is deducted from the cost of the main product. As a result, the carrying amount of the main product is not materially different from its cost.

Other Costs

15   Other costs are included in the cost of inventories only to the extent that they are incurred in bringing the inventories to their present location and condition. For example, it may be appropriate to include non-production overheads or the costs of designing products for specific customers in the cost of inventories.

16   Examples of costs excluded from the cost of inventories and recognised as expenses in the period in which they are incurred are:

(a)   abnormal amounts of wasted materials, labour or other production costs;

(b)   storage costs, unless those costs are necessary in the production process before a further production stage;

(c)   administrative overheads that do not contribute to bringing inventories to their present location and condition; and

(d)   selling costs.

17   AASB 123 *Borrowing Costs* identifies limited circumstances where borrowing costs are included in the cost of inventories.

18   An entity may purchase inventories on deferred settlement terms. When the arrangement effectively contains a financing element, that element, for example a difference between the purchase price for normal credit terms and the amount paid, is recognised as interest expense over the period of the financing.

Cost of Inventories of a Service Provider

19   To the extent that service providers have inventories, they measure them at the costs of their production. These costs consist primarily of the labour and other costs of personnel directly engaged in providing the service, including supervisory personnel, and attributable overheads. Labour and other costs relating to sales and general administrative personnel are not included but are recognised as expenses in the period in which they are incurred. The cost of inventories of a service provider does not include profit margins or non-attributable overheads that are often factored into prices charged by service providers.

Cost of Agricultural Produce Harvested from Biological Assets

20   In accordance with AASB 141 *Agriculture* inventories comprising agricultural produce that an entity has harvested from its biological assets are measured on initial recognition at their fair value less costs to sell at the point of harvest. This is the cost of the inventories at that date for application of this Standard.

Techniques for the Measurement of Cost

21   Techniques for the measurement of the cost of inventories, such as the standard cost method or the retail method, may be used for convenience if the results approximate cost. Standard costs take into account normal levels of materials and supplies, labour, efficiency and capacity utilisation. They are regularly reviewed and, if necessary, revised in the light of current conditions.

22   The retail method is often used in the retail industry for measuring inventories of large numbers of rapidly changing items with similar margins for which it is impracticable to use other costing methods. The cost of the inventory is determined by reducing the sales

value of the inventory by the appropriate percentage gross margin. The percentage used takes into consideration inventory that has been marked down to below its original selling price. An average percentage for each retail department is often used.

Cost Formulas

23 **The cost of inventories of items that are not ordinarily interchangeable and goods or services produced and segregated for specific projects shall be assigned by using specific identification of their individual costs.**

24 Specific identification of cost means that specific costs are attributed to identified items of inventory. This is the appropriate treatment for items that are segregated for a specific project, regardless of whether they have been bought or produced. However, specific identification of costs is inappropriate when there are large numbers of items of inventory that are ordinarily interchangeable. In such circumstances, the method of selecting those items that remain in inventories could be used to obtain predetermined effects on profit or loss.

25 **The cost of inventories, other than those dealt with in paragraph 23, shall be assigned by using the first-in, first-out (FIFO) or weighted average cost formula. An entity shall use the same cost formula for all inventories having a similar nature and use to the entity. For inventories with a different nature or use, different cost formulas may be justified.**

26 For example, inventories used in one operating segment may have a use to the entity different from the same type of inventories used in another operating segment. However, a difference in geographical location of inventories (or in the respective tax rules), by itself, is not sufficient to justify the use of different cost formulas.

27 The FIFO formula assumes that the items of inventory that were purchased or produced first are sold first, and consequently the items remaining in inventory at the end of the period are those most recently purchased or produced. Under the weighted average cost formula, the cost of each item is determined from the weighted average of the cost of similar items at the beginning of a period and the cost of similar items purchased or produced during the period. The average may be calculated on a periodic basis, or as each additional shipment is received, depending upon the circumstances of the entity.

Net Realisable Value

28 The cost of inventories may not be recoverable if those inventories are damaged, if they have become wholly or partially obsolete, or if their selling prices have declined. The cost of inventories may also not be recoverable if the estimated costs of completion or the estimated costs to be incurred to make the sale have increased. The practice of writing inventories down below cost to net realisable value is consistent with the view that assets shall not be carried in excess of amounts expected to be realised from their sale or use.

29 Inventories are usually written down to net realisable value item by item. In some circumstances, however, it may be appropriate to group similar or related items. This may be the case with items of inventory relating to the same product line that have similar purposes or end uses, are produced and marketed in the same geographical area, and cannot be practicably evaluated separately from other items in that product line. It is not appropriate to write inventories down on the basis of a classification of inventory, for example, finished goods, or all the inventories in a particular operating segment. Service providers generally accumulate costs in respect of each service for which a separate selling price is charged. Therefore, each such service is treated as a separate item.

30 Estimates of net realisable value are based on the most reliable evidence available at the time the estimates are made, of the amount the inventories are expected to realise. These estimates take into consideration fluctuations of price or cost directly relating to events occurring after the end of the period to the extent that such events confirm conditions existing at the end of the period.

31   Estimates of net realisable value also take into consideration the purpose for which the inventory is held. For example, the net realisable value of the quantity of inventory held to satisfy firm sales or service contracts is based on the contract price. If the sales contracts are for less than the inventory quantities held, the net realisable value of the excess is based on general selling prices. Provisions may arise from firm sales contracts in excess of inventory quantities held or from firm purchase contracts. Such provisions are dealt with under AASB 137 *Provisions, Contingent Liabilities and Contingent Assets*.

32   Materials and other supplies held for use in the production of inventories are not written down below cost if the finished products in which they will be incorporated are expected to be sold at or above cost. However, when a decline in the price of materials indicates that the cost of the finished products exceeds net realisable value, the materials are written down to net realisable value. In such circumstances, the replacement cost of the materials may be the best available measure of their net realisable value.

33   A new assessment is made of net realisable value in each subsequent period. When the circumstances that previously caused inventories to be written down below cost no longer exist or when there is clear evidence of an increase in net realisable value because of changed economic circumstances, the amount of the write-down is reversed (i.e. the reversal is limited to the amount of the original write-down) so that the new carrying amount is the lower of the cost and the revised net realisable value. This occurs, for example, when an item of inventory that is carried at net realisable value, because its selling price has declined, is still on hand in a subsequent period and its selling price has increased.

Recognition as an Expense

34   **When inventories are sold, the carrying amount of those inventories shall be recognised as an expense in the period in which the related revenue is recognised. The amount of any write-down of inventories to net realisable value and all losses of inventories shall be recognised as an expense in the period the write-down or loss occurs. The amount of any reversal of any write-down of inventories, arising from an increase in net realisable value, shall be recognised as a reduction in the amount of inventories recognised as an expense in the period in which the reversal occurs.**

Aus34.1   When inventories held for distribution by a not-for-profit entity are distributed, the carrying amount of those inventories shall be recognised as an expense. The amount of any write-down of inventories for loss of service potential and all losses of inventories shall be recognised as an expense in the period in which the write-down or loss occurs. The amount of any reversal of any write-down of inventories arising from a reversal of the circumstances that gave rise to the loss of service potential shall be recognised as a reduction in the amount of inventories recognised as an expense in the period in which the reversal occurs.

35   Some inventories may be allocated to other asset accounts, for example, inventory used as a component of self-constructed property, plant or equipment. Inventories allocated to another asset in this way are recognised as an expense during the useful life of that asset.

Disclosure

36   **The financial statements shall disclose:**

   (a)   **the accounting policies adopted in measuring inventories, including the cost formula used;**

   (b)   **the total carrying amount of inventories and the carrying amount in classifications appropriate to the entity;**

   (c)   **the carrying amount of inventories carried at fair value less costs to sell;**

   (d)   **the amount of inventories recognised as an expense during the period;**

   (e)   **the amount of any write-down of inventories recognised as an expense in the period in accordance with paragraph 34;**

(f)   the amount of any reversal of any write-down that is recognised as a reduction in the amount of inventories recognised as expense in the period in accordance with paragraph 34;

(g)   the circumstances or events that led to the reversal of a write-down of inventories in accordance with paragraph 34; and

(h)   the carrying amount of inventories pledged as security for liabilities.

Aus36.1   Notwithstanding paragraph 36, in respect of not-for-profit entities, the financial statements shall disclose:

(a)   the accounting policies adopted in measuring inventories held for distribution, including the cost formula used;

(b)   the total carrying amount of inventories held for distribution and the carrying amount in classifications appropriate to the entity;

(c)   the amount of inventories held for distribution recognised as an expense during the period in accordance with paragraph Aus34.1;

(d)   the amount of any write-down of inventories held for distribution recognised as an expense in the period in accordance with paragraph Aus34.1;

(e)   the amount of any reversal of any write-down that is recognised as a reduction in the amount of inventories held for distribution recognised as expense in the period in accordance with paragraph Aus34.1;

(f)   the circumstances or events that led to the reversal of a write-down of inventories held for distribution in accordance with paragraph Aus34.1;

(g)   the carrying amount of inventories held for distribution pledged as security for liabilities; and

(h)   the basis on which any loss of service potential of inventories held for distribution is assessed, or the bases when more than one basis is used.

37   Information about the carrying amounts held in different classifications of inventories and the extent of the changes in these assets is useful to financial statement users. Common classifications of inventories are merchandise, production supplies, materials, work in progress and finished goods. The inventories of a service provider may be described as work in progress.

38   The amount of inventories recognised as an expense during the period, which is often referred to as cost of sales, consists of those costs previously included in the measurement of inventory that has now been sold and unallocated production overheads and abnormal amounts of production costs of inventories. The circumstances of the entity may also warrant the inclusion of other amounts, such as distribution costs.

39   Some entities adopt a format for profit or loss that results in amounts being disclosed other than the cost of inventories recognised as an expense during the period. Under this format, an entity presents an analysis of expenses using a classification based on the nature of expenses. In this case, the entity discloses the costs recognised as an expense for raw materials and consumables, labour costs and other costs together with the amount of the net change in inventories for the period.

Effective Date of IAS 2

40   [Deleted by the AASB]

Withdrawal of Other Pronouncements

41   [Deleted by the AASB]

42   [Deleted by the AASB]

Transition

Aus42.1   **Not-for-profit entities shall apply paragraph Aus9.1 and measure inventories held for distribution at cost, adjusted when applicable for any loss of service potential, on a prospective basis from the beginning of the annual reporting period to which this Standard is first applied.**

Aus42.2   Under paragraph Aus42.1, not-for-profit entities shall make any necessary adjustment to the opening balance of inventories held for distribution, previously carried at the lower of cost and current replacement cost, against opening retained earnings for the current annual reporting period. Accordingly, comparative information is not adjusted.

Basis for Conclusions on AASB 2007-5

This Basis for Conclusions accompanies, but is not part of, AASB 102. The Basis for Conclusions was originally published with AASB 2007-5 Amendments to Australian Accounting Standard – Inventories Held for Distribution by Not-for-Profit Entities.

Background Relating to Standards on Inventories

BC1   For reporting periods beginning prior to 1 January 2005, under AASB 1019 *Inventories* (now superseded by AASB 102 *Inventories*), inventories were defined only in terms of items held for sale or in the process of sale. The treatment of items in the nature of inventories that were not held for sale needed to be determined by analogy because they were not explicitly covered by AASB 1019.

BC2   Inventories held for distribution by not-for-profit entities were scoped into AASB 102, issued in July 2004, and were required to be measured at the lower of cost and current replacement cost.

BC3   This is the same as the requirement in the International Public Sector Accounting Standards Board's IPSAS 12 *Inventories* issued in July 2001. (IPSAS 12 has since been revised in December 2006 for application from 1 January 2008.)

BC4   The Board notes that inventories held for distribution do not include major spare parts and stand-by equipment that qualify as property, plant and equipment, which are discussed in AASB 116 *Property, Plant and Equipment* at paragraphs 8 and 12.

Background Relating to Key Issue

BC5   A number of constituents raised issues with the Board relating to the conceptual soundness of applying the lower of cost and current replacement cost treatment to inventories held for distribution as well as the practicality of its application to certain types of inventories held for distribution.

BC6   The Board considered the view that writing down inventory held for distribution when its current replacement cost falls below cost may result in the recognition of impairments when the service potential to the entity of those inventories remains unchanged. In addition, the Board noted that the service potential to the entity of inventories held for distribution may fall, but that current replacement cost to the entity may remain higher than the original cost. The Board concluded that this is in part because the lower of cost and current replacement cost requirement focuses on financial values, whereas the service potential of inventories held for distribution by many not-for-profit entities is considered in physical terms.

BC7   The Board also considered the practical problem that current replacement costs are sometimes not readily available for many of the inventories held for distribution that have long lives because they have not been replenished for long periods. In some cases, such inventories may have maintained their service potential, but may no longer be available in the form held by the entity.

BC8   The Board noted that a for-profit entity will readily know its costs and its net realisable values, because most businesses buy and sell inventories regularly. In a not-for-profit entity that holds inventories for distribution and buys and distributes them regularly, the lower of cost and current replacement cost requirement has been viewed as the nearest available equivalent requirement.

BC9 The Board noted that the practical problems emerge when the inventories held for distribution are retained over the long term and replacement costs are not readily available. A major part of the burden is the possible need to maintain records of three prices for each type of inventory: (1) the cost; (2) the up-to-date replacement cost in case there is a need for write down; and (3) in the event that the replacement cost has previously fallen below cost, that replacement cost [carrying amount]. The Board also noted that the records of the three prices might also need to be maintained to facilitate the reversal of write downs in the event that the circumstances that previously caused inventories to be written down below cost no longer exist or when there is clear evidence of an increase in current replacement cost because of changed economic circumstances.

Alternative Solutions

BC10 The Board considered developing a proposed solution only in respect of long-lived inventories held for distribution by not-for-profit entities in order to address the practical problems raised by constituents. However, the Board concluded that it would be more appropriate to develop a solution for all types of inventories held for distribution by not-for-profit entities that addresses the issues at both the principle and practical levels. This is because the Board prefers a solution based on a high-level principle that can be applied consistently by all not-for-profit entities in a manner that best suits the character of their inventories held for distribution.

BC11 Among the possible solutions considered by the Board was applying an AASB 136 *Impairment of Assets*-style impairment test, however, it was noted that this would have many of the problems already associated with the existing requirements.

Cost Adjusted when Applicable for Any Loss of Service Potential

BC12 The Board noted that the lower of cost and net realisable value requirement in AASB 102 in respect of inventories other than those held for distribution can be viewed as being based on a notion of recognising a loss of service potential in a for-profit environment. That is, an entity that seeks to sell inventories for more than they cost generally considers the service potential of those inventories in financial terms. If net realisable value falls below cost, the entity can be viewed as suffering a loss of service potential.

BC13 The Board observed that the lower of cost and current replacement cost requirement for measuring inventories held for distribution by not-for-profit entities can be viewed as seeking to emulate the approach taken for other inventories and its focus is also on a loss of value in financial terms. However, the Board considered that this financial measure of the loss of service potential may not always be the most relevant measure in respect of inventories held for distribution by not-for-profit entities for the reasons outlined in paragraph BC6.

BC14 The Board considered that the measurement of inventories held for distribution by not-for-profit entities at cost, adjusted when applicable for any loss of service potential, is consistent with the *Framework for the Preparation and Presentation of Financial Statements*, which notes at paragraph Aus49.1:

> In respect of not-for-profit entities in the public or private sector, in pursuing their objectives, goods and services are provided that have the capacity to satisfy human wants and needs. Assets provide a means for entities to achieve their objectives. Future economic benefits or service potential is the essence of assets. Future economic benefits is synonymous with the notion of service potential, and is used in this Framework as a reference also to service potential. Future economic benefits can be described as the scarce capacity to provide benefits to the entities that use them, and is common to all assets irrespective of their physical or other form.

BC15 The Board noted that a fall in the current replacement cost of inventories held for distribution may at times indicate a loss of service potential, but that this is not necessarily always the case, and that a loss of service potential may at times be identified on other, more relevant, bases. For example, obsolescence, which may occur with or without there being a fall in current replacement cost, may be the main factor leading to a loss of service potential for many not-for-profit entities. The term 'obsolescence' covers both 'technical obsolescence' and 'functional obsolescence'. Technical obsolescence occurs when an item still functions for some or all of the tasks it was originally acquired to do, but no longer matches existing technologies. Functional obsolescence occurs when an item no longer functions the way it did when it was first acquired. In either case, a loss of service potential may need to be recognised.

BC16 The Board also considered that a problem with a purely physical service potential approach is identifying ways in which physical service potential would be measured. However, the Board concluded that many not-for-profit entities will often be more likely to monitor the service potential of their inventories held for distribution than they are to monitor the current replacement costs of those inventories. The Board considered that this is especially likely to be the case when those inventories are important to maintaining its functions or operating capability and, therefore, often in cases when it is most likely to be material to the financial statements.

BC17 The Board considers that there is a need for the circumstances of a not-for-profit entity to be the determining factor behind its manner of assessing any loss of service potential for inventories held for distribution. The measurement requirement for inventories held for distribution would require each not-for-profit entity to identify the basis (or bases) for determining any loss of service potential that best suits the circumstances relating to the entity. Different bases may apply to different inventories held for distribution within the same entity.

BC18 There was considerable support for the approach of requiring inventories held for distribution to be measured at cost, adjusted for any loss of service potential, in the submissions on Exposure Draft ED 154 *Proposed Amendments to AASB 102 – Inventories Held for Distribution by Not-for-Profit Entities*. However, some submissions expressed concerns that the lower of cost and current replacement cost requirement is being applied without difficulty by many entities and argued that it might be unnecessarily disruptive to introduce the change proposed in ED 154.

BC19 The Board noted that a current replacement cost that is lower than cost might be a common way of identifying and measuring a loss of service potential for inventories held for distribution. Accordingly, many entities are likely to continue their existing practices under a revised AASB 102, and the Board concluded few entities would be disrupted by the change.

BC20 The Board concluded that the requirement to measure inventories held for distribution at cost, adjusted when applicable for any loss of service potential, would give rise to more relevant information that better reflects the various accountabilities of not-for-profit entities. In addition, the Board concluded that the requirement is likely to be more appropriate in practical terms than the former requirement in some circumstances.

Transition

BC21 The Board considered that, in some cases, measuring at the lower of cost and current replacement cost versus measuring at cost, adjusted when applicable for any loss of service potential, would give rise to different carrying amounts for inventories held for distribution. The Board concluded that, on transition to the changed requirement, it is appropriate to require not-for-profit entities to adjust any difference prospectively against opening retained earnings and not amend comparative information on the basis that:

(a) there are likely to be practical problems associated with trying to retrospectively determine whether there have been further losses of service potential and precisely when they occurred, which may not be overcome by the impracticability override in AASB 108 *Accounting Policies, Changes in Accounting Estimates and Errors*;

(b) the relatively short period of development involved in amending AASB 102 and, therefore, the absence of a long period during which constituents would be made aware of the changes; and

(c) requiring rather than permitting the prospective transitional approach is desirable from a comparability viewpoint.

AASB 107
Statement of Cash Flows

(Compiled September 2011)

Note from the Institute of Chartered Accountants Australia

This note, prepared by the technical editors, is not part of Accounting Standard AASB 107.

Historical development

July 2004: AASB 107 'Cash Flow Statements' is the Australian equivalent of IAS 7 of the same name. It was made by the AASB on 15 July 2004 as part of the AASB's program to adopt International Financial Reporting Standards by 2005.

26 February 2007: AASB 2007-3 'Amendments to Australian Accounting Standards' was issued by the AASB. This Standard is applicable to annual reporting periods beginning on or after 1 January 2009.

30 April 2007: AASB 2007-4 'Amendments to Australian Accounting Standards' amends paragraphs 6, 18, 19, 20, Aus20.1, Aus20.2, 34, 50(b) and Appendix A paragraphs 2, 3, Direct Method Cash Flow Statement and Note 5. It added Appendix A Indirect Method Cash Flow Statement, Alternaive Presentation (Indirect Method) and Appendix B rubric, and is applicable to annual reporting periods beginning on or after 1 July 2007. Entities may elect to early-adopt it to annual reporting periods on or after 1 January 2005.

14 June 2007: AASB 2007-6 'Amendments to Australian Accounting Standards' was issued by the AASB. This Standard is applicable to annual reporting periods beginning on or after 1 January 2009.

28 June 2007: AASB 2007-7 'Amendments to Australian Accounting Standards' amends Appendix A Direct Method Cash Flow Statement and deletes paragraph Aus12.1 and is applicable to annual reporting periods beginning on or after 1 July 2007. Entities may elect to early-adopt it to annual reporting periods on or after 1 January 2005.

July 2007: Erratum amends paragraph 38 and is applicable to annual reporting periods beginning on or after 1 July 2007. Entities may elect to early-adopt it to annual reporting periods on or after 1 January 2005.

24 September 2007: AASB 2007-8 'Amendments to Australian Accounting Standards' was issued by the AASB. This Standard is applicable to annual reporting periods beginning on or after 1 January 2009.

13 December 2007: AASB 2007-10 'Further Amendments to Australian Accounting Standards arising from AASB 101' amends AASB 107, replacing the term 'financial report' with 'financial statements'. This Standard is applicable to annual reporting periods beginning on or after 1 January 2009.

6 March 2008: AASB 2008-3 'Amendments to Australian Accounting Standards arising from AASB 3 and AASB 127' amends AASB 107 for the issue of AASB 3 Revised. This Standard is applicable to annual reporting periods beginning on or after 1 July 2009.

24 July 2008: AASB 2008-5 'Amendments to Australian Accounting Standards arising from the Annual Improvements Project' amends AASB 107 in relation to cash flows relating to property, plant and equipment. This Standard is applicable to annual reporting periods beginning on or after 1 January 2009.

21 May 2009: AASB 2009-5 'Amendments to Australian Accounting Standards' is the annual improvements Standard, amending AASB 107 in relation to the classification of expenditures on unrecognised assets. This Standard applies to annual reporting periods beginning on or after 1 January 2010 and may be applied early.

---

25 June 2009: AASB 2009-6 'Amendments to Australian Accounting Standards' amends AASB 107 for editorial corrections made by the International Accounting Standards Board (IASB) to its Standards and Interpretations (IFRSs) and as a consequence of issuing revised AASB 101 'Presentation of Financial Statements'. This Standard is applicable to annual reporting periods beginning on or after 1 January 2009 that end on or after 30 June 2009.

25 June 2009: AASB 2009-7 'Amendments to Australian Accounting Standards' amends AASB 107 arising from editorial corrections by the AASB and by the International Accounting Standards Board (IASB). This Standard is applicable to annual reporting periods beginning on or after 1 July 2009.

23 October 2009: AASB 107 was reissued by the AASB, compiled to include the AASB 2007-3, AASB 2007-6, AASB 2007-8, AASB 2007-10, AASB 2008-3, AASB 2008-5, AASB 2009-5, AASB 2009-6 and AASB 2009-7 amendments and applies to annual reporting periods beginning on or after 1 July 2009 but before 1 January 2010. Early application is permitted.

On the same date the AASB reissued the version of AASB 107 applicable to annual reporting periods beginning on or after 1 January 2009 but before 1 July 2009. This version of AASB 107 has been compiled for the amending Standards applying to annual reporting periods beginning on or after 1 January 2009. This Standard applies to 31 December 2009 year ends and can be accessed from the AASB website at www.aasb.gov.au.

1 December 2009: AASB 107 was reissued by the AASB, compiled to include the AASB 2009-5 amendments and applies to annual reporting periods beginning on or after 1 January 2010.

27 October 2010: AASB 2010-5 'Further Amendments to Australian Accounting Standards' makes editorial amendments to AASB 107. This Standard is applicable to annual reporting periods beginning on or after 1 January 2011.

11 May 2011: AASB 2011-1 'Amendments to Australian Accounting Standards arising from the Trans-Tasman Convergence Project' amends AASB 107 as a result of the Trans-Tasman project to more closely align IFRSs as applied through Australian and New Zealand Standards. AASB 2011-1 deletes Australian specific disclosure requirements. Where appropriate these disclosures are now included in AASB 1054 'Australian Additional Requirements'. These Standards apply to annual reporting periods beginning on or after 1 July 2011 with early adoption permitted.

29 August 2011: AASB 2011-7 'Amendments to Australian Accounting Standards arising from the Consolidation and Joint Arrangements Standards' amends AASB 107 to give effect to many consequential changes arising from the issue of AASB 10, 11, 12, 127 and 128. This Standard applies to annual reporting periods beginning on or after 1 January 2013 and can be adopted early by for-profit entities. **These amendments are not included in this compiled Standard.**

23 September 2011: AASB 107 was reissued by the AASB, compiled to include the AASB 2010-5 and AASB 2011-1 amendments and applies to annual reporting periods ending on or after 1 July 2011 but before 1 January 2013.

References

Interpretation 1031 *Accounting for the Goods and Services Tax (GST)* applies to AASB 107.

IFRIC items not taken onto the agenda: *No. 5 Classification of treasury shares in the consolidated cash flow statement* issued in April 2003 (IFRIC), IAS 7-1 *Value added tax*, IAS 7-2 *Classifications of expenditures* and IAS 7-3 *Determination of cash equivalents* apply to AASB 107.

AASB 107 compared to IAS 7

Additions

Paragraph	Description
Aus 1.1	Which entities AASB 107 applies to.
Aus 1.2	The application date of AASB 107 (i.e. annual periods beginning 1 January 2005).
Aus 1.3	Prohibits early application of AASB 107.
Aus 1.4	Makes the requirements of AASB 107 subject to AASB 1031 'Materiality'.
Aus 1.5	Explains which Standards have been superseded by AASB 107.
Aus 1.6	Clarifies that the superseded Standards apply until AASB 107 applies.

Aus 1.7	Notice of Standard published as required on 22 July 2004.
Aus20.2	Requires a reconciliation note for those not-for-profit entities that report the net cost of services in their income statement.
Aus 54.1	Application of amendments arising from AASB 2008-3

Deletions

Paragraph	Description
2	History of IAS 7 not relevant to Australia.
53	Effective date of IAS 7 not relevant to Australia.
54	Effective date of amendments.

Contents

Compilation Details

Comparison with IAS 7

Accounting Standard
AASB 107 Statement of Cash Flows

Paragraphs

Objective	
Application	Aus1.1 – Aus1.7
Scope	1 – 3
Benefits of Cash Flow Information	4 – 5
Definitions	6
Cash and Cash Equivalents	7 – 9
Presentation of a Statement of Cash Flows	10 – 12
Operating Activities	13 – 15
Investing Activities	16
Financing Activities	17
Reporting Cash Flows from Operating Activities	18 – Aus20.2
Reporting Cash Flows from Investing and Financing Activities	21
Reporting Cash Flows on a Net Basis	22 – 24
Foreign Currency Cash Flows	25 – 28
Interest and Dividends	31 – 34
Taxes on Income	35 – 36
Investments in Subsidiaries, Associates and Joint Ventures	37 – 38
Changes in Ownership Interests in Subsidiaries and Other Businesses	39 – 42B
Non-cash Transactions	43 – 44
Components of Cash and Cash Equivalents	45 – 47
Other Disclosures	48 – 52
Effective Date	Aus54.1 – 56

Illustrative Examples:

A. Statement of Cash Flows for an Entity other than a Financial Institution

B. Statement of Cash Flows for a Financial Institution

Australian Accounting Standard AASB 107 *Statement of Cash Flows* (as amended) is set out in paragraphs Aus1.1 – 56. All the paragraphs have equal authority. Terms defined in this Standard are in *italics* the first time they appear in the Standard. AASB 107 is to be read in the context of other Australian Accounting Standards, including AASB 1048 *Interpretation and Application of Standards*, which identifies the Australian Accounting Interpretations. In the absence of explicit guidance, AASB 108 *Accounting Policies, Changes in Accounting Estimates and Errors* provides a basis for selecting and applying accounting policies.

Compilation Details

Accounting Standard AASB 107 *Statement of Cash Flows* as amended

This compiled Standard applies to annual reporting periods beginning on or after 1 July 2011 but before 1 January 2013. It takes into account amendments up to and including 11 May 2011 and was prepared on 23 September 2011 by the staff of the Australian Accounting Standards Board (AASB).

This compilation is not a separate Accounting Standard made by the AASB. Instead, it is a representation of AASB 107 (July 2004) as amended by other Accounting Standards, which are listed in the Table below.

Table of Standards

Standard	Date made	Application date *(annual reporting periods ... on or after ...)*	Application, saving or transitional provisions
AASB 107	15 Jul 2004	*(beginning)* 1 Jan 2005	
AASB 2007-3	26 Feb 2007	*(beginning)* 1 Jan 2009	see (a) below
AASB 2007-4	30 Apr 2007	*(beginning)* 1 Jul 2007	see (b) below
AASB 2007-6	14 Jun 2007	*(beginning)* 1 Jan 2009	see (c) below
AASB 2007-7	28 Jun 2007	*(beginning)* 1 Jul 2007	see (b) below
Erratum	20 Jul 2007	*(beginning)* 1 Jul 2007	see (d) below
AASB 2007-8	24 Sep 2007	*(beginning)* 1 Jan 2009	see (e) below
AASB 2007-10	13 Dec 2007	*(beginning)* 1 Jan 2009	see (e) below
AASB 2008-3	6 Mar 2008	*(beginning)* 1 Jul 2009	see (f) below
AASB 2008-5	24 Jul 2008	*(beginning)* 1 Jan 2009	see (g) below
AASB 2009-5	21 May 2009	*(beginning)* 1 Jan 2010	see (h) below
AASB 2009-6	25 Jun 2009	*(beginning)* 1 Jan 2009 and *(ending)* 30 Jun 2009	see (i) below
AASB 2009-7	25 Jun 2009	*(beginning)* 1 Jul 2009	see (j) below
AASB 2010-2	30 Jun 2010	*(beginning)* 1 Jul 2013	not compiled*
AASB 2010-5	27 Oct 2010	*(beginning)* 1 Jan 2011	see (k) below
AASB 2011-1	11 May 2011	*(beginning)* 1 Jul 2011	see (l) below
AASB 2011-7	29 Aug 2011	*(beginning)* 1 Jan 2013	not compiled*

*   The amendments made by this Standard are not included in this compilation, which presents the principal Standard as applicable to annual reporting periods beginning on or after 1 July 2011 but before 1 January 2013.

(a)   Entities may elect to apply this Standard to annual reporting periods beginning on or after 1 January 2005 but before 1 January 2009, provided that AASB 8 *Operating Segments* is also applied to such periods.

(b)   Entities may elect to apply this Standard to annual reporting periods beginning on or after 1 January 2005 but before 1 July 2007.

(c)   Entities may elect to apply this Standard to annual reporting periods beginning on or after 1 January 2005 but before 1 January 2009, provided that AASB 123 *Borrowing Costs* (June 2007) is also applied to such periods.

(d)   Entities may elect to apply this Erratum to annual reporting periods beginning on or after 1 January 2005 but before 1 July 2007.

(e)   Entities may elect to apply this Standard to annual reporting periods beginning on or after 1 January 2005 but before 1 January 2009, provided that AASB 101 *Presentation of Financial Statements* (September 2007) is also applied to such periods.

(f)   Entities may elect to apply this Standard to annual reporting periods beginning on or after 30 June 2007 but before 1 July 2009, provided that AASB 3 *Business Combinations* (March 2008) and AASB 127 *Consolidated and Separate Financial Statements* (March 2008) are also applied to such periods.

(g)   Entities may elect to apply this Standard, or its amendments to individual Standards, to annual reporting periods beginning on or after 1 January 2005 but before 1 January 2009.

(h)   Entities may elect to apply this Standard, or its amendments to individual Standards, to annual reporting periods beginning on or after 1 January 2005 but before 1 January 2010.

(i)   Entities may elect to apply this Standard to annual reporting periods beginning on or after 1 January 2005 but before 1 January 2009, provided that AASB 101 *Presentation of Financial Statements* (September 2007) is also applied to such periods, and to annual reporting periods beginning on or after 1 January 2009 that end before 30 June 2009.

(j)   Entities may elect to apply this Standard to annual reporting periods beginning before 1 July 2009 that end on or after 1 July 2008.

(k)   Entities may elect to apply this Standard to annual reporting periods beginning on or after 1 January 2005 but before 1 January 2011.

(l)   Entities may elect to apply this Standard, or its amendments to individual pronouncements, to annual reporting periods beginning on or after 1 January 2005 but before 1 July 2011, provided that AASB 1054 *Australian Additional Disclosures* is, or its relevant individual disclosure requirements are, also applied to such periods.

Table of Amendments to Standard

Paragraph affected	How affected	By ... [paragraph]
Title	amended	AASB 2007-8 [38]
	footnote added	AASB 2007-8 [39]
1	amended	AASB 2007-10 [44]
6	amended	AASB 2007-4 [35]
Aus12.1	deleted	AASB 2007-7 [11]
14	amended	AASB 2008-5 [18]
16	amended	AASB 2009-5 [13]
17	amended	AASB 2010-5 [22]
18	amended	AASB 2007-4 [26]
19	amended	AASB 2007-4 [27]
	amended	AASB 2007-8 [6]
20	amended	AASB 2007-4 [28]
	amended	AASB 2007-8 [6]
	amended	AASB 2008-3 [8]
	amended	AASB 2009-7 [11]
Aus20.1	amended	AASB 2007-4 [29]
	amended	AASB 2007-10 [45]
	deleted	AASB 2011-1 [13]
Aus20.2	amended	AASB 2007-4 [29]
	amended	AASB 2007-8 [6]
	amended	AASB 2007-10 [45]
	amended	AASB 2011-1 [14]
23	amended	AASB 2010-5 [23]
23A	added	AASB 2010-5 [23]
27	amended	AASB 2007-8 [6]
32	amended	AASB 2007-6 [12]
	amended	AASB 2007-8 [40]
34	amended	AASB 2007-4 [30]
38	amended	Erratum, Jul 2007
39-42 (and preceding heading)	amended	AASB 2008-3 [26]
42A-42B	added	AASB 2008-3 [27]
45	amended	AASB 2007-8 [6]
50(b)	added	AASB 2007-4 [31]
50(d)	amended	AASB 2007-3 [10]
53 (preceding heading)	amended	AASB 2008-5 [19]

Paragraph affected	How affected	By ... [paragraph]
54	note added	AASB 2008-3 [28]
Aus54.1	added	AASB 2008-3 [29]
55	added	AASB 2008-5 [20]
56	added	AASB 2009-5 [14]

Table of Amendments to Illustrative Examples

Paragraph affected	How affected	By ... [paragraph]
A, title, rubric, heading	amended amended	AASB 2007-4 [32, 35] AASB 2010-5 [24]
A, paragraph 2	amended amended	AASB 2007-4 [35] AASB 2007-8 [6]
A, paragraph 3	amended amended	AASB 2007-4 [35] AASB 2007-8 [6]
A, Consolidated Statement of Comprehensive Income	amended	AASB 2009-6 [36]
A, Direct Method Statement of Cash Flows	amended amended	AASB 2007-4 [35] AASB 2007-7 [12]
A, Indirect Method Statement of Cash Flows	added	AASB 2007-4 [33]
A, Note 1	amended	AASB 2008-3 [30]
A, Note 3	amended amended	AASB 2007-8 [6] AASB 2009-6 [37]
A, Note 5, Reconciliation of Net Cash ...	amended deleted	AASB 2007-4 [35] AASB 2011-1 [15]
A, Alternative Presentation (Indirect Method)	added	AASB 2007-4 [34]
B, title, rubric, heading	amended amended	AASB 2007-4 [32] AASB 2010-5 [25]

General Terminology Amendments

The following amendments are not shown in the above Tables of Amendments:

References to 'financial report(s)' were amended to 'financial statements' by AASB 2007-8 and AASB 2007-10, except in relation to specific Corporations Act references.

References to 'cash flow statement' were amended to 'statement of cash flows' by AASB 2007-8.

Other Amendments

In Appendices A and B, references to the years '20-1' and '20-2' were amended to '20X1' and '20X2' respectively by AASB 2009-6. These amendments are not shown in the above Tables of Amendments.

Comparison with IAS 7

AASB 107 and IAS 7

AASB 107 *Statement of Cash Flows* as amended incorporates IAS 7 *Statement of Cash Flows* as issued and amended by the International Accounting Standards Board (IASB). Paragraphs that have been added to this Standard (and do not appear in the text of IAS 7) are identified with the prefix "Aus", followed by the number of the relevant IASB paragraph and decimal numbering. Paragraphs that apply only to not-for-profit entities begin by identifying their limited applicability.

Compliance with IAS 7

Entities that comply with AASB 107 as amended will simultaneously be in compliance with IAS 7 as amended.

Accounting Standard AASB 107

The Australian Accounting Standards Board made Accounting Standard AASB 107 *Cash Flow Statements* under section 334 of the *Corporations Act 2001* on 15 July 2004.

This compiled version of AASB 107 applies to annual reporting periods beginning on or after 1 July 2011 but before 1 January 2013. It incorporates relevant amendments contained in other AASB Standards made by the AASB and other decisions of the AASB up to and including 11 May 2011 (see Compilation Details).

Accounting Standard AASB 107

Statement of Cash Flows[1]

Objective

Information about the cash flows of an entity is useful in providing users of financial statements with a basis to assess the ability of the entity to generate cash and cash equivalents and the needs of the entity to utilise those cash flows. The economic decisions that are taken by users require an evaluation of the ability of an entity to generate cash and cash equivalents and the timing and certainty of their generation.

The objective of this Standard is to require the provision of information about the historical changes in cash and cash equivalents of an entity by means of a statement of cash flows which classifies cash flows during the period from operating, investing and financing activities.

Application

Aus1.1   This Standard applies to:

(a)   **each entity that is required to prepare financial reports in accordance with Part 2M.3 of the Corporations Act;**

(b)   **general purpose financial statements of each reporting entity; and**

(c)   **financial statements that are, or are held out to be, general purpose financial statements.**

Aus1.2   **This Standard applies to annual reporting periods beginning on or after 1 January 2005.**

[Note: For application dates of paragraphs changed or added by an amending Standard, see Compilation Details.]

Aus1.3   **This Standard shall not be applied to annual reporting periods beginning before 1 January 2005.**

Aus1.4   **The requirements specified in this Standard apply to the financial statements where information resulting from their application is material in accordance with AASB 1031 *Materiality*.**

Aus1.5   **When applicable, this Standard supersedes:**

(a)   **AASB 1026 *Statement of Cash Flows* as notified in the *Commonwealth of Australia Gazette* No S 415, 16 October 1997; and**

(b)   **AAS 28 *Statement of Cash Flows* as issued in October 1997.**

Aus1.6   Both AASB 1026 and AAS 28 remain applicable until superseded by this Standard.

Aus1.7   Notice of this Standard was published in the *Commonwealth of Australia Gazette* No S 294, 22 July 2004.

---

1   In September 2007 the AASB amended the title of AASB 107 from *Cash Flow Statements* to *Statement of Cash Flows* as a consequence of the revision of AASB 101 *Presentation of Financial Statements* in 2007.

AASB 107   **Institute of Chartered Accountants Australia**

AASB

Scope

1   **An entity shall prepare a statement of cash flows in accordance with the requirements of this Standard and shall present it as an integral part of its financial statements for each period for which financial statements are presented.**

2   [Deleted by the AASB]

3   Users of an entity's financial statements are interested in how the entity generates and uses *cash* and *cash equivalents*. This is the case regardless of the nature of the entity's activities and irrespective of whether cash can be viewed as the product of the entity, as may be the case with a financial institution. Entities need cash for essentially the same reasons however different their principal revenue-producing activities might be. They need cash to conduct their operations, to pay their obligations, and to provide returns to their investors.

Benefits of Cash Flow Information

4   A statement of cash flows, when used in conjunction with the rest of the financial statements, provides information that enables users to evaluate the changes in net assets of an entity, its financial structure (including its liquidity and solvency) and its ability to affect the amounts and timing of *cash flows* in order to adapt to changing circumstances and opportunities. Cash flow information is useful in assessing the ability of the entity to generate cash and cash equivalents and enables users to develop models to assess and compare the present value of the future cash flows of different entities. It also enhances the comparability of the reporting of operating performance by different entities because it eliminates the effects of using different accounting treatments for the same transactions and events.

5   Historical cash flow information is often used as an indicator of the amount, timing and certainty of future cash flows. It is also useful in checking the accuracy of past assessments of future cash flows and in examining the relationship between profitability and net cash flow and the impact of changing prices.

Definitions

6   **The following terms are used in this Standard with the meanings specified.**

Cash **comprises cash on hand and demand deposits.**

Cash equivalents **are short-term, highly liquid investments that are readily convertible to known amounts of cash and which are subject to an insignificant risk of changes in value.**

Cash flows **are inflows and outflows of cash and cash equivalents.**

Financing activities **are activities that result in changes in the size and composition of the contributed equity and borrowings of the entity.**

Investing activities **are the acquisition and disposal of long-term assets and other investments not included in cash equivalents.**

Operating activities **are the principal revenue-producing activities of the entity and other activities that are not investing or financing activities.**

Cash and Cash Equivalents

7   Cash equivalents are held for the purpose of meeting short-term cash commitments rather than for investment or other purposes. For an investment to qualify as a cash equivalent it must be readily convertible to a known amount of cash and be subject to an insignificant risk of changes in value. Therefore, an investment normally qualifies as a cash equivalent only when it has a short maturity of, say, three months or less from the date of acquisition. Equity investments are excluded from cash equivalents unless they are, in substance, cash equivalents, for example in the case of preferred shares acquired within a short period of their maturity and with a specified redemption date.

8   Bank borrowings are generally considered to be *financing activities*. However, in some countries, bank overdrafts which are repayable on demand form an integral part of an entity's cash management. In these circumstances, bank overdrafts are included as a

component of cash and cash equivalents. A characteristic of such banking arrangements is that the bank balance often fluctuates from being positive to overdrawn.

9   Cash flows exclude movements between items that constitute cash or cash equivalents because these components are part of the cash management of an entity rather than part of its operating, investing and financing activities. Cash management includes the investment of excess cash in cash equivalents.

Presentation of a Statement of Cash Flows

10   **The statement of cash flows shall report cash flows during the period classified by operating, investing and financing activities.**

11   An entity presents its cash flows from operating, investing and financing activities in a manner which is most appropriate to its business. Classification by activity provides information that allows users to assess the impact of those activities on the financial position of the entity and the amount of its cash and cash equivalents. This information may also be used to evaluate the relationships among those activities.

12   A single transaction may include cash flows that are classified differently. For example, when the cash repayment of a loan includes both interest and capital, the interest element may be classified as an operating activity and the capital element is classified as a financing activity.

Operating Activities

13   The amount of cash flows arising from *operating activities* is a key indicator of the extent to which the operations of the entity have generated sufficient cash flows to repay loans, maintain the operating capability of the entity, pay dividends and make new investments without recourse to external sources of financing. Information about the specific components of historical operating cash flows is useful, in conjunction with other information, in forecasting future operating cash flows.

14   Cash flows from operating activities are primarily derived from the principal revenue-producing activities of the entity. Therefore, they generally result from the transactions and other events that enter into the determination of profit or loss. Examples of cash flows from operating activities are:

(a)   cash receipts from the sale of goods and the rendering of services;

(b)   cash receipts from royalties, fees, commissions and other revenue;

(c)   cash payments to suppliers for goods and services;

(d)   cash payments to and on behalf of employees;

(e)   cash receipts and cash payments of an insurance entity for premiums and claims, annuities and other policy benefits;

(f)   cash payments or refunds of income taxes unless they can be specifically identified with financing and *investing activities*; and

(g)   cash receipts and payments from contracts held for dealing or trading purposes.

Some transactions, such as the sale of an item of plant, may give rise to a gain or loss that is included in recognised profit or loss. The cash flows relating to such transactions are cash flows from investing activities. However, cash payments to manufacture or acquire assets held for rental to others and subsequently held for sale as described in paragraph 68A of AASB 116 *Property, Plant and Equipment* are cash flows from operating activities. The cash receipts from rents and subsequent sales of such assets are also cash flows from operating activities.

15   An entity may hold securities and loans for dealing or trading purposes, in which case they are similar to inventory acquired specifically for resale. Therefore, cash flows arising from the purchase and sale of dealing or trading securities are classified as operating activities. Similarly, cash advances and loans made by financial institutions are usually classified as operating activities since they relate to the main revenue-producing activity of that entity.

Investing Activities

16 The separate disclosure of cash flows arising from investing activities is important because the cash flows represent the extent to which expenditures have been made for resources intended to generate future income and cash flows. Only expenditures that result in a recognised asset in the statement of financial position are eligible for classification as investing activities. Examples of cash flows arising from investing activities are:

(a) cash payments to acquire property, plant and equipment, intangibles and other long-term assets. These payments include those relating to capitalised development costs and self-constructed property, plant and equipment;

(b) cash receipts from sales of property, plant and equipment, intangibles and other long-term assets;

(c) cash payments to acquire equity or debt instruments of other entities and interests in joint ventures (other than payments for those instruments considered to be cash equivalents or those held for dealing or trading purposes);

(d) cash receipts from sales of equity or debt instruments of other entities and interests in joint ventures (other than receipts for those instruments considered to be cash equivalents and those held for dealing or trading purposes);

(e) cash advances and loans made to other parties (other than advances and loans made by a financial institution);

(f) cash receipts from the repayment of advances and loans made to other parties (other than advances and loans of a financial institution);

(g) cash payments for futures contracts, forward contracts, option contracts and swap contracts except when the contracts are held for dealing or trading purposes, or the payments are classified as financing activities; and

(h) cash receipts from futures contracts, forward contracts, option contracts and swap contracts except when the contracts are held for dealing or trading purposes, or the receipts are classified as financing activities.

When a contract is accounted for as a hedge of an identifiable position, the cash flows of the contract are classified in the same manner as the cash flows of the position being hedged.

Financing Activities

17 The separate disclosure of cash flows arising from financing activities is important because it is useful in predicting claims on future cash flows by providers of capital to the entity. Examples of cash flows arising from financing activities are:

(a) cash proceeds from issuing shares or other equity instruments;

(b) cash payments to owners to acquire or redeem the entity's shares;

(c) cash proceeds from issuing debentures, loans, notes, bonds, mortgages and other short-term or long-term borrowings;

(d) cash repayments of amounts borrowed; and

(e) cash payments by a lessee for the reduction of the outstanding liability relating to a finance lease.

Reporting Cash Flows from Operating Activities

18 **An entity shall report cash flows from operating activities using either:**

(a) **the direct method, whereby major classes of gross cash receipts and gross cash payments are disclosed; or**

(b) **the indirect method, whereby profit or loss is adjusted for the effects of transactions of a non-cash nature, any deferrals or accruals of past or future operating cash receipts or payments, and items of income or expense associated with investing or financing cash flows.**

19   Entities are encouraged to report cash flows from operating activities using the direct method. The direct method provides information which may be useful in estimating future cash flows and which is not available under the indirect method. Under the direct method, information about major classes of gross cash receipts and gross cash payments may be obtained either:

(a)   from the accounting records of the entity; or

(b)   by adjusting sales, cost of sales (interest and similar income and interest expense and similar charges for a financial institution) and other items in the statement of comprehensive income for:

(i)   changes during the period in inventories and operating receivables and payables;

(ii)   other non-cash items; and

(iii)   other items for which the cash effects are investing or financing cash flows.

20   Under the indirect method, the net cash flow from operating activities is determined by adjusting profit or loss for the effects of:

(a)   changes during the period in inventories and operating receivables and payables;

(b)   non-cash items such as depreciation, provisions, deferred taxes, unrealised foreign currency gains and losses, and undistributed profits of associates; and

(c)   all other items for which the cash effects are investing or financing cash flows.

Alternatively, the net cash flow from operating activities may be presented under the indirect method by showing the revenues and expenses disclosed in the statement of comprehensive income and the changes during the period in inventories and operating receivables and payables.

Aus20.1   [Deleted by the AASB]

Aus20.2   Not-for-profit entities that use the direct method and that highlight the net cost of services in their statement of comprehensive income for the reporting period shall disclose in the complete set of financial statements a reconciliation of cash flows arising from operating activities to net cost of services as reported in the statement of comprehensive income.

Reporting Cash Flows from Investing and Financing Activities

21   **An entity shall report separately major classes of gross cash receipts and gross cash payments arising from investing and financing activities, except to the extent that cash flows described in paragraphs 22 and 24 are reported on a net basis.**

Reporting Cash Flows on a Net Basis

22   **Cash flows arising from the following operating, investing or financing activities may be reported on a net basis:**

(a)   **cash receipts and payments on behalf of customers when the cash flows reflect the activities of the customer rather than those of the entity; and**

(b)   **cash receipts and payments for items in which the turnover is quick, the amounts are large, and the maturities are short.**

23   Examples of cash receipts and payments referred to in paragraph 22(a) are:

(a)   the acceptance and repayment of demand deposits of a bank;

(b)   funds held for customers by an investment entity; and

(c)   rents collected on behalf of, and paid over to, the owners of properties.

23A   Examples of cash receipts and payments referred to in paragraph 22(b) are advances made for, and the repayment of:

    (a)   principal amounts relating to credit card customers;

    (b)   the purchase and sale of investments; and

    (c)   other short-term borrowings, for example, those which have a maturity period of three months or less.

24   **Cash flows arising from each of the following activities of a financial institution may be reported on a net basis:**

    (a)   **cash receipts and payments for the acceptance and repayment of deposits with a fixed maturity date;**

    (b)   **the placement of deposits with and withdrawal of deposits from other financial institutions; and**

    (c)   **cash advances and loans made to customers and the repayment of those advances and loans.**

Foreign Currency Cash Flows

25   **Cash flows arising from transactions in a foreign currency shall be recorded in an entity's functional currency by applying to the foreign currency amount the exchange rate between the functional currency and the foreign currency at the date of the cash flow.**

26   **The cash flows of a foreign subsidiary shall be translated at the exchange rates between the functional currency and the foreign currency at the dates of the cash flows.**

27   Cash flows denominated in a foreign currency are reported in a manner consistent with AASB 121 *The Effects of Changes in Foreign Exchange Rates*. This permits the use of an exchange rate that approximates the actual rate. For example, a weighted average exchange rate for a period may be used for recording foreign currency transactions or the translation of the cash flows of a foreign subsidiary. However, AASB 121 does not permit use of the exchange rate at the end of the reporting period when translating the cash flows of a foreign subsidiary.

28   Unrealised gains and losses arising from changes in foreign currency exchange rates are not cash flows. However, the effect of exchange rate changes on cash and cash equivalents held or due in a foreign currency is reported in the statement of cash flows in order to reconcile cash and cash equivalents at the beginning and the end of the period. This amount is presented separately from cash flows from operating, investing and financing activities and includes the differences, if any, had those cash flows been reported at end of period exchange rates.

29   [Deleted by the IASB]

30   [Deleted by the IASB]

Interest and Dividends

31   **Cash flows from interest and dividends received and paid shall each be disclosed separately. Each shall be classified in a consistent manner from period to period as either operating, investing or financing activities.**

32   The total amount of interest paid during a period is disclosed in the statement of cash flows whether it has been recognised as an expense in profit or loss or capitalised in accordance with AASB 123 *Borrowing Costs*.

33   Interest paid and interest and dividends received are usually classified as operating cash flows for a financial institution. However, there is no consensus on the classification of these cash flows for other entities. Interest paid and interest and dividends received may be classified as operating cash flows because they enter into the determination of net profit or loss. Alternatively, interest paid and interest and dividends received may be classified as financing cash flows and investing cash flows respectively, because they are costs of obtaining financial resources or returns on investments.

34   Dividends paid may be classified as a financing cash flow because they are a cost of obtaining financial resources. Alternatively, dividends paid may be classified as a component of cash flows from operating activities in order to assist users to determine the ability of an entity to pay dividends out of operating cash flows.

Taxes on Income

35   **Cash flows arising from taxes on income shall be separately disclosed and shall be classified as cash flows from operating activities unless they can be specifically identified with financing and investing activities.**

36   Taxes on income arise on transactions that give rise to cash flows that are classified as operating, investing or financing activities in a statement of cash flows. While tax expense may be readily identifiable with investing or financing activities, the related tax cash flows are often impracticable to identify and may arise in a different period from the cash flows of the underlying transaction. Therefore, taxes paid are usually classified as cash flows from operating activities. However, when it is practicable to identify the tax cash flow with an individual transaction that gives rise to cash flows that are classified as investing or financing activities the tax cash flow is classified as an investing or financing activity as appropriate. When tax cash flows are allocated over more than one class of activity, the total amount of taxes paid is disclosed.

Investments in Subsidiaries, Associates and Joint Ventures

37   When accounting for an investment in an associate or a subsidiary accounted for by use of the equity or cost method, an investor restricts its reporting in the statement of cash flows to the cash flows between itself and the investee, for example, to dividends and advances.

38   An entity which reports its interest in a jointly controlled entity (see AASB 131 *Interests in Joint Ventures*) using proportionate consolidation, includes in its consolidated statement of cash flows its proportionate share of the jointly controlled entity's cash flows. An entity which reports such an interest using the equity method includes in its statement of cash flows the cash flows in respect of its investments in the jointly controlled entity, and distributions and other payments or receipts between it and the jointly controlled entity.

Changes in Ownership Interests in Subsidiaries and Other Businesses

39   **The aggregate cash flows arising from obtaining or losing control of subsidiaries or other businesses shall be presented separately and classified as investing activities.**

40   **An entity shall disclose, in aggregate, in respect of both obtaining and losing control of subsidiaries or other businesses during the period each of the following:**

   (a)   the total consideration paid or received;

   (b)   the portion of the consideration consisting of cash and cash equivalents;

   (c)   the amount of cash and cash equivalents in the subsidiaries or other businesses over which control is obtained or lost; and

   (d)   the amount of the assets and liabilities other than cash or cash equivalents in the subsidiaries or other businesses over which control is obtained or lost, summarised by each major category.

41   The separate presentation of the cash flow effects of obtaining or losing control of subsidiaries or other businesses as single line items, together with the separate disclosure of the amounts of assets and liabilities acquired or disposed of, helps to distinguish those cash flows from the cash flows arising from the other operating, investing and financing activities. The cash flow effects of losing control are not deducted from those of obtaining control.

42   The aggregate amount of the cash paid or received as consideration for obtaining or losing control of subsidiaries or other businesses is reported in the statement of cash flows net of cash and cash equivalents acquired or disposed of as part of such transactions, events or changes in circumstances.

42A Cash flows arising from changes in ownership interests in a subsidiary that do not result in a loss of control shall be classified as cash flows from financing activities.

42B Changes in ownership interests in a subsidiary that do not result in a loss of control, such as the subsequent purchase or sale by a parent of a subsidiary's equity instruments, are accounted for as equity transactions (see AASB 127 *Consolidated and Separate Financial Statements* (as amended in March 2008)). Accordingly, the resulting cash flows are classified in the same way as other transactions with owners described in paragraph 17.

Non-cash Transactions

43 **Investing and financing transactions that do not require the use of cash or cash equivalents shall be excluded from a statement of cash flows. Such transactions shall be disclosed elsewhere in the financial statements in a way that provides all the relevant information about these investing and financing activities.**

44 Many investing and financing activities do not have a direct impact on current cash flows although they do affect the capital and asset structure of an entity. The exclusion of non-cash transactions from the statement of cash flows is consistent with the objective of a statement of cash flows as these items do not involve cash flows in the current period. Examples of non-cash transactions are:

(a) the acquisition of assets either by assuming directly related liabilities or by means of a finance lease;

(b) the acquisition of an entity by means of an equity issue; and

(c) the conversion of debt to equity.

Components of Cash and Cash Equivalents

45 **An entity shall disclose the components of cash and cash equivalents and shall present a reconciliation of the amounts in its statement of cash flows with the equivalent items reported in the statement of financial position.**

46 In view of the variety of cash management practices and banking arrangements around the world and in order to comply with AASB 101 *Presentation of Financial Statements*, an entity discloses the policy which it adopts in determining the composition of cash and cash equivalents.

47 The effect of any change in the policy for determining components of cash and cash equivalents, for example, a change in the classification of financial instruments previously considered to be part of an entity's investment portfolio, is reported in accordance with AASB 108 *Accounting Policies, Changes in Accounting Estimates and Errors*.

Other Disclosures

48 **An entity shall disclose, together with a commentary by management, the amount of significant cash and cash equivalent balances held by the entity that are not available for use by the group.**

49 There are various circumstances in which cash and cash equivalent balances held by an entity are not available for use by the group. Examples include cash and cash equivalent balances held by a subsidiary that operates in a country where exchange controls or other legal restrictions apply when the balances are not available for general use by the parent or other subsidiaries.

50 Additional information may be relevant to users in understanding the financial position and liquidity of an entity. Disclosure of this information, together with a commentary by management, is encouraged and may include:

(a) the amount of undrawn borrowing facilities that may be available for future operating activities and to settle capital commitments, indicating any restrictions on the use of these facilities;

(b) the aggregate amounts of the cash flows from each of operating, investing and financing activities related to interests in joint ventures reported using proportionate consolidation;

(c)   the aggregate amount of cash flows that represent increases in operating capacity separately from those cash flows that are required to maintain operating capacity; and

(d)   the amount of the cash flows arising from the operating, investing and financing activities of each reportable segment (see AASB 8 *Operating Segments*).

51   The separate disclosure of cash flows that represent increases in operating capacity and cash flows that are required to maintain operating capacity is useful in enabling the user to determine whether the entity is investing adequately in the maintenance of its operating capacity. An entity that does not invest adequately in the maintenance of its operating capacity may be prejudicing future profitability for the sake of current liquidity and distributions to owners.

52   The disclosure of segmental cash flows enables users to obtain a better understanding of the relationship between the cash flows of the business as a whole and those of its component parts and the availability and variability of segmental cash flows.

Effective Date

53   [Deleted by the AASB]

54   [Deleted by the AASB]

Aus54.1   AASB 2008-3 *Amendments to Australian Accounting Standards arising from AASB 3 and AASB 127* amended the requirements described in paragraphs 39-42 and added paragraphs 42A and 42B. The amendments and additions to this Standard shall be applied retrospectively.

55   Paragraph 14 was amended by AASB 2008-5 *Amendments to Australian Accounting Standards arising from the Annual Improvements Project* issued in July 2008. An entity shall apply that amendment for annual reporting periods beginning on or after 1 January 2009. Earlier application is permitted. If an entity applies the amendment for an earlier period it shall disclose that fact and apply paragraph 68A of AASB 116.

56   Paragraph 16 was amended by AASB 2009-5 *Further Amendments to Australian Accounting Standards arising from the Annual Improvements Project* issued in May 2009. An entity shall apply that amendment for annual reporting periods beginning on or after 1 January 2010. Earlier application is permitted. If an entity applies the amendment for an earlier period it shall disclose that fact.

Illustrative Examples

These illustrative examples accompany, but are not part of, AASB 107.

AASB

A Statement of Cash Flows for an Entity other than a Financial Institution

1 The examples show only current period amounts. Corresponding amounts for the preceding period are required to be presented in accordance with AASB 101 *Presentation of Financial Statements*.

2 Information from the statement of comprehensive income and statement of financial position is provided to show how the statements of cash flows under the direct method and indirect method, and the reconciliation of cash flows from operating activities to profit or loss, have been derived. Neither the statement of comprehensive income nor the statement of financial position is presented in conformity with the disclosure and presentation requirements of other Australian Accounting Standards.

3 The following additional information is also relevant for the preparation of the statements of cash flows:

- all of the shares of a subsidiary were acquired for 590. The fair values of assets acquired and liabilities assumed were as follows:

Inventories	100
Accounts receivable	100
Cash	40
Property, plant and equipment	650
Trade payables	100
Long-term debt	200

- 250 was raised from the issue of share capital and a further 250 was raised from long-term borrowings.

- interest expense was 400, of which 170 was paid during the period. Also, 100 relating to interest expense of the prior period was also paid during the period.

- dividends paid were 1,200.

- the liability for tax at the beginning and end of the period was 1,000 and 400 respectively. During the period, a further 200 tax was provided for. Withholding tax on dividends received amounted to 100.

- during the period, the group acquired property, plant and equipment with an aggregate cost of 1,250 of which 900 was acquired by means of finance leases. Cash payments of 350 were made to purchase property, plant and equipment.

- plant with original cost of 80 and accumulated depreciation of 60 was sold for 20.

- accounts receivable as at the end of 20X2 include 100 of interest receivable.

Consolidated Statement of Comprehensive Income for the period ended 20X2(a)

Sales	30,650
Cost of sales	(26,000)
Gross profit	4,650
Depreciation	(450)
Administrative and selling expenses	(910)
Interest expense	(400)
Investment income	500
Foreign exchange loss	(40)
Profit before income tax	3,350
Income tax expense	(300)
Profit for the period	3,050

(a) The entity did not recognise any components of other comprehensive income in the period ended 20X2.

Consolidated Statement of Financial Position as at the end of 20X2

		20X2		20X1
Assets				
Current Assets				
Cash and cash equivalents		230		160
Accounts receivable		1,900		1,200
Inventory		1,000		1,950
Portfolio investments		2,500		2,500
Total Current Assets		5,630		5,810
Non-current Assets				
Property, plant and equipment at cost	3,730		1,910	
Accumulated depreciation	(1,450)		(1,060)	
Property, plant and equipment net		2,280		850
Total Non-current Assets		2,280		850
Total Assets		7,910		6,660
Liabilities				
Current Liabilities				
Trade payables		250		1,890
Interest payable		230		100
Income taxes payable		400		1,000
Total Current Liabilities		880		2,990
Non-current Liabilities				
Long term debt		2,300		1,040
Total Non-current Liabilities		2,300		1,040
Total Liabilities		3,180		4,030
Net Assets		4,730		2,630
Equity				
Share capital		1,500		1,250
Retained earnings		3,230		1,380
Total Equity		4,730		2,630

Direct Method Statement of Cash Flows (paragraph 18(a))

	20X2
Cash flows from operating activities	
Cash receipts from customers	30,150
Cash paid to suppliers and employees	(27,600)
Cash generated from operations	2,550
Interest paid	(270)
Income taxes paid	(900)
Net cash from operating activities	1,380
Cash flows from investing activities	
Acquisition of subsidiary X, net of cash acquired (Note 1)	(550)
Purchase of property, plant and equipment (Note 2)	(350)
Proceeds from sale of equipment	20
Interest received	200
Dividends received	200
Net cash used in investing activities	(480)
Cash flows from financing activities	
Proceeds from issue of share capital	250
Proceeds from long-term borrowings	250
Payment of finance lease liabilities	(90)
Dividends paid [a]	(1,200)
Net cash used in financing activities	(790)
Net increase in cash and cash equivalents	110
Cash and cash equivalents at beginning of period (Note 3)	120
Cash and cash equivalents at end of period (Note 3)	230

(a) This could also be shown as an operating cash flow.

Indirect Method Statement of Cash Flows (paragraph 18(b))

		20X2
Cash flows from operating activities		
Profit before taxation	3,350	
Adjustments for:		
Depreciation	450	
Foreign exchange loss	40	
Investment income	(500)	
Interest expense	400	
	3,740	
Increase in trade and other receivables	(500)	
Decrease in inventories	1,050	
Decrease in trade payables	(1,740)	
Cash generated from operations	2,550	
Interest paid	(270)	
Income taxes paid	(900)	
Net cash from operating activities		1,380
Cash flows from investing activities		
Acquisition of subsidiary X net of cash acquired (Note 1)	(550)	
Purchase of property, plant and equipment (Note 2)	(350)	
Proceeds from sale of equipment	20	
Interest received	200	
Dividends received	200	
Net cash used in investing activities		(480)
Cash flows from financing activities		
Proceeds from issue of share capital	250	
Proceeds from long-term borrowings	250	
Payment of finance lease liabilities	(90)	
Dividends paid (a)	(1,200)	
Net cash used in financing activities		(790)
Net increase in cash and cash equivalents		110
Cash and cash equivalents at beginning of period (Note 3)		120
Cash and cash equivalents at end of period (Note 3)		230

(a) This could also be shown as an operating cash flow.

Notes to the Statement of Cash Flows (Direct Method and Indirect Method)

1 Obtaining Control of Subsidiary

During the period the Group obtained control of subsidiary X. The fair values of assets acquired and liabilities assumed were as follows:

Cash	40
Inventories	100
Accounts receivable	100
Property, plant and equipment	650
Trade payables	(100)
Long-term debt	(200)
Total purchase price paid in cash	590
Less: Cash of subsidiary X acquired	(40)
Cash paid to obtain control, net of cash acquired	550

2 Property, Plant and Equipment

During the period, the Group acquired property, plant and equipment with an aggregate cost of 1,250 of which 900 was acquired by means of finance leases. Cash payments of 350 were made to purchase property, plant and equipment.

3 Cash and Cash Equivalents

Cash and cash equivalents consist of cash on hand and balances with banks, and investments in money market instruments. Cash and cash equivalents included in the statement of cash flows comprise the following amounts in the statement of financial position:

	20X2	20X1
Cash on hand and balances with banks	40	25
Short-term investments	190	135
Cash and cash equivalents as previously reported	230	160
Effect of exchange rate changes	–	(40)
Cash and cash equivalents as restated	230	120

Cash and cash equivalents at the end of the period include deposits with banks of 100 held by a subsidiary which are not freely remissible to the holding company because of currency exchange restrictions.

The Group has undrawn borrowing facilities of 2,000 of which 700 may be used only for future expansion.

4 Segment Information

	Segment A	Segment B	Total
Cash flows from:			
Operating activities	1,520	(140)	1,380
Investing activities	(640)	160	(480)
Financing activities	(570)	(220)	(790)
	310	(200)	110

Alternative Presentation (Indirect Method)

As an alternative, in an indirect method statement of cash flows, operating profit before working capital changes is sometimes presented as follows:

Revenues excluding investment income	30,650
Operating expense excluding depreciation	(26,910)
Operating profit before working capital changes	3,740

B   Statement of Cash Flows for a Financial Institution

1   The example shows only current period amounts. Comparative amounts for the preceding period are required to be presented in accordance with AASB 101 *Presentation of Financial Statements*.

2   The example is presented using the direct method.

		20X2
Cash flows from operating activities		
Interest and commission receipts	28,447	
Interest payments	(23,463)	
Recoveries on loans previously written off	237	
Cash payments to employees and suppliers	(997)	
	4,224	
(Increase) decrease in operating assets:		
Short-term funds	(650)	
Deposits held for regulatory or monetary control purposes	234	
Funds advanced to customers	(288)	
Net increase in credit card receivables	(360)	
Other short-term negotiable securities	(120)	
Increase (decrease) in operating liabilities:		
Deposits from customers	600	
Negotiable certificates of deposit	(200)	
Net cash from operating activities before income tax	3,440	
Income taxes paid	(100)	
Net cash from operating activities		3,340
Cash flows from investing activities		
Disposal of subsidiary Y	50	
Dividends received	200	
Interest received	300	
Proceeds from sales of non-dealing securities	1,200	
Purchase of non-dealing securities	(600)	
Purchase of property, plant and equipment	(500)	
Net cash from investing activities		650
Cash flows from financing activities		
Issue of loan capital	1,000	
Issue of preference shares by subsidiary undertaking	800	
Repayment of long-term borrowings	(200)	
Net decrease in other borrowings	(1,000)	
Dividends paid	(400)	
Net cash from financing activities		200
Effects of exchange rate changes on cash and cash equivalents		600
Net increase in cash and cash equivalents		4,790
Cash and cash equivalents at beginning of period		4,050
Cash and cash equivalents at end of period		8,840

AASB 108

Accounting Policies, Changes in Accounting Estimates and Errors

(Compiled September 2011)

Note from the Institute of Chartered Accountants Australia

This note, prepared by the technical editors, is not part of Accounting Standard AASB 108.

Historical development

July 2004: AASB 108 'Accounting Policies, Changes in Accounting Estimates and Errors' is the Australian equivalent of IAS 8 of the same name. It was made by the AASB on 15 July 2004 as part of the AASB's program to adopt International Financial Reporting Standards by 2005.

April 2007: AASB 2007-4 'Amendments to Australian Accounting Standards' amends paragraph 5 and is applicable to annual reporting periods beginning on or after 1 July 2007. Entities may elect to early adopt it to annual reporting periods beginning on or after 1 January 2005.

24 September 2007: AASB 2007-8 'Amendments to Australian Accounting Standards arising from AASB 101' amends AASB 108 to align with revised AASB 101. This Standard is applicable to annual reporting periods beginning on or after 1 January 2009.

13 December 2007: AASB 2007-10 'Further Amendments to Australian Accounting Standards arising from AASB 101' amends AASB 108, replacing the term 'financial report' with 'financial statements'. This Standard is applicable to annual reporting periods beginning on or after 1 January 2009.

24 July 2008: AASB 2008-5 'Amendments to Australian Accounting Standards arising from the Annual Improvements Project' amends AASB 108 in relation to cash flows relating to the status of implementation guidance. This Standard is applicable to annual reporting periods beginning on or after 1 January 2009.

16 October 2009: AASB 108 was reissued by the AASB, compiled to include the AASB 2007-8, AASB 2007-10 and AASB 2008-5 amendments and applies to annual reporting periods beginning on or after 1 January 2009. Early application is permitted.

7 December 2009: AASB 2009-11 'Amendments to Australian Accounting Standards arising from AASB 9' amends AASB 108 to give effect to consequential changes arising from the issuance of AASB 9. This Standard is applicable to annual reporting periods beginning on or after 1 January 2013 with early adoption permitted from annual reporting periods ending on or after 31 December 2009 that begin before 1 January 2013 provided AASB 9 is also applied for the same period. The application date of AASB 2009-11 has been amended to 1 January 2015 by AASB 2012-6. **These amendments have been superseded by AASB 2010-7 and are not included in this compiled Standard.**

15 December 2009: AASB 2009-12 'Amendments to Australian Accounting Standards' amends AASB 108 for editorial corrections. This Standard is applicable to annual reporting periods beginning on or after 1 January 2011 with early adoption permitted.

1 March 2011: AASB 2010-7 'Amendments to Australian Accounting Standards arising from AASB 9 (December 2010)' as compiled amends AASB 108 to give effect to consequential changes arising from the reissue of AASB 9 in December 2010, and supersedes AASB 2009-11 which related to the previous version of AASB 9. This Standard applies to annual reporting periods beginning on or after 1 January 2013 and can be adopted early. The application date of AASB 2010-7 has been amended to 1 January 2015 by AASB 2012-6. **These amendments are not included in this compiled Standard.**

11 May 2011: AASB 2011-1 'Amendments to Australian Accounting Standards arising from the Trans-Tasman Convergence Project' amends AASB 108 as a result of the Trans-Tasman project, to more closely align IFRSs as applied through Australian and New Zealand Standards. AASB 2011-1 deletes Australian specific disclosure requirements. Where appropriate these disclosures are now included in AASB 1054 'Australian Additional Requirements'. These Standards apply to annual reporting periods beginning on or after 1 July 2011 with early adoption permitted.

---

2 September 2011: AASB 2011-8 'Amendments to Australian Accounting Standards arising from AASB 13' amends AASB 108 to give effect to a consequential change in the definition of fair value arising from the issue of AASB 13. This Standard applies to annual reporting periods beginning on or after 1 January 2013 and can be adopted early. **These amendments are not included this compiled Standard.**

23 September 2011: AASB 108 was reissued by the AASB, compiled to include the AASB 2009-12 and AASB 2011-1 amendments and applies to annual reporting periods ending on or after 1 July 2011 but before 1 January 2013.

References

Interpretation 4 *Determining Whether an Arrangement Contains a Lease,* Interpretation 5 *Rights to Interests arising from Decommissioning, Restoration and Environmental Rehabilitation Funds,* Interpretation 6 *Liabilities arising from Participating in a Specific Market – Waste Electrical and Electronic Equipment,* Interpretation 19 *Extinguishing Financial Liabilities with Equity Instruments,* Interpretation 11 *AASB 2 – Group and Treasury Share Transactions,* Interpretation 12 *Service Concession Arrangements,* Interpretation 13 *Customer Loyalty Programs,* Interpretation 14 *AASB 119 – The Limit on a Defined Benefit Asset, Minimum Funding Requirements and their interaction,* Interpretation 107 *Introduction of the Euro,* Interpretation 112 *Consolidation – Special Purpose Entities,* Interpretation 115 *Operating Leases – incentives,* Interpretation 18 *Transfers of Assets from Customers,* Interpretation 1031 *Accounting for the Goods and Services Tax (GST)* and Interpretation 1055 *Accounting for Road Earthworks* apply to AASB 108.

IFRIC item not taken onto the agenda: IAS 8-1 *Application of the IAS 8 hierarchy* applies to AASB 108.

AASB 108 compared to IAS 8

Additions

Paragraph	Description
Aus 2.1	Which entities AASB 108 applies to.
Aus 2.2	The application date of AASB 108 (i.e. annual periods beginning 1 January 2005).
Aus 2.3	Prohibits early application of AASB 108.
Aus 2.4	Makes the requirements of AASB 108 subject to AASB 1031 'Materiality'.
Aus 2.5	Explains which Standards have been superseded by AASB 108.
Aus 2.6	Clarifies that the superseded Standards apply until AASB 108 applies.
Aus 2.7	Notice of Standard published as required on 22 July 2004.

Deletions

Paragraph	Description
54	Effective date of IAS 8 not relevant to Australia.
55	Reference to superseded IAS 8.
56	Reference to superseded SIC 2 'Consistency – Capitalisation of Borrowing Costs' and SIC 18 'Consistency – Alternative Methods'.

Contents

Compilation Details

Comparison with IAS 8

Accounting Standard

AASB 108 Accounting Policies, Changes in Accounting Estimates and Errors

	Paragraphs
Objective	1 – 2
Application	Aus2.1 – Aus2.7
Scope	3 – 4
Definitions	5 – 6
Accounting Policies	
Selection and Application of Accounting Policies	7 – 12
Consistency of Accounting Policies	13
Changes in Accounting Policies	14 – 18
Applying changes in accounting policies	19 – 21
Retrospective application	22
Limitations on retrospective application	23 – 27
Disclosure	28 – 31
Changes in Accounting Estimates	32 – 38
Disclosure	39 – 40
Errors	41 – 42
Limitations on Retrospective Restatement	43 – 48
Disclosure of Prior Period Errors	49
Impracticability in Respect of Retrospective Application and Retrospective Restatement	50 – 53

Implementation Guidance on IAS 8
(available on the AASB website)

Basis for Conclusions on IAS 8
(available on the AASB website)

Australian Accounting Standard AASB 108 *Accounting Policies, Changes in Accounting Estimates and Errors* (as amended) is set out in paragraphs 1 – 53. All the paragraphs have equal authority. Terms defined in this Standard are in *italics* the first time they appear in the Standard. AASB 108 is to be read in the context of other Australian Accounting Standards, including AASB 1048 *Interpretation and Application of Standards*, which identifies the Australian Accounting Interpretations.

Compilation Details

Accounting Standard AASB 108 *Accounting Policies, Changes in Accounting Estimates and Errors* as amended

This compiled Standard applies to annual reporting periods beginning on or after 1 July 2011 but before 1 January 2013. It takes into account amendments up to and including 11 May 2011 and was prepared on 23 September 2011 by the staff of the Australian Accounting Standards Board (AASB).

This compilation is not a separate Accounting Standard made by the AASB. Instead, it is a representation of AASB 108 (July 2004) as amended by other Accounting Standards, which are listed in the Table below.

Table of Standards

Standard	Date made	Application date *(annual reporting periods … on or after …)*	Application, saving or transitional provisions
AASB 108	15 Jul 2004	*(beginning)* 1 Jan 2005	
AASB 2007-4	30 Apr 2007	*(beginning)* 1 Jul 2007	see (a) below
AASB 2007-8	24 Sep 2007	*(beginning)* 1 Jan 2009	see (b) below
AASB 2007-10	13 Dec 2007	*(beginning)* 1 Jan 2009	see (b) below
AASB 2008-5	24 Jul 2008	*(beginning)* 1 Jan 2009	see (c) below
AASB 2009-11	7 Dec 2009	*(beginning)* 1 Jan 2013	not compiled*
AASB 2009-12	15 Dec 2009	*(beginning)* 1 Jan 2011	see (d) below
AASB 2010-2	30 Jun 2010	*(beginning)* 1 Jul 2013	not compiled*
AASB 2010-7	6 Dec 2010	*(beginning)* 1 Jan 2013	not compiled*
AASB 2011-1	11 May 2011	*(beginning)* 1 Jul 2011	see (e) below
AASB 2011-8	2 Sep 2011	*(beginning)* 1 Jan 2013	not compiled*

*   The amendments made by this Standard are not included in this compilation, which presents the principal Standard as applicable to annual reporting periods beginning on or after 1 July 2011 but before 1 January 2013.

(a)   Entities may elect to apply this Standard to annual reporting periods beginning on or after 1 January 2005 but before 1 July 2007.

(b)   Entities may elect to apply this Standard to annual reporting periods beginning on or after 1 January 2005 but before 1 January 2009, provided that AASB 101 *Presentation of Financial Statements* (September 2007) is also applied to such periods.

(c)   Entities may elect to apply this Standard, or its amendments to individual Standards, to annual reporting periods beginning on or after 1 January 2005 but before 1 January 2009.

(d)   Entities may elect to apply this Standard to annual reporting periods beginning on or after 1 January 2005 but before 1 January 2011.

(e)   Entities may elect to apply this Standard, or its amendments to individual pronouncements, to annual reporting periods beginning on or after 1 January 2005 but before 1 July 2011, provided that AASB 1054 *Australian Additional Disclosures* is, or its relevant individual disclosure requirements are, also applied to such periods.

Table of Amendments

Paragraph affected	How affected	By … [paragraph]
Aus2.8	deleted	AASB 2011-1 [16]
5	amended amended	AASB 2007-4 [36] AASB 2007-8 [41]
7	amended	AASB 2008-5 [21]
8	amended	AASB 2007-10 [47]
9	amended	AASB 2008-5 [21]
10	amended	AASB 2007-10 [48]

Paragraph affected	How affected	By ... [paragraph]
11	amended	AASB 2008-5 [21]
26	amended	AASB 2007-8 [6]
32	amended	AASB 2007-10 [47]
41	amended	AASB 2007-10 [48]
42	amended	AASB 2007-10 [49]
51	amended	AASB 2007-8 [6]
	amended	AASB 2009-12 [11]

General Terminology Amendments

References to 'financial report(s)' were amended to 'financial statements' by AASB 2007-8 and AASB 2007-10, except in relation to specific Corporations Act references. These amendments are not shown in the above Table of Amendments.

Comparison with IAS 8

AASB 108 and IAS 8

AASB 108 *Accounting Policies, Changes in Accounting Estimates and Errors* as amended incorporates IAS 8 *Accounting Policies, Changes in Accounting Estimates and Errors* as issued and amended by the International Accounting Standards Board (IASB). Paragraphs that have been added to this Standard (and do not appear in the text of IAS 8) are identified with the prefix "Aus", followed by the number of the preceding IASB paragraph and decimal numbering.

Compliance with IAS 8

Entities that comply with AASB 108 as amended will simultaneously be in compliance with IAS 8 as amended.

Accounting Standard AASB 108

The Australian Accounting Standards Board made Accounting Standard AASB 108 *Accounting Policies, Changes in Accounting Estimates and Errors* under section 334 of the *Corporations Act 2001* on 15 July 2004.

This compiled version of AASB 108 applies to annual reporting periods beginning on or after 1 July 2011 but before 1 January 2013. It incorporates relevant amendments contained in other AASB Standards made by the AASB up to and including 11 May 2011 (see Compilation Details).

Accounting Standard AASB 108

Accounting Policies, Changes in Accounting Estimates and Errors

Objective

1   The objective of this Standard is to prescribe the criteria for selecting and changing *accounting policies*, together with the accounting treatment and disclosure of changes in accounting policies, changes in accounting estimates and corrections of errors. The Standard is intended to enhance the relevance and reliability of an entity's financial statements, and the comparability of those financial statements over time and with the financial statements of other entities.

2   Disclosure requirements for accounting policies, except those for changes in accounting policies, are set out in AASB 101 *Presentation of Financial Statements*.

Application

Aus2.1   **This Standard applies to:**

        (a)   **each entity that is required to prepare financial reports in accordance with Part 2M.3 of the Corporations Act;**

        (b)   **general purpose financial statements of each reporting entity; and**

        (c)   **financial statements that are, or are held out to be, general purpose financial statements.**

Aus2.2   **This Standard applies to annual reporting periods beginning on or after 1 January 2005.**

        [Note: For application dates of paragraphs changed or added by an amending Standard, see Compilation Details.]

Aus2.3   **This Standard shall not be applied to annual reporting periods beginning before 1 January 2005.**

Aus2.4   **The requirements specified in this Standard apply to the financial statements where information resulting from their application is material in accordance with AASB 1031 *Materiality*.**

Aus2.5   **When applicable, this Standard supersedes:**

        (a)   **AASB 1001 *Accounting Policies* as notified in the *Commonwealth of Australia Gazette* No S 130, 26 March 1999; and**

        (b)   **AAS 6 *Accounting Policies* as issued in March 1999.**

Aus2.6   AASB 1001 and AAS 6 remain applicable until superseded by this Standard.

Aus2.7   Notice of this Standard was published in the *Commonwealth of Australia Gazette* No S 294, 22 July 2004.

Scope

3   **This Standard shall be applied in selecting and applying accounting policies, and accounting for changes in accounting policies, changes in accounting estimates and corrections of *prior period errors*.**

4   The tax effects of corrections of prior period errors and of retrospective adjustments made to apply changes in accounting policies are accounted for and disclosed in accordance with AASB 112 *Income Taxes*.

Definitions

5   **The following terms are used in this Standard with the meanings specified.**

    Accounting policies **are the specific principles, bases, conventions, rules and practices applied by an entity in preparing and presenting financial statements.**

    A *change in accounting estimate* is an adjustment of the carrying amount of an asset or a liability, or the amount of the periodic consumption of an asset, that results from the assessment of the present status of, and expected future benefits and obligations associated with, assets and liabilities. Changes in accounting estimates result from new information or new developments and, accordingly, are not corrections of errors.

    Impracticable **– applying a requirement is impracticable when the entity cannot apply it after making every reasonable effort to do so. For a particular prior period, it is impracticable to apply a change in an accounting policy retrospectively or to make a retrospective restatement to correct an error if:**

        (a)   **the effects of the retrospective application or retrospective restatement are not determinable;**

        (b)   **the retrospective application or retrospective restatement requires assumptions about what management's intent would have been in that period; or**

AASB

(c) the retrospective application or retrospective restatement requires significant estimates of amounts and it is impossible to distinguish objectively information about those estimates that:

(i) provides evidence of circumstances that existed on the date(s) as at which those amounts are to be recognised, measured or disclosed; and

(ii) would have been available when the financial statements for that prior period were authorised for issue;

from other information.

Material – omissions or misstatements of items are material if they could, individually or collectively, influence the economic decisions that users make on the basis of the financial statements. Materiality depends on the size and nature of the omission or misstatement judged in the surrounding circumstances. The size or nature of the item, or a combination of both, could be the determining factor.

Prior period errors are omissions from, and misstatements in, the entity's financial statements for one or more prior periods arising from a failure to use, or misuse of, reliable information that:

(a) was available when financial statements for those periods were authorised for issue; and

(b) could reasonably be expected to have been obtained and taken into account in the preparation and presentation of those financial statements.

Such errors include the effects of mathematical mistakes, mistakes in applying accounting policies, oversights or misinterpretations of facts, and fraud.

Prospective application of a change in accounting policy and of recognising the effect of a change in an accounting estimate, respectively, are:

(a) applying the new accounting policy to transactions, other events and conditions occurring after the date as at which the policy is changed; and

(b) recognising the effect of the change in the accounting estimate in the current and future periods affected by the change.

Retrospective application is applying a new accounting policy to transactions, other events and conditions as if that policy had always been applied.

Retrospective restatement is correcting the recognition, measurement and disclosure of amounts of elements of financial statements as if a prior period error had never occurred.

6 Assessing whether an omission or misstatement could influence economic decisions of users, and so be material, requires consideration of the characteristics of those users. The *Framework for the Preparation and Presentation of Financial Statements* (the *Framework*) states in paragraph 25 that "users are assumed to have a reasonable knowledge of business and economic activities and accounting and a willingness to study the information with reasonable diligence." Therefore, the assessment needs to take into account how users with such attributes could reasonably be expected to be influenced in making economic decisions.

Accounting Policies

Selection and Application of Accounting Policies

7 When an Australian Accounting Standard specifically applies to a transaction, other event or condition, the accounting policy or policies applied to that item shall be determined by applying the Standard.

8 Australian Accounting Standards set out accounting policies that the AASB has concluded result in financial statements containing relevant and reliable information about the transactions, other events and conditions to which they apply. Those policies need not be applied when the effect of applying them is immaterial. However, it is inappropriate to make, or leave uncorrected, immaterial departures from Australian Accounting Standards

to achieve a particular presentation of an entity's financial position, financial performance or cash flows.

9   Australian Accounting Standards are accompanied by guidance to assist entities in applying their requirements. All such guidance states whether it is an integral part of Australian Accounting Standards. Guidance that is an integral part of Australian Accounting Standards is mandatory. Guidance that is not an integral part of Australian Accounting Standards does not contain requirements for financial statements.

10   **In the absence of an Australian Accounting Standard that specifically applies to a transaction, other event or condition, management shall use its judgement in developing and applying an accounting policy that results in information that is:**

       (a)   relevant to the economic decision-making needs of users; and

       (b)   reliable, in that the financial statements:

            (i)   represent faithfully the financial position, financial performance and cash flows of the entity;

            (ii)   reflect the economic substance of transactions, other events and conditions, and not merely the legal form;

            (iii)   are neutral, that is, free from bias;

            (iv)   are prudent; and

            (v)   are complete in all material respects.

11   **In making the judgement described in paragraph 10, management shall refer to, and consider the applicability of, the following sources in descending order:**

       (a)   the requirements in Australian Accounting Standards dealing with similar and related issues; and

       (b)   the definitions, recognition criteria and measurement concepts for assets, liabilities, income and expenses in the *Framework*.

12   **In making the judgement described in paragraph 10, management may also consider the most recent pronouncements of other standard setting bodies that use a similar conceptual framework to develop accounting standards, other accounting literature and accepted industry practices, to the extent that these do not conflict with the sources in paragraph 11.**

Consistency of Accounting Policies

13   **An entity shall select and apply its accounting policies consistently for similar transactions, other events and conditions, unless an Australian Accounting Standard specifically requires or permits categorisation of items for which different policies may be appropriate. If an Australian Accounting Standard requires or permits such categorisation, an appropriate accounting policy shall be selected and applied consistently to each category.**

Changes in Accounting Policies

14   **An entity shall change an accounting policy only if the change:**

       (a)   is required by an Australian Accounting Standard; or

       (b)   results in the financial statements providing reliable and more relevant information about the effects of transactions, other events or conditions on the entity's financial position, financial performance or cash flows.

15   Users of financial statements need to be able to compare the financial statements of an entity over time to identify trends in its financial position, financial performance and cash flows. Therefore, the same accounting policies are applied within each period and from one period to the next unless a change in accounting policy meets one of the criteria in paragraph 14.

16   The following are not changes in accounting policies:

(a)   the application of an accounting policy for transactions, other events or conditions that differ in substance from those previously occurring; and

(b)   the application of a new accounting policy for transactions, other events or conditions that did not occur previously or were immaterial.

17   The initial application of a policy to revalue assets in accordance with AASB 116 *Property, Plant and Equipment* or AASB 138 *Intangible Assets* is a change in an accounting policy to be dealt with as a revaluation in accordance with AASB 116 or AASB 138, rather than in accordance with this Standard.

18   Paragraphs 19-31 do not apply to the change in accounting policy described in paragraph 17.

Applying changes in accounting policies

19   Subject to paragraph 23:

(a)   an entity shall account for a change in accounting policy resulting from the initial application of an Australian Accounting Standard in accordance with the specific transitional provisions, if any, in that Australian Accounting Standard; and

(b)   when an entity changes an accounting policy upon initial application of an Australian Accounting Standard that does not include specific transitional provisions applying to that change, or changes an accounting policy voluntarily, it shall apply the change retrospectively.

20   For the purpose of this Standard, early application of an Australian Accounting Standard is not a voluntary change in accounting policy.

21   In the absence of an Australian Accounting Standard that specifically applies to a transaction, other event or condition, management may, in accordance with paragraph 12, apply an accounting policy from the most recent pronouncements of other standard-setting bodies that use a similar conceptual framework to develop accounting standards. If, following an amendment of such a pronouncement, the entity chooses to change an accounting policy, that change is accounted for and disclosed as a voluntary change in accounting policy.

Retrospective application

22   Subject to paragraph 23, when a change in accounting policy is applied retrospectively in accordance with paragraph 19(a) or (b), the entity shall adjust the opening balance of each affected component of equity for the earliest prior period presented and the other comparative amounts disclosed for each prior period presented as if the new accounting policy had always been applied.

Limitations on retrospective application

23   When *retrospective application* is required by paragraph 19(a) or (b), a change in accounting policy shall be applied retrospectively except to the extent that it is *impracticable* to determine either the period specific effects or the cumulative effect of the change.

24   When it is impracticable to determine the period-specific effects of changing an accounting policy on comparative information for one or more prior periods presented, the entity shall apply the new accounting policy to the carrying amounts of assets and liabilities as at the beginning of the earliest period for which retrospective application is practicable, which may be the current period, and shall make a corresponding adjustment to the opening balance of each affected component of equity for that period.

25   When it is impracticable to determine the cumulative effect, at the beginning of the current period, of applying a new accounting policy to all prior periods, the entity shall adjust the comparative information to apply the new accounting policy prospectively from the earliest date practicable.

26   When an entity applies a new accounting policy retrospectively, it applies the new accounting policy to comparative information for prior periods as far back as is practicable.

Retrospective application to a prior period is not practicable unless it is practicable to determine the cumulative effect on the amounts in both the opening and closing statements of financial position for that period. The amount of the resulting adjustment relating to periods before those presented in the financial statements is made to the opening balance of each affected component of equity of the earliest prior period presented. Usually the adjustment is made to retained earnings. However, the adjustment may be made to another component of equity (for example, to comply with an Australian Accounting Standard). Any other information about prior periods, such as historical summaries of financial data, is also adjusted as far back as is practicable.

27 When it is impracticable for an entity to apply a new accounting policy retrospectively, because it cannot determine the cumulative effect of applying the policy to all prior periods, the entity, in accordance with paragraph 25, applies the new policy prospectively from the start of the earliest period practicable. It therefore disregards the portion of the cumulative adjustment to assets, liabilities and equity arising before that date. Changing an accounting policy is permitted even if it is impracticable to apply the policy prospectively for any prior period. Paragraphs 50-53 provide guidance on when it is impracticable to apply a new accounting policy to one or more prior periods.

Disclosure

28 **When initial application of an Australian Accounting Standard has an effect on the current period or any prior period, would have such an effect except that it is impracticable to determine the amount of the adjustment, or might have an effect on future periods, an entity shall disclose:**

(a) **the title of the Australian Accounting Standard;**

(b) **when applicable, that the change in accounting policy is made in accordance with its transitional provisions;**

(c) **the nature of the change in accounting policy;**

(d) **when applicable, a description of the transitional provisions;**

(e) **when applicable, the transitional provisions that might have an effect on future periods;**

(f) **for the current period and each prior period presented, to the extent practicable, the amount of the adjustment:**

(i) **for each financial statement line item affected; and**

(ii) **if AASB 133 *Earnings per Share* applies to the entity, for basic and diluted earnings per share;**

(g) **the amount of the adjustment relating to periods before those presented, to the extent practicable; and**

(h) **if retrospective application required by paragraph 19(a) or (b) is impracticable for a particular prior period, or for periods before those presented, the circumstances that led to the existence of that condition and a description of how and from when the change in accounting policy has been applied.**

Financial statements of subsequent periods need not repeat these disclosures.

29 **When a voluntary change in accounting policy has an effect on the current period or any prior period, would have an effect on that period except that it is impracticable to determine the amount of the adjustment, or might have an effect on future periods, an entity shall disclose:**

(a) **the nature of the change in accounting policy;**

(b) **the reasons why applying the new accounting policy provides reliable and more relevant information;**

(c) for the current period and each prior period presented, to the extent practicable, the amount of the adjustment:

     (i) for each financial statement line item affected; and

     (ii) if AASB 133 applies to the entity, for basic and diluted earnings per share;

(d) the amount of the adjustment relating to periods before those presented, to the extent practicable; and

(e) if retrospective application is impracticable for a particular prior period, or for periods before those presented, the circumstances that led to the existence of that condition and a description of how and from when the change in accounting policy has been applied.

Financial statements of subsequent periods need not repeat these disclosures.

30   When an entity has not applied a new Australian Accounting Standard that has been issued but is not yet effective, the entity shall disclose:

(a) this fact; and

(b) known or reasonably estimable information relevant to assessing the possible impact that application of the new Australian Accounting Standard will have on the entity's financial statements in the period of initial application.

31   In complying with paragraph 30, an entity considers disclosing:

(a) the title of the new Australian Accounting Standard;

(b) the nature of the impending change or changes in accounting policy;

(c) the date by which application of the Australian Accounting Standard is required;

(d) the date as at which it plans to apply the Australian Accounting Standard initially; and

(e) either:

     (i) a discussion of the impact that initial application of the Australian Accounting Standard is expected to have on the entity's financial statements; or

     (ii) if that impact is not known or reasonably estimable, a statement to that effect.

Changes in Accounting Estimates

32   As a result of the uncertainties inherent in business activities, many items in financial statements cannot be measured with precision but can only be estimated. Estimation involves judgements based on the latest available, reliable information. For example, estimates may be required of:

(a) bad debts;

(b) inventory obsolescence;

(c) the fair value of financial assets or financial liabilities;

(d) the useful lives of, or expected pattern of consumption of the future economic benefits embodied in, depreciable assets; and

(e) warranty obligations.

33   The use of reasonable estimates is an essential part of the preparation of financial statements and does not undermine their reliability.

34   An estimate may need revision if changes occur in the circumstances on which the estimate was based or as a result of new information or more experience. By its nature, the revision of an estimate does not relate to prior periods and is not the correction of an error.

35   A change in the measurement basis applied is a change in an accounting policy, and is not a change in an accounting estimate. When it is difficult to distinguish a change in an

accounting policy from a change in an accounting estimate, the change is treated as a change in an accounting estimate.

36   **The effect of a change in an accounting estimate, other than a change to which paragraph 37 applies, shall be recognised prospectively by including it in profit or loss in:**

      (a)   **the period of the change, if the change affects that period only; or**

      (b)   **the period of the change and future periods, if the change affects both.**

37   **To the extent that a change in an accounting estimate gives rise to changes in assets and liabilities, or relates to an item of equity, it shall be recognised by adjusting the carrying amount of the related asset, liability or equity item in the period of the change.**

38   Prospective recognition of the effect of a change in an accounting estimate means that the change is applied to transactions, other events and conditions from the date of the change in estimate. A change in an accounting estimate may affect only the current period's profit or loss, or the profit or loss of both the current period and future periods. For example, a change in the estimate of the amount of bad debts affects only the current period's profit or loss and therefore is recognised in the current period. However, a change in the estimated useful life of, or the expected pattern of consumption of the future economic benefits embodied in, a depreciable asset affects depreciation expense for the current period and for each future period during the asset's remaining useful life. In both cases, the effect of the change relating to the current period is recognised as income or expense in the current period. The effect, if any, on future periods is recognised as income or expense in those future periods.

Disclosure

39   **An entity shall disclose the nature and amount of a change in an accounting estimate that has an effect in the current period or is expected to have an effect in future periods, except for the disclosure of the effect on future periods when it is impracticable to estimate that effect.**

40   **If the amount of the effect in future periods is not disclosed because estimating it is impracticable, an entity shall disclose that fact.**

Errors

41   Errors can arise in respect of the recognition, measurement, presentation or disclosure of elements of financial statements. Financial statements do not comply with Australian Accounting Standards if they contain either material errors or immaterial errors made intentionally to achieve a particular presentation of an entity's financial position, financial performance or cash flows. Potential current period errors discovered in that period are corrected before the financial statements are authorised for issue. However, material errors are sometimes not discovered until a subsequent period, and these prior period errors are corrected in the comparative information presented in the financial statements for that subsequent period (see paragraphs 42-47).

42   **Subject to paragraph 43, an entity shall correct material prior period errors retrospectively in the first set of financial statements authorised for issue after their discovery by:**

      (a)   **restating the comparative amounts for the prior period(s) presented in which the error occurred; or**

      (b)   **if the error occurred before the earliest prior period presented, restating the opening balances of assets, liabilities and equity for the earliest prior period presented.**

Limitations on Retrospective Restatement

43   **A prior period error shall be corrected by *retrospective restatement* except to the extent that it is impracticable to determine either the period-specific effects or the cumulative effect of the error.**

AASB 108   Institute of Chartered Accountants Australia

44   When it is impracticable to determine the period-specific effects of an error on comparative information for one or more prior periods presented, the entity shall restate the opening balances of assets, liabilities and equity for the earliest period for which retrospective restatement is practicable (which may be the current period).

45   When it is impracticable to determine the cumulative effect, at the beginning of the current period, of an error on all prior periods, the entity shall restate the comparative information to correct the error prospectively from the earliest date practicable.

46   The correction of a prior period error is excluded from profit or loss for the period in which the error is discovered. Any information presented about prior periods, including any historical summaries of financial data, is restated as far back as is practicable.

47   When it is impracticable to determine the amount of an error (e.g. a mistake in applying an accounting policy) for all prior periods, the entity, in accordance with paragraph 45, restates the comparative information prospectively from the earliest date practicable. It therefore disregards the portion of the cumulative restatement of assets, liabilities and equity arising before that date. Paragraphs 50-53 provide guidance on when it is impracticable to correct an error for one or more prior periods.

48   Corrections of errors are distinguished from changes in accounting estimates. Accounting estimates by their nature are approximations that may need revision as additional information becomes known. For example, the gain or loss recognised on the outcome of a contingency is not the correction of an error.

Disclosure of Prior Period Errors

49   In applying paragraph 42, an entity shall disclose the following:

(a)   the nature of the prior period error;

(b)   for each prior period presented, to the extent practicable, the amount of the correction:

(i)   for each financial statement line item affected; and

(ii)   if AASB 133 applies to the entity, for basic and diluted earnings per share;

(c)   the amount of the correction at the beginning of the earliest prior period presented; and

(d)   if retrospective restatement is impracticable for a particular prior period, the circumstances that led to the existence of that condition and a description of how and from when the error has been corrected.

Financial statements of subsequent periods need not repeat these disclosures.

Impracticability in Respect of Retrospective Application and Retrospective Restatement

50   In some circumstances, it is impracticable to adjust comparative information for one or more prior periods to achieve comparability with the current period. For example, data may not have been collected in the prior period(s) in a way that allows either retrospective application of a new accounting policy (including, for the purpose of paragraphs 51-53, its *prospective application* to prior periods) or retrospective restatement to correct a prior period error, and it may be impracticable to recreate the information.

51   It is frequently necessary to make estimates in applying an accounting policy to elements of financial statements recognised or disclosed in respect of transactions, other events or conditions. Estimation is inherently subjective, and estimates may be developed after the reporting period. Developing estimates is potentially more difficult when retrospectively applying an accounting policy or making a retrospective restatement to correct a prior period error, because of the longer period of time that might have passed since the affected transaction, other event or condition occurred. However, the objective of estimates related to prior periods remains the same as for estimates made in the current period, namely, for

the estimate to reflect the circumstances that existed when the transaction, other event or condition occurred.

52   Therefore, retrospectively applying a new accounting policy or correcting a prior period error requires distinguishing information that:

(a)   provides evidence of circumstances that existed on the date(s) as at which the transaction, other event or condition occurred; and

(b)   would have been available when the financial statements for that prior period were authorised for issue;

from other information. For some types of estimates (e.g. an estimate of fair value not based on an observable price or observable inputs), it is impracticable to distinguish these types of information. When retrospective application or retrospective restatement would require making a significant estimate for which it is impossible to distinguish these two types of information, it is impracticable to apply the new accounting policy or correct the prior period error retrospectively.

53   Hindsight should not be used when applying a new accounting policy to, or correcting amounts for, a prior period, either in making assumptions about what management's intentions would have been in a prior period or estimating the amounts recognised, measured or disclosed in a prior period. For example, when an entity corrects a prior period error in measuring financial assets previously classified as held-to-maturity investments in accordance with AASB 139 *Financial Instruments: Recognition and Measurement*, it does not change their basis of measurement for that period if management decided later not to hold them to maturity. In addition, when an entity corrects a prior period error in calculating its liability for employees' accumulated sick leave in accordance with AASB 119 *Employee Benefits*, it disregards information about an unusually severe influenza season during the next period that became available after the financial statements for the prior period were authorised for issue. The fact that significant estimates are frequently required when amending comparative information presented for prior periods does not prevent reliable adjustment or correction of the comparative information.

Effective Date of IAS 8

54   [Deleted by the AASB]

Withdrawal of Other Pronouncements

55   [Deleted by the AASB]

56   [Deleted by the AASB]

AASB 110
Events after the Reporting Period
(Compiled February 2010)

Note from the Institute of Chartered Accountants Australia

This note, prepared by the technical editors, is not part of Accounting Standard AASB 110.

Historical development

July 2004: AASB 110 'Events after the Balance Sheet Date' is the Australian equivalent of IAS 10 of the same name. It was made by the AASB on 15 July 2004 as part of the AASB's program to adopt International Financial Reporting Standards by 2005.

April 2007: AASB 2007-4 'Amendments to Australian AccountingStandards' amends paragraph 20 and deletes paragraph Aus6.1 and is applicable to annual reporting periods beginning on or after 1 July 2007. Entities may elect to early adopt it to annual reporting periods beginning on or after 1 January 2005.

24 September 2007: AASB 2007-8 'Amendments to Australian Accounting Standards arising from AASB 101' amends AASB 110 to align with revised AASB 101. This Standard is applicable to annual reporting periods beginning on or after 1 January 2009.

13 December 2007: AASB 2007-10 'Further Amendments to Australian Accounting Standards arising from AASB 101' amends AASB 110, replacing the term 'financial report' with 'financial statements'. This Standard is applicable to annual reporting periods beginning on or after 1 January 2009.

24 July 2008: AASB 2008-5 'Amendments to Australian Accounting Standards arising from the Annual Improvements Project' amends AASB 110 in relation to dividends declared after the end of the reporting period. This Standard is applicable to annual reporting periods beginning on or after 1 January 2009.

18 December 2008: AASB 2008-13 'Amendments to Australian Accounting Standards arising from AASB Interpretation 17 – Distributions of non-cash assets to owners' amends AASB 110 to require the disclosure of dividends that are declared after the reporting period but before the financial statements are authorised for issue. This Standard is applicable prospectively to annual reporting periods beginning on or after 1 July 2009. Retrospective application is not permitted.

25 June 2009: AASB 2009-6 'Amendments to Australian Accounting Standards' amends AASB 110 for editorial corrections made by the International Accounting Standards Board (IASB) to its Standards and Interpretations (IFRSs) and as a consequence of issuing revised AASB 101 'Presentation of Financial Statements'. This Standard is applicable to annual reporting periods beginning on or after 1 January 2009 that end on or after 30 June 2009.

30 October 2009: AASB 110 was reissued by the AASB, compiled to include the AASB 2007-8, AASB 2007-10, AASB 2008-5, AASB 2008-13 and AASB 2009-6 amendments and applies to annual reporting periods beginning on or after 1 July 2009. Early application is permitted.

On the same date the AASB reissued the version of AASB 110 applicable to annual reporting periods beginning on or after 1 January 2009 but before 1 July 2009. This version of AASB 110 has been compiled for the amending Standards applying to annual reporting periods beginning on or after 1 January 2009. This Standard applies to 31 December 2009 year ends and can be accessed from the AASB website at www.aasb.gov.au.

15 December 2009: AASB 2009-12 'Amendments to Australian Accounting Standards' amends AASB 110 for editorial corrections. This Standard is applicable to annual reporting periods beginning on or after 1 January 2011 with early adoption permitted.

23 February 2010: AASB 110 was reissued by the AASB, compiled to include the AASB 2009-12 amendments and applies to annual reporting periods ending on or after 1 January 2011.

---

2 September 2011: AASB 2011-8 'Amendments to Australian Accounting Standards arising from AASB 13' amends AASB 110 to give effect to a consequential change in the definition of fair value arising from the issue of AASB 13. This Standard applies to annual reporting periods beginning on or after 1 January 2013 and can be adopted early. **These amendments are not included in this compiled Standard.**

Reference

Interpretation 107 *Introduction of the Euro* and Interpretation 1039 *Substantive Enactment of Major Tax Bills in Australia* apply to AASB 110.

AASB 110 compared to IAS 10

Additions

Paragraph	Description
Aus 1.1	Which entities AASB 110 applies to.
Aus 1.2	The application date of AASB 110 (i.e. annual periods beginning 1 January 2005).
Aus 1.3	Prohibits early application of AASB 110.
Aus 1.4	Makes the requirements of AASB 110 subject to AASB 1031 'Materiality'.
Aus 1.5	Explains which Standards have been superseded by AASB 110.
Aus 1.6	Clarifies that the superseded Standards apply until AASB 110 applies.
Aus 1.7	Notice of Standard published as required on 22 July 2004.

Deletions

Paragraph	Description
23	Effective date of IAS 10 not relevant to Australia.

Contents

Compilation Details

Comparison with IAS 10

Accounting Standard
AASB 110 Events after the Reporting Period

	Paragraphs
Objective	1
Application	Aus1.1 – Aus1.7
Scope	2
Definitions	3 – 7
Recognition and Measurement	
Adjusting Events after the Reporting Period	8 – 9
Non-adjusting Events after the Reporting Period	10 – 11
Dividends	12 – 13
Going Concern	14 – 16
Disclosure	
Date of Authorisation for Issue	17 – 18
Updating Disclosure about Conditions at the End of the Reporting Period	19 – 20
Non-adjusting Events after the Reporting Period	21 – 22

Basis for Conclusions on IAS 10
(available on the AASB website)

Australian Accounting Standard AASB 110 *Events after the Reporting Period* (as amended) is set out in paragraphs 1 – 22. All the paragraphs have equal authority. Terms defined in this Standard are in *italics* the first time they appear in the Standard. AASB 110 is to be read in the context of other Australian Accounting Standards, including AASB 1048 *Interpretation and Application of Standards*, which identifies the Australian Accounting Interpretations. In the absence of explicit guidance, AASB 108 *Accounting Policies, Changes in Accounting Estimates and Errors* provides a basis for selecting and applying accounting policies.

Compilation Details

Accounting Standard AASB 110 *Events after the Reporting Period* as amended

This compiled Standard applies to annual reporting periods beginning on or after 1 January 2011. It takes into account amendments up to and including 15 December 2009 and was prepared on 23 February 2010 by the staff of the Australian Accounting Standards Board (AASB).

This compilation is not a separate Accounting Standard made by the AASB. Instead, it is a representation of AASB 110 (July 2004) as amended by other Accounting Standards, which are listed in the Table below.

Table of Standards

Standard	Date made	Application date *(annual reporting periods ... on or after ...)*	Application, saving or transitional provisions
AASB 110	15 Jul 2004	*(beginning)* 1 Jan 2005	
AASB 2007-4	30 Apr 2007	*(beginning)* 1 Jul 2007	see (a) below
AASB 2007-8	24 Sep 2007	*(beginning)* 1 Jan 2009	see (b) below

Standard	Date made	Application date *(annual reporting periods ... on or after ...)*	Application, saving or transitional provisions
AASB 2007-10	13 Dec 2007	*(beginning)* 1 Jan 2009	see (b) below
AASB 2008-5	24 Jul 2008	*(beginning)* 1 Jan 2009	see (c) below
AASB 2008-13	18 Dec 2008	*(beginning)* 1 Jul 2009	see (d) below
AASB 2009-6	25 Jun 2009	*(beginning)* 1 Jan 2009 and *(ending)* 30 Jun 2009	see (e) below
AASB 2009-12	15 Dec 2009	*(beginning)* 1 Jan 2011	see (f) below

(a)   Entities may elect to apply this Standard to annual reporting periods beginning on or after 1 January 2005 but before 1 July 2007.

(b)   Entities may elect to apply this Standard to annual reporting periods beginning on or after 1 January 2005 but before 1 January 2009, provided that AASB 101 *Presentation of Financial Statements* (September 2007) is also applied to such periods.

(c)   Entities may elect to apply this Standard, or its amendments to individual Standards, to annual reporting periods beginning on or after 1 January 2005 but before 1 January 2009.

(d)   Entities may elect to apply this Standard to annual reporting periods beginning on or after 1 January 2005 but before 1 July 2009, provided that AASB Interpretation 17 *Distributions of Non-cash Assets to Owners* is also applied to such periods.

(e)   Entities may elect to apply this Standard to annual reporting periods beginning on or after 1 January 2005 but before 1 January 2009, provided that AASB 101 *Presentation of Financial Statements* (September 2007) is also applied to such periods, and to annual reporting periods beginning on or after 1 January 2009 that end before 30 June 2009.

(f)   Entities may elect to apply this Standard to annual reporting periods beginning on or after 1 January 2005 but before 1 January 2011.

Table of Amendments

Paragraph affected	How affected	By ... [paragraph]
Title	amended	AASB 2007-8 [42]
1	amended	AASB 2007-10 [50]
Aus1.8	amended deleted	AASB 2007-8 [6] AASB 2009-6 [38]
3	amended	AASB 2007-10 [52]
5-6	amended	AASB 2007-10 [54]
Aus6.1	deleted	AASB 2007-4 [37]
7	amended	AASB 2007-10 [52]
11	amended	AASB 2007-10 [52]
13	amended amended amended	AASB 2007-10 [54] AASB 2008-5 [22] AASB 2008-13 [11]
16	amended	AASB 2007-10 [52]
17	amended	AASB 2007-10 [50]
18	amended	AASB 2007-10 [50, 51]
20	amended	AASB 2007-4 [38]
21	amended	AASB 2007-8 [43]

General Terminology Amendments

The following amendments are not shown in the above Table of Amendments:

References to 'financial report(s)' were amended to 'financial statements' by AASB 2007-8 and AASB 2007-10, except in relation to specific Corporations Act references.

References to 'reporting date', 'each reporting date' and 'last annual reporting date' were amended to 'end of the reporting period', 'the end of each reporting period' and 'end of the last annual reporting period' respectively by AASB 2007-8.

References to 'after the end of the reporting period' were amended to 'after the reporting period' by AASB 2009-12.

Comparison with IAS 10

AASB 110 and IAS 10

AASB 110 *Events after the Reporting Period* as amended incorporates IAS 10 *Events after the Reporting Period* as issued and amended by the International Accounting Standards Board (IASB). Paragraphs that have been added to this Standard (and do not appear in the text of IAS 10) are identified with the prefix "Aus", followed by the number of the preceding IASB paragraph and decimal numbering.

Compliance with IAS 10

Entities that comply with AASB 110 as amended will simultaneously be in compliance with IAS 10 as amended.

Accounting Standard AASB 110

The Australian Accounting Standards Board made Accounting Standard AASB 110 *Events after the Balance Sheet Date* under section 334 of the *Corporations Act 2001* on 15 July 2004.

This compiled version of AASB 110 applies to annual reporting periods beginning on or after 1 January 2011. It incorporates relevant amendments contained in other AASB Standards made by the AASB up to and including 15 December 2009 (see Compilation Details).

Accounting Standard AASB 110

Events after the Reporting Period

Objective

1   The objective of this Standard is to prescribe:

     (a)   when an entity should adjust its financial statements for *events after the reporting period*; and

     (b)   the disclosures that an entity should give about the date when the financial statements were authorised for issue and about events after the reporting period.

     The Standard also requires that an entity should not prepare its financial statements on a going concern basis if events after the reporting period indicate that the going concern assumption is not appropriate.

Application

Aus1.1   **This Standard applies to:**

     (a)   **each entity that is required to prepare financial reports in accordance with Part 2M.3 of the Corporations Act and that is a reporting entity;**

     (b)   **general purpose financial statements of each other reporting entity; and**

     (c)   **financial statements that are, or are held out to be, general purpose financial statements.**

Aus1.2   **This Standard applies to annual reporting periods beginning on or after 1 January 2005.**

[Note: For application dates of paragraphs changed or added by an amending Standard, see Compilation Details.]

Aus1.3   **This Standard shall not be applied to annual reporting periods beginning before 1 January 2005.**

Aus1.4   **The requirements specified in this Standard apply to the financial statements where information resulting from their application is material in accordance with AASB 1031 *Materiality*.**

Aus1.5   **When applicable, this Standard supersedes:**

   (a)   AASB 1002 *Events Occurring After Reporting Date* as notified in the *Commonwealth of Australia Gazette* No S 415, 16 October 1997; and

   (b)   AAS 8 *Events Occurring After Reporting Date* as issued in October 1997.

Aus1.6   Both AASB 1002 and AAS 8 remain applicable until superseded by this Standard.

Aus1.7   Notice of this Standard was published in the *Commonwealth of Australia Gazette* No S 294, 22 July 2004.

Scope

2   **This Standard shall be applied in the accounting for, and disclosure of, events after the reporting period.**

Definitions

3   **The following terms are used in this Standard with the meanings specified.**

   ***Events after the reporting period* are those events, favourable and unfavourable, that occur between the end of the reporting period and the date when the financial statements are authorised for issue. Two types of events can be identified:**

   (a)   those that provide evidence of conditions that existed at the end of the reporting period (*adjusting events after the reporting period*); and

   (b)   those that are indicative of conditions that arose after the reporting period (*non-adjusting events after the reporting period*).

4   The process involved in authorising the financial statements for issue will vary depending upon the management structure, statutory requirements and procedures followed in preparing and finalising the financial statements.

5   In some cases, an entity is required to submit its financial statements to its shareholders for approval after the financial statements have been issued. In such cases, the financial statements are authorised for issue on the date of issue, not the date when shareholders approve the financial statements.

Example

The management of an entity completes draft financial statements for the year to 31 December 20X1 on 28 February 20X2. On 18 March 20X2, the board of directors reviews the financial statements and authorises them for issue. The entity announces its profit and selected other financial information on 19 March 20X2. The financial statements are made available to shareholders and others on 1 April 20X2. The shareholders approve the financial statements at their annual meeting on 15 May 20X2 and the approved financial statements are then filed with a regulatory body on 17 May 20X2.

The financial statements are authorised for issue on 18 March 20X2 (date of board authorisation for issue).

---

6   In some cases, the management of an entity is required to issue its financial statements to a supervisory board (made up solely of non-executives) for approval. In such cases, the financial statements are authorised for issue when the management authorises them for issue to the supervisory board.

> **Example**
>
> On 18 March 20X2, the management of an entity authorises financial statements for issue to its supervisory board. The supervisory board is made up solely of non-executives and may include representatives of employees and other outside interests. The supervisory board approves the financial statements on 26 March 20X2. The financial statements are made available to shareholders and others on 1 April 20X2. The shareholders approve the financial statements at their annual meeting on 15 May 20X2 and the financial statements are then filed with a regulatory body on 17 May 20X2.
>
> *The financial statements are authorised for issue on 18 March 20X2 (date of management authorisation for issue to the supervisory board).*

7   Events after the reporting period include all events up to the date when the financial statements are authorised for issue, even if those events occur after the public announcement of a profit or of other selected financial information.

Recognition and Measurement

Adjusting Events after the Reporting Period

8   **An entity shall adjust the amounts recognised in its financial statements to reflect *adjusting events after the reporting period*.**

9   The following are examples of adjusting events after the reporting period that require an entity to adjust the amounts recognised in its financial statements, or to recognise items that were not previously recognised:

(a)   the settlement after the reporting period of a court case that confirms that the entity had a present obligation at the end of the reporting period. The entity adjusts any previously recognised provision related to this court case in accordance with AASB 137 *Provisions, Contingent Liabilities and Contingent Assets* or recognises a new provision. The entity does not merely disclose a contingent liability because the settlement provides additional evidence that would be considered in accordance with paragraph 16 of AASB 137;

(b)   the receipt of information after the reporting period indicating that an asset was impaired at the end of the reporting period, or that the amount of a previously recognised impairment loss for that asset needs to be adjusted. For example:

(i)   the bankruptcy of a customer that occurs after the reporting period usually confirms that a loss already existed at the end of the reporting period on a trade receivable and that the entity needs to adjust the carrying amount of the trade receivable; and

(ii)   the sale of inventories after the reporting period may give evidence about their net realisable value at the end of the reporting period;

(c)   the determination after the reporting period of the cost of assets purchased, or the proceeds from assets sold, before the end of the reporting period;

(d)   the determination after the reporting period of the amount of profit sharing or bonus payments, if the entity had a present legal or constructive obligation at the end of the reporting period to make such payments as a result of events before that date (see AASB 119 *Employee Benefits*); and

(e)   the discovery of fraud or errors that show that the financial statements are incorrect.

Non-adjusting Events after the Reporting Period

10   **An entity shall not adjust the amounts recognised in its financial statements to reflect *non-adjusting events after the reporting period*.**

11   An example of a non-adjusting event after the reporting period is a decline in market value of investments between the end of the reporting period and the date when the financial statements are authorised for issue. The decline in market value does not normally relate to the condition of the investments at the end of the reporting period, but reflects circumstances that have arisen subsequently. Therefore, an entity does not adjust the amounts recognised in its financial statements for the investments. Similarly, the entity does not update the amounts disclosed for the investments as at the end of the reporting period, although it may need to give additional disclosure under paragraph 21.

Dividends

12   **If an entity declares dividends to holders of equity instruments (as defined in AASB 132 *Financial Instruments: Presentation*) after the reporting period, the entity shall not recognise those dividends as a liability at the end of the reporting period.**

13   If dividends are declared after the reporting period but before the financial statements are authorised for issue, the dividends are not recognised as a liability at the end of the reporting period because no obligation exists at that time. Such dividends are disclosed in the notes in accordance with AASB 101 *Presentation of Financial Statements*.

Going Concern

14   **An entity shall not prepare its financial statements on a going concern basis if management determines after the reporting period either that it intends to liquidate the entity or to cease trading, or that it has no realistic alternative but to do so.**

15   Deterioration in operating results and financial position after the reporting period may indicate a need to consider whether the going concern assumption is still appropriate. If the going concern assumption is no longer appropriate, the effect is so pervasive that this Standard requires a fundamental change in the basis of accounting, rather than an adjustment to the amounts recognised within the original basis of accounting.

16   AASB 101 specifies required disclosures if:

   (a)   the financial statements are not prepared on a going concern basis; or

   (b)   management is aware of material uncertainties related to events or conditions that may cast significant doubt upon the entity's ability to continue as a going concern. The events or conditions requiring disclosure may arise after the reporting period.

Disclosure

Date of Authorisation for Issue

17   **An entity shall disclose the date when the financial statements were authorised for issue and who gave that authorisation. If the entity's owners or others have the power to amend the financial statements after issue, the entity shall disclose that fact.**

18   It is important for users to know when the financial statements were authorised for issue, because the financial statements do not reflect events after this date.

Updating Disclosure about Conditions at the End of the Reporting Period

19   **If an entity receives information after the reporting period about conditions that existed at the end of the reporting period, it shall update disclosures that relate to these conditions, in the light of the new information.**

20   In some cases, an entity needs to update the disclosures in its financial statements to reflect information received after the reporting period, even when the information does not affect the amounts that it recognises in its financial statements. One example of the need to update disclosures is when evidence becomes available after the reporting period about a contingent liability that existed at the end of the reporting period. In addition to considering whether it should recognise or change a provision under AASB 137, an entity updates its disclosures about the contingent liability in the light of that evidence.

Non-adjusting Events after the Reporting Period

21   **If non-adjusting events after the reporting period are material, non-disclosure could influence the economic decisions that users make on the basis of the financial statements. Accordingly, an entity shall disclose the following for each material category of non-adjusting event after the reporting period:**

   (a)   **the nature of the event; and**

   (b)   **an estimate of its financial effect, or a statement that such an estimate cannot be made.**

22 The following are examples of non-adjusting events after the reporting period that would generally result in disclosure:

(a) a major business combination after the reporting period (AASB 3 *Business Combinations* requires specific disclosures in such cases) or disposing of a major subsidiary;

(b) announcing a plan to discontinue an operation;

(c) major purchases of assets, classification of assets as held for sale in accordance with AASB 5 *Non-current Assets Held for Sale and Discontinued Operations*, other disposals of assets, or expropriation of major assets by government;

(d) the destruction of a major production plant by a fire after the reporting period;

(e) announcing, or commencing the implementation of, a major restructuring (see AASB 137);

(f) major ordinary share transactions and potential ordinary share transactions after the reporting period (AASB 133 *Earnings per Share* requires an entity to disclose a description of such transactions, other than when such transactions involve capitalisation or bonus issues, share splits or reverse share splits (all of which are required to be adjusted under AASB 133));

(g) abnormally large changes after the reporting period in asset prices or foreign exchange rates;

(h) changes in tax rates or tax laws enacted or announced after the reporting period that have a significant effect on current and deferred tax assets and liabilities (see AASB 112 *Income Taxes*);

(i) entering into significant commitments or contingent liabilities, for example, by issuing significant guarantees; and

(j) commencing major litigation arising solely out of events that occurred after the reporting period.

Effective Date of IAS 10

23 [Deleted by the AASB]

AASB 111
Construction Contracts
(Compiled October 2009)

Note from the Institute of Chartered Accountants Australia

This note, prepared by the technical editors, is not part of Accounting Standard AASB 111.

Historical development

July 2004: AASB 111 'Construction Contracts' is the Australian equivalent of IAS 11 of the same name. It was made by the AASB on 15 July 2004 as part of the AASB's program to adopt International Financial Reporting Standards by 2005.

14 June 2007: AASB 2007-6 'Amendments to Australian Accounting Standards' was issued by the AASB. This Standard is applicable to annual reporting periods beginning on or after 1 January 2009.

24 September 2007: AASB 2007-8 'Amendments to Australian Accounting Standards arising from AASB 101' amends AASB 111 to align with revised AASB 101. This Standard is applicable to annual reporting periods beginning on or after 1 January 2009.

13 December 2007: AASB 2007-10 'Further Amendments to Australian Accounting Standards arising from AASB 101' amends AASB 111, replacing the term 'financial report' with 'financial statements'. This Standard is applicable to annual reporting periods beginning on or after 1 January 2009.

22 April 2009: AASB 2009-1 'Amendments to Australian Accounting Standards Borrowing Costs of Not-for-Profit Public Sector Entities' specifies when not-for-profit public sector entities can capitalise borrowing costs attributable to contract activity. This Standard is applicable to periods beginning on or after 1 January 2009 that end on or after 30 April 2009.

25 June 2009: AASB 2009-6 'Amendments to Australian Accounting Standards' amends AASB 111 for editorial corrections made by the International Accounting Standards Board (IASB) to its Standards and Interpretations (IFRSs) and as a consequence of issuing revised AASB 101 'Presentation of Financial Statements'. This Standard is applicable to annual reporting periods beginning on or after 1 January 2009 that end on or after 30 June 2009.

30 October 2009: AASB 111 was reissued by the AASB, compiled to include the AASB 2007-6, AASB 2007-8, AASB 2007-10, AASB 2009-1 and AASB 2009-6 amendments and applies to annual reporting periods beginning on or after 1 January 2009 that end on or after 30 June 2009. Early application is permitted.

References

Interpretation 12 *Service Concession Arrangements*, Interpretation 15 *Agreements for the Construction of Real Estate,* Interpretation 127 *Evaluating the Substance of Transactions Involving the Legal Form of a Lease* and Interpretation 132 *Intangible Assets – Web Site Costs* apply to AASB 111.

IFRIC items not taken onto the agenda: No. 6 *Pre-contract costs*, No. 7 *Project accounting – contractee's accounting*, No. 8 *IAS 11 Construction Contracts and IAS 18 Revenue: Pre-completion contracts for the sale of residential properties*, IAS 11-1 *Allocation of profit in a single contract* apply to AASB 111.

AASB 111 compared to IAS 11

Additions

Paragraph	Description
Aus 1.1	Which entities AASB 111 applies to (i.e. reporting entities and general purpose financial statements).
Aus 1.2	The application date of AASB 111 (i.e. annual reporting periods beginning 1 January 2005).

Aus 1.3	Prohibits early application of AASB 111.
Aus 1.4	Makes the requirements of AASB 111 subject to AASB 1031 'Materiality'.
Aus 1.5	Explains which Australian Standards have been superseded by AASB 111.
Aus 1.6	Clarifies that the superseded Australian Standards remain in force until AASB 111 applies.
Aus 1.7	Notice of the new Standard on 22 July 2004.
Aus 18.1	Specifies when not-for-profit public sector entities can capitialise borrowing costs attributable to contract activity.

Deletions

Paragraph	*Description*
2	Reference to superseded IAS 11.
46	Effective date of IAS 11.

Contents

Compilation Details

Comparison with IAS 11

Accounting Standard
AASB 111 Construction Contracts

Paragraphs

Objective

Application   Aus1.1 – Aus1.7

Scope   1

Definitions   3 – 6

Combining and Segmenting Construction Contracts   7 – 10

Contract Revenue   11 – 15

Contract Costs   16 – 21

Recognition of Contract Revenue and Expenses   22 – 35

Recognition of Expected Losses   36 – 37

Changes in Estimates   38

Disclosure   39 – 45

Australian Guidance

Appendix: Illustrative Examples for IAS 11
(available on the AASB website)

Australian Accounting Standard AASB 111 *Construction Contracts* (as amended) is set out in paragraphs Aus1.1 – 45. All the paragraphs have equal authority. Terms defined in this Standard are in *italics* the first time they appear in the Standard. AASB 111 is to be read in the context of other Australian Accounting Standards, including AASB 1048 *Interpretation and Application of Standards*, which identifies the UIG Interpretations. In the absence of explicit guidance, AASB 108 *Accounting Policies, Changes in Accounting Estimates and Errors* provides a basis for selecting and applying accounting policies.

Compilation Details

Accounting Standard AASB 111 *Construction Contracts* as amended

This compiled Standard applies to annual reporting periods beginning on or after 1 January 2009 that end on or after 30 June 2009. It takes into account amendments up to and including 25 June 2009 and was prepared on 30 October 2009 by the staff of the Australian Accounting Standards Board (AASB).

This compilation is not a separate Accounting Standard made by the AASB. Instead, it is a representation of AASB 111 (July 2004) as amended by other Accounting Standards, which are listed in the Table below.

Table of Standards

Standard	Date made	Application date *(annual reporting periods ... on or after ...)*	Application, saving or transitional provisions
AASB 111	15 Jul 2004	*(beginning)* 1 Jan 2005	
AASB 2007-6	14 Jun 2007	*(beginning)* 1 Jan 2009	see (a) below
AASB 2007-8	24 Sep 2007	*(beginning)* 1 Jan 2009	see (b) below
AASB 2007-10	13 Dec 2007	*(beginning)* 1 Jan 2009	see (b) below
AASB 2009-1	22 Apr 2009	*(beginning)* 1 Jan 2009 and *(ending)* 30 Apr 2009	see (c) below
AASB 2009-6	25 Jun 2009	*(beginning)* 1 Jan 2009 and *(ending)* 30 Jun 2009	see (d) below

(a) Entities may elect to apply this Standard to annual reporting periods beginning on or after 1 January 2005 but before 1 January 2009, provided that AASB 123 *Borrowing Costs* (June 2007) is also applied to such periods.

(b) Entities may elect to apply this Standard to annual reporting periods beginning on or after 1 January 2005 but before 1 January 2009, provided that AASB 101 *Presentation of Financial Statements* (September 2007) is also applied to such periods.

(c) Entities may elect to apply this Standard to annual reporting periods beginning on or after 1 January 2009 that end before 30 April 2009, provided that AASB 123 *Borrowing Costs* (June 2007) is also applied to such periods.

(d) Entities may elect to apply this Standard to annual reporting periods beginning on or after 1 January 2005 but before 1 January 2009, provided that AASB 101 *Presentation of Financial Statements* (September 2007) is also applied to such periods, and to annual reporting periods beginning on or after 1 January 2009 that end before 30 June 2009.

Table of Amendments

Paragraph affected	How affected	By ... [paragraph]
Objective	amended	AASB 2007-8 [6]
Aus1.1	amended	AASB 2007-8 [7, 8]
Aus1.4	amended	AASB 2007-8 [8]
1	amended	AASB 2007-10 [55]
18	amended	AASB 2007-6 [13]
Aus18.1	added	AASB 2009-1 [6]
22-23	amended	AASB 2007-8 [6]
26	amended	AASB 2007-8 [44]
28	amended amended	AASB 2007-8 [44] AASB 2009-6 [39]
38	amended	AASB 2007-8 [44]
40	amended	AASB 2007-8 [6]

Comparison with IAS 11

AASB 111 and IAS 11

AASB 111 *Construction Contracts* as amended incorporates IAS 11 *Construction Contracts* as issued and amended by the International Accounting Standards Board (IASB). Paragraphs that have been added to this Standard (and do not appear in the text of IAS 11) are identified with the prefix "Aus", followed by the number of the relevant IASB paragraph and decimal numbering.

Compliance with IAS 11

Entities that comply with AASB 111 as amended will simultaneously be in compliance with IAS 11 as amended.

Accounting Standard AASB 111

The Australian Accounting Standards Board made Accounting Standard AASB 111 *Construction Contracts* under section 334 of the *Corporations Act 2001* on 15 July 2004.

This compiled version of AASB 111 applies to annual reporting periods beginning on or after 1 January 2009 that end on or after 30 June 2009. It incorporates relevant amendments contained in other AASB Standards made by the AASB up to and including 25 June 2009 (see Compilation Details).

Accounting Standard AASB 111
Construction Contracts

Objective

The objective of this Standard is to prescribe the accounting treatment of revenue and costs associated with construction contracts. Because of the nature of the activity undertaken in construction contracts, the date at which the contract activity is entered into and the date when the activity is completed usually fall into different reporting periods. Therefore, the primary issue in accounting for construction contracts is the allocation of contract revenue and contract costs to the reporting periods in which construction work is performed. This Standard uses the recognition criteria established in the *Framework for the Preparation and Presentation of Financial Statements* to determine when contract revenue and contract costs should be recognised as revenue and expenses in the statement of comprehensive income. It also provides practical guidance on the application of these criteria.

Application

Aus1.1　This Standard applies to:

(a)　each entity that is required to prepare financial reports in accordance with Part 2M.3 of the Corporations Act and that is a reporting entity;

(b)　general purpose financial statements of each other reporting entity; and

(c)　financial statements that are, or are held out to be, general purpose financial statements.

Aus1.2　This Standard applies to annual reporting periods beginning on or after 1 January 2005.
[Note: For application dates of paragraphs changed or added by an amending Standard, see Compilation Details.]

Aus1.3　This Standard shall not be applied to annual reporting periods beginning before 1 January 2005.

Aus1.4　The requirements specified in this Standard apply to the financial statements where information resulting from their application is material in accordance with AASB 1031 *Materiality*.

Aus1.5　When applicable, this Standard supersedes:

(a)　AASB 1009 *Construction Contracts* as notified in the *Commonwealth of Australia Gazette* No S 532, 16 December 1997; and

(b)　AAS 11 *Construction Contracts* as issued in December 1997.

Aus1.6　Both AASB 1009 and AAS 11 remain applicable until superseded by this Standard.

Aus1.7　Notice of this Standard was published in the *Commonwealth of Australia Gazette* No S 294, 22 July 2004.

Scope

1　This Standard shall be applied in accounting for construction contracts in the financial statements of contractors.

2　[Deleted by the AASB]

Definitions

3 The following terms are used in this Standard with the meanings specified.

A *construction contract* is a contract specifically negotiated for the construction of an asset or a combination of assets that are closely interrelated or interdependent in terms of their design, technology and function or their ultimate purpose or use.

A *cost plus contract* is a construction contract in which the contractor is reimbursed for allowable or otherwise defined costs, plus a percentage of these costs or a fixed fee.

A *fixed price contract* is a construction contract in which the contractor agrees to a fixed contract price, or a fixed rate per unit of output, which in some cases is subject to cost escalation clauses.

4 A construction contract may be negotiated for the construction of a single asset such as a bridge, building, dam, pipeline, road, ship or tunnel. A construction contract may also deal with the construction of a number of assets which are closely interrelated or interdependent in terms of their design, technology and function or their ultimate purpose or use; examples of such contracts include those for the construction of refineries and other complex pieces of plant or equipment.

5 For the purposes of this Standard, construction contracts include:

(a) contracts for the rendering of services which are directly related to the construction of the asset, for example, those for the services of project managers and architects; and

(b) contracts for the destruction or restoration of assets, and the restoration of the environment following the demolition of assets.

6 Construction contracts are formulated in a number of ways which, for the purposes of this Standard, are classified as *fixed price contracts* and *cost plus contracts*. Some construction contracts may contain characteristics of both a fixed price contract and a cost plus contract, for example in the case of a cost plus contract with an agreed maximum price. In such circumstances, a contractor needs to consider all the conditions in paragraphs 23 and 24 in order to determine when to recognise contract revenue and expenses.

Combining and Segmenting Construction Contracts

7 The requirements of this Standard are usually applied separately to each construction contract. However, in certain circumstances, it is necessary to apply the Standard to the separately identifiable components of a single contract or to a group of contracts together in order to reflect the substance of a contract or a group of contracts.

8 **When a contract covers a number of assets, the construction of each asset shall be treated as a separate construction contract when:**

(a) **separate proposals have been submitted for each asset;**

(b) **each asset has been subject to separate negotiation and the contractor and customer have been able to accept or reject that part of the contract relating to each asset; and**

(c) **the costs and revenues of each asset can be identified.**

9 **A group of contracts, whether with a single customer or with several customers, shall be treated as a single construction contract when:**

(a) **the group of contracts is negotiated as a single package;**

(b) **the contracts are so closely interrelated that they are, in effect, part of a single project with an overall profit margin; and**

(c) **the contracts are performed concurrently or in a continuous sequence.**

10 **A contract may provide for the construction of an additional asset at the option of the customer or may be amended to include the construction of an additional asset. The construction of the additional asset shall be treated as a separate construction contract when:**

(a)   the asset differs significantly in design, technology or function from the asset or assets covered by the original contract; or

(b)   the price of the asset is negotiated without regard to the original contract price.

Contract Revenue

11   Contract revenue shall comprise:

(a)   the initial amount of revenue agreed in the contract; and

(b)   variations in contract work, claims and incentive payments:

(i)   to the extent that it is probable that they will result in revenue; and

(ii)   they are capable of being reliably measured.

12   Contract revenue is measured at the fair value of the consideration received or receivable. The measurement of contract revenue is affected by a variety of uncertainties that depend on the outcome of future events. The estimates often need to be revised as events occur and uncertainties are resolved. Therefore, the amount of contract revenue may increase or decrease from one period to the next. For example:

(a)   a contractor and a customer may agree variations or claims that increase or decrease contract revenue in a period subsequent to that in which the contract was initially agreed;

(b)   the amount of revenue agreed in a fixed price contract may increase as a result of cost escalation clauses;

(c)   the amount of contract revenue may decrease as a result of penalties arising from delays caused by the contractor in the completion of the contract; or

(d)   when a fixed price contract involves a fixed price per unit of output, contract revenue increases as the number of units is increased.

13   A variation is an instruction by the customer for a change in the scope of the work to be performed under the contract. A variation may lead to an increase or a decrease in contract revenue. Examples of variations are changes in the specifications or design of the asset and changes in the duration of the contract. A variation is included in contract revenue when:

(a)   it is probable that the customer will approve the variation and the amount of revenue arising from the variation; and

(b)   the amount of revenue can be reliably measured.

14   A claim is an amount that the contractor seeks to collect from the customer or another party as reimbursement for costs not included in the contract price. A claim may arise from, for example, customer caused delays, errors in specifications or design, and disputed variations in contract work. The measurement of the amounts of revenue arising from claims is subject to a high level of uncertainty and often depends on the outcome of negotiations. Therefore, claims are included in contract revenue only when:

(a)   negotiations have reached an advanced stage such that it is probable that the customer will accept the claim; and

(b)   the amount that it is probable will be accepted by the customer can be measured reliably.

15   Incentive payments are additional amounts paid to the contractor if specified performance standards are met or exceeded. For example, a contract may allow for an incentive payment to the contractor for early completion of the contract. Incentive payments are included in contract revenue when:

(a)   the contract is sufficiently advanced that it is probable that the specified performance standards will be met or exceeded; and

(b)   the amount of the incentive payment can be measured reliably.

Contract Costs

16   Contract costs shall comprise:

(a)   costs that relate directly to the specific contract;

(b)   costs that are attributable to contract activity in general and can be allocated to the contract; and

(c)   such other costs as are specifically chargeable to the customer under the terms of the contract.

17   Costs that relate directly to a specific contract include:

(a)   site labour costs, including site supervision;

(b)   costs of materials used in construction;

(c)   depreciation of plant and equipment used on the contract;

(d)   costs of moving plant, equipment and materials to and from the contract site;

(e)   costs of hiring plant and equipment;

(f)   costs of design and technical assistance that is directly related to the contract;

(g)   the estimated costs of rectification and guarantee work, including expected warranty costs; and

(h)   claims from third parties.

These costs may be reduced by any incidental income that is not included in contract revenue, for example, income from the sale of surplus materials and the disposal of plant and equipment at the end of the contract.

18   Costs that may be attributable to contract activity in general and can be allocated to specific contracts include:

(a)   insurance;

(b)   costs of design and technical assistance that are not directly related to a specific contract; and

(c)   construction overheads.

Such costs are allocated using methods that are systematic and rational and are applied consistently to all costs having similar characteristics. The allocation is based on the normal level of construction activity. Construction overheads include costs such as the preparation and processing of construction personnel payroll. Costs that may be attributable to contract activity in general and can be allocated to specific contracts also include borrowing costs.

Aus18.1   In respect of not-for-profit public sector entities, costs that may be attributable to contract activity in general and can be allocated to specific contracts also include borrowing costs only when the contractor capitalises borrowing costs in accordance with AASB 123 *Borrowing Costs*.

19   Costs that are specifically chargeable to the customer under the terms of the contract may include some general administration costs and development costs for which reimbursement is specified in the terms of the contract.

20   Costs that cannot be attributed to contract activity or cannot be allocated to a contract are excluded from the costs of a construction contract. Such costs include:

(a)   general administration costs for which reimbursement is not specified in the contract;

(b)   selling costs;

(c)   research and development costs for which reimbursement is not specified in the contract; and

(d)   depreciation of idle plant and equipment that is not used on a particular contract.

21   Contract costs include the costs attributable to a contract for the period from the date of securing the contract to the final completion of the contract. However, costs that relate directly to a contract and are incurred in securing the contract are also included as part of the contract costs if they can be separately identified and measured reliably and it is

probable that the contract will be obtained. When costs incurred in securing a contract are recognised as an expense in the period in which they are incurred, they are not included in contract costs when the contract is obtained in a subsequent period.

Recognition of Contract Revenue and Expenses

22   **When the outcome of a construction contract can be estimated reliably, contract revenue and contract costs associated with the construction contract shall be recognised as revenue and expenses respectively by reference to the stage of completion of the contract activity at the end of the reporting period. An expected loss on the construction contract shall be recognised as an expense immediately in accordance with paragraph 36.**

23   **In the case of a fixed price contract, the outcome of a construction contract can be estimated reliably when all the following conditions are satisfied:**

      (a)   **total contract revenue can be measured reliably;**

      (b)   **it is probable that the economic benefits associated with the contract will flow to the entity;**

      (c)   **both the contract costs to complete the contract and the stage of contract completion at the end of the reporting period can be measured reliably; and**

      (d)   **the contract costs attributable to the contract can be clearly identified and measured reliably so that actual contract costs incurred can be compared with prior estimates.**

24   **In the case of a cost plus contract, the outcome of a construction contract can be estimated reliably when all the following conditions are satisfied:**

      (a)   **it is probable that the economic benefits associated with the contract will flow to the entity; and**

      (b)   **the contract costs attributable to the contract, whether or not specifically reimbursable, can be clearly identified and measured reliably.**

25   The recognition of revenue and expenses by reference to the stage of completion of a contract is often referred to as the percentage of completion method. Under this method, contract revenue is matched with the contract costs incurred in reaching the stage of completion, resulting in the reporting of revenue, expenses and profit which can be attributed to the proportion of work completed. This method provides useful information on the extent of contract activity and performance during a period.

26   Under the percentage of completion method, contract revenue is recognised as revenue in profit or loss in the reporting periods in which the work is performed. Contract costs are usually recognised as an expense in profit or loss in the reporting periods in which the work to which they relate is performed. However, any expected excess of total contract costs over total contract revenue for the contract is recognised as an expense immediately in accordance with paragraph 36.

27   A contractor may have incurred contract costs that relate to future activity on the contract. Such contract costs are recognised as an asset provided it is probable that they will be recovered. Such costs represent an amount due from the customer and are often classified as contract work in progress.

28   The outcome of a construction contract can only be estimated reliably when it is probable that the economic benefits associated with the contract will flow to the entity. However, when an uncertainty arises about the collectibility of an amount already included in contract revenue, and already recognised in profit or loss, the uncollectible amount or the amount in respect of which recovery has ceased to be probable is recognised as an expense rather than as an adjustment of the amount of contract revenue.

29   An entity is generally able to make reliable estimates after it has agreed to a contract which establishes:

      (a)   each party's enforceable rights regarding the asset to be constructed;

      (b)   the consideration to be exchanged; and

      (c)   the manner and terms of settlement.

It is also usually necessary for the entity to have an effective internal financial budgeting and reporting system. The entity reviews and, when necessary, revises the estimates of contract revenue and contract costs as the contract progresses. The need for such revisions does not necessarily indicate that the outcome of the contract cannot be estimated reliably.

30   The stage of completion of a contract may be determined in a variety of ways. The entity uses the method that measures reliably the work performed. Depending on the nature of the contract, the methods may include:

(a)   the proportion that contract costs incurred for work performed to date bear to the estimated total contract costs;

(b)   surveys of work performed; or

(c)   completion of a physical proportion of the contract work.

Progress payments and advances received from customers often do not reflect the work performed.

31   When the stage of completion is determined by reference to the contract costs incurred to date, only those contract costs that reflect work performed are included in costs incurred to date. Examples of contract costs which are excluded are:

(a)   contract costs that relate to future activity on the contract, such as costs of materials that have been delivered to a contract site or set aside for use in a contract but not yet installed, used or applied during contract performance, unless the materials have been made specially for the contract; and

(b)   payments made to subcontractors in advance of work performed under the subcontract.

32   **When the outcome of a construction contract cannot be estimated reliably:**

(a)   **revenue shall be recognised only to the extent of contract costs incurred that it is probable will be recoverable; and**

(b)   **contract costs shall be recognised as an expense in the period in which they are incurred.**

An expected loss on the construction contract shall be recognised as an expense immediately in accordance with paragraph 36.

33   During the early stages of a contract it is often the case that the outcome of the contract cannot be estimated reliably. Nevertheless, it may be probable that the entity will recover the contract costs incurred. Therefore, contract revenue is recognised only to the extent of costs incurred that are expected to be recoverable. As the outcome of the contract cannot be estimated reliably, no profit is recognised. However, even though the outcome of the contract cannot be estimated reliably, it may be probable that total contract costs will exceed total contract revenues. In such cases, any expected excess of total contract costs over total contract revenue for the contract is recognised as an expense immediately in accordance with paragraph 36.

34   Contract costs that are not probable of being recovered are recognised as an expense immediately. Examples of circumstances in which the recoverability of contract costs incurred may not be probable and in which contract costs may need to be recognised as an expense immediately include contracts:

(a)   that are not fully enforceable, that is, their validity is seriously in question;

(b)   the completion of which is subject to the outcome of pending litigation or legislation;

(c)   relating to properties that are likely to be condemned or expropriated;

(d)   where the customer is unable to meet its obligations; or

(e)   where the contractor is unable to complete the contract or otherwise meet its obligations under the contract.

35   **When the uncertainties that prevented the outcome of the contract being estimated reliably no longer exist, revenue and expenses associated with the construction contract shall be recognised in accordance with paragraph 22 rather than in accordance with paragraph 32.**

Recognition of Expected Losses

36   **When it is probable that total contract costs will exceed total contract revenue, the expected loss shall be recognised as an expense immediately.**

37   The amount of such a loss is determined irrespective of:

    (a)   whether work has commenced on the contract;

    (b)   the stage of completion of contract activity; or

    (c)   the amount of profits expected to arise on other contracts which are not treated as a single construction contract in accordance with paragraph 9.

Changes in Estimates

38   The percentage of completion method is applied on a cumulative basis in each reporting period to the current estimates of contract revenue and contract costs. Therefore, the effect of a change in the estimate of contract revenue or contract costs, or the effect of a change in the estimate of the outcome of a contract, is accounted for as a change in accounting estimate (see AASB 108 *Accounting Policies, Changes in Accounting Estimates and Errors*). The changed estimates are used in the determination of the amount of revenue and expenses recognised in profit or loss in the period in which the change is made and in subsequent periods.

Disclosure

39   **An entity shall disclose:**

    (a)   **the amount of contract revenue recognised as revenue in the period;**

    (b)   **the methods used to determine the contract revenue recognised in the period; and**

    (c)   **the methods used to determine the stage of completion of contracts in progress.**

40   **An entity shall disclose each of the following for contracts in progress at the end of the reporting period:**

    (a)   **the aggregate amount of costs incurred and recognised profits (less recognised losses) to date;**

    (b)   **the amount of advances received; and**

    (c)   **the amount of retentions.**

41   Retentions are amounts of progress billings that are not paid until the satisfaction of conditions specified in the contract for the payment of such amounts or until defects have been rectified. Progress billings are amounts billed for work performed on a contract whether or not they have been paid by the customer. Advances are amounts received by the contractor before the related work is performed.

42   **An entity shall present:**

    (a)   **the gross amount due from customers for contract work as an asset; and**

    (b)   **the gross amount due to customers for contract work as a liability.**

43   The gross amount due from customers for contract work is the net amount of:

    (a)   costs incurred plus recognised profits; less

    (b)   the sum of recognised losses and progress billings;

for all contracts in progress for which costs incurred plus recognised profits (less recognised losses) exceeds progress billings.

44   The gross amount due to customers for contract work is the net amount of:

    (a)   costs incurred plus recognised profits; less

    (b)   the sum of recognised losses and progress billings;

for all contracts in progress for which progress billings exceed costs incurred plus recognised profits (less recognised losses).

45   An entity discloses any contingent liabilities and contingent assets in accordance with AASB 137 *Provisions, Contingent Liabilities and Contingent Assets*. Contingent liabilities and contingent assets may arise from such items as warranty costs, claims, penalties or possible losses.

Effective Date of IAS 11

46   [Deleted by the AASB]

Australian Guidance

Australian Guidance accompanies, but is not part of, AASB 111.

Non commercial Contracts

G1   For not-for-profit entities that are construction contractors, the requirements of AASB 111 *Construction Contracts* should also be applied to non commercial construction contracts and similar arrangements that are binding on the parties to the arrangement but which do not take the form of a documented contract.

G2   A non commercial contract or similar arrangement may be either a "fixed price contract" or a "cost plus contract" (which in a non commercial context may also be referred to as a "cost based contract"). Contracts and arrangements classified as fixed price contracts may involve the funding of construction activity through indirect means such as through a general appropriation or other allocation of government funds or by general purpose grants. In contrast, contracts and arrangements classified as cost plus (or cost based) contracts may involve full or partial reimbursement of the costs incurred for the construction of the asset from the recipient of the constructed asset and/or from other parties.

AASB 112
Income Taxes

(Compiled June 2012)

Note from the Institute of Chartered Accountants Australia

This note, prepared by the technical editors, is not part of Accounting Standard AASB 112.

Historical development

15 July 2004: AASB 112 'Income Taxes' is the Australian equivalent of IAS 12 of the same name. It was made by the AASB on 15 July 2004 as part of the AASB's program to adopt International Financial Reporting Standards by 2005.

8 September 2005: AASB 2005-11 'Amendments to Australian Accounting Standards' amends paragraph 15(b) and deletes paragraph 15(c). This Standard is applicable to annual reporting periods ending on or after 31 December 2005, although entities may choose to early-adopt this Standard for annual reporting periods beginning on or after 1 January 2005.

30 April 2007: AASB 2007-4 'Amendments to Australian Accounting Standards' amends paragraphs 22, 33, 37, 59, 60, 62, 68B, 72, 78 and 81 and deletes paragraph Aus80.1 and is applicable to annual reporting periods beginning on or after 1 July 2007. Entities may elect to early-adopt it to annual reporting periods beginning on or after 1 January 2005.

24 September 2007: AASB 2007-8 'Amendments to Australian Accounting Standards arising from AASB 101' amends AASB 112 to align with revised AASB 101. This Standard is applicable to annual reporting periods beginning on or after 1 January 2009.

13 December 2007: AASB 2007-10 'Further Amendments to Australian Accounting Standards arising from AASB 101' amends AASB 112, replacing the term 'financial report' with 'financial statements'. This Standard is applicable to annual reporting periods beginning on or after 1 January 2009.

6 March 2008: AASB 2008-3 'Amendments to Australian Accounting Standards arising from AASB 3 and AASB 127' amends AASB 112 for the issue of AASB 3 Revised. This Standard is applicable to annual reporting periods beginning on or after 1 July 2009.

25 June 2009: AASB 2009-6 'Amendments to Australian Accounting Standards' amends AASB 112 for editorial corrections made by the International Accounting Standards Board (IASB) to its Standards and Interpretations (IFRSs) and as a consequence of issuing revised AASB 101 'Presentation of Financial Statements' (September 2007). This Standard is applicable to annual reporting periods beginning on or after 1 January 2009 that end on or after 30 June 2009.

25 June 2009: AASB 2009-7 'Amendments to Australian Accounting Standards' amends AASB 112 arising from editorial corrections by the AASB and by the International Accounting Standards Board (IASB). This Standard is applicable to annual reporting periods beginning on or after 1 July 2009.

5 October 2009: Erratum makes further terminology-related and editorial changes resulting from AASB 2009-6. This erratum applies to annual reporting periods beginning on or after 1 January 2009 that end on or after 30 June 2009.

30 October 2009: AASB 112 was reissued by the AASB, compiled to include the AASB 2007-8, AASB 2007-10, AASB 2008-3, AASB 2009-6, AASB 2009-7 and erratum amendments and applies to annual reporting periods beginning on or after 1 July 2009. Early application is permitted.

On the same date the AASB reissued the version of AASB 112 applicable to annual reporting periods beginning on or after 1 January 2009 but before 1 July 2009. This version of AASB 7 has been compiled for the amending Standards applying to annual reporting periods beginning on or after 1 January 2009. This Standard applies to 31 December 2009 year ends and can be accessed from the AASB website at www.aasb.gov.au.

7 December 2009: AASB 2009-11 'Amendments to Australian Accounting Standards arising from AASB 9' amends AASB 112 to give effect to consequential changes arising from the issuance of AASB 9.

AASB

This Standard is applicable to annual reporting periods beginning on or after 1 January 2013 with early adoption permitted from annual reporting periods ending on or after 31 December 2009 that begin before 1 January 2013 provided AASB 9 is also applied for the same period. The application date of AASB 2009-11 has been amended to 1 January 2015 by AASB 2012-6. **These amendments have been superseded by AASB 2010-7 and are not included in this compiled Standard.**

15 December 2009: AASB 2009-12 'Amendments to Australian Accounting Standards' amends AASB 112 for editorial corrections. This Standard is applicable to annual reporting periods beginning on or after 1 January 2011 with early adoption permitted.

27 October 2010: AASB 2010-5 'Further Amendments to Australian Accounting Standards' makes editorial amendments to AASB 112. This Standard is applicable to annual reporting periods beginning on or after 1 January 2011.

26 November 2010: AASB 112 was reissued by the AASB, compiled to include the AASB 2009-12 and AASB 2010-5 amendments and applies to annual reporting periods ending on or after 1 January 2011 but before 1 January 2013.

31 December 2010: AASB 2010-8 'Amendments to Australian Accounting Standards – Deferred Tax: Recovery of Underlying Assets' amends AASB 112 to provide a practical approach for measuring deferred tax when an investment property is valued using fair value. This Standard applies to annual reporting periods beginning on or after 1 January 2012 and can be adopted early.

1 March 2011: AASB 2010-7 'Amendments to Australian Accounting Standards arising from AASB 9 (December 2010)' as compiled amends AASB 112 to give effect to consequential changes arising from the reissue of AASB 9 in December 2010 and supersedes AASB 2009-11 which related to the previous version of AASB 9. This Standard applies to annual reporting periods beginning on or after 1 January 2013 and can be adopted early. The application date of AASB 2010-7 has been amended to 1 January 2015 by AASB 2012-6. **These amendments are not included in this compiled Standard.**

29 August 2011: AASB 2011-7 'Amendments to Australian Accounting Standards arising from the Consolidation and Joint Arrangements Standards' amends AASB 112 to give effect to many consequential changes arising from the issue of AASB 10, 11, 12, 127 and 128. This Standard applies to annual reporting periods beginning on or after 1 January 2013 and can be adopted early by for-profit entities. **These amendments are not included in this compiled Standard.**

5 September 2011: AASB 2011-9 'Amendments to Australian Accounting Standards – Presentation of Items of Other Comprehensive income' amends the presentation of items in other comprehensive income. This Standard applies to annual reporting periods beginning on or after 1 July 2012 and can be adopted early.

20 June 2012: AASB 112 was reissued by the AASB, compiled to include the AASB 2010-8 and AASB 2011-9 amendments and applies to annual reporting periods beginning on or after 1 July 2012 and can be adopted early.

References

Interpretation 7 *Applying the Restatement Approach under AASB 129 Financial Reporting in Hyperinflationary Economies*, Interpretation 1003 *Australian Petroleum Resource Rent Tax*, Interpretation 125 *Income Taxes – Changes in the Tax Status of an Entity or its Shareholders*, Interpretation 1039 *Substantive Enactment of Major Tax Bills in Australia* and Interpretation 1052 *Tax Consolidation Accounting* apply to AASB 112.

AASB item not taken onto the agenda: *Scope* applies to AASB 112.

IFRIC items not taken onto the agenda: No. 9 *Income Tax Accounting under the Tax Consolidation System – Subsidiary Leaving the Group*, No. 10 *Asset Revaluation*, No. 11 *Effective tax rates*, No. 12 *Non-depreciable/depreciable assets*, No. 13 *Income tax omnibus*, No. 15 *Classification of Interests and Penalties* and No. 16 *Estonian Dividend Tax,* IAS 12-1 *Carryforward of unused tax losses and tax credits*, IAS 12-2 *Deferred tax relating to finance leases*, IAS 12-3 *Non-amortisable intangible assets*, IAS 12-4 *Single asset entities*, IAS 12-5 *Scope*, IAS 12-6 *Deferred tax arising from unremitted foreign earnings,* IAS 112-7 *Classification of tonnage taxes*, IAS 12-10 *Rebuttable presumption to determine the manner of recovery* and IAS 12-13 IAS 12 *Income Taxes – Accounting for market value uplifts on assets that are to be introduced by a new income tax regime* apply to AASB 112.

AASB 112 compared to IAS 12

Additions

Paragraph	Description
Aus 1.1	Which entities AASB 112 applies to (i.e. reporting entities and general purpose financial statements).
Aus 1.2	The application date of AASB 112 (i.e. annual reporting periods beginning 1 January 2005).
Aus 1.3	Prohibits early application of AASB 112.
Aus 1.4	Makes the requirements of AASB 112 subject to AASB 1031 'Materiality'.
Aus 1.5	Explains which Australian Standards have been superseded by AASB 112.
Aus 1.6	Clarifies that the superseded Australian Standards remain in force until AASB 112 applies.
Aus 1.7	Notice of the new Standard published on 22 July 2004.
Aus 2.1	Clarifies that income tax equivalents of public sector entities are included within the scope of the Australian Standard.
Aus 33.1	Clarifies that non-taxable government grants received by a not-for-profit entity are recognised as income immediately and do not give rise to a deductible temporary difference and deferred tax asset.

Deletions

Paragraph	Description
81(c)(ii)	Disclosure of a numerical reconciliation between the average effective tax rate and the applicable tax rate together with the basis on which the applicable tax rate is computed.
89	Effective date of IAS 12.
90	Reference to superseded IAS 12.
91	Effective date of certain paragraphs that were added to IAS 12 subsequent to 1998.
92	Effective date of 2007 revisions to IAS 12.
95	Effective date of 2008 revisions to IAS 12.

Contents

Compilation Details

Comparison with IAS 12

**Accounting Standard
AASB 112 Income Taxes**

	Paragraphs
Objective	
Application	Aus1.1 – Aus1.7
Scope	1 – 4
Definitions	5 – 6
Tax Base	7 – 11
Recognition of Current Tax Liabilities and Current Tax Assets	12 – 14
Recognition of Deferred Tax Liabilities and Deferred Tax Assets	
Taxable Temporary Differences	15 – 18
Business Combinations	19
Assets Carried at Fair Value	20
Goodwill	21 – 21B
Initial Recognition of an Asset or Liability	22 – 23
Deductible Temporary Differences	24 – 31
Goodwill	32A
Initial Recognition of an Asset or Liability	33 – Aus33.1
Unused Tax Losses and Unused Tax Credits	34 – 36
Reassessment of Unrecognised Deferred Tax Assets	37
Investments in Subsidiaries, Branches and Associates and Interests in Joint Ventures	38 – 45
Measurement	46 – 56
Recognition of Current and Deferred Tax	57
Items Recognised in Profit or Loss	58 – 60
Items Recognised Outside Profit or Loss	61A – 65A
Deferred Tax Arising from a Business Combination	66 – 68
Current and Deferred Tax Arising from Share-based Payment Transactions	68A – 68C
Presentation	
Tax Assets and Tax Liabilities	
Offset	71 – 76
Tax Expense	
Tax Expense (Income) Related to Profit or Loss from Ordinary Activities	77
Exchange Differences on Deferred Foreign Tax Liabilities or Assets	78
Disclosure	79 – 88
Effective Date	93 – 98B

Illustrative Examples

Examples of Temporary Differences

Illustrative Computations and Presentation

Australian Accounting Standard AASB 112 *Income Taxes* (as amended) is set out in paragraphs Aus1.1 – 98B. All the paragraphs have equal authority. Paragraphs in **bold type** state the main principles. Terms defined in this Standard are in *italics* the first time they appear in the Standard. AASB 112 is to be read in the context of other Australian Accounting Standards, including AASB 1048 *Interpretation of Standards*, which identifies the Australian Accounting Interpretations. In the absence of explicit guidance, AASB 108 *Accounting Policies, Changes in Accounting Estimates and Errors* provides a basis for selecting and applying accounting policies.

Compilation Details

Accounting Standard AASB 112 *Income Taxes* as amended]

This compiled Standard applies to annual reporting periods beginning on or after 1 July 2012 but before 1 January 2013. It takes into account amendments up to and including 5 September 2011 and was prepared on 20 June 2012 by the staff of the Australian Accounting Standards Board (AASB).

This compilation is not a separate Accounting Standard made by the AASB. Instead, it is a representation of AASB 112 (July 2004) as amended by other Accounting Standards, which are listed in the Table below.

Table of Standards

Standard	Date made	Application date *(annual reporting periods ... on or after ...)*	Application, saving or transitional provisions
AASB 112	15 Jul 2004	*(beginning)* 1 Jan 2005	
AASB 2005-11	8 Sep 2005	*(ending)* 31 Dec 2005	see (a) below
AASB 2007-4	30 Apr 2007	*(beginning)* 1 Jul 2007	see (b) below
AASB 2007-8	24 Sep 2007	*(beginning)* 1 Jan 2009	see (c) below
AASB 2007-10	13 Dec 2007	*(beginning)* 1 Jan 2009	see (c) below
AASB 2008-3	6 Mar 2008	*(beginning)* 1 Jul 2009	see (d) below
AASB 2009-6	25 Jun 2009	*(beginning)* 1 Jan 2009 *and (ending)* 30 Jun 2009	see (e) below
AASB 2009-7	25 Jun 2009	*(beginning)* 1 Jul 2009	see (f) below
Erratum	5 Oct 2009	*(beginning)* 1 Jan 2009 and *(ending)* 30 Jun 2009	see (g) below
AASB 2009-11	7 Dec 2009	*(beginning)* 1 Jan 2013	not compiled*
AASB 2009-12	15 Dec 2009	*(beginning)* 1 Jan 2011	see (h) below
AASB 2010-2	30 Jun 2010	*(beginning)* 1 Jul 2013	not compiled*
AASB 2010-5	27 Oct 2010	*(beginning)* 1 Jan 2011	see (h) below
AASB 2010-7	6 Dec 2010	*(beginning)* 1 Jan 2013	not compiled*
AASB 2010-8	31 Dec 2010	*(beginning)* 1 Jan 2012	see (i) below
AASB 2011-7	29 Aug 2011	*(beginning)* 1 Jan 2013	not compiled*
AASB 2011-9	5 Sep 2011	*(beginning)* 1 Jul 2012	see (j) below

*   The amendments made by this Standard are not included in this compilation, which presents the principal Standard as applicable to annual reporting periods beginning on or after 1 July 2012 but before 1 January 2013.

(a)   Entities may elect to apply this Standard to annual reporting periods beginning on or after 1 January 2005 that end before 31 December 2005.

(b)   Entities may elect to apply this Standard to annual reporting periods beginning on or after 1 January 2005 but before 1 July 2007.

(c)   Entities may elect to apply this Standard to annual reporting periods beginning on or after 1 January 2005 but before 1 January 2009, provided that AASB 101 *Presentation of Financial Statements* (September 2007) is also applied to such periods.

(d)   Entities may elect to apply this Standard to annual reporting periods beginning on or after 30 June 2007 but before 1 July 2009, provided that AASB 3 *Business Combinations* (March 2008) and AASB 127 *Consolidated and Separate Financial Statements* (March 2008) are also applied to such periods.

(e) Entities may elect to apply this Standard to annual reporting periods beginning on or after 1 January 2005 but before 1 January 2009, provided that AASB 101 *Presentation of Financial Statements* (September 2007) is also applied to such periods, and to annual reporting periods beginning on or after 1 January 2009 that end before 30 June 2009.

(f) Entities may elect to apply this Standard to annual reporting periods beginning before 1 July 2009 that end on or after 1 July 2008.

(g) Entities may elect to apply this Erratum to annual reporting periods beginning on or after 1 January 2005, provided that AASB 2009-6 *Amendments to Australian Accounting Standards* is also applied to such periods.

(h) Entities may elect to apply this Standard to annual reporting periods beginning on or after 1 January 2005 but before 1 January 2011.

(i) Entities may elect to apply this Standard to annual reporting periods beginning on or after 1 January 2005 but before 1 January 2012.

(j) Entities may elect to apply this Standard to annual reporting periods beginning on or after 1 January 2005 but before 1 July 2012.

Table of Amendments to Standard

Paragraph affected	How affected	By ... [paragraph]
Objective	amended	AASB 2007-8 [45]
	amended	AASB 2008-3 [31]
Aus1.5	amended	AASB 2010-8 [6]
10	amended	AASB 2010-8 [7]
15	amended	AASB 2005-11 [9]
18-19	amended	AASB 2008-3 [32]
21-21B	amended	AASB 2008-3 [32]
22	amended	AASB 2007-4 [43]
	amended	AASB 2007-8 [46]
	amended	AASB 2008-3 [32]
23	amended	AASB 2007-8 [47]
26	amended	AASB 2008-3 [32]
32A (and preceding heading)	added	AASB 2008-3 [33]
33	amended	AASB 2007-4 [39]
37 (and preceding heading)	amended	AASB 2007-4 [43]
51A (examples)	amended	AASB 2010-8 [7]
51B-51E	added	AASB 2010-8 [7]
52	amended	AASB 2007-8 [48]
	amended	AASB 2009-6 [40]
	renumbered as 51A	AASB 2010-8 [7]
52B	amended	AASB 2009-12 [13]
58 (and preceding heading)	amended	AASB 2007-8 [49]
59	amended	AASB 2007-4 [43]
	amended	AASB 2007-8 [46]
60	amended	AASB 2007-4 [43]
	amended	AASB 2007-8 [46, 50]
61 (preceding heading)	amended	AASB 2007-8 [51]
61	deleted	AASB 2007-8 [52]
61A	added	AASB 2007-8 [52]
62	amended	AASB 2007-4 [43]
	amended	AASB 2007-8 [53]
	amended	AASB 2009-6 [41]
62A	added	AASB 2007-8 [53]
	amended	AASB 2009-6 [42]
63	amended	AASB 2007-8 [53]

Paragraph affected	How affected	By ... [paragraph]
64	amended	AASB 2009-6 [43]
65	amended	AASB 2007-8 [46, 54]
66-67	amended	AASB 2008-3 [34]
68	amended	AASB 2008-3 [34, 35]
68B	amended	AASB 2007-4 [43]
68C	amended	AASB 2007-8 [55]
72	amended	AASB 2007-4 [43]
77	amended	AASB 2007-8 [56]
	amended	AASB 2011-9 [18]
77A	added	AASB 2007-8 [56]
	deleted	AASB 2011-9 [18]
78	amended	AASB 2007-4 [43]
	amended	AASB 2007-10 [57]
Aus80.1	deleted	AASB 2007-4 [40]
81	amended	AASB 2007-4 [41]
	amended	AASB 2007-8 [46, 57]
	amended	AASB 2007-10 [58]
	amended	AASB 2008-3 [36]
87	amended	AASB 2007-10 [57]
88	amended	AASB 2007-8 [6]
	amended	AASB 2009-12 [13]
89 (preceding heading)	amended	Erratum, Oct 2009 [2]
92	note added	AASB 2007-8 [58]
93-94	added	AASB 2008-3 [37]
95	note added	AASB 2008-3 [37]
98	added	AASB 2010-8 [7]
98B	added	AASB 2011-9 [18]
99 (preceding heading and note)	added	AASB 2010-8 [8]

Table of Amendments to Illustrative Examples

Paragraph affected	How affected	By ... [paragraph]
Examples of Temporary Differences		
A, title, rubric, heading	amended	AASB 2010-5 [26-27]
A, 1 (preceding heading)	amended	AASB 2009-6 [44]
A, 11	amended	AASB 2009-6 [44]
A, 12	amended	AASB 2008-3 [38]
A, 18	amended	AASB 2009-6 [44]
B, 1 (preceding heading)	amended	AASB 2009-6 [44]
B, 9	amended	AASB 2008-3 [39]
Illustrative Computations and Presentation		
Heading	deleted	AASB 2010-5 [28]
Rubric	amended	AASB 2009-6 [45]
	amended	AASB 2010-5 [28]
Example 1	amended	AASB 2009-6 [45]
Example 2	amended	AASB 2007-4 [42]
	amended	AASB 2009-6 [45]
Example 3	amended	AASB 2009-6 [45]
	amended	AASB 2008-3 [40]
Example 4	amended	AASB 2009-6 [45]

Paragraph affected	How affected	By ... [paragraph]
Example 6	added	AASB 2008-3 [41]
	amended	AASB 2009-7 [12]

General Terminology Amendments

The following amendments are not shown in the above Tables of Amendments:

References to 'financial report(s)' were amended to 'financial statements' by AASB 2007-8 and AASB 2007-10, except in relation to specific Corporations Act references.

References to 'income statement' and 'balance sheet' were amended to 'statement of comprehensive income' and 'statement of financial position' respectively by AASB 2007-8.

References to 'reporting date' and 'each reporting date' were amended to 'end of the reporting period' and 'the end of each reporting period' respectively by AASB 2007-8.

Comparison with IAS 12

AASB 112 and IAS 12

AASB 112 *Income Taxes* as amended incorporates IAS 12 *Income Taxes* as issued and amended by the International Accounting Standards Board (IASB). Paragraphs that have been added to this Standard (and do not appear in the text of IAS 12) are identified with the prefix "Aus", followed by the number of the relevant IASB paragraph and decimal numbering. Paragraphs that apply only to not-for-profit entities begin by identifying their limited applicability.

Compliance with IAS 12

Entities that comply with AASB 112 as amended will simultaneously be in compliance with IAS 12 as amended.

Accounting Standard AASB 112

The Australian Accounting Standards Board made Accounting Standard AASB 112 *Income Taxes* under section 334 of the *Corporations Act 2001* on 15 July 2004.

This compiled version of AASB 112 applies to annual reporting periods beginning on or after 1 January 2012 but before 1 January 2013. It incorporates relevant amendments contained in other AASB Standards made by the AASB and other decisions of the AASB up to and including 27 October 2010 (see Compilation Details).

Accounting Standard AASB 112

Income Taxes

Objective

The objective of this Standard is to prescribe the accounting treatment for income taxes. The principal issue in accounting for income taxes is how to account for the current and future tax consequences of:

(a)   the future recovery (settlement) of the carrying amount of assets (liabilities) that are recognised in an entity's statement of financial position; and

(b)   transactions and other events of the current period that are recognised in an entity's financial statements.

It is inherent in the recognition of an asset or liability that the reporting entity expects to recover or settle the carrying amount of that asset or liability. If it is probable that recovery or settlement of that carrying amount will make future tax payments larger (smaller) than they would be if such recovery or settlement were to have no tax consequences, this Standard requires an entity to recognise a deferred tax liability (deferred tax asset), with certain limited exceptions.

This Standard requires an entity to account for the tax consequences of transactions and other events in the same way that it accounts for the transactions and other events themselves.

Thus, for transactions and other events recognised in profit or loss, any related tax effects are also recognised in profit or loss. For transactions and other events recognised outside profit or loss (either in other comprehensive income or directly in equity), any related tax effects are also recognised outside profit or loss (either in other comprehensive income or directly in equity, respectively). Similarly, the recognition of deferred tax assets and liabilities in a business combination affects the amount of goodwill arising in that business combination or the amount of the bargain purchase gain recognised.

This Standard also deals with the recognition of deferred tax assets arising from unused tax losses or unused tax credits, the presentation of income taxes in the financial statements and the disclosure of information relating to income taxes.

Application

Aus1.1   This Standard applies to:

(a)   each entity that is required to prepare financial reports in accordance with Part 2M.3 of the Corporations Act and that is a reporting entity;

(b)   general purpose financial statements of each other reporting entity; and

(c)   financial statements that are, or are held out to be, general purpose financial statements.

Aus1.2   This Standard applies to annual reporting periods beginning on or after 1 January 2005.
[Note: For application dates of paragraphs changed or added by an amending Standard, see Compilation Details.]

Aus1.3   This Standard shall not be applied to annual reporting periods beginning before 1 January 2005.

Aus1.4   The requirements specified in this Standard apply to the financial statements where information resulting from their application is material in accordance with AASB 1031 *Materiality*.

Aus1.5   When applicable, this Standard supersedes:

(a)   AASB 1020 *Accounting for Income Tax (Tax-effect Accounting)* as notified in the *Commonwealth of Australia Gazette* No S 338, 30 October 1989;

(b)   AAS 3 *Accounting for Income Tax (Tax-effect Accounting)* as issued in November 1989;

(c)   AASB 1020 *Income Taxes* as notified in the *Commonwealth of Australia Gazette* No S 595, 9 December 1999, and as amended by AASB 1020B *Amendments to Accounting Standard AASB 1020 and Australian Accounting Standard AAS 3*, which was notified in the *Commonwealth of Australia Gazette* No S 436, 19 November 2002;

(d)   AAS 3 *Income Taxes* as issued in December 1999 and as amended by AASB 1020B *Amendments to Accounting Standard AASB 1020 and Australian Accounting Standard AAS 3*, which was notified in the *Commonwealth of Australia Gazette* No S 436, 19 November 2002; and

(e)   Interpretation 121 *Income Taxes – Recovery of Revalued Non-Depreciable Assets.*

Aus1.6   Until superseded by this Standard, the following Standards remain applicable:

(a)   AASB 1020 and AAS 3 (issued in 1989); or

(b)   AASB 1020 and AAS 3 (issued in 1999, and amended in 2002).

Aus1.7   Notice of this Standard was published in the *Commonwealth of Australia Gazette* No S 294, 22 July 2004.

Scope

1   **This Standard shall be applied in accounting for income taxes.**

2   For the purposes of this Standard, income taxes include all domestic and foreign taxes which are based on *taxable profits*. Income taxes also include taxes, such as withholding taxes, which are payable by a subsidiary, associate or joint venture on distributions to the reporting entity.

Aus2.1   For public sector entities and for the purposes of this Standard, income taxes also include forms of income tax that may be payable by a public sector entity under their own enabling legislation or other authority. These forms of income tax are often referred to as "income tax equivalents".

3   [Deleted by the IASB]

4   This Standard does not deal with the methods of accounting for government grants (see AASB 120 *Accounting for Government Grants and Disclosure of Government Assistance* or, for not-for-profit entities, AASB 1004 *Contributions*) or investment tax credits. However, this Standard does deal with the accounting for *temporary differences* that may arise from such grants or investment tax credits.

Definitions

5   **The following terms are used in this Standard with the meanings specified.**

Accounting profit **is profit or loss for a period before deducting tax expense.**

Current tax **is the amount of income taxes payable (recoverable) in respect of the taxable profit (tax loss) for a period.**

Deferred tax assets **are the amounts of income taxes recoverable in future periods in respect of:**

    (a)   **deductible temporary differences;**

    (b)   **the carryforward of unused tax losses; and**

    (c)   **the carryforward of unused tax credits.**

Deferred tax liabilities **are the amounts of income taxes payable in future periods in respect of taxable temporary differences.**

Taxable profit (tax loss) **is the profit (loss) for a period, determined in accordance with the rules established by the taxation authorities, upon which income taxes are payable (recoverable).**

The *tax base* **of an asset or liability is the amount attributed to that asset or liability for tax purposes.**

Tax expense (tax income) **is the aggregate amount included in the determination of profit or loss for the period in respect of current tax and deferred tax.**

Temporary differences **are differences between the carrying amount of an asset or liability in the statement of financial position and its tax base. Temporary differences may be either:**

    (a)   *deductible temporary differences*, **which are temporary differences that will result in amounts that are deductible in determining taxable profit (tax loss) of future periods when the carrying amount of the asset or liability is recovered or settled; or**

    (b)   *taxable temporary differences*, **which are temporary differences that will result in taxable amounts in determining taxable profit (tax loss) of future periods when the carrying amount of the asset or liability is recovered or settled.**

6   *Tax expense (tax income)* comprises *current tax* expense (current tax income) and deferred tax expense (deferred tax income).

Tax Base

7   The *tax base* of an asset is the amount that will be deductible for tax purposes against any taxable economic benefits that will flow to an entity when it recovers the carrying amount of the asset. If those economic benefits will not be taxable, the tax base of the asset is equal to its carrying amount.

Examples

1   A machine cost 100. For tax purposes, depreciation of 30 has already been deducted in the current and prior periods and the remaining cost will be deductible in future periods, either as depreciation or through a deduction on disposal. Revenue generated by using the machine is taxable, any gain on disposal of the machine will be taxable and any loss on disposal will be deductible for tax purposes. *The tax base of the machine is 70.*

2   Interest receivable has a carrying amount of 100. The related interest revenue will be taxed on a cash basis. *The tax base of the interest receivable is nil.*

3   Trade receivables have a carrying amount of 100. The related revenue has already been included in taxable profit (tax loss). *The tax base of the trade receivables is 100.*

4   Dividends receivable from a subsidiary have a carrying amount of 100. The dividends are not taxable. *In substance, the entire carrying amount of the asset is deductible against the economic benefits. Consequently, the tax base of the dividends receivable is 100.*[1]

5   A loan receivable has a carrying amount of 100. The repayment of the loan will have no tax consequences. *The tax base of the loan is 100.*

---

8   The tax base of a liability is its carrying amount, less any amount that will be deductible for tax purposes in respect of that liability in future periods. In the case of revenue which is received in advance, the tax base of the resulting liability is its carrying amount, less any amount of the revenue that will not be taxable in future periods.

Examples

1   Current liabilities include accrued expenses with a carrying amount of 100. The related expense will be deducted for tax purposes on a cash basis. *The tax base of the accrued expenses is nil.*

2   Current liabilities include interest revenue received in advance, with a carrying amount of 100. The related interest revenue was taxed on a cash basis. *The tax base of the interest received in advance is nil.*

3   Current liabilities include accrued expenses with a carrying amount of 100. The related expense has already been deducted for tax purposes. *The tax base of the accrued expenses is 100.*

4   Current liabilities include accrued fines and penalties with a carrying amount of 100. Fines and penalties are not deductible for tax purposes. *The tax base of the accrued fines and penalties is 100.*[2]

5   A loan payable has a carrying amount of 100. The repayment of the loan will have no tax consequences. *The tax base of the loan is 100.*

---

9   Some items have a tax base but are not recognised as assets and liabilities in the statement of financial position. For example, research costs are recognised as an expense in determining *accounting profit* in the period in which they are incurred but may not be permitted as a deduction in determining taxable profit (tax loss) until a later period. The difference between the tax base of the research costs, being the amount the taxation authorities will permit as a deduction in future periods, and the carrying amount of nil is a *deductible temporary difference* that results in a *deferred tax asset*.

10   Where the tax base of an asset or liability is not immediately apparent, it is helpful to consider the fundamental principle upon which this Standard is based: that an entity shall, with certain limited exceptions, recognise a *deferred tax liability* (asset) whenever recovery or settlement of the carrying amount of an asset or liability would make future tax payments larger (smaller) than they would be if such recovery or settlement were to have no tax consequences. Example C following paragraph 51A illustrates circumstances

---

1   Under this analysis, there is no taxable temporary difference. An alternative analysis is that dividends receivable have a tax base of nil and that a tax rate of nil is applied to the resulting temporary difference of 100. Under both analyses, there is no deferred tax liability.

2   Under this analysis, there is no deductible temporary difference. An alternative analysis is that fines and penalties payable have a tax base of nil and that a tax rate of nil is applied to the resulting temporary difference of 100. Under both analyses, there is no deferred tax asset.

when it may be helpful to consider this fundamental principle, for example, when the tax base of an asset or liability depends on the expected manner of recovery or settlement.

11   In consolidated financial statements, temporary differences are determined by comparing the carrying amounts of assets and liabilities in the consolidated financial statements with the appropriate tax base. The tax base is determined by reference to a consolidated tax return in those jurisdictions in which such a return is filed. In other jurisdictions, the tax base is determined by reference to the tax returns of each entity in the group.

Recognition of Current Tax Liabilities and Current Tax Assets

12   **Current tax for current and prior periods shall, to the extent unpaid, be recognised as a liability. If the amount already paid in respect of current and prior periods exceeds the amount due for those periods, the excess shall be recognised as an asset.**

13   **The benefit relating to a tax loss that can be carried back to recover current tax of a previous period shall be recognised as an asset.**

14   When a tax loss is used to recover current tax of a previous period, an entity recognises the benefit as an asset in the period in which the tax loss occurs because it is probable that the benefit will flow to the entity and the benefit can be reliably measured.

Recognition of Deferred Tax Liabilities and Deferred Tax Assets

Taxable Temporary Differences

15   **A deferred tax liability shall be recognised for all** *taxable temporary differences*, **except to the extent that the deferred tax liability arises from:**

    (a)   the initial recognition of goodwill; or

    (b)   the initial recognition of an asset or liability in a transaction which:

        (i)   is not a business combination; and

        (ii)   at the time of the transaction, affects neither accounting profit nor taxable profit (tax loss).

    However, for taxable temporary differences associated with investments in subsidiaries, branches and associates, and interests in joint ventures, a deferred tax liability shall be recognised in accordance with paragraph 39.

16   It is inherent in the recognition of an asset that its carrying amount will be recovered in the form of economic benefits that flow to the entity in future periods. When the carrying amount of the asset exceeds its tax base, the amount of taxable economic benefits will exceed the amount that will be allowed as a deduction for tax purposes. This difference is a taxable temporary difference and the obligation to pay the resulting income taxes in future periods is a deferred tax liability. As the entity recovers the carrying amount of the asset, the taxable temporary difference will reverse and the entity will have taxable profit. This makes it probable that economic benefits will flow from the entity in the form of tax payments. Therefore, this Standard requires the recognition of all deferred tax liabilities, except in certain circumstances described in paragraphs 15 and 39.

Example

An asset which cost 150 has a carrying amount of 100. Cumulative depreciation for tax purposes is 90 and the tax rate is 25%.

The tax base of the asset is 60 (cost of 150 less cumulative tax depreciation of 90). To recover the carrying amount of 100, the entity must earn taxable income of 100, but will only be able to deduct tax depreciation of 60.

Consequently, the entity will pay income taxes of 10 (40 at 25%) when it recovers the carrying amount of the asset. The difference between the carrying amount of 100 and the tax base of 60 is a taxable temporary difference of 40. Therefore, the entity recognises a deferred tax liability of 10 (40 at 25%) representing the income taxes that it will pay when it recovers the carrying amount of the asset.

---

17   Some temporary differences arise when income or expense is included in accounting profit in one period but is included in taxable profit in a different period. Such temporary differences are often described as timing differences. The following are examples of temporary differences of this kind which are taxable temporary differences and which therefore result in deferred tax liabilities.

(a)   Interest revenue is included in accounting profit on a time proportion basis but may, in some jurisdictions, be included in taxable profit when cash is collected. The tax base of any receivable recognised in the statement of financial position with respect to such revenues is nil because the revenues do not affect taxable profit until cash is collected.

(b)   Depreciation used in determining taxable profit (tax loss) may differ from that used in determining accounting profit. The temporary difference is the difference between the carrying amount of the asset and its tax base which is the original cost of the asset less all deductions in respect of that asset permitted by the taxation authorities in determining taxable profit of the current and prior periods. A taxable temporary difference arises, and results in a deferred tax liability, when tax depreciation is accelerated (if tax depreciation is less rapid than accounting depreciation, a deductible temporary difference arises, and results in a deferred tax asset).

(c)   Development costs may be capitalised and amortised over future periods in determining accounting profit but deducted in determining taxable profit in the period in which they are incurred. Such development costs have a tax base of nil as they have already been deducted from taxable profit. The temporary difference is the difference between the carrying amount of the development costs and their tax base of nil.

18   Temporary differences also arise when:

(a)   the identifiable assets acquired and liabilities assumed in a business combination are recognised at their fair values in accordance with AASB 3 *Business Combinations*, but no equivalent adjustment is made for tax purposes (see paragraph 19);

(b)   assets are revalued and no equivalent adjustment is made for tax purposes (see paragraph 20);

(c)   goodwill arises in a business combination (see paragraph 21);

(d)   the tax base of an asset or liability on initial recognition differs from its initial carrying amount, for example, when an entity benefits from non-taxable government grants related to assets (see paragraphs 22, 33 and Aus33.1); or

(e)   the carrying amount of investments in subsidiaries, branches and associates or interests in joint ventures becomes different from the tax base of the investment or interest (see paragraphs 38-45).

Business Combinations

19   With limited exceptions, the identifiable assets acquired and liabilities assumed in a business combination are recognised at their fair values at the acquisition date. Temporary differences arise when the tax bases of the identifiable assets acquired and liabilities assumed are not affected by the business combination or are affected differently. For example, when the carrying amount of an asset is increased to fair value but the tax base of the asset remains at cost to the previous owner, a taxable temporary difference arises which results in a deferred tax liability. The resulting deferred tax liability affects goodwill (see paragraph 66).

Assets Carried at Fair Value

20   Australian Accounting Standards permit or require certain assets to be carried at fair value or to be revalued (see, for example, AASB 116 *Property, Plant and Equipment*, AASB 138 *Intangible Assets*, AASB 139 *Financial Instruments: Recognition and Measurement* and AASB 140 *Investment Property*). In some jurisdictions, the revaluation or other restatement of an asset to fair value affects taxable profit (tax loss) for the current period. As a result, the tax base of the asset is adjusted and no temporary difference arises.

In other jurisdictions, the revaluation or restatement of an asset does not affect taxable profit in the period of the revaluation or restatement and, consequently, the tax base of the asset is not adjusted. Nevertheless, the future recovery of the carrying amount will result in a taxable flow of economic benefits to the entity and the amount that will be deductible for tax purposes will differ from the amount of those economic benefits. The difference between the carrying amount of a revalued asset and its tax base is a temporary difference and gives rise to a deferred tax liability or asset. This is true even if:

(a) the entity does not intend to dispose of the asset. In such cases, the revalued carrying amount of the asset will be recovered through use and this will generate taxable income which exceeds the depreciation that will be allowable for tax purposes in future periods; or

(b) tax on capital gains is deferred if the proceeds of the disposal of the asset are invested in similar assets. In such cases, the tax will ultimately become payable on sale or use of the similar assets.

Goodwill

21 Goodwill arising in a business combination is measured as the excess of (a) over (b) below:

(a) the aggregate of:

(i) the consideration transferred measured in accordance with AASB 3, which generally requires acquisition-date fair value;

(ii) the amount of any non-controlling interest in the acquiree recognised in accordance with AASB 3; and

(iii) in a business combination achieved in stages, the acquisition-date fair value of the acquirer's previously held equity interest in the acquiree.

(b) the net of the acquisition-date amounts of the identifiable assets acquired and liabilities assumed measured in accordance with AASB 3.

Many taxation authorities do not allow reductions in the carrying amount of goodwill as a deductible expense in determining taxable profit. Moreover, in such jurisdictions, the cost of goodwill is often not deductible when a subsidiary disposes of its underlying business. In such jurisdictions, goodwill has a tax base of nil. Any difference between the carrying amount of goodwill and its tax base of nil is a taxable temporary difference. However, this Standard does not permit the recognition of the resulting deferred tax liability because goodwill is measured as a residual and the recognition of the deferred tax liability would increase the carrying amount of goodwill.

21A Subsequent reductions in a deferred tax liability that is unrecognised because it arises from the initial recognition of goodwill are also regarded as arising from the initial recognition of goodwill and are therefore not recognised under paragraph 15(a). For example, if in a business combination an entity recognises goodwill of CU100 that has a tax base of nil, paragraph 15(a) prohibits the entity from recognising the resulting deferred tax liability. If the entity subsequently recognises an impairment loss of CU20 for that goodwill, the amount of the taxable temporary difference relating to the goodwill is reduced from CU100 to CU80, with a resulting decrease in the value of the unrecognised deferred tax liability. That decrease in the value of the unrecognised deferred tax liability is also regarded as relating to the initial recognition of the goodwill and is therefore prohibited from being recognised under paragraph 15(a).

21B Deferred tax liabilities for taxable temporary differences relating to goodwill are, however, recognised to the extent they do not arise from the initial recognition of goodwill. For example, if in a business combination an entity recognises goodwill of CU100 that is deductible for tax purposes at a rate of 20 per cent per year starting in the year of acquisition, the tax base of the goodwill is CU100 on initial recognition and CU80 at the end of the year of acquisition. If the carrying amount of goodwill at the end of the year of acquisition remains unchanged at CU100, a taxable temporary difference of CU20 arises at the end of that year. Because that taxable temporary difference does not relate to the initial recognition of the goodwill, the resulting deferred tax liability is recognised.

Initial Recognition of an Asset or Liability

22   A temporary difference may arise on initial recognition of an asset or liability, for example if part or all of the cost of an asset will not be deductible for tax purposes. The method of accounting for such a temporary difference depends on the nature of the transaction that led to the initial recognition of the asset or liability:

(a)   in a business combination, an entity recognises any deferred tax liability or asset and this affects the amount of goodwill or bargain purchase gain it recognises (see paragraph 19).

(b)   If the transaction affects either accounting profit or taxable profit, an entity recognises any deferred tax liability or asset and recognises the resulting deferred tax expense or income in profit or loss (see paragraph 59).

(c)   If the transaction is not a business combination, and affects neither accounting profit nor taxable profit, an entity would, in the absence of the exemption provided by paragraphs 15 and 24, recognise the resulting deferred tax liability or asset and adjust the carrying amount of the asset or liability by the same amount. Such adjustments would make the financial statements less transparent. Therefore, this Standard does not permit an entity to recognise the resulting deferred tax liability or asset, either on initial recognition or subsequently (see example below). Furthermore, an entity does not recognise subsequent changes in the unrecognised deferred tax liability or asset as the asset is depreciated.

Example Illustrating Paragraph 22(c)

An entity intends to use an asset which cost 1,000 throughout its useful life of five years and then dispose of it for a residual value of nil. The tax rate is 40%. Depreciation of the asset is not deductible for tax purposes. On disposal, any capital gain would not be taxable and any capital loss would not be deductible.

As it recovers the carrying amount of the asset, the entity will earn taxable income of 1,000 and pay tax of 400. The entity does not recognise the resulting deferred tax liability of 400 because it results from the initial recognition of the asset.

In the following year, the carrying amount of the asset is 800. In earning taxable income of 800, the entity will pay tax of 320. The entity does not recognise the deferred tax liability of 320 because it results from the initial recognition of the asset.

---

23   In accordance with AASB 132 *Financial Instruments: Presentation* the issuer of a compound financial instrument (for example, a convertible bond) classifies the instrument's liability component as a liability and the equity component as equity. In some jurisdictions, the tax base of the liability component on initial recognition is equal to the initial carrying amount of the sum of the liability and equity components. The resulting taxable temporary difference arises from the initial recognition of the equity component separately from the liability component. Therefore, the exception set out in paragraph 15(b) does not apply. Consequently, an entity recognises the resulting deferred tax liability. In accordance with paragraph 61A, the deferred tax is charged directly to the carrying amount of the equity component. In accordance with paragraph 58, subsequent changes in the deferred tax liability are recognised in profit or loss as deferred tax expense (income).

Deductible Temporary Differences

24   **A deferred tax asset shall be recognised for all deductible temporary differences to the extent that it is probable that taxable profit will be available against which the deductible temporary difference can be utilised, unless the deferred tax asset arises from the initial recognition of an asset or liability in a transaction that:**

(a)   **is not a business combination; and**

(b)   **at the time of the transaction, affects neither accounting profit nor taxable profit (tax loss).**

However, for deductible temporary differences associated with investments in subsidiaries, branches and associates, and interests in joint ventures, a deferred tax asset shall be recognised in accordance with paragraph 44.

25 It is inherent in the recognition of a liability that the carrying amount will be settled in future periods through an outflow from the entity of resources embodying economic benefits. When resources flow from the entity, part or all of their amounts may be deductible in determining taxable profit of a period later than the period in which the liability is recognised. In such cases, a temporary difference exists between the carrying amount of the liability and its tax base. Accordingly, a deferred tax asset arises in respect of the income taxes that will be recoverable in the future periods when that part of the liability is allowed as a deduction in determining taxable profit. Similarly, if the carrying amount of an asset is less than its tax base, the difference gives rise to a deferred tax asset in respect of the income taxes that will be recoverable in future periods.

Example

An entity recognises a liability of 100 for accrued product warranty costs. For tax purposes, the product warranty costs will not be deductible until the entity pays claims. The tax rate is 25%.

The tax base of the liability is nil (carrying amount of 100, less the amount that will be deductible for tax purposes in respect of that liability in future periods). In settling the liability for its carrying amount, the entity will reduce its future taxable profit by an amount of 100 and, consequently, reduce its future tax payments by 25 (100 at 25%). The difference between the carrying amount of 100 and the tax base of nil is a deductible temporary difference of 100. Therefore, the entity recognises a deferred tax asset of 25 (100 at 25%), provided that it is probable that the entity will earn sufficient taxable profit in future periods to benefit from a reduction in tax payments.

---

26 The following are examples of deductible temporary differences that result in deferred tax assets:

(a) retirement benefit costs may be deducted in determining accounting profit as service is provided by the employee, but deducted in determining taxable profit either when contributions are paid to a fund by the entity or when retirement benefits are paid by the entity. A temporary difference exists between the carrying amount of the liability and its tax base; the tax base of the liability is usually nil. Such a deductible temporary difference results in a deferred tax asset as economic benefits will flow to the entity in the form of a deduction from taxable profits when contributions or retirement benefits are paid;

(b) research costs are recognised as an expense in determining accounting profit in the period in which they are incurred but may not be permitted as a deduction in determining taxable profit (tax loss) until a later period. The difference between the tax base of the research costs, being the amount the taxation authorities will permit as a deduction in future periods, and the carrying amount of nil is a deductible temporary difference that results in a deferred tax asset;

(c) with limited exceptions, an entity recognises the identifiable assets acquired and liabilities assumed in a business combination at their fair values at the acquisition date. When a liability assumed is recognised at the acquisition date but the related costs are not deducted in determining taxable profits until a later period, a deductible temporary difference arises which results in a deferred tax asset. A deferred tax asset also arises when the fair value of an identifiable asset acquired is less than its tax base. In both cases, the resulting deferred tax asset affects goodwill (see paragraph 66); and

(d) certain assets may be carried at fair value, or may be revalued, without an equivalent adjustment being made for tax purposes (see paragraph 20). A deductible temporary difference arises if the tax base of the asset exceeds its carrying amount.

27 The reversal of deductible temporary differences results in deductions in determining taxable profits of future periods. However, economic benefits in the form of reductions in tax payments will flow to the entity only if it earns sufficient taxable profits against which the deductions can be offset. Therefore, an entity recognises deferred tax assets only when it is probable that taxable profits will be available against which the deductible temporary differences can be utilised.

28   It is probable that taxable profit will be available against which a deductible temporary difference can be utilised when there are sufficient taxable temporary differences relating to the same taxation authority and the same taxable entity which are expected to reverse:

    (a)   in the same period as the expected reversal of the deductible temporary difference; or

    (b)   in periods into which a tax loss arising from the deferred tax asset can be carried back or forward.

In such circumstances, the deferred tax asset is recognised in the period in which the deductible temporary differences arise.

29   When there are insufficient taxable temporary differences relating to the same taxation authority and the same taxable entity, the deferred tax asset is recognised to the extent that:

    (a)   it is probable that the entity will have sufficient taxable profit relating to the same taxation authority and the same taxable entity in the same period as the reversal of the deductible temporary difference (or in the periods into which a tax loss arising from the deferred tax asset can be carried back or forward). In evaluating whether it will have sufficient taxable profit in future periods, an entity ignores taxable amounts arising from deductible temporary differences that are expected to originate in future periods, because the deferred tax asset arising from these deductible temporary differences will itself require future taxable profit in order to be utilised; or

    (b)   tax planning opportunities are available to the entity that will create taxable profit in appropriate periods.

30   Tax planning opportunities are actions that the entity would take in order to create or increase taxable income in a particular period before the expiry of a tax loss or tax credit carryforward. For example, in some jurisdictions, taxable profit may be created or increased by:

    (a)   electing to have interest income taxed on either a received or receivable basis;

    (b)   deferring the claim for certain deductions from taxable profit;

    (c)   selling, and perhaps leasing back, assets that have appreciated but for which the tax base has not been adjusted to reflect such appreciation; and

    (d)   selling an asset that generates non-taxable income (such as, in some jurisdictions, a government bond) in order to purchase another investment that generates taxable income.

Where tax planning opportunities advance taxable profit from a later period to an earlier period, the utilisation of a tax loss or tax credit carryforward still depends on the existence of future taxable profit from sources other than future originating temporary differences.

31   When an entity has a history of recent losses, the entity considers the guidance in paragraphs 35 and 36.

32   [Deleted by the IASB]

Goodwill

32A   If the carrying amount of goodwill arising in a business combination is less than its tax base, the difference gives rise to a deferred tax asset. The deferred tax asset arising from the initial recognition of goodwill shall be recognised as part of the accounting for a business combination to the extent that it is probable that taxable profit will be available against which the deductible temporary difference could be utilised.

Initial Recognition of an Asset or Liability

33   One case when a deferred tax asset arises on initial recognition of an asset is when a non taxable government grant related to an asset is deducted in arriving at the carrying amount of the asset but, for tax purposes, is not deducted from the asset's depreciable amount (in other words its tax base); the carrying amount of the asset is less than its tax base and this gives rise to a deductible temporary difference. Government grants may also be set up as deferred income in which case the difference between the deferred income and its

tax base of nil is a deductible temporary difference. Whichever method of presentation an entity adopts, the entity does not recognise the resulting deferred tax asset, for the reason given in paragraph 22.

Aus33.1   In respect of not-for-profit entities, a deferred tax asset will not arise on a non taxable government grant relating to an asset. Under AASB 1004 *Contributions*, a not-for-profit entity accounts for the receipt of non taxable government grants as income rather than as deferred income when those grants are controlled by the entity. As such, a temporary difference does not arise.

Unused Tax Losses and Unused Tax Credits

34   **A deferred tax asset shall be recognised for the carryforward of unused tax losses and unused tax credits to the extent that it is probable that future taxable profit will be available against which the unused tax losses and unused tax credits can be utilised.**

35   The criteria for recognising deferred tax assets arising from the carryforward of unused tax losses and tax credits are the same as the criteria for recognising deferred tax assets arising from deductible temporary differences. However, the existence of unused tax losses is strong evidence that future taxable profit may not be available. Therefore, when an entity has a history of recent losses, the entity recognises a deferred tax asset arising from unused tax losses or tax credits only to the extent that the entity has sufficient taxable temporary differences or there is convincing other evidence that sufficient taxable profit will be available against which the unused tax losses or unused tax credits can be utilised by the entity. In such circumstances, paragraph 82 requires disclosure of the amount of the deferred tax asset and the nature of the evidence supporting its recognition.

36   An entity considers the following criteria in assessing the probability that taxable profit will be available against which the unused tax losses or unused tax credits can be utilised:

(a)   whether the entity has sufficient taxable temporary differences relating to the same taxation authority and the same taxable entity, which will result in taxable amounts against which the unused tax losses or unused tax credits can be utilised before they expire;

(b)   whether it is probable that the entity will have taxable profits before the unused tax losses or unused tax credits expire;

(c)   whether the unused tax losses result from identifiable causes which are unlikely to recur; and

(d)   whether tax planning opportunities (see paragraph 30) are available to the entity that will create taxable profit in the period in which the unused tax losses or unused tax credits can be utilised.

To the extent that it is not probable that taxable profit will be available against which the unused tax losses or unused tax credits can be utilised, the deferred tax asset is not recognised.

Reassessment of Unrecognised Deferred Tax Assets

37   At the end of each reporting period, an entity reassesses unrecognised deferred tax assets. The entity recognises a previously unrecognised deferred tax asset to the extent that it has become probable that future taxable profit will allow the deferred tax asset to be recovered. For example, an improvement in trading conditions may make it more probable that the entity will be able to generate sufficient taxable profit in the future for the deferred tax asset to meet the recognition criteria set out in paragraph 24 or 34. Another example is when an entity reassesses deferred tax assets at the date of a business combination or subsequently (see paragraphs 67 and 68).

Investments in Subsidiaries, Branches and Associates and Interests in Joint Ventures

38   Temporary differences arise when the carrying amount of investments in subsidiaries, branches and associates or interests in joint ventures (namely the parent or investor's share of the net assets of the subsidiary, branch, associate or investee, including the carrying amount of goodwill) becomes different from the tax base (which is often cost) of the

investment or interest. Such differences may arise in a number of different circumstances, for example:

(a)   the existence of undistributed profits of subsidiaries, branches, associates and joint ventures;

(b)   changes in foreign exchange rates when a parent and its subsidiary are based in different countries; and

(c)   a reduction in the carrying amount of an investment in an associate to its recoverable amount.

In consolidated financial statements, the temporary difference may be different from the temporary difference associated with that investment in the parent's separate financial statements if the parent carries the investment in its separate financial statements at cost or revalued amount.

39   **An entity shall recognise a deferred tax liability for all taxable temporary differences associated with investments in subsidiaries, branches and associates, and interests in joint ventures, except to the extent that both of the following conditions are satisfied:**

         (a)   the parent, investor or venturer is able to control the timing of the reversal of the temporary difference; and

         (b)   it is probable that the temporary difference will not reverse in the foreseeable future.

40   As a parent controls the dividend policy of its subsidiary, it is able to control the timing of the reversal of temporary differences associated with that investment (including the temporary differences arising not only from undistributed profits but also from any foreign exchange translation differences). Furthermore, it would often be impracticable to determine the amount of income taxes that would be payable when the temporary difference reverses. Therefore, when the parent has determined that those profits will not be distributed in the foreseeable future, the parent does not recognise a deferred tax liability. The same considerations apply to investments in branches.

41   The non-monetary assets and liabilities of an entity are measured in its functional currency (see AASB 121 *The Effects of Changes in Foreign Exchange Rates*). If the entity's taxable profit or tax loss (and, hence, the tax base of its non-monetary assets and liabilities) is determined in a different currency, changes in the exchange rate give rise to temporary differences that result in a recognised deferred tax liability or (subject to paragraph 24) asset. The resulting deferred tax is charged or credited to profit or loss (see paragraph 58).

42   An investor in an associate does not control that entity and is usually not in a position to determine its dividend policy. Therefore, in the absence of an agreement requiring that the profits of the associate will not be distributed in the foreseeable future, an investor recognises a deferred tax liability arising from taxable temporary differences associated with its investment in the associate. In some cases, an investor may not be able to determine the amount of tax that would be payable if it recovers the cost of its investment in an associate, but can determine that it will equal or exceed a minimum amount. In such cases, the deferred tax liability is measured at this amount.

43   The arrangement between the parties to a joint venture usually deals with the sharing of the profits and identifies whether decisions on such matters require the consent of all the venturers or a specified majority of the venturers. When the venturer can control the sharing of profits and it is probable that the profits will not be distributed in the foreseeable future, a deferred tax liability is not recognised.

44   **An entity shall recognise a deferred tax asset for all deductible temporary differences arising from investments in subsidiaries, branches and associates, and interests in joint ventures, to the extent that, and only to the extent that, it is probable that:**

         (a)   the temporary difference will reverse in the foreseeable future; and

         (b)   taxable profit will be available against which the temporary difference can be utilised.

45   In deciding whether a deferred tax asset is recognised for deductible temporary differences
      associated with its investments in subsidiaries, branches and associates, and its interests
      in joint ventures, an entity considers the guidance set out in paragraphs 28 to 31.

Measurement

**46   Current tax liabilities (assets) for the current and prior periods shall be measured at
      the amount expected to be paid to (recovered from) the taxation authorities, using
      the tax rates (and tax laws) that have been enacted or substantively enacted by the
      end of the reporting period.**

**47   Deferred tax assets and liabilities shall be measured at the tax rates that are expected
      to apply to the period when the asset is realised or the liability is settled, based on tax
      rates (and tax laws) that have been enacted or substantively enacted by the end of
      the reporting period.**

48   Current and deferred tax assets and liabilities are usually measured using the tax rates
      (and tax laws) that have been enacted. However, in some jurisdictions, announcements
      of tax rates (and tax laws) by the government have the substantive effect of actual
      enactment, which may follow the announcement by a period of several months. In these
      circumstances, tax assets and liabilities are measured using the announced tax rate (and
      tax laws).

49   When different tax rates apply to different levels of taxable income, deferred tax assets
      and liabilities are measured using the average rates that are expected to apply to the
      taxable profit (tax loss) of the periods in which the temporary differences are expected to
      reverse.

50   [Deleted by the IASB]

**51   The measurement of deferred tax liabilities and deferred tax assets shall reflect the
      tax consequences that would follow from the manner in which the entity expects, at
      the end of the reporting period, to recover or settle the carrying amount of its assets
      and liabilities.**

51A   In some jurisdictions, the manner in which an entity recovers (settles) the carrying amount
      of an asset (liability) may affect either or both of:

      (a)   the tax rate applicable when the entity recovers (settles) the carrying amount of the
             asset (liability); and

      (b)   the tax base of the asset (liability).

      In such cases, an entity measures deferred tax liabilities and deferred tax assets using
      the tax rate and the tax base that are consistent with the expected manner of recovery or
      settlement.

Example A

An item of property, plant and equipment has a carrying amount of 100 and a tax base of 60. A tax rate of 20%
would apply if the item were sold and a tax rate of 30% would apply to other income.

*The entity recognises a deferred tax liability of 8 (40 at 20%) if it expects to sell the asset without further use
and a deferred tax liability of 12 (40 at 30%) if it expects to retain the asset and recover its carrying amount
through use.*

Example B

An item of property, plant and equipment with a cost of 100 and a carrying amount of 80 is revalued to 150. No equivalent adjustment is made for tax purposes. Cumulative depreciation for tax purposes is 30 and the tax rate is 30%. If the item is sold for more than cost, the cumulative tax depreciation of 30 will be included in taxable income but sale proceeds in excess of cost will not be taxable.

The tax base of the item is 70 and there is a taxable temporary difference of 80. If the entity expects to recover the carrying amount by using the item, it must generate taxable income of 150, but will only be able to deduct depreciation of 70. On this basis, there is a deferred tax liability of 24 (80 at 30%). If the entity expects to recover the carrying amount by selling the item immediately for proceeds of 150, the deferred tax liability is computed as follows:

	Taxable Temporary Difference	Tax Rate	Deferred Tax Liability
Cumulative tax depreciation	30	30%	9
Proceeds in excess of cost	50	nil	–
Total	80		9

(Note: in accordance with paragraph 61A, the additional deferred tax that arises on the revaluation is recognised in other comprehensive income.)

Example C

The facts are as in example B, except that if the item is sold for more than cost, the cumulative tax depreciation will be included in taxable income (taxed at 30%) and the sale proceeds will be taxed at 40%, after deducting an inflation-adjusted cost of 110.

If the entity expects to recover the carrying amount by using the item, it must generate taxable income of 150, but will only be able to deduct depreciation of 70. On this basis, the tax base is 70, there is a taxable temporary difference of 80 and there is a deferred tax liability of 24 (80 at 30%), as in example B.

If the entity expects to recover the carrying amount by selling the item immediately for proceeds of 150, the entity will be able to deduct the indexed cost of 110. The net proceeds of 40 will be taxed at 40%. In addition, the cumulative tax depreciation of 30 will be included in taxable income and taxed at 30%. On this basis, the tax base is 80 (110 less 30), there is a taxable temporary difference of 70 and there is a deferred tax liability of 25 (40 at 40% plus 30 at 30%). If the tax base is not immediately apparent in this example, it may be helpful to consider the fundamental principle set out in paragraph 10.

(Note: in accordance with paragraph 61A, the additional deferred tax that arises on the revaluation is recognised in other comprehensive income.)

51B   If a deferred tax liability or deferred tax asset arises from a non-depreciable asset measured using the revaluation model in AASB 116, the measurement of the deferred tax liability or deferred tax asset shall reflect the tax consequences of recovering the carrying amount of the non-depreciable asset through sale, regardless of the basis of measuring the carrying amount of that asset. Accordingly, if the tax law specifies a tax rate applicable to the taxable amount derived from the sale of an asset that differs from the tax rate applicable to the taxable amount derived from using an asset, the former rate is applied in measuring the deferred tax liability or asset related to a non-depreciable asset.

51C   If a deferred tax liability or asset arises from investment property that is measured using the fair value model in AASB 140, there is a rebuttable presumption that the carrying amount of the investment property will be recovered through sale. Accordingly, unless the presumption is rebutted, the measurement of the deferred tax liability or deferred tax asset shall reflect the tax consequences of recovering the carrying amount of the investment property entirely through sale. This presumption is rebutted if the investment property is depreciable and is held within a business model whose objective is to consume substantially all of the economic benefits embodied in the investment property over time, rather than through sale. If the presumption is rebutted, the requirements of paragraphs 51 and 51A shall be followed.

Example illustrating paragraph 51C

An investment property has a cost of 100 and fair value of 150. It is measured using the fair value model in AASB 140. It comprises land with a cost of 40 and fair value of 60 and a building with a cost of 60 and fair value of 90. The land has an unlimited useful life.

Cumulative depreciation of the building for tax purposes is 30. Unrealised changes in the fair value of the investment property do not affect taxable profit. If the investment property is sold for more than cost, the reversal of the cumulative tax depreciation of 30 will be included in taxable profit and taxed at an ordinary tax rate of 30%. For sales proceeds in excess of cost, tax law specifies tax rates of 25% for assets held for less than two years and 20% for assets held for two years or more.

Because the investment property is measured using the fair value model in AASB 140, there is a rebuttable presumption that the entity will recover the carrying amount of the investment property entirely through sale. If that presumption is not rebutted, the deferred tax reflects the tax consequences of recovering the carrying amount entirely through sale, even if the entity expects to earn rental income from the property before sale.

The tax base of the land if it is sold is 40 and there is a taxable temporary difference of 20 (60 – 40). The tax base of the building if it is sold is 30 (60 – 30) and there is a taxable temporary difference of 60 (90 – 30). As a result, the total taxable temporary difference relating to the investment property is 80 (20 + 60).

In accordance with paragraph 47, the tax rate is the rate expected to apply to the period when the investment property is realised. Thus, the resulting deferred tax liability is computed as follows, if the entity expects to sell the property after holding it for more than two years:

	Taxable Temporary Difference	*Tax Rate*	*Deferred Tax Liability*
Cumulative tax depreciation	30	30%	9
Proceeds in excess of cost	50	20%	10
Total	80		19

If the entity expects to sell the property after holding it for less than two years, the above computation would be amended to apply a rate of 25%, rather than 20%, to the proceeds in excess of cost.

If, instead, the entity holds the building within a business model whose objective is to consume substantially all of the economic benefits embodied in the building over time, rather than through sale, this presumption would be rebutted for the building. However, the land is not depreciable. Therefore the presumption of recovery through sale would not be rebutted for the land. It follows that the deferred tax liability would reflect the tax consequences of recovering the carrying amount of the building through use and the carrying amount of the land through sale.

The tax base of the building if it is used is 30 (60 – 30) and there is a taxable temporary difference of 60 (90 – 30), resulting in a deferred tax liability of 18 (60 at 30%).

The tax base of the land if it is sold is 40 and there is a taxable temporary difference of 20 (60 – 40), resulting in a deferred tax liability of 4 (20 at 20%).

As a result, if the presumption of recovery through sale is rebutted for the building, the deferred tax liability relating to the investment property is 22 (18 + 4).

51D   The rebuttable presumption in paragraph 51C also applies when a deferred tax liability or a deferred tax asset arises from measuring investment property in a business combination if the entity will use the fair value model when subsequently measuring that investment property.

51E   Paragraphs 51B-51D do not change the requirements to apply the principles in paragraphs 24-33 (deductible temporary differences) and paragraphs 34-36 (unused tax losses and unused tax credits) of this Standard when recognising and measuring deferred tax assets.

52A   In some jurisdictions, income taxes are payable at a higher or lower rate if part or all of the net profit or retained earnings is paid out as a dividend to shareholders of the entity. In some other jurisdictions, income taxes may be refundable or payable if part or all of the net profit or retained earnings is paid out as a dividend to shareholders of the entity. In these circumstances, current and deferred tax assets and liabilities are measured at the tax rate applicable to undistributed profits.

52B   In the circumstances described in paragraph 52A, the income tax consequences of dividends are recognised when a liability to pay the dividend is recognised. The income tax consequences of dividends are more directly linked to past transactions or events than to distributions to owners. Therefore, the income tax consequences of dividends are recognised in profit or loss for the period as required by paragraph 58 except to the extent that the income tax consequences of dividends arise from the circumstances described in paragraph 58(a) and (b).

Example Illustrating Paragraphs 52A and 52B

The following example deals with the measurement of current and deferred tax assets and liabilities for an entity in a jurisdiction where income taxes are payable at a higher rate on undistributed profits (50%) with an amount being refundable when profits are distributed. The tax rate on distributed profits is 35%. At the end of the reporting period, 31 December 20X1, the entity does not recognise a liability for dividends proposed or declared after the reporting period. As a result, no dividends are recognised in the year 20X1. Taxable income for 20X1 is 100,000. The net taxable temporary difference for the year 20X1 is 40,000.

The entity recognises a current tax liability and a current income tax expense of 50,000. No asset is recognised for the amount potentially recoverable as a result of future dividends. The entity also recognises a deferred tax liability and deferred tax expense of 20,000 (40,000 at 50%) representing the income taxes that the entity will pay when it recovers or settles the carrying amounts of its assets and liabilities based on the tax rate applicable to undistributed profits.

Subsequently, on 15 March 20X2 the entity recognises dividends of 10,000 from previous operating profits as a liability.

On 15 March 20X2, the entity recognises the recovery of income taxes of 1,500 (15% of the dividends recognised as a liability) as a current tax asset and as a reduction of current income tax expense for 20X2.

---

53   **Deferred tax assets and liabilities shall not be discounted.**

54   The reliable determination of deferred tax assets and liabilities on a discounted basis requires detailed scheduling of the timing of the reversal of each temporary difference. In many cases such scheduling is impracticable or highly complex. Therefore, it is inappropriate to require discounting of deferred tax assets and liabilities. To permit, but not to require, discounting would result in deferred tax assets and liabilities which would not be comparable between entities. Therefore, this Standard does not require or permit the discounting of deferred tax assets and liabilities.

55   Temporary differences are determined by reference to the carrying amount of an asset or liability. This applies even where that carrying amount is itself determined on a discounted basis, for example, in the case of retirement benefit obligations (see AASB 119 *Employee Benefits*).

56   **The carrying amount of a deferred tax asset shall be reviewed at the end of each reporting period. An entity shall reduce the carrying amount of a deferred tax asset to the extent that it is no longer probable that sufficient taxable profit will be available to allow the benefit of part or all of that deferred tax asset to be utilised. Any such reduction shall be reversed to the extent that it becomes probable that sufficient taxable profit will be available.**

Recognition of Current and Deferred Tax

57   Accounting for the current and deferred tax effects of a transaction or other event is consistent with the accounting for the transaction or event itself. Paragraphs 58 to 68C implement this principle.

Items Recognised in Profit or Loss

58   **Current and deferred tax shall be recognised as income or an expense and included in profit or loss for the period, except to the extent that the tax arises from:**

    (a)   a transaction or event which is recognised, in the same or a different period, outside profit or loss, either in other comprehensive income or directly in equity (see paragraphs 61A to 65); or

    (b)   a business combination (see paragraphs 66 to 68).

59   Most deferred tax liabilities and deferred tax assets arise where income or expense is included in accounting profit in one period, but is included in taxable profit (tax loss) in a different period. The resulting deferred tax is recognised in profit or loss. Examples are when:

    (a)   interest, royalty or dividend revenue is received in arrears and is included in accounting profit on a time apportionment basis in accordance with AASB 118 *Revenue*, but is included in taxable profit (tax loss) on a cash basis; and

(b)   costs of intangible assets have been capitalised in accordance with AASB 138 and are being amortised in profit or loss, but were deducted for tax purposes when they were incurred.

60   The carrying amount of deferred tax assets and liabilities may change even though there is no change in the amount of the related temporary differences. This can result, for example, from:

(a)   a change in tax rates or tax laws;

(b)   a reassessment of the recoverability of deferred tax assets; or

(c)   a change in the expected manner of recovery of an asset.

The resulting deferred tax is recognised in profit or loss, except to the extent that it relates to items previously recognised outside profit or loss (see paragraph 63).

Items Recognised Outside Profit or Loss

61   [Deleted by the IASB]

61A   Current tax and deferred tax shall be recognised outside profit or loss if the tax relates to items that are recognised, in the same or a different period, outside profit or loss. Therefore, current tax and deferred tax that relates to items that are recognised, in the same or a different period:

(a)   in other comprehensive income, shall be recognised in other comprehensive income (see paragraph 62); and

(b)   directly in equity, shall be recognised directly in equity (see paragraph 62A).

62   Australian Accounting Standards require or permit particular items to be recognised in other comprehensive income. Examples of such items are:

(a)   a change in carrying amount arising from the revaluation of property, plant and equipment (see AASB 116); and

(b)   [deleted by the IASB]

(c)   exchange differences arising on the translation of the financial statements of a foreign operation (see AASB 121).

(d)   [deleted by the IASB]

62A   Australian Accounting Standards require or permit particular items to be credited or charged directly to equity. Examples of such items are:

(a)   an adjustment to the opening balance of retained earnings resulting from either a change in accounting policy that is applied retrospectively or the correction of an error (see AASB 108 *Accounting Policies, Changes in Accounting Estimates and Errors*); and

(b)   amounts arising on initial recognition of the equity component of a compound financial instrument (see paragraph 23).

63   In exceptional circumstances it may be difficult to determine the amount of current and deferred tax that relates to items recognised outside profit or loss (either in other comprehensive income or directly in equity). This may be the case, for example, when:

(a)   there are graduated rates of income tax and it is impossible to determine the rate at which a specific component of taxable profit (tax loss) has been taxed;

(b)   a change in the tax rate or other tax rules affects a deferred tax asset or liability relating (in whole or in part) to an item that was previously recognised outside profit or loss; or

(c)   an entity determines that a deferred tax asset should be recognised, or should no longer be recognised in full, and the deferred tax asset relates (in whole or in part) to an item that was previously recognised outside profit or loss.

In such cases, the current and deferred tax related to items that are recognised outside profit or loss are based on a reasonable pro rata allocation of the current and deferred tax of the entity in the tax jurisdiction concerned, or other method that achieves a more appropriate allocation in the circumstances.

64   AASB 116 does not specify whether an entity should transfer each year from revaluation surplus to retained earnings an amount equal to the difference between the depreciation or amortisation on a revalued asset and the depreciation or amortisation based on the cost of that asset. If an entity makes such a transfer, the amount transferred is net of any related deferred tax. Similar considerations apply to transfers made on disposal of an item of property, plant or equipment.

65   When an asset is revalued for tax purposes and that revaluation is related to an accounting revaluation of an earlier period, or to one that is expected to be carried out in a future period, the tax effects of both the asset revaluation and the adjustment of the tax base are recognised in other comprehensive income in the periods in which they occur. However, if the revaluation for tax purposes is not related to an accounting revaluation of an earlier period, or to one that is expected to be carried out in a future period, the tax effects of the adjustment of the tax base are recognised in profit or loss.

65A   When an entity pays dividends to its shareholders, it may be required to pay a portion of the dividends to taxation authorities on behalf of shareholders. In many jurisdictions, this amount is referred to as a withholding tax. Such an amount paid or payable to taxation authorities is charged to equity as a part of the dividends.

Deferred Tax Arising from a Business Combination

66   As explained in paragraphs 19 and 26(c), temporary differences may arise in a business combination. In accordance with AASB 3, an entity recognises any resulting deferred tax assets (to the extent that they meet the recognition criteria in paragraph 24) or deferred tax liabilities as identifiable assets and liabilities at the acquisition date. Consequently, those deferred tax assets and deferred tax liabilities affect the amount of goodwill or the bargain purchase gain the entity recognises. However, in accordance with paragraph 15(a), an entity does not recognise deferred tax liabilities arising from the initial recognition of goodwill.

67   As a result of a business combination, the probability of realising a pre-acquisition deferred tax asset of the acquirer could change. An acquirer may consider it probable that it will recover its own deferred tax asset that was not recognised before the business combination. For example, the acquirer may be able to utilise the benefit of its unused tax losses against the future taxable profit of the acquiree. Alternatively, as a result of the business combination it might no longer be probable that future taxable profit will allow the deferred tax asset to be recovered. In such cases, the acquirer recognises a change in the deferred tax asset in the period of the business combination, but does not include it as part of the accounting for the business combination. Therefore, the acquirer does not take it into account in measuring the goodwill or bargain purchase gain it recognises in the business combination.

68   The potential benefit of the acquiree's income tax loss carryforwards or other deferred tax assets might not satisfy the criteria for separate recognition when a business combination is initially accounted for but might be realised subsequently. An entity shall recognise acquired deferred tax benefits that it realises after the business combination as follows:

(a)   Acquired deferred tax benefits recognised within the measurement period that result from new information about facts and circumstances that existed at the acquisition date shall be applied to reduce the carrying amount of any goodwill related to that acquisition. If the carrying amount of that goodwill is zero, any remaining deferred tax benefits shall be recognised in profit or loss.

(b)   All other acquired deferred tax benefits realised shall be recognised in profit or loss (or, if this Standard so requires, outside profit or loss).

Current and Deferred Tax Arising from Share-based Payment Transactions

68A   In some tax jurisdictions, an entity receives a tax deduction (that is, an amount that is deductible in determining taxable profit) that relates to remuneration paid in shares, share options or other equity instruments of the entity. The amount of that tax deduction may differ from the related cumulative remuneration expense, and may arise in a later reporting period. For example, in some jurisdictions, an entity may recognise an expense for the consumption of employee services received as consideration for share options granted, in accordance with AASB 2 *Share-based Payment*, and not receive a tax deduction until the share options are exercised, with the measurement of the tax deduction based on the entity's share price at the date of exercise.

68B   As with the research costs discussed in paragraphs 9 and 26(b) of this Standard, the difference between the tax base of the employee services received to date (being the amount the taxation authorities will permit as a deduction in future periods), and the carrying amount of nil, is a deductible temporary difference that results in a deferred tax asset. If the amount the taxation authorities will permit as a deduction in future periods is not known at the end of the period, it shall be estimated, based on information available at the end of the period. For example, if the amount that the taxation authorities will permit as a deduction in future periods is dependent upon the entity's share price at a future date, the measurement of the deductible temporary difference should be based on the entity's share price at the end of the period.

68C   As noted in paragraph 68A, the amount of the tax deduction (or estimated future tax deduction, measured in accordance with paragraph 68B) may differ from the related cumulative remuneration expense. Paragraph 58 of the Standard requires that current and deferred tax should be recognised as income or an expense and included in profit or loss for the period, except to the extent that the tax arises from (a) a transaction or event that is recognised, in the same or a different period, outside profit or loss, or (b) a business combination. If the amount of the tax deduction (or estimated future tax deduction) exceeds the amount of the related cumulative remuneration expense, this indicates that the tax deduction relates not only to remuneration expense but also to an equity item. In this situation, the excess of the associated current or deferred tax should be recognised directly in equity.

Presentation

Tax Assets and Tax Liabilities

69   [Deleted by the IASB]

70   [Deleted by the IASB]

Offset

71   **An entity shall offset current tax assets and current tax liabilities if, and only if, the entity:**

   (a)   **has a legally enforceable right to set off the recognised amounts; and**

   (b)   **intends either to settle on a net basis, or to realise the asset and settle the liability simultaneously.**

72   Although current tax assets and liabilities are separately recognised and measured, they are offset in the statement of financial position subject to criteria similar to those established for financial instruments in AASB 132. An entity will normally have a legally enforceable right to set off a current tax asset against a current tax liability when they relate to income taxes levied by the same taxation authority and the taxation authority permits the entity to make or receive a single net payment.

73   In consolidated financial statements, a current tax asset of one entity in a group is offset against a current tax liability of another entity in the group if, and only if, the entities concerned have a legally enforceable right to make or receive a single net payment and the entities intend to make or receive such a net payment or to recover the asset and settle the liability simultaneously.

74   An entity shall offset deferred tax assets and deferred tax liabilities if, and only if:

(a)   the entity has a legally enforceable right to set off current tax assets against current tax liabilities; and

(b)   the deferred tax assets and the deferred tax liabilities relate to income taxes levied by the same taxation authority on either:

(i)   the same taxable entity; or

(ii)   different taxable entities which intend either to settle current tax liabilities and assets on a net basis, or to realise the assets and settle the liabilities simultaneously, in each future period in which significant amounts of deferred tax liabilities or assets are expected to be settled or recovered.

75   To avoid the need for detailed scheduling of the timing of the reversal of each temporary difference, this Standard requires an entity to set off a deferred tax asset against a deferred tax liability of the same taxable entity if, and only if, they relate to income taxes levied by the same taxation authority and the entity has a legally enforceable right to set off current tax assets against current tax liabilities.

76   In rare circumstances, an entity may have a legally enforceable right of set off, and an intention to settle net, for some periods but not for others. In such rare circumstances, detailed scheduling may be required to establish reliably whether the deferred tax liability of one taxable entity will result in increased tax payments in the same period in which a deferred tax asset of another taxable entity will result in decreased payments by that second taxable entity.

Tax Expense

Tax Expense (Income) Related to Profit or Loss from Ordinary Activities

77   The tax expense (income) related to profit or loss from ordinary activities shall be presented as part of profit or loss in the statement(s) of profit or loss and other comprehensive income.

77A   [Deleted by the IASB]

Exchange Differences on Deferred Foreign Tax Liabilities or Assets

78   AASB 121 requires certain exchange differences to be recognised as income or expense but does not specify where such differences should be presented in the statement of comprehensive income. Accordingly, where exchange differences on deferred foreign tax liabilities or assets are recognised in the statement of comprehensive income, such differences may be classified as deferred tax expense (income) if that presentation is considered to be the most useful to financial statement users.

Disclosure

79   The major components of tax expense (income) shall be disclosed separately.

80   Components of tax expense (income) may include:

(a)   current tax expense (income);

(b)   any adjustments recognised in the period for current tax of prior periods;

(c)   the amount of deferred tax expense (income) relating to the origination and reversal of temporary differences;

(d)   the amount of deferred tax expense (income) relating to changes in tax rates or the imposition of new taxes;

(e)   the amount of the benefit arising from a previously unrecognised tax loss, tax credit or temporary difference of a prior period that is used to reduce current tax expense;

(f)   the amount of the benefit from a previously unrecognised tax loss, tax credit or temporary difference of a prior period that is used to reduce deferred tax expense;

(g)   deferred tax expense arising from the write-down, or reversal of a previous write-down, of a deferred tax asset in accordance with paragraph 56; and

(h) the amount of tax expense (income) relating to those changes in accounting policies and errors that are included in profit or loss in accordance with AASB 108, because they cannot be accounted for retrospectively.

81 The following shall also be disclosed separately:

(a) the aggregate current and deferred tax relating to items that are charged or credited directly to equity (see paragraph 62A);

(ab) the amount of income tax relating to each component of other comprehensive income (see paragraph 62 and AASB 101 (as revised in 2007));

(b) [deleted by the IASB];

(c) an explanation of the relationship between tax expense (income) and accounting profit in either or both of the following forms:

(i) a numerical reconciliation between tax expense (income) and the product of accounting profit multiplied by the applicable tax rate(s), disclosing also the basis on which the applicable tax rate(s) is (are) computed; or

(ii) a numerical reconciliation between the average effective tax rate and the applicable tax rate, disclosing also the basis on which the applicable tax rate is computed;

(d) an explanation of changes in the applicable tax rate(s) compared to the previous reporting period;

(e) the amount (and expiry date, if any) of deductible temporary differences, unused tax losses, and unused tax credits for which no deferred tax asset is recognised in the statement of financial position;

(f) the aggregate amount of temporary differences associated with investments in subsidiaries, branches and associates and interests in joint ventures, for which deferred tax liabilities have not been recognised (see paragraph 39);

(g) in respect of each type of temporary difference, and in respect of each type of unused tax loss and unused tax credit:

(i) the amount of the deferred tax assets and liabilities recognised in the statement of financial position for each period presented; and

(ii) the amount of the deferred tax income or expense recognised in profit or loss, if this is not apparent from the changes in the amounts recognised in the statement of financial position;

(h) in respect of discontinued operations, the tax expense relating to:

(i) the gain or loss on discontinuance; and

(ii) the profit or loss from the ordinary activities of the discontinued operation for the period, together with the corresponding amounts for each prior period presented;

(i) the amount of income tax consequences of dividends to shareholders of the entity that were proposed or declared before the financial statements were authorised for issue, but are not recognised as a liability in the financial statements;

(j) if a business combination in which the entity is the acquirer causes a change in the amount recognised for its pre-acquisition deferred tax asset (see paragraph 67), the amount of that change; and

(k) if the deferred tax benefits acquired in a business combination are not recognised at the acquisition date but are recognised after the acquisition date (see paragraph 68), a description of the event or change in circumstances that caused the deferred tax benefits to be recognised.

82   An entity shall disclose the amount of a deferred tax asset and the nature of the evidence supporting its recognition, when:

    (a)   the utilisation of the deferred tax asset is dependent on future taxable profits in excess of the profits arising from the reversal of existing taxable temporary differences; and

    (b)   the entity has suffered a loss in either the current or preceding period in the tax jurisdiction to which the deferred tax asset relates.

82A   In the circumstances described in paragraph 52A, an entity shall disclose the nature of the potential income tax consequences that would result from the payment of dividends to its shareholders. In addition, the entity shall disclose the amounts of the potential income tax consequences practically determinable and whether there are any potential income tax consequences not practically determinable.

83   [Deleted by the IASB]

84   The disclosure required by paragraph 81(c) enables users of financial statements to understand whether the relationship between tax expense (income) and accounting profit is unusual and to understand the significant factors that could affect that relationship in the future. The relationship between tax expense (income) and accounting profit may be affected by such factors as revenue that is exempt from taxation, expenses that are not deductible in determining taxable profit (tax loss), the effect of tax losses and the effect of foreign tax rates.

85   In explaining the relationship between tax expense (income) and accounting profit, an entity uses an applicable tax rate that provides the most meaningful information to the users of its financial statements. Often, the most meaningful rate is the domestic rate of tax in the country in which the entity is domiciled, aggregating the tax rate applied for national taxes with the rates applied for any local taxes which are computed on a substantially similar level of taxable profit (tax loss). However, for an entity operating in several jurisdictions, it may be more meaningful to aggregate separate reconciliations prepared using the domestic rate in each individual jurisdiction. The following example illustrates how the selection of the applicable tax rate affects the presentation of the numerical reconciliation.

Example Illustrating Paragraph 85

In 20X2, an entity has accounting profit in its own jurisdiction (country A) of 1,500 (20X1: 2,000) and in country B of 1,500 (20X1: 500). The tax rate is 30% in country A and 20% in country B. In country A, expenses of 100 (20X1: 200) are not deductible for tax purposes.

The following is an example of a reconciliation to the domestic tax rate.

	20X1	20X2
Accounting profit	2,500	3,000
Tax at the domestic rate of 30%	750	900
Tax effect of expenses that are not deductible for tax purposes	60	30
Effect of lower tax rates in country B	(50)	(150)
Tax expense	760	780

The following is an example of a reconciliation prepared by aggregating separate reconciliations for each national jurisdiction. Under this method, the effect of differences between the reporting entity's own domestic tax rate and the domestic tax rate in other jurisdictions does not appear as a separate item in the reconciliation. An entity may need to discuss the effect of significant changes in either tax rates, or the mix of profits earned in different jurisdictions, in order to explain changes in the applicable tax rate(s), as required by paragraph 81(d).

	20X1	20X2
Accounting profit	2,500	3,000
Tax at the domestic rates applicable to profits in the country concerned	700	750
Tax effect of expenses that are not deductible for tax purposes	60	30
Tax expense	760	780

---

86 The average effective tax rate is the tax expense (income) divided by the accounting profit.

87 It would often be impracticable to compute the amount of unrecognised deferred tax liabilities arising from investments in subsidiaries, branches and associates and interests in joint ventures (see paragraph 39). Therefore, this Standard requires an entity to disclose the aggregate amount of the underlying temporary differences but does not require disclosure of the deferred tax liabilities. Nevertheless, where practicable, entities are encouraged to disclose the amounts of the unrecognised deferred tax liabilities because financial statement users may find such information useful.

87A Paragraph 82A requires an entity to disclose the nature of the potential income tax consequences that would result from the payment of dividends to its shareholders. An entity discloses the important features of the income tax systems and the factors that will affect the amount of the potential income tax consequences of dividends.

87B It would sometimes not be practicable to compute the total amount of the potential income tax consequences that would result from the payment of dividends to shareholders. This may be the case, for example, where an entity has a large number of foreign subsidiaries. However, even in such circumstances, some portions of the total amount may be easily determinable. For example, in a consolidated group, a parent and some of its subsidiaries may have paid income taxes at a higher rate on undistributed profits and be aware of the amount that would be refunded on the payment of future dividends to shareholders from consolidated retained earnings. In this case, that refundable amount is disclosed. If applicable, the entity also discloses that there are additional potential income tax consequences not practicably determinable. In the parent's separate financial statements, if any, the disclosure of the potential income tax consequences relates to the parent's retained earnings.

87C An entity required to provide the disclosures in paragraph 82A may also be required to provide disclosures related to temporary differences associated with investments in subsidiaries, branches and associates or interests in joint ventures. In such cases, an entity considers this in determining the information to be disclosed under paragraph 82A. For example, an entity may be required to disclose the aggregate amount of temporary differences associated with investments in subsidiaries for which no deferred tax liabilities have been recognised (see paragraph 81(f)). If it is impracticable to compute the amounts of unrecognised deferred tax liabilities (see paragraph 87) there may be amounts of potential income tax consequences of dividends not practicably determinable related to these subsidiaries.

88 An entity discloses any tax-related contingent liabilities and contingent assets in accordance with AASB 137 *Provisions, Contingent Liabilities and Contingent Assets*. Contingent liabilities and contingent assets may arise, for example, from unresolved disputes with the taxation authorities. Similarly, where changes in tax rates or tax laws are enacted or announced after the reporting period, an entity discloses any significant effect of those changes on its current and deferred tax assets and liabilities (see AASB 110 *Events after the Reporting Period*).

Effective Date

89 [Deleted by the AASB]

90 [Deleted by the AASB]

91 [Deleted by the AASB]

92 [Deleted by the AASB]

93 **Paragraph 68 shall be applied prospectively from the effective date of AASB 3 (as revised in March 2008) to the recognition of deferred tax assets acquired in business combinations.**

94 Therefore, entities shall not adjust the accounting for prior business combinations if tax benefits failed to satisfy the criteria for separate recognition as of the acquisition date and are recognised after the acquisition date, unless the benefits are recognised within the measurement period and result from new information about facts and circumstances that

existed at the acquisition date. Other tax benefits recognised shall be recognised in profit or loss (or, if this Standard so requires, outside profit or loss).

95   [Deleted by the AASB]

98   Paragraph 52 was renumbered as 51A, paragraph 10 and the examples following paragraph 51A were amended, and paragraphs 51B and 51C and the following example and paragraphs 51D and 51E were added by AASB 2010-8 *Amendments to Australian Accounting Standards – Deferred Tax: Recovery of Underlying Assets,* issued in December 2010. An entity shall apply those amendments for annual reporting periods beginning on or after 1 January 2012. Earlier application is permitted. If an entity applies the amendments for an earlier period, it shall disclose that fact.

98B   AASB 2011-9 *Amendments to Australian Accounting Standards – Presentation of Items of Other Comprehensive Income,* issued in September 2011, amended paragraph 77 and deleted paragraph 77A. An entity shall apply those amendments when it applies AASB 101 as amended in September 2011.

Withdrawal of SIC-21

99   [Deleted by the AASB]

Illustrative Examples

These illustrative examples accompany, but are not part of, AASB 112.

Examples of Temporary Differences

A   Examples of Circumstances that give rise to Taxable Temporary Differences

All taxable temporary differences give rise to a deferred tax liability.

Transactions that affect profit or loss

1   Interest revenue is received in arrears and is included in accounting profit on a time apportionment basis but is included in taxable profit on a cash basis.

2   Revenue from the sale of goods is included in accounting profit when goods are delivered but is included in taxable profit when cash is collected. *(Note: as explained in B3 below, there is also a **deductible** temporary difference associated with any related inventory.)*

3   Depreciation of an asset is accelerated for tax purposes.

4   Development costs have been capitalised and will be amortised to the statement of comprehensive income but were deducted in determining taxable profit in the period in which they were incurred.

5   Prepaid expenses have already been deducted on a cash basis in determining the taxable profit of the current or previous periods.

Transactions that affect the statement of financial position

6   Depreciation of an asset is not deductible for tax purposes and no deduction will be available for tax purposes when the asset is sold or scrapped. *(Note: paragraph 15(b) of the Standard prohibits recognition of the resulting deferred tax liability unless the asset was acquired in a business combination, see also paragraph 22 of the Standard.)*

7   A borrower records a loan at the proceeds received (which equal the amount due at maturity), less transaction costs. Subsequently, the carrying amount of the loan is increased by amortisation of the transaction costs to accounting profit. The transaction costs were deducted for tax purposes in the period when the loan was first recognised. *(Notes: (1) the taxable temporary difference is the amount of transaction costs already deducted in determining the taxable profit of current or prior periods, less the cumulative amount amortised to accounting profit; and (2) as the initial recognition of the loan affects taxable profit, the exception in paragraph 15(b) of the Standard does not apply. Therefore, the borrower recognises the deferred tax liability.)*

8 A loan payable was measured on initial recognition at the amount of the net proceeds, net of transaction costs. The transaction costs are amortised to accounting profit over the life of the loan. Those transaction costs are not deductible in determining the taxable profit of future, current or prior periods. *(Notes: (1) the taxable temporary difference is the amount of unamortised transaction costs; and (2) paragraph 15(b) of the Standard prohibits recognition of the resulting deferred tax liability.)*

9 The liability component of a compound financial instrument (for example a convertible bond) is measured at a discount to the amount repayable on maturity (see AASB 132 *Financial Instruments: Presentation*). The discount is not deductible in determining taxable profit (tax loss).

Fair value adjustments and revaluations
10 Financial assets or investment property are carried at fair value which exceeds cost but no equivalent adjustment is made for tax purposes.

11 An entity revalues property, plant and equipment (under the revaluation model treatment in AASB 116 *Property, Plant and Equipment*) but no equivalent adjustment is made for tax purposes. *(Note: paragraph 61A of the Standard requires the related deferred tax to be recognised in other comprehensive income.)*

Business combinations and consolidation
12 The carrying amount of an asset is increased to fair value in a business combination and no equivalent adjustment is made for tax purposes. *(Note that on initial recognition, the resulting deferred tax liability increases goodwill or decreases the amount of any bargain purchase gain recognised. See paragraph 66 of the Standard.)*

13 Reductions in the carrying amount of goodwill are not deductible in determining taxable profit and the cost of the goodwill would not be deductible on disposal of the business. *(Note that paragraph 15(a) of the Standard prohibits recognition of the resulting deferred tax liability.)*

14 Unrealised losses resulting from intragroup transactions are eliminated by inclusion in the carrying amount of inventory or property, plant and equipment.

15 Retained earnings of subsidiaries, branches, associates and joint ventures are included in consolidated retained earnings, but income taxes will be payable if the profits are distributed to the reporting parent. *(Note: paragraph 39 of the Standard prohibits recognition of the resulting deferred tax liability if the parent, investor or venturer is able to control the timing of the reversal of the temporary difference and it is probable that the temporary difference will not reverse in the foreseeable future.)*

16 Investments in foreign subsidiaries, branches or associates or interests in foreign joint ventures are affected by changes in foreign exchange rates. *(Notes: (1) there may be either a taxable temporary difference or a deductible temporary difference; and (2) paragraph 39 of the Standard prohibits recognition of the resulting deferred tax liability if the parent, investor or venturer is able to control the timing of the reversal of the temporary difference and it is probable that the temporary difference will not reverse in the foreseeable future.)*

17 The non-monetary assets and liabilities of an entity are measured in its functional currency but the taxable profit or tax loss is determined in a different currency. *(Notes: (1) there may be either a taxable temporary difference or a deductible temporary difference; (2) where there is a taxable temporary difference, the resulting deferred tax liability is recognised (paragraph 41 of the Standard); and (3) the deferred tax is recognised in profit or loss, see paragraph 58 of the Standard.)*

Hyperinflation
18 Non-monetary assets are restated in terms of the measuring unit current at the end of the reporting period (see AASB 129 *Financial Reporting in Hyperinflationary Economies*) and no equivalent adjustment is made for tax purposes. *(Notes: (1) the deferred tax is recognised in profit or loss; and (2) if, in addition to the restatement, the non-monetary assets are also revalued, the deferred tax relating to the revaluation is recognised in other comprehensive income and the deferred tax relating to the restatement is recognised in profit or loss.)*

B   Examples of Circumstances that give rise to Deductible Temporary Differences

All deductible temporary differences give rise to a deferred tax asset. However, some deferred tax assets may not satisfy the recognition criteria in paragraph 24 of the Standard.

Transactions that affect profit or loss

1   Retirement benefit costs are deducted in determining accounting profit as service is provided by the employee, but are not deducted in determining taxable profit until the entity pays either retirement benefits or contributions to a fund. *(Note: similar deductible temporary differences arise where other expenses, such as product warranty costs or interest, are deductible on a cash basis in determining taxable profit.)*

2   Accumulated depreciation of an asset in the financial statements is greater than the cumulative depreciation allowed up to the end of the reporting period for tax purposes.

3   The cost of inventories sold before the end of the reporting period is deducted in determining accounting profit when goods or services are delivered but is deducted in determining taxable profit when cash is collected. *(Note: as explained in A2 above, there is also a **taxable** temporary difference associated with the related trade receivable.)*

4   The net realisable value of an item of inventory, or the recoverable amount of an item of property, plant or equipment, is less than the previous carrying amount and an entity therefore reduces the carrying amount of the asset, but that reduction is ignored for tax purposes until the asset is sold.

5   Research costs (or organisation or other start up costs) are recognised as an expense in determining accounting profit but are not permitted as a deduction in determining taxable profit until a later period.

6   Income is deferred in the statement of financial position but has already been included in taxable profit in current or prior periods.

7   A government grant which is included in the statement of financial position as deferred income will not be taxable in future periods. *(Note: paragraph 24 of the Standard prohibits the recognition of the resulting deferred tax asset, see also paragraph 33 of the Standard.)*

Fair value adjustments and revaluations

8   Financial assets or investment property are carried at fair value which is less than cost, but no equivalent adjustment is made for tax purposes.

Business combinations and consolidation

9   A liability is recognised at its fair value in a business combination, but none of the related expense is deducted in determining taxable profit until a later period. *(Note that the resulting deferred tax asset decreases goodwill or increases the amount of any bargain purchase gain recognised. See paragraph 66 of the Standard.)*

10   [Deleted by the IASB]

11   Unrealised profits resulting from intragroup transactions are eliminated from the carrying amount of assets, such as inventory or property, plant or equipment, but no equivalent adjustment is made for tax purposes.

12   Investments in foreign subsidiaries, branches or associates or interests in foreign joint ventures are affected by changes in foreign exchange rates. *(Notes: (1) there may be a taxable temporary difference or a deductible temporary difference; and (2) paragraph 44 of the Standard requires recognition of the resulting deferred tax asset to the extent, and only to the extent, that it is probable that: (a) the temporary difference will reverse in the foreseeable future; and (b) taxable profit will be available against which the temporary difference can be utilised.)*

13   The non-monetary assets and liabilities of an entity are measured in its functional currency but the taxable profit or tax loss is determined in a different currency. *(Notes: (1) there may be either a taxable temporary difference or a deductible temporary difference; (2) where there is a deductible temporary difference, the resulting deferred tax asset is recognised to the extent that it is probable that sufficient taxable profit will be available (paragraph 41*

of the Standard); and (3) the deferred tax is recognised in profit or loss, see paragraph 58 of the Standard.)

C   Examples of Circumstances where the Carrying Amount of an Asset or Liability is Equal to its Tax Base

1   Accrued expenses have already been deducted in determining an entity's current tax liability for the current or earlier periods.

2   A loan payable is measured at the amount originally received and this amount is the same as the amount repayable on final maturity of the loan.

3   Accrued expenses will never be deductible for tax purposes.

4   Accrued income will never be taxable.

Illustrative Computations and Presentation

The appendix accompanies, but is not part of, AASB 112. Extracts from statements of financial position and statements of comprehensive income are provided to show the effects on these financial statements of the transactions described below. These extracts do not necessarily conform with all the disclosure and presentation requirements of other Australian Accounting Standards.

All the examples below assume that the entities concerned have no transactions other than those described.

Example 1 – Depreciable Assets

An entity buys equipment for 10,000 and depreciates it on a straight line basis over its expected useful life of five years. For tax purposes, the equipment is depreciated at 25% a year on a straight line basis. Tax losses may be carried back against taxable profit of the previous five years. In year 0, the entity's taxable profit was 5,000. The tax rate is 40%.

The entity will recover the carrying amount of the equipment by using it to manufacture goods for resale. Therefore, the entity's current tax computation is as follows:

	Year				
	1	*2*	*3*	*4*	*5*
Taxable income	2,000	2,000	2,000	2,000	2,000
Depreciation for tax purposes	2,500	2,500	2,500	2,500	0
Taxable profit (tax loss)	(500)	(500)	(500)	(500)	2,000
Current tax expense (income) at 40%	(200)	(200)	(200)	(200)	800

The entity recognises a current tax asset at the end of years 1 to 4 because it recovers the benefit of the tax loss against the taxable profit of year 0.

The temporary differences associated with the equipment and the resulting deferred tax asset and liability and deferred tax expense and income are as follows:

	Year				
	1	*2*	*3*	*4*	*5*
Carrying Amount	8,000	6,000	4,000	2,000	0
Tax base	7,500	5,000	2,500	0	0
Taxable temporary difference	500	1,000	1,500	2,000	0
Opening deferred tax liability	0	200	400	600	800
Deferred tax expense (income)	200	200	200	200	(800)
Closing deferred tax liability	200	400	600	800	0

The entity recognises the deferred tax liability in years 1 to 4 because the reversal of the taxable temporary difference will create taxable income in subsequent years. The entity's statement of comprehensive income includes the following:

			Year		
	1	2	3	4	5
Income	2,000	2,000	2,000	2,000	2,000
Depreciation	2,000	2,000	2,000	2,000	2,000
Profit before tax	0	0	0	0	0
Current tax expense (income)	(200)	(200)	(200)	(200)	800
Deferred tax expense (income)	200	200	200	200	(800)
Total tax expense (income)	0	0	0	0	0
Net profit for the period	0	0	0	0	0

Example 2 – Deferred Tax Assets and Liabilities

The example deals with an entity over the two year period, X5 and X6. In X5, the enacted income tax rate was 40% of taxable profit. In X6, the enacted income tax rate was 35% of taxable profit.

Charitable donations are recognised as an expense when they are paid and are not deductible for tax purposes.

In X5, the entity was notified by the relevant authorities that they intend to pursue an action against the entity with respect to sulphur emissions. Although as at December X6 the action had not yet come to court the entity recognised a liability of 700 in X5 being its best estimate of the fine arising from the action. Fines are not deductible for tax purposes.

In X2, the entity incurred 1,250 of costs in relation to the development of a new product. These costs were deducted for tax purposes in X2. For accounting purposes, the entity capitalised this expenditure and amortised it on the straight line basis over five years. At 31/12/X4, the unamortised balance of these product development costs was 500.

In X5, the entity entered into an agreement with its existing employees to provide healthcare benefits to retirees. The entity recognises as an expense the cost of this plan as employees provide service. No payments to retirees were made for such benefits in X5 or X6. Healthcare costs are deductible for tax purposes when payments are made to retirees. The entity has determined that it is probable that taxable profit will be available against which any resulting deferred tax asset can be utilised.

Buildings are depreciated for accounting purposes at 5% a year on a straight line basis and at 10% a year on a straight line basis for tax purposes. Motor vehicles are depreciated for accounting purposes at 20% a year on a straight line basis and at 25% a year on a straight line basis for tax purposes. A full year's depreciation is charged for accounting purposes in the year that an asset is acquired.

At 1/1/X6, the building was revalued to 65,000 and the entity estimated that the remaining useful life of the building was 20 years from the date of the revaluation. The revaluation did not affect taxable profit in X6 and the taxation authorities did not adjust the tax base of the building to reflect the revaluation. In X6, the entity transferred 1,033 from revaluation surplus to retained earnings. This represents the difference of 1,590 between the actual depreciation on the building (3,250) and equivalent depreciation based on the cost of the building (1,660, which is the book value at 1/1/X6 of 33,200 divided by the remaining useful life of 20 years), less the related deferred tax of 557 (see paragraph 64 of the Standard).

AASB

Current Tax Expense

	X5	X6
Accounting profit	8,775	8,740
Add		
Depreciation for accounting purposes	4,800	8,250
Charitable donations	500	350
Fine for environmental pollution	700	–
Product development costs	250	250
Health care benefits	2,000	1,000
	17,025	18,590
Deduct		
Depreciation for tax purposes	(8,100)	(11,850)
Taxable Profit	8,925	6,740
Current tax expense at 40%	3,570	
Current tax expense at 35%		2,359

Carrying Amounts of Property, Plant & Equipment

Cost	Building	Motor Vehicles	Total
Balance at 31/12/X4	50,000	10,000	60,000
Additions X5	6,000	–	6,000
Balance at 31/12/X5	56,000	10,000	66,000
Elimination of accumulated depreciation on revaluation at 1/1/X6	(22,800)	–	(22,800)
Revaluation at 1/1/X6	31,800	–	31,800
Balance at 1/1/X6	65,000	10,000	75,000
Additions X6	–	15,000	15,000
	65,000	25,000	90,000
Accumulated Depreciation	*5%*	*20%*	
Balance at 31/12/X4	20,000	4,000	24,000
Depreciation X5	2,800	2,000	4,800
Balance at 31/12/X5	22,800	6,000	28,800
Revaluation at 1/1/X6	(22,800)	–	(22,800)
Balance at 1/1/X6	–	6,000	6,000
Depreciation X6	3,250	5,000	8,250
Balance at 31/12/X6	3,250	11,000	14,250
Carrying Amount			
31/12/X4	30,000	6,000	36,000
31/12/X5	33,200	4,000	37,200
31/12/X6	61,750	14,000	75,750

Tax Base of Property, Plant & Equipment

Cost	Building	Motor Vehicles	Total
Balance at 31/12/X4	50,000	10,000	60,000
Additions X5	6,000	–	6,000
Balance at 31/12/X5	56,000	10,000	66,000
Additions X6	–	15,000	15,000
Balance at 31/12/X6	56,000	25,000	81,000
Accumulated Depreciation	*10%*	*25%*	
Balance at 31/12/X4	40,000	5,000	45,000
Depreciation X5	5,600	2,500	8,100
Balance at 31/12/X5	45,600	7,500	53,100
Depreciation X6	5,600	6,250	11,850
Balance 31/12/X6	51,200	13,750	64,950
Tax Base			
31/12/X4	10,000	5,000	15,000
31/12/X5	10,400	2,500	12,900
31/12/X6	4,800	11,250	16,050

Deferred Tax Assets, Liabilities and Expense at 31/12/X4

	Carrying Amount	Tax Base	Temporary Differences
Accounts receivable	500	500	–
Inventory	2,000	2,000	–
Product development costs	500	–	500
Investments	33,000	33,000	–
Property, plant & equipment	36,000	15,000	21,000
TOTAL ASSETS	72,000	50,500	21,500
Current income taxes payable	3,000	3,000	–
Accounts payable	500	500	–
Fines payable	–	–	–
Liability for health care benefits	–	–	
Long term debt	20,000	20,000	–
Deferred income taxes	8,600	8,600	–
TOTAL LIABILITIES	32,100	32,100	
Share capital	5,000	5,000	–
Revaluation reserve	–	–	–
Retained earnings	34,900	13,400	
TOTAL LIABILITIES/EQUITY	72,000	50,500	
TEMPORARY DIFFERENCES			21,500
Deferred tax liability	21,500 at 40%		8,600
Deferred tax asset	–	–	–
Net deferred tax liability			8,600

Deferred Tax Assets, Liabilities and Expense at 31/12/X5

	Carrying Amount	Tax Base	Temporary Differences
Accounts receivable	500	500	–
Inventory	2,000	2,000	–
Product development costs	250	–	250
Investments	33,000	33,000	–
Property, plant & equipment	37,200	12,900	24,300
TOTAL ASSETS	72,950	48,400	24,550
Current income taxes payable	3,570	3,570	–
Accounts payable	500	500	–
Fines payable	700	700	–
Liability for health care benefits	2,000	–	(2,000)
Long-term debt	12,475	12,475	–
Deferred income taxes	9,020	9,020	–
TOTAL LIABILITIES	28,265	26,265	(2,000)
Share capital	5,000	5,000	–
Revaluation reserve	–	–	–
Retained earnings	39,685	17,135	
TOTAL LIABILITIES/EQUITY	72,950	48,400	
TEMPORARY DIFFERENCES			22,550
Deferred tax liability	24,550 at 40%		9,820
Deferred tax asset	(2,000) at 40%		(800)
Net deferred tax liability			9,020
Less: Opening deferred tax liability			(8,600)

Deferred tax expense (income) related to the origination and reversal
of temporary differences — **420**

Deferred Tax Assets, Liabilities and Expense at 31/12/X6

	Carrying Amount	Tax Base	Temporary Differences
Accounts receivable	500	500	–
Inventory	2,000	2,000	–
Product development costs	–	–	–
Investments	33,000	33,000	–
Property, plant & equipment	75,750	16,050	59,700
TOTAL ASSETS	111,250	51,550	59,700
Current income taxes payable	2,359	2,359	–
Accounts payable	500	500	–
Fines payable	700	700	–
Liability for health care benefits	3,000	–	(3,000)
Long term debt	12,805	12,805	–
Deferred income taxes	19,845	19,845	–
TOTAL LIABILITIES	39,209	36,209	(3,000)

	Carrying Amount	Tax Base	Temporary Differences
Share capital	5,000	5,000	–
Revaluation reserve	19,637	–	–
Retained earnings	47,404	10,341	
TOTAL LIABILITIES/EQUITY	111,250	51,550	
TEMPORARY DIFFERENCES			56,700
Deferred tax liability	59,700 at 35%		20,895
Deferred tax asset	(3,000) at 35%		(1,050)
Net deferred tax liability			19,845
Less: Opening deferred tax liability			(9,020)
Adjustment to opening deferred tax liability resulting from reduction in tax rate		22,550 at 5%	1,127
Deferred tax attributable to revaluation reserve		31,800 at 35%	(11,130)
Deferred tax expense (income) related to the origination and reversal of temporary differences			822

Illustrative Disclosure

The amounts to be disclosed in accordance with the Standard are as follows:

Major components of tax expense (income) (paragraph 79)

	X5	X6
Current tax expense	3,570	2,359
Deferred tax expense relating to the origination and reversal of temporary differences	420	822
Deferred tax expense (income) resulting from reduction in tax rate	–	(1,127)
Tax expense	3,990	2,054

Income tax relating to the components of other comprehensive income (paragraph 81(ab))

Deferred tax relating to revaluation of building	–	(11,130)

In addition, deferred tax of 557 was transferred in X6 from retained earnings to revaluation surplus. This relates to the difference between the actual depreciation on the building and equivalent depreciation based on the cost of the building.

Explanation of the relationship between tax expense and accounting profit (paragraph 81(c))

The Standard permits two alternative methods of explaining the relationship between tax expense (income) and accounting profit. Both of these formats are illustrated below.

(i)   a numerical reconciliation between tax expense (income) and the product of accounting profit multiplied by the applicable tax rate(s), disclosing also the basis on which the applicable tax rate(s) is (are) computed

	X5	X6
Accounting profit	8,775	8,740
Tax at the applicable tax rate of 35% (X5: 40%)	3,510	3,059
Tax effect of expenses that are not deductible in determining taxable profit:		
Charitable donations	200	122
Fines for environmental pollution	280	–
Reduction in opening deferred taxes resulting from reduction in tax rate	–	(1,127)
Tax expense	3,990	2,054

The applicable tax rate is the aggregate of the national income tax rate of 30% (X5: 35%) and the local income tax rate of 5%.

(ii)   a numerical reconciliation between the average effective tax rate and the applicable tax rate, disclosing also the basis on which the applicable tax rate is computed

	X5	X6
	%	%
Applicable tax rate	40.0	35.0
Tax effect of expenses that are not deductible for tax purposes:		
Charitable donations	2.3	1.4
Fines for environmental pollution	3.2	–
Effect on opening deferred taxes of reduction in tax rate	–	(12.9)
Average effective tax rate (tax expense divided by profit before tax)	45.5	23.5

The applicable tax rate is the aggregate of the national income tax rate of 30% (X5: 35%) and the local income tax rate of 5%.

An explanation of changes in the applicable tax rate(s) compared to the previous accounting period (paragraph 81(d))

In X6, the government enacted a change in the national income tax rate from 35% to 30%.

In respect of each type of temporary difference, and in respect of each type of unused tax losses and unused tax credits:

(i)   the amount of the deferred tax assets and liabilities recognised in the statement of financial position for each period presented;

(ii)   the amount of the deferred tax income or expense recognised in profit or loss for each period presented, if this is not apparent from the changes in the amounts recognised in the statement of financial position (paragraph 81(g))

	X5	X6
Accelerated depreciation for tax purposes	9,720	10,322
Liabilities for health care benefits that are deducted for tax purposes only when paid	(800)	(1,050)
Product development costs deducted from taxable profit in earlier years	100	–
Revaluation, net of related depreciation	–	10,573
Deferred tax liability	9,020	19,845

(Note: the amount of the deferred tax income or expense recognised in profit or loss for the current year is apparent from the changes in the amounts recognised in the statement of financial position)

Example 3 – Business Combinations

On 1 January X5 entity A acquired 100% of the shares of entity B at a cost of 600. At the acquisition date, the tax base in A's tax jurisdiction of A's investment in B is 600. Reductions in the carrying amount of goodwill are not deductible for tax purposes, and the cost of the goodwill would also not be deductible if B were to dispose of its underlying business. The tax rate in A's tax jurisdiction is 30% and the tax rate in B's tax jurisdiction is 40%.

The fair value of the identifiable assets acquired and liabilities assumed (excluding deferred tax assets and liabilities) by A is set out in the following table, together with their tax bases in B's tax jurisdiction and the resulting temporary differences.

	Amounts recognised at acquisition	Tax base	Temporary differences
Property, plant and equipment	270	155	115
Accounts receivable	210	210	–
Inventory	174	124	50
Retirement benefit obligations	(30)	–	(30)
Accounts payable	(120)	(120)	–
Fair value of the identifiable assets acquired and liabilities assumed, excluding deferred tax	504	369	135

The deferred tax asset arising from the retirement benefit obligations is offset against the deferred tax liabilities arising from the property, plant and equipment and inventory (see paragraph 74 of the Standard).

No deduction is available in B's tax jurisdiction for the cost of the goodwill. Therefore, the tax base of the goodwill in B's jurisdiction is nil. However, in accordance with paragraph 15(a) of the Standard, A recognises no deferred tax liability for the taxable temporary difference associated with the goodwill in B's tax jurisdiction.

The carrying amount, in A's consolidated financial statements, of its investment in B is made up as follows:

Fair value of identifiable assets acquired and liabilities assumed, excluding deferred tax	504
Deferred tax liability (135 at 40%)	(54)
Fair value of identifiable assets acquired and liabilities assumed	450
Goodwill	150
Carrying amount	600

Because, at the acquisition date, the tax base in A's tax jurisdiction of A's investment in B is 600, no temporary difference is associated in A's tax jurisdiction with the investment.

During X5, B's equity (incorporating the fair value adjustments made as a result of the business combination) changed as follows:

At 1 January X5	450
Retained earnings for X5 (net profit of 150, less dividend payable of 80)	70
At 31 December X5	520

A recognises a liability for any withholding tax or other taxes that it will incur on the accrued dividend receivable of 80.

At 31 December X5, the carrying amount of A's underlying investment in B, excluding the accrued dividend receivable, is as follows:

Net assets of B	520
Goodwill	150
Carrying amount	670

The temporary difference associated with A's underlying investment is 70. This amount is equal to the cumulative retained earnings since the acquisition date.

If A has determined that it will not sell the investment in the foreseeable future and that B will not distribute its retained earnings in the foreseeable future, no deferred tax liability is recognised in relation to A's investment in B (see paragraphs 39 and 40 of the Standard). Note that this exception would apply for an investment in an associate only if there is an agreement requiring that the profits of the associate will not be distributed in the foreseeable future (see paragraph 42 of the Standard). A discloses the amount of the temporary difference for which no deferred tax is recognised: that is, 70 (see paragraph 81(f) of the Standard).

If A expects to sell the investment in B, or that B will distribute its retained earnings in the foreseeable future, A recognises a deferred tax liability to the extent that the temporary difference is expected to reverse. The tax rate reflects the manner in which A expects to recover the carrying amount of its investment (see paragraph 51 of the Standard). A recognises the deferred tax in other comprehensive income to the extent that the deferred tax results from foreign exchange translation differences that have been recognised in other comprehensive income (paragraph 61A of the Standard). A discloses separately:

(a)   the amount of deferred tax that has been recognised in other comprehensive income (paragraph 81(ab) of the Standard); and

(b)   the amount of any remaining temporary difference which is not expected to reverse in the foreseeable future and for which, therefore, no deferred tax is recognised (see paragraph 81(f) of the Standard).

AASB

Example 4 – Compound Financial Instruments

An entity receives a non-interest-bearing convertible loan of 1,000 on 31 December X4 repayable at par on 1 January X8. In accordance with AASB 132 *Financial Instruments: Presentation*, the entity classifies the instrument's liability component as a liability and the equity component as equity. The entity assigns an initial carrying amount of 751 to the liability component of the convertible loan and 249 to the equity component. Subsequently, the entity recognises imputed discount as interest expense at an annual rate of 10% on the carrying amount of the liability component at the beginning of the year. The tax authorities do not allow the entity to claim any deduction for the imputed discount on the liability component of the convertible loan. The tax rate is 40%.

The temporary differences associated with the liability component and the resulting deferred tax liability and deferred tax expense and income are as follows:

	Year X4	X5	X6	X7
Carrying amount of liability component	751	826	909	1,000
Tax base	1,000	1,000	1,000	1,000
Taxable temporary difference	249	174	91	–
Opening deferred tax liability at 40%	0	100	70	37
Deferred tax charged to equity	100	–	–	–
Deferred tax expense (income)	–	(30)	(33)	(37)
Closing deferred tax liability at 40%	100	70	37	–

As explained in paragraph 23 of the Standard, at 31 December X4, the entity recognises the resulting deferred tax liability by adjusting the initial carrying amount of the equity component of the convertible liability. Therefore, the amounts recognised at that date are as follows:

Liability component	751
Deferred tax liability	100
Equity component (249 less 100)	149
	1,000

Subsequent changes in the deferred tax liability are recognised in profit or loss as tax income (see paragraph 23 of the Standard). Therefore, the entity's profit or loss includes the following:

	Year X4	X5	X6	X7
Interest expense (imputed discount)	–	75	83	91
Deferred tax expense (income)	–	(30)	(33)	(37)
	–	45	50	54

Example 5 – Share-based Payment Transactions

In accordance with AASB 2 *Share-based Payment*, an entity has recognised an expense for the consumption of employee services received as consideration for share options granted. A tax deduction will not arise until the options are exercised, and the deduction is based on the options' intrinsic value at exercise date.

As explained in paragraph 68B of the Standard, the difference between the tax base of the employee services received to date (being the amount the taxation authorities will permit as a deduction in future periods in respect of those services), and the carrying amount of nil, is a deductible temporary difference that results in a deferred tax asset. Paragraph 68B requires that, if the amount the taxation authorities will permit as a deduction in future periods is not known at the end of the period, it should be estimated, based on information available at the end of the period. If the amount that the taxation authorities will permit as a deduction in future periods is dependent upon the entity's share price at a future date, the measurement of the deductible temporary difference should be based on the entity's share price at the end of the period.

Therefore, in this example, the estimated future tax deduction (and hence the measurement of the deferred tax asset) should be based on the options' intrinsic value at the end of the period.

As explained in paragraph 68C of the Standard, if the tax deduction (or estimated future tax deduction) exceeds the amount of the related cumulative remuneration expense, this indicates that the tax deduction relates not only to remuneration expense but also to an equity item. In this situation, paragraph 68C requires that the excess of the associated current or deferred tax should be recognised directly in equity.

The entity's tax rate is 40%. The options were granted at the start of year 1, vested at the end of year 3 and were exercised at the end of year 5. Details of the expense recognised for employee services received and consumed in each reporting period, the number of options outstanding at each year-end, and the intrinsic value of the options at each year-end, are as follows:

	Employee services expense	Number of options at year-end	Intrinsic value per option
Year 1	188,000	50,000	5
Year 2	185,000	45,000	8
Year 3	190,000	40,000	13
Year 4	0	40,000	17
Year 5	0	40,000	20

The entity recognises a deferred tax asset and deferred tax income in years 1 – 4 and current tax income in year 5 as follows. In years 4 and 5, some of the deferred and current tax income is recognised directly in equity, because the estimated (and actual) tax deduction exceeds the cumulative remuneration expense.

Year 1

Deferred tax asset and deferred tax income:

$(50,000 \times 5 \times 1/3^* \times 40\%) =$ 33,333

* The tax base of the employee services received is based on the intrinsic value of the options, and those options were granted for three years' services. Because only one year's services have been received to date, it is necessary to multiply the option's intrinsic value by one-third to arrive at the tax base of the employee services received in year 1.

The deferred tax income is all recognised in profit or loss, because the estimated future tax deduction of 83,333 $(50,000 \times 5 \times 1/3)$ is less than the cumulative remuneration expense of 188,000.

Year 2

Deferred tax asset at year-end:

$(45,000 \times 8 \times 2/3 \times 40\%) =$	96,000
Less deferred tax asset at start of year	(33,333)
Deferred tax income for year	62,667*

* This amount consists of the following:

Deferred tax income for the temporary difference between the tax base of the employee services received during the year and their carrying amount of nil:

$(45,000 \times 8 \times 1/3 \times 40\%) =$	48,000

Tax income resulting from an adjustment to the tax base of employee services received in previous years:

(a)	increase in intrinsic value: $(45,000 \times 3 \times 1/3 \times 40\%) =$	18,000
(b)	decrease in number of options: $(5,000 \times 5 \times 1/3 \times 40\%) =$	(3,333)
	Deferred tax income for year	62,667

The deferred tax income is all recognised in profit or loss, because the estimated future tax deduction of 240,000 $(45,000 \times 8 \times 2/3)$ is less than the cumulative remuneration expense of 373,000 $(188,000 + 185,000)$.

Year 3

Deferred tax asset at year-end:

$(40,000 \times 13 \times 40\%) =$	208,000	
Less deferred tax asset at start of year	(96,000)	
Deferred tax income for year		112,000

The deferred tax income is all recognised in profit or loss, because the estimated future tax deduction of 520,000 (40,000 × 13) is less than the cumulative remuneration expense of 563,000 (188,000 + 185,000 + 190,000).

Year 4

Deferred tax asset at year-end:

$(40,000 \times 17 \times 40\%) =$	272,000	
Less deferred tax asset at start of year	(208,000)	
Deferred tax income for year		64,000

The deferred tax income is recognised partly in profit or loss and partly directly in equity as follows:

Estimated future tax deduction		
$(40,000 \times 17) =$	680,000	
Cumulative remuneration expense	563,000	
Excess tax deduction		117,000
Deferred tax income for year	64,000	
Excess recognised directly in equity		
$(117,000 \times 40\%) =$	46,800	
Recognised in profit or loss		17,200

Year 5

Deferred tax expense		
(reversal of deferred tax asset)	272,000	
Amount recognised directly in equity		
(reversal of cumulative deferred tax income recognised directly in equity)	46,800	
Amount recognised in profit or loss		225,200
Current tax income based on intrinsic value of options at exercise date		
$(40,000 \times 20 \times 40\%) =$	320,000	
Amount recognised in profit or loss		
$(563,000 \times 40\%) =$	225,200	
Amount recognised directly in equity		94,800

Summary

	Statement of comprehensive income				Statement of financial positon	
	Employee services expense	Current tax expense (income)	Deferred tax expense (income)	Total tax expense (income)	Equity	Deferred tax asset
Year 1	188,000	0	(33,333)	(33,333)	0	33,333
Year 2	185,000	0	(62,667)	(62,667)	0	96,000
Year 3	190,000	0	(112,000)	(112,000)	0	208,000
Year 4	0	0	(17,200)	(17,200)	(46,800)	272,000
Year 5	0	(225,200)	225,200	0	46,800	0
					(94,800)	
Totals	563,000	(225,200)	0	(225,200)	(94,800)	0

Example 6 – Replacement Awards in a Business Combination

On 1 January 20X1 Entity A acquired 100 per cent of Entity B. Entity A pays cash consideration of CU400 to the former owners of Entity B.

At the acquisition date Entity B had outstanding employee share options with a market-based measure of CU100. The share options were fully vested. As part of the business combination Entity B's outstanding share options are replaced by share options of Entity A (replacement awards) with a market-based measure of CU100 and an intrinsic value of CU80. The replacement awards are fully vested. In accordance with paragraphs B56-B62 of AASB 3 *Business Combinations* (as revised in March 2008), the replacement awards are part of the consideration transferred for Entity B. A tax deduction for the replacement awards will not arise until the options are exercised. The tax deduction will be based on the share options' intrinsic value at that date. Entity A's tax rate is 40 per cent. Entity A recognises a deferred tax asset of CU32 (CU80 intrinsic value × 40%) on the replacement awards at the acquisition date.

Entity A measures the identifiable net assets obtained in the business combination (excluding deferred tax assets and liabilities) at CU450. The tax base of the identifiable net assets obtained is CU300. Entity A recognises a deferred tax liability of CU60 ((CU450 – CU300) × 40%) on the identifiable net assets at the acquisition date.

Goodwill is calculated as follows:

	CU
Cash consideration	400
Market-based measure of replacement awards	100
Total consideration transferred	500
Identifiable net assets, excluding deferred tax assets and liabilities	(450)
Deferred tax asset	(32)
Deferred tax liability	60
Goodwill	**78**

Reductions in the carrying amount of goodwill are not deductible for tax purposes. In accordance with paragraph 15(a) of the Standard, Entity A recognises no deferred tax liability for the taxable temporary difference associated with the goodwill recognised in the business combination.

The accounting entry for the business combination is as follows:

	CU	CU
Dr Goodwill	78	
Dr Identifiable net assets	450	
Dr Deferred tax asset	3226	
Cr Cash		400
Cr Equity (replacement awards)		100
Cr Deferred tax liability		60

On 31 December 20X1 the intrinsic value of the replacement awards is CU120. Entity A recognises a deferred tax asset of CU48 (CU120 × 40%). Entity A recognises deferred tax income of CU16 (CU48 – CU32) from the increase in the intrinsic value of the replacement awards. The accounting entry is as follows:

	CU	CU
Dr Deferred tax asset	16	
Cr Deferred tax income		16

If the replacement awards had not been tax-deductible under current tax law, Entity A would not have recognised a deferred tax asset on the acquisition date. Entity A would have accounted for any subsequent events that result in a tax deduction related to the replacement award in the deferred tax income or expense of the period in which the subsequent event occurred.

Paragraphs B56-B62 of AASB 3 provide guidance on determining which portion of a replacement award is part of the consideration transferred in a business combination and which portion is attributable to future service and thus a post-combination remuneration expense. Deferred tax assets and liabilities on replacement awards that are post-combination expenses are accounted for in accordance with the general principles as illustrated in Example 5.

AASB 116
Property, Plant and Equipment

(Compiled October 2009)

Note from the Institute of Chartered Accountants Australia

This note, prepared by the technical editors, is not part of Accounting Standard AASB 116.

Historical development

15 July 2004: AASB 116 'Property, Plant and Equipment' is the Australian equivalent of IAS 16 of the same name. It was made by the AASB on 15 July 2004 as part of the AASB's program to adopt International Financial Reporting Standards (IFRSs) by 2005.

9 December 2004: AASB 2004-1 'Amendments to Australian Accounting Standards' amends paragraph 3, and is applicable from 1 January 2005.

6 April 2006: All Guidance accompanying, but not part of AASB 116 was removed.

7 July 2006: Reissued as a compiled Standard to incorporate amendments made by AASB 2004-1.

30 April 2007: AASB 2007-4 'Amendments to Australian Accounting Standards' amends paragraphs 3, 24, and 35 and added paragraph 28 and is applicable to annual reporting periods beginning on or after 1 July 2007. Entities may elect to early-adopt it to annual reporting periods beginning on or after 1 January 2005.

14 June 2007: AASB 2007-6 'Amendments to Australian Accounting Standards' was issued by the AASB. This Standard is applicable to annual reporting periods beginning on or after 1 January 2009.

24 September 2007: AASB 2007-8 'Amendments to Australian Accounting Standards arising from AASB 101' amends AASB 116 to align with revised AASB 101. This Standard is applicable to annual reporting periods beginning on or after 1 January 2009.

13 December 2007: AASB 2007-9 'Amendments to Australian Accounting Standards arising from the Review of AAS 27, AAS 29 and AAS 31' was issued by the AASB. This Standard is applicable to annual reporting periods beginning on or after 1 July 2008, with early adoption permitted.

13 December 2007: AASB 2007-10 'Further Amendments to Australian Accounting Standards arising from AASB 101' amends AASB 116, replacing the term 'financial report' with 'financial statements'. This Standard is applicable to annual reporting periods beginning on or after 1 January 2009.

6 March 2008: AASB 2008-3 'Amendments to Australian Accounting Standards arising from AASB 3 and AASB 127' amends AASB 116 for the issue of AASB 3 Revised. This Standard is applicable to annual reporting periods beginning on or after 1 July 2009.

24 July 2008: AASB 2008-5 'Amendments to Australian Accounting Standards arising from the Annual Improvements Project' amends AASB 116 in relation to recoverable amount and sale of assets held for rental. This Standard is applicable to annual reporting periods beginning on or after 1 January 2009.

25 June 2009: AASB 2009-6 'Amendments to Australian Accounting Standards' amends AASB 116 for editorial corrections made by the International Accounting Standards Board (IASB) to its Standards and Interpretations (IFRSs) and as a consequence of issuing revised AASB 101 'Presentation of Financial Statements'. This Standard is applicable to annual reporting periods beginning on or after 1 January 2009 that end on or after 30 June 2009.

---

30 October 2009: AASB 116 was reissued by the AASB, compiled to include the AASB 2007-6, AASB 2007-8, AASB 2007-10, AASB 2008-3, AASB 2008-5 and AASB 2009-6 amendments and applies to annual reporting periods beginning on or after 1 July 2009. Early application is permitted.

On the same date the AASB reissued the version of AASB 116 applicable to annual reporting periods beginning on or after 1 January 2009 but before 1 July 2009. This version of AASB 116 has been compiled for the amending Standards applying to annual reporting periods beginning on or after 1 January 2009. This Standard applies to 31 December 2009 year ends and can be accessed from the AASB website at www.aasb.gov.au.

5 September 2011: AASB 2011-8 'Amendments to Australian Accounting Standards arising from AASB 13' amends AASB 116 to give effect to a consequential change in the definition of fair value arising from the issue of AASB 13. This Standard applies to annual reporting periods beginning on or after 1 January 2013 and can be adopted early. **These amendments are not included in this compiled Standard.**

29 June 2012: AASB 2012-5 'Amendments to Australian Accounting Standards arising from Annual Improvements 2009–2011 Cycle' amends AASB 116 to clarify the classification of servicing equipment. This Standard applies to annual reporting periods beginning on or after 1 January 2013 and can be applied early. **These amendments are not included in this compiled Standard.**

References

Interpretation 1 *Changes in Existing Decommissioning, Restoration and Similar Liabilities*, Interpretation 4 *Determining Whether an Arrangement Contains a Lease*, Interpretation 12 *Service Concession Arrangements*, Interpretation 18 *Transfer of Assets from Customers*, Interpretation 113 *Jointly Controlled Entities – Non-Monetary Contributions by Venturers*, Interpretation 132 *Intangible Assets – Web Site Costs*, Interpretation 1031 *Accounting for the Goods and Services Tax (GST)*, Interpretation 129 *Disclosure – Service Concession Arrangements*, Interpretation 1030 *Depreciation of Long-Lived Physical Assets: Condition-Based Depreciation and Related Methods* and Interpretation 1055 *Accounting for Road Earthworks* apply to AASB 116.

The AASB items not taken onto the agenda: *Capitalised Software* applies to AASB 116.

IFRIC items not taken onto the agenda: No. 17 *Depreciation of fixed assets*, No. 18 IAS 16 *Property, Plant and Equipment and IAS 17 Leases: Depreciation of assets leased under operating leases*, IAS 16-1 *Revaluation of investment properties under construction*, IAS 16-2 IAS 16 *Property, plant and equipment – sale of assets held for rental* and IAS 16-3 *Disclosure of idle assets and construction in progress*, IAS 16-7 *Cost of testing* and IAS 16-9 *Purchase of right to use land* apply to AASB 116.

AASB 116 compared to IAS 16

Additions

Paragraph	Description
Aus 1.1	Which entities AASB 116 applies to (i.e. reporting entities and general purpose financial statements).
Aus 1.2	The application date of AASB 116 (i.e. annual reporting periods beginning 1 January 2005).
Aus 1.3	Prohibits early application of AASB 116.
Aus 1.4	Makes the requirements of AASB 116 subject to AASB 1031 'Materiality'.
Aus 1.5	Explains which Australian Standards have been superseded by AASB 116.
Aus 1.6	Clarifies that the superseded Australian Standards remain in force until AASB 116 applies.
Aus 1.7	Notice of the new Standard published on 22 July 2004.
Aus 6.1	Sets out the definition of 'not-for-profit entity'.
Aus 6.2	Examples for not-for-profits.
Aus 15.1	Initial measurement of an asset acquired for no cost by a not-for-profit entity is at fair value at the date of acquisition.

Aus 15.2	Provides examples of assets acquired for no cost by not-for-profit entities.
Aus 15.3	Clarifies that initial measurement at fair value does not constitute an election to use the revaluation model.
Aus 39.1	Net revaluation increments are brought to account by class of asset for not-for-profit entities. The net increment is recognised to the asset revaluation reserve except to the extent that it represents a reversal of a prior net decrement for the class that was recognised in the profit or loss.
Aus 40.1	Net revaluation decrements are brought to account by class of asset for not-for-profit entities. The net decrement is recognised in the profit or loss except to the extent that it represents a reversal of a prior net increment for the class that was recognised directly to equity in the asset revaluation reserve.
Aus 40.2	Clarifies that revaluation decrements and revaluation increments for not-for-profit entities must not be offset if the assets are in different classes.
Aus 77.1	The requirement to disclose the costs of assets measured under the revaluation model does not apply to not-for-profit entities.

Deletions

Paragraph	*Description*
80	Transitional provision for initial measurement for exchange of assets transactions requires prospective application.
81, 81B, 81C	Effective date of IAS 16.
82	Reference to superseded IAS 16.
83	Reference to superseded SIC Interpretations – SICs 6, 14 and 23.

AASB

Contents

Compilation Details

Comparison with IAS 16

Accounting Standard
AASB 116 Property, Plant and Equipment

	Paragraphs
Objective	1
Application	Aus1.1 – Aus1.7
Scope	2 – 5
Definitions	6 – Aus6.2
Recognition	7 – 10
Initial Costs	11
Subsequent Costs	12 – 14
Measurement at Recognition	15 – Aus15.3
Elements of Cost	16 – 22
Measurement of Cost	23 – 28
Measurement after Recognition	29
Cost Model	30
Revaluation Model	31 – 42
Depreciation	43 – 49
Depreciable Amount and Depreciation Period	50 – 59
Depreciation Method	60 – 62
Impairment	63
Compensation for Impairment	65 – 66
Derecognition	67 – 72
Disclosure	73 – 79
Effective Date	81D – 81E

Australian Implementation Guidance

Basis for Conclusions on IAS 16
(available on the AASB website)

Australian Accounting Standard AASB 116 *Property, Plant and Equipment* (as amended) is set out in paragraphs 1 – 81E. All the paragraphs have equal authority. Terms defined in this Standard are in *italics* the first time they appear in the Standard. AASB 116 is to be read in the context of other Australian Accounting Standards, including AASB 1048 *Interpretation and Application of Standards*, which identifies the Australian Accounting Interpretations. In the absence of explicit guidance, AASB 108 *Accounting Policies, Changes in Accounting Estimates and Errors* provides a basis for selecting and applying accounting policies.

Compilation Details

Accounting Standard AASB 116 *Property, Plant and Equipment* as amended

This compiled Standard applies to annual reporting periods beginning on or after 1 July 2009. It takes into account amendments up to and including 25 June 2009 and was prepared on 30 October 2009 by the staff of the Australian Accounting Standards Board (AASB).

This compilation is not a separate Accounting Standard made by the AASB. Instead, it is a representation of AASB 116 (July 2004) as amended by other Accounting Standards, which are listed in the Table below.

Table of Standards

Standard	Date made	Application date *(annual reporting periods ... on or after ...)*	Application, saving or transitional provisions
AASB 116	15 Jul 2004	*(beginning)* 1 Jan 2005	
AASB 2004-1	9 Dec 2004	*(beginning)* 1 Jan 2005	–
AASB 2007-4	30 Apr 2007	*(beginning)* 1 Jul 2007	see (a) below
AASB 2007-6	14 Jun 2007	*(beginning)* 1 Jan 2009	see (b) below
AASB 2007-8	24 Sep 2007	*(beginning)* 1 Jan 2009	see (c) below
AASB 2007-9	13 Dec 2007	*(beginning)* 1 Jul 2008	see (d) below
AASB 2007-10	13 Dec 2007	*(beginning)* 1 Jan 2009	see (c) below
AASB 2008-3	6 Mar 2008	*(beginning)* 1 Jul 2009	see (e) below
AASB 2008-5	24 Jul 2008	*(beginning)* 1 Jan 2009	see (f) below
AASB 2009-6	25 Jun 2009	*(beginning)* 1 Jan 2009 and *(ending)* 30 Jun 2009	see (g) below

(a) Entities may elect to apply this Standard to annual reporting periods beginning on or after 1 January 2005 but before 1 July 2007.

(b) Entities may elect to apply this Standard to annual reporting periods beginning on or after 1 January 2005 but before 1 January 2009, provided that AASB 123 *Borrowing Costs* (June 2007) is also applied to such periods.

(c) Entities may elect to apply this Standard to annual reporting periods beginning on or after 1 January 2005 but before 1 January 2009, provided that AASB 101 *Presentation of Financial Statements* (September 2007) is also applied to such periods.

(d) Entities may elect to apply this Standard to annual reporting periods beginning on or after 1 January 2005 but before 1 July 2008, provided that the Standards and Interpretation listed in paragraph 6 of AASB 2007-9 are also applied to such periods.

(e) Entities may elect to apply this Standard to annual reporting periods beginning on or after 30 June 2007 but before 1 July 2009, provided that AASB 3 *Business Combinations* (March 2008) and AASB 127 *Consolidated and Separate Financial Statements* (March 2008) are also applied to such periods.

(f) Entities may elect to apply this Standard, or its amendments to individual Standards, to annual reporting periods beginning on or after 1 January 2005 but before 1 January 2009.

(g) Entities may elect to apply this Standard to annual reporting periods beginning on or after 1 January 2005 but before 1 January 2009, provided that AASB 101 *Presentation of Financial Statements* (September 2007) is also applied to such periods, and to annual reporting periods beginning on or after 1 January 2009 that end before 30 June 2009.

Table of Amendments to Standard

Paragraph affected	How affected	By ... [paragraph]
1	amended	AASB 2007-10 [59]
Aus1.1	amended	AASB 2007-8 [7, 8]
Aus1.4	amended	AASB 2007-8 [8]
3	amended	AASB 2004-1 [7]
5	amended	AASB 2008-5 [23]

Paragraph affected	How affected	By ... [paragraph]
6	amended	AASB 2008-5 [23]
Aus6.2	added	AASB 2007-9 [16]
23	amended	AASB 2007-6 [14]
24	amended	AASB 2007-4 [50]
28	added	AASB 2007-4 [49]
31	amended	AASB 2007-8 [6]
35	amended	AASB 2007-4 [50]
39	amended	AASB 2007-8 [61]
Aus39.1	amended	AASB 2009-6 [46]
40	amended	AASB 2007-8 [61]
Aus40.1	amended	AASB 2009-6 [47]
41	amended	AASB 2009-6 [48]
44	amended	AASB 2008-3 [42]
68A	added	AASB 2008-5 [24]
69	amended	AASB 2008-5 [23]
73	amended amended	AASB 2007-8 [62] AASB 2007-10 [59]
74	amended amended	AASB 2007-8 [6] AASB 2007-10 [59]
75	amended	AASB 2007-10 [59]
77	amended	AASB 2009-6 [48]
79	amended	AASB 2007-10 [60]
81 (preceding heading)	amended	AASB 2008-5 [25]
81B	note added	AASB 2007-8 [63]
81C	note added	AASB 2008-3 [43]
81D	added	AASB 2008-5 [26]
81E	added	AASB 2008-5 [26]

Table of Amendments to Australian Guidance

Paragraph affected	How affected	By ... [paragraph]
G1-G11	deleted	AASB, Apr 2006 *
G1-G4	added	AASB 2007-9 [17]

*   The AASB decided at its meeting on 6 April 2006 to delete all of the Australian Guidance then accompanying,
      but not part of, AASB 116. The decision had immediate effect.

Comparison with IAS 16

AASB 116 and IAS 16

AASB 116 *Property, Plant and Equipment* as amended incorporates IAS 16 *Property, Plant and Equipment* as issued and amended by the International Accounting Standards Board (IASB). Paragraphs that have been added to this Standard (and do not appear in the text of IAS 16) are identified with the prefix "Aus", followed by the number of the preceding IASB paragraph and decimal numbering. Paragraphs that apply only to not-for-profit entities begin by identifying their limited applicability.

Compliance with IAS 16

For-profit entities that comply with AASB 116 as amended will simultaneously be in compliance with IAS 16 as amended.

AASB 116

Not-for-profit entities using the added "Aus" paragraphs in the Standard that specifically apply to not-for-profit entities may not be simultaneously complying with IAS 16. Whether a not-for-profit entity will be in compliance with IAS 16 will depend on whether the "Aus" paragraphs provide additional guidance for not-for-profit entities or contain requirements that are inconsistent with the corresponding IASB Standard and will be applied by the not-for-profit entity.

Accounting Standard AASB 116

The Australian Accounting Standards Board made Accounting Standard AASB 116 *Property, Plant and Equipment* under section 334 of the *Corporations Act 2001* on 15 July 2004.

This compiled version of AASB 116 applies to annual reporting periods beginning on or after 1 July 2009. It incorporates relevant amendments contained in other AASB Standards made by the AASB and other decisions of the AASB up to and including 25 June 2009 (see Compilation Details).

Accounting Standard AASB 116

Property, Plant and Equipment

Objective

1   The objective of this Standard is to prescribe the accounting treatment for *property, plant and equipment* so that users of the financial statements can discern information about an entity's investment in its property, plant and equipment and the changes in such investment. The principal issues in accounting for property, plant and equipment are the recognition of the assets, the determination of their *carrying amounts* and the *depreciation* charges and *impairment losses* to be recognised in relation to them.

Application

Aus1.1   **This Standard applies to:**

(a)   **each entity that is required to prepare financial reports in accordance with Part 2M.3 of the Corporations Act and that is a reporting entity;**

(b)   **general purpose financial statements of each other reporting entity; and**

(c)   **financial statements that are, or are held out to be, general purpose financial statements.**

Aus1.2   **This Standard applies to annual reporting periods beginning on or after 1 January 2005.**

[Note: For application dates of paragraphs changed or added by an amending Standard, see Compilation Details.]

Aus1.3   **This Standard shall not be applied to annual reporting periods beginning before 1 January 2005.**

Aus1.4   **The requirements specified in this Standard apply to the financial statements where information resulting from their application is material in accordance with AASB 1031 *Materiality*.**

Aus1.5   **When applicable, this Standard supersedes:**

(a)   **AASB 1015 *Acquisitions of Assets* as notified in the *Commonwealth of Australia Gazette* No S 527, 5 November 1999;**

(b)   **AASB 1021 *Depreciation* as notified in the *Commonwealth of Australia Gazette* No S 341, 29 August 1997;**

(c)   **AASB 1041 *Revaluation of Non-Current Assets* as notified in the *Commonwealth of Australia Gazette* No S 294, 19 July 2001;**

(d)   **AAS 4 *Depreciation* as issued in August 1997; and**

(e)   **AAS 21 *Acquisitions of Assets* as issued in November 1999.**

Aus1.6   AASB 1015, AASB 1021, AASB 1041, AAS 4 and AAS 21 remain applicable until superseded by this Standard.

Aus1.7   Notice of this Standard was published in the *Commonwealth of Australia Gazette* No S 294, 22 July 2004.

Scope

2   **This Standard shall be applied in accounting for property, plant and equipment except when another Standard requires or permits a different accounting treatment.**

3   This Standard does not apply to:

    (a)   property, plant and equipment classified as held for sale in accordance with AASB 5 *Non-current Assets Held for Sale and Discontinued Operations*;

    (b)   biological assets related to agricultural activity (see AASB 141 *Agriculture*);

    (c)   the recognition and measurement of exploration and evaluation assets (see AASB 6 *Exploration for and Evaluation of Mineral Resources*); or

    (d)   mineral rights and mineral reserves such as oil, natural gas and similar non-regenerative resources.

However, this Standard applies to property, plant and equipment used to develop or maintain the assets described in (b)-(d).

4   Other Australian Accounting Standards may require recognition of an item of property, plant and equipment based on an approach different from that in this Standard. For example, AASB 117 *Leases* requires an entity to evaluate its recognition of an item of leased property, plant and equipment on the basis of the transfer of risks and rewards. However, in such cases other aspects of the accounting treatment for these assets, including depreciation, are prescribed by this Standard.

5   An entity using the cost model for investment property in accordance with AASB 140 *Investment Property* shall use the cost model in this Standard.

Definitions

6   **The following terms are used in this Standard with the meanings specified.**

    Carrying amount **is the amount at which an asset is recognised after deducting any accumulated depreciation and accumulated impairment losses.**

    Cost **is the amount of cash or cash equivalents paid or the fair value of the other consideration given to acquire an asset at the time of its acquisition or construction or, where applicable, the amount attributed to that asset when initially recognised in accordance with the specific requirements of other Australian Accounting Standards, for example, AASB 2** *Share-based Payment*.

    Depreciable amount **is the cost of an asset, or other amount substituted for cost, less its residual value.**

    Depreciation **is the systematic allocation of the depreciable amount of an asset over its useful life.**

    Entity-specific **value is the present value of the cash flows an entity expects to arise from the continuing use of an asset and from its disposal at the end of its useful life or expects to incur when settling a liability.**

    Fair value **is the amount for which an asset could be exchanged between knowledgeable, willing parties in an arm's length transaction.**

    An *impairment loss* **is the amount by which the carrying amount of an asset exceeds its recoverable amount.**

    Property, plant and equipment **are tangible items that:**

    (a)   **are held for use in the production or supply of goods or services, for rental to others, or for administrative purposes; and**

    (b)   **are expected to be used during more than one period.**

Recoverable amount is the higher of an asset's fair value less costs to sell and its value in use.

The *residual value* of an asset is the estimated amount that an entity would currently obtain from disposal of the asset, after deducting the estimated costs of disposal, if the asset were already of the age and in the condition expected at the end of its useful life.

Useful life is:

(a)   the period over which an asset is expected to be available for use by an entity; or

(b)   the number of production or similar units expected to be obtained from the asset by an entity.

Aus6.1   The following term is also used in this Standard with the meaning specified.

A *not-for-profit entity* is an entity whose principal objective is not the generation of profit. A not-for-profit entity can be a single entity or a group of entities comprising the parent and each of the entities that it controls.

Aus6.2   Examples of property, plant and equipment held by not-for-profit public sector entities and for-profit government departments include, but are not limited to, infrastructure, cultural, community and heritage assets.

Recognition

7   The cost of an item of property, plant and equipment shall be recognised as an asset if, and only if:

(a)   it is probable that future economic benefits associated with the item will flow to the entity; and

(b)   the cost of the item can be measured reliably.

8   Spare parts and servicing equipment are usually carried as inventory and recognised in profit or loss as consumed. However, major spare parts and stand-by equipment qualify as property, plant and equipment when an entity expects to use them during more than one period. Similarly, if the spare parts and servicing equipment can be used only in connection with an item of property, plant and equipment, they are accounted for as property, plant and equipment.

9   This Standard does not prescribe the unit of measure for recognition, that is, what constitutes an item of property, plant and equipment. Thus, judgement is required in applying the recognition criteria to an entity's specific circumstances. It may be appropriate to aggregate individually insignificant items, such as moulds, tools and dies, and to apply the criteria to the aggregate value.

10   An entity evaluates under this recognition principle all its property, plant and equipment costs at the time they are incurred. These costs include costs incurred initially to acquire or construct an item of property, plant and equipment and costs incurred subsequently to add to, replace part of, or service it.

Initial Costs

11   Items of property, plant and equipment may be acquired for safety or environmental reasons. The acquisition of such property, plant and equipment, although not directly increasing the future economic benefits of any particular existing item of property, plant and equipment, may be necessary for an entity to obtain the future economic benefits from its other assets. Such items of property, plant and equipment qualify for recognition as assets because they enable an entity to derive future economic benefits from related assets in excess of what could be derived had it not been acquired. For example, a chemical manufacturer may install new chemical handling processes to comply with environmental requirements for the production and storage of dangerous chemicals; related plant enhancements are recognised as an asset because, without them, the entity is unable to manufacture and sell chemicals. However, the resulting carrying amount of

such an asset and related assets is reviewed for impairment in accordance with AASB 136 *Impairment of Assets*.

Subsequent Costs

12   Under the recognition principle in paragraph 7, an entity does not recognise in the carrying amount of an item of property, plant and equipment the costs of the day-to-day servicing of the item. Rather, these costs are recognised in profit or loss as incurred. Costs of day-to-day servicing are primarily the costs of labour and consumables, and may include the cost of small parts. The purpose of these expenditures is often described as for the 'repairs and maintenance' of the item of property, plant and equipment.

13   Parts of some items of property, plant and equipment may require replacement at regular intervals. For example, a furnace may require relining after a specified number of hours of use, or aircraft interiors such as seats and galleys may require replacement several times during the life of the airframe. Items of property, plant and equipment may also be acquired to make a less frequently recurring replacement, such as replacing the interior walls of a building, or to make a non-recurring replacement. Under the recognition principle in paragraph 7, an entity recognises in the carrying amount of an item of property, plant and equipment the cost of replacing part of such an item when that cost is incurred if the recognition criteria are met. The carrying amount of those parts that are replaced is derecognised in accordance with the derecognition provisions of this Standard (see paragraphs 67–72).

14   A condition of continuing to operate an item of property, plant and equipment (e.g. an aircraft) may be performing regular major inspections for faults regardless of whether parts of the item are replaced. When each major inspection is performed, its cost is recognised in the carrying amount of the item of property, plant and equipment as a replacement if the recognition criteria are satisfied. Any remaining carrying amount of the cost of the previous inspection (as distinct from physical parts) is derecognised. This occurs regardless of whether the cost of the previous inspection was identified in the transaction in which the item was acquired or constructed. If necessary, the estimated cost of a future similar inspection may be used as an indication of what the cost of the existing inspection component was when the item was acquired or constructed.

Measurement at Recognition

15   **An item of property, plant and equipment that qualifies for recognition as an asset shall be measured at its cost.**

Aus15.1   **Notwithstanding paragraph 15, in respect of *not-for-profit entities*, where an asset is acquired at no cost, or for a nominal cost, the cost is its fair value as at the date of acquisition.**

Aus15.2   In respect of not-for-profit entities, an item of property, plant and equipment may be gifted or contributed to the entity. For example, land may be contributed to a local government by a developer at no or nominal consideration to enable the local government to develop parks, roads and paths in the development. An asset may also be acquired for no or nominal consideration through the exercise of powers of sequestration. Under these circumstances the cost of the item is its fair value as at the date it is acquired.

Aus15.3   In respect of not-for-profit entities, for the purposes of this Standard, the initial recognition at fair value of an item of property, plant and equipment, acquired at no or nominal cost, consistent with the requirements of paragraph Aus15.1, does not constitute a revaluation. Accordingly, the revaluation requirements in paragraph 31, and the supporting commentary in paragraphs 32 to 35, only apply where an entity elects to revalue an item of property, plant and equipment in subsequent reporting periods.

Elements of Cost

16   The cost of an item of property, plant and equipment comprises:

   (a)   its purchase price, including import duties and non-refundable purchase taxes, after deducting trade discounts and rebates;

AASB 116

(b)　any costs directly attributable to bringing the asset to the location and condition necessary for it to be capable of operating in the manner intended by management; and

(c)　the initial estimate of the costs of dismantling and removing the item and restoring the site on which it is located, the obligation for which an entity incurs either when the item is acquired or as a consequence of having used the item during a particular period for purposes other than to produce inventories during that period.

17　Examples of directly attributable costs are:

(a)　costs of employee benefits (as defined in AASB 119 *Employee Benefits*) arising directly from the construction or acquisition of the item of property, plant and equipment;

(b)　costs of site preparation;

(c)　initial delivery and handling costs;

(d)　installation and assembly costs;

(e)　costs of testing whether the asset is functioning properly, after deducting the net proceeds from selling any items produced while bringing the asset to that location and condition (such as samples produced when testing equipment); and

(f)　professional fees.

18　An entity applies AASB 102 *Inventories* to the costs of obligations for asset dismantling, removing and restoring the site on which an item is located that are incurred during a particular period as a consequence of having used the item to produce inventories during that period. The obligations for costs accounted for in accordance with AASB 102 or AASB 116 are recognised and measured in accordance with AASB 137 *Provisions, Contingent Liabilities and Contingent Assets*.

19　Examples of costs that are not costs of an item of property, plant and equipment are:

(a)　costs of opening a new facility;

(b)　costs of introducing a new product or service (including costs of advertising and promotional activities);

(c)　costs of conducting business in a new location or with a new class of customer (including costs of staff training); and

(d)　administration and other general overhead costs.

20　Recognition of costs in the carrying amount of an item of property, plant and equipment ceases when the item is in the location and condition necessary for it to be capable of operating in the manner intended by management. Therefore, costs incurred in using or redeploying an item are not included in the carrying amount of that item. For example, the following costs are not included in the carrying amount of an item of property, plant and equipment:

(a)　costs incurred while an item capable of operating in the manner intended by management has yet to be brought into use or is operated at less than full capacity;

(b)　initial operating losses, such as those incurred while demand for the item's output builds up; and

(c)　costs of relocating or reorganising part or all of an entity's operations.

21　Some operations occur in connection with the construction or development of an item of property, plant and equipment, but are not necessary to bring the item to the location and condition necessary for it to be capable of operating in the manner intended by management. These incidental operations may occur before or during the construction or development activities. For example, income may be earned through using a building site as a car park until construction starts. Because incidental operations are not necessary to bring an item to the location and condition necessary for it to be capable of operating in the manner intended by management, the income and related expenses of incidental operations are recognised in profit or loss and included in their respective classifications of income and expense.

22   The cost of a self-constructed asset is determined using the same principles as for an acquired asset. If an entity makes similar assets for sale in the normal course of business, the cost of the asset is usually the same as the cost of constructing an asset for sale (see AASB 102). Therefore, any internal profits are eliminated in arriving at such costs. Similarly, the cost of abnormal amounts of wasted material, labour, or other resources incurred in self-constructing an asset is not included in the cost of the asset. AASB 123 *Borrowing Costs* establishes criteria for the recognition of interest as a component of the carrying amount of a self-constructed item of property, plant and equipment.

Measurement of Cost

23   The cost of an item of property, plant and equipment is the cash price equivalent at the recognition date. If payment is deferred beyond normal credit terms, the difference between the cash price equivalent and the total payment is recognised as interest over the period of credit unless such interest is capitalised in accordance with AASB 123.

24   One or more items of property, plant and equipment may be acquired in exchange for a non-monetary asset or assets, or a combination of monetary and non-monetary assets. The following discussion refers simply to an exchange of one non-monetary asset for another, but it also applies to all exchanges described in the preceding sentence. The cost of such an item of property, plant and equipment is measured at fair value unless (a) the exchange transaction lacks commercial substance or (b) the fair value of neither the asset received nor the asset given up is reliably measurable. The acquired item is measured in this way even if an entity cannot immediately derecognise the asset given up. If the acquired item is not measured at fair value, its cost is measured at the carrying amount of the asset given up.

25   An entity determines whether an exchange transaction has commercial substance by considering the extent to which its future cash flows are expected to change as a result of the transaction. An exchange transaction has commercial substance if:

     (a)   the configuration (risk, timing and amount) of the cash flows of the asset received differs from the configuration of the cash flows of the asset transferred; or

     (b)   the *entity-specific value* of the portion of the entity's operations affected by the transaction changes as a result of the exchange; and

     (c)   the difference in (a) or (b) is significant relative to the fair value of the assets exchanged.

    For the purpose of determining whether an exchange transaction has commercial substance, the entity-specific value of the portion of the entity's operations affected by the transaction shall reflect post-tax cash flows. The result of these analyses may be clear without an entity having to perform detailed calculations.

26   The fair value of an asset for which comparable market transactions do not exist is reliably measurable if (a) the variability in the range of reasonable fair value estimates is not significant for that asset or (b) the probabilities of the various estimates within the range can be reasonably assessed and used in estimating fair value. If an entity is able to determine reliably the fair value of either the asset received or the asset given up, then the fair value of the asset given up is used to measure the cost of the asset received unless the fair value of the asset received is more clearly evident.

27   The cost of an item of property, plant and equipment held by a lessee under a finance lease is determined in accordance with AASB 117.

28   The carrying amount of an item of property, plant and equipment may be reduced by government grants in accordance with AASB 120 *Accounting for Government Grants and Disclosure of Government Assistance.*

Measurement after Recognition

29   **An entity shall choose either the cost model in paragraph 30 or the revaluation model in paragraph 31 as its accounting policy and shall apply that policy to an entire class of property, plant and equipment.**

Cost Model

30 After recognition as an asset, an item of property, plant and equipment shall be carried at its cost less any accumulated depreciation and any accumulated impairment losses.

Revaluation Model

31 After recognition as an asset, an item of property, plant and equipment whose fair value can be measured reliably shall be carried at a revalued amount, being its fair value at the date of the revaluation less any subsequent accumulated depreciation and subsequent accumulated impairment losses. Revaluations shall be made with sufficient regularity to ensure that the carrying amount does not differ materially from that which would be determined using fair value at the end of the reporting period.

32 The fair value of land and buildings is usually determined from market-based evidence by appraisal that is normally undertaken by professionally qualified valuers. The fair value of items of plant and equipment is usually their market value determined by appraisal.

33 If there is no market-based evidence of fair value because of the specialised nature of the item of property, plant and equipment and the item is rarely sold, except as part of a continuing business, an entity may need to estimate fair value using an income or a depreciated replacement cost approach.

34 The frequency of revaluations depends upon the changes in fair values of the items of property, plant and equipment being revalued. When the fair value of a revalued asset differs materially from its carrying amount, a further revaluation is required. Some items of property, plant and equipment experience significant and volatile changes in fair value, thus necessitating annual revaluation. Such frequent revaluations are unnecessary for items of property, plant and equipment with only insignificant changes in fair value. Instead, it may be necessary to revalue the item only every three or five years.

35 When an item of property, plant and equipment is revalued, any accumulated depreciation at the date of the revaluation is treated in one of the following ways:

(a) restated proportionately with the change in the gross carrying amount of the asset so that the carrying amount of the asset after revaluation equals its revalued amount. This method is often used when an asset is revalued by means of applying an index to determine its depreciated replacement cost; or

(b) eliminated against the gross carrying amount of the asset and the net amount restated to the revalued amount of the asset. This method is often used for buildings.

The amount of the adjustment arising on the restatement or elimination of accumulated depreciation forms part of the increase or decrease in carrying amount that is accounted for in accordance with paragraphs 39, Aus39.1, 40, Aus40.1 and Aus40.2.

36 **If an item of property, plant and equipment is revalued, the entire class of property, plant and equipment to which that asset belongs shall be revalued.**

37 A class of property, plant and equipment is a grouping of assets of a similar nature and use in an entity's operations. The following are examples of separate classes:

(a) land;

(b) land and buildings;

(c) machinery;

(d) ships;

(e) aircraft;

(f) motor vehicles;

(g) furniture and fixtures; and

(h) office equipment.

38 The items within a class of property, plant and equipment are revalued simultaneously to avoid selective revaluation of assets and the reporting of amounts in the financial

statements that are a mixture of costs and values as at different dates. However, a class of assets may be revalued on a rolling basis provided revaluation of the class of assets is completed within a short period and provided the revaluations are kept up to date.

39   **If an asset's carrying amount is increased as a result of a revaluation, the increase shall be recognised in other comprehensive income and accumulated in equity under the heading of revaluation surplus. However, the increase shall be recognised in profit or loss to the extent that it reverses a revaluation decrease of the same asset previously recognised in profit or loss.**

Aus39.1   **Notwithstanding paragraph 39, in respect of not-for-profit entities, if the carrying amount of a class of assets is increased as a result of a revaluation, the net revaluation increase shall be recognised in other comprehensive income and accumulated in equity under the heading of revaluation surplus. However, the net revaluation increase shall be recognised in profit or loss to the extent that it reverses a net revaluation decrease of the same class of assets previously recognised in profit or loss.**

40   **If an asset's carrying amount is decreased as a result of a revaluation, the decrease shall be recognised in profit or loss. However, the decrease shall be recognised in other comprehensive income to the extent of any credit balance existing in the revaluation surplus in respect of that asset. The decrease recognised in other comprehensive income reduces the amount accumulated in equity under the heading of revaluation surplus.**

Aus40.1   **Notwithstanding paragraph 40, in respect of not-for-profit entities, if the carrying amount of a class of assets decreased as a result of a revaluation, the net revaluation decrease shall be recognised in profit or loss. However, the net revaluation decrease shall be recognised in other comprehensive income to the extent of any credit balance existing in any revaluation surplus in respect of that same class of asset. The net revaluation decrease recognised in other comprehensive income reduces the amount accumulated in equity under the heading of revaluation surplus.**

Aus40.2   **Notwithstanding paragraph 40, in respect of not-for-profit entities, revaluation increases and revaluation decreases relating to individual assets within a class of property, plant and equipment shall be offset against one another within that class but shall not be offset in respect of assets in different classes.**

41   The revaluation surplus included in equity in respect of an item of property, plant and equipment may be transferred directly to retained earnings when the asset is derecognised. This may involve transferring the whole of the surplus when the asset is retired or disposed of. However, some of the surplus may be transferred as the asset is used by an entity. In such a case, the amount of the surplus transferred would be the difference between depreciation based on the revalued carrying amount of the asset and depreciation based on the asset's original cost. Transfers from revaluation surplus to retained earnings are not made through profit or loss.

42   The effects of taxes on income, if any, resulting from the revaluation of property, plant and equipment are recognised and disclosed in accordance with AASB 112 *Income Taxes*.

Depreciation

43   **Each part of an item of property, plant and equipment with a cost that is significant in relation to the total cost of the item shall be depreciated separately.**

44   An entity allocates the amount initially recognised in respect of an item of property, plant and equipment to its significant parts and depreciates separately each such part. For example, it may be appropriate to depreciate separately the airframe and engines of an aircraft, whether owned or subject to a finance lease. Similarly, if an entity acquires property, plant and equipment subject to an operating lease in which it is the lessor, it may be appropriate to depreciate separately amounts reflected in the cost of that item that are attributable to favourable or unfavourable lease terms relative to market terms.

45   A significant part of an item of property, plant and equipment may have a useful life and a depreciation method that are the same as the *useful life* and the depreciation method of another significant part of that same item. Such parts may be grouped in determining the depreciation charge.

46 To the extent that an entity depreciates separately some parts of an item of property, plant and equipment, it also depreciates separately the remainder of the item. The remainder consists of the parts of the item that are individually not significant. If an entity has varying expectations for these parts, approximation techniques may be necessary to depreciate the remainder in a manner that faithfully represents the consumption pattern and/or useful life of its parts.

47 An entity may choose to depreciate separately the parts of an item that do not have a cost that is significant in relation to the total cost of the item.

48 **The depreciation charge for each period shall be recognised in profit or loss unless it is included in the carrying amount of another asset.**

49 The depreciation charge for a period is usually recognised in profit or loss. However, sometimes, the future economic benefits embodied in an asset are absorbed in producing other assets. In this case, the depreciation charge constitutes part of the cost of the other asset and is included in its carrying amount. For example, the depreciation of manufacturing plant and equipment is included in the costs of conversion of inventories (see AASB 102). Similarly, depreciation of property, plant and equipment used for development activities may be included in the cost of an intangible asset recognised in accordance with AASB 138 *Intangible Assets*.

Depreciable Amount and Depreciation Period

50 **The *depreciable amount* of an asset shall be allocated on a systematic basis over its useful life.**

51 **The *residual value* and the useful life of an asset shall be reviewed at least at the end of each annual reporting period and, if expectations differ from previous estimates, the change(s) shall be accounted for as a change in an accounting estimate in accordance with AASB 108 *Accounting Policies, Changes in Accounting Estimates and Errors*.**

52 Depreciation is recognised even if the fair value of the asset exceeds its carrying amount, as long as the asset's residual value does not exceed its carrying amount. Repair and maintenance of an asset do not negate the need to depreciate it.

53 The depreciable amount of an asset is determined after deducting its residual value. In practice, the residual value of an asset is often insignificant and therefore immaterial in the calculation of the depreciable amount.

54 The residual value of an asset may increase to an amount equal to or greater than the asset's carrying amount. If it does, the asset's depreciation charge is zero unless and until its residual value subsequently decreases to an amount below the asset's carrying amount.

55 Depreciation of an asset begins when it is available for use, that is, when it is in the location and condition necessary for it to be capable of operating in the manner intended by management. Depreciation of an asset ceases at the earlier of the date that the asset is classified as held for sale (or included in a disposal group that is classified as held for sale) in accordance with AASB 5 and the date that the asset is derecognised. Therefore, depreciation does not cease when the asset becomes idle or is retired from active use unless the asset is fully depreciated. However, under usage methods of depreciation the depreciation charge can be zero while there is no production.

56 The future economic benefits embodied in an asset are consumed by an entity principally through its use. However, other factors, such as technical or commercial obsolescence and wear and tear while an asset remains idle, often result in the diminution of the economic benefits that might have been obtained from the asset. Consequently, all the following factors are considered in determining the useful life of an asset:

(a) expected usage of the asset. Usage is assessed by reference to the asset's expected capacity or physical output.

(b) expected physical wear and tear, which depends on operational factors such as the number of shifts for which the asset is to be used and the repair and maintenance programme, and the care and maintenance of the asset while idle.

(c) technical or commercial obsolescence arising from changes or improvements in production, or from a change in the market demand for the product or service output of the asset.

(d) legal or similar limits on the use of the asset, such as the expiry dates of related leases.

57 The useful life of an asset is defined in terms of the asset's expected utility to the entity. The asset management policy of the entity may involve the disposal of assets after a specified time or after consumption of a specified proportion of the future economic benefits embodied in the asset. Therefore, the useful life of an asset may be shorter than its economic life. The estimation of the useful life of the asset is a matter of judgement based on the experience of the entity with similar assets.

58 Land and buildings are separable assets and are accounted for separately, even when they are acquired together. With some exceptions, such as quarries and sites used for landfill, land has an unlimited useful life and therefore is not depreciated. Buildings have a limited useful life and therefore are depreciable assets. An increase in the value of the land on which a building stands does not affect the determination of the depreciable amount of the building.

59 If the cost of land includes the costs of site dismantlement, removal and restoration, that portion of the land asset is depreciated over the period of benefits obtained by incurring those costs. In some cases, the land itself may have a limited useful life, in which case it is depreciated in a manner that reflects the benefits to be derived from it.

Depreciation Method

60 **The depreciation method used shall reflect the pattern in which the asset's future economic benefits are expected to be consumed by the entity.**

61 **The depreciation method applied to an asset shall be reviewed at least at the end of each annual reporting period and, if there has been a significant change in the expected pattern of consumption of the future economic benefits embodied in the asset, the method shall be changed to reflect the changed pattern. Such a change shall be accounted for as a change in an accounting estimate in accordance with AASB 108.**

62 A variety of depreciation methods can be used to allocate the depreciable amount of an asset on a systematic basis over its useful life. These methods include the straight-line method, the diminishing balance method and the units of production method. Straight-line depreciation results in a constant charge over the useful life if the asset's residual value does not change. The diminishing balance method results in a decreasing charge over the useful life. The units of production method results in a charge based on the expected use or output. The entity selects the method that most closely reflects the expected pattern of consumption of the future economic benefits embodied in the asset. That method is applied consistently from period to period unless there is a change in the expected pattern of consumption of those future economic benefits.

Impairment

63 To determine whether an item of property, plant and equipment is impaired, an entity applies AASB 136. That Standard explains how an entity reviews the carrying amount of its assets, how it determines the *recoverable amount* of an asset, and when it recognises, or reverses the recognition of, an impairment loss.

64 [Deleted by the IASB]

Compensation for Impairment

65 **Compensation from third parties for items of property, plant and equipment that were impaired, lost or given up shall be included in profit or loss when the compensation becomes receivable.**

66 Impairments or losses of items of property, plant and equipment, related claims for or payments of compensation from third parties and any subsequent purchase or construction

of replacement assets are separate economic events and are accounted for separately as follows:

(a) impairments of items of property, plant and equipment are recognised in accordance with AASB 136;

(b) the derecognition of items of property, plant and equipment retired or disposed of is determined in accordance with this Standard;

(c) compensation from third parties for items of property, plant and equipment that were impaired, lost or given up is included in determining profit or loss when it becomes receivable; and

(d) the cost of items of property, plant and equipment restored, purchased or constructed as replacements is determined in accordance with this Standard.

Derecognition

67 The carrying amount of an item of property, plant and equipment shall be derecognised:

(a) on disposal; or

(b) when no future economic benefits are expected from its use or disposal.

68 The gain or loss arising from the derecognition of an item of property, plant and equipment shall be included in profit or loss when the item is derecognised (unless AASB 117 requires otherwise on a sale and leaseback). Gains shall not be classified as revenue.

68A However, an entity that, in the course of its ordinary activities, routinely sells items of property, plant and equipment that it has held for rental to others shall transfer such assets to inventories at their carrying amount when they cease to be rented and become held for sale. The proceeds from the sale of such assets shall be recognised as revenue in accordance with AASB 118 *Revenue*. AASB 5 does not apply when assets that are held for sale in the ordinary course of business are transferred to inventories.

69 The disposal of an item of property, plant and equipment may occur in a variety of ways (e.g. by sale, by entering into a finance lease or by donation). In determining the date of disposal of an item, an entity applies the criteria in AASB 118 for recognising revenue from the sale of goods. AASB 117 applies to disposal by a sale and leaseback.

70 If, under the recognition principle in paragraph 7, an entity recognises in the carrying amount of an item of property, plant and equipment the cost of a replacement for part of the item, then it derecognises the carrying amount of the replaced part regardless of whether the replaced part had been depreciated separately. If it is not practicable for an entity to determine the carrying amount of the replaced part, it may use the cost of the replacement as an indication of what the cost of the replaced part was at the time it was acquired or constructed.

71 The gain or loss arising from the derecognition of an item of property, plant and equipment shall be determined as the difference between the net disposal proceeds, if any, and the carrying amount of the item.

72 The consideration receivable on disposal of an item of property, plant and equipment is recognised initially at its fair value. If payment for the item is deferred, the consideration received is recognised initially at the cash price equivalent. The difference between the nominal amount of the consideration and the cash price equivalent is recognised as interest revenue in accordance with AASB 118 reflecting the effective yield on the receivable.

Disclosure

73 The financial statements shall disclose, for each class of property, plant and equipment:

(a) the measurement bases used for determining the gross carrying amount;

(b) the depreciation methods used;

(c) the useful lives or the depreciation rates used;

(d)   the gross carrying amount and the accumulated depreciation (aggregated with accumulated impairment losses) at the beginning and end of the period; and

(e)   a reconciliation of the carrying amount at the beginning and end of the period showing:

     (i)   additions;

     (ii)   assets classified as held for sale or included in a disposal group classified as held for sale in accordance with AASB 5 and other disposals;

     (iii)   acquisitions through business combinations;

     (iv)   increases or decreases resulting from revaluations under paragraphs 31, 39, Aus39.1, 40, Aus40.1 and Aus40.2 and from impairment losses recognised or reversed in other comprehensive income in accordance with AASB 136;

     (v)   impairment losses recognised in profit or loss in accordance with AASB 136;

     (vi)   impairment losses reversed in profit or loss in accordance with AASB 136;

     (vii)   depreciation;

     (viii)   the net exchange differences arising on the translation of the financial statements from the functional currency into a different presentation currency, including the translation of a foreign operation into the presentation currency of the reporting entity; and

     (ix)   other changes.

74   The financial statements shall also disclose:

(a)   the existence and amounts of restrictions on title, and property, plant and equipment pledged as security for liabilities;

(b)   the amount of expenditures recognised in the carrying amount of an item of property, plant and equipment in the course of its construction;

(c)   the amount of contractual commitments for the acquisition of property, plant and equipment; and

(d)   if it is not disclosed separately in the statement of comprehensive income, the amount of compensation from third parties for items of property, plant and equipment that were impaired, lost or given up that is included in profit or loss.

75   Selection of the depreciation method and estimation of the useful life of assets are matters of judgement. Therefore, disclosure of the methods adopted and the estimated useful lives or depreciation rates provides users of the financial statements with information that allows them to review the policies selected by management and enables comparisons to be made with other entities. For similar reasons, it is necessary to disclose:

(a)   depreciation, whether recognised in profit or loss or as a part of the cost of other assets, during a period; and

(b)   accumulated depreciation at the end of the period.

76   In accordance with AASB 108 an entity discloses the nature and effect of a change in an accounting estimate that has an effect in the current period or is expected to have an effect in subsequent periods. For property, plant and equipment, such disclosure may arise from changes in estimates with respect to:

(a)   residual values;

(b)   the estimated costs of dismantling, removing or restoring items of property, plant and equipment;

(c)   useful lives; and

(d)   depreciation methods.

77 If items of property, plant and equipment are stated at revalued amounts, the following shall be disclosed:

(a) the effective date of the revaluation;

(b) whether an independent valuer was involved;

(c) the methods and significant assumptions applied in estimating the items' fair values;

(d) the extent to which the items' fair values were determined directly by reference to observable prices in an active market or recent market transactions on arm's length terms or were estimated using other valuation techniques;

(e) for each revalued class of property, plant and equipment, the carrying amount that would have been recognised had the assets been carried under the cost model; and

(f) the revaluation surplus, indicating the change for the period and any restrictions on the distribution of the balance to shareholders.

Aus77.1 Notwithstanding paragraph 77(e), in respect of not-for-profit entities, for each revalued class of property, plant and equipment, the requirement to disclose the carrying amount that would have been recognised had the assets been carried under the cost model does not apply.

78 In accordance with AASB 136 an entity discloses information on impaired property, plant and equipment in addition to the information required by paragraph 73(e)(iv)-(vi).

79 Users of financial statements may also find the following information relevant to their needs:

(a) the carrying amount of temporarily idle property, plant and equipment;

(b) the gross carrying amount of any fully depreciated property, plant and equipment that is still in use;

(c) the carrying amount of property, plant and equipment retired from active use and not classified as held for sale in accordance with AASB 5; and

(d) when the cost model is used, the fair value of property, plant and equipment when this is materially different from the carrying amount.

Therefore, entities are encouraged to disclose these amounts.

Transitional Provisions of IAS 16

80 [Deleted by the AASB]

Effective Date

81 [Deleted by the AASB]

81B [Deleted by the AASB]

81C [Deleted by the AASB]

81D Paragraphs 6 and 69 were amended and paragraph 68A was added by AASB 2008-5 *Amendments to Australian Accounting Standards arising from the Annual Improvements Project* issued in July 2008. An entity shall apply those amendments for annual reporting periods beginning on or after 1 January 2009. Earlier application is permitted. If an entity applies the amendments for an earlier period it shall disclose that fact and at the same time apply the related amendments to AASB 107 *Statement of Cash Flows*.

81E Paragraph 5 was amended by AASB 2008-5 *Amendments to Australian Accounting Standards arising from the Annual Improvements Project* issued in July 2008. An entity shall apply that amendment prospectively for annual reporting periods beginning on or after 1 January 2009. Earlier application is permitted if an entity also applies the amendments to paragraphs 8, 9, 22, 48, 53, 53A, 53B, 54, 57 and 85B of AASB 140 at the same time. If an entity applies the amendment for an earlier period it shall disclosure that fact.

Withdrawal of Other Pronouncements of the IASB

82   [Deleted by the AASB]

83   [Deleted by the AASB]

Australian Implementation Guidance

This guidance accompanies, but is not part of, AASB 116. This guidance is pertinent to not-for-profit public sector entities and for-profit government departments that hold heritage or cultural assets.

G1   In accordance with paragraphs 7(b), 15 and Aus15.1 of AASB 116, only those heritage and cultural assets that can be reliably measured are recognised. It depends on the circumstances as to whether the reliable measurement recognition criterion can be satisfied in relation to a particular heritage or cultural asset. Heritage and cultural assets acquired at no cost, or for a nominal cost, are required to be initially recognised at fair value as at the date of acquisition. Depending on circumstances, it may not be possible to reliably measure the fair value as at the date of acquisition of a heritage or cultural asset.

G2   Of those heritage and cultural assets that satisfy the reliable measurement criterion for initial recognition purposes, paragraph 29 of AASB 116 permits, but does not require, revaluation. However, under AASB 1049 *Whole of Government and General Government Sector Financial Reporting*, GGSs and whole of governments are required to adopt those optional treatments in Australian Accounting Standards that are aligned with the principles or rules in the Australian Bureau of Statistics Government Finance Statistics (GFS) Manual. Consequently, those entities would be required to adopt a revaluation model for heritage and cultural assets recognised under AASB 116 where the reliable measurement recognition criterion is satisfied.

G3   Furthermore, given the nature of many heritage and cultural assets that meet the recognition criteria, those assets may not have limited useful lives (for example, when the entity adopts appropriate curatorial and preservation policies), and therefore may not be subject to depreciation. However, they would be subject to impairment testing when there is an indication of impairment.

G4   The curatorial and preservation policies referred to in paragraph G3 above would typically be those developed and monitored by qualified personnel and include the following:

(a)   a clearly stated objective about the holding and preservation of items;

(b)   a well-developed plan to achieve the objective, including demonstration of how the policy will be implemented, based on advice by appropriately qualified experts;

(c)   monitoring procedures; and

(d)   periodic reviews.

In addition, there would be evidence that the policies have been adopted by the governing body of the entity.

AASB 117

Leases

(Compiled December 2009)

Note from the Institute of Chartered Accountants Australia

This note, prepared by the technical editors, is not part of Accounting Standard AASB 117.

Historical development

15 July 2004: AASB 117 'Leases' is the Australian equivalent of IAS 17 of the same name. It was made by the AASB on 15 July 2004 as part of the AASB's program to adopt International Financial Reporting Standards (IFRSs) by 2005.

5 September 2005: AASB 2005-10 'Amendments to Australian Accounting Standards' amends paragraphs 31, 35, 47, and 56. The amendments are applicable to annual reporting periods beginning on or after 1 January 2007, although entities may choose to early-adopt this Standard for annual reporting periods beginning on or after 1 January 2005.

15 February 2007: AASB 2007-2 'Amendments to Australian Accounting Standards' amends paragraphs 10, 33, and 50 and is applicable to annual reporting periods ending on or after 28 February 2007. Entities may elect to early-adopt it to annual reporting periods beginning on or after 1 January 2005.

30 April 2007: AASB 2007-4 'Amendments to Australian Accounting Standards' amends paragraphs 13 and 41 and is applicable to annual reporting periods beginning on or after 1 July 2007. Entities may elect to early-adopt it to annual reporting periods beginning on or after 1 January 2005.

24 September 2007: AASB 2007-8 'Amendments to Australian Accounting Standards' amends AASB 117, changing the term 'general purpose financial reports' to 'general purpose financial statements'. This Standard is applicable to annual reporting periods beginning on or after 1 January 2009.

21 May 2009: AASB 2009-5 'Amendments to Australian Accounting Standards' is the annual improvements Standard, amending AASB 117 in relation to the classification of leases of land and buildings. This Standard applies to annual reporting periods beginning on or after 1 January 2010 and may be applied early.

25 June 2009: AASB 2009-6 'Amendments to Australian Accounting Standards' amends AASB 117 for editorial corrections made by the International Accounting Standards Board (IASB) to its Standards and Interpretations (IFRSs) and as a consequence of issuing revised AASB 101 'Presentation of Financial Statements'. This Standard is applicable to annual reporting periods beginning on or after 1 January 2009 that end on or after 30 June 2009.

30 October 2009: AASB 117 was reissued by the AASB, compiled to include the AASB 2007-8 and AASB 2009-6 amendments and applies to annual reporting periods beginning on or after 1 January 2009 but before 1 January 2010 that end on or after 30 June 2009. Early application is permitted.

1 December 2009: AASB 117 was reissued by the AASB, compiled to include the AASB 2009-5 amendments and applies to annual reporting periods beginning on or after 1 January 2010.

5 September 2011: AASB 2011-8 'Amendments to Australian Accounting Standards arising from AASB 13' amends AASB 117 to give effect to a consequential change in the definition of fair value arising from the issue of AASB 13. This Standard applies to annual reporting periods beginning on or after 1 January 2013 and can be adopted early. **These amendments are not included in this compiled Standard.**

References

Interpretation 4 *Determining whether an Arrangement contains a Lease*, Interpretation 12 *Service Concession Arrangements*, Interpretation 115 *Operating Leases – Incentives* and Interpretation 127 *Evaluating the Substance of Transactions Involving the Legal Form of a Lease*, Interpretation 129 *Service Concession Arrangements: Disclosures*, Interpretation 132 *Intangible Assets – Web Site Costs*, apply to AASB 117.

AASB item not taken onto the agenda: *Recognition of Contingent Rentals* applies to AASB 117.

IFRIC items not taken onto the agenda: No. 17 *Depreciation of fixed assets*, No. 18 *IAS 16 Property, Plant and Equipment and IAS 17 Leases: Depreciation of assets leased under operating leases* issued in November 2004, No. 19 *Consideration of the issues addressed in UITF Abstract 36 Contracts for sale of capacity*, IAS 17-1 *Finance subleases of finance leases*, IAS 17-2 *Recognition of operating lease incentives under SIC-15*, IAS 17-3 *Time pattern of user's benefits from an operating lease*, IAS 17-4 *Leases of land that do not transfer land to the lessee*, IAS 17-5 *Recognition of contingent rentals* and IAS 17-6 *Sale and leaseback with repurchase agreements* apply to AASB 117.

AASB 117 compared to IAS 17

Additions

Paragraph	Description
Aus 1.1	Which entities AASB 117 applies to (i.e. reporting entities and general purpose financial statements).
Aus 1.2	The application date of AASB 117 (i.e. annual reporting periods beginning 1 January 2005).
Aus 1.3	Prohibits early application of AASB 117.
Aus 1.4	Makes the requirements of AASB 117 subject to AASB 1031 'Materiality'.
Aus 1.5	Explains which Australian Standards have been superseded by AASB 117.
Aus 1.6	Clarifies that the superseded Australian Standards remain in force until AASB 117 applies.
Aus 1.7	Notice of the new Standard published on 22 July 2004.

Deletions

Paragraph	Description
67	Transitional provision for entities applying IAS 17 for the first time encourages retrospective application.
68	Transitional provision for entities that applied the previous version of IAS 17.
69	Effective date of IAS 17.
70	Reference to superseded IAS 17.

Contents

Compilation Details

Comparison with IAS 17

Accounting Standard
AASB 117 Leases

	Paragraphs
Objective	1
Application	Aus1.1 – Aus1.7
Scope	2 – 3
Definitions	4 – 6
Classification of Leases	7 – 19
Leases in the Financial Statements of Lessees	
Finance Leases	
Initial recognition	20 – 24
Subsequent measurement	25 – 30
Disclosures	31 – 32
Operating Leases	33 – 34
Disclosures	35
Leases in the Financial Statements of Lessors	
Finance Leases	
Initial recognition	36 – 38
Subsequent measurement	39 – 46
Disclosures	47 – 48
Operating Leases	49 – 55
Disclosures	56 – 57
Sale and Leaseback Transactions	58 – 66
Transitional Provisions	68A
Effective Date	69A

Implementation Guidance

Basis for Conclusions on IAS 17
(available on the AASB website)

Australian Accounting Standard AASB 117 *Leases* (as amended) is set out in paragraphs 1 – 69A. All the paragraphs have equal authority. Terms defined in this Standard are in *italics* the first time they appear in the Standard. AASB 117 is to be read in the context of other Australian Accounting Standards, including AASB 1048 *Interpretation and Application of Standards*, which identifies the Australian Accounting Interpretations. In the absence of explicit guidance, AASB 108 *Accounting Policies, Changes in Accounting Estimates and Errors* provides a basis for selecting and applying accounting policies.

Compilation Details

Accounting Standard AASB 117 *Leases* as amended

This compiled Standard applies to annual reporting periods beginning on or after 1 January 2010. It takes into account amendments up to and including 25 June 2009 and was prepared on 1 December 2009 by the staff of the Australian Accounting Standards Board (AASB).

This compilation is not a separate Accounting Standard made by the AASB. Instead, it is a representation of AASB 117 (July 2004) as amended by other Accounting Standards, which are listed in the Table below.

Table of Standards

Standard	Date made	Application date *(annual reporting periods ... on or after ...)*	Application, saving or transitional provisions
AASB 117	15 Jul 2004	*(beginning)* 1 Jan 2005	
AASB 2005-10	5 Sep 2005	*(beginning)* 1 Jan 2007	see (a) below
AASB 2007-2	15 Feb 2007	*(ending)* 28 Feb 2007	see (b) below
AASB 2007-4	30 Apr 2007	*(beginning)* 1 Jul 2007	see (c) below
AASB 2007-8	24 Sep 2007	*(beginning)* 1 Jan 2009	see (d) below
AASB 2009-5	21 May 2009	*(beginning)* 1 Jan 2010	see (e) below
AASB 2009-6	25 Jun 2009	*(beginning)* 1 Jan 2009 and *(ending)* 30 Jun 2009	see (f) below

(a)　Entities may elect to apply this Standard to annual reporting periods beginning on or after 1 January 2005 but before 1 January 2007.

(b)　Entities may elect to apply the relevant amendments to annual reporting periods beginning on or after 1 January 2005 that end before 28 February 2007.

(c)　Entities may elect to apply this Standard to annual reporting periods beginning on or after 1 January 2005 but before 1 July 2007.

(d)　Entities may elect to apply this Standard to annual reporting periods beginning on or after 1 January 2005 but before 1 January 2009, provided that AASB 101 *Presentation of Financial Statements* (September 2007) is also applied to such periods.

(e)　Entities may elect to apply this Standard, or its amendments to individual Standards, to annual reporting periods beginning on or after 1 January 2005 but before 1 January 2010.

(f)　Entities may elect to apply this Standard to annual reporting periods beginning on or after 1 January 2005 but before 1 January 2009, provided that AASB 101 *Presentation of Financial Statements* (September 2007) is also applied to such periods, and to annual reporting periods beginning on or after 1 January 2009 that end before 30 June 2009.

Table of Amendments

Paragraph affected	How affected	By ... [paragraph]
Aus1.1	amended	AASB 2007-8 [7, 8]
Aus1.4	amended	AASB 2007-8 [8]
10 (footnote 1)	amended	AASB 2007-2 [10]
13	amended	AASB 2007-4 [51]
14-15	deleted	AASB 2009-5 [15]
15A	added	AASB 2009-5 [16]
20	amended	AASB 2007-8 [6]
22	amended	AASB 2007-8 [6]
23	amended	AASB 2007-8 [6]
31	amended	AASB 2005-10 [28]
	amended	AASB 2007-8 [6]
	heading added	AASB 2009-6 [50]
33 (footnote 2)	amended	AASB 2007-2 [10]

AASB

Paragraph affected	How affected	By ... [paragraph]
35	amended	AASB 2005-10 [28]
	amended	AASB 2007-8 [6]
	heading added	AASB 2009-6 [50]
36	amended	AASB 2007-8 [6]
41	amended	AASB 2007-4 [51]
47	amended	AASB 2005-10 [28]
	amended	AASB 2007-8 [6]
	heading added	AASB 2009-6 [50]
49	amended	AASB 2007-8 [6]
50 (footnote 3)	amended	AASB 2007-2 [10]
56	amended	AASB 2005-10 [28]
	heading added	AASB 2009-6 [50]
68A	added	AASB 2009-5 [16]
69A	added	AASB 2009-5 [16]

Comparison with IAS 17

AASB 117 and IAS 17

AASB 117 *Leases* as amended incorporates IAS 17 *Leases* as issued and amended by the International Accounting Standards Board (IASB). Paragraphs that have been added to this Standard (and do not appear in the text of IAS 17) are identified with the prefix "Aus", followed by the number of the preceding IASB paragraph and decimal numbering.

Compliance with IAS 17

Entities that comply with AASB 117 as amended will simultaneously be in compliance with IAS 17 as amended.

Accounting Standard AASB 117

The Australian Accounting Standards Board made Accounting Standard AASB 117 *Leases* under section 334 of the *Corporations Act 2001* on 15 July 2004.

This compiled version of AASB 117 applies to annual reporting periods beginning on or after 1 January 2010. It incorporates relevant amendments contained in other AASB Standards made by the AASB up to and including 25 June 2009 (see Compilation Details).

Accounting Standard AASB 117

Leases

Objective

1   The objective of this Standard is to prescribe, for lessees and lessors, the appropriate accounting policies and disclosure to apply in relation to leases.

Application

Aus1.1   **This Standard applies to:**

    (a)   each entity that is required to prepare financial reports in accordance with Part 2M.3 of the Corporations Act and that is a reporting entity;

    (b)   general purpose financial statements of each other reporting entity; and

    (c)   financial statements that are, or are held out to be, general purpose financial statements.

Aus1.2   This Standard applies to annual reporting periods beginning on or after
          1 January 2005.
          [Note: For application dates of paragraphs changed or added by an amending Standard,
          see Compilation Details.]

Aus1.3   This Standard shall not be applied to annual reporting periods beginning
          before 1 January 2005.

Aus1.4   The requirements specified in this Standard apply to the financial statements
          where information resulting from their application is material in accordance
          with AASB 1031 *Materiality*.

Aus1.5   When applicable, this Standard supersedes:

          (a)   Accounting Standard AASB 1008 *Leases* as notified in the *Commonwealth
                 of Australia Gazette* No S 491, 6 October 1998; and

          (b)   AAS 17 *Leases* as issued in October 1998.

Aus1.6   Both AASB 1008 and AAS 17 remain applicable until superseded by this Standard.

Aus1.7   Notice of this Standard was published in the *Commonwealth of Australia Gazette*
          No S 294, 22 July 2004.

Scope

2   This Standard shall be applied in accounting for all leases other than:

     (a)   leases to explore for or use minerals, oil, natural gas and similar
            non-regenerative resources; and

     (b)   licensing agreements for such items as motion picture films, video recordings,
            plays, manuscripts, patents and copyrights.

     However, this Standard shall not be applied as the basis of measurement for:

     (a)   property held by lessees that is accounted for as investment property
            (see AASB 140 *Investment Property*);

     (b)   investment property provided by lessors under operating leases (see AASB 140);

     (c)   biological assets held by lessees under finance leases (see AASB 141
            Agriculture); or

     (d)   biological assets provided by lessors under operating leases (see AASB 141).

3   This Standard applies to agreements that transfer the right to use assets even though
     substantial services by the lessor may be called for in connection with the operation or
     maintenance of such assets. This Standard does not apply to agreements that are contracts
     for services that do not transfer the right to use assets from one contracting party to the
     other.

Definitions

4   The following terms are used in this Standard with the meanings specified.

     The *commencement of the lease term* is the date from which the lessee is entitled to
        exercise its right to use the leased asset. It is the date of initial recognition of the
        lease (i.e. the recognition of the assets, liabilities, income or expenses resulting
        from the lease, as appropriate).

     Contingent rent is that portion of the lease payments that is not fixed in amount
        but is based on the future amount of a factor that changes other than with the
        passage of time (e.g. percentage of future sales, amount of future use, future
        price indices, future market rates of interest).

     Economic life is either:

     (a)   the period over which an asset is expected to be economically usable by one
            or more users; or

     (b)   the number of production or similar units expected to be obtained from the
            asset by one or more users.

AASB 117   Institute of Chartered Accountants Australia

Fair value is the amount for which an asset could be exchanged or a liability settled, between knowledgeable, willing parties in an arm's length transaction.

A *finance lease* is a lease that transfers substantially all the risks and rewards incidental to ownership of an asset. Title may or may not eventually be transferred.

Gross investment in the lease is the aggregate of:

(a)   the minimum lease payments receivable by the lessor under a finance lease; and

(b)   any unguaranteed residual value accruing to the lessor.

Guaranteed residual value is:

(a)   for a lessee, that part of the residual value that is guaranteed by the lessee or by a party related to the lessee (the amount of the guarantee being the maximum amount that could, in any event, become payable); and

(b)   for a lessor, that part of the residual value that is guaranteed by the lessee or by a third party unrelated to the lessor that is financially capable of discharging the obligations under the guarantee.

The *inception of the lease* is the earlier of the date of the lease agreement and the date of commitment by the parties to the principal provisions of the lease. At this date:

(a)   a lease is classified as either an operating or a finance lease; and

(b)   in the case of a finance lease, the amounts to be recognised at the commencement of the lease are determined.

Initial direct costs are incremental costs that are directly attributable to negotiating and arranging a lease, except for such costs incurred by manufacturer or dealer lessors.

The *interest rate implicit in the lease* is the discount rate that, at the inception of the lease, causes the aggregate present value of:

(a)   the minimum lease payments; and

(b)   the unguaranteed residual value

to be equal to the sum of:

(c)   the fair value of the leased asset; and

(d)   any initial direct costs of the lessor.

A *lease* is an agreement whereby the lessor conveys to the lessee in return for a payment or series of payments the right to use an asset for an agreed period of time.

The *lease term* is the non-cancellable period for which the lessee has contracted to lease the asset together with any further terms for which the lessee has the option to continue to lease the asset, with or without further payment, when at the inception of the lease it is reasonably certain that the lessee will exercise the option.

The *lessee's incremental borrowing rate of interest* is the rate of interest the lessee would have to pay on a similar lease or, if that is not determinable, the rate that, at the inception of the lease, the lessee would incur to borrow over a similar term, and with a similar security, the funds necessary to purchase the asset.

Minimum lease payments are the payments over the lease term that the lessee is or can be required to make, excluding contingent rent, costs for services and taxes to be paid by and reimbursed to the lessor, together with:

(a)   for a lessee, any amounts guaranteed by the lessee or by a party related to the lessee; or

(b)   for a lessor, any residual value guaranteed to the lessor by:

(i)   the lessee;

(ii) a party related to the lessee; or

(iii) a third party unrelated to the lessor that is financially capable of discharging the obligations under the guarantee.

However, if the lessee has an option to purchase the asset at a price that is expected to be sufficiently lower than the fair value at the date the option becomes exercisable for it to be reasonably certain, at the inception of the lease, that the option will be exercised, the minimum lease payments comprise the minimum payments payable over the lease term to the expected date of exercise of this purchase option and the payment required to exercise it.

Net investment in the lease is the gross investment in the lease discounted at the interest rate implicit in the lease.

A *non-cancellable lease* is a lease that is cancellable only:

(a)   upon the occurrence of some remote contingency;

(b)   with the permission of the lessor;

(c)   if the lessee enters into a new lease for the same or an equivalent asset with the same lessor; or

(d)   upon payment by the lessee of such an additional amount that, at inception of the lease, continuation of the lease is reasonably certain.

An *operating lease* is a lease other than a finance lease.

Unearned finance income is the difference between:

(a)   the gross investment in the lease; and

(b)   the net investment in the lease.

Unguaranteed residual value is that portion of the residual value of the leased asset, the realisation of which by the lessor is not assured or is guaranteed solely by a party related to the lessor.

Useful life is the estimated remaining period, from the commencement of the lease term, without limitation by the lease term, over which the economic benefits embodied in the asset are expected to be consumed by the entity.

5   A lease agreement or commitment may include a provision to adjust the lease payments for changes in the construction or acquisition cost of the leased property or for changes in some other measure of cost or value, such as general price levels, or in the lessor's costs of financing the lease, during the period between the inception of the lease and the commencement of the lease term. If so, the effect of any such changes shall be deemed to have taken place at the inception of the lease for the purposes of this Standard.

6   The definition of a lease includes contracts for the hire of an asset that contain a provision giving the hirer an option to acquire title to the asset upon the fulfilment of agreed conditions. These contracts are sometimes known as hire purchase contracts.

Classification of Leases

7   The classification of leases adopted in this Standard is based on the extent to which risks and rewards incidental to ownership of a leased asset lie with the lessor or the lessee. Risks include the possibilities of losses from idle capacity or technological obsolescence and of variations in return because of changing economic conditions. Rewards may be represented by the expectation of profitable operation over the asset's economic life and of gain from appreciation in value or realisation of a residual value.

8   A lease is classified as a finance lease if it transfers substantially all the risks and rewards incidental to ownership. A lease is classified as an operating lease if it does not transfer substantially all the risks and rewards incidental to ownership.

9   Because the transaction between a lessor and a lessee is based on a lease agreement between them, it is appropriate to use consistent definitions. The application of these definitions to the differing circumstances of the lessor and lessee may result in the same lease being classified differently by them. For example, this may be the case if the lessor benefits from a residual value guarantee provided by a party unrelated to the lessee.

10   Whether a lease is a finance lease or an operating lease depends on the substance of the transaction rather than the form of the contract.[1] Examples of situations that individually or in combination would normally lead to a lease being classified as a finance lease are:

    (a)   the lease transfers ownership of the asset to the lessee by the end of the lease term;

    (b)   the lessee has the option to purchase the asset at a price that is expected to be sufficiently lower than the fair value at the date the option becomes exercisable for it to be reasonably certain, at the inception of the lease, that the option will be exercised;

    (c)   the lease term is for the major part of the economic life of the asset even if title is not transferred;

    (d)   at the inception of the lease the present value of the minimum lease payments amounts to at least substantially all of the fair value of the leased asset; and

    (e)   the leased assets are of such a specialised nature that only the lessee can use them without major modifications.

11   Indicators of situations that individually or in combination could also lead to a lease being classified as a finance lease are:

    (a)   if the lessee can cancel the lease, the lessor's losses associated with the cancellation are borne by the lessee;

    (b)   gains or losses from the fluctuation in the fair value of the residual accrue to the lessee (for example, in the form of a rent rebate equalling most of the sales proceeds at the end of the lease); and

    (c)   the lessee has the ability to continue the lease for a secondary period at a rent that is substantially lower than market rent.

12   The examples and indicators in paragraphs 10 and 11 are not always conclusive. If it is clear from other features of the lease that the lease does not transfer substantially all risks and rewards incidental to ownership, the lease is classified as an operating lease. For example, this may be the case if ownership of the asset transfers at the end of the lease for a variable payment equal to its then fair value, or if there are contingent rents, as a result of which the lessee does not have substantially all such risks and rewards.

13   Lease classification is made at the inception of the lease. If at any time the lessee and the lessor agree to change the provisions of the lease, other than by renewing the lease, in a manner that would have resulted in a different classification of the lease under the criteria in paragraphs 7-12 if the changed terms had been in effect at the inception of the lease, the revised agreement is regarded as a new agreement over its term. However, changes in estimates (for example, changes in estimates of the economic life or of the residual value of the leased property), or changes in circumstances (for example, default by the lessee), do not give rise to a new classification of a lease for accounting purposes.

14   [Deleted by the IASB]

15   [Deleted by the IASB]

15A   When a lease includes both land and buildings elements, an entity assesses the classification of each element as a finance or an operating lease separately in accordance with paragraphs 7-13. In determining whether the land element is an operating or a finance lease, an important consideration is that land normally has an indefinite economic life.

---

1   See also Interpretation 127 *Evaluating the Substance of Transactions Involving the Legal Form of a Lease*, as identified in AASB 1048 *Interpretation and Application of Standards*.

16   Whenever necessary in order to classify and account for a lease of land and buildings, the minimum lease payments (including any lump-sum upfront payments) are allocated between the land and the buildings elements in proportion to the relative fair values of the leasehold interests in the land element and buildings element of the lease at the inception of the lease. If the lease payments cannot be allocated reliably between these two elements, the entire lease is classified as a finance lease, unless it is clear that both elements are operating leases, in which case the entire lease is classified as an operating lease.

17   For a lease of land and buildings in which the amount that would initially be recognised for the land element, in accordance with paragraph 20, is immaterial, the land and buildings may be treated as a single unit for the purpose of lease classification and classified as a finance or operating lease in accordance with paragraphs 7-13. In such a case, the economic life of the buildings is regarded as the economic life of the entire leased asset.

18   Separate measurement of the land and buildings elements is not required when the lessee's interest in both land and buildings is classified as an investment property in accordance with AASB 140 and the fair value model is adopted. Detailed calculations are required for this assessment only if the classification of one or both elements is otherwise uncertain.

19   In accordance with AASB 140, it is possible for a lessee to classify a property interest held under an operating lease as an investment property. If it does, the property interest is accounted for as if it were a finance lease and, in addition, the fair value model is used for the asset recognised. The lessee shall continue to account for the lease as a finance lease, even if a subsequent event changes the nature of the lessee's property interest so that it is no longer classified as investment property. This will be the case if, for example, the lessee:

   (a)   occupies the property, which is then transferred to owner-occupied property at a deemed cost equal to its fair value at the date of change in use; or

   (b)   grants a sub-lease that transfers substantially all of the risks and rewards incidental to ownership of the interest to an unrelated third party. Such a sub-lease is accounted for by the lessee as a finance lease to the third party, although it may be accounted for as an operating lease by the third party.

Leases in the Financial Statements of Lessees

Finance Leases

Initial recognition

20   **At the commencement of the lease term, lessees shall recognise finance leases as assets and liabilities in their statements of financial position at amounts equal to the fair value of the leased property or, if lower, the present value of the minimum lease payments, each determined at the inception of the lease. The discount rate to be used in calculating the present value of the minimum lease payments is the interest rate implicit in the lease, if this is practicable to determine; if not, the lessee's incremental borrowing rate shall be used. Any initial direct costs of the lessee are added to the amount recognised as an asset.**

21   Transactions and other events are accounted for and presented in accordance with their substance and financial reality and not merely with legal form. Although the legal form of a lease agreement is that the lessee may acquire no legal title to the leased asset, in the case of finance leases the substance and financial reality are that the lessee acquires the economic benefits of the use of the leased asset for the major part of its economic life in return for entering into an obligation to pay for that right an amount approximating, at the inception of the lease, the fair value of the asset and the related finance charge.

22   If such lease transactions are not reflected in the lessee's statement of financial position, the economic resources and the level of obligations of an entity are understated, thereby distorting financial ratios. Therefore, it is appropriate for a finance lease to be recognised in the lessee's statement of financial position both as an asset and as an obligation to pay future lease payments. At the commencement of the lease term, the asset and the liability for the future lease payments are recognised in the statement of financial position at the

same amounts except for any initial direct costs of the lessee that are added to the amount recognised as an asset.

23 It is not appropriate for the liabilities for leased assets to be presented in the financial statements as a deduction from the leased assets. If for the presentation of liabilities in the statement of financial position a distinction is made between current and non-current liabilities, the same distinction is made for lease liabilities.

24 Initial direct costs are often incurred in connection with specific leasing activities, such as negotiating and securing leasing arrangements. The costs identified as directly attributable to activities performed by the lessee for a finance lease are added to the amount recognised as an asset.

Subsequent measurement

25 **Minimum lease payments shall be apportioned between the finance charge and the reduction of the outstanding liability. The finance charge shall be allocated to each period during the lease term so as to produce a constant periodic rate of interest on the remaining balance of the liability. Contingent rents shall be charged as expenses in the periods in which they are incurred.**

26 In practice, in allocating the finance charge to periods during the lease term, a lessee may use some form of approximation to simplify the calculation.

27 **A finance lease gives rise to depreciation expense for depreciable assets as well as finance expense for each reporting period. The depreciation policy for depreciable leased assets shall be consistent with that for depreciable assets that are owned, and the depreciation recognised shall be calculated in accordance with AASB 116** *Property, Plant and Equipment* **and AASB 138** *Intangible Assets.* **If there is no reasonable certainty that the lessee will obtain ownership by the end of the lease term, the asset shall be fully depreciated over the shorter of the lease term and its useful life.**

28 The depreciable amount of a leased asset is allocated to each reporting period during the period of expected use on a systematic basis consistent with the depreciation policy the lessee adopts for depreciable assets that are owned. If there is reasonable certainty that the lessee will obtain ownership by the end of the lease term, the period of expected use is the useful life of the asset; otherwise the asset is depreciated over the shorter of the lease term and its useful life.

29 The sum of the depreciation expense for the asset and the finance expense for the period is rarely the same as the lease payments payable for the period, and it is, therefore, inappropriate simply to recognise the lease payments payable as an expense. Accordingly, the asset and the related liability are unlikely to be equal in amount after the commencement of the lease term.

30 To determine whether a leased asset has become impaired, an entity applies AASB 136 *Impairment of Assets.*

Disclosures

31 **Lessees shall, in addition to meeting the requirements of AASB 7** *Financial Instruments: Disclosures,* **make the following disclosures for finance leases:**

    (a) for each class of asset, the net carrying amount at the end of the reporting period;

    (b) a reconciliation between the total of future minimum lease payments at the end of the reporting period, and their present value. In addition, an entity shall disclose the total of future minimum lease payments at the end of the reporting period, and their present value, for each of the following periods:

        (i) not later than one year;

        (ii) later than one year and not later than five years;

        (iii) later than five years;

    (c) contingent rents recognised as an expense in the period;

    (d)   the total of future minimum sublease payments expected to be received under non-cancellable subleases at the end of the reporting period; and

    (e)   a general description of the lessee's material leasing arrangements including, but not limited to, the following:

        (i)   the basis on which contingent rent payable is determined;

        (ii)   the existence and terms of renewal or purchase options and escalation clauses; and

        (iii)   restrictions imposed by lease arrangements, such as those concerning dividends, additional debt, and further leasing.

32   In addition, the requirements for disclosure in accordance with AASB 116, AASB 136, AASB 138, AASB 140 and AASB 141 apply to lessees for assets leased under finance leases.

Operating Leases

33   **Lease payments under an operating lease shall be recognised as an expense on a straight-line basis over the lease term unless another systematic basis is more representative of the time pattern of the user's benefit.[2]**

34   For operating leases, lease payments (excluding costs for services such as insurance and maintenance) are recognised as an expense on a straight-line basis unless another systematic basis is representative of the time pattern of the user's benefit, even if the payments are not on that basis.

Disclosures

35   **Lessees shall, in addition to meeting the requirements of AASB 7, make the following disclosures for operating leases:**

    (a)   the total of future minimum lease payments under non-cancellable operating leases for each of the following periods:

        (i)   not later than one year;

        (ii)   later than one year and not later than five years;

        (iii)   later than five years;

    (b)   the total of future minimum sublease payments expected to be received under non-cancellable subleases at the end of the reporting period;

    (c)   lease and sublease payments recognised as an expense in the period, with separate amounts for minimum lease payments, contingent rents, and sublease payments;

    (d)   a general description of the lessee's significant leasing arrangements including, but not limited to, the following:

        (i)   the basis on which contingent rent payable is determined;

        (ii)   the existence and terms of renewal or purchase options and escalation clauses; and

        (iii)   restrictions imposed by lease arrangements, such as those concerning dividends, additional debt, and further leasing.

Leases in the Financial Statements of Lessors

Finance Leases

Initial recognition

36   **Lessors shall recognise assets held under a finance lease in their statements of financial position and present them as a receivable at an amount equal to the net investment in the lease.**

---

2   See also Interpretation 115 *Operating Leases – Incentives*, as identified in AASB 1048 *Interpretation and Application of Standards.*

AASB

37   Under a finance lease substantially all the risks and rewards incidental to legal ownership are transferred by the lessor, and thus the lease payment receivable is treated by the lessor as repayment of principal and finance income to reimburse and reward the lessor for its investment and services.

38   Initial direct costs are often incurred by lessors and include amounts such as commissions, legal fees and internal costs that are incremental and directly attributable to negotiating and arranging a lease. They exclude general overheads such as those incurred by a sales and marketing team. For finance leases other than those involving manufacturer or dealer lessors, initial direct costs are included in the initial measurement of the finance lease receivable and reduce the amount of income recognised over the lease term. The interest rate implicit in the lease is defined in such a way that the initial direct costs are included automatically in the finance lease receivable; there is no need to add them separately. Costs incurred by manufacturer or dealer lessors in connection with negotiating and arranging a lease are excluded from the definition of initial direct costs. As a result, they are excluded from the net investment in the lease and are recognised as an expense when the selling profit is recognised, which for a finance lease is normally at the commencement of the lease term.

Subsequent measurement

39   The recognition of finance income shall be based on a pattern reflecting a constant periodic rate of return on the lessor's net investment in the finance lease.

40   A lessor aims to allocate finance income over the lease term on a systematic and rational basis. This income allocation is based on a pattern reflecting a constant periodic return on the lessor's net investment in the finance lease. Lease payments relating to the period, excluding costs for services, are applied against the gross investment in the lease to reduce both the principal and the unearned finance income.

41   Estimated unguaranteed residual values used in computing the lessor's gross investment in the lease are reviewed regularly. If there has been a reduction in the estimated unguaranteed residual value, the income allocation over the lease term is revised and any reduction in respect of amounts accrued is recognised immediately.

41A   An asset under a finance lease that is classified as held for sale (or included in a disposal group that is classified as held for sale) in accordance with AASB 5 *Non-current Assets Held for Sale and Discontinued Operations* shall be accounted for in accordance with that Standard.

42   Manufacturer or dealer lessors shall recognise selling profit or loss in the period, in accordance with the policy followed by the entity for outright sales. If artificially low rates of interest are quoted, selling profit shall be restricted to that which would apply if a market rate of interest were charged. Costs incurred by manufacturer or dealer lessors in connection with negotiating and arranging a lease shall be recognised as an expense when the selling profit is recognised.

43   Manufacturers or dealers often offer to customers the choice of either buying or leasing an asset. A finance lease of an asset by a manufacturer or dealer lessor gives rise to two types of income:

    (a)   profit or loss equivalent to the profit or loss resulting from an outright sale of the asset being leased, at normal selling prices, reflecting any applicable volume or trade discounts; and

    (b)   finance income over the lease term.

44   The sales revenue recognised at the commencement of the lease term by a manufacturer or dealer lessor is the fair value of the asset, or, if lower, the present value of the minimum lease payments accruing to the lessor, computed at a market rate of interest. The cost of sale recognised at the commencement of the lease term is the cost, or carrying amount if different, of the leased property less the present value of the unguaranteed residual value. The difference between the sales revenue and the cost of sale is the selling profit, which is recognised in accordance with the entity's policy for outright sales.

45   Manufacturer or dealer lessors sometimes quote artificially low rates of interest in order to attract customers. The use of such a rate would result in an excessive portion of the total

income from the transaction being recognised at the time of sale. If artificially low rates of interest are quoted, selling profit is restricted to that which would apply if a market rate of interest were charged.

46   Costs incurred by a manufacturer or dealer lessor in connection with negotiating and arranging a finance lease are recognised as an expense at the commencement of the lease term because they are mainly related to earning the manufacturer's or dealer's selling profit.

Disclosures

47   **Lessors shall, in addition to meeting the requirements in AASB 7, disclose the following for finance leases:**

(a)   **a reconciliation between the gross investment in the lease at the end of the reporting period, and the present value of minimum lease payments receivable at the end of the reporting period. In addition, an entity shall disclose the gross investment in the lease and the present value of minimum lease payments receivable at the end of the reporting period, for each of the following periods:**

(i)   **not later than one year;**

(ii)   **later than one year and not later than five years;**

(iii)   **later than five years;**

(b)   **unearned finance income;**

(c)   **the unguaranteed residual values accruing to the benefit of the lessor;**

(d)   **the accumulated allowance for uncollectible minimum lease payments receivable;**

(e)   **contingent rents recognised as income in the period; and**

(f)   **a general description of the lessor's material leasing arrangements.**

48   As an indicator of growth it is often useful also to disclose the gross investment less unearned income in new business added during the period, after deducting the relevant amounts for cancelled leases.

Operating Leases

49   **Lessors shall present assets subject to operating leases in their statements of financial position according to the nature of the asset.**

50   **Lease income from operating leases shall be recognised in income on a straight-line basis over the lease term, unless another systematic basis is more representative of the time pattern in which use benefit derived from the leased asset is diminished.[3]**

51   Costs, including depreciation, incurred in earning the lease income are recognised as an expense. Lease income (excluding receipts for services provided such as insurance and maintenance) is recognised on a straight-line basis over the lease term even if the receipts are not on such a basis, unless another systematic basis is more representative of the time pattern in which use benefit derived from the leased asset is diminished.

52   **Initial direct costs incurred by lessors in negotiating and arranging an operating lease shall be added to the carrying amount of the leased asset and recognised as an expense over the lease term on the same basis as the lease income.**

53   **The depreciation policy for depreciable leased assets shall be consistent with the lessor's normal depreciation policy for similar assets, and depreciation shall be calculated in accordance with AASB 116 and AASB 138.**

54   To determine whether a leased asset has become impaired an entity applies AASB 136.

55   A manufacturer or dealer lessor does not recognise any selling profit on entering into an operating lease because it is not the equivalent of a sale.

---

3   See also Interpretation 115 *Operating Leases – Incentives*, as identified in AASB 1048 *Interpretation and Application of Standards*.

Disclosures

56   Lessors shall, in addition to meeting the requirements of AASB 7, disclose the following for operating leases:

(a) the future minimum lease payments under non-cancellable operating leases in the aggregate and for each of the following periods:

(i) not later than one year;

(ii) later than one year and not later than five years;

(iii) later than five years;

(b) total contingent rents recognised as income in the period; and

(c) a general description of the lessor's leasing arrangements.

57   In addition, the disclosure requirements in AASB 116, AASB 136, AASB 138, AASB 140 and AASB 141 apply to lessors for assets provided under operating leases.

Sale and Leaseback Transactions

58   A sale and leaseback transaction involves the sale of an asset and the leasing back of the same asset. The lease payment and the sale price are usually interdependent because they are negotiated as a package. The accounting treatment of a sale and leaseback transaction depends upon the type of lease involved.

59   If a sale and leaseback transaction results in a finance lease, any excess of sales proceeds over the carrying amount shall not be immediately recognised as income by a seller-lessee. Instead, it shall be deferred and amortised over the lease term.

60   If the leaseback is a finance lease, the transaction is a means whereby the lessor provides finance to the lessee, with the asset as security. For this reason it is not appropriate to regard an excess of sales proceeds over the carrying amount as income. Such excess is deferred and amortised over the lease term.

61   If a sale and leaseback transaction results in an operating lease, and it is clear that the transaction is established at fair value, any profit or loss shall be recognised immediately. If the sale price is below fair value, any profit or loss shall be recognised immediately except that, if the loss is compensated for by future lease payments at below market price, it shall be deferred and amortised in proportion to the lease payments over the period for which the asset is expected to be used. If the sale price is above fair value, the excess over fair value shall be deferred and amortised over the period for which the asset is expected to be used.

62   If the leaseback is an operating lease, and the lease payments and the sale price are at fair value, there has in effect been a normal sale transaction and any profit or loss is recognised immediately.

63   For operating leases, if the fair value at the time of a sale and leaseback transaction is less than the carrying amount of the asset, a loss equal to the amount of the difference between the carrying amount and fair value shall be recognised immediately.

64   For finance leases, no such adjustment is necessary unless there has been an impairment in value, in which case the carrying amount is reduced to recoverable amount in accordance with AASB 136.

65   Disclosure requirements for lessees and lessors apply equally to sale and leaseback transactions. The required description of material leasing arrangements leads to disclosure of unique or unusual provisions of the agreement or terms of the sale and leaseback transactions.

66   Sale and leaseback transactions may trigger the separate disclosure criteria in AASB 101 *Presentation of Financial Statements*.

Transitional Provisions

67   [Deleted by the AASB]

68   [Deleted by the AASB]

68A An entity shall reassess the classification of land elements of unexpired leases at the date it adopts the amendments referred to in paragraph 69A on the basis of information existing at the inception of those leases. It shall recognise a lease newly classified as a finance lease retrospectively in accordance with AASB 108 *Accounting Policies, Changes in Accounting Estimates and Errors*. However, if an entity does not have the information necessary to apply the amendments retrospectively, it shall:

(a) apply the amendments to those leases on the basis of the facts and circumstances existing on the date it adopts the amendments; and

(b) recognise the asset and liability related to a land lease newly classified as a finance lease at their fair values on that date; any difference between those fair values is recognised in retained earnings.

Effective Date

69 [Deleted by the AASB]

69A Paragraphs 14 and 15 were deleted, and paragraphs 15A and 68A were added as part of AASB 2009-5 *Further Amendments to Australian Accounting Standards arising from the Annual Improvements Project* issued in May 2009. An entity shall apply those amendments for annual reporting periods beginning on or after 1 January 2010. Earlier application is permitted. If an entity applies the amendments for an earlier period it shall disclose that fact.

Withdrawal of IAS 17 (revised 1997)

70 [Deleted by the AASB]

Implementation Guidance

This guidance accompanies, but is not part of, AASB 117.

Illustrative Examples of Sale and Leaseback Transactions that Result in Operating Leases

A sale and leaseback transaction that results in an operating lease may give rise to profit or a loss, the determination and treatment of which depends on the leased asset's carrying amount, fair value and selling price. The table below shows the requirements of the Standard in various circumstances.

Sale price at fair value (paragraph 61)	Carrying amount equal to fair value	Carrying amount less than fair value	Carrying amount above fair value
Profit	no profit	recognise profit immediately	not applicable
Loss	no loss	not applicable	recognise loss immediately

Sale price below fair value (paragraph 61)	Carrying amount equal to fair value	Carrying amount less than fair value	Carrying amount above fair value
Profit	no profit	recognise profit immediately	no profit (note 1)
Loss **not** compensated for by future lease payments at below market price	recognise loss immediately	recognise loss immediately	(note 1)
Loss compensated for by future lease payments at below market price	defer and amortise loss	defer and amortise loss	(note 1)

Sale price above fair value (paragraph 61)	Carrying amount equal to fair value	Carrying amount less than fair value	Carrying amount above fair value
Profit	defer and amortise profit	defer and amortise excess of sale price over fair value / recognise any excess of fair value over carrying amount immediately (note 3)	defer and amortise profit (note 2)
Loss	no loss	no loss	(note 1)

Note 1   These parts of the table represent circumstances dealt with in paragraph 63 of the Standard. Paragraph 63 requires the carrying amount of an asset to be written down to fair value where it is subject to a sale and leaseback.

Note 2   Profit is the difference between fair value and sale price because the carrying amount would have been written down to fair value in accordance with paragraph 63.

Note 3   The excess profit (the excess of sale price over fair value) is deferred and amortised over the period for which the asset is expected to be used. Any excess of fair value over the carrying amount is recognised immediately.

AASB 118
Revenue

(Compiled November 2010)

Note from the Institute of Chartered Accountants Australia

This note, prepared by the technical editors, is not part of Accounting Standard AASB 118.

Historical development

July 2004: AASB 118 'Revenue' is the Australian equivalent of IAS 18 of the same name. It was made by the AASB on 15 July 2004 as part of the AASB's program to adopt International Financial Reporting Standards (IFRSs) by 2005.

15 February 2007: AASB 2007-2 'Amendments to Australian Accounting Standards' amends paragraphs 9 and 30 and is applicable to annual reporting periods ending on or after 28 February 2007. Entities may elect to early-adopt it to annual reporting periods beginning on or after 1 January 2005.

30 April 2007: AASB 2007-4 'Amendments to Australian Accounting Standards' amends paragraphs 21 and is applicable to annual reporting periods beginning on or after 1 July 2007. Entities may elect to early-adopt it to annual reporting periods beginning on or after 1 January 2005.

24 July 2008: AASB 2008-5 'Amendments to Australian Accounting Standards arising from the Annual Improvements Project' amends AASB 118 in relation to costs of originating a loan. This Standard is applicable to annual reporting periods beginning on or after 1 January 2009.

25 July 2008: AASB 2008-7 'Amendments to Australian Accounting Standards – Cost of an Investment in a Subsidiary, Jointly Controlled Entity or Associate' amends AASB 118 to reflect that dividends declared out of pre-acquisition profits are recognised as income. This Standard is applicable to annual reporting periods beginning on or after 1 January 2009.

27 August 2008: Interpretation 15 was issued which amends the appendix to AASB 118.

21 May 2009: AASB 2009-5 'Amendments to Australian Accounting Standards' is the annual improvements Standard, amending AASB 118 in relation to determining whether an entity is acting as a principal or as an agent. This Standard applies to annual reporting periods beginning on or after 1 January 2010 and may be applied early.

30 October 2009: AASB 118 was reissued by the AASB, compiled to include the AASB 2008-5, 2008-7 and Interpretation 15 amendments. This compiled Standard applies to annual reporting periods beginning on or after 1 January 2009 but before 1 January 2010. Early application is permitted.

1 December 2009: AASB 118 was reissued by the AASB, compiled to include the AASB 2009-5 amendments and applies to annual reporting periods beginning on or after 1 January 2010.

7 December 2009: AASB 2009-11 'Amendments to Australian Accounting Standards arising from AASB 9' amends AASB 118 to give effect to consequential changes arising from the issuance of AASB 9. This Standard is applicable to annual reporting periods beginning on or after 1 January 2013 with early adoption permitted from annual reporting periods ending on or after 31 December 2009 that begin before 1 January 2013 provided AASB 9 is also applied for the same period. The application date of AASB 2009-11 has been amended to 1 January 2015 by AASB 2012-6. **These amendments have been superseded by AASB 2010-7 are not included in this compiled Standard.**

27 October 2010: AASB 2010-5 'Further Amendments to Australian Accounting Standards' makes editorial amendments to AASB 118. This Standard is applicable to annual reporting periods beginning on or after 1 January 2011.

26 November 2010: AASB 118 was reissued by the AASB, compiled to include the AASB 2010-5 amendments and applies to annual reporting periods ending on or after 1 January 2011 but before 1 January 2013.

---

1 March 2011: AASB 2010-7 'Amendments to Australian Accounting Standards arising from AASB 9 (December 2010)' as compiled amends AASB 118 to give effect to consequential changes arising from the reissue of AASB 9 in December 2010, and supersedes AASB 2009-11 which related to the previous version of AASB 9. This Standard applies to annual reporting periods beginning on or after 1 January 2013 and can be adopted early. The application date of AASB 2010-7 has been amended to 1 January 2015 by AASB 2012-6. **These amendments are not included in this compiled Standard.**

29 August 2011: AASB 2011-7 'Amendments to Australian Accounting Standards arising from the Consolidation and Joint Arrangements Standards' amends AASB 118 to give effect to many consequential changes arising from the issue of AASB 10, 11, 12, 127 and 128. This Standard applies to annual reporting periods beginning on or after 1 January 2013 and can be adopted early by for-profit entities. **These amendments are not included in this compiled Standard.**

2 September 2011: AASB 2011-8 'Amendments to Australian Accounting Standards arising from AASB 13' amends AASB 118 to give effect to a consequential change in the definition of fair value arising from the issue of AASB 13. This Standard applies to annual reporting periods beginning on or after 1 January 2013 and can be adopted early. **These amendments are not included in this compiled Standard.**

References

Interpretation 12 *Service Concession Arrangements*, Interpretation 13 *Customer Loyalty Programs*, Interpretation 15 *Agreements for the Construction of Real Estate,* Interpretation 113 *Jointly Controlled Entities – Non-Monetary Contributions by Venturers*, Interpretation 1052 *Tax Consolidation Accounting*, Interpretation 131 *Revenue – Barter Transactions Involving Advertising Services*, Interpretation 127 *Evaluating the Substance of Transactions Involving the Legal Form of a Lease*, Interpretation 1031 *Accounting for the Goods and Services Tax (GST)*, Interpretation 1038 *Contributions by Owners Made to Wholly-Owned Public Sector Entities*, Interpretation 1042 *Subscriber Acquisition Costs in the Telecommunications Industry* and Interpretation 18 *Transfers of Assets from Customers* apply to AASB 118.

AASB Rejection Statements item not taken onto the agenda: *Subscriber Acquisition Costs in the Telecommunications Industry* and *Direct Costs Affecting a Financial Instrument's Effective Interest Rate* apply to AASB 118.

IFRIC items not taken onto the agenda: No. 8 IAS 11 *Construction Contracts* and IAS 18 *Revenue: Pre-completion contracts for the sale of residential properties*, No. 20 *Extended Payment terms* and No. 21 *Prompt settlement discounts,* IAS 18-1 *Subscriber Acquisition Costs in the Telecommunications Industry,* IAS 18-2 *Guidance on identifying agency relationships*, IAS 18-9 *Financial Instruments: Recognition and Measurement – Accounting for trailing commissions* and IAS 18-10 *Receipt of a dividend of equity instrument* apply to AASB 118.

AASB 118 compared to IAS 18

Additions

Paragraph	Description
Aus 1.1	Which entities AASB 118 applies to (i.e. reporting entities and general purpose financial statements).
Aus 1.2	The application date of AASB 118 (i.e. annual reporting periods beginning 1 January 2005).
Aus 1.3	Prohibits early application of AASB 118.
Aus 1.4	Makes the requirements of AASB 118 subject to AASB 1031 'Materiality'.
Aus 1.5	Explains which Australian Standards have been superseded by AASB 118.
Aus 1.6	Clarifies that the superseded Australian Standards remain in force until AASB 118 applies.
Aus 1.7	Notice of the new Standard published on 22 July 2004.

Deletions

Paragraph	Description
2	Reference to superseded IAS 18.
37	Effective date of IAS 18.

Contents

Compilation Details

Comparison with IAS 18

Accounting Standard
AASB 118 Revenue

Paragraphs

Objective

Application   Aus1.1 – Aus1.7

Scope   1 – 6

Definitions   7 – 8

Measurement of Revenue   9 – 12

Identification of the Transaction   13

Sale of Goods   14 – 19

Rendering of Services   20 – 28

Interest, Royalties and Dividends   29 – 34

Disclosure   35 – 36

Effective Date   38

Illustrative Examples

Australian Accounting Standard AASB 118 *Revenue* (as amended) is set out in paragraphs Aus1.1 – 38. All the paragraphs have equal authority. Terms defined in this Standard are in *italics* the first time they appear in the Standard. AASB 118 is to be read in the context of other Australian Accounting Standards, including AASB 1048 *Interpretation and Application of Standards*, which identifies the Australian Accounting Interpretations. In the absence of explicit guidance, AASB 108 *Accounting Policies, Changes in Accounting Estimates and Errors* provides a basis for selecting and applying accounting policies.

Compilation Details

Accounting Standard AASB 118 *Revenue* as amended

This compiled Standard applies to annual reporting periods beginning on or after 1 January 2011 but before 1 January 2013. It takes into account amendments up to and including 27 October 2010 and was prepared on 26 November 2010 by the staff of the Australian Accounting Standards Board (AASB).

This compilation is not a separate Accounting Standard made by the AASB. Instead, it is a representation of AASB 118 (July 2004) as amended by other Accounting Standards, which are listed in the Table below.

Table of Standards

Standard	Date made	Application date *(annual reporting periods ... on or after ...)*	Application, saving or transitional provisions
AASB 118	15 Jul 2004	*(beginning)* 1 Jan 2005	
AASB 2007-2	15 Feb 2007	*(ending)* 28 Feb 2007	see (a) below
AASB 2007-4	30 Apr 2007	*(beginning)* 1 Jul 2007	see (b) below
AASB 2007-8	24 Sep 2007	*(beginning)* 1 Jan 2009	see (c) below
AASB 2008-5	24 Jul 2008	*(beginning)* 1 Jan 2009	see (d) below
AASB 2008-7	25 Jul 2008	*(beginning)* 1 Jan 2009	see (e) below

Standard	Date made	Application date *(annual reporting periods ... on or after ...)*	Application, saving or transitional provisions
Interpretation 15	27 Aug 2008	*(beginning)* 1 Jan 2009	see (e) below
AASB 2009-5	21 May 2009	*(beginning)* 1 Jan 2010	see (f) below
AASB 2009-11	7 Dec 2009	*(beginning)* 1 Jan 2013	not compiled*
AASB 2010-5	27 Oct 2010	*(beginning)* 1 Jan 2011	see (g) below

*   The amendments made by this Standard are not included in this compilation, which presents the principal Standard as applicable to annual reporting periods beginning on or after 1 January 2011 but before 1 January 2013.

(a)   Entities may elect to apply the relevant amendments to annual reporting periods beginning on or after 1 January 2005 that end before 28 February 2007.

(b)   Entities may elect to apply this Standard to annual reporting periods beginning on or after 1 January 2005 but before 1 July 2007.

(c)   Entities may elect to apply this Standard to annual reporting periods beginning on or after 1 January 2005 but before 1 January 2009, provided that AASB 101 *Presentation of Financial Statements* (September 2007) is also applied to such periods.

(d)   Entities may elect to apply this Standard, or its amendments to individual Standards, to annual reporting periods beginning on or after 1 January 2005 but before 1 January 2009.

(e)   Entities may elect to apply this pronouncement to annual reporting periods beginning on or after 1 January 2005 but before 1 January 2009.

(f)   Entities may elect to apply this Standard, or its amendments to individual Standards, to annual reporting periods beginning on or after 1 January 2005 but before 1 January 2010.

(g)   Entities may elect to apply this Standard to annual reporting periods beginning on or after 1 January 2005 but before 1 January 2011.

Table of Amendments to Standard

Paragraph affected	How affected	By ... [paragraph]
Aus1.1	amended	AASB 2007-8 [7, 8]
Aus1.4	amended	AASB 2007-8 [8]
9 (footnote 1)	amended	AASB 2007-2 [10]
11	amended	AASB 2010-5 [29]
20 (footnotes 2, 3)	amended amended	AASB 2007-2 [10] AASB 2007-8 [6]
21	amended	AASB 2007-4 [52]
32	amended	AASB 2008-7 [12]
37 (preceding heading)	amended	AASB 2008-7 [13]
38	added	AASB 2008-7 [14]

Table of Amendments to Illustrative Examples

Paragraph affected	How affected	By ... [paragraph]
Title, rubric	amended	AASB 2010-5 [30]
9	amended	Interpretation 15 [23]
14(a)	amended	AASB 2008-5 [27]
21 (and preceding heading)	added	AASB 2009-5 [17]

Comparison with IAS 18

AASB 118 and IAS 18

AASB 118 *Revenue* as amended incorporates IAS 18 *Revenue* as issued and amended by the International Accounting Standards Board (IASB). Paragraphs that have been added to this Standard (and do not appear in the text of IAS 18) are identified with the prefix "Aus", followed by the number of the relevant IASB paragraph and decimal numbering.

Compliance with IAS 18

Entities that comply with AASB 118 as amended will simultaneously be in compliance with IAS 18 as amended.

> ### Accounting Standard AASB 118
>
> The Australian Accounting Standards Board made Accounting Standard AASB 118 *Revenue* under section 334 of the *Corporations Act 2001* on 15 July 2004.
>
> This compiled version of AASB 118 applies to annual reporting periods beginning on or after 1 January 2011 but before 1 January 2013. It incorporates relevant amendments contained in other AASB Standards made by the AASB and other decisions of the AASB up to and including 27 October 2010 (see Compilation Details).

Accounting Standard AASB 118
Revenue

Objective

Income is defined in the *Framework for the Preparation and Presentation of Financial Statements* as increases in economic benefits during the reporting period in the form of inflows or enhancements of assets or decreases of liabilities that result in increases in equity, other than those relating to contributions from equity participants. Income encompasses both revenue and gains. Revenue is income that arises in the course of ordinary activities of an entity and is referred to by a variety of different names including sales, fees, interest, dividends and royalties. The objective of this Standard is to prescribe the accounting treatment of revenue arising from certain types of transactions and events.

The primary issue in accounting for revenue is determining when to recognise revenue. Revenue is recognised when it is probable that future economic benefits will flow to the entity and these benefits can be measured reliably. This Standard identifies the circumstances in which these criteria will be met and, therefore, revenue will be recognised. It also provides practical guidance on the application of these criteria.

Application

Aus1.1   This Standard applies to:

       (a)   each entity that is required to prepare financial reports in accordance with Part 2M.3 of the Corporations Act and that is a reporting entity;

       (b)   general purpose financial statements of each other reporting entity; and

       (c)   financial statements that are, or are held out to be, general purpose financial statements.

Aus1.2   This Standard applies to annual reporting periods beginning on or after 1 January 2005.

       [Note: For application dates of paragraphs changed or added by an amending Standard, see Compilation Details.]

Aus1.3   This Standard shall not be applied to annual reporting periods beginning before 1 January 2005.

Aus1.4   The requirements specified in this Standard apply to the financial statements where information resulting from their application is material in accordance with AASB 1031 *Materiality*.

Aus1.5   **When applicable, this Standard supersedes:**

(a)   AASB 1004 *Revenue* as notified in the *Commonwealth of Australia Gazette* No S 283, 17 June 1998; and

(b)   AAS 15 *Revenue* as issued in June 1998.

Aus1.6   Both AASB 1004 and AAS 15 remain applicable until superseded by this Standard.

Aus1.7   Notice of this Standard was published in the *Commonwealth of Australia Gazette* No S 294, 22 July 2004.

Scope

1   **This Standard shall be applied in accounting for revenue arising from the following transactions and events:**

(a)   **the sale of goods;**

(b)   **the rendering of services; and**

(c)   **the use by others of entity assets yielding interest, royalties and dividends.**

2   [Deleted by the AASB]

3   Goods includes goods produced by the entity for the purpose of sale and goods purchased for resale, such as merchandise purchased by a retailer or land and other property held for resale.

4   The rendering of services typically involves the performance by the entity of a contractually agreed task over an agreed period of time. The services may be rendered within a single period or over more than one period. Some contracts for the rendering of services are directly related to construction contracts, for example, those for the services of project managers and architects. Revenue arising from these contracts is not dealt with in this Standard but is dealt with in accordance with the requirements for construction contracts as specified in AASB 111 *Construction Contracts*.

5   The use by others of entity assets gives rise to revenue in the form of:

(a)   interest – charges for the use of cash or cash equivalents or amounts due to the entity;

(b)   royalties – charges for the use of long-term assets of the entity, for example, patents, trademarks, copyrights and computer software; and

(c)   dividends – distributions of profits to holders of equity investments in proportion to their holdings of a particular class of capital.

6   This Standard does not deal with revenue arising from:

(a)   lease agreements (see AASB 117 *Leases*);

(b)   dividends arising from investments which are accounted for under the equity method (see AASB 128 *Accounting for Investments in Associates*);

(c)   insurance contracts within the scope of AASB 4 *Insurance Contracts*;

(d)   changes in the fair value of financial assets and financial liabilities or their disposal (see AASB 139 *Financial Instruments: Recognition and Measurement*);

(e)   changes in the value of other current assets;

(f)   initial recognition and from changes in the fair value of biological assets related to agricultural activity (see AASB 141 *Agriculture*);

(g)   initial recognition of agricultural produce (see AASB 141); and

(h)   the extraction of mineral ores.

Definitions

7   **The following terms are used in this Standard with the meanings specified.**

Fair value **is the amount for which an asset could be exchanged, or a liability settled, between knowledgeable, willing parties in an arm's length transaction.**

Revenue **is the gross inflow of economic benefits during the period arising in the course of the ordinary activities of an entity when those inflows result in increases in equity, other than increases relating to contributions from equity participants.**

8   Revenue includes only the gross inflows of economic benefits received and receivable by the entity on its own account. Amounts collected on behalf of third parties such as sales taxes, goods and services taxes and value added taxes are not economic benefits which flow to the entity and do not result in increases in equity. Therefore, they are excluded from revenue. Similarly, in an agency relationship, the gross inflows of economic benefits include amounts collected on behalf of the principal and which do not result in increases in equity for the entity. The amounts collected on behalf of the principal are not revenue. Instead, revenue is the amount of commission.

Measurement of Revenue

9   **Revenue shall be measured at the fair value of the consideration received or receivable.[1]**

10   The amount of revenue arising on a transaction is usually determined by agreement between the entity and the buyer or user of the asset. It is measured at the fair value of the consideration received or receivable taking into account the amount of any trade discounts and volume rebates allowed by the entity.

11   In most cases, the consideration is in the form of cash or cash equivalents and the amount of revenue is the amount of cash or cash equivalents received or receivable. However, when the inflow of cash or cash equivalents is deferred, the fair value of the consideration may be less than the nominal amount of cash received or receivable. For example, an entity may provide interest-free credit to the buyer or accept a note receivable bearing a below-market interest rate from the buyer as consideration for the sale of goods. When the arrangement effectively constitutes a financing transaction, the fair value of the consideration is determined by discounting all future receipts using an imputed rate of interest. The imputed rate of interest is the more clearly determinable of either:

(a)   the prevailing rate for a similar instrument of an issuer with a similar credit rating; or

(b)   a rate of interest that discounts the nominal amount of the instrument to the current cash sales price of the goods or services.

The difference between the fair value and the nominal amount of the consideration is recognised as interest revenue in accordance with paragraphs 29 and 30 and in accordance with AASB 139.

12   When goods or services are exchanged or swapped for goods or services which are of a similar nature and value, the exchange is not regarded as a transaction which generates revenue. This is often the case with commodities like oil or milk where suppliers exchange or swap inventories in various locations to fulfil demand on a timely basis in a particular location. When goods are sold or services are rendered in exchange for dissimilar goods or services, the exchange is regarded as a transaction which generates revenue. The revenue is measured at the fair value of the goods or services received, adjusted by the amount of any cash or cash equivalents transferred. When the fair value of the goods or services received cannot be measured reliably, the revenue is measured at the fair value of the goods or services given up, adjusted by the amount of any cash or cash equivalents transferred.

Identification of the Transaction

13   The recognition criteria in this Standard are usually applied separately to each transaction. However, in certain circumstances, it is necessary to apply the recognition criteria to the separately identifiable components of a single transaction in order to reflect the substance of the transaction. For example, when the selling price of a product includes an identifiable amount for subsequent servicing, that amount is deferred and recognised as revenue over the period during which the service is performed. Conversely, the recognition criteria are applied to two or more transactions together when they are linked in such a way that the commercial effect cannot be understood without reference to the series of transactions

---

1   See also Interpretation 131 *Revenue – Barter Transactions Involving Advertising Services*, as identified in AASB 1048 *Interpretation and Application of Standards*.

as a whole. For example, an entity may sell goods and, at the same time, enter into a separate agreement to repurchase the goods at a later date, thus negating the substantive effect of the transaction; in such a case, the two transactions are dealt with together.

Sale of Goods

14   **Revenue from the sale of goods shall be recognised when all the following conditions have been satisfied:**

(a)   **the entity has transferred to the buyer the significant risks and rewards of ownership of the goods;**

(b)   **the entity retains neither continuing managerial involvement to the degree usually associated with ownership nor effective control over the goods sold;**

(c)   **the amount of revenue can be measured reliably;**

(d)   **it is probable that the economic benefits associated with the transaction will flow to the entity; and**

(e)   **the costs incurred or to be incurred in respect of the transaction can be measured reliably.**

15   The assessment of when an entity has transferred the significant risks and rewards of ownership to the buyer requires an examination of the circumstances of the transaction. In most cases, the transfer of the risks and rewards of ownership coincides with the transfer of the legal title or the passing of possession to the buyer. This is the case for most retail sales. In other cases, the transfer of risks and rewards of ownership occurs at a different time from the transfer of legal title or the passing of possession.

16   If the entity retains significant risks of ownership, the transaction is not a sale and revenue is not recognised. An entity may retain a significant risk of ownership in a number of ways. Examples of situations in which the entity may retain the significant risks and rewards of ownership are:

(a)   when the entity retains an obligation for unsatisfactory performance not covered by normal warranty provisions;

(b)   when the receipt of the revenue from a particular sale is contingent on the derivation of revenue by the buyer from its sale of the goods;

(c)   when the goods are shipped subject to installation and the installation is a significant part of the contract which has not yet been completed by the entity; and

(d)   when the buyer has the right to rescind the purchase for a reason specified in the sales contract and the entity is uncertain about the probability of return.

17   If an entity retains only an insignificant risk of ownership, the transaction is a sale and revenue is recognised. For example, a seller may retain the legal title to the goods solely to protect the collectability of the amount due. In such a case, if the entity has transferred the significant risks and rewards of ownership, the transaction is a sale and revenue is recognised. Another example of an entity retaining only an insignificant risk of ownership may be a retail sale when a refund is offered if the customer is not satisfied. Revenue in such cases is recognised at the time of sale provided the seller can reliably estimate future returns and recognises a liability for returns based on previous experience and other relevant factors.

18   Revenue is recognised only when it is probable that the economic benefits associated with the transaction will flow to the entity. In some cases, this may not be probable until the consideration is received or until an uncertainty is removed. For example, it may be uncertain that a foreign governmental authority will grant permission to remit the consideration from a sale in a foreign country. When the permission is granted, the uncertainty is removed and revenue is recognised. However, when an uncertainty arises about the collectability of an amount already included in revenue, the uncollectable amount or the amount in respect of which recovery has ceased to be probable is recognised as an expense, rather than as an adjustment of the amount of revenue originally recognised.

19   Revenue and expenses that relate to the same transaction or other event are recognised simultaneously; this process is commonly referred to as the matching of revenues

and expenses. Expenses, including warranties and other costs to be incurred after the shipment of the goods can normally be measured reliably when the other conditions for the recognition of revenue have been satisfied. However, revenue cannot be recognised when the expenses cannot be measured reliably; in such circumstances, any consideration already received for the sale of the goods is recognised as a liability.

Rendering of Services

20 **When the outcome of a transaction involving the rendering of services can be estimated reliably, revenue associated with the transaction shall be recognised by reference to the stage of completion of the transaction at the end of the reporting period. The outcome of a transaction can be estimated reliably when all the following conditions are satisfied:**

 (a) **the amount of revenue can be measured reliably;**

 (b) **it is probable that the economic benefits associated with the transaction will flow to the entity;**

 (c) **the stage of completion of the transaction at the end of the reporting period can be measured reliably; and**

 (d) **the costs incurred for the transaction and the costs to complete the transaction can be measured reliably.**[2, 3]

21 The recognition of revenue by reference to the stage of completion of a transaction is often referred to as the percentage of completion method. Under this method, revenue is recognised in the reporting periods in which the services are rendered. The recognition of revenue on this basis provides useful information on the extent of service activity and performance during a period. AASB 111 also requires the recognition of revenue on this basis. The requirements of that Standard are generally applicable to the recognition of revenue and the associated expenses for a transaction involving the rendering of services.

22 Revenue is recognised only when it is probable that the economic benefits associated with the transaction will flow to the entity. However, when an uncertainty arises about the collectability of an amount already included in revenue, the uncollectable amount, or the amount in respect of which recovery has ceased to be probable, is recognised as an expense, rather than as an adjustment of the amount of revenue originally recognised.

23 An entity is generally able to make reliable estimates after it has agreed to the following with the other parties to the transaction:

 (a) each party's enforceable rights regarding the service to be provided and received by the parties;

 (b) the consideration to be exchanged; and

 (c) the manner and terms of settlement.

It is also usually necessary for the entity to have an effective internal financial budgeting and reporting system. The entity reviews and, when necessary, revises the estimates of revenue as the service is performed. The need for such revisions does not necessarily indicate that the outcome of the transaction cannot be estimated reliably.

24 The stage of completion of a transaction may be determined by a variety of methods. An entity uses the method that measures reliably the services performed. Depending on the nature of the transaction, the methods may include:

 (a) surveys of work performed;

 (b) services performed to date as a percentage of total services to be performed; or

 (c) the proportion that costs incurred to date bear to the estimated total costs of the transaction. Only costs that reflect services performed to date are included in costs

---

2 See also Interpretation 127 *Evaluating the Substance of Transactions Involving the Legal Form of a Lease*, as identified in AASB 1048 *Interpretation and Application of Standards*.

3 See also Interpretation 131 *Revenue – Barter Transactions Involving Advertising Services*, as identified in AASB 1048 *Interpretation and Application of Standards*.

incurred to date. Only costs that reflect services performed or to be performed are included in the estimated total costs of the transaction.

Progress payments and advances received from customers often do not reflect the services performed.

25   For practical purposes, when services are performed by an indeterminate number of acts over a specified period of time, revenue is recognised on a straight-line basis over the specified period unless there is evidence that some other method better represents the stage of completion. When a specific act is much more significant than any other acts, the recognition of revenue is postponed until the significant act is executed.

26   When the outcome of the transaction involving the rendering of services cannot be estimated reliably, revenue shall be recognised only to the extent of the expenses recognised that are recoverable.

27   During the early stages of a transaction, it is often the case that the outcome of the transaction cannot be estimated reliably. Nevertheless, it may be probable that the entity will recover the transaction costs incurred. Therefore, revenue is recognised only to the extent of costs incurred that are expected to be recoverable. As the outcome of the transaction cannot be estimated reliably, no profit is recognised.

28   When the outcome of a transaction cannot be estimated reliably and it is not probable that the costs incurred will be recovered, revenue is not recognised and the costs incurred are recognised as an expense. When the uncertainties that prevented the outcome of the contract being estimated reliably no longer exist, revenue is recognised in accordance with paragraph 20 rather than in accordance with paragraph 26.

Interest, Royalties and Dividends

29   Revenue arising from the use by others of entity assets yielding interest, royalties and dividends shall be recognised on the bases set out in paragraph 30 when:

(a)   it is probable that the economic benefits associated with the transaction will flow to the entity; and

(b)   the amount of the revenue can be measured reliably.

30   Revenue shall be recognised on the following bases:

(a)   interest shall be recognised using the effective interest method as set out in AASB 139, paragraphs 9 and AG5–AG8;

(b)   royalties shall be recognised on an accrual basis in accordance with the substance of the relevant agreement; and

(c)   dividends shall be recognised when the shareholder's right to receive payment is established.

31   [Deleted by the IASB]

32   When unpaid interest has accrued before the acquisition of an interest-bearing investment, the subsequent receipt of interest is allocated between pre-acquisition and post-acquisition periods; only the post-acquisition portion is recognised as revenue.

33   Royalties accrue in accordance with the terms of the relevant agreement and are usually recognised on that basis unless, having regard to the substance of the agreement, it is more appropriate to recognise revenue on some other systematic and rational basis.

34   Revenue is recognised only when it is probable that the economic benefits associated with the transaction will flow to the entity. However, when an uncertainty arises about the collectability of an amount already included in revenue, the uncollectable amount, or the amount in respect of which recovery has ceased to be probable, is recognised as an expense, rather than as an adjustment of the amount of revenue originally recognised.

Disclosure

35   An entity shall disclose:

   (a)   the accounting policies adopted for the recognition of revenue including the methods adopted to determine the stage of completion of transactions involving the rendering of services;

   (b)   the amount of each significant category of revenue recognised during the period including revenue arising from:

   (i)   the sale of goods;

   (ii)   the rendering of services;

   (iii) interest;

   (iv)   royalties;

   (v)   dividends; and

   (c)   the amount of revenue arising from exchanges of goods or services included in each significant category of revenue.

36   An entity discloses any contingent liabilities and contingent assets in accordance with AASB 137 *Provisions, Contingent Liabilities and Contingent Assets*. Contingent liabilities and contingent assets may arise from items such as warranty costs, claims, penalties or possible losses.

Effective Date

37   [Deleted by the AASB]

38   AASB 2008-7 *Amendments to Australian Accounting Standards – Cost of an Investment in a Subsidiary, Jointly Controlled Entity or Associate*, issued in July 2008, amended paragraph 32. An entity shall apply that amendment prospectively for annual reporting periods beginning on or after 1 January 2009. Earlier application is permitted. If an entity applies the related amendments in paragraphs 4 and 37A of AASB 127 (July 2004, as amended) or paragraphs 4 and 38A of AASB 127 (March 2008, as amended) for an earlier period, it shall apply the amendment in paragraph 32 at the same time.

Illustrative Examples

These illustrative examples accompany, but are not part of, AASB 118. The examples focus on particular aspects of a transaction and are not a comprehensive discussion of all the relevant factors that might influence the recognition of revenue. The examples generally assume that the amount of revenue can be measured reliably, it is probable that the economic benefits will flow to the entity and the costs incurred or to be incurred can be measured reliably.

Sale of Goods

The law in different countries may mean the recognition criteria in this Standard are met at different times. In particular, the law may determine the point in time at which the entity transfers the significant risks and rewards of ownership. Therefore, the examples in this section of the appendix need to be read in the context of the laws relating to the sale of goods in the country in which the transaction takes place.

1   *'Bill and hold' sales, in which delivery is delayed at the buyer's request but the buyer takes title and accepts billing*

   Revenue is recognised when the buyer takes title, provided:

   (a)   it is probable that delivery will be made;

   (b)   the item is on hand, identified and ready for delivery to the buyer at the time the sale is recognised;

   (c)   the buyer specifically acknowledges the deferred delivery instructions; and

   (d)   the usual payment terms apply.

Revenue is not recognised when there is simply an intention to acquire or manufacture the goods in time for delivery.

2   *Goods shipped subject to conditions*

    (a)   *Installation and inspection*

        Revenue is normally recognised when the buyer accepts delivery, and installation and inspection are complete. However, revenue is recognised immediately upon the buyer's acceptance of delivery when:

        (i)   the installation process is simple in nature, for example the installation of a factory tested television receiver which only requires unpacking and connection of power and antennae; or

        (ii)   the inspection is performed only for purposes of final determination of contract prices, for example, shipments of iron ore, sugar or soya beans.

    (b)   *On approval when the buyer has negotiated a limited right of return*

        If there is uncertainty about the possibility of return, revenue is recognised when the shipment has been formally accepted by the buyer or the goods have been delivered and the time period for rejection has elapsed.

    (c)   *Consignment sales under which the recipient (buyer) undertakes to sell the goods on behalf of the shipper (seller)*

        Revenue is recognised by the shipper when the goods are sold by the recipient to a third party.

    (d)   *Cash on delivery sales*

        Revenue is recognised when delivery is made and cash is received by the seller or its agent.

3   *Lay away sales under which the goods are delivered only when the buyer makes the final payment in a series of instalments*

    Revenue from such sales is recognised when the goods are delivered. However, when experience indicates that most such sales are consummated, revenue may be recognised when a significant deposit is received provided the goods are on hand, identified and ready for delivery to the buyer.

4   *Orders when payment (or partial payment) is received in advance of delivery for goods not presently held in inventory, for example, the goods are still to be manufactured or will be delivered directly to the customer from a third party*

    Revenue is recognised when the goods are delivered to the buyer.

5   *Sale and repurchase agreement (other than swap transactions) under which the seller concurrently agrees to repurchase the same goods at a later date, or when the seller has a call option to repurchase, or the buyer has a put option to require the repurchase, by the seller, of the goods*

    For a sale and repurchase agreement on an asset other than a financial asset the terms of the agreement need to be analysed to ascertain whether, in substance, the seller has transferred the risks and rewards of ownership to the buyer and hence revenue is recognised. When the seller has retained the risks and rewards of ownership, even though legal title has been transferred, the transaction is a financing arrangement and does not give rise to revenue. For a sale and repurchase agreement on a financial asset, AASB 139 *Financial Instruments: Recognition and Measurement* applies.

6   *Sales to intermediate parties, such as distributors, dealers or others for resale*

    Revenue from such sales is generally recognised when the risks and rewards of ownership have passed. However, when the buyer is acting, in substance, as an agent, the sale is treated as a consignment sale.

7   *Subscriptions to publications and similar items*

    When the items involved are of similar value in each time period, revenue is recognised on a straight-line basis over the period in which the items are despatched. When the items vary in value from period to period, revenue is recognised on the basis of the sales value of the item despatched in relation to the total estimated sales value of all items covered by the subscription.

8   *Instalment sales, under which the consideration is receivable in instalments*

Revenue attributable to the sales price, exclusive of interest, is recognised at the date of sale. The sale price is the present value of the consideration, determined by discounting the instalments receivable at the imputed rate of interest. The interest element is recognised as revenue as it is earned, using the effective interest method.

9   *Real estate sales*

This example has been superseded by AASB Interpretation 15 *Agreements for the Construction of Real Estate.*

Rendering of Services

10   *Installation fees*

Installation fees are recognised as revenue by reference to the stage of completion of the installation, unless they are incidental to the sale of a product, in which case they are recognised when the goods are sold.

11   *Servicing fees included in the price of the product*

When the selling price of a product includes an identifiable amount for subsequent servicing (for example, after sales support and product enhancement on the sale of software), that amount is deferred and recognised as revenue over the period during which the service is performed. The amount deferred is that which will cover the expected costs of the services under the agreement, together with a reasonable profit on those services.

12   *Advertising commissions*

Media commissions are recognised when the related advertisement or commercial appears before the public. Production commissions are recognised by reference to the stage of completion of the project.

13   *Insurance agency commissions*

Insurance agency commissions received or receivable which do not require the agent to render further service are recognised as revenue by the agent on the effective commencement or renewal dates of the related policies. However, when it is probable that the agent will be required to render further services during the life of the policy, the commission, or part thereof, is deferred and recognised as revenue over the period during which the policy is in force.

14   *Financial service fees*

The recognition of revenue for financial service fees depends on the purposes for which the fees are assessed and the basis of accounting for any associated financial instrument. The description of fees for financial services may not be indicative of the nature and substance of the services provided. Therefore, it is necessary to distinguish between fees that are an integral part of the effective interest rate of a financial instrument, fees that are earned as services are provided, and fees that are earned on the execution of a significant act.

(a)   *Fees that are an integral part of the effective interest rate of a financial instrument*

Such fees are generally treated as an adjustment to the effective interest rate. However, when the financial instrument is measured at fair value with the change in fair value recognised in profit or loss, the fees are recognised as revenue when the instrument is initially recognised.

(i)   *Origination fees received by the entity relating to the creation or acquisition of a financial asset other than one that under AASB 139 is classified as a financial asset 'at fair value through profit or loss'*

Such fees may include compensation for activities such as evaluating the borrower's financial condition, evaluating and recording guarantees, collateral and other security arrangements, negotiating the terms of the instrument, preparing and processing documents and closing the transaction. These fees are an integral part of generating an involvement with the resulting financial instrument and, together with the related transaction costs[1] (as defined in AASB 139), are deferred and recognised as an adjustment to the effective interest rate.

    (ii)   *Commitment fees received by the entity to originate a loan when the loan commitment is outside the scope of AASB 139*

If it is probable that the entity will enter into a specific lending arrangement and the loan commitment is not within the scope of AASB 139, the commitment fee received is regarded as compensation for an ongoing involvement with the acquisition of a financial instrument and, together with the related transaction costs (as defined in AASB 139), is deferred and recognised as an adjustment to the effective interest rate. If the commitment expires without the entity making the loan, the fee is recognised as revenue on expiry. Loan commitments that are within the scope of AASB 139 are accounted for as derivatives and measured at fair value.

    (iii)   *Origination fees received on issuing financial liabilities measured at amortised cost*

These fees are an integral part of generating an involvement with a financial liability. When a financial liability is not classified as 'at fair value through profit or loss', the origination fees received are included, with the related transaction costs (as defined in AASB 139) incurred, in the initial carrying amount of the financial liability and recognised as an adjustment to the effective interest rate. An entity distinguishes fees and costs that are an integral part of the effective interest rate for the financial liability from origination fees and transaction costs relating to the right to provide services, such as investment management services.

  (b) *Fees earned as services are provided*

    (i)   *Fees charged for servicing a loan*

Fees charged by an entity for servicing a loan are recognised as revenue as the services are provided.

    (ii)   *Commitment fees to originate a loan when the loan commitment is outside the scope of AASB 139*

If it is unlikely that a specific lending arrangement will be entered into and the loan commitment is outside the scope of AASB 139, the commitment fee is recognised as revenue on a time proportion basis over the commitment period. Loan commitments that are within the scope of AASB 139 are accounted for as derivatives and measured at fair value.

    (iii)   *Investment management fees*

Fees charged for managing investments are recognised as revenue as the services are provided.

Incremental costs that are directly attributable to securing an investment management contract are recognised as an asset if they can be identified separately and measured reliably and if it is probable that they will be recovered. As in AASB 139, an incremental cost is one that would not have been incurred if the entity had not secured the investment management contract. The asset represents the entity's contractual right to benefit from providing investment management services, and is amortised as the entity recognises the related revenue. If the entity has a portfolio of investment

---

1   In AASB 2008-5 *Amendments to Australian Accounting Standards arising from the Annual Improvements Project*, issued in July 2008, the Board replaced the term 'direct costs' with 'transaction costs' as defined in paragraph 9 of AASB 139. This amendment removed an inconsistency for costs incurred in originating financial assets and liabilities that should be deferred and recognised as an adjustment to the underlying effective interest rate. 'Direct costs', as previously defined, did not require such costs to be incremental.

management contracts, it may assess their recoverability on a portfolio basis.

Some financial services contracts involve both the origination of one or more financial instruments and the provision of investment management services. An example is a long-term monthly saving contract linked to the management of a pool of equity securities. The provider of the contract distinguishes the transaction costs relating to the origination of the financial instrument from the costs of securing the right to provide investment management services.

(c) *Fees earned on the execution of a significant act*

The fees are recognised as revenue when the significant act has been completed, as in the examples below.

(i) *Commission on the allotment of shares to a client*

The commission is recognised as revenue when the shares have been allotted.

(ii) *Placement fees for arranging a loan between a borrower and an investor*

The fee is recognised as revenue when the loan has been arranged.

(iii) *Loan syndication fees*

A syndication fee received by an entity that arranges a loan and that retains no part of the loan package for itself (or retains a part at the same effective interest rate for comparable risk as other participants) is compensation for the service of syndication. Such a fee is recognised as revenue when the syndication has been completed.

15 *Admission fees*

Revenue from artistic performances, banquets and other special events is recognised when the event takes place. When a subscription to a number of events is sold, the fee is allocated to each event on a basis which reflects the extent to which services are performed at each event.

16 *Tuition fees*

Revenue is recognised over the period of instruction.

17 *Initiation, entrance and membership fees*

Revenue recognition depends on the nature of the services provided. If the fee permits only membership, and all other services or products are paid for separately, or if there is a separate annual subscription, the fee is recognised as revenue when no significant uncertainty as to its collectability exists. If the fee entitles the member to services or publications to be provided during the membership period, or to purchase goods or services at prices lower than those charged to non-members, it is recognised on a basis that reflects the timing, nature and value of the benefits provided.

18 *Franchise fees*

Franchise fees may cover the supply of initial and subsequent services, equipment and other tangible assets, and know-how. Accordingly, franchise fees are recognised as revenue on a basis that reflects the purpose for which the fees were charged. The following methods of franchise fee recognition are appropriate:

(a) *Supplies of equipment and other tangible assets*

The amount, based on the fair value of the assets sold, is recognised as revenue when the items are delivered or title passes.

(b) *Supplies of initial and subsequent services*

Fees for the provision of continuing services, whether part of the initial fee or a separate fee are recognised as revenue as the services are rendered. When the separate fee does not cover the cost of continuing services together with a reasonable profit, part of the initial fee, sufficient to cover the costs of continuing services and to provide a reasonable profit on those services, is deferred and recognised as revenue as the services are rendered.

The franchise agreement may provide for the franchisor to supply equipment, inventories, or other tangible assets, at a price lower than that charged to others or a price that does not provide a reasonable profit on those sales. In these circumstances, part of the initial fee, sufficient to cover estimated costs in excess of that price and to provide a reasonable profit on those sales, is deferred and recognised over the period the goods are likely to be sold to the franchisee. The balance of an initial fee is recognised as revenue when performance of all the initial services and other obligations required of the franchisor (such as assistance with site selection, staff training, financing and advertising) has been substantially accomplished.

The initial services and other obligations under an area franchise agreement may depend on the number of individual outlets established in the area. In this case, the fees attributable to the initial services are recognised as revenue in proportion to the number of outlets for which the initial services have been substantially completed.

If the initial fee is collectable over an extended period and there is a significant uncertainty that it will be collected in full, the fee is recognised as cash instalments are received.

(c)   *Continuing franchise fees*

Fees charged for the use of continuing rights granted by the agreement, or for other services provided during the period of the agreement, are recognised as revenue as the services are provided or the rights used.

(d)   *Agency transactions*

Transactions may take place between the franchisor and the franchisee which, in substance, involve the franchisor acting as agent for the franchisee. For example, the franchisor may order supplies and arrange for their delivery to the franchisee at no profit. Such transactions do not give rise to revenue.

19   *Fees from the development of customised software*

Fees from the development of customised software are recognised as revenue by reference to the stage of completion of the development, including completion of services provided for post delivery service support.

Interest, Royalties and Dividends

20   *Licence fees and royalties*

Fees and royalties paid for the use of an entity's assets (such as trademarks, patents, software, music copyright, record masters and motion picture films) are normally recognised in accordance with the substance of the agreement. As a practical matter, this may be on a straight-line basis over the life of the agreement, for example, when a licensee has the right to use certain technology for a specified period of time.

An assignment of rights for a fixed fee or non refundable guarantee under a non cancellable contract which permits the licensee to exploit those rights freely and the licensor has no remaining obligations to perform is, in substance, a sale. An example is a licensing agreement for the use of software when the licensor has no obligations subsequent to delivery. Another example is the granting of rights to exhibit a motion picture film in markets where the licensor has no control over the distributor and expects to receive no further revenues from the box office receipts. In such cases, revenue is recognised at the time of sale.

In some cases, whether or not a licence fee or royalty will be received is contingent on the occurrence of a future event. In such cases, revenue is recognised only when it is probable that the fee or royalty will be received, which is normally when the event has occurred.

Recognition and Measurement

21   *Determining whether an entity is acting as a principal or as an agent (2009 amendment)*

Paragraph 8 states that 'in an agency relationship, the gross inflows of economic benefits include amounts collected on behalf of the principal and which do not result in increases in equity for the entity. The amounts collected on behalf of the principal are not revenue. Instead, revenue is the amount of commission.' Determining whether an entity is acting as a principal or as an agent requires judgement and consideration of all relevant facts and circumstances.

An entity is acting as a principal when it has exposure to the significant risks and rewards associated with the sale of goods or the rendering of services. Features that indicate that an entity is acting as a principal include:

(a)   the entity has the primary responsibility for providing the goods or services to the customer or for fulfilling the order, for example by being responsible for the acceptability of the products or services ordered or purchased by the customer;

(b)   the entity has inventory risk before or after the customer order, during shipping or on return;

(c)   the entity has latitude in establishing prices, either directly or indirectly, for example by providing additional goods or services; and

(d)   the entity bears the customer's credit risk for the amount receivable from the customer.

An entity is acting as an agent when it does not have exposure to the significant risks and rewards associated with the sale of goods or the rendering of services. One feature indicating that an entity is acting as an agent is that the amount the entity earns is predetermined, being either a fixed fee per transaction or a stated percentage of the amount billed to the customer.

AASB 119
Employee Benefits

(Compiled November 2010: applicable 30 June 2013)

Note from the Institute of Chartered Accountants Australia

This note, prepared by the technical editors, is not part of Accounting Standard AASB 119.

Historical development

15 July 2004: AASB 119 'Employee Benefits' is the Australian equivalent of IAS 19 of the same name. It was made by the AASB on 15 July 2004 as part of the AASB's program to adopt International Financial Reporting Standards by 2005.

22 December 2004: A revised AASB 119 was made by the AASB and applies to annual reporting periods beginning 1 January 2006. The revised AASB 119 incorporates the IASB's December 2004 amendments to IAS 19 in respect of actuarial gains and losses, group plans and disclosures. Entities that prepare financial reports under the Corporations Act may elect to apply the revised December 2004 version of AASB 119 to earlier annual financial reporting periods beginning on or after 1 January 2005.

9 June 2005: AASB 2005-3 'Amendments to Australian Accounting Standards' deletes paragraphs Aus55.1 and Aus 55.2, and adds paragraph Australian Guidance, G20. The Standard is applicable for annual reporting periods ending on or after 31 December 2005.

6 April 2006: AASB deleted all Guidance accompanying, but not part of, AASB 119.

26 February 2007: AASB 2007-3 'Amendments to Australian Accounting Standards' was issued by the AASB. This Standard is applicable to annual reporting periods beginning on or after 1 January 2007.

30 April 2007: AASB 2007-4 'Amendments to Australian Accounting Standards' amends paragraphs Aus1.3, 7, 18, 21, 45, 58A, Aus78.1, 120A, Appendix A, and Appendix C and deletes paragraphs Aus121.1 and Aus121.2 and is applicable to annual reporting periods beginning on or after 1 July 2007. Entities may elect to early-adopt it to annual reporting periods beginning on or after 1 January 2005.

24 September 2007: AASB 2007-8 'Amendments to Australian Accounting Standards arising from AASB 101' amends AASB 119 to align with revised AASB 101. This Standard is applicable to annual reporting periods beginning on or after 1 January 2009.

13 December 2007: AASB 2007-10 'Further Amendments to Australian Accounting Standards arising from AASB 101' amends AASB 119, replacing the term 'financial report' with 'financial statements'. This Standard is applicable to annual reporting periods beginning on or after 1 January 2009.

24 July 2008: AASB 2008-5 'Amendments to Australian Accounting Standards arising from the Annual Improvements Project' amends AASB 119 in relation to curtailment and negative past service cost, plan administration costs, replacement of the term 'fall due' and guidance on contingent liabilities. This Standard is applicable to annual reporting periods beginning on or after 1 January 2009.

25 June 2009: AASB 2009-6 'Amendments to Australian Accounting Standards' amends AASB 119 for editorial corrections made by the International Accounting Standards Board (IASB) to its Standards and Interpretations (IFRSs) and as a consequence of issuing revised AASB 101 'Presentation of Financial Statements'. This Standard is applicable to annual reporting periods beginning on or after 1 January 2009 that end on or after 30 June 2009.

9 October 2009: AASB 119 was reissued by the AASB, compiled to include the AASB 2007-3, AASB 2007-8, AASB 2007-10, AASB 2008-5 and AASB 2009-6 amendments and applies to annual reporting periods beginning on or after 1 January 2009 that end on or after 30 June 2009. Early application is permitted.

---

15 December 2009: AASB 2009-12 'Amendments to Australian Accounting Standards' amends AASB 119 for editorial corrections. This Standard is applicable to annual reporting periods beginning on or after 1 January 2011 with early adoption permitted.

27 October 2010: AASB 2010-5 'Further Amendments to Australian Accounting Standards' makes editorial amendments to AASB 119. This Standard is applicable to annual reporting periods beginning on or after 1 January 2011.

26 November 2010: AASB 119 was reissued by the AASB, compiled to include the AASB 2009-12 and AASB 2010-5 amendments and applies to annual reporting periods ending on or after 1 January 2011 but before 1 July 2013.

5 September 2011: AASB 2011-8 'Amendments to Australian Accounting Standards arising from AASB 13' amends AASB 119 to give effect to a consequential change in the definition of fair value arising from the issue of AASB 13. This Standard applies to annual reporting periods beginning on or after 1 January 2013 and can be adopted early. **These amendments are not included in this compiled Standard.**

5 September 2011: AASB 119 was reissued by the AASB. This Standard applies to annual reporting periods beginning on or after 1 January 2013 and can be adopted early. **This revised Standard is included in this handbook with the footer: Applicable to periods beginning from 1 January 2013.**

References

Interpretation 14 AASB 119 – *The Limit on a Defined Benefit Asset, Minimum Funding Requirements and their interaction* applies to AASB 119.

AASB item not taken onto the agenda: *Classification of Long Service Leave Liabilities* applies to AASB 119.

IFRIC items not taken onto the agenda: No. 22 *Accounting for the Transfer to the Japanese Government of the Substitutional Portion of Employee Pension Fund Liabilities*, No. 23 *Calculation of discount rates*, No. 24 *Classification of an insured plan*, No. 25 *Employee benefits – Undiscounted vested employee benefits*, IAS 19-1 *Determining the appropriate rate to discount past employment benefit obligations*, IAS 19-2 *Employee long service leave*, IAS 19-3 *Special Wage Tax*, IAS 19-4 *Curtailments and negative past service costs*, 19-5 *Post employment benefits – Benefit allocation for defined benefit plans IAS 19*, IAS 19-6 *Changes to a plan caused by government*, IAS 19-7 *Treatment of employee contributions*, IAS 19-8 *Death in service benefit*, IAS 19-9 *Definition of plan assets*, IAS 19-10 *Pension promises based on performance hurdles*, IAS 19-14 *Settlements*, IAS 19-15 *Accounting for a statutory employee profit sharing arrangement*, IAS 19-16 *Defined Contribution Plans with Vesting Conditions IAS 19-17* and IAS 19-18 *Accounting for contribution-based promises: impact of the 2011 amendments to IAS 19* apply to AASB 119.

AASB 119 compared to IAS 19

Additions

Paragraph	Description
Aus 1.1	Which entities AASB 119 applies to (i.e. reporting entities and general purpose financial statements).
Aus 1.2	The application date of AASB 119 (i.e. annual reporting periods beginning 1 January 2005).
Aus 1.3	Prohibits early application of AASB 119.
Aus 1.4	Makes the requirements of AASB 119 subject to AASB 1031 'Materiality'.
Aus 1.5	Explains which Australian Standards have been superseded by AASB 119.
Aus 1.6	Notice of the new Standard published on 22 July 2004.
Aus 78.1	The discount rate used in the measurement of post-employment benefit obligations must be the market yield on government bonds rather than high quality corporate bonds because the market in the latter is not sufficiently active and liquid.

Deletions

Paragraph	Description
108(c)	Acquisition accounting the assets and liabilities arising from post-employment benefits includes amounts unrecognised by virtue of the transitional provision at paragraph 155(b).
153	IAS 8 applies where an entity first adopts IAS 19 for employee benefits other than those relating to defined benefit plans.
154	How to measure the transitional liability for defined benefit plans on first adopting IAS 19.
155	How to account for a transitional liability that is greater than the liability that would have been recognised at the same date under the previous accounting policy.
156	How to account for a transitional liability that is less than the liability that would have been recognised at the same date under the previous accounting policy.
157	Effective date of IAS 19.
158	Reference to superseded IAS 19.
159, 159A, 159B, 159C	Operative date for revisions to IAS 19.
160	IAS 8 applies to changes in accounting policies resulting from the application of paragraphs 159 and 159A.

Contents

Compilation Details

Comparison with IAS 19

Accounting Standard
AASB 119 Employee Benefits

	Paragraphs
Objective	
Application	Aus1.1 – Aus1.6
Scope	1 – 6
Definitions	7
Short-term Employee Benefits	8 – 9
Recognition and Measurement	
All Short-term Employee Benefits	10
Short-term Compensated Absences	11 – 16
Profit-sharing and Bonus Plans	17 – 22
Disclosure	23
Post-employment Benefits: Distinction between Defined Contribution Plans and Defined Benefit Plans	24 – 28
Multi-employer Plans	29 – 34B
State Plans	36 – 38
Insured Benefits	39 – 42
Post-employment Benefits: Defined Contribution Plans	43
Recognition and Measurement	44 – 45
Disclosure	46 – 47
Post-employment Benefits: Defined Benefit Plans	48
Recognition and Measurement	49 – 51
Accounting for the Constructive Obligation	52 – 53
Statement of Financial Position	54 – 60
Profit or Loss	61 – 62
Recognition and Measurement: Present Value of Defined Benefit Obligations and Current Service Cost	63
Actuarial Valuation Method	64 – 66
Attributing Benefit to Periods of Service	67 – 71
Actuarial Assumptions	72 – 77
Actuarial Assumptions: Discount Rate	78 – 82
Actuarial Assumptions: Salaries, Benefits and Medical Costs	83 – 91
Actuarial Gains and Losses	92 – 95
Past Service Cost	96 – 101
Recognition and Measurement: Plan Assets	
Fair Value of Plan Assets	102 – 104
Reimbursements	104A – 104D
Return on Plan Assets	105 – 107
Business Combinations	108

	Paragraphs
Curtailments and Settlements	109 – 115
Presentation	
Offset	116 – 117
Current / Non-current Distinction	118
Financial Components of Post-employment Benefit Costs	119
Disclosure	120 – 125
Other Long-term Employee Benefits	126 – 127
Recognition and Measurement	128 – 130
Disclosure	131
Termination Benefits	132
Recognition	133 – 138
Measurement	139 – 140
Disclosure	141 – 143
Effective Date	159D
Transitional Provisions	160

Guidance on Implementing AASB 119

Basis for Conclusions on IAS 19
(available on the AASB website)

Australian Accounting Standard AASB 119 *Employee Benefits* (as amended) is set out in paragraphs Aus1.1 – 160. All the paragraphs have equal authority. Terms defined in this Standard are in *italics* the first time they appear in the Standard. AASB 119 is to be read in the context of other Australian Accounting Standards, including AASB 1048 *Interpretation and Application of Standards*, which identifies the Australian Accounting Interpretations. In the absence of explicit guidance, AASB 108 *Accounting Policies, Changes in Accounting Estimates and Errors* provides a basis for selecting and applying accounting policies.

Compilation Details

Accounting Standard AASB 119 *Employee Benefits* as amended

This compiled Standard applies to annual reporting periods beginning on or after 1 January 2011 but before 1 July 2013. It takes into account amendments up to and including 27 October 2010 and was prepared on 26 November 2010 by the staff of the Australian Accounting Standards Board (AASB).

This compilation is not a separate Accounting Standard made by the AASB. Instead, it is a representation of AASB 119 (December 2004) as amended by other Accounting Standards, which are listed in the Table below.

Table of Standards

Standard	Date made	Application date (*annual reporting periods … on or after …*)	Application, saving or transitional provisions
AASB 119	22 Dec 2004	(*beginning*) 1 Jan 2006	see (a) below
AASB 2005-3	9 Jun 2005	(*beginning*) 1 Jan 2006	see (a) below
AASB 2007-3	26 Feb 2007	(*beginning*) 1 Jan 2009	see (b) below
AASB 2007-4	30 Apr 2007	(*beginning*) 1 Jul 2007	see (c) below
AASB 2007-8	24 Sep 2007	(*beginning*) 1 Jan 2009	see (d) below

AASB

Standard	Date made	Application date (*annual reporting periods ... on or after ...*)	Application, saving or transitional provisions
AASB 2007-10	13 Dec 2007	(*beginning*) 1 Jan 2009	see (d) below
AASB 2008-5	24 Jul 2008	(*beginning*) 1 Jan 2009	see (e) below
AASB 2009-6	25 Jun 2009	(*beginning*) 1 Jan 2009 and (*ending*) 30 Jun 2009	see (f) below
AASB 2009-12	15 Dec 2009	(*beginning*) 1 Jan 2011	see (g) below
AASB 2010-2	30 Jun 2010	(*beginning*) 1 Jul 2013	not compiled*
AASB 2010-5	27 Oct 2010	(*beginning*) 1 Jan 2011	see (g) below

* The amendments made by this Standard are not included in this compilation, which presents the principal Standard as applicable to annual reporting periods beginning on or after 1 January 2011 but before 1 July 2013.

(a) Entities may elect to apply this Standard to annual reporting periods beginning on or after 1 January 2005 but before 1 January 2006.

(b) Entities may elect to apply this Standard to annual reporting periods beginning on or after 1 January 2005 but before 1 January 2009, provided that AASB 8 *Operating Segments* is also applied to such periods.

(c) Entities may elect to apply this Standard to annual reporting periods beginning on or after 1 January 2005 but before 1 July 2007.

(d) Entities may elect to apply this Standard to annual reporting periods beginning on or after 1 January 2005 but before 1 January 2009, provided that AASB 101 *Presentation of Financial Statements* (September 2007) is also applied to such periods.

(e) Entities may elect to apply this Standard, or its amendments to individual Standards, to annual reporting periods beginning on or after 1 January 2005 but before 1 January 2009.

(f) Entities may elect to apply this Standard to annual reporting periods beginning on or after 1 January 2005 but before 1 January 2009, provided that AASB 101 *Presentation of Financial Statements* (September 2007) is also applied to such periods, and to annual reporting periods beginning on or after 1 January 2009 that end before 30 June 2009.

(g) Entities may elect to apply this Standard to annual reporting periods beginning on or after 1 January 2005 but before 1 January 2011.

Table of Amendments to Standard

Paragraph affected	How affected	By ... [paragraph]
Aus1.1	amended	AASB 2007-8 [7, 8]
Aus1.3	amended	AASB 2007-4 [53]
Aus1.4	amended	AASB 2007-8 [8]
7	amended amended	AASB 2007-4 [56] AASB 2008-5 [28]
8	amended	AASB 2008-5 [28]
18 (Example)	amended	AASB 2007-4 [56]
20	amended	AASB 2007-10 [61]
21	amended	AASB 2007-4 [56]
32B	amended	AASB 2008-5 [28]
45	amended	AASB 2007-4 [54]
Aus55.1	deleted	AASB 2005-3 [2]
Aus55.2	deleted	AASB 2005-3 [2]
58A	amended	AASB 2007-4 [56]
58B	amended	AASB 2010-5 [31]
65	amended	AASB 2009-6 [51]
69	amended amended	AASB 2007-8 [6] AASB 2009-6 [52]
Aus78.1	amended	AASB 2007-4 [54]
82	amended	AASB 2010-5 [32]

Paragraph affected	How affected	By ... [paragraph]
95	amended	AASB 2010-5 [32]
93A-93D	amended	AASB 2007-8 [65]
97	amended	AASB 2008-5 [28]
98	amended	AASB 2008-5 [28]
104A	amended	AASB 2007-8 [6]
104C	amended	AASB 2009-6 [53]
105	amended	AASB 2007-8 [66]
106 (Example)	amended	AASB 2007-8 [66]
111	amended	AASB 2008-5 [28]
111A	added	AASB 2008-5 [29]
115 (Example)	amended	AASB 2007-3 [11]
119	amended	AASB 2007-8 [6]
120	amended	AASB 2007-10 [62]
120A	amended	AASB 2007-4 [56]
	amended	AASB 2007-8 [67]
	amended	AASB 2007-10 [62]
	amended	AASB 2009-12 [14]
Aus121.1	deleted	AASB 2007-4 [55]
Aus121.2	deleted	AASB 2007-4 [55]
139	amended	AASB 2009-12 [14]
157 (preceding heading)	amended	AASB 2008-5 [30]
159B-159C	notes added	AASB 2009-6 [54]
159D	added	AASB 2008-5 [31]
160	added	AASB 2008-5 [31]
Aus160.1	amended	AASB 2007-10 [62]
	deleted	AASB 2008-5 [32]
161	note added	AASB 2007-8 [68]

Table of Amendments to Guidance

Paragraph or section affected	How affected	By ... [paragraph]
A	amended	AASB 2007-4 [56]
	amended	AASB 2007-8 [6]
	renamed and amended	AASB 2010-5 [33-35]
B	amended	AASB 2007-8 [6]
	amended	AASB 2009-6 [55, 56]
	renamed and amended	AASB 2010-5 [36]
C	amended	AASB 2007-4 [56]
	amended	AASB 2007-8 [6]
	amended	AASB 2009-6 [57]
	renamed and amended	AASB 2010-5 [37]
D	deleted	AASB 2009-12 [15]
Australian Guidance, G1-G19	deleted	AASB, Apr 2006 *
G20 (and preceding heading)	added	AASB 2005-3 [3]
	deleted	AASB, Apr 2006

*   The AASB decided at its meeting on 6 April 2006 to delete all of the Australian Guidance accompanying, but not part of, AASB 119. The decision had immediate effect.

General Terminology Amendments

The following amendments are not shown in the above Tables of Amendments:

References to 'balance sheet' and 'reporting date' were amended to 'statement of financial position' and 'end of the reporting period' respectively by AASB 2007-8.

Comparison with IAS 19

AASB 119 and IAS 19

AASB 119 *Employee Benefits* as amended incorporates IAS 19 *Employee Benefits* as issued and amended by the International Accounting Standards Board (IASB). Paragraphs that have been added to this Standard (and do not appear in the text of IAS 19) are identified with the prefix "Aus", followed by the number of the relevant IASB paragraph and decimal numbering.

Compliance with IAS 19

Entities that comply with AASB 119 as amended will simultaneously be in compliance with IAS 19 as amended.

Accounting Standard AASB 119

The Australian Accounting Standards Board made Accounting Standard AASB 119 *Employee Benefits* under section 334 of the Corporations Act 2001 on 22 December 2004.

This compiled version of AASB 119 applies to annual reporting periods beginning on or after 1 January 2011 but before 1 July 2013. It incorporates relevant amendments contained in other AASB Standards made by the AASB and other decisions of the AASB up to and including 27 October 2010 (see Compilation Details).

Accounting Standard AASB 119

Employee Benefits

Objective

The objective of this Standard is to prescribe the accounting and disclosure for employee benefits. The Standard requires an entity to recognise:

(a) a liability when an employee has provided service in exchange for employee benefits to be paid in the future; and

(b) an expense when the entity consumes the economic benefit arising from service provided by an employee in exchange for employee benefits.

Application

Aus1.1 **This Standard applies to:**

    (a) each entity that is required to prepare financial reports in accordance with Part 2M.3 of the Corporations Act and that is a reporting entity;

    (b) general purpose financial statements of each other reporting entity; and

    (c) financial statements that are, or are held out to be, general purpose financial statements.

Aus1.2 **This Standard applies to annual reporting periods beginning on or after 1 January 2006.**

    [Note: For application dates of paragraphs changed or added by an amending Standard, see Compilation Details.]

Aus1.3 **This Standard may be applied to annual reporting periods beginning on or after 1 January 2005 but before 1 January 2006. When an entity applies this Standard to such an annual reporting period, it shall disclose that fact.**

Aus1.4   **The requirements specified in this Standard apply to the financial statements where information resulting from their application is material in accordance with AASB 1031 *Materiality*.**

Aus1.5   **When applied or operative, this Standard supersedes AASB 119 *Employee Benefits* as notified in the *Commonwealth of Australia Gazette* No S 294, 22 July 2004.**

Aus1.6   Notice of this Standard was published in the *Commonwealth of Australia Gazette* No S 537, 22 December 2004 and No S 559, 23 December 2004.

Scope

1   **This Standard shall be applied by an employer in accounting for all *employee benefits*, except those to which AASB 2 *Share-based Payment* applies.**

2   This Standard does not deal with reporting by employee benefit plans (see AAS 25 *Financial Reporting by Superannuation Plans*).

3   The employee benefits to which this Standard applies include those provided:

     (a)   under formal plans or other formal agreements between an entity and individual employees, groups of employees or their representatives;

     (b)   under legislative requirements, or through industry arrangements, whereby entities are required to contribute to national, state, industry or other *multi-employer plans*; or

     (c)   by those informal practices that give rise to a constructive obligation. Informal practices give rise to a constructive obligation where the entity has no realistic alternative but to pay employee benefits. An example of a constructive obligation is where a change in the entity's informal practices would cause unacceptable damage to its relationship with employees.

4   Employee benefits include:

     (a)   *short-term employee benefits*, such as wages, salaries and social security contributions, paid annual leave and paid sick leave, profit-sharing and bonuses (if payable within twelve months of the end of the period) and non-monetary benefits (such as medical care, housing, cars and free or subsidised goods or services) for current employees;

     (b)   *post-employment benefits* such as pensions, other retirement benefits, post-employment life insurance and post-employment medical care;

     (c)   *other long-term employee benefits*, including long-service leave or sabbatical leave, jubilee or other long-service benefits, long term disability benefits and, if they are not payable wholly within twelve months after the end of the period, profit-sharing, bonuses and deferred compensation; and

     (d)   *termination benefits*.

     Because each category identified in (a) – (d) above has different characteristics, this Standard establishes separate requirements for each category.

5   Employee benefits include benefits provided to either employees or their dependants and may be settled by payments (or the provision of goods or services) made either directly to the employees, to their spouses, children or other dependants or to others, such as insurance companies.

6   An employee may provide services to an entity on a full-time, part time, permanent, casual or temporary basis. For the purpose of this Standard, employees include directors and other management personnel.

Definitions

7   The following terms are used in this Standard with the meanings specified.

Actuarial gains and losses comprise:

(a)   experience adjustments (the effects of differences between the previous actuarial assumptions and what has actually occurred); and

(b)   the effects of changes in actuarial assumptions.

Assets held by a long-term employee benefit fund are assets (other than non-transferable financial instruments issued by the entity) that:

(a)   are held by an entity (a fund) that is legally separate from the entity and exists solely to pay or fund employee benefits; and

(b)   are available to be used only to pay or fund employee benefits, are not available to the entity's own creditors (even in bankruptcy), and cannot be returned to the entity, unless either:

(i)   the remaining assets of the fund are sufficient to meet all the related employee benefit obligations of the plan or the entity; or

(ii)   the assets are returned to the entity to reimburse it for employee benefits already paid.

Current service cost is the increase in the present value of a defined benefit obligation resulting from employee service in the current period.

Defined benefit plans are post-employment benefit plans other than defined contribution plans.

Defined contribution plans are post-employment benefit plans under which an entity pays fixed contributions into a separate entity (a fund) and will have no legal or constructive obligation to pay further contributions if the fund does not hold sufficient assets to pay all employee benefits relating to employee service in the current and prior periods.

Employee benefits are all forms of consideration given by an entity in exchange for service rendered by employees.

Fair value is the amount for which an asset could be exchanged or a liability settled between knowledgeable, willing parties in an arm's length transaction.

Interest cost is the increase during a period in the present value of a defined benefit obligation which arises because the benefits are one period closer to settlement.

Multi-employer plans are defined contribution plans (other than state plans) or defined benefit plans (other than state plans) that:

(a)   pool the assets contributed by various entities that are not under common control; and

(b)   use those assets to provide benefits to employees of more than one entity, on the basis that contribution and benefit levels are determined without regard to the identity of the entity that employs the employees concerned.

Other long-term employee benefits are employee benefits (other than post-employment benefits and termination benefits) that are not due to be settled within twelve months after the end of the period in which the employees render the related service.

Past service cost is the change in the present value of the defined benefit obligation for employee service in prior periods, resulting in the current period from the introduction of, or changes to, post-employment benefits or other long-term employee benefits. Past service cost may be either positive (when benefits are introduced or changed so that the present value of the defined benefit obligation increases) or negative (when existing benefits are changed so that the present value of the defined benefit obligation decreases).

Plan assets comprise:

(a)   *assets held by a long-term employee benefit fund*; and

(b)   qualifying insurance policies.

Post-employment benefit plans are formal or informal arrangements under which an entity provides post employment benefits for one or more employees.

Post-employment benefits are employee benefits (other than termination benefits) which are payable after the completion of employment.

The *present value of a defined benefit obligation* is the present value, without deducting any plan assets, of expected future payments required to settle the obligation resulting from employee service in the current and prior periods.

A *qualifying insurance policy*[1] is an insurance policy issued by an insurer that is not a related party (as defined in AASB 124 *Related Party Disclosures*) of the entity, if the proceeds of the policy:

(a)   can be used only to pay or fund employee benefits under a defined benefit plan; and

(b)   are not available to the entity's own creditors (even in bankruptcy) and cannot be paid to the entity, unless either:

(i)   the proceeds represent surplus assets that are not needed for the policy to meet all the related employee benefit obligations; or

(ii) the proceeds are returned to the entity to reimburse it for employee benefits already paid.

The *return on plan assets* is interest, dividends and other revenue derived from the plan assets, together with realised and unrealised gains or losses on the plan assets, less any costs of administering the plan (other than those included in the actuarial assumptions used to measure the defined benefit obligation) and less any tax payable by the plan itself.

Short-term employee benefits are employee benefits (other than termination benefits) that are due to be settled within twelve months after the end of the period in which the employees render the related service.

Termination benefits are employee benefits payable as a result of either:

(a)   an entity's decision to terminate an employee's employment before the normal retirement date; or

(b)   an employee's decision to accept voluntary redundancy in exchange for those benefits.

Vested employee benefits are employee benefits that are not conditional on future employment.

Short-term Employee Benefits

8   Short-term employee benefits include items such as:

(a)   wages, salaries and social security contributions;

(b)   short-term compensated absences (such as paid annual leave and paid sick leave) where the compensation for the absences is due to be settled within twelve months after the end of the period in which the employees render the related employee service;

(c)   profit-sharing and bonuses payable within twelve months after the end of the period in which the employees render the related service; and

(d)   non-monetary benefits (such as medical care, housing, cars and free or subsidised goods or services) for current employees.

---

1   A qualifying insurance policy is not necessarily an insurance contract, as defined in AASB 4 *Insurance Contracts*.

9   Accounting for short-term employee benefits is generally straightforward because no actuarial assumptions are required to measure the obligation or the cost and there is no possibility of any actuarial gain or loss. Moreover, short-term employee benefit obligations are measured on an undiscounted basis.

Recognition and Measurement

All Short-term Employee Benefits

10   **When an employee has rendered service to an entity during a reporting period, the entity shall recognise the undiscounted amount of short-term employee benefits expected to be paid in exchange for that service:**

    (a)   as a liability (accrued expense), after deducting any amount already paid. If the amount already paid exceeds the undiscounted amount of the benefits, an entity shall recognise that excess as an asset (prepaid expense) to the extent that the prepayment will lead to, for example, a reduction in future payments or a cash refund; and

    (b)   as an expense, unless another Australian Accounting Standard requires or permits the inclusion of the benefits in the cost of an asset (see, for example, AASB 102 *Inventories* and AASB 116 *Property, Plant and Equipment*).

    Paragraphs 11, 14 and 17 explain how an entity shall apply this requirement to short-term employee benefits in the form of compensated absences and profit-sharing and bonus plans.

Short-term Compensated Absences

11   **An entity shall recognise the expected cost of short-term employee benefits in the form of compensated absences under paragraph 10 as follows:**

    (a)   in the case of accumulating compensated absences, when the employees render service that increases their entitlement to future compensated absences; and

    (b)   in the case of non-accumulating compensated absences, when the absences occur.

12   An entity may compensate employees for absence for various reasons including vacation, sickness and short-term disability, maternity or paternity, jury service and military service. Entitlement to compensated absences falls into two categories:

    (a)   accumulating; and

    (b)   non-accumulating.

13   Accumulating compensated absences are those that are carried forward and can be used in future periods if the current period's entitlement is not used in full. Accumulating compensated absences may be either vesting (in other words, employees are entitled to a cash payment for unused entitlement on leaving the entity) or non-vesting (when employees are not entitled to a cash payment for unused entitlement on leaving). An obligation arises as employees render service that increases their entitlement to future compensated absences. The obligation exists, and is recognised, even if the compensated absences are non-vesting, although the possibility that employees may leave before they use an accumulated non-vesting entitlement affects the measurement of that obligation.

14   **An entity shall measure the expected cost of accumulating compensated absences as the additional amount that the entity expects to pay as a result of the unused entitlement that has accumulated at the end of the reporting period.**

15   The method specified in the previous paragraph measures the obligation at the amount of the additional payments that are expected to arise solely from the fact that the benefit accumulates. In many cases, an entity may not need to make detailed computations to estimate that there is no material obligation for unused compensated absences. For example, a sick leave obligation is likely to be material only if there is a formal or informal understanding that unused paid sick leave may be taken as paid vacation.

AASB

> **Example Illustrating Paragraphs 14 and 15**
>
> An entity has 100 employees, who are each entitled to five working days of paid sick leave for each year. Unused sick leave may be carried forward for one calendar year. Sick leave is taken first out of the current year's entitlement and then out of any balance brought forward from the previous year (a LIFO basis). At 31 December 20X1, the average unused entitlement is two days per employee. The entity expects, based on past experience which is expected to continue, that 92 employees will take no more than five days of paid sick leave in 20X2 and that the remaining eight employees will take an average of six and a half days each.
>
> *The entity expects that it will pay an additional 12 days of sick pay as a result of the unused entitlement that has accumulated at 31 December 20X1 (one and a half days each, for eight employees). Therefore, the entity recognises a liability equal to 12 days of sick pay.*

16   Non-accumulating compensated absences do not carry forward: they lapse if the current period's entitlement is not used in full and do not entitle employees to a cash payment for unused entitlement on leaving the entity. This is commonly the case for sick pay (to the extent that unused past entitlement does not increase future entitlement), maternity or paternity leave and compensated absences for jury service or military service. An entity recognises no liability or expense until the time of the absence, because employee service does not increase the amount of the benefit.

Profit-sharing and Bonus Plans

17   **An entity shall recognise the expected cost of profit-sharing and bonus payments under paragraph 10 when, and only when:**

   (a)   the entity has a present legal or constructive obligation to make such payments as a result of past events; and

   (b)   a reliable estimate of the obligation can be made.

   A present obligation exists when, and only when, the entity has no realistic alternative but to make the payments.

18   Under some profit-sharing plans, employees receive a share of the profit only if they remain with the entity for a specified period. Such plans create a constructive obligation as employees render service that increases the amount to be paid if they remain in service until the end of the specified period. The measurement of such constructive obligations reflects the possibility that some employees may leave without receiving profit-sharing payments.

> **Example Illustrating Paragraph 18**
>
> A profit-sharing plan requires an entity to pay a specified proportion of its profit for the year to employees who serve throughout the year. If no employees leave during the year, the total profit-sharing payments for the year will be 3% of profit. The entity estimates that staff turnover will reduce the payments to 2.5% of profit.
>
> *The entity recognises a liability and an expense of 2.5% of profit.*

19   An entity may have no legal obligation to pay a bonus. Nevertheless, in some cases, an entity has a practice of paying bonuses. In such cases, the entity has a constructive obligation because the entity has no realistic alternative but to pay the bonus. The measurement of the constructive obligation reflects the possibility that some employees may leave without receiving a bonus.

20   An entity can make a reliable estimate of its legal or constructive obligation under a profit-sharing or bonus plan when, and only when:

   (a)   the formal terms of the plan contain a formula for determining the amount of the benefit;

   (b)   the entity determines the amounts to be paid before the financial statements are authorised for issue; or

   (c)   past practice gives clear evidence of the amount of the entity's constructive obligation.

21 An obligation under profit-sharing and bonus plans results from employee service and not from a transaction with the entity's owners. Therefore, an entity recognises the cost of profit-sharing and bonus plans not as a distribution of profit but as an expense.

22 If profit-sharing and bonus payments are not due wholly within twelve months after the end of the period in which the employees render the related service, those payments are other long-term employee benefits (see paragraphs 126-131).

Disclosure

23 Although this Standard does not require specific disclosures about short-term employee benefits, other Australian Accounting Standards may require disclosures. For example, AASB 124 requires disclosure about employee benefits for key management personnel. AASB 101 *Presentation of Financial Statements* requires disclosure of employee benefits expense.

Post-employment Benefits: Distinction between Defined Contribution Plans and Defined Benefit Plans

24 Post-employment benefits include, for example:

 (a) retirement benefits, such as pensions; and

 (b) other post-employment benefits, such as post-employment life insurance and post-employment medical care.

 Arrangements whereby an entity provides post-employment benefits are *post-employment benefit plans*. An entity applies this Standard to all such arrangements whether or not they involve the establishment of a separate entity to receive contributions and to pay benefits.

25 Post-employment benefit plans are classified as either *defined contribution plans* or *defined benefit plans*, depending on the economic substance of the plan as derived from its principal terms and conditions. Under defined contribution plans:

 (a) the entity's legal or constructive obligation is limited to the amount that it agrees to contribute to the fund. Thus, the amount of the post-employment benefits received by the employee is determined by the amount of contributions paid by an entity (and perhaps also the employee) to a post-employment benefit plan or to an insurance company, together with investment returns arising from the contributions; and

 (b) in consequence, actuarial risk (that benefits will be less than expected) and investment risk (that assets invested will be insufficient to meet expected benefits) fall on the employee.

26 Examples of cases where an entity's obligation is not limited to the amount that it agrees to contribute to the fund are when the entity has a legal or constructive obligation through:

 (a) a plan benefit formula that is not linked solely to the amount of contributions;

 (b) a guarantee, either indirectly through a plan or directly, of a specified return on contributions; or

 (c) those informal practices that give rise to a constructive obligation. For example, a constructive obligation may arise where an entity has a history of increasing benefits for former employees to keep pace with inflation even where there is no legal obligation to do so.

27 Under defined benefit plans:

 (a) the entity's obligation is to provide the agreed benefits to current and former employees; and

 (b) actuarial risk (that benefits will cost more than expected) and investment risk fall, in substance, on the entity. If actuarial or investment experience are worse than expected, the entity's obligation may be increased.

28 Paragraphs 29-42 below explain the distinction between defined contribution plans and defined benefit plans in the context of multi employer plans, state plans and insured benefits.

Multi-employer Plans

29   An entity shall classify a multi-employer plan as a defined contribution plan or a defined benefit plan under the terms of the plan (including any constructive obligation that goes beyond the formal terms). Where a multi-employer plan is a defined benefit plan, an entity shall:

(a)   account for its proportionate share of the defined benefit obligation, *plan assets* and cost associated with the plan in the same way as for any other defined benefit plan; and

(b)   disclose the information required by paragraph 120A.

30   When sufficient information is not available to use defined benefit accounting for a multi-employer plan that is a defined benefit plan, an entity shall:

(a)   account for the plan under paragraphs 44-46 as if it were a defined contribution plan;

(b)   disclose:

(i)   the fact that the plan is a defined benefit plan; and

(ii)   the reason why sufficient information is not available to enable the entity to account for the plan as a defined benefit plan; and

(c)   to the extent that a surplus or deficit in the plan may affect the amount of future contributions, disclose in addition:

(i)   any available information about that surplus or deficit;

(ii)   the basis used to determine that surplus or deficit; and

(iii)   the implications, if any, for the entity.

31   One example of a defined benefit multi-employer plan is one where:

(a)   the plan is financed on a pay-as-you-go basis such that: contributions are set at a level that is expected to be sufficient to pay the benefits falling due in the same period; and future benefits earned during the current period will be paid out of future contributions; and

(b)   employees' benefits are determined by the length of their service and the participating entities have no realistic means of withdrawing from the plan without paying a contribution for the benefits earned by employees up to the date of withdrawal. Such a plan creates actuarial risk for the entity: if the ultimate cost of benefits already earned at the end of the reporting period is more than expected, the entity will have to either increase its contributions or persuade employees to accept a reduction in benefits. Therefore, such a plan is a defined benefit plan.

32   Where sufficient information is available about a multi-employer plan which is a defined benefit plan, an entity accounts for its proportionate share of the defined benefit obligation, plan assets and post employment benefit cost associated with the plan in the same way as for any other defined benefit plan. However, in some cases, an entity may not be able to identify its share of the underlying financial position and performance of the plan with sufficient reliability for accounting purposes. This may occur if:

(a)   the entity does not have access to information about the plan that satisfies the requirements of this Standard; or

(b)   the plan exposes the participating entities to actuarial risks associated with the current and former employees of other entities, with the result that there is no consistent and reliable basis for allocating the obligation, plan assets and cost to individual entities participating in the plan.

In those cases, an entity accounts for the plan as if it were a defined contribution plan and discloses the additional information required by paragraph 30.

32A   There may be a contractual agreement between the multi-employer plan and its participants that determines how a surplus in the plan will be distributed to the participants (or the deficit funded). A participant in a multi-employer plan with such an agreement that accounts for the plan as a defined contribution plan in accordance with paragraph 30 shall recognise the asset or liability that arises from the contractual agreement and the resulting income or expense in profit or loss.

> **Example Illustrating Paragraph 32A**
>
> An entity participates in a multi-employer defined benefit plan that does not prepare plan valuations on an AASB 119 basis. It therefore accounts for the plan as if it were a defined contribution plan. A non-AASB 119 funding valuation shows a deficit of 100 million in the plan. The plan has agreed under contract a schedule of contributions with the participating employers in the plan that will eliminate the deficit over the next five years. The entity's total contributions under the contract are 8 million.
>
> *The entity recognises a liability for the contributions adjusted for the time value of money and an equal expense in profit or loss.*

32B AASB 137 *Provisions, Contingent Liabilities and Contingent Assets* requires an entity to disclose information about some contingent liabilities. In the context of a multi-employer plan, a contingent liability may arise from, for example:

    (a)   actuarial losses relating to other participating entities because each entity that participates in a multi-employer plan shares in the actuarial risks of every other participating entity; or

    (b)   any responsibility under the terms of a plan to finance any shortfall in the plan if other entities cease to participate.

33 Multi-employer plans are distinct from group administration plans. A group administration plan is merely an aggregation of single employer plans combined to allow participating employers to pool their assets for investment purposes and reduce investment management and administration costs, but the claims of different employers are segregated for the sole benefit of their own employees. Group administration plans pose no particular accounting problems because information is readily available to treat them in the same way as any other single employer plan and because such plans do not expose the participating entities to actuarial risks associated with the current and former employees of other entities. The definitions in this Standard require an entity to classify a group administration plan as a defined contribution plan or a defined benefit plan in accordance with the terms of the plan (including any constructive obligation that goes beyond the formal terms).

34 Defined benefit plans that share risks between various entities under common control, for example, a parent and its subsidiaries, are not multi-employer plans.

34A An entity participating in such a plan shall obtain information about the plan as a whole measured in accordance with AASB 119 on the basis of assumptions that apply to the plan as a whole. If there is a contractual agreement or stated policy for charging the net defined benefit cost for the plan as a whole measured in accordance with AASB 119 to individual group entities, the entity shall, in its separate or individual financial statements, recognise the net defined benefit cost so charged. If there is no such agreement or policy, the net defined benefit cost shall be recognised in the separate or individual financial statements of the group entity that is legally the sponsoring employer for the plan. The other group entities shall, in their separate or individual financial statements, recognise a cost equal to their contribution payable for the period.

34B Participation in such a plan is a related party transaction for each individual group entity. An entity shall therefore, in its separate or individual financial statements, make the following disclosures:

    (a)   the contractual agreement or stated policy for charging the net defined benefit cost or the fact that there is no such policy;

    (b)   the policy for determining the contribution to be paid by the entity;

    (c)   if the entity accounts for an allocation of the net defined benefit cost in accordance with paragraph 34A, all the information about the plan as a whole in accordance with paragraphs 120 121; and

    (d)   if the entity accounts for the contribution payable for the period in accordance with paragraph 34A, the information about the plan as a whole required in accordance with paragraphs 120A(b)-(e), (j), (n), (o), (q) and 121. The other disclosures required by paragraph 120A do not apply.

35 [Deleted by the IASB]

State Plans

36   An entity shall account for a state plan in the same way as for a multi-employer plan (see paragraphs 29 and 30).

37   State plans are established by legislation to cover all entities (or all entities in a particular category, for example, a specific industry) and are operated by national or local government or by another body (for example, an autonomous agency created specifically for this purpose) which is not subject to control or influence by the entity. Some plans established by an entity provide both compulsory benefits which substitute for benefits that would otherwise be covered under a state plan and additional voluntary benefits. Such plans are not state plans.

38   State plans are characterised as defined benefit or defined contribution in nature based on the entity's obligation under the plan. Many state plans are funded on a pay-as-you-go basis: contributions are set at a level that is expected to be sufficient to pay the required benefits falling due in the same period; future benefits earned during the current period will be paid out of future contributions. Nevertheless, in most state plans, the entity has no legal or constructive obligation to pay those future benefits: its only obligation is to pay the contributions as they fall due and if the entity ceases to employ members of the state plan, it will have no obligation to pay the benefits earned by its own employees in previous years. For this reason, state plans are normally defined contribution plans. However, in the rare cases when a state plan is a defined benefit plan, an entity applies the treatment prescribed in paragraphs 29 and 30.

Insured Benefits

39   An entity may pay insurance premiums to fund a post-employment benefit plan. The entity shall treat such a plan as a defined contribution plan unless the entity will have (either directly, or indirectly through the plan) a legal or constructive obligation to either:

   (a)   pay the employee benefits directly when they fall due; or

   (b)   pay further amounts if the insurer does not pay all future employee benefits relating to employee service in the current and prior periods.

If the entity retains such a legal or constructive obligation, the entity shall treat the plan as a defined benefit plan.

40   The benefits insured by an insurance contract need not have a direct or automatic relationship with the entity's obligation for employee benefits. Post-employment benefit plans involving insurance contracts are subject to the same distinction between accounting and funding as other funded plans.

41   Where an entity funds a post-employment benefit obligation by contributing to an insurance policy under which the entity (either directly, indirectly through the plan, through the mechanism for setting future premiums or through a related party relationship with the insurer) retains a legal or constructive obligation, the payment of the premiums does not amount to a defined contribution arrangement. It follows that the entity:

   (a)   accounts for a *qualifying insurance policy* as a plan asset (see paragraph 7); and

   (b)   recognises other insurance policies as reimbursement rights (if the policies satisfy the criteria in paragraph 104A).

42   Where an insurance policy is in the name of a specified plan participant or a group of plan participants and the entity does not have any legal or constructive obligation to cover any loss on the policy, the entity has no obligation to pay benefits to the employees and the insurer has sole responsibility for paying the benefits. The payment of fixed premiums under such contracts is, in substance, the settlement of the employee benefit obligation, rather than an investment to meet the obligation. Consequently, the entity no longer has an asset or a liability. Therefore, an entity treats such payments as contributions to a defined contribution plan.

Post-employment Benefits: Defined Contribution Plans

43   Accounting for defined contribution plans is straightforward because the entity's obligation for each period is determined by the amounts to be contributed for that period. Consequently, no actuarial assumptions are required to measure the obligation or the expense and there is no possibility of any actuarial gain or loss. Moreover, the obligations are measured on an undiscounted basis, except where they do not fall due wholly within twelve months after the end of the period in which the employees render the related service.

Recognition and Measurement

44   **When an employee has rendered service to an entity during a period, the entity shall recognise the contribution payable to a defined contribution plan in exchange for that service:**

    (a)   as a liability (accrued expense), after deducting any contribution already paid. If the contribution already paid exceeds the contribution due for service before the end of the reporting period, an entity shall recognise that excess as an asset (prepaid expense) to the extent that the prepayment will lead to, for example, a reduction in future payments or a cash refund; and

    (b)   as an expense, unless another Australian Accounting Standard requires or permits the inclusion of the contribution in the cost of an asset (see, for example, AASB 102 and AASB 116).

45   **Where contributions to a defined contribution plan do not fall due wholly within twelve months after the end of the period in which the employees render the related service, they shall be discounted using the discount rate specified in paragraphs 78 and Aus78.1.**

Disclosure

46   **An entity shall disclose the amount recognised as an expense for defined contribution plans.**

47   Where required by AASB 124 an entity discloses information about contributions to defined contribution plans for key management personnel.

Post-employment Benefits: Defined Benefit Plans

48   Accounting for defined benefit plans is complex because actuarial assumptions are required to measure the obligation and the expense and there is a possibility of *actuarial gains and losses*. Moreover, the obligations are measured on a discounted basis because they may be settled many years after the employees render the related service.

Recognition and Measurement

49   Defined benefit plans may be unfunded, or they may be wholly or partly funded by contributions by an entity, and sometimes its employees, into an entity, or fund, that is legally separate from the entity and from which the employee benefits are paid. The payment of funded benefits when they fall due depends not only on the financial position and the investment performance of the fund but also on an entity's ability (and willingness) to make good any shortfall in the fund's assets. Therefore, the entity is, in substance, underwriting the actuarial and investment risks associated with the plan. Consequently, the expense recognised for a defined benefit plan is not necessarily the amount of the contribution due for the period.

50   Accounting by an entity for defined benefit plans involves the following steps:

    (a)   using actuarial techniques to make a reliable estimate of the amount of benefit that employees have earned in return for their service in the current and prior periods. This requires an entity to determine how much benefit is attributable to the current and prior periods (see paragraphs 67-71) and to make estimates (actuarial assumptions) about demographic variables (such as employee turnover and mortality) and financial variables (such as future increases in salaries and medical costs) that will influence the cost of the benefit (see paragraphs 72-91);

    (b)   discounting that benefit using the Projected Unit Credit Method in order to determine the present value of the defined benefit obligation and the *current service cost* (see paragraphs 64-66);

    (c)   determining the *fair value* of any plan assets (see paragraphs 102-104);

    (d)   determining the total amount of actuarial gains and losses and the amount of those actuarial gains and losses to be recognised (see paragraphs 92-95);

    (e)   where a plan has been introduced or changed, determining the resulting *past service cost* (see paragraphs 96-101); and

    (f)   where a plan has been curtailed or settled, determining the resulting gain or loss (see paragraphs 109-115).

Where an entity has more than one defined benefit plan, the entity applies these procedures for each material plan separately.

51   In some cases, estimates, averages and computational shortcuts may provide a reliable approximation of the detailed computations illustrated in this Standard.

Accounting for the Constructive Obligation

52   An entity shall account not only for its legal obligation under the formal terms of a defined benefit plan, but also for any constructive obligation that arises from the entity's informal practices. Informal practices give rise to a constructive obligation where the entity has no realistic alternative but to pay employee benefits. An example of a constructive obligation is where a change in the entity's informal practices would cause unacceptable damage to its relationship with employees.

53   The formal terms of a defined benefit plan may permit an entity to terminate its obligation under the plan. Nevertheless, it is usually difficult for an entity to cancel a plan if employees are to be retained. Therefore, in the absence of evidence to the contrary, accounting for post-employment benefits assumes that an entity which is currently promising such benefits will continue to do so over the remaining working lives of employees.

Statement of Financial Position

54   The amount recognised as a defined benefit liability shall be the net total of the following amounts:

    (a)   the present value of the defined benefit obligation at the end of the reporting period (see paragraph 64);

    (b)   plus any actuarial gains (less any actuarial losses) not recognised because of the treatment set out in paragraphs 92 and 93;

    (c)   minus any past service cost not yet recognised (see paragraph 96); and

    (d)   minus the fair value at the end of the reporting period of plan assets (if any) out of which the obligations are to be settled directly (see paragraphs 102-104).

55   The present value of the defined benefit obligation is the gross obligation, before deducting the fair value of any plan assets.

56   An entity shall determine the present value of defined benefit obligations and the fair value of any plan assets with sufficient regularity that the amounts recognised in the financial statements do not differ materially from the amounts that would be determined at the end of the reporting period.

57   This Standard encourages, but does not require, an entity to involve a qualified actuary in the measurement of all material post-employment benefit obligations. For practical reasons, an entity may request a qualified actuary to carry out a detailed valuation of the obligation before the end of the reporting period. Nevertheless, the results of that valuation are updated for any material transactions and other material changes in circumstances (including changes in market prices and interest rates) up to the end of the reporting period.

58   The amount determined under paragraph 54 may be negative (an asset). An entity shall measure the resulting asset at the lower of:

    (a)   the amount determined under paragraph 54; and

(b)   the total of:

    (i)   any cumulative unrecognised net actuarial losses and past service cost (see paragraphs 92, 93 and 96); and

    (ii)   the present value of any economic benefits available in the form of refunds from the plan or reductions in future contributions to the plan. The present value of these economic benefits shall be determined using the discount rate specified in paragraph 78.

58A   The application of paragraph 58 shall not result in a gain being recognised solely as a result of an actuarial loss or past service cost in the current period or in a loss being recognised solely as a result of an actuarial gain in the current period. The entity shall therefore recognise immediately under paragraph 54 the following, to the extent that they arise while the defined benefit asset is determined in accordance with paragraph 58(b):

(a)   net actuarial losses of the current period and past service cost of the current period to the extent that they exceed any reduction in the present value of the economic benefits specified in paragraph 58(b)(ii). If there is no change or an increase in the present value of the economic benefits, the entire net actuarial losses of the current period and past service cost of the current period shall be recognised immediately under paragraph 54.

(b)   net actuarial gains of the current period after the deduction of past service cost of the current period to the extent that they exceed any increase in the present value of the economic benefits specified in paragraph 58(b)(ii). If there is no change or a decrease in the present value of the economic benefits, the entire net actuarial gains of the current period after the deduction of past service cost of the current period shall be recognised immediately under paragraph 54.

58B   Paragraph 58A applies to an entity only if it has, at the beginning or end of the reporting period, a surplus[2] in a defined benefit plan and cannot, based on the current terms of the plan, recover that surplus fully through refunds or reductions in future contributions. In such cases, past service cost and actuarial losses that arise in the period, the recognition of which is deferred under paragraph 54, will increase the amount specified in paragraph 58(b)(i). If that increase is not offset by an equal decrease in the present value of economic benefits that qualify for recognition under paragraph 58(b)(ii), there will be an increase in the net total specified by paragraph 58(b) and, hence, a recognised gain. Paragraph 58A prohibits the recognition of a gain in these circumstances. The opposite effect arises with actuarial gains that arise in the period, the recognition of which is deferred under paragraph 54, to the extent that the actuarial gains reduce cumulative unrecognised actuarial losses. Paragraph 58A prohibits the recognition of a loss in these circumstances. For examples of the application of this paragraph, see part C of the implementation guidance accompanying this Standard.

59   An asset may arise where a defined benefit plan has been overfunded or in certain cases where actuarial gains are recognised. An entity recognises an asset in such cases because:

(a)   the entity controls a resource, which is the ability to use the surplus to generate future benefits;

(b)   that control is a result of past events (contributions paid by the entity and service rendered by the employee); and

(c)   future economic benefits are available to the entity in the form of a reduction in future contributions or a cash refund, either directly to the entity or indirectly to another plan in deficit.

60   The limit in paragraph 58(b) does not override the delayed recognition of certain actuarial losses (paragraphs 92 and 93) and certain past service cost (see paragraph 96), other than as specified in paragraph 58A. Paragraph 120A(f)(iii) requires an entity to disclose any amount not recognised as an asset because of the limit in paragraph 58(b).

---

2   A surplus is an excess of the fair value of the plan assets over the present value of the defined benefit obligation.

Example Illustrating Paragraph 60

A defined benefit plan has the following characteristics:

Present value of the obligation	1,100
Fair value of plan assets	(1,190)
	(90)
Unrecognised actuarial losses	(110)
Unrecognised past service cost	(70)
Negative amount determined under paragraph 54	(270)
Present value of available future refunds and reductions in future contributions	90

The limit under paragraph 58(b) is computed as follows:

Unrecognised actuarial losses	*110*
Unrecognised past service cost	*70*
Present value of available future refunds and reductions in future contributions	*90*
Limit	*270*

The limit does not exceed the negative amount determined under paragraph 54. Therefore the entity recognises an asset of 270.

Profit or Loss

61   **An entity shall recognise the net total of the following amounts in profit or loss, except to the extent that another Australian Accounting Standard requires or permits their inclusion in the cost of an asset:**

    (a)   current service cost (see paragraphs 63-91);

    (b)   *interest cost* (see paragraph 82);

    (c)   the expected return on any plan assets (see paragraphs 105-107) and on any reimbursement rights (see paragraph 104A);

    (d)   actuarial gains and losses, as required in accordance with the entity's accounting policy (see paragraphs 92-93D);

    (e)   past service cost (see paragraph 96);

    (f)   the effect of any curtailments or settlements (see paragraphs 109 and 110); and

    (g)   the effect of the limit in paragraph 58(b), unless it is recognised outside profit or loss in accordance with paragraph 93C.

62   Other Australian Accounting Standards require the inclusion of certain employee benefit costs within the cost of assets such as inventories or property, plant and equipment (see AASB 102 and AASB 116). Any post-employment benefit costs included in the cost of such assets include the appropriate proportion of the components listed in paragraph 61.

Recognition and Measurement: Present Value of Defined Benefit Obligations and Current Service Cost

63   The ultimate cost of a defined benefit plan may be influenced by many variables, such as final salaries, employee turnover and mortality, medical cost trends and, for a funded plan, the investment earnings on the plan assets. The ultimate cost of the plan is uncertain and this uncertainty is likely to persist over a long period of time. In order to measure the present value of the post-employment benefit obligations and the related current service cost, it is necessary to:

    (a)   apply an actuarial valuation method (see paragraphs 64-66);

    (b)   attribute benefit to periods of service (see paragraphs 67-71); and

    (c)   make actuarial assumptions (see paragraphs 72-91).

Actuarial Valuation Method

64   **An entity shall use the Projected Unit Credit Method to determine the present value of its defined benefit obligations and the related current service cost and, where applicable, past service cost.**

65   The Projected Unit Credit Method (sometimes known as the accrued benefit method pro-rated on service or as the benefit/years of service method) sees each period of service as giving rise to an additional unit of benefit entitlement (see paragraphs 67-71) and measures each unit separately to build up the final obligation (see paragraphs 72-91).

Example Illustrating Paragraph 65

A lump sum benefit is payable on termination of service and equal to 1% of final salary for each year of service. The salary in year 1 is 10,000 and is assumed to increase at 7% (compound) each year. The discount rate used is 10% per year. The following table shows how the obligation builds up for an employee who is expected to leave at the end of year 5, assuming that there are no changes in actuarial assumptions. For simplicity, this example ignores the additional adjustment needed to reflect the probability that the employee may leave the entity at an earlier or later date.

Year	1	2	3	4	5
Benefit attributed to:					
– prior years	–	131	262	393	524
– current year (1% of final salary)	131	131	131	131	131
– current and prior years	131	262	393	524	655
Opening Obligation	–	89	196	324	476
Interest at 10%	–	9	20	33	48
Current Service Cost	89	98	108	119	131
Closing Obligation	89	196	324	476	655

Note:

1.   The Opening Obligation is the present value of benefit attributed to prior years.
2.   The Current Service Cost is the present value of benefit attributed to the current year.
3.   The Closing Obligation is the present value of benefit attributed to current and prior years.

---

66   An entity discounts the whole of a post-employment benefit obligation, even if part of the obligation falls due within twelve months of the end of the reporting period.

Attributing Benefit to Periods of Service

67   **In determining the present value of its defined benefit obligations and the related current service cost and, where applicable, past service cost, an entity shall attribute benefit to periods of service under the plan's benefit formula. However, if an employee's service in later years will lead to a materially higher level of benefit than in earlier years, an entity shall attribute benefit on a straight line basis from:**

     (a)   **the date when service by the employee first leads to benefits under the plan (whether or not the benefits are conditional on further service); until**

     (b)   **the date when further service by the employee will lead to no material amount of further benefits under the plan, other than from further salary increases.**

68   The Projected Unit Credit Method requires an entity to attribute benefit to the current period (in order to determine current service cost) and the current and prior periods (in order to determine the present value of defined benefit obligations). An entity attributes benefit to periods in which the obligation to provide post-employment benefits arises. That obligation arises as employees render services in return for post employment benefits which an entity expects to pay in future reporting periods. Actuarial techniques allow an entity to measure that obligation with sufficient reliability to justify recognition of a liability.

Examples Illustrating Paragraph 68

1. A defined benefit plan provides a lump-sum benefit of 100 payable on retirement for each year of service.

    A benefit of 100 is attributed to each year. The current service cost is the present value of 100. The present value of the defined benefit obligation is the present value of 100, multiplied by the number of years of service up to the end of the reporting period.

    If the benefit is payable immediately when the employee leaves the entity, the current service cost and the present value of the defined benefit obligation reflect the date at which the employee is expected to leave. Thus, because of the effect of discounting, they are less than the amounts that would be determined if the employee left at the end of the reporting period.

2. A plan provides a monthly pension of 0.2% of final salary for each year of service. The pension is payable from the age of 65.

    Benefit equal to the present value, at the expected retirement date, of a monthly pension of 0.2% of the estimated final salary payable from the expected retirement date until the expected date of death is attributed to each year of service. The current service cost is the present value of that benefit. The present value of the defined benefit obligation is the present value of monthly pension payments of 0.2% of final salary, multiplied by the number of years of service up to the end of the reporting period. The current service cost and the present value of the defined benefit obligation are discounted because pension payments begin at the age of 65.

69   Employee service gives rise to an obligation under a defined benefit plan even if the benefits are conditional on future employment (in other words they are not *vested*). Employee service before the vesting date gives rise to a constructive obligation because, at the end of each successive reporting period, the amount of future service that an employee will have to render before becoming entitled to the benefit is reduced. In measuring its defined benefit obligation, an entity considers the probability that some employees may not satisfy any vesting requirements. Similarly, although certain post-employment benefits, for example, post-employment medical benefits, become payable only if a specified event occurs when an employee is no longer employed, an obligation is created when the employee renders service that will provide entitlement to the benefit if the specified event occurs. The probability that the specified event will occur affects the measurement of the obligation, but does not determine whether the obligation exists.

Examples Illustrating Paragraph 69

1. A plan pays a benefit of 100 for each year of service. The benefits vest after ten years of service.

    A benefit of 100 is attributed to each year. In each of the first ten years, the current service cost and the present value of the obligation reflect the probability that the employee may not complete ten years of service.

2. A plan pays a benefit of 100 for each year of service, excluding service before the age of 25. The benefits vest immediately.

    No benefit is attributed to service before the age of 25 because service before that date does not lead to benefits (conditional or unconditional). A benefit of 100 is attributed to each subsequent year.

70   The obligation increases until the date when further service by the employee will lead to no material amount of further benefits. Therefore, all benefit is attributed to periods ending on or before that date. Benefit is attributed to individual reporting periods under the plan's benefit formula. However, if an employee's service in later years will lead to a materially higher level of benefit than in earlier years, an entity attributes benefit on a straight-line basis until the date when further service by the employee will lead to no material amount of further benefits. That is because the employee's service throughout the entire period will ultimately lead to benefit at that higher level.

> **Examples Illustrating Paragraph 70**
>
> 1. A plan pays a lump-sum benefit of 1,000 that vests after ten years of service. The plan provides no further benefit for subsequent service.
>
>   *A benefit of 100 (1,000 divided by ten) is attributed to each of the first ten years. The current service cost in each of the first ten years reflects the probability that the employee may not complete ten years of service. No benefit is attributed to subsequent years.*
>
> 2. A plan pays a lump-sum retirement benefit of 2,000 to all employees who are still employed at the age of 55 after twenty years of service, or who are still employed at the age of 65, regardless of their length of service.
>
>   *For employees who join before the age of 35, service first leads to benefits under the plan at the age of 35 (an employee could leave at the age of 30 and return at the age of 33, with no effect on the amount or timing of benefits). Those benefits are conditional on further service. Also, service beyond the age of 55 will lead to no material amount of further benefits. For these employees, the entity attributes benefit of 100 (2,000 divided by 20) to each year from the age of 35 to the age of 55.*
>
>   *For employees who join between the ages of 35 and 45, service beyond twenty years will lead to no material amount of further benefits. For these employees, the entity attributes benefit of 100 (2,000 divided by 20) to each of the first twenty years.*
>
>   *For an employee who joins at the age of 55, service beyond ten years will lead to no material amount of further benefits. For this employee, the entity attributes benefit of 200 (2,000 divided by 10) to each of the first ten years.*
>
>   *For all employees, the current service cost and the present value of the obligation reflect the probability that the employee may not complete the necessary period of service.*
>
> 3. A post-employment medical plan reimburses 40% of an employee's post-employment medical costs if the employee leaves after more than ten and less than twenty years of service and 50% of those costs if the employee leaves after twenty or more years of service.
>
>   *Under the plan's benefit formula, the entity attributes 4% of the present value of the expected medical costs (40% divided by ten) to each of the first ten years and 1% (10% divided by ten) to each of the second ten years. The current service cost in each year reflects the probability that the employee may not complete the necessary period of service to earn part or all of the benefits. For employees expected to leave within ten years, no benefit is attributed.*
>
> 4. A post-employment medical plan reimburses 10% of an employee's post-employment medical costs if the employee leaves after more than ten and less than twenty years of service and 50% of those costs if the employee leaves after twenty or more years of service.
>
>   *Service in later years will lead to a materially higher level of benefit than in earlier years. Therefore, for employees expected to leave after twenty or more years, the entity attributes benefit on a straight-line basis under paragraph 68. Service beyond twenty years will lead to no material amount of further benefits. Therefore, the benefit attributed to each of the first twenty years is 2.5% of the present value of the expected medical costs (50% divided by twenty).*
>
>   *For employees expected to leave between ten and twenty years, the benefit attributed to each of the first ten years is 1% of the present value of the expected medical costs. For these employees, no benefit is attributed to service between the end of the tenth year and the estimated date of leaving.*
>
>   *For employees expected to leave within ten years, no benefit is attributed.*

71 Where the amount of a benefit is a constant proportion of final salary for each year of service, future salary increases will affect the amount required to settle the obligation that exists for service before the end of the reporting period, but do not create an additional obligation. Therefore:

(a) for the purpose of paragraph 67(b), salary increases do not lead to further benefits, even though the amount of the benefits is dependent on final salary; and

(b) the amount of benefit attributed to each period is a constant proportion of the salary to which the benefit is linked.

> **Example Illustrating Paragraph 71**
>
> Employees are entitled to a benefit of 3% of final salary for each year of service before the age of 55.
>
> *Benefit of 3% of estimated final salary is attributed to each year up to the age of 55. This is the date when further service by the employee will lead to no material amount of further benefits under the plan. No benefit is attributed to service after that age.*

Actuarial Assumptions

72   **Actuarial assumptions shall be unbiased and mutually compatible.**

73   Actuarial assumptions are an entity's best estimates of the variables that will determine the ultimate cost of providing post-employment benefits. Actuarial assumptions comprise:

(a)   demographic assumptions about the future characteristics of current and former employees (and their dependants) who are eligible for benefits. Demographic assumptions deal with matters such as:

(i)   mortality, both during and after employment;

(ii)   rates of employee turnover, disability and early retirement;

(iii)   the proportion of plan members with dependants who will be eligible for benefits; and

(iv)   claim rates under medical plans; and

(b)   financial assumptions, dealing with items such as:

(i)   the discount rate (see paragraphs 78-82);

(ii)   future salary and benefit levels (see paragraphs 83-87);

(iii)   in the case of medical benefits, future medical costs, including, where material, the cost of administering claims and benefit payments (see paragraphs 88-91); and

(iv)   the expected rate of *return on plan assets* (see paragraphs 105 107).

74   Actuarial assumptions are unbiased if they are neither imprudent nor excessively conservative.

75   Actuarial assumptions are mutually compatible if they reflect the economic relationships between factors such as inflation, rates of salary increase, the return on plan assets and discount rates. For example, all assumptions which depend on a particular inflation level (such as assumptions about interest rates and salary and benefit increases) in any given future period assume the same inflation level in that period.

76   An entity determines the discount rate and other financial assumptions in nominal (stated) terms, unless estimates in real (inflation-adjusted) terms are more reliable, for example, in a hyper-inflationary economy (see AASB 129 *Financial Reporting in Hyperinflationary Economies*), or where the benefit is index-linked and there is a deep market in index-linked bonds of the same currency and term.

77   **Financial assumptions shall be based on market expectations, at the end of the reporting period, for the period over which the obligations are to be settled.**

Actuarial Assumptions: Discount Rate

78   **The rate used to discount post-employment benefit obligations (both funded and unfunded) shall be determined by reference to market yields at the end of the reporting period on high quality corporate bonds. In countries where there is no deep market in such bonds, the market yields (at the end of the reporting period) on government bonds shall be used. The currency and term of the corporate bonds or government bonds shall be consistent with the currency and estimated term of the post-employment benefit obligations.**

Aus78.1 **Notwithstanding paragraph 78, in respect of not-for-profit public sector entities, post employment benefit obligations denominated in Australian currency shall be discounted using market yields on government bonds.**

79   One actuarial assumption which has a material effect is the discount rate. The discount rate reflects the time value of money but not the actuarial or investment risk. Furthermore, the discount rate does not reflect the entity-specific credit risk borne by the entity's creditors, nor does it reflect the risk that future experience may differ from actuarial assumptions.

80   The discount rate reflects the estimated timing of benefit payments. In practice, an entity often achieves this by applying a single weighted average discount rate that reflects the estimated timing and amount of benefit payments and the currency in which the benefits are to be paid.

81   In some cases, there may be no deep market in bonds with a sufficiently long maturity to match the estimated maturity of all the benefit payments. In such cases, an entity uses current market rates of the appropriate term to discount shorter term payments, and estimates the discount rate for longer maturities by extrapolating current market rates along the yield curve. The total *present value of a defined benefit obligation* is unlikely to be particularly sensitive to the discount rate applied to the portion of benefits that is payable beyond the final maturity of the available corporate or government bonds.

82   Interest cost is computed by multiplying the discount rate as determined at the start of the period by the present value of the defined benefit obligation throughout that period, taking account of any material changes in the obligation. The present value of the obligation will differ from the liability recognised in the statement of financial position because the liability is recognised after deducting the fair value of any plan assets and because some actuarial gains and losses, and some past service costs are not recognised immediately. (Part A of the implementation guidance accompanying this Standard illustrates the computation of interest cost, among other things.)

Actuarial Assumptions: Salaries, Benefits and Medical Costs

83   **Post-employment benefit obligations shall be measured on a basis that reflects:**

     (a)   **estimated future salary increases;**

     (b)   **the benefits set out in the terms of the plan (or resulting from any constructive obligation that goes beyond those terms) at the end of the reporting period; and**

     (c)   **estimated future changes in the level of any state benefits that affect the benefits payable under a defined benefit plan, if, and only if, either:**

         (i)   **those changes were enacted before the end of the reporting period; or**

         (ii)   **past history, or other reliable evidence, indicates that those state benefits will change in some predictable manner, for example, in line with future changes in general price levels or general salary levels.**

84   Estimates of future salary increases take account of inflation, seniority, promotion and other relevant factors, such as supply and demand in the employment market.

85   If the formal terms of a plan (or a constructive obligation that goes beyond those terms) require an entity to change benefits in future periods, the measurement of the obligation reflects those changes. This is the case when, for example:

     (a)   the entity has a past history of increasing benefits, for example, to mitigate the effects of inflation, and there is no indication that this practice will change in the future; or

     (b)   actuarial gains have already been recognised in the financial statements and the entity is obliged, by either the formal terms of a plan (or a constructive obligation that goes beyond those terms) or legislation, to use any surplus in the plan for the benefit of plan participants (see paragraph 98(c)).

86   Actuarial assumptions do not reflect future benefit changes that are not set out in the formal terms of the plan (or a constructive obligation) at the end of the reporting period. Such changes will result in:

     (a)   past service cost, to the extent that they change benefits for service before the change; and

     (b)   current service cost for periods after the change, to the extent that they change benefits for service after the change.

87   Some post-employment benefits are linked to variables such as the level of state retirement benefits or state medical care. The measurement of such benefits reflects expected changes in such variables, based on past history and other reliable evidence.

88   **Assumptions about medical costs shall take account of estimated future changes in the cost of medical services, resulting from both inflation and specific changes in medical costs.**

89   Measurement of post-employment medical benefits requires assumptions about the level
      and frequency of future claims and the cost of meeting those claims. An entity estimates
      future medical costs on the basis of historical data about the entity's own experience,
      supplemented where necessary by historical data from other entities, insurance companies,
      medical providers or other sources. Estimates of future medical costs consider the effect
      of technological advances, changes in health care utilisation or delivery patterns and
      changes in the health status of plan participants.

90   The level and frequency of claims is particularly sensitive to the age, health status and
      sex of employees (and their dependants) and may be sensitive to other factors such
      as geographical location. Therefore, historical data is adjusted to the extent that the
      demographic mix of the population differs from that of the population used as a basis for
      the historical data. It is also adjusted where there is reliable evidence that historical trends
      will not continue.

91   Some post-employment health care plans require employees to contribute to the medical
      costs covered by the plan. Estimates of future medical costs take account of any such
      contributions, based on the terms of the plan at the end of the reporting period (or based
      on any constructive obligation that goes beyond those terms). Changes in those employee
      contributions result in past service cost or, where applicable, curtailments. The cost of
      meeting claims may be reduced by benefits from state or other medical providers (see
      paragraphs 83(c) and 87).

Actuarial Gains and Losses

92   **In measuring its defined benefit liability in accordance with paragraph 54, an entity
      shall, subject to paragraph 58A, recognise a portion (as specified in paragraph 93) of
      its actuarial gains and losses as income or expense if the net cumulative unrecognised
      actuarial gains and losses at the end of the previous reporting period exceeded the
      greater of:**

      **(a)   10% of the present value of the defined benefit obligation at that date (before
              deducting plan assets); and**

      (b)   10% of the fair value of any plan assets at that date.

      These limits shall be calculated and applied separately for each defined benefit plan.

93   **The portion of actuarial gains and losses to be recognised for each defined benefit
      plan is the excess determined in accordance with paragraph 92, divided by the
      expected average remaining working lives of the employees participating in that
      plan. However, an entity may adopt any systematic method that results in faster
      recognition of actuarial gains and losses, provided that the same basis is applied to
      both gains and losses and the basis is applied consistently from period to period. An
      entity may apply such systematic methods to actuarial gains and losses even if they
      are within the limits specified in paragraph 92.**

93A   **If, as permitted by paragraph 93, an entity adopts a policy of recognising actuarial
      gains and losses in the period in which they occur, it may recognise them in other
      comprehensive income, in accordance with paragraphs 93B 93D, providing it does
      so for:**

      (a)   all of its defined benefit plans; and

      (b)   all of its actuarial gains and losses.

93B   Actuarial gains and losses recognised in other comprehensive income as permitted by
      paragraph 93A shall be presented in the statement of comprehensive income.

93C   An entity that recognises actuarial gains and losses in accordance with paragraph 93A
      shall also recognise any adjustments arising from the limit in paragraph 58(b) in other
      comprehensive income.

93D   Actuarial gains and losses and adjustments arising from the limit in paragraph 58(b) that
      have been recognised in other comprehensive income shall be recognised immediately in
      retained earnings. They shall not be reclassified to profit or loss in a subsequent period.

94   Actuarial gains and losses may result from increases or decreases in either the present value of a defined benefit obligation or the fair value of any related plan assets. Causes of actuarial gains and losses include, for example:

(a)   unexpectedly high or low rates of employee turnover, early retirement or mortality or of increases in salaries, benefits (if the formal or constructive terms of a plan provide for inflationary benefit increases) or medical costs;

(b)   the effect of changes in estimates of future employee turnover, early retirement or mortality or of increases in salaries, benefits (if the formal or constructive terms of a plan provide for inflationary benefit increases) or medical costs;

(c)   the effect of changes in the discount rate; and

(d)   differences between the actual return on plan assets and the expected return on plan assets (see paragraphs 105-107).

95   In the long term, actuarial gains and losses may offset one another. Therefore, estimates of post-employment benefit obligations may be viewed as a range (or 'corridor') around the best estimate. An entity is permitted, but not required, to recognise actuarial gains and losses that fall within that range. This Standard requires an entity to recognise, as a minimum, a specified portion of the actuarial gains and losses that fall outside a 'corridor' of plus or minus 10%. [Part A of the implementation guidance accompanying this Standard illustrates the treatment of actuarial gains and losses, among other things.] The Standard also permits systematic methods of faster recognition, provided that those methods satisfy the conditions set out in paragraph 93. Such permitted methods include, for example, immediate recognition of all actuarial gains and losses, both within and outside the 'corridor'.

Past Service Cost

96   **In measuring its defined benefit liability under paragraph 54, an entity shall, subject to paragraph 58A, recognise past service cost as an expense on a straight-line basis over the average period until the benefits become vested. To the extent that the benefits are already vested immediately following the introduction of, or changes to, a defined benefit plan, an entity shall recognise past service cost immediately.**

97   Past service cost arises when an entity introduces a defined benefit plan that attributes benefits to past service or changes the benefits payable for past service under an existing defined benefit plan. Such changes are in return for employee service over the period until the benefits concerned are vested. Therefore, the entity recognises past service cost over that period, regardless of the fact that the cost refers to employee service in previous periods. The entity measures past service cost as the change in the liability resulting from the amendment (see paragraph 64). Negative past service cost arises when an entity changes the benefits attributable to past service so that the present value of the defined benefit obligation decreases.

Example Illustrating Paragraph 97

An entity operates a pension plan that provides a pension of 2% of final salary for each year of service. The benefits become vested after five years of service. On 1 January 20X5 the entity improves the pension to 2.5% of final salary for each year of service starting from 1 January 20X1. At the date of the improvement, the present value of the additional benefits for service from 1 January 20X1 to 1 January 20X5 is as follows:

Employees with more than five years' service at 1/1/X5	150
Employees with less than five years' service at 1/1/X5 (average period until vesting: three years)	120
	270

The entity recognises 150 immediately because those benefits are already vested.
The entity recognises 120 on a straight-line basis over three years from 1 January 20X5.

---

98   Past service cost excludes:

(a)   the effect of differences between actual and previously assumed salary increases on the obligation to pay benefits for service in prior years (there is no past service cost because actuarial assumptions allow for projected salaries);

(b)   underestimates and overestimates of discretionary pension increases where an entity has a constructive obligation to grant such increases (there is no past service cost because actuarial assumptions allow for such increases);

(c)   estimates of benefit improvements that result from actuarial gains that have been recognised in the financial statements if the entity is obliged, by either the formal terms of a plan (or a constructive obligation that goes beyond those terms) or legislation, to use any surplus in the plan for the benefit of plan participants, even if the benefit increase has not yet been formally awarded (the resulting increase in the obligation is an actuarial loss and not past service cost, see paragraph 85(b));

(d)   the increase in vested benefits when, in the absence of new or improved benefits, employees complete vesting requirements (there is no past service cost because the entity recognised the estimated cost of benefits as current service cost as the service was rendered); and

(e)   the effect of plan amendments that reduce benefits for future service (a curtailment).

99   An entity establishes the amortisation schedule for past service cost when the benefits are introduced or changed. It would be impracticable to maintain the detailed records needed to identify and implement subsequent changes in that amortisation schedule. Moreover, the effect is likely to be material only where there is a curtailment or settlement. Therefore, an entity amends the amortisation schedule for past service cost only if there is a curtailment or settlement.

100   Where an entity reduces benefits payable under an existing defined benefit plan, the resulting reduction in the defined benefit liability is recognised as (negative) past service cost over the average period until the reduced portion of the benefits becomes vested.

101   Where an entity reduces certain benefits payable under an existing defined benefit plan and, at the same time, increases other benefits payable under the plan for the same employees, the entity treats the change as a single net change.

Recognition and Measurement: Plan Assets

Fair Value of Plan Assets

102   The fair value of any plan assets is deducted in determining the amount recognised in the statement of financial position under paragraph 54. When no market price is available, the fair value of plan assets is estimated; for example, by discounting expected future cash flows using a discount rate that reflects both the risk associated with the plan assets and the maturity or expected disposal date of those assets (or, if they have no maturity, the expected period until the settlement of the related obligation).

103   Plan assets exclude unpaid contributions due from the entity to the fund, as well as any non-transferable financial instruments issued by the entity and held by the fund. Plan assets are reduced by any liabilities of the fund that do not relate to employee benefits, for example, trade and other payables and liabilities resulting from derivative financial instruments.

104   Where plan assets include qualifying insurance policies that exactly match the amount and timing of some or all of the benefits payable under the plan, the fair value of those insurance policies is deemed to be the present value of the related obligations, as described in paragraph 54 (subject to any reduction required if the amounts receivable under the insurance policies are not recoverable in full).

Reimbursements

104A   **When, and only when, it is virtually certain that another party will reimburse some or all of the expenditure required to settle a defined benefit obligation, an entity shall recognise its right to reimbursement as a separate asset. The entity shall measure the asset at fair value. In all other respects, an entity shall treat that asset in the same way as plan assets. In the statement of comprehensive income, the expense relating to a defined benefit plan may be presented net of the amount recognised for a reimbursement.**

104B   Sometimes, an entity is able to look to another party, such as an insurer, to pay part or all of the expenditure required to settle a defined benefit obligation. Qualifying insurance policies, as defined in paragraph 7, are plan assets. An entity accounts for qualifying insurance policies in the same way as for all other plan assets and paragraph 104A does not apply (see paragraphs 39-42 and 104).

104C When an insurance policy is not a qualifying insurance policy, that insurance policy is not a plan asset. Paragraph 104A deals with such cases: the entity recognises its right to reimbursement under the insurance policy as a separate asset, rather than as a deduction in determining the defined benefit liability recognised under paragraph 54; in all other respects, the entity treats that asset in the same way as plan assets. In particular, the defined benefit liability recognised under paragraph 54 is increased (reduced) to the extent that net cumulative actuarial gains (losses) on the defined benefit obligation and on the related reimbursement right remain unrecognised under paragraphs 92 and 93. Paragraph 120A(f)(iv) requires the entity to disclose a brief description of the link between the reimbursement right and the related obligation.

Example Illustrating Paragraphs 104A-C

Present value of obligation	1,241
Unrecognised actuarial gains	17
Liability recognised in statement of financial position	1,258
Rights under insurance policies that exactly match the amount and timing of some of the benefits payable under the plan. Those benefits have a present value of 1,092.	1,092

The unrecognised actuarial gains of 17 are the net cumulative actuarial gains on the obligation and on the reimbursement rights.

104D If the right to reimbursement arises under an insurance policy that exactly matches the amount and timing of some or all of the benefits payable under a defined benefit plan, the fair value of the reimbursement right is deemed to be the present value of the related obligation, as described in paragraph 54 (subject to any reduction required if the reimbursement is not recoverable in full).

Return on Plan Assets

105 The expected return on plan assets is one component of the expense recognised in profit or loss. The difference between the expected return on plan assets and the actual return on plan assets is an actuarial gain or loss; it is included with the actuarial gains and losses on the defined benefit obligation in determining the net amount that is compared with the limits of the 10% 'corridor' specified in paragraph 92.

106 The expected return on plan assets is based on market expectations, at the beginning of the period, for returns over the entire life of the related obligation. The expected return on plan assets reflects changes in the fair value of plan assets held during the period as a result of actual contributions paid into the fund and actual benefits paid out of the fund.

Example Illustrating Paragraph 106

At 1 January 20X1, the fair value of plan assets was 10,000 and net cumulative unrecognised gains were 760. On 30 June 20X1, the plan paid benefits of 1,900 and received contributions of 4,900. At 31 December 20X1, the fair value of plan assets was 15,000 and the present value of the defined benefit obligation was 14,792. Actuarial losses on the obligation for 20X1 were 60.

At 1 January 20X1, the entity made the following estimates, based on market prices at that date:

	%
Interest and dividend income, after tax payable by the fund	9.25
Realised and unrealised gains on plan assets (after tax)	2.00
Administration costs	(1.00)
Expected rate of return	10.25

For 20X1, the expected and actual return on plan assets are as follows:

Return on 10,000 held for 12 months at 10.25%	1,025
Return on 3,000 held for six months at 5% (equivalent to 10.25% annually, compounded every six months)	150
Expected return on plan assets for 20X1	1,175

Fair value of plan assets at 31 December 20X1	15,000
Less fair value of plan assets at 1 January 20X1	(10,000)
Less contributions received	(4,900)
Add benefits paid	1,900
Actual return on plan assets	2,000

The difference between the expected return on plan assets (1,175) and the actual return on plan assets (2,000) is an actuarial gain of 825. Therefore, the cumulative net unrecognised actuarial gains are 1,525 (760 plus 825 less 60). Under paragraph 92, the limits of the corridor are set at 1,500 (greater of: (i) 10% of 15,000 and (ii) 10% of 14,792). In the following year (20X2), the entity recognises in profit or loss an actuarial gain of 25 (1,525 less 1,500) divided by the expected average remaining working life of the employees concerned.

The expected return on plan assets for 20X2 will be based on market expectations at 1/1/X2 for returns over the entire life of the obligation.

107 In determining the expected and actual return on plan assets, an entity deducts expected administration costs, other than those included in the actuarial assumptions used to measure the obligation.

Business Combinations

108 In a business combination, an entity recognises assets and liabilities arising from post-employment benefits at the present value of the obligation less the fair value of any plan assets (see AASB 3 *Business Combinations*). The present value of the obligation includes all of the following, even if the acquiree had not recognised them at the acquisition date:

(a) actuarial gains and losses that arose before the acquisition date (whether or not they fell inside the 10% 'corridor'); and

(b) past service cost that arose from benefit changes, or the introduction of a plan, before the acquisition date.

(c) [Deleted by the AASB]

Curtailments and Settlements

109 An entity shall recognise gains or losses on the curtailment or settlement of a defined benefit plan when the curtailment or settlement occurs. The gain or loss on a curtailment or settlement shall comprise:

(a) any resulting change in the present value of the defined benefit obligation;

(b) any resulting change in the fair value of the plan assets; and

(c) any related actuarial gains and losses and past service cost that, under paragraphs 92 and 96, had not previously been recognised.

110 Before determining the effect of a curtailment or settlement, an entity shall remeasure the obligation (and the related plan assets, if any) using current actuarial assumptions (including current market interest rates and other current market prices).

111 A curtailment occurs when an entity either:

(a) is demonstrably committed to make a significant reduction in the number of employees covered by a plan; or

(b) amends the terms of a defined benefit plan so that a significant element of future service by current employees will no longer qualify for benefits, or will qualify only for reduced benefits.

A curtailment may arise from an isolated event, such as the closing of a plant, discontinuance of an operation or termination or suspension of a plan, or a reduction in the extent to which future salary increases are linked to the benefits payable for past service. Curtailments are often linked with a restructuring. When this is the case an entity accounts for a curtailment at the same time as for a related restructuring.

111A　When a plan amendment reduces benefits, only the effect of the reduction for future service is a curtailment. The effect of any reduction for past service is a negative past service cost.

112　A settlement occurs when an entity enters into a transaction that eliminates all further legal or constructive obligation for part or all of the benefits provided under a defined benefit plan, for example, when a lump-sum cash payment is made to, or on behalf of, plan participants in exchange for their rights to receive specified post-employment benefits.

113　In some cases, an entity acquires an insurance policy to fund some or all of the employee benefits relating to employee service in the current and prior periods. The acquisition of such a policy is not a settlement if the entity retains a legal or constructive obligation (see paragraph 39) to pay further amounts if the insurer does not pay the employee benefits specified in the insurance policy. Paragraphs 104A-104D deal with the recognition and measurement of reimbursement rights under insurance policies that are not plan assets.

114　A settlement occurs together with a curtailment if a plan is terminated such that the obligation is settled and the plan ceases to exist. However, the termination of a plan is not a curtailment or settlement if the plan is replaced by a new plan that offers benefits that are, in substance, identical.

115　Where a curtailment relates to only some of the employees covered by a plan, or where only part of an obligation is settled, the gain or loss includes a proportionate share of the previously unrecognised past service cost and actuarial gains and losses. The proportionate share is determined on the basis of the present value of the obligations before and after the curtailment or settlement, unless another basis is more rational in the circumstances. For example, it may be appropriate to apply any gain arising on a curtailment or settlement of the same plan to first eliminate any unrecognised past service cost relating to the same plan.

Example Illustrating Paragraph 115

An entity discontinues an operating segment and employees of the discontinued segment will earn no further benefits. This is a curtailment without a settlement. Using current actuarial assumptions (including current market interest rates and other current market prices) immediately before the curtailment, the entity has a defined benefit obligation with a net present value of 1,000 and plan assets with a fair value of 820 and net cumulative unrecognised actuarial gains of 150. The curtailment reduces the net present value of the obligation by 100 to 900.

Of the previously unrecognised actuarial gains, 10% (100/1,000) relates to the part of the obligation that was eliminated through the curtailment. Therefore, the effect of the curtailment is as follows:

	Before curtailment	*Curtailment gain*	*After curtailment*
Net present value of obligation	1,000	(100)	900
Fair value of plan assets	(820)	–	(820)
	180	(100)	80
Unrecognised actuarial gains	150	(15)	135
Net liability recognised in statement of financial position	330	(115)	215

Presentation

Offset

116　**An entity shall offset an asset relating to one plan against a liability relating to another plan when, and only when, the entity:**

　(a)　**has a legally enforceable right to use a surplus in one plan to settle obligations under the other plan; and**

　(b)　**intends either to settle the obligations on a net basis, or to realise the surplus in one plan and settle its obligation under the other plan simultaneously.**

117　The offsetting criteria are similar to those established for financial instruments in AASB 132 *Financial Instruments: Presentation.*

Current/Non-current Distinction

118　Some entities distinguish current assets and liabilities from non-current assets and liabilities. This Standard does not specify whether an entity shall distinguish current and non-current portions of assets and liabilities arising from post-employment benefits.

Financial Components of Post-employment Benefit Costs

119   This Standard does not specify whether an entity shall present current service cost, interest cost and the expected return on plan assets as components of a single item of income or expense in the statement of comprehensive income.

Disclosure

120   **An entity shall disclose information that enables users of financial statements to evaluate the nature of its defined benefit plans and the financial effects of changes in those plans during the period.**

120A **An entity shall disclose the following information about defined benefit plans:**

    (a)   **the entity's accounting policy for recognising actuarial gains and losses;**

    (b)   **a general description of the type of plan;**

    (c)   **a reconciliation of opening and closing balances of the present value of the defined benefit obligation showing separately, if applicable, the effects during the period attributable to each of the following:**

        (i)   **current service cost;**

        (ii)   **interest cost;**

        (iii)   **contributions by plan participants;**

        (iv)   **actuarial gains and losses;**

        (v)   **foreign currency exchange rate changes in plans measured in a currency different from the entity's presentation currency;**

        (vi)   **benefits paid;**

        (vii)   **past service cost;**

        (viii)   **business combinations;**

        (ix)   **curtailments; and**

        (x)   **settlements;**

    (d)   **an analysis of the defined benefit obligation into amounts arising from plans that are wholly unfunded and amounts arising from plans that are wholly or partly funded;**

    (e)   **a reconciliation of the opening and closing balances of the fair value of plan assets and of the opening and closing balances of any reimbursement right recognised as an asset in accordance with paragraph 104A showing separately, if applicable, the effects during the period attributable to each of the following:**

        (i)   **expected return on plan assets;**

        (ii)   **actuarial gains and losses;**

        (iii)   **foreign currency exchange rate changes on plans measured in a currency different from the entity's presentation currency;**

        (iv)   **contributions by the employer;**

        (v)   **contributions by plan participants;**

        (vi)   **benefits paid;**

        (vii)   **business combinations; and**

        (viii)   **settlements;**

    (f)   **a reconciliation of the present value of the defined benefit obligation in (c) and the fair value of the plan assets in (e) to the assets and liabilities recognised in the statement of financial position, showing at least:**

        (i)   **the net actuarial gains or losses not recognised in the statement of financial position (see paragraph 92);**

        (ii)   **the past service cost not recognised in the statement of financial position (see paragraph 96);**

(iii)   any amount not recognised as an asset, because of the limit in paragraph 58(b);

(iv)   the fair value at the end of the reporting period of any reimbursement right recognised as an asset in accordance with paragraph 104A (with a brief description of the link between the reimbursement right and the related obligation); and

(v)   the other amounts recognised in the statement of financial position;

(g)   the total expense recognised in profit or loss for each of the following, and the line item(s) in which they are included:

(i)   current service cost;

(ii)   interest cost;

(iii)   expected return on plan assets;

(iv)   expected return on any reimbursement right recognised as an asset in accordance with paragraph 104A;

(v)   actuarial gains and losses;

(vi)   past service cost;

(vii) the effect of any curtailment or settlement; and

(viii) the effect of the limit in paragraph 58(b);

(h)   the total amount recognised in other comprehensive income for each of the following:

(i)   actuarial gains and losses; and

(ii)   the effect of the limit in paragraph 58(b);

(i)   for entities that recognise actuarial gains and losses in other comprehensive income in accordance with paragraph 93A, the cumulative amount of actuarial gains and losses recognised in other comprehensive income;

(j)   for each major category of plan assets, which shall include, but is not limited to, equity instruments, debt instruments, property, and all other assets, the percentage or amount that each major category constitutes of the fair value of the total plan assets;

(k)   the amounts included in the fair value of plan assets for:

(i)   each category of the entity's own financial instruments; and

(ii)   any property occupied by, or other assets used by, the entity;

(l)   a narrative description of the basis used to determine the overall expected rate of return on assets, including the effect of the major categories of plan assets;

(m)   the actual return on plan assets, as well as the actual return on any reimbursement right recognised as an asset in accordance with paragraph 104A;

(n)   the principal actuarial assumptions used as at the end of the reporting period, including, when applicable:

(i)   the discount rates;

(ii)   the expected rates of return on any plan assets for the periods presented in the financial statements;

(iii)   the expected rates of return for the periods presented in the financial statements on any reimbursement right recognised as an asset in accordance with paragraph 104A;

(iv)   the expected rates of salary increases (and of changes in an index or other variable specified in the formal or constructive terms of a plan as the basis for future benefit increases);

(v)   medical cost trend rates; and

(vi)   any other material actuarial assumptions used.

An entity shall disclose each actuarial assumption in absolute terms (for example, as an absolute percentage) and not just as a margin between different percentages or other variables;

(o)   the effect of an increase of one percentage point and the effect of a decrease of one percentage point in the assumed medical cost trend rates on:

   (i)   the aggregate of the current service cost and interest cost components of net periodic post-employment medical costs; and

   (ii)   the accumulated post-employment benefit obligation for medical costs.

   For the purpose of this disclosure, all other assumptions shall be held constant. For plans operating in a high inflation environment, the disclosure shall be the effect of a percentage increase or decrease in the assumed medical cost trend rate of a significance similar to one percentage point in a low inflation environment;

(p)   the amounts for the current annual reporting period and previous four annual reporting periods of:

   (i)   the present value of the defined benefit obligation, the fair value of the plan assets and the surplus or deficit in the plan; and

   (ii)   the experience adjustments arising on:

      (A)   the plan liabilities expressed either as (1) an amount or (2) a percentage of the plan liabilities at the end of the reporting period; and

      (B)   the plan assets expressed either as (1) an amount or (2) a percentage of the plan assets at the end of the reporting period;

(q)   the employer's best estimate, as soon as it can reasonably be determined, of contributions expected to be paid to the plan during the annual reporting period beginning after the reporting period.

121   Paragraph 120A(b) requires a general description of the type of plan. Such a description distinguishes, for example, flat salary pension plans from final salary pension plans and from post-employment medical plans. The description of the plan shall include informal practices that give rise to constructive obligations included in the measurement of the defined benefit obligation in accordance with paragraph 52. Further detail is not required.

122   When an entity has more than one defined benefit plan, disclosures may be made in total, separately for each plan, or in such groupings as are considered to be the most useful. It may be useful to distinguish groupings by criteria such as the following:

(a)   the geographical location of the plans, for example, by distinguishing domestic plans from foreign plans; or

(b)   whether plans are subject to materially different risks, for example, by distinguishing flat salary pension plans from final salary pension plans and from post-employment medical plans.

When an entity provides disclosures in total for a grouping of plans, such disclosures are provided in the form of weighted averages or of relatively narrow ranges.

123   Paragraph 30 requires additional disclosures about multi-employer defined benefit plans that are treated as if they were defined contribution plans.

124   Where required by AASB 124 an entity discloses information about:

(a)   related party transactions with post-employment benefit plans; and

(b)   post-employment benefits for key management personnel.

125   Where required by AASB 137 an entity discloses information about contingent liabilities arising from post-employment benefit obligations.

Other Long-term Employee Benefits

126   Other long-term employee benefits include, for example:

(a)   long-term compensated absences such as long-service or sabbatical leave;

(b)   jubilee or other long-service benefits;

(c)   long-term disability benefits;

(d)   profit-sharing and bonuses payable twelve months or more after the end of the period in which the employees render the related service; and

(e)   deferred compensation paid twelve months or more after the end of the period in which it is earned.

127   The measurement of other long-term employee benefits is not usually subject to the same degree of uncertainty as the measurement of post employment benefits. Furthermore, the introduction of, or changes to, other long-term employee benefits rarely causes a material amount of past service cost. For these reasons, this Standard requires a simplified method of accounting for other long-term employee benefits. This method differs from the accounting required for post employment benefits as follows:

(a)   actuarial gains and losses are recognised immediately and no 'corridor' is applied; and

(b)   all past service cost is recognised immediately.

Recognition and Measurement

128   **The amount recognised as a liability for other long-term employee benefits shall be the net total of the following amounts:**

(a)   **the present value of the defined benefit obligation at the end of the reporting period (see paragraph 64);**

(b)   **minus the fair value at the end of the reporting period of plan assets (if any) out of which the obligations are to be settled directly (see paragraphs 102-104).**

In measuring the liability, an entity shall apply paragraphs 49-91, excluding paragraphs 54 and 61. An entity shall apply paragraph 104A in recognising and measuring any reimbursement right.

129   **For other long-term employee benefits, an entity shall recognise the net total of the following amounts as expense or (subject to paragraph 58) income, except to the extent that another Australian Accounting Standard requires or permits their inclusion in the cost of an asset:**

(a)   **current service cost (see paragraphs 63-91);**

(b)   **interest cost (see paragraph 82);**

(c)   **the expected return on any plan assets (see paragraphs 105-107) and on any reimbursement right recognised as an asset (see paragraph 104A);**

(d)   **actuarial gains and losses, which shall all be recognised immediately;**

(e)   **past service cost, which shall all be recognised immediately; and**

(f)   **the effect of any curtailments or settlements (see paragraphs 109 and 110).**

130   One form of other long-term employee benefit is long-term disability benefit. If the level of benefit depends on the length of service, an obligation arises when the service is rendered. Measurement of that obligation reflects the probability that payment will be required and the length of time for which payment is expected to be made. If the level of benefit is the same for any disabled employee regardless of years of service, the expected cost of those benefits is recognised when an event occurs that causes a long-term disability.

Disclosure

131   Although this Standard does not require specific disclosures about other long-term employee benefits, other Australian Accounting Standards may require disclosures, for example, where the expense resulting from such benefits is material and so would require disclosure in accordance with AASB 101. When required by AASB 124 an entity discloses information about other long-term employee benefits for key management personnel.

Termination Benefits

132   This Standard deals with termination benefits separately from other employee benefits because the event which gives rise to an obligation is the termination rather than employee service.

Recognition

133   **An entity shall recognise termination benefits as a liability and an expense when, and only when, the entity is demonstrably committed to either:**

    (a)   terminate the employment of an employee or group of employees before the normal retirement date; or

    (b)   provide termination benefits as a result of an offer made in order to encourage voluntary redundancy.

134   **An entity is demonstrably committed to a termination when, and only when, the entity has a detailed formal plan for the termination and is without realistic possibility of withdrawal. The detailed plan shall include, as a minimum:**

    (a)   the location, function, and approximate number of employees whose services are to be terminated;

    (b)   the termination benefits for each job classification or function; and

    (c)   the time at which the plan will be implemented. Implementation shall begin as soon as possible and the period of time to complete implementation shall be such that material changes to the plan are not likely.

135   An entity may be committed, by legislation, by contractual or other agreements with employees or their representatives or by a constructive obligation based on business practice, custom or a desire to act equitably, to make payments (or provide other benefits) to employees when it terminates their employment. Such payments are termination benefits. Termination benefits are typically lump-sum payments, but sometimes also include:

    (a)   enhancement of retirement benefits or of other post-employment benefits, either indirectly through an employee benefit plan or directly; and

    (b)   salary until the end of a specified notice period if the employee renders no further service that provides economic benefits to the entity.

136   Some employee benefits are payable regardless of the reason for the employee's departure. The payment of such benefits is certain (subject to any vesting or minimum service requirements) but the timing of their payment is uncertain. Although such benefits are described in some countries as termination indemnities, or termination gratuities, they are post-employment benefits, rather than termination benefits and an entity accounts for them as post-employment benefits. Some entities provide a lower level of benefit for voluntary termination at the request of the employee (in substance, a post-employment benefit) than for involuntary termination at the request of the entity. The additional benefit payable on involuntary termination is a termination benefit.

137   Termination benefits do not provide an entity with future economic benefits and are recognised as an expense immediately.

138   Where an entity recognises termination benefits, the entity may also have to account for a curtailment of retirement benefits or other employee benefits (see paragraph 109).

Measurement

139   **Where termination benefits fall due more than 12 months after the reporting period, they shall be discounted using the discount rate specified in paragraph 78.**

140   **In the case of an offer made to encourage voluntary redundancy, the measurement of termination benefits shall be based on the number of employees expected to accept the offer.**

Disclosure

141 Where there is uncertainty about the number of employees who will accept an offer of termination benefits, a contingent liability exists. As required by AASB 137 an entity discloses information about the contingent liability unless the possibility of an outflow in settlement is remote.

142 As required by AASB 101, an entity discloses the nature and amount of an expense if it is material. Termination benefits may result in an expense needing disclosure in order to comply with this requirement.

143 Where required by AASB 124 an entity discloses information about termination benefits for key management personnel.

144 – 152 [Deleted by the IASB]

Transitional Provisions of IAS 19

153 [Deleted by the AASB]

154 [Deleted by the AASB]

155 [Deleted by the AASB]

156 [Deleted by the AASB]

Effective Date

157 [Deleted by the AASB]

158 [Deleted by the AASB]

159 [Deleted by the AASB]

159A [Deleted by the AASB]

159B [Deleted by the AASB]

159C [Deleted by the AASB]

159D Paragraphs 7, 8(b), 32B, 97, 98, and 111 were amended and paragraph 111A was added by AASB 2008-5 *Amendments to Australian Accounting Standards arising from the Annual Improvements Project* issued in July 2008. An entity shall apply the amendments in paragraphs 7, 8(b) and 32B for annual reporting periods beginning on or after 1 January 2009. Earlier application is permitted. If an entity applies the amendments for an earlier period it shall disclose that fact. An entity shall apply the amendments in paragraphs 97, 98, 111 and 111A to changes in benefits that occur on or after 1 January 2009.

Transitional Provisions

160 AASB 108 applies when an entity changes its accounting policies to reflect the changes specified in paragraphs 159-159D. In applying those changes retrospectively, as required by AASB 108, the entity treats those changes as if they had been applied at the same time as the rest of this Standard. The exception is that an entity may disclose the amounts required by paragraph 120A(p) as the amounts are determined for each annual reporting period prospectively from the first annual reporting period presented in the financial statements in which the entity first applies the amendments in paragraph 120A.

Aus160.1 [Deleted by the AASB]

161 [Deleted by the AASB]

Guidance on Implementing AASB 119

This guidance accompanies, but is not part of, AASB 119.

A Illustrative Example

Extracts from statements of comprehensive income and statements of financial position are provided to show the effects of the transactions described below. These extracts do not necessarily conform with all the disclosure and presentation requirements of other Australian Accounting Standards.

Background Information

The following information is given about a funded defined benefit plan. To keep interest computations simple, all transactions are assumed to occur at the year end. The present value of the obligation and the fair value of the plan assets were both 1,000 at 1 January 20X1. Net cumulative unrecognised actuarial gains at that date were 140.

	20X1	20X2	20X3
Discount rate at start of year	10.0%	9.0%	8.0%
Expected rate of return on plan assets at start of year	12.0%	11.1%	10.3%
Current service cost	130	140	150
Benefits paid	150	180	190
Contributions paid	90	100	110
Present value of obligation at 31 December	1,141	1,197	1,295
Fair value of plan assets at 31 December	1,092	1,109	1,093
Expected average remaining working lives of employees (years)	10	10	10

In 20X2, the plan was amended to provide additional benefits with effect from 1 January 20X2. The present value as at 1 January 20X2 of additional benefits for employee service before 1 January 20X2 was 50 for vested benefits and 30 for non-vested benefits. As at 1 January 20X2, the entity estimated that the average period until the non-vested benefits would become vested was three years; the past service cost arising from additional non vested benefits is therefore recognised on a straight-line basis over three years. The past service cost arising from additional vested benefits is recognised immediately (paragraph 96 of the Standard). The entity has adopted a policy of recognising actuarial gains and losses under the minimum requirements of paragraph 93.

Changes in the Present Value of the Obligation and in the Fair Value of the Plan Assets

The first step is to summarise the changes in the present value of the obligation and in the fair value of the plan assets and use this to determine the amount of the actuarial gains or losses for the period. These are as follows:

	20X1	20X2	20X3
Present value of obligation, 1 January	1,000	1,141	1,197
Interest cost	100	103	96
Current service cost	130	140	150
Past service cost – non-vested benefits	–	30	–
Past service cost – vested benefits	–	50	–
Benefits paid	(150)	(180)	(190)
Actuarial (gain) loss on obligation (balancing figure)	61	(87)	42
Present value of obligation, 31 December	1,141	1,197	1,295

	20X1	20X2	20X3
Fair value of plan assets, 1 January	1,000	1,092	1,109
Expected return on plan assets	120	121	114
Contributions	90	100	110
Benefits paid	(150)	(180)	(190)
Actuarial gain (loss) on plan assets (balancing figure)	32	(24)	(50)
Fair value of plan assets, 31 December	1,092	1,109	1,093

Limits of the 'Corridor'

The next step is to determine the limits of the corridor and then compare these with the cumulative unrecognised actuarial gains and losses in order to determine the net actuarial gain or loss to be recognised in the following period. Under paragraph 92 of the Standard, the limits of the 'corridor' are set at the greater of:

(a)   10% of the present value of the obligation before deducting plan assets; and

(b)   10% of the fair value of any plan assets.

These limits, and the recognised and unrecognised actuarial gains and losses, are as follows:

	20X1	20X2	20X3
Net cumulative unrecognised actuarial gains (losses) at 1 January	140	107	170
Limits of 'corridor' at 1 January	100	114	120
Excess [A]	40	–	50
Average expected remaining working lives (years) [B]	10	10	10
Actuarial gain (loss) to be recognised [A/B]	4	–	5
Unrecognised actuarial gains (losses) at 1 January	140	107	170
Actuarial gain (loss) for year – obligation	(61)	87	(42)
Actuarial gain (loss) for year – plan assets	32	(24)	50
Subtotal	111	170	78
Actuarial (gain) loss recognised	(4)	–	(5)
Unrecognised actuarial gains (losses) at 31 December	107	170	73

Amounts Recognised in the Statement of Financial Position and Profit or Loss, and Related Analyses

The final step is to determine the amounts to be recognised in the statement of financial position and profit or loss, and the related analyses to be disclosed in accordance with paragraph 120A(f), (g) and (m) of the Standard (the analyses required to be disclosed in accordance with paragraphs 120A(c) and (e) are given above in the section 'Changes in the Present Value of the Obligation and in the Fair Value of the Plan Assets'). These are as follows:

	20X1	20X2	20X3
Present value of the obligation	1,141	1,197	1,295
Fair value of plan assets	(1,092)	(1,109)	(1,093)
	49	88	202
Unrecognised actuarial gains (losses)	107	170	73
Unrecognised past service cost – non-vested benefits	–	(20)	(10)
Liability recognised in statement of financial position	156	238	265

	20X1	20X2	20X3
Current service cost	130	140	150
Interest cost	100	103	96
Expected return on plan assets	(120)	(121)	(114)
Net actuarial (gain) loss recognised in year	(4)	–	(5)
Past service cost – non-vested benefits	–	10	10
Past service cost – vested benefits	–	50	–
Expense recognised in profit or loss	106	182	137
Actual return on plan assets			
Expected return on plan assets	120	121	114
Actuarial gain (loss) on plan assets	32	(24)	(50)
Actual return on plan assets	152	97	64

Note: see example illustrating paragraphs 104A-104C for presentation of reimbursements.

B Illustrative Disclosures

Extracts from notes show how the required disclosures may be aggregated in the case of a large multi-national group that provides a variety of employee benefits. These extracts do not necessarily conform with all the disclosure and presentation requirements of AASB 119 and other Australian Accounting Standards. In particular, they do not illustrate the disclosure of:

(a)   *accounting policies for employee benefits (see AASB 101 Presentation of Financial Statements). Paragraph 120A(a) of the Standard requires this disclosure to include the entity's accounting policy for recognising actuarial gains and losses;*

(b)   *a general description of the type of plan (paragraph 120A(b));*

(c)   *amounts recognised in other comprehensive income (paragraph 120A(h) and (i));*

(d)   *a narrative description of the basis used to determine the overall expected rate of return on assets (paragraph 120A(l));*

(e)   *employee benefits granted to directors and key management personnel (see AASB 124 Related Party Disclosures); or*

(f)   *share-based employee benefits (see AASB 2 Share-based Payment).*

Employee Benefit Obligations

The amounts recognised in the statement of financial position are as follows:

	Defined benefit pension plans		Post-employment medical benefits	
	20X2	20X1	20X2	20X1
Present value of funded obligations	20,300	17,400	–	–
Fair value of plan assets	(18,420)	(17,280)	–	–
	1,880	120	–	–
Present value of unfunded obligations	2,000	1,000	7,337	6,405
Unrecognised actuarial gains (losses)	(1,605)	840	(2,707)	(2,607)
Unrecognised past service cost	(450)	(650)	–	–
Net liability	1,825	1,310	4,630	3,798
Amounts in the statement of financial position:	1,825	1,400	4,630	3,798
Liabilities	–	(90)	–	–
Assets	1,825	1,310	4,630	3,798
Net liability	1,825	1,310	4,630	3,798

The pension plan assets include ordinary shares issued by [name of entity] with a fair value of 317 (20X1: 281). Plan assets also include property occupied by [name of entity] with a fair value of 200 (20X1: 185).

The amounts recognised in profit or loss are as follows:

	Defined benefit pension plans		Post-employment medical benefits	
	20X2	*20X1*	*20X2*	*20X1*
Current service cost	850	750	479	411
Interest on obligation	950	1,000	803	705
Expected return on plan assets	(900)	(650)	–	–
Net actuarial losses (gains) recognised in year	(70)	(20)	150	140
Past service cost	200	200	–	–
Losses (gains) on curtailments and settlements	175	(390)	–	–
Total, included in 'employee benefits expense'	1,205	890	1,432	1,256
	600	2,250		
Actual return on plan assets	600	2,250	–	–

Changes in the present value of the defined benefit obligation are as follows:

	Defined benefit pension plans		Post-employment medical benefits	
	20X2	*20X1*	*20X2*	*20X1*
Opening defined benefit obligation	18,400	11,600	6,405	5,439
Service cost	850	750	479	411
Interest cost	950	1,000	803	705
Actuarial losses (gains)	2,350	950	250	400
Losses (gains) on curtailments	(500)	–	–	–
Liabilities extinguished on settlements	–	(350)	–	–
Liabilities assumed in a business combination	–	5,000	–	–
Exchange differences on foreign plans	900	(150)	–	–
Benefits paid	(650)	(400)	(600)	(550)
Closing defined benefit obligation	22,300	18,400	7,337	6,405

Changes in the fair value of plan assets are as follows:

	Defined benefit pension plans	
	20X2	*20X1*
Opening fair value of plan assets	17,280	9,200
Expected return	900	650
Actuarial gains and (losses)	(300)	1,600
Assets distributed on settlements	(400)	–
Contributions by employer	700	350
Assets acquired in a business combination	–	6,000
Exchange differences on foreign plans	890	(120)
Benefits paid	(650)	(400)
	18,420	17,280

The group expects to contribute 900 to its defined benefit pension plans in 20X3.

The major categories of plan assets as a percentage of total plan assets are as follows:

	20X2	20X1
European equities	30%	35%
North American equities	16%	15%
European bonds	31%	28%
North American bonds	18%	17%
Property	5%	5%

Principal actuarial assumptions at the end of the reporting period (expressed as weighted averages):

	20X2	20X1
Discount rate at 31 December	5.0%	6.5%
Expected return on plan assets at 31 December	5.4%	7.0%
Future salary increases	5%	4%
Future pension increases	3%	2%
Proportion of employees opting for early retirement	30%	30%
Annual increase in healthcare costs	8%	8%
Future changes in maximum state healthcare benefits	3%	2%

Assumed healthcare cost trend rates have a significant effect on the amounts recognised in profit or loss. A one percentage point change in assumed healthcare cost trend rates would have the following effects:

	One percentage point increase	One percentage point decrease
Effect on the aggregate of the service cost and interest cost	190	(150)
Effect on defined benefit obligation	1,000	(900)

Amounts for the current and previous four periods are as follows:

Defined benefit pension plans

	20X2	20X1	20X0	20W9	20W8
Defined benefit obligation	(22,300)	(18,400)	(11,600)	(10,582)	(9,144)
Plan assets	18,420	17,280	9,200	8,502	10,000
Surplus/(deficit)	(3,880)	(1,120)	(2,400)	(2,080)	856
Experience adjustments on plan liabilities	(1,111)	(768)	(69)	543	(642)
Experience adjustments on plan assets	(300)	1,600	(1,078)	(2,890)	2,777

Post-employment medical benefits

	20X2	20X1	20X0	20W9	20W8
Defined benefit obligation	7,337	6,405	5,439	4,923	4,221
Experience adjustments on plan liabilities	(232)	829	490	(174)	(103)

The group also participates in an industry-wide defined benefit plan that provides pensions linked to final salaries and is funded on a pay-as-you-go basis. It is not practicable to determine the present value of the group's obligation or the related current service cost as the plan computes its obligations on a basis that differs materially from the basis used in [name of entity]'s financial statements. [describe basis] On that basis, the plan's financial statements to 30 June 20X0 show an unfunded liability of 27,525. The unfunded liability will result in future payments by participating employers. The plan has approximately 75,000 members, of whom approximately 5,000 are current or former employees of [name of entity] or their dependants. The expense recognised in profit or loss, which is equal to contributions due for the year, and is not included in the above amounts, was 230 (20X1: 215). The group's future contributions may be increased substantially if other entities withdraw from the plan.

C Illustration of the Application of Paragraph 58A

The Issue

Paragraph 58 of the Standard imposes a ceiling on the defined benefit asset that can be recognised.

58   **The amount determined under paragraph 54 may be negative (an asset). An entity shall measure the resulting asset at the lower of:**

(a)   **the amount determined under paragraph 54** [i.e. the surplus/deficit in the plan plus (minus) any unrecognised losses (gains)]**; and**

(b)   **the total of:**

(i)   **any cumulative unrecognised net actuarial losses and past service cost (see paragraphs 92, 93 and 96); and**

(ii)   **the present value of any economic benefits available in the form of refunds from the plan or reductions in future contributions to the plan. The present value of these economic benefits shall be determined using the discount rate specified in paragraph 78.**

Without paragraph 58A (see below), paragraph 58(b)(i) has the following consequence: sometimes deferring the recognition of an actuarial loss (gain) in determining the amount specified by paragraph 54 leads to a gain (loss) being recognised in profit or loss.

The following example illustrates the effect of applying paragraph 58 without paragraph 58A. The example assumes that the entity's accounting policy is not to recognise actuarial gains and losses within the 'corridor' and to amortise actuarial gains and losses outside the 'corridor'. (Whether the 'corridor' is used is not significant. The issue can arise whenever there is deferred recognition under paragraph 54.)

Example 1

Year	A Surplus in plan	B Economic benefits available (paragraph 58(b)(ii))	C Losses unrecognised under paragraph 54	D =A+C Paragraph 54	E =B+C Paragraph 58(b)	F =lower of D and E Asset ceiling, i.e. recognised asset	G Gain recognised in year 2
1	100	–	–	100	–	–	–
2	70	–	30	100	30	30	30

At the end of year 1, there is a surplus of 100 in the plan (column A in the table above), but no economic benefits are available to the entity either from refunds or reductions in future contributions[1] (column B). There are no unrecognised gains and losses under paragraph 54 (column C). So, if there were no asset ceiling, an asset of 100 would be recognised, being the amount specified by paragraph 54 (column D). The asset ceiling in paragraph 58 restricts the asset to nil (column F).

In year 2 there is an actuarial loss in the plan of 30 that reduces the surplus from 100 to 70 (column A) the recognition of which is deferred under paragraph 54 (column C). So, if there were no asset ceiling, an asset of 100 (column D) would be recognised. The asset ceiling without paragraph 58A would be 30 (column E). An asset of 30 would be recognised (column F), giving rise to a gain in income (column G) even though all that has happened is that a surplus from which the entity cannot benefit has decreased.

---

1   Based on the current terms of the plan.

A similarly counter-intuitive effect could arise with actuarial gains (to the extent that they reduce cumulative unrecognised actuarial losses).

Paragraph 58A

Paragraph 58A prohibits the recognition of gains (losses) that arise solely from past service cost and actuarial losses (gains).

> **58A** **The application of paragraph 58 shall not result in a gain being recognised solely as a result of an actuarial loss or past service cost in the current period or in a loss being recognised solely as a result of an actuarial gain in the current period. The entity shall therefore recognise immediately under paragraph 54 the following, to the extent that they arise while the defined benefit asset is determined in accordance with paragraph 58(b):**
>
> **(a)** **net actuarial losses of the current period and past service cost of the current period to the extent that they exceed any reduction in the present value of the economic benefits specified in paragraph 58(b)(ii). If there is no change or an increase in the present value of the economic benefits, the entire net actuarial losses of the current period and past service cost of the current period shall be recognised immediately under paragraph 54.**
>
> **(b)** **net actuarial gains of the current period after the deduction of past service cost of the current period to the extent that they exceed any increase in the present value of the economic benefits specified in paragraph 58(b)(ii). If there is no change or a decrease in the present value of the economic benefits, the entire net actuarial gains of the current period after the deduction of past service cost of the current period shall be recognised immediately under paragraph 54.**

Examples

The following examples illustrate the result of applying paragraph 58A. As above, it is assumed that the entity's accounting policy is not to recognise actuarial gains and losses within the 'corridor' and to amortise actuarial gains and losses outside the 'corridor'. For the sake of simplicity the periodic amortisation of unrecognised gains and losses outside the corridor is ignored in the examples.

Example 1 continued – Adjustment when there are actuarial losses and no change in the economic benefits available

	A	B	C	D $=A+C$	E $=B+C$	F $=$lower of D and E	G
Year	Surplus in plan	Economic benefits available (paragraph 58(b)(ii))	Losses unrecognised under paragraph 54	Paragraph 54	Paragraph 58(b)	Asset ceiling, i.e. recognised asset	Gain recognised in year 2
1	100	–	–	100	–	–	–
2	70	–	–	70	–	–	–

The facts are as in example 1 above. Applying paragraph 58A, there is no change in the economic benefits available to the entity[2] so the entire actuarial loss of 30 is recognised immediately under paragraph 54 (column D). The asset ceiling remains at nil (column F) and no gain is recognised.

---

2 The term 'economic benefits available to the entity' is used to refer to those economic benefits that qualify for recognition under paragraph 58(b)(ii).

AASB

In effect, the actuarial loss of 30 is recognised immediately, but is offset by the reduction in the effect of the asset ceiling.

	Statement of financial position asset under paragraph 54 (column D above)	Effect of the asset ceiling	Asset ceiling (column F above)
Year 1	100	(100)	–
Year 2	70	(70)	–
Gain/(loss)	(30)	30	–

In the above example, there is no change in the present value of the economic benefits available to the entity. The application of paragraph 58A becomes more complex when there are changes in present value of the economic benefits available, as illustrated in the following examples.

Example 2 – Adjustment when there are actuarial losses and a decrease in the economic benefits available

	A	B	C	D =A+C	E =B+C	F =lower of D and E	G
Year	Surplus in plan	Economic benefits available (paragraph 58(b)(ii))	Losses unrecognised under paragraph 54	Paragraph 54	Paragraph 58(b)	Asset ceiling, i.e. recognised asset	Gain recognised in year 2
1	60	30	40	100	70	70	–
2	25	20	50	75	70	70	–

At the end of year 1, there is a surplus of 60 in the plan (column A) and economic benefits available to the entity of 30 (column B). There are unrecognised losses of 40 under paragraph 54[3] (column C). So, if there were no asset ceiling, an asset of 100 would be recognised (column D). The asset ceiling restricts the asset to 70 (column F).

In year 2, an actuarial loss of 35 in the plan reduces the surplus from 60 to 25 (column A). The economic benefits available to the entity fall by 10 from 30 to 20 (column B). Applying paragraph 58A, the actuarial loss of 35 is analysed as follows:

Actuarial loss equal to the reduction in economic benefits	10
Actuarial loss that exceeds the reduction in economic benefits	25

In accordance with paragraph 58A, 25 of the actuarial loss is recognised immediately under paragraph 54 (column D). The reduction in economic benefits of 10 is included in the cumulative unrecognised losses that increase to 50 (column C). The asset ceiling, therefore, also remains at 70 (column E) and no gain is recognised.

In effect, an actuarial loss of 25 is recognised immediately, but is offset by the reduction in the effect of the asset ceiling.

	Statement of financial position asset under paragraph 54 (column D above)	Effect of the asset ceiling	Asset ceiling (column F above)
Year 1	100	(30)	70
Year 2	75	(5)	70
Gain/(loss)	(25)	25	–

---

3   The application of paragraph 58A allows the recognition of some actuarial gains and losses to be deferred under paragraph 54 and, hence, to be included in the calculation of the asset ceiling. For example, cumulative unrecognised actuarial losses that have built up while the amount specified by paragraph 58(b) is not lower than the amount specified by paragraph 54 will not be recognised immediately at the point that the amount specified by paragraph 58(b) becomes lower. Instead their recognition will continue to be deferred in line with the entity's accounting policy. The cumulative unrecognised losses in this example are losses the recognition of which is deferred even though paragraph 58A applies.

Example 3 – Adjustment when there are actuarial gains and a decrease in the economic benefits available to the entity

	A	B	C	D =A+C	E =B+C	F =lower of D and E	G
Year	Surplus in plan	Economic benefits available (paragraph 58(b)(ii))	Losses unrecognised under paragraph 54	Paragraph 54	Paragraph 58(b)	Asset ceiling, i.e. recognised asset	Gain recognised in year 2
1	60	30	40	100	70	70	–
2	110	25	40	150	65	65	(5)

At the end of year 1 there is a surplus of 60 in the plan (column A) and economic benefits available to the entity of 30 (column B). There are unrecognised losses of 40 under paragraph 54 that arose before the asset ceiling had any effect (column C). So, if there were no asset ceiling, an asset of 100 would be recognised (column D). The asset ceiling restricts the asset to 70 (column F).

In year 2, an actuarial gain of 50 in the plan increases the surplus from 60 to 110 (column A). The economic benefits available to the entity decrease by 5 (column B). Applying paragraph 58A, there is no increase in economic benefits available to the entity. Therefore, the entire actuarial gain of 50 is recognised immediately under paragraph 54 (column D) and the cumulative unrecognised loss under paragraph 54 remains at 40 (column C). The asset ceiling decreases to 65 because of the reduction in economic benefits. That reduction is not an actuarial loss as defined by AASB 119 and therefore does not qualify for deferred recognition.

In effect, an actuarial gain of 50 is recognised immediately, but is (more than) offset by the increase in the effect of the asset ceiling.

	Statement of financial position asset under paragraph 54 (column D above)	Effect of the asset ceiling	Asset ceiling (column F above)
Year 1	100	(30)	70
Year 2	150	(85)	65
Gain/(loss)	50	(55)	(5)

In both examples 2 and 3 there is a reduction in economic benefits available to the entity. However, in example 2 no loss is recognised whereas in example 3 a loss is recognised. This difference in treatment is consistent with the treatment of changes in the present value of economic benefits before paragraph 58A was introduced. The purpose of paragraph 58A is solely to prevent gains (losses) being recognised because of past service cost or actuarial losses (gains). As far as is possible, all other consequences of deferred recognition and the asset ceiling are left unchanged.

Example 4 – Adjustment in a period in which the asset ceiling ceases to have an effect

	A	B	C	D =A+C	E =B+C	F =lower of D and E	G
Year	Surplus in plan	Economic benefits available (paragraph 58(b)(ii))	Losses unrecognised under paragraph 54	Paragraph 54	Paragraph 58(b)	Asset ceiling, i.e. recognised asset	Gain recognised in year 2
1	60	25	40	100	65	65	–
2	(50)	0	115	65	115	65	–

At the end of year 1 there is a surplus of 60 in the plan (column A) and economic benefits are available to the entity of 25 (column B). There are unrecognised losses of 40 under paragraph 54 that arose before the asset ceiling had any effect (column C). So, if there were no asset ceiling, an asset of 100 would be recognised (column D). The asset ceiling restricts the asset to 65 (column F).

In year 2, an actuarial loss of 110 in the plan reduces the surplus from 60 to a deficit of 50 (column A). The economic benefits available to the entity decrease from 25 to 0 (column B). To apply paragraph 58A it is necessary to determine how much of the actuarial loss arises while the defined benefit asset is determined in accordance with paragraph 58(b). Once the surplus becomes a deficit, the amount determined by paragraph 54 is lower than the net total under paragraph 58(b). So, the actuarial loss that arises while the defined benefit asset is determined in accordance with paragraph 58(b) is the loss that reduces the surplus to nil, i.e. 60. The actuarial loss is, therefore, analysed as follows:

Actuarial loss that arises while the defined benefit asset is measured under paragraph 58(b):	
Actuarial loss that equals the reduction in economic benefits	25
Actuarial loss that exceeds the reduction in economic benefits	35
	60
Actuarial loss that arises while the defined benefit asset is measured under paragraph 54	50
Total actuarial loss	110

In accordance with paragraph 58A, 35 of the actuarial loss is recognised immediately under paragraph 54 (column D); 75 (25+50) of the actuarial loss is included in the cumulative unrecognised losses which increase to 115 (column C). The amount determined under paragraph 54 becomes 65 (column D) and under paragraph 58(b) becomes 115 (column E). The recognised asset is the lower of the two, i.e. 65 (column F), and no gain or loss is recognised (column G).

In effect, an actuarial loss of 35 is recognised immediately, but is offset by the reduction in the effect of the asset ceiling.

	Statement of financial position asset under paragraph 54 (column D above)	Effect of the asset ceiling	Asset ceiling (column F above)
Year 1	100	(30)	65
Year 2	65	–	65
Gain/(loss)	(35)	35	–

Notes

1   In applying paragraph 58A in situations when there is an increase in the present value of the economic benefits available to the entity, it is important to remember that the present value of the economic benefits available cannot exceed the surplus in the plan.[4]

2   In practice, benefit improvements often result in a past service cost and an increase in expected future contributions due to increased current service costs of future years. The increase in expected future contributions may increase the economic benefits available to the entity in the form of anticipated reductions in those future contributions. The prohibition against recognising a gain solely as a result of past service cost in the current period does not prevent the recognition of a gain because of an increase in economic benefits. Similarly, a change in actuarial assumptions that causes an actuarial loss may also increase expected future contributions and, hence, the economic benefits available to the entity in the form of anticipated reductions in future contributions. Again, the prohibition against recognising a gain solely as a result of an actuarial loss in the current period does not prevent the recognition of a gain because of an increase in economic benefits.

---

4   The example following paragraph 60 of AASB 119 is corrected so that the present value of available future refunds and reductions in contributions equals the surplus in the plan of 90 (rather than 100), with a further correction to make the limit 270 (rather than 280).

AASB 119

Employee Benefits

(Revised September 2011: applicable to periods beginning
from 1 January 2013)

Note from the Institute of Chartered Accountants Australia

This note, prepared by the technical editors, is not part of Accounting Standard AASB 119.

Historical development

5 September 2011: AASB 119 was reissued by the AASB. This Standard applies to annual reporting periods beginning on or after 1 January 2013 and can be adopted early.

The version of AASB 119 that applies to 30 June 2013 year ends is also included in this handbook with the footer: Applicable 30 June 2013.

References

Interpretation 14 AASB 119 – *The Limit on a Defined Benefit Asset, Minimum Funding Requirements and their interaction* applies to AASB 119.

AASB item not taken onto the agenda: *Classification of Long Service Leave Liabilities* applies to AASB 119.

IFRIC items not taken onto the agenda: No. 22 *Accounting for the Transfer to the Japanese Government of the Substitutional Portion of Employee Pension Fund Liabilities*, No. 23 *Calculation of discount rates*, No. 24 *Classification of an insured plan*, No. 25 *Employee benefits – Undiscounted vested employee benefits*, IAS 19-1 *Determining the appropriate rate to discount past employment benefit obligations*, IAS 19-2 *Employee long service leave*, IAS 19-3 *Special Wage Tax*, IAS 19-4 *Curtailments and negative past service costs*, IAS 19-5 *Post employment benefits – Benefit allocation for defined benefit plans IAS 19*, IAS 19-6 *Changes to a plan caused by government*, IAS 19-7 *Treatment of employee contributions*, IAS 19-8 *Death in service benefit*, IAS 19-9 *Definition of plan assets*, IAS 19-10 *Pension promises based on performance hurdles*, IAS 19-14 *Settlements*, IAS 19-15 *Accounting for a statutory employee profit sharing arrangement* and IAS 19-16 *Defined Contribution Plans with Vesting Conditions* apply to AASB 119.

AASB 119 compared to IAS 19

Additions

Paragraph	Description
Aus 1.1	Which entities AASB 119 applies to (i.e. reporting entities and general purpose financial statements).
Aus 1.2	The application date of AASB 119 (i.e. annual reporting periods beginning 1 January 2013).
Aus 1.3	Permits early application of AASB 119.
Aus 1.4	Makes the requirements of AASB 119 subject to AASB 1031 'Materiality'.
Aus 1.5	Explains which Australian Standards have been superseded by AASB 119.

Deletions

Paragraph	Description
172	Effective date of revised IAS 19

Contents

Preface

Comparison with IAS 19

**Introduction to IAS 19
(available on the AASB website)**

**Accounting Standard
AASB 119 Employee Benefits**

	Paragraphs
Objective	1
Application	Aus1.1–Aus1.5
Scope	2–7
Definitions	8
Short-term employee benefits	9–10
Recognition and measurement	
All short-term employee benefits	11–12
Short-term paid absences	13–18
Profit-sharing and bonus plans	19–24
Disclosure	25
Post-employment benefits: distinction between defined contribution plans and defined benefit plans	26–31
Multi-employer plans	32–39
Defined benefit plans that share risks between entities under common control	40–42
State plans	43–45
Insured benefits	46–49
Post-employment benefits: defined contribution plans	50
Recognition and measurement	51–52
Disclosure	53–54
Post-employment benefits: defined benefit plans	55
Recognition and measurement	56–60
Accounting for the constructive obligation	61–62
Statement of financial position	63–65
Recognition and measurement: present value of defined benefit obligations and current service cost	66
Actuarial valuation method	67–69
Attributing benefit to periods of service	70–74
Actuarial assumptions	75–80
Actuarial assumptions: mortality	81–82
Actuarial assumptions: discount rate	83–86
Actuarial assumptions: salaries, benefits and medical costs	87–98
Past service cost and gains and losses on settlement	99–101
Past service cost	102–108
Gains and losses on settlement	109–112
Recognition and measurement: plan assets	
Fair value of plan assets	113–115
Reimbursements	116–119

AASB

Paragraphs

Components of defined benefit cost	120–122
Net interest on the net defined benefit liability (asset)	123–126
Remeasurements of the net defined benefit liability (asset)	127–130
Presentation	
Offset	131–132
Current/non-current distinction	133
Components of defined benefit cost	134
Disclosure	135–138
Characteristics of defined benefit plans and risks associated with them	139
Explanation of amounts in the financial statements	140–144
Amount, timing and uncertainty of future cash flows	145–147
Multi-employer plans	148
Defined benefit plans that share risks between entities under common control	149–150
Disclosure requirements in other Australian Accounting Standards	151–152
Other long-term employee benefits	153–154
Recognition and measurement	155–157
Disclosure	158
Termination Benefits	159–164
Recognition	165–168
Measurement	169–170
Disclosure	171
Transition and Effective Date	173

Deleted IAS 19 Text

Basis for Conclusions on IAS 19
(available on the AASB website)

Australian Accounting Standard AASB 119 *Employee Benefits* is set out in paragraphs 1 –173. All the paragraphs have equal authority. Paragraphs in **bold type** state the main principles. AASB 119 is to be read in the context of other Australian Accounting Standards, including AASB 1048 *Interpretation of Standards*, which identifies the Australian Accounting Interpretations. In the absence of explicit guidance, AASB 108 *Accounting Policies, Changes in Accounting Estimates and Errors* provides a basis for selecting and applying accounting policies.

Preface

Introduction

The Australian Accounting Standards Board (AASB) makes Australian Accounting Standards, including Interpretations, to be applied by:

(a)   entities required by the *Corporations Act 2001* to prepare financial reports;

(b)   governments in preparing financial statements for the whole of government and the General Government Sector (GGS); and

(c)   entities in the private or public for-profit or not-for-profit sectors that are reporting entities or that prepare general purpose financial statements.

AASB 1053 *Application of Tiers of Australian Accounting Standards* establishes a differential reporting framework consisting of two tiers of reporting requirements for preparing general purpose financial statements:

(a)   Tier 1: Australian Accounting Standards; and

(b)   Tier 2: Australian Accounting Standards – Reduced Disclosure Requirements.

Tier 1 requirements incorporate International Financial Reporting Standards (IFRSs), including Interpretations, issued by the International Accounting Standards Board (IASB), with the addition of paragraphs on the applicability of each Standard in the Australian environment.

Publicly accountable for-profit private sector entities are required to adopt Tier 1 requirements, and therefore are required to comply with IFRSs. Furthermore, other for-profit private sector entities complying with Tier 1 requirements will simultaneously comply with IFRSs. Some other entities complying with Tier 1 requirements will also simultaneously comply with IFRSs.

Tier 2 requirements comprise the recognition, measurement and presentation requirements of Tier 1 but substantially reduced disclosure requirements in comparison with Tier 1.

Australian Accounting Standards also include requirements that are specific to Australian entities. These requirements may be located in Australian Accounting Standards that incorporate IFRSs or in other Australian Accounting Standards. In most instances, these requirements are either restricted to the not-for-profit or public sectors or include additional disclosures that address domestic, regulatory or other issues. These requirements do not prevent publicly accountable for-profit private sector entities from complying with IFRSs. In developing requirements for public sector entities, the AASB considers the requirements of International Public Sector Accounting Standards (IPSASs), as issued by the International Public Sector Accounting Standards Board (IPSASB) of the International Federation of Accountants.

Differences between this Standard and AASB 119 (December 2004, as amended)

Differences between this Standard and the superseded requirements under AASB 119 (December 2004, as amended) are the same as the differences between IAS 19 *Employee Benefits* (June 2011) and the superseded requirements under IAS 19 *Employee Benefits*. The main differences are summarised in the project summary and feedback statement in relation to amendments to IAS 19 *Employee Benefits*, which is available on the IASB's website at www.ifrs.org.

Reduced disclosure requirements

Disclosure requirements under Tier 2 have been determined through a separate due process – see AASB 2011-11 *Amendments to AASB 119 (September 2011) arising from Reduced Disclosure Requirements*.

Comparison with IAS 19

AASB 119 *Employee Benefits* incorporates IAS 19 *Employee Benefits* issued by the International Accounting Standards Board (IASB). Paragraphs that have been added to this Standard (and do not appear in the text of IAS 19) are identified with the prefix "Aus", followed by the number of the preceding IASB paragraph and decimal numbering. Paragraphs that apply only to not-for-profit entities begin by identifying their limited applicability.

Entities that comply with AASB 119 will simultaneously be in compliance with IAS 19.

Accounting Standard AASB 119

The Australian Accounting Standards Board makes Accounting Standard AASB 119 *Employee Benefits* under section 334 of the *Corporations Act 2001*.

Kevin M. Stevenson
Chair – AASB

Dated 5 September 2011

Accounting Standard AASB 119
Employee Benefits

Objective

1   The objective of this Standard is to prescribe the accounting and disclosure for employee benefits. The Standard requires an entity to recognise:

(a)   a liability when an employee has provided service in exchange for employee benefits to be paid in the future; and

(b)   an expense when the entity consumes the economic benefit arising from service provided by an employee in exchange for employee benefits.

Application

Aus1.1   **This Standard applies to:**

(a)   **each entity that is required to prepare financial reports in accordance with Part 2M.3 of the Corporations Act and that is a reporting entity;**

(b)   **general purpose financial statements of each other reporting entity; and**

(c)   **financial statements that are, or are held out to be, general purpose financial statements.**

Aus1.2   **This Standard applies to annual reporting periods beginning on or after 1 January 2013.**

Aus1.3   **This Standard may be applied to annual reporting periods beginning on or after 1 January 2005 but before 1 January 2013. When an entity applies this Standard to such an annual reporting period, it shall disclose that fact.**

Aus1.4   **The requirements specified in this Standard apply to the financial statements where information resulting from their application is material in accordance with AASB 1031 *Materiality*.**

Aus1.5   When applied or operative, this Standard supersedes AASB 119 *Employee Benefits* (December 2004, as amended).

Scope

2   **This Standard shall be applied by an employer in accounting for all employee benefits, except those to which AASB 2 *Share-based Payment* applies.**

3   This Standard does not deal with reporting by employee benefit plans (see AAS 25 *Financial Reporting by Superannuation Plans*).

4   The employee benefits to which this Standard applies include those provided:

(a)   under formal plans or other formal agreements between an entity and individual employees, groups of employees or their representatives;

(b)   under legislative requirements, or through industry arrangements, whereby entities are required to contribute to national, state, industry or other multi-employer plans; or

(c)   by those informal practices that give rise to a constructive obligation. Informal practices give rise to a constructive obligation where the entity has no realistic alternative but to pay employee benefits. An example of a constructive obligation is where a change in the entity's informal practices would cause unacceptable damage to its relationship with employees.

5   Employee benefits include:

(a)   short-term employee benefits, such as the following, if expected to be settled wholly before twelve months after the end of the annual reporting period in which the employees render the related services:

(i)   wages, salaries and social security contributions;

(ii)   paid annual leave and paid sick leave;

(iii)   profit-sharing and bonuses; and

(iv)   non-monetary benefits (such as medical care, housing, cars and free or subsidised goods or services) for current employees;

(b)   post-employment benefits, such as the following:

(i)   retirement benefits (eg pensions and lump sum payments on retirement); and

(ii)   other post-employment benefits, such as post-employment life insurance and post-employment medical care;

(c)   other long-term employee benefits, such as the following:

(i)   long-term paid absences such as long-service leave or sabbatical leave;

(ii)   jubilee or other long-service benefits; and

(iii)   long-term disability benefits; and

(d)   termination benefits.

6   Employee benefits include benefits provided either to employees or to their dependants or beneficiaries and may be settled by payments (or the provision of goods or services) made either directly to the employees, to their spouses, children or other dependants or to others, such as insurance companies.

7   An employee may provide services to an entity on a full-time, part-time, permanent, casual or temporary basis. For the purpose of this Standard, employees include directors and other management personnel.

Definitions

8   **The following terms are used in this Standard with the meanings specified:**

Definitions of employee benefits

Employee benefits **are all forms of consideration given by an entity in exchange for service rendered by employees or for the termination of employment.**

Short-term employee benefits **are employee benefits (other than termination benefits) that are expected to be settled wholly before twelve months after the end of the annual reporting period in which the employees render the related service.**

Post-employment benefits **are employee benefits (other than termination benefits and short-term employee benefits) that are payable after the completion of employment.**

Other long-term employee benefits **are all employee benefits other than short-term employee benefits, post-employment benefits and termination benefits.**

Termination benefits **are employee benefits provided in exchange for the termination of an employee's employment as a result of either:**

(a)   **an entity's decision to terminate an employee's employment before the normal retirement date; or**

(b)   **an employee's decision to accept an offer of benefits in exchange for the termination of employment.**

Definitions relating to classification of plans

Post-employment benefit plans **are formal or informal arrangements under which an entity provides post-employment benefits for one or more employees.**

Defined contribution plans are post-employment benefit plans under which an entity pays fixed contributions into a separate entity (a fund) and will have no legal or constructive obligation to pay further contributions if the fund does not hold sufficient assets to pay all employee benefits relating to employee service in the current and prior periods.

Defined benefit plans are post-employment benefit plans other than defined contribution plans.

Multi-employer plans are defined contribution plans (other than state plans) or defined benefit plans (other than state plans) that:

    (a)   pool the assets contributed by various entities that are not under common control; and

    (b)   use those assets to provide benefits to employees of more than one entity, on the basis that contribution and benefit levels are determined without regard to the identity of the entity that employs the employees.

Definitions relating to the net defined benefit liability (asset)

The *net defined benefit liability (asset)* is the deficit or surplus, adjusted for any effect of limiting a net defined benefit asset to the asset ceiling.

The *deficit or surplus* is:

    (a)   the present value of the defined benefit obligation less

    (b)   the fair value of plan assets (if any).

The *asset ceiling* is the present value of any economic benefits available in the form of refunds from the plan or reductions in future contributions to the plan.

The *present value of a defined benefit obligation* is the present value, without deducting any plan assets, of expected future payments required to settle the obligation resulting from employee service in the current and prior periods.

Plan assets comprise:

    (a)   assets held by a long-term employee benefit fund; and

    (b)   qualifying insurance policies.

Assets held by a long-term employee benefit fund are assets (other than non-transferable financial instruments issued by the reporting entity) that:

    (a)   are held by an entity (a fund) that is legally separate from the reporting entity and exists solely to pay or fund employee benefits; and

    (b)   are available to be used only to pay or fund employee benefits, are not available to the reporting entity's own creditors (even in bankruptcy), and cannot be returned to the reporting entity, unless either:

        (i)   the remaining assets of the fund are sufficient to meet all the related employee benefit obligations of the plan or the reporting entity; or

        (ii)   the assets are returned to the reporting entity to reimburse it for employee benefits already paid.

A *qualifying insurance policy* is an insurance policy[1] issued by an insurer that is not a related party (as defined in AASB 124 *Related Party Disclosures*) of the reporting entity, if the proceeds of the policy:

    (a)   can be used only to pay or fund employee benefits under a defined benefit plan; and

---

1   A qualifying insurance policy is not necessarily an insurance contract, as defined in AASB 4 *Insurance Contracts*.

(b) are not available to the reporting entity's own creditors (even in bankruptcy) and cannot be paid to the reporting entity, unless either:

    (i) the proceeds represent surplus assets that are not needed for the policy to meet all the related employee benefit obligations; or

    (ii) the proceeds are returned to the reporting entity to reimburse it for employee benefits already paid.

Fair value is the amount for which an asset could be exchanged or a liability settled between knowledgeable, willing parties in an arm's length transaction.

Definitions relating to defined benefit cost

Service cost comprises:

(a) *current service cost*, which is the increase in the present value of the defined benefit obligation resulting from employee service in the current period;

(b) *past service cost*, which is the change in the present value of the defined benefit obligation for employee service in prior periods, resulting from a plan amendment (the introduction or withdrawal of, or changes to, a defined benefit plan) or a curtailment (a significant reduction by the entity in the number of employees covered by a plan); and

(c) any gain or loss on settlement.

Net interest on the net defined benefit liability (asset) is the change during the period in the net defined benefit liability (asset) that arises from the passage of time.

Remeasurements of the net defined benefit liability (asset) comprise:

(a) actuarial gains and losses;

(b) the return on plan assets, excluding amounts included in net interest on the net defined benefit liability (asset); and

(c) any change in the effect of the asset ceiling, excluding amounts included in net interest on the net defined benefit liability (asset).

Actuarial gains and losses are changes in the present value of the defined benefit obligation resulting from:

(a) experience adjustments (the effects of differences between the previous actuarial assumptions and what has actually occurred); and

(b) the effects of changes in actuarial assumptions.

The *return on plan assets* is interest, dividends and other income derived from the plan assets, together with realised and unrealised gains or losses on the plan assets, less:

(a) any costs of managing plan assets; and

(b) any tax payable by the plan itself, other than tax included in the actuarial assumptions used to measure the present value of the defined benefit obligation.

A *settlement* is a transaction that eliminates all further legal or constructive obligations for part or all of the benefits provided under a defined benefit plan, other than a payment of benefits to, or on behalf of, employees that is set out in the terms of the plan and included in the actuarial assumptions.

Short-term employee benefits

9   Short-term employee benefits include items such as the following, if expected to be settled wholly before twelve months after the end of the annual reporting period in which the employees render the related services:

(a) wages, salaries and social security contributions;

(b) paid annual leave and paid sick leave;

(c)   profit-sharing and bonuses; and

(d)   non-monetary benefits (such as medical care, housing, cars and free or subsidised goods or services) for current employees.

10   An entity need not reclassify a short-term employee benefit if the entity's expectations of the timing of settlement change temporarily. However, if the characteristics of the benefit change (such as a change from a non-accumulating benefit to an accumulating benefit) or if a change in expectations of the timing of settlement is not temporary, then the entity considers whether the benefit still meets the definition of short-term employee benefits.

Recognition and measurement

All short-term employee benefits

11   **When an employee has rendered service to an entity during an accounting period, the entity shall recognise the undiscounted amount of short-term employee benefits expected to be paid in exchange for that service:**

(a)   as a liability (accrued expense), after deducting any amount already paid. If the amount already paid exceeds the undiscounted amount of the benefits, an entity shall recognise that excess as an asset (prepaid expense) to the extent that the prepayment will lead to, for example, a reduction in future payments or a cash refund.

(b)   as an expense, unless another Australian Accounting Standard requires or permits the inclusion of the benefits in the cost of an asset (see, for example, AASB 102 *Inventories* and AASB 116 *Property, Plant and Equipment*).

12   **Paragraphs 13, 16 and 19 explain how an entity shall apply paragraph 11 to short-term employee benefits in the form of paid absences and profit-sharing and bonus plans.**

Short-term paid absences

13   **An entity shall recognise the expected cost of short-term employee benefits in the form of paid absences under paragraph 11 as follows:**

(a)   in the case of accumulating paid absences, when the employees render service that increases their entitlement to future paid absences.

(b)   in the case of non-accumulating paid absences, when the absences occur.

14   An entity may pay employees for absence for various reasons including holidays, sickness and short-term disability, maternity or paternity, jury service and military service. Entitlement to paid absences falls into two categories:

(a)   accumulating; and

(b)   non-accumulating.

15   Accumulating paid absences are those that are carried forward and can be used in future periods if the current period's entitlement is not used in full. Accumulating paid absences may be either vesting (in other words, employees are entitled to a cash payment for unused entitlement on leaving the entity) or non-vesting (when employees are not entitled to a cash payment for unused entitlement on leaving). An obligation arises as employees render service that increases their entitlement to future paid absences. The obligation exists, and is recognised, even if the paid absences are non-vesting, although the possibility that employees may leave before they use an accumulated non-vesting entitlement affects the measurement of that obligation.

16   **An entity shall measure the expected cost of accumulating paid absences as the additional amount that the entity expects to pay as a result of the unused entitlement that has accumulated at the end of the reporting period.**

17   The method specified in the previous paragraph measures the obligation at the amount of the additional payments that are expected to arise solely from the fact that the benefit accumulates. In many cases, an entity may not need to make detailed computations to estimate that there is no material obligation for unused paid absences. For example, a sick

leave obligation is likely to be material only if there is a formal or informal understanding that unused paid sick leave may be taken as paid annual leave.

> **Example illustrating paragraphs 16 and 17**
>
> An entity has 100 employees, who are each entitled to five working days of paid sick leave for each year. Unused sick leave may be carried forward for one calendar year. Sick leave is taken first out of the current year's entitlement and then out of any balance brought forward from the previous year (a LIFO basis). At 31 December 20X1 the average unused entitlement is two days per employee. The entity expects, on the basis of experience that is expected to continue, that 92 employees will take no more than five days of paid sick leave in 20X2 and that the remaining eight employees will take an average of six and a half days each.
>
> *The entity expects that it will pay an additional twelve days of sick pay as a result of the unused entitlement that has accumulated at 31 December 20X1 (one and a half days each, for eight employees). Therefore, the entity recognises a liability equal to twelve days of sick pay.*

18   Non-accumulating paid absences do not carry forward: they lapse if the current period's entitlement is not used in full and do not entitle employees to a cash payment for unused entitlement on leaving the entity. This is commonly the case for sick pay (to the extent that unused past entitlement does not increase future entitlement), maternity or paternity leave and paid absences for jury service or military service. An entity recognises no liability or expense until the time of the absence, because employee service does not increase the amount of the benefit.

Profit-sharing and bonus plans

19   **An entity shall recognise the expected cost of profit-sharing and bonus payments under paragraph 11 when, and only when:**

(a)   **the entity has a present legal or constructive obligation to make such payments as a result of past events; and**

(b)   **a reliable estimate of the obligation can be made.**

A present obligation exists when, and only when, the entity has no realistic alternative but to make the payments.

20   Under some profit-sharing plans, employees receive a share of the profit only if they remain with the entity for a specified period. Such plans create a constructive obligation as employees render service that increases the amount to be paid if they remain in service until the end of the specified period. The measurement of such constructive obligations reflects the possibility that some employees may leave without receiving profit-sharing payments.

> **Example illustrating paragraph 20**
>
> A profit-sharing plan requires an entity to pay a specified proportion of its profit for the year to employees who serve throughout the year. If no employees leave during the year, the total profit-sharing payments for the year will be 3 per cent of profit. The entity estimates that staff turnover will reduce the payments to 2.5 per cent of profit.
>
> *The entity recognises a liability and an expense of 2.5 per cent of profit.*

21   An entity may have no legal obligation to pay a bonus. Nevertheless, in some cases, an entity has a practice of paying bonuses. In such cases, the entity has a constructive obligation because the entity has no realistic alternative but to pay the bonus. The measurement of the constructive obligation reflects the possibility that some employees may leave without receiving a bonus.

22   An entity can make a reliable estimate of its legal or constructive obligation under a profit-sharing or bonus plan when, and only when:

(a)   the formal terms of the plan contain a formula for determining the amount of the benefit;

(b)   the entity determines the amounts to be paid before the financial statements are authorised for issue; or

(c)   past practice gives clear evidence of the amount of the entity's constructive obligation.

AASB 119

Applicable to periods beginning from 1 January 2013

23   An obligation under profit-sharing and bonus plans results from employee service and not from a transaction with the entity's owners. Therefore, an entity recognises the cost of profit-sharing and bonus plans not as a distribution of profit but as an expense.

24   If profit-sharing and bonus payments are not expected to be settled wholly before twelve months after the end of the annual reporting period in which the employees render the related service, those payments are other long-term employee benefits (see paragraphs 153–158).

Disclosure

25   Although this Standard does not require specific disclosures about short-term employee benefits, other Australian Accounting Standards may require disclosures. For example, AASB 124 requires disclosures about employee benefits for key management personnel. AASB 101 *Presentation of Financial Statements* requires disclosure of employee benefits expense.

Post-employment benefits: distinction between defined contribution plans and defined benefit plans

26   Post-employment benefits include items such as the following:

    (a)   retirement benefits (eg pensions and lump sum payments on retirement); and

    (b)   other post-employment benefits, such as post-employment life insurance and post-employment medical care.

Arrangements whereby an entity provides post-employment benefits are post-employment benefit plans. An entity applies this Standard to all such arrangements whether or not they involve the establishment of a separate entity to receive contributions and to pay benefits.

27   Post-employment benefit plans are classified as either defined contribution plans or defined benefit plans, depending on the economic substance of the plan as derived from its principal terms and conditions.

28   Under defined contribution plans the entity's legal or constructive obligation is limited to the amount that it agrees to contribute to the fund. Thus, the amount of the post-employment benefits received by the employee is determined by the amount of contributions paid by an entity (and perhaps also the employee) to a post-employment benefit plan or to an insurance company, together with investment returns arising from the contributions. In consequence, actuarial risk (that benefits will be less than expected) and investment risk (that assets invested will be insufficient to meet expected benefits) fall, in substance, on the employee.

29   Examples of cases where an entity's obligation is not limited to the amount that it agrees to contribute to the fund are when the entity has a legal or constructive obligation through:

    (a)   a plan benefit formula that is not linked solely to the amount of contributions and requires the entity to provide further contributions if assets are insufficient to meet the benefits in the plan benefit formula;

    (b)   a guarantee, either indirectly through a plan or directly, of a specified return on contributions; or

    (c)   those informal practices that give rise to a constructive obligation. For example, a constructive obligation may arise where an entity has a history of increasing benefits for former employees to keep pace with inflation even where there is no legal obligation to do so.

30   Under defined benefit plans:

    (a)   the entity's obligation is to provide the agreed benefits to current and former employees; and

    (b)   actuarial risk (that benefits will cost more than expected) and investment risk fall, in substance, on the entity. If actuarial or investment experience are worse than expected, the entity's obligation may be increased.

31   Paragraphs 32–49 explain the distinction between defined contribution plans and defined benefit plans in the context of multi-employer plans, defined benefit plans that share risks between entities under common control, state plans and insured benefits.

Multi-employer plans

32   An entity shall classify a multi-employer plan as a defined contribution plan or a defined benefit plan under the terms of the plan (including any constructive obligation that goes beyond the formal terms).

33   If an entity participates in a multi-employer defined benefit plan, unless paragraph 34 applies, it shall:

(a)   account for its proportionate share of the defined benefit obligation, plan assets and cost associated with the plan in the same way as for any other defined benefit plan; and

(b)   disclose the information required by paragraphs 135–148 (excluding paragraph 148(d)).

34   When sufficient information is not available to use defined benefit accounting for a multi-employer defined benefit plan, an entity shall:

(a)   account for the plan in accordance with paragraphs 51 and 52 as if it were a defined contribution plan; and

(b)   disclose the information required by paragraph 148.

35   One example of a multi-employer defined benefit plan is one where:

(a)   the plan is financed on a pay-as-you-go basis: contributions are set at a level that is expected to be sufficient to pay the benefits falling due in the same period; and future benefits earned during the current period will be paid out of future contributions; and

(b)   employees' benefits are determined by the length of their service and the participating entities have no realistic means of withdrawing from the plan without paying a contribution for the benefits earned by employees up to the date of withdrawal. Such a plan creates actuarial risk for the entity: if the ultimate cost of benefits already earned at the end of the reporting period is more than expected, the entity will have either to increase its contributions or to persuade employees to accept a reduction in benefits. Therefore, such a plan is a defined benefit plan.

36   Where sufficient information is available about a multi-employer defined benefit plan, an entity accounts for its proportionate share of the defined benefit obligation, plan assets and post-employment cost associated with the plan in the same way as for any other defined benefit plan. However, an entity may not be able to identify its share of the underlying financial position and performance of the plan with sufficient reliability for accounting purposes. This may occur if:

(a)   the plan exposes the participating entities to actuarial risks associated with the current and former employees of other entities, with the result that there is no consistent and reliable basis for allocating the obligation, plan assets and cost to individual entities participating in the plan; or

(b)   the entity does not have access to sufficient information about the plan to satisfy the requirements of this Standard.

In those cases, an entity accounts for the plan as if it were a defined contribution plan and discloses the information required by paragraph 148.

37   There may be a contractual agreement between the multi-employer plan and its participants that determines how the surplus in the plan will be distributed to the participants (or the deficit funded). A participant in a multi-employer plan with such an agreement that accounts for the plan as a defined contribution plan in accordance with paragraph 34 shall recognise the asset or liability that arises from the contractual agreement and the resulting income or expense in profit or loss.

Example illustrating paragraph 37

An entity participates in a multi-employer defined benefit plan that does not prepare plan valuations on an AASB 119 basis. It therefore accounts for the plan as if it were a defined contribution plan. A non-AASB 119 funding valuation shows a deficit of CU100 million[2] in the plan. The plan has agreed under contract a schedule of contributions with the participating employers in the plan that will eliminate the deficit over the next five years. The entity's total contributions under the contract are CU8 million.

The entity recognises a liability for the contributions adjusted for the time value of money and an equal expense in profit or loss.

---

38   Multi-employer plans are distinct from group administration plans. A group administration plan is merely an aggregation of single employer plans combined to allow participating employers to pool their assets for investment purposes and reduce investment management and administration costs, but the claims of different employers are segregated for the sole benefit of their own employees. Group administration plans pose no particular accounting problems because information is readily available to treat them in the same way as any other single employer plan and because such plans do not expose the participating entities to actuarial risks associated with the current and former employees of other entities. The definitions in this Standard require an entity to classify a group administration plan as a defined contribution plan or a defined benefit plan in accordance with the terms of the plan (including any constructive obligation that goes beyond the formal terms).

39   **In determining when to recognise, and how to measure, a liability relating to the wind-up of a multi-employer defined benefit plan, or the entity's withdrawal from a multi-employer defined benefit plan, an entity shall apply AASB 137 *Provisions, Contingent Liabilities and Contingent Assets*.**

Defined benefit plans that share risks between entities under common control

40   Defined benefit plans that share risks between entities under common control, for example, a parent and its subsidiaries, are not multi-employer plans.

41   An entity participating in such a plan shall obtain information about the plan as a whole measured in accordance with this Standard on the basis of assumptions that apply to the plan as a whole. If there is a contractual agreement or stated policy for charging to individual group entities the net defined benefit cost for the plan as a whole measured in accordance with this Standard, the entity shall, in its separate or individual financial statements, recognise the net defined benefit cost so charged. If there is no such agreement or policy, the net defined benefit cost shall be recognised in the separate or individual financial statements of the group entity that is legally the sponsoring employer for the plan. The other group entities shall, in their separate or individual financial statements, recognise a cost equal to their contribution payable for the period.

42   Participation in such a plan is a related party transaction for each individual group entity. An entity shall therefore, in its separate or individual financial statements, disclose the information required by paragraph 149.

State plans

43   **An entity shall account for a state plan in the same way as for a multi-employer plan (see paragraphs 32–39).**

44   State plans are established by legislation to cover all entities (or all entities in a particular category, for example, a specific industry) and are operated by national or local government or by another body (for example, an autonomous agency created specifically for this purpose) that is not subject to control or influence by the reporting entity. Some plans established by an entity provide both compulsory benefits, as a substitute for benefits that would otherwise be covered under a state plan, and additional voluntary benefits. Such plans are not state plans.

---

2   In this Standard monetary amounts are denominated in 'currency units (CU)'

45 State plans are characterised as defined benefit or defined contribution, depending on the entity's obligation under the plan. Many state plans are funded on a pay-as-you-go basis: contributions are set at a level that is expected to be sufficient to pay the required benefits falling due in the same period; future benefits earned during the current period will be paid out of future contributions. Nevertheless, in most state plans the entity has no legal or constructive obligation to pay those future benefits: its only obligation is to pay the contributions as they fall due and if the entity ceases to employ members of the state plan, it will have no obligation to pay the benefits earned by its own employees in previous years. For this reason, state plans are normally defined contribution plans. However, when a state plan is a defined benefit plan an entity applies paragraphs 32–39.

Insured benefits

46 **An entity may pay insurance premiums to fund a post-employment benefit plan. The entity shall treat such a plan as a defined contribution plan unless the entity will have (either directly, or indirectly through the plan) a legal or constructive obligation either:**

(a) **to pay the employee benefits directly when they fall due; or**

(b) **to pay further amounts if the insurer does not pay all future employee benefits relating to employee service in the current and prior periods.**

If the entity retains such a legal or constructive obligation, the entity shall treat the plan as a defined benefit plan.

47 The benefits insured by an insurance policy need not have a direct or automatic relationship with the entity's obligation for employee benefits. Post-employment benefit plans involving insurance policies are subject to the same distinction between accounting and funding as other funded plans.

48 Where an entity funds a post-employment benefit obligation by contributing to an insurance policy under which the entity (either directly, indirectly through the plan, through the mechanism for setting future premiums or through a related party relationship with the insurer) retains a legal or constructive obligation, the payment of the premiums does not amount to a defined contribution arrangement. It follows that the entity:

(a) accounts for a qualifying insurance policy as a plan asset (see paragraph 8); and

(b) recognises other insurance policies as reimbursement rights (if the policies satisfy the criterion in paragraph 116).

49 Where an insurance policy is in the name of a specified plan participant or a group of plan participants and the entity does not have any legal or constructive obligation to cover any loss on the policy, the entity has no obligation to pay benefits to the employees and the insurer has sole responsibility for paying the benefits. The payment of fixed premiums under such contracts is, in substance, the settlement of the employee benefit obligation, rather than an investment to meet the obligation. Consequently, the entity no longer has an asset or a liability. Therefore, an entity treats such payments as contributions to a defined contribution plan.

Post-employment benefits: defined contribution plans

50 Accounting for defined contribution plans is straightforward because the reporting entity's obligation for each period is determined by the amounts to be contributed for that period. Consequently, no actuarial assumptions are required to measure the obligation or the expense and there is no possibility of any actuarial gain or loss. Moreover, the obligations are measured on an undiscounted basis, except where they are not expected to be settled wholly before twelve months after the end of the annual reporting period in which the employees render the related service.

Recognition and measurement

51 When an employee has rendered service to an entity during a period, the entity shall recognise the contribution payable to a defined contribution plan in exchange for that service:

  (a) as a liability (accrued expense), after deducting any contribution already paid. If the contribution already paid exceeds the contribution due for service before the end of the reporting period, an entity shall recognise that excess as an asset (prepaid expense) to the extent that the prepayment will lead to, for example, a reduction in future payments or a cash refund.

  (b) as an expense, unless another Australian Accounting Standard requires or permits the inclusion of the contribution in the cost of an asset (see, for example, AASB 102 and AASB 116).

52 When contributions to a defined contribution plan are not expected to be settled wholly before twelve months after the end of the annual reporting period in which the employees render the related service, they shall be discounted using the discount rate specified in paragraph 83.

Disclosure

53 An entity shall disclose the amount recognised as an expense for defined contribution plans.

54 Where required by AASB 124 an entity discloses information about contributions to defined contribution plans for key management personnel.

Post-employment benefits: defined benefit plans

55 Accounting for defined benefit plans is complex because actuarial assumptions are required to measure the obligation and the expense and there is a possibility of actuarial gains and losses. Moreover, the obligations are measured on a discounted basis because they may be settled many years after the employees render the related service.

Recognition and measurement

56 Defined benefit plans may be unfunded, or they may be wholly or partly funded by contributions by an entity, and sometimes its employees, into an entity, or fund, that is legally separate from the reporting entity and from which the employee benefits are paid. The payment of funded benefits when they fall due depends not only on the financial position and the investment performance of the fund but also on an entity's ability, and willingness, to make good any shortfall in the fund's assets. Therefore, the entity is, in substance, underwriting the actuarial and investment risks associated with the plan. Consequently, the expense recognised for a defined benefit plan is not necessarily the amount of the contribution due for the period.

57 Accounting by an entity for defined benefit plans involves the following steps:

  (a) determining the deficit or surplus. This involves:

    (i)   using an actuarial technique, the projected unit credit method, to make a reliable estimate of the ultimate cost to the entity of the benefit that employees have earned in return for their service in the current and prior periods (see paragraphs 67–69). This requires an entity to determine how much benefit is attributable to the current and prior periods (see paragraphs 70–74) and to make estimates (actuarial assumptions) about demographic variables (such as employee turnover and mortality) and financial variables (such as future increases in salaries and medical costs) that will affect the cost of the benefit (see paragraphs 75–98).

    (ii) discounting that benefit in order to determine the present value of the defined benefit obligation and the current service cost (see paragraphs 67–69 and 83–86).

    (iii) deducting the fair value of any plan assets (see paragraphs 113–115) from the present value of the defined benefit obligation.

AASB 119   **Institute of Chartered Accountants Australia**
Applicable to periods beginning from 1 January 2013

(b)   determining the amount of the net defined benefit liability (asset) as the amount of the deficit or surplus determined in (a), adjusted for any effect of limiting a net defined benefit asset to the asset ceiling (see paragraph 64).

(c)   determining amounts to be recognised in profit or loss:

   (i)   current service cost (see paragraphs 70–74).

   (ii)   any past service cost and gain or loss on settlement (see paragraphs 99–112).

   (iii)   net interest on the net defined benefit liability (asset) (see paragraphs 123–126).

(d)   determining the remeasurements of the net defined benefit liability (asset), to be recognised in other comprehensive income, comprising:

   (i)   actuarial gains and losses (see paragraphs 128 and 129);

   (ii)   return on plan assets, excluding amounts included in net interest on the net defined benefit liability (asset) (see paragraph 130); and

   (iii)   any change in the effect of the asset ceiling (see paragraph 64), excluding amounts included in net interest on the net defined benefit liability (asset).

Where an entity has more than one defined benefit plan, the entity applies these procedures for each material plan separately.

58   **An entity shall determine the net defined benefit liability (asset) with sufficient regularity that the amounts recognised in the financial statements do not differ materially from the amounts that would be determined at the end of the reporting period.**

59   This Standard encourages, but does not require, an entity to involve a qualified actuary in the measurement of all material post-employment benefit obligations. For practical reasons, an entity may request a qualified actuary to carry out a detailed valuation of the obligation before the end of the reporting period. Nevertheless, the results of that valuation are updated for any material transactions and other material changes in circumstances (including changes in market prices and interest rates) up to the end of the reporting period.

60   In some cases, estimates, averages and computational short cuts may provide a reliable approximation of the detailed computations illustrated in this Standard.

Accounting for the constructive obligation

61   **An entity shall account not only for its legal obligation under the formal terms of a defined benefit plan, but also for any constructive obligation that arises from the entity's informal practices. Informal practices give rise to a constructive obligation where the entity has no realistic alternative but to pay employee benefits. An example of a constructive obligation is where a change in the entity's informal practices would cause unacceptable damage to its relationship with employees.**

62   The formal terms of a defined benefit plan may permit an entity to terminate its obligation under the plan. Nevertheless, it is usually difficult for an entity to terminate its obligation under a plan (without payment) if employees are to be retained. Therefore, in the absence of evidence to the contrary, accounting for post-employment benefits assumes that an entity that is currently promising such benefits will continue to do so over the remaining working lives of employees.

Statement of financial position

63   **An entity shall recognise the net defined benefit liability (asset) in the statement of financial position.**

64   **When an entity has a surplus in a defined benefit plan, it shall measure the net defined benefit asset at the lower of:**

   (a)   the surplus in the defined benefit plan; and

   (b)   the asset ceiling, determined using the discount rate specified in paragraph 83.

65   A net defined benefit asset may arise where a defined benefit plan has been overfunded or
      where actuarial gains have arisen. An entity recognises a net defined benefit asset in such
      cases because:

(a)   the entity controls a resource, which is the ability to use the surplus to generate
      future benefits;

(b)   that control is a result of past events (contributions paid by the entity and service
      rendered by the employee); and

(c)   future economic benefits are available to the entity in the form of a reduction in
      future contributions or a cash refund, either directly to the entity or indirectly to
      another plan in deficit. The asset ceiling is the present value of those future benefits.

Recognition and measurement: present value of defined benefit obligations and current service cost

66   The ultimate cost of a defined benefit plan may be influenced by many variables, such
      as final salaries, employee turnover and mortality, employee contributions and medical
      cost trends. The ultimate cost of the plan is uncertain and this uncertainty is likely to
      persist over a long period of time. In order to measure the present value of the post-
      employment benefit obligations and the related current service cost, it is necessary:

(a)   to apply an actuarial valuation method (see paragraphs 67–69);

(b)   to attribute benefit to periods of service (see paragraphs 70–74); and

(c)   to make actuarial assumptions (see paragraphs 75–98).

Actuarial valuation method

67   **An entity shall use the projected unit credit method to determine the present value
      of its defined benefit obligations and the related current service cost and, where
      applicable, past service cost.**

68   The projected unit credit method (sometimes known as the accrued benefit method
      pro-rated on service or as the benefit/years of service method) sees each period of service
      as giving rise to an additional unit of benefit entitlement (see paragraphs 70–74) and
      measures each unit separately to build up the final obligation (see paragraphs 75–98).

Example illustrating paragraph 68

A lump sum benefit is payable on termination of service and equal to 1 per cent of final salary for each
year of service. The salary in year 1 is CU10,000 and is assumed to increase at 7 per cent (compound)
each year. The discount rate used is 10 per cent per year. The following table shows how the obligation
builds up for an employee who is expected to leave at the end of year 5, assuming that there are no
changes in actuarial assumptions. For simplicity, this example ignores the additional adjustment needed
to reflect the probability that the employee may leave the entity at an earlier or later date.

Year	1	2	3	4	5
	CU	CU	CU	CU	CU
Benefit attributed to:					
– prior years	0	131	262	393	524
– current year (1% of final salary)	131	131	131	131	131
– current and prior years	131	262	393	524	655
Opening obligation	–	89	196	324	476
Interest at 10%	–	9	20	33	48
Current service cost	89	98	108	119	131
Closing obligation	89	196	324	476	655

Note:

1   *The opening obligation is the present value of the benefit attributed to prior years.*

2   *The current service cost is the present value of the benefit attributed to the current year.*

3   *The closing obligation is the present value of the benefit attributed to current and prior years.*

---

69 An entity discounts the whole of a post-employment benefit obligation, even if part of the obligation is expected to be settled before twelve months after the reporting period.

Attributing benefit to periods of service

70 **In determining the present value of its defined benefit obligations and the related current service cost and, where applicable, past service cost, an entity shall attribute benefit to periods of service under the plan's benefit formula. However, if an employee's service in later years will lead to a materially higher level of benefit than in earlier years, an entity shall attribute benefit on a straight-line basis from:**

(a) **the date when service by the employee first leads to benefits under the plan (whether or not the benefits are conditional on further service) until**

(b) **the date when further service by the employee will lead to no material amount of further benefits under the plan, other than from further salary increases.**

71 The projected unit credit method requires an entity to attribute benefit to the current period (in order to determine current service cost) and the current and prior periods (in order to determine the present value of defined benefit obligations). An entity attributes benefit to periods in which the obligation to provide post-employment benefits arises. That obligation arises as employees render services in return for post-employment benefits that an entity expects to pay in future reporting periods. Actuarial techniques allow an entity to measure that obligation with sufficient reliability to justify recognition of a liability.

Examples illustrating paragraph 71

1 A defined benefit plan provides a lump sum benefit of CU100 payable on retirement for each year of service.

A benefit of CU100 is attributed to each year. The current service cost is the present value of CU100. The present value of the defined benefit obligation is the present value of CU100, multiplied by the number of years of service up to the end of the reporting period.

If the benefit is payable immediately when the employee leaves the entity, the current service cost and the present value of the defined benefit obligation reflect the date at which the employee is expected to leave. Thus, because of the effect of discounting, they are less than the amounts that would be determined if the employee left at the end of the reporting period.

2 A plan provides a monthly pension of 0.2 per cent of final salary for each year of service. The pension is payable from the age of 65.

Benefit equal to the present value, at the expected retirement date, of a monthly pension of 0.2 per cent of the estimated final salary payable from the expected retirement date until the expected date of death is attributed to each year of service. The current service cost is the present value of that benefit. The present value of the defined benefit obligation is the present value of monthly pension payments of 0.2 per cent of final salary, multiplied by the number of years of service up to the end of the reporting period. The current service cost and the present value of the defined benefit obligation are discounted because pension payments begin at the age of 65.

---

72 Employee service gives rise to an obligation under a defined benefit plan even if the benefits are conditional on future employment (in other words they are not vested). Employee service before the vesting date gives rise to a constructive obligation because, at the end of each successive reporting period, the amount of future service that an employee will have to render before becoming entitled to the benefit is reduced. In measuring its defined benefit obligation, an entity considers the probability that some employees may not satisfy any vesting requirements. Similarly, although some post-employment benefits, for example, post-employment medical benefits, become payable only if a specified event occurs when an employee is no longer employed, an obligation is created when the employee renders service that will provide entitlement to the benefit if the specified event occurs. The probability that the specified event will occur affects the measurement of the obligation, but does not determine whether the obligation exists.

Examples illustrating paragraph 72

1   A plan pays a benefit of CU100 for each year of service. The benefits vest after ten years of service.

A benefit of CU100 is attributed to each year. In each of the first ten years, the current service cost and the present value of the obligation reflect the probability that the employee may not complete ten years of service.

2   A plan pays a benefit of CU100 for each year of service, excluding service before the age of 25. The benefits vest immediately.

No benefit is attributed to service before the age of 25 because service before that date does not lead to benefits (conditional or unconditional). A benefit of CU100 is attributed to each subsequent year.

---

73   The obligation increases until the date when further service by the employee will lead to no material amount of further benefits. Therefore, all benefit is attributed to periods ending on or before that date. Benefit is attributed to individual accounting periods under the plan's benefit formula. However, if an employee's service in later years will lead to a materially higher level of benefit than in earlier years, an entity attributes benefit on a straight-line basis until the date when further service by the employee will lead to no material amount of further benefits. That is because the employee's service throughout the entire period will ultimately lead to benefit at that higher level.

Examples illustrating paragraph 73

1   A plan pays a lump sum benefit of CU1,000 that vests after ten years of service. The plan provides no further benefit for subsequent service.

A benefit of CU100 (CU1,000 divided by ten) is attributed to each of the first ten years.

The current service cost in each of the first ten years reflects the probability that the employee may not complete ten years of service. No benefit is attributed to subsequent years.

2   A plan pays a lump sum retirement benefit of CU2,000 to all employees who are still employed at the age of 55 after twenty years of service, or who are still employed at the age of 65, regardless of their length of service.

For employees who join before the age of 35, service first leads to benefits under the plan at the age of 35 (an employee could leave at the age of 30 and return at the age of 33, with no effect on the amount or timing of benefits). Those benefits are conditional on further service. Also, service beyond the age of 55 will lead to no material amount of further benefits. For these employees, the entity attributes benefit of CU100 (CU2,000 divided by twenty) to each year from the age of 35 to the age of 55.

For employees who join between the ages of 35 and 45, service beyond twenty years will lead to no material amount of further benefits. For these employees, the entity attributes benefit of CU100 (CU2,000 divided by twenty) to each of the first twenty years.

For an employee who joins at the age of 55, service beyond ten years will lead to no material amount of further benefits. For this employee, the entity attributes benefit of CU200 (CU2,000 divided by ten) to each of the first ten years.

For all employees, the current service cost and the present value of the obligation reflect the probability that the employee may not complete the necessary period of service.

3   A post-employment medical plan reimburses 40 per cent of an employee's post-employment medical costs if the employee leaves after more than ten and less than twenty years of service and 50 per cent of those costs if the employee leaves after twenty or more years of service.

Under the plan's benefit formula, the entity attributes 4 per cent of the present value of the expected medical costs (40 per cent divided by ten) to each of the first ten years and 1 per cent (10 per cent divided by ten) to each of the second ten years. The current service cost in each year reflects the probability that the employee may not complete the necessary period of service to earn part or all of the benefits. For employees expected to leave within ten years, no benefit is attributed.

4   A post-employment medical plan reimburses 10 per cent of an employee's post-employment medical costs if the employee leaves after more than ten and less than twenty years of service and 50 per cent of those costs if the employee leaves after twenty or more years of service.

Service in later years will lead to a materially higher level of benefit than in earlier years. Therefore, for employees expected to leave after twenty or more years, the entity attributes benefit on a straight-line basis under paragraph 71. Service beyond twenty years will lead to no material amount of further benefits. Therefore, the benefit attributed to each of the first twenty years is 2.5 per cent of the present value of the expected medical costs (50 per cent divided by twenty).

continued

AASB

> For employees expected to leave between ten and twenty years, the benefit attributed to each of the first ten years is 1 per cent of the present value of the expected medical costs.
>
> For these employees, no benefit is attributed to service between the end of the tenth year and the estimated date of leaving.
>
> For employees expected to leave within ten years, no benefit is attributed.

74 Where the amount of a benefit is a constant proportion of final salary for each year of service, future salary increases will affect the amount required to settle the obligation that exists for service before the end of the reporting period, but do not create an additional obligation. Therefore:

(a) for the purpose of paragraph 70(b), salary increases do not lead to further benefits, even though the amount of the benefits is dependent on final salary; and

(b) the amount of benefit attributed to each period is a constant proportion of the salary to which the benefit is linked.

> **Example illustrating paragraph 74**
>
> Employees are entitled to a benefit of 3 per cent of final salary for each year of service before the age of 55.
>
> Benefit of 3 per cent of estimated final salary is attributed to each year up to the age of 55. This is the date when further service by the employee will lead to no material amount of further benefits under the plan. No benefit is attributed to service after that age.

Actuarial assumptions

75 Actuarial assumptions shall be unbiased and mutually compatible.

76 Actuarial assumptions are an entity's best estimates of the variables that will determine the ultimate cost of providing post-employment benefits. Actuarial assumptions comprise:

(a) demographic assumptions about the future characteristics of current and former employees (and their dependants) who are eligible for benefits. Demographic assumptions deal with matters such as:

    (i) mortality (see paragraphs 81 and 82);

    (ii) rates of employee turnover, disability and early retirement;

    (iii) the proportion of plan members with dependants who will be eligible for benefits;

    (iv) the proportion of plan members who will select each form of payment option available under the plan terms; and

    (v) claim rates under medical plans.

(b) financial assumptions, dealing with items such as:

    (i) the discount rate (see paragraphs 83–86);

    (ii) benefit levels, excluding any cost of the benefits to be met by employees, and future salary (see paragraphs 87–95);

    (iii) in the case of medical benefits, future medical costs, including claim handling costs (ie the costs that will be incurred in processing and resolving claims, including legal and adjuster's fees) (see paragraphs 96–98); and

    (iv) taxes payable by the plan on contributions relating to service before the reporting date or on benefits resulting from that service.

77 Actuarial assumptions are unbiased if they are neither imprudent nor excessively conservative.

78 Actuarial assumptions are mutually compatible if they reflect the economic relationships between factors such as inflation, rates of salary increase and discount rates. For example, all assumptions that depend on a particular inflation level (such as assumptions about interest rates and salary and benefit increases) in any given future period assume the same inflation level in that period.

79   An entity determines the discount rate and other financial assumptions in nominal (stated) terms, unless estimates in real (inflation-adjusted) terms are more reliable, for example, in a hyperinflationary economy (see AASB 129 *Financial Reporting in Hyperinflationary Economies*), or where the benefit is index-linked and there is a deep market in index-linked bonds of the same currency and term.

80   **Financial assumptions shall be based on market expectations, at the end of the reporting period, for the period over which the obligations are to be settled.**

Actuarial assumptions: mortality

81   **An entity shall determine its mortality assumptions by reference to its best estimate of the mortality of plan members both during and after employment.**

82   In order to estimate the ultimate cost of the benefit an entity takes into consideration expected changes in mortality, for example by modifying standard mortality tables with estimates of mortality improvements.

Actuarial assumptions: discount rate

83   **The rate used to discount post-employment benefit obligations (both funded and unfunded) shall be determined by reference to market yields at the end of the reporting period on high quality corporate bonds. In countries where there is no deep market in such bonds, the market yields (at the end of the reporting period) on government bonds shall be used. The currency and term of the corporate bonds or government bonds shall be consistent with the currency and estimated term of the post-employment benefit obligations.**

Aus83.1   **Notwithstanding paragraph 83, in respect of not-for-profit public sector entities, post employment benefit obligations denominated in Australian currency shall be discounted using market yields on government bonds.**

84   One actuarial assumption that has a material effect is the discount rate. The discount rate reflects the time value of money but not the actuarial or investment risk. Furthermore, the discount rate does not reflect the entity-specific credit risk borne by the entity's creditors, nor does it reflect the risk that future experience may differ from actuarial assumptions.

85   The discount rate reflects the estimated timing of benefit payments. In practice, an entity often achieves this by applying a single weighted average discount rate that reflects the estimated timing and amount of benefit payments and the currency in which the benefits are to be paid.

86   In some cases, there may be no deep market in bonds with a sufficiently long maturity to match the estimated maturity of all the benefit payments. In such cases, an entity uses current market rates of the appropriate term to discount shorter-term payments, and estimates the discount rate for longer maturities by extrapolating current market rates along the yield curve. The total present value of a defined benefit obligation is unlikely to be particularly sensitive to the discount rate applied to the portion of benefits that is payable beyond the final maturity of the available corporate or government bonds.

Actuarial assumptions: salaries, benefits and medical costs

87   **An entity shall measure its defined benefit obligations on a basis that reflects:**

   (a)   **the benefits set out in the terms of the plan (or resulting from any constructive obligation that goes beyond those terms) at the end of the reporting period;**

   (b)   **any estimated future salary increases that affect the benefits payable;**

   (c)   **the effect of any limit on the employer's share of the cost of the future benefits;**

   (d)   **contributions from employees or third parties that reduce the ultimate cost to the entity of those benefits; and**

AASB

    (e)   estimated future changes in the level of any state benefits that affect the benefits payable under a defined benefit plan, if, and only if, either:

        (i)   those changes were enacted before the end of the reporting period; or

        (ii)   historical data, or other reliable evidence, indicate that those state benefits will change in some predictable manner, for example, in line with future changes in general price levels or general salary levels.

88   Actuarial assumptions reflect future benefit changes that are set out in the formal terms of a plan (or a constructive obligation that goes beyond those terms) at the end of the reporting period. This is the case if, for example:

    (a)   the entity has a history of increasing benefits, for example, to mitigate the effects of inflation, and there is no indication that this practice will change in the future;

    (b)   the entity is obliged, by either the formal terms of a plan (or a constructive obligation that goes beyond those terms) or legislation, to use any surplus in the plan for the benefit of plan participants (see paragraph 108(c)); or

    (c)   benefits vary in response to a performance target or other criteria. For example, the terms of the plan may state that it will pay reduced benefits or require additional contributions from employees if the plan assets are insufficient. The measurement of the obligation reflects the best estimate of the effect of the performance target or other criteria.

89   Actuarial assumptions do not reflect future benefit changes that are not set out in the formal terms of the plan (or a constructive obligation) at the end of the reporting period. Such changes will result in:

    (a)   past service cost, to the extent that they change benefits for service before the change; and

    (b)   current service cost for periods after the change, to the extent that they change benefits for service after the change.

90   Estimates of future salary increases take account of inflation, seniority, promotion and other relevant factors, such as supply and demand in the employment market.

91   Some defined benefit plans limit the contributions that an entity is required to pay. The ultimate cost of the benefits takes account of the effect of a limit on contributions. The effect of a limit on contributions is determined over the shorter of:

    (a)   the estimated life of the entity; and

    (b)   the estimated life of the plan.

92   Some defined benefit plans require employees or third parties to contribute to the cost of the plan. Contributions by employees reduce the cost of the benefits to the entity. An entity considers whether third-party contributions reduce the cost of the benefits to the entity, or are a reimbursement right as described in paragraph 116. Contributions by employees or third parties are either set out in the formal terms of the plan (or arise from a constructive obligation that goes beyond those terms), or are discretionary. Discretionary contributions by employees or third parties reduce service cost upon payment of these contributions to the plan.

93   Contributions from employees or third parties set out in the formal terms of the plan either reduce service cost (if they are linked to service), or reduce remeasurements of the net defined benefit liability (asset) (eg if the contributions are required to reduce a deficit arising from losses on plan assets or actuarial losses). Contributions from employees or third parties in respect of service are attributed to periods of service as a negative benefit in accordance with paragraph 70 (ie the net benefit is attributed in accordance with that paragraph).

94   Changes in employee or third-party contributions in respect of service result in:

    (a)   current and past service cost (if changes in employee contributions are not set out in the formal terms of a plan and do not arise from a constructive obligation); or

    (b)   actuarial gains and losses (if changes in employee contributions are set out in the formal terms of a plan, or arise from a constructive obligation).

95   Some post-employment benefits are linked to variables such as the level of state retirement benefits or state medical care. The measurement of such benefits reflects the best estimate of such variables, based on historical data and other reliable evidence.

96   **Assumptions about medical costs shall take account of estimated future changes in the cost of medical services, resulting from both inflation and specific changes in medical costs.**

97   Measurement of post-employment medical benefits requires assumptions about the level and frequency of future claims and the cost of meeting those claims. An entity estimates future medical costs on the basis of historical data about the entity's own experience, supplemented where necessary by historical data from other entities, insurance companies, medical providers or other sources. Estimates of future medical costs consider the effect of technological advances, changes in health care utilisation or delivery patterns and changes in the health status of plan participants.

98   The level and frequency of claims is particularly sensitive to the age, health status and sex of employees (and their dependants) and may be sensitive to other factors such as geographical location. Therefore, historical data are adjusted to the extent that the demographic mix of the population differs from that of the population used as a basis for the data. They are also adjusted where there is reliable evidence that historical trends will not continue.

Past service cost and gains and losses on settlement

99   **Before determining past service cost, or a gain or loss on settlement, an entity shall remeasure the net defined benefit liability (asset) using the current fair value of plan assets and current actuarial assumptions (including current market interest rates and other current market prices) reflecting the benefits offered under the plan before the plan amendment, curtailment or settlement.**

100   An entity need not distinguish between past service cost resulting from a plan amendment, past service cost resulting from a curtailment and a gain or loss on settlement if these transactions occur together. In some cases, a plan amendment occurs before a settlement, such as when an entity changes the benefits under the plan and settles the amended benefits later. In those cases an entity recognises past service cost before any gain or loss on settlement.

101   A settlement occurs together with a plan amendment and curtailment if a plan is terminated with the result that the obligation is settled and the plan ceases to exist. However, the termination of a plan is not a settlement if the plan is replaced by a new plan that offers benefits that are, in substance, the same.

Past service cost

102   Past service cost is the change in the present value of the defined benefit obligation resulting from a plan amendment or curtailment.

103   **An entity shall recognise past service cost as an expense at the earlier of the following dates:**

      (a)   when the plan amendment or curtailment occurs; and

      (b)   when the entity recognises related restructuring costs (see AASB 137) or termination benefits (see paragraph 165).

104   A plan amendment occurs when an entity introduces, or withdraws, a defined benefit plan or changes the benefits payable under an existing defined benefit plan.

105   A curtailment occurs when an entity significantly reduces the number of employees covered by a plan. A curtailment may arise from an isolated event, such as the closing of a plant, discontinuance of an operation or termination or suspension of a plan.

106   Past service cost may be either positive (when benefits are introduced or changed so that the present value of the defined benefit obligation increases) or negative (when benefits are withdrawn or changed so that the present value of the defined benefit obligation decreases).

107 Where an entity reduces benefits payable under an existing defined benefit plan and, at the same time, increases other benefits payable under the plan for the same employees, the entity treats the change as a single net change.

108 Past service cost excludes:

(a) the effect of differences between actual and previously assumed salary increases on the obligation to pay benefits for service in prior years (there is no past service cost because actuarial assumptions allow for projected salaries);

(b) underestimates and overestimates of discretionary pension increases when an entity has a constructive obligation to grant such increases (there is no past service cost because actuarial assumptions allow for such increases);

(c) estimates of benefit improvements that result from actuarial gains or from the return on plan assets that have been recognised in the financial statements if the entity is obliged, by either the formal terms of a plan (or a constructive obligation that goes beyond those terms) or legislation, to use any surplus in the plan for the benefit of plan participants, even if the benefit increase has not yet been formally awarded (there is no past service cost because the resulting increase in the obligation is an actuarial loss, see paragraph 88); and

(d) the increase in vested benefits (ie benefits that are not conditional on future employment, see paragraph 72) when, in the absence of new or improved benefits, employees complete vesting requirements (there is no past service cost because the entity recognised the estimated cost of benefits as current service cost as the service was rendered).

Gains and losses on settlement

109 The gain or loss on a settlement is the difference between:

(a) the present value of the defined benefit obligation being settled, as determined on the date of settlement; and

(b) the settlement price, including any plan assets transferred and any payments made directly by the entity in connection with the settlement.

110 An entity shall recognise a gain or loss on the settlement of a defined benefit plan when the settlement occurs.

111 A settlement occurs when an entity enters into a transaction that eliminates all further legal or constructive obligation for part or all of the benefits provided under a defined benefit plan (other than a payment of benefits to, or on behalf of, employees in accordance with the terms of the plan and included in the actuarial assumptions). For example, a one-off transfer of significant employer obligations under the plan to an insurance company through the purchase of an insurance policy is a settlement; a lump sum cash payment, under the terms of the plan, to plan participants in exchange for their rights to receive specified post-employment benefits is not.

112 In some cases, an entity acquires an insurance policy to fund some or all of the employee benefits relating to employee service in the current and prior periods. The acquisition of such a policy is not a settlement if the entity retains a legal or constructive obligation (see paragraph 46) to pay further amounts if the insurer does not pay the employee benefits specified in the insurance policy. Paragraphs 116–119 deal with the recognition and measurement of reimbursement rights under insurance policies that are not plan assets.

Recognition and measurement: plan assets

Fair value of plan assets

113 The fair value of any plan assets is deducted from the present value of the defined benefit obligation in determining the deficit or surplus. When no market price is available, the fair value of plan assets is estimated, for example, by discounting expected future cash flows using a discount rate that reflects both the risk associated with the plan assets and the maturity or expected disposal date of those assets (or, if they have no maturity, the expected period until the settlement of the related obligation).

114   Plan assets exclude unpaid contributions due from the reporting entity to the fund, as well as any non-transferable financial instruments issued by the entity and held by the fund. Plan assets are reduced by any liabilities of the fund that do not relate to employee benefits, for example, trade and other payables and liabilities resulting from derivative financial instruments.

115   Where plan assets include qualifying insurance policies that exactly match the amount and timing of some or all of the benefits payable under the plan, the fair value of those insurance policies is deemed to be the present value of the related obligations (subject to any reduction required if the amounts receivable under the insurance policies are not recoverable in full).

Reimbursements

116   **When, and only when, it is virtually certain that another party will reimburse some or all of the expenditure required to settle a defined benefit obligation, an entity shall:**

    (a)   **recognise its right to reimbursement as a separate asset. The entity shall measure the asset at fair value.**

    (b)   **disaggregate and recognise changes in the fair value of its right to reimbursement in the same way as for changes in the fair value of plan assets (see paragraphs 124 and 125). The components of defined benefit cost recognised in accordance with paragraph 120 may be recognised net of amounts relating to changes in the carrying amount of the right to reimbursement.**

117   Sometimes, an entity is able to look to another party, such as an insurer, to pay part or all of the expenditure required to settle a defined benefit obligation. Qualifying insurance policies, as defined in paragraph 8, are plan assets. An entity accounts for qualifying insurance policies in the same way as for all other plan assets and paragraph 116 is not relevant (see paragraphs 46–49 and 115).

118   When an insurance policy held by an entity is not a qualifying insurance policy, that insurance policy is not a plan asset. Paragraph 116 is relevant to such cases: the entity recognises its right to reimbursement under the insurance policy as a separate asset, rather than as a deduction in determining the defined benefit deficit or surplus. Paragraph 140(b) requires the entity to disclose a brief description of the link between the reimbursement right and the related obligation.

119   If the right to reimbursement arises under an insurance policy that exactly matches the amount and timing of some or all of the benefits payable under a defined benefit plan, the fair value of the reimbursement right is deemed to be the present value of the related obligation (subject to any reduction required if the reimbursement is not recoverable in full).

Components of defined benefit cost

120   **An entity shall recognise the components of defined benefit cost, except to the extent that another Australian Accounting Standard requires or permits their inclusion in the cost of an asset, as follows:**

    (a)   **service cost (see paragraphs 66–112) in profit or loss;**

    (b)   **net interest on the net defined benefit liability (asset) (see paragraphs 123–126) in profit or loss; and**

    (c)   **remeasurements of the net defined benefit liability (asset) (see paragraphs 127–130) in other comprehensive income.**

121   Other Australian Accounting Standards require the inclusion of some employee benefit costs within the cost of assets, such as inventories and property, plant and equipment (see AASB 102 and AASB 116). Any post-employment benefit costs included in the cost of such assets include the appropriate proportion of the components listed in paragraph 120.

122   **Remeasurements of the net defined benefit liability (asset) recognised in other comprehensive income shall not be reclassified to profit or loss in a subsequent period.**

However, the entity may transfer those amounts recognised in other comprehensive income within equity.

Net interest on the net defined benefit liability (asset)

123   **Net interest on the net defined benefit liability (asset) shall be determined by multiplying the net defined benefit liability (asset) by the discount rate specified in paragraph 83, both as determined at the start of the annual reporting period, taking account of any changes in the net defined benefit liability (asset) during the period as a result of contribution and benefit payments.**

124   Net interest on the net defined benefit liability (asset) can be viewed as comprising interest income on plan assets, interest cost on the defined benefit obligation and interest on the effect of the asset ceiling mentioned in paragraph 64.

125   Interest income on plan assets is a component of the return on plan assets, and is determined by multiplying the fair value of the plan assets by the discount rate specified in paragraph 83, both as determined at the start of the annual reporting period, taking account of any changes in the plan assets held during the period as a result of contributions and benefit payments. The difference between the interest income on plan assets and the return on plan assets is included in the remeasurement of the net defined benefit liability (asset).

126   Interest on the effect of the asset ceiling is part of the total change in the effect of the asset ceiling, and is determined by multiplying the effect of the asset ceiling by the discount rate specified in paragraph 83, both as determined at the start of the annual reporting period. The difference between that amount and the total change in the effect of the asset ceiling is included in the remeasurement of the net defined benefit liability (asset).

Remeasurements of the net defined benefit liability (asset)

127   Remeasurements of the net defined benefit liability (asset) comprise:

(a)   actuarial gains and losses (see paragraphs 128 and 129);

(b)   the return on plan assets (see paragraph 130), excluding amounts included in net interest on the net defined benefit liability (asset) (see paragraph 125); and

(c)   any change in the effect of the asset ceiling, excluding amounts included in net interest on the net defined benefit liability (asset) (see paragraph 126).

128   Actuarial gains and losses result from increases or decreases in the present value of the defined benefit obligation because of changes in actuarial assumptions and experience adjustments. Causes of actuarial gains and losses include, for example:

(a)   unexpectedly high or low rates of employee turnover, early retirement or mortality or of increases in salaries, benefits (if the formal or constructive terms of a plan provide for inflationary benefit increases) or medical costs;

(b)   the effect of changes to assumptions concerning benefit payment options;

(c)   the effect of changes in estimates of future employee turnover, early retirement or mortality or of increases in salaries, benefits (if the formal or constructive terms of a plan provide for inflationary benefit increases) or medical costs; and

(d)   the effect of changes in the discount rate.

129   Actuarial gains and losses do not include changes in the present value of the defined benefit obligation because of the introduction, amendment, curtailment or settlement of the defined benefit plan, or changes to the benefits payable under the defined benefit plan. Such changes result in past service cost or gains or losses on settlement.

130   In determining the return on plan assets, an entity deducts the costs of managing the plan assets and any tax payable by the plan itself, other than tax included in the actuarial assumptions used to measure the defined benefit obligation (paragraph 76). Other administration costs are not deducted from the return on plan assets.

Presentation

Offset

131   An entity shall offset an asset relating to one plan against a liability relating to another plan when, and only when, the entity:

    (a)   has a legally enforceable right to use a surplus in one plan to settle obligations under the other plan; and

    (b)   intends either to settle the obligations on a net basis, or to realise the surplus in one plan and settle its obligation under the other plan simultaneously.

132   The offsetting criteria are similar to those established for financial instruments in AASB 132 *Financial Instruments: Presentation*.

Current/non-current distinction

133   Some entities distinguish current assets and liabilities from non-current assets and liabilities. This Standard does not specify whether an entity should distinguish current and non-current portions of assets and liabilities arising from post-employment benefits.

Components of defined benefit cost

134   Paragraph 120 requires an entity to recognise service cost and net interest on the net defined benefit liability (asset) in profit or loss. This Standard does not specify how an entity should present service cost and net interest on the net defined benefit liability (asset). An entity presents those components in accordance with AASB 101.

Disclosure

135   An entity shall disclose information that:

    (a)   explains the characteristics of its defined benefit plans and risks associated with them (see paragraph 139);

    (b)   identifies and explains the amounts in its financial statements arising from its defined benefit plans (see paragraphs 140–144); and

    (c)   describes how its defined benefit plans may affect the amount, timing and uncertainty of the entity's future cash flows (see paragraphs 145–147).

136   To meet the objectives in paragraph 135, an entity shall consider all the following:

    (a)   the level of detail necessary to satisfy the disclosure requirements;

    (b)   how much emphasis to place on each of the various requirements;

    (c)   how much aggregation or disaggregation to undertake; and

    (d)   whether users of financial statements need additional information to evaluate the quantitative information disclosed.

137   If the disclosures provided in accordance with the requirements in this Standard and other Australian Accounting Standards are insufficient to meet the objectives in paragraph 135, an entity shall disclose additional information necessary to meet those objectives. For example, an entity may present an analysis of the present value of the defined benefit obligation that distinguishes the nature, characteristics and risks of the obligation. Such a disclosure could distinguish:

    (a)   between amounts owing to active members, deferred members, and pensioners.

    (b)   between vested benefits and accrued but not vested benefits.

    (c)   between conditional benefits, amounts attributable to future salary increases and other benefits.

138   An entity shall assess whether all or some disclosures should be disaggregated to distinguish plans or groups of plans with materially different risks. For example, an entity may disaggregate disclosure about plans showing one or more of the following features:

    (a)   different geographical locations.

    (b)   different characteristics such as flat salary pension plans, final salary pension plans or post-employment medical plans.

AASB 119   Institute of Chartered Accountants Australia
Applicable to periods beginning from 1 January 2013

AASB

    (c)   different regulatory environments.

    (d)   different reporting segments.

    (e)   different funding arrangements (eg wholly unfunded, wholly or partly funded).

Characteristics of defined benefit plans and risks associated with them

139   An entity shall disclose:

    (a)   information about the characteristics of its defined benefit plans, including:

        (i)   the nature of the benefits provided by the plan (eg final salary defined benefit plan or contribution-based plan with guarantee).

        (ii)   a description of the regulatory framework in which the plan operates, for example the level of any minimum funding requirements, and any effect of the regulatory framework on the plan, such as the asset ceiling (see paragraph 64).

        (iii)   a description of any other entity's responsibilities for the governance of the plan, for example responsibilities of trustees or of board members of the plan.

    (b)   a description of the risks to which the plan exposes the entity, focused on any unusual, entity-specific or plan-specific risks, and of any significant concentrations of risk. For example, if plan assets are invested primarily in one class of investments, eg property, the plan may expose the entity to a concentration of property market risk.

    (c)   a description of any plan amendments, curtailments and settlements.

Explanation of amounts in the financial statements

140   An entity shall provide a reconciliation from the opening balance to the closing balance for each of the following, if applicable:

    (a)   the net defined benefit liability (asset), showing separate reconciliations for:

        (i)   plan assets.

        (ii)   the present value of the defined benefit obligation.

        (iii)   the effect of the asset ceiling.

    (b)   any reimbursement rights. An entity shall also describe the relationship between any reimbursement right and the related obligation.

141   Each reconciliation listed in paragraph 140 shall show each of the following, if applicable:

    (a)   current service cost.

    (b)   interest income or expense.

    (c)   remeasurements of the net defined benefit liability (asset), showing separately:

        (i)   the return on plan assets, excluding amounts included in interest in (b).

        (ii)   actuarial gains and losses arising from changes in demographic assumptions (see paragraph 76(a)).

        (iii)   actuarial gains and losses arising from changes in financial assumptions (see paragraph 76(b)).

        (iv)   changes in the effect of limiting a net defined benefit asset to the asset ceiling, excluding amounts included in interest in (b). An entity shall also disclose how it determined the maximum economic benefit available, ie whether those benefits would be in the form of refunds, reductions in future contributions or a combination of both.

    (d)   past service cost and gains and losses arising from settlements. As permitted by paragraph 100, past service cost and gains and losses arising from settlements need not be distinguished if they occur together.

    (e)   the effect of changes in foreign exchange rates.

(f)   contributions to the plan, showing separately those by the employer and by plan participants.

(g)   payments from the plan, showing separately the amount paid in respect of any settlements.

(h)   the effects of business combinations and disposals.

142   An entity shall disaggregate the fair value of the plan assets into classes that distinguish the nature and risks of those assets, subdividing each class of plan asset into those that have a quoted market price in an active market (as defined in AASB 13 *Fair Value Measurement*[3]) and those that do not. For example, and considering the level of disclosure discussed in paragraph 136, an entity could distinguish between:

(a)   cash and cash equivalents;

(b)   equity instruments (segregated by industry type, company size, geography etc);

(c)   debt instruments (segregated by type of issuer, credit quality, geography etc);

(d)   real estate (segregated by geography etc);

(e)   derivatives (segregated by type of underlying risk in the contract, for example, interest rate contracts, foreign exchange contracts, equity contracts, credit contracts, longevity swaps etc);

(f)   investment funds (segregated by type of fund);

(g)   asset-backed securities; and

(h)   structured debt.

143   An entity shall disclose the fair value of the entity's own transferable financial instruments held as plan assets, and the fair value of plan assets that are property occupied by, or other assets used by, the entity.

144   An entity shall disclose the significant actuarial assumptions used to determine the present value of the defined benefit obligation (see paragraph 76). Such disclosure shall be in absolute terms (eg as an absolute percentage, and not just as a margin between different percentages and other variables). When an entity provides disclosures in total for a grouping of plans, it shall provide such disclosures in the form of weighted averages or relatively narrow ranges.

Amount, timing and uncertainty of future cash flows

145   An entity shall disclose:

(a)   a sensitivity analysis for each significant actuarial assumption (as disclosed under paragraph 144) as of the end of the reporting period, showing how the defined benefit obligation would have been affected by changes in the relevant actuarial assumption that were reasonably possible at that date.

(b)   the methods and assumptions used in preparing the sensitivity analyses required by (a) and the limitations of those methods.

(c)   changes from the previous period in the methods and assumptions used in preparing the sensitivity analyses, and the reasons for such changes.

146   An entity shall disclose a description of any asset-liability matching strategies used by the plan or the entity, including the use of annuities and other techniques, such as longevity swaps, to manage risk.

147   To provide an indication of the effect of the defined benefit plan on the entity's future cash flows, an entity shall disclose:

(a)   a description of any funding arrangements and funding policy that affect future contributions.

(b)   the expected contributions to the plan for the next annual reporting period.

---

3   If an entity has not yet applied AASB 13, it may refer to paragraph AG71 of AASB 139 *Financial Instruments: Recognition and Measurement*, or paragraph B.5.4.3 of AASB 9 *Financial Instruments* (December 2010), if applicable.

AASB

    (c)   information about the maturity profile of the defined benefit obligation. This will include the weighted average duration of the defined benefit obligation and may include other information about the distribution of the timing of benefit payments, such as a maturity analysis of the benefit payments.

Multi-employer plans

148   If an entity participates in a multi-employer defined benefit plan, it shall disclose:

    (a)   a description of the funding arrangements, including the method used to determine the entity's rate of contributions and any minimum funding requirements.

    (b)   a description of the extent to which the entity can be liable to the plan for other entities' obligations under the terms and conditions of the multi-employer plan.

    (c)   a description of any agreed allocation of a deficit or surplus on:

        (i)   wind-up of the plan; or

        (ii)   the entity's withdrawal from the plan.

    (d)   if the entity accounts for that plan as if it were a defined contribution plan in accordance with paragraph 34, it shall disclose the following, in addition to the information required by (a)–(c) and instead of the information required by paragraphs 139–147:

        (i)   the fact that the plan is a defined benefit plan.

        (ii)   the reason why sufficient information is not available to enable the entity to account for the plan as a defined benefit plan.

        (iii)   the expected contributions to the plan for the next annual reporting period.

        (iv)   information about any deficit or surplus in the plan that may affect the amount of future contributions, including the basis used to determine that deficit or surplus and the implications, if any, for the entity.

        (v)   an indication of the level of participation of the entity in the plan compared with other participating entities. Examples of measures that might provide such an indication include the entity's proportion of the total contributions to the plan or the entity's proportion of the total number of active members, retired members, and former members entitled to benefits, if that information is available.

Defined benefit plans that share risks between entities under common control

149   If an entity participates in a defined benefit plan that shares risks between entities under common control, it shall disclose:

    (a)   the contractual agreement or stated policy for charging the net defined benefit cost or the fact that there is no such policy.

    (b)   the policy for determining the contribution to be paid by the entity.

    (c)   if the entity accounts for an allocation of the net defined benefit cost as noted in paragraph 41, all the information about the plan as a whole required by paragraphs 135–147.

    (d)   if the entity accounts for the contribution payable for the period as noted in paragraph 41, the information about the plan as a whole required by paragraphs 135–137, 139, 142–144 and 147(a) and (b).

150   The information required by paragraph 149(c) and (d) can be disclosed by cross-reference to disclosures in another group entity's financial statements if:

    (a)   that group entity's financial statements separately identify and disclose the information required about the plan; and

    (b)   that group entity's financial statements are available to users of the financial statements on the same terms as the financial statements of the entity and at the same time as, or earlier than, the financial statements of the entity.

Disclosure requirements in other Australian Accounting Standards

151   Where required by AASB 124 an entity discloses information about:

     (a)   related party transactions with post-employment benefit plans; and

     (b)   post-employment benefits for key management personnel.

152   Where required by AASB 137 an entity discloses information about contingent liabilities arising from post-employment benefit obligations.

Other long-term employee benefits

153   Other long-term employee benefits include items such as the following, if not expected to be settled wholly before twelve months after the end of the annual reporting period in which the employees render the related service:

     (a)   long-term paid absences such as long-service or sabbatical leave;

     (b)   jubilee or other long-service benefits;

     (c)   long-term disability benefits;

     (d)   profit-sharing and bonuses; and

     (e)   deferred remuneration.

154   The measurement of other long-term employee benefits is not usually subject to the same degree of uncertainty as the measurement of post-employment benefits. For this reason, this Standard requires a simplified method of accounting for other long-term employee benefits. Unlike the accounting required for post-employment benefits, this method does not recognise remeasurements in other comprehensive income.

Recognition and measurement

155   In recognising and measuring the surplus or deficit in an other long-term employee benefit plan, an entity shall apply paragraphs 56–98 and 113–115. An entity shall apply paragraphs 116–119 in recognising and measuring any reimbursement right.

156   For other long-term employee benefits, an entity shall recognise the net total of the following amounts in profit or loss, except to the extent that another Australian Accounting Standard requires or permits their inclusion in the cost of an asset:

     (a)   service cost (see paragraphs 66–112);

     (b)   net interest on the net defined benefit liability (asset) (see paragraphs 123–126); and

     (c)   remeasurements of the net defined benefit liability (asset) (see paragraphs 127–130).

157   One form of other long-term employee benefit is long-term disability benefit. If the level of benefit depends on the length of service, an obligation arises when the service is rendered. Measurement of that obligation reflects the probability that payment will be required and the length of time for which payment is expected to be made. If the level of benefit is the same for any disabled employee regardless of years of service, the expected cost of those benefits is recognised when an event occurs that causes a long-term disability.

Disclosure

158   Although this Standard does not require specific disclosures about other long-term employee benefits, other Australian Accounting Standards may require disclosures. For example, AASB 124 requires disclosures about employee benefits for key management personnel. AASB 101 requires disclosure of employee benefits expense.

Termination benefits

159   This Standard deals with termination benefits separately from other employee benefits because the event that gives rise to an obligation is the termination of employment rather than employee service. Termination benefits result from either an entity's decision to terminate the employment or an employee's decision to accept an entity's offer of benefits in exchange for termination of employment.

160 Termination benefits do not include employee benefits resulting from termination of employment at the request of the employee without an entity's offer, or as a result of mandatory retirement requirements, because those benefits are post-employment benefits. Some entities provide a lower level of benefit for termination of employment at the request of the employee (in substance, a post-employment benefit) than for termination of employment at the request of the entity. The difference between the benefit provided for termination of employment at the request of the employee and a higher benefit provided at the request of the entity is a termination benefit.

161 The form of the employee benefit does not determine whether it is provided in exchange for service or in exchange for termination of the employee's employment. Termination benefits are typically lump sum payments, but sometimes also include:

(a) enhancement of post-employment benefits, either indirectly through an employee benefit plan or directly.

(b) salary until the end of a specified notice period if the employee renders no further service that provides economic benefits to the entity.

162 Indicators that an employee benefit is provided in exchange for services include the following:

(a) the benefit is conditional on future service being provided (including benefits that increase if further service is provided).

(b) the benefit is provided in accordance with the terms of an employee benefit plan.

163 Some termination benefits are provided in accordance with the terms of an existing employee benefit plan. For example, they may be specified by statute, employment contract or union agreement, or may be implied as a result of the employer's past practice of providing similar benefits. As another example, if an entity makes an offer of benefits available for more than a short period, or there is more than a short period between the offer and the expected date of actual termination, the entity considers whether it has established a new employee benefit plan and hence whether the benefits offered under that plan are termination benefits or post-employment benefits. Employee benefits provided in accordance with the terms of an employee benefit plan are termination benefits if they both result from an entity's decision to terminate an employee's employment and are not conditional on future service being provided.

164 Some employee benefits are provided regardless of the reason for the employee's departure. The payment of such benefits is certain (subject to any vesting or minimum service requirements) but the timing of their payment is uncertain. Although such benefits are described in some jurisdictions as termination indemnities or termination gratuities, they are post-employment benefits rather than termination benefits, and an entity accounts for them as post-employment benefits.

Recognition

165 An entity shall recognise a liability and expense for termination benefits at the earlier of the following dates:

(a) when the entity can no longer withdraw the offer of those benefits; and

(b) when the entity recognises costs for a restructuring that is within the scope of AASB 137 and involves the payment of termination benefits.

166 For termination benefits payable as a result of an employee's decision to accept an offer of benefits in exchange for the termination of employment, the time when an entity can no longer withdraw the offer of termination benefits is the earlier of:

(a) when the employee accepts the offer; and

(b) when a restriction (eg a legal, regulatory or contractual requirement or other restriction) on the entity's ability to withdraw the offer takes effect. This would be when the offer is made, if the restriction existed at the time of the offer.

167   For termination benefits payable as a result of an entity's decision to terminate an employee's employment, the entity can no longer withdraw the offer when the entity has communicated to the affected employees a plan of termination meeting all of the following criteria:

(a)   Actions required to complete the plan indicate that it is unlikely that significant changes to the plan will be made.

(b)   The plan identifies the number of employees whose employment is to be terminated, their job classifications or functions and their locations (but the plan need not identify each individual employee) and the expected completion date.

(c)   The plan establishes the termination benefits that employees will receive in sufficient detail that employees can determine the type and amount of benefits they will receive when their employment is terminated.

168   When an entity recognises termination benefits, the entity may also have to account for a plan amendment or a curtailment of other employee benefits (see paragraph 103).

Measurement

169   **An entity shall measure termination benefits on initial recognition, and shall measure and recognise subsequent changes, in accordance with the nature of the employee benefit, provided that if the termination benefits are an enhancement to post-employment benefits, the entity shall apply the requirements for post-employment benefits. Otherwise:**

(a)   **if the termination benefits are expected to be settled wholly before twelve months after the end of the annual reporting period in which the termination benefit is recognised, the entity shall apply the requirements for short-term employee benefits.**

(b)   **if the termination benefits are not expected to be settled wholly before twelve months after the end of the annual reporting period, the entity shall apply the requirements for other long-term employee benefits.**

170   Because termination benefits are not provided in exchange for service, paragraphs 70–74 relating to the attribution of the benefit to periods of service are not relevant.

Example illustrating paragraphs 159–170

Background

As a result of a recent acquisition, an entity plans to close a factory in ten months and, at that time, terminate the employment of all of the remaining employees at the factory. Because the entity needs the expertise of the employees at the factory to complete some contracts, it announces a plan of termination as follows.

Each employee who stays and renders service until the closure of the factory will receive on the termination date a cash payment of CU30,000. Employees leaving before closure of the factory will receive CU10,000.

There are 120 employees at the factory. At the time of announcing the plan, the entity expects 20 of them to leave before closure. Therefore, the total expected cash outflows under the plan are CU3,200,000 (ie 20 × CU10,000 + 100 × CU30,000). As required by paragraph 160, the entity accounts for benefits provided in exchange for termination of employment as termination benefits and accounts for benefits provided in exchange for services as short-term employee benefits.

Termination benefits

The benefit provided in exchange for termination of employment is CU10,000. This is the amount that an entity would have to pay for terminating the employment regardless of whether the employees stay and render service until closure of the factory or they leave before closure. Even though the employees can leave before closure, the termination of all employees' employment is a result of the entity's decision to close the factory and terminate their employment (ie all employees will leave employment when the factory closes). Therefore the entity recognises a liability of CU1,200,000 (ie 120 × CU10,000) for the termination benefits provided in accordance with the employee benefit plan at the earlier of when the plan of termination is announced and when the entity recognises the restructuring costs associated with the closure of the factory.

continued

AASB 119
Applicable to periods beginning from 1 January 2013
     Institute of Chartered Accountants Australia

> *Benefits provided in exchange for service*
>
> The incremental benefits that employees will receive if they provide services for the full ten-month period are in exchange for services provided over that period. The entity accounts for them as short-term employee benefits because the entity expects to settle them before twelve months after the end of the annual reporting period. In this example, discounting is not required, so an expense of CU200,000 (ie CU2,000,000 ÷ 10) is recognised in each month during the service period of ten months, with a corresponding increase in the carrying amount of the liability.

Disclosure

171 Although this Standard does not require specific disclosures about termination benefits, other Australian Accounting Standards may require disclosures. For example, AASB 124 requires disclosures about employee benefits for key management personnel. AASB 101 requires disclosure of employee benefits expense.

Transition and effective date

172 [Deleted by the AASB – see paragraphs Aus1.2 and Aus1.3]

173 An entity shall apply this Standard retrospectively, in accordance with AASB 108 *Accounting Policies, Changes in Accounting Estimates and Errors*, except that:

(a) an entity need not adjust the carrying amount of assets outside the scope of this Standard for changes in employee benefit costs that were included in the carrying amount before the date of initial application. The date of initial application is the beginning of the earliest prior period presented in the first financial statements in which the entity adopts this Standard.

(b) in financial statements for periods beginning before 1 January 2014, an entity need not present comparative information for the disclosures required by paragraph 145 about the sensitivity of the defined benefit obligation.

Deleted IAS 19 Text

Deleted IAS 19 text is not part of AASB 119.

Paragraph 172

An entity shall apply this Standard for annual periods beginning on or after 1 January 2013. Earlier application is permitted. If an entity applies this Standard for an earlier period, it shall disclose that fact.

AASB 120
Accounting for Government Grants and Disclosure of Government Assistance

(Compiled June 2012)

Note from the Institute of Chartered Accountants Australia

This note, prepared by the technical editors, is not part of Accounting Standard AASB 120.

Historical development

July 2004: AASB 120 'Accounting for Government Grants and Disclosure of Government Assistance' is the Australian equivalent of IAS 20 of the same name. It was made by the AASB on 15 July 2004 as part of the AASB's program to adopt International Financial Reporting Standards by 2005.

15 February 2007: AASB 2007-2 'Amendments to Australian Accounting Standards' amends paragraph 3 and is applicable to annual reporting periods ending on or after 28 February 2007, with early adoption permitted for annual reporting periods beginning on or after 1 January 2005.

30 April 2007: AASB 2007-4 'Amendments to Australian Accounting Standards' amends paragraphs 23, 24, 26, 28, 29, 31 and 36 and adds paragraphs 25, 27, and 30. It is applicable to annual reporting periods beginning on or after 1 July 2007, with early adoption permitted for annual reporting periods beginning on or after 1 January 2005.

24 September 2007: AASB 2007-8 'Amendments to Australian Accounting Standards arising from AASB 101' amends AASB 120 to align with revised AASB 101. This Standard is applicable to annual reporting periods beginning on or after 1 January 2009.

13 December 2007: AASB 2007-10 'Further Amendments to Australian Accounting Standards arising from AASB 101' amends AASB 120, primarily replacing the term 'financial report' with 'financial statements'. This Standard is applicable to annual reporting periods beginning on or after 1 January 2009.

24 July 2008: AASB 2008-5 'Amendments to Australian Accounting Standards arising from the Annual Improvements Project' amends AASB 120 in relation to government loans with a below-market rate of interest and consistency of terminology with other Australian Accounting Standards. This Standard is applicable to annual reporting periods beginning on or after 1 January 2009.

6 November 2009: AASB 120 was reissued by the AASB, compiled to include the AASB 2007-8, AASB 2007-10 and AASB 2008-5 amendments. This compiled Standard applies to annual reporting periods beginning on or after 1 January 2009.

1 March 2011: AASB 2010-7 'Amendments to Australian Accounting Standards arising from AASB 9 (December 2010)' as compiled amends AASB 120 to give effect to consequential changes arising from the reissue of AASB 9 in December 2010. This Standard applies to annual reporting periods beginning on or after 1 January 2013 and can be adopted early. **These amendments are not included in this compiled Standard.**

2 September 2011: AASB 2011-8 'Amendments to Australian Accounting Standards arising from AASB 13' amends AASB 120 to give effect to a consequential change in the definition of fair value arising from the issue of AASB 13. This Standard applies to annual reporting periods beginning on or after 1 January 2013 and can be adopted early. **These amendments are not included in this compiled Standard.**

5 September 2011: AASB 2011-9 'Amendments to Australian Accounting Standards – Presentation of Items of Other Comprehensive income' amends the presentation of items in other comprehensive income. This Standard applies to annual reporting periods beginning on or after 1 July 2012 and can be adopted early.

20 June 2012: AASB 120 was reissued by the AASB, compiled to include the AASB 2011-9 amendments and applies to annual reporting periods beginning on or after 1 July 2012 but before 1 January 2013 and can be adopted early.

References

Interpretation 110 *Government Assistance – No Specific Relation to Operating Activities* and Interpretation 12 *Service Concession Arrangements* apply to AASB 120.

IFRIC items not taken onto the agenda: No. 14 *Discounting of current taxes payable* applies to AASB 120.

AASB 120 compared to IAS 20

Additions

Paragraph	Description
Aus 1.1	Which entities AASB 120 applies to (i.e. reporting entities and general purpose financial statements of for-profit entities only).
Aus 1.2	The application date of AASB 120 (i.e. annual reporting periods beginning 1 January 2005).
Aus 1.3	Prohibits early application of AASB 120.
Aus 1.4	Makes the requirements of AASB 120 subject to AASB 1031 'Materiality'.
Aus 1.5	Explains which Australian Standards have been superseded by AASB 120.
Aus 1.6	Clarifies that the superseded Australian Standards remain in force until AASB 120 applies.
Aus 1.7	Notice of the new Standard published on 22 July 2004.

Deletions

Paragraph	Description
40	Transitional provisions on first time application.
41	Effective date of IAS 20.
42	Effective date of 2007 revisions to IAS 20.

Contents

Compilation Details

Comparison with IAS 20

Accounting Standard
AASB 120 Accounting for Government Grants and Disclosure of Government Assistance

	Paragraphs
Application	Aus1.1 – Aus1.7
Scope	1 – 2
Definitions	3 – 6
Government Grants	7 – 22
Non-monetary Government Grants	23
Presentation of Grants Related to Assets	24 – 28
Presentation of Grants Related to Income	29 – 31
Repayment of Government Grants	32 – 33
Government Assistance	34 – 38
Disclosure	39
Effective Date	43 – 46

Australian Accounting Standard AASB 120 *Accounting for Government Grants and Disclosure of Government Assistance* (as amended) is set out in paragraphs Aus1.1 – 46. All the paragraphs have equal authority. Paragraphs in **bold type** state the main principles. Terms defined in this Standard are in *italics* the first time they appear in the Standard. AASB 120 is to be read in the context of other Australian Accounting Standards, including AASB 1048 *Interpretation of Standards*, which identifies the Australian Accounting Interpretations. In the absence of explicit guidance, AASB 108 *Accounting Policies, Changes in Accounting Estimates and Errors* provides a basis for selecting and applying accounting policies.

Compilation Details

Accounting Standard AASB 120 *Accounting for Government Grants and Disclosure of Government Assistance* as amended

This compiled Standard applies to annual reporting periods beginning on or after 1 July 2012 but before 1 January 2013. It takes into account amendments up to and including 5 September 2011 and was prepared on 20 June 2012 by the staff of the Australian Accounting Standards Board (AASB).

This compilation is not a separate Accounting Standard made by the AASB. Instead, it is a representation of AASB 120 (July 2004) as amended by other Accounting Standards, which are listed in the Table below.

Table of Standards

Standard	Date made	Application date *(annual reporting periods ... on or after ...)*	Application, saving or transitional provisions
AASB 120	15 Jul 2004	*(beginning)* 1 Jan 2005	
AASB 2007-2	15 Feb 2007	*(ending)* 28 Feb 2007	see (a) below
AASB 2007-4	30 Apr 2007	*(beginning)* 1 Jul 2007	see (b) below
AASB 2007-8	24 Sep 2007	*(beginning)* 1 Jan 2009	see (c) below
AASB 2007-10	13 Dec 2007	*(beginning)* 1 Jan 2009	see (c) below
AASB 2008-5	24 Jul 2008	*(beginning)* 1 Jan 2009	see (d) below

Standard	Date made	Application date *(annual reporting periods ... on or after ...)*	Application, saving or transitional provisions
AASB 2010-7	31 Dec 2010	*(beginning)* 1 Jan 2013	not compiled*
AASB 2011-8	2 Sep 2011	*(beginning)* 1 Jan 2013	not compiled*
AASB 2011-9	5 Sep 2011	*(beginning)* 1 Jul 2012	see (e) below

*   The amendments made by this Standard are not included in this compilation, which presents the principal Standard as applicable to annual reporting periods beginning on or after 1 July 2012 but before 1 January 2013.

(a)   Entities may elect to apply the relevant amendments to annual reporting periods beginning on or after 1 January 2005 that end before 28 February 2007.

(b)   Entities may elect to apply this Standard to annual reporting periods beginning on or after 1 January 2005 but before 1 July 2007.

(c)   Entities may elect to apply this Standard to annual reporting periods beginning on or after 1 January 2005 but before 1 January 2009, provided that AASB 101 *Presentation of Financial Statements* (September 2007) is also applied to such periods.

(d)   Entities may elect to apply this Standard, or its amendments to individual Standards, to annual reporting periods beginning on or after 1 January 2005 but before 1 January 2009.

(e)   Entities may elect to apply this Standard to annual reporting periods beginning on or after 1 January 2005 but before 1 July 2012.

Table of Amendments

Paragraph affected	How affected	By ... [paragraph]
Title	footnote added	AASB 2008-5 [37]
Aus1.1	amended	AASB 2007-8 [7, 8]
Aus1.4	amended	AASB 2007-8 [8]
2	amended	AASB 2008-5 [37]
3 (footnote 1)	amended	AASB 2007-2 [10]
5	amended	AASB 2007-10 [63]
10A	added	AASB 2008-5 [33]
12-13	amended	AASB 2008-5 [37]
14	amended	AASB 2007-8 [6, 69]
	amended	AASB 2008-5 [37]
15	amended	AASB 2007-8 [69]
	amended	AASB 2008-5 [37]
16-18	amended	AASB 2008-5 [37]
20-22	amended	AASB 2008-5 [37]
23	amended	AASB 2007-4 [57]
24	amended	AASB 2007-4 [58]
	amended	AASB 2007-8 [6]
25	added	AASB 2007-4 [58]
26	amended	AASB 2007-4 [58]
	amended	AASB 2008-5 [37]
27	added	AASB 2007-4 [58]
	amended	AASB 2008-5 [37]
28	amended	AASB 2007-4 [58]
	amended	AASB 2007-8 [6, 70]
29	amended	AASB 2007-4 [59]
	amended	AASB 2007-8 [6]
	amended	AASB 2011-9 [19]
29A	added	AASB 2007-8 [71]
	deleted	AASB 2011-9 [19]

Paragraph affected	How affected	By ... [paragraph]
30	added	AASB 2007-4 [59]
31	amended	AASB 2007-4 [59]
32	amended	AASB 2007-4 [60]
	amended	AASB 2008-5 [37]
37	deleted	AASB 2008-5 [34]
41 (preceding heading)	amended	AASB 2008-5 [35]
42	note added	AASB 2007-8 [72]
43	added	AASB 2008-5 [36]
46	added	AASB 2011-9 [19]

Comparison with IAS 20

AASB 120 and IAS 20

AASB 120 *Accounting for Government Grants and Disclosure of Government Assistance* as amended incorporates IAS 20 *Accounting for Government Grants and Disclosure of Government Assistance* as issued and amended by the International Accounting Standards Board (IASB). Paragraphs that have been added to this Standard (and do not appear in the text of IAS 20) are identified with the prefix "Aus", followed by the number of the relevant IASB paragraph and decimal numbering.

Compliance with IAS 20

For-profit entities that comply with AASB 120 as amended will simultaneously be in compliance with IAS 20 as amended.

Accounting Standard AASB 120

The Australian Accounting Standards Board made Accounting Standard AASB 120 *Accounting for Government Grants and Disclosure of Government Assistance* under section 334 of the *Corporations Act 2001* on 15 July 2004.

This compiled version of AASB 120 applies to annual reporting periods beginning on or after 1 July 2012 but before 1 January 2013. It incorporates relevant amendments contained in other AASB Standards made by the AASB up to and including 5 September 2011 (see Compilation Details).

Accounting Standard AASB 120

Accounting for Government Grants and Disclosure of Government Assistance[1]

Application

Aus1.1   **This Standard applies to:**

(a)   **each for-profit entity that is required to prepare financial reports in accordance with Part 2M.3 of the Corporations Act and that is a reporting entity;**

(b)   **general purpose financial statements of each other for-profit reporting entity; and**

---

1   As part of AASB 2008-5 *Amendments to Australian Accounting Standards arising from the Annual Improvements Project* issued in July 2008 the Board amended terminology used in this Standard to be consistent with other Australian Accounting Standards as follows:

(a)   'taxable income' was amended to 'taxable profit or tax loss',

(b)   'recognised as income/expense' was amended to 'recognised in profit or loss',

(c)   'credited directly to shareholders' interests/equity' was amended to 'recognised outside profit or loss', and

(d)   'revision to an accounting estimate' was amended to 'change in accounting estimate'.

	(c)	financial statements of a for-profit entity that are, or are held out to be, general purpose financial statements.

Aus1.2   This Standard applies to annual reporting periods beginning on or after 1 January 2005.

[Note: For application dates of paragraphs changed or added by an amending Standard, see Compilation Details.]

Aus1.3   This Standard shall not be applied to annual reporting periods beginning before 1 January 2005.

Aus1.4   The requirements specified in this Standard apply to the financial statements where information resulting from their application is material in accordance with AASB 1031 *Materiality*.

Aus1.5   When applicable, this Standard supersedes AASB 1004 *Revenue* as notified in the *Commonwealth of Australia Gazette* No S 283, 17 June 1998.

Aus1.6   AASB 1004 issued in June 1998 remains applicable until superseded by this Standard.

Aus1.7   Notice of this Standard was published in the *Commonwealth of Australia Gazette* No S 294, 22 July 2004.

Scope

1   This Standard shall be applied in accounting for, and in the disclosure of, *government grants* and in the disclosure of other forms of *government assistance*.

2   This Standard does not deal with:

(a)   the special problems arising in accounting for government grants in financial statements reflecting the effects of changing prices or in supplementary information of a similar nature.

(b)   government assistance that is provided for an entity in the form of benefits that are available in determining taxable profit or tax loss, or are determined or limited on the basis of income tax liability. Examples of such benefits are income tax holidays, investment tax credits, accelerated depreciation allowances and reduced income tax rates.

(c)   government participation in the ownership of the entity.

(d)   government grants covered by AASB 141 *Agriculture*.

Definitions

3   The following terms are used in this Standard with the meanings specified.

Fair value is the amount for which an asset could be exchanged between a knowledgeable, willing buyer and a knowledgeable, willing seller in an arm's length transaction.

Forgivable loans are loans which the lender undertakes to waive repayment of under certain prescribed conditions.

Government refers to government, government agencies and similar bodies whether local, national or international.

Government assistance is action by government designed to provide an economic benefit specific to an entity or range of entities qualifying under certain criteria. Government assistance for the purpose of this Standard does not include benefits provided only indirectly through action affecting general trading conditions, such as the provision of infrastructure in development areas or the imposition of trading constraints on competitors.

Government grants are assistance by government in the form of transfers of resources to an entity in return for past or future compliance with certain conditions relating to the operating activities of the entity. They exclude those forms of government assistance which cannot reasonably have a value placed upon them and transactions with government which cannot be distinguished from the normal trading transactions of the entity.[2]

Grants related to assets are government grants whose primary condition is that an entity qualifying for them should purchase, construct or otherwise acquire long-term assets. Subsidiary conditions may also be attached restricting the type or location of the assets or the periods during which they are to be acquired or held.

Grants related to income are government grants other than those related to assets.

4   Government assistance takes many forms varying both in the nature of the assistance given and in the conditions which are usually attached to it. The purpose of the assistance may be to encourage an entity to embark on a course of action which it would not normally have taken if the assistance was not provided.

5   The receipt of government assistance by an entity may be significant for the preparation of the financial statements for two reasons. Firstly, if resources have been transferred, an appropriate method of accounting for the transfer must be found. Secondly, it is desirable to give an indication of the extent to which the entity has benefited from such assistance during the reporting period. This facilitates comparison of an entity's financial statements with those of prior periods and with those of other entities.

6   Government grants are sometimes called by other names such as subsidies, subventions, or premiums.

Government Grants

7   **Government grants, including non-monetary grants at *fair value*, shall not be recognised until there is reasonable assurance that:**

(a)   **the entity will comply with the conditions attaching to them; and**

(b)   **the grants will be received.**

8   A government grant is not recognised until there is reasonable assurance that the entity will comply with the conditions attaching to it, and that the grant will be received. Receipt of a grant does not of itself provide conclusive evidence that the conditions attaching to the grant have been or will be fulfilled.

9   The manner in which a grant is received does not affect the accounting method to be adopted in regard to the grant. Thus a grant is accounted for in the same manner whether it is received in cash or as a reduction of a liability to the government.

10   *A forgivable loan* from government is treated as a government grant when there is reasonable assurance that the entity will meet the terms for forgiveness of the loan.

10A   The benefit of a government loan at a below-market rate of interest is treated as a government grant. The loan shall be recognised and measured in accordance with AASB 139 *Financial Instruments: Recognition and Measurement*. The benefit of the below-market rate of interest shall be measured as the difference between the initial carrying value of the loan determined in accordance with AASB 139 and the proceeds received. The benefit is accounted for in accordance with this Standard. The entity shall consider the conditions and obligations that have been, or must be, met when identifying the costs for which the benefit of the loan is intended to compensate.

11   Once a government grant is recognised, any related contingent liability or contingent asset is treated in accordance with AASB 137 *Provisions, Contingent Liabilities and Contingent Assets*.

12   **Government grants shall be recognised in profit or loss on a systematic basis over the periods in which the entity recognises as expenses the related costs for which the grants are intended to compensate.**

13   There are two broad approaches to the accounting for government grants: the capital approach, under which a grant is recognised outside profit or loss, and the income approach, under which a grant is recognised in profit or loss over one or more periods.

---

2   See also Interpretation 110 *Government Assistance – No Specific Relation to Operating Activities*, as identified in AASB 1048 *Interpretation and Application of Standards*.

14   Those in support of the capital approach argue as follows:

     (a)   government grants are a financing device and should be dealt with as such in the statement of financial position rather than be recognised in profit or loss to offset the items of expense that they finance. Because no repayment is expected, such grants should be recognised outside profit or loss.

     (b)   it is inappropriate to recognise government grants in profit or loss, because they are not earned but represent an incentive provided by government without related costs.

15   Arguments in support of the income approach are as follows:

     (a)   because government grants are receipts from a source other than shareholders, they should not be recognised directly in equity but should be recognised in profit or loss in appropriate periods.

     (b)   government grants are rarely gratuitous. The entity earns them through compliance with their conditions and meeting the envisaged obligations. They should therefore be recognised in profit or loss over the periods in which the entity recognises as expenses the related costs for which the grant is intended to compensate.

     (c)   because income and other taxes are expenses, it is logical to deal also with government grants, which are an extension of fiscal policies, in profit or loss.

16   It is fundamental to the income approach that government grants should be recognised in profit or loss on a systematic basis over the periods in which the entity recognises as expenses the related costs for which the grant is intended to compensate. Recognition of government grants in profit or loss on a receipts basis is not in accordance with the accrual accounting assumption (see AASB 101 *Presentation of Financial Statements*) and would be acceptable only if no basis existed for allocating a grant to periods other than the one in which it was received.

17   In most cases the periods over which an entity recognises the costs or expenses related to a government grant are readily ascertainable. Thus grants in recognition of specific expenses are recognised in profit or loss in the same period as the relevant expenses. Similarly, grants related to depreciable assets are usually recognised in profit or loss over the periods and in the proportions in which depreciation expense on those assets is recognised.

18   Grants related to non-depreciable assets may also require the fulfilment of certain obligations and would then be recognised in profit or loss over the periods that bear the cost of meeting the obligations. As an example, a grant of land may be conditional upon the erection of a building on the site and it may be appropriate to recognise the grant in profit or loss over the life of the building.

19   Grants are sometimes received as part of a package of financial or fiscal aids to which a number of conditions are attached. In such cases, care is needed in identifying the conditions giving rise to costs and expenses which determine the periods over which the grant will be earned. It may be appropriate to allocate part of a grant on one basis and part on another.

20   **A government grant that becomes receivable as compensation for expenses or losses already incurred or for the purpose of giving immediate financial support to the entity with no future related costs shall be recognised in profit or loss of the period in which it becomes receivable.**

21   In some circumstances, a government grant may be awarded for the purpose of giving immediate financial support to an entity rather than as an incentive to undertake specific expenditures. Such grants may be confined to a particular entity and may not be available to a whole class of beneficiaries. These circumstances may warrant recognising a grant in profit or loss of the period in which the entity qualifies to receive it, with disclosure to ensure that its effect is clearly understood.

22   A government grant may become receivable by an entity as compensation for expenses or losses incurred in a previous period. Such a grant is recognised in profit or loss of the

period in which it becomes receivable, with disclosure to ensure that its effect is clearly understood.

Non-monetary Government Grants

23   A government grant may take the form of a transfer of a non-monetary asset, such as land or other resources, for the use of the entity. In these circumstances it is usual to assess the fair value of the non-monetary asset and to account for both grant and asset at that fair value. An alternative course that is sometimes followed is to record both asset and grant at a nominal amount.

Presentation of Grants Related to Assets

24   **Government *grants related to assets*, including non-monetary grants at fair value, shall be presented in the statement of financial position either by setting up the grant as deferred income or by deducting the grant in arriving at the carrying amount of the asset.**

25   Two methods of presentation in financial statements of grants (or the appropriate portions of grants) related to assets are regarded as acceptable alternatives.

26   One method recognises the grant as deferred income that is recognised in profit or loss on a systematic basis over the useful life of the asset.

27   The other method deducts the grant in calculating the carrying amount of the asset. The grant is recognised in profit or loss over the life of a depreciable asset as a reduced depreciation expense.

28   The purchase of assets and the receipt of related grants can cause major movements in the cash flow of an entity. For this reason and in order to show the gross investment in assets, such movements are often disclosed as separate items in the statement of cash flows regardless of whether or not the grant is deducted from the related asset for presentation purposes in the statement of financial position.

Presentation of Grants Related to Income

29   *Grants related to income* are presented as part of profit or loss, either separately or under a general heading such as 'Other income'; alternatively, they are deducted in reporting the related expense.

29A   [Deleted by the IASB]

30   Supporters of the first method claim that it is inappropriate to net income and expense items and that separation of the grant from the expense facilitates comparison with other expenses not affected by a grant. For the second method it is argued that the expenses might well not have been incurred by the entity if the grant had not been available and presentation of the expense without offsetting the grant may therefore be misleading.

31   Both methods are regarded as acceptable for the presentation of grants related to income. Disclosure of the grant may be necessary for a proper understanding of the financial statements. Disclosure of the effect of the grants on any item of income or expense which is required to be separately disclosed is usually appropriate.

Repayment of Government Grants

32   **A government grant that becomes repayable shall be accounted for as a change in accounting estimate (see AASB 108 *Accounting Policies, Changes in Accounting Estimates and Errors*). Repayment of a grant related to income shall be applied first against any unamortised deferred credit recognised in respect of the grant. To the extent that the repayment exceeds any such deferred credit, or when no deferred credit exists, the repayment shall be recognised immediately in profit or loss. Repayment of a grant related to an asset shall be recognised by increasing the carrying amount of the asset or reducing the deferred income balance by the amount repayable. The cumulative additional depreciation that would have been recognised in profit or loss to date in the absence of the grant shall be recognised immediately in profit or loss.**

33   Circumstances giving rise to repayment of a grant related to an asset may require consideration to be given to the possible impairment of the new carrying amount of the asset.

Government Assistance

34   Excluded from the definition of government grants in paragraph 3 are certain forms of government assistance which cannot reasonably have a value placed upon them and transactions with government which cannot be distinguished from the normal trading transactions of the entity.

35   Examples of assistance that cannot reasonably have a value placed upon them are free technical or marketing advice and the provision of guarantees. An example of assistance that cannot be distinguished from the normal trading transactions of the entity is a government procurement policy that is responsible for a portion of the entity's sales. The existence of the benefit might be unquestioned but any attempt to segregate the trading activities from government assistance could well be arbitrary.

36   The significance of the benefit in the above examples may be such that disclosure of the nature, extent and duration of the assistance is necessary in order that the financial statements may not be misleading.

37   [Deleted by the IASB]

38   In this Standard, government assistance does not include the provision of infrastructure by improvement to the general transport and communication network and the supply of improved facilities such as irrigation or water reticulation which is available on an ongoing indeterminate basis for the benefit of an entire local community.

Disclosure

39   The following matters shall be disclosed:

   (a)   the accounting policy adopted for government grants, including the methods of presentation adopted in the financial statements;

   (b)   the nature and extent of government grants recognised in the financial statements and an indication of other forms of government assistance from which the entity has directly benefited; and

   (c)   unfulfilled conditions and other contingencies attaching to government assistance that has been recognised.

Transitional Provisions

40   [Deleted by the AASB]

Effective Date

41   [Deleted by the AASB]

42   [Deleted by the AASB]

43   Paragraph 37 was deleted and paragraph 10A added by AASB 2008-5 *Amendments to Australian Accounting Standards arising from the Annual Improvements Project* issued in July 2008. An entity shall apply those amendments prospectively to government loans received in annual reporting periods beginning on or after 1 January 2009. Earlier application is permitted. If an entity applies the amendments for an earlier period it shall disclose that fact.

46   AASB 2011-9 *Amendments to Australian Accounting Standards – Presentation of Items of Other Comprehensive Income*, issued in September 2011, amended paragraph 29 and deleted paragraph 29A. An entity shall apply those amendments when it applies AASB 101 as amended in September 2011.

AASB 121
The Effects of Changes in Foreign Exchange Rates

(Compiled June 2012)

Note from the Institute of Chartered Accountants Australia

This note, prepared by the technical editors, is not part of Accounting Standard AASB 121.

Historical development

15 July 2004: AASB 121 'The Effects of Changes in Foreign Exchange Rates' is the Australian equivalent of IAS 21 of the same name. It was made by the AASB on 15 July 2004 as part of the AASB's program to adopt International Financial Reporting Standards (IFRSs) by 2005.

1 December 2004: AASB 2004-2 'Amendments to Australian Accounting Standards' adds paragraph Aus38.1. The Standard is applicable to annual reporting periods beginning on or after 1 January 2005.

18 January 2006: AASB 2006-1 provides that a monetary item can be denominated in any currency and still be part of the reporting entity's net investment in a foreign operation.

15 February 2007: AASB 2007-2 'Amendments to Australian Accounting Standards' amends paragraph 3 and is applicable to annual reporting periods ending on or after 28 February 2007, with early adoption permitted for annual reporting periods beginning on or after 1 January 2005.

30 April 2007: AASB 2007-4 'Amendments to Australian Accounting Standards' deletes paragraph Aus53.1 and is applicable to annual reporting periods beginning on or after 1 July 2007, with early adoption permitted for annual reporting periods beginning on or after 1 January 2005.

July 2007: Erratum amends paragraphs 3, 33, 44 and 46 and is applicable for annual reporting periods beginning on or after 1 July 2007, with early adoption permitted for annual reporting periods beginning on or after 1 January 2005.

24 September 2007: AASB 2007-8 'Amendments to Australian Accounting Standards arising from AASB 101' amends AASB 121 to align with revised AASB 101. This Standard is applicable to annual reporting periods beginning on or after 1 January 2009.

13 December 2007: AASB 2007-10 'Further Amendments to Australian Accounting Standards arising from AASB 101' amends AASB 121, replacing the term 'financial report' with 'financial statements'. This Standard is applicable to annual reporting periods beginning on or after 1 January 2009..

6 March 2008: AASB 2008-3 'Amendments to Australian Accounting Standards arising from AASB 3 and AASB 127' amends AASB 121 for the issue of AASB 3 Revised. This Standard is applicable to annual reporting periods beginning on or after 1 July 2009.

25 July 2008: AASB 2008-7 'Amendments to Australian Accounting Standards – Cost of an Investment in a Subsidiary, Jointly Controlled Entity or Associate' amends AASB 121 to reflect that dividends declared out of pre-acquisition profits are recognised as income. This Standard is applicable to annual reporting periods beginning on or after 1 January 2009.

25 June 2009: AASB 2009-6 'Amendments to Australian Accounting Standards' amends AASB 121 for editorial corrections made by the International Accounting Standards Board (IASB) to its Standards and Interpretations (IFRSs) and as a consequence of issuing revised AASB 101 'Presentation of Financial Statements'. This Standard is applicable to annual reporting periods beginning on or after 1 January 2009 that end on or after 30 June 2009.

5 October 2009: Erratum makes further terminology-related and editorial changes resulting from AASB 2009-6. This erratum applies to annual reporting periods beginning on or after 1 January 2009 that end on or after 30 June 2009.

2 November 2009: AASB 121 was reissued by the AASB, compiled to include the AASB 2007-8, AASB 2007-10, AASB 2008-3, AASB 2008-7, AASB 2009-6 and erratum amendments and applies to annual reporting periods beginning on or after 1 July 2009.

---

7 December 2009: AASB 2009-11 'Amendments to Australian Accounting Standards arising from AASB 9' amends AASB 121 to give effect to consequential changes arising from the issuance of AASB 9. This Standard is applicable to annual reporting periods beginning on or after 1 January 2013 with early adoption permitted from annual reporting periods ending on or after 31 December 2009 that begin before 1 January 2013 provided AASB 9 is also applied for the same period. The application date of AASB 2009-11 has been amended to 1 January 2015 by AASB 2012-6. **These amendments have been superseded by AASB 2010-7 and are not included in this compiled Standard.**

2 June 2010: AASB 2010-3 'Amendments to Australian Accounting Standards arising from the Annual Improvements Project' amends AASB 121 in relation to transition requirements for amendments arising as a result of AASB 127. This Standard is applicable to annual reporting periods beginning on or after 1 July 2010 with early adoption permitted.

7 September 2010: AASB 121 was reissued by the AASB, compiled to include the AASB 2010-3 amendments and applies to annual reporting periods beginning on or after 1 July 2010 but before 1 January 2013.

27 October 2010: AASB 2010-5 'Further Amendments to Australian Accounting Standards' makes editorial amendments to AASB 121. This Standard is applicable to annual reporting periods beginning on or after 1 January 2011.

1 March 2011: AASB 2010-7 'Amendments to Australian Accounting Standards arising from AASB 9 (December 2010)' as compiled amends AASB 121 to give effect to consequential changes arising from the reissue of AASB 9 in December 2010, and supersedes AASB 2009-11 which related to the previous version of AASB 9. This Standard applies to annual reporting periods beginning on or after 1 January 2013 and can be adopted early. The application date of AASB 2010-7 has been amended to 1 January 2015 by AASB 2012-6. **These amendments are not included in this compiled Standard.**

11 May 2011: AASB 2011-1 'Amendments to Australian Accounting Standards arising from the Trans-Tasman Convergence Project' amends AASB 121 as a result of the Trans-Tasman project, to more closely align IFRSs as applied through Australian and New Zealand Standards. AASB 2011-1 deletes Australian specific disclosure requirements. Where appropriate these disclosures are now included in AASB 1054 'Australian Additional Requirements'. These Standards apply to annual reporting periods beginning on or after 1 July 2011 with early adoption permitted.

29 August 2011: AASB 2011-7 'Amendments to Australian Accounting Standards arising from the Consolidation and Joint Arrangements Standards' amends AASB 121 to give effect to many consequential changes arising from the issue of AASB 10, 11, 12, 127 and 128. This Standard applies to annual reporting periods beginning on or after 1 January 2013 and can be adopted early by for-profit entities. **These amendments are not included in this compiled Standard.**

5 September 2011: AASB 2011-8 'Amendments to Australian Accounting Standards arising from AASB 13' amends AASB 121 to give effect to a consequential change in the definition of fair value arising from the issue of AASB 13. This Standard applies to annual reporting periods beginning on or after 1 January 2013 and can be adopted early. **These amendments are not included in this compiled Standard.**

5 September 2011: AASB 2011-9 'Amendments to Australian Accounting Standards – Presentation of Items of Other Comprehensive income' amends the presentation of items in other comprehensive income. This Standard applies to annual reporting periods beginning on or after 1 July 2012 and can be adopted early.

23 September 2011: AASB 121 was reissued by the AASB, compiled to include the AASB 2010-5 and AASB 2011-1 amendments and applies to annual reporting periods ending on or after 1 July 2011 but before 1 July 2012.

20 June 2012: AASB 121 was reissued by the AASB, compiled to include the AASB 2011-9 amendments and applies to annual reporting periods beginning on or after 1 July 2012 and can be adopted early.

References

Interpretation 107 *Introduction of the Euro* and Interpretation 16 *Hedges of a Net Investment in a Foreign Operation* apply to AASB 121.

IFRIC items not taken onto the agenda: No. 26 *Exchange Rate for Re-measuring Foreign Currency Transactions and Translation of Foreign Operations under IAS 21,* IAS 21-2 *Determination of functional currency of an investment holding company* and IAS 21-3 *Repayments of investment and foreign currency translation reserve* apply to AASB 121.

AASB 121 compared to IAS 21

Additions

Paragraph	*Description*
Aus 2.1	Which entities AASB 121 applies to (i.e. reporting entities and general purpose financial statements).
Aus 2.2	The application date of AASB 121 (i.e. annual reporting periods beginning 1 January 2005).
Aus 2.3	Prohibits early application of AASB 121.
Aus 2.4	Makes the requirements of AASB 121 subject to AASB 1031 'Materiality'.
Aus 2.5	Explains which Australian Standards have been superseded by AASB 121.
Aus 2.6	Clarifies that the superseded Australian Standards remain in force until AASB 121 applies.
Aus 2.7	Notice of the new Standard published on 22 July 2004.

Deletions

Paragraph	*Description*
58	Effective date of IAS 21.
59	Transitional provision in respect of accounting for the acquisition of a foreign operation.
60	First time application for all other changes to be accounted for in accordance with IAS 8 'Accounting Policies, Changes in Accounting Estimates and Errors'.
61	Reference to superseded IAS 21.
62	Reference to superseded SIC Interpretations – SICs 11, 19 and 30.

Contents

Compilation Details

Comparison with IAS 21

Accounting Standard
AASB 121 The Effects of Changes in Foreign Exchange Rates

Paragraphs

Objective	1 – 2
Application	Aus2.1 – Aus2.7
Scope	3 – 7
Definitions	8
Elaboration on the Definitions	
Functional Currency	9 – 14
Net Investment in a Foreign Operation	15 – 15A
Monetary Items	16
Summary of the Approach Required by this Standard	17 – 19
Reporting Foreign Currency Transactions in the Functional Currency	
Initial Recognition	20 – 22
Reporting at the Ends of Subsequent Reporting Periods	23 – 26
Recognition of Exchange Differences	27 – 34
Change in Functional Currency	35 – 37
Use of a Presentation Currency other than the Functional Currency	
Translation to the Presentation Currency	38 – 43
Translation of a Foreign Operation	44 – 47
Disposal or Partial Disposal of a Foreign Operation	48 – 49
Tax Effects of All Exchange Differences	50
Disclosure	51 – 57
Effective Date and Transition	60B – 60H

Basis for conclusions on IAS 21
(available on the AASB website)

Australian Accounting Standard AASB 121 *The Effects of Changes in Foreign Exchange Rates* (as amended) is set out in paragraphs 1 – 60H. All the paragraphs have equal authority. Paragraphs in **bold type** state the main principles. Terms defined in this Standard are in *italics* the first time they appear in the Standard. AASB 121 is to be read in the context of other Australian Accounting Standards, including AASB 1048 *Interpretation of Standards*, which identifies the Australian Accounting Interpretations. In the absence of explicit guidance, AASB 108 *Accounting Policies, Changes in Accounting Estimates and Errors* provides a basis for selecting and applying accounting policies.

Compilation Details

Accounting Standard AASB 121 *The Effects of Changes in Foreign Exchange Rates* as amended

This compiled Standard applies to annual reporting periods beginning on or after 1 July 2012 but before 1 January 2013. It takes into account amendments up to and including 5 September 2011 and was prepared on 20 June 2012 by the staff of the Australian Accounting Standards Board (AASB).

This compilation is not a separate Accounting Standard made by the AASB. Instead, it is a representation of AASB 121 (July 2004) as amended by other Accounting Standards, which are listed in the Table below.

Table of Standards

Standard	Date made	Application date *(annual reporting periods ... on or after ...)*	Application, saving or transitional provisions
AASB 121	15 Jul 2004	*(beginning)* 1 Jan 2005	
AASB 2004-2	1 Dec 2004	*(beginning)* 1 Jan 2005	–
AASB 2006-1	18 Jan 2006	*(ending)* 31 Dec 2006	see (a) below
AASB 2007-2	15 Feb 2007	*(ending)* 28 Feb 2007	see (b) below
AASB 2007-4	30 Apr 2007	*(beginning)* 1 Jul 2007	see (c) below
Erratum	20 Jul 2007	*(beginning)* 1 Jul 2007	see (d) below
AASB 2007-8	24 Sep 2007	*(beginning)* 1 Jan 2009	see (e) below
AASB 2007-10	13 Dec 2007	*(beginning)* 1 Jan 2009	see (e) below
AASB 2008-3	6 Mar 2008	*(beginning)* 1 Jul 2009	see (f) below
AASB 2008-7	25 Jul 2008	*(beginning)* 1 Jan 2009	see (g) below
AASB 2009-6	25 Jun 2009	*(beginning)* 1 Jan 2009 and *(ending)* 30 Jun 2009	see (h) below
Erratum	5 Oct 2009	*(beginning)* 1 Jan 2009 and *(ending)* 30 Jun 2009	see (i) below
AASB 2009-11	7 Dec 2009	*(beginning)* 1 Jan 2013	not compiled*
AASB 2010-3	23 Jun 2010	*(beginning)* 1 Jul 2010	see (j) below
AASB 2010-2	30 Jun 2010	*(beginning)* 1 Jul 2013	not compiled*
AASB 2010-5	27 Oct 2010	*(beginning)* 1 Jan 2011	see (k) below
AASB 2010-7	6 Dec 2010	*(beginning)* 1 Jan 2013	not compiled*
AASB 2011-1	11 May 2011	*(beginning)* 1 Jul 2011	see (l) below
AASB 2011-7	29 Aug 2011	*(beginning)* 1 Jan 2013	not compiled*
AASB 2011-8	2 Sep 2011	*(beginning)* 1 Jan 2013	not compiled*
AASB 2011-9	5 Sep 2011	*(beginning)* 1 Jul 2012	see (m) below

* The amendments made by this Standard are not included in this compilation, which presents the principal Standard as applicable to annual reporting periods beginning on or after 1 July 2012 but before 1 January 2013.

(a) Entities may elect to apply this Standard to annual reporting periods beginning on or after 1 January 2005 that end before 31 December 2006.

(b) Entities may elect to apply the relevant amendments to annual reporting periods beginning on or after 1 January 2005 that end before 28 February 2007.

(c) Entities may elect to apply this Standard to annual reporting periods beginning on or after 1 January 2005 but before 1 July 2007.

(d) Entities may elect to apply this Erratum to annual reporting periods beginning on or after 1 January 2005 but before 1 July 2007.

(e) Entities may elect to apply this Standard to annual reporting periods beginning on or after 1 January 2005 but before 1 January 2009, provided that AASB 101 *Presentation of Financial Statements* (September 2007) is also applied to such periods.

(f) Entities may elect to apply this Standard to annual reporting periods beginning on or after 30 June 2007 but before 1 July 2009, provided that AASB 3 *Business Combinations* (March 2008) and AASB 127 *Consolidated and Separate Financial Statements* (March 2008) are also applied to such periods.

(g) Entities may elect to apply this Standard to annual reporting periods beginning on or after 1 January 2005 but before 1 January 2009.

(h) Entities may elect to apply this Standard to annual reporting periods beginning on or after 1 January 2005 but before 1 January 2009, provided that AASB 101 *Presentation of Financial Statements* (September 2007) is also applied to such periods, and to annual reporting periods beginning on or after 1 January 2009 that end before 30 June 2009.

(i) Entities may elect to apply this Erratum to annual reporting periods beginning on or after 1 January 2005, provided that AASB 2009-6 *Amendments to Australian Accounting Standards* is also applied to such periods.

(j) Entities may elect to apply this Standard to annual reporting periods beginning on or after 1 January 2005 but before 1 July 2010.

(k) Entities may elect to apply this Standard to annual reporting periods beginning on or after 1 January 2005 but before 1 January 2011.

(l) Entities may elect to apply this Standard, or its amendments to individual pronouncements, to annual reporting periods beginning on or after 1 January 2005 but before 1 July 2011, provided that AASB 1054 *Australian Additional Disclosures* is, or its relevant individual disclosure requirements are, also applied to such periods.

(m) Entities may elect to apply this Standard to annual reporting periods beginning on or after 1 January 2005 but before 1 July 2012.

Table of Amendments

Paragraph affected	How affected	By ... [paragraph]
1	amended	AASB 2007-10 [64]
3	amended	AASB 2007-2 [10]
	amended	Erratum, Jul 2007
	amended	AASB 2010-5 [38]
7	amended	AASB 2007-8 [6]
	amended	AASB 2009-6 [58]
8	amended	AASB 2007-8 [6]
	amended	AASB 2007-10 [66]
14	amended	AASB 2007-10 [66]
15A	added	AASB 2006-1 [5]
23 (and preceding heading)	amended	AASB 2007-8 [6]
	amended	Erratum, Oct 2009 [3]
25	amended	AASB 2007-8 [6]
27	amended	AASB 2007-8 [74]
	amended	AASB 2010-5 [39]
28	amended	AASB 2007-10 [67]
30-31	amended	AASB 2007-8 [75]
32	amended	AASB 2007-8 [76]
33	amended	AASB 2006-1 [6]
	amended	Erratum, Jul 2007
	amended	AASB 2007-8 [77]
37	amended	AASB 2007-8 [78]
Aus38.1	added	AASB 2004-2 [10]
	deleted	AASB 2011-1 [17]
39	amended	AASB 2007-8 [6, 79-81]
	amended	AASB 2011-9 [20]
41	amended	AASB 2007-8 [6, 82]
	amended	AASB 2008-3 [8]
42	amended	AASB 2007-8 [6]
44	amended	Erratum, Jul 2007
45	amended	AASB 2007-8 [82]

Paragraph affected	How affected	By ... [paragraph]
46	amended	Erratum, Jul 2007
	amended	AASB 2007-8 [6, 82]
48	amended	AASB 2007-8 [82]
	heading amended	AASB 2008-3 [44]
48A-48D	added	AASB 2008-3 [44]
49	amended	AASB 2008-7 [15]
	amended	AASB 2008-3 [44]
52	amended	AASB 2007-8 [82]
Aus53.1	deleted	AASB 2007-4 [61]
55	amended	AASB 2009-6 [59]
58 (preceding heading)	amended	AASB 2009-6 [60]
58A	note added	AASB 2009-6 [61]
59 (preceding heading)	deleted	AASB 2009-6 [62]
60A	note added	AASB 2007-8 [83]
60B	note added	AASB 2008-3 [45]
	paragraph added (in place of note)	AASB 2010-3 [9]
60D	added	AASB 2010-3 [9]
60H	added	AASB 2011-9 [20]

General Terminology Amendments

The following amendments are not shown in the above Table of Amendments:

References to 'financial report(s)' were amended to 'financial statements' by AASB 2007-8 and AASB 2007-10, except in relation to specific Corporations Act references.

Comparison with IAS 21

AASB 121 and IAS 21

AASB 121 *The Effects of Changes in Foreign Exchange Rates* as amended incorporates IAS 21 *The Effects of Changes in Foreign Exchange Rates* as issued and amended by the International Accounting Standards Board (IASB). Paragraphs that have been added to this Standard (and do not appear in the text of IAS 21) are identified with the prefix "Aus", followed by the number of the preceding IASB paragraph and decimal numbering.

Compliance with IAS 21

Entities that comply with AASB 121 as amended will simultaneously be in compliance with IAS 21 as amended.

Accounting Standard AASB 121

The Australian Accounting Standards Board made Accounting Standard AASB 121 *The Effects of Changes in Foreign Exchange Rates* under section 334 of the *Corporations Act 2001* on 15 July 2004.

This compiled version of AASB 121 applies to annual reporting periods beginning on or after 1 July 2012 but before 1 January 2013. It incorporates relevant amendments contained in other AASB Standards made by the AASB and other decisions of the AASB up to and including 5 September 2011 (see Compilation Details).

Accounting Standard AASB 121

The Effects of Changes in Foreign Exchange Rates

Objective

1 An entity may carry on foreign activities in two ways. It may have transactions in foreign currencies or it may have *foreign operations*. In addition, an entity may present its financial statements in a *foreign currency*. The objective of this Standard is to prescribe how to include foreign currency transactions and foreign operations in the financial statements of an entity and how to translate financial statements into a *presentation currency*.

2 The principal issues are which *exchange rate(s)* to use and how to report the effects of changes in exchange rates in the financial statements.

Application

Aus2.1 **This Standard applies to:**

(a) **each entity that is required to prepare financial reports in accordance with Part 2M.3 of the Corporations Act and that is a reporting entity;**

(b) **general purpose financial statements of each other reporting entity; and**

(c) **financial statements that are, or are held out to be, general purpose financial statements.**

Aus2.2 **This Standard applies to annual reporting periods beginning on or after 1 January 2005.**

[Note: For application dates of paragraphs changed or added by an amending Standard, see Compilation Details.]

Aus2.3 **This Standard shall not be applied to annual reporting periods beginning before 1 January 2005.**

Aus2.4 **The requirements specified in this Standard apply to the financial statements where information resulting from their application is material in accordance with AASB 1031 *Materiality*.**

Aus2.5 **When applicable, this Standard supersedes AASB 1012 *Foreign Currency Translation* as notified in the *Commonwealth of Australia Gazette* No S 586, 17 November 2000.**

Aus2.6 AASB 1012 remains applicable until superseded by this Standard.

Aus2.7 Notice of this Standard was published in the *Commonwealth of Australia Gazette* No S 294, 22 July 2004.

Scope

3 **This Standard shall be applied:[1]**

(a) **in accounting for transactions and balances in foreign currencies, except for those derivative transactions and balances that are within the scope of AASB 139 *Financial Instruments: Recognition and Measurement*;**

(b) **in translating the results and financial position of foreign operations that are included in the financial statements of the entity by consolidation, proportionate consolidation or the equity method; and**

(c) **in translating an entity's results and financial position into a presentation currency.**

4 AASB 139 applies to many foreign currency derivatives and, accordingly, these are excluded from the scope of this Standard. However, those foreign currency derivatives that are not within the scope of AASB 139 (e.g. some foreign currency derivatives that are embedded in other contracts) are within the scope of this Standard. In addition, this Standard applies when an entity translates amounts relating to derivatives from its *functional currency* to its presentation currency.

---

1 See also Interpretation 107 *Introduction of the Euro*, as identified in AASB 1048 *Interpretation of Standards*.

5   This Standard does not apply to hedge accounting for foreign currency items, including the hedging of a net investment in a foreign operation. AASB 139 applies to hedge accounting.

6   This Standard applies to the presentation of an entity's financial statements in a foreign currency and sets out requirements for the resulting financial statements to be described as complying with Australian equivalents to IFRSs. For translations of financial information into a foreign currency that do not meet these requirements, this Standard specifies information to be disclosed.

7   This Standard does not apply to the presentation in a statement of cash flows of the cash flows arising from transactions in a foreign currency, or to the translation of cash flows of a foreign operation (see AASB 107 *Statement of Cash Flows*).

Definitions

8   **The following terms are used in this Standard with the meanings specified.**

Closing rate **is the spot exchange rate at the end of the reporting period.**

Exchange difference **is the difference resulting from translating a given number of units of one currency into another currency at different exchange rates.**

Exchange rate **is the ratio of exchange for two currencies.**

Fair value **is the amount for which an asset could be exchanged, or a liability settled, between knowledgeable, willing parties in an arm's length transaction.**

Foreign currency **is a currency other than the functional currency of the entity.**

Foreign operation **is an entity that is a subsidiary, associate, joint venture or branch of a reporting entity, the activities of which are based or conducted in a country or currency other than those of the reporting entity.**

Functional currency **is the currency of the primary economic environment in which the entity operates.**

A *group* **is a parent and all its subsidiaries.**

Monetary items **are units of currency held and assets and liabilities to be received or paid in a fixed or determinable number of units of currency.**

Net investment in a foreign operation **is the amount of the reporting entity's interest in the net assets of that operation.**

Presentation currency **is the currency in which the financial statements are presented.**

Spot exchange rate **is the exchange rate for immediate delivery.**

Elaboration on the Definitions

Functional Currency

9   The primary economic environment in which an entity operates is normally the one in which it primarily generates and expends cash. An entity considers the following factors in determining its functional currency:

(a)   the currency:

(i)   that mainly influences sales prices for goods and services (this will often be the currency in which sales prices for its goods and services are denominated and settled); and

(ii)   of the country whose competitive forces and regulations mainly determine the sales price of its goods and services;

(b)   the currency that mainly influences labour, material and other costs of providing goods or services (this will often be the currency in which such costs are denominated and settled).

10   The following factors may also provide evidence of an entity's functional currency:

(a)   the currency in which funds from financing activities (i.e. issuing debt and equity instruments) are generated;

(b)   the currency in which receipts from operating activities are usually retained.

11 The following additional factors are considered in determining the functional currency of a foreign operation, and whether its functional currency is the same as that of the reporting entity (the reporting entity, in this context, being the entity that has the foreign operation as its subsidiary, branch, associate or joint venture):

(a) whether the activities of the foreign operation are carried out as an extension of the reporting entity, rather than being carried out with a significant degree of autonomy. An example of the former is when the foreign operation only sells goods imported from the reporting entity and remits the proceeds to it. An example of the latter is when the operation accumulates cash and other *monetary items*, incurs expenses, generates income and arranges borrowings, all substantially in its local currency;

(b) whether transactions with the reporting entity are a high or low proportion of the foreign operation's activities;

(c) whether cash flows from the activities of the foreign operation directly affect the cash flows of the reporting entity and are readily available for remittance to it;

(d) whether cash flows from the activities of the foreign operation are sufficient to service existing and normally expected debt obligations without funds being made available by the reporting entity.

12 When the above indicators are mixed and the functional currency is not obvious, management uses its judgement to determine the functional currency that most faithfully represents the economic effects of the underlying transactions, events and conditions. As part of this approach, management gives priority to the primary indicators in paragraph 9 before considering the indicators in paragraphs 10 and 11, which are designed to provide additional supporting evidence to determine an entity's functional currency.

13 An entity's functional currency reflects the underlying transactions, events and conditions that are relevant to it. Accordingly, once determined, the functional currency is not changed unless there is a change in those underlying transactions, events and conditions.

14 If the functional currency is the currency of a hyperinflationary economy, the entity's financial statements are restated in accordance with AASB 129 *Financial Reporting in Hyperinflationary Economies*. An entity cannot avoid restatement in accordance with AASB 129 by, for example, adopting as its functional currency a currency other than the functional currency determined in accordance with this Standard (such as the functional currency of its parent).

Net Investment in a Foreign Operation
15 An entity may have a monetary item that is receivable from or payable to a foreign operation. An item for which settlement is neither planned nor likely to occur in the foreseeable future is, in substance, a part of the entity's net investment in that foreign operation, and is accounted for in accordance with paragraphs 32 and 33. Such monetary items may include long-term receivables or loans. They do not include trade receivables or trade payables.

15A The entity that has a monetary item receivable from or payable to a foreign operation described in paragraph 15 may be any subsidiary of the group. For example, an entity has two subsidiaries, A and B. Subsidiary B is a foreign operation. Subsidiary A grants a loan to Subsidiary B. Subsidiary A's loan receivable from Subsidiary B would be part of the entity's net investment in Subsidiary B if settlement of the loan is neither planned nor likely to occur in the foreseeable future. This would also be true if Subsidiary A were itself a foreign operation.

Monetary Items
16 The essential feature of a monetary item is a right to receive (or an obligation to deliver) a fixed or determinable number of units of currency. Examples include: pensions and other employee benefits to be paid in cash; provisions that are to be settled in cash; and cash dividends that are recognised as a liability. Similarly, a contract to receive (or deliver) a variable number of the entity's own equity instruments or a variable amount of assets in which the *fair value* to be received (or delivered) equals a fixed or determinable number of units of currency is a monetary item. Conversely, the essential feature of a non-monetary item is the absence of a right to receive (or an obligation to deliver) a fixed

or determinable number of units of currency. Examples include: amounts prepaid for goods and services (e.g. prepaid rent); goodwill; intangible assets; inventories; property, plant and equipment; and provisions that are to be settled by the delivery of a non-monetary asset.

Summary of the Approach Required by this Standard

17   In preparing financial statements, each entity – whether a stand-alone entity, an entity with foreign operations (such as a parent) or a foreign operation (such as a subsidiary or branch) – determines its functional currency in accordance with paragraphs 9-14. The entity translates foreign currency items into its functional currency and reports the effects of such translation in accordance with paragraphs 20-37 and 50.

18   Many reporting entities comprise a number of individual entities (e.g. a *group* is made up of a parent and one or more subsidiaries). Various types of entities, whether members of a group or otherwise, may have investments in associates or joint ventures. They may also have branches. It is necessary for the results and financial position of each individual entity included in the reporting entity to be translated into the currency in which the reporting entity presents its financial statements. This Standard permits the presentation currency of a reporting entity to be any currency (or currencies). The results and financial position of any individual entity within the reporting entity whose functional currency differs from the presentation currency are translated in accordance with paragraphs 38-50.

19   This Standard also permits a stand-alone entity preparing financial statements or an entity preparing separate financial statements in accordance with AASB 127 *Consolidated and Separate Financial Statements* to present its financial statements in any currency (or currencies). If the entity's presentation currency differs from its functional currency, its results and financial position are also translated into the presentation currency in accordance with paragraphs 38-50.

Reporting Foreign Currency Transactions in the Functional Currency

Initial Recognition

20   A foreign currency transaction is a transaction that is denominated or requires settlement in a foreign currency, including transactions arising when an entity:

(a)   buys or sells goods or services whose price is denominated in a foreign currency;

(b)   borrows or lends funds when the amounts payable or receivable are denominated in a foreign currency; or

(c)   otherwise acquires or disposes of assets, or incurs or settles liabilities, denominated in a foreign currency.

21   **A foreign currency transaction shall be recorded, on initial recognition in the functional currency, by applying to the foreign currency amount the *spot exchange rate* between the functional currency and the foreign currency at the date of the transaction.**

22   The date of a transaction is the date on which the transaction first qualifies for recognition in accordance with Australian equivalents to IFRSs. For practical reasons, a rate that approximates the actual rate at the date of the transaction is often used, for example, an average rate for a week or a month might be used for all transactions in each foreign currency occurring during that period. However, if exchange rates fluctuate significantly, the use of the average rate for a period is inappropriate.

Reporting at the Ends of Subsequent Reporting Periods

23   **At each end of the reporting period:**

(a)   **foreign currency monetary items shall be translated using the *closing rate*;**

(b)   **non-monetary items that are measured in terms of historical cost in a foreign currency shall be translated using the exchange rate at the date of the transaction; and**

    (c)   **non-monetary items that are measured at fair value in a foreign currency shall be translated using the exchange rates at the date when the fair value was determined.**

24   The carrying amount of an item is determined in conjunction with other relevant Standards. For example, property, plant and equipment may be measured in terms of fair value or historical cost in accordance with AASB 116 *Property, Plant and Equipment*. Whether the carrying amount is determined on the basis of historical cost or on the basis of fair value, if the amount is determined in a foreign currency it is then translated into the functional currency in accordance with this Standard.

25   The carrying amount of some items is determined by comparing two or more amounts. For example, the carrying amount of inventories is the lower of cost and net realisable value in accordance with AASB 102 *Inventories*. Similarly, in accordance with AASB 136 *Impairment of Assets*, the carrying amount of an asset for which there is an indication of impairment is the lower of its carrying amount before considering possible impairment losses and its recoverable amount. When such an asset is non-monetary and is measured in a foreign currency, the carrying amount is determined by comparing:

    (a)   the cost or carrying amount, as appropriate, translated at the exchange rate at the date when that amount was determined (i.e. the rate at the date of the transaction for an item measured in terms of historical cost); and

    (b)   the net realisable value or recoverable amount, as appropriate, translated at the exchange rate at the date when that value was determined (e.g. the closing rate at the end of the reporting period).

The effect of this comparison may be that an impairment loss is recognised in the functional currency but would not be recognised in the foreign currency, or vice versa.

26   When several exchange rates are available, the rate used is that at which the future cash flows represented by the transaction or balance could have been settled if those cash flows had occurred at the measurement date. If exchangeability between two currencies is temporarily lacking, the rate used is the first subsequent rate at which exchanges could be made.

Recognition of Exchange Differences

27   As noted in paragraphs 3(a) and 5, AASB 139 applies to hedge accounting for foreign currency items. The application of hedge accounting requires an entity to account for some *exchange differences* differently from the treatment of exchange differences required by this Standard. For example, AASB 139 requires that exchange differences on monetary items that qualify as hedging instruments in a cash flow hedge are recognised initially in other comprehensive income to the extent the hedge is effective.

28   **Exchange differences arising on the settlement of monetary items or on translating monetary items at rates different from those at which they were translated on initial recognition during the period or in previous financial statements, shall be recognised in profit or loss in the period in which they arise, except as described in paragraph 32.**

29   When monetary items arise from a foreign currency transaction and there is a change in the exchange rate between the transaction date and the date of settlement, an exchange difference results. When the transaction is settled within the same reporting period as that in which it occurred, all the exchange difference is recognised in that period. However, when the transaction is settled in a subsequent reporting period, the exchange difference recognised in each period up to the date of settlement is determined by the change in exchange rates during each period.

30   **When a gain or loss on a non-monetary item is recognised in other comprehensive income, any exchange component of that gain or loss shall be recognised in other comprehensive income. Conversely, when a gain or loss on a non-monetary item is recognised in profit or loss, any exchange component of that gain or loss shall be recognised in profit or loss.**

31   Other Australian Accounting Standards require some gains and losses to be recognised in other comprehensive income. For example, AASB 116 requires some gains and losses arising on a revaluation of property, plant and equipment to be recognised in other comprehensive income. When such an asset is measured in a foreign currency, paragraph 23(c) of this Standard requires the revalued amount to be translated using the rate at the date the value is determined, resulting in an exchange difference that is also recognised in other comprehensive income.

32   Exchange differences arising on a monetary item that forms part of a reporting entity's *net investment in a foreign operation* (see paragraph 15) shall be recognised in profit or loss in the separate financial statements of the reporting entity or the individual financial statements of the foreign operation as appropriate. In the financial statements that includes the foreign operation and the reporting entity (e.g. the consolidated financial statements when the foreign operation is a subsidiary), such exchange differences shall be recognised initially in other comprehensive income and reclassified from equity to profit or loss on disposal of the net investment in accordance with paragraph 48.

33   When a monetary item forms part of a reporting entity's net investment in a foreign operation and is denominated in the functional currency of the reporting entity, an exchange difference arises in the foreign operation's individual financial statements in accordance with paragraph 28. If such an item is denominated in the functional currency of the foreign operation, an exchange difference arises in the reporting entity's separate financial statements in accordance with paragraph 28. If such an item is denominated in a currency other than the functional currency of either the reporting entity or the foreign operation, an exchange difference arises in the reporting entity's separate financial statements and in the foreign operation's individual financial statements in accordance with paragraph 28. Such exchange differences are recognised in other comprehensive income in the financial statements that include the foreign operation and the reporting entity (i.e. financial statements in which the foreign operation is consolidated, proportionately consolidated or accounted for using the equity method).

34   When an entity keeps its books and records in a currency other than its functional currency, at the time the entity prepares its financial statements, all amounts are translated into the functional currency in accordance with paragraphs 20-26. This produces the same amounts in the functional currency as would have occurred had the items been recorded initially in the functional currency. For example, monetary items are translated into the functional currency using the closing rate, and non-monetary items that are measured on a historical cost basis are translated using the exchange rate at the date of the transaction that resulted in their recognition.

Change in Functional Currency

35   When there is a change in an entity's functional currency, the entity shall apply the translation procedures applicable to the new functional currency prospectively from the date of the change.

36   As noted in paragraph 13, the functional currency of an entity reflects the underlying transactions, events and conditions that are relevant to the entity. Accordingly, once the functional currency is determined, it can be changed only if there is a change to those underlying transactions, events and conditions. For example, a change in the currency that mainly influences the sales prices of goods and services may lead to a change in an entity's functional currency.

37   The effect of a change in functional currency is accounted for prospectively. In other words, an entity translates all items into the new functional currency using the exchange rate at the date of the change. The resulting translated amounts for non-monetary items are treated as their historical cost. Exchange differences arising from the translation of a foreign operation previously recognised in other comprehensive income in accordance with paragraphs 32 and 39(c) are not reclassified from equity to profit or loss until the disposal of the operation.

Use of a Presentation Currency other than the Functional Currency

Translation to the Presentation Currency

38   An entity may present its financial statements in any currency (or currencies). If the presentation currency differs from the entity's functional currency, it translates its results and financial position into the presentation currency. For example, when a group contains individual entities with different functional currencies, the results and financial position of each entity are expressed in a common currency so that the consolidated financial statements may be presented.

39   **The results and financial position of an entity whose functional currency is not the currency of a hyperinflationary economy shall be translated into a different presentation currency using the following procedures:**

   (a)   assets and liabilities for each statement of financial position presented (i.e. including comparatives) shall be translated at the closing rate at the date of that statement of financial position;

   (b)   income and expenses for each statement of comprehensive income or separate income statement presented (i.e. including comparatives) shall be translated at exchange rates at the dates of the transactions; and

   (c)   all resulting exchange differences shall be recognised in other comprehensive income.

40   For practical reasons, a rate that approximates the exchange rates at the dates of the transactions, for example an average rate for the period, is often used to translate income and expense items. However, if exchange rates fluctuate significantly, the use of the average rate for a period is inappropriate.

41   The exchange differences referred to in paragraph 39(c) result from:

   (a)   translating income and expenses at the exchange rates at the dates of the transactions and assets and liabilities at the closing rate; and

   (b)   translating the opening net assets at a closing rate that differs from the previous closing rate.

   These exchange differences are not recognised in profit or loss because the changes in exchange rates have little or no direct effect on the present and future cash flows from operations. The cumulative amount of the exchange differences is presented in a separate component of equity until disposal of the foreign operation. When the exchange differences relate to a foreign operation that is consolidated but not wholly-owned, accumulated exchange differences arising from translation and attributable to non-controlling interests are allocated to, and recognised as part of, non-controlling interests in the consolidated statement of financial position.

42   **The results and financial position of an entity whose functional currency is the currency of a hyperinflationary economy shall be translated into a different presentation currency using the following procedures:**

   (a)   all amounts (i.e. assets, liabilities, equity items, income and expenses, including comparatives) shall be translated at the closing rate at the date of the most recent statement of financial position, except that

   (b)   when amounts are translated into the currency of a non-hyperinflationary economy, comparative amounts shall be those that were presented as current year amounts in the relevant prior year financial statements (i.e. not adjusted for subsequent changes in the price level or subsequent changes in exchange rates).

43   **When an entity's functional currency is the currency of a hyperinflationary economy, the entity shall restate its financial statements in accordance with AASB 129 before applying the translation method set out in paragraph 42, except for comparative amounts that are translated into a currency of a non-hyperinflationary economy (see paragraph 42(b)). When the economy ceases to be hyperinflationary and the**

entity no longer restates its financial statements in accordance with AASB 129, it shall use as the historical costs for translation into the presentation currency the amounts restated to the price level at the date the entity ceased restating its financial statements.

Translation of a Foreign Operation

44   Paragraphs 45-47, in addition to paragraphs 38-43, apply when the results and financial position of a foreign operation are translated into a presentation currency so that the foreign operation can be included in the financial statements of the reporting entity by consolidation, proportionate consolidation or the equity method.

45   The incorporation of the results and financial position of a foreign operation with those of the reporting entity follows normal consolidation procedures, such as the elimination of intragroup balances and intragroup transactions of a subsidiary (see AASB 127 and AASB 131 *Interests in Joint Ventures*). However, an intragroup monetary asset (or liability), whether short-term or long-term, cannot be eliminated against the corresponding intragroup liability (or asset) without showing the results of currency fluctuations in the consolidated financial statements. This is because the monetary item represents a commitment to convert one currency into another and exposes the reporting entity to a gain or loss through currency fluctuations. Accordingly, in the consolidated financial statements of the reporting entity, such an exchange difference is recognised in profit or loss or, if it arises from the circumstances described in paragraph 32, it is recognised in other comprehensive income and accumulated in a separate component of equity until the disposal of the foreign operation.

46   When the financial statements of a foreign operation are as of a date different from that of the reporting entity, the foreign operation often prepares additional statements as of the same date as the reporting entity's financial statements. When this is not done, AASB 127 allows the use of a different date provided that the difference is no greater than three months and adjustments are made for the effects of any significant transactions or other events that occur between the different dates. In such a case, the assets and liabilities of the foreign operation are translated at the exchange rate at the end of the reporting period of the foreign operation. Adjustments are made for significant changes in exchange rates up to the end of the reporting period of the reporting entity in accordance with AASB 127. The same approach is used in applying the equity method to associates and joint ventures and in applying proportionate consolidation to joint ventures in accordance with AASB 128 *Investments in Associates* and AASB 131.

47   **Any goodwill arising on the acquisition of a foreign operation and any fair value adjustments to the carrying amounts of assets and liabilities arising on the acquisition of that foreign operation shall be treated as assets and liabilities of the foreign operation. Thus they shall be expressed in the functional currency of the foreign operation and shall be translated at the closing rate in accordance with paragraphs 39 and 42.**

Disposal or Partial Disposal of a Foreign Operation

48   **On the disposal of a foreign operation, the cumulative amount of the exchange differences relating to that foreign operation, recognised in other comprehensive income and accumulated in a separate component of equity, shall be reclassified from equity to profit or loss (as a reclassification adjustment) when the gain or loss on disposal is recognised (see AASB 101 *Presentation of Financial Statements* (as revised in 2007)).**

48A   In addition to the disposal of an entity's entire interest in a foreign operation, the following are accounted for as disposals even if the entity retains an interest in the former subsidiary, associate or jointly controlled entity:

(a)   the loss of control of a subsidiary that includes a foreign operation;

(b)   the loss of significant influence over an associate that includes a foreign operation; and

(c)   the loss of joint control over a jointly controlled entity that includes a foreign operation.

48B On disposal of a subsidiary that includes a foreign operation, the cumulative amount of the exchange differences relating to that foreign operation that have been attributed to the non-controlling interests shall be derecognised, but shall not be reclassified to profit or loss.

48C On the partial disposal of a subsidiary that includes a foreign operation, the entity shall re-attribute the proportionate share of the cumulative amount of the exchange differences recognised in other comprehensive income to the non-controlling interests in that foreign operation. In any other partial disposal of a foreign operation the entity shall reclassify to profit or loss only the proportionate share of the cumulative amount of the exchange differences recognised in other comprehensive income.

48D A partial disposal of an entity's interest in a foreign operation is any reduction in an entity's ownership interest in a foreign operation, except those reductions in paragraph 48A that are accounted for as disposals.

49 An entity may dispose or partially dispose of its interest in a foreign operation through sale, liquidation, repayment of share capital or abandonment of all, or part of, that entity. The payment of a dividend is part of a disposal only when it constitutes a return of the investment, for example when the dividend is paid out of pre-acquisition profits. A write-down of the carrying amount of a foreign operation, either because of its own losses or because of an impairment recognised by the investor, does not constitute a partial disposal. Accordingly, no part of the foreign exchange gain or loss recognised in other comprehensive income is reclassified to profit or loss at the time of a write-down.

Tax Effects of All Exchange Differences

50 Gains and losses on foreign currency transactions and exchange differences arising on translating the results and financial position of an entity (including a foreign operation) into a different currency may have tax effects. AASB 112 *Income Taxes* applies to these tax effects.

Disclosure

51 **In paragraphs 53 and 55-57 references to 'functional currency' apply, in the case of a group, to the functional currency of the parent.**

52 **An entity shall disclose:**

(a) **the amount of exchange differences recognised in profit or loss except for those arising on financial instruments measured at fair value through profit or loss in accordance with AASB 139; and**

(b) **net exchange differences recognised in other comprehensive income and accumulated in a separate component of equity, and a reconciliation of the amount of such exchange differences at the beginning and end of the period.**

53 **When the presentation currency is different from the functional currency, that fact shall be stated, together with disclosure of the functional currency and the reason for using a different presentation currency.**

54 **When there is a change in the functional currency of either the reporting entity or a significant foreign operation, that fact and the reason for the change in functional currency shall be disclosed.**

55 **When an entity presents its financial statements in a currency that is different from its functional currency, it shall describe the financial statements as complying with Australian equivalents to IFRSs only if they comply with all the requirements of Australian equivalents to IFRSs including the translation method set out in paragraphs 39 and 42.**

56 An entity sometimes presents its financial statements or other financial information in a currency that is not its functional currency without meeting the requirements of paragraph 55. For example, an entity may convert into another currency only selected items from its financial statements. Or, an entity whose functional currency is not the currency of a hyperinflationary economy may convert the financial statements into

another currency by translating all items at the most recent closing rate. Such conversions are not in accordance with Australian equivalents to IFRSs and the disclosures set out in paragraph 57 are required.

57   **When an entity displays its financial statements or other financial information in a currency that is different from either its functional currency or its presentation currency and the requirements of paragraph 55 are not met, it shall:**

  (a)   **clearly identify the information as supplementary information to distinguish it from the information that complies with Australian equivalents to IFRSs;**

  (b)   **disclose the currency in which the supplementary information is displayed; and**

  (c)   **disclose the entity's functional currency and the method of translation used to determine the supplementary information.**

Effective Date and Transition

58   [Deleted by the AASB]

58A   [Deleted by the AASB]

59   [Deleted by the AASB]

60   [Deleted by the AASB]

60A   [Deleted by the AASB]

60B   AASB 2008-3 *Amendments to Australian Accounting Standards arising from AASB 3 and AASB 127* added paragraphs 48A-48D and amended paragraph 49. An entity shall apply those amendments prospectively for annual reporting periods beginning on or after 1 July 2009. If an entity applies AASB 127 (amended 2008) for an earlier period, the amendments shall be applied for that earlier period.

60D   Paragraph 60B was added by AASB 2010-3 *Amendments to Australian Accounting Standards arising from the Annual Improvements Project* issued in June 2010. An entity shall apply the amendments noted in paragraph 60B prospectively for annual reporting periods beginning on or after 1 July 2010. Earlier application is permitted.

60H   AASB 2011-9 *Amendments to Australian Accounting Standards – Presentation of Items of Other Comprehensive Income*, issued in September 2011, amended paragraph 39. An entity shall apply that amendment when it applies AASB 101 as amended in September 2011.

Withdrawal of Other Pronouncements of the IASB

61   [Deleted by the AASB]

62   [Deleted by the AASB]

AASB 123
Borrowing Costs

(Compiled November 2009)

Note from the Institute of Chartered Accountants Australia

This commentary, prepared by the technical editors, is not part of Accounting Standard AASB 123.

Historical development

July 2004: AASB 123 'Borrowing Costs' is the Australian equivalent of IAS 23 of the same name. It was made by the AASB on 15 July 2004 as part of the AASB's program to adopt International Financial Reporting Standards (IFRSs) by 2005.

June 2007: AASB 123 'Borrowing Costs' was reissued by the AASB based on revised IAS 23 of the same name, and is applicable to annual reporting periods beginning on or after 1 January 2009, with early adoption permitted for annual reporting periods beginning on or after 1 January 2005 but before 1 January 2009. The revised Standard requires the capitalisation of all borrowing costs directly attributable to the acquitisition, construction or production of a qualifying asset. All other borrowing costs are immediatley recognised as expenses. The revised Standard differs from the July 2004 version of the Standard which permitted a choice between capitalising and expensing borrowing costs attributable to a qualifying asset.

24 July 2008: AASB 2008-5 'Amendments to Australian Accounting Standards arising from the Annual Improvements Project' amends AASB 123 in relation to components of borrowing costs. This Standard is applicable to annual reporting periods beginning on or after 1 January 2009.

22 April 2009: AASB 2009-1 'Amendments to Australian Accounting Standards – Borrowing Costs of Not for Profit Entities' amends AASB 123 so a not-for-profit public sector entity may choose to expense borrowing costs. This Standard is applicable to periods beginning on or after 1 January 2009 that end on or after 30 April 2009.

25 June 2009: AASB 2009-6 'Amendments to Australian Accounting Standards' amends AASB 123 for editorial corrections made by the International Accounting Standards Board (IASB) to its Standards and Interpretations (IFRSs) and as a consequence of issuing revised AASB 101 'Presentation of Financial Statements'. This Standard is applicable to annual reporting periods beginning on or after 1 January 2009 that end on or after 30 June 2009.

4 November 2009: AASB 123 was reissued by the AASB, compiled to include the AASB 2008-5, AASB 2009-1 and AASB 2009-6 amendments and applies to annual reporting periods beginning on or after 1 January 2009.

References

Interpretation 1 *Changes in Existing Decommissioning Restoration and Similar Liabilities* and Interpretation 12 *Service Concession Arrangements* apply to AASB 123.

IFRIC items not taken onto the agenda: IAS 23-1 *Foreign Exchange and capitalisable borrowing costs* and IAS 23-2 apply to AASB 123.

AASB 120 compared to IAS 20

Additions

Paragraph	Description
Aus 1.1	Which entities AASB 123 applies to (i.e. reporting entities and general purpose financial reports).
Aus 1.2	The application date of AASB 123 (i.e. annual reporting periods beginning 1 January 2009).
Aus 1.3	Permits early application of AASB 123.

Aus 1.4	Makes the requirements of AASB 123 subject to AASB 1031 'Materiality'.
Aus 1.5	Explains which Australian Standards have been superseded by AASB 123.
Deletions	
Paragraph	*Description*
29	Effective date of IAS 23.
30	Withdrawal of previous IAS 23.

Contents

Compilation Details

Comparison with IAS 23

Accounting Standard
AASB 123 Borrowing Costs

	Paragraphs
Core Principle	1 – Aus1.0
Application	Aus1.1 – Aus1.5
Scope	2 – 4
Definitions	5 – 7
Recognition	8 – 9
Borrowing Costs Eligible for Capitalisation	10 – 15
Excess of the Carrying Amount of the Qualifying Asset over Recoverable Amount	16
Commencement of Capitalisation	17 – 19
Suspension of Capitalisation	20 – 21
Cessation of Capitalisation	22 – 25
Disclosure	26 – Aus26.1
Transitional Provisions	27 – 28
Effective Date	29A

Deleted IAS 23 Text

Basis for Conclusions on IAS 23
(available on the AASB website)

Australian Accounting Standard AASB 123 *Borrowing Costs* (as amended) is set out in paragraphs 1 – 29A. All the paragraphs have equal authority. Paragraphs in **bold type** state the main principles. Terms defined in this Standard are in *italics* the first time they appear in the Standard. AASB 123 is to be read in the context of other Australian Accounting Standards, including AASB 1048 *Interpretation and Application of Standards*, which identifies the Australian Accounting Interpretations. In the absence of explicit guidance, AASB 108 *Accounting Policies, Changes in Accounting Estimates and Errors* provides a basis for selecting and applying accounting policies.

Compilation Details

Accounting Standard AASB 123 *Borrowing Costs* as amended

This compiled Standard applies to annual reporting periods beginning on or after 1 January 2009 that end on or after 30 June 2009. It takes into account amendments up to and including 25 June 2009 and was prepared on 4 November 2009 by the staff of the Australian Accounting Standards Board (AASB).

This compilation is not a separate Accounting Standard made by the AASB. Instead, it is a representation of AASB 123 (June 2007) as amended by other Accounting Standards, which are listed in the Table below.

Table of Standards

Standard	Date made	Application date *(annual reporting periods ... on or after ...)*	Application, saving or transitional provisions
AASB 123	14 Jun 2007	*(beginning)* 1 Jan 2009	see (a) below
AASB 2007-8	24 Sep 2007	*(beginning)* 1 Jan 2009	see (b) below
AASB 2008-5	24 Jul 2008	*(beginning)* 1 Jan 2009	see (c) below
AASB 2009-1	22 Apr 2009	*(beginning)* 1 Jan 2009 and *(ending)* 30 Apr 2009	see (d) below
AASB 2009-6	25 Jun 2009	*(beginning)* 1 Jan 2009 and *(ending)* 30 Jun 2009	see (e) below

(a)   Entities may elect to apply this Standard to annual reporting periods beginning on or after 1 January 2005 but before 1 January 2009.

(b)   Entities may elect to apply this Standard to annual reporting periods beginning on or after 1 January 2005 but before 1 January 2009, provided that AASB 101 *Presentation of Financial Statements* (September 2007) is also applied to such periods.

(c)   Entities may elect to apply this Standard, or its amendments to individual Standards, to annual reporting periods beginning on or after 1 January 2005 but before 1 January 2009.

(d)   Entities may elect to apply this Standard to annual reporting periods beginning on or after 1 January 2009 that end before 30 April 2009, provided that AASB 123 *Borrowing Costs* (June 2007) is also applied to such periods.

(e)   Entities may elect to apply this Standard to annual reporting periods beginning on or after 1 January 2005 but before 1 January 2009, provided that AASB 101 *Presentation of Financial Statements* (September 2007) is also applied to such periods, and to annual reporting periods beginning on or after 1 January 2009 that end before 30 June 2009.

Table of Amendments

Paragraph affected	How affected	By ... [paragraph]
Aus1.0	added	AASB 2009-1 [7]
Aus1.1	amended	AASB 2007-8 [7, 8]
Aus1.4	amended	AASB 2007-8 [8]
6	amended amended	AASB 2008-5 [38] AASB 2009-6 [63]
Aus8.1	added	AASB 2009-1 [8]
Aus8.2	added	AASB 2009-1 [8]
Aus26.1	added	AASB 2009-1 [9]
29 (preceding heading)	amended	AASB 2008-5 [39]
29A	added	AASB 2008-5 [40]

Comparison with IAS 23

AASB 123 and IAS 23

AASB 123 *Borrowing Costs* as amended incorporates IAS 23 *Borrowing Costs* as issued and amended by the International Accounting Standards Board (IASB). Paragraphs that have been added to this Standard (and do not appear in the text of IAS 23) are identified with the prefix "Aus", followed by the number of the preceding IASB paragraph and decimal numbering. Paragraphs that apply only to not-for-profit entities begin by identifying their limited applicability.

Compliance with IAS 23

For-profit entities that comply with AASB 123 as amended will simultaneously be in compliance with IAS 23 as amended.

Not-for-profit entities using the added "Aus" paragraphs in the Standard that specifically apply to not-for-profit entities may not be simultaneously complying with IAS 23. Whether a not-for-profit entity will be in compliance with IAS 23 will depend on whether the "Aus" paragraphs provide additional guidance for not-for-profit entities or contain requirements that are inconsistent with the corresponding IASB Standard and will be applied by the not-for-profit entity.

Accounting Standard AASB 123

The Australian Accounting Standards Board made Accounting Standard AASB 123 *Borrowing Costs* under section 334 of the *Corporations Act 2001* on 14 June 2007.

This compiled version of AASB 123 applies to annual reporting periods beginning on or after 1 January 2009 that end on or after 30 June 2009. It incorporates relevant amendments contained in other AASB Standards made by the AASB up to and including 25 June 2009 (see Compilation Details).

Accounting Standard AASB 123

Borrowing Costs

Core Principle

1   **Borrowing costs that are directly attributable to the acquisition, construction or production of a qualifying asset form part of the cost of that asset. Other borrowing costs are recognised as an expense.**

Aus1.0   **In respect of not-for-profit public sector entities[1], borrowing costs may be expensed in accordance with paragraph Aus8.1.**

Application

Aus1.1   **This Standard applies to:**

    (a)   **each entity that is required to prepare financial reports in accordance with Part 2M.3 of the Corporations Act and that is a reporting entity;**

    (b)   **general purpose financial statements of each other reporting entity; and**

    (c)   **financial statements that are, or are held out to be, general purpose financial statements.**

Aus1.2   **This Standard applies to annual reporting periods beginning on or after 1 January 2009.**

    [Note: For application dates of paragraphs changed or added by an amending Standard, see Compilation Details.]

Aus1.3   **This Standard may be applied to annual reporting periods beginning on or after 1 January 2005 but before 1 January 2009. When an entity applies this Standard to such an annual reporting period, it shall disclose that fact.**

Aus1.4   **The requirements specified in this Standard apply to the financial statements where information resulting from their application is material in accordance with AASB 1031 *Materiality*.**

Aus1.5   **When applicable, this Standard supersedes AASB 123 *Borrowing Costs* as notified in the *Commonwealth of Australia Gazette* No S 294, 22 July 2004.**

Scope

2   **An entity shall apply this Standard in accounting for borrowing costs.**

3   The Standard does not deal with the actual or imputed cost of equity, including preferred capital not classified as a liability.

4   An entity is not required to apply the Standard to borrowing costs directly attributable to the acquisition, construction or production of:

    (a)   a qualifying asset measured at fair value, for example a biological asset; or

    (b)   inventories that are manufactured, or otherwise produced, in large quantities on a repetitive basis.

---

[1]   In April 2009, the AASB agreed to reintroduce the expense option for not-for-profit public sector entities. The AASB currently has a project on the application of AASB 123 to not-for-profit public sector entities.

Definitions

5   This Standard uses the following terms with the meanings specified:

Borrowing costs are interest and other costs that an entity incurs in connection with the borrowing of funds.

A *qualifying asset* is an asset that necessarily takes a substantial period of time to get ready for its intended use or sale.

6   Borrowing costs may include:

(a)   interest expense calculated using the effective interest method as described in AASB 139 *Financial Instruments: Recognition and Measurement*;

(b)   [deleted by the IASB]

(c)   [deleted by the IASB]

(d)   finance charges in respect of finance leases recognised in accordance with AASB 117 *Leases*; and

(e)   exchange differences arising from foreign currency borrowings to the extent that they are regarded as an adjustment to interest costs.

7   Depending on the circumstances, any of the following may be qualifying assets:

(a)   inventories

(b)   manufacturing plants

(c)   power generation facilities

(d)   intangible assets

(e)   investment properties.

Financial assets, and inventories that are manufactured, or otherwise produced, over a short period of time, are not qualifying assets. Assets that are ready for their intended use or sale when acquired are not qualifying assets.

Recognition

8   An entity shall capitalise borrowing costs that are directly attributable to the acquisition, construction or production of a qualifying asset as part of the cost of that asset. An entity shall recognise other borrowing costs as an expense in the period in which it incurs them.

Aus8.1   A not-for-profit public sector entity may elect to recognise borrowing costs as an expense in the period in which they are incurred regardless of how the borrowings are applied.

Aus8.2   In respect of not-for-profit public sector entities, paragraphs 9-26, 27 and 28 apply only when an entity elects to capitalise borrowing costs that are directly attributable to the acquisition, construction or production of a qualifying asset as part of the cost of that asset.

9   Borrowing costs that are directly attributable to the acquisition, construction or production of a qualifying asset are included in the cost of that asset. Such borrowing costs are capitalised as part of the cost of the asset when it is probable that they will result in future economic benefits to the entity and the costs can be measured reliably. When an entity applies AASB 129 *Financial Reporting in Hyperinflationary Economies*, it recognises as an expense the part of borrowing costs that compensates for inflation during the same period in accordance with paragraph 21 of that Standard.

Borrowing Costs Eligible for Capitalisation

10   The borrowing costs that are directly attributable to the acquisition, construction or production of a qualifying asset are those borrowing costs that would have been avoided if the expenditure on the qualifying asset had not been made. When an entity borrows funds specifically for the purpose of obtaining a particular qualifying asset, the borrowing costs that directly relate to that qualifying asset can be readily identified.

AASB

11   It may be difficult to identify a direct relationship between particular borrowings and a qualifying asset and to determine the borrowings that could otherwise have been avoided. Such a difficulty occurs, for example, when the financing activity of an entity is co-ordinated centrally. Difficulties also arise when a group uses a range of debt instruments to borrow funds at varying rates of interest, and lends those funds on various bases to other entities in the group. Other complications arise through the use of loans denominated in or linked to foreign currencies, when the group operates in highly inflationary economies, and from fluctuations in exchange rates. As a result, the determination of the amount of borrowing costs that are directly attributable to the acquisition of a qualifying asset is difficult and the exercise of judgement is required.

12   **To the extent that an entity borrows funds specifically for the purpose of obtaining a qualifying asset, the entity shall determine the amount of borrowing costs eligible for capitalisation as the actual borrowing costs incurred on that borrowing during the period less any investment income on the temporary investment of those borrowings.**

13   The financing arrangements for a qualifying asset may result in an entity obtaining borrowed funds and incurring associated borrowing costs before some or all of the funds are used for expenditures on the qualifying asset. In such circumstances, the funds are often temporarily invested pending their expenditure on the qualifying asset. In determining the amount of borrowing costs eligible for capitalisation during a period, any investment income earned on such funds is deducted from the borrowing costs incurred.

14   **To the extent that an entity borrows funds generally and uses them for the purpose of obtaining a qualifying asset, the entity shall determine the amount of borrowing costs eligible for capitalisation by applying a capitalisation rate to the expenditures on that asset. The capitalisation rate shall be the weighted average of the borrowing costs applicable to the borrowings of the entity that are outstanding during the period, other than borrowings made specifically for the purpose of obtaining a qualifying asset. The amount of borrowing costs that an entity capitalises during a period shall not exceed the amount of borrowing costs it incurred during that period.**

15   In some circumstances, it is appropriate to include all borrowings of the parent and its subsidiaries when computing a weighted average of the borrowing costs; in other circumstances, it is appropriate for each subsidiary to use a weighted average of the borrowing costs applicable to its own borrowings.

Excess of the Carrying Amount of the Qualifying Asset Over Recoverable Amount

16   When the carrying amount or the expected ultimate cost of the qualifying asset exceeds its recoverable amount or net realisable value, the carrying amount is written down or written off in accordance with the requirements of other Standards. In certain circumstances, the amount of the write-down or write-off is written back in accordance with those other Standards.

Commencement of Capitalisation

17   **An entity shall begin capitalising borrowing costs as part of the cost of a qualifying asset on the commencement date. The commencement date for capitalisation is the date when the entity first meets all of the following conditions:**

(a)   **it incurs expenditures for the asset;**

(b)   **it incurs borrowing costs; and**

(c)   **it undertakes activities that are necessary to prepare the asset for its intended use or sale.**

18   Expenditures on a qualifying asset include only those expenditures that have resulted in payments of cash, transfers of other assets or the assumption of interest-bearing liabilities. Expenditures are reduced by any progress payments received and grants received in connection with the asset (see AASB 120 *Accounting for Government Grants and Disclosure of Government Assistance*). The average carrying amount of the asset during a period, including borrowing costs previously capitalised, is normally a reasonable approximation of the expenditures to which the capitalisation rate is applied in that period.

19   The activities necessary to prepare the asset for its intended use or sale encompass more than the physical construction of the asset. They include technical and administrative work prior to the commencement of physical construction, such as the activities associated with obtaining permits prior to the commencement of the physical construction. However, such activities exclude the holding of an asset when no production or development that changes the asset's condition is taking place. For example, borrowing costs incurred while land is under development are capitalised during the period in which activities related to the development are being undertaken. However, borrowing costs incurred while land acquired for building purposes is held without any associated development activity do not qualify for capitalisation.

Suspension of Capitalisation

20   An entity shall suspend capitalisation of borrowing costs during extended periods in which it suspends active development of a qualifying asset.

21   An entity may incur borrowing costs during an extended period in which it suspends the activities necessary to prepare an asset for its intended use or sale. Such costs are costs of holding partially completed assets and do not qualify for capitalisation. However, an entity does not normally suspend capitalising borrowing costs during a period when it carries out substantial technical and administrative work. An entity also does not suspend capitalising borrowing costs when a temporary delay is a necessary part of the process of getting an asset ready for its intended use or sale. For example, capitalisation continues during the extended period that high water levels delay construction of a bridge, if such high water levels are common during the construction period in the geographical region involved.

Cessation of Capitalisation

22   An entity shall cease capitalising borrowing costs when substantially all the activities necessary to prepare the qualifying asset for its intended use or sale are complete.

23   An asset is normally ready for its intended use or sale when the physical construction of the asset is complete even though routine administrative work might still continue. If minor modifications, such as the decoration of a property to the purchaser's or user's specification, are all that are outstanding, this indicates that substantially all the activities are complete.

24   When an entity completes the construction of a qualifying asset in parts and each part is capable of being used while construction continues on other parts, the entity shall cease capitalising borrowing costs when it completes substantially all the activities necessary to prepare that part for its intended use or sale.

25   A business park comprising several buildings, each of which can be used individually, is an example of a qualifying asset for which each part is capable of being usable while construction continues on other parts. An example of a qualifying asset that needs to be complete before any part can be used is an industrial plant involving several processes which are carried out in sequence at different parts of the plant within the same site, such as a steel mill.

Disclosure

26   An entity shall disclose:

      (a)   the amount of borrowing costs capitalised during the period; and

      (b)   the capitalisation rate used to determine the amount of borrowing costs eligible for capitalisation.

Aus26.1   A not-for-profit public sector entity shall disclose the accounting policy adopted for borrowing costs.

Transitional Provisions

27 **When application of this Standard constitutes a change in accounting policy, an entity shall apply the Standard to borrowing costs relating to qualifying assets for which the commencement date for capitalisation is on or after the application date.**

28 **However, an entity may designate any date before the application date and apply the Standard to borrowing costs relating to all qualifying assets for which the commencement date for capitalisation is on or after that date.**

Effective Date

29 [Deleted by the AASB]

29A Paragraph 6 is amended by AASB 2008-5 *Amendments to Australian Accounting Standards arising from the Annual Improvements Project* issued in July 2008. An entity shall apply that amendment for annual reporting periods beginning on or after 1 January 2009. Earlier application is permitted. If an entity applies the amendment for an earlier period it shall disclose that fact.

Withdrawal of IAS 23 (revised 1993)

30 [Deleted by the AASB]

Deleted IAS 23 Text

Deleted IAS 23 text is not part of AASB 123.

Paragraph 29

An entity shall apply the Standard for annual periods beginning on or after 1 January 2009. Earlier application is permitted. If an entity applies the Standard from a date before 1 January 2009, it shall disclose that fact.

Paragraph 30

This Standard supersedes IAS 23 *Borrowing Costs* revised in 1993.

AASB 124
Related Party Disclosures
(Revised December 2009)

Note from the Institute of Chartered Accountants Australia

This note, prepared by the technical editors, is not part of Accounting Standard AASB 124.

Historical development

15 July 2004: AASB 124 'Related Party Disclosures' is the Australian equivalent of IAS 24 of the same name. It was made by the AASB on 15 July 2004 as part of the AASB's program to adopt International Financial Reporting Standards (IFRSs) by 2005.

22 December 2004: AASB 2004-3 'Amendments to Australian Accounting Standards' amends paragraph 20 as a consequence of the reissue of AASB 119 'Employee Benefits'(December 2004). The Standard is applicable to annual reporting periods beginning on or after 1 January 2006, but is applicable from 1 January 2005 for entities who choose to early-adopt AASB 119 and AASB 2004-3.

20 December 2005: Reissued to include the requirements of AASB 1046 'Director and Executive Disclosures by Disclosing Entities' (withdrawn). In order to achieve IFRS compliance by parent entities, the relief available to parent entities under AASB 1046 is no longer provided under AASB 124. There are also changes to definitions – with reference to key management personnel rather than specified executives – disclosures, and layout. The more detailed disclosures by disclosing entities of compensation of individuals as required by AASB 1046 remain under AASB 124.

24 September 2007: AASB 2007-8 'Amendments to Australian Accounting Standards arising from AASB 101' amends AASB 124 to align with revised AASB 101. This Standard is applicable to annual reporting periods beginning on or after 1 January 2009.

13 December 2007: AASB 2007-10 'Further Amendments to Australian Accounting Standards arising from AASB 101' amends AASB 124, replacing the term 'financial report' with 'financial statements'. This Standard is applicable to annual reporting periods beginning on or after 1 January 2009.

6 June 2008: AASB 2008-4 'Amendments to Australian Accounting Standard – Key Management Personnel Disclosures by Disclosing Entities' excludes disclosing entities that are companies from the application of AASB 124 paragraphs Aus25.2 to Aus25.6, Aus25.7.1 and Aus25.7.2, as the requirements for these entities are now incorporated into the Corporations law. These amendments are applicable to annual reporting periods ending on or after 30 June 2008.

7 November 2008: AASB 124 was reissued by the AASB compiled to include the AASB 2008-4 amendments.

4 November 2009: AASB 124 was reissued by the AASB, compiled to include the AASB 2007-8 and AASB 2007-10 amendments and applies to annual reporting periods beginning on or after 1 January 2009. Early application is permitted for annual reporting periods beginning on or after 30 June 2007 that end before 30 June 2008.

15 December 2009: a revised version of AASB 124 was issued by the AASB, simplifying and clarifying the definition and meaning of a related party and providing a partial exemption from the disclosure requirements for government related entities. This Standard applies to annual reporting periods beginning on or after 1 January 2011.

7 July 2011: AASB 2011-4 'Amendments to Australian Accounting Standards to Remove Individual Key Management Personnel Disclosure Requirements' amends AASB 124 to remove the individual key management personnel disclosures. This Standard applies to annual reporting periods beginning on or after 1 January 2013 and cannot be adopted early. **These amendments are not included in the revised version of AASB 124.**

AASB

29 August 2011: AASB 2011-7 'Amendments to Australian Accounting Standards arising from the Consolidation and Joint Arrangements Standards' amends AASB 124 to give effect to many consequential changes arising from the issue of AASB 10, 11, 12, 127 and 128. This Standard applies to annual reporting periods beginning on or after 1 January 2013 and can be adopted early by for-profit entities. **These amendments are not included in the revised version of AASB 124.**

5 September 2011: AASB 2011-10 'Amendments to Australian Accounting Standards arising from AASB 119 (September 2011)' amends AASB 124 to give effect to a consequential change arising from the issue of AASB 119. This Standard applies to annual reporting periods beginning on or after 1 January 2013 and can be adopted early. **These amendments are not included in the revised version of AASB 124.**

References

IFRIC items not taken onto the agenda: No. 27 *Identifying and disclosing related party transactions by state-owned business entities*, No. 28 *Disclosure of emoluments to key management personnel* and No. 29 *Interpretation of the term 'information' in IAS 24 paragraph 17* apply to AASB 124.

AASB 124 compared to IAS 24

Additions

Paragraph	Description
Aus 1.1	Objective of paragraph Aus 29.1 to Aus 29.9.3 is to require disclosing entities to disclose additional information.
Aus 1.2	Which entities paragraphs 1 to 28 apply to (i.e. reporting entities and general purpose financial statements).
Aus 1.3	Exempts not-for-profit public sector entities from paragraphs 1 to 28 of the Standard.
Aus 1.4	Paragraphs Aus 29.1 to Aus 29.9.3 apply to disclosing entities.
Aus 1.4.1	Paragraphs Aus 29.2 to Aus 29.6 and 29.7.1 and Aus 29.7.2 do not apply to disclosing entities that are companies.
Aus 1.5	The disclosures required by paragraphs Aus 29.1 to Aus 29.9.3 are not required by a parent entity when consolidated financial statements are presented.
Aus 1.6	The application date of AASB 124 (i.e. annual reporting periods (beginning on or after 1 January 2011).
Aus 1.7	Permits early application of AASB 124.
Aus 1.8	Makes the requirements of AASB 124 paragraph 1 − 28 subject to AASB 1031 'Materiality'.
Aus 1.9	Deems the disclosures required by paragraphs Aus 29.1 to Aus 29.9.3 to be material.
Aus 1.10	Explains which Australian Standards have been superseded by AASB 124.
Aus 9.1	Additional Australian definitions for 'director', 'disclosing entity', and 'remuneration'.
Aus 9.1.1	Explains the term compensation.
Aus 29.1 to Aus 29.9.3	Require additional disclosures by disclosing entities in relation to directors and executives, other than paragraphs 29.2 to Aus 29.6 and Aus 29.7.1 and Aus 29.7.2 do not apply to disclosing entities that are companies.

Deletions

Paragraph	Description
29	Reference to superseded IAS 24.

Contents

Preface

Comparison with IAS 24

Accounting Standard
AASB 124 Related Party Disclosures

	Paragraphs
Objective	1 – Aus1.1
Application	Aus1.2 – Aus1.10
Scope	2 – 4
Purpose of Related Party Disclosures	5 – 8
Definitions	9 – 12
Disclosures	
All Entities	13 – 24
Government-related Entities	25 – 27
Effective Date and Transition	28
Other Key Management Personnel Disclosures by Disclosing Entities	Aus29.1 – Aus29.3
Compensation	Aus29.4
Principles of Compensation	Aus29.5
Modification of Terms of Share-based Payment Transactions	Aus29.6
Equity Instruments	Aus25.7.2
Different Classes to be Separately Identified	Aus29.7
Options and Rights Provided as Compensation	Aus29.7.1
Equity Instruments Provided on Exercise of Options and Rights Granted as Compensation	Aus29.7.2
Options and Rights Holdings	Aus29.7.3
Equity Holdings and Transactions	Aus29.7.4 – Aus29.7.5
Loans	Aus29.8 – Aus29.8.2
Other Transactions and Balances	Aus29.9 – Aus29.9.3

Illustrative Examples

Basis for conclusions on IAS 24
(available on the AASB website)

Australian Accounting Standard AASB 124 *Related Party Disclosures* is set out in paragraphs 1 – Aus29.9.3. All the paragraphs have equal authority. Paragraphs in **bold type** state the main principles. AASB 124 is to be read in the context of other Australian Accounting Standards, including AASB 1048 *Interpretation and Application of Standards*, which identifies the Australian Accounting Interpretations. In the absence of explicit guidance, AASB 108 *Accounting Policies, Changes in Accounting Estimates and Errors* provides a basis for selecting and applying accounting policies.

Preface

Introduction

The Australian Accounting Standards Board (AASB) makes Australian Accounting Standards, including Interpretations, to be applied by:

(a) entities required by the *Corporations Act 2001* to prepare financial reports;

(b) governments in preparing financial statements for the whole of government and the General Government Sector (GGS); and

(c) entities in the private or public for-profit or not-for-profit sectors that are reporting entities or that prepare general purpose financial statements.

Australian Accounting Standards incorporate International Financial Reporting Standards (IFRSs), including Interpretations, issued by the International Accounting Standards Board (IASB), with the addition of paragraphs on the applicability of each Standard in the Australian environment.

Australian Accounting Standards also include requirements that are specific to Australian entities. These requirements may be located in Australian Accounting Standards that incorporate IFRSs or in other Australian Accounting Standards. In most instances, these requirements are either restricted to the not-for-profit or public sectors or include additional disclosures that address domestic, regulatory or other issues. In developing requirements for public sector entities, the AASB considers the requirements of International Public Sector Accounting Standards (IPSASs), as issued by the International Public Sector Accounting Standards Board (IPSASB) of the International Federation of Accountants.

Private sector for-profit entities complying with Australian Accounting Standards will simultaneously comply with IFRSs. Many other entities complying with Australian Accounting Standards will also simultaneously comply with IFRSs.

Differences between this Standard and AASB 124 (December 2005, as amended)

The main changes from AASB 124 as issued in December 2005 (as amended) are described below.

(a) The definition of a related party is simplified, clarifying its intended meaning and eliminating inconsistencies from the definition, including:

(i) the definition now identifies a subsidiary and an associate with the same investor as related parties of each other;

(ii) entities significantly influenced by one person and entities significantly influenced by a close member of the family of that person are no longer related parties of each other; and

(iii) the definition now identifies that, whenever a person or entity has both joint control over a second entity and joint control or significant influence over a third party, the second and third entities are related to each other.

(b) A partial exemption is provided from the disclosure requirements for government-related entities. Entities that are related by virtue of being controlled by the same government can provide reduced related party disclosures.

Comparison with IAS 24

Paragraphs 1 to 28 of AASB 124 *Related Party Disclosures* incorporate IAS 24 *Related Party Disclosures* issued by the International Accounting Standards Board (IASB). Paragraphs that have been added to this Standard (and do not appear in the text of IAS 24) are identified with the prefix "Aus", followed by the number of the preceding IASB paragraph and decimal numbering. Paragraphs that apply only to not-for-profit entities begin by identifying their limited applicability. Paragraphs Aus29.1 to Aus29.9.3 require disclosing entities to provide additional information about individual key management personnel that are not required by IAS 24.

Entities that comply with AASB 124 will simultaneously be in compliance with IAS 24.

Compliance with the additional individual key management personnel disclosure requirements in paragraphs Aus29.1 to Aus29.9.3 of AASB 124 is not needed for IFRS compliance.

Accounting Standard AASB 124

The Australian Accounting Standards Board makes Accounting Standard AASB 124 *Related Party Disclosures* under section 334 of the *Corporations Act 2001*.

Dated 15 December 2009

Kevin M. Stevenson
Chair – AASB

Accounting Standard AASB 124
Related Party Disclosures

Objective

1   The objective of this Standard is to ensure that an entity's financial statements contain the disclosures necessary to draw attention to the possibility that its financial position and profit or loss may have been affected by the existence of related parties and by transactions and outstanding balances, including commitments, with such parties.

Aus1.1   The objective of paragraphs Aus29.1 to Aus29.9.3 of this Standard is to require *disclosing entities* to disclose additional information relating to individual *key management personnel*.

Application

Aus1.2   This Standard applies to:

(a)   each entity that is required to prepare financial reports in accordance with Part 2M.3 of the Corporations Act and that is a reporting entity;

(b)   general purpose financial statements of each other reporting entity; and

(c)   financial statements that are, or are held out to be, general purpose financial statements.

Aus1.3   Paragraphs 1 to 28 of this Standard do not apply to general purpose financial statements of not-for-profit public sector entities.

Aus1.4   Subject to paragraphs Aus1.4.1 and Aus1.5, paragraphs Aus29.1 to Aus29.9.3 of this Standard apply to each disclosing entity, or group of which a disclosing entity is the parent, that is required to prepare financial reports in accordance with Part 2M.3 of the Corporations Act.

Aus1.4.1   Paragraphs Aus29.2 to Aus29.6 and Aus29.7.1 and Aus29.7.2 of this Standard do not apply to disclosing entities that are companies.

Aus1.5   An entity that is the parent entity in a group and presents its separate financial statements together with the consolidated financial statements in accordance with AASB 127 *Consolidated and Separate Financial Statements* need not provide in its separate financial statements the disclosures required by paragraphs Aus29.1 to Aus29.9.3 of this Standard.

Aus1.6   This Standard applies to annual reporting periods beginning on or after 1 January 2011.

Aus1.7   This Standard may be applied to annual reporting periods beginning on or after 1 January 2005 but before 1 January 2011. When an entity applies this Standard to such an annual reporting period, it shall disclose that fact and at the same time apply the amendments to AASB 8 *Operating Segments* as made by AASB 2009-12 *Amendments to Australian Accounting Standards*.

AASB

Aus1.8	The requirements specified in paragraphs 1 to 28 of this Standard apply to the financial statements where information resulting from their application is material in accordance with AASB 1031 *Materiality*.
Aus1.9	The disclosures required by paragraphs Aus29.1 to Aus29.9.3 of this Standard are deemed material.
Aus1.10	When applied or operative, this Standard supersedes AASB 124 *Related Party Disclosures* issued in December 2005, as amended.

Scope

2   This Standard shall be applied in:

    (a)   identifying related party relationships and transactions;

    (b)   identifying outstanding balances, including commitments, between an entity and its related parties;

    (c)   identifying the circumstances in which disclosure of the items in (a) and (b) is required; and

    (d)   determining the disclosures to be made about those items.

3   This Standard requires disclosure of related party relationships, transactions and outstanding balances, including commitments, in the consolidated and separate financial statements of a parent, venturer or investor presented in accordance with AASB 127. This Standard also applies to individual financial statements.

4   Related party transactions and outstanding balances with other entities in a group are disclosed in an entity's financial statements. Intragroup related party transactions and outstanding balances are eliminated in the preparation of consolidated financial statements of the group.

Purpose of Related Party Disclosures

5   Related party relationships are a normal feature of commerce and business. For example, entities frequently carry on parts of their activities through subsidiaries, joint ventures and associates. In those circumstances, the entity has the ability to affect the financial and operating policies of the investee through the presence of control, joint control or significant influence.

6   A related party relationship could have an effect on the profit or loss and financial position of an entity. Related parties may enter into transactions that unrelated parties would not. For example, an entity that sells goods to its parent at cost might not sell on those terms to another customer. Also, transactions between related parties may not be made at the same amounts as between unrelated parties.

7   The profit or loss and financial position of an entity may be affected by a related party relationship even if related party transactions do not occur. The mere existence of the relationship may be sufficient to affect the transactions of the entity with other parties. For example, a subsidiary may terminate relations with a trading partner on acquisition by the parent of a fellow subsidiary engaged in the same activity as the former trading partner. Alternatively, one party may refrain from acting because of the significant influence of another – for example, a subsidiary may be instructed by its parent not to engage in research and development.

8   For these reasons, knowledge of an entity's transactions, outstanding balances, including commitments, and relationships with related parties may affect assessments of its operations by users of financial statements, including assessments of the risks and opportunities facing the entity.

Definitions

9   The following terms are used in this Standard with the meanings specified:

A *related party* is a person or entity that is related to the entity that is preparing its financial statements (in this Standard referred to as the 'reporting entity').

(a)   A person or a close member of that person's family is related to a reporting entity if that person:

    (i)   has control or joint control over the reporting entity;

    (ii)   has significant influence over the reporting entity; or

    (iii)   is a member of the key management personnel of the reporting entity or of a parent of the reporting entity.

(b)   An entity is related to a reporting entity if any of the following conditions applies:

    (i)   The entity and the reporting entity are members of the same group (which means that each parent, subsidiary and fellow subsidiary is related to the others).

    (ii)   One entity is an associate or joint venture of the other entity (or an associate or joint venture of a member of a group of which the other entity is a member).

    (iii)   Both entities are joint ventures of the same third party.

    (iv)   One entity is a joint venture of a third entity and the other entity is an associate of the third entity.

    (v)   The entity is a post-employment benefit plan for the benefit of employees of either the reporting entity or an entity related to the reporting entity. If the reporting entity is itself such a plan, the sponsoring employers are also related to the reporting entity.

    (vi)   The entity is controlled or jointly controlled by a person identified in (a).

    (vii)   A person identified in (a)(i) has significant influence over the entity or is a member of the key management personnel of the entity (or of a parent of the entity).

A *related party transaction* is a transfer of resources, services or obligations between a reporting entity and a related party, regardless of whether a price is charged.

Close members of the family of a person are those family members who may be expected to influence, or be influenced by, that person in their dealings with the entity and include:

(a)   that person's children and spouse or domestic partner;

(b)   children of that person's spouse or domestic partner; and

(c)   dependants of that person or that person's spouse or domestic partner.

Compensation includes all employee benefits (as defined in AASB 119 *Employee Benefits*) including employee benefits to which AASB 2 *Share-based Payment* applies. Employee benefits are all forms of consideration paid, payable or provided by the entity, or on behalf of the entity, in exchange for services rendered to the entity. It also includes such consideration paid on behalf of a parent of the entity in respect of the entity. Compensation includes:

(a)   short-term employee benefits, such as wages, salaries and social security contributions, paid annual leave and paid sick leave, profit-sharing and bonuses (if payable within twelve months of the end of the period) and non-monetary benefits (such as medical care, housing, cars and free or subsidised goods or services) for current employees;

(b)   post-employment benefits such as pensions, other retirement benefits, post-employment life insurance and post-employment medical care;

(c) other long-term employee benefits, including long-service leave or sabbatical leave, jubilee or other long-service benefits, long-term disability benefits and, if they are not payable wholly within twelve months after the end of the period, profit-sharing, bonuses and deferred compensation;

(d) termination benefits; and

(e) share-based payment.

Control is the power to govern the financial and operating policies of an entity so as to obtain benefits from its activities.

Joint control is the contractually agreed sharing of control over an economic activity.

Key management personnel are those persons having authority and responsibility for planning, directing and controlling the activities of the entity, directly or indirectly, including any director (whether executive or otherwise) of that entity.

Significant influence is the power to participate in the financial and operating policy decisions of an entity, but is not control over those policies. Significant influence may be gained by share ownership, statute or agreement.

Government refers to government, government agencies and similar bodies whether local, national or international.

A *government-related entity* is an entity that is controlled, jointly controlled or significantly influenced by a government.

Aus9.1   The following terms are also used in this Standard with the meaning specified.

Director means:

(a) a person who is a director under the Corporations Act; and

(b) in the case of entities governed by bodies not called a board of directors, a person who, regardless of the name that is given to the position, is appointed to the position of member of the governing body, council, commission or authority.

Disclosing entity is defined in the Corporations Act.

Remuneration is *compensation* as defined in this Standard.

Aus9.1.1   Although the defined term 'compensation' is used in this Standard rather than the term '*remuneration*', both words refer to the same concept and all references in the Corporations Act to the remuneration of directors and executives is taken as referring to compensation as defined and explained in this Standard.

10   In considering each possible related party relationship, attention is directed to the substance of the relationship and not merely the legal form.

11   In the context of this Standard, the following are not related parties:

(a) two entities simply because they have a director or other member of key management personnel in common or because a member of key management personnel of one entity has significant influence over the other entity.

(b) two venturers simply because they share joint control over a joint venture.

(c)   (i)   providers of finance,

     (ii)   trade unions,

     (iii)   public utilities, and

     (iv)   departments and agencies of a government that does not control, jointly control or significantly influence the reporting entity,

simply by virtue of their normal dealings with an entity (even though they may affect the freedom of action of an entity or participate in its decision-making process).

(d) a customer, supplier, franchisor, distributor or general agent with whom an entity transacts a significant volume of business, simply by virtue of the resulting economic dependence.

12   In the definition of a related party, an associate includes subsidiaries of the associate and a joint venture includes subsidiaries of the joint venture. Therefore, for example, an associate's subsidiary and the investor that has significant influence over the associate are related to each other.

Disclosures

All Entities

13   **Relationships between a parent and its subsidiaries shall be disclosed irrespective of whether there have been transactions between them. An entity shall disclose the name of its parent and, if different, the ultimate controlling party. If neither the entity's parent nor the ultimate controlling party produces consolidated financial statements available for public use, the name of the next most senior parent that does so shall also be disclosed.**

Aus13.1   **When any of the parent entities and/or ultimate controlling parties named in accordance with paragraph 13 is incorporated or otherwise constituted outside Australia, an entity shall:**

(a)   **identify which of those entities is incorporated overseas and where; and**

(b)   **disclose the name of the ultimate controlling entity incorporated within Australia.**

14   To enable users of financial statements to form a view about the effects of related party relationships on an entity, it is appropriate to disclose the related party relationship when control exists, irrespective of whether there have been transactions between the related parties.

15   The requirement to disclose related party relationships between a parent and its subsidiaries is in addition to the disclosure requirements in AASB 127, AASB 128 *Investments in Associates* and AASB 131 *Interests in Joint Ventures*.

16   Paragraph 13 refers to the next most senior parent. This is the first parent in the group above the immediate parent that produces consolidated financial statements available for public use.

17   **An entity shall disclose key management personnel compensation in total and for each of the following categories:**

(a)   **short-term employee benefits;**

(b)   **post-employment benefits;**

(c)   **other long-term benefits;**

(d)   **termination benefits; and**

(e)   **share-based payment.**

18   **If an entity has had related party transactions during the periods covered by the financial statements, it shall disclose the nature of the related party relationship as well as information about those transactions and outstanding balances, including commitments, necessary for users to understand the potential effect of the relationship on the financial statements. These disclosure requirements are in addition to those in paragraph 17. At a minimum, disclosures shall include:**

(a)   **the amount of the transactions;**

(b)   **the amount of outstanding balances, including commitments, and:**

(i)   **their terms and conditions, including whether they are secured, and the nature of the consideration to be provided in settlement; and**

(ii)   **details of any guarantees given or received;**

(c)   **provisions for doubtful debts related to the amount of outstanding balances; and**

(d)   **the expense recognised during the period in respect of bad or doubtful debts due from related parties.**

19 The disclosures required by paragraph 18 shall be made separately for each of the following categories:

(a) the parent;

(b) entities with joint control or significant influence over the entity;

(c) subsidiaries;

(d) associates;

(e) joint ventures in which the entity is a venturer;

(f) key management personnel of the entity or its parent; and

(g) other related parties.

20 The classification of amounts payable to, and receivable from, related parties in the different categories as required in paragraph 19 is an extension of the disclosure requirement in AASB 101 *Presentation of Financial Statements* for information to be presented either in the statement of financial position or in the notes. The categories are extended to provide a more comprehensive analysis of related party balances and apply to related party transactions.

21 The following are examples of transactions that are disclosed if they are with a related party:

(a) purchases or sales of goods (finished or unfinished);

(b) purchases or sales of property and other assets;

(c) rendering or receiving of services;

(d) leases;

(e) transfers of research and development;

(f) transfers under licence agreements;

(g) transfers under finance arrangements (including loans and equity contributions in cash or in kind);

(h) provision of guarantees or collateral;

(i) commitments to do something if a particular event occurs or does not occur in the future, including executory contracts[1] (recognised and unrecognised); and

(j) settlement of liabilities on behalf of the entity or by the entity on behalf of that related party.

22 Participation by a parent or subsidiary in a defined benefit plan that shares risks between group entities is a transaction between related parties (see paragraph 34B of AASB 119).

23 Disclosures that related party transactions were made on terms equivalent to those that prevail in arm's length transactions are made only if such terms can be substantiated.

24 **Items of a similar nature may be disclosed in aggregate except when separate disclosure is necessary for an understanding of the effects of related party transactions on the financial statements of the entity.**

Government-related Entities

25 **A reporting entity is exempt from the disclosure requirements of paragraph 18 in relation to related party transactions and outstanding balances, including commitments, with:**

(a) **a government that has control, joint control or significant influence over the reporting entity; and**

(b) **another entity that is a related party because the same government has control, joint control or significant influence over both the reporting entity and the other entity.**

---

1 AASB 137 *Provisions, Contingent Liabilities and Contingent Assets* defines executory contracts as contracts under which neither party has performed any of its obligations or both parties have partially performed their obligations to an equal extent.

26   If a reporting entity applies the exemption in paragraph 25, it shall disclose the following about the transactions and related outstanding balances referred to in paragraph 25:

(a)   the name of the government and the nature of its relationship with the reporting entity (i.e. control, joint control or significant influence);

(b)   the following information in sufficient detail to enable users of the entity's financial statements to understand the effect of related party transactions on its financial statements:

(i)   the nature and amount of each individually significant transaction; and

(ii)   for other transactions that are collectively, but not individually, significant, a qualitative or quantitative indication of their extent. Types of transactions include those listed in paragraph 21.

27   In using its judgement to determine the level of detail to be disclosed in accordance with the requirements in paragraph 26(b), the reporting entity shall consider the closeness of the related party relationship and other factors relevant in establishing the level of significance of the transaction such as whether it is:

(a)   significant in terms of size;

(b)   carried out on non-market terms;

(c)   outside normal day-to-day business operations, such as the purchase and sale of businesses;

(d)   disclosed to regulatory or supervisory authorities;

(e)   reported to senior management;

(f)   subject to shareholder approval.

Effective Date and Transition

28   An entity shall apply this Standard retrospectively for annual reporting periods beginning on or after 1 January 2011. Earlier application is permitted, either of the whole Standard or of the partial exemption in paragraphs 25 to 27 for government-related entities. If an entity applies either the whole Standard or that partial exemption for a period beginning before 1 January 2011, it shall disclose that fact.

Withdrawal of IAS 24 (2003)

29   [Deleted by the AASB]

Other Key Management Personnel Disclosures by Disclosing Entities

Aus29.1   Paragraphs Aus29.2 to Aus29.9.3 of this Standard apply to each disclosing entity (subject to parent entity relief) that is required to prepare financial reports in accordance with Part 2M.3 of the Corporations Act. However, paragraphs Aus29.2 to Aus29.6 and Aus29.7.1 and Aus29.7.2 of this Standard do not apply to disclosing entities that are companies. The disclosures required of disclosing entities by paragraphs Aus29.2 to Aus29.9.3 are in addition to those required by paragraphs 1 to 28.

Aus29.2   The following details about each key management person shall be disclosed:

(a)   the name of the person;

(b)   the position held; and

(c)   where the period of responsibility is less than the reporting period, the date or dates identifying the period of responsibility.

Aus29.3   If any of the following changes occur after the reporting period and prior to the date when the financial statements are authorised for issue, the name, position and date for each person involved shall be disclosed for:

       (a)   each change in the chief executive officer and *directors* of the entity; and

       (b)   the retirement of any key management person (other than a director or chief executive officer).

Compensation

Aus29.4   For each key management person, the following components of the categories required by paragraph 17, shall be disclosed:

       (a)   short-term employee benefits. Amounts in this category shall be divided into at least the following components:

            (i)   cash salary, fees and short-term compensated absences;

            (ii)   short-term cash profit-sharing and other bonuses;

            (iii) non-monetary benefits; and

            (iv) other short-term employee benefits;

       (b)   post-employment benefits. Amounts in this category shall be divided into at least the following components:

            (i)   pension and superannuation benefits; and

            (ii)   other post-employment benefits;

       (c)   other long-term employee benefits, separately identifying amounts attributable to long-term incentive plans;

       (d)   termination benefits; and

       (e)   share-based payment. Amounts in this category shall be divided into at least the following components:

            (i)   equity-settled share-based payment transactions:

                (A)   shares and units;

                (B)   options and rights;

            (ii)   cash-settled share-based payment transactions; and

            (iii) all other forms of share-based payment compensation (including hybrids).

Principles of Compensation

Aus29.5   The following details concerning the compensation of each key management person shall be disclosed:

       (a)   discussion of board policy for determining the nature and amount of compensation of key management personnel of the entity;

       (b)   discussion of the relationship between such policy and the entity's performance;

       (c)   if an element of the compensation of a key management person is dependent on the satisfaction of a performance condition:

            (i)   a detailed summary of the performance condition;

            (ii)   an explanation of why the performance condition was chosen;

            (iii) a summary of the methods used in assessing whether the performance condition is satisfied and an explanation of why those methods were chosen; and

        (iv) if the performance condition involves a comparison with factors external to the entity:

            (A) a summary of the factors to be used in making the comparison; and

            (B) if any of the factors relates to the performance of another entity, of two or more other entities or an index in which the securities of an entity or entities are included – the identity of that entity, of each of those entities or of the index;

(d) for each grant of a cash bonus, performance-related bonus or share-based payment compensation benefit, whether part of a specific contract for services or not, the terms and conditions of each grant affecting compensation in this or future reporting periods, including:

    (i) the grant date;

    (ii) the nature of the compensation granted;

    (iii) the service and performance criteria used to determine the amount of compensation; and

    (iv) if there has been any alteration of the terms or conditions of the grant since the grant date, the date, details and effect of each alteration;

(e) for each contract for services between the key management person and the disclosing entity (or any of its subsidiaries), such further explanations as are necessary in addition to those prescribed in subparagraphs (c) and (d) to provide an understanding of how the amount of compensation in the current reporting period was determined and how the terms of the contract affect compensation in future periods;

(f) if an element of the compensation consists of securities of a body and that element is not dependent on the satisfaction of a performance condition – an explanation of why that element of the compensation is not dependent on the satisfaction of a performance condition;

(g) an explanation of the relative proportions of those elements of the person's compensation that are related to performance and those elements of the person's compensation that are not; and

(h) if the person is employed by the entity under a contract – the duration of the contract, the periods of notice required to terminate the contract and the termination payments provided for under the contract.

Modification of Terms of Share-based Payment Transactions

Aus29.6   Where the terms of share-based payment transactions (including options or rights) granted as compensation to a key management person have been altered or modified by the issuing entity during the reporting period, the following details shall be disclosed for each such person:

(a) the date of each alteration of the terms;

(b) the market price of the underlying equity instrument at the date of alteration;

(c) the terms of the grant immediately prior to alteration, including the number and class of the underlying equity instruments, exercise price, time remaining until expiry and each other condition in the terms affecting the vesting or exercise of the option or other right;

(d) the new terms; and

(e) the difference between the total of the fair value of the options or other rights affected by the alteration immediately before the alteration and the total of the fair value of those options or other rights immediately after the alteration.

Equity Instruments

Different Classes to be Separately Identified

Aus29.7   All disclosures required by paragraphs Aus29.7.1 to Aus29.7.5 refer to equity instruments issued or issuable by the disclosing entity and any of its subsidiaries and shall be separated into each class of equity instrument identifying each class by:

    (a)   the name of the issuing entity;

    (b)   the class of equity instrument; and

    (c)   if the instrument is an option or right, the class and number of equity instruments for which it may be exercised.

Options and Rights Provided as Compensation

Aus29.7.1   The following details of options and rights over equity instruments provided as compensation to each key management person shall be disclosed:

    (a)   the number of options and the number of rights that, during the reporting period, have:

        (i)   been granted; and

        (ii) vested;

    (b)   particulars of the terms and conditions of each grant made during the reporting period, including:

        (i)   the fair value per option or right at grant date;

        (ii)   the exercise price per share or unit;

        (iii) the amount, if any, paid or payable by the recipient;

        (iv)   the expiry date;

        (v)   the date or dates when the options or rights may be exercised; and

        (vi)   a summary of the service and performance criteria that must be met before the beneficial interest vests in the person.

Equity Instruments Provided on Exercise of Options and Rights Granted as Compensation

Aus29.7.2   The following details of the equity instruments provided as a result of the exercise during the reporting period of options and rights granted as compensation to each key management person shall be disclosed:

    (a)   the number of equity instruments;

    (b)   when the number of options or rights exercised differs from the number of equity instruments disclosed under (a), the number of options or rights exercised;

    (c)   the amount paid per instrument; and

    (d)   the amount unpaid per instrument.

Options and Rights Holdings

Aus29.7.3   In respect of options and rights held, whether directly, indirectly or beneficially, by each key management person, a close member of the family of that person, or an entity over which either of these persons have, directly or indirectly, control, joint control or significant influence, disclosure shall be made of the number:

    (a)   held at the start of the reporting period;

    (b)   granted during the reporting period as compensation;

    (c)   exercised during the reporting period;

    (d)   resulting from any other change during the reporting period;

    (e)   held at the end of the reporting period;

(f)   vested at the end of the reporting period;

(g)   vested and exercisable at the end of the reporting period; and

(h)   vested and unexercisable at the end of the reporting period.

Equity Holdings and Transactions

Aus29.7.4   In respect of equity instruments (other than options and rights) held directly, indirectly or beneficially by each key management person, a close member of the family of that person, or an entity over which either of these persons have, directly or indirectly, control, joint control or significant influence, disclosure shall be made of the number:

(a)   held at the start of the reporting period;

(b)   granted during the reporting period as compensation;

(c)   received during the reporting period on exercise of options or rights;

(d)   resulting from any other change during the reporting period;

(e)   held at the end of the reporting period; and

(f)   if any such are included in the number disclosed under subparagraph (e) above, held nominally at the end of the reporting period.

Aus29.7.5   If transactions involving equity instruments, other than share-based payment compensation, have occurred between a key management person, a close member of the family of that person, or an entity over which either of these persons have, directly or indirectly, control, joint control or significant influence and the issuing entity during the reporting period, the nature of each different type of transaction shall be disclosed where the terms or conditions were more favourable than those which it is reasonable to expect the entity would have adopted if dealing at arm's length with an unrelated person. For each such transaction, the details of the terms and conditions shall be disclosed.

Loans

Aus29.8   The details required by paragraph Aus29.8.1 shall be disclosed separately in respect of each aggregate of loans made, guaranteed or secured, directly or indirectly, by the disclosing entity and any of its subsidiaries to:

(a)   all key management personnel, close members of the family of those personnel, or entities over which any of these persons have, directly or indirectly, control, joint control or significant influence; and

(b)   each key management person, a close member of the family of that person, or an entity over which either of these persons have, directly or indirectly, control, joint control or significant influence, by name whose aggregate loan amount exceeded $100,000 at any time during the reporting period.

Aus29.8.1   In respect of each aggregate of loans to key management personnel and to each key management person as required by paragraph Aus29.8, the following details shall be disclosed:

(a)   the amount outstanding at the start of the reporting period;

(b)   the amount of interest paid and payable in respect of the reporting period to the disclosing entity and any of its subsidiaries;

(c)   the difference between the amount disclosed in accordance with subparagraph (b) above and the amount of interest that would have been charged on an arm's-length basis;

(d)   each write-down and each allowance for doubtful receivables recognised by the disclosing entity and any of its subsidiaries;

(e)   the amount outstanding at the end of the reporting period;

(f)   for each key management person only, the highest amount of indebtedness during the reporting period;

(g)   for key management personnel only, the number of persons included in the group aggregate at the end of the reporting period; and

(h)   a summary of the terms and conditions of the loans.

Aus29.8.2   For the purposes of paragraphs Aus29.8 and Aus29.8.1 loans do not include loans involved in transactions that are in substance options, including non-recourse loans.

Other Transactions and Balances

Aus29.9   In respect of transactions during the reporting period between the disclosing entity and any of its subsidiaries and key management personnel, a close member of the family of those personnel, or an entity over which any of these persons have, directly or indirectly, control, joint control or significant influence, other than transactions covered by paragraphs Aus29.4 to Aus29.8.1 or excluded by paragraph Aus29.9.3, the following details shall be disclosed:

(a)   each type of transaction of different nature;

(b)   the terms and conditions of each type of transaction or, where there are different categories of terms and conditions within each type, the terms and conditions of each category of transaction; and

(c)   for each type of transaction or, where there are different categories within each type, each category of transaction:

    (i)   the names of the persons involved; and

    (ii)   the aggregate amount recognised.

Aus29.9.1   In respect of each aggregate amount disclosed in accordance with paragraph Aus29.9, the following details shall be disclosed:

(a)   the total of amounts recognised as revenue, separately identifying where applicable the total amounts recognised as:

    (i)   interest revenue; and

    (ii)   dividend revenue;

(b)   the total of amounts recognised as expense, separately identifying where applicable the total amounts recognised as:

    (i)   interest expense; and

    (ii)   write-downs of receivables and allowances made for doubtful receivables; and

(c)   any further disclosures necessary to provide an understanding of the effects of the transactions on the financial statements.

Aus29.9.2   In respect of assets and liabilities at the end of the reporting period recognised in relation to transactions identified in accordance with paragraph Aus29.9, disclosure shall be made of:

(a)   the total of all assets, classified into current and non-current assets and, where applicable, any allowance for doubtful receivables at the end of the reporting period; and

(b)   the total of all liabilities, classified into current and non-current liabilities.

Aus29.9.3   Transactions with and amounts receivable from or payable to a key management person, a close member of the family of that person, or an entity over which either of these persons have, directly or indirectly, control, joint control or significant influence, are excluded from the requirements of paragraphs Aus29.9 to Aus29.9.2 when:

(a)   they occur within a normal employee, customer or supplier relationship on terms and conditions no more favourable than those that it is reasonable to expect the entity would have adopted if dealing at arm's length with an unrelated person;

(b)   information about them does not have the potential to affect adversely decisions about the allocation of scarce resources made by users of the financial statements, or the discharge of accountability by the key management person; and

(c)   they are trivial or domestic in nature.

Illustrative Examples

The following examples accompany, but are not part of, AASB 124 Related Party Disclosures.

They illustrate:

*   *the partial exemption for government-related entities; and*
*   *how the definition of a related party would apply in specified circumstances.*

In the examples, references to 'financial statements' relate to the individual, separate or consolidated financial statements.

Partial Exemption for Government-related Entities

Example 1 – Exemption from Disclosure (paragraph 25)

IE1   Government G directly or indirectly controls Entities 1 and 2 and Entities A, B, C and D. Person X is a member of the key management personnel of Entity 1.

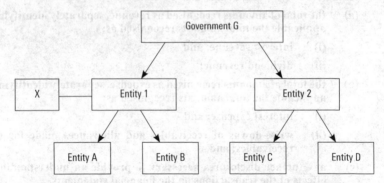

IE2   For Entity A's financial statements, the exemption in paragraph 25 applies to:

(a)   transactions with Government G; and

(b)   transactions with Entities 1 and 2 and Entities B, C and D.

However, that exemption does not apply to transactions with Person X.

Disclosure Requirements when Exemption Applies (paragraph 26)

IE3   In Entity A's financial statements, an example of disclosure to comply with paragraph 26(b)(i) for **individually** significant transactions could be:

AASB

Example of disclosure for individually significant transaction carried out on non market terms

On 15 January 20X1 Entity A, a utility company in which Government G indirectly owns 75 per cent of outstanding shares, sold a 10 hectare piece of land to another government-related utility company for CU5 million.[1] On 31 December 20X0 a plot of land in a similar location, of a similar size and with similar characteristics, was sold for CU3 million. There had not been any appreciation or depreciation of the land in the intervening period. See note X [of the financial statements] for disclosure of government assistance as required by AASB 120 *Accounting for Government Grants and Disclosure of Government Assistance* and notes Y and Z [of the financial statements] for compliance with other relevant Australian Accounting Standards.

Example of disclosure for individually significant transaction because of size of transaction

In the year ended December 20X1 Government G provided Entity A, a utility company in which Government G indirectly owns 75 per cent of outstanding shares, with a loan equivalent to 50 per cent of its funding requirement, repayable in quarterly instalments over the next five years. Interest is charged on the loan at a rate of 3 per cent, which is comparable to that charged on Entity A's bank loans.[2] See notes Y and Z [of the financial statements] for compliance with other relevant Australian Accounting Standards.

Example of disclosure of collectively significant transactions

In Entity A's financial statements, an example of disclosure to comply with paragraph 26(b) (ii) for **collectively** significant transactions could be:

Government G, indirectly, owns 75 per cent of Entity A's outstanding shares. Entity A's significant transactions with Government G and other entities controlled, jointly controlled or significantly influenced by Government G are [a large portion of its sales of goods and purchases of raw materials] or [about 50 per cent of its sales of goods and about 35 per cent of its purchases of raw materials].

The company also benefits from guarantees by Government G of the company's bank borrowing. See note X [of the financial statements] for disclosure of government assistance as required by AASB 120 *Accounting for Government Grants and Disclosure of Government Assistance* and notes Y and Z [of the financial statements] for compliance with other relevant Australian Accounting Standards.

Definition of a Related Party

*The references are to subparagraphs of the definition of a **related party** in paragraph 9 of AASB 124.*

Example 2 – Associates and Subsidiaries

IE4   Parent entity has a controlling interest in Subsidiaries A, B and C and has significant influence over Associates 1 and 2. Subsidiary C has significant influence over Associate 3.

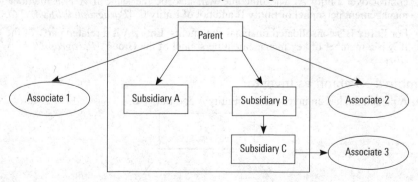

---

1   In these examples monetary amounts are denominated in 'currency units (CU)'.

2   If the reporting entity had concluded that this transaction constituted government assistance it would have needed to consider the disclosure requirements in AASB 120.

IE5   For Parent's separate financial statements, Subsidiaries A, B and C and Associates 1, 2 and 3 are related parties. [*Paragraph 9(b)(i) and (ii)*]

IE6   For Subsidiary A's financial statements, Parent, Subsidiaries B and C and Associates 1, 2 and 3 are related parties. For Subsidiary B's separate financial statements, Parent, Subsidiaries A and C and Associates 1, 2 and 3 are related parties. For Subsidiary C's financial statements, Parent, Subsidiaries A and B and Associates 1, 2 and 3 are related parties. [*Paragraph 9(b) (i) and (ii)*]

IE7   For the financial statements of Associates 1, 2 and 3, Parent and Subsidiaries A, B and C are related parties. Associates 1, 2 and 3 are not related to each other. [*Paragraph 9(b)(ii)*]

IE8   For Parent's consolidated financial statements, Associates 1, 2 and 3 are related to the Group. [*Paragraph 9(b)(ii)*]

Example 3 – Key Management Personnel

IE9   A person, X, has a 100 per cent investment in Entity A and is a member of the key management personnel of Entity C. Entity B has a 100 per cent investment in Entity C.

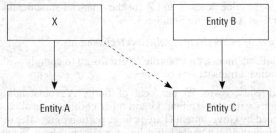

IE10   For Entity C's financial statements, Entity A is related to Entity C because X controls Entity A and is a member of the key management personnel of Entity C. [*Paragraph 9(b) (vi) – (a)(iii)*]

IE11   For Entity C's financial statements, Entity A is also related to Entity C if X is a member of the key management personnel of Entity B and not of Entity C. [*Paragraph 9(b)(vi) – (a) (iii)*]

IE12   Furthermore, the outcome described in paragraphs IE10 and IE11 will be the same if X has joint control over Entity A. [*Paragraph 9(b)(vi)-(a)(iii)*] (If X had only significant influence over Entity A and not control or joint control, then Entities A and C would not be related to each other.)

IE13   For Entity A's financial statements, Entity C is related to Entity A because X controls A and is a member of Entity C's key management personnel. [*Paragraph 9(b)(vii) – (a)(i)*]

IE14   Furthermore, the outcome described in paragraph IE13 will be the same if X has joint control over Entity A. The outcome will also be the same if X is a member of key management personnel of Entity B and not of Entity C. [*Paragraph 9(b)(vii) – (a)(i)*]

IE15   For Entity B's consolidated financial statements, Entity A is a related party of the Group if X is a member of key management personnel of the Group. [*Paragraph 9(b) (vi) – (a) (iii)*]

Example 4 – Person as Investor

IE16   A person, X, has an investment in Entity A and Entity B.

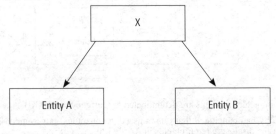

IE17 For Entity A's financial statements, if X controls or jointly controls Entity A, Entity B is related to Entity A when X has control, joint control or significant influence over Entity B. [*Paragraph 9(b)(vi) – (a)(i) and 9(b)(vii) – (a)(i)*]

IE18 For Entity B's financial statements, if X controls or jointly controls Entity A, Entity A is related to Entity B when X has control, joint control or significant influence over Entity B. [*Paragraph 9(b)(vi) – (a)(i) and 9(b)(vi) – (a)(ii)*]

IE19 If X has significant influence over both Entity A and Entity B, Entities A and B are not related to each other.

Example 5 – Close Members of the Family Holding Investments

IE20 A person, X, is the domestic partner of Y. X has an investment in Entity A and Y has an investment in Entity B.

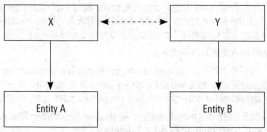

IE21 For Entity A's financial statements, if X controls or jointly controls Entity A, Entity B is related to Entity A when Y has control, joint control or significant influence over Entity B. [*Paragraph 9(b)(vi) – (a)(i) and 9(b)(vii) – (a)(i)*]

IE22 For Entity B's financial statements, if X controls or jointly controls Entity A, Entity A is related to Entity B when Y has control, joint control or significant influence over Entity B. [*Paragraph 9(b)(vi) – (a)(i) and 9(b)(vi) – (a)(ii)*]

IE23 If X has significant influence over Entity A and Y has significant influence over Entity B, Entities A and B are not related to each other.

Example 6 – Entity with Joint Control

IE24 Entity A has both (i) joint control over Entity B and (ii) joint control or significant influence over Entity C.

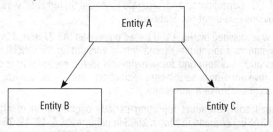

IE25 For Entity B's financial statements, Entity C is related to Entity B. [*Paragraph 9(b)(iii) and (iv)*]

IE26 Similarly, for Entity C's financial statements, Entity B is related to Entity C. [*Paragraph 9(b)(iii) and (iv)*]

AASB 127
Consolidated and Separate Financial Statements
(Compiled September 2011: applicable 30 June 2013)

Note from the Institute of Chartered Accountants Australia

This note, prepared by the technical editors, is not part of Accounting Standard AASB 127.

Historical development

15 July 2004: AASB 127 'Consolidated and Separate Financial Statements' is the Australian equivalent of IAS 27 of the same name. It was made by the AASB on 15 July 2004 as part of the AASB's program to adopt International Financial Reporting Standards by 2005.

6 April 2006: Removal of Australian Guidance.

15 February 2007: AASB 2007-2 'Amendments to Australian Accounting Standards' amends paragraph 13 and is applicable to annual reporting periods ending on or after 28 February 2007, with early adoption permitted for annual reporting periods beginning on or after 1 January 2005.

26 February 2007: AASB 2007-3 'Amendments to Australian Accounting Standards' is applicable for annual reporting periods beginning on or after 1 January 2009.

30 April 2007: AASB 2007-4 'Amendments to Australian Accounting Standards' amends paragraphs 3, 4, 6, 7, 38, 39, 42 and Aus42.1. It adds paragraphs Aus6.1, 8, 9, 10, Aus10.1, 11 and 41 and deletes paragraphs Aus9.1, Aus27.1, Aus40.1 and Aus42.2. It is applicable for annual reporting periods beginning on or after 1 July 2007, with early adoption permitted for annual reporting periods beginning on or after 1 January 2005.

July 2007: Erratum amends paragraph IG7 and is applicable to annual reporting periods beginning on or after 1 July 2007, with early adoption permitted for annual reporting periods beginning on or after 1 January 2005.

13 December 2007: AASB 2007-9 'Amendments to Australian Accounting Standards arising from the Review of AAS 27, AAS 29 and AAS 31' was issued by the AASB. This Standard is applicable to annual reporting periods beginning on or after 1 July 2008, with early adoption permitted.

March 2008: AASB 127 'Consolidated and Separate Financial Statements' was issued by the AASB superseding the previous version of the Standard.

AASB 127 (revised) was reissued by the AASB based on revised IAS 27 issued by the IASB. The main objective of the revision was to reduce alternatives in accounting for subsidiaries in consolidated financial statements and in accounting for investments in the separate financial statements of a parent, venturer or investor. The amendments related primarily to accounting for non-controlling interests and the loss of control of a subsidiary.

This Standard is applicable to annual reporting periods beginning on or after 1 January 2005. The amendments to AASB 127 made in March 2008 in paragraphs 4, 18, 19, 26-37 and 41(e) and (f) are applicable for annual periods beginning on or after 1 July 2009.

24 July 2008: AASB 2008-5 'Amendments to Australian Accounting Standards arising from the Annual Improvements Project' amends AASB 127 in relation to measurement of a subsidiary held for sale in separate financial statements. This Standard is applicable to annual reporting periods beginning on or after 1 January 2009.

25 July 2008: AASB 2008-7 'Amendments to Australian Accounting Standards – Cost of an Investment in a Subsidiary, Jointly Controlled Entity or Associate' amends AASB 127 to reflect that dividends declared out of pre-acquisition profits are recognised as income. This Standard is applicable to annual reporting periods beginning on or after 1 January 2009.

29 September 2009: AASB 127 revised was reissued by the AASB, compiled to include the AASB 2008-5 and AASB 2008-7 amendments. This compiled Standard applies to annual reporting periods beginning on or after 1 July 2009. Early application is permitted.

On the same date the previous version of AASB 127 was reissued by the AASB, applicable to annual reporting periods beginning on or after 1 January 2009 but before 1 July 2009. This version of AASB 127 has been compiled for the amending Standards applying to annual reporting periods beginning on or after 1 January 2009. This Standard applies to 31 December 2009 year end and can be accessed from the AASB website at www.aasb.gov.au.

7 December 2009: AASB 2009-11 'Amendments to Australian Accounting Standards arising from AASB 9' amends AASB 127 to give effect to consequential changes arising from the issuance of AASB 9. This Standard is applicable to annual reporting periods beginning on or after 1 January 2013 with early adoption permitted from annual reporting periods ending on or after 31 December 2009 that begin before 1 January 2013 provided AASB 9 is also applied for the same period. The application date of AASB 2009-11 has been amended to 1 January 2015 by AASB 2012-6. **These amendments have been superseded by AASB 2010-7 and are not included in this compiled Standard.**

1 March 2011: AASB 2010-7 'Amendments to Australian Accounting Standards arising from AASB 9 (December 2010)' as compiled amends AASB 127 to give effect to consequential changes arising from the reissue of AASB 9 in December 2010, and supersedes AASB 2009-11 which related to the previous version of AASB 9. This Standard applies to annual reporting periods beginning on or after 1 January 2013 and can be adopted early. The application date of AASB 2010-7 has been amended to 1 January 2015 by AASB 2012-6. **These amendments are not included in this compiled Standard.**

11 July 2011: AASB 2011-5 'Amendments to Australian Accounting Standards – Extending Relief from Consolidation, the Equity Method and Proportionate Consolidation' amends AASB 127 to give relief from consolidating and equity accounting in certain situations. These Standards apply to annual reporting periods beginning on or after 1 July 2011 with early adoption permitted.

29 August 2011: A revised version of AASB 127 was issued by the AASB, applicable to annual reporting periods beginning 1 January 2013. **This revised Standard is included in this handbook with the footer: Applicable to periods beginning from 1 January 2013.**

23 September 2011: AASB 127 was reissued by the AASB, compiled to include the AASB 2011-5 amendments and applies to annual reporting periods beginning on or after 1 July 2011 but before 1 July 2012. **This compiled Standard is included in this handbook with the footer: Applicable 30 June 2013.**

References

Interpretation 5 *Rights to Interests arising from Decommissioning, Restoration and Environmental Rehabilitation Funds*, Interpretation 1052 *Tax Consolidation Accounting*, Interpretation 112 *Consolidation – Special Purpose Entities*, and Interpretation 17 *Distributions of Non-cash Assets to Owners* apply to AASB 127.

IFRIC items not taken onto the agenda: No. 31 *The effects of rights of veto on control*, No. 33 *Reciprocal interests*, IAS 27-1 *Separate financial statements issued before consolidated financial statements*, IAS 27-2 *SIC 12 Consolidation – Special purpose entities – Relinquishment of control*, IAS 27-8 *Transaction costs for non-controlling interests*, IAS 27-9 *Presentation of comparatives when applying the 'pooling of interests' method*, IAS 29-10 *Combined financial statements and redefining the reporting entity*, IAS 27-11 *Put options written over non-controlling interests* and IAS 27-13 *Group reorganisation in separate financial statements* apply to AASB 127.

AASB 127 (applicable 30 June 2013) compared to IAS 27 (applicable 30 June 2013)

Additions

Paragraph	Description
Aus 1.1	Which entities AASB 127 applies to (i.e. reporting entities and general purpose financial statements).
Aus 1.2	The application date of AASB 127 (i.e. annual reporting periods beginning 1 January 2005 other than for the March 2008 amendments, i.e. 1 July 2009).
Aus 1.3	Makes the requirements of AASB 127 subject to AASB 1031 'Materiality'.
Aus 1.4	Explains which Australian Standards have been superseded by AASB 127.
Aus 1.5	Specifies that reporting entities include governments.

Aus 6.1	Specifies that for reporting under the Corporations Act, consolidated financial statements and separate financial statements are required to be presented together.
Aus 9.1	Clarifies that AASB 127 does not necessarily deem the parent of a public sector group of entities that is a reporting entity (e.g. a government and its controlled entities) to be a reporting entity.
Aus10.1	Clarifies a parent which is a not-for-profit entity need not prepare consolidated financial statement in certain circumstances.
Aus10.2	Requires the ultimate Australian parent to prepare consolidated financial statements when either the parent and/or the group is a reporting entity.
Aus 17.1 to Aus 17.10	Discusses the application of the Standard to the public sector.
Aus 43.1	Requires certain disclosures for public sector entities if the parent financial statements are not prepared.
Aus 45.1	Transitional requirements for public sector entities relating to the March 2008 amendments.
Australian application guidance	Summarises the circumstances in which the exemption from presenting consolidated financial statements may be available to a parent entity.

Deletions

Paragraph	*Description*
44	Effective date of IAS 27.
46	Reference to superseded IAS 27.

Contents

Compilation Details

Comparison with IAS 27

Accounting Standard
AASB 127 Consolidated and Separate Financial Statements

Paragraphs

Application	Aus1.1 – Aus1.5
Scope	1 – 3
Definitions	4 – 8
Presentation of consolidated financial statements	9 – 11
Scope of consolidated financial statements	12 – 17
Factors indicating control in the public sector	Aus17.1 – Aus17.2
Accountability of the other entity to Parliament, or to the Executive, or to a particular Minister	Aus17.3
Residual financial interest in the net assets of the other entity by the government	Aus17.4
General implications of the concept of control in the public sector	Aus17.5 – Aus17.9
Control versus day-to-day management by government	Aus17.10
Consolidation procedures	18 – 31
Loss of control	32 – 37
Accounting for investments in subsidiaries, jointly controlled entities and associates in separate financial statements	38 – 40
Disclosure	41 – Aus43.1
Effective date and transition	45 – 45C

Implementation Guidance

Australian Application Advice

Deleted IAS 27 Text

Basis for Conclusions on IAS 27
(available on the AASB website)

AASB

Australian Accounting Standard AASB 127 *Consolidated and Separate Financial Statements* (as amended) is set out in paragraphs Aus1.1 – 45C. All the paragraphs have equal authority. Paragraphs in **bold type** state the main principles. Terms defined in this Standard are in *italics* the first time they appear in the Standard. AASB 127 is to be read in the context of other Australian Accounting Standards, including AASB 1048 *Interpretation and Application of Standards*, which identifies the Australian Accounting Interpretations. In the absence of explicit guidance, AASB 108 *Accounting Policies, Changes in Accounting Estimates and Errors* provides a basis for selecting and applying accounting policies.

Compilation Details

Accounting Standard AASB 127 *Consolidated and Separate Financial Statements* as amended

This compiled Standard applies to annual reporting periods beginning on or after 1 July 2011 but before 1 January 2013. It takes into account amendments up to and including 20 July 2011 and was prepared on 23 September 2011 by the staff of the Australian Accounting Standards Board (AASB).

This compilation is not a separate Accounting Standard made by the AASB. Instead, it is a representation of AASB 127 (March 2008) as amended by other Accounting Standards, which are listed in the Table below.

Table of Standards

Standard	Date made	Application date *(annual reporting periods ... on or after ...)*	Application, saving or transitional provisions
AASB 127	6 Mar 2008	*(beginning)* 1 Jul 2009	see (a) below
AASB 2008-5	24 Jul 2008	*(beginning)* 1 Jan 2009	see (b) below
AASB 2008-7	25 Jul 2008	*(beginning)* 1 Jan 2009	see (c) below
AASB 2009-11	7 Dec 2009	*(beginning)* 1 Jan 2013	not compiled*
AASB 2010-2	30 Jun 2010	*(beginning)* 1 Jul 2013	not compiled*
AASB 2010-7	6 Dec 2010	*(beginning)* 1 Jan 2013	not compiled*
AASB 2011-5	20 Jul 2011	*(beginning)* 1 Jul 2011	see (d) below
AASB 2011-6	20 Jul 2011	*(beginning)* 1 Jul 2013	not compiled*

*   The amendments made by this Standard are not included in this compilation, which presents the principal Standard as applicable to annual reporting periods beginning on or after 1 July 2011 but before 1 January 2013. The principal Standard has been superseded by AASB 10 *Consolidated Financial Statements* and AASB 127 *Separate Financial Statements*, which apply to annual reporting periods beginning on or after 1 January 2013.

(a)   Entities may elect to apply this Standard to annual reporting periods beginning on or after 1 January 2005 but before 1 July 2009.

(b)   Entities may elect to apply this Standard, or its amendments to individual Standards, to annual reporting periods beginning on or after 1 January 2005 but before 1 January 2009.

(c)   Entities may elect to apply this Standard to annual reporting periods beginning on or after 1 January 2005 but before 1 January 2009.

(d)   Entities may elect to apply this Standard to annual reporting periods beginning on or after 1 January 2005 but before 1 July 2011.

Table of Amendments

Paragraph affected	How affected	By ... [paragraph]
4	amended	AASB 2008-7 [20]
8	amended	AASB 2011-5 [8]
9	amended	AASB 2011-5 [9]
Aus10.1	renumbered as Aus10.2 added	AASB 2011-5 [6] AASB 2011-5 [7]
Aus10.2	amended	AASB 2011-5 [6]
11	amended	AASB 2011-5 [8]
38	amended	AASB 2008-5 [43]
38A-38C	added	AASB 2008-7 [21]
39	amended	AASB 2011-5 [8]
42	amended	AASB 2011-5 [8]

Paragraph affected	How affected	By ... [paragraph]
45A	added	AASB 2008-5 [44]
45B, 45C	added	AASB 2008-7 [22]

Table of Amendments to Australian Application Guidance

Paragraph affected	How affected	By ... [paragraph]
AG1	added	AASB 2011-5 [10]

Comparison with IAS 27

AASB 127 and IAS 27

AASB 127 *Consolidated and Separate Financial Statements* as amended incorporates IAS 27 *Consolidated and Separate Financial Statements* as issued and amended by the International Accounting Standards Board (IASB). Paragraphs that have been added to this Standard (and do not appear in the text of IAS 27) are identified with the prefix "Aus", generally followed by the number of the relevant IASB paragraph and decimal numbering. Paragraphs that have limited application begin by identifying their applicability.

Compliance with IAS 27

Entities other than public sector entities that comply with AASB 127 as amended will simultaneously be in compliance with IAS 27 as amended.

Accounting Standard AASB 127

The Australian Accounting Standards Board made Accounting Standard AASB 127 *Consolidated and Separate Financial Statements* under section 334 of the *Corporations Act 2001* on 6 March 2008.

This compiled version of AASB 127 applies to annual reporting periods beginning on or after 1 July 2011 but before 1 January 2013. It incorporates relevant amendments contained in other AASB Standards made by the AASB up to and including 20 July 2011 (see Compilation Details).

Accounting Standard AASB 127

Consolidated and Separate Financial Statements

Application

Aus1.1 This Standard applies to:

    (a) each entity that is required to prepare financial reports in accordance with Part 2M.3 of the Corporations Act and that is a reporting entity;

    (b) general purpose financial statements of each other reporting entity; and

    (c) financial statements that are, or are held out to be, general purpose financial statements.

Aus1.2 This Standard applies to annual reporting periods beginning on or after 1 January 2005. Adoption of this Standard prior to 1 January 2005 is not permitted. Paragraphs 45 and Aus45.1 specify the application of the amendments to AASB 127 made in March 2008.

    [Note: For application dates of paragraphs changed or added by an amending Standard, see Compilation Details.]

Aus1.3 The requirements specified in this Standard apply to the financial statements where information resulting from their application is material in accordance with AASB 1031 *Materiality*.

Aus1.4   When applied or operative, this Standard supersedes AASB 127 *Consolidated and Separate Financial Statements* issued in July 2004 and amended to December 2007.

Aus1.5   As defined in AASB 101 *Presentation of Financial Statements*, reporting entities include local governments, governments and most, if not all, government departments.

Scope

1   **This Standard shall be applied in the preparation and presentation of consolidated financial statements for a group of entities under the control of a parent.**

2   This Standard does not deal with methods of accounting for business combinations and their effects on consolidation, including goodwill arising on a business combination (see AASB 3 *Business Combinations*).

3   **This Standard shall also be applied in accounting for investments in subsidiaries, jointly controlled entities and associates when an entity elects, or is required by local regulations, to present separate financial statements.**

Definitions

4   **The following terms are used in this Standard with the meanings specified:**

> *Consolidated financial statements* **are the financial statements of a group presented as those of a single economic entity.**

> *Control* **is the power to govern the financial and operating policies of an entity so as to obtain benefits from its activities.**

> **A** *group* **is a parent and all its subsidiaries.**

> *Non-controlling interest* **is the equity in a subsidiary not attributable, directly or indirectly, to a parent.**

> **A** *parent* **is an entity that has one or more subsidiaries.**

> *Separate financial statements* **are those presented by a parent, an investor in an associate or a venturer in a jointly controlled entity, in which the investments are accounted for on the basis of the direct equity interest rather than on the basis of the reported results and net assets of the investees.**

> **A** *subsidiary* **is an entity, including an unincorporated entity such as a partnership, that is controlled by another entity (known as the parent).**

5   A parent or its subsidiary may be an investor in an associate or a venturer in a jointly controlled entity. In such cases, consolidated financial statements prepared and presented in accordance with this Standard are also prepared so as to comply with AASB 128 *Investments in Associates* and AASB 131 *Interests in Joint Ventures*.

6   For an entity described in paragraph 5, separate financial statements are those prepared and presented in addition to the financial statements referred to in paragraph 5. Separate financial statements need not be appended to, or accompany, those statements.

Aus6.1   Notwithstanding paragraph 6, for the purpose of reporting under the Corporations Act, consolidated financial statements and separate financial statements are required to be presented together.

7   The financial statements of an entity that does not have a subsidiary, associate or venturer's interest in a jointly controlled entity are not separate financial statements.

8   A parent that is exempted in accordance with paragraphs 10-Aus10.2 from presenting consolidated financial statements may present separate financial statements as its only financial statements.

Presentation of consolidated financial statements

9   **A parent, other than a parent described in paragraph 10 or Aus10.1, as modified by paragraph Aus10.2, shall present consolidated financial statements in which it consolidates its investments in subsidiaries in accordance with this Standard.**

AASB

Aus9.1   In certain instances in the public sector a group of entities (e.g. a government and its controlled entities) is a reporting entity, but the parent may not be explicitly identified for financial reporting purposes. This Standard does not deem a parent in such a group to be a separate reporting entity. Furthermore, this Standard does not require the preparation of separate financial statements for the parent, but does require consolidated financial statements to be presented.

10   A parent need not present consolidated financial statements if and only if:

    (a)   the parent is itself a wholly-owned subsidiary, or is a partially-owned subsidiary of another entity and its other owners, including those not otherwise entitled to vote, have been informed about, and do not object to, the parent not presenting consolidated financial statements;

    (b)   the parent's debt or equity instruments are not traded in a public market (a domestic or foreign stock exchange or an over-the-counter market, including local and regional markets);

    (c)   the parent did not file, nor is it in the process of filing, its financial statements with a securities commission or other regulatory organisation for the purpose of issuing any class of instruments in a public market; and

    (d)   the ultimate or any intermediate parent of the parent produces consolidated financial statements available for public use that comply with International Financial Reporting Standards.

Aus10.1   Notwithstanding paragraph 10(d), a parent that meets the criteria in paragraphs 10(a), 10(b) and 10(c) need not present consolidated financial statements if its ultimate or any intermediate parent produces consolidated financial statements available for public use and the parent and its ultimate or intermediate parent are both not-for-profit entities complying with Australian Accounting Standards.

Aus10.2   Notwithstanding paragraphs 10 and Aus10.1, the ultimate Australian parent shall present consolidated financial statements that consolidate its investments in subsidiaries in accordance with this Standard when either the parent or the group is a reporting entity or both the parent and the group are reporting entities.

11   A parent that elects in accordance with paragraphs 10-Aus10.2 not to present consolidated financial statements, and presents only separate financial statements, complies with paragraphs 38-43.

Scope of consolidated financial statements

12   Consolidated financial statements shall include all subsidiaries of the parent.[1]

13   Control is presumed to exist when the parent owns, directly or indirectly through subsidiaries, more than half of the voting power of an entity unless, in exceptional circumstances, it can be clearly demonstrated that such ownership does not constitute control. Control also exists when the parent owns half or less of the voting power of an entity when there is:[2]

    (a)   power over more than half of the voting rights by virtue of an agreement with other investors;

    (b)   power to govern the financial and operating policies of the entity under a statute or an agreement;

    (c)   power to appoint or remove the majority of the members of the board of directors or equivalent governing body and control of the entity is by that board or body; or

    (d)   power to cast the majority of votes at meetings of the board of directors or equivalent governing body and control of the entity is by that board or body.

---

1   If on acquisition a subsidiary meets the criteria to be classified as held for sale in accordance with AASB 5 *Non-current Assets Held for Sale and Discontinued Operations*, it shall be accounted for in accordance with that Standard.

2   See also Interpretation 112 *Consolidation – Special Purpose Entities*, as identified in AASB 1048 *Interpretation and Application of Standards.*

14   An entity may own share warrants, share call options, debt or equity instruments that are convertible into ordinary shares, or other similar instruments that have the potential, if exercised or converted, to give the entity voting power or reduce another party's voting power over the financial and operating policies of another entity (potential voting rights). The existence and effect of potential voting rights that are currently exercisable or convertible, including potential voting rights held by another entity, are considered when assessing whether an entity has the power to govern the financial and operating policies of another entity. Potential voting rights are not currently exercisable or convertible when, for example, they cannot be exercised or converted until a future date or until the occurrence of a future event.

15   In assessing whether potential voting rights contribute to control, the entity examines all facts and circumstances (including the terms of exercise of the potential voting rights and any other contractual arrangements whether considered individually or in combination) that affect potential voting rights, except the intention of management and the financial ability to exercise or convert such rights.

16   A subsidiary is not excluded from consolidation simply because the investor is a venture capital organisation, mutual fund, unit trust or similar entity.

17   A subsidiary is not excluded from consolidation because its business activities are dissimilar from those of the other entities within the group. Relevant information is provided by consolidating such subsidiaries and disclosing additional information in the consolidated financial statements about the different business activities of subsidiaries. For example, the disclosures required by AASB 8 *Operating Segments* help to explain the significance of different business activities within the group.

Factors indicating control in the public sector

Paragraphs Aus17.1-Aus17.10 of this Standard apply only to public sector entities.

Aus17.1   This Standard does not attempt to identify all groups in the public sector that should prepare financial statements. Instead, it describes the factors that are considered in determining whether one entity has the power to govern the financial and operating policies of another entity, whether a group exists and whether that group constitutes a reporting entity. In addition, the Standard identifies the accounting techniques that are employed when the financial statements of a number of separate entities are to be combined. This approach avoids the prescriptive designation of artificial reporting entities and the resulting preparation of meaningless consolidated financial statements.

Aus17.2   In the public sector, a parent/subsidiary relationship could be established in the manner outlined in paragraph 13 or, as is more frequently the case, control of another entity by the government may be indicated by the following two factors:

(a)   the other entity is accountable to Parliament, or to the Executive, or to a particular Minister; and

(b)   the government has the residual financial interest in the net assets of the other entity.

Accountability of the other entity to Parliament, or to the Executive, or to a particular Minister

Aus17.3   The existence of one, or a combination of a number of the following circumstances, indicate that an entity is accountable to Parliament, or to the Executive, or to a particular Minister:

(a)   the existence of a Ministerial or other government power that enables the government to give directions to the governing body of that entity so that the entity acts as an agent of the government to achieve government policy objectives;

(b)   Ministerial approval is required for operating budgets;

(c)   the government has the ability to veto operating and capital budgets of that entity;

AASB

(d)   the government has broad discretion, under existing legislation, to appoint or remove a majority of members of the governing body of that entity. This would include for example, the power of the Minister or a central authority to appoint and remove members of the board of management. The governing body of an entity cannot maintain financial and operating policies that do not have the support of a government if the government has the power under existing legislation to appoint or remove a majority of members of the governing body of the entity. In these circumstances, the government has the power to govern the financial and operating policies so as to meet its own objectives. For control to exist through the power to appoint or remove a majority of members of the governing body of another entity, a government must have broad discretion over their appointment and removal. For example, if the power to appoint or remove a majority of members of the governing body requires an amendment to the current legislation or the creation of new legislation, then the government's power is not presently exercisable and control does not exist. Also, where the power of the government to remove members of the governing body of another entity only arises under certain restricted circumstances (for example, for reasons relating to a lack of probity), the government would not have the power to govern the financial and operating policies of the entity by virtue of that power (although it may have the power in respect of the financial and operating policies through some other means);

(e)   the entity is required to submit to Parliament reports on operations that include audited financial statements; such requirements arising either under the general reporting requirements of legislation concerned with financial reporting and/or audit of public sector entities or under that entity's enabling legislation; or

(f)   the mandate of the entity is established, or limited, by its enabling legislation. The definition of control requires only that the government's power to govern the financial and operating policies of another entity is sufficient to enable the government to obtain benefits from the entity's activities. Enabling legislation relating to the other entity which establishes the broad financial and operating policies of the entity is sufficient to ensure control by the government. However, the impact of enabling legislation also needs to be evaluated in the light of other prevailing circumstances. For example, a marketing board whose mandate is created, and limited, by legislation is not controlled by a government if the legislation unequivocally assigns power to govern financial and operating policies to other entities such as relevant commodity producers, and the government does not have the power to appoint or remove a majority of members of the governing body.

Residual financial interest in the net assets of the other entity by the government

Aus17.4   The existence of the following circumstances indicates whether the government has a residual financial interest in the net assets of the other entity:

(a)   the government is exposed to the residual liabilities of the entity; or

(b)   the government has the right to receive the residual net assets of the entity if that entity is dissolved.

General implications of the concept of control in the public sector

Aus17.5   In the public sector, reporting entities may include Ministerial portfolios, Ministerial departments, statutory authorities or other entities. In some cases the reporting entity may comprise a parent and a number of controlled entities, and in other cases the reporting entity may be the parent or the controlled entity itself.

Aus17.6   A government will usually control the statutory authorities or corporations that it has established, because the legislation will normally address the financial and operating policies necessary to enable the entity to work with the government in achieving its objectives.

Aus17.7   In determining the existence of a group in the public sector, consideration should be given to the controlling entity's ability to deploy the resources under its control and whether there are restrictions on the allocation of funds between activities under its authority. In addition, the ability of the entities to operate for the benefit of the controlling entity is a central characteristic of a group. If an entity is precluded from operating for the benefit of the controlling entity, for example, through the existence of separate administrations, it is clear that the entity would not be included in the group. A Minister may have responsibility for more than one function. Those functions may be encompassed in a single portfolio or administered through a number of portfolios. The specification of separate objectives for each function will usually be an indication of the existence of separate economic entities, regardless of whether the functions are combined in the one portfolio or administered separately through more than one portfolio. Similarly, the financial statements of individual local governments would not be aggregated for the purpose of preparing financial statements in each State or Territory because the combination of such local government bodies would fail to satisfy the definition of a group.

Aus17.8   For a government to control an entity, it must have the power to require an entity's assets to be deployed towards achieving government objectives. This may mean, but need not require, that the government can do, or require the entity to do, one or more of the following with the controlled entity's assets:

     (a)   exchange them;

     (b)   use them to provide goods and services consistent with the government's objectives;

     (c)   charge for their use;

     (d)   use them to settle liabilities; or

     (e)   hold them.

Aus17.9   Accordingly, a government does not control another entity where:

     (a)   it cannot dominate the financial and operating policies of the entity that are necessary to enable the entity to operate towards achieving government objectives, notwithstanding that both entities have similar objectives. For example, a government and a charitable entity funded by that government may share common objectives with respect to care of the homeless. However, the charitable entity is not controlled by the government when its governing body maintains discretion as to how its resources are to be deployed and whether it will accept resources from the government;

     (b)   it cannot benefit from the resources or residual resources of the entity, notwithstanding that it may have the power to govern the entity's financial and operating policies. For example, where a government acts as a trustee for a trust and its relationship with the trust does not extend beyond the normal responsibilities of a trustee, the government does not control the trust as it cannot deploy the resources or residual resources of the trust for its own benefit;

     (c)   it influences, rather than governs, the financial and operating policies required to enable the entity to operate towards achieving the government's objectives. The wide ranging powers of governments mean that they can influence the financial and operating policies of many entities, particularly those which are financially dependent on government funding. However, where the governing bodies of those entities maintain discretion with respect to whether they will accept resources from the government, or the manner in which their resources are to be deployed, they are not controlled by the government. For example, this will normally be the case with religious organisations that provide aged-care services. While these organisations may receive government grants for capital construction and operating costs, and the government providing the grant may require them to comply with certain service standards and restrictions on user fees, they will not

AASB

usually be controlled by the government because their governing body will maintain the ultimate discretion about whether assets are deployed to those services. Furthermore, while private schools, private hospitals, individual local governments and universities may be financially dependent, to a greater or lesser degree, on governments or agencies thereof, they would not be considered to be controlled by those governments or agencies for the purposes of this Standard. Therefore, this Standard does not require that the financial statements of such entities be consolidated with the financial statements of a government or government agency;

(d) it merely has the power to regulate the behaviour of the entity by use of its legislative powers. The power of government to establish the regulatory environment within which entities operate and to impose conditions or sanctions on their operations does not of itself constitute control of the assets deployed by those entities. For example, governments regulate the operations of entities operating in the gaming industry, but those entities are not controlled by government unless the assets or residual assets of those entities can be deployed for the benefit of government; or

(e) its ability to redeploy the assets of another entity for its own benefit is not presently exercisable. For example, under existing legislative arrangements, State and Territory governments do not control local governments because:

(i) they cannot sell the assets of a local government and redeploy the proceeds from the sale towards the State or Territory budget; and

(ii) the governing body of the local government, whether an elected council or administrators appointed by a government, is bound to deploy its assets for the benefit of the local community (and not the State or Territory government).

Control versus day-to-day management by government

Aus17.10 The existence of control for the purpose of this Standard does not require that the government has responsibility over the day-to-day operations of an entity, or the manner in which professional functions are performed by the entity. For example, the legislation governing the establishment and operation of an independent statutory office (such as that of the Auditor-General) sets out the broad parameters within which the office is required to operate, and enables the office to operate in a manner consistent with the objectives set by Parliament for the operation of government. Similarly, notwithstanding the operational independence of the judiciary from the Parliament, the legislative framework within which the judiciary operates is established in a manner consistent with the objectives set by Parliament for the administration of justice. In addition, the government retains the right to the residual assets of statutory offices and judicial entities. Notwithstanding the absence of responsibility for the day-to-day operations of such entities, or the manner in which professional functions are performed in those entities, their assets, liabilities, revenues and expenses are included in the financial statements of the relevant government.

Consolidation procedures

18 In preparing consolidated financial statements, an entity combines the financial statements of the parent and its subsidiaries line by line by adding together like items of assets, liabilities, equity, income and expenses. In order that the consolidated financial statements present financial information about the group as that of a single economic entity, the following steps are then taken:

(a) the carrying amount of the parent's investment in each subsidiary and the parent's portion of equity of each subsidiary are eliminated (see AASB 3, which describes the treatment of any resultant goodwill);

(b) non-controlling interests in the profit or loss of consolidated subsidiaries for the reporting period are identified; and

(c)   non-controlling interests in the net assets of consolidated subsidiaries are identified separately from the parent's ownership interests in them. Non-controlling interests in the net assets consist of:

       (i)   the amount of those non-controlling interests at the date of the original combination calculated in accordance with AASB 3; and

       (ii)   the non-controlling interests' share of changes in equity since the date of the combination.

19   When potential voting rights exist, the proportions of profit or loss and changes in equity allocated to the parent and non-controlling interests are determined on the basis of present ownership interests and do not reflect the possible exercise or conversion of potential voting rights.

20   Intragroup balances, transactions, income and expenses shall be eliminated in full.

21   Intragroup balances and transactions, including income, expenses and dividends, are eliminated in full. Profits and losses resulting from intragroup transactions that are recognised in assets, such as inventory and fixed assets, are eliminated in full. Intragroup losses may indicate an impairment that requires recognition in the consolidated financial statements. AASB 112 *Income Taxes* applies to temporary differences that arise from the elimination of profits and losses resulting from intragroup transactions.

22   The financial statements of the parent and its subsidiaries used in the preparation of the consolidated financial statements shall be prepared as of the same date. When the end of the reporting period of the parent is different from that of a subsidiary, the subsidiary prepares, for consolidation purposes, additional financial statements as of the same date as the financial statements of the parent unless it is impracticable to do so.

23   When, in accordance with paragraph 22, the financial statements of a subsidiary used in the preparation of consolidated financial statements are prepared as of a date different from that of the parent's financial statements, adjustments shall be made for the effects of significant transactions or events that occur between that date and the date of the parent's financial statements. In any case, the difference between the end of the reporting period of the subsidiary and that of the parent shall be no more than three months. The length of the reporting periods and any difference between the ends of the reporting periods shall be the same from period to period.

24   Consolidated financial statements shall be prepared using uniform accounting policies for like transactions and other events in similar circumstances.

25   If a member of the group uses accounting policies other than those adopted in the consolidated financial statements for like transactions and events in similar circumstances, appropriate adjustments are made to its financial statements in preparing the consolidated financial statements.

26   The income and expenses of a subsidiary are included in the consolidated financial statements from the acquisition date as defined in AASB 3. Income and expenses of the subsidiary shall be based on the values of the assets and liabilities recognised in the parent's consolidated financial statements at the acquisition date. For example, depreciation expense recognised in the consolidated statement of comprehensive income after the acquisition date shall be based on the fair values of the related depreciable assets recognised in the consolidated financial statements at the acquisition date. The income and expenses of a subsidiary are included in the consolidated financial statements until the date when the parent ceases to control the subsidiary.

27   Non-controlling interests shall be presented in the consolidated statement of financial position within equity, separately from the equity of the owners of the parent.

28   Profit or loss and each component of other comprehensive income are attributed to the owners of the parent and to the non-controlling interests. Total comprehensive income is attributed to the owners of the parent and to the non-controlling interests even if this results in the non-controlling interests having a deficit balance.

29   If a subsidiary has outstanding cumulative preference shares that are classified as equity and are held by non-controlling interests, the parent computes its share of profit or loss after adjusting for the dividends on such shares, whether or not dividends have been declared.

30   **Changes in a parent's ownership interest in a subsidiary that do not result in a loss of control are accounted for as equity transactions (i.e. transactions with owners in their capacity as owners).**

31   In such circumstances the carrying amounts of the controlling and non-controlling interests shall be adjusted to reflect the changes in their relative interests in the subsidiary. Any difference between the amount by which the non-controlling interests are adjusted and the fair value of the consideration paid or received shall be recognised directly in equity and attributed to the owners of the parent.

Loss of control

32   A parent can lose control of a subsidiary with or without a change in absolute or relative ownership levels. This could occur, for example, when a subsidiary becomes subject to the control of a government, court, administrator or regulator. It also could occur as a result of a contractual agreement.

33   A parent might lose control of a subsidiary in two or more arrangements (transactions). However, sometimes circumstances indicate that the multiple arrangements should be accounted for as a single transaction. In determining whether to account for the arrangements as a single transaction, a parent shall consider all of the terms and conditions of the arrangements and their economic effects. One or more of the following may indicate that the parent should account for the multiple arrangements as a single transaction:

(a)   They are entered into at the same time or in contemplation of each other.

(b)   They form a single transaction designed to achieve an overall commercial effect.

(c)   The occurrence of one arrangement is dependent on the occurrence of at least one other arrangement.

(d)   One arrangement considered on its own is not economically justified, but it is economically justified when considered together with other arrangements. An example is when one disposal of shares is priced below market and is compensated for by a subsequent disposal priced above market.

34   **If a parent loses control of a subsidiary, it:**

(a)   **derecognises the assets (including any goodwill) and liabilities of the subsidiary at their carrying amounts at the date when control is lost;**

(b)   **derecognises the carrying amount of any non-controlling interests in the former subsidiary at the date when control is lost (including any components of other comprehensive income attributable to them);**

(c)   **recognises:**

(i)   **the fair value of the consideration received, if any, from the transaction, event or circumstances that resulted in the loss of control; and**

(ii)   **if the transaction that resulted in the loss of control involves a distribution of shares of the subsidiary to owners in their capacity as owners, that distribution;**

(d)   **recognises any investment retained in the former subsidiary at its fair value at the date when control is lost;**

(e)   **reclassifies to profit or loss, or transfers directly to retained earnings if required in accordance with other Australian Accounting Standards, the amounts identified in paragraph 35; and**

(f)   **recognises any resulting difference as a gain or loss in profit or loss attributable to the parent.**

35   If a parent loses control of a subsidiary, the parent shall account for all amounts recognised in other comprehensive income in relation to that subsidiary on the same basis as would be required if the parent had directly disposed of the related assets or liabilities. Therefore, if a gain or loss previously recognised in other comprehensive income would be reclassified to profit or loss on the disposal of the related assets or liabilities, the parent reclassifies the gain or loss from equity to profit or loss (as a reclassification adjustment) when it loses control of the subsidiary. For example, if a subsidiary has available-for-sale financial assets and the parent loses control of the subsidiary, the parent shall reclassify to profit or loss the gain or loss previously recognised in other comprehensive income in relation to those assets. Similarly, if a revaluation surplus previously recognised in other comprehensive income would be transferred directly to retained earnings on the disposal of the asset, the parent transfers the revaluation surplus directly to retained earnings when it loses control of the subsidiary.

36   **On the loss of control of a subsidiary, any investment retained in the former subsidiary and any amounts owed by or to the former subsidiary shall be accounted for in accordance with other Australian Accounting Standards from the date when control is lost.**

37   The fair value of any investment retained in the former subsidiary at the date when control is lost shall be regarded as the fair value on initial recognition of a financial asset in accordance with AASB 139 *Financial Instruments: Recognition and Measurement* or, when appropriate, the cost on initial recognition of an investment in an associate or jointly controlled entity.

Accounting for investments in subsidiaries, jointly controlled entities and associates in separate financial statements

38   **When an entity prepares separate financial statements, it shall account for investments in subsidiaries, jointly controlled entities and associates either:**

   (a)   at cost, or

   (b)   in accordance with AASB 139.

   The entity shall apply the same accounting for each category of investments. Investments accounted for at cost shall be accounted for in accordance with AASB 5 *Non-current Assets Held for Sale and Discontinued Operations* when they are classified as held for sale (or included in a disposal group that is classified as held for sale) in accordance with AASB 5. The measurement of investments accounted for in accordance with AASB 139 is not changed in such circumstances.

38A   **An entity shall recognise a dividend from a subsidiary, jointly controlled entity or associate in profit or loss in its separate financial statements when its right to receive the dividend is established.**

38B   When a parent reorganises the structure of its group by establishing a new entity as its parent in a manner that satisfies the following criteria:

   (a)   the new parent obtains control of the original parent by issuing equity instruments in exchange for existing equity instruments of the original parent;

   (b)   the assets and liabilities of the new group and the original group are the same immediately before and after the reorganisation; and

   (c)   the owners of the original parent before the reorganisation have the same absolute and relative interests in the net assets of the original group and the new group immediately before and after the reorganisation

   and the new parent accounts for its investment in the original parent in accordance with paragraph 38(a) in its separate financial statements, the new parent shall measure cost at the carrying amount of its share of the equity items shown in the separate financial statements of the original parent at the date of the reorganisation.

AASB

38C   Similarly, an entity that is not a parent might establish a new entity as its parent in a manner that satisfies the criteria in paragraph 38B. The requirements in paragraph 38B apply equally to such reorganisations. In such cases, references to 'original parent' and 'original group' are to the 'original entity'.

39   This Standard does not mandate which entities produce separate financial statements available for public use. Paragraphs 38 and 40-43 apply when an entity prepares separate financial statements that comply with Australian Accounting Standards. The entity also produces consolidated financial statements available for public use as required by paragraph 9, unless the exemption provided in paragraphs 10-Aus10.2 is applicable.

40   **Investments in jointly controlled entities and associates that are accounted for in accordance with AASB 139 in the consolidated financial statements shall be accounted for in the same way in the investor's separate financial statements.**

Disclosure

41   **The following disclosures shall be made in consolidated financial statements:**

     (a)   **the nature of the relationship between the parent and a subsidiary when the parent does not own, directly or indirectly through subsidiaries, more than half of the voting power;**

     (b)   **the reasons why the ownership, directly or indirectly through subsidiaries, of more than half of the voting or potential voting power of an investee does not constitute control;**

     (c)   **the end of the reporting period of the financial statements of a subsidiary when such financial statements are used to prepare consolidated financial statements and are as of a date or for a period that is different from that of the parent's financial statements, and the reason for using a different date or period;**

     (d)   **the nature and extent of any significant restrictions (e.g. resulting from borrowing arrangements or regulatory requirements) on the ability of subsidiaries to transfer funds to the parent in the form of cash dividends or to repay loans or advances;**

     (e)   **a schedule that shows the effects of any changes in a parent's ownership interest in a subsidiary that do not result in a loss of control on the equity attributable to owners of the parent; and**

     (f)   **if control of a subsidiary is lost, the parent shall disclose the gain or loss, if any, recognised in accordance with paragraph 34, and:**

         (i)   **the portion of that gain or loss attributable to recognising any investment retained in the former subsidiary at its fair value at the date when control is lost; and**

         (ii)   **the line item(s) in the statement of comprehensive income in which the gain or loss is recognised (if not presented separately in the statement of comprehensive income).**

42   **When separate financial statements are prepared for a parent that, in accordance with paragraphs 10-Aus10.2, elects not to prepare consolidated financial statements, those separate financial statements shall disclose:**

     (a)   **the fact that the financial statements are separate financial statements; that the exemption from consolidation has been used; the name and country of incorporation or residence of the entity whose consolidated financial statements that comply with International Financial Reporting Standards have been produced for public use; and the address where those consolidated financial statements are obtainable;**

     (b)   **a list of significant investments in subsidiaries, jointly controlled entities and associates, including the name, country of incorporation or residence,**

proportion of ownership interest and, if different, proportion of voting power held; and

(c)   a description of the method used to account for the investments listed under (b).

43   When a parent (other than a parent covered by paragraph 42), venturer with an interest in a jointly controlled entity or an investor in an associate prepares separate financial statements, those separate financial statements shall disclose:

(a)   the fact that the statements are separate financial statements and the reasons why those statements are prepared if not required by law;

(b)   a list of significant investments in subsidiaries, jointly controlled entities and associates, including the name, country of incorporation or residence, proportion of ownership interest and, if different, proportion of voting power held; and

(c)   a description of the method used to account for the investments listed under (b);

and shall identify the financial statements prepared in accordance with paragraph 9 of this Standard or AASB 128 and AASB 131 to which they relate.

Aus43.1   In respect of not-for-profit public sector entities, where a group of entities is a reporting entity, but separate financial statements for the parent are not prepared, the notes to the consolidated financial statements shall disclose a list of significant subsidiaries, including:

(a)   the name;

(b)   country of incorporation or residence (where other than Australia); and

(c)   proportion of ownership interest and, if different, proportion of voting power held.

Effective date and transition

44   [Deleted by the AASB]

45   An entity shall apply the amendments to AASB 127 made in March 2008 in paragraphs 4, 18, 19, 26-37 and 41(e) and (f) for annual periods beginning on or after 1 July 2009. Earlier application is permitted. However, an entity shall not apply these amendments for annual periods beginning before 1 July 2009 unless it also applies AASB 3 (as revised in March 2008). If an entity applies the amendments before 1 July 2009, it shall disclose that fact. An entity shall apply the amendments retrospectively, with the following exceptions:

(a)   the amendment to paragraph 28 for attributing total comprehensive income to the owners of the parent and to the non-controlling interests even if this results in the non-controlling interests having a deficit balance. Therefore, an entity shall not restate any profit or loss attribution for reporting periods before the amendment is applied.

(b)   the requirements in paragraphs 30 and 31 for accounting for changes in ownership interests in a subsidiary after control is obtained. Therefore, the requirements in paragraphs 30 and 31 do not apply to changes that occurred before an entity applies the amendments.

(c)   the requirements in paragraphs 34-37 for the loss of control of a subsidiary. An entity shall not restate the carrying amount of an investment in a former subsidiary if control was lost before it applies those amendments. In addition, an entity shall not recalculate any gain or loss on the loss of control of a subsidiary that occurred before the amendments are applied.

Aus45.1   Paragraphs Aus17.1-Aus17.10 may be applied to annual reporting periods beginning on or after 1 January 2005 but beginning before 1 July 2008,

> provided there is early adoption for the same annual reporting period of the
> following pronouncements, as applicable:
>
> (a) AASB 1004 *Contributions*;
>
> (b) AASB 1049 *Whole of Government and General Government Sector Financial Reporting*;
>
> (c) AASB 1050 *Administered Items*;
>
> (d) AASB 1051 *Land Under Roads*;
>
> (e) AASB 1052 *Disaggregated Disclosures*; and
>
> (f) AASB Interpretation 1038 *Contributions by Owners Made to Wholly-Owned Public Sector Entities*.

45A Paragraph 38 was amended by AASB 2008-5 *Amendments to Australian Accounting Standards arising from the Annual Improvements Project* issued in July 2008. An entity shall apply that amendment for annual reporting periods beginning on or after 1 January 2009, prospectively from the date at which it first applied AASB 5. Earlier application is permitted. If an entity applies the amendment for an earlier period it shall disclose that fact.

45B AASB 2008-7 *Amendments to Australian Accounting Standards – Cost of an Investment in a Subsidiary, Jointly Controlled Entity or Associate*, issued in July 2008, deleted the definition of the cost method from paragraph 4 and added paragraph 38A. An entity shall apply those amendments prospectively for annual reporting periods beginning on or after 1 January 2009. Earlier application is permitted. If an entity applies the changes for an earlier period, it shall disclose that fact and apply the related amendments to AASB 118, AASB 121 and AASB 136 at the same time.

45C AASB 2008-7 *Amendments to Australian Accounting Standards – Cost of an Investment in a Subsidiary, Jointly Controlled Entity or Associate*, issued in July 2008, added paragraphs 38B and 38C. An entity shall apply those paragraphs prospectively to reorganisations occurring in annual reporting periods beginning on or after 1 January 2009. Earlier application is permitted. In addition, an entity may elect to apply paragraphs 38B and 38C retrospectively to past reorganisations within the scope of those paragraphs. However, if an entity restates any reorganisation to comply with paragraph 38B or 38C, it shall restate all later reorganisations within the scope of those paragraphs. If an entity applies paragraph 38B or 38C for an earlier period, it shall disclose that fact.

Withdrawal of IAS 27 (2003)

46 [Deleted by the AASB]

Implementation Guidance

Guidance on implementing AASB 127 *Consolidated and Separate Financial Statements*, AASB 128 *Investments in Associates* and AASB 131 *Interests in Joint Ventures*

This guidance accompanies AASB 127, AASB 128 and AASB 131, but is not part of them.

Consideration of potential voting rights

Introduction

IG1   Paragraphs 14, 15 and 19 of AASB 127 *Consolidated and Separate Financial Statements* (as amended in March 2008) and paragraphs 8 and 9 of AASB 128 *Investments in Associates* require an entity to consider the existence and effect of all potential voting rights that are currently exercisable or convertible. They also require all facts and circumstances that affect potential voting rights to be examined, except the intention of management and the financial ability to exercise or convert potential voting rights. Because the definition of joint control in paragraph 3 of AASB 131 *Interests in Joint Ventures* depends upon the definition of control, and because that Standard is linked to AASB 128 for application of the equity method, this guidance is also relevant to AASB 131.

Guidance

IG2   Paragraph 4 of AASB 127 defines control as the power to govern the financial and operating policies of an entity so as to obtain benefits from its activities. Paragraph 2 of AASB 128 defines significant influence as the power to participate in the financial and operating policy decisions of the investee but not to control those policies. Paragraph 3 of AASB 131 defines joint control as the contractually agreed sharing of control over an economic activity. In these contexts, power refers to the ability to do or effect something. Consequently, an entity has control, joint control or significant influence when it currently has the ability to exercise that power, regardless of whether control, joint control or significant influence is actively demonstrated or is passive in nature. Potential voting rights held by an entity that are currently exercisable or convertible provide this ability. The ability to exercise power does not exist when potential voting rights lack economic substance (e.g. the exercise price is set in a manner that precludes exercise or conversion in any feasible scenario). Consequently, potential voting rights are considered when, in substance, they provide the ability to exercise power.

IG3   Control and significant influence also arise in the circumstances described in paragraph 13 of AASB 127 and paragraphs 6 and 7 of AASB 128 respectively, which include consideration of the relative ownership of voting rights. AASB 131 depends on AASB 127 and AASB 128 and references to AASB 127 and AASB 128 from this point onwards should be read as being relevant to AASB 131. Nevertheless it should be borne in mind that joint control involves contractual sharing of control and this contractual aspect is likely to be the critical determinant. Potential voting rights such as share call options and convertible debt are capable of changing an entity's voting power over another entity – if the potential voting rights are exercised or converted, then the relative ownership of the ordinary shares carrying voting rights changes. Consequently, the existence of control (the definition of which permits only one entity to have control of another entity) and significant influence are determined only after assessing all the factors described in paragraph 13 of AASB 127 and paragraphs 6 and 7 of AASB 128 respectively, and considering the existence and effect of potential voting rights. In addition, the entity examines all facts and circumstances that affect potential voting rights except the intention of management and the financial ability to exercise or convert such rights. The intention of management does not affect the existence of power and the financial ability of an entity to exercise or convert potential voting rights is difficult to assess.

IG4   An entity may initially conclude that it controls or significantly influences another entity after considering the potential voting rights that it can currently exercise or convert.

However, the entity may not control or significantly influence the other entity when potential voting rights held by other parties are also currently exercisable or convertible. Consequently, an entity considers all potential voting rights held by it and by other parties that are currently exercisable or convertible when determining whether it controls or significantly influences another entity. For example, all share call options are considered, whether held by the entity or another party. Furthermore, the definition of control in paragraph 4 of AASB 127 permits only one entity to have control of another entity. Therefore, when two or more entities each hold significant voting rights, both actual and potential, the factors in paragraph 13 of AASB 127 are reassessed to determine which entity has control.

IG5 The proportion allocated to the parent and non-controlling interests in preparing consolidated financial statements in accordance with AASB 127, and the proportion allocated to an investor that accounts for its investment using the equity method in accordance with AASB 128, are determined solely on the basis of present ownership interests. The proportion allocated is determined taking into account the eventual exercise of potential voting rights and other derivatives that, in substance, give access at present to the economic benefits associated with an ownership interest.

IG6 In some circumstances an entity has, in substance, a present ownership as a result of a transaction that gives it access to the economic benefits associated with an ownership interest. In such circumstances, the proportion allocated is determined taking into account the eventual exercise of those potential voting rights and other derivatives that give the entity access to the economic benefits at present.

IG7 AASB 139 *Financial Instruments: Recognition and Measurement* does not apply to interests in subsidiaries, associates and jointly controlled entities that are consolidated, accounted for using the equity method or proportionately consolidated in accordance with AASB 127, AASB 128 and AASB 131 respectively. When instruments containing potential voting rights in substance currently give access to the economic benefits associated with an ownership interest, and the investment is accounted for in one of the above ways, the instruments are not subject to the requirements of AASB 139. In all other cases, instruments containing potential voting rights are accounted for in accordance with AASB 139.

Illustrative examples

IG8 The five examples below each illustrate one aspect of a potential voting right. In applying AASB 127, AASB 128 or AASB 131, an entity considers all aspects. The existence of control, significant influence and joint control can be determined only after assessing the other factors described in AASB 127, AASB 128 and AASB 131. For the purpose of these examples, however, those other factors are presumed not to affect the determination, even though they may affect it when assessed.

Example 1: Options are out of the money

Entities A and B own 80 per cent and 20 per cent respectively of the ordinary shares that carry voting rights at a general meeting of shareholders of Entity C. Entity A sells one-half of its interest to Entity D and buys call options from Entity D that are exercisable at any time at a premium to the market price when issued, and if exercised would give Entity A its original 80 per cent ownership interest and voting rights.

Though the options are out of the money, they are currently exercisable and give Entity A the power to continue to set the operating and financial policies of Entity C, because Entity A could exercise its options now. The existence of the potential voting rights, as well as the other factors described in paragraph 13 of AASB 127, are considered and it is determined that Entity A controls Entity C.

Example 2: Possibility of exercise or conversion

Entities A, B and C own 40 per cent, 30 per cent and 30 per cent respectively of the ordinary shares that carry voting rights at a general meeting of shareholders of Entity D. Entity A also owns call options that are exercisable at any time at the fair value of the underlying shares and if exercised would give it an additional 20 per cent of the voting rights in Entity D and reduce Entity B's and Entity C's interests to 20 per cent each.

If the options are exercised, Entity A will have control over more than one-half of the voting power. The existence of the potential voting rights, as well as the other factors described in paragraph 13 of AASB 127 and paragraphs 6 and 7 of AASB 128, are considered and it is determined that Entity A controls Entity D.

Example 3: Other rights that have the potential to increase an entity's voting power or reduce another entity's voting power

Entities A, B and C own 25 per cent, 35 per cent and 40 per cent respectively of the ordinary shares that carry voting rights at a general meeting of shareholders of Entity D. Entities B and C also have share warrants that are exercisable at any time at a fixed price and provide potential voting rights. Entity A has a call option to purchase these share warrants at any time for a nominal amount. If the call option is exercised, Entity A would have the potential to increase its ownership interest, and thereby its voting rights, in Entity D to 51 per cent (and dilute Entity B's interest to 23 per cent and Entity C's interest to 26 per cent).

Although the share warrants are not owned by Entity A, they are considered in assessing control because they are currently exercisable by Entities B and C. Normally, if an action (e.g. purchase or exercise of another right) is required before an entity has ownership of a potential voting right, the potential voting right is not regarded as held by the entity. However, the share warrants are, in substance, held by Entity A, because the terms of the call option are designed to ensure Entity A's position. The combination of the call option and share warrants gives Entity A the power to set the operating and financial policies of Entity D, because Entity A could currently exercise the option and share warrants. The other factors described in paragraph 13 of AASB 127 and paragraphs 6 and 7 of AASB 128 are also considered, and it is determined that Entity A, not Entity B or C, controls Entity D.

Example 4: Management intention

Entities A, B and C each own 33⅓ per cent of the ordinary shares that carry voting rights at a general meeting of shareholders of Entity D. Entities A, B and C each have the right to appoint two directors to the board of Entity D. Entity A also owns call options that are exercisable at a fixed price at any time and if exercised would give it all the voting rights in Entity D. The management of Entity A does not intend to exercise the call options, even if Entities B and C do not vote in the same manner as Entity A. The existence of the potential voting rights, as well as the other factors described in paragraph 13 of AASB 127 and paragraphs 6 and 7 of AASB 128, are considered and it is determined that Entity A controls Entity D. The intention of Entity A's management does not influence the assessment.

Example 5: Financial ability

Entities A and B own 55 per cent and 45 per cent respectively of the ordinary shares that carry voting rights at a general meeting of shareholders of Entity C. Entity B also holds debt instruments that are convertible into ordinary shares of Entity C. The debt can be converted at a substantial price, in comparison with Entity B's net assets, at any time and if converted would require Entity B to borrow additional funds to make the payment. If the debt were to be converted, Entity B would hold 70 per cent of the voting rights and Entity A's interest would reduce to 30 per cent.

Although the debt instruments are convertible at a substantial price, they are currently convertible and the conversion feature gives Entity B the power to set the operating and financial policies of Entity C. The existence of the potential voting rights, as well as the other factors described in paragraph 13 of AASB 127, are considered and it is determined that Entity B, not Entity A, controls Entity C. The financial ability of Entity B to pay the conversion price does not influence the assessment.

Australian Application Guidance

This guidance accompanies, but is not part of, AASB 127.

Exemption from Presenting Consolidated Financial Statements

AG1 The following table summarises the circumstances in which the exemption from presenting consolidated financial statements set out in paragraphs 10-Aus10.2 of this Standard may be available to a parent entity. The exemption is available only if the requirements of those paragraphs are satisfied. For example, the exemption is not available to a parent entity if it is a disclosing entity.

Same type of entity		
Ultimate or Intermediate Parent	FP	NFP
Parent	FP	NFP
Exemption for the parent	Available*	Available

Different type of entity		
Ultimate or Intermediate Parent	FP	NFP
Parent	NFP	FP
Exemption for the parent	Available*	Not available^

FP = For-profit entity

NFP = Not-for-profit entity

* The exemption would not be available by reference to the intermediate parent when it is a for-profit public sector entity unable to claim compliance with IFRSs – see paragraph Aus16.2 of AASB 101 Presentation of Financial Statements.

^ When the parent entity's NFP ultimate or intermediate parent is able to claim compliance with IFRSs, the exemption is available.

Deleted IAS 27 Text

Deleted IAS 27 text is not part of AASB 127.

Paragraph 44

An entity shall apply this Standard for annual periods beginning on or after 1 January 2005. Earlier application is encouraged. If an entity applies this Standard for a period beginning before 1 January 2005, it shall disclose that fact.

Paragraph 46

This Standard supersedes IAS 27 *Consolidated and Separate Financial Statements* (as revised in 2003).

AASB 127

Separate Financial Statements

(Revised August 2011: applicable to periods beginning
from 1 January 2013)

Note from the Institute of Chartered Accountants Australia

This note, prepared by the technical editors, is not part of Accounting Standard AASB 127.

Historical development

29 August 2011: A revised version of AASB 127 was issued applicable to annual reporting periods beginning 1 January 2013. Together with new AASB 10, AASB 11 and AASB 12 and revised AASB 128, these Standards changes group accounting.

This revised Standard is included here with the footer: Applicable to periods beginning from 1 January 2013.

10 September 2012: AASB 2012-7 'Amendments to Australian Accounting Standards arising from Reduced Disclosure Requirements' amends AASB 127 in relation to reduced disclosure requirements and applies to annual reporting periods beginning on or after 1 July 2013. **These amendments are not included in this compiled Standard.**

References

AASB 127 compared to IAS 27

Additions

Paragraph	Description
Aus 1.1	Which entities AASB 127 applies to (i.e. reporting entities and general purpose financial statements).
Aus 1.2	The application date of AASB 127 (i.e. annual reporting periods beginning 1 January 2013).
Aus 1.3	Permits early application by for-profit entities.
Aus 1.4	Makes the requirements of AASB 127 subject to AASB 1031 'Materiality'.
Aus 1.5	Explains which Australian Standards have been superseded by AASB 127.
Aus 16.1	Explains application to not-for-profit parents.

Deletions

Paragraph	Description
18	Effective date of IAS 27.
20	Reference to superseded IAS 27.

Contents

Preface

Comparison with IAS 27

Accounting Standard
AASB 127 Separate Financial Statements

	Paragraphs
Objective	1
Application	Aus1.1 – Aus1.5
Scope	2 – 3
Definitions	4 – 8
Preparation of separate financial statements	9 – 14
Disclosure	15 – 17
Effective date and transition	
References to AASB 9	19

Deleted IAS 27 Text

Basis for Conclusions on IAS 27
(available on the AASB website)

Australian Accounting Standard AASB 127 *Separate Financial Statements* is set out in paragraphs 1 – 19. All the paragraphs have equal authority. Paragraphs in **bold type** state the main principles. AASB 127 is to be read in the context of other Australian Accounting Standards, including AASB 1048 *Interpretation of Standards*, which identifies the Australian Accounting Interpretations. In the absence of explicit guidance, AASB 108 *Accounting Policies, Changes in Accounting Estimates and Errors* provides a basis for selecting and applying accounting policies.

Preface

Introduction

The Australian Accounting Standards Board (AASB) makes Australian Accounting Standards, including Interpretations, to be applied by:

(a)   entities required by the *Corporations Act 2001* to prepare financial reports;

(b)   governments in preparing financial statements for the whole of government and the General Government Sector (GGS); and

(c)   entities in the private or public for-profit or not-for-profit sectors that are reporting entities or that prepare general purpose financial statements.

AASB 1053 *Application of Tiers of Australian Accounting Standards* establishes a differential reporting framework consisting of two tiers of reporting requirements for preparing general purpose financial statements:

(a)   Tier 1: Australian Accounting Standards; and

(b)   Tier 2: Australian Accounting Standards – Reduced Disclosure Requirements.

Tier 1 requirements incorporate International Financial Reporting Standards (IFRSs), including Interpretations, issued by the International Accounting Standards Board (IASB), with the addition of paragraphs on the applicability of each Standard in the Australian environment.

Publicly accountable for-profit private sector entities are required to adopt Tier 1 requirements, and therefore are required to comply with IFRSs. Furthermore, other for-profit private sector entities complying with Tier 1 requirements will simultaneously comply with IFRSs. Some other entities complying with Tier 1 requirements will also simultaneously comply with IFRSs.

Tier 2 requirements comprise the recognition, measurement and presentation requirements of Tier 1 and substantially reduced disclosure requirements in comparison to Tier 1.

Australian Accounting Standards also include requirements that are specific to Australian entities. These requirements may be located in Australian Accounting Standards that incorporate IFRSs or in other Australian Accounting Standards. In most instances, these requirements are either restricted to the not-for-profit or public sectors or include additional disclosures that address domestic, regulatory or other issues. These requirements do not prevent publicly accountable for-profit private sector entities from complying with IFRSs. In developing requirements for public sector entities, the AASB considers the requirements of International Public Sector Accounting Standards (IPSASs), as issued by the International Public Sector Accounting Standards Board (IPSASB) of the International Federation of Accountants.

Implications for not-for-profit entities

This Standard applies to both for-profit and not-for-profit entities. However, prior to the 1 January 2013 mandatory application date of this Standard, the AASB will consider whether this Standard should be modified for application by not-for-profit entities having regard to its *Processes for Modifying IFRSs for PBE/NFP*. In light of this, not-for-profit entities are not permitted to apply this Standard prior to the mandatory application date.

Reduced disclosure requirements

Disclosure requirements under Tier 2 will be determined through a separate due process with amendments being made subsequently to this Standard as required.

Comparison with IAS 27

AASB 127 *Separate Financial Statements* incorporates IAS 27 *Separate Financial Statements* issued by the International Accounting Standards Board (IASB). Paragraphs that have been added to this Standard (and do not appear in the text of IAS 27) are identified with the prefix "Aus", followed by the number of the preceding IASB paragraph and decimal numbering.

For-profit entities that comply with AASB 127 will simultaneously be in compliance with IAS 27.

Not-for-profit entities using the added "Aus" paragraphs in the Standard that specifically apply to not-for-profit entities may not be simultaneously complying with IAS 27.

Accounting Standard AASB 127

The Australian Accounting Standards Board makes Accounting Standard AASB 127 *Separate Financial Statements* under section 334 of the *Corporations Act 2001*.

Kevin M. Stevenson
Chair – AASB

Dated 29 August 2011

Accounting Standard AASB 127

Separate Financial Statements

Objective

1   The objective of this Standard is to prescribe the accounting and disclosure requirements for investments in subsidiaries, joint ventures and associates when an entity prepares separate financial statements.

Application

Aus1.1   This Standard applies to:

   (a)   each entity that is required to prepare financial reports in accordance with Part 2M.3 of the Corporations Act and that is a reporting entity;

   (b)   general purpose financial statements of each other reporting entity; and

   (c)   financial statements that are, or are held out to be, general purpose financial statements.

Aus1.2   This Standard applies to annual reporting periods beginning on or after 1 January 2013.

Aus1.3   This Standard may be applied by for-profit entities, but not by not-for-profit entities, to annual reporting periods beginning on or after 1 January 2005 but before 1 January 2013. If a for-profit entity applies this Standard to such an annual reporting period, it shall disclose that fact and apply AASB 10 *Consolidated Financial Statements*, AASB 11 *Joint Arrangements*, AASB 12 *Disclosure of Interests in Other Entities* and AASB 128 *Investments in Associates and Joint Ventures* (August 2011) at the same time.

Aus1.4   The requirements specified in this Standard apply to the financial statements where information resulting from their application is material in accordance with AASB 1031 *Materiality*.

Aus1.5   When applied or operative, this Standard, together with AASB 10, supersedes AASB 127 *Consolidated and Separate Financial Statements* (March 2008, as amended).

Scope

2   This Standard shall be applied in accounting for investments in subsidiaries, joint ventures and associates when an entity elects, or is required by local regulations, to present separate financial statements.

3   This Standard does not mandate which entities produce separate financial statements. It applies when an entity prepares separate financial statements that comply with Australian Accounting Standards.

Definitions

4   The following terms are used in this Standard with the meanings specified:

Consolidated financial statements are the financial statements of a group in which the assets, liabilities, equity, income, expenses and cash flows of the parent and its subsidiaries are presented as those of a single economic entity.

Separate financial statements are those presented by a parent (ie an investor with control of a subsidiary) or an investor with joint control of, or significant influence over, an investee, in which the investments are accounted for at cost or in accordance with AASB 9 *Financial Instruments*.

5   The following terms are defined in Appendix A of AASB 10 *Consolidated Financial Statements*, Appendix A of AASB 11 *Joint Arrangements* and paragraph 3 of AASB 128 *Investments in Associates and Joint Ventures*:

- associate
- control of an investee
- group
- joint control
- joint venture
- joint venturer
- parent
- significant influence
- subsidiary.

6   Separate financial statements are those presented in addition to consolidated financial statements or in addition to financial statements in which investments in associates or joint ventures are accounted for using the equity method, other than in the circumstances set out in paragraph 8. Separate financial statements need not be appended to, or accompany, those statements.

7   Financial statements in which the equity method is applied are not separate financial statements. Similarly, the financial statements of an entity that does not have a subsidiary, associate or joint venturer's interest in a joint venture are not separate financial statements.

8   An entity that is exempted in accordance with paragraphs 4(a), Aus4.1 and Aus4.2 of AASB 10 from consolidation or paragraphs 17 and Aus17.1 of AASB 128 (August 2011) from applying the equity method may present separate financial statements as its only financial statements.

Preparation of separate financial statements

9   **Separate financial statements shall be prepared in accordance with all applicable Standards, except as provided in paragraph 10.**

10   **When an entity prepares separate financial statements, it shall account for investments in subsidiaries, joint ventures and associates either:**

        (a)   at cost, or

        (b)   in accordance with AASB 9.

        The entity shall apply the same accounting for each category of investments. Investments accounted for at cost shall be accounted for in accordance with AASB 5 *Non-current Assets Held for Sale and Discontinued Operations* **when they are classified as held for sale (or included in a disposal group that is classified as held for sale). The measurement of investments accounted for in accordance with AASB 9 is not changed in such circumstances.**

11   If an entity elects, in accordance with paragraph 18 of AASB 128 (August 2011), to measure its investments in associates or joint ventures at fair value through profit or loss in accordance with AASB 9, it shall also account for those investments in the same way in its separate financial statements.

12   **An entity shall recognise a dividend from a subsidiary, a joint venture or an associate in profit or loss in its separate financial statements when its right to receive the dividend is established.**

13   When a parent reorganises the structure of its group by establishing a new entity as its parent in a manner that satisfies the following criteria:

        (a)   the new parent obtains control of the original parent by issuing equity instruments in exchange for existing equity instruments of the original parent;

        (b)   the assets and liabilities of the new group and the original group are the same immediately before and after the reorganisation; and

        (c)   the owners of the original parent before the reorganisation have the same absolute and relative interests in the net assets of the original group and the new group immediately before and after the reorganisation,

        and the new parent accounts for its investment in the original parent in accordance with paragraph 10(a) in its separate financial statements, the new parent shall measure cost at the carrying amount of its share of the equity items shown in the separate financial statements of the original parent at the date of the reorganisation.

14   Similarly, an entity that is not a parent might establish a new entity as its parent in a manner that satisfies the criteria in paragraph 13. The requirements in paragraph 13 apply equally to such reorganisations. In such cases, references to 'original parent' and 'original group' are to the 'original entity'.

Disclosure

15   **An entity shall apply all applicable Standards when providing disclosures in its separate financial statements, including the requirements in paragraphs 16–17.**

16   **When a parent, in accordance with paragraphs 4(a), Aus4.1 and Aus4.2 of AASB 10, elects not to prepare consolidated financial statements and instead prepares separate financial statements, it shall disclose in those separate financial statements:**

        (a)   the fact that the financial statements are separate financial statements; that the exemption from consolidation has been used; the name and principal place of business (and country of incorporation, if different) of the entity whose consolidated financial statements that comply with International Financial

Reporting Standards have been produced for public use; and the address where those consolidated financial statements are obtainable.

    (b)   a list of significant investments in subsidiaries, joint ventures and associates, including:

        (i)   the name of those investees.

        (ii)   the principal place of business (and country of incorporation, if different) of those investees.

        (iii)   its proportion of the ownership interest (and its proportion of the voting rights, if different) held in those investees.

    (c)   a description of the method used to account for the investments listed under (b).

Aus16.1   When a not-for-profit parent, in accordance with paragraphs 4(a), Aus4.1 and Aus4.2 of AASB 10, elects not to prepare consolidated financial statements and instead prepares separate financial statements, it shall disclose in those separate financial statements the disclosures specified in paragraph 16, with the exception that the reference in paragraph 16(a) to 'International Financial Reporting Standards' is replaced by a reference to 'Australian Accounting Standards'.

17   When a parent (other than a parent covered by paragraph 16 or Aus16.1) or an investor with joint control of, or significant influence over, an investee prepares separate financial statements, the parent or investor shall identify the financial statements prepared in accordance with AASB 10, AASB 11 or AASB 128 (August 2011) to which they relate. The parent or investor shall also disclose in its separate financial statements:

    (a)   the fact that the statements are separate financial statements and the reasons why those statements are prepared if not required by law.

    (b)   a list of significant investments in subsidiaries, joint ventures and associates, including:

        (i)   the name of those investees.

        (ii)   the principal place of business (and country of incorporation, if different) of those investees.

        (iii)   its proportion of the ownership interest (and its proportion of the voting rights, if different) held in those investees.

    (c)   a description of the method used to account for the investments listed under (b).

The parent or investor shall also identify the financial statements prepared in accordance with AASB 10, AASB 11 or AASB 128 (August 2011) to which they relate.

Effective date and transition

18   [Deleted by the AASB – see paragraphs Aus1.2 and Aus1.3]

References to AASB 9

19   If an entity applies this Standard but does not yet apply AASB 9, any reference to AASB 9 shall be read as a reference to AASB 139 *Financial Instruments: Recognition and Measurement.*

Withdrawal of IAS 27 (2008)

20   [Deleted by the AASB – see paragraph Aus1.5]

Deleted IAS 27 Text

Deleted IAS 27 text is not part of AASB 127.

Paragraph 18

An entity shall apply this Standard for annual periods beginning on or after 1 January 2013. Earlier application is permitted. If an entity applies this Standard earlier, it shall disclose that fact and apply IFRS 10, IFRS 11, IFRS 12 *Disclosure of Interests in Other Entities* and IAS 28 (as amended in 2011) at the same time.

Paragraph 20

This Standard is issued concurrently with IFRS 10. Together, the two IFRSs supersede IAS 27 *Consolidated and Separate Financial Statements* (as amended in 2008).

AASB 128

Investments in Associates

(Compiled September 2011: applicable 30 June 2013)

AASB

Note from the Institute of Chartered Accountants Australia

This note, prepared by the technical editors, is not part of Accounting Standard AASB 128.

Historical development

15 July 2004: AASB 128 'Investments in Associates' is the Australian equivalent of IAS 28 of the same name. It was made by the AASB on 15 July 2004 as part of the AASB's program to adopt International Financial Reporting Standards (IFRSs) by 2005.

6 April 2006: Removal of Australian Guidance.

30 April 2007: AASB 2007-4 'Amendments to Australian Accounting Standards' amends paragraph 2, adds paragraphs 3, 4, 5 and 13(b) and deletes paragraphs Aus 14.1 and Aus 37.1. It is applicable for annual reporting periods beginning on or after 1 July 2007, with early adoption permitted for annual reporting periods beginning on or after 1 January 2005.

28 June 2007: AASB 2007-7 'Amendments to Australian Accounting Standards' amends paragraph 35 and is applicable for annual reporting periods beginning on or after 1 July 2007, with early adoption permitted for annual reporting periods beginning on or after 1 January 2005.

24 September 2007: AASB 2007-8 'Amendments to Australian Accounting Standards' is applicable for annual reporting periods beginning on or after 1 January 2009.

13 December 2007: AASB 2007-10 'Further Amendments to Australian Accounting Standards arising from AASB 101' amends AASB 128, replacing the term 'financial report' with 'financial statements'. This Standard is applicable to annual reporting periods beginning on or after 1 January 2009.

6 March 2008: AASB 2008-3 'Amendments to Australian Accounting Standards arising from AASB 3 and AASB 127' amends AASB 128 for the issue of AASB 3 Revised. This Standard is applicable to annual reporting periods beginning on or after 1 July 2009.

24 July 2008: AASB 2008-5 'Amendments to Australian Accounting Standards arising from the Annual Improvements Project' amends AASB 128 in relation to required disclosures when investments in associates are accounted for at fair value through profit or loss, and the impairment of an investment in an associate. This Standard is applicable to annual reporting periods beginning on or after 1 January 2009.

4 November 2009: AASB 128 was reissued by the AASB, compiled to include the AASB 2007-8, AASB 2007-10, AASB 2008-3 and AASB 2008-5 amendments and applies to annual reporting periods beginning on or after 1 July 2009. Early application is permitted.

On the same date the AASB reissued the version of AASB 128 applicable to annual reporting periods beginning on or after 1 January 2009 but before 1 July 2009. This version of AASB 128 has been compiled for the amending Standards applying to annual reporting periods beginning on or after 1 January 2009. This Standard applies to 31 December 2009 year end.

7 December 2009: AASB 2009-11 'Amendments to Australian Accounting Standards arising from AASB 9' amends AASB 128 to give effect to consequential changes arising from the issuance of AASB 9. This Standard is applicable to annual reporting periods beginning on or after 1 January 2013 with early adoption permitted from annual reporting periods ending on or after 31 December 2009 that begin before 1 January 2013 provided AASB 9 is also applied for the same period. The application date of AASB 2009-11 has been amended to 1 January 2015 by AASB 2012-6. **These amendments have been superseded by AASB 2010-7 and are not included in this compiled Standard.**

---

2 June 2010: AASB 2010-3 'Amendments to Australian Accounting Standards arising from the Annual Improvements Project' amends AASB 128 in relation to transition requirements for amendments arising as a result of AASB 127. This Standard is applicable to annual reporting periods beginning on or after 1 July 2010 with early adoption permitted.

7 September 2010: AASB 128 was reissued by the AASB, compiled to include the AASB 2010-3 amendments and applies to annual reporting periods beginning on or after 1 July 2010 but before 1 January 2013.

1 March 2011: AASB 2010-7 'Amendments to Australian Accounting Standards arising from AASB 9 (December 2010)' as compiled amends AASB 128 to give effect to consequential changes arising from the reissue of AASB 9 in December 2010 and supersedes AASB 2009-11 which related to the previous version of AASB 9. This Standard applies to annual reporting periods beginning on or after 1 January 2013 and can be adopted early. The application date of AASB 2010-7 has been amended to 1 January 2015 by AASB 2012-6. **These amendments are not included in this compiled Standard.**

11 May 2011: AASB 2011-1 'Amendments to Australian Accounting Standards arising from the Trans-Tasman Convergence Project' amends AASB 128 as a result of the Trans-Tasman project, to more closely align IFRSs as applied through Australian and New Zealand Standards. AASB 2011-1 deletes Australian specific disclosure requirements. Where appropriate these disclosures are now included in AASB 1054 'Australian Additional Requirements'. These Standards apply to annual reporting periods beginning on or after 1 July 2011 with early adoption permitted.

11 July 2011: AASB 2011-5 'Amendments to Australian Accounting Standards – Extending Relief from Consolidation, the Equity Method and Proportionate Consolidation' amends AASB 128 to give relief from consolidating and equity accounting in certain situations. These Standards apply to annual reporting periods beginning on or after 1 July 2011 with early adoption permitted.

29 August 2011: A revised version of AASB 128 was issued by the AASB, applicable to annual reporting periods beginning 1 January 2013. **This revised Standard is included in this handbook with the footer: Applicable to periods beginning from 1 January 2013.**

2 September 2011: AASB 2011-8 'Amendments to Australian Accounting Standards arising from AASB 13' amends AASB 128 to give effect to a consequential change in the definition of fair value arising from the issue of AASB 13. This Standard applies to annual reporting periods beginning on or after 1 January 2013 and can be adopted early. **These amendments are not included this compiled Standard.**

23 September 2011: AASB 128 was reissued by the AASB, compiled to include the AASB 2001-1 and AASB 2011-5 amendments and applies to annual reporting periods beginning on or after 1 July 2011 but before 1 July 2012. **This compiled Standard is included in this handbook with the footer: Applicable 30 June 2013.**

References

Interpretation 5 *Rights to Interests arising from Decommissioning, Restoration and Environmental Rehabilitation Funds* applies to AASB 128.

IFRIC items not taken onto the agenda: No. 31 *The effects of rights of veto on control* issued in August 2002, IAS 28-1, IAS 28-2 *Venture capital consolidations and partial use of fair value through profit or loss*, IAS 28-3 *Impairment of investments in associates,* No. 33 *Reciprocal interests* reissued in April 2005, No. 34 *Equity method application* issued in April 2003, No. 35 *Investments in associates – investments after discontinuing equity accounting* issued in February 2002, IAS 28-1, IAS 28-2 *Venture capital consolidations and partial use of fair value through profit or loss* and IAS 28-3 *Impairment of investments in associates* apply to AASB 128.

AASB 128 (applicable 30 June 2013) compared to IAS 28 (applicable 30 June 2013)

Additions

Paragraph	Description
Aus 1.1	Which entities AASB 128 applies to (i.e. reporting entities and general purpose financial statements).
Aus 1.2	The application date of AASB 128 (i.e. annual reporting periods beginning 1 January 2005).

Aus 1.3	Prohibits early application of AASB 128.
Aus 1.4	Makes the requirements of AASB 128 subject to AASB 1031 'Materiality'.
Aus 1.5	Explains which Australian Standards have been superseded by AASB 128.
Aus 1.6	Clarifies that the superseded Australian Standards remain in force until AASB 128 applies.
Aus 1.7	Notice of the new Standard published on 22 July 2004.
Aus13.1	Clarifies an investor which is a not-for-profit entity need not apply equity accounting in certain circumstances.

Deletions

Paragraph	*Description*
41, 41A	Effective date of IAS 28.
42	Reference to superseded IAS 28.
43	Reference to superseded SIC Interpretations – SICs 3, 20 and 33.

Contents

Compilation Details

Comparison with IAS 28

Accounting Standard
AASB 128 Investments in Associates

	Paragraphs
Application	Aus1.1 – Aus1.7
Scope	1
Definitions	2 – 5
Significant Influence	6 – 10
Equity Method	11 – 12
Application of the Equity Method	13 – 30
Impairment Losses	31 – 34
Separate Financial Statements	35 – 36
Disclosure	37 – 40
Effective Date and Transition	41B – 41E

Implementation Guidance
(see AASB 127 *Consolidated and Separate Financial Statements*)

Basis for Conclusions on IAS 28
(available on the AASB website)

Australian Accounting Standard AASB 128 *Investments in Associates* (as amended) is set out in paragraphs Aus1.1 – 41E. All the paragraphs have equal authority. Terms defined in this Standard are in *italics* the first time they appear in the Standard. AASB 128 is to be read in the context of other Australian Accounting Standards, including AASB 1048 *Interpretation of Standards*, which identifies the Australian Accounting Interpretations. In the absence of explicit guidance, AASB 108 *Accounting Policies, Changes in Accounting Estimates and Errors* provides a basis for selecting and applying accounting policies.

Compilation Details

Accounting Standard AASB 128 *Investments in Associates* as amended

This compiled Standard applies to annual reporting periods beginning on or after 1 July 2011 but before 1 January 2013. It takes into account amendments up to and including 20 July 2011 and was prepared on 23 September 2011 by the staff of the Australian Accounting Standards Board (AASB).

This compilation is not a separate Accounting Standard made by the AASB. Instead, it is a representation of AASB 128 (July 2004) as amended by other Accounting Standards, which are listed in the Table below.

Table of Standards

Standard	Date made	Application date *(annual reporting periods ... on or after ...)*	Application, saving or transitional provisions
AASB 128	15 Jul 2004	*(beginning)* 1 Jan 2005	
AASB 2007-4	30 Apr 2007	*(beginning)* 1 Jul 2007	see (a) below
AASB 2007-7	28 Jun 2007	*(beginning)* 1 Jul 2007	see (a) below
AASB 2007-8	24 Sep 2007	*(beginning)* 1 Jan 2009	see (b) below
AASB 2007-10	13 Dec 2007	*(beginning)* 1 Jan 2009	see (b) below
AASB 2008-3	6 Mar 2008	*(beginning)* 1 Jul 2009	see (c) below
AASB 2008-5	24 Jul 2008	*(beginning)* 1 Jan 2009	see (d) below
AASB 2009-11	7 Dec 2009	*(beginning)* 1 Jan 2013	not compiled*
AASB 2010-3	23 Jun 2010	*(beginning)* 1 Jul 2010	see (e) below
AASB 2010-2	30 Jun 2010	*(beginning)* 1 Jul 2013	not compiled*
AASB 2010-7	6 Dec 2010	*(beginning)* 1 Jan 2013	not compiled*
AASB 2011-1	11 May 2011	*(beginning)* 1 Jul 2011	see (f) below
AASB 2011-5	20 Jul 2011	*(beginning)* 1 Jul 2011	see (g) below
AASB 2011-6	20 Jul 2011	*(beginning)* 1 Jul 2013	not compiled*
AASB 2011-8	2 Sep 2011	*(beginning)* 1 Jan 2013	not compiled*

* The amendments made by this Standard are not included in this compilation, which presents the principal Standard as applicable to annual reporting periods beginning on or after 1 July 2011 but before 1 January 2013. The principal Standard has been superseded by AASB 128 *Investments in Associates and Joint Ventures*, which applies to annual reporting periods beginning on or after 1 January 2013.

(a) Entities may elect to apply this Standard to annual reporting periods beginning on or after 1 January 2005 but before 1 July 2007.

(b) Entities may elect to apply this Standard to annual reporting periods beginning on or after 1 January 2005 but before 1 January 2009, provided that AASB 101 *Presentation of Financial Statements* (September 2007) is also applied to such periods.

(c) Entities may elect to apply this Standard to annual reporting periods beginning on or after 30 June 2007 but before 1 July 2009, provided that AASB 3 *Business Combinations* (March 2008) and AASB 127 *Consolidated and Separate Financial Statements* (March 2008) are also applied to such periods.

(d) Entities may elect to apply this Standard, or its amendments to individual Standards, to annual reporting periods beginning on or after 1 January 2005 but before 1 January 2009.

(e) Entities may elect to apply this Standard to annual reporting periods beginning on or after 1 January 2005 but before 1 July 2010.

(f) Entities may elect to apply this Standard, or its amendments to individual pronouncements, to annual reporting periods beginning on or after 1 January 2005 but before 1 July 2011, provided that AASB 1054 *Australian Additional Disclosures* is, or its relevant individual disclosure requirements are, also applied to such periods.

(g) Entities may elect to apply this Standard to annual reporting periods beginning on or after 1 January 2005 but before 1 July 2011, provided that AASB 2007-4 *Amendments to Australian Accounting Standards arising from ED 151 and Other Amendments* is also applied to such periods.

Table of Amendments

Paragraph affected	How affected	By ... [paragraph]
Aus1.1	amended	AASB 2007-8 [7, 8]
Aus1.4	amended	AASB 2007-8 [8]
Aus1.8	amended	AASB 2007-8 [8]
	deleted	AASB 2011-1 [18]
1	amended	AASB 2008-5 [45]
2	amended	AASB 2007-4 [70]
3	added	AASB 2007-4 [71]
4	added	AASB 2007-4 [71]
5	added	AASB 2007-4 [71]
	amended	AASB 2011-5 [17]
11	amended	AASB 2007-8 [88]
13	amended	AASB 2007-4 [71]
	amended	AASB 2007-10 [72]
	amended	AASB 2011-5 [17]
Aus13.1	added	AASB 2011-5 [18]
Aus14.1	deleted	AASB 2007-4 [72]
18-19	amended	AASB 2008-3 [46]
19A	added	AASB 2008-3 [47]
23	amended	AASB 2008-3 [48]
24	amended	AASB 2007-8 [88]
25	amended	AASB 2007-8 [88]
33	amended	AASB 2008-5 [45]
35	amended	AASB 2007-7 [13]
	amended	AASB 2008-3 [49]
37	amended	AASB 2007-8 [88]
Aus37.1	deleted	AASB 2007-4 [72]
39	amended	AASB 2007-8 [88]
41 (preceding heading)	amended	AASB 2008-5 [46]
41A	note added	AASB 2007-8 [89]
41B	note added	AASB 2008-3 [50]
	paragraph added (in place of note)	AASB 2010-3 [10]
41C	added	AASB 2008-5 [47]
41E	added	AASB 2010-3 [10]

Comparison with IAS 28

AASB 128 and IAS 28

AASB 128 *Investments in Associates* as amended incorporates IAS 28 *Investments in Associates* as issued and amended by the International Accounting Standards Board (IASB). Paragraphs that have been added to this Standard (and do not appear in the text of IAS 28) are identified with the prefix "Aus", followed by the number of the relevant IASB paragraph and decimal numbering.

Compliance with IAS 28

Entities that comply with AASB 128 as amended will simultaneously be in compliance with IAS 28 as amended.

> ## Accounting Standard AASB 128
>
> The Australian Accounting Standards Board made Accounting Standard AASB 128 *Investments in Associates* under section 334 of the *Corporations Act 2001* on 15 July 2004.
>
> This compiled version of AASB 128 applies to annual reporting periods beginning on or after 1 July 2011 but before 1 January 2013. It incorporates relevant amendments contained in other AASB Standards made by the AASB up to and including 20 July 2011 (see Compilation Details).

Accounting Standard AASB 128

Investments in Associates

Application

Aus1.1   This Standard applies to:

(a)   each entity that is required to prepare financial reports in accordance with Part 2M.3 of the Corporations Act and that is a reporting entity;

(b)   general purpose financial statements of each other reporting entity; and

(c)   financial statements that are, or are held out to be, general purpose financial statements.

Aus1.2   This Standard applies to annual reporting periods beginning on or after 1 January 2005.

[Note: For application dates of paragraphs changed or added by an amending Standard, see Compilation Details.]

Aus1.3   This Standard shall not be applied to annual reporting periods beginning before 1 January 2005.

Aus1.4   The requirements specified in this Standard apply to the financial statements where information resulting from their application is material in accordance with AASB 1031 *Materiality*.

Aus1.5   When applicable, this Standard supersedes:

(a)   AASB 1016 *Accounting for Investments in Associates* as notified in the *Commonwealth of Australia Gazette* No S 415, 25 August 1998 as amended by AASB 1016A *Amendments to Accounting Standard AASB 1016* as notified in the *Commonwealth of Australia Gazette* No S 502, 15 October 1998; and

(b)   AAS 14 *Accounting for Investments in Associates* as issued in May 1997.

Aus1.6   Both AASB 1016 and AAS 14 remain applicable until superseded by this Standard.

Aus1.7   Notice of this Standard was published in the *Commonwealth of Australia Gazette* No S 294, 22 July 2004.

Scope

1   This Standard shall be applied in accounting for investments in associates. However, it does not apply to investments in associates held by:

(a)   venture capital organisations, or

(b)   mutual funds, unit trusts and similar entities including investment-linked insurance funds

that upon initial recognition are designated as at fair value through profit or loss or are classified as held for trading and accounted for in accordance with AASB 139 *Financial Instruments: Recognition and Measurement*. Such investments shall be measured at fair value in accordance with AASB 139, with changes in fair value recognised in profit or loss in the period of the change. An entity holding such an investment shall make the disclosures required by paragraph 37(f).

Definitions

2   The following terms are used in this Standard with the meanings specified.

An *associate* is an entity, including an unincorporated entity such as a partnership, over which the investor has significant influence and that is neither a subsidiary nor an interest in a joint venture.

Consolidated financial statements are the financial statements of a group presented as those of a single economic entity.

Control is the power to govern the financial and operating policies of an entity so as to obtain benefits from its activities.

The *equity method* is a method of accounting whereby the investment is initially recognised at cost and adjusted thereafter for the post-acquisition change in the investor's share of net assets of the investee. The profit or loss of the investor includes the investor's share of the profit or loss of the investee.

Joint control is the contractually agreed sharing of control over an economic activity, and exists only when the strategic financial and operating decisions relating to the activity require the unanimous consent of the parties sharing control (the venturers).

Separate financial statements are those presented by a parent, an investor in an associate or a venturer in a jointly controlled entity, in which the investments are accounted for on the basis of the direct equity interest rather than on the basis of the reported results and net assets of the investees.

Significant influence is the power to participate in the financial and operating policy decisions of the investee but is not control or *joint control* over those policies.

A *subsidiary* is an entity, including an unincorporated entity such as a partnership, that is controlled by another entity (known as the parent).

3   Financial statements in which the *equity method* is applied are not *separate financial statements*, nor are the financial statements of an entity that does not have a *subsidiary*, associate or venturer's interest in a joint venture.

4   Separate financial statements are those presented in addition to *consolidated financial statements*, financial statements in which investments are accounted for using the equity method and financial statements in which venturers' interests in joint ventures are proportionately consolidated. Separate financial statements may or may not be appended to, or accompany, those financial statements.

5   Entities that are exempted in accordance with paragraphs 10–Aus10.2 of AASB 127 *Consolidated and Separate Financial Statements* from consolidation, paragraph 2 of AASB 131 *Interests in Joint Ventures* from applying proportionate consolidation or paragraph 13(c) of this Standard from applying the equity method may present separate financial statements as their only financial statements.

Significant Influence

6   If an investor holds, directly or indirectly (e.g. through subsidiaries), 20% or more of the voting power of the investee, it is presumed that the investor has *significant influence*, unless it can be clearly demonstrated that this is not the case. Conversely, if the investor holds, directly or indirectly (e.g. through subsidiaries), less than 20 per cent of the voting power of the investee, it is presumed that the investor does not have significant influence, unless such influence can be clearly demonstrated. A substantial or majority ownership by another investor does not necessarily preclude an investor from having significant influence.

7   The existence of significant influence by an investor is usually evidenced in one or more of the following ways:

(a)   representation on the board of directors or equivalent governing body of the investee;

(b)   participation in policy-making processes, including participation in decisions about dividends or other distributions;

(c)   material transactions between the investor and the investee;

(d)   interchange of managerial personnel; or

(e)   provision of essential technical information.

8   An entity may own share warrants, share call options, debt or equity instruments that are convertible into ordinary shares, or other similar instruments that have the potential, if exercised or converted, to give the entity additional voting power or reduce another party's voting power over the financial and operating policies of another entity (i.e. potential voting rights). The existence and effect of potential voting rights that are currently exercisable or convertible, including potential voting rights held by other entities, are considered when assessing whether an entity has significant influence. Potential voting rights are not currently exercisable or convertible when, for example, they cannot be exercised or converted until a future date or until the occurrence of a future event.

9   In assessing whether potential voting rights contribute to significant influence, the entity examines all facts and circumstances (including the terms of exercise of the potential voting rights and any other contractual arrangements whether considered individually or in combination) that affect potential rights except the intention of management and the financial ability to exercise or convert.

10   An entity loses significant influence over an investee when it loses the power to participate in the financial and operating policy decisions of that investee. The loss of significant influence can occur with or without a change in absolute or relative ownership levels. It could occur, for example, when an associate becomes subject to the *control* of a government, court, administrator or regulator. It could also occur as a result of a contractual agreement.

Equity Method

11   Under the equity method, the investment in an associate is initially recognised at cost and the carrying amount is increased or decreased to recognise the investor's share of the profit or loss of the investee after the date of acquisition. The investor's share of the profit or loss of the investee is recognised in the investor's profit or loss. Distributions received from an investee reduce the carrying amount of the investment. Adjustments to the carrying amount may also be necessary for changes in the investor's proportionate interest in the investee arising from changes in the investee's other comprehensive income. Such changes include those arising from the revaluation of property, plant and equipment and from foreign exchange translation differences. The investor's share of those changes is recognised in other comprehensive income of the investor (see AASB 101 *Presentation of Financial Statements* (as revised in 2007)).

12   When potential voting rights exist, the investor's share of profit or loss of the investee and of changes in the investee's equity is determined on the basis of present ownership interests and does not reflect the possible exercise or conversion of potential voting rights.

Application of the Equity Method

13   **An investment in an associate shall be accounted for using the equity method except when:**

(a)   the investment is classified as held for sale in accordance with AASB 5 *Non-current Assets Held for Sale and Discontinued Operations*; or

(b)   the exception in paragraph 10 or Aus10.1, as modified by paragraph Aus10.2, of AASB 127 allowing a parent that also has an interest in an associate not to present consolidated financial statements, applies; or

(c)   all of the following apply:

(i)   the investor is a wholly-owned subsidiary, or is a partially-owned subsidiary of another entity and its other owners, including those not otherwise entitled to vote, have been informed about, and do not object to, the investor not applying the equity method;

(ii)   the investor's debt or equity instruments are not traded in a public market (a domestic or foreign stock exchange or an over-the-counter market, including local and regional markets);

(iii)   the investor did not file, nor is it in the process of filing, its financial statements with a securities commission or other regulatory organisation, for the purpose of issuing any class of instruments in a public market; and

(iv)   the ultimate Australian or any intermediate parent of the investor produces consolidated financial statements available for public use that comply with International Financial Reporting Standards.

Aus13.1   Notwithstanding paragraph 13(c)(iv), an investor that meets the criteria in paragraphs 13(c)(i), 13(c)(ii) and 13(c)(iii) need not apply the equity method in accounting for an interest in an associate if its ultimate or any intermediate parent produces consolidated financial statements available for public use and the investor and its ultimate or intermediate parent are both not-for-profit entities complying with Australian Accounting Standards.

14   Investments described in paragraph 13(a) shall be accounted for in accordance with AASB 5.

15   When an investment in an associate previously classified as held for sale no longer meets the criteria to be so classified, it shall be accounted for using the equity method as from the date of its classification as held for sale. Financial statements for the periods since classification as held for sale shall be amended accordingly.

16   [Deleted by the IASB]

17   The recognition of income on the basis of distributions received may not be an adequate measure of the income earned by an investor on an investment in an associate because the distributions received may bear little relation to the performance of the associate. Because the investor has significant influence over the associate, the investor has an interest in the associate's performance and, as a result, the return on its investment. The investor accounts for this interest by extending the scope of its financial statements to include its share of profits or losses of such an associate. As a result, application of the equity method provides more informative reporting of the net assets and profit or loss of the investor.

18   An investor shall discontinue the use of the equity method from the date when it ceases to have significant influence over an associate and shall account for the investment in accordance with AASB 139 from that date, provided the associate does not become a subsidiary or a joint venture as defined in AASB 131. On the loss of significant influence, the investor shall measure at fair value any investment the investor retains in the former associate. The investor shall recognise in profit or loss any difference between:

(a)   the fair value of any retained investment and any proceeds from disposing of the part interest in the associate; and

(b)   the carrying amount of the investment at the date when significant influence is lost.

19   When an investment ceases to be an associate and is accounted for in accordance with AASB 139, the fair value of the investment at the date when it ceases to be an associate shall be regarded as its fair value on initial recognition as a financial asset in accordance with AASB 139.

19A   If an investor loses significant influence over an associate, the investor shall account for all amounts recognised in other comprehensive income in relation to that associate on the same basis as would be required if the associate had directly disposed of the related assets or liabilities. Therefore, if a gain or loss previously recognised in other comprehensive income by an associate would be reclassified to profit or loss on the disposal of the related assets or liabilities, the investor reclassifies the gain or loss from equity to profit or loss (as a reclassification adjustment) when it loses significant influence over the associate. For example, if an associate has available-for-sale financial assets and the investor loses significant influence over the associate, the investor shall reclassify to profit or loss the gain or loss previously recognised in other comprehensive income in relation to those assets. If an investor's ownership interest in an associate is reduced, but the investment continues to be an associate, the investor shall reclassify to profit or loss only a proportionate amount of the gain or loss previously recognised in other comprehensive income.

20 Many of the procedures appropriate for the application of the equity method are similar to the consolidation procedures described in AASB 127 *Consolidated and Separate Financial Statements*. Furthermore, the concepts underlying the procedures used in accounting for the acquisition of a subsidiary are also adopted in accounting for the acquisition of an investment in an associate.

21 A group's share in an associate is the aggregate of the holdings in that associate by the parent and its subsidiaries. The holdings of the group's other associates or joint ventures are ignored for this purpose. When an associate has subsidiaries, associates, or joint ventures, the profits or losses and net assets taken into account in applying the equity method are those recognised in the associate's financial statements (including the associate's share of the profits or losses and net assets of its associates and joint ventures), after any adjustments necessary to give effect to uniform accounting policies (see paragraphs 26 and 27).

22 Profits and losses resulting from 'upstream' and 'downstream' transactions between an investor (including its consolidated subsidiaries) and an associate are recognised in the investor's financial statements only to the extent of unrelated investors' interests in the associate. 'Upstream' transactions are, for example, sales of assets from an associate to the investor. 'Downstream' transactions are, for example, sales of assets from the investor to an associate. The investor's share in the associate's profits and losses resulting from these transactions is eliminated.

23 An investment in an associate is accounted for using the equity method from the date on which it becomes an associate. On acquisition of the investment any difference between the cost of the investment and the investor's share of the net fair value of the associate's identifiable assets and liabilities is accounted for as follows:

(a) goodwill relating to an associate is included in the carrying amount of the investment. Amortisation of that goodwill is not permitted.

(b) any excess of the investor's share of the net fair value of the associate's identifiable assets and liabilities over the cost of the investment is included as income in the determination of the investor's share of the associate's profit or loss in the period in which the investment is acquired.

Appropriate adjustments to the investor's share of the associate's profits or losses after acquisition are also made to account, for example, for depreciation of the depreciable assets, based on their fair values at the acquisition date. Similarly, appropriate adjustments to the investor's share of the associate's profits or losses after acquisition are made for impairment losses recognised by the associate, such as for goodwill or property, plant and equipment.

24 **The most recent available financial statements of the associate are used by the investor in applying the equity method. When the end of the reporting period of the investor is different from that of the associate, the associate prepares, for the use of the investor, financial statements as of the same date as the financial statements of the investor unless it is impracticable to do so.**

25 **When, in accordance with paragraph 24, the financial statements of an associate used in applying the equity method are prepared as of a different date from that of the investor, adjustments shall be made for the effects of significant transactions or events that occur between that date and the date of the investor's financial statements. In any case, the difference between the end of the reporting period of the associate and that of the investor shall be no more than three months. The length of the reporting periods and any difference between the ends of the reporting periods shall be the same from period to period.**

26 **The investor's financial statements shall be prepared using uniform accounting policies for like transactions and events in similar circumstances.**

27 If an associate uses accounting policies other than those of the investor for like transactions and events in similar circumstances, adjustments shall be made to conform the associate's

accounting policies to those of the investor when the associate's financial statements are used by the investor in applying the equity method.

28   If an associate has outstanding cumulative preference shares that are held by parties other than the investor and classified as equity, the investor computes its share of profits or losses after adjusting for the dividends on such shares, whether or not the dividends have been declared.

29   If an investor's share of losses of an associate equals or exceeds its interest in the associate, the investor discontinues recognising its share of further losses. The interest in an associate is the carrying amount of the investment in the associate under the equity method together with any long-term interests that, in substance, form part of the investor's net investment in the associate. For example, an item for which settlement is neither planned nor likely to occur in the foreseeable future is, in substance, an extension of the entity's investment in that associate. Such items may include preference shares and long-term receivables or loans but do not include trade receivables, trade payables or any long-term receivables for which adequate collateral exists, such as secured loans. Losses recognised under the equity method in excess of the investor's investment in ordinary shares are applied to the other components of the investor's interest in an associate in the reverse order of their seniority (i.e. priority in liquidation).

30   After the investor's interest is reduced to zero, additional losses are provided for, and a liability is recognised, only to the extent that the investor has incurred legal or constructive obligations or made payments on behalf of the associate. If the associate subsequently reports profits, the investor resumes recognising its share of those profits only after its share of the profits equals the share of losses not recognised.

Impairment Losses

31   After application of the equity method, including recognising the associate's losses in accordance with paragraph 29, the investor applies the requirements of AASB 139 to determine whether it is necessary to recognise any additional impairment loss with respect to the investor's net investment in the associate.

32   The investor also applies the requirements of AASB 139 to determine whether any additional impairment loss is recognised with respect to the investor's interest in the associate that does not constitute part of the net investment and the amount of that impairment loss.

33   Because goodwill that forms part of the carrying amount of an investment in an associate is not separately recognised, it is not tested for impairment separately by applying the requirements for impairment testing goodwill in AASB 136 *Impairment of Assets*. Instead, the entire carrying amount of the investment is tested for impairment in accordance with AASB 136 as a single asset, by comparing its recoverable amount (higher of value in use and fair value less costs to sell) with its carrying amount, whenever application of the requirements in AASB 139 indicates that the investment may be impaired. An impairment loss recognised in those circumstances is not allocated to any asset, including goodwill, that forms part of the carrying amount of the investment in the associate. Accordingly, any reversal of that impairment loss is recognised in accordance with AASB 136 to the extent that the recoverable amount of the investment subsequently increases. In determining the value in use of the investment, an entity estimates:

(a)   its share of the present value of the estimated future cash flows expected to be generated by the associate, including the cash flows from the operations of the associate and the proceeds on the ultimate disposal of the investment; or

(b)   the present value of the estimated future cash flows expected to arise from dividends to be received from the investment and from its ultimate disposal.

Under appropriate assumptions, both methods give the same result.

34   The recoverable amount of an investment in an associate is assessed for each associate, unless the associate does not generate cash inflows from continuing use that are largely independent of those from other assets of the entity.

Separate Financial Statements

35   An investment in an associate shall be accounted for in the investor's separate financial statements in accordance with paragraphs 38-43 of AASB 127.

36   This Standard does not mandate which parent entities produce separate financial statements available for public use.

Disclosure

37   The following disclosures shall be made:

(a)   the fair value of investments in associates for which there are published price quotations;

(b)   summarised financial information of associates, including the aggregated amounts of assets, liabilities, revenues and profit or loss;

(c)   the reasons why the presumption that an investor does not have significant influence is overcome if the investor holds, directly or indirectly through subsidiaries, less than 20% of the voting or potential voting power of the investee but concludes that it has significant influence;

(d)   the reasons why the presumption that an investor has significant influence is overcome if the investor holds, directly or indirectly through subsidiaries, 20% or more of the voting or potential voting power of the investee but concludes that it does not have significant influence;

(e)   the end of the reporting period of the financial statements of an associate, when such financial statements are used in applying the equity method and are as of a date or for a period that is different from that of the investor, and the reason for using a different date or different period;

(f)   the nature and extent of any significant restrictions (e.g. resulting from borrowing arrangements or regulatory requirements) on the ability of associates to transfer funds to the investor in the form of cash dividends, or repayment of loans or advances;

(g)   the unrecognised share of losses of an associate, both for the period and cumulatively, if an investor has discontinued recognition of its share of losses of an associate;

(h)   the fact that an associate is not accounted for using the equity method in accordance with paragraph 13; and

(i)   summarised financial information of associates, either individually or in groups, that are not accounted for using the equity method, including the amounts of total assets, total liabilities, revenues and profit or loss.

38   Investments in associates accounted for using the equity method shall be classified as non-current assets. The investor's share of the profit or loss of such associates, and the carrying amount of those investments, shall be separately disclosed. The investor's share of any discontinued operations of such associates shall also be separately disclosed.

39   The investor's share of changes recognised in other comprehensive income by the associate shall be recognised by the investor in other comprehensive income.

40   In accordance with AASB 137 *Provisions, Contingent Liabilities and Contingent Assets*, the investor shall disclose:

(a)   its share of the contingent liabilities of an associate incurred jointly with other investors; and

(b)   those contingent liabilities that arise because the investor is severally liable for all or part of the liabilities of the associate.

Effective Date and Transition

41   [Deleted by the AASB]

41A   [Deleted by the AASB]

41B   AASB 2008-3 *Amendments to Australian Accounting Standards arising from AASB 3 and AASB 127* amended paragraphs 18, 19 and 35 and added paragraph 19A. An entity shall apply the amendment to paragraph 35 retrospectively and the amendments to paragraphs 18 and 19 and paragraph 19A prospectively for annual reporting periods beginning on or after 1 July 2009. If an entity applies AASB 127 (amended 2008) for an earlier period, the amendments shall be applied for that earlier period.

41C   Paragraphs 1 and 33 were amended by AASB 2008-5 *Amendments to Australian Accounting Standards arising from the Annual Improvements Project* issued in July 2008. An entity shall apply those amendments for annual reporting periods beginning on or after 1 January 2009. Earlier application is permitted. If an entity applies the amendments for an earlier period it shall disclose that fact and apply for that earlier period the amendments to paragraph 3 of AASB 7 *Financial Instruments: Disclosures*, paragraph 1 of AASB 131 and paragraph 4 of AASB 132 *Financial Instruments: Presentation* issued in July 2008. An entity is permitted to apply the amendments prospectively.

41E   Paragraph 41B was added by AASB 2010-3 *Amendments to Australian Accounting Standards arising from the Annual Improvements Project* issued in June 2010. An entity shall apply the amendment to paragraph 35 retrospectively and the amendments to paragraphs 18 and 19 and paragraph 19A prospectively for annual reporting periods beginning on or after 1 July 2010. Earlier application is permitted. If an entity applies the amendment before 1 July 2010 it shall disclose that fact.

Withdrawal of Other IASB Pronouncements

42   [Deleted by the AASB]

43   [Deleted by the AASB]

AASB 128

Investments in Associates and Joint Ventures

(Revised August 2011: applicable to periods beginning
from 1 January 2013)

AASB

Note from the Institute of Chartered Accountants Australia

This note, prepared by the technical editors, is not part of Accounting Standard AASB 128.

Historical development

29 August 2011: A revised version of AASB 128 was issued applicable to annual reporting period beginning 1 January 2013. Together with AASB 10, AASB 11, AASB 12 and revised AASB 127, this Standard changes group accounting.

This Standard is included in this handbook with the footer: Applicable to periods beginning from 1 January 2013.

References

AASB 128 compared to IAS 28

Additions

Paragraph	Description
Aus 1.1	Which entities AASB 128 applies to (i.e. reporting entities and general purpose financial statements).
Aus 1.2	The application date of AASB 128 (i.e. annual reporting periods beginning 1 January 2013).
Aus 1.3	permits early application of AASB 128 by for-profit entities.
Aus 1.4	Makes the requirements of AASB 128 subject to AASB 1031 'Materiality'.
Aus 1.5	Explains which Australian Standards have been superseded by AASB 128.
Aus 17.1	Explains application for not-for-profit entities.

Deletions

Paragraph	Description
45	Effective date of IAS 28.
47	Reference to superseded IAS 28.

Contents

Preface

Comparison with IAS 28

Introduction to IAS 28
(available on the AASB website)

Accounting Standard
AASB 128 Investments in Associates and Joint Ventures

Paragraphs

Objective	1
Application	Aus1.1 – Aus1.5
Scope	2
Definitions	3 – 4
Significant influence	5 – 9
Equity method	10 – 15
Application of the equity method	16
Exemptions from applying the equity method	17 – 19
Classification as held for sale	20 – 21
Discontinuing the use of the equity method	22 – 24
Changes in ownership interest	25
Equity method procedures	26 – 39
Impairment losses	40 – 43
Separate financial statements	44
Effective date and transition	
References to AASB 9	46

Deleted IAS 28 Text

Basis for Conclusions on paragraph Aus17.1
(see Basis for Conclusions on AASB 20115)

Basis for Conclusions on IAS 28
(available on the AASB website)

Australian Accounting Standard AASB 128 *Investments in Associates and Joint Ventures* is set out in paragraphs 1 – 46. All the paragraphs have equal authority. Paragraphs in **bold type** state the main principles. AASB 128 is to be read in the context of other Australian Accounting Standards, including AASB 1048 *Interpretation of Standards*, which identifies the Australian Accounting Interpretations. In the absence of explicit guidance, AASB 108 *Accounting Policies, Changes in Accounting Estimates and Errors* provides a basis for selecting and applying accounting policies.

Preface

Introduction

The Australian Accounting Standards Board (AASB) makes Australian Accounting Standards, including Interpretations, to be applied by:

(a)   entities required by the *Corporations Act 2001* to prepare financial reports;

(b)   governments in preparing financial statements for the whole of government and the General Government Sector (GGS); and

(c)   entities in the private or public for-profit or not-for-profit sectors that are reporting entities or that prepare general purpose financial statements.

AASB 1053 *Application of Tiers of Australian Accounting Standards* establishes a differential reporting framework consisting of two tiers of reporting requirements for preparing general purpose financial statements:

(a)   Tier 1: Australian Accounting Standards; and

(a)   Tier 2: Australian Accounting Standards – Reduced Disclosure Requirements.

Tier 1 requirements incorporate International Financial Reporting Standards (IFRSs), including Interpretations, issued by the International Accounting Standards Board (IASB), with the addition of paragraphs on the applicability of each Standard in the Australian environment.

Publicly accountable for-profit private sector entities are required to adopt Tier 1 requirements, and therefore are required to comply with IFRSs. Furthermore, other for-profit private sector entities complying with Tier 1 requirements will simultaneously comply with IFRSs. Some other entities complying with Tier 1 requirements will also simultaneously comply with IFRSs.

Tier 2 requirements comprise the recognition, measurement and presentation requirements of Tier 1 and substantially reduced disclosure requirements in comparison to Tier 1.

Australian Accounting Standards also include requirements that are specific to Australian entities. These requirements may be located in Australian Accounting Standards that incorporate IFRSs or in other Australian Accounting Standards. In most instances, these requirements are either restricted to the not-for-profit or public sectors or include additional disclosures that address domestic, regulatory or other issues. These requirements do not prevent publicly accountable for-profit private sector entities from complying with IFRSs. In developing requirements for public sector entities, the AASB considers the requirements of International Public Sector Accounting Standards (IPSASs), as issued by the International Public Sector Accounting Standards Board (IPSASB) of the International Federation of Accountants.

Implications for not-for-profit entities

This Standard applies to both for-profit and not-for-profit entities. However, prior to the 1 January 2013 mandatory application date of this Standard, the AASB will consider whether this Standard should be modified for application by not-for-profit entities having regard to its *Process for Modifying IFRSs for PBE/NFP*. In light of this, not-for-profit entities are not permitted to apply this Standard prior to the mandatory application date.

Comparison with IAS 28

AASB 128 *Investments in Associates and Joint Ventures* incorporates IAS 28 *Investments in Associates and Joint Ventures* issued by the International Accounting Standards Board (IASB). Paragraphs that have been added to this Standard (and do not appear in the text of IAS 28) are identified with the prefix "Aus", followed by the number of the preceding IASB paragraph and decimal numbering.

For-profit entities that comply with AASB 128 will simultaneously be in compliance with IAS 28.

Not-for-profit entities using the added "Aus" paragraphs in this Standard that specifically apply to not-for-profit entities may not be simultaneously complying with IAS 28.

Accounting Standard AASB 128

The Australian Accounting Standards Board makes Accounting Standard AASB 128 *Investments in Associates and Joint Ventures* under section 334 of the *Corporations Act 2001*.

Dated 29 August 2011

Kevin M. Stevenson
Chair – AASB

Accounting Standard AASB 128

Investments in Associates and Joint Ventures

Objective

1   The objective of this Standard is to prescribe the accounting for investments in associates and to set out the requirements for the application of the equity method when accounting for investments in associates and joint ventures.

Application

Aus1.1   This Standard applies to:

(a)   each entity that is required to prepare financial reports in accordance with Part 2M.3 of the Corporations Act and that is a reporting entity;

(b)   general purpose financial statements of each other reporting entity; and

(c)   financial statements that are, or are held out to be, general purpose financial statements.

Aus1.2   This Standard applies to annual reporting periods beginning on or after 1 January 2013.

Aus1.3   This Standard may be applied by for-profit entities, but not by not-for-profit entities, to annual reporting periods beginning on or after 1 January 2005 but before 1 January 2013. If a for-profit entity applies this Standard to such an annual reporting period, it shall disclose that fact and apply AASB 10 *Consolidated Financial Statements*, AASB 11 *Joint Arrangements*, AASB 12 *Disclosure of Interests in Other Entities* and AASB 127 *Separate Financial Statements* (August 2011), at the same time.

Aus1.4   The requirements specified in this Standard apply to the financial statements where information resulting from their application is material in accordance with AASB 1031 *Materiality*.

Aus1.5   When applied or operative, this Standard supersedes AASB 128 *Investments in Associates* (July 2004, as amended).

Scope

2   This Standard shall be applied by all entities that are investors with joint control of, or significant influence over, an investee.

Definitions

3   The following terms are used in this Standard with the meanings specified:

An *associate* is an entity over which the investor has significant influence.

Consolidated financial statements are the financial statements of a group in which assets, liabilities, equity, income, expenses and cash flows of the parent and its subsidiaries are presented as those of a single economic entity.

The *equity method* is a method of accounting whereby the investment is initially recognised at cost and adjusted thereafter for the post-acquisition change in the investor's share of the investee's net assets. The investor's profit or loss includes its share of the investee's profit or loss and the investor's other comprehensive income includes its share of the investee's other comprehensive income.

A *joint arrangement* is an arrangement of which two or more parties have joint control.

Joint control is the contractually agreed sharing of control of an arrangement, which exists only when decisions about the relevant activities require the unanimous consent of the parties sharing control.

A *joint venture* is a joint arrangement whereby the parties that have joint control of the arrangement have rights to the net assets of the arrangement.

A *joint venturer* is a party to a joint venture that has joint control of that joint venture.

Significant influence is the power to participate in the financial and operating policy decisions of the investee but is not control or joint control of those policies.

4   The following terms are defined in paragraph 4 of AASB 127 *Separate Financial Statements* and in Appendix A of AASB 10 *Consolidated Financial Statements* and are used in this Standard with the meanings specified in the Standards in which they are defined:

- control of an investee
- group
- parent
- separate financial statements
- subsidiary.

Significant influence

5   If an entity holds, directly or indirectly (e.g. through subsidiaries), 20 per cent or more of the voting power of the investee, it is presumed that the entity has significant influence, unless it can be clearly demonstrated that this is not the case. Conversely, if the entity holds, directly or indirectly (e.g. through subsidiaries), less than 20 per cent of the voting power of the investee, it is presumed that the entity does not have significant influence, unless such influence can be clearly demonstrated. A substantial or majority ownership by another investor does not necessarily preclude an entity from having significant influence.

6   The existence of significant influence by an entity is usually evidenced in one or more of the following ways:

(a)   representation on the board of directors or equivalent governing body of the investee;

(b)   participation in policy-making processes, including participation in decisions about dividends or other distributions;

(c)   material transactions between the entity and its investee;

(d)   interchange of managerial personnel; or

(e)   provision of essential technical information.

7   An entity may own share warrants, share call options, debt or equity instruments that are convertible into ordinary shares, or other similar instruments that have the potential, if exercised or converted, to give the entity additional voting power or to reduce another party's voting power over the financial and operating policies of another entity (ie potential voting rights). The existence and effect of potential voting rights that are currently exercisable or convertible, including potential voting rights held by other entities, are considered when assessing whether an entity has significant influence. Potential voting rights are not currently exercisable or convertible when, for example, they cannot be exercised or converted until a future date or until the occurrence of a future event.

8   In assessing whether potential voting rights contribute to significant influence, the entity examines all facts and circumstances (including the terms of exercise of the potential voting rights and any other contractual arrangements whether considered individually or in combination) that affect potential rights, except the intentions of management and the financial ability to exercise or convert those potential rights.

9   An entity loses significant influence over an investee when it loses the power to participate in the financial and operating policy decisions of that investee. The loss of significant influence can occur with or without a change in absolute or relative ownership levels. It could occur, for example, when an associate becomes subject to the control of a government, court, administrator or regulator. It could also occur as a result of a contractual arrangement.

Equity method

10   Under the equity method, on initial recognition the investment in an associate or a joint venture is recognised at cost, and the carrying amount is increased or decreased to recognise the investor's share of the profit or loss of the investee after the date of acquisition. The investor's share of the investee's profit or loss is recognised in the investor's profit or loss. Distributions received from an investee reduce the carrying amount of the investment. Adjustments to the carrying amount may also be necessary for changes in the investor's proportionate interest in the investee arising from changes in the investee's other comprehensive income. Such changes include those arising from the revaluation of property, plant and equipment and from foreign exchange translation differences. The investor's share of those changes is recognised in the investor's other comprehensive income (see AASB 101 *Presentation of Financial Statements*).

11   The recognition of income on the basis of distributions received may not be an adequate measure of the income earned by an investor on an investment in an associate or a joint venture because the distributions received may bear little relation to the performance of the associate or joint venture. Because the investor has joint control of, or significant influence over, the investee, the investor has an interest in the associate's or joint venture's performance and, as a result, the return on its investment. The investor accounts for this interest by extending the scope of its financial statements to include its share of the profit or loss of such an investee. As a result, application of the equity method provides more informative reporting of the investor's net assets and profit or loss.

12   When potential voting rights or other derivatives containing potential voting rights exist, an entity's interest in an associate or a joint venture is determined solely on the basis of existing ownership interests and does not reflect the possible exercise or conversion of potential voting rights and other derivative instruments, unless paragraph 13 applies.

13   In some circumstances, an entity has, in substance, an existing ownership as a result of a transaction that currently gives it access to the returns associated with an ownership interest. In such circumstances, the proportion allocated to the entity is determined by taking into account the eventual exercise of those potential voting rights and other derivative instruments that currently give the entity access to the returns.

14   AASB 9 *Financial Instruments* does not apply to interests in associates and joint ventures that are accounted for using the equity method. When instruments containing potential voting rights in substance currently give access to the returns associated with an ownership interest in an associate or a joint venture, the instruments are not subject to AASB 9. In all other cases, instruments containing potential voting rights in an associate or a joint venture are accounted for in accordance with AASB 9.

15   Unless an investment, or a portion of an investment, in an associate or a joint venture is classified as held for sale in accordance with AASB 5 *Non-current Assets Held for Sale and Discontinued Operations*, the investment, or any retained interest in the investment not classified as held for sale, shall be classified as a non-current asset.

Application of the equity method

16   An entity with joint control of, or significant influence over, an investee shall account for its investment in an associate or a joint venture using the equity method except when that investment qualifies for exemption in accordance with paragraphs 17–19.

Exemptions from applying the equity method

17   An entity need not apply the equity method to its investment in an associate or a joint venture if the entity is a parent that is exempt from preparing consolidated financial

statements by the scope exception in paragraphs 4(a), Aus4.1 and Aus4.2 of AASB 10 or if all the following apply:

(a) The entity is a wholly-owned subsidiary, or is a partially-owned subsidiary of another entity and its other owners, including those not otherwise entitled to vote, have been informed about, and do not object to, the entity not applying the equity method.

(b) The entity's debt or equity instruments are not traded in a public market (a domestic or foreign stock exchange or an over-the-counter market, including local and regional markets).

(c) The entity did not file, nor is it in the process of filing, its financial statements with a securities commission or other regulatory organisation, for the purpose of issuing any class of instruments in a public market.

(d) The ultimate or any intermediate parent of the entity produces consolidated financial statements available for public use that comply with IFRSs.

Aus17.1 Notwithstanding paragraph 17(d), an investor that meets the criteria in paragraphs 17(a), 17(b) and 17(c) need not apply the equity method in accounting for an interest in an associate or joint venture if its ultimate or any intermediate parent produces consolidated financial statements available for public use and the investor or the joint venturer and its ultimate or intermediate parent are both not-for-profit entities complying with Australian Accounting Standards.

18 When an investment in an associate or a joint venture is held by, or is held indirectly through, an entity that is a venture capital organisation, or a mutual fund, unit trust and similar entities including investment-linked insurance funds, the entity may elect to measure investments in those associates and joint ventures at fair value through profit or loss in accordance with AASB 9.

19 When an entity has an investment in an associate, a portion of which is held indirectly through a venture capital organisation, or a mutual fund, unit trust and similar entities including investment-linked insurance funds, the entity may elect to measure that portion of the investment in the associate at fair value through profit or loss in accordance with AASB 9 regardless of whether the venture capital organisation, or the mutual fund, unit trust and similar entities including investment-linked insurance funds, has significant influence over that portion of the investment. If the entity makes that election, the entity shall apply the equity method to any remaining portion of its investment in an associate that is not held through a venture capital organisation, or a mutual fund, unit trust and similar entities including investment-linked insurance funds.

Classification as held for sale

20 An entity shall apply AASB 5 to an investment, or a portion of an investment, in an associate or a joint venture that meets the criteria to be classified as held for sale. Any retained portion of an investment in an associate or a joint venture that has not been classified as held for sale shall be accounted for using the equity method until disposal of the portion that is classified as held for sale takes place. After the disposal takes place, an entity shall account for any retained interest in the associate or joint venture in accordance with AASB 9 unless the retained interest continues to be an associate or a joint venture, in which case the entity uses the equity method.

21 When an investment, or a portion of an investment, in an associate or a joint venture previously classified as held for sale no longer meets the criteria to be so classified, it shall be accounted for using the equity method retrospectively as from the date of its classification as held for sale. Financial statements for the periods since classification as held for sale shall be amended accordingly.

Discontinuing the use of the equity method

22 **An entity shall discontinue the use of the equity method from the date when its investment ceases to be an associate or a joint venture as follows:**

(a) **If the investment becomes a subsidiary, the entity shall account for its investment in accordance with AASB 3** *Business Combinations* **and AASB 10.**

    (b)   **If the retained interest in the former associate or joint venture is a financial asset, the entity shall measure the retained interest at fair value. The fair value of the retained interest shall be regarded as its fair value on initial recognition as a financial asset in accordance with AASB 9. The entity shall recognise in profit or loss any difference between:**

        (i)   **the fair value of any retained interest and any proceeds from disposing of a part interest in the associate or joint venture; and**

        (ii)   **the carrying amount of the investment at the date the equity method was discontinued.**

    (c)   **When an entity discontinues the use of the equity method, the entity shall account for all amounts previously recognised in other comprehensive income in relation to that investment on the same basis as would have been required if the investee had directly disposed of the related assets or liabilities.**

23   Therefore, if a gain or loss previously recognised in other comprehensive income by the investee would be reclassified to profit or loss on the disposal of the related assets or liabilities, the entity reclassifies the gain or loss from equity to profit or loss (as a reclassification adjustment) when the equity method is discontinued. For example, if an associate or a joint venture has cumulative exchange differences relating to a foreign operation and the entity discontinues the use of the equity method, the entity shall reclassify to profit or loss the gain or loss that had previously been recognised in other comprehensive income in relation to the foreign operation.

24   **If an investment in an associate becomes an investment in a joint venture or an investment in a joint venture becomes an investment in an associate, the entity continues to apply the equity method and does not remeasure the retained interest.**

Changes in ownership interest

25   If an entity's ownership interest in an associate or a joint venture is reduced, but the entity continues to apply the equity method, the entity shall reclassify to profit or loss the proportion of the gain or loss that had previously been recognised in other comprehensive income relating to that reduction in ownership interest if that gain or loss would be required to be reclassified to profit or loss on the disposal of the related assets or liabilities.

Equity method procedures

26   Many of the procedures that are appropriate for the application of the equity method are similar to the consolidation procedures described in AASB 10. Furthermore, the concepts underlying the procedures used in accounting for the acquisition of a subsidiary are also adopted in accounting for the acquisition of an investment in an associate or a joint venture.

27   A group's share in an associate or a joint venture is the aggregate of the holdings in that associate or joint venture by the parent and its subsidiaries. The holdings of the group's other associates or joint ventures are ignored for this purpose. When an associate or a joint venture has subsidiaries, associates or joint ventures, the profit or loss, other comprehensive income and net assets taken into account in applying the equity method are those recognised in the associate's or joint venture's financial statements (including the associate's or joint venture's share of the profit or loss, other comprehensive income and net assets of its associates and joint ventures), after any adjustments necessary to give effect to uniform accounting policies (see paragraphs 35 and 36).

28   Gains and losses resulting from 'upstream' and 'downstream' transactions between an entity (including its consolidated subsidiaries) and its associate or joint venture are recognised in the entity's financial statements only to the extent of unrelated investors' interests in the associate or joint venture. 'Upstream' transactions are, for example, sales of assets from an associate or a joint venture to the investor. 'Downstream' transactions are, for example, sales or contributions of assets from the investor to its associate or its joint venture. The investor's share in the associate's or joint venture's gains or losses resulting from these transactions is eliminated.

29   When downstream transactions provide evidence of a reduction in the net realisable value of the assets to be sold or contributed, or of an impairment loss of those assets, those losses shall be recognised in full by the investor. When upstream transactions provide evidence of a reduction in the net realisable value of the assets to be purchased or of an impairment loss of those assets, the investor shall recognise its share in those losses.

30   The contribution of a non-monetary asset to an associate or a joint venture in exchange for an equity interest in the associate or joint venture shall be accounted for in accordance with paragraph 28, except when the contribution lacks commercial substance, as that term is described in AASB 116 *Property, Plant and Equipment*. If such a contribution lacks commercial substance, the gain or loss is regarded as unrealised and is not recognised unless paragraph 31 also applies. Such unrealised gains and losses shall be eliminated against the investment accounted for using the equity method and shall not be presented as deferred gains or losses in the entity's consolidated statement of financial position or in the entity's statement of financial position in which investments are accounted for using the equity method.

31   If, in addition to receiving an equity interest in an associate or a joint venture, an entity receives monetary or non-monetary assets, the entity recognises in full in profit or loss the portion of the gain or loss on the non-monetary contribution relating to the monetary or non-monetary assets received.

32   An investment is accounted for using the equity method from the date on which it becomes an associate or a joint venture. On acquisition of the investment, any difference between the cost of the investment and the entity's share of the net fair value of the investee's identifiable assets and liabilities is accounted for as follows:

(a)   Goodwill relating to an associate or a joint venture is included in the carrying amount of the investment. Amortisation of that goodwill is not permitted.

(b)   Any excess of the entity's share of the net fair value of the investee's identifiable assets and liabilities over the cost of the investment is included as income in the determination of the entity's share of the associate or joint venture's profit or loss in the period in which the investment is acquired.

Appropriate adjustments to the entity's share of the associate's or joint venture's profit or loss after acquisition are made in order to account, for example, for depreciation of the depreciable assets based on their fair values at the acquisition date. Similarly, appropriate adjustments to the entity's share of the associate's or joint venture's profit or loss after acquisition are made for impairment losses such as for goodwill or property, plant and equipment.

33   **The most recent available financial statements of the associate or joint venture are used by the entity in applying the equity method. When the end of the reporting period of the entity is different from that of the associate or joint venture, the associate or joint venture prepares, for the use of the entity, financial statements as of the same date as the financial statements of the entity unless it is impracticable to do so.**

34   **When, in accordance with paragraph 33, the financial statements of an associate or a joint venture used in applying the equity method are prepared as of a date different from that used by the entity, adjustments shall be made for the effects of significant transactions or events that occur between that date and the date of the entity's financial statements. In any case, the difference between the end of the reporting period of the associate or joint venture and that of the entity shall be no more than three months. The length of the reporting periods and any difference between the ends of the reporting periods shall be the same from period to period.**

35   **The entity's financial statements shall be prepared using uniform accounting policies for like transactions and events in similar circumstances.**

36   If an associate or a joint venture uses accounting policies other than those of the entity for like transactions and events in similar circumstances, adjustments shall be made to make the associate's or joint venture's accounting policies conform to those of the entity when the associate's or joint venture's financial statements are used by the entity in applying the equity method.

37   If an associate or a joint venture has outstanding cumulative preference shares that are held by parties other than the entity and are classified as equity, the entity computes its share of profit or loss after adjusting for the dividends on such shares, whether or not the dividends have been declared.

38   If an entity's share of losses of an associate or a joint venture equals or exceeds its interest in the associate or joint venture, the entity discontinues recognising its share of further losses. The interest in an associate or a joint venture is the carrying amount of the investment in the associate or joint venture determined using the equity method together with any long-term interests that, in substance, form part of the entity's net investment in the associate or joint venture. For example, an item for which settlement is neither planned nor likely to occur in the foreseeable future is, in substance, an extension of the entity's investment in that associate or joint venture. Such items may include preference shares and long-term receivables or loans, but do not include trade receivables, trade payables or any long-term receivables for which adequate collateral exists, such as secured loans. Losses recognised using the equity method in excess of the entity's investment in ordinary shares are applied to the other components of the entity's interest in an associate or a joint venture in the reverse order of their seniority (ie priority in liquidation).

39   After the entity's interest is reduced to zero, additional losses are provided for, and a liability is recognised, only to the extent that the entity has incurred legal or constructive obligations or made payments on behalf of the associate or joint venture. If the associate or joint venture subsequently reports profits, the entity resumes recognising its share of those profits only after its share of the profits equals the share of losses not recognised.

Impairment losses

40   After application of the equity method, including recognising the associate's or joint venture's losses in accordance with paragraph 38, the entity applies AASB 139 *Financial Instruments: Recognition and Measurement* to determine whether it is necessary to recognise any additional impairment loss with respect to its net investment in the associate or joint venture.

41   The entity also applies AASB 139 to determine whether any additional impairment loss is recognised with respect to its interest in the associate or joint venture that does not constitute part of the net investment and the amount of that impairment loss.

42   Because goodwill that forms part of the carrying amount of an investment in an associate or a joint venture is not separately recognised, it is not tested for impairment separately by applying the requirements for impairment testing goodwill in AASB 136 *Impairment of Assets*. Instead, the entire carrying amount of the investment is tested for impairment in accordance with AASB 136 as a single asset, by comparing its recoverable amount (higher of value in use and fair value less costs to sell) with its carrying amount, whenever application of AASB 139 indicates that the investment may be impaired. An impairment loss recognised in those circumstances is not allocated to any asset, including goodwill, that forms part of the carrying amount of the investment in the associate or joint venture. Accordingly, any reversal of that impairment loss is recognised in accordance with AASB 136 to the extent that the recoverable amount of the investment subsequently increases. In determining the value in use of the investment, an entity estimates:

(a)   its share of the present value of the estimated future cash flows expected to be generated by the associate or joint venture, including the cash flows from the operations of the associate or joint venture and the proceeds from the ultimate disposal of the investment; or

(b)   the present value of the estimated future cash flows expected to arise from dividends to be received from the investment and from its ultimate disposal.

Using appropriate assumptions, both methods give the same result.

43   The recoverable amount of an investment in an associate or a joint venture shall be assessed for each associate or joint venture, unless the associate or joint venture does not generate cash inflows from continuing use that are largely independent of those from other assets of the entity.

Separate financial statements

44 An investment in an associate or a joint venture shall be accounted for in the entity's separate financial statements in accordance with paragraph 10 of AASB 127 (August 2011).

Effective date and transition

45 [Deleted by the AASB – see paragraphs Aus1.2 and Aus1.3]

References to AASB 9

46 If an entity applies this Standard but does not yet apply AASB 9, any reference to AASB 9 shall be read as a reference to AASB 139.

Withdrawal of IAS 28 (2003)

47 [Deleted by the AASB – see paragraph Aus1.5]

Deleted IAS 28 Text

Deleted IAS 28 text is not part of AASB 128.

Paragraph 45

An entity shall apply this Standard for annual periods beginning on or after 1 January 2013. Earlier application is permitted. If an entity applies this Standard earlier, it shall disclose that fact and apply IFRS 10, IFRS 11 *Joint Arrangements*, IFRS 12 *Disclosure of Interests in Other Entities* and IAS 27 (as amended in 2011) at the same time.

Paragraph 47

This Standard supersedes IAS 28 *Investments in Associates* (as revised in 2003).

AASB 129
Financial Reporting in Hyperinflationary Economies

(Compiled November 2009)

Note from the Institute of Chartered Accountants Australia

This note, prepared by the technical editors, is not part of Accounting Standard AASB 129.

Historical development

July 2004: AASB 129 'Financial Reporting in Hyperinflationary Economies' is the Australian equivalent of IAS 29 of the same name. It was made by the AASB on 15 July 2004 as part of the AASB's program to adopt International Financial Reporting Standards (IFRSs) by 2005.

30 April 2007: AASB 2007-4 'Amendments to Australian Accounting Standards' amends paragraphs 34 and 35 and is applicable for annual reporting periods beginning on or after 1 July 2007, with early adoption permitted for annual reporting periods beginning on or after 1 January 2005.

24 September 2007: AASB 2007-8 'Amendments to Australian Accounting Standards arising from AASB 101' amends AASB 129 to align with revised AASB 101. This Standard is applicable to annual reporting periods beginning on or after 1 January 2009.

13 December 2007: AASB 2007-10 'Further Amendments to Australian Accounting Standards arising from AASB 101' amends AASB 129, replacing the term 'financial report' with 'financial statements'. This Standard is applicable to annual reporting periods beginning on or after 1 January 2009.

24 July 2008: AASB 2008-5 'Amendments to Australian Accounting Standards arising from the Annual Improvements Project' amends AASB 129 to change the terms in AASB 129 to be consistent with other accounting Standards. This Standard is applicable to annual reporting periods beginning on or after 1 January 2009.

25 June 2009: AASB 2009-6 'Amendments to Australian Accounting Standards' amends AASB 129 for editorial corrections made by the International Accounting Standards Board (IASB) to its Standards and Interpretations (IFRSs) and as a consequence of issuing revised AASB 101 'Presentation of Financial Statements'. This Standard is applicable to annual reporting periods beginning on or after 1 January 2009 that end on or after 30 June 2009.

6 November 2009: AASB 129 was reissued by the AASB, compiled to include the AASB 2007-8, AASB 2007-10, AASB 2008-5 and AASB 2009-6 amendments and applies to annual reporting periods beginning on or after 1 January 2009 that end on or after 30 June 2009. Early application is permitted.

References

Interpretation 7 *Applying the Restatement Approach under AASB 129 Financial Reporting in Hyperinflationary Economies* applies to AASB 129.

IFRIC item not taken onto the agenda: No. 31 *Hyperinflation* issued in November 2002 applies to AASB 129.

AASB 129 compared to IAS 29

Additions

Paragraph	Description
Aus 1.1	Which entities AASB 129 applies to (i.e. reporting entities and general purpose financial statements).
Aus 1.2	The application date of AASB 129, (i.e. annual reporting periods beginning 1 January 2005).
Aus 1.3	Prohibits early application of AASB 129.

Aus 1.4 Makes the requirements of AASB 129 subject to AASB 1031 'Materiality'.

Aus 1.5 Notice of the new Standard published on 22 July 2004.

Deletions

Paragraph *Description*

41 Effective date of IAS 29.

Contents

Compilation Details

Comparison with IAS 29

Accounting Standard
AASB 129 Financial Reporting in Hyperinflationary Economies

	Paragraphs
Application	Aus1.1 – Aus1.5
Scope	1 – 4
The Restatement of Financial Statements	5 – 10
Historical Cost Financial Statements	
Statement of Financial Position	11 – 25
Statement of Comprehensive Income	26
Gain or Loss on Net Monetary Position	27 – 28
Current Cost Financial Statements	
Statement of Financial Position	29
Statement of Comprehensive Income	30
Gain or Loss on Net Monetary Position	31
Taxes	32
Statement of Cash Flows	33
Corresponding Figures	34
Consolidated Financial Statements	35 – 36
Selection and Use of the General Price Index	37
Economies Ceasing to be Hyperinflationary	38
Disclosures	39 – 40

Australian Accounting Standard AASB 129 *Financial Reporting in Hyperinflationary Economies* (as amended) is set out in paragraphs Aus1.1 – 40. All the paragraphs have equal authority. AASB 129 is to be read in the context of other Australian Accounting Standards, including AASB 1048 *Interpretation and Application of Standards*, which identifies the Australian Accounting Interpretations. In the absence of explicit guidance, AASB 108 *Accounting Policies, Changes in Accounting Estimates and Errors* provides a basis for selecting and applying accounting policies.

Compilation Details

Accounting Standard AASB 129 *Financial Reporting in Hyperinflationary Economies* as amended

This compiled Standard applies to annual reporting periods beginning on or after 1 January 2009 that end on or after 30 June 2009. It takes into account amendments up to and including 25 June 2009 and was prepared on 6 November 2009 by the staff of the Australian Accounting Standards Board (AASB).

This compilation is not a separate Accounting Standard made by the AASB. Instead, it is a representation of AASB 129 (July 2004) as amended by other Accounting Standards, which are listed in the Table below.

Table of Standards

Standard	Date made	Application date *(annual reporting periods ... on or after ...)*	Application, saving or transitional provisions
AASB 129	15 Jul 2004	*(beginning)* 1 Jan 2005	
AASB 2007-4	30 Apr 2007	*(beginning)* 1 Jul 2007	see (a) below
AASB 2007-8	24 Sep 2007	*(beginning)* 1 Jan 2009	see (b) below
AASB 2007-10	13 Dec 2007	*(beginning)* 1 Jan 2009	see (b) below
AASB 2008-5	24 Jul 2008	*(beginning)* 1 Jan 2009	see (c) below
AASB 2009-6	25 Jun 2009	*(beginning)* 1 Jan 2009 and *(ending)* 30 Jun 2009	see (d) below

(a)   Entities may elect to apply this Standard to annual reporting periods beginning on or after 1 January 2005 but before 1 July 2007.

(b)   Entities may elect to apply this Standard to annual reporting periods beginning on or after 1 January 2005 but before 1 January 2009, provided that AASB 101 *Presentation of Financial Statements* (September 2007) is also applied to such periods.

(c)   Entities may elect to apply this Standard, or its amendments to individual Standards, to annual reporting periods beginning on or after 1 January 2005 but before 1 January 2009.

(d)   Entities may elect to apply this Standard to annual reporting periods beginning on or after 1 January 2005 but before 1 January 2009, provided that AASB 101 *Presentation of Financial Statements* (September 2007) is also applied to such periods, and to annual reporting periods beginning on or after 1 January 2009 that end before 30 June 2009.

Table of Amendments

Paragraph affected	How affected	By ... [paragraph]
Title	footnote added	AASB 2008-5 [48]
Aus1.1	amended	AASB 2007-8 [7, 8]
Aus1.4	amended	AASB 2007-8 [8]
4	amended	AASB 2007-10 [73]
6	amended	AASB 2008-5 [48]
8	amended	AASB 2008-5 [48]
14	amended	AASB 2008-5 [48]
15	amended	AASB 2008-5 [48]
19	amended	AASB 2008-5 [48]
20	amended	AASB 2008-5 [48]
25	amended	AASB 2009-6 [64]
27	amended	AASB 2007-8 [90]
28	amended amended	AASB 2007-8 [91] AASB 2008-5 [48]
33 (and preceding heading)	amended	AASB 2007-8 [6]

Paragraph affected	How affected	By ... [paragraph]
34	amended	AASB 2007-4 [73]
35	amended	AASB 2007-4 [73]
36	amended	AASB 2007-8 [92]
38	amended	AASB 2007-10 [73]

General Terminology Amendments

The following amendments are not shown in the above Table of Amendments:

References to 'income statement', 'balance sheet' and 'reporting date' were amended to 'statement of comprehensive income', 'statement of financial position' and 'end of the reporting period' respectively by AASB 2007-8.

Comparison with IAS 29

AASB 129 and IAS 29

AASB 129 *Financial Reporting in Hyperinflationary Economies* as amended incorporates IAS 29 *Financial Reporting in Hyperinflationary Economies* as issued and amended by the International Accounting Standards Board (IASB). Paragraphs that have been added to this Standard (and do not appear in the text of IAS 29) are identified with the prefix "Aus", followed by the number of the relevant IASB paragraph and decimal numbering.

Compliance with IAS 29

Entities that comply with AASB 129 as amended will simultaneously be in compliance with IAS 29 as amended.

Accounting Standard AASB 129

The Australian Accounting Standards Board made Accounting Standard AASB 129 *Financial Reporting in Hyperinflationary Economies* under section 334 of the *Corporations Act 2001* on 15 July 2004.

This compiled version of AASB 129 applies to annual reporting periods beginning on or after 1 January 2009 that end on or after 30 June 2009. It incorporates relevant amendments contained in other AASB Standards made by the AASB up to and including 25 June 2009 (see Compilation Details).

Accounting Standard AASB 129

Financial Reporting in Hyperinflationary Economies[1]

Application

Aus1.1   This Standard applies to:

    (a)   each entity that is required to prepare financial reports in accordance with Part 2M.3 of the Corporations Act and that is a reporting entity;

    (b)   general purpose financial statements of each other reporting entity; and

    (c)   financial statements that are, or are held out to be, general purpose financial statements.

Aus1.2   This Standard applies to annual reporting periods beginning on or after 1 January 2005.

    [Note: For application dates of paragraphs changed or added by an amending Standard, see Compilation Details.]

---

1   As part of AASB 2008-5 *Amendments to Australian Accounting Standards arising from the Annual Improvements Project* issued in July 2008, the Board changed the terms used in AASB 129 to be consistent with other Australian Accounting Standards as follows: (a) 'market value' was amended to 'fair value', and (b) 'results of operations' and 'net income' were amended to 'profit or loss'.

Aus1.3   This Standard shall not be applied to annual reporting periods beginning before 1 January 2005.

Aus1.4   The requirements specified in this Standard apply to the financial statements where information resulting from their application is material in accordance with AASB 1031 *Materiality*.

Aus1.5   Notice of this Standard was published in the *Commonwealth of Australia Gazette* No S 294, 22 July 2004.

Scope

1   This Standard shall be applied to the individual financial statements, including the consolidated financial statements, of any entity whose functional currency is the currency of a hyperinflationary economy.

2   In a hyperinflationary economy, reporting of operating results and financial position in the local currency without restatement is not useful. Money loses purchasing power at such a rate that comparison of amounts from transactions and other events that have occurred at different times, even within the same accounting period, is misleading.

3   This Standard does not establish an absolute rate at which hyperinflation is deemed to arise. It is a matter of judgement when restatement of financial statements in accordance with this Standard becomes necessary. Hyperinflation is indicated by characteristics of the economic environment of a country which include, but are not limited to, the following:

(a)   the general population prefers to keep its wealth in non-monetary assets or in a relatively stable foreign currency. Amounts of local currency held are immediately invested to maintain purchasing power;

(b)   the general population regards monetary amounts not in terms of the local currency but in terms of a relatively stable foreign currency. Prices may be quoted in that currency;

(c)   sales and purchases on credit take place at prices that compensate for the expected loss of purchasing power during the credit period, even if the period is short;

(d)   interest rates, wages and prices are linked to a price index; and

(e)   the cumulative inflation rate over three years is approaching, or exceeds, 100%.

4   It is preferable that all entities that report in the currency of the same hyperinflationary economy apply this Standard from the same date. Nevertheless, this Standard applies to the financial statements of any entity from the beginning of the reporting period in which it identifies the existence of hyperinflation in the country in whose currency it reports.

The Restatement of Financial Statements

5   Prices change over time as the result of various specific or general political, economic and social forces. Specific forces such as changes in supply and demand and technological changes may cause individual prices to increase or decrease significantly and independently of each other. In addition, general forces may result in changes in the general level of prices and therefore in the general purchasing power of money.

6   Entities that prepare financial statements on the historical cost basis of accounting do so without regard either to changes in the general level of prices or to increases in specific prices of recognised assets or liabilities. The exceptions to this are those assets and liabilities that the entity is required, or chooses, to measure at fair value. For example, property, plant and equipment may be revalued to fair value and biological assets are generally required to be measured at fair value. Some entities, however, present financial statements that are based on a current cost approach that reflects the effects of changes in the specific prices of assets held.

7   In a hyperinflationary economy, financial statements, whether they are based on a historical cost approach or a current cost approach, are useful only if they are expressed in terms of the measuring unit current at the end of the reporting period. As a result, this Standard applies to the primary financial statements of entities reporting in the currency

of a hyperinflationary economy. Presentation of the information required by this Standard as a supplement to unrestated financial statements is not permitted. Furthermore, separate presentation of the financial statements before restatement is discouraged.

8   **The financial statements of an entity whose functional currency is the currency of a hyperinflationary economy, whether they are based on a historical cost approach or a current cost approach, shall be stated in terms of the measuring unit current at the end of the reporting period. The corresponding figures for the previous period required by AASB 101 *Presentation of Financial Statements* (as revised in 2007) and any information in respect of earlier periods shall also be stated in terms of the measuring unit current at the end of the reporting period. For the purpose of presenting comparative amounts in a different presentation currency, paragraphs 42(b) and 43 of AASB 121 *The Effects of Changes in Foreign Exchange Rates* apply.**

9   **The gain or loss on the net monetary position shall be included in net income and separately disclosed.**

10   The restatement of financial statements in accordance with this Standard requires the application of certain procedures as well as judgement. The consistent application of these procedures and judgements from period to period is more important than the precise accuracy of the resulting amounts included in the restated financial statements.

Historical Cost Financial Statements

Statement of Financial Position

11   Statement of financial position amounts not already expressed in terms of the measuring unit current at the end of the reporting period are restated by applying a general price index.

12   Monetary items are not restated because they are already expressed in terms of the monetary unit current at the end of the reporting period. Monetary items are money held and items to be received or paid in money.

13   Assets and liabilities linked by agreement to changes in prices, such as index linked bonds and loans, are adjusted in accordance with the agreement in order to ascertain the amount outstanding at the end of the reporting period. These items are carried at this adjusted amount in the restated statement of financial position.

14   All other assets and liabilities are non-monetary. Some non-monetary items are carried at amounts current at the end of the reporting period, such as net realisable value and fair value, so they are not restated. All other non-monetary assets and liabilities are restated.

15   Most non-monetary items are carried at cost or cost less depreciation; hence they are expressed at amounts current at their date of acquisition. The restated cost, or cost less depreciation, of each item is determined by applying to its historical cost and accumulated depreciation the change in a general price index from the date of acquisition to the end of the reporting period. For example, property, plant and equipment, inventories of raw materials and merchandise, goodwill, patents, trademarks and similar assets are restated from the dates of their purchase. Inventories of partly-finished and finished goods are restated from the dates on which the costs of purchase and of conversion were incurred.

16   Detailed records of the acquisition dates of items of property, plant and equipment may not be available or capable of estimation. In these rare circumstances, it may be necessary, in the first period of application of this Standard, to use an independent professional assessment of the value of the items as the basis for their restatement.

17   A general price index may not be available for the periods for which the restatement of property, plant and equipment is required by this Standard. In these circumstances, it may be necessary to use an estimate based, for example, on the movements in the exchange rate between the functional currency and a relatively stable foreign currency.

18   Some non-monetary items are carried at amounts current at dates other than that of acquisition or that of the statement of financial position, for example, property, plant and equipment that has been revalued at some earlier date. In these cases, the carrying amounts are restated from the date of the revaluation.

19   The restated amount of a non-monetary item is reduced, in accordance with appropriate Australian Accounting Standards, when it exceeds its recoverable amount. For example,

restated amounts of property, plant and equipment, goodwill, patents and trademarks are reduced to recoverable amount and restated amounts of inventories are reduced to net realisable value.

20 An investee that is accounted for under the equity method may report in the currency of a hyperinflationary economy. The statement of financial position and statement of comprehensive income of such an investee are restated in accordance with this Standard in order to calculate the investor's share of its net assets and profit or loss. When the restated financial statements of the investee are expressed in a foreign currency they are translated at closing rates.

21 The impact of inflation is usually recognised in borrowing costs. It is not appropriate both to restate the capital expenditure financed by borrowing and to capitalise that part of the borrowing costs that compensates for the inflation during the same period. This part of the borrowing costs is recognised as an expense in the period in which the costs are incurred.

22 An entity may acquire assets under an arrangement that permits it to defer payment without incurring an explicit interest charge. Where it is impracticable to impute the amount of interest, such assets are restated from the payment date and not the date of purchase.

23 [Deleted by the IASB]

24 At the beginning of the first period of application of this Standard, the components of owners' equity, except retained earnings and any revaluation surplus, are restated by applying a general price index from the dates the components were contributed or otherwise arose. Any revaluation surplus that arose in previous periods is eliminated. Restated retained earnings are derived from all the other amounts in the restated statement of financial position.

25 At the end of the first period and in subsequent periods, all components of owners' equity are restated by applying a general price index from the beginning of the period or the date of contribution, if later. The movements for the period in owners' equity are disclosed in accordance with AASB 101.

Statement of Comprehensive Income

26 This Standard requires that all items in the statement of comprehensive income are expressed in terms of the measuring unit current at the end of the reporting period. Therefore all amounts need to be restated by applying the change in the general price index from the dates when the items of income and expenses were initially recorded in the financial statements.

Gain or Loss on Net Monetary Position

27 In a period of inflation, an entity holding an excess of monetary assets over monetary liabilities loses purchasing power and an entity with an excess of monetary liabilities over monetary assets gains purchasing power to the extent the assets and liabilities are not linked to a price level. This gain or loss on the net monetary position may be derived as the difference resulting from the restatement of non-monetary assets, owners' equity and items in the statement of comprehensive income and the adjustment of index linked assets and liabilities. The gain or loss may be estimated by applying the change in a general price index to the weighted average for the period of the difference between monetary assets and monetary liabilities.

28 The gain or loss on the net monetary position is included in profit or loss. The adjustment to those assets and liabilities linked by agreement to changes in prices made in accordance with paragraph 13 is offset against the gain or loss on net monetary position. Other income and expense items, such as interest income and expense, and foreign exchange differences related to invested or borrowed funds, are also associated with the net monetary position. Although such items are separately disclosed, it may be helpful if they are presented together with the gain or loss on net monetary position in the statement of comprehensive income.

Current Cost Financial Statements

Statement of Financial Position

29   Items stated at current cost are not restated because they are already expressed in terms of the measuring unit current at the end of the reporting period. Other items in the statement of financial position are restated in accordance with paragraphs 11 to 25.

Statement of Comprehensive Income

30   The current cost statement of comprehensive income, before restatement, generally reports costs current at the time at which the underlying transactions or events occurred. Cost of sales and depreciation are recorded at current costs at the time of consumption; sales and other expenses are recorded at their money amounts when they occurred. Therefore all amounts need to be restated into the measuring unit current at the end of the reporting period by applying a general price index.

Gain or Loss on Net Monetary Position

31   The gain or loss on the net monetary position is accounted for in accordance with paragraphs 27 and 28.

Taxes

32   The restatement of financial statements in accordance with this Standard may give rise to differences between the carrying amount of individual assets and liabilities in the statement of financial position and their tax bases. These differences are accounted for in accordance with AASB 112 *Income Taxes*.

Statement of Cash Flows

33   This Standard requires that all items in the statement of cash flows are expressed in terms of the measuring unit current at the end of the reporting period.

Corresponding Figures

34   Corresponding figures for the previous reporting period, whether they were based on a historical cost approach or a current cost approach, are restated by applying a general price index so that the comparative financial statements are presented in terms of the measuring unit current at the end of the reporting period. Information that is disclosed in respect of earlier periods is also expressed in terms of the measuring unit current at the end of the reporting period. For the purpose of presenting comparative amounts in a different presentation currency, paragraphs 42(b) and 43 of AASB 121 apply.

Consolidated Financial Statements

35   A parent that reports in the currency of a hyperinflationary economy may have subsidiaries that also report in the currencies of hyperinflationary economies. The financial statements of any such subsidiary need to be restated by applying a general price index of the country in whose currency it reports before they are included in the consolidated financial statements issued by its parent. Where such a subsidiary is a foreign subsidiary, its restated financial statements are translated at closing rates. The financial statements of subsidiaries that do not report in the currencies of hyperinflationary economies are dealt with in accordance with AASB 121.

36   If financial statements with different ends of the reporting periods are consolidated, all items, whether non-monetary or monetary, need to be restated into the measuring unit current at the date of the consolidated financial statements.

Selection and Use of the General Price Index

37   The restatement of financial statements in accordance with this Standard requires the use of a general price index that reflects changes in general purchasing power. It is preferable that all entities that report in the currency of the same economy use the same index.

Economies Ceasing to be Hyperinflationary

38   When an economy ceases to be hyperinflationary and an entity discontinues the preparation and presentation of financial statements prepared in accordance with this Standard, it shall treat the amounts expressed in the measuring unit current at the end of the previous reporting period as the basis for the carrying amounts in its subsequent financial statements.

Disclosures

39   The following disclosures shall be made:

(a)   the fact that the financial statements and the corresponding figures for previous periods have been restated for the changes in the general purchasing power of the functional currency and, as a result, are stated in terms of the measuring unit current at the end of the reporting period;

(b)   whether the financial statements are based on a historical cost approach or a current cost approach; and

(c)   the identity and level of the price index at the end of the reporting period and the movement in the index during the current and the previous reporting period.

40   The disclosures required by this Standard are needed to make clear the basis of dealing with the effects of inflation in the financial statements. They are also intended to provide other information necessary to understand that basis and the resulting amounts.

Effective Date of IAS 29

41   [Deleted by the AASB]

AASB 131
Interests in Joint Ventures

(Compiled September 2011)

Note from the Institute of Chartered Accountants Australia

This note, prepared by the technical editors, is not part of Accounting Standard AASB 131.

Historical development

15 July 2004: AASB 131 'Interests in Joint Ventures' is the Australian equivalent of IAS 31 of the same name. It was made by the AASB on 15 July 2004 as part of the AASB's program to adopt International Financial Reporting Standards by 2005.

22 December 2004: AASB 2004-2 'Amendments to Australian Accounting Standards' amends paragraph 2, and 48 and is applicable to annual reporting periods beginning on or after 1 January 2005.

15 February 2007: AASB 2007-2 'Amendments to Australian Accounting Standards' amends paragraphs 2 and 48 and is applicable to annual reporting periods ending on or after 28 February 2007. Entities may elect to early-adopt it to annual reporting periods beginning on or after 1 January 2005.

30 April 2007: AASB 2007-4 'Amendments to Australian Accounting Standards' allows a jointly controlled entity to be accounted for using the proportionate consolidation method. AASB 2007-4 amends paragraphs 3, 38, 43 and 46, adds paragraphs 4, 5, 6, 30-37, 39, 40, 56 and 57 and deletes paragraphs Aus38.1 and Aus57.1-Aus57.5. It is applicable to annual reporting periods beginning on or after 1 July 2007. Entities may elect to early-adopt it to annual reporting periods beginning on or after 1 January 2005.

24 September 2007: AASB 2007-8 'Amendments to Australian Accounting Standards' amends AASB 131, changing the term 'general purpose financial reports' to 'general purpose financial statements'. This Standard is applicable to annual reporting periods beginning on or after 1 January 2009.

13 December 2007: AASB 2007-10 'Further Amendments to Australian Accounting Standards arising from AASB 101' amends AASB 131, replacing the term 'financial report' with 'financial statements'. This Standard is applicable to annual reporting periods beginning on or after 1 January 2009.

6 March 2008: AASB 2008-3 'Amendments to Australian Accounting Standards arising from AASB 3 and AASB 127' amends AASB 131 for the issue of AASB 3 Revised. This Standard is applicable to annual reporting periods beginning on or after 1 July 2009.

24 July 2008: AASB 2008-5 'Amendments to Australian Accounting Standards arising from the Annual Improvements Project' amends AASB 131 in relation to required disclosures for certain joint ventures. This Standard is applicable to annual reporting periods beginning on or after 1 January 2009.

6 November 2009: AASB 131 was reissued by the AASB, compiled to include the AASB 2007-8, AASB 2007-10, AASB 2008-3 and AASB 2008-5 amendments and applies to annual reporting periods beginning on or after 1 July 2009. Early application is permitted.

7 December 2009: AASB 2009-11 'Amendments to Australian Accounting Standards arising from AASB 9' amends AASB 131 to give effect to consequential changes arising from the issuance of AASB 9. This Standard is applicable to annual reporting periods beginning on or after 1 January 2013 with early adoption permitted from annual reporting periods ending on or after 31 December 2009 that begin before 1 January 2013 provided AASB 9 is also applied for the same period. The application date of AASB 2009-11 has been amended to 1 January 2015 by AASB 2012-6. **These amendments have been superseded by AASB 2010-7 and are not included in this compiled Standard.**

---

2 June 2010: AASB 2010-3 'Amendments to Australian Accounting Standards arising from the Annual Improvements Project' amends AASB 131 in relation to transition requirements for amendments arising as a result of AASB 127. This Standard is applicable to annual reporting periods beginning on or after 1 July 2010 with early adoption permitted.

7 September 2010: AASB 131 was reissued by the AASB, compiled to include the AASB 2010-3 amendments and applies to annual reporting periods beginning on or after 1 July 2010 but before 1 January 2013.

1 March 2011: AASB 2010-7 'Amendments to Australian Accounting Standards arising from AASB 9 (December 2010)' as compiled amends AASB 131 to give effect to consequential changes arising from the reissue of AASB 9 in December 2010, and supersedes AASB 2009-11, which related to the previous version of AASB 9. This Standard applies to annual reporting periods beginning on or after 1 January 2013 and can be adopted early. The application date of AASB 2010-7 has been amended to 1 January 2015 by AASB 2012-6. **These amendments are not included in this compiled Standard.**

11 July 2011: AASB 2011-5 'Amendments to Australian Accounting Standards - Extending Relief from Consolidation, the Equity Method and Proportionate Consolidation' amends AASB 131 to give relief from consolidating and equity accounting in certain situations. These Standards apply to annual reporting periods beginning on or after 1 July 2011 with early adoption permitted.

5 September 2011: AASB 2011-8 'Amendments to Australian Accounting Standards arising from AASB 13' amends AASB 131 to give effect to a consequential change in the definition of fair value arising from the issue of AASB 13. This Standard applies to annual reporting periods beginning on or after 1 January 2013 and can be adopted early. **These amendments are not included this compiled Standard.**

23 September 2011: AASB 131 was reissued by the AASB, compiled to include the AASB 2011-5 amendments and applies to annual reporting periods ending on or after 1 July 2011 but before 1 January 2013.

AASB 131 will be replaced by AASB 11 for periods beginning from 1 January 2013.

Reference

Interpretation 5 *Rights to Interests arising from Decommissioning, Restoration and Environmental Rehabilitation Funds* and Interpretation 113 *Jointly Controlled Entities – Non-Monetary Contributions by Venturers* apply to AASB 131.

AASB 131 compared to IAS 31

Additions

Paragraph	Description
Aus 1.1	Which entities AASB 131 applies to (i.e. reporting entities and general purpose financial statements).
Aus 1.2	The application date of AASB 131 (i.e. annual reporting periods beginning 1 January 2005).
Aus 1.3	Prohibits early application of AASB 131.
Aus 1.4	Makes the requirements of AASB 131 subject to AASB 1031 'Materiality'.
Aus 1.5	Explains which Australian Standards have been superseded by AASB 131.
Aus 1.6	Clarifies that the superseded Australian Standards remain in force until AASB 131 applies.
Aus 1.7	Notice of the new Standard published on 22 July 2004.
Aus 2.1	Clarifies a venturer in a not-for-profit group that meets certain conditions need not apply proportionate consolidation or the equity method of accounting.

Deletions

Paragraph	Description
58	Effective date of IAS 31.
59	Withdrawal of previous version of IAS 31.

Contents

Compilation Details

Comparison with IAS 131

Accounting Standard
AASB 131 Interests in Joint Ventures

	Paragraphs
Application	Aus1.1 – Aus1.7
Scope	1 – Aus2.1
Definitions	3 – 6
Forms of Joint Venture	7
Joint Control	8
Contractual Arrangement	9 – 12
Jointly Controlled Operations	13 – 17
Jointly Controlled Assets	18 – 23
Jointly Controlled Entities	24 – 29
Financial Statements of a Venturer	
Proportionate Consolidation	30 – 37
Equity Method	38 – 41
Exceptions to Proportionate Consolidation and Equity Method	42 – 45B
Separate Financial Statements of a Venturer	46 – 47
Transactions Between a Venturer and a Joint Venture	48 – 50
Reporting Interests in Joint Ventures in the Financial Statements of an Investor	51
Operators of Joint Ventures	52 – 53
Disclosure	
Interests in Joint Ventures	54 – 57
Effective Date and Transition	58A – 58D

Implementation Guidance
(see AASB 127 *Consolidated and Separate Financial Statements*)

Basis for Conclusions on IAS 31
(available on the AASB website)

Australian Accounting Standard AASB 131 *Interests in Joint Ventures* (as amended) is set out in paragraphs Aus1.1 – 58D. All the paragraphs have equal authority. Terms defined in this Standard are in *italics* the first time they appear in the Standard. AASB 131 is to be read in the context of other Australian Accounting Standards, including AASB 1048 *Interpretation of Standards*, which identifies the Australian Accounting Interpretations. In the absence of explicit guidance, AASB 108 *Accounting Policies, Changes in Accounting Estimates and Errors* provides a basis for selecting and applying accounting policies.

Compilation Details

Accounting Standard AASB 131 *Interests in Joint Ventures* as amended

AASB

This compiled Standard applies to annual reporting periods beginning on or after 1 July 2011 but before 1 January 2013. It takes into account amendments up to and including 20 July 2011 and was prepared on 23 September 2011 by the staff of the Australian Accounting Standards Board (AASB).

This compilation is not a separate Accounting Standard made by the AASB. Instead, it is a representation of AASB 131 (July 2004) as amended by other Accounting Standards, which are listed in the Table below.

Table of Standards

Standard	Date made	Application date *(annual reporting periods ... on or after ...)*	Application, saving or transitional provisions
AASB 131	15 Jul 2004	*(beginning)* 1 Jan 2005	
AASB 2004-2	22 Dec 2004	*(beginning)* 1 Jan 2005	–
AASB 2007-2	15 Feb 2007	*(ending)* 28 Feb 2007	see (a) below
AASB 2007-4	30 Apr 2007	*(beginning)* 1 Jul 2007	see (b) below
AASB 2007-8	24 Sep 2007	*(beginning)* 1 Jan 2009	see (c) below
AASB 2007-10	13 Dec 2007	*(beginning)* 1 Jan 2009	see (c) below
AASB 2008-3	6 Mar 2008	*(beginning)* 1 Jul 2009	see (d) below
AASB 2008-5	24 Jul 2008	*(beginning)* 1 Jan 2009	see (e) below
AASB 2009-11	7 Dec 2009	*(beginning)* 1 Jan 2013	not compiled*
AASB 2010-3	23 Jun 2010	*(beginning)* 1 Jul 2010	see (f) below
AASB 2010-2	30 Jun 2010	*(beginning)* 1 Jul 2013	not compiled*
AASB 2010-7	6 Dec 2010	*(beginning)* 1 Jan 2013	not compiled*
AASB 2011-5	20 Jul 2011	*(beginning)* 1 Jul 2011	see (g) below
AASB 2011-6	20 Jul 2011	*(beginning)* 1 Jul 2013	not compiled*
AASB 2011-8	2 Sep 2011	*(beginning)* 1 Jan 2013	not compiled*

* The amendments made by this Standard are not included in this compilation, which presents the principal Standard as applicable to annual reporting periods beginning on or after 1 July 2011 but before 1 January 2013. The principal Standard has been superseded by AASB 11 *Joint Arrangements*, which applies to annual reporting periods beginning on or after 1 January 2013.

(a) Entities may elect to apply the relevant amendments to annual reporting periods beginning on or after 1 January 2005 that end before 28 February 2007.

(b) Entities may elect to apply this Standard to annual reporting periods beginning on or after 1 January 2005 but before 1 July 2007.

(c) Entities may elect to apply this Standard to annual reporting periods beginning on or after 1 January 2005 but before 1 January 2009, provided that AASB 101 *Presentation of Financial Statements* (September 2007) is also applied to such periods.

(d) Entities may elect to apply this Standard to annual reporting periods beginning on or after 30 June 2007 but before 1 July 2009, provided that AASB 3 *Business Combinations* (March 2008) and AASB 127 *Consolidated and Separate Financial Statements* (March 2008) are also applied to such periods.

(e) Entities may elect to apply this Standard, or its amendments to individual Standards, to annual reporting periods beginning on or after 1 January 2005 but before 1 January 2009.

(f) Entities may elect to apply this Standard to annual reporting periods beginning on or after 1 January 2005 but before 1 July 2010.

(g) Entities may elect to apply this Standard to annual reporting periods beginning on or after 1 January 2005 but before 1 July 2011, provided that AASB 2007-4 *Amendments to Australian Accounting Standards arising from ED 151 and Other Amendments* is also applied to such periods.

Table of Amendments

Paragraph affected	How affected	By ... [paragraph]
Aus1.1	amended	AASB 2007-8 [7, 8]
Aus1.4	amended	AASB 2007-8 [8]
1	amended amended	AASB 2007-10 [74] AASB 2008-5 [49]
2	amended amended amended amended	AASB 2004-2 [12] AASB 2007-4 [76] AASB 2007-10 [74] AASB 2011-5 [19]
Aus2.1	added	AASB 2011-5 [20]
3	amended	AASB 2007-4 [77]
4	added	AASB 2007-4 [78]
5	added	AASB 2007-4 [78]
6	added amended	AASB 2007-4 [78] AASB 2011-5 [19]
30 (preceding heading)	added amended	AASB 2007-4 [79] AASB 2007-10 [74]
30-32	added	AASB 2007-4 [80]
33	added amended	AASB 2007-4 [80] AASB 2007-8 [6]
34-37	added	AASB 2007-4 [80]
38	amended	AASB 2007-4 [81]
Aus38.1	deleted	AASB 2007-4 [82]
39	added	AASB 2007-4 [81]
40	added	AASB 2007-4 [81]
42 (preceding heading)	amended	AASB 2007-4 [83]
43	amended	AASB 2007-4 [81]
Aus43.1	deleted	AASB 2007-4 [82]
45	amended	AASB 2008-3 [51]
45A-45B	added	AASB 2008-3 [52]
46	amended amended	AASB 2007-4 [84] AASB 2008-3 [53]
48 (footnote 1)	amended	AASB 2007-2 [10]
51 (preceding heading)	amended	AASB 2007-10 [74]
56	added	AASB 2007-4 [85]
57	added	AASB 2007-4 [85]
Aus57.1-Aus57.5	deleted	AASB 2007-4 [86]
58 (preceding heading)	amended	AASB 2008-5 [50]
58A	note added paragraph added (in place of note)	AASB 2008-3 [54] AASB 2010-3 [11]
58B	added	AASB 2008-5 [51]
58D	added	AASB 2010-3 [11]

Comparison with IAS 31

AASB 131 and IAS 31

AASB 131 *Interests in Joint Ventures* as amended incorporates IAS 31 *Interests in Joint Ventures* as issued and amended by the International Accounting Standards Board (IASB). Paragraphs that have been added to this Standard (and do not appear in the text of IAS 31) are identified with the prefix "Aus", followed by the number of the relevant IASB paragraph and decimal numbering.

Compliance with IAS 31

Entities that comply with AASB 131 as amended will simultaneously be in compliance with IAS 31 as amended.

Accounting Standard AASB 131

The Australian Accounting Standards Board made Accounting Standard AASB 131 *Interests in Joint Ventures* under section 334 of the *Corporations Act 2001* on 15 July 2004.

This compiled version of AASB 131 applies to annual reporting periods beginning on or after 1 July 2011 but before 1 January 2013. It incorporates relevant amendments contained in other AASB Standards made by the AASB up to and including 20 July 2011 (see Compilation Details).

Accounting Standard AASB 131

Interests in Joint Ventures

Application

Aus1.1   This Standard applies to:

(a)   **each entity that is required to prepare financial reports in accordance with Part 2M.3 of the Corporations Act and that is a reporting entity;**

(b)   **general purpose financial statements of each other reporting entity; and**

(c)   **financial statements that are, or are held out to be, general purpose financial statements.**

Aus1.2   **This Standard applies to annual reporting periods beginning on or after 1 January 2005.**
[Note: For application dates of paragraphs changed or added by an amending Standard, see Compilation Details.]

Aus1.3   **This Standard shall not be applied to annual reporting periods beginning before 1 January 2005.**

Aus1.4   **The requirements specified in this Standard apply to the financial statements where information resulting from their application is material in accordance with AASB 1031 *Materiality*.**

Aus1.5   **When applicable, this Standard supersedes:**

(a)   **AASB 1006 *Interests in Joint Ventures* as notified in the *Commonwealth of Australia Gazette* No S 575, 7 December 1998; and**

(b)   **AAS 19 *Interests in Joint Ventures* as issued in December 1998.**

Aus1.6   Both AASB 1006 and AAS 19 remain applicable until superseded by this Standard.

Aus1.7   Notice of this Standard was published in the *Commonwealth of Australia Gazette* No S 294, 22 July 2004.

Scope

1   This Standard shall be applied in accounting for interests in *joint ventures* and the reporting of joint venture assets, liabilities, income and expenses in the financial statements of *venturers* and investors, regardless of the structures or forms under which the joint venture activities take place. However, it does not apply to venturers' interests in jointly controlled entities held by:

(a)   venture capital organisations; or

(b)   mutual funds, unit trusts and similar entities including investment-linked insurance funds

that upon initial recognition are designated as at fair value through profit or loss or are classified as held for trading and accounted for in accordance with AASB 139 *Financial Instruments: Recognition and Measurement*. Such investments shall be measured at fair value in accordance with AASB 139, with changes in fair value recognised in profit or loss in the period of the change. A venturer holding such an interest shall make the disclosures required by paragraphs 55 and 56.

2   A venturer with an interest in a jointly controlled entity is exempted from paragraphs 30 (*proportionate consolidation*) and 38 (*equity method*) when it meets the following conditions:

(a)   the interest is classified as held for sale in accordance with AASB 5 *Non-current Assets Held for Sale and Discontinued Operations*; or

(b)   the exception in paragraph 10 or Aus10.1, as modified by paragraph Aus10.2, of AASB 127 *Consolidated and Separate Financial Statements* allowing a parent that also has an interest in a jointly controlled entity not to present consolidated financial statements is applicable; or

(c)   all of the following apply:

(i)   the venturer is a wholly-owned subsidiary, or is a partially-owned subsidiary of another entity and its owners, including those not otherwise entitled to vote, have been informed about, and do not object to, the venturer not applying proportionate consolidation or the equity method;

(ii)   the venturer's debt or equity instruments are not traded in a public market (a domestic or foreign stock exchange or an over-the-counter market, including local and regional markets);

(iii)   the venturer did not file, nor is it in the process of filing, its financial statements with a securities commission or other regulatory organisation, for the purpose of issuing any class of instruments in a public market; and

(iv)   the ultimate Australian or any intermediate parent of the venturer produces consolidated financial statements available for public use that comply with International Financial Reporting Standards.

Aus2.1   Notwithstanding paragraph 2(c)(iv), a venturer that meets the criteria in paragraphs 2(c)(i), 2(c)(ii) and 2(c)(iii) need not apply proportionate consolidation or the equity method in accounting for an interest in a jointly controlled entity if its ultimate or any intermediate parent produces consolidated financial statements available for public use and the venturer and its ultimate or intermediate parent are both not-for-profit entities complying with Australian Accounting Standards.

Definitions

3   The following terms are used in this Standard with the meanings specified.

Control is the power to govern the financial and operating policies of an economic activity so as to obtain benefits from it.

The *equity method* is a method of accounting whereby an interest in a jointly controlled entity is initially recorded at cost and adjusted thereafter for the post-acquisition change in the venturer's share of net assets of the jointly controlled entity. The profit or loss of the venturer includes the venturer's share of the profit or loss of the jointly controlled entity.

An *investor in a joint venture* is a party to a joint venture and does not have joint control over that joint venture.

Joint control is the contractually agreed sharing of control over an economic activity and exists only when the strategic financial and operating decisions relating to the activity require the unanimous consent of the parties sharing control (the venturers).

A *joint venture* is a contractual arrangement whereby two or more parties undertake an economic activity that is subject to joint control.

Proportionate consolidation is a method of accounting whereby a venturer's share of each of the assets, liabilities, income and expenses of a jointly controlled entity is combined line by line with similar items in the venturer's financial statements or reported as separate line items in the venturer's financial statements.

Separate financial statements are those presented by a parent, an investor in an associate or a venturer in a jointly controlled entity, in which the investments are accounted for on the basis of the direct equity interest rather than on the basis of the reported results and net assets of the investees.

Significant influence is the power to participate in the financial and operating policy decisions of an economic activity but is not control or joint control over those policies.

A *venturer* is a party to a joint venture and has joint control over that joint venture.

4   Financial statements in which proportionate consolidation or the equity method is applied are not *separate financial statements*, nor are the financial statements of an entity that does not have a subsidiary, associate or venturer's interest in a jointly controlled entity.

5   Separate financial statements are those presented in addition to consolidated financial statements, financial statements in which investments are accounted for using the equity method and financial statements in which venturers' interests in joint ventures are proportionately consolidated. Separate financial statements need not be appended to, or accompany, those statements.

6   Entities that are exempted in accordance with paragraphs 10-Aus10.2 of AASB 127 from consolidation, paragraph 13(c) of AASB 128 *Investments in Associates* from applying the equity method or paragraph 2 of this Standard from applying proportionate consolidation or the equity method may present separate financial statements as their only financial statements.

Forms of Joint Venture

7   Joint ventures take many different forms and structures. This Standard identifies three broad types—jointly controlled operations, jointly controlled assets and jointly controlled entities—that are commonly described as, and meet the definition of, joint ventures. The following characteristics are common to all joint ventures:

(a)   two or more venturers are bound by a contractual arrangement; and

(b)   the contractual arrangement establishes *joint control*.

Joint Control

8   Joint control may be precluded when an investee is in legal reorganisation or in bankruptcy, or operates under severe long-term restrictions on its ability to transfer funds to the venturer. If joint control is continuing, these events are not enough in themselves to justify not accounting for joint ventures in accordance with this Standard.

Contractual Arrangement

9   The existence of a contractual arrangement distinguishes interests that involve joint control from investments in associates in which the investor has *significant influence* (see AASB 128 *Investments in Associates*). Activities that have no contractual arrangement to establish joint control are not joint ventures for the purposes of this Standard.

10   The contractual arrangement may be evidenced in a number of ways, for example by a contract between the venturers or minutes of discussions between the venturers. In some cases, the arrangement is incorporated in the articles or other by-laws of the joint venture. Whatever its form, the contractual arrangement is usually in writing and deals with such matters as:

   (a)   the activity, duration and reporting obligations of the joint venture;

   (b)   the appointment of the board of directors or equivalent governing body of the joint venture and the voting rights of the venturers;

   (c)   capital contributions by the venturers; and

   (d)   the sharing by the venturers of the output, income, expenses or results of the joint venture.

11   The contractual arrangement establishes joint control over the joint venture. Such a requirement ensures that no single venturer is in a position to *control* the activity unilaterally.

12   The contractual arrangement may identify one venturer as the operator or manager of the joint venture. The operator does not control the joint venture but acts within the financial and operating policies that have been agreed by the venturers in accordance with the contractual arrangement and delegated to the operator. If the operator has the power to govern the financial and operating policies of the economic activity, it controls the venture and the venture is a subsidiary of the operator and not a joint venture.

Jointly Controlled Operations

13   The operation of some joint ventures involves the use of the assets and other resources of the venturers rather than the establishment of a corporation, partnership or other entity, or a financial structure that is separate from the venturers themselves. Each venturer uses its own property, plant and equipment and carries its own inventories. It also incurs its own expenses and liabilities and raises its own finance, which represent its own obligations. The joint venture activities may be carried out by the venturer's employees alongside the venturer's similar activities. The joint venture agreement usually provides a means by which the revenue from the sale of the joint product and any expenses incurred in common are shared among the venturers.

14   An example of a jointly controlled operation is when two or more venturers combine their operations, resources and expertise to manufacture, market and distribute jointly a particular product, such as an aircraft. Different parts of the manufacturing process are carried out by each of the venturers. Each venturer bears its own costs and takes a share of the revenue from the sale of the aircraft, such share being determined in accordance with the contractual arrangement.

15   In respect of its interests in jointly controlled operations, a venturer shall recognise in its financial statements:

   (a)   the assets that it controls and the liabilities that it incurs; and

   (b)   the expenses that it incurs and its share of the income that it earns from the sale of goods or services by the joint venture.

16   Because the assets, liabilities, income and expenses are recognised in the financial statements of the venturer, no adjustments or other consolidation procedures are required in respect of these items when the venturer presents consolidated financial statements.

17   Separate accounting records may not be required for the joint venture itself and financial statements may not be prepared for the joint venture. However, the venturers may prepare management accounts so that they may assess the performance of the joint venture.

Jointly Controlled Assets

18   Some joint ventures involve the joint control, and often the joint ownership, by the venturers of one or more assets contributed to, or acquired for the purpose of, the joint venture and dedicated to the purposes of the joint venture. The assets are used to obtain benefits for the venturers. Each venturer may take a share of the output from the assets and each bears an agreed share of the expenses incurred.

19   These joint ventures do not involve the establishment of a corporation, partnership or other entity, or a financial structure that is separate from the venturers themselves. Each venturer has control over its share of future economic benefits through its share of the jointly controlled asset.

20   Many activities in the oil, gas and mineral extraction industries involve jointly controlled assets. For example, a number of oil production companies may jointly control and operate an oil pipeline. Each venturer uses the pipeline to transport its own product in return for which it bears an agreed proportion of the expenses of operating the pipeline. Another example of a jointly controlled asset is when two entities jointly control a property, each taking a share of the rents received and bearing a share of the expenses.

21   In respect of its interest in jointly controlled assets, a venturer shall recognise in its financial statements:

   (a)   its share of the jointly controlled assets, classified according to the nature of the assets;

   (b)   any liabilities that it has incurred;

   (c)   its share of any liabilities incurred jointly with the other venturers in relation to the joint venture;

   (d)   any income from the sale or use of its share of the output of the joint venture, together with its share of any expenses incurred by the joint venture; and

   (e)   any expenses that it has incurred in respect of its interest in the joint venture.

22   In respect of its interest in jointly controlled assets, each venturer includes in its accounting records and recognises in its financial statements:

   (a)   its share of the jointly controlled assets, classified according to the nature of the assets rather than as an investment. For example, a share of a jointly controlled oil pipeline is classified as property, plant and equipment.

   (b)   any liabilities that it has incurred, for example those incurred in financing its share of the assets.

   (c)   its share of any liabilities incurred jointly with other venturers in relation to the joint venture.

   (d)   any income from the sale or use of its share of the output of the joint venture, together with its share of any expenses incurred by the joint venture.

   (e)   any expenses that it has incurred in respect of its interest in the joint venture, for example those related to financing the venturer's interest in the assets and selling its share of the output.

Because the assets, liabilities, income and expenses are recognised in the financial statements of the venturer, no adjustments or other consolidation procedures are required in respect of these items when the venturer presents consolidated financial statements.

23   The treatment of jointly controlled assets reflects the substance and economic reality and, usually, the legal form of the joint venture. Separate accounting records for the joint venture itself may be limited to those expenses incurred in common by the venturers and ultimately borne by the venturers according to their agreed shares. Financial statements may not be prepared for the joint venture, although the venturers may prepare management accounts so that they may assess the performance of the joint venture.

Jointly Controlled Entities

24   A jointly controlled entity is a joint venture that involves the establishment of a corporation, partnership or other entity in which each venturer has an interest. The entity operates in the same way as other entities, except that a contractual arrangement between the venturers establishes joint control over the economic activity of the entity.

25   A jointly controlled entity controls the assets of the joint venture, incurs liabilities and expenses and earns income. It may enter into contracts in its own name and raise finance for the purposes of the joint venture activity. Each venturer is entitled to a share of the profits of the jointly controlled entity, although some jointly controlled entities also involve a sharing of the output of the joint venture.

26   A common example of a jointly controlled entity is when two entities combine their activities in a particular line of business by transferring the relevant assets and liabilities into a jointly controlled entity. Another example is when an entity commences a business in a foreign country in conjunction with the government or other agency in that country, by establishing a separate entity that is jointly controlled by the entity and the government or agency.

27   Many jointly controlled entities are similar in substance to those joint ventures referred to as jointly controlled operations or jointly controlled assets. For example, the venturers may transfer a jointly controlled asset, such as an oil pipeline, into a jointly controlled entity, for tax or other reasons. Similarly, the venturers may contribute into a jointly controlled entity assets that will be operated jointly. Some jointly controlled operations also involve the establishment of a jointly controlled entity to deal with particular aspects of the activity, for example, the design, marketing, distribution or after-sales service of the product.

28   A jointly controlled entity maintains its own accounting records and prepares and presents financial statements in the same way as other entities in conformity with Australian equivalents to IFRSs.

29   Each venturer usually contributes cash or other resources to the jointly controlled entity. These contributions are included in the accounting records of the venturer and recognised in its financial statements as an investment in the jointly controlled entity.

Financial Statements of a Venturer

Proportionate Consolidation

30   **A venturer shall recognise its interest in a jointly controlled entity using proportionate consolidation or the alternative method described in paragraph 38. When proportionate consolidation is used, one of the two reporting formats identified below shall be used.**

31   A venturer recognises its interest in a jointly controlled entity using one of the two reporting formats for proportionate consolidation irrespective of whether it also has investments in subsidiaries or whether it describes its financial statements as consolidated financial statements.

32   When recognising an interest in a jointly controlled entity, it is essential that a venturer reflects the substance and economic reality of the arrangement, rather than the joint venture's particular structure or form. In a jointly controlled entity, a venturer has control over its share of future economic benefits through its share of the assets and liabilities of the venture. This substance and economic reality are reflected in the consolidated financial statements of the venturer when the venturer recognises its interests in the assets, liabilities, income and expenses of the jointly controlled entity by using one of the two reporting formats for proportionate consolidation described in paragraph 34.

33 The application of proportionate consolidation means that the statement of financial position of the venturer includes its share of the assets that it controls jointly and its share of the liabilities for which it is jointly responsible. The statement of comprehensive income of the venturer includes its share of the income and expenses of the jointly controlled entity. Many of the procedures appropriate for the application of proportionate consolidation are similar to the procedures for the consolidation of investments in subsidiaries, which are set out in AASB 127.

34 Different reporting formats may be used to give effect to proportionate consolidation. The venturer may combine its share of each of the assets, liabilities, income and expenses of the jointly controlled entity with the similar items, line by line, in its financial statements. For example, it may combine its share of the jointly controlled entity's inventory with its inventory and its share of the jointly controlled entity's property, plant and equipment with its property, plant and equipment. Alternatively, the venturer may include separate line items for its share of the assets, liabilities, income and expenses of the jointly controlled entity in its financial statements. For example, it may show its share of a current asset of the jointly controlled entity separately as part of its current assets; it may show its share of the property, plant and equipment of the jointly controlled entity separately as part of its property, plant and equipment. Both these reporting formats result in the reporting of identical amounts of profit or loss and of each major classification of assets, liabilities, income and expenses; both formats are acceptable for the purposes of this Standard.

35 Whichever format is used to give effect to proportionate consolidation, it is inappropriate to offset any assets or liabilities by the deduction of other liabilities or assets or any income or expenses by the deduction of other expenses or income, unless a legal right of set-off exists and the offsetting represents the expectation as to the realisation of the asset or the settlement of the liability.

36 **A venturer shall discontinue the use of proportionate consolidation from the date on which it ceases to have joint control over a jointly controlled entity.**

37 A venturer discontinues the use of proportionate consolidation from the date on which it ceases to share in the control of a jointly controlled entity. This may happen, for example, when the venturer disposes of its interest or when such external restrictions are placed on the jointly controlled entity that the venturer no longer has joint control.

Equity Method

38 **As an alternative to proportionate consolidation described in paragraph 30, a venturer shall recognise its interest in a jointly controlled entity using the equity method.**

39 A venturer recognises its interest in a jointly controlled entity using the equity method irrespective of whether it also has investments in subsidiaries or whether it describes its financial statements as consolidated financial statements.

40 Some venturers recognise their interests in jointly controlled entities using the equity method, as described in AASB 128. The use of the equity method is supported by those who argue that it is inappropriate to combine controlled items with jointly controlled items and by those who believe that venturers have significant influence, rather than joint control, in a jointly controlled entity. This Standard does not recommend the use of the equity method because proportionate consolidation better reflects the substance and economic reality of a venturer's interest in a jointly controlled entity, that is to say, control over the venturer's share of the future economic benefits. Nevertheless, this Standard permits the use of the equity method, as an alternative treatment, when recognising interests in jointly controlled entities.

41 **A venturer shall discontinue the use of the equity method from the date on which it ceases to have joint control over, or have significant influence in, a jointly controlled entity.**

Exceptions to Proportionate Consolidation and Equity Method

42 **Interests in jointly controlled entities that are classified as held for sale in accordance with AASB 5 *Non-current Assets Held for Sale and Discontinued Operations* shall be accounted for in accordance with that Standard.**

43   When an interest in a jointly controlled entity previously classified as held for sale no longer meets the criteria to be so classified, it shall be accounted for using proportionate consolidation or the equity method as from the date of its classification as held for sale. Financial statements for the periods since classification as held for sale shall be amended accordingly.

44   [Deleted by the IASB]

45   **When an investor ceases to have joint control over an entity, it shall account for any remaining investment in accordance with AASB 139 from that date, provided that the former jointly controlled entity does not become a subsidiary or associate. From the date when a jointly controlled entity becomes a subsidiary of an investor, the investor shall account for its interest in accordance with AASB 127 and AASB 3 *Business Combinations* (as revised in March 2008). From the date when a jointly controlled entity becomes an associate of an investor, the investor shall account for its interest in accordance with AASB 128. On the loss of joint control, the investor shall measure at fair value any investment the investor retains in the former jointly controlled entity. The investor shall recognise in profit or loss any difference between:**

      (a)   the fair value of any retained investment and any proceeds from disposing of the part interest in the jointly controlled entity; and

      (b)   the carrying amount of the investment at the date when joint control is lost.

45A   **When an investment ceases to be a jointly controlled entity and is accounted for in accordance with AASB 139, the fair value of the investment when it ceases to be a jointly controlled entity shall be regarded as its fair value on initial recognition as a financial asset in accordance with AASB 139.**

45B   If an investor loses joint control of an entity, the investor shall account for all amounts recognised in other comprehensive income in relation to that entity on the same basis as would be required if the jointly controlled entity had directly disposed of the related assets or liabilities. Therefore, if a gain or loss previously recognised in other comprehensive income would be reclassified to profit or loss on the disposal of the related assets or liabilities, the investor reclassifies the gain or loss from equity to profit or loss (as a reclassification adjustment) when the investor loses joint control of the entity. For example, if a jointly controlled entity has available-for-sale financial assets and the investor loses joint control of the entity, the investor shall reclassify to profit or loss the gain or loss previously recognised in other comprehensive income in relation to those assets. If an investor's ownership interest in a jointly controlled entity is reduced, but the investment continues to be a jointly controlled entity, the investor shall reclassify to profit or loss only a proportionate amount of the gain or loss previously recognised in other comprehensive income.

Separate Financial Statements of a Venturer

46   **An interest in a jointly controlled entity shall be accounted for in a venturer's separate financial statements in accordance with paragraphs 38-43 of AASB 127.**

47   This Standard does not mandate which entities produce separate financial statements available for public use.

Transactions between a Venturer and a Joint Venture

48   **When a venturer contributes or sells assets to a joint venture, recognition of any portion of a gain or loss from the transaction shall reflect the substance of the transaction. While the assets are retained by the joint venture, and provided the venturer has transferred the significant risks and rewards of ownership, the venturer shall recognise only that portion of the gain or loss that is attributable to the interests of the other venturers.[1] The venturer shall recognise the full amount of any loss when the contribution or sale provides evidence of a reduction in the net realisable value of current assets or an impairment loss.**

---

1   See also Interpretation 113 *Jointly Controlled Entities—Non-Monetary Contributions by Venturers*, as identified in AASB 1048 *Interpretation of Standards*.

49   When a venturer purchases assets from a joint venture, the venturer shall not recognise its share of the profits of the joint venture from the transaction until it resells the assets to an independent party. A venturer shall recognise its share of the losses resulting from these transactions in the same way as profits except that losses shall be recognised immediately when they represent a reduction in the net realisable value of current assets or an impairment loss.

50   To assess whether a transaction between a venturer and a joint venture provides evidence of impairment of an asset, the venturer determines the recoverable amount of the asset in accordance with AASB 136 *Impairment of Assets*. In determining value in use, the venturer estimates future cash flows from the asset on the basis of continuing use of the asset and its ultimate disposal by the joint venture.

Reporting Interests in Joint Ventures in the Financial Statements of an Investor

51   An *investor in a joint venture* that does not have joint control shall account for that investment in accordance with AASB 139 or, if it has significant influence in the joint venture, in accordance with AASB 128.

Operators of Joint Ventures

52   Operators or managers of a joint venture shall account for any fees in accordance with AASB 118 *Revenue*.

53   One or more venturers may act as the operator or manager of a joint venture. Operators are usually paid a management fee for such duties. The fees are accounted for by the joint venture as an expense.

Disclosure

Interests in Joint Ventures

54   A venturer shall disclose the aggregate amount of the following contingent liabilities, unless the probability of loss is remote, separately from the amount of other contingent liabilities:

(a)   any contingent liabilities that the venturer has incurred in relation to its interests in joint ventures and its share in each of the contingent liabilities that have been incurred jointly with other venturers;

(b)   its share of the contingent liabilities of the joint ventures themselves for which it is contingently liable; and

(c)   those contingent liabilities that arise because the venturer is contingently liable for the liabilities of the other venturers of a joint venture.

55   A venturer shall disclose the aggregate amount of the following commitments in respect of its interests in joint ventures separately from other commitments:

(a)   any capital commitments of the venturer in relation to its interests in joint ventures and its share in the capital commitments that have been incurred jointly with other venturers; and

(b)   its share of the capital commitments of the joint ventures themselves.

56   A venturer shall disclose a listing and description of interests in significant joint ventures and the proportion of ownership interest held in jointly controlled entities. A venturer that recognises its interests in jointly controlled entities using the line-by-line reporting format for proportionate consolidation or the equity method shall disclose the aggregate amounts of each of current assets, long-term assets, current liabilities, long-term liabilities, income and expenses related to its interests in joint ventures.

57   A venturer shall disclose the method it uses to recognise its interests in jointly controlled entities.

Effective Date and Transition

58   [Deleted by the AASB]

58A   AASB 2008-3 *Amendments to Australian Accounting Standards arising from AASB 3 and AASB 127* amended paragraphs 45 and 46 and added paragraphs 45A and 45B. An entity shall apply the amendment to paragraph 46 retrospectively and the amendment to paragraph 45 and paragraphs 45A and 45B_prospectively for annual reporting periods beginning on or after 1 July 2009. If an entity applies AASB 127 (amended 2008) for an earlier period, the amendments shall be applied for that earlier period.

58B   Paragraph 1 was amended by AASB 2008-5 *Amendments to Australian Accounting Standards arising from the Annual Improvements Project* issued in July 2008. An entity shall apply that amendment for annual reporting periods beginning on or after 1 January 2009. Earlier application is permitted. If an entity applies the amendment for an earlier period it shall disclose that fact and apply for that earlier period the amendments to paragraph 3 of AASB 7 *Financial Instruments: Disclosures*, paragraph 1 of AASB 128 and paragraph 4 of AASB 132 *Financial Instruments: Presentation* issued in July 2008. An entity is permitted to apply the amendment prospectively.

58D   Paragraph 58A was added by AASB 2010-3 *Amendments to Australian Accounting Standards arising from the Annual Improvements Project* issued in June 2010. An entity shall apply the amendment to paragraph 46 retrospectively and the amendment to paragraph 45 and paragraphs 45A and 45B_prospectively for annual reporting periods beginning on or after 1 July 2010. Earlier application is permitted. If an entity applies the amendment before 1 July 2010 it shall disclose that fact.

Withdrawal of IAS 31 (revised 2000)

59   [Deleted by the AASB]

AASB 132
Financial Instruments: Presentation
(Compiled June 2012)

Note from the Institute of Chartered Accountants Australia

This note, prepared by the technical editors, is not part of Accounting Standard AASB 132.

Historical development

15 July 2004: AASB 132 'Financial Instruments: Disclosure and Presentation' is the Australian equivalent to IAS 32 of the same name. It was made by the AASB on 15 July 2004 as part of the AASB's program to adopt International Financial Reporting Standards (IFRSs) by 2005.

9 June 2005: AASB 2005-4 'Amendments to Australian Accounting Standards' amends paragraphs 66, 94, and AG40. The amendments are applicable to annual reporting periods beginning on or after 1 January 2006, with early adoption permitted for annual reporting periods beginning on or after 1 January 2005. If an entity applies the amendments contained in AASB 2005-4 to AASB 139 for an earlier period, the amendments to AASB 132 shall be applied for that earlier period.

5 September 2005: AASB 2005-10 'Amendments to Australian Accounting Standards' amends the Standard's title and paragraphs 2, 3, 4(a), 40, 47, 50 and AG39. The Standard deletes paragraphs 1, Aus3.5, 5, 7, 51 to 95 inclusive, AG24 and AG40. The disclosure requirements contained in the deleted paragraphs 51 to 95 of AASB 132 will be superseded by AASB 7 'Financial Instruments: Disclosures'. The Standard is applicable to annual reporting periods beginning on or after 1 January 2007, with early adoption permitted for annual reporting periods beginning on or after 1 January 2005.

6 September 2005: AASB 2005-9 'Amendments to Australian Accounting Standards' amends paragraphs 4(d) and 12. The amendments are applicable to annual reporting periods beginning on or after 1 January 2006, with early adoption permitted for annual reporting periods beginning on or after 1 January 2005.

8 September 2005: AASB 2005-11 'Amendments to Australian Accounting Standards' amends paragraphs 35, AG8 and AG 40. The amendments are applicable to annual reporting periods ending on or after 31 December 2005, with early adoption permitted for annual reporting periods beginning on or after 1 January 2005.

30 April 2007: AASB 2007-4 'Amendments to Australian Accounting Standards' amends paragraphs 2, AG2, AG12 and AG29 and is applicable to annual reporting periods beginning on or after 1 July 2007. Entities may elect to early-adopt it to annual reporting periods beginning on or after 1 January 2005.

24 September 2007: AASB 2007-8 'Amendments to Australian Accounting Standards arising from AASB 101' amends AASB 132 to align with revised AASB 101. This Standard is applicable to annual reporting periods beginning on or after 1 January 2009.

5 March 2008: AASB 2008-2 'Amendments to Australian Accounting Standards – Puttable Financial Instruments and Obligations arising on Liquidation' classifies as equity instruments certain puttable financial instruments. This Standard is applicable to annual reporting periods beginning on or after 1 January 2009.

6 March 2008: AASB 2008-3 'Amendments to Australian Accounting Standards arising from AASB 3 and AASB 127' amends AASB 132 for the issue of AASB 3 Revised. This Standard is applicable to annual reporting periods beginning on or after 1 July 2009.

24 July 2008: AASB 2008-5 'Amendments to Australian Accounting Standards arising from the Annual Improvements Project' amends AASB 132 to clarify investments accounted for in accordance with AASB 139 must also apply AASB 132. This Standard is applicable to annual reporting periods beginning on or after 1 January 2009.

---

25 June 2009: AASB 2009-6 'Amendments to Australian Accounting Standards' amends AASB 132 for editorial corrections made by the International Accounting Standards Board (IASB) to its Standards and Interpretations (IFRSs) and as a consequence of issuing revised AASB 101 'Presentation of Financial Statements'. This Standard is applicable to annual reporting periods beginning on or after 1 January 2009 that end on or after 30 June 2009.

25 September 2009: the AASB reissued the version of AASB 132 applicable to annual reporting periods beginning on or after 1 January 2009 but before 1 July 2009. This version of AASB 132 has been compiled for the amending Standards applying to annual reporting periods beginning on or after 1 January 2009. This Standard applies to 31 December 2009 year end.

20 October 2009: AASB 2009-10 'Amendments to Australian Accounting Standards – Classification of Rights Issues' amends AASB 132 to clarify the classification of rights, options or warrants. This Standard is applicable to annual reporting periods beginning on or after 1 February 2010. Early adoption is permitted.

2 November 2009: AASB 132 was reissued by the AASB, compiled to include the AASB 2007-8, AASB 2008-2, AASB 2008-3, AASB 2008-5 and AASB 2009-6 amendments and applies to annual reporting periods beginning on or after 1 July 2009 but before 1 February 2010. Early application is permitted.

7 December 2009: AASB 2009-11 'Amendments to Australian Accounting Standards arising from AASB 9' amends AASB 132 to give effect to consequential changes arising from the issuance of AASB 9. This Standard is applicable to annual reporting periods beginning on or after 1 January 2013 with early adoption permitted from annual reporting periods ending on or after 31 December 2009 that begin before 1 January 2013 provided AASB 9 is also applied for the same period. The application date of AASB 2009-11 has been amended to 1 January 2015 by AASB 2012-6. **These amendments have been superseded by AASB 2017-7 and are not included in this compiled Standard.**

2 June 2010: AASB 2010-3 'Amendments to Australian Accounting Standards arising from the Annual Improvements Project' amends AASB 132 in relation to transition requirements for contingent consideration from a business combination that occurred before the effective date of the revised AASB 3. This Standard is applicable to annual reporting periods beginning on or after 1 July 2010 with early adoption permitted.

7 September 2010: AASB 132 was reissued by the AASB, compiled to include the AASB 2010-3 amendments and applies to annual reporting periods beginning on or after 1 July 2010 but before 1 January 2013.

27 October 2010: AASB 2010-5 'Further Amendments to Australian Accounting Standards' makes editorial amendments to AASB 132. This Standard is applicable to annual reporting periods beginning on or after 1 January 2011.

1 March 2011: AASB 2010-7 'Amendments to Australian Accounting Standards arising from AASB 9 (December 2010)' as compiled amends AASB 132 to give effect to consequential changes arising from the reissue of AASB 9 in December 2010, and supersedes AASB 2009-11, which related to the previous version of AASB 9. This Standard applies to annual reporting periods beginning on or after 1 January 2013 and can be adopted early. The application date of AASB 2010-7 has been amended to 1 January 2015 by AASB 2012-6. **These amendments are not included in this compiled Standard.**

11 May 2011: AASB 2011-1 'Amendments to Australian Accounting Standards arising from the Trans-Tasman Convergence Project' amends AASB 132 as a result of the Trans-Tasman project, to more closely align IFRSs as applied through Australian and New Zealand Standards. AASB 2011-1 deletes Australian-specific disclosure requirements. Where appropriate these disclosures are now included in AASB 1054 'Australian Additional Requirements'. These Standards apply to annual reporting periods beginning on or after 1 July 2011 with early adoption permitted.

29 August 2011: AASB 2011-7 'Amendments to Australian Accounting Standards arising from the Consolidation and Joint Arrangements Standards' amends AASB 132 to give effect to many consequential changes arising from the issue of AASB 10, 11, 12, 127 and 128. This Standard applies to annual reporting periods beginning on or after 1 January 2013 and can be adopted early by for-profit entities. **These amendments are not included in this compiled Standard.**

2 September 2011: AASB 2011-8 'Amendments to Australian Accounting Standards arising from AASB 13' amends AASB 132 to give effect to a consequential change in the definition of fair value arising from the issue of AASB 13. This Standard applies to annual reporting periods beginning on or after 1 January 2013 and can be adopted early. **These amendments are not included in this compiled Standard.**

5 September 2011: AASB 2011-9 'Amendments to Australian Accounting Standards – Presentation of Items of Other Comprehensive income' amends the presentation of items in other comprehensive income. This Standard applies to annual reporting periods beginning on or after 1 July 2012 and can be adopted early.

23 September 2011: AASB 132 was reissued by the AASB, compiled to include the AASB 2010-5 and AASB 2011-1 amendments and applies to annual reporting periods ending on or after 1 July 2011 but before 1 July 2012.

20 June 2012: AASB 132 was reissued by the AASB, compiled to include the AASB 2011-9 amendments and applies to annual reporting periods beginning on or after 1 July 2012 but before 1 January 2013. It can be adopted early.

29 June 2012: AASB 2012-2 'Amendments to Australian Accounting Standards – Disclosures – Offsetting Financial Assets and Financial Liabilities' amends AASB 132 to refer to extended AASB 7 disclosures in relation to the effect of netting arrangements and applies to reporting periods beginning on or after 1 January 2013. **These amendments are not included in this compiled Standard.**

29 June 2012: AASB 2012-3 'Amendments to Australian Accounting Standards – Offsetting Financial Assets and Financial Liabilities' amends AASB 132 to add application guidance relating to offsetting and applies to reporting periods beginning on or after 1 January 2014. **These amendments are not included in this compiled Standard.**

29 June 2012: AASB 2012-5 'Amendments to Australian Accounting Standards arising from Annual Improvements 2009–2011 Cycle' amends AASB 132 in relation to the tax effect of distribution to holders of equity instruments. This Standard applies to annual reporting periods beginning on or after 1 January 2013 and can be adopted early. **These amendments are not included in this compiled Standard.**

References

Interpretation 2 *Members' Shares in Co-operative Entities and Similar Instruments*, Interpretation 19 *Extinguishing Financial Liabilities with Equity Instruments,* Interpretation 11 *AASB 2-Group and Treasury Share Transactions*, Interpretation 12 *Service Concession Arrangements* and Interpretation 1038 *Contributions by Owners made to Wholly-Owned Public Sector Entities* apply to AASB 132.

AASB item not taken onto the agenda: *Classification of Long Service Leave Liabilities* applies to AASB 132.

IFRIC items not taken onto the agenda: No. 44 *Discretionary Distributions and Economic Compulsion*, No. 45 *Own shares that are held for trading purposes*, No. 46 *The Meaning of Other than Temporary Impairment and its Application to Certain Investments*, No. 48 *Classification of non-redeemable preference shares*, IAS 32-1 *Changes in the contractual terms of an existing equity instrument resulting in it being reclassified to a financial liability*, IAS 32-2 *Classification of a financial instrument as liability or equity*, IAS 32-3 *Foreign currency instruments exchangeable into equity instruments of the parent entity of the issuer*, IAS 32-4 *Puts and forwards held by minority interests,* IAS 32-6 *Transaction costs to be deducted from equity*, IAS 32R-1 *IAS 32 Financial Instruments: Presentation – Classification of puttable and perpetual instruments*, IAS 32-8 *Application of the 'fixed for fixed' condition* and IAS 32-9 *Shareholder discretion* apply to AASB 132.

AASB 132 compared to IAS 32

Additions

Paragraph	Description
Aus 3.1	Which entities AASB 132 applies to (i.e. reporting entities and general purpose financial statements).
Aus 3.2	The application date of AASB 132 (i.e. annual reporting periods beginning 1 January 2005).

Aus 3.3	Prohibits early application of AASB 132.
Aus 3.4	Makes the requirements of AASB 132 subject to AASB 1031 'Materiality'.
Aus 3.6	Explains which Australian Standards have been superseded by AASB 132.
Aus 3.7	Clarifies that the superseded Australian Standards remain in force until AASB 132 applies.
Aus 3.8	Notice of the new Standard published on 22 July 2004.

Deletions

Paragraph	*Description*
96, 96A	Effective date of IAS 32. Earlier application permitted but IAS 32 and IAS 39 must be applied together.
97, 97A	IAS 32 must be applied retrospectively on initial application.
98	Reference to superseded IAS 32.
99	Reference to superseded SIC Interpretations – SICs 5, 16 and 17.
100	Reference to withdrawn draft SIC Interpretation D34.

Contents

Compilation Details

Comparison with IAS 32

Accounting Standard
AASB 132 Financial Instruments: Presentation

Paragraphs

Objective 2 – 3

Application Aus3.1 – Aus3.8

Scope 4 – 10

Definitions 11 – 14

Presentation

    Liabilities and Equity 15 – 16

        Puttable Instruments 16A – 16B

        Instruments, or Components of Instruments, that Impose on the
Entity an Obligation to Deliver to Another Party a Pro Rata
Share of the Net Assets of the Entity Only on Liquidation 16C – 16D

        Reclassification of Puttable Instruments and Instruments that
Impose on the Entity an Obligation to Deliver to Another
Party a Pro Rata Share of the Net Assets of the Entity Only
on Liquidation 16E – 16F

        No Contractual Obligation to Deliver Cash or Another Financial Asset 17 – 20

        Settlement in the Entity's Own Equity Instruments 21 – 24

        Contingent Settlement Provisions 25

        Settlement Options 26 – 27

    Compound Financial Instruments 28 – 32

    Treasury Shares 33 – 34

    Interest, Dividends, Losses and Gains 35 – 41

    Offsetting a Financial Asset and a Financial Liability 42 – 50

Effective Date and Transition 96B – 97K

Appendix: Application Guidance AG1 – AG2

    Definitions

        Financial Assets and Financial Liabilities AG3 – AG12

        Equity Instruments AG13 – AG14

        The Class of Instruments that is Subordinate to
All Other Classes AG14A – AG14D

        Total Expected Cash Flows Attributable to the Instrument
over the Life of the Instrument AG14E

        Transactions Entered into by an Instrument Holder Other than
as Owner of the Entity AG14F – AG14I

        No Other Financial Instrument or Contract with Total Cash
Flows that Substantially Fixes or Restricts the Residual
Return to the Instrument Holder AG14J

        Derivative Financial Instruments AG15 – AG19

        Contracts to Buy or Sell Non-Financial Items AG20 – AG23

AASB

Paragraphs

Presentation

  Liabilities and Equity

    No Contractual Obligation to Deliver Cash or Another
Financial Asset .... AG25 – AG26

    Settlement in the Entity's Own Equity Instruments AG27

    Contingent Settlement Provisions AG28

    Treatment in Consolidated Financial Statements .... AG29 – AG29A

  Compound Financial Instruments .... AG30 – AG35

  Treasury Shares AG36

  Interest, Dividends, Losses and Gains AG37

  Offsetting a Financial Asset and a Financial Liability .... AG38 – AG39

Illustrative Examples

Basis for Conclusions on IAS 32
(available on the AASB website)

Australian Accounting Standard AASB 132 *Financial Instruments: Presentation* (as amended) is set out in paragraphs 2 – 97K and the Appendix. All the paragraphs have equal authority. Paragraphs in **bold type** state the main principles. Terms defined in this Standard are in *italics* the first time they appear in the Standard. AASB 132 is to be read in the context of other Australian Accounting Standards, including AASB 1048 *Interpretation of Standards*, which identifies the Australian Accounting Interpretations. In the absence of explicit guidance, AASB 108 *Accounting Policies, Changes in Accounting Estimates and Errors* provides a basis for selecting and applying accounting policies.

Compilation Details

Accounting Standard AASB 132 *Financial Instruments: Presentation* as amended

This compiled Standard applies to annual reporting periods beginning on or after 1 July 2012 but before 1 January 2013. It takes into account amendments made up to and including 5 September 2011 and was prepared on 20 June 2012 by the staff of the Australian Accounting Standards Board (AASB).

This compilation is not a separate Accounting Standard made by the AASB. Instead, it is a representation of AASB 132 (July 2004) as amended by other Accounting Standards, which are listed in the Table below.

Table of Standards

Standard	Date made	Application date *(annual reporting periods … on or after …)*	Application, saving or transitional provisions
AASB 132	15 Jul 2004	*(beginning)* 1 Jan 2005	
AASB 2005-4	9 Jun 2005	*(beginning)* 1 Jan 2006	see (a) below
AASB 2005-9	6 Sep 2005	*(beginning)* 1 Jan 2006	see (b) below
AASB 2005-10	5 Sep 2005	*(beginning)* 1 Jan 2007	see (c) below
AASB 2005-11	8 Sep 2005	*(ending)* 31 Dec 2005	see (d) below
Erratum	24 Feb 2006	*(ending)* 24 Feb 2006	see (e) below
AASB 2007-4	30 Apr 2007	*(beginning)* 1 Jul 2007	see (f) below
AASB 2007-8	24 Sep 2007	*(beginning)* 1 Jan 2009	see (g) below
AASB 2008-2	5 Mar 2008	*(beginning)* 1 Jan 2009	see (h) below
AASB 2008-3	6 Mar 2008	*(beginning)* 1 Jul 2009	see (i) below

Standard	Date made	Application date *(annual reporting periods ... on or after ...)*	Application, saving or transitional provisions
AASB 2008-5	24 Jul 2008	*(beginning)* 1 Jan 2009	see (j) below
AASB 2009-6	25 Jun 2009	*(beginning)* 1 Jan 2009 and *(ending)* 30 Jun 2009	see (k) below
AASB 2009-10	20 Oct 2009	*(beginning)* 1 Feb 2010	see (l) below
AASB 2009-11	7 Dec 2009	*(beginning)* 1 Jan 2013	not compiled*
AASB 2010-3	23 Jun 2010	*(beginning)* 1 Jul 2010	see (m) below
AASB 2010-5	27 Oct 2010	*(beginning)* 1 Jan 2011	see (n) below
AASB 2010-7	6 Dec 2010	*(beginning)* 1 Jan 2013	not compiled*
AASB 2011-1	11 May 2011	*(beginning)* 1 Jul 2011	see (o) below
AASB 2011-7	29 Aug 2011	*(beginning)* 1 Jan 2013	not compiled*
AASB 2011-8	2 Sep 2011	*(beginning)* 1 Jan 2013	not compiled*
AASB 2011-9	5 Sep 2011	*(beginning)* 1 Jul 2012	see (p) below

*   The amendments made by this Standard are not included in this compilation, which presents the principal Standard as applicable to annual reporting periods beginning on or after 1 July 2012 but before 1 January 2013.

(a)   Entities may elect to apply this Standard to annual reporting periods beginning on or after 1 January 2005 but before 1 January 2006. Entities that elect to apply the amendments in AASB 2005-4 in respect of AASB 139 *Financial Instruments: Recognition and Measurement* to such periods must also apply the amendments made to AASB 132 by AASB 2005-4.

(b)   Entities may elect to apply this Standard to annual reporting periods beginning on or after 1 January 2005 but before 1 January 2006.

(c)   Entities may elect to apply this Standard to annual reporting periods beginning on or after 1 January 2005 but before 1 January 2007.

(d)   Entities may elect to apply this Standard to annual reporting periods beginning on or after 1 January 2005 that end before 31 December 2005.

(e)   Entities may elect to apply this Erratum to annual reporting periods beginning on or after 1 January 2005 that end before 24 February 2006.

(f)   Entities may elect to apply this Standard to annual reporting periods beginning on or after 1 January 2005 but before 1 July 2007.

(g)   Entities may elect to apply this Standard to annual reporting periods beginning on or after 1 January 2005 but before 1 January 2009, provided that AASB 101 *Presentation of Financial Statements* (September 2007) is also applied to such periods.

(h)   Entities may elect to apply this Standard to annual reporting periods beginning on or after 1 January 2005 but before 1 January 2009.

(i)   Entities may elect to apply this Standard to annual reporting periods beginning on or after 30 June 2007 but before 1 July 2009, provided that AASB 3 *Business Combinations* (March 2008) and AASB 127 *Consolidated and Separate Financial Statements* (March 2008) are also applied to such periods.

(j)   Entities may elect to apply this Standard, or its amendments to individual Standards, to annual reporting periods beginning on or after 1 January 2005 but before 1 January 2009.

(k)   Entities may elect to apply this Standard to annual reporting periods beginning on or after 1 January 2005 but before 1 January 2009, provided that AASB 101 *Presentation of Financial Statements* (September 2007) is also applied to such periods, and to annual reporting periods beginning on or after 1 January 2009 that end before 30 June 2009.

(l)   Entities may elect to apply this Standard to annual reporting periods beginning on or after 1 January 2005 but before 1 February 2010.

(m)   Entities may elect to apply this Standard to annual reporting periods beginning on or after 1 January 2005 but before 1 July 2010.

(n)   Entities may elect to apply this Standard to annual reporting periods beginning on or after 1 January 2005 but before 1 January 2011.

(o)   Entities may elect to apply this Standard, or its amendments to individual pronouncements, to annual reporting periods beginning on or after 1 January 2005 but before 1 July 2011, provided that AASB 1054 *Australian Additional Disclosures* is, or its relevant individual disclosure requirements are, also applied to such periods.

(p)   Entities may elect to apply this Standard to annual reporting periods beginning on or after 1 January 2005 but before 1 July 2012.

Table of Amendments to Standard

Paragraph affected	How affected	By ... [paragraph]
Title	amended	AASB 2005-10 [6]
1	deleted	AASB 2005-10 [7]
2	amended	AASB 2005-10 [7]
	amended	AASB 2007-4 [89]
3	amended	AASB 2005-10 [7]
Aus3.1	amended	AASB 2007-8 [7, 8]
Aus3.4	amended	AASB 2007-8 [8]
Aus3.5	deleted	AASB 2005-10 [8]
4	amended	AASB 2005-9 [23]
	amended	AASB 2005-10 [9]
	amended	Erratum, Feb 2006
	amended	AASB 2008-5 [52]
	amended	AASB 2008-3 [55]
5	deleted	AASB 2005-10 [10]
7	deleted	AASB 2005-10 [10]
11 (preceding heading)	amended	AASB 2007-4 [89]
11	amended	AASB 2008-2 [13-15]
	amended	AASB 2009-10 [6]
	amended	AASB 2010-5 [40]
12	amended	AASB 2005-9 [24]
15 (preceding heading)	amended	AASB 2008-2 [16]
16	amended	AASB 2008-2 [17]
	amended	AASB 2009-10 [6]
16A (and preceding heading)	added	AASB 2008-2 [18]
	amended	AASB 2009-6 [65]
16B	added	AASB 2008-2 [18]
16C (and preceding heading)	added	AASB 2008-2 [18]
	amended	AASB 2009-6 [65]
16D	added	AASB 2008-2 [18]
16E (and preceding heading)	added	AASB 2008-2 [18]
	amended	AASB 2009-6 [66]
16F	added	AASB 2008-2 [18]
	amended	AASB 2009-6 [66]
17	amended	AASB 2008-2 [19]
18	amended	AASB 2007-8 [93]
	amended	AASB 2008-2 [19]
19	amended	AASB 2008-2 [19]
22	amended	AASB 2008-2 [20]
22A	added	AASB 2008-2 [21]
	amended	AASB 2009-6 [66]
23	amended	AASB 2008-2 [22]
25	amended	AASB 2008-2 [23]
	amended	AASB 2009-6 [66]
29	amended	AASB 2007-8 [94]
33 (preceding heading)	amended	AASB 2011-1 [19]
34	amended	AASB 2007-8 [6]
35	amended	AASB 2005-11 [10]

Paragraph affected	How affected	By ... [paragraph]
40	amended	AASB 2005-10 [11]
	amended	AASB 2007-8 [95]
	amended	AASB 2011-9 [21]
41-42	amended	AASB 2007-8 [6]
44	amended	AASB 2007-8 [6]
47	amended	AASB 2005-10 [12]
50	amended	AASB 2005-10 [13]
51-95	deleted	AASB 2005-10 [14]
66	amended	AASB 2005-4 [15]
94	amended	AASB 2005-4 [16]
	amended	Erratum, Feb 2006
96 (preceding heading)	amended	AASB 2008-2 [24]
96A	note added	AASB 2008-2 [25]
96B	added	AASB 2008-2 [26]
96C	added	AASB 2008-2 [26]
	amended	AASB 2010-5 [41]
97A	note added	AASB 2007-8 [96]
97B	note added	AASB 2008-3 [56]
	paragraph added	AASB 2010-3 [12]
	(in place of note)	
97C	added	AASB 2008-2 [27]
97D	added	AASB 2008-5 [54]
97E	added	AASB 2009-10 [6]
97G	added	AASB 2010-3 [12]
97K	added	AASB 2011-9 [21]
AG2	amended	AASB 2007-4 [89]
AG8	amended	AASB 2005-11 [11]
AG12	amended	AASB 2007-4 [89]
AG13-AG14	amended	AASB 2008-2 [28]
AG14A-AG14E (and preceding headings)	added	AASB 2008-2 [29]
AG14F (and preceding heading)	added	AASB 2008-2 [29]
	amended	AASB 2009-6 [67]
AG14G-AG14I	added	AASB 2008-2 [29]
AG14J (and preceding heading)	added	AASB 2008-2 [29]
AG24	deleted	AASB 2005-10 [15]
AG27	amended	AASB 2008-2 [30]
AG29	amended	AASB 2007-4 [89]
	amended	AASB 2008-3 [8]
AG29A	added	AASB 2008-2 [31]
AG31	amended	AASB 2007-8 [97]
AG36	amended	AASB 2007-8 [6]
AG39	amended	AASB 2005-10 [15]
	amended	AASB 2007-8 [98]
AG40	amended	AASB 2005-4 [17]
	amended	AASB 2005-11 [12]
	deleted	AASB 2005-10 [15]

Table of Amendments to Illustrative Examples

Paragraph affected	How affected	By ... [paragraph]
IE1	amended	AASB 2008-2 [32]
IE10	amended	AASB 2009-6 [68]
IE32	amended	AASB 2007-8 [6]
	amended	AASB 2009-6 [69]
IE33	amended	AASB 2007-8 [6]
	amended	AASB 2008-2 [33]
	amended	AASB 2009-6 [70]
IE45	amended	AASB 2007-8 [6]
	amended	AASB 2009-6 [71]

Comparison with IAS 32

AASB 132 and IAS 32

AASB 132 *Financial Instruments: Presentation* as amended incorporates IAS 32 *Financial Instruments: Presentation* as issued and amended by the International Accounting Standards Board (IASB). Paragraphs that have been added to this Standard (and do not appear in the text of IAS 32) are identified with the prefix "Aus", followed by the number of the preceding IASB paragraph and decimal numbering.

Compliance with IAS 32

Entities that comply with AASB 132 as amended will simultaneously be in compliance with IAS 32 as amended.

Accounting Standard AASB 132

The Australian Accounting Standards Board made Accounting Standard AASB 132 *Financial Instruments: Disclosure and Presentation* under section 334 of the *Corporations Act 2001* on 15 July 2004.

This compiled version of AASB 132 applies to annual reporting periods beginning on or after 1 July 2012 but before 1 January 2013. It incorporates relevant amendments contained in other AASB Standards made by the AASB and other decisions of the AASB up to and including 5 September 2011 (see Compilation Details).

Accounting Standard AASB 132

Financial Instruments: Presentation

Objective

1   [Deleted by the IASB]

2   The objective of this Standard is to establish principles for presenting *financial instruments* as liabilities or equity and for offsetting *financial assets* and *financial liabilities*. It applies to the classification of financial instruments, from the perspective of the issuer, into financial assets, financial liabilities and *equity instruments*; the classification of related interest, dividends, losses and gains; and the circumstances in which financial assets and financial liabilities should be offset.

3   The principles in this Standard complement the principles for recognising and measuring financial assets and financial liabilities in AASB 139 *Financial Instruments: Recognition and Measurement*, and for disclosing information about them in AASB 7 *Financial Instruments: Disclosures*.

Application

Aus3.1   This Standard applies to:

(a)   each entity that is required to prepare financial reports in accordance with Part 2M.3 of the Corporations Act and that is a reporting entity;

(b)   general purpose financial statements of each other reporting entity; and

(c)   financial statements that are, or are held out to be, general purpose financial statements.

Aus3.2   This Standard applies to annual reporting periods beginning on or after 1 January 2005

[Note: For application dates of paragraphs changed or added by an amending Standard, see Compilation Details.]

Aus3.3   This Standard shall not be applied to annual reporting periods beginning before 1 January 2005.

Aus3.4   The requirements specified in this Standard apply to the financial statements where information resulting from their application is material in accordance with AASB 1031 *Materiality*.

Aus3.5   [Deleted by the AASB]

Aus3.6   When applicable, this Standard supersedes:

(a)   AASB 1033 *Presentation and Disclosure of Financial Instruments* as notified in the *Commonwealth of Australia Gazette* No S 516, 29 October 1999; and

(b)   AAS 33 *Presentation and Disclosure of Financial Instruments* as issued in October 1999.

Aus3.7   Both AASB 1033 and AAS 33 remain applicable until superseded by this Standard.

Aus3.8   Notice of this Standard was published in the *Commonwealth of Australia Gazette* No S 294, 22 July 2004.

Scope

4   This Standard shall be applied by all entities to all types of financial instruments except:

(a)   those interests in subsidiaries, associates, or joint ventures that are accounted for in accordance with AASB 127 *Consolidated and Separate Financial Statements*, AASB 128 *Investments in Associates* or AASB 131 *Interests in Joint Ventures*. However, in some cases, AASB 127, AASB 128 or AASB 131 permits an entity to account for an interest in a subsidiary, associate or joint venture using AASB 139; in those cases, entities shall apply the requirements of this Standard. Entities shall also apply this Standard to all derivatives linked to interests in subsidiaries, associates or joint ventures;

(b)   employers' rights and obligations under employee benefit plans, to which AASB 119 *Employee Benefits* applies;

(c)   [deleted by the IASB]

(d)   insurance contracts as defined in AASB 4 *Insurance Contracts*. However, this Standard applies to derivatives that are embedded in insurance contracts if AASB 139 requires the entity to account for them separately. Moreover, an issuer shall apply this Standard to financial guarantee contracts if the issuer applies AASB 139 in recognising and measuring the contracts, but shall apply AASB 1023 *General Insurance Contracts* if the issuer elects, in accordance with paragraph 2.2(f) of AASB 1023, to apply AASB 1023 in recognising and measuring them;

(e)   financial instruments that are within the scope of AASB 4 because they contain a discretionary participation feature. The issuer of these instruments is exempt from applying to these features paragraphs 15-32 and AG25-AG35 of this

Standard regarding the distinction between financial liabilities and equity instruments. However, these instruments are subject to all other requirements of this Standard. Furthermore, this Standard applies to derivatives that are embedded in these instruments (see AASB 139); and

(f)   financial instruments, contracts and obligations under share-based payment transactions to which AASB 2 *Share-based Payment* applies, except for:

(i)   contracts within the scope of paragraphs 8-10 of this Standard, to which this Standard applies; or

(ii)   paragraphs 33 and 34 of this Standard, which shall be applied to treasury shares purchased, sold, issued or cancelled in connection with employee share option plans, employee share purchase plans, and all other share-based payment arrangements.

5   [Deleted by the IASB]

6   [Deleted by the IASB]

7   [Deleted by the IASB]

8   This Standard shall be applied to those contracts to buy or sell a non-financial item that can be settled net in cash or another financial instrument, or by exchanging financial instruments, as if the contracts were financial instruments, with the exception of contracts that were entered into and continue to be held for the purpose of the receipt or delivery of a non-financial item in accordance with the entity's expected purchase, sale, or usage requirements.

9   There are various ways in which a contract to buy or sell a non-financial item can be settled net in cash or another financial instrument or by exchanging financial instruments. These include:

(a)   when the terms of the contract permit either party to settle it net in cash or another financial instrument or by exchanging financial instruments;

(b)   when the ability to settle net in cash or another financial instrument, or by exchanging financial instruments, is not explicit in the terms of the contract, but the entity has a practice of settling similar contracts net in cash or another financial instrument, or by exchanging financial instruments (whether with the counterparty, by entering into offsetting contracts or by selling the contract before its exercise or lapse);

(c)   when, for similar contracts, the entity has a practice of taking delivery of the underlying and selling it within a short period after delivery for the purpose of generating a profit from short-term fluctuations in price or dealer's margin; and

(d)   when the non-financial item that is the subject of the contract is readily convertible to cash.

A contract to which (b) or (c) applies is not entered into for the purpose of the receipt or delivery of the non-financial item in accordance with the entity's expected purchase, sale or usage requirements, and, accordingly, is within the scope of this Standard. Other contracts to which paragraph 8 applies are evaluated to determine whether they were entered into and continue to be held for the purpose of the receipt or delivery of the non-financial item in accordance with the entity's expected purchase, sale or usage requirement, and, accordingly, whether they are within the scope of this Standard.

10   A written option to buy or sell a non-financial item that can be settled net in cash or another financial instrument, or by exchanging financial instruments, in accordance with paragraph 9(a) or (d) is within the scope of this Standard. Such a contract cannot be entered into for the purpose of the receipt or delivery of the non-financial item in accordance with the entity's expected purchase, sale or usage requirements.

Definitions (see also paragraphs AG3-AG23)

11   The following terms are used in this Standard with the meanings specified.

A *financial instrument* is any contract that gives rise to a financial asset of one entity and a financial liability or equity instrument of another entity.

A *financial asset* is any asset that is:

(a)   cash;

(b)   an equity instrument of another entity;

(c)   a contractual right:

  (i)   to receive cash or another financial asset from another entity; or

  (ii) to exchange financial assets or financial liabilities with another entity under conditions that are potentially favourable to the entity; or

(d)   a contract that will or may be settled in the entity's own equity instruments and is:

  (i)   a non-derivative for which the entity is or may be obliged to receive a variable number of the entity's own equity instruments; or

  (ii) a derivative that will or may be settled other than by the exchange of a fixed amount of cash or another financial asset for a fixed number of the entity's own equity instruments. For this purpose the entity's own equity instruments do not include puttable financial instruments classified as equity instruments in accordance with paragraphs 16A and 16B, instruments that impose on the entity an obligation to deliver to another party a pro rata share of the net assets of the entity only on liquidation and are classified as equity instruments in accordance with paragraphs 16C and 16D, or instruments that are contracts for the future receipt or delivery of the entity's own equity instruments.

A *financial liability* is any liability that is:

(a)   a contractual obligation:

  (i)   to deliver cash or another financial asset to another entity; or

  (ii) to exchange financial assets or financial liabilities with another entity under conditions that are potentially unfavourable to the entity; or

(b)   a contract that will or may be settled in the entity's own equity instruments and is:

  (i)   a non-derivative for which the entity is or may be obliged to deliver a variable number of the entity's own equity instruments; or

  (ii) a derivative that will or may be settled other than by the exchange of a fixed amount of cash or another financial asset for a fixed number of the entity's own equity instruments. For this purpose, rights, options or warrants to acquire a fixed number of the entity's own equity instruments for a fixed amount of any currency are equity instruments if the entity offers the rights, options or warrants pro rata to all of its existing owners of the same class of its own non-derivative equity instruments. Also, for these purposes the entity's own equity instruments do not include puttable financial instruments that are classified as equity instruments in accordance with paragraphs 16A and 16B, instruments that impose on the entity an obligation to deliver to another party a pro rata share of the net assets of the entity only on liquidation and are classified as equity instruments in accordance with paragraphs 16C and 16D, or instruments that are contracts for the future receipt or delivery of the entity's own equity instruments.

> As an exception, an instrument that meets the definition of a financial liability is classified as an equity instrument if it has all the features and meets the conditions in paragraphs 16A and 16B or paragraphs 16C and 16D.

> An *equity instrument* is any contract that evidences a residual interest in the assets of an entity after deducting all of its liabilities.

> *Fair value* is the amount for which an asset could be exchanged, or a liability settled, between knowledgeable, willing parties in an arm's length transaction.

> A *puttable instrument* is a financial instrument that gives the holder the right to put the instrument back to the issuer for cash or another financial asset or is automatically put back to the issuer on the occurrence of an uncertain future event or the death or retirement of the instrument holder.

12   The following terms are defined in paragraph 9 of AASB 139 and are used in this Standard with the meaning specified in AASB 139:

       (a)   amortised cost of a financial asset or financial liability;

       (b)   available-for-sale financial assets;

       (c)   derecognition;

       (d)   derivative;

       (e)   effective interest method;

       (f)   financial asset or financial liability at fair value through profit or loss;

       (g)   financial guarantee contract;

       (h)   firm commitment;

       (i)   forecast transaction;

       (j)   hedge effectiveness;

       (k)   hedged item;

       (l)   hedging instrument;

       (m)   held-to-maturity investments;

       (n)   loans and receivables;

       (o)   regular way purchase or sale; and

       (p)   transaction costs.

13   In this Standard, 'contract' and 'contractual' refer to an agreement between two or more parties that has clear economic consequences that the parties have little, if any, discretion to avoid, usually because the agreement is enforceable by law. Contracts, and thus financial instruments, may take a variety of forms and need not be in writing.

14   In this Standard, 'entity' includes individuals, partnerships, incorporated bodies, trusts and government agencies.

Presentation

Liabilities and Equity (see also paragraphs AG13-AG14J and AG25-AG29A)

15   **The issuer of a financial instrument shall classify the instrument, or its component parts, on initial recognition as a financial liability, a financial asset or an equity instrument in accordance with the substance of the contractual arrangement and the definitions of a financial liability, a financial asset and an equity instrument.**

16   When an issuer applies the definitions in paragraph 11 to determine whether a financial instrument is an equity instrument rather than a financial liability, the instrument is an equity instrument if, and only if, both conditions (a) and (b) below are met.

       (a)   The instrument includes no contractual obligation:

            (i)   to deliver cash or another financial asset to another entity; or

            (ii)   to exchange financial assets or financial liabilities with another entity under conditions that are potentially unfavourable to the issuer.

(b)   If the instrument will or may be settled in the issuer's own equity instruments, it is:

    (i)   a non-derivative that includes no contractual obligation for the issuer to deliver a variable number of its own equity instruments; or

    (ii)   a derivative that will be settled only by the issuer exchanging a fixed amount of cash or another financial asset for a fixed number of its own equity instruments. For this purpose, rights, options or warrants to acquire a fixed number of the entity's own equity instruments for a fixed amount of any currency are equity instruments if the entity offers the rights, options or warrants pro rata to all of its existing owners of the same class of its own non-derivative equity instruments. Also for these purposes the issuer's own equity instruments do not include instruments that have all the features and meet the conditions described in paragraphs 16A and 16B or paragraphs 16C and 16D, or instruments that are contracts for the future receipt or delivery of the issuer's own equity instruments.

A contractual obligation, including one arising from a derivative financial instrument, that will or may result in the future receipt or delivery of the issuer's own equity instruments, but does not meet conditions (a) and (b) above, is not an equity instrument. As an exception, an instrument that meets the definition of a financial liability is classified as an equity instrument if it has all the features and meets the conditions in paragraphs 16A and 16B or paragraphs 16C and 16D.

Puttable Instruments

16A   A puttable financial instrument includes a contractual obligation for the issuer to repurchase or redeem that instrument for cash or another financial asset on exercise of the put. As an exception to the definition of a financial liability, an instrument that includes such an obligation is classified as an equity instrument if it has all the following features:

(a)   It entitles the holder to a pro rata share of the entity's net assets in the event of the entity's liquidation. The entity's net assets are those assets that remain after deducting all other claims on its assets. A pro rata share is determined by:

    (i)   dividing the entity's net assets on liquidation into units of equal amount; and

    (ii)   multiplying that amount by the number of the units held by the financial instrument holder.

(b)   The instrument is in the class of instruments that is subordinate to all other classes of instruments. To be in such a class the instrument:

    (i)   has no priority over other claims to the assets of the entity on liquidation; and

    (ii)   does not need to be converted into another instrument before it is in the class of instruments that is subordinate to all other classes of instruments.

(c)   All financial instruments in the class of instruments that is subordinate to all other classes of instruments have identical features. For example, they must all be puttable, and the formula or other method used to calculate the repurchase or redemption price is the same for all instruments in that class.

(d)   Apart from the contractual obligation for the issuer to repurchase or redeem the instrument for cash or another financial asset, the instrument does not include any contractual obligation to deliver cash or another financial asset to another entity, or to exchange financial assets or financial liabilities with another entity under conditions that are potentially unfavourable to the entity, and it is not a contract that will or may be settled in the entity's own equity instruments as set out in subparagraph (b) of the definition of a financial liability.

(e)   The total expected cash flows attributable to the instrument over the life of the instrument are based substantially on the profit or loss, the change in the recognised net assets or the change in the fair value of the recognised and unrecognised net assets of the entity over the life of the instrument (excluding any effects of the instrument).

16B   For an instrument to be classified as an equity instrument, in addition to the instrument having all the above features, the issuer must have no other financial instrument or contract that has:

(a)   total cash flows based substantially on the profit or loss, the change in the recognised net assets or the change in the fair value of the recognised and unrecognised net assets of the entity (excluding any effects of such instrument or contract); and

(b)   the effect of substantially restricting or fixing the residual return to the puttable instrument holders.

For the purposes of applying this condition, the entity shall not consider non-financial contracts with a holder of an instrument described in paragraph 16A that have contractual terms and conditions that are similar to the contractual terms and conditions of an equivalent contract that might occur between a non-instrument holder and the issuing entity. If the entity cannot determine that this condition is met, it shall not classify the puttable instrument as an equity instrument.

Instruments, or Components of Instruments, that Impose on the Entity an Obligation to Deliver to Another Party a Pro Rata Share of the Net Assets of the Entity Only on Liquidation

16C   Some financial instruments include a contractual obligation for the issuing entity to deliver to another entity a pro rata share of its net assets only on liquidation. The obligation arises because liquidation either is certain to occur and outside the control of the entity (for example, a limited life entity) or is uncertain to occur but is at the option of the instrument holder. As an exception to the definition of a financial liability, an instrument that includes such an obligation is classified as an equity instrument if it has all the following features:

(a)   It entitles the holder to a pro rata share of the entity's net assets in the event of the entity's liquidation. The entity's net assets are those assets that remain after deducting all other claims on its assets. A pro rata share is determined by:

(i)   dividing the net assets of the entity on liquidation into units of equal amount; and

(ii)   multiplying that amount by the number of the units held by the financial instrument holder.

(b)   The instrument is in the class of instruments that is subordinate to all other classes of instruments. To be in such a class the instrument:

(i)   has no priority over other claims to the assets of the entity on liquidation; and

(ii)   does not need to be converted into another instrument before it is in the class of instruments that is subordinate to all other classes of instruments.

(c)   All financial instruments in the class of instruments that is subordinate to all other classes of instruments must have an identical contractual obligation for the issuing entity to deliver a pro rata share of its net assets on liquidation.

16D   For an instrument to be classified as an equity instrument, in addition to the instrument having all the above features, the issuer must have no other financial instrument or contract that has:

(a)   total cash flows based substantially on the profit or loss, the change in the recognised net assets or the change in the fair value of the recognised and unrecognised net assets of the entity (excluding any effects of such instrument or contract); and

(b)   the effect of substantially restricting or fixing the residual return to the instrument holders.

For the purposes of applying this condition, the entity shall not consider non-financial contracts with a holder of an instrument described in paragraph 16C that have contractual terms and conditions that are similar to the contractual terms and conditions of an equivalent contract that might occur between a non-instrument holder and the issuing entity. If the entity cannot determine that this condition is met, it shall not classify the instrument as an equity instrument.

Reclassification of Puttable Instruments and Instruments that Impose on the Entity an Obligation to Deliver to Another Party a Pro Rata Share of the Net Assets of the Entity Only on Liquidation

16E An entity shall classify a financial instrument as an equity instrument in accordance with paragraphs 16A and 16B or paragraphs 16C and 16D from the date when the instrument has all the features and meets the conditions set out in those paragraphs. An entity shall reclassify a financial instrument from the date when the instrument ceases to have all the features or meet all the conditions set out in those paragraphs. For example, if an entity redeems all its issued non-puttable instruments and any puttable instruments that remain outstanding have all the features and meet all the conditions in paragraphs 16A and 16B, the entity shall reclassify the puttable instruments as equity instruments from the date when it redeems the non-puttable instruments.

16F An entity shall account as follows for the reclassification of an instrument in accordance with paragraph 16E:

(a) It shall reclassify an equity instrument as a financial liability from the date when the instrument ceases to have all the features or meet the conditions in paragraphs 16A and 16B or paragraphs 16C and 16D. The financial liability shall be measured at the instrument's fair value at the date of reclassification. The entity shall recognise in equity any difference between the carrying value of the equity instrument and the fair value of the financial liability at the date of reclassification.

(b) It shall reclassify a financial liability as equity from the date when the instrument has all the features and meets the conditions set out in paragraphs 16A and 16B or paragraphs 16C and 16D. An equity instrument shall be measured at the carrying value of the financial liability at the date of reclassification.

No Contractual Obligation to Deliver Cash or Another Financial Asset (paragraph 16(a))

17 With the exception of the circumstances described in paragraphs 16A and 16B or paragraphs 16C and 16D, a critical feature in differentiating a financial liability from an equity instrument is the existence of a contractual obligation of one party to the financial instrument (the issuer) either to deliver cash or another financial asset to the other party (the holder) or to exchange financial assets or financial liabilities with the holder under conditions that are potentially unfavourable to the issuer. Although the holder of an equity instrument may be entitled to receive a pro rata share of any dividends or other distributions of equity, the issuer does not have a contractual obligation to make such distributions because it cannot be required to deliver cash or another financial asset to another party.

18 The substance of a financial instrument, rather than its legal form, governs its classification in the entity's statement of financial position. Substance and legal form are commonly consistent, but not always. Some financial instruments take the legal form of equity but are liabilities in substance and others may combine features associated with equity instruments and features associated with financial liabilities. For example:

(a) a preference share that provides for mandatory redemption by the issuer for a fixed or determinable amount at a fixed or determinable future date, or gives the holder the right to require the issuer to redeem the instrument at or after a particular date for a fixed or determinable amount, is a financial liability; and

(b) a financial instrument that gives the holder the right to put it back to the issuer for cash or another financial asset (a 'puttable instrument') is a financial liability, except for those instruments classified as equity instruments in accordance with paragraphs 16A and 16B or paragraphs 16C and 16D. The financial instrument is a financial liability even when the amount of cash or other financial assets is determined on the basis of an index or other item that has the potential to increase or decrease. The existence of an option for the holder to put the instrument back to the issuer for cash or another financial asset means that the puttable instrument meets the definition of a financial liability, except for those instruments classified as equity instruments in accordance with paragraphs 16A and 16B or paragraphs 16C and 16D. For example, open-ended mutual funds, unit trusts, partnerships and some co-operative entities may provide their unitholders or members with

AASB 132

a right to redeem their interests in the issuer at any time for cash, which results in the unitholders' or members' interests being classified as financial liabilities, except for those instruments classified as equity instruments in accordance with paragraphs 16A and 16B or paragraphs 16C and 16D. However, classification as a financial liability does not preclude the use of descriptors such as 'net asset value attributable to unitholders' and 'change in net asset value attributable to unitholders' in the financial statements of an entity that has no contributed equity (such as some mutual funds and unit trusts, see Illustrative Example 7) or the use of additional disclosure to show that total members' interests comprise items such as reserves that meet the definition of equity and puttable instruments that do not (see Illustrative Example 8).

19   If an entity does not have an unconditional right to avoid delivering cash or another financial asset to settle a contractual obligation, the obligation meets the definition of a financial liability, except for those instruments classified as equity instruments in accordance with paragraphs 16A and 16B or paragraphs 16C and 16D. For example:

    (a)   a restriction on the ability of an entity to satisfy a contractual obligation, such as lack of access to foreign currency or the need to obtain approval for payment from a regulatory authority, does not negate the entity's contractual obligation or the holder's contractual right under the instrument; and

    (b)   a contractual obligation that is conditional on a counterparty exercising its right to redeem is a financial liability because the entity does not have the unconditional right to avoid delivering cash or another financial asset.

20   A financial instrument that does not explicitly establish a contractual obligation to deliver cash or another financial asset may establish an obligation indirectly through its terms and conditions. For example:

    (a)   a financial instrument may contain a non-financial obligation that must be settled if, and only if, the entity fails to make distributions or to redeem the instrument. If the entity can avoid a transfer of cash or another financial asset only by settling the non-financial obligation, the financial instrument is a financial liability; and

    (b)   a financial instrument is a financial liability if it provides that on settlement the entity will deliver either:

        (i)   cash or another financial asset; or

        (ii)   its own shares whose value is determined to exceed substantially the value of the cash or other financial asset.

    Although the entity does not have an explicit contractual obligation to deliver cash or another financial asset, the value of the share settlement alternative is such that the entity will settle in cash. In any event, the holder has in substance been guaranteed receipt of an amount that is at least equal to the cash settlement option (see paragraph 21).

Settlement in the Entity's Own Equity Instruments (paragraph 16(b))

21   A contract is not an equity instrument solely because it may result in the receipt or delivery of the entity's own equity instruments. An entity may have a contractual right or obligation to receive or deliver a number of its own shares or other equity instruments that varies so that the *fair value* of the entity's own equity instruments to be received or delivered equals the amount of the contractual right or obligation. Such a contractual right or obligation may be for a fixed amount or an amount that fluctuates in part or in full in response to changes in a variable other than the market price of the entity's own equity instruments (e.g. an interest rate, a commodity price or a financial instrument price). Two examples are (a) a contract to deliver as many of the entity's own equity instruments as are equal in value to CU100,[1] and (b) a contract to deliver as many of the entity's own equity instruments as are equal in value to the value of 100 ounces of gold. Such a contract is a financial liability of the entity even though the entity must or can settle it by delivering its own equity instruments. It is not an equity instrument because the entity uses a variable

---

1   In this Standard, monetary amounts are denominated in 'currency units' (CU).

AASB

number of its own equity instruments as a means to settle the contract. Accordingly, the contract does not evidence a residual interest in the entity's assets after deducting all of its liabilities.

22 Except as stated in paragraph 22A, a contract that will be settled by the entity (receiving or) delivering a fixed number of its own equity instruments in exchange for a fixed amount of cash or another financial asset is an equity instrument. For example, an issued share option that gives the counterparty a right to buy a fixed number of the entity's shares for a fixed price or for a fixed stated principal amount of a bond is an equity instrument. Changes in the fair value of a contract arising from variations in market interest rates that do not affect the amount of cash or other financial assets to be paid or received, or the number of equity instruments to be received or delivered, on settlement of the contract do not preclude the contract from being an equity instrument. Any consideration received (such as the premium received for a written option or warrant on the entity's own shares) is added directly to equity. Any consideration paid (such as the premium paid for a purchased option) is deducted directly from equity. Changes in the fair value of an equity instrument are not recognised in the financial statements.

22A If the entity's own equity instruments to be received, or delivered, by the entity upon settlement of a contract are puttable financial instruments with all the features and meeting the conditions described in paragraphs 16A and 16B, or instruments that impose on the entity an obligation to deliver to another party a pro rata share of the net assets of the entity only on liquidation with all the features and meeting the conditions described in paragraphs 16C and 16D, the contract is a financial asset or a financial liability. This includes a contract that will be settled by the entity receiving or delivering a fixed number of such instruments in exchange for a fixed amount of cash or another financial asset.

23 With the exception of the circumstances described in paragraphs 16A and 16B or paragraphs 16C and 16D, a contract that contains an obligation for an entity to purchase its own equity instruments for cash or another financial asset gives rise to a financial liability for the present value of the redemption amount (for example, for the present value of the forward repurchase price, option exercise price or other redemption amount). This is the case even if the contract itself is an equity instrument. One example is an entity's obligation under a forward contract to purchase its own equity instruments for cash. When the financial liability is recognised initially under AASB 139, its fair value (the present value of the redemption amount) is reclassified from equity. Subsequently, the financial liability is measured in accordance with AASB 139. If the contract expires without delivery, the carrying amount of the financial liability is reclassified to equity. An entity's contractual obligation to purchase its own equity instruments gives rise to a financial liability for the present value of the redemption amount even if the obligation to purchase is conditional on the counterparty exercising a right to redeem (e.g. a written put option that gives the counterparty the right to sell an entity's own equity instruments to the entity for a fixed price).

24 A contract that will be settled by the entity delivering or receiving a fixed number of its own equity instruments in exchange for a variable amount of cash or another financial asset is a financial asset or financial liability. An example is a contract for the entity to deliver 100 of its own equity instruments in return for an amount of cash calculated to equal the value of 100 ounces of gold.

Contingent Settlement Provisions

25 A financial instrument may require the entity to deliver cash or another financial asset, or otherwise to settle it in such a way that it would be a financial liability, in the event of the occurrence or non-occurrence of uncertain future events (or on the outcome of uncertain circumstances) that are beyond the control of both the issuer and the holder of the instrument, such as a change in a stock market index, consumer price index, interest rate or taxation requirements, or the issuer's future revenues, net income or debt-to-equity ratio. The issuer of such an instrument does not have the unconditional right to avoid

delivering cash or another financial asset (or otherwise to settle it in such a way that it would be a financial liability). Therefore, it is a financial liability of the issuer unless:

(a)   the part of the contingent settlement provision that could require settlement in cash or another financial asset (or otherwise in such a way that it would be a financial liability) is not genuine;

(b)   the issuer can be required to settle the obligation in cash or another financial asset (or otherwise to settle it in such a way that it would be a financial liability) only in the event of liquidation of the issuer; or

(c)   the instrument has all the features and meets the conditions in paragraphs 16A and 16B.

Settlement Options

26   **When a derivative financial instrument gives one party a choice over how it is settled (e.g. the issuer or the holder can choose settlement net in cash or by exchanging shares for cash), it is a financial asset or a financial liability unless all of the settlement alternatives would result in it being an equity instrument.**

27   An example of a derivative financial instrument with a settlement option that is a financial liability is a share option that the issuer can decide to settle net in cash or by exchanging its own shares for cash. Similarly, some contracts to buy or sell a non-financial item in exchange for the entity's own equity instruments are within the scope of this Standard because they can be settled either by delivery of the non-financial item or net in cash or another financial instrument (see paragraphs 8-10). Such contracts are financial assets or financial liabilities and not equity instruments.

Compound Financial Instruments
(see also paragraphs AG30-AG35 and Illustrative Examples 9-12)

28   **The issuer of a non-derivative financial instrument shall evaluate the terms of the financial instrument to determine whether it contains both a liability and an equity component. Such components shall be classified separately as financial liabilities, financial assets or equity instruments in accordance with paragraph 15.**

29   An entity recognises separately the components of a financial instrument that (a) creates a financial liability of the entity and (b) grants an option to the holder of the instrument to convert it into an equity instrument of the entity. For example, a bond or similar instrument convertible by the holder into a fixed number of ordinary shares of the entity is a compound financial instrument. From the perspective of the entity, such an instrument comprises two components: a financial liability (a contractual arrangement to deliver cash or another financial asset) and an equity instrument (a call option granting the holder the right, for a specified period of time, to convert it into a fixed number of ordinary shares of the entity). The economic effect of issuing such an instrument is substantially the same as issuing simultaneously a debt instrument with an early settlement provision and warrants to purchase ordinary shares, or issuing a debt instrument with detachable share purchase warrants. Accordingly, in all cases, the entity presents the liability and equity components separately in its statement of financial position.

30   Classification of the liability and equity components of a convertible instrument is not revised as a result of a change in the likelihood that a conversion option will be exercised, even when exercise of the option may appear to have become economically advantageous to some holders. Holders may not always act in the way that might be expected because, for example, the tax consequences resulting from conversion may differ among holders. Furthermore, the likelihood of conversion will change from time to time. The entity's contractual obligation to make future payments remains outstanding until it is extinguished through conversion, maturity of the instrument, or some other transaction.

31   AASB 139 deals with the measurement of financial assets and financial liabilities. Equity instruments are instruments that evidence a residual interest in the assets of an entity after deducting all of its liabilities. Therefore, when the initial carrying amount of a compound financial instrument is allocated to its equity and liability components, the equity component is assigned the residual amount after deducting from the fair value of the instrument as a whole the amount separately determined for the liability component.

AASB 132

The value of any derivative features (such as a call option) embedded in the compound financial instrument other than the equity component (such as an equity conversion option) is included in the liability component. The sum of the carrying amounts assigned to the liability and equity components on initial recognition is always equal to the fair value that would be ascribed to the instrument as a whole. No gain or loss arises from initially recognising the components of the instrument separately.

32 Under the approach described in paragraph 31, the issuer of a bond convertible into ordinary shares first determines the carrying amount of the liability component by measuring the fair value of a similar liability (including any embedded non-equity derivative features) that does not have an associated equity component. The carrying amount of the equity instrument represented by the option to convert the instrument into ordinary shares is then determined by deducting the fair value of the financial liability from the fair value of the compound financial instrument as a whole.

Treasury Shares (see also paragraph AG36)

33 **If an entity reacquires its own equity instruments, those instruments ('treasury shares') shall be deducted from equity. No gain or loss shall be recognised in the profit or loss on the purchase, sale, issue or cancellation of an entity's own equity instruments. Such treasury shares may be acquired and held by the entity or by other members of the consolidated group. Consideration paid or received shall be recognised directly in equity.**

34 The amount of treasury shares held is disclosed separately either in the statement of financial position or in the notes, in accordance with AASB 101 *Presentation of Financial Statements*. An entity provides disclosure in accordance with AASB 124 *Related Party Disclosures* if the entity reacquires its own equity instruments from related parties.

Interest, Dividends, Losses and Gains (see also paragraph AG37)

35 **Interest, dividends, losses and gains relating to a financial instrument or a component that is a financial liability shall be recognised as income or expense in profit or loss. Distributions to holders of an equity instrument shall be debited by the entity directly to equity, net of any related income tax benefit. Transaction costs of an equity transaction shall be accounted for as a deduction from equity, net of any related income tax benefit.**

36 The classification of a financial instrument as a financial liability or an equity instrument determines whether interest, dividends, losses and gains relating to that instrument are recognised as income or expense in profit or loss. Thus, dividend payments on shares wholly recognised as liabilities are recognised as expenses in the same way as interest on a bond. Similarly, gains and losses associated with redemptions or refinancings of financial liabilities are recognised in profit or loss, whereas redemptions or refinancings of equity instruments are recognised as changes in equity. Changes in the fair value of an equity instrument are not recognised in the financial statements.

37 An entity typically incurs various costs in issuing or acquiring its own equity instruments. Those costs might include registration and other regulatory fees, amounts paid to legal, accounting and other professional advisers, printing costs and stamp duties. The transaction costs of an equity transaction are accounted for as a deduction from equity (net of any related income tax benefit) to the extent they are incremental costs directly attributable to the equity transaction that otherwise would have been avoided. The costs of an equity transaction that is abandoned are recognised as an expense.

38 Transaction costs that relate to the issue of a compound financial instrument are allocated to the liability and equity components of the instrument in proportion to the allocation of proceeds. Transaction costs that relate jointly to more than one transaction (e.g. costs of a concurrent offering of some shares and a stock exchange listing of other shares) are allocated to those transactions using a basis of allocation that is rational and consistent with similar transactions.

39 The amount of transaction costs accounted for as a deduction from equity in the period is disclosed separately under AASB 101. The related amount of income taxes recognised

directly in equity is included in the aggregate amount of current and deferred income tax credited or charged to equity that is disclosed under AASB 112 *Income Taxes*.

40   Dividends classified as an expense may be presented in the statement(s) of profit or loss and other comprehensive income either with interest on other liabilities or as a separate item. In addition to the requirements of this Standard, disclosure of interest and dividends is subject to the requirements of AASB 101 and AASB 7. In some circumstances, because of the differences between interest and dividends with respect to matters such as tax deductibility, it is desirable to disclose them separately in the statement(s) of profit or loss and other comprehensive income. Disclosures of the tax effects are made in accordance with AASB 112.

41   Gains and losses related to changes in the carrying amount of a financial liability are recognised as income or expense in profit or loss even when they relate to an instrument that includes a right to the residual interest in the assets of the entity in exchange for cash or another financial asset (see paragraph 18(b)). Under AASB 101 the entity presents any gain or loss arising from remeasurement of such an instrument separately in the statement of comprehensive income when it is relevant in explaining the entity's performance.

Offsetting a Financial Asset and a Financial Liability (see also paragraphs AG38 and AG39)

42   **A financial asset and a financial liability shall be offset and the net amount presented in the statement of financial position when, and only when, an entity:**

   (a)   currently has a legally enforceable right to set off the recognised amounts; and

   (b)   intends either to settle on a net basis, or to realise the asset and settle the liability simultaneously.

   In accounting for a transfer of a financial asset that does not qualify for derecognition, the entity shall not offset the transferred asset and the associated liability (see AASB 139, paragraph 36).

43   This Standard requires the presentation of financial assets and financial liabilities on a net basis when doing so reflects an entity's expected future cash flows from settling two or more separate financial instruments. When an entity has the right to receive or pay a single net amount and intends to do so, it has, in effect, only a single financial asset or financial liability. In other circumstances, financial assets and financial liabilities are presented separately from each other consistently with their characteristics as resources or obligations of the entity.

44   Offsetting a recognised financial asset and a recognised financial liability and presenting the net amount differs from the derecognition of a financial asset or a financial liability. Although offsetting does not give rise to recognition of a gain or loss, the derecognition of a financial instrument not only results in the removal of the previously recognised item from the statement of financial position but also may result in recognition of a gain or loss.

45   A right of set-off is a debtor's legal right, by contract or otherwise, to settle or otherwise eliminate all or a portion of an amount due to a creditor by applying against that amount an amount due from the creditor. In unusual circumstances, a debtor may have a legal right to apply an amount due from a third party against the amount due to a creditor provided that there is an agreement between the three parties that clearly establishes the debtor's right of set-off. Because the right of set-off is a legal right, the conditions supporting the right may vary from one legal jurisdiction to another and the laws applicable to the relationships between the parties need to be considered.

46   The existence of an enforceable right to set off a financial asset and a financial liability affects the rights and obligations associated with a financial asset and a financial liability and may affect an entity's exposure to credit and liquidity risk. However, the existence of the right, by itself, is not a sufficient basis for offsetting. In the absence of an intention to exercise the right or to settle simultaneously, the amount and timing of an entity's future cash flows are not affected. When an entity intends to exercise the right or to settle simultaneously, presentation of the asset and liability on a net basis reflects more appropriately the amounts and timing of the expected future cash flows, as well as the risks to which those cash flows are exposed. An intention by one or both parties to settle

on a net basis without the legal right to do so is not sufficient to justify offsetting because the rights and obligations associated with the individual financial asset and financial liability remain unaltered.

47 An entity's intentions with respect to settlement of particular assets and liabilities may be influenced by its normal business practices, the requirements of the financial markets and other circumstances that may limit the ability to settle net or to settle simultaneously. When an entity has a right of set-off, but does not intend to settle net or to realise the asset and settle the liability simultaneously, the effect of the right on the entity's credit risk exposure is disclosed in accordance with paragraph 36 of AASB 7.

48 Simultaneous settlement of two financial instruments may occur through, for example, the operation of a clearing house in an organised financial market or a face-to-face exchange. In these circumstances the cash flows are, in effect, equivalent to a single net amount and there is no exposure to credit or liquidity risk. In other circumstances, an entity may settle two instruments by receiving and paying separate amounts, becoming exposed to credit risk for the full amount of the asset or liquidity risk for the full amount of the liability. Such risk exposures may be significant even though relatively brief. Accordingly, realisation of a financial asset and settlement of a financial liability are treated as simultaneous only when the transactions occur at the same moment.

49 The conditions set out in paragraph 42 are generally not satisfied and offsetting is usually inappropriate when:

(a) several different financial instruments are used to emulate the features of a single financial instrument (a 'synthetic instrument');

(b) financial assets and financial liabilities arise from financial instruments having the same primary risk exposure (e.g. assets and liabilities within a portfolio of forward contracts or other derivative instruments) but involve different counterparties;

(c) financial or other assets are pledged as collateral for non-recourse financial liabilities;

(d) financial assets are set aside in trust by a debtor for the purpose of discharging an obligation without those assets having been accepted by the creditor in settlement of the obligation (e.g. a sinking fund arrangement); or

(e) obligations incurred as a result of events giving rise to losses are expected to be recovered from a third party by virtue of a claim made under an insurance contract.

50 An entity that undertakes a number of financial instrument transactions with a single counterparty may enter into a 'master netting arrangement' with that counterparty. Such an agreement provides for a single net settlement of all financial instruments covered by the agreement in the event of default on, or termination of, any one contract. These arrangements are commonly used by financial institutions to provide protection against loss in the event of bankruptcy or other circumstances that result in a counterparty being unable to meet its obligations. A master netting arrangement commonly creates a right of set-off that becomes enforceable and affects the realisation or settlement of individual financial assets and financial liabilities only following a specified event of default or in other circumstances not expected to arise in the normal course of business. A master netting arrangement does not provide a basis for offsetting unless both of the criteria in paragraph 42 are satisfied. When financial assets and financial liabilities subject to a master netting arrangement are not offset, the effect of the arrangement on an entity's exposure to credit risk is disclosed in accordance with paragraph 36 of AASB 7.

Disclosure

51-95 [Deleted by the IASB]

Effective Date and Transition

96 [Deleted by the AASB]

96A [Deleted by the AASB]

96B AASB 2008-2 *Amendments to Australian Accounting Standards – Puttable Financial Instruments and Obligations arising on Liquidation* introduced a limited scope exception; therefore, an entity shall not apply the exception by analogy.

96C The classification of instruments under this exception shall be restricted to the accounting for such an instrument under AASB 7, AASB 101, AASB 132 and AASB 139. The instrument shall not be considered an equity instrument under other guidance, for example AASB 2.

97 [Deleted by the AASB]

97A [Deleted by the AASB]

97B AASB 2008-3 *Amendments to Australian Accounting Standards arising from AASB 3 and AASB 127* deleted paragraph 4(c). An entity shall apply that amendment for annual reporting periods beginning on or after 1 July 2009. If an entity applies AASB 3 (revised 2008) for an earlier period, the amendment shall also be applied for that earlier period. However, the amendment does not apply to contingent consideration that arose from a business combination for which the acquisition date preceded the application of AASB 3 (revised 2008). Instead, an entity shall account for such consideration in accordance with paragraphs 65A-65E of AASB 3 (as amended in 2010).

97C When applying the amendments made in AASB 2008-2, an entity is required to split a compound financial instrument with an obligation to deliver to another party a pro rata share of the net assets of the entity only on liquidation into separate liability and equity components. If the liability component is no longer outstanding, a retrospective application of those amendments to AASB 132 would involve separating two components of equity. The first component would be in retained earnings and represent the cumulative interest accreted on the liability component. The other component would represent the original equity component. Therefore, an entity need not separate these two components if the liability component is no longer outstanding at the date of application of the amendments.

97D Paragraph 4 was amended by AASB 2008-5 *Amendments to Australian Accounting Standards arising from the Annual Improvements Project* issued in July 2008. An entity shall apply that amendment for annual reporting periods beginning on or after 1 January 2009. Earlier application is permitted. If an entity applies the amendment for an earlier period it shall disclose that fact and apply for that earlier period the amendments to paragraph 3 of AASB 7, paragraph 1 of AASB 128 and paragraph 1 of AASB 131 issued in July 2008. An entity is permitted to apply the amendment prospectively.

97E Paragraphs 11 and 16 were amended by AASB 2009-10 *Amendments to Australian Accounting Standards – Classification of Rights Issues* issued in October 2009. An entity shall apply that amendment for annual reporting periods beginning on or after 1 February 2010. Earlier application is permitted. If an entity applies the amendment for an earlier period, it shall disclose that fact.

97G Paragraph 97B was added by AASB 2010-3 *Amendments to Australian Accounting Standards arising from the Annual Improvements Project* issued in June 2010. An entity shall apply the last two sentences of paragraph 97B for annual reporting periods beginning on or after 1 July 2010. Earlier application is permitted.

97K AASB 2011-9 *Amendments to Australian Accounting Standards – Presentation of Items of Other Comprehensive Income*, issued in September 2011, amended paragraph 40. An entity shall apply that amendment when it applies AASB 101 as amended in September 2011.

Withdrawal of Other Pronouncements

98 [Deleted by the AASB]

99 [Deleted by the AASB]

100 [Deleted by the AASB]

Appendix
Application Guidance

The Appendix is an integral part of AASB 132.

AG1 This Application Guidance explains the application of particular aspects of the Standard.

AG2 The Standard does not deal with the recognition or measurement of financial instruments. Requirements about the recognition and measurement of financial assets and financial liabilities are set out in AASB 139.

Definitions (paragraphs 11-14)

Financial Assets and Financial Liabilities

AG3 Currency (cash) is a financial asset because it represents the medium of exchange and is therefore the basis on which all transactions are measured and recognised in financial statements. A deposit of cash with a bank or similar financial institution is a financial asset because it represents the contractual right of the depositor to obtain cash from the institution or to draw a cheque or similar instrument against the balance in favour of a creditor in payment of a financial liability.

AG4 Common examples of financial assets representing a contractual right to receive cash in the future and corresponding financial liabilities representing a contractual obligation to deliver cash in the future are:

(a) trade accounts receivable and payable;

(b) notes receivable and payable;

(c) loans receivable and payable; and

(d) bonds receivable and payable.

In each case, one party's contractual right to receive (or obligation to pay) cash is matched by the other party's corresponding obligation to pay (or right to receive).

AG5 Another type of financial instrument is one for which the economic benefit to be received or given up is a financial asset other than cash. For example, a note payable in government bonds gives the holder the contractual right to receive and the issuer the contractual obligation to deliver government bonds, not cash. The bonds are financial assets because they represent obligations of the issuing government to pay cash. The note is, therefore, a financial asset of the note holder and a financial liability of the note issuer.

AG6 'Perpetual' debt instruments (such as 'perpetual bonds', debentures and capital notes) normally provide the holder with the contractual right to receive payments on account of interest at fixed dates extending into the indefinite future, either with no right to receive a return of principal or a right to a return of principal under terms that make it very unlikely or very far in the future. For example, an entity may issue a financial instrument requiring it to make annual payments in perpetuity equal to a stated interest rate of 8 per cent applied to a stated par or principal amount of CU1,000.[2] Assuming 8 per cent to be the market rate of interest for the instrument when issued, the issuer assumes a contractual obligation to make a stream of future interest payments having a fair value (present value) of CU1,000 on initial recognition. The holder and issuer of the instrument have a financial asset and a financial liability, respectively.

AG7 A contractual right or contractual obligation to receive, deliver or exchange financial instruments is itself a financial instrument. A chain of contractual rights or contractual obligations meets the definition of a financial instrument if it will ultimately lead to the receipt or payment of cash or to the acquisition or issue of an equity instrument.

---

2 In this guidance, monetary amounts are denominated in 'currency units' (CU).

AG8   The ability to exercise a contractual right or the requirement to satisfy a contractual obligation may be absolute, or it may be contingent on the occurrence of a future event. For example, a financial guarantee is a contractual right of the lender to receive cash from the guarantor, and a corresponding contractual obligation of the guarantor to pay the lender, if the borrower defaults. The contractual right and obligation exist because of a past transaction or event (assumption of the guarantee), even though the lender's ability to exercise its right and the requirement for the guarantor to perform under its obligation are both contingent on a future act of default by the borrower. A contingent right and obligation meet the definition of a financial asset and a financial liability, even though such assets and liabilities are not always recognised in the financial statements. Some of these contingent rights and obligations may be insurance contracts within the scope of AASB 4 *Insurance Contracts*.

AG9   Under AASB 117 *Leases* a finance lease is regarded as primarily an entitlement of the lessor to receive, and an obligation of the lessee to pay, a stream of payments that are substantially the same as blended payments of principal and interest under a loan agreement. The lessor accounts for its investment in the amount receivable under the lease contract rather than the leased asset itself. An operating lease, on the other hand, is regarded as primarily an uncompleted contract committing the lessor to provide the use of an asset in future periods in exchange for consideration similar to a fee for a service. The lessor continues to account for the leased asset itself rather than any amount receivable in the future under the contract. Accordingly, a finance lease is regarded as a financial instrument and an operating lease is not regarded as a financial instrument (except as regards individual payments currently due and payable).

AG10   Physical assets (such as inventories, property, plant and equipment), leased assets, and intangible assets (such as patents and trademarks) are not financial assets. Control of such physical and intangible assets creates an opportunity to generate an inflow of cash or another financial asset, but it does not give rise to a present right to receive cash or another financial asset.

AG11   Assets (such as prepaid expenses) for which the future economic benefit is the receipt of goods or services, rather than the right to receive cash or another financial asset, are not financial assets. Similarly, items such as deferred revenue and most warranty obligations are not financial liabilities because the outflow of economic benefits associated with them is the delivery of goods and services rather than a contractual obligation to pay cash or another financial asset.

AG12   Liabilities or assets that are not contractual (such as income taxes that are created as a result of statutory requirements imposed by governments) are not financial liabilities or financial assets. Accounting for income taxes is dealt with in AASB 112. Similarly, constructive obligations, as defined in AASB 137 *Provisions, Contingent Liabilities and Contingent Assets*, do not arise from contracts and are not financial liabilities.

Equity Instruments

AG13   Examples of equity instruments include non-puttable ordinary shares, some puttable instruments (see paragraphs 16A and 16B), some instruments that impose on the entity an obligation to deliver to another party a pro rata share of the net assets of the entity only on liquidation (see paragraphs 16C and 16D), some types of preference shares (see paragraphs AG25 and AG26), and warrants or written call options that allow the holder to subscribe for or purchase a fixed number of non-puttable ordinary shares in the issuing entity in exchange for a fixed amount of cash or another financial asset. An entity's obligation to issue or purchase a fixed number of its own equity instruments in exchange for a fixed amount of cash or another financial asset is an equity instrument of the entity (except as stated in paragraph 22A). However, if such a contract contains an obligation for the entity to pay cash or another financial asset (other than a contract classified as equity in accordance with paragraphs 16A and 16B or paragraphs 16C and 16D), it also gives rise to a liability for the present value of the redemption amount (see paragraph AG27(a)).

An issuer of non-puttable ordinary shares assumes a liability when it formally acts to make a distribution and becomes legally obliged to the shareholders to do so. This may be the case following the declaration of a dividend or when the entity is being wound up and any assets remaining after the satisfaction of liabilities become distributable to shareholders.

AG14 A purchased call option or other similar contract acquired by an entity that gives it the right to reacquire a fixed number of its own equity instruments in exchange for delivering a fixed amount of cash or another financial asset is not a financial asset of the entity (except as stated in paragraph 22A). Instead, any consideration paid for such a contract is deducted from equity.

The Class of Instruments that is Subordinate to All Other Classes (paragraphs 16A(b) and 16C(b))

AG14A One of the features of paragraphs 16A and 16C is that the financial instrument is in the class of instruments that is subordinate to all other classes.

AG14B When determining whether an instrument is in the subordinate class, an entity evaluates the instrument's claim on liquidation as if it were to liquidate on the date when it classifies the instrument. An entity shall reassess the classification if there is a change in relevant circumstances. For example, if the entity issues or redeems another financial instrument, this may affect whether the instrument in question is in the class of instruments that is subordinate to all other classes.

AG14C An instrument that has a preferential right on liquidation of the entity is not an instrument with an entitlement to a pro rata share of the net assets of the entity. For example, an instrument has a preferential right on liquidation if it entitles the holder to a fixed dividend on liquidation, in addition to a share of the entity's net assets, when other instruments in the subordinate class with a right to a pro rata share of the net assets of the entity do not have the same right on liquidation.

AG14D If an entity has only one class of financial instruments, that class shall be treated as if it were subordinate to all other classes.

Total Expected Cash Flows Attributable to the Instrument over the Life of the Instrument (paragraph 16A(e))

AG14E The total expected cash flows of the instrument over the life of the instrument must be substantially based on the profit or loss, change in the recognised net assets or fair value of the recognised and unrecognised net assets of the entity over the life of the instrument. Profit or loss and the change in the recognised net assets shall be measured in accordance with relevant Australian Accounting Standards.

Transactions Entered into by an Instrument Holder Other than as Owner of the Entity (paragraphs 16A and 16C)

AG14F The holder of a puttable financial instrument or an instrument that imposes on the entity an obligation to deliver to another party a pro rata share of the net assets of the entity only on liquidation may enter into transactions with the entity in a role other than that of an owner. For example, an instrument holder may also be an employee of the entity. Only the cash flows and the contractual terms and conditions of the instrument that relate to the instrument holder as an owner of the entity shall be considered when assessing whether the instrument should be classified as equity under paragraph 16A or paragraph 16C.

AG14G An example is a limited partnership that has limited and general partners. Some general partners may provide a guarantee to the entity and may be remunerated for providing that guarantee. In such situations, the guarantee and the associated cash flows relate to the instrument holders in their role as guarantors and not in their roles as owners of the entity. Therefore, such a guarantee and the associated cash flows would not result in the general partners being considered subordinate to the limited partners, and would be disregarded when assessing whether the contractual terms of the limited partnership instruments and the general partnership instruments are identical.

AG14H   Another example is a profit or loss sharing arrangement that allocates profit or loss to the instrument holders on the basis of services rendered or business generated during the current and previous years. Such arrangements are transactions with instrument holders in their role as non-owners and should not be considered when assessing the features listed in paragraph 16A or paragraph 16C. However, profit or loss sharing arrangements that allocate profit or loss to instrument holders based on the nominal amount of their instruments relative to others in the class represent transactions with the instrument holders in their roles as owners and should be considered when assessing the features listed in paragraph 16A or paragraph 16C.

AG14I   The cash flows and contractual terms and conditions of a transaction between the instrument holder (in the role as a non-owner) and the issuing entity must be similar to an equivalent transaction that might occur between a non-instrument holder and the issuing entity.

No Other Financial Instrument or Contract with Total Cash Flows that Substantially Fixes or Restricts the Residual Return to the Instrument Holder (paragraphs 16B and 16D)

AG14J   A condition for classifying as equity a financial instrument that otherwise meets the criteria in paragraph 16A or paragraph 16C is that the entity has no other financial instrument or contract that has (a) total cash flows based substantially on the profit or loss, the change in the recognised net assets or the change in the fair value of the recognised and unrecognised net assets of the entity and (b) the effect of substantially restricting or fixing the residual return. The following instruments, when entered into on normal commercial terms with unrelated parties, are unlikely to prevent instruments that otherwise meet the criteria in paragraph 16A or paragraph 16C from being classified as equity:

(a)   instruments with total cash flows substantially based on specific assets of the entity;

(b)   instruments with total cash flows based on a percentage of revenue;

(c)   contracts designed to reward individual employees for services rendered to the entity;

(d)   contracts requiring the payment of an insignificant percentage of profit for services rendered or goods provided.

Derivative Financial Instruments

AG15   Financial instruments include primary instruments (such as receivables, payables and equity instruments) and derivative financial instruments (such as financial options, futures and forwards, interest rate swaps and currency swaps). Derivative financial instruments meet the definition of a financial instrument and, accordingly, are within the scope of this Standard.

AG16   Derivative financial instruments create rights and obligations that have the effect of transferring between the parties to the instrument one or more of the financial risks inherent in an underlying primary financial instrument. On inception, derivative financial instruments give one party a contractual right to exchange financial assets or financial liabilities with another party under conditions that are potentially favourable, or a contractual obligation to exchange financial assets or financial liabilities with another party under conditions that are potentially unfavourable. However, they generally do not result in a transfer of the underlying primary financial instrument on inception of the contract, nor does such a transfer necessarily take place on maturity of the contract.[3] Some instruments embody both a right and an obligation to make an exchange. Because the terms of the exchange are determined on inception of the derivative instrument, as prices in financial markets change those terms may become either favourable or unfavourable.

---

3   This is true of most, but not all derivatives, for example, in some cross-currency interest rate swaps principal is exchanged on inception (and re-exchanged on maturity).

AASB

AG17   A put or call option to exchange financial assets or financial liabilities (i.e. financial instruments other than an entity's own equity instruments) gives the holder a right to obtain potential future economic benefits associated with changes in the fair value of the financial instrument underlying the contract. Conversely, the writer of an option assumes an obligation to forgo potential future economic benefits or bear potential losses of economic benefits associated with changes in the fair value of the underlying financial instrument. The contractual right of the holder and obligation of the writer meet the definition of a financial asset and a financial liability, respectively. The financial instrument underlying an option contract may be any financial asset, including shares in other entities and interest bearing instruments. An option may require the writer to issue a debt instrument, rather than transfer a financial asset, but the instrument underlying the option would constitute a financial asset of the holder if the option were exercised. The option-holder's right to exchange the financial asset under potentially favourable conditions and the writer's obligation to exchange the financial asset under potentially unfavourable conditions are distinct from the underlying financial asset to be exchanged upon exercise of the option. The nature of the holder's right and of the writer's obligation are not affected by the likelihood that the option will be exercised.

AG18   Another example of a derivative financial instrument is a forward contract to be settled in six months' time in which one party (the purchaser) promises to deliver CU1,000,000 cash in exchange for CU1,000,000 face amount of fixed rate government bonds, and the other party (the seller) promises to deliver CU1,000,000 face amount of fixed rate government bonds in exchange for CU1,000,000 cash. During the six months, both parties have a contractual right and a contractual obligation to exchange financial instruments. If the market price of the government bonds rises above CU1,000,000, the conditions will be favourable to the purchaser and unfavourable to the seller; if the market price falls below CU1,000,000, the effect will be the opposite. The purchaser has a contractual right (a financial asset) similar to the right under a call option held and a contractual obligation (a financial liability) similar to the obligation under a put option written; the seller has a contractual right (a financial asset) similar to the right under a put option held and a contractual obligation (a financial liability) similar to the obligation under a call option written. As with options, these contractual rights and obligations constitute financial assets and financial liabilities separate and distinct from the underlying financial instruments (the bonds and cash to be exchanged). Both parties to a forward contract have an obligation to perform at the agreed time, whereas performance under an option contract occurs only if and when the holder of the option chooses to exercise it.

AG19   Many other types of derivative instruments embody a right or obligation to make a future exchange, including interest rate and currency swaps, interest rate caps, collars and floors, loan commitments, note issuance facilities and letters of credit. An interest rate swap contract may be viewed as a variation of a forward contract in which the parties agree to make a series of future exchanges of cash amounts, one amount calculated with reference to a floating interest rate and the other with reference to a fixed interest rate. Futures contracts are another variation of forward contracts, differing primarily in that the contracts are standardised and traded on an exchange.

Contracts to Buy or Sell Non-Financial Items (paragraphs 8-10)

AG20   Contracts to buy or sell non-financial items do not meet the definition of a financial instrument because the contractual right of one party to receive a non-financial asset or service and the corresponding obligation of the other party do not establish a present right or obligation of either party to receive, deliver or exchange a financial asset. For example, contracts that provide for settlement only by the receipt or delivery of a non-financial item (e.g. an option, futures or forward contract on silver) are not financial instruments. Many commodity contracts are of this type. Some are standardised in form and traded on organised markets in much the same fashion as some derivative financial instruments. For example, a commodity futures contract may be bought and sold readily for cash because it is listed for trading on an exchange and may change hands many times. However, the parties buying and selling the contract are, in effect, trading the underlying commodity. The ability to buy or sell a commodity contract for cash, the ease with which it may be bought or sold and the possibility of negotiating a cash settlement of the obligation to receive or deliver the commodity do not alter the fundamental character of the contract in a way that creates a financial instrument. Nevertheless, some contracts to buy or sell non-financial items that can be settled net or by exchanging financial instruments, or in which the non-financial item is readily convertible to cash, are within the scope of the Standard as if they were financial instruments (see paragraph 8).

AG21   A contract that involves receipt or delivery of physical assets does not give rise to a financial asset of one party and a financial liability of the other party unless any corresponding payment is deferred past the date on which the physical assets are transferred. Such is the case with the purchase or sale of goods on trade credit.

AG22   Some contracts are commodity-linked, but do not involve settlement through the physical receipt or delivery of a commodity. They specify settlement through cash payments that are determined according to a formula in the contract, rather than through payment of fixed amounts. For example, the principal amount of a bond may be calculated by applying the market price of oil prevailing at the maturity of the bond to a fixed quantity of oil. The principal is indexed by reference to a commodity price, but is settled only in cash. Such a contract constitutes a financial instrument.

AG23   The definition of a financial instrument also encompasses a contract that gives rise to a non-financial asset or non-financial liability in addition to a financial asset or financial liability. Such financial instruments often give one party an option to exchange a financial asset for a non-financial asset. For example, an oil-linked bond may give the holder the right to receive a stream of fixed periodic interest payments and a fixed amount of cash on maturity, with the option to exchange the principal amount for a fixed quantity of oil. The desirability of exercising this option will vary from time to time depending on the fair value of oil relative to the exchange ratio of cash for oil (the exchange price) inherent in the bond. The intentions of the bondholder concerning the exercise of the option do not affect the substance of the component assets. The financial asset of the holder and the financial liability of the issuer make the bond a financial instrument, regardless of the other types of assets and liabilities also created.

AG24   [Deleted by the IASB]

Presentation

Liabilities and Equity (paragraphs 15-27)

No Contractual Obligation to Deliver Cash or Another Financial Asset (paragraphs 17-20)

AG25   Preference shares may be issued with various rights. In determining whether a preference share is a financial liability or an equity instrument, an issuer assesses the particular rights attaching to the share to determine whether it exhibits the fundamental characteristic of a financial liability. For example, a preference share that provides for redemption on a specific date or at the option of the holder contains a financial liability because the issuer has an obligation to transfer financial assets to the holder of the share. The potential inability of an issuer to satisfy an obligation to redeem a preference share when contractually required to do so, whether because of a lack of funds, a statutory restriction or insufficient profits or reserves, does not negate the obligation. An option of the issuer to redeem the shares for cash does not satisfy the definition of a financial liability because the issuer does not have a present obligation to transfer financial assets to the shareholders. In this case, redemption of the shares is solely at the discretion of the issuer. An obligation may arise, however, when the issuer of the shares exercises its option, usually by formally notifying the shareholders of an intention to redeem the shares.

AG26 When preference shares are non-redeemable, the appropriate classification is determined by the other rights that attach to them. Classification is based on an assessment of the substance of the contractual arrangements and the definitions of a financial liability and an equity instrument. When distributions to holders of the preference shares, whether cumulative or non-cumulative, are at the discretion of the issuer, the shares are equity instruments. The classification of a preference share as an equity instrument or a financial liability is not affected by, for example:

(a) a history of making distributions;

(b) an intention to make distributions in the future;

(c) a possible negative impact on the price of ordinary shares of the issuer if distributions are not made (because of restrictions on paying dividends on the ordinary shares if dividends are not paid on the preference shares);

(d) the amount of the issuer's reserves;

(e) an issuer's expectation of a profit or loss for a period; or

(f) an ability or inability of the issuer to influence the amount of its profit or loss for the period.

Settlement in the Entity's Own Equity Instruments (paragraphs 21-24)

AG27 The following examples illustrate how to classify different types of contracts on an entity's own equity instruments.

(a) A contract that will be settled by the entity receiving or delivering a fixed number of its own shares for no future consideration, or exchanging a fixed number of its own shares for a fixed amount of cash or another financial asset, is an equity instrument (except as stated in paragraph 22A). Accordingly, any consideration received or paid for such a contract is added directly to or deducted directly from equity. One example is an issued share option that gives the counterparty a right to buy a fixed number of the entity's shares for a fixed amount of cash. However, if the contract requires the entity to purchase (redeem) its own shares for cash or another financial asset at a fixed or determinable date or on demand, the entity also recognises a financial liability for the present value of the redemption amount (with the exception of instruments that have all the features and meet the conditions in paragraphs 16A and 16B or paragraphs 16C and 16D). One example is an entity's obligation under a forward contract to repurchase a fixed number of its own shares for a fixed amount of cash.

(b) An entity's obligation to purchase its own shares for cash gives rise to a financial liability for the present value of the redemption amount even if the number of shares that the entity is obliged to repurchase is not fixed or if the obligation is conditional on the counterparty exercising a right to redeem (except as stated in paragraphs 16A and 16B or paragraphs 16C and 16D). One example of a conditional obligation is an issued option that requires the entity to repurchase its own shares for cash if the counterparty exercises the option.

(c) A contract that will be settled in cash or another financial asset is a financial asset or financial liability even if the amount of cash or another financial asset that will be received or delivered is based on changes in the market price of the entity's own equity (except as stated in paragraphs 16A and 16B or paragraphs 16C and 16D). One example is a net cash-settled share option.

(d) A contract that will be settled in a variable number of the entity's own shares whose value equals a fixed amount or an amount based on changes in an underlying variable (e.g. a commodity price) is a financial asset or a financial liability. An example is a written option to buy gold that, if exercised, is settled net in the entity's own instruments by the entity delivering as many of those instruments as are equal to the value of the option contract. Such a contract is a financial asset or financial liability even if the underlying variable is the entity's own share price rather than gold. Similarly, a contract that will be settled in a fixed number of the entity's own shares, but the rights attaching to those shares will be varied so that the settlement value equals a fixed amount or an amount based on changes in an underlying variable, is a financial asset or a financial liability.

Contingent Settlement Provisions (paragraph 25)

AG28   Paragraph 25 requires that if a part of a contingent settlement provision that could require settlement in cash or another financial asset (or in another way that would result in the instrument being a financial liability) is not genuine, the settlement provision does not affect the classification of a financial instrument. Thus, a contract that requires settlement in cash or a variable number of the entity's own shares only on the occurrence of an event that is extremely rare, highly abnormal and very unlikely to occur is an equity instrument. Similarly, settlement in a fixed number of an entity's own shares may be contractually precluded in circumstances that are outside the control of the entity, but if these circumstances have no genuine possibility of occurring, classification as an equity instrument is appropriate.

Treatment in Consolidated Financial Statements

AG29   In consolidated financial statements, an entity presents non-controlling interests – that is, the interests of other parties in the equity and income of its subsidiaries – in accordance with AASB 101 and AASB 127. When classifying a financial instrument (or a component of it) in consolidated financial statements, an entity considers all terms and conditions agreed between members of the group and the holders of the instrument in determining whether the group as a whole has an obligation to deliver cash or another financial asset in respect of the instrument or to settle it in a manner that results in liability classification. When a subsidiary in a group issues a financial instrument and a parent or other group entity agrees additional terms directly with the holders of the instrument (e.g. a guarantee), the group may not have discretion over distributions or redemption. Although the subsidiary may appropriately classify the instrument without regard to these additional terms in its individual financial statements, the effect of other agreements between members of the group and the holders of the instrument is considered to ensure that consolidated financial statements reflect the contracts and transactions entered into by the group as a whole. To the extent that there is such an obligation or settlement provision, the instrument (or the component of it that is subject to the obligation) is classified as a financial liability in consolidated financial statements.

AG29A   Some types of instruments that impose a contractual obligation on the entity are classified as equity instruments in accordance with paragraphs 16A and 16B or paragraphs 16C and 16D. Classification in accordance with those paragraphs is an exception to the principles otherwise applied in this Standard to the classification of an instrument. This exception is not extended to the classification of non-controlling interests in the consolidated financial statements. Therefore, instruments classified as equity instruments in accordance with either paragraphs 16A and 16B or paragraphs 16C and 16D in the separate or individual financial statements that are non-controlling interests are classified as liabilities in the consolidated financial statements of the group.

Compound Financial Instruments (paragraphs 28-32)

AG30   Paragraph 28 applies only to issuers of non-derivative compound financial instruments. Paragraph 28 does not deal with compound financial instruments from the perspective of holders. AASB 139 deals with the separation of embedded derivates from the perspective of holders of compound financial instruments that contain debt and equity features.

AG31   A common form of compound financial instrument is a debt instrument with an embedded conversion option, such as a bond convertible into ordinary shares of the issuer, and without any other embedded derivative features. Paragraph 28 requires the issuer of such a financial instrument to present the liability component and the equity component separately in the statement of financial position, as follows.

    (a)   The issuer's obligation to make scheduled payments of interest and principal is a financial liability that exists as long as the instrument is not converted. On initial recognition, the fair value of the liability component is the present value of the contractually determined stream of future cash flows discounted at the rate of interest applied at that time by the market to instruments of comparable credit status and providing substantially the same cash flows, on the same terms, but without the conversion option.

    (b)   The equity instrument is an embedded option to convert the liability into equity of the issuer. The fair value of the option comprises its time value and its intrinsic value, if any. This option has value on initial recognition even when it is out of the money.

AG32   On conversion of a convertible instrument at maturity, the entity derecognises the liability component and recognises it as equity. The original equity component remains as equity (although it may be transferred from one line item within equity to another). There is no gain or loss on conversion at maturity.

AG33   When an entity extinguishes a convertible instrument before maturity through an early redemption or repurchase in which the original conversion privileges are unchanged, the entity allocates the consideration paid and any transaction costs for the repurchase or redemption to the liability and equity components of the instrument at the date of the transaction. The method used in allocating the consideration paid and transaction costs to the separate components is consistent with that used in the original allocation to the separate components of the proceeds received by the entity when the convertible instrument was issued, in accordance with paragraphs 28-32.

AG34   Once the allocation of the consideration is made, any resulting gain or loss is treated in accordance with accounting principles applicable to the related component, as follows:

    (a)   the amount of gain or loss relating to the liability component is recognised in profit or loss; and

    (b)   the amount of consideration relating to the equity component is recognised in equity.

AG35   An entity may amend the terms of a convertible instrument to induce early conversion, for example by offering a more favourable conversion ratio or paying other additional consideration in the event of conversion before a specified date. The difference, at the date the terms are amended, between the fair value of the consideration the holder receives on conversion of the instrument under the revised terms and the fair value of the consideration the holder would have received under the original terms is recognised as a loss in profit or loss.

Treasury Shares (paragraphs 33 and 34)

AG36   An entity's own equity instruments are not recognised as a financial asset regardless of the reason for which they are reacquired. Paragraph 33 requires an entity that reacquires its own equity instruments to deduct those equity instruments from equity. However, when an entity holds its own equity on behalf of others, for example, a financial institution holding its own equity on behalf of a client, there is an agency relationship and as a result those holdings are not included in the entity's statement of financial position.

Interest, Dividends, Losses and Gains (paragraphs 35-41)

AG37   The following example illustrates the application of paragraph 35 to a compound instrument. Assume that a non-cumulative preference share is mandatorily redeemable for cash in five years, but that dividends are payable at the discretion of the entity before the redemption date. Such an instrument is a compound financial instrument, with the liability component being the present value of the redemption amount. The unwinding of the discount on this component is recognised in profit or loss and classified as interest expense. Any dividends paid relate to the equity component and, accordingly, are recognised as a distribution of profit or loss. A similar treatment would apply if the redemption was not mandatory but at the option of the holder, or if the share was mandatorily convertible into a variable number of ordinary shares calculated to equal a fixed amount or an amount based on changes in an underlying variable (e.g. commodity). However, if any unpaid dividends are added to the redemption amount, the entire instrument is a liability. In such a case, any dividends are classified as interest expense.

Offsetting a Financial Asset and a Financial Liability (paragraphs 42-50)

AG38   To offset a financial asset and a financial liability, an entity must have a currently enforceable legal right to set off the recognised amounts. An entity may have a conditional right to set off recognised amounts, such as in a master netting agreement or in some forms of non-recourse debt, but such rights are enforceable only on the occurrence of some future event, usually a default of the counterparty. Thus, such an arrangement does not meet the conditions for offset.

AG39   The Standard does not provide special treatment for so-called 'synthetic instruments', which are groups of separate financial instruments acquired and held to emulate the characteristics of another instrument. For example, a floating rate long-term debt combined with an interest rate swap that involves receiving floating payments and making fixed payments synthesises a fixed rate long-term debt. Each of the individual financial instruments that together constitute a synthetic instrument represents a contractual right or obligation with its own terms and conditions and each may be transferred or settled separately. Each financial instrument is exposed to risks that may differ from the risks to which other financial instruments are exposed. Accordingly, when one financial instrument in a synthetic instrument is an asset and another is a liability, they are not offset and presented in an entity's statement of financial position on a net basis unless they meet the criteria for offsetting in paragraph 42.

Disclosure

Financial Assets and Financial Liabilities at Fair Value Through Profit or Loss (paragraph 94(f))

AG40   [Deleted by the IASB]

Illustrative Examples

Contents

Paragraphs

Accounting for Contracts on Equity Instruments of an Entity IE1

Example 1: Forward to buy shares IE2 – IE6

Example 2: Forward to sell shares IE7 – IE11

Example 3: Purchased call option on shares IE12 – IE16

Example 4: Written call option on shares IE17 – IE21

Example 5: Purchased put option on shares IE22 – IE26

Example 6: Written put option on shares IE27 – IE31

Entities such as Mutual Funds and Co-operatives whose Share Capital is not Equity as Defined in AASB 132

Example 7: Entities with no equity IE32

Example 8: Entities with some equity IE33

Accounting for Compound Financial Instruments

Example 9: Separation of a compound financial instrument on initial recognition IE34 – IE36

Example 10: Separation of a compound financial instrument with multiple embedded derivative features IE37 – IE38

Example 11: Repurchase of a convertible instrument IE39 – IE46

Example 12: Amendment of the terms of a convertible instrument to induce early conversion IE47 – IE50

Illustrative Examples

The examples accompany, but are not part of, AASB 132.

Accounting for Contracts on Equity Instruments of an Entity

IE1 The following examples[1] illustrate the application of paragraphs 15-27 and AASB 139 to the accounting for contracts on an entity's own equity instruments (other than the financial instruments specified in paragraphs 16A and 16B or paragraphs 16C and 16D).

Example 1: Forward to buy shares

IE2 This example illustrates the journal entries for forward purchase contracts on an entity's own shares that will be settled (a) net in cash, (b) net in shares or (c) by delivering cash in exchange for shares. It also discusses the effect of settlement options (see (d) below). To simplify the illustration, it is assumed that no dividends are paid on the underlying shares (i.e. the 'carry return' is zero) so that the present value of the forward price equals the spot price when the fair value of the forward contract is zero. The fair value of the forward has been computed as the difference between the market share price and the present value of the fixed forward price.

---

1 In these examples, monetary amounts are denominated in 'currency units' (CU).

Assumptions:

Contract date	1 February 2002
Maturity date	31 January 2003
Market price per share on 1 February 2002	CU100
Market price per share on 31 December 2002	CU110
Market price per share on 31 January 2003	CU106
Fixed forward price to be paid on 31 January 2003	CU104
Present value of forward price on 1 February 2002	CU100
Number of shares under forward contract	1,000
Fair value of forward on 1 February 2002	CU0
Fair value of forward on 31 December 2002	CU6,300
Fair value of forward on 31 January 2003	CU2,000

(a)   Cash for cash ('net cash settlement')

IE3   In this subsection, the forward purchase contract on the entity's own shares will be settled net in cash, that is, there is no receipt or delivery of the entity's own shares upon settlement of the forward contract.

On 1 February 2002, Entity A enters into a contract with Entity B to receive the fair value of 1,000 of Entity A's own outstanding ordinary shares as of 31 January 2003 in exchange for a payment of CU104,000 in cash (i.e. CU104 per share) on 31 January 2003. The contract will be settled net in cash. Entity A records the following journal entries.

1 February 2002

The price per share when the contract is agreed on 1 February 2002 is CU100. The initial fair value of the forward contract on 1 February 2002 is zero.

No entry is required because the fair value of the derivative is zero and no cash is paid or received.

31 December 2002

On 31 December 2002, the market price per share has increased to CU110 and, as a result, the fair value of the forward contract has increased to CU6,300.

Dr	Forward asset	CU6,300
Cr	Gain	CU6,300

To record the increase in the fair value of the forward contract.

31 January 2003

On 31 January 2003, the market price per share has decreased to CU106. The fair value of the forward contract is CU2,000 ([CU106 × 1,000] – CU104,000).

On the same day, the contract is settled net in cash. Entity A has an obligation to deliver CU104,000 to Entity B and Entity B has an obligation to deliver CU106,000 (CU106 × 1,000) to Entity A, so Entity B pays the net amount of CU2,000 to Entity A.

Dr	Loss	CU4,300
Cr	Forward asset	CU4,300

To record the decrease in the fair value of the forward contract
(i.e. CU4,300 = CU6,300 – CU2,000).

| Dr | Cash | CU2,000 | |
| Cr | Forward asset | | CU2,000 |

To record the settlement of the forward contract.

(b) Shares for shares ('net share settlement')

IE4 Assume the same facts as in (a) except that settlement will be made net in shares instead of net in cash. Entity A's journal entries are the same as those shown in (a) above, except for recording the settlement of the forward contract, as follows:

31 January 2003

The contract is settled net in shares. Entity A has an obligation to deliver CU104,000 (CU104 × 1,000) worth of its shares to Entity B and Entity B has an obligation to deliver CU106,000 (CU106 × 1,000) worth of shares to Entity A. Thus, Entity B delivers a net amount of CU2,000 (CU106,000 – CU104,000) worth of shares to Entity A, that is, 18.9 shares (CU2,000 ÷ CU106).

| Dr | Equity | CU2,000 | |
| Cr | Forward asset | | CU2,000 |

To record the settlement of the forward contract.

(c) Cash for shares ('gross physical settlement')

IE5 Assume the same facts as in (a) except that settlement will be made by delivering a fixed amount of cash and receiving a fixed number of Entity A's shares. Similarly to (a) and (b) above, the price per share that Entity A will pay in one year is fixed at CU104. Accordingly, Entity A has an obligation to pay CU104,000 in cash to Entity B (CU104 × 1,000) and Entity B has an obligation to deliver 1,000 of Entity A's outstanding shares to Entity A in one year. Entity A records the following journal entries.

1 February 2002

| Dr | Equity | CU100,000 | |
| Cr | Liability | | CU100,000 |

To record the obligation to deliver CU104,000 in one year at its present value of CU100,000 discounted using an appropriate interest rate (see AASB 139, paragraph AG64).

31 December 2002

| Dr | Interest expense | CU3,660 | |
| Cr | Liability | | CU3,660 |

To accrue interest in accordance with the effective interest method on the liability for the share redemption amount.

31 January 2003

| Dr | Interest expense | CU340 | |
| Cr | Liability | | CU340 |

To accrue interest in accordance with the effective interest method on the liability for the share redemption amount.

Entity A delivers CU104,000 in cash to Entity B and Entity B delivers 1,000 of Entity A's shares to Entity A.

| Dr | Liability | CU104,000 | |
| Cr | Cash | | CU104,000 |

To record the settlement of the obligation to redeem Entity A's own shares for cash.

(d)   Settlement options

IE6   The existence of settlement options (such as net in cash, net in shares or by an exchange of cash and shares) has the result that the forward repurchase contract is a financial asset or a financial liability. If one of the settlement alternatives is to exchange cash for shares ((c) above), Entity A recognises a liability for the obligation to deliver cash, as illustrated in (c) above. Otherwise, Entity A accounts for the forward contract as a derivative.

Example 2: Forward to sell shares

IE7   This example illustrates the journal entries for forward sale contracts on an entity's own shares that will be settled (a) net in cash, (b) net in shares or (c) by receiving cash in exchange for shares. It also discusses the effect of settlement options (see (d) below). To simplify the illustration, it is assumed that no dividends are paid on the underlying shares (*i.e.* the 'carry return' is zero) so that the present value of the forward price equals the spot price when the fair value of the forward contract is zero. The fair value of the forward has been computed as the difference between the market share price and the present value of the fixed forward price.

Assumptions:

Contract date	1 February 2002
Maturity date	31 January 2003
Market price per share on 1 February 2002	CU100
Market price per share on 31 December 2002	CU110
Market price per share on 31 January 2003	CU106
Fixed forward price to be received on 31 January 2003	CU104
Present value of forward price on 1 February 2002	CU100
Number of shares under forward contract	1,000
Fair value of forward on 1 February 2002	CU0
Fair value of forward on 31 December 2002	CU(6,300)
Fair value of forward on 31 January 2003	CU(2,000)

(a)   Cash for cash ('net cash settlement')

IE8   On 1 February 2002, Entity A enters into a contract with Entity B to pay the fair value of 1,000 of Entity A's own outstanding ordinary shares as of 31 January 2003 in exchange for CU104,000 in cash (*i.e.* CU104 per share) on 31 January 2003. The contract will be settled net in cash. Entity A records the following journal entries.

1 February 2002

No entry is required because the fair value of the derivative is zero and no cash is paid or received.

31 December 2002

Dr	Loss	CU6,300	
Cr	Forward liability		CU6,300

To record the decrease in the fair value of the forward contract.

31 January 2003

Dr	Forward liability	CU4,300	
Cr	Gain		CU4,300

To record the increase in the fair value of the forward contract
(i.e. CU4,300 = CU6,300 – CU2,000).

The contract is settled net in cash. Entity B has an obligation to deliver CU104,000 to Entity A, and Entity A has an obligation to deliver CU106,000 (CU106 × 1,000) to Entity B. Thus, Entity A pays the net amount of CU2,000 to Entity B.

Dr	Forward liability	CU2,000	
Cr	Cash		CU2,000

To record the settlement of the forward contract.

(b) Shares for shares ('net share settlement')

IE9   Assume the same facts as in (a) except that settlement will be made net in shares instead of net in cash. Entity A's journal entries are the same as those shown in (a), except:

31 January 2003

The contract is settled net in shares. Entity A has a right to receive CU104,000 (CU104 × 1,000) worth of its shares and an obligation to deliver CU106,000 (CU106 × 1,000) worth of its shares to Entity A. Thus, Entity A delivers a net amount of CU2,000 (CU106,000 – CU104,000) worth of its shares to Entity B, that is, 18.9 shares (CU2,000 ÷ CU106).

Dr	Forward liability	CU2,000	
Cr	Equity		CU2,000

To record the settlement of the forward contract. The issue of the entity's own shares is treated as an equity transaction.

(c) Shares for cash ('gross physical settlement')

IE10   Assume the same facts as in (a), except that settlement will be made by receiving a fixed amount of cash and delivering a fixed number of the entity's own shares. Similarly to (a) and (b) above, the price per share that Entity A will receive in one year is fixed at CU104. Accordingly, Entity A has a right to receive CU104,000 in cash (CU104 × 1,000) and an obligation to deliver 1,000 of its own shares in one year. Entity A records the following journal entries.

1 February 2002

No entry is made on 1 February. No cash is paid or received because the forward has an initial fair value of zero. A forward contract to deliver a fixed number of Entity A's own shares in exchange for a fixed amount of cash or another financial asset meets the definition of an equity instrument because it cannot be settled otherwise than through the delivery of shares in exchange for cash.

31 December 2002

No entry is made on 31 December because no cash is paid or received and a contract to deliver a fixed number of Entity A's own shares in exchange for a fixed amount of cash meets the definition of an equity instrument of the entity.

31 January 2003

On 31 January 2003, Entity A receives CU104,000 in cash and delivers 1,000 shares.

Dr	Cash	CU104,000	
Cr	Equity		CU104,000

To record the settlement of the forward contract.

(d) Settlement options

IE11   The existence of settlement options (such as net in cash, net in shares or by an exchange of cash and shares) has the result that the forward contract is a financial asset or a financial liability. It does not meet the definition of an equity instrument because it can be settled otherwise than by Entity A repurchasing a fixed number of its own shares in exchange for paying a fixed amount of cash or another financial asset. Entity A recognises a derivative asset or liability, as illustrated in (a) and (b) above. The accounting entry to be made on settlement depends on how the contract is actually settled.

Example 3: Purchased call option on shares

IE12 This example illustrates the journal entries for a purchased call option right on the entity's own shares that will be settled (a) net in cash, (b) net in shares or (c) by delivering cash in exchange for the entity's own shares. It also discusses the effect of settlement options (see (d) below):

Assumptions:

Contract date	1 February 2002
Exercise date	31 January 2003
	(European terms, i.e. it can be exercised only at maturity)
Exercise right holder	Reporting entity (Entity A)
Market price per share on 1 February 2002	CU100
Market price per share on 31 December 2002	CU104
Market price per share on 31 January 2003	CU104
Fixed exercise price to be paid on 31 January 2003	CU102
Number of shares under option contract	1,000
Fair value of option on 1 February 2002	CU5,000
Fair value of option on 31 December 2002	CU3,000
Fair value of option on 31 January 2003	CU2,000

(a)   Cash for cash ('net cash settlement')

IE13 On 1 February 2002, Entity A enters into a contract with Entity B that gives Entity B the obligation to deliver, and Entity A the right to receive the fair value of 1,000 of Entity A's own ordinary shares as of 31 January 2003 in exchange for CU102,000 in cash (i.e. CU102 per share) on 31 January 2003, if Entity A exercises that right. The contract will be settled net in cash. If Entity A does not exercise its right, no payment will be made. Entity A records the following journal entries.

1 February 2002

The price per share when the contract is agreed on 1 February 2002 is CU100. The initial fair value of the option contract on 1 February 2002 is CU5,000, which Entity A pays to Entity B in cash on that date. On that date, the option has no intrinsic value, only time value, because the exercise price of CU102 exceeds the market price per share of CU100 and it would therefore not be economic for Entity A to exercise the option. In other words, the call option is out of the money.

Dr	Call option asset	CU5,000
Cr	Cash	CU5,000

To recognise the purchased call option.

31 December 2002

On 31 December 2002, the market price per share has increased to CU104. The fair value of the call option has decreased to CU3,000, of which CU2,000 is intrinsic value ([CU104 – CU102] × 1,000), and CU1,000 is the remaining time value.

Dr	Loss	CU2,000
Cr	Call option asset	CU2,000

To record the decrease in the fair value of the call option.

31 January 2003

On 31 January 2003, the market price per share is still CU104. The fair value of the call option has decreased to CU2,000, which is all intrinsic value ([CU104 – CU102] × 1,000) because no time value remains.

Dr	Loss	CU1,000	
Cr	Call option asset		CU1,000

To record the decrease in the fair value of the call option.

On the same day, Entity A exercises the call option and the contract is settled net in cash. Entity B has an obligation to deliver CU104,000 (CU104 × 1,000) to Entity A in exchange for U102,000 (CU102 × 1,000) from Entity A, so Entity A receives a net amount of CU2,000.

Dr	Cash	CU2,000	
Cr	Call option asset		CU2,000

To record the settlement of the option contract.

(b)   Shares for shares ('net share settlement')

IE14   Assume the same facts as in (a) except that settlement will be made net in shares instead of net in cash. Entity A's journal entries are the same as those shown in (a) except for recording the settlement of the option contract as follows:

31 January 2003

Entity A exercises the call option and the contract is settled net in shares. Entity B has an obligation to deliver CU104,000 (CU104 × 1,000) worth of Entity A's shares to Entity A in exchange for CU102,000 (CU102 × 1,000) worth of Entity A's shares. Thus, Entity B delivers the net amount of CU2,000 worth of shares to Entity A, that is, 19.2 shares (CU2,000 ÷ CU104).

Dr	Equity	CU2,000	
Cr	Call option asset		CU2,000

To record the settlement of the option contract. The settlement is accounted for as a treasury share transaction (i.e. no gain or loss).

(c)   Cash for shares ('gross physical settlement')

IE15   Assume the same facts as in (a) except that settlement will be made by receiving a fixed number of shares and paying a fixed amount of cash, if Entity A exercises the option. Similarly to (a) and (b) above, the exercise price per share is fixed at CU102. Accordingly, Entity A has a right to receive 1,000 of Entity A's own outstanding shares in exchange for CU102,000 (CU102 × 1,000) in cash, if Entity A exercises its option. Entity A records the following journal entries.

1 February 2002

Dr	Equity	CU5,000	
Cr	Cash		CU5,000

To record the cash paid in exchange for the right to receive Entity A's own shares in one year for a fixed price. The premium paid is recognised in equity.

31 December 2002

No entry is made on 31 December because no cash is paid or received and a contract that gives a right to receive a fixed number of Entity A's own shares in exchange for a fixed amount of cash meets the definition of an equity instrument of the entity.

31 January 2003

Entity A exercises the call option and the contract is settled gross. Entity B has an obligation to deliver 1,000 of Entity A's shares in exchange for CU102,000 in cash.

Dr	Equity	CU102,000	
Cr	Cash		CU102,000

To record the settlement of the option contract.

(d)   Settlement options

IE16   The existence of settlement options (such as net in cash, net in shares or by an exchange of cash and shares) has the result that the call option is a financial asset. It does not meet the definition of an equity instrument because it can be settled otherwise than by Entity A repurchasing a fixed number of its own shares in exchange for paying a fixed amount of cash or another financial asset. Entity A recognises a derivative asset, as illustrated in (a) and (b) above. The accounting entry to be made on settlement depends on how the contract is actually settled.

Example 4: Written call option on shares

IE17   This example illustrates the journal entries for a written call option obligation on the entity's own shares that will be settled (a) net in cash, (b) net in shares or (c) by delivering cash in exchange for shares. It also discusses the effect of settlement options (see (d) below).

Assumptions:

Contract date	1 February 2002
Exercise date	31 January 2003 (European terms, i.e. it can be exercised only at maturity)
Exercise right holder	Counterparty (Entity B)
Market price per share on 1 February 2002	CU100
Market price per share on 31 December 2002	CU104
Market price per share on 31 January 2003	CU104
Fixed exercise price to be received on 31 January 2003	CU102
Number of shares under option contract	1,000
Fair value of option on 1 February 2002	CU5,000
Fair value of option on 31 December 2002	CU3,000
Fair value of option on 31 January 2003	CU2,000

(a)   Cash for cash ('net cash settlement')

IE18   Assume the same facts as in Example 3(a) above except that Entity A has written a call option on its own shares instead of having purchased a call option on them. Accordingly, on 1 February 2002 Entity A enters into a contract with Entity B that gives Entity B the right to receive and Entity A the obligation to pay the fair value of 1,000 of Entity A's own ordinary shares as of 31 January 2003 in exchange for CU102,000 in cash (i.e. CU102 per share) on 31 January 2003, if Entity B exercises that right. The contract will be settled net in cash. If Entity B does not exercise its right, no payment will be made. Entity A records the following journal entries.

1 February 2002

Dr	Cash	CU5,000	
Cr	Call option obligation		CU5,000

To recognise the written call option.

31 December 2002

| Dr | Call option obligation | CU2,000 | |
| Cr | Gain | | CU2,000 |

To record the decrease in the fair value of the call option.

31 January 2003

| Dr | Call option obligation | CU1,000 | |
| Cr | Gain | | CU1,000 |

To record the decrease in the fair value of the option.

On the same day, Entity B exercises the call option and the contract is settled net in cash. Entity A has an obligation to deliver CU104,000 (CU104 × 1,000) to Entity B in exchange for CU102,000 (CU102 × 1,000) from Entity B, so Entity A pays a net amount of CU2,000.

| Dr | Call option obligation | CU2,000 | |
| Cr | Cash | | CU2,000 |

To record the settlement of the option contract.

(b)   Shares for shares ('net share settlement')

IE19   Assume the same facts as in (a) except that settlement will be made net in shares instead of net in cash. Entity A's journal entries are the same as those shown in (a), except for recording the settlement of the option contract, as follows:

31 January 2003

Entity B exercises the call option and the contract is settled net in shares. Entity A has an obligation to deliver CU104,000 (CU104 × 1,000) worth of Entity A's shares to Entity B in exchange for CU102,000 (CU102 × 1,000) worth of Entity A's shares. Thus, Entity A delivers the net amount of CU2,000 worth of shares to Entity B, that is, 19.2 shares (CU2,000 ÷ CU104).

| Dr | Call option obligation | CU2,000 | |
| Cr | Equity | | CU2,000 |

To record the settlement of the option contract. The settlement is accounted for as an equity transaction.

(c)   Cash for shares ('gross physical settlement')

IE20   Assume the same facts as in (a) except that settlement will be made by delivering a fixed number of shares and receiving a fixed amount of cash, if Entity B exercises the option. Similarly to (a) and (b) above, the exercise price per share is fixed at CU102. Accordingly, Entity B has a right to receive 1,000 of Entity A's own outstanding shares in exchange for CU102,000 (CU102 × 1,000) in cash, if Entity B exercises its option. Entity A records the following journal entries.

1 February 2002

| Dr | Cash | CU5,000 | |
| Cr | Equity | | CU5,000 |

To record the cash received in exchange for the obligation to deliver a fixed number of Entity A's own shares in one year for a fixed price. The premium received is recognised in equity. Upon exercise, the call would result in the issue of a fixed number of shares in exchange for a fixed amount of cash.

31 December 2002

No entry is made on 31 December because no cash is paid or received and a contract to deliver a fixed number of Entity A's own shares in exchange for a fixed amount of cash meets the definition of an equity instrument of the entity.

31 January 2003

Entity B exercises the call option and the contract is settled gross. Entity A has an obligation to deliver 1,000 shares in exchange for CU102,000 in cash.

Dr	Cash	CU102,000	
Cr	Equity		CU102,000

To record the settlement of the option contract.

(d) Settlement options

IE21 The existence of settlement options (such as net in cash, net in shares or by an exchange of cash and shares) has the result that the call option is a financial liability. It does not meet the definition of an equity instrument because it can be settled otherwise than by Entity A issuing a fixed number of its own shares in exchange for receiving a fixed amount of cash or another financial asset. Entity A recognises a derivative liability, as illustrated in (a) and (b) above. The accounting entry to be made on settlement depends on how the contract is actually settled.

Example 5: Purchased put option on shares

IE22 This example illustrates the journal entries for a purchased put option on the entity's own shares that will be settled (a) net in cash, (b) net in shares or (c) by delivering cash in exchange for shares. It also discusses the effect of settlement options (see (d) below).

Assumptions:

Contract date	1 February 2002
Exercise date	31 January 2003 (European terms, i.e. it can be exercised only at maturity)
Exercise right holder	Reporting entity (Entity A)
Market price per share on 1 February 2002	CU100
Market price per share on 31 December 2002	CU95
Market price per share on 31 January 2003	CU95
Fixed exercise price to be received on 31 January 2003	CU98
Number of shares under option contract	1,000
Fair value of option on 1 February 2002	CU5,000
Fair value of option on 31 December 2002	CU4,000
Fair value of option on 31 January 2003	CU3,000

(a) Cash for cash ('net cash settlement')

IE23 On 1 February 2002, Entity A enters into a contract with Entity B that gives Entity A the right to sell, and Entity B the obligation to buy the fair value of 1,000 of Entity A's own outstanding ordinary shares as of 31 January 2003 at a strike price of CU98,000 (i.e. CU98 per share) on 31 January 2003, if Entity A exercises that right. The contract will be settled net in cash. If Entity A does not exercise its right, no payment will be made. Entity A records the following journal entries.

1 February 2002

The price per share when the contract is agreed on 1 February 2002 is CU100. The initial fair value of the option contract on 1 February 2002 is CU5,000, which Entity A pays to Entity B in cash on that date. On that date, the option has no intrinsic value, only time value, because the exercise price of CU98 is less than the market price per share of CU100. Therefore it would not be economic for Entity A to exercise the option. In other words, the put option is out of the money.

Dr	Put option asset	CU5,000	
Cr	Cash		CU5,000

To recognise the purchased put option.

31 December 2002

On 31 December 2002 the market price per share has decreased to CU95. The fair value of the put option has decreased to CU4,000, of which CU3,000 is intrinsic value ([CU98 – CU95] × 1,000) and CU1,000 is the remaining time value.

Dr	Loss	CU1,000	
Cr	Put option asset		CU1,000

To record the decrease in the fair value of the put option.

31 January 2003

On 31 January 2003 the market price per share is still CU95. The fair value of the put option has decreased to CU3,000, which is all intrinsic value ([CU98 – CU95] × 1,000) because no time value remains.

Dr	Loss	CU1,000	
Cr	Put option asset		CU1,000

To record the decrease in the fair value of the option.

On the same day, Entity A exercises the put option and the contract is settled net in cash. Entity B has an obligation to deliver CU98,000 to Entity A and Entity A has an obligation to deliver CU95,000 (CU95 × 1,000) to Entity B, so Entity B pays the net amount of CU3,000 to Entity A.

Dr	Cash	CU3,000	
Cr	Put option asset		CU3,000

To record the settlement of the option contract.

(b) Shares for shares ('net share settlement')

IE24 Assume the same facts as in (a) except that settlement will be made net in shares instead of net in cash. Entity A's journal entries are the same as shown in (a), except:

31 January 2003

Entity A exercises the put option and the contract is settled net in shares. In effect, Entity B has an obligation to deliver CU98,000 worth of Entity A's shares to Entity A, and Entity A has an obligation to deliver CU95,000 worth of Entity A's shares (CU95 × 1,000) to Entity B, so Entity B delivers the net amount of CU3,000 worth of shares to Entity A, that is, 31.6 shares (CU3,000 ÷ CU95).

Dr	Equity	CU3,000	
Cr	Put option asset		CU3,000

To record the settlement of the option contract.

(c) Cash for shares ('gross physical settlement')

IE25 Assume the same facts as in (a) except that settlement will be made by receiving a fixed amount of cash and delivering a fixed number of Entity A's shares, if Entity A exercises the option. Similarly to (a) and (b) above, the exercise price per share is fixed at CU98. Accordingly, Entity B has an obligation to pay CU98,000 in cash to Entity A (CU98 × 1,000) in exchange for 1,000 of Entity A's outstanding shares, if Entity A exercises its option. Entity A records the following journal entries.

1 February 2002

| Dr | Equity | CU5,000 | |
| Cr | Cash | | CU5,000 |

To record the cash received in exchange for the right to deliver Entity A's own shares in one year for a fixed price. The premium paid is recognised directly in equity. Upon exercise, it results in the issue of a fixed number of shares in exchange for a fixed price.

31 December 2002

No entry is made on 31 December because no cash is paid or received and a contract to deliver a fixed number of Entity A's own shares in exchange for a fixed amount of cash meets the definition of an equity instrument of Entity A.

31 January 2003

Entity A exercises the put option and the contract is settled gross. Entity B has an obligation to deliver CU98,000 in cash to Entity A in exchange for 1,000 shares.

| Dr | Cash | CU98,000 | |
| Cr | Equity | | CU98,000 |

To record the settlement of the option contract.

(d)   *Settlement options*

IE26   The existence of settlement options (such as net in cash, net in shares or by an exchange of cash and shares) has the result that the put option is a financial asset. It does not meet the definition of an equity instrument because it can be settled otherwise than by Entity A issuing a fixed number of its own shares in exchange for receiving a fixed amount of cash or another financial asset. Entity A recognises a derivative asset, as illustrated in (a) and (b) above. The accounting entry to be made on settlement depends on how the contract is actually settled.

Example 6: Written put option on shares

IE27   This example illustrates the journal entries for a written put option on the entity's own shares that will be settled (a) net in cash, (b) net in shares or (c) by delivering cash in exchange for shares. It also discusses the effect of settlement options (see (d) below).

Assumptions:

Contract date	1 February 2002
Exercise date	31 January 2003 (European terms, i.e. it can be exercised only at maturity)
Exercise right holder	Counterparty (Entity B)
Market price per share on 1 February 2002	CU100
Market price per share on 31 December 2002	CU95
Market price per share on 31 January 2003	CU95
Fixed exercise price to be paid on 31 January 2003	CU98
Present value of exercise price on 1 February 2002	CU95
Number of shares under option contract	1,000
Fair value of option on 1 February 2002	CU5,000
Fair value of option on 31 December 2002	CU4,000
Fair value of option on 31 January 2003	CU3,000

(a)   *Cash for cash ('net cash settlement')*

IE28   Assume the same facts as in Example 5(a) above, except that Entity A has written a put option on its own shares instead of having purchased a put option on its own shares.

Accordingly, on 1 February 2002, Entity A enters into a contract with Entity B that gives Entity B the right to receive and Entity A the obligation to pay the fair value of 1,000 of Entity A's outstanding ordinary shares as of 31 January 2003 in exchange for CU98,000 in cash (i.e. CU98 per share) on 31 January 2003, if Entity B exercises that right. The contract will be settled net in cash. If Entity B does not exercise its right, no payment will be made. Entity A records the following journal entries.

1 February 2002

Dr	Cash	CU5,000	
Cr	Put option liability		CU5,000

To recognise the written put option.

31 December 2002

Dr	Put option liability	CU1,000	
Cr	Gain		CU1,000

To record the decrease in the fair value of the put option.

31 January 2003

Dr	Put option liability	CU1,000	
Cr	Gain		CU1,000

To record the decrease in the fair value of the put option.

On the same day, Entity B exercises the put option and the contract is settled net in cash. Entity A has an obligation to deliver CU98,000 to Entity B, and Entity B has an obligation to deliver CU95,000 (CU95 × 1,000) to Entity A. Thus, Entity A pays the net amount of CU3,000 to Entity B.

Dr	Put option liability	CU3,000	
Cr	Cash		CU3,000

To record the settlement of the option contract.

(b)   Shares for shares ('net share settlement')

IE29   Assume the same facts as in (a) except that settlement will be made net in shares instead of net in cash. Entity A's journal entries are the same as those in (a), except for the following:

31 January 2003

Entity B exercises the put option and the contract is settled net in shares. In effect, Entity A has an obligation to deliver CU98,000 worth of shares to Entity B, and Entity B has an obligation to deliver CU95,000 worth of Entity A's shares (CU95 x 1,000) to Entity A. Thus, Entity A delivers the net amount of CU3,000 worth of Entity A's shares to Entity B, that is, 31.6 shares (3,000 ÷ 95).

Dr	Put option liability	CU3,000	
Cr	Equity		CU3,000

To record the settlement of the option contract. The issue of Entity A's own shares is accounted for as an equity transaction.

(c)   Cash for shares ('gross physical settlement')

IE30   Assume the same facts as in (a) except that settlement will be made by delivering a fixed amount of cash and receiving a fixed number of shares, if Entity B exercises the option. Similarly to (a) and (b) above, the exercise price per share is fixed at CU98. Accordingly, Entity A has an obligation to pay CU98,000 in cash to Entity B (CU98 × 1,000) in exchange for 1,000 of Entity A's outstanding shares, if Entity B exercises its option. Entity A records the following journal entries.

1 February 2002

| Dr | Cash | CU5,000 | |
| Cr | Equity | | CU5,000 |

To recognise the option premium received of CU5,000 in equity.

| Dr | Equity | CU95,000 | |
| Cr | Liability | | CU95,000 |

To recognise the present value of the obligation to deliver CU98,000 in one year, that is, CU95,000, as a liability.

31 December 2002

| Dr | Interest expense | CU2,750 | |
| Cr | Liability | | CU2,750 |

To accrue interest in accordance with the effective interest method on the liability for the share redemption amount.

31 January 2003

| Dr | Interest expense | CU250 | |
| Cr | Liability | | CU250 |

To accrue interest in accordance with the effective interest method on the liability for the share redemption amount.

On the same day, Entity B exercises the put option and the contract is settled gross. Entity A has an obligation to deliver CU98,000 in cash to Entity B in exchange for CU95,000 worth of shares (CU95 × 1,000).

| Dr | Liability | CU98,000 | |
| Cr | Cash | | CU98,000 |

To record the settlement of the option contract.

(d)   **Settlement options**

IE31   The existence of settlement options (such as net in cash, net in shares or by an exchange of cash and shares) has the result that the written put option is a financial liability. If one of the settlement alternatives is to exchange cash for shares ((c) above), Entity A recognises a liability for the obligation to deliver cash, as illustrated in (c) above. Otherwise, Entity A accounts for the put option as a derivative liability.

Entities such as Mutual Funds and Co-operatives whose Share Capital is not Equity as Defined in AASB 132

Example 7: Entities with no equity

IE32   The following example illustrates a format of a statement of comprehensive income and statement of financial position that may be used by entities such as mutual funds that do not have equity as defined in AASB 132. Other formats are possible.

Statement of comprehensive income for the year ended 31 December 20x1

	20x1	20x0
	CU	CU
Revenue	2,956	1,718
Expenses (classified by nature or function)	(644)	(614)
Profit from operating activities	2,312	1,104
Finance costs – other finance costs	(47)	(47)
– distributions to unitholders	(50)	(50)
Change in net assets attributable to unitholders	2,215	1,007

Statement of financial position at 31 December 20x1

	20x1		20x0	
	CU	CU	CU	CU
Assets				
Non-current assets				
(classified in accordance with AASB 101				
Presentation of Financial Statements)	91,374		78,484	
Total non-current assets		91,374		78,484
Current assets				
(classified in accordance with AASB 101)	1,422		1,769	
Total current assets		1,422		1,769
Total assets		92,796		80,253
Liabilities				
Current liabilities				
(classified in accordance with AASB 101)	647		66	
Total current liabilities		(647)		(66)
Non-current liabilities excluding				
net assets attributable to unitholders				
(classified in accordance with AASB 101)	280		136	
		(280)		(136)
Net assets attributable to unitholders		91,869		80,051

Example 8: Entities with some equity

IE33 The following example illustrates a format of a statement of comprehensive income and statement of financial position that may be used by entities whose share capital is not equity as defined in AASB 132 because the entity has an obligation to repay the share capital on demand but does not have all the features or meet the conditions in paragraphs 16A and 16B or paragraphs 16C and 16D. Other formats are possible.

Statement of comprehensive income for the year ended 31 December 20x1

	20x1	20x0
	CU	CU
Revenue	472	498
Expenses (classified by nature or function)	(367)	(396)
Profit from operating activities	105	102
Finance costs – other finance costs	(4)	(4)
– distributions to members	(50)	(50)
Change in net assets attributable to members	51	48

Statement of financial position at 31 December 20x1

	20x1		20x0	
	CU	CU	CU	CU
Assets				
Non-current assets				
(classified in accordance with AASB 101)	908		830	
Total non-current assets		908		830
Current assets (classified in accordance with				
AASB 101)	383		350	
Total current assets		383		350
Total assets		1,291		1,180

	20x1		20x0
	CU	CU	CU	CU

Liabilities

Current liabilities (classified in accordance with AASB 101)	372		338	
Share capital repayable on demand	202		161	
Total current liabilities		(574)		(499)
Total assets less current liabilities		717		681
Non-current liabilities (classified in accordance with AASB 101)	187		196	
		187		196
Other Components of Equity²				
Reserves for example, revaluation surplus, retained earnings etc	530		485	
		530		485
		717		681
Memorandum Note – Total Members' Interests				
Share capital repayable on demand		202		161
Reserves		530		485
		732		646

Accounting for Compound Financial Instruments

Example 9: Separation of a compound financial instrument on initial recognition

IE34 Paragraph 28 describes how the components of a compound financial instrument are separated by the entity on initial recognition. The following example illustrates how such a separation is made.

IE35 An entity issues 2,000 convertible bonds at the start of year 1. The bonds have a three-year term, and are issued at par with a face value of CU1,000 per bond, giving total proceeds of CU2,000,000. Interest is payable annually in arrears at a nominal annual interest rate of 6 per cent. Each bond is convertible at any time up to maturity into 250 ordinary shares. When the bonds are issued, the prevailing market interest rate for similar debt without conversion options is 9 per cent.

IE36 The liability component is measured first, and the difference between the proceeds of the bond issue and the fair value of the liability is assigned to the equity component. The present value of the liability component is calculated using a discount rate of 9 per cent, the market interest rate for similar bonds having no conversion rights, as shown below.

	CU
Present value of the principal – CU2,000,000 payable at the end of three years	1,544,367
Present value of the interest – CU120,000 payable annually in arrears for three years	303,755
Total liability component	1,848,122
Equity component (by deduction)	151,878
Proceeds of the bond issue	2,000,000

---

2   In this example, the entity has no obligation to deliver a share of its reserves to its members.

Example 10: Separation of a compound financial instrument with multiple embedded derivative features

IE37 The following example illustrates the application of paragraph 31 to the separation of the liability and equity components of a compound financial instrument with multiple embedded derivative features.

IE38 Assume that the proceeds received on the issue of a callable convertible bond are CU60. The value of a similar bond without a call or equity conversion option is CU57. Based on an option pricing model, it is determined that the value to the entity of the embedded call feature in a similar bond without an equity conversion option is CU2. In this case, the value allocated to the liability component under paragraph 31 is CU55 (CU57 – CU2) and the value allocated to the equity component is CU5 (CU60 – CU55).

Example 11: Repurchase of a convertible instrument

IE39 The following example illustrates how an entity accounts for a repurchase of a convertible instrument. For simplicity, at inception, the face amount of the instrument is assumed to be equal to the aggregate carrying amount of its liability and equity components in the financial statements, *that is,* no original issue premium or discount exists. Also, for simplicity, tax considerations have been omitted from the example.

IE40 On 1 January 1999, Entity A issued a 10 per cent convertible debenture with a face value of CU1,000 maturing on 31 December 2008. The debenture is convertible into ordinary shares of Entity A at a conversion price of CU25 per share. Interest is payable half-yearly in cash. At the date of issue, Entity A could have issued nonconvertible debt with a ten-year term bearing a coupon interest rate of 11 per cent.

IE41 In the financial statements of Entity A the carrying amount of the debenture was allocated on issue as follows:

	CU
Liability component	
Present value of 20 half-yearly interest payments of CU50, discounted at 11%	597
Present value of CU1,000 due in 10 years, discounted at 11%, compounded half-yearly	343
	940
Equity component	
(difference between CU1,000 total proceeds and CU940 allocated above)	60
Total proceeds	1,000

IE42 On 1 January 2004, the convertible debenture has a fair value of CU1,700.

IE43 Entity A makes a tender offer to the holder of the debenture to repurchase the debenture for CU1,700, which the holder accepts. At the date of repurchase, Entity A could have issued non-convertible debt with a five-year term bearing a coupon interest rate of 8 per cent.

IE44 The repurchase price is allocated as follows:

	Carrying Value	Fair Value	Difference
Liability component:	**CU**	**CU**	**CU**
Present value of 10 remaining half-yearly interest payments of CU50, discounted at 11% and 8%, respectively	377	405	
Present value of CU1,000 due in 5 years, discounted at 11% and 8%, compounded half-yearly, respectively	585	676	
	962	1,081	(119)

	Carrying Value	Fair Value	Difference
Equity component	60	619[3]	(559)
Total	1,022	1,700	(678)

IE45   Entity A recognises the repurchase of the debenture as follows:

Dr	Liability component	CU962	
Dr	Debt settlement expense (profit or loss)	CU119	
Cr	Cash		CU1,081

To recognise the repurchase of the liability component.

Dr	Equity	CU619	
Cr	Cash		CU619

To recognise the cash paid for the equity component.

IE46   The equity component remains as equity, but may be transferred from one line item within equity to another.

Example 12: Amendment of the terms of a convertible instrument to induce early conversion

IE47   The following example illustrates how an entity accounts for the additional consideration paid when the terms of a convertible instrument are amended to induce early conversion.

IE48   On 1 January 1999, Entity A issued a 10 per cent convertible debenture with a face value of CU1,000 with the same terms as described in Example 11. On 1 January 2000, to induce the holder to convert the convertible debenture promptly, Entity A reduces the conversion price to CU20 if the debenture is converted before 1 March 2000 (i.e. within 60 days).

IE49   Assume the market price of Entity A's ordinary shares on the date the terms are amended is CU40 per share. The fair value of the incremental consideration paid by Entity A is calculated as follows:

*Number of ordinary shares to be issued to debenture holders under **amended** conversion terms:*

Face amount	CU1,000
New conversion price	/CU20 per share
Number of ordinary shares to be issued on conversion	50 shares

*Number of ordinary shares to be issued to debenture holders under **original** conversion terms:*

Face amount	CU1,000
Original conversion price	/CU25 per share
Number of ordinary shares issued upon conversion	40 shares

*Number of **incremental** ordinary shares issued upon conversion* — 10 shares

Value of incremental ordinary shares issued upon conversion

CU40 per share × 10 incremental shares	CU400

IE50   The incremental consideration of CU400 is recognised as a loss in profit or loss.

---

3   This amount represents the differences between the fair value amount allocated to the liability component and the repurchase price of CU1,700.

AASB 133
Earnings per Share

(Compiled June 2012)

Note from the Institute of Chartered Accountants Australia

This note, prepared by the technical editors, is not part of the Accounting Standard AASB 133.

Historical development

15 July 2004: AASB 133 'Earnings Per Share' is the Australian equivalent of IAS 33 of the same name. It was made by the AASB on 15 July 2004 as part of the AASB's program to adopt International Financial Reporting Standards (IFRSs) by 2005.

5 September 2005: AASB 2005-10 'Amendments to Australian Accounting Standards' amends paragraph 72. The Standard is applicable to annual reporting periods beginning on or after 1 January 2007, with early adoption permitted for annual reporting periods beginning on or after 1 January 2005.

8 September 2005: AASB 2005-11 'Amendments to Australian Accounting Standards' amends paragraphs 24 and 25, and is applicable to annual reporting periods ending on or after 31 December 2005. Early adoption of the Standard is permitted for annual reporting periods beginning on or after 1 January 2005.

30 April 2007: AASB 2007-4 'Amendments to Australian Accounting Standards' amends paragraphs Aus 1.1, 53, 68, 73 and Examples 8 and 12, and deletes paragraphs Aus 63.1-Aus 63.5 and Aus 70.1. It is applicable for annual reporting periods beginning on or after 1 July 2007. Entities may elect to early-adopt it to annual reporting periods beginning on or after 1 January 2005.

24 September 2007: AASB 2007-8 'Amendments to Australian Accounting Standards arising from AASB 101' amends AASB 133 to align with revised AASB 101. This Standard is applicable to annual reporting periods beginning on or after 1 January 2009.

13 December 2007: AASB 2007-10 'Further Amendments to Australian Accounting Standards arising from AASB 101' amends AASB 133, replacing the term 'financial report' with 'financial statements'. This Standard is applicable to annual reporting periods beginning on or after 1 January 2009.

6 March 2008: AASB 2008-3 'Amendments to Australian Accounting Standards arising from AASB 3 and AASB 127' amends AASB 133 for the issue of AASB 3 Revised. This Standard is applicable to annual reporting periods beginning on or after 1 July 2009.

25 June 2009: AASB 2009-6 'Amendments to Australian Accounting Standards' amends AASB 133 for editorial corrections made by the International Accounting Standards Board (IASB) to its Standards and Interpretations (IFRSs) and as a consequence of issuing revised AASB 101 'Presentation of Financial Statements'. This Standard is applicable to annual reporting periods beginning on or after 1 January 2009 that end on or after 30 June 2009.

2 November 2009: AASB 133 was reissued by the AASB, compiled to include the AASB 2007-8, AASB 2007-10, AASB 2008-3 and AASB 2009-6 amendments and applies to annual reporting periods beginning on or after 1 July 2009. Early application is permitted.

On the same date the AASB reissued the version of AASB 133 applicable to annual reporting periods beginning on or after 1 January 2009 but before 1 July 2009. This version of AASB 133 has been compiled for the amending Standards applying to annual reporting periods beginning on or after 1 January 2009. This Standard applies to 31 December 2009 year ends and can be accessed from the AASB website at www.aasb.gov.au.

15 December 2009: AASB 2009-12 'Amendments to Australian Accounting Standards' amends AASB 133 for editorial corrections. This Standard is applicable to annual reporting periods beginning on or after 1 January 2011 with early adoption permitted.

---

27 October 2010: AASB 2010-5 'Further Amendments to Australian Accounting Standards' makes editorial amendments to AASB 133. This Standard is applicable to annual reporting periods beginning on or after 1 January 2011.

26 November 2010: AASB 133 was reissued by the AASB, compiled to include the AASB 2009-12 and AASB 2010-5 amendments and applies to annual reporting periods ending on or after 1 January 2011 but before 1 July 2013.

29 August 2011: AASB 2011-7 'Amendments to Australian Accounting Standards arising from the Consolidation and Joint Arrangements Standards' amends AASB 133 to give effect to many consequential changes arising from the issue of AASB 10, 11, 12, 127 and 128. This Standard applies to annual reporting periods beginning on or after 1 January 2013 and can be adopted early by for-profit entities. **These amendments are not included in this compiled Standard.**

5 September 2011: AASB 2011-8 'Amendments to Australian Accounting Standards arising from AASB 13' amends AASB 133 to give effect to a consequential change in the definition of fair value arising from the issue of AASB 13. This Standard applies to annual reporting periods beginning on or after 1 January 2013 and can be adopted early. **These amendments are not included in this compiled Standard.**

5 September 2011: AASB 2011-9 'Amendments to Australian Accounting Standards – Presentation of Items of Other Comprehensive income' amends the presentation of items in other comprehensive income. This Standard applies to annual reporting periods beginning on or after 1 July 2012 and can be adopted early.

20 June 2012: AASB 133 was reissued by the AASB, compiled to include the AASB 2011-9 amendments and applies to annual reporting periods beginning on or after 1 July 2012 but before 1 January 2013. It can be adopted early.

AASB 133 compared to IAS 33

Additions

Paragraph	Description
Aus 1.1	Which entities AASB 133 applies to (i.e. reporting entities required to prepare Corporations Act financial reports that have listed ordinary shares or that are in the process of listing and any entity that voluntarily discloses earning per share).
Aus 1.2	The application date of AASB 133 (i.e. annual reporting periods beginning 1 January 2005).
Aus 1.3	Prohibits early application of AASB 133.
Aus 1.4	Makes the requirements of AASB 133 subject to AASB 1031 'Materiality'.
Aus 1.5	Explains which Australian Standards have been superseded by AASB 133.
Aus 1.6	Clarifies that the relief available to disclosing entities other than companies in relation to earning per share disclosures is also superseded by AASB 133.
Aus 1.7	Clarifies that the superseded Australian Standards remain in force until AASB 133 applies.
Aus 1.8	Notice of the new Standard published on 22 July 2004.

Deletions

Paragraph	Description
2	Scope paragraph of IAS 33 applies the Standard to entities' ordinary shares or potential ordinary shares that are publicly traded or in the process of becoming so.
74, 74A	Effective date of IAS 33.
75	Reference to superseded IAS 33.
76	Reference to superseded SIC Interpretations – SIC 24 'Earnings Per Share – Financial Instruments and Other Contracts that May Be Settled in Shares'.

Contents

Compilation Details

Comparison with IAS 33

Accounting Standard
AASB 133 Earnings per Share

	Paragraphs
Objective	1
Application	Aus1.1 – Aus1.8
Scope	3 – 4A
Definitions	5 – 8
Measurement	
Basic Earnings per Share	9 – 11
Earnings	12 – 18
Shares	19 – 29
Diluted Earnings per Share	30 – 32
Earnings	33 – 35
Shares	36 – 40
Dilutive Potential Ordinary Shares	41 – 44
Options, warrants and their equivalents	45 – 48
Convertible instruments	49 – 51
Contingently issuable shares	52 – 57
Contracts that may be settled in ordinary shares or cash	58 – 61
Purchased options	62
Written put options	63
Retrospective Adjustments	64 – 65
Presentation	66 – 69
Disclosure	70 – 73A
Effective Date of IAS 33	74D

Appendix: Application Guidance

Illustrative Examples

Basis for Conclusions on IAS 33
(available on the AASB website)

> Australian Accounting Standard AASB 133 *Earnings per Share* (as amended) is set out in paragraphs 1 – 74D and the Appendix. All the paragraphs have equal authority. Paragraphs in **bold type** state the main principles. Terms defined in this Standard are in *italics* the first time they appear in the Standard. AASB 133 is to be read in the context of other Australian Accounting Standards, including AASB 1048 *Interpretation of Standards*, which identifies the Australian Accounting Interpretations. In the absence of explicit guidance, AASB 108 *Accounting Policies, Changes in Accounting Estimates and Errors* provides a basis for selecting and applying accounting policies.

Compilation Details

Accounting Standard AASB 133 *Earnings per Share* as amended

This compiled Standard applies to annual reporting periods beginning on or after 1 July 2012 but before 1 January 2013. It takes into account amendments up to and including 5 September 2011 and was prepared on 20 June 2012 by the staff of the Australian Accounting Standards Board (AASB).

This compilation is not a separate Accounting Standard made by the AASB. Instead, it is a representation of AASB 133 (July 2004) as amended by other Accounting Standards, which are listed in the Table below.

Table of Standards

Standard	Date made	Application date (*annual reporting periods ... on or after ...*)	Application, saving or transitional provisions
AASB 133	15 Jul 2004	(*beginning*) 1 Jan 2005	
AASB 2005-10	5 Sep 2005	(*beginning*) 1 Jan 2007	see (a) below
AASB 2005-11	8 Sep 2005	(*ending*) 31 Dec 2005	see (b) below
AASB 2007-4	30 Apr 2007	(*beginning*) 1 Jul 2007	see (c) below
AASB 2007-8	24 Sep 2007	(*beginning*) 1 Jan 2009	see (d) below
AASB 2007-10	13 Dec 2007	(*beginning*) 1 Jan 2009	see (d) below
AASB 2008-3	6 Mar 2008	(*beginning*) 1 Jul 2009	see (e) below
AASB 2009-6	25 Jun 2009	(*beginning*) 1 Jan 2009 and (*ending*) 30 Jun 2009	see (f) below
AASB 2009-12	15 Dec 2009	(*beginning*) 1 Jan 2011	see (g) below
AASB 2010-2	30 Jun 2010	(*beginning*) 1 Jul 2013	not compiled*
AASB 2010-5	27 Oct 2010	(*beginning*) 1 Jan 2011	see (g) below
AASB 2011-7	29 Aug 2011	(beginning) 1 Jan 2013	not compiled*
AASB 2011-8	2 Sep 2011	(beginning) 1 Jan 2013	not compiled*
AASB 2011-9	5 Sep 2011	(beginning) 1 Jul 2012	see (h) below

* The amendments made by this Standard are not included in this compilation, which presents the principal Standard as applicable to annual reporting periods beginning on or after 1 July 2012 but before 1 January 2013.

(a) Entities may elect to apply this Standard to annual reporting periods beginning on or after 1 January 2005 but before 1 January 2007.

(b) Entities may elect to apply this Standard to annual reporting periods beginning on or after 1 January 2005 that end before 31 December 2005.

(c) Entities may elect to apply this Standard to annual reporting periods beginning on or after 1 January 2005 but before 1 July 2007.

(d) Entities may elect to apply this Standard to annual reporting periods beginning on or after 1 January 2005 but before 1 January 2009, provided that AASB 101 *Presentation of Financial Statements* (September 2007) is also applied to such periods.

(e) Entities may elect to apply this Standard to annual reporting periods beginning on or after 30 June 2007 but before 1 July 2009, provided that AASB 3 *Business Combinations* (March 2008) and AASB 127 *Consolidated and Separate Financial Statements* (March 2008) are also applied to such periods.

(f) Entities may elect to apply this Standard to annual reporting periods beginning on or after 1 January 2005 but before 1 January 2009, provided that AASB 101 *Presentation of Financial Statements* (September 2007) is also applied to such periods, and to annual reporting periods beginning on or after 1 January 2009 that end before 30 June 2009.

(g) Entities may elect to apply this Standard to annual reporting periods beginning on or after 1 January 2005 but before 1 January 2011.

(h) Entities may elect to apply this Standard to annual reporting periods beginning on or after 1 January 2005 but before 1 July 2012.

Table of Amendments to Standard

Paragraph affected	How affected	By … [paragraph]
Aus1.1	amended	AASB 2007-4 [90]
Aus1.4	amended	AASB 2007-8 [8]
4	amended	AASB 2007-8 [99]
4A	added	AASB 2007-8 [100]
	amended	AASB 2011-9 [22]
13	amended	AASB 2007-8 [101]
22	amended	AASB 2007-8 [6]
	amended	AASB 2008-3 [57]
24	amended	AASB 2005-11 [13]
25	deleted	AASB 2005-11 [13]
63	amended	AASB 2007-4 [92]
Aus63.1-Aus63.5	deleted	AASB 2007-4 [91]
64	amended	AASB 2007-8 [6]
	amended	AASB 2007-10 [75]
	amended	AASB 2009-12 [16]
66	amended	AASB 2007-8 [6]
67	amended	AASB 2007-8 [6, 102]
67A	added	AASB 2007-8 [103]
	amended	AASB 2009-6 [73]
	amended	AASB 2011-9 [22]
68	amended	AASB 2007-4 [92]
	amended	AASB 2007-8 [6]
68A	added	AASB 2009-6 [74]
	amended	AASB 2011-9 [22]
70	amended	AASB 2007-8 [6]
	amended	AASB 2009-12 [16]
Aus70.1	deleted	AASB 2007-4 [91]
71	amended	AASB 2007-8 [6]
	amended	AASB 2009-12 [16]
72	amended	AASB 2005-10 [29]
73	amended	AASB 2007-4 [92]
	amended	AASB 2007-8 [6]
73A	added	AASB 2007-8 [103]
	amended	AASB 2011-9 [22]
74A	note added	AASB 2007-8 [103]
74D	added	AASB 2011-9 [22]
Appendix, A1	amended	AASB 2008-3 [8]

Table of Amendments to Illustrative Examples

Paragraph affected	How affected	By … [paragraph]
Example 4	amended	AASB 2007-8 [6]
Example 8	amended	AASB 2007-4 [92]
Example 12	amended	AASB 2007-4 [92]
	amended	AASB 2007-8 [6]
	amended	AASB 2009-6 [75]
	amended	AASB 2010-5 [42]

General Terminology Amendments

References to 'equity holders' were amended to 'owners' by AASB 2007-8. References to 'owners' were amended back to 'equity holders' by AASB 2009-6. These amendments are not shown in the above Tables of Amendments.

Comparison with IAS 33

AASB 133 and IAS 33

AASB 133 *Earnings per Share* as amended incorporates IAS 33 *Earnings per Share* as issued and amended by the International Accounting Standards Board (IASB). Paragraphs that have been added to this Standard (and do not appear in the text of IAS 33) are identified with the prefix "Aus", followed by the number of the preceding IASB paragraph and decimal numbering.

Compliance with IAS 33

Entities that comply with AASB 133 as amended will simultaneously be in compliance with IAS 33 as amended.

Accounting Standard AASB 133

The Australian Accounting Standards Board made Accounting Standard AASB 133 *Earnings per Share* under section 334 of the *Corporations Act 2001* on 15 July 2004.

This compiled version of AASB 133 applies to annual reporting periods beginning on or after 1 July 2012 but before 1 January 2013. It incorporates relevant amendments contained in other AASB Standards made by the AASB up to and including 5 September 2011 (see Compilation Details).

Accounting Standard AASB 133

Earnings per Share

Objective

1   The objective of this Standard is to prescribe principles for the determination and presentation of earnings per share, so as to improve performance comparisons between different entities in the same reporting period and between different reporting periods for the same entity. Even though earnings per share data have limitations because of the different accounting policies that may be used for determining 'earnings', a consistently determined denominator enhances financial reporting. The focus of this Standard is on the denominator of the earnings per share calculation.

Application

Aus1.1   **This Standard applies to each entity that is required to prepare financial reports in accordance with Part 2M.3 of the Corporations Act and that is:**

        (a)   a reporting entity whose *ordinary shares* or *potential ordinary shares* are publicly traded; or

        (b)   a reporting entity that is in the process of issuing ordinary shares or potential ordinary shares in public markets; or

        (c)   an entity that discloses earnings per share.

Aus1.2   **This Standard applies to annual reporting periods beginning on or after 1 January 2005.**

        [Note: For application dates of paragraphs changed or added by an amending Standard, see Compilation Details.]

Aus1.3   **This Standard shall not be applied to annual reporting periods beginning before 1 January 2005.**

Aus1.4   **The requirements specified in this Standard apply to the financial statements where information resulting from their application is material in accordance with AASB 1031** *Materiality.*

Aus1.5   **When applicable, this Standard supersedes AASB 1027** *Earnings per Share* **as notified in the** *Commonwealth of Australia Gazette***, No S 236, 29 June 2001.**

Aus1.6   When applicable, this Standard also supersedes the relief provided in paragraph 10 of AASB 1030 *Application of Accounting Standards to Financial Year Accounts and Consolidated Accounts of Disclosing Entities other than Companies* in respect of disclosing entities other than:

(a)   companies; and

(b)   other bodies corporate;

listed on the Australian Stock Exchange.

Aus1.7   AASB 1027 remains applicable until superseded by this Standard.

Aus1.8   Notice of this Standard was published in the *Commonwealth of Australia Gazette* No S 294, 22 July 2004.

Scope

2   [Deleted by the AASB]

3   **An entity that discloses earnings per share shall calculate and disclose earnings per share in accordance with this Standard.**

4   **When an entity presents both consolidated financial statements and separate financial statements prepared in accordance with AASB 127** *Consolidated and Separate Financial Statements***, the disclosures required by this Standard need be presented only on the basis of the consolidated information. An entity that chooses to disclose earnings per share based on its separate financial statements shall present such earnings per share information only in its statement of comprehensive income. An entity shall not present such earnings per share information in the consolidated financial statements.**

4A   **If an entity presents items of profit or loss in a separate statement as described in paragraph 10A of AASB 101** *Presentation of Financial Statements* **(as amended in 2011), it presents earnings per share only in that separate statement.**

Definitions

5   **The following terms are used in this Standard with the meanings specified.**

Antidilution **is an increase in earnings per share or a reduction in loss per share resulting from the assumption that convertible instruments are converted, that options or warrants are exercised, or that ordinary shares are issued upon the satisfaction of specified conditions.**

Contingently issuable ordinary **shares are ordinary shares issuable for little or no cash or other consideration upon the satisfaction of specified conditions in a contingent share agreement.**

A *contingent share agreement* **is an agreement to issue shares that is dependent on the satisfaction of specified conditions.**

Dilution **is a reduction in earnings per share or an increase in loss per share resulting from the assumption that convertible instruments are converted, that options or warrants are exercised, or that ordinary shares are issued upon the satisfaction of specified conditions.**

Options, warrants and their equivalents **are financial instruments that give the holder the right to purchase ordinary shares.**

An *ordinary share* **is an equity instrument that is subordinate to all other classes of equity instruments.**

A *potential ordinary share* **is a financial instrument or other contract that may entitle its holder to ordinary shares.**

Put options on ordinary shares are contracts that give the holder the right to sell ordinary shares at a specified price for a given period.

6   Ordinary shares participate in profit for the period only after other types of shares such as preference shares have participated. An entity may have more than one class of ordinary shares. Ordinary shares of the same class have the same rights to receive dividends.

7   Examples of potential ordinary shares are:

   (a)   financial liabilities or equity instruments, including preference shares, that are convertible into ordinary shares;

   (b)   options and warrants;

   (c)   shares that would be issued upon the satisfaction of conditions resulting from contractual arrangements, such as the purchase of a business or other assets.

8   Terms defined in AASB 132 *Financial Instruments: Presentation* are used in this Standard with the meanings specified in paragraph 11 of AASB 132, unless otherwise noted. AASB 132 defines financial instrument, financial asset, financial liability, equity instrument and fair value, and provides guidance on applying those definitions.

Measurement

Basic Earnings per Share

9   **An entity shall calculate basic earnings per share amounts for profit or loss attributable to ordinary equity holders of the parent entity and, if presented, profit or loss from continuing operations attributable to those equity holders.**

10   **Basic earnings per share shall be calculated by dividing profit or loss attributable to ordinary equity holders of the parent entity (the numerator) by the weighted average number of ordinary shares outstanding (the denominator) during the period.**

11   The objective of basic earnings per share information is to provide a measure of the interests of each ordinary share of a parent entity in the performance of the entity over the reporting period.

Earnings

12   **For the purpose of calculating basic earnings per share, the amounts attributable to ordinary equity holders of the parent entity in respect of:**

   (a)   **profit or loss from continuing operations attributable to the parent entity; and**

   (b)   **profit or loss attributable to the parent entity**

   shall be the amounts in (a) and (b) adjusted for the after-tax amounts of preference dividends, differences arising on the settlement of preference shares, and other similar effects of preference shares classified as equity.

13   All items of income and expense attributable to ordinary equity holders of the parent entity that are recognised in a period, including tax expense and dividends on preference shares classified as liabilities, are included in the determination of profit or loss for the period attributable to ordinary equity holders of the parent entity (see AASB 101).

14   The after-tax amount of preference dividends that is deducted from profit or loss is:

   (a)   the after-tax amount of any preference dividends on non-cumulative preference shares declared in respect of the period; and

   (b)   the after-tax amount of the preference dividends for cumulative preference shares required for the period, whether or not the dividends have been declared. The amount of preference dividends for the period does not include the amount of any preference dividends for cumulative preference shares paid or declared during the current period in respect of previous periods.

15   Preference shares that provide for a low initial dividend to compensate an entity for selling the preference shares at a discount, or an above market dividend in later periods to compensate investors for purchasing preference shares at a premium, are sometimes referred to as increasing rate preference shares. Any original issue discount or premium on increasing rate preference shares is amortised to retained earnings using the effective

interest method and treated as a preference dividend for the purposes of calculating earnings per share.

16 Preference shares may be repurchased under an entity's tender offer to the holders. The excess of the fair value of the consideration paid to the preference shareholders over the carrying amount of the preference shares represents a return to the holders of the preference shares and a charge to retained earnings for the entity. This amount is deducted in calculating profit or loss attributable to ordinary equity holders of the parent entity.

17 Early conversion of convertible preference shares may be induced by an entity through favourable changes to the original conversion terms or the payment of additional consideration. The excess of the fair value of the ordinary shares or other consideration paid over the fair value of the ordinary shares issuable under the original conversion terms is a return to the preference shareholders, and is deducted in calculating profit or loss attributable to ordinary equity holders of the parent entity.

18 Any excess of the carrying amount of preference shares over the fair value of the consideration paid to settle them is added in calculating profit or loss attributable to ordinary equity holders of the parent entity.

Shares

19 For the purpose of calculating basic earnings per share, the number of ordinary shares shall be the weighted average number of ordinary shares outstanding during the period.

20 Using the weighted average number of ordinary shares outstanding during the period reflects the possibility that the amount of shareholders' capital varied during the period as a result of a larger or smaller number of shares being outstanding at any time. The weighted average number of ordinary shares outstanding during the period is the number of ordinary shares outstanding at the beginning of the period, adjusted by the number of ordinary shares bought back or issued during the period multiplied by a time-weighting factor. The time-weighting factor is the number of days that the shares are outstanding as a proportion of the total number of days in the period; a reasonable approximation of the weighted average is adequate in many circumstances.

21 Shares are usually included in the weighted average number of shares from the date consideration is receivable (which is generally the date of their issue), for example:

(a) ordinary shares issued in exchange for cash are included when cash is receivable;

(b) ordinary shares issued on the voluntary reinvestment of dividends on ordinary or preference shares are included when dividends are reinvested;

(c) ordinary shares issued as a result of the conversion of a debt instrument to ordinary shares are included from the date that interest ceases to accrue;

(d) ordinary shares issued in place of interest or principal on other financial instruments are included from the date that interest ceases to accrue;

(e) ordinary shares issued in exchange for the settlement of a liability of the entity are included from the settlement date;

(f) ordinary shares issued as consideration for the acquisition of an asset other than cash are included as of the date on which the acquisition is recognised; and

(g) ordinary shares issued for the rendering of services to the entity are included as the services are rendered.

The timing of the inclusion of ordinary shares is determined by the terms and conditions attaching to their issue. Due consideration is given to the substance of any contract associated with the issue.

22 Ordinary shares issued as part of the consideration transferred in a business combination are included in the weighted average number of shares from the acquisition date. This is because the acquirer incorporates into its statement of comprehensive income the acquiree's profits and losses from that date.

23   Ordinary shares that will be issued upon the conversion of a mandatorily convertible instrument are included in the calculation of basic earnings per share from the date the contract is entered into.

24   Contingently issuable shares are treated as outstanding and are included in the calculation of basic earnings per share only from the date when all necessary conditions are satisfied (i.e. the events have occurred). Shares that are issuable solely after the passage of time are not contingently issuable shares, because the passage of time is a certainty. Outstanding ordinary shares that are contingently returnable (i.e. subject to recall) are not treated as outstanding and are excluded from the calculation of basic earnings per share until the date the shares are no longer subject to recall.

25   [Deleted by the IASB]

26   **The weighted average number of ordinary shares outstanding during the period and for all periods presented shall be adjusted for events, other than the conversion of potential ordinary shares, that have changed the number of ordinary shares outstanding without a corresponding change in resources.**

27   Ordinary shares may be issued, or the number of ordinary shares outstanding may be reduced, without a corresponding change in resources. Examples include:

   (a)   a capitalisation or bonus issue (sometimes referred to as a stock dividend);

   (b)   a bonus element in any other issue, for example a bonus element in a rights issue to existing shareholders;

   (c)   a share split; and

   (d)   a reverse share split (consolidation of shares).

28   In a capitalisation or bonus issue or a share split, ordinary shares are issued to existing shareholders for no additional consideration. Therefore, the number of ordinary shares outstanding is increased without an increase in resources. The number of ordinary shares outstanding before the event is adjusted for the proportionate change in the number of ordinary shares outstanding as if the event had occurred at the beginning of the earliest period presented. For example, on a two-for-one bonus issue, the number of ordinary shares outstanding before the issue is multiplied by three to obtain the new total number of ordinary shares, or by two to obtain the number of additional ordinary shares.

29   A consolidation of ordinary shares generally reduces the number of ordinary shares outstanding without a corresponding reduction in resources. However, when the overall effect is a share repurchase at fair value, the reduction in the number of ordinary shares outstanding is the result of a corresponding reduction in resources. An example is a share consolidation combined with a special dividend. The weighted average number of ordinary shares outstanding for the period in which the combined transaction takes place is adjusted for the reduction in the number of ordinary shares from the date the special dividend is recognised.

Diluted Earnings per Share

30   **An entity shall calculate diluted earnings per share amounts for profit or loss attributable to ordinary equity holders of the parent entity and, if presented, profit or loss from continuing operations attributable to those equity holders.**

31   **For the purpose of calculating diluted earnings per share, an entity shall adjust profit or loss attributable to ordinary equity holders of the parent entity, and the weighted average number of shares outstanding, for the effects of all dilutive potential ordinary shares.**

32   The objective of diluted earnings per share is consistent with that of basic earnings per share, to provide a measure of the interest of each ordinary share in the performance of an entity, while giving effect to all dilutive potential ordinary shares outstanding during the period. As a result:

   (a)   profit or loss attributable to ordinary equity holders of the parent entity is increased by the after-tax amount of dividends and interest recognised in the period in respect of the dilutive potential ordinary shares and is adjusted for any other changes in income or expense that would result from the conversion of the dilutive potential ordinary shares; and

(b)   the weighted average number of ordinary shares outstanding is increased by the weighted average number of additional ordinary shares that would have been outstanding assuming the conversion of all dilutive potential ordinary shares.

Earnings

33   **For the purpose of calculating diluted earnings per share, an entity shall adjust profit or loss attributable to ordinary equity holders of the parent entity, as calculated in accordance with paragraph 12, by the after-tax effect of:**

   (a)   **any dividends or other items related to dilutive potential ordinary shares deducted in arriving at profit or loss attributable to ordinary equity holders of the parent entity as calculated in accordance with paragraph 12;**

   (b)   **any interest recognised in the period related to dilutive potential ordinary shares; and**

   (c)   **any other changes in income or expense that would result from the conversion of the dilutive potential ordinary shares.**

34   After the potential ordinary shares are converted into ordinary shares, the items identified in paragraph 33(a)-(c) no longer arise. Instead, the new ordinary shares are entitled to participate in profit or loss attributable to ordinary equity holders of the parent entity. Therefore, profit or loss attributable to ordinary equity holders of the parent entity calculated in accordance with paragraph 12 is adjusted for the items identified in paragraph 33(a)-(c) and any related taxes. The expenses associated with potential ordinary shares include transaction costs and discounts accounted for in accordance with the effective interest method (see paragraph 9 of AASB 139 *Financial Instruments: Recognition and Measurement*).

35   The conversion of potential ordinary shares may lead to consequential changes in income or expenses. For example, the reduction of interest expense related to potential ordinary shares and the resulting increase in profit or reduction in loss may lead to an increase in the expense related to a non-discretionary employee profit-sharing plan. For the purpose of calculating diluted earnings per share, profit or loss attributable to ordinary equity holders of the parent entity is adjusted for any such consequential changes in income or expense.

Shares

36   **For the purpose of calculating diluted earnings per share, the number of ordinary shares shall be the weighted average number of ordinary shares calculated in accordance with paragraphs 19 and 26, plus the weighted average number of ordinary shares that would be issued on the conversion of all the dilutive potential ordinary shares into ordinary shares. Dilutive potential ordinary shares shall be deemed to have been converted into ordinary shares at the beginning of the period or, if later, the date of the issue of the potential ordinary shares.**

37   Dilutive potential ordinary shares shall be determined independently for each period presented. The number of dilutive potential ordinary shares included in the year-to-date period is not a weighted average of the dilutive potential ordinary shares included in each interim computation.

38   Potential ordinary shares are weighted for the period they are outstanding. Potential ordinary shares that are cancelled or allowed to lapse during the period are included in the calculation of diluted earnings per share only for the portion of the period during which they are outstanding. Potential ordinary shares that are converted into ordinary shares during the period are included in the calculation of diluted earnings per share from the beginning of the period to the date of conversion; from the date of conversion, the resulting ordinary shares are included in both basic and diluted earnings per share.

39   The number of ordinary shares that would be issued on conversion of dilutive potential ordinary shares is determined from the terms of the potential ordinary shares. When more than one basis of conversion exists, the calculation assumes the most advantageous conversion rate or exercise price from the standpoint of the holder of the potential ordinary shares.

40   A subsidiary, joint venture or associate may issue to parties other than the parent, venturer or investor potential ordinary shares that are convertible into either ordinary shares of the subsidiary, joint venture or associate, or ordinary shares of the parent, venturer or investor (the reporting entity). If these potential ordinary shares of the subsidiary, joint venture or associate have a dilutive effect on the basic earnings per share of the reporting entity, they are included in the calculation of diluted earnings per share.

Dilutive Potential Ordinary Shares

41   **Potential ordinary shares shall be treated as dilutive when, and only when, their conversion to ordinary shares would decrease earnings per share or increase loss per share from continuing operations.**

42   An entity uses profit or loss from continuing operations attributable to the parent entity as the control number to establish whether potential ordinary shares are dilutive or antidilutive. Profit or loss from continuing operations attributable to the parent entity is adjusted in accordance with paragraph 12 and excludes items relating to discontinued operations.

43   Potential ordinary shares are antidilutive when their conversion to ordinary shares would increase earnings per share or decrease loss per share from continuing operations. The calculation of diluted earnings per share does not assume conversion, exercise, or other issue of potential ordinary shares that would have an antidilutive effect on earnings per share.

44   In determining whether potential ordinary shares are dilutive or antidilutive, each issue or series of potential ordinary shares is considered separately rather than in aggregate. The sequence in which potential ordinary shares are considered may affect whether they are dilutive. Therefore, to maximise the *dilution* of basic earnings per share, each issue or series of potential ordinary shares is considered in sequence from the most dilutive to the least dilutive, that is, dilutive potential ordinary shares with the lowest 'earnings per incremental share' are included in the diluted earnings per share calculation before those with a higher earnings per incremental share. Options and warrants are generally included first because they do not affect the numerator of the calculation.

Options, warrants and their equivalents

45   **For the purpose of calculating diluted earnings per share, an entity shall assume the exercise of dilutive options and warrants of the entity. The assumed proceeds from these instruments shall be regarded as having been received from the issue of ordinary shares at the average market price of ordinary shares during the period. The difference between the number of ordinary shares issued and the number of ordinary shares that would have been issued at the average market price of ordinary shares during the period shall be treated as an issue of ordinary shares for no consideration.**

46   Options and warrants are dilutive when they would result in the issue of ordinary shares for less than the average market price of ordinary shares during the period. The amount of the dilution is the average market price of ordinary shares during the period minus the issue price. Therefore, to calculate diluted earnings per share, potential ordinary shares are treated as consisting of both the following:

   (a)   a contract to issue a certain number of the ordinary shares at their average market price during the period. Such ordinary shares are assumed to be fairly priced and to be neither dilutive nor antidilutive. They are ignored in the calculation of diluted earnings per share; and

   (b)   a contract to issue the remaining ordinary shares for no consideration. Such ordinary shares generate no proceeds and have no effect on profit or loss attributable to ordinary shares outstanding. Therefore, such shares are dilutive and are added to the number of ordinary shares outstanding in the calculation of diluted earnings per share.

47   Options and warrants have a dilutive effect only when the average market price of ordinary shares during the period exceeds the exercise price of the options or warrants (i.e. they are 'in the money'). Previously reported earnings per share are not retroactively adjusted to reflect changes in prices of ordinary shares.

47A For share options and other share-based payment arrangements to which AASB 2 *Share-based Payment* applies, the issue price referred to in paragraph 46 and the exercise price referred to in paragraph 47 shall include the fair value of any goods or services to be supplied to the entity in the future under the share option or other share-based payment arrangement.

48 Employee share options with fixed or determinable terms and non vested ordinary shares are treated as options in the calculation of diluted earnings per share, even though they may be contingent on vesting. They are treated as outstanding on the grant date. Performance-based employee share options are treated as contingently issuable shares because their issue is contingent upon satisfying specified conditions in addition to the passage of time.

Convertible instruments

49 The dilutive effect of convertible instruments shall be reflected in diluted earnings per share in accordance with paragraphs 33 and 36.

50 Convertible preference shares are antidilutive whenever the amount of the dividend on such shares declared in or accumulated for the current period per ordinary share obtainable on conversion exceeds basic earnings per share. Similarly, convertible debt is antidilutive whenever its interest (net of tax and other changes in income or expense) per ordinary share obtainable on conversion exceeds basic earnings per share.

51 The redemption or induced conversion of convertible preference shares may affect only a portion of the previously outstanding convertible preference shares. In such cases, any excess consideration referred to in paragraph 17 is attributed to those shares that are redeemed or converted for the purpose of determining whether the remaining outstanding preference shares are dilutive. The shares redeemed or converted are considered separately from those shares that are not redeemed or converted.

Contingently issuable shares

52 As in the calculation of basic earnings per share, *contingently issuable ordinary shares* are treated as outstanding and included in the calculation of diluted earnings per share if the conditions are satisfied (i.e. the events have occurred). Contingently issuable shares are included from the beginning of the period (or from the date of the contingent share agreement, if later). If the conditions are not satisfied, the number of contingently issuable shares included in the diluted earnings per share calculation is based on the number of shares that would be issuable if the end of the period were the end of the contingency period. Restatement is not permitted if the conditions are not met when the contingency period expires.

53 If attainment or maintenance of a specified amount of earnings for a period is the condition for contingent issue and if that amount has been attained at the end of the reporting period but must be maintained beyond the end of the reporting period for an additional period, then the additional ordinary shares are treated as outstanding, if the effect is dilutive, when calculating diluted earnings per share. In that case, the calculation of diluted earnings per share is based on the number of ordinary shares that would be issued if the amount of earnings at the end of the reporting period were the amount of earnings at the end of the contingency period. Because earnings may change in a future period, the calculation of basic earnings per share does not include such contingently issuable ordinary shares until the end of the contingency period because not all necessary conditions have been satisfied.

54 The number of ordinary shares contingently issuable may depend on the future market price of the ordinary shares. In that case, if the effect is dilutive, the calculation of diluted earnings per share is based on the number of ordinary shares that would be issued if the market price at the end of the reporting period were the market price at the end of the contingency period. If the condition is based on an average of market prices over a period of time that extends beyond the end of the reporting period, the average for the period of time that has lapsed is used. Because the market price may change in a future period, the calculation of basic earnings per share does not include such contingently issuable ordinary shares until the end of the contingency period because not all necessary conditions have been satisfied.

55   The number of ordinary shares contingently issuable may depend on future earnings and
      future prices of the ordinary shares. In such cases, the number of ordinary shares included
      in the diluted earnings per share calculation is based on both conditions (i.e. earnings to
      date and the current market price at the end of the reporting period). Contingently issuable
      ordinary shares are not included in the diluted earnings per share calculation unless both
      conditions are met.

56   In other cases, the number of ordinary shares contingently issuable depends on a condition
      other than earnings or market price (e.g. the opening of a specific number of retail stores).
      In such cases, assuming that the present status of the condition remains unchanged until
      the end of the contingency period, the contingently issuable ordinary shares are included
      in the calculation of diluted earnings per share according to the status at the end of the
      reporting period.

57   Contingently issuable potential ordinary shares (other than those covered by a contingent
      share agreement, such as contingently issuable convertible instruments) are included in
      the diluted earnings per share calculation as follows:

      (a)   an entity determines whether the potential ordinary shares may be assumed to be
             issuable on the basis of the conditions specified for their issue in accordance with
             the contingent ordinary share provisions in paragraphs 52-56; and

      (b)   if those potential ordinary shares should be reflected in diluted earnings per share,
             an entity determines their impact on the calculation of diluted earnings per share
             by following the provisions for options and warrants in paragraphs 45-48, the
             provisions for convertible instruments in paragraphs 49-51, the provisions for
             contracts that may be settled in ordinary shares or cash in paragraphs 58-61, or
             other provisions, as appropriate.

      However, exercise or conversion is not assumed for the purpose of calculating diluted
      earnings per share unless exercise or conversion of similar outstanding potential ordinary
      shares that are not contingently issuable is assumed.

Contracts that may be settled in ordinary shares or cash

58   **When an entity has issued a contract that may be settled in ordinary shares or in
      cash at the entity's option, the entity shall presume that the contract will be settled
      in ordinary shares, and the resulting potential ordinary shares shall be included in
      diluted earnings per share if the effect is dilutive.**

59   When such a contract is presented for accounting purposes as an asset or a liability, or
      has an equity component and a liability component, the entity shall adjust the numerator
      for any changes in profit or loss that would have resulted during the period if the contract
      had been classified wholly as an equity instrument. That adjustment is similar to the
      adjustments required in paragraph 33.

60   **For contracts that may be settled in ordinary shares or cash at the holder's option,
      the more dilutive of cash settlement and share settlement shall be used in calculating
      diluted earnings per share.**

61   An example of a contract that may be settled in ordinary shares or in cash is a debt
      instrument that, on maturity, gives the entity the unrestricted right to settle the principal
      amount in cash or in its own ordinary shares. Another example is a written put option that
      gives the holder a choice of settling in ordinary shares or in cash.

Purchased options

62   Contracts such as purchased *put options* and purchased call options (i.e. options held
      by the entity on its own ordinary shares) are not included in the calculation of diluted
      earnings per share because including them would be antidilutive. The put option would be
      exercised only if the exercise price were higher than the market price and the call option
      would be exercised only if the exercise price were lower than the market price.

Written put options

63   **Contracts that require the entity to repurchase its own shares, such as written put
      options and forward purchase contracts, are reflected in the calculation of diluted
      earnings per share if the effect is dilutive. If these contracts are 'in the money' during**

the period (i.e. the exercise or settlement price is above the average market price for that period), the potential dilutive effect on earnings per share shall be calculated as follows:

(a) it shall be assumed that at the beginning of the period sufficient ordinary shares will be issued (at the average market price during the period) to raise proceeds to satisfy the contract;

(b) it shall be assumed that the proceeds from the issue are used to satisfy the contract (i.e. to buy back ordinary shares); and

(c) the incremental ordinary shares (the difference between the number of ordinary shares assumed issued and the number of ordinary shares received from satisfying the contract) shall be included in the calculation of diluted earnings per share.

Retrospective Adjustments

64   If the number of ordinary or potential ordinary shares outstanding increases as a result of a capitalisation, bonus issue or share split, or decreases as a result of a reverse share split, the calculation of basic and diluted earnings per share for all periods presented shall be adjusted retrospectively. If these changes occur after the reporting period but before the financial statements are authorised for issue, the per share calculations for those and any prior period financial statements presented shall be based on the new number of shares. The fact that per share calculations reflect such changes in the number of shares shall be disclosed. In addition, basic and diluted earnings per share of all periods presented shall be adjusted for the effects of errors and adjustments resulting from changes in accounting policies, accounted for retrospectively.

65   An entity does not restate diluted earnings per share of any prior period presented for changes in the assumptions used in earnings per share calculations or for the conversion of potential ordinary shares into ordinary shares.

Presentation

66   An entity shall present in the statement of comprehensive income basic and diluted earnings per share for profit or loss from continuing operations attributable to the ordinary equity holders of the parent entity and for profit or loss attributable to the ordinary equity holders of the parent entity for the period for each class of ordinary shares that has a different right to share in profit for the period. An entity shall present basic and diluted earnings per share with equal prominence for all periods presented.

67   Earnings per share is presented for every period for which a statement of comprehensive income is presented. If diluted earnings per share is reported for at least one period, it shall be reported for all periods presented, even if it equals basic earnings per share. If basic and diluted earnings per share are equal, dual presentation can be accomplished in one line in the statement of comprehensive income.

67A If an entity presents items of profit or loss in a separate statement as described in paragraph 10A of AASB 101 (as amended in 2011), it presents basic and diluted earnings per share, as required in paragraphs 66 and 67, in that separate statement.

68   An entity that reports a discontinued operation shall disclose the basic and diluted amounts per share for the discontinued operation either in the statement of comprehensive income or in the notes.

68A If an entity presents items of profit or loss in a separate statement as described in paragraph 10A of AASB 101 (as amended in 2011), it presents basic and diluted earnings per share for the discontinued operation, as required in paragraph 68, in that separate statement or in the notes.

69   An entity shall present basic and diluted earnings per share, even if the amounts are negative (i.e. a loss per share).

Disclosure

70   An entity shall disclose the following:

    (a)   the amounts used as the numerators in calculating basic and diluted earnings per share, and a reconciliation of those amounts to profit or loss attributable to the parent entity for the period. The reconciliation shall include the individual effect of each class of instruments that affects earnings per share;

    (b)   the weighted average number of ordinary shares used as the denominator in calculating basic and diluted earnings per share, and a reconciliation of these denominators to each other. The reconciliation shall include the individual effect of each class of instruments that affects earnings per share;

    (c)   instruments (including contingently issuable shares) that could potentially dilute basic earnings per share in the future, but were not included in the calculation of diluted earnings per share because they are antidilutive for the period(s) presented; and

    (d)   a description of ordinary share transactions or potential ordinary share transactions, other than those accounted for in accordance with paragraph 64, that occur after the reporting period and that would have changed significantly the number of ordinary shares or potential ordinary shares outstanding at the end of the period if those transactions had occurred before the end of the reporting period.

71   Examples of transactions in paragraph 70(d) include:

    (a)   an issue of shares for cash;

    (b)   an issue of shares when the proceeds are used to repay debt or preference shares outstanding at the end of the reporting period;

    (c)   the redemption of ordinary shares outstanding;

    (d)   the conversion or exercise of potential ordinary shares outstanding at the end of the reporting period into ordinary shares;

    (e)   an issue of options, warrants, or convertible instruments; and

    (f)   the achievement of conditions that would result in the issue of contingently issuable shares.

Earnings per share amounts are not adjusted for such transactions occurring after the reporting period because such transactions do not affect the amount of capital used to produce profit or loss for the period.

72   Financial instruments and other contracts generating potential ordinary shares may incorporate terms and conditions that affect the measurement of basic and diluted earnings per share. These terms and conditions may determine whether any potential ordinary shares are dilutive and, if so, the effect on the weighted average number of shares outstanding and any consequent adjustments to profit or loss attributable to ordinary equity holders. The disclosure of the terms and conditions of such financial instruments and other contracts is encouraged, if not otherwise required (see AASB 7 *Financial Instruments: Disclosures*).

73   If an entity discloses, in addition to basic and diluted earnings per share, amounts per share using a reported component of the statement of comprehensive income other than one required by this Standard, such amounts shall be calculated using the weighted average number of ordinary shares determined in accordance with this Standard. Basic and diluted amounts per share relating to such a component shall be disclosed with equal prominence and presented in the notes. An entity shall indicate the basis on which the numerator(s) is (are) determined, including whether amounts per share are before tax or after tax. If a component of the statement of comprehensive income is used that is not reported as a line item in the statement of comprehensive income, a reconciliation shall be provided between the component used and a line item that is reported in the statement of comprehensive income.

73A Paragraph 73 applies also to an entity that discloses, in addition to basic and diluted earnings per share, amounts per share using a reported item of profit or loss, other than one required by this Standard.

Effective Date of IAS 33

74 [Deleted by the AASB]

74A [Deleted by the AASB]

74D AASB 2011-9 *Amendments to Australian Accounting Standards – Presentation of Items of Other Comprehensive Income*, issued in September 2011, amended paragraphs 4A, 67A, 68A and 73A. An entity shall apply those amendments when it applies AASB 101 as amended in September 2011.

75 [Deleted by the AASB]

76 [Deleted by the AASB]

Appendix

Application Guidance

This Appendix is an integral part of AASB 133.

Profit or loss attributable to the parent entity

A1 For the purpose of calculating earnings per share based on the consolidated financial statements, profit or loss attributable to the parent entity refers to profit or loss of the consolidated entity after adjusting for non-controlling interests.

Rights issues

A2 The issue of ordinary shares at the time of exercise or conversion of potential ordinary shares does not usually give rise to a bonus element. This is because the potential ordinary shares are usually issued for full value, resulting in a proportionate change in the resources available to the entity. In a rights issue, however, the exercise price is often less than the fair value of the shares. Therefore, as noted in paragraph 27(b), such a rights issue includes a bonus element. If a rights issue is offered to all existing shareholders, the number of ordinary shares to be used in calculating basic and diluted earnings per share for all periods before the rights issue is the number of ordinary shares outstanding before the issue, multiplied by the following factor:

$$\frac{\text{Fair value per share immediately before the exercise of rights}}{\text{Theoretical ex-rights fair value per share}}$$

The theoretical ex-rights fair value per share is calculated by adding the aggregate market value of the shares immediately before the exercise of the rights to the proceeds from the exercise of the rights, and dividing by the number of shares outstanding after the exercise of the rights. Where the rights are to be publicly traded separately from the shares before the exercise date, fair value for the purposes of this calculation is established at the close of the last day on which the shares are traded together with the rights.

Control number

A3 To illustrate the application of the control number notion described in paragraphs 42 and 43, assume that an entity has profit from continuing operations attributable to the parent entity of CU4,800[1], a loss from discontinued operations attributable to the parent entity of (CU7,200), a loss attributable to the parent entity of (CU2,400), and 2,000 ordinary shares and 400 potential ordinary shares outstanding. The entity's basic earnings per share is CU2.40 for continuing operations, (CU3.60) for discontinued operations and (CU1.20) for the loss. The 400 potential ordinary shares are included in the diluted earnings per share calculation because the resulting CU2.00 earnings per share for continuing operations is

---

1 In this guidance, monetary amounts are denominated in 'currency units' (CU).

dilutive, assuming no profit or loss impact of those 400 potential ordinary shares. Because profit from continuing operations attributable to the parent entity is the control number, the entity also includes those 400 potential ordinary shares in the calculation of the other earnings per share amounts, even though the resulting earnings per share amounts are antidilutive to their comparable basic earnings per share amounts, that is, the loss per share is less [(CU3.00) per share for the loss from discontinued operations and (CU1.00) per share for the loss for the period].

Average market price of ordinary shares

A4   For the purpose of calculating diluted earnings per share, the average market price of ordinary shares assumed to be issued is calculated on the basis of the average market price of the ordinary shares during the period. Theoretically, every market transaction for an entity's ordinary shares could be included in the determination of the average market price. As a practical matter, however, a simple average of weekly or monthly prices is usually adequate.

A5   Generally, closing market prices are adequate for calculating the average market price. When prices fluctuate widely, however, an average of the high and low prices usually produces a more representative price. The method used to calculate the average market price is used consistently unless it is no longer representative because of changed conditions. For example, an entity that uses closing market prices to calculate the average market price for several years of relatively stable prices might change to an average of high and low prices if prices start fluctuating greatly and the closing market prices no longer produce a representative average price.

Options, warrants and their equivalents

A6   Options or warrants to purchase convertible instruments are assumed to be exercised to purchase the convertible instrument whenever the average prices of both the convertible instrument and the ordinary shares obtainable upon conversion are above the exercise price of the options or warrants. However, exercise is not assumed unless conversion of similar outstanding convertible instruments, if any, is also assumed.

A7   Options or warrants may permit or require the tendering of debt or other instruments of the entity (or its parent or a subsidiary) in payment of all or a portion of the exercise price. In the calculation of diluted earnings per share, those options or warrants have a dilutive effect if (a) the average market price of the related ordinary shares for the period exceeds the exercise price or (b) the selling price of the instrument to be tendered is below that at which the instrument may be tendered under the option or warrant agreement and the resulting discount establishes an effective exercise price below the market price of the ordinary shares obtainable upon exercise. In the calculation of diluted earnings per share, those options or warrants are assumed to be exercised and the debt or other instruments are assumed to be tendered. If tendering cash is more advantageous to the option or warrant holder and the contract permits tendering cash, tendering of cash is assumed. Interest (net of tax) on any debt assumed to be tendered is added back as an adjustment to the numerator.

A8   Similar treatment is given to preference shares that have similar provisions or to other instruments that have conversion options that permit the investor to pay cash for a more favourable conversion rate.

A9   The underlying terms of certain options or warrants may require the proceeds received from the exercise of those instruments to be applied to redeem debt or other instruments of the entity (or its parent or a subsidiary). In the calculation of diluted earnings per share, those options or warrants are assumed to be exercised and the proceeds applied to purchase the debt at its average market price rather than to purchase ordinary shares. However, the excess proceeds received from the assumed exercise over the amount used for the assumed purchase of debt are considered (i.e. assumed to be used to buy back ordinary shares) in the diluted earnings per share calculation. Interest (net of tax) on any debt assumed to be purchased is added back as an adjustment to the numerator.

Written put options

A10 To illustrate the application of paragraph 63, assume that an entity has outstanding 120 written put options on its ordinary shares with an exercise price of CU35. The average market price of its ordinary shares for the period is CU28. In calculating diluted earnings per share, the entity assumes that it issued 150 shares at CU28 per share at the beginning of the period to satisfy its put obligation of CU4,200. The difference between the 150 ordinary shares issued and the 120 ordinary shares received from satisfying the put option (30 incremental ordinary shares) is added to the denominator in calculating diluted earnings per share.

Instruments of subsidiaries, joint ventures or associates

A11 Potential ordinary shares of a subsidiary, joint venture or associate convertible into either ordinary shares of the subsidiary, joint venture or associate, or ordinary shares of the parent, venturer or investor (the reporting entity) are included in the calculation of diluted earnings per share as follows:

(a) instruments issued by a subsidiary, joint venture or associate that enable their holders to obtain ordinary shares of the subsidiary, joint venture or associate are included in calculating the diluted earnings per share data of the subsidiary, joint venture or associate. Those earnings per share are then included in the reporting entity's earnings per share calculations based on the reporting entity's holding of the instruments of the subsidiary, joint venture or associate; and

(b) instruments of a subsidiary, joint venture or associate that are convertible into the reporting entity's ordinary shares are considered among the potential ordinary shares of the reporting entity for the purpose of calculating diluted earnings per share. Likewise, options or warrants issued by a subsidiary, joint venture or associate to purchase ordinary shares of the reporting entity are considered among the potential ordinary shares of the reporting entity in the calculation of consolidated diluted earnings per share.

A12 For the purpose of determining the earnings per share effect of instruments issued by a reporting entity that are convertible into ordinary shares of a subsidiary, joint venture or associate, the instruments are assumed to be converted and the numerator (profit or loss attributable to ordinary equity holders of the parent entity) adjusted as necessary in accordance with paragraph 33. In addition to those adjustments, the numerator is adjusted for any change in the profit or loss recorded by the reporting entity (such as dividend income or equity method income) that is attributable to the increase in the number of ordinary shares of the subsidiary, joint venture or associate outstanding as a result of the assumed conversion. The denominator of the diluted earnings per share calculation is not affected because the number of ordinary shares of the reporting entity outstanding would not change upon assumed conversion.

Participating equity instruments and two-class ordinary shares

A13 The equity of some entities includes:

(a) instruments that participate in dividends with ordinary shares according to a predetermined formula (for example, two for one) with, at times, an upper limit on the extent of participation (for example, up to, but not beyond, a specified amount per share); and

(b) a class of ordinary shares with a different dividend rate from that of another class of ordinary shares but without prior or senior rights.

A14 For the purpose of calculating diluted earnings per share, conversion is assumed for those instruments described in paragraph A13 that are convertible into ordinary shares if the effect is dilutive. For those instruments that are not convertible into a class of ordinary shares, profit or loss for the period is allocated to the different classes of shares and participating equity instruments in accordance with their dividend rights or other rights to participate in undistributed earnings.

To calculate basic and diluted earnings per share:

(a)   profit or loss attributable to ordinary equity holders of the parent entity is adjusted (a profit reduced and a loss increased) by the amount of dividends declared in the period for each class of shares and by the contractual amount of dividends (or interest on participating bonds) that must be paid for the period (for example, unpaid cumulative dividends);

(b)   the remaining profit or loss is allocated to ordinary shares and participating equity instruments to the extent that each instrument shares in earnings as if all of the profit or loss for the period had been distributed. The total profit or loss allocated to each class of equity instrument is determined by adding together the amount allocated for dividends and the amount allocated for a participation feature; and

(c)   the total amount of profit or loss allocated to each class of equity instrument is divided by the number of outstanding instruments to which the earnings are allocated to determine the earnings per share for the instrument.

For the calculation of diluted earnings per share, all potential ordinary shares assumed to have been issued are included in outstanding ordinary shares.

Partly paid shares

A15   Where ordinary shares are issued but not fully paid, they are treated in the calculation of basic earnings per share as a fraction of an ordinary share to the extent that they were entitled to participate in dividends during the period relative to a fully paid ordinary share.

A16   To the extent that partly paid shares are not entitled to participate in dividends during the period they are treated as the equivalent of warrants or options in the calculation of diluted earnings per share. The unpaid balance is assumed to represent proceeds used to purchase ordinary shares. The number of shares included in diluted earnings per share is the difference between the number of shares subscribed and the number of shares assumed to be purchased.

Illustrative Examples

Contents

These examples accompany, but are not part of, AASB 133.

Example 1   Increasing Rate Preference Shares

Example 2   Weighted Average Number of Ordinary Shares

Example 3   Bonus Issue

Example 4   Rights Issue

Example 5   Effects of Share Options on Diluted Earnings per Share

Example 5A   Determining the Exercise Price of Employee Share Options

Example 6   Convertible Bonds

Example 7   Contingently Issuable Shares

Example 8   Convertible Bonds Settled in Shares or Cash at the Issuer's Option

Example 9   Calculation of Weighted Average Number of Shares: Determining the Order in Which to Include Dilutive Instruments

Example 10   Instruments of a Subsidiary: Calculation of Basic and Diluted Earnings per Share

Example 11   Participating Equity Instruments and Two-Class Ordinary Shares

Example 12   Calculation and Presentation of Basic and Diluted Earnings per Share (Comprehensive Example)

Example 1 – Increasing Rate Preference Shares
Reference: AASB 133, paragraphs 12 and 15

Entity D issued non-convertible, non-redeemable class A cumulative preference shares of CU100 par value on 1 January 20X1. The class A preference shares are entitled to a cumulative annual dividend of CU7 per share starting in 20X4.

At the time of issue, the market rate dividend yield on the class A preference shares was 7 per cent a year. Thus, Entity D could have expected to receive proceeds of approximately CU100 per class A preference share if the dividend rate of CU7 per share had been in effect at the date of issue.

In consideration of the dividend payment terms, however, the class A preference shares were issued at CU81.63 per share, that is, at a discount of CU18.37 per share. The issue price can be calculated by taking the present value of CU100, discounted at 7 per cent over a three-year period.

Because the shares are classified as equity, the original issue discount is amortised to retained earnings using the effective interest method and treated as a preference dividend for earnings per share purposes. To calculate basic earnings per share, the following imputed dividend per class A preference share is deducted to determine the profit or loss attributable to ordinary equity holders of the parent entity:

Year	Carrying amount of class A preference shares 1 January	Imputed Dividend[1]	Carrying amount of class A preference shares 31 December[2]	Dividend paid
	CU	CU	CU	CU
20X1	81.63	5.71	87.34	–
20X2	87.34	6.12	93.46	–
20X3	93.46	6.54	100.00	–
Thereafter:	100.00	7.00	107.00	(7.00)

Example 2 – Weighted Average Number of Ordinary Shares
Reference: AASB 133, paragraphs 19-21

		Shares issued	Treasury shares[3]	Shares outstanding
1 January 20X1	Balance at beginning of year	2,000	300	1,700
31 May 20X1	Issue of new shares for cash	800	–	2,500
1 December 20X1	Purchase of treasury shares for cash	–	250	2,250
31 December 20X1	Balance at year-end	2,800	550	2,250

Calculation of weighted average:

$(1{,}700 \times 5/12) + (2{,}500 \times 6/12) + (2{,}250 \times 1/12) = 2{,}146$ shares *or*

$(1{,}700 \times 12/12) + (800 \times 7/12) - (250 \times 1/12) = 2{,}146$ shares

---

1   At 7%.

2   This is before dividend payment.

3   Treasury shares are equity instruments re-acquired and held by the issuing entity itself or by its subsidiaries.

Example 3 – Bonus Issue

Reference: AASB 133, paragraphs 26, 27(a) and 28

Profit attributable to ordinary equity holders of the parent entity 20X0   CU180
Profit attributable to ordinary equity holders of the parent entity 20X1   CU600
Ordinary shares outstanding until 30 September 20X1   200

Bonus issue 1 October 20X1   2 ordinary shares for each
                                                  ordinary share outstanding at
                                                  30 September 20X1
                                                  200 × 2 = 400

Basic earnings per share 20X1 $\dfrac{CU600}{(200 + 400)} = CU1.00$

Basic earnings per share 20X0 $\dfrac{CU180}{(200 + 400)} = CU0.30$

Because the bonus issue was without consideration, it is treated as if it had occurred before the beginning of 20X0, the earliest period presented.

Example 4 – Rights Issue

Reference: AASB 133, paragraphs 26, 27(b) and A2

	20X0	20X1	20X2
Profit attributable to ordinary equity holders of the parent entity	CU1,100	CU1,500	CU1,800

Shares outstanding before rights issue   500 shares

Rights issue   One new share for each five outstanding shares
                                          (100 new shares total)

                                          Exercise price: CU5.00

                                          Date of rights issue: 1 January 20X1

                                          Last date to exercise rights: 1 March 20X1

Market price of one ordinary share
  immediately before exercise on
  1 March 20X1:   CU11.00

End of the reporting period   31 December

Calculation of theoretical ex-rights value per share

$$\frac{\text{Fair value of all outstanding shares before the exercise of rights} + \text{total amount received from exercise of rights}}{\text{Number of shares outstanding before exercise} + \text{number of shares issued in the exercise}}$$

$$\frac{(CU11.00 \times 500 \text{ shares}) + (CU5.00 \times 100 \text{ shares})}{500 \text{ shares} + 100 \text{ shares}}$$

Theoretical ex-rights value per share = CU10.00

Calculation of adjustment factor

$$\frac{\text{Fair value per share before exercise of rights}}{\text{Theoretical ex-rights value per share}} \qquad \frac{CU11.00}{CU10.00} = 1.10$$

Calculation of basic earnings per share

		20X0	20X1	20X2
20X0 basic EPS as originally reported:	CU1,100 ÷ 500 shares	CU2.20		
20X0 basic EPS restated for rights issue:	$\dfrac{\text{CU1,100}}{(500 \text{ shares} \times 1.1)}$	CU2.00		
20X1 basic EPS including effects of rights issue:	$\dfrac{\text{CU1,500}}{(500 \times 1.1 \times 2/12) + (600 \times 10/12)}$		CU2.54	
20X2 basic EPS:	CU1,800 ÷ 600 shares			CU3.00

Example 5 – Effects of Share Options on Diluted Earnings per Share

Reference: AASB 133, paragraphs 45-47

Profit attributable to ordinary equity holders of the parent entity for year 20X1	CU1,200,000
Weighted average number of ordinary shares outstanding during year 20X1	500,000 shares
Average market price of one ordinary share during year 20X1	CU20.00
Weighted average number of shares under option during year 20X1	100,000 shares
Exercise price for shares under option during year 20X1	CU15.00

Calculation of earnings per share

	Earnings CU	Shares	Per share CU
Profit attributable to ordinary equity holders of the parent entity for year 20X1	1,200,000		
Weighted average shares outstanding during year 20X1		500,000	
Basic earnings per share			2.40
Weighted average number of shares under option		100,000	
Weighted average number of shares that would have been issued at average market price: $(100,000 \times \text{CU15.00}) \div \text{CU20.00}$	[4]	(75,000)	
Diluted earnings per share	1,200,000	525,000	2.29

---

4   Earnings have not increased because the total number of shares has increased only by the number of shares (25,000) deemed to have been issued for no consideration (see paragraph 46(b) of the Standard).

Example 5A – Determining the Exercise Price of Employee Share Options

Weighted average number of unvested share options per employee	1,000

Weighted average amount per employee to be recognised over the remainder of the vesting period for employee services to be rendered as consideration for the share options, determined in accordance with AASB 2 *Share-based Payment*

	CU1,200
Cash exercise price of unvested share options	CU15

Calculation of adjusted exercise price

Fair value of services yet to be rendered per employee:	CU1,200
Fair value of services yet to be rendered per option: (CU1,200 ÷ 1,000)	
	CU1.20
Total exercise price of share options: (CU15.00 + CU1.20)	CU16.20

Example 6 – Convertible Bonds[5]

Reference: AASB 133, paragraphs 33, 34, 36 and 49

Profit attributable to ordinary equity holders of the parent entity	CU1,004
Ordinary shares outstanding	1,000
Basic earnings per share	CU1.00
Convertible bonds	100
Each block of 10 bonds is convertible into three ordinary shares	
Interest expense for the current year relating to the liability component of the convertible bonds	CU10
Current and deferred tax relating to that interest expense	CU4

Note: the interest expense includes amortisation of the discount arising on initial recognition of the liability component (see AASB 132 *Financial Instruments: Presentation*).

Adjusted profit attributable to ordinary equity holders of the parent entity	CU1,004 + CU10 – CU4 = CU1,010
Number of ordinary shares resulting from conversion of bonds	30
Number of ordinary shares used to calculate diluted earnings per share	1,000 + 30 = 1,030
Diluted earnings per share	$\dfrac{CU1,010}{1,030}$ = CU0.98

---

5   This example does not illustrate the classification of the components of convertible financial instruments as liabilities and equity or the classification of related interest and dividends as expenses and equity as required by AASB 132.

Example 7 – Contingently Issuable Shares
Reference: AASB 133, paragraphs 19, 24, 36, 37, 41-43 and 52

Ordinary shares outstanding during 20X1	1,000,000 (there were no options, warrants or convertible instruments outstanding during the period)

An agreement related to a recent business combination provides for the issue of additional ordinary shares based on the following conditions:

	5,000 additional ordinary shares for each new retail site opened during 20X1
	1,000 additional ordinary shares for each CU1,000 of consolidated profit in excess of CU2,000,000 for the year ended 31 December 20X1
Retail sites opened during the year:	One on 1 May 20X1
	One on 1 September 20X1
Consolidated year-to-date profit attributable to ordinary equity holders of the parent entity:	CU1,100,000 as of 31 March 20X1
	CU2,300,000 as of 30 June 20X1
	CU1,900,000 as of 30 September 20X1 (including a CU450,000 loss from a discontinuing operation)
	CU2,900,000 as of 31 December 20X1

Basic earnings per share

	First quarter	Second quarter	Third quarter	Fourth quarter	Full year
Numerator (CU)	1,100,000	1,200,000	(400,000)	1,000,000	2,900,000
Denominator:					
Ordinary shares outstanding	1,000,000	1,000,000	1,000,000	1,000,000	1,000,000
Retail site contingency	–	3,333[a]	6,667[b]	10,000	5,000[c]
Earnings contingency[d]	–	–	–	–	–
Total shares	1,000,000	1,003,333	1,006,667	1,010,000	1,005,000
Basic earnings per share (CU)	1.10	1.20	(0.40)	0.99	2.89

(a)   5,000 shares × 2/3

(b)   5,000 shares + (5,000 shares × 1/3)

(c)   (5,000 shares × 8/12) + (5,000 shares × 4/12)

(d)   The earnings contingency has no effect on basic earnings per share because it is not certain that the condition is satisfied until the end of the contingency period. The effect is negligible for the fourth-quarter and full-year calculations because it is not certain that the condition is met until the last day of the period.

Diluted earnings per share

	First quarter	Second quarter	Third quarter	Fourth quarter	Full year
Numerator (CU)	1,100,000	1,200,000	(400,000)	1,000,000	2,900,000
Denominator:					
Ordinary shares outstanding	1,000,000	1,000,000	1,000,000	1,000,000	1,000,000
Retail site contingency	–	5,000	10,000	10,000	10,000
Earnings contingency	–[(e)]	300,000[(f)]	–[(g)]	900,000[(h)]	900,000[(h)]
Total shares	1,000,000	1,305,000	1,010,000	1,910,000	1,910,000
Diluted earnings per share (CU)	1.10	0.92	(0.40)[(i)]	0.52	1.52

Example 8 – Convertible Bonds Settled in Shares or Cash at the Issuer's Option

Reference: AASB 133, paragraphs 31-33, 36, 58 and 59

An entity issues 2,000 convertible bonds at the beginning of Year 1. The bonds have a three-year term, and are issued at par with a face value of CU1,000 per bond, giving total proceeds of CU2,000,000. Interest is payable annually in arrears at a nominal annual interest rate of 6 per cent. Each bond is convertible at any time up to maturity into 250 ordinary shares. The entity has an option to settle the principal amount of the convertible bonds in ordinary shares or in cash.

When the bonds are issued, the prevailing market interest rate for similar debt without a conversion option is 9 per cent. At the issue date, the market price of one ordinary share is CU3. Income tax is ignored.

Profit attributable to ordinary equity holders of the parent entity Year 1	CU1,000,000
Ordinary shares outstanding	1,200,000
Convertible bonds outstanding	2,000
Allocation of proceeds of bond issue:	
Liability component	CU1,848,122[6]
Equity component	CU151,878
	CU2,000,000

The liability and equity components would be determined in accordance with AASB 132. These amounts are recognised as the initial carrying amounts of the liability and equity components. The amount assigned to the issuer conversion option equity element is an addition to equity and is not adjusted.

(e)   Company A does not have year-to-date profit exceeding CU2,000,000 at 31 March 20X1. This Standard does not permit projecting future earnings levels and including the related contingent shares.

(f)   [(CU2,300,000 – CU2,000,000) ÷ 1,000] × 1,000 shares = 300,000 shares.

(g)   Year-to-date profit is less than CU2,000,000.

(h)   [(CU2,900,000 – CU2,000,000) ÷ 1,000] × 1,000 shares = 900,000 shares.

(i)   Because the loss during the third quarter is attributable to a loss from a discontinuing operation, the *antidilution* rules do not apply. The control number (i.e. profit or loss from continuing operations attributable to the equity holders of the parent entity) is positive. Accordingly, the effect of potential ordinary shares is included in the calculation of diluted earnings per share.

6   This represents the present value of the principal and interest discounted at 9% – CU2,000,000 payable at the end of three years; CU120,000 payable annually in arrears for three years.

Basic earnings per share Year 1:

$$\frac{CU1,000,000}{1,200,000} = CU0.83 \text{ per ordinary share}$$

Diluted earnings per share Year 1:

It is presumed that the issuer will settle the contract by the issue of ordinary shares. The dilutive effect is therefore calculated in accordance with paragraph 59 of the Standard.

$$\frac{CU1,000,000 + CU166,331^{(a)}}{1,200,000 + 500,000^{(b)}} = CU0.69 \text{ per ordinary share}$$

Example 9 – Calculation of Weighted Average Number of Shares: Determining the Order in Which to Include Dilutive Instruments[7]

Primary reference: AASB 133, paragraph 44

Secondary reference: AASB 133, paragraphs 10, 12, 19, 31-33, 36, 41-47, 49 and 50

Earnings	CU
Profit from continuing operations attributable to the parent entity	16,400,000
Less dividends on preference shares	(6,400,000)
Profit from continuing operations attributable to ordinary equity holders of the parent entity	10,000,000
Loss from discontinued operations attributable to the parent entity	(4,000,000)
Profit attributable to ordinary equity holders of the parent entity	6,000,000
Ordinary shares outstanding	2,000,000
Average market price of one ordinary share during year	CU75.00

Potential Ordinary Shares

Options	100,000 with exercise price of CU60.00
Convertible preference shares	800,000 shares with a par value of CU100 entitled to a cumulative dividend of CU8 per share. Each preference share is convertible to two ordinary shares.
5% convertible bonds	Nominal amount CU100,000,000. Each CU1,000 bond is convertible to 20 ordinary shares. There is no amortisation of premium or discount affecting the determination of interest expense.
Tax rate	40%

(a) Profit is adjusted for the accretion of CU166,331 (CU1,848,122 × 9%) of the liability because of the passage of time.

(b) 500,000 ordinary shares = 250 ordinary shares × 2000 convertible bonds.

7 This example does not illustrate the classification of the components of convertible financial instruments as liabilities and equity or the classification of related interest and dividends as expenses and equity as required by AASB 132.

Increase in Earnings Attributable to Ordinary Equity Holders on Conversion of Potential Ordinary Shares

		Increase in earnings	Increase in number of ordinary shares	Earnings per incremental share
		CU		CU
Options				
Increase in earnings		Nil		
Incremental shares issued for no consideration	100,000 × (CU75 – CU60) ÷ CU75		20,000	Nil
Convertible preference shares				
Increase in profit	CU800,000 × 100 × .08	6,400,000		
Incremental shares	2 × 800,000		1,600,000	4.00
5% convertible bonds				
Increase in profit	CU100,000,000 × 0.05 × (1 – 0.40)	3,000,000		
Incremental shares	100,000 × 20		2,000,000	1.50

The order in which to include the dilutive instruments is therefore:

(1) Options

(2) 5% convertible bonds

(3) Convertible preference shares

Calculation of Diluted Earnings per Share

	Profit from continuing operations attributable to ordinary equity holders of the parent entity (control number)	Ordinary shares	Per share	
	CU		CU	
As reported	10,000,000	2,000,000	5.00	
Options	–	20,000		
	10,000,000	2,020,000	4.95	Dilutive
5% convertible bonds	3,000,000	2,000,000		
	13,000,000	4,020,000	3.23	Dilutive
Convertible preference shares	6,400,000	1,600,000		
	19,400,000	5,620,000	3.45	Antidilutive

Because diluted earnings per share is increased when taking the convertible preference shares into account (from CU3.23 to CU3.45), the convertible preference shares are antidilutive and are ignored in the calculation of diluted earnings per share. Therefore, diluted earnings per share for profit from continuing operations is CU3.23:

	Basic EPS CU	*Diluted EPS* CU
Profit from continuing operations attributable to ordinary equity holders of the parent entity	5.00	3.23
Loss from discontinued operations attributable to ordinary equity holders of the parent entity	(2.00)[a]	(0.99)[b]
Profit attributable to ordinary equity holders of the parent entity	3.00[c]	2.24[d]

Example 10 – Instruments of a Subsidiary: Calculation of Basic and Diluted Earnings per Share[8]

Reference: AASB 133, paragraphs 40, A11 and A12

Parent:

Profit attributable to ordinary equity holders of the parent entity	CU12,000 (excluding any earnings of, or dividends paid by, the subsidiary)
Ordinary shares outstanding	10,000
Instruments of subsidiary owned by the parent	800 ordinary shares
	30 warrants exercisable to purchase ordinary shares of subsidiary
	300 convertible preference shares

(a)   (CU4,000,000) ÷ 2,000,000 = (CU2.00)

(b)   (CU4,000,000) ÷ 4,020,000 = (CU0.99)

(c)   CU6,000,000 ÷ 2,000,000 = CU3.00

(d)   (CU6,000,000 + CU3,000,000)/ 4,020,000 = CU2.24

8   This example does not illustrate the classification of the components of convertible financial instruments as liabilities and equity or the classification of related interest and dividends as expenses and equity as required by AASB 132.

Subsidiary:

Profit	CU5,400
Ordinary shares outstanding	1,000
Warrants	150, exercisable to purchase ordinary shares of the subsidiary
Exercise price	CU10
Average market price of one ordinary share	CU20
Convertible preference shares	400, each convertible into one ordinary share
Dividends on preference shares	CU1 per share

No inter-company eliminations or adjustments were necessary except for dividends.

For the purposes of this illustration, income taxes have been ignored.

Subsidiary's earnings per share

Basic EPS   CU5.00   calculated: $\dfrac{CU5,400^{(a)} - CU400^{(b)}}{1,000^{(c)}}$

Diluted EPS   CU3.66   calculated: $\dfrac{CU5,400^{(d)}}{(1,000 + 75^{(e)} + 400^{(f)})}$

Consolidated earnings per share

Basic EPS   CU1.63 calculated: $\dfrac{CU12,000^{(g)} + CU4,300^{(h)}}{10,000^{(i)}}$

Diluted EPS   CU1.61 calculated: $\dfrac{CU12,000 + CU2,928^{(j)} + CU55^{(k)} + CU1,098^{(l)}}{10,000}$

(a) Subsidiary's profit attributable to ordinary equity holders.

(b) Dividends paid by subsidiary on convertible preference shares.

(c) Subsidiary's ordinary shares outstanding.

(d) Subsidiary's profit attributable to ordinary equity holders (CU5,000) increased by CU400 preference dividends for the purpose of calculating diluted earnings per share.

(e) Incremental shares from warrants, calculated: [(CU20 – CU10) ÷ CU20] × 150.

(f) Subsidiary's ordinary shares assumed outstanding from conversion of convertible preference shares, calculated: 400 convertible preference shares × conversion factor of 1.

(g) Parent's profit attributable to ordinary equity holders of the parent entity.

(h) Portion of subsidiary's profit to be included in consolidated basic earnings per share, calculated: (800 × CU5.00) + (300 × CU1.00).

(i) Parent's ordinary shares outstanding.

(j) Parent's proportionate interest in subsidiary's earnings attributable to ordinary shares, calculated: (800 ÷ 1,000) × (1,000 shares × CU3.66 per share).

(k) Parent's proportionate interest in subsidiary's earnings attributable to warrants, calculated: (30 ÷ 150) × (75 incremental shares × CU3.66 per share).

(l) Parent's proportionate interest in subsidiary's earnings attributable to convertible preference shares, calculated: (300 ÷ 400) × (400 shares from conversion × CU3.66 per share).

Example 11 – Participating Equity Instruments and Two-Class Ordinary Shares[9]

Reference: AASB 133, paragraphs A13 and A14

Profit attributable to equity holders of the parent entity	CU100,000
Ordinary shares outstanding	10,000
Non-convertible preference shares	6,000
Non-cumulative annual dividend on preference shares (before any dividend is paid on ordinary shares)	CU5.50 per share

After ordinary shares have been paid a dividend of CU2.10 per share, the preference shares participate in any additional dividends on a 20:80 ratio with ordinary shares (i.e. after preference and ordinary shares have been paid dividends of CU5.50 and CU2.10 per share, respectively, preference shares participate in any additional dividends at a rate of one-fourth of the amount paid to ordinary shares on a per-share basis).

Dividends on preference shares paid	CU33,000	(CU5.50 per share)
Dividends on ordinary shares paid	CU21,000	(CU2.10 per share)

Basic earnings per share is calculated as follows:

	CU	CU
Profit attributable to equity holders of the parent entity		100,000
Less dividends paid:		
Preference	33,000	
Ordinary	21,000	(54,000)
Undistributed earnings		46,000

Allocation of undistributed earnings:

Allocation per ordinary share = A

Allocation per preference share = B; B = 1/4 A

$$(A \times 10,000) + (1/4 \times A \times 6,000) = CU46,000$$
$$A = CU46,000 \div (10,000 + 1,500)$$
$$A = CU4.00$$
$$B = 1/4 A$$
$$B = CU1.00$$

Basic per share amounts:

	Preference shares	Ordinary shares
Distributed earnings	CU5.50	CU2.10
Undistributed earnings	CU1.00	CU4.00
Totals	CU6.50	CU6.10

---

9 This example does not illustrate the classification of the components of convertible financial instruments as liabilities and equity or the classification of related interest and dividends as expenses and equity as required by AASB 132.

Example 12 – Calculation and Presentation of Basic and Diluted Earnings per Share (Comprehensive Example)[10]

This example illustrates the quarterly and annual calculations of basic and diluted earnings per share in the year 20X1 for Company A, which has a complex capital structure. The control number is profit or loss from continuing operations attributable to the parent entity. Other facts assumed are as follows:

Average market price of ordinary shares: The average market prices of ordinary shares for the calendar year 20X1 were as follows:

First quarter	CU49
Second quarter	CU60
Third quarter	CU67
Fourth quarter	CU67

The average market price of ordinary shares from 1 July to 1 September 20X1 was CU65.

Ordinary shares: The number of ordinary shares outstanding at the beginning of 20X1 was 5,000,000. On 1 March 20X1, 200,000 ordinary shares were issued for cash.

Convertible bonds: In the last quarter of 20X0, 5 per cent convertible bonds with a principal amount of CU12,000,000 due in 20 years were sold for cash at CU1,000 (par). Interest is payable twice a year, on 1 November and 1 May. Each CU1,000 bond is convertible into 40 ordinary shares. No bonds were converted in 20X0. The entire issue was converted on 1 April 20X1 because the issue was called by Company A.

Convertible preference shares: In the second quarter of 20X0, 800,000 convertible preference shares were issued for assets in a purchase transaction. The quarterly dividend on each convertible preference share is CU0.05, payable at the end of the quarter for shares outstanding at that date. Each share is convertible into one ordinary share. Holders of 600,000 convertible preference shares converted their preference shares into ordinary shares on 1 June 20X1.

Warrants: Warrants to buy 600,000 ordinary shares at CU55 per share for a period of five years were issued on 1 January 20X1. All outstanding warrants were exercised on 1 September 20X1.

Options: Options to buy 1,500,000 ordinary shares at CU75 per share for a period of 10 years were issued on 1 July 20X1. No options were exercised during 20X1 because the exercise price of the options exceeded the market price of the ordinary shares.

Tax rate: The tax rate was 40 per cent for 20X1.

20X1	Profit (loss) from continuing operations attributable to the parent entity[(a)]	Profit (loss) attributable to the parent entity
	CU	CU
First quarter	5,000,000	5,000,000
Second quarter	6,500,000	6,500,000
Third quarter	1,000,000	(1,000,000) [(b)]
Fourth quarter	(700,000)	(700,000)
Full year	11,800,000	9,800,000

---

10 This example does not illustrate the classification of the components of convertible financial instruments as liabilities and equity or the classification of related interest and dividends as expenses and equity as required by AASB 132.

(a) This is the control number (before adjusting for preference dividends).

(b) Company A had a CU2,000,000 loss (net of tax) from discontinued operations in the third quarter.

First Quarter 20X1

Basic EPS calculation	CU
Profit from continuing operations attributable to the parent entity	5,000,000
Less: preference share dividends	(40,000)(c)
Profit attributable to ordinary equity holders of the parent entity	4,960,000

Dates	Shares Outstanding	Fraction of period	Weighted-average shares
1 January – 28 February	5,000,000	2/3	3,333,333
Issue of ordinary shares on 1 March	200,000		
1 March – 31 March	5,200,000	1/3	1,733,333
Weighted-average shares			5,066,666
Basic EPS			**CU0.98**

Diluted EPS calculation	
Profit attributable to ordinary equity holders of the parent entity	CU4,960,000
Plus: profit impact of assumed conversions	
Preference share dividends	CU40,000(d)
Interest on 5% convertible bonds	CU90,000(e)
Effect of assumed conversions	CU130,000
Profit attributable to ordinary equity holders of the parent entity including assumed conversions	CU5,090,000
Weighted-average shares	5,066,666
Plus: incremental shares from assumed conversions	
Warrants	0(f)
Convertible preference shares	800,000
5% convertible bonds	480,000
Dilutive potential ordinary shares	1,280,000
Adjusted weighted-average shares	6,346,666
Diluted EPS	**CU0.80**

Second Quarter 20X1

Basic EPS calculation	CU
Profit from continuing operations attributable to the parent entity	6,500,000
Less: preference share dividends	(10,000)(g)
Profit attributable to ordinary equity holders of the parent entity	6,490,000

(c)   800,000 shares × CU0.05

(d)   800,000 shares × CU0.05

(e)   (CU12,000,000 × 5%) ÷ 4; less taxes at 40%

(f)   The warrants were not assumed to be exercised because they were antidilutive in the period (CU55 [exercise price] > CU49 [average price]).

(g)   200,000 shares × CU0.05

Dates	Shares outstanding	Fraction of period	Weighted-average shares
1 April	5,200,000		
Conversion of 5% bonds on 1 April	480,000		
1 April – 31 May	5,680,000	2/3	3,786,666
Conversion of preference shares on 1 June	600,000		
1 June – 30 June	6,280,000	1/3	2,093,333
Weighted-average shares			5,880,000
Basic EPS			**CU1.10**

Diluted EPS calculation

Profit attributable to ordinary equity holders of the parent entity	CU6,490,000
Plus: profit impact of assumed conversions	
Preference share dividends	CU10,000[h]
Effect of assumed conversions	CU10,000
Profit attributable to ordinary equity holders of the parent entity including assumed conversions	CU6,500,000
Weighted-average shares	5,880,000
Plus: incremental shares from assumed conversions	
Warrants	50,000[i]
Convertible preference shares	600,000[j]
Dilutive potential ordinary shares	650,000
Adjusted weighted-average shares	6,530,000
Diluted EPS	**CU1.00**

Third Quarter 20X1

Basic EPS calculation	CU
Profit from continuing operations attributable to the parent entity	1,000,000
Less: preference share dividends	(10,000)
Profit from continuing operations attributable to ordinary equity holders of the parent entity	990,000
Loss from discontinued operation attributable to the parent entity	(2,000,000)
Loss attributable to ordinary equity holders of the parent entity	(1,010,000)

(h) 200,000 shares × CU0.05

(i) CU55 × 600,000 = CU33,000,000; CU33,000,000 ÷ CU60 = 550,000; 600,000 − 550,000 = 50,000 shares
OR [(CU60 - CU55) ÷ CU60] × 600,000 shares = 50,000 shares

(j) (800,000 shares × 2/3) + (200,000 shares × 1/3)

Institute of Chartered Accountants Australia

Dates	Shares outstanding	Fraction of period	Weighted-average shares
1 July – 31 August	6,280,000	2/3	4,186,666
Exercise of warrants on 1 September	600,000		
1 September – 30 September	6,880,000	1/3	2,293,333
Weighted-average shares			6,480,000

Basic EPS

Profit from continuing operations	**CU0.15**
Loss from discontinued operations	**(CU0.31)**
Loss	**(CU0.16)**

Diluted EPS calculation

Profit from continuing operations attributable to ordinary equity holders of the parent entity		CU990,000
Plus: profit impact of assumed conversions		
Preference share dividends	CU10,000	
Effect of assumed conversions		CU10,000
Profit from continuing operations attributable to ordinary equity holders of the parent entity including assumed conversions		CU1,000,000
Loss from discontinued operations attributable to the parent entity		(CU2,000,000)
Loss attributable to ordinary equity holders of the parent entity including assumed conversions		(CU1,000,000)
Weighted-average shares		6,480,000
Plus: incremental shares from assumed conversions		
Warrants	61,538 [(k)]	
Convertible preference shares	200,000	
Dilutive potential ordinary shares		261,538
Adjusted weighted-average shares		6,741,538

Diluted EPS

Profit from continuing operations	**CU0.15**
Loss from discontinued operations	**(CU0.30)**
Loss	**(CU0.15)**

Note: The incremental shares from assumed conversions are included in calculating the diluted per-share amounts for the loss from discontinued operations even though they are antidilutive. This is because the control number (profit from continuing operations attributable to ordinary equity holders of the parent entity, adjusted for preference dividends) is positive (i.e. profit, rather than loss).

(k) $[(CU65 - CU55) \div CU65] \times 600,000 = 92,308$ shares; $92,308 \times 2/3 = 61,538$ shares

Fourth Quarter 20X1

	CU
Basic and diluted EPS calculation	
Loss from continuing operations attributable to the parent entity	(700,000)
Add: preference share dividends	(10,000)
Loss attributable to ordinary equity holders of the parent entity	(710,000)

Dates	Shares outstanding	Fraction of period	Weighted-average shares
1 October – 31 December	6,880,000	3/3	6,880,000
Weighted-average shares			6,880,000

Basic and diluted EPS

Loss attributable to ordinary equity holders of the parent entity	*(CU0.10)*

Note: The incremental shares from assumed conversions are not included in calculating the diluted per-share amounts because the control number (loss from continuing operations attributable to ordinary equity holders of the parent entity adjusted for preference dividends) is negative (i.e. a loss, rather than profit).

Full year 20X1

	CU
Basic EPS calculation	
Profit from continuing operations attributable to the parent entity	11,800,000
Less: preference share dividends	(70,000)
Profit from continuing operations attributable to ordinary equity holders of the parent entity	11,730,000
Loss from discontinued operations attributable to the parent entity	(2,000,000)
Profit attributable to ordinary equity holders of the parent entity	9,730,000

Dates	Shares Outstanding	Fraction of period	Weighted-average shares
1 January – 28 February	5,000,000	2/12	833,333
Issue of ordinary shares on 1 March	200,000		
1 March – 31 March	5,200,000	1/12	433,333
Conversion of 5% bonds on 1 April	480,000		
1 April – 31 May	5,680,000	2/12	946,667
Conversion of preference shares on 1 June	600,000		
1 June – 31 August	6,280,000	3/12	1,570,000
Exercise of warrants on 1 September	600,000		
1 September – 31 December	6,880,000	4/12	2,293,333
Weighted-average shares			6,076,667

Basic EPS

Profit from continuing operations	*CU1.93*
Loss from discontinued operations	*(CU0.33)*
Profit	*CU1.60*

Diluted EPS calculation

Profit from continuing operations attributable to ordinary equity holders of the parent entity		CU11,730,000
Plus: profit impact of assumed conversions		
Preference share dividends	CU70,000	
Interest on 5% convertible bonds	CU90,000[(l)]	
Effect of assumed conversions		CU160,000
Profit from continuing operations attributable to ordinary equity holders of the parent entity including assumed conversions		CU11,890,000
Loss from discontinued operations attributable to the parent entity		(CU2,000,000)
Profit attributable to ordinary equity holders of the parent entity including assumed conversions		CU9,890,000
Weighted-average shares		6,076,667
Plus: incremental shares from assumed conversions		
Warrants	14,880[(m)]	
Convertible preference shares	450,000[(n)]	
5% convertible bonds	120,000[(o)]	
Dilutive potential ordinary shares		584,880
Adjusted weighted-average shares		6,661,547

Diluted EPS

Profit from continuing operations	*CU1.78*
Loss from discontinued operations	*(CU0.30)*
Profit	*CU1.48*

(l)   (CU12,000,000 × 5%) ÷ 4; less taxes at 40%

(m)   [(CU57.125* − CU55) ÷ CU57.125] × 600,000 = 22,320 shares;
      22,320 × 8/12 = 14,880 shares
      * The average market price from 1 January 20X1 to 1 September 20X1.

(n)   (800,000 shares × 5/12) + (200,000 shares × 7/12)

(o)   480,000 shares × 3/12

The following illustrates how Company A might present its earnings per share data in its statement of comprehensive income. Note that the amounts per share for the loss from discontinued operations are not required to be presented in the statement of comprehensive income.

	For the year ended 20X1 CU
Earnings per ordinary share	
Profit from continuing operations	1.93
Loss from discontinued operations	(0.33)
Profit	1.60
Diluted earnings per ordinary share	
Profit from continuing operations	1.78
Loss from discontinued operations	(0.30)
Profit	1.48

The following table includes the quarterly and annual earnings per share data for Company A. The purpose of this table is to illustrate that the sum of the four quarters' earnings per share data will not necessarily equal the annual earnings per share data. The Standard does not require disclosure of this information.

	First quarter CU	Second quarter CU	Third quarter CU	Fourth quarter CU	Full year CU
Basic EPS					
Profit (loss) from continuing operations	0.98	1.10	0.15	(0.10)	1.93
Loss from discontinued operations	–	–	(0.31)	–	(0.33)
Profit (loss)	0.98	1.10	(0.16)	(0.10)	1.60
Diluted EPS					
Profit (loss) from continuing operations	0.80	1.00	0.15	(0.10)	1.78
Loss from discontinued operations	–	–	(0.30)	–	(0.30)
Profit (loss)	0.80	1.00	(0.15)	(0.10)	1.48

AASB 134
Interim Financial Reporting

(Compiled June 2012)

Note from the Institute of Chartered Accountants Australia

This note, prepared by the technical editors, is not part of Accounting Standard AASB 134.

Historical development

15 July 2004: AASB 134 'Interim Financial Reporting' is the Australian equivalent of IAS 34 of the same name. It was made by the AASB on 15 July 2004 as part of the AASB's program to adopt International Financial Reporting Standards (IFRSs) by 2005.

22 December 2005: AASB 2004-2 'Amendments to Australian Accounting Standards' amends paragraph Aus14.2, and is applicable to annual reporting periods beginning on or after 1 January 2005.

29 June 2005: AASB 2005-7 'Amendments to Australian Accounting Standards' deletes paragraph Aus21.1, and is applicable to annual reporting periods ending on or after 30 June 2005. Early adoption of this Standard is permitted for interim reporting periods beginning on or after 1 January 2005.

13 December 2006: AASB 2006-4 'Amendments to Australian Accounting Standards' amends paragraph Aus 1.3, adds Aus 2.1 and is applicable to annual reporting periods ending on or after 31 December 2006.

26 February 2007: AASB 2007-3 'Amendments to Australian Accounting Standards' was issued by the AASB. This Standard is applicable for annual reporting periods beginning on or after 1 January 2009.

30 April 2007: AASB 2007-4 'Amendments to Australian Accounting Standards' amends paragraphs 8 and 24, adds paragraph 14, and deletes Aus14.1, Aus14.2, Aus16.1-Aus16.4, Aus18.1, Aus21.1 and Aus27.1-Aus27.2. It is applicable to annual reporting periods beginning on or after 1 July 2007. Entities may elect to early-adopt it to annual reporting periods beginning on or after 1 January 2005.

24 September 2007: AASB 2007-8 'Amendments to Australian Accounting Standards arising from AASB 101' amends AASB 134 to align with revised AASB 101. This Standard is applicable to annual reporting periods beginning on or after 1 January 2009.

13 December 2007: AASB 2007-10 'Further Amendments to Australian Accounting Standards arising from AASB 101' amends AASB 134, replacing the term 'financial report' with 'financial statements'. This Standard is applicable to annual reporting periods beginning on or after 1 January 2009.

6 March 2008: AASB 2008-3 'Amendments to Australian Accounting Standards arising from AASB 3 and AASB 127' amends AASB 134 for the issue of AASB 3 Revised. This Standard is applicable to annual reporting periods beginning on or after 1 July 2009.

24 July 2008: AASB 2008-5 'Amendments to Australian Accounting Standards arising from the Annual Improvements Project' amends AASB 134 in relation to earnings per share disclosures in interim financial reports. This Standard is applicable to annual reporting periods beginning on or after 1 January 2009.

25 June 2009: AASB 2009-6 'Amendments to Australian Accounting Standards' amends AASB 134 for editorial corrections made by the International Accounting Standards Board (IASB) to its Standards and Interpretations (IFRSs) and as a consequence of issuing revised AASB 101 'Presentation of Financial Statements'. This Standard is applicable to annual reporting periods beginning on or after 1 January 2009 that end on or after 30 June 2009.

6 November 2009: AASB 134 was reissued by the AASB, compiled to include the AASB 2007-3, AASB 2007-8, AASB 2007-10, AASB 2008-3, AASB 2008-5 and AASB 2009-6 amendments and applies to annual reporting periods beginning on or after 1 July 2009. Early application is permitted.

---

23 June 2010: AASB 2010-4 'Further Amendments to Australian Accounting Standards arising from the Annual Improvements Project' amends AASB 134 in relation to significant events and transactions. This Standard is applicable to annual reporting periods beginning on or after 1 January 2011, with early adoption permitted for annual reporting periods beginning on or after 1 January 2005 but before 1 January 2011.

27 October 2010: AASB 2010-5 'Further Amendments to Australian Accounting Standards' makes editorial amendments to AASB 134. This Standard is applicable to annual reporting periods beginning on or after 1 January 2011.

11 May 2011: AASB 2011-1 'Amendments to Australian Accounting Standards arising from the Trans-Tasman Convergence Project' amends AASB 134 as a result of the Trans-Tasman project, to more closely align IFRSs as applied through Australian and New Zealand Standards. AASB 2011-1 deletes Australian specific disclosure requirements. Where appropriate these disclosures are now included in AASB 1054 'Australian Additional Requirements'. These Standards apply to annual reporting periods beginning on or after 1 July 2011 with early adoption permitted.

29 August 2011: AASB 2011-7 'Amendments to Australian Accounting Standards arising from the Consolidation and Joint Arrangements Standards' amends AASB 134 to give effect to many consequential changes arising from the issue of AASB 10, 11, 12, 127 and 128. This Standard applies to annual reporting periods beginning on or after 1 January 2013 and can be adopted early by for-profit entities. **These amendments are not included in this compiled this compiled Standard.**

2 September 2011: AASB 2011-8 'Amendments to Australian Accounting Standards arising from AASB 13' amends AASB 134 to give effect to a consequential change in the definition of fair value arising from the issue of AASB 13. This Standard applies to annual reporting periods beginning on or after 1 January 2013 and can be adopted early. **These amendments are not included in this compiled Standard.**

5 September 2011: AASB 2011-9 'Amendments to Australian Accounting Standards – Presentation of Items of Other Comprehensive Income' amends the presentation of items in other comprehensive income. This Standard applies to annual reporting periods beginning on or after 1 July 2012 and can be adopted early.

5 September 2011: AASB 2011-10 'Amendments to Australian Accounting Standards arising from AASB 119 (September 2011)' amends AASB 134 to give effect to a consequential change arising from the issue of AASB 119. This Standard applies to annual reporting periods beginning on or after 1 January 2013 and can be adopted early. **These amendments are not included in this compiled Standard.**

23 September 2011: AASB 134 was reissued by the AASB, compiled to include the AASB 2010-4, AASB 2010-5 and AASB 2011-1 amendments and applies to annual reporting periods ending on or after 1 July 2011 but before 1 July 2012.

20 June 2012: AASB 134 was reissued by the AASB, compiled to include the AASB 2011-9 amendments and applies to annual reporting periods beginning on or after 1 July 2012 but before 1 January 2013 and can be adopted early.

29 June 2012: AASB 2012-5 'Amendments to Australian Accounting Standards arising from Annual Improvements 2009–2011 Cycle' amends AASB 134 in relation to interim financial reporting and segment information for total assets and liabilities. This Standard applies to annual reporting periods beginning on or after 1 January 2013 and can be applied early. **These amendments are not included in this compiled Standard.**

References

Interpretation 10 *Interim Financial Reporting and Impairment*.

IFRIC item not taken onto the agenda: IAS 34-2 *Interim fair value disclosures* applies to AASB 134.

AASB 134 compared to IAS 34

Additions

Paragraph	Description
Aus 1.1	Which entities AASB 134 applies to (i.e. disclosing entities required to prepare half-year financial reports under the Corporations Act and other interim financial reports that are general purpose financial statements).
Aus 1.2	Further explanation of the Corporations Act requirement for half-year financial reports and voluntary interim financial reports.
Aus 1.3	Clarifies that interim financial reports that are special purpose financial statements or lack the characteristics of general purpose financial statements are not dealt with by AASB 134.
Aus 1.4	The application date of AASB 134 (i.e. interim reporting periods beginning 1 January 2005).
Aus 1.5	Prohibits early application of AASB 134.
Aus 1.6	Makes the requirements of AASB 134 subject to AASB 1031 'Materiality'.
Aus 1.7	Explains which Australian Standards have been superseded by AASB 134.
Aus 1.8	Clarifies that the superseded Australian Standards remain in force until AASB 134 applies.
Aus 1.9	Notice of the new Standard published on 22 July 2004.
Aus 2.1	Standard does not apply to interim financial reports for the General Government sector of each government.

Deletions

Paragraph	Description
46	Effective date of IAS 34.
47	Effective date of 2007 revisions to IAS 34.
48	Effective date of 2008 revisions to IAS 34.

AASB

Contents

Compilation Details

Comparison with IAS 34

Accounting Standard
AASB 134 Interim Financial Reporting

Paragraphs

Objective

Application   Aus1.1 – Aus1.9

Scope   1 – 3

Definitions   4

Content of an Interim Financial Report   5 – 7

    Minimum Components of an Interim Financial Report   8 – 8A

    Form and Content of Interim Financial Statements   9 – 14

    Significant Events and Transactions   15 – 15C

    Other Disclosures   16A

    Disclosure of Compliance with Australian Accounting Standards   19

    Periods for which Interim Financial Statements are
        Required to be Presented   20 – 22

    Materiality   23 – 25

Disclosure in Annual Financial Statements   26 – 27

Recognition and Measurement

    Same Accounting Policies as Annual   28 – 36

    Revenues Received Seasonally, Cyclically, or Occasionally   37 – 38

    Costs Incurred Unevenly During the Annual Reporting Period   39

    Applying the Recognition and Measurement Principles   40

    Use of Estimates   41 – 42

Restatement of Previously Reported Interim Periods   43 – 45

Effective Date of IAS 34   49 – 51

Illustrative Examples

    A. Illustration of Periods Required to be Presented

    B. Examples of Applying the Recognition and Measurement Principles

    C. Examples of the Use of Estimates

Australian Accounting Standard AASB 134 *Interim Financial Reporting* (as amended) is set out in paragraphs Aus1.1 – 51. All the paragraphs have equal authority. Paragraphs in **bold type** state the main principles. Terms defined in this Standard are in *italics* the first time they appear in the Standard. AASB 134 is to be read in the context of other Australian Accounting Standards including AASB 1048 *Interpretation of Standards*, which identifies the Australian Accounting Interpretations. In the absence of explicit guidance, AASB 108 *Accounting Policies, Changes in Accounting Estimates and Errors* provides a basis for selecting and applying accounting policies.

Compilation Details

Accounting Standard AASB 134 *Interim Financial Reporting* as amended

This compiled Standard applies to annual reporting periods beginning on or after 1 July 2012 but before 1 January 2013. It takes into account amendments up to and including 5 September 2011 and was prepared on 20 June 2012 by the staff of the Australian Accounting Standards Board (AASB).

This compilation is not a separate Accounting Standard made by the AASB. Instead, it is a representation of AASB 134 (July 2004) as amended by other Accounting Standards, which are listed in the Table below.

Table of Standards

Standard	Date made	Application date *(interim reporting periods ... on or after ...)*	Application, saving or transitional provisions
AASB 134	15 July 2004	*(beginning)* 1 Jan 2005	
AASB 2004-2	22 Dec 2004	*(beginning)* 1 Jan 2005	–
AASB 2005-7	29 June 2005	*(ending)* 30 June 2005	see (a) below
AASB 2006-4	13 Dec 2006	*(ending)* 31 Dec 2006	–
AASB 2007-3	26 Feb 2007	*(beginning)* 1 Jan 2009	see (b) below
AASB 2007-4	30 Apr 2007	*(beginning)* 1 Jul 2007	see (c) below
AASB 2007-8	24 Sep 2007	*(beginning)* 1 Jan 2009	see (d) below
AASB 2007-10	13 Dec 2007	*(beginning)* 1 Jan 2009	see (d) below
AASB 2008-3	6 Mar 2008	*(beginning)* 1 Jul 2009	see (e) below
AASB 2008-5	24 Jul 2008	*(beginning)* 1 Jan 2009	see (f) below
AASB 2009-6	25 Jun 2009	*(beginning)* 1 Jan 2009 and *(ending)* 30 Jun 2009	see (g) below
AASB 2010-4	23 Jun 2010	*(beginning)* 1 Jan 2011	see (h) below
AASB 2010-2	30 Jun 2010	*(beginning)* 1 Jul 2013	not compiled*
AASB 2010-5	27 Oct 2010	*(beginning)* 1 Jan 2011	see (h) below
AASB 2011-1	11 May 2010	*(beginning)* 1 Jul 2011	see (i) below
AASB 2011-8	2 Sep 2011	*(beginning)* 1 Jan 2013	not compiled*
AASB 2011-9	5 Sep 2011	*(beginning)* 1 Jul 2012	see (j) below
AASB 2011-10	5 Sep 2011	*(beginning)* 1 Jan 2013	not compiled*

*   The amendments made by this Standard are not included in this compilation, which presents the principal Standard as applicable to annual reporting periods beginning on or after 1 July 2012 but before 1 January 2013.

(a)   Entities may elect to apply this Standard to interim reporting periods beginning on or after 1 January 2005 that end before 30 June 2005.

(b)   Entities may elect to apply this Standard to annual reporting periods beginning on or after 1 January 2005 but before 1 January 2009, provided that AASB 8 *Operating Segments* is also applied to such periods.

(c)   Entities may elect to apply this Standard to annual reporting periods beginning on or after 1 January 2005 but before 1 July 2007.

(d)   Entities may elect to apply this Standard to annual reporting periods beginning on or after 1 January 2005 but before 1 January 2009, provided that AASB 101 *Presentation of Financial Statements* (September 2007) is also applied to such periods.

(e)   Entities may elect to apply this Standard to annual reporting periods beginning on or after 30 June 2007 but before 1 July 2009, provided that AASB 3 *Business Combinations* (March 2008) and AASB 127 *Consolidated and Separate Financial Statements* (March 2008) are also applied to such periods.

(f)   Entities may elect to apply this Standard, or its amendments to individual Standards, to annual reporting periods beginning on or after 1 January 2005 but before 1 January 2009.

(g) Entities may elect to apply this Standard to annual reporting periods beginning on or after 1 January 2005 but before 1 January 2009, provided that AASB 101 *Presentation of Financial Statements* (September 2007) is also applied to such periods, and to annual reporting periods beginning on or after 1 January 2009 that end before 30 June 2009.

(h) Entities may elect to apply this Standard to annual reporting periods beginning on or after 1 January 2005 but before 1 January 2011.

(i) Entities may elect to apply this Standard, or its amendments to individual pronouncements, to annual reporting periods beginning on or after 1 January 2005 but before 1 July 2011, provided that AASB 1054 *Australian Additional Disclosures* is, or its relevant individual disclosure requirements are, also applied to such periods.

(j) Entities may elect to apply this Standard to annual reporting periods beginning on or after 1 January 2005 but before 1 July 2012.

Table of Amendments to Standard

Paragraph affected	How affected	By ... [paragraph]
Objective	amended	AASB 2007-10 [76]
Aus1.1	amended	AASB 2007-8 [7, 8]
	amended	AASB 2007-10 [77]
Aus1.2	amended	AASB 2007-8 [8, 104]
	amended	AASB 2007-10 [77]
Aus1.3	amended	AASB 2006-4 [4]
	amended	AASB 2007-8 [7, 8]
	amended	AASB 2007-10 [77]
Aus1.6	amended	AASB 2007-8 [8]
	amended	AASB 2007-10 [77]
1	amended	AASB 2007-10 [77]
	amended	AASB 2011-1 [20]
2	amended	AASB 2007-10 [77]
Aus2.1	added	AASB 2006-4 [5]
4	amended	AASB 2007-8 [105]
5	amended	AASB 2007-8 [105]
6-7	amended	AASB 2007-10 [77]
8	amended	AASB 2007-4 [95]
	amended	AASB 2007-8 [105]
	amended	AASB 2011-9 [23]
8A	added	AASB 2007-8 [106]
	amended	AASB 2011-9 [23]
9	amended	AASB 2007-10 [77]
	heading amended	AASB 2007-10 [80]
10	amended	AASB 2007-10 [77]
11	amended	AASB 2007-8 [107]
	amended	AASB 2008-5 [55]
11A	added	AASB 2007-8 [108]
	amended	AASB 2011-9 [23]
12	amended	AASB 2007-8 [6, 109]
	amended	AASB 2010-5 [43]
13	deleted	AASB 2007-8 [110]
	note added	AASB 2007-10 [78]
14	added	AASB 2007-4 [93]
Aus14.1	deleted	AASB 2007-4 [94]
Aus14.2	amended	AASB 2004-2 [14]
	deleted	AASB 2007-4 [94]
15 (preceding heading)	amended	AASB 2010-4 [12]
15	amended	AASB 2007-8 [6]
	amended	AASB 2010-4 [12]

AASB

Paragraph affected	How affected	By ... [paragraph]
15A-15C	added	AASB 2010-4 [12]
16	amended	AASB 2007-3 [13]
	amended	AASB 2007-8 [111]
	amended	AASB 2007-10 [79]
	amended	AASB 2008-3 [58]
	deleted	AASB 2010-4 [12]
16A (and preceding heading)	added	AASB 2010-4 [12]
Aus16.1-Aus16.4	deleted	AASB 2007-4 [94]
17	amended	AASB 2007-8 [6]
	deleted	AASB 2010-4 [12]
18	amended	AASB 2007-10 [77]
	deleted	AASB 2010-4 [12]
Aus18.1	deleted	AASB 2007-4 [94]
19	amended	AASB 2009-6 [76]
20	amended	AASB 2007-8 [6, 112]
	heading amended	AASB 2007-10 [80]
	amended	AASB 2009-6 [77]
	amended	AASB 2011-9 [23]
21	amended	AASB 2007-8 [113]
Aus21.1	deleted	AASB 2005-7 [6]
22	amended	AASB 2010-5 [44]
24	amended	AASB 2007-4 [95]
	amended	AASB 2007-10 [80]
26 (and preceding heading)	amended	AASB 2007-10 [79]
27	amended	AASB 2007-10 [79]
	amended	AASB 2009-6 [78]
Aus27.1-Aus27.2	deleted	AASB 2007-4 [94]
28	amended	AASB 2007-10 [80]
29	amended	AASB 2007-10 [80, 81]
30	amended	AASB 2007-8 [114]
	amended	AASB 2007-10 [82]
31	amended	AASB 2007-8 [6, 115]
32	amended	AASB 2007-8 [116]
33	amended	AASB 2007-8 [6]
34	amended	AASB 2007-10 [80]
35	amended	AASB 2007-10 [77]
36	amended	AASB 2007-10 [83]
40	amended	AASB 2010-5 [45]
42	amended	AASB 2010-5 [46]
47	note added	AASB 2007-8 [117]
48	note added	AASB 2008-3 [59]
49	added	AASB 2010-4 [12]
51	added	AASB 2011-9 [23]

Table of Amendments to Illustrative Examples

Paragraph affected	How affected	By ... [paragraph]
A, title, rubric, heading	amended	AASB 2010-5 [47, 48]
A1	amended	AASB 2007-8 [6]
A2	amended	AASB 2007-8 [6]

Paragraph affected	How affected	By ... [paragraph]
B, title, rubric, heading	amended	AASB 2010-5 [49]
B3	amended	AASB 2007-8 [6]
	amended	AASB 2009-6 [79]
B7	amended	AASB 2010-5 [50]
B8	amended	AASB 2007-8 [6]
B10	amended	AASB 2007-8 [6]
	amended	AASB 2009-6 [79]
B11	amended	AASB 2009-6 [79]
B13	amended	AASB 2007-10 [79]
B25	amended	AASB 2009-6 [79]
B28	amended	AASB 2009-6 [79]
B30	amended	AASB 2007-10 [80]
	amended	AASB 2009-6 [79]
B33	amended	AASB 2007-8 [6]
	amended	AASB 2010-5 [51]
C, title, rubric, heading	amended	AASB 2010-5 [52]
C2	amended	AASB 2009-6 [80]
C4	amended	AASB 2007-8 [6]
C5	amended	AASB 2009-6 [80]
C7	amended	AASB 2009-6 [80]

Comparison with IAS 34

AASB 134 and IAS 34

AASB 134 *Interim Financial Reporting* as amended incorporates IAS 34 *Interim Financial Reporting* as issued and amended by the International Accounting Standards Board (IASB). Paragraphs that have been added to this Standard (and do not appear in the text of IAS 34) are identified with the prefix "Aus", followed by the number of the relevant IASB paragraph and decimal numbering.

Compliance with IAS 34

Entities that comply with AASB 134 as amended will simultaneously be in compliance with IAS 34 as amended.

Accounting Standard AASB 134

The Australian Accounting Standards Board made Accounting Standard AASB 134 *Interim Financial Reporting* under section 334 of the *Corporations Act 2001* on 15 July 2004.

This compiled version of AASB 134 applies to annual reporting periods beginning on or after 1 July 2012 but before 1 January 2013. It incorporates relevant amendments contained in other AASB Standards made by the AASB up to and including 5 September 2011 (see Compilation Details).

Accounting Standard AASB 134

Interim Financial Reporting

Objective

The objective of this Standard is to prescribe the minimum content of an interim financial report and to prescribe the principles for recognition and measurement in complete or condensed financial statements for an interim period. Timely and reliable interim financial reporting improves the ability of investors, creditors, and others to understand an entity's capacity to generate earnings and cash flows and its financial condition and liquidity.

Application

Aus1.1   **This Standard applies to:**

(a)   **each disclosing entity required to prepare half-year financial reports in accordance with Part 2M.3 of the Corporations Act;**

(b)   *interim financial reports* **that are general purpose financial statements of each other reporting entity; and**

(c)   **interim financial reports that are, or are held out to be, general purpose financial statements.**

Aus1.2   Under the Corporations Act, disclosing entities are required to prepare half-year financial reports. Disclosing entities may also voluntarily prepare other general purpose interim financial reports. This Standard prescribes the form and content of general purpose interim financial reports, including half-year financial reports prepared by disclosing entities.

Aus1.3   Interim financial reports that are intended to be special purpose financial reports do not fall within the scope of this Standard. However, interim financial reports that are purported to be special purpose financial reports but have the characteristics of general purpose financial statements fall within the scope of this Standard. Interim financial reports that are widely available but lack the characteristics of general purpose financial statements are not regarded as general purpose financial statements. An example is selected interim summary financial information, such as turnover and profit, voluntarily released by some entities. In some cases, professional judgement is needed to determine whether particular interim financial reports are general purpose financial statements.

Aus1.4   **This Standard applies to *interim periods* beginning on or after 1 January 2005.** [Note: For application dates of paragraphs changed or added by an amending Standard, see Compilation Details.]

Aus1.5   **This Standard shall not be applied to interim periods beginning before 1 January 2005.**

Aus1.6   **The requirements specified in this Standard apply to the interim financial report where information resulting from their application is material in accordance with AASB 1031 *Materiality*.**

Aus1.7   **When applicable, this Standard supersedes AASB 1029 *Interim Financial Reporting* as notified in the *Commonwealth of Australia Gazette* No S 534, 5 October 2000.**

Aus1.8   AASB 1029 remains applicable until superseded by this Standard.

Aus1.9   Notice of this Standard was published in the *Commonwealth of Australia Gazette* No S 294, 22 July 2004.

Scope

1   This Standard does not mandate which entities should be required to publish interim financial reports, how frequently, or how soon after the end of an interim period. However, governments, securities regulators, stock exchanges, and accountancy bodies often require entities whose debt or equity securities are publicly traded to publish interim financial reports. This Standard applies if an entity is required or elects to publish an interim financial report in accordance with Australian Accounting Standards. The International Accounting Standards Committee[1] encourages publicly traded entities to provide interim financial reports that conform to the recognition, measurement, and disclosure principles set out in this Standard. Specifically, publicly traded entities are encouraged:

(a)   to provide interim financial reports at least as of the end of the first half of their annual reporting period; and

(b)   to make their interim financial reports available not later than 60 days after the end of the interim period.

---

1   The International Accounting Standards Committee was succeeded by the International Accounting Standards Board, which began operations in 2001.

2   Each financial report, annual or interim, is evaluated on its own for conformity to
        Australian Accounting Standards. The fact that an entity may not have provided interim
        financial reports during a particular annual reporting period or may have provided interim
        financial reports that do not comply with this Standard does not prevent the entity's
        annual financial statements from conforming to Australian Accounting Standards if they
        otherwise do so.

**Aus2.1   This Standard does not apply to interim financial reports for the General
        Government Sector of each government.**

3   If an entity's interim financial report is described as complying with Australian Accounting
        Standards, it must comply with all of the requirements of this Standard. Paragraph 19
        requires certain disclosures in that regard.

Definitions

4   **The following terms are used in this Standard with the meanings specified.**

        Interim financial report **means a financial report containing either a complete set
        of financial statements (as described in AASB 101** *Presentation of Financial
        Statements* **(as revised in 2007)) or a set of condensed financial statements
        (as described in this Standard) for an interim period.**

        Interim period **is a reporting period shorter than a full annual reporting period.**

Content of an Interim Financial Report

5   AASB 101 (as revised in 2007) defines a complete set of financial statements as including
        the following components:

        (a)   a statement of financial position as at the end of the period;

        (b)   a statement of comprehensive income for the period;

        (c)   a statement of changes in equity for the period;

        (d)   a statement of cash flows for the period;

        (e)   notes, comprising a summary of significant accounting policies and other explanatory
                information; and

        (f)   a statement of financial position as at the beginning of the earliest comparative period
                when an entity applies an accounting policy retrospectively or makes a retrospective
                restatement of items in its financial statements, or when it reclassifies items in its
                financial statements.

6   In the interest of timeliness and cost considerations and to avoid repetition of information
        previously reported, an entity may be required to or may elect to provide less information
        at interim dates as compared with its annual financial statements. This Standard defines
        the minimum content of an interim financial report as including condensed financial
        statements and selected explanatory notes. The interim financial report is intended to
        provide an update on the latest complete set of annual financial statements. Accordingly,
        it focuses on new activities, events, and circumstances and, except for comparatives, does
        not duplicate information previously reported.

7   Nothing in this Standard is intended to prohibit or discourage an entity from publishing
        a complete set of financial statements (as described in AASB 101) as its interim financial
        report, rather than condensed financial statements and selected explanatory notes. Nor does
        this Standard prohibit or discourage an entity from including in condensed interim financial
        statements more than the minimum line items or selected explanatory notes as set out in
        this Standard. The recognition and measurement guidance in this Standard applies also to
        complete financial statements for an interim period, and such statements would include all
        of the disclosures required by this Standard (particularly the selected note disclosures in
        paragraph 16) and those required by other Australian Accounting Standards.

Minimum Components of an Interim Financial Report

8   **An interim financial report shall include, at a minimum, the following components:**

        (a)   **a condensed statement of financial position;**

AASB 134   Institute of Chartered Accountants Australia

AASB

    (b)   a condensed statement or condensed statements of profit or loss and other comprehensive income;

    (c)   a condensed statement of changes in equity;

    (d)   a condensed statement of cash flows; and

    (e)   selected explanatory notes.

8A   If an entity presents items of profit or loss in a separate statement as described in paragraph 10A of AASB 101 (as amended in 2011), it presents interim condensed information from that statement.

Form and Content of Interim Financial Statements

9   If an entity publishes a complete set of financial statements in its interim financial report, the form and content of those statements shall conform to the requirements of AASB 101 for a complete set of financial statements.

10   If an entity publishes a set of condensed financial statements in its interim financial report, those condensed statements shall include, at a minimum, each of the headings and subtotals that were included in its most recent annual financial statements and the selected explanatory notes as required by this Standard. Additional line items or notes shall be included if their omission would make the condensed interim financial statements misleading.

11   In the statement that presents the components of profit or loss for an interim period, an entity shall present basic and diluted earnings per share for that period when the entity is within the scope of AASB 133 *Earnings per Share*[2].

11A   If an entity presents items of profit or loss in a separate statement as described in paragraph 10A of AASB 101 (as amended in 2011), it presents basic and diluted earnings per share in that statement.

12   AASB 101 (as revised in 2007) provides guidance on the structure of financial statements. The Implementation Guidance for IAS 1 illustrates ways in which the statement of financial position, statement of comprehensive income and statement of changes in equity may be presented.

13   [Deleted by the IASB]

14   An interim financial report is prepared on a consolidated basis if the entity's most recent annual financial statements were consolidated statements. The parent's separate financial statements are not consistent or comparable with the consolidated statements in the most recent annual financial report. If an entity's annual financial report included the parent's separate financial statements in addition to consolidated financial statements, this Standard neither requires nor prohibits the inclusion of the parent's separate statements in the entity's interim financial report.

Significant Events and Transactions

15   An entity shall include in its interim financial report an explanation of events and transactions that are significant to an understanding of the changes in financial position and performance of the entity since the end of the last annual reporting period. Information disclosed in relation to those events and transactions shall update the relevant information presented in the most recent annual financial report.

15A   A user of an entity's interim financial report will have access to the most recent annual financial report of that entity. Therefore, it is unnecessary for the notes to an interim financial report to provide relatively insignificant updates to the information that was reported in the notes in the most recent annual financial report.

---

2   This paragraph was amended by AASB 2008-5 *Amendments to Australian Accounting Standards arising from the Annual Improvements Project* issued in July 2008 to clarify the scope of AASB 134.

15B   The following is a list of events and transactions for which disclosures would be required
        if they are significant; the list is not exhaustive:

   (a)   the write-down of inventories to net realisable value and the reversal of such a write-
           down;

   (b)   recognition of a loss from the impairment of financial assets, property, plant and
           equipment, intangible assets, or other assets, and the reversal of such an impairment
           loss;

   (c)   the reversal of any provisions for the costs of restructuring;

   (d)   acquisitions and disposals of items of property, plant and equipment;

   (e)   commitments for the purchase of property, plant and equipment;

   (f)   litigation settlements;

   (g)   corrections of prior period errors;

   (h)   changes in the business or economic circumstances that affect the fair value of the
           entity's financial assets and financial liabilities, whether those assets or liabilities
           are recognised at fair value or amortised cost;

   (i)   any loan default or breach of a loan agreement that has not been remedied on or
           before the end of the reporting period;

   (j)   related party transactions;

   (k)   transfers between levels of the fair value hierarchy used in measuring the fair value
           of financial instruments;

   (l)   changes in the classification of financial assets as a result of a change in the purpose
           or use of those assets; and

   (m)   changes in contingent liabilities or contingent assets.

15C   Individual Australian Accounting Standards provide guidance regarding disclosure
        requirements for many of the items listed in paragraph 15B. When an event or transaction
        is significant to an understanding of the changes in an entity's financial position or
        performance since the last annual reporting period, its interim financial report should
        provide an explanation of and an update to the relevant information included in the
        financial statements of the last annual reporting period.

Other Disclosures

16   [Deleted by the IASB]

16A   **In addition to disclosing significant events and transactions in accordance with
        paragraphs 15-15C, an entity shall include the following information, in the notes
        to its interim financial statements, if not disclosed elsewhere in the interim financial
        report. The information shall normally be reported on an annual reporting period-
        to-date basis.**

   (a)   **a statement that the same accounting policies and methods of computation are
           followed in the interim financial statements as compared with the most recent
           annual financial statements or, if those policies or methods have been changed,
           a description of the nature and effect of the change;**

   (b)   **explanatory comments about the seasonality or cyclicality of interim
           operations;**

   (c)   **the nature and amount of items affecting assets, liabilities, equity, net income
           or cash flows that are unusual because of their nature, size or incidence;**

   (d)   **the nature and amount of changes in estimates of amounts reported in prior
           interim periods of the current annual reporting period or changes in estimates
           of amounts reported in prior annual reporting periods;**

   (e)   **issues, repurchases and repayments of debt and equity securities;**

   (f)   **dividends paid (aggregate or per share) separately for ordinary shares and
           other shares;**

(g)   the following segment information (disclosure of segment information is required in an entity's interim financial report only if AASB 8 *Operating Segments* requires that entity to disclose segment information in its annual financial statements):

    (i)   revenues from external customers, if included in the measure of segment profit or loss reviewed by the chief operating decision maker or otherwise regularly provided to the chief operating decision maker;

    (ii)   intersegment revenues, if included in the measure of segment profit or loss reviewed by the chief operating decision maker or otherwise regularly provided to the chief operating decision maker;

    (iii)   a measure of segment profit or loss;

    (iv)   total assets for which there has been a material change from the amount disclosed in the last annual financial statements;

    (v)   a description of differences from the last annual financial statements in the basis of segmentation or in the basis of measurement of segment profit or loss;

    (vi)   a reconciliation of the total of the reportable segments' measures of profit or loss to the entity's profit or loss before tax expense (tax income) and discontinued operations. However, if an entity allocates to reportable segments items such as tax expense (tax income), the entity may reconcile the total of the segments' measures of profit or loss to profit or loss after those items. Material reconciling items shall be separately identified and described in that reconciliation;

(h)   events after the interim period that have not been reflected in the financial statements for the interim period; and

(i)   the effect of changes in the composition of the entity during the interim period, including business combinations, obtaining or losing control of subsidiaries and long-term investments, restructurings, and discontinued operations. In the case of business combinations, the entity shall disclose the information required by AASB 3 *Business Combinations*.

17   [Deleted by the IASB]

18   [Deleted by the IASB]

Disclosure of Compliance with Australian Accounting Standards

19   If an entity's interim financial report is in compliance with this Standard, that fact shall be disclosed. An interim financial report shall not be described as complying with Australian Accounting Standards unless it complies with all the requirements of Australian Accounting Standards.

Periods for which Interim Financial Statements are Required to be Presented

20   Interim reports shall include interim financial statements (condensed or complete) for periods as follows:

(a)   statement of financial position as of the end of the current interim period and a comparative statement of financial position as of the end of the immediately preceding annual reporting period;

(b)   statements of profit or loss and other comprehensive income for the current interim period and cumulatively for the current annual reporting period to date, with comparative statements of profit or loss and other comprehensive income for the comparable interim periods (current and annual reporting period-to-date) of the immediately preceding annual reporting period. As permitted by AASB 101 (as amended in 2011), an interim report may present for each period a statement or statements of profit or loss and other comprehensive income;

(c)   statement of changes in equity cumulatively for the current annual reporting period to date, with a comparative statement for the comparable annual reporting period-to-date period of the immediately preceding annual reporting period; and

(d)   statement of cash flows cumulatively for the current annual reporting period to date, with a comparative statement for the comparable annual reporting period-to-date period of the immediately preceding annual reporting period.

21   For an entity whose business is highly seasonal, financial information for the twelve months up to the end of the interim period and comparative information for the prior twelve-month period may be useful. Accordingly, entities whose business is highly seasonal are encouraged to consider reporting such information in addition to the information called for in the preceding paragraph.

22   Part A of the illustrative examples accompanying this Standard illustrates the periods required to be presented by an entity that reports half-yearly and an entity that reports quarterly.

Materiality

23   **In deciding how to recognise, measure, classify, or disclose an item for interim financial reporting purposes, materiality shall be assessed in relation to the interim period financial data. In making assessments of materiality, it shall be recognised that interim measurements may rely on estimates to a greater extent than measurements of annual financial data.**

24   In deciding whether an item is material, its nature and amount usually need to be evaluated together. AASB 1031 *Materiality* provides guidance on the role of materiality in making judgements in the preparation and presentation of financial statements. AASB 101 and AASB 108 *Accounting Policies, Changes in Accounting Estimates and Errors* define an item as material if its omission or misstatement could influence the economic decisions of users of the financial statements. AASB 101 requires separate disclosure of material items, including (for example) discontinued operations, and AASB 108 requires disclosure of changes in accounting estimates, errors and changes in accounting policies.

25   While judgement is always required in assessing materiality, this Standard bases the recognition and disclosure decision on data for the interim period by itself for reasons of understandability of the interim figures. Thus, for example, unusual items, changes in accounting policies or estimates, and errors are recognised and disclosed on the basis of materiality in relation to interim period data to avoid misleading inferences that might result from non-disclosure. The overriding goal is to ensure that an interim financial report includes all information that is relevant to understanding an entity's financial position and performance during the interim period.

Disclosure in Annual Financial Statements

26   **If an estimate of an amount reported in an interim period is changed significantly during the final interim period of the annual reporting period but a separate financial report is not published for that final interim period, the nature and amount of that change in estimate shall be disclosed in a note in the annual financial statements for that annual reporting period.**

27   AASB 108 requires disclosure of the nature and (if practicable) the amount of a change in estimate that either has a material effect in the current period or is expected to have a material effect in subsequent periods. Paragraph 16(d) of this Standard requires similar disclosure in an interim financial report. Examples include changes in estimate in the final interim period relating to inventory write-downs, restructurings, or impairment losses that were reported in an earlier interim period of the annual reporting period. The disclosure required by the preceding paragraph is consistent with the AASB 108 requirement and is intended to be narrow in scope – relating only to the change in estimate. An entity is not required to include additional interim period financial information in its annual financial statements.

Recognition and Measurement

Same Accounting Policies as Annual

28   **An entity shall apply the same accounting policies in its interim financial statements as are applied in its annual financial statements, except for accounting policy changes made after the date of the most recent annual financial statements that are to be reflected in the next annual financial statements. However, the frequency of an entity's reporting (annual, half-yearly, or quarterly) shall not affect the measurement of its annual results. To achieve that objective, measurements for interim reporting purposes shall be made on an annual reporting period-to-date basis.**

29   Requiring that an entity apply the same accounting policies in its interim financial statements as in its annual statements may seem to suggest that interim period measurements are made as if each interim period stands alone as an independent reporting period. However, by providing that the frequency of an entity's reporting should not affect the measurement of its annual results, paragraph 28 acknowledges that an interim period is a part of a larger annual reporting period. Annual reporting period-to-date measurements may involve changes in estimates of amounts reported in prior interim periods of the current annual reporting period. But the principles for recognising assets, liabilities, income and expenses for interim periods are the same as in annual financial statements.

30   To illustrate:

    (a)   the principles for recognising and measuring losses from inventory write-downs, restructurings, or impairments in an interim period are the same as those that an entity would follow if it prepared only annual financial statements. However, if such items are recognised and measured in one interim period and the estimate changes in a subsequent interim period of that annual reporting period, the original estimate is changed in the subsequent interim period either by accrual of an additional amount of loss or by reversal of the previously recognised amount;

    (b)   a cost that does not meet the definition of an asset at the end of an interim period is not deferred in the statement of financial position either to await future information as to whether it has met the definition of an asset or to smooth earnings over interim periods within an annual reporting period; and

    (c)   income tax expense is recognised in each interim period based on the best estimate of the weighted average annual income tax rate expected for the full annual reporting period. Amounts accrued for income tax expense in one interim period may have to be adjusted in a subsequent interim period of that annual reporting period if the estimate of the annual income tax rate changes.

31   Under the *Framework for the Preparation and Presentation of Financial Statements* (the *Framework*), recognition is the "process of incorporating in the statement of financial position or statement of comprehensive income an item that meets the definition of an element and satisfies the criteria for recognition". The definitions of assets, liabilities, income and expenses are fundamental to recognition, at the end of both annual and interim financial reporting periods.

32   For assets, the same tests of future economic benefits apply at interim dates and at the end of an entity's annual reporting period. Costs that, by their nature, would not qualify as assets at the end of an annual reporting period would not qualify at interim dates either. Similarly, a liability at the end of an interim reporting period must represent an existing obligation at that date, just as it must at the end of an annual reporting period.

33   An essential characteristic of income (revenue) and expenses is that the related inflows and outflows of assets and liabilities have already taken place. If those inflows or outflows have taken place, the related revenue and expense are recognised; otherwise they are not recognised. The *Framework* says that "expenses are recognised in the statement of comprehensive income when a decrease in future economic benefits related to a decrease in an asset or an increase of a liability has arisen that can be measured reliably.... [The] *Framework* does not allow the recognition of items in the statement of financial position which do not meet the definition of assets or liabilities".

34   In measuring the assets, liabilities, income, expenses and cash flows reported in its financial statements, an entity that reports only annually is able to take into account information that becomes available throughout the annual reporting period. Its measurements are, in effect, on an annual reporting period-to-date basis.

35   An entity that reports half-yearly uses information available by mid-year or shortly thereafter in making the measurements in its financial statements for the first six-month period and information available by the end of the annual reporting period or shortly thereafter for the twelve-month period. The twelve-month measurements will reflect possible changes in estimates of amounts reported for the first six-month period. The amounts reported in the interim financial report for the first six-month period are not retrospectively adjusted. Paragraphs 16(d) and 26 require, however, that the nature and amount of any significant changes in estimates be disclosed.

36   An entity that reports more frequently than half-yearly measures income and expenses on an annual reporting period-to-date basis for each interim period using information available when each set of financial statements is being prepared. Amounts of income and expenses reported in the current interim period will reflect any changes in estimates of amounts reported in prior interim periods of the annual reporting period. The amounts reported in prior interim periods are not retrospectively adjusted. Paragraphs 16(d) and 26 require, however, that the nature and amount of any significant changes in estimates be disclosed.

Revenues Received Seasonally, Cyclically, or Occasionally

37   **Revenues that are received seasonally, cyclically, or occasionally within an annual reporting period shall not be anticipated or deferred as of an interim date if anticipation or deferral would not be appropriate at the end of the entity's annual reporting period.**

38   Examples include dividend revenue, royalties and government grants. Additionally, some entities consistently earn more revenues in certain interim periods of an annual reporting period than in other interim periods, for example, seasonal revenues of retailers. Such revenues are recognised when they occur.

Costs Incurred Unevenly During the Annual Reporting Period

39   **Costs that are incurred unevenly during an entity's annual reporting period shall be anticipated or deferred for interim reporting purposes if, and only if, it is also appropriate to anticipate or defer that type of cost at the end of each annual reporting period.**

Applying the Recognition and Measurement Principles

40   Part B of the illustrative examples accompanying this Standard provides examples of applying the general recognition and measurement principles set out in paragraphs 28-39.

Use of Estimates

41   **The measurement procedures to be followed in an interim financial report shall be designed to ensure that the resulting information is reliable and that all material financial information that is relevant to an understanding of the financial position or performance of the entity is appropriately disclosed. While measurements in both annual and interim financial reports are often based on reasonable estimates, the preparation of interim financial reports generally will require a greater use of estimation methods than annual financial reports.**

42   Part C of the illustrative examples accompanying this Standard provides examples of the use of estimates in interim periods.

Restatement of Previously Reported Interim Periods

43   **A change in accounting policy, other than one for which the transition is specified by a new Australian Accounting Standard, shall be reflected by:**

        (a)   **restating the financial statements of prior interim periods of the current annual reporting period and the comparable interim periods of any prior annual**

reporting periods that will be restated in the annual financial statements in accordance with AASB 108; or

(b) when it is impracticable to determine the cumulative effect at the beginning of the annual reporting period of applying a new accounting policy to all prior periods, adjusting the financial statements of prior interim periods of the current annual reporting period, and comparable interim periods of prior annual reporting periods to apply the new accounting policy prospectively from the earliest date practicable.

44 One objective of the preceding principle is to ensure that a single accounting policy is applied to a particular class of transactions throughout an entire annual reporting period. Under AASB 108, a change in accounting policy is reflected by retrospective application, with restatement of prior period financial data as far back as is practicable. However, if the cumulative amount of the adjustment relating to prior annual reporting periods is impracticable to determine, then under AASB 108 the new policy is applied prospectively from the earliest date practicable. The effect of the principle in paragraph 43 is to require that within the current annual reporting period any change in accounting policy is applied either retrospectively or, if that is not practicable, prospectively, from no later than the beginning of the annual reporting period.

45 To allow accounting changes to be reflected as of an interim date within the annual reporting period would allow two differing accounting policies to be applied to a particular class of transactions within a single annual reporting period. The result would be interim allocation difficulties, obscured operating results, and complicated analysis and understandability of interim period information.

Effective Date of IAS 34

46 [Deleted by the AASB]

47 [Deleted by the AASB]

48 [Deleted by the AASB]

49 Paragraph 15 was amended, paragraphs 15A-15C and 16A were added and paragraphs 16, 17 and 18 were deleted by AASB 2010-4 *Further Amendments to Australian Accounting Standards arising from the Annual Improvements Project* issued in June 2010. An entity shall apply those amendments for annual reporting periods beginning on or after 1 January 2011. Earlier application is permitted. If an entity applies the amendments for an earlier period it shall disclose that fact.

51 AASB 2011-9 *Amendments to Australian Accounting Standards – Presentation of Items of Other Comprehensive Income*, issued in September 2011, amended paragraphs 8, 8A, 11A and 20. An entity shall apply those amendments when it applies AASB 101 as amended in September 2011.

Illustrative Examples

These illustrative examples accompany, but are not part of, AASB 134.

A   Illustration of Periods Required to be Presented

The following examples illustrate application of the principle in paragraph 20.

Entity Publishes Interim Financial Reports Half-Yearly

A1   The entity's annual reporting period ends 31 December (calendar year). The entity will present the following financial statements (condensed or complete) in its half-yearly interim financial report as of 30 June 2001:

Statement of Financial Position:

| At | 30 June 2001 | 31 December 2000 |

Statement of Comprehensive Income:

| 6 months ending | 30 June 2001 | 30 June 2000 |

Statement of Cash Flows:

| 6 months ending | 30 June 2001 | 30 June 2000 |

Statement of Changes in Equity:

| 6 months ending | 30 June 2001 | 30 June 2000 |

Entity Publishes Interim Financial Reports Quarterly

A2   The entity's annual reporting period ends 31 December (calendar year). The entity will present the following financial statements (condensed or complete) in its quarterly interim financial report as of 30 June 2001:

Statement of Financial Position:

| At | 30 June 2001 | 31 December 2000 |

Statement of Comprehensive Income:

| 6 months ending | 30 June 2001 | 30 June 2000 |
| 3 months ending | 30 June 2001 | 30 June 2000 |

Statement of Cash Flows:

| 6 months ending | 30 June 2001 | 30 June 2000 |

Statement of Changes in Equity:

| 6 months ending | 30 June 2001 | 30 June 2000 |

B   Examples of Applying the Recognition and Measurement Principles

The following are examples of applying the general recognition and measurement principles set out in paragraphs 28-39.

Employer Payroll Taxes and Insurance Contributions

B1   If employer payroll taxes or contributions to government-sponsored insurance funds are assessed on an annual basis, the employer's related expense is recognised in interim periods using an estimated average annual effective payroll tax or contribution rate, even though a large portion of the payments may be made early in the annual reporting period. A common example is an employer payroll tax or insurance contribution that is imposed up to a certain maximum level of earnings per employee. For higher income employees, the maximum income is reached before the end of each annual reporting period, and the employer makes no further payments through to the end of each annual reporting period.

Major Planned Periodic Maintenance or Overhaul

B2   The cost of a planned major periodic maintenance or overhaul or other seasonal expenditure that is expected to occur late in the annual reporting period is not anticipated for interim reporting purposes unless an event has caused the entity to have a legal or constructive obligation. The mere intention or necessity to incur expenditure related to the future is not sufficient to give rise to an obligation.

Provisions

B3 A provision is recognised when an entity has no realistic alternative but to make a transfer of economic benefits as a result of an event that has created a legal or constructive obligation. The amount of the obligation is adjusted upward or downward, with a corresponding loss or gain recognised in profit or loss, if the entity's best estimate of the amount of the obligation changes.

B4 This Standard requires that an entity apply the same criteria for recognising and measuring a provision at an interim date as it would at the end of its annual reporting period. The existence or non-existence of an obligation to transfer benefits is not a function of the length of the reporting period. It is a question of fact.

Year-End Bonuses

B5 The nature of year-end bonuses varies widely. Some are earned simply by continued employment during a time period. Some bonuses are earned based on a monthly, quarterly, or annual measure of operating result. They may be purely discretionary, contractual, or based on years of historical precedent.

B6 A bonus is anticipated for interim reporting purposes if, and only if, (a) the bonus is a legal obligation or past practice would make the bonus a constructive obligation for which the entity has no realistic alternative but to make the payments, and (b) a reliable estimate of the obligation can be made. AASB 119 *Employee Benefits* provides guidance.

Contingent Lease Payments

B7 Contingent lease payments can be an example of a legal or constructive obligation that is recognised as a liability. If a lease provides for contingent payments based on the lessee achieving a certain level of annual sales, an obligation can arise in the interim periods of the annual reporting period before the required annual level of sales has been achieved, if that required level of sales is expected to be achieved and the entity, therefore, has no realistic alternative but to make the future lease payment.

Intangible Assets

B8 An entity will apply the definition and recognition criteria for an intangible asset in the same way in an interim period as in an annual period. Costs incurred before the recognition criteria for an intangible asset are met are recognised as an expense. Costs incurred after the specific point in time at which the criteria are met are recognised as part of the cost of an intangible asset. 'Deferring' costs as assets in an interim statement of financial position in the hope that the recognition criteria will be met later in the annual reporting period is not justified.

Pensions

B9 Pension cost for an interim period is calculated on an annual reporting period-to-date basis by using the actuarially determined pension cost rate at the end of the prior annual reporting period, adjusted for significant market fluctuations since that time and for significant curtailments, settlements, or other significant one-time events.

Vacations, Holidays, and Other Short-term Compensated Absences

B10 Accumulating compensated absences are those that are carried forward and can be used in future periods if the current period's entitlement is not used in full. AASB 119 *Employee Benefits* requires that an entity measure the expected cost of and obligation for accumulating compensated absences at the amount the entity expects to pay as a result of the unused entitlement that has accumulated at the end of the reporting period. That principle is also applied at the end of interim financial reporting periods. Conversely, an entity recognises no expense or liability for non-accumulating compensated absences at the end of an interim reporting period, just as it recognises none at the end of an annual reporting period.

Other Planned but Irregularly Occurring Costs

B11   An entity's budget may include certain costs expected to be incurred irregularly during the annual reporting period, such as charitable contributions and employee training costs. Those costs generally are discretionary even though they are planned and tend to recur from year to year. Recognising an obligation at the end of an interim financial reporting period for such costs that have not yet been incurred generally is not consistent with the definition of a liability.

Measuring Interim Income Tax Expense

B12   Interim period income tax expense is accrued using the tax rate that would be applicable to expected total annual earnings, that is, the estimated average annual effective income tax rate applied to the pretax income of the interim period.

B13   This is consistent with the basic concept set out in paragraph 28 that the same accounting recognition and measurement principles shall be applied in an interim financial report as are applied in annual financial statements. Income taxes are assessed on an annual basis. Interim period income tax expense is calculated by applying to an interim period's pre-tax income the tax rate that would be applicable to expected total annual earnings, that is, the estimated average annual effective income tax rate. That estimated average annual rate would reflect a blend of the progressive tax rate structure expected to be applicable to the full annual reporting period's earnings including enacted or substantively enacted changes in the income tax rates scheduled to take effect later in the annual reporting period. AASB 112 *Income Taxes* provides guidance on substantively enacted changes in tax rates. The estimated average annual income tax rate would be re-estimated on an annual reporting period-to-date basis, consistent with paragraph 28 of this Standard. Paragraph 16(d) requires disclosure of a significant change in estimate.

B14   To the extent practicable, a separate estimated average annual effective income tax rate is determined for each taxing jurisdiction and applied individually to the interim period pre-tax income of each jurisdiction. Similarly, if different income tax rates apply to different categories of income (such as capital gains or income earned in particular industries), to the extent practicable a separate rate is applied to each individual category of interim period pre-tax income. While that degree of precision is desirable, it may not be achievable in all cases, and a weighted average of rates across jurisdictions or across categories of income is used if it is a reasonable approximation of the effect of using more specific rates.

B15   To illustrate the application of the foregoing principle, an entity reporting quarterly expects to earn 10,000 pre-tax each quarter and operates in a jurisdiction with a tax rate of 20 per cent on the first 20,000 of annual earnings and 30 per cent on all additional earnings. Actual earnings match expectations. The following table shows the amount of income tax expense that is reported in each quarter:

	1st Quarter	2nd Quarter	3rd Quarter	4th Quarter	Annual
Tax expense	2,500	2,500	2,500	2,500	10,000

10,000 of tax is expected to be payable for the full annual reporting period on 40,000 of pre-tax income.

B16   As another illustration, an entity reports quarterly, earns 15,000 pre-tax profit in the first quarter but expects to incur losses of 5,000 in each of the three remaining quarters (thus having zero income for the annual reporting period), and operates in a jurisdiction in which its estimated average annual income tax rate is expected to be 20 per cent. The following table shows the amount of income tax expense (income tax revenue) that is reported in each quarter:

	1st Quarter	2nd Quarter	3rd Quarter	4th Quarter	Annual
Tax expense	3,000	(1,000)	(1,000)	(1,000)	0

Difference in Annual Reporting Period and Tax Year

B17   If the annual reporting period and the income tax year differ, income tax expense for the interim periods of that annual reporting period is measured using separate weighted average estimated effective tax rates for each of the income tax years applied to the portion of pre-tax income earned in each of those income tax years.

B18   To illustrate, an entity's annual reporting period ends 30 June and it reports quarterly. Its taxable year ends 31 December. For the annual reporting period that begins 1 July, Year 1 and ends 30 June, Year 2, the entity earns 10,000 pre-tax each quarter. The estimated average annual income tax rate is 30 per cent in Year 1 and 40 per cent in Year 2.

	Quarter Ending 30 Sept. Year 1	Quarter Ending 31 Dec. Year 1	Quarter Ending 31 Mar. Year 2	Quarter Ending 30 June Year 2	Year Ending 30 June Year 2
Tax expense	3,000	3,000	4,000	4,000	14,000

Tax Credits

B19   Some tax jurisdictions give taxpayers credits against the tax payable based on amounts of capital expenditures, exports, research and development expenditures, or other bases. Anticipated tax benefits of this type for the annual reporting period are generally reflected in computing the estimated annual effective income tax rate, because those credits are granted and calculated on an annual basis under most tax laws and regulations. On the other hand, tax benefits that relate to a one-time event are recognised in computing income tax expense in that interim period, in the same way that special tax rates applicable to particular categories of income are not blended into a single effective annual tax rate. Moreover, in some jurisdictions tax benefits or credits, including those related to capital expenditures and levels of exports, while reported on the income tax return, are more similar to a government grant and are recognised in the interim period in which they arise.

Tax Loss and Tax Credit Carrybacks and Carryforwards

B20   The benefits of a tax loss carryback are reflected in the interim period in which the related tax loss occurs. AASB 112 provides that the "benefit relating to a tax loss that can be carried back to recover current tax of a previous period shall be recognised as an asset". A corresponding reduction of tax expense or increase of tax income is also recognised.

B21   AASB 112 provides that "a deferred tax asset shall be recognised for the carryforward of unused tax losses and unused tax credits to the extent that it is probable that future taxable profit will be available against which the unused tax losses and unused tax credits can be utilised". AASB 112 provides criteria for assessing the probability of taxable profit against which the unused tax losses and credits can be utilised. Those criteria are applied at the end of each interim period and, if they are met, the effect of the tax loss carryforward is reflected in the computation of the estimated average annual effective income tax rate.

B22   To illustrate, an entity that reports quarterly has an operating loss carryforward of 10,000 for income tax purposes at the start of the current annual reporting period for which a deferred tax asset has not been recognised. The entity earns 10,000 in the first quarter of the current annual reporting period and expects to earn 10,000 in each of the three remaining quarters. Excluding the carryforward, the estimated average annual income tax rate is expected to be 40 per cent. Tax expense is as follows:

	1st Quarter	2nd Quarter	3rd Quarter	4th Quarter	Annual
Tax expense	3,000	3,000	3,000	3,000	12,000

Contractual or Anticipated Purchase Price Changes

B23   Volume rebates or discounts and other contractual changes in the prices of raw materials, labour, or other purchased goods and services are anticipated in interim periods, by both the payer and the recipient, if it is probable that they have been earned or will take effect. Thus, contractual rebates and discounts are anticipated but discretionary rebates and discounts are not anticipated because the resulting asset or liability would not satisfy the conditions in the *Framework* that an asset must be a resource controlled by the entity as a result of a past event and that a liability must be a present obligation whose settlement is expected to result in an outflow of resources.

Depreciation and Amortisation

B24   Depreciation and amortisation for an interim period is based only on assets owned during that interim period. It does not take into account asset acquisitions or dispositions planned for later in the annual reporting period.

Inventories

B25   Inventories are measured for interim financial reporting by the same principles as at the end of an annual reporting period. AASB 102 *Inventories* establishes standards for recognising and measuring inventories. Inventories pose particular problems at the end of any financial reporting period because of the need to determine inventory quantities, costs, and net realisable values. Nonetheless, the same measurement principles are applied for interim inventories. To save cost and time, entities often use estimates to measure inventories at interim dates to a greater extent than at the end of annual reporting periods. Following are examples of how to apply the net realisable value test at an interim date and how to treat manufacturing variances at interim dates.

Net Realisable Value of Inventories

B26   The net realisable value of inventories is determined by reference to selling prices and related costs to complete and dispose at interim dates. An entity will reverse a write-down to net realisable value in a subsequent interim period only if it would be appropriate to do so at the end of each annual reporting period.

B27   [Deleted by the IASB]

Interim Period Manufacturing Cost Variances

B28   Price, efficiency, spending, and volume variances of a manufacturing entity are recognised in income at the end of interim reporting periods to the same extent that those variances are recognised in income at the end of an annual reporting period. Deferral of variances that are expected to be absorbed by the end of the annual reporting period is not appropriate because it could result in reporting inventory at the interim date at more or less than its portion of the actual cost of manufacture.

Foreign Currency Translation Gains and Losses

B29   Foreign currency translation gains and losses are measured for interim financial reporting by the same principles as at the end of each annual reporting period.

B30   AASB 121 *The Effects of Changes in Foreign Exchange Rates* specifies how to translate the financial statements for foreign operations into the presentation currency, including guidelines for using average or closing foreign exchange rates and guidelines for recognising the resulting adjustments in profit or loss or in other comprehensive income. Consistently with AASB 121, the actual average and closing rates for the interim period are used. Entities do not anticipate some future changes in foreign exchange rates in the remainder of the current annual reporting period in translating foreign operations at an interim date.

B31   If AASB 121 requires translation adjustments to be recognised as income or expense in the period in which they arise, that principle is applied during each interim period. Entities do not defer some foreign currency translation adjustments at an interim date if the adjustment is expected to reverse before the end of each annual reporting period.

Interim Financial Reporting in Hyperinflationary Economies

B32 Interim financial reports in hyperinflationary economies are prepared by the same principles as at the end of an annual reporting period.

B33 AASB 129 *Financial Reporting in Hyperinflationary Economies* requires that the financial statements of an entity that reports in the currency of a hyperinflationary economy be stated in terms of the measuring unit current at the end of the reporting period, and the gain or loss on the net monetary position is included in net income. Also, comparative financial data reported for prior periods are restated to the current measuring unit.

B34 Entities follow those same principles at interim dates, thereby presenting all interim data in the measuring unit as of the end of the interim period, with the resulting gain or loss on the net monetary position included in the interim period's net income. Entities do not annualise the recognition of the gain or loss. Nor do they use an estimated annual inflation rate in preparing an interim financial report in a hyperinflationary economy.

Impairment of Assets

B35 AASB 136 *Impairment of Assets* requires that an impairment loss be recognised if the recoverable amount has declined below carrying amount.

B36 This Standard requires that an entity apply the same impairment testing, recognition and reversal criteria at an interim date as it would at the end of its annual reporting period. That does not mean, however, that an entity must necessarily make a detailed impairment calculation at the end of each interim period. Rather, an entity will review for indications of significant impairment since the end of the most recent annual reporting period to determine whether such a calculation is needed.

C Examples of the Use of Estimates

The following examples illustrate application of the principle in paragraph 41.

C1 **Inventories:** Full stock-taking and valuation procedures may not be required for inventories at interim dates, although it may be done at the end of an annual reporting period. It may be sufficient to make estimates at interim dates based on sales margins.

C2 **Classifications of current and non-current assets and liabilities:** Entities may do a more thorough investigation for classifying assets and liabilities as current or non-current at the end of annual reporting periods than at interim dates.

C3 **Provisions:** Determination of the appropriate amount of a provision (such as a provision for warranties, environmental costs and site restoration costs) may be complex and often costly and timeconsuming. Entities sometimes engage outside experts to assist in the annual calculations. Making similar estimates at interim dates often entails updating of the prior annual provision rather than the engaging of outside experts to do a new calculation.

C4 **Pensions:** AASB 119 *Employee Benefits* requires that an entity determine the present value of defined benefit obligations and the market value of plan assets at the end of each reporting period and encourages an entity to involve a professionally qualified actuary in measurement of the obligations. For interim reporting purposes, reliable measurement is often obtainable by extrapolation of the latest actuarial valuation.

C5 **Income taxes:** Entities may calculate income tax expense and deferred income tax liability at annual dates by applying the tax rate for each individual jurisdiction to measures of income for each jurisdiction. Paragraph 14 of Appendix B acknowledges that while that degree of precision is desirable at the end of interim reporting periods as well, it may not be achievable in all cases, and a weighted average of rates across jurisdictions or across categories of income is used if it is a reasonable approximation of the effect of using more specific rates.

C6 **Contingencies:** The measurement of contingencies may involve the opinions of legal experts or other advisers. Formal reports from independent experts are sometimes obtained with respect to contingencies. Such opinions about litigation, claims, assessments and other contingencies and uncertainties may or may not also be needed at interim dates.

C7   **Revaluations and fair value accounting:** AASB 116 *Property, Plant and Equipment* allows an entity to choose as its accounting policy the revaluation model whereby items of property, plant and equipment are revalued to fair value. Similarly, AASB 140 *Investment Property* requires an entity to determine the fair value of investment property. For those measurements, an entity may rely on professionally qualified valuers at the end of annual reporting periods though not at the end of interim reporting periods.

C8   **Intercompany reconciliations:** Some intercompany balances that are reconciled on a detailed level in preparing consolidated financial statements at the end of an annual reporting period might be reconciled at a less detailed level in preparing consolidated financial statements at an interim date.

C9   **Specialised industries:** Because of complexity, costliness, and time, interim period measurements in specialised industries might be less precise than at the end of an annual reporting period. An example would be calculation of insurance reserves by insurance companies.

AASB 136
Impairment of Assets

(Compiled December 2009)

Note from the Institute of Chartered Accountants Australia

This note, prepared by the technical editors, is not part of Accounting Standard AASB 136.

Historical development

July 2004: AASB 136 'Impairment of Assets' is the Australian equivalent of IAS 36 of the same name. It was made by the AASB on 15 July 2004 as part of the AASB's program to adopt International Financial Reporting Standards (IFRSs) by 2005.

26 February 2007: AASB 2007-3 'Amendments to Australian Accounting Standards' was issued by the AASB. This Standard is applicable for annual reporting periods beginning on or after 1 January 2009.

30 April 2007: AASB 2007-4 'Amendments to Australian Accounting Standards' amends paragraph 28 and is applicable to annual reporting periods beginning on or after 1 July 2007. Entities may elect to early-adopt it to annual reporting periods beginning on or after 1 January 2005.

24 September 2007: AASB 2007-8 'Amendments to Australian Accounting Standards arising from AASB 101' amends AASB 136 to align with revised AASB 101. This Standard is applicable to annual reporting periods beginning on or after 1 January 2009.

13 December 2007: AASB 2007-10 'Further Amendments to Australian Accounting Standards arising from AASB 101' amends AASB 136, replacing the term 'financial report' with 'financial statements'. This Standard is applicable to annual reporting periods beginning on or after 1 January 2009.

6 March 2008: AASB 2008-3 'Amendments to Australian Accounting Standards arising from AASB 3 and AASB 127' amends AASB 136 for the issue of AASB 3 Revised. This Standard is applicable to annual reporting periods beginning on or after 1 July 2009.

24 July 2008: AASB 2008-5 'Amendments to Australian Accounting Standards arising from the Annual Improvements Project' amends AASB 136 in relation to the disclosure of estimates used to determine recoverable amount. This Standard is applicable to annual reporting periods beginning on or after 1 January 2009.

25 July 2008: AASB 2008-7 'Amendments to Australian Accounting Standards – Cost of an Investment in a Subsidiary, Jointly Controlled Entity or Associate' amends AASB 136 to include recognising a dividend from a subsidiary, jointly controlled entity or associate as an indication that the investment may be impaired. This Standard is applicable to annual reporting periods beginning on or after 1 January 2009.

21 May 2009: AASB 2009-5 'Amendments to Australian Accounting Standards' is the annual improvements Standard, amending AASB 5 in relation to the unit of accounting for goodwill impairment test. This Standard applies to annual reporting periods beginning on or after 1 January 2010 and may be applied early.

25 June 2009: AASB 2009-6 'Amendments to Australian Accounting Standards' amends AASB 136 for editorial corrections made by the International Accounting Standards Board (IASB) to its Standards and Interpretations (IFRSs) and as a consequence of issuing revised AASB 101 *Presentation of Financial Statements* (September 2007). This Standard is applicable to annual reporting periods beginning on or after 1 January 2009 that end on or after 30 June 2009.

25 June 2009: AASB 2009-7 'Amendments to Australian Accounting Standards' amends AASB 136 arising from editorial corrections by the AASB and by the International Accounting Standards Board (IASB). This Standard is applicable to annual reporting periods beginning on or after 1 July 2009.

---

23 October 2009: AASB 136 was reissued by the AASB, compiled to include the AASB 2007-3, AASB 2007-8, AASB 2007-10, AASB 2008-3, AASB 2008-5, AASB 2008-7, AASB 2009-5, AASB 2009-6 and AASB 2009-7 amendments and applies to annual reporting periods beginning on or after 1 July 2009 but before 1 January 2010. Early application is permitted.

On the same date the AASB reissued the version of AASB 136 applicable to annual reporting periods beginning on or after 1 January 2009 but before 1 July 2009. This version of AASB 136 has been compiled for the amending Standards applying to annual reporting periods beginning on or after 1 January 2009. This Standard applies to 31 December 2009 year ends.

1 December 2009: AASB 136 was reissued by the AASB, compiled to include the AASB 2009-5 amendments and applies to annual reporting periods beginning on or after 1 January 2010.

7 December 2009: AASB 2009-11 'Amendments to Australian Accounting Standards arising from AASB 9' amends AASB 136 to give effect to consequential changes arising from the issuance of AASB 9. This Standard is applicable to annual reporting periods beginning on or after 1 January 2013 with early adoption permitted from annual reporting periods ending on or after 31 December 2009 that begin before 1 January 2013 provided AASB 9 is also applied for the same period. The application date of AASB 2009-11 has been amended to 1 January 2015 by AASB 2012-6. **These amendments have been superseded by AASB 2010-7 and are not included in this compiled Standard.**

1 March 2011: AASB 2010-7 'Amendments to Australian Accounting Standards arising from AASB 9 (December 2010)' as compiled amends AASB 136 to give effect to consequential changes arising from the reissue of AASB 9 in December 2010 and supersedes AASB 2009-11, which related to the previous version of AASB 9. This Standard applies to annual reporting periods beginning on or after 1 January 2013 and can be adopted early. The application date of AASB 2010-7 has been amended to 1 January 2015 by AASB 2012-6. **These amendments are not included in this compiled Standard.**

29 August 2011: AASB 2011-7 'Amendments to Australian Accounting Standards arising from the Consolidation and Joint Arrangements Standards' amends AASB 136 to give effect to many consequential changes arising from the issue of AASB 10, 11, 12, 127 and 128. This Standard applies to annual reporting periods beginning on or after 1 January 2013 and can be adopted early by for-profit entities. **These amendments are not included in this compiled Standard.**

5 September 2011: AASB 2011-8 'Amendments to Australian Accounting Standards arising from AASB 13' amends AASB 136 to give effect to a consequential change in the definition of fair value arising from the issue of AASB 13. This Standard applies to annual reporting periods beginning on or after 1 January 2013 and can be adopted early. **These amendments are not included in this compiled Standard.**

References

Interpretation 1 *Changes in Existing Decommissioning Restoration and Similar Liabilities*, Interpretation 10 *Interim Financial Reporting and Impairment*, Interpretation 12 *Service Concession Arrangements*, Interpretation 132 *Intangible Assets – Web Site Costs,* Interpretation 1042 *Subscriber Acquisition Costs in the Telecommunications Industry* apply to AASB 136.

IFRIC items not taken onto the agenda: No. 37 *The inclusion/exclusion from value in use of cash flows expected to arise from a future restructuring*, No. 38 *Impairment of undeveloped reserves by entities engaged in extractive activities,* No. 39 *Provisions – onerous contracts*, IAS 36-1 *Identifying cash generating units in the retail industry* and IAS 36-2 *Calculation of value in use* apply to AASB 136.

AASB 136 compared to IAS 36

Additions

Paragraph	Description
Aus 1.1	Which entities AASB 136 applies to (i.e. reporting entities and general purpose financial statements).
Aus 1.2	The application date of AASB 136 (i.e. annual reporting periods beginning 1 January 2005).
Aus 1.3	Prohibits early application of AASB 136.
Aus 1.4	Makes the requirements of AASB 136 subject to AASB 1031 'Materiality'.

Aus 1.5	Explains which Australian Standards have been superseded by AASB 136.
Aus 1.6	Clarifies that the superseded Australian Standards remain in force until AASB 136 applies.
Aus 1.7	Notice of the new Standard published on 22 July 2004.
Aus 6.1	Clarifies that in the case of an asset of not-for-profit entity, value in use means depreciated replacement cost.
Aus 6.2	Sets out the not-for-profit definitions of 'not-for-profit entity' and 'depreciated replacement cost'.
Aus 32.1	Requires that a not-for-profit entity determine value in use of an asset using the depreciated replacement cost of the asset if the future economic benefits of the asset are not primarily dependent on net cash inflows and the asset would be replaced if the entity were deprived of it.
Aus 32.2	Clarifies how depreciated replacement cost is measured by reference to the lowest cost at which the gross future economic benefits of the asset could currently be obtained in normal course of business.
Aus 61.1	Clarifies that for a not-for-profit entity any impairment loss on a revalued asset must be recognised directly against the asset revaluation reserve to the extent of any amount that stands to the credit of the asset's class in the reserve.
Aus 120.1	Clarifies that for a not-for-profit entity the reversal of an impairment loss on a revalued asset is credited to the asset revaluation reserve except to the extent that an impairment loss on the same class of asset was previously recognised in the profit or loss.

Deletions

Paragraph	Description
138	Effective date and transitional provision of IAS 36 based on election in IFRS 3 'Business Combinations'
139	Effective date and transitional provision of IAS 36 in cases other than paragraph 138.
140	Application to transactions before required date is encouraged but IFRS 3 and IAS 38 'Intangible Assets' must be applied at the same time.
141	Reference to superseded IAS 36.

Contents

Compilation Details

Comparison with IAS 36

Accounting Standard
AASB 136 Impairment of Assets

	Paragraphs
Objective	1
Application	Aus1.1 – Aus1.7
Scope	2 – 5
Definitions	6 – Aus6.2
Identifying an Asset that may be Impaired	7 – 17
Measuring Recoverable Amount	18 – 23
Measuring the Recoverable Amount of an Intangible Asset with an Indefinite Useful Life	24
Fair Value less Costs to Sell	25 – 29
Value in Use	30 – Aus32.2
Basis for Estimates of Future Cash Flows	33 – 38
Composition of Estimates of Future Cash Flows	39 – 53
Foreign Currency Future Cash Flows	54
Discount Rate	55 – 57
Recognising and Measuring an Impairment Loss	58 – 64
Cash-generating Units and Goodwill	65
Identifying the Cash-generating Unit to Which an Asset Belongs	66 – 73
Recoverable Amount and Carrying Amount of a Cash-generating Unit	74 – 79
Goodwill	
Allocating Goodwill to Cash-generating Units	80 – 87
Testing Cash-generating Units with Goodwill for Impairment	88 – 90
Timing of Impairment Tests	96 – 99
Corporate Assets	100 – 103
Impairment Loss for a Cash-generating Unit	104 – 108
Reversing an Impairment Loss	109 – 116
Reversing an Impairment Loss for an Individual Asset	117 – 121
Reversing an Impairment Loss for a Cash-generating Unit	122 – 123
Reversing an Impairment Loss for Goodwill	124 – 125
Disclosure	126 – 133
Estimates used to Measure Recoverable Amounts of Cash-generating Units Containing Goodwill or Intangible Assets with Indefinite Useful Lives	134 – 137
Transitional Provisions and Effective Date	140C – 140E

Appendix:

A. Using Present Value Techniques to Measure Value in Use

C. Impairment Testing Cash-generating Units with Goodwill and Non-controlling Interests

Illustrative Examples

Basis for Conclusions on IAS 36
(available on the AASB website)

> Australian Accounting Standard AASB 136 *Impairment of Assets* (as amended) is set out in paragraphs 1 – 140E and Appendices A and C. All the paragraphs have equal authority. Terms defined in this Standard are in *italics* the first time they appear in the Standard. AASB 136 is to be read in the context of other Australian Accounting Standards, including AASB 1048 *Interpretation and Application of Standards*, which identifies the Australian Accounting Interpretations. In the absence of explicit guidance, AASB 108 *Accounting Policies, Changes in Accounting Estimates and Errors* provides a basis for selecting and applying accounting policies.

Compilation Details

Accounting Standard AASB 136 *Impairment of Assets* as amended

This compiled Standard applies to annual reporting periods beginning on or after 1 January 2010. It takes into account amendments up to and including 25 June 2009 and was prepared on 1 December 2009 by the staff of the Australian Accounting Standards Board (AASB).

This compilation is not a separate Accounting Standard made by the AASB. Instead, it is a representation of AASB 136 (July 2004) as amended by other Accounting Standards, which are listed in the Table below.

Table of Standards

Standard	Date made	Application date *(annual reporting periods ... on or after ...)*	Application, saving or transitional provisions
AASB 136	15 Jul 2004	*(beginning)* 1 Jan 2005	
AASB 2007-3	26 Feb 2007	*(beginning)* 1 Jan 2009	see (a) below
AASB 2007-4	30 Apr 2007	*(beginning)* 1 Jul 2007	see (b) below
AASB 2007-8	24 Sep 2007	*(beginning)* 1 Jan 2009	see (c) below
AASB 2007-10	13 Dec 2007	*(beginning)* 1 Jan 2009	see (c) below
AASB 2008-3	6 Mar 2008	*(beginning)* 1 Jul 2009	see (d) below
AASB 2008-5	24 Jul 2008	*(beginning)* 1 Jan 2009	see (e) below
AASB 2008-7	25 Jul 2008	*(beginning)* 1 Jan 2009	see (f) below
AASB 2009-5	21 May 2009	*(beginning)* 1 Jan 2010	see (g) below
AASB 2009-6	25 Jun 2009	*(beginning)* 1 Jan 2009 and *(ending)* 30 Jun 2009	see (h) below
AASB 2009-7	25 Jun 2009	*(beginning)* 1 Jul 2009	see (i) below

(a) Entities may elect to apply this Standard to annual reporting periods beginning on or after 1 January 2005 but before 1 January 2009, provided that AASB 8 *Operating Segments* is also applied to such periods.

(b) Entities may elect to apply this Standard to annual reporting periods beginning on or after 1 January 2005 but before 1 July 2007.

(c) Entities may elect to apply this Standard to annual reporting periods beginning on or after 1 January 2005 but before 1 January 2009, provided that AASB 101 *Presentation of Financial Statements* (September 2007) is also applied to such periods.

(d) Entities may elect to apply this Standard to annual reporting periods beginning on or after 30 June 2007 but before 1 July 2009, provided that AASB 3 *Business Combinations* (March 2008) and AASB 127 *Consolidated and Separate Financial Statements* (March 2008) are also applied to such periods.

(e) Paragraph 59 of this Standard specifies application provisions. Entities may elect to apply this Standard, or its amendments to individual Standards, to annual reporting periods beginning on or after 1 January 2005 but before 1 January 2009.

(f) Entities may elect to apply this Standard to annual reporting periods beginning on or after 1 January 2005 but before 1 January 2009.

(g) Entities may elect to apply this Standard, or its amendments to individual Standards, to annual reporting periods beginning on or after 1 January 2005 but before 1 January 2010.

(h) Entities may elect to apply this Standard to annual reporting periods beginning on or after 1 January 2005 but before 1 January 2009, provided that AASB 101 *Presentation of Financial Statements* (September 2007) is also applied to such periods, and to annual reporting periods beginning on or after 1 January 2009 that end before 30 June 2009.

(i) Entities may elect to apply this Standard to annual reporting periods beginning before 1 July 2009 that end on or after 1 July 2008.

Table of Amendments to Standard

Paragraph affected	How affected	By ... [paragraph]
Aus1.1	amended	AASB 2007-8 [7, 8]
Aus1.4	amended	AASB 2007-8 [8]
2	amended	AASB 2008-5 [56]
5	amended	AASB 2008-5 [56]
6	amended amended	AASB 2007-10 [84] AASB 2008-3 [60]
9	amended	AASB 2007-8 [6]
12	amended	AASB 2008-7 [23]
27	amended	AASB 2007-8 [6]
28	amended	AASB 2007-4 [96]
61	amended	AASB 2007-8 [118]
Aus61.1	amended	AASB 2009-6 [81]
65	amended	AASB 2008-3 [61]
80	amended amended	AASB 2007-3 [14] AASB 2009-5 [18]
81	amended	AASB 2008-3 [62]
85	amended	AASB 2008-3 [62]
91-95 (and preceding heading)	deleted	AASB 2008-3 [63]
110	amended	AASB 2007-8 [6]
120	amended	AASB 2007-8 [118]
Aus120.1	amended	AASB 2009-6 [82]
126	amended	AASB 2007-8 [6, 119]
129	amended amended	AASB 2007-3 [15] AASB 2007-8 [119]
130	amended	AASB 2007-3 [16]
133	amended	AASB 2007-8 [6]
134	amended	AASB 2008-5 [56]
138 (and preceding heading)	amended note amended	AASB 2008-5 [57] AASB 2008-3 [64]
140A	note added	AASB 2007-8 [120]
140B	note added	AASB 2008-3 [65]
140C	added	AASB 2008-5 [58]
140D	added	AASB 2008-7 [24]
140E	added	AASB 2009-5 [19]
Appendix C	added	AASB 2008-3 [66]

Table of Amendments to Illustrative Examples

Paragraph affected	How affected	By ... [paragraph]
IE62-IE64 (and preceding headings)	amended	AASB 2008-3 [67]
IE65 (and preceding heading)	amended	AASB 2008-3 [67]
	amended	AASB 2009-7 [13]
IE66-IE68 (and preceding heading)	amended	AASB 2008-3 [67]
IE68A-IE68J (and preceding headings)	added	AASB 2008-3 [68]
IE80	amended	AASB 2007-3 [Appx]
IE89	amended	AASB 2007-10 [84]

Comparison with IAS 36

AASB 136 and IAS 36

AASB 136 *Impairment of Assets* as amended incorporates IAS 36 *Impairment of Assets* as issued and amended by the International Accounting Standards Board (IASB). Paragraphs that have been added to this Standard (and do not appear in the text of IAS 36) are identified with the prefix "Aus", followed by the number of the preceding IASB paragraph and decimal numbering. Paragraphs that apply only to not-for-profit entities begin by identifying their limited applicability.

Compliance with IAS 36

For-profit entities that comply with AASB 136 as amended will simultaneously be in compliance with IAS 36 as amended.

Not-for-profit entities using the added "Aus" paragraphs in the Standard that specifically apply to not-for-profit entities may not be simultaneously complying with IAS 36. Whether a not-for-profit entity will be in compliance with IAS 36 will depend on whether the "Aus" paragraphs provide additional guidance for not-for-profit entities or contain requirements that are inconsistent with the corresponding IASB Standard and will be applied by the not-for-profit entity.

Accounting Standard AASB 136

The Australian Accounting Standards Board made Accounting Standard AASB 136 *Impairment of Assets* under section 334 of the *Corporations Act 2001* on 15 July 2004.

This compiled version of AASB 136 applies to annual reporting periods beginning on or after 1 January 2010. It incorporates relevant amendments contained in other AASB Standards made by the AASB up to and including 25 June 2009 (see Compilation Details).

Accounting Standard AASB 136

Impairment of Assets

Objective

1   The objective of this Standard is to prescribe the procedures that an entity applies to ensure that its assets are carried at no more than their *recoverable amount*. An asset is carried at more than its recoverable amount if its *carrying amount* exceeds the amount to be recovered through use or sale of the asset. If this is the case, the asset is described as impaired and the Standard requires the entity to recognise an *impairment loss*. The Standard also specifies when an entity should reverse an impairment loss and prescribes disclosures.

Application

Aus1.1 This Standard applies to:

(a) each entity that is required to prepare financial reports in accordance with Part 2M.3 of the Corporations Act and that is a reporting entity;

(b) general purpose financial statements of each other reporting entity; and

(c) financial statements that are, or are held out to be, general purpose financial statements.

Aus1.2 This Standard applies to annual reporting periods beginning on or after 1 January 2005.

[Note: For application dates of paragraphs changed or added by an amending Standard, see Compilation Details.]

Aus1.3 This Standard shall not be applied to annual reporting periods beginning before 1 January 2005.

Aus1.4 The requirements specified in this Standard apply to the financial statements where information resulting from their application is material in accordance with AASB 1031 *Materiality*.

Aus1.5 When applicable, this Standard supersedes:

(a) AASB 1010 *Recoverable Amount of Non-Current Assets* as notified in the *Commonwealth of Australia Gazette* No S 657, 24 December 1999; and

(b) AAS 10 *Recoverable Amount of Non-Current Assets* as issued in December 1999.

Aus1.6 Both AASB 1010 and AAS 10 remain applicable until superseded by this Standard.

Aus1.7 Notice of this Standard was published in the *Commonwealth of Australia Gazette* No S 294, 22 July 2004.

Scope

2 This Standard shall be applied in accounting for the impairment of all assets, other than:

(a) inventories (see AASB 102 *Inventories*);

(b) assets arising from construction contracts (see AASB 111 *Construction Contracts*);

(c) deferred tax assets (see AASB 112 *Income Taxes*);

(d) assets arising from employee benefits (see AASB 119 *Employee Benefits*);

(e) financial assets that are within the scope of AASB 139 *Financial Instruments: Recognition and Measurement*;

(f) investment property that is measured at fair value (see AASB 140 *Investment Property*);

(g) biological assets related to agricultural activity that are measured at fair value less costs to sell (see AASB 141 *Agriculture*);

(h) deferred acquisition costs, and intangible assets, arising from an insurer's contractual rights under insurance contracts within the scopes of AASB 4 *Insurance Contracts*, AASB 1023 *General Insurance Contracts* and AASB 1038 *Life Insurance Contracts*; and

(i) non-current assets (or disposal groups) classified as held for sale in accordance with AASB 5 *Non-current Assets Held for Sale and Discontinued Operations*.

3 This Standard does not apply to inventories, assets arising from construction contracts, deferred tax assets, assets arising from employee benefits, or assets classified as held for sale (or included in a disposal group that is classified as held for sale) because existing Standards applicable to these assets contain requirements for recognising and measuring these assets.

AASB

4　　This Standard applies to financial assets classified as:

(a)　　subsidiaries, as defined in AASB 127 *Consolidated and Separate Financial Statements*;

(b)　　associates, as defined in AASB 128 *Investments in Associates*; and

(c)　　joint ventures, as defined in AASB 131 *Interests in Joint Ventures*.

For impairment of other financial assets, refer to AASB 139.

5　　This Standard does not apply to financial assets within the scope of AASB 139, investment property measured at fair value in accordance with AASB 140, or biological assets related to agricultural activity measured at fair value less costs to sell in accordance with AASB 141. However, this Standard applies to assets that are carried at revalued amount (i.e. fair value) in accordance with other Australian Accounting Standards, such as the revaluation model in AASB 116 *Property, Plant and Equipment*. Identifying whether a revalued asset may be impaired depends on the basis used to determine fair value:

(a)　　if the asset's fair value is its market value, the only difference between the asset's fair value and its fair value less costs to sell is the direct incremental costs to dispose of the asset:

(i)　　if the disposal costs are negligible, the recoverable amount of the revalued asset is necessarily close to, or greater than, its revalued amount (i.e. fair value). In this case, after the revaluation requirements have been applied, it is unlikely that the revalued asset is impaired and recoverable amount need not be estimated;

(ii)　　if the disposal costs are not negligible, the fair value less costs to sell of the revalued asset is necessarily less than its fair value. Therefore, the revalued asset will be impaired if its *value in use* is less than its revalued amount (i.e. fair value). In this case, after the revaluation requirements have been applied, an entity applies this Standard to determine whether the asset may be impaired; and

(b)　　if the asset's fair value is determined on a basis other than its market value, its revalued amount (i.e. fair value) may be greater or lower than its recoverable amount. Hence, after the revaluation requirements have been applied, an entity applies this Standard to determine whether the asset may be impaired.

Definitions

6　　**The following terms are used in this Standard with the meanings specified.**

An *active market* is a market in which all the following conditions exist:

(a)　　the items traded within the market are homogeneous;

(b)　　willing buyers and sellers can normally be found at any time; and

(c)　　prices are available to the public.

***Carrying amount* is the amount at which an asset is recognised after deducting any accumulated depreciation (amortisation) and accumulated impairment losses thereon.**

A *cash-generating unit* is the smallest identifiable group of assets that generates cash inflows that are largely independent of the cash inflows from other assets or groups of assets.

***Corporate assets* are assets other than goodwill that contribute to the future cash flows of both the cash-generating unit under review and other cash-generating units.**

***Costs of disposal* are incremental costs directly attributable to the disposal of an asset or cash-generating unit, excluding finance costs and income tax expense.**

***Depreciable amount* is the cost of an asset, or other amount substituted for cost in the financial statements, less its residual value.**

> *Depreciation (Amortisation)* is the systematic allocation of the depreciable amount of an asset over its useful life.[1]
>
> *Fair value less costs to sell* is the amount obtainable from the sale of an asset or cash-generating unit in an arm's length transaction between knowledgeable, willing parties, less the costs of disposal.
>
> An *impairment loss* is the amount by which the carrying amount of an asset or a cash-generating unit exceeds its recoverable amount.
>
> The *recoverable amount* of an asset or a cash-generating unit is the higher of its fair value less costs to sell and its value in use.
>
> *Useful life* is either:
>
> > (a)   the period of time over which an asset is expected to be used by the entity; or
> >
> > (b)   the number of production or similar units expected to be obtained from the asset by the entity.
>
> *Value in use* is the present value of the future cash flows expected to be derived from an asset or cash-generating unit.

Aus6.1   Notwithstanding paragraph 6, in respect of *not-for-profit entities*, value in use is *depreciated replacement cost* of an asset when the future economic benefits of the asset are not primarily dependent on the asset's ability to generate net cash inflows and where the entity would, if deprived of the asset, replace its remaining future economic benefits.

Aus6.2   The following terms are also used in this Standard with the meaning specified.

> A *not-for-profit entity* is an entity whose principal objective is not the generation of profit. A not-for-profit entity can be a single entity or a group of entities comprising the parent and each of the entities that it controls.
>
> *Depreciated replacement cost* is the current replacement cost of an asset less, where applicable, accumulated depreciation calculated on the basis of such cost to reflect the already consumed or expired future economic benefits of the asset.

Identifying an Asset that may be Impaired

7   Paragraphs 8-17 specify when recoverable amount shall be determined. These requirements use the term 'an asset' but apply equally to an individual asset or a *cash-generating unit*. The remainder of this Standard is structured as follows:

(a)   paragraphs 18-57 set out the requirements for measuring recoverable amount. These requirements also use the term 'an asset' but apply equally to an individual asset and a cash-generating unit;

(b)   paragraphs 58-108 set out the requirements for recognising and measuring impairment losses. Recognition and measurement of impairment losses for individual assets other than goodwill are dealt with in paragraphs 58-64. Paragraphs 65-108 deal with the recognition and measurement of impairment losses for cash-generating units and goodwill;

(c)   paragraphs 109-116 set out the requirements for reversing an impairment loss recognised in prior periods for an asset or a cash-generating unit. Again, these requirements use the term 'an asset' but apply equally to an individual asset or a cash-generating unit. Additional requirements for an individual asset are set out in paragraphs 117-121, for a cash-generating unit in paragraphs 122 and 123, and for goodwill in paragraphs 124 and 125; and

(d)   paragraphs 126-133 specify the information to be disclosed about impairment losses and reversals of impairment losses for assets and cash-generating units.

---

1   In the case of an intangible asset, the term 'amortisation' is generally used instead of 'depreciation'. The two terms have the same meaning.

Paragraphs 134-137 specify additional disclosure requirements for cash-generating units to which goodwill or intangible assets with indefinite useful lives have been allocated for impairment testing purposes.

8   An asset is impaired when its carrying amount exceeds its recoverable amount. Paragraphs 12-14 describe some indications that an impairment loss may have occurred. If any of those indications is present, an entity is required to make a formal estimate of recoverable amount. Except as described in paragraph 10, this Standard does not require an entity to make a formal estimate of recoverable amount if no indication of an impairment loss is present.

9   **An entity shall assess at the end of each reporting period whether there is any indication that an asset may be impaired. If any such indication exists, the entity shall estimate the recoverable amount of the asset.**

10   **Irrespective of whether there is any indication of impairment, an entity shall also:**

(a)   **test an intangible asset with an indefinite *useful life* or an intangible asset not yet available for use for impairment annually by comparing its carrying amount with its recoverable amount. This impairment test may be performed at any time during an annual period, provided it is performed at the same time every year. Different intangible assets may be tested for impairment at different times. However, if such an intangible asset was initially recognised during the current annual period, that intangible asset shall be tested for impairment before the end of the current annual period; and**

(b)   **test goodwill acquired in a business combination for impairment annually in accordance with paragraphs 80-99.**

11   The ability of an intangible asset to generate sufficient future economic benefits to recover its carrying amount is usually subject to greater uncertainty before the asset is available for use than after it is available for use. Therefore, this Standard requires an entity to test for impairment, at least annually, the carrying amount of an intangible asset that is not yet available for use.

12   **In assessing whether there is any indication that an asset may be impaired, an entity shall consider, as a minimum, the following indications:**

External sources of information

(a)   **during the period, an asset's market value has declined significantly more than would be expected as a result of the passage of time or normal use;**

(b)   **significant changes with an adverse effect on the entity have taken place during the period, or will take place in the near future, in the technological, market, economic or legal environment in which the entity operates or in the market to which an asset is dedicated;**

(c)   **market interest rates or other market rates of return on investments have increased during the period, and those increases are likely to affect the discount rate used in calculating an asset's value in use and decrease the asset's recoverable amount materially;**

(d)   **the carrying amount of the net assets of the entity is more than its market capitalisation;**

Internal sources of information

(e)   **evidence is available of obsolescence or physical damage of an asset;**

(f)   **significant changes with an adverse effect on the entity have taken place during the period, or are expected to take place in the near future, in the extent to which, or manner in which, an asset is used or is expected to be used. These changes include the asset becoming idle, plans to discontinue or restructure the operation to which an asset belongs, plans to dispose of an asset before the previously** expected date, and reassessing the useful life of an asset as finite rather than indefinite;[2] and

(g)   evidence is available from internal reporting that indicates that the economic performance of an asset is, or will be, worse than expected.

Dividend from a subsidiary, jointly controlled entity or associate

(h)   for an investment in a subsidiary, jointly controlled entity or associate, the investor recognises a dividend from the investment and evidence is available that:

    (i)   the carrying amount of the investment in the separate financial statements exceeds the carrying amounts in the consolidated financial statements of the investee's net assets, including associated goodwill; or

    (ii)   the dividend exceeds the total comprehensive income of the subsidiary, jointly controlled entity or associate in the period the dividend is declared.

13   The list in paragraph 12 is not exhaustive. An entity may identify other indications that an asset may be impaired and these would also require the entity to determine the asset's recoverable amount or, in the case of goodwill, perform an impairment test in accordance with paragraphs 80-99.

14   Evidence from internal reporting that indicates that an asset may be impaired includes the existence of:

(a)   cash flows for acquiring the asset, or subsequent cash needs for operating or maintaining it, that are significantly higher than those originally budgeted;

(b)   actual net cash flows or operating profit or loss flowing from the asset that are significantly worse than those budgeted;

(c)   a significant decline in budgeted net cash flows or operating profit, or a significant increase in budgeted loss, flowing from the asset; or

(d)   operating losses or net cash outflows for the asset, when current period amounts are aggregated with budgeted amounts for the future.

15   As indicated in paragraph 10, this Standard requires an intangible asset with an indefinite useful life or not yet available for use and goodwill to be tested for impairment, at least annually. Apart from when the requirements in paragraph 10 apply, the concept of materiality applies in identifying whether the recoverable amount of an asset needs to be estimated. For example, if previous calculations show that an asset's recoverable amount is significantly greater than its carrying amount, the entity need not re-estimate the asset's recoverable amount if no events have occurred that would eliminate that difference. Similarly, previous analysis may show that an asset's recoverable amount is not sensitive to one (or more) of the indications listed in paragraph 12.

16   As an illustration of paragraph 15, if market interest rates or other market rates of return on investments have increased during the period, an entity is not required to make a formal estimate of an asset's recoverable amount in the following cases:

(a)   if the discount rate used in calculating the asset's value in use is unlikely to be affected by the increase in these market rates. For example, increases in short-term interest rates may not have a material effect on the discount rate used for an asset that has a long remaining useful life;

(b)   if the discount rate used in calculating the asset's value in use is likely to be affected by the increase in these market rates but previous sensitivity analysis of recoverable amount shows that:

    (i)   it is unlikely that there will be a material decrease in recoverable amount because future cash flows are also likely to increase (e.g. in some cases, an

---

2   Once an asset meets the criteria to be classified as held for sale (or is included in a disposal group that is classified as held for sale), it is excluded from the scope of this Standard and is accounted for in accordance with AASB 5 *Non-current Assets Held for Sale and Discontinued Operations*.

> entity may be able to demonstrate that it adjusts its revenues to compensate for any increase in market rates); or
>
> (ii) the decrease in recoverable amount is unlikely to result in a material impairment loss.

17 If there is an indication that an asset may be impaired, this may indicate that the remaining useful life, the *depreciation (amortisation)* method or the residual value for the asset needs to be reviewed and adjusted in accordance with the Standard applicable to the asset, even if no impairment loss is recognised for the asset.

Measuring Recoverable Amount

18 This Standard defines recoverable amount as the higher of an asset's or cash-generating unit's fair value less costs to sell and its value in use. Paragraphs 19-57 set out the requirements for measuring recoverable amount. These requirements use the term 'an asset' but apply equally to an individual asset or a cash-generating unit.

19 It is not always necessary to determine both an asset's fair value less costs to sell and its value in use. If either of these amounts exceeds the asset's carrying amount, the asset is not impaired and it is not necessary to estimate the other amount.

20 It may be possible to determine fair value less costs to sell, even if an asset is not traded in an *active market*. However, sometimes it will not be possible to determine fair value less costs to sell because there is no basis for making a reliable estimate of the amount obtainable from the sale of the asset in an arm's length transaction between knowledgeable and willing parties. In this case, the entity may use the asset's value in use as its recoverable amount.

21 If there is no reason to believe that an asset's value in use materially exceeds its fair value less costs to sell, the asset's fair value less costs to sell may be used as its recoverable amount. This will often be the case for an asset that is held for disposal. This is because the value in use of an asset held for disposal will consist mainly of the net disposal proceeds, as the future cash flows from continuing use of the asset until its disposal are likely to be negligible.

22 Recoverable amount is determined for an individual asset, unless the asset does not generate cash inflows that are largely independent of those from other assets or groups of assets. If this is the case, recoverable amount is determined for the cash-generating unit to which the asset belongs (see paragraphs 65-103), unless either:

(a) the asset's fair value less costs to sell is higher than its carrying amount; or

(b) the asset's value in use can be estimated to be close to its fair value less costs to sell and fair value less costs to sell can be determined.

23 In some cases, estimates, averages and computational short cuts may provide reasonable approximations of the detailed computations illustrated in this Standard for determining fair value less costs to sell or value in use.

Measuring the Recoverable Amount of an Intangible Asset with an Indefinite Useful Life

24 Paragraph 10 requires an intangible asset with an indefinite useful life to be tested for impairment annually by comparing its carrying amount with its recoverable amount, irrespective of whether there is any indication that it may be impaired. However, the most recent detailed calculation of such an asset's recoverable amount made in a preceding period may be used in the impairment test for that asset in the current period, provided all of the following criteria are met:

(a) if the intangible asset does not generate cash inflows from continuing use that are largely independent of those from other assets or groups of assets and is therefore tested for impairment as part of the cash-generating unit to which it belongs, the assets and liabilities making up that unit have not changed significantly since the most recent recoverable amount calculation;

(b) the most recent recoverable amount calculation resulted in an amount that exceeded the asset's carrying amount by a substantial margin; and

(c)   based on an analysis of events that have occurred and circumstances that have
        changed since the most recent recoverable amount calculation, the likelihood that
        a current recoverable amount determination would be less than the asset's carrying
        amount is remote.

Fair Value less Costs to Sell

25   The best evidence of an asset's fair value less costs to sell is a price in a binding sale
      agreement in an arm's length transaction, adjusted for incremental costs that would be
      directly attributable to the disposal of the asset.

26   If there is no binding sale agreement but an asset is traded in an active market, fair value
      less costs to sell is the asset's market price less the *costs of disposal*. The appropriate
      market price is usually the current bid price. When current bid prices are unavailable,
      the price of the most recent transaction may provide a basis from which to estimate fair
      value less costs to sell, provided that there has not been a significant change in economic
      circumstances between the transaction date and the date as at which the estimate is made.

27   If there is no binding sale agreement or active market for an asset, fair value less costs to
      sell is based on the best information available to reflect the amount that an entity could
      obtain, at the end of the reporting period, from the disposal of the asset in an arm's length
      transaction between knowledgeable, willing parties, after deducting the costs of disposal.
      In determining this amount, an entity considers the outcome of recent transactions for
      similar assets within the same industry. Fair value less costs to sell does not reflect a
      forced sale, unless management is compelled to sell immediately.

28   Costs of disposal, other than those that have been recognised as liabilities, are deducted in
      determining fair value less costs to sell. Examples of such costs are legal costs, stamp duty
      and similar transaction taxes, costs of removing the asset, and direct incremental costs
      to bring an asset into condition for its sale. However, termination benefits (as defined in
      AASB 119) and costs associated with reducing or reorganising a business following the
      disposal of an asset are not direct incremental costs to dispose of the asset.

29   Sometimes, the disposal of an asset would require the buyer to assume a liability and
      only a single fair value less costs to sell is available for both the asset and the liability.
      Paragraph 78 explains how to deal with such cases.

Value in Use

30   **The following elements shall be reflected in the calculation of an asset's value in use:**

      (a)   an estimate of the future cash flows the entity expects to derive from the asset;

      **(b)   expectations about possible variations in the amount or timing of those future
                cash flows;**

      **(c)   the time value of money, represented by the current market risk-free rate of
                interest;**

      (d)   the price for bearing the uncertainty inherent in the asset; and

      **(e)   other factors, such as illiquidity, that market participants would reflect in
                pricing the future cash flows the entity expects to derive from the asset.**

31   Estimating the value in use of an asset involves the following steps:

      (a)   estimating the future cash inflows and outflows to be derived from continuing use
              of the asset and from its ultimate disposal; and

      (b)   applying the appropriate discount rate to those future cash flows.

32   The elements identified in paragraph 30(b), (d) and (e) can be reflected either as adjustments
      to the future cash flows or as adjustments to the discount rate. Whichever approach an
      entity adopts to reflect expectations about possible variations in the amount or timing of
      future cash flows, the result shall be to reflect the expected present value of the future
      cash flows, that is the weighted average of all possible outcomes. The Appendix provides
      additional guidance on the use of present value techniques in measuring an asset's value
      in use.

Aus32.1 Notwithstanding paragraphs 30, 31 and 32, in respect of not-for-profit entities, where the future economic benefits of an asset are not primarily dependent on the asset's ability to generate net cash inflows and where the entity would, if deprived of the asset, replace its remaining future economic benefits, value in use shall be determined as the depreciated replacement cost of the asset.

Aus32.2 Depreciated replacement cost is defined as the current replacement cost of an asset less, where applicable, accumulated depreciation calculated on the basis of such cost to reflect the already consumed or expired future economic benefits of the asset. The current replacement cost of an asset is its cost measured by reference to the lowest cost at which the gross future economic benefits of that asset could currently be obtained in the normal course of business.

Basis for Estimates of Future Cash Flows

33 In measuring value in use an entity shall:

    (a) base cash flow projections on reasonable and supportable assumptions that represent management's best estimate of the range of economic conditions that will exist over the remaining useful life of the asset. Greater weight shall be given to external evidence;

    (b) base cash flow projections on the most recent financial budgets/forecasts approved by management, but shall exclude any estimated future cash inflows or outflows expected to arise from future restructurings or from improving or enhancing the asset's performance. Projections based on these budgets/forecasts shall cover a maximum period of five years, unless a longer period can be justified; and

    (c) estimate cash flow projections beyond the period covered by the most recent budgets/forecasts by extrapolating the projections based on the budgets/forecasts using a steady or declining growth rate for subsequent years, unless an increasing rate can be justified. This growth rate shall not exceed the long-term average growth rate for the products, industries, or country or countries in which the entity operates, or for the market in which the asset is used, unless a higher rate can be justified.

34 Management assesses the reasonableness of the assumptions on which its current cash flow projections are based by examining the causes of differences between past cash flow projections and actual cash flows. Management shall ensure that the assumptions on which its current cash flow projections are based are consistent with past actual outcomes, provided the effects of subsequent events or circumstances that did not exist when those actual cash flows were generated make this appropriate.

35 Detailed, explicit and reliable financial budgets/forecasts of future cash flows for periods longer than five years are generally not available. For this reason, management's estimates of future cash flows are based on the most recent budgets/forecasts for a maximum of five years. Management may use cash flow projections based on financial budgets/forecasts over a period longer than five years if it is confident that these projections are reliable and it can demonstrate its ability, based on past experience, to forecast cash flows accurately over that longer period.

36 Cash flow projections until the end of an asset's useful life are estimated by extrapolating the cash flow projections based on the financial budgets/forecasts using a growth rate for subsequent years. This rate is steady or declining, unless an increase in the rate matches objective information about patterns over a product or industry lifecycle. If appropriate, the growth rate is zero or negative.

37 When conditions are favourable, competitors are likely to enter the market and restrict growth. Therefore, entities will have difficulty in exceeding the average historical growth rate over the long term (say, twenty years) for the products, industries, or country or countries in which the entity operates, or for the market in which the asset is used.

38 In using information from financial budgets/forecasts, an entity considers whether the information reflects reasonable and supportable assumptions and represents management's best estimate of the set of economic conditions that will exist over the remaining useful life of the asset.

Composition of Estimates of Future Cash Flows

39   **Estimates of future cash flows shall include:**

    (a)   **projections of cash inflows from the continuing use of the asset;**

    (b)   **projections of cash outflows that are necessarily incurred to generate the cash inflows from continuing use of the asset (including cash outflows to prepare the asset for use) and can be directly attributed, or allocated on a reasonable and consistent basis, to the asset; and**

    (c)   **net cash flows, if any, to be received (or paid) for the disposal of the asset at the end of its useful life.**

40   Estimates of future cash flows and the discount rate reflect consistent assumptions about price increases attributable to general inflation. Therefore, if the discount rate includes the effect of price increases attributable to general inflation, future cash flows are estimated in nominal terms. If the discount rate excludes the effect of price increases attributable to general inflation, future cash flows are estimated in real terms (but include future specific price increases or decreases).

41   Projections of cash outflows include those for the day-to-day servicing of the asset as well as future overheads that can be attributed directly, or allocated on a reasonable and consistent basis, to the use of the asset.

42   When the carrying amount of an asset does not yet include all the cash outflows to be incurred before it is ready for use or sale, the estimate of future cash outflows includes an estimate of any further cash outflow that is expected to be incurred before the asset is ready for use or sale. For example, this is the case for a building under construction or for a development project that is not yet completed.

43   To avoid double-counting, estimates of future cash flows do not include:

    (a)   cash inflows from assets that generate cash inflows that are largely independent of the cash inflows from the asset under review (e.g. financial assets such as receivables); and

    (b)   cash outflows that relate to obligations that have been recognised as liabilities (e.g. payables, pensions or provisions).

44   **Future cash flows shall be estimated for the asset in its current condition. Estimates of future cash flows shall not include estimated future cash inflows or outflows that are expected to arise from:**

    (a)   **a future restructuring to which an entity is not yet committed; or**

    (b)   **improving or enhancing the asset's performance.**

45   Because future cash flows are estimated for the asset in its current condition, value in use does not reflect:

    (a)   future cash outflows or related cost savings (e.g. reductions in staff costs) or enefits that are expected to arise from a future restructuring to which an entity is not yet committed; or

    (b)   future cash outflows that will improve or enhance the asset's performance or the related cash inflows that are expected to arise from such outflows.

46   A restructuring is a programme that is planned and controlled by management and materially changes either the scope of the business undertaken by an entity or the manner in which the business is conducted. AASB 137 *Provisions, Contingent Liabilities and Contingent Assets* contains guidance clarifying when an entity is committed to a restructuring.

47   When an entity becomes committed to a restructuring, some assets are likely to be affected by this restructuring. Once the entity is committed to the restructuring:

    (a)   its estimates of future cash inflows and cash outflows for the purpose of determining value in use reflect the cost savings and other benefits from the restructuring (based on the most recent financial budgets/forecasts approved by management); and

    (b)   its estimates of future cash outflows for the restructuring are included in a restructuring provision in accordance with AASB 137.

Illustrative Example 5 illustrates the effect of a future restructuring on a value in use calculation.

48 Until an entity incurs cash outflows that improve or enhance the asset's performance, estimates of future cash flows do not include the estimated future cash inflows that are expected to arise from the increase in economic benefits associated with the cash outflow (see Illustrative Example 6).

49 Estimates of future cash flows include future cash outflows necessary to maintain the level of economic benefits expected to arise from the asset in its current condition. When a cash-generating unit consists of assets with different estimated useful lives, all of which are essential to the ongoing operation of the unit, the replacement of assets with shorter lives is considered to be part of the day-to-day servicing of the unit when estimating the future cash flows associated with the unit. Similarly, when a single asset consists of components with different estimated useful lives, the replacement of components with shorter lives is considered to be part of the day-to-day servicing of the asset when estimating the future cash flows generated by the asset.

50 **Estimates of future cash flows shall not include:**

(a)   cash inflows or outflows from financing activities; or

(b)   income tax receipts or payments.

51 Estimated future cash flows reflect assumptions that are consistent with the way the discount rate is determined. Otherwise, the effect of some assumptions will be counted twice or ignored. Because the time value of money is considered by discounting the estimated future cash flows, these cash flows exclude cash inflows or outflows from financing activities. Similarly, because the discount rate is determined on a pre-tax basis, future cash flows are also estimated on a pre-tax basis.

52 **The estimate of net cash flows to be received (or paid) for the disposal of an asset at the end of its useful life shall be the amount that an entity expects to obtain from the disposal of the asset in an arm's length transaction between knowledgeable, willing parties, after deducting the estimated costs of disposal.**

53 The estimate of net cash flows to be received (or paid) for the disposal of an asset at the end of its useful life is determined in a similar way to an asset's fair value less costs to sell, except that, in estimating those net cash flows:

(a)   an entity uses prices prevailing at the date of the estimate for similar assets that have reached the end of their useful life and have operated under conditions similar to those in which the asset will be used; and

(b)   the entity adjusts those prices for the effect of both future price increases due to general inflation and specific future price increases or decreases. However, if estimates of future cash flows from the asset's continuing use and the discount rate exclude the effect of general inflation, the entity also excludes this effect from the estimate of net cash flows on disposal.

Foreign Currency Future Cash Flows

54 Future cash flows are estimated in the currency in which they will be generated and then discounted using a discount rate appropriate for that currency. An entity translates the present value using the spot exchange rate at the date of the value in use calculation.

Discount Rate

55 **The discount rate (rates) shall be a pre-tax rate (rates) that reflect(s) current market assessments of:**

(a)   the time value of money; and

(b)   the risks specific to the asset for which the future cash flow estimates have not been adjusted.

56 A rate that reflects current market assessments of the time value of money and the risks specific to the asset is the return that investors would require if they were to choose an investment that would generate cash flows of amounts, timing and risk profile equivalent to those that the entity expects to derive from the asset. This rate is estimated from the rate implicit in current market transactions for similar assets or from the weighted average

cost of capital of a listed entity that has a single asset (or a portfolio of assets) similar in terms of service potential and risks to the asset under review. However, the discount rate(s) used to measure an asset's value in use shall not reflect risks for which the future cash flow estimates have been adjusted. Otherwise, the effect of some assumptions will be double-counted.

57   When an asset-specific rate is not directly available from the market, an entity uses surrogates to estimate the discount rate. The Appendix provides additional guidance on estimating the discount rate in such circumstances.

Recognising and Measuring an Impairment Loss

58   Paragraphs 59-64 set out the requirements for recognising and measuring impairment losses for an individual asset other than goodwill. Recognising and measuring impairment losses for cash-generating units and goodwill are dealt with in paragraphs 65-108.

59   **If, and only if, the recoverable amount of an asset is less than its carrying amount, the carrying amount of the asset shall be reduced to its recoverable amount. That reduction is an impairment loss.**

60   **An impairment loss shall be recognised immediately in profit or loss, unless the asset is carried at revalued amount in accordance with another Standard (e.g. in accordance with the revaluation model in AASB 116). Any impairment loss of a revalued asset shall be treated as a revaluation decrease in accordance with that other Standard.**

61   An impairment loss on a non-revalued asset is recognised in profit or loss. However, an impairment loss on a revalued asset is recognised in other comprehensive income to the extent that the impairment loss does not exceed the amount in the revaluation surplus for that same asset. Such an impairment loss on a revalued asset reduces the revaluation surplus for that asset.

Aus61.1   Notwithstanding paragraph 61, in respect of not-for-profit entities, an impairment loss on a revalued asset is recognised in other comprehensive income to the extent that the impairment loss does not exceed the amount in the revaluation surplus for the class of asset. Such an impairment loss on a revalued asset reduces the revaluation surplus for the class of asset.

62   **When the amount estimated for an impairment loss is greater than the carrying amount of the asset to which it relates, an entity shall recognise a liability if, and only if, that is required by another Standard.**

63   **After the recognition of an impairment loss, the depreciation (amortisation) charge for the asset shall be adjusted in future periods to allocate the asset's revised carrying amount, less its residual value (if any), on a systematic basis over its remaining useful life.**

64   If an impairment loss is recognised, any related deferred tax assets or liabilities are determined in accordance with AASB 112 by comparing the revised carrying amount of the asset with its tax base (see Illustrative Example 3).

Cash-generating Units and Goodwill

65   Paragraphs 66-108 and Appendix C set out the requirements for identifying the cash-generating unit to which an asset belongs and determining the carrying amount of, and recognising impairment losses for, cash-generating units and goodwill.

Identifying the Cash-generating Unit to Which an Asset Belongs

66   **If there is any indication that an asset may be impaired, recoverable amount shall be estimated for the individual asset. If it is not possible to estimate the recoverable amount of the individual asset, an entity shall determine the recoverable amount of the cash-generating unit to which the asset belongs (the asset's cash-generating unit).**

67   The recoverable amount of an individual asset cannot be determined if:

(a)   the asset's value in use cannot be estimated to be close to its fair value less costs to sell (e.g. when the future cash flows from continuing use of the asset cannot be estimated to be negligible); and

(b)   the asset does not generate cash inflows that are largely independent of those from other assets.

In such cases, value in use and, therefore, recoverable amount, can be determined only for the asset's cash-generating unit.

> **Example**
>
> A mining entity owns a private railway to support its mining activities. The private railway could be sold only for scrap value and it does not generate cash inflows that are largely independent of the cash inflows from the other assets of the mine.
>
> *It is not possible to estimate the recoverable amount of the private railway because its value in use cannot be determined and is probably different from scrap value. Therefore, the entity estimates the recoverable amount of the cash-generating unit to which the private railway belongs, that is, the mine as a whole.*

68   As defined in paragraph 6, an asset's cash-generating unit is the smallest group of assets that includes the asset and generates cash inflows that are largely independent of the cash inflows from other assets or groups of assets. Identification of an asset's cash-generating unit involves judgement. If recoverable amount cannot be determined for an individual asset, an entity identifies the lowest aggregation of assets that generate largely independent cash inflows.

> **Example**
>
> A bus company provides services under contract with a municipality that requires minimum service on each of five separate routes. Assets devoted to each route and the cash flows from each route can be identified separately. One of the routes operates at a significant loss.
>
> *Because the entity does not have the option to curtail any one bus route, the lowest level of identifiable cash inflows that are largely independent of the cash inflows from other assets or groups of assets is the cash inflows generated by the five routes together. The cash-generating unit for each route is the bus company as a whole.*

69   Cash inflows are inflows of cash and cash equivalents received from parties external to the entity. In identifying whether cash inflows from an asset (or group of assets) are largely independent of the cash inflows from other assets (or groups of assets), an entity considers various factors including how management monitors the entity's operations (such as by product lines, businesses, individual locations, districts or regional areas) or how management makes decisions about continuing or disposing of the entity's assets and operations. Illustrative Example 1 gives examples of identification of a cash-generating unit.

70   **If an active market exists for the output produced by an asset or group of assets, that asset or group of assets shall be identified as a cash-generating unit, even if some or all of the output is used internally. If the cash inflows generated by any asset or cash-generating unit are affected by internal transfer pricing, an entity shall use management's best estimate of future price(s) that could be achieved in arm's length transactions in estimating:**

(a)   **the future cash inflows used to determine the asset's or cash-generating unit's value in use; and**

(b)   **the future cash outflows used to determine the value in use of any other assets or cash-generating units that are affected by the internal transfer pricing.**

71   Even if part or all of the output produced by an asset or a group of assets is used by other units of the entity (e.g. products at an intermediate stage of a production process), this asset or group of assets forms a separate cash-generating unit if the entity could sell the output on an active market. This is because the asset or group of assets could generate cash inflows that would be largely independent of the cash inflows from other assets or groups of assets. In using information based on financial budgets/forecasts that relates to such a cash-generating unit, or to any other asset or cash-generating unit affected

by internal transfer pricing, an entity adjusts this information if internal transfer prices do not reflect management's best estimate of future prices that could be achieved in arm's length transactions.

72   **Cash-generating units shall be identified consistently from period to period for the same asset or types of assets, unless a change is justified.**

73   If an entity determines that an asset belongs to a cash-generating unit different from that in previous periods, or that the types of assets aggregated for the asset's cash-generating unit have changed, paragraph 130 requires disclosures about the cash-generating unit, if an impairment loss is recognised or reversed for the cash-generating unit.

Recoverable Amount and Carrying Amount of a Cash-generating Unit

74   The recoverable amount of a cash-generating unit is the higher of the cash-generating unit's fair value less costs to sell and its value in use. For the purpose of determining the recoverable amount of a cash-generating unit, any reference in paragraphs 19-57 to 'an asset' is read as a reference to 'a cash-generating unit'.

75   **The carrying amount of a cash-generating unit shall be determined on a basis consistent with the way the recoverable amount of the cash-generating unit is determined.**

76   The carrying amount of a cash-generating unit:

(a)   includes the carrying amount of only those assets that can be attributed directly, or allocated on a reasonable and consistent basis, to the cash-generating unit and will generate the future cash inflows used in determining the cash-generating unit's value in use; and

(b)   does not include the carrying amount of any recognised liability, unless the recoverable amount of the cash-generating unit cannot be determined without consideration of this liability.

This is because fair value less costs to sell and value in use of a cash-generating unit are determined excluding cash flows that relate to assets that are not part of the cash-generating unit and liabilities that have been recognised (see paragraphs 28 and 43).

77   When assets are grouped for recoverability assessments, it is important to include in the cash-generating unit all assets that generate or are used to generate the relevant stream of cash inflows. Otherwise, the cash-generating unit may appear to be fully recoverable when in fact an impairment loss has occurred. In some cases, although some assets contribute to the estimated future cash flows of a cash-generating unit, they cannot be allocated to the cash-generating unit on a reasonable and consistent basis. This might be the case for goodwill or *corporate assets* such as head office assets. Paragraphs 80-103 explain how to deal with these assets in testing a cash-generating unit for impairment.

78   It may be necessary to consider some recognised liabilities to determine the recoverable amount of a cash-generating unit. This may occur if the disposal of a cash-generating unit would require the buyer to assume the liability. In this case, the fair value less costs to sell (or the estimated cash flow from ultimate disposal) of the cash-generating unit is the estimated selling price for the assets of the cash-generating unit and the liability together, less the costs of disposal. To perform a meaningful comparison between the carrying amount of the cash-generating unit and its recoverable amount, the carrying amount of the liability is deducted in determining both the cash-generating unit's value in use and its carrying amount.

> **Example**
>
> A company operates a mine in a country where legislation requires that the owner must restore the site on completion of its mining operations. The cost of restoration includes the replacement of the overburden, which must be removed before mining operations commence. A provision for the costs to replace the overburden was recognised as soon as the overburden was removed. The amount provided was recognised as part of the cost of the mine and is being depreciated over the mine's useful life. The carrying amount of the provision for restoration costs is CU500,[3] which is equal to the present value of the restoration costs.
>
> The entity is testing the mine for impairment. The cash-generating unit for the mine is the mine as a whole. The entity has received various offers to buy the mine at a price of around CU800. This price reflects the fact that the buyer will assume the obligation to restore the overburden. Disposal costs for the mine are negligible. The value in use of the mine is approximately CU1,200, excluding restoration costs. The carrying amount of the mine is CU1,000.
>
> *The cash-generating unit's fair value less costs to sell is CU800. This amount considers restoration costs that have already been provided for. As a consequence, the value in use for the cash-generating unit is determined after consideration of the restoration costs and is estimated to be CU700 (CU1,200 less CU500). The carrying amount of the cash-generating unit is CU500, which is the carrying amount of the mine (CU1,000) less the carrying amount of the provision for restoration costs (CU500). Therefore, the recoverable amount of the cash-generating unit exceeds its carrying amount.*

79   For practical reasons, the recoverable amount of a cash-generating unit is sometimes determined after consideration of assets that are not part of the cash-generating unit (e.g. receivables or other financial assets) or liabilities that have been recognised (e.g. payables, pensions and other provisions). In such cases, the carrying amount of the cash-generating unit is increased by the carrying amount of those assets and decreased by the carrying amount of those liabilities.

Goodwill

Allocating Goodwill to Cash-generating Units

80   **For the purpose of impairment testing, goodwill acquired in a business combination shall, from the acquisition date, be allocated to each of the acquirer's cash-generating units, or groups of cash-generating units, that is expected to benefit from the synergies of the combination, irrespective of whether other assets or liabilities of the acquiree are assigned to those units or groups of units. Each unit or group of units to which the goodwill is so allocated shall:**

    (a)   represent the lowest level within the entity at which the goodwill is monitored for internal management purposes; and

    (b)   not be larger than an operating segment as defined by paragraph 5 of AASB 8 *Operating Segments* before aggregation.

81   Goodwill recognised in a business combination is an asset representing the future economic benefits arising from other assets acquired in a business combination that are not individually identified and separately recognised. Goodwill does not generate cash flows independently of other assets or groups of assets, and often contributes to the cash flows of multiple cash-generating units. Goodwill sometimes cannot be allocated on a non-arbitrary basis to individual cash-generating units, but only to groups of cash-generating units. As a result, the lowest level within the entity at which the goodwill is monitored for internal management purposes sometimes comprises a number of cash-generating units to which the goodwill relates, but to which it cannot be allocated. References in paragraphs 83-99 and Appendix C to a cash-generating unit to which goodwill is allocated should be read as references also to a group of cash-generating units to which goodwill is allocated.

82   Applying the requirements in paragraph 80 results in goodwill being tested for impairment at a level that reflects the way an entity manages its operations and with which the goodwill would naturally be associated. Therefore, the development of additional reporting systems is typically not necessary.

---

3   In this Standard, monetary amounts are denominated in 'currency units' (CU).

83   A cash-generating unit to which goodwill is allocated for the purpose of impairment testing may not coincide with the level at which goodwill is allocated in accordance with AASB 121 *The Effects of Changes in Foreign Exchange Rates* for the purpose of measuring foreign currency gains and losses. For example, if an entity is required by AASB 121 to allocate goodwill to relatively low levels for the purpose of measuring foreign currency gains and losses, it is not required to test the goodwill for impairment at that same level unless it also monitors the goodwill at that level for internal management purposes.

84   **If the initial allocation of goodwill acquired in a business combination cannot be completed before the end of the annual period in which the business combination is effected, that initial allocation shall be completed before the end of the first annual period beginning after the acquisition date.**

85   In accordance with AASB 3 *Business Combinations*, if the initial accounting for a business combination can be determined only provisionally by the end of the period in which the combination is effected, the acquirer:

        (a)   accounts for the combination using those provisional values; and

        (b)   recognises any adjustments to those provisional values as a result of completing the initial accounting within the measurement period, which shall not exceed twelve months from the acquisition date.

        In such circumstances, it might also not be possible to complete the initial allocation of the goodwill recognised in the combination before the end of the annual period in which the combination is effected. When this is the case, the entity discloses the information required by paragraph 133.

86   **If goodwill has been allocated to a cash-generating unit and the entity disposes of an operation within that unit, the goodwill associated with the operation disposed of shall be:**

        (a)   **included in the carrying amount of the operation when determining the gain or loss on disposal; and**

        (b)   **measured on the basis of the relative values of the operation disposed of and the portion of the cash-generating unit retained, unless the entity can demonstrate that some other method better reflects the goodwill associated with the operation disposed of.**

Example

An entity sells for CU100 an operation that was part of a cash-generating unit to which goodwill has been allocated. The goodwill allocated to the unit cannot be identified or associated with an asset group at a level lower than that unit, except arbitrarily. The recoverable amount of the portion of the cash-generating unit retained is CU300.

Because the goodwill allocated to the cash-generating unit cannot be non-arbitrarily identified or associated with an asset group at a level lower than that unit, the goodwill associated with the operation disposed of is measured on the basis of the relative values of the operation disposed of and the portion of the unit retained. Therefore, 25 per cent of the goodwill allocated to the cash-generating unit is included in the carrying amount of the operation that is sold.

---

87   **If an entity reorganises its reporting structure in a way that changes the composition of one or more cash-generating units to which goodwill has been allocated, the goodwill shall be reallocated to the units affected. This reallocation shall be performed using a relative value approach similar to that used when an entity disposes of an operation within a cash-generating unit, unless the entity can demonstrate that some other method better reflects the goodwill associated with the reorganised units.**

Example

Goodwill had previously been allocated to cash-generating unit A. The goodwill allocated to A cannot be identified or associated with an asset group at a level lower than A, except arbitrarily. A is to be divided and integrated into three other cash-generating units, B, C and D.

Because the goodwill allocated to A cannot be non-arbitrarily identified or associated with an asset group at a level lower than A, it is reallocated to units B, C and D on the basis of the relative values of the three portions of A before those portions are integrated with B, C and D.

Testing Cash-generating Units with Goodwill for Impairment

88 When, as described in paragraph 81, goodwill relates to a cash-generating unit but has not been allocated to that unit, the unit shall be tested for impairment, whenever there is an indication that the unit may be impaired, by comparing the unit's carrying amount, excluding any goodwill, with its recoverable amount. Any impairment loss shall be recognised in accordance with paragraph 104.

89 If a cash-generating unit described in paragraph 88 includes in its carrying amount an intangible asset that has an indefinite useful life or is not yet available for use and that asset can be tested for impairment only as part of the cash-generating unit, paragraph 10 requires the unit also to be tested for impairment annually.

90 A cash-generating unit to which goodwill has been allocated shall be tested for impairment annually, and whenever there is an indication that the unit may be impaired, by comparing the carrying amount of the unit, including the goodwill, with the recoverable amount of the unit. If the recoverable amount of the unit exceeds the carrying amount of the unit, the unit and the goodwill allocated to that unit shall be regarded as not impaired. If the carrying amount of the unit exceeds the recoverable amount of the unit, the entity shall recognise the impairment loss in accordance with paragraph 104.

91-95 [Deleted by the IASB]

Timing of Impairment Tests

96 The annual impairment test for a cash-generating unit to which goodwill has been allocated may be performed at any time during an annual period, provided the test is performed at the same time every year. Different cash-generating units may be tested for impairment at different times. However, if some or all of the goodwill allocated to a cash-generating unit was acquired in a business combination during the current annual period, that unit shall be tested for impairment before the end of the current annual period.

97 If the assets constituting the cash-generating unit to which goodwill has been allocated are tested for impairment at the same time as the unit containing the goodwill, they shall be tested for impairment before the unit containing the goodwill. Similarly, if the cash-generating units constituting a group of cash-generating units to which goodwill has been allocated are tested for impairment at the same time as the group of units containing the goodwill, the individual units shall be tested for impairment before the group of units containing the goodwill.

98 At the time of impairment testing a cash-generating unit to which goodwill has been allocated, there may be an indication of an impairment of an asset within the unit containing the goodwill. In such circumstances, the entity tests the asset for impairment first, and recognises any impairment loss for that asset before testing for impairment the cash-generating unit containing the goodwill. Similarly, there may be an indication of an impairment of a cash-generating unit within a group of units containing the goodwill. In such circumstances, the entity tests the cash-generating unit for impairment first, and recognises any impairment loss for that unit, before testing for impairment the group of units to which the goodwill is allocated.

99 The most recent detailed calculation made in a preceding period of the recoverable amount of a cash-generating unit to which goodwill has been allocated may be used in the impairment test of that unit in the current period provided all of the following criteria are met:

(a) the assets and liabilities making up the unit have not changed significantly since the most recent recoverable amount calculation;

(b) the most recent recoverable amount calculation resulted in an amount that exceeded the carrying amount of the unit by a substantial margin; and

(c) based on an analysis of events that have occurred and circumstances that have changed since the most recent recoverable amount calculation, the likelihood that a current recoverable amount determination would be less than the current carrying amount of the unit is remote.

Corporate Assets

100   Corporate assets include group or divisional assets such as the building of a headquarters or a division of the entity, EDP equipment or a research centre. The structure of an entity determines whether an asset meets this Standard's definition of corporate assets for a particular cash-generating unit. The distinctive characteristics of corporate assets are that they do not generate cash inflows independently of other assets or groups of assets and their carrying amount cannot be fully attributed to the cash-generating unit under review.

101   Because corporate assets do not generate separate cash inflows, the recoverable amount of an individual corporate asset cannot be determined unless management has decided to dispose of the asset. As a consequence, if there is an indication that a corporate asset may be impaired, recoverable amount is determined for the cash-generating unit or group of cash-generating units to which the corporate asset belongs, and is compared with the carrying amount of this cash-generating unit or group of cash-generating units. Any impairment loss is recognised in accordance with paragraph 104.

102   **In testing a cash-generating unit for impairment, an entity shall identify all the corporate assets that relate to the cash-generating unit under review. If a portion of the carrying amount of a corporate asset:**

   (a)   **can be allocated on a reasonable and consistent basis to that unit, the entity shall compare the carrying amount of the unit, including the portion of the carrying amount of the corporate asset allocated to the unit, with its recoverable amount. Any impairment loss shall be recognised in accordance with paragraph 104.**

   (b)   **cannot be allocated on a reasonable and consistent basis to that unit, the entity shall:**

      (i)   **compare the carrying amount of the unit, excluding the corporate asset, with its recoverable amount and recognise any impairment loss in accordance with paragraph 104;**

      (ii)   **identify the smallest group of cash-generating units that includes the cash-generating unit under review and to which a portion of the carrying amount of the corporate asset can be allocated on a reasonable and consistent basis; and**

      (iii) **compare the carrying amount of that group of cash-generating units, including the portion of the carrying amount of the corporate asset allocated to that group of units, with the recoverable amount of the group of units. Any impairment loss shall be recognised in accordance with paragraph 104.**

103   Illustrative Example 8 illustrates the application of these requirements to corporate assets.

Impairment Loss for a Cash-generating Unit

104   **An impairment loss shall be recognised for a cash-generating unit (the smallest group of cash-generating units to which goodwill or a corporate asset has been allocated) if, and only if, the recoverable amount of the unit (group of units) is less than the carrying amount of the unit (group of units). The impairment loss shall be allocated to reduce the carrying amount of the assets of the unit (group of units) in the following order:**

   (a)   **first, to reduce the carrying amount of any goodwill allocated to the cash-generating unit (group of units); and**

   (b)   **then, to the other assets of the unit (group of units) pro rata on the basis of the carrying amount of each asset in the unit (group of units).**

   These reductions in carrying amounts shall be treated as impairment losses on individual assets and recognised in accordance with paragraph 60.

105 In allocating an impairment loss in accordance with paragraph 104, an entity shall not reduce the carrying amount of an asset below the highest of:

    (a)   its fair value less costs to sell (if determinable);

    (b)   its value in use (if determinable); and

    (c)   zero.

The amount of the impairment loss that would otherwise have been allocated to the asset shall be allocated pro rata to the other assets of the unit (group of units).

106 If it is not practicable to estimate the recoverable amount of each individual asset of a cash-generating unit, this Standard requires an arbitrary allocation of an impairment loss between the assets of that unit, other than goodwill, because all assets of a cash-generating unit work together.

107 If the recoverable amount of an individual asset cannot be determined (see paragraph 67):

    (a)   an impairment loss is recognised for the asset if its carrying amount is greater than the higher of its fair value less costs to sell and the results of the allocation procedures described in paragraphs 104 and 105; and

    (b)   no impairment loss is recognised for the asset if the related cash-generating unit is not impaired. This applies even if the asset's fair value less costs to sell is less than its carrying amount.

Example

A machine has suffered physical damage but is still working, although not as well as before it was damaged. The machine's fair value less costs to sell is less than its carrying amount. The machine does not generate independent cash inflows. The smallest identifiable group of assets that includes the machine and generates cash inflows that are largely independent of the cash inflows from other assets is the production line to which the machine belongs. The recoverable amount of the production line shows that the production line taken as a whole is not impaired.

Assumption 1: budgets/forecasts approved by management reflect no commitment of management to replace the machine.

The recoverable amount of the machine alone cannot be estimated because the machine's value in use:

    (a)   may differ from its fair value less costs to sell; and

    (b)   can be determined only for the cash-generating unit to which the machine belongs (the production line).

The production line is not impaired. Therefore, no impairment loss is recognised for the machine. Nevertheless, the entity may need to reassess the depreciation period or the depreciation method for the machine. Perhaps a shorter depreciation period or a faster depreciation method is required to reflect the expected remaining useful life of the machine or the pattern in which economic benefits are expected to be consumed by the entity.

Assumption 2: budgets/forecasts approved by management reflect a commitment of management to replace the machine and sell it in the near future. Cash flows from continuing use of the machine until its disposal are estimated to be negligible.

The machine's value in use can be estimated to be close to its fair value less costs to sell. Therefore, the recoverable amount of the machine can be determined and no consideration is given to the cash-generating unit to which the machine belongs (i.e. the production line). Because the machine's fair value less costs to sell is less than its carrying amount, an impairment loss is recognised for the machine.

---

108 After the requirements in paragraphs 104 and 105 have been applied, a liability shall be recognised for any remaining amount of an impairment loss for a cash-generating unit if, and only if, that is required by another Standard.

Reversing an Impairment Loss

109 Paragraphs 110-116 set out the requirements for reversing an impairment loss recognised for an asset or a cash-generating unit in prior periods. These requirements use the term 'an asset' but apply equally to an individual asset or a cash-generating unit. Additional requirements for an individual asset are set out in paragraphs 117-121, for a cash-generating unit in paragraphs 122 and 123 and for goodwill in paragraphs 124 and 125.

110   An entity shall assess at the end of each reporting period whether there is any indication that an impairment loss recognised in prior periods for an asset other than goodwill may no longer exist or may have decreased. If any such indication exists, the entity shall estimate the recoverable amount of that asset.

111   In assessing whether there is any indication that an impairment loss recognised in prior periods for an asset other than goodwill may no longer exist or may have decreased, an entity shall consider, as a minimum, the following indications:

External sources of information

(a)   the asset's market value has increased significantly during the period;

(b)   significant changes with a favourable effect on the entity have taken place during the period, or will take place in the near future, in the technological, market, economic or legal environment in which the entity operates or in the market to which the asset is dedicated;

(c)   market interest rates or other market rates of return on investments have decreased during the period, and those decreases are likely to affect the discount rate used in calculating the asset's value in use and increase the asset's recoverable amount materially;

Internal sources of information

(d)   significant changes with a favourable effect on the entity have taken place during the period, or are expected to take place in the near future, in the extent to which, or manner in which, the asset is used or is expected to be used. These changes include costs incurred during the period to improve or enhance the asset's performance or restructure the operation to which the asset belongs; and

(e)   evidence is available from internal reporting that indicates that the economic performance of the asset is, or will be, better than expected.

112   Indications of a potential decrease in an impairment loss in paragraph 111 mainly mirror the indications of a potential impairment loss in paragraph 12.

113   If there is an indication that an impairment loss recognised for an asset other than goodwill may no longer exist or may have decreased, this may indicate that the remaining useful life, the depreciation (amortisation) method or the residual value may need to be reviewed and adjusted in accordance with the Standard applicable to the asset, even if no impairment loss is reversed for the asset.

114   An impairment loss recognised in prior periods for an asset other than goodwill shall be reversed if, and only if, there has been a change in the estimates used to determine the asset's recoverable amount since the last impairment loss was recognised. If this is the case, the carrying amount of the asset shall, except as described in paragraph 117, be increased to its recoverable amount. That increase is a reversal of an impairment loss.

115   A reversal of an impairment loss reflects an increase in the estimated service potential of an asset, either from use or from sale, since the date when an entity last recognised an impairment loss for that asset. Paragraph 130 requires an entity to identify the change in estimates that causes the increase in estimated service potential. Examples of changes in estimates include:

(a)   a change in the basis for recoverable amount (i.e. whether recoverable amount is based on fair value less costs to sell or value in use);

(b)   if recoverable amount was based on value in use, a change in the amount or timing of estimated future cash flows or in the discount rate; or

(c)   if recoverable amount was based on fair value less costs to sell, a change in estimate of the components of fair value less costs to sell.

116   An asset's value in use may become greater than the asset's carrying amount simply because the present value of future cash inflows increases as they become closer.

However, the service potential of the asset has not increased. Therefore, an impairment loss is not reversed just because of the passage of time (sometimes called the 'unwinding' of the discount), even if the recoverable amount of the asset becomes higher than its carrying amount.

Reversing an Impairment Loss for an Individual Asset

117 The increased carrying amount of an asset other than goodwill attributable to a reversal of an impairment loss shall not exceed the carrying amount that would have been determined (net of amortisation or depreciation) had no impairment loss been recognised for the asset in prior years.

118 Any increase in the carrying amount of an asset other than goodwill above the carrying amount that would have been determined (net of amortisation or depreciation) had no impairment loss been recognised for the asset in prior years is a revaluation. In accounting for such a revaluation, an entity applies the Standard applicable to the asset.

119 A reversal of an impairment loss for an asset other than goodwill shall be recognised immediately in profit or loss, unless the asset is carried at revalued amount in accordance with another Standard (e.g. the revaluation model in AASB 116). Any reversal of an impairment loss of a revalued asset shall be treated as a revaluation increase in accordance with that other Standard.

120 A reversal of an impairment loss on a revalued asset is recognised in other comprehensive income and increases the revaluation surplus for that asset. However, to the extent that an impairment loss on the same revalued asset was previously recognised in profit or loss, a reversal of that impairment loss is also recognised in profit or loss.

Aus120.1 Notwithstanding paragraph 120, in respect of not-for-profit entities, a reversal of an impairment loss on a revalued asset is recognised in other comprehensive income and increases the revaluation surplus. However, to the extent that an impairment loss on the same class of asset was previously recognised in profit or loss, a reversal of that impairment loss is also recognised in profit or loss.

121 After a reversal of an impairment loss is recognised, the depreciation (amortisation) charge for the asset shall be adjusted in future periods to allocate the asset's revised carrying amount, less its residual value (if any), on a systematic basis over its remaining useful life.

Reversing an Impairment Loss for a Cash-generating Unit

122 A reversal of an impairment loss for a cash-generating unit shall be allocated to the assets of the unit, except for goodwill, pro rata with the carrying amounts of those assets. These increases in carrying amounts shall be treated as reversals of impairment losses for individual assets and recognised in accordance with paragraph 119.

123 In allocating a reversal of an impairment loss for a cash-generating unit in accordance with paragraph 122, the carrying amount of an asset shall not be increased above the lower of:

(a) its recoverable amount (if determinable); and

(b) the carrying amount that would have been determined (net of amortisation or depreciation) had no impairment loss been recognised for the asset in prior periods.

The amount of the reversal of the impairment loss that would otherwise have been allocated to the asset shall be allocated pro rata to the other assets of the unit, except for goodwill.

Reversing an Impairment Loss for Goodwill

124 An impairment loss recognised for goodwill shall not be reversed in a subsequent period.

125 AASB 138 *Intangible Assets* prohibits the recognition of internally generated goodwill. Any increase in the recoverable amount of goodwill in the periods following the recognition of an impairment loss for that goodwill is likely to be an increase in internally

generated goodwill, rather than a reversal of the impairment loss recognised for the acquired goodwill.

Disclosure

126   An entity shall disclose the following for each class of assets:

   (a)   the amount of impairment losses recognised in profit or loss during the period and the line item(s) of the statement of comprehensive income in which those impairment losses are included;

   (b)   the amount of reversals of impairment losses recognised in profit or loss during the period and the line item(s) of the statement of comprehensive income in which those impairment losses are reversed;

   (c)   the amount of impairment losses on revalued assets recognised in other comprehensive income during the period; and

   (d)   the amount of reversals of impairment losses on revalued assets recognised in other comprehensive income during the period.

127   A class of assets is a grouping of assets of similar nature and use in an entity's operations.

128   The information required in paragraph 126 may be presented with other information disclosed for the class of assets. For example, this information may be included in a reconciliation of the carrying amount of property, plant and equipment, at the beginning and end of the period, as required by AASB 116.

129   An entity that reports segment information in accordance with AASB 8 shall disclose the following for each reportable segment:

   (a)   the amount of impairment losses recognised in profit or loss and in other comprehensive income during the period; and

   (b)   the amount of reversals of impairment losses recognised in profit or loss and in other comprehensive income during the period.

130   An entity shall disclose the following for each material impairment loss recognised or reversed during the period for an individual asset, including goodwill, or a cash-generating unit:

   (a)   the events and circumstances that led to the recognition or reversal of the impairment loss;

   (b)   the amount of the impairment loss recognised or reversed; and

   (c)   for an individual asset:

      (i)   the nature of the asset; and

      (ii)   if the entity reports segment information in accordance with AASB 8, the reportable segment to which the asset belongs;

   (d)   for a cash-generating unit:

      (i)   a description of the cash generating unit (such as whether it is a product line, a plant, a business operation, a geographical area, or a reportable segment as defined in AASB 8);

      (ii)   the amount of the impairment loss recognised or reversed by class of assets and, if the entity reports segment information in accordance with AASB 8, by reportable segment; and

      (iii) if the aggregation of assets for identifying the cash-generating unit has changed since the previous estimate of the cash-generating unit's recoverable amount (if any), a description of the current and former way of aggregating assets and the reasons for changing the way the cash-generating unit is identified; and

   (e)   whether the recoverable amount of the asset (cash-generating unit) is its fair value less costs to sell or its value in use;

(f)   if recoverable amount is fair value less costs to sell, the basis used to determine fair value less costs to sell (such as whether fair value was determined by reference to an active market); and

(g)   if recoverable amount is value in use, the discount rate(s) used in the current estimate and previous estimate (if any) of value in use.

131   An entity shall disclose the following information for the aggregate impairment losses and the aggregate reversals of impairment losses recognised during the period for which no information is disclosed in accordance with paragraph 130:

(a)   the main classes of assets affected by impairment losses and the main classes of assets affected by reversals of impairment losses; and

(b)   the main events and circumstances that led to the recognition of these impairment losses and reversals of impairment losses.

132   An entity is encouraged to disclose assumptions used to determine the recoverable amount of assets (cash-generating units) during the period. However, paragraph 134 requires an entity to disclose information about the estimates used to measure the recoverable amount of a cash-generating unit when goodwill or an intangible asset with an indefinite useful life is included in the carrying amount of that unit.

133   If, in accordance with paragraph 84, any portion of the goodwill acquired in a business combination during the period has not been allocated to a cash-generating unit (group of units) at the end of the reporting period, the amount of the unallocated goodwill shall be disclosed together with the reasons why that amount remains unallocated.

Estimates used to Measure Recoverable Amounts of Cash-generating Units Containing Goodwill or Intangible Assets with Indefinite Useful Lives

134   An entity shall disclose the information required by (a)-(f) for each cash-generating unit (group of units) for which the carrying amount of goodwill or intangible assets with indefinite useful lives allocated to that unit (group of units) is significant in comparison with the entity's total carrying amount of goodwill or intangible assets with indefinite useful lives:

(a)   the carrying amount of goodwill allocated to the unit (group of units);

(b)   the carrying amount of intangible assets with indefinite useful lives allocated to the unit (group of units);

(c)   the basis on which the unit's (group of units') recoverable amount has been determined (i.e. value in use or fair value less costs to sell);

(d)   if the unit's (group of units') recoverable amount is based on value in use:

    (i)   a description of each key assumption on which management has based its cash flow projections for the period covered by the most recent budgets/forecasts. Key assumptions are those to which the unit's (group of units') recoverable amount is most sensitive;

    (ii)   a description of management's approach to determining the value(s) assigned to each key assumption, whether those value(s) reflect past experience or, if appropriate, are consistent with external sources of information, and, if not, how and why they differ from past experience or external sources of information;

    (iii)   the period over which management has projected cash flows based on financial budgets/forecasts approved by management and, when a period greater than five years is used for a cash-generating unit (group of units), an explanation of why that longer period is justified;

    (iv)   the growth rate used to extrapolate cash flow projections beyond the period covered by the most recent budgets/forecasts, and the justification for using any growth rate that exceeds the long-term average growth rate for the products, industries, or country or countries in which the entity operates, or for the market to which the unit (group of units) is dedicated; and

    (v)   the discount rate(s) applied to the cash flow projections;

(e)   if the unit's (group of units') recoverable amount is based on fair value less costs to sell, the methodology used to determine fair value less costs to sell. If fair value less costs to sell is not determined using an observable market price for the unit (group of units), the following information shall also be disclosed:

    (i)   a description of each key assumption on which management has based its determination of fair value less costs to sell. Key assumptions are those to which the unit's (group of units') recoverable amount is most sensitive.

    (ii)   a description of management's approach to determining the value (or values) assigned to each key assumption, whether those values reflect past experience or, if appropriate, are consistent with external sources of information, and, if not, how and why they differ from past experience or external sources of information.

If fair value less costs to sell is determined using discounted cash flow projections, the following information shall also be disclosed:

    (iii)   the period over which management has projected cash flows;

    (iv)   the growth rate used to extrapolate cash flow projections;

    (v)   the discount rate(s) applied to the cash flow projections;

(f)   if a reasonably possible change in a key assumption on which management has based its determination of the unit's (group of units') recoverable amount would cause the unit's (group of units') carrying amount to exceed its recoverable amount:

    (i)   the amount by which the unit's (group of units') recoverable amount exceeds its carrying amount;

    (ii)   the value assigned to the key assumption; and

    (iii)   the amount by which the value assigned to the key assumption must change, after incorporating any consequential effects of that change on the other variables used to measure recoverable amount, in order for the unit's (group of units') recoverable amount to be equal to its carrying amount.

135   If some or all of the carrying amount of goodwill or intangible assets with indefinite useful lives is allocated across multiple cash-generating units (groups of units), and the amount so allocated to each unit (group of units) is not significant in comparison with the entity's total carrying amount of goodwill or intangible assets with indefinite useful lives, that fact shall be disclosed, together with the aggregate carrying amount of goodwill or intangible assets with indefinite useful lives allocated to those units (groups of units). In addition, if the recoverable amounts of any of those units (groups of units) are based on the same key assumption(s) and the aggregate carrying amount of goodwill or intangible assets with indefinite useful lives allocated to them is significant in comparison with the entity's total carrying amount of goodwill or intangible assets with indefinite useful lives, an entity shall disclose that fact, together with:

(a)   the aggregate carrying amount of goodwill allocated to those units (groups of units);

(b)   the aggregate carrying amount of intangible assets with indefinite useful lives allocated to those units (groups of units);

(c)   a description of the key assumption(s);

(d)   a description of management's approach to determining the value(s) assigned to the key assumption(s), whether those value(s) reflect past experience or, if appropriate, are consistent with external sources of information, and, if not, how and why they differ from past experience or external sources of information;

(e) if a reasonably possible change in the key assumption(s) would cause the aggregate of the units' (groups of units') carrying amounts to exceed the aggregate of their recoverable amounts:

   (i) the amount by which the aggregate of the units' (groups of units') recoverable amounts exceeds the aggregate of their carrying amounts;

   (ii) the value(s) assigned to the key assumption(s); and

   (iii) the amount by which the value(s) assigned to the key assumption(s) must change, after incorporating any consequential effects of the change on the other variables used to measure recoverable amount, in order for the aggregate of the units' (groups of units') recoverable amounts to be equal to the aggregate of their carrying amounts.

136   The most recent detailed calculation made in a preceding period of the recoverable amount of a cash-generating unit (group of units) may, in accordance with paragraph 24 or 99, be carried forward and used in the impairment test for that unit (group of units) in the current period provided specified criteria are met. When this is the case, the information for that unit (group of units) that is incorporated into the disclosures required by paragraphs 134 and 135 relate to the carried forward calculation of recoverable amount.

137   Illustrative Example 9 illustrates the disclosures required by paragraphs 134 and 135.

Transitional Provisions and Effective Date

138   [Deleted by the IASB]

139   [Deleted by the AASB]

140   [Deleted by the AASB]

140A [Deleted by the AASB]

140B [Deleted by the AASB]

140C Paragraph 134(e) was amended by AASB 2008-5 *Amendments to Australian Accounting Standards arising from the Annual Improvements Project* issued in July 2008. An entity shall apply that amendment for annual reporting periods beginning on or after 1 January 2009. Earlier application is permitted. If an entity applies the amendment for an earlier period it shall disclose that fact.

140D AASB 2008-7 *Amendments to Australian Accounting Standards – Cost of an Investment in a Subsidiary, Jointly Controlled Entity or Associate*, issued in July 2008, added paragraph 12(h). An entity shall apply that amendment prospectively for annual reporting periods beginning on or after 1 January 2009. Earlier application is permitted. If an entity applies the related amendments in paragraphs 4 and 37A of AASB 127 (July 2004, as amended) or paragraphs 4 and 38A of AASB 127 (March 2008, as amended) for an earlier period, it shall apply the amendment in paragraph 12(h) at the same time.

140E AASB 2009-5 *Further Amendments to Australian Accounting Standards arising from the Annual Improvements Project*, issued in May 2009, amended paragraph 80(b). An entity shall apply that amendment prospectively for annual reporting periods beginning on or after 1 January 2010. Earlier application is permitted. If an entity applies the amendment for an earlier period it shall disclose that fact.

Withdrawal of IAS 36 (issued 1998)

141   [Deleted by the AASB]

Appendix A

Using Present Value Techniques to Measure Value in Use

This appendix is an integral part of AASB 136. It provides guidance on the use of present value techniques in measuring value in use. Although the guidance uses the term 'asset', it equally applies to a group of assets forming a cash-generating unit.

The Components of a Present Value Measurement

A1   The following elements together capture the economic differences between assets:

(a)   an estimate of the future cash flow, or in more complex cases, series of future cash flows the entity expects to derive from the asset;

(b)   expectations about possible variations in the amount or timing of those cash flows;

(c)   the time value of money, represented by the current market risk-free rate of interest;

(d)   the price for bearing the uncertainty inherent in the asset; and

(e)   other, sometimes unidentifiable, factors (such as illiquidity) that market participants would reflect in pricing the future cash flows the entity expects to derive from the asset.

A2   This appendix contrasts two approaches to computing present value, either of which may be used to estimate the value in use of an asset, depending on the circumstances. Under the 'traditional' approach, adjustments for factors (b)-(e) described in paragraph A1 are embedded in the discount rate. Under the 'expected cash flow' approach, factors (b), (d) and (e) cause adjustments in arriving at risk-adjusted expected cash flows. Whichever approach an entity adopts to reflect expectations about possible variations in the amount or timing of future cash flows, the result should be to reflect the expected present value of the future cash flows, that is, the weighted average of all possible outcomes.

General Principles

A3   The techniques used to estimate future cash flows and interest rates will vary from one situation to another depending on the circumstances surrounding the asset in question. However, the following general principles govern any application of present value techniques in measuring assets.

(a)   Interest rates used to discount cash flows should reflect assumptions that are consistent with those inherent in the estimated cash flows. Otherwise, the effect of some assumptions will be double-counted or ignored. For example, a discount rate of 12 per cent might be applied to contractual cash flows of a loan receivable. That rate reflects expectations about future defaults from loans with particular characteristics. That same 12 per cent rate should not be used to discount expected cash flows because those cash flows already reflect assumptions about future defaults.

(b)   Estimated cash flows and discount rates should be free from both bias and factors unrelated to the asset in question. For example, deliberately understating estimated net cash flows to enhance the apparent future profitability of an asset introduces a bias into the measurement.

(c)   Estimated cash flows or discount rates should reflect the range of possible outcomes rather than a single most likely, minimum or maximum possible amount.

Traditional and Expected Cash Flow Approaches to Present Value

Traditional Approach

A4   Accounting applications of present value have traditionally used a single set of estimated cash flows and a single discount rate, often described as 'the rate commensurate with the risk'. In effect, the traditional approach assumes that a single discount rate convention can incorporate all the expectations about the future cash flows and the appropriate risk premium. Therefore, the traditional approach places most of the emphasis on selection of the discount rate.

A5   In some circumstances, such as those in which comparable assets can be observed in the marketplace, a traditional approach is relatively easy to apply. For assets with contractual cash flows, it is consistent with the manner in which marketplace participants describe assets, as in 'a 12 per cent bond'.

A6   However, the traditional approach may not appropriately address some complex measurement problems, such as the measurement of non-financial assets for which no market for the item or a comparable item exists. A proper search for 'the rate commensurate with the risk' requires analysis of at least two items – an asset that exists in the marketplace and has an observed interest rate and the asset being measured. The appropriate discount rate for the cash flows being measured must be inferred from the observable rate of interest in that other asset. To draw that inference, the characteristics of the other asset's cash flows must be similar to those of the asset being measured. Therefore, the measurer must do the following:

(a)   identify the set of cash flows that will be discounted;

(b)   identify another asset in the marketplace that appears to have similar cash flow characteristics;

(c)   compare the cash flow sets from the two items to ensure that they are similar (e.g. are both sets contractual cash flows, or is one contractual and the other an estimated cash flow?);

(d)   evaluate whether there is an element in one item that is not present in the other (e.g. is one less liquid than the other?); and

(e)   evaluate whether both sets of cash flows are likely to behave (i.e. vary) in a similar fashion in changing economic conditions.

Expected Cash Flow Approach

A7   The expected cash flow approach is, in some situations, a more effective measurement tool than the traditional approach. In developing a measurement, the expected cash flow approach uses all expectations about possible cash flows instead of the single most likely cash flow. For example, a cash flow might be CU100, CU200 or CU300 with probabilities of 10 per cent, 60 per cent and 30 per cent, respectively. The expected cash flow is CU220. The expected cash flow approach thus differs from the traditional approach by focusing on direct analysis of the cash flows in question and on more explicit statements of the assumptions used in the measurement.

A8   The expected cash flow approach also allows use of present value techniques when the timing of cash flows is uncertain. For example, a cash flow of CU1,000 may be received in one year, two years or three years with probabilities of 10 per cent, 60 per cent and 30 per cent, respectively. The example below shows the computation of expected present value in that situation.

Present value of CU1,000 in 1 year at 5%	CU952.38	
Probability	10.00%	CU95.24
Present value of CU1,000 in 2 years at 5.25%	CU902.73	
Probability	60.00%	CU541.64
Present value of CU1,000 in 3 years at 5.50%	CU851.61	
Probability	30.00%	CU255.48
Expected present value		CU892.36

A9   The expected present value of CU892.36 differs from the traditional notion of a best estimate of CU902.73 (the 60 per cent probability). A traditional present value computation applied to this example requires a decision about which of the possible timings of cash flows to use and, accordingly, would not reflect the probabilities of other timings. This is because the discount rate in a traditional present value computation cannot reflect uncertainties in timing.

A10   The use of probabilities is an essential element of the expected cash flow approach. Some question whether assigning probabilities to highly subjective estimates suggests greater precision than, in fact, exists. However, the proper application of the traditional approach (as described in paragraph A6) requires the same estimates and subjectivity without providing the computational transparency of the expected cash flow approach.

A11   Many estimates developed in current practice already incorporate the elements of expected cash flows informally. In addition, accountants often face the need to measure an asset using limited information about the probabilities of possible cash flows. For example, an accountant might be confronted with the following situations:

   (a)   the estimated amount falls somewhere between CU50 and CU250, but no amount in the range is more likely than any other amount. Based on that limited information, the estimated expected cash flow is CU150 [(50 + 250)/2];

   (b)   the estimated amount falls somewhere between CU50 and CU250, and the most likely amount is CU100. However, the probabilities attached to each amount are unknown. Based on that limited information, the estimated expected cash flow is CU133.33 [(50 + 100 + 250)/3]; and

   (c)   the estimated amount will be CU50 (10 per cent probability), CU250 (30 per cent probability), or CU100 (60 per cent probability). Based on that limited information, the estimated expected cash flow is CU140 [(50 × 0.10) + (250 × 0.30) + (100 × 0.60)].

In each case, the estimated expected cash flow is likely to provide a better estimate of value in use than the minimum, most likely or maximum amount taken alone.

A12   The application of an expected cash flow approach is subject to a cost-benefit constraint. In some cases, an entity may have access to extensive data and may be able to develop many cash flow scenarios. In other cases, an entity may not be able to develop more than general statements about the variability of cash flows without incurring substantial cost. The entity needs to balance the cost of obtaining additional information against the additional reliability that information will bring to the measurement.

A13   Some maintain that expected cash flow techniques are inappropriate for measuring a single item or an item with a limited number of possible outcomes. They offer an example of an asset with two possible outcomes: a 90 per cent probability that the cash flow will be CU10 and a 10 per cent probability that the cash flow will be CU1,000. They observe that the expected cash flow in that example is CU109 and criticise that result as not representing either of the amounts that may ultimately be paid.

A14   Assertions like the one just outlined reflect underlying disagreement with the measurement objective. If the objective is accumulation of costs to be incurred, expected cash flows may not produce a representationally faithful estimate of the expected cost. However, this Standard is concerned with measuring the recoverable amount of an asset. The recoverable amount of the asset in this example is not likely to be CU10, even though that is the most likely cash flow. This is because a measurement of CU10 does not incorporate the uncertainty of the cash flow in the measurement of the asset. Instead, the uncertain cash flow is presented as if it were a certain cash flow. No rational entity would sell an asset with these characteristics for CU10.

Discount Rate

A15   Whichever approach an entity adopts for measuring the value in use of an asset, interest rates used to discount cash flows should not reflect risks for which the estimated cash flows have been adjusted. Otherwise, the effect of some assumptions will be double-counted.

A16   When an asset-specific rate is not directly available from the market, an entity uses surrogates to estimate the discount rate. The purpose is to estimate, as far as possible, a market assessment of:

   (a)   the time value of money for the periods until the end of the asset's useful life; and

   (b)   factors (b), (d) and (e) described in paragraph A1, to the extent those factors have not caused adjustments in arriving at estimated cash flows.

AASB

A17 As a starting point in making such an estimate, the entity might take into account the following rates:

    (a)   the entity's weighted average cost of capital determined using techniques such as the Capital Asset Pricing Model;

    (b)   the entity's incremental borrowing rate; and

    (c)   other market borrowing rates.

A18 However, these rates must be adjusted:

    (a)   to reflect the way that the market would assess the specific risks associated with the asset's estimated cash flows; and

    (b)   to exclude risks that are not relevant to the asset's estimated cash flows or for which the estimated cash flows have been adjusted.

    Consideration should be given to risks such as country risk, currency risk and price risk.

A19 The discount rate is independent of the entity's capital structure and the way the entity financed the purchase of the asset, because the future cash flows expected to arise from an asset do not depend on the way in which the entity financed the purchase of the asset.

A20 Paragraph 55 requires the discount rate used to be a pre-tax rate. Therefore, when the basis used to estimate the discount rate is post-tax, that basis is adjusted to reflect a pre-tax rate.

A21 An entity normally uses a single discount rate for the estimate of an asset's value in use. However, an entity uses separate discount rates for different future periods where value in use is sensitive to a difference in risks for different periods or to the term structure of interest rates.

Appendix C

This appendix is an integral part of the Standard.

Impairment Testing Cash-generating Units with Goodwill and Non-controlling Interests

C1 In accordance with AASB 3 (as revised in March 2008), the acquirer measures and recognises goodwill as of the acquisition date as the excess of (a) over (b) below:

    (a)   the aggregate of:

        (i)   the consideration transferred measured in accordance with AASB 3, which generally requires acquisition-date fair value;

        (ii)   the amount of any non-controlling interest in the acquiree measured in accordance with AASB 3; and

        (iii)   in a business combination achieved in stages, the acquisition-date fair value of the acquirer's previously held equity interest in the acquiree.

    (b)   the net of the acquisition-date amounts of the identifiable assets acquired and liabilities assumed measured in accordance with AASB 3.

Allocation of Goodwill

C2 Paragraph 80 of this Standard requires goodwill acquired in a business combination to be allocated to each of the acquirer's cash-generating units, or groups of cash-generating units, expected to benefit from the synergies of the combination, irrespective of whether other assets or liabilities of the acquiree are assigned to those units, or groups of units. It is possible that some of the synergies resulting from a business combination will be allocated to a cash-generating unit in which the non-controlling interest does not have an interest.

Testing for Impairment

C3 Testing for impairment involves comparing the recoverable amount of a cash-generating unit with the carrying amount of the cash-generating unit.

C4 If an entity measures non-controlling interests as its proportionate interest in the net identifiable assets of a subsidiary at the acquisition date, rather than at fair value, goodwill attributable to non-controlling interests is included in the recoverable amount of the related cash-generating unit but is not recognised in the parent's consolidated financial statements. As a consequence, an entity shall gross up the carrying amount of goodwill allocated to the unit to include the goodwill attributable to the non-controlling interest. This adjusted carrying amount is then compared with the recoverable amount of the unit to determine whether the cash-generating unit is impaired.

Allocating an Impairment Loss

C5 Paragraph 104 requires any identified impairment loss to be allocated first to reduce the carrying amount of goodwill allocated to the unit and then to the other assets of the unit pro rata on the basis of the carrying amount of each asset in the unit.

C6 If a subsidiary, or part of a subsidiary, with a non-controlling interest is itself a cash-generating unit, the impairment loss is allocated between the parent and the non-controlling interest on the same basis as that on which profit or loss is allocated.

C7 If a subsidiary, or part of a subsidiary, with a non-controlling interest is part of a larger cash-generating unit, goodwill impairment losses are allocated to the parts of the cash-generating unit that have a non-controlling interest and the parts that do not. The impairment losses should be allocated to the parts of the cash-generating unit on the basis of:

(a) to the extent that the impairment relates to goodwill in the cash-generating unit, the relative carrying values of the goodwill of the parts before the impairment; and

(b) to the extent that the impairment relates to identifiable assets in the cash-generating unit, the relative carrying values of the net identifiable assets of the parts before the impairment. Any such impairment is allocated to the assets of the parts of each unit pro rata on the basis of the carrying amount of each asset in the part.

In those parts that have a non-controlling interest, the impairment loss is allocated between the parent and the non-controlling interest on the same basis as that on which profit or loss is allocated.

C8 If an impairment loss attributable to a non-controlling interest relates to goodwill that is not recognised in the parent's consolidated financial statements (see paragraph C4), that impairment is not recognised as a goodwill impairment loss. In such cases, only the impairment loss relating to the goodwill that is allocated to the parent is recognised as a goodwill impairment loss.

C9 Illustrative Example 7 illustrates the impairment testing of a non-wholly-owned cash-generating unit with goodwill.

Illustrative Examples

Contents

		Paragraphs
1	Identification of Cash-generating Units	
	A – Retail Store Chain	IE1 – IE4
	B – Plant for an Intermediate Step in a Production Process	IE5 – IE10
	C – Single Product Entity	IE11 – IE16
	D – Magazine Titles	IE17 – IE19
	E – Building Half-Rented to Others and Half-Occupied for Own Use	IE20 – IE22
2	Calculation of Value in Use and Recognition of an Impairment Loss	IE23 – IE32
3	Deferred Tax Effects	
	A – Deferred Tax Effects of the Recognition of an Impairment Loss	IE33 – IE35
	B – Recognition of an Impairment Loss Creates a Deferred Tax Asset	IE36 – IE37
4	Reversal of an Impairment Loss	IE38 – IE43
5	Treatment of a Future Restructuring	IE44 – IE53
6	Treatment of Future Costs	IE54 – IE61
7	Impairment Testing Cash-generating Units with Goodwill and Non-controlling Interests	
	A – Non-controlling Interests Measured Initially as a Proportionate Share of the Net Identifiable Assets	IE62 – IE68
	B – Non-controlling Interests Measured Initially at Fair Value and the Related Subsidiary is a Stand-alone Cash-generating Unit	IE68A – IE68E
	C – Non-controlling Interests Measured Initially at Fair Value and the Related Subsidiary is part of a Larger Cash-generating Unit	IE68F – IE68J
8	Allocation of Corporate Assets	IE69 – IE79
9	Disclosures about Cash-generating Units with Goodwill or Intangible Assets with Indefinite Useful Lives	IE80 – IE89

Illustrative Examples

These examples accompany, but are not part of, AASB 136. All the examples assume that the entities concerned have no transactions other than those described. In the examples monetary amounts are determined in 'currency units' (CU).

Example 1 – Identification of Cash-generating Units

The purpose of this example is:

(a)   to indicate how cash-generating units are identified in various situations; and

(b)   to highlight certain factors that an entity may consider in identifying the cash-generating unit to which an asset belongs.

A – Retail Store Chain

Background

IE1   Store X belongs to a retail store chain M. X makes all its retail purchases through M's purchasing centre. Pricing, marketing, advertising and human resources policies (except for hiring X's cashiers and sales staff) are decided by M. M also owns five other stores in the same city as X (although in different neighbourhoods) and 20 other stores in other cities. All stores are managed in the same way as X. X and four other stores were purchased five years ago and goodwill was recognised.

What is the cash-generating unit for X (X's cash-generating unit)?

Analysis

IE2 In identifying X's cash-generating unit, an entity considers whether, for example:

    (a) internal management reporting is organised to measure performance on a store-by-store basis; and

    (b) the business is run on a store-by-store profit basis or on a region/city basis.

IE3 All M's stores are in different neighbourhoods and probably have different customer bases. So, although X is managed at a corporate level, X generates cash inflows that are largely independent of those of M's other stores. Therefore, it is likely that X is a cash-generating unit.

IE4 If X's cash-generating unit represents the lowest level within M at which the goodwill is monitored for internal management purposes, M applies to that cash generating unit the impairment test described in paragraph 90 of AASB 136. If information about the carrying amount of goodwill is not available and monitored for internal management purposes at the level of X's cash-generating unit, M applies to that cash-generating unit the impairment test described in paragraph 88 of AASB 136.

B – Plant for an Intermediate Step in a Production Process

Background

IE5 A significant raw material used for plant Y's final production is an intermediate product bought from plant X of the same entity. X's products are sold to Y at a transfer price that passes all margins to X. Eighty per cent of Y's final production is sold to customers outside of the entity. Sixty per cent of X's final production is sold to Y and the remaining 40 per cent is sold to customers outside of the entity.

For each of the following cases, what are the cash-generating units for X and Y?

    Case 1: X could sell the products it sells to Y in an active market. Internal transfer prices are higher than market prices.

    Case 2: There is no active market for the products X sells to Y.

Analysis

Case 1

IE6 X could sell its products in an active market and, so, generate cash inflows that would be largely independent of the cash inflows from Y. Therefore, it is likely that X is a separate cash-generating unit, although part of its production is used by Y (see paragraph 70 of AASB 136).

IE7 It is likely that Y is also a separate cash-generating unit. Y sells 80 per cent of its products to customers outside of the entity. Therefore, its cash inflows can be regarded as largely independent.

IE8 Internal transfer prices do not reflect market prices for X's output. Therefore, in determining value in use of both X and Y, the entity adjusts financial budgets/forecasts to reflect management's best estimate of future prices that could be achieved in arm's length transactions for those of X's products that are used internally (see paragraph 70 of AASB 136).

Case 2

IE9 It is likely that the recoverable amount of each plant cannot be assessed independently of the recoverable amount of the other plant because:

    (a) the majority of X's production is used internally and could not be sold in an active market. So, cash inflows of X depend on demand for Y's products. Therefore, X cannot be considered to generate cash inflows that are largely independent of those of Y; and

    (b) the two plants are managed together.

IE10 As a consequence, it is likely that X and Y together are the smallest group of assets that generates cash inflows that are largely independent.

C – Single Product Entity

Background

IE11 Entity M produces a single product and owns plants A, B and C. Each plant is located in a different continent. A produces a component that is assembled in either B or C. The combined capacity of B and C is not fully utilised. M's products are sold worldwide from either B or C. For example, B's production can be sold in C's continent if the products can be delivered faster from B than from C. Utilisation levels of B and C depend on the allocation of sales between the two sites.

For each of the following cases, what are the cash-generating units for A, B and C?

Case 1:   There is an active market for A's products.

Case 2:   There is no active market for A's products.

Analysis

Case 1

IE12 It is likely that A is a separate cash-generating unit because there is an active market for its products (see Example B - Plant for an Intermediate Step in a Production Process, Case 1).

IE13 Although there is an active market for the products assembled by B and C, cash inflows for B and C depend on the allocation of production across the two sites. It is unlikely that the future cash inflows for B and C can be determined individually. Therefore, it is likely that B and C together are the smallest identifiable group of assets that generates cash inflows that are largely independent.

IE14 In determining the value in use of A and B plus C, M adjusts financial budgets/forecasts to reflect its best estimate of future prices that could be achieved in arm's length transactions for A's products (see paragraph 70 of AASB 136).

Case 2

IE15 It is likely that the recoverable amount of each plant cannot be assessed independently because:

(a)   there is no active market for A's products. Therefore, A's cash inflows depend on sales of the final product by B and C; and

(b)   although there is an active market for the products assembled by B and C, cash inflows for B and C depend on the allocation of production across the two sites. It is unlikely that the future cash inflows for B and C can be determined individually.

IE16 As a consequence, it is likely that A, B and C together (i.e. M as a whole) are the smallest identifiable group of assets that generates cash inflows that are largely independent.

D – Magazine Titles

Background

IE17 A publisher owns 150 magazine titles of which 70 were purchased and 80 were self-created. The price paid for a purchased magazine title is recognised as an intangible asset. The costs of creating magazine titles and maintaining the existing titles are recognised as an expense when incurred. Cash inflows from direct sales and advertising are identifiable for each magazine title. Titles are managed by customer segments. The level of advertising income for a magazine title depends on the range of titles in the customer segment to which the magazine title relates. Management has a policy to abandon old titles before the end of their economic lives and replace them immediately with new titles for the same customer segment.

What is the cash-generating unit for an individual magazine title?

Analysis

IE18 It is likely that the recoverable amount of an individual magazine title can be assessed. Even though the level of advertising income for a title is influenced, to a certain extent, by the other titles in the customer segment, cash inflows from direct sales and advertising are identifiable for each title. In addition, although titles are managed by customer segments, decisions to abandon titles are made on an individual title basis.

IE19   Therefore, it is likely that individual magazine titles generate cash inflows that are largely independent of each other and that each magazine title is a separate cash-generating unit.

E – Building Half-Rented to Others and Half-Occupied for Own Use

Background

IE20   M is a manufacturing company. It owns a headquarters building that used to be fully occupied for internal use. After down-sizing, half of the building is now used internally and half rented to third parties. The lease agreement with the tenant is for five years.

       What is the cash-generating unit of the building?

Analysis

IE21   The primary purpose of the building is to serve as a corporate asset, supporting M's manufacturing activities. Therefore, the building as a whole cannot be considered to generate cash inflows that are largely independent of the cash inflows from the entity as a whole. So, it is likely that the cash-generating unit for the building is M as a whole.

IE22   The building is not held as an investment. Therefore, it would not be appropriate to determine the value in use of the building based on projections of future market related rents.

Example 2 – Calculation of Value in Use and Recognition of an Impairment Loss

In this example, tax effects are ignored.

Background and Calculation of Value in Use

IE23   At the end of 20X0, entity T acquires entity M for CU10,000. M has manufacturing plants in three countries.

       Schedule 1. Data at the end of 20X0

End of 20X0	Allocation of purchase price	Fair value of identifiable assets	Goodwill*
	CU	CU	CU
Activities in Country A	3,000	2,000	1,000
Activities in Country B	2,000	1,500	500
Activities in Country C	5,000	3,500	1,500
Total	10,000	7,000	3,000

* Activities in each country represent the lowest level at which the goodwill is monitored for internal management purposes (determined as the difference between the purchase price of the activities in each country, as specified in the purchase agreement, and the fair value of the identifiable assets).

IE23A   Because goodwill has been allocated to the activities in each country, each of those activities must be tested for impairment annually or more frequently if there is any indication that it may be impaired (see paragraph 90 of AASB 136).

IE24   The recoverable amounts (i.e. higher of value in use and fair value less costs to sell) of the cash-generating units are determined on the basis of value in use calculations. At the end of 20X0 and 20X1, the value in use of each cash-generating unit exceeds its carrying amount. Therefore the activities in each country and the goodwill allocated to those activities are regarded as not impaired.

IE25   At the beginning of 20X2, a new government is elected in Country A. It passes legislation significantly restricting exports of T's main product. As a result, and for the foreseeable future, T's production in Country A will be cut by 40 per cent.

IE26   The significant export restriction and the resulting production decrease require T also to estimate the recoverable amount of the Country A operations at the beginning of 20X2.

IE27   T uses straight-line depreciation over a 12-year life for the Country A identifiable assets and anticipates no residual value.

IE28 To determine the value in use for the Country A cash-generating unit (see Schedule 2), T:

(a) prepares cash flow forecasts derived from the most recent financial budgets/ forecasts for the next five years (years 20X2-20X6) approved by management;

(b) estimates subsequent cash flows (years 20X7-20Y2) based on declining growth rates. The growth rate for 20X7 is estimated to be 3 per cent. This rate is lower than the average long-term growth rate for the market in Country A; and

(c) selects a 15 per cent discount rate, which represents a pre-tax rate that reflects current market assessments of the time value of money and the risks specific to the Country A cash-generating unit.

Recognition and Measurement of Impairment Loss

IE29 The recoverable amount of the Country A cash-generating unit is CU1,360.

IE30 T compares the recoverable amount of the Country A cash-generating unit with its carrying amount (see Schedule 3).

IE31 Because the carrying amount exceeds the recoverable amount by CU1,473, T recognises an impairment loss of CU1,473 immediately in profit or loss. The carrying amount of the goodwill that relates to the Country A operations is reduced to zero before reducing the carrying amount of other identifiable assets within the Country A cash-generating unit (see paragraph 104 of AASB 136).

IE32 Tax effects are accounted for separately in accordance with AASB 112 *Income Taxes* (see Illustrative Example 3A).

Schedule 2. Calculation of the value in use of the Country A cash-generating unit at the beginning of 20X2

Year	Long-term growth rates	Future cash flows CU	Present value factor at 15% discount rate$	Discounted future cash flows CU
20X2 (n=1)		230*	0.86957	200
20X3		253*	0.75614	191
20X4		273*	0.65752	180
20X5		290*	0.57175	166
20X6		304*	0.49718	151
20X7	3%	313†	0.43233	135
20X8	−2%	307†	0.37594	115
20X9	−6%	289†	0.32690	94
20Y0	−15%	245†	0.28426	70
20Y1	−25%	184†	0.24719	45
20Y2	−67%	61†	0.21494	13
Value in use				1,360

* Based on management's best estimate of net cash flow projections (after the 40% cut).

† Based on an extrapolation from preceding year cash flow using declining growth rates.

§ The present value factor is calculated as $k = 1/(1+a)^n$, where a = discount rate and n = period of discount.

Schedule 3. Calculation and allocation of the impairment loss for the Country A cash-generating unit at the beginning of 20X2

Beginning of 20X2	Goodwill CU	Identifiable assets CU	Total CU
Historical cost	1,000	2,000	3,000
Accumulated depreciation (20X1)	–	(167)	(167)
Carrying amount	1,000	1,833	2,833
Impairment loss	(1,000)	(473)	(1,473)
Carrying amount after impairment loss	–	1,360	1,360

Example 3 – Deferred Tax Effects

A – Deferred Tax Effects of the Recognition of an Impairment Loss

Use the data for entity T as presented in Example 2, with supplementary information as provided in this example.

IE33   At the beginning of 20X2, the tax base of the identifiable assets of the Country A cash-generating unit is CU900. Impairment losses are not deductible for tax purposes. The tax rate is 40 per cent.

IE34   The recognition of an impairment loss on the assets of the Country A cash-generating unit reduces the taxable temporary difference related to those assets. The deferred tax liability is reduced accordingly.

Beginning of 20X2	Identifiable assets before impairment loss CU	Impairment loss CU	Identifiable assets after impairment loss CU
Carrying amount (Example 2)	1,833	(473)	1,360
Tax base	900	–	900
Taxable temporary difference	933	(473)	460
Deferred tax liability at 40%	373	(189)	184

IE35   In accordance with AASB 112, no deferred tax relating to the goodwill was recognised initially. Therefore, the impairment loss relating to the goodwill does not give rise to a deferred tax adjustment.

B – Recognition of an Impairment Loss Creates a Deferred Tax Asset

IE36   An entity has an identifiable asset with a carrying amount of CU1,000. Its recoverable amount is CU650. The tax rate is 30 per cent and the tax base of the asset is CU800. Impairment losses are not deductible for tax purposes. The effect of the impairment loss is as follows:

	Before impairment CU	Effect of impairment CU	After impairment CU
Carrying amount	1,000	(350)	650
Tax base	800	–	800
Taxable (deductible) temporary difference	200	(350)	(150)
Deferred tax liability (asset) at 30%	60	(105)	(45)

IE37   In accordance with AASB 112, the entity recognises the deferred tax asset to the extent that it is probable that taxable profit will be available against which the deductible temporary difference can be utilised.

Example 4 – Reversal of an Impairment Loss

Use the data for entity T as presented in Example 2, with supplementary information as provided in this example. In this example, tax effects are ignored.

Background

IE38 In 20X3, the government is still in office in Country A, but the business situation is improving. The effects of the export laws on T's production are proving to be less drastic than initially expected by management. As a result, management estimates that production will increase by 30 per cent. This favourable change requires T to re-estimate the recoverable amount of the net assets of the Country A operations (see paragraphs 110 and 111 of AASB 136). The cash-generating unit for the net assets of the Country A operations is still the Country A operations.

IE39 Calculations similar to those in Example 2 show that the recoverable amount of the Country A cash-generating unit is now CU1,910.

Reversal of Impairment Loss

IE40 T compares the recoverable amount and the net carrying amount of the Country A cash-generating unit.

Schedule 1. Calculation of the carrying amount of the Country A cash-generating unit at the end of 20X3

	Goodwill CU	Identifiable assets CU	Total CU
Beginning of 20X2 (Example 2)			
Historical cost	1,000	2,000	3,000
Accumulated depreciation	–	(167)	(167)
Impairment loss	(1,000)	(473)	(1,473)
Carrying amount after impairment loss	–	1,360	1,360
End of 20X3			
Additional depreciation (2 years)*	–	(247)	(247)
Carrying amount	–	1,113	1,113
Recoverable amount			1,910
Excess of recoverable amount over carrying amount			797

* After recognition of the impairment loss at the beginning of 20X2, T revised the depreciation charge for the Country A identifiable assets (from CU166.7 per year to CU123.6 per year), based on the revised carrying amount and remaining useful life (11 years).

IE41 There has been a favourable change in the estimates used to determine the recoverable amount of the Country A net assets since the last impairment loss was recognised. Therefore, in accordance with paragraph 114 of AASB 136, T recognises a reversal of the impairment loss recognised in 20X2.

IE42 In accordance with paragraphs 122 and 123 of AASB 136, T increases the carrying amount of the Country A identifiable assets by CU387 (see Schedule 3), that is, up to the lower of recoverable amount (CU1,910) and the identifiable assets' depreciated historical cost (CU1,500) (see Schedule 2). This increase is recognised immediately in profit or loss.

IE43 In accordance with paragraph 124 of AASB 136, the impairment loss on goodwill is not reversed.

Schedule 2. Determination of the depreciated historical cost of the Country A identifiable assets at the end of 20X3

End of 20X3	Identifiable assets CU
Historical cost	2,000
Accumulated depreciation *(166.7 × 3 years)*	(500)
Depreciated historical cost	1,500
Carrying amount (Schedule 1)	1,113
Difference	387

Schedule 3. Carrying amount of the Country A assets at the end of 20X3

End of 20X3	Goodwill CU	Identifiable assets CU	Total CU
Gross carrying amount	1,000	2,000	3,000
Accumulated amortisation	–	(414)	(414)
Accumulated impairment loss	(1,000)	(473)	(1,473)
Carrying amount	–	1,113	1,113
Reversal of impairment loss	0	387	387
Carrying amount after reversal of impairment loss	–	1,500	1,500

Example 5 – Treatment of a Future Restructuring

In this example, tax effects are ignored.

Background

IE44   At the end of 20X0, entity K tests a plant for impairment. The plant is a cash-generating unit. The plant's assets are carried at depreciated historical cost. The plant has a carrying amount of CU3,000 and a remaining useful life of 10 years.

IE45   The plant's recoverable amount (i.e. higher of value in use and fair value less costs to sell) is determined on the basis of a value in use calculation. Value in use is calculated using a pre-tax discount rate of 14 per cent.

IE46   Management approved budgets reflect that:

(a)   at the end of 20X3, the plant will be restructured at an estimated cost of CU100. Since K is not yet committed to the restructuring, a provision has not been recognised for the future restructuring costs; and

(b)   there will be future benefits from this restructuring in the form of reduced future cash outflows.

IE47   At the end of 20X2, K becomes committed to the restructuring. The costs are still estimated to be CU100 and a provision is recognised accordingly. The plant's estimated future cash flows reflected in the most recent management approved budgets are given in paragraph IE51 and a current discount rate is the same as at the end of 20X0.

IE48   At the end of 20X3, actual restructuring costs of CU100 are incurred and paid. Again, the plant's estimated future cash flows reflected in the most recent management approved budgets and a current discount rate are the same as those estimated at the end of 20X2.

At the End of 20X0

Schedule 1. Calculation of the plant's value in use at the end of 20X0

Year	Future cash flows CU	Discounted at 14% CU
20X1	300	263
20X2	280	215
20X3	420*	283
20X4	520†	308
20X5	350†	182
20X6	420†	191
20X7	480†	192
20X8	480†	168
20X9	460†	141
20X10	400†	108
Value in use		2,051

* Excludes estimated restructuring costs reflected in management budgets.

† Excludes estimated benefits expected from the restructuring reflected in management budgets.

IE49 The plant's recoverable amount (i.e. value in use) is less than its carrying amount. Therefore, K recognises an impairment loss for the plant.

Schedule 2. Calculation of the impairment loss at the end of 20X0

	Plant CU
Carrying amount before impairment loss	3,000
Recoverable amount (Schedule 1)	2,051
Impairment loss	(949)
Carrying amount after impairment loss	2,051

At the End of 20X1

IE50 No event occurs that requires the plant's recoverable amount to be re-estimated. Therefore, no calculation of the recoverable amount is required to be performed.

At the End of 20X2

IE51 The entity is now committed to the restructuring. Therefore, in determining the plant's value in use, the benefits expected from the restructuring are considered in forecasting cash flows. This results in an increase in the estimated future cash flows used to determine value in use at the end of 20X0. In accordance with paragraphs 110 and 111 of AASB 136, the recoverable amount of the plant is re-determined at the end of 20X2.

Schedule 3. Calculation of the plant's value in use at the end of 20X2

Year	Future cash flows CU	Discounted at 14% CU
20X3	420*	368
20X4	570†	439
20X5	380†	256
20X6	450†	266
20X7	510†	265
20X8	510†	232

Year	Future cash flows CU	Discounted at 14% CU
20X9	480†	192
20X10	410†	144
Value in use		2,162

* Excludes estimated restructuring costs because a liability has already been recognised.

† Includes estimated benefits expected from the restructuring reflected in management budgets.

IE52 The plant's recoverable amount (value in use) is higher than its carrying amount (see Schedule 4). Therefore, K reverses the impairment loss recognised for the plant at the end of 20X0.

Schedule 4. Calculation of the reversal of the impairment loss at the end of 20X2

	Plant CU
Carrying amount at the end of 20X0 (Schedule 2)	2,051
End of 20X2	
Depreciation charge (for 20X1 and 20X2 – Schedule 5)	(410)
Carrying amount before reversal	1,641
Recoverable amount (Schedule 3)	2,162
Reversal of the impairment loss	521
Carrying amount after reversal	2,162
Carrying amount: depreciated historical cost (Schedule 5)	2,400*

* The reversal does not result in the carrying amount of the plant exceeding what its carrying amount would have been at depreciated historical cost. Therefore, the full reversal of the impairment loss is recognised.

IE53 There is a cash outflow of CU100 when the restructuring costs are paid. Even though a cash outflow has taken place, there is no change in the estimated future cash flows used to determine value in use at the end of 20X2. Therefore, the plant's recoverable amount is not calculated at the end of 20X3.

Schedule 5. Summary of the carrying amount of the plant

End of year	Depreciated historical cost CU	Recoverable amount CU	Adjusted depreciation charge CU	Impairment loss CU	Carrying amount after impairment CU
20X0	3,000	2,051	0	(949)	2,051
20X1	2,700	nc	(205)	0	1,846
20X2	2,400	2,162	(205)	521	2,162
20X3	2,100	nc	(270)	0	1,892

nc = not calculated as there is no indication that the impairment loss may have increased/decreased.

Example 6 – Treatment of Future Costs

In this example, tax effects are ignored.

Background

IE54 At the end of 20X0, entity F tests a machine for impairment. The machine is a cash-generating unit. It is carried at depreciated historical cost and its carrying amount is CU150,000. It has an estimated remaining useful life of 10 years.

IE55 The machine's recoverable amount (i.e. higher of value in use and fair value less costs to sell) is determined on the basis of a value in use calculation. Value in use is calculated using a pre-tax discount rate of 14 per cent.

IE56 Management approved budgets reflect:

(a) estimated costs necessary to maintain the level of economic benefit expected to arise from the machine in its current condition; and

(b) that in 20X4, costs of CU25,000 will be incurred to enhance the machine's performance by increasing its productive capacity.

IE57 At the end of 20X4, costs to enhance the machine's performance are incurred. The machine's estimated future cash flows reflected in the most recent management approved budgets are given in paragraph IE60 and a current discount rate is the same as at the end of 20X0.

At the End of 20X0

Schedule 1. Calculation of the machine's value in use at the end of 20X0

Year	Future cash flows CU	Discounted at 14% CU
20X1	22,165*	19,443
20X2	21,450*	16,505
20X3	20,550*	13,871
20X4	24,725*†	14,639
20X5	25,325*§	13,153
20X6	24,825*§	11,310
20X7	24,123*§	9,640
20X8	25,533*§	8,951
20X9	24,234*§	7,452
20X10	22,850*§	6,164
Value in use		121,128

* Includes estimated costs necessary to maintain the level of economic benefit expected to arise from the machine in its current condition

† Excludes estimated costs to enhance the machine's performance reflected in management budgets.

§ Excludes estimated benefits expected from enhancing the machine's performance reflected in management budgets.

IE58 The machine's recoverable amount (value in use) is less than its carrying amount. Therefore, F recognises an impairment loss for the machine.

Schedule 2. Calculation of the impairment loss at the end of 20X0

	Machine CU
Carrying amount before impairment loss	150,000
Recoverable amount (Schedule 1)	121,128
Impairment loss	(28,872)
Carrying amount after impairment loss	121,128

Years 20X1 – 20X3

IE59 No event occurs that requires the machine's recoverable amount to be re-estimated. Therefore, no calculation of recoverable amount is required to be performed.

At the End of 20X4

IE60 The costs to enhance the machine's performance are incurred. Therefore, in determining the machine's value in use, the future benefits expected from enhancing the machine's performance are considered in forecasting cash flows. This results in an increase in the estimated future cash flows used to determine value in use at the end of 20X0.

As a consequence, in accordance with paragraphs 110 and 111 of AASB 136, the recoverable amount of the machine is recalculated at the end of 20X4.

Schedule 3. Calculation of the machine's value in use at the end of 20X4

Year	Future cash flows* CU	Discounted at 14% CU
20X5	30,321	26,597
20X6	32,750	25,200
20X7	31,721	21,411
20X8	31,950	18,917
20X9	33,100	17,191
20X10	27,999	12,756
Value in use		122,072

* Includes estimated benefits expected from enhancing the machine's performance reflected in management budgets.

IE61 The machine's recoverable amount (i.e. value in use) is higher than the machine's carrying amount and depreciated historical cost (see Schedule 4). Therefore, K reverses the impairment loss recognised for the machine at the end of 20X0 so that the machine is carried at depreciated historical cost.

Schedule 4. Calculation of the reversal of the impairment loss at the end of 20X4

	Machine CU
Carrying amount at the end of 20X0 (Schedule 2)	121,128
End of 20X4	
Depreciation charge (20X1 to 20X4 – Schedule 5)	(48,452)
Costs to enhance the asset's performance	25,000
Carrying amount before reversal	97,676
Recoverable amount (Schedule 3)	122,072
Reversal of the impairment loss	17,324
Carrying amount after reversal	115,000
Carrying amount: depreciated historical cost (Schedule 5)	115,000*

* The value in use of the machine exceeds what its carrying amount would have been at depreciated historical cost. Therefore, the reversal is limited to an amount that does not result in the carrying amount of the machine exceeding depreciated historical cost.

Schedule 5. Summary of the carrying amount of the machine

Year	Depreciated historical cost CU	Recoverable amount CU	Adjusted depreciation charge CU	Impairment loss CU	Carrying amount after impairment CU
20X0	150,000	121,128	0	(28,872)	121,128
20X1	135,000	nc	(12,113)	0	109,015
20X2	120,000	nc	(12,113)	0	96,902
20X3	105,000	nc	(12,113)	0	84,789
20X4	90,000		(12,113)		
enhancement	25,000		—		
	115,000	122,072	(12,113)	17,324	115,000
20X5	95,833	nc	(19,167)	0	95,833

nc = not calculated as there is no indication that the impairment loss may have increased/decreased.

Example 7 – Impairment Testing Cash-generating Units with Goodwill and Non-controlling Interests

Example 7A – Non-controlling Interests Measured Initially as a Proportionate Share of the Net Identifiable Assets

In this example, tax effects are ignored.

AASB

Background

IE62 Parent acquires an 80 per cent ownership interest in Subsidiary for CU2,100 on 1 January 20X3. At that date, Subsidiary's net identifiable assets have a fair value of CU1,500. Parent chooses to measure the non-controlling interests as the proportionate interest of Subsidiary's net identifiable assets of CU300 (20% of CU1,500). Goodwill of CU900 is the difference between the aggregate of the consideration transferred and the amount of the non-controlling interests (CU2,100 + CU300) and the net identifiable assets (CU1,500).

IE63 The assets of Subsidiary together are the smallest group of assets that generate cash inflows that are largely independent of the cash inflows from other assets or groups of assets. Therefore Subsidiary is a cash-generating unit. Because other cash-generating units of Parent are expected to benefit from the synergies of the combination, the goodwill of CU500 related to those synergies has been allocated to other cash-generating units within Parent. Because the cash-generating unit comprising Subsidiary includes goodwill within its carrying amount, it must be tested for impairment annually, or more frequently if there is an indication that it may be impaired (see paragraph 90 of AASB 136).

IE64 At the end of 20X3, Parent determines that the recoverable amount of cash-generating unit Subsidiary is CU1,000. The carrying amount of the net assets of Subsidiary, excluding goodwill, is CU1,350.

Testing Subsidiary (Cash-generating Unit) for Impairment

IE65 Goodwill attributable to non-controlling interests is included in Subsidiary's recoverable amount of CU1,000 but has not been recognised in Parent's consolidated financial statements. Therefore, in accordance with paragraph C4 of Appendix C of AASB 136, the carrying amount of Subsidiary is grossed up to include goodwill attributable to the non-controlling interests, before being compared with the recoverable amount of CU1,000. Goodwill attributable to Parent's 80 per cent interest in Subsidiary at the acquisition date is CU400 after allocating CU500 to other cash-generating units within Parent. Therefore, goodwill attributable to the 20 per cent non-controlling interests in Subsidiary at the acquisition date is CU100.

Schedule 1. Testing Y for impairment at the end of 20X3

End of 20X3	Goodwill of Subsidiary	Net identifiable assets	Total
	CU	CU	CU
Carrying amount	400	1,350	1,750
Unrecognised non-controlling interests	100	–	100
Adjusted carrying amount	500	1,350	1,850
Recoverable amount			1,000
Impairment loss			850

Allocating the Impairment Loss

IE66 In accordance with paragraph 104 of AASB 136, the impairment loss of CU850 is allocated to the assets in the unit by first reducing the carrying amount of goodwill.

IE67 Therefore, CU500 of the CU850 impairment loss for the unit is allocated to the goodwill. In accordance with paragraph C6 of Appendix C of AASB 136, if the partially-owned subsidiary is itself a cash-generating unit, the goodwill impairment loss is allocated to the controlling and non-controlling interests on the same basis as that on which profit or loss is allocated. In this example, profit or loss is allocated on the basis of relative ownership interests. Because the goodwill is recognised only to the extent of Parent's 80 per cent ownership interest in Subsidiary, Parent recognises only 80 per cent of that goodwill impairment loss (i.e. CU400).

IE68 The remaining impairment loss of CU350 is recognised by reducing the carrying amounts of Subsidiary's identifiable assets (see Schedule 2).

Schedule 2. Allocation of the impairment loss for Subsidiary at the end of 20X3

End of 20X3	Goodwill	Net identifiable assets	Total
	CU	CU	CU
Carrying amount	400	1,350	1,750
Impairment loss	(400)	(350)	(750)
Carrying amount after impairment loss	–	1,000	1,000

Example 7B – Non-controlling Interests Measured Initially at Fair Value and the Related Subsidiary is a Stand-alone Cash-generating Unit

In this example, tax effects are ignored.

Background

IE68A Parent acquires an 80 per cent ownership interest in Subsidiary for CU2,100 on 1 January 20X3. At that date, Subsidiary's net identifiable assets have a fair value of CU1,500. Parent chooses to measure the non-controlling interests at fair value, which is CU350. Goodwill of CU950 is the difference between the aggregate of the consideration transferred and the amount of the non-controlling interests (CU2,100 + CU350) and the net identifiable assets (CU1,500).

IE68B The assets of Subsidiary together are the smallest group of assets that generate cash inflows that are largely independent of the cash inflows from other assets or groups of assets. Therefore, Subsidiary is a cash-generating unit. Because other cash-generating units of Parent are expected to benefit from the synergies of the combination, the goodwill of CU500 related to those synergies has been allocated to other cash-generating units within Parent. Because Subsidiary includes goodwill within its carrying amount, it must be tested for impairment annually, or more frequently if there is an indication that it might be impaired (see paragraph 90 of AASB 136).

Testing Subsidiary for Impairment

IE68C At the end of 20X3, Parent determines that the recoverable amount of cash-generating unit Subsidiary is CU1,650. The carrying amount of the net assets of Subsidiary, excluding goodwill, is CU1,350.

Schedule 1. Testing Subsidiary for impairment at the end of 20X3

End of 20X3	Goodwill	Net identifiable assets	Total
	CU	CU	CU
Carrying amount	450	1,350	1,800
Recoverable amount			1,650
Impairment loss			150

Allocating the Impairment Loss

IE68D In accordance with paragraph 104 of AASB 136, the impairment loss of CU150 is allocated to the assets in the unit by first reducing the carrying amount of goodwill.

IE68E Therefore, the full amount of impairment loss of CU150 for the unit is allocated to the goodwill. In accordance with paragraph C6 of Appendix C of AASB 136, if the partially-owned subsidiary is itself a cash-generating unit, the goodwill impairment loss is allocated to the controlling and non-controlling interests on the same basis as that on which profit or loss is allocated.

Example 7C – Non-controlling Interests Measured Initially at Fair Value and the Related Subsidiary is part of a Larger Cash-generating Unit

In this example, tax effects are ignored.

Background

IE68F Suppose that, for the business combination described in paragraph IE68A of Example 7B, the assets of Subsidiary will generate cash inflows together with other assets or groups of assets of Parent. Therefore, rather than Subsidiary being the cash-generating unit for the purposes of impairment testing, Subsidiary becomes part of a larger cash-generating unit, Z. Other cash-generating units of Parent are also expected to benefit from the synergies of the combination. Therefore, goodwill related to those synergies, in the amount of CU500, has been allocated to those other cash-generating units. Z's goodwill related to previous business combinations is CU800.

IE68G Because Z includes goodwill within its carrying amount, both from Subsidiary and from previous business combinations, it must be tested for impairment annually, or more frequently if there is an indication that it might be impaired (see paragraph 90 of AASB 136).

Testing Subsidiary for Impairment

IE68H At the end of 20X3, Parent determines that the recoverable amount of cash-generating unit Z is CU3,300. The carrying amount of the net assets of Z, excluding goodwill, is CU2,250.

Schedule 3. Testing Z for impairment at the end of 20X3

End of 20X3	Goodwill CU	Net identifiable assets CU	Total CU
Carrying amount	1,250	2,250	3,500
Recoverable amount			3,300
Impairment loss			200

Allocating the Impairment Loss

IE68I In accordance with paragraph 104 of AASB 136, the impairment loss of CU200 is allocated to the assets in the unit by first reducing the carrying amount of goodwill. Therefore, the full amount of impairment loss of CU200 for cash-generating unit Z is allocated to the goodwill. In accordance with paragraph C7 of Appendix C of AASB 136, if the partially-owned Subsidiary forms part of a larger cash-generating unit, the goodwill impairment loss would be allocated first to the parts of the cash-generating unit, Z, and then to the controlling and non-controlling interests of the partially-owned Subsidiary.

IE68J Parent allocates the impairment loss to the parts of the cash-generating unit on the basis of the relative carrying values of the goodwill of the parts before the impairment. In this example Subsidiary is allocated 36 per cent of the impairment (450/1,250). The impairment loss is then allocated to the controlling and non-controlling interests on the same basis as that on which profit or loss is allocated.

Example 8 – Allocation of Corporate Assets

In this example, tax effects are ignored.

Background

IE69 Entity M has three cash-generating units: A, B and C. The carrying amounts of those units do not include goodwill. There are adverse changes in the technological environment in which M operates. Therefore, M conducts impairment tests of each of its cash-generating units. At the end of 20X0, the carrying amounts of A, B and C are CU100, CU150 and CU200 respectively.

IE70   The operations are conducted from a headquarters. The carrying amount of the headquarters is CU200: a headquarters building of CU150 and a research centre of CU50. The relative carrying amounts of the cash-generating units are a reasonable indication of the proportion of the headquarters building devoted to each cash-generating unit. The carrying amount of the research centre cannot be allocated on a reasonable basis to the individual cash-generating units.

IE71   The remaining estimated useful life of cash-generating unit A is 10 years. The remaining useful lives of B, C and the headquarters are 20 years. The headquarters is depreciated on a straight-line basis.

IE72   The recoverable amount (i.e. higher of value in use and fair value less costs to sell) of each cash-generating unit is based on its value in use. Value in use is calculated using a pre-tax discount rate of 15 per cent.

Identification of Corporate Assets

IE73   In accordance with paragraph 102 of AASB 136, M first identifies all the corporate assets that relate to the individual cash-generating units under review. The corporate assets are the headquarters building and the research centre.

IE74   M then decides how to deal with each of the corporate assets:

(a)   the carrying amount of the headquarters building can be allocated on a reasonable and consistent basis to the cash-generating units under review; and

(b)   the carrying amount of the research centre cannot be allocated on a reasonable and consistent basis to the individual cash-generating units under review.

Allocation of Corporate Assets

IE75   The carrying amount of the headquarters building is allocated to the carrying amount of each individual cash-generating unit. A weighted allocation basis is used because the estimated remaining useful life of A's cash-generating unit is 10 years, whereas the estimated remaining useful lives of B and C's cash-generating units are 20 years.

Schedule 1. Calculation of a weighted allocation of the carrying amount of the headquarters building

End of 20X0	A CU	B CU	C CU	Total CU
Carrying amount	100	150	200	450
Useful life	10 years	20 years	20 years	
Weighting based on useful life	1	2	2	
Carrying amount after weighting	100	300	400	800
Pro-rata allocation of the building	12%	38%	50%	100%
	(100/800)	(300/800)	(400/800)	
Allocation of the carrying amount of the building (based on pro-rata above)	19	56	75	150
Carrying amount (after allocation of the building)	119	206	275	600

Determination of Recoverable Amount and Calculation of Impairment Losses

IE76   Paragraph 102 of AASB 136 requires first that the recoverable amount of each individual cash-generating unit be compared with its carrying amount, including the portion of the carrying amount of the headquarters building allocated to the unit, and any resulting impairment loss recognised. Paragraph 102 of AASB 136 then requires the recoverable amount of M as a whole (i.e. the smallest group of cash-generating units that includes the research centre) to be compared with its carrying amount, including both the headquarters building and the research centre.

Schedule 2. Calculation of A, B, C and M's value in use at the end of 20X0

Year	A Future cash flows CU	A Discount at 15% CU	B Future cash flows CU	B Discount at 15% CU	C Future cash flows CU	C Discount at 15% CU	M Future cash flows CU	M Discount at 15% CU
1	18	16	9	8	10	9	39	34
2	31	23	16	12	20	15	72	54
3	37	24	24	16	34	22	105	69
4	42	24	29	17	44	25	128	73
5	47	24	32	16	51	25	143	71
6	52	22	33	14	56	24	155	67
7	55	21	34	13	60	22	162	61
8	55	18	35	11	63	21	166	54
9	53	15	35	10	65	18	167	48
10	48	12	35	9	66	16	169	42
11			36	8	66	14	132	28
12			35	7	66	12	131	25
13			35	6	66	11	131	21
14			33	5	65	9	128	18
15			30	4	62	8	122	15
16			26	3	60	6	115	12
17			22	2	57	5	108	10
18			18	1	51	4	97	8
19			14	1	43	3	85	6
20			10	1	35	2	71	4
Value in use		199		164		271		720*

* It is assumed that the research centre generates additional future cash flows for the entity as a whole. Therefore, the sum of the value in use of each individual cash-generating unit is less than the value in use of the business as a whole. The additional cash flows are not attributable to the headquarters building.

Schedule 3. Impairment testing A, B and C

End of 20X0	A CU	B CU	C CU
Carrying amount (after allocation of the building) (Schedule 1)	119	206	275
Recoverable amount (Schedule 2)	199	164	271
Impairment loss	0	(42)	(4)

IE77 The next step is to allocate the impairment losses between the assets of the cash-generating units and the headquarters building.

Schedule 4. Allocation of the impairment losses for cash-generating units B and C

Cash-generating unit	B CU	C CU
To headquarters building	(12) *(42 × 56/206)*	(1) *(4 × 75/275)*
To assets in cash-generating unit	(30) *(42 × 150/206)*	(3) *(4 × 200/275)*
	(42)	(4)

IE78   Because the research centre could not be allocated on a reasonable and consistent basis to A, B and C's cash-generating units, M compares the carrying amount of the smallest group of cash-generating units to which the carrying amount of the research centre can be allocated (i.e. M as a whole) to its recoverable amount.

Schedule 5. Impairment testing the smallest group of cash-generating units to which the carrying amount of the research centre can be allocated (i.e. M as a whole)

End of 20X0	A CU	B CU	C CU	Building CU	Research centre CU	M CU
Carrying amount	100	150	200	150	50	650
Impairment loss arising from the first step of the test	–	(30)	(3)	(13)	–	(46)
Carrying amount after the first step of the test	100	120	197	137	50	604
Recoverable amount (Schedule 2)						720
Impairment loss for the 'larger' cash-generating unit						0

IE79   Therefore, no additional impairment loss results from the application of the impairment test to M as a whole. Only an impairment loss of CU46 is recognised as a result of the application of the first step of the test to A, B and C.

Example 9 – Disclosures about Cash-generating Units with Goodwill or Intangible Assets with Indefinite Useful Lives

The purpose of this example is to illustrate the disclosures required by paragraphs 134 and 135 of AASB 136.

Background

IE80   Entity M is a multinational manufacturing firm that uses geographical segments for reporting segment information. M's three reportable segments are Europe, North America and Asia. Goodwill has been allocated for impairment testing purposes to three individual cash-generating units – two in Europe (units A and B) and one in North America (unit C) – and to one group of cash-generating units (comprising operation XYZ) in Asia. Units A, B and C and operation XYZ each represent the lowest level within M at which the goodwill is monitored for internal management purposes.

IE81   M acquired unit C, a manufacturing operation in North America, in December 20X2. Unlike M's other North American operations, C operates in an industry with high margins and high growth rates, and with the benefit of a 10-year patent on its primary product. The patent was granted to C just before M's acquisition of C. As part of accounting for the acquisition of C, M recognised, in addition to the patent, goodwill of CU3,000 and a brand name of CU1,000. M's management has determined that the brand name has an indefinite useful life. M has no other intangible assets with indefinite useful lives.

IE82 The carrying amounts of goodwill and intangible assets with indefinite useful lives allocated to units A, B and C and to operation XYZ are as follows:

	Goodwill CU	Intangible assets with indefinite useful lives CU
A	350	
B	450	
C	3,000	1,000
XYZ	1,200	
Total	5,000	1,000

IE83 During the year ending 31 December 20X3, M determines that there is no impairment of any of its cash-generating units or group of cash-generating units containing goodwill or intangible assets with indefinite useful lives. The recoverable amounts (i.e. higher of value in use and fair value less costs to sell) of those units and group of units are determined on the basis of value in use calculations. M has determined that the recoverable amount calculations are most sensitive to changes in the following assumptions:

Units A and B	Unit C	Operation XYZ
Gross margin during the budget period (budget period is 4 years)	5-year US government bond rate during the budget period (budget period is 5 years)	Gross margin during the budget period (budget period is 5 years)
Raw materials price inflation during the budget period	Raw materials price inflation during the budget period	Japanese yen/US dollar exchange rate during the budget period
Units A and B	Unit C	Operation XYZ
Market share during the budget period	Market share during the budget period	Market share during the budget period
Growth rate used to extrapolate cash flows beyond the budget period	Growth rate used to extrapolate cash flows beyond the budget period	Growth rate used to extrapolate cash flows beyond the budget period

IE84 Gross margins during the budget period for A, B and XYZ are estimated by M based on average gross margins achieved in the period immediately before the start of the budget period, increased by 5 per cent per year for anticipated efficiency improvements. A and B produce complementary products and are operated by M to achieve the same gross margins.

IE85 Market shares during the budget period are estimated by M based on average market shares achieved in the period immediately before the start of the budget period, adjusted each year for any anticipated growth or decline in market shares. M anticipates that:

(a) market shares for A and B will differ, but will each grow during the budget period by 3 per cent per year as a result of ongoing improvements in product quality;

(b) C's market share will grow during the budget period by 6 per cent per year as a result of increased advertising expenditure and the benefits from the protection of the 10-year patent on its primary product; and

(c) XYZ's market share will remain unchanged during the budget period as a result of the combination of ongoing improvements in product quality and an anticipated increase in competition.

IE86 A and B purchase raw materials from the same European suppliers, whereas C's raw materials are purchased from various North American suppliers. Raw materials price inflation during the budget period is estimated by M to be consistent with forecast consumer price indices published by government agencies in the relevant European and North American countries.

IE87　The 5-year US government bond rate during the budget period is estimated by M to be consistent with the yield on such bonds at the beginning of the budget period. The Japanese yen/US dollar exchange rate is estimated by M to be consistent with the average market forward exchange rate over the budget period.

IE88　M uses steady growth rates to extrapolate beyond the budget period cash flows for A, B, C and XYX. The growth rates for A, B and XYZ are estimated by M to be consistent with publicly available information about the long-term average growth rates for the markets in which A, B and XYZ operate. However, the growth rate for C exceeds the long-term average growth rate for the market in which C operates. M's management is of the opinion that this is reasonable in the light of the protection of the 10-year patent on C's primary product.

IE89　M includes the following disclosure in the notes to its financial statements for the year ending 31 December 20X3.

Impairment Tests for Goodwill and Intangible Assets with Indefinite Lives

Goodwill has been allocated for impairment testing purposes to three individual cash-generating units – two in Europe (units A and B) and one in North America (unit C) – and to one group of cash-generating units (comprising operation XYZ) in Asia. The carrying amount of goodwill allocated to unit C and operation XYZ is significant in comparison with the total carrying amount of goodwill, but the carrying amount of goodwill allocated to each of units A and B is not. Nevertheless, the recoverable amounts of units A and B are based on some of the same key assumptions, and the aggregate carrying amount of goodwill allocated to those units is significant.

Operation XYZ

The recoverable amount of operation XYZ has been determined based on a value in use calculation. That calculation uses cash flow projections based on financial budgets approved by management covering a five-year period, and a discount rate of 8.4 per cent. Cash flows beyond that five-year period have been extrapolated using a steady 6.3 per cent growth rate. This growth rate does not exceed the long-term average growth rate for the market in which XYZ operates. Management believes that any reasonably possible change in the key assumptions on which XYZ's recoverable amount is based would not cause XYZ's carrying amount to exceed its recoverable amount.

Unit C

The recoverable amount of unit C has also been determined based on a value in use calculation. That calculation uses cash flow projections based on financial budgets approved by management covering a five-year period, and a discount rate of 9.2 per cent. C's cash flows beyond the five-year period are extrapolated using a steady 12 per cent growth rate. This growth rate exceeds by 4 percentage points the long-term average growth rate for the market in which C operates. However, C benefits from the protection of a 10-year patent on its primary product, granted in December 20X2. Management believes that a 12 per cent growth rate is reasonable in the light of that patent. Management also believes that any reasonably possible change in the key assumptions on which C's recoverable amount is based would not cause C's carrying amount to exceed its recoverable amount.

Units A and B

The recoverable amounts of units A and B have been determined on the basis of value in use calculations. Those units produce complementary products, and their recoverable amounts are based on some of the same key assumptions. Both value in use calculations use cash flow projections based on financial budgets approved by management covering a four-year period, and a discount rate of 7.9 per cent. Both sets of cash flows beyond the four-year period are extrapolated using a steady 5 per cent growth rate. This growth rate does not exceed the long-term average growth rate for the market in which A and B operate. Cash flow projections during the budget period for both A and B are also based on the same expected gross margins during the budget period and the same raw materials price inflation during the budget period. Management believes that any reasonably possible change in any of these key assumptions would not cause the aggregate carrying amount of A and B to exceed the aggregate recoverable amount of those units.

	Operation XYZ	Unit C	Units A and B (in aggregate)
Carrying amount of goodwill	CU1,200	CU3,000	CU800
Carrying amount of brand name with indefinite useful life	–	CU1,000	–

Key assumptions used in value in use calculations *

	Operation XYZ	Unit C	Units A and B (in aggregate)
• Key assumption	• **Budgeted gross margins**	• **5-year US government bond rate**	• **Budgeted gross margins**
• Basis for determining value(s) assigned to key assumption	• Average gross margins achieved in period immediately before the budget period, increased for expected efficiency improvements.	• Yield on 5-year US government bonds at the beginning of the budget period.	• Average gross margins achieved in period immediately before the budget period, increased for expected efficiency improvements.
	• Values assigned to key assumption reflect past experience, except for efficiency improvements. Management believes improvements of 5% per year are reasonably achievable.	• Value assigned to key assumption is consistent with external sources of information.	• Values assigned to key assumption reflect past experience, except for efficiency improvements. Management believes improvements of 5% per year are reasonably achievable.
• Key assumption	• **Japanese yen/US dollar exchange rate during the budget period**	• **Raw materials price inflation**	• **Raw materials price inflation**
• Basis for determining value(s) assigned to key assumption	• Average market forward exchange rate over the budget period.	• Forecast consumer price indices during the budget period for North American countries from which raw materials are purchased.	• Forecast consumer price indices during the budget period for European countries from which raw materials are purchased.
	• Value assigned to key assumption is consistent with external sources of information.	• Value assigned to key assumption is consistent with external sources of information.	• Value assigned to key assumption is consistent with external sources of information.

	Operation XYZ	*Unit C*	*Units A and B (in aggregate)*
• **Key assumption**	• **Budgeted market share**	• **Budgeted market share**	
• Basis for determining value(s) assigned to key assumption	• Average market share in period immediately before the budget period.	• Average market share in period immediately before the budget period, increased each year for anticipated growth in market share.	
	• Value assigned to key assumption reflects past experience. No change in market share expected as a result of ongoing product quality improvements coupled with anticipated increase in competition.	• Management believes market share growth of 6% per year is reasonably achievable due to increased advertising expenditure, the benefit from the protection of the 10-year patent on C's primary product, and the expected synergies to be achieved from operating C as part of M's North American segment.	

* The key assumptions shown in this table for units A and B are only those that are used in the recoverable amount calculations for both units.

AASB 137
Provisions, Contingent Liabilities and Contingent Assets

(Compiled November 2010)

Note from the Institute of Chartered Accountants Australia

This note, prepared by the technical editors, is not part of Accounting Standard AASB 137.

Historical development

15 July 2004: AASB 137 'Provisions, Contingent Liabilities and Contingent Assets' is the Australian equivalent of IAS 37 of the same name. It was made by the AASB on 15 July 2004 as part of the AASB's program to adopt International Financial Reporting Standards (IFRSs) by 2005.

6 April 2006: Removal of Australian Guidance.

30 April 2007: AASB 2007-4 'Amendments to Australian Accounting Standards' amends the objective, paragraphs 41 and C, Example 2A and is applicable to annual reporting periods beginning on or after 1 July 2007. Entities may elect to early-adopt it to annual reporting periods beginning on or after 1 January 2005.

24 September 2007: AASB 2007-8 'Amendments to Australian Accounting Standards' was issued by the AASB. This Standard is applicable for annual reporting periods beginning on or after 1 January 2009.

13 December 2007: AASB 2007-9 'Amendments to Australian Accounting Standards arising from the Review of AAS 27, AAS 29 and AAS 31' was issued by the AASB. This Standard is applicable to annual reporting periods beginning on or after 1 July 2008, with early adoption permitted.

13 December 2007: AASB 2007-10 'Further Amendments to Australian Accounting Standards arising from AASB 101' amends AASB 137, replacing the term 'financial report' with 'financial statements'. This Standard is applicable to annual reporting periods beginning on or after 1 January 2009.

6 March 2008: AASB 2008-3 'Amendments to Australian Accounting Standards arising from AASB 3 and AASB 127' amends AASB 137 for the issue of AASB 3 Revised. This Standard is applicable to annual reporting periods beginning on or after 1 July 2009.

7 November 2008: Compiled AASB 137 was issued by the AASB, compiled to include the AASB 2007-9 amendments.

25 June 2009: AASB 2009-6 'Amendments to Australian Accounting Standards' amends AASB 137 for editorial corrections made by the International Accounting Standards Board (IASB) to its Standards and Interpretations (IFRSs) and as a consequence of issuing revised AASB 101 'Presentation of Financial Statements'. This Standard is applicable to annual reporting periods beginning on or after 1 January 2009 that end on or after 30 June 2009.

23 October 2009: The AASB reissued the version of AASB 137 applicable to annual reporting periods beginning on or after 1 January 2009 but before 1 July 2009. This version of AASB 137 has been compiled for the amending Standards applying to annual reporting periods beginning on or after 1 January 2009. This Standard applies to 31 December 2009 year ends and can be accessed from the AASB website at www.aasb.gov.au.

26 October 2009: AASB 137 was reissued by the AASB, compiled to include the AASB 2007-8, AASB 2007-10, AASB 2008-3 and AASB 2009-6 amendments and applies to annual reporting periods beginning on or after 1 July 2009. Early application is permitted.

15 December 2009: AASB 2009-12 'Amendments to Australian Accounting Standards' amends AASB 137 for editorial corrections. This Standard is applicable to annual reporting periods beginning on or after 1 January 2011 with early adoption permitted.

27 October 2010: AASB 2010-5 'Further Amendments to Australian Accounting Standards' makes editorial amendments to AASB 137. This Standard is applicable to annual reporting periods beginning on or after 1 January 2011.

26 November 2010: AASB 137 was reissued by the AASB, compiled to include the AASB 2009-12 and AASB 2010-5 amendments and applies to annual reporting periods ending on or after 1 January 2011 but before 1 July 2013.

1 March 2011: AASB 2010-7 'Amendments to Australian Accounting Standards arising from AASB 9 (December 2010)' as compiled amends AASB 137 to give effect to consequential changes arising from the reissue of AASB 9 in December 2010 and supersedes AASB 2009-11, which related to the previous version of AASB 9. This Standard applies to annual reporting periods beginning on or after 1 January 2013 and can be adopted early. The application date of AASB 2010-7 has been amended to 1 January 2015 by AASB 2012-6. **These amendments are not included in this compiled Standard.**

References

Interpretation 1 *Changes in Existing Decommissioning, Restoration and Similar Liabilities*, Interpretation 5 *Rights to Interests arising from Decommissioning, Restoration and Environmental Rehabilitation Funds*, Interpretation 6 *Liabilities arising from Participating in a Specific Market – Waste Electrical & Electronic Equipment*, Interpretation 1019 *The Superannuation Contributions Surcharge*, Interpretation 12 *Service Concession Arrangements*, Interpretation 13 *Customer Loyalty Programs*, Interpretation 14 *AASB 119 – The Limit on a Defined Benefit Asset, Minimum Funding Requirements and their interaction*, Interpretation 127 *Evaluating the Substance of Transactions Involving the Legal Form of a Lease*, Interpretation 129 *Service Concession Arrangements: Disclosures*, Interpretation 1030 *Depreciation of Long Lived Physical Assets: Condition-Based Depreciation and Related Methods*, Interpretation 1047 *Professional Indemnity Claims Liabilities in Medical Defence Organisations* and Interpretation 1052 *Tax Consolidation Accounting* apply to AASB 137.

IFRIC items not taken onto the agenda: No. 39 *Provisions – Onerous Contracts*, No. 40 *Onerous Contracts – Operating Leases and Other Executory Contracts*, No. 41 *Provisions – examples of constructive obligations*, No. 56 *The seller's contingent consideration*, IAS 37-1 *Obligations to repair/maintain another entity's property, plant and equipment*, IAS 37-2 *Deposits on returnable containers* and *IAS 37-3 IAS 37 Provisions, Contingent Liabilities and Contingent Assets/IAS 38 Intangible Assets – Regulatory assets and liabilities* apply to AASB 137.

AASB 137 compared to IAS 37

Additions

Paragraph	Description
Aus 1.1	Which entities AASB 137 applies to (i.e. reporting entities and general purpose financial statements).
Aus 1.2	The application date of AASB 137 (i.e. annual reporting periods beginning 1 January 2005).
Aus 1.3	Prohibits early application of AASB 137.
Aus 1.4	Makes the requirements of AASB 137 subject to AASB 1031 'Materiality'.
Aus 1.5	Explains which Australian Standards have been superseded by AASB 137.
Aus 1.6	Clarifies that the superseded Australian Standards remain in force until AASB 137 applies.
Aus 1.7	Notice of the new Standard published on 22 July 2004.
Aus 26.1 – Aus 26.2	Recognition of liabilities for government.

Deletions

Paragraph	Description
93	Transitional provisions for first time application of IAS 37.
95	Effective date of IAS 37.

Contents

Compilation Details

Comparison With IAS 37

Accounting Standard
AASB 137 Provisions, Contingent Liabilities and Contingent Assets

Paragraphs

Objective	
Application	Aus1.1 – Aus1.7
Scope	1 – 9
Definitions	10
Provisions and Other Liabilities	11
Relationship between Provisions and Contingent Liabilities	12 – 13
Recognition	
Provisions	14
Present Obligation	15 – 16
Past Event	17 – 22
Probable Outflow of Resources Embodying Economic Benefits	23 – 24
Reliable Estimate of the Obligation	25 – 26
Recognition of Liabilities Arising from Local Government and Government Existing Public Policies, Budget Policies, Election Promises or Statements of Intent	Aus26.1 – Aus26.2
Contingent Liabilities	27 – 30
Contingent Assets	31 – 35
Measurement	
Best Estimate	36 – 41
Risks and Uncertainties	42 – 44
Present Value	45 – 47
Future Events	48 – 50
Expected Disposal of Assets	51 – 52
Reimbursements	53 – 58
Changes in Provisions	59 – 60
Use of Provisions	61 – 62
Application of the Recognition and Measurement Rules	
Future Operating Losses	63 – 65
Onerous Contracts	66 – 69
Restructuring	70 – 83
Disclosure	84 – 92

Guidance on implementing AASB 137

A. Tables – Provisions, Contingent Liabilities, Contingent Assets and Reimbursements

B. Decision Tree

C. Examples: Recognition

D. Examples: Disclosures

Australian Accounting Standard AASB 137 *Provisions, Contingent Liabilities and Contingent Assets* (as amended) is set out in paragraphs Aus1.1 – 92. All the paragraphs have equal authority. Terms defined in this Standard are in *italics* the first time they appear in the Standard. AASB 137 is to be read in the context of other Australian Accounting Standards, including AASB 1048 *Interpretation of Standards*, which identifies the Australian Accounting Interpretations. In the absence of explicit guidance, AASB 108 *Accounting Policies, Changes in Accounting Estimates and Errors* provides a basis for selecting and applying accounting policies.

Compilation Details

Accounting Standard AASB 137 *Provisions, Contingent Liabilities and Contingent Assets* as amended

This compiled Standard applies to annual reporting periods beginning on or after 1 January 2011 but before 1 July 2013. It takes into account amendments up to and including 27 October 2010 and was prepared on 26 November 2010 by the staff of the Australian Accounting Standards Board (AASB).

This compilation is not a separate Accounting Standard made by the AASB. Instead, it is a representation of AASB 137 (July 2004) as amended by other Accounting Standards, which are listed in the Table below.

Table of Standards

Standard	Date made	Application date *(annual reporting periods ... on or after ...)*	Application, saving or transitional provisions
AASB 137	15 Jul 2004	*(beginning)* 1 Jan 2005	
AASB 2007-4	30 Apr 2007	*(beginning)* 1 Jul 2007	see (a) below
AASB 2007-8	24 Sep 2007	*(beginning)* 1 Jan 2009	see (b) below
AASB 2007-9	13 Dec 2007	*(beginning)* 1 Jul 2008	see (c) below
AASB 2007-10	13 Dec 2007	*(beginning)* 1 Jan 2009	see (b) below
AASB 2008-3	6 Mar 2008	*(beginning)* 1 Jul 2009	see (d) below
AASB 2009-6	25 Jun 2009	*(beginning)* 1 Jan 2009 and *(ending)* 30 Jun 2009	see (e) below
AASB 2009-12	15 Dec 2009	*(beginning)* 1 Jan 2011	see (f) below
AASB 2010-2	30 Jun 2010	*(beginning)* 1 Jul 2013	not compiled*
AASB 2010-5	27 Oct 2010	*(beginning)* 1 Jan 2011	see (f) below

*   The amendments made by this Standard are not included in this compilation, which presents the principal Standard as applicable to annual reporting periods beginning on or after 1 January 2011 but before 1 July 2013.

(a)   Entities may elect to apply this Standard to annual reporting periods beginning on or after 1 January 2005 but before 1 July 2007.

(b)   Entities may elect to apply this Standard to annual reporting periods beginning on or after 1 January 2005 but before 1 January 2009, provided that AASB 101 *Presentation of Financial Statements* (September 2007) is also applied to such periods.

(c)   Entities may elect to apply this Standard to annual reporting periods beginning on or after 1 January 2005 but before 1 July 2008, provided that the Standards and Interpretation listed in paragraph 6 of AASB 2007-9 are also applied to such periods.

(d)   Entities may elect to apply this Standard to annual reporting periods beginning on or after 30 June 2007 but before 1 July 2009, provided that AASB 3 *Business Combinations* (March 2008) and AASB 127 *Consolidated and Separate Financial Statements* (March 2008) are also applied to such periods.

(e)   Entities may elect to apply this Standard to annual reporting periods beginning on or after 1 January 2005 but before 1 January 2009, provided that AASB 101 *Presentation of Financial Statements* (September 2007) is also applied to such periods, and to annual reporting periods beginning on or after 1 January 2009 that end before 30 June 2009.

(f)   Entities may elect to apply this Standard to annual reporting periods beginning on or after 1 January 2005 but before 1 January 2011.

Table of Amendments to Standard

Paragraph affected	How affected	By ... [paragraph]
Objective	amended	AASB 2007-4 [97]
Aus1.1	amended	AASB 2007-8 [7, 8]
Aus1.4	amended	AASB 2007-8 [8]
5	amended	AASB 2008-3 [69]
16	amended amended	AASB 2009-12 [17] AASB 2010-5 [53]
18	amended amended	AASB 2007-8 [6] AASB 2007-10 [85]
25	amended amended	AASB 2007-8 [122] AASB 2007-10 [88]
Aus26.1-Aus26.2 (and preceding heading)	added	AASB 2007-9 [20]
30	amended	AASB 2007-10 [88]
33	amended	AASB 2007-10 [86]
35	amended	AASB 2007-10 [88]
38	amended	AASB 2009-12 [17]
41	amended	AASB 2007-4 [97]
46	amended	AASB 2009-12 [17]
54	amended	AASB 2007-8 [6]
75	amended amended amended amended	AASB 2007-8 [6] AASB 2007-10 [88] AASB 2009-6 [83] AASB 2009-12 [17]

Table of Amendments to Guidance

Paragraph affected	How affected	By ... [paragraph]
A, title, rubric, heading	amended	AASB 2010-5 [54-55]
A, Reimbursements	amended	AASB 2007-8 [6]
B, title, rubric, heading	amended	AASB 2010-5 [56]
C, title, rubric, heading	amended	AASB 2010-5 [57]
C, Example 2A	amended	AASB 2007-4 [97]
C, Example 6	amended	AASB 2009-6 [84]
C, Example 10	amended amended	AASB 2007-10 [87, 88] AASB 2009-6 [84]
D, title, rubric, heading	amended	AASB 2010-5 [58]

General Terminology Amendments

References to 'reporting date' and 'each reporting date' were amended to 'end of the reporting period' and 'the end of each reporting period' respectively by AASB 2007-8. These amendments are not shown in the above Tables of Amendments.

Comparison with IAS 37

AASB 137 and IAS 37

AASB 137 *Provisions, Contingent Liabilities and Contingent Assets* as amended incorporates IAS 37 *Provisions, Contingent Liabilities and Contingent Assets* as issued and amended by the International Accounting Standards Board (IASB). Paragraphs that have been added to this Standard (and do not appear in the text of IAS 37) are identified with the prefix "Aus", followed by the number of the relevant IASB paragraph and decimal numbering.

Compliance with IAS 37

Entities that comply with AASB 137 as amended will simultaneously be in compliance with IAS 37 as amended.

Accounting Standard AASB 137

The Australian Accounting Standards Board made Accounting Standard AASB 137 *Provisions, Contingent Liabilities and Contingent Assets* under section 334 of the *Corporations Act 2001* on 15 July 2004.

This compiled version of AASB 137 applies to annual reporting periods beginning on or after 1 January 2011 but before 1 July 2013. It incorporates relevant amendments contained in other AASB Standards made by the AASB up to and including 27 October 2010 (see Compilation Details).

Accounting Standard AASB 137

Provisions, Contingent Liabilities and Contingent Assets

Objective

The objective of this Standard is to ensure that appropriate recognition criteria and measurement bases are applied to provisions, contingent liabilities and contingent assets and that sufficient information is disclosed in the notes to enable users to understand their nature, timing and amount.

Application

Aus1.1   This Standard applies to:

    (a)   **each entity that is required to prepare financial reports in accordance with Part 2M.3 of the Corporations Act and that is a reporting entity;**

    (b)   **general purpose financial statements of each other reporting entity; and**

    (c)   **financial statements that are, or are held out to be, general purpose financial statements.**

Aus1.2   **This Standard applies to annual reporting periods beginning on or after 1 January 2005.**

    [Note: For application dates of paragraphs changed or added by an amending Standard, see Compilation Details.]

Aus1.3   **This Standard shall not be applied to annual reporting periods beginning before 1 January 2005.**

Aus1.4   **The requirements specified in this Standard apply to the financial statements where information resulting from their application is material in accordance with AASB 1031 *Materiality*.**

Aus1.5   **When applicable, this Standard supersedes AASB 1044 *Provisions, Contingent Liabilities and Contingent Assets* as notified in the *Commonwealth of Australia Gazette* No S 450, 26 October 2001.**

Aus1.6   AASB 1044 remains applicable until superseded by this Standard.

Aus1.7 Notice of this Standard was published in the *Commonwealth of Australia Gazette* No S 294, 22 July 2004.

Scope

1 **This Standard shall be applied by all entities in accounting for *provisions*, *contingent liabilities* and *contingent assets*, except:**

   (a) **those resulting from executory contracts, except where the contract is onerous[1]; and**

   (b) **[Deleted by the IASB];**

   (c) **those covered by another Australian Accounting Standard.**

2 This Standard does not apply to financial instruments (including guarantees) that are within the scope of AASB 139 *Financial Instruments: Recognition and Measurement*.

3 Executory contracts are contracts under which neither party has performed any of its obligations or both parties have partially performed their obligations to an equal extent. This Standard does not apply to executory contracts unless they are onerous.

4 [Deleted by the IASB]

5 When another Australian Accounting Standard deals with a specific type of provision, contingent liability or contingent asset, an entity applies that Standard instead of this Standard. For example, some types of provisions are addressed in Standards on:

   (a) construction contracts (see AASB 111 *Construction Contracts*);

   (b) income taxes (see AASB 112 *Income Taxes*);

   (c) leases (see AASB 117 *Leases*). However, as AASB 117 contains no specific requirements to deal with operating leases that have become onerous, this Standard applies to such cases;

   (d) employee benefits (see AASB 119 *Employee Benefits*); and

   (e) insurance contracts (see AASB 4 *Insurance Contracts*, AASB 1023 *General Insurance Contracts*, and AASB 1038 *Life Insurance Contracts*). However, this Standard applies to provisions, contingent liabilities and contingent assets of an insurer, other than those arising from its contractual obligations and rights under insurance contracts within the scopes of AASB 4, AASB 1023 or AASB 1038.

6 Some amounts treated as provisions may relate to the recognition of revenue, for example where an entity gives guarantees in exchange for a fee. This Standard does not address the recognition of revenue. AASB 118 *Revenue* identifies the circumstances in which revenue is recognised and provides practical guidance on the application of the recognition criteria. This Standard does not change the requirements of AASB 118.

7 This Standard defines provisions as *liabilities* of uncertain timing or amount. In some countries the term 'provision' is also used in the context of items such as depreciation, impairment of assets and doubtful debts: these are adjustments to the carrying amounts of assets and are not addressed in this Standard.

8 Other Australian Accounting Standards specify whether expenditures are treated as assets or as expenses. These issues are not addressed in this Standard. Accordingly, this Standard neither prohibits nor requires capitalisation of the costs recognised when a provision is made.

9 This Standard applies to provisions for *restructuring* (including discontinued operations). When a restructuring meets the definition of a discontinued operation, additional disclosures may be required by AASB 5 *Non-current Assets Held for Sale and Discontinued Operations*.

---

1 'Onerous contract' is a defined term.

Definitions

10   The following terms are used in this Standard with the meanings specified.

A *constructive obligation* is an obligation that derives from an entity's actions where:

(a)   by an established pattern of past practice, published policies or a sufficiently specific current statement, the entity has indicated to other parties that it will accept certain responsibilities; and

(b)   as a result, the entity has created a valid expectation on the part of those other parties that it will discharge those responsibilities.

A *contingent asset* is a possible asset that arises from past events and whose existence will be confirmed only by the occurrence or non-occurrence of one or more uncertain future events not wholly within the control of the entity.

A *contingent liability* is:

(a)   a possible obligation that arises from past events and whose existence will be confirmed only by the occurrence or non-occurrence of one or more uncertain future events not wholly within the control of the entity; or

(b)   a present obligation that arises from past events but is not recognised because:

(i)   it is not probable that an outflow of resources embodying economic benefits will be required to settle the obligation; or

(ii)   the amount of the obligation cannot be measured with sufficient reliability.

A *legal obligation* is an obligation that derives from:

(a)   a contract (through its explicit or implicit terms);

(b)   legislation; or

(c)   other operation of law.

A *liability* is a present obligation of the entity arising from past events, the settlement of which is expected to result in an outflow from the entity of resources embodying economic benefits.

An *obligating event* is an event that creates a legal or constructive obligation that results in an entity having no realistic alternative to settling that obligation.

An *onerous contract* is a contract in which the unavoidable costs of meeting the obligations under the contract exceed the economic benefits expected to be received under it.

A *provision* is a liability of uncertain timing or amount.

A *restructuring* is a programme that is planned and controlled by management, and materially changes either:

(a)   the scope of a business undertaken by an entity; or

(b)   the manner in which that business is conducted.

Provisions and Other Liabilities

11   Provisions can be distinguished from other liabilities such as trade payables and accruals because there is uncertainty about the timing or amount of the future expenditure required in settlement. By contrast:

(a)   trade payables are liabilities to pay for goods or services that have been received or supplied and have been invoiced or formally agreed with the supplier; and

(b)   accruals are liabilities to pay for goods or services that have been received or supplied but have not been paid, invoiced or formally agreed with the supplier, including amounts due to employees (for example, amounts relating to accrued vacation pay).

Although it is sometimes necessary to estimate the amount or timing of accruals, the uncertainty is generally much less than for provisions.

Accruals are often reported as part of trade and other payables, whereas provisions are reported separately.

Relationship between Provisions and Contingent Liabilities

12 In a general sense, all provisions are contingent because they are uncertain in timing or amount. However, within this Standard the term 'contingent' is used for liabilities and assets that are not recognised because their existence will be confirmed only by the occurrence or non-occurrence of one or more uncertain future events not wholly within the control of the entity. In addition, the term 'contingent liability' is used for liabilities that do not meet the recognition criteria.

13 This Standard distinguishes between:

(a) provisions – which are recognised as liabilities (assuming that a reliable estimate can be made) because they are present obligations and it is probable that an outflow of resources embodying economic benefits will be required to settle the obligations; and

(b) contingent liabilities – which are not recognised as liabilities because they are either:

(i) possible obligations, as it has yet to be confirmed whether the entity has a present obligation that could lead to an outflow of resources embodying economic benefits; or

(ii) present obligations that do not meet the recognition criteria in this Standard (because either it is not probable that an outflow of resources embodying economic benefits will be required to settle the obligation, or a sufficiently reliable estimate of the amount of the obligation cannot be made).

Recognition

Provisions

14 **A provision shall be recognised when:**

(a) **an entity has a present obligation (legal or constructive) as a result of a past event;**

(b) **it is probable that an outflow of resources embodying economic benefits will be required to settle the obligation; and**

(c) **a reliable estimate can be made of the amount of the obligation.**

If these conditions are not met, no provision shall be recognised.

Present Obligation

15 **In rare cases it is not clear whether there is a present obligation. In these cases, a past event is deemed to give rise to a present obligation if, taking account of all available evidence, it is more likely than not that a present obligation exists at the end of the reporting period.**

16 In almost all cases it will be clear whether a past event has given rise to a present obligation. In rare cases, for example in a lawsuit, it may be disputed either whether certain events have occurred or whether those events result in a present obligation. In such a case, an entity determines whether a present obligation exists at the end of the reporting period by taking account of all available evidence, including, for example, the opinion of experts. The evidence considered includes any additional evidence provided by events after the reporting period. On the basis of such evidence:

(a) where it is more likely than not that a present obligation exists at the end of the reporting period, the entity recognises a provision (if the recognition criteria are met); and

(b)   where it is more likely that no present obligation exists at the end of the reporting period, the entity discloses a contingent liability, unless the possibility of an outflow of resources embodying economic benefits is remote (see paragraph 86).

Past Event

17   A past event that leads to a present obligation is called an *obligating event*. For an event to be an obligating event, it is necessary that the entity has no realistic alternative to settling the obligation created by the event. This is the case only:

(a)   where the settlement of the obligation can be enforced by law;[2] or

(b)   in the case of a *constructive obligation*, where the event (which may be an action of the entity) creates valid expectations in other parties that the entity will discharge the obligation.

18   Financial statements deal with the financial position of an entity at the end of its reporting period and not its possible position in the future. Therefore, no provision is recognised for costs that need to be incurred to operate in the future. The only liabilities recognised in an entity's statement of financial position are those that exist at the end of the reporting period.

19   It is only those obligations arising from past events existing independently of an entity's future actions (that is, the future conduct of its business) that are recognised as provisions. Examples of such obligations are penalties or clean-up costs for unlawful environmental damage, both of which would lead to an outflow of resources embodying economic benefits in settlement regardless of the future actions of the entity. Similarly, an entity recognises a provision for the decommissioning costs of an oil installation or a nuclear power station to the extent that the entity is obliged to rectify damage already caused. In contrast, because of commercial pressures or legal requirements, an entity may intend or need to carry out expenditure to operate in a particular way in the future (for example, by fitting smoke filters in a certain type of factory). Because the entity can avoid the future expenditure by its future actions, for example by changing its method of operation, it has no present obligation for that future expenditure and no provision is recognised.

20   An obligation always involves another party to whom the obligation is owed. It is not necessary, however, to know the identity of the party to whom the obligation is owed – indeed the obligation may be to the public at large. Because an obligation always involves a commitment to another party, it follows that a management or board decision does not give rise to a constructive obligation at the end of the reporting period unless the decision has been communicated before the end of the reporting period to those affected by it in a sufficiently specific manner to raise a valid expectation in them that the entity will discharge its responsibilities.

21   An event that does not give rise to an obligation immediately may do so at a later date, because of changes in the law or because an act (for example, a sufficiently specific public statement) by the entity gives rise to a constructive obligation. For example, when environmental damage is caused there may be no obligation to remedy the consequences. However, the causing of the damage will become an obligating event when a new law requires the existing damage to be rectified or when the entity publicly accepts responsibility for rectification in a way that creates a constructive obligation.

22   Where details of a proposed new law have yet to be finalised, an obligation arises only when the legislation is virtually certain to be enacted as drafted. For the purpose of this Standard, such an obligation is treated as a *legal obligation*. Differences in circumstances surrounding enactment make it impossible to specify a single event that would make the enactment of a law virtually certain. In many cases it will be impossible to be virtually certain of the enactment of a law until it is enacted.

Probable Outflow of Resources Embodying Economic Benefits

23   For a *liability* to qualify for recognition there must be not only a present obligation but also the probability of an outflow of resources embodying economic benefits to settle

---

2   'Legal obligation' is a defined term.

that obligation. For the purpose of this Standard[3], an outflow of resources or other event is regarded as probable if the event is more likely than not to occur, that is, the probability that the event will occur is greater than the probability that it will not. Where it is not probable that a present obligation exists, an entity discloses a contingent liability, unless the possibility of an outflow of resources embodying economic benefits is remote (see paragraph 86).

24   Where there are a number of similar obligations (for example, product warranties or similar contracts) the probability that an outflow will be required in settlement is determined by considering the class of obligations as a whole. Although the likelihood of outflow for any one item may be small, it may well be probable that some outflow of resources will be needed to settle the class of obligations as a whole. If that is the case, a provision is recognised (if the other recognition criteria are met).

Reliable Estimate of the Obligation

25   The use of estimates is an essential part of the preparation of financial statements and does not undermine their reliability. This is especially true in the case of provisions, which by their nature are more uncertain than most other items in the statement of financial position. Except in extremely rare cases, an entity will be able to determine a range of possible outcomes and can therefore make an estimate of the obligation that is sufficiently reliable to use in recognising a provision.

26   In the extremely rare case where no reliable estimate can be made, a liability exists that cannot be recognised. That liability is disclosed as a contingent liability (see paragraph 86).

Recognition of Liabilities Arising from Local Government and Government Existing Public Policies, Budget Policies, Election Promises or Statements of Intent

Aus26.1   This paragraph and paragraph Aus26.2 relate to the recognition by a local government, government department or government of a liability arising from a local government or government existing public policy, budget policy, election promise or statement of intent. The intention to make payments to other parties, whether advised in the form of a local government or government budget policy, election promise or statement of intent, does not of itself create a present obligation which is binding. A liability would be recognised only when the entity is committed in the sense that it has little or no discretion to avoid the sacrifice of future economic benefits. For example, a government does not have a present obligation to sacrifice future economic benefits for social welfare payments that might arise in future reporting periods. A present obligation for social welfare payments arises only when entitlement conditions are satisfied for payment during a particular payment period. Similarly, a government does not have a present obligation to sacrifice future economic benefits under multi-year public policy agreements until the grantee meets conditions such as grant eligibility criteria, or has provided the services or facilities required under the grant agreement. In such cases, only amounts outstanding in relation to current or previous periods satisfy the definition of liabilities.

Aus26.2   Some such transactions or events may give rise to legal, social, political or economic consequences which leave little, if any, discretion to avoid a sacrifice of future economic benefits. In such circumstances, the definition of a liability is satisfied. An example of such an event is the occurrence of a disaster, where a government has a clear and formal policy to provide financial aid to victims of such disasters. In this circumstance, the government has little discretion to avoid the sacrifice of future economic benefits. However, the liability is recognised only when the amount of financial aid to be provided can be measured reliably.

---

3   The interpretation of 'probable' in this Standard as 'more likely than not' does not necessarily apply in other Australian Accounting Standards.

Contingent Liabilities

27   **An entity shall not recognise a contingent liability.**

28   A contingent liability is disclosed, as required by paragraph 86, unless the possibility of an outflow of resources embodying economic benefits is remote.

29   Where an entity is jointly and severally liable for an obligation, the part of the obligation that is expected to be met by other parties is treated as a contingent liability. The entity recognises a provision for the part of the obligation for which an outflow of resources embodying economic benefits is probable, except in the extremely rare circumstances where no reliable estimate can be made.

30   Contingent liabilities may develop in a way not initially expected. Therefore, they are assessed continually to determine whether an outflow of resources embodying economic benefits has become probable. If it becomes probable that an outflow of future economic benefits will be required for an item previously dealt with as a contingent liability, a provision is recognised in the financial statements of the period in which the change in probability occurs (except in the extremely rare circumstances where no reliable estimate can be made).

Contingent Assets

31   **An entity shall not recognise a contingent asset.**

32   Contingent assets usually arise from unplanned or other unexpected events that give rise to the possibility of an inflow of economic benefits to the entity. An example is a claim that an entity is pursuing through legal processes, where the outcome is uncertain.

33   Contingent assets are not recognised in financial statements since this may result in the recognition of income that may never be realised. However, when the realisation of income is virtually certain, then the related asset is not a contingent asset and its recognition is appropriate.

34   A contingent asset is disclosed, as required by paragraph 89, where an inflow of economic benefits is probable.

35   Contingent assets are assessed continually to ensure that developments are appropriately reflected in the financial statements. If it has become virtually certain that an inflow of economic benefits will arise, the asset and the related income are recognised in the financial statements of the period in which the change occurs. If an inflow of economic benefits has become probable, an entity discloses the contingent asset (see paragraph 89).

Measurement

Best Estimate

36   **The amount recognised as a provision shall be the best estimate of the expenditure required to settle the present obligation at the end of the reporting period.**

37   The best estimate of the expenditure required to settle the present obligation is the amount that an entity would rationally pay to settle the obligation at the end of the reporting period or to transfer it to a third party at that time. It will often be impossible or prohibitively expensive to settle or transfer an obligation at the end of the reporting period. However, the estimate of the amount that an entity would rationally pay to settle or transfer the obligation gives the best estimate of the expenditure required to settle the present obligation at the end of the reporting period.

38   The estimates of outcome and financial effect are determined by the judgement of the management of the entity, supplemented by experience of similar transactions and, in some cases, reports from independent experts. The evidence considered includes any additional evidence provided by events after the reporting period.

39   Uncertainties surrounding the amount to be recognised as a provision are dealt with by various means according to the circumstances. Where the provision being measured involves a large population of items, the obligation is estimated by weighting all possible outcomes by their associated probabilities. The name for this statistical method of estimation is 'expected value'. The provision will therefore be different depending on

whether the probability of a loss of a given amount is, for example, 60 per cent or 90 per cent. Where there is a continuous range of possible outcomes, and each point in that range is as likely as any other, the mid-point of the range is used.

Example

An entity sells goods with a warranty under which customers are covered for the cost of repairs of any manufacturing defects that become apparent within the first six months after purchase. If minor defects were detected in all products sold, repair costs of 1 million would result. If major defects were detected in all products sold, repair costs of 4 million would result. The entity's past experience and future expectations indicate that, for the coming year, 75 per cent of the goods sold will have no defects, 20 per cent of the goods sold will have minor defects and 5 per cent of the goods sold will have major defects. In accordance with paragraph 24, an entity assesses the probability of an outflow for the warranty obligations as a whole.

The expected value of the cost of repairs is:

(75% of nil) + (20% of 1m) + (5% of 4m) = 400,000

---

40   Where a single obligation is being measured, the individual most likely outcome may be the best estimate of the liability. However, even in such a case, the entity considers other possible outcomes. Where other possible outcomes are either mostly higher or mostly lower than the most likely outcome, the best estimate will be a higher or lower amount. For example, if an entity has to rectify a serious fault in a major plant that it has constructed for a customer, the individual most likely outcome may be for the repair to succeed at the first attempt at a cost of 1,000, but a provision for a larger amount is made if there is a significant chance that further attempts will be necessary.

41   The provision is measured before tax, as the tax consequences of the provision, and changes in it, are dealt with under AASB 112.

Risks and Uncertainties

42   **The risks and uncertainties that inevitably surround many events and circumstances shall be taken into account in reaching the best estimate of a provision.**

43   Risk describes variability of outcome. A risk adjustment may increase the amount at which a liability is measured. Caution is needed in making judgements under conditions of uncertainty, so that income or assets are not overstated and expenses or liabilities are not understated. However, uncertainty does not justify the creation of excessive provisions or a deliberate overstatement of liabilities. For example, if the projected costs of a particularly adverse outcome are estimated on a prudent basis, that outcome is not then deliberately treated as more probable than is realistically the case. Care is needed to avoid duplicating adjustments for risk and uncertainty with consequent overstatement of a provision.

44   Disclosure of the uncertainties surrounding the amount of the expenditure is made under paragraph 85(b).

Present Value

45   **Where the effect of the time value of money is material, the amount of a provision shall be the present value of the expenditures expected to be required to settle the obligation.**

46   Because of the time value of money, provisions relating to cash outflows that arise soon after the reporting period are more onerous than those where cash outflows of the same amount arise later. Provisions are therefore discounted, where the effect is material.

47   **The discount rate (or rates) shall be a pre-tax rate (or rates) that reflect(s) current market assessments of the time value of money and the risks specific to the liability. The discount rate(s) shall not reflect risks for which future cash flow estimates have been adjusted.**

Future Events

48   **Future events that may affect the amount required to settle an obligation shall be reflected in the amount of a provision where there is sufficient objective evidence that they will occur.**

49   Expected future events may be particularly important in measuring provisions. For example, an entity may believe that the cost of cleaning up a site at the end of its life will be reduced by future changes in technology. The amount recognised reflects a reasonable expectation of technically qualified, objective observers, taking account of all available evidence as to the technology that will be available at the time of the clean-up. Thus it is appropriate to include, for example, expected cost reductions associated with increased experience in applying existing technology or the expected cost of applying existing technology to a larger or more complex clean-up operation than has previously been carried out. However, an entity does not anticipate the development of a completely new technology for cleaning up unless it is supported by sufficient objective evidence.

50   The effect of possible new legislation is taken into consideration in measuring an existing obligation when sufficient objective evidence exists that the legislation is virtually certain to be enacted. The variety of circumstances that arise in practice makes it impossible to specify a single event that will provide sufficient, objective evidence in every case. Evidence is required both of what legislation will demand and of whether it is virtually certain to be enacted and implemented in due course. In many cases sufficient objective evidence will not exist until the new legislation is enacted.

Expected Disposal of Assets

51   **Gains from the expected disposal of assets shall not be taken into account in measuring a provision.**

52   Gains on the expected disposal of assets are not taken into account in measuring a provision, even if the expected disposal is closely linked to the event giving rise to the provision. Instead, an entity recognises gains on expected disposals of assets at the time specified by the Standard dealing with the assets concerned.

Reimbursements

53   **Where some or all of the expenditure required to settle a provision is expected to be reimbursed by another party, the reimbursement shall be recognised when, and only when, it is virtually certain that reimbursement will be received if the entity settles the obligation. The reimbursement shall be treated as a separate asset. The amount recognised for the reimbursement shall not exceed the amount of the provision.**

54   **In the statement of comprehensive income, the expense relating to a provision may be presented net of the amount recognised for a reimbursement.**

55   Sometimes, an entity is able to look to another party to pay part or all of the expenditure required to settle a provision (for example, through insurance contracts, indemnity clauses or suppliers' warranties). The other party may either reimburse amounts paid by the entity or pay the amounts directly.

56   In most cases the entity will remain liable for the whole of the amount in question so that the entity would have to settle the full amount if the third party failed to pay for any reason. In this situation, a provision is recognised for the full amount of the liability, and a separate asset for the expected reimbursement is recognised when it is virtually certain that reimbursement will be received if the entity settles the liability.

57   In some cases, the entity will not be liable for the costs in question if the third party fails to pay. In such a case the entity has no liability for those costs and they are not included in the provision.

58   As noted in paragraph 29, an obligation for which an entity is jointly and severally liable is a contingent liability to the extent that it is expected that the obligation will be settled by the other parties.

Changes in Provisions

59   **Provisions shall be reviewed at the end of each reporting period and adjusted to reflect the current best estimate. If it is no longer probable that an outflow of resources embodying economic benefits will be required to settle the obligation, the provision shall be reversed.**

60   Where discounting is used, the carrying amount of a provision increases in each period to reflect the passage of time. This increase is recognised as borrowing cost.

Use of Provisions

61 **A provision shall be used only for expenditures for which the provision was originally recognised.**

62 Only expenditures that relate to the original provision are set against it. Setting expenditures against a provision that was originally recognised for another purpose would conceal the impact of two different events.

Application of the Recognition and Measurement Rules

Future Operating Losses

63 **Provisions shall not be recognised for future operating losses.**

64 Future operating losses do not meet the definition of a liability in paragraph 10 and the general recognition criteria set out for provisions in paragraph 14.

65 An expectation of future operating losses is an indication that certain assets of the operation may be impaired. An entity tests these assets for impairment under AASB 136 *Impairment of Assets*.

Onerous Contracts

66 **If an entity has a contract that is onerous, the present obligation under the contract shall be recognised and measured as a provision.**

67 Many contracts (for example, some routine purchase orders) can be cancelled without paying compensation to the other party, and therefore there is no obligation. Other contracts establish both rights and obligations for each of the contracting parties. Where events make such a contract onerous, the contract falls within the scope of this Standard and a liability exists which is recognised. Executory contracts that are not onerous fall outside the scope of this Standard.

68 This Standard defines an *onerous contract* as a contract in which the unavoidable costs of meeting the obligations under the contract exceed the economic benefits expected to be received under it. The unavoidable costs under a contract reflect the least net cost of exiting from the contract, which is the lower of the cost of fulfilling it and any compensation or penalties arising from failure to fulfil it.

69 Before a separate provision for an onerous contract is established, an entity recognises any impairment loss that has occurred on assets dedicated to that contract (see AASB 136).

Restructuring

70 The following are examples of events that may fall under the definition of restructuring:

    (a)   sale or termination of a line of business;

    (b)   the closure of business locations in a country or region or the relocation of business activities from one country or region to another;

    (c)   changes in management structure, for example, eliminating a layer of management; and

    (d)   fundamental reorganisations that have a material effect on the nature and focus of the entity's operations.

71 A provision for restructuring costs is recognised only when the general recognition criteria for provisions set out in paragraph 14 are met. Paragraphs 72-83 set out how the general recognition criteria apply to restructurings.

72 **A constructive obligation to restructure arises only when an entity:**

    (a) **has a detailed formal plan for the restructuring identifying at least:**

        (i) **the business or part of a business concerned;**

        (ii) **the principal locations affected;**

        (iii) **the location, function, and approximate number of employees who will be compensated for terminating their services;**

(iv)   the expenditures that will be undertaken; and

(v)   when the plan will be implemented; and

(b)   has raised a valid expectation in those affected that it will carry out the restructuring by starting to implement that plan or announcing its main features to those affected by it.

73   Evidence that an entity has started to implement a restructuring plan would be provided, for example, by dismantling plant or selling assets or by the public announcement of the main features of the plan. A public announcement of a detailed plan to restructure constitutes a constructive obligation to restructure only if it is made in such a way and in sufficient detail (that is, setting out the main features of the plan) that it gives rise to valid expectations in other parties such as customers, suppliers and employees (or their representatives) that the entity will carry out the restructuring.

74   For a plan to be sufficient to give rise to a constructive obligation when communicated to those affected by it, its implementation needs to be planned to begin as soon as possible and to be completed in a timeframe that makes significant changes to the plan unlikely. If it is expected that there will be a long delay before the restructuring begins or that the restructuring will take an unreasonably long time, it is unlikely that the plan will raise a valid expectation on the part of others that the entity is at present committed to restructuring, because the timeframe allows opportunities for the entity to change its plans.

75   A management or board decision to restructure taken before the end of the reporting period does not give rise to a constructive obligation at the end of the reporting period unless the entity has, before the end of the reporting period:

(a)   started to implement the restructuring plan; or

(b)   announced the main features of the restructuring plan to those affected by it in a sufficiently specific manner to raise a valid expectation in them that the entity will carry out the restructuring.

If an entity starts to implement a restructuring plan, or announces its main features to those affected, only after the reporting period, disclosure is required under AASB 110 *Events after the Reporting Period*, if the restructuring is material and non-disclosure could influence the economic decisions that users make on the basis of the financial statements.

76   Although a constructive obligation is not created solely by a management decision, an obligation may result from other earlier events together with such a decision. For example, negotiations with employee representatives for termination payments, or with purchasers for the sale of an operation, may have been concluded subject only to board approval. Once that approval has been obtained and communicated to the other parties, the entity has a constructive obligation to restructure, if the conditions of paragraph 72 are met.

77   In some countries, the ultimate authority is vested in a board whose membership includes representatives of interests other than those of management (for example, employees) or notification to such representatives may be necessary before the board decision is taken. Because a decision by such a board involves communication to these representatives, it may result in a constructive obligation to restructure.

78   No obligation arises for the sale of an operation until the entity is committed to the sale, that is, there is a binding sale agreement.

79   Even when an entity has taken a decision to sell an operation and announced that decision publicly, it cannot be committed to the sale until a purchaser has been identified and there is a binding sale agreement. Until there is a binding sale agreement, the entity will be able to change its mind and indeed will have to take another course of action if a purchaser cannot be found on acceptable terms. When the sale of an operation is envisaged as part of a restructuring, the assets of the operation are reviewed for impairment, under AASB 136. When a sale is only part of a restructuring, a constructive obligation can arise for the other parts of the restructuring before a binding sale agreement exists.

80   A restructuring provision shall include only the direct expenditures arising from the restructuring, which are those that are both:

(a)   necessarily entailed by the restructuring; and

(b)   not associated with the ongoing activities of the entity.

81   A restructuring provision does not include such costs as:

(a)   retraining or relocating continuing staff;

(b)   marketing; or

(c)   investment in new systems and distribution networks.

These expenditures relate to the future conduct of the business and are not liabilities for restructuring at the end of the reporting period. Such expenditures are recognised on the same basis as if they arose independently of a restructuring.

82   Identifiable future operating losses up to the date of a restructuring are not included in a provision, unless they relate to an onerous contract as defined in paragraph 10.

83   As required by paragraph 51, gains on the expected disposal of assets are not taken into account in measuring a restructuring provision, even if the sale of assets is envisaged as part of the restructuring.

Disclosure

84   For each class of provision, an entity shall disclose:

(a)   the carrying amount at the beginning and end of the period;

(b)   additional provisions made in the period, including increases to existing provisions;

(c)   amounts used (that is, incurred and charged against the provision) during the period;

(d)   unused amounts reversed during the period; and

(e)   the increase during the period in the discounted amount arising from the passage of time and the effect of any change in the discount rate.

Comparative information is not required.

85   An entity shall disclose the following for each class of provision:

(a)   a brief description of the nature of the obligation and the expected timing of any resulting outflows of economic benefits;

(b)   an indication of the uncertainties about the amount or timing of those outflows. Where necessary to provide adequate information, an entity shall disclose the major assumptions made concerning future events, as addressed in paragraph 48; and

(c)   the amount of any expected reimbursement, stating the amount of any asset that has been recognised for that expected reimbursement.

86   Unless the possibility of any outflow in settlement is remote, an entity shall disclose for each class of contingent liability at the end of the reporting period a brief description of the nature of the contingent liability and, where practicable:

(a)   an estimate of its financial effect, measured under paragraphs 36-52;

(b)   an indication of the uncertainties relating to the amount or timing of any outflow; and

(c)   the possibility of any reimbursement.

87   In determining which provisions or contingent liabilities may be aggregated to form a class, it is necessary to consider whether the nature of the items is sufficiently similar for a single statement about them to fulfil the requirements of paragraphs 85(a) and (b) and 86(a) and (b). Thus, it may be appropriate to treat as a single class of provision amounts relating to warranties of different products, but it would not be appropriate to treat as a single class amounts relating to normal warranties and amounts that are subject to legal proceedings.

88   Where a provision and a contingent liability arise from the same set of circumstances, an entity makes the disclosures required by paragraphs 84-86 in a way that shows the link between the provision and the contingent liability.

89   **Where an inflow of economic benefits is probable, an entity shall disclose a brief description of the nature of the contingent assets at the end of the reporting period, and, where practicable, an estimate of their financial effect, measured using the principles set out for provisions in paragraphs 36-52.**

90   It is important that disclosures for contingent assets avoid giving misleading indications of the likelihood of income arising.

91   **Where any of the information required by paragraphs 86 and 89 is not disclosed because it is not practicable to do so, that fact shall be stated.**

92   **In extremely rare cases, disclosure of some or all of the information required by paragraphs 84-89 can be expected to prejudice seriously the position of the entity in a dispute with other parties on the subject matter of the provision, contingent liability or contingent asset. In such cases, an entity need not disclose the information, but shall disclose the general nature of the dispute, together with the fact that, and reason why, the information has not been disclosed.**

Transitional Provisions
93   [Deleted by the AASB]
94   [Deleted by the IASB]

Effective Date of IAS 37
95   [Deleted by the AASB]
96   [Deleted by the IASB]

Guidance on Implementing AASB 137

This guidance accompanies, but is not part of, AASB 137.

A Tables – Provisions, Contingent Liabilities,Contingent Assets and Reimbursements
The purpose of these tables is to summarise the main requirements of the Standard.

Provisions and Contingent Liabilities

Where, as a result of past events, there may be an outflow of resources embodying future economic benefits in settlement of: (a) a present obligation; or (b) a possible obligation whose existence will be confirmed only by the occurrence or non-occurrence of one or more uncertain future events not wholly within the control of the entity.		
There is a present obligation that probably requires an outflow of resources.	There is a possible obligation or a present obligation that may, but probably will not, require an outflow of resources.	There is a possible obligation or a present obligation where the likelihood of an outflow of resources is remote.
A provision is recognised (paragraph 14).	No provision is recognised (paragraph 27).	No provision is recognised (paragraph 27).
Disclosures are required for the provision (paragraphs 84 and 85).	Disclosures are required for the contingent liability (paragraph 86).	No disclosure is required (paragraph 86).

A contingent liability also arises in the extremely rare case where there is a liability that cannot be recognised because it cannot be measured reliably. Disclosures are required for the contingent liability.

Contingent Assets

Where, as a result of past events, there is a possible asset whose existence will be confirmed only by the occurrence or non-occurrence of one or more uncertain future events not wholly within the control of the entity.		
The inflow of economic benefits is virtually certain.	The inflow of economic benefits is probable, but not virtually certain.	The inflow is not probable.
The asset is not contingent (paragraph 33).	No asset is recognised (paragraph 31).	No asset is recognised (paragraph 31).
	Disclosures are required (paragraph 89).	No disclosure is required (paragraph 89).

Reimbursements

Some or all of the expenditure required to settle a provision is expected to be reimbursed by another party.		
The entity has no obligation for the part of the expenditure to be reimbursed by the other party.	The obligation for the amount expected to be reimbursed remains with the entity and it is virtually certain that reimbursement will be received if the entity settles the provision.	The obligation for the amount expected to be reimbursed remains with the entity and the reimbursement is not virtually certain if the entity settles the provision.
The entity has no liability for the amount to be reimbursed (paragraph 57).	The reimbursement is recognised as a separate asset in the statement of financial position and may be offset against the expense in the statement of comprehensive income. The amount recognised for the expected reimbursement does not exceed the liability (paragraphs 53 and 54).	The expected reimbursement is not recognised as an asset (paragraph 53).
No disclosure is required.	The reimbursement is disclosed together with the amount recognised for the reimbursement (paragraph 85(c)).	The expected reimbursement is disclosed (paragraph 85(c)).

B Decision Tree

The purpose of this diagram is to summarise the main recognition requirements of the Standard for provisions and contingent liabilities.

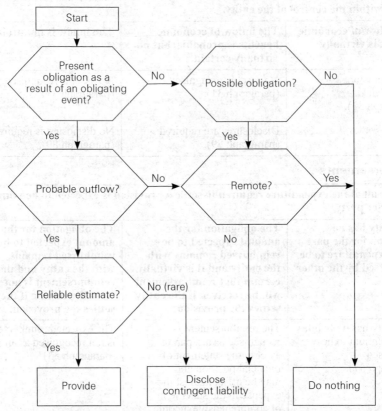

Note: in rare cases, it is not clear whether there is a present obligation. In these cases, a past event is deemed to give rise to a present obligation if, taking account of all available evidence, it is more likely than not that a present obligation exists at the end of the reporting period (paragraph 15 of the Standard).

C Examples: Recognition

All the entities in the examples have 31 December year-ends. In all cases, it is assumed that a reliable estimate can be made of any outflows expected. In some examples the circumstances described may have resulted in impairment of the assets – this aspect is not dealt with in the examples.

The cross-references provided in the examples indicate paragraphs of the Standard that are particularly relevant.

References to 'best estimate' are to the present value amount, where the effect of the time value of money is material.

Example 1 Warranties

A manufacturer gives warranties at the time of sale to purchasers of its product. Under the terms of the contract for sale the manufacturer undertakes to make good, by repair or replacement, manufacturing defects that become apparent within three years from the date of sale. On past experience, it is probable (that is, more likely than not) that there will be some claims under the warranties.

Present obligation as a result of a past obligating event – The obligating event is the sale of the product with a warranty, which gives rise to a legal obligation.

An outflow of resources embodying economic benefits in settlement – Probable for the warranties as a whole (see paragraph 24).

Conclusion – A provision is recognised for the best estimate of the costs of making good under the warranty products sold before the end of the reporting period (see paragraphs 14 and 24).

Example 2A Contaminated Land – Legislation Virtually Certain to be Enacted

An entity in the oil industry causes contamination but cleans up only when required to do so under the laws of the particular country in which it operates. One country in which it operates has had no legislation requiring cleaning up, and the entity has been contaminating land in that country for several years. At 31 December 2000, it is virtually certain that a draft law requiring a clean-up of land already contaminated will be enacted shortly after the year-end.

Present obligation as a result of a past obligating event – The obligating event is the contamination of the land because of the virtual certainty of legislation requiring cleaning up.

An outflow of resources embodying economic benefits in settlement – Probable.

Conclusion – A provision is recognised for the best estimate of the costs of the clean-up (see paragraphs 14 and 22).

Example 2B Contaminated Land and Constructive Obligation

An entity in the oil industry causes contamination and operates in a country where there is no environmental legislation. However, the entity has a widely published environmental policy in which it undertakes to clean up all contamination that it causes. The entity has a record of honouring this published policy.

Present obligation as a result of a past obligating event – The obligating event is the contamination of the land, which gives rise to a constructive obligation because the conduct of the entity has created a valid expectation on the part of those affected by it that the entity will clean up contamination.

An outflow of resources embodying economic benefits in settlement – Probable.

Conclusion – A provision is recognised for the best estimate of the costs of clean-up (see paragraphs 10 (the definition of a constructive obligation), 14 and 17).

Example 3 Offshore Oilfield

An entity operates an offshore oilfield where its licensing agreement requires it to remove the oil rig at the end of production and restore the seabed. Ninety per cent of the eventual costs relate to the removal of the oil rig and restoration of damage caused by building it, and 10 per cent arise through the extraction of oil. At the end of the reporting period, the rig has been constructed but no oil has been extracted.

Present obligation as a result of a past obligating event – The construction of the oil rig creates a legal obligation under the terms of the licence to remove the rig and restore the seabed and is thus an obligating event. At the end of the reporting period, however, there is no obligation to rectify the damage that will be caused by extraction of the oil.

An outflow of resources embodying economic benefits in settlement – Probable.

Conclusion – A provision is recognised for the best estimate of 90 per cent of the eventual costs that relate to the removal of the oil rig and restoration of damage caused by building it (see paragraph 14). These costs are included as part of the cost of the oil rig. The 10 per cent of costs that arise through the extraction of oil are recognised as a liability when the oil is extracted.

Example 4 Refunds Policy

A retail store has a policy of refunding purchases by dissatisfied customers, even though it is under no legal obligation to do so. Its policy of making refunds is generally known.

Present obligation as a result of a past obligating event – The obligating event is the sale of the product, which gives rise to a constructive obligation because the conduct of the store has created a valid expectation on the part of its customers that the store will refund purchases.

An outflow of resources embodying economic benefits in settlement – Probable, a proportion of goods are returned for refund (see paragraph 24).

Conclusion – A provision is recognised for the best estimate of the costs of refunds (see paragraphs 10 (the definition of a constructive obligation), 14, 17 and 24).

Example 5A Closure of a Division – No Implementation Before End of the Reporting Period

On 12 December 2000, the board of an entity decided to close down a division. Before the end of the reporting period (31 December 2000) the decision was not communicated to any of those affected and no other steps were taken to implement the decision.

Present obligation as a result of a past obligating event – There has been no obligating event and so there is no obligation.

Conclusion – No provision is recognised (see paragraphs 14 and 72).

Example 5B Closure of a Division – Communication/Implementation Before End of the Reporting Period

On 12 December 2000, the board of an entity decided to close down a division making a particular product. On 20 December 2000, a detailed plan for closing down the division was agreed by the board; letters were sent to customers warning them to seek an alternative source of supply and redundancy notices were sent to the staff of the division.

Present obligation as a result of a past obligating event – The obligating event is the communication of the decision to the customers and employees, which gives rise to a constructive obligation from that date, because it creates a valid expectation that the division will be closed.

An outflow of resources embodying economic benefits in settlement – Probable.

Conclusion – A provision is recognised at 31 December 2000 for the best estimate of the costs of closing the division (see paragraphs 14 and 72).

Example 6 Legal Requirement to Fit Smoke Filters

Under new legislation, an entity is required to fit smoke filters to its factories by 30 June 2000. The entity has not fitted the smoke filters.

(a)   At 31 December 1999, the end of the reporting period

Present obligation as a result of a past obligating event – There is no obligation because there is no obligating event either for the costs of fitting smoke filters or for fines under the legislation.

Conclusion – No provision is recognised for the cost of fitting the smoke filters (see paragraphs 14 and 17-19).

(b)   At 31 December 2000, the end of the reporting period

Present obligation as a result of a past obligating event – There is still no obligation for the costs of fitting smoke filters because no obligating event has occurred (the fitting of the filters). However, an obligation might arise to pay fines or penalties under the legislation because the obligating event has occurred (the non-compliant operation of the factory).

An outflow of resources embodying economic benefits in settlement – Assessment of probability of incurring fines and penalties by non-compliant operation depends on the details of the legislation and the stringency of the enforcement regime.

Conclusion – No provision is recognised for the costs of fitting smoke filters. However, a provision is recognised for the best estimate of any fines and penalties that are more likely than not to be imposed (see paragraphs 14 and 17-19).

Example 7 Staff Retraining as a Result of Changes in the Income Tax System

The government introduces a number of changes to the income tax system. As a result of these changes, an entity in the financial services sector will need to retrain a large proportion of its administrative and sales workforce in order to ensure continued compliance with financial services regulation. At the end of the reporting period, no retraining of staff has taken place.

Present obligation as a result of a past obligating event – There is no obligation because no obligating event (retraining) has taken place.

Conclusion – No provision is recognised (see paragraphs 14 and 17-19).

Example 8 An Onerous Contract

An entity operates profitably from a factory that it has leased under an operating lease. During December 2000, the entity relocates its operations to a new factory. The lease on the old factory continues for the next four years, it cannot be cancelled and the factory cannot be re-let to another user.

Present obligation as a result of a past obligating event – The obligating event is the signing of the lease contract, which gives rise to a legal obligation.

An outflow of resources embodying economic benefits in settlement – When the lease becomes onerous, an outflow of resources embodying economic benefits is probable. (Until the lease becomes onerous, the entity accounts for the lease under AASB 117 *Leases*).

Conclusion – A provision is recognised for the best estimate of the unavoidable lease payments (see paragraphs 5(c), 14 and 66).

Example 9 A Single Guarantee

On 31 December 1999, Entity A gives a guarantee of certain borrowings of Entity B, whose financial condition at that time is sound. During 2000, the financial condition of Entity B deteriorates and at 30 June 2000, Entity B files for protection from its creditors.

This contract meets the definition of an insurance contract in AASB 4 *Insurance Contracts*. AASB 4 permits the issuer to continue its existing accounting policies for insurance contracts if specified minimum requirements are satisfied. AASB 4 also permits changes in accounting policies that meet specified criteria. The following is an example of an accounting policy that AASB 4 permits.

(a)   At 31 December 1999

Present obligation as a result of a past obligating event – The obligating event is the giving of the guarantee, which gives rise to a legal obligation.

An outflow of resources embodying economic benefits in settlement – No outflow of benefits is probable at 31 December 1999.

Conclusion – The guarantee is recognised at fair value.

(b)   At 31 December 2000

Present obligation as a result of a past obligating event – The obligating event is the giving of the guarantee, which gives rise to a legal obligation.

An outflow of resources embodying economic benefits in settlement – At 31 December 2000, it is probable that an outflow of resources embodying economic benefits will be required to settle the obligation.

Conclusion – The guarantee is subsequently measured at the higher of (a) the best estimate of the obligation (see paragraphs 14 and 23), and (b) the amount initially recognised less, when appropriate, cumulative amortisation in accordance with AASB 118 *Revenue*.

Note: Where an entity gives guarantees in exchange for a fee, revenue is recognised under AASB 118.

Example 10 A Court Case

After a wedding in 2000, ten people died, possibly as a result of food poisoning from products sold by the entity. Legal proceedings are started seeking damages from the entity but it disputes liability. Up to the date of authorisation of the financial statements for the year to 31 December 2000 for issue, the entity's lawyers advise that it is probable that the entity will not be found liable.

However, when the entity prepares the financial statements for the year to 31 December 2001, its lawyers advise that, owing to developments in the case, it is probable that the entity will be found liable.

(a)   At 31 December 2000

Present obligation as a result of a past obligating event – On the basis of the evidence available when the financial statements were approved, there is no obligation as a result of past events.

Conclusion – No provision is recognised (see paragraphs 15 and 16). The matter is disclosed as a contingent liability unless the probability of any outflow is regarded as remote (paragraph 86).

(b)   At 31 December 2001

Present obligation as a result of a past obligating event   On the basis of the evidence available, there is a present obligation.

An outflow of resources embodying economic benefits in settlement – Probable.

Conclusion – A provision is recognised for the best estimate of the amount to settle the obligation (paragraphs 14-16).

Example 11 Repairs and Maintenance

Some assets require, in addition to routine maintenance, substantial expenditure every few years for major refits or refurbishment and the replacement of major components. AASB 116 *Property, Plant and Equipment* gives guidance on allocating expenditure on an asset to its component parts where these components have different useful lives or provide benefits in a different pattern.

Example 11A Refurbishment Costs – No Legislative Requirement

A furnace has a lining that needs to be replaced every five years for technical reasons. At the end of the reporting period, the lining has been in use for three years.

Present obligation as a result of a past obligating event – There is no present obligation.

Conclusion – No provision is recognised (see paragraphs 14 and 17-19).

The cost of replacing the lining is not recognised because, at the end of the reporting period, no obligation to replace the lining exists independently of the company's future actions – even the intention to incur the expenditure depends on the company deciding to continue operating the furnace or to replace the lining. Instead of a provision being recognised, the depreciation of the lining takes account of its consumption, that is, it is depreciated over five years. The re-lining costs then incurred are capitalised with the consumption of each new lining shown by depreciation over the subsequent five years.

Example 11B Refurbishment Costs – Legislative Requirement

An airline is required by law to overhaul its aircraft once every three years.

Present obligation as a result of a past obligating event – There is no present obligation.

Conclusion – No provision is recognised (see paragraphs 14 and 17-19).

The costs of overhauling aircraft are not recognised as a provision for the same reasons as the cost of replacing the lining is not recognised as a provision in example 11A. Even a legal requirement to overhaul does not make the costs of overhaul a liability, because no obligation exists to overhaul the aircraft independently of the entity's future actions – the entity could avoid the future expenditure by its future actions, for example, by selling the aircraft. Instead of a provision being recognised, the depreciation of the aircraft takes account of the future incidence of maintenance costs, that is, an amount equivalent to the expected maintenance costs is depreciated over three years.

D Examples: Disclosures

Two examples of the disclosures required by paragraph 85 are provided below.

Example 1 Warranties

A manufacturer gives warranties at the time of sale to purchasers of its three product lines. Under the terms of the warranty, the manufacturer undertakes to repair or replace items that fail to perform satisfactorily for two years from the date of sale. At the end of the reporting period, a provision of 60,000 has been recognised. The provision has not been discounted as the effect of discounting is not material. The following information is disclosed:

A provision of 60,000 has been recognised for expected warranty claims on products sold during the last three annual reporting periods. It is expected that the majority of this expenditure will be incurred in the next annual reporting period, and all will be incurred within two years of the end of the reporting period.

Example 2 Decommissioning Costs

In 2000, an entity involved in nuclear activities recognises a provision for decommissioning costs of 300 million. The provision is estimated using the assumption that decommissioning will take place in 60-70 years' time. However, there is a possibility that it will not take place until 100-110 years' time, in which case the present value of the costs will be significantly reduced. The following information is disclosed:

A provision of 300 million has been recognised for decommissioning costs. These costs are expected to be incurred between 2060 and 2070; however, there is a possibility that decommissioning will not take place until 2100-2110. If the costs were measured based upon the expectation that they would not be incurred until 2100-2110 the provision would be reduced to 136 million. The provision has been estimated using existing technology, at current prices, and discounted using a real discount rate of 2 per cent.

An example is given below of the disclosures required by paragraph 92 where some of the information required is not given because it can be expected to prejudice seriously the position of the entity.

Example 3 Disclosure Exemption

An entity is involved in a dispute with a competitor, who is alleging that the entity has infringed patents and is seeking damages of 100 million. The entity recognises a provision for its best estimate of the obligation, but discloses none of the information required by paragraphs 84 and 85 of the Standard. The following information is disclosed:

Litigation is in process against the company relating to a dispute with a competitor who alleges that the company has infringed patents and is seeking damages of 100 million. The information usually required by AASB 137 Provisions, Contingent Liabilities and Contingent Assets is not disclosed on the grounds that it can be expected to prejudice seriously the outcome of the litigation. The directors are of the opinion that the claim can be successfully resisted by the company.

AASB 138
Intangible Assets

(Compiled October 2009)

Note from the Institute of Chartered Accountants Australia

This note, prepared by the technical editors, is not part of Accounting Standard AASB 138.

Historical development

15 July 2004: AASB 138 'Intangible Assets' is the Australian equivalent of IAS 38 of the same name. It was made by the AASB on 15 July 2004 as part of the AASB's program to adopt International Financial Reporting Standards (IFRSs) by 2005.

9 December 2004: AASB 2004-1 'Amendments to Australian Accounting Standards' amends paragraph 2, and is applicable from 1 January 2005.

30 April 2007: AASB 2007-4 'Amendments to Australian Accounting Standards' amends paragraphs 2, 3, 28, 33, 44, 66, 68, 69, 83, 97, 108, 109 and 113 and is applicable for annual reporting periods beginning on or after 1 July 2007. Entities may elect to early-adopt it to annual reporting periods beginning on or after 1 January 2005.

28 June 2007: AASB 2007-6 'Amendments to Australian Accounting Standards' was issued by the AASB. This Standard is applicable for annual reporting periods beginning on or after 1 January 2009.

24 September 2007: AASB 2007-8 'Amendments to Australian Accounting Standards' was issued by the AASB. This Standard is applicable for annual reporting periods beginning on or after 1 January 2009.

13 December 2007: AASB 2007-10 'Further Amendments to Australian Accounting Standards arising from AASB 101' amends AASB 138, replacing the term 'financial report' with 'financial statements'. This Standard is applicable to annual reporting periods beginning on or after 1 January 2009.

6 March 2008: AASB 2008-3 'Amendments to Australian Accounting Standards arising from AASB 3 and AASB 127' amends AASB 138 for the issue of AASB 3 revised. This Standard is applicable to annual reporting periods beginning on or after 1 July 2009.

24 July 2008: AASB 2008-5 'Amendments to Australian Accounting Standards arising from the Annual Improvements Project' amends AASB 138 in relation to advertising and promotional activities and the units of production method of amortisation. This Standard is applicable to annual reporting periods beginning on or after 1 January 2009.

25 June 2009: AASB 2009-4 'Amendments to Australian Accounting Standards arising from the Annual Improvements Project' amends AASB 138 in relation to measuring the fair value of an intangible asset acquired in a business combination. This Standard is applicable to annual reporting periods beginning on or after 1 July 2009 with early adoption permitted.

25 June 2009: AASB 2009-6 'Amendments to Australian Accounting Standards' amends AASB 138 for editorial corrections made by the International Accounting Standards Board (IASB) to its Standards and Interpretations (IFRSs) and as a consequence of issuing revised AASB 101 'Presentation of Financial Statements'. This Standard is applicable to annual reporting periods beginning on or after 1 January 2009 that end on or after 30 June 2009.

30 October 2009: AASB 138 was reissued by the AASB, compiled to include the AASB 2007-6, AASB 2007-8, AASB 2007-10, AASB 2008-3, AASB 2008-5, AASB 2009-4 and AASB 2009-6 amendments and applies to annual reporting periods beginning on or after 1 July 2009. Early application is permitted.

On the same date the AASB reissued the version of AASB 138 applicable to annual reporting periods beginning on or after 1 January 2009 but before 1 July 2009. This version of AASB 138 has been compiled for the amending Standards applying to annual reporting periods beginning on or after 1 January 2009. This Standard applies to 31 December 2009 year ends and can be accessed from the AASB website at www.aasb.gov.au.

---

29 August 2011: AASB 2011-7 'Amendments to Australian Accounting Standards arising from the Consolidation and Joint Arrangements Standards' amends AASB 138 to give effect to many consequential changes arising from the issue of AASB 10, 11, 12, 127 and 128. This Standard applies to annual reporting periods beginning on or after 1 January 2013 and can be adopted early by for-profit entities. **These amendments are not included in this compiled Standard.**

5 September 2011: AASB 2011-8 'Amendments to Australian Accounting Standards arising from AASB 13' amends AASB 138 to give effect to a consequential change in the definition of fair value arising from the issue of AASB 13. This Standard applies to annual reporting periods beginning on or after 1 January 2013 and can be adopted early. **These amendments are not included in this compiled Standard.**

References

Interpretation 4 *Determining Whether an Arrangement Contains a Lease*, Interpretation 12 *Service Concession Arrangements*, Interpretation 129 *Service Concession Arrangements: Disclosures*, Interpretation 1031 *Accounting for the Goods and Services Tax (GST)*, Interpretation 132 *Intangible Assets – Web Site Costs* and Interpretation 1042 *Subscriber Acquisition Costs in the Telecommunications Industry* apply to AASB 138.

AASB item not taken onto the agenda: *Capitalised Software* applies to AASB 138.

IFRIC items not taken onto the agenda: No. 42 *Costs of acquiring or developing content for electronic databases*, No. 43 *Subscriber acquisition costs*, IAS 38-1 *Regulatory asset*, IAS 38-2 *Classification and accounting for SIM cards*, IAS 38-3 *Adoption of IAS 38 (revised 2004)*, IAS 38-6 *Compliance costs for REACH*, IAS 38-7 *Accounting for sales costs* and IAS 38-8 *Amortisation method* apply to AASB 138.

AASB 138 compared to IAS 38

Additions

Paragraph	Description
Aus 1.1	Which entities AASB 138 applies to (i.e. reporting entities and general purpose financial statements).
Aus 1.2	The application date of AASB 138 (i.e. annual reporting periods beginning 1 January 2005).
Aus 1.3	Prohibits early application of AASB 138.
Aus 1.4	Makes the requirements of AASB 138 subject to AASB 1031 'Materiality'.
Aus 1.5	Explains which Australian Standards have been superseded by AASB 138.
Aus 1.6	Clarifies that the superseded Australian Standards remain in force until AASB 138 applies.
Aus 1.7	Notice of the new Standard published on 22 July 2004.
Aus 24.1	Where a not-for-profit entity acquires an intangible asset at no cost or nominal cost its deemed cost for initial measurement is fair value at the date of acquisition.
Aus 85.1	Net revaluation increments are brought to account by class of asset for not-for-profit entities. The net increment is recognised to the asset revaluation reserve except to the extent that it represents a reversal of a prior net decrement for the class that was recognised in the profit or loss.
Aus 86.1	Net revaluation decrements are brought to account by class of asset for not-for-profit entities. The net decrement is recognised in the profit or loss except to the extent that it represents a reversal of a prior net increment for the class that was recognised directly to equity in the asset revaluation reserve.
Aus 86.2	Clarifies that revaluation decrements and revaluation increments for not-for-profit entities must not be offset if the assets are in different classes.
Aus 124.1	The requirement to disclose the costs of intangible assets measured under the revaluation model does not apply to not-for-profit entities.

AASB

Deletions

Paragraph	*Description*
129	Effective date and transitional provision of IAS 38 based on election in IFRS 3 'Business Combinations'.
130,130A, 130B	Effective date and transitional provision of IAS 38 in cases other than paragraph 129.
131	Explanation of what is means to apply IAS 38 requirements prospectively as set out in paragraph 129.
132	Application to transactions before required date is encouraged but IFRS 3 and IAS 36 'Impairment of Assets' must be applied at the same time.
133	Reference to superseded IAS 38.

Contents

Compilation Details

Comparison with IAS 38

**Accounting Standard
AASB 138 Intangible Assets**

Paragraphs

Objective	1
Application	Aus1.1 – 1.7
Scope	2 – 7
Definitions	8
Intangible Assets	9 – 10
Identifiability	11 – 12
Control	13 – 16
Future Economic Benefits	17
Recognition and Measurement	18 – Aus24.1
Separate Acquisition	25 – 32
Acquisition as Part of a Business Combination	33 – 34
Measuring the Fair Value of an Intangible Asset Acquired in a Business Combination	35 – 41
Subsequent Expenditure on an Acquired In-process Research and Development Project	42 – 43
Acquisition by way of a Government Grant	44
Exchanges of Assets	45 – 47
Internally Generated Goodwill	48 – 50
Internally Generated Intangible Assets	51 – 53
Research Phase	54 – 56
Development Phase	57 – 64
Cost of an Internally Generated Intangible Asset	65 – 67
Recognition of an Expense	68 – 70
Past Expenses not to be Recognised as an Asset	71
Measurement after Recognition	72 – 73
Cost Model	74
Revaluation Model	75 – 87
Useful Life	88 – 96
Intangible Assets with Finite Useful Lives	
Amortisation Period and Amortisation Method	97 – 99
Residual Value	100 – 103
Review of Amortisation Period and Amortisation Method	104 – 106
Intangible Assets with Indefinite Useful Lives	107 – 108
Review of Useful Life Assessment	109 – 110
Recoverability of the Carrying Amount – Impairment Losses	111
Retirements and Disposals	112 – 117
Disclosure	
General	118 – 123
Intangible Assets Measured after Recognition using the Revaluation Model	124 – 125
Research and Development Expenditure	126 – 127

Paragraphs

Other Information   128
Transitional Provisions and Effective Date   130C – 130E

Illustrative Examples
Assessing the Useful Lives of Intangible Assets

Basis for conclusions on IAS 38
(available on the AASB website)

Australian Accounting Standard AASB 138 *Intangible Assets* (as amended) is set out in paragraphs 1 – 130E.
All the paragraphs have equal authority. Terms defined in this Standard are in *italics* the first time they appear
in the Standard. AASB 138 is to be read in the context of other Australian Accounting Standards, including
AASB 1048 *Interpretation and Application of Standards*, which identifies the Australian Accounting
Interpretations. In the absence of explicit guidance, AASB 108 *Accounting Policies, Changes in Accounting
Estimates and Errors* provides a basis for selecting and applying accounting policies.

Compilation Details

Accounting Standard AASB 138 *Intangible Assets* as amended

This compiled Standard applies to annual reporting periods beginning on or after 1 July 2009.
It takes into account amendments up to and including 25 June 2009 and was prepared on
30 October 2009 by the staff of the Australian Accounting Standards Board (AASB).

This compilation is not a separate Accounting Standard made by the AASB. Instead, it is a
representation of AASB 138 (July 2004) as amended by other Accounting Standards, which are
listed in the Table below.

Table of Standards

Standard	Date made	Application date *(annual reporting periods ... on or after ...)*	Application, saving or transitional provisions
AASB 138	15 Jul 2004	*(beginning)* 1 Jan 2005	
AASB 2004-1	9 Dec 2004	*(beginning)* 1 Jan 2005	–
AASB 2007-4	30 Apr 2007	*(beginning)* 1 Jul 2007	see (a) below
AASB 2007-6	14 Jun 2007	*(beginning)* 1 Jan 2009	see (b) below
AASB 2007-8	24 Sep 2007	*(beginning)* 1 Jan 2009	see (c) below
AASB 2007-10	13 Dec 2007	*(beginning)* 1 Jan 2009	see (c) below
AASB 2008-3	6 Mar 2008	*(beginning)* 1 Jul 2009	see (d) below
AASB 2008-5	24 Jul 2008	*(beginning)* 1 Jan 2009	see (e) below
AASB 2009-4	21 May 2009	*(beginning)* 1 Jul 2009	see (f) below
AASB 2009-6	25 Jun 2009	*(beginning)* 1 Jan 2009 and *(ending)* 30 Jun 2009	see (g) below

(a)   Entities may elect to apply this Standard to annual reporting periods beginning on or after 1 January 2005 but
      before 1 July 2007.

(b)   Entities may elect to apply this Standard to annual reporting periods beginning on or after 1 January 2005 but
      before 1 January 2009, provided that AASB 123 *Borrowing Costs* (June 2007) is also applied to such periods.

(c)   Entities may elect to apply this Standard to annual reporting periods beginning on or after 1 January 2005
      but before 1 January 2009, provided that AASB 101 *Presentation of Financial Statements* (September 2007)
      is also applied to such periods.

(d)   Entities may elect to apply this Standard to annual reporting periods beginning on or after 30 June 2007
      but before 1 July 2009, provided that AASB 3 *Business Combinations* (March 2008) and AASB 127
      Consolidated and Separate Financial Statements (March 2008) are also applied to such periods.

AASB

(e) Entities may elect to apply this Standard, or its amendments to individual Standards, to annual reporting periods beginning on or after 1 January 2005 but before 1 January 2009.

(f) Entities may elect to apply this Standard, or its amendments to individual pronouncements, to annual reporting periods beginning on or after 1 January 2005 but before 1 July 2009.

(g) Entities may elect to apply this Standard to annual reporting periods beginning on or after 1 January 2005 but before 1 January 2009, provided that AASB 101 *Presentation of Financial Statements* (September 2007) is also applied to such periods, and to annual reporting periods beginning on or after 1 January 2009 that end before 30 June 2009.

Table of Amendments to Standard

Paragraph affected	How affected	By ... [paragraph]
Aus1.1	amended	AASB 2007-8 [7, 8]
Aus1.4	amended	AASB 2007-8 [8]
2	amended	AASB 2004-1 [8]
	amended	AASB 2007-4 [99]
3	amended	AASB 2007-4 [99]
8	amended	AASB 2007-8 [6]
	amended	AASB 2008-3 [70]
11	amended	AASB 2007-10 [89]
	amended	AASB 2008-3 [71]
12	amended	AASB 2008-3 [71]
25	amended	AASB 2008-3 [71]
28	amended	AASB 2007-4 [99]
32	amended	AASB 2007-6 [15]
33	amended	AASB 2007-4 [99]
	amended	AASB 2008-3 [71]
34-35	amended	AASB 2008-3 [71]
36-37	amended	AASB 2009-4 [10]
38	deleted	AASB 2008-3 [72]
40-41	amended	AASB 2009-4 [10]
44	amended	AASB 2007-4 [98]
66	amended	AASB 2007-4 [99]
67 (Example)	amended	AASB 2007-8 [6]
68	amended	AASB 2007-4 [99]
	amended	AASB 2008-3 [73]
69	amended	AASB 2007-4 [99]
	amended	AASB 2008-5 [60]
	amended	AASB 2008-3 [73]
69A	added	AASB 2008-5 [61]
70	amended	AASB 2008-5 [60]
73	amended	AASB 2007-10 [89]
75	amended	AASB 2007-8 [6]
83	amended	AASB 2007-4 [99]
85	amended	AASB 2007-8 [123]
Aus85.1	amended	AASB 2009-6 [85]
86	amended	AASB 2007-8 [123]
Aus86.1	amended	AASB 2009-6 [86]
87	amended	AASB 2007-8 [124]
	amended	AASB 2009-6 [87]
94	amended	AASB 2008-3 [74]
97	amended	AASB 2007-4 [99]

Paragraph affected	How affected	By ... [paragraph]
98	amended	AASB 2008-5 [60]
108	amended	AASB 2007-4 [99]
109	amended	AASB 2007-4 [99]
113	amended	AASB 2007-4 [99]
115A	added	AASB 2008-3 [75]
118	amended	AASB 2007-8 [6, 125]
119	amended	AASB 2007-10 [89]
122	amended	AASB 2007-10 [89]
124	amended	AASB 2009-6 [87]
129 (and preceding heading)	amended note amended	AASB 2008-5 [62] AASB 2008-3 [76]
130A	note added	AASB 2009-6 [88]
130B	note added	AASB 2007-8 [126]
130C	note added added	AASB 2008-3 [77] AASB 2009-4 [11]
130D	added	AASB 2008-5 [63]
130E	added	AASB 2009-4 [11]
131 (preceding heading)	added	AASB 2009-6 [89]
132 (preceding heading)	added	AASB 2009-6 [90]

Table of Amendments to Illustrative Examples

Paragraph affected	How affected	By ... [paragraph]
Examples 1-3	amended	AASB 2007-8 [6]

Comparison with IAS 38

AASB 138 and IAS 38

AASB 138 *Intangible Assets* as amended incorporates IAS 38 *Intangible Assets* as issued and amended by the International Accounting Standards Board (IASB). Paragraphs that have been added to this Standard (and do not appear in the text of IAS 38) are identified with the prefix "Aus", followed by the number of the preceding IASB paragraph and decimal numbering. Paragraphs that apply only to not-for-profit entities begin by identifying their limited applicability.

Compliance with IAS 38

For-profit entities that comply with AASB 138 as amended will simultaneously be in compliance with IAS 38 as amended.

Not-for-profit entities using the added "Aus" paragraphs in the Standard that specifically apply to not-for-profit entities may not be simultaneously complying with IAS 38. Whether a not-for-profit entity will be in compliance with IAS 38 will depend on whether the "Aus" paragraphs provide additional guidance for not-for-profit entities or contain requirements that are inconsistent with the corresponding IASB Standard and will be applied by the not-for-profit entity.

Accounting Standard AASB 138

The Australian Accounting Standards Board made Accounting Standard AASB 138 *Intangible Assets* under section 334 of the *Corporations Act 2001* on 15 July 2004.

This compiled version of AASB 138 applies to annual reporting periods beginning on or after 1 July 2009. It incorporates relevant amendments contained in other AASB Standards made by the AASB up to and including 25 June 2009 (see Compilation Details).

Accounting Standard AASB 138
Intangible Assets

Objective

1   The objective of this Standard is to prescribe the accounting treatment for *intangible assets* that are not dealt with specifically in another Standard. This Standard requires an entity to recognise an intangible asset if, and only if, specified criteria are met. The Standard also specifies how to measure the *carrying amount* of intangible assets and requires specified disclosures about intangible assets.

Application

Aus1.1   **This Standard applies to:**

     (a)   **each entity that is required to prepare financial reports in accordance with Part 2M.3 of the Corporations Act and that is a reporting entity;**

     (b)   **general purpose financial statements of each other reporting entity; and**

     (c)   **financial statements that are, or are held out to be, general purpose financial statements.**

Aus1.2   **This Standard applies to annual reporting periods beginning on or after 1 January 2005.**

     [Note: For application dates of paragraphs changed or added by an amending Standard, see Compilation Details.]

Aus1.3   **This Standard shall not be applied to annual reporting periods beginning before 1 January 2005.**

Aus1.4   **The requirements specified in this Standard apply to the financial statements where information resulting from their application is material in accordance with AASB 1031 *Materiality*.**

Aus1.5   **When applicable, this Standard supersedes the following, to the extent that they relate to the accounting for intangible assets:**

     (a)   **AASB 1010 *Recoverable Amount of Non-Current Assets* as notified in the *Commonwealth of Australia Gazette* No S 657, 24 December 1999;**

     (b)   **AASB 1011 *Accounting for Research and Development Costs* as notified in the *Commonwealth of Australia Gazette* No S 99, 29 May 1987;**

     (c)   **AASB 1013 *Accounting for Goodwill* as notified in the *Commonwealth of Australia Gazette* No S 206, 14 June 1996;**

     (d)   **AASB 1015 *Acquisitions of Assets* as notified in the *Commonwealth of Australia Gazette* No S 527, 5 November 1999;**

     (e)   **AASB 1021 *Depreciation* as notified in the *Commonwealth of Australia Gazette* No S 341, 29 August 1997;**

     (f)   **AASB 1041 *Revaluation of Non-Current Assets* as notified in the *Commonwealth of Australia Gazette* No S 294, 19 July 2001;**

     (g)   **AAS 4 *Depreciation* as issued in August 1997;**

     (h)   **AAS 10 *Recoverable Amount of Non-Current Assets* as issued in December 1999;**

     (i)   **AAS 13 *Accounting for Research and Development Costs* as issued in March 1983;**

     (j)   **AAS 18 *Accounting for Goodwill* as issued in June 1996; and**

     (k)   **AAS 21 *Acquisitions of Assets* as issued in November 1999.**

Aus1.6   Each of the Standards identified in Aus1.5(a)-(k) remain applicable until superseded by this Standard.

Aus1.7   Notice of this Standard was published in the *Commonwealth of Australia Gazette* No S 294, 22 July 2004.

Scope

2   This Standard shall be applied in accounting for intangible assets, except:

    (a)   intangible assets that are within the scope of another Australian Accounting Standard;

    (b)   financial assets, as defined in AASB 132 *Financial Instruments: Presentation*;

    (c)   the recognition and measurement of exploration and evaluation assets (see AASB 6 *Exploration for and Evaluation of Mineral Resources*); and

    (d)   expenditure on the development and extraction of minerals, oil, natural gas and similar non-regenerative resources.

3   If another Standard prescribes the accounting for a specific type of intangible asset, an entity applies that Standard instead of this Standard. For example, this Standard does not apply to:

    (a)   intangible assets held by an entity for sale in the ordinary course of business (see AASB 102 *Inventories* and AASB 111 *Construction Contracts*);

    (b)   deferred tax assets (see AASB 112 *Income Taxes*);

    (c)   leases that are within the scope of AASB 117 *Leases*;

    (d)   *assets* arising from employee benefits (see AASB 119 *Employee Benefits*);

    (e)   financial assets as defined in AASB 132. The recognition and measurement of some financial assets are covered by AASB 127 *Consolidated and Separate Financial Statements*, AASB 128 *Investments in Associates* and AASB 131 *Interests in Joint Ventures*;

    (f)   goodwill acquired in a business combination (see AASB 3 *Business Combinations*);

    (g)   deferred acquisition costs, and intangible assets, arising from an insurer's contractual rights under insurance contracts within the scope of AASB 4 *Insurance Contracts*. AASB 4 sets out specific disclosure requirements for those deferred acquisition costs but not for those intangible assets. Therefore, the disclosure requirements in this Standard apply to those intangible assets; and

    (h)   non-current intangible assets classified as held for sale (or included in a disposal group that is classified as held for sale) in accordance with AASB 5 *Non-current Assets Held for Sale and Discontinued Operations*.

4   Some intangible assets may be contained in or on a physical substance such as a compact disc (in the case of computer software), legal documentation (in the case of a licence or patent) or film. In determining whether an asset that incorporates both intangible and tangible elements should be treated under AASB 116 *Property, Plant and Equipment* or as an intangible asset under this Standard, an entity uses judgement to assess which element is more significant. For example, computer software for a computer-controlled machine tool that cannot operate without that specific software is an integral part of the related hardware and it is treated as property, plant and equipment. The same applies to the operating system of a computer. When the software is not an integral part of the related hardware, computer software is treated as an intangible asset.

5   This Standard applies to, among other things, expenditure on advertising, training, start-up, *research and development* activities. Research and development activities are directed to the development of knowledge. Therefore, although these activities may result in an asset with physical substance (e.g. a prototype), the physical element of the asset is secondary to its intangible component, that is, the knowledge embodied in it.

6   In the case of a finance lease, the underlying asset may be either tangible or intangible. After initial recognition, a lessee accounts for an intangible asset held under a finance lease in accordance with this Standard. Rights under licensing agreements for items such as motion picture films, video recordings, plays, manuscripts, patents and copyrights are excluded from the scope of AASB 117 and are within the scope of this Standard.

7   Exclusions from the scope of a Standard may occur if activities or transactions are so specialised that they give rise to accounting issues that may need to be dealt with in a different way. Such issues arise in the accounting for expenditure on the exploration for, or development and extraction of, oil, gas and mineral deposits in extractive industries and

in the case of insurance contracts. Therefore, this Standard does not apply to expenditure on such activities and contracts. However, this Standard applies to other intangible assets used (such as computer software), and other expenditure incurred (such as start-up costs), in extractive industries or by insurers.

Definitions

8   **The following terms are used in this Standard with the meanings specified.**

An *active market* is a market in which all the following conditions exist:

(a)   the items traded in the market are homogeneous;

(b)   willing buyers and sellers can normally be found at any time; and

(c)   prices are available to the public.

Amortisation is the systematic allocation of the depreciable amount of an intangible asset over its useful life.

An *asset* is a resource:

(a)   controlled by an entity as a result of past events; and

(b)   from which future economic benefits are expected to flow to the entity.

Carrying amount is the amount at which an asset is recognised in the statement of financial position after deducting any accumulated amortisation and accumulated impairment losses thereon.

Cost is the amount of cash or cash equivalents paid or the fair value of other consideration given to acquire an asset at the time of its acquisition or construction, or, when applicable, the amount attributed to that asset when initially recognised in accordance with the specific requirements of other Australian Accounting Standards, for example AASB 2 Share-based Payment.

Depreciable amount is the cost of an asset, or other amount substituted for cost, less its residual value.

Development is the application of research findings or other knowledge to a plan or design for the production of new or substantially improved materials, devices, products, processes, systems or services before the start of commercial production or use.

Entity-specific value is the present value of the cash flows an entity expects to arise from the continuing use of an asset and from its disposal at the end of its useful life or expects to incur when settling a liability.

Fair value of an asset is the amount for which that asset could be exchanged between knowledgeable, willing parties in an arm's length transaction.

An *impairment loss* is the amount by which the carrying amount of an asset exceeds its recoverable amount.

An *intangible asset* is an identifiable non-monetary asset without physical substance.

Monetary assets are money held and assets to be received in fixed or determinable amounts of money.

Research is original and planned investigation undertaken with the prospect of gaining new scientific or technical knowledge and understanding.

The *residual value* of an intangible asset is the estimated amount that an entity would currently obtain from disposal of the asset, after deducting the estimated costs of disposal, if the asset were already of the age and in the condition expected at the end of its useful life.

Useful life is:

(a)   the period over which an asset is expected to be available for use by an entity; or

(b)   the number of production or similar units expected to be obtained from the asset by an entity.

Intangible Assets

9   Entities frequently expend resources, or incur liabilities, on the acquisition, development, maintenance or enhancement of intangible resources such as scientific or technical knowledge, design and implementation of new processes or systems, licences, intellectual property, market knowledge and trademarks (including brand names and publishing titles). Common examples of items encompassed by these broad headings are computer software, patents, copyrights, motion picture films, customer lists, mortgage servicing rights, fishing licences, import quotas, franchises, customer or supplier relationships, customer loyalty, market share and marketing rights.

10   Not all the items described in paragraph 9 meet the definition of an intangible asset, that is, identifiability, control over a resource and existence of future economic benefits. If an item within the scope of this Standard does not meet the definition of an intangible asset, expenditure to acquire it or generate it internally is recognised as an expense when it is incurred. However, if the item is acquired in a business combination, it forms part of the goodwill recognised at the acquisition date (see paragraph 68).

Identifiability

11   The definition of an intangible asset requires an intangible asset to be identifiable to distinguish it from goodwill. Goodwill recognised in a business combination is an asset representing the future economic benefits arising from other assets acquired in a business combination that are not individually identified and separately recognised. The future economic benefits may result from synergy between the identifiable assets acquired or from assets that, individually, do not qualify for recognition in the financial statements.

12   An asset is identifiable if it either:

   (a)   is separable, i.e. is capable of being separated or divided from the entity and sold, transferred, licensed, rented or exchanged, either individually or together with a related contract, identifiable asset or liability, regardless of whether the entity intends to do so; or

   (b)   arises from contractual or other legal rights, regardless of whether those rights are transferable or separable from the entity or from other rights and obligations.

Control

13   An entity controls an asset if the entity has the power to obtain the future economic benefits flowing from the underlying resource and to restrict the access of others to those benefits. The capacity of an entity to control the future economic benefits from an intangible asset would normally stem from legal rights that are enforceable in a court of law. In the absence of legal rights, it is more difficult to demonstrate control. However, legal enforceability of a right is not a necessary condition for control because an entity may be able to control the future economic benefits in some other way.

14   Market and technical knowledge may give rise to future economic benefits. An entity controls those benefits if, for example, the knowledge is protected by legal rights such as copyrights, a restraint of trade agreement (where permitted) or by a legal duty on employees to maintain confidentiality.

15   An entity may have a team of skilled staff and may be able to identify incremental staff skills leading to future economic benefits from training. The entity may also expect that the staff will continue to make their skills available to the entity. However, an entity usually has insufficient control over the expected future economic benefits arising from a team of skilled staff and from training for these items to meet the definition of an intangible asset. For a similar reason, specific management or technical talent is unlikely to meet the definition of an intangible asset, unless it is protected by legal rights to use it and to obtain the future economic benefits expected from it, and it also meets the other parts of the definition.

16   An entity may have a portfolio of customers or a market share and expect that, because of its efforts in building customer relationships and loyalty, the customers will continue to trade with the entity. However, in the absence of legal rights to protect, or other ways to control, the relationships with customers or the loyalty of the customers to the entity, the

entity usually has insufficient control over the expected economic benefits from customer relationships and loyalty for such items (e.g. portfolio of customers, market shares, customer relationships and customer loyalty) to meet the definition of intangible assets. In the absence of legal rights to protect customer relationships, exchange transactions for the same or similar non-contractual customer relationships (other than as part of a business combination) provide evidence that the entity is nonetheless able to control the expected future economic benefits flowing from the customer relationships. Because such exchange transactions also provide evidence that the customer relationships are separable, those customer relationships meet the definition of an intangible asset.

Future Economic Benefits

17   The future economic benefits flowing from an intangible asset may include revenue from the sale of products or services, cost savings, or other benefits resulting from the use of the asset by the entity. For example, the use of intellectual property in a production process may reduce future production costs rather than increase future revenues.

Recognition and Measurement

18   The recognition of an item as an intangible asset requires an entity to demonstrate that the item meets:

(a)   the definition of an intangible asset (see paragraphs 8-17); and

(b)   the recognition criteria (see paragraphs 21-23).

This requirement applies to costs incurred initially to acquire or internally generate an intangible asset and those incurred subsequently to add to, replace part of, or service it.

19   Paragraphs 25-32 deal with the application of the recognition criteria to separately acquired intangible assets, and paragraphs 33-43 deal with their application to intangible assets acquired in a business combination. Paragraph 44 deals with the initial measurement of intangible assets acquired by way of a government grant, paragraphs 45-47 with exchanges of intangible assets, and paragraphs 48-50 with the treatment of internally generated goodwill. Paragraphs 51-67 deal with the initial recognition and measurement of internally generated intangible assets.

20   The nature of intangible assets is such that, in many cases, there are no additions to such an asset or replacements of part of it. Accordingly, most subsequent expenditures are likely to maintain the expected future economic benefits embodied in an existing intangible asset rather than meet the definition of an intangible asset and the recognition criteria in this Standard. In addition, it is often difficult to attribute subsequent expenditure directly to a particular intangible asset rather than to the business as a whole. Therefore, only rarely will subsequent expenditure – expenditure incurred after the initial recognition of an acquired intangible asset or after completion of an internally generated intangible asset – be recognised in the carrying amount of an asset. Consistently with paragraph 63, subsequent expenditure on brands, mastheads, publishing titles, customer lists and items similar in substance (whether externally acquired or internally generated) is always recognised in profit or loss as incurred. This is because such expenditure cannot be distinguished from expenditure to develop the business as a whole.

21   **An intangible asset shall be recognised if, and only if:**

(a)   **it is probable that the expected future economic benefits that are attributable to the asset will flow to the entity; and**

(b)   **the *cost* of the asset can be measured reliably.**

22   **An entity shall assess the probability of expected future economic benefits using reasonable and supportable assumptions that represent management's best estimate of the set of economic conditions that will exist over the *useful life* of the asset.**

23   An entity uses judgement to assess the degree of certainty attached to the flow of future economic benefits that are attributable to the use of the asset on the basis of the evidence available at the time of initial recognition, giving greater weight to external evidence.

24   **An intangible asset shall be measured initially at cost.**

Aus24.1   **Notwithstanding paragraph 24, in respect of not-for-profit entities, where an asset is acquired at no cost, or for a nominal cost, the cost is its *fair value* as at the date of acquisition.**

Separate Acquisition

25   Normally, the price an entity pays to acquire separately an intangible asset will reflect expectations about the probability that the expected future economic benefits embodied in the asset will flow to the entity. In other words, the entity expects there to be an inflow of economic benefits, even if there is uncertainty about the timing or the amount of the inflow. Therefore, the probability recognition criterion in paragraph 21(a) is always considered to be satisfied for separately acquired intangible assets.

26   In addition, the cost of a separately acquired intangible asset can usually be measured reliably. This is particularly so when the purchase consideration is in the form of cash or other *monetary assets*.

27   The cost of a separately acquired intangible asset comprises:

   (a)   its purchase price, including import duties and non-refundable purchase taxes, after deducting trade discounts and rebates; and

   (b)   any directly attributable cost of preparing the asset for its intended use.

28   Examples of directly attributable costs are:

   (a)   costs of employee benefits (as defined in AASB 119) arising directly from bringing the asset to its working condition;

   (b)   professional fees arising directly from bringing the asset to its working condition; and

   (c)   costs of testing whether the asset is functioning properly.

29   Examples of expenditures that are not part of the cost of an intangible asset are:

   (a)   costs of introducing a new product or service (including costs of advertising and promotional activities);

   (b)   costs of conducting business in a new location or with a new class of customer (including costs of staff training); and

   (c)   administration and other general overhead costs.

30   Recognition of costs in the carrying amount of an intangible asset ceases when the asset is in the condition necessary for it to be capable of operating in the manner intended by management. Therefore, costs incurred in using or redeploying an intangible asset are not included in the carrying amount of that asset. For example, the following costs are not included in the carrying amount of an intangible asset:

   (a)   costs incurred while an asset capable of operating in the manner intended by management has yet to be brought into use; and

   (b)   initial operating losses, such as those incurred while demand for the asset's output builds up.

31   Some operations occur in connection with the development of an intangible asset, but are not necessary to bring the asset to the condition necessary for it to be capable of operating in the manner intended by management. These incidental operations may occur before or during the development activities. Because incidental operations are not necessary to bring an asset to the condition necessary for it to be capable of operating in the manner intended by management, the income and related expenses of incidental operations are recognised immediately in profit or loss, and included in their respective classifications of income and expense.

32   If payment for an intangible asset is deferred beyond normal credit terms, its cost is the cash price equivalent. The difference between this amount and the total payments is recognised as interest expense over the period of credit unless it is capitalised in accordance with AASB 123 *Borrowing Costs*.

Acquisition as Part of a Business Combination

33   In accordance with AASB 3 *Business Combinations* (as revised in March 2008), if an intangible asset is acquired in a business combination, the cost of that intangible asset is its fair value at the acquisition date. The fair value of an intangible asset will reflect expectations about the probability that the expected future economic benefits embodied in the asset will flow to the entity. In other words, the entity expects there to be an inflow of economic benefits, even if there is uncertainty about the timing or the amount of the inflow. Therefore, the probability recognition criterion in paragraph 21(a) is always considered to be satisfied for intangible assets acquired in business combinations. If an asset acquired in a business combination is separable or arises from contractual or other legal rights, sufficient information exists to measure reliably the fair value of the asset. Thus, the reliable measurement criterion in paragraph 21(b) is always considered to be satisfied for intangible assets acquired in business combinations.

34   In accordance with this Standard and AASB 3 (as revised in March 2008), an acquirer recognises at the acquisition date, separately from goodwill, an intangible asset of the acquiree, irrespective of whether the asset had been recognised by the acquiree before the business combination. This means that the acquirer recognises as an asset separately from goodwill an in-process research and development project of the acquiree if the project meets the definition of an intangible asset. An acquiree's in-process research and development project meets the definition of an intangible asset when it:

(a)   meets the definition of an asset; and

(b)   is identifiable, i.e. is separable or arises from contractual or other legal rights.

Measuring the Fair Value of an Intangible Asset Acquired in a Business Combination

35   If an intangible asset acquired in a business combination is separable or arises from contractual or other legal rights, sufficient information exists to measure reliably the fair value of the asset. When, for the estimates used to measure an intangible asset's fair value, there is a range of possible outcomes with different probabilities, that uncertainty enters into the measurement of the asset's fair value.

36   An intangible asset acquired in a business combination might be separable, but only together with a related contract, identifiable asset or liability. In such cases, the acquirer recognises the intangible asset separately from goodwill, but together with the related item.

37   The acquirer may recognise a group of complementary intangible assets as a single asset provided the individual assets in the group have similar useful lives. For example, the terms 'brand' and 'brand name' are often used as synonyms for trademarks and other marks. However, the former are general marketing terms that are typically used to refer to a group of complementary assets such as a trademark (or service mark) and its related trade name, formulas, recipes and technological expertise.

38   [Deleted by the IASB]

39   Quoted market prices in an *active market* provide the most reliable estimate of the fair value of an intangible asset (see also paragraph 78). The appropriate market price is usually the current bid price. If current bid prices are unavailable, the price of the most recent similar transaction may provide a basis from which to estimate fair value, provided that there has not been a significant change in economic circumstances between the transaction date and the date at which the asset's fair value is estimated.

40   If no active market exists for an intangible asset, its fair value is the amount that the entity would have paid for the asset, at the acquisition date, in an arm's length transaction between knowledgeable and willing parties, on the basis of the best information available. In determining this amount, an entity considers the outcome of recent transactions for similar assets. For example, an entity may apply multiples reflecting current market transactions to factors that drive the profitability of the asset (such as revenue, operating profit or earnings before interest, tax, depreciation and amortisation).

41   Entities that are involved in the purchase and sale of intangible assets may have developed techniques for estimating their fair values indirectly. These techniques may be used for initial measurement of an intangible asset acquired in a business combination if their

objective is to estimate fair value and if they reflect current transactions and practices in the industry to which the asset belongs. These techniques include, for example:

(a)   discounting estimated future net cash flows from the asset; or

(b)   estimating the costs the entity avoids by owning the intangible asset and not needing:

   (i)   to license it from another party in an arm's length transaction (as in the 'relief from royalty' approach, using discounted net cash flows); or

   (ii)   to recreate or replace it (as in the cost approach).

Subsequent Expenditure on an Acquired In-process Research and Development Project

42   Research or development expenditure that:

(a)   relates to an in-process research or development project acquired separately or in a business combination and recognised as an intangible asset; and

(b)   is incurred after the acquisition of that project,

shall be accounted for in accordance with paragraphs 54-62.

43   Applying the requirements in paragraphs 54-62 means that subsequent expenditure on an in-process research or development project acquired separately or in a business combination and recognised as an intangible asset is:

(a)   recognised as an expense when incurred if it is research expenditure;

(b)   recognised as an expense when incurred if it is development expenditure that does not satisfy the criteria for recognition as an intangible asset in paragraph 57; and

(c)   added to the carrying amount of the acquired in-process research or development project if it is development expenditure that satisfies the recognition criteria in paragraph 57.

Acquisition by way of a Government Grant

44   In some cases, an intangible asset may be acquired free of charge, or for nominal consideration, by way of a government grant. This may happen when a government transfers or allocates to an entity intangible assets such as airport landing rights, licences to operate radio or television stations, import licences or quotas or rights to access other restricted resources. In accordance with AASB 120 *Accounting for Government Grants and Disclosure of Government Assistance*, an entity may choose to recognise both the intangible asset and the grant initially at fair value.[1] If an entity chooses not to recognise the asset initially at fair value, the entity recognises the asset initially at a nominal amount (the other treatment permitted by AASB 120) plus any expenditure that is directly attributable to preparing the asset for its intended use.

Exchanges of Assets

45   One or more intangible assets may be acquired in exchange for a non-monetary asset or assets, or a combination of monetary and non-monetary assets. The following discussion refers simply to an exchange of one non-monetary asset for another, but it also applies to all exchanges described in the preceding sentence. The cost of such an intangible asset is measured at fair value unless (a) the exchange transaction lacks commercial substance or (b) the fair value of neither the asset received nor the asset given up is reliably measurable. The acquired asset is measured in this way even if an entity cannot immediately derecognise the asset given up. If the acquired asset is not measured at fair value, its cost is measured at the carrying amount of the asset given up.

46   An entity determines whether an exchange transaction has commercial substance by considering the extent to which its future cash flows are expected to change as a result of the transaction. An exchange transaction has commercial substance if:

---

1   AASB 120 only applies to for-profit entities. Not-for-profit entities are required to recognise the intangible asset and the grant initially at fair value in accordance with AASB 1004 *Contributions*.

(a) the configuration (i.e. risk, timing and amount) of the cash flows of the asset received differs from the configuration of the cash flows of the asset transferred; or

(b) the *entity-specific value* of the portion of the entity's operations affected by the transaction changes as a result of the exchange; and

(c) the difference in (a) or (b) is significant relative to the fair value of the assets exchanged.

For the purpose of determining whether an exchange transaction has commercial substance, the entity-specific value of the portion of the entity's operations affected by the transaction shall reflect post-tax cash flows. The result of these analyses may be clear without an entity having to perform detailed calculations.

47 Paragraph 21(b) specifies that a condition for the recognition of an intangible asset is that the cost of the asset can be measured reliably. The fair value of an intangible asset for which comparable market transactions do not exist is reliably measurable if (a) the variability in the range of reasonable fair value estimates is not significant for that asset or (b) the probabilities of the various estimates within the range can be reasonably assessed and used in estimating fair value. If an entity is able to determine reliably the fair value of either the asset received or the asset given up, then the fair value of the asset given up is used to measure cost unless the fair value of the asset received is more clearly evident.

Internally Generated Goodwill

48 **Internally generated goodwill shall not be recognised as an asset.**

49 In some cases, expenditure is incurred to generate future economic benefits, but it does not result in the creation of an intangible asset that meets the recognition criteria in this Standard. Such expenditure is often described as contributing to internally generated goodwill. Internally generated goodwill is not recognised as an asset because it is not an identifiable resource (i.e. it is not separable nor does it arise from contractual or other legal rights) controlled by the entity that can be measured reliably at cost.

50 Differences between the market value of an entity and the carrying amount of its identifiable net assets at any time may capture a range of factors that affect the value of the entity. However, such differences do not represent the cost of intangible assets controlled by the entity.

Internally Generated Intangible Assets

51 It is sometimes difficult to assess whether an internally generated intangible asset qualifies for recognition because of problems in:

(a) identifying whether and when there is an identifiable asset that will generate expected future economic benefits; and

(b) determining the cost of the asset reliably. In some cases, the cost of generating an intangible asset internally cannot be distinguished from the cost of maintaining or enhancing the entity's internally generated goodwill or of running day-to-day operations.

Therefore, in addition to complying with the general requirements for the recognition and initial measurement of an intangible asset, an entity applies the requirements and guidance in paragraphs 52-67 to all internally generated intangible assets.

52 To assess whether an internally generated intangible asset meets the criteria for recognition, an entity classifies the generation of the asset into:

(a) a research phase; and

(b) a development phase.

Although the terms 'research' and 'development' are defined, the terms 'research phase' and 'development phase' have a broader meaning for the purpose of this Standard.

53 If an entity cannot distinguish the research phase from the development phase of an internal project to create an intangible asset, the entity treats the expenditure on that project as if it were incurred in the research phase only.

Research Phase

54   No intangible asset arising from research (or from the research phase of an internal project) shall be recognised. Expenditure on research (or on the research phase of an internal project) shall be recognised as an expense when it is incurred.

55   In the research phase of an internal project, an entity cannot demonstrate that an intangible asset exists that will generate probable future economic benefits. Therefore, this expenditure is recognised as an expense when it is incurred.

56   Examples of research activities are:

    (a)   activities aimed at obtaining new knowledge;

    (b)   the search for, evaluation and final selection of, applications of research findings or other knowledge;

    (c)   the search for alternatives for materials, devices, products, processes, systems or services; and

    (d)   the formulation, design, evaluation and final selection of possible alternatives for new or improved materials, devices, products, processes, systems or services.

Development Phase

57   An intangible asset arising from development (or from the development phase of an internal project) shall be recognised if, and only if, an entity can demonstrate all of the following:

    (a)   the technical feasibility of completing the intangible asset so that it will be available for use or sale;

    (b)   its intention to complete the intangible asset and use or sell it;

    (c)   its ability to use or sell the intangible asset;

    (d)   how the intangible asset will generate probable future economic benefits. Among other things, the entity can demonstrate the existence of a market for the output of the intangible asset or the intangible asset itself or, if it is to be used internally, the usefulness of the intangible asset;

    (e)   the availability of adequate technical, financial and other resources to complete the development and to use or sell the intangible asset; and

    (f)   its ability to measure reliably the expenditure attributable to the intangible asset during its development.

58   In the development phase of an internal project, an entity can, in some instances, identify an intangible asset and demonstrate that the asset will generate probable future economic benefits. This is because the development phase of a project is further advanced than the research phase.

59   Examples of development activities are:

    (a)   the design, construction and testing of pre-production or pre-use prototypes and models;

    (b)   the design of tools, jigs, moulds and dies involving new technology;

    (c)   the design, construction and operation of a pilot plant that is not of a scale economically feasible for commercial production; and

    (d)   the design, construction and testing of a chosen alternative for new or improved materials, devices, products, processes, systems or services.

60   To demonstrate how an intangible asset will generate probable future economic benefits, an entity assesses the future economic benefits to be received from the asset using the principles in AASB 136 *Impairment of Assets*. If the asset will generate economic benefits only in combination with other assets, the entity applies the concept of cash-generating units in AASB 136.

61   Availability of resources to complete, use and obtain the benefits from an intangible asset can be demonstrated by, for example, a business plan showing the technical, financial and

other resources needed and the entity's ability to secure those resources. In some cases, an entity demonstrates the availability of external finance by obtaining a lender's indication of its willingness to fund the plan.

62   An entity's costing systems can often measure reliably the cost of generating an intangible asset internally, such as salary and other expenditure incurred in securing copyrights or licences or developing computer software.

63   **Internally generated brands, mastheads, publishing titles, customer lists and items similar in substance shall not be recognised as intangible assets.**

64   Expenditure on internally generated brands, mastheads, publishing titles, customer lists and items similar in substance cannot be distinguished from the cost of developing the business as a whole. Therefore, such items are not recognised as intangible assets.

Cost of an Internally Generated Intangible Asset

65   The cost of an internally generated intangible asset for the purpose of paragraph 24 is the sum of expenditure incurred from the date when the intangible asset first meets the recognition criteria in paragraphs 21, 22 and 57. Paragraph 71 prohibits reinstatement of expenditure previously recognised as an expense.

66   The cost of an internally generated intangible asset comprises all directly attributable costs necessary to create, produce, and prepare the asset to be capable of operating in the manner intended by management. Examples of directly attributable costs are:

(a)   costs of materials and services used or consumed in generating the intangible asset;

(b)   costs of employee benefits (as defined in AASB 119) arising from the generation of the intangible asset;

(c)   fees to register a legal right; and

(d)   amortisation of patents and licences that are used to generate the intangible asset.

AASB 123 specifies criteria for the recognition of interest as an element of the cost of an internally generated intangible asset.

67   The following are not components of the cost of an internally generated intangible asset:

(a)   selling, administrative and other general overhead expenditure unless this expenditure can be directly attributed to preparing the asset for use;

(b)   identified inefficiencies and initial operating losses incurred before the asset achieves planned performance; and

(c)   expenditure on training staff to operate the asset.

Example illustrating paragraph 65

An entity is developing a new production process. During 20X5, expenditure incurred was CU1,000,[2] of which CU900 was incurred before 1 December 20X5 and CU100 was incurred between 1 December 20X5 and 31 December 20X5. The entity is able to demonstrate that, at 1 December 20X5, the production process met the criteria for recognition as an intangible asset. The recoverable amount of the know-how embodied in the process (including future cash outflows to complete the process before it is available for use) is estimated to be CU500.

At the end of 20X5, the production process is recognised as an intangible asset at a cost of CU100 (expenditure incurred since the date when the recognition criteria were met, i.e. 1 December 20X5). The CU900 expenditure incurred before 1 December 20X5 is recognised as an expense because the recognition criteria were not met until 1 December 20X5. This expenditure does not form part of the cost of the production process recognised in the statement of financial position.

During 20X6, expenditure incurred is CU2,000. At the end of 20X6, the recoverable amount of the know-how embodied in the process (including future cash outflows to complete the process before it is available for use) is estimated to be CU1,900.

At the end of 20X6, the cost of the production process is CU2,100 (CU100 expenditure recognised at the end of 20X5 plus CU2,000 expenditure recognised in 20X6). The entity recognises an impairment loss of CU200 to adjust the carrying amount of the process before impairment loss (CU2,100) to its recoverable amount (CU1,900). This impairment loss will be reversed in a subsequent period if the requirements for the reversal of an impairment loss in AASB 136 are met.

---

2   In this Standard, monetary amounts are denominated in 'currency units' (CU).

Recognition of an Expense

68   Expenditure on an intangible item shall be recognised as an expense when it is incurred unless:

(a)   it forms part of the cost of an intangible asset that meets the recognition criteria (see paragraphs 18-67); or

(b)   the item is acquired in a business combination and cannot be recognised as an intangible asset. If this is the case, it forms part of the amount recognised as goodwill at the acquisition date (see AASB 3).

69   In some cases, expenditure is incurred to provide future economic benefits to an entity, but no intangible asset or other asset is acquired or created that can be recognised. In these cases, the expenditure is recognised as an expense when it is incurred. For example, expenditure on research is recognised as an expense when it is incurred (see paragraph 54), except when it forms part of a business combination. Other examples of expenditure that is recognised as an expense when it is incurred include:

(a)   expenditure on start-up activities (i.e. start-up costs), unless this expenditure is included in the cost of an item of property, plant and equipment in accordance with AASB 116. Start-up costs may consist of establishment costs such as legal and secretarial costs incurred in establishing a legal entity, expenditure to open a new facility or business (i.e. pre-opening costs) or expenditures for starting new operations or launching new products or processes (i.e. pre-operating costs);

(b)   expenditure on training activities;

(c)   expenditure on advertising and promotional activities (including mail order catalogues);

(d)   expenditure on relocating or reorganising part or all of an entity.

69A   An entity has a right to access goods when it owns them. Similarly, it has a right to access goods when they have been constructed by a supplier in accordance with the terms of a supply contract and the entity could demand delivery of them in return for payment. Services are received when they are performed by a supplier in accordance with a contract to deliver them to the entity and not when the entity uses them to deliver another service, for example, to deliver an advertisement to customers.

70   Paragraph 68 does not preclude an entity from recognising a prepayment as an asset when payment for goods has been made in advance of the entity obtaining a right to access those goods. Similarly, paragraph 68 does not preclude an entity from recognising a prepayment as an asset when payment for services has been made in advance of the entity receiving those services.

Past Expenses not to be Recognised as an Asset

71   Expenditure on an intangible item that was initially recognised as an expense shall not be recognised as part of the cost of an intangible asset at a later date.

Measurement after Recognition

72   An entity shall choose either the cost model in paragraph 74 or the revaluation model in paragraph 75 as its accounting policy. If an intangible asset is accounted for using the revaluation model, all the other assets in its class shall also be accounted for using the same model, unless there is no active market for those assets.

73   A class of intangible assets is a grouping of assets of a similar nature and use in an entity's operations. The items within a class of intangible assets are revalued simultaneously to avoid selective revaluation of assets and the reporting of amounts in the financial statements representing a mixture of costs and values as at different dates.

Cost Model

74   After initial recognition, an intangible asset shall be carried at its cost less any accumulated amortisation and any accumulated *impairment losses*.

Revaluation Model

75   After initial recognition, an intangible asset shall be carried at a revalued amount, being its fair value at the date of the revaluation less any subsequent accumulated amortisation and any subsequent accumulated impairment losses. For the purpose of revaluations under this Standard, fair value shall be determined by reference to an active market. Revaluations shall be made with such regularity that at the end of the reporting period the carrying amount of the asset does not differ materially from its fair value.

76   The revaluation model does not allow:

(a)   the revaluation of intangible assets that have not previously been recognised as assets; or

(b)   the initial recognition of intangible assets at amounts other than cost.

77   The revaluation model is applied after an asset has been initially recognised at cost. However, if only part of the cost of an intangible asset is recognised as an asset because the asset did not meet the criteria for recognition until part of the way through the process (see paragraph 65), the revaluation model may be applied to the whole of that asset.

78   It is uncommon for an active market with the characteristics described in paragraph 8 to exist for an intangible asset, although this may happen. For example, in some jurisdictions, an active market may exist for freely transferable taxi licences, fishing licences or production quotas. However, an active market cannot exist for brands, newspaper mastheads, music and film publishing rights, patents or trademarks, because each such asset is unique. Also, although intangible assets are bought and sold, contracts are negotiated between individual buyers and sellers, and transactions are relatively infrequent. For these reasons, the price paid for one asset may not provide sufficient evidence of the fair value of another. Moreover, prices are often not available to the public.

79   The frequency of revaluations depends on the volatility of the fair values of the intangible assets being revalued. If the fair value of a revalued asset differs materially from its carrying amount, a further revaluation is necessary. Some intangible assets may experience significant and volatile movements in fair value, thus necessitating annual revaluation. Such frequent revaluations are unnecessary for intangible assets with only insignificant movements in fair value.

80   If an intangible asset is revalued, any accumulated amortisation at the date of the revaluation is either:

(a)   restated proportionately with the change in the gross carrying amount of the asset so that the carrying amount of the asset after revaluation equals its revalued amount; or

(b)   eliminated against the gross carrying amount of the asset and the net amount restated to the revalued amount of the asset.

81   If an intangible asset in a class of revalued intangible assets cannot be revalued because there is no active market for this asset, the asset shall be carried at its cost less any accumulated amortisation and impairment losses.

82   If the fair value of a revalued intangible asset can no longer be determined by reference to an active market, the carrying amount of the asset shall be its revalued amount at the date of the last revaluation by reference to the active market less any subsequent accumulated amortisation and any subsequent accumulated impairment losses.

83   The fact that an active market no longer exists for a revalued intangible asset may indicate that the asset may be impaired and that it needs to be tested in accordance with AASB 136.

84   If the fair value of the asset can be determined by reference to an active market at a subsequent measurement date, the revaluation model is applied from that date.

85   If an intangible asset's carrying amount is increased as a result of a revaluation, the increase shall be recognised in other comprehensive income and accumulated in equity under the heading of revaluation surplus. However, the increase shall be recognised

in profit or loss to the extent that it reverses a revaluation decrease of the same asset previously recognised in profit or loss.

Aus85.1   Notwithstanding paragraph 85, in respect of not-for-profit entities, if the carrying amount of a class of assets is increased as a result of a revaluation, the net revaluation increase shall be recognised in other comprehensive income and accumulated in equity under the heading of revaluation surplus. However, the net revaluation increase shall be recognised in profit or loss to the extent that it reverses a net revaluation decrease of the same class of assets previously recognised in profit or loss.

86   If an intangible asset's carrying amount is decreased as a result of a revaluation, the decrease shall be recognised in profit or loss. However, the decrease shall be recognised in other comprehensive income to the extent of any credit balance in the revaluation surplus in respect of that asset. The decrease recognised in other comprehensive income reduces the amount accumulated in equity under the heading of revaluation surplus.

Aus86.1   Notwithstanding paragraph 86, in respect of not-for-profit entities, if the carrying amount of a class of assets decreased as a result of a revaluation, the net revaluation decrease shall be recognised in profit or loss. However, the net revaluation decrease shall be recognised in other comprehensive income to the extent of any credit balance existing in any revaluation surplus in respect of that same class of assets. The net revaluation decrease recognised in other comprehensive income reduces the amount accumulated in equity under the heading of revaluation surplus.

Aus86.2   In respect of not-for-profit entities, revaluation increases and revaluation decreases relating to individual assets within a class of intangible assets shall be offset against one another within that class but shall not be offset in respect of assets in different classes.

87   The cumulative revaluation surplus included in equity may be transferred directly to retained earnings when the surplus is realised. The whole surplus may be realised on the retirement or disposal of the asset. However, some of the surplus may be realised as the asset is used by the entity; in such a case, the amount of the surplus realised is the difference between amortisation based on the revalued carrying amount of the asset and amortisation that would have been recognised based on the asset's historical cost. The transfer from revaluation surplus to retained earnings is not made through profit or loss.

Useful Life

88   An entity shall assess whether the useful life of an intangible asset is finite or indefinite and, if finite, the length of, or number of production or similar units constituting, that useful life. An intangible asset shall be regarded by the entity as having an indefinite useful life when, based on an analysis of all of the relevant factors, there is no foreseeable limit to the period over which the asset is expected to generate net cash inflows for the entity.

89   The accounting for an intangible asset is based on its useful life. An intangible asset with a finite useful life is amortised (see paragraphs 97-106), and an intangible asset with an indefinite useful life is not (see paragraphs 107-110). The Illustrative Examples accompanying this Standard illustrate the determination of useful life for different intangible assets, and the subsequent accounting for those assets based on the useful life determinations.

90   Many factors are considered in determining the useful life of an intangible asset, including:

   (a)   the expected usage of the asset by the entity and whether the asset could be managed efficiently by another management team;

   (b)   typical product life cycles for the asset and public information on estimates of useful lives of similar assets that are used in a similar way;

   (c)   technical, technological, commercial or other types of obsolescence;

(d)   the stability of the industry in which the asset operates and changes in the market demand for the products or services output from the asset;

(e)   expected actions by competitors or potential competitors;

(f)   the level of maintenance expenditure required to obtain the expected future economic benefits from the asset and the entity's ability and intention to reach such a level;

(g)   the period of control over the asset and legal or similar limits on the use of the asset, such as the expiry dates of related leases; and

(h)   whether the useful life of the asset is dependent on the useful life of other assets of the entity.

91   The term 'indefinite' does not mean 'infinite'. The useful life of an intangible asset reflects only that level of future maintenance expenditure required to maintain the asset at its standard of performance assessed at the time of estimating the asset's useful life, and the entity's ability and intention to reach such a level. A conclusion that the useful life of an intangible asset is indefinite should not depend on planned future expenditure in excess of that required to maintain the asset at that standard of performance.

92   Given the history of rapid changes in technology, computer software and many other intangible assets are susceptible to technological obsolescence. Therefore, it is likely that their useful life is short.

93   The useful life of an intangible asset may be very long or even indefinite. Uncertainty justifies estimating the useful life of an intangible asset on a prudent basis, but it does not justify choosing a life that is unrealistically short.

94   **The useful life of an intangible asset that arises from contractual or other legal rights shall not exceed the period of the contractual or other legal rights, but may be shorter depending on the period over which the entity expects to use the asset. If the contractual or other legal rights are conveyed for a limited term that can be renewed, the useful life of the intangible asset shall include the renewal period(s) only if there is evidence to support renewal by the entity without significant cost. The useful life of a reacquired right recognised as an intangible asset in a business combination is the remaining contractual period of the contract in which the right was granted and shall not include renewal periods.**

95   There may be both economic and legal factors influencing the useful life of an intangible asset. Economic factors determine the period over which future economic benefits will be received by the entity. Legal factors may restrict the period over which the entity controls access to these benefits. The useful life is the shorter of the periods determined by these factors.

96   Existence of the following factors, among others, indicates that an entity would be able to renew the contractual or other legal rights without significant cost:

(a)   there is evidence, possibly based on experience, that the contractual or other legal rights will be renewed. If renewal is contingent upon the consent of a third party, this includes evidence that the third party will give its consent;

(b)   there is evidence that any conditions necessary to obtain renewal will be satisfied; and

(c)   the cost to the entity of renewal is not significant when compared with the future economic benefits expected to flow to the entity from renewal.

If the cost of renewal is significant when compared with the future economic benefits expected to flow to the entity from renewal, the 'renewal' cost represents, in substance, the cost to acquire a new intangible asset at the renewal date.

Intangible Assets with Finite Useful Lives

Amortisation Period and Amortisation Method

97   **The *depreciable amount* of an intangible asset with a finite useful life shall be allocated on a systematic basis over its useful life. Amortisation shall begin when the asset is available for use, that is, when it is in the location and condition necessary for**

it to be capable of operating in the manner intended by management. Amortisation shall cease at the earlier of the date that the asset is classified as held for sale (or included in a disposal group that is classified as held for sale) in accordance with AASB 5 and the date that the asset is derecognised. The amortisation method used shall reflect the pattern in which the asset's future economic benefits are expected to be consumed by the entity. If that pattern cannot be determined reliably, the straight-line method shall be used. The amortisation charge for each period shall be recognised in profit or loss unless this or another Standard permits or requires it to be included in the carrying amount of another asset.

98   A variety of amortisation methods can be used to allocate the depreciable amount of an asset on a systematic basis over its useful life. These methods include the straight-line method, the diminishing balance method and the unit of production method. The method used is selected on the basis of the expected pattern of consumption of the expected future economic benefits embodied in the asset and is applied consistently from period to period, unless there is a change in the expected pattern of consumption of those future economic benefits.

99   Amortisation is usually recognised in profit or loss. However, sometimes the future economic benefits embodied in an asset are absorbed in producing other assets. In this case, the amortisation charge constitutes part of the cost of the other asset and is included in its carrying amount. For example, the amortisation of intangible assets used in a production process is included in the carrying amount of inventories (see AASB 102 *Inventories*).

Residual Value

100   The *residual value* of an intangible asset with a finite useful life shall be assumed to be zero unless:

(a)   there is a commitment by a third party to purchase the asset at the end of its useful life; or

(b)   there is an active market for the asset and:

(i)   residual value can be determined by reference to that market; and

(ii)   it is probable that such a market will exist at the end of the asset's useful life.

101   The depreciable amount of an asset with a finite useful life is determined after deducting its residual value. A residual value other than zero implies that an entity expects to dispose of the intangible asset before the end of its economic life.

102   An estimate of an asset's residual value is based on the amount recoverable from disposal using prices prevailing at the date of the estimate for the sale of a similar asset that has reached the end of its useful life and has operated under conditions similar to those in which the asset will be used. The residual value is reviewed at least at the end of each annual reporting period. A change in the asset's residual value is accounted for as a change in an accounting estimate in accordance with AASB 108 *Accounting Policies, Changes in Accounting Estimates and Errors*.

103   The residual value of an intangible asset may increase to an amount equal to or greater than the asset's carrying amount. If it does, the asset's amortisation charge is zero unless and until its residual value subsequently decreases to an amount below the asset's carrying amount.

Review of Amortisation Period and Amortisation Method

104   The amortisation period and the amortisation method for an intangible asset with a finite useful life shall be reviewed at least at the end of each annual reporting period. If the expected useful life of the asset is different from previous estimates, the amortisation period shall be changed accordingly. If there has been a change in the expected pattern of consumption of the future economic benefits embodied in the asset, the amortisation method shall be changed to reflect the changed pattern. Such changes shall be accounted for as changes in accounting estimates in accordance with AASB 108.

105   During the life of an intangible asset, it may become apparent that the estimate of its useful life is inappropriate. For example, the recognition of an impairment loss may indicate that the amortisation period needs to be changed.

106   Over time, the pattern of future economic benefits expected to flow to an entity from an intangible asset may change. For example, it may become apparent that a diminishing balance method of amortisation is appropriate rather than a straight-line method. Another example is if use of the rights represented by a licence is deferred pending action on other components of the business plan. In this case, economic benefits that flow from the asset may not be received until later periods.

Intangible Assets with Indefinite Useful Lives

107   **An intangible asset with an indefinite useful life shall not be amortised.**

108   In accordance with AASB 136, an entity is required to test an intangible asset with an indefinite useful life for impairment by comparing its recoverable amount with its carrying amount:

(a)   annually, and

(b)   whenever there is an indication that the intangible asset may be impaired.

Review of Useful Life Assessment

109   **The useful life of an intangible asset that is not being amortised shall be reviewed each period to determine whether events and circumstances continue to support an indefinite useful life assessment for that asset. If they do not, the change in the useful life assessment from indefinite to finite shall be accounted for as a change in an accounting estimate in accordance with AASB 108.**

110   In accordance with AASB 136, reassessing the useful life of an intangible asset as finite rather than indefinite is an indicator that the asset may be impaired. As a result, the entity tests the asset for impairment by comparing its recoverable amount, determined in accordance with AASB 136, with its carrying amount, and recognising any excess of the carrying amount over the recoverable amount as an impairment loss.

Recoverability of the Carrying Amount – Impairment Losses

111   To determine whether an intangible asset is impaired, an entity applies AASB 136. That Standard explains when and how an entity reviews the carrying amount of its assets, how it determines the recoverable amount of an asset and when it recognises or reverses an impairment loss.

Retirements and Disposals

112   **An intangible asset shall be derecognised:**

(a)   **on disposal; or**

(b)   **when no future economic benefits are expected from its use or disposal.**

113   **The gain or loss arising from the derecognition of an intangible asset shall be determined as the difference between the net disposal proceeds, if any, and the carrying amount of the asset. It shall be recognised in profit or loss when the asset is derecognised (unless AASB 117 requires otherwise on a sale and leaseback). Gains shall not be classified as revenue.**

114   The disposal of an intangible asset may occur in a variety of ways (e.g. by sale, by entering into a finance lease, or by donation). In determining the date of disposal of such an asset, an entity applies the criteria in AASB 118 *Revenue* for recognising revenue from the sale of goods. AASB 117 applies to disposal by a sale and leaseback.

115   If in accordance with the recognition principle in paragraph 21 an entity recognises in the carrying amount of an asset the cost of a replacement for part of an intangible asset, then it derecognises the carrying amount of the replaced part. If it is not practicable for an entity to determine the carrying amount of the replaced part, it may use the cost of the replacement as an indication of what the cost of the replaced part was at the time it was acquired or internally generated.

115A   In the case of a reacquired right in a business combination, if the right is subsequently reissued (sold) to a third party, the related carrying amount, if any, shall be used in determining the gain or loss on reissue.

116   The consideration receivable on disposal of an intangible asset is recognised initially at its fair value. If payment for the intangible asset is deferred, the consideration received is recognised initially at the cash price equivalent. The difference between the nominal amount of the consideration and the cash price equivalent is recognised as interest revenue in accordance with AASB 118 reflecting the effective yield on the receivable.

117   Amortisation of an intangible asset with a finite useful life does not cease when the intangible asset is no longer used, unless the asset has been fully depreciated or is classified as held for sale (or included in a disposal group that is classified as held for sale) in accordance with AASB 5.

Disclosure

General

118   **An entity shall disclose the following for each class of intangible assets, distinguishing between internally generated intangible assets and other intangible assets:**

   (a)   **whether the useful lives are indefinite or finite and, if finite, the useful lives or the amortisation rates used;**

   (b)   **the amortisation methods used for intangible assets with finite useful lives;**

   (c)   **the gross carrying amount and any accumulated amortisation (aggregated with accumulated impairment losses) at the beginning and end of the period;**

   (d)   **the line item(s) of the statement of comprehensive income in which any amortisation of intangible assets is included;**

   (e)   **a reconciliation of the carrying amount at the beginning and end of the period showing:**

      (i)   **additions, indicating separately those from internal development, those acquired separately, and those acquired through business combinations;**

      (ii)   **assets classified as held for sale or included in a disposal group classified as held for sale in accordance with AASB 5 and other disposals;**

      (iii)   **increases or decreases during the period resulting from revaluations under paragraphs 75, 85 and 86 and from impairment losses recognised or reversed in other comprehensive income in accordance with AASB 136 (if any);**

      (iv)   **impairment losses recognised in profit or loss during the period in accordance with AASB 136 (if any);**

      (v)   **impairment losses reversed in profit or loss during the period in accordance with AASB 136 (if any);**

      (vi)   **any amortisation recognised during the period;**

      (vii)   **net exchange differences arising on the translation of the financial statements into the presentation currency, and on the translation of a foreign operation into the presentation currency of the entity; and**

      (viii)   **other changes in the carrying amount during the period.**

119   A class of intangible assets is a grouping of assets of a similar nature and use in an entity's operations. Examples of separate classes may include:

   (a)   brand names;

   (b)   mastheads and publishing titles;

   (c)   computer software;

   (d)   licences and franchises;

   (e)   copyrights, patents and other industrial property rights, service and operating rights;

(f) recipes, formulae, models, designs and prototypes; and

(g) intangible assets under development.

The classes mentioned above are disaggregated (aggregated) into smaller (larger) classes if this results in more relevant information for the users of the financial statements.

120 An entity discloses information on impaired intangible assets in accordance with AASB 136 in addition to the information required by paragraph 118(e)(iii)-(v).

121 AASB 108 requires an entity to disclose the nature and amount of a change in an accounting estimate that has a material effect in the current period or is expected to have a material effect in subsequent periods. Such disclosure may arise from changes in:

(a) the assessment of an intangible asset's useful life;

(b) the amortisation method; or

(c) residual values.

122 An entity shall also disclose:

(a) **for an intangible asset assessed as having an indefinite useful life, the carrying amount of that asset and the reasons supporting the assessment of an indefinite useful life. In giving these reasons, the entity shall describe the factor(s) that played a significant role in determining that the asset has an indefinite useful life;**

(b) **a description, the carrying amount and remaining amortisation period of any individual intangible asset that is material to the entity's financial statements;**

(c) **for intangible assets acquired by way of a government grant and initially recognised at fair value (see paragraph 44):**

(i) **the fair value initially recognised for these assets;**

(ii) **their carrying amount; and**

(iii) **whether they are measured after recognition under the cost model or the revaluation model;**

(d) **the existence and carrying amounts of intangible assets whose title is restricted and the carrying amounts of intangible assets pledged as security for liabilities; and**

(e) **the amount of contractual commitments for the acquisition of intangible assets.**

123 When an entity describes the factor(s) that played a significant role in determining that the useful life of an intangible asset is indefinite, the entity considers the list of factors in paragraph 90.

Intangible Assets Measured after Recognition using the Revaluation Model

124 If intangible assets are accounted for at revalued amounts, an entity shall disclose the following:

(a) **by class of intangible assets:**

(i) **the effective date of the revaluation;**

(ii) **the carrying amount of revalued intangible assets; and**

(iii) **the carrying amount that would have been recognised had the revalued class of intangible assets been measured after recognition using the cost model in paragraph 74;**

(b) **the amount of the revaluation surplus that relates to intangible assets at the beginning and end of the period, indicating the changes during the period and any restrictions on the distribution of the balance to shareholders; and**

(c) **the methods and significant assumptions applied in estimating the assets' fair values.**

Aus124.1 Notwithstanding paragraph 124(a)(iii), in respect of not-for-profit entities, for each revalued class of intangible assets, the requirement to disclose the

> carrying amount that would have been recognised had the assets been carried under the cost model does not apply.

125 It may be necessary to aggregate the classes of revalued assets into larger classes for disclosure purposes. However, classes are not aggregated if this would result in the combination of a class of intangible assets that includes amounts measured under both the cost and revaluation models.

Research and Development Expenditure

126 **An entity shall disclose the aggregate amount of research and development expenditure recognised as an expense during the period.**

127 Research and development expenditure comprises all expenditure that is directly attributable to research or development activities (see paragraphs 66 and 67 for guidance on the type of expenditure to be included for the purpose of the disclosure requirement in paragraph 126).

Other Information

128 An entity is encouraged, but not required, to disclose the following information:

(a) a description of any fully amortised intangible asset that is still in use; and

(b) a brief description of significant intangible assets controlled by the entity but not recognised as assets because they did not meet the recognition criteria in this Standard.

Transitional Provisions and Effective Date

129 [Deleted by the IASB]

130 [Deleted by the AASB]

130A [Deleted by the AASB]

130B [Deleted by the AASB]

130C AASB 2008-3 *Amendments to Australian Accounting Standards Arising from AASB 3 and AASB 127* amended paragraphs 12, 33-35, 68, 69 and 94, deleted paragraph 38 and added paragraph 115A. AASB 2009-4 *Amendments to Australian Accounting Standards arising from the Annual Improvements Project*, issued in May 2009, amended paragraphs 36 and 37. An entity shall apply those amendments prospectively for annual reporting periods beginning on or after 1 July 2009. Therefore, amounts recognised for intangible assets and goodwill in prior business combinations shall not be adjusted. If an entity applies AASB 3 (revised 2008) for an earlier period, it shall apply the amendments for that earlier period and disclose that fact.

130D Paragraphs 69, 70 and 98 were amended and paragraph 69A was added by AASB 2008-5 *Amendments to Australian Accounting Standards arising from the Annual Improvements Project* issued in July 2008. An entity shall apply those amendments for annual reporting periods beginning on or after 1 January 2009. Earlier application is permitted. If an entity applies the amendments for an earlier period it shall disclose that fact.

130E AASB 2009-4 *Amendments to Australian Accounting Standards arising from the Annual Improvements Project*, issued in May 2009, amended paragraphs 40 and 41. An entity shall apply those amendments prospectively for annual reporting periods beginning on or after 1 July 2009. Earlier application is permitted. If an entity applies the amendments for an earlier period it shall disclose that fact.

Exchanges of Similar Assets

131 [Deleted by the AASB]

Early Application

132 [Deleted by the AASB]

Withdrawal of IAS 38 (Issued 1998)

133 [Deleted by the AASB]

Illustrative Examples

These examples accompany, but are not part of, AASB 138.

Assessing the Useful Lives of Intangible Assets

The following guidance provides examples on determining the useful life of an intangible asset in accordance with AASB 138.

Each of the following examples describes an acquired intangible asset, the facts and circumstances surrounding the determination of its useful life, and the subsequent accounting based on that determination.

Example 1 An acquired customer list

A direct-mail marketing company acquires a customer list and expects that it will be able to derive benefit from the information on the list for at least one year, but no more than three years. The customer list would be amortised over management's best estimate of its useful life, say 18 months. Although the direct-mail marketing company may intend to add customer names and other information to the list in the future, the expected benefits of the acquired customer list relate only to the customers on that list at the date it was acquired. The customer list also would be reviewed for impairment in accordance with AASB 136 Impairment of Assets by assessing at the end of each reporting period whether there is any indication that the customer list may be impaired.

Example 2 An acquired patent that expires in 15 years

The product protected by the patented technology is expected to be a source of net cash inflows for at least 15 years. The entity has a commitment from a third party to purchase that patent in five years for 60 per cent of the fair value of the patent at the date it was acquired, and the entity intends to sell the patent in five years.

The patent would be amortised over its five-year useful life to the entity, with a residual value equal to the present value of 60 per cent of the patent's fair value at the date it was acquired. The patent would also be reviewed for impairment in accordance with AASB 136 by assessing at the end of each reporting period whether there is any indication that it may be impaired.

Example 3 An acquired copyright that has a remaining legal life of 50 years

An analysis of consumer habits and market trends provides evidence that the copyrighted material will generate net cash inflows for only 30 more years.

The copyright would be amortised over its 30-year estimated useful life. The copyright also would be reviewed for impairment in accordance with AASB 136 by assessing at the end of each reporting period whether there is any indication that it may be impaired.

Example 4 An acquired broadcasting licence that expires in five years

The broadcasting licence is renewable every 10 years if the entity provides at least an average level of service to its customers and complies with the relevant legislative requirements. The licence may be renewed indefinitely at little cost and has been renewed twice before the most recent acquisition. The acquiring entity intends to renew the licence indefinitely and evidence supports its ability to do so. Historically, there has been no compelling challenge to the licence renewal. The technology used in broadcasting is not expected to be replaced by another technology at any time in the foreseeable future. Therefore, the licence is expected to contribute to the entity's net cash inflows indefinitely.

The broadcasting licence would be treated as having an indefinite useful life because it is expected to contribute to the entity's net cash inflows indefinitely. Therefore, the licence would not be amortised until its useful life is determined to be finite. The licence would be tested for impairment in accordance with AASB 136 annually and whenever there is an indication that it may be impaired.

Example 5 The broadcasting licence in Example 4

The licensing authority subsequently decides that it will no longer renew broadcasting licences, but rather will auction the licences. At the time the licensing authority's decision is made, the entity's broadcasting licence has three years until it expires. The entity expects that the licence will continue to contribute to net cash inflows until the licence expires.

Because the broadcasting licence can no longer be renewed, its useful life is no longer indefinite. Thus, the acquired licence would be amortised over its remaining three-year useful life and immediately tested for impairment in accordance with AASB 136.

Example 6 An acquired airline route authority between two European cities that expires in three years

The route authority may be renewed every five years, and the acquiring entity intends to comply with the applicable rules and regulations surrounding renewal. Route authority renewals are routinely granted at a minimal cost and historically have been renewed when the airline has complied with the applicable rules and regulations. The acquiring entity expects to provide service indefinitely between the two cities from its hub airports and expects that the related supporting infrastructure (airport gates, slots, and terminal facility leases) will remain in place at those airports for as long as it has the route authority. An analysis of demand and cash flows supports those assumptions.

Because the facts and circumstances support the acquiring entity's ability to continue providing air service indefinitely between the two cities, the intangible asset related to the route authority is treated as having an indefinite useful life. Therefore, the route authority would not be amortised until its useful life is determined to be finite. It would be tested for impairment in accordance with AASB 136 annually and whenever there is an indication that it may be impaired.

Example 7 An acquired trademark used to identify and distinguish a leading consumer product that has been a market-share leader for the past eight years

The trademark has a remaining legal life of five years but is renewable every 10 years at little cost. The acquiring entity intends to renew the trademark continuously and evidence supports its ability to do so. An analysis of (1) product life cycle studies, (2) market, competitive and environmental trends, and (3) brand extension opportunities provides evidence that the trademarked product will generate net cash inflows for the acquiring entity for an indefinite period.

The trademark would be treated as having an indefinite useful life because it is expected to contribute to net cash inflows indefinitely. Therefore, the trademark would not be amortised until its useful life is determined to be finite. It would be tested for impairment in accordance with AASB 136 annually and whenever there is an indication that it may be impaired.

Example 8 A trademark acquired 10 years ago that distinguishes a leading consumer product

The trademark was regarded as having an indefinite useful life when it was acquired because the trademarked product was expected to generate net cash inflows indefinitely. However, unexpected competition has recently entered the market and will reduce future sales of the product. Management estimates that net cash inflows generated by the product will be 20% less for the foreseeable future. However, management expects that the product will continue to generate net cash inflows indefinitely at those reduced amounts.

As a result of the projected decrease in future net cash inflows, the entity determines that the estimated recoverable amount of the trademark is less than its carrying amount, and an impairment loss is recognised. Because it is still regarded as having an indefinite useful life, the trademark would continue not to be amortised but would be tested for impairment in accordance with AASB 136 annually and whenever there is an indication that it may be impaired.

Example 9 A trademark for a line of products that was acquired several years ago in a business combination

At the time of the business combination the acquiree had been producing the line of products for 35 years with many new models developed under the trademark. At the acquisition date the acquirer expected to continue producing the line, and an analysis of various economic factors indicated there was no limit to the period the trademark would contribute to net cash inflows. Consequently, the trademark was not amortised by the acquirer. However, management has recently decided that production of the product line will be discontinued over the next four years.

Because the useful life of the acquired trademark is no longer regarded as indefinite, the carrying amount of the trademark would be tested for impairment in accordance with AASB 136 and amortised over its remaining four-year useful life.

AASB 139
Financial Instruments:
Recognition and Measurement
(Compiled November 2010)

Note from the Institute of Chartered Accountants Australia

This note, prepared by the technical editors, is not part of Accounting Standard AASB 139.

Historical development

15 July 2004: AASB 139 'Financial Instruments: Recognition and Measurement' was made on 15 July 2004 as part of the AASB's program to adopt International Financial Reporting Standards (IFRSs) by 2005. AASB 139 is the equivalent of IAS 39 of the same name.

22 December 2004: AASB 2004-2 'Amendments to Australian Accounting Standards' adds paragraph AG76A to AASB 139, and is applicable to annual reporting periods beginning on or after 1 January 2005.

5 May 2005: AASB 2005-1 'Amendments to Australian Accounting Standards' amends paragraphs 80, (heading following paragraph) 102, AG99A, and AG99B, and adds paragraphs 108A, 108B, AG99C, AG99D, AG113 and preceding heading. The Standard is applicable to annual reporting periods beginning on or after 1 January 2006, with early adoption permitted for annual reporting periods beginning on or after 1 January 2005.

9 June 2005: AASB 2005-4 'Amendments to Australian Accounting Standards' amends paragraphs 9 'Definitions of Four Categories of Financial Instruments' part (b), 12, 13, and 105. AASB 2005-4 adds paragraphs 11A, 48A, 105A to 105D, AG4B and preceding headings, AG4C to AG4K, AG33A and preceding heading, and AG33B. The Standard is applicable to annual reporting periods beginning on or after 1 January 2006, with early adoption permitted for annual reporting periods beginning on or after 1 January 2005.

9 June 2005: AASB 2005-5 'Amendments to Australian Accounting Standards' amends paragraphs 2(h), 2(i), and adds paragraph 2(j). This Standard is applicable to annual reporting periods beginning on or after 1 January 2006. The application date of AASB 2005-5 is linked to UIG Interpretations 4 and 5: when an entity adopts these UIG Interpretations for annual reporting periods beginning on or after 1 January 2005 but before 1 January 2006, this Standard is also applied as appropriate for that earlier period.

5 September 2005: AASB 2005-10 'Amendments to Australian Accounting Standards' amends paragraphs 1, 9 (definition of 'financial liability at fair value through profit and loss', first paragraph of part (b)(ii)), 45, and 48. The Standard is applicable to annual reporting periods beginning on or after 1 January 2007, with early adoption permitted for annual reporting periods beginning on or after 1 January 2005.

6 September 2005: AASB 2005-9 'Amendments to Australian Accounting Standards' amends paragraphs 2(e), 2(h), 4, 47, and AG4. The Standard also adds paragraphs 9 (heading and a definition of 'a financial guarantee contract'), 103A note, 103B note, AG3A and AG4A and deletes paragraph 3. The Standard is applicable to annual reporting periods beginning on or after 1 January 2006, with early adoption permitted for annual reporting periods beginning on or after 1 January 2005.

8 September 2005: AASB 2005-11 'Amendments to Australian Accounting Standards' amends paragraphs AG52 (fifth paragraph of the text box) and AG66. The Standard is applicable to annual reporting periods ending on or after 31 December 2005, with early adoption permitted for annual reporting periods beginning on or after 1 January 2005 and ending before 31 December 2005.

15 February 2007: AASB 2007-3 'Amendments to Australian Accounting Standards' amends paragraph 15 and is applicable for annual reporting periods ending on or after 28 February 2007. Entities may elect to early-adopt it to annual reporting periods beginning on or after 1 January 2005.

---

30 April 2007: AASB 2007-4 'Amendments to Australian Accounting Standards' amends paragraphs 9, 47, AG1, AG2, AG3, AG4E, AG29, AG33, AG46, AG53, AG79, AG82 and AG125 and is applicable for annual reporting periods beginning on or after 1 July 2007. Entities may elect to early-adopt it to annual reporting periods beginning on or after 1 January 2005.

24 September 2007: AASB 2007-8 'Amendments to Australian Accounting Standards' was issued by the AASB. This Standard is applicable for annual reporting periods beginning on or after 1 January 2009.

13 December 2007: AASB 2007-10 'Further Amendments to Australian Accounting Standards arising from AASB 101' amends AASB 139, replacing the term 'financial report' with 'financial statements'. This Standard is applicable to annual reporting periods beginning on or after 1 January 2009.

5 March 2008: AASB 2008-2 'Amendments to Australian Accounting Standards – Puttable Financial Instruments and Obligations arising on Liquidation' classifies as equity instruments certain puttable financial instruments. This Standard is applicable to annual reporting periods beginning on or after 1 January 2009.

6 March 2008: AASB 2008-3 'Amendments to Australian Accounting Standards arising from AASB 3 and AASB 127' amends AASB 139 for the issue of AASB 3 Revised. This Standard is applicable to annual reporting periods beginning on or after 1 July 2009.

24 July 2008: AASB 2008-5 'Amendments to Australian Accounting Standards arising from the Annual Improvements Project' amends AASB 139 in relation to reclassification of derivatives into or out of the classification of 'at fair value through profit or loss', designating and documenting hedges at the segment level and the applicable effective interest rate on cessation of fair value hedge accounting. This Standard is applicable to annual reporting periods beginning on or after 1 January 2009.

27 August 2008: AASB 2008-8 'Amendments to Australian Accounting Standards – Eligible Hedged Items' amends AASB 139 to clarify how the principles that determine whether a hedged risk or portion of cash flows is eligible for designation as a hedged item, should be applied in particular situations. This Standard is applicable to annual reporting periods beginning on or after 1 July 2009.

22 October 2008: AASB 2008-10 'Amendments to Australian Accounting Standards – Reclassification of Financial Assets' was issued by the AASB. The amendment aligns the disclosures in AASB 7 with the amendments to AASB 139, which permit an entity to reclassify some financial assets, in certain circumstances. This Standard is applicable from 1 July 2008. Early adoption is not permitted.

7 November 2008: Compiled AASB 139 was issued by the AASB.

18 December 2008: AASB 2008-12 'Amendments to Australian Accounting Standards – Reclassification of Financial Assets – Effective Date and Transition' was issued by the AASB, clarifying the amendments in AASB 2008-10 are applicable on or after 1 July 2008.

22 April 2009: AASB 2009-3 'Amendments to Australian Accounting Standards' clarifies the requirements in relation to the treatment of embedded derivatives within a host contract that is reclassified out of the fair value through profit or loss category in accordance with the amendments made to AASB 139 in October 2008. This Standard is applicable to annual reporting periods ending on or after 30 June 2009.

21 May 2009: AASB 2009-5 'Amendments to Australian Accounting Standards' is the annual improvements Standard, amending AASB 139 in relation to treating loan prepayment penalties as closely related embedded derivatives, and clarify the scope of exemption for business combination contracts and cash flow hedge accounting. This Standard applies to annual reporting periods beginning on or after 1 January 2010 and may be applied early.

25 June 2009: AASB 2009-6 'Amendments to Australian Accounting Standards' amends AASB 139 for editorial corrections made by the International Accounting Standards Board (IASB) to its Standards and Interpretations (IFRSs) and as a consequence of issuing revised AASB 101 'Presentation of Financial Statements' (September 2007). This Standard is applicable to annual reporting periods beginning on or after 1 January 2009 that end on or after 30 June 2009.

25 June 2009: AASB 2009-7 'Amendments to Australian Accounting Standards' amends AASB 139 arising from editorial corrections by the AASB and by the International Accounting Standards Board (IASB). This Standard is applicable to annual reporting periods beginning on or after 1 July 2009.

5 October 2009: Erratum makes further terminology-related and editorial changes resulting from AASB 2009-6. This erratum applies to annual reporting periods beginning on or after 1 January 2009 that end on or after 30 June 2009.

6 October 2009: AASB 139 was reissued by the AASB, applying to annual reporting periods beginning on or after 1 January 2009 but before 1 July 2009 that end on or after 30 June 2009. Early application is not permitted. This version of AASB 139 has been compiled for the amending Standards apply to annual reporting periods beginning on or after 1 January 2009. This Standard applies to 31 December 2009 year ends.

9 October 2009: AASB 139 was reissued by the AASB, compiled to include the AASB 2007-8, 2007-10, 2008-2, 2008-3, 2008-5, 2008-8, 2009-3, 2009-6, 2009-7 and Erratum (October 2009) amendments. This compiled Standard applies to annual reporting periods beginning on or after 1 July 2009 but before 1 January 2010. Early application is permitted only for annual reporting periods ending on or after 30 June 2009.

7 December 2009: AASB 2009-11 'Amendments to Australian Accounting Standards arising from AASB 9' amends AASB 139 to give effect to consequential changes arising from the issuance of AASB 9. This Standard is applicable to annual reporting periods beginning on or after 1 January 2013 with early adoption permitted from annual reporting periods ending on or after 31 December 2009 that begin before 1 January 2013 provided AASB 9 is also applied for the same period. The application date of AASB 2009-11 has been amended to 1 January 2015 by AASB 2012-6. **These amendments have been superseded by AASB 2010-7 and are not included in this compiled Standard.**

15 December 2009: AASB 2009-12 'Amendments to Australian Accounting Standards' amends AASB 139 for editorial corrections. This Standard is applicable to annual reporting periods beginning on or after 1 January 2011 with early adoption permitted.

2 June 2010: AASB 2010-3 'Amendments to Australian Accounting Standards arising from the Annual Improvements Project' amends AASB 139 in relation to transition requirements for contingent consideration from a business combination that occurred before the effective date of the revised AASB 3. This Standard is applicable to annual reporting periods beginning on or after 1 July 2010 with early adoption permitted.

7 September 2010: AASB 139 was reissued by the AASB, compiled to include the AASB 2009-5 and AASB 2010-3 amendments, and applies to annual reporting periods beginning on or after 1 July 2010 but before 1 January 2011.

27 October 2010: AASB 2010-5 'Further Amendments to Australian Accounting Standards' makes editorial amendments to AASB 139. This Standard is applicable to annual reporting periods beginning on or after 1 January 2011.

26 November 2010: AASB 139 was reissued by the AASB, compiled to include the AASB 2009-12 and AASB 2010-5 amendments, and applies to annual reporting periods ending on or after 1 January 2011 but before 1 January 2013.

1 March 2011: AASB 2010-7 'Amendments to Australian Accounting Standards arising from AASB 9 (December 2010)' as compiled amends AASB 139 to give effect to consequential changes arising from the reissue of AASB 9 in December 2010, and supersedes AASB 2009-11, which related to the previous version of AASB 9. This Standard applies to annual reporting periods beginning on or after 1 January 2013 and can be adopted early. The application date of AASB 2010-7 has been amended to 1 January 2015 by AASB 2012-6. **These amendments are not included in this compiled Standard.**

29 August 2011: AASB 2011-7 'Amendments to Australian Accounting Standards arising from the Consolidation and Joint Arrangements Standards' amends AASB 139 to give effect to many consequential changes arising from the issue of AASB 10, 11, 12, 127 and 128. This Standard applies to annual reporting periods beginning on or after 1 January 2013 and can be adopted early by for-profit entities. **These amendments are not included in this compiled Standard.**

2 September 2011: AASB 2011-8 'Amendments to Australian Accounting Standards arising from AASB 13' amends AASB 139 to give effect to a consequential change in the definition of fair value arising from the issue of AASB 13. This Standard applies to annual reporting periods beginning on or after 1 January 2013 and can be adopted early. **These amendments are not included in this compiled Standard.**

A new accounting Standard: AASB 9 *Financial Instruments* will replace AASB 139. AASB 9 was issued by the AASB in December 2009 and amended in December 2009 and is applicable for periods beginning on or after 1 January 2015 with early adoption permitted.

References

Interpretation 2 Members' *Shares in Co-operative Entities and Similar Instruments*, Interpretation 5 *Rights to Interests arising from Decommissioning, Restoration and Environmental Rehabilitation Funds*, Interpretation 9 *Reassessment of Embedded Derivatives*, Interpretation 19 *Extinguishing Financial Liabilities with Equity Instruments*, Interpretation 10 *Interim Financial Reporting and Impairment*, Interpretation 12 *Service Concession Arrangements*, Interpretation 16 *Hedges of a Net Investment in a Foreign Operation*, Interpretation 19 *Extinguishing Financial Liabilities with Equity Instruments*, Interpretation 107 *Introduction of the Euro* and Interpretation 127 *Evaluating the Substance of Transactions Involving the Legal Form of a Lease* apply to AASB 139.

AASB item not taken onto the agenda: *Direct costs affecting a financial instrument's effective interest rate* applies to AASB 138.

IFRIC items not taken onto the agenda: No. 20 *Extended Payment terms* issued in July 2004, No. 44 *Discretionary Distributions and Economic Compulsion*, No. 45 *Own shares that are held for trading purposes*, No. 46 *The Meaning of Other than Temporary Impairment and its Application to Certain Investments*, No. 47 *The Closely Related Criterion for Embedded Derivatives in IAS 39*, No. 48 *Classification of non-redeemable preference shares*, No. 49 *Impairment: Accounting for Incurred Losses under IAS 39*, No. 50 *Effective Interest Rates* issued in October 2004, No. 51 *Commodity Price Risk Hedging*, No. 52 *Single Instrument Designated as a Hedge of More than One Type of Risk*, No. 56 *The seller's contingent consideration*, IAS 39-1 *Hedge effectiveness tests – vacillations in effectiveness/timing of tests*, IAS 39-2 *Impairment of an Equity Security*, IAS 39-3 *Meaning of delivery*, IAS 39-4 *Retention of servicing rights*; IAS 39-5 *Revolving structures*, IAS 39-6 *Valuation of electricity derivatives*, IAS 39-7 *Testing of hedge effectiveness on a cumulative basis*, IAS 39-8 *IAS 39 Financial Instruments: Recognition and Measurement—Definition of a derivative: Indexation on own EBITDA or own revenue*, IAS 39-9 *IAS 39 Financial Instruments: Recognition and Measurement—Short Trading*, IAS 39-10 IAS 39 *Financial Instruments: Recognition and Measurement*, IAS 27 *Consolidated and Separate Financial Statements—Financial Instruments puttable at an amount other than Fair Value*, IAS 39-11 *Written options in retail energy contracts*, IAS 39-12 *Assessing hedge effectiveness of an interest rate swap in a cash flow hedge*, IAS 39-13 *Gaming transactions*, IAS 39-14 *Hedging multiple risks with a single derivative hedging instrument*, IAS 39-15 *Hedging future cash flows with purchased options*, IAS 39-16 *Scope of IAS 39 paragraph 2(g)*, IAS 39-17 *Guidance on effective interest rate*, IAS 39-18 *Accounting for trailing commissions*, IAS 39-19 *Valuation of restricted securities*, IAS 39-20, IAS 39-21 *Participation rights and calculation of the effective interest rate*, IAS 39-22 *Classification of failed loan syndications*, IAS 39-23 *Hedging using more than one derivative as the hedging instrument*, IAS 39-24 *Meaning of 'Significant or prolonged'*, IAS 39-25 *Unit of account for forward contracts with volumetric optionality*, IAS 39-27 *Impairment of financial assets reclassified from available-for-sale to loans and receivables*, IAS 39-31A *Derecognition of financial instruments upon modification* and IAS 39-31A *Classification of a GDP-linked security* apply to AASB 139.

AASB 139 compared to IAS 39

Additions

Paragraph	Description
Aus 1.1	Which entities AASB 139 applies to (i.e. reporting entities and general purpose financial statements).
Aus 1.2	The application date of AASB 139 (i.e. annual reporting periods beginning 1 January 2005).
Aus 1.3	Prohibits application of AASB 139 before 1 January 2005.
Aus 1.4	Makes the requirements of AASB 139 subject to AASB 1031 'Materiality'.
Aus 1.5	Notice of the new Standard published on 22 July 2004.

Deletions

Paragraph	Description
103	Effective date of IAS 39.
104	IAS 39 must be applied retrospectively except as set out in paragraphs 105–108.
106	The derecognition requirements at paragraphs 15–37 and Appendix A paragraphs AG36–AG52 must be applied prospectively except as allowed by paragraph 107.
107	The derecognition requirements at paragraphs 15–37 and Appendix A paragraphs AG36–AG52 may be applied retrospectively from a date of the entity's choosing provided timely information is available.
	The carrying amount of non-financial assets and non-financial liabilities must not be adjusted to exclude gains and losses related to cash flow hedges that were recognised before IAS 39 applied.
109	Reference to superseded IAS 39.
110	Reference to superseded Implementation Guidance for IAS 39.

Contents

Compilation Details

Comparison With IAS 39

Accounting Standard
AASB 139 Financial Instruments: Recognition and Measurement

	Paragraphs
Objective	1
Application	Aus1.1 – Aus1.5
Scope	2 – 7
Definitions	8 – 9
Embedded Derivatives	10 – 13
Recognition and Derecognition	
Initial Recognition	14
Derecognition of a Financial Asset	15 – 23
Transfers that Qualify for Derecognition	24 – 28
Transfers that Do Not Qualify for Derecognition	29
Continuing Involvement in Transferred Assets	30 – 35
All Transfers	36 – 37
Regular Way Purchase or Sale of a Financial Asset	38
Derecognition of a Financial Liability	39 – 42
Measurement	
Initial Measurement of Financial Assets and Financial Liabilities	43 – 44
Subsequent Measurement of Financial Assets	45 – 46
Subsequent Measurement of Financial Liabilities	47
Fair Value Measurement Considerations	48 – 49
Reclassifications	50 – 54
Gains and Losses	55 – 57
Impairment and Uncollectibility of Financial Assets	58 – 62
Financial Assets Carried at Amortised Cost	63 – 65
Financial Assets Carried at Cost	66
Available-for-Sale Financial Assets	67 – 70
Hedging	71
Hedging Instruments	
Qualifying Instruments	72 – 73
Designation of Hedging Instruments	74 – 77
Hedged Items	
Qualifying Items	78 – 80
Designation of Financial Items as Hedged Items	81 – 81A
Designation of Non-Financial Items as Hedged Items	82
Designation of Groups of Items as Hedged Items	83 – 84
Hedge Accounting	85 – 88

	Paragraphs
Fair Value Hedges	89 – 94
Cash Flow Hedges	95 – 101
Hedges of a Net Investment	102
Effective Date and Transition	103D – 108C

Appendix A:

Application Guidance	
Scope	AG1 – AG4A
Definitions	
Designation as at Fair Value through Profit or Loss	AG4B – AG4K
Effective Interest Rate	AG5 – AG8
Derivatives	AG9 – AG12A
Transaction Costs	AG13
Financial Assets and Financial Liabilities Held for Trading	AG14 – AG15
Held-to-Maturity Investments	AG16 – AG25
Loans and Receivables	AG26
Embedded Derivatives	AG27 – AG33
Instruments containing Embedded Derivatives	AG33A – AG33B
Recognition and Derecognition	
Initial Recognition	AG34 – AG35
Derecognition of a Financial Asset	AG36 – AG44
Transfers that Qualify for Derecognition	AG45 – AG46
Transfers that Do Not Qualify for Derecognition	AG47
Continuing Involvement in Transferred Assets	AG48
All Transfers	AG49 – AG50
Examples	AG51 – AG52
Regular Way Purchase or Sale of a Financial Asset	AG53 – AG56
Derecognition of a Financial Liability	AG57 – AG63
Measurement	
Initial Measurement of Financial Assets and Financial Liabilities	AG64 – AG65
Subsequent Measurement of Financial Assets	AG66 – AG68
Fair Value Measurement Considerations	AG69 – AG70
Active Market: Quoted Price	AG71 – AG73
No Active Market: Valuation Technique	AG74 – AG79
No Active Market: Equity Instruments	AG80 – AG81
Inputs to Valuation Techniques	AG82
Gains and Losses	AG83
Impairment and Uncollectibility of Financial Assets	
Financial Assets Carried at Amortised Cost	AG84 – AG92
Interest Income After Impairment Recognition	AG93

	Paragraphs
Hedging	
Hedging Instruments	
Qualifying Instruments	AG94 – AG97
Hedged Items	
Qualifying Items	AG98 – AG99F
Designation of Non-Financial Items as Hedged Items	AG100
Designation of Groups of Items as Hedged Items	AG101
Hedge Accounting	AG102 – AG104
Assessing Hedge Effectiveness	AG105 – AG113
Fair Value Hedge Accounting for a Portfolio Hedge of Interest Rate Risk	AG114 – AG132
Transition	AG133

Illustrative Example

Implementation Guidance
(available on the AASB website)

Basis for Conclusions on IAS 39
(available on the AASB website)

Australian Accounting Standard AASB 139 *Financial Instruments: Recognition and Measurement* (as amended) is set out in paragraphs 1 – 108C and Appendix A. All the paragraphs have equal authority. Terms defined in this Standard are in *italics* the first time they appear in the Standard. AASB 139 is to be read in the context of other Australian Accounting Standards, including AASB 1048 *Interpretation of Standards*, which identifies the Australian Accounting Interpretations. In the absence of explicit guidance, AASB 108 *Accounting Policies, Changes in Accounting Estimates and Errors* provides a basis for selecting and applying accounting policies.

Compilation Details

Accounting Standard AASB 139 *Financial Instruments: Recognition and Measurement* as amended

This compiled Standard applies to annual reporting periods beginning on or after 1 January 2011 but before 1 January 2013. It takes into account amendments up to and including 27 October 2010 and was prepared on 26 November 2010 by the staff of the Australian Accounting Standards Board (AASB).

This compilation is not a separate Accounting Standard made by the AASB. Instead, it is a representation of AASB 139 (July 2004) as amended by other Accounting Standards, which are listed in the Table below.

Table of Standards

Standard	Date made	Application date *(annual reporting periods ... on or after ...)*	Application, saving or transitional provisions
AASB 139	15 Jul 2004	*(beginning)* 1 Jan 2005	
AASB 2004-2	22 Dec 2004	*(beginning)* 1 Jan 2005	–
AASB 2005-1	5 May 2005	*(beginning)* 1 Jan 2006	see (a) below
AASB 2005-4	9 Jun 2005	*(beginning)* 1 Jan 2006	see (a) below
AASB 2005-5	9 Jun 2005	*(beginning)* 1 Jan 2006	see (a) below
AASB 2005-9	6 Sep 2005	*(beginning)* 1 Jan 2006	see (a) below
AASB 2005-10	5 Sep 2005	*(beginning)* 1 Jan 2007	see (b) below

Standard	Date made	Application date *(annual reporting periods ... on or after ...)*	Application, saving or transitional provisions
AASB 2005-11	8 Sep 2005	*(ending)* 31 Dec 2005	see (c) below
Erratum	24 Feb 2006	*(ending)* 24 Feb 2006	see (d) below
AASB 2007-2	15 Feb 2007	*(ending)* 28 Feb 2007	see (e) below
AASB 2007-4	30 Apr 2007	*(beginning)* 1 Jul 2007	see (f) below
AASB 2007-8	24 Sep 2007	*(beginning)* 1 Jan 2009	see (g) below
AASB 2007-10	13 Dec 2007	*(beginning)* 1 Jan 2009	see (g) below
AASB 2008-2	5 Mar 2008	*(beginning)* 1 Jan 2009	see (h) below
AASB 2008-3	6 Mar 2008	*(beginning)* 1 Jul 2009	see (i) below
AASB 2008-5	24 Jul 2008	*(beginning)* 1 Jan 2009	see (j) below
AASB 2008-8	27 Aug 2008	*(beginning)* 1 Jul 2009	see (k) below
AASB 2008-10	22 Oct 2008	*(ending)* 1 Jul 2008	see (l) below
AASB 2008-12	18 Dec 2008	*(ending)* 1 Jul 2008	see (l) below
AASB 2009-3	22 Apr 2009	*(ending)* 30 Jun 2009	see (l) below
AASB 2009-5	21 May 2009	*(beginning)* 1 Jan 2010	see (m) below
AASB 2009-6	25 Jun 2009	*(beginning)* 1 Jan 2009 and *(ending)* 30 Jun 2009	see (n) below
AASB 2009-7	25 Jun 2009	*(beginning)* 1 Jul 2009	see (o) below
Erratum	5 Oct 2009	*(beginning)* 1 Jan 2009 and *(ending)* 30 Jun 2009	see (p) below
AASB 2009-11	7 Dec 2009	*(beginning)* 1 Jan 2013	not compiled*
AASB 2009-12	15 Dec 2009	*(beginning)* 1 Jan 2011	see (q) below
AASB 2010-3	23 Jun 2010	*(beginning)* 1 Jul 2010	see (r) below
AASB 2010-5	27 Oct 2010	*(beginning)* 1 Jan 2011	see (q) below

*   The amendments made by this Standard are not included in this compilation, which presents the principal Standard as applicable to annual reporting periods beginning on or after 1 January 2011 but before 1 January 2013.

(a)   Entities may elect to apply this Standard to annual reporting periods beginning on or after 1 January 2005 but before 1 January 2006.

(b)   Entities may elect to apply this Standard to annual reporting periods beginning on or after 1 January 2005 but before 1 January 2007.

(c)   Entities may elect to apply this Standard to annual reporting periods beginning on or after 1 January 2005 that end before 31 December 2005.

(d)   Entities may elect to apply this Erratum to annual reporting periods beginning on or after 1 January 2005 that end before 24 February 2006.

(e)   Entities may elect to apply the relevant amendments to annual reporting periods beginning on or after 1 January 2005 that end before 28 February 2007.

(f)   Entities may elect to apply this Standard to annual reporting periods beginning on or after 1 January 2005 but before 1 July 2007.

(g)   Entities may elect to apply this Standard to annual reporting periods beginning on or after 1 January 2005 but before 1 January 2009, provided that AASB 101 *Presentation of Financial Statements* (September 2007) is also applied to such periods.

(h)   Entities may elect to apply this Standard to annual reporting periods beginning on or after 1 January 2005 but before 1 January 2009.

(i)   Entities may elect to apply this Standard to annual reporting periods beginning on or after 30 June 2007 but before 1 July 2009, provided that AASB 3 *Business Combinations* (March 2008) and AASB 127 *Consolidated and Separate Financial Statements* (March 2008) are also applied to such periods.

(j)   Entities may elect to apply this Standard, or its amendments to individual Standards, to annual reporting periods beginning on or after 1 January 2005 but before 1 January 2009.

(k)   Entities may elect to apply this Standard to annual reporting periods beginning on or after 1 January 2005 but before 1 July 2009.

(l)   Entities are not permitted to apply this Standard to earlier annual reporting periods.

(m) Entities may elect to apply this Standard, or its amendments to individual Standards, to annual reporting periods beginning on or after 1 January 2005 but before 1 January 2010.

(n)   Entities may elect to apply this Standard to annual reporting periods beginning on or after 1 January 2005 but before 1 January 2009, provided that AASB 101 *Presentation of Financial Statements* (September 2007) is also applied to such periods, and to annual reporting periods beginning on or after 1 January 2009 that end before 30 June 2009.

(o)   Entities may elect to apply this Standard to annual reporting periods beginning before 1 July 2009 that end on or after 1 July 2008.

(p)   Entities may elect to apply this Erratum to annual reporting periods beginning on or after 1 January 2005, provided that AASB 2009-6 *Amendments to Australian Accounting Standards* is also applied to such periods.

(q)   Entities may elect to apply this Standard to annual reporting periods beginning on or after 1 January 2005 but before 1 January 2011.

(r)   Entities may elect to apply this Standard to annual reporting periods beginning on or after 1 January 2005 but before 1 July 2010.

Table of Amendments

Paragraph affected	How affected	By ... [paragraph]
1	amended	AASB 2005-10 [30]
Aus1.1	amended	AASB 2007-8 [7, 8]
Aus1.4	amended	AASB 2007-8 [8]
2	amended	AASB 2005-5 [11]
	amended	AASB 2005-9 [15]
	amended	Erratum, Feb 2006
	amended	AASB 2008-2 [34]
	amended	AASB 2008-3 [78]
	amended	AASB 2009-5 [20]
3	deleted	AASB 2005-9 [16]
4	amended	AASB 2005-9 [17]
8	amended	Erratum, Feb 2006
9	amended	AASB 2005-4 [7]
	amended	AASB 2005-9 [18]
	amended	AASB 2005-10 [31]
	amended	AASB 2007-4 [101]
	amended	AASB 2008-5 [64]
	amended	AASB 2009-6 [91]
11	amended	AASB 2007-8 [128]
11A	added	AASB 2005-4 [8]
12	amended	AASB 2005-4 [9]
	amended	AASB 2007-8 [129]
	amended	AASB 2009-3 [5]
13	amended	AASB 2005-4 [9]
14	amended	AASB 2007-8 [130]
15	amended	AASB 2007-2 [10]
19	amended	AASB 2007-8 [6]
45	amended	AASB 2005-10 [32]
	amended	AASB 2007-8 [6]
47	amended	AASB 2005-9 [19]
	amended	AASB 2007-4 [101]
48	amended	AASB 2005-10 [33]
48A	added	AASB 2005-4 [10]
50	amended	AASB 2008-10 [6]
50A	added	AASB 2008-5 [65]
50B-50F	added	AASB 2008-10 [7]

AASB

Paragraph affected	How affected	By ... [paragraph]
54	amended	AASB 2007-8 [131]
55	amended	AASB 2007-8 [131]
	amended	AASB 2009-6 [92]
57	amended	AASB 2010-5 [59]
58	amended	AASB 2007-8 [6]
67	amended	AASB 2007-8 [6]
68	amended	AASB 2007-8 [132]
73	amended	AASB 2008-5 [64]
80	amended	AASB 2005-1 [6]
	amended	AASB 2009-5 [20]
88	amended	Erratum, Feb 2006
95	amended	AASB 2007-8 [133]
97	amended	AASB 2007-8 [134]
	amended	AASB 2009-5 [20]
98	amended	AASB 2007-8 [135]
100	amended	AASB 2007-8 [135]
	amended	AASB 2009-5 [20]
101	amended	AASB 2007-8 [136]
102	amended	AASB 2007-8 [137]
	amended	AASB 2008-3 [79]
103	amended	AASB 2005-1 [7]
(preceding heading)	amended	AASB 2008-5 [66]
	amended	AASB 2009-3 [6]
103A-103B	note added	AASB 2005-9 [20]
103C	note added	AASB 2007-8 [138]
103D	note added	AASB 2008-3 [80]
	paragraph added (in place of note)	AASB 2010-3 [13]
103E	note added	AASB 2008-3 [80]
103F	note added	AASB 2008-2 [35]
103G	note added	AASB 2008-8 [5]
Aus103H-Aus103I	added	AASB 2008-12 [5]
Aus103H	renumbered as 103H and amended	AASB 2009-7 [14]
Aus103I	renumbered as 103I and amended	AASB 2009-7 [15]
103J	added	AASB 2009-3 [6]
103K	added	AASB 2009-5 [21]
103N	added	AASB 2010-3 [13]
105	amended	AASB 2005-4 [11]
	amended	AASB 2007-8 [139]
105A-105D	added	AASB 2005-4 [11]
107A	note added	AASB 2009-6 [93]
108	added	AASB 2007-8 [139]
108A-108B	added	AASB 2005-1 [8]
108C	added	AASB 2008-5 [67]
	amended	AASB 2009-5 [20]
AG1	amended	AASB 2007-4 [101]
AG2	amended	AASB 2007-4 [101]
AG3	amended	AASB 2007-4 [100,101]

Paragraph affected	How affected	By ... [paragraph]
AG4	renumbered as AG3A renumbered from AG4A amended amended	AASB 2005-9 [21] AASB 2007-8 [140]
AG4A	renumbered as AG4 added amended	AASB 2005-9 [21] AASB 2005-9 [22] AASB 2007-10 [90]
AG4B-AG4K (and headings)	added	AASB 2005-4 [12]
AG4C	amended	AASB 2007-10 [90]
AG4D	amended	AASB 2007-10 [90]
AG4E	amended amended	AASB 2007-4 [101] AASB 2007-8 [140]
AG4I	amended	AASB 2007-4 [101]
AG8	amended amended amended	AASB 2008-10 [8] AASB 2008-12 [6] AASB 2008-5 [64]
AG23	amended	Erratum, Feb 2006
AG25	amended amended	AASB 2007-8 [6] Erratum, Oct 2009 [4]
AG29	amended	AASB 2007-4 [101]
AG30	amended	AASB 2009-5 [20]
AG32	amended	AASB 2007-8 [6]
AG33	amended	AASB 2007-4 [101]
AG33A-AG33B (and preceding heading)	added	AASB 2005-4 [13]
AG46	amended	AASB 2007-4 [101]
AG51	amended amended	Erratum, Feb 2006 AASB 2007-8 [142]
AG52	amended amended	AASB 2005-11 [14] AASB 2009-6 [94]
AG53	amended	AASB 2007-4 [101]
AG64	amended	Erratum, Feb 2006
AG66	amended	AASB 2005-11 [15]
AG67	amended amended	AASB 2007-8 [143] AASB 2009-6 [95]
AG71	amended	AASB 2007-8 [6]
AG76A	added	AASB 2004-2 [16]
AG77	amended	Erratum, Feb 2006
AG79	amended	AASB 2007-4 [101]
AG82	amended	AASB 2007-4 [101]
AG86	amended amended	AASB 2007-8 [6] AASB 2007-10 [91]
AG87	amended	AASB 2009-12 [18]
AG99A-AG99B	renumbered as AG99C-AG99D added	AASB 2005-1 [9]
AG99B	amended	AASB 2007-8 [144]
AG99BA	added	AASB 2008-8 [6]
AG99E-AG99F	added	AASB 2008-8 [7]

Paragraph affected	How affected	By ... [paragraph]
AG106	amended	AASB 2007-10 [90]
AG110A–AG110B	added	AASB 2008-8 [8]
AG125	amended	AASB 2007-4 [101]
AG129	amended	AASB 2007-8 [145]
AG133 (and preceding heading)	added	AASB 2005-1 [10]

General Terminology Amendments

The following amendments are not shown in the above Table of Amendments:

References to 'income statement', 'balance sheet' and 'separate balance sheet line item' were amended to 'statement of comprehensive income', 'statement of financial position' and 'separate line item in the statement of financial position' respectively by AASB 2007-8.

References to 'recognised in equity' and 'recognised directly in equity' were amended to 'recognised in other comprehensive income' by AASB 2007-8.

References in the Illustrative Example to 'statement of comprehensive income' were amended to 'profit or loss' by AASB 2009-6.

Comparison with IAS 39

AASB 139 and IAS 39

AASB 139 *Financial Instruments: Recognition and Measurement* as amended incorporates IAS 39 *Financial Instruments: Recognition and Measurement* as issued and amended by the International Accounting Standards Board (IASB). Paragraphs that have been added to this Standard (and do not appear in the text of IAS 39) are identified with the prefix "Aus", followed by the number of the preceding IASB paragraph and decimal numbering.

Compliance with IAS 39

Entities that comply with AASB 139 as amended will simultaneously be in compliance with IAS 39 as amended.

Accounting Standard AASB 139

The Australian Accounting Standards Board made Accounting Standard AASB 139 *Financial Instruments: Recognition and Measurement* under section 334 of the *Corporations Act 2001* on 15 July 2004.

This compiled version of AASB 139 applies to annual reporting periods beginning on or after 1 January 2011 but before 1 January 2013. It incorporates relevant amendments contained in other AASB Standards made by the AASB and other decisions of the AASB up to and including 27 October 2010 (see Compilation Details).

Accounting Standard AASB 139

Financial Instruments: Recognition and Measurement

Objective

1 The objective of this Standard is to establish principles for recognising and measuring financial assets, financial liabilities and some contracts to buy or sell non-financial items. Requirements for presenting information about financial instruments are in AASB 132 *Financial Instruments: Presentation*. Requirements for disclosing information about financial instruments are in AASB 7 *Financial Instruments: Disclosures*.

Application

Aus1.1   This Standard applies to:

(a)   each entity that is required to prepare financial reports in accordance with Part 2M.3 of the Corporations Act and that is a reporting entity;

(b)   general purpose financial statements of each other reporting entity; and

(c)   financial statements that are, or are held out to be, general purpose financial statements.

Aus1.2   This Standard applies to annual reporting periods beginning on or after 1 January 2005.

[Note: For application dates of paragraphs changed or added by an amending Standard, see Compilation Details.]

Aus1.3   This Standard shall not be applied to annual reporting periods beginning before 1 January 2005.

Aus1.4   The requirements specified in this Standard apply to the financial statements where information resulting from their application is material in accordance with AASB 1031 *Materiality*.

Aus1.5   Notice of this Standard was published in the *Commonwealth of Australia Gazette* No S 294, 22 July 2004.

Scope

2   This Standard shall be applied by all entities to all types of financial instruments except:

(a)   those interests in subsidiaries, associates and joint ventures that are accounted for under AASB 127 *Consolidated and Separate Financial Statements*; AASB 128 *Investments in Associates*; or AASB 131 *Interests in Joint Ventures*. However, entities shall apply this Standard to an interest in a subsidiary, associate or joint venture that according to AASB 127, AASB 128 or AASB 131 is accounted for under this Standard. Entities shall also apply this Standard to *derivatives* on an interest in a subsidiary, associate or joint venture unless the derivative meets the definition of an equity instrument of the entity in AASB 132;

(b)   rights and obligations under leases to which AASB 117 *Leases* applies. However:

(i)   lease receivables recognised by a lessor are subject to the *derecognition* and impairment provisions of this Standard (see paragraphs 15-37 and 58, 59, 63-65 and Appendix A paragraphs AG36-AG52 and AG84-AG93);

(ii)   finance lease payables recognised by a lessee are subject to the derecognition provisions of this Standard (see paragraphs 39-42 and Appendix A paragraphs AG57-AG63); and

(iii)   derivatives that are embedded in leases are subject to the embedded derivatives provisions of this Standard (see paragraphs 10-13 and Appendix A paragraphs AG27-AG33);

(c)   employers' rights and obligations under employee benefit plans, to which AASB 119 *Employee Benefits* applies;

(d)   financial instruments issued by the entity that meet the definition of an equity instrument in AASB 132 (including options and warrants) or that are required to be classified as an equity instrument in accordance with paragraphs 16A and 16B or paragraphs 16C and 16D of AASB 132. However, the holder of such equity instruments shall apply this Standard to those instruments, unless they meet the exception in (a) above;

(e)   rights and obligations arising under (i) an insurance contract as defined in AASB 4 *Insurance Contracts*, other than an issuer's rights and obligations arising under an insurance contract that meets the definition of a financial guarantee contract in paragraph 9, or (ii) a contract that is within the scope of AASB 4 because it contains a discretionary participation feature. However, this Standard applies to a derivative that is embedded in a contract within the scope of AASB 4 if the derivative is not itself a contract within the scope of AASB 4 (see paragraphs 10-13 and Appendix A paragraphs AG27-AG33). Moreover, if an issuer of financial guarantee contracts has previously asserted explicitly that it regards such contracts as insurance contracts and has used accounting applicable to insurance contracts, the issuer may elect to apply either this Standard or AASB 1023 *General Insurance Contracts* to such financial guarantee contracts (see paragraphs AG4 and AG4A). The issuer may make that election contract by contract, but the election for each contract is irrevocable;

(f)   [Deleted by the IASB]

(g)   any forward contracts between an acquirer and a selling shareholder to buy or sell an acquiree that will result in a business combination at a future acquisition date. The term of the forward contract should not exceed a reasonable period normally necessary to obtain any required approvals and to complete the transaction;

(h)   loan commitments other than those loan commitments described in paragraph 4. An issuer of loan commitments shall apply AASB 137 *Provisions, Contingent Liabilities and Contingent Assets* to loan commitments that are not within the scope of this Standard. However, all loan commitments are subject to the derecognition provisions of this Standard (see paragraphs 15-42 and Appendix A paragraphs AG36-AG63);

(i)   financial instruments, contracts and obligations under share-based payment transactions to which AASB 2 *Share-based Payment* applies, except for contracts within the scope of paragraphs 5-7 of this Standard, to which this Standard applies; and

(j)   rights to payments to reimburse the entity for expenditure it is required to make to settle a liability that it recognises as a provision in accordance with AASB 137, or for which, in an earlier period, it recognised a provision in accordance with AASB 137.

3   [Deleted by the IASB]

4   The following loan commitments are within the scope of this Standard:

(a)   loan commitments that the entity designates as financial liabilities at fair value through profit or loss. An entity that has a past practice of selling the assets resulting from its loan commitments shortly after origination shall apply this Standard to all its loan commitments in the same class;

(b)   loan commitments that can be settled net in cash or by delivering or issuing another financial instrument. These loan commitments are derivatives. A loan commitment is not regarded as settled net merely because the loan is paid out in instalments (e.g. a mortgage construction loan that is paid out in instalments in line with the progress of construction); and

(c)   commitments to provide a loan at a below-market interest rate. Paragraph 47(d) specifies the subsequent measurement of liabilities arising from these loan commitments.

5   This Standard shall be applied to those contracts to buy or sell a non-financial item that can be settled net in cash or in another financial instrument, or by exchanging financial instruments, as if the contracts were financial instruments, with the exception of contracts that were entered into and continue to be held for the purpose of receipt or delivery of a non-financial item in accordance with the entity's expected purchase, sale, or usage requirements.

6   There are various ways in which a contract to buy or sell a non-financial item can be settled net in cash or another financial instrument or by exchanging financial instruments. These include:

(a)   when the terms of the contract permit either party to settle it net in cash or in another financial instrument or by exchanging financial instruments;

(b)   when the ability to settle net in cash or in another financial instrument, or by exchanging financial instruments, is not explicit in the terms of the contract, but the entity has a practice of settling similar contracts net in cash or another financial instrument or by exchanging financial instruments (whether with the counterparty, by entering into offsetting contracts or by selling the contract before its exercise or lapse);

(c)   when, for similar contracts, the entity has a practice of taking delivery of the underlying and selling it within a short period after delivery for the purpose of generating a profit from short-term fluctuations in price or dealer's margin; and

(d)   when the non-financial item that is the subject of the contract is readily convertible to cash.

A contract to which (b) and (c) applies is not entered into for the purpose of the receipt or delivery of the non-financial item in accordance with the entity's expected purchase, sale or usage requirements, and accordingly, is within the scope of this Standard. Other contracts to which paragraph 5 applies are evaluated to determine whether they were entered into and continue to be held for the purpose of the receipt or delivery of the non-financial item in accordance with the entity's expected purchase, sale or usage requirements, and accordingly, whether they are within the scope of this Standard.

7   A written option to buy or sell a non-financial item that can be settled net in cash or another financial instrument, or by exchanging financial instruments, in accordance with paragraph 6(a) or (d) is within the scope of this Standard. Such a contract cannot be entered into for the purpose of the receipt or delivery of the non-financial item in accordance with the entity's expected purchase, sale or usage requirements.

Definitions

8   The terms defined in AASB 132 are used in this Standard with the meanings specified in paragraph 11 of AASB 132. AASB 132 defines the following terms:

(a)   financial instrument;

(b)   financial asset;

(c)   financial liability; and

(d)   equity instrument;

and provides guidance on applying those definitions.

9   **The following terms are used in this Standard with the meanings specified.**

Definition of a Derivative

A *derivative* **is a financial instrument or other contract within the scope of this Standard (see paragraphs 2-7) with all three of the following characteristics:**

(a)   **its value changes in response to the change in a specified interest rate, financial instrument price, commodity price, foreign exchange rate, index of prices or rates, credit rating or credit index, or other variable, provided in the case of a non-financial variable that the variable is not specific to a party to the contract (sometimes called the 'underlying');**

(b)   **it requires no initial net investment or an initial net investment that is smaller than would be required for other types of contracts that would be expected to have a similar response to changes in market factors; and**

(c)   **it is settled at a future date.**

Definitions of Four Categories of Financial Instruments

A *financial asset or financial liability at fair value through profit or loss* is a financial asset or financial liability that meets either of the following conditions:

(a) it is classified as held for trading. A financial asset or financial liability is classified as held for trading if:

    (i) it is acquired or incurred principally for the purpose of selling or repurchasing it in the near term;

    (ii) on initial recognition it is part of a portfolio of identified financial instruments that are managed together and for which there is evidence of a recent actual pattern of short-term profit-taking; or

    (iii) it is a derivative (except for a derivative that is a financial guarantee contract or a designated and effective hedging instrument);

(b) upon initial recognition it is designated by the entity as at fair value through profit or loss. An entity may use this designation only when permitted by paragraph 11A, or when doing so results in more relevant information, because either:

    (i) it eliminates or significantly reduces a measurement or recognition inconsistency (sometimes referred to as 'an accounting mismatch') that would otherwise arise from measuring assets or liabilities or recognising the gains and losses on them on different bases; or

    (ii) a group of financial assets, financial liabilities or both is managed and its performance is evaluated on a fair value basis, in accordance with a documented risk management or investment strategy, and information about the group is provided internally on that basis to the entity's key management personnel (as defined in AASB 124 *Related Party Disclosures*), for example the entity's board of directors and chief executive officer.

In AASB 7, paragraphs 9-11 and B4 require the entity to provide disclosures about financial assets and financial liabilities it has designated as at fair value through profit or loss, including how it has satisfied these conditions. For instruments qualifying in accordance with (ii) above, that disclosure includes a narrative description of how designation as at fair value through profit or loss is consistent with the entity's documented risk management or investment strategy.

Investments in equity instruments that do not have a quoted market price in an active market, and whose fair value cannot be reliably measured (see paragraph 46(c) and Appendix A paragraphs AG80 and AG81), shall not be designated as at fair value through profit or loss.

It should be noted that paragraphs 48, 48A, 49 and Appendix A paragraphs AG69-AG82, which set out requirements for determining a reliable measure of the fair value of a financial asset or financial liability, apply equally to all items that are measured at fair value, whether by designation or otherwise, or whose fair value is disclosed.

Held-to-maturity investments are non-derivative financial assets with fixed or determinable payments and fixed maturity that an entity has the positive intention and ability to hold to maturity (see Appendix A paragraphs AG16-AG25) other than:

(a) those that the entity upon initial recognition designates as at fair value through profit or loss;

(b) those that the entity designates as available for sale; and

(c) those that meet the definition of loans and receivables.

An entity shall not classify any financial assets as held to maturity if the entity has, during the current annual reporting period or during the two preceding annual reporting periods, sold or reclassified more than an insignificant amount of held-to-maturity investments before maturity (more than insignificant in relation to the total amount of held-to-maturity investments) other than sales or reclassifications that:

    (i)   are so close to maturity or the financial asset's call date (e.g. less than three months before maturity) that changes in the market rate of interest would not have a significant effect on the financial asset's fair value;

    (ii)   occur after the entity has collected substantially all of the financial asset's original principal through scheduled payments or prepayments; or

    (iii) are attributable to an isolated event that is beyond the entity's control, is non-recurring and could not have been reasonably anticipated by the entity.

Loans and receivables are non-derivative financial assets with fixed or determinable payments that are not quoted in an active market, other than:

    (a)   those that the entity intends to sell immediately or in the near term, which shall be classified as held for trading, and those that the entity upon initial recognition designates as at fair value through profit or loss;

    (b)   those that the entity upon initial recognition designates as available for sale; or

    (c)   those for which the holder may not recover substantially all of its initial investment, other than because of credit deterioration, which shall be classified as available for sale.

An interest acquired in a pool of assets that are not loans or receivables (e.g. an interest in a mutual fund or a similar fund) is not a loan or receivable.

Available-for-sale financial assets are those non-derivative financial assets that are designated as available for sale or that are not classified as (a) loans and receivables, (b) held-to-maturity investments or (c) financial assets at fair value through profit or loss.

Definition of a Financial Guarantee Contract

A *financial guarantee contract* is a contract that requires the issuer to make specified payments to reimburse the holder for a loss it incurs because a specified debtor fails to make payment when due in accordance with the original or modified terms of a debt instrument.

Definitions Relating to Recognition and Measurement

The *amortised cost of a financial asset or financial liability* is the amount at which the financial asset or financial liability is measured at initial recognition minus principal repayments, plus or minus the cumulative amortisation using the effective interest method of any difference between that initial amount and the maturity amount, and minus any reduction (directly or through the use of an allowance account) for impairment or uncollectibility.

The *effective interest method* is a method of calculating the amortised cost of a financial asset or a financial liability (or group of financial assets or financial liabilities) and of allocating the interest income or interest expense over the relevant period. The effective interest rate is the rate that exactly discounts estimated future cash payments or receipts through the expected life of the financial instrument or, when appropriate, a shorter period to the net carrying amount of the financial asset or financial liability. When calculating the effective interest rate, an entity shall estimate cash flows considering all contractual terms of the financial instrument (e.g., prepayment, call and similar options) but shall not consider future credit losses. The calculation includes all fees and points paid or received between parties to the contract that are an integral part of the effective interest rate (see AASB 118 *Revenue*), transaction costs, and all other premiums or discounts. There is a presumption that the cash flows and the expected life of a group of similar financial instruments can be estimated reliably. However, in those rare cases when it is not possible to estimate reliably the cash flows or the expected life of a financial instrument (or group of financial instruments), the entity shall use the contractual cash flows over the full contractual term of the financial instrument (or group of financial instruments).

Derecognition means the removal of a previously recognised financial asset or financial liability from an entity's statement of financial position.

Fair value is the amount for which an asset could be exchanged or a liability settled, between knowledgeable, willing parties in an arm's length transaction.[1]

A *regular way purchase or sale* is a purchase or sale of a financial asset under a contract whose terms require delivery of the asset within the time frame established generally by regulation or convention in the marketplace concerned.

Transaction costs are incremental costs that are directly attributable to the acquisition, issue or disposal of a financial asset or financial liability (see Appendix A paragraph AG13). An incremental cost is one that would not have been incurred if the entity had not acquired, issued or disposed of the financial instrument.

Definitions Relating to Hedge Accounting

A *firm commitment* is a binding agreement for the exchange of a specified quantity of resources at a specified price on a specified future date or dates.

A *forecast transaction* is an uncommitted but anticipated future transaction.

A *hedging instrument* is a designated derivative or (for a hedge of the risk of changes in foreign currency exchange rates only) a designated non-derivative financial asset or non-derivative financial liability whose fair value or cash flows are expected to offset changes in the fair value or cash flows of a designated hedged item (paragraphs 72-77 and Appendix A paragraphs AG94-AG97 elaborate on the definition of a hedging instrument).

A *hedged item* is an asset, liability, firm commitment, highly probable forecast transaction or net investment in a foreign operation that (a) exposes the entity to risk of changes in fair value or future cash flows and (b) is designated as being hedged (paragraphs 78-84 and Appendix A paragraphs AG98-AG101 elaborate on the definition of hedged items).

Hedge effectiveness is the degree to which changes in fair value or cash flows attributable to a hedged risk are offset by changes in the fair value or cash flows of the hedging instrument (see Appendix A paragraphs AG105-AG113).

Embedded Derivatives

10   An embedded derivative is a component of a hybrid (combined) instrument that also includes a non-derivative host contract – with the effect that some of the cash flows of the combined instrument vary in a way similar to a stand-alone derivative. An embedded derivative causes some or all of the cash flows that otherwise would be required by the contract to be modified according to a specified interest rate, financial instrument price, commodity price, foreign exchange rate, index of prices or rates, credit rating or credit index, or other variable. A derivative that is attached to a financial instrument but is contractually transferable independently of that instrument, or has a different counterparty from that instrument, is not an embedded derivative, but a separate financial instrument.

11   An embedded derivative shall be separated from the host contract and accounted for as a derivative under this Standard if, and only if:

(a)   the economic characteristics and risks of the embedded derivative are not closely related to the economic characteristics and risks of the host contract (see Appendix A paragraphs AG30 and AG33);

---

1   Paragraphs 48-49 and AG69-AG82 of Appendix A contain requirements for determining the fair value of a financial asset or financial liability.

(b)   a separate instrument with the same terms as the embedded derivative would meet the definition of a derivative; and

(c)   the hybrid (combined) instrument is not measured at fair value with changes in fair value recognised in profit or loss (i.e. a derivative that is embedded in a *financial asset or financial liability at fair value through profit or loss* is not separated).

If an embedded derivative is separated, the host contract shall be accounted for under this Standard if it is a financial instrument, and in accordance with other appropriate Standards if it is not a financial instrument. This Standard does not address whether an embedded derivative shall be presented separately in the statement of financial position.

11A   Notwithstanding paragraph 11, if a contract contains one or more embedded derivatives, an entity may designate the entire hybrid (combined) contract as a financial asset or financial liability at fair value through profit or loss unless:

(a)   the embedded derivative(s) does not significantly modify the cash flows that otherwise would be required by the contract; or

(b)   it is clear with little or no analysis when a similar hybrid (combined) instrument is first considered that separation of the embedded derivative(s) is prohibited, such as a prepayment option embedded in a loan that permits the holder to prepay the loan for approximately its amortised cost.

12   If an entity is required by this Standard to separate an embedded derivative from its host contract, but is unable to measure the embedded derivative separately either at acquisition or at the end of a subsequent financial reporting period, it shall designate the entire hybrid (combined) contract as at fair value through profit or loss. Similarly, if an entity is unable to measure separately the embedded derivative that would have to be separated on reclassification of a hybrid (combined) contract out of the fair value through profit or loss category, that reclassification is prohibited. In such circumstances the hybrid (combined) contract remains classified as at fair value through profit or loss in its entirety.

13   If an entity is unable to determine reliably the fair value of an embedded derivative on the basis of its terms and conditions (for example, because the embedded derivative is based on an unquoted equity instrument), the fair value of the embedded derivative is the difference between the fair value of the hybrid (combined) instrument and the fair value of the host contract, if those can be determined under this Standard. If the entity is unable to determine the fair value of the embedded derivative using this method, paragraph 12 applies and the hybrid (combined) instrument is designated as at fair value through profit or loss.

Recognition and Derecognition

Initial Recognition

14   An entity shall recognise a financial asset or a financial liability in its statement of financial position when, and only when, the entity becomes a party to the contractual provisions of the instrument. (See paragraph 38 with respect to regular way purchases of financial assets.)

Derecognition of a Financial Asset

15   In consolidated financial statements, paragraphs 16-23 and Appendix A paragraphs AG34-AG52 are applied at a consolidated level. Hence, an entity first consolidates all subsidiaries in accordance with AASB 127 and the Interpretation 112 *Consolidation – Special Purpose Entities* as identified in AASB 1048 *Interpretation of Standards*, and then applies paragraphs 16-23 and Appendix A paragraphs AG34-AG52 to the resulting group.

16   Before evaluating whether, and to what extent, derecognition is appropriate under paragraphs 17-23, an entity determines whether those paragraphs should be applied

to a part of a financial asset (or a part of a group of similar financial assets) or a financial asset (or a group of similar financial assets) in its entirety, as follows:

(a) Paragraphs 17-23 are applied to a part of a financial asset (or a part of a group of similar financial assets) if, and only if, the part being considered for derecognition meets one of the following three conditions:

(i) The part comprises only specifically identified cash flows from a financial asset (or a group of similar financial assets). For example, when an entity enters into an interest rate strip whereby the counterparty obtains the right to the interest cash flows, but not the principal cash flows from a debt instrument, paragraphs 17-23 are applied to the interest cash flows.

(ii) The part comprises only a fully proportionate (pro rata) share of the cash flows from a financial asset (or a group of similar financial assets). For example, when an entity enters into an arrangement whereby the counterparty obtains the rights to a 90 per cent share of all principal and interest cash flows of a debt instrument, paragraphs 17-23 are applied to 90 per cent of those cash flows. If there is more than one counterparty, each counterparty is not required to have a proportionate share of the cash flows provided that the transferring entity has a fully proportionate share.

(iii) The part comprises only a fully proportionate (pro rata) share of specifically identified cash flows from a financial asset (or a group of similar financial assets). For example, when an entity enters into an arrangement whereby the counterparty obtains the rights to a 90 per cent share of interest cash flows from a financial asset, paragraphs 17-23 are applied to 90 per cent of those interest cash flows. If there is more than one counterparty, each counterparty is not required to have a proportionate share of the specifically identified cash flows provided that the transferring entity has a fully proportionate share.

(b) In all other cases, paragraphs 17-23 are applied to the financial asset in its entirety (or to the group of similar financial assets in their entirety). For example, when an entity transfers (i) the rights to the first or the last 90 per cent of cash collections from a financial asset (or a group of financial assets), or (ii) the rights to 90 per cent of the cash flows from a group of receivables, but provides a guarantee to compensate the buyer for any credit losses up to 8 per cent of the principal amount of the receivables, paragraphs 17-23 are applied to the financial asset (or a group of similar financial assets) in its entirety.

In paragraphs 17-26, the term 'financial asset' refers to either a part of a financial asset (or a part of a group of similar financial assets) as identified in (a) above or, otherwise, a financial asset (or a group of similar financial assets) in its entirety.

17 An entity shall derecognise a financial asset when, and only when:

(a) the contractual rights to the cash flows from the financial asset expire; or

(b) it transfers the financial asset as set out in paragraphs 18 and 19 and the transfer qualifies for derecognition in accordance with paragraph 20.

(See paragraph 38 for regular way sales of financial assets.)

18 An entity transfers a financial asset if, and only if, it either:

(a) transfers the contractual rights to receive the cash flows of the financial asset; or

(b) retains the contractual rights to receive the cash flows of the financial asset, but assumes a contractual obligation to pay the cash flows to one or more recipients in an arrangement that meets the conditions in paragraph 19.

19 When an entity retains the contractual rights to receive the cash flows of a financial asset (the 'original asset'), but assumes a contractual obligation to pay those cash flows to one or more entities (the 'eventual recipients'), the entity treats the transaction as

a transfer of a financial asset if, and only if, all of the following three conditions are met.

(a)   The entity has no obligation to pay amounts to the eventual recipients unless it collects equivalent amounts from the original asset. Short-term advances by the entity with the right of full recovery of the amount lent plus accrued interest at market rates do not violate this condition.

(b)   The entity is prohibited by the terms of the transfer contract from selling or pledging the original asset other than as security to the eventual recipients for the obligation to pay them cash flows.

(c)   The entity has an obligation to remit any cash flows it collects on behalf of the eventual recipients without material delay. In addition, the entity is not entitled to reinvest such cash flows, except for investments in cash or cash equivalents (as defined in AASB 107 *Statement of Cash Flows*) during the short settlement period from the collection date to the date of required remittance to the eventual recipients, and interest earned on such investments is passed to the eventual recipients.

20   When an entity transfers a financial asset (see paragraph 18), it shall evaluate the extent to which it retains the risks and rewards of ownership of the financial asset. In this case:

(a)   if the entity transfers substantially all the risks and rewards of ownership of the financial asset, the entity shall derecognise the financial asset and recognise separately as assets or liabilities any rights and obligations created or retained in the transfer;

(b)   if the entity retains substantially all the risks and rewards of ownership of the financial asset, the entity shall continue to recognise the financial asset;

(c)   if the entity neither transfers nor retains substantially all the risks and rewards of ownership of the financial asset, the entity shall determine whether it has retained control of the financial asset. In this case:

      (i)   if the entity has not retained control, it shall derecognise the financial asset and recognise separately as assets or liabilities any rights and obligations created or retained in the transfer;

      (ii)   if the entity has retained control, it shall continue to recognise the financial asset to the extent of its continuing involvement in the financial asset (see paragraph 30).

21   The transfer of risks and rewards (see paragraph 20) is evaluated by comparing the entity's exposure, before and after the transfer, with the variability in the amounts and timing of the net cash flows of the transferred asset. An entity has retained substantially all the risks and rewards of ownership of a financial asset if its exposure to the variability in the present value of the future net cash flows from the financial asset does not change significantly as a result of the transfer (e.g. because the entity has sold a financial asset subject to an agreement to buy it back at a fixed price or the sales price plus a lender's return). An entity has transferred substantially all the risks and rewards of ownership of a financial asset if its exposure to such variability is no longer significant in relation to the total variability in the present value of the future net cash flows associated with the financial asset (e.g. because the entity has sold a financial asset subject only to an option to buy it back at its fair value at the time of repurchase or has transferred a fully proportionate share of the cash flows from a larger financial asset in an arrangement, such as a loan sub-participation, that meets the conditions in paragraph 19).

22   Often it will be obvious whether the entity has transferred or retained substantially all risks and rewards of ownership and there will be no need to perform any computations. In other cases, it will be necessary to compute and compare the entity's exposure to the variability in the present value of the future net cash flows before and after the transfer. The computation and comparison is made using as the discount rate an appropriate current market interest rate. All reasonably possible variability in net cash flows is considered, with greater weight being given to those outcomes that are more likely to occur.

23   Whether the entity has retained control (see paragraph 20(c)) of the transferred asset depends on the transferee's ability to sell the asset. If the transferee has the practical ability to sell the asset in its entirety to an unrelated third party and is able to exercise that ability unilaterally and without needing to impose additional restrictions on the transfer, the entity has not retained control. In all other cases, the entity has retained control.

Transfers that Qualify for Derecognition (see paragraphs 20(a) and (c)(i))

24   **If an entity transfers a financial asset in a transfer that qualifies for derecognition in its entirety and retains the right to service the financial asset for a fee, it shall recognise either a servicing asset or a servicing liability for that servicing contract. If the fee to be received is not expected to compensate the entity adequately for performing the servicing, a servicing liability for the servicing obligation shall be recognised at its fair value. If the fee to be received is expected to be more than adequate compensation for the servicing, a servicing asset shall be recognised for the servicing right at an amount determined on the basis of an allocation of the carrying amount of the larger financial asset in accordance with paragraph 27.**

25   **If, as a result of a transfer, a financial asset is derecognised in its entirety but the transfer results in the entity obtaining a new financial asset or assuming a new financial liability, or a servicing liability, the entity shall recognise the new financial asset, financial liability or servicing liability at fair value.**

26   **On derecognition of a financial asset in its entirety, the difference between:**

   (a)   **the carrying amount; and**

   (b)   **the sum of (i) the consideration received (including any new asset obtained less any new liability assumed) and (ii) any cumulative gain or loss that had been recognised in other comprehensive income (see paragraph 55(b));**

   shall be recognised in profit or loss.

27   **If the transferred asset is part of a larger financial asset (e.g. when an entity transfers interest cash flows that are part of a debt instrument, see paragraph 16(a)) and the part transferred qualifies for derecognition in its entirety, the previous carrying amount of the larger financial asset shall be allocated between the part that continues to be recognised and the part that is derecognised, based on the relative fair values of those parts on the date of the transfer. For this purpose, a retained servicing asset shall be treated as a part that continues to be recognised. The difference between:**

   (a)   **the carrying amount allocated to the part derecognised; and**

   (b)   **the sum of (i) the consideration received for the part derecognised (including any new asset obtained less any new liability assumed) and (ii) any cumulative gain or loss allocated to it that had been recognised in other comprehensive income (see paragraph 55(b));**

   shall be recognised in profit or loss. A cumulative gain or loss that had been recognised in other comprehensive income is allocated between the part that continues to be recognised and the part that is derecognised based on the relative fair values of those parts.

28   **When an entity allocates the previous carrying amount of a larger financial asset between the part that continues to be recognised and the part that is derecognised, the fair value of the part that continues to be recognised needs to be determined. When the entity has a history of selling parts similar to the part that continues to be recognised or other market transactions exist for such parts, recent prices of actual transactions provide the best estimate of its fair value. When there are no price quotes or recent market transactions to support the fair value of the part that continues to be recognised, the best estimate of the fair value is the difference between the fair value of the larger financial asset as a whole and the consideration received from the transferee for the part that is derecognised.**

Transfers that Do Not Qualify for Derecognition (see paragraph 20(b))

29   **If a transfer does not result in derecognition because the entity has retained substantially all the risks and rewards of ownership of the transferred asset, the entity**

shall continue to recognise the transferred asset in its entirety and shall recognise a financial liability for the consideration received. In subsequent periods, the entity shall recognise any income on the transferred asset and any expense incurred on the financial liability.

Continuing Involvement in Transferred Assets (see paragraph 20(c)(ii))

30   If an entity neither transfers nor retains substantially all the risks and rewards of ownership of a transferred asset, and retains control of the transferred asset, the entity continues to recognise the transferred asset to the extent of its continuing involvement. The extent of the entity's continuing involvement in the transferred asset is the extent to which it is exposed to changes in the value of the transferred asset. For example:

(a)   when the entity's continuing involvement takes the form of guaranteeing the transferred asset, the extent of the entity's continuing involvement is the lower of (i) the amount of the asset and (ii) the maximum amount of the consideration received that the entity could be required to repay ('the guarantee amount');

(b)   when the entity's continuing involvement takes the form of a written or purchased option (or both) on the transferred asset, the extent of the entity's continuing involvement is the amount of the transferred asset that the entity may repurchase. However, in case of a written put option on an asset that is measured at fair value, the extent of the entity's continuing involvement is limited to the lower of the fair value of the transferred asset and the option exercise price (see paragraph AG48); and

(c)   when the entity's continuing involvement takes the form of a cash-settled option or similar provision on the transferred asset, the extent of the entity's continuing involvement is measured in the same way as that which results from non-cash settled options as set out in (b) above.

31   When an entity continues to recognise an asset to the extent of its continuing involvement, the entity also recognises an associated liability. Despite the other measurement requirements in this Standard, the transferred asset and the associated liability are measured on a basis that reflects the rights and obligations that the entity has retained. The associated liability is measured such that the net carrying amount of the transferred asset and the associated liability is:

(a)   the amortised cost of the rights and obligations retained by the entity, if the transferred asset is measured at amortised cost; or

(b)   equal to the fair value of the rights and obligations retained by the entity when measured on a stand-alone basis, if the transferred asset is measured at fair value.

32   The entity shall continue to recognise any income arising on the transferred asset to the extent of its continuing involvement and shall recognise any expense incurred on the associated liability.

33   For the purpose of subsequent measurement, recognised changes in the fair value of the transferred asset and the associated liability are accounted for consistently with each other in accordance with paragraph 55, and shall not be offset.

34   If an entity's continuing involvement is in only a part of a financial asset (e.g. when an entity retains an option to repurchase part of a transferred asset, or retains a residual interest that does not result in the retention of substantially all the risks and rewards of ownership and the entity retains control), the entity allocates the previous carrying amount of the financial asset between the part it continues to recognise under continuing involvement, and the part it no longer recognises based on the relative fair values of those parts on the date of the transfer. For this purpose, the requirements of paragraph 28 apply. The difference between:

(a)   the carrying amount allocated to the part that is no longer recognised; and

(b)   the sum of (i) the consideration received for the part no longer recognised and (ii) any cumulative gain or loss allocated to it that had been recognised in other comprehensive income (see paragraph 55(b));

shall be recognised in profit or loss. A cumulative gain or loss that had been recognised in other comprehensive income is allocated between the part that continues to be recognised and the part that is no longer recognised on the basis of the relative fair values of those parts.

35   If the transferred asset is measured at amortised cost, the option in this Standard to designate a financial liability as at fair value through profit or loss is not applicable to the associated liability.

All Transfers

36   If a transferred asset continues to be recognised, the asset and the associated liability shall not be offset. Similarly, the entity shall not offset any income arising from the transferred asset with any expense incurred on the associated liability (see AASB 132, paragraph 42).

37   If a transferor provides non-cash collateral (such as debt or equity instruments) to the transferee, the accounting for the collateral by the transferor and the transferee depends on whether the transferee has the right to sell or repledge the collateral and on whether the transferor has defaulted. The transferor and transferee shall account for the collateral as follows.

    (a)   If the transferee has the right by contract or custom to sell or repledge the collateral, then the transferor shall reclassify that asset in its statement of financial position (e.g. as a loaned asset, pledged equity instruments or repurchase receivable) separately from other assets.

    (b)   If the transferee sells collateral pledged to it, it shall recognise the proceeds from the sale and a liability measured at fair value for its obligation to return the collateral.

    (c)   If the transferor defaults under the terms of the contract and is no longer entitled to redeem the collateral, it shall derecognise the collateral, and the transferee shall recognise the collateral as its asset initially measured at fair value or, if it has already sold the collateral, derecognise its obligation to return the collateral.

    (d)   Except as provided in (c), the transferor shall continue to carry the collateral as its asset, and the transferee shall not recognise the collateral as an asset.

Regular Way Purchase or Sale of a Financial Asset

38   A *regular way purchase or sale* of financial assets shall be recognised and derecognised, as applicable, using trade date accounting or settlement date accounting (see Appendix A paragraphs AG53-AG56).

Derecognition of a Financial Liability

39   An entity shall remove a financial liability (or a part of a financial liability) from its statement of financial position when, and only when, it is extinguished – that is, when the obligation specified in the contract is discharged or cancelled or expires.

40   An exchange between an existing borrower and lender of debt instruments with substantially different terms shall be accounted for as an extinguishment of the original financial liability and the recognition of a new financial liability. Similarly, a substantial modification of the terms of an existing financial liability or a part of it (whether or not attributable to the financial difficulty of the debtor) shall be accounted for as an extinguishment of the original financial liability and the recognition of a new financial liability.

41   The difference between the carrying amount of a financial liability (or part of a financial liability) extinguished or transferred to another party and the consideration paid, including any non-cash assets transferred or liabilities assumed, shall be recognised in profit or loss.

42   If an entity repurchases a part of a financial liability, the entity shall allocate the previous carrying amount of the financial liability between the part that continues to be recognised and the part that is derecognised based on the relative fair values of those parts on the date

of the repurchase. The difference between (a) the carrying amount allocated to the part derecognised and (b) the consideration paid, including any non-cash assets transferred or liabilities assumed, for the part derecognised shall be recognised in profit or loss.

Measurement

Initial Measurement of Financial Assets and Financial Liabilities

43 **When a financial asset or financial liability is recognised initially, an entity shall measure it at its fair value plus, in the case of a financial asset or financial liability not at fair value through profit or loss, *transaction costs* that are directly attributable to the acquisition or issue of the financial asset or financial liability.**

44 When an entity uses settlement date accounting for an asset that is subsequently measured at cost or amortised cost, the asset is recognised initially at its fair value on the trade date (see Appendix A paragraphs AG53-AG56).

Subsequent Measurement of Financial Assets

45 For the purpose of measuring a financial asset after initial recognition, this Standard classifies financial assets into the following four categories defined in paragraph 9:

(a) financial assets at fair value through profit or loss;

(b) *held-to-maturity investments*;

(c) *loans and receivables*; and

(d) *available-for-sale financial assets*.

These categories apply to measurement and profit or loss recognition under this Standard. The entity may use other descriptors for these categories or other categorisations when presenting information in the financial statements. The entity shall disclose in the notes the information required by AASB 7.

46 **After initial recognition, an entity shall measure financial assets, including derivatives that are assets, at their fair values, without any deduction for transaction costs it may incur on sale or other disposal, except for the following financial assets:**

(a) **loans and receivables as defined in paragraph 9, which shall be measured at amortised cost using the *effective interest method*;**

(b) **held-to-maturity investments as defined in paragraph 9, which shall be measured at amortised cost using the effective interest method; and**

(c) **investments in equity instruments that do not have a quoted market price in an active market and whose fair value cannot be reliably measured and derivatives that are linked to and must be settled by delivery of such unquoted equity instruments, which shall be measured at cost (see Appendix A paragraphs AG80 and AG81).**

Financial assets that are designated as *hedged items* are subject to measurement under the hedge accounting requirements in paragraphs 89-102. All financial assets except those measured at fair value through profit or loss are subject to review for impairment in accordance with paragraphs 58-70, and Appendix A paragraphs AG84-AG93.

Subsequent Measurement of Financial Liabilities

47 **After initial recognition, an entity shall measure all financial liabilities at amortised cost using the effective interest method, except for:**

(a) **financial liabilities at fair value through profit or loss. Such liabilities, including derivatives that are liabilities, shall be measured at fair value except for a derivative liability that is linked to and must be settled by delivery of an unquoted equity instrument whose fair value cannot be reliably measured which shall be measured at cost;**

(b) **financial liabilities that arise when a transfer of a financial asset does not qualify for derecognition or when the continuing involvement approach** applies. Paragraphs 29 and 31 apply to the measurement of such financial liabilities;

(c)   financial guarantee contracts as defined in paragraph 9. After initial recognition, an issuer of such a contract shall (unless paragraph 47(a) or (b) applies) measure it at the higher of:

      (i)   the amount determined in accordance with AASB 137; and

      (ii)   the amount initially recognised (see paragraph 43) less, when appropriate, cumulative amortisation recognised in accordance with AASB 118; and

(d)   commitments to provide a loan at a below-market interest rate. After initial recognition, an issuer of such a commitment shall (unless paragraph 47(a) applies) measure it at the higher of:

      (i)   the amount determined in accordance with AASB 137; and

      (ii)   the amount initially recognised (see paragraph 43) less, when appropriate, cumulative amortisation recognised in accordance with AASB 118.

Financial liabilities that are designated as hedged items are subject to the hedge accounting requirements in paragraphs 89-102.

Fair Value Measurement Considerations

48   In determining the fair value of a financial asset or a financial liability for the purpose of applying this Standard, AASB 132 or AASB 7, an entity shall apply paragraphs AG69-AG82 of Appendix A.

48A   The best evidence of fair value is quoted prices in an active market. If the market for a financial instrument is not active, an entity establishes fair value by using a valuation technique. The objective of using a valuation technique is to establish what the transaction price would have been on the measurement date in an arm's length exchange motivated by normal business considerations. Valuation techniques include using recent arm's length market transactions between knowledgeable, willing parties, if available, reference to the current fair value of another instrument that is substantially the same, discounted cash flow analysis and option pricing models. If there is a valuation technique commonly used by market participants to price the instrument and that technique has been demonstrated to provide reliable estimates of prices obtained in actual market transactions, the entity uses that technique. The chosen valuation technique makes maximum use of market inputs and relies as little as possible on entity-specific inputs. It incorporates all factors that market participants would consider in setting a price and is consistent with accepted economic methodologies for pricing financial instruments. Periodically, an entity calibrates the valuation technique and tests it for validity using prices from any observable current market transactions in the same instrument (i.e. without modification or repackaging) or based on any available observable market data.

49   The fair value of a financial liability with a demand feature (e.g. a demand deposit) is not less than the amount payable on demand, discounted from the first date that the amount could be required to be paid.

Reclassifications

50   An entity:

(a)   shall not reclassify a derivative out of the fair value through profit or loss category while it is held or issued;

(b)   shall not reclassify any financial instrument out of the fair value through profit or loss category if upon initial recognition it was designated by the entity as at fair value through profit or loss; and

(c)   may, if a financial asset is no longer held for the purpose of selling or repurchasing it in the near term (notwithstanding that the financial asset may have been acquired or incurred principally for the purpose of selling or repurchasing it in the near term), reclassify that financial asset out of the fair

value through profit or loss category if the requirements in paragraph 50B or 50D are met.

An entity shall not reclassify any financial instrument into the fair value through profit or loss category after initial recognition.

50A   The following changes in circumstances are not reclassifications for the purposes of paragraph 50:

    (a)   a derivative that was previously a designated and effective hedging instrument in a cash flow hedge or net investment hedge no longer qualifies as such;

    (b)   a derivative becomes a designated and effective hedging instrument in a cash flow hedge or net investment hedge;

    (c)   financial assets are reclassified when an insurance company changes its accounting policies in accordance with paragraph 45 of AASB 4.

50B   A financial asset to which paragraph 50(c) applies (except a financial asset of the type described in paragraph 50D) may be reclassified out of the fair value through profit or loss category only in rare circumstances.

50C   If an entity reclassifies a financial asset out of the fair value through profit or loss category in accordance with paragraph 50B, the financial asset shall be reclassified at its fair value on the date of reclassification. Any gain or loss already recognised in profit or loss shall not be reversed. The fair value of the financial asset on the date of reclassification becomes its new cost or amortised cost, as applicable.

50D   A financial asset to which paragraph 50(c) applies that would have met the definition of loans and receivables (if the financial asset had not been required to be classified as held for trading at initial recognition) may be reclassified out of the fair value through profit or loss category if the entity has the intention and ability to hold the financial asset for the foreseeable future or until maturity.

50E   A financial asset classified as available for sale that would have met the definition of loans and receivables (if it had not been designated as available for sale) may be reclassified out of the available-for-sale category to the loans and receivables category if the entity has the intention and ability to hold the financial asset for the foreseeable future or until maturity.

50F   If an entity reclassifies a financial asset out of the fair value through profit or loss category in accordance with paragraph 50D or out of the available-for-sale category in accordance with paragraph 50E, it shall reclassify the financial asset at its fair value on the date of reclassification. For a financial asset reclassified in accordance with paragraph 50D, any gain or loss already recognised in profit or loss shall not be reversed. The fair value of the financial asset on the date of reclassification becomes its new cost or amortised cost, as applicable. For a financial asset reclassified out of the available-for-sale category in accordance with paragraph 50E, any previous gain or loss on that asset that has been recognised in other comprehensive income in accordance with paragraph 55(b) shall be accounted for in accordance with paragraph 54.

51   **If, as a result of a change in intention or ability, it is no longer appropriate to classify an investment as held-to-maturity, it shall be reclassified as available for sale and remeasured at fair value, and the difference between its carrying amount and fair value shall be accounted for in accordance with paragraph 55(b).**

52   **Whenever sales or reclassifications of more than an insignificant amount of held-to-maturity investments do not meet any of the conditions in paragraph 9, any remaining held-to-maturity investments shall be reclassified as available for sale. On such reclassification, the difference between their carrying amount and fair value shall be accounted for in accordance with paragraph 55(b).**

53   **If a reliable measure becomes available for a financial asset or financial liability for which such a measure was previously not available, and the asset or liability is required to be measured at fair value if a reliable measure is available (see paragraphs 46(c) and 47), the asset or liability shall be remeasured at fair value, and the difference between its carrying amount and fair value shall be accounted for in accordance with paragraph 55.**

54   If, as a result of a change in intention or ability or in the rare circumstance that a reliable measure of fair value is no longer available (see paragraphs 46(c) and 47) or because the 'two preceding annual reporting periods' referred to in paragraph 9 have passed, it becomes appropriate to carry a financial asset or financial liability at cost or amortised cost rather than at fair value, the fair value carrying amount of the financial asset or the financial liability on that date becomes its new cost or amortised cost, as applicable. Any previous gain or loss on that asset that has been recognised in other comprehensive income in accordance with paragraph 55(b) shall be accounted for as follows.

    (a)   In the case of a financial asset with a fixed maturity, the gain or loss shall be amortised to profit or loss over the remaining life of the held-to-maturity investment using the effective interest method. Any difference between the new amortised cost and maturity amount shall also be amortised over the remaining life of the financial asset using the effective interest method, similar to the amortisation of a premium and a discount. If the financial asset is subsequently impaired, any gain or loss that has been recognised in other comprehensive income is reclassified from equity to profit or loss in accordance with paragraph 67.

    (b)   In the case of a financial asset that does not have a fixed maturity, the gain or loss shall be recognised in profit or loss when the financial asset is sold or otherwise disposed of. If the financial asset is subsequently impaired any previous gain or loss that has been recognised in other comprehensive income is reclassified from equity to profit or loss in accordance with paragraph 67.

Gains and Losses

55   A gain or loss arising from a change in the fair value of a financial asset or financial liability that is not part of a hedging relationship (see paragraphs 89-102) shall be recognised, as follows.

    (a)   A gain or loss on a financial asset or financial liability classified as at fair value through profit or loss shall be recognised in profit or loss.

    (b)   A gain or loss on an available-for-sale financial asset shall be recognised in other comprehensive income, except for impairment losses (see paragraphs 67-70) and foreign exchange gains and losses (see Appendix A paragraph AG83), until the financial asset is derecognised. At that time, the cumulative gain or loss previously recognised in other comprehensive income shall be reclassified from equity to profit or loss as a reclassification adjustment (see AASB 101 *Presentation of Financial Statements* (as revised in 2007)). However, interest calculated using the effective interest method (see paragraph 9) is recognised in profit or loss (see AASB 118). Dividends on an available-for-sale equity instrument are recognised in profit or loss when the entity's right to receive payment is established (see AASB 118).

56   For financial assets and financial liabilities carried at amortised cost (see paragraphs 46 and 47), a gain or loss is recognised in profit or loss when the financial asset or financial liability is derecognised or impaired, and through the amortisation process. However, for financial assets or financial liabilities that are hedged items (see paragraphs 78-84, and Appendix A paragraphs AG98-AG101) the accounting for the gain or loss shall follow paragraphs 89-102.

57   If an entity recognises financial assets using settlement date accounting (see paragraph 38 and Appendix A paragraphs AG53-AG56), any change in the fair value of the asset to be received during the period between the trade date and the settlement date is not recognised for assets carried at cost or amortised cost (other than impairment losses). For assets carried at fair value, however, the change in fair value shall be recognised in profit or loss or in other comprehensive income, as appropriate under paragraph 55.

Impairment and Uncollectibility of Financial Assets

58   **An entity shall assess at the end of each reporting period whether there is any objective evidence that a financial asset or group of financial assets is impaired. If any such evidence exists, the entity shall apply paragraph 63 (for financial assets carried at amortised cost), paragraph 66 (for financial assets carried at cost) or paragraph 67 (for available-for-sale financial assets) to determine the amount of any impairment loss.**

59   A financial asset or a group of financial assets is impaired and impairment losses are incurred if, and only if, there is objective evidence of impairment as a result of one or more events that occurred after the initial recognition of the asset (a 'loss event') and that loss event (or events) has an impact on the estimated future cash flows of the financial asset or group of financial assets that can be reliably estimated. It may not be possible to identify a single, discrete event that caused the impairment. Rather the combined effect of several events may have caused the impairment. Losses expected as a result of future events, no matter how likely, are not recognised. Objective evidence that a financial asset or group of assets is impaired includes observable data that comes to the attention of the holder of the asset about the following loss events:

(a)   significant financial difficulty of the issuer or obligor;

(b)   a breach of contract, such as a default or delinquency in interest or principal payments;

(c)   the lender, for economic or legal reasons relating to the borrower's financial difficulty, granting to the borrower a concession that the lender would not otherwise consider;

(d)   it becoming probable that the borrower will enter bankruptcy or other financial reorganisation;

(e)   the disappearance of an active market for that financial asset because of financial difficulties; or

(f)   observable data indicating that there is a measurable decrease in the estimated future cash flows from a group of financial assets since the initial recognition of those assets, although the decrease cannot yet be identified with the individual financial assets in the group, including:

   (i)   adverse changes in the payment status of borrowers in the group (e.g. an increased number of delayed payments or an increased number of credit card borrowers who have reached their credit limit and are paying the minimum monthly amount); or

   (ii)   national or local economic conditions that correlate with defaults on the assets in the group (e.g. an increase in the unemployment rate in the geographical area of the borrowers, a decrease in property prices for mortgages in the relevant area, a decrease in oil prices for loan assets to oil producers, or adverse changes in industry conditions that affect the borrowers in the group).

60   The disappearance of an active market because an entity's financial instruments are no longer publicly traded is not evidence of impairment. A downgrade of an entity's credit rating is not, of itself, evidence of impairment, although it may be evidence of impairment when considered with other available information. A decline in the fair value of a financial asset below its cost or amortised cost is not necessarily evidence of impairment (e.g. a decline in the fair value of an investment in a debt instrument that results from an increase in the risk-free interest rate).

61   In addition to the types of events in paragraph 59, objective evidence of impairment for an investment in an equity instrument includes information about significant changes with an adverse effect that have taken place in the technological, market, economic or legal environment in which the issuer operates, and indicates that the cost of the investment in the equity instrument may not be recovered. A significant or prolonged decline in the fair value of an investment in an equity instrument below its cost is also objective evidence of impairment.

62   In some cases the observable data required to estimate the amount of an impairment loss on a financial asset may be limited or no longer fully relevant to current circumstances. For example, this may be the case when a borrower is in financial difficulties and there are few available historical data relating to similar borrowers. In such cases, the entity uses its experienced judgement to estimate the amount of any impairment loss. Similarly, an entity uses its experienced judgement to adjust observable data for a group of financial assets to reflect current circumstances (see paragraph AG89). The use of reasonable estimates is an essential part of the preparation of financial statements and does not undermine their reliability.

Financial Assets Carried at Amortised Cost

63   **If there is objective evidence that an impairment loss on loans and receivables or held-to-maturity investments carried at amortised cost has been incurred, the amount of the loss is measured as the difference between the asset's carrying amount and the present value of estimated future cash flows (excluding future credit losses that have not been incurred) discounted at the financial asset's original effective interest rate (i.e. the effective interest rate computed at initial recognition). The carrying amount of the asset shall be reduced either directly or through use of an allowance account. The amount of the loss shall be recognised in profit or loss.**

64   An entity first assesses whether objective evidence of impairment exists individually for financial assets that are individually significant, and individually or collectively for financial assets that are not individually significant (see paragraph 59). If an entity determines that no objective evidence of impairment exists for an individually assessed financial asset, whether significant or not, it includes the asset in a group of financial assets with similar credit risk characteristics and collectively assesses them for impairment. Assets that are individually assessed for impairment and for which an impairment loss is or continues to be recognised are not included in a collective assessment of impairment.

65   **If, in a subsequent period, the amount of the impairment loss decreases and the decrease can be related objectively to an event occurring after the impairment was recognised (such as an improvement in the debtor's credit rating), the previously recognised impairment loss shall be reversed either directly or by adjusting an allowance account. The reversal shall not result in a carrying amount of the financial asset that exceeds what the amortised cost would have been had the impairment not been recognised at the date the impairment is reversed. The amount of the reversal shall be recognised in profit or loss.**

Financial Assets Carried at Cost

66   **If there is objective evidence that an impairment loss has been incurred on an unquoted equity instrument that is not carried at fair value because its fair value cannot be reliably measured, or on a derivative asset that is linked to and must be settled by delivery of such an unquoted equity instrument, the amount of the impairment loss is measured as the difference between the carrying amount of the financial asset and the present value of estimated future cash flows discounted at the current market rate of return for a similar financial asset (see paragraph 46(c) and Appendix A paragraphs AG80 and AG81). Such impairment losses shall not be reversed.**

Available-for-Sale Financial Assets

67   **When a decline in the fair value of an available-for-sale financial asset has been recognised in other comprehensive income and there is objective evidence that the asset is impaired (see paragraph 59), the cumulative loss that had been recognised in other comprehensive income shall be reclassified from equity to profit or loss as a reclassification adjustment even though the financial asset has not been derecognised.**

68   **The amount of the cumulative loss that is reclassified from equity to profit or loss under paragraph 67 shall be the difference between the acquisition cost (net of any principal repayment and amortisation) and current fair value, less any impairment loss on that financial asset previously recognised in profit or loss.**

69   **Impairment losses recognised in profit or loss for an investment in an equity instrument classified as available for sale shall not be reversed through profit or loss.**

70   If, in a subsequent period, the fair value of a debt instrument classified as available
      for sale increases and the increase can be objectively related to an event occurring
      after the impairment loss was recognised in profit or loss, the impairment loss shall
      be reversed, with the amount of the reversal recognised in profit or loss.

Hedging

71   If there is a designated hedging relationship between a *hedging instrument* and
      a hedged item as described in paragraphs 85-88 and Appendix A paragraphs
      AG102-AG104, accounting for the gain or loss on the hedging instrument and the
      hedged item shall follow paragraphs 89-102.

Hedging Instruments

Qualifying Instruments

72   This Standard does not restrict the circumstances in which a derivative may be designated
      as a hedging instrument provided the conditions in paragraph 88 are met, except for some
      written options (see Appendix A paragraph AG94). However, a non-derivative financial
      asset or non-derivative financial liability may be designated as a hedging instrument only
      for a hedge of a foreign currency risk.

73   For hedge accounting purposes, only instruments that involve a party external to the
      reporting entity (i.e. external to the group or individual entity that is being reported on) can
      be designated as hedging instruments. Although individual entities within a consolidated
      group or divisions within an entity may enter into hedging transactions with other
      entities within the group or divisions within the entity, any such intragroup transactions
      are eliminated on consolidation. Therefore, such hedging transactions do not qualify for
      hedge accounting in the consolidated financial statements of the group. However, they
      may qualify for hedge accounting in the individual or separate financial statements of
      individual entities within the group provided that they are external to the individual entity
      that is being reported on.

Designation of Hedging Instruments

74   There is normally a single fair value measure for a hedging instrument in its entirety, and
      the factors that cause changes in fair value are co-dependent. Thus, a hedging relationship
      is designated by an entity for a hedging instrument in its entirety. The only exceptions
      permitted are:

      (a)   separating the intrinsic value and time value of an option contract and designating
             as the hedging instrument only the change in intrinsic value of an option and
             excluding change in its time value; and

      (b)   separating the interest element and the spot price of a forward contract.

      These exceptions are permitted because the intrinsic value of the option and the premium
      on the forward can generally be measured separately. A dynamic hedging strategy that
      assesses both the intrinsic value and time value of an option contract can qualify for hedge
      accounting.

75   A proportion of the entire hedging instrument, such as 50 per cent of the notional amount,
      may be designated as the hedging instrument in a hedging relationship. However, a
      hedging relationship may not be designated for only a portion of the time period during
      which a hedging instrument remains outstanding.

76   A single hedging instrument may be designated as a hedge of more than one type of
      risk provided that (a) the risks hedged can be identified clearly; (b) the effectiveness
      of the hedge can be demonstrated; and (c) it is possible to ensure that there is specific
      designation of the hedging instrument and different risk positions.

77   Two or more derivatives, or proportions of them (or, in the case of a hedge of currency
      risk, two or more non-derivatives or proportions of them, or a combination of derivatives
      and non-derivatives or proportions of them), may be viewed in combination and jointly
      designated as the hedging instrument, including when the risk(s) arising from some
      derivatives offset(s) those arising from others. However, an interest rate collar or other
      derivative instrument that combines a written option and a purchased option does not

qualify as a hedging instrument if it is, in effect, a net written option (for which a net premium is received). Similarly, two or more instruments (or proportions of them) may be designated as the hedging instrument only if none of them is a written option or a net written option.

Hedged Items

Qualifying Items

78   A hedged item can be a recognised asset or liability, an unrecognised firm commitment, a highly probable forecast transaction or a net investment in a foreign operation. The hedged item can be (a) a single asset, liability, firm commitment, highly probable forecast transaction or net investment in a foreign operation, (b) a group of assets, liabilities, firm commitments, highly probable forecast transactions or net investments in foreign operations with similar risk characteristics or (c) in a portfolio hedge of interest rate risk only, a portion of the portfolio of financial assets or financial liabilities that share the risk being hedged.

79   Unlike loans and receivables, a held-to-maturity investment cannot be a hedged item with respect to interest-rate risk or prepayment risk because designation of an investment as held to maturity requires an intention to hold the investment until maturity without regard to changes in the fair value or cash flows of such an investment attributable to changes in interest rates. However, a held-to-maturity investment can be a hedged item with respect to risks from changes in foreign currency exchange rates and credit risk.

80   For hedge accounting purposes, only assets, liabilities, firm commitments or highly probable forecast transactions that involve a party external to the entity can be designated as hedged items. It follows that hedge accounting can be applied to transactions between entities in the same group only in the individual or separate financial statements of those entities and not in the consolidated financial statements of the group. As an exception, the foreign currency risk of an intragroup monetary item (e.g. a payable/receivable between two subsidiaries) may qualify as a hedged item in the consolidated financial statements if it results in an exposure to foreign exchange rate gains or losses that are not fully eliminated on consolidation in accordance with AASB 121 *The Effects of Changes in Foreign Exchange Rates*. In accordance with AASB 121, foreign exchange rate gains and losses on intragroup monetary items are not fully eliminated on consolidation when the intragroup monetary item is transacted between two group entities that have different functional currencies. In addition, the foreign currency risk of a highly probable forecast intragroup transaction may qualify as a hedged item in consolidated financial statements provided that the transaction is denominated in a currency other than the functional currency of the entity entering into that transaction and the foreign currency risk will affect consolidated profit or loss.

Designation of Financial Items as Hedged Items

81   If the hedged item is a financial asset or financial liability, it may be a hedged item with respect to the risks associated with only a portion of its cash flows or fair value (such as one or more selected contractual cash flows or portions of them or a percentage of the fair value) provided that effectiveness can be measured. For example, an identifiable and separately measurable portion of the interest rate exposure of an interest-bearing asset or interest-bearing liability may be designated as the hedged risk (such as a risk-free interest rate or benchmark interest rate component of the total interest rate exposure of a hedged financial instrument).

81A   In a fair value hedge of the interest rate exposure of a portfolio of financial assets or financial liabilities (and only in such a hedge), the portion hedged may be designated in terms of an amount of a currency (e.g. an amount of dollars, euro, pounds or rand) rather than as individual assets (or liabilities). Although the portfolio may, for risk management purposes, include assets and liabilities, the amount designated is an amount of assets or an amount of liabilities. Designation of a net amount including assets and liabilities is not permitted. The entity may hedge a portion of the interest rate risk associated with this designated amount. For example, in the case of a hedge of a portfolio containing prepayable assets, the entity may hedge the change in fair value that is attributable to a change in the hedged interest rate on the basis of expected, rather than contractual, repricing dates. When the portion hedged is based on expected repricing dates, the effect that changes in the hedged interest rate have on those expected repricing dates shall be included when determining the change in the fair value of the hedged item. Consequently, if a portfolio that contains prepayable items is hedged with a nonprepayable derivative, ineffectiveness arises if the dates on which items in the hedged portfolio are expected to prepay are revised, or actual prepayment dates differ from those expected.

Designation of Non-Financial Items as Hedged Items

82　　If the hedged item is a non-financial asset or non-financial liability, it shall be designated as a hedged item (a) for foreign currency risks, or (b) in its entirety for all risks, because of the difficulty of isolating and measuring the appropriate portion of the cash flows or fair value changes attributable to specific risks other than foreign currency risks.

Designation of Groups of Items as Hedged Items

83　　Similar assets or similar liabilities shall be aggregated and hedged as a group only if the individual assets or individual liabilities in the group share the risk exposure that is designated as being hedged. Furthermore, the change in fair value attributable to the hedged risk for each individual item in the group shall be expected to be approximately proportional to the overall change in fair value attributable to the hedged risk of the group of items.

84　　Because an entity assesses *hedge effectiveness* by comparing the change in the fair value or cash flow of a hedging instrument (or group of similar hedging instruments) and a hedged item (or group of similar hedged items), comparing a hedging instrument with an overall net position (e.g. the net of all fixed rate assets and fixed rate liabilities with similar maturities), rather than with a specific hedged item, does not qualify for hedge accounting.

Hedge Accounting

85　　Hedge accounting recognises the offsetting effects on profit or loss of changes in the fair values of the hedging instrument and the hedged item.

86　　Hedging relationships are of three types:

(a)　*fair value hedge*: a hedge of the exposure to changes in fair value of a recognised asset or liability or an unrecognised firm commitment, or an identified portion of such an asset, liability, or firm commitment, that is attributable to a particular risk and could affect profit or loss;

(b)　*cash flow hedge*: a hedge of the exposure to variability in cash flows that (i) is attributable to a particular risk associated with a recognised asset or liability (such as all or some future interest payments on variable rate debt) or a highly probable forecast transaction and (ii) could affect profit or loss; and

(c)　*hedge of a net investment in a foreign operation* as defined in AASB 121.

87　　A hedge of the foreign currency risk of a firm commitment may be accounted for as a fair value hedge or as a cash flow hedge.

88　　A hedging relationship qualifies for hedge accounting under paragraphs 89-102 if, and only if, all of the following conditions are met.

(a)　At the inception of the hedge there is formal designation and documentation of the hedging relationship and the entity's risk management objective and strategy for undertaking the hedge. That documentation shall include identification of the hedging instrument, the hedged item or transaction, the nature of the risk being hedged and how the entity will assess the hedging instrument's effectiveness in offsetting the exposure to changes in the hedged item's fair value or cash flows attributable to the hedged risk.

(b)　The hedge is expected to be highly effective (see Appendix A paragraphs AG105-AG113) in achieving offsetting changes in fair value or cash flows attributable to the hedged risk, consistently with the originally documented risk management strategy for that particular hedging relationship.

AASB

(c)   For cash flow hedges, a forecast transaction that is the subject of the hedge must be highly probable and must present an exposure to variations in cash flows that could ultimately affect profit or loss.

(d)   The effectiveness of the hedge can be reliably measured, that is, the fair value or cash flows of the hedged item that are attributable to the hedged risk and the fair value of the hedging instrument can be reliably measured (see paragraphs 46 and 47 and Appendix A paragraphs AG80 and AG81 for guidance on determining fair value).

(e)   The hedge is assessed on an ongoing basis and determined actually to have been highly effective throughout the reporting periods for which the hedge was designated.

Fair Value Hedges

89   If a fair value hedge meets the conditions in paragraph 88 during the period, it shall be accounted for as follows:

(a)   the gain or loss from remeasuring the hedging instrument at fair value (for a derivative hedging instrument) or the foreign currency component of its carrying amount measured in accordance with AASB 121 (for a non-derivative hedging instrument) shall be recognised in profit or loss; and

(b)   the gain or loss on the hedged item attributable to the hedged risk shall adjust the carrying amount of the hedged item and be recognised in profit or loss. This applies if the hedged item is otherwise measured at cost. Recognition of the gain or loss attributable to the hedged risk in profit or loss applies if the hedged item is an available-for-sale financial asset.

89A   For a fair value hedge of the interest rate exposure of a portion of a portfolio of financial assets or financial liabilities (and only in such a hedge), the requirement in paragraph 89(b) may be met by presenting the gain or loss attributable to the hedged item either:

(a)   in a single separate line item within assets, for those repricing time periods for which the hedged item is an asset; or

(b)   in a single separate line item within liabilities, for those repricing time periods for which the hedged item is a liability.

The separate line items referred to in (a) and (b) above shall be presented next to financial assets or financial liabilities. Amounts included in these line items shall be removed from the statement of financial position when the assets or liabilities to which they relate are derecognised.

90   If only particular risks attributable to a hedged item are hedged, recognised changes in the fair value of the hedged item unrelated to the hedged risk are recognised as set out in paragraph 55.

91   An entity shall discontinue prospectively the hedge accounting specified in paragraph 89 if:

(a)   the hedging instrument expires or is sold, terminated or exercised (for this purpose, the replacement or rollover of a hedging instrument into another hedging instrument is not an expiration or termination if such replacement or rollover is part of the entity's documented hedging strategy);

(b)   the hedge no longer meets the criteria for hedge accounting in paragraph 88; or

(c)   the entity revokes the designation.

92   Any adjustment arising from paragraph 89(b) to the carrying amount of a hedged financial instrument for which the effective interest method is used (or, in the case of a portfolio hedge of interest rate risk, to the separate line item in the statement of financial position described in paragraph 89A) shall be amortised to profit or loss.

Amortisation may begin as soon as an adjustment exists and shall begin no later than when the hedged item ceases to be adjusted for changes in its fair value attributable to the risk being hedged. The adjustment is based on a recalculated effective interest rate at the date amortisation begins. However, if, in the case of a fair value hedge of the interest rate exposure of a portfolio of financial assets or financial liabilities (and only in such a hedge), amortising using a recalculated effective interest rate is not practicable, the adjustment shall be amortised using a straight-line method. The adjustment shall be amortised fully by maturity of the financial instrument or, in the case of a portfolio hedge of interest rate risk, by expiry of the relevant repricing time period.

93   When an unrecognised firm commitment is designated as a hedged item, the subsequent cumulative change in the fair value of the firm commitment attributable to the hedged risk is recognised as an asset or liability with a corresponding gain or loss recognised in profit or loss (see paragraph 89(b)). The changes in the fair value of the hedging instrument are also recognised in profit or loss.

94   When an entity enters into a firm commitment to acquire an asset or assume a liability that is a hedged item in a fair value hedge, the initial carrying amount of the asset or liability that results from the entity meeting the firm commitment is adjusted to include the cumulative change in the fair value of the firm commitment attributable to the hedged risk that was recognised in the statement of financial position.

Cash Flow Hedges
95   If a cash flow hedge meets the conditions in paragraph 88 during the period, it shall be accounted for as follows:

(a)   the portion of the gain or loss on the hedging instrument that is determined to be an effective hedge (see paragraph 88) shall be recognised in other comprehensive income; and

(b)   the ineffective portion of the gain or loss on the hedging instrument shall be recognised in profit or loss.

96   More specifically, a cash flow hedge is accounted for as follows:

(a)   the separate component of equity associated with the hedged item is adjusted to the lesser of the following (in absolute amounts):

(i)   the cumulative gain or loss on the hedging instrument from inception of the hedge; and

(ii)   the cumulative change in fair value (present value) of the expected future cash flows on the hedged item from inception of the hedge;

(b)   any remaining gain or loss on the hedging instrument or designated component of it (i.e. not an effective hedge) is recognised in profit or loss; and

(c)   if an entity's documented risk management strategy for a particular hedging relationship excludes from the assessment of hedge effectiveness a specific component of the gain or loss or related cash flows on the hedging instrument (see paragraphs 74, 75 and 88(a)), that excluded component of gain or loss is recognised in accordance with paragraph 55.

97   If a hedge of a forecast transaction subsequently results in the recognition of a financial asset or a financial liability, the associated gains or losses that were recognised in other comprehensive income in accordance with paragraph 95 shall be reclassified from equity to profit or loss as a reclassification adjustment (see AASB 101 (as revised in 2007)) in the same period or periods during which the hedged forecast cashflows affect profit or loss (such as in the periods that interest income or interest expense is recognised). However, if an entity expects that all or a portion of a loss recognised in other comprehensive income will not be recovered in one or more future periods, it shall reclassify into profit or loss as a reclassification adjustment the amount that is not expected to be recovered.

98   If a hedge of a forecast transaction subsequently results in the recognition of a non-financial asset or a non-financial liability, or a forecast transaction for a non-financial

asset or non-financial liability becomes a firm commitment for which fair value hedge accounting is applied, then the entity shall adopt (a) or (b) below:

(a) it reclassifies the associated gains and losses that were recognised in other comprehensive income in accordance with paragraph 95 to profit or loss as a reclassification adjustment (see AASB 101 (revised 2007)) in the same period or periods during which the asset acquired or liability assumed affects profit or loss (such as in the periods that depreciation expense or cost of sales is recognised). However, if an entity expects that all or a portion of a loss recognised in other comprehensive income will not be recovered in one or more future periods, it shall reclassify from equity to profit or loss as a reclassification adjustment the amount that is not expected to be recovered; or

(b) it removes the associated gains and losses that were recognised in other comprehensive income in accordance with paragraph 95, and includes them in the initial cost or other carrying amount of the asset or liability.

99 An entity shall adopt either (a) or (b) in paragraph 98 as its accounting policy and shall apply it consistently to all hedges to which paragraph 98 relates.

100 For cash flow hedges other than those covered by paragraphs 97 and 98, amounts that had been recognised in other comprehensive income shall be reclassified from equity to profit or loss as a reclassification adjustment (see AASB 101 (revised 2007)) in the same period or periods during which the hedged forecast cash flows affect profit or loss (for example, when a forecast sale occurs).

101 In any of the following circumstances, an entity shall discontinue prospectively the hedge accounting specified in paragraphs 95-100.

(a) The hedging instrument expires or is sold, terminated or exercised (for this purpose, the replacement or rollover of a hedging instrument into another hedging instrument is not an expiration or termination if such replacement or rollover is part of the entity's documented hedging strategy). In this case, the cumulative gain or loss on the hedging instrument that has been recognised in other comprehensive income from the period when the hedge was effective (see paragraph 95(a)) shall remain separately in equity until the forecast transaction occurs. When the transaction occurs, paragraphs 97, 98 or 100 applies.

(b) The hedge no longer meets the criteria for hedge accounting in paragraph 88. In this case, the cumulative gain or loss on the hedging instrument that has been recognised in other comprehensive income from the period when the hedge was effective (see paragraph 95(a)) shall remain separately in equity until the forecast transaction occurs. When the transaction occurs, paragraphs 97, 98 or 100 applies.

(c) The forecast transaction is no longer expected to occur, in which case any related cumulative gain or loss on the hedging instrument that has been recognised in other comprehensive income from the period when the hedge was effective (see paragraph 95(a)) shall be reclassified from equity to profit or loss as a reclassification adjustment. A forecast transaction that is no longer highly probable (see paragraph 88(c)) may still be expected to occur.

(d) The entity revokes the designation. For hedges of a forecast transaction, the cumulative gain or loss on the hedging instrument that has been recognised in other comprehensive income from the period when the hedge was effective (see paragraph 95(a)) shall remain separately in equity until the forecast transaction occurs or is no longer expected to occur. When the transaction occurs, paragraphs 97, 98 or 100 applies. If the transaction is no longer expected to occur, the cumulative gain or loss that had been recognised in other comprehensive income shall be reclassified from equity to profit or loss as a reclassification adjustment.

Hedges of a Net Investment

102   Hedges of a net investment in a foreign operation, including a hedge of a monetary item that is accounted for as part of the net investment (see AASB 121), shall be accounted for similarly to cash flow hedges:

(a)   the portion of the gain or loss on the hedging instrument that is determined to be an effective hedge (see paragraph 88) shall be recognised in other comprehensive income; and

(b)   the ineffective portion shall be recognised in profit or loss.

The gain or loss on the hedging instrument relating to the effective portion of the hedge that has been recognised in other comprehensive income shall be reclassified from equity to profit or loss as a reclassification adjustment (see AASB 101 (revised 2007)) in accordance with paragraphs 48-49 of AASB 121 on the disposal or partial disposal of the foreign operation.

Effective Date and Transition

103   [Deleted by the AASB]

103A   [Deleted by the AASB]

103B   [Deleted by the AASB]

103C   [Deleted by the AASB]

103D   AASB 2008-3 *Amendments to Australian Accounting Standards arising from AASB 3 and AASB 127* deleted paragraph 2(f). An entity shall apply that amendment for annual reporting periods beginning on or after 1 July 2009. If an entity applies AASB 3 (revised 2008) for an earlier period, the amendment shall also be applied for that earlier period. However, the amendment does not apply to contingent consideration that arose from a business combination for which the acquisition date preceded the application of AASB 3 (revised 2008). Instead, an entity shall account for such consideration in accordance with paragraphs 65A-65E of AASB 3 (as amended in 2010).

103E   [Deleted by the AASB]

103F   [Deleted by the AASB]

103G   [Deleted by the AASB]

103H   AASB 2008-10 *Amendments to Australian Accounting Standards – Reclassification of Financial Assets*, issued in October 2008, amended paragraphs 50 and AG8, and added paragraphs 50B-50F. An entity shall apply those amendments on or after 1 July 2008. An entity shall not reclassify a financial asset in accordance with paragraph 50B, 50D or 50E before 1 July 2008. Any reclassification of a financial asset made on or after 1 November 2008 shall take effect only from the date when the reclassification is made. Any reclassification of a financial asset in accordance with paragraph 50B, 50D or 50E shall not be applied retrospectively before 1 July 2008.

103I   AASB 2008-12 *Amendments to Australian Accounting Standards – Reclassification of Financial Assets – Effective Date and Transition*, issued in December 2008, added paragraph 103H. An entity shall apply that amendment on or after 1 July 2008.

103J   An entity shall apply paragraph 12, as amended by AASB 2009-3 *Amendments to Australian Accounting Standards – Embedded Derivatives*, issued in April 2009, for annual reporting periods ending on or after 30 June 2009.

103K   AASB 2009-5 *Further Amendments to Australian Accounting Standards arising from the Annual Improvements Project*, issued in May 2009, amended paragraphs 2(g), 97, 100 and AG30(g). An entity shall apply the amendments to paragraphs 2(g), 97 and 100 prospectively to all unexpired contracts for annual reporting periods beginning on or after 1 January 2010. An entity shall apply the amendment to paragraph AG30(g) for annual reporting periods beginning on or after 1 January 2010. Earlier application is permitted. If an entity applies the amendment for an earlier period it shall disclose that fact.

103N   Paragraph 103D was added by AASB 2010-3 *Amendments to Australian Accounting Standards arising from the Annual Improvements Project* issued in June 2010. An entity shall apply the last two sentences of paragraph 103D for annual reporting periods beginning on or after 1 July 2010. Earlier application is permitted.

104 [Deleted by the AASB]

105 When this Standard is first applied, an entity is permitted to designate a previously recognised financial asset as available for sale. For any such financial asset, the entity shall recognise all cumulative changes in fair value in a separate component of equity until subsequent derecognition or impairment, when the entity shall reclassify that cumulative gain or loss from equity to profit or loss as a reclassification adjustment (see AASB 101 (revised 2007)). The entity shall also:

(a) restate the financial asset using the new designation in the comparative financial statements; and

(b) disclose the fair value of the financial assets at the date of designation and their classification and carrying amount in the previous financial statements.

105A An entity shall apply paragraphs 11A, 48A, AG4B-AG4K, AG33A and AG33B and the amendments made to paragraphs 9, 12 and 13 of this Standard by AASB 2005-4 for annual periods beginning on or after 1 January 2006. Earlier application is encouraged.

105B An entity that first applies paragraphs 11A, 48A, AG4B-AG4K, AG33A and AG33B and the amendments made to paragraphs 9, 12 and 13 of this Standard by AASB 2005-4 in its annual period beginning before 1 January 2006:

(a) is permitted, when those new and amended paragraphs are first applied, to designate as at fair value through profit or loss any previously recognised financial asset or financial liability that then qualifies for such designation. When the annual period begins before 1 September 2005, such designations need not be completed until 1 September 2005 and may also include financial assets and financial liabilities recognised between the beginning of that annual period and 1 September 2005. Notwithstanding paragraph 91, any financial assets and financial liabilities designated as at fair value through profit or loss in accordance with this subparagraph that were previously designated as the hedged item in fair value hedge accounting relationships shall be de-designated from those relationships at the same time they are designated as at fair value through profit or loss;

(b) shall disclose the fair value of any financial assets or financial liabilities designated in accordance with subparagraph (a) at the date of designation and their classification and carrying amount in the previous financial statements;

(c) shall de-designate any financial asset or financial liability previously designated as at fair value through profit or loss if it does not qualify for such designation in accordance with those new and amended paragraphs. When a financial asset or financial liability will be measured at amortised cost after de-designation, the date of de-designation is deemed to be its date of initial recognition; and

(d) shall disclose the fair value of any financial assets or financial liabilities de-designated in accordance with subparagraph (c) at the date of de-designation and their new classifications.

105C An entity that first applies paragraphs 11A, 48A, AG4B-AG4K, AG33A and AG33B and the amendments made to paragraphs 9, 12 and 13 of this Standard by AASB 2005-4 in its annual period beginning on or after 1 January 2006:

(a) shall de-designate any financial asset or financial liability previously designated as at fair value through profit or loss only if it does not qualify for such designation in accordance with those new and amended paragraphs. When a financial asset or financial liability will be measured at amortised cost after de-designation, the date of de-designation is deemed to be its date of initial recognition;

(b)   shall not designate as at fair value through profit or loss any previously recognised financial assets or financial liabilities; and

(c)   shall disclose the fair value of any financial assets or financial liabilities de-designated in accordance with subparagraph (a) at the date of de-designation and their new classifications.

105D An entity shall restate its comparative financial statements using the new designations in paragraph 105B or 105C provided that, in the case of a financial asset, financial liability, or group of financial assets, financial liabilities or both, designated as at fair value through profit or loss, those items or groups would have met the criteria in paragraph 9(b)(i), 9(b)(ii) or 11A at the beginning of the comparative period or, if acquired after the beginning of the comparative period, would have met the criteria in paragraph 9(b)(i), 9(b)(ii) or 11A at the date of initial recognition.

106   [Deleted by the AASB]

107   [Deleted by the AASB]

107A [Deleted by the AASB]

108   An entity shall not adjust the carrying amount of non-financial assets and non-financial liabilities to exclude gains and losses related to cash flow hedges that were included in the carrying amount before the beginning of the financial year in which this Standard is first applied. At the beginning of the financial period in which this Standard is first applied, any amount recognised outside profit or loss (in other comprehensive income or directly in equity) for a hedge of a firm commitment that under this Standard is accounted for as a fair value hedge shall be reclassified as an asset or liability, except for a hedge of foreign currency risk that continues to be treated as a cash flow hedge.

108A An entity shall apply the last sentence of paragraph 80, and paragraphs AG99A and AG99B, for annual periods beginning on or after 1 January 2006. Earlier application is encouraged. If an entity has designated as the hedged item an external forecast transaction that:

(a)   is denominated in the functional currency of the entity entering into the transaction;

(b)   gives rise to an exposure that will have an effect on consolidated profit or loss (i.e. is denominated in a currency other than the group's presentation currency); and

(c)   would have qualified for hedge accounting had it not been denominated in the functional currency of the entity entering into it;

it may apply hedge accounting in the consolidated financial statements in the period(s) before the date of application of the last sentence of paragraph 80, and paragraphs AG99A and AG99B.

108B An entity need not apply paragraph AG99B to comparative information relating to periods before the date of application of the last sentence of paragraph 80 and paragraph AG99A.

108C Paragraphs 9, 73 and AG8 were amended and paragraph 50A added by AASB 2008-5 *Amendments to Australian Accounting Standards arising from the Annual Improvements Project* issued in July 2008. Paragraph 80 was amended by AASB 2009-5 *Further Amendments to Australian Accounting Standards arising from the Annual Improvements Project* issued in May 2009. An entity shall apply those amendments for annual reporting periods beginning on or after 1 January 2009. An entity shall apply the amendments in paragraphs 9 and 50A as of the date and in the manner it applied the 2005 amendments described in paragraph 105A. Earlier application of all the amendments is permitted. If an entity applies the amendments for an earlier period it shall disclose that fact.

Withdrawal of Other Pronouncements

109   [Deleted by the AASB]

110   [Deleted by the AASB]

Appendix A
Application Guidance

This Appendix is an integral part of AASB 139.

Scope (paragraph 2-7)

AG1 Some contracts require a payment based on climatic, geological or other physical variables. (Those based on climatic variables are sometimes referred to as 'weather derivatives'.) If those contracts are not within the scope of AASB 4, they are within the scope of this Standard.

AG2 This Standard does not change the requirements relating to employee benefit plans that comply with AAS 25 *Financial Reporting by Superannuation Plans* and royalty agreements based on the volume of sales or service revenues that are accounted for under AASB 118.

AG3 Sometimes, an entity makes what it views as a 'strategic investment' in equity instruments issued by another entity, with the intention of establishing or maintaining a long-term operating relationship with the entity in which the investment is made. The investor entity uses AASB 128 to determine whether the equity method of accounting is appropriate for such an investment. Similarly, the investor entity uses AASB 131 to determine whether proportionate consolidation or the equity method is appropriate for such an investment. If neither the equity method nor proportionate consolidation is appropriate, the entity applies this Standard to that strategic investment.

AG3A This Standard applies to the financial assets and financial liabilities of insurers other than rights and obligations that paragraph 2(e) excludes because they arise under contracts within the scope of AASB 4.

AG4 Financial guarantee contracts may have various legal forms, such as a guarantee, some types of letter of credit, a credit default contract or an insurance contract. Their accounting treatment does not depend on their legal form. The following are examples of the appropriate treatment (see paragraph 2(e)).

(a) Although a financial guarantee contract meets the definition of an insurance contract in AASB 4 if the risk transferred is significant, the issuer applies this Standard. Nevertheless, if the issuer has previously asserted explicitly that it regards such contracts as insurance contracts and has used accounting applicable to insurance contracts, the issuer may elect to apply either this Standard or AASB 1023 to such financial guarantee contracts. If this Standard applies, paragraph 43 requires the issuer to recognise a financial guarantee contract initially at fair value. If the financial guarantee contract was issued to an unrelated party in a stand-alone arm's length transaction, its fair value at inception is likely to equal the premium received, unless there is evidence to the contrary. Subsequently, unless the financial guarantee contract was designated at inception as at fair value through profit or loss or unless paragraphs 29-37 and AG47-AG52 apply (when a transfer of a financial asset does not qualify for derecognition or the continuing involvement approach applies), the issuer measures it at the higher of:

(i) the amount determined in accordance with AASB 137; and

(ii) the amount initially recognised less, when appropriate, cumulative amortisation recognised in accordance with AASB 118 (see paragraph 47(c)).

(b) Some credit-related guarantees do not, as a precondition for payment, require that the holder is exposed to, and has incurred a loss on, the failure of the debtor to make payments on the guaranteed asset when due. An example of such a guarantee is one that requires payments in response to changes in a specified credit rating or credit index. Such guarantees are not financial guarantee contracts, as defined in this Standard, and are not insurance contracts, as defined in AASB 4. Such guarantees are derivatives and the issuer applies this Standard to them.

(c) If a financial guarantee contract was issued in connection with the sale of goods, the issuer applies AASB 118 in determining when it recognises the revenue from the guarantee and from the sale of goods.

AG4A   Assertions that an issuer regards contracts as insurance contracts are typically found throughout the issuer's communications with customers and regulators, contracts, business documentation and financial statements. Furthermore, insurance contracts are often subject to accounting requirements that are distinct from the requirements for other types of transaction, such as contracts issued by banks or commercial companies. In such cases, an issuer's financial statements typically include a statement that the issuer has used those accounting requirements.

Definitions (paragraphs 8 and 9)

Designation as at Fair Value through Profit or Loss

AG4B   Paragraph 9 of this Standard allows an entity to designate a financial asset, a financial liability, or a group of financial instruments (financial assets, financial liabilities or both) as at fair value through profit or loss provided that doing so results in more relevant information.

AG4C   The decision of an entity to designate a financial asset or financial liability as at fair value through profit or loss is similar to an accounting policy choice (although, unlike an accounting policy choice, it is not required to be applied consistently to all similar transactions). When an entity has such a choice, paragraph 14(b) of AASB 108 *Accounting Policies, Changes in Accounting Estimates and Errors* requires the chosen policy to result in the financial statements providing reliable and more relevant information about the effects of transactions, other events and conditions on the entity's financial position, financial performance or cash flows. In the case of designation as at fair value through profit or loss, paragraph 9 sets out the two circumstances when the requirement for more relevant information will be met. Accordingly, to choose such designation in accordance with paragraph 9, the entity needs to demonstrate that it falls within one (or both) of these two circumstances.

Paragraph 9(b)(i): Designation eliminates or significantly reduces a measurement or recognition inconsistency that would otherwise arise

AG4D   Under AASB 139, measurement of a financial asset or financial liability and classification of recognised changes in its value are determined by the item's classification and whether the item is part of a designated hedging relationship. Those requirements can create a measurement or recognition inconsistency (sometimes referred to as an 'accounting mismatch') when, for example, in the absence of designation as at fair value through profit or loss, a financial asset would be classified as available for sale (with most changes in fair value recognised in other comprehensive income) and a liability the entity considers related would be measured at amortised cost (with changes in fair value not recognised). In such circumstances, an entity may conclude that its financial statements would provide more relevant information if both the asset and the liability were classified as at fair value through profit or loss.

AG4E   The following examples show when this condition could be met. In all cases, an entity may use this condition to designate financial assets or financial liabilities as at fair value through profit or loss only if it meets the principle in paragraph 9(b)(i).

(a) An entity has liabilities whose cash flows are contractually based on the performance of assets that would otherwise be classified as available for sale. For example, an insurer may have liabilities containing a discretionary participation feature that pay benefits based on realised and/or unrealised investment returns of a specified pool of the insurer's assets. If the measurement of those liabilities reflects current market prices, classifying the assets as at fair value through profit or loss means that changes in the fair value of the financial assets are recognised in profit or loss in the same period as related changes in the value of the liabilities.

(b) An entity has liabilities under insurance contracts whose measurement incorporates current information (as permitted by AASB 4, paragraph 24), and financial assets it considers related that would otherwise be classified as available for sale or measured at amortised cost.

(c) An entity has financial assets, financial liabilities or both that share a risk, such as interest rate risk, that gives rise to opposite changes in fair value that tend to offset each other. However, only some of the instruments would be measured at fair value through profit or loss (i.e. are derivatives, or are classified as held for trading). It may also be the case that the requirements for hedge accounting are not met, for example because the requirements for effectiveness in paragraph 88 are not met.

(d) An entity has financial assets, financial liabilities or both that share a risk, such as interest rate risk, that gives rise to opposite changes in fair value that tend to offset each other and the entity does not qualify for hedge accounting because none of the instruments is a derivative. Furthermore, in the absence of hedge accounting there is a significant inconsistency in the recognition of gains and losses. For example:

(i) the entity has financed a portfolio of fixed rate assets that would otherwise be classified as available for sale with fixed rate debentures whose changes in fair value tend to offset each other. Reporting both the assets and the debentures at fair value through profit or loss corrects the inconsistency that would otherwise arise from measuring the assets at fair value with changes recognised in other comprehensive income and the debentures at amortised cost; or

(ii) the entity has financed a specified group of loans by issuing traded bonds whose changes in fair value tend to offset each other. If, in addition, the entity regularly buys and sells the bonds but rarely, if ever, buys and sells the loans, reporting both the loans and the bonds at fair value through profit or loss eliminates the inconsistency in the timing of recognition of gains and losses that would otherwise result from measuring them both at amortised cost and recognising a gain or loss each time a bond is repurchased.

AG4F   In cases such as those described in the preceding paragraph, to designate, at initial recognition, the financial assets and financial liabilities not otherwise so measured as at fair value through profit or loss may eliminate or significantly reduce the measurement or recognition inconsistency and produce more relevant information. For practical purposes, the entity need not enter into all of the assets and liabilities giving rise to the measurement or recognition inconsistency at exactly the same time. A reasonable delay is permitted provided that each transaction is designated as at fair value through profit or loss at its initial recognition and, at that time, any remaining transactions are expected to occur.

AG4G   It would not be acceptable to designate only some of the financial assets and financial liabilities giving rise to the inconsistency as at fair value through profit or loss if to do so would not eliminate or significantly reduce the inconsistency and would therefore not result in more relevant information. However, it would be acceptable to designate only some of a number of similar financial assets or similar financial liabilities if doing so achieves a significant reduction (and possibly a greater reduction than other allowable designations) in the inconsistency. For example, assume an entity has a number of similar financial liabilities that sum to CU100[1] and a number of similar financial assets that sum to CU50 but are measured on a different basis. The entity may significantly reduce the measurement inconsistency by designating at initial recognition all of the assets but only some of the liabilities (e.g. individual liabilities with a combined total of CU45) as at fair

---

1   In this Standard, monetary amounts are denominated in 'currency units' (CU).

value through profit or loss. However, because designation as at fair value through profit or loss can be applied only to the whole of a financial instrument, the entity in this example must designate one or more liabilities in their entirety. It could not designate either a component of a liability (e.g. changes in value attributable to only one risk, such as changes in a benchmark interest rate) or a proportion (i.e. percentage) of a liability.

Paragraph 9(b)(ii): A group of financial assets, financial liabilities or both is managed and its performance is evaluated on a fair value basis, in accordance with a documented risk management or investment strategy

AG4H   An entity may manage and evaluate the performance of a group of financial assets, financial liabilities or both in such a way that measuring that group at fair value through profit or loss results in more relevant information. The focus in this instance is on the way the entity manages and evaluates performance, rather than on the nature of its financial instruments.

AG4I   The following examples show when this condition could be met. In all cases, an entity may use this condition to designate financial assets or financial liabilities as at fair value through profit or loss only if it meets the principle in paragraph 9(b)(ii).

     (a)   The entity is a venture capital organisation, mutual fund, unit trust or similar entity whose business is investing in financial assets with a view to profiting from their total return in the form of interest or dividends and changes in fair value. AASB 128 and AASB 131 allow such investments to be excluded from their scope provided they are measured at fair value through profit or loss. An entity may apply the same accounting policy to other investments managed on a total return basis but over which its influence is insufficient for them to be within the scope of AASB 128 or AASB 131.

     (b)   The entity has financial assets and financial liabilities that share one or more risks and those risks are managed and evaluated on a fair value basis in accordance with a documented policy of asset and liability management. An example could be an entity that has issued 'structured products' containing multiple embedded derivatives and manages the resulting risks on a fair value basis using a mix of derivative and non-derivative financial instruments. A similar example could be an entity that originates fixed interest rate loans and manages the resulting benchmark interest rate risk using a mix of derivative and non-derivative financial instruments.

     (c)   The entity is an insurer that holds a portfolio of financial assets, manages that portfolio so as to maximise its total return (i.e. interest or dividends and changes in fair value), and evaluates its performance on that basis. The portfolio may be held to back specific liabilities, equity or both. If the portfolio is held to back specific liabilities, the condition in paragraph 9(b)(ii) may be met for the assets regardless of whether the insurer also manages and evaluates the liabilities on a fair value basis. The condition in paragraph 9(b)(ii) may be met when the insurer's objective is to maximise total return on the assets over the longer term even if amounts paid to holders of participating contracts depend on other factors such as the amount of gains realised in a shorter period (e.g. a year) or are subject to the insurer's discretion.

AG4J   As noted above, this condition relies on the way the entity manages and evaluates performance of the group of financial instruments under consideration. Accordingly, (subject to the requirement of designation at initial recognition) an entity that designates financial instruments as at fair value through profit or loss on the basis of this condition shall so designate all eligible financial instruments that are managed and evaluated together.

AG4K   Documentation of the entity's strategy need not be extensive but should be sufficient to demonstrate compliance with paragraph 9(b)(ii). Such documentation is not required for each individual item, but may be on a portfolio basis. For example, if the performance management system for a department – as approved by the entity's key management personnel – clearly demonstrates that its performance is evaluated on a total return basis, no further documentation is required to demonstrate compliance with paragraph 9(b)(ii).

Effective Interest Rate

AG5   In some cases, financial assets are acquired at a deep discount that reflects incurred credit losses. Entities include such incurred credit losses in the estimated cash flows when computing the effective interest rate.

AG6   When applying the effective interest method, an entity generally amortises any fees, points paid or received, transaction costs, other premiums or discounts included in the calculation of the effective interest rate over the expected life of the instrument. However, a shorter period is used if this is the period to which the fees, points paid or received, transaction costs, premiums or discounts relate. This will be the case when the variable to which the fees, points paid or received, transaction costs, premiums or discounts relate, is repriced to market rates before the expected maturity of the instrument. In such a case, the appropriate amortisation period is the period to the next such repricing date. For example, if a premium or discount on a floating rate instrument reflects interest that has accrued on the instrument since interest was last paid or changes in market rates since the floating interest rate was reset to market rates, it will be amortised to the next date when the floating interest is reset to market rates. This is because the premium or discount relates to the period to the next interest reset date because, at that date, the variable to which the premium or discount relates (i.e. interest rates) is reset to market rates. If, however, the premium or discount results from a change in the credit spread over the floating rate specified in the instrument, or other variables that are not reset to market rates, it is amortised over the expected life of the instrument.

AG7   For floating rate financial assets and floating rate financial liabilities, periodic re-estimation of cash flows to reflect movements in market rates of interest alters the effective interest rate. If a floating rate financial asset or floating rate financial liability is recognised initially at an amount equal to the principal receivable or payable on maturity, re-estimating the future interest payments normally has no significant effect on the carrying amount of the asset or liability.

AG8   If an entity revises its estimates of payments or receipts, the entity shall adjust the carrying amount of the financial asset or financial liability (or group of financial instruments) to reflect actual and revised estimated cash flows. The entity recalculates the carrying amount by computing the present value of estimated future cash flows at the financial instrument's original effective interest rate or, when applicable, the revised effective interest rate calculated in accordance with paragraph 92. The adjustment is recognised in profit or loss as income or expense. If a financial asset is reclassified in accordance with paragraph 50B, 50D or 50E, and the entity subsequently increases its estimates of future cash receipts as a result of increased recoverability of those cash receipts, the effect of that increase shall be recognised as an adjustment to the effective interest rate from the date of the change in estimate rather than as an adjustment to the carrying amount of the asset at the date of the change in estimate.

Derivatives

AG9   Typical examples of derivatives are futures and forward, swap and option contracts. A derivative usually has a notional amount, which is an amount of currency, a number of shares, a number of units of weight or volume or other units specified in the contract. However, a derivative instrument does not require the holder or writer to invest or receive the notional amount at the inception of the contract. Alternatively, a derivative could require a fixed payment or payment of an amount that can change (but not proportionally with a change in the underlying) as a result of some future event that is unrelated to a notional amount. For example, a contract may require a fixed payment of CU1,000[2] if six-month LIBOR increases by 100

---

2   In this Standard, monetary amounts are denominated in 'currency units' (CU).

basis points. Such a contract is a derivative even though a notional amount is not specified.

AG10   The definition of a derivative in this Standard includes contracts that are settled gross by delivery of the underlying item (e.g. a forward contract to purchase a fixed rate debt instrument). An entity may have a contract to buy or sell a non-financial item that can be settled net in cash or another financial instrument or by exchanging financial instruments (e.g. a contract to buy or sell a commodity at a fixed price at a future date). Such a contract is within the scope of this Standard unless it was entered into and continues to be held for the purpose of delivery of a non-financial item in accordance with the entity's expected purchase, sale or usage requirements (see paragraphs 5-7).

AG11   One of the defining characteristics of a derivative is that it has an initial net investment that is smaller than would be required for other types of contracts that would be expected to have a similar response to changes in market factors. An option contract meets that definition because the premium is less than the investment that would be required to obtain the underlying financial instrument to which the option is linked. A currency swap that requires an initial exchange of different currencies of equal fair values meets the definition because it has a zero initial net investment.

AG12   A regular way purchase or sale gives rise to a fixed price commitment between trade date and settlement date that meets the definition of a derivative. However, because of the short duration of the commitment it is not recognised as a derivative financial instrument. Rather, this Standard provides for special accounting for such regular way contracts (see paragraphs 38 and AG53-AG56).

AG12A   The definition of a derivative refers to non-financial variables that are not specific to a party to the contract. These include an index of earthquake losses in a particular region and an index of temperatures in a particular city. Non-financial variables specific to a party to the contract include the occurrence or non-occurrence of a fire that damages or destroys an asset of a party to the contract. A change in the fair value of a non-financial asset is specific to the owner if the fair value reflects not only changes in market prices for such assets (a financial variable) but also the condition of the specific non-financial asset held (a non-financial variable). For example, if a guarantee of the residual value of a specific car exposes the guarantor to the risk of changes in the car's physical condition, the change in that residual value is specific to the owner of the car.

Transaction Costs

AG13   Transaction costs include fees and commissions paid to agents (including employees acting as selling agents), advisers, brokers, and dealers, levies by regulatory agencies and securities exchanges, and transfer taxes and duties. Transaction costs do not include debt premiums or discounts, financing costs or internal administrative or holding costs.

Financial Assets and Financial Liabilities Held for Trading

AG14   Trading generally reflects active and frequent buying and selling, and financial instruments held for trading generally are used with the objective of generating a profit from short-term fluctuations in price or dealer's margin.

AG15   Financial liabilities held for trading include:

(a)   derivative liabilities that are not accounted for as hedging instruments;

(b)   obligations to deliver financial assets borrowed by a short seller (i.e. an entity that sells financial assets it has borrowed and does not yet own);

(c)   financial liabilities that are incurred with an intention to repurchase them in the near term (e.g. a quoted debt instrument that the issuer may buy back in the near term depending on changes in its fair value); and

(d)   financial liabilities that are part of a portfolio of identified financial instruments that are managed together and for which there is evidence of a recent pattern of short-term profit-taking.

The fact that a liability is used to fund trading activities does not in itself make that liability one that is held for trading.

Held-to-Maturity Investments

AG16   An entity does not have a positive intention to hold to maturity an investment in a financial asset with a fixed maturity if:

    (a)   the entity intends to hold the financial asset for an undefined period;

    (b)   the entity stands ready to sell the financial asset (other than if a situation arises that is non-recurring and could not have been reasonably anticipated by the entity) in response to changes in market interest rates or risks, liquidity needs, changes in the availability of and the yield on alternative investments, changes in financing sources and terms or changes in foreign currency risk; or

    (c)   the issuer has a right to settle the financial asset at an amount significantly below its amortised cost.

AG17   A debt instrument with a variable interest rate can satisfy the criteria for a held-to-maturity investment. Equity instruments cannot be held-to-maturity investments either because they have an indefinite life (such as ordinary shares) or because the amounts the holder may receive can vary in a manner that is not predetermined (such as for share options, warrants, and similar rights). With respect to the definition of held-to-maturity investments, fixed or determinable payments and fixed maturity mean that a contractual arrangement defines the amounts and dates of payments to the holder, such as interest and principal payments. A significant risk of non-payment does not preclude classification of a financial asset as held to maturity as long as its contractual payments are fixed or determinable and the other criteria for that classification are met. If the terms of a perpetual debt instrument provide for interest payments for an indefinite period, the instrument cannot be classified as held to maturity because there is no maturity date.

AG18   The criteria for classification as a held-to-maturity investment are met for a financial asset that is callable by the issuer if the holder intends and is able to hold it until it is called or until maturity and the holder would recover substantially all of its carrying amount. The call option of the issuer, if exercised, simply accelerates the asset's maturity. However, if the financial asset is callable on a basis that would result in the holder not recovering substantially all of its carrying amount, the financial asset cannot be classified as a held-to-maturity investment. The entity considers any premium paid and capitalised transaction costs in determining whether the carrying amount would be substantially recovered.

AG19   A financial asset that is puttable (i.e. the holder has the right to require that the issuer repay or redeem the financial asset before maturity) cannot be classified as a held-to-maturity investment because paying for a put feature in a financial asset is inconsistent with expressing an intention to hold the financial asset until maturity.

AG20   For most financial assets, fair value is a more appropriate measure than amortised cost. The held-to-maturity classification is an exception, but only if the entity has a positive intention and the ability to hold the investment to maturity. When an entity's actions cast doubt on its intention and ability to hold such investments to maturity, paragraph 9 precludes the use of the exception for a reasonable period of time.

AG21   A disaster scenario that is only remotely possible, such as a run on a bank or a similar situation affecting an insurer, is not something that is assessed by an entity in deciding whether it has the positive intention and ability to hold an investment to maturity.

AG22   Sales before maturity could satisfy the condition in paragraph 9 – and therefore not raise a question about the entity's intention to hold other investments to maturity – if they are attributable to any of the following:

    (a)   a significant deterioration in the issuer's creditworthiness. For example, a sale following a downgrade in a credit rating by an external rating agency would not necessarily raise a question about the entity's intention to hold other investments to maturity if the downgrade provides evidence of a significant deterioration in the issuer's creditworthiness judged by reference to the credit rating at initial recognition. Similarly, if an entity uses internal ratings for assessing exposures, changes in those internal ratings may help to identify issuers for which there has been a significant deterioration in creditworthiness, provided the entity's approach to assigning internal ratings and changes in those ratings give a consistent, reliable, and objective measure of the credit quality of the issuers. If there is evidence that a financial asset is impaired (see paragraphs 58 and 59), the deterioration in creditworthiness is often regarded as significant;

(b) a change in tax law that eliminates or significantly reduces the tax-exempt status of interest on the held-to-maturity investment (but not a change in tax law that revises the marginal tax rates applicable to interest income);

(c) a major business combination or major disposition (such as a sale of a segment) that necessitates the sale or transfer of held-to-maturity investments to maintain the entity's existing interest rate risk position or credit risk policy (although the business combination is an event within the entity's control, the changes to its investment portfolio to maintain an interest rate risk position or credit risk policy may be consequential rather than anticipated);

(d) a change in statutory or regulatory requirements significantly modifying either what constitutes a permissible investment or the maximum level of particular types of investments, thereby causing an entity to dispose of a held-to-maturity investment;

(e) a significant increase in the industry's regulatory capital requirements that causes the entity to downsize by selling held-to-maturity investments; or

(f) a significant increase in the risk weights of held-to-maturity investments used for regulatory risk-based capital purposes.

AG23 An entity does not have a demonstrated ability to hold to maturity an investment in a financial asset with a fixed maturity if:

(a) it does not have the financial resources available to continue to finance the investment until maturity; or

(b) it is subject to an existing legal or other constraint that could frustrate its intention to hold the financial asset to maturity. (However, an issuer's call option does not necessarily frustrate an entity's intention to hold a financial asset to maturity – see paragraph AG18.)

AG24 Circumstances other than those described in paragraphs AG16-AG23 can indicate that an entity does not have a positive intention or the ability to hold an investment to maturity.

AG25 An entity assesses its intention and ability to hold its held-to-maturity investments to maturity not only when those financial assets are initially recognised, but also at the end of each subsequent reporting period.

Loans and Receivables

AG26 Any non-derivative financial asset with fixed or determinable payments (including loan assets, trade receivables, investments in debt instruments, and deposits held in banks) could potentially meet the definition of loans and receivables. However, a financial asset that is quoted in an active market (such as a quoted debt instrument, see paragraph AG71) does not qualify for classification as a loan or receivable. Financial assets that do not meet the definition of loans and receivables may be classified as held-to-maturity investments if they meet the conditions for that classification (see paragraphs 9 and AG16-AG25). On initial recognition of a financial asset that would otherwise be classified as a loan or receivable, an entity may designate it as a financial asset at fair value through profit or loss, or available for sale.

Embedded Derivatives (paragraphs 10-13)

AG27 If a host contract has no stated or predetermined maturity and represents a residual interest in the net assets of an entity, then its economic characteristics and risks are those of an equity instrument, and an embedded derivative would need to possess equity characteristics related to the same entity to be regarded as closely related. If the host contract is not an equity instrument and meets the definition of a financial instrument, then its economic characteristics and risks are those of a debt instrument.

AG28 An embedded non-option derivative (such as an embedded forward or swap) is separated from its host contract on the basis of its stated or implied substantive terms, so as to result in it having a fair value of zero at initial recognition. An embedded option-based derivative (such as an embedded put, call, cap, floor or swaption) is separated from its host contract on the basis of the stated terms of the option feature. The initial carrying amount of the host instrument is the residual amount after separating the embedded derivative.

AG29 Generally, multiple embedded derivatives in a single instrument are treated as a single compound embedded derivative. However, embedded derivatives that are classified as equity (see AASB 132) are accounted for separately from those classified as assets or liabilities. In addition, if an instrument has more than one embedded derivative and those derivatives relate to different risk exposures and are readily separable and independent of each other, they are accounted for separately from each other.

AG30 The economic characteristics and risks of an embedded derivative are not closely related to the host contract (paragraph 11(a)) in the following examples. In these examples, assuming the conditions in paragraph 11(b) and (c) are met, an entity accounts for the embedded derivative separately from the host contract.

(a) A put option embedded in an instrument that enables the holder to require the issuer to reacquire the instrument for an amount of cash or other assets that varies on the basis of the change in an equity or commodity price or index is not closely related to a host debt instrument.

(b) A call option embedded in an equity instrument that enables the issuer to reacquire that equity instrument at a specified price is not closely related to the host equity instrument from the perspective of the holder (from the issuer's perspective, the call option is an equity instrument provided it meets the conditions for that classification under AASB 132, in which case it is excluded from the scope of this Standard).

(c) An option or automatic provision to extend the remaining term to maturity of a debt instrument is not closely related to the host debt instrument unless there is a concurrent adjustment to the approximate current market rate of interest at the time of the extension. If an entity issues a debt instrument and the holder of that debt instrument writes a call option on the debt instrument to a third party, the issuer regards the call option as extending the term to maturity of the debt instrument provided the issuer can be required to participate in or facilitate the remarketing of the debt instrument as a result of the call option being exercised.

(d) Equity-indexed interest or principal payments embedded in a host debt instrument or insurance contract – by which the amount of interest or principal is indexed to the value of equity instruments – are not closely related to the host instrument because the risks inherent in the host and the embedded derivative are dissimilar.

(e) Commodity-indexed interest or principal payments embedded in a host debt instrument or insurance contract – by which the amount of interest or principal is indexed to the price of a commodity (such as gold) – are not closely related to the host instrument because the risks inherent in the host and the embedded derivative are dissimilar.

(f)   An equity conversion feature embedded in a convertible debt instrument is not closely related to the host debt instrument from the perspective of the holder of the instrument (from the issuer's perspective, the equity conversion option is an equity instrument and excluded from the scope of this Standard provided it meets the conditions for that classification under AASB 132).

(g)   A call, put, or prepayment option embedded in a host debt contract or host insurance contract is not closely related to the host contract unless:

     (i)   the option's exercise price is approximately equal on each exercise date to the amortised cost of the host debt instrument or the carrying amount of the host insurance contract; or

     (ii)   the exercise price of a prepayment option reimburses the lender for an amount up to the approximate present value of lost interest for the remaining term of the host contract. Lost interest is the product of the principal amount prepaid multiplied by the interest rate differential. The interest rate differential is the excess of the effective interest rate of the host contract over the effective interest rate the entity would receive at the prepayment date if it reinvested the principal amount prepaid in a similar contract for the remaining term of the host contract.

      The assessment of whether the call or put option is closely related to the host debt contract is made before separating the equity element of a convertible debt instrument in accordance with AASB 132.

(h)   Credit derivatives that are embedded in a host debt instrument and allow one party (the 'beneficiary') to transfer the credit risk of a particular reference asset, which it may not own, to another party (the 'guarantor') are not closely related to the host debt instrument. Such credit derivatives allow the guarantor to assume the credit risk associated with the reference asset without directly owning it.

AG31   An example of a hybrid instrument is a financial instrument that gives the holder a right to put the financial instrument back to the issuer in exchange for an amount of cash or other financial assets that varies on the basis of the change in an equity or commodity index that may increase or decrease (a 'puttable instrument'). Unless the issuer on initial recognition designates the puttable instrument as a financial liability at fair value through profit or loss, it is required to separate an embedded derivative (i.e. the indexed principal payment) under paragraph 11 because the host contract is a debt instrument under paragraph AG27 and the indexed principal payment is not closely related to a host debt instrument under paragraph AG30(a). Because the principal payment can increase and decrease, the embedded derivative is a non-option derivative whose value is indexed to the underlying variable.

AG32   In the case of a puttable instrument that can be put back at any time for cash equal to a proportionate share of the net asset value of an entity (such as units of an open-ended mutual fund or some unit-linked investment products), the effect of separating an embedded derivative and accounting for each component is to measure the combined instrument at the redemption amount that is payable at the end of the reporting period if the holder exercised its right to put the instrument back to the issuer.

AG33   The economic characteristics and risks of an embedded derivative are closely related to the economic characteristics and risks of the host contract in the following examples. In these examples, an entity does not account for the embedded derivative separately from the host contract.

(a)   An embedded derivative in which the underlying is an interest rate or interest rate index that can change the amount of interest that would otherwise be paid or received on an interest-bearing host debt contract or insurance contract is closely related to the host contract unless the combined instrument can be settled in such a way that the holder would not recover substantially all of its recognised investment or the embedded derivative could at least double the holder's initial rate of return on the host contract and could result in a rate of return that is at least twice what the market return would be for a contract with the same terms as the host contract.

(b) An embedded floor or cap on the interest rate on a debt contract or insurance contract is closely related to the host contract, provided the cap is at or above the market rate of interest and the floor is at or below the market rate of interest when the contract is issued, and the cap or floor is not leveraged in relation to the host contract. Similarly, provisions included in a contract to purchase or sell an asset (e.g. a commodity) that establish a cap and a floor on the price to be paid or received for the asset are closely related to the host contract if both the cap and floor were out of the money at inception and are not leveraged.

(c) An embedded foreign currency derivative that provides a stream of principal or interest payments that are denominated in a foreign currency and is embedded in a host debt instrument (e.g. a dual currency bond) is closely related to the host debt instrument. Such a derivative is not separated from the host instrument because AASB 121 requires foreign currency gains and losses on monetary items to be recognised in profit or loss.

(d) An embedded foreign currency derivative in a host contract that is an insurance contract or is not a financial instrument (such as a contract for the purchase or sale of a non-financial item where the price is denominated in a foreign currency) is closely related to the host contract provided it is not leveraged, does not contain an option feature, and requires payments denominated in one of the following currencies:

(i) the functional currency of any substantial party to the contract;

(ii) the currency in which the price of the related good or service that is acquired or delivered is routinely denominated in commercial transactions around the world (such as the US dollar for crude oil transactions); or

(iii) a currency that is commonly used in contracts to purchase or sell non-financial items in the economic environment in which the transaction takes place (e.g. a relatively stable and liquid currency that is commonly used in local business transactions or external trade).

(e) An embedded prepayment option in an interest-only or principal-only strip is closely related to the host contract provided the host contract (i) initially resulted from separating the right to receive contractual cash flows of a financial instrument that, in and of itself, did not contain an embedded derivative, and (ii) does not contain any terms not present in the original host debt contract.

(f) An embedded derivative in a host lease contract is closely related to the host contract if the embedded derivative is (i) an inflation-related index such as an index of lease payments to a consumer price index (provided that the lease is not leveraged and the index relates to inflation in the entity's own economic environment), (ii) contingent rentals based on related sales or (iii) a contingent rental based on variable interest rates.

(g) A unit-linking feature embedded in a host financial instrument or host insurance contract is closely related to the host instrument or host contract if the unit-denominated payments are measured at current unit values that reflect the fair values of the assets of the fund. A unit-linking feature is a contractual term that requires payments denominated in units of an internal or external investment fund.

(h) A derivative embedded in an insurance contract is closely related to the host insurance contract if the embedded derivative and host insurance contract are so interdependent that an entity cannot measure the embedded derivative separately (i.e. without considering the host contract).

Instruments containing Embedded Derivatives

AG33A   When an entity becomes a party to a hybrid (combined) instrument that contains one or more embedded derivatives, paragraph 11 requires the entity to identify any such embedded derivative, assess whether it is required to be separated from the host contract and, for those that are required to be separated, measure the derivatives at fair value at initial recognition and subsequently. These requirements can be more complex, or result in less reliable measures, than measuring the entire instrument at fair value through profit or loss. For that reason this Standard permits the entire instrument to be designated as at fair value through profit or loss.

AG33B   Such designation may be used whether paragraph 11 requires the embedded derivatives to be separated from the host contract or prohibits such separation. However, paragraph 11A would not justify designating the hybrid (combined) instrument as at fair value through profit or loss in the cases set out in paragraph 11A(a) and (b) because doing so would not reduce complexity or increase reliability.

Recognition and Derecognition (paragraphs 14-42)

Initial Recognition (paragraph 14)

AG34   As a consequence of the principle in paragraph 14, an entity recognises all of its contractual rights and obligations under derivatives in its statement of financial position as assets and liabilities, respectively, except for derivatives that prevent a transfer of financial assets from being accounted for as a sale (see paragraph AG49). If a transfer of a financial asset does not qualify for derecognition, the transferee does not recognise the transferred asset as its asset (see paragraph AG50).

AG35   The following are examples of applying the principle in paragraph 14.

    (a)   Unconditional receivables and payables are recognised as assets or liabilities when the entity becomes a party to the contract and, as a consequence, has a legal right to receive or a legal obligation to pay cash.

    (b)   Assets to be acquired and liabilities to be incurred as a result of a firm commitment to purchase or sell goods or services are generally not recognised until at least one of the parties has performed under the agreement. For example, an entity that receives a firm order does not generally recognise an asset (and the entity that places the order does not recognise a liability) at the time of the commitment but, rather, delays recognition until the ordered goods or services have been shipped, delivered or rendered. If a firm commitment to buy or sell non-financial items is within the scope of this Standard under paragraphs 5-7, its net fair value is recognised as an asset or liability on the commitment date (see (c) below). In addition, if a previously unrecognised firm commitment is designated as a hedged item in a fair value hedge, any change in the net fair value attributable to the hedged risk is recognised as an asset or liability after the inception of the hedge (see paragraphs 93 and 94).

    (c)   A forward contract that is within the scope of this Standard (see paragraphs 2-7) is recognised as an asset or a liability on the commitment date, rather than on the date on which settlement takes place. When an entity becomes a party to a forward contract, the fair values of the right and obligation are often equal, so that the net fair value of the forward is zero. If the net fair value of the right and obligation are not zero, the contract is recognised as an asset or liability.

    (d)   Option contracts that are within the scope of this Standard (see paragraphs 2-7) are recognised as assets or liabilities when the holder or writer becomes a party to the contract.

    (e)   Planned future transactions, no matter how likely, are not assets and liabilities because the entity has not become a party to a contract.

Derecognition of a Financial Asset (paragraphs 15-37)

AG36   The following flowchart illustrates the evaluation of whether and to what extent a financial asset is derecognised.

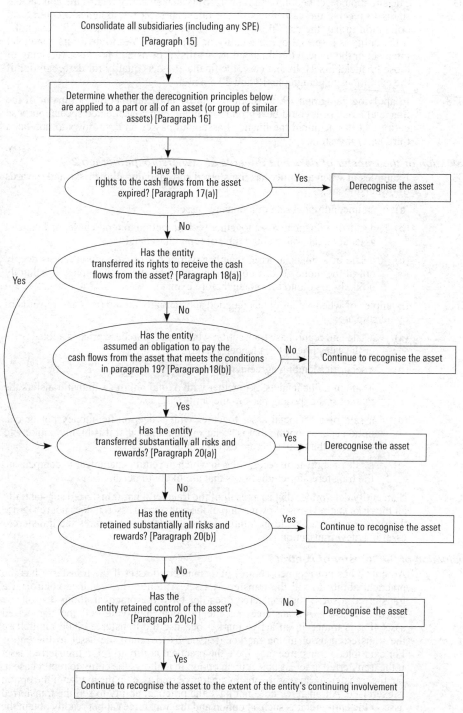

Arrangements under which an entity retains the contractual rights to receive the cash flows of a financial asset but assumes a contractual obligation to pay the cash flows to one or more recipients (paragraph 18(b))

AG37   The situation described in paragraph 18(b) (when an entity retains the contractual rights to receive the cash flows of the financial asset but assumes a contractual obligation to pay the cash flows to one or more recipients) occurs, for example, if the entity is a special purpose entity or trust, and issues to investors beneficial interests in the underlying financial assets that it owns and provides servicing of those financial assets. In that case, the financial assets qualify for derecognition if the conditions in paragraphs 19 and 20 are met.

AG38   In applying paragraph 19, the entity could be, for example, the originator of the financial asset, or it could be a group that includes a consolidated special purpose entity that has acquired the financial asset and passes on cash flows to unrelated third party investors.

Evaluation of the transfer of risks and rewards of ownership (paragraph 20)

AG39   Examples of when an entity has transferred substantially all the risks and rewards of ownership are:

(a)   an unconditional sale of a financial asset;

(b)   a sale of a financial asset together with an option to repurchase the financial asset at its fair value at the time of repurchase; and

(c)   a sale of a financial asset together with a put or call option that is deeply out of the money (i.e. an option that is so far out of the money it is highly unlikely to go into the money before expiry).

AG40   Examples of when an entity has retained substantially all the risks and rewards of ownership are:

(a)   a sale and repurchase transaction where the repurchase price is a fixed price or the sales price plus a lender's return;

(b)   a securities lending agreement;

(c)   a sale of a financial asset together with a total return swap that transfers the market risk exposure back to the entity;

(d)   a sale of a financial asset together with a deep-in-the-money put or call option (i.e. an option that is so far in the money that it is highly unlikely to go out of the money before expiry); and

(e)   a sale of short-term receivables in which the entity guarantees to compensate the transferee for credit losses that are likely to occur.

AG41   If an entity determines that as a result of the transfer it has transferred substantially all the risks and rewards of ownership of the transferred asset, it does not recognise the transferred asset again in a future period, unless it reacquires the transferred asset in a new transaction.

Evaluation of the transfer of control

AG42   An entity has not retained control of a transferred asset if the transferee has the practical ability to sell the transferred asset. An entity has retained control of a transferred asset if the transferee does not have the practical ability to sell the transferred asset. A transferee has the practical ability to sell the transferred asset if it is traded in an active market because the transferee could repurchase the transferred asset in the market if it needs to return the asset to the entity. For example, a transferee may have the practical ability to sell a transferred asset if the transferred asset is subject to an option that allows the entity to repurchase it, but the transferee can readily obtain the transferred asset in the market if the option is exercised. A transferee does not have the practical ability to sell the transferred asset if the entity retains such an option and the transferee cannot readily obtain the transferred asset in the market if the entity exercises its option.

AG43   The transferee has the practical ability to sell the transferred asset only if the transferee can sell the transferred asset in its entirety to an unrelated third party and is able to exercise that ability unilaterally and without imposing additional restrictions on the transfer. The critical question is what the transferee is able to do in practice, not what contractual rights the transferee has concerning what it can do with the transferred asset or what contractual prohibitions exist. In particular:

(a)   a contractual right to dispose of the transferred asset has little practical effect if there is no market for the transferred asset; and

(b)   an ability to dispose of the transferred asset has little practical effect if it cannot be exercised freely. For that reason:

(i)   the transferee's ability to dispose of the transferred asset must be independent of the actions of others (i.e. it must be a unilateral ability); and

(ii)   the transferee must be able to dispose of the transferred asset without needing to attach restrictive conditions or "strings" to the transfer (e.g. conditions about how a loan asset is serviced or an option giving the transferee the right to repurchase the asset).

AG44   That the transferee is unlikely to sell the transferred asset does not, of itself, mean that the transferor has retained control of the transferred asset. However, if a put option or guarantee constrains the transferee from selling the transferred asset, then the transferor has retained control of the transferred asset. For example, if a put option or guarantee is sufficiently valuable it constrains the transferee from selling the transferred asset because the transferee would, in practice, not sell the transferred asset to a third party without attaching a similar option or other restrictive conditions. Instead, the transferee would hold the transferred asset so as to obtain payments under the guarantee or put option. Under these circumstances the transferor has retained control of the transferred asset.

Transfers that Qualify for Derecognition

AG45   An entity may retain the right to a part of the interest payments on transferred assets as compensation for servicing those assets. The part of the interest payments that the entity would give up upon termination or transfer of the servicing contract is allocated to the servicing asset or servicing liability. The part of the interest payments that the entity would not give up is an interest-only strip receivable. For example, if the entity would not give up any interest upon termination or transfer of the servicing contract, the entire interest spread is an interest-only strip receivable. For the purposes of applying paragraph 27, the fair values of the servicing asset and interest-only strip receivable are used to allocate the carrying amount of the receivables between the part of the asset that is derecognised and the part that continues to be recognised. If there is no servicing fee specified or the fee to be received is not expected to compensate the entity adequately for performing the servicing, a liability for the servicing obligation is recognised at fair value.

AG46   In estimating the fair values of the part that continues to be recognised and the part that is derecognised for the purposes of applying paragraph 27, an entity applies the fair value measurement requirements in paragraphs 48-49 and AG68-AG82 in addition to paragraph 28.

Transfers that Do Not Qualify for Derecognition

AG47   The following is an application of the principle outlined in paragraph 29. If a guarantee provided by the entity for default losses on the transferred asset prevents a transferred asset from being derecognised because the entity has retained substantially all the risks and rewards of ownership of the transferred asset, the transferred asset continues to be recognised in its entirety and the consideration received is recognised as a liability.

Continuing Involvement in Transferred Assets

AG48   The following are examples of how an entity measures a transferred asset and the associated liability under paragraph 30.

All assets

(a)   If a guarantee provided by an entity to pay for default losses on a transferred asset prevents the transferred asset from being derecognised to the extent of the continuing involvement, the transferred asset at the date of the transfer is measured at the lower of (i) the carrying amount of the asset and (ii) the maximum amount of the consideration received in the transfer that the entity could be required to repay ('the guarantee amount'). The associated liability is initially measured at the guarantee amount plus the fair value of the guarantee (which is normally the consideration received for the guarantee). Subsequently, the initial fair value of the guarantee is recognised in profit or loss on a time proportionate basis (see AASB 118) and the carrying value of the asset is reduced by any impairment losses.

Assets measured at amortised cost

(b)   If a put option obligation written by an entity or call option right held by an entity prevents a transferred asset from being derecognised and the entity measures the transferred asset at amortised cost, the associated liability is measured at its cost (i.e. the consideration received) adjusted for the amortisation of any difference between that cost and the amortised cost of the transferred asset at the expiration date of the option. For example, assume that the amortised cost and carrying amount of the asset on the date of the transfer is CU98 and that the consideration received is CU95. The amortised cost of the asset on the option exercise date will be CU100. Then the initial carrying amount of the associated liability is CU95 and the difference between CU95 and CU100 is recognised in profit or loss using the effective interest method. If the option is exercised, any difference between the carrying amount of the associated liability and the exercise price is recognised in profit or loss.

Assets measured at fair value

(c)   If a call option right retained by an entity prevents a transferred asset from being derecognised and the entity measures the transferred asset at fair value, the asset continues to be measured at its fair value. The associated liability is measured at (i) the option exercise price less the time value of the option if the option is in or at the money or (ii), the fair value of the transferred asset less the time value of the option if the option is out of the money. The adjustment to the measurement of the associated liability ensures that the net carrying amount of the asset and the associated liability is the fair value of the call option right. For example, if the fair value of the underlying asset is CU80, the option exercise price is CU95, and the time value of the option is CU5, then the carrying amount of the associated liability is CU75 (CU80 – CU5) and the carrying amount of the transferred asset is CU80 (i.e. its fair value).

(d)   If a put option written by an entity prevents a transferred asset from being derecognised and the entity measures the transferred asset at fair value, the associated liability is measured at the option exercise price plus the time value of the option. The measurement of the asset at fair value is limited to the lower of the fair value and the option exercise price because the entity has no right to increases in the fair value of the transferred asset above the exercise price of the option. This ensures that the net carrying amount of the asset and the associated liability is the fair value of the put option obligation. For example, if the fair value of the underlying asset is CU120, the option exercise price is CU100, and the time value of the option is CU5, then the carrying amount of the associated liability is CU105 (CU100 + CU5) and the carrying amount of the asset is CU100 (in this case the option exercise price).

(e)   If a collar, in the form of a purchased call and written put, prevents a transferred asset from being derecognised and the entity measures the asset at fair value, it continues to measure the asset at fair value. The associated liability is measured at (i) the sum of the call exercise price and fair value of the put option less the time value of the call option, if the call option is in or at the money or (ii) the sum of the fair value of the asset and the fair value of the put option less the time value of the call option if the call option is out of the money. The adjustment to the associated liability ensures that the net carrying amount of the asset and the associated liability is the fair value of the options held and written by the entity. For example, assume an entity transfers a financial asset that is measured at fair value while simultaneously purchasing a call with an exercise price of CU120 and writing a put with an exercise price of CU80. Assume also that the fair value of the asset is CU100 at the date of the transfer. The time value of the put and call are CU1 and CU5 respectively. In this case, the entity recognises an asset of CU100 (the fair value of the asset) and a liability of CU96 [(CU100 + CU1) – CU5]. This gives a net asset value of CU4, which is the fair value of the options held and written by the entity.

All Transfers

AG49   To the extent that a transfer of a financial asset does not qualify for derecognition, the transferor's contractual rights or obligations related to the transfer are not accounted for separately as derivatives if recognising both the derivative and either the transferred asset or the liability arising from the transfer would result in recognising the same rights or obligations twice. For example, a call option retained by the transferor may prevent a transfer of financial assets from being accounted for as a sale. In that case, the call option is not separately recognised as a derivative asset.

AG50   To the extent that a transfer of a financial asset does not qualify for derecognition, the transferee does not recognise the transferred asset as its asset. The transferee derecognises the cash or other consideration paid and recognises a receivable from the transferor. If the transferor has both a right and an obligation to reacquire control of the entire transferred asset for a fixed amount (such as under a repurchase agreement), the transferee may account for its receivable as a loan or receivable.

Examples

AG51   The following examples illustrate the application of the derecognition principles of this Standard.

(a)   *Repurchase agreements and securities lending.* If a financial asset is sold under an agreement to repurchase it at a fixed price or at the sales price plus a lender's return or if it is loaned under an agreement to return it to the transferor, it is not derecognised because the transferor retains substantially all the risks and rewards of ownership. If the transferee obtains the right to sell or pledge the asset, the transferor reclassifies the asset in its statement of financial position, for example, as a loaned asset or repurchase receivable.

(b)   *Repurchase agreements and securities lending – Assets that are substantially the same.* If a financial asset is sold under an agreement to repurchase the same or substantially the same asset at a fixed price or at the sales price plus a lender's return or if a financial asset is borrowed or loaned under an agreement to return the same or substantially the same asset to the transferor, it is not derecognised because the transferor retains substantially all the risks and rewards of ownership.

(c)   *Repurchase agreements and securities lending – Right of substitution.* If a repurchase agreement at a fixed repurchase price or a price equal to the sale price plus a lender's return, or a similar securities lending transaction, provides the transferee with a right to substitute assets that are similar and of equal fair value to the transferred asset at the repurchase date, the asset sold or lent under a repurchase or securities lending transaction is not derecognised because the transferor retains substantially all the risks and rewards of ownership.

(d)   *Repurchase right of first refusal at fair value.* If an entity sells a financial asset and retains only a right of first refusal to repurchase the transferred asset at fair value if the transferee subsequently sells it, the entity derecognises the asset because it has transferred substantially all the risks and rewards of ownership.

(e) *Wash sale transaction.* The repurchase of a financial asset shortly after it has been sold is sometimes referred to as a wash sale. Such a repurchase does not preclude derecognition provided that the original transaction met the derecognition requirements. However, if an agreement to sell a financial asset is entered into concurrently with an agreement to repurchase the same asset at a fixed price or the sales price plus a lender's return, then the asset is not derecognised.

(f) *Put options and call options that are deeply in the money.* If a transferred financial asset can be called back by the transferor and the call option is deeply in the money, the transfer does not qualify for derecognition because the transferor has retained substantially all the risks and rewards of ownership. Similarly, if the financial asset can be put back by the transferee and the put option is deeply in the money, the transfer does not qualify for derecognition because the transferor has retained substantially all the risks and rewards of ownership.

(g) *Put options and call options that are deeply out of the money.* A financial asset that is transferred subject only to a deep out-of-the-money put option held by the transferee or a deep out-of-the-money call option held by the transferor is derecognised. This is because the transferor has transferred substantially all the risks and rewards of ownership.

(h) *Readily obtainable assets subject to a call option that is neither deeply in the money nor deeply out of the money.* If an entity holds a call option on an asset that is readily obtainable in the market and the option is neither deeply in the money nor deeply out of the money, the asset is derecognised. This is because the entity (i) has neither retained nor transferred substantially all the risks and rewards of ownership and (ii) has not retained control. However, if the asset is not readily obtainable in the market, derecognition is precluded to the extent of the amount of the asset that is subject to the call option because the entity has retained control of the asset.

(i) *A not readily obtainable asset subject to a put option written by an entity that is neither deeply in the money or deeply out of the money.* If an entity transfers a financial asset that is not readily obtainable in the market, and writes a put option that is not deeply out of the money, the entity neither retains nor transfers substantially all the risks and rewards of ownership because of the written put option. The entity retains control of the asset if the put option is sufficiently valuable to prevent the transferee from selling the asset, in which case the asset continues to be recognised to the extent of the transferor's continuing involvement (see paragraph AG44). The entity transfers control of the asset if the put option is not sufficiently valuable to prevent the transferee from selling the asset, in which case the asset is derecognised.

(j) *Assets subject to a fair value put or call option or a forward repurchase agreement.* A transfer of a financial asset that is subject only to a put or call option or a forward repurchase agreement that has an exercise or repurchase price equal to the fair value of the financial asset at the time of repurchase results in derecognition because of the transfer of substantially all the risks and rewards of ownership.

(k) *Cash settled call or put options.* An entity evaluates the transfer of a financial asset that is subject to a put or call option or a forward repurchase agreement that will be settled net in cash to determine whether it has retained or transferred substantially all the risks and rewards of ownership. If the entity has not retained substantially all the risks and rewards of ownership of the transferred asset, it determines whether it has retained control of the transferred asset. That the put or the call or the forward repurchase agreement is settled net in cash does not automatically mean that the entity has transferred control (see paragraphs AG44 and (g), (h) and (i) above).

(l)   *Removal of accounts provision.* A removal of accounts provision is an unconditional repurchase (call) option that gives an entity the right to reclaim assets transferred subject to some restrictions. Provided that such an option results in the entity neither retaining nor transferring substantially all the risks and rewards of ownership, it precludes derecognition only to the extent of the amount subject to repurchase (assuming that the transferee cannot sell the assets). For example, if the carrying amount and proceeds from the transfer of loan assets are CU100,000 and any individual loan could be called back but the aggregate amount of loans that could be repurchased could not exceed CU10,000, CU90,000 of the loans would qualify for derecognition.

(m)   *Clean-up calls.* An entity, which may be a transferor, that services transferred assets may hold a clean-up call to purchase remaining transferred assets when the amount of outstanding assets falls to a specified level at which the cost of servicing those assets becomes burdensome in relation to the benefits of servicing. Provided that such a clean-up call results in the entity neither retaining nor transferring substantially all the risks and rewards of ownership and the transferee cannot sell the assets, it precludes derecognition only to the extent of the amount of the assets that is subject to the call option.

(n)   *Subordinated retained interests and credit guarantees.* An entity may provide the transferee with credit enhancement by subordinating some amount or all of its interest retained in the transferred asset. Alternatively, an entity may agree to provide the transferee with credit enhancement in the form of a credit guarantee that could be unlimited or limited to a specified amount. If the entity retains substantially all the risks and rewards of ownership of the transferred asset, the asset continues to be recognised in its entirety. If the entity retains some, but not substantially all, of the risks and rewards of ownership and has retained control, derecognition is precluded to the extent of the amount of cash or other assets that the entity could be required to pay.

(o)   *Total return swaps.* An entity may sell a financial asset to a transferee and enter into a total return swap with the transferee, whereby all of the interest payment cash flows from the underlying asset are remitted to the entity in exchange for a fixed payment or variable rate payment and any increases or declines in the fair value of the underlying asset are absorbed by the entity. In such a case, derecognition of all of the asset is prohibited.

(p)   *Interest rate swaps.* An entity may transfer to a transferee a fixed rate financial asset and enter into an interest rate swap with the transferee to receive a fixed interest rate and pay a variable interest rate based on a notional amount that is equal to the principal amount of the transferred financial asset. The interest rate swap does not preclude derecognition of the transferred asset provided the payments on the swap are not conditional on payments being made on the transferred asset.

(q)   *Amortising interest rate swaps.* An entity may transfer to a transferee a fixed rate financial asset that is paid off over time, and enter into an amortising interest rate swap with the transferee to receive a fixed interest rate and pay a variable interest rate based on a notional amount. If the notional amount of the swap amortises so that it equals the principal amount of the transferred financial asset outstanding at any point in time, the swap would generally result in the entity retaining substantial prepayment risk, in which case the entity either continues to recognise all of the transferred asset or continues to recognise the transferred asset to the extent of its continuing involvement.

Conversely, if the amortisation of the notional amount of the swap is not linked to the principal amount outstanding of the transferred asset, such a swap would not result in the entity retaining prepayment risk on the asset. Hence would not preclude derecognition of the transferred asset provided the payments on the swap are not conditional on interest payments being made on the transferred asset and the swap does not result in the entity retaining any other significant risks and rewards of ownership on the transferred asset.

AG52   This paragraph illustrates the application of the continuing involvement approach when the entity's continuing involvement is in a part of a financial asset.

Assume an entity has a portfolio of prepayable loans whose coupon and effective interest rate is 10% and whose principal amount and amortised cost is CU10,000. It enters into a transaction in which, in return for a payment of CU9,115, the transferee obtains the right to CU9,000 of any collections of principal plus interest at 9.5%. The entity retains rights to CU1,000 of any collections of principal plus interest thereon at 10%, plus the excess spread of 0.5% on the remaining CU9,000 of principal. Collections from prepayments are allocated between the entity and the transferee proportionately in the ratio of 1:9, but any defaults are deducted from the entity's interest of CU1,000 until that interest is exhausted. The fair value of the loans at the date of the transaction is CU10,100 and the estimated fair value of the excess spread of 0.5% is CU40.

The entity determines that it has transferred some significant risk and rewards of ownership (e.g., significant prepayment risk) but has also retained some significant risks and rewards of ownership (because of its subordinated retained interest) and has retained control. It therefore applies the continuing involvement approach.

To apply this Standard, the entity analyses the transaction as (a) a retention of a fully proportionate retained interest of CU1,000, plus (b) the subordination of that retained interest to provide credit enhancement to the transferee for credit losses.

The entity calculates that CU9,090 (90% x CU10,100) of the consideration received of CU9,115 represents the consideration for a fully proportionate 90% share. The remainder of the consideration received, of CU25, represents consideration received for subordinating its retained interest to provide credit enhancement to the transferee for credit losses. In addition, the excess spread of 0.5% represents consideration received for the credit enhancement. Accordingly the total consideration received for the credit enhancement is CU 65 (CU25 + CU40).

The entity calculates the gain or loss on the sale of the 90 percent share of cash flows. Assuming that separate fair values of the 90 per cent part transferred and the 10 per cent part retained are not available at the date of the transfer, the entity allocates the carrying amount of the asset in accordance with paragraph 28 as follows:

	Estimated Fair Value	Percentage	Allocated Carrying Amount
Portion Transferred	9,090	90%	9,000
Portion Retained	1,010	10%	1,000
Total	**10,100**		**10,000**

The entity computes its gain or loss on the sale of the 90 per cent share of the cash flows by deducting the allocated carrying amount of the portion transferred from the consideration received that is, as CU90 (CU9,090 – CU9,000). The carrying amount of the portion retained by the entity is CU1,000.

In addition, the entity recognises the continuing involvement that results from the subordination of its retained interest for credit losses. Accordingly, it recognises an asset of CU 1,000 (the maximum amount of the cash flows it would not receive under the subordination), and an associated liability of CU1,065 (which is the maximum amount of the cash flows it would not receive under the subordination, CU1,000 plus the fair value of the subordination of CU65).

continued

The entity uses all of the above information to account for the transaction as follows:

	Debit	Credit
Original Asset	–	9,000
Asset recognised for subordination or the residual interest	1,000	–
Asset for the consideration received in the form of excess spread	40	–
Profit or loss (gain on transfer)	–	90
Liability	–	1,065
Cash Received	9,115	–
Total	**10,155**	**10,115**

Immediately following the transaction, the carrying amount of the asset is CU2,040 composing CU1,000 representing the allocated cost of the portion retained and CU1,040 representing the entity's additional continuing involvement from the subordination of its retained interest for credit losses (which includes the excess spread of CU40).

In subsequent periods, the entity recognises the consideration received for the credit enhancement (CU65) on a time proportion basis, accrues interest on the recognised asset using the effective interest method and recognises any credit impairment on the recognised assets. As an example of the latter, assume that in the following year there is a credit impairment loss on the underlying loans of CU300. The entity reduces its recognised asset by CU600 (CU300 relating to its retained interest and CU300 relating to the additional continuing involvement that arises from the subordination of its retained interest for credit losses), and reduces its recognised liability by CU300. The net result is a charge to profit or loss for credit impairment of CU300.

Regular Way Purchase or Sale of a Financial Asset (paragraph 38)

AG53   A regular way purchase or sale of financial assets is recognised using either trade date accounting or settlement date accounting as described in paragraphs AG55 and AG56. The method used is applied consistently for all purchases and sales of financial assets that belong to the same category of financial assets defined in paragraph 9. For this purpose assets that are held for trading form a separate category from assets designated at fair value through profit or loss.

AG54   A contract that requires or permits net settlement of the change in the value of the contract is not a regular way contract. Instead, such a contract is accounted for as a derivative in the period between the trade date and the settlement date.

AG55   The trade date is the date that an entity commits itself to purchase or sell an asset. Trade date accounting refers to (a) the recognition of an asset to be received and the liability to pay for it on the trade date and (b) derecognition of an asset that is sold, recognition of any gain or loss on disposal, and the recognition of a receivable from the buyer for payment on the trade date. Generally, interest does not start to accrue on the asset and corresponding liability until the settlement date when title passes.

AG56   The settlement date is the date that an asset is delivered to or by an entity. Settlement date accounting refers to (a) the recognition of an asset on the day it is received by the entity and (b) the derecognition of an asset and recognition of any gain or loss on disposal on the day that it is delivered by the entity. When settlement date accounting is applied an entity accounts for any change in the fair value of the asset to be received during the period between the trade date and the settlement date in the same way as it accounts for the acquired asset. In other words, the change in value is not recognised for assets carried at cost or amortised cost; it is recognised in profit or loss for assets designated as financial assets at fair value through profit or loss; and it is recognised in other comprehensive income for assets classified as available for sale.

Derecognition of a Financial Liability (paragraphs 39-42)

AG57   A financial liability (or part of it) is extinguished when the debtor either:

(a)   discharges the liability (or part of it) by paying the creditor, normally with cash, other financial assets, goods or services; or

(b)   is legally released from primary responsibility for the liability (or part of it) either by process of law or by the creditor (if the debtor has given a guarantee this condition may still be met).

AG58   If an issuer of a debt instrument repurchases that instrument, the debt is extinguished even if the issuer is a market maker in that instrument or intends to resell it in the near term.

AG59   Payment to a third party, including a trust (sometimes called 'in-substance defeasance'), does not, by itself, relieve the debtor of its primary obligation to the creditor, in the absence of legal release.

AG60   If a debtor pays a third party to assume an obligation and notifies its creditor that the third party has assumed its debt obligation, the debtor does not derecognise the debt obligation unless the condition in paragraph AG57(b) is met. If the debtor pays a third party to assume an obligation and obtains a legal release from its creditor, the debtor has extinguished the debt. However, if the debtor agrees to make payments on the debt to the third party or direct to its original creditor, the debtor recognises a new debt obligation to the third party.

AG61   Although legal release, whether judicially or by the creditor, results in derecognition of a liability, the entity may recognise a new liability if the derecognition criteria in paragraphs 15-37 are not met for the financial assets transferred. If those criteria are not met, the transferred assets are not derecognised, and the entity recognises a new liability relating to the transferred assets.

AG62   For the purpose of paragraph 40, the terms are substantially different if the discounted present value of the cash flows under the new terms, including any fees paid net of any fees received and discounted using the original effective interest rate, is at least 10 per cent different from the discounted present value of the remaining cash flows of the original financial liability. If an exchange of debt instruments or modification of terms is accounted for as an extinguishment, any costs or fees incurred are recognised as part of the gain or loss on the extinguishment. If the exchange or modification is not accounted for as an extinguishment, any costs or fees incurred adjust the carrying amount of the liability and are amortised over the remaining term of the modified liability.

AG63   In some cases, a creditor releases a debtor from its present obligation to make payments, but the debtor assumes a guarantee obligation to pay if the party assuming primary responsibility defaults. In this circumstance the debtor:

(a)   recognises a new financial liability based on the fair value of its obligation for the guarantee; and

(b)   recognises a gain or loss based on the difference between (i) any proceeds paid and (ii) the carrying amount of the original financial liability less the fair value of the new financial liability.

Measurement (paragraphs 43-70)

Initial Measurement of Financial Assets and Financial Liabilities (paragraph 43)

AG64   The fair value of a financial instrument on initial recognition is normally the transaction price (i.e. the fair value of the consideration given or received, see also paragraph AG76). However, if part of the consideration given or received is for something other than the financial instrument, the fair value of the financial instrument is estimated, using a valuation technique (see paragraphs AG74-AG79). For example, the fair value of a long-term loan or receivable that carries no interest can be estimated as the present value of all future cash receipts discounted using the prevailing market rate(s) of interest for a similar instrument (similar as to currency, term, type of interest rate, and other factors) with a similar credit rating. Any additional amount lent is an expense or a reduction of income unless it qualifies for recognition as some other type of asset.

AG65   If an entity originates a loan that bears an off-market interest rate (e.g. 5 per cent when the market rate for similar loans is 8 per cent), and receives an up-front fee as compensation, the entity recognises the loan at its fair value, i.e. net of the fee it receives. The entity accretes the discount to profit or loss using the effective interest rate method.

Subsequent Measurement of Financial Assets (paragraphs 45 and 46)

AG66   If a financial instrument that was previously recognised as a financial asset is measured at fair value and its fair value falls below zero, it is a financial liability measured in accordance with paragraph 47.

AG67   The following example illustrates the accounting for transaction costs on the initial and subsequent measurement of an available-for-sale financial asset. An asset is acquired for CU100 plus a purchase commission of CU2. Initially, the asset is recognised at CU102. The end of the reporting period occurs one day later, when the quoted market price of the asset is CU100. If the asset were sold, a commission of CU3 would be paid. On that date, the asset is measured at CU100 (without regard to the possible commission on sale) and a loss of CU2 is recognised in other comprehensive income. If the available-for-sale financial asset has fixed or determinable payments, the transaction costs are amortised to profit or loss using the effective interest method. If the available-for-sale financial asset does not have fixed or determinable payments, the transaction costs are recognised in profit or loss when the asset is derecognised or becomes impaired.

AG68   Instruments that are classified as loans and receivables are measured at amortised cost without regard to the entity's intention to hold them to maturity.

Fair Value Measurement Considerations (paragraphs 48-49)

AG69   Underlying the definition of fair value is a presumption that an entity is a going concern without any intention or need to liquidate, to curtail materially the scale of its operations or to undertake a transaction on adverse terms. Fair value is not, therefore, the amount that an entity would receive or pay in a forced transaction, involuntary liquidation or distress sale. However, fair value reflects the credit quality of the instrument.

AG70   This Standard uses the terms "bid price" and "asking price" (sometimes referred to as "current offer price") in the context of quoted market prices, and the term "the bid-ask spread" to include only transaction costs. Other adjustments to arrive at fair value (e.g. for counterparty credit risk) are not included in the term "bid-ask spread".

Active Market: Quoted Price

AG71   A financial instrument is regarded as quoted in an active market if quoted prices are readily and regularly available from an exchange, dealer, broker, industry group, pricing service or regulatory agency, and those prices represent actual and regularly occurring market transactions on an arm's length basis. Fair value is defined in terms of a price agreed by a willing buyer and a willing seller in an arm's length transaction. The objective of determining fair value for a financial instrument that is traded in an active market is to arrive at the price at which a transaction would occur at the end of the reporting period in that instrument (i.e. without modifying or repackaging the instrument) in the most advantageous active market to which the entity has immediate access. However, the entity adjusts the price in the more advantageous market to reflect any differences in counterparty credit risk between instruments traded in that market and the one being valued. The existence of published price quotations in an active market is the best evidence of fair value and when they exist they are used to measure the financial asset or financial liability.

AG72   The appropriate quoted market price for an asset held or liability to be issued is usually the current bid price and, for an asset to be acquired or liability held, the asking price. When an entity has assets and liabilities with offsetting market risks, it may use mid-market prices as a basis for establishing fair values for the offsetting risk positions and apply the bid or asking price to the net open position as appropriate. When current bid and asking prices are unavailable, the price of the most recent transaction provides evidence of the current fair value as long as there has not been a significant change in economic circumstances since the time of the transaction. If conditions have changed since the time of the transaction (e.g. a change in the risk-free interest rate following the most recent price quote for a corporate bond), the fair value reflects the change in conditions by reference to current prices or rates for similar financial instruments, as appropriate. Similarly, if the entity can demonstrate that the last transaction price is not fair value (e.g. because it reflected the amount that an entity would receive or pay in a forced transaction, involuntary liquidation or distress sale), that price is adjusted. The fair value of a portfolio of financial instruments is the product of the number of units of the instrument and its quoted market price. If a published price quotation in an active market does not exist for a financial instrument in its entirety, but active markets exist for its component parts, fair value is determined on the basis of the relevant market prices for the component parts.

AG73   If a rate (rather than a price) is quoted in an active market, the entity uses that market-quoted rate as an input into a valuation technique to determine fair value. If the market-quoted rate does not include credit risk or other factors that market participants would include in valuing the instrument, the entity adjusts for those factors.

No Active Market: Valuation Technique

AG74   If the market for a financial instrument is not active, an entity establishes fair value by using a valuation technique. Valuation techniques include using recent arm's length market transactions between knowledgeable, willing parties, if available, reference to the current fair value of another instrument that is substantially the same, discounted cash flow analysis, and option pricing models. If there is a valuation technique commonly used by market participants to price the instrument and that technique has been demonstrated to provide reliable estimates of prices obtained in actual market transactions, the entity uses that technique.

AG75   The objective of using a valuation technique is to establish what the transaction price would have been on the measurement date in an arm's length exchange motivated by normal business considerations. Fair value is estimated on the basis of the results of a valuation technique that makes maximum use of market inputs, and relies as little as possible on entity-specific inputs. A valuation technique would be expected to arrive at a realistic estimate of the fair value if (a) it reasonably reflects how the market could be expected to price the instrument and (b) the inputs to the valuation technique reasonably represent market expectations and measures of the risk-return factors inherent in the financial instrument.

AG76   Therefore, a valuation technique (a) incorporates all factors that market participants would consider in setting a price and (b) is consistent with accepted economic methodologies for pricing financial instruments. Periodically, an entity calibrates the valuation technique and tests it for validity using prices from any observable current market transactions in the same instrument (i.e. without modification or repackaging) or based on any available observable market data. An entity obtains market data consistently in the same market where the instrument was originated or purchased. The best evidence of the fair value of a financial instrument at initial recognition is the transaction price (i.e. the fair value of the consideration given or received) unless the fair value of that instrument is evidenced by comparison with other observable current market transactions in the same instrument (i.e. without modification or repackaging) or based on a valuation technique whose variables include only data from observable markets.

AASB

AG76A   The subsequent measurement of the financial asset or financial liability and the subsequent recognition of gains and losses shall be consistent with the requirements of this Standard. The application of paragraph AG76 may result in no gain or loss being recognised on the initial recognition of a financial asset or financial liability. In such a case, AASB 139 requires that a gain or loss shall be recognised after initial recognition only to the extent that it arises from a change in a factor (including time) that market participants would consider in setting a price.

AG77   The initial acquisition or origination of a financial asset or incurrence of a financial liability is a market transaction that provides a foundation for estimating the fair value of the financial instrument. In particular, if the financial instrument is a debt instrument (such as a loan), its fair value can be determined by reference to the market conditions that existed at its acquisition or origination date and current market conditions or interest rates currently charged by the entity or by others for similar debt instruments (i.e. similar remaining maturity, cash flow pattern, currency, credit risk, collateral, and interest basis). Alternatively, provided there is no change in the credit risk of the debtor and applicable credit spreads after the origination of the debt instrument, an estimate of the current market interest rate may be derived by using a benchmark interest rate reflecting a better credit quality than the underlying debt instrument, holding the credit spread constant, and adjusting for the change in the benchmark interest rate from the origination date. If conditions have changed since the most recent market transaction, the corresponding change in the fair value of the financial instrument being valued is determined by reference to current prices or rates for similar financial instruments, adjusted as appropriate, for any differences from the instrument being valued.

AG78   The same information may not be available at each measurement date. For example, at the date that an entity makes a loan or acquires a debt instrument that is not actively traded, the entity has a transaction price that is also a market price. However, no new transaction information may be available at the next measurement date and, although the entity can determine the general level of market interest rates, it may not know what level of credit or other risk market participants would consider in pricing the instrument on that date. An entity may not have information from recent transactions to determine the appropriate credit spread over the basic interest rate to use in determining a discount rate for a present value computation. It would be reasonable to assume, in the absence of evidence to the contrary, that no changes have taken place in the spread that existed at the date the loan was made. However, the entity would be expected to make reasonable efforts to determine whether there is evidence that there has been a change in such factors. When evidence of a change exists, the entity would consider the effects of the change in determining the fair value of the financial instrument.

AG79   In applying discounted cash flow analysis, an entity uses one or more discount rates equal to the prevailing rates of return for financial instruments having substantially the same terms and characteristics, including the credit quality of the instrument, the remaining term over which the contractual interest rate is fixed, the remaining term to repayment of the principal and the currency in which payments are to be made. Short-term receivables and payables with no stated interest rate may be measured at the original invoice amount if the effect of discounting is immaterial.

No Active Market: Equity Instruments

AG80   The fair value of investments in equity instruments that do not have a quoted market price in an active market and derivatives that are linked to and must be settled by delivery of such an unquoted equity instrument (see paragraphs 46(c) and 47) is reliably measurable if (a) the variability in the range of reasonable fair value estimates is not significant for that instrument or (b) the probabilities of the various estimates within the range can be reasonably assessed and used in estimating fair value.

AG81   There are many situations in which the variability in the range of reasonable fair value estimates of investments in equity instruments that do not have a quoted market price and derivatives that are linked to and must be settled by delivery of such an unquoted equity instrument (see paragraphs 46(c) and 47) is likely not to be significant. Normally it is possible to estimate the fair value of a financial asset that an entity has acquired from an outside party. However, if the range of reasonable fair value estimates is significant and the probabilities of the various estimates cannot be reasonably assessed, an entity is precluded from measuring the instrument at fair value.

Inputs to Valuation Techniques

AG82   An appropriate technique for estimating the fair value of a particular financial instrument would incorporate observable market data about the market conditions and other factors that are likely to affect the instrument's fair value. The fair value of a financial instrument will be based on one or more of the following factors (and perhaps others).

(a)   *The time value of money (i.e. interest at the basic or risk-free rate).* Basic interest rates can usually be derived from observable government bond prices and are often quoted in financial publications. These rates typically vary with the expected dates of the projected cash flows along a yield curve of interest rates for different time horizons. For practical reasons, an entity may use a well-accepted and readily observable general rate, such as LIBOR or a swap rate, as the benchmark rate. (Because a rate such as LIBOR is not the risk-free interest rate, the credit risk adjustment appropriate to the particular financial instrument is determined on the basis of its credit risk in relation to the credit risk in this benchmark rate.) In some countries, the central government's bonds may carry a significant credit risk and may not provide a stable benchmark basic interest rate for instruments denominated in that currency. Some entities in these countries may have a better credit standing and a lower borrowing rate than the central government. In such a case, basic interest rates may be more appropriately determined by reference to interest rates for the highest rated corporate bonds issued in the currency of that jurisdiction.

(b)   *Credit risk.* The effect on fair value of credit risk (i.e. the premium over the basic interest rate for credit risk) may be derived from observable market prices for traded instruments of different credit quality or from observable interest rates charged by lenders for loans of various credit ratings.

(c)   *Foreign currency exchange prices.* Active currency exchange markets exist for most major currencies, and prices are quoted daily in financial publications.

(d)   *Commodity prices.* There are observable market prices for many commodities.

(e)   *Equity prices.* Prices (and indexes of prices) of traded equity instruments are readily observable in some markets. Present value based techniques may be used to estimate the current market price of equity instruments for which there are no observable prices.

(f)   *Volatility (i.e. magnitude of future changes in price of the financial instrument or other item).* Measures of the volatility of actively traded items can normally be reasonably estimated on the basis of historical market data or by using volatilities implied in current market prices.

(g)   *Prepayment risk and surrender risk.* Expected prepayment patterns for financial assets and expected surrender patterns for financial liabilities can be estimated on the basis of historical data. (The fair value of a financial liability that can be surrendered by the counterparty cannot be less than the present value of the surrender amount, see paragraph 49.)

(h)   *Servicing costs of a financial asset or a financial liability.* Costs of servicing can be estimated using comparisons with current fees charged by other market participants. If the costs of servicing a financial asset or financial liability are significant and other market participants would face comparable costs, the issuer would consider them in determining the fair value of that financial asset or financial liability. It is likely that the fair value at inception of a contractual right to future fees equals the origination costs paid for them, unless future fees and related costs are out of line with market comparables.

Gains and Losses (paragraphs 55-57)

AG83   An entity applies AASB 121 to financial assets and financial liabilities that are monetary items in accordance with AASB 121 and denominated in a foreign currency. Under AASB 121, any foreign exchange gains and losses on monetary assets and monetary liabilities are recognised in profit or loss. An exception is a monetary item that is designated as a hedging instrument in either a cash flow hedge (see paragraphs 95-101) or a hedge of a net investment (see paragraph 102). For the purpose of recognising foreign exchange gains and losses under AASB 121, a monetary available-for-sale financial asset is treated as if it were carried at amortised cost in the foreign currency. Accordingly, for such a financial asset, exchange differences resulting from changes in amortised cost are recognised in profit or loss and other changes in carrying amount are recognised in accordance with paragraph 55(b). For available-for-sale financial assets that are not monetary items under AASB 121 (e.g. equity instruments), the gain or loss that is recognised in other comprehensive income under paragraph 55(b) includes any related foreign exchange component. If there is a hedging relationship between a non-derivative monetary asset and a non-derivative monetary liability, changes in the foreign currency component of those financial instruments are recognised in profit or loss.

Impairment and Uncollectibility of Financial Assets (paragraphs 58-70)

Financial Assets Carried at Amortised Cost (paragraphs 63-65)

AG84   Impairment of a financial asset carried at amortised cost is measured using the financial instrument's original effective interest rate because discounting at the current market rate of interest would, in effect, impose fair value measurement on financial assets that are otherwise measured at amortised cost. If the terms of a loan, receivable or held-to-maturity investment are renegotiated or otherwise modified because of financial difficulties of the borrower or issuer, impairment is measured using the original effective interest rate before the modification of terms. Cash flows relating to short-term receivables are not discounted if the effect of discounting is immaterial. If a loan, receivable or held-to-maturity investment has a variable interest rate, the discount rate for measuring any impairment loss under paragraph 63 is the current effective interest rate(s) determined under the contract. As a practical expedient, a creditor may measure impairment of a financial asset carried at amortised cost on the basis of an instrument's fair value using an observable market price. The calculation of the present value of the estimated future cash flows of a collateralised financial asset reflects the cash flows that may result from foreclosure less costs for obtaining and selling the collateral, whether or not foreclosure is probable.

AG85   The process for estimating impairment considers all credit exposures, not only those of low credit quality. For example, if an entity uses an internal credit grading system it considers all credit grades, not only those reflecting a severe credit deterioration.

AG86   The process for estimating the amount of an impairment loss may result either in a single amount or in a range of possible amounts. In the latter case, the entity recognises an impairment loss equal to the best estimate within the range[3], taking into account all relevant information available before the financial statements are issued about conditions existing at the end of the reporting period.

AG87   For the purpose of a collective evaluation of impairment, financial assets are grouped on the basis of similar credit risk characteristics that are indicative of the debtor's ability to pay all amounts due according to the contractual terms (e.g. on the basis of a credit risk evaluation or grading process that considers asset type, industry, geographical location, collateral type, past-due status, and other relevant factors).

---

3   AASB 137, paragraph 39 contains guidance on how to determine the best estimate in a range of possible outcomes.

The characteristics chosen are relevant to the estimation of future cash flows for groups of such assets by being indicative of the debtors' ability to pay all amounts due according to the contractual terms of the assets being evaluated. However, loss probabilities and other loss statistics differ at a group level between (a) assets that have been individually evaluated for impairment and found not to be impaired and (b) assets that have not been individually evaluated for impairment, with the result that a different amount of impairment may be required. If an entity does not have a group of assets with similar risk characteristics, it does not make the additional assessment.

AG88   Impairment losses recognised on a group basis represent an interim step pending the identification of impairment losses on individual assets in the group of financial assets that are collectively assessed for impairment. As soon as information is available that specifically identifies losses on individually impaired assets in a group, those assets are removed from the group.

AG89   Future cash flows in a group of financial assets that are collectively evaluated for impairment are estimated on the basis of historical loss experience for assets with credit risk characteristics similar to those in the group. Entities that have no entity-specific loss experience or insufficient experience use peer group experience for comparable groups of financial assets. Historical loss experience is adjusted on the basis of current observable data to reflect the effects of current conditions that did not affect the period on which the historical loss experience is based and to remove the effects of conditions in the historical period that do not exist currently. Estimates of changes in future cash flows reflect and are directionally consistent with changes in related observable data from period to period (such as changes in unemployment rates, property prices, commodity prices, payment status or other factors that are indicative of incurred losses in the group and their magnitude). The methodology and assumptions used for estimating future cash flows are reviewed regularly to reduce any differences between loss estimates and actual loss experience.

AG90   As an example of applying paragraph AG89, an entity may determine, on the basis of historical experience, that one of the main causes of default on credit card loans is the death of the borrower. The entity may observe that the death rate is unchanged from one year to the next. Nevertheless, some of the borrowers in the entity's group of credit card loans may have died in that year, indicating that an impairment loss has occurred on those loans, even if, at the year-end, the entity is not yet aware which specific borrowers have died. It would be appropriate for an impairment loss to be recognised for these 'incurred but not reported' losses. However, it would not be appropriate to recognise an impairment loss for deaths that are expected to occur in a future period, because the necessary loss event (the death of the borrower) has not yet occurred.

AG91   When using historical loss rates in estimating future cash flows, it is important that information about historical loss rates is applied to groups that are defined in a manner consistent with the groups for which the historical loss rates were observed. Therefore, the method used should enable each group to be associated with information about past loss experience in groups of assets with similar credit risk characteristics and relevant observable data that reflect current conditions.

AG92   Formula-based approaches or statistical methods may be used to determine impairment losses in a group of financial assets (e.g. for smaller balance loans) as long as they are consistent with the requirements in paragraphs 63-65 and AG87-AG91. Any model used would incorporate the effect of the time value of money, consider the cash flows for all of the remaining life of an asset (not only the next year), consider the age of the loans within the portfolio and not give rise to an impairment loss on initial recognition of a financial asset.

Interest Income After Impairment Recognition

AG93   Once a financial asset or a group of similar financial assets has been written down as a result of an impairment loss, interest income is thereafter recognised using the rate of interest used to discount the future cash flows for the purpose of measuring the impairment loss.

Hedging (paragraphs 71-102)

Hedging Instruments (paragraphs 72-77)

Qualifying Instruments (paragraphs 72 and 73)

AG94   The potential loss on an option that an entity writes could be significantly greater than the potential gain in value of a related hedged item. In other words, a written option is not effective in reducing the profit or loss exposure of a hedged item. Therefore, a written option does not qualify as a hedging instrument unless it is designated as an offset to a purchased option, including one that is embedded in another financial instrument (e.g. a written call option used to hedge a callable liability). In contrast, a purchased option has potential gains equal to or greater than losses and therefore has the potential to reduce profit or loss exposure from changes in fair values or cash flows. Accordingly, it can qualify as a hedging instrument.

AG95   A held-to-maturity investment carried at amortised cost may be designated as a hedging instrument in a hedge of foreign currency risk.

AG96   An investment in an unquoted equity instrument that is not carried at fair value because its fair value cannot be reliably measured or a derivative that is linked to and must be settled by delivery of such an unquoted equity instrument (see paragraphs 46(c) and 47) cannot be designated as a hedging instrument.

AG97   An entity's own equity instruments are not financial assets or financial liabilities of the entity and, therefore, cannot be designated as hedging instruments.

Hedged Items (paragraphs 78-84)

Qualifying Items (paragraphs 78-80)

AG98   A firm commitment to acquire a business in a business combination cannot be a hedged item, except for foreign exchange risk, because the other risks being hedged cannot be specifically identified and measured. These other risks are general business risks.

AG99   An equity method investment cannot be a hedged item in a fair value hedge because the equity method recognises in profit or loss the investor's share of the associate's profit or loss, rather than changes in the investment's fair value. For a similar reason, an investment in a consolidated subsidiary cannot be a hedged item in a fair value hedge because consolidation recognises in profit or loss the subsidiary's profit or loss, rather than changes in the investment's fair value. A hedge of a net investment in a foreign operation is different because it is a hedge of the foreign currency exposure, not a fair value hedge of the change in the value of the investment.

AG99A   Paragraph 80 states that in consolidated financial statements the foreign currency risk of a highly probable forecast intragroup transaction may qualify as a hedged item in a cash flow hedge, provided the transaction is denominated in a currency other than the functional currency of the entity entering into that transaction and the foreign currency risk will affect consolidated profit or loss. For this purpose an entity can be a parent, subsidiary, associate, joint venture or branch. If the foreign currency risk of a forecast intragroup transaction does not affect consolidated profit or loss, the intragroup transaction cannot qualify as a hedged item. This is usually the case for royalty payments, interest payments or management charges between members of the same group unless there is a related external transaction. However, when the foreign currency risk of a forecast intragroup transaction will affect consolidated profit or loss, the intragroup transaction can qualify as a hedged item. An example is forecast sales or purchases of inventories between members of the same group if there is an onward sale of the inventory to a party external to the group. Similarly, a forecast intragroup sale of plant and equipment from the group entity that manufactured it to a group entity that will use the plant and equipment in its operations may affect consolidated profit or loss. This could occur, for example, because the plant and equipment will be depreciated by the purchasing entity and the amount initially recognised for the plant and equipment may change if the forecast intragroup transaction is denominated in a currency other than the functional currency of the purchasing entity.

AG99B   If a hedge of a forecast intragroup transaction qualifies for hedge accounting, any gain or loss that is recognised in other comprehensive income in accordance with paragraph 95(a) shall be reclassified from equity to profit or loss as a reclassification adjustment in the same period or periods during which the foreign currency risk of the hedged transaction affects consolidated profit or loss.

AG99BA   An entity can designate all changes in the cash flows or fair value of a hedged item in a hedging relationship. An entity can also designate only changes in the cash flows or fair value of a hedged item above or below a specified price or other variable (a one-sided risk). The intrinsic value of a purchased option hedging instrument (assuming that it has the same principal terms as the designated risk), but not its time value, reflects a one-sided risk in a hedged item. For example, an entity can designate the variability of future cash flow outcomes resulting from a price increase of a forecast commodity purchase. In such a situation, only cash flow losses that result from an increase in the price above the specified level are designated. The hedged risk does not include the time value of a purchased option because the time value is not a component of the forecast transaction that affects profit or loss (paragraph 86(b)).

AG99C   If a portion of the cash flows of a financial asset or financial liability is designated as the hedged item, that designated portion must be less than the total cash flows of the asset or liability. For example, in the case of a liability whose effective interest rate is below LIBOR, an entity cannot designate (a) a portion of the liability equal to the principal amount plus interest at LIBOR and (b) a negative residual portion. However, the entity may designate all of the cash flows of the entire financial asset or financial liability as the hedged item and hedge them for only one particular risk (e.g. only for changes that are attributable to changes in LIBOR). For example, in the case of a financial liability whose effective interest rate is 100 basis points below LIBOR, an entity can designate as the hedged item the entire liability (i.e. principal plus interest at LIBOR minus 100 basis points) and hedge the change in the fair value or cash flows of that entire liability that is attributable to changes in LIBOR. The entity may also choose a hedge ratio of other than one to one in order to improve the effectiveness of the hedge as described in paragraph AG100.

AG99D   In addition, if a fixed rate financial instrument is hedged some time after its origination and interest rates have changed in the meantime, the entity can designate a portion equal to a benchmark rate that is higher than the contractual rate paid on the item. The entity can do so provided that the benchmark rate is less than the effective interest rate calculated on the assumption that the entity had purchased the instrument on the day it first designates the hedged item. For example, assume an entity originates a fixed rate financial asset of CU100 that has an effective interest rate of 6 per cent at a time when LIBOR is 4 per cent. It begins to hedge that asset some time later when LIBOR has increased to 8 per cent and the fair value of the asset has decreased to CU90. The entity calculates that if it had purchased the asset on the date it first designates it as the hedged item for its then fair value of CU90, the effective yield would have been 9.5 per cent. Because LIBOR is less than this effective yield, the entity can designate a LIBOR portion of 8 per cent that consists partly of the contractual interest cash flows and partly of the difference between the current fair value (i.e. CU90) and the amount repayable on maturity (i.e. CU100).

AG99E   Paragraph 81 permits an entity to designate something other than the entire fair value change or cash flow variability of a financial instrument. For example:

(a)   all of the cash flows of a financial instrument may be designated for cash flow or fair value changes attributable to some (but not all) risks; or

(b)   some (but not all) of the cash flows of a financial instrument may be designated for cash flow or fair value changes attributable to all or only some risks (i.e. a 'portion' of the cash flows of the financial instrument may be designated for changes attributable to all or only some risks).

AG99F To be eligible for hedge accounting, the designated risks and portions must be separately identifiable components of the financial instrument, and changes in the cash flows or fair value of the entire financial instrument arising from changes in the designated risks and portions must be reliably measurable. For example:

(a) for a fixed rate financial instrument hedged for changes in fair value attributable to changes in a risk-free or benchmark interest rate, the risk-free or benchmark rate is normally regarded as both a separately identifiable component of the financial instrument and reliably measurable.

(b) inflation is not separately identifiable and reliably measurable and cannot be designated as a risk or a portion of a financial instrument unless the requirements in (c) are met.

(c) a contractually specified inflation portion of the cash flows of a recognised inflation-linked bond (assuming there is no requirement to account for an embedded derivative separately) is separately identifiable and reliably measurable as long as other cash flows of the instrument are not affected by the inflation portion.

Designation of Non-Financial Items as Hedged Items (paragraph 82)

AG100 Changes in the price of an ingredient or component of a non-financial asset or non-financial liability generally do not have a predictable, separately measurable effect on the price of the item that is comparable to the effect of, say, a change in market interest rates or the price of a bond. Thus, a non-financial asset or non-financial liability is a hedged item only in its entirety or for exchange risk. If there is a difference between the terms of the hedging instrument and the hedged item (such as for a hedge of the forecast purchase of Brazilian coffee using a forward contract to purchase Colombian coffee on otherwise similar terms), the hedging relationship nonetheless can qualify as a hedge relationship provided all the conditions in paragraph 88 are met, including that the hedge is expected to be highly effective. For this purpose, the amount of the hedging instrument may be greater or less than that of the hedged item if this improves the effectiveness of the hedging relationship. For example, a regression analysis could be performed to establish a statistical relationship between the hedged item (e.g. a transaction in Brazilian coffee) and the hedging instrument (e.g. a transaction in Colombian coffee). If there is a valid statistical relationship between the two variables (i.e. between the unit prices of Brazilian coffee and Colombian coffee), the slope of the regression line can be used to establish the hedge ratio that will maximise expected effectiveness. For example, if the slope of the regression line is 1.02, a hedge ratio based on 0.98 quantities of hedged items to 1.00 quantities of the hedging instrument maximises expected effectiveness. However, the hedging relationship may result in ineffectiveness that is recognised in profit or loss during the term of the hedging relationship.

Designation of Groups of Items as Hedged Items (paragraphs 83 and 84)

AG101 A hedge of an overall net position (e.g. the net of all fixed rate assets and fixed rate liabilities with similar maturities), rather than of a specific hedged item, does not qualify for hedge accounting. However, almost the same effect on profit or loss of hedge accounting for this type of hedging relationship can be achieved by designating as the hedged item part of the underlying items. For example, if a bank has CU100 of assets and CU90 of liabilities with risks and terms of a similar nature and hedges the net CU10 exposure, it can designate as the hedged item CU10 of those assets. This designation can be used if such assets and liabilities are fixed rate instruments, in which case it is a fair value hedge, or if they are variable rate instruments, in which case it is a cash flow hedge. Similarly, if an entity has a firm commitment to make a purchase in a foreign currency of CU100 and a firm commitment to make a sale in the foreign currency of CU90, it can hedge the net amount of CU10 by acquiring a derivative and designating it as a hedging instrument associated with CU10 of the firm purchase commitment of CU100.

Hedge Accounting (paragraphs 85-102)

AG102   An example of a fair value hedge is a hedge of exposure to changes in the fair value of a fixed rate debt instrument as a result of changes in interest rates. Such a hedge could be entered into by the issuer or by the holder.

AG103   An example of a cash flow hedge is use of a swap to change floating rate debt to fixed rate debt (i.e. a hedge of a future transaction where the future cash flows being hedged are the future interest payments).

AG104   A hedge of a firm commitment (e.g. a hedge of the change in fuel price relating to an unrecognised contractual commitment by an electric utility to purchase fuel at a fixed price) is a hedge of an exposure to a change in fair value. Accordingly, such a hedge is a fair value hedge. However, under paragraph 87 a hedge of the foreign currency risk of a firm commitment could alternatively be accounted for as a cash flow hedge.

Assessing Hedge Effectiveness

AG105   A hedge is regarded as highly effective only if both of the following conditions are met.

(a)   At the inception of the hedge and in subsequent periods, the hedge is expected to be highly effective in achieving offsetting changes in fair value or cash flows attributable to the hedged risk during the period for which the hedge is designated. Such an expectation can be demonstrated in various ways, including a comparison of past changes in the fair value or cash flows of the hedged item that are attributable to the hedged risk with past changes in the fair value or cash flows of the hedging instrument, or by demonstrating a high statistical correlation between the fair value or cash flows of the hedged item and those of the hedging instrument. The entity may choose a hedge ratio of other than one to one in order to improve the effectiveness of the hedge as described in paragraph AG100.

(b)   The actual results of the hedge are within a range of 80-125 per cent. For example, if actual results are such that the loss on the hedging instrument is CU120 and the gain on the cash instruments CU100, offset can be measured by 120/100, which is 120 per cent, or by 100/120, which is 83 per cent. In this example, assuming the hedge meets the condition in (a), the entity would conclude that the hedge has been highly effective.

AG106   Effectiveness is assessed, at a minimum, at the time an entity prepares its annual or interim financial statements.

AG107   This Standard does not specify a single method for assessing hedge effectiveness. The method an entity adopts for assessing hedge effectiveness depends on its risk management strategy. For example, if the entity's risk management strategy is to adjust the amount of the hedging instrument periodically to reflect changes in the hedged position, the entity needs to demonstrate that the hedge is expected to be highly effective only for the period until the amount of the hedging instrument is next adjusted. In some cases, an entity adopts different methods for different types of hedges. An entity's documentation of its hedging strategy includes its procedures for assessing effectiveness. Those procedures state whether the assessment includes all of the gain or loss on a hedging instrument or whether the instrument's time value is excluded.

AG107A   If an entity hedges less than 100 per cent of the exposure on an item, such as 85 per cent, it shall designate the hedged item as being 85 per cent of the exposure and shall measure ineffectiveness based on the change in that designated 85 per cent exposure. However, when hedging the designated 85 per cent exposure, the entity may use a hedge ratio of other than one to one if that improves the expected effectiveness of the hedge, as explained in paragraph AG100.

AG108   If the principal terms of the hedging instrument and of the hedged asset, liability, firm commitment or highly probable forecast transaction are the same, the changes in fair value and cash flows attributable to the risk being hedged may be likely to offset each other fully, both when the hedge is entered into and afterwards.

For example, an interest rate swap is likely to be an effective hedge if the notional and principal amounts, term, repricing dates, dates of interest and principal receipts and payments, and basis for measuring interest rates are the same for the hedging instrument and the hedged item. In addition, a hedge of a highly probable forecast purchase of a commodity with a forward contract is likely to be highly effective if:

(a) the forward contract is for the purchase of the same quantity of the same commodity at the same time and location as the hedged forecast purchase;

(b) the fair value of the forward contract at inception is zero; and

(c) either the change in the discount or premium on the forward contract is excluded from the assessment of effectiveness and recognised in profit or loss or the change in expected cash flows on the highly probable forecast transaction is based on the forward price for the commodity.

AG109　Sometimes the hedging instrument offsets only part of the hedged risk. For example, a hedge would not be fully effective if the hedging instrument and hedged item are denominated in different currencies that do not move in tandem. Also, a hedge of interest rate risk using a derivative would not be fully effective if part of the change in the fair value of the derivative is attributable to the counterparty's credit risk.

AG110　To qualify for hedge accounting, the hedge must relate to a specific identified and designated risk, and not merely to the entity's general business risks, and must ultimately affect the entity's profit or loss. A hedge of the risk of obsolescence of a physical asset or the risk of expropriation of property by a government is not eligible for hedge accounting; effectiveness cannot be measured because those risks are not measurable reliably.

AG110A　Paragraph 74(a) permits an entity to separate the intrinsic value and time value of an option contract and designate as the hedging instrument only the change in the intrinsic value of the option contract. Such a designation may result in a hedging relationship that is perfectly effective in achieving offsetting changes in cash flows attributable to a hedged one-sided risk of a forecast transaction, if the principal terms of the forecast transaction and hedging instrument are the same.

AG110B　If an entity designates a purchased option in its entirety as the hedging instrument of a one-sided risk arising from a forecast transaction, the hedging relationship will not be perfectly effective. This is because the premium paid for the option includes time value and, as stated in paragraph AG99BA, a designated one-sided risk does not include the time value of an option. Therefore, in this situation, there will be no offset between the cash flows relating to the time value of the option premium paid and the designated hedged risk.

AG111　In the case of interest rate risk, hedge effectiveness may be assessed by preparing a maturity schedule for financial assets and financial liabilities that shows the net interest rate exposure for each time period, provided that the net exposure is associated with a specific asset or liability (or a specific group of assets or liabilities or a specific portion of them) giving rise to the net exposure, and hedge effectiveness is assessed against that asset or liability.

AG112　In assessing the effectiveness of a hedge, an entity generally considers the time value of money. The fixed interest rate on a hedged item need not exactly match the fixed interest rate on a swap designated as a fair value hedge. Nor does the variable interest rate on an interest-bearing asset or liability need to be the same as the variable interest rate on a swap designated as a cash flow hedge. A swap's fair value derives from its net settlements. The fixed and variable rates on a swap can be changed without affecting the net settlement if both are changed by the same amount.

AG113　If an entity does not meet hedge effectiveness criteria, the entity discontinues hedge accounting from the last date on which compliance with hedge effectiveness was demonstrated. However, if the entity identifies the event or change in circumstances that caused the hedging relationship to fail the effectiveness criteria, and demonstrates that the hedge was effective before the event or change in circumstances occurred, the entity discontinues hedge accounting from the date of the event or change in circumstances.

Fair Value Hedge Accounting for a Portfolio Hedge of Interest Rate Risk

AG114   For a fair value hedge of interest rate risk associated with a portfolio of financial assets or financial liabilities, an entity would meet the requirements of this Standard if it complies with the procedures set out in (a)-(i) and paragraphs AG115-AG132 below.

(a)   As part of its risk management process the entity identifies a portfolio of items whose interest rate risk it wishes to hedge. The portfolio may comprise only assets, only liabilities or both assets and liabilities. The entity may identify two or more portfolios (e.g. the entity may group its available-for-sale assets into a separate portfolio), in which case it applies the guidance below to each portfolio separately.

(b)   The entity analyses the portfolio into repricing time periods based on expected, rather than contractual, repricing dates. The analysis into repricing time periods may be performed in various ways including scheduling cash flows into the periods in which they are expected to occur, or scheduling notional principal amounts into all periods until repricing is expected to occur.

(c)   On the basis of this analysis, the entity decides the amount it wishes to hedge. The entity designates as the hedged item an amount of assets or liabilities (but not a net amount) from the identified portfolio equal to the amount it wishes to designate as being hedged. This amount also determines the percentage measure that is used for testing effectiveness in accordance with paragraph AG126(b).

(d)   The entity designates the interest rate risk it is hedging. This risk could be a portion of the interest rate risk in each of the items in the hedged position, such as a benchmark interest rate (e.g. LIBOR).

(e)   The entity designates one or more hedging instruments for each repricing time period.

(f)   Using the designations made in (c)-(e) above, the entity assesses at inception and in subsequent periods, whether the hedge is expected to be highly effective during the period for which the hedge is designated.

(g)   Periodically, the entity measures the change in the fair value of the hedged item (as designated in (c)) that is attributable to the hedged risk (as designated in (d)), on the basis of the expected repricing dates determined in (b). Provided that the hedge is determined actually to have been highly effective when assessed using the entity's documented method of assessing effectiveness, the entity recognises the change in fair value of the hedged item as a gain or loss in profit or loss and in one of two line items in the statement of financial position as described in paragraph 89A. The change in fair value need not be allocated to individual assets or liabilities.

(h)   The entity measures the change in fair value of the hedging instrument(s) (as designated in (e)) and recognises it as a gain or loss in profit or loss. The fair value of the hedging instrument(s) is recognised as an asset or liability in the statement of financial position.

(i)   Any ineffectiveness[4] will be recognised in profit or loss as the difference between the change in fair value referred to in (g) and that referred to in (h).

AG115   This approach is described in more detail below. The approach shall be applied only to a fair value hedge of the interest rate risk associated with a portfolio of financial assets or financial liabilities.

---

4   The same materiality considerations apply in this context as apply throughout Australian Accounting Standards.

AG116   The portfolio identified in paragraph AG114(a) could contain assets and liabilities. Alternatively, it could be a portfolio containing only assets, or only liabilities. The portfolio is used to determine the amount of the assets or liabilities the entity wishes to hedge. However, the portfolio is not itself designated as the hedged item.

AG117   In applying paragraph AG114(b), the entity determines the expected repricing date of an item as the earlier of the dates when that item is expected to mature or to reprice to market rates. The expected repricing dates are estimated at the inception of the hedge and throughout the term of the hedge, based on historical experience and other available information, including information and expectations regarding prepayment rates, interest rates and the interaction between them. Entities that have no entity-specific experience or insufficient experience use peer group experience for comparable financial instruments. These estimates are reviewed periodically and updated in the light of experience. In the case of a fixed rate item that is prepayable, the expected repricing date is the date on which the item is expected to prepay unless it reprices to market rates on an earlier date. For a group of similar items, the analysis into time periods based on expected repricing dates may take the form of allocating a percentage of the group, rather than individual items, to each time period. An entity may apply other methodologies for such allocation purposes. For example, it may use a prepayment rate multiplier for allocating amortising loans to time periods based on expected repricing dates. However, the methodology for such an allocation shall be in accordance with the entity's risk management procedures and objectives.

AG118   As an example of the designation set out in paragraph AG114(c), if in a particular repricing time period an entity estimates that it has fixed rate assets of CU100 and fixed rate liabilities of CU80 and decides to hedge all of the net position of CU20, it designates as the hedged item assets in the amount of CU20 (a portion of the assets).[5] The designation is expressed as an 'amount of a currency' (e.g. an amount of dollars, euro, pounds or rand) rather than as individual assets. It follows that all of the assets (or liabilities) from which the hedged amount is drawn – that is all of the CU100 of assets in the above example – must be:

(a)   items whose fair value changes in response to changes in the interest rate being hedged; and

(b)   items that could have qualified for fair value hedge accounting if they had been designated as hedged individually. In particular, because the Standard[6] specifies that the fair value of a financial liability with a demand feature (such as demand deposits and some types of time deposits) is not less than the amount payable on demand, discounted from the first date that the amount could be required to be paid, such an item cannot qualify for fair value hedge accounting for any time period beyond the shortest period in which the holder can demand payment. In the above example, the hedged position is an amount of assets. Hence, such liabilities are not a part of the designated hedged item, but are used by the entity to determine the amount of the asset that is designated as being hedged. If the position the entity wished to hedge was an amount of liabilities, the amount representing the designated hedged item must be drawn from fixed rate liabilities other than liabilities that the entity can be required to repay in an earlier time period, and the percentage measure used for assessing hedge effectiveness in accordance with paragraph AG126(b) would be calculated as a percentage of these other liabilities. For example, assume that an entity estimates that in a particular repricing time period it has fixed rate liabilities of CU100, comprising CU40 of demand deposits and CU60 of liabilities with no demand feature, and CU70 of fixed rate assets. If the entity decides to hedge all of the net position

---

5   This Standard permits an entity to designate any amount of the available qualifying assets or liabilities, that is, in this example any amount of assets between CU0 and CU100.

6   See paragraph 49.

of CU30, it designates as the hedged item liabilities of CU30 or 50 per cent[7] of the liabilities with no demand feature.

AG119   The entity also complies with the other designation and documentation requirements set out in paragraph 88(a). For a portfolio hedge of interest rate risk, this designation and documentation specifies the entity's policy for all of the variables that are used to identify the amount that is hedged and how effectiveness is measured, including the following:

(a)   which assets and liabilities are to be included in the portfolio hedge and the basis to be used for removing them from the portfolio;

(b)   how the entity estimates repricing dates, including what interest rate assumptions underlie estimates of prepayment rates and the basis for changing those estimates. The same method is used for both the initial estimates made at the time an asset or liability is included in the hedged portfolio and for any later revisions to those estimates;

(c)   the number and duration of repricing time periods;

(d)   how often the entity will test effectiveness and which of the two methods in paragraph AG126 it will use;

(e)   the methodology used by the entity to determine the amount of assets or liabilities that are designated as the hedged item and, accordingly, the percentage measure used when the entity tests effectiveness using the method described in paragraph AG126(b); and

(f)   when the entity tests effectiveness using the method described in paragraph AG126(b), whether the entity will test effectiveness for each repricing time period individually, for all time periods in aggregate, or by using some combination of the two.

The policies specified in designating and documenting the hedging relationship shall be in accordance with the entity's risk management procedures and objectives. Changes in policies shall not be made arbitrarily. They shall be justified on the basis of changes in market conditions and other factors and be founded on and consistent with the entity's risk management procedures and objectives.

AG120   The hedging instrument referred to in paragraph AG114(e) may be a single derivative or a portfolio of derivatives all of which contain exposure to the hedged interest rate risk designated in paragraph AG114(d) (e.g. a portfolio of interest rate swaps all of which contain exposure to LIBOR). Such a portfolio of derivatives may contain offsetting risk positions. However, it may not include written options or net written options, because the Standard[8] does not permit such options to be designated as hedging instruments (except when a written option is designated as an offset to a purchased option). If the hedging instrument hedges the amount designated in paragraph AG114(c) for more than one repricing time period, it is allocated to all of the time periods that it hedges. However, the whole of the hedging instrument must be allocated to those repricing time periods because the Standard[9] does not permit a hedging relationship to be designated for only a portion of the time period during which a hedging instrument remains outstanding.

AG121   When the entity measures the change in the fair value of a prepayable item in accordance with paragraph AG114(g), a change in interest rates affects the fair value of the prepayable item in two ways: it affects the fair value of the contractual cash flows and the fair value of the prepayment option that is contained in a prepayable item. Paragraph 81 of the Standard permits an entity to designate a portion of a financial asset or financial liability, sharing a common risk exposure, as the hedged item, provided effectiveness can be measured. For prepayable items, paragraph 81A permits this to be achieved by designating the hedged item in terms of the change

---

7      $CU30 \div (CU100 - CU40) = 50$ per cent.

8   See paragraphs 77 and AG94.

9   See paragraph 75.

AASB

in the fair value that is attributable to changes in the designated interest rate on the basis of expected, rather than contractual, repricing dates. However, the effect that changes in the hedged interest rate have on those expected repricing dates shall be included when determining the change in the fair value of the hedged item. Consequently, if the expected repricing dates are revised (e.g. to reflect a change in expected prepayments), or if actual repricing dates differ from those expected, ineffectiveness will arise as described in paragraph AG126. Conversely, changes in expected repricing dates that (a) clearly arise from factors other than changes in the hedged interest rate, (b) are uncorrelated with changes in the hedged interest rate and (c) can be reliably separated from changes that are attributable to the hedged interest rate (e.g. changes in prepayment rates clearly arising from a change in demographic factors or tax regulations rather than changes in interest rate) are excluded when determining the change in the fair value of the hedged item, because they are not attributable to the hedged risk. If there is uncertainty about the factor that gave rise to the change in expected repricing dates or the entity is not able to separate reliably the changes that arise from the hedged interest rate from those that arise from other factors, the change is assumed to arise from changes in the hedged interest rate.

AG122   The Standard does not specify the techniques used to determine the amount referred to in paragraph AG114(g), namely the change in the fair value of the hedged item that is attributable to the hedged risk. If statistical or other estimation techniques are used for such measurement, management must expect the result to approximate closely that which would have been obtained from measurement of all the individual assets or liabilities that constitute the hedged item. It is not appropriate to assume that changes in the fair value of the hedged item equal changes in the value of the hedging instrument.

AG123   Paragraph 89A requires that if the hedged item for a particular repricing time period is an asset, the change in its value is presented in a separate line item within assets. Conversely, if the hedged item for a particular repricing time period is a liability, the change in its value is presented in a separate line item within liabilities. These are the separate line items referred to in paragraph AG114(g). Specific allocation to individual assets (or liabilities) is not required.

AG124   Paragraph AG114(i) notes that ineffectiveness arises to the extent that the change in the fair value of the hedged item that is attributable to the hedged risk differs from the change in the fair value of the hedging derivative. Such a difference may arise for a number of reasons, including:

(a)   actual repricing dates being different from those expected, or expected repricing dates being revised;

(b)   items in the hedged portfolio becoming impaired or being derecognised;

(c)   the payment dates of the hedging instrument and the hedged item being different; and

(d)   other causes (e.g. when a few of the hedged items bear interest at a rate below the benchmark rate for which they are designated as being hedged, and the resulting ineffectiveness is not so great that the portfolio as a whole fails to qualify for hedge accounting).

Such ineffectiveness[10] shall be identified and recognised in profit or loss.

AG125   Generally, the effectiveness of the hedge will be improved:

(a)   if the entity schedules items with different prepayment characteristics in a way that takes account of the differences in prepayment behaviour;

(b)   when the number of items in the portfolio is larger. When only a few items are contained in the portfolio, relatively high ineffectiveness is likely if one of the items prepays earlier or later than expected. Conversely, when the portfolio contains many items, the prepayment behaviour can be predicted more accurately;

---

10   The same materiality considerations apply in this context as apply throughout Australian Accounting Standards.

   (c)   when the repricing time periods used are narrower (e.g. 1-month as opposed to 3-month repricing time periods). Narrower repricing time periods reduce the effect of any mismatch between the repricing and payment dates (within the repricing time period) of the hedged item and those of the hedging instrument; and

   (d)   the greater the frequency with which the amount of the hedging instrument is adjusted to reflect changes in the hedged item (e.g. because of changes in prepayment expectations).

AG126   An entity tests effectiveness periodically. If estimates of repricing dates change between one date on which an entity assesses effectiveness and the next, it shall calculate the amount of effectiveness either:

   (a)   as the difference between the change in the fair value of the hedging instrument (see paragraph AG114(h)) and the change in the value of the entire hedged item that is attributable to changes in the hedged interest rate (including the effect that changes in the hedged interest rate have on the fair value of any embedded prepayment option); or

   (b)   using the following approximation. The entity:

       (i)   calculates the percentage of the assets (or liabilities) in each repricing time period that was hedged, on the basis of the estimated repricing dates at the last date it tested effectiveness;

      (ii)   applies this percentage to its revised estimate of the amount in that repricing time period to calculate the amount of the hedged item based on its revised estimate;

     (iii)   calculates the change in the fair value of its revised estimate of the hedged item that is attributable to the hedged risk and presents it as set out in paragraph AG114(g);

     (iv)   recognises ineffectiveness equal to the difference between the amount determined in (iii) and the change in the fair value of the hedging instrument (see paragraph AG114(h)).

AG127   When measuring effectiveness, the entity distinguishes revisions to the estimated repricing dates of existing assets (or liabilities) from the origination of new assets (or liabilities), with only the former giving rise to ineffectiveness. All revisions to estimated repricing dates (other than those excluded in accordance with paragraph AG121), including any reallocation of existing items between time periods, are included when revising the estimated amount in a time period in accordance with paragraph AG126(b)(ii) and hence when measuring effectiveness. Once ineffectiveness has been recognised as set out above, the entity establishes a new estimate of the total assets (or liabilities) in each repricing time period, including new assets (or liabilities) that have been originated since it last tested effectiveness, and designates a new amount as the hedged item and a new percentage as the hedged percentage. The procedures set out in paragraph AG126(b) are then repeated at the next date it tests effectiveness.

AG128   Items that were originally scheduled into a repricing time period may be derecognised because of earlier than expected prepayment or writeoffs caused by impairment or sale. When this occurs, the amount of change in fair value included in the separate line item referred to in paragraph AG114(g) that relates to the derecognised item shall be removed from the statement of financial position, and included in the gain or loss that arises on derecognition of the item. For this purpose, it is necessary to know the repricing time period(s) into which the derecognised item was scheduled, because this determines the repricing time period(s) from which to remove it and hence the amount to remove from the separate line item referred to in paragraph AG114(g). When an item is derecognised, if it can be determined in which time period it was included, it is removed from that time period. If not, it is removed from the earliest time period if the derecognition resulted from higher than expected prepayments, or allocated to all time periods containing the derecognised item on a systematic and rational basis if the item was sold or became impaired.

AG129   In addition, any amount relating to a particular time period that has not been derecognised when the time period expires is recognised in profit or loss at that time (see paragraph 89A). For example, assume an entity schedules items into three repricing time periods. At the previous redesignation, the change in fair value reported in the single line item in the statement of financial position was an asset of CU25. That amount represents amounts attributable to periods 1, 2 and 3 of CU7, CU8 and CU10, respectively. At the next redesignation, the assets attributable to period 1 have been either realised or rescheduled into other periods. Therefore, CU7 is derecognised from the statement of financial position and recognised in profit or loss. CU8 and CU10 are now attributable to periods 1 and 2, respectively. These remaining periods are then adjusted, as necessary, for changes in fair value as described in paragraph AG114(g).

AG130   As an illustration of the requirements of the previous two paragraphs, assume that an entity scheduled assets by allocating a percentage of the portfolio into each repricing time period. Assume also that it scheduled CU100 into each of the first two time periods. When the first repricing time period expires, CU110 of assets are derecognised because of expected and unexpected repayments. In this case, all of the amount contained in the separate line item referred to in paragraph AG114(g) that relates to the first time period is removed from the statement of financial position, plus 10 per cent of the amount that relates to the second time period.

AG131   If the hedged amount for a repricing time period is reduced without the related assets (or liabilities) being derecognised, the amount included in the separate line item referred to in paragraph AG114(g) that relates to the reduction shall be amortised in accordance with paragraph 92.

AG132   An entity may wish to apply the approach set out in paragraphs AG114-AG131 to a portfolio hedge that had previously been accounted for as a cash flow hedge in accordance with AASB 139. Such an entity would revoke the previous designation of a cash flow hedge in accordance with paragraph 101(d), and apply the requirements set out in that paragraph. It would also redesignate the hedge as a fair value hedge and apply the approach set out in paragraphs AG114-AG131 prospectively to subsequent reporting periods.

Transition (paragraphs 103-108B)

AG133   An entity may have designated a forecast intragroup transaction as a hedged item at the start of an annual period beginning on or after 1 January 2005 (or, for the purpose of restating comparative information the start of an earlier comparative period) in a hedge that would qualify for hedge accounting in accordance with this Standard (as amended by the last sentence of paragraph 80). Such an entity may use that designation to apply hedge accounting in consolidated financial statements from the start of the annual period beginning on or after 1 January 2005 (or the start of the earlier comparative period). Such an entity shall also apply paragraphs AG99A and AG99B from the start of the annual period beginning on or after 1 January 2005. However, in accordance with paragraph 108B, it need not apply paragraph AG99B to comparative information for earlier periods.

Illustrative Example

This example accompanies, but is not part of, AASB 139.

Facts

IE1   On 1 January 20x1, Entity A identifies a portfolio comprising assets and liabilities whose interest rate risk it wishes to hedge. The liabilities include demandable deposit liabilities that the depositor may withdraw at any time without notice. For risk management purposes, the entity views all of the items in the portfolio as fixed rate items.

IE2   For risk management purposes, Entity A analyses the assets and liabilities in the portfolio into repricing time periods based on expected repricing dates. The entity uses monthly time periods and schedules items for the next five years (i.e. it has 60 separate monthly time periods).[1] The assets in the portfolio are prepayable assets that Entity A allocates into time periods based on the expected prepayment dates, by allocating a percentage of all of the assets, rather than individual items, into each time period. The portfolio also includes demandable liabilities that the entity expects, on a portfolio basis, to repay between one month and five years and, for risk management purposes, are scheduled into time periods on this basis. On the basis of this analysis, Entity A decides what amount it wishes to hedge in each time period.

IE3   This example deals only with the repricing time period expiring in three months' time, that is the time period maturing on 31 March 20x1 (a similar procedure would be applied for each of the other 59 time periods). Entity A has scheduled assets of CU100 million and liabilities of CU80 million into this time period. All of the liabilities are repayable on demand.

IE4   Entity A decides, for risk management purposes, to hedge the net position of CU20 million and accordingly enters into an interest rate swap[2] on 1 January 20x1 to pay a fixed rate and receive LIBOR, with a notional principal amount of CU20 million and a fixed life of three months.

IE5   This Example makes the following simplifying assumptions:

     (a)   the coupon on the fixed leg of the swap is equal to the fixed coupon on the asset;

     (b)   the coupon on the fixed leg of the swap becomes payable on the same dates as the interest payments on the asset; and

     (c)   the interest on the variable leg of the swap is the overnight LIBOR rate. As a result, the entire fair value change of the swap arises from the fixed leg only, because the variable leg is not exposed to changes in fair value due to changes in interest rates.

     In cases when these simplifying assumptions do not hold, greater ineffectiveness will arise.

     (The ineffectiveness arising from (a) could be eliminated by designating as the hedged item a portion of the cash flows on the asset that are equivalent to the fixed leg of the swap.)

IE6   It is also assumed that Entity A tests effectiveness on a monthly basis.

---

1   In this Example principal cash flows have been scheduled into time periods but the related interest cash flows have been included when calculating the change in the fair value of the hedged item. Other methods of scheduling assets and liabilities are also possible. Also, in this Example, monthly repricing time periods have been used. An entity may choose narrower or wider time periods.

2   This Example uses a swap as the hedging instrument. An entity may use forward rate agreements or other derivatives as hedging instruments.

IE7   The fair value of an equivalent non-prepayable asset of CU20 million, ignoring changes in value that are not attributable to interest rate movements, at various times during the period of the hedge is as follows.

	1 Jan 20x1	31 Jan 20x1	1 Feb 20x1	28 Feb 20x1	31 Mar 20x1
Fair value (asset) (CU)	20,000,000	20,047,408	20,047,408	20,023,795	Nil

IE8   The fair value of the swap at various times during the period of the hedge is as follows.

	1 Jan 20x1	31 Jan 20x1	1 Feb 20x1	28 Feb 20x1	31 Mar 20x1
Fair value (liability) (CU)	Nil	(47,408)	(47,408)	(23,795)	Nil

Accounting Treatment

IE9   On 1 January 20x1, Entity A designates as the hedged item an amount of CU20 million of assets in the three-month time period. It designates as the hedged risk the change in the value of the hedged item (i.e. the CU20 million of assets) that is attributable to changes in LIBOR. It also complies with the other designation requirements set out in paragraphs 88(d) and AG119 of the Standard.

IE10   Entity A designates as the hedging instrument the interest rate swap described in paragraph IE4.

End of month 1 (31 January 20x1)

IE11   On 31 January 20x1 (at the end of month 1) when Entity A tests effectiveness, LIBOR has decreased. Based on historical prepayment experience, Entity A estimates that, as a consequence, prepayments will occur faster than previously estimated. As a result it re-estimates the amount of assets scheduled into this time period (excluding new assets originated during the month) as CU96 million.

IE12   The fair value of the designated interest rate swap with a notional principal of CU20 million is (CU47,408)[3] (the swap is a liability).

IE13   Entity A computes the change in the fair value of the hedged item, taking into account the change in estimated prepayments, as follows.

     (a)   First, it calculates the percentage of the initial estimate of the assets in the time period that was hedged. This is 20 per cent (CU20 million ÷ CU100 million).

     (b)   Second, it applies this percentage (20 per cent) to its revised estimate of the amount in that time period (CU96 million) to calculate the amount that is the hedged item based on its revised estimate. This is CU19.2 million.

     (c)   Third, it calculates the change in the fair value of this revised estimate of the hedged item (CU19.2 million) that is attributable to changes in LIBOR. This is CU45,511 (CU47,408[4] × (CU19.2 million ÷ CU20 million)).

---

3   See paragraph IE8.
4   That is, CU20,047,408 – CU20,000,000. See paragraph IE7.

IE14 Entity A makes the following accounting entries relating to this time period:

Dr Cash CU172,097
Cr Profit or loss (interest income)[5]   CU172,097

To recognise the interest received on the hedged amount (CU19.2 million).

Dr Profit or loss (interest expense) CU179,268
Cr Profit or loss (interest income)   CU179,268
Cr Cash   Nil

To recognise the interest received and paid on the swap designated as the hedging instrument.

Dr Profit or loss (loss) CU47,408
Cr Derivative liability   CU47,408

To recognise the change in the fair value of the swap.

Dr Separate line item in the statement
of financial position CU45,511
Cr Profit or loss (gain)   CU45,511

To recognise the change in the fair value of the hedged amount.

IE15 The net result on profit or loss (excluding interest income and interest expense) is to recognise a loss of (CU1,897). This represents ineffectiveness in the hedging relationship that arises from the change in estimated prepayment dates.

Beginning of month 2

IE16 On 1 February 20x1 Entity A sells a proportion of the assets in the various time periods. Entity A calculates that it has sold 8⅓ per cent of the entire portfolio of assets. Because the assets were allocated into time periods by allocating a percentage of the assets (rather than individual assets) into each time period, Entity A determines that it cannot ascertain into which specific time periods the sold assets were scheduled. Hence it uses a systematic and rational basis of allocation. Based on the fact that it sold a representative selection of the assets in the portfolio, Entity A allocates the sale proportionately over all time periods.

IE17 On this basis, Entity A computes that it has sold 8⅓ per cent of the assets allocated to the three month time period, that is CU8 million (8⅓ per cent of CU96 million). The proceeds received are CU8,018,400, equal to the fair value of the assets.[6] On derecognition of the assets, Entity A also removes from the separate line item in the statement of financial position an amount that represents the change in the fair value of the hedged assets that it has now sold. This is 8⅓ per cent of the total line item balance of CU45,511, that is CU3,793.

IE18 Entity A makes the following accounting entries to recognise the sale of the asset and the removal of part of the balance in the separate line item in the statement of financial position.

Dr Cash CU8,018,400
Cr Asset   CU8,000,000
Cr Separate line item in the
statement of financial position   CU3,793
Cr Profit or loss (gain)   CU14,607

To recognise the sale of the asset at fair value and to recognise a gain on sale.

Because the change in the amount of the assets is not attributable to a change in the hedged interest rate no ineffectiveness arises.

---

5   This Example does not show how amounts of interest income and interest expense are calculated.

6   The amount realised on sale of the asset is the fair value of a prepayable asset, which is less than the fair value of the equivalent non-prepayable asset shown in paragraph IE7.

IE19   Entity A now has CU88 million of assets and CU80 million of liabilities in this time period. Hence the net amount Entity A wants to hedge is now CU8 million and, accordingly, it designates CU8 million as the hedged amount.

IE20   Entity A decides to adjust the hedging instrument by designating only a proportion of the original swap as the hedging instrument. Accordingly, it designates as the hedging instrument CU8 million or 40 per cent of the notional amount of the original swap with a remaining life of two months and a fair value of CU18,963.[7] It also complies with the other designation requirements in paragraphs 88(a) and AG119 of the Standard. The CU12 million of the notional amount of the swap that is no longer designated as the hedging instrument is either classified as held for trading with changes in fair value recognised in profit or loss, or is designated as the hedging instrument in a different hedge.[8]

IE21   As at 1 February 20x1 and after accounting for the sale of assets, the separate line item in the statement of financial position is CU41,718 (CU45,511 – CU3,793), which represents the cumulative change in fair value of CU17.6 million[9] of assets. However, as at 1 February 20x1, Entity A is hedging only CU8 million of assets that have a cumulative change in fair value of CU18,963.[10] The remaining separate line item in the statement of financial position of CU22,755[11] relates to an amount of assets that Entity A still holds but is no longer hedging. Accordingly Entity A amortises this amount over the remaining life of the time period, that is it amortises CU22,755 over two months.

IE22   Entity A determines that it is not practicable to use a method of amortisation based on a recalculated effective yield and hence uses a straight-line method.

End of month 2 (28 February 20x1)

IE23   On 28 February 20x1 when Entity A next tests effectiveness, LIBOR is unchanged. Entity A does not revise its prepayment expectations. The fair value of the designated interest rate swap with a notional principal of CU8 million is (CU9,518)[12] (the swap is a liability). Also, Entity A calculates the fair value of the CU8 million of the hedged assets as at 28 February 20x1 as CU8,009,518.[13]

---

7   CU47,408 × 40 per cent.

8   The entity could instead enter into an offsetting swap with a notional principal of CU12 million to adjust its position and designate as the hedging instrument all CU20 million of the existing swap and all CU12 million of the new offsetting swap.

9   CU19.2 million – (8⅓ % × CU19.2 million).

10   CU41,718 × (CU8 million ÷ CU17.6 million).

11   CU41,718 – CU18,963.

12   CU23,795 [see paragraph IE8] × [CU8 million ÷ CU20 million).

13   CU20,023,795 [see paragraph IE7] × (CU8 million ÷ CU20 million).

IE24   Entity A makes the following accounting entries relating to the hedge in this time
        period:

Dr   Cash   CU71,707
Cr   Profit or loss (interest income)   CU71,707

To recognise the interest received on the hedged amount (CU8 million).

Dr   Profit or loss (interest expense)   CU71,707
Cr   Profit or loss (interest income)   CU62,115
Cr   Cash   CU9,592

*To recognise the interest received and paid on the portion of the swap designated
as the hedging instrument (CU8 million).*

Dr   Derivative liability   CU9,445
Cr   Profit or loss (gain)   CU9,445

*To recognise the change in the fair value of the portion of the swap designated
as the hedging instrument (CU8 million) (CU9,518 – CU18,963)*

Dr   Profit or loss (loss)   CU9,445
Cr   Separate line item in the statement of financial position   CU9,445

*To recognise the change in the fair value of the hedged amount
(CU8,009,518 – CU8,018,963).*

IE25   The net effect on profit or loss (excluding interest income and interest expense)
        is nil reflecting that the hedge is fully effective.

IE26   Entity A makes the following accounting entry to amortise the line item balance for
        this time period:

Dr   Profit or loss (loss)   CU11,378
Cr   Separate line item in the statement of financial position   CU11,378[14]

To recognise the amortisation charge for the period.

End of month 3

IE27   During the third month there is no further change in the amount of assets or
        liabilities in the three-month time period. On 31 March 20x1 the assets and the
        swap mature and all balances are recognised in profit or loss.

IE28   Entity A makes the following accounting entries relating to this time period:

Dr   Cash   CU8,071,707
Cr   Asset (statement of financial position)   CU8,000,000
Cr   Profit or loss (interest income)   CU71,707

*To recognise the interest and cash received on maturity of the hedged amount
(CU8 million).*

Dr   Profit or loss (interest expense)   CU71,707
Cr   Profit or loss (interest income)   CU62,115
Cr   Cash   CU9,592

*To recognise the interest received and paid on the portion of the swap designated
as the hedging instrument (CU8 million).*

Dr   Derivative liability   CU9,518
Cr   Profit or loss (gain)   CU9,518

---

14   CU22,755 ÷ 2.

AASB

To recognise the expiry of the portion of the swap designated as the hedging instrument (CU8 million).

Dr   Profit or loss (loss)   CU9,518

Cr   Separate line item in the statement of financial position   CU9,518

To remove the remaining line item balance on expiry of the time period.

IE29   The net effect on profit or loss (excluding interest income and interest expense) is nil reflecting that the hedge is fully effective.

IE30   Entity A makes the following accounting entry to amortise the line item balance for this time period:

Dr   Profit or loss (loss)   CU11,377

Cr   Separate line item in the statement of financial position   CU11,377[15]

To recognise the amortisation charge for the period.

Summary

IE31   The tables below summarise:

(a)   changes in the separate line item in the statement of financial position;

(b)   the fair value of the derivative;

(c)   the profit or loss effect of the hedge for the entire three-month period of the hedge; and

(d)   interest income and interest expense relating to the amount designated as hedged.

Description	1 Jan 20x1 CU	31 Jan 20x1 CU	1 Feb 20x1 CU	28 Feb 20x1 CU	31 Mar 20x1 CU
Amount of asset hedged	20 million	19.2 million	8 million	8 million	8 million

(a) Changes in the separate line item in the statement of financial position

	1 Jan 20x1	31 Jan 20x1	1 Feb 20x1	28 Feb 20x1	31 Mar 20x1
Brought forward:					
Balance to be amortised	Nil	Nil	Nil	22,755	11,377
Remaining balance	Nil	Nil	45,511	18,963	9,518
Less: Adjustment on sale of asset	Nil	Nil	(3,793)	Nil	Nil
Adjustment for change in fair value of the hedged asset	Nil	45,511	Nil	(9,445)	(9,518)
Amortisation	Nil	Nil	Nil	(11,378)	(11,377)
Carried forward:					
Balance to be amortised	**Nil**	**Nil**	**22,755**	**11,377**	**Nil**
Remaining balance	**Nil**	**45,511**	**18,963**	**9,518**	**Nil**

(b) The fair value of the derivative

	1 Jan 20x1	31 Jan 20x1	1 Feb 20x1	28 Feb 20x1	31 Mar 20x1
CU20,000,000	Nil	47,408	-	-	-
CU12,000,000	Nil	-	28,445	No longer designated as the hedging instrument.	
CU8,000,000	Nil	-	18,963	9,518	Nil
Total	**Nil**	**47,408**	**47,408**	**9,518**	**Nil**

---

15   CU22,755 ÷ 2.

(c) Profit or loss effect of the hedge

	1 Jan 20x1	31 Jan 20x1	1 Feb 20x1	28 Feb 20x1	31 Mar 20x1
Change in line item: asset	Nil	45,511	N/A	(9,445)	(9,518)
Change in derivative fair value	Nil	(47,408)	N/A	9,445	9,518
Net effect	Nil	(1,897)	N/A	Nil	Nil
Amortisation	Nil	Nil	N/A	(11,378)	(11,377)

In addition, there is a gain on sale of assets of CU14,607 at 1 February 20x1.

(d) Interest income and interest expense relating to the amount designated as hedged

Profit or loss recognised for the amount hedged	1 Jan 20x1	31 Jan 20x1	1 Feb 20x1	28 Feb 20x1	31 Mar 20x1
Interest income					
- on the asset	Nil	172,097	N/A	71,707	71,707
- on the swap	Nil	179,268	N/A	62,115	62,115
Interest expense					
- on the swap	Nil	(179,268)	N/A	(71,707)	(71,707)

AASB 140
Investment Property
(Compiled November 2010)

Note from the Institute of Chartered Accountants Australia

This note, prepared by the technical editors, is not part of Accounting Standard AASB 140.

Historical development

July 2004: AASB 140 'Investment Property' is the Australian equivalent of IAS 40 of the same name. It was made by the AASB on 15 July 2004 as part of the AASB's program to adopt International Financial Reporting Standards (IFRSs) by 2005.

24 September 2007: AASB 2007-8 'Amendments to Australian Accounting Standards arising from AASB 101' amends AASB 140 to align with revised AASB 101. This Standard is applicable to annual reporting periods beginning on or after 1 January 2009.

13 December 2007: AASB 2007-10 'Further Amendments to Australian Accounting Standards arising from AASB 101' amends AASB 140, replacing the term 'financial report' with 'financial statements'. This Standard is applicable to annual reporting periods beginning on or after 1 January 2009.

24 July 2008: AASB 2008-5 'Amendments to Australian Accounting Standards arising from the Annual Improvements Project' amends AASB 140 in relation to property under construction or development for future use as investment property, consistency of terminology with AASB 108 and investment property held under lease. This Standard is applicable to annual reporting periods beginning on or after 1 January 2009.

25 June 2009: AASB 2009-6 'Amendments to Australian Accounting Standards' amends AASB 140 for editorial corrections made by the International Accounting Standards Board (IASB) to its Standards and Interpretations (IFRSs) and as a consequence of issuing revised AASB 101 'Presentation of Financial Statements'. This Standard is applicable to annual reporting periods beginning on or after 1 January 2009 that end on or after 30 June 2009.

4 November 2009: AASB 140 was reissued by the AASB, compiled to include the AASB 2007-8, AASB 2007-10, AASB 2008-5 and AASB 2009-6 amendments and applies to annual reporting periods beginning on or after 1 January 2009 that end on or after 30 June 2009. Early application is permitted.

27 October 2010: AASB 2010-5 'Further Amendments to Australian Accounting Standards' makes editorial amendments to AASB 140. This Standard is applicable to annual reporting periods beginning on or after 1 January 2011.

26 November 2010: AASB 140 was reissued by the AASB, compiled to include the AASB 2010-5 amendments and applies to annual reporting periods ending on or after 1 January 2011 but before 1 July 2013.

29 August 2011: AASB 2011-7 'Amendments to Australian Accounting Standards arising from the Consolidation and Joint Arrangements Standards' amends AASB 140 to give effect to many consequential changes arising from the issue of AASB 10, 11, 12, 127 and 128. This Standard applies to annual reporting periods beginning on or after 1 January 2013 and can be adopted early by for-profit entities. **These amendments are not included in this compiled Standard.**

2 September 2011: AASB 2011-8 'Amendments to Australian Accounting Standards arising from AASB 13' amends AASB 140 to give effect to a consequential change in the definition of fair value arising from the issue of AASB 13. This Standard applies to annual reporting periods beginning on or after 1 January 2013 and can be adopted early. **These amendments are not included in this compiled Standard.**

21 March 2012: AASB 2012-1 'Amendments to Australian Accounting Standards – Fair Value Measurement – Reduced Disclosure Requirements' amends AASB 140 to establish and amend reduced disclosure requirements arising from AASB 13 'Fair Value Measurement'. **These amendments are not included in this compiled Standard.**

References

Interpretation 121 *Income Taxes – Recovery of Revalued Non-Depreciable Assets* applies to AASB 140.

AASB 140 compared to IAS 40

Additions

Paragraph	Description
Aus 1.1	Which entities AASB 140 applies to (i.e. reporting entities and general purpose financial statements).
Aus 1.2	The application date of AASB 140 (i.e. annual reporting periods beginning 1 January 2005).
Aus 1.3	Prohibits early application of AASB 140.
Aus 1.4	Makes the requirements of AASB 140 subject to AASB 1031 'Materiality'.
Aus 1.5	Notice of the new Standard published on 22 July 2004.
Aus 9.1	Clarifies that the property of not-for-profit entities held to meet service delivery objectives rather than earn rental or capital appreciation does not meet the definition of investment property and must be accounted for under AASB 116 'Property, Plant and Equipment'.
Aus 20.1	Where a not-for-profit entity acquires an investment property at no cost or nominal cost its deemed cost for initial measurement is fair value at the date of acquisition.

Deletions

Paragraph	Description
80	Transitional provisions where eligible property interests held under operating leases are treated as investment property on first time application.
81	Further explanation that the IAS 40 transitional provisions are different to the general retrospective approach required by IAS 8 'Accounting Policies, Changes in Accounting Estimates and Errors'.
82	Clarifies that the amount standing to the credit of an asset revaluation reserve for investment property forms part of the adjustment to opening retained profits on first time application of IAS 40.
83	Clarifies that IAS 8 applies on first time application of IAS 40 if an entity chooses the cost model for its investment property and includes the reclassification of any amount standing to the credit of the asset revaluation reserve.
84	Transitional provision for initial measurement for exchange of assets transactions requires prospective application.
85, 85A	Effective date of IAS 40.
86	Reference to superseded IAS 40.

Contents

Compilation Details

Comparison with IAS 40

Accounting Standard
AASB 140 Investment Property

	Paragraphs
Objective	1
Application	Aus1.1 – Aus1.5
Scope	2 – 4
Definitions	5 – 15
Recognition	16 – 19
Measurement at Recognition	20 – 29
Measurement after Recognition	
Accounting Policy	30 – 32C
Fair Value Model	33 – 52
Inability to Determine Fair Value Reliably	53 – 55
Cost Model	56
Transfers	57 – 65
Disposals	66 – 73
Disclosure	
Fair Value Model and Cost Model	74 – 75
Fair Value Model	76 – 78
Cost Model	79
Effective Date	85B

Basis for Conclusions on IAS 40
(available on the AASB website)

Australian Accounting Standard AASB 140 *Investment Property* (as amended) is set out in paragraphs 1 – 85B. All the paragraphs have equal authority. Terms defined in this Standard are in *italics* the first time they appear in the Standard. AASB 140 is to be read in the context of other Australian Accounting Standards, including AASB 1048 Interpretation and Application of Standards, which identifies the Australian Accounting Interpretations. In the absence of explicit guidance, AASB 108 *Accounting Policies, Changes in Accounting Estimates and Errors* provides a basis for selecting and applying accounting policies.

Compilation Details

Accounting Standard AASB 140 *Investment Property* as amended

This compiled Standard applies to annual reporting periods beginning on or after 1 January 2011 but before 1 July 2013. It takes into account amendments up to and including 27 October 2010 and was prepared on 26 November 2010 by the staff of the Australian Accounting Standards Board (AASB).

This compilation is not a separate Accounting Standard made by the AASB. Instead, it is a representation of AASB 140 (July 2004) as amended by other Accounting Standards, which are listed in the Table below.

Table of Standards

Standard	Date made	Application date (*annual reporting periods ... on or after ...*)	Application, saving or transitional provisions
AASB 140	15 Jul 2004	(*beginning*) 1 Jan 2005	
AASB 2007-8	24 Sep 2007	(*beginning*) 1 Jan 2009	see (a) below
AASB 2007-10	13 Dec 2007	(*beginning*) 1 Jan 2009	see (a) below
AASB 2008-5	24 Jul 2008	(*beginning*) 1 Jan 2009	see (b) below
AASB 2009-6	25 Jun 2009	(*beginning*) 1 Jan 2009 and (*ending*) 30 Jun 2009	see (c) below
AASB 2010-2	30 Jun 2010	(*beginning*) 1 Jul 2013	not compiled*
AASB 2010-5	27 Oct 2010	(*beginning*) 1 Jan 2011	see (d) below

* The amendments made by this Standard are not included in this compilation, which presents the principal Standard as applicable to annual reporting periods beginning on or after 1 January 2011 but before 1 July 2013.

(a) Entities may elect to apply this Standard to annual reporting periods beginning on or after 1 January 2005 but before 1 January 2009, provided that AASB 101 *Presentation of Financial Statements* (September 2007) is also applied to such periods.

(b) Entities may elect to apply this Standard, or its amendments to individual Standards, to annual reporting periods beginning on or after 1 January 2005 but before 1 January 2009.

(c) Entities may elect to apply this Standard to annual reporting periods beginning on or after 1 January 2005 but before 1 January 2009, provided that AASB 101 *Presentation of Financial Statements* (September 2007) is also applied to such periods, and to annual reporting periods beginning on or after 1 January 2009 that end before 30 June 2009.

(d) Entities may elect to apply this Standard to annual reporting periods beginning on or after 1 January 2005 but before 1 January 2011.

Table of Amendments

Paragraph affected	How affected	By ... [paragraph]
Aus1.1	amended	AASB 2007-8 [7, 8]
Aus1.4	amended	AASB 2007-8 [8]
3	amended	AASB 2007-10 [92]
5	amended	AASB 2007-8 [6]
8	amended	AASB 2008-5 [68]
9	amended	AASB 2008-5 [68]
22	deleted	AASB 2008-5 [69]
31	amended amended	AASB 2007-10 [92] AASB 2008-5 [68]
38	amended	AASB 2007-8 [6]
42	amended	AASB 2007-8 [6]
48	amended	AASB 2008-5 [68]

Paragraph affected	How affected	By ... [paragraph]
50	amended	AASB 2008-5 [68]
53	amended	AASB 2008-5 [68]
53A-53B	added	AASB 2008-5 [70]
54	amended	AASB 2008-5 [68]
56	amended	AASB 2009-6 [97]
57	amended	AASB 2008-5 [68]
58	amended	AASB 2007-8 [6]
62	amended	AASB 2007-8 [146]
	amended	AASB 2009-6 [98]
66	amended	AASB 2007-8 [6]
67	amended	AASB 2010-5 [60]
75	amended	AASB 2007-10 [92]
85 (preceding heading)	amended	AASB 2008-5 [71]
85A	note added	AASB 2007-8 [147]
85B	added	AASB 2008-5 [72]

Comparison with IAS 40

AASB 140 and IAS 40

AASB 140 *Investment Property* as amended incorporates IAS 40 *Investment Property* as issued and amended by the International Accounting Standards Board (IASB). Paragraphs that have been added to this Standard (and do not appear in the text of IAS 40) are identified with the prefix "Aus", followed by the number of the preceding IASB paragraph and decimal numbering. Paragraphs that apply only to not-for-profit entities begin by identifying their limited applicability.

Compliance with IAS 40

For-profit entities that comply with AASB 140 as amended will simultaneously be in compliance with IAS 40 as amended.

Not-for-profit entities using the added Australian paragraph Aus20.1 will not simultaneously be in compliance with the requirements of IAS 40. Not-for-profit entities not using added Australian paragraph Aus20.1 will be able to claim compliance with IAS 40.

Accounting Standard AASB 140

The Australian Accounting Standards Board made Accounting Standard AASB 140 *Investment Property* under section 334 of the *Corporations Act 2001* on 15 July 2004.

This compiled version of AASB 140 applies to annual reporting periods beginning on or after 1 January 2011 but before 1 July 2013. It incorporates relevant amendments contained in other AASB Standards made by the AASB up to and including 27 October 2010 (see Compilation Details).

Accounting Standard AASB 140
Investment Property

Objective

1   The objective of this Standard is to prescribe the accounting treatment for *investment property* and related disclosure requirements.

Application

Aus1.1   **This Standard applies to:**

(a)   **each entity that is required to prepare financial reports in accordance with Part 2M.3 of the Corporations Act and that is a reporting entity;**

(b)   **general purpose financial statements of each other reporting entity; and**

(c)   **financial statements that are, or are held out to be, general purpose financial statements.**

Aus1.2   **This Standard applies to annual reporting periods beginning on or after 1 January 2005.**

[Note: For application dates of paragraphs changed or added by an amending Standard, see Compilation Details.]

Aus1.3   **This Standard shall not be applied to annual reporting periods beginning before 1 January 2005.**

Aus1.4   **The requirements specified in this Standard apply to the financial statements where information resulting from their application is material in accordance with AASB 1031** *Materiality.*

Aus1.5   Notice of this Standard was published in the *Commonwealth of Australia Gazette* No S 294, 22 July 2004.

Scope

2   **This Standard shall be applied in the recognition, measurement and disclosure of investment property.**

3   Among other things, this Standard applies to the measurement in a lessee's financial statements of investment property interests held under a lease accounted for as a finance lease and to the measurement in a lessor's financial statements of investment property provided to a lessee under an operating lease. This Standard does not deal with matters covered in AASB 117 *Leases*, including:

(a)   classification of leases as finance leases or operating leases;

(b)   recognition of lease income from investment property (see also AASB 118 *Revenue*);

(c)   measurement in a lessee's financial statements of property interests held under a lease accounted for as an operating lease;

(d)   measurement in a lessor's financial statements of its net investment in a finance lease;

(e)   accounting for sale and leaseback transactions; and

(f)   disclosure about finance leases and operating leases.

4   This Standard does not apply to:

(a)   biological assets related to agricultural activity (see AASB 141 *Agriculture*); and

(b)   mineral rights and mineral reserves such as oil, natural gas and similar non-regenerative resources.

Definitions

5   The following terms are used in this Standard with the meanings specified.

Carrying amount is the amount at which an asset is recognised in the statement of financial position.

Cost is the amount of cash or cash equivalents paid or the fair value of other consideration given to acquire an asset at the time of its acquisition or construction or, where applicable, the amount attributed to that asset when initially recognised in accordance with the specific requirements of other Standards, for example, AASB 2 *Share-based Payment*.

Fair value is the amount for which an asset could be exchanged between knowledgeable, willing parties in an arm's length transaction.

Investment property is property (land or a building – or part of a building – or both) held (by the owner or by the lessee under a finance lease) to earn rentals or for capital appreciation or both, rather than for:

(a)   use in the production or supply of goods or services or for administrative purposes; or

(b)   sale in the ordinary course of business.

Owner-occupied property is property held (by the owner or by the lessee under a finance lease) for use in the production or supply of goods or services or for administrative purposes.

6   A property interest that is held by a lessee under an operating lease may be classified and accounted for as investment property if, and only if, the property would otherwise meet the definition of an investment property and the lessee uses the *fair value* model set out in paragraphs 33–55 for the asset recognised. This classification alternative is available on a property-by-property basis. However, once this classification alternative is selected for one such property interest held under an operating lease, all property classified as investment property shall be accounted for using the fair value model. When this classification alternative is selected, any interest so classified is included in the disclosures required by paragraphs 74–78.

7   Investment property is held to earn rentals or for capital appreciation or both. Therefore, an investment property generates cash flows largely independently of the other assets held by an entity. This distinguishes investment property from *owner-occupied* property. The production or supply of goods or services (or the use of property for administrative purposes) generates cash flows that are attributable not only to property, but also to other assets used in the production or supply process. AASB 116 *Property, Plant and Equipment* applies to owner-occupied property.

8   The following are examples of investment property:

(a)   land held for long-term capital appreciation rather than for short-term sale in the ordinary course of business;

(b)   land held for a currently undetermined future use (if an entity has not determined that it will use the land as owner-occupied property or for short-term sale in the ordinary course of business, the land is regarded as held for capital appreciation);

(c)   a building owned by the entity (or held by the entity under a finance lease) and leased out under one or more operating leases;

(d)   a building that is vacant but is held to be leased out under one or more operating leases; and

(e)   property that is being constructed or developed for future use as investment property.

9   The following are examples of items that are not investment property and are therefore outside the scope of this Standard:

    (a)   property intended for sale in the ordinary course of business or in the process of construction or development for such sale (see AASB 102 *Inventories*), for example, property acquired exclusively with a view to subsequent disposal in the near future or for development and resale;

    (b)   property being constructed or developed on behalf of third parties (see AASB 111 *Construction Contracts*);

    (c)   owner-occupied property (see AASB 116), including (among other things) property held for future use as owner-occupied property, property held for future development and subsequent use as owner-occupied property, property occupied by employees (whether or not the employees pay rent at market rates) and owner-occupied property awaiting disposal;

    (d)   [deleted by the IASB]

    (e)   property that is leased to another entity under a finance lease.

Aus9.1   In respect of not-for-profit entities, property may be held to meet service delivery objectives rather than to earn rental or for capital appreciation. In such situations the property will not meet the definition of investment property and will be accounted for under AASB 116, for example:

    (a)   property held for strategic purposes; and

    (b)   property held to provide a social service, including those which generate cash inflows where the rental revenue is incidental to the purpose for holding the property.

10   Some properties comprise a portion that is held to earn rentals or for capital appreciation and another portion that is held for use in the production or supply of goods or services or for administrative purposes. If these portions could be sold separately (or leased out separately under a finance lease), an entity accounts for the portions separately. If the portions could not be sold separately, the property is investment property only if an insignificant portion is held for use in the production or supply of goods or services or for administrative purposes.

11   In some cases, an entity provides ancillary services to the occupants of a property it holds. An entity treats such a property as investment property if the services are insignificant to the arrangement as a whole. An example is when the owner of an office building provides security and maintenance services to the lessees who occupy the building.

12   In other cases, the services provided are significant. For example, if an entity owns and manages a hotel, services provided to guests are significant to the arrangement as a whole. Therefore, an owner-managed hotel is owner-occupied property, rather than investment property.

13   It may be difficult to determine whether ancillary services are so significant that a property does not qualify as investment property. For example, the owner of a hotel sometimes transfers some responsibilities to third parties under a management contract. The terms of such contracts vary widely. At one end of the spectrum, the owner's position may, in substance, be that of a passive investor. At the other end of the spectrum, the owner may simply have outsourced day-to-day functions while retaining significant exposure to variation in the cash flows generated by the operations of the hotel.

14   Judgement is needed to determine whether a property qualifies as investment property. An entity develops criteria so that it can exercise that judgement consistently in accordance with the definition of investment property and with the related guidance in paragraphs 7-13. Paragraph 75(c) requires an entity to disclose these criteria when classification is difficult.

15   In some cases, an entity owns property that is leased to, and occupied by, its parent or another subsidiary. The property does not qualify as investment property in the consolidated

financial statements, because the property is owner-occupied from the perspective of the group. However, from the perspective of the entity that owns it, the property is investment property if it meets the definition in paragraph 5. Therefore, the lessor treats the property as investment property in its individual financial statements.

Recognition

16   **Investment property shall be recognised as an asset when, and only when:**

(a)   **it is probable that the future economic benefits that are associated with the investment property will flow to the entity; and**

(b)   **the *cost* of the investment property can be measured reliably.**

17   An entity evaluates under this recognition principle all its investment property costs at the time they are incurred. These costs include costs incurred initially to acquire an investment property and costs incurred subsequently to add to, replace part of, or service a property.

18   Under the recognition principle in paragraph 16, an entity does not recognise in the *carrying amount* of an investment property the costs of the day-to-day servicing of such a property. Rather, these costs are recognised in profit or loss as incurred. Costs of day-to-day servicing are primarily the cost of labour and consumables, and may include the cost of minor parts. The purpose of these expenditures is often described as for the 'repairs and maintenance' of the property.

19   Parts of investment properties may have been acquired through replacement. For example, the interior walls may be replacements of original walls. Under the recognition principle, an entity recognises in the carrying amount of an investment property the cost of replacing part of an existing investment property at the time that cost is incurred if the recognition criteria are met. The carrying amount of those parts that are replaced is derecognised in accordance with the derecognition provisions of this Standard.

Measurement at Recognition

20   **An investment property shall be measured initially at its cost. Transaction costs shall be included in the initial measurement.**

Aus20.1   **Notwithstanding paragraph 20, in respect of not-for-profit entities, where an investment property is acquired at no cost or for nominal cost, its cost shall be deemed to be its fair value as at the date of acquisition.**

21   The cost of a purchased investment property comprises its purchase price and any directly attributable expenditure. Directly attributable expenditure includes, for example, professional fees for legal services, property transfer taxes and other transaction costs.

22   [Deleted by the IASB]

23   The cost of an investment property is not increased by:

(a)   start-up costs (unless they are necessary to bring the property to the condition necessary for it to be capable of operating in the manner intended by management);

(b)   operating losses incurred before the investment property achieves the planned level of occupancy; or

(c)   abnormal amounts of wasted material, labour or other resources incurred in constructing or developing the property.

24   If payment for an investment property is deferred, its cost is the cash price equivalent. The difference between this amount and the total payments is recognised as interest expense over the period of credit.

25   **The initial cost of a property interest held under a lease and classified as an investment property shall be as prescribed for a finance lease by paragraph 20 of AASB 117 *Leases*, that is, the asset shall be recognised at the lower of the fair value of the leased property and the present value of the minimum lease payments. An equivalent amount shall be recognised as a liability in accordance with that same paragraph.**

26   Any premium paid for a lease is treated as part of the minimum lease payments for this purpose, and is therefore included in the cost of the lease, but is excluded from the liability. If a property interest held under a lease is classified as investment property, the item accounted for at fair value is that interest and not the underlying property. Guidance on determining the fair value of a property interest is set out for the fair value model in paragraphs 33 52. That guidance is also relevant to the determination of fair value when that value is used as cost for initial recognition purposes.

27   One or more investment properties may be acquired in exchange for a non-monetary asset or assets, or a combination of monetary and non-monetary assets. The following discussion refers simply to an exchange of one non-monetary asset for another, but it also applies to all the exchanges described in the preceding sentence. The cost of such an investment property is measured at fair value unless (a) the exchange transaction lacks commercial substance or (b) the fair value of neither the asset received nor the asset given up is reliably measurable. The acquired asset is measured in this way even if an entity cannot immediately derecognise the asset given up. If the acquired asset is not measured at fair value, its cost is measured at the carrying amount of the asset given up.

28   An entity determines whether an exchange transaction has commercial substance by considering the extent to which its future cash flows are expected to change as a result of the transaction. An exchange transaction has commercial substance if:

(a)   the configuration (risk, timing and amount) of the cash flows of the asset received differs from the configuration of the cash flows of the asset transferred; or

(b)   the entity-specific value of the portion of the entity's operations affected by the transaction changes as a result of the exchange; and

(c)   the difference in (a) or (b) is significant relative to the fair value of the assets exchanged.

For the purpose of determining whether an exchange transaction has commercial substance, the entity-specific value of the portion of the entity's operations affected by the transaction shall reflect post-tax cash flows. The result of these analyses may be clear without an entity having to perform detailed calculations.

29   The fair value of an asset for which comparable market transactions do not exist is reliably measurable if (a) the variability in the range of reasonable fair value estimates is not significant for that asset or (b) the probabilities of the various estimates within the range can be reasonably assessed and used in estimating fair value. If the entity is able to determine reliably the fair value of either the asset received or the asset given up, then the fair value of the asset given up is used to measure cost unless the fair value of the asset received is more clearly evident.

Measurement after Recognition

Accounting Policy

30   **With the exceptions noted in paragraphs 32A and 34, an entity shall choose as its accounting policy either the fair value model in paragraphs 33 to 55 or the cost model in paragraph 56 and shall apply that policy to all of its investment property.**

31   AASB 108 *Accounting Policies, Changes in Accounting Estimates and Errors* states that a voluntary change in accounting policy shall be made only if the change results in the financial statements providing reliable and more relevant information about the effects of transactions, other events or conditions on the entity's financial position, financial performance or cash flows. It is highly unlikely that a change from the fair value model to the cost model will result in a more relevant presentation.

32   This Standard requires all entities to determine the fair value of investment property for the purpose of either measurement (if the entity uses the fair value model) or disclosure (if it uses the cost model). An entity is encouraged, but not required, to determine the fair value of investment property on the basis of a valuation by an independent valuer who holds a recognised and relevant professional qualification and has recent experience in the location and category of the investment property being valued.

32A An entity may:

    (a) choose either the fair value model or the cost model for all investment property backing liabilities that pay a return linked directly to the fair value of, or returns from, specified assets including that investment property; and

    (b) choose either the fair value model or the cost model for all other investment property, regardless of the choice in (a).

32B Some insurers and other entities operate an internal property fund that issues notional units, with some units held by investors in linked contracts and others held by the entity. Paragraph 32A does not permit an entity to measure the property held by the fund partly at cost and partly at fair value.

32C If an entity chooses different models for the two categories described in paragraph 32A, sales of investment property between pools of assets measured using different models shall be recognised at fair value and the cumulative change in fair value shall be recognised in profit or loss. Accordingly, if an investment property is sold from a pool in which the fair value model is used into a pool in which the cost model is used, the property's fair value at the date of the sale becomes its deemed cost.

Fair Value Model

33 After initial recognition, an entity that chooses the fair value model shall measure all of its investment property at fair value, except in the cases described in paragraph 53.

34 When a property interest held by a lessee under an operating lease is classified as an investment property under paragraph 6, paragraph 30 is not elective; the fair value model shall be applied.

35 A gain or loss arising from a change in the fair value of investment property shall be recognised in profit or loss for the period in which it arises.

36 The fair value of investment property is the price at which the property could be exchanged between knowledgeable, willing parties in an arm's length transaction (see paragraph 5). Fair value specifically excludes an estimated price inflated or deflated by special terms or circumstances such as atypical financing, sale and leaseback arrangements, special considerations or concessions granted by anyone associated with the sale.

37 An entity determines fair value without any deduction for transaction costs it may incur on sale or other disposal.

38 The fair value of investment property shall reflect market conditions at the end of the reporting period.

39 Fair value is time-specific as of a given date. Because market conditions may change, the amount reported as fair value may be incorrect or inappropriate if estimated as of another time. The definition of fair value also assumes simultaneous exchange and completion of the contract for sale without any variation in price that might be made in an arm's length transaction between knowledgeable, willing parties if exchange and completion are not simultaneous.

40 The fair value of investment property reflects, among other things, rental income from current leases and reasonable and supportable assumptions that represent what knowledgeable, willing parties would assume about rental income from future leases in the light of current conditions. It also reflects, on a similar basis, any cash outflows (including rental payments and other outflows) that could be expected in respect of the property. Some of those outflows are reflected in the liability whereas others relate to outflows that are not recognised in the financial statements until a later date (e.g. periodic payments such as contingent rents).

41 Paragraph 25 specifies the basis for initial recognition of the cost of an interest in a leased property. Paragraph 33 requires the interest in the leased property to be re-measured, if necessary, to fair value. In a lease negotiated at market rates, the fair value of an interest in a leased property at acquisition, net of all expected lease payments (including those relating to recognised liabilities), should be zero. This fair value does not change regardless of whether, for accounting purposes, a leased asset and liability are recognised at fair value

or at the present value of minimum lease payments, in accordance with paragraph 20 of AASB 117. Thus, remeasuring a leased asset from cost in accordance with paragraph 25 to the fair value in accordance with paragraph 33 should not give rise to any initial gain or loss, unless fair value is measured at different times. This could occur when an election to apply the fair value model is made after initial recognition.

42   The definition of fair value refers to "knowledgeable, willing parties". In this context, "knowledgeable" means that both the willing buyer and the willing seller are reasonably informed about the nature and characteristics of the investment property, its actual and potential uses, and market conditions at the end of the reporting period. A willing buyer is motivated, but not compelled, to buy. This buyer is neither over-eager nor determined to buy at any price. The assumed buyer would not pay a higher price than a market comprising knowledgeable, willing buyers and sellers would require.

43   A willing seller is neither an over-eager nor a forced seller, prepared to sell at any price, nor one prepared to hold out for a price not considered reasonable in current market conditions. The willing seller is motivated to sell the investment property at market terms for the best price obtainable. The factual circumstances of the actual investment property owner are not a part of this consideration because the willing seller is a hypothetical owner (e.g. a willing seller would not take into account the particular tax circumstances of the actual investment property owner).

44   The definition of fair value refers to an arm's length transaction. An arm's length transaction is one between parties that do not have a particular or special relationship that makes prices of transactions uncharacteristic of market conditions. The transaction is presumed to be between unrelated parties, each acting independently.

45   The best evidence of fair value is given by current prices in an active market for similar property in the same location and condition and subject to similar lease and other contracts. An entity takes care to identify any differences in the nature, location or condition of the property, or in the contractual terms of the leases and other contracts relating to the property.

46   In the absence of current prices in an active market of the kind described in paragraph 45, an entity considers information from a variety of sources, including:

(a)   current prices in an active market for properties of different nature, condition or location (or subject to different lease or other contracts), adjusted to reflect those differences;

(b)   recent prices of similar properties on less active markets, with adjustments to reflect any changes in economic conditions since the date of the transactions that occurred at those prices; and

(c)   discounted cash flow projections based on reliable estimates of future cash flows, supported by the terms of any existing lease and other contracts and (when possible) by external evidence such as current market rents for similar properties in the same location and condition, and using discount rates that reflect current market assessments of the uncertainty in the amount and timing of the cash flows.

47   In some cases, the various sources listed in the previous paragraph may suggest different conclusions about the fair value of an investment property. An entity considers the reasons for those differences, in order to arrive at the most reliable estimate of fair value within a range of reasonable fair value estimates.

48   In exceptional cases, there is clear evidence when an entity first acquires an investment property (or when an existing property first becomes investment property after a change in use) that the variability in the range of reasonable fair value estimates will be so great, and the probabilities of the various outcomes so difficult to assess, that the usefulness of a single estimate of fair value is negated. This may indicate that the fair value of the property will not be reliably determinable on a continuing basis (see paragraph 53).

49   Fair value differs from value in use, as defined in AASB 136 *Impairment of Assets*. Fair value reflects the knowledge and estimates of knowledgeable, willing buyers and sellers. In contrast, value in use reflects the entity's estimates, including the effects of factors that may be specific to the entity and not applicable to entities in general.

For example, fair value does not reflect any of the following factors to the extent that they would not be generally available to knowledgeable, willing buyers and sellers:

(a)   additional value derived from the creation of a portfolio of properties in different locations;

(b)   synergies between investment property and other assets;

(c)   legal rights or legal restrictions that are specific only to the current owner; and

(d)   tax benefits or tax burdens that are specific to the current owner.

50   In determining the carrying amount of investment property under the fair value model, an entity does not double-count assets or liabilities that are recognised as separate assets or liabilities. For example:

(a)   equipment such as lifts or air-conditioning is often an integral part of a building and is generally included in the fair value of the investment property, rather than recognised separately as property, plant and equipment;

(b)   if an office is leased on a furnished basis, the fair value of the office generally includes the fair value of the furniture, because the rental income relates to the furnished office. When furniture is included in the fair value of investment property, an entity does not recognise that furniture as a separate asset;

(c)   the fair value of investment property excludes prepaid or accrued operating lease income, because the entity recognises it as a separate liability or asset; and

(d)   the fair value of investment property held under a lease reflects expected cash flows (including contingent rent that is expected to become payable). Accordingly, if a valuation obtained for a property is net of all payments expected to be made, it will be necessary to add back any recognised lease liability, to arrive at the carrying amount of the investment property using the fair value model.

51   The fair value of investment property does not reflect future capital expenditure that will improve or enhance the property and does not reflect the related future benefits from this future expenditure.

52   In some cases, an entity expects that the present value of its payments relating to an investment property (other than payments relating to recognised liabilities) will exceed the present value of the related cash receipts. An entity applies AASB 137 *Provisions, Contingent Liabilities and Contingent Assets* to determine whether to recognise a liability and, if so, how to measure it.

Inability to Determine Fair Value Reliably

53   **There is a rebuttable presumption that an entity can reliably determine the fair value of an investment property on a continuing basis. However, in exceptional cases, there is clear evidence when an entity first acquires an investment property (or when an existing property first becomes investment property after a change in use) that the fair value of the investment property is not reliably determinable on a continuing basis. This arises when, and only when, comparable market transactions are infrequent and alternative reliable estimates of fair value (for example, based on discounted cash flow projections) are not available. If an entity determines that the fair value of an investment property under construction is not reliably determinable but expects the fair value of the property to be reliably determinable when construction is complete, it shall measure that investment property under construction at cost until either its fair value becomes reliably determinable or construction is completed (whichever is earlier). If an entity determines that the fair value of an investment property (other than an investment property under construction) is not reliably determinable on a continuing basis, the entity shall measure that investment property using the cost model in AASB 116. The residual value of the investment property shall be assumed to be zero. The entity shall apply AASB 116 until disposal of the investment property.**

53A   Once an entity becomes able to measure reliably the fair value of an investment property under construction that has previously been measured at cost, it shall measure that property at its fair value. Once construction of that property is complete, it is presumed that fair value can be measured reliably. If this is not the case, in accordance with paragraph 53, the property shall be accounted for using the cost model in accordance with AASB 116.

53B   The presumption that the fair value of investment property under construction can be measured reliably can be rebutted only on initial recognition. An entity that has measured an item of investment property under construction at fair value may not conclude that the fair value of the completed investment property cannot be determined reliably.

54   In the exceptional cases when an entity is compelled, for the reason given in paragraph 53, to measure an investment property using the cost model in accordance with AASB 116, it measures at fair value all its other investment property including investment property under construction. In these cases, although an entity may use the cost model for one investment property, the entity shall continue to account for each of the remaining properties using the fair value model.

55   **If an entity has previously measured an investment property at fair value, it shall continue to measure the property at fair value until disposal (or until the property becomes owner-occupied property or the entity begins to develop the property for subsequent sale in the ordinary course of business) even if comparable market transactions become less frequent or market prices become less readily available.**

Cost Model

56   **After initial recognition, an entity that chooses the cost model shall measure all of its investment properties in accordance with AASB 116's requirements for that model, other than those that meet the criteria to be classified as held for sale (or are included in a disposal group that is classified as held for sale) in accordance with AASB 5 *Non-current Assets Held for Sale and Discontinued Operations*. Investment properties that meet the criteria to be classified as held for sale (or are included in a disposal group that is classified as held for sale) shall be measured in accordance with AASB 5.**

Transfers

57   **Transfers to, or from, investment property shall be made when, and only when, there is a change in use, evidenced by:**

       (a)   commencement of owner-occupation, for a transfer from investment property to owner-occupied property;

       (b)   commencement of development with a view to sale, for a transfer from investment property to inventories;

       (c)   end of owner-occupation, for a transfer from owner-occupied property to investment property; or

       (d)   commencement of an operating lease to another party, for a transfer from inventories to investment property.

       (e)   [deleted by the IASB]

58   Paragraph 57(b) requires an entity to transfer a property from investment property to inventories when, and only when, there is a change in use, evidenced by commencement of development with a view to sale. When an entity decides to dispose of an investment property without development, it continues to treat the property as an investment property until it is derecognised (eliminated from the statement of financial position) and does not treat it as inventory. Similarly, if an entity begins to redevelop an existing investment property for continued future use as investment property, the property remains an investment property and is not reclassified as owner-occupied property during the redevelopment.

59   Paragraphs 60 65 apply to recognition and measurement issues that arise when an entity uses the fair value model for investment property. When an entity uses the cost model, transfers between investment property, owner-occupied property and inventories do not change the carrying amount of the property transferred and they do not change the cost of that property for measurement or disclosure purposes.

60 For a transfer from investment property carried at fair value to owner-occupied property or inventories, the property's deemed cost for subsequent accounting in accordance with AASB 116 or AASB 102 *Inventories* shall be its fair value at the date of change in use.

61 If an owner-occupied property becomes an investment property that will be carried at fair value, an entity shall apply AASB 116 up to the date of change in use. The entity shall treat any difference at that date between the carrying amount of the property in accordance with AASB 116 and its fair value in the same way as a revaluation in accordance with AASB 116.

62 Up to the date when an owner-occupied property becomes an investment property carried at fair value, an entity depreciates the property and recognises any impairment losses that have occurred. The entity treats any difference at that date between the carrying amount of the property in accordance with AASB 116 and its fair value in the same way as a revaluation in accordance with AASB 116. In other words:

(a) any resulting decrease in the carrying amount of the property is recognised in profit or loss. However, to the extent that an amount is included in revaluation surplus for that property, the decrease is recognised in other comprehensive income and reduces the revaluation surplus within equity; and

(b) any resulting increase in the carrying amount is treated as follows:

(i) to the extent that the increase reverses a previous impairment loss for that property, the increase is recognised in profit or loss. The amount recognised in profit or loss does not exceed the amount needed to restore the carrying amount to the carrying amount that would have been determined (net of depreciation) had no impairment loss been recognised; and

(ii) any remaining part of the increase is recognised in other comprehensive income and increases the revaluation surplus within equity. On subsequent disposal of the investment property, the revaluation surplus included in equity may be transferred to retained earnings. The transfer from revaluation surplus to retained earnings is not made through profit or loss.

63 For a transfer from inventories to investment property that will be carried at fair value, any difference between the fair value of the property at that date and its previous carrying amount shall be recognised in profit or loss.

64 The treatment of transfers from inventories to investment property that will be carried at fair value is consistent with the treatment of sales of inventories.

65 When an entity completes the construction or development of a self-constructed investment property that will be carried at fair value, any difference between the fair value of the property at that date and its previous carrying amount shall be recognised in profit or loss.

Disposals

66 An investment property shall be derecognised (eliminated from the statement of financial position) on disposal or when the investment property is permanently withdrawn from use and no future economic benefits are expected from its disposal.

67 The disposal of an investment property may be achieved by sale or by entering into a finance lease. In determining the date of disposal for investment property, an entity applies the criteria in AASB 118 *Revenue* for recognising revenue from the sale of goods and considers the related guidance in the illustrative examples accompanying AASB 118. AASB 117 applies to a disposal effected by entering into a finance lease and to a sale and leaseback.

68 If, in accordance with the recognition principle in paragraph 16, an entity recognises in the carrying amount of an asset the cost of a replacement for part of an investment property, then it derecognises the carrying amount of the replaced part. For investment property accounted for using the cost model, a replaced part may not be a part that was depreciated separately. If it is not practicable for an entity to determine the carrying amount of the replaced part, it may use the cost of the replacement as an indication of what the cost

of the replaced part was at the time it was acquired or constructed. In accordance with the fair value model, the fair value of the investment property may already reflect that the part to be replaced has lost its value. In other cases it may be difficult to discern how much fair value shall be reduced for the part being replaced. An alternative to reducing fair value for the replaced part, when it is not practical to do so, is to include the cost of the replacement in the carrying amount of the asset and then to reassess the fair value, as would be required for additions not involving replacement.

69   **Gains or losses arising from the retirement or disposal of investment property shall be determined as the difference between the net disposal proceeds and the carrying amount of the asset and shall be recognised in profit or loss (unless AASB 117 requires otherwise on a sale and leaseback) in the period of the retirement or disposal.**

70   The consideration receivable on disposal of an investment property is recognised initially at fair value. In particular, if payment for an investment property is deferred, the consideration received is recognised initially at the cash price equivalent. The difference between the nominal amount of the consideration and the cash price equivalent is recognised as interest revenue in accordance with AASB 118 using the effective interest method.

71   An entity applies AASB 137 *Provisions, Contingent Liabilities and Contingent Assets* or other Standards, as appropriate, to any liabilities that it retains after disposal of an investment property.

72   **Compensation from third parties for investment property that was impaired, lost or given up shall be recognised in profit or loss when the compensation becomes receivable.**

73   Impairments or losses of investment property, related claims for or payments of compensation from third parties and any subsequent purchase or construction of replacement assets are separate economic events and are accounted for separately as follows:

     (a)   impairments of investment property are recognised in accordance with AASB 136;

     (b)   retirements or disposals of investment property are recognised in accordance with paragraphs 66-71 of this Standard;

     (c)   compensation from third parties for investment property that was impaired, lost or given up is recognised in profit or loss when it becomes receivable; and

     (d)   the cost of assets restored, purchased or constructed as replacements is determined in accordance with paragraphs 20-29 of this Standard.

Disclosure

Fair Value Model and Cost Model

74   The disclosures below apply in addition to those in AASB 117. In accordance with AASB 117, the owner of an investment property provides lessors' disclosures about leases into which it has entered. An entity that holds an investment property under a finance or operating lease provides lessees' disclosures for finance leases and lessors' disclosures for any operating leases into which it has entered.

75   **An entity shall disclose:**

     (a)   **whether it applies the fair value or the cost model;**

     (b)   **if it applies the fair value model, whether, and in what circumstances, property interests held under operating leases are classified and accounted for as investment property;**

     (c)   **when classification is difficult (see paragraph 14), the criteria it uses to distinguish investment property from owner-occupied property and from property held for sale in the ordinary course of business;**

     (d)   **the methods and significant assumptions applied in determining the fair value of investment property, including a statement whether the determination of fair value was supported by market evidence or was more heavily based on** other factors (which the entity shall disclose) because of the nature of the property and lack of comparable market data;

(e) the extent to which the fair value of investment property (as measured or disclosed in the financial statements) is based on a valuation by an independent valuer who holds a recognised and relevant professional qualification and has recent experience in the location and category of the investment property being valued. If there has been no such valuation, that fact shall be disclosed;

(f) the amounts recognised in profit or loss for:

    (i) rental income from investment property;

    (ii) direct operating expenses (including repairs and maintenance) arising from investment property that generated rental income during the period;

    (iii) direct operating expenses (including repairs and maintenance) arising from investment property that did not generate rental income during the period; and

    (iv) the cumulative change in fair value recognised in profit or loss on a sale of investment property from a pool of assets in which the cost model is used into a pool in which the fair value model is used (see paragraph 32C);

(g) the existence and amounts of restrictions on the realisability of investment property or the remittance of income and proceeds of disposal; and

(h) contractual obligations to purchase, construct or develop investment property or for repairs, maintenance or enhancements.

Fair Value Model

76 In addition to the disclosures required by paragraph 75, an entity that applies the fair value model in paragraphs 33 55 shall disclose a reconciliation between the carrying amounts of investment property at the beginning and end of the period, showing the following:

(a) additions, disclosing separately those additions resulting from acquisitions and those resulting from subsequent expenditure recognised in the carrying amount of an asset;

(b) additions resulting from acquisitions through business combinations;

(c) assets classified as held for sale or included in a disposal group in accordance with AASB 5 and other disposals;

(d) net gains or losses from fair value adjustments;

(e) the net exchange differences arising on the translation of the financial statements into a different presentation currency, and on translation of a foreign operation into the presentation currency of the reporting entity;

(f) transfers to and from inventories and owner-occupied property; and

(g) other changes.

77 When a valuation obtained for investment property is adjusted significantly for the purpose of the financial statements, for example to avoid double-counting of assets or liabilities that are recognised as separate assets and liabilities as described in paragraph 50, the entity shall disclose a reconciliation between the valuation obtained and the adjusted valuation included in the financial statements, showing separately the aggregate amount of any recognised lease obligations that have been added back, and any other significant adjustments.

78 In the exceptional cases referred to in paragraph 53, when an entity measures investment property using the cost model in AASB 116, the reconciliation required by paragraph 76 shall disclose amounts relating to that investment property separately

from amounts relating to other investment property. In addition, an entity shall disclose:

(a)   a description of the investment property;

(b)   an explanation of why fair value cannot be determined reliably;

(c)   if possible, the range of estimates within which fair value is highly likely to lie; and

(d)   on disposal of investment property not carried at fair value:

    (i)   the fact that the entity has disposed of investment property not carried at fair value;

    (ii)   the carrying amount of that investment property at the time of sale; and

    (iii)   the amount of gain or loss recognised.

Cost Model

79   In addition to the disclosures required by paragraph 75, an entity that applies the cost model in paragraph 56 shall disclose:

(a)   the depreciation methods used;

(b)   the useful lives or the depreciation rates used;

(c)   the gross carrying amount and the accumulated depreciation (aggregated with accumulated impairment losses) at the beginning and end of the period;

(d)   a reconciliation of the carrying amount of investment property at the beginning and end of the period, showing the following:

    (i)   additions, disclosing separately those additions resulting from acquisitions and those resulting from subsequent expenditure recognised as an asset;

    (ii)   additions resulting from acquisitions through business combinations;

    (iii)   assets classified as held for sale or included in a disposal group in accordance with AASB 5 and other disposals;

    (iv)   depreciation;

    (v)   the amount of impairment losses recognised, and the amount of impairment losses reversed, during the period in accordance with AASB 136;

    (vi)   the net exchange differences arising on the translation of the financial statements into a different presentation currency, and on translation of a foreign operation into the presentation currency of the reporting entity;

    (vii)   transfers to and from inventories and owner-occupied property; and

    (viii) other changes; and

(e)   the fair value of investment property. In the exceptional cases described in paragraph 53, when an entity cannot determine the fair value of the investment property reliably, it shall disclose:

    (i)   a description of the investment property;

    (ii)   an explanation of why fair value cannot be determined reliably; and

    (iii)   if possible, the range of estimates within which fair value is highly likely to lie.

Transitional Provisions

80   [Deleted by the AASB]

81   [Deleted by the AASB]

82   [Deleted by the AASB]

83   [Deleted by the AASB]

84   [Deleted by the AASB]

Effective Date

85   [Deleted by the AASB]

85A   [Deleted by the AASB]

85B   Paragraphs 8, 9, 48, 53, 54 and 57 were amended, paragraph 22 was deleted and paragraphs 53A and 53B were added by AASB 2008-5 *Amendments to Australian Accounting Standards arising from the Annual Improvements Project* issued in July 2008. An entity shall apply those amendments prospectively for annual reporting periods beginning on or after 1 January 2009. An entity is permitted to apply the amendments to investment property under construction from any date before 1 January 2009 provided that the fair values of investment properties under construction were determined at those dates. Earlier application is permitted. If an entity applies the amendments for an earlier period it shall disclose that fact and at the same time apply the amendments to paragraphs 5 and 81E of AASB 116 *Property, Plant and Equipment*.

Withdrawal of IAS 40 (2000)

86   [Deleted by the AASB]

AASB 141
Agriculture

(Compiled October 2009)

Note from the Institute of Chartered Accountants Australia

This note, prepared by the technical editors, is not part of Accounting Standard AASB 141.

Historical development

15 July 2004: AASB 141 'Agriculture' is the Australian equivalent of IAS 41 of the same name. It was made by the AASB on 15 July 2004 as part of the AASB's program to adopt International Financial Reporting Standards (IFRSs) by 2005.

22 December 2004: AASB 2004-2 'Amendments to Australian Accounting Standards' amends paragraph 50, and is applicable to annual reporting periods beginning on or after 1 January 2005. The amending Standard was issued by the AASB following a review of IFRSs and the Australian equivalents.

6 April 2006: Removal of Australian Guidance.

7 July 2006: Compiled version of the Standard was issued, incorporating amendments contained in AASB 2004-2 and AASB 2005-11.

30 April 2007: AASB 2007-4 'Amendments to Australian Accounting Standards' deletes paragraphs Aus 43.1 and Aus 49.1 and is applicable for annual reporting periods beginning on or after 1 July 2007. Entities may elect to early-adopt it to annual reporting periods beginning on or after 1 January 2005.

24 September 2007: AASB 2007-8 'Amendments to Australian Accounting Standards' was issued by the AASB. This Standard is applicable for annual reporting periods beginning on or after 1 January 2009.

13 December 2007: AASB 2007-10 'Further Amendments to Australian Accounting Standards arising from AASB 101' amends AASB 141, replacing the term 'financial report' with 'financial statements'. This Standard is applicable to annual reporting periods beginning on or after 1 January 2009.

24 July 2008: AASB 2008-5 'Amendments to Australian Accounting Standards arising from the Annual Improvements Project' amends AASB 141 in relation to the discount rate for fair value calculations, additional biological transformation, examples of agricultural produce and products and point-of-sale costs. This Standard is applicable to annual reporting periods beginning on or after 1 January 2009.

25 June 2009: AASB 2009-6 'Amendments to Australian Accounting Standards' amends AASB 141 for editorial corrections made by the International Accounting Standards Board (IASB) to its Standards and Interpretations (IFRSs) and as a consequence of issuing revised AASB 101 'Presentation of Financial Statements' (September 2007). This Standard is applicable to annual reporting periods beginning on or after 1 January 2009 that end on or after 30 June 2009.

5 October 2009: Erratum makes further terminology-related and editorial changes resulting from AASB 2009-6. This erratum applies to annual reporting periods beginning on or after 1 January 2009 that end on or after 30 June 2009.

6 October 2009: AASB 141 was reissued by the AASB, compiled to include the AASB 2007-8, AASB 2007-10, AASB 2008-5, AASB 2009-6 and Erratum (October 2009) amendments. This compiled Standard applies to annual reporting periods beginning on or after 1 January 2009 that end on or after 30 June 2009. Early application is permitted.

29 August 2011: AASB 2011-7 'Amendments to Australian Accounting Standards arising from the Consolidation and Joint Arrangements Standards' amends AASB 141 to give effect to many consequential changes arising from the issue of AASB 10, 11, 12, 127 and 128. This Standard applies to annual reporting periods beginning on or after 1 January 2013 and can be adopted early by for-profit entities. **These amendments are not included in this compiled Standard.**

---

5 September 2011: AASB 2011-8 'Amendments to Australian Accounting Standards arising from AASB 13' amends AASB 141 to give effect to a consequential change in the definition of fair value arising from the issue of AASB 13. This Standard applies to annual reporting periods beginning on or after 1 January 2013 and can be adopted early. **These amendments are not included in this compiled Standard.**

21 March 2012: AASB 2012-1 'Amendments to Australian Accounting Standards – Fair Value Measurement – Reduced Disclosure Requirements' amends AASB 141 to establish and amend reduced disclosure requirements arising from AASB 13 'Fair Value Measurement'. **These amendments are not included in this compiled Standard.**

Reference

IFRIC item not taken onto the agenda: IAS 41-2 *Discount rate assumptions used in fair value calculations* applies to AASB 141.

AASB 141 compared to IAS 41

Additions

Paragraph	Description
Aus 1.1	Which entities AASB 141 applies to (i.e. reporting entities and general purpose financial statements).
Aus 1.2	The application date of AASB 141 (i.e. annual reporting periods beginning 1 January 2005).
Aus 1.3	Prohibits early application of AASB 141.
Aus 1.4	Makes the requirements of AASB 141 subject to AASB 1031 'Materiality'.
Aus 1.5	Explains which Australian Standards have been superseded by AASB 141.
Aus 1.6	Clarifies that the superseded Australian Standards remain in force until AASB 141 applies.
Aus 1.7	Notice of the new Standard published on 22 July 2004.
Aus 38.1	Clarifies that not-for-profit entities recognise government grants for biological assets in accordance with AASB 1004 'Contributions'.

Deletions

Paragraph	Description
58	Effective date of IAS 41.
59	First time application to be accounted for in accordance with IAS 8 'Accounting Policies, Changes in Accounting Estimates and Errors'.

Contents

Compilation Details

Comparison with IAS 41

Accounting Standard
AASB 141 Agriculture

	Paragraphs
Objective	
Application	Aus1.1 – Aus1.7
Scope	1 – 4
Definitions	
Agriculture-related Definitions	5 – 7
General Definitions	8 – 9
Recognition and Measurement	10 – 25
Gains and Losses	26 – 29
Inability to Measure Fair Value Reliably	30 – 33
Government Grants	34 – Aus38.1
Disclosure	
General	40 – 53
Additional Disclosures for Biological Assets where Fair Value Cannot be Measured Reliably	54 – 56
Government Grants	57
Effective Date and Transition	60

Appendix: Illustrative Examples
(available on the AASB website)

Basis for Conclusions on IAS 41
(available on the AASB website)

Australian Accounting Standard AASB 141 *Agriculture* (as amended) is set out in paragraphs Aus1.1 – 60. All the paragraphs have equal authority. Terms defined in this Standard are in *italics* the first time they appear in the Standard. AASB 141 is to be read in the context of other Australian Accounting Standards, including AASB 1048 *Interpretation and Application of Standards*, which identifies the Australian Accounting Interpretations. In the absence of explicit guidance, AASB 108 *Accounting Policies, Changes in Accounting Estimates and Errors* provides a basis for selecting and applying accounting policies.

Compilation Details

Accounting Standard AASB 141 *Agriculture* as amended

This compiled Standard applies to annual reporting periods beginning on or after 1 January 2009 that end on or after 30 June 2009. It takes into account amendments up to and including 5 October 2009 and was prepared on 6 October 2009 by the staff of the Australian Accounting Standards Board (AASB).

This compilation is not a separate Accounting Standard made by the AASB. Instead, it is a representation of AASB 141 (July 2004) as amended by other Accounting Standards, which are listed in the Table below.

Table of Standards

Standard	Date made	Application date *(annual reporting periods ... on or after ...)*	Application, saving or transitional provisions
AASB 141	15 Jul 2004	*(beginning)* 1 Jan 2005	
AASB 2004-2	22 Dec 2004	*(beginning)* 1 Jan 2005	–
AASB 2005-11	8 Sep 2005	*(ending)* 31 Dec 2005	see (a) below
AASB 2007-4	30 Apr 2007	*(beginning)* 1 Jul 2007	see (b) below
AASB 2007-8	24 Sep 2007	*(beginning)* 1 Jan 2009	see (c) below
AASB 2007-10	13 Dec 2007	*(beginning)* 1 Jan 2009	see (c) below
AASB 2008-5	24 Jul 2008	*(beginning)* 1 Jan 2009	see (d) below
AASB 2009-6	25 Jun 2009	*(beginning)* 1 Jan 2009 and *(ending)* 30 Jun 2009	see (e) below
Erratum	5 Oct 2009	*(beginning)* 1 Jan 2009 and *(ending)* 30 Jun 2009	see (f) below

(a) Entities may elect to apply this Standard for annual reporting periods beginning on or after 1 January 2005 that end before 31 December 2005.

(b) Entities may elect to apply this Standard to annual reporting periods beginning on or after 1 January 2005 but before 1 July 2007.

(c) Entities may elect to apply this Standard to annual reporting periods beginning on or after 1 January 2005 but before 1 January 2009, provided that AASB 101 *Presentation of Financial Statements* (September 2007) is also applied to such periods.

(d) Paragraph 78 of this Standard specifies application provisions. Entities may elect to apply this Standard, or its amendments to individual Standards, to annual reporting periods beginning on or after 1 January 2005 but before 1 January 2009.

(e) Entities may elect to apply this Standard to annual reporting periods beginning on or after 1 January 2005 but before 1 January 2009, provided that AASB 101 *Presentation of Financial Statements* (September 2007) is also applied to such periods, and to annual reporting periods beginning on or after 1 January 2009 that end before 30 June 2009.

(f) Entities may elect to apply this Erratum to annual reporting periods beginning on or after 1 January 2005, provided that AASB 2009-6 *Amendments to Australian Accounting Standards* is also applied to such periods.

Table of Amendments to Standard

Paragraph affected	How affected	By ... [paragraph]
Objective	amended	AASB 2005-11 [16]
Aus1.1	amended	AASB 2007-8 [7, 8]
Aus1.4	amended	AASB 2007-8 [8]
1	amended	AASB 2009-6 [99]
4-6	amended	AASB 2008-5 [74]
8	amended	AASB 2007-8 [6]
12	amended	AASB 2007-8 [6]
14	deleted	AASB 2008-5 [75]

Paragraph affected	How affected	By ... [paragraph]
17	amended	AASB 2008-5 [74]
18	amended	AASB 2007-8 [6]
20-21	amended	AASB 2008-5 [74]
24	amended	AASB 2007-8 [6]
	amended	Erratum, Oct 2009 [5]
34-36	amended	AASB 2008-5 [74]
Aus43.1	deleted	AASB 2007-4 [102]
46	amended	AASB 2007-10 [93]
Aus49.1	deleted	AASB 2007-4 [102]
50	amended	AASB 2004-2 [18]
	amended	AASB 2007-10 [94]
58 (preceding heading)	amended	AASB 2008-5 [76]
60	added	AASB 2008-5 [77]

Table of Amendments to Illustrative Examples

Paragraph affected	How affected	By ... [paragraph]
Appendix A	deleted	AASB, Apr 2006*

* The AASB decided at its meeting on 6 April 2006 to delete all of the Australian Illustrative Examples accompanying, but not part of, AASB 141. The decision had immediate effect.

General Terminology Amendments

The following amendments are not shown in the above Tables of Amendments:

References to 'estimated point-of-sale costs' and 'point-of-sale costs' were amended to 'costs to sell' by AASB 2008-5.

Comparison with IAS 41

AASB 141 and IAS 41

AASB 141 *Agriculture* as amended incorporates IAS 41 *Agriculture* as issued and amended by the International Accounting Standards Board (IASB). Paragraphs that have been added to this Standard (and do not appear in the text of IAS 41) are identified with the prefix "Aus", followed by the number of the relevant IASB paragraph and decimal numbering. Paragraphs that apply only to not for profit entities begin by identifying their limited applicability.

Compliance with IAS 41

For profit entities that comply with AASB 141 as amended will simultaneously be in compliance with IAS 41 as amended. Not for profit entities using the added "Aus" paragraphs in the Standard that specifically apply to not for profit entities may not be simultaneously complying with IAS 41. Whether a not for profit entity will be in compliance with IAS 41 will depend on whether the "Aus" paragraphs provide additional guidance for not for profit entities or contain requirements that are inconsistent with the corresponding IASB Standard and will be applied by the not for profit entity.

Accounting Standard AASB 141

The Australian Accounting Standards Board made Accounting Standard AASB 141 *Agriculture* under section 334 of the *Corporations Act 2001* on 15 July 2004.

This compiled version of AASB 141 applies to annual reporting periods beginning on or after 1 January 2009 that end on or after 30 June 2009. It incorporates relevant amendments contained in other AASB Standards made by the AASB and other decisions of the AASB up to and including 5 October 2009 (see Compilation Details).

Accounting Standard AASB 141
Agriculture

Objective

The objective of this Standard is to prescribe the accounting treatment and disclosures related to agricultural activity.

Application

Aus1.1   **This Standard applies to:**

         (a)   each entity that is required to prepare financial reports in accordance with Part 2M.3 of the Corporations Act and that is a reporting entity;

         (b)   general purpose financial statements of each other reporting entity; and

         (c)   financial statements that are, or are held out to be, general purpose financial statements.

Aus1.2   **This Standard applies to annual reporting periods beginning on or after 1 January 2005.**

         [Note: For application dates of paragraphs changed or added by an amending Standard, see Compilation Details.]

Aus1.3   **This Standard shall not be applied to annual reporting periods beginning before 1 January 2005.**

Aus1.4   **The requirements specified in this Standard apply to the financial statements where information resulting from their application is material in accordance with AASB 1031** *Materiality.*

Aus1.5   **When applicable, this Standard supersedes:**

         (a)   AASB 1037 *Self-Generating and Regenerating Assets* **as notified in the** *Commonwealth of Australia Gazette* **No S 390, 7 August 1998 and as amended by AASB 1037A** *Amendments to Accounting Standard* **AASB 1037, which was notified in the** *Commonwealth of Australia Gazette* **No S 314, 8 July 1999; and**

         (b)   AAS 35 *Self-Generating and Regenerating Assets* **as issued in August 1998 and as amended by AAS 35A** *Amendments to Australian Accounting Standard AAS 35,* **which was issued in July 1999.**

Aus1.6   AASB 1037, AASB 1037A, AAS 35 and AAS 35A remain applicable until superseded by this Standard.

Aus1.7   Notice of this Standard was published in the *Commonwealth of Australia Gazette* No S 294, 22 July 2004.

Scope

1   **This Standard shall be applied to account for the following when they relate to agricultural activity:**

         (a) ** *biological assets*;**

         (b) ** *agricultural produce* **at the point of *harvest***; and**

         (c) ** *government grants* **covered by paragraphs 34 and 35.

2   This Standard does not apply to:

         (a)   land related to agricultural activity (see AASB 116 *Property, Plant and Equipment* and AASB 140 *Investment Property*); and

         (b)   intangible assets related to agricultural activity (see AASB 138 *Intangible Assets*).

3   This Standard is applied to agricultural produce, which is the harvested product of the entity's biological assets, only at the point of harvest. Thereafter, AASB 102 *Inventories* or another applicable Standard is applied. Accordingly, this Standard does not deal with the processing of agricultural produce after harvest; for example, the processing of grapes

into wine by a vintner who has grown the grapes. While such processing may be a logical and natural extension of agricultural activity, and the events taking place may bear some similarity to *biological transformation*, such processing is not included within the definition of agricultural activity in this Standard.

4   The table below provides examples of biological assets, agricultural produce, and products that are the result of processing after harvest:

Biological assets	Agricultural produce	Products that are the result of processing after harvest
Sheep	Wool	Yarn, carpet
Trees in a plantation forest	Felled trees	Logs, lumber
Plants	Cotton	Thread, clothing
	Harvested cane	Sugar
Dairy cattle	Milk	Cheese
Pigs	Carcass	Sausages, cured hams
Bushes	Leaf	Tea, cured tobacco
Vines	Grapes	Wine
Fruit trees	Picked fruit	Processed fruit

Definitions

Agriculture-related Definitions

5   **The following terms are used in this Standard with the meanings specified.**

Agricultural activity is the management by an entity of the biological transformation and harvest of biological assets for sale or for conversion into agricultural produce or into additional biological assets.

Agricultural produce is the harvested product of the entity's biological assets.

A **biological asset** is a living animal or plant.

Biological transformation comprises the processes of growth, degeneration, production, and procreation that cause qualitative or quantitative changes in a biological asset.

Costs to sell are the incremental costs directly attributable to the disposal of an asset, excluding finance costs and income taxes.

A **group of biological assets** is an aggregation of similar living animals or plants.

Harvest is the detachment of produce from a biological asset or the cessation of a biological asset's life processes.

6   Agricultural activity covers a diverse range of activities; for example, raising livestock, forestry, annual or perennial cropping, cultivating orchards and plantations, floriculture, and aquaculture (including fish farming). Certain common features exist within this diversity:

(a)   *Capability to change.* Living animals and plants are capable of biological transformation;

(b)   *Management of change.* Management facilitates biological transformation by enhancing, or at least stabilising, conditions necessary for the process to take place (for example, nutrient levels, moisture, temperature, fertility, and light). Such management distinguishes agricultural activity from other activities. For example, harvesting from unmanaged sources (such as ocean fishing and deforestation) is not agricultural activity; and

(c)   *Measurement of change.* The change in quality (for example, genetic merit, density, ripeness, fat cover, protein content, and fibre strength) or quantity (for example, progeny, weight, cubic metres, fibre length or diameter, and number of buds) brought about by biological transformation or harvest is measured and monitored as a routine management function.

7   Biological transformation results in the following types of outcomes:

(a)   asset changes through (i) growth (an increase in quantity or improvement in quality of an animal or plant); (ii) degeneration (a decrease in the quantity or deterioration in quality of an animal or plant); or (iii) procreation (creation of additional living animals or plants); or

(b)   production of agricultural produce such as latex, tea leaf, wool, and milk.

General Definitions

8   **The following terms are used in this Standard with the meanings specified.**

An *active market* is a market where all the following conditions exist:

(a)   **the items traded within the market are homogeneous;**

(b)   **willing buyers and sellers can normally be found at any time; and**

(c)   **prices are available to the public.**

***Carrying amount* is the amount at which an asset is recognised in the statement of financial position.**

***Fair value* is the amount for which an asset could be exchanged, or a liability settled, between knowledgeable, willing parties in an arm's length transaction.**

Government grants* are as defined in AASB 120 *Accounting for Government Grants and Disclosure of Government Assistance.

9   The *fair value* of an asset is based on its present location and condition. As a result, for example, the fair value of cattle at a farm is the price for the cattle in the relevant market less the transport and other costs of getting the cattle to that market.

Recognition and Measurement

10   **An entity shall recognise a biological asset or agricultural produce when, and only when:**

(a)   **the entity controls the asset as a result of past events;**

(b)   **it is probable that future economic benefits associated with the asset will flow to the entity; and**

(c)   **the fair value or cost of the asset can be measured reliably.**

11   In agricultural activity, control may be evidenced by, for example, legal ownership of cattle and the branding or otherwise marking of the cattle on acquisition, birth, or weaning. The future benefits are normally assessed by measuring the significant physical attributes.

12   **A biological asset shall be measured on initial recognition and at the end of each reporting period at its fair value less costs to sell, except for the case described in paragraph 30 where the fair value cannot be measured reliably.**

13   **Agricultural produce harvested from an entity's biological assets shall be measured at its fair value less costs to sell at the point of harvest. Such measurement is the cost at that date when applying AASB 102 or another applicable Standard.**

14   [Deleted by the IASB]

15   The determination of fair value for a biological asset or agricultural produce may be facilitated by grouping biological assets or agricultural produce according to significant attributes; for example, by age or quality. An entity selects the attributes corresponding to the attributes used in the market as a basis for pricing.

16   Entities often enter into contracts to sell their biological assets or agricultural produce at a future date. Contract prices are not necessarily relevant in determining fair value, because fair value reflects the current market in which a willing buyer and seller would enter into a transaction. As a result, the fair value of a biological asset or agricultural produce is not adjusted because of the existence of a contract. In some cases, a contract for the sale of a biological asset or agricultural produce may be an onerous contract, as defined in

AASB 137 *Provisions, Contingent Liabilities and Contingent Assets*. AASB 137 applies to onerous contracts.

17   If an active market exists for a biological asset or agricultural produce in its present location and condition, the quoted price in that market is the appropriate basis for determining the fair value of that asset. If an entity has access to different active markets, the entity uses the most relevant one. For example, if an entity has access to two active markets, it would use the price existing in the market expected to be used.

18   If an active market does not exist, an entity uses one or more of the following, when available, in determining fair value:

(a)   the most recent market transaction price, provided that there has not been a significant change in economic circumstances between the date of that transaction and the end of the reporting period;

(b)   market prices for similar assets with adjustment to reflect differences; and

(c)   sector benchmarks such as the value of an orchard expressed per export tray, bushel, or hectare, and the value of cattle expressed per kilogram of meat.

19   In some cases, the information sources listed in paragraph 18 may suggest different conclusions as to the fair value of a biological asset or agricultural produce. An entity considers the reasons for those differences, in order to arrive at the most reliable estimate of fair value within a relatively narrow range of reasonable estimates.

20   In some circumstances, market-determined prices or values may not be available for a biological asset in its present condition. In these circumstances, an entity uses the present value of expected net cash flows from the asset discounted at a current market-determined rate in determining fair value.

21   The objective of a calculation of the present value of expected net cash flows is to determine the fair value of a biological asset in its present location and condition. An entity considers this in determining an appropriate discount rate to be used and in estimating expected net cash flows. In determining the present value of expected net cash flows, an entity includes the net cash flows that market participants would expect the asset to generate in its most relevant market.

22   An entity does not include any cash flows for financing the assets, taxation, or re-establishing biological assets after harvest (for example, the cost of replanting trees in a plantation forest after harvest).

23   In agreeing an arm's length transaction price, knowledgeable, willing buyers and sellers consider the possibility of variations in cash flows. It follows that fair value reflects the possibility of such variations. Accordingly, an entity incorporates expectations about possible variations in cash flows into either the expected cash flows, or the discount rate, or some combination of the two. In determining a discount rate, an entity uses assumptions consistent with those used in estimating the expected cash flows, to avoid the effect of some assumptions being double-counted or ignored.

24   Cost may sometimes approximate fair value, particularly when:

(a)   little biological transformation has taken place since initial cost incurrence (for example, for fruit tree seedlings planted immediately prior to the end of a reporting period); or

(b)   the impact of the biological transformation on price is not expected to be material (for example, for the initial growth in a 30-year pine plantation production cycle).

25   Biological assets are often physically attached to land (for example, trees in a plantation forest). There may be no separate market for biological assets that are attached to the land but an active market may exist for the combined assets, that is, for the biological assets, raw land, and land improvements, as a package. An entity may use information regarding the combined assets to determine fair value for the biological assets. For example, the fair value of raw land and land improvements may be deducted from the fair value of the combined assets to arrive at the fair value of biological assets.

Gains and Losses

26   **A gain or loss arising on initial recognition of a biological asset at fair value less costs to sell and from a change in fair value less costs to sell of a biological asset shall be included in profit or loss for the period in which it arises.**

27   A loss may arise on initial recognition of a biological asset, because costs to sell are deducted in determining fair value less costs to sell of a biological asset. A gain may arise on initial recognition of a biological asset, such as when a calf is born.

28   **A gain or loss arising on initial recognition of agricultural produce at fair value less costs to sell shall be included in profit or loss for the period in which it arises.**

29   A gain or loss may arise on initial recognition of agricultural produce as a result of harvesting.

Inability to Measure Fair Value Reliably

30   **There is a presumption that fair value can be measured reliably for a biological asset. However, that presumption can be rebutted only on initial recognition for a biological asset for which market determined prices or values are not available and for which alternative estimates of fair value are determined to be clearly unreliable. In such a case, that biological asset shall be measured at its cost less any accumulated depreciation and any accumulated impairment losses. Once the fair value of such a biological asset becomes reliably measurable, an entity shall measure it at its fair value less costs to sell. Once a non current biological asset meets the criteria to be classified as held for sale (or is included in a disposal group that is classified as held for sale) in accordance with AASB 5 *Non current Assets Held for Sale and Discontinued Operations*, it is presumed that fair value can be measured reliably.**

31   The presumption in paragraph 30 can be rebutted only on initial recognition. An entity that has previously measured a biological asset at its fair value less costs to sell continues to measure the biological asset at its fair value less costs to sell until disposal.

32   In all cases, an entity measures agricultural produce at the point of harvest at its fair value less costs to sell. This Standard reflects the view that the fair value of agricultural produce at the point of harvest can always be measured reliably.

33   In determining cost, accumulated depreciation and accumulated impairment losses, an entity considers AASB 102, AASB 116, and AASB 136 *Impairment of Assets*.

Government Grants

34   **An unconditional government grant related to a biological asset measured at its fair value less costs to sell shall be recognised in profit or loss when, and only when, the government grant becomes receivable.**

35   **If a government grant related to a biological asset measured at its fair value less costs to sell is conditional, including when a government grant requires an entity not to engage in specified agricultural activity, an entity shall recognise the government grant in profit or loss when, and only when, the conditions attaching to the government grant are met.**

36   Terms and conditions of government grants vary. For example, a grant may require an entity to farm in a particular location for five years and require the entity to return all of the grant if it farms for a period shorter than five years. In this case, the grant is not recognised in profit or loss until the five years have passed. However, if the terms of the grant allow part of it to be retained according to the time that has elapsed, the entity recognises that part in profit or loss as time passes.

37   If a government grant relates to a biological asset measured at its cost less any accumulated depreciation and any accumulated impairment losses (see paragraph 30), AASB 120 is applied.

38   This Standard requires a different treatment from AASB 120, if a government grant relates to a biological asset measured at its fair value less costs to sell or a government grant requires an entity not to engage in specified agricultural activity. AASB 120 is applied

only to a government grant related to a biological asset measured at its cost less any accumulated depreciation and any accumulated impairment losses.

Aus38.1   **Notwithstanding paragraphs 34-38, not-for-profit entities recognise government grants related to a biological asset in accordance with AASB 1004 *Contributions*.**

Disclosure

39   [Deleted by the IASB]

General

40   **An entity shall disclose the aggregate gain or loss arising during the current period on initial recognition of biological assets and agricultural produce and from the change in fair value less costs to sell of biological assets.**

41   **An entity shall provide a description of each group of *biological assets*.**

42   The disclosure required by paragraph 41 may take the form of a narrative or quantified description.

43   An entity is encouraged to provide a quantified description of each group of biological assets, distinguishing between consumable and bearer biological assets or between mature and immature biological assets, as appropriate. For example, an entity may disclose the carrying amounts of consumable biological assets and bearer biological assets by group. An entity may further divide those carrying amounts between mature and immature assets. These distinctions provide information that may be helpful in assessing the timing of future cash flows. An entity discloses the basis for making any such distinctions.

44   Consumable biological assets are those that are to be harvested as agricultural produce or sold as biological assets. Examples of consumable biological assets are livestock intended for the production of meat, livestock held for sale, fish in farms, crops such as maize and wheat, and trees being grown for lumber. Bearer biological assets are those other than consumable biological assets; for example, livestock from which milk is produced, grape vines, fruit trees, and trees from which firewood is harvested while the tree remains. Bearer biological assets are not agricultural produce but, rather, are self-regenerating.

45   Biological assets may be classified either as mature biological assets or immature biological assets. Mature biological assets are those that have attained harvestable specifications (for consumable biological assets) or are able to sustain regular harvests (for bearer biological assets).

46   **If not disclosed elsewhere in information published with the financial statements, an entity shall describe:**
   (a)   **the nature of its activities involving each group of biological assets; and**
   (b)   **non-financial measures or estimates of the physical quantities of:**
       (i)   **each group of the entity's biological assets at the end of the period; and**
       (ii)   **output of agricultural produce during the period.**

47   **An entity shall disclose the methods and significant assumptions applied in determining the fair value of each group of agricultural produce at the point of harvest and each group of biological assets.**

48   **An entity shall disclose the fair value less costs to sell of agricultural produce harvested during the period, determined at the point of harvest.**

49   **An entity shall disclose:**
   (a)   **the existence and carrying amounts of biological assets whose title is restricted, and the carrying amounts of biological assets pledged as security for liabilities;**
   (b)   **the amount of commitments for the development or acquisition of biological assets; and**
   (c)   **financial risk management strategies related to agricultural activity.**

50　An entity shall present a reconciliation of changes in the *carrying amount* of biological assets between the beginning and the end of the current period. The reconciliation shall include:

(a)　the gain or loss arising from changes in fair value less costs to sell;

(b)　increases due to purchases;

(c)　decreases attributable to sales and biological assets classified as held for sale (or included in a disposal group that is classified as held for sale) in accordance with AASB 5;

(d)　decreases due to harvest;

(e)　increases resulting from business combinations;

(f)　net exchange differences arising on the translation of financial statements into a different presentation currency, and on the translation of a foreign operation into the presentation currency of the reporting entity; and

(g)　other changes.

51　The fair value less costs to sell of a biological asset can change due to both physical changes and price changes in the market. Separate disclosure of physical and price changes is useful in appraising current period performance and future prospects, particularly when there is a production cycle of more than one year. In such cases, an entity is encouraged to disclose, by group or otherwise, the amount of change in fair value less costs to sell included in profit or loss due to physical changes and due to price changes. This information is generally less useful when the production cycle is less than one year (for example, when raising chickens or growing cereal crops).

52　Biological transformation results in a number of types of physical change – growth, degeneration, production, and procreation, each of which is observable and measurable. Each of those physical changes has a direct relationship to future economic benefits. A change in fair value of a biological asset due to harvesting is also a physical change.

53　Agricultural activity is often exposed to climatic, disease, and other natural risks. If an event occurs that gives rise to a material item of income or expense, the nature and amount of that item are disclosed in accordance with AASB 101 *Presentation of Financial Statements*. Examples of such an event include an outbreak of a virulent disease, a flood, a severe drought or frost, and a plague of insects.

Additional Disclosures for Biological Assets where Fair Value Cannot be Measured Reliably

54　If an entity measures biological assets at their cost less any accumulated depreciation and any accumulated impairment losses (see paragraph 30) at the end of the period, the entity shall disclose for such biological assets:

(a)　a description of the biological assets;

(b)　an explanation of why fair value cannot be measured reliably;

(c)　if possible, the range of estimates within which fair value is highly likely to lie;

(d)　the depreciation method used;

(e)　the useful lives or the depreciation rates used; and

(f)　the gross carrying amount and the accumulated depreciation (aggregated with accumulated impairment losses) at the beginning and end of the period.

55　If, during the current period, an entity measures biological assets at their cost less any accumulated depreciation and any accumulated impairment losses (see paragraph 30), an entity shall disclose any gain or loss recognised on disposal of such biological assets and the reconciliation required by paragraph 50 shall disclose amounts related to such biological assets separately. In addition, the reconciliation shall include the following amounts included in profit or loss related to those biological assets:

(a)　impairment losses;

(b)　reversals of impairment losses; and

(c)　depreciation.

56 If the fair value of biological assets previously measured at their cost less any accumulated depreciation and any accumulated impairment losses becomes reliably measurable during the current period, an entity shall disclose for those biological assets:

   (a) description of the biological assets;

   (b) an explanation of why fair value has become reliably measurable; and

   (c) the effect of the change.

Government Grants

57 An entity shall disclose the following related to agricultural activity covered by this Standard:

   (a) the nature and extent of government grants recognised in the financial statements;

   (b) unfulfilled conditions and other contingencies attaching to government grants; and

   (c) significant decreases expected in the level of government grants.

Effective Date and Transition

58 [Deleted by the AASB]

59 [Deleted by the AASB]

60 Paragraphs 5, 6, 17, 20 and 21 were amended and paragraph 14 deleted by AASB 2008-5 *Amendments to Australian Accounting Standards arising from the Annual Improvements Project* issued in July 2008. An entity shall apply those amendments prospectively for annual reporting periods beginning on or after 1 January 2009. Earlier application is permitted. If an entity applies the amendments for an earlier period it shall disclose that fact.

AASB 1004
Contributions

(Revised December 2007)

Note from the Institute of Chartered Accountants Australia

This note, prepared by the technical editors, is not part of Accounting Standard AASB 1004.

Historical development

1986: Approved Accounting Standard ASRB 1004 'Disclosure of Operating Revenue' was issued by Australia's (then) Accounting Standards Review Board (ASRB) in 1986 and as its name indicates the Standard was concerned only with revenue disclosures.

June 1998: The AASB reissued the Standard in June 1998 as AASB 1004 'Revenue'. The purpose of the 1998 version of the Standard extended to prescribing the rules for the recognition and measurement of revenue arising from various types of transactions and events.

July 2004: The AASB reissued the Standard in July 2004 as AASB 1004 'Contributions'. The purpose of the 2004 version of the Standard is to ensure that the pre-2005 Australian GAAP applicable to accounting for contributions by not-for-profit entities continues to apply in 2005 and later years.

For-profit entities' revenues and contributions received/receivable relating to annual reporting periods on or after 1 January 2005 are subject to the stable platform of 2005 Australian equivalents to International Financial Reporting Standards (IFRS), namely AASB 118 'Revenue' and AASB 120 'Accounting for Government Grants and Disclosure of Government Assistance'.

13 December 2007: AASB 1004 'Contributions' was reissued by the AASB.

In October and December 2007 the AASB issued new and revised AASB 1004 'Contributions', AASB 1049 'Whole of Government and General Government Sector Financial Reporting', AASB 1050 'Administered Items', AASB 1051 'Land Under Roads', AASB 1052 'Disaggregated Disclosures', AASB Interpretation 1038 'Contributions by Owners Made to Wholly-Owned Public Sector Entities', AASB 2007-9 'Amendments to Australian Accounting Standards arising from the Review of AAS 27, AAS 29 and AAS 31'. These revisions result from a short-term review, primarily focused on relocating, where necessary, the requirements in AASs 27, 29 and 31, substantively unamended (with some exceptions), into topic-based Standards.

These Standards, and Interpretation, apply to annual reporting periods beginning on or after 1 July 2008, with early adoption permitted. These Standards supersede AAS 27, AAS 29 and AAS 31.

29 August 2011: AASB 2011-7 'Amendments to Australian Accounting Standards arising from the Consolidation and Joint Arrangements Standards' amends AASB 1004 to give effect to many consequential changes arising from the issue of AASB 10, 11, 12, 127 and 128. This Standard applies to annual reporting periods beginning on or after 1 January 2013 and can be adopted early by for-profit entities. **These amendments are not included in this revised Standard.**

5 September 2011: AASB 2011-8 'Amendments to Australian Accounting Standards arising from AASB 13' amends AASB 1004 to give effect to a consequential change in the definition of fair value arising from the issue of AASB 13. This Standard applies to annual reporting periods beginning on or after 1 January 2013 and can be adopted early. **These amendments are not included in this revised Standard.**

Reference

Interpretation 1038 *Contributions by Owners Made to Wholly-Owned Public Sector Entities* applies to AASB 1004.

Contents

Preface

Comparison with International Pronouncements

Accounting Standard
AASB 1004 Contributions

	Paragraphs
Application	1 – 10
Measurement of Contributions	11
Recognition of Contributions of Assets	12 – 15
Liabilities Forgiven	16 – 17
Disclosures	18
Recognition of Contributions, other than Contributions by Owners, by Local Governments, Government Departments, GGSs or Whole of Governments	
Contributions	19 – 26
Control over Assets	27 – 30
Taxes Collected by Government Departments and Parliamentary Appropriations to Government Departments	
Taxes Collected by Government Departments	31
Parliamentary Appropriations to Government Departments	32 – 38
Liabilities of Government Departments Assumed by Other Entities	39 – 43
Contributions of Services	44 – 47
Contributions by Owners and Distributions to Owners of Local Governments, Government Departments and Whole of Governments	48 – 53
Restructure of Administrative Arrangements	54 – 59
Disclosure of Contributions	60 – 62
Additional Government Department Disclosures	63
Compliance with Parliamentary Appropriations and Other Externally-Imposed Requirements	64 – 68

Appendices

A. Defined Terms

B. Comparison of AASB 1004 with AASs 27, 29 and 31

Basis for Conclusions

Australian Accounting Standard AASB 1004 *Contributions* is set out in paragraphs 1 – 68 and Appendix A. All the paragraphs have equal authority. Paragraphs in **bold type** state the main principles. AASB 1004 is to be read in the context of other Australian Accounting Standards, including AASB 1048 *Interpretation and Application of Standards*, which identifies the Australian Accounting Interpretations. In the absence of explicit guidance, AASB 108 *Accounting Policies, Changes in Accounting Estimates and Errors* provides a basis for selecting and applying accounting policies.

Preface

Background

Australian Accounting Standards incorporate International Financial Reporting Standards (IFRSs), as issued by the International Accounting Standards Board (IASB), with the addition of paragraphs on the applicability of the Standard in the Australian environment.

Some Australian Accounting Standards also include requirements that are specific to Australian entities. In most instances, these requirements are restricted to not-for-profit entities, including public sector entities, or include additional disclosures that address domestic, regulatory or other issues.

Reasons for Revising this Standard

AAS 27 *Financial Reporting by Local Governments*, AAS 29 *Financial Reporting by Government Departments* and AAS 31 *Financial Reporting by Governments* were first issued in 1991, 1993 and 1996 respectively. While AASs 27, 29 and 31 had been subject to a number of limited reviews since then, the requirements in these Standards needed a comprehensive review because:

(a)   there had been significant developments in Australian financial reporting, in particular adopting IFRSs within Australian Accounting Standards, for reporting periods beginning on or after 1 January 2005. As a result of these developments, uncertainties emerged as to the application of cross-references to other Australian Accounting Standards and the override provisions in AASs 27, 29 and 31 that made the requirements in AASs 27, 29 and 31 take precedence over other requirements;

(b)   local governments, government departments and governments were subject to requirements that differed from requirements applicable to other not-for-profit entities and for-profit entities contained in Australian Accounting Standards. An objective of the Board is to put in place transaction-neutral standards that will treat like transactions and events consistently;

(c)   the Board had made significant progress in its project on the harmonisation of Generally Accepted Accounting Principles (GAAP) and Government Finance Statistics (GFS) so far as it relates to the General Government Sector (GGS) and the whole of government of the federal, state and territory governments. It was therefore particularly timely to review the requirements in AAS 31;

(d)   they did not reflect contemporary accounting thought; and

(e)   they did not reflect the current style of writing standards, which is to specify principles rather than rules, and requirements rather than encouragements.

The Board intends to continue with its policy of developing a common accounting standards framework for both for-profit and not-for-profit entities whilst acknowledging differences in some areas. The Board is committed to having a platform of topic-based transaction-neutral Standards that will apply to the public sector.

Review of AASs 27, 29 and 31

The Board initiated a project for reviewing the requirements in AASs 27, 29 and 31, divided into two phases comprising a short-term and a longer-term review.

The primary focus in the short-term review has been on relocating, where necessary, the requirements in AASs 27, 29 and 31, substantively unamended (with some exceptions), into topic-based Standards.

In the longer term the focus will be on improving the requirements for each topic-based issue where necessary. The longer-term review will be carried out in stages as outlined in the AASB's Public Sector Policy Paper *Australian Accounting Standards and Public Sector Entities*. A review by the AASB of non-exchange income, which will incorporate a review of contributions, is in progress at the time of revising this Standard.

AASB 1004 in the Context of the Review of AASs 27, 29 and 31

The Board decided to relocate the requirements on contributions from AASs 27, 29 and 31, substantively unamended (with some exceptions, as noted in Appendix B), into AASB 1004.

The Board outlined its short-term proposals in Exposure Draft ED 156 *Proposals Arising from the Short-term Review of the Requirements in AAS 27, AAS 29 and AAS 31*, which was issued in June 2007.

Main Features of this Standard

Application Date

This Standard is applicable to annual reporting periods beginning on or after 1 July 2008. Early adoption is permitted for annual reporting periods beginning on or after 1 January 2005, but before 1 July 2008, provided there is early adoption for the same annual reporting period of the following pronouncements being issued at about the same time, as applicable:

(a)   AASB 1049 *Whole of Government and General Government Sector Financial Reporting*;

(b)   AASB 1050 *Administered Items*;

(c)   AASB 1051 *Land Under Roads*;

(d)   AASB 1052 *Disaggregated Disclosures*;

(e)   AASB 2007-9 *Amendments to Australian Accounting Standards arising from the Review of AASs 27, 29 and 31*; and

(f)   AASB Interpretation 1038 *Contributions by Owners Made to Wholly-Owned Public Sector Entities*.

Main Requirements

This Standard:

(a)   in its application to contributions to not-for-profit entities:

        (i)   requires income to be measured at the fair value of the contributions received or receivable (paragraph 11);

        (ii)   requires income from a contribution to be recognised when an entity obtains control of the contribution or right to receive the contribution, it is probable the economic benefits comprising the contribution will flow to the entity, and the amount can be measured reliably (paragraphs 12-15);

        (iii)   requires the gross amount of a liability forgiven by a credit provider to be recognised by the borrower as income (paragraphs 16 and 17); and

        (iv)   requires certain disclosures relating to contributions of assets and forgiveness of liabilities (paragraph 18);

(b)   in its application to local governments, government departments that are reporting entities, GGSs and whole of governments:

        (i)   provides guidance on the recognition of contributions other than contributions by owners (paragraphs 19-30);

        (ii)   requires contributions of services to be recognised under certain circumstances (paragraphs 44-47); and

        (iii)   requires certain disclosures in relation to contributions recognised as income (paragraphs 60-62);

(c)   in its application to local governments, government departments that are reporting entities, and whole of governments, requires recognised contributions by and distributions to owners to be accounted for as a direct adjustment to equity (paragraphs 48-53);

(d)   in its application to government controlled not-for-profit entities and for-profit government departments that are reporting entities:

        (i)   defines restructures of administrative arrangements and specifies that they are in the nature of transactions with owners in their capacity as owners to be recognised on a net basis (Appendix A and paragraphs 54-56);

      (ii)   requires a transferee in a restructure of administrative arrangements to disclose, where practicable, the expenses and income attributable to transferred activities for the reporting period, showing separately those expenses and income recognised by the transferor during the reporting period (paragraph 57); and

      (iii)   requires certain other disclosures relating to restructures of administrative arrangements (paragraphs 58 and 59); and

(e)   in its application to government departments that are reporting entities:

      (i)   provides guidance on the treatment of taxes collected by a government department (paragraph 31);

      (ii)   provides guidance on the treatment of parliamentary appropriations (paragraphs 32-38);

      (iii)   specifies requirements relating to the assumption of a government department's liability by another entity (paragraphs 39-43);

      (iv)   requires disclosure of appropriations by class and liabilities that were assumed during the reporting period by the government or other entity (paragraph 63); and

      (v)   specifies requirements relating to disclosure of compliance with parliamentary appropriations and other externally imposed requirements (paragraphs 64-68).

Comparison with International Pronouncements

This Standard retains the requirements in AASB 1004 *Contributions* (as issued in July 2004) and incorporates relevant paragraphs from AAS 27 *Financial Reporting by Local Governments*, AAS 29 *Financial Reporting by Government Departments* and AAS 31 *Financial Reporting by Governments* in substantially unamended form (with some exceptions, as noted in Appendix B). Accordingly, the development of this Standard did not involve consideration of International Public Sector Accounting Standards (IPSASs) issued by the International Public Sector Accounting Standards Board or International Financial Reporting Standards (IFRSs) issued by the International Accounting Standards Board.

A review by the AASB of accounting for non-exchange income (which will incorporate a review of contributions) is in progress at the time of issue of this Standard. That review will involve consideration of international pronouncements.

AASB 1004 and IPSASs

Not-for-profit entities that comply with the requirements of AASB 1004 may not simultaneously be in compliance with the requirements of IPSAS 23 *Revenue from Non-Exchange Transactions (Taxes and Transfers)*. This is because the requirements in AASB 1004 are different from those in IPSAS 23. The more significant differences include:

(a)   IPSAS 23 applies to all public sector entities other than government business enterprises, whereas the various requirements in AASB 1004 apply as detailed in the table at paragraph 6;

(b)   IPSAS 23 requires an inflow of resources from a non-exchange transaction (such as a contribution) recognised as an asset to be recognised as revenue, except to the extent that a liability is recognised in respect of the same inflow. Conditions on a transferred asset give rise to a present obligation on initial recognition that is to be recognised as a liability provided it meets the liability recognition criteria. AASB 1004, on the other hand, requires contributions, other than contributions by owners, to be recognised as income when the transferee local government, government department, General Government Sector (GGS) or whole of government obtains control over them, irrespective of whether restrictions or conditions are imposed on the use of the contributions;

(c)   under IPSAS 23 an entity may, but is not required to, recognise services in-kind as revenue and as an asset. Under AASB 1004, contributions of services to local governments, government departments, GGSs and whole of governments are recognised as income when, and only when, the fair value of those services can be reliably determined, and the services would have been purchased if they had not been donated; and

(d)   AASB 1004 includes a number of disclosure requirements that are not included in IPSAS 23, such as the requirement for government departments to disclose information relating to compliance with parliamentary appropriations and other externally imposed requirements.

AASB 1004 and IFRSs

Not-for-profit entities that comply with the requirements of AASB 1004 may not simultaneously be in compliance with the requirements of IAS 20 *Accounting for Government Grants and Disclosure of Government Assistance*. This is because the recognition criteria in AASB 1004 are different from those in IAS 20.

AASB 1004 requires contributions received or receivable to be recognised immediately as revenue when:

(a)   the entity obtains control of the contribution or the right to receive the contribution;

(b)   it is probable that the economic benefits comprising the contribution will flow to the entity; and

(c)   the amount of the contribution can be measured reliably.

In contrast, IAS 20 requires government grants to be recognised as income on a systematic basis over the periods necessary to match them with the related costs which they are intended to compensate or by deducting the grant in arriving at the carrying amount of the asset when there is reasonable assurance that:

(a)   the entity will comply with the conditions attaching to them; and

(b)   the grants will be received.

Accounting Standard AASB 1004

The Australian Accounting Standards Board makes Accounting Standard AASB 1004 *Contributions*.

Dated 13 December 2007

D.G. Boymal
Chair – AASB

Accounting Standard AASB 1004

Contributions

Application

1   **Subject to paragraphs 2 to 5, this Standard applies to:**

    (a)   **each not-for-profit entity that is required to prepare financial reports in accordance with Part 2M.3 of the Corporations Act and that is a reporting entity;**

    (b)   **general purpose financial statements of each other not-for-profit entity that is a reporting entity;**

    (c)   **financial statements of not-for-profit entities that are, or are held out to be, general purpose financial statements; and**

    (d)   **financial statements of General Government Sectors (GGSs) prepared in accordance with AASB 1049 *Whole of Government and General Government Sector Financial Reporting*.**

2   **Paragraphs 31 to 43 and 63 to 68 only apply to government departments that are reporting entities.**

3   **Paragraphs 19 to 30, 44 to 47 and 60 to 62 only apply to local governments, government departments that are reporting entities, GGSs and whole of governments.**

4   **Paragraphs 48 to 53 only apply to local governments, government departments that are reporting entities, and whole of governments.**

5   **Paragraphs 54 to 59 only apply to government controlled not-for-profit entities and for-profit government departments that are reporting entities.**

6   The following table identifies which paragraphs are applicable to each type of entity to which this Standard applies:

Type of entity to which the paragraph is applicable	Content of paragraphs	Para No.
Not-for-profit private sector entities	Measurement of contributions	11
	Recognition of contributions of assets	12 – 15
	Liabilities forgiven	16 – 17
	Disclosures	18
Not-for-profit government departments	Measurement of contributions	11
	Recognition of contributions of assets	12 – 15
	Liabilities forgiven	16 – 17
	Disclosures	18
	Recognition of contributions other than contributions by owners	19 – 30
	Taxes collected by government departments	31
	Parliamentary appropriations	32 – 38
	Liabilities of government departments assumed by other entities	39 – 43
	Contributions of services	44 – 47
	Contributions by owners and distributions to owners	48 – 53
	Restructure of administrative arrangements	54 – 59
	Disclosure of contributions	60 – 62
	Government department disclosures	63
	Compliance with parliamentary appropriations and other externally imposed requirements	64 – 68
For-profit government departments	Recognition of contributions other than contributions by owners	19 – 30
	Taxes collected by government departments	31
	Parliamentary appropriations	32 – 38
	Liabilities of government departments assumed by other entities	39 – 43
	Contributions of services	44 – 47
	Contributions by owners and distributions to owners	48 – 53
	Restructure of administrative arrangements	54 – 59
	Disclosure of contributions	60 – 62
	Government department disclosures	63
	Compliance with parliamentary appropriations and other externally imposed requirements	64 – 68
Other government controlled not-for-profit entities	Measurement of contributions	11
	Recognition of contributions of assets	12 – 15
	Liabilities forgiven	16 – 17
	Disclosures	18
	Restructure of administrative arrangements	54 – 59

Type of entity to which the paragraph is applicable	Content of paragraphs	Para No.
Local governments	Measurement of contributions	11
	Recognition of contributions of assets	12 – 15
	Liabilities forgiven	16 – 17
	Disclosures	18
	Recognition of contributions other than contributions by owners	19 – 30
	Contributions of services	44 – 47
	Contributions by owners and distributions to owners	48 – 53
	Disclosure of contributions	60 – 62
Whole of governments	Measurement of contributions	11
	Recognition of contributions of assets	12 – 15
	Liabilities forgiven	16 – 17
	Disclosures	18
	Recognition of contributions other than contributions by owners	19 – 30
	Contributions of services	44 – 47
	Contributions by owners and distributions to owners	48 – 53
	Disclosure of contributions	60 – 62
GGSs	Measurement of contributions	11
	Recognition of contributions of assets	12 – 15
	Liabilities forgiven	16 – 17
	Disclosures	18
	Recognition of contributions other than contributions by owners	19 – 30
	Contributions of services	44 – 47
	Disclosure of contributions	60 – 62

7   This Standard applies to annual reporting periods beginning on or after 1 July 2008.

8   This Standard may be applied to annual reporting periods beginning on or after 1 January 2005 but before 1 July 2008, provided there is early adoption for the same annual reporting period of the following pronouncements being issued at about the same time, as applicable:

    (a)   AASB 1049 *Whole of Government and General Government Sector Financial Reporting*;

    (b)   AASB 1050 *Administered Items*;

    (c)   AASB 1051 *Land Under Roads*;

    (d)   AASB 1052 *Disaggregated Disclosures*;

    (e)   AASB 2007-9 *Amendments to Australian Accounting Standards arising from the Review of AASs 27, 29 and 31*; and

    (f)   AASB Interpretation 1038 *Contributions by Owners Made to Wholly-Owned Public Sector Entities*.

9   The requirements specified in this Standard apply to the complete set of financial statements where information resulting from their application is material in accordance with AASB 1031 *Materiality*.

10   When applicable, this Standard, together with the Standards referred to in paragraph 8, supersede:

    (a)   AASB 1004 *Contributions* as notified in the *Commonwealth of Australia Gazette* No S 294, 22 July 2004;

    (b)   AAS 27 *Financial Reporting by Local Governments*, as amended;

(c) AAS 29 *Financial Reporting by Government Departments*, as amended; and

(d) AAS 31 *Financial Reporting by Governments*, as amended.

Measurement of Contributions

11 Income shall be measured at the fair value of the contributions received or receivable.

Recognition of Contributions of Assets

12 Income arising from the contribution of an asset to the entity shall be recognised when, and only when, all the following conditions have been satisfied:

(a) the entity obtains control of the contribution or the right to receive the contribution;

(b) it is probable that the economic benefits comprising the contribution will flow to the entity; and

(c) the amount of the contribution can be measured reliably.

13 A contribution occurs when an entity receives an asset, including the right to receive cash or other forms of asset without directly giving approximately equal value to the other party or parties to the transfer; that is, when there is a *non reciprocal transfer*. Contributions would, for example, include donated assets. Contributions that are income exclude *contributions by owners*.

14 In some cases it may be difficult to determine whether the entity has control of a contribution or the right to receive a contribution. One such case could be economic benefits expected to be received under a multi-year public policy agreement. The entity does not obtain control of a contribution under such an agreement until it has met conditions or provided services or facilities that make it eligible to receive a contribution. On this basis, under multi-year public policy agreements, income would be recognised only in relation to contributions received or receivable under policy agreements. Another example is where a donor pledges a donation to an entity. If the pledge is not enforceable against the donor, the entity does not control the contribution.

15 In some cases it may be difficult to determine whether the entity is giving approximately equal value to the other parties to a transfer. This is particularly the case where, for example, fees are charged by a not-for-profit entity for the potential use of a general pool of facilities. In circumstances where clubs and professional associations charge fees in return for contributors being able to enjoy the use of facilities, receive publications or practice in a particular vocation for a defined period, an exchange transaction can be presumed and the fees would not be treated as contributions. The recipient of the fees would have a contractual or constructive obligation to refund some or all fees if it were unable to provide the facilities or services. In circumstances where the benefits to contributors are only nominal, such as acknowledgment letters, general information about the entity's activities and satisfaction of contributors' altruistic goals, the fees are in the nature of contributions.

Liabilities Forgiven

16 The gross amount of a liability forgiven by a credit provider shall be recognised by the borrower as income.

17 Where equity is substituted for a liability, this is not treated as a forgiveness.

Disclosures

18 The following information shall be disclosed:

(a) contributions of assets, including cash and non-monetary assets; and

(b) the forgiveness of liabilities.

Recognition of Contributions, other than Contributions by Owners, by Local Governments, Government Departments, GGSs or Whole of Governments

Paragraphs 19 to 30 of this Standard apply only to local governments, government departments, GGSs and whole of governments.

Contributions

19   Contributions, other than contributions by owners, to a local government, government department, GGS or whole of government are received in the form of involuntary transfers, such as rates, taxes and fines, and voluntary transfers, such as grants and donations. In the case of government departments, parliamentary appropriations, other than those that give rise to a liability or that are in the nature of a contribution by owners, may also be a type of contribution.

20   This Standard requires contributions, other than contributions by owners, to be recognised as income when the transferee local government, government department, GGS or whole of government obtains control over them, irrespective of whether restrictions or conditions are imposed on the use of the contributions. The transferee does not have a present obligation to sacrifice future economic benefits to the transferor, even though the transferee has a fiduciary responsibility to use the assets effectively and efficiently in pursuing its objectives. This fiduciary responsibility pertains to all assets and does not, of itself, create a present obligation to make sacrifices of future economic benefits to external parties. Accordingly, the receipt of contributions does not give rise to a liability.

21   For transfers to a local government, government department, GGS or whole of government to create a present obligation on that entity to make future sacrifices of economic benefits to external parties, the transfers must be reciprocal. Where assets are provided on the condition that the local government, government department, GGS or whole of government is to make a reciprocal transfer of economic benefits, and that transfer has not occurred prior to the reporting date, a liability is recognised as at the reporting date in respect of such amounts.

22   Reciprocal transfers are transfers in which the transferor and transferee directly receive and sacrifice approximately equal value. Examples of reciprocal transfers are sales of goods and services, the provision of loan funds, and the provision of employee services. A reciprocal transfer also occurs where, for example, assets are provided to a government department on the condition that the government department renders particular services to the transferor of the assets and, if the services are not rendered, those assets are required to be remitted directly to the transferor. Another example of a reciprocal transfer is where a user charge is provided to a local government in advance for repairs to a private road, where the charge would be repayable directly to the provider or providers if the works were not performed.

23   For a transaction to be reciprocal, the transferor must have a right to receive the benefits directly. It is not sufficient that the transferor receives benefits indirectly as a result of the transfer. For example, when a government provides a grant to a local government, it does not receive value directly in exchange, although it (or those it represents) would indirectly receive a benefit as a result of the local government deploying the grant in providing goods or services to beneficiaries that the grantor government represents.

24   While involuntary transfers to local governments, government departments, GGSs and whole of governments may result in the provision of some goods or services to the transferor, they do not give the transferor a claim to receive directly benefits of approximately equal value. The receipt and sacrifice of approximately equal value may occur, but only by coincidence. For example, governments are not obliged to provide commensurate benefits, in the form of goods or services, to particular taxpayers in return for their taxes. For this reason, involuntary transfers are non-reciprocal transfers.

25   There could be instances where a transfer of economic benefits comprises a reciprocal component and a non-reciprocal component. For example, where another entity transfers a building to a local government, government department, GGS or whole of government at a price that intentionally is significantly lower than its fair value, the transfer is in part

reciprocal (to the extent that approximately equal value is received directly in exchange) and in part non reciprocal. In this circumstance, because a reciprocal transaction is involved, any unsatisfied obligation to provide consideration in return for the building is a liability of the local government, government department, GGS or whole of government.

26   If a local government, government department, GGS or whole of government failed to meet the specific conditions attaching to a contribution of assets and part or all of the contribution is required to be repaid, a liability and an expense would need to be recognised for the amount payable. In this circumstance, the transferee has a present obligation to the transferor that has arisen as a result of a past event: the failure of the transferee to meet the conditions for retention of the contribution.

Control over Assets

27   Control of amounts in the nature of voluntary transfers arises when the transferee can benefit from funds transferred to it and deny or regulate the access of others to those benefits. Therefore, control arises when, for example, government departments can use funds granted or transferred to purchase goods and services or retain those funds for future purchases.

28   The timing of gaining control over assets acquired from voluntary non-reciprocal transfers, such as grants and donations, depends upon the arrangements between the transferor and the transferee. For example, where a State Government receives a single-year grant from the Commonwealth Government to provide services in the following reporting period, the State Government obtains control over the grant when the grant eligibility criteria have been satisfied or the services or facilities under the grant agreement (if any) have been provided, which may coincide with the date of its receipt. This is because when the State Government satisfies grant eligibility criteria or provides services or facilities under any grant agreement, it has the capacity to benefit from the grant and can deny or regulate the access of others to it. Correspondingly, in this circumstance, the Commonwealth Government would recognise an expense at the same time.

29   In the case of multi-year grant agreements from a government to another level of government or a government department, the transferee government or government department does not control the contributed assets, and therefore should not recognise revenues, until the transferor government has a present obligation that is binding. For example, the transferee government or government department does not gain control of assets under a multi-year public policy grant agreement until it has met conditions such as grant eligibility criteria or provided the services or facilities that make it eligible to receive a contribution. On this basis, under multi-year public policy agreements, income would be recognised only in relation to grants received or receivable under any grant agreement.

30   Control over assets acquired from involuntary non-reciprocal transfers, such as rates, taxes and fines, is obtained when the underlying transaction or other event giving rise to control of the future economic benefits occurs. For example, taxes are recognised when the underlying transaction or event that gives rise to the GGS's or whole of government's right to collect the tax occurs and can be measured reliably. In some cases an inability to reliably measure taxes when the underlying transactions or events occur means that they may need to be recognised at a later time. In most cases, taxes will be recognised in the reporting period in which the tax assessments are due to be issued or during which the tax collections are received. For this reason, the disclosure of policies adopted for recognising taxes will enhance the understandability and comparability of information relating to them. Where the transfers arise from a periodical charge, such as a land tax, a government obtains control over the assets on the day on which the government becomes entitled to levy the land tax. Control over assets acquired from local government rates would be obtained at the commencement of the rating period or, where earlier, upon receipt.

Taxes Collected by Government Departments and Parliamentary Appropriations to Government Departments

Paragraphs 31 to 38 of this Standard apply only to government departments.

Taxes Collected by Government Departments

31   It is unlikely that taxes, for example, income tax, will qualify as income of the agency responsible for their collection. This is because the agency responsible for collecting taxes does not normally control the future economic benefits embodied in tax collections (see AASB 1050). Taxes are recognised when the definition of, and recognition criteria for, income is met. Accordingly, taxes which are controlled by the tax collection agency and which satisfy the recognition criteria for income specified in paragraph 12 of this Standard qualify for recognition as income in the reporting period during which control is obtained. This means that taxes are treated in the same manner as described in paragraph 30.

Parliamentary Appropriations to Government Departments

32   **Parliamentary appropriations over which a government department gains control during the reporting period shall be recognised as:**

    (a)   income of that reporting period where the appropriation:

        (i)   satisfies the definition of income in the *Framework for the Preparation and Presentation of Financial Statements* (the *Framework*); and

        (ii)   satisfies the recognition criteria for income;

    (b)   a direct adjustment to equity where the appropriation satisfies the definition of a contribution by owners; or

    (c)   a liability of the government department where the appropriation:

        (i)   satisfies the definition of liabilities in the *Framework*; and

        (ii)   satisfies the recognition criteria for liabilities in the *Framework*.

33   Parliamentary appropriations may be designated as recurrent appropriations, capital or works and services appropriations or other appropriations. Irrespective of the designation given to a parliamentary appropriation, its recognition as income, a contribution by owners or a liability requires an evaluation of the characteristics of the parliamentary appropriation by reference to the definitions of income, contributions by owners and liabilities. This ensures that the substance, rather than the form, of the parliamentary appropriation is reported.

Parliamentary Appropriations as Income

34   The parliamentary appropriation process currently adopted in some jurisdictions in Australia is such that government departments do not gain control of funds appropriated for their use until obligations are incurred or expenditures are made by the government department. In these jurisdictions, appropriations recognised as income are in the nature of a recovery of costs incurred for the acquisition of goods and services or for amounts otherwise expended. As such, a government department usually only controls amounts appropriated by parliament for its use during the reporting period where those amounts have been expended or are required to meet obligations incurred during that reporting period.

35   However, the nature of parliamentary appropriations, and the circumstances that give rise to a government department's control of such appropriations, can vary across different jurisdictions in Australia, and may vary for different types of appropriations within a particular jurisdiction. In addition, a government department's authority and ability to maintain separate bank accounts and to retain funds that have been appropriated for its use but that have not been expended during a reporting period can change over time. Similarly, the nature and content of appropriation legislation, the manner in which government departments' activities are funded, and the mechanisms by which parliament and the government ensure that the government departments' use of public funds is appropriate and consistent with government priorities as sanctioned by parliament, can

change over time. These changes can affect a government department's ability to control amounts appropriated for its use. Accordingly, the extent to which amounts appropriated for a government department's use are recognised as income of a particular reporting period is determined by reference to the characteristics of the appropriation process and the circumstances in which the government department obtains control of appropriated amounts.

36   Where the nature of parliamentary appropriations is such that a government department's control over appropriations is not dependent on expenditure or the incurrence of obligations or the completion of agreed outputs, services or facilities, the government department's control of the appropriated amounts occurs at the earliest of:

(a)   the commencement of the period to which the appropriation applies;

(b)   the receipt of the appropriated funds; and

(c)   the date on which the government department's authority to expend appropriated funds becomes effective.

37   Where a government department controls amounts appropriated to it for transfer to other parties, those amounts give rise to assets and income when the government department gains control of those appropriations. Where a government department controls the appropriations and the conditions for transfer to beneficiaries are satisfied during the reporting period but the amounts have not been transferred as at the reporting date, the government department recognises a liability in respect of such amounts. Where amounts are to be transferred in future reporting periods and the conditions for transfer are also to be satisfied in future reporting periods, the government department does not recognise a liability as at the reporting date in respect of such amounts.

38   Parliamentary appropriations made to enable a tax collection agency to perform its services are income of that agency. This is because the agency has the authority to deploy the appropriated funds for the achievement of its objectives and, consequently, controls the assets arising from the appropriation.

Liabilities of Government Departments Assumed by Other Entities

Paragraphs 39 to 43 of this Standard apply only to government departments.

39   **A liability of a government department that is assumed by the government or other entity shall be accounted for as follows:**

(a)   **on initial incurrence of the liability by the government department, the government department shall recognise a liability and an expense;**

(b)   **on assumption of the liability by the government or other entity, the government department shall extinguish the liability and:**

(i)   **when the assumption is not in the nature of a contribution by owners, the government department shall recognise income of an amount equivalent to the liability assumed; or**

(ii)   **when the assumption of the liability is in the nature of a contribution by owners, the government department shall make a direct adjustment to equity of an amount equivalent to the liability assumed.**

40   The obligation to make payments to employees in respect of long-service leave and other employee benefits may rest with the government, a central agency or other entity. However, the costs of long-service leave and other employee benefits are part of the cost of the goods and services provided by the government department for which those employees work. Employment contracts or employment arrangements may be such that a government or other entity, rather than the government department, directly incurs the obligation to settle liabilities that arise in respect of benefits of the government department's employees. Alternatively, it may be that the government department initially incurs the obligation to settle such liabilities, and the government or other entity then assumes that obligation.

41   A government or other entity may initially incur, and then settle, obligations in respect of the wages, salaries and other costs of the employees of a government department during

the reporting period. Similarly, other expenses of operating the government department during the reporting period, such as building occupancy expenses, may be incurred and settled by the government or other entity. In such cases, the government department does not recognise a liability when the expenses are initially incurred. Rather, the government department recognises income equivalent to the fair value of the employee services or other assets it receives, and recognises expenses of the same amount to reflect that the economic benefits represented by those employee services or other benefits have been consumed by the government department. For employee services, this normally occurs when the services are provided, but in some instances the costs of these services forms part of the cost of acquiring an asset.

42   When an employee transfers from one government department to another government department, the liability in respect of employee benefits accrued up to the transfer date is usually transferred to the transferee government department. In such cases, the transferor government department may make a payment to the transferee government department for the employee's accrued benefits. When an employee transfers from one government department to another government department:

(a)   the transferor government department extinguishes any liability for employee benefits recognised in respect of the employee, and recognises income equivalent to the liability extinguished. When a payment is made or is to be made by the transferor government department in consideration for the assumption of the liability by the transferee government department, the transferor government department extinguishes the liability and recognises a decrease in assets (cash) or an increase in liabilities (cash payable). When the payment is less than the total amount of the liability, the transferor government department recognises income equal to the amount of that shortfall; and

(b)   the transferee government department recognises an expense and a liability in respect of any present obligations to pay accrued employee benefits in the future that are assumed as a consequence of the transfer. When a payment is made or is to be made to the transferee government department in consideration for the assumption of the liability, the transferee government department recognises the liability assumed and an increase in assets (cash or cash receivable). When the payment is less than the total amount of the liability for employee entitlements assumed, the transferee government department recognises an expense equal to the amount of that shortfall.

43   As noted in paragraphs 39 to 41, a government may initially incur or subsequently assume all obligations to make payments to employees of a government department in respect of long-service leave and other employee benefits. In such cases, the transfer of employees between government departments will not give rise to the need for the transferee government department to recognise expenses and liabilities or for the transferor government department to extinguish liabilities and recognise income as outlined in paragraph 42.

Contributions of Services

Paragraphs 44 to 47 of this Standard apply only to local governments, government departments, GGSs and whole of governments.

44   **Contributions of services to local governments, government departments, GGSs and whole of governments shall be recognised as income when and only when:**

(a)   **the fair value of those services can be reliably determined; and**

(b)   **the services would have been purchased if they had not been donated.**

45   Local governments, government departments, GGSs and whole of governments may receive contributions of goods or services free of charge or for nominal consideration by way of gift or donation. The assets and income recognised by the recipient in respect of such contributions, subject to the requirements of paragraph 12 of this Standard, are measured at the fair value of the goods or services received. This ensures that the operating statement reports the change in resources controlled by the recipient as a result

of the operations for the reporting period, and that the statement of financial position reports the assets and liabilities of the recipient as at the reporting date.

46 Some donated services, while useful, may not be central to the delivery of the outputs of the local government, government department, GGS or whole of government. In these cases, it is unlikely that the recipient would purchase the services if they were not donated. Recognition of the fair value of those services as income and expenses is not relevant to assessments of the cost of services provided by, or the financial performance of, the recipient. Accordingly, this Standard requires that contributed services only be recognised when the services would be purchased if not donated and when their fair value can be measured reliably.

47 In some cases, the gaining of control over the assets that result from contributions and the consumption of the future economic benefits embodied in those assets will be simultaneous. For example, donated services give rise to income and an asset of the recipient and, simultaneously, an expense as the future economic benefits embodied in the asset are consumed. Therefore, the net effect of the contribution of services is the recognition of income and an expense. Such recognition is important if the operating statement is to reflect fully the cost of services provided during the reporting period and the sources and amounts of the entity's income. Such information is useful in assessing the cost efficiency of an entity's performance and the amounts and sources of likely future resource requirements.

Contributions by Owners and Distributions to Owners of Local Governments, Government Departments and Whole of Governments

Paragraphs 48 to 53 of this Standard apply only to local governments, government departments and whole of governments.

48 **Contributions by owners shall be recognised as a direct adjustment to equity when the contributed assets qualify for recognition.**

49 **Distributions to owners shall be recognised as a direct adjustment to equity when the associated reduction in assets, rendering of services or increase in liabilities qualifies for recognition.**

50 It is important to distinguish contributions by owners from other contributions. It may be argued that contributions that are provided on the condition that they be expended on assets that increase the capacity of the entity to provide particular services should be classified as contributions of equity. However, such contributions would be contributions by owners, as defined in Appendix A to this Standard, only when the contributor establishes by way of the contribution a financial interest in the net assets of the entity that:

    (a) conveys entitlement both to a financial return on the contribution and to distributions of any excess of assets over liabilities in the event of the entity being wound up; and/or

    (b) can be sold, transferred or redeemed.

51 Contributions by owners are examples of non-reciprocal transfers. Examples of contributions by owners (and distributions to owners) are non-reciprocal transfers between a government department and the controlling government acting in its capacity as owner. Transactions with owners in their capacity as owners are not common in a local government context. A local government may on occasions receive contributions by owners, as defined in Appendix A to this Standard, such as investments in the capital of companies controlled by the governing body of the local government. Such contributions would need to be recognised as contributions of equity.

52 Contributions by owners can occur upon establishment of the entity or at a subsequent stage of the entity's existence. Contributions by owners can be in the form of cash, nonmonetary assets such as property, plant and equipment, or the provision of services. In some instances, the contribution may result from the conversion of the entity's liabilities into equity.

53   Reductions in equity as a result of distributions to owners (either dividends or returns of capital) can be in the form of a transfer of assets, a rendering of services or an increase in liabilities. Distributions from government departments to governments are made at the discretion of the government.

Restructure of Administrative Arrangements

Paragraphs 54 to 59 of this Standard apply only to government controlled not-for-profit entities and for-profit government departments.

54   **In relation to a *restructure of administrative arrangements*, a government controlled not-for-profit transferor entity or a for-profit government department transferor entity shall recognise distributions to owners and a government controlled not-for-profit transferee entity or a for-profit government department transferee entity shall recognise contributions by owners in respect of assets transferred.**

55   **In relation to a restructure of administrative arrangements, a government controlled not-for-profit transferor entity or a for-profit government department transferor entity shall recognise contributions by owners and a government controlled not-for-profit transferee entity or a for-profit government department transferee entity shall recognise distributions to owners in respect of liabilities transferred.**

56   **When both assets and liabilities are transferred as a consequence of a restructure of administrative arrangements, a government controlled not-for-profit transferor entity or a for-profit government department transferor entity and a government controlled not-for-profit transferee entity or a for-profit government department transferee entity shall recognise a net contribution by owners or distribution to owners, as applicable.**

57   **When activities are transferred as a consequence of a restructure of administrative arrangements, a government controlled not-for-profit transferee entity or a for-profit government department transfe`ree entity shall disclose the expenses and income attributable to the transferred activities for the reporting period, showing separately those expenses and items of income recognised by the transferor during the reporting period. If disclosure of this information would be impracticable, that fact shall be disclosed, together with an explanation of why this is the case.**

58   **For each material transfer, the assets and liabilities transferred as a consequence of a restructure of administrative arrangements during the reporting period shall be disclosed by class, and the counterparty transferor/transferee entity shall be identified. With respect to transfers that are individually immaterial, the assets and liabilities transferred shall be disclosed on an aggregate basis.**

59   The disclosures required by paragraph 58 will assist users to identify the assets and liabilities recognised or derecognised as a result of a restructure of administrative arrangements separately from other assets and liabilities and to identify the transferor/transferee entity.

Disclosure of Contributions

Paragraphs 60 to 62 of this Standard apply only to local governments, government departments, GGSs and whole of governments.

60   **The complete set of financial statements shall disclose, separately by way of note, the amounts and nature of:**

      (a)   contributions recognised as income during the reporting period in respect of which expenditure in a manner specified by a transferor contributor had yet to be made as at the reporting date, details of those contributions and the conditions attaching to them;

      (b)   contributions recognised as income during the reporting period that were provided specifically for the provision of goods or services over a future period;

      (c)   contributions recognised as income during the reporting period that were obtained in respect of a future rating or taxing period identified by the local

government, GGS or whole of government for the purpose of establishing a rate or tax;

(d) the nature of the amounts referred to in (a), (b) and (c) above and, in respect of (b) and (c) above, the periods to which they relate; and

(e) contributions recognised as income in a previous reporting period that were obtained in respect of the current reporting period.

61 Where a local government, government department, GGS or whole of government receives contributions on the condition that the related assets shall be expended in a particular manner or used over a particular period, and those conditions are undischarged in part or in full as at the reporting date, the entity will have a strong fiduciary responsibility in relation to the deployment of those contributed assets. As noted in paragraph 20, this fiduciary responsibility does not constitute a liability. However, information about the contributions, including the conditions, is relevant to users of the complete set of financial statements, particularly in assessing performance and the discharge of accountability obligations. Accordingly, this Standard requires disclosure of those conditions where they are yet to be discharged, in part or in full, as at the reporting date. In addition, disclosure of contributions recognised as income in a previous reporting period that were provided specifically in respect of the current reporting period will provide information relevant to users' assessments of the entity's recovery of the cost of goods and services it has provided during the current reporting period.

62 **The complete set of financial statements shall disclose separately the fair value of goods and services received free of charge, or for nominal consideration, that are recognised during the reporting period.**

Additional Government Department Disclosures

Paragraph 63 of this Standard applies only to government departments.

63 **The complete set of financial statements of a government department shall disclose separately:**

(a) appropriations, by class; and

(b) liabilities that were assumed during the reporting period by the government or other entity.

Compliance with Parliamentary Appropriations and Other Externally-Imposed Requirements

Paragraphs 64 to 68 of this Standard apply only to government departments.

64 **The complete set of financial statements of a government department shall disclose separately:**

(a) a summary of the recurrent, capital or other major categories of appropriations, disclosing separately:

(i) the original amounts appropriated for the reporting period; and

(ii) the total amounts appropriated for the reporting period;

(b) amounts authorised other than by way of appropriation and advanced separately by the Treasurer, other minister or other legislative authority for the reporting period;

(c) the expenditures for the reporting period in respect of each of the items disclosed in (a) and (b) above;

(d) the reasons for any material variances between the amounts appropriated or otherwise authorised and the associated expenditures for the reporting period; and

(e) the nature and probable financial effect of any non compliance by the government department with externally-imposed requirements for the reporting period, not already disclosed by virtue of (d) above, and that are relevant to assessments of the government department's performance, financial position or financing and investing activities.

65   The information disclosed about compliance with externally-imposed requirements shall be in a form that is relevant to users of that information, and that reflects the following:

    (a)   the operating characteristics of the government department;

    (b)   the structure of the appropriations;

    (c)   any other requirements that are imposed externally on the government department; and

    (d)   the general purpose nature of the complete set of financial statements.

66   For the purposes of economic decision making, including assessments of accountability, this Standard requires that users of the complete set of financial statements be provided with information about the amounts appropriated or otherwise authorised for a government department's use, and whether the government department's expenditures were as authorised. When spending limits imposed by parliamentary appropriation or other authorisation have not been complied with, information regarding the amount of, and reasons for, the non compliance is relevant for assessing the performance of management, the likely consequences of non-compliance, and the ability of the government department to continue to provide services at a similar or different level in the future.

67   Broad summaries of the major categories of appropriations and associated expenditures, rather than detailed reporting of appropriations line-item by line-item for each activity, is sufficient for most users of a government department's complete set of financial statements. Determining the level of detail and the structure of the summarised information is a matter of judgement. The detailed information about compliance with spending mandates required by certain users should be provided in special purpose financial statements.

68   In addition to requirements to comply with expenditure limits imposed by parliamentary appropriations, government departments are subject to a range of legislative, regulatory and other externally-imposed requirements governing their operations. Knowledge of non compliance with such requirements is relevant for accountability purposes and may affect users' assessments of the government department's performance and likely future operations. It may also influence decisions about resources to be allocated to that government department in the future.

Appendix A
Defined Terms

This Appendix is an integral part of AASB 1004.

Contributions   Non-reciprocal transfers to the entity.

Contributions by owners   Future economic benefits that have been contributed to the entity by parties external to the entity, other than those which result in liabilities of the entity, that give rise to a financial interest in the net assets of the entity which:

    (a)   conveys entitlement both to distributions of future economic benefits by the entity during its life, such distributions being at the discretion of the ownership group or its representatives, and to distributions of any excess of assets over liabilities in the event of the entity being wound up; and/or

    (b)   can be sold, transferred or redeemed.

Non-reciprocal transfer   A transfer in which the entity receives assets or services or has liabilities extinguished without directly giving approximately equal value in exchange to the other party or parties to the transfer.

AASB

Restructure of administrative arrangements	The reallocation or reorganisation of assets, liabilities, activities and responsibilities amongst the entities that the government controls that occurs as a consequence of a rearrangement in the way in which activities and responsibilities as prescribed under legislation or other authority are allocated between the government's controlled entities.
	The scope of the requirements relating to restructures of administrative arrangements is limited to the transfer of a business (as defined in AASB 3 *Business Combinations*). The requirements do not apply to, for example, a transfer of an individual asset or a group of assets that is not a business.

Appendix B
Comparison of AASB 1004 with AAS 27, AAS 29 and AAS 31

This Appendix accompanies, but is not part of, AASB 1004.

Paragraphs 19 to 68 of this Standard broadly reproduce the requirements relating to contributions contained in AAS 27 *Financial Reporting by Local Governments*, AAS 29 *Financial Reporting by Government Departments* and AAS 31 *Financial Reporting by Governments*, with some exceptions. The more significant exceptions include:

(a) requirements in this Standard relating to recognition of contributions other than contributions by owners (paragraphs 19 to 30), contributions of services (paragraphs 44 to 47) and disclosure of contributions (paragraphs 60 to 62) have been extended to apply to General Government Sectors (GGSs);

(b) requirements in this Standard relating to recognition of non-reciprocal transfers (paragraph 30), including material from AAS 31 (paragraph 15.2.1) have been extended beyond whole of governments to local governments, government departments and GGSs;

(c) requirements in this Standard relating to recognition and disclosure of contributions of services (paragraphs 44 to 47, and 62) have been extended beyond government departments to local governments, government departments, GGSs and whole of governments;

(d) requirements in this Standard relating to the disclosure of contributions (paragraph 60) are more detailed than those that applied to government departments under AAS 29 and governments under AAS 31;

(e) guidance in this Standard relating to contributions by owners and distributions to owners of local governments, government departments and whole of governments (paragraphs 48 to 53) has been amended to make it consistent with Interpretation 1038 *Contributions by Owners Made to Wholly-Owned Public Sector Entities*; and

(f) requirements in this Standard relating to restructures of administrative arrangements (paragraphs 54 to 59) require that transfers of resources resulting from such restructures are to be treated as movements in owner's equity by government controlled not-for-profit entities and for-profit government departments that are transferees or transferors. This contrasts with the treatment under superseded AAS 29 and Interpretation 1038 that would have required treatment of the resource transfers as revenues or expenses in some circumstances. This Standard also includes a definition of 'restructure of administrative arrangements" (Appendix A).

The following table provides source references to paragraphs 19 – 68 of this Standard, most of which were derived from AASs 27, 29 and 31. It is provided to facilitate an understanding of, and assist in the application of, the requirements in this Standard.

Paragraphs in AASB 1004	Relevant source paragraphs in AASs 27, 29 and 31
19, 20, first sentence 21	60, 64-65 of AAS 27, 10.12.1 – 10.12.3 of AAS 29 and 14.1.1 – 14.1.3 of AAS 31
Second sentence of 21	67 of AAS 27 and 10.12.4 of AAS 29
22 – 23	61 of AAS 27, 10.12.2 and 10.12.4 of AAS 29 and 14.1.8 and 14.1.9 of AAS 31
24	62 of AAS 27 and 14.1.10 of AAS 31
25	14.1.11 of AAS 31
26	69 of AAS 27, 10.12.7 of AAS 29 and 14.1.4 of AAS 31
27	10.5.5 of AAS 29
28 – 29	10.12.5 of AAS 29 and 14.1.6 and 14.1.7 of AAS 31
30	68 of AAS 27, 10.5.10 of AAS 29 and 14.1.5 and 15.2.1 of AAS 31
31	10.5.9 of AAS 29
32	10.5 of AAS 29
33	10.5.1 of AAS 29
34 – 36	10.5.6 and 10.5.7 of AAS 29
37	10.5.17 of AAS 29
38	10.5.10 of AAS 29
39 – 43	8.2, 8.2.1 and 8.2.3 – 8.2.5 of AAS 29
44	10.12 of AAS 29
45	10.12.6 of AAS 29
46	10.12.9 of AAS 29
47	10.12.8 of AAS 29
48 – 53	63 and 70 of AAS 27, 11.1 – 11.2.4 of AAS 29 and 14.1.12 and 14.1.13 of AAS 31
54 – 59	7.4, 7.4.2 and 10.6 – 10.9.3 of AAS 29
60 – 61	92 and 93 of AAS 27 and 12.4 and 12.4.1 of AAS 29
62	12.2(d) of AAS 29
63	12.2(b) and (c) of AAS 29
64	12.6 of AAS 29
65	12.6.3 of AAS 29
66	12.6.2 of AAS 29
67	12.6.3 of AAS 29
68	12.6.4 of AAS 29

Basis for Conclusions

This Basis for Conclusions accompanies, but is not part of, AASB 1004.

Introduction

BC1 This Basis for Conclusions summarises the Board's considerations in revising AASB 1004 *Contributions* in the context of the Board's short-term review of the requirements in AAS 27 *Financial Reporting by Local Governments*, AAS 29 *Financial Reporting by Government Departments* and AAS 31 *Financial Reporting by Governments*.

Background

BC2 The Board considered it timely to review the requirements in AASs 27, 29 and 31, in particular to:

(a) review the extent to which local governments, government departments and governments should continue to be subject to requirements that differ from requirements applicable to other not-for-profit entities and for-profit entities contained in Australian Accounting Standards. The Board concluded that differences should be removed, where appropriate and timely, to improve the overall quality of financial reporting;

(b) bring requirements applicable to local governments, government departments and governments up-to-date with contemporary accounting thought;

(c) consider the implications of the outcomes of its project on the harmonisation of Generally Accepted Accounting Principles (GAAP) and Government Finance Statistics (GFS), in particular, on the requirements in AAS 31;

(d) decide whether the encouragements in AASs 27, 29 and 31 should be made mandatory or removed; and

(e) remove uncertainty in the application of cross-references to other Australian Accounting Standards and the override provisions in AASs 27, 29 and 31 that made the requirements in AASs 27, 29 and 31 take precedence over other requirements.

BC3 The Board considered the following alternative mechanisms for implementing the approach of updating and improving the requirements for local governments, government departments and governments:

(a) review the requirements in AASs 27, 29 and 31 and, where appropriate:

(i) amend other Australian Accounting Standards to pick up any issues that are addressed in AASs 27, 29 and 31 that are not adequately addressed in the latest Australian Accounting Standards and have them apply to local governments, government departments and governments; or

(ii) create public sector specific topic-based Standards;

and consequently withdraw AASs 27, 29 and 31; or

(b) review AASs 27, 29 and 31 and re-issue them in light of the latest Australian Accounting Standards, retaining/amending where necessary any issues that are addressed in AASs 27, 29 and 31 that are not adequately addressed in the latest Australian Accounting Standards.

BC4 The Board chose alternative (a) given the improvements in the quality of financial reporting by local governments, government departments and governments since AASs 27, 29 and 31 were first issued.

BC5 Where the Board identified that the material in AASs 27, 29 and 31 could be improved within time and resource constraints, improvements have been made. Much of the material in AASs 27, 29 and 31 has been retained substantively unamended. Improvements will be progressed in due course in line with the AASB's Public Sector Policy Paper *Australian Accounting Standards and Public Sector Entities*.

BC6 The first stage of the short-term review of the requirements in AASs 27, 29 and 31 was the preparation of a paragraph-by-paragraph analysis of each of AASs 27, 29 and 31, listing each paragraph of each Standard alongside corresponding Standards or other pronouncements that would apply to local governments, government departments or governments in the absence of AASs 27, 29 and 31. The Board's conclusions and rationale for the treatment of each paragraph in the context of the review were also provided in the analysis. The Board's primary focus was on dealing with the requirements from the three Standards in such a way as to not leave a vacuum.

BC7   Each paragraph from AASs 27, 29 and 31 was classified as being:

  (a)   no longer needed or adequately dealt with in other Standards;

  (b)   more appropriately dealt with in other Standards; or

  (c)   not adequately and/or appropriately dealt with in other Standards and therefore should be retained or improved and incorporated into other Standards.

The paragraph-by-paragraph analyses considered by the AASB in developing the Exposure Draft ED 156 *Proposals Arising from the Short-term Review of the Requirements in AAS 27, AAS 29 and AAS 31* that gave rise to this Standard are available on the AASB website. They support, but do not form part of, this Basis for Conclusions.

BC8   In reviewing the paragraphs, the Board noted that some material in AASs 27, 29 and 31 would, under the current style of writing Standards, be located in a separate Basis for Conclusions. Given the short-term nature of the review of AASs 27, 29 and 31, the Board concluded that explanations of technical issues that both originated in and are being relocated from AASs 27, 29 and 31 should, when appropriate, be located in the body of the Standard to which they are relocated.

BC9   The Board decided not to retain the illustrative general purpose financial reports provided in AASs 27, 29 and 31, because their purpose, which was to provide an educational tool in the initial stages of accrual reporting by local governments, government departments and governments is no longer needed.

BC10 The remainder of this Basis for Conclusions focuses on issues specific to contributions.

Contributions

General Approach

BC11 The Board decided to broadly retain the material on contributions from AASs 27, 29 and 31 and locate it in separate sections within AASB 1004 because it was not adequately covered in existing Australian Accounting Standards.

BC12 The Board concluded that, in the short term, minimal changes should be made to the content of the material. The Board considered that it is appropriate to review the requirements and guidance for contributions as part of a longer-term project as outlined in the AASB's Public Sector Policy Paper. A review by the Board of non-exchange income, which will incorporate a review of contributions, is in progress at the time of revision of this Standard.

BC13 The Board considered two options for relocating the requirements on contributions into AASB 1004:

  (a)   merging the AASs 27, 29 and 31 paragraphs into the then existing AASB 1004 requirements; or

  (b)   adding the AASs 27, 29 and 31 paragraphs into the existing AASB 1004 as separate sections.

The paragraphs in AASs 27, 29 and 31 containing guidance about contributions were very detailed and contained a large amount of commentary whereas the then existing guidance in AASB 1004 was significantly less detailed. The Board concluded that merging the requirements in AASs 27, 29 and 31 with the AASB 1004 requirements would, in effect, require the redrafting of the entire Standard, which is beyond the scope of this project. The integration approach was also considered more likely to raise controversial revenue recognition issues for all not-for-profit entities that, as noted in paragraph BC12, the Board will deal with as a separate longer-term project applicable to a broader range of entities.

BC14 The Board also considered whether the guidance from AASs 27, 29 and 31 should be merged into a single set of generic requirements or expressed separately for local governments, government departments or governments. The Board concluded that the three sets of guidance from AASs 27, 29 and 31 were sufficiently similar to be merged to form one set of requirements – noting that such an approach results in some changes for some entities. One area where this occurs is the disclosure of contributions, where government departments and governments are now required to make disclosures not previously required, because AAS 27 was more onerous than AASs 29 and 31.

BC15 The Board decided to include specific references to the application of this Standard to General Government Sectors (GGSs) to support/clarify the AASB 1049 *Financial Reporting of General Government Sectors by Governments* requirement for GGSs to adopt other Australian Accounting Standards, including this Standard. As this Standard has many parts, applicable to different groups of entities, the Board considered it would aid users to explicitly refer to GGSs in paragraph 1(d) and throughout this Standard.

BC16 In addition, the Board decided to extend the application of the requirements relating to 'contributions of services' to apply beyond government departments to local governments, GGSs and whole of governments, for consistency across these types of entities.

BC17 Because the guidance from AASs 27, 29 and 31 partly overlapped with the guidance in the superseded AASB 1004, the Board amended the requirements to reduce duplication.

BC18 The Board considered whether the paragraphs of AAS 29 that address the accounting for parliamentary appropriations, which are only applicable to government departments, should be incorporated into this Standard as a separate section. The Board noted the view that the requirements are no longer needed given the nature of current arrangements between governments and government departments for parliamentary appropriations compared with past arrangements and government departments' familiarity with accrual accounting. However, the Board concluded that the paragraphs should be retained, in keeping with Board's short-term intention of retaining the guidance from AASs 27, 29 and 31 where there are no comparable requirements in existing Australian Accounting Standards and thereby avoid creating a vacuum.

BC19 Paragraph 15.2.1 of AAS 31 dealt with the disclosure of policies adopted for recognising tax revenues. Given the nature of the commentary, the Board concluded that it would be most logical to locate the contents of this paragraph in paragraph 30 of this Standard within the area that relates to recognition of 'contributions, other than contributions by owners, by local governments, government departments, GGSs or whole of governments' and within the section 'control over assets' in a paragraph that discusses control over assets acquired from involuntary non-reciprocal transfers, such as rates, taxes and fines. In doing this, the Board decided to extend the requirements beyond whole of governments to local governments, government departments and GGSs.

Liabilities Assumed by Other Entities

BC20 The Board decided to substantially retain the guidance in AAS 29 relating to the treatment of liabilities assumed by other entities in the financial statements of a government department. The Board concluded that, although the superseded AASB 1004 specified requirements for liabilities that are forgiven, it did not explicitly deal with liabilities that are assumed by other entities.

BC21 The Board considered whether to align the requirements in paragraphs 8.2, 8.2.1 and 8.2.3-8.2.5 of AAS 29 for derecognition of liabilities with the corresponding requirements in AASB 139 *Financial Instruments: Recognition and Measurement*. The Board noted that the AAS 29 requirements, which reflected a symmetrical accounting approach, may not be consistent with the criteria for derecognition of a liability in AASB 139, which does not necessarily result in symmetry and refers to liabilities arising from contracts. Given the relationship between an entity assuming a government department's liability (such as the controlling government) and the government department, the Board concluded that the symmetrical accounting adopted in AAS 29 is appropriate for derecognition of liabilities.

Government Department Disclosures Relating to Revenue

BC22 The Board decided that it would be most logical to incorporate the requirements from paragraphs 12.2(b)-(d) of AAS 29 relating to disclosure requirements for certain revenue items (that is, appropriations by class; liabilities that were assumed during the reporting period by the government or other entity; and the fair value of goods and services received free of charge, or for nominal consideration, and recognised during the reporting period) into this Standard. This is because they are disclosures of items of revenue that, for the purpose of the short-term review, are considered to be sufficiently related to the scope of the superseded AASB 1004.

BC23 The Board decided to limit the requirements in paragraphs 12.2(b) and (c) of AAS 29 to government departments, in keeping with its approach of retaining AASs 27, 29 and 31 requirements in the short term. In keeping with the Board's decision to extend the application of the section on 'contribution of services' to apply beyond government departments to local governments, GGSs and whole of governments (see paragraph BC16), the Board concluded that the disclosure requirements in paragraph 12.2(d) of AAS 29 relating to revenue disclosures about contributions of services should also be extended to apply to local governments, GGSs and whole of governments. Furthermore, the Board concluded that the paragraph in question should be amended to refer to recognised contributions of services to be consistent with the requirements under which not all contributions received would be required to be recognised.

Restructures of Administrative Arrangements

BC24 The Board considered it timely to amend the requirements in paragraphs 7.4, 7.4.2 and 10.6-10.9.3 of AAS 29 for restructures of administrative arrangements as part of the short-term review of AAS 29 and in light of the existing definition of contributions by owners that is contained in this Standard. The Board decided to define restructures of administrative arrangements and to specify that they are in the nature of transactions with owners in their capacity as owners to be recognised on a net basis. In particular, the Board concluded that a transfer of net assets arising as a consequence of a restructure of administrative arrangements is faithfully represented as a distribution to owners by the transferor and a contribution by owners by the transferee. The Board also noted that this would result in greater consistency in accounting for restructures of administrative arrangements. The Board concluded that this approach is preferable to the superseded approach whereby transfers need to be designated as contributions by owners at the time of the transfer to be treated as such. The Board noted that this would result in a significant change in the current AAS 29 requirements as the possibility of treating a transfer as a revenue/expense item would no longer be available, and would give rise to amendments to Interpretation 1038 *Contributions by Owners Made to Wholly-Owned Public Sector Entities* to make it consistent with this Standard. Consistent with the short-term nature of the review of AASs 27, 29 and 31, the Board intends making amendments to Interpretation 1038 to make it consistent with this Standard. In the longer term, the Board intends to undertake a fundamental review of Interpretation 1038.

BC25 The Board concluded that the effect of the requirements should be expanded beyond government departments to include all government controlled not-for-profit public sector entities and for-profit government departments, noting that this would increase the consistency with the scope of Interpretation 1038 which applies to all wholly-owned public sector entities that prepare general purpose financial statements, not just government departments. This will assist in harmonising requirements and guidance in relation to contributions by owners. It is not intended that the amended requirements for restructures of administrative arrangements necessarily apply in analogous circumstances. For example, it is not intended that the amended requirements apply in the accounting for restructures of commonly-controlled private sector entities.

BC26 Although assets and/or liabilities assumed by another entity as a consequence of a restructure of administrative arrangements were not explicitly dealt with in the superseded AASB 1004, the Board concluded that this Standard is an appropriate location for this material as it is the Standard that is best suited to dealing with contributions, including contributions by owners, to not-for-profit reporting entities and for-profit government departments.

BC27 In addition, in accordance with its decision to issue AASB 2005-6 *Amendments to Australian Accounting Standards [AASB 3]*, the Board concluded that AASB 3 *Business Combinations* is not an appropriate Standard in which to locate specific requirements relating to restructures of administrative arrangements because business combinations involving entities or businesses under common control are now excluded from the scope of AASB 3. However, a cross-reference from AASB 3 to AASB 1004 is provided to assist in understanding the relationship between the two Standards.

BC28 The Board also concluded that it is not necessary at this time to explicitly address the measurement basis to be adopted for transferred assets and liabilities due to a restructure of administrative arrangements. An asset acquired by a government controlled not-for-profit entity or a for-profit government department as a consequence of a restructure of administrative arrangements is considered to be a contribution by owners. Not specifying the measurement basis is consistent with Interpretation 1038, which also does not specify the measurement basis to be adopted with respect to contributions by owners or distributions to owners. In addition, AASB 3 does not address the measurement issue for a restructure of entities under common control. The Board also noted that measurement requirements in AASB 116 *Property, Plant and Equipment* (including paragraph Aus15.1) do not apply to assets transferred under a restructure of administrative arrangements because they are acquired by the transferee as part of a business. The Board acknowledges that, as the proposed amendments do not specify the measurement basis to be adopted, assets and liabilities transferred in the course of a restructure of administrative arrangements could be measured at fair value or book value.

BC29 The Board noted that the scope of the requirements relating to restructures of administrative arrangements is limited to the transfer of a business (as defined in AASB 3). The Board does not intend the requirements to apply where, for example, an individual asset or a group of assets that are not a business are transferred, noting that transfers of an individual asset and a group of assets are scoped out by the definition of a business in AASB 3.

Compliance with Parliamentary Appropriations and Other Externally-Imposed Requirements by Government Departments

BC30 The Board noted that issues relating to compliance with parliamentary appropriations and other externally-imposed requirements are important for government accountability. Accordingly, the Board concluded that the requirements in paragraphs 12.6 and 12.6.2-12.6.4 of AAS 29 for disclosure of compliance with parliamentary appropriations and other externally imposed requirements should be retained.

BC31 The Board concluded that the requirements for the disclosure by government departments of compliance with parliamentary appropriations and other externally-imposed requirements are sufficiently related to the topic of contributions to be incorporated into this Standard.

BC32 Consistent with the short-term nature of the project, the requirements are to be limited to government departments rather than applying them more broadly to not-for-profit public sector entities. In due course, the Board will consider extending the application of the requirements.

BC33 The Board concluded that it is appropriate to not retain paragraph 12.6.1 of AAS 29, which explains the meaning of parliamentary appropriations, as it is no longer necessary.

AASB 1023
General Insurance Contracts

(Compiled November 2010)

Note from the Institute of Chartered Accountants Australia

This note, prepared by the technical editors, is not part of Accounting Standard AASB 1023.

Historical development

1990: ASRB 1023 'Financial Reporting of General Insurance Activities' was issued by Australia's (then) Accounting Standards Review Board in 1990.

1996: The AASB reissued AASB 1023 in 1996 to amend the claims development disclosures required by the Standard.

15 July 2004: The AASB reissued the Standard in July 2004 as AASB 1023 'General Insurance Contracts' to incorporate the requirements of IFRS 4 'Insurance Contracts' that apply to general insurance contracts. The 2004 version of AASB 1023 forms part of the stable platform of 2005 Australian equivalents to International Financial Reporting Standards (IFRSs).

3 June 2005: AASB 2005-2 'Amendments to Australian Accounting Standards' amends paragraphs 5.1.10, 9.1, 17.1(a) to 17.1(c), 17.2, 17.8, 17.8.1 and 17.9.1. The Standard deletes paragraphs 17.1(d) to (f), and adds paragraph 17.8. The Standard is applicable to annual reporting periods beginning on or after 1 January 2005.

9 June 2005: AASB 2005-4 'Amendments to Australian Accounting Standards' amends paragraphs 15.2,15.2.1, 15.2.2, 15.5, 15.5.2, 16.1 and 16.1.1. The Standard is applicable to annual reporting periods beginning on or after 1 January 2005.

5 September 2005: AASB 2005-10 'Amendments to Australian Accounting Standards' amends paragraphs 17.7, 17.7.1, 17.7.3, 17.9.1 and 18.3, and adds paragraphs 17.7.5 and 17.8. This Standard is applicable to annual reporting periods beginning on or after 1 January 2007 with early adoption permitted for annual reporting periods beginning on or after 1 January 2005.

6 September 2005: AASB 2005-9 'Amendments to Australian Accounting Standards' amends paragraphs 2.2(f), Appendix 17(e) and Appendix 18(e). This Standard is applicable to annual reporting periods beginning on or after 1 January 2006, with early adoption permitted for annual reporting periods beginning on or after 1 January 2005.

6 May 2006: Compiled version of the Standard was issued, incorporating amendments contained in AASB 2005-2, AASB 2005-4, AASB 2005-9, AASB 2005-10 and AASB 2005-12.

26 February 2007: AASB 2007-3 'Amendments to Australian Accounting Standards' was issued by the AASB. This Standard is applicable for annual reporting periods beginning on or after 1 January 2009.

30 April 2007: AASB 2007-4 'Amendments to Australian Accounting Standards' amends paragraphs 2.2, 13.3.1, 15.2, 15.5, 17.2, 17.8 and19.1 and is applicable to annual reporting periods beginning on or after 1 July 2007. Entities may elect to early-adopt it to annual reporting periods beginning on or after 1 January 2005.

24 September 2007: AASB 2007-8 'Amendments to Australian Accounting Standards' amends AASB 1023, changing the term 'general purpose financial reports' to 'general purpose financial statements'. This Standard is applicable to annual reporting periods beginning on or after 1 January 2009.

13 December 2007: AASB 2007-10 'Further Amendments to Australian Accounting Standards arising from AASB 101' amends AASB 1023, replacing the term 'financial report' with 'financial statements'. This Standard is applicable to annual reporting periods beginning on or after 1 January 2009.

AASB

24 July 2008: AASB 2008-5 'Amendments to Australian Accounting Standards arising from the Annual Improvements Project' amends AASB 1023 in relation to investments not classified for sale under AASB 5. This Standard is applicable to annual reporting periods beginning on or after 1 January 2009.

22 April 2009: AASB 2009-2 'Amendments to Australian Accounting Standards – Improving Disclosures about Financial Instruments' amends AASB 1023 to require enhanced disclosures about fair value measurements and liquidity risk. This Standard is applicable to annual reporting periods beginning on or after 1 January 2009 that end on or after 30 April 2009.

25 June 2009: AASB 2009-6 'Amendments to Australian Accounting Standards' amends AASB 1023 for editorial corrections made by the International Accounting Standards Board (IASB) to its Standards and Interpretations (IFRSs) and as a consequence of issuing revised AASB 101 *Presentation of Financial Statements* (September 2007). This Standard is applicable to annual reporting periods beginning on or after 1 January 2009 that end on or after 30 June 2009.

5 October 2009: Erratum makes further terminology-related and editorial changes resulting from AASB 2009-6. This erratum applies to annual reporting periods beginning on or after 1 January 2009 that end on or after 30 June 2009.

6 October 2009: AASB 1023 was reissued by the AASB, compiled to include the AASB 2007-3, AASB 2007-8, AASB 2007-10, AASB 2008-5, AASB 2009-2, AASB 2009-6 and Erratum (October 2009) amendments. This compiled Standard applies to annual reporting periods beginning on or after 1 January 2009 that end on or after 30 June 2009. Early application is permitted.

7 December 2009: AASB 2009-11 'Amendments to Australian Accounting Standards arising from AASB 9' amends AASB 1023 to give effect to consequential changes arising from the issuance of AASB 9. This Standard is applicable to annual reporting periods beginning on or after 1 January 2013 with early adoption permitted from annual reporting periods ending on or after 31 December 2009 that begin before 1 January 2013 provided AASB 9 is also applied for the same period. The application date of AASB 2009-11 has been amended to 1 January 2015 by AASB 2012-6. **These amendments have been superseded by AASB 2010-7 and are not included in this compiled Standard.**

15 December 2009: AASB 2009-12 'Amendments to Australian Accounting Standards' amends AASB 1023 for editorial corrections. This Standard is applicable to annual reporting periods beginning on or after 1 January 2011 with early adoption permitted.

27 October 2010: AASB 2010-5 'Further Amendments to Australian Accounting Standards' makes editorial amendments to AASB 1023. This Standard is applicable to annual reporting periods beginning on or after 1 January 2011.

26 November 2010: AASB 1023 was reissued by the AASB, compiled to include the AASB 2009-12 and AASB 2010-5 amendments and applies to annual reporting periods ending on or after 1 January 2011 but before 1 January 2013.

1 March 2011: AASB 2010-7 'Amendments to Australian Accounting Standards arising from AASB 9 (December 2010)' as compiled amends AASB 1023 to give effect to consequential changes arising from the reissue of AASB 9 in December 2010 and supersedes AASB 2009-11, which related to the previous version of AASB 9. This Standard applies to annual reporting periods beginning on or after 1 January 2013 and can be adopted early. The application date of AASB 2010-7 has been amended to 1 January 2015 by AASB 2012-6. **These amendments are not included in this compiled Standard.**

29 August 2011: AASB 2011-7 'Amendments to Australian Accounting Standards arising from the Consolidation and Joint Arrangements Standards' amends AASB 1023 to give effect to many consequential changes arising from the issue of AASB 10, 11, 12, 127 and 128. This Standard applies to annual reporting periods beginning on or after 1 January 2013 and can be adopted early by for-profit entities. **These amendments are not included in this compiled Standard.**

5 September 2011: AASB 2011-8 'Amendments to Australian Accounting Standards arising from AASB 13' amends AASB 1023 to give effect to a consequential change in the definition of fair value arising from the issue of AASB 13. This Standard applies to annual reporting periods beginning on or after 1 January 2013 and can be adopted early. **These amendments are not included in this compiled Standard.**

Reference

Interpretation 1047 *Professional Indemnity Claims Liabilities in Medical Defence Organisations* applies to AASB 1023.

Contents

Compilation Details

Comparison with IFRS 4

Accounting Standard
AASB 1023 General Insurance Contracts

	Paragraphs
Application	1.1 – 1.7
Scope	
General Insurance Contracts	2.1 – 2.1.5
Transactions Outside the Scope of this Standard	2.2
Embedded Derivatives	2.3.1 – 2.3.2
Deposit Components	2.4.1 – 2.4.4
Purpose of Standard	3.1
Premium Revenue	
Classification	4.1.1 – 4.1.3
Recognition	4.2 – 4.2.7
Measurement	4.3 – 4.4.12
Unclosed Business	4.5 – 4.5.2
Outstanding Claims Liability	
Recognition and Measurement	5.1 – 5.1.3
Central Estimate	5.1.4 – 5.1.5
Risk Margin	5.1.6 – 5.1.11
Expected Future Payments	5.2 – 5.2.12
Discount Rates	6.1 – 6.1.3
Unearned Premium Liability	7.1 – 7.1.1
Acquisition Costs	8.1 – 8.1.3
Liability Adequacy Test	9.1 – 9.1.6
Outwards Reinsurance Expense	10.1 – 10.1.5
Reinsurance Recoveries and Non-reinsurance Recoveries	11.1 – 11.1.3
Impairment of Reinsurance Assets	12.1.1
Portfolio Transfers and Business Combinations	13.1 – 13.3.4
Underwriting Pools and Coinsurance	14.1 – 14.2
Assets Backing General Insurance Liabilities	
Fair Value Approach	15.1.1
Measurement	15.2 – 15.5.2
Non-insurance Contracts Regulated under the *Insurance Act 1973*	16.1 – 16.2
Disclosures	
Statement of Comprehensive Income	17.1 – 17.1.2
Statement of Financial Position	17.2 – 17.3
Non-insurance Contracts	17.4 – 17.4.1
Insurance Contracts – Explanation of Recognised Amounts	17.6 – 17.6.6

	Paragraphs
Nature and Extent of Risks Arising from Insurance Contracts	17.7 – 17.7.5
Liability Adequacy Test	17.8
Other Disclosures	17.9.1
Transitional Provisions	18.1 – 18.3.1
Definitions	19.1 – 19.2

Appendix: Definition of an Insurance Contract

> Australian Accounting Standard AASB 1023 *General Insurance Contracts* (as amended) is set out in paragraphs 1.1 – 19.2 and the Appendix. All the paragraphs have equal authority. Paragraphs in **bold type** state the main principles. Terms defined in this Standard are in *italics* the first time they appear in the Standard. AASB 1023 is to be read in the context of other Australian Accounting Standards including AASB 1048 *Interpretation of Standards*, which identifies the Australian Accounting Interpretations. In the absence of explicit guidance, AASB 108 *Accounting Policies, Changes in Accounting Estimates and Errors* provides a basis for selecting and applying accounting policies.

Compilation Details

Accounting Standard AASB 1023 *General Insurance Contracts* as amended

This compiled Standard applies to annual reporting periods beginning on or after 1 January 2011 but before 1 January 2013. It takes into account amendments up to and including 27 October 2010 and was prepared on 26 November 2010 by the staff of the Australian Accounting Standards Board (AASB).

This compilation is not a separate Accounting Standard made by the AASB. Instead, it is a representation of AASB 1023 (July 2004) as amended by other Accounting Standards, which are listed in the Table below.

Table of Standards

Standard	Date made	Application date (*annual reporting periods ... on or after ...*)	Application, saving or transitional provisions
AASB 1023	15 Jul 2004	*(beginning)* 1 Jan 2005	
AASB 2005-2	3 Jun 2005	*(beginning)* 1 Jan 2005	
AASB 2005-4	9 Jun 2005	*(beginning)* 1 Jan 2006	see (a) below
AASB 2005-9	6 Sep 2005	*(beginning)* 1 Jan 2006	see (a) below
AASB 2005-10	5 Sep 2005	*(beginning)* 1 Jan 2007	see (b) below
AASB 2005-12	8 Dec 2005	*(ending)* 31 Dec 2005	see (c) below
AASB 2007-3	26 Feb 2007	*(beginning)* 1 Jan 2009	see (d) below
AASB 2007-4	30 Apr 2007	*(beginning)* 1 Jul 2007	see (e) below
AASB 2007-8	24 Sep 2007	*(beginning)* 1 Jan 2009	see (f) below
AASB 2007-10	13 Dec 2007	*(beginning)* 1 Jan 2009	see (f) below
AASB 2008-5	24 Jul 2008	*(beginning)* 1 Jan 2009	see (g) below
AASB 2009-2	22 Apr 2009	*(beginning)* 1 Jan 2009 and *(ending)* 30 Apr 2009	see (h) below
AASB 2009-6	25 Jun 2009	*(beginning)* 1 Jan 2009 and *(ending)* 30 Jun 2009	see (i) below
Erratum	5 Oct 2009	*(beginning)* 1 Jan 2009 and *(ending)* 30 Jun 2009	see (j) below

Standard	Date made	Application date *(annual reporting periods ... on or after ...)*	Application, saving or transitional provisions
AASB 2009-11	7 Dec 2009	*(beginning)* 1 Jan 2013	not compiled*
AASB 2009-12	15 Dec 2009	*(beginning)* 1 Jan 2011	see (k) below
AASB 2010-5	27 Oct 2010	*(beginning)* 1 Jan 2011	see (k) below

* The amendments made by this Standard are not included in this compilation, which presents the principal Standard as applicable to annual reporting periods beginning on or after 1 January 2011 but before 1 January 2013.

(a) Entities may elect to apply this Standard to annual reporting periods beginning on or after 1 January 2005 but before 1 January 2006.

(b) Entities may elect to apply this Standard to annual reporting periods beginning on or after 1 January 2005 but before 1 January 2007.

(c) Entities may elect to apply this Standard to annual reporting periods beginning on or after 1 January 2005 that end before 31 December 2005.

(d) Entities may elect to apply this Standard to annual reporting periods beginning on or after 1 January 2005 but before 1 January 2009, provided that AASB 8 *Operating Segments* is also applied to such periods.

(e) Entities may elect to apply this Standard to annual reporting periods beginning on or after 1 January 2005 but before 1 July 2007.

(f) Entities may elect to apply this Standard to annual reporting periods beginning on or after 1 January 2005 but before 1 January 2009, provided that AASB 101 *Presentation of Financial Statements* (September 2007) is also applied to such periods.

(g) Entities may elect to apply this Standard, or its amendments to individual Standards, to annual reporting periods beginning on or after 1 January 2005 but before 1 January 2009.

(h) Entities may elect to apply this Standard to annual reporting periods beginning on or after 1 January 2005 but before 1 January 2009 and to annual reporting periods beginning on or after 1 January 2009 that end before 30 April 2009.

(i) Entities may elect to apply this Standard to annual reporting periods beginning on or after 1 January 2005 but before 1 January 2009, provided that AASB 101 *Presentation of Financial Statements* (September 2007) is also applied to such periods, and to annual reporting periods beginning on or after 1 January 2009 that end before 30 June 2009.

(j) Entities may elect to apply this Erratum to annual reporting periods beginning on or after 1 January 2005, provided that AASB 2009-6 *Amendments to Australian Accounting Standards* is also applied to such periods.

(k) Entities may elect to apply this Standard to annual reporting periods beginning on or after 1 January 2005 but before 1 January 2011.

Table of Amendments

Paragraph affected	How affected	By ... [paragraph]
2.2	amended	AASB 2005-9 [12, 25]
	amended	AASB 2007-4 [104]
4.2.5	amended	AASB 2009-12 [19]
4.4.8	amended	AASB 2009-12 [19]
4.5.2	amended	AASB 2007-10 [95]
	amended	AASB 2009-12 [19]
5.1.10	amended	AASB 2005-2 [7]
5.2.4	amended	AASB 2009-12 [19]
6.1.3	amended	Erratum, Oct 2009 [6]
9.1	amended	AASB 2005-2 [8]
9.1.1	deleted	AASB 2005-2 [9]
9.1.2	renumbered as 9.1.1	AASB 2005-2 [10]
	added	AASB 2005-2 [11]
9.1.5	amended	AASB 2005-2 [12]
13.3.1	amended	AASB 2007-4 [104]
15.2	amended	AASB 2005-4 [21]
15.2.1	amended	AASB 2005-4 [21]

Paragraph affected	How affected	By ... [paragraph]
15.2.2	amended	AASB 2005-4 [22]
15.5	amended	AASB 2005-4 [23]
	amended	AASB 2005-12 [14]
	amended	AASB 2007-4 [104]
	amended	AASB 2008-5 [79]
15.5.2	amended	AASB 2005-4 [24]
	amended	AASB 2008-5 [79]
15.5.3	deleted	AASB 2005-12 [15]
16.1	amended	AASB 2005-4 [25]
16.1.1	amended	AASB 2005-4 [25]
17.1(a), (b) & (c)	deleted	AASB 2005-2 [13]
17.1(d)	renumbered as 17.1(a)	AASB 2005-2 [14]
17.1(e)	renumbered as 17.1(b)	AASB 2005-2 [15]
17.1(f)	amended	AASB 2005-2 [16]
	renumbered as 17.1(c)	
17.2	amended	AASB 2005-2 [17]
	amended	AASB 2007-4 [104]
17.5 (and preceding heading)	deleted	AASB 2007-3 [17]
17.5.1	deleted	AASB 2007-3 [17]
17.7 (and preceding heading)	amended	AASB 2005-10 [41]
17.7.1	amended	AASB 2005-10 [41]
	amended	AASB 2009-2 [13]
17.7.3	amended	AASB 2005-10 [42]
17.7.4	amended	AASB 2009-6 [100]
17.7.5	added	AASB 2005-10 [43]
17.8 (and preceding heading)	added	AASB 2005-2 [18]
	amended	AASB 2007-4 [104]
17.8.1	renumbered as 17.9.1	AASB 2005-2 [19]
17.9.1	amended	AASB 2005-10 [44]
18.3	amended	AASB 2005-10 [45]
19.1	amended	AASB 2007-4 [103,104]
	amended	AASB 2010-5 [61]
19.2	added	AASB 2010-5 [62]
Appendix, 1	amended	AASB 2010-5 [63]
Appendix, 8	amended	AASB 2010-5 [63]
Appendix, 17(e)	amended	AASB 2005-9 [13, 25]
Appendix, 18(e)	amended	AASB 2005-9 [14]

General Terminology Amendments

The following amendments are not shown in the above Table of Amendments:

References to 'financial report(s)' were amended to 'financial statements' by AASB 2007-8 and AASB 2007-10, except in relation to specific Corporations Act references and interim financial reports.

References to 'income statement' and 'balance sheet' were amended to 'statement of comprehensive income' and 'statement of financial position' respectively by AASB 2007-8.

References to 'reporting date' and 'each reporting date' were amended to 'end of the reporting period' and 'the end of each reporting period' respectively by AASB 2007-8.

Comparison with IFRS 4

AASB 1023 and IFRS 4

AASB 1023 *General Insurance Contracts* as amended incorporates the limited improvements to accounting for insurance contracts required by IFRS 4 *Insurance Contracts*.

General insurers applying this Standard and Australian equivalents to IFRSs will be compliant with IFRSs.

IFRS 4 is being implemented in Australia using three Accounting Standards:

(a) AASB 4 *Insurance Contracts* (the Australian equivalent to IFRS 4), which applies to fixed-fee service contracts that meet the definition of an insurance contract;

(b) AASB 1023, which applies to general insurance contracts; and

(c) AASB 1038 *Life Insurance Contracts*, which applies to life insurance contracts.

IFRS 4 applies to all insurance contracts and financial instruments with discretionary participation features, whereas AASB 1023 only applies to general insurance contracts as well as certain aspects of accounting for assets that back general insurance liabilities. Whereas IFRS 4 only includes limited improvements to accounting for insurance contracts and disclosure requirements, AASB 1023 addresses all aspects of the recognition, measurement and disclosure of general insurance contracts.

IFRS 4 allows insurers to use a practice described as "shadow accounting". The revised AASB 1023 does not allow shadow accounting.

Accounting Standard AASB 1023

The Australian Accounting Standards Board made Accounting Standard AASB 1023 *General Insurance Contracts* under section 334 of the *Corporations Act 2001* on 15 July 2004.

This compiled version of AASB 1023 applies to annual reporting periods beginning on or after 1 January 2011 but before 1 January 2013. It incorporates relevant amendments contained in other AASB Standards made by the AASB and other decisions of the AASB up to and including 27 October 2010 (see Compilation Details).

Accounting Standard AASB 1023

General Insurance Contracts

1 Application

1.1 **This Standard applies to:**

(a) **each entity that is required to prepare financial reports in accordance with Part 2M.3 of the Corporations Act and that is a reporting entity;**

(b) **general purpose financial statements of each other reporting entity; and**

(c) **financial statements that are, or are held out to be, general purpose financial statements.**

1.2 **This Standard applies to annual reporting periods beginning on or after 1 January 2005.**

[Note: For application dates of paragraphs changed or added by an amending Standard, see Compilation Details.]

1.3 **This Standard shall not be applied to annual reporting periods beginning before 1 January 2005.**

1.4 **The requirements specified in this Standard apply to the financial statements where information resulting from their application is material in accordance with AASB 1031 *Materiality*.**

1.4.1 The requirements specified in this Standard apply to the financial statements where information resulting from their application is material, in accordance with AASB 1031.

An example of the application of materiality is that disclosures about *general insurance contracts* in the context of a group that includes a *general insurer* are required where the general insurance business is material in the context of the group.

1.4.2   For the purposes of AASB 134 *Interim Financial Reporting*, the determination of the *outstanding claims liability* does not necessarily require a full actuarial valuation. In accordance with AASB 134, the outstanding claims liability would need to be determined on a reliable basis, would be based on reasonable estimates, would include a full review of all assumptions, and would not be materially different from the outstanding claims liability determined by a full actuarial valuation.

1.5   When applicable, this Standard supersedes:

    (a)   Accounting Standard AASB 1023 *Financial Reporting of General Insurance Activities* as approved by notice published in the *Commonwealth of Australia Gazette* No S 415, 6 November 1996; and

    (b)   AAS 26 *Financial Reporting of General Insurance Activities* issued in November 1996.

1.6   Both AASB 1023 (issued in November 1996) and AAS 26 remain applicable until superseded by this Standard.

1.7   Notice of this Standard was published in the *Commonwealth of Australia Gazette* No S 294, 22 July 2004.

2 Scope

General Insurance Contracts

2.1   This Standard applies to:

    (a)   general insurance contracts (including *general reinsurance contracts*) that a general insurer issues and to general reinsurance contracts that it holds;

    (b)   certain assets backing general insurance liabilities;

    (c)   *financial liabilities* and *financial assets* that arise under non-insurance contracts; and

    (d)   certain assets backing financial liabilities that arise under non-insurance contracts.

2.1.1   There are various types of *insurance contract*. This Standard deals with general insurance contracts (including general reinsurance contracts). General insurance contracts are defined as insurance contracts that are not *life insurance contracts*.

2.1.2   This Standard applies to general insurance contracts issued by Registered Health Benefits Organisations (RHBOs) registered under the *National Health Act 1953*. RHBOs apply this Standard to contracts that meet the definition of a general insurance contract and to certain assets backing general insurance liabilities.

2.1.3   For ease of reference, this Standard describes any entity that issues an insurance contract as an *insurer*, whether or not the issuer is regarded as an insurer for legal, regulatory or supervisory purposes.

2.1.4   A *reinsurance contract* is a type of insurance contract. Accordingly, all references in this Standard to insurance contracts also apply to reinsurance contracts.

2.1.5   *Weather derivatives* that meet the definition of a general insurance contract under this Standard are treated under this Standard. A contract that requires payment based on climatic, geological or other physical variables only where there is an adverse effect on the contract holder is a weather derivative that is an insurance contract. To meet the definition of a general insurance contract, the physical variable specified in the contract will be specific to a party to the contract.

Transactions Outside the Scope of this Standard

2.2 This Standard does not apply to:

(a) life insurance contracts (see AASB 1038 *Life Insurance Contracts*);

(b) product warranties issued directly by a manufacturer, dealer or retailer (see AASB 118 *Revenue* and AASB 137 *Provisions, Contingent Liabilities and Contingent Assets*);

(c) employers' assets and liabilities under employee benefit plans (see AASB 119 *Employee Benefits* and AASB 2 *Share-based Payment*) and retirement benefit obligations reported by defined benefit retirement plans (see AAS 25 *Financial Reporting by Superannuation Plans*);

(d) contingent consideration payable or receivable in a business combination (see AASB 3 *Business Combinations*);

(e) contractual rights or contractual obligations that are contingent on the future use of, or right to use, a non-financial item (for example, some license fees, royalties, contingent lease payments and similar items), as well as a lessee's residual value guarantee embedded in a finance lease (see AASB 117 *Leases*, AASB 118 and AASB 138 *Intangible Assets*);

(f) *financial guarantee contracts* unless the issuer has previously asserted explicitly that it regards such contracts as insurance contracts and has used accounting applicable to insurance contracts, in which case the issuer may elect to apply either AASB 139 *Financial Instruments: Recognition and Measurement*, AASB 132 *Financial Instruments: Presentation* and AASB 7 *Financial Instruments: Disclosures* or this Standard to such financial guarantee contracts. The issuer may make that election contract by contract, but the election for each contract is irrevocable;

(g) *direct insurance contracts* that the entity holds (that is direct insurance contracts in which the entity is a *policyholder*). However, a *cedant* shall apply this Standard to reinsurance contracts that it holds; and

(h) fixed-fee service contracts, that meet the definition of an insurance contract, if the level of service depends on an uncertain event, for example maintenance contracts or roadside assistance contracts (see AASB 4 *Insurance Contracts*).

Embedded Derivatives

2.3.1 AASB 139 requires an entity to separate some embedded derivatives from their host contract, measure them at *fair value* and include changes in their fair value in the statement of comprehensive income. AASB 139 applies to derivatives embedded in a general insurance contract unless the embedded derivative is itself a general insurance contract.

2.3.2 As an exception to the requirement in AASB 139, an insurer need not separate, and measure at fair value, a policyholder's option to surrender an insurance contract for a fixed amount (or for an amount based on a fixed amount and an interest rate) even if the exercise price differs from the carrying amount of the host *insurance liability*. However, the requirement in AASB 139 applies to a put option or cash surrender option embedded in an insurance contract if the surrender value varies in response to the change in a financial variable (such as an equity or commodity price or index), or a non-financial variable that is not specific to a party to the contract. Furthermore, that requirement also applies if the holder's ability to exercise a put option or cash surrender option is triggered by a change in such a variable (for example, a put option that can be exercised if a stock market index reaches a specified level).

Deposit Components

2.4.1 Some general insurance contracts contain both an insurance component and a *deposit component*. In some cases, an insurer is required or permitted to *unbundle* those components.

(a)   Unbundling is required if both the following conditions are met:

   (i)   the insurer can measure the deposit component (including any embedded surrender options) separately (that is, without considering the insurance component); and

   (ii)   the insurer's accounting policies do not otherwise require it to recognise all obligations and rights arising from the deposit component.

(b)   Unbundling is permitted, but not required, if the insurer can measure the deposit component separately as in paragraph 2.4.1(a)(i) but its accounting policies require it to recognise all obligations and rights arising from the deposit component, regardless of the basis used to measure those rights and obligations.

(c)   Unbundling is prohibited if an insurer cannot measure the deposit component separately as in paragraph 2.4.1(a)(i).

2.4.2   The following is an example of a case when an insurer's accounting policies do not require it to recognise all obligations arising from a deposit component. A cedant receives compensation for losses from a *reinsurer*, but the contract obliges the cedant to repay the compensation in future years. That obligation arises from a deposit component. If the cedant's accounting policies would otherwise permit it to recognise the compensation as income without recognising the resulting obligation, unbundling is required.

2.4.3   A general insurer, in considering the need to unbundle the deposit component of the general insurance contract, would consider all expected cash flows over the period of the contract and would consider the substance of the contract. For example, while some financial reinsurance contracts may require annual renewal, in substance they may be expected to be renewed for a number of years.

2.4.4   To unbundle a general insurance contract, an insurer shall:

(a)   apply this Standard to the insurance component; and

(b)   apply AASB 139 to the deposit component. When applying AASB 139, an insurer shall designate the deposit component as "at fair value through profit or loss", on first application of this Standard or on initial recognition of the deposit component.

3 Purpose of Standard

3.1   The purpose of this Standard is to:

(a)   specify the manner of accounting for general insurance contracts consistent with AASB 4;

(b)   specify certain aspects of accounting for assets backing general insurance liabilities;

(c)   specify certain aspects of accounting for non-insurance contracts; and

(d)   require disclosure of information relating to general insurance contracts.

4 Premium Revenue

Classification

4.1.1   *Premium* revenue comprises:

(a)   premiums from direct business, that is, premiums paid by a policyholder (that is neither an insurer nor reinsurer) to a general insurer; and

(b)   premiums from reinsurance business, that is, premiums received by a reinsurer from an insurer or from another reinsurer.

4.1.2   Premiums from direct business arise from contracts when a policyholder transfers significant *insurance risk* to an insurer.

4.1.3   Premiums from reinsurance business arise from contracts when an insurer or reinsurer transfers significant insurance risk to another reinsurer.

AASB

Recognition

4.2 **Premium revenue shall be recognised from the *attachment date* as soon as there is a basis on which it can be reliably estimated.**

4.2.1 The amount of premium is determined by a general insurer or reinsurer so as to cover anticipated *claims*, reinsurance premiums, administrative, acquisition and other costs, and a profit component (having regard to expected income from the investment of premiums). The amounts collected in respect of these components are income of an insurer on the basis that they are collected in consideration for the insurer rendering services by indemnifying those insured against specified losses.

4.2.2 For certain classes of general insurance business, government authorities may require the payment of levies and charges. For example, workers' compensation insurance levies, annual licence fees and fire brigade charges may apply. Such levies and charges are expenses of the insurer, rather than government charges directly upon those insured. The insurer is not acting simply as a collector of these levies and charges. Although not compelled to collect these amounts from those insured, the insurer is entitled to include in premiums an amount to cover the estimated amount of the levies and charges. The insurer is usually responsible for paying the levies and charges at a later date. The amount paid by the insurer does not depend on the amounts collected from those insured in relation to the levies and charges. Therefore, the amounts collected to meet levies and charges are income of the insurer. The insurer accrues for all levies and charges expected under the general insurance contracts written in the period.

4.2.3 In most States, stamp duty is charged on individual general insurance contracts and is separately identified by insurers on policy documents. The insurer is normally required to collect and pass on to the government an equivalent amount. Because such stamp duty is a tax collected on behalf of a third party and there is no choice on the part of the insurer but to collect the duty from the insured, it is not income of the insurer. Similarly, Goods and Services Tax (GST) is not income of the insurer.

4.2.4 Premium revenue needs to be recognised from the date of the attachment of risk in relation to each general insurance contract because insurers earn premium revenue by assuming insurance risks from that date on behalf of those insured. However, for reasons of practicality, many general insurers use bases of recognition that attempt to approximate this date. Such bases are acceptable provided that they do not result in the recognition of a materially different amount of premium revenue in a particular reporting period than would be the case if recognition occurred from the date of attachment of risk for each general insurance contract.

4.2.5 In recognising premium from the attachment date, an insurer may recognise premiums relating to general insurance contracts when the contract period commences after the reporting period, commonly referred to as premiums in advance. The attachment date is the date from which an insurer accepts risk. An insurer may accept risk prior to the date a contract commences: for example, it is not unusual for insurers to issue renewals, and for renewals to be paid for by policyholders, prior to the commencement date of an insurance contract. For commercial lines insurance, where the policyholder may be using the services of an insurance broker, the renewal terms could be agreed by both the insurer and policyholder prior to the commencement date and before the policyholder has paid the premium. In this situation, there may also have been a transfer of risk. As premiums in advance relate entirely to insurance cover to be provided in a future period, premiums in advance are recognised as part of the unearned premium liability. Premiums in advance are considered as part of the *liability adequacy test* required by section 9.

Reinsurance premiums

4.2.6 From the perspective of the reinsurer, reinsurance premiums accepted are akin to premiums accepted by a direct insurer. The reinsurer recognises *inwards reinsurance* premiums ceded to it as revenue in the same way as a direct insurer treats the acceptance of direct premiums as revenue.

4.2.7 Premiums accepted by the reinsurer are recognised from the attachment date, that is, the date from which the reinsurer bears its proportion of the relevant risks underwritten by the cedant. Reinsurers usually use bases of recognition that approximate the dates of bearing the risks. For example, the reinsurer may assume that its acceptance of risks occurs from the middle of the period for which the aggregate ceded premiums are advised by the cedant. This approach is acceptable provided that the premiums received or receivable in respect of the reporting period are recognised in that period, whether or not the periodic advice from the cedant has been received.

Measurement

4.3   Premium revenue shall be recognised in the statement of comprehensive income from the attachment date:

(a)   over the period of the general insurance contract for direct business; or

(b)   over the period of indemnity for reinsurance business;

in accordance with the pattern of the incidence of risk expected under the general insurance contract.

4.4   In the case of business where the premium is subject to later adjustment, the adjusted premium shall be used, where possible, as the basis for recognising premium revenue. Where this is not possible, the *deposit premium*, adjusted for any other relevant information, shall be recognised as the premium revenue, provided that it is expected that this amount will not be materially different from the actual amount of premium.

4.4.1   Premium revenue is recognised in the statement of comprehensive income when it has been earned. An insurance contract involves the transfer of significant insurance risk. The insurer estimates the pattern of the incidence of risk over the period of the contract for direct business, or over the period of indemnity for reinsurance business, and the premium revenue is recognised in accordance with this pattern. This results in the allocation of the premium revenue and the *claims incurred* expense and hence the gross underwriting result over the period of the contract for direct business, or over the period of indemnity for reinsurance business, in accordance with the pattern of the incidence of risk.

4.4.2   Measuring premium revenue involves the following steps:

(a)   estimating the total amount of premium revenue expected under the contract;

(b)   estimating the total amount of *claims expenses* expected under the contract and estimating when the claims are expected to arise;

(c)   estimating the pattern of the incidence of risk from the result of (b); and

(d)   recognising the premium revenue under the contract identified in (a) when it will be earned, that is, in accordance with the pattern of the incidence of risk determined in (c).

4.4.3   For some general insurance contracts, especially complex multi-year reinsurance contracts, these estimations involve the use of significant judgement. The estimates are reassessed at the end of each reporting period. This prospective estimate of all of the income and expenses expected under the contract is also necessary for the purposes of the liability adequacy test. Refer to section 9.

Direct business

4.4.4   For most direct general insurance contracts the specified period of the contract is one year. For many direct insurance contracts the pattern of the incidence of risk will be linear, that is, the risk of events occurring that will give rise to claims is evenly spread throughout the contract period. For these contracts the premium revenue will be earned evenly over the period of the contract. However, for some direct insurance contracts the risk of events occurring that will give rise to claims is not evenly spread throughout the contract. For example, with motor insurance contracts, the risk of events occurring that will give rise to claims may be subject to seasonal factors.

4.4.5   Insurers estimate the pattern of the incidence of risk expected under the general insurance contracts from the attachment date. An insurer may be able to reliably estimate the pattern for a particular type of insurance business based upon past experience. However, when there have been changes in the nature of the cover provided, or, when there has been a change in loss experience, the insurer reflects this in the estimations.

Reinsurance business

4.4.6 Reinsurers recognise reinsurance premiums over the period of indemnity provided by the reinsurance contract in accordance with the pattern of the incidence of risk. For a typical twelve-month proportional treaty, such as a quota share treaty, written on a "risks attaching basis", the period of indemnity will be twenty-four months, as the proportional treaty will indemnify the direct insurer (or, for retrocession, the reinsurer) for losses arising under direct policies written during the twelve-month contract period. Hence, an underlying annual direct contract written on the last day of the reinsurance contract has twelve months of insurance cover beyond the last day of the reinsurance contract. The reinsurer estimates the pattern of the incidence of risk over the twenty-four-month indemnity period.

4.4.7 The reinsurer may be able to reliably estimate the pattern for a particular type of reinsurance business based upon past experience. The reinsurer is likely to seek information from the cedant to estimate the pattern of the incidence of loss expected. When there have been changes in the nature of the cover provided or when there has been a change in loss experience the insurer will need to reflect this in the estimations.

4.4.8 To determine the pattern of the incidence of risk, reinsurers first determine the total reinsurance premiums expected under the contract. The premiums receivable under reinsurance treaties often depend on the volume of business written by the cedant after the reporting period but before the treaty expiry date. This is always true of proportional (quota share and surplus) treaties that span the end of the reporting period, and is often true of non-proportional treaties. For such treaties, to estimate the total premium revenue expected under the reinsurance contract, the reinsurer estimates the inwards reinsurance premium it will receive under the contract by estimating the gross premium revenue that the cedant is likely to receive. The reinsurer is likely to estimate this by communicating with the cedant, and by reviewing past experience.

4.4.9 For a typical non-proportional treaty, such as an excess of loss treaty, the period of indemnity is usually the same as the contract period. For example, an excess of loss treaty could indemnify a cedant for all claims incurred above the excess (either individual claims or in aggregate) during the contract period, or for all claims made during the contract period. For some of these contracts the pattern of the incidence of risk is likely to be linear and hence for these contracts the premium revenue expected under the contract is earned evenly over the contract period.

4.4.10 With a non-proportional treaty the reinsurer estimates the total liabilities that are likely to arise under the underlying insurance contracts to enable an estimation of the total inwards reinsurance premium revenue expected under the contract. Where relevant, the reinsurer estimates whether the cedant is likely to want to reinstate the contract, in which case the reinsurer considers the additional reinstatement premiums it is expected to receive and the extent that they may have been earned at the end of the reporting period. A reinsurer liaises closely with the cedant, reviews any market information on significant losses or events that may have arisen, for example a hailstorm or earthquake, and reviews past experience.

4.4.11 Some reinsurance contracts might involve an experience account. Whilst such contracts may require annual renewal, in substance the contract period is likely to be greater than one year. In estimating the total inwards reinsurance premium expected under the contract and in estimating the total reinsurance claims, to determine the pattern of the incidence of risk, the reinsurer considers the probability-weighted expected cash flows over the expected period of the contract, and discounts these cash flows to reflect the time value of money. Section 6 discusses the determination of discount rates. In determining the expected cash flows, the reinsurer considers any cash flows such as profit commissions and commission rebates.

Adjusted premiums

4.4.12 For some classes of insurance it is usual for the premium to be adjusted as a result of events and information that only become known during or after the insurance contract period. For example, marine cargo insurance is a type of "adjustable" business for which a deposit premium is paid at the beginning of the contract period and subsequently adjusted on the basis of a cargo declaration.

Unclosed Business

4.5   Premium revenue relating to unclosed business shall be recognised in accordance with paragraphs 4.2, 4.3 and 4.4.

4.5.1   Frequently, there is insufficient information available at the end of a reporting period to enable a general insurer to accurately identify the business written close to the end of the reporting period for which the date of attachment of risk is prior to the end of the reporting period. This is often referred to as unclosed business. Consistent with the principle stated in paragraph 4.2, that premium revenue is to be recognised from the attachment date, all unclosed business is estimated and the premium relating to unclosed business included in premium revenue.

4.5.2   Estimates of the amount of unclosed business can be made using information from prior periods adjusted for the impact of recent trends and events. In addition, information about unclosed business may become available after the reporting period and before the financial statements are authorised for issue and may enable more reliable estimates to be made.

5 Outstanding Claims Liability

Recognition and Measurement

5.1   An outstanding claims liability shall be recognised in respect of direct business and reinsurance business and shall be measured as the central estimate of the present value of the expected future payments for claims incurred with an additional risk margin to allow for the inherent uncertainty in the central estimate.

5.1.1   The recognition and measurement approach requires estimation of the probability-weighted expected cost (discounted to a present value) of settling claims incurred, and the addition of a risk margin to reflect inherent uncertainty in the central estimate.

5.1.2   The longer the expected period from the end of the reporting period to settlement, the more likely it is that the ultimate cost of settlement will be affected by inflationary factors likely to occur during the period to settlement. These factors include changes in specific price levels, for example, trends in average periods of incapacity and in the amounts of court awards for successful claims. For claims expected to be settled within one year of the end of the reporting period, the impact of inflationary factors might not be material.

5.1.3   For claims expected to be settled within one year of the end of the reporting period, where the amount of the expected future payments does not differ materially from the present value of those payments, insurers would not need to discount the expected future payments.

Central Estimate

5.1.4   In estimating the outstanding claims liability, a central estimate is adopted. If all the possible values of the outstanding claims liability are expressed as a statistical distribution, the central estimate is the mean of that distribution.

5.1.5   In estimating the outstanding claims liability, an insurer may make use of case estimates of individual reported claims that remain unsettled at the end of the reporting period. An insurer may base case estimates on the most likely claim costs. Where the range in potential outcomes is small, the likely cost may be close to the mean cost. However, where the potential range in outcomes is large and where the probability distribution may be highly skewed, the most likely cost, or the mode, could be below the mean and hence below the central estimate. In this situation, the insurer would need to increase the case estimates accordingly to ensure that they represent the central estimate.

Risk Margin

5.1.6   The outstanding claims liability includes, in addition to the central estimate of the present value of the expected future payments, a risk margin that relates to the inherent uncertainty in the central estimate of the present value of the expected future payments.

5.1.7   Risk margins are determined on a basis that reflects the insurer's business. Regard is had to the robustness of the valuation models, the reliability and volume of available data, past experience of the insurer and the industry and the characteristics of the classes of business written.

5.1.8 The risk margin is applied to the net outstanding claims for the entity as a whole. The overall net uncertainty has regard to:

(a) the uncertainty in the gross outstanding claims liability;

(b) the effect of reinsurance on (a); and

(c) the uncertainty in reinsurance and other recoveries due.

5.1.9 In practice, however, outstanding claims liabilities are often estimated on a class-by-class basis, including an assessment of the uncertainty in each class and the determination of a risk margin by class of business. When these estimates are combined for all classes, the central estimates are combined, however the risk margin for all classes when aggregated may be determined by some insurers to be less than the sum of the individual risk margins. The extent of the difference that some insurers may decide to recognise is likely to depend upon the degree of diversification between the different classes and the degree of correlation between the experiences of these classes.

5.1.10 For the purposes of the liability adequacy test, required by section 9, the risk margin for the entity as a whole is apportioned across portfolios of contracts that are subject to broadly similar risks and are managed together as a single portfolio.

5.1.11 Risk margins adopted for regulatory purposes may be appropriate risk margins for the purposes of this Standard, or they may be an appropriate starting point in determining such risk margins.

Expected Future Payments

5.2 The expected future payments shall include:

(a) amounts in relation to unpaid reported claims;

(b) claims incurred but not reported (IBNR);

(c) claims incurred but not enough reported (IBNER); and

(d) costs, including claims handling costs, which the insurer expects to incur in settling these incurred claims.

5.2.1 It is important to identify the components of the ultimate cost to an insurer of settling incurred claims, for the purposes of determining the claims expense for the reporting period and determining the outstanding claims liability as at the end of the reporting period. These components comprise the policy benefit amounts required to be paid to or on behalf of those insured, and claims handling costs, that is, costs associated with achieving settlements with those insured. Claims handling costs include costs that can be associated directly with individual claims, such as legal and other professional fees, and costs that can only be indirectly associated with individual claims, such as claims administration costs.

5.2.2 Policy benefit amounts and direct claims handling costs are expenses of an insurer, representing the consumption or loss of economic benefits. The outstanding claims liability includes unpaid policy benefits and direct claims handling costs relating to claims arising during current and prior reporting periods, as they are outgoings that an insurer is presently obliged to meet as a result of past events.

5.2.3 Indirect claims handling costs incurred during the reporting period are also expenses of an insurer, and include a portion of the indirect claims handling costs to be paid in the future, being that portion which relates to handling claims incurred during the reporting period. The outstanding claims liability includes these unpaid indirect claims handling costs.

5.2.4 It is important to ensure that claims are recognised as expenses and liabilities for the correct reporting period. For contracts written on a claims incurred basis, claims arise from *insured events* that occur during the insurance contract period. Some events will occur and give rise to claims that are reported to the insurer and settled within the same reporting period. Other reported claims may be unsettled at the end of a particular reporting period. In addition, there may be events that give rise to claims that, at the end of a reporting period, have yet to be reported to the insurer. The latter are termed claims incurred but not reported (IBNR claims). The insurer also considers the need to recognise a liability for claims that may be re-opened after the reporting period.

5.2.5   For contracts written on a claims made basis, claims arise in respect of claims reported during the insurance contract period. The insured event that gave rise to the claim could have occurred in a previous period. While claims made insurance contracts should theoretically only give rise to outstanding claims liabilities and IBNER claims (see paragraph 5.2.10), as claims cannot be incurred but not reported under such a contract, this may not be the case for reinsurers. A reinsurer may have reinsured a claims made contract on a claims incurred basis. In this case whilst a loss or other event would be reported to the direct insurer during the period of insurance to generate a valid claim, the reinsurer may not have received information about the claim but would have an IBNR liability. Similarly, a reinsurer may have issued a claims made reinsurance contract but may need to consider that not all notices of claims may have been reported by the direct insurer. Insurers and reinsurers should also consider court rulings that may impact on the way claims made contracts are interpreted.

5.2.6   Claims arising from events that occur during a reporting period and which are settled during that same period are expenses of that period. In addition, a liability and corresponding expense is recognised for reported claims arising from events of the reporting period that have yet to be settled. This involves a process of estimation that includes assessment of individual claims and past claims experience.

5.2.7   When, based on knowledge of the business, IBNR claims are expected to exist, an estimate is made of the amount of the claims that will arise therefrom. This involves recognition of a liability and corresponding expense for the reporting period. As in the case of reported but unsettled claims, an estimate of the amount of the current claims incurred but not reported is based on past experience and takes into account any changes in circumstances, such as recent catastrophic events that may have occurred during the reporting period and changes in the volume or mix of insurance contracts underwritten, that may affect the pattern of unreported claims.

5.2.8   Some insurers use estimations or formulae, related to the amount of outstanding claims and based on the past experience of the insurer and the industry, to arrive at an estimate of direct and indirect claims handling costs.

5.2.9   Claims expense and the outstanding claims liability are adjusted on the basis of information, including re-opened claims, that becomes available after the initial recognition of claims, to enable the insurer to make a more accurate estimate of the ultimate cost of settlement. This is often referred to as claims development. As is the case with other liabilities, the effect of the adjustments to the liability for outstanding claims and to claims expense is recognised in the statement of comprehensive income when the information becomes available.

5.2.10   Where further information becomes available about reported claims and reveals that the ultimate cost of settling claims has been under-estimated, the upwards adjustment to claims expense and to the liability for outstanding claims is often referred to as claims incurred but not enough reported (IBNER claims). Where further information reveals that the ultimate cost of settling claims has been over-estimated, the adjustment is sometimes referred to as negative IBNER claims.

5.2.11   Appropriate allowance is made for *future claim* cost escalation when determining the central estimate of the present value of the expected future payments. Future claims payments may increase over current levels as a result of wage or price inflation, and as a result of superimposed inflation (cost increases) due to court awards, environmental factors or economic or other causes.

5.2.12   With inwards reinsurance claims the reinsurer will receive periodic advices from each cedant. These may include aggregate information relating to the claims liability. The reinsurer measures its outstanding claims liability on the basis of this information and its past experience of the claims payments made under reinsurance arrangements. The reinsurer also considers market knowledge of losses and other events such as hailstorms or earthquakes.

6 Discount Rates

6.1 The outstanding claims liability shall be discounted for the time value of money using risk-free discount rates that are based on current observable, objective rates that relate to the nature, structure and term of the future obligations.

6.1.1 The discount rates adopted are not intended to reflect risks inherent in the liability cash flows, which might be allowed for by a reduction in the discount rate in a fair value measurement, nor are they intended to reflect the insurance and other non-financial risks and uncertainties reflected in the outstanding claims liability. The discount rates are not intended to include allowance for the cost of any options or guarantees that are separately measured within the outstanding claims liability.

6.1.2 Typically, government bond rates may be appropriate discount rates for the purposes of this Standard, or they may be an appropriate starting point in determining such discount rates.

6.1.3 The portion of the increase in the liability for outstanding claims from the end of the previous reporting period to the end of the current reporting period which is due to discounted claims not yet settled being one period closer to settlement, ought, conceptually, to be recognised as interest expense of the current reporting period. However, it is considered that the costs of distinguishing this component of the increase in the outstanding claims liability exceed the benefits that may be gained from its disclosure. Thus, such increase is included in claims expense for the current reporting period.

7 Unearned Premium Liability

7.1 Premium that has not been recognised in the statement of comprehensive income is premium that is unearned and shall be recognised in the statement of financial position as an unearned premium liability.

7.1.1 The unearned premium liability is to meet the costs, including the claims handling costs, of future claims that will arise under current general insurance contracts and the deferred acquisition costs that will be recognised as an expense in the statement of comprehensive income in future reporting periods.

8 Acquisition Costs

8.1 Acquisition costs incurred in obtaining and recording general insurance contracts shall be deferred and recognised as assets where they can be reliably measured and where it is probable that they will give rise to premium revenue that will be recognised in the statement of comprehensive income in subsequent reporting periods. Deferred acquisition costs shall be amortised systematically in accordance with the expected pattern of the incidence of risk under the related general insurance contracts.

8.1.1 Acquisition costs are incurred in obtaining and recording general insurance contracts. They include commission or brokerage paid to agents or brokers for obtaining business for the insurer, selling and underwriting costs such as advertising and risk assessment, the administrative costs of recording policy information and premium collection costs.

8.1.2 Because such costs are usually incurred at acquisition whilst the pattern of earnings occurs throughout the contract periods, which may extend beyond the end of the reporting period, those acquisition costs which lead to obtaining future benefits for the insurer are recognised as assets.

8.1.3 For an asset to be recognised, it will be probable that the future economic benefits will eventuate, and that it possesses a cost or other value that can be measured reliably. Direct acquisition costs such as commission or brokerage are readily measurable. However, it may be difficult to reliably measure indirect costs that give rise to premium revenue, such as administration costs, because it is difficult to associate them with particular insurance contracts.

9 Liability Adequacy Test

9.1 The adequacy of the unearned premium liability shall be assessed by considering current estimates of the present value of the expected future cash flows relating to

future claims arising from the rights and obligations under current general insurance contracts. If the present value of the expected future cash flows relating to future claims arising from the rights and obligations under current general insurance contracts, plus an additional risk margin to reflect the inherent uncertainty in the central estimate, exceed the unearned premium liability less related intangible assets and related deferred acquisition costs, then the unearned premium liability is deficient. The entire deficiency shall be recognised in the statement of comprehensive income. In recognising the deficiency in the statement of comprehensive income the insurer shall first write-down any related intangible assets and then the related deferred acquisition costs. If an additional liability is required this shall be recognised in the statement of financial position as an unexpired risk liability. The liability adequacy test for the unearned premium liability shall be performed at the level of a portfolio of contracts that are subject to broadly similar risks and are managed together as a single portfolio.

9.1.1 In determining the present value of the expected future cash flows relating to future claims arising from the rights and obligations under current general insurance contracts, the insurer applies sections 5 and 6 and includes an appropriate risk margin to reflect inherent uncertainty in the central estimate, as set out in paragraphs 5.1.6 to 5.1.11.

9.1.2 Whilst the probability of adequacy adopted in performing the liability adequacy test may be the same or similar to the probability of adequacy adopted in determining the outstanding claims liability, this Standard does not require the same or similar probabilities of adequacy. However, the users of financial statements need to be presented with information explaining any differences in probabilities of adequacy adopted, and insurers are required to disclose the reasons for any differences in accordance with paragraph 17.8(e).

9.1.3 The unearned premium liability may include premiums in advance as described in paragraph 4.2.5. Insurers also consider whether there are any additional general insurance contracts, where the premium revenue is not recognised in the unearned premium liability, under which the insurer has a constructive obligation to settle future claims that may arise. That is, there may be general insurance contracts where there has not been a transfer of risk, as described in paragraph 4.2.5, but where a constructive obligation has arisen. The cash flows expected under these contracts are considered as part of the liability adequacy test.

9.1.4 In reviewing expected future cash flows, the insurer takes into account both future cash flows under insurance contracts it has issued and the related reinsurance.

9.1.5 The related intangible assets referred to in paragraph 9.1 are those that arise under paragraph 13.3.1(b). As the liability adequacy test for the unearned premium liability is performed at the level of portfolios of contracts that are subject to broadly similar risks and are managed together as a single portfolio, the intangible asset is allocated on a reasonable basis across these portfolios.

9.1.6 As the liability adequacy test applies to deferred acquisition costs and to intangible assets, these assets are excluded from the scope of AASB 136 *Impairment of Assets*.

10 Outwards Reinsurance Expense

10.1 **Premium ceded to reinsurers shall be recognised by the cedant as outwards reinsurance expense in the statement of comprehensive income from the attachment date over the period of indemnity of the reinsurance contract in accordance with the expected pattern of the incidence of risk.**

10.1.1 It is common for general insurers or reinsurers to reinsure a portion of the risks that they accept. To secure reinsurance cover, the cedant passes on a portion of the premiums received to a reinsurer. This is known as outwards reinsurance expense.

10.1.2 The cedant accounts for direct insurance and reinsurance transactions on a gross basis, so that the extent and effectiveness of the reinsurance arrangements are apparent to the users of the financial statements, and an indication of the insurer's risk management performance is provided to users. The gross amount of premiums earned by the cedant during the reporting period is recognised as income because it undertakes to indemnify the full amount of the specified losses of those it has insured, regardless of the reinsurance arrangements. Correspondingly, the cedant recognises the gross amount of claims expense in the reporting period because it is obliged to meet the full cost of successful claims by those it has insured.

10.1.3 Accordingly, premium ceded to reinsurers is recognised in the statement of comprehensive income as an expense of the cedant on the basis that it is an outgoing incurred in undertaking the business of direct insurance underwriting, and is not to be netted off against premium revenue.

10.1.4 Outwards reinsurance expense is recognised in the statement of comprehensive income consistently with the recognition of reinsurance recoveries under the reinsurance contract. For proportional reinsurance the estimate of outwards reinsurance expense is based upon the gross premium of the underlying direct insurance contract. For non-proportional reinsurance the cedant estimates the total claims that are likely to be made under the contract and hence whether it needs to recognise additional outwards reinsurance expense under a minimum and deposit arrangement or whether it needs to recognise reinstatement premiums expense.

10.1.5 Some reinsurance contracts purchased by a cedant might involve an experience account. Whilst these contracts may require annual renewal, in substance, the contract period is likely to be greater than one year. In estimating the outwards reinsurance expense and reinsurance recoveries to be recognised in the reporting period the cedant considers the probability-weighted expected cash flows over the expected period of indemnity and discounts the cash flows to reflect the time value of money. In determining the discount rates to be adopted, an insurer applies the same principles that are used to determine the discount rates for outstanding claims liabilities outlined in section 6. In considering all expected cash flows the reinsurer considers any profit commissions and commission rebates.

11 Reinsurance Recoveries and Non-reinsurance Recoveries

11.1 Reinsurance recoveries received or receivable in relation to the outstanding claims liability and non-reinsurance recoveries received or receivable shall be recognised as income of the cedant and shall not be netted off against the claims expense or outwards reinsurance expense in the statement of comprehensive income, or the outstanding claims liability or unearned premium liability in the statement of financial position.

11.1.1 The reinsurance recoveries receivable in the statement of financial position may not be received for some time. The reinsurance recoveries receivable are discounted on a basis consistent with the discounting of the outstanding claims liabilities outlined in section 6.

11.1.2 An insurer may also be entitled to non-reinsurance recoveries under the insurance contract such as salvage, subrogation and sharing arrangements with other insurers. Non-reinsurance recoveries are not offset against gross claims, but are recognised as income or assets, in the same way as, but separately from, reinsurance recoveries. The non-reinsurance recoveries receivable in the statement of financial position may not be received for some time. The non-reinsurance recoveries receivable are discounted on a basis consistent with the discounting of the outstanding claims liabilities outlined in section 6.

11.1.3 Amounts that reduce the liability to the policyholder, such as excesses or allowances for contributory negligence, are not non-reinsurance recoveries and are offset against the gross claims.

12 Impairment of Reinsurance Assets

12.1.1 If a cedant's *reinsurance asset* is impaired, the cedant shall reduce its carrying amount accordingly and recognise that impairment in the statement of comprehensive income. A reinsurance asset is impaired if, and only if:

(a)   there is objective evidence, as a result of an event that occurred after initial recognition of the reinsurance asset, that the cedant may not receive amounts due to it under the terms of the contract; and

(b)   that event has a reliably measurable impact on the amounts that the cedant will
       receive from the reinsurer.

13 Portfolio Transfers and Business Combinations

**13.1   Where the responsibility in relation to claims on transferred insurance business
         remains with the transferring insurer, the transfer shall be treated by the transferring
         insurer and the accepting insurer as reinsurance business.**

13.1.1 Portfolio transfer is a term used to describe the process by which premiums and claims are
        transferred from one insurer to another. Transfers may be completed in a number of ways
        in relation to claims arising from events that occurred before the transfer. The receiving
        insurer may take responsibility in relation to all claims under the agreement or treaty that
        have not yet been paid, or it may take responsibility only in relation to those claims arising
        from events that occur after the date of transfer.

13.1.2 In relation to the transfer of insurance business, while the acquiring insurer agrees to meet
        the claims of those insured from a particular time, the contractual responsibility of the
        original insurer to meet those claims normally remains.

13.1.3 In relation to the withdrawal of a reinsurer from a reinsurance treaty arrangement, the
        contractual responsibility of the reinsurer to the direct insurer in relation to outstanding
        claims may be passed back to the direct insurer with a return of any premium relating
        to unexpired risk, or may be retained by the withdrawing reinsurer. In the former case,
        the direct insurer may choose to reinsure the outstanding claims with another reinsurer.
        This assuming reinsurer would be ceded premium for bearing liability in relation to
        existing outstanding claims.

13.1.4 Where the responsibility in relation to claims on transferred insurance business remains
        with the transferring insurer:

(a)   the transferring insurer recognises the transferred premium revenue and the relevant
       outstanding claims in the same way as other outwards reinsurance business; and

(b)   the accepting insurer recognises the premium revenue ceded to it and the relevant
       outstanding claims in the same way as other inwards reinsurance business.

**13.2   Where the responsibility in relation to claims on transferred insurance business
         passes from the transferring insurer to the accepting insurer, the transfer shall be
         accounted for as a portfolio withdrawal by the transferring insurer and as a portfolio
         assumption by the accepting insurer.**

**13.3   A portfolio withdrawal shall be accounted for by the transferring insurer by
         eliminating the liabilities and assets connected with the risks transferred. A portfolio
         assumption shall be accounted for by the accepting insurer by recognising the
         relevant amount of unexpired premium revenue and the outstanding claims for
         which the transferring insurer is no longer responsible.**

13.3.1 To comply with AASB 3, an insurer shall, at the acquisition date, measure at fair value
        the insurance liabilities assumed and *insurance assets* acquired in a business combination.
        However, an insurer is permitted, but not required, to use an expanded presentation that
        splits the fair value of acquired insurance contracts into two components:

(a)   a liability measured in accordance with the insurer's accounting policies for general
       insurance contracts that it issues; and

(b)   an intangible asset, representing the difference between:

  (i)   the fair value of the contractual insurance rights acquired and insurance
         obligations assumed; and

  (ii)   the amount described in paragraph 13.3.1(a).

         The subsequent measurement of this asset shall be consistent with the
         measurement of the related insurance liability.

13.3.2 An insurer acquiring a portfolio of general insurance contracts may use an expanded
        presentation described in paragraph 13.3.1.

13.3.3 The intangible assets described in paragraphs 13.3.1 and 13.3.2 are excluded from the scope of AASB 136 and from the scope of AASB 138 in respect of recognition and measurement. AASB 136 and AASB 138 apply to customer lists and customer relationships reflecting the expectation of future contracts that are not part of the contractual insurance rights and contractual insurance obligations that existed at the date of a business combination or portfolio transfer.

13.3.4 AASB 138 includes specific disclosure requirements in relation to this intangible asset.

14 Underwriting Pools and Coinsurance

14.1 Insurance business allocated through underwriting pools and coinsurance arrangements, by an entity acting as agent, shall be accounted for by the accepting insurer as direct insurance business.

14.1.1 Direct insurers or reinsurers may form underwriting pools or enter coinsurance arrangements as vehicles for jointly insuring particular risks or types of risks. Premiums, claims and other expenses are usually shared in agreed ratios by insurers involved in these arrangements.

14.1.2 Many underwriting pools and coinsurance arrangements involve the acceptance of risks by an entity acting as an agent for pool members or coinsurers. The entity receives premiums and pays claims and expenses, and allocates shares of the business to each pool member or coinsurer in agreed ratios. As the entity acting as agent is not an insurer, the business allocated to pool members and coinsurers is not reinsurance business. Pool members and coinsurers treat such business allocated to them as direct insurance business.

14.2 Business directly underwritten by a member of an underwriting pool or coinsurance arrangement shall be treated as direct insurance business and the portion of the risk reinsured by other pool members or coinsurers, determined by reference to the extent of the shares in the pool or arrangement of other pool members or coinsurers, shall be treated as outwards reinsurance. The pool member's or coinsurer's share of insurance business that other insurers place in the pool or arrangement shall be treated as inwards reinsurance.

15 Assets Backing General Insurance Liabilities

Fair Value Approach

15.1.1 Paragraphs 15.2 to 15.5 address the measurement of certain assets backing general insurance liabilities or financial liabilities that arise under non-insurance contracts. The fair value approach to the measurement of assets backing general insurance liabilities or financial liabilities that arise under non-insurance contracts is consistent with the present value measurement approach for general insurance liabilities, and the fair value measurement for financial liabilities that arise under non-insurance contracts, required by this Standard. Where assets are not backing general insurance liabilities or financial liabilities that arise under non-insurance contracts, general insurers apply the applicable accounting standards making use of any measurement choices available.

Measurement

15.2 Financial assets that:

    (a)   **are within the scope of AASB 139;**

    (b)   **back general insurance liabilities; and**

    (c)   **are permitted to be designated as "at fair value through profit or loss" under AASB 139;**

shall be designated as "at fair value through profit or loss" under AASB 139 on first application of this Standard, or on initial recognition.

15.2.1 An insurer applies AASB 139 to its financial assets. Under AASB 139 a financial asset at fair value through profit or loss is a financial asset that meets either of the following conditions:

    (a)   it is classified as held for trading; or

(b)   it is designated as "at fair value through profit or loss" upon initial recognition. An entity may use this designation when it is a contract with an embedded derivative and paragraph 11A of AASB 139 allows the entity to measure the contract as "at fair value through profit or loss"; or when doing so results in more relevant information, because either:

        (i)   it eliminates or significantly reduces a measurement or recognition inconsistency (sometimes referred to as 'an accounting mismatch') that would otherwise arise from measuring assets or liabilities or recognising the gains and losses on them on different bases; or

        (ii)   a group of financial assets, financial liabilities or both is managed and its performance is evaluated on a fair value basis, in accordance with a documented risk management or investment strategy, and information about the group is provided internally on that basis to the entity's key management personnel (as defined in AASB 124 *Related Party Disclosures*), for example the entity's board of directors and chief executive officer.

AASB 1 *First-time Adoption of Australian Accounting Standards* permits entities to designate financial assets as "at fair value through profit or loss" on first application of the Standard.

15.2.2 The view adopted in this Standard is that financial assets, within the scope of AASB 139 that back general insurance liabilities, are permitted to be measured at fair value through profit or loss under AASB 139. This is because the measurement of general insurance liabilities under this Standard incorporates current information and measuring the financial assets backing these general insurance liabilities at fair value, eliminates or significantly reduces a potential measurement inconsistency which would arise if the assets were classified as available for sale or measured at amortised cost.

15.3   Investment property within the scope of AASB 140 *Investment Property* and that backs general insurance liabilities shall be measured using the fair value model under AASB 140.

15.4   Property, plant and equipment that is within the scope of AASB 116 *Property, Plant and Equipment* and that backs general insurance liabilities, shall be measured using the revaluation model under AASB 116.

15.4.1 An insurer applies AASB 116 to its property, plant and equipment. Under AASB 116 property includes owner-occupied property and property being constructed or developed for future use as investment property. Under AASB 116, the cost model, for measurement subsequent to initial recognition, is to carry property, plant and equipment at cost. However, AASB 116 also has a revaluation model: an entity, subsequent to initial recognition, may carry its property, plant and equipment assets at a revalued amount, being its fair value at the date of the revaluation less any subsequent accumulated depreciation and subsequent accumulated impairment losses.

15.4.2 Those property, plant and equipment assets that are within the scope of AASB 116 and that the insurer considers back general insurance liabilities are measured using the revaluation model under AASB 116.

15.5   When preparing *separate financial statements*, those investments in subsidiaries, jointly controlled entities and associates that:

(a)   are defined by AASB 127 *Consolidated and Separate Financial Statements*, AASB 128 *Investments in Associates* and AASB 131 *Interests in Joint Ventures*;

(b)   back general insurance liabilities; and

(c)   are permitted to be designated as "at fair value through profit or loss" under AASB 139;

shall be designated as "at fair value through profit or loss" under AASB 139, on first application of this Standard or on initial recognition.

15.5.1 An insurer applies AASB 127 to its investments in subsidiaries, jointly controlled entities and associates when preparing separate financial statements. Under AASB 127, in the parent's own financial statements, the investments in subsidiaries, jointly controlled entities and associates can either be accounted for at cost or in accordance with AASB 139.

15.5.2 In the parent's separate financial statements, investments in subsidiaries, jointly controlled entities and associates that are within the scope of AASB 127, that the insurer considers back general insurance liabilities, and that are permitted to be designated as "at fair value through profit or loss" under AASB 139, are designated as "at fair value through profit or loss" under AASB 139, on first application of this Standard or on initial recognition.

16 Non-insurance Contracts Regulated under the *Insurance Act 1973*

16.1 Non-insurance contracts regulated under the *Insurance Act 1973* shall be treated under AASB 139 to the extent that they give rise to financial assets and financial liabilities. However, the financial assets and the financial liabilities that arise under these contracts shall be designated as "at fair value through profit or loss", on first application of this Standard, or on initial recognition of the financial assets or financial liabilities, where this is permitted under AASB 139.

16.1.1 In relation to non-insurance contracts regulated under the Insurance Act, an insurer applies AASB 139 to its financial assets and financial liabilities. Under AASB 139 a financial asset or financial liability at fair value through profit or loss is a financial asset or financial liability that meets either of the following conditions:

(a)   it is classified as held for trading; or

(b)   it is designated as "at fair value through profit or loss" upon initial recognition. An entity may use this designation when it is a contract with an embedded derivative and paragraph 11A of AASB 139 allows the entity to measure the contract as "at fair value through profit or loss"; or when doing so results in more relevant information, because either:

(i)   it eliminates or significantly reduces a measurement or recognition inconsistency (sometimes referred to as 'an accounting mismatch') that would otherwise arise from measuring assets or liabilities or recognising the gains and losses on them on different bases; or

(ii)   a group of financial assets, financial liabilities or both is managed and its performance is evaluated on a fair value basis, in accordance with a documented risk management or investment strategy, and information about the group is provided internally on that basis to the entity's key management personnel (as defined in AASB 124 *Related Party Disclosures*), for example the entity's board of directors and chief executive officer.

AASB 1 *First-time Adoption of Australian Accounting Standards* permits entities to designate financial assets and financial liabilities as "at fair value through profit or loss" on first application of the Standard.

16.2   Paragraphs 15.2, 15.3, 15.4 and 15.5 shall also be applied to the measurement of assets that back financial liabilities that arise under non-insurance contracts.

17 Disclosures

Statement of Comprehensive Income

17.1   In relation to the statement of comprehensive income, the financial statements shall disclose:

(a)   **the underwriting result for the reporting period, determined as the amount obtained by deducting the sum of claims expense, outwards reinsurance premium expense and underwriting expenses from the sum of direct and inwards reinsurance premium revenues and recoveries revenue;**

(b)   *net claims incurred* **shall be disclosed, showing separately:**

(i)   **the amount relating to risks borne in the current reporting period; and**

(ii)   **the amount relating to a reassessment of risks borne in all previous reporting periods.**

An explanation shall be provided where net claims incurred relating to a reassessment of risks borne in previous reporting periods are material; and

      (c)   in respect of 17.1(b)(i) and 17.1(b)(ii), the following components shall be separately disclosed:

          (i)   gross claims incurred – undiscounted;

          (ii)   reinsurance and other recoveries – undiscounted; and

          (iii)   discount movements shown separately for (i) and (ii).

17.1.1 This Standard requires the underwriting result for the reporting period to be disclosed. This disclosure gives an indication of an insurer's underwriting performance, including the extent to which underwriting activities rely on investment income for the payment of claims.

17.1.2 Based on the total movement in net claims incurred, it may appear that there has not been a material reassessment of risks borne in previous periods, however, there may be material movements at a business segment level, that mitigate each other. For example, the insurer may have seen a material deterioration in its motor portfolio, which has been mitigated by material savings in the professional indemnity portfolio, such that when both portfolios are aggregated there appears to have been little change in the reporting period. In such circumstances, the insurer provides an explanation of the reassessments that took place in the net claims incurred for previous periods during the reporting period at the business segment level.

Statement of Financial Position

17.2   The financial statements shall disclose in relation to the outstanding claims liability:

      (a)   the central estimate of the expected present value of future payments for claims incurred;

      (b)   the component related to the risk margin;

      (c)   the percentage risk margin adopted in determining the outstanding claims liability (determined from (a) and (b) above);

      (d)   the probability of adequacy intended to be achieved through adoption of the risk margin; and

      (e)   the process used to determine the risk margin, including the way in which diversification of risks has been allowed for.

17.3   An insurer shall disclose the process used to determine which assets back general insurance liabilities and which assets back financial liabilities arising under non-insurance contracts.

Non-insurance Contracts

17.4   Where a general insurer has issued a non-insurance contract or holds a non-insurance contract as a cedant, and that non-insurance contract has a material financial impact on the statement of comprehensive income, statement of financial position or cash flows, the general insurer shall disclose:

      (a)   the nature of the non-insurance contract;

      (b)   the recognised assets, liabilities, income, expense and cash flows arising from the non-insurance contract; and

      (c)   information that helps users to understand the amount, timing and uncertainty of future cash flows from the non-insurance contract.

17.4.1 In applying paragraph 17.4 a non-insurance contract shall be considered together with any related contracts or side letters, when determining the need for disclosure, and in making the disclosures required.

17.5   [Deleted by the AASB]

17.5.1 [Deleted by the AASB]

Insurance Contracts – Explanation of Recognised Amounts

17.6 **An insurer shall disclose information that identifies and explains the amounts in its financial statements arising from insurance contracts.**

17.6.1 To comply with paragraph 17.6, an insurer shall disclose:

    (a)   its accounting policies for insurance contracts and related assets, liabilities, income and expense;

    (b)   the recognised assets, liabilities, income, expense and cash flows arising from insurance contracts. Furthermore, if the insurer is a cedant, it shall disclose:

        (i)   gains and losses recognised in the statement of comprehensive income on buying reinsurance; and

        (ii)   if the cedant defers and amortises gains and losses arising on buying reinsurance, the amortisation for the period and the amounts remaining unamortised at the beginning and end of the period;

    (c)   the process used to determine the assumptions that have the greatest effect on the measurement of the recognised amounts described in (b). When practicable, an insurer shall also give quantified disclosure of those assumptions;

    (d)   the effect of changes in assumptions used to measure insurance assets and insurance liabilities, showing separately the effect of each change that has a material effect on the financial statements; and

    (e)   reconciliations of changes in insurance liabilities, reinsurance assets and, if any, related deferred acquisition costs.

17.6.2 In applying paragraph 17.6.1(b), the recognised assets and liabilities arising from insurance contracts would normally include:

    (a)   gross outstanding claims liability;

    (b)   reinsurance recoveries receivable arising from the outstanding claims liability;

    (c)   gross unearned premium liability;

    (d)   reinsurance recoveries receivable arising from the unearned premium liability;

    (e)   unexpired risk liability;

    (f)   other reinsurance recoveries receivable;

    (g)   other recoveries receivable;

    (h)   outwards reinsurance expense asset or liability;

    (i)   direct premium revenue receivable;

    (j)   inwards reinsurance premium revenue receivable;

    (k)   deferred acquisition cost asset; and

    (l)   intangible assets relating to acquired insurance contracts.

17.6.3 In applying paragraph 17.6.1(b), the recognised income and expenses arising from insurance contracts would normally include:

    (a)   direct premium revenue;

    (b)   inwards reinsurance premium revenue (including retrocessions);

    (c)   reinsurance and other recoveries revenue;

    (d)   direct claims expense;

    (e)   reinsurance claims expense;

    (f)   outwards reinsurance premium expense (including retrocessions);

    (g)   acquisition costs expense; and

    (h)   other underwriting expenses, including claims handling expenses.

17.6.4 When an insurer is presenting the disclosures required by paragraphs 17.6.1(c) and 17.6.1(d) the insurer determines the level and extent of disclosure that is appropriate having regard to its circumstances and the qualitative characteristics of financial statements under the *Framework for the Preparation and Presentation of Financial Statements* of understandability, relevance, reliability and comparability.

17.6.5 For an insurer that is involved in a large number of insurance classes, across different jurisdictions, disclosure by class of business is likely to be voluminous and may not be understandable to the user of the financial statements. Furthermore, for such an insurer, disclosure for the entity as a whole is also likely to be at too high a level of aggregation to be relevant or comparable. It is expected that for most insurers disclosure at the major business segment level would normally be most appropriate. The insurer may believe that disclosure of a range of values would be relevant to the users of the financial statements.

17.6.6 Some of the assumptions that would normally have the greatest effect on the measurement of the recognised amounts described in paragraph 17.6.1(b), are discount rates, inflation rates, average weighted term to settlement from the claims reporting date, average claim frequency, average claim size and expense rates. The insurer determines whether these assumptions shall be disclosed given the requirements of paragraphs 17.6 and 17.6.1.

Nature and Extent of Risks Arising from Insurance Contracts

17.7 An insurer shall disclose information that enables users of its financial statements to evaluate the nature and extent of risks arising from insurance contracts.

17.7.1 To comply with paragraph 17.7, an insurer shall disclose:

(a) its objectives, policies and processes for managing risks arising from insurance contracts and the methods used to manage those risks;

(b) information about *insurance risk* (both before and after risk mitigation by reinsurance), including information about:

(i) sensitivity to insurance risk (see paragraph 17.7.5);

(ii) concentrations of insurance risk, including a description of how management determines concentrations and a description of the shared characteristic that identifies each concentration (e.g. type of insured event, geographical area, or currency); and

(iii) actual claims compared with previous estimates (i.e. claims development). The disclosure about claims development shall go back to the period when the earliest material claim arose for which there is still uncertainty about the amount and timing of the claims payments, but need not go back more than ten years. An insurer need not disclose this information for claims for which uncertainty about the amount and timing of claims payments is typically resolved within one year;

(c) information about credit risk, liquidity risk and market risk that paragraphs 31 - 42 of AASB 7 *Financial Instruments: Disclosures* would require if the insurance contracts were within the scope of AASB 7. However:

(i) an insurer need not provide the maturity analyses required by paragraphs 39(a) and (b) of AASB 7 if it discloses information about the estimated timing of the net cash outflows resulting from recognised insurance liabilities instead. This may take the form of an analysis, by estimated timing, of the amounts recognised in the statement of financial position; and

(ii) if an insurer uses an alternative method to manage sensitivity to market conditions, such as an embedded value analysis, it may use that sensitivity analysis to meet the requirement in paragraph 40(a) of AASB 7. Such an insurer shall also provide the disclosures required by paragraph 41 of AASB 7; and

(d) information about exposures to market risk arising from embedded derivatives contained in a host insurance contract if the insurer is not required to, and does not, measure the embedded derivatives at fair value.

17.7.2 For an insurer that is involved in a large number of insurance classes, across different jurisdictions, disclosure by class of business is likely to be voluminous and may not be understandable to the user of the financial statements. Furthermore, for such an insurer disclosure for the entity as a whole would normally be at too high a level of aggregation to be relevant or comparable. It is expected that for most insurers disclosure at the major business segment level would normally be most appropriate.

17.7.3 The claims development disclosure required by paragraph 17.7.1(b)(iii) only applies to classes of business where claims are not typically resolved within one year. The insurer, in disclosing claims development, ensures it is clear to the reader of the financial statements, which classes of business, or which segments of the business, are covered by the disclosures and which classes of business, or which segments of the business, are not covered by the disclosures.

17.7.4 IG Example 5 in the *Guidance on Implementing IFRS 4* Insurance Contracts, provides one possible format to meet the claims development disclosure requirements of this Standard. Such a format may be particularly appropriate for longer tail classes of business where the long tail nature of the claims is a significant aspect in the development of the claims, as this format illustrates the development of claims over a number of years. If this format is adopted, disclosure by accident year, gross and net of reinsurance, of undiscounted claims would normally be most relevant to the users of financial statements. The insurer explains the information presented. This includes whether the claims are discounted or undiscounted, gross or net of reinsurance and by accident year or underwriting year.

17.7.5 To comply with paragraph 17.7.1(b)(i), an insurer shall disclose either (a) or (b) as follows:

(a) a sensitivity analysis that shows how profit or loss and equity would have been affected had changes in the relevant risk variable that were reasonably possible at the end of the reporting period occurred; the methods and assumptions used in preparing the sensitivity analysis; and any changes from the previous period in the methods and assumptions used. However, if an insurer uses an alternative method to manage sensitivity to market conditions, such as an embedded value analysis, it may meet this requirement by disclosing that alternative sensitivity analysis and the disclosures required by paragraph 41 of AASB 7; and

(b) qualitative information about sensitivity, and information about those terms and conditions of insurance contracts that have a material effect on the amount, timing and uncertainty of the insurer's future cash flows.

Liability Adequacy Test

17.8 **In relation to the liability adequacy test in section 9, the financial statements shall disclose:**

(a) **where a deficiency has been identified, the amounts underlying the calculation performed, that is:**

(i) **unearned premium liability;**

(ii) **related reinsurance asset;**

(iii) **deferred acquisition costs;**

(iv) **intangible assets;**

(v) **present value of expected future cash flows for future claims, showing expected reinsurance recoveries separately; and**

(vi) **deficiency;**

(b) **any write-down of deferred acquisition costs under the liability adequacy test;**

(c) **any write-down of intangible assets under the liability adequacy test;**

(d) **in relation to the present value of expected future cash flows for future claims:**

(i) **the central estimate of the present value of expected future cash flows;**

(ii) **the component of present value of expected future cash flows related to the risk margin;**

(iii) **the percentage risk margin adopted in determining the present value of expected future cash flows (determined from (i) and (ii) above);**

(iv)   the probability of adequacy intended to be achieved through adoption of the risk margin; and

(v)   the process used to determine the risk margin, including the way in which diversification of risks has been allowed for;

(e)   where the probability of adequacy disclosed in paragraph 17.2(d) is not the same or similar to the probability of adequacy disclosed in paragraph 17.8(d)(iv), the reasons for the difference; and

(f)   where a surplus has been identified, the fact that the liability adequacy test identified a surplus.

Other Disclosures

17.9.1 This Standard addresses disclosure requirements in relation to general insurance contracts. Other Australian Accounting Standards may be relevant to a general insurer's financial statements. In particular, the disclosure requirements in AASB 7 would normally be relevant to general insurers.

18 Transitional Provisions

18.1   An entity need not apply the disclosure requirements in this Standard to comparative information that relates to annual periods beginning before 1 January 2005, except for the disclosures required by paragraphs 17.6.1(a) and 17.6.1(b) about accounting policies, and recognised assets, liabilities, income and expense and cash flows.

18.2   Where an entity applies the disclosure requirements in this Standard to comparative information that relates to annual periods beginning before 1 January 2005, if it is impracticable to apply a particular requirement of this Standard to comparative information that relates to annual periods beginning before 1 January 2005, an entity shall disclose that fact. AASB 108 *Accounting Policies, Changes in Accounting Estimates and Errors* explains the term "impracticable".

18.3   In applying paragraph 17.7.1(b)(iii), an entity need not disclose information about claims development that occurred earlier than five years before the end of the first annual reporting period in which it applies this Standard. Furthermore, if it is impracticable, when an entity first applies this Standard, to prepare information about claims development that occurred before the beginning of the earliest period for which an entity presents full comparative information that complies with this Standard, the entity shall disclose that fact.

18.3.1 There are also references to transitional measurement requirements in paragraphs 15.2.1, 15.2.2, 15.5, 15.5.2, 16.1 and 16.1.1.

19 Definitions

19.1   In this Standard:

attachment date means, for a direct insurer, the date as from which the insurer accepts risk from the insured under an insurance contract or endorsement or, for a reinsurer, the date from which the reinsurer accepts risk from the direct insurer or another reinsurer under a reinsurance arrangement

cedant means the policyholder under a reinsurance contract

claim means a demand by any party external to the entity for payment by the insurer on account of an alleged loss resulting from an insured event or events, that have occurred, alleged to be covered by an insurance contract

claims expense means the charge to the statement of comprehensive income for the reporting period and represents the sum of claims settled and claims management expenses relating to claims incurred in the period and the movement in the gross outstanding claims liability in the period

claims incurred means claims that have occurred prior to the end of the reporting period, whether reported or unreported at the end of the reporting period *deposit component* means a contractual component that is not accounted for as a derivative under AASB 139 *Financial Instruments: Recognition and Measurement* and would be within the scope of AASB 139 if it were a separate instrument

deposit premium means the premium charged by the insurer at the inception of a contract under which the final premium depends on conditions prevailing over the contract period and so is not determined until the expiry of that period

direct insurance contract means an insurance contract that is not a reinsurance contract

fair value means the amount for which an asset could be exchanged, or a liability settled, between knowledgeable, willing parties in an arm's length transaction

financial risk means the risk of a possible future change in one or more of a specified interest rate, financial instrument price, commodity price, foreign exchange rate, index of prices or rates, a credit rating or credit index or other variable, provided in the case of a non-financial variable that the variable is not specific to a party to the contract

future claims means claims in respect of insured events that are expected to occur in future reporting periods under policies where the attachment date is prior to the end of the reporting period

general insurance contract means an insurance contract that is not a life insurance contract

general insurer means an insurer that writes general insurance contracts

general reinsurance contract means a reinsurance contract that is not a *life reinsurance contract*

insurance asset means an insurer's net contractual rights under an insurance contract

insurance contract means a contract under which one party (the insurer) accepts significant insurance risk from another party (the policyholder) by agreeing to compensate the policyholder if a specified uncertain future event *(*the insured event*)* adversely affects the policyholder

(Refer to Appendix for additional guidance in applying this definition.)

insurance liability means an insurer's net contractual obligations under an insurance contract

insurance risk means risk, other than financial risk, transferred from the holder of a contract to the issuer

insured event means an uncertain future event covered by an insurance contract and creates insurance risk

insurer means the party that has an obligation under an insurance contract to compensate a policyholder if an insured event occurs

inwards reinsurance means reinsurance contracts written by reinsurers

liability adequacy test means an assessment of whether the carrying amount of an insurance liability needs to be increased (or the carrying amount of the related deferred acquisition costs or related intangible assets decreased) based on a review of future cash flows

life insurance contract means an insurance contract, or a financial instrument with a discretionary participation feature, regulated under the *Life Insurance Act 1995*, and similar contracts issued by entities operating outside Australia

life reinsurance contract means a life insurance contract issued by one insurer (the reinsurer*)* to compensate another insurer (the cedant) for losses on one or more contracts issued by the cedant

net claims incurred means direct claims costs net of reinsurance and other recoveries, and indirect claims handling costs, determined on a discounted basis

non-insurance contract **means a contract regulated under the *Insurance Act 1973*, and similar contracts issued by entities operating outside Australia, which fails to meet the definition of an insurance contract under this Standard**

(An example of a non-insurance contract might be a type of complex financial reinsurance contract.)

outstanding claims liability **means all unpaid claims and related claims handling expenses relating to claims incurred prior to the end of the reporting period**

policyholder **means a party that has a right to compensation under an insurance contract if an insured event occurs**

premium **means the amount charged in relation to accepting risk from the insured, but does not include amounts collected on behalf of third parties**

reinsurance assets **means a cedant's net contractual rights under a reinsurance contract**

reinsurance contract **means an insurance contract issued by one insurer (the reinsurer) to compensate another insurer (the cedant) for losses on one or more contracts issued by the cedant**

reinsurer **means the party that has an obligation under a reinsurance contract to compensate a cedant if an insured event occurs**

separate financial statements **are those presented by a parent, an investor in an associate or a venturer in a jointly controlled entity, in which the investments are accounted for on the basis of the direct equity interest rather than on the basis of the reported results and net assets of the investees**

unbundle **means to treat the components of a contract as if they were separate contracts**

weather derivative **means a contract that requires payment based on climatic, geological or other physical variables**

19.2   The following terms are defined in AASB 132 or AASB 139 and are used in this Standard with the meaning specified in those Standards:

(a)   financial asset;

(b)   financial guarantee contract;

(c)   financial instrument; and

(d)   financial liability.

Appendix

Definition of an Insurance Contract

This Appendix is an integral part of AASB 1023.

1   This Appendix gives guidance on the definition of an insurance contract in section 19 of the Standard. It addresses the following issues:

     (a)   the term 'uncertain future event' (paragraphs 2-4);

     (b)   payments in kind (paragraphs 5-6);

     (c)   insurance risk and other risks (paragraphs 7-16);

     (d)   examples of insurance contracts (paragraphs 17-20);

     (e)   significant insurance risk (paragraphs 21-26); and

     (f)   changes in the level of insurance risk (paragraphs 27 and 28).

Uncertain Future Event

2   Uncertainty (or risk) is the essence of an insurance contract. Accordingly, at least one of the following is uncertain at the inception of an insurance contract:

     (a)   whether an insured event will occur;

     (b)   when it will occur; or

     (c)   how much the insurer will need to pay if it occurs.

3   In some insurance contracts, the insured event is the discovery of a loss during the term of the contract, even if the loss arises from an event that occurred before the inception of the contract. In other insurance contracts, the insured event is an event that occurs during the term of the contract, even if the resulting loss is discovered after the end of the contract term.

4   Some insurance contracts cover events that have already occurred, but whose financial effect is still uncertain. An example is a reinsurance contract that covers the direct insurer against adverse development of claims already reported by policyholders. In such contracts, the insured event is the discovery of the ultimate cost of those claims.

Payments in Kind

5   Some insurance contracts require or permit payments to be made in kind. An example is when the insurer replaces a stolen article directly, instead of reimbursing the policyholder. Another example is when an insurer uses its own hospitals and medical staff to provide medical services covered by the contracts.

6   Some fixed-fee service contracts in which the level of service depends on an uncertain event meet the definition of an insurance contract in this Standard but are not regulated as insurance contracts in some countries. One example is a maintenance contract in which the service provider agrees to repair specified equipment after a malfunction. The fixed service fee is based on the expected number of malfunctions, but it is uncertain whether a particular machine will break down. The malfunction of the equipment adversely affects its owner and the contract compensates the owner (in kind, rather than cash). Another example is a contract for car breakdown services in which the provider agrees, for a fixed annual fee, to provide roadside assistance or tow the car to a nearby garage. The latter contract could meet the definition of an insurance contract even if the provider does not agree to carry out repairs or replace parts.

Distinction between Insurance Risk and Other Risks

7   The definition of an insurance contract refers to insurance risk, which this Standard defines as risk, other than *financial risk*, transferred from the holder of a contract to the issuer. A contract that exposes the issuer to financial risk without significant insurance risk is not an insurance contract.

8   The definition of financial risk in section 19 of the Standard includes a list of financial and non-financial variables. That list includes non-financial variables that are not specific to a party to the contract, such as an index of earthquake losses in a particular region or an index of temperatures in a particular city. It excludes non-financial variables that are specific to a party to the contract, such as the occurrence or non-occurrence of a fire that damages or destroys an asset of that party. Furthermore, the risk of changes in the fair value of a non-financial asset is not a financial risk if the fair value reflects not only changes in market prices for such assets (a financial variable) but also the condition of a specific non-financial asset held by a party to a contract (a non-financial variable). For example, if a guarantee of the residual value of a specific car exposes the guarantor to the risk of changes in the car's physical condition, that risk is insurance risk, not financial risk.

9   Some contracts expose the issuer to financial risk, in addition to significant insurance risk. For example, many life insurance contracts both guarantee a minimum rate of return to policyholders (creating financial risk) and promise death benefits that at some times significantly exceed the policyholder's account balance (creating insurance risk in the form of mortality risk). Such contracts are insurance contracts.

10   Under some contracts, an insured event triggers the payment of an amount linked to a price index. Such contracts are insurance contracts, provided the payment that is contingent on the insured event can be significant. The link to the price index is an embedded derivative, but it also transfers insurance risk. If the resulting transfer of insurance risk is significant, the embedded derivative meets the definition of an insurance contract, in which case it need not be separated and measured at fair value (see paragraph 2.3.1 of this Standard).

11   The definition of insurance risk refers to risk that the insurer accepts from the policyholder. In other words, insurance risk is a pre-existing risk transferred from the policyholder to the insurer. Thus, a new risk created by the contract is not insurance risk.

12   The definition of an insurance contract refers to an adverse effect on the policyholder. The definition does not limit the payment by the insurer to an amount equal to the financial impact of the adverse event. For example, the definition does not exclude 'new-for-old' coverage that pays the policyholder sufficient to permit replacement of a damaged old asset by a new asset.

13   Some contracts require a payment if a specified uncertain event occurs, but do not require an adverse effect on the policyholder as a precondition for payment. Such a contract is not an insurance contract even if the holder uses the contract to mitigate an underlying risk exposure. For example, if the holder uses a derivative to hedge an underlying non financial variable that is correlated with cash flows from an asset of the entity, the derivative is not an insurance contract because payment is not conditional on whether the holder is adversely affected by a reduction in the cash flows from the asset. Conversely, the definition of an insurance contract refers to an uncertain event for which an adverse effect on the policyholder is a contractual precondition for payment. This contractual precondition does not require the insurer to investigate whether the event actually caused an adverse effect, but permits the insurer to deny payment if it is not satisfied that the event caused an adverse effect.

14   Lapse or persistency risk (i.e. the risk that the counterparty will cancel the contract earlier or later than the issuer had expected in pricing the contract) is not insurance risk because the payment to the counterparty is not contingent on an uncertain future event that adversely affects the counterparty. Similarly, expense risk (i.e. the risk of unexpected increases in the administrative costs associated with the servicing of a contract, rather than in costs associated with insured events) is not insurance risk because an unexpected increase in expenses does not adversely affect the counterparty.

15   Therefore, a contract that exposes the issuer to lapse risk, persistency risk or expense risk is not an insurance contract unless it also exposes the issuer to insurance risk. However, if the issuer of that contract mitigates that risk by using a second contract to transfer part of that risk to another party, the second contract exposes that other party to insurance risk.

16   An insurer can accept significant insurance risk from the policyholder only if the insurer is an entity separate from the policyholder. In the case of a mutual insurer, the mutual

accepts risk from each policyholder and pools that risk. Although policyholders bear that pooled risk collectively in their capacity as owners, the mutual has still accepted the risk that is the essence of an insurance contract.

Examples of General Insurance Contracts

17   The following are examples of contracts that are general insurance contracts, if the transfer of insurance risk is significant:

(a)   insurance against theft or damage to property;

(b)   insurance against product liability, professional liability, civil liability or legal expenses;

(c)   medical cover;

(d)   surety bonds, fidelity bonds, performance bonds and bid bonds (i.e. contracts that provide compensation if another party fails to perform a contractual obligation, for example an obligation to construct a building);

(e)   credit insurance that provides for specified payments to be made to reimburse the holder for a loss it incurs because a specified debtor fails to make payment when due under the original or modified terms of a debt instrument. These contracts could have various legal forms, such as that of a guarantee, some types of letter of credit, a credit derivative default contract or an insurance contract. However, although these contracts meet the definition of an insurance contract, they also meet the definition of a financial guarantee contract in AASB 139 and are within the scope of AASB 7 and AASB 139, not this Standard (see paragraph 2.2(f)). Nevertheless, if an issuer of financial guarantee contracts has previously asserted explicitly that it regards such contracts as insurance contracts and has used accounting applicable to insurance contracts, the issuer may elect to apply either AASB 139 and AASB 7 or this Standard to such financial guarantee contracts;

(f)   product warranties. Product warranties issued by another party for goods sold by a manufacturer, dealer or retailer are within the scope of this Standard. However, product warranties issued directly by a manufacturer, dealer or retailer are outside its scope, because they are within the scope of AASB 118 *Revenue* and AASB 137 *Provisions, Contingent Liabilities and Contingent Assets*;

(g)   title insurance (i.e. insurance against the discovery of defects in title to land that were not apparent when the insurance contract was written). In this case, the insured event is the discovery of a defect in the title, not the defect itself;

(h)   travel assistance (i.e. compensation in cash or in kind to policyholders for losses suffered while they are travelling). Paragraphs 5 and 6 of this Appendix discuss some contracts of this kind;

(i)   catastrophe bonds that provide for reduced payments of principal, interest or both if a specified event adversely affects the issuer of the bond (unless the specified event does not create significant insurance risk, for example if the event is a change in an interest rate or foreign exchange rate);

(j)   insurance swaps and other contracts that require a payment based on changes in climatic, geological or other physical variables that are specific to a party to the contract; and

(k)   reinsurance contracts.

18   The following are examples of items that are not general insurance contracts:

(a)   contracts that have the legal form of insurance, but pass all significant insurance risk back to the policyholder through non-cancellable and enforceable mechanisms that adjust future payments by the policyholder as a direct result of insured losses, for example some financial reinsurance contracts or some group contracts (such contracts are normally non-insurance *financial instruments* or service contracts, see paragraphs 19 and 20 of this Appendix);

(b) self-insurance, in other words retaining a risk that could have been covered by insurance (there is no insurance contract because there is no agreement with another party);

(c) contracts (such as gambling contracts) that require a payment if a specified uncertain future event occurs, but do not require, as a contractual precondition for payment, that the event adversely affects the policyholder. However, this does not preclude the specification of a predetermined payout to quantify the loss caused by a specified event such as an accident;

(d) derivatives that expose one party to financial risk but not insurance risk, because they require that party to make payment based solely on changes in one or more of a specified interest rate, financial instrument price, commodity price, foreign exchange rate, index of prices or rates, credit rating or credit index or other variable, provided in the case of a non-financial variable that the variable is not specific to a party to the contract (see AASB 139);

(e) a credit-related guarantee (or letter of credit, credit derivative default contract or credit insurance contract) that requires payments even if the holder has not incurred a loss on the failure of the debtor to make payments when due (see AASB 139);

(f) contracts that require a payment based on a climatic, geological or other physical variable that is not specific to a party to the contract (commonly described as weather derivatives);

(g) catastrophe bonds that provide for reduced payments of principal, interest or both, based on a climatic, geological or other physical variable that is not specific to a party to the contract; and

(h) life insurance contracts.

19 If the contracts described in paragraph 18 of this Appendix create financial assets or financial liabilities, they are within the scope of AASB 139. Among other things, this means that the parties to the contract use what is sometimes called deposit accounting, which involves the following:

(a) one party recognises the consideration received as a financial liability, rather than as revenue; and

(b) the other party recognises the consideration paid as a financial asset, rather than as an expense.

20 If the contracts described in paragraph 18 of this Appendix do not create financial assets or financial liabilities, AASB 118 applies. Under AASB 118, revenue associated with a transaction involving the rendering of services is recognised by reference to the stage of completion of the transaction if the outcome of the transaction can be estimated reliably.

Significant Insurance Risk

21 A contract is an insurance contract only if it transfers significant insurance risk. Paragraphs 7 to 20 of this Appendix discuss insurance risk. The following paragraphs discuss the assessment of whether insurance risk is significant.

22 Insurance risk is significant if, and only if, an insured event could cause an insurer to pay significant additional benefits in any scenario, excluding scenarios that lack commercial substance (i.e. have no discernible effect on the economics of the transaction). If significant additional benefits would be payable in scenarios that have commercial substance, the condition in the previous sentence may be met even if the insured event is extremely unlikely or even if the expected (i.e. probability-weighted) present value of contingent cash flows is a small proportion of the expected present value of all the remaining contractual cash flows.

23 The additional benefits described in paragraph 22 of this Appendix refer to amounts that exceed those that would be payable if no insured event occurred (excluding scenarios

that lack commercial substance). Those additional amounts include claims handling and claims assessment costs, but exclude:

(a) the loss of the ability to charge the policyholder for future services;

(b) a payment conditional on an event that does not cause a significant loss to the holder of the contract. For example, consider a contract that requires the issuer to pay one million currency units if an asset suffers physical damage causing an insignificant economic loss of one currency unit to the holder. In this contract, the holder transfers to the insurer the insignificant risk of losing one currency unit. At the same time, the contract creates non-insurance risk that the issuer will need to pay 999,999 currency units if the specified event occurs. Because the issuer does not accept significant insurance risk from the holder, this contract is not an insurance contract; and

(c) possible reinsurance recoveries. The insurer accounts for these separately.

24 An insurer shall assess the significance of insurance risk contract by contract, rather than by reference to materiality to the financial statements[1]. Thus, insurance risk may be significant even if there is a minimal probability of material losses for a whole book of contracts. This contract-by-contract assessment makes it easier to classify a contract as an insurance contract. However, if a relatively homogeneous book of small contracts is known to consist of contracts that all transfer insurance risk, an insurer need not examine each contract within that book to identify a few non-derivative contracts that transfer insignificant insurance risk.

25 Paragraph 22 of this Appendix refers to additional benefits. These additional benefits could include a requirement to pay benefits earlier if the insured event occurs earlier and the payment is not adjusted for the time value of money.

26 If an insurance contract is unbundled into a deposit component and an insurance component, the significance of insurance risk transfer is assessed by reference to the insurance component. The significance of insurance risk transferred by an embedded derivative is assessed by reference to the embedded derivative.

Changes in the Level of Insurance Risk

27 Some contracts do not transfer any insurance risk to the issuer at inception, although they do transfer insurance risk at a later time.

28 A contract that qualifies as an insurance contract remains an insurance contract until all rights and obligations are extinguished or expire.

---

1 For this purpose, contracts entered into simultaneously with a single counterparty (or contracts that are otherwise interdependent) form a single contract.

AASB 1031
Materiality

(Compiled February 2010)

Note from the Institute of Chartered Accountants Australia

This note, prepared by the technical editors, is not part of Accounting Standard AASB 1031.

Historical development

September 1995: AASB 1031 'Materiality' was issued by the AASB in September 1995.

July 2004: The AASB reissued the Standard in July 2004 with minor amendments made in relation to its application and terminology. The purpose of the 2004 version of AASB 1031 is to provide guidance on materiality in addition to that found in the Australian equivalent of the IASB Framework so that the meaning of materiality remains well explained in the Australian context.

24 September 2007: AASB 2007-8 'Amendments to Australian Accounting Standards' amends AASB 1031, changing the term 'general purpose financial reports' to 'general purpose financial statements'. This Standard is applicable to annual reporting periods beginning on or after 1 January 2009.

13 December 2007: AASB 2007-10 'Further Amendments to Australian Accounting Standards arising from AASB 101' amends AASB 1031, replacing the term 'financial report' with 'financial statements'. This Standard is applicable to annual reporting periods beginning on or after 1 January 2009.

7 October 2009: AASB 1031 was reissued by the AASB, compiled to include the AASB 2007-8 and 2007-10 amendments. This compiled Standard applies to annual reporting periods beginning on or after 1 January 2009. Early application is permitted.

15 December 2009: AASB 2009-12 'Amendments to Australian Accounting Standards' amends AASB 1031 for editorial corrections. This Standard is applicable to annual reporting periods beginning on or after 1 January 2011 with early adoption permitted.

23 February 2010: AASB 1031 was reissued by the AASB, compiled to include the AASB 2009-12 amendments and applies to annual reporting periods ending on or after 1 January 2011.

Contents

Compilation Details

Accounting Standard
AASB 1031 Materiality

	Paragraphs
Objective	1
Application	2 – 6
Purpose	7 – 8
Application of Materiality	9 – 19

Appendix: Defined Term

Australian Accounting Standard AASB 1031 *Materiality* (as amended) is set out in paragraphs 1 – 19 and the Appendix. All the paragraphs have equal authority. Paragraphs in **bold type** state the main principles. Terms defined in this Standard are in *italics* the first time they appear in the Standard. AASB 1031 is to be read in the context of other Australian Accounting Standards, including AASB 1048 *Interpretation and Application of Standards*, which identifies the Australian Accounting Interpretations. In the absence of explicit guidance, AASB 108 *Accounting Policies, Changes in Accounting Estimates and Errors* provides a basis for selecting and applying accounting policies.

Compilation Details

Accounting Standard AASB 1031 *Materiality* as amended

This compiled Standard applies to annual reporting periods beginning on or after 1 January 2011. It takes into account amendments up to and including 15 December 2009 and was prepared on 23 February 2010 by the staff of the Australian Accounting Standards Board (AASB).

This compilation is not a separate Accounting Standard made by the AASB. Instead, it is a representation of AASB 1031 (July 2004) as amended by other Accounting Standards, which are listed in the Table below.

Table of Standards

Standard	Date made	Application date (*annual reporting periods ... on or after ...*)	Application, saving or transitional provisions
AASB 1031	15 Jul 2004	(*beginning*) 1 Jan 2005	see (a) below
AASB 2007-8	24 Sep 2007	(*beginning*) 1 Jan 2009	see (b) below
AASB 2007-10	13 Dec 2007	(*beginning*) 1 Jan 2009	see (b) below
AASB 2009-12	15 Dec 2009	(*beginning*) 1 Jan 2011	see (c) below

(a) Entities may elect to apply this Standard to annual reporting periods beginning before 1 January 2005.

(b) Entities may elect to apply this Standard to annual reporting periods beginning on or after 1 January 2005 but before 1 January 2009 provided that AASB 101 *Presentation of Financial Statements* (September 2007) is also applied to such periods.

(c) Entities may elect to apply this Standard to annual reporting periods beginning on or after 1 January 2005 but before 1 January 2011.

Table of Amendments

Paragraph affected	How affected	By … [paragraph]
1	amended	AASB 2007-10 [97]
2	amended	AASB 2007-8 [8]
	amended	AASB 2007-10 [98]
7-9	amended	AASB 2007-10 [97]
12	amended	AASB 2007-8 [6]
	amended	AASB 2009-12 [20]
13-14	amended	AASB 2007-8 [6]
15	amended	AASB 2007-10 [97]
16	amended	AASB 2007-8 [6]
17	amended	AASB 2007-10 [97]
18	amended	AASB 2007-8 [6]
	amended	AASB 2007-10 [97]
Appendix	amended	AASB 2007-10 [97]

Accounting Standard AASB 1031

The Australian Accounting Standards Board made Accounting Standard AASB 1031 *Materiality* under section 334 of the *Corporations Act 2001* on 15 July 2004.

This compiled version of AASB 1031 applies to annual reporting periods beginning on or after 1 January 2011. It incorporates relevant amendments contained in other AASB Standards made by the AASB up to and including 15 December 2009 (see Compilation Details).

Accounting Standard AASB 1031

Materiality

Objective

1 The objective of this Standard is to:

    (a) define materiality;

    (b) explain the role of materiality in making judgements in the preparation and presentation of the financial statements; and

    (c) require the standards specified in other Australian Accounting Standards to be applied when information resulting from their application is *material*.

Application

2 **This Standard applies to each entity preparing financial statements in accordance with Australian Accounting Standards.**

3 **This Standard applies to annual reporting periods beginning on or after 1 January 2005.**
[Note: For application dates of paragraphs changed or added by an amending Standard, see Compilation Details.]

4 **This Standard may be applied to annual reporting periods beginning before 1 January 2005. An entity that is required to prepare financial reports in accordance with Part 2M.3 of the Corporations Act may apply this Standard to annual reporting periods beginning before 1 January 2005, when an election has been made in accordance with subsection 334(5) of the Corporations Act.**

5 **When applied or operative, this Standard supersedes:**

    (a) AASB 1031 *Materiality* as notified in the *Commonwealth of Australia Gazette* No S 357, 22 September 1995; and

    (b) AAS 5 *Materiality* as issued in September 1995.

6   Notice of this Standard was published in the *Commonwealth of Australia Gazette* No S 294, 22 July 2004.

Purpose

7   Financial reporting encompasses the provision of financial statements and related financial and other information. Financial statements are the principal means of communicating financial information about a reporting entity to users. In order to meet the objective of general purpose financial reporting, information provided in the financial statements needs to be useful to users for making and evaluating decisions about the allocation of resources and possess the qualitative characteristics specified in the *Framework for the Preparation and Presentation of Financial Statements*.

8   General purpose financial reporting involves making decisions about the information to be included in general purpose financial statements and how it is presented. In making these judgements, considerations of materiality play an essential part. This is because the inclusion of information which is not material or the exclusion of information which is material may impair the usefulness of the information provided to users.

Application of Materiality

9   **The standards specified in other Australian Accounting Standards apply to the financial statements when information resulting from their application is material. Information is material if its omission, misstatement or non-disclosure has the potential, individually or collectively, to:**

     (a)   influence the economic decisions of users taken on the basis of the financial statements; or

     (b)   affect the discharge of accountability by the management or governing body of the entity.

10   The notion of materiality influences whether an item or an aggregate of items is required to be recognised, measured or disclosed in accordance with the requirements of an Australian Accounting Standard. When an item or an aggregate of items is not material, application of the materiality notion does not mean that those items would not be recognised, measured or disclosed, but rather that the entity would not be required to recognise, measure or disclose those items in accordance with the requirements of an Australian Accounting Standard.

11   In addition to guiding the application of the recognition, measurement and disclosure requirements, the notion of materiality guides the margin of error that is acceptable in the amount attributed to an item or an aggregate of items and the degree of precision required in estimating the amount of an item or an aggregate of items.

12   In deciding whether an item or an aggregate of items is material, the size and nature of the omission or misstatement of the items usually need to be evaluated together. In particular circumstances, either the nature or the amount of an item or an aggregate of items could be the determining factor. For example:

     (a)   in the context of error corrections or adjustments for events occurring after the reporting period, materiality based on amount alone is sufficient to require a correction or an adjustment to be made; and

     (b)   it may be necessary to treat as material an item or an aggregate of items which would not be judged material on the basis of the amount involved, because of their nature. This may apply when:

           (i)   transactions occur between an entity and parties who have a fiduciary responsibility in relation to that entity, such as those transactions outlined in AASB 124 *Related Party Disclosures* and AASB 1046 *Director and Executive Disclosures by Disclosing Entities*; or

           (ii) restrictions on the powers and operations of the entity affect the risks and uncertainties relating to an item, for example, legal restrictions imposed by governments on assets held in foreign countries; or

(iii)   an entity expands its operations into a new segment which affects the assessment of the risks and opportunities facing the entity; or

(iv)   a change in circumstances puts the entity in danger of breaching a financial covenant.

13   In determining whether the amount of an item or an aggregate of items is material:

(a)   the amount of an item or an aggregate of items relating to the statement of financial position is compared with the more appropriate of:

(i)   the recorded amount of equity; and

(ii)   the appropriate asset or liability class total; or

(b)   the amount of an item or an aggregate of items relating to the statement of comprehensive income is compared with the more appropriate of the:

(i)   profit or loss and the appropriate income or expense amount for the current reporting period; and

(ii)   average profit or loss and the average of the appropriate income or expense amounts for a number of reporting periods (including the current reporting period); or

(c)   the amount of an item or an aggregate of items relating to the statement of cash flows is compared with the more appropriate of the:

(i)   net cash provided by or used in the operating, investing, financing or other activities as appropriate, for the current reporting period; and

(ii)   average net cash provided by or used in the operating, investing, financing or other activities as appropriate, for a number of reporting periods (including the current reporting period).

14   As not-for-profit entities are primarily concerned with the achievement of objectives other than the generation of profit, such as service delivery, it may not be appropriate to assess materiality for statement of comprehensive income items by reference to profit or loss or average profit or loss in the manner outlined in paragraph 13(b). In these cases, the guidance set out in paragraphs 17-19 is more appropriate to consider. A not for profit entity is an entity whose principal objective is not the generation of profit. A not for profit entity can be a single entity or a group of entities comprising the parent and each of the entities that it controls.

15   Quantitative thresholds used as guidance for determining the materiality of the amount of an item or an aggregate of items shall, of necessity, be drawn at arbitrary levels. Materiality is a matter of professional judgement influenced by the characteristics of the entity and the perceptions as to who are, or are likely to be, the users of the financial statements, and their information needs. Materiality judgements can only be properly made by those who have the facts. In this context, the following quantitative thresholds may be used as guidance in considering the materiality of the amount of items included in the comparisons referred to in paragraph 13 of this Standard:

(a)   an amount which is equal to or greater than 10 per cent of the appropriate base amount may be presumed to be material unless there is evidence or convincing argument to the contrary; and

(b)   an amount which is equal to or less than 5 per cent of the appropriate base amount may be presumed not to be material unless there is evidence, or convincing argument, to the contrary.

16   In relation to items or an aggregate of items in the statement of comprehensive income, an amount as referred to in paragraph 15 is an amount after allowing for any income tax effect when the base amount has itself been determined after allowing for any income tax effect.

17   In practice materiality judgements are typically made on the basis described in paragraph 13. However, further indications of materiality may be evident from making assessments of the items in an absolute and a relative context. This may necessitate disclosure of

information in the financial statements about items which are not considered material in amount in accordance with paragraph 13.

18 In absolute terms, consideration is given to the financial statements as a whole. In particular, consideration is given to factors which may indicate deviations from normal activities such as the reversal of a trend, turning a profit into a loss or creating or eliminating the margin of solvency in a statement of financial position. For example, when the entity's financial position has deteriorated, and the entity has revalued items of property, plant or equipment upwards, information regarding the revaluation of those assets would be likely to be material, and thus the accounting and disclosure requirements specified in AASB 116 *Property, Plant and Equipment* would apply, even though the revaluation amount may not be material by comparison with the recorded amount of equity.

19 In relative terms, items are compared to any directly related items. The amount of an item may not be material when judged on the basis described in paragraph 13, but its size in relation to a related item may indicate that information about it is material. For example, the amount of interest revenue would be compared with the amount of the relevant loans. Such a comparison may indicate that information about the interest is material because its amount is much lower (or higher) than expected, having regard to the loan balance and applicable interest rates.

Appendix

Defined Term

This appendix is an integral part of AASB 1031.

Material   Omissions or misstatements of items are material if they could, individually or collectively, influence the economic decisions of users taken on the basis of the financial statements. Materiality depends on the size and nature of the omission or misstatement judged in the surrounding circumstances. The size or nature of the item, or a combination of both, could be the determining factor.

AASB 1038
Life Insurance Contracts
(Compiled November 2010)

Note from the Institute of Chartered Accountants Australia

This note, prepared by the technical editors, is not part of Accounting Standard AASB 1038.

Historical development

1998: ASRB 1038 'Life Insurance Business' was issued by the AASB in 1998.

July 2004: The AASB reissued the Standard in July 2004 as AASB 1038 'Life Insurance Contracts' to incorporate the requirements of IFRS 4 'Insurance Contracts' that apply to life insurance contracts. The 2004 version of AASB 1038 forms part of the stable platform of 2005 Australian equivalents to International Financial Reporting Standards (IFRSs).

9 June 2005: AASB 2005-4 'Amendments to Australian Accounting Standards' amends paragraphs 10.2, 10.2.1, 10.2.2, 10.5, 10.6, 10.7, 10.7.2, 12.1, 12.1.1, and adds paragraph 12.1.2. The Standard is applicable to annual reporting periods beginning on or after 1 January 2005.

5 September 2005: AASB 2005-10 'Amendments to Australian Accounting Standards' amends paragraphs 2.1.6, 15.1, 15.1.1, 15.1.2, 17.5.5(c), 17.13.1, 19.3, and adds paragraphs 15.1.3 and 17.5.5(d). This Standard is applicable to annual reporting periods beginning on or after 1 January 2007 with early adoption permitted for annual reporting periods beginning on or after 1 January 2005.

5 May 2006: Compiled version of the Standard was issued, incorporating amendments contained in AASB 2005-4, AASB 2005-10 and AASB 2005-12.

26 February 2007: AASB 2007-3 'Amendments to Australian Accounting Standards' was issued by the AASB. This Standard is applicable for annual reporting periods beginning on or after 1 January 2009.

30 April 2007: AASB 2007-4 'Amendments to Australian Accounting Standards' amends paragraphs 1.1, 10.2, 10.3, 10.5, 12.1.2, 14.1.4, 14.1.5, 15.1, 15.1.1, 15.1.3, 17.5.5, 18.2.1, 20.1 and Appendix, 16 is applicable to annual reporting periods beginning on or after 1 July 2007. Entities may elect to early-adopt it to annual reporting periods beginning on or after 1 January 2005.

24 September 2007: AASB 2007-8 'Amendments to Australian Accounting Standards' amends AASB 1038, changing the term 'general purpose financial reports' to 'general purpose financial statements'. This Standard is applicable to annual reporting periods beginning on or after 1 January 2009.

13 December 2007: AASB 2007-10 'Further Amendments to Australian Accounting Standards arising from AASB 101' amends AASB 1038, replacing the term 'financial report' with 'financial statements'. This Standard is applicable to annual reporting periods beginning on or after 1 January 2009.

24 July 2008: AASB 2008-5 'Amendments to Australian Accounting Standards arising from the Annual Improvements Project' amends AASB 1038 in relation to investments not classified for sale under AASB 5. This Standard is applicable to annual reporting periods beginning on or after 1 January 2009.

22 April 2009: AASB 2009-2 'Amendments to Australian Accounting Standards – Improving Disclosures about Financial Instruments' amends AASB 1038 to require enhanced disclosures about fair value measurements and liquidity risk. This Standard is applicable to annual reporting periods beginning on or after 1 January 2009 that end on or after 30 April 2009.

---

25 June 2009: AASB 2009-6 'Amendments to Australian Accounting Standards' amends AASB 1038 for editorial corrections made by the International Accounting Standards Board (IASB) to its Standards and Interpretations (IFRSs) and as a consequence of issuing revised AASB 101 *Presentation of Financial Statements* (September 2007). This Standard is applicable to annual reporting periods beginning on or after 1 January 2009 that end on or after 30 June 2009.

5 October 2009: Erratum makes further terminology-related and editorial changes resulting from AASB 2009-6. This erratum applies to annual reporting periods beginning on or after 1 January 2009 that end on or after 30 June 2009.

6 October 2009: AASB 1038 was reissued by the AASB, compiled to include the AASB 2007-3, AASB 2007-8, AASB 2007-10, AASB 2008-5, AASB 2009-2, AASB 2009-6 and Erratum (October 2009) amendments. This compiled Standard applies to annual reporting periods beginning on or after 1 January 2009 that end on or after 30 June 2009. Early application is permitted.

7 December 2009: AASB 2009-11 'Amendments to Australian Accounting Standards arising from AASB 9' amends AASB 1038 to give effect to consequential changes arising from the issuance of AASB 9. This Standard is applicable to annual reporting periods beginning on or after 1 January 2013 with early adoption permitted from annual reporting periods ending on or after 31 December 2009 that begin before 1 January 2013 provided AASB 9 is also applied for the same period. The application date of AASB 2009-11 has been amended to 1 January 2015 by AASB 2012-6. **These amendments have been superseded by AASB 2010-7 and are not included in this compiled Standard.**

27 October 2010: AASB 2010-5 'Further Amendments to Australian Accounting Standards' makes editorial amendments to AASB 1038. This Standard is applicable to annual reporting periods beginning on or after 1 January 2011.

26 November 2010: AASB 1038 was reissued by the AASB, compiled to include the AASB 2010-5 amendments and applies to annual reporting periods ending on or after 1 January 2011.

1 March 2011: AASB 2010-7 'Amendments to Australian Accounting Standards arising from AASB 9 (December 2010)' as compiled amends AASB 1038 to give effect to consequential changes arising from the reissue of AASB 9 in December 2010 and supersedes AASB 2009-11, which related to the previous version of AASB 9. This Standard applies to annual reporting periods beginning on or after 1 January 2013 and can be adopted early. The application date of AASB 2010-7 has been amended to 1 January 2015 by AASB 2012-6. **These amendments are not included in this compiled Standard.**

29 August 2011: AASB 2011-7 'Amendments to Australian Accounting Standards arising from the Consolidation and Joint Arrangements Standards' amends AASB 1038 to give effect to many consequential changes arising from the issue of AASB 10, 11, 12, 127 and 128. This Standard applies to annual reporting periods beginning on or after 1 January 2013 and can be adopted early by for-profit entities. **These amendments are not included in this compiled Standard.**

2 September 2011: AASB 2011-8 'Amendments to Australian 'Accounting Standards arising from AASB 13' amends AASB 1038 to give effect to a consequential change in the definition of fair value arising from the issue of AASB 13. This Standard applies to annual reporting periods beginning on or after 1 January 2013 and can be adopted early. **These amendments are not included in this compiled Standard.**

Contents

Compilation Details

Comparison with IFRS 4

Accounting Standard
AASB 1038 Life Insurance Contracts

	Paragraphs
Application	1.1 – 1.7
Scope	
Life Insurance Contracts	2.1 – 2.1.6
Embedded Derivatives	2.2.1 – 2.2.3
Deposit Components	2.3.1 – 2.3.4
Purpose of Standard	3.1
Entity and Consolidation Issues	
The Life Insurer Entity	4.1 – 4.1.2
Financial Statements of Groups that Include a Life Insurer Subsidiary	4.2 – 4.2.2
Premiums and Claims	5.1 – 5.2.3
Reinsurance	
Reporting by Cedants	6.1 – 6.1.2
Reporting by Reinsurers	6.2 – 6.2.1
Impairment of Reinsurance Assets	7.1.1
Life Insurance Liabilities	
Present Value and Best Estimates	8.1 – 8.1.6
Acquisition Costs	8.1.7 – 8.1.8
Recognition of Planned Margins as Revenues	8.2 – 8.2.2
Differences between Actual and Assumed Experience	8.3 – 8.3.2
Changes to Underlying Assumptions	8.4 – 8.5.3
Changes to Discount Rates and Related Economic Assumptions	8.5.4 – 8.5.5
Liability Adequacy Test	8.6 – 8.6.4
Discount Rates	8.7 – 8.8.2
Financial Instruments with Discretionary Participation Features	8.9
Participating Benefits	9.1 – 9.2.5
Assets Backing Life Insurance Liabilities or Life Investment Contract Liabilities	
Fair Value Approach	10.1.1
Measurement	10.2 – 10.6.1
Separate Financial Statements	10.7 – 10.7.2
Imputed Inflows and Outflows	11.1 – 11.1.3
Life Investment Contracts	12.1 – 12.1.2
Life Insurance Contracts Acquired in a Business Combination or Portfolio Transfer	13.1.1 – 13.1.5
Life Insurance Contracts Disclosure – Explanation of Recognised Amounts	14.1 – 14.1.7
Nature and Extent of Risks Arising from Life Insurance Contracts	15.1 – 15.1.3
Other Disclosures Relating to Life Insurance Contracts	16.1 – 16.1.1

	Paragraphs
Disclosures Relating to Life Insurance Contracts and Life Investment Contracts	
Financial Performance	17.1 – 17.2
Restrictions on Assets	17.3 – 17.3.1
Guaranteed or Assured Returns of Funds Invested	17.4 – 17.4.1
Equity	17.5 – 17.5.5
Solvency Information	17.8 – 17.8.1
Managed Funds and Other Fiduciary Activities	17.9
Actuarial Information	17.10
Assets Backing Life Insurance Liabilities or Life Investment Contract Liabilities	17.11
Other Disclosures	17.12.1 – 17.13.1
Disaggregated Information	
Statutory Funds and the Shareholder Fund	18.1 – 18.1.1
Investment-linked and Non-investment-linked Business	18.2 – 18.2.1
Imputed Inflows and Outflows	18.3 – 18.3.1
Transitional Provisions	19.1 – 19.3.1
Definitions	20.1 – 20.2

Appendix:

Definition of an Insurance Contract

Australian Accounting Standard AASB 1038 *Life Insurance Contracts* (as amended) is set out in paragraphs 1.1 – 20.2 and the Appendix. All the paragraphs have equal authority. Paragraphs in **bold type** state the main principles. Terms defined in this Standard are in *italics* the first time they appear in the Standard. AASB 1038 is to be read in the context of other Australian Accounting Standards including AASB 1048 *Interpretation and Application of Standards*, which identifies the Australian Accounting Interpretations. In the absence of explicit guidance, AASB 108 *Accounting Policies, Changes in Accounting Estimates and Errors* provides a basis for selecting and applying accounting policies.

Compilation Details

Accounting Standard AASB 1038 *Life Insurance Contracts* as amended

This compiled Standard applies to annual reporting periods beginning on or after 1 January 2011 but before 1 January 2013. It takes into account amendments up to and including 27 October 2010 and was prepared on 26 November 2010 by the staff of the Australian Accounting Standards Board (AASB).

This compilation is not a separate Accounting Standard made by the AASB. Instead, it is a representation of AASB 1038 (July 2004) as amended by other Accounting Standards, which are listed in the Table below.

Table of Standards

Standard	Date made	Application date (*annual reporting periods ... on or after ...*)	Application, saving or transitional provisions
AASB 1038	15 Jul 2004	(*beginning*) 1 Jan 2005	
AASB 2005-4	9 Jun 2005	(*beginning*) 1 Jan 2006	see (a) below
AASB 2005-10	5 Sep 2005	(*beginning*) 1 Jan 2007	see (b) below
AASB 2005-12	8 Dec 2005	(*ending*) 31 Dec 2005	see (c) below

Standard	Date made	Application date (*annual reporting periods … on or after …*)	Application, saving or transitional provisions
AASB 2007-3	26 Feb 2007	(*beginning*) 1 Jan 2009	see (d) below
AASB 2007-4	30 Apr 2007	(*beginning*) 1 Jul 2007	see (e) below
AASB 2007-8	24 Sep 2007	(*beginning*) 1 Jan 2009	see (f) below
AASB 2007-10	13 Dec 2007	(*beginning*) 1 Jan 2009	see (f) below
AASB 2008-5	24 Jul 2008	(*beginning*) 1 Jan 2009	see (g) below
AASB 2009-2	22 Apr 2009	(*beginning*) 1 Jan 2009 and (ending) 30 Apr *2009*	see (h) below
AASB 2009-6	25 Jun 2009	(*beginning*) 1 Jan 2009 and (*ending*) 30 Jun 2009	see (i) below
AASB 2009-11	7 Dec 2009	(*beginning*) 1 Jan 2013	not compiled*
Erratum	5 Oct 2009	(*beginning*) 1 Jan 2009 and (*ending*) 30 Jun 2009	see (j) below
AASB 2010-5	27 Oct 2010	(*beginning*) 1 Jan 2011	see (k) below

*   The amendments made by this Standard are not included in this compilation, which presents the principal Standard as applicable to annual reporting periods beginning on or after 1 January 2011 but before 1 January 2013.

(a)   Entities may elect to apply this Standard to annual reporting periods beginning on or after 1 January 2005 but before 1 January 2006.

(b)   Entities may elect to apply this Standard to annual reporting periods beginning on or after 1 January 2005 but before 1 January 2007.

(c)   Entities may elect to apply this Standard to annual reporting periods beginning on or after 1 January 2005 that end before 31 December 2005.

(d)   Entities may elect to apply this Standard to annual reporting periods beginning on or after 1 January 2005 but before 1 January 2009, provided that AASB 8 *Operating Segments* is also applied to such periods.

(e)   Entities may elect to apply this Standard to annual reporting periods beginning on or after 1 January 2005 but before 1 July 2007.

(f)   Entities may elect to apply this Standard to annual reporting periods beginning on or after 1 January 2005 but before 1 January 2009, provided that AASB 101 *Presentation of Financial Statements* (September 2007) is also applied to such periods.

(g)   Entities may elect to apply this Standard, or its amendments to individual Standards, to annual reporting periods beginning on or after 1 January 2005 but before 1 January 2009.

(h)   Entities may elect to apply this Standard to annual reporting periods beginning on or after 1 January 2005 but before 1 January 2009 and to annual reporting periods beginning on or after 1 January 2009 that end before 30 April 2009.

(i)   Entities may elect to apply this Standard to annual reporting periods beginning on or after 1 January 2005 but before 1 January 2009, provided that AASB 101 *Presentation of Financial Statements* (September 2007) is also applied to such periods, and to annual reporting periods beginning on or after 1 January 2009 that end before 30 June 2009.

(j)   Entities may elect to apply this Erratum to annual reporting periods beginning on or after 1 January 2005, provided that AASB 2009-6 *Amendments to Australian Accounting Standards* is also applied to such periods.

(k)   Entities may elect to apply this Standard to annual reporting periods beginning on or after 1 January 2005 but before 1 January 2011.

Table of Amendments

Paragraph affected	How affected	By … [paragraph]
1.1	amended amended	AASB 2007-4 [105] AASB 2007-10 [99]
2.1.6	amended	AASB 2005-10 [46]
4.1.2	amended	AASB 2005-12 [5]
5.2.4	deleted	Erratum, Oct 2009 [7]
8.4.2	amended	Erratum, Oct 2009 [8]
9.2.2	amended	AASB 2005-12 [6]

Paragraph affected	How affected	By ... [paragraph]
10.1.1	amended	AASB 2009-6 [101]
10.2	amended	AASB 2005-4 [26]
	amended	AASB 2007-4 [109]
10.2.1	amended	AASB 2005-4 [26]
10.2.2	amended	AASB 2005-4 [27]
10.3	amended	AASB 2007-4 [109]
10.5	amended	AASB 2005-4 [28]
	amended	AASB 2005-12 [7]
10.6	amended	AASB 2005-4 [29]
	amended	AASB 2005-12 [8]
10.7	amended	AASB 2005-4 [30]
	amended	AASB 2008-5 [80]
10.7.2	amended	AASB 2005-4 [31]
	amended	AASB 2008-5 [80]
10.7.3	deleted	AASB 2005-12 [9]
12.1	amended	AASB 2005-4 [32]
12.1.1	renumbered as 12.1.2	AASB 2005-4 [33]
	added	
12.1.2	amended	AASB 2007-4 [109]
	amended	AASB 2010-5 [64]
14.1.4	amended	AASB 2007-4 [109]
14.1.5	amended	AASB 2007-4 [109]
15.1 (and preceding heading)	amended	AASB 2005-10 [47]
	amended	AASB 2007-4 [109]
15.1.1	amended	AASB 2005-10 [47]
	amended	AASB 2007-4 [109]
	amended	AASB 2009-2 [14]
15.1.2	amended	AASB 2005-10 [49]
15.1.3 (and preceding heading)	added	AASB 2005-10 [48]
	amended	AASB 2007-4 [109]
17.5.2	amended	AASB 2005-12 [10]
17.5.3	amended	AASB 2005-12 [11]
17.5.4	amended	AASB 2005-12 [12]
17.5.5	amended	AASB 2005-10 [50, 51]
	amended	AASB 2005-12 [13]
	amended	AASB 2007-4 [106, 107, 109]
17.13.1	amended	AASB 2005-10 [52]
18.2.1	amended	AASB 2007-4 [109]
18.2.2 (and preceding heading)	deleted	AASB 2007-3 [18]
19.3	amended	AASB 2005-10 [53]
20.1	amended	AASB 2007-4 [108]
	amended	AASB 2010-5 [65]
20.2	added	AASB 2010-5 [66]
Appendix, 16	amended	AASB 2007-4 [109]

General Terminology Amendments

The following amendments are not shown in the above Table of Amendments:

References to 'financial report(s)' were amended to 'financial statements' by AASB 2007-8 and AASB 2007-10, except in relation to specific Corporations Act references and interim financial reports.

References to 'income statement' and 'balance sheet' were amended to 'statement of comprehensive income' and 'statement of financial position' respectively by AASB 2007-8.

References to 'reporting date' and 'each reporting date' were amended to 'end of the reporting period' and 'the end of each reporting period' respectively by AASB 2007-8.

Comparison with IFRS 4

AASB 1038 and IFRS 4

AASB 1038 *Life Insurance Contracts* as amended incorporates the limited improvements to accounting for insurance contracts required by IFRS 4 *Insurance Contracts*.

Life insurers applying this Standard and Australian equivalents to other IFRSs will therefore be compliant with IFRSs.

IFRS 4 is being implemented in Australia using three Accounting Standards:

(a)   AASB 4 *Insurance Contracts* (the Australian equivalent to IFRS 4), which applies to fixed-fee service contracts that meet the definition of an insurance contract;

(b)   AASB 1023 *General Insurance Contracts*, which applies to general insurance contracts; and

(c)   AASB 1038, which applies to life insurance contracts.

IFRS 4 applies to all insurance contracts and financial instruments with discretionary participation features, whereas AASB 1038 applies to life insurance contracts and financial instruments with discretionary participation features, certain aspects of accounting for life investment contracts as well as certain aspects of accounting for assets that back life insurance liabilities or life investment contract liabilities.

Whereas IFRS 4 only includes limited improvements to accounting for insurance contracts and disclosure requirements, AASB 1038 addresses all aspects of the recognition, measurement and disclosure of life insurance contracts.

IFRS 4 allows insurers to use a practice described as "shadow accounting". The revised AASB 1038 does not allow shadow accounting.

Accounting Standard AASB 1038

The Australian Accounting Standards Board made Accounting Standard AASB 1038 *Life Insurance Contracts* under section 334 of the *Corporations Act 2001* on 15 July 2004.

This compiled version of AASB 1038 applies to annual reporting periods beginning on or after 1 January 2011 but before 1 January 2013. It incorporates relevant amendments contained in other AASB Standards made by the AASB and other decisions of the AASB up to and including 27 October 2010 (see Compilation Details).

Accounting Standard AASB 1038

Life Insurance Contracts

1 Application

1.1 This Standard applies to each entity that is:

    (a)   a *life insurer*; or

    (b)   the parent in a group that includes a life insurer;

when the entity:

    (c)   is a reporting entity that is required to prepare financial reports in accordance with Part 2M.3 of the Corporations Act;

    (d)   is an other reporting entity and prepares general purpose financial statements; or

    (e)   prepares financial statements that are, or are held out to be, general purpose financial statements.

1.1.1   This Standard applies to the consolidated financial statements of a group in relation to a life insurer subsidiary. Paragraph 4.2 is of particular relevance in this case.

1.2 This Standard applies to annual reporting periods beginning on or after 1 January 2005.
[Note: For application dates of paragraphs changed or added by an amending Standard, see Compilation Details.]

1.3 This Standard shall not be applied to annual reporting periods beginning before 1 January 2005.

1.4 The requirements specified in this Standard apply to the financial statements where information resulting from their application is material in accordance with AASB 1031 *Materiality*.

1.4.1   The requirements specified in this Standard apply to the financial statements where information resulting from their application is material, in accordance with AASB 1031. An example of the application of materiality is that disclosures about *life insurance contracts* in the context of a group that includes a life insurer are required where the *life insurance business* is material in the context of the group.

1.4.2   For the purposes of AASB 134 *Interim Financial Reporting*, the determination of *policy liabilities* does not necessarily require a full actuarial valuation. In accordance with AASB 134, policy liabilities would need to be determined on a reliable basis, would be based on reasonable estimates, would include a full review of all assumptions, and would not be materially different from the policy liabilities determined by a full actuarial valuation.

1.5 When operative, this Standard supersedes AASB 1038 *Life Insurance Business* as approved by public notice in the *Commonwealth of Australia Gazette* No 546, 19 November 1998.

1.6   AASB 1038 (issued in November 1998) remains applicable until superseded by this Standard.

1.7   Notice of this Standard was published in the *Commonwealth of Australia Gazette* No S 294, 22 July 2004.

2 Scope

Life Insurance Contracts

2.1 This Standard applies to:

    (a)   life insurance contracts (including *life reinsurance contracts*) that a life insurer issues and to life reinsurance contracts that it holds;

(b)   certain aspects of accounting for *life investment contracts* that a life insurer issues, or, in the case of a life investment contract that is reinsured, that it holds; and

(c)   certain assets backing *life insurance liabilities* or *life investment contract liabilities*.

2.1.1   A life insurance contract is:

(a)   an *insurance contract*, as defined by this Standard, regulated under the *Life Insurance Act 1995*, or similar contracts issued by entities operating outside Australia; or

(b)   a *financial instrument with a discretionary participation feature*, which is regulated under the Life Insurance Act, or similar contracts issued by entities operating outside Australia.

2.1.2   All other insurance contracts are *general insurance contracts* and are treated under AASB 023 *General Insurance Contracts* or AASB 4 *Insurance Contracts*.

2.1.3   A life insurer is defined as an *insurer* or *reinsurer*, registered under the Life Insurance Act, who issues life insurance contracts or life investment contracts, or a similar entity operating outside Australia.

2.1.4   This Standard applies to life insurance contracts issued by friendly societies registered under the Life Insurance Act. Private health insurance contracts that are issued under the *National Health Act 1953* by friendly societies registered under the Life Insurance Act are excluded from the scope of this Standard. Private health insurance contracts issued under the National Health Act are treated under AASB 1023.

2.1.5   Life insurers often sell contracts that do not meet the definition of a life insurance contract in this Standard. These contracts are referred to as life investment contracts for the purposes of this Standard. Section 12 addresses the requirements in relation to life investment contracts.

2.1.6   A financial instrument with a discretionary participation feature, issued by a life insurer, is defined as a life insurance contract for the purposes of this Standard and in measuring the life insurance liability, issuers of such instruments would apply paragraph 8.9. AASB 7 *Financial Instruments: Disclosures* addresses additional disclosure in relation to these financial instruments.

Embedded Derivatives

2.2.1   AASB 139 *Financial Instruments: Recognition and Measurement* requires an entity to separate some embedded derivatives from their host contract, measure them at fair value and include changes in their *fair value* in the statement of comprehensive income. AASB 139 applies to derivatives embedded in a life insurance contract unless the embedded derivative is itself a life insurance contract.

2.2.2   As an exception to the requirement in AASB 139, an insurer need not separate, and measure at fair value, a *policyholder's* option to surrender an insurance contract for a fixed amount (or for an amount based on a fixed amount and an interest rate) even if the exercise price differs from the carrying amount of the host *insurance liability*. However, the requirement in AASB 139 applies to a put option or cash surrender option embedded in an insurance contract if the surrender value varies in response to the change in a financial variable (such as an equity or commodity price or index), or a non-financial variable that is not specific to a party to the contract. Furthermore, that requirement also applies if the holder's ability to exercise a put option or cash surrender option is triggered by a change in such a variable (for example, a put option that can be exercised if a stock market index reaches a specified level).

2.2.3   Paragraph 2.2.2 applies equally to options to surrender a financial instrument containing a discretionary participation feature.

Deposit Components

2.3.1   Some life insurance contracts contain both an insurance component and a *deposit component*. In some cases, an insurer is permitted to *unbundle* those components.

2.3.2 Unbundling is permitted if the insurer can measure the deposit component separately.

2.3.3 If a life insurer cannot measure the deposit component separately, an insurer shall not unbundle the deposit component.

2.3.4 To unbundle a life insurance contract, a life insurer:

(a) treats the life insurance component as a life insurance contract in accordance with this Standard;

(b) subject to (c), treats the deposit component as a life investment contract in accordance with this Standard; and

(c) where the deposit component includes a discretionary participation feature, treats this component as a separate life insurance contract in accordance with this Standard.

3 Purpose of Standard

3.1 The purpose of this Standard is to:

(a) **prescribe the accounting methods to be used for reporting on life insurance contracts consistent with AASB 4 *Insurance Contracts*, and the accounting methods to be used for certain aspects of life investment contracts;**

(b) **prescribe the accounting methods to be used in accounting for assets backing life insurance liabilities or life investment contract liabilities; and**

(c) **require disclosures about life insurance contracts and disclosures about certain aspects of life investment contracts.**

4 Entity and Consolidation Issues

The Life Insurer Entity

4.1 A life insurer shall recognise in its financial statements the assets, liabilities, income, expenses and equity of the entity, whether they are designated as relating to policyholders or to shareholders.

4.1.1 Life insurers may have both policyholders and shareholders with a financial interest in the entity. It is sometimes argued that the interests of policyholders and the interests of shareholders form the bases of separate entities that should prepare separate primary financial statements. However, the view adopted in this Standard is that the interests of policyholders and shareholders are intertwined and form the basis of a single entity. The boundaries of this entity are defined by control. The directors of the life insurer, in pursuing its objectives, govern the decision-making in relation to the financial and operating policies of the life insurer, which includes the assets of the entity, whether they are designated as relating to policyholders or to shareholders.

4.1.2 Equity in a shareholder-owned life insurer will generally comprise only shareholder equity. Although participants in the industry commonly refer to "policyholder retained profits", in relation to Australian business such amounts are unvested policyholder benefits liabilities. Under Australian legislation, "policyholder retained profits" relating to Australian life insurance business are paid to policyholders, although the timing of the payment is at the discretion of the life insurer. A life insurer may have unallocated surplus that is in the nature of "policyholder equity" if it is a friendly society or has foreign life insurance operations in a jurisdiction that permits retained profits to remain unallocated between policyholders and shareholders, and the policyholders' component has yet to be determined. A key factor in evaluating the classification as liability or equity of retained profits in a friendly society is the benefit fund rules of each particular benefit fund. If the rules of a benefit fund were such that all retained profits by default are for the benefit of policyholders, such retained profits would be classed as policyholder benefit liabilities.

Financial Statements of Groups that Include a Life Insurer Subsidiary

4.2 The consolidated financial statements of a group that includes a life insurer subsidiary shall recognise all of the assets, liabilities, income and expenses of that subsidiary, whether they are designated as relating to the policyholders or to the shareholders

of that life insurer. The life insurance contracts, life investment contracts and assets of a life insurer subsidiary and its group recognised in the consolidated financial statements of a group shall be measured in accordance with this Standard.

4.2.1   For the same reasons that a life insurer entity is considered to comprise both policyholder and shareholder interests, the view adopted in this Standard is that the parent controls the interests of both policyholders and shareholders and, accordingly, the consolidated financial statements of the group include all of those interests. The parent of a life insurer effectively uses all of the resources of shareholders and policyholders in achieving its objectives and effectively controls policyholder interests for the benefit of both policyholders and shareholders.

4.2.2   Some life insurers are subsidiaries of entities other than life insurers, such as banks, and some are subsidiaries of other life insurers. The character of the parent of a life insurer has no bearing on whether consolidated financial statements, prepared in accordance with paragraph 4.2, are required.

5 Premiums and Claims

5.1   Subject to paragraph 5.2, insurance components of life insurance contract premiums are income and insurance components of life insurance contract claims are expenses and shall be recognised separately in the statement of comprehensive income. Deposit components of life insurance contract premiums are not income and deposit components of life insurance contract claims are not expenses and shall be recognised as changes in life insurance liabilities.

5.2   For life insurance contracts where unbundling of the deposit component is prohibited under paragraph 2.3.3, premiums shall be recognised as income and claims shall be recognised as expenses.

5.2.1   A wide variety of products are offered by life insurers – risk or insurance products, investment products and numerous hybrids of these two products. There will be hybrid products that fall within the scope of this Standard that have both deposit and insurance components.

5.2.2   Premiums may comprise amounts that give rise to:

    (a)   income that is earned by providing services, including the bearing of risks; and

    (b)   amounts that are akin to deposits and which qualify for recognition as liabilities.

5.2.3   Similarly, claims may comprise amounts that give rise to:

    (a)   expenses that are incurred in providing services, including the bearing of risks; and

    (b)   amounts that are akin to withdrawals from deposits and which qualify for recognition as reductions in liabilities.

6 Reinsurance

Reporting by Cedants

6.1   A *cedant* shall recognise:

    (a)   premiums ceded to reinsurers as reinsurance expenses;

    (b)   claim recoveries and commissions from reinsurers as income; and

    (c)   claim recoveries and other inflows not yet received from a reinsurer as an asset.

6.1.1   Life insurers may reinsure some of their business. The cedant remains responsible for the total amount of successful claims of policyholders and, through reinsurance arrangements, may be entitled to recover amounts relating to some of those claims.

6.1.2   *Reinsurance contracts* are considered to be separate transactions from the original life insurance contracts and therefore give rise to separately recognisable amounts. The cedant recognises the gross amount of premiums received in accordance with paragraphs 5.1 and 5.2 and, where portions of the policies are reinsured, the ceded premiums are recognised as expenses (except where they would otherwise be recognised as deposits, if not reinsured).

Any recoveries from reinsurers are recognised as income by the cedant (except for any amounts representing the return of deposits). Consistent with this approach, the gross amount of life insurance liabilities is recognised as a liability and claim recoveries not yet received from a reinsurer are recognised as a receivable by the cedant.

Reporting by Reinsurers

6.2 Inwards reinsurance premiums and outwards reinsurance claims shall be recognised by the accepting reinsurer as for premiums and claims in accordance with paragraphs 5.1 and 5.2. Life insurance liabilities assumed shall be recognised as a liability by the accepting reinsurer in accordance with section 8.

6.2.1 From the perspective of the reinsurer, reinsurance premiums accepted are recognised in the same way as the cedant treats the acceptance of premiums under a *direct insurance contract*. Correspondingly, claims paid and payable to direct insurers are recognised as expenses by the reinsurer. Consistent with these treatments, life insurance liabilities assumed are recognised as a liability by the accepting reinsurer.

7 Impairment of Reinsurance Assets

7.1.1 If a cedant's *reinsurance asset* is impaired, the cedant shall reduce its carrying amount accordingly and recognise that impairment in the statement of comprehensive income. A reinsurance asset is impaired if, and only if:

(a) there is objective evidence, as a result of an event that occurred after initial recognition of the reinsurance asset, that the cedant may not receive amounts due to it under the terms of the contract; and

(b) that event has a reliably measurable impact on the amounts that the cedant will receive from the reinsurer.

8 Life Insurance Liabilities

Present Value and Best Estimates

8.1 Obligations arising from life insurance contracts (life insurance liabilities) shall be recognised as liabilities and shall be measured at the end of each reporting period as:

(a) **the net present value of future receipts from and payments to policyholders, including participating benefits, allowing for the possibility of discontinuance before the end of insurance contract periods, plus planned margins of revenues over expenses relating to services yet to be provided to policyholders, on the basis of assumptions that are best estimates and using a discount rate determined in accordance with paragraphs 8.7 or 8.8; or**

(b) **the accumulated benefits to policyholders after allowing for the portion of *acquisition costs* expected to be recouped where the result would not be materially different from the application of paragraph 8.1(a).**

8.1.1 The participating benefits component of life insurance liabilities includes previously vested benefits and future supportable bonuses. In addition to life insurance liabilities, there may be other liabilities that relate to participating policyholders. Insurance contract benefits attributable to participating policyholders that are not yet vested with specific policyholders are recognised as liabilities. These are further discussed in section 9.

8.1.2 Premiums are generally received in advance of the provision of services to policyholders, including the payment of claims. In return for premiums, life insurers provide services sometimes over long periods. Entering into a life insurance contract is considered to be the event that gives rise to future benefits and present obligations under a policy.

8.1.3 Where there are a number of variables relating to future uncertainties, a net present value approach to measuring life insurance liabilities is likely to provide the most appropriate measurement basis. The obligations under these more complex contracts are generally measured as the present value of the expected inflows, such as premiums and fees, and outflows, such as claims and other expenses, based on assumptions relating to whole populations of policyholders, and taking into account applicable taxation.

8.1.4   An accumulation approach involves accruing the entitlements in policyholders' records at the end of the reporting period. If the fees expected to be charged by the life insurer to the policyholder in each future reporting period are expected to equal or exceed any expenses incurred by the life insurer, the life insurance liability calculated under the accumulation approach would not be materially different from that obtained using the approach in paragraph 8.1(a).

8.1.5   The ultimate cost of meeting claims under many life insurance contracts depends on the frequency of occurrence of particular future events such as death and surrender and in some cases may depend upon other factors such as the future levels of investment returns. Assumptions need to be made about these future events. In order to ensure that life insurance liabilities are measured reliably, such assumptions need to be "best estimates".

8.1.6   Best estimate assumptions used in determining the present value of life insurance liabilities, such as the best estimate of the bonus rate, are made on the basis of the assets available to the life insurer at the end of the reporting period and do not include any allowance for future contributions by owners and other funds which may be provided in the future to support the business.

Acquisition Costs

8.1.7   Life insurance contracts written in one reporting period often give rise to benefits to the life insurer in subsequent reporting periods, such as future management fees and surrender penalties. Therefore, there are future benefits associated with the costs of acquiring life insurance contracts, and such costs are often substantial.

8.1.8   In the life insurance industry, acquisition costs are usually recognised as expenses in the reporting period in which they are incurred. This is generally offset by identifying a portion of the planned margins included in life insurance liabilities as relating to the recovery of acquisition costs. The most useful and reliable information available about the acquisition costs that will give rise to future economic benefits is the amount of future charges for acquisition costs identified as part of the process of determining life insurance liabilities.

Recognition of Planned Margins as Revenues

8.2   Planned margins of revenues over expenses for life insurance contracts shall be recognised in the statement of comprehensive income over the reporting periods during which the services, to which those margins relate, are provided to policyholders, and the revenues, relating to those services, are received.

8.2.1   In setting premium rates, life insurers will include planned margins of revenues over expenses. As noted in paragraph 8.1.2, premiums are generally received in advance of the provision of services to policyholders.

8.2.2   In this Standard, planned margins are recognised in the statement of comprehensive income when, and only when, the life insurer has performed the services necessary to establish a valid claim to those margins and has received the revenues relating to those services. To ensure that planned margins are recognised during the reporting period in which the relevant services are provided, life insurance liabilities include a component relating to those margins. These margins are then "released" based on one or more factors or "profit carriers" which correspond to the performance of services and the earning of the margins. In relation to many products, the profit carrier might be premiums or claims.

Differences between Actual and Assumed Experience

8.3   Except in relation to investment earnings rate assumptions for participating business, the effect of changes in life insurance liabilities resulting from a difference between actual and assumed experience determined during the reporting period shall be recognised in the statement of comprehensive income as income or expenses in the reporting period in which the changes occur.

8.3.1   The assumed patterns and frequencies of events used in determining life insurance liabilities are compared with actual events in each reporting period to assess their accuracy. The effects of differences between actual and assumed experience represents decreases or increases in the expected payments to policyholders and are income or expenses of the reporting period in which the differences occur. For example, where the assumed costs of death claims under a renewable term life product line are greater than the actual costs for a reporting period, income equal to the difference is recognised in the statement of comprehensive income for the current reporting period.

8.3.2 The recognition of the net amount of changes in life insurance liabilities resulting from a difference between actual and assumed experience identified during the reporting period as income or an expense is consistent with the use of assumptions that are best estimates as at the end of each reporting period.

Changes to Underlying Assumptions

8.4 Assumptions used for measuring life insurance liabilities shall be reviewed for each reporting period. Where the review leads to changes in assumptions, with the exception of new business, the changes shall be deemed to occur at the end of the reporting period.

8.4.1 Assumptions used for measuring new business may be deemed to have occurred at the beginning of the reporting period, or at the date of commencement of the new business or at the end of the reporting period.

8.4.2 In preparing interim financial reports, the end of the reporting period is the end of the interim reporting period. Accordingly, changes in assumptions are deemed to occur at the end of the interim reporting period.

8.5 The financial effects of changes to the assumptions underlying the measurement of life insurance liabilities made during the reporting period shall be recognised in the statement of comprehensive income over the future reporting periods during which services are provided to policyholders, except that:

(a) any estimated excess of the present value of future expenses over the present value of future revenues for a group of related products arising during the reporting period shall be recognised as an expense of the reporting period;

(b) the reversal of an expense previously recognised in accordance with paragraph 8.5(a) shall be recognised as income of the reporting period in which the reversal of the loss is recognised;

(c) the effects of a change to adopted discount rates and related economic assumptions caused by changes in investment market and general economic conditions shall be recognised as income or expense of the reporting period in which the change occurs; and

(d) material calculation errors and similar errors shall be treated in accordance with AASB 108 *Accounting Policies, Changes in Accounting Estimates and Errors.*

8.5.1 The assumptions underlying the measurement of life insurance liabilities are reviewed at the end of each reporting period. Based on past experience and revised expectations about the future, it may become apparent that particular assumptions are not consistent with likely future experience and need to be changed. Such changes are effectively a reassessment of the likely patterns and frequencies of future events. The normal revision of assumptions is not considered to be an error.

8.5.2 Apart from the circumstances identified in paragraph 8.5, changes to underlying assumptions are effectively recognised over future reporting periods by adjusting the planned margins included in life insurance liabilities. If the effect of a changed assumption is a decrease in the present value of present obligations to policyholders, the planned margin is increased. If the effect is an increase in the present value of obligations to policyholders, the planned margin is reduced. The overall amount of life insurance liabilities is not affected by these changes to underlying assumptions, as long as the planned margin of revenues over expenses is not eliminated.

8.5.3 Material calculation errors and similar errors are treated in accordance with AASB 108. Under AASB 108, except to the extent that it is impracticable to determine either the period-specific effects or the cumulative effect of the error, an entity corrects material prior period errors retrospectively in the first financial statements authorised for issue after their discovery by:

(a)   restating the comparative amounts for the prior period(s) presented in which the error occurred; or

(b)   if the error occurred before the earliest prior period presented, restating the opening balances of assets, liabilities and equity for the earliest prior period presented.

Changes to Discount Rates and Related Economic Assumptions

8.5.4   As with other assumptions, the discount rates and related economic assumptions used in determining life insurance liabilities are reviewed at the end of each reporting period. The effects of a change to adopted discount rates and related economic assumptions caused by changes in investment market and economic conditions are recognised in the reporting period in which the change is made. For a life insurer with a typical spread of investments, if market yields fall, investment values generally rise and the resulting increases in investment values are recognised as income in the reporting period in which they occur. Where the discount rates are adjusted in line with such falls in market rates, life insurance liabilities for such contracts will increase and an expense will be recognised, having an offsetting (but not usually matching) effect on the increased investment values.

8.5.5   In relation to participating business (which is discussed in section 9), the effect of a change to the assumptions about discount rates, explained in paragraph 8.5.4, is a result of adjusting the best estimate of life insurance liabilities, including future participating benefits. For example, if market rates of return rise, investment values generally fall and the resulting decreases in investment values are recognised as an expense in the reporting period in which they occur. The fall in investment values will clearly impact on the ability of the life insurer to support future participating benefits. These are likely to be reduced, with an offsetting effect on the reduced investment values.

Liability Adequacy Test

8.6   Life insurers shall perform a *liability adequacy test*.

8.6.1   Situations may arise where the present value of the planned margin of revenues over expenses for a group of related products will be adjusted as a result of changing underlying assumptions to the extent that the planned margin is eliminated and becomes a planned loss. That is, a review of expected future cash flows indicates that the present value of estimated future expenses for a group of related products exceeds the present value of estimated future revenues. In such circumstances, the excess of the present value of expenses over revenues arising during the reporting period is recognised in the statement of comprehensive income in the reporting period in which the assessment is made. The loss reflects a higher present obligation due to adverse future experience, which is now expected in future years. Whilst the future cash flows giving rise to the loss are yet to occur, this treatment is justified on the basis that entering into life insurance contracts is an event that gives rise to a present obligation to meet the expected future claims.

8.6.2   A group of related products, for the purpose of the calculating the planned margin, performing the liability adequacy test and for disclosure, would be products that have substantially the same contractual terms and were priced on the basis of substantially the same assumptions.

8.6.3   In reviewing expected future cash flows, the insurer takes into account both future cash flows under insurance contracts it has issued and the related reinsurance contracts.

8.6.4   Where an intangible asset has arisen under paragraph 13.1.1(b), a loss arises when the present value of planned margins of revenues over expenses is less than the related intangible asset. This test is to be performed for groups of related products and the intangible asset is allocated, on a reasonable basis, across these groups. Any loss is recognised as an expense in the statement of comprehensive income. In recognising the loss in the statement of comprehensive income, the life insurer first writes down the related intangible asset and then reflects any additional liability in the life insurance liabilities.

Discount Rates

8.7 To the extent that the benefits under life insurance contracts are not contractually linked to the performance of the assets held, the life insurance liabilities shall be discounted for the time value of money using risk-free discount rates based on current observable, objective rates that relate to the nature, structure and term of the future obligations.

8.8 To the extent that the benefits under life insurance contracts are contractually linked to the performance of the assets held, the life insurance liabilities shall be discounted using discount rates based on the market returns on assets backing life insurance liabilities.

8.8.1 In applying paragraph 8.7, the discount rates adopted are not intended to reflect risks inherent in the liability cash flows, which might be allowed for by a reduction in the discount rate in a fair value measurement, nor are they intended to reflect the insurance and other non-financial risks and uncertainties reflected in the life insurance liabilities. The discount rates are not intended to include allowance for the cost of any options or guarantees that are separately measured as part of the life insurance liabilities.

8.8.2 In applying paragraph 8.7, typically, government bond rates may be appropriate discount rates for the purposes of this Standard, or they may be an appropriate starting point in determining such discount rates.

Financial Instruments with Discretionary Participation Features

8.9 Financial instruments with discretionary participation features are life insurance contracts for the purposes of this Standard and shall be treated in accordance with paragraphs 8.1 to 8.8 and section 9.

9 Participating Benefits

9.1 Except for transfers from unvested policyholder benefits liabilities, participating benefits vested in policyholders in relation to the reporting period shall be recognised in the statement of comprehensive income as expenses for the reporting period. Such benefits which remain payable as at the end of the reporting period shall be recognised as a component of life insurance liabilities.

9.2 Participating benefits that have been allocated in relation to the reporting period to participating policyholders generally, but that have not yet vested in specific policyholders, shall be recognised as expenses for the reporting period. Amounts that have been allocated to participating policyholders generally, but that have not vested in specific policyholders as at the end of the reporting period, shall be recognised as unvested policyholder benefits liabilities.

9.2.1 Some life insurers sell participating business. Participating policyholders are generally eligible to receive the same types of benefits as other policyholders and, in addition, are entitled to participate in the profits relating to participating business. For example, a participating policyholder may receive a low contractually determined rate of return on savings together with term life cover and, in addition, receive benefits that depend on the investment performance of the pool of assets associated with participating policies and on the risk experience of participating policyholders. These additional benefits are often called bonuses and are at the discretion of the life insurer. In some reporting periods the life insurer may withhold a portion of the "profits" from the pool of participating business and recognise these "profits" as unvested policyholder benefits liabilities. In other reporting periods the life insurer may "top up" the vested benefits to participating policyholders. Such vesting of benefits is often done to provide a reasonably level vesting of benefits over time, despite volatility in periodic profits from participating business.

9.2.2 It is sometimes argued that the discretionary nature of participating benefits means that they should be treated as appropriations of profit in the same way as dividends to shareholders. Because life insurance liabilities relating to all types of policyholders are recognised as liabilities under the Life Insurance Act (excluding some contracts issued by friendly societies), it is appropriate for the participating benefits vested in relation to the reporting period, other than transfers from unvested policyholder benefits liabilities, to be recognised as expenses of the reporting period.

9.2.3   Mutual life insurers are effectively owned by their policyholder members. Nevertheless, the mutual life insurer also has obligations to its policyholders. These obligations are classified as policy liabilities. Benefits vested in a mutual life insurer's policyholders, other than transfers from unvested policyholder benefits liabilities, are also to be recognised as expenses in the reporting period in which they are vested.

9.2.4   For financial reporting purposes, participating benefits vested in policyholders in a reporting period but not yet paid are included in life insurance liabilities and are measured at net present values. In the case of investment account participating business this may be approximately the same as the amount actually allocated to policyholder accounts. In the case of traditional participating business, there may be a significant difference between the net present value and the face value of the amount vested in policyholders. The net present value is relevant for financial reporting purposes because it is the best estimate of the net present value of the amount that the life insurer expects to pay out in the future using information based on experience up to the end of the reporting period.

9.2.5   Where a life insurer "tops up" the vested benefits from previously recognised unvested policyholder benefits liabilities, a transfer between liabilities is recognised. If a life insurer tops up the vested benefits for participating policyholders other than from unvested policyholder benefits liabilities, the amount of the "top up" is recognised as an expense of the reporting period in which the additional benefits are vested.

10 Assets Backing Life Insurance Liabilities or Life Investment Contract Liabilities

Fair Value Approach

10.1.1 Paragraphs 10.2 to 10.7.2 address the measurement of certain assets backing life insurance liabilities or life investment contract liabilities. The fair value approach to the measurement of assets backing life insurance liabilities or life investment contract liabilities is consistent with the present value measurement approach for life insurance liabilities required by this Standard and the fair value measurement approach for life investment contract liabilities required by this Standard. Where assets are not backing life insurance liabilities or life investment contract liabilities life insurers apply the applicable accounting standards making use of any measurement choices available.

Measurement

10.2   *Financial assets* that:

    (a)   **are within the scope of AASB 139;**

    (b)   **back life insurance liabilities or life investment contract liabilities; and**

    (c)   **are permitted to be designated as "at fair value through profit or loss" under AASB 139;**

    shall be designated as "at fair value through profit or loss" under AASB 139 on first application of this Standard, or on initial recognition.

10.2.1 An insurer applies AASB 139 to its financial assets. Under AASB 139 a financial asset at fair value through profit or loss is a financial asset that meets either of the following conditions:

    (a)   it is classified as held for trading; or

    (b)   it is designated as "at fair value through profit or loss" upon initial recognition. An entity may use this designation when it is a contract with an embedded derivative and paragraph 11A of AASB 139 allows the entity to measure the contract as "at fair value through profit or loss"; or when doing so results in more relevant information, because either:

        (i)   it eliminates or significantly reduces a measurement or recognition inconsistency (sometimes referred to as 'an accounting mismatch') that would otherwise arise from measuring assets or liabilities or recognising the gains and losses on them on different bases; or

(ii) a group of financial assets, *financial liabilities* or both is managed and its performance is evaluated on a fair value basis, in accordance with a documented risk management or investment strategy, and information about the group is provided internally on that basis to the entity's key management personnel (as defined in AASB 124 *Related Party Disclosures*), for example the entity's board of directors and chief executive officer.

AASB 1 *First-time Adoption of Australian Equivalents to International Financial Reporting Standards* permits entities to designate financial assets as "at fair value through profit or loss" on first application of the Standard.

10.2.2 The view adopted in this Standard is that, in all but rare cases, financial assets within the scope of AASB 139 that back life insurance liabilities or life investment contract liabilities are permitted to be measured at fair value through profit or loss under AASB 139. This is because the measurement of life insurance liabilities under this Standard incorporates current information and measuring the financial assets backing these life insurance liabilities at fair value eliminates or significantly reduces a potential measurement inconsistency which would arise if the assets were classified as available for sale or measured at amortised cost. In addition, under AASB 139, a group of financial assets may be designated as at fair value through profit or loss where it is both managed and its performance is evaluated on a fair value basis, in accordance with a documented risk management or investment strategy. In the vast majority of cases, financial assets backing life investment contract liabilities and financial assets backing life insurance liabilities would be managed and their performance would be evaluated on a fair value basis, in accordance with a documented risk management or investment strategy.

10.3 Investment property that is within the scope of AASB 140 *Investment Property* and that backs life insurance liabilities or life investment contract liabilities shall be measured at fair value using the fair value model under AASB 140.

10.4 Property, plant and equipment that is within the scope of AASB 116 *Property, Plant and Equipment* and that backs life insurance liabilities or life investment contract liabilities shall be measured using the revaluation model under AASB 116.

10.4.1 An insurer applies AASB 116 to its property, plant and equipment. Under AASB 116 property includes owner-occupied property and property being constructed or developed for future use as investment property. Under AASB 116, the cost model, for measurement subsequent to initial recognition, is to carry property, plant and equipment at cost. However, AASB 116 has a revaluation model: an entity, subsequent to initial recognition, may carry its property, plant and equipment assets at a revalued amount, being its fair value at the date of the revaluation less any subsequent accumulated depreciation and subsequent accumulated impairment losses.

10.4.2 Those property, plant and equipment assets that are within the scope of AASB 116 and that the insurer considers back life insurance liabilities or life investment contract liabilities are measured using the revaluation model under AASB 116, that is, they are measured at fair value with increases in fair value credited directly to equity and decreases recognised as an expense, unless they reverse a previous increase.

10.5 Investments in associates that:

(a) are defined by AASB 128 *Investments in Associates*;

(b) back either life insurance liabilities or life investment contract liabilities;

(c) are held by mutual funds, unit trusts and similar entities including *investment-linked* insurance funds; and

(d) are permitted to be designated as "at fair value through profit or loss" under AASB 139;

shall be designated as "at fair value through profit or loss" under AASB 139 on first application of this Standard, or on initial recognition.

10.5.1 An insurer applies AASB 128 to its investments in associates. AASB 128 requires investments in associates to be accounted for using the equity method but it does not apply to investments in associates held by mutual funds, unit trusts and similar entities including investment-linked insurance funds that are treated under AASB 139 and designated as "at fair value through profit or loss".

10.6   **Venturers' interests in jointly controlled entities that:**

   (a)   **are defined by AASB 131** *Interests in Joint Ventures***;**

   (b)   **back either life insurance liabilities or life investment contract liabilities;**

   (c)   **are held by mutual funds, unit trusts and similar entities including investment-linked insurance funds; and**

   (d)   **are permitted to be designated as "at fair value through profit or loss" under AASB 139;**

   shall be designated as "at fair value through profit or loss" under AASB 139, on first application of this Standard, or on initial recognition.

10.6.1   Entities apply AASB 131 to interests in joint ventures. AASB 131 requires investments in joint ventures to be proportionately consolidated or to be accounted for using the equity method. However, AASB 131 does not apply to venturers' interests in jointly controlled entities held by mutual funds, unit trusts and similar entities including investment-linked insurance funds that are treated under AASB 139 and designated as "at fair value through profit or loss".

Separate Financial Statements

10.7   **When preparing** *separate financial statements***, those investments in subsidiaries, jointly controlled entities and associates that:**

   (a)   **are within the scope of AASB 127** *Consolidated and Separate Financial Statements***;**

   (b)   **back life insurance liabilities or life investment contract liabilities; and**

   (c)   **are permitted to be designated as "at fair value through profit or loss" under AASB 139;**

   shall be designated as "at fair value through profit or loss" under AASB 139, on first application of this Standard or on initial recognition.

10.7.1   An insurer applies AASB 127 to its investments in subsidiaries, jointly controlled entities and associates when preparing separate financial statements. Under AASB 127, in the parent's separate financial statements, the investments in subsidiaries, jointly controlled entities and associates can either be accounted for at cost or in accordance with AASB 139.

10.7.2   In the parent's separate financial statements, investments in subsidiaries, jointly controlled entities and associates, that are within the scope of AASB 127, that the insurer considers back life insurance liabilities or life investment contract liabilities, and that are permitted to be designated as "at fair value through profit or loss" under AASB 139, are designated as "at fair value through profit or loss" under AASB 139, on first application of this Standard or on initial recognition.

11 Imputed Inflows and Outflows

11.1   **Subject to paragraph 18.3, a life insurer shall recognise imputed inflows and outflows as income and expenses when, and only when, such imputed flows relate to transactions with external entities.**

11.1.1   Life insurers often impute inflows and outflows to different classes of policyholders in order to help ensure that they are treated equitably. For example, a life insurer may own the buildings that it occupies. The funds of a particular group of policyholders are used to acquire and operate such buildings whilst a wider group of policyholders and shareholders may benefit from the use of the buildings. In the owner-occupied building example, the life insurer imputes an inflow of rent income to the policyholders whose funds are used to acquire and operate the buildings and imputes an outflow of rent cost to the other policyholders and to shareholders.

11.1.2   In cases where there are no transactions with external entities, such as with owner-occupied buildings, the life insurer is dealing with itself. There is no transaction or other past event that gives rise to income or an expense. Any inflows and outflows imputed for internal management purposes would be eliminated in preparing external financial statements except in relation to the disaggregated disclosures required by paragraphs 18.1 and 18.2.

11.1.3 In some cases, life insurers impute inflows and outflows where external entities are involved. For example, life insurers often lend funds to their employees at concessional rates of interest with the funds being provided by a particular group of policyholders, whilst other policyholders and any shareholders benefit from the services provided by those employees. Because external parties are involved, such imputed inflows and outflows are recognised as income and expenses when they can be reliably measured.

12 Life Investment Contracts

12.1 Life investment contract liabilities, that are permitted to be designated as "at fair value through profit or loss" under AASB 139, shall be designated as "at fair value through profit or loss" under AASB 139 on first application of this Standard, or on initial recognition.

12.1.1 The view adopted in this Standard is that, in all but rare cases, life investment contract liabilities within the scope of AASB 139 are permitted to be measured at fair value through profit or loss under AASB 139. This is because, when a life investment contract liability is backed by a financial asset measured at fair value through profit or loss, designating the life investment contract liability at fair value through profit or loss eliminates or significantly reduces a potential measurement inconsistency which would arise if the life investment contract liability were measured at amortised cost. In addition, in the vast majority of cases, life investment contract liabilities would be managed and their performance would be evaluated on a fair value basis, in accordance with a documented risk management or investment strategy.

12.1.2 Some life investment contracts involve both the origination of one or more financial instruments and the provision of management services. Life investment contract liabilities arise under the financial instrument element and are treated under AASB 139. The management services element, including associated acquisition costs, is treated under AASB 118 *Revenue*; this element may also give rise to assets and liabilities. Life insurers shall refer to paragraph 14(b)(iii) in the illustrative examples accompanying AASB 118.

13 Life Insurance Contracts Acquired in a Business Combination or Portfolio Transfer

13.1.1 To comply with AASB 3 *Business Combinations*, an insurer shall, at the acquisition date, measure at fair value the insurance liabilities assumed and *insurance assets* acquired in a business combination. However, an insurer is permitted, but not required, to use an expanded presentation that splits the fair value of acquired insurance contracts into two components:

(a) a liability measured in accordance with the insurer's accounting policies for life insurance contracts that it issues; and

(b) an intangible asset, representing the difference between:

  (i) the fair value of the contractual insurance rights acquired and insurance obligations assumed; and

  (ii) the amount described in paragraph 13.1.1(a).

The subsequent measurement of this asset shall be consistent with the measurement of the related life insurance liability.

13.1.2 An insurer acquiring a portfolio of life insurance contracts may use an expanded presentation described in paragraph 13.1.1.

13.1.3 The intangible assets described in paragraphs 13.1.1 and 13.1.2 are excluded from the scope of AASB 136 *Impairment of Assets* and from the scope of AASB 138 *Intangible Assets* in respect of recognition and measurement. AASB 136 and AASB 138 apply to customer lists and customer relationships reflecting the expectation of future contracts that are not part of the contractual insurance rights and contractual insurance obligations that existed at the date of a business combination or portfolio transfer.

13.1.4 AASB 138 includes disclosure requirements in relation to this intangible asset.

13.1.5 Where a life insurer recognises an intangible asset under paragraph 13.1.1(b), this intangible asset is considered when performing the liability adequacy test referred to in paragraph 8.6.

14 Life Insurance Contracts Disclosure – Explanation of Recognised Amounts

14.1   A life insurer shall disclose information that identifies and explains the amounts in its financial statements arising from life insurance contracts.

14.1.1 To comply with paragraph 14.1, a life insurer shall disclose:

(a)   its accounting policies for life insurance contracts and related assets, liabilities, income and expense;

(b)   the recognised assets, liabilities, income, expense and cash flows arising from life insurance contracts. Furthermore, if the life insurer is a cedant, it shall disclose:

(i)   gains and losses recognised in profit or loss at the time of buying reinsurance; and

(ii)   if the cedant defers and amortises gains and losses arising at the time of buying reinsurance, the amortisation for the period and the amounts remaining unamortised at the beginning and end of the period;

(c)   the process used to determine the assumptions that have the greatest effect on the measurement of the recognised amounts described in (b). When practicable, a life insurer shall also give quantified disclosure of those assumptions;

(d)   the effect of changes in assumptions used to measure life insurance assets and life insurance liabilities, showing separately the effect of each change that has a material effect on the financial statements; and

(e)   reconciliations of changes in life insurance liabilities and reinsurance assets.

14.1.2 When applying paragraph 14.1.1(b) and disclosing recognised income arising from life insurance contracts, life insurers would normally disclose income from direct and reinsurance business. In accordance with the principles embodied in this Standard, with the exception of premium revenue recognised in accordance with paragraph 5.1, all revenues are recognised and disclosed before the effects of any transfers to or from life insurance liabilities. Disclosure of the effects of transfers to and from life insurance liabilities is required by paragraph 14.1.1(e).

14.1.3 In accordance with the principles embodied in this Standard, with the exception of claims expense recognised in accordance with paragraph 5.1, all expenses are recognised and disclosed before the effects of any transfers to or from life insurance liabilities. Disclosure of the effects of transfers to and from life insurance liabilities is required by paragraph 14.1.1(e).

14.1.4 To disclose and explain the expenses arising from life insurance contracts, life insurers would normally disclose:

(a)   outwards reinsurance expense;

(b)   operating expenses:

(i)   claims expense;

(ii)   policy acquisition expenses, separated into material components including commission;

(iii)   policy maintenance expenses; and

(iv)   investment management expenses; and

(c)   the basis for the apportionment of operating expenses between:

(i)   life insurance contract acquisition;

(ii)   life insurance contract maintenance;

(iii)   investment management expenses;

       (iv)   life investment contract acquisition;

       (v)   life investment contract maintenance; and

       (vi)   other expenses.

14.1.5 When applying paragraphs 14.1.1(c) and 14.1.1(d) and disclosing the process used to determine assumptions, quantified disclosure of assumptions and the effect of changes in assumptions, the life insurer would normally show the impact of changes in assumptions on future profit margins and life insurance liabilities. The assumptions that would normally have the greatest effect on the measurement of recognised amounts described in paragraph 14.1.1(b) are:

(a)   discount rates and inflation rates;

(b)   profit carriers used for each major product group;

(c)   future maintenance and investment management expenses, the rate of inflation applicable to them and any automatic indexation of benefits and premiums;

(d)   rates of taxation;

(e)   mortality and morbidity, by reference to the identity of the tables;

(f)   rates of discontinuance;

(g)   surrender values;

(h)   rates of growth of unit prices in respect of unit-linked benefits;

(i)   rates of future supportable participating benefits; and

(j)   the crediting policy adopted in determining future supportable participating benefits.

14.1.6 When applying paragraph 14.1.1(b) and disclosing the recognised liabilities arising from life insurance contracts, life insurers would normally disclose the following components of life insurance liabilities:

(a)   future policy benefits, including participating benefits;

(b)   balance of future expenses;

(c)   planned margins of revenues over expenses;

(d)   future charges for acquisition costs; and

(e)   balance of future revenues.

14.1.7 When a life insurer is presenting the disclosures required by paragraphs 14.1.1(c) and 14.1.1(d) the insurer determines the level and extent of disclosure that is appropriate having regard to its circumstances and the qualitative characteristics of financial statements under the *Framework for the Preparation and Presentation of Financial Statements* of understandability, relevance, reliability and comparability.

15 Nature and Extent of Risks Arising from Life Insurance Contracts

15.1 A life insurer shall disclose information that enables users of its financial statements to evaluate the nature and extent of risks arising from life insurance contracts.

15.1.1 To comply with paragraph 15.1, a life insurer shall disclose:

(a)   its objectives, policies and processes for managing risks arising from life insurance contracts and the methods used to manage those risks;

(b)   information about *insurance risk* (both before and after risk mitigation by reinsurance), including information about:

    (i)   sensitivity to insurance risk (see paragraph 15.1.3);

    (ii)   concentrations of insurance risk, including a description of how management determines concentrations and a description of the shared characteristic that identifies each concentration (e.g. type of *insured event*, geographical area, or currency); and

      (iii)   actual claims compared with previous estimates (i.e. claims development). The disclosure about claims development shall go back to the period when the earliest material claim arose for which there is still uncertainty about the amount and timing of the claims payments, but need not go back more than ten years. A life insurer need not disclose this information for claims for which uncertainty about the amount and timing of claims payments is typically resolved within one year;

  (c)   information about credit risk, liquidity risk and market risk that paragraphs 31-42 of AASB 7 would require if the life insurance contracts were within the scope of AASB 7. However:

      (i)   a life insurer need not provide the maturity analyses required by paragraphs 39(a) and (b) of AASB 7 if it discloses information about the estimated timing of the net cash outflows resulting from recognised insurance liabilities instead. This may take the form of an analysis, by estimated timing, of the amounts recognised in the statement of financial position; and

      (ii)   if a life insurer uses an alternative method to manage sensitivity to market conditions, such as an embedded value analysis, it may use that sensitivity analysis to meet the requirement in paragraph 40(a) of AASB 7. Such a life insurer shall also provide the disclosures required by paragraph 41 of AASB 7; and

  (d)   information about exposures to market risk arising from embedded derivatives contained in a host insurance contract if the life insurer is not required to, and does not, measure the embedded derivatives at fair value.

15.1.2 The claims development disclosure required by paragraph 15.1.1(b)(iii) only applies to classes of business where claims are not typically resolved within one year. For many life insurance products this disclosure would not normally be required. Furthermore, claims development disclosure would not normally be needed for annuity contracts, for example, because each periodic payment arises, in effect, from a separate claim about which there is no uncertainty.

15.1.3 To comply with paragraph 15.1.1(b)(i), a life insurer shall disclose either (a) or (b) as follows:

  (a)   a sensitivity analysis that shows how profit or loss and equity would have been affected had changes in the relevant risk variable that were reasonably possible at the end of the reporting period occurred; the methods and assumptions used in preparing the sensitivity analysis; and any changes from the previous period in the methods and assumptions used. However, if a life insurer uses an alternative method to manage sensitivity to market conditions, such as an embedded value analysis, it may meet this requirement by disclosing that alternative sensitivity analysis and the disclosures required by paragraph 41 of AASB 7; and

  (b)   qualitative information about sensitivity, and information about those terms and conditions of life insurance contracts that have a material effect on the amount, timing and uncertainty of the life insurer's future cash flows.

16 Other Disclosures Relating to Life Insurance Contracts

16.1 Where any premiums and any claims are separated into their revenue, expense and change in life insurance liability components in accordance with paragraph 5.1, total premiums and total claims shall be disclosed.

16.1.1 The mix of products written by a life insurer will vary between life insurers. Comparability between life insurers is enhanced by the disclosure of total premiums and total claims.

17 Disclosures Relating to Life Insurance Contracts and Life Investment Contracts

Financial Performance

17.1 The following components of profit or loss shall be shown, separated between policyholder and shareholder interests:

    (a) profit related to movement in life insurance liabilities;

    (b) profit related to movement in life investment contract liabilities and movement in assets or liabilities arising in respect of the management services element of life investment contracts;

    (c) investment earnings on assets in excess of policy liabilities; and

    (d) other items, separated into material components.

17.2 The following components of profit related to movements in life insurance liabilities, life investment contract liabilities and assets or liabilities arising in respect of the management services element of life investment contracts shall be shown:

    (a) planned margins of revenues over expenses;

    (b) the difference between actual and assumed experience;

    (c) the effects of changes to underlying assumptions;

    (d) loss recognition on groups of related products or reversal of previously recognised losses required by paragraph 8.6; and

    (e) other movements, separated into material components.

Restrictions on Assets

17.3 Restrictions attaching to assets held for the benefit of policyholders shall be disclosed.

17.3.1 There are a number of restrictions on the use of assets invested for policyholders in *statutory funds*. It is important that these restrictions be disclosed so that users of the financial statements can assess their impact.

Guaranteed or Assured Returns of Funds Invested

17.4 A life insurer shall separately disclose:

    (a) in respect of contracts with discretionary participation features, the amount of policy liabilities that relates to the *guaranteed element*;

    (b) in respect of investment-linked contracts, the amount of policy liabilities subject to investment performance guarantees; and

    (c) in respect of any other contracts not addressed in (a) or (b) with a fixed or guaranteed termination value, the amount of the current termination values.

17.4.1 Many life insurers issue contracts that provide some form of guarantee or assurance about the return of funds invested. It is useful for users of life insurers' financial statements to have information about the extent of such guarantees or assurances, since they involve the life insurer bearing investment risks on behalf of policyholders.

Equity

17.5 The following components of equity shall be disclosed:

    (a) retained earnings wholly attributable to shareholders; and

    (b) retained earnings where the allocation between participating policyholders and shareholders has yet to be determined.

17.5.1 Information about the different components of retained earnings is useful in meeting the accountability obligations of the life insurer for the whole business and in showing the relative positions of the major stakeholders.

17.5.2 A life insurer that has issued participating business may have "retained profits" generated from that business. In relation to Australian participating policyholders, these "retained profits" are liabilities in accordance with the Life Insurance Act. However, in friendly societies or foreign life insurance operations, "retained profits" may exist which have yet to be allocated between policyholders and shareholders. Such "retained profits" are separately disclosed. It is relevant to note that "retained profits" directly attributable to shareholders may reside in both statutory funds and a shareholder fund.

17.5.3   Where, in friendly societies or foreign life operations, "retained profits" exist, which have yet to be allocated and which are treated as equity then the insurer applies paragraphs 17.5.4 and 17.5.5 to this participating business.

17.5.4   Where a life insurance contract with a discretionary participation feature is issued by a friendly society or foreign life operation, the issuer of such a contract:

    (a)   may, but need not, recognise the guaranteed element separately from the discretionary participation feature. If the issuer does not recognise them separately, it classifies the whole contract as a liability. If the issuer classifies them separately, it classifies the guaranteed element as a liability;

    (b)   shall, if it recognises the discretionary participation feature separately from the guaranteed element, classify that feature as either a liability or a separate component of equity. This Standard does not specify how the issuer determines whether that feature is a liability or equity. The issuer may split that feature into liability and equity components and shall use a consistent accounting policy for that split. The issuer shall not classify that feature as an intermediate category that is neither liability nor equity;

    (c)   may recognise all premiums received as revenue without separating any portion that relates to the equity component. The resulting changes in the guaranteed element and in the portion of the discretionary participation feature classified as a liability shall be recognised in profit or loss. If part of the entire discretionary participation feature is classified in equity, a portion of profit or loss may be attributable to that feature (in the same way that a portion may be attributable to minority interests). The issuer shall recognise the portion of profit or loss attributable to any equity component of a discretionary participation feature as an allocation of profit or loss, not as expense or income (see AASB 101 *Presentation of Financial Statements*);

    (d)   shall, if the contract contains an embedded derivative within the scope of AASB 139, apply AASB 139 to that embedded derivative; and

    (e)   shall, in all respects not described in paragraphs 14-20 of AASB 4 and paragraphs 34(a)-(d) of AASB 4, continue its existing accounting policies for such contracts, unless it changes those accounting policies in a way that complies with paragraphs 21-30 of AASB 4.

17.5.5   The requirements in paragraph 17.5.4 also apply to a life investment contract issued by a friendly society or foreign life insurer that contains a discretionary participation feature. In addition:

    (a)   if the issuer classifies the entire discretionary participation feature as a liability, it shall apply the liability adequacy test in paragraph 8.6 to the whole contract (i.e. both the guaranteed element and the discretionary participation feature). The issuer need not determine the amount that would result from applying AASB 139 to the guaranteed element;

    (b)   if the issuer classifies part or all of the discretionary participation feature as a separate component of equity, the liability recognised for the whole contract shall not be less than the amount that would result from applying AASB 139 to the guaranteed element. That amount shall include the intrinsic value of an option to surrender the contract, but need not include its time value if paragraph 2.2.2 exempts that option from measurement at fair value. The issuer need not disclose the amount that would result from applying AASB 139 to the guaranteed element, nor need it present that amount separately. Furthermore, the issuer need not determine that amount if the total liability recognised is clearly higher;

    (c)   although these contracts are financial instruments, the issuer may continue to recognise the premiums for those contracts as revenue and recognise as an expense the resulting increase in the carrying amount of the liability, subject to the requirements of paragraphs 5.1 and 5.2; and

(d)   although these contracts are financial instruments, an issuer applying paragraph 20(b) of AASB 7 to contracts with a discretionary participation feature shall disclose the total interest expense recognised in profit or loss, but need not calculate such interest expense using the effective interest method.

Solvency Information

17.8   **A life insurer shall disclose the regulatory solvency position of each statutory fund. A group shall disclose the regulatory solvency position of each life insurer in the group.**

17.8.1   Under the Life Insurance Act, life insurers are required to hold reserves in excess of the amount of policy liabilities. These additional reserves are necessary to support the life insurer's capital requirements under its business plan and to provide a cushion against adverse experience in managing long-term risks. Because solvency is an important aspect of a life insurer's financial position, information about it is useful to users of financial statements.

Managed Funds and Other Fiduciary Activities

17.9   **The nature and amount of the life insurer's activities relating to managed funds and trust activities, and whether arrangements exist to ensure that such activities are managed independently from its other activities, shall be disclosed.**

Actuarial Information

17.10   **The following shall be disclosed in notes:**

(a)   **if other than the end of the reporting period, the effective date of the actuarial report on policy liabilities and solvency reserves;**

(b)   **the name and qualifications of the actuary;**

(c)   **whether the amount of policy liabilities has been determined in accordance with the requirements of the Life Insurance Act; and**

(d)   **whether the actuary is satisfied as to the accuracy of the data from which the amount of policy liabilities has been determined.**

Assets Backing Life Insurance Liabilities or Life Investment Contract Liabilities

17.11   **An insurer shall disclose the process used to determine which assets back life insurance liabilities or life investment contract liabilities.**

Other Disclosures

17.12.1 Australian Accounting Standards and the Life Insurance Act differ in their requirements. Accordingly, life insurers are encouraged to disclose a reconciliation between:

(a)   the profit for the reporting period reported under Australian Accounting Standards and the profit for the reporting period reported under the Life Insurance Act; and

(b)   the retained earnings at the end of the reporting period in accordance with Australian Accounting Standards and the retained earnings at the end of the reporting period in accordance with the Life Insurance Act.

17.13.1 This Standard addresses disclosure requirements in relation to life insurance contracts and certain disclosure requirements in relation to life investment contracts. Other Australian Accounting Standards may be relevant to a life insurer's financial statements. In particular, the disclosure requirements in AASB 7 would normally be relevant to life insurers.

18 Disaggregated Information

Statutory Funds and the Shareholder Fund

18.1   For each statutory fund and for the shareholder fund the following shall be disclosed:

    (a)   investment assets;

    (b)   other assets;

    (c)   life insurance liabilities;

    (d)   life investment contract liabilities and assets or liabilities arising in respect of the management services element of life investment contracts;

    (e)   liabilities other than life insurance liabilities or life investment contract liabilities;

    (f)   retained earnings, showing the amount directly attributable to shareholders and other retained earnings;

    (g)   premium revenue split between life insurance contracts and life investment contracts;

    (h)   investment income;

    (i)   claims expense split between life insurance contracts and life investment contracts;

    (j)   other operating expenses;

    (k)   investment income paid or allocated to policyholders;

    (l)   profit or loss before tax;

    (m)   profit or loss after tax; and

    (n)   transfers to or from other funds.

18.1.1 Disaggregated information for each life fund and the shareholder fund is useful because, under Australian legislation, each life insurer may have more than one fund and, in general, the assets of each life fund are only available to meet the liabilities and expenses of that life fund.

Investment-linked and Non-investment-linked Business

18.2   A life insurer shall disclose the information required by paragraphs 18.1(a) to 18.1(m) disaggregated between those amounts relating to investment-linked business and those relating to *non-investment-linked business*.

18.2.1 The risks and potential rewards for a life insurer differ substantially as between investment-linked business and non-investment-linked business. Accordingly, disaggregated information about these is considered to be useful in assessing the financial performance and financial position of a life insurer. The information required by paragraph 18.2 is for the entity's life insurance business as a whole; it is not required for each life fund.

18.2.2 [Deleted by the AASB]

Imputed Inflows and Outflows

18.3   Disclosures required by paragraphs 18.1 and 18.2 shall include all imputed inflows and outflows as income and expenses where they can be reliably measured.

18.3.1 As discussed in paragraph 11.1.1, life insurers often impute inflows and outflows to different classes of policyholders and shareholders to help ensure that they are treated equitably. Whereas, in relation to the statement of comprehensive income and the statement of financial position, paragraph 11.1 only permits the recognition of imputed inflows and outflows relating to transactions with external parties, paragraph 18.3 requires all imputed inflows and outflows to be included in the disaggregated information to reflect the performance of each segment of the life insurer.

19 Transitional Provisions

19.1   An entity need not apply the disclosure requirements in this Standard to comparative information that relates to annual periods beginning before 1 January 2005, except for the disclosures required by paragraphs 14.1.1(a) and 14.1.1(b) about accounting policies, and recognised assets, liabilities, income and expense and cash flows.

19.2   When an entity applies the disclosure requirements in this Standard to comparative information that relates to annual periods beginning before 1 January 2005, if it is impracticable to apply a particular requirement of this Standard to comparative information that relates to annual periods beginning before 1 January 2005, an entity shall disclose that fact. AASB 108 explains the term "impracticable".

19.3   In applying paragraph 15.1.1(b)(iii), an entity need not disclose information about claims development that occurred earlier than five years before the end of the first annual reporting period in which it applies this Standard. Furthermore, if it is impracticable, when an entity first applies this Standard, to prepare information about claims development that occurred before the beginning of the earliest period for which an entity presents full comparative information that complies with this Standard, the entity shall disclose that fact.

19.3.1 There are also references to transitional measurement requirements in paragraphs 10.2-10.2.2, 10.5, 10.6, 10.7, 10.7.2 and 12.1.

20 Definitions

20.1   In this Standard:

acquisition costs means the fixed and variable costs of acquiring new business, including commissions and similar distribution costs, and costs of accepting, issuing and initially recording policies

(Acquisition costs relate to the costs incurred in acquiring specific life insurance contracts during the reporting period. They do not include the general growth and development costs incurred by a life insurer.)

cedant means the policyholder under a life reinsurance contract

deposit component means a contractual component that is not accounted for as a derivative under AASB 139 *Financial Instruments: Recognition and Measurement* and would be within the scope of AASB 139 if it were a separate instrument

direct insurance contract means an insurance contract that is not a reinsurance contract

discretionary participation feature means a contractual right to receive, as a supplement to *guaranteed benefits*, additional benefits:

(a)   that are likely to be a significant portion of the total contractual benefits;

(b)   whose amount or timing is contractually at the discretion of the issuer; and

(c)   that are contractually based on:

(i)   the performance of a specified pool of contracts or a specified type of contract;

(ii)   realised and/or unrealised investment returns on a specified pool of assets held by the issuer; or

(iii)   the profit or loss of the company, fund or other entity that issues the contract

fair value means the amount for which an asset could be exchanged, or a liability settled, between knowledgeable, willing parties in an arm's length transaction

financial risk means the risk of a possible future change in one or more of a specified interest rate, financial instrument price, commodity price, foreign exchange rate, index of prices or rates, a credit rating or credit index or other variable, provided in the case of a non-financial variable that the variable is not specific to a party to the contract

general insurance contract means an insurance contract that is not a life insurance contract

guaranteed benefits means payments or other benefits to which a particular policyholder or investor has an unconditional right that is not subject to the contractual discretion of the issuer

guaranteed element means an obligation to pay guaranteed benefits included in a contract that contains a discretionary participation feature

insurance asset means an insurer's net contractual rights under an insurance contract

insurance contract means a contract under which one party (the insurer) accepts significant insurance risk from another party (the policyholder) by agreeing to compensate the policyholder if a specified uncertain future event (the insured event) adversely affects the policyholder

(Refer to Appendix for additional guidance in applying this definition.)

insurance liability means an insurer's net contractual obligations under an insurance contract

insurance risk means risk, other than financial risk, transferred from the holder of a contract to the issuer

insured event means an uncertain future event covered by an insurance contract and creates insurance risk

insurer means the party that has an obligation under an insurance contract to compensate a policyholder if an insured event occurs

investment-linked means where the benefit amount under a life insurance contract or life investment contract is directly linked to the market value of the investments held in the particular investment-linked fund

liability adequacy test means an assessment of whether the carrying amount of an insurance liability needs to be increased (or the carrying amount of the related deferred acquisition costs or related intangible assets decreased) based on a review of future cash flows

life insurance business means all life insurance contract and life investment contract business conducted by a life insurer

life insurance contract means an insurance contract, or a financial instrument with a discretionary participation feature, regulated under the Life Insurance Act, and similar contracts issued by entities operating outside Australia

(Private health insurance contracts issued under the *National Health Act 1953* but written by friendly societies registered under the Life Insurance Act, are not life insurance contracts but are general insurance contracts.)

life insurance liability means a life insurer's net contractual obligations under a life insurance contract

life insurer means an entity registered under the *Life Insurance Act 1995*, that issues life insurance contracts or life investment contracts, and similar entities operating outside Australia

life investment contract means a contract which is regulated under the *Life Insurance Act 1995* but which does not meet the definition of a life insurance contract in this Standard, and similar contracts issued by entities operating outside Australia

life investment contract liability means a life insurer's net contractual obligations under a life investment contract which arise under the financial instrument component of a life investment contract

life reinsurance contract means a life insurance contract issued by one insurer (the reinsurer) to compensate another insurer (the cedant) for losses on one or more contracts issued by the cedant

non-investment-linked business means life insurance business other than investment-linked business

policyholder means a party that has a right to compensation under an insurance contract if an insured event occurs

policy liability means a liability that arises under a life insurance contract or a life investment contract including any asset or liability arising in respect of the management services element of a life investment contract

reinsurance assets means a cedant's net contractual rights under a reinsurance contract

reinsurance contract means an insurance contract issued by one insurer (the reinsurer) to compensate another insurer (the cedant) for losses on one or more contracts issued by the cedant

reinsurer means the party that has an obligation under a reinsurance contract to compensate a cedant if an insured event occurs

separate financial statements are those presented by a parent, an investor in an associate or a venturer in a jointly controlled entity, in which the investments are accounted for on the basis of the direct equity interest rather than on the basis of the reported results and net assets of the investees

statutory fund means a statutory fund under the *Life Insurance Act 1995*

unbundle means to account for the components of a contract as if they were separate contracts

20.2 The following terms are defined in AASB 132 *Financial Instruments: Presentation* and are used in this Standard with the meaning specified in AASB 132:

(a)   financial asset;

(b)   financial instrument; and

(c)   financial liability.

Appendix

Definition of an Insurance Contract

This appendix is an integral part of AASB 1038.

1   This Appendix gives guidance on the definition of an insurance contract in section 20 of this Standard. It addresses the following issues:

(a)   the term 'uncertain future event' (paragraphs 2-4);

(b)   insurance risk and other risks (paragraphs 5-14);

(c)   examples of life insurance contracts (paragraphs 15-18);

(d)   significant insurance risk (paragraphs 19-25); and

(e)   changes in the level of insurance risk (paragraphs 26 and 27).

Uncertain Future Event

2   Uncertainty (or risk) is the essence of an insurance contract. Accordingly, at least one of the following is uncertain at the inception of an insurance contract:

(a)   whether an insured event will occur;

(b)   when it will occur; or

(c)   how much the insurer will need to pay if it occurs.

3   In some insurance contracts, the insured event is the discovery of a loss during the term of the contract, even if the loss arises from an event that occurred before the inception of the contract. In other insurance contracts, the insured event is an event that occurs

during the term of the contract, even if the resulting loss is discovered after the end of the contract term.

4   Some insurance contracts cover events that have already occurred, but whose financial effect is still uncertain. An example is a reinsurance contract that covers the direct insurer against adverse development of claims already reported by policyholders. In such contracts, the insured event is the discovery of the ultimate cost of those claims.

Distinction between Insurance Risk and Other Risks

5   The definition of an insurance contract refers to insurance risk, which this Standard defines as risk, other than *financial risk*, transferred from the holder of a contract to the issuer. A contract that exposes the issuer to financial risk without significant insurance risk is not an insurance contract.

6   The definition of financial risk in section 20 of this Standard includes a list of financial and non-financial variables. That list includes non-financial variables that are not specific to a party to the contract, such as an index of earthquake losses in a particular region or an index of temperatures in a particular city. It excludes non financial variables that are specific to a party to the contract.

7   Some contracts expose the issuer to financial risk, in addition to significant insurance risk. For example, many life insurance contracts both guarantee a minimum rate of return to policyholders (creating financial risk) and promise death benefits that at some times significantly exceed the policyholder's account balance (creating insurance risk in the form of mortality risk). Such contracts are insurance contracts.

8   Under some contracts, an insured event triggers the payment of an amount linked to a price index. Such contracts are insurance contracts, provided the payment that is contingent on the insured event can be significant. For example, a life-contingent annuity linked to a cost-of-living index transfers insurance risk because payment is triggered by an uncertain event – the survival of the annuitant. The link to the price index is an embedded derivative, but it also transfers insurance risk. If the resulting transfer of insurance risk is significant, the embedded derivative meets the definition of an insurance contract, in which case it need not be separated and measured at fair value (see paragraph 2.2.1 of this Standard).

9   The definition of insurance risk refers to risk that the insurer accepts from the policyholder. In other words, insurance risk is a pre existing risk transferred from the policyholder to the insurer. Thus, a new risk created by the contract is not insurance risk.

10   The definition of an insurance contract refers to an adverse effect on the policyholder. The definition does not limit the payment by the insurer to an amount equal to the financial impact of the adverse event. For example, the definition does not limit payment under a term life insurance contract to the financial loss suffered by the deceased's dependants, nor does it preclude the payment of predetermined amounts to quantify the loss caused by death or an accident.

11   Some contracts require a payment if a specified uncertain event occurs, but do not require an adverse effect on the policyholder as a precondition for payment. Such a contract is not an insurance contract even if the holder uses the contract to mitigate an underlying risk exposure. For example, if the holder uses a derivative to hedge an underlying non-financial variable that is correlated with cash flows from an asset of the entity, the derivative is not an insurance contract because payment is not conditional on whether the holder is adversely affected by a reduction in the cash flows from the asset. Conversely, the definition of an insurance contract refers to an uncertain event for which an adverse effect on the policyholder is a contractual precondition for payment. This contractual precondition does not require the insurer to investigate whether the event actually caused an adverse effect, but permits the insurer to deny payment if it is not satisfied that the event caused an adverse effect.

12   Lapse or persistency risk (i.e. the risk that the counterparty will cancel the contract earlier or later than the issuer had expected in pricing the contract) is not insurance risk because the payment to the counterparty is not contingent on an uncertain future event that adversely affects the counterparty. Similarly, expense risk (i.e. the risk of unexpected increases in the administrative costs associated with the servicing of a contract, rather

than in costs associated with insured events) is not insurance risk because an unexpected increase in expenses does not adversely affect the counterparty.

13   Therefore, a contract that exposes the issuer to lapse risk, persistency risk or expense risk is not an insurance contract unless it also exposes the issuer to insurance risk. However, if the issuer of that contract mitigates that risk by using a second contract to transfer part of that risk to another party, the second contract exposes that other party to insurance risk.

14   An insurer can accept significant insurance risk from the policyholder only if the insurer is an entity separate from the policyholder. In the case of a mutual insurer, the mutual accepts risk from each policyholder and pools that risk. Although policyholders bear that pooled risk collectively in their capacity as owners, the mutual has still accepted the risk that is the essence of an insurance contract.

Examples of Life Insurance Contracts

15   The following are examples of contracts that are life insurance contracts, if the transfer of insurance risk is significant:

(a)   life insurance contracts (although death is certain, it is uncertain when death will occur or, for some types of life insurance, whether death will occur within the period covered by the insurance);

(b)   life-contingent annuities and pensions (i.e. contracts that provide compensation for the uncertain future event – the survival of the annuitant or pensioner – to assist the annuitant or pensioner in maintaining a given standard of living, which would otherwise be adversely affected by his or her survival); and

(c)   life reinsurance contracts.

16   The following are examples of items that are not life insurance contracts:

(a)   investment contracts that are governed under the *Life Insurance Act 1995* but do not expose the insurer to significant insurance risk, for example life insurance contracts in which the insurer bears no significant mortality risk (such contracts are non-insurance financial instruments or service contracts: see paragraphs 17 and 18 of this Appendix);

(b)   contracts that have the legal form of insurance, but pass all significant insurance risk back to the policyholder through non-cancellable and enforceable mechanisms that adjust future payments by the policyholder as a direct result of insured losses, for example some financial reinsurance contracts or some group contracts (such contracts are normally non-insurance financial instruments or service contracts: see paragraphs 17 and 18 of this Appendix);

(c)   self-insurance, in other words retaining a risk that could have been covered by insurance (there is no insurance contract because there is no agreement with another party);

(d)   contracts (such as gambling contracts) that require a payment if a specified uncertain future event occurs, but do not require, as a contractual precondition for payment, that the event adversely affects the policyholder. However, this does not preclude the specification of a predetermined payout to quantify the loss caused by a specified event such as death or an accident;

(e)   derivatives that expose one party to financial risk but not insurance risk, because they require that party to make payment based solely on changes in one or more of a specified interest rate, financial instrument price, commodity price, foreign exchange rate, index of prices or rates, credit rating or credit index or other variable, provided in the case of a non-financial variable that the variable is not specific to a party to the contract (see AASB 139); and

(f)   general insurance contracts.

17   If the contracts described in paragraph 16 of this Appendix create financial assets or financial liabilities, they are within the scope of AASB 139. Among other things, this

means that the parties to the contract use what is sometimes called deposit accounting, which involves the following:

(a)   one party recognises the consideration received as a financial liability, rather than as revenue; and

(b)   the other party recognises the consideration paid as a financial asset, rather than as an expense.

18   If the contracts described in paragraph 16 of this Appendix do not create financial assets or financial liabilities, AASB 118 applies. Under AASB 118, revenue associated with a transaction involving the rendering of services is recognised by reference to the stage of completion of the transaction if the outcome of the transaction can be estimated reliably.

Significant Insurance Risk

19   A contract is an insurance contract only if it transfers significant insurance risk. Paragraphs 5 to 14 of this Appendix discuss insurance risk. The following paragraphs discuss the assessment of whether insurance risk is significant.

20   Insurance risk is significant if, and only if, an insured event could cause an insurer to pay significant additional benefits in any scenario, excluding scenarios that lack commercial substance (i.e. have no discernible effect on the economics of the transaction). If significant additional benefits would be payable in scenarios that have commercial substance, the condition in the previous sentence may be met even if the insured event is extremely unlikely or even if the expected (i.e. probability-weighted) present value of contingent cash flows is a small proportion of the expected present value of all the remaining contractual cash flows.

21   The additional benefits described in paragraph 20 of this Appendix refer to amounts that exceed those that would be payable if no insured event occurred (excluding scenarios that lack commercial substance). Those additional amounts include claims handling and claims assessment costs, but exclude:

(a)   the loss of the ability to charge the policyholder for future services. For example, in an investment-linked life insurance contract, the death of the policyholder means that the insurer can no longer perform investment management services and collect a fee for doing so. However, this economic loss for the insurer does not reflect insurance risk, just as a mutual fund manager does not take on insurance risk in relation to the possible death of the client. Therefore, the potential loss of future investment management fees is not relevant in assessing how much insurance risk is transferred by a contract;

(b)   waiver on death of charges that would be made on cancellation or surrender. Because the contract brought those charges into existence, the waiver of these charges does not compensate the policyholder for a pre-existing risk. Hence, they are not relevant in assessing how much insurance risk is transferred by a contract;

(c)   a payment conditional on an event that does not cause a significant loss to the holder of the contract. For example, consider a contract that requires the issuer to pay one million currency units if an asset suffers physical damage causing an insignificant economic loss of one currency unit to the holder. In this contract, the holder transfers to the insurer the insignificant risk of losing one currency unit. At the same time, the contract creates non-insurance risk that the issuer will need to pay 999,999 currency units if the specified event occurs. Because the issuer does not accept significant insurance risk from the holder, this contract is not an insurance contract; and

(d)   possible reinsurance recoveries. The insurer accounts for these separately.

22   An insurer shall assess the significance of insurance risk contract by contract, rather than by reference to materiality to the financial statements[1]. Thus, insurance risk may be significant even if there is a minimal probability of material losses for a whole book of

---

1   For this purpose, contracts entered into simultaneously with a single counterparty (or contracts that are otherwise interdependent) form a single contract.

AASB

contracts. This contract-by-contract assessment makes it easier to classify a contract as an insurance contract. However, if a relatively homogeneous book of small contracts is known to consist of contracts that all transfer insurance risk, an insurer need not examine each contract within that book to identify a few non-derivative contracts that transfer insignificant insurance risk.

23 It follows from paragraphs 20 to 22 of this Appendix that if a contract pays a death benefit exceeding the amount payable on survival, the contract is an insurance contract unless the additional death benefit is insignificant (judged by reference to the contract rather than to an entire book of contracts). As noted in paragraph 21(b) of this Appendix, the waiver on death of cancellation or surrender charges is not included in this assessment if this waiver does not compensate the policyholder for a pre-existing risk. Similarly, an annuity contract that pays out regular sums for the rest of a policyholder's life is an insurance contract, unless the aggregate life contingent payments are insignificant.

24 Paragraph 20 of this Appendix refers to additional benefits. These additional benefits could include a requirement to pay benefits earlier if the insured event occurs earlier and the payment is not adjusted for the time value of money. An example is whole life insurance for a fixed amount (in other words, insurance that provides a fixed death benefit whenever the policyholder dies, with no expiry date for the cover). It is certain that the policyholder will die, but the date of death is uncertain. The insurer will suffer a loss on those individual contracts for which policyholders die early, even if there is no overall loss on the whole book of contracts.

25 If an insurance contract is unbundled into a deposit component and an insurance component, the significance of insurance risk transfer is assessed by reference to the insurance component. The significance of insurance risk transferred by an embedded derivative is assessed by reference to the embedded derivative.

Changes in the Level of Insurance Risk

26 Some contracts do not transfer any insurance risk to the issuer at inception, although they do transfer insurance risk at a later time. For example, consider a contract that provides a specified investment return and includes an option for the policyholder to use the proceeds of the investment on maturity to buy a life-contingent annuity at the current annuity rates charged by the insurer to other new annuitants when the policyholder exercises the option. The contract transfers no insurance risk to the issuer until the option is exercised, because the insurer remains free to price the annuity on a basis that reflects the insurance risk transferred to the insurer at that time. However, if the contract specifies the annuity rates (or a basis for setting the annuity rates), the contract transfers insurance risk to the issuer at inception.

27 A contract that qualifies as an insurance contract remains an insurance contract until all rights and obligations are extinguished or expire.

AASB 1039
Concise Financial Reports

(Compiled June 2012)

Note from the Institute of Chartered Accountants Australia

This note, prepared by the technical editors, is not part of Accounting Standard AASB 1039.

Historical development

June 2002: AASB 1039 'Concise Financial Reports' was issued by the AASB in June 2002.

April 2005: The AASB reissued the Standard in April 2005 to incorporate the changes resulting from the adoption of Australian equivalents to International Financial Reporting Standards (IFRSs) and the CLERP 9 amendments to the *Corporations Act 2001* (Cth). The revised AASB 1039 is applicable to annual reporting periods ending on or after 31 December 2005, with early adoption prohibited for annual reporting periods beginning before 1 January 2005.

27 August 2008: AASB 1039 was reissued with consequential amendments arising from Accounting Standards AASB 101 and AASB 8. This Standard is applicable for annual reporting periods beginning on or after 1 January 2009.

25 June 2009: AASB 2009-6 'Amendments to Australian Accounting Standards' amends AASB 1039 for editorial corrections made by the International Accounting Standards Board (IASB) to its Standards and Interpretations (IFRSs) and as a consequence of issuing revised AASB 101 'Presentation of Financial Statements'. This Standard is applicable to annual reporting periods beginning on or after 1 January 2009 that end on or after 30 June 2009.

2 November 2009: AASB 1039 was reissued by the AASB, compiled to include the AASB 2009-6 amendments and applies to annual reporting periods beginning on or after 1 January 2009 that end on or after 30 June 2009. Early application is permitted.

5 September 2011: AASB 2011-9 'Amendments to Australian Accounting Standards – Presentation of Items of Other Comprehensive income' amends the presentation of items in other comprehensive income. This Standard applies to annual reporting periods beginning on or after 1 July 2012 and can be adopted early.

20 June 2012: AASB 1039 was reissued by the AASB, compiled to include the AASB 2011-9 amendments and applies to annual reporting periods beginning on or after 1 July 2012 and can be adopted early.

Contents

Compilation Details

Accounting Standard
AASB 1039 Concise Financial Reports

	Paragraph
Application	1 – 5
Operative Date	6 – 8
Purpose of Standard	9 – 11
Preparation and Presentation	12 – 17
Financial Statements	18 – 27
Specific Disclosures	28 – 32
Relationship to Financial Report	33
Comparative Information	34 – 35
Definitions	36 – 37

Australian Accounting Standard AASB 1039 *Concise Financial Reports* (as amended) is set out in paragraphs 1 – 37. All the paragraphs have equal authority. Paragraphs in **bold type** state the main principles. AASB 1039 is to be read in the context of other Australian Accounting Standards, including AASB 1048 *Interpretation and Application of Standards*, which identifies the Australian Accounting Interpretations. In the absence of explicit guidance, AASB 108 *Accounting Policies, Changes in Accounting Estimates* and Errors provides a basis for selecting and applying accounting policies.

Compilation Details

Accounting Standard AASB 1039 *Concise Financial Reports* as amended

This compiled Standard applies to annual reporting periods beginning on or after 1 July 2012. It takes into account amendments up to and including 5 September 2011 and was prepared on 20 June 2012 by the staff of the Australian Accounting Standards Board (AASB).

This compilation is not a separate Accounting Standard made by the AASB. Instead, it is a representation of AASB 1039 (August 2008) as amended by other Accounting Standards, which are listed in the Table below.

Table of Standards

Standard	Date made	Application date *(annual reporting periods … on or after …)*	Application, saving or transitional provisions
AASB 1039	27 Aug 2008	*(beginning)* 1 Jan 2009	see (a) below
AASB 2009-6	25 Jun 2009	*(beginning)* 1 Jan 2009 and *(ending)* 30 Jun 2009	see (b) below
AASB 2011-9	5 Sept 2011	*(beginning)* 1 Jul 2012	see (c) below

(a) Entities may elect to apply this Standard to annual reporting periods beginning on or after 1 January 2005 but before 1 January 2009, provided that AASB 101 *Presentation of Financial Statements* (September 2007) and AASB 8 *Operating Segments* are also applied to such periods.

(b) Entities may elect to apply this Standard to annual reporting periods beginning on or after 1 January 2005 but before 1 January 2009, provided that AASB 101 *Presentation of Financial Statements* (September 2007) is also applied to such periods, and to annual reporting periods beginning on or after 1 January 2009 that end before 30 June 2009.

(c) Entities may elect to apply this Standard to annual reporting periods beginning on or after 1 January 2005 but before 1 July 2012.

Table of Amendments

Paragraph affected	How affected	By ... [paragraph]
18-19	amended	AASB 2011-9 [24]
27	amended	AASB 2011-9 [24]
31	amended	AASB 2009-6 [102]

Accounting Standard AASB 1039

The Australian Accounting Standards Board made Accounting Standard AASB 1039 *Concise Financial Reports* under section 334 of the *Corporations Act 2001* on 27 August 2008.

This compiled version of AASB 1039 applies to annual reporting periods beginning on or after 1 July 2012. It incorporates relevant amendments contained in other AASB Standards made by the AASB up to and including 5 September 2011 (see Compilation Details).

Accounting Standard AASB 1039
Concise Financial Reports

Application

1   **This Standard applies to a concise financial report prepared by an entity in accordance with paragraph 314(2)(a) in Part 2M.3 of the Corporations Act.**

2   Under the Corporations Act a company, registered scheme or disclosing entity can elect to send to its members for a financial year a concise report, which includes a concise financial report, instead of the financial report.

3   **Where an entity is the parent of a group, this Standard applies to the consolidated financial statements of the entity and the notes to those statements, and does not require that parent financial information be provided.**

4   If the entity provides parent financial information in addition to consolidated financial information, the parent financial information is also subject to the requirements of this Standard.

5   **The requirements specified in this Standard apply to the concise financial report where information resulting from their application is material in accordance with AASB 1031 *Materiality*.**

Operative Date

6   **This Standard applies to annual reporting periods beginning on or after 1 January 2009.**

     [Note: For application dates of paragraphs changed or added by an amending Standard, see Compilation Details.]

7   **This Standard may be applied to annual reporting periods beginning on or after 1 January 2005 but before 1 January 2009 provided that AASB 101 *Presentation of Financial Statements* (September 2007) and AASB 8 *Operating Segments* are also applied to the period. If an entity adopts this Standard for an earlier period, it shall disclose that fact.**

8   **When applied or operative, this Standard supersedes AASB 1039 *Concise Financial Reports* made on 14 April 2005.**

Purpose of Standard

9   **The purpose of this Standard is to specify the minimum content of a concise financial report.**

10   The requirements of the Corporations Act relating to concise financial reports are based on the view that a concise financial report can provide members with information relevant to evaluating the business, without giving them fully detailed accounting disclosures.

For some members, the provision of less detailed information is expected to be sufficient to meet their needs for an understanding of the financial performance, financial position and financing and investing activities of the company, registered scheme or disclosing entity.

11   The minimum content required by this Standard is intended also to provide sufficient information to permit members to identify if and when they consider it would be useful to obtain more comprehensive and detailed information by requesting a copy of the financial report.

Preparation and Presentation

12   **The financial statements and specific disclosures (identified in paragraphs 28 to 32 of this Standard) required in a concise financial report shall be derived from the financial report of the entity. Any other information included in a concise financial report shall be consistent with the financial report of the entity.**

13   In order to achieve consistency and comparability with information included in the financial report, this Standard requires the accounting policies relating to recognition and measurement applied in the preparation of a concise financial report to be the same as those adopted in the preparation of the financial report.

14   This Standard prescribes the minimum information to be disclosed in a concise financial report but does not prescribe the format in which that information is presented. The format for the presentation of information in a concise financial report is developed having regard to the particular circumstances of the entity and the presentation of relevant, reliable, understandable and comparable information about the entity's financial performance, financial position and financing and investing activities. Entities are encouraged to develop a format that best meets the information needs of their members.

15   The consistency required by paragraph 12 means that information voluntarily included in the concise financial report is determined in accordance with the treatment adopted in the financial report. When the information in the financial report was determined in accordance with an Accounting Standard, the same treatment is adopted in the concise financial report.

16   **The nature and estimated magnitude of particular items are disclosed if it is likely that the concise financial report would be misleading without such disclosures.**

17   The content of a concise financial report specified in this Standard constitutes the minimum level of disclosure. Where there are particular features of the operations and activities of the entity that are significant, the entity may need to provide additional information in the concise financial report in order to comply with paragraph 16. Similarly, members benefit from industry-specific disclosures, for example, disclosure of additional information by mining companies in relation to exploration and evaluation expenditure and decommissioning costs, and by banks and other financial institutions in relation to doubtful debts.

Financial Statements

18   **A concise financial report shall include the following financial statements:**

   (a)   a statement of profit or loss and other comprehensive income for the annual reporting period;

   (b)   a statement of financial position as at the end of the annual reporting period;

   (c)   a statement of cash flows for the annual reporting period; and

   (d)   a statement of changes in equity for the annual reporting period.

19   In accordance with paragraph 10A of AASB 101 *Presentation of Financial Statements*, an entity may present all items of income and expense recognised in a period in a single statement of profit or loss and other comprehensive income or present the profit or loss section in a separate statement of profit or loss.

20   **Each financial statement shall be presented as it is in the financial report, in accordance with other Accounting Standards, except for the omission of cross-references to notes to the financial statements in the financial report.**

21   All the notes to the financial statements required by other Accounting Standards are not required in the concise financial report. For example, this Standard does not require an entity that uses the direct method in the statement of cash flows to provide a reconciliation of cash flows arising from operating activities to profit or loss. However, information required in some notes by other Accounting Standards is required when specified in this Standard.

22   It is recommended that the financial statements in the concise financial report be cross-referenced, where appropriate, to disclosures included in the concise financial report.

23   When the entity is a parent and only the consolidated financial statements are presented, the lack of financial statements for the parent would not be regarded as contravening paragraph 21.

24   The financial statements of entities other than listed companies shall be accompanied by discussion and analysis to assist the understanding of members.

25   Listed companies are not required by this Standard to provide discussion and analysis in the concise financial report because, unlike other entities, they are required by section 299A of the Corporations Act to provide an operational and financial report in the Directors' Report that is part of the concise report. Paragraph 24 only exempts listed companies from the statutory obligation to provide discussion and analysis of the financial statements. It does not prohibit a listed company from providing any discussion and analysis that it considers would assist a reader to understand the financial statements in the concise financial report.

26   The information reported in the financial statements will be enhanced by a discussion and analysis of the principal factors affecting the financial performance, financial position and financing and investing activities of the entity. The extent of the discussion and analysis provided will vary from entity to entity, and from year to year, as is necessary in the circumstances to help compensate for the brevity of the concise financial report compared with the financial report.

27   In most situations, the content of the discussion and analysis would cover at least the following areas:

    (a)   in relation to the statement of profit or loss and other comprehensive income:

        (i)   trends in revenues;

        (ii)   the effects of significant economic or other events on the operations of the entity;

        (iii)   the main influences on costs of operations; and

        (iv)   measures of financial performance such as return on sales, return on assets and return on equity;

    (b)   in relation to the statement of financial position:

        (i)   changes in the composition of assets;

        (ii)   the relationship between debt and equity; and

        (iii)   significant movements in assets, liabilities and equity items;

    (c)   in relation to the statement of cash flows:

        (i)   changes in cash flows from operations;

        (ii)   financing of capital expenditure programs; and

        (iii)   servicing and repayment of borrowings; and

    (d)   in relation to the statement of changes in equity:

        (i)   changes in the composition of the components of equity; and

        (ii)   causes of significant changes in subscribed capital, such as rights issues, share buy-backs or capital reductions.

Specific Disclosures

28   When the entity has prepared its financial report on the basis that the entity is not a going concern, or where the going concern basis has become inappropriate after the reporting date, this fact shall be disclosed.

29   The following information shall be disclosed for each reportable segment identified in the financial report in accordance with AASB 8 *Operating Segments*:

(a)   revenues from sales to external customers and revenues from transactions with other operating segments of the same entity if the specified amounts are included in the measure of segment profit or loss reviewed by the chief operating decision maker or are otherwise regularly provided to the chief operating decision maker, even if not included in that measure of segment profit or loss;

(b)   a measure of profit or loss;

(c)   a measure of total assets; and

(d)   a measure of liabilities if such amount is regularly provided to the chief operating decision maker.

30   The following items for the period shall be disclosed even if the amounts are zero (since these items are material by their nature):

(a)   the amount of sales revenue recognised and included in revenue in accordance with AASB 118 *Revenue*;

(b)   the amount of dividends, in aggregate and per share, in respect of each class of shares included in equity, identifying:

(i)   dividends paid during the period and date of payment; and

(ii)   dividends proposed or declared before the financial report was authorised for issue, and the expected date of payment, separately identifying, where relevant, those recognised from those not recognised as a distribution to equity holders during the period;

(c)   in respect of each dividend disclosed in accordance with paragraph 30(b) of this Standard, the amount, in aggregate and per share, of the dividend that:

(i)   has been or will be franked and the tax rate at which the dividend has been or will be franked; and

(ii)   has not been or will not be franked; and

(d)   where the entity is required to comply with AASB 133 *Earnings per Share*, the amount of basic earnings per share and diluted earnings per share.

31   The following items shall be disclosed:

(a)   the presentation currency used;

(b)   in respect of each event occurring after the reporting date that does not relate to conditions existing at the reporting date, the information required by paragraph 21 of AASB 110 *Events after the Reporting Period*; and

(c)   where there is a change in accounting policy or estimates from those used in the preceding reporting period, or a correction of a prior period error, which has a material effect in the current reporting period or is expected to have a material effect in a subsequent reporting period, the information required about such a change or correction by the relevant Accounting Standards that are applicable to the current reporting period.

32   The concise financial report for the period when an entity first adopts Australian equivalents to IFRSs shall provide directions as to the location in the financial report of the reconciliations and other disclosures required by paragraphs 39 and 40 of AASB 1 *First-time Adoption of Australian Equivalents to International Financial Reporting Standards*. A summary of this information shall be included in the concise financial report.

Relationship to Financial Report

33   The first page of the concise financial report shall prominently display advice to the effect that:

   (a)   the concise financial report is an extract from the financial report;

   (b)   the financial statements and specific disclosures included in the concise financial report have been derived from the financial report;

   (c)   the concise financial report cannot be expected to provide as full an understanding of the financial performance, financial position and financing and investing activities of the entity as the financial report; and

   (d)   further financial information can be obtained from the financial report and that the financial report is available, free of charge, on request to the entity.

Comparative Information

34   Any requirements relating to comparative information in other Accounting Standards that have been adopted in the preparation of the financial report are applicable in this Standard.

35   When disclosure is not required with respect to the current reporting period for an item in paragraphs 28 to 32 of this Standard but was required in the preceding reporting period, it is still necessary to disclose the comparative information.

Definitions

36   In this Standard, technical terms have the same meaning as in the relevant Accounting Standards applied in the preparation of the financial report for the current reporting period.

37   The terms 'concise report', 'concise financial report', 'financial report', 'listed company' and 'members' have the meanings as given or used in Chapter 2M of the Corporations Act.

AASB 1048
Interpretation of Standards

(Reissued June 2012)

AASB

Note from the Institute of Chartered Accountants Australia

This note, prepared by the technical editors, is not part of Accounting Standard AASB 1048.

Historical development

January 2004: AASB 1048 'Interpretation and Application of Standards' was issued by the AASB in January 2004. The principal aim of the Standard is to give regulatory status to the pronouncements of the Urgent Issues Group, known as the UIG Interpretations.

AASB 1048 separates UIG Interpretations into two groups. The first group (shown at Table 1) includes those that correspond to IASB Interpretations. The second group (shown at Table 2) includes other Interpretations that are relevant in the Australian context.

AASB 1048 is a service Standard that will be reissued when necessary to bring its tables up-to-date for the most recent UIG Interpretations.

December 2004: AASB 1048 was reissued by the AASB in December 2004.

September 2005: AASB 1048 was reissued by the AASB in September 2005 and is applicable to annual reporting periods ending on or after 31 December 2005.

5 April 2006: AASB 1048 was reissued to incorporate UIG Interpretation 7, UIG Interpretation 8 and UIG Interpretation 9.

July 2006: The AASB took over responsibility for issuing Interpretations from the UIG. The Interpretations are now known collectively as the 'Australian Accounting Interpretations', and each Interpretation referred to as 'Interpretation' rather than 'UIG' Interpretation or 'AASB Interpretation'.

December 2006: AASB 1048 was reissued to incorporate Interpretation 10.

March 2007: AASB 1048 was reissued to incorporate Interpretations 11 and 12, and revised Interpretations 4 and 129.

September 2007: AASB 1048 was reissued to incorporate Interpretations 13 and 14, and revised Interpretations 1, 12 and 113.

September 2008: AASB 1048 was reissued to incorporate changes to Interpretations 2, 9, 107 and for new Interpretations 15, 16, 1003 and 1038.

March 2009: AASB 1048 was reissued to incorporate Interpretations 17 and 18.

30 June 2010: AASB 1048 was reissued to incorporate Interpretation 19 and to reflect amended versions of Interpretations where applicable.

29 June 2012: AASB 1048 was reissued to incorporate Interpretation 20 and to reflect current Interpretations where applicable.

Contents

Preface

Comparison with International Pronouncements

Accounting Standard
AASB 1048 Interpretation of Standards

Paragraphs

Objective	1
Application	2 – 6
Scope	7 – 8
Australian Interpretations corresponding to IASB Interpretations	9 – 10
Other Australian Interpretations	11 – 12

> Australian Accounting Standard AASB 1048 *Interpretation of Standards* is set out in paragraphs 1 – 12. All the paragraphs have equal authority. In the absence of explicit guidance, AASB 108 *Accounting Policies, Changes in Accounting Estimates and Errors* provides a basis for selecting and applying accounting policies.

Preface

Introduction

The Australian Accounting Standards Board (AASB) makes Australian Accounting Standards, including Interpretations, to be applied by:

(a)   entities required by the *Corporations Act 2001* to prepare financial reports;

(b)   governments in preparing financial statements for the whole of government and the General Government Sector (GGS); and

(c)   entities in the private or public for-profit or not-for-profit sectors that are reporting entities or that prepare general purpose financial statements.

AASB 1053 *Application of Tiers of Australian Accounting Standards* establishes a differential reporting framework consisting of two tiers of reporting requirements for preparing general purpose financial statements:

(a)   Tier 1: Australian Accounting Standards; and

(b)   Tier 2: Australian Accounting Standards – Reduced Disclosure Requirements.

Tier 1 requirements incorporate International Financial Reporting Standards (IFRSs), including Interpretations, issued by the International Accounting Standards Board (IASB), with the addition of paragraphs on the applicability of each Standard in the Australian environment.

Publicly accountable for-profit private sector entities are required to adopt Tier 1 requirements, and therefore are required to comply with IFRSs. Furthermore, other for-profit private sector entities complying with Tier 1 requirements will simultaneously comply with IFRSs. Some other entities complying with Tier 1 requirements will also simultaneously comply with IFRSs.

Tier 2 requirements comprise the recognition, measurement and presentation requirements of Tier 1 but substantially reduced disclosure requirements in comparison with Tier 1.

Australian Accounting Standards also include requirements that are specific to Australian entities. These requirements may be located in Australian Accounting Standards that incorporate IFRSs or in other Australian Accounting Standards. In most instances, these requirements are either restricted to the not-for-profit or public sectors or include additional disclosures that address domestic, regulatory or other issues. These requirements do not prevent publicly accountable for-profit private sector entities from complying with IFRSs. In developing requirements for public sector entities, the AASB considers the requirements of International Public Sector Accounting Standards (IPSASs), as issued by the International Public Sector Accounting Standards Board (IPSASB) of the International Federation of Accountants.

Reasons for Issuing AASB 1048

Australian Accounting Standards that apply to annual reporting periods beginning on or after 1 January 2005 include IFRSs, which comprise Accounting Standards and Interpretations. The adoption of IFRSs in Australia is in accordance with a strategic direction made by the Financial Reporting Council (FRC).

This Standard clarifies that all Australian Interpretations have the same authoritative status. Those that incorporate the IASB Interpretations must be applied to achieve compliance with IFRSs. Australian Interpretations issued by the AASB comprise both AASB and UIG Interpretations. UIG Interpretations were developed by the Urgent Issues Group, a former committee of the AASB.

Need for a Service Standard

In the Australian context, Australian Interpretations do not have the same legal status as Standards (delegated legislation) and are treated as 'external documents' by the *Acts Interpretation Act 1901* and the *Legislative Instruments Act 2003*. Although references in one Standard to a second Standard are ambulatory (automatically moving forward to refer to the most recently-issued version of the second Standard), references in a Standard to external documents are stationary (being fixed in time to refer to the contents of the external document when the Standard was issued). A simple reference to an Australian Interpretation in a Standard can refer only to the Interpretation that existed when the Standard was issued. It cannot refer to any revised version of the Interpretation that may exist at a later reporting date. However, a Standard can refer to a second Standard and, when the first Standard is applied at a later reporting date, the reference will be to the then-current version of the second Standard, even if it has been reissued since the first Standard was issued.

The service Standard approach involves issuing this Standard to list the Australian Interpretations, and referring to this Standard in every other Standard where necessary to refer to an Interpretation. This enables references to the Interpretations in all other Standards to be updated by reissuing the service Standard.

This approach preserves the status of Australian Interpretations as 'external documents' referred to in a Standard, with the contents fixed in time to that existing when the Standard takes effect. It does not treat the Interpretations as delegated legislation or confer ambulatory status on the reference. In each Standard where there is a need to refer to an Australian Interpretation, the reference will be to this Standard, phrased as "Interpretation [number] [title] as identified in AASB 1048" (or similar). This reference, being to another Standard, is ambulatory and will refer to the version of this Standard that is in force from time to time. AASB 1048 itself will contain the direct references to the external documents and will be reissued periodically.

This approach to clarifying the status of Australian Interpretations ensures there is no difference between the status in the hierarchy accorded to Interpretations in IAS 8 *Accounting Policies, Changes in Accounting Estimates and Errors* compared with AASB 108 *Accounting Policies, Changes in Accounting Estimates and Errors*.

Main Features of this Standard

This Standard (issued in June 2012) supersedes the previous version of AASB 1048, issued in June 2010.

Application Date

This Standard is applicable to annual reporting periods ending on or after 30 June 2012 (see paragraph 3). To be consistent with the position for IFRSs as adopted in Australia, early adoption of this Standard is not permitted for annual reporting periods beginning before 1 January 2005. However, early adoption is otherwise permitted as specified in paragraph 4, subject to paragraphs 10 and 12.

Main Requirements

This Standard identifies the Australian Interpretations and classifies them into two groups: those that correspond to an IASB Interpretation and those that do not. Entities are required to apply each relevant Australian Interpretation in preparing financial statements that are within the scope of the Standard.

In respect of the first group (Table 1), it is necessary for those Australian Interpretations, where relevant, to be applied in order for an entity to be able to make an explicit and unreserved statement of compliance with IFRSs. The IASB defines IFRSs to include the IFRIC and the SIC Interpretations.

In the second group (Table 2), this Standard lists the other Australian Interpretations, which do not correspond to the IASB Interpretations, to assist financial statement preparers and users to identify the other authoritative pronouncements necessary for compliance in the Australian context.

The Standard will be reissued when necessary to keep the Tables up to date.

Changes from AASB 1048 (June 2010)

The main differences between the previous version of AASB 1048 and this version are as follows:

(a)   the removal from Tables 1 and 2 in paragraphs 9 and 11 of the Standard of the versions of Interpretations that do not apply to any of the reporting periods to which this Standard mandatorily applies (see paragraph 3); and

(b)   the addition of one Interpretation incorporating an IFRIC Interpretation to Table 1, as set out in the following table.

Principal Addition to Table 1

Interpretation *Issue Date*	Title	Application Date (annual reporting periods)	IFRIC or SIC Interp'n
20 *November 2011*	Stripping Costs in the Production Phase of a Surface Mine	(beginning) 1 January 2013	IFRIC 20

Amended versions of Interpretations since June 2010 have also been added to Table 1 and Table 2, where applicable to any reporting period to which this Standard mandatorily applies.

Comparison with International Pronouncements

AASB 1048 and IASB Pronouncements

There is no International Accounting Standards Board (IASB) Standard that directly corresponds to AASB 1048. However, Table 1 in AASB 1048 (see paragraph 9) contains a list of Australian Interpretations identifying the corresponding IASB Interpretations.

Compliance with IFRSs

For-profit entities that comply with the Australian Interpretations designated in this Standard as corresponding to the IASB Interpretations will simultaneously be in compliance with the Interpretations referred to by the IASB in its definition of International Financial Reporting Standards (IFRSs). Such compliance is one of the prerequisites that needs to be met before an entity can make an explicit and unreserved statement of compliance with IFRSs, as described in AASB 101 *Presentation of Financial Statements*.

Accounting Standard AASB 1048

The Australian Accounting Standards Board makes Accounting Standard AASB 1048 *Interpretation of Standards* under section 334 of the *Corporations Act 2001*.

Kevin M. Stevenson
Chair – AASB

Dated 29 June 2012

Accounting Standard AASB 1048

Interpretation of Standards

AASB

Objective

1 The objective of this Standard is to provide an up-to-date listing of Australian Interpretations and to ensure the effectiveness of references in Australian Accounting Standards to Australian Interpretations. AASB and UIG Interpretations are referred to collectively in this Standard as Australian Interpretations.

Application

2 **This Standard applies to:**

(a) **each entity that is required to prepare financial reports in accordance with Part 2M.3 of the Corporations Act;**

(b) **general purpose financial statements of each reporting entity; and**

(c) **financial statements that are, or are held out to be, general purpose financial statements.**

3 **This Standard applies to annual reporting periods ending on or after 30 June 2012.**

4 **This Standard may be applied to annual reporting periods beginning on or after 1 January 2005 that end before 30 June 2012.**

5 **The requirements specified in this Standard apply to the financial statements where information resulting from their application is material in accordance with AASB 1031 *Materiality*.**

6 **When applicable, this Standard supersedes AASB 1048 *Interpretation of Standards* as issued in June 2010.**

Scope

7 This Standard refers to all Australian Interpretations currently approved by the AASB and applicable to any period[1] specified in paragraph 3, classified according to whether or not they correspond to Interpretations adopted by the International Accounting Standards Board (IASB).

8 For ease of presentation, the Australian Interpretations are set out in two separate tables: in paragraph 9, Table 1 lists those corresponding to IASB Interpretations and, in paragraph 11, Table 2 lists the other Interpretations. Each reference to an Interpretation in a row in each of the Tables 1 and 2 is to be treated as a separate provision of this Standard.

Australian Interpretations corresponding to IASB Interpretations

9 **An entity shall apply each relevant Australian Interpretation listed in Table 1 below.**

Table 1: Australian Interpretations corresponding to IASB Interpretations

Interpretation *Issue Date*	Title	Application Date (annual reporting periods)	IFRIC or SIC Interp'n
1 *June 2009* [as amended to]	Changes in Existing Decommissioning, Restoration and Similar Liabilities	(beginning) 1 January 2009	IFRIC 1
2 *June 2012* [as amended to]	Members' Shares in Co-operative Entities and Similar Instruments	(beginning) 1 July 2013	IFRIC 2

---

1 Periods no longer than 18 months.

Interpretation _Issue Date_	Title	Application Date (annual reporting periods)	IFRIC or SIC Interp'n
2 _June 2012_ [as amended to]	Members' Shares in Co-operative Entities and Similar Instruments	(beginning) 1 January 2013	IFRIC 2
2 _May 2011_ [as amended to]	Members' Shares in Co-operative Entities and Similar Instruments	(beginning) 1 July 2011	IFRIC 2
2 _December 2009_ [as amended to]	Members' Shares in Co-operative Entities and Similar Instruments	(beginning) 1 January 2011	IFRIC 2
4 _September 2011_ [as amended to]	Determining whether an Arrangement contains a Lease	(beginning) 1 July 2013	IFRIC 4
4 _September 2011_ [as amended to]	Determining whether an Arrangement contains a Lease	(beginning) 1 January 2013	IFRIC 4
4 _December 2009_ [as amended to]	Determining whether an Arrangement contains a Lease	(beginning) 1 January 2011	IFRIC 4
5 _August 2011_ [as amended to]	Rights to Interests arising from Decommissioning, Restoration and Environmental Rehabilitation Funds	(beginning) 1 July 2013	IFRIC 5
5 _August 2011_ [as amended to]	Rights to Interests arising from Decommissioning, Restoration and Environmental Rehabilitation Funds	(beginning) 1 January 2013	IFRIC 5
5 _September 2007_ [as amended to]	Rights to Interests arising from Decommissioning, Restoration and Environmental Rehabilitation Funds	(beginning) 1 January 2009	IFRIC 5
6 _September 2007_ [as amended to]	Liabilities arising from Participating in a Specific Market – Waste Electrical and Electronic Equipment	(beginning) 1 January 2009	IFRIC 6
7 _October 2009_ [as amended to]	Applying the Restatement Approach under AASB 129 _Financial Reporting in Hyperinflationary Economies_	(beginning) 1 January 2009	IFRIC 7
9 _August 2011_ [as amended to]	Reassessment of Embedded Derivatives	(beginning) 1 January 2013	IFRIC 9
9 _May 2009_ [as amended to]	Reassessment of Embedded Derivatives	(beginning) 1 July 2009	IFRIC 9
10 _December 2010_ [as amended to]	Interim Financial Reporting and Impairment	(beginning) 1 January 2013	IFRIC 10
10 _October 2009_ [as amended to]	Interim Financial Reporting and Impairment	(beginning) 1 January 2009	IFRIC 10
12 _September 2011_ [as amended to]	Service Concession Arrangements	(beginning) 1 January 2013	IFRIC 12

Interpretation Issue Date	Title	Application Date (annual reporting periods)	IFRIC or SIC Interp'n
12 June 2009 [as amended to]	Service Concession Arrangements	(beginning) 1 January 2009	IFRIC 12
13 September 2011 [as amended to]	Customer Loyalty Programmes	(beginning) 1 January 2013	IFRIC 13
13 June 2010 [as amended to]	Customer Loyalty Programmes	(beginning) 1 January 2011	IFRIC 13
14 September 2011 [as amended to]	AASB 119 – The Limit on a Defined Benefit Asset, Minimum Funding Requirements and their Interaction	(beginning) 1 January 2013	IFRIC 14
14 December 2009 [as amended to]	AASB 119 – The Limit on a Defined Benefit Asset, Minimum Funding Requirements and their Interaction	(beginning) 1 January 2011	IFRIC 14
15 June 2010 [as amended to]	Agreements for the Construction of Real Estate	(beginning) 1 July 2013	IFRIC 15
15 August 2008	Agreements for the Construction of Real Estate	(beginning) 1 January 2009	IFRIC 15
16 August 2011 [as amended to]	Hedges of a Net Investment in a Foreign Operation	(beginning) 1 January 2013	IFRIC 16
16 December 2009 [as amended to]	Hedges of a Net Investment in a Foreign Operation	(beginning) 1 January 2011	IFRIC 16
17 September 2011 [as amended to]	Distributions of Non-cash Assets to Owners	(beginning) 1 July 2013	IFRIC 17
17 September 2011 [as amended to]	Distributions of Non-cash Assets to Owners	(beginning) 1 January 2013	IFRIC 17
17 June 2009 [as amended to]	Distributions of Non-cash Assets to Owners	(beginning) 1 July 2009	IFRIC 17
18 March 2009	Transfers of Assets from Customers	(ending) 1 July 2009	IFRIC 18
19 September 2011 [as amended to]	Extinguishing Financial Liabilities with Equity Instruments	(beginning) 1 January 2013	IFRIC 19
19 December 2009	Extinguishing Financial Liabilities with Equity Instruments	(beginning) 1 July 2010	IFRIC 19
20 November 2011	Stripping Costs in the Production Phase of a Surface Mine	(beginning) 1 January 2013	IFRIC 20
107 June 2009 [as amended to]	Introduction of the Euro	(beginning) 1 July 2009	SIC-7
110 September 2007 [as amended to]	Government Assistance – No Specific Relation to Operating Activities	(beginning) 1 January 2009	SIC-10

Interpretation *Issue Date*	Title	Application Date (annual reporting periods)	IFRIC or SIC Interp'n
112 *May 2011* [as amended to]	Consolidation – Special Purpose Entities	(beginning) 1 July 2011	SIC-12
112 *October 2010* [as amended to]	Consolidation – Special Purpose Entities	(beginning) 1 January 2011	SIC-12
113 *May 2011* [as amended to]	Jointly Controlled Entities – Non- Monetary Contributions by Venturers	(beginning) 1 July 2011	SIC-13
113 *September 2007* [as amended to]	Jointly Controlled Entities – Non- Monetary Contributions by Venturers	(beginning) 1 January 2009	SIC-13
115 *October 2010* [as amended to]	Operating Leases – Incentives	(beginning) 1 January 2011	SIC-15
121 *September 2007* [as amended to]	Income Taxes – Recovery of Revalued Non-Depreciable Assets	(beginning) 1 January 2009	SIC-21
125 *June 2009* [as amended to]	Income Taxes – Changes in the Tax Status of an Entity or its Shareholders	(beginning) 1 January 2009	SIC-25
127 *December 2010* [as amended to]	Evaluating the Substance of Transactions Involving the Legal Form of a Lease	(beginning) 1 July 2013	SIC-27
127 *December 2010* [as amended to]	Evaluating the Substance of Transactions Involving the Legal Form of a Lease	(beginning) 1 January 2013	SIC-27
127 *October 2010* [as amended to]	Evaluating the Substance of Transactions Involving the Legal Form of a Lease	(beginning) 1 January 2011	SIC-27
129 *June 2010* [as amended to]	Service Concession Arrangements: Disclosures	(beginning) 1 July 2013	SIC-29
129 *June 2009* [as amended to]	Service Concession Arrangements: Disclosures	(beginning) 1 January 2009	SIC-29
131 *September 2011* [as amended to]	Revenue – Barter Transactions Involving Advertising Services	(beginning) 1 January 2013	SIC-31
131 *September 2007* [as amended to]	Revenue – Barter Transactions Involving Advertising Services	(beginning) 1 January 2009	SIC-31
132 *September 2011* [as amended to]	Intangible Assets – Web Site Costs	(beginning) 1 January 2013	SIC-32
132 *October 2010* [as amended to]	Intangible Assets – Web Site Costs	(beginning) 1 January 2011	SIC-32

10 The principal application date listed in Table 1 for each Interpretation is a reference to annual reporting periods beginning or ending (as indicated) on or after the date specified. An entity may elect to apply an individual Interpretation to annual reporting periods in advance of that stated for the Interpretation in Table 1, subject to the early application requirements of the Interpretation. However, an Interpretation shall not be applied to annual reporting periods beginning before 1 January 2005.

Other Australian Interpretations

11 **An entity shall apply each relevant Australian Interpretation listed in Table 2 below.**

Table 2: Other Australian Interpretations

Interpretation *Issue Date*	Title	**Application Date** (annual reporting periods)
1003 *November 2007*	Australian Petroleum Resource Rent Tax	(ending) 30 June 2008
1019 *December 2007* [as amended to]	The Superannuation Contributions Surcharge	(beginning) 1 January 2009
1030 *September 2007* [as amended to]	Depreciation of Long-Lived Physical Assets: Condition-Based Depreciation and Related Methods	(beginning) 1 January 2009
1031 *December 2007* [as amended to]	Accounting for the Goods and Services Tax (GST)	(beginning) 1 January 2009
1038 *December 2007*	Contributions by Owners Made to Wholly-Owned Public Sector Entities	(beginning) 1 July 2008
1039 *December 2009* [as amended to]	Substantive Enactment of Major Tax Bills in Australia	(beginning) 1 January 2011
1042 *October 2010* [as amended to]	Subscriber Acquisition Costs in the Telecommunications Industry	(beginning) 1 January 2011
1047 *December 2007* [as amended to]	Professional Indemnity Claims Liabilities in Medical Defence Organisations	(beginning) 1 January 2009
1052 *June 2010* [as amended to]	Tax Consolidation Accounting	(beginning) 1 July 2013
1052 *December 2009* [as amended to]	Tax Consolidation Accounting	(beginning) 1 January 2011
1055 *December 2007* [as amended to]	Accounting for Road Earthworks	(beginning) 1 January 2009

12 The principal application date listed in Table 2 for each Interpretation is a reference to annual reporting periods beginning or ending (as indicated) on or after the date specified. An entity may elect to apply an individual Interpretation to annual reporting periods in advance of that stated for the Interpretation in Table 2, subject to the early application requirements of the Interpretation. However, an Interpretation shall not be applied to annual reporting periods beginning before 1 January 2005.

AASB 1049

Whole of Government and General Government Sector Financial Reporting

(Compiled June 2012)

Note from the Institute of Chartered Accountants Australia

This note, prepared by the technical editors, is not part of Accounting Standard AASB 1049.

Historical development

September 2006: AASB 1049 'Financial Reporting of General Government Sectors by Governments' was issued by the AASB.

October 2007: AASB 1049 'Whole of Government and General Government Sector Financial Reporting' was issued by the AASB, replacing the pervious version of AASB 1049 for financial reporting periods beginning on or after 1 July 2008. Early adoption is permitted. The issue of this Standard is part of the AASB's implementation of the FRC's strategic direction that the AASB should harmonise Government Finance Statistics (GFS) and Generally Accepted Accounting Principles (GAAP) reporting,

September 2008: AASB 2008-9 'Amendments to AASB 1049 for Consistency with AABS 1049' amends AASB 1049 to align it with revised AABS 101. This Standard is applicable to annual reporting periods beginning on or after 1 January 2009.

10 August 2009: AASB 1049 was reissued by the AASB, compiled to include the AASB 2008-9 amendments and applies to annual reporting periods beginning on or after 1 January 2009. Early application is permitted.

20 May 2011: AASB 2011-3 'Amendments to Australian Accounting Standards – Orderly Adoption of Changes to the ABS GFS Manual and Related Amendments' amends AASB 1049 as a result of the AASB's post-implementation review of AASB 1049, in relation to the definition of the ABS GFS Manual, relief from adopting the latest version of the ABS GFS Manual and related disclosures. This Standard applies to annual reporting periods beginning on or after 1 July 2012 and can be adopted early.

5 September 2011: AASB 2011-9 'Amendments to Australian Accounting Standards – Presentation of Items of Other Comprehensive Income' amends the presentation of items in other comprehensive income. This Standard applies to annual reporting periods beginning on or after 1 July 2012 and can be adopted early.

5 September 2011: AASB 2011-10 'Amendments to Australian Accounting Standards arising from AASB 119 (September 2011)' amends AASB 1049 to give effect to a consequential change arising from the issue of AASB 119. This Standard applies to annual reporting periods beginning on or after 1 January 2013 and can be adopted early. **These amendments are not included in this compiled Standard.**

14 December 2011: AASB 2011-13 'Amendments to Australian Accounting Standard – Improvements to AASB 1049' amends AASB 1049 to clarify the alignment of GGS and whole of government financial statements. This Standard applies to annual reporting periods beginning on or after 1 July 2012, with early adoption permitted

20 June 2012: AASB 1049 was reissued by the AASB, compiled to include the AASB 2011-9, AASB 2011-3 and AASB 2011-13 amendments and applies to annual reporting periods beginning on or after 1 July 2012 but before 1 January 2013. Early application is permitted.

Contents

Compilation Details

Comparison with IASB Pronouncements

Accounting Standard
AASB 1049 Whole of Government and General Government
Sector Financial Reporting

Paragraphs

Objective	1
Application	2 – 6
Financial Statements to be Prepared	7 – 8
Compliance with Australian Accounting Standards and the ABS GFS Manual	9 – 18D
Presentation and Scope of GGS Financial Statements	19
GGS Investment in PNFC Sector and PFC Sector Entities	20 – 23
GGS Investment in Jointly Controlled Entities and Associates	24
Whole of Government and GGS Statements of Financial Position	27 – 28
Whole of Government and GGS Statements of Comprehensive Income	29 – 34
Whole of Government and GGS Statements of Changes in Equity	34A – 34B
Whole of Government and GGS Statements of Cash Flows	35 – 37
Illustrative Examples	38
Notes	
Summary of Significant Accounting Policies	39 – 40
Other Explanatory Notes	41 – 47
Functional Information	48 – 51
Whole of Government Sector Information	52 – 58
Budgetary Information	59 – 65

Appendix
A. Defined Terms

Basis for Conclusions on AASB 1049

Basis for Conclusions on AASB 2008-9

Basis for Conclusions on AASB 2011-3

Basis for Conclusions on AASB 2011-13

Illustrative Examples

A. Whole of Government Statement of Comprehensive Income, Statement of Financial Position, Statement of Changes in Equity, Statement of Cash Flows and Selected Notes

B. General Government Sector Statement of Comprehensive Income, Statement of Financial Position, Statement of Changes in Equity, Statement of Cash Flows and Selected Notes

C. Extract from the Note Containing the Summary of Significant Accounting Policies of a General Government Sector

D. Key Technical Terms Used in the Complete Sets of Financial Statements

Australian Accounting Standard AASB 1049 *Whole of Government and General Government Sector Financial Reporting* (as amended) is set out in paragraphs 1 – 65 and Appendix A. All the paragraphs have equal authority. Paragraphs in **bold type** state the main principles. Terms defined in this Standard are in *italics* the first time they appear in the Standard. AASB 1049 is to be read in the context of other Australian Accounting Standards, including AASB 1048 *Interpretation of Standards*, which identifies the Australian Accounting Interpretations. In the absence of explicit guidance, AASB 108 *Accounting Policies, Changes in Accounting Estimates and Errors* provides a basis for selecting and applying accounting policies.

Compilation Details

Accounting Standard AASB 1049 *Whole of Government and General Government Sector* as amended

This compiled Standard applies to annual reporting periods beginning on or after 1 July 2012 but before 1 January 2013. It takes into account amendments up to and including 14 December 2011 and was prepared on 20 June 2012 by the staff of the Australian Accounting Standards Board (AASB).

This compilation is not a separate Accounting Standard made by the AASB. Instead, it is a representation of AASB 1049 (October 2007) as amended by other Accounting Standards, which are listed in the Table below.

Table of Standards

Standard	Date made	Application date *(annual reporting periods ... on or after ...)*	Application, saving or transitional provisions
AASB 1049	30 Oct 2007	*(beginning)* 1 Jul 2008	see (a) below
AASB 2008-9	24 Sep 2008	*(beginning)* 1 Jan 2009	see (b) below
AASB 2011-3	20 May 2011	*(beginning)* 1 Jul 2012	see (c) below
AASB 2011-9	5 Sep 2011	*(beginning)* 1 Jul 2012	see (d) below
AASB 2011-10	5 Sep 2011	*(beginning)* 1 Jan 2013	not compiled*
AASB 2011-13	14 Dec 2011	*(beginning)* 1 Jul 2012	see (e) below

* The amendments made by this Standard are not included in this compilation, which presents the principal Standard as applicable to annual reporting periods beginning on or after 1 July 2012 but before 1 January 2013.

(a) Entities may elect to apply this Standard to annual reporting periods beginning before 1 July 2008.

(b) Entities may elect to apply this Standard to annual reporting periods beginning on or after 1 January 2005 but before 1 January 2009, provided that AASB 101 *Presentation of Financial Statements* (September 2007) is also applied to such periods.

(c) Entities may elect to apply this Standard to annual reporting periods beginning on or after 1 January 2009 but before 1 July 2012.

(d) Entities may elect to apply this Standard to annual reporting periods beginning on or after 1 January 2005 but before 1 July 2012.

(e) Entities may elect to apply this Standard to annual reporting periods beginning on or after 1 January 2009 but before 1 July 2012, provided that AASB 2011-3 *Amendments to Australian Accounting Standards – Orderly Adoption of Changes to the ABS GFS Manual and Related Amendments* is also applied to such periods.

Table of Amendments to Standard

Paragraph affected	How affected	By ... [paragraph]
1	amended	AASB 2008-9 [5]
3-6	amended	AASB 2008-9 [6]
7	amended amended	AASB 2008-9 [7] AASB 2011-13 [8]
8	amended	AASB 2011-13 [9]
9 (preceding heading)	amended	AASB 2011-13 [10]
10	amended	AASB 2008-9 [8]

Paragraph affected	How affected	By ... [paragraph]
12	amended	AASB 2008-9 [9]
13	amended	AASB 2011-13 [11]
13A	added	AASB 2011-13 [11]
13B	added	AASB 2011-3 [7]
14	amended	AASB 2008-9 [10]
15	amended	AASB 2008-9 [5, 11]
16-17	amended	AASB 2008-9 [12]
18	amended	AASB 2011-13 [12]
18A-18D	added	AASB 2011-13 [12]
19	amended	AASB 2008-9 [13]
20	amended	AASB 2008-9 [14]
23	amended amended	AASB 2008-9 [15] AASB 2011-13 [13]
25 (and preceding heading)	deleted	AASB 2008-9 [16]
26	deleted	AASB 2008-9 [16]
27 (and preceding heading)	amended	AASB 2008-9 [5, 17]
29 (and preceding heading)	amended	AASB 2008-9 [18]
30	amended	AASB 2011-13 [14]
30A	added	AASB 2011-13 [14]
31	amended	AASB 2011-13 [14]
33	amended amended	AASB 2008-9 [19] AASB 2011-9 [25]
34	amended	AASB 2008-9 [20]
34A (and preceding heading)	added	AASB 2008-9 [21]
34B	added amended	AASB 2008-9 [21] AASB 2011-13 [15]
35 (and preceding heading)	amended	AASB 2008-9 [5, 22]
37	amended	AASB 2008-9 [5]
38	amended	AASB 2008-9 [23]
39	amended amended amended	AASB 2008-9 [24] AASB 2011-3 [8] AASB 2011-13 [16]
39A	added	AASB 2011-3 [8]
40	amended	AASB 2008-9 [24]
41	amended amended	AASB 2008-9 [25] AASB 2011-13 [17]
42	amended	AASB 2011-13 [18]
43	amended	AASB 2008-9 [26]
44	amended amended	AASB 2008-9 [27] AASB 2011-13 [19]
45	amended	AASB 2008-9 [28]
47	amended	AASB 2008-9 [29]
48	amended amended	AASB 2008-9 [30] AASB 2011-13 [20]
50	amended	AASB 2011-13 [20]
51	amended	AASB 2008-9 [31]
52	amended amended	AASB 2008-9 [32] AASB 2011-13 [21]

Paragraph affected	How affected	By ... [paragraph]
53	amended	AASB 2008-9 [32]
54	amended	AASB 2008-9 [33]
55	amended	AASB 2011-13 [22]
58	amended	AASB 2008-9 [34]
59	amended	AASB 2008-9 [35]
	amended	AASB 2011-13 [23]
63	amended	AASB 2011-13 [23]
64	amended	AASB 2008-9 [36]
	amended	AASB 2011-13 [23]
65	amended	AASB 2008-9 [37]
65A	added	AASB 2008-9 [38]
	deleted	AASB 2011-13 [24]
66-70	deleted	AASB 2011-13 [24]
Appendix A	amended	AASB 2008-9 [39]
	amended	AASB 2011-3 [9]

Table of Amendments to Illustrative Examples

Paragraph affected	How affected	By ... [paragraph]
Illustrative Examples	amended	AASB 2008-9 [40]
	amended	AASB 2011-3 [10-12]
	amended	AASB 2011-9 [26-27]
	amended	AASB 2011-13 [25-32]

General Terminology Amendments

The following amendments made by AASB 2008-9 are not shown in the above Tables of Amendments:

References to 'financial report(s)' were amended to 'financial statements', except in relation to specific Corporations Act references.

References to 'balance sheet(s)' and 'cash flow statement(s)' were amended to 'statement(s) of financial position' and 'statement(s) of cash flows' respectively, except in relation to ABS GFS Manual references.

References to 'operating statement(s)' were amended to 'statement(s) of comprehensive income'.

The phrases 'on the face(s) of', 'movements in equity' and 'transactions with owners as owners' were amended to 'in', 'changes in equity' and 'transactions with owners in their capacity as owners' respectively.

The following amendments made by AASB 2011-13 are not shown in the above Tables of Amendments:

References to 'other non-owner changes in equity' and 'other changes in equity' were amended to 'other comprehensive income'.

Comparison with
IASB Pronouncements

AASB 1049 and International Financial Reporting Standards

There is no specific Standard issued by the International Accounting Standards Board dealing with whole of government financial statements and GGS financial statements.

Many of the issues addressed in this Standard are addressed in International Financial Reporting Standards (IFRSs). To the extent this Standard incorporates by cross-reference other Australian Accounting Standards, those Standards provide a comparison of this Standard with IFRSs.

In addition, in some significant respects, this Standard amends the requirements of other Australian Accounting Standards for the purposes of whole of government financial statements and GGS financial statements, and thereby differs from the requirements in IFRSs. In relation to whole of government financial statements and GGS financial statements, differences relate to the presentation of the financial statements, especially the statement of comprehensive income, and notes. In relation to GGS financial statements, a difference relates to the specification of the entities to be consolidated and the consequential accounting for investments in controlled entities in other sectors that are not consolidated.

Accounting Standard AASB 1049

The Australian Accounting Standards Board made Accounting Standard AASB 1049 *Whole of Government and General Government Sector Financial Reporting* on 30 October 2007.

This compiled version of AASB 1049 applies to annual reporting periods beginning on or after 1 July 2012 but before 1 January 2013. It incorporates relevant amendments contained in other AASB Standards made by the AASB up to and including 14 December 2011 (see Compilation Details).

Accounting Standard AASB 1049

Whole of Government and General Government Sector Financial Reporting

Objective

1   The objective of this Standard is to specify requirements for *whole of government general purpose financial statements* and *General Government Sector (GGS)* financial statements of each *government*. This Standard requires compliance with other applicable Australian Accounting Standards except as specified in this Standard. It also requires disclosure of additional information such as reconciliations to *key fiscal aggregates* determined in accordance with the *ABS GFS Manual* and, for the whole of government, sector information (GGS, *Public Non-Financial Corporations (PNFC) sector* and *Public Financial Corporations (PFC) sector*). Whole of government financial statements and GGS financial statements prepared in accordance with this Standard provide users with:

     (a)   information about the stewardship by each government and accountability for the resources entrusted to it;

     (b)   information about the financial position, performance and cash flows of each government and its sectors; and

     (c)   information that facilitates assessments of the macro-economic impact of each government and its sectors.

Application

2   **This Standard applies to each government's whole of government general purpose financial statements and GGS financial statements.**

3   **This Standard applies to annual reporting periods beginning on or after 1 January 2009.**

     [Note: For application dates of paragraphs changed or added by an amending Standard, see Compilation Details.]

4   **This Standard may be applied to annual reporting periods beginning before 1 January 2009, provided there is early adoption for the same annual reporting period of AASB 101 *Presentation of Financial Statements* (September 2007).**

5   **The requirements specified in this Standard apply where information resulting from their application is material in accordance with AASB 1031 *Materiality*.**

6   When applicable, this Standard supersedes AASB 1049 *Financial Reporting of General Government Sectors by Governments* (October 2007).

Financial Statements to be Prepared

7   **A government shall prepare both whole of government financial statements and GGS financial statements, whether presented together or separately in accordance with the requirements of this Standard.**

8   **A government shall, at all times, make its GGS financial statements available at the same time that its whole of government financial statements are made available.**

Compliance with Australian Accounting Standards and the ABS GFS Manual

9   **Unless otherwise specified in this Standard, the whole of government financial statements and the GGS financial statements shall adopt the same accounting policies and be prepared in a manner consistent with other applicable Australian Accounting Standards.**

10   With limited significant exceptions, this Standard requires the definition, recognition, measurement, classification, consolidation, presentation and disclosure requirements specified in other applicable Australian Accounting Standards to be adopted. This Standard only requires a different treatment from another applicable Australian Accounting Standard when the requirements of this Standard directly conflict with the requirements of that other Standard. In particular, in relation to the GGS, in conflict with AASB 127 *Consolidated and Separate Financial Statements*, paragraph 19 prohibits the consolidation of controlled entities in other sectors.

11   Where an Australian Accounting Standard:

     (a)   explicitly excludes from its scope not-for-profit entities, such as AASB 114 *Segment Reporting* (and AASB 8 *Operating Segments*)[1]; or

     (b)   explicitly excludes from its scope not-for-profit public sector entities, such as AASB 124 *Related Party Disclosures*; or

     (c)   only applies to certain entities, such as listed companies, that are required to prepare financial reports in accordance with Part 2M.3 of the *Corporations Act 2001*, such as AASB 133 *Earnings per Share*;

the whole of government financial statements and the GGS financial statements are not required to adopt the requirements of that Standard.

12   Paragraph Aus15.4 of AASB 101 applies to the whole of government. It does not apply to the GGS. Accordingly, the GGS is not required to disclose that its financial statements are general purpose financial statements or special purpose financial statements.

13   **In satisfying paragraph 9 of this Standard, subject to paragraph 13A, where compliance with the ABS GFS Manual would not conflict with Australian Accounting Standards, the principles and rules in the ABS GFS Manual shall be applied. In particular, certain Australian Accounting Standards allow optional treatments within their scope. Those optional treatments in Australian Accounting Standards aligned with the principles or rules in the ABS GFS Manual shall be applied.**

13A   **A government is not required to early adopt Australian Accounting Standards.**

13B   **For the purpose of this Standard, a government shall apply the version of the ABS GFS Manual effective at the beginning of the previous annual reporting period or any version effective at a later date, as the basis for GFS information included in the financial statements under this Standard. The date on which amendments to the ABS GFS Manual become effective is, for the purpose of this Standard, the publication date if no effective date is specified by the ABS.**

---

1   AASB 8 (February 2007) is operative on or after 1 January 2009, with early adoption allowed. When applicable, AASB 8 supersedes AASB 114.

14 Examples of particular optional treatments in Australian Accounting Standards that paragraph 13 of this Standard has the effect of limiting, include:

(a) assets within the scope of AASB 116 *Property, Plant and Equipment*, AASB 138 *Intangible Assets* or AASB 140 *Investment Property* that may be measured at cost or at fair value. Those assets that are assets under the ABS GFS Manual that are within the scope of those Standards are required to be measured at fair value because the ABS GFS Manual requires those assets to be measured at market value.

However, the fair value options allowed under AASB 116, AASB 138 and AASB 140 are not amended by paragraph 13 of this Standard. If the fair value of an asset cannot be reliably measured in accordance with an Australian Accounting Standard that allows a choice between fair value and cost, then that asset is to be measured at cost. Where historical cost is adopted because fair value cannot be measured reliably, historical cost is not characterised as fair value. Also, for example, the requirement for the fair value of an intangible asset to be determined by reference to an active market under AASB 138 continues to apply;

(b) certain financial instruments that may be measured at fair value or on another basis under AASB 139 *Financial Instruments: Recognition and Measurement*. Where financial instruments meet the criteria for measurement at fair value under AASB 139, they are required to be measured at fair value where the ABS GFS Manual requires market value as the measurement basis.

Although fair value measurement in the statement of financial position may be mandated through paragraph 13 of this Standard, the accounting for changes in fair value in the statement of comprehensive income is not mandated by paragraph 13. Rather, changes in fair value are classified in the statement of comprehensive income in accordance with AASB 139. AASB 139 anticipates certain financial assets being classified as either:

(i) 'fair value through profit or loss', with changes in fair value included in operating result; or

(ii) 'available-for-sale', with changes in fair value included in the other comprehensive income section of the statement of comprehensive income;

(c) actuarial gains and losses relating to defined benefit superannuation plans that may be recognised in full through operating result (which is part of comprehensive result), recognised in full through other comprehensive income (which is also part of comprehensive result), or partially deferred using a 'corridor approach' under AASB 119 *Employee Benefits*. For the purpose of this Standard, the option to partially defer using a 'corridor approach' is not available because it is not acceptable under the ABS GFS Manual. The other two options are available;

(d) investments in jointly controlled entities that may be accounted for using the equity method of accounting or proportionate consolidation under AASB 131 *Interests in Joint Ventures*. Because proportionate consolidation is inconsistent with the ABS GFS Manual's principles and rules, paragraph 13 of this Standard has the effect of not allowing proportionate consolidation to be adopted;

(e) cash flows from operating activities that may be reported using either the direct method or the indirect method in the statement of cash flows under AASB 107 *Statement of Cash Flows*. Because the direct method is consistent with the format of the cash flow statement under the ABS GFS Manual, paragraph 13 of this Standard has the effect of requiring the direct method to be adopted;

(f) dividends paid by entities within the PNFC sector and PFC sector that may be classified by those sectors as a financing cash flow or as a component of cash flows from operating activities under AASB 107. Because classification as a financing cash flow is consistent with the format of the cash flow statement under the ABS GFS Manual, paragraph 13 of this Standard has the effect of requiring classification of dividends paid as a financing cash flow; and

(g) government grants accounted for by entities within the PNFC sector and PFC sector in accordance with AASB 120 *Accounting for Government Grants and*

Disclosure of Government Assistance. In accordance with paragraphs 52(b)(i) and 53 of this Standard, information about the PNFC sector and PFC sector disclosed for the whole of government is prepared in a manner consistent with the accounting policies adopted in the whole of government statement of financial position, statement of comprehensive income, statement of changes in equity and statement of cash flows. Therefore, the options in AASB 120 are not adopted and instead the principles in AASB 1004 *Contributions* are applied.

15   Certain Australian Accounting Standards do not prescribe specific treatments for all items and issues within their scope. An example is AASB 101, which specifies only the minimum line items to be presented in the statement of financial position and requires additional line items, headings and subtotals to be presented when such presentation is relevant to an understanding of the entity's financial position. The ABS GFS Manual specifies principles and rules for the presentation of a balance sheet prepared for GFS purposes. Those ABS GFS Manual principles and rules are required to be applied in the presentation of the whole of government statement of financial position and the GGS statement of financial position to the extent that they do not conflict with AASB 101.

16   **Subject to paragraphs 41(a)(i)(A) and 52(b)(ii)(A) of this Standard, key fiscal aggregates that are disclosed for the whole of government or the GGS, either because they are required by this Standard or a government elects to provide additional information, shall be measured in a manner that is consistent with amounts recognised in the corresponding statement of financial position, statement of comprehensive income, statement of changes in equity and statement of cash flows.**

17   This Standard requires certain information that is relevant to an assessment of the macro-economic impact of:

(a)   a whole of government and GGS to be included in the statements of financial position, statements of comprehensive income and statements of cash flows (see paragraphs 28, 32 and 37); and

(b)   a government's sectors to be included in the sector statements of financial position, statements of comprehensive income and statements of cash flows required to be disclosed for the whole of government by paragraph 52(b)(i).

This Standard requires the information to be determined in a manner consistent with other amounts recognised in the statement of financial position, statement of comprehensive income, statement of changes in equity and statement of cash flows. Corresponding amounts, determined in accordance with the ABS GFS Manual, are required to be disclosed in the notes where they differ from the amounts presented in the statement of financial position, statement of comprehensive income and statement of cash flows (see paragraphs 41(a)(i)(A) and 52(b)(ii)(A)).

18   A government may elect to disclose key fiscal aggregates (as defined) or other information additional to the requirements of this Standard. If a government elects to make additional disclosures, they are made in a way that does not detract from the information prescribed in this Standard.

18A   Examples of additional disclosures that may be made voluntarily include the classification of *other economic flows* consistent with Table 7.4 of the ABS publication *Australian System of Government Finance Statistics: Concepts, Sources and Methods, 2005* (ABS Catalogue No. 5514.0) and additional key fiscal aggregates, such as change in *net worth* due to revaluations and change in net worth due to other changes in the volume of assets.

18B   Consistent with the requirements in paragraph 16 of this Standard, additional key fiscal aggregates are measured in a manner consistent with recognised amounts. Consistent with paragraphs 41(a)(i) and 52(b)(ii) of this Standard, where they differ, corresponding key fiscal aggregates measured in accordance with the ABS GFS Manual are disclosed, together with a reconciliation of the two measures of each key fiscal aggregate.

18C   Fiscal aggregates that are not measured in a manner consistent with recognised amounts or the ABS GFS Manual may be disclosed, but are not presented as key fiscal aggregates.

18D   If a government elects to disclose aggregates that are not key fiscal aggregates, they are made in a way that clearly differentiates them from key fiscal aggregates.

Presentation and Scope of GGS Financial Statements

19   A government shall present GGS financial statements in which it consolidates only entities that are within the GGS, using the consolidation procedures specified in AASB 127.

GGS Investment in PNFC Sector and PFC Sector Entities

20   A GGS equity investment in a government controlled entity that is within the PNFC sector or PFC sector shall be recognised as an asset in the GGS statement of financial position. It shall be measured:

    (a)   at fair value, where fair value is reliably measurable; or

    (b)   at the government's proportional share of the carrying amount of net assets of the PNFC sector or PFC sector entity before consolidation eliminations, where fair value is not reliably measurable and the carrying amount of net assets before consolidation eliminations is not less than zero; or

    (c)   at zero, where fair value is not reliably measurable and the carrying amount of net assets of the PNFC sector or PFC sector entity before consolidation eliminations is less than zero.

    Any change in the carrying amount of the investment from period to period shall be accounted for as if the change in carrying amount is a change in fair value and accounted for in a manner consistent with the requirements in AASB 139.

21   If the carrying amount of net assets of a PNFC sector or PFC sector entity is less than zero, a liability may need to be recognised by the GGS to the extent a present obligation exists.

22   Income from GGS investments in controlled entities in the PNFC sector and PFC sector is accounted for in accordance with AASB 118 *Revenue* and AASB 139. Dividends are classified as revenue consistent with AASB 118. A change in the carrying amount of the investment over the reporting period that does not arise from the government acquiring or disposing of an interest or undistributed dividends is classified as a gain or loss. The gain or loss is included in the operating result or other comprehensive income, depending on whether the investment is classified in the same manner as 'fair value through profit or loss' investments or in the same manner as 'available-for-sale' investments consistent with the principles in AASB 139.

23   For the purposes of determining the carrying amount of net assets of entities within the PNFC sector and PFC sector recognised and measured in accordance with paragraph 20(b):

    (a)   each PNFC sector and PFC sector entity's accounting policies are adjusted to align with the accounting policies adopted for the whole of government for the same period;

    (b)   intersector balances between the GGS and entities within the PNFC sector and PFC sector are not eliminated; and

    (c)   individual amounts for each PNFC sector and PFC sector entity are presented in aggregate.

GGS Investment in Jointly Controlled Entities and Associates

24   Investments in jointly controlled entities and associates shall be measured using the equity method of accounting, unless the investment is classified as held for sale in accordance with AASB 5 *Non-current Assets Held for Sale and Discontinued Operations*, in which case AASB 5 is applied.

25   [Deleted]

26   [Deleted]

Whole of Government and GGS Statements of Financial Position

27   The whole of government statement of financial position and the GGS statement of financial position, and notes thereto, shall be presented in a manner consistent with the requirements in AASB 101.

28   Net worth shall be presented in the whole of government statement of financial position and GGS statement of financial position, measured in a manner consistent with other amounts recognised in the respective statements of financial position.

Whole of Government and GGS Statements of Comprehensive Income

29   The whole of government statement of comprehensive income and GGS statement of comprehensive income, and notes thereto, shall be presented in a manner consistent with the requirements for a single statement of comprehensive income in AASB 101.

30   For the purpose of presentation, all amounts relating to an item included in the determination of comprehensive result (total change in net worth [before transactions with owners in their capacity as owners]) shall be classified as *transactions* or other economic flows in a manner that is consistent with applying the principles in the ABS GFS Manual from the GAAP perspective.

30A   In accordance with paragraph 30:

     (a)   where GAAP and GFS both recognise the item in the reporting period, amounts relating to that item shall be classified in accordance with the ABS GFS Manual; and

     (b)   where GAAP recognises an item that GFS does not recognise in the reporting period, subject to paragraph 55(b), amounts relating to that item shall be classified by applying GFS principles to the underlying event giving rise to the amounts, as if the amounts were recognised under GFS, using an analogous GFS item.

31   The following examples illustrate how the approach in paragraphs 30 and 30A applies to particular items:

     (a)   in both a whole of government and GGS financial reporting context, where GAAP and GFS both recognise the item in the reporting period:

         (i)   net profit/(loss) from associates potentially comprises two components under GFS classification – dividends from associates and the remainder. Accordingly, dividends are classified as transactions and the remainder is classified as other economic flows. Such dividends are not included in the line item that includes dividends from entities other than associates;

         (ii)   changes in the fair value of financial instruments measured at fair value, that do not arise from undistributed interest or dividends, are classified as other economic flows, irrespective of whether the instruments are classified as 'fair value through profit or loss' or 'available-for-sale';

         (iii)   actuarial gains and losses relating to defined benefit superannuation plans are classified as other economic flows, irrespective of whether they are included in the calculation of operating result or the other comprehensive income section of the statement of comprehensive income;

         (iv)   changes in the fair value of investment property potentially comprise two components under GFS classification – consumption of capital and price changes. Accordingly, the expense arising from consumption of capital is classified as transactions and the gains and losses arising from price changes are classified as other economic flows. Although the consumption of capital may be considered to be similar in nature to depreciation, it is not included in the line item that includes depreciation; and

         (v)   bad debts expense is classified as transactions to the extent it is mutually agreed, otherwise it is classified as other economic flows; and

(b)   in both a whole of government and GGS financial reporting context, where GAAP recognises an item that GFS does not recognise in the reporting period:

(i)   income that arises from the amortisation of a prepayment received for a licence involving the licensee having rights over a specified period of time (that GFS treated in a previous period as a sale of intangible asset) is classified as transactions, by analogy with the GFS classification of the amortisation of a prepayment received for a service to be rendered;

(ii)   doubtful debts expense that arises from the impairment of loans and receivables is classified as other economic flows, by analogy with the GFS classification of revaluation of financial assets;

(iii)   an expense that arises from the initial recognition of the difference between the fair value of a concessionary loan and the transaction price (the loan proceeds) is classified as transactions, by analogy with the GFS classification of subsidies; and

(iv)   an expense that arises from the initial recognition of a provision for decommissioning costs for which there is no counterparty that recognises a related financial asset is classified as transactions, by analogy with the GFS classification of an expense arising from the initial recognition of a liability. Subsequent changes in the measurement of such provisions arising from changes in estimates of the expenditure required to settle the present obligation are classified as other economic flows, by analogy with the GFS classification of revaluation of liabilities; and

(c)   in a GGS financial reporting context, dividends from PNFC sector and PFC sector entities are classified as transactions to the extent the ABS GFS Manual accounts for them as dividends and otherwise as other economic flows.

In some cases the approach in paragraphs 30 and 30A facilitates the reduction of differences between GAAP and GFS, particularly at the key fiscal aggregate level. Illustrative Examples A and B illustrate the classification between transactions and other economic flows for some of the items listed above and other possible circumstances where items recognised in the whole of government statement of comprehensive income and the GGS statement of comprehensive income do not have GFS equivalents.

32   **The following shall be presented in the whole of government statement of comprehensive income and the GGS statement of comprehensive income:**

(a)   *net operating balance;*

(b)   **total change in net worth (before transactions with owners in their capacity as owners, where they exist); and**

(c)   *net lending/(borrowing)* **and its derivation from net operating balance;**

measured in a manner consistent with other amounts recognised in the respective statements of comprehensive income.

33   Under AASB 101, an entity may present a single statement of profit or loss and other comprehensive income, with profit or loss and other comprehensive income presented in two sections. The sections shall be presented together, with the profit or loss section presented first followed directly by the other comprehensive income section. An entity may present the profit or loss section in a separate statement of profit or loss. If so, the separate statement of profit or loss shall immediately precede the statement presenting comprehensive income. This Standard requires a single statement of profit or loss and other comprehensive income option to be adopted, and therefore requires all recognised income and expenses to be included in a single statement that presents the comprehensive result (total change in net worth [before transactions with owners in their capacity as owners, where they exist]).

34   As noted in paragraph 14(c), actuarial gains and losses relating to defined benefit superannuation plans may be recognised in full either through operating result or in full through other comprehensive income.

Whole of Government and GGS Statements of Changes in Equity

34A   The whole of government statement of changes in equity and the GGS statement of changes in equity, and notes thereto, shall be presented in a manner consistent with the requirements in AASB 101.

34B   Generally, transactions with owners in their capacity as owners do not arise in a GGS context because there is no ownership group identified for the GGS. They may arise in a whole of government context in relation to partly-owned subsidiaries. They may also arise between PNFC sector and PFC sector entities and their owner, the GGS.

Whole of Government and GGS Statements of Cash Flows

35   The whole of government statement of cash flows and the GGS statement of cash flows, and notes thereto, shall be presented in a manner consistent with the requirements in AASB 107.

36   Cash flows relating to investing in financial assets for policy purposes and for liquidity management purposes shall be presented separately, determined in a manner consistent with the ABS GFS Manual, in the whole of government statement of cash flows and the GGS statement of cash flows.

37   The whole of government statement of cash flows and the GGS statement of cash flows shall also include *cash surplus/(deficit)* and its derivation, measured in a manner consistent with other amounts recognised in the respective statements of cash flows, without the deduction of the value of assets acquired under finance leases and similar arrangements.

Illustrative Examples

38   An example of an acceptable whole of government statement of financial position, statement of comprehensive income, statement of changes in equity and statement of cash flows format and GGS statement of financial position, statement of comprehensive income, statement of changes in equity and statement of cash flows format that are in accordance with this Standard is provided in Illustrative Examples A and B respectively.

Notes

Summary of Significant Accounting Policies

39   In addition to the disclosures required by other Australian Accounting Standards in the note containing the summary of significant accounting policies, the following disclosures shall be made prominently in that note:

     (a)   for the whole of government and the GGS:

         (i)   a statement that the financial statements are prepared in accordance with this Standard;

         (ii)   a reference to the version of the ABS GFS Manual used as the basis for GFS information included in the financial statements, and when an entity has not applied the most recent version of the ABS GFS Manual:

             (A)   this fact; and

             (B)   known or reasonably estimable information relevant to assessing the possible impact that application of the latest version of the ABS GFS Manual will have on the financial statements in the period of initial application; and

         (iii)   where the GGS financial statements and whole of government financial statements are presented separately from each other, a cross-reference to each other; and

     (b)   for the GGS only:

         (i)   a statement of the purpose for which the GGS financial statements are prepared;

     (ii)   a description of the GGS; and

     (iii)   a description of how the GGS financial statements differ from the whole of government financial statements in terms of the treatment of the government's investments in PNFC sector and PFC sector entities.

39A   In complying with paragraph 39(a)(ii), an entity considers disclosing:

    (a)   the version of the latest ABS GFS Manual;

    (b)   the nature of the impending change or changes in the ABS GFS Manual;

    (c)   the date by which application of the latest version of the ABS GFS Manual is required;

    (d)   the date as at which it plans to apply the latest version of the ABS GFS Manual initially; and

    (e)   either:

      (i)   a discussion of the impact that initial application of the latest version of the ABS GFS Manual is expected to have on the entity's financial statements; or

      (ii)   if that impact is not known or reasonably estimable, a statement to that effect.

40   An example of the information to be included in the summary of significant accounting policies disclosed for the GGS in accordance with paragraph 39 is provided in Illustrative Example C.

Other Explanatory Notes

41   **In addition to the disclosures required to be made in other explanatory notes in accordance with other applicable Australian Accounting Standards, the following disclosures shall be made:**

    (a)   for the whole of government and the GGS:

      (i)   where the key fiscal aggregates measured in accordance with the ABS GFS Manual differ from the key fiscal aggregates provided pursuant to paragraph 16 of this Standard:

        (A)   the key fiscal aggregates measured in accordance with the ABS GFS Manual; and

        (B)   a reconciliation of the two measures of key fiscal aggregates and an explanation of the differences; and

      (ii)   where the key fiscal aggregates measured in accordance with the ABS GFS Manual do not differ from the key fiscal aggregates provided pursuant to paragraph 16, a statement of that fact; and

      (iii)   explanations of key technical terms used; and

    (b)   for the GGS:

      (i)   a list of entities within the GGS, and any changes to that list that have occurred since the previous reporting date and the reasons for those changes;

      (ii)   a list of significant investments in PNFC sector and PFC sector entities, including:

        (A)   the name;

        (B)   proportion of ownership interest and, if different, proportion of voting power held; and

        (C)   the measurement basis adopted for the amount recognised in accordance with paragraph 20; and

      (iii)   the aggregate amount of dividends and other distributions to owners in their capacity as owners from PNFC sector and PFC sector entities to the GGS and the aggregate amount of the comprehensive result attributable to the GGS of the PNFC sector and PFC sector entities disclosed in the

whole of government statement of comprehensive income by sector for the reporting period.

42   In relation to the requirements in paragraph 41(a)(i), differences in the key fiscal aggregates determined under the ABS GFS Manual and pursuant to paragraph 16 of this Standard arise from differences in definition, recognition, measurement and certain classification requirements. Each difference gives rise to the need for disclosure of a reconciliation and an explanation of the difference. Examples of such differences include:

(a)   in a whole of government and GGS context:

(i)   doubtful debts – although the ABS GFS Manual recognises bad debts written off, it does not recognise write-downs of accounts receivable in relation to doubtful debts;

(ii)   provisions recognised as liabilities – in the absence of a counter-party recognising a related financial asset, the ABS GFS Manual does not recognise a liability arising from a constructive obligation;

(iii)   inventories – under the ABS GFS Manual, inventories are measured at current prices, whereas under AASB 102 *Inventories* (as amended by AASB 2007-5 *Amendments to Australian Accounting Standard – Inventories Held for Distribution by Not-for-Profit Entities*), depending on their nature, inventories are measured at the lower of cost and net realisable value or at cost adjusted when applicable for any loss of service potential; and

(iv)   investments in associates – under the ABS GFS Manual, those assets are measured at current prices where current prices exist, whereas under AASB 128 *Investments in Associates* the equity method of accounting generally applies; and

(b)   in a whole of government context only:

(i)   non-controlling interest in controlled entities – under the ABS GFS Manual, minority interest is classified as a liability and measured at current prices, whereas under AASB 127 non-controlling interest that is classified as equity is not remeasured; and

(ii)   outgoing dividends – under the ABS GFS Manual, outgoing dividends are classified as an expense, whereas under AASB 101 a dividend is treated as a distribution to owners.

Illustrative Examples A and B illustrate some of these and other possible circumstances where differences arise and the manner in which they are reflected in reconciliation notes.

43   In relation to the whole of government, for the purpose of paragraph 41(a)(i)(A), the ABS GFS Manual key fiscal aggregate that corresponds to the requirement in paragraph 32(b) to present 'total change in net worth before transactions with owners in their capacity as owners' is 'total change in net worth' (after transactions with owners in their capacity as owners). Accordingly, the reconciliation required to be disclosed for the whole of government by paragraph 41(a)(i)(B) is from 'total change in net worth before transactions with owners in their capacity as owners' as presented in accordance with paragraph 32(b) to 'total change in net worth' measured in accordance with the ABS GFS Manual. As noted in paragraph 34B, transactions with owners in their capacity as owners do not arise in a GGS context.

44   Some differences between GAAP and GFS requirements relate to differences in classification or differences in consolidation eliminations that do not cause a difference in measurements of key fiscal aggregates and therefore do not need to be included in the reconciliation notes. However, they do give rise to the need for explanations of the differences to be disclosed. Examples of such differences include:

(a)   for both the whole of government and the GGS:

(i)   AASB 132 *Financial Instruments: Presentation* classifies certain prepaid expenses as non-financial assets, whereas the ABS GFS Manual classifies them as financial assets;

(ii)   AASB 137 *Provisions, Contingent Liabilities and Contingent Assets* may classify an amount within provisions, whereas the ABS GFS Manual classifies them as accounts payable; and

(iii)   paragraph 31(a)(iv) of this Standard notes that consumption of capital of investment property is classified separately from depreciation, whereas the ABS GFS Manual classifies it as depreciation; and

(b)   for the whole of government, consolidation eliminations. Under the ABS GFS Manual, certain transactions between the GGS and entities within the PNFC sector and PFC sector are not eliminated on whole of government consolidation, whereas under AASB 127 intragroup transactions that are not, in substance, transactions with external parties are eliminated in full. The GFS treatment has the effect of 'grossing up' both GFS revenue and GFS expenses by equal amounts and though the key fiscal aggregates remain the same, the differences in GAAP and GFS revenues and expenses should be disclosed. For example, a GGS may compensate a PNFC sector entity for a community service obligation, imposed by the GGS, that requires the PNFC sector entity to provide free services to a cohort of private individuals. The compensation provided by the GGS to the PNFC sector entity is not eliminated for whole of government reporting under the ABS GFS Manual (instead it is 'rerouted' through the household sector of the economy and therefore treated as an expense of the GGS to the household sector, and an expense of the household sector to the PNFC sector entity, and therefore revenue of the PNFC sector entity).

45   The GGS is not subject to the disclosures required by paragraphs 41, 42, 43 and Aus43.1 of AASB 127 relating to investments in subsidiaries, jointly controlled entities and associates. The requirements in those paragraphs are either addressed elsewhere in this Standard or are not significant for GGS financial reporting.

46   In relation to the requirement in paragraph 41(a)(iii) to disclose explanations of key technical terms, key technical terms include:

(a)   transactions;

(b)   other economic flows;

(c)   net operating balance;

(d)   net lending/(borrowing);

(e)   financial assets;

(f)   non-financial assets;

(g)   net worth;

(h)   cash surplus/(deficit);

(i)   operating result;

(j)   comprehensive result (total change in net worth [before transactions with owners in their capacity as owners]);

(k)   total change in net worth; and

(l)   net debt.

An example of the disclosures required by paragraph 41(a)(iii) is provided in Illustrative Example D.

47   Paragraph 112 of AASB 101 requires additional information to be provided in notes that is not presented in the statement of financial position, statement of comprehensive income, statement of changes in equity and statement of cash flows but is relevant to an understanding of them. Consistent with this, the components of aggregate numbers presented in those statements, including key fiscal aggregates, are disclosed in the notes where relevant.

Functional Information

48   In respect of each broad function identified in Table 2.6 "Government Purpose Classification: Major Groups" of the ABS publication *Australian System of Government Finance Statistics: Concepts, Sources and Methods, 2005* (ABS Catalogue No. 5514.0), the whole of government and the GGS shall disclose by way of note:

(a)   a description of that function;

(b)   the carrying amount of assets recognised in the respective statements of financial position that are reliably attributable to that function; and

(c)   expenses, excluding losses, included in operating result in the respective statements of comprehensive income for the reporting period that are reliably attributable to that function.

49   The information provided by way of note in accordance with paragraph 48 shall be aggregated. A reconciliation of the aggregate amount of expenses, excluding losses, included in operating result to the aggregate of expenses from transactions recognised in the statement of comprehensive income shall be disclosed.

50   Paragraph 48 requires disclosure of information about the recognised expenses, excluding losses, included in operating result and assets that are reliably attributable to broad functions determined to at least the ABS GFS Manual two-digit level of classification shown in Table 2.6 of the ABS publication *Australian System of Government Finance Statistics: Concepts, Sources and Methods, 2005* (ABS Catalogue No. 5514.0). Disclosure of this information assists users in identifying the resources committed to particular functions and the costs of service delivery that are reliably attributable to those functions. Functional classification of financial information, where it can be determined reliably, will also assist users in assessing the significance of financial or non-financial performance indicators reported by the government.

51   AASB 114 (AASB 8) does not apply to the whole of government or the GGS. The bases used in the ABS GFS Manual for identifying functions do not necessarily accord with the criteria for identifying segments contained in AASB 114 (AASB 8). However, AASB 114 (AASB 8) may be useful in identifying the expenses, excluding losses, included in operating result and assets that are reliably attributable to each function. An example of the disclosures required by paragraphs 48(b) and 48(c) in respect of each function of the whole of government and the GGS is provided in Illustrative Examples A and B respectively.

Whole of Government Sector Information

52   The whole of government shall disclose by way of note, in respect of the GGS, PNFC sector and PFC sector as defined in the ABS GFS Manual:

(a)   a description of each sector;

(b)   for each sector:

(i)   a statement of financial position, statement of comprehensive income, statement of changes in equity and statement of cash flows that are consistent with the whole of government's corresponding financial statements prepared in accordance with this Standard;

(ii)   where the key fiscal aggregates measured in accordance with the ABS GFS Manual differ from the key fiscal aggregates determined in a manner consistent with paragraph 16 of this Standard:

(A)   the key fiscal aggregates measured in accordance with the ABS GFS Manual; and

(B)   a reconciliation of the two measures of key fiscal aggregates and an explanation of the differences; and

(iii) where the key fiscal aggregates measured in accordance with the ABS GFS Manual do not differ from the key fiscal aggregates determined in a manner consistent with paragraph 16, a statement of that fact; and

(c)   a reconciliation between the information disclosed for the sectors in total and the corresponding information in the whole of government's statement of financial position, statement of comprehensive income, statement of changes in equity and statement of cash flows (see, for example, Illustrative Example A).

53 Sector information prepared in accordance with paragraph 52(b) is determined before consolidation eliminations. Accordingly, GGS investments in PNFC sector and PFC sector entities are included in the GGS information that is disclosed for the whole of government. They are measured at the carrying amount of net assets disclosed by the whole of government for the PNFC sector and PFC sector.

54 Notes to the sector statements of financial position, statements of comprehensive income, statements of changes in equity and statements of cash flows, other than those required by paragraph 52, are not required to be disclosed.

55 In relation to the requirements in paragraph 52(b)(ii), differences in the key fiscal aggregates determined under the ABS GFS Manual and consistent with paragraph 16 of this Standard arise from differences in definition, recognition, measurement and certain classification requirements. Each difference gives rise to the need for disclosure of a reconciliation and an explanation of the difference. Examples of such differences for the PNFC sector and the PFC sector include those identified in paragraph 42 of this Standard, as well as:

(a) ownership interest in PNFC sector and PFC sector entities – in contrast to Australian Accounting Standards, under the ABS GFS Manual, the carrying amount of ownership interest in PNFC sector and PFC sector entities is deducted in the determination of net worth of those sectors. In particular:

(i) where the market value of ownership interest in PNFC sector and PFC sector entities is reliably measurable, GFS deducts it in determining net worth of those sectors. Accordingly, negative GFS net worth arises if the market value exceeds the recognised carrying amount of net assets. Under Australian Accounting Standards, the market value of ownership interest is not recognised; and

(ii) where ownership interest in PNFC sector and PFC sector entities is measured by GFS at the carrying amount of net assets, GFS net worth is nil. Under Australian Accounting Standards, the carrying amount of net assets is not deducted in determining net worth; and

(b) deferred tax assets and deferred tax liabilities of PNFC sector and PFC sector entities – the ABS GFS Manual does not recognise deferred tax assets and deferred tax liabilities that are recognised by PNFC sector and PFC sector entities in accordance with AASB 112 *Income Taxes*. Like the approach in paragraph 61A of AASB 112, a deferred tax revenue or expense recognised in accordance with AASB 112 is classified in the statement of comprehensive income as a transaction or an other economic flow consistent with the underlying event giving rise to the related deferred tax asset or liability. For example, when a deferred tax liability arises from the revaluation of an asset, the related deferred tax expense is classified as an other economic flow because the asset revaluation itself is recognised as an other economic flow.

56 For the purpose of paragraph 52(b)(ii)(A), the ABS GFS Manual key fiscal aggregate that corresponds to the requirement implicit in paragraph 52(b)(i) to present 'total change in net worth before transactions with owners in their capacity as owners' for the PNFC sector and PFC sector is 'total change in net worth' (after transactions with owners in their capacity as owners). Accordingly, the reconciliation required to be disclosed by paragraph 52(b)(ii)(B) is from 'total change in net worth before transactions with owners in their capacity as owners' as presented in accordance with paragraph 52(b)(i) to 'total change in net worth' measured in accordance with the ABS GFS Manual.

57 A government may choose to disclose sectors in addition to the GGS, PNFC sector and PFC sector. For example, a government may disclose information about the total non-financial public sector, comprising the GGS and PNFC sector. Where that is the case, the additional sectors are disclosed on a comparable basis to the information disclosed for the GGS, PNFC sector and PFC sector.

58   The sector statements of financial position, statements of comprehensive income, statements of changes in equity and statements of cash flows could be presented in a single schedule that includes an adjustments column or row to facilitate reconciliation to the corresponding whole of government statements in accordance with paragraph 52(c). Alternatively, those sector financial statements may be presented in columns, with or without an adjustments column, in the whole of government statement of financial position, statement of comprehensive income, statement of changes in equity and statement of cash flows. Where an adjustments column is not provided in those whole of government financial statements, the reconciliation required by paragraph 52(c) is provided in the notes. Disclosure of the individual eliminations between the sectors is not required.

Budgetary Information

59   **Where a whole of government or GGS budgeted:**

   (a)   statement of financial position;

   (b)   statement of comprehensive income;

   (c)   statement of changes in equity; or

   (d)   statement of cash flows;

   is presented to parliament, the whole of government or GGS, respectively, shall disclose for the reporting period:

   (e)   that original budgeted financial statement presented to parliament, presented on a basis that is consistent with the presentation and classification bases prescribed for financial statements by this Standard; and

   (f)   explanations of major variances between the actual amounts presented in the financial statements and corresponding original budget amounts.

60   **Comparative budgetary information in respect of the previous period need not be disclosed.**

61   The original budget is the first budget presented to parliament in respect of the reporting period. Amendments made to the budget by the executive are not reflected in the budgetary information that is required to be disclosed under paragraph 59.

62   Any revised budget that is presented to parliament during the reporting period may be disclosed in addition to the original budget.

63   For the purpose of this Standard, governments are required to report the financial information required by paragraph 59 about their original budgets for the reporting period that are presented to parliament. This facilitates users of financial statements (including taxpayers) making and evaluating decisions about the allocation of scarce resources and for assessing the discharge of a government's accountability. The budget information is disclosed on the same presentation and classification bases, as the financial statements, to facilitate a comparison of actual outcomes against the budget.

64   The whole of government and GGS statements of financial position, statements of comprehensive income, statements of changes in equity and statements of cash flows include information about the government, as determined in accordance with this Standard. To the extent the presentation and classification bases adopted in the first budget presented to parliament are not consistent with the corresponding financial statements, the budget presented to parliament is restated for budget disclosure purposes to align with the presentation and classification bases specified in this Standard. As the presentation and classification bases adopted in the budget are consistent with the financial statements, budget information may be presented in the statement of financial position, statement of comprehensive income, statement of changes in equity and statement of cash flows.

65   The explanations of major variances required to be disclosed by paragraph 59(f) are those relevant to an assessment of the discharge of accountability and to an analysis of performance of government. They include high-level explanations of the causes of major variances rather than merely the nature of the variances.

Appendix A
Defined Terms

AASB

This appendix is an integral part of AASB 1049.

ABS GFS Manual	Australian Bureau of Statistics (ABS) publications *Australian System of Government Finance Statistics: Concepts, Sources and Methods, 2005* (ABS Catalogue No. 5514.0) and *Amendments to Australian System of Government Finance Statistics, 2005* (ABS Catalogue No. 5514.0) published on the ABS website.
cash surplus/(deficit)	Net cash flows from operating activities plus net cash flows from acquisition and disposal of non-financial assets less distributions paid less value of assets acquired under finance leases and similar arrangements. Defined in the ABS GFS Manual (paragraph 2.124).
General Government Sector (GGS)	Institutional sector comprising all *government units* and *non-profit institutions* controlled and mainly financed by government. Defined in the ABS GFS Manual (Glossary, page 256).
government	The Australian Government, the Government of the Australian Capital Territory, New South Wales, the Northern Territory, Queensland, South Australia, Tasmania, Victoria or Western Australia.
government units	Unique kinds of legal entities established by political processes which have legislative, judicial or executive authority over other *institutional units* within a given area and which: (i) provide goods and services to the community and/or individuals free of charge or at prices that are not economically significant; and (ii) redistribute income and wealth by means of taxes and other compulsory transfers. Defined in the ABS GFS Manual (Glossary, page 257).
institutional unit	An economic entity that is capable, in its own right, of owning assets, incurring liabilities and engaging in economic activities and in transactions with other entities. Defined in the ABS GFS Manual (Glossary, page 257).
key fiscal aggregates	Referred to as analytical balances in the ABS GFS Manual, are data identified in the ABS GFS Manual as useful for macro-economic analysis purposes, including assessing the impact of a government and its sectors on the economy. They are: opening net worth, net operating balance, net lending/(borrowing), change in net worth due to revaluations, change in net worth due to other changes in the volume of assets, total change in net worth, closing net worth and cash surplus/(deficit).
net lending/(borrowing)	The financing requirement of government, calculated as the net operating balance less the net acquisition of non-financial assets. A positive result reflects a net lending position and a negative result reflects a net borrowing position. Based on the definition in the ABS GFS Manual (Glossary, page 259).

net operating balance	This is calculated as income from transactions minus expenses from transactions. Based on the definition in the ABS GFS Manual (Glossary, page 259).
net worth	Assets less liabilities and shares/contributed capital. For the GGS, net worth is assets less liabilities since shares and contributed capital is zero. It is an economic measure of wealth and reflects the contribution of governments to the wealth of Australia. Defined in the ABS GFS Manual (Glossary, page 259).
non-profit institution	A legal or social entity that is created for the purpose of producing or distributing goods and services but is not permitted to be a source of income, profit or other financial gain for the units that establish, control or finance it. Defined in the ABS GFS Manual (Glossary, page 260).
other economic flows	Changes in the volume or value of an asset or liability that do not result from transactions (i.e. revaluations and other changes in the volume of assets). Defined in the ABS GFS Manual (Glossary, page 260).
Public Financial Corporations (PFC) sector	Institutional sector comprising resident government controlled corporations and *quasi-corporations* mainly engaged in financial intermediation or provision of auxiliary financial services. Based on the definition in the ABS GFS Manual (Glossary, page 261).
Public Non-Financial Corporations (PNFC) sector	Institutional sector comprising resident government controlled corporations and quasi-corporations mainly engaged in the production of market goods and/or non-financial services. Based on the definition in the ABS GFS Manual (Glossary, page 261).
quasi-corporation	An unincorporated enterprise that functions as if it were a corporation, has the same relationship with its owner as a corporation, and keeps a separate set of accounts. Defined in the ABS GFS Manual (Glossary, page 261).
transactions	Interactions between two institutional units by mutual agreement or actions within a unit that it is analytically useful to treat as transactions. Defined in the ABS GFS Manual (Glossary, page 263).
whole of government general purpose financial statements (also referred to as 'whole of government financial statements' in this Standard)	General purpose financial statements prepared by a government that are prepared in accordance with Australian Accounting Standards, including AASB 127 *Consolidated and Separate Financial Statements*, and thereby separately recognise assets, liabilities, income, expenses and cash flows of all entities under the control of the government on a line-by-line basis.

Basis for Conclusions on AASB 1049

Whole of Government and General Government Sector Financial Reporting

This Basis for Conclusions accompanies, but is not part of, AASB 1049.

Introduction

BC1   The Preface to this Standard outlines the broad strategic direction issued to the Australian Accounting Standards Board (AASB) by the Financial Reporting Council (FRC) that gave rise to AASB 1049 *Whole of Government and General Government Sector Financial Reporting*. This Basis for Conclusions summarises the Board's considerations in developing the Standard. It focuses on the issues that the Board considers to be of greatest significance.

BC2   In developing the Standard, the Board first considered GAAP/GFS harmonisation issues from a General Government Sector (GGS) perspective. This resulted in the issue of AASB 1049 *Financial Reporting of General Government Sectors by Governments* in September 2006. It included a requirement that a government not make its GGS financial report available prior to its whole of government financial report being made available. The Board became aware that no jurisdiction intended to early adopt AASB 1049 (September 2006) because of this requirement, combined with concern that the whole of government accounting basis (then specified in AAS 31 *Financial Reporting by Governments*) was, at the time, different from the GGS accounting basis (specified in AASB 1049).

BC3   In addressing this concern, the Board considered the extent to which the principles in AASB 1049 (September 2006) should apply to whole of government financial reporting. The Board concluded that the requirements for GAAP/GFS harmonised whole of government financial reports, incorporating requirements for information about the GGS, the Public Non-Financial Corporations (PNFC) sector and the Public Financial Corporations (PFC) sector, should be based on the principles in AASB 1049 (September 2006). This reflects the relationship between the GGS of a government, the other sectors of a government and the whole of government and is a response to an assessment of user needs. Given the relationship between the GGS and whole of government, an alternative approach that would result in fundamentally different accounting bases for GGS financial reports and whole of government financial reports has the potential to confuse some users.

BC4   The Board developed a separate Exposure Draft (ED 155 *Financial Reporting by Whole of Governments*) for the purpose of exposing its proposals for GAAP/GFS harmonisation requirements for whole of government financial reporting, rather than present the proposals integrated with the requirements in AASB 1049 (September 2006). However, the Board indicated its intention in ED 155 that the Standard to be developed would be an amended AASB 1049 that specifies, in an integrated way, the GAAP/GFS harmonised requirements for GGS financial reports and whole of government financial reports. The Board concluded that a single integrated Standard is justified on the basis that:

(a)   it more effectively acknowledges the strong relationship between whole of government financial reports and GGS financial reports. An integrated Standard is consistent with the requirement that GGS financial reports not be made available prior to the release of whole of government financial reports (see paragraphs BC18-BC20);

(b)   it is more consistent with a topic-based approach to setting Standards; and

(c)   it imposes a greater discipline on the Board to ensure that the requirements are expressed in the same way for GGS and whole of government, and only differ where intended.

GGS Financial Reports

Preparation of GGS Financial Reports [Paragraphs 2 and 7]

The Nature of a GGS Financial Report

BC5 Due to the unique circumstances related to the GGS, its relationship to the whole of government (see paragraphs BC18-BC20) and its macro-economic significance, the Board concluded that a Standard should require the preparation of financial reports of a federal, state or territory government's GGS. The Board also supported the GGS presenting a financial report on the basis that whole of government financial reports are to be available at the same time as the GGS financial report (see paragraph BC18).

BC6 The Board concluded that it is not necessary to specify whether the GGS is a reporting entity and whether the GGS financial report prepared in accordance with the Standard is a general purpose financial report (GPFR) because the Standard itself prescribes the particular requirements for the scope of the GGS and the form and content of the GGS financial report.

GGS Financial Report Prepared on a Partial Consolidation Basis

BC7 It is inherent in the definition of a GGS that government controlled entities within the PNFC sector and PFC sector are not consolidated in the GGS financial report (see paragraphs BC11-BC13). Only government controlled entities that fall within the boundary of a GGS are consolidated. Accordingly, the Board concluded that a government should produce a GGS financial report on a partial consolidation basis (see paragraph 19).

BC8 This focus on the GGS and consequently the partial consolidation approach is consistent with, to some extent, the 'through the eyes of management' approach adopted in AASB 8 *Operating Segments*. The information used to manage a government includes GGS information prepared on a partial consolidated basis because, essentially, the GGS equates to the budget sector of Australian governments, and reporting of budget outcomes is a major focus.

BC9 The Board's decisions reflect that:

(a) the GGS is a significant sector of a government that warrants prominence in financial reporting;

(b) GGS financial information is relevant to users and is widely distributed;

(c) GGS financial information should be made available to the public in a manner that meets the key characteristics of comparability, understandability, relevance, reliability and timeliness set out in AASB *Framework for the Preparation and Presentation of Financial Statements*; and

(d) GGS financial information is necessary to provide a link to GGS budgets, which are a means by which governments outline their taxing policies and resource allocation decisions (see paragraphs BC57-BC62).

BC10 An alternative view considered by the Board is that, because a GGS is a sector of the whole of government, GGS financial information prepared on a partial consolidation basis should only be included in the whole of government GPFR (see also paragraph BC20). When that GGS financial information is presented in a financial report that is separate from the whole of government GPFR, it should be characterised as a special purpose financial report. However, as explained in paragraph BC6, the Board decided that, because the Standard prescribes the form and content of the GGS financial report, it is not necessary to take such an approach.

Accounting for GGS Investments in PNFC Sector and PFC Sector Entities in GGS Financial Reports [Paragraphs 19 and 20]

BC11 The issue of the accounting for GGS investments in PNFC sector and PFC sector entities in the GGS financial report is closely related to the basis on which the GGS financial report is prepared and to the issue of partial consolidation (see paragraphs BC7-BC10).

BC12 The Board decided that, consistent with GFS principles and rules, entities that are controlled by a government, but are not part of the GGS of the government, should be recognised in the GGS financial report as investments.

BC13 Furthermore, the Board concluded that GGS controlling investments in PNFC sector and PFC sector entities should be measured at, depending on circumstances, fair value, the government's proportional share of the carrying amount of net assets (as a surrogate for fair value) or zero. Measurement at fair value, or at the government's proportional share of the carrying amount of net assets where fair value is not reliably measurable, is consistent with GFS. Not allowing investments to be measured below zero is consistent with the principles elsewhere in GAAP (for example, AASB 128 *Investments in Associates* does not allow negative investment values when using the equity method).

BC14 When a GGS's controlling investment in a PNFC sector or PFC sector entity is measured at the government's proportional share of the carrying amount of net assets, for consistency with GFS principles, it should be accounted for as a financial asset consistent with AASB 139 *Financial Instruments: Recognition and Measurement*, rather than as if it were an investment in an associate accounted for using the equity method of accounting.

Accounting for GGS Investments in Jointly Controlled Entities and Associates in GGS Financial Reports [Paragraph 24]

BC15 The Board concluded that investments in jointly controlled entities and associates should be measured using the equity method of accounting, except when the investment is classified as held for sale in accordance with AASB 5 *Non-current Assets Held for Sale and Discontinued Operations*. This is on the basis that, consistent with paragraph 19 of this Standard that prescribes the use of the consolidation procedures in AASB 127 *Consolidated and Separate Financial Statements*, the GGS financial report is treated as if it is a consolidated financial report rather than as 'separate financial statements', as defined in AASB 127.

Disclosures about the GGS in the Summary of Significant Accounting Policies Note [Paragraph 39(b)]

BC16 The Board concluded that additional disclosures relating to the nature of the GGS and its relationship to the whole of government financial report should be made as part of the note in the GGS financial report containing the summary of significant accounting policies. These disclosures are intended to help overcome concerns that users might perceive the GGS financial report as being a substitute for the whole of government financial report. Furthermore, the disclosures are intended to help users understand the nature of the GGS and its financial reports to provide a greater link to the budget outcome reports, to the extent they focus solely on the GGS.

Other Disclosures Specific to the GGS [Paragraph 41(b)]

BC17 Given this Standard encompasses GFS concepts and definitions for the GGS, the Board considered it appropriate to require additional disclosures to be included in the GGS financial report. The additional disclosures include:

(a) a list of entities within the GGS and any changes to that list since the previous reporting date and reasons for the changes (paragraph 41(b)(i)). This disclosure informs users of the controlled entities that have been consolidated into the GGS financial report and, for the purposes of year to year comparisons, the changes to the list of entities. The reasons for changes should be capable of being traced back to the ABS GFS Manual definition of the GGS and should reflect a fundamental change to the nature of an entity's functions and purpose;

(b) a list of significant investments in PNFC sector and PFC sector entities (paragraph 41(b)(ii)). This disclosure informs users of the controlled entities that have not been consolidated into the GGS financial report and the effect of GGS management decisions to retain or divest these investments and their effect on the balance sheet of the GGS; and

(c) the aggregate amount of dividends and other distributions to owners as owners from PNFC sector and PFC sector entities to the GGS and the aggregate amount of the comprehensive result of the PNFC sector and PFC sector entities that is attributable to the GGS for the reporting period (paragraph 41(b)(iii)). This disclosure provides further information about the relationship between the GGS and PNFC sector and PFC sector entities.

Relationship between GGS Financial Reports and Whole of Government Financial Reports [Paragraphs 8 and 39(b)(iv)]

BC18 As noted in paragraph BC2, the Board concluded that, because of the relationship between the GGS (partially consolidated) financial report and the whole of government (fully consolidated) financial report, the GGS financial report should not be made available prior to the whole of government financial report being made available. Furthermore, the GGS financial report should include a cross-reference to the whole of government financial report (see paragraph 39(b)(iv)). This approach ensures that GGS financial reports are given due prominence within an appropriate context. That context is the whole of government financial reports that provide information about all the resources controlled by the government.

BC19 Board consultations indicated that most jurisdictions would be able to meet the requirement for the whole of government financial report to be available at the time the GGS financial report is prepared in the short term. One jurisdiction faced a number of impediments, including legislative provisions, to achieving completion of the whole of government financial report at the same time as a GGS financial report could be prepared. The Board therefore decided to specify a mandatory operative date for the Standard of the year beginning 1 July 2008, and to allow early adoption (see paragraphs 3 and 4). The Board's decision not to permit the preparation and presentation of GGS financial reports at an earlier date than for the whole of government financial report is consistent, by analogy, with the requirements in AASB 127 that parent entity financial reports cannot be prepared and presented unless consolidated financial statements are available.

BC20 Prior to this Standard, Australian Accounting Standards only anticipated that sectors of a whole of government (including the GGS) might be disclosed in the whole of government financial report in the form of disaggregated information. That is, separate financial reporting of a GGS was not contemplated. The Board considered whether, consistent with this disaggregated information approach, the proposals in International Public Sector Accounting Standards Board (IPSASB) Exposure Draft ED 28 *Disclosure of Financial Information about the General Government Sector*, since reflected in IPSAS 22 *Disclosure of Financial Information About the General Government Sector*, should be adopted in Australia. When a government elects to disclose information about its GGS in its whole of government financial reports, IPSAS 22 requires the information to conform with the accounting policies of the whole of government financial report (which are not GAAP/GFS harmonised) except for consolidation requirements and the accounting for investments in controlled PNFC sector and PFC sector entities. The Board concluded that such an approach would not adequately facilitate the presentation of GGS information and GFS information with appropriate prominence.

Whole of Government Financial Reports

Specification of Requirements for Whole of Government Financial Reports

BC21 AAS 31 was first issued in 1996 and specified requirements for general purpose financial reporting by governments. Since then, AAS 31 had only been subject to limited reviews, the most recent in June 1998.[1] The Board considered it timely to undertake a comprehensive review of the requirements in AAS 31 through two concurrent and interrelated AASB projects:

(a) the GAAP/GFS Harmonisation project; and

(b) the Short-term Review of the Requirements in AAS 27 *Financial Reporting by Local Governments*, AAS 29 *Financial Reporting by Government Departments* and AAS 31 *Financial Reporting by Governments*.

BC22 This Standard, which is a result of the GAAP/GFS Harmonisation project, together with the new, amending and revised Standards being developed from the Short-term Review of the Requirements in AASs 27, 29 & 31, supersede AAS 31.

---

1 Although AAS 31A *Amendments to the Transitional Provisions in AAS 31* was issued in December 1999 and AASB 1045 *Land Under Roads: Amendments to AAS 27A, AAS 29 & AAS 31* was issued in October 2002, they only had the effect of extending the transitional provisions for land under roads.

AASB

BC23 This Standard requires governments to prepare GPFRs that adopt applicable Australian Accounting Standards, except when otherwise specified (see paragraph 9). The Short-term Review of the Requirements in AASs 27, 29 & 31 retains or amends the AAS 31 requirements by amending, where appropriate, the Australian Accounting Standards that this Standard requires to be adopted by governments. The Bases for Conclusions accompanying Exposure Draft ED 156 *Proposals Arising from the Short-term Review of the Requirements in AAS 27, AAS 29 and AAS 31* and to accompany the resulting new, amending or revised Standards, contain the Board's rationale for its treatment of the requirements in AAS 31. This Basis for Conclusions provides the Board's rationale for adopting GAAP/GFS harmonisation principles for whole of governments.

BC24 The Board concluded that adopting the GAAP/GFS harmonisation principles in this Standard would help ensure that the multiple needs of users for both GAAP and GFS based information prepared under a harmonised framework at a whole of government level (incorporating sector information) are satisfied.

Preparation of Whole of Government Financial Reports [Paragraphs 2 and 7]

BC25 Due to the nature of governments, the Board concluded that a Standard should continue to specify requirements for the preparation of whole of government GPFRs of the federal and each state and territory government.

Consolidation of Non-resident Entities

BC26 Generally, the controlled entities that are not consolidated within the GGS would be consolidated under both GAAP and GFS in whole of government financial reports, and therefore one of the more controversial aspects dealt with in the context of GGS financial reporting (see paragraphs BC5-BC13) does not arise in the context of whole of government. However, a different kind of non-consolidation issue conceivably arises. Under GAAP, irrespective of residency, all controlled entities are consolidated. Under GFS, controlled non-residents are not consolidated. For example, an off-shore subsidiary of a PNFC sector entity or PFC sector entity is not consolidated under GFS because it is not part of the Australian economic territory. Instead GFS records the parent PNFC sector or PFC sector entity as having an equity investment in the non-resident subsidiary and deriving dividend income from it. The non-resident subsidiary is an institutional unit in the economic territory of the other economy that would be part of that other economy's private sector.

BC27 The Board concluded that, consistent with AASB 127, all controlled entities should be consolidated on a line-by-line basis in whole of government financial reports. If material, the GFS non-consolidation of non-resident subsidiaries would be shown as a reconciling difference (see paragraphs BC40(c) and BC52). The Board noted that Australian jurisdictions either do not have non-resident subsidiaries or have immaterial non-resident subsidiaries. Given that the issue is not significant in practice, the Board concluded that it is not necessary for the Standard to explicitly refer to the issue.

Consolidation of PNFC Sector and PFC Sector Entities

BC28 The Board noted that under AASB 1049 (September 2006), and carried over with some clarification into this Standard, the GGS recognises its investment in PNFC sector and PFC sector entities at, depending on circumstances, fair value, proportional share of the carrying amount of net assets (as a surrogate for fair value) or zero (see paragraph BC13).

BC29 The Board considered the whole of government consolidation implications of GGS investments in PNFC sector and PFC sector entities potentially being measured at fair value in GGS financial reports. The Board noted that if the whole of government financial report were to consolidate PNFC sector and PFC sector entities at fair value, this would result in the recognition of, among other things, internally generated goodwill. The Board concluded that it is not appropriate for a government to recognise internally generated goodwill, noting that internally generated goodwill is also not recognised under GFS. Accordingly, the Board concluded that PNFC sector and PFC sector entities should be consolidated at the carrying amount of their net assets on a line-by-line basis, determined in a manner consistent with GAAP/GFS harmonisation principles.

BC30 The Board noted that no PNFC sector and PFC sector entities in any Australian jurisdiction currently have traded shares and therefore the principle in this Standard would be expected to result in the investments being measured at the carrying amount of net assets, which is consistent with GFS in these circumstances. Therefore, the question of consolidating PNFC sector and PFC sector entities at fair value is not expected to arise frequently in practice.

Disclosure of Whole of Government Sector Information [Paragraph 52]

PNFC Sector and PFC Sector Information as Note Disclosure in Whole of Government Financial Reports

BC31 The Board concluded that financial statements for the GGS, PNFC sector and PFC sector and reconciliations between GFS and GAAP measures of key fiscal aggregates for each sector should be disclosed in the whole of government financial report. The Board concluded that such information, together with related information, is sufficient to satisfy user needs in a general purpose financial reporting context and therefore it is not necessary to require the preparation of separate PNFC sector and PFC sector financial reports. To facilitate a presentation format that provides sufficient prominence to the various sectors relative to each other and the whole of government, the Board concluded that the sector financial statements could be presented:

(a) as a table in the notes to the whole of government financial statements comprising all sectors, an adjustments column and the whole of government; or

(b) on the face of the government's financial statements.

BC32 The Board considered whether to make the sector information disclosure requirements less onerous by only requiring disclosure of sector financial statements prepared on a GFS basis. The Board noted that this would in some respects broadly align with the 'through the eyes of management' approach adopted in AASB 8. However, the Board concluded that this approach should not be adopted because:

(a) sectors are different in nature from operating segments;

(b) such an approach would not be consistent with the approach to GAAP/GFS harmonisation adopted for the GGS financial report; and

(c) there would be a potential for user confusion if GGS financial reports adopt an accounting basis fundamentally different from that used for the GGS financial information presented in the whole of government financial report.

BC33 The Board also considered whether to not require disclosure of reconciliations of GAAP and GFS measures of key fiscal aggregates for the PNFC sector and PFC sector (see paragraph BC52), noting a view expressed by some that having to provide such information is onerous for preparers. The Board concluded that such information is useful for a significant group of users and therefore should be included in the whole of government financial report.

BC34 The Board noted that a government may choose to present information about additional sectors, such as the total non-financial public sector (comprising the GGS and PNFC sector). The Board concluded that it is not necessary to prescribe the disclosure of additional sectors, because the GGS, PNFC sector and PFC sector comprise a comprehensive disaggregation of the whole of government. However, where a government elects to disclose information about additional sectors, this should be made on a comparable basis. This ensures that information contained in the financial report is consistent.

GGS Investment in PNFC Sector and PFC Sector Entities

BC35 The Board addressed the question of whether the GGS information disclosed in the whole of government financial report should be consistent with the GGS financial report or the whole of government consolidated amounts. It therefore considered whether GGS investments in PNFC sector and PFC sector entities should be disclosed, and how they should be measured (fair value, carrying amount of net assets or zero). The Board noted that if a GGS investment in PNFC sector and PFC sector entities were to be measured at fair value in the whole of government financial report's sector information disclosures, there would be a disconnect between that amount and the carrying amount of net assets disclosed for the PNFC sector and PFC sector.

BC36 The Board concluded that GGS investments in PNFC sector and PFC sector entities should be included in the sector information disclosures, and be measured at the carrying amount of net assets disclosed for the PNFC sector and PFC sector in the whole of government financial report. The Board notes that it is conceivable, although unlikely in practice, that information about the GGS investment in PNFC and PFC sectors in the GGS financial report might differ from the GGS financial information disclosed in the whole of government financial report. This is appropriate given the different contexts in which the two sets of GGS information are presented. GGS financial reports treat the GGS as akin to a separate reporting entity whereas the GGS information disclosed in whole of government financial reports treats the GGS as a sector of a reporting entity.

Issues Common to Whole of Government Financial Reports and GGS Financial Reports

GAAP or GFS [Paragraph 9]

BC37 The Board considered whether GAAP or GFS principles should prevail for financial reporting purposes. The Board concluded that GAAP definition, recognition and measurement principles should be applied in accordance with other Australian Accounting Standards, unless otherwise specified, to accommodate GFS principles. In particular, in the interests of GAAP/GFS harmonisation, the Board concluded that GAAP presentation principles should be modified to accommodate GFS principles. Although this issue was considered in a GGS context, the Board concluded that there is no reason to adopt a different approach in a whole of government context.

BC38 An alternative approach to adopting GAAP with limited exceptions would have been to decide, for the purposes of preparing financial reports, that the GFS framework should apply. Making that declaration in a Standard would mean that GFS would become part of GAAP. However, the Board formed the view that its objective of promulgating an Australian Accounting Standard that provides useful information in a financial reporting context could be achieved without overriding entirely the GAAP framework. Accordingly, the Board's starting point was the principles and framework of GAAP, and the Board concluded that to simply adopt GFS in the Standard would be an inappropriate approach. To have adopted the GFS framework and principles as the starting point for the development of a Standard within the GAAP context, would have required the Board to become closely involved with all elements of the GFS framework. This would include any ongoing changes to the GFS framework, over which the Board has no control.

BC39 The Board's decision to adopt GAAP with limited exceptions was made on the basis that the accounting prescribed under Australian Accounting Standards is appropriate for events that occur within the not-for-profit sector, including the government. The Board noted that, in developing those Australian Accounting Standards, where the International Financial Reporting Standards (IFRSs) upon which the Standards are based do not sufficiently deal with not-for-profit circumstances, Aus paragraphs have been or will be inserted by the Board or separate Standards have been or will be issued to deal with those circumstances.

BC40 The Board's conclusion facilitates GAAP/GFS harmonisation for whole of government financial reports and GGS financial reports by:

(a) amending presentation requirements to encompass a comprehensive operating statement (paragraphs 29 and 52(b)(i)) that retains the GAAP classification system but overlays it with a transactions/other economic flows classification system based on GFS (paragraphs 30 and 52(b)(i));

(b) expanding disclosure requirements to accommodate, on the face of the statements, key fiscal aggregates under GFS (paragraphs 28, 32, 37 and 52(b)(i)) and the distinction between cash flows relating to investing in financial assets for policy purposes and for liquidity management purposes adopted by GFS (paragraphs 36 and 52(b)(i)); and

(c) specifying supplementary disclosure requirements, including GFS measures of key fiscal aggregates, reconciliations between GAAP and GFS measures of key fiscal aggregates and explanations of differences between GAAP and GFS (paragraphs 41 and 52) – (see paragraphs BC48-BC53).

BC41 The Board decided to utilise the GFS principles related to the distinction between transactions and other economic flows for presentation purposes in the operating statement as it facilitates GAAP/GFS harmonisation in a number of areas – especially at the key fiscal aggregates level. The Board formed the view that applying the GFS principles in this way is possible without breaching the principles of GAAP because the GAAP classification system has been retained but overlayed with the GFS classification system. Furthermore, GAAP disclosure requirements have been retained.

BC42 In a whole of government context, including the disclosure of information about the PNFC sector and PFC sector, the Board considered the manner in which transactions with owners as owners should be treated. It concluded that, because they are different in nature from amounts recognised on the face of the operating statement, such transactions should be disclosed in the notes or a separate statement. However, consistent with AASB 1049 (September 2006) and paragraph 97(b) and (c) of AASB 101 *Presentation of Financial Statements*, and subject to paragraph 93B of AASB 119 *Employee Benefits*, movements in reserves should be disclosed in notes, on the face of the operating statement or in a separate statement.

Limitation of GAAP Options [Paragraph 13]

BC43 The Board concluded that, where other Australian Accounting Standards allow optional treatments, only those treatments that align with GFS should be applied. The Board concluded that this is appropriate because it results in the selection of the accounting policies that advance the objective of GAAP/GFS harmonisation. The Board noted that this would in turn improve consistency and comparability between jurisdictions. Although this issue was considered in a GGS context, the Board concluded that there is no reason to adopt a different approach in a whole of government context.

BC44 This approach, which results in mandating a particular accounting policy or limiting an otherwise broader choice of policies, is a crucial element of GAAP/GFS harmonisation as it facilitates the adoption of GFS treatments within the GAAP framework.

BC45 A contrary view considered by the Board is that all Australian Accounting Standards should apply, without exception, including the full range of optional treatments in those Standards. Under this view, any optional treatments available under GAAP would be available even where they do not align with GFS. It was also suggested that mandating particular optional treatments undermines the transaction neutrality principle. The Board rejected this view as not supporting the objective of GAAP/GFS harmonisation.

Adoption of ABS GFS Manual [Paragraph 13]

BC46 The Board concluded that this Standard should cross-reference to the GFS Manual published by the ABS as amended from time to time, rather than the International Monetary Fund's *Government Finance Statistics Manual 2001* (IMF GFSM 2001). It did so, notwithstanding the context of international harmonisation, on the basis that:

(a) the ABS has a similar role to the role that the Board plays for GAAP. That is, the ABS GFS Manual refines the generic requirements of IMF GFSM 2001 into more specific and relevant requirements for the Australian context, and the Board refines the requirements of IFRSs in issuing Australian Accounting Standards in relation to not-for-profit entities. [Chapter 7 of the ABS GFS Manual includes a section on the relationship of the ABS GFS Manual to IMF GFSM 2001];

(b) there is no compelling reason for preferring IMF GFSM 2001 over the ABS GFS Manual. Both the IMF and the ABS are independent authorities; and

(c) Australia remains ahead of international developments in the field of GAAP/GFS harmonisation.

Although this issue was considered in a GGS context, the Board concluded that there is no reason to adopt a different approach in a whole of government context.

BC47 The reference to the ABS GFS Manual is an ambulatory reference, rather than a static one. This means that the ABS GFS Manual referred to is that which may be amended from time to time. In the absence of an ambulatory reference, it may be necessary for the Board to revise its Standard more frequently than would otherwise be the case.

Presentation of Key Fiscal Aggregates
[Paragraphs 16, 28, 32, 37, 41(a)(i) and 52(b)(ii)]

BC48 The Board concluded that, as well as requiring presentation of the usual GAAP aggregates, the Standard should require or allow certain GFS named key fiscal aggregates to be presented on the face of the financial statements. Although this issue was considered in a GGS context, the Board concluded that there is no reason to adopt a different approach in a whole of government context. These aggregates reflect some of the reporting features of the GFS system by including indicators of the macro-economic impact of a particular government's policy decisions on the economy as a whole, and its overall financing impact on capital markets. These GFS aggregates are important to an understanding of a GGS and a whole of government (including its sectors) and therefore they should be displayed with an appropriate level of prominence in the financial reports.

BC49 The Board concluded that the key fiscal aggregates should be measured in a manner consistent with other amounts recognised on the face of the financial statements. The Board was mindful of the potential distortion of what might be regarded by some as 'pure GFS' measures of key fiscal aggregates. Nevertheless, the Board considered that the approach adopted increases understanding as to the manner in which the key fiscal aggregates are derived and interconnected with the existing GAAP concepts.

BC50 Depending on the jurisdiction concerned, it is possible that the measurement differences will not be of great significance, and the Board expects that, over time, several of the measurement differences will be resolved. In any event, measurement differences are included in the reconciliations and explanations required by paragraphs 41(a)(i)(B) and 52(b)(ii)(B) (see paragraph BC52).

BC51 The Board also noted some concerns about the GFS nomenclature being used to describe the key fiscal aggregates. Despite these concerns, the same GFS nomenclature has been retained on the basis that to do otherwise would require the introduction of further definitions and terminology that could cause confusion for users. This approach is consistent with the Board's expectation that, over time, several of the differences will be resolved. The Board further noted that GAAP and GFS already share other terminology, such as assets and depreciation, despite being subject to different definition, recognition and measurement requirements.

BC52 Following the Board's decision to require the presentation of the key fiscal aggregates on the face of the financial statements, the Board also concluded that it is appropriate to stipulate certain disclosure requirements. Where the key fiscal aggregates presented on the face of the financial statements differ from those measured in accordance with the ABS GFS Manual, a reconciliation of the two measures and/or an explanation of the differences is required to be disclosed so that users are informed about the relationship between GAAP and GFS.

BC53 The level of prominence of these disclosures is not prescribed in the Standard.

Disclosure of Functional Information [Paragraphs 48 and 49]

BC54 The Board concluded that disaggregated/functional information disclosure requirements should be limited to expenses (excluding losses) recognised in operating result and assets. It noted that this disaggregation provides information that is useful in understanding the disbursement of the overall resources of a government. Although this issue was considered in a GGS context, the Board concluded that there is no reason to adopt a different approach in a whole of government context.

BC55 In drawing this conclusion, the Board took into account that AASB 114 *Segment Reporting* (and AASB 8) does not apply to not-for-profit entities. The Board is monitoring the implementation of the International Accounting Standards Board (IASB) and the IPSASB Standards on segment reporting, and this may lead to an amendment to the requirements for not-for-profit entities more generally.

BC56 The Board noted that governments are already providing comparable disaggregated information of GFS expenses and net acquisitions of GFS non-financial assets as part of their GFS reporting requirements and it does not appear to be unduly onerous. The Standard makes it clear that disaggregation should only occur where it can be reliably attributable to a function.

Budgetary Information [Paragraph 59]

BC57 The FRC's broad strategic direction makes specific mention of budgetary information. The direction is, among other things, to achieve an Australian Accounting Standard "... in which the outcome statements are directly comparable with the relevant budget statements".

BC58 The Board concluded that the Standard should require disclosure of certain budgetary information where budgetary information is presented to parliament, including the original budgeted financial statements. The Board also concluded that explanations of major variances between the actual amounts presented on the face of the financial statements and corresponding budget amounts should be disclosed. Although this issue was considered in a GGS context, the Board concluded that there is no reason to adopt a different approach in a whole of government context. In doing so, the Board noted that Australian Accounting Standards, including this Standard, do not prescribe the preparation of a budget. The Board also noted that governments typically budget on a GGS basis rather than on a whole of government basis.

BC59 The Board concluded that the 'presented' budget is more relevant to users than the 'adopted' budget. The presented budget is the one most widely publicised and, accordingly, is the primary reference point for any assessment of the reliability of budgeting, identification of major variances and assessment of the quality of stewardship in relation to the period. Therefore, this Standard mandates inclusion of the first budget presented to parliament. This Standard also allows for revised budgeted financial statements to be disclosed, acknowledging that revised budgets may occur late in the financial period and their disclosure can play a role in demonstrating an aspect of stewardship.

BC60 The Board concluded that the requirement for disclosure of explanations of major variances should be a key feature within the Standard. It did so on the basis that the information is useful and relevant to users and that merely recording the amount of the variance is not sufficient to meet accountability needs. An explanation of major variances is critical if users are to find comparisons between actual and budget valuable input to their analysis of the performance of government. A similar requirement exists within the New Zealand Accounting Standard NZ IAS 1 *Presentation of Financial Statements* (paragraphs NZ41.1 and NZ41.2) – see also paragraph 70 of NZ FRS-42 *Prospective Financial Statements*.

BC61 This is not an area in which the IASB has developed an IFRS. The Board considered IPSAS 24 *Presentation of Budget Information in Financial Statements* and concluded that it does not provide an appropriate basis for budgetary reporting in the Australian environment, particularly because it gives primacy to the budget basis over the accounting basis and contemplates explanations of variances being disclosed outside the financial report.

BC62 The Board also noted that, as part of the Uniform Presentation Framework, typically Australian jurisdictions publish GGS budget information together with budget information relating to the PNFC sector (and the Non-Financial Public Sector, comprising the GGS and PNFC sector) but not the PFC sector. The Board considered whether sector-based budgetary information should be required to be disclosed in the whole of government financial report. The Board concluded that because the PNFC sector and PFC sector are not required by Australian Accounting Standards to prepare separate financial reports, a requirement to disclose budget information for the PNFC sector and PFC sector in whole of government financial reports would be onerous and of limited use to users even if that budget information is presented to parliament. The Board also noted that GGS budgetary information is required to be disclosed in GGS financial reports in accordance with this Standard. Accordingly, the Board concluded that sector-based budgetary information should not be required to be disclosed in whole of government financial reports.

Performance Indicators

BC63 The proposals in Exposure Draft ED 142 *Financial Reporting of General Government Sectors by Governments* (issued July 2005) relating to performance indicators were modelled on the requirements that were contained within AAS 27, AAS 29 and AAS 31 at that time. Most respondents to ED 142 supported the principles but seemed to interpret the proposals as potentially mandating disclosure of performance indicators in the GGS financial reports. Many claimed it would be premature to mandate disclosure of performance indicators.

BC64 The Board decided to not retain the proposed requirements and guidance for either whole of government financial reports or GGS financial reports. It intends to consider issues relating to performance indicators more comprehensively in a separate project in due course.

Transitional Requirements [Paragraphs 66-68]

BC65 Consistent with the general approach adopted in this Standard, the Board decided that the requirements relating to changes in accounting policies in AASB 108 *Accounting Policies, Changes in Accounting Estimates and Errors* should apply to the first financial report prepared in accordance with this Standard and that it is not necessary to specify such a requirement in this Standard.

BC66 The Board noted that jurisdictions adopted Australian equivalents to IFRSs for their whole of government financial reports for annual reporting periods ending on 30 June 2006 (under AAS 31 and AASB 1 *First-time Adoption of Australian Equivalents to International Financial Reporting Standards*) and AASB 1049 requires the date of transition of the GGS to be the date of transition used in the whole of government financial reports. The Board also noted that all jurisdictions intended deferring adopting AASB 1049 (September 2006) until a whole of government harmonised Standard is in place (see paragraph BC2). Accordingly, the Board concluded that it is only necessary to provide specific transitional requirements in a whole of government GAAP/GFS harmonised Standard to the extent necessary to facilitate consistency between GGS and whole of government financial reporting and between GAAP and GFS.

BC67 The Board concluded that AASB 1 should be applied by GGSs in their first financial report prepared in accordance with this Standard, with certain exceptions.

BC68 As noted in paragraph BC66, the Board concluded that, in relation to the GGS, the date of transition should be the date of transition used in the whole of government financial report and that the whole of government elections under AASB 1 that align with GFS should be adopted by the GGS. This is on the basis that the GGS is part of the whole of government. The Board noted that to do otherwise would inappropriately give rise to potential differences between the amounts in the GGS financial report and the whole of government financial report.

BC69 The Board concluded that GGSs should be relieved from the disclosure requirements on transition, including the reconciliation from previous GAAP to Australian equivalents to IFRSs, in paragraphs 38 to 46 of AASB 1. The Board considers that the disclosures would not be relevant given that the date of transition of the GGS is the same as the date of transition used in the whole of government financial report, which is likely to be two or three years earlier than the first time the GGS applies this Standard.

BC70 The Board also concluded that GGSs and whole of governments should be subject to the other aspects of AASB 1 to enable governments to avail themselves of the various forms of optional relief provided under AASB 1 to facilitate GAAP/GFS harmonisation. The extent to which that relief is available is limited to some extent by the operation of paragraphs 13, 66 and 68(c) of this Standard.

Basis For Conclusions on AASB 2008-9

This Basis for Conclusions accompanies, but is not part of, AASB 1049. The Basis for Conclusions was originally published with AASB 2008-9 Amendments to AASB 1049 for Consistency with AASB 101 (September 2008).

Background

BC1   This Basis for Conclusions summarises the Australian Accounting Standards Board's considerations in reaching the conclusions in this Standard. Individual Board members gave greater weight to some factors than to others.

Significant Issues

BC2   AASB 101 *Presentation of Financial Statements* (as issued in October 2006) required the presentation of an income statement that included items of income and expense recognised in profit or loss. It required items of income and expense not recognised in profit or loss to be presented in the statement of changes in equity, potentially together with owner changes in equity. Revised AASB 101 (issued September 2007) includes requirements for income and expenses to be presented in one statement (a statement of comprehensive income) or in two statements (a separate income statement and a statement of comprehensive income), separately from owner changes in equity. As a result of these changes, revised AASB 101 more closely aligned with the principles in AASB 1049 (issued October 2007), and it became possible for AASB 1049 to rely more heavily on the principles in AASB 101 by cross-reference rather than express requirements directly in AASB 1049. The changes help reinforce the approach taken in AASB 1049 of relying on other Standards rather than re-expressing the principles in those Standards directly in AASB 1049.

BC3   The Board noted that a consequence of relying on the revised AASB 101 is a requirement to present a statement of changes in equity. Previously, AASB 1049 contemplated information pertinent to a statement of changes in equity being presented in a note or a separate statement to the extent the information is not included in the statement of comprehensive income. This is because of the way in which superseded AASB 101 treated such items. For example, superseded AASB 101 required changes in reserves to be presented in what was then a statement of changes in equity (which included components of comprehensive income) or in the notes. It also contemplated transactions with owners in their capacity as owners being presented in the statement of changes in equity or in the notes. Revised AASB 101 requires changes in reserves and transactions with owners in their capacity as owners to be presented in the statement of changes in equity. Therefore, this Standard amends AASB 1049 to require the presentation of a statement of changes in equity.

BC4   With minor exceptions, the Board decided to align the terminology used in AASB 1049 with the terminology in revised AASB 101 to ensure greater consistency across the suite of Australian Accounting Standards. The reference to 'comprehensive result' and 'operating result' is retained, despite revised AASB 101's use of the terms 'total comprehensive income' and 'profit or loss'. The Board concluded that, for the purpose of the Standard, the terms 'comprehensive result' and 'operating result' are more appropriate in a not-for-profit public sector context.

BC5   Consistent with revised AASB 101, the financial statement titles 'balance sheet', 'operating statement' and 'cash flow statement' have been replaced by 'statement of financial position', 'statement of comprehensive income' and 'statement of cash flows' respectively. However, the Board notes that, consistent with the flexibility on statement titles allowed for in revised AASB 101, whole of governments and GGSs would not be restricted by AASB 1049 to using the titles used in AASB 1049.

BC6   The Board decided that the transitional requirements in the revised AASB 1049 should not be available to governments that have previously applied AASB 1049 as issued in October 2007. This is because the transitional requirements should only be available once, on the initial transition to GAAP/GFS harmonisation.

BC7   Following feedback on AASB 1049 from constituents the Board decided to clarify that:

(a)   the whole of government statement of comprehensive income disclosures referred to in paragraph 41(b)(iii) of AASB 1049 relate to the sector statements of comprehensive income that are disclosed for the whole of government; and

(b)   the budget information disclosure requirements in paragraph 59 of AASB 1049 only relate to the budgeted financial statement(s) that were initially presented to parliament.

BC8   To assist in implementing the changes to AASB 1049 the Board decided to incorporate the changes into the Illustrative Examples in the Standard, including the addition of illustrations of the statement of changes in equity.

BC9   Following feedback from constituents on ED 163 the Board decided:

(a)   to require that, where the revised AASB 1049 is applied to annual reporting periods beginning before 1 January 2009, there is early adoption for the same annual reporting period of AASB 101 (September 2007). This will help to ensure consistency in application of the two Standards; and

(b)   to illustrate the statement of changes in equity for the whole of government by sector in a down-the-page, rather than an across-the-page, format in an attempt to make it more understandable.

Basis for Conclusions on AASB 2011-3

This Basis for Conclusions accompanies, but is not part of, AASB 1049. The Basis for Conclusions was originally published with AASB 2011-3 Amendments to Australian Accounting Standards – Orderly Adoption of Changes to the ABS GFS Manual and Related Amendments *(May 2011).*

Background

BC1   This Basis for Conclusions summarises the Australian Accounting Standards Board (AASB) considerations in reaching the conclusions in this Standard. Individual Board members gave greater weight to some factors than to others.

BC2   Given the substantial change to financial reporting brought about by AASB 1049 *Whole of Government and General Government Sector Financial Reporting* (October 2007), the Board decided to undertake a post-implementation review of that Standard. The objective was to identify any material issues at an operational level with a view to improving financial reporting. The post-implementation review included consideration of the consistency of application of AASB 1049 across jurisdictions.

BC3   Various methods were used to identify the AASB 1049 implementation issues, some of which are the subject of this Standard. These methods included consulting with personnel with AASB 1049 implementation experience from each jurisdiction's Department of Treasury and Finance and Auditor-General's Office.

BC4   After reviewing the implementation issues identified, the Board proposed amendments to AASB 1049 in Exposure Draft ED 211 *Proposed Amendments to AASB 1049* (Issued in March 2011). The Exposure Draft was structured to focus on two sets of proposals:

(a)   Part 1, open for a 30-day comment period, relates to the definition of the ABS GFS Manual, relief from adopting the latest version of the ABS GFS Manual, and related disclosures; and

(b)   Part 2, open for a 90-day comment period, relates to other proposals.

Part 1 had a 30-day comment period because of the Board's aim to provide relief as early as possible from the requirement to adopt the latest version of the ABS GFS Manual, so that the relief would be available for the reporting period ending on 30 June 2011. Therefore, this Standard arises from the Part 1 proposals in ED 211. The second set of proposals will be considered in due course.

Issues Giving Rise to Amendments to AASB 1049

Orderly Adoption of Changes to the ABS GFS Manual
[paragraphs 13B, 39(a)(ii) & 39A]

BC5 The Board considered how best to draft requirements into AASB 1049 that would help facilitate the orderly adoption of future amendments to the ABS GFS Manual for the purposes of GAAP/GFS harmonised financial reporting. The Board noted that there are potentially two broad aspects to this issue:

(a) the manner in which a change to the ABS GFS Manual should be initially adopted in the GAAP/GFS harmonised financial statements for the purposes of determining GFS information included in those statements; and

(b) the time lag to allow between the change being issued and it becoming mandatory for the GAAP/GFS harmonised financial statements.

BC6 In relation to the manner in which a change in the ABS GFS Manual should be initially adopted, the Board noted that if AASB 1049 were to override, or even merely clarify, GFS transitional arrangements, it would arguably go beyond the Board's role, and potentially result in the Board interpreting or effectively modifying the ABS GFS Manual. To avoid this, consistent with the approach in AASB 1049, the Board decided that AASB 1049 should adopt the ABS GFS Manual as it is. The Board noted that to do otherwise would create the potential for there to be a permanent difference between the amounts presented as GFS in the financial statements and amounts published by the ABS. However, the Board noted this decision only pertains to GFS information, and therefore GAAP requirements (including those relating to retrospectivity in AASB 108 *Accounting Policies, Changes in Accounting Estimates and Errors*) apply, unamended, to the manner in which a change in accounting policy is initially adopted.

BC7 In relation to time lag, the Board noted that providing relief through a 'time lag' has the potential to give rise to temporary differences between the amounts presented as GFS in the financial statements and amounts published by the ABS. After considering alternative approaches on how to give an effective time lag between the issue of an amendment to the ABS GFS Manual and when it becomes mandatory for GAAP/GFS harmonised financial reporting purposes, the Board decided AASB 1049 should specify that references to the ABS GFS Manual are to the version of the Manual effective at the beginning of the previous annual reporting period or any version effective at a later date. The Board decided to allow jurisdictions to adopt a version of the ABS GFS Manual for AASB 1049 financial reporting purposes, even if that version was not effective until after the beginning of the reporting period, consistent with the Board's usual policy of allowing early adoption of Australian Accounting Standards.

BC8 The Board noted that this approach is broadly aligned with the Board's normal approach to specifying transitional requirements for changes to GAAP because it:

(a) specifies, albeit in an ambulatory two year lagged way, a mandatory operative date for changes to the ABS GFS Manual;

(b) provides a reasonable time for entities to implement changes to the ABS GFS Manual that could affect comparative information; and

(c) allows, but does not require, entities to adopt changes to the ABS GFS Manual prior to mandatory operative dates.

BC9 The Board also noted that this approach would warrant an amendment to paragraph 39 of AASB 1049, to help ensure users are informed about the version of the ABS GFS Manual adopted as the basis for GFS information included in financial statements. Consequently, amendments are made to Illustrative Example C 'Extract from the Note Containing the Summary of Significant Accounting Policies of a General Government Sector', which provides an illustration of disclosures required by paragraph 39. Also, consistent with paragraph 30 of AASB 108 relating to new but not yet effective Standards, the Board decided that AASB 1049 should require the disclosure of information about the latest version of the ABS GFS Manual that has not yet had an impact on the financial statements.

BC10 To address concerns about uncertainties that arise from the ABS potentially not specifying effective dates for amendments to the ABS GFS Manual, the Board decided to clarify that the date on which amendments to the ABS GFS Manual become effective is, for the purpose of AASB 1049, the publication date if no effective date is specified by the ABS.

Definition of the ABS GFS Manual [Appendix A]

BC11 The Board decided that the ABS GFS Manual continues to be the appropriate authoritative source for GFS matters that are pertinent to general purpose financial reporting. After consulting with the ABS, which had clarified the boundaries of the ABS GFS Manual on its website since ED 211 was issued, the Board also decided the ABS GFS Manual should be defined as "Australian Bureau of Statistics publications *Australian System of Government Finance Statistics: Concepts, Sources and Methods, 2005* (ABS Catalogue No. 5514.0) and *Amendments to Australian System of Government Finance Statistics, 2005* (ABS Catalogue No. 5514.0) published on the ABS website". Consequently, amendments are made to the illustrated explanation of the key technical term 'Government Finance Statistics (GFS)' provided in Illustrative Example D 'Key Technical Terms Used in the Complete Sets of Financial Statements' to make it consistent with the revised definition of the ABS GFS Manual.

Basis for Conclusions on AASB 2011-13

This Basis for Conclusions accompanies, but is not part of, AASB 1049. The Basis for Conclusions was originally published with AASB 2011-13 Amendments to Australian Accounting Standard – Improvements to AASB 1049 *(December 2011).*

Background

BC1 This Basis for Conclusions summarises the Australian Accounting Standards Board (AASB) considerations in reaching the conclusions in this Standard. Individual Board members gave greater weight to some factors than to others.

BC2 Given the substantial change to financial reporting brought about by AASB 1049 *Whole of Government and General Government Sector Financial Reporting* (October 2007, as amended), the Board decided to undertake a post-implementation review of that Standard. The objective was to identify any material issues at an operational level with a view to improving financial reporting. The post-implementation review included consideration of the consistency of application of AASB 1049 across jurisdictions.

BC3 Various methods were used to identify the AASB 1049 implementation issues that gave rise to the amendments in this Standard. These methods included consulting with personnel with AASB 1049 implementation experience from each jurisdiction's Department of Treasury and Finance and Auditor-General's Office.

BC4 The Board noted that the post-implementation review work to date has not identified any major flaws in the Standard. However, the Board identified a number of aspects of AASB 1049 where improvements could be made. After reviewing the implementation issues identified, the Board issued Exposure Draft ED 211 *Proposed Amendments to AASB 1049* containing proposals to amend AASB 1049 to clarify some of its requirements.

BC5 The Board issued AASB 2011-3 *Amendments to Australian Accounting Standards – Orderly Adoption of Changes to the ABS GFS Manual and Related Amendments* [AASB 1049] in May 2011. The amendments in AASB 2011-3 arise from the proposals in ED 211 relating to the definition of the ABS GFS Manual, and related disclosures. AASB 2011-3 was issued early so that the relief would be available for the reporting period ending on 30 June 2011.

BC6 The amendments in this Standard arise from the remaining proposals in ED 211, with the bases for amendments outlined in paragraphs BC7-BC22. In addition, the Board decided that some issues raised in the post-implementation review did not warrant amendments to AASB 1049, on the bases outlined in paragraphs BC23-BC40.

Issues giving Rise to Amendments to AASB 1049

Alignment to terminology used in AASB 101

BC7 Consistent with the terminology used in AASB 101 *Presentation of Financial Statements*, wherever the term 'other non-owner changes in equity' or 'other changes in equity' is used in AASB 1049 to refer to the other comprehensive income section in the statement of comprehensive income, the Board decided to amend the term to 'other comprehensive income'.

Preparation of GGS and Whole of Government Financial Statements [paragraph 7][1]

BC8 Consistent with the original intention of paragraph 7 of AASB 1049 (see for example paragraphs BC5 and BC25 of AASB 1049) the Board decided to clarify within the body of the Standard that both whole of government and GGS financial statements are required to be prepared. The amendment addresses the concern that some could conceivably interpret AASB 1049 as merely specifying requirements for financial statements if they are prepared.

Relative Timing and Cross-Referencing of GGS and Whole of Government Financial Statements [paragraphs 8, 39(a) and 39(b)]

BC9 AASB 1049 previously allowed GGS financial statements to be made available later than whole of government financial statements being made available. Where the GGS financial statements were presented separately from the whole of government financial statements, a cross-reference from the GGS financial statements to the whole of government financial statements was required to be made. The Board decided that AASB 1049 should be amended to require, at all times, GGS and whole of government financial statements to be made available at the same time and cross-referenced to each other. This is on the basis that:

(a) GGS financial statements provide useful information (e.g. budgetary information) for users, and users should receive such information on a timely basis;

(b) GGS financial statements provide a bridge between a government's budget and its whole of government financial statements; and

(c) given that GGS is a sector of whole of government, whole of government financial statements provide a context to the GGS financial statements.

Adoption of Options in GAAP that align with GFS [paragraphs 13-15]

Early Adoption of New or Revised Standards

BC10 The Board noted that paragraph 13 of AASB 1049 could be interpreted as requiring early adoption of a new or revised Standard if its adoption is more in line with GFS than the requirements of the Standard being superseded. The Board decided that such an interpretation is not the intention of paragraph 13 as it would potentially undermine the Board's intention of facilitating the orderly adoption of new or revised requirements. Accordingly, the Board decided to amend AASB 1049 to clarify that AASB 1049, in mandating a particular accounting policy or limiting an otherwise broader choice of policies for the objective of GAAP/GFS harmonisation, does not require that a new or revised Standard must be adopted early, even if early adoption would more quickly allow alignment with GFS.

Disclosure of Key Fiscal Aggregates

Presentation of Additional Fiscal Aggregates [paragraphs 16 & 18]

BC11 The Board noted that AASB 1049 allows jurisdictions to disclose fiscal aggregates that are additional to the key fiscal aggregates required by AASB 1049. However, the Board noted the concern that, in practice, these other fiscal aggregates are not necessarily clearly distinguished from those key fiscal aggregates in the financial statements. To address this concern, the Board decided that AASB 1049 should be amended to require a clear

---

1 References to paragraphs in the headings of this Basis for Conclusions are to paragraphs in AASB 1049.

differentiation between key fiscal aggregates and other fiscal aggregates, to help avoid potential confusion for users.

Disclosure of Other Measures of Key Fiscal Aggregates
[paragraphs 16, 18, 41(a)(i) & 52(b)(ii)]

BC12 AASB 1049 previously only allowed key fiscal aggregates measured in a manner consistent with recognised amounts or the ABS GFS Manual to be disclosed. Other measures of key fiscal aggregates were not allowed to be disclosed. The Board decided that AASB 1049 should be amended to allow disclosure of other measures of key fiscal aggregates (i.e. not measured in a manner consistent with recognised amounts or the ABS GFS Manual) on the basis that preparers should not be prevented from disclosing information they believe is useful to users, as long as it does not detract from the information required by the Standard. Accordingly, paragraphs 41(a)(i) and 52(b)(ii) have been amended by removing the requirement that prohibits the disclosure of other measures of key fiscal aggregates. Furthermore, the amendments to paragraph 18 in AASB 1049 clarify that other measures of key fiscal aggregates should not be presented as key fiscal aggregates, to help avoid potential confusion for users.

Determination of the Amount to be Recognised for GGS Investments in PNFC and PFC Sector Entities [paragraphs 20(c), 21 & 23(c)]

BC13 Paragraph 20 of AASB 1049 requires GGS controlling investments in PNFC sector and PFC sector entities to be measured at, depending on circumstances, fair value, or the government's proportional share of the carrying amount of net assets, or zero. Therefore, an investment is not recognised at an amount below zero. As noted in paragraph BC13 of AASB 1049 measurement at fair value, or at the government's proportional share of the carrying amount of net assets where fair value is not reliably measurable, is consistent with GFS. That paragraph also notes that not allowing investments to be measured below zero is consistent with the principles elsewhere in GAAP (for example, AASB 128 *Investments in Associates* does not allow negative investment values when using the equity method).

BC14 With that background, in relation to paragraph 20 of AASB 1049, the Board noted the view of some practitioners that paragraph 23(c) of AASB 1049 is inconsistent with paragraph 20(c) because paragraph 23(c), which refers to 'net basis', implies individual amounts may be less than zero whereas paragraph 20(c) requires individual amounts to be not less than zero for the purposes of measuring a GGS equity investment in a PNFC sector or PFC sector entity. Consistent with the rationale in paragraph BC13 of AASB 1049, the Board decided the last sentence of paragraph 23(c) should be amended to be consistent with paragraph 20(c).

Classification of Items between Transactions and Other Economic Flows [paragraphs 30, 31 & 55(b)]

BC15 The Board acknowledged the view that paragraph 30 should be amended to provide further guidance for the classification of items between transactions and other economic flows to help facilitate greater consistency in its application by jurisdictions, particularly for circumstances where items arising under GAAP are not recognised under GFS in the reporting period. The Board noted that for circumstances where items arising under GAAP are also recognised under GFS in the reporting period, the principle for classification between transactions and other economic flows are already in AASB 1049. The Board decided to amend AASB 1049 to clarify the principle for classification between transactions and other economic flows in circumstances where items arising under GAAP are not recognised under GFS in the reporting period. In addition, to assist in applying the clarified principle, the Board decided to provide additional examples of how the clarified principles would apply in particular circumstances.

BC16 Related to this issue, the Board considered whether classification of GAAP items that are also recognised under GFS in the reporting period should be grouped together, and presented separately in the statement of comprehensive income from classification of GAAP items that are not recognised under GFS in the reporting period. However, the Board decided against imposing such a requirement, on the basis that it was not identified as an issue in the post-implementation review of AASB 1049.

Defence Weapons Platforms [paragraphs 31(a)(v) and 44(a)(iv) of AASB 1049, and the Illustrative Examples A and B accompanying AASB 1049]

BC17 Consistent with the ABS GFS Manual, which now recognises and measures defence weapons platforms in the same way as other non-financial assets, the relevant paragraphs in AASB 1049 and the relevant sections of the Illustrative Examples accompanying AASB 1049 are amended. There would now be no convergence difference between GAAP and GFS in relation to defence weapons platforms.

Transactions with Owners as Owners in a GGS Context [paragraph 34B]

BC18 The Board noted that, although not common, transactions with owners in their capacity as owners that are not eliminated on consolidation could arise because of non-controlling interest attributable to entities outside the GGS. Therefore, the Board decided that paragraph 34B should be amended to acknowledge that this could occur.

Interpretation of 'presented on a basis that is consistent with' in the Context of Budgetary Information [paragraphs 59(e), 63 & 64]

BC19 Paragraph 59(e) of AASB 1049 required disclosure of the original budgeted financial statements, presented on a basis that is consistent with the basis prescribed for the financial statements by AASB 1049. The Board noted that some practitioners questioned the meaning of 'presented on a basis that is consistent with'. In particular, it was questioned whether the budget would be required to be recast solely for presentation and classification or whether the requirement extends to recognition and measurement. The Board noted the practical difficulties of recasting for recognition and measurement differences – e.g. retrospectively determining 'budgeted' fair values when hindsight is likely to influence such a determination. Therefore, the Board decided that paragraph 59(e) of AASB 1049 should be amended to clarify that the budget should be recast solely for presentation and classification matters, not for recognition and measurement matters. This amendment gave rise to consequential amendments to paragraphs 63 and 64 to focus them on presentation and classification.

BC20 In relation to the requirement in paragraph 59(f) to disclose explanations of major variances between actual and budget amounts, the Board noted that variances might arise from recognition and measurement principles adopted in the budget being different from the recognition and measurement principles adopted in the financial statements.

Transitional Requirements [paragraphs 65A, 66, 67, 68, 69 & 70]

BC21 The Board noted it is no longer necessary to specify transitional requirements because all jurisdictions have previously first-time adopted AASB 1049 for their whole of government and GGS financial statements.

Tax-effect Accounting by GGS [Explanatory Note r(ii) to the Illustrative Examples accompanying AASB 1049]

BC22 The Board noted that of those jurisdictions that recognise deferred tax liabilities at the PNFC/PFC level, only some reflect corresponding amounts in the GGS statement of financial position as deferred tax assets. The Board also noted:

(a) the view that, from a GAAP perspective, such 'mirror' accounting can be justified given the amount is known in a 'closed system' (i.e. the taxpayer and taxing authority are within the government); and

(b) the question of whether the amounts are in the nature of a tax or distribution to owners as owners.

After considering these issues, the Board considered whether to remove the text in square brackets in Explanatory Note r(ii) on the basis that the subject matter of that text is beyond the scope of the GAAP/GFS Harmonisation project. However, the Board noted that the tax regime assumed is in the context of an illustrative example and thus is non-prescriptive.

The Board decided to retain the text, on the basis that it provides a useful explanation of why there is no convergence difference for GGS in relation to deferred tax balances as illustrated in Example A, with some editorial amendments to the text to clarify that the tax regime assumed is for the purpose of an illustrative example.

Significant Issues that did not give rise to Amendments to AASB 1049

Purpose of the GGS Financial Report [paragraphs 12 & BC6]

BC23 The Board noted that paragraph 12 does not require disclosure of whether GGS financial statements are general purpose financial statements or special purpose financial statements and considered whether the absence of such a requirement gives rise to implementation issues. The Board decided AASB 1049 should not be amended in relation to this issue at this time because the AASB 1049 approach to the issue has not created insurmountable practical problems for jurisdictions, particularly because, in practice, GGS financial statements are not presented separately from the general purpose financial statements of the whole of government. The Board notes that, in due course, it may be appropriate to revisit the way AASB 1049 deals with the issue, depending on the outcome of future work to be undertaken on the Board's Differential Reporting project.

Adoption of Options in GAAP that align with GFS [paragraphs 13 & 14]

Examples of Particular Optional Treatments in GAAP

BC24 The Board noted the view that the Board should fully analyse optional treatments in GAAP and specify directly in AASB 1049 those treatments to be adopted, to avoid the need for preparers to refer directly to the ABS GFS Manual. The Board decided that the relatively principles-based approach in AASB 1049 should be retained, rather than including an exhaustive list of GAAP options that align with GFS, on the basis that it is not the Board's role to interpret GFS. Also, the Board decided to monitor the development of any further guidance by other interested parties on this issue and expressed a willingness to collaborate with Treasuries and the ABS in developing such guidance if Treasuries decide to develop separate guidance.

BC25 The Board noted that some practitioners questioned the application of paragraph 12 of AASB 108 *Accounting Policies, Changes in Accounting Estimates and Errors* in the context of aligning optional treatments in GAAP with GFS and whether the wording in that paragraph of 'most recent pronouncements of other standard setting bodies' included the ABS GFS Manual.

Paragraph 12 of AASB 108 states:

"In making the judgement described in paragraph 10, management may also consider the most recent pronouncements of other standard setting bodies that use a similar conceptual framework to develop accounting standards, other accounting literature and accepted industry practices, to the extent that these do not conflict with the sources in paragraph 11."

The Board decided that the ABS GFS Manual should not be included in the AASB 108 hierarchy, on the basis that GFS, per se, is not a part of GAAP.

Presentation of the Whole of Government/GGS Statements of Financial Position [paragraph 15]

BC26 The Board noted that the Illustrative Examples accompanying AASB 1049 subclassify non-financial assets between 'produced' and 'non-produced' categories even though the ABS GFS Manual does not explicitly require such a subclassification. The Board decided it is not necessary to amend AASB 1049 to remove the subclassification because the Illustrative Examples are not prescriptive.

BC27 The Board also noted the view that AASB 1049 should be amended to clarify requirements relating to the presentation of statements of financial position based on liquidity. However, the Board decided it is not necessary to amend AASB 1049 in relation to this issue because the principles in AASB 1049 are sufficiently clear and the Illustrative Examples are not prescriptive.

Presentation of Operating Result on the Face [paragraph 29]

BC28 The Board noted the view that AASB 1049 should be amended to allow the operating result (a GAAP subtotal) not to be presented on the face of the single statement of comprehensive income on the basis that its presentation on the face clutters the statement. This is consistent with a view that users are most interested in the 'net result from transactions – net operating balance', and that including the 'operating result' on the face has the potential to confuse users. However, the Board decided that paragraph 29 should continue to require jurisdictions to present the operating result on the face of the single statement of comprehensive income because, consistent with the fundamental basis upon which AASB 1049 was developed, such a presentation is required by AASB 101.

Treatment of Non-cash Items in relation to Cash Flow Statements [paragraphs 18 & 37]

BC29 The Board noted that some jurisdictions present the value of assets acquired under finance leases and similar arrangements on the face of the cash flow statements. The Board also noted the concern expressed by some about such non-cash flows being included in cash flow statements. However, the Board decided it is not necessary to amend AASB 1049 for this issue because it is already obvious in GAAP (including AASB 1049) that an entity should clearly distinguish between information that is and is not cash flow information.

GAAP/GFS Reconciliation Requirements [paragraphs 41(a)(i)(B) & 52(b)(ii)(B)]

BC30 The Board noted that AASB 1049 requires disclosure of reconciliations of GAAP and GFS measures of certain key fiscal aggregates, and an explanation of the differences. The Board also noted the view that such disclosures are unnecessary and therefore that the reconciliation requirement should be removed. However, the Board decided paragraphs 41(a)(i)(B) and 52(b)(ii)(B) should continue to require the reconciliations and explanations because they provide useful information for users in the context of GAAP/GFS harmonisation and the reconciliation schedule is a critical part of AASB 1049.

BC31 On a related issue, the Board considered whether it is necessary to amend AASB 1049 to explicitly address the circumstances where GFS amounts determined by the ABS differ from and are published after amounts disclosed as GFS amounts in the financial statements. The question arises as to which GFS amounts should be reconciled to in the comparative information disclosed in the following year's financial statements. The Board decided that it is not necessary to explicitly address this issue in AASB 1049, noting that the GFS amounts previously reported in the financial statements would be the relevant amounts.

Disclosure of the Aggregates of Dividends and Other Distributions to Owners as Owners [paragraph 41(b)(iii)]

BC32 The Board noted that paragraph 41(b)(iii) requires the GGS financial statements to disclose the aggregate amount of dividends and other distributions to owners as owners from PNFC sector and PFC sector entities to the GGS. The Board also noted the suggestion that the wording in paragraph 41(b)(iii) should be amended because it is unclear as to what is meant by 'other distributions'. The Board decided paragraph 41(b)(iii) should not be amended in relation to this issue on the basis that there is apparently no significant issue in complying with the requirement in paragraph 41(b)(iii). The Board particularly noted it is a matter of professional judgement based on circumstances whether income tax equivalent income is in the nature of a distribution to owners as owners.

BC33 The Board noted the view that paragraph 41(b)(iii) should be amended to require the disclosure of contributions from the GGS in its capacity as owner to PNFC sector and PFC sector entities to enable derivation of 'net distributions'. However, the Board noted that typically such information is already disclosed and therefore it is not necessary for AASB 1049 to mandate it.

Carrying Amounts of Assets Attributable to Functions [paragraphs 48(b), 50 & 51]

BC34 The Board noted that AASB 1049 requires disclosure of the carrying amount of recognised assets that are reliably attributable to each function (paragraph 48(b)). The Board also noted that the relevance of such a disclosure when it is not based on an ABS GFS Manual concept was questioned by some. The Board decided paragraph 48(b) should continue to require the disclosure on the basis that the disclosure would assist users in identifying resources committed to particular functions relative to the costs of service delivery that are reliably attributable to those functions, which facilitates comparisons between jurisdictions. The Board also noted that, in due course, its Disaggregated Disclosures project will address, amongst other things, issues raised in the post-implementation review of AASB 1049. The Board noted that retaining the requirement would avoid the risk of otherwise removing the requirement and then potentially reinstating it as a result of the Disaggregated Disclosures project.

'Expenses, excluding Losses, included in Operating Result' by Function [paragraphs 48(c), 50 & 51]

BC35 Consistent with the decision to retain the requirement in AASB 1049 to disclose carrying amount of recognised assets that are reliably attributable to each function (see paragraph BC34), the Board decided to retain the requirement to disclose 'expenses, excluding losses, included in operating result' (paragraph 48(c)).

BC36 The Board noted that 'expenses excluding losses' is not explicitly described in AASB 1049. Furthermore, the Board noted the view that inclusion of this term in the functional information could confuse users (and preparers) as there is no clear definition of what is intended to be included in the calculation and that the phrase should be replaced with the phrase 'expenses from transactions', which would avoid the reconciliation required by paragraph 49. However, the Board decided paragraph 48(c) should not be amended for the following reasons:

(a) if the reference to 'excluding losses' were omitted, it would seem to be anomalous to include losses, but not gains, given that gains and losses relating to an item might be netted off; and

(b) 'expenses excluding losses' more closely aligns with GAAP than 'expenses from transactions', because 'expenses from transactions' does not include GAAP expenses classified as other economic flows.

Explanations of Variances from Budget [paragraphs 59(f) & 65]

BC37 The Board noted that the AASB 1049 requirement to include explanations of variances between budgeted and actual financial information was questioned by some practitioners for two primary reasons:

(a) the requirement to explain variances is unnecessary as the variance explanations are not relevant to users because variance explanations are more relevant at entity level and the reasons for changes in budgetary assumptions are explained every time the budgets are updated; and

(b) the inclusion of unaudited budgetary information within the audited financial statements results in audit report comments in relation to budget information within the statements. In particular, whilst audit of variances between budgeted and actual data is possible at the higher levels, at a lower level there is insufficient evidence available to make assessments.

BC38 The Board decided not to amend paragraph 59(f) in relation to this issue on the basis that disclosure of variance information provides useful information for users and facilitates the discharge of accountability by governments. Paragraph BC60 of AASB 1049 contains the Board's rationale for the requirement for disclosure of explanations of major variances between the actual amounts presented on the face of the financial statements and corresponding budget amounts.

Capital Management Disclosures

BC39 The Board considered whether the exemption provided by paragraph Aus1.7 of AASB 101 for whole of governments and GGSs from presenting certain capital management disclosures required by paragraphs 134-136 of AASB 101 should be retained or removed.

BC40 The Board decided it would be inappropriate to reconsider the exemption as part of the post-implementation review of AASB 1049, on the basis that the issue should be considered in the context of a broader range of not-for-profit entities than whole of governments and GGSs.

Illustrative Examples

The following examples accompany, but are not part of, AASB 1049.

A Whole of Government Statement of Comprehensive Income, Statement of Financial Position, Statement of Changes in Equity, Statement of Cash Flows and Selected Notes

B General Government Sector Statement of Comprehensive Income, Statement of Financial Position, Statement of Changes in Equity, Statement of Cash Flows and Selected Notes

C Extract from the Note Containing the Summary of Significant Accounting Policies of a General Government Sector

D Key Technical Terms Used in the Complete Sets of Financial Statements

Illustrative Examples A and B provide examples of acceptable formats for whole of government and GGS financial statements respectively, that are consistent with the requirements of this Standard and the assumptions made for the purpose of the illustrations. They also illustrate an acceptable style and format for reconciliation notes and functional information. Furthermore, sector information is illustrated for the whole of government in Illustrative Example A.

The styles and formats illustrated are not mandatory. Other styles and formats may be equally appropriate if they meet the requirements of this Standard.

To assist an understanding of the illustrations, particularly in relation to differences between GAAP and GFS, explanatory notes are provided at the end of Illustrative Example B and relate to both Illustrative Examples A and B. They do not form part of the illustrative financial statements or notes.

Illustrative Examples A and B do not purport to identify all possible differences between GAAP and GFS, nor to present in the financial statements all the line items as might be required by a different set of assumptions. Additionally, they do not illustrate the disclosure of comparative period information or the notes required by paragraphs 39[1], 41 (except the relevant reconciliation notes)[2], 52(a) and the explanation of differences required by 52(b)(ii)(B). They also do not illustrate the disclosure requirements of budgetary information (paragraphs 59-65), nor all the disclosures required by other Australian Accounting Standards.

The amounts used are based on assumptions made for illustrative purposes only.

---

1 Illustrative Example C provides an example of the information to be included in the summary of significant accounting policies of the GGS in accordance with paragraph 39(b).

2 Illustrative Example D provides an example of the information to be included in the other explanatory notes of the whole of government and GGS regarding explanations of key technical terms in accordance with paragraph 41(a)(iii).

Illustrative Example A

Whole of Government Statement of Comprehensive Income, Statement of Financial Position, Statement of Changes in Equity, Statement of Cash Flows and Selected Notes

Statement of Comprehensive Income for the Whole of Government of the ABC Government for the Year Ended 30 June 20XX

	Notes	$m
Revenue from Transactions		
Taxation revenue		209,178
Other revenue		
Interest, other than swap interest		3,298
Dividends from associates (part of share of net profit/(loss) from associates)		3
Sales of goods and services		12,862
Other current revenues		2,792
		228,133
Expenses from Transactions		
Employee benefits expense		
Wages, salaries and supplements		(20,866)
Superannuation		(2,477)
Use of goods and services		(40,710)
Depreciation		(3,823)
Interest, other than swap interest and superannuation interest expenses		(4,841)
Subsidy expenses		(5,253)
Grants		(69,494)
Social benefits		(71,730)
Superannuation net interest expenses		(4,902)
Loss on write-off of financial assets at fair value through operating result		(380)
		(224,476)
NET RESULT FROM TRANSACTIONS – NET OPERATING BALANCE		**3,657**
Other Economic Flows – Included in Operating Result		
Other revenue		
Net swap interest revenue		577
Net foreign exchange gains		2,120
Net gain on sale of non-financial assets		343
Net gain on financial assets or liabilities at fair value through operating result		265
Net actuarial gains[a]		866
Amortisation of non-produced assets		(119)
Doubtful debts		(604)
Share of net profit/(loss) from associates, excluding dividends		(26)
		3,422
OPERATING RESULT		**7,079**
Other Economic Flows – Other Comprehensive Income		
Items that will not be reclassified to operating result		
Revaluations		1,589
Items that may be reclassified subsequently to operating result		
Net gain on financial assets measured at fair value		2,946
		4,535
COMPREHENSIVE RESULT – TOTAL CHANGE IN NET WORTH BEFORE TRANSACTIONS WITH OWNERS IN THEIR CAPACITY AS OWNERS		**11,614**

	Notes	$m
KEY FISCAL AGGREGATES		
NET LENDING/(BORROWING)	S2	**5,100**
plus Net acquisition/(disposal) of non-financial assets from transactions		(1,443)
NET OPERATING BALANCE	S1	**3,657**
plus Net other economic flows		7,957
TOTAL CHANGE IN NET WORTH BEFORE TRANSACTIONS WITH OWNERS IN THEIR CAPACITY AS OWNERS	S3	**11,614**

a   Explanatory note: As noted in paragraph 14(c) of this Standard, an alternative treatment of net actuarial gains relating to defined benefit superannuation plans [consistent with paragraph 93B of AASB 119 *Employee Benefits*] would be to recognise them in full through other comprehensive income (which is part of comprehensive result).

Statement of Financial Position for the Whole of Government of the ABC Government as at 30 June 20XX

	Notes	$m
Assets		
Financial Assets		
Cash and deposits		14,070
Accounts receivable		18,080
Securities other than shares		78,438
Loans		9,956
Advances		7,758
Shares and other equity		
Investments accounted for using equity method		695
Investments in other entities		1,142
		130,139
Non-Financial Assets		
Produced assets		
Inventories		5,346
Machinery and equipment		67,014
Buildings and structures		16,654
Intangibles		1,380
Valuables		6,867
Non-produced assets		
Land		9,876
Intangibles		1,193
		108,330
TOTAL ASSETS		**238,469**
Liabilities		
Deposits held		81,311
Accounts payable		5,080
Securities other than shares		21,520
Borrowing		9,346
Superannuation		89,858
Provisions		30,298
TOTAL LIABILITIES		**237,413**
NET ASSETS/(LIABILITIES)		**1,056**
Accumulated surplus/(deficit)		(33,041)
Other reserves		34,097
NET WORTH	T	**1,056**

Statement of Changes in Equity for the Whole of Government of the ABC Government for the Year Ended 30 June 20XX

	Accumulated surplus/(deficit)	Asset revaluation reserve	Accumulated net gain on financial assets	Total equity
	$m	$m	$m	$m
Equity at 1 July 20XX-1	(40,120)	16,887	12,675	(10,558)
Total comprehensive result	7,079	1,589	2,946	11,614
EQUITY AT 30 JUNE 20XX	(33,041)	18,476	15,621	1,056

Statement of Cash Flows for the Whole of Government of the ABC Government for the Year Ended 30 June 20XX

	Notes	$m
Cash Flows from Operating Activities		
Cash received		
Taxes received		206,343
Sales of goods and services		10,624
Interest, excluding swap interest		3,298
Dividends from associates		3
Other receipts		3,161
		223,429
Cash paid		
Payments to and on behalf of employees		(19,996)
Purchases of goods and services		(41,019)
Interest, excluding swap interest		(4,841)
Subsidies		(5,253)
Grants		(69,494)
Social benefits		(70,597)
Other payments		(4,123)
		(215,323)
NET CASH FLOWS FROM OPERATING ACTIVITES		**8,106**
Cash Flows from Investing Activities		
Non-Financial Assets		
Sales of non-financial assets		3,036
Purchases of new non-financial assets		(5,238)
Net cash flows from investments in non-financial assets		(2,202)
Financial Assets (Policy Purposes)		
Purchases of investments		(1,641)
Net cash flows from investments in financial assets (policy purposes)		(1,641)
Financial Assets (Liquidity Management Purposes)		
Sales of investments		1,778
Purchases of investments		(9,084)
Net cash flows from investments in financial assets (liquidity management purposes)		(7,306)
NET CASH FLOWS FROM INVESTING ACTIVITIES		**(11,149)**

	Notes	$m
Cash Flows from Financing Activities		
Cash received		
Borrowing		9,692
Deposits received		6,947
Swap interest		3,617
Other financing		2,857
		23,113
Cash paid		
Borrowing		(15,325)
Deposits paid		(1,841)
Swap interest		(3,040)
Other financing		(1,870)
		(22,076)
NET CASH FLOWS FROM FINANCING ACTIVITIES		**1,037**
NET INCREASE IN CASH AND CASH EQUIVALENTS		**(2,006)**
Cash and cash equivalents at beginning of year		16,076
CASH AND CASH EQUIVALENTS AT END OF YEAR		**14,070**
KEY FISCAL AGGREGATE		
Net cash flows from operating activities		8,106
Net cash flows from investments in non-financial assets		(2,202)
CASH SURPLUS/(DEFICIT)	U	**5,904**

R1 Statement of Comprehensive Income for the Whole of Government by Sector of the ABC Government for the Year Ended 30 June 20XX

	Notes	GGS $m	PNFC sector $m	PFC sector $m	Eliminations $m	Whole of Government $m
Revenue from Transactions						
Taxation revenue		209,178			-	209,178
Other revenue						
Interest, other than swap interest		1,304	113	3,969	(2,088)	3,298
Dividends and income tax from other sector entities		1,399	-	-	(1,399)	-
Dividends from associates (part of share of net profit/(loss) from associates)		1	2	-	-	3
Sales of goods and services		4,314	6,079	3,677	(1,208)	12,862
Other current revenues		2,684	130	176	(198)	2,792
		218,880	6,324	7,822	(4,893)	228,133
Expenses from Transactions						
Employee benefits expense						
Wages, salaries and supplements		(14,178)	(6,302)	(386)	-	(20,866)
Superannuation		(2,069)	(395)	(13)	-	(2,477)
Use of goods and services		(37,898)	(2,855)	(550)	593	(40,710)
Depreciation		(3,672)	(125)	(26)	-	(3,823)
Interest, other than swap interest and superannuation interest expenses		(4,201)	(513)	(2,215)	2,088	(4,841)
Subsidy expenses		(5,742)	-	-	489	(5,253)
Grants		(69,692)	-	-	198	(69,494)
Social benefits		(71,856)	-	-	126	(71,730)
Income tax expenses		-	(200)	(151)	351	-
Superannuation net interest expenses		(4,898)	(3)	(1)	-	(4,902)
Loss on write-off of financial assets at fair value through operating result		(380)	-	-	-	(380)
		(214,586)	(10,393)	(3,342)	3,845	(224,476)
NET RESULT FROM TRANSACTIONS – NET OPERATING BALANCE		4,294	(4,069)	4,480	(1,048)	3,657

AASB

	Notes	GGS $m	PNFC sector $m	PFC sector $m	Eliminations $m	Whole of Government $m
Other Economic Flows – Included in Operating Result						
Other revenue						
Net swap interest revenue		340	69	168	-	577
Dividends from other sector entities		300	-	-	(300)	-
Net foreign exchange gains/(losses)		599	(3)	1,524	-	2,120
Net gain on sale of non-financial assets		200	145	(2)	-	343
Net gain on financial assets or liabilities at fair value through operating result		220	-	45	-	265
Net actuarial gains		840	21	5	-	866
Amortisation of non-produced assets		(75)	(43)	(1)	-	(119)
Doubtful debts		(500)	(63)	(41)	-	(604)
Share of net profit/(loss) from associates, excluding dividends		(51)	25	-	-	(26)
		1,873	151	1,698	(300)	3,422
OPERATING RESULT		6,167	(3,918)	6,178	(1,348)	7,079
Other Economic Flows – Other Comprehensive Income						
Items that will not be reclassified to operating result						
Revaluations		1,552	20	17		1,589
Items that may be reclassified subsequently to operating result						
Net gain on equity investments in other sector entities measured at proportional share of the carrying amount of net assets/(liabilities)		1,072	-	-	(1,072)	-
Net gain on financial assets measured at fair value		1,000	15	1,931	-	2,946
		3,624	35	1,948	(1,072)	4,535
COMPREHENSIVE RESULT – TOTAL CHANGE IN NET WORTH BEFORE TRANSACTIONS WITH OWNERS IN THEIR CAPACITY AS OWNERS		9,791	(3,883)	8,126	(2,420)	11,614

AASB

KEY FISCAL AGGREGATES

	Notes	GGS $m	PNFC sector $m	PFC sector $m	Eliminations $m	Whole of Government $m
NET LENDING/(BORROWING)	S2	**4,967**	**(3,347)**	**4,528**	**(1,048)**	**5,100**
plus Net acquisition/(disposal) of non-financial assets from transactions		(673)	(722)	(48)	-	(1,443)
NET OPERATING BALANCE	S1	**4,294**	**(4,069)**	**4,480**	**(1,048)**	**3,657**
plus Net other economic flows		5,497	186	3,646	(1,372)	7,957
TOTAL CHANGE IN NET WORTH BEFORE TRANSACTIONS WITH OWNERS IN THEIR CAPACITY AS OWNERS	S3	**9,791**	**(3,883)**	**8,126**	**(2,420)**	**11,614**

R2 Statement of Financial Position for the Whole of Government by Sector of the ABC Government as at 30 June 20XX

Assets

Financial Assets

	GGS $m	PNFC sector $m	PFC sector $m	Eliminations $m	Whole of Government $m
Cash and deposits	10,591	939	2,540	-	14,070
Accounts receivable	16,748	764	2,557	(1,989)	18,080
Securities other than shares	24,188	457	104,293	(50,500)	78,438
Loans	10,302	15	98	(459)	9,956
Advances	7,758	-	-	-	7,758
Shares and other equity					
Investments accounted for using equity method	365	330	-	-	695
Investments in other entities (excluding sector entities)	-	357	785	-	1,142
Investments in other sector entities	32,759	-	-	(32,759)	-
	102,711	2,862	110,273	(85,707)	130,139

Non-Financial Assets

Produced assets

	GGS $m	PNFC sector $m	PFC sector $m	Eliminations $m	Whole of Government $m
Inventories	4,832	502	12	-	5,346
Machinery and equipment	54,367	12,546	101	-	67,014
Buildings and structures	14,152	1,821	681	-	16,654
Intangibles	1,250	115	15	-	1,380
Valuables	6,442	358	67	-	6,867

	Notes	GGS $m	PNFC sector $m	PFC sector $m	Eliminations $m	Whole of Government $m
Non-produced assets						
Land		5,196	4,327	353	-	9,876
Intangibles		747	428	18	-	1,193
		86,986	20,097	1,247	-	108,330
TOTAL ASSETS		**189,697**	**22,959**	**111,520**	**(85,707)**	**238,469**
Liabilities						
Deposits held		364	10	80,937	-	81,311
Accounts payable		5,253	150	1,666	(1,989)	5,080
Securities other than shares		60,650	500	10,870	(50,500)	21,520
Borrowing		6,246	359	3,200	(459)	9,346
Deferred tax liability		-	506	-	(506)	-
Superannuation		88,540	768	550	-	89,858
Provisions		28,094	659	1,545	-	30,298
TOTAL LIABILITIES		**189,147**	**2,952**	**98,768**	**(53,454)**	**237,413**
NET ASSETS/(LIABILITIES)		**550**	**20,007**	**12,752**	**(32,253)**	**1,056**
Contributed Equity		-	6,900	350	(7,250)	-
Accumulated surplus/(deficit)		(20,324)	10,857	863	(24,437)	(33,041)
Other reserves		20,874	2,250	11,539	(566)	34,097
NET WORTH	T	**550**	**20,007**	**12,752**	**(32,253)**	**1,056**

R3 Statement of Changes in Equity for the Whole of Government by Sector of the ABC Government for the Year Ended 30 June 20XX

	Equity at 1 July 20XX-1 $m	Total comprehensive result $m	Dividends $m	Equity at 30 June 20XX $m
GGS				
Accumulated surplus/(deficit)	(26,491)	6,167	-	(20,324)
Asset revaluation reserve	12,161	1,552	-	13,713
Accumulated net gain on equity investments in other sector entities measured at proportional share of the carrying amount of net assets/(liabilities)	500	1,072	-	1,572
Accumulated net gain on financial assets measured at fair value	4,589	1,000	-	5,589
	(9,241)	9,791	-	550
PNFC sector				
Contributed equity	6,900	-	-	6,900
Accumulated surplus/(deficit)	15,334	(3,918)	(559)	10,857
Asset revaluation reserve	2,030	20	-	2,050
Accumulated net gain on financial assets measured at fair value	185	15	-	200
	24,449	(3,883)	(559)	20,007
PFC sector				
Contributed equity	350	-	-	350
Accumulated surplus/(deficit)	(4,526)	6,178	(789)	863
Asset revaluation reserve	1,690	17	-	1,707
Accumulated net gain on financial assets measured at fair value	7,901	1,931	-	9,832
	5,415	8,126	(789)	12,752
Eliminations	(31,181)	(2,420)	1,348	(32,253)
Total Whole of Government	**(10,558)**	**11,614**	**-**	**1,056**

Explanatory Note: Shares and contributed equity do not exist in a GGS context.

R4   Statement of Cash Flows for the Whole of Government by Sector of the ABC Government for the Year Ended 30 June 20XX

	Notes	GGS $m	PNFC sector $m	PFC sector $m	Eliminations $m	Whole of Government $m
Cash Flows from Operating Activities						
Cash received						
Taxes received		206,343	-	-	-	206,343
Sales of goods and services		4,314	5,615	1,899	(1,204)	10,624
Interest, excluding swap interest		1,304	113	3,969	(2,088)	3,298
Dividends and income tax receipts		1,399	-	-	(1,399)	-
Dividends from associates		1	2	-	-	3
Other receipts		2,935	275	159	(208)	3,161
		216,296	6,005	6,027	(4,899)	223,429
Cash paid						
Income tax paid		-	(200)	(151)	351	-
Payments to and on behalf of employees		(16,247)	(3,397)	(352)	-	(19,996)
Purchases of goods and services		(37,898)	(3,151)	(559)	589	(41,019)
Interest, excluding swap interest		(4,201)	(513)	(2,215)	2,088	(4,841)
Subsidies		(5,742)	-	-	489	(5,253)
Grants		(69,692)	-	-	198	(69,494)
Social benefits		(70,723)	-	-	126	(70,597)
Other payments		(2,134)	(1,157)	(842)	10	(4,123)
		(206,637)	(8,418)	(4,119)	3,851	(215,323)
NET CASH FLOWS FROM OPERATING ACTIVITES		**9,659**	**(2,413)**	**1,908**	**(1,048)**	**8,106**
Cash Flows from Investing Activities						
Non-Financial Assets						
Sales of non-financial assets		1,734	1,234	68	-	3,036
Purchases of new non-financial assets		(4,504)	(689)	(45)	-	(5,238)
Net cash flows from investments in non-financial assets		(2,770)	545	23	-	(2,202)

	Notes	GGS $m	PNFC sector $m	PFC sector $m	Eliminations $m	Whole of Government $m
Financial Assets (Policy Purposes)						
Dividends received out of proceeds from sale of PNFC sector assets		300	-	-	(300)	-
Purchases of investments		(1,641)	-	-	-	(1,641)
Net cash flows from investments in financial assets (policy purposes)		(1,341)	-	-	(300)	(1,641)
Financial Assets (Liquidity Management Purposes)						
Sales of investments		500	45	1,977	(744)	1,778
Purchases of investments		(3,500)	(5)	(9,934)	4,355	(9,084)
Net cash flows from investments in financial assets (liquidity management purposes)		(3,000)	40	(7,957)	3,611	(7,306)
NET CASH FLOWS FROM INVESTING ACTIVITIES		**(7,111)**	**585**	**(7,934)**	**3,311**	**(11,149)**
Cash Flows from Financing Activities						
Cash received						
Borrowing		13,597	450	-	(4,355)	9,692
Deposits received		899	20	6,028	-	6,947
Swap interest		1,912	110	1,595	-	3,617
Other financing		233	169	2,455	-	2,857
		16,641	749	10,078	(4,355)	23,113
Cash paid						
Borrowing		(15,032)	(677)	(360)	744	(15,325)
Deposits paid		(213)	(7)	(1,621)	-	(1,841)
Swap interest		(1,572)	(41)	(1,427)	-	(3,040)
Dividends paid out of proceeds from sale of assets		-	(300)	-	300	-
Other dividends paid		-	(259)	(789)	1,048	-
Other financing		(765)	(990)	(115)	-	(1,870)
		(17,582)	(2,274)	(4,312)	2,092	(22,076)

	Notes	GGS $m	PNFC sector $m	PFC sector $m	Eliminations $m	Whole of Government $m	Explanatory Notes
NET CASH FLOWS FROM FINANCING ACTIVITIES		(941)	(1,525)	5,766	(2,263)	1,037	
NET INCREASE IN CASH AND CASH EQUIVALENTS		**1,607**	**(3,353)**	**(260)**	-	**(2,006)**	
Cash and cash equivalents at beginning of year		8,984	4,292	2,800	-	16,076	
CASH AND CASH EQUIVALENTS AT END OF YEAR		**10,591**	**939**	**2,540**	-	**14,070**	
KEY FISCAL AGGREGATE							
Net cash flows from operating activities		9,659	(2,413)	1,908	(1,048)	8,106	
Net cash flows from investments in non-financial assets		(2,770)	545	23	-	(2,202)	
Dividends paid out of proceeds from sale of assets		-	(300)	-	300	-	
Other dividends paid		-	(259)	(789)	1,048	-	
CASH SURPLUS/(DEFICIT)	U	**6,889**	**(2,427)**	**1,142**	**300**	**5,904**	

Note S1 – Reconciliation to GFS Net Operating Balance*

	GGS $m	PNFC sector $m	PFC sector $m	Eliminations $m	Whole of Government $m	Explanatory Notes
Net result from transactions – net operating balance	4,294	(4,069)	4,480	(1,048)	3,657	a
Convergence differences						
Use of goods and services – development costs	(45)	(41)	-	-	(86)	b
Depreciation – development costs	6	5	-	-	11	c
Social benefits	94	-	-	-	94	d
Dividends to GGS from other sector entities	-	(259)	(789)	1,048	-	
Total convergence differences	55	(295)	(789)	1,048	19	
GFS NET OPERATING BALANCE	**4,349**	**(4,364)**	**3,691**	-	**3,676**	e

* Determined in accordance with the ABS GFS Manual.

Note S2 – Reconciliation to GFS Net Lending/(Borrowing)*

	Notes	GGS $m	PNFC sector $m	PFC sector $m	Eliminations $m	Whole of Government $m	Explanatory Notes
Net lending/(borrowing)		4,967	(3,347)	4,528	(1,048)	5,100	
Convergence differences							
Relating to net operating balance	S1	55	(295)	(789)	1,048	19	
Relating to net acquisition/(disposal) of non-financial assets from transactions		(100)	(7)	(1)	-	(108)	f
Total convergence differences		(45)	(302)	(790)	1,048	(89)	
GFS NET LENDING/(BORROWING)		**4,922**	**(3,649)**	**3,738**	**-**	**5,011**	

Note S3 – Reconciliation to GFS Total Change in Net Worth*

	Notes	GGS $m	PNFC sector $m	PFC sector $m	Eliminations $m	Whole of Government $m	Explanatory Notes
Comprehensive result – total change in net worth before transactions with owners in their capacity as owners		9,791	(3,883)	8,126	(2,420)	11,614	
Convergence differences							
Relating to net operating balance	S1	55	(295)	(789)	1,048	19	g
Relating to other economic flows							
Dividends to GGS out of proceeds from sale of PNFC sector assets		(300)	-	-	300	-	
Doubtful debts		500	63	41	-	604	h
Net gain on equity investments in other sector entities measured at proportional share of the carrying amount of net assets/(liabilities)		390	-	-	(390)	-	i
Share of net profit/(loss) from associates (excluding dividends)		51	-	-	-	51	j
Revaluations – market value of investments		(55)	-	-	-	(55)	k(i)
Revaluations – intangible assets		130	12	-	-	142	k(ii)
Revaluations – property		-	10	-	(10)	-	k(iii)

	Notes	GGS $m	PNFC sector $m	PFC sector $m	Eliminations $m	Whole of Government $m	Explanatory Notes
Remeasurement of shares and other contributed capital		-	4,093	(7,378)	3,285	-	l
Total convergence differences		771	3,883	(8,126)	4,233	761	
GFS TOTAL CHANGE IN NET WORTH		**10,562**	**-**	**-**	**1,813**	**12,375**	

* Determined in accordance with the ABS GFS Manual.

Note T – Reconciliation to GFS Net Worth*

	Notes	GGS $m	PNFC sector $m	PFC sector $m	Eliminations $m	Whole of Government $m	Explanatory Notes
Net worth		550	20,007	12,752	(32,253)	1,056	
Convergence differences							
Assets							
Accounts receivable		1,800	165	298	-	2,263	m
Shares and other equity		36	-	-	-	36	n
Investments accounted for using equity method		900	-	-	(900)	-	o
Investments in other sector entities							
Non-financial assets							
Machinery and equipment		(30,745)	-	-	-	(30,745)	
Intangible assets – research and development		(400)	(69)	-	-	(469)	p(i)
Intangible assets – no active market		150	-	-	-	150	p(ii)
Liabilities							
Provisions		94	-	-	-	94	q(i)
Deferred tax liability		-	506	-	(506)	-	q(ii)
Shares and other contributed capital		-	(20,609)	(13,050)	33,659	-	r
Total convergence differences		(28,165)	(20,007)	(12,752)	32,253	(28,671)	
GFS NET WORTH		**(27,615)**	**-**	**-**	**-**	**(27,615)**	s

AASB

Note U – Reconciliation to GFS Cash Surplus/(Deficit)*

	Notes	GGS $m	PNFC sector $m	PFC sector $m	Eliminations $m	Whole of Government $m	Explanatory Notes
Cash surplus/(deficit)		6,889	(2,427)	1,142	300	5,904	t
Convergence difference							
Adjustments to cash flows from investments in non-financial assets							
Finance leases and similar arrangements		(4)	-	-	-	(4)	u
GFS CASH SURPLUS/(DEFICIT)		**6,885**	**(2,427)**	**1,142**	**300**	**5,900**	

* Determined in accordance with the ABS GFS Manual.

Disaggregated Information

Z   Functional Classification for Whole of Government

	Expenses, excluding losses, included in operating result 20XX $m	Assets 20XX $m
General public services	(52,194)	10,009
Defence	(13,018)	55,759
Public order and safety	(2,521)	5,587
Education	(14,156)	8,645
Health	(32,569)	2,002
Social security and welfare	(70,139)	4,045
Housing and community amenities	(1,727)	5,533
Recreation and culture	(2,291)	3,003
Fuel and energy	(1,546)	990
Agriculture, forestry, fishing and hunting	(3,711)	2,572
Mining and mineral resources, other than fuels; manufacturing; and construction	(3,756)	2,515
Transport and communications	(9,509)	37,051
Other economic affairs	(1,502)	1,046
Other purposes [b]	(15,576)	99,712
TOTAL	**(224,215)**	**238,469**

b   Explanatory note: For the purpose of this illustration, financial assets that are not allocated
     to other functions are included in the 'Other purposes' function.

*Reconciliation of 'expenses, excluding losses, included in the
operating result' to 'expenses from transactions' in the statement
of comprehensive income*

	20XX $m
Expenses from transactions	224,476
Less: loss on write-off of financial assets at fair value through operating result	(380)
	224,096
Plus: amortisation of non-produced assets	119
Expenses, excluding losses, included in operating result	224,215

Illustrative Example B

General Government Sector Statement of Comprehensive Income, Statement of Financial Position, Statement of Changes in Equity, Statement of Cash Flows and Selected Notes

Statement of Comprehensive Income for the General Government Sector of the ABC Government for the Year Ended 30 June 20XX

	Notes	$m
Revenue from Transactions		
Taxation revenue		209,178
Other revenue		
Interest, other than swap interest		1,304
Dividends and income tax from other sector entities		1,399
Dividends from associates (part of share of net profit/(loss) from associates)		1
Sales of goods and services		4,314
Other current revenues		2,684
		218,880
Expenses from Transactions		
Employee benefits expense		
Wages, salaries and supplements		(14,178)
Superannuation		(2,069)
Use of goods and services		(37,898)
Depreciation		(3,672)
Interest, other than swap interest and superannuation interest expenses		(4,201)
Subsidy expenses		(5,742)
Grants		(69,692)
Social benefits		(71,856)
Superannuation net interest expenses		(4,898)
Loss on write-off of financial assets at fair value through operating result		(380)
		(214,586)
NET RESULT FROM TRANSACTIONS – NET OPERATING BALANCE		**4,294**
Other Economic Flows – Included in Operating Result		
Other revenue		
Net swap interest revenue		340
Dividends from other sector entities		300
Net foreign exchange gains		599
Net gain on sale of non-financial assets		200
Net gain on financial assets or liabilities at fair value through operating result		220
Net actuarial gainsa		840
Amortisation of non-produced assets		(75)
Doubtful debts		(500)
Share of net profit/(loss) from associates, excluding dividends		(51)
		1,873
OPERATING RESULT		**6,167**

	Notes	$m
Other Economic Flows – Other Comprehensive Income		
Items that will not be reclassified to operating result		
Revaluations		1,552
Items that may be reclassified subsequently to operating result		
Net gain on equity investments in other sector entities measured at proportional share of carrying amount of net assets/(liabilities)		1,072
Net gain on financial assets measured at fair value		1,000
		3,624
COMPREHENSIVE RESULT – TOTAL CHANGE IN NET WORTH		**9,791**
KEY FISCAL AGGREGATES		
NET LENDING/(BORROWING)	S2	**4,967**
plus Net acquisition/(disposal) of non-financial assets from transactions		(673)
NET OPERATING BALANCE	S1	**4,294**
plus Net other economic flows		5,497
TOTAL CHANGE IN NET WORTH	S3	**9,791**

a   Explanatory note: As noted in paragraph 14(c) of this Standard, an alternative treatment of net actuarial gains relating to defined benefit superannuation plans [consistent with paragraph 93B of AASB 119 *Employee Benefits*] would be to recognise them in full through other comprehensive income (which is part of comprehensive result).

Statement of Financial Position for the General Government Sector of the ABC Government as at 30 June 20XX

	Notes	$m
Assets		
Financial Assets		
Cash and deposits		10,591
Accounts receivable		16,748
Securities other than shares		24,188
Loans		10,302
Advances		7,758
Shares and other equity		
Investments accounted for using equity method		365
Investments in other sector entities		32,759
		102,711
Non-Financial Assets		
Produced assets		
Inventories		4,832
Machinery and equipment		54,367
Buildings and structures		14,152
Intangibles		1,250
Valuables		6,442
Non-produced assets		
Land		5,196
Intangibles		747
		86,986
TOTAL ASSETS		**189,697**

	Notes	$m
Liabilities		
Deposits held		364
Accounts payable		5,253
Securities other than shares		60,650
Borrowing		6,246
Superannuation		88,540
Provisions		28,094
TOTAL LIABILITIES		**189,147**
NET ASSETS/(LIABILITIES)		**550**
Accumulated surplus/(deficit)		(20,324)
Other reserves		20,874
NET WORTH	T	**550**

Statement of Changes in Equity for the General Government Sector of the ABC Government for the Year Ended 30 June 20XX

	Accumulated surplus/ (deficit)	Asset revaluation reserve	Accumulated net gain on equity investments in other sector entities	Accumulated net gain on other financial assets	Total equity
	$m	$m	$m	$m	$m
Equity at 1 July 20XX-1	(26,491)	12,161	500	4,589	(9,241)
Total comprehensive result	6,167	1,552	1,072	1,000	9,791
EQUITY AT 30 JUNE 20XX	**(20,324)**	**13,713**	**1,572**	**5,589**	**550**

Statement of Cash Flows for the General Government Sector of the ABC Government for the Year Ended 30 June 20XX

	Notes	$m
Cash Flows from Operating Activities		
Cash received		
Taxes received		206,343
Sales of goods and services		4,314
Interest, excluding swap interest		1,304
Dividends and income tax receipts		1,399
Dividends from associates		1
Other receipts		2,935
		216,296
Cash paid		
Payments to and on behalf of employees		(16,247)
Purchases of goods and services		(37,898)
Interest, excluding swap interest		(4,201)
Subsidies		(5,742)
Grants		(69,692)
Social benefits		(70,723)
Other payments		(2,134)
		(206,637)
NET CASH FLOWS FROM OPERATING ACTIVITIES		**9,659**

	Notes	$m
Cash Flows from Investing Activities		
Non-Financial Assets		
Sales of non-financial assets		1,734
Purchases of new non-financial assets		(4,504)
Net cash flows from investments in non-financial assets		(2,770)
Financial Assets (Policy Purposes)		
Dividends received out of proceeds from sale of PNFC sector assets		300
Purchases of investments		(1,641)
Net cash flows from investments in financial assets (policy purposes)		(1,341)
Financial Assets (Liquidity Management Purposes)		
Sales of investments		500
Purchases of investments		(3,500)
Net cash flows from investments in financial assets (liquidity management purposes)		(3,000)
NET CASH FLOWS FROM INVESTING ACTIVITIES		**(7,111)**
Cash Flows from Financing Activities		
Cash received		
Borrowing		13,597
Deposits received		899
Swap interest		1,912
Other financing		233
		16,641
Cash paid		
Borrowing		(15,032)
Deposits paid		(213)
Swap interest		(1,572)
Other financing		(765)
		(17,582)
NET CASH FLOWS FROM FINANCING ACTIVITIES		**(941)**
NET INCREASE IN CASH AND CASH EQUIVALENTS		**1,607**
Cash and cash equivalents at beginning of year		8,984
CASH AND CASH EQUIVALENTS AT END OF YEAR		**10,591**
KEY FISCAL AGGREGATE		
Net cash flows from operating activities		9,659
Net cash flows from investments in non-financial assets		(2,770)
CASH SURPLUS/(DEFICIT)	U	**6,889**

Note S1 – Reconciliation to GFS Net Operating Balance*

	Notes	$m	Explanatory Notes
Net result from transactions – net operating balance		4,294	
Convergence differences			
Use of goods and services – development costs		(45)	a
Depreciation – development costs		6	b
Social benefits		94	c
Total convergence differences		55	
GFS NET OPERATING BALANCE		**4,349**	e

Note S2 – Reconciliation to GFS Net Lending/ (Borrowing)*

Net lending/(borrowing)		4,967	
Convergence differences			
Relating to net operating balance	S1	55	
Relating to net acquisition/(disposal) of non-financial assets from transactions		(100)	f
Total convergence differences		(45)	
GFS NET LENDING/(BORROWING)		**4,922**	

Note S3 – Reconciliation to GFS Total Change in Net Worth*

Comprehensive result – total change in net worth		9,791	
Convergence differences			
Relating to net operating balance	S1	55	
Relating to other economic flows			
Dividends to GGS out of proceeds from sale of PNFC sector assets		(300)	g
Doubtful debts		500	h
Net gain on equity investments in other sector entities measured at proportional share of the carrying amount of net assets/(liabilities)		390	i
Share of net profit/(loss) from associates (excluding dividends)		51	j
Revaluations – market value of investments		(55)	k(i)
Revaluations – intangible assets		130	k(ii)
Total convergence differences		771	
GFS TOTAL CHANGE IN NET WORTH		**10,562**	

* Determined in accordance with the ABS GFS Manual

Note T – Reconciliation to GFS Net Worth*

	Notes	$m	Explanatory Notes
Net worth		550	
Convergence differences			
Assets			
Accounts receivable		1,800	m
Shares and other equity			
Investments accounted for using equity method		36	n
Investments in other sector entities		900	o
Non-financial assets			
Machinery and equipment		(30,745)	
Intangible assets – research and development		(400)	p(i)
Intangible assets – no active market		150	p(ii)
Liabilities			
Provisions		94	q(i)
Total convergence differences		(28,165)	
GFS NET WORTH		**(27,615)**	s

Note U – Reconciliation to GFS Cash Surplus/ (Deficit)*

	Notes	$m	Explanatory Notes
Cash surplus/(deficit)		6,889	
Convergence differences			
Adjustments to cash flows from investments in non-financial assets			
Finance leases and similar arrangements		(4)	t
GFS CASH SURPLUS/(DEFICIT)		**6,885**	u

* Determined in accordance with the ABS GFS Manual.

Disaggregated Information

Z Functional Classification for General Government Sector

	Expenses, excluding losses, included in operating result 20XX $m	Assets 20XX $m
General public services	(50,661)	7,149
Defence	(13,018)	55,759
Public order and safety	(2,401)	3,991
Education	(13,482)	6,175
Health	(31,971)	1,430
Social security and welfare	(69,036)	2,899
Housing and community amenities	(1,645)	3,952
Recreation and culture	(2,182)	2,145
Fuel and energy	(1,473)	707
Agriculture, forestry, fishing and hunting	(3,535)	1,837
Mining and mineral resources, other than fuels; manufacturing; and construction	(3,578)	1,797
Transport and communications	(4,295)	13,418
Other economic affairs	(1,431)	747
Other purposes [b]	(15,573)	87,691
TOTAL	(214,281)	189,697

b Explanatory note: For the purpose of this illustration, financial assets that are not allocated to other functions are included in the 'Other purposes' function.

Reconciliation of 'expenses, excluding losses, included in operating result' to 'expenses from transactions' in the statement of comprehensive income

	20XX $m
Expenses from transactions	214,586
Less: loss on write-off of financial assets at fair value through operating result	(380)
	214,206
Plus: amortisation of non-produced assets	75
Expenses, excluding losses, included in operating result	214,281

Explanatory Notes Supporting Illustrative Examples A and B

The following notes are for explanatory purposes only, and do not form part of the financial statements or accompanying notes illustrated in Illustrative Examples A or B.

The notes provide explanations of the convergence differences between the key fiscal aggregates presented in each of the financial statements and GFS measures of the key fiscal aggregates for the whole of government (including the sectors) and GGS.

Convergence Differences relating to the Statements of Comprehensive Income

Net Operating Balance

a **Expenses from Transactions – Use of Goods and Services**

The convergence difference of ($45m) in the GGS and ($41m) in the PNFC sector arises because GFS expenses certain development costs and classifies them as expenses from transactions. However, the development costs are not recognised as expenses from transactions in the statement of comprehensive income because they are recognised as intangible assets upon acquisition. GFS treats goods and services used for research and development as use of goods and services expenses from transactions, rather than as acquisitions of intangible assets, even though some development activities are expected to bring benefits for more than one year (refer also to Note (b)).

The total difference of ($86m) flows through to the whole of government amounts.

b   Expenses from Transactions – Depreciation

The convergence difference of $6m in the GGS and $5m in the PNFC sector arises because GFS recognises a smaller amortisation of produced intangibles than is recognised as an expense from transactions in the statement of comprehensive income. GFS treats goods and services used for research and development as use of goods and services expense from transactions, rather than as acquisitions of intangible assets, even though some development activities may bring benefits for more than one year (refer also to Note (a)).

The total difference of $11m flows through to the whole of government amounts.

c   Expenses from Transactions – Social Benefits

The convergence difference of $94m in the GGS arises because GFS does not recognise a liability relating to the potential beneficiaries of a social benefit scheme who had not registered for benefits as at the reporting date. Therefore, GFS does not recognise the associated expense from transactions, whereas such an amount is recognised in the statement of comprehensive income and classified as expenses from transactions.

This difference flows through to the whole of government amounts.

d   Dividends to GGS from Other Sector Entities

The convergence difference comprises ($259m) in the PNFC sector and ($789m) in the PFC sector because GFS treats dividends to owners as an expense, whereas such an amount is not recognised as an expense in the statement of comprehensive income because it is treated as a distribution to owners and therefore a direct debit to equity.

The total difference of ($1,048m) does not flow through to the whole of government amounts as it arises from intersector transactions.

e   Other Differences Included in the GFS Net Operating Balance

A classification difference arises in the whole of government and the GGS, because GFS classifies the debt security written off by mutual agreement of $380m as a capital grant expense from transactions, whereas, although it is recognised as an expense from transactions in the statement of comprehensive income, it is classified as loss on write-off of financial assets at fair value through operating result. [For the purpose of Illustrative Examples A and B, the debt security is assumed to have satisfied the criteria in AASB 139 *Financial Instruments: Recognition and Measurement* for classification as a 'fair value through profit or loss' financial asset.] The write-off arose from the Government agreeing to forgive the outstanding debt of a Country. The classification difference has no impact on the amount of the GFS Net Operating Balance.

A GGS/PNFC elimination difference arises in respect of the treatment of $25m of the social benefits. Under GFS, certain transactions between the GGS and entities within the PNFC and PFC sectors are not eliminated on consolidation, whereas under AASB 127 *Consolidated and Separate Financial Statements* intragroup transactions that are not in substance transactions with external parties are eliminated in full. The GFS treatment has the effect of 'grossing up' both GFS 'revenue from transactions – other current revenues' and GFS 'expenses from transactions – grants' of the whole of government by equal amounts even though the key fiscal aggregates remain the same. [For the purpose of this illustration, it is assumed the GGS has compensated a PNFC entity for $25m of community service obligations, imposed by the GGS, that requires the PNFC entity to provide free services to a cohort of private individuals.] The compensation provided by the GGS to the PNFC entity is not eliminated under GFS (instead it is 'rerouted' through the household sector of the economy and therefore treated as an expense of the GGS to the household sector, and an expense of the household sector to the PNFC entity and therefore revenue of the PNFC entity). This convergence difference has no impact on the amount of the whole of government's GFS Net Operating Balance. This difference does not affect the GGS or the PNFC and PFC sectors but impacts the total of revenues and expenses in the whole of government statement of comprehensive income.

Net Lending/(Borrowing)

f   **Net Acquisition/(Disposal) of Non-Financial Assets from Transactions**

The convergence differences are explained as follows:

	Statement of Comprehensive Income $m	GFS $m	Convergence Difference $m	For explanations see notes
GGS				
Gross fixed capital formation	3,932	1,847	2,085	(a)
Depreciation	(3,747)	(1,562)	(2,185)	(b)#
Change in inventory	300	300	-	
Other transactions in non-financial assets	(1,158)	(1,158)	-	
Net acquisition/(disposal) of non-financial assets from transactions	(673)	(573)	(100)	
PNFC Sector				
Gross fixed capital formation	342	301	41	(a)
Depreciation	(168)	(120)	(48)	(b)#
Change in inventory	(9)	(9)	-	
Other transactions in non-financial assets	(887)	(887)	-	
Net acquisition/(disposal) of non-financial assets from transactions	(722)	(715)	(7)	
PFC Sector				
Gross fixed capital formation	18	18	-	
Depreciation	(27)	(26)	(1)	#
Change in inventory	2	2	-	
Other transactions in non-financial assets	(41)	(41)	-	
Net acquisition/(disposal) of non-financial assets from transactions	(48)	(47)	(1)	
Whole of Government				
Gross fixed capital formation	4,292	2,166	2,126	(a)
Depreciation	(3,942)	(1,708)	(2,234)	(b)#
Change in inventory	293	293	-	
Other transactions in non-financial assets	(2,086)	(2,086)	-	
Net acquisition/(disposal) of non-financial assets from transactions	(1,443)	(1,335)	(108)	

\# Depreciation shown in the statement of comprehensive income column includes both depreciation and amortisation from non-produced assets. Note (b) explains the convergence difference so far as it relates to the item described as depreciation in the statement of comprehensive income. The convergence differences shown in this note also include the amounts for 'amortisation of non-produced assets' presented in the statement of comprehensive income of $75m for the GGS, $43m for the PNFC sector and $1m for the PFC sector.

Net Other Economic Flows

g   **Other Economic Flows – Included in Operating Result – Other Revenue – Dividends to GGS from the sale of PNFC sector assets**

The convergence difference of ($300m) arises in the GGS because GFS classifies $300m of the distributions from other sector entities as a transaction in financial assets (that is, as a withdrawal of equity because it is funded from proceeds from sale of assets), whereas the statement of comprehensive income recognises it as dividend revenue and classifies it as other economic flows (refer also to Note i).

This difference does not flow through to the whole of government amounts as it arises from intersector transactions.

h **Other Economic Flows – Included in Operating Result – Doubtful Debts**

The convergence differences of $500m in the GGS, $63m in the PNFC sector and $41m in the PFC sector arise because GFS does not recognise doubtful debts, whereas the statement of comprehensive income recognises doubtful debts and classifies it as other economic flows. In this example, no bad debts were written off from doubtful debts. GFS recognises amounts written off when there is mutual agreement with debtors as capital grants expenses in the period of the write-off, and recognises those written off unilaterally by the government as other economic flows also in the period of the write-off.

The total difference of $604m flows through to the whole of government amounts.

i **Other Economic Flows – Other Non-Owner[3] Changes in Equity – Net Gain on Equity Investments in Other Sector Entities Measured at Proportional Share of the Carrying Amount of Net Assets/(Liabilities)**

The convergence differences comprise:

$90m in the GGS: The carrying amount of net assets (and therefore the change in carrying amount of net assets) of other sector entities determined under GFS principles and rules differs from the carrying amount of net assets (and therefore the change in carrying amount of net assets) of the subsidiaries recognised in the statement of financial position (being the carrying amount of net assets determined before elimination of intersector balances).

The difference is therefore equivalent to the total of those convergence differences affecting the total change in net worth impacting either through the net operating balance (itemised in Note S1 of Illustrative Example A) or other economic flows (other than transactions with owners in their capacity as owners in the form of dividends paid – itemised in Note S3 of Illustrative Example A). The components are:

	$m
Use of goods and services – development costs [PNFC]	(41)
Depreciation – development costs [PNFC]	5
Doubtful debts [PNFC]	63
Doubtful debts [PFC]	41
Revaluations – intangible assets [PNFC]	12
Revaluations – property [PNFC]	10
TOTAL	90

$300m in the GGS: GFS treats this amount as a distribution from other sector entities classified as a transaction in financial assets (that is, as a withdrawal of equity because it is funded from proceeds from sale of assets), whereas the statement of comprehensive income recognises it as dividend revenue and classifies it as other economic flows (refer also to Note g). Under GFS, the holding gain on other sector entities is determined after taking into account additions to and withdrawals from equity that have occurred.

The total difference of $390m does not flow through to the whole of government amounts as it arises from intersector items.

j **Other Economic Flows – Included in Operating Result – Share of Net Profit/(Loss) from Associates (Excluding Dividends)**

The convergence difference of $51m arises in the GGS because GFS does not recognise the share of the associate's loss (excluding dividends), whereas consistent with the equity method of accounting, it is recognised as an expense of $51m and classified as an other economic flow and dividends are recognised as a revenue of $1m and classified as a transaction in the statement of comprehensive income. GFS recognises the decrease in the market value of investments in associates of $55m as an other economic flow (refer to

---

3   The term 'Non-Owner' is not needed in a GGS context compared with the whole of government context. In a whole of government context the term is used in Illustrative Example A in relation to the PNFC and PFC sector financial statements to distinguish between transactions that occur between the GGS (as owner) and the PNFC/PFC sectors and other types of transactions.

Note k(ii)), and the dividends on such investments of $1m as dividend revenue from transactions.

This difference flows through to the whole of government amounts.

k   **Other Economic Flows – Other Non-Owner[4] Changes in Equity – Revaluations**

The convergence differences comprise:

k(i)   ($55m) in the GGS because GFS recognises the decrease in the market value of investments in associates of $55m as an other economic flow, whereas it is not recognised in the statement of comprehensive income. Consistent with the equity method of accounting, the statement of comprehensive income recognises the share of the associate's loss of $50m as a loss of $51m classified as other economic flows and revenue (from dividends) of $1m (refer also to Note j).

This difference flows through to the whole of government amounts.

k(ii) $130m in the GGS and $12m in the PNFC sector because GFS recognises the net increase in the revalued intangible assets as an other economic flow, whereas it is not recognised in the statement of comprehensive income. In accordance with paragraph 81 of AASB 138 *Intangible Assets*, the intangible assets in this example are not revalued because there is no active market for them.

The total difference of $142m flows through to the whole of government amounts.

k(iii) $10m in the PNFC sector because while GFS recognises the gross increase in the revalued asset (in Illustrative Example A, assumed to have arisen from an upward asset revaluation of properties), it does not recognise as an offset part of the increase in the revalued asset as being due to a corresponding increase in the deferred tax liability. (Refer also to Note q(ii))

This difference does not flow through to the whole of government amounts as the whole of government does not have a deferred tax liability.

l   **Remeasurement of Shares and Other Contributed Capital**

The convergence differences of $4,093m in the PNFC sector and ($7,378m) in the PFC sector arise because GFS measures net worth as assets less liabilities less share capital/ contributed capital (remeasured). Because in Illustrative Example A PNFC and PFC sectors are 100 per cent owned by the GGS, the GFS net worth, and therefore the GFS change in net worth, of these sectors is zero. In effect, all of the convergence differences that impact on the comprehensive result are netted off for the PNFC and PFC sectors against the GFS remeasurement of shares and other contributed capital.

The total difference of ($3,285m) does not flow through to the whole of government amounts as they relate to the GGS ownership interest in PNFC/PFC sectors.

Convergence Differences relating to the Statements of Financial Position

Net Worth

m   **Assets – Financial Assets – Accounts Receivable**

The convergence differences of $1,800m in the GGS, $165m in the PNFC sector and $298m in the PFC sector arise because GFS does not recognise doubtful debts, whereas a provision for doubtful debts is recognised in the statement of financial position.

This total difference of $2,263m flows through to the whole of government amounts.

n   **Assets – Financial Assets – Shares and Other Equity – Investments Accounted for Using Equity Method**

The convergence difference of $36m arises in the GGS because GFS recognises the net decrease in the market value of investments in associates, whereas the equity method of accounting is applied in the calculation of the carrying amount recognised in the statement of financial position.

This difference flows through to the whole of government amounts.

---

4   The term 'Non-Owner' is not needed in a GGS context compared with the whole of government context. In a whole of government context the term is used in Illustrative Example A in relation to the PNFC and PFC sector financial statements to distinguish between transactions that occur between the GGS (as owner) and the PNFC/PFC sectors and other types of transactions.

o **Assets – Financial Assets – Shares and Other Equity – GGS Investments in Other Sector Entities**

The convergence difference of $900m arises in the GGS in relation to the measurement of equity investments in other sector entities measured at proportional share of the carrying amount of net assets/(liabilities), due to different definition, recognition and measurement principles and rules for certain assets and liabilities under GFS.

The difference is therefore equivalent to the total of those convergence differences affecting Net Worth (as itemised in Note T). The components are:

	$m
Amounts receivable [PNFC]	165
Amounts receivable [PFC]	298
Intangible assets – research and development [PNFC]	(69)
Deferred tax liability [PNFC]	506
TOTAL	900

This difference does not flow through to the whole of government amounts as it arises from an intersector item.

p **Assets – Non-Financial Assets – Produced Assets – Intangibles**

The convergence differences comprise:

p(i) ($400m) in the GGS and ($69m) in the PNFC sector because GFS treats research and development costs as use of goods and services expenses from transactions, whereas some are treated as acquisitions of intangible assets for the statement of financial position because some development activities are expected to bring benefits for more than one year.

This total difference of ($469m) flows through to the whole of government amounts.

p(ii) $150m in the GGS because GFS recognises the revaluation of certain intangible assets, whereas those intangible assets have not been revalued in the statement of financial position because there is no active market (in accordance with paragraph 81 of AASB 138).

This difference flows through to the whole of government amounts.

q **Liabilities – Provisions**

The convergence differences comprise:

q(i) $94m in the GGS because GFS does not recognise certain provisions that are recognised in the statement of financial position as liabilities (for example, to the extent that they arise from constructive obligations for which there is no counterparty recognising a related financial asset).

This difference flows through to the whole of government amounts.

q(ii) $506m in the PNFC sector because GFS does not recognise the deferred tax liability.

This difference does not flow through to the whole of government amounts as it arises from a PNFC sector liability that is not a whole of government liability.

[Note: Depending on the arrangements operating in a particular jurisdiction, a GGS, as an income tax collector, may not be able to recognise a related revenue unless it meets the criteria in AASB 1004 *Contributions*. Under the tax regime assumed for the purpose of this example, the GGS, as the tax collector, does not recognise deferred tax balances because the tax events associated with the PNFC sector's deferred tax balances have not occurred, even though from the PNFC sector's viewpoint, the event is the recognition of the underlying assets and/or liabilities in accordance with AASB 112 *Income Taxes*. This treatment in the GGS accords with GFS, which does not recognise deferred tax assets. Therefore, no convergence difference arises.]

r **Shares and Other Contributed Capital**

The convergence differences of ($20,609m) in the PNFC sector and ($13,050m) in the PFC sector arise because GFS measures net worth as assets less liabilities less shares/contributed capital, whereas shares/contributed capital are not deducted in the determination of GAAP net worth. Because in this example GFS measures shares/contributed capital of the PNFC and PFC sectors at the carrying amount of net assets of those sectors, PNFC and PFC sector GFS net worth is nil.

The total difference of ($33,659m) does not flow through to the whole of government amounts as they relate to the GGS ownership interest in the PNFC and PFC sectors.

s   **Classification Difference Included in the GFS Net Worth**

A classification difference arises in the GGS because GFS classifies $28,000m of the $28,094m of provisions as other accounts payable. The classification difference has no impact on the amount of the GFS Net Worth.

This difference flows through to whole of government amounts.

Convergence Differences relating to the Statements of Cash Flows

Cash Surplus/(Deficit)

t   **Cash Flows from Investments in Non-Financial Assets**

The convergence difference of ($4m) in the GGS arises because GFS recognises a notional cash outflow relating to new finance leases and similar arrangements in calculating cash surplus/(deficit), whereas the statement of cash flows does not recognise notional cash flows.

This difference flows through to the whole of government amounts.

u   **Classification Differences Included in the GFS Cash Surplus/(Deficit)**

For the whole of government and GGS, amounts of $41,019m and $37,898m respectively have been recognised as payments for purchases of goods and services from operating activities in the statement of cash flows. Under GFS, the corresponding amounts are $41,105m and $39,943m respectively.

The convergence difference of $45m in the GGS is due to capitalised development costs that are classified as purchases of non-financial assets – which are investing activities in the statement of cash flows.

For the PNFC sector, an amount of $3,151m has been recognised as payments for purchases of goods and services from operating activities in the statement of cash flows. Under GFS, the corresponding amount is $3,192m.

The convergence difference of $41m comprises capitalised development costs that are classified as purchases of non-financial assets – which are classified as investing activities in the statement of cash flows.

The total convergence difference of $86m flows through to whole of government.

These classification differences have no impact on the amount of the GFS Cash Surplus/(Deficit).

Illustrative Example C

Extract from the Note Containing the Summary of Significant Accounting Policies of a General Government Sector

> The following is an example of an extract from Note 1 of the financial statements for a year subsequent to the first year of adoption of this Standard, consistent with the requirements of paragraph 39. This example assumes that the GGS financial statements are presented separately from the whole of government financial statements, and that the most recent version of the ABS GFS Manual has been applied.

The financial statements of the General Government Sector (GGS) of *[name of the Government]* have been prepared in accordance with AASB 1049 *Whole of Government and General Government Sector Financial Reporting*, which requires compliance with all Australian Accounting Standards except those identified below. The purpose of the financial statements is to provide users with information about the stewardship by the Government in relation to its GGS and accountability for the resources entrusted to it; information about the financial position, changes in net assets/(liabilities), performance and cash flows of the Government's GGS; and information that facilitates assessments of the macro-economic impact of the Government's GGS.

The GGS of *[name of the Government]* is a component of the Whole of Government of *[name of the Government]*. The GGS is determined in accordance with the principles and rules contained in the Australian Bureau of Statistics publications:

(a)   *Australian System of Government Finance Statistics: Concepts, Sources and Methods, 2005* (ABS Catalogue No. 5514.0); and

(b)   *Amendments to Australian System of Government Finance Statistics, 2005* (ABS Catalogue No. 5514.0)

published on the ABS website on *[publication date, or refer to effective date if specified by the ABS]* (ABS GFS Manual). The GGS consists of all government units and non-profit institutions controlled and mainly financed by government. Government units are legal entities established by political processes that have legislative, judicial, or executive authority over other units and which provide goods and services to the community or to individuals on a non-market basis; and make transfer payments to redistribute income and wealth. Non-profit institutions are created for the purpose of producing or distributing goods and services but are not a source of income, profit or other financial gain for the government.

The Standard under which the GGS financial statements are prepared does not require full application of AASB 127 *Consolidated and Separate Financial Statements* and AASB 139 *Financial Instruments: Recognition and Measurement*. Assets, liabilities, income, expenses and cash flows of government controlled entities that are in the Public Non-Financial Corporations sector and the Public Financial Corporations sector are not separately recognised in the GGS of *[name of the Government's]* financial statements. Instead, the GGS financial statements recognise an asset, being the controlling equity investment in those entities, and recognise a gain or loss relating to changes in the carrying amount of that asset, measured in accordance with AASB 1049. Readers are referred to the Whole of Government general purpose financial statements of *[name of the Government]* for the year ended 30 June 20XX for financial information that separately recognises assets, liabilities, income, expenses and cash flows of all entities under the control of the *[name of the Government]*.

The ABS GFS Manual also provides the basis upon which Government Finance Statistics (GFS) information that is contained in the financial statements is prepared. In particular, notes disclosing key fiscal aggregates of net worth, net operating balance, total change in net worth, net lending/(borrowing) and cash surplus/(deficit) determined using the principles and rules in the ABS GFS Manual are included in the financial statements, together with a reconciliation of those key fiscal aggregates to the corresponding key fiscal aggregates recognised in the financial statements.

Illustrative Example D

Key Technical Terms Used in the Complete Sets of Financial Statements

This illustration provides an example of the presentation of explanations of selected key technical terms used in the Whole of Government and GGS Financial Statements and Selected Notes (Illustrative Examples A and B), as required by paragraph 41(a)(iii) of this Standard.

This illustration presents generic explanations, suitable in both a whole of government and GGS context, except where indicated. In instances where the generic definition is not necessarily appropriate, further guidance has been provided.

Cash surplus/(deficit) is net cash flows from operating activities plus net cash flows from acquisition and disposal of non-financial assets and less distributions paid. GFS cash surplus/(deficit) also deducts the value of assets acquired under finance leases and similar arrangements.

Comprehensive result (total change in net worth before transactions with owners in their capacity as owners)[5] is the net result of all items of income and expense recognised for the period. It is the aggregate of operating result and other comprehensive income, other than transactions with owners in their capacity as owners.

Convergence difference is the difference between the amounts recognised in the financial statements compared with the amounts determined for GFS purposes as a result of differences in definition, recognition, measurement, classification and consolidation principles and rules.

Financial asset is any asset that is:

(a)   cash;

(b)   an equity instrument of another entity;

(c)   a contractual right:

    (i)   to receive cash or another financial asset from another entity; or

    (ii)   to exchange financial assets or financial liabilities with another entity under conditions that are potentially favourable to the entity; or

(d)   a contract that will or may be settled in the entity's own equity instruments and is:

    (i)   a non-derivative for which the entity is or may be obliged to receive a variable number of the entity's own equity instruments; or

    (ii)   a derivative that will or may be settled other than by the exchange of a fixed amount of cash or another financial asset for a fixed number of the entity's own equity instruments. For this purpose the entity's own equity instruments do not include instruments that are themselves contracts for the future receipt or delivery of the entity's own equity instruments.

General Government Sector (GGS) is the institutional sector comprising all government units and non-profit institutions controlled and mainly financed by government.

Government Finance Statistics (GFS) enable policymakers and analysts to study developments in the financial operations, financial position and liquidity situation of the government. More details about the GFS can be found in the Australian Bureau of Statistics (ABS) publications *Australian System of Government Finance Statistics: Concepts, Sources and Methods, 2005* (ABS Catalogue No. 5514.0) and *Amendments to Australian System of Government Finance Statistics, 2005* (ABS Catalogue No. 5514.0) published on the ABS website.

Gross fixed capital formation is the value of acquisition less disposals of new and existing produced assets that can be used in production, other than inventories.

Mutually agreed bad debts are financial assets written off where there was prior knowledge and consent by the counterparties.

Net acquisition/(disposal) of non-financial assets from transactions is gross fixed capital formation less depreciation plus changes in inventories plus other transactions in non-financial assets.

Net actuarial gains includes actuarial gains and losses on defined benefit superannuation plans.

Net cash flows from investments in financial assets (liquidity management purposes) is cash receipts from liquidation or repayment of investments in financial assets for liquidity management purposes less cash payments for such investments. Investment for liquidity management purposes means making funds available to others with no policy intent and with the aim of earning a commercial rate of return.

Net cash flows from investments in financial assets (policy purposes) is cash receipts from the repayment and liquidation of investments in financial assets for policy purposes less cash

---

5   Explanatory note: The term 'transactions with owners in their capacity as owners' is most pertinent in a whole of government context. Such transactions may occur between the GGS, as owner, and the PNFC/PFC sectors and are therefore required to be disclosed in the sector information included in the whole of government financial statements. In addition, transactions with owners in their capacity as owners may occur in a whole of government context in relation to partly-owned subsidiaries. Accordingly, the GGS financial statements could use the alternative term 'Comprehensive result (total change in net worth)' defined as the net result of all items of income and expense recognised for the period. It is the aggregate of operating result and other changes in equity.

payments for acquiring financial assets for policy purposes. Acquisition of financial assets for policy purposes is distinguished from investments in financial assets (liquidity management purposes) by the underlying government motivation for acquiring the assets. Acquisition of financial assets for policy purposes is motivated by government policies such as encouraging the development of certain industries or assisting citizens affected by natural disaster.

Net gain on equity investments in other sector entities measured at proportional share of the carrying amount of net assets/(liabilities) comprises the net gains relating to the equity held by the GGS in other sector entities. It arises from a change in the carrying amount of net assets of the subsidiaries. The net gains are measured based on the proportional share of the subsidiary's carrying amount of net assets/(liabilities) before elimination of intersector balances.

Net lending/(borrowing) is net operating balance minus the net acquisition/(disposal) of non-financial assets. It is also equal to transactions in the net acquisition/(disposal) of financial assets minus the net incurrence of liabilities. It indicates the extent to which financial resources are placed at the disposal of the rest of the economy or the utilisation of financial resources generated by the rest of the economy. It is an indicator of the financial impact on the rest of the economy.

Net other economic flows is the net change in the volume or value of assets and liabilities that does not result from transactions.

Net result from transactions – net operating balance is revenue from transactions minus expenses from transactions. It is a summary measure of the ongoing sustainability of operations. It excludes gains and losses resulting from changes in price levels and other changes in the volume of assets. It is the component of the change in net worth that is due to transactions and can be attributed directly to government policies.

Net worth is assets less liabilities and shares/contributed capital. For the GGS, net worth is assets less liabilities, since shares and contributed capital do not exist in a GGS context[6]. It is an economic measure of wealth and reflects the contribution to the wealth of Australia. The change in net worth is the preferred measure for assessing the sustainability of fiscal activities.

Non-financial assets are all assets that are not 'financial assets'.

Non-produced assets are assets needed for production that have not themselves been produced. They include land, subsoil assets, and certain intangible assets.

Non-produced intangibles are intangible assets needed for production that have not themselves been produced. They include constructs of society such as patents.

Operating result is a measure of financial performance of the operations for the period. It is the net result of items of revenue, gains and expenses (including losses) recognised for the period, excluding those that are classified as 'other comprehensive income'.

Other current revenues refers to current revenue other than current revenue from taxes, sales of goods and services, and property income. It includes revenue from fines other than penalties imposed by tax authorities.

Other economic flows – see definition of 'net other economic flows' above.

Other sector entities are government controlled entities that are not part of the GGS.

Public Financial Corporations (PFC) sector is the institutional sector comprising resident government controlled corporations and quasi-corporations mainly engaged in financial intermediation or provision of auxiliary financial services.

Public Non-Financial Corporations (PNFC) sector is the institutional sector comprising resident government controlled corporations and quasi-corporations mainly engaged in the production of market goods and/or non-financial services.

Quasi-corporation is an unincorporated enterprise that functions as if it were a corporation, has the same relationship with its owner as a corporation, and keeps a separate set of accounts.

Securities other than shares are negotiable financial instruments serving as evidence of the obligations to settle by means of providing cash, a financial instrument, or some other item of

---

6   Explanatory note: The reference to shares/contributed capital is most pertinent in a whole of government context. As an alternative, the GGS financial statements could define 'net worth' as 'assets less liabilities' because shares and contributed capital do not exist in a GGS context.

economic value. The security normally specifies a schedule for interest payments and principal repayments. Some examples are: bills, bonds and debentures, commercial paper, and securitised mortgage loans.

Social benefits are transfers in cash or in kind to relieve households of the burden of a defined set of social risks. Social risks are events or circumstances that may adversely affect the welfare of households either by imposing additional demands on their resources or by reducing their incomes.

Transactions are interactions between two units by mutual agreement or an action within a unit that is analytically useful to treat as a transaction.

Unilaterally determined bad debts are financial assets written off without an agreement with the debtor in cases such as bankruptcy of the debtor.

Use of goods and services is the total value of goods and services used in production, and use of goods acquired for resale. Goods and services acquired for use as direct in-kind transfers to households or as grants are excluded.

Valuables are produced goods of considerable value that are acquired and held primarily as stores of value over time and are not used primarily for purposes of production or consumption. They include works of art not used primarily in museums to produce services for the public.

Wages, salaries and supplements consist of all uncapitalised compensation of employees except for superannuation. It includes pay in cash or in-kind.

Whole of government financial statements are financial statements that are prepared in accordance with Australian Accounting Standards, including AASB 127 *Consolidated and Separate Financial Statements*, and thereby separately recognise assets, liabilities, income, expenses, and cash flows of all entities under the control of the government on a line-by-line basis.

AASB 1050
Administered Items

(Issued December 2007)

Note from the Institute of Chartered Accountants Australia

This note, prepared by the technical editors, is not part of Accounting Standard AASB 1050.

Historical development

13 December 2007: AASB 1050 'Administered Items' was issued by the AASB.

In October and December 2007 the AASB issued new and revised AASB 1004 'Contributions', AASB 1049 'Whole of Government and General Government Sector Financial Reporting', AASB 1050 'Administered Items', AASB 1051 'Land Under Roads', AASB 1052 'Disaggregated Disclosures', AASB Interpretation 1038 'Contributions by Owners Made to Wholly-Owned Public Sector Entities' and AASB 2007-9 'Amendments to Australian Accounting Standards arising from the Review of AAS 27, AAS 29 and AAS 31'. These revisions result from a short-term review, primarily focused on relocating, where necessary, the requirements in AASs 27, 29 and 31, substantively unamended (with some exceptions), into topic-based Standards.

These Standards and Interpretation apply to annual reporting periods beginning on or after 1 July 2008, with early adoption permitted. These Standards supersede AAS 27, AAS 29 and AAS 31.

Contents

Preface

Comparison with International Pronouncements

Accounting Standard
AASB 1050 Administered Items

Paragraphs

Objective 1

Application 2 – 6

Disclosure of Administered Income, Expenses, Assets and Liabilities 7 – 14

Taxes 15 – 16

Transfer Payments 17 – 23

Accounting Basis 24

Display of Information about Administered Items 25

Appendix

A. Comparison of AASB 1050 with AAS 29

Basis for Conclusions

Australian Accounting Standard AASB 1050 *Administered Items* is set out in paragraphs 1 – 25. All the paragraphs have equal authority. Paragraphs in **bold type** state the main principles. AASB 1050 is to be read in the context of other Australian Accounting Standards, including AASB 1048 *Interpretation and Application of Standards*, which identifies the Australian Accounting Interpretations. In the absence of explicit guidance, AASB 108 *Accounting Policies, Changes in Accounting Estimates and Errors* provides a basis for selecting and applying accounting policies.

Preface

Background

Australian Accounting Standards incorporate International Financial Reporting Standards (IFRSs), as issued by the International Accounting Standards Board (IASB), with the addition of paragraphs on the applicability of the Standard in the Australian environment.

Some Australian Accounting Standards also include requirements that are specific to Australian entities. In most instances, these requirements are restricted to not-for-profit entities, including public sector entities, or include additional disclosures that address domestic, regulatory or other issues.

Reasons for Issuing this Standard

AAS 27 *Financial Reporting by Local Governments*, AAS 29 *Financial Reporting by Government Departments* and AAS 31 *Financial Reporting by Governments* were first issued in 1991, 1993 and 1996 respectively. While AASs 27, 29 and 31 had been subject to a number of limited reviews since then, the requirements in these Standards needed a comprehensive review because:

(a) there had been significant developments in Australian financial reporting, in particular adopting IFRSs within Australian Accounting Standards, for reporting periods beginning on or after 1 January 2005. As a result of these developments, uncertainties emerged as to the application of cross-references to other Australian Accounting Standards and the override provisions in AASs 27, 29 and 31 that made the requirements in AASs 27, 29 and 31 take precedence over other requirements;

(b)   local governments, government departments and governments were subject to requirements that differed from requirements applicable to other not-for-profit entities and for-profit entities contained in Australian Accounting Standards. An objective of the Board is to put in place transaction-neutral standards that will treat like transactions and events consistently;

(c)   the Board had made significant progress in its project on the harmonisation of Generally Accepted Accounting Principles (GAAP) and Government Finance Statistics (GFS) so far as it relates to the General Government Sector and the whole of government of the federal, state and territory governments. It was therefore particularly timely to review the requirements in AAS 31;

(d)   they did not reflect contemporary accounting thought; and

(e)   they did not reflect the current style of writing standards, which is to specify principles rather than rules, and requirements rather than encouragements.

The Board intends to continue with its policy of developing a common accounting standards framework for both for-profit and not-for-profit entities whilst acknowledging differences in some areas. The Board is committed to having a platform of topic-based transaction-neutral Standards that will apply to the public sector.

Review of AASs 27, 29 and 31

The Board initiated a project for reviewing the requirements in AASs 27, 29 and 31, divided into two phases comprising a short-term and a longer-term review.

The primary focus in the short term review has been on relocating, where necessary, the requirements in AASs 27, 29 and 31, substantively unamended (with some exceptions), into topic-based Standards.

In the longer term the focus will be on improving the requirements for each topic-based issue where necessary. The longer-term review will be carried out in stages as outlined in the AASB's Public Sector Policy Paper *Australian Accounting Standards and Public Sector Entities*.

AASB 1050 in the Context of the Review of AASs 27, 29 and 31

The Board decided to relocate the requirements for the disclosure of administered items from AAS 29, substantively unamended (with some exceptions, as noted in Appendix A), into a new topic-based Standard.

The Board outlined its short-term proposals in Exposure Draft ED 156 *Proposals Arising from the Short-term Review of the Requirements in AAS 27, AAS 29 and AAS 31*, which was issued in June 2007.

Main Features of this Standard

Application Date

This Standard is applicable to annual reporting periods beginning on or after 1 July 2008. Early adoption is permitted for annual reporting periods beginning on or after 1 January 2005, but before 1 July 2008, provided there is early adoption for the same annual reporting period of the following pronouncements being issued at about the same time, as applicable:

(a)   AASB 1004 *Contributions*;

(b)   AASB 1049 *Whole of Government and General Government Sector Financial Reporting*;

(c)   AASB 1051 *Land Under Roads*;

(d)   AASB 1052 *Disaggregated Disclosures*;

(e)   AASB 2007-9 *Amendments to Australian Accounting Standards arising from the Review of AASs 27, 29 and 31*; and

(f)   AASB Interpretation 1038 *Contributions by Owners Made to Wholly-Owned Public Sector Entities*.

AASB

Main Requirements

This Standard only applies to general purpose financial statements of government departments. The main requirements are for a government department to:

(a)   disclose administered income, showing separately each major class of income; and in respect of each major class of income, the amounts reliably attributable to each of the government department's activities and the amounts not attributable to activities (paragraph 7(a));

(b)   disclose administered expenses, showing separately each major class of expense; and in respect of each major class of expense, the amounts reliably attributable to each of the government department's activities and the amounts not attributable to activities (paragraph 7(b));

(c)   apply the principles of AASB 1052 in disclosing administered income and expenses reliably attributable to activities (paragraph 8);

(d)   disclose administered assets and administered liabilities, showing separately each major class of asset and liability (paragraph 7(c) and (d));

(e)   disclose, in relation to transfers that are not controlled by the government department, the details of the broad categories of recipients and the amounts transferred to those recipients (paragraph 22); and

(f)   report administered income, expenses, assets and liabilities on the same basis adopted for the recognition of the elements of the financial statements (paragraph 24).

Comparison with International Pronouncements

This Standard contains relevant requirements for the disclosure of administered items by government departments that have been relocated from AAS 29 *Financial Reporting by Government Departments* in substantially unamended form (with some exceptions, as noted in Appendix A). Accordingly, the development of this Standard did not involve consideration of International Public Sector Accounting Standards (IPSASs) issued by the International Public Sector Accounting Standards Board (IPSASB) or International Financial Reporting Standards (IFRSs) issued by the International Accounting Standards Board (IASB).

The longer-term review of accounting for administered items will involve consideration of international pronouncements.

AASB 1050 and IPSASs

At the date of issue, this Standard has no corresponding IPSAS dealing specifically with administered items. Consistent with this Standard, paragraph 12 of IPSAS 9 *Revenue from Exchange Transactions* notes that amounts collected on behalf of third parties in a custodial or agency relationship are excluded from revenue.

The IPSASB is undertaking a project to develop a public sector conceptual framework. Administered items is a topic that will be addressed as part of that project.

AASB 1050 and IFRSs

At the date of issue, this Standard has no corresponding IFRS dealing specifically with administered items. Consistent with this Standard, paragraph 8 of IAS 18 *Revenue* notes that amounts collected on behalf of third parties in an agency relationship are not revenue. In addition, where a bank is engaged in significant trust activities (which excludes safe custody functions), paragraph 55 of IAS 30 *Disclosures in the Financial Statements of Banks and Similar Financial Institutions* (superseded by IFRS 7 *Financial Instruments: Disclosures* from 1 January 2007) requires the disclosure of that fact and an indication of the extent of those activities.

Accounting Standard AASB 1050

The Australian Accounting Standards Board makes Accounting Standard AASB 1050 *Administered Items*.

D.G. Boymal
Chair – AASB

Dated 13 December 2007

Accounting Standard AASB 1050
Administered Items

Objective

1   The objective of this Standard is to specify requirements for government departments
relating to administered items. Disclosures made in accordance with this Standard
provide users with information relevant to assessing the performance of a government
department, including accountability for resources entrusted to it.

Application

2   This Standard applies to general purpose financial statements of government
departments.

3   This Standard applies to annual reporting periods beginning on or after 1 July 2008.

4   This Standard may be applied to annual reporting periods beginning on or after
1 January 2005 but before 1 July 2008, provided there is early adoption for the same
annual reporting period of the following pronouncements being issued at about the
same time, as applicable:

(a)   AASB 1004 *Contributions*;

(b)   AASB 1049 *Whole of Government and General Government Sector Financial
Reporting*;

(c)   AASB 1051 *Land Under Roads*;

(d)   AASB 1052 *Disaggregated Disclosures*;

(e)   AASB 2007-9 *Amendments to Australian Accounting Standards arising from
the Review of AASs 27, 29 and 31*; and

(f)   AASB Interpretation 1038 *Contributions by Owners Made to Wholly-Owned
Public Sector Entities*.

5   The requirements specified in this Standard apply to the complete set of financial
statements where information resulting from their application is material in
accordance with AASB 1031 *Materiality*.

6   When applicable, this Standard, together with the Standards referred to in
paragraph 4, supersede AAS 29 *Financial Reporting by Government Departments* as
issued in June 1998, as amended.

Disclosure of Administered Income, Expenses, Assets and Liabilities

7   A government department shall disclose the following in its complete set of financial
statements in relation to activities administered by the government department:

(a)   administered income, showing separately:

(i)   each major class of income; and

(ii)   in respect of each major class of income, the amounts reliably
attributable to each of the government department's activities and the
amounts not attributable to activities;

(b)   administered expenses, showing separately:

(i)   each major class of expense; and

(ii)   in respect of each major class of expense, the amounts reliably
attributable to each of the government department's activities and the
amounts not attributable to activities;

(c)   administered assets, showing separately each major class of asset; and

(d)   administered liabilities, showing separately each major class of liability.

8 AASB 1052 specifies requirements for the disclosure of income and expenses attributable to a government department's activities. The principles in that Standard are applied in disclosing administered income and expenses reliably attributable to activities in accordance with paragraphs 7(a)(ii) and 7(b)(ii) of this Standard.

9 A government department's operating statement only recognises income and expenses of the government department. Similarly, a government department's statement of financial position only recognises assets that the government department controls and liabilities that involve a future sacrifice of the government department's assets.

10 Items recognised in the statement of financial position include the assets and liabilities of the trusts that the government department controls and from whose activities the government department obtains benefits.

11 The responsibilities of a government department may encompass the levying or collection of taxes, fines and fees, the provision of goods and services at a charge to recipients, and the transfer of funds to eligible beneficiaries. These activities may give rise to income and expenses that are not attributable to the government department. This occurs, for example, where the government department is unable to use for its own purposes the proceeds of user charges, taxes, fines and fees it collects without further authorisation, or where the transfer of funds to eligible beneficiaries does not involve a reduction in the assets recognised in the government department's statement of financial position. In addition, the government department may manage government assets in the capacity of an agent and may incur liabilities that, for example, while involving a future disbursement from the Consolidated Revenue Fund or other Fund will not involve a sacrifice of the assets that the government department controls as at the end of the reporting period. This administered income and these administered expenses, assets and liabilities are not recognised in the government department's operating statement or statement of financial position.

12 A government department's ability to control all, or a portion of, the proceeds of the user charges, fines and fees it levies may be subject to complex arrangements. Consistent with those arrangements, where a government department does not control any of the proceeds of the user charges, fines and fees that it levies, it does not recognise any of the proceeds of those user charges, fines and fees as income. Similarly, where, as a result of automatic appropriations or other authority, a government department controls some but not all of the proceeds of user charges, fines and fees, the department recognises as income only those amounts that it controls.

13 If taxes, fines, fees and other amounts that are not controlled by a government department were to be recognised as assets or income by the collecting government department, users could incorrectly assume that these amounts were available for the government department's use.

14 The tax revenues, user charges, fines and fees administered by a government department and the amount of funds transferred to eligible beneficiaries are an important indicator of the government department's performance in achieving its objectives. Therefore, paragraph 7 requires disclosure of income and expenses administered by a government department that are not recognised in the government department's operating statement. Disclosure of this information by major class and by activity facilitates an assessment of activity costs and cost recoveries, and is therefore relevant to parliamentary decision making and enhances the discharge of accountability obligations. Even though a government department does not control such items, the effective and efficient administration of these items is an important role of the government department.

Taxes

15 It is unlikely that taxes, for example, income tax, will qualify as income of the agency responsible for their collection, for example, the Australian Taxation Office, or the central agency responsible for management of the Consolidated Revenue Fund, Trust Fund or other Fund, for example, Treasury. This is because the agency responsible for collecting taxes does not normally control the future economic benefits embodied in tax collections. Similarly, Treasury may be responsible for bank accounts into which tax collections are deposited, but until parliament has 'appropriated funds' for Treasury use or authorised the Treasury to make payments, the Treasury will not control those tax revenues.

16   Parliamentary appropriations made to enable the tax collection agency to perform its services are income of that agency. This is because the agency has the authority to deploy the appropriated funds for the achievement of its objectives and, consequently, controls the assets arising from the appropriation.

Transfer Payments

17   A government department does not recognise as income and expenses those amounts that the government department is responsible for transferring to eligible beneficiaries, consistent with legislation or other authority, but that the government department does not control. If these amounts were recognised as income on receipt by the government department and as expenses on payment by the government department, users could incorrectly assume that the government department controlled these amounts. Nevertheless, this Standard requires such amounts to be disclosed in the complete set of financial statements because that information may be relevant for understanding the government department's financial performance, including assessments of accountability. Even though a government department does not control such items, their effective and efficient administration is an important role of the government department.

18   Consistent with a government department's objectives and with legislation or other authority, amounts appropriated to government departments may include amounts to be transferred to third parties or recoupment of such amounts previously transferred by the government department. Such transfers may encompass payments for unemployment benefits, family allowances, age and invalid pensions, disaster relief, and grants and subsidies made to other governments or to other government or private sector entities.

19   Whether a government department recognises the amounts appropriated for transfer during the reporting period as income, and the amounts transferred during that reporting period as expenses, depends on whether the government department controls the assets to be transferred, and whether the amounts subsequently transferred constitute a reduction in the net assets of the government department.

20   Where amounts are transferred to eligible beneficiaries and the identity of the beneficiaries and the amounts to be transferred to them are determined by reference to legislation or other authority, it is unlikely that the government department controls the funds to be transferred. The government department is merely the agent responsible for the administration of the transfer process. As such, the government department does not benefit from the assets held for transfer, nor does it have the capacity to deny or regulate the access of eligible beneficiaries to the assets. Accordingly, the government department does not recognise assets and income in respect of amounts appropriated for transfer, nor expenses in respect of the amounts subsequently transferred.

21   Although transfers not controlled by a government department do not qualify for recognition in the financial statements, information about their nature and amount is relevant for understanding the government department's financial performance.

22   Details of the broad categories of recipients and the amounts transferred to those recipients shall be disclosed in the government department's complete set of financial statements.

23   In some cases it may not be clear whether the government department controls amounts to be transferred to eligible beneficiaries. For example, amounts may be appropriated to a government department for subsequent transfer, but the government department can exercise significant discretion in determining the amount or timing of payment, the identity of beneficiaries and the conditions under which the payments are to be made. In such cases, preparers and auditors use their judgement in deciding whether the government department controls the amounts to be transferred.

Accounting Basis

24   To facilitate the assessment of the costs incurred and the cost recoveries generated as a result of the government department's activities, administered income, expenses, assets and liabilities are reported on the same basis adopted for the recognition of the elements of the financial statements.

Display of Information about Administered Items

25 The manner in which administered transactions are displayed in the financial statements of a government department will depend on the administrative arrangements adopted by the controlling government, and may therefore vary from jurisdiction to jurisdiction. For example, in some jurisdictions it may be appropriate for administered transactions to be displayed as a separate schedule to the operating statement and/or the statement of financial position. In other jurisdictions, a government department's accountability for administered transactions may mean that it is appropriate for administered transactions to be displayed with, but clearly distinguishable from, the government department's operating statement and/or statement of financial position.

Appendix A
Comparison of AASB 1050 with AAS 29

This Appendix accompanies, but is not part of, AASB 1050.

This Standard reproduces the requirements relating to administered items contained in AAS 29, except that:

(a) paragraph 5.2.5 of AAS 29 encouraged disclosure of items collected or distributed on behalf of another entity or held in legal custody that are neither administered nor controlled. This Standard does not contain such an encouragement;

(b) in relation to transfer payments, paragraph 10.5.15 of AAS 29 noted that transfer payments not controlled by a government department do not qualify for recognition. However, the paragraph contemplated disclosure of the broad categories of recipients and the amounts transferred to those recipients. Paragraph 22 of this Standard requires such disclosures;

(c) paragraph 12.9.4 of AAS 29 encouraged the disclosure of information about administered assets and administered liabilities on an activity basis. This Standard does not contain such an encouragement; and

(d) paragraph 8 of this Standard requires the principles in AASB 1052 *Disaggregated Disclosures* to be applied in disclosing administered income and expenses reliably attributable to activities. AAS 29 did not include such a specific requirement.

The following table provides source references to paragraphs 7 – 25 of this Standard, most of which were derived from AAS 29. It is provided to facilitate an understanding of, and assist in the application of, the requirements in this Standard.

Paragraph in AASB 1050	Relevant source paragraph/s in AAS 29
7	12.9
8	New paragraph
9	12.9.1
10	5.2.5
11	12.9.2
12	10.4.2
13	6.3.11
14	12.9.3 and last sentence of 6.3.11
15	10.5.9
16	First two sentences of paragraph 10.5.10
17	6.3.12
18	10.5.11
19	10.5.12
20	10.5.13
21 – 22	10.5.15
23	10.5.16
24	12.9.6
25	12.9.5

Basis for Conclusions

This Basis for Conclusions accompanies, but is not part of, AASB 1050.

Introduction

BC1 This Basis for Conclusions summarises the Board's considerations in developing this Standard in the context of the Board's short-term review of the requirements in AAS 27 *Financial Reporting by Local Governments*, AAS 29 *Financial Reporting by Government Departments* and AAS 31 *Financial Reporting by Governments*.

Background

BC2 The Board considered it timely to review the requirements in AASs 27, 29 and 31, in particular to:

    (a) review the extent to which local governments, government departments and governments should continue to be subject to requirements that differ from requirements applicable to other not-for-profit entities and for-profit entities contained in Australian Accounting Standards. The Board concluded that differences should be removed, where appropriate and timely, to improve the overall quality of financial reporting;

    (b) bring requirements applicable to local governments, government departments and governments up-to-date with contemporary accounting thought;

    (c) consider the implications of the outcomes of its project on the harmonisation of Generally Accepted Accounting Principles (GAAP) and Government Finance Statistics (GFS), in particular on the requirements in AAS 31;

    (d) decide whether the encouragements in AASs 27, 29 and 31 should be made mandatory or removed; and

    (e) remove uncertainty in the application of cross-references to other Australian Accounting Standards and the override provisions in AASs 27, 29 and 31 that made the requirements in AASs 27, 29 and 31 take precedence over other requirements.

BC3 The Board considered the following alternative mechanisms for implementing the approach of updating and improving the requirements for local governments, government departments and governments:

    (a) review the requirements in AASs 27, 29 and 31 and where appropriate:

        (i) amend other Australian Accounting Standards to pick up any issues that are addressed in AASs 27, 29 and 31 that are not adequately addressed in the latest Australian Accounting Standards and have them apply to local governments, government departments and governments; or

        (ii) create public sector specific topic-based Standards;

    and consequently withdraw AASs 27, 29 and 31; or

    (b) review AASs 27, 29 and 31 and re-issue them in light of the latest Australian Accounting Standards, retaining/amending where necessary any issues that are addressed in AASs 27, 29 and 31 that are not adequately addressed in the latest Australian Accounting Standards.

BC4 The Board chose alternative (a), given the improvements in the quality of financial reporting by local governments, government departments and governments since AASs 27, 29 and 31 were first issued.

BC5 Where the Board identified that the material in AASs 27, 29 and 31 could be improved within time and resource constraints, improvements have been made. Much of the material in AASs 27, 29 and 31 has been retained substantively unamended. Improvements will be progressed in due course in line with the AASB's Public Sector Policy Paper *Australian Accounting Standards and Public Sector Entities*.

BC6 The first stage of the short-term review of the requirements in AASs 27, 29 and 31 was the preparation of a paragraph-by-paragraph analysis of each of AASs 27, 29 and 31, listing each paragraph of each Standard alongside corresponding Standards or other pronouncements that would apply to local governments, government departments or governments in the absence of AASs 27, 29 and 31. The Board's conclusions and rationale for the treatment of each paragraph in the context of the review were also provided in the analysis. The Board's primary focus was on dealing with the requirements from the three Standards in such a way as to not leave a vacuum.

BC7　Each paragraph from AASs 27, 29 and 31 was classified as being:

(a)　no longer needed or adequately dealt with in other Standards;

(b)　more appropriately dealt with in other Standards; or

(c)　not adequately and/or appropriately dealt with in other Standards and therefore should be retained or improved and incorporated into other Standards.

The paragraph-by-paragraph analyses considered by the AASB in developing the Exposure Draft ED 156 *Proposals Arising from the Short-term Review of the Requirements in AAS 27, AAS 29 and AAS 31* that gave rise to this Standard are available on the AASB website. They support, but do not form part of, this Basis for Conclusions.

BC8　In reviewing the paragraphs, the Board noted that some material in AASs 27, 29 and 31 would, under the current style of writing Standards, be located in a separate Basis for Conclusions. For example, paragraph 6.3.12 of AAS 29 provides a rationale for the disclosure of information about administered items. Given the short-term nature of the review of AASs 27, 29 and 31, the Board concluded that explanations of technical issues that both originated in and are being relocated from AASs 27, 29 and 31 should, when appropriate, be located in the body of the Standard to which the relevant requirements are being relocated.

BC9　The Board decided not to retain the illustrative general purpose financial reports provided in AASs 27, 29 and 31, because their purpose, which was to provide an educational tool in the initial stages of accrual reporting by local governments, government departments and governments, is no longer needed.

BC10 The remainder of this Basis for Conclusions focuses on issues specific to administered items.

Administered Items

Location of Requirements

BC11 Consistent with paragraphs BC3(a)(ii) and BC7(c), the Board decided to retain the existing requirements and guidance relating to administered items from AAS 29 and include them, substantively unchanged (although see paragraphs BC15 – BC17 below).

BC12 As an alternative, the Board considered locating the material in an existing Standard such as AASB 101 *Presentation of Financial Statements*. However, the Board concluded that:

(a)　the material is sufficiently dissimilar from the other requirements of AASB 101 to warrant a separate Standard; and

(b)　a new Standard on administered items would make the requirements easily identifiable by those financial report preparers and auditors most affected by the requirements.

Short-term Retention of Acknowledged Inadequacies

BC13 The Board noted that some of the acknowledged inadequacies in AAS 29 are retained, including the lack of extensive guidance for identifying administered items and the potential inadequate prominence given to administered items in a complete set of financial statements. The Board decided that this is justified on the basis that this Standard is a short-term measure until such time as the Board undertakes a longer-term project on administered items as part of a broader review.

Application Limited to Government Departments

BC14 The Board concluded that it is appropriate for government departments, including for-profit government departments, to be subject to this Standard, consistent with the range of entities that were subject to AAS 29. The Board also concluded that it is appropriate to limit the application of this Standard to government departments because extending the application of the requirements as part of the short-term review would delay the short-term project and impinge on the issues to be addressed in the longer term. The Board noted that, as a part of the Board's fundamental longer-term review of the requirements in AAS 29, consideration will be given to the different treatments available that would result in administered items being given more prominence and disclosed in more detail in the general purpose financial statements of government departments and other entities.

Treatment of Encouragements in AAS 29

BC15 In line with paragraph BC2(d), the Board considered whether the encouragement in paragraph 5.2.5 of AAS 29 should be removed or amended to require items collected or distributed on behalf of another entity or held in legal custody that are neither administered nor controlled to be disclosed. The Board concluded that the encouragement should be removed. This is in acknowledgement of the implementation difficulties related to the lack of clarity in the short term about the definition of 'items that a government department collects or distributes on behalf of another entity that are neither controlled nor administered items'. The Board noted that this issue will be addressed as part of the planned longer-term more fundamental review of requirements relating to administered items.

BC16 Also consistent with paragraph BC2(d), the Board decided that, although transfers not controlled by a government department (such as, in general, pensions paid to beneficiaries) do not qualify for recognition, details of the broad categories of recipients and the amounts transferred to those recipients should be required to be disclosed in a complete set of financial statements (see paragraph 22 of this Standard). This is because the resulting information is relevant for understanding the government department's financial performance.

BC17 Paragraph 12.9.4 of AAS 29 encouraged the disclosure of information about administered assets and administered liabilities on an activity basis. Again, consistent with paragraph BC2(d), the Board concluded that the encouragement should be removed, noting that its removal does not create a vacuum.

Other Changes to Requirements in AAS 29

BC18 The Board decided to delete the following sentence in paragraph 12.9.6 of AAS 29: "In some jurisdictions, this may mean that the basis adopted by a government department for reporting administered items may differ from the basis adopted by the government itself". The Board considers this sentence to be redundant, given that government departments are typically directed to adopt particular policies by their controlling government.

AASB 1051
Land Under Roads

(Issued December 2007)

AASB

Note from the Institute of Chartered Accountants Australia

This note, prepared by the technical editors, is not part of Accounting Standard AASB 1051.

Historical development

13 December 2007: AASB 1051 'Land Under Roads' was issued by the AASB.

In October and December 2007 the AASB issued new and revised AASB 1004 'Contributions', AASB 1049 'Whole of Government and General Government Sector Financial Reporting', AASB 1050 'Administered Items', AASB 1051 'Land Under Roads', AASB 1052 'Disaggregated Disclosures', AASB Interpretation 1038 'Contributions by Owners Made to Wholly-Owned Public Sector Entities' and AASB 2007-9 'Amendments to Australian Accounting Standards arising from the Review of AAS 27, AAS 29 and AAS 31'. These revisions result from a short-term review, primarily focused on relocating, where necessary, the requirements in AASs 27, 29 and 31, substantively unamended (with some exceptions), into topic-based Standards.

These Standards and Interpretation apply to annual reporting periods beginning on or after 1 July 2008, with early adoption permitted. These Standards supersede AAS 27, AAS 29 and AAS 31.

Contents

Preface

Comparison with International Pronouncements

Accounting Standard
AASB 1051 Land Under Roads

Paragraphs

Objective   1

Application   2 – 6

Land Under Roads   7 – 15

Appendices:

A. Defined Terms

B. Comparison of AASB 1051 with AASs 27, 29 and 31

C. Implementation Guidance

Basis for Conclusions

Australian Accounting Standard AASB 1051 *Land Under Roads* is set out in paragraphs 1 – 15 and Appendix A. All the paragraphs have equal authority. Paragraphs in **bold type** state the main principles. Terms defined in this Standard are in *italics* the first time they appear in the Standard. AASB 1051 is to be read in the context of other Australian Accounting Standards, including AASB 1048 *Interpretation and Application of Standards*, which identifies the Australian Accounting Interpretations. In the absence of explicit guidance, AASB 108 *Accounting Policies, Changes in Accounting Estimates and Errors* provides a basis for selecting and applying accounting policies.

Preface

Background

Australian Accounting Standards incorporate International Financial Reporting Standards (IFRSs), as issued by the International Accounting Standards Board (IASB), with the addition of paragraphs on the applicability of the Standard in the Australian environment.

Some Australian Accounting Standards also include requirements that are specific to Australian entities. In most instances, these requirements are restricted to not-for-profit entities, including public sector entities, or include additional disclosures that address domestic, regulatory or other issues.

Reasons for Issuing this Standard

AAS 27 *Financial Reporting by Local Governments*, AAS 29 *Financial Reporting by Government Departments* and AAS 31 *Financial Reporting by Governments* were first issued in 1991, 1993 and 1996 respectively. While AASs 27, 29 and 31 had been subject to a number of limited reviews since then, the requirements in these Standards needed a comprehensive review because:

(a)   there had been significant developments in Australian financial reporting, in particular adopting IFRSs within Australian Accounting Standards, for reporting periods beginning on or after 1 January 2005. As a result of these developments, uncertainties emerged as to the application of cross-references to other Australian Accounting Standards and the override provisions in AASs 27, 29 and 31 that made the requirements in AASs 27, 29 and 31 take precedence over other requirements;

(b)   local governments, government departments and governments were subject to requirements that differed from requirements applicable to other not-for-profit entities and for-profit entities contained in Australian Accounting Standards. An objective of the Board is to put in place transaction-neutral standards that will treat like transactions and events consistently;

(c)   the Board had made significant progress in its project on the harmonisation of Generally Accepted Accounting Principles (GAAP) and Government Finance Statistics (GFS) so far as it relates to the General Government Sector (GGS) and the whole of government of the federal, state and territory governments. It was therefore particularly timely to review the requirements in AAS 31;

(d)   they did not reflect contemporary accounting thought; and

(e)   they did not reflect the current style of drafting standards, which is to specify principles rather than rules, and requirements rather than encouragements.

The Board intends to continue with its policy of developing a common accounting standards framework for both for-profit and not-for-profit entities whilst acknowledging differences in some areas. The Board is committed to having a platform of topic-based transaction-neutral Standards that will apply to the public sector.

Review of AASs 27, 29 and 31

The Board initiated a project for reviewing the requirements in AASs 27, 29 and 31, divided into two phases comprising a short-term and a longer-term review.

The primary focus in the short-term has been on relocating, where necessary, the requirements in AASs 27, 29 and 31, substantively unamended (with some exceptions), into topic-based Standards.

In the longer term the focus will be on improving the requirements for each topic-based issue where necessary. The longer-term review will be carried out in stages as outlined in the AASB's Public Sector Policy Paper *Australian Accounting Standards and Public Sector Entities*.

AASB 1051 in the Context of the Review of AASs 27, 29 and 31

The Board outlined proposals for transitional requirements relating to land under roads in Exposure Draft ED 156 *Proposals Arising from the Short-term Review of the Requirements in AAS 27, AAS 29 and AAS 31*, which was issued in June 2007. In the light of responses to ED 156, the Board decided to make substantial changes to those proposals. The Board also decided to locate the amended requirements into a new topic-based Standard.

Main Features of this Standard

Application Date

This Standard is applicable to annual reporting periods beginning on or after 1 July 2008. Early adoption is permitted for annual reporting periods beginning on or after 1 January 2005, but before 1 July 2008, provided there is early adoption for the same annual reporting period of the following pronouncements being issued at about the same time, as applicable:

(a)   AASB 1004 *Contributions*;

(b)   AASB 1049 *Whole of Government and General Government Sector Financial Reporting*;

(c)   AASB 1050 *Administered Items*;

(d)   AASB 1052 *Disaggregated Disclosures*;

(e)   AASB 2007-9 *Amendments to Australian Accounting Standards arising from the Review of AASs 27, 29 and 31*; and

(f)   AASB Interpretation 1038 *Contributions by Owners Made to Wholly-Owned Public Sector Entities*.

Main Requirements

This Standard, which applies to general purpose financial statements of local governments, government departments, GGSs and whole of governments:

(a)   allows an entity to elect to recognise (including continue to recognise or recognise for the first time), subject to satisfaction of asset recognition criteria, or not to recognise (including continue to not recognise or to derecognise) as an asset, land under roads acquired before the end of the first reporting period ending on or after 31 December 2007. A final election is to be made effective as at the first day of the next reporting period following the end of the first reporting period ending on or after 31 December 2007;

(b)   requires that any adjustments that arise from an election be made against accumulated surplus (deficiency);

(c)   requires an entity to disclose its accounting policy for land under roads acquired before the end of the first reporting period ending on or after 31 December 2007;

(d)   allows an entity, in relation to land under roads acquired before the end of the first reporting period ending on or after 31 December 2007, to elect to adopt the fair value (as at the date of that election) or a previous revaluation under the "fair value or revaluation as deemed cost" exemptions contained in AASB 1 *First-time Adoption of Australian Equivalents to International Financial Reporting Standards*, as if it were adopting Australian equivalents to IFRSs for the first time. This applies where an entity recognises that land under roads after the entity's first-time adoption of Australian equivalents to IFRSs. The election must be made effective as at the first day of the next reporting period following the end of the first reporting period ending on or after 31 December 2007; and

(e)   clarifies that the principles in other Standards (including AASB 116 *Property, Plant and Equipment*) apply to land under roads, except to the extent that this Standard requires or permits otherwise, including the requirement that land under roads acquired after the end of the first reporting period ending on or after 31 December 2007 is accounted for in accordance with AASB 116.

Comparison with International Pronouncements

AASB 1051 and International Public Sector Accounting Standards

International Public Sector Accounting Standards (IPSASs) are issued by the International Public Sector Accounting Standards Board (IPSASB).

Land under roads falls within the scope of IPSAS 17 *Property, Plant and Equipment* (issued December 2001, amended February 2007).

IPSAS 17 does not require recognition of land under roads (and other property, plant and equipment) for reporting periods beginning on a date within five years following the date of first adoption of accrual accounting in accordance with IPSASs. However, at the expiry of the transitional period, holdings of land under roads must be recognised where they satisfy the recognition criteria. The effect of the initial recognition of land under roads is accounted for as an adjustment to the opening balance of accumulated surpluses or deficits. When an entity elects to not recognise land under roads within the transitional period, certain disclosures must be made.

This Standard does not require the recognition of land under roads acquired before the end of the first reporting period ending on or after 31 December 2007. If an entity decides to recognise such land then, under this Standard, the entity may elect, in certain circumstances, to apply the fair value or a previous revaluation under the "fair value or revaluation as deemed cost" exemptions in AASB 1 *First-time Adoption of Australian Equivalents to International Financial Reporting Standards*. In contrast, IPSAS 17 requires an entity that adopts accrual accounting for the first time in accordance with IPSASs to initially recognise land under roads at cost or fair value. For items acquired at no cost, or for a nominal cost, cost is the item's fair value as at the date of acquisition.

Land under roads acquired after the end of the first reporting period ending on or after 31 December 2007 is accounted for under AASB 116 *Property, Plant and Equipment*. AASB 116 contains a comparison with the corresponding IPSAS 17.

AASB

AASB 1051 and International Financial Reporting Standards

Land under roads falls within the scope of IAS 16 *Property, Plant and Equipment*, which does not contain requirements or choices equivalent to this Standard for land under roads acquired before the end of the first reporting period ending on or after 31 December 2007.

Land under roads acquired after the end of the first reporting period ending on or after 31 December 2007 is accounted for under AASB 116. AASB 116 contains a comparison with the corresponding IAS 16.

This Standard allows an entity to elect, in certain circumstances, to apply the fair value or a previous revaluation under the "fair value or revaluation as deemed cost exemptions" in AASB 1. AASB 1 contains a comparison with the corresponding IFRS 1 *First-time Adoption of International Financial Reporting Standards*.

Accounting Standard AASB 1051

The Australian Accounting Standards Board makes Accounting Standard AASB 1051 *Land Under Roads*.

Dated 13 December 2007

D.G. Boymal
Chair – AASB

Accounting Standard AASB 1051

Land Under Roads

Objective

1   The objective of this Standard is to specify the requirements for financial reporting of *land under roads* by local governments, government departments, General Government Sectors (GGSs) and whole of governments.

Application

2   **This Standard applies to general purpose financial statements of local governments, government departments and whole of governments, and financial statements of GGSs.**

3   **This Standard applies to annual reporting periods beginning on or after 1 July 2008.**

4   **This Standard may be applied to annual reporting periods beginning on or after 1 January 2005 but before 1 July 2008, provided there is early adoption for the same annual reporting period of the following pronouncements being issued at about the same time, as applicable:**

   (a)   **AASB 1004 *Contributions*;**

   (b)   **AASB 1049 *Whole of Government and General Government Sector Financial Reporting*;**

   (c)   **AASB 1050 *Administered Items*;**

   (d)   **AASB 1052 *Disaggregated Disclosures*;**

   (e)   **AASB 2007-9 *Amendments to Australian Accounting Standards arising from the Review of AASs 27, 29 and 31*; and**

   (f)   **AASB Interpretation 1038 *Contributions by Owners Made to Wholly-Owned Public Sector Entities*.**

5   **The requirements specified in this Standard apply to the financial statements where information resulting from their application is material in accordance with AASB 1031 *Materiality*.**

6   **When applicable, this Standard, together with the Standards referred to in paragraph 4, supersede:**

   (a)   **AAS 27 *Financial Reporting by Local Governments* as issued in June 1996, as amended;**

(b)   AAS 29 *Financial Reporting by Government Departments* as issued in June 1998, as amended; and

(c)   AAS 31 *Financial Reporting by Governments* as issued in June 1998, as amended.

Land Under Roads

7   Other Australian Accounting Standards (including AASB 116 *Property, Plant and Equipment*) apply to land under roads, except to the extent that this Standard requires or permits otherwise.

8   An entity may elect to recognise (including continue to recognise or to recognise for the first time), subject to satisfaction of the asset recognition criteria, or not to recognise (including continue not to recognise or to derecognise) as an asset, land under roads acquired before the end of the first reporting period ending on or after 31 December 2007.

9   An entity shall make a final election under paragraph 8 effective as at the first day of the next reporting period following the end of the first reporting period ending on or after 31 December 2007. Any adjustments that arise from a final election that is made effective as at that first day shall be made against the opening balance of accumulated surplus (deficiency) of that next reporting period.

10   Adjustments arising under paragraph 9 include those relating to a revision of recognised amounts of previously recognised land under roads acquired before the end of the first reporting period ending on or after 31 December 2007, made to reflect a reassessment of the factors used to determine those recognised amounts. Any adjustments that arise from an election that is made effective:

(a)   before the first day of the next reporting period following the end of the first reporting period ending on or after 31 December 2007, is made against accumulated surplus (deficiency) of the earliest prior period presented, and therefore comparative data is adjusted; and

(b)   on the first day of the next reporting period following the end of the first reporting period ending on or after 31 December 2007, is made against the opening balance of accumulated surplus (deficiency) of that next reporting period, and therefore comparative data is not adjusted.

11   An entity shall disclose its accounting policy for land under roads acquired before the end of the first reporting period ending on or after 31 December 2007, in each reporting period to which this Standard is applied.

12   The nature and net amount of each adjustment made in accordance with paragraph 9 shall be disclosed.

13   Where an entity recognises land under roads in accordance with paragraphs 8 and 9, but after the entity's first-time adoption of Australian equivalents to International Financial Reporting Standards (IFRSs), the entity may, in relation to land under roads, elect to adopt the fair value (as at the date of that election) or a previous revaluation under the "fair value or revaluation as deemed cost" exemptions contained in AASB 1 *First-time Adoption of Australian Equivalents to International Financial Reporting Standards*, as if it were adopting Australian equivalents to IFRSs for the first time.

14   Paragraph 13 enables an entity that recognises land under roads acquired before the end of the first reporting period ending on or after 31 December 2007, after its first-time adoption of Australian equivalents to IFRSs and under paragraphs 8 and 9, to elect to:

(a)   measure the fair value of land under roads as at the date of the election made under paragraph 13 and use that fair value as the deemed cost;

(b)   use an earlier revaluation of land under roads as its deemed cost; or

(c)   use an earlier deemed cost of land under roads established from an event-driven fair value measurement as its deemed cost.

15   Land under roads acquired after the end of the first reporting period ending on or after 31 December 2007 is accounted for in accordance with AASB 116.

Appendix A

Defined Terms

This Appendix is an integral part of AASB 1051.

land under roads   Land under roadways, and road reserves, including land under footpaths, nature strips and median strips.

Appendix B

Comparison of AASB 1051 with AASs 27, 29 and 31

This Appendix accompanies, but is not part of, AASB 1051.

The requirements of this Standard differ from the requirements contained in AASs 27 *Financial Reporting by Local Governments*, AAS 29 *Financial Reporting by Government Departments* and AAS 31 *Financial Reporting by Governments* (as amended), and expresses the requirements generically. The main differences between AASB 1051 and AASs 27, 29 and 31 (as amended) are:

(a)   this Standard extends indefinitely the relief from the requirement to recognise land under roads acquired before the end of the first reporting period ending on or after 31 December 2007. AASs 27, 29 and 31 provided recognition relief only for a transitional period;

(b)   AASs 27, 29 and 31 encouraged entities to recognise land under roads as an asset wherever it can be measured reliably. Consistent with the AASB's policy of not including encouragements within Standards, this encouragement has not been included in this Standard;

(c)   this Standard notes that AASB 116 *Property, Plant and Equipment* applies to land under roads acquired after the end of the first reporting period ending on or after 31 December 2007. AASs 27, 29 and 31 would have required that AASB 116 be retrospectively applied to land under roads after the end of the transitional period;

(d)   in certain circumstances this Standard allows an entity, in relation to land under roads acquired before the end of the first reporting period ending on or after 31 December 2007, to elect to adopt the fair value (as at the date of that election) or a previous revaluation under the "fair value or revaluation as deemed cost" exemptions contained in AASB 1 *First-time Adoption of Australian Equivalents to International Financial Reporting Standards*, as if it were adopting Australian equivalents to IFRSs for the first time. AASs 27, 29 and 31 did not contain this relief;

(e)   AASs 29 and 31 did not explicitly require that, if the recognised amounts of land under roads acquired before the end of the first reporting period ending on or after 31 December 2007 are revised, up until the first day of the next reporting period, to reflect a reassessment of the factors used to determine those recognised amounts, the net amount of the resultant adjustments be made against accumulated surplus (deficiency) in the reporting periods in which the recognised amounts are revised; and

(f)   this Standard extends the requirements to General Government Sectors.

Appendix C

Implementation Guidance

This Appendix accompanies, but is not part of, AASB 1051.

The following diagram illustrates the effect of the requirements in this Standard for land under roads acquired before 1 July 2008, assuming an entity with a 1 July 2008 to 30 June 2009 reporting period makes a final election under paragraphs 8 and 9 as at 1 July 2008. (Note that land under roads acquired after 30 June 2008 is accounted for in accordance with AASB 116.)

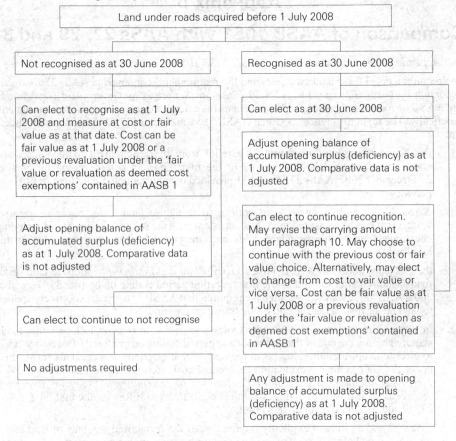

Basis for Conclusions

This Basis for Conclusions accompanies, but is not part of, AASB 1051.

Introduction

BC1 This Basis for Conclusions summarises the Board's considerations in developing this Standard in the context of the Board's short-term review of the requirements in AAS 27 *Financial Reporting by Local Governments*, AAS 29 *Financial Reporting by Government Departments* and AAS 31 *Financial Reporting by Governments*.

Background

BC2 The Board considered it timely to review the requirements in AASs 27, 29 and 31, in particular to:

(a) review the extent to which local governments, government departments and governments should continue to be subject to requirements that differ from requirements applicable to other not-for-profit entities and for-profit entities contained in Australian Accounting Standards. The Board concluded that differences should be removed, where appropriate and timely, to improve the overall quality of financial reporting;

(b) bring requirements applicable to local governments, government departments and governments up-to-date with contemporary accounting thought;

(c) consider the implications of the outcomes of its project on the harmonisation of Generally Accepted Accounting Principles (GAAP) and Government Finance Statistics (GFS), in particular on the requirements in AAS 31;

(d) decide whether the encouragements in AASs 27, 29 and 31 should be made mandatory or removed; and

(e) remove uncertainty in the application of cross-references to other Australian Accounting Standards and the override provisions in AASs 27, 29 and 31 that made the requirements in AASs 27, 29 and 31 take precedence over other requirements.

BC3 The Board considered the following alternative mechanisms for implementing the approach of updating and improving the requirements for local governments, government departments and governments:

(a) review the requirements in AASs 27, 29 and 31 and where appropriate:

(i) amend other Australian Accounting Standards to pick up any issues that are addressed in AASs 27, 29 and 31 that are not adequately addressed in the latest Australian Accounting Standards and have them apply to local governments, government departments and governments; or

(ii) create public sector specific topic-based Standards;

and consequently withdraw AASs 27, 29 and 31; or

(b) review AASs 27, 29 and 31 and re-issue them in light of the latest Australian Accounting Standards, retaining/amending where necessary any issues that are addressed in AASs 27, 29 and 31 that are not adequately addressed in the latest Australian Accounting Standards.

BC4 The Board chose alternative (a) given the improvements in the quality of financial reporting by local governments, government departments and governments since AASs 27, 29 and 31 were first issued.

BC5 Where the Board identified that the material in AASs 27, 29 and 31 could be improved within time and resource constraints, improvements have been made. Much of the material in AASs 27, 29 and 31 has been retained substantively unamended. Improvements will be progressed in due course in line with the AASB's Public Sector Policy Paper *Australian Accounting Standards and Public Sector Entities*.

BC6 The first stage of the short-term review of the requirements in AASs 27, 29 and 31 was the preparation of a paragraph-by-paragraph analysis of each of AASs 27, 29 and 31, listing each paragraph of each Standard alongside corresponding Standards or other pronouncements that would apply to local governments, government departments or governments in the absence of AASs 27, 29 and 31. The Board's conclusions and rationale for the treatment of each paragraph in the context of the review were also provided in the analysis. The Board's primary focus was on dealing with the requirements from the three Standards in such a way as to not leave a vacuum.

BC7   Each paragraph from AASs 27, 29 and 31 was classified as being:

(a)   no longer needed or adequately dealt with in other Standards;

(b)   more appropriately dealt with in other Standards; or

(c)   not adequately and/or appropriately dealt with in other Standards and therefore should be retained or improved and incorporated into other Standards.

The paragraph-by-paragraph analyses considered by the AASB in developing the Exposure Draft ED 156 *Proposals Arising from the Short-term Review of the Requirements in AAS 27, AAS 29 and AAS 31* that gave rise to this Standard are available on the AASB website. They support, but do not form part of, this Basis for Conclusions.

BC8   In reviewing the paragraphs, the Board noted that some material in AASs 27, 29 and 31 would, under the current style of writing Standards, be located in a separate Basis for Conclusions. Given the short-term nature of the review of AASs 27, 29 and 31, the Board concluded that explanations of technical issues that both originated in and are being relocated from AASs 27, 29 and 31 should, when appropriate, be located in the body of the Standard to which the relevant requirements are being relocated.

BC9   The Board decided not to retain the illustrative general purpose financial reports provided in AASs 27, 29 and 31, because their purpose, which was to provide an educational tool in the initial stages of accrual reporting by local governments, government departments and governments, is no longer needed.

BC10 The remainder of this Basis for Conclusions focuses on issues specific to land under roads.

Land Under Roads

BC11 The Board decided to issue this Standard as part of the short-term review of the requirements in AASs 27, 29 and 31 and to amend the previous transitional relief for land under roads, to allow entities to elect whether to recognise land under roads acquired before the end of the first reporting period ending on or after 31 December 2007. This decision is in acknowledgement of the potentially onerous demands on entities if they were to be required to retrospectively identify, assess the recognition criteria, recognise and measure land under roads previously acquired.

BC12 The Board decided that a final election relating to the recognition of land under roads acquired before the end of the first reporting period ending on or after 31 December 2007 should be made effective as at the first day of the next reporting period. The final election can be made at any time prior to the completion of the financial statements for that next reporting period, but will be effective as at the first day of that period. The Board also decided that, to facilitate the transition to the new requirements, any adjustments arising from an election be made against accumulated surplus (deficiency); and that there would be no requirement to adjust comparative data for earlier periods when the election is made effective as at that first day. The Board noted that the extent to which an entity could change its recognition policy after that date would be constrained by the requirements of AASB 108 *Accounting Policies, Changes in Accounting Estimates and Errors* relating to voluntary change in accounting policy. Accordingly, subsequent changes to the accounting policy relating to the recognition of land under roads acquired before the end of the first reporting period ending on or after 31 December 2007 could only be made to recognise land under roads that it previously elected to not recognise (or, conceivably, vice versa) if that change could be justified based on paragraph 14 of AASB 108.

BC13 Consistent with the entities that were subject to AASs 27, 29 and 31, this Standard applies to local governments, government departments (including for-profit government departments), and whole of governments. In addition, the application of this Standard extends to General Government Sectors (GGSs), which facilitates consistency in financial reporting by GGSs and whole of governments.

AASB

BC14 In relation to GGSs and whole of governments, the Board considered the relationship between this Standard and the principle in AASB 1049 *Whole of Government and General Government Sector Financial Reporting* that GGSs and whole of governments should adopt optional treatments in Australian Accounting Standards that align with the principles or rules in the Australian Bureau of Statistics (ABS) Government Finance Statistics (GFS) Manual. The Board noted that the recognition relief provided in this Standard for land under roads is potentially inconsistent with GFS principles. However, the Board also noted that land under roads is not recognised under GFS in practice in certain circumstances, depending on the availability of information pertinent to measurement. Accordingly, the Board concluded that the impact of AASB 1049 relative to this Standard on the recognition of land under roads would be expected to be limited.

BC15 Accordingly, the Board decided that the broad principle adopted in AASB 1049 that a GAAP option should be adopted where it aligns with GFS should be retained without an exception for land under roads. In making this decision, the Board also noted that any difference between GFS principles and practice is beyond the control of the AASB, and that land under roads does not create unique issues in a GAAP/GFS harmonisation context.

BC16 The Board concluded that, in principle, land under roads is property and therefore falls within the scope of AASB 116. Accordingly, it is appropriate that land under roads acquired after the end of the first reporting period ending on or after 31 December 2007 is accounted for in accordance with AASB 116. In making this decision, the Board noted that AASB 116, including paragraph Aus15.1, requires:

(a) assets acquired at no cost, or for a nominal cost, to be initially measured at fair value as at the date of acquisition where fair value can be measured reliably; and

(b) requires assets acquired at a cost to be initially measured at cost, but does not require adoption of the revaluation model. The Board also noted that issues relating to reliable measurement of fair value are not unique to land under roads and therefore could be dealt with in the same manner in which issues for other classes of assets are dealt with under AASB 116.

BC17 The Board also concluded that further requirements should replicate, in certain circumstances, the fair value or a previous revaluation (in accordance with, for example, AASB 1041 *Revaluation of Non-Current Assets* or AASB 116 *Property, Plant and Equipment*) under the "fair value or revaluation as deemed cost" exemptions in AASB 1 *First-time Adoption of Australian Equivalents to International Financial Reporting Standards* on the basis that this would facilitate the initial recognition of land under roads under AASB 116. The requirements would be used when a local government, government department, GGS or whole of government elects to recognise and measure land under roads acquired before the end of the first reporting period ending on or after 31 December 2007 under paragraphs 8 and 9 of this Standard, after its first-time adoption of Australian equivalents to International Financial Reporting Standards.

AASB 1052
Disaggregated Disclosures

(Issued December 2007)

Note from the Institute of Chartered Accountants Australia

This note, prepared by the technical editors, is not part of Accounting Standard AASB 1052.

Historical development

13 December 2007: AASB 1052 'Disaggregated Disclosures' was issued by the AASB.

In October and December 2007 the AASB issued new and revised AASB 1004 'Contributions', AASB 1049 'Whole of Government and General Government Sector Financial Reporting', AASB 1050 'Administered Items', AASB 1051 'Land Under Roads', AASB 1052 'Disaggregated Disclosures', AASB Interpretation 1038 'Contributions by Owners Made to Wholly-Owned Public Sector Entities' and AASB 2007-9 'Amendments to Australian Accounting Standards arising from the Review of AAS 27, AAS 29 and AAS 31'. These revisions result from a short-term review, primarily focused on relocating, where necessary, the requirements in AASs 27, 29 and 31, substantively unamended (with some exceptions), into topic-based Standards.

These Standards and Interpretations apply to annual reporting periods beginning on or after 1 July 2008, with early adoption permitted. These Standards supersede AAS 27, AAS 29 and AAS 31.

Contents

Preface

Comparison with International Pronouncements

Accounting Standard
AASB 1052 Disaggregated Disclosures

	Paragraphs
Objective	1 – 2
Application	3 – 10
Classification According to Function or Activity by Local Governments	11 – 14
Disclosure of Service Costs and Achievements by Government Departments	15 – 19
Identifying Major Activities of Government Departments	20 – 21

Appendix
A. Comparison of AASB 1052 with AASs 27 and 29

Basis for Conclusions

Australian Accounting Standard AASB 1052 *Disaggregated Disclosures* is set out in paragraphs 1 to 21. All the paragraphs have equal authority. Paragraphs in **bold type** state the main principles. AASB 1052 is to be read in the context of other Australian Accounting Standards, including AASB 1048 *Interpretation and Application of Standards*, which identifies the Australian Accounting Interpretations. In the absence of explicit guidance, AASB 108 *Accounting Policies, Changes in Accounting Estimates and Errors* provides a basis for selecting and applying accounting policies.

Preface

Background

Australian Accounting Standards incorporate International Financial Reporting Standards (IFRSs), as issued by the International Accounting Standards Board (IASB), with the addition of paragraphs on the applicability of the Standard in the Australian environment.

Some Australian Accounting Standards also include requirements that are specific to Australian entities. In most instances, these requirements are restricted to not-for-profit entities, including public sector entities, or include additional disclosures that address domestic, regulatory or other issues.

Reasons for Issuing this Standard

AAS 27 *Financial Reporting by Local Governments*, AAS 29 *Financial Reporting by Government Departments* and AAS 31 *Financial Reporting by Governments* were first issued in 1991, 1993 and 1996 respectively. While AASs 27, 29 and 31 had been subject to a number of limited reviews since then, the requirements in these Standards needed a comprehensive review because:

(a) there had been significant developments in Australian financial reporting, in particular adopting International Financial Reporting Standards (IFRSs) within Australian Accounting Standards, for reporting periods beginning on or after 1 January 2005. As a result of these developments, uncertainties emerged as to the application of cross-references to other Australian Accounting Standards and the override provisions in AASs 27, 29 and 31 that made the requirements in AASs 27, 29 and 31 take precedence over other requirements;

(b) local governments, government departments and governments were subject to requirements that differed from requirements applicable to other not-for-profit entities and for-profit entities contained in Australian Accounting Standards. An objective of the Board is to put in place transaction-neutral Standards that will treat like transactions and events consistently;

(c)   the Board had made significant progress in its project on the harmonisation of Generally Accepted Accounting Principles (GAAP) and Government Finance Statistics (GFS) so far as it relates to the General Government Sector (GGS) and the whole of government of the federal, state and territory governments. It was therefore particularly timely to review the requirements in AAS 31;

(d)   they did not reflect contemporary accounting thought; and

(e)   they did not reflect the current style of writing standards, which is to specify principles rather than rules, and requirements rather than encouragements.

The Board intends to continue with its policy of developing a common accounting standards framework for both for-profit and not-for-profit entities whilst acknowledging differences in some areas. The Board is committed to having a platform of topic-based transaction-neutral Standards that will apply to the public sector.

Review of AASs 27, 29 and 31

The Board initiated a project for reviewing the requirements in AASs 27, 29 and 31, divided into two phases comprising a short-term and a longer-term review.

The primary focus in the short term has been on relocating, where necessary, the requirements in AASs 27, 29 and 31, substantively unamended (with some exceptions), into topic-based Standards.

In the longer term the focus will be on improving the requirements for each topic-based issue where necessary. The longer-term review will be carried out in stages as outlined in the AASB's Public Sector Policy Paper *Australian Accounting Standards and Public Sector Entities*.

AASB 1052 in the Context of the Review of AASs 27, 29 and 31

The Board decided to relocate the requirements relating to reporting of disaggregated information by local governments from AAS 27 and government departments from AAS 29, substantively unamended (with some exceptions, as noted in Appendix A), into a new topic-based Standard.

The Board outlined its short-term proposals in Exposure Draft ED 156 *Proposals Arising from the Short-term Review of the Requirements in AAS 27, AAS 29 and AAS 31*, which was issued in June 2007.

Main Features of this Standard

Application Date

This Standard is applicable to annual reporting periods beginning on or after 1 July 2008. Early adoption is permitted for annual reporting periods beginning on or after 1 January 2005, but before 1 July 2008, provided there is early adoption for the same annual reporting period of the following pronouncements being issued at about the same time, as applicable:

(a)   AASB 1004 *Contributions*;

(b)   AASB 1049 *Whole of Government and General Government Sector Financial Reporting*;

(c)   AASB 1050 *Administered Items*;

(d)   AASB 1051 *Land Under Roads*;

(e)   AASB 2007-9 *Amendments to Australian Accounting Standards arising from the Review of AASs 27, 29 and 31*; and

(f)   AASB Interpretation 1038 *Contributions by Owners Made to Wholly-Owned Public Sector Entities*.

Main Requirements

This Standard, which only applies to general purpose financial statements of local governments and government departments, requires disclosure of:

(a)   financial information by function or activity by local governments; and

(b)   financial information about service costs and achievements by government departments.

In relation to local governments, this Standard requires disclosure of:

(a)   the nature and objective of each function/activity;

(b)   the carrying amounts of assets reliably attributable to each function/activity;

(c)   income (with component revenues from related grants disclosed separately as a component thereof) and expenses for the reporting period that are reliably attributable to each function/activity; and

(d)   a reconciliation of the above disclosures to related information in the complete set of financial statements.

In relation to government departments, this Standard requires disclosure of:

(a)   in summarised form, the identity and purpose of each major activity undertaken;

(b)   if not otherwise disclosed in, or in conjunction with, the government department's complete set of financial statements, a summary of the government department's objectives;

(c)   expenses that are reliably attributable to each major activity, showing separately each major class of expenses;

(d)   income that is reliably attributable to each major activity, showing separately user charges, income from government and other income by major class of income; and

(e)   the assets deployed and liabilities incurred that are reliably attributable to each major activity.

Comparison with International Pronouncements

This Standard contains relevant requirements relating to reporting of disaggregated information by local governments and government departments that have been relocated from AAS 27 *Financial Reporting by Local Governments* and AAS 29 *Financial Reporting by Government Departments* in substantially unamended form (with some exceptions, as noted in Appendix A). Accordingly, the development of this Standard did not involve consideration of International Public Sector Accounting Standards (IPSASs) issued by the International Public Sector Accounting Standards Board or International Financial Reporting Standards (IFRSs) issued by the International Accounting Standards Board.

The longer-term review of disaggregated disclosures for local governments and government departments will involve consideration of International pronouncements.

AASB 1052 and IPSASs

IPSAS 18 *Segment Reporting* addresses segment reporting issues and specifies requirements for all public sector entities other than government business enterprises. It contains more detailed requirements and guidance than this Standard. For example, IPSAS 18:

(a)   defines a segment as a distinguishable activity or group of activities of an entity for which it is appropriate to separately report financial information for the purpose of evaluating the entity's past performance in achieving its objectives and for making decisions about the future allocation of resources;

(b)   provides detailed guidance on determining segments;

(c)   requires specific disclosures about segments, including segment revenue, expenses, assets, liabilities and capital expenditure; and

(d)   requires specific disclosures for assets that are jointly used by two or more segments.

AASB 1052 and IFRSs

IAS 14 *Segment Reporting*, which is superseded when applicable by IFRS 8 *Operating Segments*, does not apply to the general purpose financial statements of local governments and government departments. IAS 14 and IFRS 8 specify requirements that differ substantially from the requirements in this Standard.

Accounting Standard AASB 1052

The Australian Accounting Standards Board makes Accounting Standard AASB 1052 *Disaggregated Disclosures*.

Dated 13 December 2007

D.G. Boymal
Chair – AASB

Accounting Standard AASB 1052

Disaggregated Disclosures

Objective

1   The objective of this Standard is to specify principles for reporting:

(a)   financial information by function or activity by local governments; and

(b)   financial information about service costs and achievements by government departments.

2   Disclosures made in accordance with this Standard provide users with information relevant to assessing the performance of a local government or government department, including accountability for resources entrusted to it.

Application

3   **Subject to paragraphs 4 and 5, this Standard applies to general purpose financial statements of local governments and government departments.**

4   **Paragraphs 11 to 14 only apply to general purpose financial statements of local governments.**

5   **Paragraphs 15 to 21 only apply to general purpose financial statements of government departments.**

6   **This Standard applies to annual reporting periods beginning on or after 1 July 2008.**

7   **This Standard may be applied to annual reporting periods beginning on or after 1 January 2005 but before 1 July 2008, provided there is early adoption for the same annual reporting period of the following pronouncements being issued at about the same time, as applicable:**

(a)   **AASB 1004 *Contributions*;**

(b)   **AASB 1049 *Whole of Government and General Government Sector Financial Reporting*;**

(c)   **AASB 1050 *Administered Items*;**

(d)   **AASB 1051 *Land Under Roads*;**

(e)   **AASB 2007-9 *Amendments to Australian Accounting Standards arising from the Review of AASs 27, 29 and 31*; and**

(f)   **AASB Interpretation 1038 *Contributions by Owners Made to Wholly-Owned Public Sector Entities*.**

8   This Standard does not specify disaggregated disclosure requirements for whole of governments or General Government Sectors (GGSs). The requirements for disaggregated disclosures for whole of governments and GGSs are contained in AASB 1049.

9   **The requirements specified in this Standard apply to the complete set of financial statements where information resulting from their application is material in accordance with AASB 1031 *Materiality*.**

10   When applicable, this Standard, together with the Standards referred to in paragraph 7, supersede:

    (a)   AAS 27 *Financial Reporting by Local Governments* as issued in June 1996, as amended; and

    (b)   AAS 29 *Financial Reporting by Government Departments* as issued in June 1998, as amended.

Classification According to Function or Activity by Local Governments

Paragraphs 11 to 14 only apply to local governments.

11   The complete set of financial statements of a local government shall disclose in respect of each broad function or activity:

    (a)   by way of note:

        (i)   the nature and objectives of that function/activity; and

        (ii)   the carrying amount of assets that are reliably attributable to that function/activity; and

    (b)   by way of note or otherwise:

        (i)   income for the reporting period that is reliably attributable to that function/activity, with component revenues from related grants disclosed separately as a component thereof; and

        (ii)   expenses for the reporting period that are reliably attributable to that function/activity.

12   The information provided by way of note in accordance with paragraph 11 shall be aggregated and reconciled to agree with the related information in the financial statements of the local government.

13   This Standard requires disclosure of information about the assets, income and expenses of the local government according to the broad functions or activities of the local government, whether they be related to service delivery or undertaken for commercial objectives. Disclosure of this information assists users in identifying the resources committed to particular functions/activities of the local government, the costs of service delivery that are reliably attributable to those functions/activities, and the extent to which the local government has recovered those costs from income that is reliably attributable to those functions/activities. Function/activity classification of financial information will also assist users in assessing the significance of any financial or non-financial performance indicators reported by the local government.

14   AASB 114 *Segment Reporting* and AASB 8 *Operating Segments* are not applicable to local governments. The bases considered appropriate for identifying broad functions or activities of local governments would not necessarily accord with the criteria for identification of segments contained in those Standards. However, preparers of the complete set of financial statements may find that the guidance contained in those Standards is useful in identifying the income, expenses and assets that are reliably attributable to the broad functions or activities of the local government.

Disclosure of Service Costs and Achievements by Government Departments

Paragraphs 15 to 21 only apply to government departments.

15   The complete set of financial statements of a government department shall disclose:

    (a)   in summarised form, the identity and purpose of each major activity undertaken by the government department during the reporting period;

    (b)   if not otherwise disclosed in, or in conjunction with, the government department's complete set of financial statements, a summary of the government department's objectives;

(c)   expenses reliably attributable to each of the activities identified in (a) above, showing separately each major class of expenses; and

(d)   income reliably attributable to each of the activities identified in (a) above, showing separately user charges, income from government and other income by major class of income.

16   **The complete set of financial statements of a government department shall also disclose the assets deployed and liabilities incurred that are reliably attributable to each of the activities identified in paragraph 15(a).**

17   Government departments are required to achieve service delivery as well as financial objectives. Accordingly, a government department's performance is assessed by reference to the effectiveness, economy and efficiency with which the government department achieves its service delivery and financial objectives. Financial information is therefore only a subset of the information necessary to enable an adequate assessment of a government department's performance. Accordingly, the complete set of financial statements is presented as part of an annual report that discloses information about such matters as the government department's objectives and service delivery achievements during the reporting period. To enhance the quality of information available for assessing performance, paragraph 15 requires that a summary of the government department's objectives be disclosed in the complete set of financial statements where the government department's annual report does not include this disclosure.

18   Paragraphs 15 and 16 require disclosure of information about the expenses, income, assets and liabilities attributable to the major activities of a government department for the reporting period. This information is relevant in assessing the effectiveness, efficiency and economy of operations and of resource allocation decisions. It is also necessary for reviewing existing expenditure commitments and service delivery arrangements, and for considering the long-term funding implications of new initiatives.

19   However, in some instances it may not be possible to reliably attribute all expenses, income, assets and liabilities to each of the major activities of a government department. Paragraphs 15 and 16 require that the complete set of financial statements of a government department only disclose, on an activity by activity basis, information about the expenses, income, assets and liabilities that can be reliably attributed to major activities.

Identifying Major Activities of Government Departments

20   Judgement is required to identify those activities of a government department that warrant separate disclosure in the complete set of financial statements. Exercising this judgement involves a consideration of the following:

(a)   the objectives of the government department;

(b)   the likely users of the general purpose financial statements;

(c)   the activity level that may be relevant to users' assessments of the performance of the government department; and

(d)   the concept of materiality as set out in the *Framework for the Preparation and Presentation of Financial Statements* and AASB 1031.

21   AASB 1050 also contains requirements relating to the disclosure of administered income and expenses attributable to a government department's activities. The principles in this Standard are used in satisfying the requirements in AASB 1050.

Appendix A

Comparison of AASB 1052 with AASs 27 and 29

This Appendix accompanies, but is not part of, AASB 1052.

This Standard reproduces the material relating to disaggregated disclosures contained in AAS 27 and AAS 29, except that:

(a)   Appendix 1 to AAS 27 contained an illustrative example of the disclosures required in respect of the broad functions/activities of a local government. This Standard does not provide an illustration;

(b)   AAS 29 (paragraph 12.7.2) encouraged a government department to disclose the assets deployed and liabilities incurred that are reliably attributable to each of its activities. This Standard (paragraph 16) requires such disclosure; and

(c)   this Standard (paragraph 21) notes that its principles are used in satisfying the requirement in AASB 1050 Administered Items to disclose administered income and expenses attributable to a government department's activities. AASs 27 and 29 contained no such reference.

The following table provides source references to paragraphs 11 – 21 of this Standard, most of which were derived from AASs 27 and 29. It is provided to facilitate an understanding of, and assist in the application of, the requirements in this Standard.

Paragraphs in AASB 1052	Relevant source paragraphs in AASs 27 & 29
11 – 14	86 – 89 of AAS 27
15 – 20	12.7 – 12.7.4 of AAS 29
21	New paragraph

Basis for Conclusions

This Basis for Conclusions accompanies, but is not part of, AASB 1052.

Introduction

BC1   This Basis for Conclusions summarises the Board's considerations in developing this Standard in the context of the Board's short-term review of the requirements in AAS 27 *Financial Reporting by Local Governments*, AAS 29 *Financial Reporting by Government Departments* and AAS 31 *Financial Reporting by Governments*.

Background

BC2   The Board considered it timely to review the requirements in AASs 27, 29 and 31, in particular to:

(a)   review the extent to which local governments, government departments and governments should continue to be subject to requirements that differ from requirements applicable to other not-for-profit entities and for-profit entities contained in Australian Accounting Standards. The Board concluded that differences should be removed, where appropriate and timely, to improve the overall quality of financial reporting;

(b)   bring requirements applicable to local governments, government departments and governments up-to-date with contemporary accounting thought;

(c)   consider the implications of the outcomes of its project on the harmonisation of Generally Accepted Accounting Principles (GAAP) and Government Finance Statistics (GFS), in particular on the requirements in AAS 31;

(d)   decide whether the encouragements in AASs 27, 29 and 31 should be made mandatory or removed; and

(e)   remove uncertainty in the application of cross-references to other Australian Accounting Standards and the override provisions in AASs 27, 29 and 31 that made the requirements in AASs 27, 29 and 31 take precedence over other requirements.

BC3   The Board considered the following alternative mechanisms for implementing the approach of updating and improving the requirements for local governments, government departments and governments:

   (a)   review the requirements in AASs 27, 29 and 31 and where appropriate:

      (i)   amend other Australian Accounting Standards to pick up any issues that are addressed in AASs 27, 29 and 31 that are not adequately addressed in the latest Australian Accounting Standards and have them apply to local governments, government departments and governments; or

      (ii)   create public sector specific topic-based Standards;

      and consequently withdraw AASs 27, 29 and 31; or

   (b)   review AASs 27, 29 and 31 and re-issue them in light of the latest Australian Accounting Standards, retaining/amending where necessary any issues that are addressed in AASs 27, 29 and 31 that are not adequately addressed in the latest Australian Accounting Standards.

BC4   The Board chose alternative (a) given the improvements in the quality of financial reporting by local governments, government departments and governments since AASs 27, 29 and 31 were first issued.

BC5   Where the Board identified that the material in AASs 27, 29 and 31 could be improved within time and resource constraints, improvements have been made. Much of the material in AASs 27, 29 and 31 has been retained substantively unamended. Improvements will be progressed in due course in line with the AASB's Public Sector Policy Paper *Australian Accounting Standards and Public Sector Entities*.

BC6   The first stage of the short-term review of the requirements in AASs 27, 29 and 31 was the preparation of a paragraph-by-paragraph analysis of each of AASs 27, 29 and 31, listing each paragraph of each Standard alongside corresponding Standards or other pronouncements that would apply to local governments, government departments or governments in the absence of AASs 27, 29 and 31. The Board's conclusions and rationale for the treatment of each paragraph in the context of the review were also provided in the analysis. The Board's primary focus was on dealing with the requirements from the three Standards in such a way as to not leave a vacuum.

BC7   Each paragraph from AASs 27, 29 and 31 was classified as being:

   (a)   no longer needed or adequately dealt with in other Standards;

   (b)   more appropriately dealt with in other Standards; or

   (c)   not adequately and/or appropriately dealt with in other Standards and therefore should be retained or improved and incorporated into other Standards.

   The paragraph-by-paragraph analyses considered by the AASB in developing the Exposure Draft ED 156 *Proposals Arising from the Short-term Review of the Requirements in AAS 27, AAS 29 and AAS 31* that gave rise to this Standard are available on the AASB website. They support, but do not form part of, this Basis for Conclusions.

BC8   In reviewing the paragraphs, the Board noted that some material in AASs 27, 29 and 31 would, under the current style of writing Standards, be located in a separate Basis for Conclusions. Given the short-term nature of the review of AASs 27, 29 and 31, the Board concluded that explanations of technical issues that both originated in and are being relocated from AASs 27, 29 and 31 should, when appropriate, be located in the body of the Standard to which they are relocated.

BC9   The Board decided not to retain the illustrative general purpose financial reports provided in AASs 27, 29 and 31, because their purpose, which was to provide an educational tool in the initial stages of accrual reporting by local governments, government departments and governments, is no longer needed.

BC10 The remainder of this Basis for Conclusions focuses on issues specific to disaggregated disclosures.

Disaggregated Disclosures

BC11 The Board decided to retain, substantially unchanged, the requirements relating to segment-like reporting from paragraphs 86 to 89 of AAS 27 and paragraphs 12.7 to 12.7.4 of AAS 29 and relocate them into a separate new topic-based Standard. Because of the differing requirements, the Board concluded that they should be expressed separately for local governments and government departments. A longer-term separate project on disaggregated disclosures for local governments and government departments will be progressed in due course.

BC12 The Board considered relocating the material into AASB 114 *Segment Reporting* (and subsequently AASB 8 *Operating Segments*), but rejected this option consistent with its intention to retain requirements substantively unchanged in the short term. The guidance in AASB 114 (and AASB 8), which is not applicable to not-for-profit entities or for-profit government departments, comprehensively addresses segment reporting issues and specifies requirements that differ substantially from those required under AASs 27, 29 and 31.

BC13 The Board considered whether for-profit government departments should be subject to AASB 114 (and AASB 8) rather than this Standard. The Board noted that for-profit government departments typically do not exist in practice. Consistent with the general approach to the short-term review of AASs 27, 29 and 31, and because AAS 29 applied to government departments, including for-profit government departments, the Board decided that for-profit government departments should continue to adopt policies that are consistent with not-for-profit government departments to the extent previously required by AAS 29. This approach will be reviewed as part of the Board's longer-term consideration of the definition of government departments in the context of the reporting entity concept.

BC14 Paragraph 12.7.2 of AAS 29 encouraged the disclosure of information about assets deployed and liabilities incurred in relation to each major activity undertaken by a government department. Consistent with paragraph BC2(d), the Board decided that, in relation to disaggregated information, assets deployed and liabilities incurred in relation to and reliably attributable to each major activity undertaken by a government department should be required to be disclosed (see paragraph 16). The information is relevant in assessing the effectiveness, efficiency and economy of operations and of resource allocation decisions.

BC15 The Board decided not to retain the requirements relating to segment-like reporting from paragraphs 15.12 to 15.12.2 of AAS 31. It is not necessary for this Standard to specify disaggregated disclosure requirements for governments, as AASB 1049 *Whole of Government and General Government Sector Financial Reporting* addresses disaggregated disclosure requirements for governments.

AASB 1053
Application of Tiers of Australian Accounting Standards

(Issued June 2010)

Note from the Institute of Chartered Accountants Australia

This note, prepared by the technical editors, is not part of Accounting Standard AASB 1053.

Historical development

30 June 2010: AASB 1053 was issued to implement the two-tier arrangement of the AASB's Reduced Disclosure Regime.

This Standard is applicable to annual reporting periods beginning on or after 1 July 2013. This Standard may be adopted early.

The AASB has issued a number of amending Standards to incorporate reduced disclosure requirements into the existing Accounting Standards and Interpretations.

Relevant accounting standards in this handbook are:

- AASB 2010-2 'Amendments to Australian Accounting Standards arising from Reduced Disclosure Requirements'

- AASB 2011-2 'Amendments to Australian Accounting Standards arising from the Trans-Tasman Convergence Project – Reduced Disclosure Requirements'

- AASB 2011-6 'Amendments to Australian Accounting Standards – Extending Relief from Consolidation, the Equity Method and Proportionate Consolidation – Reduced Disclosure Requirements'

- AASB 2011-11 'Amendments to AASB 119 (September 2011) arising from Reduced Disclosure Requirements'.

- AASB 2012-1 ' Amendments to Australian Accounting Standards – Fair Value Measurement – Reduced Disclosure Requirements'

- AASB 2012-7 'Amendments to Australian Accounting Standards arising from Reduced Disclosure Requirements'

For up-to-date information and compiled RDR versions of Australian Accounting Standards for early adopters, refer to the AASB website at www.aasb.gov.au.

Contents

Preface

Comparison with IFRS for SMEs

Accounting Standard
AASB 1053 Application of Tiers of Australian Accounting Standards

	Paragraphs
Objective	1
Application	2 – 6
Tiers of Reporting Requirements	7 – 10
Application of Australian Accounting Standards under the Differential Reporting Framework	
Application of Tier 1 Reporting Requirements	11 – 12
Application of Tier 2 Reporting Requirements	13 – 16
Transition	17
Transition from Special Purpose Financial Statements to Tier 1 or Tier 2	18 – 20
Transition between Tiers	21 – 23

Appendices:

A Defined Terms

B Public Accountability

C Transition

Basis for Conclusions

Australian Accounting Standard AASB 1053 *Application of Tiers of Australian Accounting Standards* is set out in paragraphs 1 – 23 and Appendices A and B. All the paragraphs have equal authority. Paragraphs in **bold type** state the main principles. AASB 1053 is to be read in the context of other Australian Accounting Standards, including AASB 1048 *Interpretation of Standards*, which identifies the Australian Accounting Interpretations. In the absence of explicit guidance, AASB 108 *Accounting Policies, Changes in Accounting Estimates and Errors* provides a basis for selecting and applying accounting policies.

Preface

Introduction

The Australian Accounting Standards Board (AASB) makes Australian Accounting Standards, including Interpretations, to be applied by:

(a)   entities required by the *Corporations Act 2001* to prepare financial reports;

(b)   governments in preparing financial statements for the whole of government and the General Government Sector (GGS); and

(c)   entities in the private or public for-profit or not-for-profit sectors that are reporting entities or that prepare general purpose financial statements.

When appropriate, Australian Accounting Standards incorporate International Financial Reporting Standards (IFRSs), including Interpretations, issued by the International Accounting Standards Board (IASB), with the addition of paragraphs on the applicability of each Standard in the Australian environment.

Australian Accounting Standards also include requirements that are specific to Australian entities. These requirements may be located in Australian Accounting Standards that incorporate IFRSs or in other Australian Accounting Standards. In most instances, these requirements are either restricted to the not-for-profit or public sectors or include additional disclosures that address domestic, regulatory or other issues. In developing requirements for public sector entities, the AASB considers the requirements of International Public Sector Accounting Standards (IPSASs), as issued by the International Public Sector Accounting Standards Board (IPSASB) of the International Federation of Accountants.

References in this Standard to 'Australian Accounting Standards – Reduced Disclosure Requirements' relate to the second Tier of requirements for general purpose financial statements (Tier 2), to distinguish them from references to 'Australian Accounting Standards' that relate to the first Tier of requirements for preparing general purpose financial statements (Tier 1).

Private sector for-profit entities complying with Tier 1 requirements will simultaneously comply with IFRSs. Many other entities complying with Tier 1 requirements will also simultaneously comply with IFRSs.

Reasons for Issuing this Standard

This Standard establishes a differential financial reporting framework consisting of two Tiers of reporting requirements for preparing general purpose financial statements:

(a)   Tier 1: Australian Accounting Standards; and

(b)   Tier 2: Australian Accounting Standards – Reduced Disclosure Requirements.

Tier 2 comprises the recognition, measurement and presentation requirements of Tier 1 and substantially reduced disclosures corresponding to those requirements.

The following entities apply Tier 1 requirements in preparing general purpose financial statements:

(a)   for-profit entities in the private sector that have public accountability (as defined in this Standard); and

(b)   the Australian Government and State, Territory and Local Governments.

The following entities apply either Tier 2 or Tier 1 requirements in preparing general purpose financial statements:

(a)   for-profit private sector entities that do not have public accountability;

(b)   all not-for-profit private sector entities; and

(c)   public sector entities other than the Australian Government and State, Territory and Local Governments[1].

Whilst Tier 2 requirements would be available to all not-for-profit private sector entities and most public sector entities, regulators might exercise a power to require the application of Tier 1 requirements by the entities they regulate.

Comparison with IFRS for SMEs

The disclosures required by Tier 2 and the disclosures required by the IASB's *International Financial Reporting Standard for Small and Medium-sized Entities* (*IFRS for SMEs*) are highly similar. However, Tier 2 requirements and the *IFRS for SMEs* are not directly comparable as a consequence of Tier 2 including recognition and measurement requirements corresponding to those in IFRSs, whereas the *IFRS for SMEs* includes limited modifications to those requirements.

In addition, the recognition, measurement and disclosure requirements that apply in accordance with Tier 2 are to be revised as Australian Accounting Standards are revised, whereas the *IFRS for SMEs* is expected to be revised only periodically for revisions of IFRSs.

---

1   AASB 1049 *Whole of Government and General Government Sector Financial Reporting* applies to the GGS financial statements of the Australian Government and State and Territory Governments. Unless otherwise specified in AASB 1049, GGS financial statements are required to adopt the same accounting policies, including in relation to disclosures, as the whole of government general purpose financial statements. Accordingly, the reduction in disclosures allowed by Tier 2 is not available to GGSs (or whole of governments).

AASB

Accounting Standard AASB 1053

The Australian Accounting Standards Board makes Accounting Standard AASB 1053 *Application of Tiers of Australian Accounting Standards* under section 334 of the *Corporations Act 2001*.

Kevin M. Stevenson
Chair – AASB

Dated 30 June 2010

Accounting Standard AASB 1053

Application of Tiers of Australian Accounting Standards

Objective

1   The objective of this Standard is to set out the application of Tiers of Australian Accounting Standards to different categories of entities preparing *general purpose financial statements*.

Application

2   This Standard applies to[1]:

(a)   **each entity that is required to prepare financial reports in accordance with Part 2M.3 of the Corporations Act;**

(b)   **general purpose financial statements of each *reporting entity*;**

(c)   **financial statements that are, or are held out to be, general purpose financial statements; and**

(d)   **financial statements of General Government Sectors (GGSs) prepared in accordance with AASB 1049 *Whole of Government and General Government Sector Financial Reporting*.**

3   **This Standard applies to annual reporting periods beginning on or after 1 July 2013.**

4   **This Standard may be applied to annual reporting periods beginning on or after 1 July 2009 but before 1 July 2013. When an entity applies this Standard to such an annual reporting period it shall disclose that fact.**

5   When an entity elects to early adopt this Standard for an annual reporting period beginning on or after 1 July 2009 but before 1 July 2013 and prepares Tier 2 general purpose financial statements, it shall also adopt the relevant Standards that specify Tier 2 reporting requirements.

6   **The requirements specified in this Standard apply to the financial statements where information resulting from their application is material in accordance with AASB 1031 *Materiality*.**

Tiers of Reporting Requirements

7   Australian Accounting Standards consist of two Tiers of reporting requirements for preparing general purpose financial statements:

(a)   Tier 1: Australian Accounting Standards; and

(b)   Tier 2: Australian Accounting Standards – Reduced Disclosure Requirements.

8   Tier 1 incorporates International Financial Reporting Standards (IFRSs) issued by the International Accounting Standards Board (IASB) and include requirements that are specific to Australian entities.

---

1   This application paragraph does not amend the application paragraphs of other Standards that are restricted to reporting entities

9   Tier 2 comprises the recognition and measurement requirements of Tier 1 but substantially reduced disclosure requirements. Except for the presentation of a third statement of financial position under Tier 1^2, the presentation requirements under Tier 1 and Tier 2 are the same.

10   Each Australian Accounting Standard specifies the entities to which it applies and, where necessary, sets out disclosure requirements from which Tier 2 entities are exempt.

Application of Australian Accounting Standards under the Differential Reporting Framework

Application of Tier 1 Reporting Requirements

11   **Tier 1 reporting requirements shall apply to the general purpose financial statements of the following types of entities:**

  (a)   **for-profit private sector entities that have *public accountability*; and**

  (b)   **the Australian Government and State, Territory and Local Governments.**

12   **Subject to AASB 1049, GGSs of the Australian Government and State and Territory Governments shall apply Tier 1 reporting requirements.**

Application of Tier 2 Reporting Requirements

13   **The following types of entities shall, as a minimum, apply Tier 2 reporting requirements in preparing general purpose financial statements:**

  (a)   **for-profit private sector entities that do not have public accountability;**

  (b)   **not-for-profit private sector entities; and**

  (c)   **public sector entities, whether for-profit or not-for-profit, other than the Australian Government and State, Territory and Local Governments.**

  These types of entities may elect to apply Tier 1 reporting requirements in preparing general purpose financial statements.

14   Entities applying Tier 2 reporting requirements would not be able to state compliance with IFRSs.

15   Whilst Tier 2 reporting requirements are available under this Standard to non-publicly accountable for-profit private sector entities, not-for-profit private sector entities and public sector entities (both for-profit or not-for-profit) other than those required to apply Tier 1 reporting requirements, regulators might exercise a power to require the application of Tier 1 reporting requirements.

16   Disclosures under Tier 2 reporting requirements are the minimum disclosures required to be included in general purpose financial statements. Entities may include additional disclosures using Tier 1 reporting requirements as a guide if, in their judgement, such additional disclosures are consistent with the objective of general purpose financial statements.

Transition

17   Some of the disclosure requirements in AASB 1 *First-time Adoption of Australian Accounting Standards* have been excluded from Tier 2 reporting requirements. Accordingly, entities adopting Tier 2 reporting requirements for the first time that are required to apply AASB 1 shall comply with the reduced disclosure requirements in AASB 1, including for the purposes of paragraph 18.

---

2   Under AASB 101 *Presentation of Financial Statements*, a complete set of financial statements includes a statement of financial position as at the beginning of the earliest comparative period when an entity applies an accounting policy retrospectively or makes a retrospective restatement of items in its financial statements, or when it reclassifies items in its financial statements.

AASB

Transition from Special Purpose Financial Statements to Tier 1 or Tier 2

18   An entity that prepared its most recent previous financial statements in the form of special purpose financial statements and:

(a)   did not apply the recognition and measurement requirements of applicable Australian Accounting Standards; or

(b)   applied the recognition and measurement requirements of applicable Australian Accounting Standards selectively;

shall apply all the relevant requirements of AASB 1 on transition to either Tier 1 or Tier 2.

19   An entity that prepared its most recent previous financial statements in the form of special purpose financial statements and applied all the recognition and measurement requirements of applicable Australian Accounting Standards, including the recognition and measurement requirements of AASB 1, shall:

(a)   on transition to Tier 2, not apply AASB 1; and

(b)   on transition to Tier 1, apply AASB 1.

20   In relation to paragraph 19(b), entities claiming compliance with IFRSs need to apply the full disclosure requirements of AASB 1. Not-for-profit entities applying Aus paragraphs claiming compliance with Australian Accounting Standards, but not necessarily compliance with IFRSs, also need to apply the full disclosure requirements of AASB 1.

Transition between Tiers

21   An entity transitioning from Tier 2 to Tier 1 shall:

(a)   apply AASB 1, if it is claiming compliance with IFRSs; and

(b)   not apply AASB 1, if it is a not-for-profit entity not claiming compliance with IFRSs.

22   In relation to paragraph 21(a), entities claiming compliance with IFRSs (which would include all for-profit entities applying Tier 1 reporting requirements) need to apply the full requirements of AASB 1, as in previously applying Tier 2 reporting requirements, they have only applied some of the disclosure requirements of AASB 1.

23   An entity transitioning from Tier 1 to Tier 2 shall not apply AASB 1.

Appendix A
Defined Terms

This appendix is an integral part of AASB 1053.

The following terms have the meanings specified:

> **General purpose financial statements** are those intended to meet the needs of users who are not in a position to require an entity to prepare reports tailored to their particular information needs.

> **Public accountability** means accountability to those existing and potential resource providers and others external to the entity who make economic decisions but are not in a position to demand reports tailored to meet their particular information needs.

> A for-profit private sector entity has public accountability if:

>> (a)   its debt or equity instruments are traded in a public market or it is in the process of issuing such instruments for trading in a public market (a domestic or foreign stock exchange or an over-the-counter market, including local and regional markets); or

>> (b)   it holds assets in a fiduciary capacity for a broad group of outsiders as one of its primary businesses. This is typically the case for banks, credit unions, insurance companies, securities brokers/dealers, mutual funds and investment banks.

> **Reporting entity** means an entity in respect of which it is reasonable to expect the existence of users who rely on the entity's general purpose financial statements for information that will be useful to them for making and evaluating decisions about the allocation of resources. A reporting entity can be a single entity or a group comprising a parent and all of its subsidiaries.

Appendix B
Public Accountability

This appendix is an integral part of AASB 1053.

B1   Public accountability is defined in Appendix A. The notion of public accountability is consistent with the notion adopted by the IASB in its *International Financial Reporting Standard for Small and Medium-sized Entities (IFRS for SMEs).* It is different from the notion of public accountability in the general sense of the term that is often employed in relation to not-for-profit, including public sector, entities.

B2   The following for-profit entities are deemed to have public accountability:

> (a)   disclosing entities, even if their debt or equity instruments are not traded in a public market or are not in the process of being issued for trading in a public market;

> (b)   co-operatives that issue debentures;

> (c)   registered managed investment schemes;

> (d)   superannuation plans regulated by the Australian Prudential Regulation Authority (APRA) other than Small APRA Funds as defined by APRA Superannuation Circular No. II.E.1 *Regulation of Small APRA Funds,* December 2000; and

> (e)   authorised deposit-taking institutions.

Appendix C

Transition

This appendix accompanies, but is not part of, AASB 1053.

It is intended to facilitate the application of transitional provisions in paragraphs 17 to 23 of the Standard for transitioning from special purpose financial statements (SPFSs) to general purpose financial statements (GPFSs) and between Tiers.

Chart 1: Moving from SPFSs to GPFSs

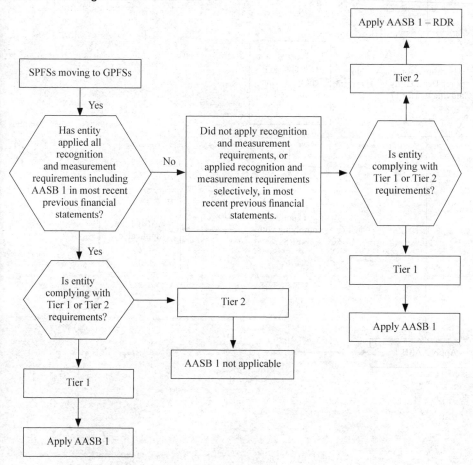

Chart 2: Moving between Tiers

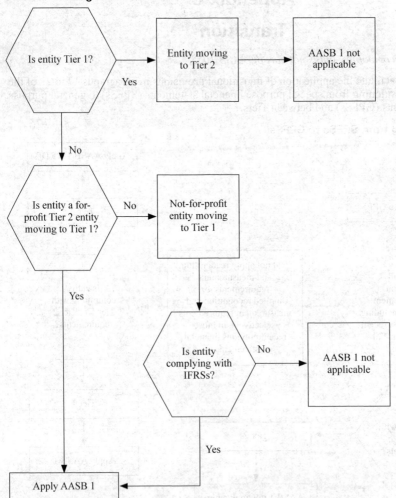

Basis for Conclusions

The Basis for Conclusions accompanies, but is not part of, AASB 1053.

BC1   This Basis for Conclusions summarises the Australian Accounting Standards Board's considerations in reaching the conclusions in AASB 1053 *Application of Tiers of Australian Accounting Standards*. It also provides a context for the Board's decisions about disclosures from which 'Tier 2' entities are exempt, which are reflected in AASB 2010-2 *Amendments to Australian Accounting Standards arising from Reduced Disclosure Requirements*. It focuses on the issues that the Board considers to be of greatest significance. Individual Board members gave greater weight to some factors than to others.

Background to Differential Reporting in Australia

BC2   A form of differential reporting has been incorporated in Accounting Standards in Australia since the early 1990s. The concept of 'reporting entity' is at the core of this differential reporting regime. Statement of Accounting Concepts SAC 1 *Definition of the Reporting Entity* deals with the reporting entity concept. The AASB *Glossary of Defined Terms* includes the definition of a reporting entity[1] as:

> An entity in respect of which it is reasonable to expect the existence of users who rely on the entity's general purpose financial statement for information that will be useful to them for making and evaluating decisions about the allocation of resources. A reporting entity can be a single entity or a group comprising a parent and all of its subsidiaries.

BC3   Most Australian Accounting Standards include the requirements of corresponding International Financial Reporting Standards (IFRSs) and have the following application paragraph:

> This Standard applies to:
>
> (a)   each entity that is required to prepare financial reports in accordance with Part 2M.3 of the Corporations Act and that is a reporting entity;
>
> (b)   general purpose financial statements of each other reporting entity; and
>
> (c)   financial statements that are, or are held out to be, general purpose financial statements.

Prior to AASB 1053, for-profit and not-for-profit (NFP) entities falling within the scope of this application paragraph were subject to all the recognition, measurement, presentation and disclosure requirements of those Standards. These entities included entities incorporated under the *Corporations Act 2001* that are reporting entities.

BC4   Under the Corporations Act, disclosing entities, public companies (including companies limited by guarantee), large proprietary companies and registered schemes must prepare and lodge financial statements that comply with accounting standards. Large proprietary companies are those companies that meet at least two of the three size thresholds set out in the Corporations Act relating to:

(a)   the consolidated revenue for the financial year of the company and the entities it controls (if any);

(b)   the value of the consolidated gross assets at the end of the financial year of the company and the entities it controls (if any); and

(c)   the number of employees of the company and the entities it controls (if any) at the end of the financial year.

These Corporations Act size thresholds effectively remove the external reporting obligations for small proprietary companies.[2]

---

1   This definition is included in paragraph Aus7.2 of AASB 101 *Presentation of Financial Statements.*

2   Under Sections 292(2), 293 and 294 of the Corporations Act, small proprietary companies must prepare and lodge financial reports in certain circumstances such as when the Australian Securities and Investments Commission (ASIC) directs them, or they are controlled by a foreign company, or 5% of shareholders vote to have a financial report.

BC5   Accordingly, prior to AASB 1053, a reporting burden that is less than compliance with full Australian Accounting Standards was only available to non-reporting entities in the preparation of financial statements that are not general purpose financial statements. The financial statements of non-reporting entities are classified as special purpose financial statements and, like general purpose financial statements, are subject to true and fair view requirements of the Corporations Act where they fall within the scope of that Act.

BC6   Entities eligible for this reduced reporting burden included those incorporated under the Corporations Act that are not reporting entities but are required to prepare financial statements. Only AASB 101 *Presentation of Financial Statements*, AASB 107 *Statement of Cash Flows*, AASB 108 *Accounting Policies, Changes in Accounting Estimates and Errors*, AASB 1031 *Materiality* and AASB 1048 *Interpretation of Standards* apply to such entities, by virtue of the application paragraphs in those Standards.

BC7   The Australian Securities and Investment Commission (ASIC) has expressed the view[3] that non-reporting entities required to prepare financial statements in accordance with Chapter 2M of the Corporations Act should comply with the recognition and measurement requirements of all accounting standards. Under ASIC's view, the only 'relief' for these entities is not having to apply the disclosure requirements contained in Standards other than AASB 101, AASB 107 and AASB 108.

BC8   In addition to AASB pronouncements that incorporate IFRSs, there are Australian Accounting Standards (including Interpretations) that apply specifically to some or all NFP entities, including:

(a)   AASB 1004 *Contributions*;

(b)   AASB 1049 *Whole of Government and General Government Sector Financial Reporting*;

(c)   AASB 1050 *Administered Items*;

(d)   AASB 1051 *Land Under Roads*;

(e)   AASB 1052 *Disaggregated Disclosures*; and

(f)   AASB Interpretation 1038 *Contributions by Owners Made to Wholly-owned Public Sector Entities*.

BC9   Prior to AASB 1053, entities not incorporated under the Corporations Act, (which include many NFP entities and most public sector entities), were required to apply, where applicable, the recognition, measurement, presentation and disclosure requirements of these and other Australian Accounting Standards if they were reporting entities or holding out financial statements to be general purpose financial statements.

The Need to Review the Differential Reporting Framework

BC10   The Board identified a number of concerns with the differential reporting framework that existed prior to AASB 1053. These concerns included that:

(a)   costs of preparing general purpose financial statements for some entities were greater than benefits for the users of those general purpose financial statements, because the framework resulted in requirements for general purpose financial statements that were overly burdensome for many entities; and

(b)   user needs were not being satisfied for other entities, because the framework was being applied in a way that some entities (which should prepare general purpose financial statements) were being treated as non-reporting entities and preparing only special purpose financial statements.

---

3   ASIC Regulatory Guide 85 *Reporting requirements for non-reporting entities.*

BC11   When it was initially considering these concerns, the Board noted that the International Accounting Standards Board (IASB) was developing an *IFRS for SMEs* that would result in general purpose financial statements that would not be compliant with IFRSs. Accordingly, the Board decided that, in revising its differential reporting framework, it was appropriate for the Board to also consider requirements for general purpose financial statements that differ from (full) Australian Accounting Standards. The Financial Reporting Council has been kept apprised of these developments.

BC12   The Board issued a number of consultative documents containing its proposals for addressing the concerns noted in paragraph BC10. These documents were, in sequence:

(a)   Invitation to Comment ITC 12 *Request for Comment on a Proposed Revised Differential Reporting Regime for Australia and IASB Exposure Draft of A Proposed IFRS for Small and Medium-sized Entities* – issued in May 2007;

(b)   Consultation Paper *Differential Financial Reporting – Reducing Disclosure Requirements (A Proposed Reduced Disclosure Regime for Non-publicly Accountable For-profit Private Sector Entities and Certain Entities in the Not-for-profit Private Sector and Public Sector)* – issued in February 2010; and

(c)   Exposure Draft ED 192 *Differential Reporting Framework* – also issued in February 2010.

BC13   These consultative documents contained proposals relating to both of the concerns (a) and (b) noted in paragraph BC10 above. The Board refined its ITC 12 proposals in the light of comments it received on the ITC, and reflected its revised proposals in the Consultation Paper and accompanying ED 192. After considering constituent comments on ED 192, the Board decided to issue AASB 1053 in response to concern (a), and to undertake further research prior to deciding how it would deal with concern (b).

BC14   In relation to concern (b), many constituents agreed with the manner in which the Board proposed to address the concern, which was to change the focus from reporting entity to general purpose financial statements and clarify the meaning of general purpose financial statements in an Australian context. This was on the grounds that:

(a)   the application of reporting entity involves a high degree of subjectivity and the term is open to differing interpretations; and

(b)   the use of reporting entity for differential reporting is not universally understood.

This group was of the view that the use of the reporting entity concept does not provide the intended result, and the uncertainty surrounding its application reduces its usefulness as a robust criterion for differential reporting purposes.

BC15   In contrast, other constituents expressed the view that the concept of reporting entity works well and should be retained as one aspect of differential reporting. They commented that they have not seen evidence of major problems with its application. This group, therefore, considered that those entities that currently claim to be non-reporting entities and prepare special purpose financial statements do not have dependent users and the evidence does not support a view that there is a systemic problem with reporting entities claiming a non-reporting entity status to evade their reporting responsibilities under Australian Accounting Standards.

BC16   The Board concluded that, in the light of these contrasting claims, further research should be carried out on the impact of the ED 192 proposals on those entities currently preparing special purpose financial statements. This is primarily with a view to ensuring that those entities currently appropriately preparing special purpose financial statements are not disadvantaged by the proposals. Consistent with this, the Board decided that, under the first stage of revisions to the differential reporting framework, concern (a) should be addressed. The Board's approach to dealing with concern (a) leaves the current differential reporting framework based on the reporting entity concept and general purpose financial statements intact, including the requirement for entities required to prepare financial reports in accordance with Part 2M.3 of the Corporations Act to apply AASB 101, AASB 107, AASB 108, AASB 1031 and AASB 1048, by virtue of the application paragraphs in those Standards.

BC17   The remainder of this Basis for Conclusions focuses on the basis for the Board's conclusions relating to concern (a).

Different Tiers of Requirements for General Purpose Financial Statements

BC18   The Board decided to retain full IFRSs as adopted in Australia as the first Tier (Tier 1) of reporting requirements, and make it mandatory for a relatively small number of entities in the private and public sectors in their preparation of general purpose financial statements. These entities are limited to publicly accountable entities in the for-profit private sector and Governments in the public sector (see paragraphs BC25 and BC52). Accordingly, AASB 1053 does not reduce the reporting burden of those entities. Retention of full IFRSs as adopted in Australia requirements for these entities is consistent with the approach adopted by the IASB to require certain entities to continue to comply with full IFRSs in order to claim IFRS compliance.

BC19   The Board decided to introduce a second Tier (Tier 2) of requirements to substantially reduce the burden of financial reporting for other entities in both the private and public sectors in their preparation of general purpose financial statements. Tier 2 retains the recognition, measurement and presentation requirements[4] of full IFRSs as adopted in Australia, but requires disclosures that are substantially reduced when compared with those required under full IFRSs as adopted in Australia.

BC20   The Board regards AASB 1053 as a pragmatic and substantive response to the need to reduce the burden of disclosure requirements on Australian reporting entities. However, the Board does not regard it as a complete or final answer to that need. In addition to the further research referred to in paragraph BC16 above, the Board intends continuing its deliberations on revising the differential reporting framework with a view to ongoing improvements (including having regard to decisions made by the IASB in relation to its *IFRS for SMEs* – see paragraph BC98). The Board concluded that the reforms in AASB 1053 should not be delayed while consideration of other possible areas of reform continues. The Board notes that important reforms are also being considered to reduce the complexity of full IFRSs, including in the area of financial instruments, which would help reduce reporting complexities when adopted in Australia, including for entities that would be subject to Tier 1 requirements. The IASB is expected to move beyond financial instruments in its efforts to simplify requirements and the AASB will continue to encourage and support those efforts.

BC21   The new Tier 2 requirements do not change the current AASB policy of the same transactions and other events being subject to the same accounting requirements to the extent feasible (that is, transaction neutrality), for all entities preparing general purpose financial statements (whether for-profit or NFP).

BC22   The Board considered whether a third tier of reporting requirements for general purpose financial statements should be introduced to provide simpler financial reporting requirements for smaller NFP entities since those entities might find the adoption of Tier 2 requirements overly burdensome on cost-benefit grounds. The Board noted that many NFP entities in the private sector are established as companies limited by guarantee under the Corporations Act or as associations under relevant Incorporated Associations Acts in each State and Territory. Moreover, many non-trading cooperatives are regulated by State or Territory Acts. Having regard to this legislation, the Board noted that a reason for contemplating the need for a third tier was that there is generally no NFP equivalent to the outright exemption from reporting that exists for small proprietary companies (see paragraph BC4 above).

---

4   Except for presentation of a third balance sheet required under Tier 1.

BC23   The Board noted that while there is some support from constituents for creating a third tier, there are different views about the requirements of such a tier and the way entities applying those requirements should be identified. The Board also considered the proposals for reporting relief in the Discussion Paper published by the Australian Government in June 2007 titled *Financial Reporting by Unlisted Public Companies* in relation to the creation of a third tier of reporting requirements for companies limited by guarantee[5].

BC24   The Board decided not to introduce a third tier of reporting requirements on the basis that:

(a)   the Government intended to alleviate the reporting burden of small companies limited by guarantee through amendments to the Corporations Act; and

(b)   Tier 2 requirements for preparing general purpose financial statements would help reduce the disclosure burden of NFP entities significantly.

Applicability of the Different Tiers to For-Profit Entities

Public Accountability

BC25   The Board concluded that for-profit entities that are publicly accountable (as defined in *International Financial Reporting Standard for Small and Medium-sized Entities [IFRS for SMEs]*) should be required to apply full IFRSs as adopted in Australia. This is on the basis of consistency with international reporting requirements in the for-profit private sector. The Board noted that, since Australia has adopted full IFRSs, it would be logical to use the public accountability notion used by the IASB in determining which entities in the for-profit sector should apply Australian Accounting Standards in full.

BC26   The Board acknowledged constituents' comments about some aspects of the definition of public accountability that the application of the definition in some cases may involve interpretation or judgement. Some respondents to ED 192 noted it would be helpful for the Board to clarify certain terms used in the definition. These include the term 'public market' referred to in the first leg of the definition and the terms 'fiduciary', 'broad', 'outsiders' and 'primary business' referred to in the second leg of the definition. However, the Board noted it is not a policy of the Board to further interpret the IASB's terms and definitions. Accordingly, the Board decided that, instead of interpreting the terms in the definition, AASB 1053 should identify entities that the Board deems to be publicly accountable in the Australian context, to supplement the IASB's definition of public accountability (see Appendix B of AASB 1053).

BC27   In relation to identifying entities that should be deemed to be publicly accountable in the Australian context, some respondents to ED 192 questioned whether captive insurers should be classified as publicly accountable since, in their view, there is unlikely to be a broad group of outsiders involved. The Board noted that the nature of captive insurers varies. Some only provide insurance to subsidiaries within their group while others also insure joint venture businesses. Some captive insurers, such as association captive insurers, can insure a wide range of members. Those that provide insurance to subsidiaries within groups may also deal with outsiders. For example, they may offer products that have public beneficiaries (such as public or product liability, or professional indemnity).

BC28   The Board concluded that, whilst it expects that most insurance companies will be publicly accountable, there may be certain general insurers, such as some captive insurers, that may not be publicly accountable. Accordingly, the Board did not deem all regulated insurance entities as publicly accountable.

BC29   Some respondents to ED 192 also questioned whether Small Australian Prudential Regulation Authority (APRA) Funds (SAFs) should be deemed to be publicly

---

5   The outcome of the proposals in the Discussion Paper are included in the *Corporations Amendment (Corporate Reporting Reform) Act 2010*.

accountable, given the small number of members and the limited users of their financial statements.

BC30   The Board noted that SAFs are usually similar in size to self-managed super funds (SMSFs) but, unlike SMSFs (which are regulated by the Australian Taxation Office [ATO]), are regulated by APRA because they do not meet all conditions to be a SMSF. The Board noted there may be users (such as regulators and trustees) of the financial statements of SAFs who can command information they need and the outsiders for whom the SAF holds assets in a fiduciary capacity. Accordingly, those users do not seem to constitute a broad group and the Board decided not to deem SAFs as publicly accountable.

BC31   Furthermore, some respondents questioned whether all entities holding an Australian Financial Services Licence (AFSL) would meet the definition of publicly accountable.

BC32   The Board noted that AFSL holders undertake a range of activities and are a diverse group of entities. The Board concluded that whether an AFSL holder is publicly accountable depends on the circumstances, including the nature of the services they provide. Therefore, it would not be appropriate for the Board to deem AFSL holders as publicly accountable or not publicly accountable.

Size Thresholds

BC33   The Board proposed in ITC 12 that for-profit entities that do not satisfy the definition of a publicly accountable entity, nevertheless may be viewed as being 'important' from a public interest perspective because of their large size, and should be subject to Tier 1 requirements. The size thresholds proposed were:

- Consolidated revenue for the financial year of the entity and the entities it controls (if any) of $500m.

- Consolidated assets at financial year end of the entity and the entities it controls (if any) of $250m.

BC34   The Board considered constituents' comments on the issue and decided not to require entities that are 'important' because of their large size to adopt Tier 1 requirements on the grounds that:

(a)   size thresholds are arbitrary;

(b)   using public accountability (as defined by the IASB) for the for-profit sector in Australia would be consistent with international requirements;

(c)   large non-publicly accountable entities would still be required to prepare high-quality general purpose financial statements under the requirements of Tier 2; and

(d)   keeping size thresholds that identify 'important' entities up-to-date would entail additional maintenance and monitoring costs.

For-Profit Entities in the Public Sector

BC35   The Board noted that the definition of public accountability it has adopted has a for-profit private sector orientation as it is based on the definition included in the *IFRS for SMEs*. The Board noted that the nature of for-profit entities in the public sector may differ from that in the private sector in that many Government Business Enterprises (GBEs) also undertake social policy obligations. Moreover, the ownership group in many for-profit public sector entities is not a broad group. The Board noted that, although these entities are typically seen as publicly accountable in the general sense of the term, they do not typically fall under the definition of public accountability used for the private sector.

BC36   Some respondents to ED 192 expressed the view that GBEs should be included in Tier 1 because of their commercial significance and their participation in markets in competition with private sector for-profit entities. Others noted that, while it is acknowledged there is a relatively high level of public interest in relation to GBEs, it is also important that those public sector entities that compete with private sector entities in Tier 2 are not disadvantaged through the application of more onerous financial reporting requirements.

BC37   Some respondents supported an approach where GBEs would by default be classified as Tier 2 entities, with the caveat that the public sector entity that 'regulates' the respective entities would determine whether individual entities should apply the disclosure requirements of Tier 1. This approach, it was noted, could result in GBEs achieving the same level of financial reporting as for-profit private sector entities of similar nature and size.

BC38   The Board concluded that, consistent with the role of other regulators under the revised differential reporting framework (see paragraphs BC40-BC41), the determination of the Tiers of reporting requirements under which for-profit public sector entities should report would best be left to relevant public sector regulators in each jurisdiction.

Entities Eligible for Tier 2 Requirements can Elect to Adopt Tier 1 Requirements

BC39   The Board concluded that an entity that is eligible to adopt Tier 2 requirements should be permitted to adopt Tier 1 requirements. This is on the basis that:

    (a)   a relevant regulator may decide that in certain circumstances it is more beneficial to the users of financial statements, including the public at large, to include more comprehensive information in the general purpose financial statements;

    (b)   a subsidiary may be required to apply Tier 1 requirements by its parent; and

    (c)   some entities may find it more convenient or beneficial to continue to apply Tier 1 requirements in their circumstances. Examples include entities:

       (i)   contemplating future listing on the stock exchange;

       (ii)   planning to engage in activities as their primary business that would classify them as holders of assets in a fiduciary capacity for a broad group of outsiders; and

       (iii)   preferring to state compliance with full IFRSs because they are primarily engaged in international business.

The Role of Other Regulators

BC40   The Board noted that other regulators, legislators and stakeholders play an important role in the application of Standards, including providing exemptions in certain circumstances. For example, as noted in paragraph BC4, small proprietary companies are exempted from financial reporting under the Corporations Act.

BC41   The Board noted that some respondents to ITC 12 expressed concern about possible inconsistencies in practice that may arise if the Board were to specify rules rather than principles for determining which Tier of reporting is applicable to which entities. This is due to complexities involved in determining the application of different Tiers of reporting requirements to entities of different sizes and with varying levels of economic, social and political significance across different economic sectors. To help avoid these inconsistencies and to facilitate the application of different Tiers of reporting requirements in an effective and efficient manner, the Board decided that other regulators, legislators or stakeholders should have a role in determining the application of Standards under the revised framework. Accordingly, the Board decided that, except for the cases where a clear-cut and timeless application criterion can be used by the Board or a clear-cut judgement can be made based on relevant factors, the application issue would best be dealt with by other regulators, legislators and stakeholders (see, for example, paragraphs BC39(a) and (b)).

Applicability of the Different Tiers to NFP Entities

Public Accountability

BC42   The Board considered whether the notion of public accountability as defined by the IASB could usefully be applied to the NFP sector. It noted that, although there are some who argue that the IASB definition of public accountability may cover some NFP entities on the grounds that they hold funds in a fiduciary capacity for a broad group of outsiders, the IASB definition has a for-profit context that makes it unsuitable for the NFP sector.

BC43   The Board also considered using a modified definition of public accountability in the NFP sector context. The Board noted the disparate views among constituents about whether such a notion can effectively be modified and used to identify entities falling under different reporting Tiers in the NFP sector.

BC44   The Board noted that some constituents believe that the level of public accountability, for example, for each charity, depends on a number of entity-specific factors, which reduce the usefulness of 'public accountability' as a stand-alone criterion for differential reporting purposes in the NFP sector. Some constituents argued that the degree of public accountability of a charity has a direct relationship to the following.

(a)   *Sources of funds*: for example, if the sources of funds are public donations (particularly those that are tax deductible by the donor) or government grants, then a high degree of public accountability is expected. Voluntary labour may be regarded as a form of donation and, therefore, a high degree of public accountability might be expected when significant voluntary labour is involved. Generally the level of public accountability is high where public funds are involved, such as when community or social activities are carried out on behalf of government. However, when the source of funds is an individual or a corporation, a much lower degree of public accountability is expected on the basis that the individual or corporation involved can probably access the financial information they need. A moderate level of public accountability may be envisaged when the sources of funds are grants from foundations or sponsors.

(b)   *Number of stakeholders in the entity*: the wider the spectrum of stakeholders, the higher the expected level of public accountability.

(c)   *Scale of operations and geographical coverage*: generally charities active at the national or international level are seen as being publicly accountable at a high level.

BC45   The Board concluded that a modified definition of public accountability in the NFP private sector context would not provide a robust basis for identifying entities falling under different reporting Tiers since NFP private sector entities, (with the likely exception of smaller member-based entities), are typically seen as having differing degrees of public accountability in the general sense of the term.

BC46   The Board reached a similar conclusion about whether a definition of public accountability could provide a robust basis for identifying NFP public sector entities falling under different reporting Tiers. This is on the basis that these entities are regarded as publicly accountable in the general sense of the term.

Size Thresholds

BC47   The Board proposed in ITC 12 that NFP entities that prepare general purpose financial statements that exceed nominated size thresholds should be required to apply Tier 1 requirements. The size thresholds proposed were:

- Consolidated revenue for the financial year of the entity and the entities it controls (if any) of $25m.

- Consolidated assets at the end of the financial year of the entity and the entities it controls (if any) of $12.5m.

BC48   Some respondents to ITC 12 preferred the use of size thresholds in comparison to the use of a modified notion of public accountability as the basis for identifying reporting Tiers on the grounds that it is relatively objective and would provide consistency in identifying entities that fall under different Tiers. However, other respondents were concerned about using size thresholds, citing the following reasons:

(a)   size thresholds are arbitrary;

(b)   size thresholds will become outdated over time; and

(c)   particularly in the public sector, unless jurisdiction-specific thresholds are prescribed, it would lead to similar entities applying different requirements across different State and Territory jurisdictions.

BC49   There were also differences of view between respondents as to the amounts of the appropriate thresholds. Some thought the thresholds noted in paragraph BC47 are too low and should be raised to be comparable to 'important' entity thresholds contemplated for the for-profit sector noted in paragraph BC33. Others thought the thresholds being contemplated are too high, which would mean that too few NFP entities would apply full IFRSs as adopted in Australia. Yet others thought that the ratio of thresholds (revenue twice the assets) is not appropriate for many asset-rich entities in the NFP sector.

BC50   Respondents' comments on the comparability of thresholds between private and public sector NFP entities and their difference from those contemplated for 'important' entities in the for-profit sector did not reflect any convergence of views. Some respondents thought that public sector NFP entities are inherently of greater public interest than private sector NFP entities. Others thought that the thresholds should take account of the fact that the resources at the disposal of public sector NFP entities are generally significantly greater than those at the disposal of private sector NFP entities. Some expressed the view that public interest would not differ between the for-profit and NFP sectors. Others expressed the view that entities within the public sector are all of public interest and expressed concern that size thresholds would give a misleading perception of an increase in public interest proportional to an increase in an entity's size.

BC51   Consistent with the Board's conclusions in relation to size thresholds for for-profit entities, the Board concluded that size thresholds do not provide a robust basis for differential reporting purposes in a NFP context because of the complexities involved and that the disadvantages of using size thresholds would exceed any advantages that may arise from their use. The Board also noted that keeping size thresholds up-to-date would entail additional maintenance and monitoring costs.

Governments

BC52   The Board concluded that the Australian Government and State, Territory and Local Governments should be subject to Tier 1 requirements. This is on the basis that these entities clearly satisfy the criteria cited in paragraph BC63 as a whole, including in particular their coercive power to tax, rate or levy. Consistent with this conclusion, the Board also decided that General Government Sectors of the Australian Government and State and Territory Governments should continue to apply AASB 1049 *Whole of Government and General Government Sector Financial Reporting*, without the reduction in disclosures provided by Tier 2.

Public Sector NFP Universities

BC53   ED 192 proposed that universities in the public sector should be subject to Tier 1 requirements. Some respondents concurred with the proposal on the grounds that universities in the public sector are government funded. However, others had reservations, which included the following:

(a)   since universities are statutory bodies (in some jurisdictions), then they should be subject to the same reporting requirements that apply to other statutory bodies in the relevant jurisdiction – that is, the decision as to whether universities should be subject to Tier 1 or Tier 2 requirements should be left to the local regulator;

(b)   while it is acknowledged they are large entities, there would appear to be no conceptual reason mandating the classification of universities under Tier 1 – for example, they have no coercive power to tax, rate or levy;

(c)   funding by government or receipt of voluntary donations, by itself, does not suffice to classify universities as Tier 1 entities since many other public sector entities fall in the same category; and

(d)   the proposal would not be consistent with transaction-neutrality principles, because it would result in public sector NFP universities being treated differently from private sector universities.

BC54　　The Board noted that because universities differ from jurisdiction to jurisdiction, it may not enable regulators in those jurisdictions to apply criteria that they regard as appropriate in their circumstances, if the Board were to make a universal decision on the reporting Tier under which they fall. Accordingly the Board decided that universities should be allowed to apply Tier 2 requirements in preparing their general purpose financial statements unless a relevant public sector regulator requires the application of Tier 1 requirements.

Private Sector NFP Entities

BC55　　The Board considered the issue of possible subclassifications of different types of NFP entities within the NFP sector for differential reporting purposes. The Board noted commentators' views on ITC 14 *Proposed Definition and Guidance for Not-for-Profit Entities* that NFP entities can generally be identified as being in one of three categories based on the nature of their operations and sources of funding:

(a)　　charities;

(b)　　member-based entities; and

(c)　　public sector entities;

and that there may be a need for a fourth 'other' category to cater for entities such as schools and religious organisations. The Board noted the significant disparities in the size of entities within each of the above categories.

BC56　　Some constituents argued that the disclosures required by full IFRSs (or the *IFRS for SMEs*) would not satisfy the information needs of users of financial statements of, for example, charities. These Standards, it was noted, have a for-profit focus while the nature of charities' activities is such that not all disclosures in these Standards are pertinent to the needs of users of the financial statements of charities. Moreover, there are disclosures that relate to the nature of operations of charities and specific issues of public interest that are not required by these Standards and that may be within the scope of financial reporting. It was argued that the stakeholders of a charity are interested in the accountability of the entity in achieving objectives stated in the entity's mission statement using funds provided by those stakeholders. They noted that donors, grantors and other contributors who provide resources in the form of money or voluntary services and the public at large (which includes the beneficiaries of charitable activity) are all interested in the accountability of charities.

BC57　　The Board noted that a similar view exists in regard to all NFP entities. This view links accountability to the objective of each NFP entity and advocates disclosure of particular performance-related information to help inform a wide range of stakeholders about the way a NFP entity is utilising its resources in achieving its purpose.

BC58　　The Board decided that there should not be subclassifications of different types of entities in the NFP sector other than between private and public sector entities, for differential reporting purposes. In arriving at this decision, the Board noted that:

(a)　　in a transaction-neutral reporting environment, subclassifications should not make a reporting difference as far as the recognition and measurement of transactions are concerned; and

(b)　　a choice between Tier 1 and Tier 2 requirements would provide different levels of disclosures appropriate for entities with different levels of activities.

BC59　　The Board noted that its conclusion on this matter does not rule out specific projects directed at particular types of NFP entities and decided that its separate project on Disclosures by Private Sector Not-for-Profit Entities should be the vehicle through which it determines whether disclosures in addition to those required by full IFRSs as adopted in Australia should be required of Tier 1 or Tier 2 NFP entities. The Board also noted that much of the information relating to the extent to which a NFP entity has achieved its purpose set out in its mission statement may not be of a financial nature.

Entities Eligible for Tier 2 Requirements can Elect to Adopt Tier 1 Requirements

BC60   The Board concluded that a NFP entity that is eligible to adopt Tier 2 requirements should be permitted to adopt Tier 1 requirements. This is on the basis that, as noted in relation to the for-profit sector in paragraph BC39, in some jurisdictions, a relevant regulator may decide that in certain circumstances it is more beneficial to the users of financial statements, including the public at large, to include more comprehensive information in the general purpose financial statements. A NFP entity may also find it beneficial to choose to apply Tier 1 requirements in order to claim compliance with full IFRSs as adopted in Australia with a view to enhancing its credibility internationally, in particular in relation to major users of financial statements such as donors and governments.

The Role of Other Regulators

BC61   The Board acknowledges that, although AASB 1053 allows the vast majority of entities in the NFP sector to adopt Tier 2 requirements, other regulators may decide that some of those entities should adopt Tier 1 requirements.

BC62   Some respondents to ED 192 particularly commented that, while they welcome the choice that the Board has provided to public sector regulators in determining which of the Tiers should be followed by entities other than those required by the Board to apply Tier 1 requirements, the Board should develop non-mandatory guidance, in the form of qualitative criteria, to help public sector regulators consistently identify entities falling under each of the two Tiers of reporting requirements.

BC63   The Board explored the possibility of providing guidance, noting there are a range of qualitative factors that could be considered, including the following:

     (a)   *the entity's coercive power to obtain public funds*: the Board noted this notion of coercive power is a narrow criterion and on its own would be helpful only in a limited number of cases for jurisdictions in identifying entities falling under each Tier;

     (b)   *level of public funds used by the entity*: entities in the public sector vary in the degree to which they are publicly funded, the discretion over the distribution or expenditure of public funds, and the nature of that spending (for example, operational compared with income redistribution);

     (c)   *risk profile*: generally, risk in the public sector is a reference to uncertainty in achieving an organisation's objectives and more comprehensive disclosures may be warranted where an entity is seen as having a high risk profile;

     (d)   *level of complexity*: the level of complexity of public sector entities varies with the nature, diversity and range of their activities, which may also point to the existence of a wide range of stakeholders; and

     (e)   *financial profile*: the financial profile of a public sector entity may point to its economic significance and ability in providing services, which would in turn have an impact on the level of public interest.

BC64   The Board noted that, while each of the above factors may be a useful indicator to help regulators in identifying entities that should disclose more comprehensive information in their general purpose financial statements, no single criterion, by itself, would be likely to provide a conclusive basis for a jurisdiction to distinguish between Tier 1 and Tier 2 entities in the public sector.

BC65   The Board noted these factors as a whole were taken into account in its decision to classify the Australian Government and State, Territory and Local Governments as Tier 1 entities (see paragraph BC52). Accordingly, the Board concluded that these factors as a whole would be likely to benefit regulators across public sector jurisdictions in identifying the population of entities that could be of greater interest to users of general purpose financial statements, including the public at large. The Board noted regulators may develop their own size thresholds to identify those entities about which there would be sufficient interest to justify applying Tier 1 requirements. To arrive at consistent results, the Board noted it might be appropriate to use a number of different size indicators such as total assets, revenue, and number of employees as the basis for thresholds.

Tier 2 Requirements

BC66   The Board decided to adopt the Reduced Disclosure Requirements (RDR) reflected in AASB 1053, rather than the *IFRS for SMEs*, as Tier 2 requirements. The Board noted that the two approaches are fundamentally different because the RDR involve applying the same recognition and measurement requirements as Tier 1, whereas the *IFRS for SMEs* modifies the recognition and measurement requirements of full IFRSs. In deciding between the RDR and the *IFRS for SMEs*, the Board also considered whether entities subject to Tier 2 requirements should be provided with an option of adopting the RDR or the *IFRS for SMEs*.

Reasons for Not Adopting *IFRS for SMEs*

BC67   Constituents' comments on the *IFRS for SMEs* were mixed. While many supported its reduction in disclosure requirements, they expressed concern about introducing recognition and measurement requirements that are different from those included in full IFRSs.

BC68   There was also concern expressed about the differences in the hierarchies for determining accounting policies under the *IFRS for SMEs* and full IFRSs in the absence of a specific requirement. It was noted that the hierarchy adopted in the *IFRS for SMEs* would lead to disparities in the choice of accounting policies by different entities as it gives precedence to the Conceptual Framework over full IFRSs as the source of guidance for determining accounting policies in the absence of a specific requirement.

BC69   Other respondents noted the additional initial and ongoing costs of training and education for two sets of standards both for the profession and at the tertiary level.

BC70   In its submission to the IASB on the proposed *IFRS for SMEs*, the AASB noted that the *IFRS for SMEs* in its proposed form would not be a stand-alone document and that to meet its stand-alone objective more topics and more treatment options would need to be included from full IFRSs.

BC71   Based on comments received from constituents, the AASB commented in its submission to the IASB that:

> Some subsidiaries of publicly accountable entities would find it burdensome to apply the proposed *IFRS for SMEs* in preparing their general purpose financial statements. They would need to prepare financial information based on the recognition and measurement requirements of full IFRSs for the purposes of the parent entity consolidation. If such subsidiaries are not themselves publicly accountable but apply full IFRSs (as they are already applying full IFRS recognition and measurement for consolidation purposes), they are required to disclose information that is onerous to prepare and is often of no benefit to users. If they were to adopt the *IFRS for SMEs* as proposed, they could choose to refer to a full IFRS for an option that is not included in the *IFRS for SMEs*. However, they are then required to follow the disclosure requirements of that full IFRS. A stand-alone *IFRS for SMEs* that includes only the absolute minimum necessary disclosures, more topics and more of the treatment options from full IFRSs may alleviate the problem. However, it seems likely that subsidiaries within large groups would be involved in a wider range of activities and transactions than an equivalent SME that is not part of a group. Accordingly, it may be necessary for the IASB to consider permitting subsidiaries of publicly accountable entities to prepare general purpose financial statements by applying all the recognition and measurement requirements of full IFRSs, but permitting reduced disclosures similar to those required by the *IFRS for SMEs*.

BC72   However, the *IFRS for SMEs*, published in July 2009, did not address many of the Australian constituents' concerns. The *IFRS for SMEs* changes some of the full IFRS recognition and measurement accounting policy options by mandating or eliminating a particular option or introducing 'new' options. That means some of the full IFRS recognition and measurement accounting policy options are not available to SMEs and there are some that differ from comparable full IFRS recognition and measurement requirements.

BC73   The AASB discussed the *IFRS for SMEs* with a view to assessing its suitability as Tier 2 requirements. The AASB noted that there are concerns about adopting the *IFRS for SMEs* in Australia for the following reasons:

    (a)   some of the accounting policy options that have been removed would be the favoured accounting policies for many Australian entities;

    (b)   changes to full IFRS recognition and measurement requirements under the *IFRS for SMEs* and the absence of some accounting policy options from the *IFRS for SMEs* would force subsidiaries to adjust accounting policies for consolidation purposes when parents apply full IFRSs;

    (c)   entities applying the *IFRS for SMEs* would be deprived of improvements and simplifications as they become available at the full IFRS level because the IASB has stated that it will only update the *IFRS for SMEs* once there have been two years of broad adoption and, thereafter, every three years;

    (d)   possible benefits that might result from comparability with overseas entities applying the *IFRS for SMEs* would:

        (i)   depend on how widely adopted it becomes;

        (ii)   be limited because entities seeking to access international capital markets would generally apply full IFRSs; and

        (iii)   be mitigated due to a loss of comparability across all types of entities' general purpose financial statements within Australia;

    (e)   having different streams of recognition and measurement requirements involves different streams of knowledge, such that education and training at the tertiary level and within the accounting profession would become more costly;

    (f)   there would be start up costs because entities preparing general purpose financial statements have already made the effort to apply full IFRSs;

    (g)   adoption of the *IFRS for SMEs* may be seen as a retrograde step in a country that has already adopted full IFRS recognition and measurement accounting policy options;

    (h)   the actual changes in recognition and measurement requirements in the *IFRS for SMEs* would not produce any real economies for Australian SMEs; and

    (i)   in the event that an entity moves to, or from, full IFRSs, there would be costs involved in migrating from the recognition and measurement requirements of one Tier of reporting to another.

BC74   The Board concluded that the *IFRS for SMEs* is not presently a suitable set of requirements for Tier 2 in Australia. However, the Board decided it will continue to monitor and contribute to further changes in the *IFRS for SMEs* and that it is open to the possibility of adopting the *IFRS for SMEs* in future should the changes in that Standard make it practicable in an integrated for-profit/NFP sector reporting environment.

BC75   The Board noted that the introduction of the RDR as Tier 2 is supported by a majority of respondents to ED 192 who have also provided reasons for not supporting the adoption of the *IFRS for SMEs* as Tier 2 in place of the RDR or as an alternative alongside it.

Approach to Determining Disclosure Requirements under the RDR

BC76   In determining the RDR, the Board sought to balance the need to reduce disclosures with the need to satisfy the objective of general purpose financial statements. From amongst a number of possible approaches to determining disclosure requirements under the RDR, the Board decided to adopt an approach that:

(a) draws on the *IFRS for SMEs* to identify disclosures in cases where the recognition and measurement accounting policy options available or requirements under the RDR align with those under the *IFRS for SMEs*; and

(b) applies 'user need' and 'cost-benefit' principles (that is, the same basic principles used by the IASB in determining disclosures under the *IFRS for SMEs*) to arrive at reduced disclosure requirements in cases where the recognition and measurement accounting policy options or requirements under the RDR differ from those under the *IFRS for SMEs*.

In applying this approach, the Board concluded that satisfying the objective of general purpose financial statements should be the overriding basis for determining the disclosures under the RDR whether or not the recognition and measurement accounting policy options available or required under that regime align with those provided under the *IFRS for SMEs*. The Board applied this approach to each disclosure requirement in each Australian Accounting Standard. The results are reflected in AASB 2010-2.

BC77   The Board noted that its approach would help minimise the cost of determining and maintaining disclosures under the RDR.

BC78   Consistent with the IASB's approach in the *IFRS for SMEs*, the AASB concluded that users of general purpose financial statements of non-publicly accountable for-profit entities are particularly interested in information about:

(a) short-term cash flows and about obligations, commitments or contingencies, whether or not recognised as liabilities;

(b) liquidity and solvency;

(c) measurement uncertainties;

(d) the entity's accounting policy choices;

(e) disaggregations of amounts presented in the financial statements; and

(f) transactions and other events and conditions encountered by such entities.

BC79   The Board also concluded that, in addition to the particular information needs of users of non-publicly accountable for-profit entities noted in paragraph BC78, the information needs of the users of general purpose financial statements of NFP entities in both the private and public sectors would be satisfied by adopting a similar approach, having regard to the specific needs of users of NFP, including public sector, entity financial statements. The AASB uses its *Process for Modifying IFRSs for PBE/NFP* in assessing the need for specific requirements relating to NFP entities.

BC80   The Board noted that, although the *IFRS for SMEs* has been developed to apply to for-profit private sector entities, broadly it is considered reasonable to rely on the judgements made in developing the *IFRS for SMEs* in respect of both for-profit and NFP (including public sector) entities in Australia given that IFRSs are generally applied to all types of Australian entities.

Application of Standards

BC81   AASB 2010-2 specifies the disclosures in each Australian Accounting Standard from which Tier 2 entities are exempted. However, some Standards are equally applicable to both Tier 1 and Tier 2 entities. Accordingly, such Standards do not provide reduced disclosures for Tier 2 entities. Examples are AASB 118 *Revenue* and AASB 1004 *Contributions*.

BC82   Some Standards apply only to Tier 1 entities, but Tier 2 entities may elect to use them. Examples are AASB 8 *Operating Segments* and AASB 133 *Earnings per Share*, which generally apply only to entities that access public capital markets, as stated in their application paragraphs.

BC83   AASB 134 *Interim Financial Reporting* applies to disclosing entities' half-year financial statements. Consistent with the Board's approach to other Standards in respect of annual general purpose financial statements, other Tier 1 entities and

Tier 2 entities that elect to prepare interim general purpose financial statements would be required to apply AASB 134 (which specifies reduced disclosure requirements under Tier 2), by virtue of the application paragraph in that Standard.

BC84   Entities applying AASB 134 may prepare condensed interim financial statements or present a complete set of financial statements as interim financial statements. Tier 2 entities are exempted from some disclosures when preparing condensed financial statements and would apply Tier 2 requirements in AASB 101 when preparing a complete set of financial statements as their interim financial statements.

BC85   There are also Standards that are only applicable to Tier 1 entities, and Tier 2 entities cannot elect to apply them in preparing financial statements. These Standards are identified by virtue of their application paragraphs. Currently the only example is AASB 1049 *Whole of Government and General Government Sector Financial Reporting*.

BC86   In considering possible reductions in disclosure requirements of:

(a)   AASB 4 *Insurance Contracts*, AASB 1023 *General Insurance Contracts* and AASB 1038 *Life Insurance Contracts* for insurers that might not be publicly accountable, such as potentially some captive insurers (see paragraphs BC27-BC28); and

(b)   AAS 25 *Financial Reporting by Superannuation Plans* for superannuation plans that might not be publicly accountable, such as SAFs (see paragraphs BC29-BC30);

the Board noted that such decisions should be made after applying further due process, including public exposure of proposed reductions. This is because ED 192 did not include proposed reduced disclosures for AASB 4, AASB 1023, AASB 1038 and AAS 25. In particular, the Board considered it would need to consult widely about whether some life insurers could be given relief from disclosures under AASB 1038 because the Board's initial view is that life insurance is of high public interest and comprehensive information on life insurance is needed by users of general purpose financial statements.

BC87   The Board noted that, until the above due process is completed, all insurers and superannuation plans preparing general purpose financial statements would continue to apply these Standards in full. Accordingly, if there are any Tier 2 insurers or superannuation plans preparing general purpose financial statements, the only benefits of reduced disclosure requirements available to them would be through the reduced disclosures in other Standards.

Transition

BC88   The Board considered the transitional requirements for entities adopting Tier 2 requirements for the first time and moving between Tiers. The Board identified three main scenarios for transition that should be dealt with in AASB 1053:

(a)   transition by an entity that prepared its most recent previous financial statements in the form of special purpose financial statements to Tier 1 or Tier 2;

(b)   transition by an entity applying Tier 1 to Tier 2; and

(c)   transition by an entity applying Tier 2 to Tier 1.

BC89   The Board noted that, for transitioning from special purpose financial statements to general purpose financial statements, an assessment of whether the preparer has applied recognition and measurement requirements in its most recent previous financial statements is of paramount importance. Accordingly, an entity that has applied recognition and measurement requirements of Australian Accounting Standards selectively or not at all in its special purpose financial statements should be treated differently from one that has applied the recognition and measurement requirements of applicable Australian Accounting Standards, including those of AASB 1 *First-time Adoption of Australian Accounting Standards*.

BC90   AASB 1 includes disclosure requirements. Entities transitioning from special purpose financial statements to Tier 2 are exempted from some of the disclosure requirements in that Standard, using the principles applied in determining disclosures under Tier 2 (see paragraph BC78).

BC91   Entities transitioning from Tier 1 to Tier 2 would not apply AASB 1. However, entities transitioning from Tier 2 to Tier 1 would need to apply AASB 1 in full to claim compliance with IFRSs, as under Tier 2 they would only have applied some of the disclosure requirements of AASB 1. This is consistent with the Board's policy that for-profit entities complying with Australian Accounting Standards simultaneously comply with IFRSs.

BC92   Entities that transition to Tier 1 need to apply AASB 1 in full in order to be able to claim compliance with IFRSs, in accordance with AASB 101, including making an unreserved statement of compliance as required by AASB 101.

BC93   The Board considered whether entities transitioning between Tiers for which compliance with IFRSs is not pertinent, in particular NFP entities that are subject to Aus paragraphs, should be subject to AASB 1 on transition. The Board concluded that AASB 1 is not applicable in those circumstances because, at the time of transition between Tiers, Australian Accounting Standards or Australian Accounting Standards – Reduced Disclosure Requirements, which have common recognition and measurement requirements, have previously been complied with. Accordingly, it would not be appropriate to imply, through application of AASB 1, that the basis of accounting has changed.

Operative Date

BC94   The Board concluded that mandatory application of Tier 2 requirements should be annual reporting periods beginning on or after 1 July 2013. The Board noted a long transitional period is particularly required to allow entities that prepare special purpose financial statements to make necessary preparations for transitioning to Tier 2 requirements should they choose to prepare general purpose financial statements under Tier 2. The Board considered it would be beneficial to have a relatively long transition period to allow these entities to prepare their internal reporting systems for transition.

BC95   However, the Board decided to allow early adoption of Tier 2 requirements for those entities that want to avail themselves of the reduced disclosure requirements under that Tier before the mandatory application date of 1 July 2013. Early adoption is permitted for annual reporting periods that begin on or after 1 July 2009 but before 1 July 2013. The Board decided not to permit early adoption for annual reporting periods that begin before 1 July 2009 due to the difficulty of identifying relevant Standards applying to those earlier periods and making consistent judgments as to which disclosures in those Standards would be applicable under Tier 2.

BC96   The Board also noted that a long transition period would potentially enable any outcome of the second stage of the project to be made operative from the same date as the first stage, to facilitate minimal disruption on transition. The Board will not decide whether the second stage should be progressed until the results of the research project it has commissioned are known.

BC97   The transition period is also consistent with the Board's normal policy regarding transition periods for its Standards. The Board concluded that making Tier 2 requirements mandatory from the date of issue of relevant Standards may inappropriately require entities that currently apply Tier 1 to select that Tier and make disclosures related to that selection rather than continue their current accounting disclosures that comply with current GAAP.

Maintenance of Tier 2 Requirements

BC98   The Board decided that Tier 2 requirements should be maintained on a continuous basis, rather than waiting for the IASB to update its *IFRS for SMEs*, which the IASB plans to undertake only every few years, by which time there would be an accumulation of possible changes. The AASB intends that each future Exposure

Draft or Invitation to Comment involving changes to Tier 1 that includes disclosure proposals would seek comment about which disclosures should be included in Tier 2, and may include the AASB's proposed reduced disclosures.

Post-implementation Review

BC99   The Board decided that Tier 2 requirements should be subject to review and revision taking account of implementation experience and international developments.

BC100   The Board plans to monitor implementation experience with Tier 2 requirements and use it as a basis for providing feedback to the IASB to assist with its further deliberations on differential reporting matters and to help shape future amendments to the *IFRS for SMEs*.

Trans-Tasman Convergence

BC101   AASB 1053 was developed in the context of the Prime Ministers of Australia and New Zealand having signed on 20 August 2009 a Joint Statement of Intent that agreed on a framework of Outcome Proposals for developing cross-border economic initiatives. A range of shared Outcome Proposals have been identified across a wide range of business law areas, including in relation to financial reporting. The outcomes are expected to accelerate and deepen trans-Tasman regulatory integration as part of a broader single economic market initiative. Outcome Proposals relating to financial reporting include:

For-profit entities

(a)   "Profit entities are able to use a single set of accounting standards and prepare only one set of financial statements (timeframe: short term – within two years)"

(b)   "Trans-Tasman companies have to prepare only one set of financial statements to one set of standards (timeframe: short term – within two years)"

Not-for-profit entities

"Not-for-profit entities are able to use a single set of accounting standards and prepare only one set of financial statements (timeframe: medium term – within five years)".

BC102   These Outcome Proposals are intended to reduce compliance costs for entities operating across the Tasman and support trans-Tasman investment through the consistency of financial statements. The use of full IFRSs as the foundation standards in both countries provides a sound basis for achieving the above Outcome Proposals. However, further harmonisation in regard to financial reporting by entities other than those that are required to apply full IFRSs as adopted in Australia would be necessary to achieve the Outcome Proposals. This would be achieved by convergence of the differential reporting frameworks in the two countries.

BC103   New Zealand already adopts a differential reporting regime (that is different from the regime in Australia both before and after AASB 1053), which is expected to undergo restructuring in the light of the New Zealand Ministry of Economic Development review of standard setting arrangements. Close monitoring of these developments by the two countries would help identify an appropriate approach to converge the differential reporting frameworks in the two countries in due course.

BC104   The convergence of differential reporting frameworks is likely to be conducted in stages, with the first stage relating to for-profit private sector entities. New Zealand is expected to employ a notion of public accountability that is close to the IASB's definition to distinguish between for-profit entities that apply NZ IFRSs and those that can avail themselves of concessions under the differential reporting framework. The AASB noted that the use of the IASB's notion of public accountability under Tier 2 requirements in Australia provides common ground to discuss the harmonisation of the two countries' differential reporting frameworks in regard to for-profit private sector entities.

AASB 1054

Australian Additional Disclosures

(Issued May 2011)

Note from the Institute of Chartered Accountants Australia

This note, prepared by the technical editors, is not part of Accounting Standard AASB 1054.

Historical development

11 May 2011: AASB 1054 'Australian Additional Disclosures' was issued as part of the Trans-Tasman Convergence Project. This Standard sets out the Australian-specific disclosure requirements that are in addition to disclosure requirements in International Financial Reporting Standards. Previously these disclosures were included in other AASB Standards.

This Standard applies to annual reporting periods beginning on or after 1 July 2011 and can be adopted early.

Contents

Preface
Comparison with IFRSs
Accounting Standard
AASB 1054 Australian Additional Disclosures

	Paragraphs
Objective	1
Application	2 – 5
Definitions	6
Compliance with Australian Accounting Standards	7
Reporting Framework	8
General Purpose or Special Purpose Financial Statements	9
Audit Fees	10 – 11
Imputation Credits	12 – 15
Reconciliation of Net Operating Cash Flow to Profit (Loss)	16

Basis for Conclusions

Australian Accounting Standard AASB 1054 *Australian Additional Disclosures* is set out in paragraphs 1 – 16. All the paragraphs have equal authority. Paragraphs in **bold type** state the main principles. AASB 1054 is to be read in the context of other Australian Accounting Standards, including AASB 1048 *Interpretation of Standards*, which identifies the Australian Accounting Interpretations. In the absence of explicit guidance, AASB 108 *Accounting Policies, Changes in Accounting Estimates and Errors* provides a basis for selecting and applying accounting policies.

Preface

Introduction

The Australian Accounting Standards Board (AASB) makes Australian Accounting Standards, including Interpretations, to be applied by:

(a)   entities required by the *Corporations Act 2001* to prepare financial reports;

(b)   governments in preparing financial statements for the whole of government and the General Government Sector (GGS); and

(c)   entities in the private or public for-profit or not-for-profit sectors that are reporting entities or that prepare general purpose financial statements.

When appropriate, Australian Accounting Standards incorporate International Financial Reporting Standards (IFRSs), including Interpretations, issued by the International Accounting Standards Board (IASB), with the addition of paragraphs on the applicability of each Standard in the Australian environment.

Australian Accounting Standards also include requirements that are specific to Australian entities. These requirements may be located in Australian Accounting Standards that incorporate IFRSs or in other Australian Accounting Standards. In most instances, these requirements are either restricted to the not-for-profit or public sectors or include additional disclosures that address domestic, regulatory or other issues. In developing requirements for public sector entities, the AASB considers the requirements of International Public Sector Accounting Standards (IPSASs), as issued by the International Public Sector Accounting Standards Board (IPSASB) of the International Federation of Accountants.

AASB 1053 *Application of Tiers of Australian Accounting Standards* establishes a differential reporting framework consisting of two tiers of reporting requirements for preparing general purpose financial statements:

(a)   Tier 1: Australian Accounting Standards; and

(b)   Tier 2: Australian Accounting Standards – Reduced Disclosure Requirements.

Private sector for-profit entities complying with Tier 1 requirements will simultaneously comply with IFRSs. Many other entities complying with Tier 1 will also simultaneously comply with IFRSs.

Main Features of this Standard

This Standard sets out the Australian-specific disclosures for entities that have adopted Australian Accounting Standards. This Standard contains disclosure requirements that are additional to IFRSs.

This Standard results from the proposals that were included in Exposure Draft AASB ED 200B/ FRSB ED 122 *Proposed Separate Disclosure Standards*, published in July 2010.

The AASB and the Financial Reporting Standards Board (FRSB) of the New Zealand Institute of Chartered Accountants jointly issued AASB ED 200B/FRSB ED 122 for the purpose of harmonising Australian Accounting Standards and New Zealand equivalents to IFRSs (NZ IFRSs), with a focus on eliminating differences between the Standards in each jurisdiction relating to for-profit entities.

This Standard is a consequence of Phase 1 of the joint Trans-Tasman Convergence project of the AASB and the FRSB.

Trans-Tasman Convergence Project

At the October 2009 joint meeting, the AASB and the FRSB formalised a project for harmonising differences between the Australian Accounting Standards and NZ IFRSs.

The Boards have been working on convergence issues for some years to promote harmonisation of financial reporting standards across the Tasman. The Boards' efforts were given impetus by the Joint Prime Ministerial Statement of Intent and the Single Economic Market Outcome Proposals issued by the then Prime Ministers of both countries in August 2009, which was revised in June 2010.

The specific outcome sought is to enable entities, from an accounting standards perspective, to prepare only one set of financial statements that would be recognised in both jurisdictions. The relevant timeframe for achieving this outcome, in relation to for-profit entities, is by the end of 2011. The Joint Prime Ministerial Statement of Intent notes that such an outcome would allow a reduction in compliance costs for entities operating across the Tasman and it would support Trans-Tasman investment through the consistency of financial statements.

The project is divided into the following three phases:

(a)   Phase 1 has addressed the harmonisation of financial reporting requirements across the Tasman in relation to for-profit entities that assert compliance with IFRSs. The Boards were keen to first address differences from IFRSs and between Australian and New Zealand Standards as they apply to for-profit entities, on the basis that such entities are the most likely to claim compliance with IFRSs and trade across the Tasman;

(b)   a possible Phase 2 would specifically address differences affecting private not-for-profit entities; and

(c)   a possible Phase 3 would address differential reporting and qualifying entity differences.

Whilst for-profit entities currently applying Tier 1 Australian Accounting Standards and New Zealand Financial Reporting Standards are able to make an explicit and unreserved statement of compliance with IFRSs, the Boards decided to bring the alignment to IFRSs even closer than present, by eliminating any unnecessary variation from the wording of IFRSs. In particular, the Boards decided to use the IFRSs as the basis for eliminating Trans-Tasman differences. This is on the basis that if one jurisdiction did not see a need to modify the relevant IFRS and has not experienced adverse consequences, the other jurisdiction should consider the removal of the modification.

Accordingly for Phase 1, the Boards utilised the following principles in removing the differences between the Australian and New Zealand Standards:

(a)   eliminate differences from IFRSs, where possible; and

(b)   in cases where a disclosure requirement additional to IFRSs is of such importance that it should be retained, the additional disclosure requirement has been harmonised with the equivalent requirement in the other jurisdiction to the extent possible and relocated to a new Standard.

At the conclusion of Phase 1, the Boards decided to issue the following for each jurisdiction:

(a)   an amending standard containing the necessary amendments to the jurisdiction's Standards; and

(b)   a standard containing the jurisdiction-specific disclosures that are in addition to IFRSs. In reaching their decision on the location of additional disclosures, the Boards placed emphasis on bringing the wording of Australian and New Zealand Standards closer to IFRSs.

Accordingly, the AASB made:

(a)   AASB 2011-1 *Amendments to Australian Accounting Standards arising from the Trans-Tasman Convergence Project*; and

(b)   this Standard, which contains the Australian-specific disclosures that are in addition to IFRSs.

The FRSB prepared:

(a)   Harmonisation Amendments to New Zealand equivalents to International Financial Reporting Standards; and

(b)   FRS-44 *New Zealand Additional Disclosures*.

Application Date

This Standard is applicable to annual reporting periods beginning on or after 1 July 2011. Early adoption is permitted for annual reporting periods beginning on or after 1 January 2005 but before 1 July 2011, provided that AASB 2011-1 is also adopted early for the same period.

Specific disclosure requirements may individually be adopted early. When an entity elects to early adopt a disclosure requirement in this Standard, it shall also early adopt the relevant amendments in AASB 2011-1.

Main Requirements

This Standard includes definitions of 'annual reporting period' and 'special purpose financial statements'.

This Standard requires disclosure about:

(a)   compliance with Australian Accounting Standards;

(b)   the statutory basis or reporting framework for the financial statements;

(c)   whether the financial statements are general purpose or special purpose;

(d)   audit fees;

(e)   imputation credits; and

(f)   reconciliation of net operating cash flow to profit (loss).

Implications for Not-for-Profit Entities

This Standard applies to both for-profit entities and not-for-profit entities. This Standard does not include paragraphs that apply only to not-for-profit entities.

Implications for RDR Entities

Amendments to this Standard to introduce reduced disclosure requirements for entities preparing general purpose financial statements under Australian Accounting Standards – Reduced Disclosure Requirements for annual reporting periods beginning on or after 1 July 2013 are included in AASB 2011-2 *Amendments to Australian Accounting Standards arising from the Trans-Tasman Convergence Project – Reduced Disclosure Requirements*.

Comparison with IFRSs

AASB 1054 *Australian Additional Disclosures* includes disclosure requirements and definitions which are additional to International Financial Reporting Standards issued by the International Accounting Standards Board (IASB).

Compliance with AASB 1054 is not needed for IFRS compliance.

Accounting Standard AASB 1054

The Australian Accounting Standards Board makes Accounting Standard AASB 1054 *Australian Additional Disclosures* under section 334 of the *Corporations Act 2001*.

Kevin M. Stevenson
Chair – AASB

Dated 11 May 2011

Accounting Standard AASB 1054

Australian Additional Disclosures

Objective

1   The objective of this Standard is to set out Australian-specific disclosure requirements that are in addition to disclosure requirements in International Financial Reporting Standards.

Application

2   **This Standard applies to:**

     (a)   **each entity that is required to prepare financial reports in accordance with Part 2M.3 of the Corporations Act;**

     (b)   **general purpose financial statements of each reporting entity; and**

     (c)   **financial statements that are, or are held out to be, general purpose financial statements.**

3   **This Standard applies to *annual reporting periods* beginning on or after 1 July 2011.**

4   **This Standard, or individual disclosure requirements, may be applied to annual reporting periods beginning on or after 1 January 2005 but before 1 July 2011, provided that AASB 2011-1 *Amendments to Australian Accounting Standards arising from the Trans-Tasman Convergence Project*, or its relevant individual amendments, is also adopted early for the same period. When an entity applies this Standard, or individual disclosure requirements, to such an annual reporting period, it shall disclose that fact.**

5   **The requirements specified in this Standard apply to the financial statements where information resulting from their application is material in accordance with AASB 1031 *Materiality*.**

Definitions

6   The following terms are used in this Standard with the meanings specified.

         Annual reporting period means the financial year or similar period to which annual financial statements relate.

         Special purpose financial statements are financial statements other than general purpose financial statements.

Compliance with Australian Accounting Standards

7   An entity whose financial statements comply with Australian Accounting Standards shall make an explicit and unreserved statement of such compliance in the notes. An entity shall not describe financial statements as complying with Australian Accounting Standards unless they comply with all the requirements of Australian Accounting Standards.

Reporting Framework

8   An entity shall disclose in the notes:

(a)   the statutory basis or other reporting framework, if any, under which the financial statements are prepared; and

(b)   whether, for the purposes of preparing the financial statements, it is a for-profit or not-for-profit entity.

General Purpose or Special Purpose Financial Statements

9   An entity shall disclose in the notes whether the financial statements are general purpose financial statements or *special purpose financial statements*.

Audit Fees

10   An entity shall disclose fees to each auditor or reviewer, including any network firm, separately for:

(a)   the audit or review of the financial statements; and

(b)   all other services performed during the reporting period.

11   For paragraph 10(b) above, an entity shall describe the nature of other services.

Imputation Credits

12   The term 'imputation credits' is used in paragraphs 13-15 to also mean 'franking credits'. The disclosures required by paragraphs 13 and 15 shall be made separately in respect of any New Zealand imputation credits and any Australian imputation credits.

13   An entity shall disclose the amount of imputation credits available for use in subsequent reporting periods.

14   For the purposes of determining the amount required to be disclosed in accordance with paragraph 13, entities may have:

(a)   imputation credits that will arise from the payment of the amount of the provision for income tax;

(b)   imputation debits that will arise from the payment of dividends recognised as a liability at the reporting date; and

(c)   imputation credits that will arise from the receipt of dividends recognised as receivables at the reporting date.

15   Where there are different classes of investors with different entitlements to imputation credits, disclosures shall be made about the nature of those entitlements for each class where this is relevant to an understanding of them.

Reconciliation of Net Operating Cash Flow to Profit (Loss)

16   When an entity uses the direct method to present its statement of cash flows, the financial statements shall provide a reconciliation of the net cash flow from operating activities to profit (loss).

Basis for Conclusions

This Basis for Conclusions accompanies, but is not part of, AASB 1054.

Background

BC1   This Basis for Conclusions summarises the considerations of the Australian Accounting Standards Board and the Financial Reporting Standards Board (FRSB) of the New Zealand Institute of Chartered Accountants (NZICA) in reaching the conclusions in AASB 1054. It also provides a context for the Boards' decisions about harmonising the disclosure requirements. It focuses on the issues that the Boards consider to be of greatest significance. Individual Board members gave greater weight to some factors than to others.

Location of Additional Disclosures

BC2   The Boards discussed the merits of locating the additional domestic disclosure requirements in a separate disclosure standard compared with locating them within topic-based standards, which is the current practice. Some members supported a separate disclosure standard largely on the basis that it would facilitate the topic-based standards being identical to International Financial Reporting Standards (IFRSs). Other members expressed a preference for locating additional disclosures within topic-based standards for ease of use. On balance, with the benefit of constituent responses to AASB ED 200B/ FRSB ED 122 *Proposed Separate Disclosure Standards*, the Boards decided to locate the additional disclosures in separate disclosure standards on the basis that they view bringing the wording of Australian and New Zealand Standards closer to IFRSs as one of the greatest benefits of the Trans-Tasman Convergence project.

Definitions

BC3   The definition of 'annual reporting period' has been retained on the basis that it is used in application paragraphs of AASB Standards, consistent with terminology in the Australian *Corporations Act 2001*.

BC4   The definition of 'special purpose financial statements' has been retained on the basis that it is used in a disclosure requirement related to the AASB's differential reporting framework.

Audit Fees

BC5   The AASB and the FRSB have relocated and amended the audit fee disclosure requirements contained in AASB 101 *Presentation of Financial Statements* and NZ IAS 1 *Presentation of Financial Statements* to their respective separate disclosure Standards and harmonised the disclosure requirements across both jurisdictions.

BC6   The AASB and the FRSB consider that the disclosure of audit fees is a matter of accountability and, given that the accountability environment is similar in both jurisdictions, they should have the same audit fee disclosure requirements. The Boards also took the opportunity to simplify the disclosure requirements on the basis that in recent times both preparers and users have indicated that disclosures in financial statements have become overly complex.

BC7   The AASB and FRSB noted the usefulness of the notion of 'related practice' in audit fee disclosures in AASB 101 and decided to incorporate a similar notion that is common to both jurisdictions in the harmonised disclosures. Accordingly, the Boards decided to include the notion of 'network firm' from APES 110 *Code of Ethics for Professional Accountants* issued by Accounting and Professional Ethical Standards Board (APESB) (February 2008) and *Code of Ethics: Independence in Assurance Engagements* issued by the NZICA (September 2008). The Boards also decided not to define or provide explanatory material for 'network firm' on the basis that the notion is generally understood and preparers and auditors could refer to the relevant APESB and NZICA pronouncements.

BC8 The AASB and FRSB note that disclosures are made in the context of the scope of the entity reporting. Accordingly, in the case of a group, disclosures made in accordance with paragraph 10 would include fees paid by the parent and its subsidiaries for each of the parent and its subsidiaries.

Imputation Credits

BC9 The AASB and the FRSB have relocated the imputation credit disclosure requirements contained in AASB 101 and NZ IAS 12 *Income Taxes* to their respective separate disclosure Standards and to harmonise the disclosure requirements across both jurisdictions.

BC10 The AASB and the FRSB noted that Australia and New Zealand are among a limited number of jurisdictions that have an imputation tax regime and acknowledge the decision usefulness of information about imputation credits to users of financial information. Accordingly, the AASB and the FRSB decided that these disclosure requirements should be retained.

BC11 Given that both jurisdictions have disclosure requirements about imputation credits, and that the imputation regimes in each jurisdiction are highly similar, the Boards have harmonised the wording across both jurisdictions. The Boards also took the opportunity to simplify the disclosure requirements on the basis that in recent times both preparers and users have indicated that disclosures in financial statements have become overly complex.

Reconciliation of Net Operating Cash Flow to Profit (Loss)

BC12 The AASB and the FRSB have relocated the requirement to disclose a reconciliation of net operating cash flow to profit or loss when an entity uses the direct method to present its statement of cash flows [that were contained in AASB 107 *Statement of Cash Flows* and NZ IAS 7 *Statement of Cash Flows*] to their respective separate disclosure standards and to harmonise the disclosure requirements across both jurisdictions.

BC13 The Boards, in forming the view to retain the requirement for a reconciliation of net operating cash flow to profit or loss, acknowledged the weight of comments received on AASB ED 200B/FRSB ED 122 from constituents who opposed the proposal to remove this requirement.

BC14 The Boards noted that the IASB has recently considered requiring a reconciliation of net operating cash flow to profit or loss in the context of its Financial Statement Presentation project.

AASB 2010-2

Amendments to Australian Accounting Standards arising from Reduced Disclosure Requirements

(Issued June 2010)

Note from the Institute of Chartered Accountants Australia

This note, prepared by the technical editors, is not part of Accounting Standard AASB 2010-2.

Historical development

30 June 2010: AASB 2010-2 was issued to make amendments to many of the existing AASB Standards and Interpretations to introduce the Reduced Disclosure Requirements (RDR) into these pronouncements.

This Standard is applicable to annual reporting periods beginning on or after 1 July 2013. This Standard may be adopted early.

Contents

Preface

Accounting Standard

AASB 2010-2 Amendments to Australian Accounting Standards
arising from Reduced Disclosure Requirements

Paragraphs

Objective	1
Application	2 – 11
Amendments to AASB 1	12 – 14
Amendments to AASB 2	15
Amendments to AASB 3	16
Amendments to AASB 5	17
Amendments to AASB 7	18
Amendments to AASB 8	19
Amendments to AASB 101	20 – 23
Amendments to AASB 102	24
Amendments to AASB 107	25
Amendments to AASB 108	26 – 27
Amendments to AASB 110	28
Amendments to AASB 111	29
Amendments to AASB 112	30
Amendments to AASB 116	31
Amendments to AASB 117	32
Amendments to AASB 119	33
Amendments to AASB 121	34
Amendments to AASB 123	35
Amendments to AASB 124	36
Amendments to AASB 127	37
Amendments to AASB 128	38
Amendments to AASB 131	39
Amendments to AASB 133	40
Amendments to AASB 134	41
Amendments to AASB 136	42
Amendments to AASB 137	43
Amendments to AASB 138	44
Amendments to AASB 140	45
Amendments to AASB 141	46
Amendments to AASB 1050	47
Amendments to AASB 1052	48
Amendments to Interpretation 2	49
Amendments to Interpretation 4	50
Amendments to Interpretation 5	51

Paragraphs

Amendments to Interpretation 15   52
Amendments to Interpretation 17   53
Amendments to Interpretation 127   54
Amendments to Interpretation 129   55
Amendments to Interpretation 1052   56

Appendix:

Early Application of Australian Accounting Standards – Reduced Disclosure
Requirements

Australian Accounting Standard AASB 2010-2 *Amendments to Australian Accounting Standards arising from Reduced Disclosure Requirements* is set out in paragraphs 1 – 56 and the Appendix. All the paragraphs have equal authority.

Preface

Standards Amended by AASB 2010-2

This Standard makes amendments to many Australian Accounting Standards, including Interpretations, to introduce reduced disclosure requirements to the pronouncements for application by certain types of entities in preparing general purpose financial statements.

Main Features of this Standard

Application Date

This Standard applies to annual reporting periods beginning on or after 1 July 2013. Earlier application is permitted for annual reporting periods beginning on or after 1 July 2009 but before 1 July 2013, provided that AASB 1053 *Application of Tiers of Australian Accounting Standards* is also applied for the period.

Main Requirements

This Standard gives effect to Australian Accounting Standards – Reduced Disclosure Requirements. AASB 1053 provides further information regarding the differential reporting framework and the two tiers of reporting requirements for preparing general purpose financial statements.

Accounting Standard AASB 2010-2

Australian Accounting Standards Board makes Accounting Standard AASB 2010-2 *Amendments to Australian Accounting Standards arising from Reduced Disclosure Requirements* under section 334 of the *Corporations Act 2001*.

Kevin M. Stevenson
Chair – AASB

Dated 30 June 2010

Accounting Standard AASB 2010-2

Amendments to Australian Accounting Standards arising from Reduced Disclosure Requirements

Objective

1   The objective of this Standard is to make amendments to:

    (a)   AASB 1 *First-time Adoption of Australian Accounting Standards*;

    (b)   AASB 2 *Share-based Payment*;

    (c)   AASB 3 *Business Combinations*;

    (d)   AASB 5 *Non-current Assets Held for Sale and Discontinued Operations*;

    (e)   AASB 7 *Financial Instruments: Disclosures*;

    (f)   AASB 8 *Operating Segments*;

    (g)   AASB 101 *Presentation of Financial Statements*;

    (h)   AASB 102 *Inventories*;

    (i)   AASB 107 *Statement of Cash Flows*;

    (j)   AASB 108 *Accounting Policies, Changes in Accounting Estimates and Errors*;

    (k)   AASB 110 *Events after the Reporting Period*;

    (l)   AASB 111 *Construction Contracts*;

    (m)   AASB 112 *Income Taxes*;

    (n)   AASB 116 *Property, Plant and Equipment*;

    (o)   AASB 117 *Leases*;

    (p)   AASB 119 *Employee Benefits*;

    (q)   AASB 121 *The Effects of Changes in Foreign Exchange Rates*;

    (r)   AASB 123 *Borrowing Costs*;

    (s)   AASB 124 *Related Party Disclosures*;

    (t)   AASB 127 *Consolidated and Separate Financial Statements*;

    (u)   AASB 128 *Investments in Associates*;

    (v)   AASB 131 *Interests in Joint Ventures*;

    (w)   AASB 133 *Earnings per Share*;

    (x)   AASB 134 *Interim Financial Reporting*;

    (y)   AASB 136 *Impairment of Assets*;

    (z)   AASB 137 *Provisions, Contingent Liabilities and Contingent Assets*;

    (aa)   AASB 138 *Intangible Assets*;

    (bb)   AASB 140 *Investment Property*;

    (cc)   AASB 141 *Agriculture*;

    (dd)   AASB 1050 *Administered Items*;

    (ee)   AASB 1052 *Disaggregated Disclosures*;

    (ff)   Interpretation 2 *Members' Shares in Co-operative Entities and Similar Instruments*;

    (gg)   Interpretation 4 *Determining whether an Arrangement contains a Lease*;

    (hh)   Interpretation 5 *Rights to Interests arising from Decommissioning, Restoration and Environmental Rehabilitation Funds*;

    (ii)   Interpretation 15 *Agreements for the Construction of Real Estate*;

(jj)   Interpretation 17 *Distributions of Non-cash Assets to Owners*;

(kk)   Interpretation 127 *Evaluating the Substance of Transactions Involving the Legal Form of a Lease*;

(ll)   Interpretation 129 *Service Concession Arrangements: Disclosures*; and

(mm) Interpretation 1052 *Tax Consolidation Accounting*;

as a consequence of the adoption of a revised differential financial reporting framework.

Application

2   Subject to paragraphs 3-8, this Standard applies to:

(a)   each entity that is required to prepare financial reports in accordance with Part 2M.3 of the Corporations Act and that is a reporting entity;

(b)   general purpose financial statements of each other reporting entity; and

(c)   financial statements that are, or are held out to be, general purpose financial statements.

3   In respect of AASB 8, this Standard applies to:

(a)   each for-profit entity that is required to prepare financial reports in accordance with Part 2M.3 of the Corporations Act and that is a reporting entity;

(b)   general purpose financial statements of each other for-profit reporting entity other than for-profit government departments; and

(c)   financial statements of a for-profit entity other than for-profit government departments that are, or are held out to be, general purpose financial statements;

in respect of:

(d)   the separate or individual financial statements of an entity:

(i)   whose debt or equity instruments are traded in a public market (a domestic or foreign stock exchange or an over-the-counter market, including local and regional markets); or

(ii)   that files, or is in the process of filing, its financial statements with a securities commission or other regulatory organisation for the purpose of issuing any class of instruments in a public market; and

(e)   the consolidated financial statements of a group with a parent:

(i)   whose debt or equity instruments are traded in a public market (a domestic or foreign stock exchange or an over-the-counter market, including local and regional markets); or

(ii)   that files, or is in the process of filing, the consolidated financial statements with a securities commission or other regulatory organisation for the purpose of issuing any class of instruments in a public market.

4   In respect of AASB 101, AASB 107 and AASB 108, this Standard applies to:

(a)   each entity that is required to prepare financial reports in accordance with Part 2M.3 of the Corporations Act;

(b)   general purpose financial statements of each reporting entity; and

(c)   financial statements that are, or are held out to be, general purpose financial statements.

5   In respect of AASB 133, this Standard applies to each entity that is required to prepare financial reports in accordance with Part 2M.3 of the Corporations Act and that is:

(a)   a reporting entity whose ordinary shares or potential ordinary shares are publicly traded; or

AASB

(b)   a reporting entity that is in the process of issuing ordinary shares or potential ordinary shares in public markets; or

(c)   an entity that discloses earnings per share.

6   In respect of AASB 134, this Standard applies to:

    (a)   each disclosing entity required to prepare half-year financial reports in accordance with Part 2M.3 of the Corporations Act;

    (b)   interim financial reports that are general purpose financial statements of each other reporting entity; and

    (c)   interim financial reports that are, or are held out to be, general purpose financial statements.

7   In respect of AASB 1050, this Standard applies to general purpose financial statements of government departments.

8   In respect of AASB 1052, this Standard applies to general purpose financial statements of local governments and government departments.

9   This Standard applies to annual reporting periods beginning on or after 1 July 2013.

10   This Standard shall be applied when AASB 1053 *Application of Tiers of Australian Accounting Standards* is applied. This Standard may be applied to annual reporting periods beginning on or after 1 July 2009 but before 1 July 2013 provided AASB 1053 is also adopted early for the same period. When an entity applies this Standard to such an annual reporting period, it shall disclose that fact.

11   This Standard uses underlining, striking out and other typographical material to identify some of the amendments to a Standard, in order to make the amendments more understandable. However, the amendments made by this Standard do not include that underlining, striking out or other typographical material.

Amendments to AASB 1

12   The following subheading and paragraphs are added to AASB 1:

Reduced Disclosure Requirements

Aus1.6   **The following do not apply to entities preparing general purpose financial statements under Australian Accounting Standards – Reduced Disclosure Requirements:**

    (a)   **paragraphs 21-23, 24(b), 24(c) and 25-33; and**

    (b)   **in paragraph 24, the text "To comply with paragraph 23,".**

    Entities applying Australian Accounting Standards – Reduced Disclosure Requirements may elect to comply with some or all of these excluded requirements.

Aus1.7   The requirements that do not apply to entities preparing general purpose financial statements under Australian Accounting Standards – Reduced Disclosure Requirements are identified in this Standard by shading of the relevant text.

Aus1.8   **The RDR paragraph in this Standard applies only to entities preparing general purpose financial statements under Australian Accounting Standards – Reduced Disclosure Requirements.**

RDR21.1   In respect of entities applying Australian Accounting Standards – Reduced Disclosure Requirements, to comply with AASB 101, an entity's first Australian-Accounting-Standards-Redu**ced-Disclosure-Requirements financial statements shall include at least two statements of financial position, two statements of comprehensive income, two separate income statements (if presented), two statements of cash flows and two statements of changes in equity and related notes, including comparative information.**

13   Footnote1 to paragraph 1 is amended as follows (new text is underlined):

> 1   The term 'Australian Accounting Standards' refers to Standards (including Interpretations) made by the AASB that apply to any reporting period beginning on or after 1 January 2005. In this context, the term encompasses Australian Accounting Standards – Reduced Disclosure Requirements, which some entities are permitted to apply in accordance with AASB 1053 *Application of Tiers of Australian Accounting Standards* in preparing general purpose financial statements.

14   Paragraph Aus3.1 is amended as follows (new text is underlined and deleted text is struck through):

> Aus3.1   The conditions specified in paragraph 3 for the application of this Standard are satisfied when the first financial statements after this Standard becomes effective contain a statement that the financial statements comply with Australian Accounting Standards, in accordance with paragraph ~~Aus15.2~~ Aus15.1 of AASB 101.

Amendments to AASB 2

15   The following subheading and paragraphs are added to AASB 2:

Reduced Disclosure Requirements

> Aus1.6   **The following do not apply to entities preparing general purpose financial statements under Australian Accounting Standards – Reduced Disclosure Requirements:**
>
> > (a)   **paragraphs 45(c), 45(d), 46, 47(a), 47(b), 47(c)(ii), 47(c)(iii) and 48-52; and**
> >
> > (b)   **in paragraph 47, the text "to give effect to the principle in paragraph 46,".**
>
> **Entities applying Australian Accounting Standards – Reduced Disclosure Requirements may elect to comply with some or all of these excluded requirements.**

> Aus1.7   The requirements that do not apply to entities preparing general purpose financial statements under Australian Accounting Standards – Reduced Disclosure Requirements are identified in this Standard by shading of the relevant text.

> Aus1.8   **RDR paragraphs in this Standard apply only to entities preparing general purpose financial statements under Australian Accounting Standards – Reduced Disclosure Requirements.**

> RDR46.1   **For equity-settled share-based payment arrangements, an entity applying Australian Accounting Standards – Reduced Disclosure Requirements shall disclose information about how it measured the fair value of goods or services received or the fair value of the equity instruments granted. If a valuation methodology was used, the entity shall disclose the method and its reason for choosing it.**

> RDR46.2   **For cash-settled share-based payment arrangements, an entity applying Australian Accounting Standards – Reduced Disclosure Requirements shall disclose information about how the liability was measured.**

> RDR50.1   **An entity applying Australian Accounting Standards – Reduced Disclosure Requirements shall disclose the following information about the effect of share-based payment transactions on the entity's profit or loss for the period and on its financial position:**
>
> > (a)   **the total expense recognised in profit or loss for the period; and**
> >
> > (b)   **the total carrying amount at the end of the period of liabilities arising from share-based payment transactions.**

Amendments to AASB 3

16   The following subheading and paragraphs are added to AASB 3:

Reduced Disclosure Requirements

Aus1.7   **The following do not apply to entities preparing general purpose financial statements under Australian Accounting Standards – Reduced Disclosure Requirements:**

(a)   **paragraphs 59-63, Aus63.6-Aus63.9, B64(d), B64(e), B64(h), B64(k), B64(l), B64(m), B64(n)(ii), B64(o)(ii), B64(q), B65, B66, B67(a)-(c) and B67(e);**

(b)   **in the heading before paragraph B64, the text "(application of paragraphs 59 and 61)";**

(c)   **in paragraph B64, the text "To meet the objective in paragraph 59,";**

(d)   **in paragraph B64(j), the sentence "If a contingent liability ... liability cannot be measured reliably."; and**

(e)   **in paragraph B67, the text "To meet the objective in paragraph 61,".**

Entities applying Australian Accounting Standards – Reduced Disclosure Requirements may elect to comply with some or all of these excluded requirements.

Aus1.8   The requirements that do not apply to entities preparing general purpose financial statements under Australian Accounting Standards – Reduced Disclosure Requirements are identified in this Standard by shading of the relevant text, except for comparative disclosures subject to RDR paragraphs.

Aus1.9   **RDR paragraphs in this Standard apply only to entities preparing general purpose financial statements under Australian Accounting Standards – Reduced Disclosure Requirements.**

RDRB65.1 For individually immaterial business combinations occurring during the reporting period that are material collectively, an acquirer applying Australian Accounting Standards – Reduced Disclosure Requirements shall disclose in aggregate the information required by paragraphs B64(f), B64(g), B64(i), B64(n)(i), B64(o)(i) and B64(p) and the first sentence of paragraph B64(j).

RDRB67.1 An entity applying Australian Accounting Standards – Reduced Disclosure Requirements is not required to disclose the reconciliation specified in paragraph B67(d) for prior periods.

Amendments to AASB 5

17   The following subheading and paragraphs are added to AASB 5:

Reduced Disclosure Requirements

Aus1.9   **The following do not apply to entities preparing general purpose financial statements under Australian Accounting Standards – Reduced Disclosure Requirements:**

(a)   **paragraphs 33(b), 33(d), 41(d) and 42; and**

(b)   **the second and third sentence in paragraph 35, including paragraphs 35(a)-(c).**

Entities applying Australian Accounting Standards – Reduced Disclosure Requirements may elect to comply with some or all of these excluded requirements.

Aus1.10   The requirements that do not apply to entities preparing general purpose financial statements under Australian Accounting Standards – Reduced Disclosure Requirements are identified in this Standard by shading of the relevant text.

Amendments to AASB 7

18   The following subheading and paragraphs are added to AASB 7:

Reduced Disclosure Requirements

Aus2.9   **The following do not apply to entities preparing general purpose financial statements under Australian Accounting Standards – Reduced Disclosure Requirements:**

    (a)   **paragraphs 6, 9-11B, 12C, 15, 18, 19, 20(c), 20(d), 20A, 25-27, 27A, 27B, 30(b)-(e), 31-42, B1-B4 and B7-B28;**

    (b)   **in paragraph 8(a), the text ", showing separately ... AASB 9";**

    (c)   **in paragraph 8(e), the text ", showing separately ... AASB 139";**

    (d)   **in paragraph 20(a)(i), the text ", showing separately ... AASB 9";**

    (e)   **in paragraph 20(a)(v), the text ", showing separately ... AASB 139";**

    (f)   **in paragraph 23(d), the text ", showing the ... income"; and**

    (g)   **the fourth sentence in paragraph 28, including paragraphs 28(a) and (b).**

Entities applying Australian Accounting Standards – Reduced Disclosure Requirements may elect to comply with some or all of these excluded requirements.

Aus2.10   The requirements that do not apply to entities preparing general purpose financial statements under Australian Accounting Standards – Reduced Disclosure Requirements are identified in this Standard by shading of the relevant text.

Aus2.11   **RDR paragraphs in this Standard apply only to entities preparing general purpose financial statements under Australian Accounting Standards – Reduced Disclosure Requirements.**

RDR18.1   For *loans payable* recognised at the end of the reporting period for which there is a breach of terms or default of principal, interest, sinking fund, or redemption terms that has not been remedied by the end of the reporting period, an entity applying Australian Accounting Standards – Reduced Disclosure Requirements shall disclose the following:

    (a)   details of that breach or default;

    (b)   the carrying amount of the related loans payable at the end of the reporting period; and

    (c)   whether the breach or default was remedied, or the terms of the loans payable were renegotiated, before the financial statements were authorised for issue.

RDR27.1   An entity applying Australian Accounting Standards – Reduced Disclosure Requirements shall disclose, for all financial assets and financial liabilities that are measured at fair value, the basis for determining fair value, for example quoted market price in an active market or a valuation technique. When a valuation technique is used, the entity shall disclose the assumptions applied in determining fair value for each class of financial assets or financial liabilities. For example, if applicable, an entity discloses information about the assumptions relating to prepayment rates, rates of estimated credit losses, and interest rates or discount rates.

Amendments to AASB 8

19   The following subheading and paragraphs are added to AASB 8:

Reduced Disclosure Requirements

Aus2.6   The requirements that do not apply to entities preparing general purpose financial statements under Australian Accounting Standards – Reduced Disclosure Requirements are identified in this Standard by shading of the relevant text. By virtue of paragraph Aus2.1 this Standard applies to Tier 1 entities preparing general purpose financial statements in accordance with Australian Accounting Standards. Entities applying Australian Accounting Standards – Reduced Disclosure Requirements may elect to comply with some or all of the excluded requirements.

Amendments to AASB 101

20   The following subheading and paragraphs are added to AASB 101:

Reduced Disclosure Requirements

Aus1.8   **The following do not apply to entities preparing general purpose financial statements under Australian Accounting Standards – Reduced Disclosure Requirements:**

    (a)   paragraphs 10(f), 15, 16, Aus16.1, Aus16.3, 39(c), 42(b), 61, 65, 80A, 90-92, 94, 104, 131 and 134-Aus138.6;

    (b)   the second sentence in paragraph 39; and

    (c)   in paragraph 107, the text ", and the related amount per share".

    Entities applying Australian Accounting Standards – Reduced Disclosure Requirements may elect to comply with some or all of these excluded requirements.

Aus1.9   The requirements that do not apply to entities preparing general purpose financial statements under Australian Accounting Standards – Reduced Disclosure Requirements are identified in this Standard by shading of the relevant text.

Aus1.10   **RDR paragraphs in this Standard apply only to entities preparing general purpose financial statements under Australian Accounting Standards – Reduced Disclosure Requirements.**

RDR15.1   **Financial statements shall present fairly the financial position, financial performance and cash flows of an entity applying Australian Accounting Standards – Reduced Disclosure Requirements. Fair presentation requires the faithful representation of the effects of transactions, other events and conditions in accordance with the definitions and recognition criteria for assets, liabilities, income and expenses set out in the *Framework*. The application of Australian Accounting Standards – Reduced Disclosure Requirements, with additional disclosure when necessary, is presumed to result in financial statements that achieve a fair presentation.**

RDR16.1   **An entity whose financial statements comply with Australian Accounting Standards – Reduced Disclosure Requirements shall make an explicit and unreserved statement of such compliance in the notes. An entity shall not describe financial statements as complying with Australian Accounting Standards – Reduced Disclosure Requirements unless they comply with all the requirements of Australian Accounting Standards – Reduced Disclosure Requirements. Entities applying Australian Accounting Standards – Reduced Disclosure Requirements would not be able to state compliance with IFRSs.**

21   Paragraph Aus15.1 is renumbered as Aus15.3 and amended as follows (new text is underlined and deleted text is struck through):

Aus15.3   **The Corporations Act requires an entity's financial report to comply with ~~Australian Accounting Standards~~ accounting standards made by the AASB and, if necessary to give a true and fair view, to disclose further information ~~to be disclosed~~ in the notes.**

22   Paragraph Aus15.2 is renumbered as Aus15.1 and amended as follows (new text is underlined):

Aus15.1   **An entity shall disclose in the notes a statement whether the financial statements have been prepared in accordance with Australian Accounting Standards or Australian Accounting Standards – Reduced Disclosure Requirements.**

23   Paragraph Aus15.3 is renumbered as Aus15.2 and amended as follows (new text is underlined and deleted text is struck through):

Aus15.2   The financial reporting framework applied in the preparation of the financial statements is identified in the summary of accounting policies so that users understand the basis on which the financial statements ~~has~~ have been prepared. In addition to stating whether the financial statements have been prepared in accordance with Australian Accounting Standards or Australian Accounting Standards – Reduced Disclosure Requirements, it may also be appropriate to indicate the relevant statutory and other requirements adopted in the preparation of the financial statements.

Amendments to AASB 102

24   The following subheading and paragraphs are added to AASB 102:

Reduced Disclosure Requirements

Aus1.8   **Paragraphs 36(c), 36(g) and Aus36.1(f) of this Standard do not apply to entities preparing general purpose financial statements under Australian Accounting Standards – Reduced Disclosure Requirements. Entities applying Australian Accounting Standards – Reduced Disclosure Requirements may elect to comply with some or all of these excluded requirements.**

Aus1.9   The requirements that do not apply to entities preparing general purpose financial statements under Australian Accounting Standards – Reduced Disclosure Requirements are identified in this Standard by shading of the relevant text.

Amendments to AASB 107

25   The following subheading and paragraphs are added to AASB 107:

Reduced Disclosure Requirements

Aus1.8   **Paragraphs Aus20.1, Aus20.2, 40, 41, 46, 50(d) and 52 of this Standard do not apply to entities preparing general purpose financial statements under Australian Accounting Standards – Reduced Disclosure Requirements. Entities applying Australian Accounting Standards – Reduced Disclosure Requirements may elect to comply with some or all of these excluded requirements.**

Aus1.9   The requirements that do not apply to entities preparing general purpose financial statements under Australian Accounting Standards – Reduced Disclosure Requirements are identified in this Standard by shading of the relevant text.

Amendments to AASB 108

26   The following subheading and paragraphs are added to AASB 108:

Reduced Disclosure Requirements

Aus2.9   **Paragraphs 28(b), 28(d), 28(e), 28(h), 30, 31 and 40 of this Standard do not apply to entities preparing general purpose financial statements under Australian Accounting Standards – Reduced Disclosure Requirements. Entities applying Australian Accounting Standards – Reduced Disclosure Requirements may elect to comply with some or all of these excluded requirements.**

Aus2.10   The requirements that do not apply to entities preparing general purpose financial statements under Australian Accounting Standards – Reduced Disclosure Requirements are identified in this Standard by shading of the relevant text.

Aus2.11   **The RDR paragraph in this Standard applies only to entities preparing general purpose financial statements under Australian Accounting Standards – Reduced Disclosure Requirements.**

RDR28.1   **An entity applying Australian Accounting Standards – Reduced Disclosure Requirements shall disclose an explanation if it is impracticable to determine the amounts required to be disclosed by paragraph 28(f)(i) or 28(g).**

27   Paragraph 7 is amended as follows (new text is underlined):

7   **When an Australian Accounting Standard[1] specifically applies to a transaction, other event or condition, the accounting policy or policies applied to that item shall be determined by applying the Standard.**

> 1   The term 'Australian Accounting Standards' refers to Standards (including Interpretations) made by the AASB that apply to any reporting period beginning on or after 1 January 2005. In this context, the term encompasses Australian Accounting Standards – Reduced Disclosure Requirements, which some entities are permitted to apply in accordance with AASB 1053 *Application of Tiers of Australian Accounting Standards* in preparing general purpose financial statements.

Amendments to AASB 110

28   The following subheading and paragraphs are added to AASB 110:

Reduced Disclosure Requirements

Aus1.8   **The following do not apply to entities preparing general purpose financial statements under Australian Accounting Standards – Reduced Disclosure Requirements:**

        (a)   **paragraphs 13, 19 and 20; and**

        (b)   **in paragraph 22(a), the text "(AASB 3 … in such cases)".**

        Entities applying Australian Accounting Standards – Reduced Disclosure Requirements may elect to comply with some or all of these excluded requirements.

Aus1.9   The requirements that do not apply to entities preparing general purpose financial statements under Australian Accounting Standards – Reduced Disclosure Requirements are identified in this Standard by shading of the relevant text.

Amendments to AASB 111

29   The following subheading and paragraphs are added to AASB 111:

Reduced Disclosure Requirements

Aus1.8   **Paragraphs 40, 41 and 45 of this Standard do not apply to entities preparing general purpose financial statements under Australian Accounting Standards – Reduced Disclosure Requirements. Entities applying Australian Accounting Standards – Reduced Disclosure**

Requirements may elect to comply with some or all of these excluded requirements.

Aus1.9   The requirements that do not apply to entities preparing general purpose financial statements under Australian Accounting Standards – Reduced Disclosure Requirements are identified in this Standard by shading of the relevant text.

Amendments to AASB 112

30   The following subheading and paragraphs are added to AASB 112:

Reduced Disclosure Requirements

Aus1.8   **The following do not apply to entities preparing general purpose financial statements under Australian Accounting Standards – Reduced Disclosure Requirements:**

     (a)   paragraphs 81(ab), 81(f), 81(i)-(k), 82 and 87-87C; and

     (b)   the second sentence in paragraph 82A.

     Entities applying Australian Accounting Standards – Reduced Disclosure Requirements may elect to comply with some or all of these excluded requirements.

Aus1.9   The requirements that do not apply to entities preparing general purpose financial statements under Australian Accounting Standards – Reduced Disclosure Requirements are identified in this Standard by shading of the relevant text.

Aus1.10   **The RDR paragraph in this Standard applies only to entities preparing general purpose financial statements under Australian Accounting Standards – Reduced Disclosure Requirements.**

RDR81.1   **An entity applying Australian Accounting Standards – Reduced Disclosure Requirements shall disclose the aggregate amount of current and deferred income tax relating to items recognised in other comprehensive income.**

Amendments to AASB 116

31   The following subheading and paragraphs are added to AASB 116:

Reduced Disclosure Requirements

Aus1.8   **Paragraphs 73(e)(viii), 74(b), 74(d), 77(e), Aus77.1 and 79 of this Standard do not apply to entities preparing general purpose financial statements under Australian Accounting Standards – Reduced Disclosure Requirements. Entities applying Australian Accounting Standards – Reduced Disclosure Requirements may elect to comply with some or all of these excluded requirements.**

Aus1.9   The requirements that do not apply to entities preparing general purpose financial statements under Australian Accounting Standards – Reduced Disclosure Requirements are identified in this Standard by shading of the relevant text, except for comparative disclosures subject to RDR paragraphs.

Aus1.10   **The RDR paragraph in this Standard applies only to entities preparing general purpose financial statements under Australian Accounting Standards – Reduced Disclosure Requirements.**

RDR73.1   **An entity applying Australian Accounting Standards – Reduced Disclosure Requirements is not required to disclose the reconciliation specified in paragraph 73(e) for prior periods.**

Amendments to AASB 117

32   The following subheading and paragraphs are added to AASB 117:

Reduced Disclosure Requirements

Aus1.8   **The following do not apply to entities preparing general purpose financial statements under Australian Accounting Standards – Reduced Disclosure Requirements:**

     (a)   **paragraphs 31(c), 31(d), 35(b) and 48;**

     (b)   **in paragraph 31(b), the text "a reconciliation … present value." and, in the second sentence, the text "In addition, an entity shall disclose" and "and their present value,";**

     (c)   **in paragraph 35(c), the text ", with separate amounts … sublease payments"; and**

     (d)   **in paragraph 56(a), the words "in the aggregate and".**

     Entities applying Australian Accounting Standards – Reduced Disclosure Requirements may elect to comply with some or all of these excluded requirements.

Aus1.9   The requirements that do not apply to entities preparing general purpose financial statements under Australian Accounting Standards – Reduced Disclosure Requirements are identified in this Standard by shading of the relevant text.

Amendments to AASB 119

33   The following subheading and paragraphs are added to AASB 119:

Reduced Disclosure Requirements

Aus1.7   **The following do not apply to entities preparing general purpose financial statements under Australian Accounting Standards – Reduced Disclosure Requirements:**

     (a)   **paragraphs 30(c)(ii), 34B, 47, 120, 120A(c), 120A(d), 120A(e)(i)-(iii), 120A(e)(vii), 120A(e)(viii), 120A(l), 120A(n)(iii), 120A(o)-(q), 124(b) and 143;**

     (b)   **the third sentence in paragraph 23;**

     (c)   **in paragraph 120A(g), the text "for each of … in paragraph 58(b)";**

     (d)   **in paragraph 120A(m), the text ", as well as … paragraph 104A"; and**

     (e)   **the second sentence in paragraph 131.**

     Entities applying Australian Accounting Standards – Reduced Disclosure Requirements may elect to comply with some or all of these excluded requirements.

Aus1.8   The requirements that do not apply to entities preparing general purpose financial statements under Australian Accounting Standards – Reduced Disclosure Requirements are identified in this Standard by shading of the relevant text, except for comparative disclosures subject to RDR paragraphs.

Aus1.9   **RDR paragraphs in this Standard apply only to entities preparing general purpose financial statements under Australian Accounting Standards – Reduced Disclosure Requirements.**

RDR120A.1   **An entity applying Australian Accounting Standards – Reduced Disclosure Requirements shall disclose a reconciliation of opening and closing balances of the defined benefit obligation showing separately benefits paid and all other changes. These disclosures may be made in**

total, separately for each plan, or in such groupings as are considered to be the most useful.

RDR120A.2   **An entity applying Australian Accounting Standards – Reduced Disclosure Requirements is not required to disclose the reconciliations specified in paragraphs 120A(e) and RDR120A.1 for prior periods.**

Amendments to AASB 121

34   The following subheading and paragraphs are added to AASB 121:

Reduced Disclosure Requirements

Aus2.8   **Paragraphs 55-57 of this Standard do not apply to entities preparing general purpose financial statements under Australian Accounting Standards – Reduced Disclosure Requirements. Entities applying Australian Accounting Standards – Reduced Disclosure Requirements may elect to comply with some or all of these excluded requirements.**

Aus2.9   The requirements that do not apply to entities preparing general purpose financial statements under Australian Accounting Standards – Reduced Disclosure Requirements are identified in this Standard by shading of the relevant text.

Amendments to AASB 123

35   The following subheading and paragraphs are added to AASB 123:

Reduced Disclosure Requirements

Aus1.6   **Paragraph 26(b) of this Standard does not apply to entities preparing general purpose financial statements under Australian Accounting Standards – Reduced Disclosure Requirements. Entities applying Australian Accounting Standards – Reduced Disclosure Requirements may elect to comply with this excluded requirement.**

Aus1.7   The requirement that does not apply to entities preparing general purpose financial statements under Australian Accounting Standards – Reduced Disclosure Requirements are identified in this Standard by shading of the relevant text.

Amendments to AASB 124

36   The following subheading and paragraphs are added to AASB 124:

Reduced Disclosure Requirements

Aus1.11   **The following do not apply to entities preparing general purpose financial statements under Australian Accounting Standards – Reduced Disclosure Requirements:**

(a)   **paragraphs Aus13.1, 26, 27 and Aus29.1-Aus29.9.3;**

(b)   **in paragraph 17, the text "and for each of … (e) share-based payment"; and**

(c)   **in paragraph 22, the text "(see paragraph 34B of AASB 119)".**

Entities applying Australian Accounting Standards – Reduced Disclosure Requirements may elect to comply with some or all of these excluded requirements.

Aus1.12   The requirements that do not apply to entities preparing general purpose financial statements under Australian Accounting Standards – Reduced Disclosure Requirements are identified in this Standard by shading of the relevant text.

Amendments to AASB 127

37   The following subheading and paragraphs are added to AASB 127:

Reduced Disclosure Requirements

Aus1.6   **The following do not apply to entities preparing general purpose financial statements under Australian Accounting Standards – Reduced Disclosure Requirements:**

      (a)   **paragraphs 41(b), 41(e), 41(f), 42, 43(b), 43(c) and Aus43.1; and**

      (b)   **in paragraph 43, the text "(other than a parent covered by paragraph 42)".**

      Entities applying Australian Accounting Standards – Reduced Disclosure Requirements may elect to comply with some or all of these excluded requirements.

Aus1.7   The requirements that do not apply to entities preparing general purpose financial statements under Australian Accounting Standards – Reduced Disclosure Requirements are identified in this Standard by shading of the relevant text.

Aus1.8   **The RDR paragraph in this Standard applies only to entities preparing general purpose financial statements under Australian Accounting Standards – Reduced Disclosure Requirements.**

RDR43.1   **A parent, venturer with an interest in a jointly controlled entity or an investor in an associate, that prepares separate financial statements applying Australian Accounting Standards – Reduced Disclosure Requirements, shall disclose a description of the methods used to account for the investments in subsidiaries, jointly controlled entities and associates.**

Amendments to AASB 128

38   The following subheading and paragraphs are added to AASB 128:

Reduced Disclosure Requirements

Aus1.9   **Paragraphs 37(b)-(i) of this Standard do not apply to entities preparing general purpose financial statements under Australian Accounting Standards – Reduced Disclosure Requirements. Entities applying Australian Accounting Standards – Reduced Disclosure Requirements may elect to comply with some or all of these excluded requirements.**

Aus1.10   The requirements that do not apply to entities preparing general purpose financial statements under Australian Accounting Standards – Reduced Disclosure Requirements are identified in this Standard by shading of the relevant text.

Amendments to AASB 131

39   The following subheading and paragraphs are added to AASB 131:

Reduced Disclosure Requirements

Aus1.8   **Paragraph 56 of this Standard does not apply to entities preparing general purpose financial statements under Australian Accounting Standards – Reduced Disclosure Requirements. Entities applying Australian Accounting Standards – Reduced Disclosure Requirements may elect to comply with this excluded requirement.**

Aus1.9   The requirement that does not apply to entities preparing general purpose financial statements under Australian Accounting Standards – Reduced Disclosure Requirements is identified in this Standard by shading of the relevant text.

Amendments to AASB 133

40   The following subheading and paragraphs are added to AASB 133:

Reduced Disclosure Requirements

Aus1.9   The requirements that do not apply to entities preparing general purpose financial statements under Australian Accounting Standards – Reduced Disclosure Requirements are identified in this Standard by shading of the relevant text. By virtue of paragraph Aus1.1 this Standard applies to Tier 1 entities preparing general purpose financial statements in accordance with Australian Accounting Standards. Entities applying Australian Accounting Standards – Reduced Disclosure Requirements may elect to comply with some or all of the excluded requirements.

Amendments to AASB 134

41   The following subheading and paragraphs are added to AASB 134:

Reduced Disclosure Requirements

Aus1.10   The following do not apply to entities preparing general purpose financial statements under Australian Accounting Standards – Reduced Disclosure Requirements:

(a)   paragraphs 5(f), 16(g), 19 and 21; and

(b)   in paragraph 16(i), the sentence ". In the case of ... required by AASB 3 *Business Combinations*".

Entities applying Australian Accounting Standards – Reduced Disclosure Requirements may elect to comply with some or all of these excluded requirements.

Aus1.11   The requirements that do not apply to entities preparing general purpose financial statements under Australian Accounting Standards – Reduced Disclosure Requirements are identified in this Standard by shading of the relevant text.

Aus1.12   The RDR paragraph in this Standard applies only to entities preparing general purpose financial statements under Australian Accounting Standards – Reduced Disclosure Requirements.

RDR19.1   If an entity's interim financial report is in compliance with this Standard as it applies to entities applying the Australian Accounting Standards – Reduced Disclosure Requirements, that fact shall be disclosed. An interim financial report shall not be described as complying with Australian Accounting Standards – Reduced Disclosure Requirements unless it complies with all of the requirements of Australian Accounting Standards – Reduced Disclosure Requirements.

Amendments to AASB 136

42   The following subheading and paragraphs are added to AASB 136:

Reduced Disclosure Requirements

Aus1.8   Paragraphs 129-137 of this Standard do not apply to entities preparing general purpose financial statements under Australian Accounting Standards – Reduced Disclosure Requirements. Entities applying Australian Accounting Standards – Reduced Disclosure Requirements may elect to comply with some or all of these excluded requirements.

Aus1.9   The requirements that do not apply to entities preparing general purpose financial statements under Australian Accounting Standards – Reduced Disclosure Requirements are identified in this Standard by shading of the relevant text.

Amendments to AASB 137

43   The following subheading and paragraphs are added to AASB 137:

Reduced Disclosure Requirements

Aus1.8   **The following do not apply to entities preparing general purpose financial statements under Australian Accounting Standards – Reduced Disclosure Requirements:**

     (a)   **paragraphs 84(b), 84(e) and 85(c);**

     (b)   **in paragraph 75, the text "If an entity starts to … of the financial statements."; and**

     (c)   **in paragraph 85(b), the text ". Where necessary … paragraph 48".**

     Entities applying Australian Accounting Standards – Reduced Disclosure Requirements may elect to comply with some or all of these excluded requirements.

Aus1.9   The requirements that do not apply to entities preparing general purpose financial statements under Australian Accounting Standards – Reduced Disclosure Requirements are identified in this Standard by shading of the relevant text.

Amendments to AASB 138

44   The following subheading and paragraphs are added to AASB 138:

Reduced Disclosure Requirements

Aus1.8   **Paragraphs 118(e)(vii), 120, 124(a)(iii), Aus124.1 and 128 of this Standard do not apply to entities preparing general purpose financial statements under Australian Accounting Standards – Reduced Disclosure Requirements. Entities applying Australian Accounting Standards – Reduced Disclosure Requirements may elect to comply with some or all of these excluded requirements.**

Aus1.9   The requirements that do not apply to entities preparing general purpose financial statements under Australian Accounting Standards – Reduced Disclosure Requirements are identified in this Standard by shading of the relevant text, except for comparative disclosures subject to RDR paragraphs.

Aus1.10   **The RDR paragraph in this Standard applies only to entities preparing general purpose financial statements under Australian Accounting Standards – Reduced Disclosure Requirements.**

RDR118.1 **An entity applying Australian Accounting Standards – Reduced Disclosure Requirements is not required to disclose the reconciliations specified in paragraph 118(e) for prior periods.**

Amendments to AASB 140

45   The following subheading and paragraphs are added to AASB 140:

Reduced Disclosure Requirements

Aus1.6   **The following do not apply to entities preparing general purpose financial statements under Australian Accounting Standards – Reduced Disclosure Requirements:**

     (a)   **paragraphs 75(b), 75(c), 75(f), 76(e), 77, 79(d)(vi), 79(d)(vii) and 79(e);**

     (b)   **in paragraph 75(d), the text ", including a statement … market data";**

     (c)   **in paragraph 76(a), the text ", disclosing separately … an asset"; and**

     (d)   **in paragraph 79(d)(i), the text ", disclosing separately … an asset".**

Entities applying Australian Accounting Standards – Reduced Disclosure Requirements may elect to comply with some or all of these excluded requirements.

Aus1.7   The requirements that do not apply to entities preparing general purpose financial statements under Australian Accounting Standards – Reduced Disclosure Requirements are identified in this Standard by shading of the relevant text, except for comparative disclosures subject to RDR paragraphs.

Aus1.8   **The RDR paragraph in this Standard applies only to entities preparing general purpose financial statements under Australian Accounting Standards – Reduced Disclosure Requirements.**

RDR76.1   **An entity applying Australian Accounting Standards – Reduced Disclosure Requirements is not required to disclose the reconciliation specified in paragraph 76 for prior periods.**

Amendments to AASB 141

46   The following subheading and paragraphs are added to AASB 141:

Reduced Disclosure Requirements

Aus1.8   **Paragraphs 40, 43-46, 48, 49, 51-53, 54(c), 55, 56 and 57(c) of this Standard do not apply to entities preparing general purpose financial statements under Australian Accounting Standards – Reduced Disclosure Requirements. Entities applying Australian Accounting Standards – Reduced Disclosure Requirements may elect to comply with some or all of these excluded requirements.**

Aus1.9   The requirements that do not apply to entities preparing general purpose financial statements under Australian Accounting Standards – Reduced Disclosure Requirements are identified in this Standard by shading of the relevant text.

Aus1.10   **The RDR paragraph in this Standard applies only to entities preparing general purpose financial statements under Australian Accounting Standards – Reduced Disclosure Requirements.**

RDR50.1   **An entity applying Australian Accounting Standards – Reduced Disclosure Requirements is not required to disclose the reconciliation specified in paragraph 50 for prior periods.**

Amendments to AASB 1050

47   The following subheading and paragraphs are added to AASB 1050:

Reduced Disclosure Requirements

6A   **The following do not apply to entities preparing general purpose financial statements under Australian Accounting Standards – Reduced Disclosure Requirements:**

(a)   **paragraphs 7(a)(ii), 7(b)(ii) and 8; and**

(b)   **in paragraph 14, the words "and by activity" in the third sentence.**

Entities applying Australian Accounting Standards – Reduced Disclosure Requirements may elect to comply with some or all of these excluded requirements.

6B   The requirements that do not apply to entities preparing general purpose financial statements under Australian Accounting Standards – Reduced Disclosure Requirements are identified in this Standard by shading of the relevant text.

Amendments to AASB 1052

48   The following subheading and paragraphs are added to AASB 1052:

Reduced Disclosure Requirements

10A   **Paragraphs 11-21 of this Standard do not apply to entities preparing general purpose financial statements under Australian Accounting Standards – Reduced Disclosure Requirements. Entities applying Australian Accounting Standards – Reduced Disclosure Requirements may elect to comply with some or all of these excluded requirements.**

10B   The requirements that do not apply to entities preparing general purpose financial statements under Australian Accounting Standards – Reduced Disclosure Requirements are identified in this Standard by shading of the relevant text.

Amendments to Interpretation 2

49   The following subheading and paragraphs are added to Interpretation 2:

Reduced Disclosure Requirements

Aus13.5   **Paragraph 13 of this Interpretation does not apply to entities preparing general purpose financial statements under Australian Accounting Standards – Reduced Disclosure Requirements. Entities applying Australian Accounting Standards – Reduced Disclosure Requirements may elect to comply with this excluded requirement.**

Aus13.6   The requirement that does not apply to entities preparing general purpose financial statements under Australian Accounting Standards – Reduced Disclosure Requirements is identified in this Interpretation by shading of the relevant text.

Amendments to Interpretation 4

50   The following subheading and paragraphs are added to Interpretation 4:

Reduced Disclosure Requirements

Aus15.6   **The text ", but: … elements in the arrangement" in paragraph 15(b) of this Interpretation does not apply to entities preparing general purpose financial statements under Australian Accounting Standards – Reduced Disclosure Requirements. Entities applying Australian Accounting Standards – Reduced Disclosure Requirements may elect to comply with this excluded requirement.**

Aus15.7   The requirement that does not apply to entities preparing general purpose financial statements under Australian Accounting Standards – Reduced Disclosure Requirements is identified in this Interpretation by shading of the relevant text.

Amendments to Interpretation 5

51   The following subheading and paragraphs are added to Interpretation 5:

Reduced Disclosure Requirements

Aus13.5   **Paragraphs 11 and 13 of this Interpretation do not apply to entities preparing general purpose financial statements under Australian Accounting Standards – Reduced Disclosure Requirements. Entities applying Australian Accounting Standards – Reduced Disclosure Requirements may elect to comply with one or both of these excluded requirements.**

Aus13.6   The requirements that do not apply to entities preparing general purpose financial statements under Australian Accounting Standards – Reduced Disclosure Requirements are identified in this Interpretation by shading of the relevant text.

Amendments to Interpretation 15

52   The following subheading and paragraphs are added to Interpretation 15:

Reduced Disclosure Requirements

Aus23.5   **Paragraphs 20 and 21 of this Interpretation do not apply to entities preparing general purpose financial statements under Australian Accounting Standards – Reduced Disclosure Requirements. Entities applying Australian Accounting Standards – Reduced Disclosure Requirements may elect to comply with one or both of these excluded requirements.**

Aus23.6   The requirements that do not apply to entities preparing general purpose financial statements under Australian Accounting Standards – Reduced Disclosure Requirements are identified in this Interpretation by shading of the relevant text.

Amendments to Interpretation 17

53   The following subheading and paragraphs are added to Interpretation 17:

Reduced Disclosure Requirements

Aus17.5   **Paragraphs 16 and 17 of this Interpretation do not apply to entities preparing general purpose financial statements under Australian Accounting Standards – Reduced Disclosure Requirements. Entities applying Australian Accounting Standards – Reduced Disclosure Requirements may elect to comply with one or both of these excluded requirements.**

Aus17.6   The requirements that do not apply to entities preparing general purpose financial statements under Australian Accounting Standards – Reduced Disclosure Requirements are identified in this Interpretation by shading of the relevant text.

Amendments to Interpretation 127

54   The following subheading and paragraphs are added to Interpretation 127:

Reduced Disclosure Requirements

Aus11.7   **Paragraphs 10 and 11 of this Interpretation do not apply to entities preparing general purpose financial statements under Australian Accounting Standards – Reduced Disclosure Requirements. Entities applying Australian Accounting Standards – Reduced Disclosure Requirements may elect to comply with one or both of these excluded requirements.**

Aus11.8   The requirements that do not apply to entities preparing general purpose financial statements under Australian Accounting Standards – Reduced Disclosure Requirements are identified in this Interpretation by shading of the relevant text.

Amendments to Interpretation 129

55   The following subheading and paragraphs are added to Interpretation 129:

Reduced Disclosure Requirements

Aus7.6   **Paragraphs 6, 6A and 7 of this Interpretation do not apply to entities preparing general purpose financial statements under Australian Accounting Standards – Reduced Disclosure Requirements. Entities applying Australian Accounting Standards – Reduced Disclosure Requirements may elect to comply with some or all of these excluded requirements.**

Aus7.7   The requirements that do not apply to entities preparing general purpose financial statements under Australian Accounting Standards – Reduced

Disclosure Requirements are identified in this Interpretation by shading of the relevant text.

Amendments to Interpretation 1052

56   The following subheading and paragraphs are added to Interpretation 1052:

Reduced Disclosure Requirements

23A   **The following do not apply to entities preparing general purpose financial statements under Australian Accounting Standards – Reduced Disclosure Requirements:**

    (a)   paragraph 16; and

    (b)   the first and second sentence in paragraph 59.

    Entities applying Australian Accounting Standards – Reduced Disclosure Requirements may elect to comply with some or all of these excluded requirements.

23B   The requirements that do not apply to entities preparing general purpose financial statements under Australian Accounting Standards – Reduced Disclosure Requirements are identified in this Interpretation by shading of the relevant text.

Appendix

Early Application of Australian Accounting Standards – Reduced Disclosure Requirements

This Appendix is an integral part of this Standard.

A1   The Australian Accounting Standards – Reduced Disclosure Requirements may be applied early to annual reporting periods beginning on or after 1 July 2009 but before 1 July 2013. The amendments set out in paragraphs 12-56 of this Standard also apply to all the versions of pronouncements applicable to such periods when the Australian Accounting Standards – Reduced Disclosure Requirements are applied early, with the exception of AASB 7 *Financial Instruments: Disclosures* and AASB 124 *Related Party Disclosures*. The amendments to those Standards are set out below.

Amendments Applying from 1 July 2009

Amendments to AASB 7

A2   The following subheading and paragraphs are added to the versions of AASB 7 that apply to annual reporting periods beginning on or after 1 July 2009 but before 1 July 2013:

Reduced Disclosure Requirements

Aus2.9   **The following do not apply to entities preparing general purpose financial statements under Australian Accounting Standards – Reduced Disclosure Requirements:**

    (a)   paragraphs 6, 9-11, 12A(b), 12A(e), 15, 18, 19, 20(c), 20(d), 25-27, 27A, 27B, 30(b)-(e), 31-42, B1-B4 and B7-B28;

    (b)   in paragraph 8(a), the text ", showing separately ... AASB 139";

    (c)   in paragraph 8(e), the text ", showing separately ... AASB 139";

    (d)   in paragraph 20(a)(i), the text ", showing separately ... AASB 139";

    (e)   in paragraph 23(d), the text ", showing the ... income"; and

    (f)   the fourth sentence in paragraph 28, including paragraphs 28(a) and (b).

    Entities applying Australian Accounting Standards – Reduced Disclosure Requirements may elect to comply with some or all of these excluded requirements.

Aus2.10   **RDR paragraphs in this Standard apply only to entities preparing general purpose financial statements under Australian Accounting Standards – Reduced Disclosure Requirements.**

Aus2.11   The requirements that do not apply to entities preparing general purpose financial statements under Australian Accounting Standards – Reduced Disclosure Requirements are identified in this Standard by shading of the relevant text.

RDR18.1   For *loans payable* recognised at the end of the reporting period for which there is a breach of terms or default of principal, interest, sinking fund, or redemption of terms that has not been remedied by the end of the reporting period, an entity preparing general purpose financial statements under Australian Accounting Standards – Reduced Disclosure Requirements shall disclose the following:

     (a)   details of that breach or default;

     (b)   the carrying amount of the related loans payable at the end of the reporting period; and

     (c)   whether the breach or default was remedied, or the terms of the loans payable were renegotiated, before the financial statements were authorised for issue.

RDR27.1   An entity applying Australian Accounting Standards – Reduced Disclosure Requirements shall disclose, for all financial assets and financial liabilities that are measured at fair value, the basis for determining fair value, for example quoted market price in an active market or a valuation technique. When a valuation technique is used, the entity shall disclose the assumptions applied in determining fair value for each class of financial assets or financial liabilities. For example, if applicable, an entity discloses information about the assumptions relating to prepayment rates, rates of estimated credit losses, and interest rates or discount rates.

A3   The version of AASB 7 that applies to annual reporting periods beginning on or after 1 January 2013 but before 1 July 2013 is also the version that applies to periods beginning on or after 1 July 2013. Therefore, the amendments set out in paragraph 18 of this Standard also apply to that version of AASB 7 when Australian Accounting Standards – Reduced Disclosure Requirements are applied early to annual reporting periods beginning on or after 1 January 2013 but before 1 July 2013.

Amendments to AASB 124

A4   The following subheading and paragraphs are added to the version of AASB 124 that applies to annual reporting periods beginning on or after 1 July 2009 that begin before 1 January 2011:

Reduced Disclosure Requirements

Aus1.12   **The following do not apply to entities preparing general purpose financial statements under Australian Accounting Standards – Reduced Disclosure Requirements:**

     (a)   **paragraphs Aus12.1 and Aus25.1-Aus25.9.3;**

     (g)   **in paragraph 16, the text "and for each of … (e) share-based payment"; and**

     (h)   **in paragraph 20, the text "(see paragraph 34B … December 2004)".**

Entities applying Australian Accounting Standards – Reduced Disclosure Requirements may elect to comply with some or all of these excluded requirements.

Aus1.13   The requirements that do not apply to entities preparing general purpose financial statements under Australian Accounting Standards – Reduced Disclosure Requirements are identified in this Standard by shading of the relevant text.

A5　　The version of AASB 124 that applies to annual reporting periods beginning on or after 1 January 2011 but before 1 July 2013 is also the version that applies to periods beginning on or after 1 July 2013. Therefore, the amendments set out in paragraph 36 of this Standard also apply to that version of AASB 124 when Australian Accounting Standards – Reduced Disclosure Requirements are applied early to annual reporting periods beginning on or after 1 January 2011 but before 1 July 2013.

AASB 2010-7

Amendments to Australian Accounting Standards arising from AASB 9 (December 2010)

[AASB 1, 3, 4, 5, 7, 101, 102, 108, 112, 118, 120, 121, 127, 128, 131, 132, 136, 137, 139, 1023 & 1038 and Interpretations 2, 5, 10, 12, 19 & 127]

(Compiled October 2012)

Note from the Institute of Chartered Accountants Australia

This note, prepared by the technical editors, is not part of Accounting Standard AASB 2010-7.

Historical development

6 December 2010: AASB 2010-7 was issued amending AASB 1, 3, 4 , 5, 7, 101, 102, 108, 112, 118, 120, 121, 127, 128, 131, 132, 136, 137, 139, 1023 & 1038 and Interpretations 2, 5, 10, 12, 19 & 127 arising from the issue of revised AASB 9 'Financial Instruments' in December 2010. AASB 2010-7 supersedes AASB 2009-11, which relates to the December 2009 version of AASB 9.

This Standard is applicable to annual reporting periods beginning on or after 1 January 2013 with early application permitted.

1 March 2011: Compiled AASB 2010-7 was issued, amended by AASB 2010-10 'Further Amendments to Accounting Standards – Removal of Fixed Dates for First-time Adopters'.

Compiled AASB 2010-7 is applicable to annual reporting periods beginning on or after 1 January 2013 with early application permitted.

10 September 2012: AASB 2012-6 'Amendments to Australian Accounting Standards – Mandatory Effective Date of AASB 9 and Transition Disclosures' amends the mandatory effective date of AASB 2010-7 to annual reporting periods beginning on or after 1 January 2015 instead of 1 January 2013.

31 October 2012: AASB 2010-7 was issued by the AASB, compiled to include the AASB 2012-6 amendments. This Standard applies to annual reporting periods beginning on or after 1 January 2015 and can be adopted early.

Contents

Preface

Compilation Details

Accounting Standard
AASB 2010-7 Amendments to Australian Accounting Standards
arising from AASB 9 (December 2010)

	Paragraphs
Objective	1
Application	2 – 8
Amendments to AASB 1	9 – 12
Amendments to AASB 3	13
Amendments to AASB 4	14 – 16
Amendments to AASB 5	17
Amendments to AASB 7	18 – 21
Amendments to AASB 101	22
Amendments to AASB 102	23
Amendments to AASB 108	24
Amendments to AASB 112	25
Amendments to AASB 118	26 – 27
Amendments to AASB 120	28
Amendments to AASB 121	29
Amendments to AASB 127	30 – 31
Amendments to AASB 128	32
Amendments to AASB 131	33
Amendments to AASB 132	34 – 37
Amendments to AASB 136	38
Amendments to AASB 137	39 – 40
Amendments to AASB 139	41 – 55
Amendments to AASB 1023	56 – 57
Amendments to AASB 1038	58 – 59
Amendments to Interpretation 2	60 – 62
Amendments to Interpretation 5	63 – 64
Amendments to Interpretation 10	65 – 66
Amendments to Interpretation 12	67 – 69
Amendments to Interpretation 19	70 – 71
Amendments to Interpretation 127	72 – 74

Appendix: Early Application

Australian Accounting Standard AASB 2010-7 *Amendments to Australian Accounting Standards arising from AASB 9 (December 2010)* (as amended) is set out in paragraphs 1 – 74. All the paragraphs have equal authority.

Compilation Details

Accounting Standard AASB 2010-7 *Amendments to Australian Accounting Standards arising from AASB 9 (December 2010)* as amended

This compiled Standard applies to annual reporting periods beginning on or after 1 January 2015. It takes into account amendments up to and including 10 September 2012 and was prepared on 31 October 2012 by the staff of the Australian Accounting Standards Board (AASB).

This compilation is not a separate Accounting Standard made by the AASB. Instead, it is a representation of AASB 2010-7 (December 2010) as amended by other Accounting Standards, which are listed in the table below.

Table of Standards

Standard	Date made	Application date *(annual reporting periods ... on or after ...)*	Application, saving or transitional provisions
AASB 2010-7	6 Dec 2010	(beginning) 1 Jan 2015	see (a) below
AASB 2010-10	31 Dec 2010	(beginning) 1 Jan 2013	see (b) below
AASB 2012-6	10 Sept 2012	(beginning) 1 Jan 2013	see (c) below

(a) AASB 2010-7 applies to annual reporting periods beginning on or after 1 January 2015 (instead of 1 January 2013) as a result of amendments made by AASB 2012-6 *Amendments to Australian Accounting Standards – Mandatory Effective Date of AASB 9 and Transition Disclosures*.

(b) Entities may elect to apply this Standard from any date between 6 and 31 December 2010, for entities initially applying this Standard before 1 January 2011, or to annual reporting periods beginning on or after 1 January 2011.

(c) Entities may elect to apply the amendments to AASB 2010-7 in this Standard as set out in note (b).

Table of Amendments

Paragraph affected	How affected	By ... [paragraph]
5-7	amended	AASB 2012-6 [16]
10	amended	AASB 2010-10 [8]
	amended	AASB 2012-6 [18]
11	amended	AASB 2010-10 [9]
	amended	AASB 2012-6 [19, 20]
18	amended	AASB 2012-6 [21]
22	amended	AASB 2012-6 [22]
30-33	deleted	AASB 2012-6 [17]
34	amended	AASB 2012-6 [23]
38	amended	AASB 2012-6 [24]
48	amended	AASB 2012-6 [25]
50	amended	AASB 2012-6 [26]
62	amended	AASB 2012-6 [27]
71	amended	AASB 2012-6 [28]

Accounting Standard AASB 2010-7

The Australian Accounting Standards Board made Accounting Standard *AASB 2010-7 Amendments to Australian Accounting Standards arising from AASB 9 (December 2010)* under section 334 of the *Corporations Act 2001* on 6 December 2010.

This compiled version of AASB 2010-7 applies to annual reporting periods beginning on or after 1 January 2015. It incorporates relevant amendments contained in other AASB Standards made by the AASB up to and including 10 September 2012 (see Compilation Details).

Accounting Standard AASB 2010-7

Amendments to Australian Accounting Standards arising from AASB 9 (December 2010)

Objective

1   The objective of this Standard is to make amendments to:

(a)   AASB 1 *First-time Adoption of Australian Accounting Standards*;

(b)   AASB 3 *Business Combinations*;

(c)   AASB 4 *Insurance Contracts*;

(d)   AASB 5 *Non-current Assets Held for Sale and Discontinued Operations*;

(e)   AASB 7 *Financial Instruments: Disclosures*;

(f)   AASB 101 *Presentation of Financial Statements*;

(g)   AASB 102 *Inventories*;

(h)   AASB 108 *Accounting Policies, Changes in Accounting Estimates and Errors*;

(i)   AASB 112 *Income Taxes*;

(j)   AASB 118 *Revenue*;

(k)   AASB 120 *Accounting for Government Grants and Disclosure of Government Assistance*;

(l)   AASB 121 *The Effects of Changes in Foreign Exchange Rates*;

(m)   AASB 127 *Consolidated and Separate Financial Statements*;

(n)   AASB 128 *Investments in Associates*;

(o)   AASB 131 *Interests in Joint Ventures*;

(p)   AASB 132 *Financial Instruments: Presentation*;

(q)   AASB 136 *Impairment of Assets*;

(r)   AASB 137 *Provisions, Contingent Liabilities and Contingent Assets*;

(s)   AASB 139 *Financial Instruments: Recognition and Measurement*;

(t)   AASB 1023 *General Insurance Contracts*;

(u)   AASB 1038 *Life Insurance Contracts*;

(v)   Interpretation 2 *Members' Shares in Co-operative Entities and Similar Instruments*;

(w)   Interpretation 5 *Rights to Interests arising from Decommissioning, Restoration and Environmental Rehabilitation Funds*;

(x)   Interpretation 10 *Interim Financial Reporting and Impairment*;

(y)   Interpretation 12 *Service Concession Arrangements*;

(z)   Interpretation 19 *Extinguishing Financial Liabilities with Equity Instruments*; and

(aa)   Interpretation 127 *Evaluating the Substance of Transactions Involving the Legal Form of a Lease*;

as a consequence of the issuance of AASB 9 *Financial Instruments* in December 2010.

Application

2   **Subject to paragraphs 3 and 4, this Standard applies to:**

(a)   **each entity that is required to prepare financial reports in accordance with Part 2M.3 of the Corporations Act and that is a reporting entity;**

(b)   **general purpose financial statements of each other reporting entity; and**

(c)   **financial statements that are, or are held out to be, general purpose financial statements.**

3   **In respect of AASB 101 and AASB 108, this Standard applies to:**

    (a)   **each entity that is required to prepare financial reports in accordance with Part 2M.3 of the Corporations Act;**

    (b)   **general purpose financial statements of each reporting entity; and**

    (c)   **financial statements that are, or are held out to be, general purpose financial statements.**

4   **In respect of AASB 1038, this Standard applies to each entity that is:**

    (a)   **a life insurer; or**

    (b)   **the parent in a group that includes a life insurer;**

    when the entity:

    (c)   **is a reporting entity that is required to prepare financial reports in accordance with Part 2M.3 of the Corporations Act;**

    (d)   **is an other reporting entity and prepares general purpose financial statements; or**

    (e)   **prepares financial statements that are, or are held out to be, general purpose financial statements.**

5   **This Standard applies to annual reporting periods beginning on or after 1 January 2015.**

6   **Earlier application is permitted from:**

    (a)   **any date between the issue of this Standard and 31 December 2010, for entities initially applying this Standard before 1 January 2011; or**

    (b)   **the beginning of the first reporting period in which the entity adopts this Standard, for entities initially applying this Standard on or after 1 January 2011.**

    However, if an entity elects to apply this Standard early and has not already applied AASB 9 and AASB 2009-11 *Amendments to Australian Accounting Standards arising from AASB 9* **issued in December 2009 (as amended), it must apply all of the requirements in AASB 9 (December 2010) at the same time. If an entity applies this Standard in its financial statements for a period beginning before 1 January 2015, it shall disclose that fact.**

7   When applied or operative, this Standard supersedes AASB 2009-11 *Amendments to Australian Accounting Standards arising from AASB 9*. However, for annual reporting periods ending on or after 31 December 2009 that begin before 1 January 2015, an entity may elect to apply AASB 9 (December 2009) instead of applying AASB 9 (December 2010) and therefore will apply the amendments to other Australian Accounting Standards in AASB 2009-11 instead of this Standard.

8   **This Standard uses underlining, striking out and other typographical material to identify some of the amendments to a Standard or an Interpretation, in order to make the amendments more understandable. However, the amendments made by this Standard do not include that underlining, striking out or other typographical material.**

Amendments to AASB 1

9   Paragraph 29 is amended to read as follows, paragraph 39B is deleted and paragraphs 29A and 39G are added:

    29   An entity is permitted to designate a previously recognised financial asset as a financial asset measured at fair value through profit or loss in accordance with paragraph D19A. The entity shall disclose the fair value of financial assets so designated at the date of designation and their classification and carrying amount in the previous financial statements.

29A An entity is permitted to designate a previously recognised financial liability as a financial liability at fair value through profit or loss in accordance with paragraph D19. The entity shall disclose the fair value of financial liabilities so designated at the date of designation and their classification and carrying amount in the previous financial statements.

39B [Deleted by the IASB]

39G AASB 2010-7 *Amendments to Australian Accounting Standards arising from AASB 9 (December 2010)*, issued in December 2010, amended paragraphs 29, B1-B5, D1(j), D14, D15, D19 and D20, added paragraphs 29A, B8, B9, D19A-D19D, E1 and E2 and deleted paragraph 39B. An entity shall apply those amendments when it applies AASB 9 as issued in December 2010.

10 In Appendix B, paragraphs B1-B5 are amended to read as follows, and a heading and paragraph B8, and a heading and paragraph B9 are added:

B1 An entity shall apply the following exceptions:

    (a)   derecognition of financial assets and financial liabilities (paragraphs B2 and B3);

    (b)   hedge accounting (paragraphs B4-B6);

    (c)   non-controlling interests (paragraph B7);

    (d)   classification and measurement of financial assets (paragraph B8);

    (e)   embedded derivatives (paragraph B9); and

    (f)   government loans (paragraphs B10-B12).

Derecognition of financial assets and financial liabilities

B2 Except as permitted by paragraph B3, a first-time adopter shall apply the derecognition requirements in AASB 9 *Financial Instruments* prospectively for transactions occurring on or after the date of transition to Australian Accounting Standards. For example, if a first-time adopter derecognised non-derivative financial assets or non-derivative financial liabilities in accordance with its previous GAAP as a result of a transaction that occurred before the date of transition to Australian Accounting Standards, it shall not recognise those assets and liabilities in accordance with Australian Accounting Standards (unless they qualify for recognition as a result of a later transaction or event).

B3 Despite paragraph B2, an entity may apply the derecognition requirements in AASB 9 retrospectively from a date of the entity's choosing, provided that the information needed to apply AASB 9 to financial assets and financial liabilities derecognised as a result of past transactions was obtained at the time of initially accounting for those transactions.

Hedge accounting

B4 As required by AASB 9, at the date of transition to Australian Accounting Standards an entity shall:

    (a)   measure all derivatives at fair value; and

    (b)   eliminate all deferred losses and gains arising on derivatives that were reported in accordance with previous GAAP as if they were assets or liabilities.

B5 An entity shall not reflect in its opening Australian-Accounting-Standards statement of financial position a hedging relationship of a type that does not qualify for hedge accounting in accordance with AASB 139 (for example, many hedging relationships where the hedging instrument is a cash instrument or written option; or where the hedged item is a net position). However, if an entity designated a net position as a hedged item in accordance with previous GAAP, it may designate an individual item within that net position as a hedged item in accordance with Australian Accounting Standards, provided that it does so no later than the date of transition to Australian Accounting Standards.

Classification and measurement of financial assets

B8   An entity shall assess whether a financial asset meets the conditions in paragraph 4.1.2 of AASB 9 on the basis of the facts and circumstances that exist at the date of transition to Australian Accounting Standards.

Embedded derivatives

B9   A first-time adopter shall assess whether an embedded derivative is required to be separated from the host contract and accounted for as a derivative on the basis of the conditions that existed at the later of the date it first became a party to the contract and the date a reassessment is required by paragraph B4.3.11 of AASB 9.

11   In Appendix D, paragraphs D1(j), D14, D15, D19 and D20 are amended to read as follows and paragraphs D19A-D19D are added:

D1   An entity may elect to use one or more of the following exemptions:

      (a)   ...

      (j)   designation of previously recognised financial instruments (paragraphs D19-D19D);

      (k)   ...

D14   When an entity prepares separate financial statements, AASB 127 requires it to account for its investments in subsidiaries, jointly controlled entities and associates either:

      (a)   at cost; or

      (b)   in accordance with AASB 9.

D19   AASB 9 permits a financial liability (provided it meets certain criteria) to be designated as a financial liability at fair value through profit or loss. Despite this requirement an entity is permitted to designate, at the date of transition to Australian Accounting Standards, any financial liability as at fair value through profit or loss provided the liability meets the criteria in paragraph 4.2.2 of AASB 9 at that date.

D19A   An entity may designate a financial asset as measured at fair value through profit or loss in accordance with paragraph 4.1.5 of AASB 9 on the basis of the facts and circumstances that exist at the date of transition to Australian Accounting Standards.

D19B   An entity may designate an investment in an equity instrument as at fair value through other comprehensive income in accordance with paragraph 5.7.5 of AASB 9 on the basis of the facts and circumstances that exist at the date of transition to Australian Accounting Standards.

D19C   If it is impracticable (as defined in AASB 108) for an entity to apply retrospectively the effective interest method or the impairment requirements in paragraphs 58-65 and AG84-AG93 of AASB 139, the fair value of the financial asset at the date of transition to Australian Accounting Standards shall be the new amortised cost of that financial asset at the date of transition to Australian Accounting Standards.

D19D   An entity shall determine whether the treatment in paragraph 5.7.7 of AASB 9 would create an accounting mismatch in profit or loss on the basis of the facts and circumstances that exist at the date of transition to Australian Accounting Standards.

Fair value measurement of financial assets or financial liabilities at initial recognition

D20   Despite the requirements of paragraphs 7 and 9, an entity may apply the requirements in the last sentence of paragraph B5.4.8 and in paragraph B5.4.9 of AASB 9 prospectively to transactions entered into on or after the date of transition to Australian Accounting Standards.

12   In Appendix E, a heading and paragraphs E1 and E2 are added:

Exemption from the requirement to restate comparative information for AASB 9

E1   In its first Australian-Accounting-Standards financial statements, an entity that (a) adopts Australian Accounting Standards for annual periods beginning before 1 January 2012 and (b) applies AASB 9 shall present at least one year of comparative information. However, this comparative information need not comply with AASB 7 *Financial Instruments: Disclosures* or AASB 9, to the extent that the disclosures required by AASB 7 relate to items within the scope of AASB 9. For such entities, references to the 'date of transition to Australian Accounting Standards' shall mean, in the case of AASB 7 and AASB 9 only, the beginning of the first Australian-Accounting-Standards reporting period.

E2   An entity that chooses to present comparative information that does not comply with AASB 7 and AASB 9 in its first year of transition shall:

    (a)   apply the recognition and measurement requirements of its previous GAAP in place of the requirements of AASB 9 to comparative information about items within the scope of AASB 9.

    (b)   disclose this fact together with the basis used to prepare this information.

    (c)   treat any adjustment between the statement of financial position at the comparative period's reporting date (i.e. the statement of financial position that includes comparative information under previous GAAP) and the statement of financial position at the start of the *first Australian-Accounting-Standards reporting period* (i.e. the first period that includes information that complies with AASB 7 and AASB 9) as arising from a change in accounting policy and give the disclosures required by paragraph 28(a)-(e) and (f)(i) of AASB 108. Paragraph 28(f)(i) applies only to amounts presented in the statement of financial position at the comparative period's reporting date.

    (d)   apply paragraph 17(c) of AASB 101 to provide additional disclosures when compliance with the specific requirements in Australian Accounting Standards is insufficient to enable users to understand the impact of particular transactions, other events and conditions on the entity's financial position and financial performance.

Amendments to AASB 3

13   Paragraphs 16, 42, 53, 56 and 58(b) are amended to read as follows, paragraph 64A is deleted and paragraph 64D is added:

16   In some situations, Australian Accounting Standards provide for different accounting depending on how an entity classifies or designates a particular asset or liability. Examples of classifications or designations that the acquirer shall make on the basis of the pertinent conditions as they exist at the acquisition date include but are not limited to:

    (a)   classification of particular financial assets and liabilities as measured at fair value or at amortised cost, in accordance with AASB 9 *Financial Instruments*;

    (b)   designation of a derivative instrument as a hedging instrument in accordance with AASB 139; and

    (c)   assessment of whether an embedded derivative should be separated from a host contract in accordance with AASB 9 (which is a matter of 'classification' as this Standard uses that term).

42   In a business combination achieved in stages, the acquirer shall remeasure its previously held equity interest in the acquiree at its acquisition-date fair value and recognise the resulting gain or loss, if any, in profit or loss or other comprehensive income, as appropriate. In prior reporting periods, the acquirer may have recognised changes in the value of its equity interest in the acquiree in other comprehensive income.

If so, the amount that was recognised in other comprehensive income shall be recognised on the same basis as would be required if the acquirer had disposed directly of the previously held equity interest.

53 Acquisition-related costs are costs the acquirer incurs to effect a business combination. Those costs include finder's fees; advisory, legal, accounting, valuation and other professional or consulting fees; general administrative costs, including the costs of maintaining an internal acquisitions department; and costs of registering and issuing debt and equity securities. The acquirer shall account for acquisition-related costs as expenses in the periods in which the costs are incurred and the services are received, with one exception. The costs to issue debt or equity securities shall be recognised in accordance with AASB 132 and AASB 9.

56 After initial recognition and until the liability is settled, cancelled or expires, the acquirer shall measure a contingent liability recognised in a business combination at the higher of:

(a) the amount that would be recognised in accordance with AASB 137; and

(b) the amount initially recognised less, if appropriate, cumulative amortisation recognised in accordance with AASB 118 *Revenue*.

This requirement does not apply to contracts accounted for in accordance with AASB 9.

58 Some changes ...

(b) Contingent consideration classified as an asset or a liability that:

(i) is a financial instrument and is within the scope of AASB 9 shall be measured at fair value, with any resulting gain or loss recognised either in profit or loss or in other comprehensive income in accordance with AASB 9.

(ii) is not within the scope of AASB 9 shall be accounted for in accordance with AASB 137 or other Australian Accounting Standards as appropriate.

64A [Deleted by the IASB]

64D AASB 2010-7 *Amendments to Australian Accounting Standards arising from AASB 9 (December 2010)*, issued in December 2010, amended paragraphs 16, 42, 53, 56 and 58(b) and deleted paragraph 64A. An entity shall apply those amendments when it applies AASB 9 as issued in December 2010.

Amendments to AASB 4

14 Paragraphs 3, 4(d), 7, 8, 12, 34(d), 35 and 45 are amended to read as follows, paragraph 41C is deleted and paragraph 41D is added:

3 This Standard does not address other aspects of accounting by insurers, such as accounting for financial assets held by insurers and financial liabilities issued by insurers (see AASB 132 *Financial Instruments: Presentation*, AASB 139 *Financial Instruments: Recognition and Measurement*, AASB 7 and AASB 9 *Financial Instruments*), except in the transitional provisions in paragraph 45.

4 An entity shall not apply this Standard to:

(a) ...

(d) *financial guarantee contracts* unless the issuer has previously asserted explicitly that it regards such contracts as insurance contracts and has used accounting applicable to insurance contracts, in which case the issuer may elect to apply either AASB 132, AASB 7 and AASB 9 or AASB 1023 to such financial guarantee contracts. The issuer may make that election contract by contract, but the election for each contract is irrevocable;

(e) ...

7 AASB 9 requires an entity to separate some embedded derivatives from their host contract, measure them at fair value and include changes in their *fair value* in profit

or loss. AASB 9 applies to derivatives embedded in an insurance contract unless the embedded derivative is itself an insurance contract.

8   As an exception to the requirements in AASB 9, an insurer need not separate, and measure at fair value, a policyholder's option to surrender an insurance contract for a fixed amount (or for an amount based on a fixed amount and an interest rate), even if the exercise price differs from the carrying amount of the host *insurance liability*. However, the requirements in AASB 9 do apply to a put option or cash surrender option embedded in an insurance contract if the surrender value varies in response to the change in a financial variable (such as an equity or commodity price or index), or a non-financial variable that is not specific to a party to the contract. Furthermore, those requirements also apply if the holder's ability to exercise a put option or cash surrender option is triggered by a change in such a variable (for example, a put option that can be exercised if a stock market index reaches a specified level).

12   To unbundle a contract, an insurer shall:

     (a)   apply this Standard to the insurance component; and

     (b)   apply AASB 9 to the deposit component.

34   Some insurance contracts contain a discretionary participation feature as well as a *guaranteed element*. The issuer of such a contract:

     (a)   ...

     (d)   shall, if the contract contains an embedded derivative within the scope of AASB 9, apply AASB 9 to that embedded derivative; and

     (e)   ...

Discretionary participation features in financial instruments

35   The requirements in paragraph 34 also apply to a financial instrument that contains a discretionary participation feature. In addition:

     (a)   if the issuer classifies the entire discretionary participation feature as a liability, it shall apply the liability adequacy test in paragraphs 15-19 to the whole contract (i.e. both the guaranteed element and the discretionary participation feature). The issuer need not determine the amount that would result from applying AASB 9 to the guaranteed element.

     (b)   if the issuer classifies part or all of that feature as a separate component of equity, the liability recognised for the whole contract shall not be less than the amount that would result from applying AASB 9 to the guaranteed element. That amount shall include the intrinsic value of an option to surrender the contract, but need not include its time value if paragraph 9 exempts that option from measurement at fair value. The issuer need not disclose the amount that would result from applying AASB 9 to the guaranteed element, nor need it present that amount separately. Furthermore, the issuer need not determine that amount if the total liability recognised is clearly higher;

     (c)   ...

41C   [Deleted by the IASB]

41D   AASB 2010-7 *Amendments to Australian Accounting Standards arising from AASB 9 (December 2010)*, issued in December 2010, amended paragraphs 3, 4(d), 7, 8, 12, 34(d), 35, 45 and B18-B20 and Appendix A and deleted paragraph 41C. An entity shall apply those amendments when it applies AASB 9 as issued in December 2010.

45   Despite paragraph 4.4.1 of AASB 9, when an insurer changes its accounting policies for insurance liabilities, it is permitted, but not required, to reclassify some or all of its financial assets so that they are measured at fair value. This reclassification is permitted if an insurer changes accounting policies when it first applies this Standard and if it makes a subsequent policy change permitted by paragraph 22. The reclassification is a change in accounting policy and AASB 108 applies.

15   In Appendix A the defined term 'deposit component' is amended to read as follows:

deposit component   A contractual component that is not accounted for as a derivative under AASB 9 and would be within the scope of AASB 9 if it were a separate instrument.

16   In Appendix B, paragraphs B18-B20 are amended to read as follows:

B18   The following are examples of contracts that are insurance contracts, if the transfer of insurance risk is significant:

   (a)   ...

   (g)   credit insurance that provides for specified payments to be made to reimburse the holder for a loss it incurs because a specified debtor fails to make payment when due under the original or modified terms of a debt instrument. These contracts could have various legal forms, such as that of a guarantee, some types of letter of credit, a credit derivative default contract or an insurance contract. However, although these contracts meet the definition of an insurance contract, they also meet the definition of a financial guarantee contract in AASB 9 and are within the scope of AASB 132[1] and AASB 9, not this Standard (see paragraph 4(d)). Nevertheless, if an issuer of financial guarantee contracts has previously asserted explicitly that it regards such contracts as insurance contracts and has used accounting applicable to insurance contracts, the issuer may elect to apply either AASB 1321 and AASB 9 or AASB 1023 to such financial guarantee contracts;

   _____
   1   When an entity applies AASB 7, the reference to AASB 132 is replaced by a reference to AASB 7.

   (h)   ...

B19   The following are examples of items that are not insurance contracts:

   (a)   ...

   (e)   derivatives that expose one party to financial risk but not insurance risk, because they require that party to make payment based solely on changes in one or more of a specified interest rate, financial instrument price, commodity price, foreign exchange rate, index of prices or rates, credit rating or credit index or other variable, provided in the case of a non-financial variable that the variable is not specific to a party to the contract (see AASB 9);

   (f)   a credit-related guarantee (or letter of credit, credit derivative default contract or credit insurance contract) that requires payments even if the holder has not incurred a loss on the failure of the debtor to make payments when due (see AASB 9);

   (g)   ...

B20   If the contracts described in paragraph B19 create financial assets or financial liabilities, they are within the scope of AASB 9. Among other things, this means ...

Amendments to AASB 5

17   Paragraph 5 is amended to read as follows and paragraph 44F is added:

   5   The measurement provisions of this Standard[3] do not apply to the following assets, which are covered by the Australian Accounting Standards listed, either as individual assets or as part of a disposal group:

   (a)   ...

   (c)   financial assets within the scope of AASB 9 *Financial Instruments*;

   (d)   ...

   _____
   3   Other than paragraphs 18 and 19, which require the assets in question to be measured in accordance with other applicable Australian Accounting Standards.

44F   AASB 2010-7 *Amendments to Australian Accounting Standards arising from AASB 9 (December 2010)*, issued in December 2010, amended paragraph 5. An entity shall apply that amendment when it applies AASB 9 as issued in December 2010.

Amendments to AASB 7

18   Paragraphs 2-5, 8-10, 11, 14, 20, 28 and 30 are amended to read as follows, paragraphs 12, 12A, 29(b) and 44H are deleted and a heading and paragraphs 10A, 11A, 11B, 12B-12D, 20A, 44I, 44J, 44N and 44S-44W are added:

2   The principles in this Standard complement the principles for recognising, measuring and presenting financial assets and financial liabilities in AASB 132 *Financial Instruments: Presentation* and AASB 9 *Financial Instruments*.

Scope

3   This Standard shall be applied by all entities to all types of financial instruments, except:

    (a)   those interests in subsidiaries, associates or joint ventures that are accounted for in accordance with AASB 10 *Consolidated Financial Statements*, AASB 127 *Separate Financial Statements* or AASB 128 *Investments in Associates and Joint Ventures*. However, in some cases, AASB 127 or AASB 128 permits an entity to account for an interest in a subsidiary, associate or joint venture using AASB 9; in those cases, entities shall apply the requirements of this Standard and, for those interests measured at fair value, the requirements of AASB 13 *Fair Value Measurement*. Entities shall also apply this Standard to all derivatives linked to interests in subsidiaries, associates or joint ventures unless the derivative meets the definition of an equity instrument in AASB 132;

    (b)   ...

    (d)   insurance contracts as defined in AASB 4 *Insurance Contracts*. However, this Standard applies to derivatives that are embedded in insurance contracts if AASB 9 requires the entity to account for them separately. Moreover, an issuer shall apply this Standard to *financial guarantee contracts* if the issuer applies AASB 9 in recognising and measuring the contracts, but shall apply AASB 4 if the issuer elects, in accordance with paragraph 4(d) of AASB 4, to apply AASB 4 in recognising and measuring them;

    (e)   ...

4   This Standard applies to recognised and unrecognised financial instruments. Recognised financial instruments include financial assets and financial liabilities that are within the scope of AASB 9. Unrecognised financial instruments include some financial instruments that, although outside the scope of AASB 9, are within the scope of this Standard (such as some loan commitments).

5   This Standard applies to contracts to buy or sell a non-financial item that are within the scope of AASB 9.

8   The carrying amounts of each of the following categories, as specified in AASB 9, shall be disclosed either in the statement of financial position or in the notes:

    (a)   financial assets measured at fair value through profit or loss, showing separately (i) those designated as such upon initial recognition and (ii) those mandatorily measured at fair value in accordance with AASB 9;

    (b)-(d)[deleted by the IASB]

    (e)   financial liabilities at fair value through profit or loss, showing separately (i) those designated as such upon initial recognition and (ii) those that meet the definition of held for trading in AASB 9;

    (f)   financial assets measured at amortised cost;

    (g)   financial liabilities measured at amortised cost; and

    (h)   financial assets measured at fair value through other comprehensive income.

Financial assets or financial liabilities at fair value through profit or loss

9   If the entity has designated as measured at fair value a financial asset (or group of financial assets) that would otherwise be measured at amortised cost, it shall disclose:

   (a)   the maximum exposure to *credit risk* (see paragraph 36(a)) of the financial asset (or group of financial assets) at the end of the reporting period;

   (b)   the amount by which any related credit derivatives or similar instruments mitigate that maximum exposure to credit risk;

   (c)   the amount of change, during the period and cumulatively, in the fair value of the financial asset (or group of financial assets) that is attributable to changes in the credit risk of the financial asset determined either:

          (i)   ...

   (d)   the amount of the change in the fair value of any related credit derivatives or similar instruments that has occurred during the period and cumulatively since the financial asset was designated.

10   If the entity has designated a financial liability as at fair value through profit or loss in accordance with paragraph 4.2.2 of AASB 9 and is required to present the effects of changes in that liability's credit risk in other comprehensive income (see paragraph 5.7.7 of AASB 9), it shall disclose:

   (a)   the amount of change, cumulatively, in the fair value of the financial liability that is attributable to changes in the credit risk of that liability (see paragraphs B5.7.13-B5.7.20 of AASB 9 for guidance on determining the effects of changes in a liability's credit risk);

   (b)   the difference between the financial liability's carrying amount and the amount the entity would be contractually required to pay at maturity to the holder of the obligation;

   (c)   any transfers of the cumulative gain or loss within equity during the period including the reason for such transfers; and

   (d)   if a liability is derecognised during the period, the amount (if any) presented in other comprehensive income that was realised at derecognition.

10A   If an entity has designated a financial liability as at fair value through profit or loss in accordance with paragraph 4.2.2 of AASB 9 and is required to present all changes in the fair value of that liability (including the effects of changes in the credit risk of the liability) in profit or loss (see paragraphs 5.7.7 and 5.7.8 of AASB 9), it shall disclose:

   (a)   the amount of change, during the period and cumulatively, in the fair value of the financial liability that is attributable to changes in the credit risk of that liability (see paragraphs B5.7.13-B5.7.20 of AASB 9 for guidance on determining the effects of changes in a liability's credit risk); and

   (b)   the difference between the financial liability's carrying amount and the amount the entity would be contractually required to pay at maturity to the holder of the obligation.

11   The entity shall also disclose:

   (a)   a detailed description of the methods used to comply with the requirements in paragraphs 9(c), 10(a) and 10A(a) and paragraph 5.7.7(a) of AASB 9, including an explanation of why the method is appropriate;

   (b)   if the entity believes that the disclosure it has given, either in the statement of financial position or in the notes, to comply with the requirements in paragraph 9(c), 10(a) or 10A(a) or paragraph 5.7.7(a) of AASB 9 does not faithfully represent the change in the fair value of the financial asset or financial liability attributable to changes in its credit risk, the reasons for reaching this conclusion and the factors it believes are relevant; and

(c)   a detailed description of the methodology or methodologies used to determine whether presenting the effects of changes in a liability's credit risk in other comprehensive income would create or enlarge an accounting mismatch in profit or loss (see paragraphs 5.7.7 and 5.7.8 of AASB 9). If an entity is required to present the effects of changes in a liability's credit risk in profit or loss (see paragraph 5.7.8 of AASB 9), the disclosure must include a detailed description of the economic relationship described in paragraph B5.7.6 of AASB 9.

Financial assets measured at fair value through other comprehensive income

11A   If an entity has designated investments in equity instruments to be measured at fair value through other comprehensive income, as permitted by paragraph 5.7.5 of AASB 9, it shall disclose:

(a)   which investments in equity instruments have been designated to be measured at fair value through other comprehensive income;

(b)   the reasons for using this presentation alternative;

(c)   the fair value of each such investment at the end of the reporting period;

(d)   dividends recognised during the period, showing separately those related to investments derecognised during the reporting period and those related to investments held at the end of the reporting period; and

(e)   any transfers of the cumulative gain or loss within equity during the period including the reason for such transfers.

11B   If an entity derecognised investments in equity instruments measured at fair value through other comprehensive income during the reporting period, it shall disclose:

(a)   the reasons for disposing of the investments;

(b)   the fair value of the investments at the date of derecognition; and

(c)   the cumulative gain or loss on disposal.

12B   An entity shall disclose if, in the current or previous reporting periods, it has reclassified any financial assets in accordance with paragraph 4.4.1 of AASB 9. For each such event, an entity shall disclose:

(a)   the date of reclassification;

(b)   a detailed explanation of the change in business model and a qualitative description of its effect on the entity's financial statements; and

(c)   the amount reclassified into and out of each category.

12C   For each reporting period following reclassification until derecognition, an entity shall disclose for assets reclassified so that they are measured at amortised cost in accordance with paragraph 4.4.1 of AASB 9:

(a)   the effective interest rate determined on the date of reclassification; and

(b)   the interest income or expense recognised.

12D   If an entity has reclassified financial assets so that they are measured at amortised cost since its last annual reporting date, it shall disclose:

(a)   the fair value of the financial assets at the end of the reporting period; and

(b)   the fair value gain or loss that would have been recognised in profit or loss during the reporting period if the financial assets had not been reclassified.

14   An entity shall disclose:

(a)   the carrying amount of financial assets it has pledged as collateral for liabilities or contingent liabilities, including amounts that have been reclassified in accordance with paragraph 3.3.23(a) of AASB 9; and

(b)   the terms and conditions relating to its pledge.

20   An entity shall disclose the following items of income, expense, gains or losses either in the statement of comprehensive income or in the notes:

(a)   net gains or net losses on:

(i)   financial assets or financial liabilities measured at fair value through profit or loss, showing separately those on financial assets or financial liabilities designated as such upon initial recognition, and those on financial assets or financial liabilities that are mandatorily measured at fair value in accordance with AASB 9 (e.g. financial liabilities that meet the definition of held for trading in AASB 9). For financial liabilities designated as at fair value through profit or loss, an entity shall show separately the amount of gain or loss recognised in other comprehensive income and the amount recognised in profit or loss;

(ii)-(iv) [deleted by the IASB]

(v)   financial liabilities measured at amortised cost;

(vi)   financial assets measured at amortised cost; and

(vii) financial assets measured at fair value through other comprehensive income;

(b)   total interest income and total interest expense (calculated using the effective interest method) for financial assets that are measured at amortised cost or financial liabilities not at fair value through profit or loss;

(c)   fee income and expense (other than amounts included in determining the effective interest rate) arising from:

(i)   financial assets measured at amortised cost or financial liabilities that are not at fair value through profit or loss; and

(ii)   trust and other fiduciary activities that result in the holding or investing of assets on behalf of individuals, trusts, retirement benefit plans, and other institutions;

(d)   interest income on impaired financial assets accrued in accordance with paragraph AG93 of AASB 139; and

(e)   ...

20A   An entity shall disclose an analysis of the gain or loss recognised in the statement of comprehensive income arising from the derecognition of financial assets measured at amortised cost, showing separately gains and losses arising from derecognition of those financial assets. This disclosure shall include the reasons for derecognising those financial assets.

28   In some cases, an entity does not recognise a gain or loss on initial recognition of a financial asset or financial liability because the fair value is neither evidenced by a quoted price in an active market for an identical asset or liability (i.e. a Level 1 input) nor based on a valuation technique that uses only data from observable markets (see paragraph B5.1.2A of AASB 9). In such cases, the entity shall disclose by class of financial asset or financial liability:

(a)   its accounting policy for recognising in profit or loss the difference between the fair value at initial recognition and the transaction price to reflect a change in factors (including time) that market participants would take into account when pricing the asset or liability (see paragraph B5.1.2A(b) of AASB 9).

(b)   the aggregate difference yet to be recognised in profit or loss at the beginning and end of the period and a reconciliation of changes in the balance of this difference.

(c)   why the entity concluded that the transaction price was not the best evidence of fair value, including a description of the evidence that supports the fair value.

29   Disclosures of fair value are not required:

        (a)   ...

        (b)   [deleted by the IASB]

        (c)   ...

30   In the case described in paragraph 29(c), an entity shall disclose information to help users of the financial statements make their own judgements about the extent of possible differences between the carrying amount of those contracts and their fair value, including:

        (a)   ...

44H   [Deleted by the IASB]

44I   When an entity first applies AASB 9, it shall disclose for each class of financial assets and financial liabilities at the date of initial application:

        (a)   the original measurement category and carrying amount determined in accordance with AASB 139;

        (b)   the new measurement category and carrying amount determined in accordance with AASB 9; and

        (c)   the amount of any financial assets and financial liabilities in the statement of financial position that were previously designated as measured at fair value through profit or loss but are no longer so designated, distinguishing between those that AASB 9 requires an entity to reclassify and those that an entity elects to reclassify.

     An entity shall present these quantitative disclosures in tabular format unless another format is more appropriate.

44J   When an entity first applies AASB 9, it shall disclose qualitative information to enable users to understand:

        (a)   how it applied the classification requirements in AASB 9 to those financial assets whose classification has changed as a result of applying AASB 9; and

        (b)   the reasons for any designation or de-designation of financial assets or financial liabilities as measured at fair value through profit or loss.

44N   AASB 2010-7 *Amendments to Australian Accounting Standards arising from AASB 9 (December 2010)*, issued in December 2010, amended paragraphs 2-5, 8-10, 11, 14, 20, 28, 30, Appendix A, B1, B5, B10(a), B22 and B27, added paragraphs 10A, 11A, 11B, 12B-12D, 20A, 44I and 44J, and deleted paragraphs 12, 12A, 29(b), 44H, B4 and Appendix D. An entity shall apply those amendments when it applies AASB 9 as issued in December 2010.

44S   When an entity first applies the classification and measurement requirements of AASB 9, it shall present the disclosures set out in paragraphs 44T-44W of this Standard if it elects to, or is required to, provide these disclosures in accordance with paragraph 7.2.14 of AASB 9.

44T   If required by paragraph 44S, at the date of initial application of AASB 9 an entity shall disclose the changes in the classifications of financial assets and financial liabilities, showing separately:

        (a)   the changes in the carrying amounts on the basis of their measurement categories in accordance with AASB 139 (ie not resulting from a change in measurement attribute on transition to AASB 9); and

        (b)   the changes in the carrying amounts arising from a change in measurement attribute on transition to AASB 9.

     The disclosures in this paragraph need not be made after the annual reporting period in which AASB 9 is initially applied.

44U   In the reporting period in which AASB 9 is initially applied, an entity shall disclose the following for financial assets and financial liabilities that have been reclassified so that they are measured at amortised cost as a result of the transition to AASB 9:

    (a)   the fair value of the financial assets or financial liabilities at the end of the reporting period;

    (b)   the fair value gain or loss that would have been recognised in profit or loss or other comprehensive income during the reporting period if the financial assets or financial liabilities had not been reclassified;

    (c)   the effective interest rate determined on the date of reclassification; and

    (d)   the interest income or expense recognised.

If an entity treats the fair value of a financial asset or a financial liability as its amortised cost at the date of initial application (see paragraph 7.2.10 of AASB 9), the disclosures in (c) and (d) of this paragraph shall be made for each reporting period following reclassification until derecognition. Otherwise, the disclosures in this paragraph need not be made after the reporting period containing the date of initial application.

44V   If an entity presents the disclosures set out in paragraphs 44S-44U at the date of initial application of AASB 9, those disclosures, and the disclosures in paragraph 28 of AASB 108 during the reporting period containing the date of initial application, must permit reconciliation between:

    (a)   the measurement categories in accordance with AASB 139 and AASB 9; and

    (b)   the line items presented in the statements of financial position.

44W   If an entity presents the disclosures set out in paragraphs 44S-44U at the date of initial application of AASB 9, those disclosures, and the disclosures in paragraph 25 of this Standard at the date of initial application, must permit reconciliation between:

    (a)   the measurement categories presented in accordance with AASB 139 and AASB 9; and

    (b)   the class of financial instrument at the date of initial application.

19   In Appendix A, the last paragraph is amended to read as follows:

The following terms are defined in paragraph 11 of AASB 132, paragraph 9 of AASB 139 or Appendix A of AASB 9 and are used in the Standard with the meaning specified in AASB 132, AASB 139 and AASB 9.

    (a)   amortised cost of a financial asset or financial liability;

    (b)   derecognition;

    (c)   derivative;

    (d)   effective interest method;

    (e)   equity instrument;

    (f)   fair value;

    (g)   financial asset;

    (h)   financial guarantee contract;

    (i)   financial instrument;

    (j)   financial liability;

    (k)   financial liability at fair value through profit or loss;

    (l)   forecast transaction;

    (m)   hedging instrument;

    (n)   held for trading;

    (o)   reclassification date; and

    (p)   regular way purchase or sale.

20   In Appendix B, paragraph B4 is deleted and paragraphs B1, B5, B10(a), B22 and B27 are amended to read as follows:

B1   Paragraph 6 requires an entity to group financial instruments into classes that are appropriate to the nature of the information disclosed and that take into account the characteristics of those financial instruments. The classes described in paragraph 6 are determined by the entity and are, thus, distinct from the categories of financial instruments specified in AASB 9 (which determine how financial instruments are measured and where changes in fair value are recognised).

B5   Paragraph 21 requires disclosure of the measurement basis (or bases) used in preparing the financial statements and the other accounting policies used that are relevant to an understanding of the financial statements. For financial instruments, such disclosure may include:

    (a)   for financial liabilities designated as at fair value through profit or loss:

        (i)   the nature of the financial liabilities the entity has designated as at fair value through profit or loss;

        (ii)   the criteria for so designating such financial liabilities on initial recognition; and

        (iii)   how the entity has satisfied the conditions in paragraph 4.2.2 of AASB 9 for such designation.

    (aa)   for financial assets designated as measured at fair value through profit or loss:

        (i)   the nature of the financial assets the entity has designated as measured at fair value through profit or loss; and

        (ii)   how the entity has satisfied the criteria in paragraph 4.1.5 of AASB 9 for such designation.

    (b)   [deleted by the IASB]

    (c)   whether regular way purchases and sales of financial assets are accounted for at trade date or at settlement date (see paragraph 3.1.2 of AASB 9).

    (d)   ...

B10   Activities that give rise to credit risk and the associated maximum exposure to credit risk include, but are not limited to:

    (a)   granting loans to customers and placing deposits with other entities. In these cases, the maximum exposure to credit risk is the carrying amount of the related financial assets;

    (b)   ...

B22   *Interest rate risk* arises on interest-bearing financial instruments recognised in the statement of financial position (e.g. debt instruments acquired or issued) and on some financial instruments not recognised in the statement of financial position (e.g. some loan commitments).

B27   In accordance with paragraph 40(a), the sensitivity of profit or loss (that arises, for example, from instruments measured at fair value through profit or loss) is disclosed separately from the sensitivity of other comprehensive income (that arises, for example, from investments in equity instruments whose changes in fair value are presented in other comprehensive income).

21   Appendix D is deleted.

Amendments to AASB 101

22   In paragraph 7, the definition of 'other comprehensive income' and paragraphs 68,
71, 82, 93, 95 and 123 are amended to read as follows, paragraph 139E is deleted and
paragraph 139G is added:

7   **The following terms are used in this Standard with the meanings specified:**

Other comprehensive income **comprises items of income and expense
(including reclassification adjustments) that are not recognised in profit or
loss as required or permitted by other Australian Accounting Standards.**

The components of other comprehensive income include:

(a)   ...

(d)   gains and losses from investments in equity instruments measured at
fair value through other comprehensive income in accordance with
paragraph 5.7.5 of AASB 9 *Financial Instruments*;

(e)   the effective portion of gains and losses on hedging instruments in a
cash flow hedge (see AASB 139 *Financial Instruments: Recognition and
Measurement*); and

(f)   for particular liabilities designated as at fair value through profit or loss,
the amount of the change in fair value that is attributable to changes in the
liability's credit risk (see paragraph 5.7.7 of AASB 9).

...

68   The operating cycle of an entity ... Current assets also include assets held primarily
for the purpose of trading (examples include some financial assets that meet the
definition of held for trading in AASB 9) and the current portion of non-current
financial assets.

71   Other current liabilities are not settled as part of the normal operating cycle, but
are due for settlement within twelve months after the reporting period or held
primarily for the purpose of trading. Examples are some financial liabilities that
meet the definition of held for trading in AASB 9, bank overdrafts, and the current
portion of non-current financial liabilities, dividends payable, income taxes and
other non-trade payables. Financial liabilities that provide financing on a long-term
basis (i.e. are not part of the working capital used in the entity's normal operating
cycle) and are not due for settlement within twelve months after the reporting
period are non-current liabilities, subject to paragraphs 74 and 75.

82   **In addition to items required by other Australian Accounting Standards, the
profit or loss section or the statement of profit or loss shall include line items
that present the following amounts for the period:**

(a)   **revenue;**

(aa)   **gains and losses arising from the derecognition of financial assets
measured at amortised cost;**

(b)   **finance costs;**

(c)   **share of the profit or loss of associates and joint ventures accounted for
using the equity method;**

(ca)   **if a financial asset is reclassified so that it is measured at fair value, any
gain or loss arising from a difference between the previous carrying
amount and its fair value at the reclassification date (as defined
in AASB 9);**

(d)   **...**

93   Other Australian Accounting Standards specify whether and when amounts
previously recognised in other comprehensive income are reclassified to profit
or loss. Such reclassifications are referred to in this Standard as reclassification
adjustments. A reclassification adjustment is included with the related component
of other comprehensive income in the period that the adjustment is reclassified to

profit or loss. These amounts may have been recognised in other comprehensive income ...

95   Reclassification adjustments arise, for example, on disposal of a foreign operation (see AASB 121) and when a hedged forecast transaction affects profit or loss (see paragraph 100 of AASB 139 in relation to cash flow hedges).

123   In the process of applying the entity's accounting policies, management makes various judgements, apart from those involving estimations, that can significantly affect the amounts it recognises in the financial statements. For example, management makes judgements in determining:

    (a)   [deleted by the IASB]

    (b)   ...

139E [Deleted by the IASB]

139G AASB 2010-7 *Amendments to Australian Accounting Standards arising from AASB 9 (December 2010)*, issued in December 2010, amended paragraphs 7, 68, 71, 82, 93, 95 and 123 and deleted paragraph 139E. An entity shall apply those amendments when it applies AASB 9 as issued in December 2010.

Amendments to AASB 102

23   Paragraph 2(b) is amended to read as follows, paragraph 40A is deleted and paragraph 40B is added:

    2   **This Standard applies to all inventories, except:**

       (a)   **...**

       (b)   **financial instruments (see AASB 132** *Financial Instruments: Presentation* **and AASB 9** *Financial Instruments***); and**

       (c)   **...**

    40A [Deleted by the IASB]

    40B AASB 2010-7 *Amendments to Australian Accounting Standards arising from AASB 9 (December 2010)*, issued in December 2010, amended paragraph 2(b) and deleted paragraph 40A. An entity shall apply those amendments when it applies AASB 9 as issued in December 2010.

Amendments to AASB 108

24   Paragraph 53 is amended to read as follows, paragraph 54A is deleted and paragraph 54B is added:

    53   Hindsight should not be used when applying a new accounting policy to, or correcting amounts for, a prior period, either in making assumptions about what management's intentions would have been in a prior period or estimating the amounts recognised, measured or disclosed in a prior period. For example, when an entity corrects a prior period error in calculating its liability for employees' accumulated sick leave in accordance with AASB 119 *Employee Benefits*, it disregards information about an unusually severe influenza season during the next period that became available after the financial statements for the prior period were authorised for issue. The fact that significant estimates are frequently required when amending comparative information presented for prior periods does not prevent reliable adjustment or correction of the comparative information.

    54A [Deleted by the IASB]

    54B AASB 2010-7 *Amendments to Australian Accounting Standards arising from AASB 9 (December 2010)*, issued in December 2010, amended paragraph 53 and deleted paragraph 54A. An entity shall apply those amendments when it applies AASB 9 as issued in December 2010.

Amendments to AASB 112

25   Paragraph 20 is amended to read as follows, paragraph 96 is deleted and paragraph 97 is added:

      20   Australian Accounting Standards permit or require certain assets to be carried at fair value or to be revalued (see, for example, AASB 116 *Property, Plant and Equipment*, AASB 138 *Intangible Assets*, AASB 140 *Investment Property* and AASB 9 *Financial Instruments*). In some jurisdictions, the revaluation or other restatement of an asset to fair value affects taxable profit (tax loss) for the current period. As a result, ...

      96   [Deleted by the IASB]

      97   AASB 2010-7 *Amendments to Australian Accounting Standards arising from AASB 9 (December 2010)*, issued in December 2010, amended paragraph 20 and deleted paragraph 96. An entity shall apply those amendments when it applies AASB 9 as issued in December 2010.

Amendments to AASB 118

26   Paragraphs 6(d) and 11 are amended to read as follows, paragraph 39 is deleted and paragraph 40 is added:

      6   This Standard does not deal with revenue arising from:

           (a)   ...

           (d)   changes in the fair value of financial assets and financial liabilities or their disposal (see AASB 9 *Financial Instruments*);

           (e)   ...

      11   In most cases ... The difference between the fair value and the nominal amount of the consideration is recognised as interest revenue in accordance with paragraphs 29 and 30 and in accordance with AASB 9.

      39   [Deleted by the IASB]

      40   AASB 2010-7 *Amendments to Australian Accounting Standards arising from AASB 9 (December 2010)*, issued in December 2010, amended paragraphs 6(d) and 11 and deleted paragraph 39. An entity shall apply those amendments when it applies AASB 9 as issued in December 2010.

27   In the Illustrative Examples, paragraphs 5 and 14 are amended to read as follows:

      5   ...

      For a sale and repurchase agreement on an asset other than a financial asset, the terms of the agreement need to be analysed to ascertain whether, in substance, the seller has transferred the risks and rewards of ownership to the buyer and hence revenue is recognised. When the seller has retained the risks and rewards of ownership, even though legal title has been transferred, the transaction is a financing arrangement and does not give rise to revenue. For a sale and repurchase agreement on a financial asset, AASB 9 *Financial Instruments* applies.

      14   *Financial service fees*

           ...

           (a)   *Fees that are an integral part of the effective interest rate of a financial instrument*

                ...

                (i)   *Origination fees received by the entity relating to the creation or acquisition of a financial asset other than one that under AASB 9 is measured at fair value through profit or loss*

                    Such fees may include compensation for activities such as evaluating the borrower's financial condition, evaluating and recording guarantees, collateral and other security arrangements, negotiating the terms of the instrument, preparing and processing documents and closing the transaction. These fees are an integral part of generating an involvement with the resulting financial instrument and, together with the related transaction costs[1] (as defined in AASB 139), are deferred and recognised as an adjustment to the effective interest rate.

---

1   In AASB 2008-5 *Amendments to Australian Accounting Standards arising from the Annual Improvements Project*, issued in July 2008, the Board replaced the term 'direct costs' with 'transaction costs' as defined in paragraph 9 of AASB 139. This amendment removed an inconsistency for costs incurred in originating financial assets and liabilities that should be deferred and recognised as an adjustment to the underlying effective interest rate. 'Direct costs', as previously defined, did not require such costs to be incremental.

    (ii)   *Commitment fees received by the entity to originate a loan when the loan commitment is outside the scope of AASB 9*

If it is probable that the entity will enter into a specific lending arrangement and the loan commitment is not within the scope of AASB 9, the commitment fee received is regarded as compensation for an ongoing involvement with the acquisition of a financial instrument and, together with the related transaction costs (as defined in AASB 139), is deferred and recognised as an adjustment to the effective interest rate. If the commitment expires without the entity making the loan, the fee is recognised as revenue on expiry. Loan commitments that are within the scope of AASB 9 are accounted for as derivatives and measured at fair value.

    (iii)   *Origination fees received on issuing financial liabilities measured at amortised cost*

These fees are an integral part of generating an involvement with a financial liability. When a financial liability is not classified as at fair value through profit or loss, the origination fees received are included, with the related transaction costs (as defined in AASB 139) incurred, in the initial carrying amount of the financial liability and recognised as an adjustment to the effective interest rate. An entity distinguishes fees and costs that are an integral part of the effective interest rate for the financial liability from origination fees and transaction costs relating to the right to provide services, such as investment management services.

  (b)   *Fees earned as services are provided*

    (i)   ...

    (ii)   *Commitment fees to originate a loan when the loan commitment is outside the scope of AASB 9*

If it is unlikely that a specific lending arrangement will be entered into and the loan commitment is outside the scope of AASB 9, the commitment fee is recognised as revenue on a time proportion basis over the commitment period. Loan commitments that are within the scope of AASB 9 are accounted for as derivatives and measured at fair value.

    (iii)   ...

Amendments to AASB 120

28   Paragraph 10A is amended to read as follows and paragraph 44 is added:

    10A   The benefit of a government loan at a below-market rate of interest is treated as a government grant. The loan shall be recognised and measured in accordance with AASB 9 *Financial Instruments*. The benefit of the below-market rate of interest shall be measured as the difference between the initial carrying value of the loan determined in accordance with AASB 9 and the proceeds received.

The benefit is accounted for in accordance with this Standard. The entity shall consider the conditions and obligations that have been, or must be, met when identifying the costs for which the benefit of the loan is intended to compensate.

44   AASB 2010-7 *Amendments to Australian Accounting Standards arising from AASB 9 (December 2010)*, issued in December 2010, amended paragraph 10A. An entity shall apply that amendment when it applies AASB 9 as issued in December 2010.

Amendments to AASB 121

29   Paragraphs 3(a), 4 and 52(a) are amended to read as follows, paragraph 60C is deleted and paragraph 60E is added:

3   **This Standard shall be applied:**[1]

(a)   **in accounting for transactions and balances in foreign currencies, except for those derivative transactions and balances that are within the scope of AASB 9 *Financial Instruments*;**

(b)   **...**

---

1   See also Interpretation 107 *Introduction of the Euro*, as identified in AASB 1048 *Interpretation of Standards*.

4   AASB 9 applies to many foreign currency derivatives and, accordingly, these are excluded from the scope of this Standard. However, those foreign currency derivatives that are not within the scope of AASB 9 (e.g. some foreign currency derivatives that are embedded in other contracts) are within the scope of this Standard. In addition, this Standard applies when an entity translates amounts relating to derivatives from its functional currency to its presentation currency.

52   **An entity shall disclose:**

(a)   **the amount of exchange differences recognised in profit or loss except for those arising on financial instruments measured at fair value through profit or loss in accordance with AASB 9; and**

(b)   **...**

60C [Deleted by the IASB]

60E AASB 2010-7 *Amendments to Australian Accounting Standards arising from AASB 9 (December 2010)*, issued in December 2010, amended paragraphs 3(a), 4 and 52(a) and deleted paragraph 60C. An entity shall apply those amendments when it applies AASB 9 as issued in December 2010.

Amendments to AASB 127

30-31 [Deleted – see early application Appendix]

Amendments to AASB 128

32   [Deleted – see early application Appendix]

Amendments to AASB 131

33   [Deleted – see early application Appendix]

Amendments to AASB 132

34   Paragraphs 3, 4, 12, 23, 31, 42 and 96C are amended to read as follows, paragraph 97F is deleted and paragraph 97H is added:

3   The principles in this Standard complement the principles for recognising and measuring financial assets and financial liabilities in AASB 9 *Financial Instruments*, and for disclosing information about them in AASB 7 *Financial Instruments: Disclosures*.

Scope

4   This Standard shall be applied by all entities to all types of financial instruments except:

     (a)   those interests in subsidiaries, associates or joint ventures that are accounted for in accordance with AASB 10 *Consolidated Financial Statements*, AASB 127 *Separate Financial Statements* or AASB 128 *Investments in Associates and Joint Ventures*. However, in some cases, AASB 127 or AASB 128 permits an entity to account for an interest in a subsidiary, associate or joint venture using AASB 9; in those cases, entities shall apply the requirements of this Standard. Entities shall also apply this Standard to all derivatives linked to interests in subsidiaries, associates or joint ventures;

     (b)   ...

     (d)   insurance contracts as defined in AASB 4 *Insurance Contracts*. However, this Standard applies to derivatives that are embedded in insurance contracts if AASB 9 requires the entity to account for them separately. Moreover, an issuer shall apply this Standard to financial guarantee contracts if the issuer applies AASB 9 in recognising and measuring the contracts, but shall apply AASB 4 if the issuer elects, in accordance with paragraph 4(d) of AASB 4, to apply AASB 4 in recognising and measuring them;

     (e)   financial instruments that are within the scope of AASB 4 because they contain a discretionary participation feature. The issuer of these instruments is exempt from applying to these features paragraphs 15-32 and AG25-AG35 of this Standard regarding the distinction between financial liabilities and equity instruments. However, these instruments are subject to all other requirements of this Standard. Furthermore, this Standard applies to derivatives that are embedded in these instruments (see AASB 9); and

12   The following terms are defined in Appendix A of AASB 9 or paragraph 9 of AASB 139 and are used in this Standard with the meaning specified in AASB 139 and AASB 9.

     (a)   amortised cost of a financial asset or financial liability;

     (b)   derecognition;

     (c)   derivative;

     (d)   effective interest method;

     (e)   financial guarantee contract;

     (f)   financial liability at fair value through profit or loss;

     (g)   firm commitment;

     (h)   forecast transaction;

     (i)   hedge effectiveness;

     (j)   hedged item;

     (k)   hedging instrument;

     (l)   held for trading;

     (m)   regular way purchase or sale; and

     (n)   transaction costs.

23   With the exception of the circumstances described in paragraphs 16A and 16B or paragraphs 16C and 16D, a contract that contains an obligation for an entity to purchase its own equity instruments for cash or another financial asset gives rise to a financial liability for the present value of the redemption amount (for example, for the present value of the forward repurchase price, option exercise price

or other redemption amount). This is the case even if the contract itself is an equity instrument. One example is an entity's obligation under a forward contract to purchase its own equity instruments for cash. The financial liability is recognised initially at the present value of the redemption amount, and is reclassified from equity. Subsequently, the financial liability is measured in accordance with AASB 9. If the contract expires without delivery, the carrying amount of the financial liability is reclassified to equity. An entity's contractual obligation to purchase its own equity instruments gives rise to a financial liability for the present value of the redemption amount even if the obligation to purchase is conditional on the counterparty exercising a right to redeem (eg a written put option that gives the counterparty the right to sell an entity's own equity instruments to the entity for a fixed price).

31   AASB 9 deals with the measurement of financial assets and financial liabilities. Equity instruments ...

42   ...

In accounting for a transfer of a financial asset that does not qualify for derecognition, the entity shall not offset the transferred asset and the associated liability (see AASB 9, paragraph 3.2.22).

96C   The classification of instruments under this exception shall be restricted to the accounting for such an instrument under AASB 101, AASB 132, AASB 139, AASB 7 and AASB 9. The instrument shall not be considered an equity instrument under other guidance, for example AASB 2.

97F   [Deleted by the IASB]

97H   AASB 2010-7 *Amendments to Australian Accounting Standards arising from AASB 9 (December 2010)*, issued in December 2010, amended paragraphs 3, 4, 12, 23, 31, 42, 96C, AG2 and AG30 and deleted paragraph 97F. An entity shall apply those amendments when it applies AASB 9 as issued in December 2010.

35   In the Appendix, paragraphs AG2 and AG30 are amended to read as follows:

AG2   The Standard does not deal with the recognition or measurement of financial instruments. Requirements about the recognition and measurement of financial assets and financial liabilities are set out in AASB 9.

AG30 Paragraph 28 applies only to issuers of non-derivative compound financial instruments. Paragraph 28 does not deal with compound financial instruments from the perspective of holders. AASB 9 deals with the classification and measurement of financial assets that are compound financial instruments from the holder's perspective.

36   Paragraph IE1 is amended to read as follows:

IE1   The following examples[1] illustrate the application of paragraphs 15-27 and AASB 9 to the accounting for contracts on an entity's own equity instruments (other than the financial instruments specified in paragraphs 16A and 16B or paragraphs 16C and 16D).

---

1   In these examples, monetary amounts are denominated in 'currency units' (CU).

37   In the example in paragraph IE5, the caption below the first journal entry is amended to read as follows:

To record the obligation to deliver CU104,000 in one year at its present value of CU100,000 discounted using an appropriate interest rate (see AASB 9, paragraph B5.1.1).

Amendments to AASB 136

38   Paragraphs 2(e) and 5 are amended to read as follows, paragraph 140F is deleted and paragraph 140G is added:

    2   ...

        (e)   **financial assets that are within the scope of AASB 9** *Financial Instruments*;

        (f)   ...

    5   This Standard does not apply to financial assets within the scope of AASB 9, investment property measured at fair value within the scope of AASB 140, or biological assets related to agricultural activity measured at fair value less costs to sell within the scope of AASB 141. However, ...

    140F   [Deleted by the IASB]

    140G   AASB 2010-7 *Amendments to Australian Accounting Standards arising from AASB 9 (December 2010)*, issued in December 2010, amended paragraphs 2(e) and 5 and deleted paragraph 140F. An entity shall apply those amendments when it applies AASB 9 as issued in December 2010.

Amendments to AASB 137

39   Paragraph 2 is amended to read as follows and paragraph 97 is added:

    2   This Standard does not apply to financial instruments (including guarantees) that are within the scope of AASB 9 *Financial Instruments*.

    97   AASB 2010-7 *Amendments to Australian Accounting Standards arising from AASB 9 (December 2010)*, issued in December 2010, amended paragraph 2. An entity shall apply that amendment when it applies AASB 9 as issued in December 2010.

40   Example 9 is amended to read as follows:

On 31 December 1999, Entity A gives a guarantee of certain borrowings of Entity B, whose financial condition at that time is sound. During 2000, the financial condition of Entity B deteriorates and at 30 June 2000 Entity B files for protection from its creditors.

This contract meets the definition of an insurance contract in AASB 4 *Insurance Contracts*, but is within the scope of AASB 9 *Financial Instruments*, because it also meets the definition of a financial guarantee contract in AASB 9. If an issuer has previously asserted explicitly that it regards such contracts as insurance contracts and has used accounting applicable to insurance contracts, the issuer may elect to apply either AASB 4 or AASB 9 to such financial guarantee contracts. AASB 4 permits the issuer to continue its existing accounting policies for insurance contracts if specified minimum requirements are satisfied. AASB 4 also permits changes in accounting policies that meet specified criteria. The following is an example of an accounting policy that AASB 4 permits and that also complies with the requirements in AASB 9 for financial guarantee contracts within the scope of AASB 9.

    ...

Amendments to AASB 139

41   Paragraph 1 is deleted.

42   Paragraphs 2 and 4 are amended to read as follows:

    2   **This Standard shall be applied by all entities to all types of financial instruments except:**

        (a)   ...

        (b)   **rights and obligations under leases to which AASB 117** *Leases* **applies. However:**

              (i)   **lease receivables recognised by a lessor are subject to the derecognition and impairment provisions of this Standard;**

    (ii)   finance lease payables recognised by a lessee are subject to the derecognition provisions of this Standard; and

    (iii)   derivatives that are embedded in leases are subject to the embedded derivatives provisions of this Standard;

(c)   ...

(e)   rights and obligations arising under (i) an insurance contract as defined in AASB 4 *Insurance Contracts*, other than an issuer's rights and obligations arising under an insurance contract that meets the definition of a financial guarantee contract in Appendix A of AASB 9, or (ii) a contract that is within the scope of AASB 4 because it contains a discretionary participation feature. However, this Standard applies to a derivative that is embedded in a contract within the scope of AASB 4 if the derivative is not itself a contract within the scope of AASB 4. Moreover, if an issuer of financial guarantee contracts has previously asserted explicitly that it regards such contracts as insurance contracts and has used accounting applicable to insurance contracts, the issuer may elect to apply either this Standard or AASB 4 to such financial guarantee contracts (see paragraphs AG4 and AG4A). The issuer may make that election contract by contract, but the election for each contract is irrevocable;

(f)   ...

(h)   loan commitments other than those loan commitments described in paragraph 4. An issuer of loan commitments shall apply AASB 137 *Provisions, Contingent Liabilities and Contingent* Assets to loan commitments that are not within the scope of this Standard. However, all loan commitments are subject to the derecognition provisions of this Standard;

(i)   financial instruments, contracts and obligations under share-based payment transactions to which AASB 2 *Share-based Payment* applies, except for contracts within the scope of paragraphs 5-7 of this Standard, to which this Standard applies; and

(j)   ...

4   The following loan commitments are within the scope of this Standard:

(a)   loan commitments that the entity designates as financial liabilities at fair value through profit or loss (see paragraph 4.2.2 of AASB 9). An entity that has a past practice of selling the assets resulting from its loan commitments shortly after origination shall apply this Standard to all its loan commitments in the same class;

(b)   ...

(c)   commitments to provide a loan at a below market interest rate (see paragraph 4.2.1 of AASB 9).

43   Paragraph 8 is amended to read as follows:

8   The terms defined in AASB 9 and AASB 132 are used in this Standard with the meanings specified in Appendix A of AASB 9 and paragraph 11 of AASB 132. AASB 9 and AASB 132 define the following terms:

    (a)   derecognition;

    (b)   derivative;

    (c)   equity instrument;

    (d)   fair value;

    (e)   financial asset;

    (f)   financial guarantee contract;

      (g)   financial instrument; and

      (h)   financial liability;

      and provide guidance on applying those definitions.

44   In paragraph 9, the titles and definitions for 'Definition of a Derivative', 'Definitions of Four Categories of Financial Instruments' and 'Definition of a Financial Guarantee Contract' are deleted. In 'Definitions Relating to Recognition and Measurement', the definitions 'Derecognition', 'Fair value' and 'A regular way purchase or sale' are deleted.

45   Paragraphs 10-57 are deleted.

46   Paragraphs 61 and 66-70 and the headings above paragraphs 63, 66 and 67 are deleted.

47   The heading 'Impairment and uncollectibility of financial assets' above paragraph 58, and paragraphs 58 and 63 are amended to read as follows:

Impairment and uncollectibility of financial assets measured at amortised cost

58   **An entity shall assess at the end of each reporting period whether there is any objective evidence that a financial asset or group of financial assets measured at amortised cost is impaired. If any such evidence exists, the entity shall apply paragraph 63 to determine the amount of any impairment loss.**

63   **If there is objective evidence that an impairment loss on financial assets measured at amortised cost has been incurred, the amount of the loss is measured as ...**

48   Paragraph 79 is deleted and paragraphs 88(d), 89(b), 90 and 96(c) are amended to read as follows:

88   **A hedging relationship qualifies for hedge accounting under paragraphs 89-102 if, and only if, all the following conditions are met.**

      (a)   **...**

      (d)   **The effectiveness of the hedge can be reliably measured, i.e. the fair value or cash flows of the hedged item that are attributable to the hedged risk and the fair value of the hedging instrument can be reliably measured.**

      (e)   **...**

Fair value hedges

89   **If a fair value hedge meets the conditions in paragraph 88 during the period, it shall be accounted for as follows:**

      (a)   **...**

      (b)   **the gain or loss on the hedged item attributable to the hedged risk shall adjust the carrying amount of the hedged item and be recognised in profit or loss. This applies if the hedged item is otherwise measured at cost.**

90   If only particular risks attributable to a hedged item are hedged, recognised changes in the fair value of the hedged item unrelated to the hedged risk are recognised as set out in paragraph 5.7.1 of AASB 9.

96   More specifically, a cash flow hedge is accounted for as follows:

      (a)   ...

      (c)   if an entity's documented risk management strategy for a particular hedging relationship excludes from the assessment of hedge effectiveness a specific component of the gain or loss or related cash flows on the hedging instrument (see paragraphs 74, 75 and 88(a)), that excluded component of gain or loss is recognised in accordance with paragraph 5.7.1 of AASB 9.

49   Paragraphs 103K, 104 and 108C are amended to read as follows, paragraphs 103H-103J,
       103L, 103M and 105-105D are deleted and paragraph 103O is added:

       103K AASB 2009-5 *Further Amendments to Australian Accounting Standards
             arising from the Annual Improvements Project*, issued in May 2009, amended
             paragraphs 2(g), 97 and 100. An entity shall apply the amendments to those
             paragraphs prospectively to all unexpired contracts for annual periods beginning
             on or after 1 January 2010. Earlier application is permitted. If an entity applies the
             amendment for an earlier period it shall disclose that fact.

       103L [Deleted by the IASB]

       103M [Deleted by the IASB]

       103O AASB 2010-7 *Amendments to Australian Accounting Standards arising from
             AASB 9 (December 2010)*, issued in December 2010, amended paragraphs 2, 4,
             8, 9, 58, 63, 88(d), 89(b), 90, 96(c), 103K, 104, 108C, AG3-AG4, AG8, AG84,
             AG95, AG114(a) and AG118(b) and deleted paragraphs 1, 10-57, 61, 66-70, 79,
             103H-103J, 103L, 103M, 105-105D, AG4B-AG4K, AG9-AG12A, AG14-AG15,
             AG27-AG83 and AG96. An entity shall apply those amendments when it applies
             AASB 9 as issued in December 2010.

       104   This Standard shall be applied retrospectively except as specified in paragraph 108.
             The opening balance of retained earnings for the earliest prior period presented
             and all other comparative amounts shall be adjusted as if this Standard had always
             been in use unless restating the information would be impracticable. If restatement
             is impracticable, the entity shall disclose that fact and indicate the extent to which
             the information was restated.

       108C Paragraphs 73 and AG8 were amended by AASB 2008-5 *Amendments to Australian
             Accounting Standards arising from the Annual Improvements Project* issued in
             July 2008. Paragraph 80 was amended by AASB 2009-5 *Further Amendments to
             Australian Accounting Standards arising from the Annual Improvements Project*
             issued in May 2009. An entity shall apply those amendments for annual periods
             beginning on or after 1 January 2009. Earlier application of all the amendments is
             permitted. If an entity applies the amendments for an earlier period it shall disclose
             that fact.

50   In Appendix A, paragraphs AG3-AG4 are amended to read as follows.

       AG3   ... If the equity method is not appropriate, the entity applies this Standard and
             AASB 9 to that strategic investment.

       AG3A This Standard and AASB 9 apply to the financial assets and financial liabilities
             of insurers, other than rights and obligations that paragraph 2(e) excludes because
             they arise under contracts within the scope of AASB 4.

       AG4   Financial guarantee contracts may have various legal forms, such as...

             (a)   Although a financial guarantee contract meets the definition of an insurance
                   contract in AASB 4 if the risk transferred is significant, the issuer applies this
                   Standard and AASB 9. Nevertheless, if the issuer has previously asserted
                   explicitly that it regards such contracts as insurance contracts and has used
                   accounting applicable to insurance contracts, the issuer may elect to apply
                   either this Standard and AASB 9 or AASB 4 to such financial guarantee
                   contracts. If this Standard and AASB 9 apply, paragraph 5.1.1 of AASB 9
                   requires the issuer to recognise a financial guarantee contract initially at fair
                   value. If the financial guarantee contract was issued to an unrelated party in a
                   stand-alone arm's length transaction, its fair value at inception is likely to equal
                   the premium received, unless there is evidence to the contrary. Subsequently,
                   unless the financial guarantee contract was designated at inception as at
                   fair value through profit or loss or unless paragraphs 3.2.15-3.2.23 and
                   B3.2.12-B3.2.17 of AASB 9 apply (when a transfer of a financial asset

        does not qualify for derecognition or the continuing involvement approach applies), the issuer measures it at the higher of:

    (i)   the amount determined in accordance with AASB 137; and

    (ii)   the amount initially recognised less, when appropriate, cumulative amortisation recognised in accordance with AASB 118 (see paragraph 4.2.1(c) of AASB 9).

    (b)   Some credit-related guarantees do not, as a precondition for payment, require that the holder is exposed to, and has incurred a loss on, the failure of the debtor to make payments on the guaranteed asset when due. An example of such a guarantee is one that requires payments in response to changes in a specified credit rating or credit index. Such guarantees are not financial guarantee contracts as defined in AASB 9, and are not insurance contracts as defined in AASB 4. Such guarantees are derivatives and the issuer applies this Standard and AASB 9 to them.

    (c)   ...

51   In Appendix A, paragraphs AG4B-AG4K, AG9-AG12A and AG14-AG15 are deleted and paragraph AG8 is amended to read as follows:

AG8   If an entity revises its estimates of payments or receipts, the entity shall adjust the carrying amount of the financial asset or financial liability (or group of financial instruments) to reflect actual and revised estimated cash flows. The entity recalculates the carrying amount by computing the present value of estimated future cash flows at the financial instrument's original effective interest rate or, when applicable, the revised effective interest rate calculated in accordance with paragraph 92. The adjustment is recognised in profit or loss as income or expense.

52   In Appendix A, paragraphs AG27-AG83 are deleted.

53   In Appendix A, the heading 'Impairment and uncollectibility of financial assets (paragraphs 58-70)' above paragraph AG84 and paragraph AG84 are amended to read as follows:

Impairment and uncollectibility of financial assets measured at amortised cost (paragraphs 58-65)

AG84   Impairment of a financial asset measured at amortised cost is measured using the financial instrument's original effective interest rate because discounting at the current market rate of interest would, in effect, impose fair value measurement on financial assets that are otherwise measured at amortised cost. If the terms of a financial asset measured at amortised cost are renegotiated or otherwise modified because of financial difficulties of the borrower or issuer, impairment is measured using the original effective interest rate before the modification of terms. Cash flows relating to short-term receivables are not discounted if the effect of discounting is immaterial. If a financial asset measured at amortised cost has a variable interest rate, the discount rate for measuring any impairment loss under paragraph 63 is the current effective interest rate(s) determined under the contract. As a practical expedient, a creditor may measure impairment of a financial asset measured at amortised cost on the basis of an instrument's fair value using an observable market price. The calculation of the present value of the estimated future cash flows of a collateralised financial asset reflects the cash flows that may result from foreclosure less costs for obtaining and selling the collateral, whether or not foreclosure is probable.

54   In Appendix A, paragraph AG96 and the first footnote to paragraph AG118(b) are deleted and paragraphs AG95, AG114(a) and AG118(b) are amended to read as follows:

AG95   A financial asset measured at amortised cost may be designated as a hedging instrument in a hedge of foreign currency risk.

AG96   [Deleted by the IASB]

AG114   For a fair value hedge of interest rate risk associated with a portfolio of financial assets or financial liabilities, an entity would meet the requirements of this Standard if it complies with the procedures set out in (a)-(i) and paragraphs AG115-AG132 below.

     (a)   As part of its risk management process the entity identifies a portfolio of items whose interest rate risk it wishes to hedge. The portfolio may comprise only assets, only liabilities or both assets and liabilities. The entity may identify two or more portfolios, in which case it applies the guidance below to each portfolio separately.

     (b)   …

AG118   As an example of the designation set out …

     (a)   …

     (b)   items that could have qualified for fair value hedge accounting if they had been designated as hedged individually. In particular, because AASB 9 specifies that the fair value of a financial liability with a demand feature (such as …

55   The heading above paragraph AG133 is amended to read as follows:

Transition (paragraphs 103-108C)

Amendments to AASB 1023

56   In paragraphs 2.3.2, 2.4.4, 15.2, 15.5, 15.5.1 15.5.2 and 16.1, and in paragraphs 17, 18 and 19 of the Appendix, the references to 'AASB 139' are replaced with 'AASB 9'.

57   Paragraphs 2.2(f), 2.3.1, 15.2.1, 15.2.2, 16.1.1 and 19.1 are amended, paragraph 18.4 is deleted and paragraphs 16.1.2, 16.1.3 and 18.5 are added as follows:

2.2   **This Standard does not apply to:**

     (a)   **…**

     (f)   *financial guarantee contracts* **unless … the issuer may elect to apply either AASB 9** *Financial Instruments,* **AASB 132** *Financial Instruments: Presentation* **and AASB 7** *Financial Instruments: Disclosures* **or this Standard to such financial guarantee contracts. …**

     (g)   **…**

   2.3.1   AASB 9 *Financial Instruments* requires hybrid contracts that contain financial asset hosts to be classified and measured in their entirety in accordance with the requirements in paragraphs 4.1.1-4.1.5 of that Standard. However, AASB 139 requires an entity to separate some embedded derivatives from their financial liability hosts contract, measure them at *fair value* and include changes in their fair value in the statement of comprehensive income. AASB 139 applies to derivatives embedded in a general insurance contract unless the embedded derivative is itself a general insurance contract.

   15.2.1   An insurer applies AASB 139 to its financial assets. Under AASB 139 a financial asset is classified and measured at fair value through profit or loss when is a financial asset that meets either of the following conditions:

     (a)   it does not meet the criteria specified in paragraph 4.1.2 of AASB 9 to be is classified as held for trading at amortised cost; or

     (b)   it is designated as "at fair value through profit or loss" upon initial recognition in accordance with paragraph 4.1.5 of AASB 9. An entity may use this designation when it is a contract with an embedded derivative and paragraph 11A of AASB 139 allows the entity to measure the contract as "at fair value through profit or loss"; or when doing so results in more relevant information, because either:

         (i)   it eliminates or significantly reduces a measurement or recognition inconsistency (sometimes referred to as 'an accounting mismatch') that would otherwise arise from measuring assets or liabilities or recognising the gains and losses on them on different bases; or

(ii) a group of financial assets, financial liabilities or both is managed and its performance is evaluated on a fair value basis, in accordance with a documented risk management or investment strategy, and information about the group is provided internally on that basis to the entity's key management personnel (as defined in AASB 124 *Related Party Disclosures*), for example the entity's board of directors and chief executive officer.

...

15.2.2 The view adopted in this Standard is that financial assets, within the scope of AASB ~~139~~ that back general insurance liabilities, are permitted to be measured at fair value through profit or loss under AASB ~~139~~. This is because the measurement of general insurance liabilities under this Standard incorporates current information and measuring the financial assets backing these general insurance liabilities at fair value, eliminates or significantly reduces a potential measurement inconsistency which would arise if the assets were classified ~~as available for sale or~~ <u>and</u> measured at amortised cost.

16.1.1 In relation to non-insurance contracts regulated under the Insurance Act, an insurer applies AASB ~~139~~ to its financial assets and financial liabilities. ~~Under AASB 139 a financial asset or financial liability at fair value through profit or loss is a financial asset or financial liability that meets either of the following conditions:~~

~~(a) it is classified as held for trading; or~~

~~(b) it is designated as "at fair value through profit or loss" upon initial recognition. An entity may use this designation when it is a contract with an embedded derivative and paragraph 11A of AASB 139 allows the entity to measure the contract as "at fair value through profit or loss"; or when doing so results in more relevant information, because either:~~

~~(i) it eliminates or significantly reduces a measurement or recognition inconsistency (sometimes referred to as 'an accounting mismatch') that would otherwise arise from measuring assets or liabilities or recognising the gains and losses on them on different bases; or~~

~~(ii) a group of financial assets, financial liabilities or both is managed and its performance is evaluated on a fair value basis, in accordance with a documented risk management or investment strategy, and information about the group is provided internally on that basis to the entity's key management personnel (as defined in AASB 124 *Related Party Disclosures*), for example the entity's board of directors and chief executive officer.~~

~~AASB 1 *First-time Adoption of Australian Accounting Standards* permits entities to designate financial assets and financial liabilities as "at fair value through profit or loss" on first application of the Standard.~~

16.1.2 <u>Under AASB 9 a financial asset is classified and measured at fair value through profit or loss when:</u>

(a) <u>it does not meet the criteria specified in paragraph 4.1.2 of AASB 9 to be classified at amortised cost; or</u>

(b) <u>it is designated as "at fair value through profit or loss" upon initial recognition in accordance with paragraph 4.1.5 of AASB 9.</u>

<u>AASB 1 *First-time Adoption of Australian Accounting Standards* permits entities to designate financial assets as "at fair value through profit or loss" on first application of the Standard.</u>

16.1.3 Under AASB 9 a financial liability at fair value through profit or loss is a financial liability that meets either of the following conditions:

(a)   it meets the definition of held for trading; or

(b)   it is designated as "at fair value through profit or loss" upon initial recognition in accordance with paragraph 4.2.2, because either:

(i)   it eliminates or significantly reduces a measurement or recognition inconsistency (sometimes referred to as 'an accounting mismatch') that would otherwise arise from measuring assets or liabilities or recognising the gains and losses on them on different bases; or

(ii)   a group of financial liabilities or financial assets and financial liabilities is managed and its performance is evaluated on a fair value basis, in accordance with a documented risk management or investment strategy, and information about the group is provided internally on that basis to the entity's key management personnel (as defined in AASB 124 *Related Party Disclosures*), for example the entity's board of directors and chief executive officer.

An entity may also use this designation when it is a contract with an embedded derivative and paragraph 4.3.3 of AASB 9 allows the entity to measure the hybrid contract as "at fair value through profit or loss".

AASB 1 *First-time Adoption of Australian Accounting Standards* permits entities to designate financial liabilities as "at fair value through profit or loss" on first application of the Standard.

18.4   **[Deleted by the AASB]**

18.5   AASB 2010-7 *Amendments to Australian Accounting Standards arising from AASB 9 (December 2010)*, **issued in December 2010, amended paragraphs 2.2(f), 2.3.1, 2.3.2, 2.4.4, 15.2, 15.2.1, 15.2.2, 15.5, 15.5.1, 15.5.2, 16.1, 16.1.1 and 19.1, and paragraphs 17, 18 and 19 in the Appendix to AASB 1023 and added paragraphs 16.1.2 and 16.1.3. An entity shall apply those amendments when it applies AASB 9 as issued in December 2010.**

19.1   **In this Standard:**

...

deposit component **means a contractual component that is not accounted for as a derivative under AASB 9** *Financial Instruments* **and would be within the scope of AASB 9 if it were a separate instrument**

...

Amendments to AASB 1038

58   In paragraphs 2.2.2, 10.2, 10.5, 10.5.1, 10.6, 10.6.1, 10.7, 10.7.1, 10.7.2, 12.1, 12.1.1, 12.1.2, 17.5.4 and 17.5.5, and paragraphs 16 and 17 in the Appendix, the references to 'AASB 139' are replaced with 'AASB 9'.

59   Paragraphs 2.2.1, 10.2.1 and 10.2.2 and 20.1 are amended, paragraph 19.4 is deleted and paragraph 19.5 is added as follows:

2.2.1   AASB 9 *Financial Instruments* requires hybrid contracts that contain financial asset hosts to be classified and measured in their entirety in accordance with the requirements in paragraphs 4.1.1-4.1.5 of that Standard. However, AASB ~~139~~ ~~*Financial Instruments: Recognition and Measurement*~~ requires an entity to separate some embedded derivatives from their financial liability hosts ~~contract,~~ measure them at *fair value* and include changes in their fair value in the statement of comprehensive income. AASB ~~139~~ applies to derivatives embedded in a life insurance contract unless the embedded derivative is itself a life insurance contract.

10.2.1 An insurer applies AASB ~~139~~ to its financial assets. Under AASB ~~139~~ a financial asset <u>is classified and measured</u> at fair value through profit or loss <u>when</u> ~~is a financial asset that meets either of the following conditions~~:

    (a)   it ~~is classified as held for trading~~ does not meet the criteria specified in paragraph 4.1.2 of AASB 9 to be classified at amortised cost; or

    (b)   it is designated as "at fair value through profit or loss" upon initial recognition in accordance with paragraph 4.1.5 of AASB 9. ~~An entity may use this designation when it is a contract with an embedded derivative and paragraph 11A of AASB 139 allows the entity to measure the contract as "at fair value through profit or loss"; or when doing so results in more relevant information, because either:~~

        ~~(i)   it eliminates or significantly reduces a measurement or recognition inconsistency (sometimes referred to as 'an accounting mismatch') that would otherwise arise from measuring assets or liabilities or recognising the gains and losses on them on different bases; or~~

        ~~(ii)   a group of financial assets, financial liabilities or both is managed and its performance is evaluated on a fair value basis, in accordance with a documented risk management or investment strategy, and information about the group is provided internally on that basis to the entity's key management personnel (as defined in AASB 124 *Related Party Disclosures*), for example the entity's board of directors and chief executive officer.~~

AASB 1 *First-time Adoption of Australian Accounting Standards* permits entities to designate financial assets as "at fair value through profit or loss" on first application of the Standard.

10.2.2 The view adopted in this Standard is that, in all but rare cases, financial assets within the scope of AASB ~~139~~ that back life insurance liabilities or life investment contract liabilities are permitted to be measured at fair value through profit or loss under AASB ~~139~~. This is because the measurement of life insurance liabilities under this Standard incorporates current information and measuring the financial assets backing these life insurance liabilities at fair value eliminates or significantly reduces a potential measurement inconsistency which would arise if the assets were classified ~~as available for sale or~~ <u>and</u> measured at amortised cost. ~~In addition, under AASB 139, a group of financial assets may be designated as at fair value through profit or loss where it is both managed and its performance is evaluated on a fair value basis, in accordance with a documented risk management or investment strategy. In the vast majority of cases, financial assets backing life investment contract liabilities and financial assets backing life insurance liabilities would be managed and their performance would be evaluated on a fair value basis, in accordance with a documented risk management or investment strategy.~~

19.4   **[Deleted by the AASB]**

19.5   **AASB 2010-7 *Amendments to Australian Accounting Standards arising from AASB 9 (December 2010)*, issued in December 2010, amended paragraphs 2.2.1, 2.2.2, 10.2, 10.2.1, 10.2.2, 10.5, 10.5.1, 10.6, 10.6.1, 10.7, 10.7.1, 10.7.2, 12.1, 12.1.1, 12.1.2, 17.5.4, 17.5.5 and 20.1 and paragraphs 16 and 17 in the Appendix. An entity shall apply those amendments when it applies AASB 9 as issued in December 2010.**

20.1   **In this Standard:**

    ...

    ***deposit component* means a contractual component that is not accounted for as a derivative under AASB ~~139~~ *Financial Instruments: Recognition and Measurement* and would be within the scope of AASB ~~139~~ *Financial Instruments: Recognition and Measurement* if it were a separate instrument**

    ...

Amendments to Interpretation 2

60   Below the heading 'References', the reference to AASB 139 is deleted and a reference to AASB 9 *Financial Instruments* is added.

61   Paragraph 15 is added:

15   AASB 2010-7 *Amendments to Australian Accounting Standards arising from AASB 9 (December 2010)*, issued in December 2010, amended paragraphs A8 and A10. An entity shall apply those amendments when it applies AASB 9 as issued in December 2010.

62   In the Appendix, paragraph A10 is amended to read as follows:

A10   Following the change in its governing charter the co-operative entity can now be required to redeem a maximum of 25 per cent of its outstanding shares or a maximum of 50,000 shares at CU20 each. Accordingly, on 1 January 20x3 the co-operative entity classifies as financial liabilities an amount of CU1,000,000 being the maximum amount payable on demand under the redemption provisions, as determined in accordance with paragraph 5.4.3 of AASB 9. It therefore transfers on 1 January 20x3 from equity to financial liabilities an amount of CU200,000, leaving CU2,000,000 classified as equity. In this example the entity does not recognise a gain or loss on the transfer.

Amendments to Interpretation 5

63   Below the heading 'References', the reference to AASB 139 is deleted and a reference to AASB 9 *Financial Instruments* is added.

64   Paragraph 5 is amended to read as follows and paragraph 14A is added:

5   A residual interest in a fund that extends beyond a right to reimbursement, such as a contractual right to distributions once all the decommissioning has been completed or on winding up the fund, may be an equity instrument within the scope of AASB 9 and is not within the scope of this Interpretation.

14A   AASB 2010-7 *Amendments to Australian Accounting Standards arising from AASB 9 (December 2010)*, issued in December 2010, amended paragraph 5. An entity shall apply that amendment when it applies AASB 9 as issued in December 2010.

Amendments to Interpretation 10

65   Below the heading 'References', the reference to AASB 139 is deleted and a reference to AASB 9 *Financial Instruments* is added.

66   Paragraphs 5, 6 and 11 are deleted, paragraphs 1, 2, 7 and 8 are amended to read as follows and paragraph 12 is added:

1   An entity is required to assess goodwill for impairment at the end of each reporting period, and, if required, to recognise an impairment loss at that date in accordance with AASB 136 *Impairment of Assets*. However, …

2   The Interpretation addresses the interaction between the requirements of AASB 134 *Interim Financial Reporting* and the recognition of impairment losses on goodwill in AASB 136, and the effect of that interaction on subsequent interim and annual financial statements.

7   The Interpretation addresses the following issue:

Should an entity reverse impairment losses recognised in an interim period on goodwill if a loss would not have been recognised, or a smaller loss would have been recognised, had an impairment assessment been made only at the end of a subsequent reporting period?

Consensus

8   An entity shall not reverse an impairment loss recognised in a previous interim period in respect of goodwill.

11   [Deleted by the IASB]

12   AASB 2010-7 *Amendments to Australian Accounting Standards arising from AASB 9 (December 2010)*, issued in December 2010, amended paragraphs 1, 2, 7 and 8 and deleted paragraphs 5, 6 and 11. An entity shall apply those amendments when it applies AASB 9 as issued in December 2010.

Amendments to Interpretation 12

67   Below the heading 'References', the reference to AASB 139 is deleted and a reference to AASB 9 *Financial Instruments* is added.

68   Paragraphs 23-25 are amended to read as follows, paragraph 28A is deleted and paragraph 28B is added:

23   AASB 132 *Financial Instruments: Presentation* and AASB 7 *Financial Instruments: Disclosures* and AASB 9 *Financial Instruments* apply to the financial asset recognised under paragraphs 16 and 18.

24   The amount due from or at the direction of the grantor is accounted for in accordance with AASB 9 as:

(a)   at amortised cost; or

(b)   measured at fair value through profit or loss.

25   If the amount due from the grantor is accounted for at amortised cost, AASB 9 requires interest calculated using the effective interest method to be recognised in profit or loss.

28A   [Deleted by the IASB]

28B   AASB 2010-7 *Amendments to Australian Accounting Standards arising from AASB 9 (December 2010)*, issued in December 2010, amended paragraphs 23-25 and deleted paragraph 28A. An entity shall apply those amendments when it applies AASB 9 as issued in December 2010.

69   Paragraphs IE7 and IE28 are amended to read as follows:

IE7   AASB 9 *Financial Instruments* may require the entity to measure the amounts due from the grantor at amortised cost, unless the entity designates those amounts as measured at fair value through profit or loss. If the receivable is measured at amortised cost in accordance with AASB 9, it is measured initially at fair value and subsequently at amortised cost, i.e. the amount initially recognised plus the cumulative interest on that amount calculated using the effective interest method minus repayments.

IE28   AASB 9 *Financial Instruments* may require the entity to measure the amount due from or at the direction of the grantor in exchange for the construction services at amortised cost. If the receivable is measured at amortised cost in accordance with AASB 9, it is measured initially at fair value and subsequently at amortised cost, i.e. the amount initially recognised plus the cumulative interest on that amount minus repayments.

Amendments to Interpretation 19

70   Below the heading 'References', the reference to AASB 139 is deleted and a reference to AASB 9 *Financial Instruments* is added.

71   Paragraphs 4(a), 5, 9 and 10 are amended to read as follows and paragraph 14 is added:

4   This Interpretation addresses the following issues:

(a)   Are an entity's equity instruments issued to extinguish all or part of a financial liability 'consideration paid' in accordance with paragraph 3.3.3 of AASB 9?

(b)   ...

Consensus

5   The issue of an entity's equity instruments to a creditor to extinguish all or part of a financial liability is consideration paid in accordance with paragraph 3.3.3 of AASB 9. An entity shall remove a financial liability (or part of a financial liability) from its statement of financial position when, and only when, it is extinguished in accordance with paragraph 3.3.1 of AASB 9.

9   The difference between the carrying amount of the financial liability (or part of a financial liability) extinguished, and the consideration paid, shall be recognised in profit or loss, in accordance with paragraph 3.3.3 of AASB 9. The equity instruments issued shall be recognised initially and measured at the date the financial liability (or part of that liability) is extinguished.

10   When only part of the financial liability is extinguished, consideration shall be allocated in accordance with paragraph 8. The consideration allocated to the remaining liability shall form part of the assessment of whether the terms of that remaining liability have been substantially modified. If the remaining liability has been substantially modified, the entity shall account for the modification as the extinguishment of the original liability and the recognition of a new liability as required by paragraph 3.3.2 of AASB 9.

14   AASB 2010-7 *Amendments to Australian Accounting Standards arising from AASB 9 (December 2010)*, issued in December 2010, amended paragraphs 4(a), 5, 7, 9 and 10. An entity shall apply those amendments when it applies AASB 9 as issued in December 2010.

Amendments to Interpretation 127

72   Below the heading 'References', the reference to AASB 139 is deleted and a reference to AASB 9 *Financial Instruments* is added.

73   In the Consensus, paragraph 7 is amended to read as follows:

7   Other obligations of an arrangement, including any guarantees provided and obligations incurred upon early termination, shall be accounted for under AASB 137 *Provisions, Contingent Liabilities and Contingent Assets*, AASB 1023 *General Insurance Contracts* or AASB 9 *Financial Instruments*, depending on the terms.

74   Paragraphs 14 and 15 are amended to read as follows:

14   When an entity ... A financial asset and a financial liability, or a portion of either, are derecognised only when the requirements of paragraphs 3.2.1-3.2.23, 3.3.1-3.3.4, B3.2.1-B3.2.17 and B3.3.1-B3.3.7 of AASB 9 are met.

15   AASB 1023 provides guidance for recognising and measuring financial guarantees and similar instruments that provide for payments to be made if the debtor fails to make payments when due, if that contract transfers significant insurance risk to the issuer. Financial guarantee contracts that provide for payments to be made in response to changes in relation to a variable (sometimes referred to as an 'underlying') are subject to AASB 139.[1]

---

1   In December 2009 and December 2010 the AASB issued amendments to some of the requirements of AASB 139 and relocated them to AASB 9 *Financial Instruments*. AASB 9 applies to all items within the scope of AASB 139.

Appendix

Early Application

This appendix is an integral part of this Standard.

A1   Australian Accounting Standards AASB 9 *Financial Instruments* (December 2010) and AASB 2010-7 *Amendments to Australian Accounting Standards arising from AASB 9* (December 2010) may be applied early to annual reporting periods beginning before 1 January 2015 from:

    (a)   any date between 6 and 31 December 2010, for entities initially applying the Standards before 1 January 2011; or

    (b)   the beginning of the first reporting period in which the entity adopts the Standards, for entities initially applying the Standards on or after 1 January 2011.

Amendments to AASB 127, AASB 128 and AASB 131

A2   If AASB 9 (December 2010) and AASB 2010-7 are applied early to annual reporting periods that begin before 1 January 2013, AASB 127 *Consolidated and Separate Financial Statements*, AASB 128 *Investments in Associates* and AASB 131 *Interests in Joint Ventures* are applicable, provided that AASB 10 *Consolidated Financial Statements* and the other Standards that supersede those Standards for periods beginning on or after 1 January 2013 are not also applied early to such periods.

A3   In the circumstances set out in paragraph A2, versions of AASB 127, AASB 128 and AASB 131 are amended as originally set out in paragraphs 30-33 of AASB 2010-7 (as issued in December 2010).

A4   If AASB 13 *Fair Value Measurement* is also applied in the circumstances set out in paragraph A2, paragraph 1 of versions of AASB 128 and AASB 131 is amended by deleting the sentence 'An entity shall measure such investments at fair value through profit or loss in accordance with AASB 9.'

AASB 2011-2

Amendments to Australian Accounting Standards arising from the Trans-Tasman Convergence Project – Reduced Disclosure Requirements

[AASB 101 & AASB 1054]

(Issued May 2011)

Note from the Institute of Chartered Accountants Australia

This note, prepared by the technical editors, is not part of Accounting Standard AASB 2011-2.

Historical development

11 May 2011: AASB 2011-2 was issued amending AASB 101 and AASB 1054 to reflect the outcomes of the Trans-Tasman Convergence Project for entities applying the Reduced Disclosure Requirements (RDR).

This Standard is applicable to annual reporting periods beginning on or after 1 July 2013, with early adoption permitted.

Contents

Preface

Accounting Standard
AASB 2011-2 Amendments to Australian Accounting Standards arising
from the Trans-Tasman Convergence Project – Reduced Disclosure Requirements

	Paragraphs
Objective	1
Application	2 – 5
Amendments to AASB 101	6 – 7
Amendments to AASB 1054	8

> Australian Accounting Standard AASB 2011-2 *Amendments to Australian Accounting Standards arising from the Trans-Tasman Convergence Project – Reduced Disclosure Requirements* is set out in paragraphs 1 – 8. All the paragraphs have equal authority.

Preface

Standards Amended by AASB 2011-2

This Standard makes amendments to the following Australian Accounting Standards:

1.   AASB 101 *Presentation of Financial Statements*

2.   AASB 1054 *Australian Additional Disclosures*,

to establish reduced disclosure requirements for entities preparing general purpose financial statements under Australian Accounting Standards – Reduced Disclosure Requirements in relation to the Australian additional disclosures arising from the Trans-Tasman Convergence Project.

Main Features of this Standard

Amendments to AASB 101

In June 2010, the AASB issued AASB 2010-2 *Amendments to Australian Accounting Standards arising from Reduced Disclosure Requirements* that introduced reduced disclosure requirements (RDR) to many Australian Accounting Standards, including AASB 101.

In May 2011, the AASB issued AASB 2011-1 *Amendments to Australian Accounting Standards arising from the Trans-Tasman Convergence Project* and AASB 1054 as outcomes of the Trans-Tasman Convergence project. AASB 1054 contains the Australian-specific disclosures that are in addition to International Financial Reporting Standards. AASB 2011-1 contains the related amendments to other Australian Accounting Standards. For example, some of the disclosure requirements previously in paragraphs Aus15.1-Aus15.3 and other paragraphs of AASB 101 are now included in AASB 1054 instead.

This Standard revises the RDR amendments originally specified in AASB 2010-2 for AASB 101 to reflect the deletion of certain disclosure requirements from AASB 101.

Amendments to AASB 1054

This Standard makes amendments to AASB 1054 to introduce reduced disclosure requirements to that Standard for entities preparing general purpose financial statements under Australian Accounting Standards – Reduced Disclosure Requirements. These reflect the reduced disclosure requirements originally specified in AASB 2010-2 for AASB 101 disclosures that are now in AASB 1054.

Application Date

This Standard is applicable to annual reporting periods beginning on or after 1 July 2013. Early adoption is permitted for annual reporting periods beginning on or after 1 July 2009 but before 1 July 2013, provided that the following are also adopted for the same period:

(a)   AASB 1053 *Application of Tiers of Australian Accounting Standards*;

(b)   AASB 1054; and

(c)   AASB 2011-1.

Accounting Standard AASB 2011-2

The Australian Accounting Standards Board makes Accounting Standard AASB 2011-2 *Amendments to Australian Accounting Standards arising from the Trans-Tasman Convergence Project – Reduced Disclosure Requirements* under section 334 of the *Corporations Act 2001*.

Kevin M. Stevenson
Dated 11 May 2011   Chair – AASB

Accounting Standard AASB 2011-2

Amendments to Australian Accounting Standards arising from the Trans-Tasman Convergence Project – Reduced Disclosure Requirements

Objective

1   The objective of this Standard is to make amendments to:
   (a)   AASB 101 *Presentation of Financial Statements*; and
   (b)   AASB 1054 *Australian Additional Disclosures*;

   to establish reduced disclosure requirements for entities preparing general purpose financial statements under Australian Accounting Standards – Reduced Disclosure Requirements for the Australian additional disclosures arising from the Trans-Tasman Convergence Project.

Application

2   **This Standard applies to:**
   (a)   each entity that is required to prepare financial reports in accordance with Part 2M.3 of the Corporations Act;
   (b)   general purpose financial statements of each reporting entity; and
   (c)   financial statements that are, or are held out to be, general purpose financial statements.

3   **This Standard applies to annual reporting periods beginning on or after 1 July 2013.**

4   **This Standard shall be applied when AASB 1053 *Application of Tiers of Australian Accounting Standards* is applied. This Standard may be applied to annual reporting periods beginning on or after 1 July 2009 but before 1 July 2013 provided the following are also adopted for the same period:**
   (a)   AASB 1053;
   (b)   AASB 1054; and
   (c)   AASB 2011-1 *Amendments to Australian Accounting Standards arising from the Trans-Tasman Convergence Project*.

   When an entity applies this Standard to such an annual reporting period, it shall disclose that fact.

5   **This Standard uses underlining, striking out and other typographical material to identify some of the amendments to a Standard, in order to make the amendments**

more understandable. However, the amendments made by this Standard do not include that underlining, striking out or other typographical material.

Amendments to AASB 101

6   Paragraph Aus1.8 is amended as follows (new text is underlined and deleted text is struck through):

> **Aus1.8**   **The following do not apply to entities preparing general purpose financial statements under Australian Accounting Standards – Reduced Disclosure Requirements:**
>
> (a)   **paragraphs 10(f), 15, 16, ~~Aus16.1,~~ Aus16.3, 39(c), 42(b), 61, 65, 80A, 90-92, 94, 104, 131 and 134-<u>138</u> ~~Aus138.6~~;**
>
> (b)   **the second sentence in paragraph 39; and**
>
> (c)   **in paragraph 107, the text ", and the related amount <u>of dividends</u> per share".**
>
> **Entities applying Australian Accounting Standards – Reduced Disclosure Requirements may elect to comply with some or all of these excluded requirements.**

7   Paragraph RDR16.1 is amended as follows (deleted text is struck through):

> **RDR16.1**   ~~An entity whose financial statements comply with Australian Accounting Standards – Reduced Disclosure Requirements shall make an explicit and unreserved statement of such compliance in the notes. An entity shall not describe financial statements as complying with Australian Accounting Standards – Reduced Disclosure Requirements unless they comply with all the requirements of Australian Accounting Standards – Reduced Disclosure Requirements.~~ **Entities applying Australian Accounting Standards – Reduced Disclosure Requirements would not be able to state compliance with IFRSs.**

Amendments to AASB 1054

8   The following subheading and paragraphs are added to AASB 1054:

Reduced Disclosure Requirements

> **5A**   **Paragraphs 10-16 of this Standard do not apply to entities preparing general purpose financial statements under Australian Accounting Standards – Reduced Disclosure Requirements. Entities applying Australian Accounting Standards – Reduced Disclosure Requirements may elect to comply with some or all of these excluded requirements.**
>
> 5B   The requirements that do not apply to entities preparing general purpose financial statements under Australian Accounting Standards – Reduced Disclosure Requirements are identified in this Standard by shading of the relevant text.
>
> **5C**   **RDR paragraphs in this Standard apply only to entities preparing general purpose financial statements under Australian Accounting Standards – Reduced Disclosure Requirements.**
>
> > **RDR7.1**   **An entity whose financial statements comply with Australian Accounting Standards – Reduced Disclosure Requirements shall make an explicit and unreserved statement of such compliance in the notes. An entity shall not describe financial statements as complying with Australian Accounting Standards – Reduced Disclosure Requirements unless they comply with all the requirements of Australian Accounting Standards – Reduced Disclosure Requirements.**

AASB 2011-4

Amendments to Australian Accounting Standards to Remove Individual Key Management Personnel Disclosure Requirements

[AASB 124]

(Issued July 2011)

Note from the Institute of Chartered Accountants Australia

This note, prepared by the technical editors, is not part of Accounting Standard AASB 2011-4.

Historical development

7 July 2011: AASB 2011-4 was issued removing the individual key management personnel disclosures from AASB 124.

This Standard is applicable to annual reporting periods beginning on or after 1 July 2013. Early adoption is not permitted.

Contents

Preface

Accounting Standard
AASB 2011-4 Amendments to Australian Accounting Standards to Remove Individual Key Management Personnel Disclosure Requirements

	Paragraphs
Objective	1
Application	2 – 3
Amendments to AASB 124	4 – 6

Basis for Conclusions

Australian Accounting Standard AASB 2011-4 *Amendments to Australian Accounting Standards to Remove Individual Key Management Personnel Disclosure Requirements* is set out in paragraphs 1 – 6. All the paragraphs have equal authority.

Preface

Standards Amended by AASB 2011-4

This Standard makes amendments to Australian Accounting Standard AASB 124 *Related Party Disclosures*.

These amendments arise from a decision of the AASB to remove the individual key management personnel (KMP) disclosures from AASB 124 on the basis they:

- are not part of International Financial Reporting Standards (IFRSs), which include requirements to disclose aggregate (rather than individual) amounts of KMP compensation;

- are not included in New Zealand accounting standards and, accordingly, their removal is consistent with meeting the 2010 Outcome Proposal of the Australian and New Zealand governments that for-profit entities are able to use a single set of accounting standards and prepare only one set of financial statements;

- are considered by the AASB to be more in the nature of governance disclosures that are better dealt with as part of the *Corporations Act 2001*;

- were originally included in AASB 124 when fewer similar disclosure requirements were included in the Corporations Act and, in many respects, relate to similar disclosure requirements currently in that Act and therefore detract from the clarity of the requirements applying in this area; and

- could be considered (during the transition period for this Amending Standard) for inclusion in the Corporations Act or other legislation to the extent they presently go beyond the requirements in legislation and are considered appropriate in light of government policy.

Accounting Standard AASB 2011-4

The Australian Accounting Standards Board makes Accounting Standard AASB 2011-4 *Amendments to Australian Accounting Standards to Remove Individual Key Management Personnel Disclosure Requirements* under section 334 of the *Corporations Act 2001*.

Dated 7 July 2011

Kevin M. Stevenson
Chair – AASB

Accounting Standard AASB 2011-4

Amendments to Australian Accounting Standards to Remove Individual Key Management Personnel Disclosure Requirements

Objective

1   The objective of this Standard is to make amendments to AASB 124 *Related Party Disclosures* to remove individual key management personnel disclosure requirements.

Application

2   **This Standard applies to each disclosing entity, or group of which a disclosing entity is the parent, that is required to prepare financial reports in accordance with Part 2M.3 of the Corporations Act.**

3   **This Standard applies to annual reporting periods beginning on or after 1 July 2013. Early adoption of this Standard is not permitted.**

Amendments to AASB 124

4   Paragraphs Aus1.1, Aus1.4, Aus1.4.1, Aus1.5, Aus1.9 and paragraphs Aus29.1 to Aus29.9.3, including headings associated with paragraphs Aus29.1 to Aus29.9.3, are deleted from AASB 124.

5   Paragraph Aus1.3 is amended to read as follows:

     Aus1.3   This Standard does not apply to general purpose financial statements of not-for-profit public sector entities.

6   Paragraph Aus1.8 is amended to read as follows:

     Aus1.8   The requirements of this Standard apply to the financial statements where information resulting from their application is material in accordance with AASB 1031 *Materiality*.

Basis for Conclusions

Background

BC1   This Basis for Conclusions summarises the AASB's considerations in deciding that the disclosure requirements regarding individual key management personnel (KMP) should be removed from AASB 124 *Related Party Disclosures*. Individual AASB members gave greater weight to some factors than to others.

Additional Australian requirements

BC2   The AASB adopts International Financial Reporting Standards (IFRSs) by incorporating them into Australian Accounting Standards and publicly accountable for-profit entities are required to apply them in preparing their general purpose financial statements. (Public accountability is defined in AASB 1053 *Application of Tiers of Australian Accounting Standards* and includes listed and other disclosing entities.) The AASB includes some disclosure requirements that are in addition to the IFRSs, but aims to keep these to a minimum on the basis that the IFRSs represent best international practice for general purpose financial reporting of publicly accountable for-profit entities.

BC3   Prior to adopting IFRSs in 2005, the AASB had on issue AASB 1046 *Director and Executive Disclosures by Disclosing Entities*, which included disclosure requirements in respect of the compensation, equity holdings and loans of individual KMP. When IFRSs were adopted, these requirements were largely

AASB

carried forward for disclosing entities as 'Aus' paragraphs in AASB 124, which incorporates IAS 24 *Related Party Disclosures*.

BC4   Section 300A of the *Corporations Act 2001* and Regulation 2M.3.03 were amended in 2007 to require disclosing entities that are companies to report individual remuneration information in the directors' report.[1] The AASB responded by amending AASB 124 to relieve disclosing entities that are companies from complying with the paragraphs in AASB 124 that have been included in the Corporations Act and Regulation 2M.3.03, following a due process that involved issuing ED 162 *Proposed Amendments to Key Management Personnel Disclosures by Disclosing Entities* in April 2008 for public comment. The resulting amendment avoided requiring each disclosing entity that is a company to disclose this information twice – in its directors' report and in its financial statements.[2] The existing AASB 124 retains Australian-specific individual KMP disclosure requirements on remuneration in relation to disclosing entities other than companies, and on equity holdings, loans, and other transactions and balances in relation to all disclosing entities.

Constituent views

BC5   A number of constituents who commented on ED 162 encouraged the Board to consider removing all the individual KMP disclosure requirements (Aus paragraphs) from AASB 124. Accordingly, in ED 200A *Proposals to Harmonise Australian and New Zealand Standards in Relation to Entities Applying IFRSs as Adopted in Australia and New Zealand* (issued in July 2010) the AASB specifically sought comment on whether the individual KMP disclosure requirements should be retained or removed. All of those who responded to this question supported their removal.

BC6   The views expressed by constituents on ED 162 and ED 200A were largely based on two factors:

    (a)   a view that individual KMP disclosures are a governance matter that would be most appropriately dealt with directly by the Government through the Corporations Act; and

    (b)   a desire to remove as much Australian specific text from the AASB's Standards that incorporate IFRSs so that those Standards replicate as closely as possible the content of the IFRSs as issued by the IASB.

BC7   Constituents have also raised concerns about the potential for confusion because all of the AASB 124 individual KMP disclosures apply to disclosing entities that are not companies, while only a subset of those disclosures apply to disclosing entities that are companies (as explained in paragraph BC4).

New Zealand Convergence

BC8   The AASB and the New Zealand accounting standard setter have been converging their standards over recent years. A key aim is to meet the Outcome Proposals set by the Australian and New Zealand governments, which include enabling for-profit entities to use a single set of accounting standards and prepare only one set of financial statements for both jurisdictions.[3] The New Zealand accounting standards also incorporate IFRSs and do not contain additional individual KMP disclosure requirements.

BC9   The AASB concluded that it is in the interests of trans-Tasman convergence, and achieving the Outcome Proposals, to remove the individual KMP disclosure requirements from Australian Accounting Standards.

---

1   Corporations Act Regulation 2M.6.04 permitted listed companies to avoid making the same disclosures twice; however, the Corporations Amendment Regulations 2007 (No. 2) removed that regulation.

2   AASB 2008-4 *Amendments to Australian Accounting Standard – Key Management Personnel Disclosures by Disclosing Entities*.

3   More information is available from the Trans-Tasman Outcomes Implementation Group website – www.treasury.gov.au/ttoig.

BC10   The AASB noted that the Australian Treasury and New Zealand Ministry of Economic Development are aware that the legislative requirements regarding individual KMP disclosures may need to be changed in order to align them across the two jurisdictions.

Nature of Disclosures

BC11   The AASB 1046 disclosure requirements (noted in paragraph BC3) that were carried forward when Australia adopted IFRSs were, in part, the product of an earlier policy of removing disclosure requirements from corporations legislation and including them in accounting standards. In the years since adopting IFRSs, there has been more emphasis on including governance-type disclosures directly in legislation.

BC12   More disclosure requirements have been added to Section 300A of the Corporations Act regarding disclosures about individual KMP as well as a requirement for a remuneration report for listed companies since the AASB first made the Standards incorporating IFRSs.

BC13   The AASB concluded that the IAS 24 requirements (included in AASB 124) to disclose amounts of aggregate KMP compensation as well as treating KMP as related parties for the purposes of the other disclosure requirements are sufficient in the context of the role of accounting standards in meeting the objective of general purpose financial reporting.[4]

Timing

BC14   The amendments to AASB 124 to remove the disclosure requirements regarding individual KMP are applicable to annual reporting periods beginning on or after 1 July 2013, and early adoption is not permitted. Accordingly, relevant disclosing entities will need to comply with the disclosure requirements for at least another two years.

BC15   The AASB concluded that the transition period should be sufficient to allow the relevant government agencies to consider whether there is a need to amend their existing requirements relating to individual KMP and, if so, the manner in which they should be amended. In particular, the AASB was mindful of allowing sufficient time to conduct any relevant public consultation in view of other developments that are taking place in connection with governance disclosure requirements.

---

4   The objective of financial reporting is currently identified in SAC 2 *Objective of General Purpose Financial Reporting and Framework for the Preparation and Presentation of Financial Statements.*

AASB 2011-6

Amendments to Australian Accounting Standards – Extending Relief from Consolidation, the Equity Method and Proportionate Consolidation – Reduced Disclosure Requirements

[AASB 127, AASB 128 & AASB 131]

(Issued July 2011)

Note from the Institute of Chartered Accountants Australia

This note, prepared by the technical editors, is not part of Accounting Standard AASB 2011-6.

Historical development

20 July 2011: AASB 2011-6 was issued amending AASB 127, 128 and 131 to extend relief from consolidation, the equity method and proportionate consolidation in certain circumstances to entities applying the Reduced Disclosure Requirements (RDR).

This Standard is applicable to annual reporting periods beginning on or after 1 July 2013, with early adoption permitted.

Contents

Preface

Accounting Standard
AASB 2011-6 Amendments to Australian Accounting Standards – Extending Relief From Consolidation, the Equity Method and Proportionate Consolidation – Reduced Disclosure Requirements

	Paragraphs
Objective	1
Application	2 – 5
Amendments to AASB 127	6 – 7
Amendment to AASB 128	8
Amendment to AASB 131	9

Basis for Conclusions

Australian Accounting Standard AASB 2011-6 *Amendments to Australian Accounting Standards – Extending Relief from Consolidation, the Equity Method and Proportionate Consolidation – Reduced Disclosure Requirements* is set out in paragraphs 1 – 9. All the paragraphs have equal authority.

Preface

Standards Amended by AASB 2011-6

This Standard makes amendments to the following Australian Accounting Standards:

1.   AASB 127 *Consolidated and Separate Financial Statements*

2.   AASB 128 *Investments in Associates*

3.   AASB 131 *Interests in Joint Ventures*.

These amendments result from the proposals that were included in Exposure Draft ED 205 *Extending Relief from Consolidation, the Equity Method and Proportionate Consolidation*.

Existing Relief from Consolidation, the Equity Method and Proportionate Consolidation

Paragraph 10 of AASB 127 provides relief from preparing consolidated financial statements if, and only if, the parent entity satisfies the following criteria:

(a)   the parent is itself a wholly-owned subsidiary, or is a partially-owned subsidiary of another entity and its other owners, including those not otherwise entitled to vote, have been informed about, and do not object to, the parent not presenting consolidated financial statements;

(b)   the parent's debt or equity instruments are not traded in a public market (a domestic or foreign stock exchange or an over-the-counter market, including local and regional markets);

(c)   the parent did not file, nor is it in the process of filing, its financial statements with a securities commission or other regulatory organisation for the purpose of issuing any class of instruments in a public market; and

(d)   the parent entity's ultimate parent or an intermediate parent of the parent entity produced consolidated financial statements that are compliant with International Financial Reporting Standards (IFRS).

A similar option is available in paragraph 13(c) of AASB 128 for investors to obtain relief from applying the equity method of accounting when accounting for investments in associates and in paragraph 2(c) of AASB 131 for venturers to obtain relief from the equity method and proportionate consolidation when accounting for interests in joint ventures.

AASB 2011-5 *Amendments to Australian Accounting Standards – Extending Relief from Consolidation, the Equity Method and Proportionate Consolidation* extended this relief to not-for-profit entities in certain circumstances.

With the introduction of the Australian Accounting Standards – Reduced Disclosure Requirements (RDR), entities applying RDR are not able to produce financial statements that are IFRS compliant. In these circumstances, relief from consolidation, the equity method and proportionate consolidation is not available under the existing requirements.

Main Features of this Standard

The amendments made by this Standard (AASB 2011-6) are amendments to AASB 127, AASB 128 and AASB 131 as already amended by AASB 2011 5.

Extending the Relief

The AASB considers that the relief from consolidation, the equity method and proportionate consolidation should also be available in certain circumstances to a parent entity, investor or venturer where the ultimate or any intermediate parent entity prepares consolidated financial statements that are not compliant with IFRS as a result of applying Australian Accounting Standards – Reduced Disclosure Requirements. Therefore, this Standard extends that relief provided that the parent entity, investor or venturer:

(a)   is an entity complying with Australian Accounting Standards – Reduced Disclosure Requirements;

(b)   has an ultimate or intermediate parent that prepares consolidated financial statements in accordance with Australian Accounting Standards or Australian Accounting Standards – Reduced Disclosure Requirements; and

(c)   meets the relevant criteria in paragraphs 10(a) to 10(c) of AASB 127, paragraphs 13(c)(i) to 13(c)(iii) of AASB 128 or paragraphs 2(c)(i) to 2(c)(iii) of AASB 131.

Accordingly, this Standard extends the relief from consolidation, the equity method and proportionate consolidation by removing the requirement for the consolidated financial statements prepared by the ultimate or any intermediate parent entity to be IFRS compliant, provided that the parent entity, investor or venturer and the ultimate or intermediate parent entity comply with Australian Accounting Standards or Australian Accounting Standards – Reduced Disclosure Requirements, as stated above.

This approach is based on the view that financial statement users would be able to satisfy their information needs through the consolidated financial statements prepared by the parent higher up in the group.

Application Date

This Standard applies to annual reporting periods beginning on or after 1 July 2013.

This Standard may be applied to annual reporting periods beginning on or after 1 July 2009 but before 1 July 2013, provided that AASB 1053 *Application of Tiers of Australian Accounting Standards* is also adopted early for the same period. The date limitation on early application reflects the limitation on the early application of the reduced disclosure requirements under AASB 1053.

Accounting Standard AASB 2011-6

The Australian Accounting Standards Board makes Accounting Standard AASB 2011-6 *Amendments to Australian Accounting Standards – Extending Relief from Consolidation, the Equity Method and Proportionate Consolidation – Reduced Disclosure Requirements* under section 334 of the *Corporations Act 2001*.

Kevin M. Stevenson
Dated 20 July 2011   Chair – AASB

Accounting Standard AASB 2011-6

Amendments to Australian Accounting Standards – Extending Relief from Consolidation, the Equity Method and Proportionate Consolidation – Reduced Disclosure Requirements

Objective

1   The objective of this Standard is to make amendments to:

(a)   AASB 127 *Consolidated and Separate Financial Statements*;

(b)   AASB 128 *Investments in Associates*; and

(c)   AASB 131 *Interests in Joint Ventures*;

to extend the circumstances in which an entity can obtain relief from consolidation, the equity method or proportionate consolidation.

Application

2   **This Standard applies to:**

(a)   **each entity that is required to prepare financial reports in accordance with Part 2M.3 of the Corporations Act and that is a reporting entity;**

(b)   **general purpose financial statements of each other reporting entity; and**

(c)   **financial statements that are, or are held out to be, general purpose financial statements.**

3   **This Standard applies to annual reporting periods beginning on or after 1 July 2013.**

4   **This Standard may be applied to annual reporting periods beginning on or after 1 July 2009 but before 1 July 2013, provided that AASB 1053 *Application of Tiers of Australian Accounting Standards* is also adopted early for the same period. When an entity applies this Standard to such an annual reporting period, it shall disclose that fact.**

5   **This Standard uses underlining, striking out and other typographical material to identify some of the amendments to a Standard, in order to make the amendments more understandable. However, the amendments made by this Standard do not include that underlining, striking out or other typographical material.**

Amendments to AASB 127

6   Paragraph Aus10.1 is amended as follows (new text is underlined):

Aus10.1   Notwithstanding paragraph 10(d), a parent that meets the criteria in paragraphs 10(a), 10(b) and 10(c) need not present consolidated financial statements if its ultimate or any intermediate parent produces consolidated financial statements available for public use and:

(a)   the parent and its ultimate or intermediate parent are:

(i)   both not-for-profit entities complying with Australian Accounting Standards; or

(ii)   both entities complying with Australian Accounting Standards – Reduced Disclosure Requirements; or

(b)   the parent is an entity complying with Australian Accounting Standards – Reduced Disclosure Requirements and its ultimate or intermediate parent is a not-for-profit entity complying with Australian Accounting Standards.

7   In the Australian Application Guidance accompanying AASB 127, the table in paragraph AG1 is deleted and the following table inserted:

Same type of entity – same tier

Ultimate or Intermediate Parent	FP – Tier 1	FP – Tier 2	NFP – Tier 1	NFP – Tier 2
Parent	FP – Tier 1	FP – Tier 2	NFP – Tier 1	NFP – Tier 2
Exemption	Available*	Available	Available	Available

Same type of entity – different tier

Ultimate or Intermediate Parent	FP – Tier 1	FP – Tier 2	NFP – Tier 1	NFP – Tier 2
Parent	FP – Tier 2	FP – Tier 1	NFP – Tier 2	NFP – Tier 1
Exemption	Available*	Not available	Available	Not available

Different type of entity – same tier

Ultimate or Intermediate Parent	FP – Tier 1	FP – Tier 2	NFP – Tier 1	NFP – Tier 2
Parent	NFP – Tier 1	NFP – Tier 2	FP – Tier 1	FP – Tier 2
Exemption	Available*	Available	Not available^	Available

Different type of entity – different tier

Ultimate or Intermediate Parent	FP – Tier 1	FP – Tier 2	NFP – Tier 1	NFP – Tier 2
Parent	NFP – Tier 2	NFP – Tier 1	FP – Tier 2	FP – Tier 1
Exemption	Available*	Not available	Available	Not available

FP = For-profit entity

NFP = Not-for-profit entity

*   The exemption would not be available by reference to the intermediate parent when it is a for-profit public sector entity unable to claim compliance with IFRSs – see paragraph Aus16.2 of AASB 101 *Presentation of Financial Statements*.

^   When the parent entity's NFP ultimate or intermediate parent is able to claim compliance with IFRSs, the exemption is available.

Australian Accounting Standards consist of two tiers of reporting requirements for preparing general purpose financial statements:

(a)   Tier 1: Australian Accounting Standards; and

(b)   Tier 2: Australian Accounting Standards – Reduced Disclosure Requirements.

Amendment to AASB 128

8   Paragraph Aus13.1 is amended as follows (new text is underlined):

Aus13.1   **Notwithstanding paragraph 13(c)(iv), an investor that meets the criteria in paragraphs 13(c)(i), 13(c)(ii) and 13(c)(iii) need not apply the equity method in accounting for an interest in an associate if its ultimate or any intermediate parent produces consolidated financial statements available for public use and:**

    (a)   the investor and its ultimate or intermediate parent are:

        (i)   both not-for-profit entities complying with Australian Accounting Standards; or

        (ii)   both entities complying with Australian Accounting Standards – Reduced Disclosure Requirements; or

    (b)   the investor is an entity complying with Australian Accounting Standards – Reduced Disclosure Requirements and its ultimate or intermediate parent is a not-for-profit entity complying with Australian Accounting Standards.

Amendment to AASB 131

9   Paragraph Aus2.1 is amended as follows (new text is underlined):

Aus2.1   **Notwithstanding paragraph 2(c)(iv), a venturer that meets the criteria in paragraphs 2(c)(i), 2(c)(ii) and 2(c)(iii) need not apply proportionate consolidation or the equity method in accounting for an interest in a jointly controlled entity if its ultimate or any intermediate parent produces consolidated financial statements available for public use and:**

         (a)   the venturer and its ultimate or intermediate parent are:

             (i)   both not-for-profit entities complying with Australian Accounting Standards; or

             (ii)   both entities complying with Australian Accounting Standards – Reduced Disclosure Requirements; or

         (b)   the venturer is an entity complying with Australian Accounting Standards – Reduced Disclosure Requirements and its ultimate or intermediate parent is a not-for-profit entity complying with Australian Accounting Standards.

Basis for Conclusions

The Basis for Conclusions accompanies, but is not part of, AASB 2011-6.

Introduction

BC1   This Basis for Conclusions summarises the Australian Accounting Standards Board's considerations in reaching the conclusions in AASB 2011-5 Amendments to Australian Accounting Standards – Extending Relief from *Consolidation, the Equity Method and Proportionate Consolidation* and AASB 2011-6 *Amendments to Australian Accounting Standards – Extending Relief from Consolidation, the Equity Method and Proportionate Consolidation – Reduced Disclosure Requirements.* Individual Board members gave greater weight to some factors than to others.

Background

BC2   Paragraph 10 of AASB 127 *Consolidated and Separate Financial Statements* (in common with IAS 27 *Consolidated and Separate Financial Statements*) provides relief from preparing consolidated financial statements for parents that meet four criteria, including having an ultimate parent or an intermediate parent that prepares IFRS-compliant consolidated financial statements (paragraph 10(d)).

BC3   Due to the addition of Aus paragraphs in IFRSs as adopted in Australia, the financial statements of some entities applying Australian Accounting Standards are not IFRS compliant. This means that a parent that has an ultimate parent or other intermediate parent that prepares non-IFRS-compliant consolidated financial statements does not have access to the exemption from consolidation provided in paragraph 10 of AASB 127, even if the criteria in paragraphs 10(a) to 10(c) are met.

BC4   Similarly, investors need not apply the equity method when they meet the four criteria in paragraph 13(c) of AASB 128 *Investments in Associates* and venturers need not apply proportionate consolidation or the equity method when they meet the four criteria in paragraph 2(c) of AASB 131 *Interests in Joint Ventures*. The criteria in paragraph 10 of AASB 127, paragraph 13(c) of AASB 128 and paragraph 2(c) of AASB 131 are similar.

BC5   Consequently, the exemptions from the equity method and proportionate consolidation are also not available under those paragraphs to an investor or a venturer when its ultimate parent or intermediate parent prepares non-IFRS-compliant consolidated financial statements.

Amendments to AAS – Extending Relief from Consolidation,   **1513**
the Equity Method and Proportionate Consolidation, etc

AASB

BC6   The AASB issued Exposure Draft ED 205 *Extending Relief from Consolidation, the Equity Method and Proportionate Consolidation* in September 2010. The AASB considered the submissions received from constituents and confirmed the principal approach proposed in the Exposure Draft.

New Zealand Approach

BC7   During its development of ED 205, the AASB noted that a related issue was considered by the Financial Reporting Standards Board (FRSB) of the New Zealand Institute of Chartered Accountants in December 2008. This concerned the requirement in paragraph 10(d) of NZ IAS 27 *Consolidated and Separate Financial Statements* that the parent's financial statements must be 'available for public use'. Due to the reporting requirements in New Zealand, not all entities are required to file their financial statements with the Companies Office. Hence, when a parent of a group is not required to submit its financial statements, any intermediate subsidiaries were unable to use the paragraph 10 exemption. As a result, the FRSB inserted paragraph NZ 3.1 into NZ IAS 27 so that entities that qualify for differential reporting concessions were not required to comply with paragraph 10(d). In order to qualify for the exemption not to present consolidated financial statements, qualifying entities were still required to comply with all the other conditions in paragraph 10.

BC8   In addition, the AASB noted that the FRSB had inserted a similar exemption into NZ IAS 28 *Investments in Associates* (paragraph NZ 1.2) and NZ IAS 31 *Interests in Joint Ventures* (paragraph NZ 1.1), extending the relief from application of the equity method by investors and proportionate consolidation or the equity method by venturers.

BC9   The AASB did not follow the FRSB's specific approach for qualifying entities, given the different issues faced by the two Boards and the different financial reporting framework in New Zealand, including its differential reporting framework that involves modifications to the recognition and measurement requirements of IFRSs.

Extending the Exemptions

BC10   The AASB considered the limitations on the exemptions and developed a view that relief from consolidation, the equity method and proportionate consolidation should be extended to a not-for-profit or Tier 2 parent, investor or venturer if it:

(a)   has a parent higher up in the group that prepares consolidated financial statements (whether or not IFRS-compliant) that are available for public use and:

(i)   those consolidated financial statements incorporate the information that would otherwise have been presented in the parent's consolidated financial statements or the investor's or venturer's financial statements; or

(ii)   the parent, investor or venturer is an entity complying with Australian Accounting Standards – Reduced Disclosure Requirements ('Tier 2'); and

(b)   meets the criteria in paragraphs 10(a) to 10(c) of AASB 127, paragraphs 13(c)(i) to 13(c)(iii) of AASB 128 or paragraphs 2(c)(i) to 2(c)(iii) of AASB 131, as relevant.

BC11   This view is based on the principle that financial statement users would be able to satisfy their information needs through the consolidated financial statements prepared by the parent higher up in the group. However, the AASB decided that such relief should not be available in relation to the General Government Sector (GGS) of each Federal, State and Territory Government due to the unique circumstances related to the GGS, its relationship to the whole of government and its macro-economic significance. The AASB also decided that the partial consolidation basis for GGS financial statements required by AASB 1049 *Whole of Government and General Government Sector Financial Reporting* would not be amended.

BC12   Consistent with IAS 27, IAS 28 *Investments in Associates* and IAS 31 *Interests in Joint Ventures*, the AASB decided that the existing relief provided under paragraph 10 of AASB 127, paragraph 13(c) of AASB 128 and paragraph 2(c) of AASB 131 should be retained. The extension of relief on the basis set out in paragraph BC10 does not change the present requirements for relief when the ultimate or intermediate parent is a for-profit Tier 1 entity – that entity is still required to prepare IFRS-compliant consolidated financial statements.

Not-For-Profit Ultimate or Intermediate Parent

BC13   When the ultimate or intermediate parent is a not-for-profit Tier 1 entity, and the parent, investor or venturer is a for-profit Tier 1 entity, the relief is not available where there are differences in the basis of accounting between the not-for-profit and for-profit entities as a result of the not-for-profit entity applying Standards or Aus paragraphs that contain requirements that are inconsistent with IFRS requirements. Extending relief to the for-profit Tier 1 parent, investor or venturer in this case would be beyond the scope of the relief available under IFRSs. However, the relief is available when the not-for-profit entity is not required to apply such inconsistent requirements. This is indicated by footnote to the table in paragraph AG1 of the Australian application guidance added to AASB 127. In this case, the for-profit Tier 1 entity would be able to claim compliance with IFRSs in that the relief is within the scope of the relief available under IFRSs.

BC14   The AASB considered the extension of relief to a for-profit Tier 2 parent, investor or venturer that has a not-for-profit ultimate or intermediate parent. The table in the Basis for Conclusions in ED 205 proposed that relief should be available to a parent, investor or venturer in these circumstances, which appears to be inconsistent with the circumstances addressed in paragraph BC13. The AASB considered three approaches to addressing the apparent inconsistency:

     (a)   amend the table proposed in ED 205 to indicate that the relief would not be available;

     (b)   retain the approach proposed in ED 205, that the relief would be available, and extend the justification in the Basis for Conclusions for this position; or

     (c)   retain the approach proposed in ED 205 with no amendment to the justification.

BC15   The AASB adopted the approach in paragraph BC14(b), extending the relief, based on its judgement that the relief would be reasonable for Tier 2 parents, investors or venturers despite any differences in the basis of accounting in the consolidated financial statements of the ultimate or intermediate parent that are publicly available. Typically, the not-for-profit ultimate or intermediate parent would not be able to claim compliance with IFRSs, and the Tier 2 parent, investor or venturer could not do so.

For-Profit Public Sector Entities

BC16   The AASB decided that relief would not be available to a parent entity merely because the intermediate parent preparing consolidated financial statements is a for-profit Tier 1 public sector entity unable to claim compliance with IFRSs. This decision was made on the basis that a for-profit public sector entity may apply requirements in particular Standards, such as AASB 1004 *Contributions*, and Aus paragraphs in other Australian Accounting Standards that are inconsistent with an IFRS requirement. However, relief may be available to the parent entity on another basis permitted by the Standard.

BC17   Relief is (or is not) available to a for-profit public sector entity as the parent, investor or venturer on the same basis as for any other for-profit parent, investor or venturer.

Amendments to AAS – Extending Relief from Consolidation, **1515**
the Equity Method and Proportionate Consolidation, etc

AASB

Other Changes

BC18   The AASB also decided that, consistent with paragraph 10(d) of AASB 127, the references to 'Australian equivalents to IFRSs' in paragraph 13(c)(iv) of AASB 128 and paragraph 2(c)(iv) of AASB 131 should be amended to 'International Financial Reporting Standards'.

BC19   The AASB decided to include the summary table set out in the Basis for Conclusions in the Exposure Draft as Australian application guidance accompanying, but not part of, the amended AASB 127. Whereas the table in the Exposure Draft addressed relief in relation to both not-for-profit entities and entities applying reduced disclosure requirements under AASB 1053 *Application of Tiers of Australian Accounting Standards*, the table added to the AASB 127 guidance by AASB 2011-5 addresses not-for-profit entities but not reduced disclosure requirements.

Reduced Disclosure Requirements

BC20   Exposure Draft ED 205, in addition to addressing relief for not-for-profit entities, also proposed the extension of relief to entities applying Australian Accounting Standards – Reduced Disclosure Requirements under AASB 1053. The AASB decided that relief should be extended to Tier 2 entities, either on the same basis as for not-for-profit entities or as addressed in paragraphs BC14 and BC15. Accounting Standard AASB 2011 6 provides this relief. That Standard also expands the table in the Australian application guidance accompanying AASB 127 to address entities applying reduced disclosure requirements.

BC21   Whereas AASB 2011-5 applies to annual reporting periods beginning on or after 1 July 2011, AASB 2011-6 applies to annual reporting periods beginning on or after 1 July 2013, being the application date of the reduced disclosure requirements under AASB 1053. Accordingly, two amending Standards were prepared to reflect the different application dates. Early application of each Standard is permitted. Early application of AASB 2011-6 requires early application of AASB 1053.

AASB 2011-7

Amendments to Australian Accounting Standards arising from the Consolidation and Joint Arrangements Standards

[AASB 1, 2, 3, 5, 7, 101, 107, 112, 118, 121, 124, 132, 133, 136, 138, 139, 1023 & 1038 and Interpretations 5, 9, 16 & 17]

(Issued October 2012)

Note from the Institute of Chartered Accountants Australia

This note, prepared by the technical editors, is not part of Accounting Standard AASB 2011-7.

Historical development

29 August 2011: AASB 2011-7 was issued amending AASB 1, 2, 3, 5, 7, 9, 2009-11, 101, 107, 112, 118, 121, 124, 132, 133, 136, 138, 139, 1023 & 1038 and Interpretations 5, 9, 16 & 17 to give effect to consequential changes arising from the issue of AASB 10 'Consolidated Financial Statements', AASB 11 'Joint Arrangements', AASB 12 'Disclosures of Interests in Other Entities', AASB 127 'Separate Financial Statements' and AASB 128 'Investments in Associates and Joint Ventures'.

This Standard is applicable to annual reporting periods beginning on or after 1 January 2013 and can be applied early by for-profit entities, provided AASB 10, AASB 11, AASB 12, AASB 127 and AASB 128 are adopted at the same time.

10 September 2012: AASB 2012-6 'Amendments to Australian Accounting Standards – Mandatory Effective Date of AASB 9 and Transition Disclosures' amends AASB 2011-7 consequential to the change to the mandatory effective date of AASB 9 to annual reporting periods beginning on or after 1 January 2015 instead of 1 January 2013.

31 October 2012: AASB 2010-7 was issued by the AASB, compiled to include the 2012-6 amendments. This Standard applies to annual reporting periods beginning on or after 1 January 2013 and can be adopted early.

Contents

AASB

Compilation Details

Accounting Standard
AASB 2011-7 Amendments to Australian Accounting Standards
arising from the Consolidation and Joint Arrangements Standards

	Paragraphs
Objective	1
Application	2 – 8
Amendments to AASB 1	9 –14
Amendments to AASB 2	15 – 17
Amendments to AASB 3	18 – 20
Amendments to AASB 5	21 – 22
Amendments to AASB 7	23 – 24
Amendments to AASB 101	27
Amendments to AASB 107	28 – 30
Amendments to AASB 112	31 – 34
Amendments to AASB 118	35 – 36
Amendments to AASB 121	37 – 39
Amendments to AASB 124	40 – 44
Amendments to AASB 132	45 – 46
Amendments to AASB 133	47
Amendments to AASB 136	48 – 49
Amendments to AASB 138	50
Amendments to AASB 139	51 – 52
Amendments to AASB 1023	53 – 54
Amendments to AASB 1038	55 – 56
Amendments to Interpretation 5	57 – 59
Amendments to Interpretation 9	60 – 61
Amendment to Interpretation 16	62
Amendments to Interpretation 17	63 – 66

Appendix: Early Application of the Consolidation and Joint Arrangements Standards

---

Australian Accounting Standard AASB 2011-7 *Amendments to Australian Accounting Standards arising from the Consolidation and Joint Arrangements Standards* (as amended) is set out in paragraphs 1 – 66 and the Appendix. All the paragraphs have equal authority.

Compilation Details

Accounting Standard AASB 2011-7 *Amendments to Australian Accounting Standards arising from the Consolidation and Joint Arrangements Standards* as amended

This compiled Standard applies to annual reporting periods beginning on or after 1 January 2013. It takes into account amendments up to and including 10 September 2012 and was prepared on 31 October 2012 by the staff of the Australian Accounting Standards Board (AASB).

This compilation is not a separate Accounting Standard made by the AASB. Instead, it is a representation of AASB 2011-7 (August 2011) as amended by other Accounting Standards, which are listed in the Table below.

Table of Standards

Standard	Date made	Application date *(annual reporting periods ... on or after ...)*	Application, saving or transitional provisions
AASB 2011-7	29 Aug 2011	(beginning) 1 Jan 2013	see (a) below
AASB 2012-6	10 Sep 2012	(beginning) 1 Jan 2013	see (b) below

(a) Entities may elect to apply this Standard to annual reporting periods beginning on or after 1 January 2005 but before 1 January 2013, with certain exceptions.

(b) Entities may elect to apply this Standard to annual reporting periods ending on or after 31 December 2009 that begin before 1 January 2013, with certain exceptions.

Table of Amendments

Paragraph affected	How affected	By ... [paragraph]
1	amended	AASB 2012-6 [29]
7	amended	AASB 2012-6 [30]
23	amended	AASB 2012-6 [31]
25-26	deleted	AASB 2012-6 [29]
27	amended	AASB 2012-6 [33]
45	amended	AASB 2012-6 [34]
51-52	amended	AASB 2012-6 [36]
52A	added	AASB 2012-6 [36]
55	amended	AASB 2012-6 [38]
A1	amended	AASB 2012-6 [29]
A2	deleted	AASB 2012-6 [29]
A4	deleted	AASB 2012-6 [32]
A5-A7	deleted	AASB 2012-6 [29]
A9	amended	AASB 2012-6 [35]
A10-A12	deleted	AASB 2012-6 [37]

Accounting Standard AASB 2011-7

The Australian Accounting Standards Board made Accounting Standard AASB 2011-7 *Amendments to Australian Accounting Standards arising from the Consolidation and Joint Arrangements Standards* under section 334 of the *Corporations Act 2001* on 29 August 2011.

This compiled version of AASB 2011-7 applies to annual reporting periods beginning on or after 1 January 2013. It incorporates relevant amendments contained in other AASB Standards made by the AASB up to and including 10 September 2012 (see Compilation Details).

Amendments to Australian Accounting Standards arising   **1519**
from the Consolidation and Joint Arrangements Standards

AASB

Accounting Standard AASB 2011-7

Amendments to Australian Accounting Standards arising from the Consolidation and Joint Arrangements Standards

Objective

1   The objective of this Standard is to make amendments to:

(a)   AASB 1 *First-time Adoption of Australian Accounting Standards*;

(b)   AASB 2 *Share-based Payment*;

(c)   AASB 3 *Business Combinations*;

(d)   AASB 5 *Non-current Assets Held for Sale and Discontinued Operations*;

(e)   AASB 7 *Financial Instruments: Disclosures*;

(f)-(h) [deleted]

(i)   AASB 101 *Presentation of Financial Statements*;

(j)   AASB 107 *Statement of Cash Flows*;

(k)   AASB 112 *Income Taxes*;

(l)   AASB 118 *Revenue*;

(m)   AASB 121 *The Effects of Changes in Foreign Exchange Rates*;

(n)   AASB 124 *Related Party Disclosures*;

(o)   AASB 132 *Financial Instruments: Presentation*;

(p)   AASB 133 *Earnings per Share*;

(q)   AASB 136 *Impairment of Assets*;

(r)   AASB 138 *Intangible Assets*;

(s)   AASB 139 *Financial Instruments: Recognition and Measurement*;

(t)   AASB 1023 *General Insurance Contracts*;

(u)   AASB 1038 *Life Insurance Contracts*;

(v)   Interpretation 5 *Rights to Interests arising from Decommissioning, Restoration and Environmental Rehabilitation Funds*;

(w)   Interpretation 9 *Reassessment of Embedded Derivatives*;

(x)   Interpretation 16 *Hedges of a Net Investment in a Foreign Operation*; and

(y)   Interpretation 17 *Distributions of Non-cash Assets to Owners*;

as a consequence of the issuance of AASB 10 *Consolidated Financial Statements*, AASB 11 *Joint Arrangements*, AASB 12 *Disclosure of Interests in Other Entities*, AASB 127 *Separate Financial Statements* and AASB 128 *Investments in Associates and Joint Ventures* in August 2011.

Application

2   **Subject to paragraphs 3-5, this Standard applies to:**

(a)   **each entity that is required to prepare financial reports in accordance with Part 2M.3 of the Corporations Act and that is a reporting entity;**

(b)   **general purpose financial statements of each other reporting entity; and**

(c)   **financial statements that are, or are held out to be, general purpose financial statements.**

3   In respect of AASB 101 and AASB 107, this Standard applies to:

(a)   each entity that is required to prepare financial reports in accordance with Part 2M.3 of the Corporations Act;

(b)   general purpose financial statements of each reporting entity; and

(c)   financial statements that are, or are held out to be, general purpose financial statements.

4   In respect of AASB 133, this Standard applies to each entity that is required to prepare financial reports in accordance with Part 2M.3 of the Corporations Act and that is:

(a)   a reporting entity whose ordinary shares or potential ordinary shares are publicly traded; or

(b)   a reporting entity that is in the process of issuing ordinary shares or potential ordinary shares in public markets; or

(c)   an entity that discloses earnings per share.

5   In respect of AASB 1038, this Standard applies to each entity that is:

(a)   a life insurer; or

(b)   the parent in a group that includes a life insurer;

when the entity:

(c)   is a reporting entity that is required to prepare financial reports in accordance with Part 2M.3 of the Corporations Act;

(d)   is an other reporting entity and prepares general purpose financial statements; or

(e)   prepares financial statements that are, or are held out to be, general purpose financial statements.

6   This Standard applies to annual reporting periods beginning on or after 1 January 2013.

[Note: For application dates of paragraphs changed or added by an amending Standard, see Compilation Details.]

7   This Standard shall be applied when AASB 10, AASB 11, AASB 12, AASB 127 (August 2011) and AASB 128 (August 2011) are applied. This Standard may be applied by for-profit entities, but not by not-for-profit entities, to annual reporting periods beginning on or after 1 January 2005 but before 1 January 2013, except that the amendments to AASB 3 may be applied early only to annual reporting periods beginning on or after 30 June 2007 but before 1 January 2013. If a for-profit entity applies this Standard to an annual reporting period beginning on or after 1 January 2005 but before 1 January 2013, it shall disclose that fact and apply AASB 10, AASB 11, AASB 12, AASB 127 (August 2011) and AASB 128 (August 2011) at the same time.

8   This Standard uses underlining, striking out and other typographical material to identify some of the amendments to a Standard or an Interpretation, in order to make the amendments more understandable. However, the amendments made by this Standard do not include that underlining, striking out or other typographical material.

Amendments to Australian Accounting Standards arising   **1521**
from the Consolidation and Joint Arrangements Standards

AASB

Amendments to AASB 1

9   In paragraphs 31, D1(g), D14 and D15 and in the headings before paragraphs 31 and D14, 'jointly controlled entity' is amended to 'joint venture' and 'jointly controlled entities' is amended to 'joint ventures'.

10   Paragraph 39I is added as follows:

> 39I   AASB 2011-7 *Amendments to Australian Accounting Standards arising from the Consolidation and Joint Arrangements Standards*, issued in August 2011, amended paragraphs 31, B7, C1, D1, D14 and D15 and added paragraph D31. An entity shall apply those amendments when it applies AASB 10 *Consolidated Financial Statements* and AASB 11 *Joint Arrangements*.

11   Paragraph B7 is amended as follows (new text is underlined and deleted text is struck through):

> B7   A first-time adopter shall apply the following requirements of ~~AASB 127 Consolidated and Separate Financial Statements (as amended in 2008)~~ AASB 10 prospectively from the date of transition to Australian Accounting Standards:
>
> (a)   the requirement in paragraph ~~28~~ B94 that total comprehensive income is attributed to the owners of the parent and to the non-controlling interests even if this results in the non-controlling interests having a deficit balance;
>
> (b)   the requirements in paragraphs ~~30 and 31~~ 23 and B93 for accounting for changes in the parent's ownership interest in a subsidiary that do not result in a loss of control; and
>
> (c)   the requirements in paragraphs ~~34-37~~ B97-B99 for accounting for a loss of control over a subsidiary, and the related requirements of paragraph 8A of AASB 5 *Non-current Assets Held for Sale and Discontinued Operations*.
>
> However, if a first-time adopter elects to apply AASB 3 ~~Business Combinations (as revised in 2008)~~ retrospectively to past business combinations, it ~~also~~ shall also apply ~~AASB 127 (as amended in 2008)~~ AASB 10 in accordance with paragraph C1 of this Standard.

12   Paragraph C1 is amended as follows (new text is underlined and deleted text is struck through):

> C1   A first-time adopter may elect not to apply AASB 3 ~~Business Combinations (as revised in 2008)~~ retrospectively to past business combinations (business combinations that occurred before the date of transition to Australian Accounting Standards). However, if a first-time adopter restates any business combination to comply with AASB 3 ~~(as revised in 2008)~~, it shall restate all later business combinations and shall also apply ~~AASB 127 Consolidated and Separate Financial Statements (as amended in 2008)~~ AASB 10 from that same date. For example, if a first-time adopter elects to restate a business combination that occurred on 30 June 20X6, it shall restate all business combinations that occurred on 30 June 20X6 and the date of transition to Australian Accounting Standards, and it shall also apply ~~AASB 127 (amended 2008)~~ AASB 10 from 30 June 20X6.

13   Paragraph D1 is amended as follows (new text is underlined and deleted text is struck through):

> D1   An entity may elect to use one or more of the following exemptions:
>
> (a)   ...
>
> (p)   extinguishing financial liabilities with equity instruments (paragraph D25); ~~and~~
>
> (q)   severe hyperinflation (paragraphs D26-D30)~~.~~ ; and
>
> (r)   joint arrangements (paragraph D31).
>
> An entity shall not apply these exemptions by analogy to other items.

14   After paragraph D30, a heading and paragraph D31 are added as follows:

Joint arrangements

D31   A first-time adopter may apply the transition provisions in AASB 11 with the following exception. When changing from proportionate consolidation to the equity method, a first-time adopter shall test for impairment the investment in accordance with AASB 136 as at the beginning of the earliest period presented, regardless of whether there is any indication that the investment may be impaired. Any resulting impairment shall be recognised as an adjustment to retained earnings at the beginning of the earliest period presented.

Amendments to AASB 2

15   In paragraph 5, 'AASB 131 *Interests in Joint Ventures*' is amended to 'AASB 11 *Joint Arrangements*'.

16   Paragraph 63A is added as follows:

63A   AASB 2011-7 *Amendments to Australian Accounting Standards arising from the Consolidation and Joint Arrangements Standards*, issued in August 2011, amended paragraph 5 and Appendix A. An entity shall apply those amendments when it applies AASB 10 *Consolidated Financial Statements* and AASB 11.

17   In Appendix A, the footnote to the definition of 'share-based payment arrangement' is amended as follows (new text is underlined and deleted text is struck through):

3   A 'group' is defined in ~~paragraph 4~~ Appendix A of ~~AASB 127~~ AASB 10 *Consolidated ~~and Separate~~ Financial Statements* as 'a parent and ~~all~~ its subsidiaries' from the perspective of the reporting entity's ultimate parent.

Amendments to AASB 3

18   Paragraph 7 is amended (new text is underlined and deleted text is struck through) and paragraph 64E is added as follows:

7   The guidance in ~~AASB 127~~ AASB 10 *Consolidated Financial Statements* shall be used to identify the acquirer – the entity that obtains control of another entity, i.e. the acquiree. If a business combination has occurred but applying the guidance in ~~AASB 127~~ AASB 10 does not clearly indicate which of the combining entities is the acquirer, the factors in paragraphs B14-B18 shall be considered in making that determination.

64E   AASB 2011-7 *Amendments to Australian Accounting Standards arising from the Consolidation and Joint Arrangements Standards*, issued in August 2011, amended paragraphs 7, B13, B63(e) and Appendix A. An entity shall apply those amendments when it applies AASB 10.

19   In Appendix A, the definition of 'control' is deleted.

20   Paragraphs B13 and B63(e) are amended as follows (new text is underlined and deleted text is struck through):

B13   The guidance in ~~AASB 127~~ AASB 10 *Consolidated ~~and Separate~~ Financial Statements* shall be used to identify the acquirer – the entity that obtains control of the acquiree. If a business combination has occurred but applying the guidance in ~~AASB 127~~ AASB 10 does not clearly indicate which of the combining entities is the acquirer, the factors in paragraphs B14-B18 shall be considered in making that determination.

B63   Examples of other Australian Accounting Standards that provide guidance on subsequently measuring and accounting for assets acquired and liabilities assumed or incurred in a business combination include:

(a)   ...

(e)   ~~AASB 127 (as amended in March 2008)~~ AASB 10 provides guidance on accounting for changes in a parent's ownership interest in a subsidiary after control is obtained.

Amendments to Australian Accounting Standards arising   **1523**
from the Consolidation and Joint Arrangements Standards

AASB

Amendments to AASB 5

21   Paragraph 28 is amended as follows (new text is underlined):

    28   The entity shall include any required adjustment to the carrying amount of a non-current asset that ceases to be classified as held for sale in profit or loss [footnote omitted] from continuing operations in the period in which the criteria in paragraphs 7-9 are no longer met. <u>Financial statements for the periods since classification as held for sale shall be amended accordingly if the disposal group or non-current asset that ceases to be classified as held for sale is a subsidiary, joint operation, joint venture, associate, or a portion of an interest in a joint venture or an associate.</u> The entity shall present that adjustment in the same caption in the statement of comprehensive income used to present a gain or loss, if any, recognised in accordance with paragraph 37.

22   Paragraph 44G is added as follows:

    44G   AASB 2011-7 *Amendments to Australian Accounting Standards arising from the Consolidation and Joint Arrangements Standards*, issued in August 2011, amended paragraph 28. An entity shall apply that amendment when it applies AASB 11 *Joint Arrangements*.

Amendments to AASB 7

23   Paragraph 3(a) is amended as follows (new text is underlined and deleted text is struck through):

    3   **This Standard shall be applied by all entities to all types of financial instruments, except:**

       (a)   **those interests in subsidiaries, associates or joint ventures that are accounted for in accordance with <u>AASB 10 *Consolidated Financial Statements*,</u> AASB 127 ~~*Consolidated and*~~ *Separate Financial Statements*~~;~~ or AASB 128 *Investments in Associates <u>and Joint Ventures</u>* ~~or AASB 131 Interests in Joint Ventures~~. However, in some cases, AASB 127~~;~~ <u>or</u> AASB 128 ~~or AASB 131~~ permits an entity to account for an interest in a subsidiary, associate or joint venture using AASB 139; in those cases, ...**

24   Paragraph 44O is added as follows:

    44O   AASB 2011-7 *Amendments to Australian Accounting Standards arising from the Consolidation and Joint Arrangements Standards*, issued in August 2011, amended paragraph 3. An entity shall apply that amendment when it applies AASB 10 and AASB 11 *Joint Arrangements*.

Amendments to AASB 9 (December 2010)

25-26   [deleted]

Amendments to AASB 101

27   Paragraphs 4, 119, 123 and 124 are amended (new text is underlined and deleted text is struck through) and paragraph 139H is added as follows:

    4   This Standard does not apply to the structure and content of condensed interim financial statements prepared in accordance with AASB 134 *Interim Financial Reporting*. However, paragraphs 15-35 apply to such financial statements. This Standard applies equally to all entities, including those that present consolidated financial statements <u>in accordance with AASB 10 *Consolidated Financial Statements*</u> and those that present separate financial statements ~~as defined~~ in <u>accordance with</u> AASB 127 ~~*Consolidated and*~~ *Separate Financial Statements*.

    119   ... An example is disclosure of whether ~~a venturer recognises its interest in a jointly controlled entity using proportionate consolidation or the equity method (see AASB 131 Interests in Joint Ventures)~~ <u>an entity applies the fair value or cost model to its investment property (see AASB 140 *Investment Property*)</u>. Some Australian Accounting Standards specifically require disclosure of particular accounting

policies, including choices made by management between different policies they allow. …

123 In the process of applying the entity's accounting policies, management makes various judgements, apart from those involving estimations, that can significantly affect the amounts it recognises in the financial statements. For example, management makes judgements in determining:

(a) whether financial assets are held-to-maturity investments;

(b) when substantially all the significant risks and rewards of ownership of financial assets and lease assets are transferred to other entities; and

(c) whether, in substance, particular sales of goods are financing arrangements and therefore do not give rise to revenue; and.

(d) ~~whether the substance of the relationship between the entity and a special purpose entity indicates that the entity controls the special purpose entity.~~

124 Some of the disclosures made in accordance with paragraph 122 are required by other Australian Accounting Standards. For example, ~~AASB 127 requires an entity to disclose the reasons why the entity's ownership interest does not constitute control, in respect of an investee that is not a subsidiary even though more than half of its voting or potential voting power is owned directly or indirectly through subsidiaries~~ AASB 12 *Disclosure of Interests in Other Entities* requires an entity to disclose the judgements it has made in determining whether it controls another entity. AASB 140 *Investment Property* requires …

139H AASB 2011-7 *Amendments to Australian Accounting Standards arising from the Consolidation and Joint Arrangements Standards*, issued in August 2011, amended paragraphs 4, 119, 123 and 124. An entity shall apply those amendments when it applies AASB 10 and AASB 12.

Amendments to AASB 107

28 Paragraphs 37, 38 and 42B are amended as follows (new text is underlined and deleted text is struck through):

37 When accounting for an investment in an associate, a joint venture or a subsidiary accounted for by use of the equity or cost method, an investor restricts its reporting in the statement of cash flows to the cash flows between itself and the investee, for example, to dividends and advances.

38 ~~An entity which reports its interest in a jointly controlled entity (see AASB 131 Interests in Joint Ventures) using proportionate consolidation, includes in its consolidated statement of cash flows its proportionate share of the jointly controlled entity's cash flows.~~ An entity ~~which~~ that reports its ~~such an~~ interest in an associate or a joint venture using the equity method includes in its statement of cash flows the cash flows in respect of its investments in the ~~jointly controlled entity~~ associate or joint venture, and distributions and other payments or receipts between it and the ~~jointly controlled entity~~ associate or joint venture.

42B Changes in ownership interests in a subsidiary that do not result in a loss of control, such as the subsequent purchase or sale by a parent of a subsidiary's equity instruments, are accounted for as equity transactions (see ~~AASB 127~~ AASB 10 *Consolidated ~~and Separate~~ Financial Statements* ~~(as amended in March 2008)~~). Accordingly, …

29 Paragraph 50(b) is deleted and a note added as follows:

50 Additional information …

(a)   …

(b)   [deleted by the IASB]

(c)   …

Amendments to Australian Accounting Standards arising   **1525**
from the Consolidation and Joint Arrangements Standards

AASB

30   Paragraph 57 is added as follows:

> 57   AASB 2011-7 *Amendments to Australian Accounting Standards arising from the Consolidation and Joint Arrangements Standards*, issued in August 2011, amended paragraphs 37, 38 and 42B and deleted paragraph 50(b). An entity shall apply those amendments when it applies AASB 10 and AASB 11 *Joint Arrangements*.

Amendments to AASB 112

31   In paragraphs 2, 15, 18(e), 24, 38, 44, 45, 81(f), 87 and 87C and the heading before paragraph 38, 'joint venture' is amended to 'joint arrangement' and 'joint ventures' is amended to 'joint arrangements'.

32   Paragraph 39 is amended as follows (new text is underlined and deleted text is struck through):

> **39**   **An entity shall recognise a deferred tax liability for all taxable temporary differences associated with investments in subsidiaries, branches and associates, and interests in joint ventures arrangements, except to the extent that both of the following conditions are satisfied:**
>
> > **(a)**   **the parent, investor, or joint venturer or joint operator is able to control the timing of the reversal of the temporary difference; and**
> >
> > **(b)**   **...**

33   Paragraph 43 is amended as follows (new text is underlined and deleted text is struck through):

> 43   The arrangement between the parties to a joint venture arrangement usually deals with the sharing distribution of the profits and identifies whether decisions on such matters require the consent of all the venturers parties or a specified majority group of the venturers parties. When the joint venturer or joint operator can control the timing of the distribution of its share of the sharing of profits of the joint arrangement and it is probable that its share of the profits will not be distributed in the foreseeable future, a deferred tax liability is not recognised.

34   Paragraph 98A is added as follows:

> 98A   AASB 2011-7 *Amendments to Australian Accounting Standards arising from the Consolidation and Joint Arrangements Standards*, issued in August 2011, amended paragraphs 2, 15, 18(e), 24, 38, 39, 43-45, 81(f), 87 and 87C. An entity shall apply those amendments when it applies AASB 11 *Joint Arrangements*.

Amendments to AASB 118

35   Paragraph 6(b) is amended as follows (new text is underlined and deleted text is struck through):

> 6   This Standard does not deal with revenue arising from:
>
> > (a)   ...
> >
> > (b)   dividends arising from investments which are accounted for under the equity method (see AASB 128 *Accounting for Investments in Associates and Joint Ventures*);
> >
> > (c)   ...

36   Paragraph 41 is added as follows:

> 41   AASB 2011-7 *Amendments to Australian Accounting Standards arising from the Consolidation and Joint Arrangements Standards*, issued in August 2011, amended paragraph 6(b). An entity shall apply that amendment when it applies AASB 11 *Joint Arrangements*.

Amendments to AASB 121

37   In the definition of 'foreign operation' in paragraph 8 and in paragraphs 11 and 18, 'joint venture' is amended to 'joint arrangement' and 'joint ventures' is amended to 'joint arrangements'.

38   In paragraphs 3(b) and 44 'proportionate consolidation' and in paragraph 33 'proportionately consolidated' are deleted.

39   Paragraphs 19, 45, 46 and 48A are amended (new text is underlined and deleted text is struck through) and paragraph 60F is added as follows:

> 19   This Standard also permits a stand-alone entity preparing financial statements or an entity preparing separate financial statements in accordance with AASB 127 ~~Consolidated and~~ *Separate Financial Statements* to present its financial statements in any currency (or currencies). If the …

> 45   The incorporation of the results and financial position of a foreign operation with those of the reporting entity follows normal consolidation procedures, such as the elimination of intragroup balances and intragroup transactions of a subsidiary (see ~~AASB 127~~ *AASB 10 Consolidated Financial Statements* ~~and AASB 131 Interests in Joint Ventures~~). However, …

> 46   When the financial statements of a foreign operation are as of a date different from that of the reporting entity, the foreign operation often prepares additional statements as of the same date as the reporting entity's financial statements. When this is not done, ~~AASB 127~~ AASB 10 allows the use of a different date provided that the difference is no greater than three months and adjustments are made for the effects of any significant transactions or other events that occur between the different dates. In such a case, the assets and liabilities of the foreign operation are translated at the exchange rate at the end of the reporting period of the foreign operation. Adjustments are made for significant changes in exchange rates up to the end of the reporting period of the reporting entity in accordance with ~~AASB 127~~ AASB 10. The same approach is used in applying the equity method to associates and joint ventures ~~and in applying proportionate consolidation to joint ventures~~ in accordance with AASB 128 *Investments in Associates* ~~and AASB 131~~ (August 2011).

> 48A   In addition to the disposal of an entity's entire interest in a foreign operation, the following partial disposals are accounted for as disposals ~~even if the entity retains an interest in the former subsidiary, associate or jointly controlled entity~~:

>> (a)   when the partial disposal involves the loss of control of a subsidiary that includes a foreign operation, regardless of whether the entity retains a non-controlling interest in its former subsidiary after the partial disposal; and

>> (b)   when the retained interest after the partial disposal of an interest in ~~the loss of significant influence over an~~ a joint arrangement or a partial disposal of an interest in an associate that includes a foreign operation is a financial asset that includes a foreign operation.~~; and~~

>> ~~(c)   the loss of joint control over a jointly controlled entity that includes a foreign operation.~~

> 60F   AASB 2011-7 *Amendments to Australian Accounting Standards arising from the Consolidation and Joint Arrangements Standards*, issued in August 2011, amended paragraphs 3(b), 8, 11, 18, 19, 33, 44-46 and 48A. An entity shall apply those amendments when it applies AASB 10 and AASB 11 *Joint Arrangements*.

Amendments to AASB 124

40   Paragraph 3 is amended as follows (new text is underlined and deleted text is struck through):

> **3   This Standard requires disclosure of related party relationships, transactions and outstanding balances, including commitments, in the consolidated and separate financial statements of a parent~~, venturer~~ or investors with joint control of, or significant influence over, an investee presented in accordance with AASB 10 *Consolidated Financial Statements* or AASB 127 ~~Consolidated and~~ *Separate Financial Statements*. This Standard also applies to individual financial statements.**

AASB

41   In paragraph 9, the definitions of 'control', 'joint control' and 'significant influence' are deleted and a sentence is added as follows:

The terms 'control', 'joint control' and 'significant influence' are defined in AASB 10, AASB 11 *Joint Arrangements* **and AASB 128** *Investments in Associates and Joint Ventures* **and are used in this Standard with the meanings specified in those Standards.**

42   In paragraph 9, the definition of 'related party' is amended as follows (new text is underlined and deleted text is struck through):

A *related party* **is a person or entity that is related to the entity that is preparing its financial statements (in this Standard referred to as the 'reporting entity').**

    (a)   **A person or a close member of that person's family is related to a reporting entity if that person:**

    (i)   **has control or joint control** ~~over~~ <u>of</u> **the reporting entity;**

    (ii)   **...**

43   Paragraph 11(b) is amended as follows (new text is underlined and deleted text is struck through):

    11   In the context of this Standard, the following are not related parties:

        (a)   ...

        (b)   two <u>joint</u> venturers simply because they share joint control ~~over~~ <u>of</u> a joint venture.

        (c)   ...

44   Paragraphs 15, 19 and 25 are amended (new text is underlined and deleted text is struck through) and paragraph 28A is added as follows:

    15   The requirement to disclose related party relationships between a parent and its subsidiaries is in addition to the disclosure requirements in AASB 127 <u>and</u>~~,~~ ~~AASB 128~~ *~~Investments in Associates~~* ~~and AASB 131~~ *~~Interests in Joint Ventures~~* <u>AASB 12</u> <u>*Disclosure of Interests in Other Entities*</u>.

    19   **The disclosures required by paragraph 18 shall be made separately for each of the following categories:**

        (a)   **the parent;**

        (b)   **entities with joint control <u>of,</u> or significant influence over<u>,</u> the entity;**

        (c)   **subsidiaries;**

        (d)   **associates;**

        (e)   **joint ventures in which the entity is a <u>joint</u> venturer;**

        (f)   **key management personnel of the entity or its parent; and**

        (g)   **other related parties.**

    25   **A reporting entity is exempt from the disclosure requirements of paragraph 18 in relation to related party transactions and outstanding balances, including commitments, with:**

        (a)   **a government that has control<u>,</u> <u>or</u> joint control <u>of,</u> or significant influence over<u>,</u> the reporting entity; and**

        (b)   **another entity that is a related party because the same government has control<u>,</u> <u>or</u> joint control <u>of;</u> or significant influence over<u>,</u> both the reporting entity and the other entity.**

    28A   AASB 2011-7 *Amendments to Australian Accounting Standards arising from the Consolidation and Joint Arrangements Standards*, issued in August 2011, amended paragraphs 3, 9, 11(b), 15, 19(b) and (e) and 25. An entity shall apply those amendments when it applies AASB 10, AASB 11 and AASB 12.

Amendments to AASB 132

45   Paragraph 4(a) is amended (new text is underlined and deleted text is struck through) and paragraph 97I is added as follows:

> **4**   **This Standard shall be applied by all entities to all types of financial instruments except:**
>
> > **(a)   those interests in subsidiaries, associates or joint ventures that are accounted for in accordance with <u>AASB 10 *Consolidated Financial Statements,*</u> AASB 127 ~~*Consolidated and*~~ Separate Financial Statements; or AASB 128 *Investments in Associates <u>and Joint Ventures</u> ~~or AASB 131 Interests in Joint Ventures~~*. However, in some cases, AASB 127; <u>or AASB 128</u> ~~or AASB 131~~ permits an entity to account for an interest in a subsidiary, associate or joint venture using AASB 139; in those cases, ...**

> 97I   AASB 2011-7 *Amendments to Australian Accounting Standards arising from the Consolidation and Joint Arrangements Standards*, issued in August 2011, amended paragraphs 4(a) and AG29. An entity shall apply those amendments when it applies AASB 10 and AASB 11 *Joint Arrangements*.

46   In the Appendix, paragraph AG29 is amended as follows:

> AG29 In consolidated financial statements, an entity presents non-controlling interests – that is, the interests of other parties in the equity and income of its subsidiaries – in accordance with AASB 101 and ~~AASB 127~~ <u>AASB 10</u>. When ...

Amendments to AASB 133

47   Paragraphs 4, 40 and A11 are amended (new text is underlined and deleted text is struck through) and paragraph 74B is added as follows:

> **4**   **When an entity presents both consolidated financial statements and separate financial statements prepared in accordance with <u>AASB 10 *Consolidated Financial Statements* and</u> AASB 127 ~~*Consolidated and*~~ Separate Financial Statements, <u>respectively</u>, the disclosures required by this Standard need be presented only on the basis of the consolidated information. An ...**

> 40   A subsidiary, joint venture or associate may issue to parties other than the parent; ~~venturer~~ or investor<u>s with joint control of, or significant influence over, the investee</u> potential ordinary shares that are convertible into either ordinary shares of the subsidiary, joint venture or associate, or ordinary shares of the parent; <u>or investors with joint control of, or significant influence</u> (the reporting entity) <u>over, the investee</u> ~~venturer or investor~~. If these potential ordinary shares of the subsidiary, joint venture or associate have a dilutive effect on the basic earnings per share of the reporting entity, they are included in the calculation of diluted earnings per share.

> 74B   AASB 2011-7 *Amendments to Australian Accounting Standards arising from the Consolidation and Joint Arrangements Standards*, issued in August 2011, amended paragraphs 4, 40 and A11. An entity shall apply those amendments when it applies AASB 10 and AASB 11 *Joint Arrangements*.

> A11   Potential ordinary shares of a subsidiary, joint venture or associate convertible into either ordinary shares of the subsidiary, joint venture or associate, or ordinary shares of the parent; <u>or investors with joint control of, or significant influence</u> (the reporting entity) <u>over, the investee</u> ~~venturer or investor~~ are included in the calculation of diluted earnings per share as follows: ...

Amendments to AASB 136

48   In the heading before paragraph 12(h) and in paragraph 12(h), 'jointly controlled entity' is amended to 'joint venture'.

49   Paragraph 4 is amended (new text is underlined and deleted text is struck through) and paragraph 140H is added as follows:

     4   This Standard applies to financial assets classified as:

         (a)   subsidiaries, as defined in ~~AASB 127~~ AASB 10 *Consolidated ~~and Separate~~ Financial Statements*;

         (b)   associates, as defined in AASB 128 *Investments in Associates and Joint Ventures*; and

         (c)   joint ventures, as defined in ~~AASB 131 Interests in Joint Ventures~~ AASB 11 *Joint Arrangements*.

         …

   140H   AASB 2011-7 *Amendments to Australian Accounting Standards arising from the Consolidation and Joint Arrangements Standards*, issued in August 2011, amended paragraph 4, the heading above paragraph 12(h) and paragraph 12(h). An entity shall apply those amendments when it applies AASB 10 and AASB 11.

Amendments to AASB 138

50   Paragraph 3(e) is amended (new text is underlined and deleted text is struck through) and paragraph 130F is added as follows:

     3   If another Standard prescribes the accounting for a specific type of intangible asset, an entity applies that Standard instead of this Standard. For example, this Standard does not apply to:

         (a)   …

         (e)   financial assets as defined in AASB 132. The recognition and measurement of some financial assets are covered by AASB 10 *Consolidated Financial Statements*, AASB 127 ~~Consolidated and~~ *Separate Financial Statements*; and AASB 128 *Investments in Associates and Joint Ventures* ~~and AASB 131 Interests in Joint Ventures~~;

         (f)   …

   130F   AASB 2011-7 *Amendments to Australian Accounting Standards arising from the Consolidation and Joint Arrangements Standards*, issued in August 2011, amended paragraph 3(e). An entity shall apply that amendment when it applies AASB 10 and AASB 11 *Joint Arrangements*.

Amendments to AASB 139

51   Paragraphs 2(a) and AG36-AG38 are amended (new text is underlined and deleted text is struck through) and paragraph 103P is added as follows:

     2   **This Standard shall be applied by all entities to all types of financial instruments except:**

         (a)   **those interests in subsidiaries, associates and joint ventures that are accounted for ~~under~~ in accordance with AASB 10 *Consolidated Financial Statements*, AASB 127 ~~Consolidated and~~ *Separate Financial Statements*; or AASB 128 *Investments in Associates and Joint Ventures*; ~~or AASB 131 Interests in Joint Ventures~~. However, entities shall apply this Standard to an interest in a subsidiary, associate or joint venture that according to AASB 127; or AASB 128 ~~or AASB 131~~ is accounted for under this Standard. …**

   103P   AASB 2011-7 *Amendments to Australian Accounting Standards arising from the Consolidation and Joint Arrangements Standards*, issued in August 2011, amended paragraphs 2(a), 15, AG3, AG4I(a) and AG36-AG38. An entity shall apply those amendments when it applies AASB 10 and AASB 11.

In paragraph AG36, '(including any SPE)' in the first box of the flowchart is deleted.

AG37 The situation described in paragraph 18(b) (when an entity retains the contractual rights to receive the cash flows of the financial asset but assumes a contractual obligation to pay the cash flows to one or more recipients) occurs, for example, if the entity is a ~~special purpose entity or~~ trust, and issues to investors beneficial interests in the underlying financial assets that it owns and provides servicing of those financial assets. In that case, the financial assets qualify for derecognition if the conditions in paragraphs 19 and 20 are met.

AG38 In applying paragraph 19, the entity could be, for example, the originator of the financial asset, or it could be a group that includes a ~~consolidated special purpose entity~~ <u>subsidiary</u> that has acquired the financial asset and passes on cash flows to unrelated third party investors.

52   Paragraphs 15 and AG3 are amended to read as follows:

    15   In consolidated financial statements, paragraphs 16-23 and Appendix A paragraphs AG34-AG52 are applied at a consolidated level. Hence, an entity first consolidates all subsidiaries in accordance with AASB 10, and then applies paragraphs 16-23 and Appendix A paragraphs AG34-AG52 to the resulting group.

    AG3   Sometimes, an entity makes what it views as a 'strategic investment' in equity instruments issued by another entity, with the intention of establishing or maintaining a long-term operating relationship with the entity in which the investment is made. The investor or joint venturer entity uses AASB 128 to determine whether the equity method of accounting is appropriate for such an investment. If the equity method is not appropriate, the entity applies this Standard to that strategic investment.

52A   Paragraph AG4I(a) is amended to read as follows:

    AG4I   The following examples show when this condition could be met. …

        (a)   The entity is a venture capital organisation, mutual fund, unit trust or similar entity whose business is investing in financial assets with a view to profiting from their total return in the form of interest or dividends and changes in fair value. AASB 128 allows such investments to be measured at fair value through profit or loss in accordance with this Standard. An entity may apply the same accounting policy to other investments managed on a total return basis but over which its influence is insufficient for them to be within the scope of AASB 128.

        (b)   …

Amendments to AASB 1023

53   Paragraph 15.5 is amended as follows (new text is underlined and deleted text is struck through):

    15.5   **When preparing *separate financial statements*, those investments in subsidiaries, ~~jointly controlled entities~~ <u>joint ventures</u> and associates that:**

        (a)   **are defined by <u>AASB 10</u> ~~AASB 127~~ *Consolidated ~~and Separate~~ Financial Statements*, <u>AASB 11 *Joint Arrangements* and</u> AASB 128 *Investments in Associates <u>and Joint Ventures</u>* ~~and AASB 131 *Interests in Joint Ventures*~~;**

        (b)   …

54   In paragraphs 15.5.1 and 15.5.2, 'jointly controlled entities' is amended to 'joint ventures'.

Amendments to AASB 1038

55   Paragraphs 10.5-10.7 are amended as follows (new text is underlined and deleted text is struck through):

    10.5   **Investments in associates that:**

        (a)   **are defined by AASB 128 *Investments in Associates <u>and Joint Ventures</u>*;**

        (b)   …

10.5.1 An insurer applies AASB 128 to its investments in associates. AASB 128 requires investments in associates to be accounted for using the equity method. When but ~~it does not apply to~~ investments in associates are held by mutual funds, unit trusts and similar entities including investment-linked insurance funds, AASB 128 permits the investments in those associates to be measured at fair value through profit or loss in accordance with AASB 139 ~~that are treated under AASB 139 and designated as "at fair value through profit or loss"~~.

10.6 **Venturers' interests in ~~jointly controlled entities~~ joint ventures that:**

    (a)   **are defined by ~~AASB 131 *Interests in Joint Ventures*~~ AASB 11 *Joint Arrangements*;**

    (b)   **...**

10.6.1 ~~Entities apply AASB 131 to interests in joint ventures. AASB 131 requires investments in joint ventures to be proportionately consolidated or to be accounted for using the equity method.~~ AASB 11 requires a joint venturer to recognise its interest in a joint venture as an investment and to account for that investment using the equity method in accordance with AASB 128 unless exempted from applying that method. ~~However, AASB 131 does not apply to venturers' interests in jointly controlled entities held by~~ AASB 128 permits mutual funds, unit trusts and similar entities including investment-linked insurance funds to measure investments in joint ventures at fair value through profit or loss in accordance with AASB 139 ~~that are treated under AASB 139 and designated as "at fair value through profit or loss"~~.

10.7 **When preparing *separate financial statements*, those investments in subsidiaries, ~~jointly controlled entities~~ joint ventures and associates that:**

    (a)   **are within the scope of AASB 127 ~~*Consolidated and*~~ *Separate Financial Statements*;**

    (b)   **...**

56   In paragraphs 10.7.1 and 10.7.2, 'jointly controlled entities' is amended to 'joint ventures'.

Amendments to Interpretation 5

57   Paragraphs 8 and 9 are amended as follows (new text is underlined and deleted text is struck through):

8   The contributor shall determine whether it has control, or joint control of, or significant influence over, the fund by reference to ~~AASB 127~~ AASB 10 *Consolidated ~~and Separate~~ Financial Statements*, AASB 11 *Joint Arrangements* and AASB 128 *Investments in Associates and Joint Ventures*, ~~AASB 131 *Interests in Joint Ventures*~~ and UIG Interpretation 112 ~~*Consolidation — Special Purpose Entities*~~. If it does, the contributor shall account for its interest in the fund in accordance with those Standards.

9   If a contributor does not have control, or joint control of, or significant influence over, the fund, the contributor shall recognise the right to receive reimbursement from the fund as a reimbursement in accordance with AASB 137 *Provisions, Contingent Liabilities and Contingent Assets*. This reimbursement shall be measured at the lower of:

    (a)   ...

58   The heading 'Effective Date of IFRIC 5' before paragraph 14 is amended to 'Effective Date'.

59   Paragraph 14B is added as follows:

14B   AASB 2011-7 *Amendments to Australian Accounting Standards arising from the Consolidation and Joint Arrangements Standards*, issued in August 2011, amended paragraphs 8 and 9. An entity shall apply those amendments when it applies AASB 10 and AASB 11.

Amendments to Interpretation 9

60　In paragraph 5(c), 'AASB 131 Interests in Joint Ventures' is amended to 'AASB 11 *Joint Arrangements*'.

61　Paragraph 12 is added as follows:

12　AASB 2011-7 *Amendments to Australian Accounting Standards arising from the Consolidation and Joint Arrangements Standards*, issued in August 2011, amended paragraph 5(c). An entity shall apply that amendment when it applies AASB 11.

Amendment to Interpretation 16

62　The footnote to paragraph 2 is amended as follows (new text is underlined and deleted text is struck through):

1　This will be the case for consolidated financial statements, financial statements in which investments <u>such as associates or joint ventures</u> are accounted for using the equity method, ~~financial statements in which venturers' interests in joint ventures are proportionately consolidated (subject to change as proposed in ED 157 *Joint Arrangements* published by the Australian Accounting Standards Board, being equivalent to ED 9 *Joint Arrangements* published by the International Accounting Standards Board in September 2007)~~ and financial statements that include a branch <u>or a joint operation as defined in AASB 11 *Joint Arrangements*</u>.

Amendments to Interpretation 17

63　Paragraph 7 is amended as follows (new text is underlined and deleted text is struck through):

7　In accordance with paragraph 5, this Interpretation does not apply when an entity distributes some of its ownership interests in a subsidiary but retains control of the subsidiary. The entity making a distribution that results in the entity recognising a non-controlling interest in its subsidiary accounts for the distribution in accordance with ~~AASB 127 (as amended in 2008)~~ <u>AASB 10</u>.

64　The heading 'Effective Date of IFRIC 17' before paragraph 18 is amended to 'Effective Date'.

65　Paragraph 19 is added as follows:

19　AASB 2011-7 *Amendments to Australian Accounting Standards arising from the Consolidation and Joint Arrangements Standards*, issued in August 2011, amended paragraph 7. An entity shall apply that amendment when it applies AASB 10.

66　In the Illustrative Examples accompanying Interpretation 17, paragraph IE4 is amended as follows (new text is underlined and deleted text is struck through):

IE4　However, if Company A distributes to its shareholders shares of Subsidiary B representing only a non-controlling interest in Subsidiary B and retains control of Subsidiary B, the transaction is not within the scope of the Interpretation. Company A accounts for the distribution in accordance with ~~AASB 127~~ <u>AASB 10</u> *Consolidated ~~and Separate~~ Financial Statements* ~~(as amended in 2008)~~. Company A controls Company B both before and after the transaction.

Amendments to Australian Accounting Standards arising   **1533**
from the Consolidation and Joint Arrangements Standards

AASB

Appendix

Early Application of the Consolidation and Joint Arrangements Standards

This Appendix is an integral part of this Standard.

A1   Australian Accounting Standards AASB 10 *Consolidated Financial Statements*, AASB 11 *Joint Arrangements*, AASB 12 *Disclosure of Interests in Other Entities*, AASB 127 *Separate Financial Statements* (August 2011) and AASB 128 *Investments in Associates and Joint Ventures* (August 2011) may be applied early to annual reporting periods beginning on or after 1 January 2005 but before 1 January 2013. The amendments set out in paragraphs 9-66 of this Standard also apply to all the versions of the pronouncements applicable to such periods when AASB 10, AASB 11, AASB 12, AASB 127 (August 2011) and AASB 128 (August 2011) are applied early, with the exception of:

    (a)   AASB 3 *Business Combinations* (July 2004, as amended);

    (b)   AASB 7 *Financial Instruments: Disclosures*;

    (c)   AASB 132 *Financial Instruments: Presentation*;

    (d)   [deleted];

    (e)   AASB 1023 *General Insurance Contracts*; and

    (f)   AASB 1038 *Life Insurance Contracts*.

    The early-application amendments to those Standards (other than AASB 3) are set out in this Appendix. The amendments are presented in relation to the annual reporting periods to which various versions of those Standards apply mandatorily. However, most versions may also be applied to earlier annual reporting periods as stated in each version.

A2   [deleted]

Amendments to AASB 7

A3   Paragraph 3(a) is amended (new text is underlined and deleted text is struck through) and paragraph 44O is added to the versions of AASB 7 that apply to annual reporting periods beginning on or after 1 January 2007 but before 1 January 2009, as follows:

    3   **This Standard shall be applied by all entities to all types of financial instruments, except:**

       (a)   **those interests in subsidiaries, associates or joint ventures that are accounted for in accordance with <u>AASB 10 *Consolidated Financial Statements*,</u> AASB 127** ~~Consolidated and~~ **Separate Financial Statements** ~~,~~ **<u>or</u> AASB 128** *Investments in Associates <u>and Joint Ventures</u>* ~~or AASB 131 Interests in Joint Ventures~~**. However, in some cases, AASB 127** ~~,~~ **<u>or</u> AASB 128** ~~or AASB 131~~ **permits an entity to account for an interest in a subsidiary, associate or joint venture using AASB 139; in those cases, entities shall apply the disclosure requirements in <u>AASB 12</u>** <u>*Disclosure of Interests in Other Entities*</u> **or AASB 127** ~~, AASB 128 or AASB 131~~ **in addition to those in this Standard. ...**

    44O   AASB 2011-7 *Amendments to Australian Accounting Standards arising from the Consolidation and Joint Arrangements Standards*, issued in August 2011, amended paragraph 3. An entity shall apply that amendment when it applies AASB 10 and AASB 11 *Joint Arrangements*.

A4   [deleted]

Amendment to AASB 9 (December 2009)

A5   [deleted]

Amendments to AASB 2009-11

A6-A7   [deleted]

Amendments to AASB 132

A8 Paragraphs 4(a) and AG29 are amended to read as follows and paragraph 97I is added to the versions of AASB 132 that apply to annual reporting periods beginning on or after 1 January 2005 but before 1 January 2009:

4 **This Standard shall be applied by all entities to all types of financial instruments except:**

(a) **those interests in subsidiaries, associates or joint ventures that are accounted for in accordance with AASB 10** *Consolidated Financial Statements*, **AASB 127** *Separate Financial Statements* **or AASB 128** *Investments in Associates and Joint Ventures*. **However, in some cases, AASB 127 or AASB 128 permits an entity to account for an interest in a subsidiary, associate or joint venture using AASB 139; in those cases, entities shall apply the disclosure requirements in AASB 12** *Disclosure of Interests in Other Entities* **or AASB 127 in addition to those in this Standard. ...**

97I AASB 2011-7 *Amendments to Australian Accounting Standards arising from the Consolidation and Joint Arrangements Standards*, issued in August 2011, amended paragraphs 4(a) and AG29. An entity shall apply those amendments when it applies AASB 10 and AASB 11 *Joint Arrangements*.

AG29 In consolidated financial statements, an entity presents minority interests – that is, the interests of other parties in the equity and income of its subsidiaries – in accordance with AASB 101 and AASB 10. When classifying a financial instrument ...

A9 Paragraphs 4(a) and AG29 are amended to read as follows and paragraph 97I is added to the versions of AASB 132 that apply to annual reporting periods beginning on or after 1 January 2009 but before 1 July 2009, as follows:

4 **This Standard shall be applied by all entities to all types of financial instruments except:**

(a) **those interests in subsidiaries, associates or joint ventures that are accounted for in accordance with AASB 10** *Consolidated Financial Statements*, **AASB 127** *Separate Financial Statements* **or AASB 128** *Investments in Associates and Joint Ventures*. **However, in some cases, AASB 127 or AASB 128 permits an entity to account for an interest in a subsidiary, associate or joint venture using AASB 139; in those cases, ...**

97I AASB 2011-7 *Amendments to Australian Accounting Standards arising from the Consolidation and Joint Arrangements Standards*, issued in August 2011, amended paragraphs 4(a) and AG29. An entity shall apply those amendments when it applies AASB 10 and AASB 11 *Joint Arrangements*.

AG29 In consolidated financial statements, an entity presents ... the interests of other parties in the equity and income of its subsidiaries – in accordance with AASB 101 and AASB 10. When classifying a financial instrument ...

Amendments to AASB 139

A10-A12 [deleted]

Amendments to Australian Accounting Standards arising   **1535**
from the Consolidation and Joint Arrangements Standards

AASB

Amendments to AASB 1023

A13   Paragraph 15.5 is amended to read as follows in the versions of AASB 1023 that apply to annual reporting periods beginning on or after 1 January 2005 but before 1 January 2013:

> **15.5 When preparing** *separate financial statements*, **those investments in subsidiaries, joint ventures and associates that:**
>
>   **(a)**   **are defined by AASB 10** *Consolidated Financial Statements*, **AASB 11** *Joint Arrangements* **and AASB 128** *Investments in Associates and Joint Ventures*;
>
>   **(b)**   ...

A14   In paragraphs 15.5.1 and 15.5.2 in the versions of AASB 1023 that apply to annual reporting periods beginning on or after 1 January 2005 but before 1 January 2013, 'jointly controlled entities' is amended to 'joint ventures'.

Amendments to AASB 1038

A15   Paragraphs 10.5-10.7 are amended to read as follows in the versions of AASB 1038 that apply to annual reporting periods beginning on or after 1 January 2005 but before 1 January 2013:

> **10.5 Investments in associates that:**
>
>   **(a)**   **are defined by AASB 128** *Investments in Associates and Joint Ventures*;
>
>   **(b)**   ...
>
> 10.5.1 An insurer applies AASB 128 to its investments in associates. AASB 128 requires investments in associates to be accounted for using the equity method. When investments in associates are held by mutual funds, unit trusts and similar entities including investment-linked insurance funds, the investments in those associates are permitted to be measured at fair value through profit or loss in accordance with AASB 139.
>
> **10.6 Venturers' interests in joint ventures that:**
>
>   **(a)**   **are defined by AASB 11** *Joint Arrangements*;
>
>   **(b)**   ...
>
> 10.6.1 AASB 11 requires a joint venturer to recognise its interest in a joint venture as an investment and to account for that investment using the equity method in accordance with AASB 128 unless exempted from applying that method. Mutual funds, unit trusts and similar entities including investment-linked insurance funds are permitted to measure investments in joint ventures at fair value through profit or loss in accordance with AASB 139.
>
> **10.7 When preparing** *separate financial statements*, **those investments in subsidiaries, joint ventures and associates that:**
>
>   **(a)**   **are within the scope of AASB 127** *Separate Financial Statements*;
>
>   **(b)**   ...

A16   In paragraphs 10.7.1 and 10.7.2 in the versions of AASB 1038 that apply to annual reporting periods beginning on or after 1 January 2005 but before 1 January 2013, 'jointly controlled entities' is amended to 'joint ventures'.

AASB 2011-8

Amendments to Australian Accounting Standards arising from AASB 13

[AASB 1, 2, 3, 4, 5, 7, 9, 101, 102, 108, 110, 116, 117, 118, 119, 120, 121, 128, 131, 132, 133, 134, 136, 138, 139, 140, 141, 1004, 1023 & 1038 and Interpretations 2, 4, 12, 13, 14, 17, 19, 131 & 132]

(Issued November 2012)

Note from the Institute of Chartered Accountants Australia

This note, prepared by the technical editors, is not part of Accounting Standard AASB 2011-8.

Historical development

2 September 2011: AASB 2011-8 was issued amending AASB 1, 2, 3, 4, 5, 7, 9, 2009-11, 2010-7, 101, 102, 108, 110, 116, 117, 118, 119, 120, 121, 128, 131, 132, 133, 134, 136, 138, 139, 140, 141, 1004, 1023 & 1038 and Interpretations 2, 4, 12, 13, 14, 17, 19, 131 & 132 arising from the issue of AASB 13 'Fair Value Measurement'. AASB 13 defines 'fair value' and the requirements when measuring the fair value of assets and liabilties.

This Standard is applicable to annual reporting periods beginning on or after 1 January 2013 with early adoption permitted.

5 September 2011: AASB 2011-10 'Amendments to Australian Accounting Standards arising from AASB 119 (September 2011)' amends AASB 2011-8 consequential to the issue of AASB 119. This Standard is applicable to annual reporting periods beginning on or after 1 January 2013 and can be adopted early.

10 September 2012: AASB 2012-6 'Amendments to Australian Accounting Standards – Mandatory Effective Date of AASB 9 and Transition Disclosures' amends AASB 2011-8 consequential to the change to the mandatory effective date of AASB 9 to annual reporting periods beginning on or after 1 January 2015 instead of 1 January 2013.

16 November 2012: AASB 2011-8 was reissued by the AASB, compiled to include the AASB 2011-10 and AASB 2012-6 amendments. This Standard is applicable to annual reporting periods beginning on or after 1 January 2013 and can be adopted early.

Contents

Compilation Details

**Accounting Standard
AASB 2011-8 Amendments to Australian Accounting Standards
arising from AASB 13**

	Paragraphs
Objective	1
Application	2 – 11
Change in Definition	12 – 13
Amendments to AASB 1	14 – 16
Amendment to AASB 2	17
Amendments to AASB 3	18 – 20
Amendment to AASB 4	21
Amendment to AASB 5	22
Amendments to AASB 7	23 – 27
Amendments to AASB 101	38 – 39
Amendments to AASB 102	40 – 41
Amendments to AASB 108	42 – 43
Amendments to AASB 110	44 – 45
Amendments to AASB 116	46 – 49
Amendment to AASB 117	50
Amendment to AASB 118	51
Amendments to AASB 119	52 – 53
Amendment to AASB 120	54
Amendments to AASB 121	55 – 56
Amendments to AASB 132	57 – 59
Amendments to AASB 133	60 – 62
Amendments to AASB 134	63 – 66
Amendments to AASB 136	67 – 75
Amendments to AASB 138	76 – 83
Amendments to AASB 139	84 – 86
Amendments to AASB 140	87 – 95
Amendments to AASB 141	96 – 100
Amendments to AASB 1004	101 – 102
Amendment to AASB 1023	103
Amendment to AASB 1038	104
Amendments to Interpretation 2	105 – 108
Amendments to Interpretation 4	109 – 110
Amendments to Interpretation 12	111
Amendments to Interpretation 13	112 – 117
Amendments to Interpretation 14	118
Amendments to Interpretation 17	119 – 121

AASB

	Paragraphs
Amendments to Interpretation 19	122 – 125
Amendment to Interpretation 131	126
Amendment to Interpretation 132	127

Appendix: Early Application of AASB 13

Implementation Guidance – Amendments
(available on the AASB website)

Bases For Conclusions – Amendments
(available on the AASB website)

Australian Accounting Standard AASB 2011-8 *Amendments to Australian Accounting Standards arising from AASB 13* (as amended) is set out in paragraphs 1 – 127 and the Appendix. All the paragraphs have equal authority.

Compilation Details

Accounting Standard AASB 2011-8 *Amendments to Australian Accounting Standards arising from AASB 13* as amended

This compiled Standard applies to annual reporting periods beginning on or after 1 January 2013. It takes into account amendments up to and including 10 September 2012 and was prepared on 16 November 2012 by the staff of the Australian Accounting Standards Board (AASB).

This compilation is not a separate Accounting Standard made by the AASB. Instead, it is a representation of AASB 2011-8 (September 2011) as amended by other Accounting Standards, which are listed in the Table below.

Table of Standards

Standard	Date made	Application date *(annual reporting periods ... on or after ...)*	Application, saving or transitional provisions
AASB 2011-8	2 Sep 2011	(beginning) 1 Jan 2013	see (a) below
AASB 2011-10	5 Sep 2011	(beginning) 1 Jan 2013	see (b) below
AASB 2012-6	10 Sep 2012	(beginning) 1 Jan 2013	see (b) below

(a) Entities may elect to apply this Standard to annual reporting periods beginning on or after 1 January 2005 but before 1 January 2013, with certain exceptions.

(b) Entities may elect to apply this Standard to annual reporting periods beginning on or after 1 January 2005 but before 1 January 2013, provided that AASB 119 Employee Benefits (September 2011) is also applied to such periods.

(c) Entities may elect to apply this Standard to annual reporting periods ending on or after 31 December 2009 that begin before 1 January 2013, with certain exceptions.

Table of Amendments

Paragraph affected	How affected	By ... [paragraph]
1	amended	AASB 2012-6 [39]
10	amended	AASB 2012-6 [40]
16	amended	AASB 2012-6 [42, 43]
25	amended	AASB 2012-6 [45]

Paragraph affected	How affected	By ... [paragraph]
25A	added	AASB 2012-6 [46]
26	amended	AASB 2012-6 [47]
28-37	deleted	AASB 2012-6 [39]
52-53	amended	AASB 2011-10 [22]
57	amended	AASB 2012-6 [49]
84-86	amended	AASB 2012-6 [51]
86A	added	AASB 2012-6 [51]
108	amended	AASB 2012-6 [53]
123	amended	AASB 2012-6 [55]
A2	amended	AASB 2012-6 [41]
A3	deleted	AASB 2012-6 [39]
A5	deleted	AASB 2012-6 [44]
A7	deleted	AASB 2012-6 [44]
A8-A9	deleted	AASB 2012-6 [48]
A11	deleted	AASB 2012-6 [48]
A12-A25	deleted	AASB 2012-6 [39]
A28	deleted	AASB 2012-6 [50]
A29-A30	deleted	AASB 2012-6 [52]
A32	deleted	AASB 2012-6 [52]
A34	deleted	AASB 2012-6 [52]
A35	deleted	AASB 2012-6 [54]
A36	deleted	AASB 2012-6 [56]

Accounting Standard AASB 2011-8

The Australian Accounting Standards Board made Accounting Standard AASB 2011-8 *Amendments to Australian Accounting Standards arising from AASB 13* under section 334 of the *Corporations Act 2001* on 2 September 2011.

This compiled version of AASB 2011-8 applies to annual reporting periods beginning on or after 1 January 2013. It incorporates relevant amendments contained in other AASB Standards made by the AASB up to and including 10 September 2012 (see Compilation Details).

Accounting Standard AASB 2011-8

Amendments to Australian Accounting Standards arising from AASB 13

Objective

1   The objective of this Standard is to make amendments to:

(a)   AASB 1 *First-time Adoption of Australian Accounting Standards*;

(b)   AASB 2 *Share-based Payment*;

(c)   AASB 3 *Business Combinations*;

(d)   AASB 4 *Insurance Contracts*;

(e)   AASB 5 *Non-current Assets Held for Sale and Discontinued Operations*;

(f)   AASB 7 *Financial Instruments: Disclosures*;

(g)-(j) [deleted]

(k)   AASB 101 *Presentation of Financial Statements*;

(l)   AASB 102 *Inventories*;

(m)   AASB 108 *Accounting Policies, Changes in Accounting Estimates and Errors*;

(n)   AASB 110 *Events after the Reporting Period*;

(o)   AASB 116 *Property, Plant and Equipment*;

(p)   AASB 117 *Leases*;

(q)   AASB 118 *Revenue*;

(r)   AASB 119 *Employee Benefits*;

(s)   AASB 120 *Accounting for Government Grants and Disclosure of Government Assistance*;

(t)   AASB 121 *The Effects of Changes in Foreign Exchange Rates*;

(u)   AASB 128 *Investments in Associates*;

(v)   AASB 131 *Interests in Joint Ventures*;

(w)   AASB 132 *Financial Instruments: Presentation*;

(x)   AASB 133 *Earnings per Share*;

(y)   AASB 134 *Interim Financial Reporting*;

(z)   AASB 136 *Impairment of Assets*;

(aa)   AASB 138 *Intangible Assets*;

(bb)   AASB 139 *Financial Instruments: Recognition and Measurement*;

(cc)   AASB 140 *Investment Property*;

(dd)   AASB 141 *Agriculture*;

(ee)   AASB 1004 *Contributions*;

(ff)   AASB 1023 *General Insurance Contracts*;

(gg)   AASB 1038 *Life Insurance Contracts*;

(hh)   Interpretation 2 *Members' Shares in Co-operative Entities and Similar Instruments*;

(ii)   Interpretation 4 *Determining whether an Arrangement contains a Lease*;

(jj)   Interpretation 12 *Service Concession Arrangements*;

(kk)   Interpretation 13 *Customer Loyalty Programmes*;

(ll)   Interpretation 14 *AASB 119 – The Limit on a Defined Benefit Asset, Minimum Funding Requirements and their Interaction*;

(mm)   Interpretation 17 *Distributions of Non-cash Assets to Owners*;

(nn)   Interpretation 19 *Extinguishing Financial Liabilities with Equity Instruments*;

(oo)   Interpretation 131 *Revenue – Barter Transactions Involving Advertising Services*; and

(pp)   Interpretation 132 *Intangible Assets – Web Site Costs*;

as a consequence of the issuance of AASB 13 *Fair Value Measurement* in September 2011.

Application

2   **Subject to paragraphs 3–8, this Standard applies to:**

    (a)   **each entity that is required to prepare financial reports in accordance with Part 2M.3 of the Corporations Act and that is a reporting entity;**

    (b)   **general purpose financial statements of each other reporting entity; and**

    (c)   **financial statements that are, or are held out to be, general purpose financial statements.**

3   **In respect of AASB 101 and AASB 108, this Standard applies to:**

    (a)   **each entity that is required to prepare financial reports in accordance with Part 2M.3 of the Corporations Act;**

   (b)   general purpose financial statements of each reporting entity; and

   (c)   financial statements that are, or are held out to be, general purpose financial statements.

4   In respect of AASB 120, this Standard applies to:

   (a)   each for-profit entity that is required to prepare financial reports in accordance with Part 2M.3 of the Corporations Act and that is a reporting entity;

   (b)   general purpose financial statements of each other for-profit reporting entity; and

   (c)   financial statements of a for-profit entity that are, or are held out to be, general purpose financial statements.

5   In respect of AASB 133, this Standard applies to each entity that is required to prepare financial reports in accordance with Part 2M.3 of the Corporations Act and that is:

   (a)   a reporting entity whose ordinary shares or potential ordinary shares are publicly traded; or

   (b)   a reporting entity that is in the process of issuing ordinary shares or potential ordinary shares in public markets; or

   (c)   an entity that discloses earnings per share.

6   In respect of AASB 134, this Standard applies to:

   (a)   each disclosing entity required to prepare half-year financial reports in accordance with Part 2M.3 of the Corporations Act;

   (b)   interim financial reports that are general purpose financial statements of each other reporting entity; and

   (c)   interim financial reports that are, or are held out to be, general purpose financial statements.

7   In respect of AASB 1004, this Standard applies to:

   (a)   each not-for-profit entity that is required to prepare financial reports in accordance with Part 2M.3 of the Corporations Act and that is a reporting entity;

   (b)   general purpose financial statements of each other not-for-profit entity that is a reporting entity;

   (c)   financial statements of not-for-profit entities that are, or are held out to be, general purpose financial statements; and

   (d)   financial statements of General Government Sectors (GGSs) prepared in accordance with AASB 1049 *Whole of Government and General Government Sector Financial Reporting*.

8   In respect of AASB 1038, this Standard applies to each entity that is:

   (a)   a life insurer; or

   (b)   the parent in a group that includes a life insurer;

when the entity:

   (c)   is a reporting entity that is required to prepare financial reports in accordance with Part 2M.3 of the Corporations Act;

   (d)   is an other reporting entity and prepares general purpose financial statements; or

   (e)   prepares financial statements that are, or are held out to be, general purpose financial statements.

9   This Standard applies to annual reporting periods beginning on or after 1 January 2013.

[Note: For application dates of paragraphs changed or added by an amending Standard, see Compilation Details.]

10   This Standard shall be applied when AASB 13 is applied. This Standard may be applied to annual reporting periods beginning on or after 1 January 2005 but before 1 January 2013, except that the amendments to AASB 3 may be applied early only to annual reporting periods beginning on or after 30 June 2007 but before 1 January 2013. If an entity applies this Standard to an annual reporting period beginning on or after 1 January 2005 but before 1 January 2013, it shall disclose that fact and apply AASB 13 at the same time.

11   This Standard uses underlining, striking out and other typographical material to identify some of the amendments to a Standard or an Interpretation, in order to make the amendments more understandable. However, the amendments made by this Standard do not include that underlining, striking out or other typographical material.

Change in Definition

12   In AASB 1, AASB 3, AASB 4, AASB 5, AASB 9, AASB 1023 and AASB 1038, the definition of 'fair value' is replaced with:

> *Fair value* is the price that would be received to sell an asset or paid to transfer a liability in an orderly transaction between market participants at the measurement date. (See AASB 13.)

13   In AASB 102, AASB 116, AASB 118, AASB 119, AASB 120, AASB 121, AASB 132 and AASB 140, the definition of 'fair value' is replaced with:

> *Fair value* is the price that would be received to sell an asset or paid to transfer a liability in an orderly transaction between market participants at the measurement date. (See AASB 13 *Fair Value Measurement*.)

Amendments to AASB 1

14   Paragraph 19 is deleted.

15   Paragraph 39J is added as follows:

> 39J   AASB 2011-8 *Amendments to Australian Accounting Standards arising from AASB 13*, issued in September 2011, deleted paragraph 19, amended the definition of fair value in Appendix A and amended paragraphs D15 and D20. An entity shall apply those amendments when it applies AASB 13 *Fair Value Measurement*.

16   Paragraphs D15 and D20 are amended as follows (new text is underlined and deleted text is struck through):

> D15   If a first-time adopter measures such an investment at cost in accordance with AASB 127, it shall measure that investment at one of the following amounts in its separate opening Australian-Accounting-Standards statement of financial position:
>
> (a)   ...
>
> (b)   deemed cost. The deemed cost of such an investment shall be its:
>
> > (i)   fair value ~~(determined in accordance with AASB 139)~~ at the entity's date of transition to Australian Accounting Standards in its separate financial statements; or
> >
> > (ii)   ...
>
> D20   Notwithstanding the requirements of paragraphs 7 and 9, an entity may apply the requirements in ~~the last sentence~~ paragraph AG76(a) of AASB 139 ~~paragraph AG76 and in paragraph AG76A~~ prospectively to transactions entered into on or after the date of transition to Australian Accounting Standards.

AASB

Amendment to AASB 2

17   Paragraph 6A is added as follows:

    6A   This Standard uses the term 'fair value' in a way that differs in some respects from the definition of fair value in AASB 13 *Fair Value Measurement*. Therefore, when applying AASB 2 an entity measures fair value in accordance with this Standard, not AASB 13.

Amendments to AASB 3

18   Paragraphs 20, 29, 33 and 47 are amended as follows (new text is underlined and deleted text is struck through):

    20   ~~Paragraphs B41–B45 provide guidance on measuring the fair value of particular identifiable assets and a non-controlling interest in an acquiree.~~ Paragraphs 24–31 specify the types of identifiable assets and liabilities that include items for which this Standard provides limited exceptions to the measurement principle.

    29   The acquirer shall measure the value of a reacquired right recognised as an intangible asset on the basis of the remaining contractual term of the related contract regardless of whether market participants would consider potential contractual renewals ~~in determining~~ <u>when measuring</u> its fair value. Paragraphs B35 and B36 provide related application guidance.

    33   … To determine the amount of goodwill in a business combination in which no consideration is transferred, the acquirer shall use the acquisition-date fair value of the acquirer's interest in the acquiree ~~determined using a valuation technique~~ in place of the acquisition-date fair value of the consideration transferred (paragraph 32(a)(i)). …

    47   … For example, unless an intervening event that changed its fair value can be identified, the sale of an asset to a third party shortly after the acquisition date for an amount that differs significantly from its provisional fair value ~~determined~~ <u>measured</u> at that date is likely to indicate an error in the provisional amount.

19   Paragraph 64F is added as follows:

    64F   AASB 2011-8 *Amendments to Australian Accounting Standards arising from AASB 13*, issued in September 2011, amended paragraphs 20, 29, 33, 47, amended the definition of fair value in Appendix A and amended paragraphs B22, B40, B43–B46, B49 and B64. An entity shall apply those amendments when it applies AASB 13 *Fair Value Measurement*.

20   In Appendix B, paragraphs B22 and B40, B43–B46, B49 and B64 are amended as follows (new text is underlined and deleted text is struck through):

    B22   Because the consolidated financial statements represent the continuation of the financial statements of the legal subsidiary except for its capital structure, the consolidated financial statements reflect:

        (a)   …

        (d)   the amount recognised as issued equity interests in the consolidated financial statements determined by adding the issued equity interest of the legal subsidiary (the accounting acquirer) outstanding immediately before the business combination to the fair value of the legal parent (accounting acquiree) ~~determined in accordance with this Standard~~. However, …

        (e)   …

    B40   The identifiability criteria determine whether an intangible asset is recognised separately from goodwill. However, the criteria neither provide guidance for measuring the fair value of an intangible asset nor restrict the assumptions used in ~~estimating~~ <u>measuring</u> the fair value of an intangible asset. For example, the acquirer would take into account <u>the</u> assumptions that market participants would ~~consider~~ <u>use when pricing the intangible asset</u>, such as expectations of future contract renewals, in measuring fair value. …

B43 ~~For~~ To protect its competitive <u>position</u>, or <u>for</u> other reasons, the acquirer may intend not to use an acquired <u>non-financial</u> asset <u>actively</u>, ~~for example, a research and development intangible asset~~, or it may <u>not</u> intend to use the asset ~~in a way that is different from the way in which other market participants would use it~~ <u>according to its highest and best use. For example, that might be the case for an acquired research and development intangible asset that the acquirer plans to use defensively by preventing others from using it.</u> Nevertheless, the acquirer shall measure the <u>fair value of the non-financial</u> asset ~~at fair value determined in accordance with~~ <u>assuming</u> its <u>highest and best</u> use by ~~other~~ market participants <u>in accordance with the appropriate valuation premise, both initially and when measuring fair value less costs of disposal for subsequent impairment testing.</u>

B44 This Standard allows the acquirer to measure a non-controlling interest in the acquiree at its fair value at the acquisition date. Sometimes an acquirer will be able to measure the acquisition-date fair value of a non-controlling interest on the basis of <u>a quoted price in an</u> active market ~~prices~~ for the equity shares (<u>i.e. those</u> not held by the acquirer<u>).</u> In other situations, however, <u>a quoted price in</u> an active market ~~price~~ for the equity shares will not be available. In those situations, the acquirer would measure the fair value of the non-controlling interest using <u>an</u>other valuation technique<u>s</u>.

B45 The fair values of the acquirer's interest in the acquiree and the non-controlling interest on a per-share basis might differ. The main difference is likely to be the inclusion of a control premium in the per-share fair value of the acquirer's interest in the acquiree or, conversely, the inclusion of a discount for lack of control (also referred to as a ~~minority~~ <u>non-controlling interest</u> discount) in the per-share fair value of the non-controlling interest <u>if market participants would take into account such a premium or discount when pricing the non-controlling interest</u>.

B46 In a business combination achieved without the transfer of consideration, the acquirer must substitute the acquisition-date fair value of its interest in the acquiree for the acquisition-date fair value of the consideration transferred to measure goodwill or a gain on a bargain purchase (see paragraphs 32–34). ~~The acquirer should measure the acquisition-date fair value of its interest in the acquiree using one or more valuation techniques that are appropriate in the circumstances and for which sufficient data are available. If more than one valuation technique is used, the acquirer should evaluate the results of the techniques, considering the relevance and reliability of the inputs used and the extent of the available data.~~

B49 A fair value measurement of a mutual entity should include the assumptions that market participants would make about future member benefits as well as any other relevant assumptions market participants would make about the mutual entity. For example, ~~an estimated cash flow model~~ <u>a present value technique</u> may be used to ~~determine~~ <u>measure</u> the fair value of a mutual entity. The cash flows used as inputs to the model should be based on the expected cash flows of the mutual entity, which are likely to reflect reductions for member benefits, such as reduced fees charged for goods and services.

B64 To meet the objective in paragraph 59, the acquirer shall disclose the following information for each business combination that occurs during the reporting period:

(a)   …

(f)   the acquisition-date fair value of the total consideration transferred and the acquisition-date fair value of each major class of consideration, such as:

  (i)   …

  (iv)   equity interests of the acquirer, including the number of instruments or interests issued or issuable and the method of ~~determining~~ <u>measuring</u> the fair value of those instruments or interests.

(g)   …

(o)   for each business combination in which the acquirer holds less than 100 per cent of the equity interests in the acquiree at the acquisition date:

        (i)   ...

        (ii)   for each non-controlling interest in an acquiree measured at fair value, the valuation technique(s) and ~~key model~~ significant inputs used ~~for determining~~ to measure that value.

    (p)   ...

Amendment to AASB 4

21   Paragraph 41E is added as follows:

    41E   AASB 2011-8 *Amendments to Australian Accounting Standards arising from AASB 13*, issued in September 2011, amended the definition of fair value in Appendix A. An entity shall apply that amendment when it applies AASB 13 *Fair Value Measurement*.

Amendment to AASB 5

22   Paragraph 44H is added as follows:

    44H   AASB 2011-8 *Amendments to Australian Accounting Standards arising from AASB 13*, issued in September 2011, amended the definition of fair value in Appendix A. An entity shall apply that amendment when it applies AASB 13 *Fair Value Measurement*.

Amendments to AASB 7

23   Paragraph 3 is amended as follows (new text is underlined):

    3   **This Standard shall be applied by all entities to all types of financial instruments, except:**

        (a)   **... in those cases, entities shall apply the requirements of this Standard and, for those interests measured at fair value, the requirements of AASB 13** *Fair Value Measurement*. **...**

        (b)   **...**

24   Paragraphs 27–27B are deleted.

25   Paragraph 28 is amended as follows (new text is underlined and deleted text is struck through):

    28   ~~If the market for a financial instrument is not active, an entity establishes its fair value using a valuation technique (see paragraphs AG74–AG79 of AASB 139). Nevertheless, the best evidence of fair value at initial recognition is the transaction price (i.e. the fair value of the consideration given or received), unless conditions described in paragraph AG76 of AASB 139 are met. It follows that there could be a difference between the fair value at initial recognition and the amount that would be determined at that date using the valuation technique. If such a difference exists, an entity shall disclose, by class of financial instrument:~~ In some cases, an entity does not recognise a gain or loss on initial recognition of a financial asset or financial liability because the fair value is neither evidenced by a quoted price in an active market for an identical asset or liability (i.e. a Level 1 input) nor based on a valuation technique that uses only data from observable markets (see paragraph AG76 of AASB 139). In such cases, the entity shall disclose by class of financial asset or financial liability:

        (a)   its accounting policy for recognising in profit or loss the ~~that~~ difference between the fair value at initial recognition and the transaction price ~~in profit or loss~~ to reflect a change in factors (including time) that market participants would ~~consider in setting a price~~ take into account when pricing the asset or liability (see paragraph ~~AG76A~~ AG76(b) of AASB 139). ~~; and~~

        (b)   ...

        (c)   why the entity concluded that the transaction price was not the best evidence of fair value, including a description of the evidence that supports the fair value.

25A Paragraph 29 is amended as follows (new text is underlined and deleted text is struck through):

   29   Disclosures of fair value are not required:

   (a)   ...

   (b)   for an investment in equity instruments that do not have a quoted ~~market price~~ in an active market for an identical instrument (i.e. a Level 1 input), or derivatives linked to such equity instruments, that is measured at cost in accordance with AASB 139 because its fair value cannot otherwise be measured reliably; or

   (c)   ...

26 Paragraph 44P is added as follows:

   44P   AASB 2011-8 *Amendments to Australian Accounting Standards arising from AASB 13*, issued in September 2011, amended paragraphs 3, 28 and 29 and Appendix A and deleted paragraphs 27–27B. An entity shall apply those amendments when it applies AASB 13.

27 In Appendix A, the definition of 'other price risk' is amended as follows (new text is underlined and deleted text is struck through):

   other price risk   The risk that the fair value or future cash flows of a financial instrument will fluctuate because of changes in market prices (other than those arising from **interest rate risk** or **currency risk**), whether those changes are caused by factors specific to the individual financial instrument or its issuer~~,~~ or by factors affecting all similar financial instruments traded in the market.

Amendments to AASB 9 (December 2010)

28-37 [deleted]

Amendments to AASB 101

38 Paragraphs 128 and 133 are amended as follows (new text is underlined and deleted text is struck through):

   128   The disclosures in paragraph 125 are not required for assets and liabilities with a significant risk that their carrying amounts might change materially within the next financial year if, at the end of the reporting period, they are measured at fair value based on ~~recently observed market prices~~ a quoted price in an active market for an identical asset or liability. Such fair values might change materially within the next financial year but these changes would not arise from assumptions or other sources of estimation uncertainty at the end of the reporting period.

   133   Other Australian Accounting Standards require the disclosure of some of the assumptions that would otherwise be required in accordance with paragraph 125. For example, AASB 137 requires disclosure, in specified circumstances, of major assumptions concerning future events affecting classes of provisions. ~~AASB 7~~ AASB 13 *Fair Value Measurement* requires disclosure of significant assumptions (including the valuation technique(s) and inputs) the entity uses when measuring ~~in estimating~~ the fair values of ~~financial~~ assets and financial liabilities that are carried at fair value. ~~AASB 116 requires disclosure of significant assumptions that the entity uses in estimating the fair values of revalued items of property, plant and equipment.~~

39 Paragraph 139I is added as follows:

   139I   AASB 2011-8 *Amendments to Australian Accounting Standards arising from AASB 13*, issued in September 2011, amended paragraphs 128 and 133. An entity shall apply those amendments when it applies AASB 13.

Amendments to AASB 102

40   Paragraph 7 is amended as follows (new text is underlined and deleted text is struck through):

> 7   Net realisable value refers to the net amount that an entity expects to realise from the sale of inventory in the ordinary course of business. ~~Fair value reflects the amount for which the same inventory could be exchanged between knowledgeable and willing buyers and sellers in the marketplace.~~ <u>Fair value reflects the price at which an orderly transaction to sell the same inventory in the principal (or most advantageous) market for that inventory would take place between market participants at the measurement date.</u> The former is an entity-specific value; the latter is not. Net realisable value for inventories may not equal fair value less costs to sell.

41   Paragraph 40C is added as follows:

> 40C   AASB 2011-8 *Amendments to Australian Accounting Standards arising from AASB 13*, issued in September 2011, amended the definition of fair value in paragraph 6 and amended paragraph 7. An entity shall apply those amendments when it applies AASB 13.

Amendments to AASB 108

42   Paragraph 52 is amended as follows (new text is underlined and deleted text is struck through):

> 52   Therefore, retrospectively applying a new accounting policy or correcting a prior period error requires distinguishing information that:
>
> (a)   provides evidence of circumstances that existed on the date(s) as at which the transaction, other event or condition occurred; and
>
> (b)   would have been available when the financial statements for that prior period were authorised for issue;
>
> from other information. For some types of estimates (e.g. ~~an estimate~~ of a fair value <u>measurement that uses significant unobservable</u> ~~not based on an observable price or observable~~ inputs), it is impracticable to distinguish these types of information. When retrospective application or retrospective restatement would require making a significant estimate for which it is impossible to distinguish these two types of information, it is impracticable to apply the new accounting policy or correct the prior period error retrospectively.

43   Paragraph 54C is added as follows:

> 54C   AASB 2011-8 *Amendments to Australian Accounting Standards arising from AASB 13*, issued in September 2011, amended paragraph 52. An entity shall apply that amendment when it applies AASB 13 *Fair Value Measurement*.

Amendments to AASB 110

44   In paragraph 11, 'market value' is amended to 'fair value'.

45   Paragraph 23A is added as follows:

> 23A   AASB 2011-8 *Amendments to Australian Accounting Standards arising from AASB 13*, issued in September 2011, amended paragraph 11. An entity shall apply that amendment when it applies AASB 13 *Fair Value Measurement*.

Amendments to AASB 116

46   Paragraph 26 is amended as follows (new text is underlined and deleted text is struck through):

> 26   The fair value of an asset ~~for which comparable market transactions do not exist~~ is reliably measurable if (a) the variability in the range of reasonable fair value ~~estimates~~ <u>measurements</u> is not significant for that asset or (b) the probabilities of the various estimates within the range can be reasonably assessed and used ~~in estimating~~ <u>when measuring</u> fair value. If an entity is able to ~~determine~~ <u>measure</u>

reliably the fair value of either the asset received or the asset given up, then the fair value of the asset given up is used to measure the cost of the asset received unless the fair value of the asset received is more clearly evident.

47   Paragraphs 32 and 33 are deleted.

48   Paragraphs 35 and 77 are amended as follows (new text is underlined and deleted text is struck through):

35   When an item of property, plant and equipment is revalued, any accumulated depreciation at the date of the revaluation is treated in one of the following ways:

(a)   restated proportionately with the change in the gross carrying amount of the asset so that the carrying amount of the asset after revaluation equals its revalued amount. This method is often used when an asset is revalued by means of applying an index to determine its ~~depreciated~~ replacement cost (see AASB 13); or

(b)   ...

77   **If items of property, plant and equipment are stated at revalued amounts, the following shall be disclosed <u>in addition to the disclosures required by AASB 13</u>:**

(a)   ...

(c)   [deleted by the IASB] ~~the methods and significant assumptions applied in estimating the items' fair values;~~

(d)   [deleted by the IASB] ~~the extent to which the items' fair values were determined directly by reference to observable prices in an active market or recent market transactions on arm's length terms or were estimated using other valuation techniques;~~

(e)   ...

49   Paragraph 81F is added as follows:

81F   AASB 2011-8 *Amendments to Australian Accounting Standards arising from AASB 13*, issued in September 2011, amended the definition of fair value in paragraph 6, amended paragraphs 26, 35 and 77 and deleted paragraphs 32 and 33. An entity shall apply those amendments when it applies AASB 13.

Amendment to AASB 117

50   Paragraph 6A is added as follows:

6A   AASB 117 uses the term 'fair value' in a way that differs in some respects from the definition of fair value in AASB 13 *Fair Value Measurement*. Therefore, when applying AASB 117 an entity measures fair value in accordance with AASB 117, not AASB 13.

Amendment to AASB 118

51   Paragraph 42 is added as follows:

42   AASB 2011-8 *Amendments to Australian Accounting Standards arising from AASB 13*, issued in September 2011, amended the definition of fair value in paragraph 7. An entity shall apply that amendment when it applies AASB 13.

Amendments to AASB 119

52   Paragraph 113 is amended as follows (new text is underlined and deleted text is struck through):

113   The fair value of any plan assets is deducted in determining the deficit or surplus. ~~When no market price is available, the fair value of plan assets is estimated; for example, by discounting expected future cash flows using a discount rate that reflects both the risk associated with the plan assets and the maturity or expected disposal date of those assets (or, if they have no maturity, the expected period until the settlement of the related obligation).~~

53   Paragraph 174 is added as follows:

    174   AASB 2011-8 *Amendments to Australian Accounting Standards arising from AASB 13*, issued in September 2011, amended the definition of fair value in paragraph 8 and amended paragraph 113. An entity shall apply those amendments when it applies AASB 13.

Amendment to AASB 120

54   Paragraph 45 is added as follows:

    45   AASB 2011-8 *Amendments to Australian Accounting Standards arising from AASB 13*, issued in September 2011, amended the definition of fair value in paragraph 3. An entity shall apply that amendment when it applies AASB 13.

Amendments to AASB 121

55   Paragraph 23(c) is amended as follows (new text is underlined and deleted text is struck through):

23   ...

    (c)   **non-monetary items that are measured at fair value in a foreign currency shall be translated using the exchange rates at the date when the fair value was** ~~determined~~ **measured.**

56   Paragraph 60G is added as follows:

    60G   AASB 2011-8 *Amendments to Australian Accounting Standards arising from AASB 13*, issued in September 2011, amended the definition of fair value in paragraph 8 and amended paragraph 23. An entity shall apply those amendments when it applies AASB 13.

Amendments to AASB 132

57   Paragraph 23 is amended as follows (new text is underlined and deleted text is struck through):

    23   ... One example is an entity's obligation under a forward contract to purchase its own equity instruments for cash. ~~When the~~ The financial liability is recognised initially at ~~under AASB 139, its~~ fair value ~~(~~the present value of the redemption amount~~)~~, and is reclassified from equity. ...

58   Paragraph 97J is added as follows:

    97J   AASB 2011-8 *Amendments to Australian Accounting Standards arising from AASB 13*, issued in September 2011, amended the definition of fair value in paragraph 11 and amended paragraphs 23 and AG31. An entity shall apply those amendments when it applies AASB 13.

59   In the Application Guidance, paragraph AG31 is amended as follows (deleted text is struck through):

    AG31 A common form of compound financial instrument is a debt instrument with an embedded conversion option, such as a bond convertible into ordinary shares of the issuer, and without any other embedded derivative features. Paragraph 28 requires the issuer of such a financial instrument to present the liability component and the equity component ... as follows:

    (a)   ...

    (b)   The equity instrument is an embedded option to convert the liability into equity of the issuer. ~~The fair value of the option comprises its time value and its intrinsic value, if any.~~ This option has value on initial recognition even when it is out of the money.

Amendments to AASB 133

60   Paragraphs 8 and 47A are amended as follows (new text is underlined and deleted text is struck through):

    8   Terms defined in AASB 132 *Financial Instruments: Presentation* are used in this Standard with the meanings specified in paragraph 11 of AASB 132, unless otherwise noted. AASB 132 defines financial instrument, financial asset, financial liability, and equity instrument and fair value, and provides guidance on applying those definitions. AASB 13 *Fair Value Measurement* defines fair value and sets out requirements for applying that definition.

    47A   For share options and other share-based payment arrangements to which AASB 2 *Share-based Payment* applies, the issue price referred to in paragraph 46 and the exercise price referred to in paragraph 47 shall include the fair value (measured in accordance with AASB 2) of any goods or services to be supplied to the entity in the future under the share option or other share-based payment arrangement.

61   Paragraph 74C is added as follows:

    74C   AASB 2011-8 *Amendments to Australian Accounting Standards arising from AASB 13*, issued in September 2011, amended paragraphs 8, 47A and A2. An entity shall apply those amendments when it applies AASB 13.

62   In Appendix A, paragraph A2 is amended as follows (new text is underlined and deleted text is struck through):

    A2   The issue of ordinary shares at the time of exercise or conversion of potential ordinary shares does not usually give rise to a bonus element. This is because the potential ordinary shares are usually issued for full fair value, resulting in a proportionate change in the resources available to the entity. In a rights issue, however, the exercise price is often less than the fair value of the shares. ... The theoretical ex-rights fair value per share is calculated by adding the aggregate market fair value of the shares immediately before the exercise of the rights to the proceeds from the exercise of the rights, and dividing by the number of shares outstanding after the exercise of the rights. Where the rights are to be publicly traded separately from the shares before the exercise date, fair value for the purposes of this calculation is established measured at the close of the last day on which the shares are traded together with the rights.

Amendments to AASB 134

63   Paragraph 16A is amended as follows (new text is underlined and deleted text is struck through):

    16A   In addition to disclosing significant events and transactions in accordance with paragraphs 15–15C, an entity shall include the following information, in the notes to its interim financial statements, if not disclosed elsewhere in the interim financial report. The information shall normally be reported on an annual reporting period-to-date basis.

        (a)   ...

        (h)   events after the interim period that have not been reflected in the financial statements for the interim period; and

        (i)   the effect of changes in the composition of the entity ... disclose the information required by AASB 3 *Business Combinations*:: and

        (j)   for financial instruments, the disclosures about fair value required by paragraphs 91–93(h), 94–96, 98 and 99 of AASB 13 *Fair Value Measurement* and paragraphs 25, 26 and 28–30 of AASB 7 *Financial Instruments: Disclosures*.

64   The heading 'Effective Date of IAS 34' before paragraph 46 is amended to 'Effective Date'.

65   Paragraph 50 is added as follows:

     50   AASB 2011-8 *Amendments to Australian Accounting Standards arising from AASB 13*, issued in September 2011, added paragraph 16A(j) and amended paragraphs C4 and C7 in the illustrative examples. An entity shall apply those amendments when it applies AASB 13.

66   In the Illustrative Examples accompanying AASB 134, paragraphs C4 and C7 are amended as follows (new text is underlined and deleted text is struck through):

     C4   **Pensions:** AASB 119 *Employee Benefits* requires ~~that~~ an entity <u>to</u> determine the present value of defined benefit obligations and the ~~market~~ <u>fair</u> value of plan assets at …

     C7   **Revaluations and fair value accounting:** AASB 116 *Property, Plant and Equipment* allows an entity to choose as its accounting policy the revaluation model whereby items of property, plant and equipment are revalued to fair value. Similarly, AASB 140 *Investment Property* requires an entity to ~~determine~~ <u>measure</u> the fair value of investment property. …

Amendments to AASB 136

67   In AASB 136 and the accompanying Illustrative Examples, all references to 'fair value less costs to sell' are replaced with 'fair value less costs of disposal', except in relation to AASB 141.

68   Paragraph 5 is amended as follows (new text is underlined and deleted text is struck through):

     5   This Standard does not apply to … investment property measured at fair value ~~in accordance with~~ <u>within the scope of</u> AASB 140, or biological assets related to agricultural activity measured at fair value … ~~in accordance with~~ <u>within the scope of</u> AASB 141. However, this Standard applies to assets that are carried at revalued amount (i.e. fair value <u>at the date of the revaluation less any subsequent accumulated depreciation and subsequent accumulated impairment losses</u>) in accordance with other Australian Accounting Standards, such as the revaluation models in AASB 116 *Property, Plant and Equipment* <u>and AASB 138 *Intangible Assets*. The only difference between an asset's fair value and its fair value less costs of disposal is the direct incremental costs attributable to the disposal of the asset.</u> ~~Identifying whether a revalued asset may be impaired depends on the basis used to determine fair value:~~

       (a)   ~~if the asset's fair value is its market value, the only difference between the asset's fair value and its fair value less costs to sell is the direct incremental costs to dispose of the asset:~~

          ~~(i)~~   ~~if~~ <u>If</u> the disposal costs are negligible, the recoverable amount of the revalued asset is necessarily close to, or greater than, its revalued amount ~~(i.e. fair value)~~. In this case, after the revaluation requirements have been applied, it is unlikely that the revalued asset is impaired and recoverable amount need not be estimated~~;~~.

          ~~(ii)~~   ~~if the disposal costs are not negligible, the fair value less costs to sell of the revalued asset is necessarily less than its fair value. Therefore, the revalued asset will be impaired if its value in use is less than its revalued amount (i.e. fair value). In this case, after the revaluation requirements have been applied, an entity applies this Standard to determine whether the asset may be impaired; and~~

       (b)   <u>[deleted by the IASB]</u> ~~if the asset's fair value is determined on a basis other than its market value, its revalued amount (i.e. fair value) may be greater or lower than its recoverable amount. Hence, after the revaluation requirements have been applied, an entity applies this Standard to determine whether the asset may be impaired.~~

  (c) If the disposal costs are not negligible, the fair value less costs of disposal of the revalued asset is necessarily less than its fair value. Therefore, the revalued asset will be impaired if its *value in use* is less than its revalued amount. In this case, after the revaluation requirements have been applied, an entity applies this Standard to determine whether the asset may be impaired.

69 Paragraph 6 is amended (new text is underlined and deleted text is struck through) as follows (as a consequence of the amendment to the definition of fair value less costs to sell, all references to 'fair value less costs to sell' in AASB 136 are replaced with 'fair value less costs of disposal'):

 6 **The following terms are used in this Standard with the meanings specified.**

  ~~An *active market* is a market in which all the following conditions exist:~~

   ~~(a) the items traded within the market are homogeneous;~~

   ~~(b) willing buyers and sellers can normally be found at any time; and~~

   ~~(c) prices are available to the public.~~

  ...

  Fair value ~~*less costs to sell*~~ **is the amount obtainable from the sale of an** ~~asset or cash-generating unit in an arm's length transaction between knowledgeable, willing parties, less the costs of disposal~~ **is the price that would be received to sell an asset or paid to transfer a liability in an orderly transaction between market participants at the measurement date. (See AASB 13** *Fair Value Measurement*.**)**

70 Paragraphs 12, 20 and 22 are amended as follows (new text is underlined and deleted text is struck through):

 12 **In assessing whether there is any indication that an asset may be impaired, an entity shall consider, as a minimum, the following indications:**

  External sources of information

  (a) ~~during the period,~~ **there are observable indications that the** ~~an~~ **asset's** ~~market~~ **value has declined** **during the period** **significantly more than would be expected as a result of the passage of time or normal use;**

  (b) ...

 20 It may be possible to ~~determine~~ measure fair value less costs ~~to sell~~ of disposal, even if ~~there is not~~ a quoted price in an active market for an identical asset ~~is not traded in an~~ *active market*. However, sometimes it will not be possible to ~~determine~~ measure fair value less costs ~~to sell~~ of disposal because there is no basis for making a reliable estimate of the ~~amount obtainable from the sale of the asset in an arm's length transaction between knowledgeable and willing parties~~ price at which an orderly transaction to sell the asset would take place between market participants at the measurement date under current market conditions. In this case, the entity may use the asset's value in use as its recoverable amount.

 22 Recoverable amount is determined for an individual asset ... unless either:

  (a) ...

  (b) the asset's value in use can be estimated to be close to its fair value less costs ~~to sell~~ of disposal and fair value less costs ~~to sell~~ of disposal can be ~~determined~~ measured.

71 Paragraphs 25–27 are deleted.

72 Paragraph 28 is amended as follows (new text is underlined and deleted text is struck through):

 28 Costs of disposal, other than those that have been recognised as liabilities, are deducted in ~~determining~~ measuring fair value less costs ~~to sell~~ of disposal. Examples ...

73   Paragraph 53A is added as follows:

    53A   Fair value differs from value in use. Fair value reflects the assumptions market participants would use when pricing the asset. In contrast, value in use reflects the effects of factors that may be specific to the entity and not applicable to entities in general. For example, fair value does not reflect any of the following factors to the extent that they would not be generally available to market participants:

        (a)   additional value derived from the grouping of assets (such as the creation of a portfolio of investment properties in different locations);

        (b)   synergies between the asset being measured and other assets;

        (c)   legal rights or legal restrictions that are specific only to the current owner of the asset; and

        (d)   tax benefits or tax burdens that are specific to the current owner of the asset.

74   Paragraphs 78, 105, 111, 130 and 134 are amended as follows (new text is underlined and deleted text is struck through):

    78   It may be necessary to consider some recognised liabilities to determine the recoverable amount of a cash-generating unit. This may occur if the disposal of a cash-generating unit would require the buyer to assume the liability. In this case, the fair value less costs ~~to sell~~ of disposal (or the estimated cash flow from ultimate disposal) of the cash-generating unit is the ~~estimated selling~~ price to sell ~~for~~ the assets of the cash-generating unit and the liability together, less the costs of disposal. To perform a meaningful comparison between the carrying amount of the cash-generating unit and its recoverable amount, the carrying amount of the liability is deducted in determining both the cash-generating unit's value in use and its carrying amount.

    105   **In allocating an impairment loss in accordance with paragraph 104, an entity shall not reduce the carrying amount of an asset below the highest of:**

        (a)   **its fair value less costs ~~to sell~~ of disposal (if ~~determinable~~ measurable);**

        (b)   **...**

    111   **In assessing whether there is any indication that an impairment loss recognised in prior periods for an asset other than goodwill may no longer exist or may have decreased, an entity shall consider, as a minimum, the following indications:**

    External sources of information

        (a)   **there are observable indications that the asset's ~~market~~ value has increased significantly during the period;**

        (b)   **...**

    130   **An entity shall disclose the following for each material impairment loss recognised or reversed during the period for an individual asset, including goodwill, or a cash-generating unit:**

        (a)   **...**

        (f)   **if recoverable amount is fair value less costs ~~to sell~~ of disposal, the basis used to ~~determine~~ measure fair value less costs ~~to sell~~ of disposal (such as whether fair value was ~~determined~~ measured by reference to a quoted price in an active market for an identical asset). An entity is not required to provide the disclosures required by AASB 13; and**

        (g)   **...**

134   An entity shall disclose the information required by (a)–(f) for each cash-
generating unit (group of units) for which the carrying amount of goodwill
or intangible assets with indefinite useful lives allocated to that unit (group of
units) is significant in comparison with the entity's total carrying amount of
goodwill or intangible assets with indefinite useful lives:

(a)   ...

(c)   the recoverable amount of the unit (or group of units) and the basis
on which the unit's (group of units') recoverable amount has been
determined (i.e. value in use or fair value less costs ~~to sell~~ of disposal);

(d)   if the unit's (group of units') recoverable amount is based on value in use:

(i)   ~~a description of~~ each key assumption on which management has
based its cash flow projections for the period covered by the most
recent budgets/forecasts. Key assumptions are those to which the
unit's (group of units') recoverable amount is most sensitive;

(ii)   ...

(e)   if the unit's (group of units') recoverable amount is based on fair value
less costs ~~to sell~~ of disposal, the ~~methodology~~ valuation technique(s) used
to ~~determine~~ measure fair value less costs ~~to sell~~ of disposal. An entity
is not required to provide the disclosures required by AASB 13. If fair
value less costs ~~to sell~~ of disposal is not ~~determined~~ measured using
~~an observable market~~ a quoted price for ~~the~~ an identical unit (group
of units), an entity shall disclose the following information ~~shall also be
disclosed~~:

(i)   ~~a description of~~ each key assumption on which management has
based its determination of fair value less costs ~~to sell~~ of disposal.
Key assumptions are those to which the unit's (group of units')
recoverable amount is most sensitive.

(ii)   ...

(iiA)   the level of the fair value hierarchy (see AASB 13) within which
the fair value measurement is categorised in its entirety (without
giving regard to the observability of 'costs of disposal').

(iiB)   if there has been a change in valuation technique, the change and
the reason(s) for making it.

If fair value less costs ~~to sell~~ of disposal is ~~determined~~ measured using
discounted cash flow projections, an entity shall disclose the following
information ~~shall also be disclosed~~:

(iii)   the period over which management has projected cash flows;

(iv)   the growth rate used to extrapolate cash flow projections;

(v)   the discount rate(s) applied to the cash flow projections;

(f)   ...

75   Paragraph 140I is added as follows:

140I   AASB 2011-8 *Amendments to Australian Accounting Standards arising from
AASB 13*, issued in September 2011, amended paragraphs 5, 6, 12, 20, 22, 28,
78, 105, 111, 130 and 134, deleted paragraphs 25–27 and added paragraph 53A.
An entity shall apply those amendments when it applies AASB 13.

Amendments to AASB 138

76   Paragraph 8 is amended as follows (new text is underlined and deleted text is struck through):

     8   **The following terms are used in this Standard with the meanings specified.**

         ~~An *active market* is a market in which all the following conditions exist:~~

           ~~(a) the items traded in the market are homogeneous;~~

           ~~(b) willing buyers and sellers can normally be found at any time; and~~

           ~~(c) prices are available to the public.~~

         ...

         Fair value ~~*of an asset* is the amount for which that asset could be exchanged between knowledgeable, willing parties in an arm's length transaction~~ <u>is the price that would be received to sell an asset or paid to transfer a liability in an orderly transaction between market participants at the measurement date. (See AASB 13 *Fair Value Measurement*.)</u>

77   Paragraph 33 is amended as follows (new text is underlined):

     33   In accordance with AASB 3 *Business Combinations* (as revised in March 2008), if an intangible asset is acquired in a business combination, the cost of that intangible asset is its fair value at the acquisition date. The fair value of an intangible asset will reflect <u>market participants'</u> expectations <u>at the acquisition date</u> about the probability that the expected future economic benefits embodied in the asset will flow to the entity. ...

78   The heading above paragraph 35 is amended as follows (deleted text is struck through):

     ~~Measuring the Fair Value of an~~ Intangible Asset Acquired in a Business Combination

79   Paragraphs 39–41 are deleted.

80   Paragraphs 47, 50, 75, 78, 82, 84 and 100 are amended as follows (new text is underlined and deleted text is struck through):

     47   Paragraph 21(b) specifies that a condition for the recognition of an intangible asset is that the cost of the asset can be measured reliably. The fair value of an intangible asset ~~for which comparable market transactions do not exist~~ is reliably measurable if (a) the variability in the range of reasonable fair value ~~estimates~~ <u>measurements</u> is not significant for that asset or (b) the probabilities of the various estimates within the range can be reasonably assessed and used ~~in estimating~~ <u>when measuring</u> fair value. If an entity is able to ~~determine~~ <u>measure</u> reliably the fair value of either the asset received or the asset given up, then the fair value of the asset given up is used to measure cost unless the fair value of the asset received is more clearly evident.

     50   Differences between the ~~market~~ <u>fair</u> value of an entity and the carrying amount of its identifiable net assets at any time may capture a range of factors that affect the <u>fair</u> value of the entity. However, such differences do not represent the cost of intangible assets controlled by the entity.

     75   **... For the purpose of revaluations under this Standard, fair value shall be ~~determined~~ <u>measured</u> by reference to an active market. ...**

     78   It is uncommon for an active market ~~with the characteristics described in paragraph 8~~ to exist for an intangible asset, although this may happen. ...

     82   **If the fair value of a revalued intangible asset can no longer be ~~determined~~ <u>measured</u> by reference to an active market, the carrying amount of the asset shall be its revalued amount at the date of the last revaluation by reference to the active market less any subsequent accumulated amortisation and any subsequent accumulated impairment losses.**

     84   If the fair value of the asset can be ~~determined~~ <u>measured</u> by reference to an active market at a subsequent measurement date, the revaluation model is applied from that date.

    100   The *residual value* of an intangible asset with a finite useful life shall be assumed to be zero unless:

        (a)   ...

        (b)   there is an active market <u>(as defined in AASB 13)</u> for the asset and:

             (i)   ...

81   Paragraph 124 is amended as follows (new text is underlined and deleted text is struck through):

    124   If intangible assets are accounted for at revalued amounts, an entity shall disclose the following:

        (a)   by class of intangible assets:

             (i)   ...

             (iii)   the carrying amount ... paragraph 74; <u>and</u>

        (b)   the amount of ... shareholders~~; and~~ <u>.</u>

        (c)   [deleted by the IASB] ~~the methods and significant assumptions applied in estimating the assets' fair values.~~

82   Paragraph 130E is deleted.

83   Paragraph 130G is added as follows:

    130G AASB 2011-8 *Amendments to Australian Accounting Standards arising from AASB 13*, issued in September 2011, amended paragraphs 8, 33, 47, 50, 75, 78, 82, 84, 100 and 124 and deleted paragraphs 39–41 and 130E. An entity shall apply those amendments when it applies AASB 13.

Amendments to AASB 139

84   Paragraph 9 is amended (new text is underlined and deleted text is struck through) as follows:

    9   **The following terms are used in this Standard with the meanings specified.**

       ...

       It should be noted that <u>AASB 13 *Fair Value Measurement*</u> ~~paragraphs 48, 48A, 49 and Appendix A paragraphs AG69–AG82, which~~ set<u>s</u> out <u>the</u> requirements for ~~determining a reliable measure of~~ <u>measuring</u> the fair value of a financial asset or financial liability, ~~apply equally to all items that are measured at fair value,~~ whether by designation or otherwise, or whose fair value is disclosed.

       ...

85   Paragraphs 9, 13, 28, 47, 88, AG52, AG76, AG76A, AG80, AG81 and AG96 are amended (new text is underlined and deleted text is struck through), paragraphs 43A and 103Q are added, and paragraphs 48–49, AG69–AG75, AG77–AG79 and AG82 and their related headings are deleted as follows:

    9   **The following terms are used in this Standard with the meanings specified.**

       ...

       Fair value **is the ~~amount for which an asset could be exchanged, or a liability settled, between knowledgeable, willing parties in an arm's length transaction.~~[†] <u>price that would be received to sell an asset or paid to transfer a liability in an orderly transaction between market participants at the measurement date. (See AASB 13.)</u>**

       ...

    The footnote to the definition of fair value is deleted.

      13   If an entity is unable to ~~determine~~ <u>measure</u> reliably the fair value of an embedded derivative on the basis of its terms and conditions (... because the embedded derivative is based on an ~~unquoted~~ equity instrument <u>that does not have a quoted price in an active market for an identical instrument, i.e. a Level 1 input</u>), the

fair value of the embedded derivative is the difference between the fair value of ... and the fair value of the host contract, if those can be determined under this Standard. If the entity is unable to ~~determine~~ measure the fair value of the embedded derivative using this method, paragraph 12 applies ...

28 When an entity allocates the previous carrying amount of a larger financial asset between the part that continues to be recognised and the part that is derecognised, the fair value of the part that continues to be recognised needs to be ~~determined~~ measured. ...

43A However, if the fair value of the financial asset or financial liability at initial recognition differs from the transaction price, an entity shall apply paragraph AG76.

47 After initial recognition, an entity shall measure all financial liabilities at amortised cost using the effective interest method, except for:

(a) financial liabilities at fair value through profit or loss. Such liabilities, including derivatives that are liabilities, shall be measured at fair value except for a derivative liability that is linked to and must be settled by delivery of an ~~unquoted~~ equity instrument <u>that does not have a quoted price in an active market for an identical instrument (i.e. a Level 1 input)</u> whose fair value cannot <u>otherwise</u> be reliably measured, which shall be measured at cost;

(b) ...

88 A hedging relationship qualifies for hedge accounting under paragraphs 89–102 if, and only if, all ~~of~~ the following conditions are met.

(a) ...

(d) The effectiveness of the hedge can be reliably measured, that is, the fair value or cash flows of the hedged item that are attributable to the hedged risk and the fair value of the hedging instrument can be reliably measured ~~(see paragraphs 46 and 47 and Appendix A paragraphs AG80 and AG81 for guidance on determining fair value).~~

(e) ...

103Q AASB 2011-8 *Amendments to Australian Accounting Standards arising from AASB 13*, issued in September 2011, amended paragraphs 9, 13, 28, 47, 88, AG46, AG52, AG64, AG76, AG76A, AG80, AG81 and AG96, added paragraph 43A, and deleted paragraphs 48–49, AG69–AG75, AG77–AG79, and AG82 and their related headings. An entity shall apply those amendments when it applies AASB 13.

AG52 This paragraph illustrates the application of the continuing involvement approach when the entity's continuing involvement is in a part of a financial asset.

> Assume an entity has a portfolio of prepayable loans ... The fair value of the loans at the date of the transaction is CU10,100 and the ~~estimated~~ fair value of the excess spread of 0.5% is CU40.
>
> ...
>
> The entity calculates the gain or loss on the sale of the 90 per cent share of cash flows. Assuming that separate fair values ... are not available at the date of the transfer, the entity allocates the carrying amount of the asset in accordance with paragraph 28 as follows:
>
> | | ~~Estimated~~ Fair Value | Percentage | Allocated Carrying Amount |
> | --- | --- | --- | --- |
> | Portion Transferred | 9,090 | 90% | 9,000 |
> | Portion Retained | 1,010 | 10% | 1,000 |
> | **Total** | **10,100** | | **10,000** |
>
> ...

AG76 ~~Therefore, a valuation technique (a) incorporates all factors that market participants would consider in setting a price and (b) is consistent with accepted economic methodologies for pricing financial instruments. Periodically, an entity calibrates the valuation technique and tests it for validity using prices from any observable current market transactions in the same instrument (i.e. without modification or repackaging) or based on any available observable market data. An entity obtains market data consistently in the same market where the instrument was originated or purchased.~~ The best evidence of the fair value of a financial instrument at initial recognition is <u>normally</u> the transaction price (i.e. the fair value of the consideration given or received<u>, see also AASB 13</u>). <u>If an entity determines that the fair value at initial recognition differs from the transaction price as mentioned in paragraph 43A, the entity shall account for</u> ~~unless the fair value of~~ that instrument <u>at that date as follows:</u>

  <u>(a)</u> <u>at the measurement required by paragraph 43 if that fair value</u> is evidenced by ~~comparison with other observable current market transactions in the same instrument (i.e. without modification or repackaging)~~ <u>a quoted price in an active market for an identical asset or liability (i.e. a Level 1 input)</u> or based on a valuation technique ~~whose variables include~~ <u>that uses</u> only data from observable markets. <u>An entity shall recognise the difference between the fair value at initial recognition and the transaction price as a gain or loss.</u>

  <u>(b)</u> <u>in all other cases, at the measurement required by paragraph 43, adjusted to defer the difference between the fair value at initial recognition and the transaction price. After initial recognition, the entity shall recognise that deferred difference as a gain or loss only to the extent that it arises from a change in a factor (including time) that market participants would take into account when pricing the asset or liability.</u>

AG76A The subsequent measurement of the financial asset or financial liability and the subsequent recognition of gains and losses shall be consistent with the requirements of this Standard. ~~The application of paragraph AG76 may result in no gain or loss being recognised on the initial recognition of a financial asset or financial liability. In such a case, AASB 139 requires that a gain or loss shall be recognised after initial recognition only to the extent that it arises from a change in a factor (including time) that market participants would consider in setting a price.~~

AG80 The fair value of investments in equity instruments that do not have a quoted ~~market~~ price in an active market <u>for an identical instrument (i.e. a Level 1 input)</u> and derivatives that are linked to and must be settled by delivery of such an ~~unquoted~~ equity instrument (see paragraphs 46(c) and 47) is reliably measurable if (a) the variability in the range of reasonable fair value ~~estimates~~ <u>measurements</u> is not significant for that instrument or (b) the probabilities of the various estimates within the range can be reasonably assessed and used ~~in estimating~~ <u>when measuring</u> fair value.

AG81 There are many situations in which the variability in the range of reasonable fair value ~~estimates~~ <u>measurements</u> of investments in equity instruments that do not have a quoted ~~market~~ price <u>in an active market for an identical instrument (i.e. a Level 1 input)</u> and derivatives that are linked to and must be settled by delivery of such an ~~unquoted~~ equity instrument (see paragraphs 46(c) and 47) is likely not to be significant. Normally it is possible to ~~estimate~~ <u>measure</u> the fair value of a financial asset that an entity has acquired from an outside party. However, if the range of reasonable fair value ~~estimates~~ <u>measurements</u> is significant and the probabilities of the various estimates cannot be reasonably assessed, an entity is precluded from measuring the instrument at fair value.

AG96 An investment in an ~~unquoted~~ equity instrument that <u>does not have a quoted price in an active market for an identical instrument (i.e. a Level 1 input)</u> is not carried at fair value because its fair value cannot <u>otherwise</u> be reliably measured or a derivative that is linked to and must be settled by delivery of such an ~~unquoted~~

equity instrument (see paragraphs 46(c) and 47) cannot be designated as a hedging instrument.

86   Paragraph AG46 is amended (new text is underlined and deleted text is struck through) as follows:

     AG46   ~~In estimating~~ When measuring the fair values of the part that continues to be recognised and the part that is derecognised for the purposes of applying paragraph 27, an entity applies the fair value measurement requirements in AASB 13 ~~paragraphs 48–49 and AG68–AG82~~ in addition to paragraph 28.

86A   Paragraph AG64 is amended (new text is underlined and deleted text is struck through) as follows:

     AG64   The fair value of a financial instrument on initial recognition is normally the transaction price (i.e. the fair value of the consideration given or received, see also AASB 13 and paragraph AG76). However, if part of the consideration given or received is for something other than the financial instrument, an entity shall measure the fair value of the financial instrument ~~is estimated, using a valuation technique (see paragraphs AG74–AG79)~~. For example, the fair value of a long-term loan or receivable that carries no interest can be ~~estimated~~ measured as the present value of all future cash receipts discounted using the prevailing market rate(s) of interest for a similar instrument …

Amendments to AASB 140

87   Paragraphs 26, 29 and 32 are amended as follows (new text is underlined and deleted text is struck through):

     26   … Guidance on ~~determining~~ measuring the fair value of a property interest is set out for the fair value model in paragraphs ~~33–52~~ 33–35, 40, 41, 48, 50 and 52 and in AASB 13. That guidance is also relevant to the ~~determination~~ measurement of fair value when that value is used as cost for initial recognition purposes.

     29   The fair value of an asset ~~for which comparable market transactions do not exist~~ is reliably measurable if (a) the variability in the range of reasonable fair value ~~estimates~~ measurements is not significant for that asset or (b) the probabilities of the various estimates within the range can be reasonably assessed and used ~~in estimating~~ when measuring fair value. If the entity is able to ~~determine~~ measure reliably the fair value of either the asset received or the asset given up, then the fair value of the asset given up is used to measure cost unless the fair value of the asset received is more clearly evident.

     32   This Standard requires all entities to ~~determine~~ measure the fair value of investment property, for the purpose of either measurement (if the entity uses the fair value model) or disclosure (if it uses the cost model). An entity is encouraged, but not required, to ~~determine~~ measure the fair value of investment property on the basis of a valuation by an independent valuer who holds a recognised and relevant professional qualification and has recent experience in the location and category of the investment property being valued.

88   Paragraphs 36–39 are deleted.

89   Paragraphs 40 is amended as follows (new text is underlined and deleted text is struck through):

     40   When measuring the ~~The~~ fair value of investment property in accordance with AASB 13, an entity shall ensure that the fair value reflects, among other things, rental income from current leases and ~~reasonable and supportable~~ other assumptions that ~~represent what knowledgeable, willing parties~~ market participants would ~~assume~~ use when pricing the investment property ~~about rental income from future leases in the light of~~ under current market conditions. ~~It also reflects, on a similar basis, any cash outflows (including rental payments and other outflows) that could be expected in respect of the property. Some of those outflows are reflected in the liability whereas others relate to outflows that are not recognised in the financial statements until a later date (e.g. periodic payments such as contingent rents).~~

90   Paragraphs 42–47, 49, 51 and 75(d) are deleted.

91   Paragraph 48 is amended as follows (new text is underlined and deleted text is struck through):

    48   In exceptional cases, there is clear evidence when an entity first acquires an investment property (or when an existing property first becomes investment property …) that the variability in the range of reasonable fair value ~~estimates~~ measurements will be so great, and the probabilities of the various outcomes so difficult to assess, that the usefulness of a single ~~estimate~~ measure of fair value is negated. This may indicate that the fair value of the property will not be reliably ~~determinable~~ measurable on a continuing basis (see paragraph 53).

92   The heading above paragraph 53 and paragraphs 53 and 53B are amended as follows (new text is underlined and deleted text is struck through):

Inability to ~~Determine~~ Measure Fair Value Reliably

    53   **There is a rebuttable presumption that an entity can reliably ~~determine~~ measure the fair value of an investment property on a continuing basis. However, in exceptional cases, there is clear evidence when an entity first acquires an investment property (or when an existing property first becomes investment property …) that the fair value of the investment property is not reliably ~~determinable~~ measurable on a continuing basis. This arises when, and only when, the market for comparable ~~market~~ properties is inactive (e.g. there are few recent transactions, price quotations are not current or observed transaction prices indicate that the seller was forced to sell) ~~are infrequent~~ and alternative reliable ~~estimates~~ measurements of fair value (for example, based on discounted cash flow projections) are not available. If an entity determines that the fair value of an investment property under construction is not reliably determinable measurable but expects the fair value of the property to be reliably ~~determinable~~ measurable when construction is complete, it shall measure that investment property under construction at cost until either its fair value becomes reliably ~~determinable~~ measurable or construction is completed (whichever is earlier). If an entity determines that the fair value of an investment property (other than an investment property under construction) is not reliably ~~determinable~~ measurable on a continuing basis, the entity shall measure that investment property using the cost model in AASB 116. The residual value of the investment property shall be assumed to be zero. The entity shall apply AASB 116 until disposal of the investment property.**

    53B   … An entity that has measured an item of investment property under construction at fair value may not conclude that the fair value of the completed investment property cannot be ~~determined~~ measured reliably.

93   Paragraphs 78 and 79 are amended as follows (new text is underlined and deleted text is struck through):

    78   **In the exceptional cases referred to in paragraph 53, when an entity measures investment property using the cost model in AASB 116, the reconciliation required by paragraph 76 shall disclose amounts relating to that investment property separately from amounts relating to other investment property. In addition, an entity shall disclose:**

        (a)   **…**

        (b)   **an explanation of why fair value cannot be ~~determined~~ measured reliably;**

        (c)   **…**

    79   **In addition to the disclosures required by paragraph 75, an entity that applies the cost model in paragraph 56 shall disclose:**

        (a)   **…**

> (e)   the fair value of investment property. In the exceptional cases described in paragraph 53, when an entity cannot ~~determine~~ <u>measure</u> the fair value of the investment property reliably, it shall disclose:
>
> > (i)   ...
> >
> > (ii)   an explanation of why fair value cannot be ~~determined~~ <u>measured</u> reliably; and
> >
> > (iii)   ...

94   Paragraph 85B is amended as follows (new text is underlined and deleted text is struck through):

> 85B   ... An entity is permitted to apply the amendments to investment property under construction from any date before 1 January 2009 provided that the fair values of investment properties under construction were ~~determined~~ <u>measured</u> at those dates. ...

95   Paragraph 85C is added as follows:

> 85C   AASB 2011-8 *Amendments to Australian Accounting Standards arising from AASB 13*, issued in September 2011, amended the definition of fair value in paragraph 5, amended paragraphs 26, 29, 32, 40, 48, 53, 53B, 78, 79 and 85B, and deleted paragraphs 36–39, 42–47, 49, 51 and 75(d). An entity shall apply those amendments when it applies AASB 13.

Amendments to AASB 141

96   Paragraphs 8, 15 and 16 are amended as follows (new text is underlined and deleted text is struck through):

> 8   **The following terms are used in this Standard with the meanings specified.**
>
> > ~~An *active market* is a market where all the following conditions exist:~~
> >
> > ~~(a)   the items traded within the market are homogeneous;~~
> >
> > ~~(b)   willing buyers and sellers can normally be found at any time; and~~
> >
> > ~~(c)   prices are available to the public.~~
> >
> > ...
>
> *Fair value* is the ~~amount for which an asset could be exchanged, or a liability settled, between knowledgeable, willing parties in an arm's length transaction~~ <u>price that would be received to sell an asset or paid to transfer a liability in an orderly transaction between market participants at the measurement date. (See AASB 13 *Fair Value Measurement*.)</u>

> 15   The ~~determination of~~ fair value <u>measurement of</u> ~~for~~ a biological asset or agricultural produce may be facilitated by grouping biological assets or agricultural produce according to significant attributes; for example, by age or quality. ...

> 16   Entities often enter into contracts to sell their biological assets or agricultural produce at a future date. Contract prices are not necessarily relevant in ~~determining~~ <u>measuring</u> fair value, because fair value reflects the current market <u>conditions</u> in which ~~a willing buyer and seller~~ <u>market participant buyers and sellers</u> would enter into a transaction. ...

97   Paragraphs 9, 17–21 and 23 are deleted.

98   Paragraphs 25 and 30 are amended as follows (new text is underlined and deleted text is struck through):

> 25   ... An entity may use information regarding the combined assets to ~~determine~~ <u>measure the</u> fair value ~~for~~ <u>of</u> the biological assets. ...

> 30   **There is a presumption that fair value can be measured reliably for a biological asset. However, that presumption can be rebutted only on initial recognition for a biological asset for which <u>quoted</u> market~~-determined~~ prices ~~or values~~ are not available and for which alternative ~~estimates of~~ fair value <u>measurements</u> are determined to be clearly unreliable. ...**

99　　Paragraphs 47 and 48 are deleted.

100　Paragraph 61 is added as follows:

　　　61　　AASB 2011-8 *Amendments to Australian Accounting Standards arising from AASB 13*, issued in September 2011, amended paragraphs 8, 15, 16, 25 and 30 and deleted paragraphs 9, 17–21, 23, 47 and 48. An entity shall apply those amendments when it applies AASB 13.

Amendments to AASB 1004

101　Paragraph 11 is amended as follows (new text is underlined):

　　　11　　Income shall be measured at the fair value <u>(see AASB 13 *Fair Value Measurement*)</u> of the *contributions* received or receivable.

102　Paragraph 44 is amended as follows (new text is underlined and deleted text is struck through):

　　　44　　Contributions of services to local governments, government departments, GGSs and whole of governments shall be recognised as income when and only when:

　　　　　(a)　　the fair value of those services can be reliably ~~determined~~ <u>measured</u>; and

　　　　　(b)　　...

Amendment to AASB 1023

103　Paragraph 15.3 is amended as follows (new text is underlined):

　　　15.3　Investment property within the scope of AASB 140 *Investment Property* and that backs general insurance liabilities shall be measured using the fair value model under <u>AASB 140 and AASB 13 *Fair Value Measurement*</u>.

Amendment to AASB 1038

104　Paragraph 10.3 is amended as follows (new text is underlined):

　　　10.3　Investment property that is within the scope of AASB 140 *Investment Property* and that backs life insurance liabilities or life investment contract liabilities shall be measured at fair value using the fair value model under AASB 140 <u>and AASB 13 *Fair Value Measurement*</u>.

Amendments to Interpretation 2

105　Below the heading 'References', a reference to Accounting Standard AASB 13 *Fair Value Measurement* is added.

106　The heading 'Effective Date of IFRIC 2' before paragraph 14 is amended to 'Effective Date'.

107　Paragraph 16 is added as follows:

　　　16　　AASB 2011-8 *Amendments to Australian Accounting Standards arising from AASB 13*, issued in September 2011, amended paragraph A8. An entity shall apply that amendment when it applies AASB 13.

108　In the Appendix, paragraph A8 is amended as follows (new text is underlined and deleted text is struck through):

　　　A8　　Members' shares in excess of the prohibition against redemption are financial liabilities. The co-operative entity measures this financial liability at fair value at initial recognition. Because these shares are redeemable on demand, the co-operative entity ~~determines~~ <u>measures</u> the fair value of such financial liabilities <u>in accordance with paragraph 47 of AASB 13</u> ~~as required by paragraph 49 of AASB 139 *Financial Instruments: Recognition and Measurement*~~, which states: 'The fair value of a financial liability with a demand feature (eg a demand deposit) is not less than the amount payable on demand ...' Accordingly, the co-operative entity classifies as financial liabilities the maximum amount payable on demand under the redemption provisions.

Amendments to Interpretation 4

109   Below the heading 'References', a reference to Accounting Standard AASB 13 *Fair Value Measurement* is added.

110   In paragraph 15(a), 'fair value' is footnoted as follows:

AASB 117 uses the term 'fair value' in a way that differs in some respects from the definition of fair value in AASB 13. Therefore, when applying AASB 117 an entity measures fair value in accordance with AASB 117, not AASB 13.

Amendments to Interpretation 12

111   In the Illustrative Examples accompanying Interpretation 12, paragraphs IE15 and IE31 are amended as follows (new text is underlined and deleted text is struck through):

IE15   During the construction phase of the arrangement the operator's asset (representing its accumulating right to be paid for providing construction services) is classified as an intangible asset (licence to charge users of the infrastructure). The operator estimates measures the fair value of its consideration received to be as equal to the forecast construction costs plus 5 per cent margin, which the operator concludes i consistent with the rate that a market participant would require as compensation for providing the construction services and for assuming the risk associated with the construction costs. It is also assumed that …

IE31   During the construction phase of the arrangement the operator's asset (representing its accumulating right to be paid for providing construction services) is classified as a right to receive a licence to charge users of the infrastructure. The operator estimates measures the fair value of its consideration received or receivable as equal to the forecast construction costs plus 5 per cent, which the operator concludes is consistent with the rate that a market participant would require as compensation for providing the construction services and for assuming the risk associated with the construction costs. It is also assumed that …

Amendments to Interpretation 13

112   Below the heading 'References', a reference to Accounting Standard AASB 13 *Fair Value Measurement* is added.

113   Paragraph 6 is amended as follows (deleted text is struck through):

6   The consideration allocated to the award credits shall be measured by reference to their fair value, i.e. the amount for which the award credits could be sold separately.

114   The heading 'Effective Date' before paragraph 10 is amended to 'Effective date and transition', and the heading 'Transition' before paragraph 11 is deleted.

115   Paragraph 10B is added as follows:

10B   AASB 2011-8 *Amendments to Australian Accounting Standards arising from AASB 13*, issued in September 2011, amended paragraphs 6 and AG1–AG3. An entity shall apply those amendments when it applies AASB 13.

116   In the Application Guidance, paragraphs AG1–AG3 are amended as follows (new text is underlined and deleted text is struck through):

AG1   Paragraph 6 of the consensus requires the consideration allocated to award credits to be measured by reference to their fair value, i.e. the amount for which the award credits could be sold separately. If the fair value there is not directly observable a quoted market price for an identical award credit, it fair value must be estimated measured using another valuation technique.

AG2   An entity may estimate measure the fair value of award credits by reference to the fair value of the awards for which they could be redeemed. The fair value … :

(a)   the … initial sale; and

(b) the proportion of award credits that are not expected to be redeemed by customers.; and

(c) non-performance risk.

If customers can choose from a range of different awards, the fair value of the award credits will reflects the fair values of the range of available awards, weighted in proportion to the frequency with which each award is expected to be selected.

AG3 In some circumstances, other ~~estimation~~ valuation techniques may be ~~available~~ used. For example, if a third party will supply the awards and the entity pays the third party for each award credit it grants, it could ~~estimate~~ measure the fair value of the award credits by reference to the amount it pays the third party, adding a reasonable profit margin. Judgement is required to select and apply the ~~estimation~~ valuation technique that satisfies the requirements of paragraph 6 of the consensus and is most appropriate in the circumstances.

117 In the Illustrative Examples accompanying Interpretation 13, paragraphs IE1 and IE3 are amended as follows (new text is underlined and deleted text is struck through):

IE1 A grocery retailer operates a customer loyalty programme. It grants programme members loyalty points when they spend a specified amount on groceries. Programme members can redeem the points for further groceries. The points have no expiry date. In one period, the entity grants 100 points. Management ~~estimates~~ measures the fair value of groceries for which each loyalty point can be redeemed as 1.25 currency units (CU1.25). This amount takes into account ~~an~~ management's estimate of the discount that ~~management~~ market participants would assume when pricing the award credits. That discount takes into account market participants' expectations of the discount that ~~expects~~ would otherwise be offered to customers who have not earned award credits from an initial sale. In addition, management estimates that market participants would ~~expects~~ only 80 of these points to be redeemed. Therefore, the fair value of each point is CU1, being the fair value of the award for each loyalty point granted of CU1.25 reduced to take into account points not expected to be redeemed ((80 points/100 points) × CU1.25 = CU1). Accordingly, management defers recognition of revenue of CU100. Throughout the example, management determines that non-performance risk has an immaterial effect on the measurement of its obligation under the programme.

IE3 In the second year, management revises its estimate of market participants' expectations. It now expects 90 points to be redeemed altogether.

Amendments to Interpretation 14

118 In the Illustrative Examples accompanying Interpretation 14, all references to 'market value' of assets are replaced with 'fair value'.

Amendments to Interpretation 17

119 Below the heading 'References', a reference to Accounting Standard AASB 13 *Fair Value Measurement* is added.

120 Paragraph 17 is amended as follows (new text is underlined and deleted text is struck through):

17 If, after the end of a reporting period but before the financial statements are authorised for issue, an entity declares a dividend to distribute a non-cash asset, it shall disclose:

(a) …

(c) the ~~estimated~~ fair value of the asset to be distributed as of the end of the reporting period, if it is different from its carrying amount, and the information about the method(s) used to ~~determine~~ measure that fair value required by ~~AASB 7 paragraph 27(a) and (b)~~ paragraphs 93(b), (d), (g) and (i) and 99 of AASB 13.

121   Paragraph 20 is added as follows:

     20   AASB 2011-8 *Amendments to Australian Accounting Standards arising from AASB 13*, issued in September 2011, amended paragraph 17. An entity shall apply that amendment when it applies AASB 13.

Amendments to Interpretation 19

122   Below the heading 'References', a reference to Accounting Standard AASB 13 *Fair Value Measurement* is added.

123   Paragraph 7 is amended as follows (new text is underlined and deleted text is struck through):

     7   If the fair value of the equity instruments issued cannot be reliably measured then the equity instruments shall be measured to reflect the fair value of the financial liability extinguished. In measuring the fair value of a financial liability extinguished that includes a demand feature (eg a demand deposit), paragraph ~~49~~ 47 of ~~AASB 139~~ AASB 13 is not applied.

124   The heading 'Effective date of IFRIC 19' before paragraph 12 is amended to 'Effective date and transition', and the heading 'Transition' before paragraph 13 is deleted.

125   Paragraph 15 is added as follows:

     15   AASB 2011-8 *Amendments to Australian Accounting Standards arising from AASB 13*, issued in September 2011, amended paragraph 7. An entity shall apply that amendment when it applies AASB 13.

Amendment to Interpretation 131

126   In paragraph 8, the first sentence is footnoted as follows:

AASB 13 *Fair Value Measurement*, issued in September 2011, defines fair value and contains the requirements for measuring fair value.

Amendment to Interpretation 132

127   In paragraph 18, the first reference to 'an active market' is footnoted as follows:

AASB 13 *Fair Value Measurement*, issued in September 2011, defines fair value and contains the requirements for measuring fair value. AASB 13 defines an active market.

Appendix

Early Application of AASB 13

This appendix is an integral part of AASB 2011-8.

A1   Australian Accounting Standard AASB 13 *Fair Value Measurement* may be applied early to annual reporting periods beginning on or after 1 January 2005 but before 1 January 2013. The amendments set out in paragraphs 12–127 of this Standard also apply, as far as possible, to all the versions of the pronouncements applicable to such periods when AASB 13 is applied early.

A2   However, the early-application amendments to the following pronouncements are set out in this Appendix:

     (a)   AASB 1 *First-time Adoption of Australian Accounting Standards* (May 2009);

     (b)   AASB 7 *Financial Instruments: Disclosures*;

     (c)   AASB 128 *Investments in Associates*;

     (d)   AASB 131 *Interests in Joint Ventures*;

     (e)   [Deleted]

     (f)   AASB 139 *Financial Instruments: Recognition and Measurement*.

     (g)   [Deleted]

     (h)   [Deleted]

The amendments are presented in relation to the annual reporting periods to which various versions of those pronouncements apply mandatorily. However, most versions may also be applied to earlier annual reporting periods as stated in each version.

A3   [Deleted]

Change in Definition

A4   The changes to the definition of 'fair value' in paragraphs 12 and 13 of this Standard apply in early application cases and are not repeated in the amendments set out in this Appendix.

Amendments to AASB 1 (May 2009)

A5   [Deleted]

A6   Paragraph D20 is amended as follows (new text is underlined and deleted text is struck through) in the versions of AASB 1 that apply to annual reporting periods beginning on or after 1 July 2009 but before 1 July 2011:

> D20   Notwithstanding the requirements of paragraphs 7 and 9, an entity may apply the requirements in ~~the last sentence~~ paragraph AG76(a) of AASB 139 ~~paragraph AG76 and in paragraph AG76A~~, in either of the following ways:
>
>   (a)   ...

A7   [Deleted]

Amendments to AASB 7

A8-A9   [Deleted]

A10   Paragraph 3 is amended as follows (new text is underlined) in the versions of AASB 7 that apply to annual reporting periods beginning on or after 1 January 2007 but before 1 January 2009:

> 3   **This Standard shall be applied by all entities to all types of financial instruments, except:**
>
>   (a)   **... in addition to those in this Standard. <u>For those interests measured at fair value, entities shall apply the requirements of AASB 13</u> _Fair Value Measurement._ Entities shall also apply ...**
>
>   (b)   **...**

A11   [Deleted]

Amendments to AASB 9 (December 2009)

A12   [Deleted]

Amendments to AASB 2009-11

A13-A22   [Deleted]

Amendments to AASB 2010-7

A23-A25   [Deleted]

Amendments to AASB 128

A26   Paragraphs 1 and 37 are amended (new text is underlined and deleted text is struck through) and paragraph 41G is added in the versions of AASB 128 that apply to annual reporting periods beginning on or after 1 January 2005 but before 1 January 2013, as follows:

> 1   **This Standard shall be applied in accounting for investments in associates. However, it does not apply to investments in associates held by:**
>
>   (a)   **venture capital organisations, or**
>
>   (b)   **mutual funds, unit trusts and similar entities including investment-linked insurance funds**

that upon initial recognition are designated as at fair value through profit or loss or are classified as held for trading and accounted for in accordance with AASB 139 *Financial Instruments: Recognition and Measurement*. For such ~~Such~~ investments ~~shall be measured at fair value in accordance with AASB 139~~, an entity shall recognise with changes in fair value ~~recognised~~ in profit or loss ...

37   The following disclosures shall be made:

(a)   the fair value of investments in associates for which there are ~~published price quotations~~ quoted market prices;

(b)   ...

41G   AASB 2011-8 *Amendments to Australian Accounting Standards arising from AASB 13*, issued in September 2011, amended paragraphs 1 and 37. An entity shall apply those amendments when it applies AASB 13 *Fair Value Measurement*.

Amendments to AASB 131

A27   Paragraph 1 is amended (new text is underlined and deleted text is struck through) and paragraph 58F is added in the versions of AASB 131 that apply to annual reporting periods beginning on or after 1 January 2005 but before 1 January 2013, as follows:

1   This Standard shall be applied in accounting for interests in *joint ventures* and the reporting of joint venture assets, liabilities, income and expenses ... of *venturers* and investors, regardless of the structures or forms under which the joint venture activities take place. However, it does not apply to venturers' interests in jointly controlled entities held by:

(a)   venture capital organisations, or

(b)   mutual funds, unit trusts and similar entities including investment-linked insurance funds

that upon initial recognition are designated as at fair value through profit or loss or are classified as held for trading and accounted for in accordance with AASB 139 *Financial Instruments: Recognition and Measurement*. For such ~~Such~~ investments ~~shall be measured at fair value in accordance with AASB 139~~, an entity shall recognise ~~with~~ changes in fair value ~~recognised~~ in profit or loss ...

58F   AASB 2011-8 *Amendments to Australian Accounting Standards arising from AASB 13*, issued in September 2011, amended paragraph 1. An entity shall apply that amendment when it applies AASB 13 *Fair Value Measurement*.

Amendments to AASB 132

A28   [Deleted]

Amendments to AASB 139

A29-A30   [Deleted]

A31   Paragraph AG46 is amended (new text is underlined and deleted text is struck through) in the versions of AASB 139 that apply to annual reporting periods beginning on or after 1 January 2005 but before 1 January 2007, as follows:

AG46 ~~In estimating~~ When measuring the fair values of the part that continues to be recognised and the part that is derecognised for the purposes of applying paragraph 27, an entity applies the fair value measurement requirements in AASB 13 ~~paragraphs 48, 49 and AG68–AG82~~ in addition to paragraph 28.

A32   [Deleted]

A33   Paragraph AG64 is amended (new text is underlined and deleted text is struck through) in the versions of AASB 139 that apply to annual reporting periods beginning on or after 1 January 2005 that end before 24 February 2006, as follows:

> AG64 The fair value of a financial instrument on initial recognition is normally the transaction price (i.e. the fair value of the consideration given or received, see also <u>AASB 13 and paragraph</u> AG76. However, if part of the consideration given or received is for something other than the financial instrument, <u>an entity shall measure</u> the fair value of the financial instrument ~~is estimated, using a valuation technique (see paragraphs AG74 and AG79)~~. For example, the fair value of an originated long-term loan or receivable that carries no interest can be ~~estimated~~ <u>measured</u> as the present value of all future cash receipts discounted using the prevailing market rate(s) of interest for a similar instrument …

A34   [Deleted]

Amendments to Interpretation 2

A35   [Deleted]

Amendments to Interpretation 19

A36   [Deleted]

AASB 2011-10

Amendments to Australian Accounting Standards arising from AASB 119 (September 2011)

[AASB 1, AASB 8, AASB 101, AASB 124, AASB 134, AASB 1049 & AASB 2011-8, and Interpretation 14]

(Issued September 2011)

Note from the Institute of Chartered Accountants Australia

This note, prepared by the technical editors, is not part of Accounting Standard AASB 2011-10.

Historical development

5 September 2011: AASB 2011-10 was issued amending AASB 1, AASB 8, AASB 101, AASB 124, AASB 134, AASB 1049 & AASB 2011-8, and Interpretation 14 consequential to the issue of revised AASB 119.

This Standard is applicable to annual reporting periods beginning on or after 1 January 2013 with early adoption permitted.

AASB 2011-10

Contents

Preface

Accounting Standard
Amendments to Australian Accounting Standards
arising from AASB 119 (September 2011)

	Paragraphs
Objective	1
Application	2 – 9
Amendments to AASB 1	10 – 12
Amendment to AASB 8	13
Amendments to AASB 101	14 – 15
Amendment to AASB 124	16
Amendments to AASB 134	17
Amendments to AASB 1049	18 – 21
Amendments to AASB 2011-8	22
Amendments to Interpretation 14	23

> Australian Accounting Standard AASB 2011-10 *Amendments to Australian Accounting Standards arising from AASB 119* (September 2011) is set out in paragraphs 1 – 23. All the paragraphs have equal authority.

Preface

Standards Amended by AASB 2011-10

This Standard makes amendments to the following Australian Accounting Standards and Interpretation:

1. AASB 1 *First-time Adoption of Australian Accounting Standards*
2. AASB 8 *Operating Segments*
3. AASB 101 *Presentation of Financial Statements*
4. AASB 124 *Related Party Disclosures*
5. AASB 134 *Interim Financial Reporting*
6. AASB 1049 *Whole of Government and General Government Sector Financial Reporting*
7. AASB 2011-8 *Amendments to Australian Accounting Standards arising from AASB 13*
8. Interpretation 14 AASB 119 – *The Limit on a Defined Benefit Asset, Minimum Funding Requirements and their Interaction*

These amendments arise from the issuance of AASB 119 *Employee Benefits* in September 2011.

Accounting Standard AASB 2011-10

The Australian Accounting Standards Board makes Accounting Standard AASB 2011-10 *Amendments to Australian Accounting Standards arising from AASB 119 (September 2011)* under section 334 of the *Corporations Act 2001*.

Kevin M. Stevenson
Chair – AASB

Dated 5 September 2011

Accounting Standard AASB 2011-10

Amendments to Australian Accounting Standards Arising from AASB 119 (September 2011)

Objective

1   The objective of this Standard is to make amendments to:

(a)   AASB 1 *First-time Adoption of Australian Accounting Standards*;

(b)   AASB 8 *Operating Segments*;

(c)   AASB 101 *Presentation of Financial Statements*;

(d)   AASB 124 *Related Party Disclosures*;

(e)   AASB 134 *Interim Financial Reporting*;

(f)   AASB 1049 *Whole of Government and General Government Sector Financial Reporting*;

(g)   AASB 2011-8 *Amendments to Australian Accounting Standards arising from AASB 13*; and

(h)   Interpretation 14 AASB 119 – *The Limit on a Defined Benefit Asset, Minimum Funding Requirements and their Interaction*;

as a consequence of the issuance of AASB 119 *Employee Benefits* in September 2011.

Application

2   **Subject to paragraphs 3–6, this Standard applies to:**

(a)   **each entity that is required to prepare financial reports in accordance with Part 2M.3 of the Corporations Act and that is a reporting entity;**

(b)   **general purpose financial statements of each other reporting entity; and**

(c)   **financial statements that are, or are held out to be, general purpose financial statements.**

3   **In respect of AASB 8, this Standard applies to:**

(a)   **each for-profit entity that is required to prepare financial reports in accordance with Part 2M.3 of the Corporations Act and that is a reporting entity;**

(b)   **general purpose financial statements of each other for-profit reporting entity other than for-profit government departments; and**

(c)   **financial statements of a for-profit entity other than for-profit government departments that are, or are held out to be, general purpose financial statements.**

4   **In respect of AASB 101, this Standard applies to:**

(a)   **each entity that is required to prepare financial reports in accordance with Part 2M.3 of the Corporations Act;**

(b)   **general purpose financial statements of each reporting entity; and**

(c)   **financial statements that are, or are held out to be, general purpose financial statements.**

5   **In respect of AASB 134, this Standard applies to:**

(a)   **each disclosing entity required to prepare half-year financial reports in accordance with Part 2M.3 of the Corporations Act;**

(b)   **interim financial reports that are general purpose financial statements of each other reporting entity; and**

(c)   **interim financial reports that are, or are held out to be, general purpose financial statements.**

6	In respect of AASB 1049, this Standard applies to each government's whole of government general purpose financial statements and General Government Sector financial statements.

7	This Standard applies to annual reporting periods beginning on or after 1 January 2013.

8	This Standard shall be applied when AASB 119 (September 2011) is applied. This Standard may be applied to annual reporting periods beginning on or after 1 January 2005 but before 1 January 2013 provided AASB 119 (September 2011) is applied for the same period. If an entity applies this Standard to such an annual reporting period, it shall disclose that fact.

9	This Standard uses underlining, striking out and other typographical material to identify some of the amendments to a Standard or an Interpretation, in order to make the amendments more understandable. However, the amendments made by this Standard do not include that underlining, striking out or other typographical material.

Amendments to AASB 1

10	Paragraph 39L is added as follows:

AASB 2011-10 *Amendments to Australian Accounting Standards arising from AASB 119* (September 2011) amended paragraph D1, deleted paragraphs D10 and D11 and added paragraph E5. An entity shall apply those amendments when it applies AASB 119 (September 2011).

11	In Appendix D (Exemptions from other Australian Accounting Standards), the heading above paragraph D10 and paragraphs D10 and D11 are deleted and paragraph D1 is amended (new text is underlined and deleted text is struck through) as follows:

D1	An entity may elect to use one or more of the following exemptions:

(a)	…

(e)	[deleted by the IASB] ~~employee benefits (paragraphs D10 and D11);~~

(f)	…

12	In Appendix E (Short-term exemptions from Australian Accounting Standards), a heading and paragraph E5 are added as follows:

Employee benefits

E5	A first-time adopter may apply the transition provisions in paragraph 173(b) of AASB 119.

Amendment to AASB 8

13	Paragraph 24 is amended (new text is underlined and deleted text is struck through) as follows:

24	An entity shall disclose the following about each reportable segment if the specified amounts are included in the measure of segment assets reviewed by the chief operating decision maker or are otherwise regularly provided to the chief operating decision maker, even if not included in the measure of segment assets:

(a)	…

(b)	the amounts of additions to non-current assets1 other than financial instruments, deferred tax assets, ~~post-employment~~ net defined benefit assets (see AASB 119 *Employee Benefits* ~~paragraphs 54–58~~) and rights arising under insurance contracts.

[footnote omitted]

Amendments to AASB 101

14 In paragraph 7, the definition of 'other comprehensive income' is amended (new text is underlined and deleted text is struck through) as follows:

> 7 ...
>
> > *Other comprehensive income* comprises items of income and expense (including reclassification adjustments) that are not recognised in profit or loss as required or permitted by other Australian Accounting Standards.
> >
> > The components of other comprehensive income include:
> >
> > (a) changes in revaluation surplus (see AASB 116 *Property, Plant and Equipment* and AASB 138 *Intangible Assets*);
> >
> > (b) remeasurements of ~~actuarial gains and losses on~~ defined benefit plans ~~recognised in accordance with paragraph 93A of~~ (see AASB 119 *Employee Benefits*);
> >
> > (c) ...

15 Paragraph 96 is amended (new text is underlined and deleted text is struck through), and paragraph 139K is added as follows:

> 96 Reclassification adjustments do not arise on changes in revaluation surplus recognised in accordance with AASB 116 or AASB 138 or on remeasurements of ~~actuarial gains and losses on~~ defined benefit plans recognised in accordance with ~~paragraph 93A of~~ AASB 119. These components are recognised in other comprehensive income and are not reclassified to profit or loss in subsequent periods. Changes in revaluation surplus may be transferred to retained earnings in subsequent periods as the asset is used or when it is derecognised (see AASB 116 and AASB 138). ~~Actuarial gains and losses are reported in retained earnings in the period that they are recognised as other comprehensive income (see AASB 119).~~

> 139K AASB 2011-10 *Amendments to Australian Accounting Standards arising from AASB 119 (September 2011)* amended the definition of 'other comprehensive income' in paragraph 7 and paragraph 96. An entity shall apply those amendments when it applies AASB 119 (September 2011).

Amendment to AASB 124

16 Paragraph 22 is amended (new text is underlined and deleted text is struck through) as follows:

> 22 Participation by a parent or subsidiary in a defined benefit plan that shares risks between group entities is a transaction between related parties (see paragraph ~~34B~~ 42 of AASB 119 (September 2011)).

Amendments to AASB 134

17 In the Illustrative Examples accompanying AASB 134, paragraphs B9 and B10 are amended (new text is underlined and deleted text is struck through) as follows:

> B9 Pension cost for an interim period is calculated on an annual reporting period-to-date basis by using the actuarially determined pension cost rate at the end of the prior annual reporting period, adjusted for significant market fluctuations since that time and for ~~significant curtailments, settlements, or other~~ significant ~~one-time~~ one-off events, such as plan amendments, curtailments and settlements.

> B10 Accumulating ~~compensated~~ paid absences are those that are carried forward and can be used in future periods if the current period's entitlement is not used in full. AASB 119 *Employee Benefits* requires that an entity measure the expected cost of and obligation for accumulating ~~compensated~~ paid absences at the amount the entity expects to pay as a result of the unused entitlement that has accumulated at the end of the reporting period. That principle is also applied at the end of interim financial reporting periods. Conversely, an entity recognises no expense or liability for non-accumulating ~~compensated~~ paid absences at the end of an interim reporting period, just as it recognises none at the end of an annual reporting period.

Amendments to AASB 1049

18   Paragraphs 14 and 31 are amended (new text is underlined and deleted text is struck through) as follows:

14   Examples of particular optional treatments in Australian Accounting Standards that paragraph 13 of this Standard has the effect of limiting, include:

(a)   …

(c)   ~~actuarial gains and losses relating to defined benefit superannuation plans that may be recognised in full through operating result (which is part of comprehensive result), recognised in full through other non-owner changes in equity (which is also part of comprehensive result), or partially deferred using a 'corridor approach' under AASB 119 Employee Benefits. For the purpose of this Standard, the option to partially defer using a 'corridor approach' is not available because it is not acceptable under the ABS GFS Manual. The other two options are available;~~ [deleted]

(d)   …

31   The following examples illustrate how the approach in paragraph 30 applies to particular items:

(a)   in both a whole of government and GGS financial reporting context:

(i)   …

(iii)   ~~actuarial gains and losses~~ <u>remeasurements of the defined benefit liability (asset)</u> relating to defined benefit superannuation plans are classified as other economic flows, ~~irrespective of whether they are included in the calculation of operating result or the other non-owner changes in equity section of the statement of comprehensive income~~;

(iv)   …

19   Paragraph 34 is deleted and a note added as follows:

34   ~~As noted in paragraph 14(c), actuarial gains and losses relating to defined benefit superannuation plans may be recognised in full either through operating result or in full through other non-owner changes in equity.~~ [Deleted]

20   In the Illustrative Examples accompanying AASB 1049, Illustrative Example A is amended (new text is underlined and deleted text is struck through) as follows:

ILLUSTRATIVE EXAMPLE A

…

Statement of Comprehensive Income for the Whole of Government of the ABC Government for the Year Ended 30 June 20XX

	Notes	$m

…

Other Economic Flows – Included in Operating Result

…

~~Net actuarial gains~~[a] <u>Remeasurements</u> <u>of the defined benefit liability</u>		866

…

~~a Explanatory note: As noted in paragraph 14(c) of this Standard, an alternative treatment of net actuarial gains relating to defined benefit superannuation plans [consistent with paragraph 93B of AASB 119 *Employee Benefits*] would be to recognise them in full through other non-owner changes in equity (which is part of comprehensive result).~~

…

R1 Statement of Comprehensive Income for the Whole of Government by Sector of the ABC Government for the Year Ended 30 June 20XX

	Notes	GGS sector $m	PNFC sector $m	PFC sector $m	Eliminations $m	Whole of Government $m
...						
~~Net actuarial gains~~						
Remeasurements of the defined benefit liability		840	21	5	–	866
...						

21   Illustrative Example B is amended (new text is underlined and deleted text is struck through) as follows:

ILLUSTRATIVE EXAMPLE B

Statement of Comprehensive Income for the General Government Sector of the ABC Government for the Year Ended 30 June 20XX

	Notes	$m
...		

Other Economic Flows – Included in Operating Result

...		
~~Net actuarial gains~~[a] Remeasurements of the defined benefit liability		840
...		

a ~~Explanatory note: As noted in paragraph 14(c) of this Standard, an alternative treatment of net actuarial gains relating to defined benefit superannuation plans [consistent with paragraph 93B of AASB 119 *Employee Benefits*] would be to recognise them in full through other non-owner changes in equity (which is part of comprehensive result).~~

...

Amendments to AASB 2011-8

22   Paragraphs 52 and 53 are amended (new text is underlined and deleted text is struck through) as follows:

   52   Paragraphs ~~50 and 102 are~~ 113 is amended as follows:

      ~~50   Accounting by an entity for defined benefit plans involves the following steps:~~

         ~~(a)~~   ...

         ~~(c)~~ determining measuring the fair value of any plan assets ~~(see paragraphs 102–104)~~;

         ~~(d)~~ ...

         ...

      ~~102~~ 113   The fair value of any plan assets is deducted in determining the deficit or surplus. ~~amount recognised in the statement of financial position in accordance with~~ under paragraph 54. ~~When no market price is available, the fair value of plan assets is estimated; for example, by discounting expected future cash flows using a discount rate that reflects both the risk associated with the plan assets and the maturity or expected disposal date of those assets (or, if they have no maturity, the expected period until the settlement of the related obligation).~~

53   Paragraph ~~162~~ 174 is added as follows:

~~162~~174   AASB 2011-8 *Amendments to Australian Accounting Standards arising from AASB 13*, issued in September 2011, amended the definition of fair value in paragraph ~~7~~ 8 and amended paragraphs ~~50 and 102~~ 113. An entity shall apply those amendments when it applies AASB 13.

Amendments to Interpretation 14

23   Paragraphs 25 and 26 are deleted, paragraphs 1, 6, 17 and 24 are amended (new text is underlined and deleted text is struck through) and paragraph 27C is added as follows:

1   Paragraph ~~58~~ 64 of Accounting Standard AASB 119 *Employee Benefits* limits the measurement of a net defined benefit asset to the lower of the surplus in the defined benefit plan and the asset ceiling. Paragraph 8 of AASB 119 defines the asset ceiling as 'the present value of any economic benefits available in the form of refunds from the plan or reductions in future contributions to the plan' ~~plus unrecognised gains and losses~~. Questions have arisen about when refunds or reductions in future contributions should be regarded as available, particularly when a minimum funding requirement exists.

6   The issues addressed in this Interpretation are:

   (a)   when refunds or reductions in future contributions should be regarded as available in accordance with the definition of the asset ceiling in paragraph 8 ~~paragraph 58~~ of AASB 119;

   (b)   ...

17   An entity shall determine the future service costs using assumptions consistent with those used to determine the defined benefit obligation and with the situation that exists at the end of the reporting period as determined by AASB 119. Therefore, an entity shall assume no change to the benefits to be provided by a plan in the future until the plan is amended and shall assume a stable workforce in the future unless the entity ~~is demonstrably committed at the end of the reporting period to~~ makes a reduction in the number of employees covered by the plan. In the latter case, the assumption about the future workforce shall include the reduction. ...

24   To the extent that the contributions payable will not be available after they are paid into the plan, the entity shall recognise a liability when the obligation arises. The liability shall reduce the net defined benefit asset or increase the net defined benefit liability so that no gain or loss is expected to result from applying paragraph ~~58~~ 64 of AASB 119 when the contributions are paid.

27C   AASB 2011-10 *Amendments to Australian Accounting Standards arising from AASB 119 (September 2011)* amended paragraphs 1, 6, 17 and 24 and deleted paragraphs 25 and 26. An entity shall apply those amendments when it applies AASB 119 (September 2011).

7   In the Illustrative Examples accompanying Interpretation 14, Illustrative Examples 1–4 are amended (new text is underlined and deleted text is struck through) as follows:

IE1   ...

Market value of assets	1,200
Present value of defined benefit obligation under AASB 119	(1,100)
Surplus	100
~~Defined benefit asset (before consideration of the minimum funding requirement)~~[a]	~~100~~

~~(a) For simplicity, it is assumed that there are no unrecognised amounts.~~

IE2   Paragraph 24 of AASB Interpretation 14 requires the entity to recognise a liability to the extent that the contributions payable are not fully available. Payment of the contributions of 200 will increase the AASB 119 surplus from 100 to 300. Under the rules of the plan this amount will be fully refundable to the entity with no associated costs. Therefore, no liability is recognised for the obligation to pay the contributions <u>and the net defined benefit asset is 100</u>.

IE3   ...

Market value of assets	1,000
Present value of defined benefit obligation under AASB 119	(1,100)
Deficit	(100)
~~Defined benefit (liability) (before consideration of the minimum funding requirement)~~[a]	~~(100)~~

~~(a) For simplicity, it is assumed that there are no unrecognised amounts.~~

IE7   Therefore, <u>the net defined benefit liability is 180, comprising the deficit of 100 plus the additional liability of 80 resulting from the requirements in paragraph 24 of AASB Interpretation 14.</u> ~~the entity increases the defined benefit liability by 80. As required by paragraph 26 of AASB Interpretation 14, 80 is recognised immediately in accordance with the entity's adopted policy for recognising the effect of the limit in paragraph 58 and the entity recognises a net liability of 180 in the statement of financial position.~~ No other liability is recognised in respect of the statutory obligation to pay contributions of 300.

Summary

Market value of assets	1,000
Present value of defined benefit obligation under AASB 119	(1,100)
Deficit	(100)
~~Defined benefit liability (before consideration of the minimum finding requirement)~~[a]	~~100~~
~~Adjustment in respect of minimum funding requirement~~	
Effect of the asset ceiling	(80)
Net <u>defined benefit</u> liability ~~recognised in the statement of financial position~~	(180)

~~(a) For simplicity, it is assumed that there are no unrecognised amounts.~~

IE8   When the contributions of 300 are paid, the net <u>defined benefit</u> asset ~~recognised in the statement of financial position~~ will be 120.

IE10   Plan C also has an AASB 119 surplus at the end of the reporting period of 50, which cannot be refunded to the entity under any circumstances. ~~There are no unrecognised amounts.~~

IE14   When these contributions are paid into the plan, ~~the present value of~~ the AASB 119 surplus (i.e. the fair value of assets less the present value of the defined benefit obligation) would, other things being equal, increase from 50 to 350 (300 + 50).

IE19   Paragraph 24 of AASB Interpretation 14 requires the entity to recognise a liability to the extent that the additional contributions payable will not be fully available. Therefore, the ~~entity reduces the defined benefit asset by~~ <u>effect of the asset ceiling is</u> 294

(50 + 300 – 56).

IE20 ~~As required by paragraph 26 of AASB Interpretation 14, the 294 is recognised immediately in accordance with the entity's adopted policy for recognising the effect of the limit in paragraph 58 and~~ <u>T</u>the entity recognises a net <u>defined benefit</u> liability of 244 in the statement of financial position. No other liability is recognised in respect of the obligation to make contributions to fund the minimum funding shortfall.

Summary

Surplus	<u>50</u>
Net ~~D~~defined benefit asset (before consideration of the minimum funding requirement)	50
~~Adjustment in respect of minimum funding requirement~~	
Effect of the asset ceiling	(294)
Net <u>defined benefit</u> liability ~~recognised in the statement of financial position~~[a]	<u>(244)</u>

~~(a) For simplicity, it is assumed that there are no unrecognised amounts.~~

IE21 When the contributions of 300 are paid into the plan, the net <u>defined benefit</u> asset ~~recognised in the statement of financial position~~ will become 56 (300 – 244).

IE23 Plan D has an AASB 119 surplus of 35 at the beginning of 20X1. ~~There are no cumulative unrecognised net actuarial losses and past service costs.~~ This example assumes that the discount rate and expected return on assets are 0 per cent, and that the plan cannot refund the surplus to the entity under any circumstances but can use the surplus for reductions of future contributions.

IE27 Assuming a discount rate of 0 per cent, the present value of the economic benefit available as a reduction in future contributions is equal to 30. Thus in accordance with paragraph ~~58~~ <u>64</u> of AASB 119 the entity recognises ~~an~~ <u>net</u> <u>defined benefit</u> asset of 30 (because this is lower than the AASB 119 surplus of 65).

AASB 2011-11

Amendments to AASB 119 (September 2011) arising from Reduced Disclosure Requirements

(Issued September 2011)

AASB

Note from the Institute of Chartered Accountants Australia

This note, prepared by the technical editors, is not part of Accounting Standard AASB 2011-11.

Historical development

5 September 2011: AASB 2011-11 was issued amending AASB 119 (September 2011) to incorporate Reduced Disclosure Requirements (RDR).

This Standard is applicable to annual reporting periods beginning on or after 1 July 2013 with early application permitted.

Contents

Preface

Accounting Standard
Amendments to AASB 119 (September 2011)
arising from Reduced Disclosure Requirements

	Paragraphs
Objective	1
Application	2–4
Amendments to AASB 119 (September 2011)	5

> Australian Accounting Standard AASB 2011-11 *Amendments to AASB 119 (September 2011) arising from Reduced Disclosure Requirements* is set out in paragraphs 1–5. All the paragraphs have equal authority.

Preface

Standards Amended by AASB 2011-11

This Standard makes amendments to AASB 119 *Employee Benefits* (September 2011), to incorporate reduced disclosure requirements into the Standard for entities applying Tier 2 requirements in preparing general purpose financial statements.

These amendments arise from the issuance of AASB 119 (September 2011).

Main Features of this Standard

Application Date

This Standard applies to annual reporting periods beginning on or after 1 July 2013. Earlier application is permitted for annual reporting periods beginning on or after 1 July 2009 but before 1 July 2013, provided that AASB 1053 *Application of Tiers of Australian Accounting Standards* is also applied for the period.

Main Requirements

This Standard gives effect to Australian Accounting Standards – Reduced Disclosure Requirements for AASB 119 (September 2011). AASB 1053 provides further information regarding the differential reporting framework and the two tiers of reporting requirements for preparing general purpose financial statements.

Accounting Standard AASB 2011-11

The Australian Accounting Standards Board makes Accounting Standard AASB 2011-11 *Amendments to AASB 119 (September 2011) arising from Reduced Disclosure Requirements* under section 334 of the *Corporations Act 2001*.

Dated 5 September 2011

Kevin M. Stevenson
Chair – AASB

Accounting Standard AASB 2011-11

Amendments to AASB 119 (September 2011) arising from Reduced Disclosure Requirements

Objective

1   The objective of this Standard is to make amendments to AASB 119 *Employee Benefits* (September 2011) to incorporate reduced disclosure requirements for entities applying Tier 2 requirements in preparing general purpose financial statements.

Application

2   **This Standard applies to:**

   (a)   **each entity that is required to prepare financial reports in accordance with Part 2M.3 of the Corporations Act and that is a reporting entity;**

   (b)   **general purpose financial statements of each other reporting entity; and**

   (c)   **financial statements that are, or are held out to be, general purpose financial statements.**

3   **This Standard applies to annual reporting periods beginning on or after 1 July 2013.**

4   **This Standard shall be applied when AASB 1053 *Application of Tiers of Australian Accounting Standards* is applied. This Standard may be applied to annual reporting periods beginning on or after 1 July 2009 but before 1 July 2013 provided AASB 1053 is also adopted early for the same period. When an entity applies this Standard to such an annual reporting period, it shall disclose that fact.**

Amendments to AASB 119 (September 2011)

5   The following subheading and paragraphs are added to AASB 119 (September 2011):

Reduced Disclosure Requirements

Aus1.6   **The following do not apply to entities preparing general purpose financial statements under Australian Accounting Standards – Reduced Disclosure Requirements:**

   (a)   **in paragraph 25, the text "For example, AASB 124 requires disclosures about employee benefits for key management personnel. AASB 101 *Presentation of Financial Statements* requires disclosure of employee benefits expense.";**

   (b)   **paragraphs 54, 135(c), 137, 139(c), 141(a)-(e), 141(h), footnote 3 to paragraph 142, 145-147, 148(d)(v) and 149-151;**

   (c)   **in paragraph 139(a), the text ", including:" and associated paragraphs (i)-(iii);**

   (d)   **in paragraph 140(b), the text "An entity shall also describe the relationship between any reimbursement right and the related obligation.";**

   (e)   **in paragraph 141(f), the text ", showing separately those by the employer and by plan participants";**

   (f)   **in paragraph 141(g), the text ", showing separately the amount paid in respect of any settlements";**

   (g)   **in paragraph 142, the text ", subdividing each class of plan asset into those that have a quoted market price in an active market (as defined in AASB 13 *Fair Value Measurement*³) and those that do not. For example, and considering the level of disclosure discussed in paragraph 136, an entity could distinguish between:" and associated paragraphs (a)-(h);**

(h)   in paragraph 144, the text "Such disclosure shall be in absolute terms (e.g. as an absolute percentage, and not just as a margin between different percentages and other variables). When an entity provides disclosures in total for a grouping of plans, it shall provide such disclosures in the form of weighted averages or relatively narrow ranges."

(i)   in paragraph 148(d)(iv), the text ", including the basis used to determine that deficit or surplus";

(j)   in paragraph 158, the text "AASB 124 requires disclosures about employee benefits for key management personnel."; and

(k)   in paragraph 171, the text "AASB 124 requires disclosures about employee benefits for key management personnel."

Entities applying Australian Accounting Standards – Reduced Disclosure Requirements may elect to comply with some or all of these excluded requirements.

Aus1.7   The requirements that do not apply to entities preparing general purpose financial statements under Australian Accounting Standards – Reduced Disclosure Requirements are identified in this Standard by shading of the relevant text.

Aus1.8   The RDR paragraph in this Standard applies only to entities preparing general purpose financial statements under Australian Accounting Standards – Reduced Disclosure Requirements.

RDR140.1   An entity applying Australian Accounting Standards – Reduced Disclosure Requirements is not required to disclose the reconciliations specified in paragraphs 140 and 141 for prior periods.

AASB 2011-12

Amendments to Australian Accounting Standards arising from Interpretation 20

(Issued November 2011)

Note from the Institute of Chartered Accountants Australia

This note, prepared by the technical editors, is not part of Accounting Standard AASB 2011-12.

Historical development

14 November 2011: AASB 2011-12 was issued amending AASB 1 in relation to Interpretation 20 'Stripping Costs in the Production Phase of a Surface Mine'.

Contents

Preface

Accounting Standard

AASB 2011-12 Amendments to Australian Accounting Standards
arising from Interpretation 20

	Paragraphs
Objective	1
Application	2 – 4
Amendments to AASB 1	5 – 7

> Australian Accounting Standard AASB 2011-12 *Amendments to Australian Accounting Standards arising from Interpretation 20* is set out in paragraphs 1 – 7. All the paragraphs have equal authority.

Preface

Standards Amended by AASB 2011-12

This Standard makes amendments to Australian Accounting Standard AASB 1 *First-time Adoption of Australian Accounting Standards*.

These amendments arise from the issuance of IFRIC Interpretation 20 *Stripping Costs in the Production Phase of a Surface Mine*.

Application date

This Standard applies to annual reporting periods beginning on or after 1 January 2013. This Standard is applied when AASB Interpretation 20 is applied. Earlier application is permitted for annual reporting periods beginning on or after 1 January 2005 but before 1 January 2013.

Accounting Standard AASB 2011-12

The Australian Accounting Standards Board makes Accounting Standard AASB 2011-12 *Amendments to Australian Accounting Standards arising from Interpretation 20* under section 334 of the *Corporations Act 2001*.

Dated: 14 November 2011

Kevin M. Stevenson
Chair – AASB

Accounting Standard AASB 2011-12

Amendments to Australian Accounting Standards arising from Interpretation 20

Objective

1   The objective of this Standard is to make amendments to AASB 1 *First-time Adoption of Australian Accounting Standards* as a consequence of the issuance of IFRIC Interpretation 20 by the International Accounting Standards Board in October 2011.

Application

2   **This Standard applies to:**

   (a)   each entity that is required to prepare financial reports in accordance with Part 2M.3 of the Corporations Act and that is a reporting entity;

   (b)   general purpose financial statements of each other reporting entity; and

   (c)   financial statements that are, or are held out to be, general purpose financial statements.

3   This Standard applies to annual reporting periods beginning on or after 1 January 2013.

4   This Standard shall be applied when Interpretation 20 is applied. This Standard may be applied to annual reporting periods beginning on or after 1 January 2005 but before 1 January 2013 provided Interpretation 20 is also adopted early for the same period. When an entity applies this Standard to such an annual reporting period, it shall disclose that fact.

Amendments to AASB 1

5   In Appendix D, paragraph D1 is amended as follows (new text is underlined and deleted text is struck through):

    D1   An entity may elect to use one or more of the following exemptions:

        (a)   share-based payment transactions (paragraphs D2 and D3);

        ...

        (m)   financial assets or intangible assets accounted for in accordance with Interpretation 12 *Service Concession Arrangements* (paragraph D22);

        (n)   borrowing costs (paragraph D23);

        (o)   transfers of assets from customers (paragraph D24);

        (p)   extinguishing financial liabilities with equity instruments (paragraph D25);

        (q)   severe hyperinflation (paragraphs D26–D30); ~~and~~

        (r)   joint arrangements (paragraph D31)~~.~~; and

        (s)   stripping costs in the production phase of a surface mine (paragraph D32).

6   After paragraph D31 a heading and paragraph D32 are added:

Stripping costs in the production phase of a surface mine

    D32   A first-time adopter may apply the transitional provisions set out in paragraphs A2 to A4 of AASB Interpretation 20 *Stripping Costs in the Production Phase of a Surface Mine* as identified in AASB 1048.

7   After paragraph 39L paragraph 39M is added:

    39M   AASB 2011-12 *Amendments to Australian Accounting Standards arising from AASB Interpretation 20* added paragraph D32 and amended paragraph D1. An entity shall apply that amendment when it applies AASB Interpretation 20 *Stripping Costs in the Production Phase of a Surface Mine* as identified in AASB 1048.

AASB 2012-1

Amendments to Australian Accounting Standards – Fair Value Measurement – Reduced Disclosure Requirements

[AASB 3, AASB 7, AASB 13, AASB 140 and AASB 141]

(Issued March 2012)

Note from the Institute of Chartered Accountants Australia

This note, prepared by the technical editors, is not part of Accounting Standard AASB 2012-1.

Historical development

21 March 2012: AASB 2012-1 was issued amending AASBs 3, 7, 13, 140 and 141 to apply the AASB's reduced disclosure regime arising from AASB 13 *Fair Value Measurement*.

AASB

Contents

Preface

Accounting Standard

AASB 2012-1 Amendments to Australian Accounting Standards – Fair Value Measurement – Reduced Disclosure Requirements

	Paragraphs
Objective	1
Application	2 – 4
Amendment to AASB 3	5
Amendments to AASB 7	6 – 7
Amendments to AASB 13	8
Amendments to AASB 140	9
Amendment to AASB 141	10

> Australian Accounting Standard AASB 2012-1 *Amendments to Australian Accounting Standards – Fair Value Measurement – Reduced Disclosure Requirements* is set out in paragraphs 1 – 10. All the paragraphs have equal authority.

Preface

Introduction

This Standard makes amendments to the Australian Accounting Standards (including some amended by AASB 2010-2 *Amendments to Australian Accounting Standards arising from Reduced Disclosure Requirements*) listed in paragraph 1 of the Standard.

These amendments arise from the proposals that were included in Exposure Draft ED 219 *AASB 13* Fair Value Measurement *and AASB 2011-8* Amendments to Australian Accounting Standards arising from AASB 13: *Tier 2 Proposals* and result from the application of the AASB's 'Tier 2 Disclosure Principles'.

Main Features of this Standard

Application Date

This Standard applies to annual reporting periods beginning on or after 1 July 2013. Earlier application is permitted for annual reporting periods beginning on or after 1 July 2009 but before 1 July 2013, provided that the following are also adopted for the same period:

(a)   AASB 1053 *Application of Tiers of Australian Accounting Standards*;

(b)   AASB 13 *Fair Value Measurement*; and

(c)   AASB 2011-8 *Amendments to Australian Accounting Standards arising from AASB 13*.

Main Requirements

This Standard establishes and amends reduced disclosure requirements for entities preparing general purpose financial statements under Australian Accounting Standards – Reduced Disclosure Requirements for additional and amended disclosures arising from AASB 13 and the consequential amendments implemented through AASB 2011-8.

Accounting Standard AASB 2012-1

The Australian Accounting Standards Board makes Accounting Standard AASB 2012-1 *Amendments to Australian Accounting Standards – Fair Value Measurement – Reduced Disclosure Requirements* under section 334 of the *Corporations Act 2001*.

Dated 21 March 2012

Kevin M. Stevenson
Chair – AASB

Accounting Standard AASB 2012-1

Amendments to Australian Accounting Standards – Fair Value Measurement – Reduced Disclosure Requirements

Objective

1   The objective of this Standard is to make amendments to:

(a)   AASB 3 *Business Combinations*;

(b)   AASB 7 *Financial Instruments: Disclosures*;

(c)   AASB 13 *Fair Value Measurement*;

(d)   AASB 140 *Investment Property*; and

(e)   AASB 141 *Agriculture*;

to establish reduced disclosure requirements for entities preparing general purpose financial statements under Australian Accounting Standards – Reduced Disclosure Requirements for additional and amended disclosures arising from AASB 13 and the consequential amendments implemented through AASB 2011-8 *Amendments to Australian Accounting Standards arising from AASB 13*.

Application

2   **This Standard applies to:**

(a)   **each entity that is required to prepare financial reports in accordance with Part 2M.3 of the Corporations Act and that is a reporting entity;**

(b)   **general purpose financial statements of each other reporting entity; and**

(c)   **financial statements that are, or are held out to be, general purpose financial statements.**

3   **This Standard applies to annual reporting periods beginning on or after 1 July 2013.**

4   **This Standard shall be applied when AASB 1053 *Application of Tiers of Australian Accounting Standards* is applied. This Standard may be applied to annual reporting periods beginning on or after 1 July 2009 but before 1 July 2013, provided the following are also adopted for the same period:**

(a)   **AASB 1053;**

(b)   **AASB 13; and**

(c)   **AASB 2011-8.**

When an entity applies this Standard to such an annual reporting period, it shall disclose that fact.

Amendment to AASB 3

5   In paragraph Aus1.7(a), the reference to paragraph B64(o)(ii) is deleted.

Amendments to AASB 7

6   In paragraph Aus2.9(a), the reference to paragraphs 25-27 is amended to paragraphs 25-28, and the references to paragraphs 27A and 27B are deleted.

7   Paragraphs Aus2.9(g) and RDR27.1 are deleted. Consequently, the word "and" is added at the end of paragraph Aus2.9(e) and in paragraph Aus2.9(f) the text "; and" is replaced by a full stop.

Amendments to AASB 13

8   The following subheading and paragraphs are added:

Reduced Disclosure Requirements

Aus4.5   **The text "both of" in the lead in of paragraph 91 and paragraphs 91(b), 93(b)-(i), 95 and 97-99 of this Standard do not apply to entities preparing general purpose financial statements under Australian Accounting Standards – Reduced Disclosure Requirements. Entities applying Australian Accounting Standards – Reduced Disclosure Requirements may elect to comply with some or all of these excluded requirements.**

Aus4.6   The requirements that do not apply to entities preparing general purpose financial statements under Australian Accounting Standards – Reduced Disclosure Requirements are identified in this Standard by shading of the relevant text.

Amendments to AASB 140

9   Paragraph Aus1.6(b) is deleted, and paragraphs Aus1.6(c) and (d) are renumbered as paragraphs Aus1.6(b) and (c) respectively.

Amendment to AASB 141

10   In paragraph Aus1.8, the reference to paragraph 48 is deleted.

AASB 2012-2

Amendments to Australian Accounting Standards – Disclosures – Offsetting Financial Assets and Financial Liabilities

[AASB 7 and AASB 132]

(Issued June 2012)

Note from the Institute of Chartered Accountants Australia

This note, prepared by the technical editors, is not part of Accounting Standard AASB 2012-2.

Historical development

29 June 2012: AASB 2012-2 was issued amending AASBs 7 and 132 to provide users of financial statements with information about netting arrangements, including rights of set-off related to an entity's financial instruments and the effects of such rights on its statement of financial position.

Contents

Preface

Accounting Standard

AASB 2012-2 Amendments to Australian Accounting Standards – Disclosures – Offsetting Financial Assets And Financial Liabilities

	Paragraphs
Objective	1
Application	2 – 4
Amendments to AASB 7	5 – 7
Amendment to AASB 132	8

IASB Implementation Guidance – Amendments
(available on the AASB website)

IASB Basis For Conclusions – Amendments
(available on the AASB website)

Australian Accounting Standard AASB 2012-2 *Amendments to Australian Accounting Standards – Disclosures – Offsetting Financial Assets and Financial Liabilities* is set out in paragraphs 1 – 8. All the paragraphs have equal authority.

Preface

Introduction

This Standard makes amendments to Australian Accounting Standards AASB 7 *Financial Instruments: Disclosures* and AASB 132 *Financial Instruments: Presentation*.

These amendments arise from the issuance of *Disclosures – Offsetting Financial Assets and Financial Liabilities* (Amendments to IFRS 7) by the International Accounting Standards Board in December 2011.

Main Features of this Standard

Application Date

This Standard applies to annual reporting periods beginning on or after 1 January 2013 and interim periods within those annual reporting periods.

Main Requirements

This Standard amends the required disclosures in AASB 7 to include information that will enable users of an entity's financial statements to evaluate the effect or potential effect of netting arrangements, including rights of set-off associated with the entity's recognised financial assets and recognised financial liabilities, on the entity's financial position.

This Standard also amends AASB 132 to refer to the additional disclosures added to AASB 7 by this Standard.

A subsequent Standard will establish reduced disclosure requirements for entities preparing general purpose financial statements under Australian Accounting Standards – Reduced Disclosure Requirements in relation to the disclosures added to AASB 7 by this Standard.

Accounting Standard AASB 2012-2

The Australian Accounting Standards Board makes Accounting Standard AASB 2012-2 *Amendments to Australian Accounting Standards – Disclosures – Offsetting Financial Assets and Financial Liabilities* under section 334 of the *Corporations Act 2001*.

Dated 29 June 2012

Kevin M. Stevenson
Chair – AASB

Accounting Standard AASB 2012-2

Amendments to Australian Accounting Standards – Disclosures – Offsetting Financial Assets and Financial Liabilities

Objective

1   The objective of this Standard is to make amendments to:

(a)   AASB 7 *Financial Instruments: Disclosures*; and

(b)   AASB 132 *Financial Instruments: Presentation*;

as a consequence of the issuance of International Financial Reporting Standard *Disclosures – Offsetting Financial Assets and Financial Liabilities* (Amendments to IFRS 7) by the International Accounting Standards Board in December 2011.

Application

2   **This Standard applies to:**

(a)   **each entity that is required to prepare financial reports in accordance with Part 2M.3 of the Corporations Act and that is a reporting entity;**

(b)   **general purpose financial statements of each other reporting entity; and**

(c)   **financial statements that are, or are held out to be, general purpose financial statements.**

3   **This Standard applies to annual reporting periods beginning on or after 1 January 2013 and interim periods within those annual reporting periods.**

4   **This Standard uses underlining, striking out and other typographical material to identify some of the amendments to a Standard, in order to make the amendments more understandable. However, the amendments made by this Standard do not include that underlining, striking out or other typographical material.**

Amendments to AASB 7

5   A heading and paragraphs 13A-13F are added after paragraph 13 as follows:

Offsetting financial assets and financial liabilities

13A   The disclosures in paragraphs 13B-13E supplement the other disclosure requirements of this Standard and are required for all recognised financial instruments that are set off in accordance with paragraph 42 of AASB 132. These disclosures also apply to recognised financial instruments that are subject to an enforceable master netting arrangement or similar agreement, irrespective of whether they are set off in accordance with paragraph 42 of AASB 132.

13B   An entity shall disclose information to enable users of its financial statements to evaluate the effect or potential effect of netting arrangements on the entity's financial position. This includes the effect or potential effect of rights of set-off associated with the entity's recognised financial assets and recognised financial liabilities that are within the scope of paragraph 13A.

Amendments to Australian Accounting Standards – Disclosures   1593
– Offsetting Financial Assets and Financial Liabilities

AASB

13C   To meet the objective in paragraph 13B, an entity shall disclose, at the end of the reporting period, the following quantitative information separately for recognised financial assets and recognised financial liabilities that are within the scope of paragraph 13A:

(a)   the gross amounts of those recognised financial assets and recognised financial liabilities;

(b)   the amounts that are set off in accordance with the criteria in paragraph 42 of AASB 132 when determining the net amounts presented in the statement of financial position;

(c)   the net amounts presented in the statement of financial position;

(d)   the amounts subject to an enforceable master netting arrangement or similar agreement that are not otherwise included in paragraph 13C(b), including:

(i)   amounts related to recognised financial instruments that do not meet some or all of the offsetting criteria in paragraph 42 of AASB 132; and

(ii)   amounts related to financial collateral (including cash collateral); and

(e)   the net amount after deducting the amounts in (d) from the amounts in (c) above.

The information required by this paragraph shall be presented in a tabular format, separately for financial assets and financial liabilities, unless another format is more appropriate.

13D   The total amount disclosed in accordance with paragraph 13C(d) for an instrument shall be limited to the amount in paragraph 13C(c) for that instrument.

13E   An entity shall include a description in the disclosures of the rights of set-off associated with the entity's recognised financial assets and recognised financial liabilities subject to enforceable master netting arrangements and similar agreements that are disclosed in accordance with paragraph 13C(d), including the nature of those rights.

13F   If the information required by paragraphs 13B-13E is disclosed in more than one note to the financial statements, an entity shall cross-refer between those notes.

6   Paragraph 44R is added as follows:

44R   AASB 2012-2 *Amendments to Australian Accounting Standards – Disclosures – Offsetting Financial Assets and Financial Liabilities*, issued in June 2012, added paragraphs 13A-13F and B40-B53. An entity shall apply those amendments for annual reporting periods beginning on or after 1 January 2013 and interim periods within those annual reporting periods. An entity shall provide the disclosures required by those amendments retrospectively.

7   Paragraphs B40-B53 and related headings are added as follows:

Offsetting financial assets and financial liabilities (paragraphs 13A-13F)

Scope (paragraph 13A)

B40   The disclosures in paragraphs 13B-13E are required for all recognised financial instruments that are set off in accordance with paragraph 42 of AASB 132. In addition, financial instruments are within the scope of the disclosure requirements in paragraphs 13B-13E if they are subject to an enforceable master netting arrangement or similar agreement that covers similar financial instruments and transactions, irrespective of whether the financial instruments are set off in accordance with paragraph 42 of AASB 132.

B41   The similar agreements referred to in paragraphs 13A and B40 include derivative clearing agreements, global master repurchase agreements, global master securities lending agreements, and any related rights to financial collateral. The similar financial instruments and transactions referred to in paragraph B40 include derivatives, sale and repurchase agreements, reverse sale and repurchase agreements, securities borrowing, and securities lending agreements. Examples of financial instruments that are not within the scope of paragraph 13A are loans and customer deposits at the same institution (unless they are set off in the statement of financial position), and financial instruments that are subject only to a collateral agreement.

Disclosure of quantitative information for recognised financial assets and recognised financial liabilities within the scope of paragraph 13A (paragraph 13C)

B42 Financial instruments disclosed in accordance with paragraph 13C may be subject to different measurement requirements (for example, a payable related to a repurchase agreement may be measured at amortised cost, while a derivative will be measured at fair value). An entity shall include instruments at their recognised amounts and describe any resulting measurement differences in the related disclosures.

Disclosure of the gross amounts of recognised financial assets and recognised financial liabilities within the scope of paragraph 13A (paragraph 13C(a))

B43 The amounts required by paragraph 13C(a) relate to recognised financial instruments that are set off in accordance with paragraph 42 of AASB 132. The amounts required by paragraph 13C(a) also relate to recognised financial instruments that are subject to an enforceable master netting arrangement or similar agreement irrespective of whether they meet the offsetting criteria. However, the disclosures required by paragraph 13C(a) do not relate to any amounts recognised as a result of collateral agreements that do not meet the offsetting criteria in paragraph 42 of AASB 132. Instead, such amounts are required to be disclosed in accordance with paragraph 13C(d).

Disclosure of the amounts that are set off in accordance with the criteria in paragraph 42 of AASB 132 (paragraph 13C(b))

B44 Paragraph 13C(b) requires that entities disclose the amounts set off in accordance with paragraph 42 of AASB 132 when determining the net amounts presented in the statement of financial position. The amounts of both the recognised financial assets and the recognised financial liabilities that are subject to set-off under the same arrangement will be disclosed in both the financial asset and financial liability disclosures. However, the amounts disclosed (in, for example, a table) are limited to the amounts that are subject to set-off. For example, an entity may have a recognised derivative asset and a recognised derivative liability that meet the offsetting criteria in paragraph 42 of AASB 132. If the gross amount of the derivative asset is larger than the gross amount of the derivative liability, the financial asset disclosure table will include the entire amount of the derivative asset (in accordance with paragraph 13C(a)) and the entire amount of the derivative liability (in accordance with paragraph 13C(b)). However, while the financial liability disclosure table will include the entire amount of the derivative liability (in accordance with paragraph 13C(a)), it will only include the amount of the derivative asset (in accordance with paragraph 13C(b)) that is equal to the amount of the derivative liability.

Disclosure of the net amounts presented in the statement of financial position (paragraph 13C(c))

B45 If an entity has instruments that meet the scope of these disclosures (as specified in paragraph 13A), but that do not meet the offsetting criteria in paragraph 42 of AASB 132, the amounts required to be disclosed by paragraph 13C(c) would equal the amounts required to be disclosed by paragraph 13C(a).

B46 The amounts required to be disclosed by paragraph 13C(c) must be reconciled to the individual line item amounts presented in the statement of financial position.

Amendments to Australian Accounting Standards – Disclosures   1595
– Offsetting Financial Assets and Financial Liabilities

AASB

For example, if an entity determines that the aggregation or disaggregation of individual financial statement line item amounts provides more relevant information, it must reconcile the aggregated or disaggregated amounts disclosed in paragraph 13C(c) back to the individual line item amounts presented in the statement of financial position.

Disclosure of the amounts subject to an enforceable master netting arrangement or similar agreement that are not otherwise included in paragraph 13C(b) (paragraph 13C(d))

B47   Paragraph 13C(d) requires that entities disclose amounts that are subject to an enforceable master netting arrangement or similar agreement that are not otherwise included in paragraph 13C(b). Paragraph 13C(d)(i) refers to amounts related to recognised financial instruments that do not meet some or all of the offsetting criteria in paragraph 42 of AASB 132 (for example, current rights of set-off that do not meet the criterion in paragraph 42(b) of AASB 132, or conditional rights of set-off that are enforceable and exercisable only in the event of default, or only in the event of insolvency or bankruptcy of any of the counterparties).

B48   Paragraph 13C(d)(ii) refers to amounts related to financial collateral, including cash collateral, both received and pledged. An entity shall disclose the fair value of those financial instruments that have been pledged or received as collateral. The amounts disclosed in accordance with paragraph 13C(d)(ii) should relate to the actual collateral received or pledged and not to any resulting payables or receivables recognised to return or receive back such collateral.

Limits on the amounts disclosed in paragraph 13C(d) (paragraph 13D)

B49   When disclosing amounts in accordance with paragraph 13C(d), an entity must take into account the effects of over-collateralisation by financial instrument. To do so, the entity must first deduct the amounts disclosed in accordance with paragraph 13C(d)(i) from the amount disclosed in accordance with paragraph 13C(c). The entity shall then limit the amounts disclosed in accordance with paragraph 13C(d)(ii) to the remaining amount in paragraph 13C(c) for the related financial instrument. However, if rights to collateral can be enforced across financial instruments, such rights can be included in the disclosure provided in accordance with paragraph 13D.

Description of the rights of set-off subject to enforceable master netting arrangements and similar agreements (paragraph 13E)

B50   An entity shall describe the types of rights of set-off and similar arrangements disclosed in accordance with paragraph 13C(d), including the nature of those rights. For example, an entity shall describe its conditional rights. For instruments subject to rights of set-off that are not contingent on a future event but that do not meet the remaining criteria in paragraph 42 of AASB 132, the entity shall describe the reason(s) why the criteria are not met. For any financial collateral received or pledged, the entity shall describe the terms of the collateral agreement (for example, when the collateral is restricted).

Disclosure by type of financial instrument or by counterparty

B51   The quantitative disclosures required by paragraph 13C(a)-(e) may be grouped by type of financial instrument or transaction (for example, derivatives, repurchase and reverse repurchase agreements or securities borrowing and securities lending agreements).

B52   Alternatively, an entity may group the quantitative disclosures required by paragraph 13C(a)-(c) by type of financial instrument, and the quantitative disclosures required by paragraph 13C(c)-(e) by counterparty. If an entity provides the required information by counterparty, the entity is not required to identify the counterparties by name. However, designation of counterparties (Counterparty A, Counterparty B, Counterparty C, etc) shall remain consistent from year to year for the years presented to maintain comparability. Qualitative disclosures shall be considered so that further information can be given about the types of counterparties. When disclosure of the amounts in paragraph 13C(c)-(e) is provided by counterparty, amounts that are individually significant in terms of total counterparty amounts shall be separately disclosed and the remaining individually insignificant counterparty amounts shall be aggregated into one line item.

Other

B53 The specific disclosures required by paragraphs 13C-13E are minimum requirements. To meet the objective in paragraph 13B an entity may need to supplement them with additional (qualitative) disclosures, depending on the terms of the enforceable master netting arrangements and related agreements, including the nature of the rights of set-off, and their effect or potential effect on the entity's financial position.

Amendment to AASB 132

8 Paragraph 43 is amended as follows (new text is underlined):

43 This Standard requires the presentation of financial assets and financial liabilities on a net basis when doing so reflects an entity's expected future cash flows from settling two or more separate financial instruments. When an entity has the right to receive or pay a single net amount and intends to do so, it has, in effect, only a single financial asset or financial liability. In other circumstances, financial assets and financial liabilities are presented separately from each other consistently with their characteristics as resources or obligations of the entity. An entity shall disclose the information required in paragraphs 13B-13E of AASB 7 for recognised financial instruments that are within the scope of paragraph 13A of AASB 7.

AASB 2012-3

Amendments to Australian Accounting Standards – Offsetting Financial Assets and Financial Liabilities

[AASB 132]

(Issued June 2012)

Note from the Institute of Chartered Accountants Australia

This note, prepared by the technical editors, is not part of Accounting Standard AASB 2012-3.

Historical development

29 June 2012: AASB 2012-3 was issued amending AASB 132 to address inconsistencies in the application of the offsetting criteria.

Contents

Preface

Accounting Standard

AASB 2012-3 Amendments to Australian Accounting Standards – Offsetting Financial Assets and Financial Liabilities

	Paragraphs
Objective	1
Application	2 – 4
Amendments to AASB 132	5 – 7

IASB Basis For Conclusions – Amendments
(available on the AASB website)

Australian Accounting Standard AASB 2012-3 *Amendments to Australian Accounting Standards – Offsetting Financial Assets and Financial Liabilities* is set out in paragraphs 1 – 7. All the paragraphs have equal authority.

Preface

Introduction

This Standard makes amendments to Australian Accounting Standard AASB 132 *Financial Instruments: Presentation*.

These amendments arise from the issuance of *Offsetting Financial Assets and Financial Liabilities* (Amendments to IAS 32) by the International Accounting Standards Board in December 2011.

Main Features of this Standard

Application Date

This Standard applies to annual reporting periods beginning on or after 1 January 2014. Earlier application is permitted for annual reporting periods beginning on or after 1 January 2005 but before 1 January 2014, provided that AASB 2012-2 *Amendments to Australian Accounting Standards – Disclosures – Offsetting Financial Assets and Financial Liabilities* is also applied.

Main Requirements

This Standard adds application guidance to AASB 132 to address inconsistencies identified in applying some of the offsetting criteria of AASB 132, including clarifying the meaning of "currently has a legally enforceable right of set-off" and that some gross settlement systems may be considered equivalent to net settlement.

Accounting Standard AASB 2012-3

The Australian Accounting Standards Board makes Accounting Standard AASB 2012-3 *Amendments to Australian Accounting Standards – Offsetting Financial Assets and Financial Liabilities* under section 334 of the *Corporations Act 2001*.

Kevin M. Stevenson
Chair – AASB

Dated 29 June 2012

Accounting Standard AASB 2012-3

Amendments to Australian Accounting Standards – Offsetting Financial Assets and Financial Liabilities

Objective

1   The objective of this Standard is to make amendments to AASB 132 *Financial Instruments: Presentation* as a consequence of the issuance of International Financial Reporting Standard *Offsetting Financial Assets and Financial Liabilities* (Amendments to IAS 32) by the International Accounting Standards Board in December 2011.

Application

2   This Standard applies to:

(a)   each entity that is required to prepare financial reports in accordance with Part 2M.3 of the Corporations Act and that is a reporting entity;

(b)   general purpose financial statements of each other reporting entity; and

(c)   financial statements that are, or are held out to be, general purpose financial statements.

3   This Standard applies to annual reporting periods beginning on or after 1 January 2014.

4   This Standard may be applied to annual reporting periods beginning on or after 1 January 2005 but before 1 January 2014. When an entity applies this Standard to such an annual reporting period, it shall disclose that fact and shall also make the disclosures required by AASB 2012-2 *Amendments to Australian Accounting Standards – Disclosures – Offsetting Financial Assets and Financial Liabilities* issued in June 2012.

Amendments to AASB 132

5   Paragraph 97L is added as follows:

97L   AASB 2012-3 *Amendments to Australian Accounting Standards – Offsetting Financial Assets and Financial Liabilities*, issued in June 2012, deleted paragraph AG38 and added paragraphs AG38A-AG38F. An entity shall apply those amendments for annual reporting periods beginning on or after 1 January 2014. An entity shall apply those amendments retrospectively. Earlier application is permitted. If an entity applies those amendments from an earlier date, it shall disclose that fact and shall also make the disclosures required by AASB 2012-2 *Amendments to Australian Accounting Standards – Disclosures – Offsetting Financial Assets and Financial Liabilities* issued in June 2012.

6   Paragraph AG38 is deleted and a note added as follows:

AG38 [Deleted by the IASB]

7   Paragraphs AG38A-AG38F and related headings are added as follows:

Criterion that an entity 'currently has a legally enforceable right to set off the recognised amounts' (paragraph 42(a))

AG38A   A right of set-off may be currently available or it may be contingent on a future event (for example, the right may be triggered or exercisable only on the occurrence of some future event, such as the default, insolvency or bankruptcy of one of the counterparties). Even if the right of set-off is not contingent on a future event, it may only be legally enforceable in the normal course of business, or in the event of default, or in the event of insolvency or bankruptcy, of one or all of the counterparties.

AG38B To meet the criterion in paragraph 42(a), an entity must currently have a legally enforceable right of set-off. This means that the right of set-off:

(a) must not be contingent on a future event; and

(b) must be legally enforceable in all of the following circumstances:

(i) the normal course of business;

(ii) the event of default; and

(iii) the event of insolvency or bankruptcy

of the entity and all of the counterparties.

AG38C The nature and extent of the right of set-off, including any conditions attached to its exercise and whether it would remain in the event of default or insolvency or bankruptcy, may vary from one legal jurisdiction to another. Consequently, it cannot be assumed that the right of set-off is automatically available outside of the normal course of business. For example, the bankruptcy or insolvency laws of a jurisdiction may prohibit, or restrict, the right of set-off in the event of bankruptcy or insolvency in some circumstances.

AG38D The laws applicable to the relationships between the parties (for example, contractual provisions, the laws governing the contract, or the default, insolvency or bankruptcy laws applicable to the parties) need to be considered to ascertain whether the right of set-off is enforceable in the normal course of business, in an event of default, and in the event of insolvency or bankruptcy, of the entity and all of the counterparties (as specified in paragraph AG38B(b)).

Criterion that an entity 'intends either to settle on a net basis, or to realise the asset and settle the liability simultaneously' (paragraph 42(b))

AG38E To meet the criterion in paragraph 42(b) an entity must intend either to settle on a net basis or to realise the asset and settle the liability simultaneously. Although the entity may have a right to settle net, it may still realise the asset and settle the liability separately.

AG38F If an entity can settle amounts in a manner such that the outcome is, in effect, equivalent to net settlement, the entity will meet the net settlement criterion in paragraph 42(b). This will occur if, and only if, the gross settlement mechanism has features that eliminate or result in insignificant credit and liquidity risk, and that will process receivables and payables in a single settlement process or cycle. For example, a gross settlement system that has all of the following characteristics would meet the net settlement criterion in paragraph 42(b):

(a) financial assets and financial liabilities eligible for set-off are submitted at the same point in time for processing;

(b) once the financial assets and financial liabilities are submitted for processing, the parties are committed to fulfil the settlement obligation;

(c) there is no potential for the cash flows arising from the assets and liabilities to change once they have been submitted for processing (unless the processing fails – see (d) below);

(d) assets and liabilities that are collateralised with securities will be settled on a securities transfer or similar system (for example, delivery versus payment), so that if the transfer of securities fails, the processing of the related receivable or payable for which the securities are collateral will also fail (and vice versa);

(e) any transactions that fail, as outlined in (d), will be re-entered for processing until they are settled;

(f)   settlement is carried out through the same settlement institution (for example, a settlement bank, a central bank or a central securities depository); and

(g)   an intraday credit facility is in place that will provide sufficient overdraft amounts to enable the processing of payments at the settlement date for each of the parties, and it is virtually certain that the intraday credit facility will be honoured if called upon.

AASB 2012-4

Amendments to Australian Accounting Standards – Government Loans

[AASB 1]

(Issued June 2012)

Note from the Institute of Chartered Accountants Australia

This note, prepared by the technical editors, is not part of Accounting Standard AASB 2012-4.

Historical development

29 June 2012: AASB 2012-4 was issued amending AASB 1 to provide relief to first-time adopters of IFRSs from requirements in AASB 120.

Contents

Preface

Accounting Standard

AASB 2012-4 Amendments To Australian Accounting Standards – Government Loans

Paragraphs

Objective   1

Application   2 – 5

Amendments to AASB 1   6 – 8

IASB Implementation Guidance – Amendments
(available on the AASB website)

IASB Basis For Conclusions – Amendments
(available on the AASB website)

> Australian Accounting Standard AASB 2012-4 *Amendments to Australian Accounting Standards – Government Loans* is set out in paragraphs 1 – 8. All the paragraphs have equal authority.

Preface

Introduction

This Standard makes amendments to Australian Accounting Standard AASB 1 *First-time Adoption of Australian Accounting Standards*.

These amendments arise primarily from the issuance of *Government Loans* (Amendments to IFRS 1) by the International Accounting Standards Board in March 2012.

Main Features of this Standard

Application Date

This Standard applies to annual reporting periods beginning on or after 1 January 2013. Earlier application is permitted for annual reporting periods beginning on or after 1 January 2005 but before 1 January 2013.

Main Requirements

This Standard adds an exception to the retrospective application of Australian Accounting Standards to require that first-time adopters apply the requirements in AASB 139 *Financial Instruments: Recognition and Measurement* (or AASB 9 *Financial Instruments*) and AASB 120 *Accounting for Government Grants and Disclosure of Government Assistance* prospectively to government loans existing at the date of transition to Australian Accounting Standards. This means that first-time adopters would not recognise the corresponding benefit of the government loan received at a below-market rate of interest as a government grant. However, entities may choose to apply the requirements of AASB 139 (or AASB 9) and AASB 120 to government loans retrospectively if the information needed to do so had been obtained at the time of initially accounting for that loan. These amendments give first-time adopters the same relief as existing preparers of Australian-Accounting-Standards financial statements.

Accounting Standard AASB 2012-4

The Australian Accounting Standards Board makes Accounting Standard AASB 2012-4 *Amendments to Australian Accounting Standards – Government Loans* under section 334 of the *Corporations Act 2001*.

Kevin M. Stevenson
Dated 29 June 2012   Chair – AASB

Accounting Standard AASB 2012-4

Amendments To Australian Accounting Standards – Government Loans

Objective

1   The objective of this Standard is to make amendments to AASB 1 *First-time Adoption of Australian Accounting Standards* as a consequence of the issuance of International Financial Reporting Standard *Government Loans* (Amendments to IFRS 1) by the International Accounting Standards Board in March 2012.

Application

2   **This Standard applies to:**

(a)   **each entity that is required to prepare financial reports in accordance with Part 2M.3 of the Corporations Act and that is a reporting entity;**

(b)   **general purpose financial statements of each other reporting entity; and**

(c)   **financial statements that are, or are held out to be, general purpose financial statements.**

3   **This Standard applies to annual reporting periods beginning on or after 1 January 2013.**

4   **This Standard may be applied to annual reporting periods beginning on or after 1 January 2005 but before 1 January 2013. When an entity applies this Standard to such an annual reporting period, it shall disclose that fact.**

5   **This Standard uses underlining, striking out and other typographical material to identify some of the amendments to AASB 1, in order to make the amendments more understandable. However, the amendments made by this Standard do not include that underlining, striking out or other typographical material.**

Amendments to AASB 1

6   Paragraphs 39N and 39O are added as follows:

39N   AASB 2012-4 *Amendments to Australian Accounting Standards – Government Loans*, issued in June 2012, amended paragraph B1 and added paragraphs B10-B12. An entity shall apply those paragraphs for annual reporting periods beginning on or after 1 January 2013. Earlier application is permitted.

39O   Paragraphs B10 and B11 refer to AASB 9. If an entity applies this Standard but does not yet apply AASB 9, the references in paragraphs B10 and B11 to AASB 9 shall be read as references to AASB 139 *Financial Instruments: Recognition and Measurement*.

7   Paragraph B1 is amended as follows (new text is underlined and deleted text is struck through):

B1   An entity shall apply the following exceptions:

(a)   derecognition of financial assets and financial liabilities (paragraphs B2 and B3);

(b)   hedge accounting (paragraphs B4-B6);

(c)   non-controlling interests (paragraph B7); <u>and</u>

~~(d)   classification and measurement of financial assets (paragraph B8); and~~

~~(e)   embedded derivatives (paragraph B9).~~

<u>(f)   government loans (paragraphs B10-B12).</u>

8   Paragraphs B10-B12 and a related heading are added as follows:

Government loans

B10   A first-time adopter shall classify all government loans received as a financial liability or an equity instrument in accordance with AASB 132 *Financial Instruments: Presentation*. Except as permitted by paragraph B11, a first-time adopter shall apply the requirements in AASB 9 *Financial Instruments* and AASB 120 *Accounting for Government Grants and Disclosure of Government Assistance* prospectively to government loans existing at the date of transition to Australian Accounting Standards and shall not recognise the corresponding benefit of the government loan at a below-market rate of interest as a government grant. Consequently, if a first-time adopter did not, under its previous GAAP, recognise and measure a government loan at a below-market rate of interest on a basis consistent with Australian-Accounting-Standards requirements, it shall use its previous GAAP carrying amount of the loan at the date of transition to Australian Accounting Standards as the carrying amount of the loan in the opening Australian-Accounting-Standards statement of financial position. An entity shall apply AASB 9 to the measurement of such loans after the date of transition to Australian Accounting Standards.

B11   Despite paragraph B10, an entity may apply the requirements in AASB 9 and AASB 120 retrospectively to any government loan originated before the date of transition to Australian Accounting Standards, provided that the information needed to do so had been obtained at the time of initially accounting for that loan.

B12   The requirements and guidance in paragraphs B10 and B11 do not preclude an entity from being able to use the exemptions described in paragraphs D19-D19D relating to the designation of previously recognised financial instruments at fair value through profit or loss.

AASB 2012-5

Amendments to Australian Accounting Standards arising from Annual Improvements 2009 – 2011 Cycle

[AASB 1, AASB 101, AASB 116, AASB 132 & AASB 134 and Interpretation 2]

(Issued June 2012)

Note from the Institute of Chartered Accountants Australia

This note, prepared by the technical editor, is not part of Accounting Standard AASB 2012-5.

Historical development

29 June 2012: AASB 2012-5 was issued amending AASBs 1, 101, 116, 132 & 134 and Interpretation 2. Most of the changes in AASB 2012-5 are not expected to have significant impact in Australia.

Contents

Preface

Accounting Standard

AASB 2012-5 Amendments to Australian Accounting Standards arising from Annual Improvements 2009–2011 Cycle

	Paragraphs
Objective	1
Application	2 – 7
Amendments to AASB 1	8 – 10
Amendments to AASB 101	11
Amendments to AASB 116	12
Amendments to AASB 132	13
Amendments to AASB 134	14 – 15
Amendments to Interpretation 2	16

IASB Bases For Conclusions – Amendments
(available on the AASB website)

> Australian Accounting Standard AASB 2012-5 *Amendments to Australian Accounting Standards arising from Annual Improvements 2009–2011 Cycle* is set out in paragraphs 1 – 16. All the paragraphs have equal authority.

Preface

Introduction

This Standard makes amendments to the Australian Accounting Standards and Interpretation listed in paragraph 1 of the Standard.

These amendments are a consequence of the annual improvements process, which provides a vehicle for making non-urgent but necessary amendments to Standards.

These amendments result from proposals that were included in Exposure Draft ED 213 *Improvements to IFRSs* published in July 2011 and follow the issuance of *Annual Improvements to IFRSs 2009–2011 Cycle* issued by the International Accounting Standards Board in May 2012.

Main Features of this Standard

Application Date

This Standard is applicable to annual reporting periods beginning on or after 1 January 2013. Earlier application is permitted for annual reporting periods beginning on or after 1 January 2005 but before 1 January 2013.

The insertion of early application conditions in the individual Standards and Interpretation means that the amendments (or sets of amendments) to each of those Standards and Interpretation can be applied separately.

Main Requirements

The subjects of the principal amendments to the Standards and Interpretation are set out below:

Australian Accounting Standard or Interpretation	Subject of amendment
AASB 1 *First-time Adoption of Australian Accounting Standards*	Repeated application of AASB 1
	Borrowing costs

Australian Accounting Standard or Interpretation	Subject of amendment
AASB 101 *Presentation of Financial Statements*	Clarification of the requirements for comparative information
AASB 116 *Property, Plant and Equipment*	Classification of servicing equipment
AASB 132 *Financial Instruments: Presentation*; and Interpretation 2 *Members' Shares in Co-operative Entities and Similar Instruments*	Tax effect of distribution to holders of equity instruments
AASB 134 *Interim Financial Reporting*	Interim financial reporting and segment information for total assets and liabilities

Accounting Standard AASB 2012-5

The Australian Accounting Standards Board makes Accounting Standard AASB 2012-5 *Amendments to Australian Accounting Standards arising from Annual Improvements 2009–2011 Cycle* under section 334 of the *Corporations Act 2001*.

Dated 29 June 2012

Kevin M. Stevenson
Chair – AASB

Accounting Standard AASB 2012-5

Amendments to Australian Accounting Standards arising from Annual Improvements 2009–2011 Cycle

Objective

1   The objective of this Standard is to make amendments to:

(a)   AASB 1 *First-time Adoption of Australian Accounting Standards*;

(b)   AASB 101 *Presentation of Financial Statements*;

(c)   AASB 116 *Property, Plant and Equipment*;

(d)   AASB 132 *Financial Instruments: Presentation*;

(e)   AASB 134 *Interim Financial Reporting*; and

(f)   Interpretation 2 *Members' Shares in Co-operative Entities and Similar Instruments*;

as a consequence of the issuance of International Financial Reporting Standard *Annual Improvements to IFRSs 2009–2011 Cycle* by the International Accounting Standards Board in May 2012.

Application

2   **Subject to paragraphs 3 and 4, this Standard applies to:**

(a)   **each entity that is required to prepare financial reports in accordance with Part 2M.3 of the Corporations Act and that is a reporting entity;**

(b)   **general purpose financial statements of each other reporting entity; and**

(c)   **financial statements that are, or are held out to be, general purpose financial statements.**

3   **In respect of AASB 101, this Standard applies to:**

(a)   **each entity that is required to prepare financial reports in accordance with Part 2M.3 of the Corporations Act;**

(b)   **general purpose financial statements of each reporting entity; and**

(c)   **financial statements that are, or are held out to be, general purpose financial statements.**

4   In respect of AASB 134, this Standard applies to:

    (a)   each disclosing entity required to prepare half-year financial reports in accordance with Part 2M.3 of the Corporations Act;

    (b)   interim financial reports that are general purpose financial statements of each other reporting entity; and

    (c)   interim financial reports that are, or are held out to be, general purpose financial statements.

5   This Standard applies to annual reporting periods beginning on or after 1 January 2013.

6   This Standard may be applied to annual reporting periods beginning on or after 1 January 2005 but before 1 January 2013. The insertion of early application conditions in the individual Standards and Interpretation means that the amendments (or sets of amendments) to each of those Standards and Interpretation can be applied separately from the other amendments provided the particular early application conditions are satisfied.

7   This Standard uses underlining, striking out and other typographical material to identify some of the amendments to a Standard or an Interpretation, in order to make the amendments more understandable. However, the amendments made by this Standard do not include that underlining, striking out or other typographical material.

Amendments to AASB 1

8   Paragraphs 4A, 4B, 23A, 23B and 39P are added as follows:

    4A   Notwithstanding the requirements in paragraphs 2-Aus3.2, an entity that has applied Australian Accounting Standards or IFRSs in a previous reporting period, but whose most recent previous annual financial statements did not contain an explicit and unreserved statement of compliance with Australian Accounting Standards or IFRSs, must either apply this Standard or else apply Australian Accounting Standards retrospectively in accordance with AASB 108 *Accounting Policies, Changes in Accounting Estimates and Errors* as if the entity had never stopped applying Australian Accounting Standards or IFRSs.

    4B   When an entity does not elect to apply this Standard in accordance with paragraph 4A, the entity shall nevertheless apply the disclosure requirements in paragraphs 23A and 23B of AASB 1, in addition to the disclosure requirements in AASB 108.

    23A   An entity that has applied Australian Accounting Standards or IFRSs in a previous period, as described in paragraph 4A, shall disclose:

        (a)   the reason it stopped applying Australian Accounting Standards or IFRSs; and

        (b)   the reason it is resuming or commencing the application of Australian Accounting Standards.

    23B   When an entity, in accordance with paragraph 4A, does not elect to apply AASB 1, the entity shall explain the reasons for electing to apply Australian Accounting Standards as if it had never stopped applying Australian Accounting Standards or IFRSs.

    39P   AASB 2012-5 *Amendments to Australian Accounting Standards arising from Annual Improvements 2009–2011 Cycle*, issued in June 2012, added paragraphs 4A, 4B, 23A and 23B. An entity shall apply that amendment retrospectively in accordance with AASB 108 *Accounting Policies, Changes in Accounting Estimates and Errors* for annual reporting periods beginning on or after 1 January 2013. Earlier application is permitted. If an entity applies that amendment for an earlier period it shall disclose that fact.

9   Paragraph D23 is amended as follows (new text is underlined and deleted text is struck through) and paragraph 39Q is added:

D23   ~~A first-time adopter may apply the transitional provisions set out in paragraphs 27 and 28 of AASB 123~~ *Borrowing Costs*, ~~as revised in 2007. In those paragraphs references to the application date shall be interpreted as 1 January 2009 or the date of transition to Australian Accounting Standards, whichever is later.~~ A first-time adopter can elect to apply the requirements of AASB 123 *Borrowing Costs* from the date of transition or from an earlier date as permitted by paragraph 28 of AASB 123. From the date on which an entity that applies this exemption begins to apply AASB 123, the entity:

(a)   shall not restate the borrowing cost component that was capitalised under previous GAAP and that was included in the carrying amount of assets at that date; and

(b)   shall account for borrowing costs incurred on or after that date in accordance with AASB 123, including those borrowing costs incurred on or after that date on qualifying assets already under construction.

39Q   AASB 2012-5 *Amendments to Australian Accounting Standards arising from Annual Improvements 2009–2011 Cycle*, issued in June 2012, amended paragraph D23. An entity shall apply that amendment retrospectively in accordance with AASB 108 *Accounting Policies, Changes in Accounting Estimates and Errors* for annual reporting periods beginning on or after 1 January 2013. Earlier application is permitted. If an entity applies that amendment for an earlier period it shall disclose that fact.

10   Paragraph 21 is amended as follows (new text is underlined and deleted text is struck through) and paragraph 39R is added:

21   ~~To comply with AASB 101, an~~ An entity's first Australian-Accounting-Standards financial statements shall include at least three statements of financial position, two statements of profit or loss and other comprehensive income, two separate statements of profit or loss (if presented), two statements of cash flows and two statements of changes in equity and related notes, including comparative information for all statements presented.

39R   AASB 2012-5 *Amendments to Australian Accounting Standards arising from Annual Improvements 2009–2011 Cycle*, issued in June 2012, amended paragraph 21. An entity shall apply that amendment retrospectively in accordance with AASB 108 *Accounting Policies, Changes in Accounting Estimates and Errors* for annual reporting periods beginning on or after 1 January 2013. Earlier application is permitted. If an entity applies that amendment for an earlier period it shall disclose that fact.

Amendments to AASB 101

11   Paragraphs 10, 38 and 41 are amended as follows (new text is underlined and deleted text is struck through). Paragraphs 39 and 40 are deleted (and notes added). Paragraphs 38A-38D, 40A-40D and 139L and related headings are added.

10   A complete set of financial statements comprises:

(a)   ...

(e)   notes, comprising a summary of significant accounting policies and other explanatory information;~~ and~~

(ea)   comparative information in respect of the preceding period as specified in paragraphs 38 and 38A; and

(f)   a statement of financial position as at the beginning of the ~~earliest comparative~~ preceding period when an entity applies an accounting policy retrospectively or makes a retrospective restatement of items in its financial statements, or when it reclassifies items in its financial statements in accordance with paragraphs 40A-40D.

...

Minimum Comparative Information

38   Except when Australian Accounting Standards permit or require otherwise, an entity shall ~~disclose~~ <u>present</u> comparative information in respect of the ~~previous~~ <u>preceding</u> period for all amounts reported in the current period's financial statements. An entity shall include comparative information for narrative and descriptive information ~~when~~ <u>if</u> it is relevant to ~~an~~ understanding ~~of~~ the current period's financial statements.

38A   **An entity shall present, as a minimum, two statements of financial position, two statements of profit or loss and other comprehensive income, two separate statements of profit or loss (if presented), two statements of cash flows and two statements of changes in equity, and related notes.**

38B   In some cases, narrative information provided in the financial statements for the preceding period(s) continues to be relevant in the current period. For example, an entity discloses in the current period details of a legal dispute, the outcome of which was uncertain at the end of the preceding period and is yet to be resolved. Users may benefit from the disclosure of information that the uncertainty existed at the end of the preceding period and from the disclosure of information about the steps that have been taken during the period to resolve the uncertainty.

Additional Comparative Information

38C   An entity may present comparative information in addition to the minimum comparative financial statements required by Australian Accounting Standards, as long as that information is prepared in accordance with Australian Accounting Standards. This comparative information may consist of one or more statements referred to in paragraph 10, but need not comprise a complete set of financial statements. When this is the case, the entity shall present related note information for those additional statements.

38D   For example, an entity may present a third statement of profit or loss and other comprehensive income (thereby presenting the current period, the preceding period and one additional comparative period). However, the entity is not required to present a third statement of financial position, a third statement of cash flows or a third statement of changes in equity (ie an additional financial statement comparative). The entity is required to present, in the notes to the financial statements, the comparative information related to that additional statement of profit or loss and other comprehensive income.

39   [Deleted by the IASB]

40   [Deleted by the IASB]

Change in Accounting Policy, Retrospective Restatement or Reclassification

40A   **An entity shall present a third statement of financial position as at the beginning of the preceding period in addition to the minimum comparative financial statements required in paragraph 38A if:**

    (a)   **it applies an accounting policy retrospectively, makes a retrospective restatement of items in its financial statements or reclassifies items in its financial statements; and**

    (b)   **the retrospective application, retrospective restatement or the reclassification has a material effect on the information in the statement of financial position at the beginning of the preceding period.**

40B   In the circumstances described in paragraph 40A, an entity shall present three statements of financial position as at:

    (a)   the end of the current period;

    (b)   the end of the preceding period; and

    (c)   the beginning of the preceding period.

40C   When an entity is required to present an additional statement of financial position in accordance with paragraph 40A, it must disclose the information required by paragraphs 41-44 and AASB 108. However, it need not present the related notes to the opening statement of financial position as at the beginning of the preceding period.

40D   The date of that opening statement of financial position shall be as at the beginning of the preceding period regardless of whether an entity's financial statements present comparative information for earlier periods (as permitted in paragraph 38C).

41   ~~When the~~ **If an entity changes the presentation or classification of items in its financial statements, ~~the entity~~ it shall reclassify comparative amounts unless reclassification is impracticable. When ~~the~~ an entity reclassifies comparative amounts, ~~the entity~~ it shall disclose (including as at the beginning of the preceding period):**

   (a) ...

139L   AASB 2012-5 *Amendments to Australian Accounting Standards arising from Annual Improvements 2009–2011 Cycle*, issued in June 2012, amended paragraphs 10, 38 and 41, deleted paragraphs 39 and 40 and added paragraphs 38A-38D and 40A-40D. An entity shall apply that amendment retrospectively in accordance with AASB 108 *Accounting Policies, Changes in Accounting Estimates and Errors* for annual reporting periods beginning on or after 1 January 2013. Earlier application is permitted. If an entity applies that amendment for an earlier period it shall disclose that fact.

Amendments to AASB 116

12   Paragraph 8 is amended as follows (new text is underlined and deleted text is struck through) and paragraph 81G is added:

   8   ~~Spare~~ Items such as spare parts, stand-by equipment and servicing equipment are recognised in accordance with this Standard ~~are usually carried as inventory and recognised in profit or loss as consumed. However, major spare parts and stand-by equipment qualify as property, plant and equipment~~ when they meet the definition of property, plant and equipment. Otherwise, such items are classified as inventory. ~~an entity expects to use them during more than one period. Similarly, if the spare parts and servicing equipment can be used only in connection with an item of property, plant and equipment, they are accounted for as property, plant and equipment.~~

   81G   AASB 2012-5 *Amendments to Australian Accounting Standards arising from Annual Improvements 2009–2011 Cycle*, issued in June 2012, amended paragraph 8. An entity shall apply that amendment retrospectively in accordance with AASB 108 *Accounting Policies, Changes in Accounting Estimates and Errors* for annual reporting periods beginning on or after 1 January 2013. Earlier application is permitted. If an entity applies that amendment for an earlier period it shall disclose that fact.

Amendments to AASB 132

13   Paragraphs 35, 37 and 39 are amended as follows (new text is underlined and deleted text is struck through) and paragraphs 35A and 97M are added:

   35   Interest, dividends, losses and gains relating to a financial instrument or a component that is a financial liability shall be recognised as income or expense in profit or loss. Distributions to holders of an equity instrument shall be recognised ~~debited~~ by the entity directly ~~to~~ in equity~~, net of any related income tax benefit~~. Transaction costs of an equity transaction shall be accounted for as a deduction from equity~~, net of any related income tax benefit~~.

   35A   Income tax relating to distributions to holders of an equity instrument and to transaction costs of an equity transaction shall be accounted for in accordance with AASB 112 *Income Taxes*.

37   An entity typically incurs various costs in issuing or acquiring its own equity instruments. Those costs might include registration and other regulatory fees, amounts paid to legal, accounting and other professional advisers, printing costs and stamp duties. The transaction costs of an equity transaction are accounted for as a deduction from equity ~~(net of any related income tax benefit)~~ to the extent they are incremental costs directly attributable to the equity transaction that otherwise would have been avoided. The costs of an equity transaction that is abandoned are recognised as an expense.

39   The amount of transaction costs accounted for as a deduction from equity in the period is disclosed separately ~~under~~ in accordance with AASB 101. ~~The related amount of income taxes recognised directly in equity is included in the aggregate amount of current and deferred income tax credited or charged to equity that is disclosed under AASB 112 Income Taxes.~~

97M   AASB 2012-5 *Amendments to Australian Accounting Standards arising from Annual Improvements 2009–2011 Cycle*, issued in June 2012, amended paragraphs 35, 37 and 39 and added paragraph 35A. An entity shall apply that amendment retrospectively in accordance with AASB 108 *Accounting Policies, Changes in Accounting Estimates and Errors* for annual reporting periods beginning on or after 1 January 2013. Earlier application is permitted. If an entity applies that amendment for an earlier period it shall disclose that fact.

Amendments to AASB 134

14   Paragraph 5 is amended as follows (new text is underlined and deleted text is struck through) and paragraph 52 is added:

5   AASB 101 ~~(as revised in 2007)~~ defines a complete set of financial statements as including the following components:

     (a)   …

     (b)   a statement of profit or loss and other comprehensive income for the period;

     (c)   …

     (e)   notes, comprising a summary of significant accounting policies and other explanatory information; ~~and~~

     (ea)   comparative information in respect of the preceding period as specified in paragraphs 38 and 38A of AASB 101; and

     (f)   a statement of financial position as at the beginning of the ~~earliest comparative~~ preceding period when an entity applies an accounting policy retrospectively or makes a retrospective restatement of items in its financial statements, or when it reclassifies items in its financial statements in accordance with paragraphs 40A-40D of AASB 101.

An entity may use titles for the statements other than those used in this Standard. For example, an entity may use the title 'statement of comprehensive income' instead of 'statement of profit or loss and other comprehensive income'.

52   AASB 2012-5 *Amendments to Australian Accounting Standards arising from Annual Improvements 2009–2011 Cycle*, issued in June 2012, amended paragraph 5. An entity shall apply that amendment retrospectively in accordance with AASB 108 *Accounting Policies, Changes in Accounting Estimates and Errors* for annual reporting periods beginning on or after 1 January 2013. Earlier application is permitted. If an entity applies that amendment for an earlier period it shall disclose that fact.

15   Paragraph 16A is amended as follows (new text is underlined and deleted text is struck through) and paragraph 53 is added:

16A   **In addition to disclosing significant events and transactions in accordance with paragraphs 15-15C, an entity shall include the following information, in the notes to its interim financial statements, if not disclosed elsewhere in the** interim financial report. The information shall normally be reported on an annual reporting period-to-date basis.

(a)   ...

(g)   the following segment information (disclosure of segment information is required in an entity's interim financial report only if AASB 8 *Operating Segments* requires that entity to disclose segment information in its annual financial statements):

   (i)   ...

   (iv)   <u>a measure of</u> total assets <u>and liabilities for a particular reportable segment if such amounts are regularly provided to the chief operating decision maker and if</u> ~~for which~~ there has been a material change from the amount disclosed in the last annual financial statements <u>for that reportable segment</u>;

   (v)   ...

(h)   ...

53   AASB 2012-5 *Amendments to Australian Accounting Standards arising from Annual Improvements 2009–2011 Cycle*, issued in June 2012, amended paragraph 16A. An entity shall apply that amendment retrospectively in accordance with AASB 108 *Accounting Policies, Changes in Accounting Estimates and Errors* for annual reporting periods beginning on or after 1 January 2013. Earlier application is permitted. If an entity applies that amendment for an earlier period it shall disclose that fact.

Amendments to Interpretation 2

16   Paragraph 11 is amended as follows (new text is underlined and deleted text is struck through) and paragraph 17 is added:

   11   As required by paragraph 35 of AASB 132, distributions to holders of equity instruments are recognised directly in equity~~, net of any income tax benefits~~. Interest, dividends and other returns relating to financial instruments classified as financial liabilities are expenses, regardless of whether those amounts paid are legally characterised as dividends, interest or otherwise.

   17   AASB 2012-5 *Amendments to Australian Accounting Standards arising from Annual Improvements 2009–2011 Cycle*, issued in June 2012, amended paragraph 11. An entity shall apply that amendment retrospectively in accordance with AASB 108 *Accounting Policies, Changes in Accounting Estimates and Errors* for annual reporting periods beginning on or after 1 January 2013. If an entity applies the amendment to AASB 132 as a part of AASB 2012-5 for an earlier period, the amendment in paragraph 11 shall be applied for that earlier period.

AASB 2012-7

Amendments to Australian Accounting Standards arising from Reduced Disclosure Requirements

[AASB 7, AASB 12, AASB 101 and AASB 127]

(Issued September 2012)

Note from the Institute of Chartered Accountants Australia

This note, prepared by the technical editors, is not part of Accounting Standard AASB 2012-7.

Historical development

10 September 2012: AASB 2012-7 was issued amending AASB 7, 12, 101 and 127 following recent changes to the disclosure requirements in these standards.

Contents

Preface

Accounting Standard

AASB 2012-7 Amendments to Australian Accounting Standards arising from Reduced Disclosure Requirements

Paragraphs

Objective 1

Application 2 – 6

Amendments to AASB 7 7 – 8

Amendments to AASB 12 9

Amendments to AASB 101 10

Amendments to AASB 127 11

Australian Accounting Standard AASB 2012-7 *Amendments to Australian Accounting Standards arising from Reduced Disclosure Requirements* is set out in paragraphs 1 – 11. All the paragraphs have equal authority.

Preface

Introduction

This Standard makes amendments to the Australian Accounting Standards listed in paragraph 1 of this Standard to incorporate reduced disclosure requirements into the Standards for entities preparing general purpose financial statements under Australian Accounting Standards – Reduced Disclosure Requirements.

These amendments result from the application of the AASB's 'Tier 2 Disclosure Principles' and are based on the proposals that were included in the following Exposure Drafts:

(a) ED 207 *Amendments to AASB 7: Tier 2*;

(b) ED 209 *Offsetting Financial Assets and Financial Liabilities (proposed amendments to AASB 7 and AASB 132, and proposal relating to Tier 2 disclosure requirements)*;

(c) ED 213 *Improvements to IFRSs*;

(d) ED 216 *AASB 12* Disclosure of Interests in Other Entities: *Tier 2 proposals*;

(e) ED 217 *AASB 127* Separate Financial Statements: *Tier 2 proposals*; and

(f) ED 218 *Presentation of Items of Other Comprehensive Income: Tier 2 Proposals*.

Main Features of this Standard

Application Date

This Standard applies to annual reporting periods beginning on or after 1 July 2013. Earlier application of the Standard (or its amendments to individual Standards) is permitted for annual reporting periods beginning on or after 1 July 2009 but before 1 July 2013, provided that the Standards listed in paragraph 5 of this Standard (as relevant) are also adopted for the same period.

Main Requirements

This Standard adds to or amends the Australian Accounting Standards – Reduced Disclosure Requirements for AASB 7 *Financial Instruments: Disclosures*, AASB 12 *Disclosure of Interests in Other Entities*, AASB 101 *Presentation of Financial Statements* and AASB 127 *Separate Financial Statements*. AASB 1053 *Application of Tiers of Australian Accounting Standards* provides further information regarding the differential reporting framework and the two tiers of reporting requirements for preparing general purpose financial statements.

AASB

Accounting Standard AASB 2012-7

The Australian Accounting Standards Board makes Accounting Standard AASB 2012-7 *Amendments to Australian Accounting Standards arising from Reduced Disclosure Requirements* under section 334 of the *Corporations Act 2001*.

Kevin M. Stevenson
Dated 10 September 2012   Chair – AASB

Accounting Standard AASB 2012-7

Amendments To Australian Accounting Standards Arising From Reduced Disclosure Requirements

Objective

1   The objective of this Standard is to make amendments to:

     (a)   AASB 7 *Financial Instruments: Disclosures*;

     (b)   AASB 12 *Disclosure of Interests in Other Entities*;

     (c)   AASB 101 *Presentation of Financial Statements*; and

     (d)   AASB 127 *Separate Financial Statements*;

     to establish reduced disclosure requirements for entities preparing general purpose financial statements under Australian Accounting Standards – Reduced Disclosure Requirements for additional and amended disclosures arising from:

     (e)   AASB 2010-6 *Amendments to Australian Accounting Standards – Disclosures on Transfers of Financial Assets*;

     (f)   AASB 12;

     (g)   AASB 127;

     (h)   AASB 2011-9 *Amendments to Australian Accounting Standards – Presentation of Items of Other Comprehensive Income*;

     (i)   AASB 2012-2 *Amendments to Australian Accounting Standards – Disclosures – Offsetting Financial Assets and Financial Liabilities*;

     (j)   AASB 2012-5 *Amendments to Australian Accounting Standards arising from Annual Improvements 2009–2011 Cycle*; and

     (k)   AASB 2012-6 *Amendments to Australian Accounting Standards – Mandatory Effective Date of AASB 9 and Transition Disclosures*.

Application

2   **Subject to paragraph 3, this Standard applies to:**

     (a)   **each entity that is required to prepare financial reports in accordance with Part 2M.3 of the Corporations Act and that is a reporting entity;**

     (a)   **general purpose financial statements of each other reporting entity; and**

     (b)   **financial statements that are, or are held out to be, general purpose financial statements.**

3   **In respect of AASB 101, this Standard applies to:**

     (a)   **each entity that is required to prepare financial reports in accordance with Part 2M.3 of the Corporations Act;**

     (b)   **general purpose financial statements of each reporting entity; and**

     (c)   **financial statements that are, or are held out to be, general purpose financial statements.**

4   This Standard applies to annual reporting periods beginning on or after 1 July 2013.

5   This Standard, or its amendments to individual Standards, may be applied to annual
reporting periods beginning on or after 1 July 2009 but before 1 July 2013, provided
that AASB 1053 *Application of Tiers of Australian Accounting Standards* and the
following Standards (as relevant) are also adopted for the same period:

(a)   amendments to AASB 7 – AASB 2010-6, AASB 2012-2 and AASB 2012-6;

(b)   amendments to AASB 12 – AASB 12;

(c)   amendments to AASB 101 – AASB 2011-9 and AASB 2012-5; and

(d)   amendments to AASB 127 – AASB 127.

When an entity applies this Standard, or its amendments to individual Standards,
to such an annual reporting period, it shall disclose that fact.

6   This Standard uses underlining, striking out and other typographical material to
identify some of the amendments to a Standard in order to make the amendments
more understandable. However, the amendments made by this Standard do not
include that underlining, striking out or other typographical material.

Amendments to AASB 7

7   Paragraph Aus2.9 is amended as follows (new text is underlined and deleted text is struck
through):

Aus2.9   The following do not apply to entities preparing general purpose
financial statements under Australian Accounting Standards – Reduced
Disclosure Requirements:

(a)   paragraphs 6, 9-11B, 9-11, 12A(b), 12A(e), 12C, 13A-13F, 15, 18,
19, 20(c), 20(d), 20A, 25-28, 30(b)-(e), 31-42, 42C, 42D(d), 42D(e),
42E(a), 42E(b), 42E(d)-(f), 42F-42H, B1-B4, and B7-B28 B7-B29
and B33-B53;

(b)   in paragraph 8(a), the text ", showing separately … AASB 9
AASB 139";

(c)   in paragraph 8(e), the text ", showing separately … AASB 139";

(d)   in paragraph 20(a)(i), the text ", showing separately … AASB 9
AASB 139";

(e)   in paragraph 20(a)(v), the text ", showing separately …
AASB 139"; and

(f)   in paragraph 23(d), the text ", showing the … income".; and

(g)   in paragraph 42D(f), the text "the total carrying amount of the
original assets before the transfer,".

…

8   The following footnote is added at the end of the first sentence of paragraph B32:

A cross-reference to a paragraph that contains disclosure requirements that do not
apply to entities preparing general purpose financial statements under Australian
Accounting Standards – Reduced Disclosure Requirements does not amend the
requirements for such entities.

Amendments to AASB 12

9   The following subheading and paragraphs are added:

Reduced Disclosure Requirements

Aus4.6   The following do not apply to entities preparing general purpose
financial statements under Australian Accounting Standards – Reduced
Disclosure Requirements:

        (a)   paragraphs 9(a), 9(d), 9(e), 10(a)(ii), 10(b)(ii)-(iv), 11(b), 12, 13(a)
                   (ii), 13(b), 14, 16, 18, 19, 20(b), 21(a)(ii), 21(b)(ii), 21(c), 22, 24(b),
                   25, 27-29, B10-B17, B25 and B26; and

        (b)   in paragraph 26, the text "qualitative and quantitative".

Entities applying Australian Accounting Standards – Reduced Disclosure
Requirements may elect to comply with some or all of these excluded
requirements.

Aus4.7   The requirements that do not apply to entities preparing general purpose
financial statements under Australian Accounting Standards – Reduced
Disclosure Requirements are identified in this Standard by shading of the
relevant text.

Amendments to AASB 101

10   Paragraph Aus1.8 is amended as follows (new text is underlined and deleted text is struck
through):

Aus1.8   The following do not apply to entities preparing general purpose
financial statements under Australian Accounting Standards – Reduced
Disclosure Requirements:

        (a)   paragraphs 10(f), 15, 16, Aus16.3, ~~39(c)~~, 40A-40D, 42(b), 61, 65,
                   80A, ~~90-92,~~ 90, 92, 94, 104, 131 and 134-138; and

        ~~(b)   the second sentence in paragraph 39; and~~

        (~~c~~b)   in paragraph 107, the text ", and the related amount of dividends
                   per share".

     ...

Amendments to AASB 127

11   The following subheading and paragraphs are added:

Reduced Disclosure Requirements

Aus1.6   The following do not apply to entities preparing general purpose
financial statements under Australian Accounting Standards – Reduced
Disclosure Requirements:

        (a)   paragraphs 16, Aus16.1, 17(b) and 17(c);

        (b)   in paragraph 17, the text "(other than a parent covered by
                   paragraph 16 or Aus16.1)"; and

        (c)   in paragraph 17(a), the text "and the reasons why those
                   statements are prepared if not required by law".

Entities applying Australian Accounting Standards – Reduced
Disclosure Requirements may elect to comply with some or all of these
excluded requirements.

Aus1.7   The requirements that do not apply to entities preparing general purpose
financial statements under Australian Accounting Standards – Reduced
Disclosure Requirements are identified in this Standard by shading of the
relevant text.

Aus1.8   The RDR paragraph in this Standard applies only to entities preparing
general purpose financial statements under Australian Accounting
Standards – Reduced Disclosure Requirements.

RDR17.1   A parent or an investor with joint control of, or significant influence
over, an investee, that prepares separate financial statements applying
Australian Accounting Standards – Reduced Disclosure Requirements,
shall disclose the methods used to account for the investment when the
investment is significant.

AAS 25

Financial Reporting by Superannuation Plans

(Compiled May 2006)

Prepared by the Australian Accounting Research Foundation and by the Australian Accounting Standards Board.

Issued by the Australian Accounting Research Foundation on behalf of the Australian Society of Certified Practising Accountants and The Institute of Chartered Accountants in Australia.

Note from the Institute of Chartered Accountants Australia

This note, prepared by the technical editors, is not part of Australian Accounting Standard AAS 25.

Historical development

August 1990: AAS 25 'Financial Reporting by Superannuation Plans' was issued by the Australian Accounting Research Foundation (AARF) in August 1990.

May 1992: AAS 25 was reissued by the AARF in May 1992 to make various amendments, which included adding transitional provisions for the initial application of the Standard and revising the requirements for comparative information.

March 1993: AAS 25 was reissued by the AARF again in March 1993 to make minor changes in response to industry experience with the Standard. These changes included clarifying the commentary on how superannuation plans may be constituted and removing certain disclosure requirements.

15 May 2006: Compiled version of the Standard was issued, incorporating amendments contained in AASB 2005-13.

The AASB is working on a project to replace AAS 25. For up-to-date information, refer to the AASB website at www.aasb.gov.au.

Contents

Compilation Details

Accounting Standard
AAS 25 Financial Reporting by Superannuation Plans

	Paragraphs
Citation	1
Accounting Standards and Commentary	2
Application and Operative Date	3–4
Statement of Purpose	5–7
Application of Materiality	8–9
Definitions	10
Superannuation plans	11
Defined contribution and defined benefit plans	12
Reporting Entity	13–15
Users of financial reports of superannuation plans	16–18
Financial reporting by superannuation plans	19–20
General Purpose Financial Reports	21–23
Liabilities	24
Accrued benefits	25–26
Assets	27
Employer undertakings or guarantees to fund benefit payments	28
Revenues	29
Expenses	30
Defined contribution plans – reporting format	31
Defined benefit plans – reporting format	32–33
Availability of financial reports and related information	34–36
Measurement of Assets	37–41
Insurance of members' benefits	42–43
Changes in the Net Market Value of Assets	44–48
Measurement of Accrued Benefits	49–50B
Defined contribution plans	51
Defined benefit plans	52–53
Measurement of Benefits Accrued During the Reporting Period – Defined Contribution Plans	54
Measurement of Benefits Accrued During the Measurement Period – Defined Benefit Plans	55–56
Disclosure Requirements	
Defined contribution plans	
Statement of financial position	57
Operating statement	58
Statement of cash flows	59
Defined benefit plans	
Statement of net assets	60
Statement of changes in net assets	61

AAS

Paragraphs

Alternative reporting format   62

Actuarial information   63–64

Vested benefits   65

Plans Whose Only Assets are Endowment, Whole of Life or
Other Long-term Insurance Policies which Match and Fully Guarantee
the Benefits to be Paid to Individual Members   66

Other Information   67

Transitional Provisions – General

Initial adjustments   68

Comparative amounts   69

Transitional Provisions – Defined Contribution Plans

Alternative reporting format   70–71

Statement of net assets   72

Statement of changes in net assets   73

Transitional Provisions – Defined Benefit Plans

Accrued benefits   74–75

Compatibility with International Accounting Standard IAS 26

Appendices

1   Example of a Financial Report for a Defined Contribution Superannuation Plan (Prepared in Conformity with the Full Provisions of this Standard)

2   Example of a Financial Report for a Defined Contribution Superannuation Plan (Prepared in Conformity with the Transitional Provisions set out in Paragraphs 70 to 73)

3   Example of a Financial Report for a Defined Benefit Superannuation Plan which Elects to Prepare a Statement of Net Assets and a Statement of Changes in Net Assets

4   Example of a Financial Report for a Defined Benefit Superannuation Plan which Elects to Prepare an Operating Statement, a Statement of Financial Position and a Statement of Cash Flows

Compilation Details

Accounting Standard AASB 25 *Financial Reporting by Superannuation Plans* as amended

This compilation takes into account amendments up to and including 19 December 2005 and was prepared on 15 May 2006 by the staff of the Australian Accounting Standards Board (AASB).

This compilation is not a separate Accounting Standard made by the AASB. Instead, it is a representation of AAS 25 (March 1993) as amended by other Accounting Standards, which are listed in the Table below.

Table of Standards

Standard	Date made	Application date (*annual reporting periods ... on or after ...*)	Application, saving or transitional provisions
AAS 25	March 1993	*(ending)* 30 Jun 1993	
AASB 2005-13	19 Dec 2005	*(ending)* 31 Dec 2005	see (a) below

(a)   Entities may elect to apply this Standard to annual reporting periods beginning on or after 1 January 2005 that end before 31 December 2005.

Table of Amendments

Paragraph affected	How affected	By ... [paragraph]
49 (and preceding heading)	amended	AASB 2005-13 [5, 6]
50A	added	AASB 2005-13 [7]
50B	added	AASB 2005-13 [7]
51	amended	AASB 2005-13 [8]
57	amended	AASB 2005-13 [9]
58	amended	AASB 2005-13 [10]
60	amended	AASB 2005-13 [11]
61	amended	AASB 2005-13 [12]

Accounting Standard AAS 25

The Australian Accounting Standards Board made Accounting Standard AAS 25 *Financial Reporting by Superannuation Plans* in March 1993.

This compiled version of AAS 25 incorporates subsequent amendments contained in other AASB Standards made by the AASB up to and including 19 December 2005 (see Compilation Details).

Australian Accounting Standard AAS 25

Financial Reporting by Superannuation Plans

Citation

1   This Standard may be cited as Australian Accounting Standard AAS 25 "Financial Reporting by Superannuation Plans".

Accounting Standards and Commentary

2   The accounting standards set out in this Standard are shown in bold print. Commentary is shown in normal print immediately after the accounting standard(s) to which it relates, as an aid to the interpretation of the accounting standard(s).

Application and Operative Date

Standards

3   **This Standard:**

(a)   **applies to general purpose financial reports of each superannuation plan in the private or public sector that is a reporting entity, in relation to its first reporting period that ends on or after 30 June 1993, and later reporting periods;**
[Note: For application dates of paragraphs changed or added by an amending Standard, see Compilation Details.]

(b)   **may be applied by an entity specified in paragraph 3(a) to a reporting period that ends before 30 June 1993;**

(c)   **when operative, supersedes Australian Accounting Standard AAS 25 "Financial Reporting by Superannuation Plans" as issued in May 1992.**

4   **A superannuation plan which is not a reporting entity shall, when it prepares a financial report which it purports to be a general purpose financial report, apply this Standard as if it is a reporting entity.**

Statement of Purpose

Standards

5   The purpose of this Standard is:

    (a)   to specify the manner in which superannuation plans should account for particular transactions and events;

    (b)   to specify the format(s) of superannuation plan financial statements; and

    (c)   to require disclosure of certain information in the financial report of superannuation plans.

Commentary

6   Statement of Accounting Concepts SAC 2 "Objective of General Purpose Financial Reporting" states that general purpose financial reports shall provide information useful to users for making and evaluating decisions about the allocation of scarce resources. Financial reports which highlight investment performance and include disclosure of information about the assets and liabilities of the plan, the benefits generated by the plan during the period, its financing and investing activities and compliance with provisions of the trust deed will be relevant to plan members and other users for making and evaluating decisions on the allocation of scarce resources. In addition, such financial reports will be necessary if trustees and administrators are to discharge their responsibility to be accountable to plan members.

7   The Standard does not deal with accounting in an employer's financial reports for employee entitlements, including retirement benefits. This will be the subject of a separate Standard.

Application of Materiality

Standards

8   **The accounting standards set out in this Standard shall, in accordance with Australian Accounting Standard AAS 5 "Materiality in Financial Statements", apply to financial reports where such application is of material consequence. Information about a superannuation plan will be material if its omission, non-disclosure or misstatement has the potential to adversely affect:**

    (a)   **decisions about the allocation of scarce resources made by users of the financial report; or**

    (b)   **the discharge of accountability by the management or governing body of the superannuation plan.**

Commentary

9   In deciding whether an item is material, its nature and amount usually need to be evaluated together.

Definitions

Standards

10   For the purposes of this Standard:

    "accrued benefits" means benefits the plan is presently obliged to transfer in the future to members and beneficiaries as a result of membership of the plan up to the reporting date and, in the case of defined contribution plans, encompasses benefits which have been allocated to individual members' accounts and benefits not yet so allocated;

    "beneficiaries" means those persons who are currently receiving, or are currently entitled to receive, benefits from the superannuation plan;

    "defined benefit plan" means a superannuation plan where the amounts to be paid to one or more members, if they were to remain members until normal retirement age, are specified, or are determined, at least in part, by reference to a formula based on their years of membership and/or salary levels, and encompasses all plans other than defined contribution plans;

"defined contribution plan" means a superannuation plan where the amounts to be paid to members, if they were to remain members until normal retirement age, are determined by reference to accumulated contributions made to the plan, together with investment earnings thereon;

"entity" means any legal, administrative, or fiduciary arrangement, organisational structure or other party (including a person) having the capacity to deploy scarce resources in order to achieve objectives;

"general purpose financial report" means a financial report intended to meet the information needs common to users who are unable to command the preparation of reports tailored so as to satisfy, specifically, all of their information needs;

"members" means those persons in respect of whom contributions are made, or have been made, under the terms of a superannuation plan, and who, as a consequence, expect to receive benefits from the plan;

"net market value" means the amount which could be expected to be received from the disposal of an asset in an orderly market after deducting costs expected to be incurred in realising the proceeds of such a disposal;

"reporting date" means the end of the reporting period to which the financial report relates;

"reporting entity" means an entity (including an economic entity) in respect of which it is reasonable to expect the existence of users dependent on general purpose financial reports for information which will be useful to them for making and evaluating decisions about the allocation of scarce resources;

"superannuation plan" means an arrangement whereby it is agreed, between trustees and employers, employees or self-employed persons, that benefits be provided upon the retirement of plan members or upon their resignation, death, disablement or other specified event(s); and

"vested benefits" means benefits, the members' rights to which, under the terms of a superannuation plan, are not conditional upon continued plan membership or any factor other than resignation from the plan.

Superannuation plans

Commentary

11   A superannuation plan may be constituted as either a separate entity or a number of separate entities established to administer aspects of the plan. Examples of the latter may exist where a superannuation plan operates through two separate administrative entities, one of which manages members' contributions and the other of which administers the payment of benefits. For the purposes of this Standard, a superannuation plan is regarded as a distinct entity whether it is constituted as either a separate entity or a number of separate but interconnected entities, and irrespective of the reporting obligations attaching to those entities and the strategy employed to fund the benefits. Where the superannuation plan includes a number of separate entities, this Standard requires the identity of those entities to be disclosed. This Standard, therefore, applies regardless of whether a separate pool of assets from which benefits are paid is created, whether benefits are to be met with the proceeds of insurance contracts and whether there are trustees. It also applies where a nominee holds investments on behalf of the plan. However, the full provisions of this Standard do not apply to superannuation plans whose only assets (other than temporary deposits at call with a bank) are endowment, whole of life or other long-term insurance policies which match and fully guarantee the benefits to be paid to individual members.

Defined contribution and defined benefit plans

Commentary

12   This Standard applies to general purpose financial reports of defined contribution plans and defined benefit plans. The characteristic which distinguishes defined contribution plans from defined benefit plans is the manner in which the benefits to be paid at normal retirement age are to be determined. In the case of defined contribution plans, the amounts to be paid to members at normal retirement age are determined by reference

to the accumulated contributions made by, and/or on behalf of, members, together with investment earnings thereon. In the case of defined benefit plans, the amounts to be paid to one or more members at normal retirement age are specified or are determined, at least in part, by reference to members' years of membership and/or salary levels or, in the case of defined benefit unit plans, the number of units purchased. Defined benefit plans encompass all plans other than defined contribution plans. As such, for the purposes of this Standard, those plans which exhibit features of both defined contribution and defined benefit plans, are classified as defined benefit plans.

Reporting Entity

Standards

13   **Each superannuation plan that is a reporting entity shall prepare, at least annually, a general purpose financial report and shall make it available to members. General purpose financial reports of superannuation plans shall be prepared inconformity with Statements of Accounting Concepts and Australian Accounting Standards, except to the extent that the standards set out in this Standard differ from the requirements set out in those Statements and Standards.**

Commentary

14   Paragraphs 19 to 37 of Statement of Accounting Concepts SAC 1 "Definition of the Reporting Entity" provide guidance for determining whether an entity is a reporting entity. An entity is not a reporting entity merely because it prepares a financial report pursuant to legislation or some other requirement.

15   Miscellaneous Professional Statement APS 1 "Conformity with Statements of Accounting Concepts and Accounting Standards "requires general purpose financial reports to be prepared in accordance with Accounting Standards and Statements of Accounting Concepts. APS 1 also requires that to the extent of any incompatibility between an Accounting Standard and a Statement of Accounting Concepts, the requirements of the Standard prevail.

Users of financial reports of superannuation plans

Commentary

16   The primary purpose of a superannuation plan is to provide benefits on the retirement of plan members. In expectation of such benefits, contributions are made by, and/or on behalf of, members. Members will therefore have a particular interest in the performance of trustees and administrators in managing the resources under their control and in the ability of the plan to generate, and distribute when due, an adequate level of benefits.

17   Plan members are likely to be the primary users of financial reports of superannuation plans. Other users may include potential members and beneficiaries of the plan, employers, trustees and plan administrators, trade unions, investors (and financial analysts and other advisers) concerned with an entity's potential obligations in respect of the plan, regulators, and other members of the community.

18   The interests of these other users will also be related to the provision of information to assist in making and evaluating decisions about the allocation of scarce resources and in assessing the rendering of accountability by trustees and administrators. They are likely to require the disclosure of information similar to that required by members. For example, employers and, in respect of public sector plans, taxpayers and ratepayers are likely to have a particular interest in assessing the adequacy of assets currently available for distribution as benefits and the performance of the plan during the reporting period in accumulating assets for the benefit of members and beneficiaries. Taxpayers and ratepayers would also be likely to have a particular interest, in respect of public sector defined benefit plans, in the extent to which the plans' obligations to members and beneficiaries have been funded and in any undertakings that have been made in respect of future funding.

Financial reporting by superannuation plans

Commentary

19 Members, or other users with a legitimate interest in financial information about a superannuation plan, may be unable to command the disclosure of financial information specific to their own needs. Such users must rely on any financial report(s) prepared in respect of the plan for the disclosure of financial information. In such cases the superannuation plan is a reporting entity and is required to prepare a general purpose financial report. This Standard requires that general purpose financial reports of superannuation plans be prepared in accordance with the accrual basis of accounting and establishes financial reporting requirements which will enhance the relevance and reliability, and therefore usefulness, of those reports.

20 While this Standard requires that general purpose financial reports be prepared by all superannuation plans that are reporting entities, it places no reporting requirements on plans which are not reporting entities. Consistent with the concept of a reporting entity as defined in paragraph 10, it is likely that:

(a) single member plans; and

(b) plans where plan members are employed by entities other than public companies, and the plan members and the owners of the employer entity are an identical group;

would not normally be identified as reporting entities, and therefore would not normally be required to prepare general purpose financial reports. This is because it is likely that members of these types of plans will have access to, or be able to command the disclosure of, the information they require.

General Purpose Financial Reports

Standards

21 **The general purpose financial report of a defined contribution superannuation plan, except for those plans identified in paragraph 66 and unless the transitional provisions set out in paragraph 70 are applied, shall include a statement of financial position, an operating statement, a statement of cash flows and notes thereto.**

22 **The general purpose financial report of a defined benefit superannuation plan, except for those plans identified in paragraph 66, shall include either:**

(a) **a statement of net assets, a statement of changes in net assets and notes thereto; or**

(b) **a statement of financial position, an operating statement, a statement of cash flows and notes thereto -this reporting format is available only if accrued benefits are measured as at the end of each reporting period.**

23 **The financial report of a superannuation plan shall, where financial reports have been prepared for more than one reporting period, include the corresponding amounts for the corresponding preceding reporting period.**

Liabilities

Commentary

24 Liabilities arise when, as a result of past transactions or other past events, an entity has a present obligation to make a disposition of economic benefits to other entities in the future. Liabilities of a superannuation plan may include the liability for accrued benefits, income tax liabilities and sundry liabilities. Sundry liabilities may include accounts payable, borrowings, pre-paid contributions and, in the case of defined contribution plans, other liabilities arising from benefits which have been forfeited and which have not been designated for the benefit of existing plan members as at the reporting date. For defined contribution plans, benefits which have been forfeited and have not been designated for the benefit of existing plan members may encompass amounts held for the benefit of future members, amounts to be returned to employers and amounts held as an offset to future employer contributions.

Accrued benefits

Commentary

25   The position adopted in this Standard is that benefits which have accrued to members and beneficiaries as a result of membership of the plan up to the reporting date constitute a liability of the superannuation plan. This is because a superannuation plan has a present obligation to transfer assets (pay benefits) to plan members and beneficiaries at a future date as a result of past transactions or other past events.

26   The transactions or events which give rise to a superannuation plan's present obligation to pay benefits result from membership of the plan. In the case of defined contribution plans those transactions or events are the contributions made by, and/or on behalf of, members and employers. In the case of defined benefit plans, members have, during their period of membership of the plan, provided the services in respect of which the benefits are considered payable.

Assets

Commentary

27   The assets of a superannuation plan may include the following:

(a)   contributions receivable, being amounts due to the plan at the reporting date from employer(s), members and any other contributors;

(b)   investments of the plan, which may include equity or debt securities and real estate;

(c)   cash and other monetary assets; and

(d)   other assets, including those which are used in the operation of the plan.

Employer undertakings or guarantees to fund benefit payments

Commentary

28   Assets arise when, as a result of past transactions or events, the entity controls future economic benefits or service potential. A government or other employer may undertake, or guarantee, to provide funds to meet benefit payments as they fall due. Such undertakings or guarantees will ensure that the plan, whether or not fully funded, will be able to meet its obligations to pay benefits to members. However, the economic benefits represented by resources to be provided to the plan at some time in the future under the terms of any undertaking or guarantee are not controlled by the plan at the reporting date, and, therefore, cannot be treated as if they were assets of the plan as at that date.

Revenues

Commentary

29   Revenues of a superannuation plan may include investment revenue, contributions revenue and other revenue. Investment revenue may include interest and dividends, the proceeds of insurance policies other than term insurance, property rentals and, consistent with the standards set out in paragraph 44, changes in the net market value of investments. Contributions revenue will include members' and employers' contributions, gross of any tax. Other revenue will include payments received in respect of term insurance policies and changes in the net market value of other assets.

Expenses

Commentary

30   Expenses of a superannuation plan may include benefits accruing to plan members and beneficiaries as a result of membership of the plan during the period, general administration expenses, expenses directly related to investment activities, income tax expense (including capital gains tax) determined in accordance with the provisions of Australian Accounting Standard AAS 3 "Accounting for Income Tax (Tax-effect Accounting)" and other expenses. General administration expenses may include premiums paid or payable in respect of term insurance policies and insurance policies referred to in paragraph 43, salaries of administrators and others, and other operating expenses.

Defined contribution plans – reporting format

Commentary

31   This Standard requires, unless the transitional provisions set out in paragraph 70 are applied, defined contribution plans to prepare a financial report similar to general purpose financial reports prepared and presented annually by other reporting entities. Those financial reports usually include a statement of financial position (balance sheet), operating (profit and loss) statement, statement of cash flows and notes thereto. An illustrative example is provided in Appendix 1 of this Standard.

Defined benefit plans – reporting format

Commentary

32   Where accrued benefits of a defined benefit superannuation plan are measured as at the end of each reporting period, this Standard allows adoption of either of the two alternative reporting formats set out in paragraph 22. Where accrued benefits are not measured as at the end of each reporting period, the option in respect of reporting formats is removed and plans are required to adopt the reporting format outlined in paragraph 22(a). This Standard therefore requires that the financial report of a defined benefit plan comprise either:

(a)   a statement of net assets, a statement of changes in net assets and notes thereto, including a note which discloses the amount of accrued benefits, and, where accrued benefits have been remeasured during the reporting period, changes therein. The financial statements will therefore highlight assets available to meet accrued benefits and the changes in those assets as a result of investment and other activities of the plan during the reporting period, and accrued benefits, and any changes therein, will be reported in the notes thereto; or

(b)   a statement of financial position (balance sheet) which includes the liability for accrued benefits on the face of that statement, an operating statement, a statement of cash flows and notes thereto. The financial statements will therefore highlight changes in assets as a result of investment and other activities of the plan during the reporting period, major categories of cash flows occurring during the reporting period, the benefits which have accrued to members and beneficiaries during the period and whether, at reporting date, the assets of the plan are greater or less than accrued benefits and other liabilities.

33   An illustrative example of the financial report of a defined benefit superannuation plan prepared in accordance with the standards set out in paragraph 22(a) is provided in Appendix 3 of this Standard. An illustrative example of the financial report of a defined benefit superannuation plan prepared in accordance with the standards set out in paragraph 22(b) is provided in Appendix 4 of this Standard.

Availability of financial reports and related information

Commentary

34   The Occupational Superannuation Standards Regulations require superannuation plans to prepare and distribute to members financial information relating to individual benefit entitlements.

35   The provision of information about individual benefits is important. However, statements relating to an individual's benefits need to be read in conjunction with a financial report prepared for the plan as a whole and, in the case of defined benefit plans, a copy or summary of the latest actuarial report. A general purpose financial report will highlight the plan's performance in accumulating assets for the benefit of members and beneficiaries during the reporting period. The report will aid members and other users in assessing such matters as the plan's ability to generate an adequate level of benefits in the future and to pay benefits at the time members withdraw from the plan or on termination or liquidation of the plan. This Standard requires that the general purpose financial report be distributed, or otherwise be made readily available, to members.

36   Though not required by this Standard, it is recommended that the financial statements included in general purpose financial reports be supported by a report of the trustees of the plan. That report should include comment on the investment performance and policies of the plan, highlight significant features of the operations of the plan and confirm that requirements of the trust deed had been complied with, or identify those requirements which had not been complied with. The trustees' report should also include a formal statement as to the fairness of presentation of the financial report prepared in respect of the plan.

Measurement of Assets

Standards

37   **Assets of a defined contribution plan and a defined benefit plan shall be measured at net market values as at the reporting date.**

Commentary

38   This Standard requires that, in the preparation of the financial report, the assets of superannuation plans are to be measured at net market value, as defined in paragraph 10. Where a market does not exist for long-term monetary assets, the calculation of net market value will require the determination of a present value by application of a current, market-determined, risk-adjusted discount rate. In establishing net market values of assets it may be necessary to exercise judgement in respect of determining such matters as:

(a)   the costs expected to be incurred in realising the proceeds of any disposals (consistent with the provisions of Australian Accounting Standard AAS 5 "Materiality in Financial Statements", where such costs are not expected to be material, assets can be measured at gross market value. In addition, as a practical measure, the expected cost of disposal may be estimated by application of an average rate over all assets);

(b)   the likely proceeds to be realised from the disposal of assets for which market prices are not publicly quoted or otherwise readily available; and

(c)   the appropriate discount factor to be applied to long-term monetary assets.

39   The primary function of superannuation plans is to act as a vehicle for the accumulation of assets to pay benefits to members and beneficiaries. Measuring assets at net market value as at the reporting date provides more relevant information to users about the resources available to pay benefits than does the cost basis of measurement. The net market value basis of measurement is therefore required by this Standard. Information about the assets available to pay benefits will be relevant to an assessment of, in the case of defined benefit plans, the plan's ability to meet its obligations to members and beneficiaries and, in the case of defined contribution plans, the plan's ability to provide an adequate level of benefits for members and beneficiaries.

40   It is sometimes argued that, when net market values of assets are used, averaging techniques to "smooth" the effects of fluctuations in the market values of assets should be employed. Such smoothing may be important in establishing the manner in which the plan is to be funded in the long term, however, for financial reporting purposes, assets are to be measured as at the reporting date. The measurement of assets on this basis is necessary to facilitate comparability of financial reports from one period to the next, and with the financial reports of other plans. It is also necessary to ensure that assets included in financial reports, and changes in the net market values of those assets, are measured on a basis which is both consistent and verifiable. Accordingly, for financial reporting purposes, smoothing techniques are not be applied to the measurement of assets.

41   The requirement to measure all assets of a superannuation plan at net market value means that in the case of depreciable assets, such as fixtures and fittings, the provisions of Australian Accounting Standard AAS 4 "Depreciation of Non-Current Assets" do not apply.

Insurance of members' benefits

Commentary

42   Where plans invest in insurance policies, other than term insurance or policies of the type referred to in paragraph 43, to meet members' benefits, those insurance policies are to be valued at net market value. In determining the net market value of insurance policies, reference should be made to the insurer's assessment of the present value of the insurance policy, or where relevant, the actuarially determined assessment of the amount recoverable from the insurer. Where, at the reporting date, it is intended to surrender a policy, the policy should be valued at surrender value.

43   A plan may purchase long-term insurance policies which match, and fully guarantee, the benefits to be paid to individual members. Where those policies have been purchased in the name or names of individual members and the plan has no further obligations in respect of payment of benefits to those members, the acquisition costs of the policy should be treated as the cost of discharging the obligations at the time of purchase. Such policies should not be included in the statement of financial position. Where such policies constitute all the assets of a plan, the plan is relieved from all obligations in respect of payment of benefits to members. In such cases this Standard requires the plan to report only the information identified in paragraph 66.

Changes in the Net Market Value of Assets

Standards

44   **For a defined contribution plan and a defined benefit plan, the change in the net market value of a plan's assets since the beginning of the reporting period shall be included as a component of revenue for the reporting period.**

Commentary

45   Assets available to pay benefits are generated by the accumulation and investment of contributions made by, and/or on behalf of, members, and earnings thereon. Accordingly, an assessment of the performance of a superannuation plan involves consideration of the overall change in the amount of assets available to pay benefits over the reporting period and the manner in which that change was achieved. To reflect the overall change in the amount of assets available to pay benefits, this Standard requires that periodic changes in the net market value of plan assets be recognised as revenue in the financial statements of the plan.

46   The requirement to include changes in the net market value of assets as a component of revenue means that where an operating (profit and loss) statement is prepared in respect of any superannuation plan, the provisions of Australian Accounting Standard AAS 10 "Accounting for the Revaluation of Non-Current Assets" and, if the plan holds inventories other than marketable securities, Australian Accounting Standard AAS 2 "Measurement and Presentation of Inventories in the Context of the Historical Cost System", do not apply.

47   Consistent with the standards set out in paragraph 44, revenue will include changes in net market values of investments and other assets held at the reporting date and, in respect of investments and other assets realised during the period, the difference between the carrying amount of the investment or other asset as at the beginning of the reporting period (or when acquired, if acquired after the beginning of the reporting period) and its net market value when realised.

48   The requirement to include changes in net market values of assets realised during the reporting period in revenue means that a gain or loss on the disposal of non-current assets will not result – in concept assets will be revalued to net market value immediately prior to their disposal, changes in net market value will be included in revenue and no gain or loss on disposal will result.

Measurement of Accrued Benefits and Financial Liabilities

Standards

49   Accrued benefits of a defined contribution plan shall be shown as an amount equivalent to the difference between the carrying amount of the assets and the sum of all other liabilities.

50   Accrued benefits of a defined benefit plan shall be measured, except where the transitional provisions set out in paragraph 74 are applied, using actuarial assumptions and valuations where appropriate, as the present value of expected future payments arising from membership of the plan up to the measurement date. The present value of expected future benefit payments shall be determined by discounting the gross benefit payments at a current, market-determined, risk-adjusted discount rate appropriate to the plan. Where comprehensive actuarial reviews are undertaken on a triennial or less frequent basis, accrued benefits shall be measured as part of each comprehensive actuarial review and may be, but are not required to be, measured in periods between those reviews. Where comprehensive actuarial reviews are undertaken on a triennial or more frequent basis, accrued benefits shall be measured on at least a triennial basis, and may be, but are not required to be, measured on a more frequent basis.

50A   Financial liabilities[1] of a defined contribution plan and a defined benefit plan shall be measured at net market values as at the reporting date.

50B   For a defined contribution plan and a defined benefit plan, the change in net market values of the plan's financial liabilities since the beginning of the reporting period shall be included in the profit or loss for the reporting period.

Defined contribution plans

Commentary

51   The liability of a defined contribution plan for accrued benefits is to be shown as the difference between the carrying amount of plan assets and the sum of all other liabilities. All other liabilities may include income tax liabilities, financial liabilities including those liabilities arising from forfeited benefits, which have not been designated for the benefit of existing plan members as at the reporting date. Accrued benefits may encompass amounts which have been allocated to members' accounts at reporting date and amounts which have not yet been so allocated. This Standard therefore acknowledges that, at the reporting date, accrued benefits may encompass amounts allocated to individual members' accounts and the balances of income equalisation, or similar, accounts.

Defined benefit plans

Commentary

52   It is common practice for trustees of plans to obtain comprehensive actuarial valuations for funding purposes at least triennially. The Occupational Superannuation Standards Regulations require actuarial investigations to be carried out at least every three years. This Standard requires accrued benefits of a defined benefit superannuation plan to be measured as part of each comprehensive actuarial review where those reviews are undertaken on a triennial, or less frequent, basis, but does not require accrued benefits to be measured at more frequent intervals than the triennial comprehensive actuarial review. This Standard does not prohibit accrued benefits from being measured for financial reporting purposes in periods between the triennial comprehensive actuarial review. However, consistent with the requirements of this Standard, accrued benefits are required to be measured as at each reporting date if the reporting format outlined in paragraph 22(b) is adopted.

---

1   Financial liabilities, including credit balances of hedging instruments and derivatives, are the financial liabilities that would otherwise be included within the scope of AASB 132 *Financial Instruments: Disclosure and Presentation* and AASB 139 *Financial Instruments: Recognition and Measurement*. Some of the sundry liabilities, as referred to in paragraph 24 of this Standard, are financial liabilities.

53   The liability of a defined benefit plan for accrued benefits is to be calculated on the basis of the present value of expected future benefit payments which arise from membership of the plan up to the measurement date. The expected benefit payments to be made in the future will need to be determined by application of a valuation method based upon certain actuarial assumptions. Those assumptions will incorporate consideration of such factors as future salary levels, mortality rates, membership turnover and the expected value of benefits to be paid as a result of early withdrawal from membership of the plan. The gross amount of the expected future benefit payments, in respect of membership up to the measurement date, will then be discounted to present value by a current, market-determined, risk-adjusted discount rate appropriate to the plan. Relevant actuarial assumptions used in the course of the actuarial review could be used in the measurement of accrued benefits for financial reporting purposes. However, actuarial valuation methods conventionally focus on the funding of benefits, irrespective of whether they stem from past or future membership, and employ long-term, average discount rates. However, for financial reporting purposes, the present value of expected future benefit payments should not include benefits which have not yet accrued and should be discounted at the rate of return that the plan anticipates it could achieve if, at the measurement date, sufficient funds were available to meet accrued benefits as they fall due. Therefore, this Standard specifies that for financial reporting purposes, the amount of benefit payments expected to be made in the future is to be based on membership of the plan up to the measurement date; and is to be discounted at a rate determined by reference to a current, market-determined, risk-adjusted rate of return appropriate to the plan.

Measurement of Benefits Accrued During the Reporting Period – Defined Contribution Plans

Standards

54   The amount of the benefits that has been accrued by a defined contribution plan during the reporting period shall be measured as the difference between revenues and direct investment, general administration, income tax and any other expenses incurred during the reporting period in generating benefits for plan members and beneficiaries.

Measurement of Benefits Accrued During the Measurement Period – Defined Benefit Plans

Standards

55   **In respect of defined benefit plans, the amount of benefits accrued during the measurement period shall:**

   (a)   where accrued benefits are measured as at the end of each reporting period, be measured as the sum of the net change in the amount of accrued benefits between the beginning of the reporting period and the end of the reporting period and the amount of any benefits paid to plan beneficiaries during the reporting period; and

   (b)   where accrued benefits are not measured as at the end of each reporting period but have been measured during the reporting period, be measured as the sum of the net change in the amount of accrued benefits and the amount of any benefits paid to plan beneficiaries during the period between the current and immediately preceding measurement dates.

Commentary

56   Where accrued benefits of a defined benefit plan have not been measured during the reporting period, no amount will be reported as benefits accrued during the measurement period. The measurement period refers to the period between the two most recent dates as at which accrued benefits were measured.

Disclosure Requirements

Defined contribution plans

Statement of financial position

Standards

57   The statement of financial position of a defined contribution plan shall disclose:

     (a)   the assets of the plan, showing separately investments and other assets by class of assets;

     (b)   the liabilities of the plan, showing separately the liability for accrued benefits and other liabilities by class of liabilities;

     (c)   separately, by way of note or otherwise, the amount of accrued benefits allocated to members' accounts and the amount not yet so allocated; and

     (d)   by way of note:

         (i)   changes in the liability for accrued benefits;

         (ii)   vested benefits;

         (iii)   any benefits which have been guaranteed, the identity of the guarantor(s), the nature of the guarantee(s) and any changes from the corresponding preceding reporting period;

         (iv)   the method adopted in determining net market value for each class of asset disclosed; and

         (v)   the method adopted in determining net market value for financial liabilities.

Operating statement

Standards

58   The operating statement of a defined contribution plan shall disclose, by way of note or otherwise:

     (a)   revenue of the superannuation plan, showing separately:

         (i)   investment revenue and its individual components, including changes in net market values for each class of investment;

         (ii)   amounts contributed by employers;

         (iii)   amounts contributed by members; and

         (iv)   other revenue, including proceeds from term insurance policies and changes in net market values of assets other than investments;

     (b)   direct investment, general administration and income tax expenses;

     (c)   the amount of benefits that has been accrued during the reporting period, measured in accordance with the standards set out in paragraph 54; and

     (d)   by way of note:

         (i)   separately, the change during the reporting period in net market values of investments held at the reporting date, other assets held at the reporting date, investments realised during the reporting period and other assets realised during the reporting period; and

         (ii)   the rate(s) or other basis of contributions by employers and members during the reporting period, and any change in the rate(s) or other basis of contributions from the corresponding preceding reporting period; and

     (e)   changes in net market values of financial liabilities that have been recognised in the profit or loss for the reporting period.

Statement of cash flows

Standards

59   The statement of cash flows of a defined contribution plan shall be prepared in accordance with Australian Accounting Standard AAS 28 "Statement of Cash Flows", and shall include separate disclosure of the amount of benefits paid to members during the reporting period.

Defined benefit plans

Statement of net assets

Standards

60   The statement of net assets of a defined benefit plan shall disclose:

(a)   the assets of the plan, showing separately investments and other assets by class of assets;

(b)   the liabilities of the plan, showing separately each class of liability but excluding the liability for accrued benefits;

(c)   net assets available to pay benefits; and

(d)   by way of note:

(i)   the liability for accrued benefits and the date as at which the liability was measured;

(ii)   where accrued benefits have been measured during the reporting period, the benefits which have accrued since the last measurement date, measured in accordance with the standards set out in paragraph 55;

(iii)   vested benefits;

(iv)   any benefits which have been guaranteed, the identity of the guarantor(s), the nature of the guarantee(s) and any changes from the corresponding preceding reporting period;

(v)   the method adopted in determining net market value for each class of asset disclosed; and

(vi)   the method adopted in determining net market value for financial liabilities.

Statement of changes in net assets

Standards

61   The statement of changes in net assets of a defined benefit plan shall disclose:

(a)   the amount of net assets available to pay benefits as at the beginning and end of the reporting period;

(b)   amounts contributed by employers;

(c)   amounts contributed by members;

(d)   investment revenue, showing separately its individual components, including changes in net market value for each class of investment;

(e)   changes in net market value of assets other than investments;

(f)   other revenue, showing separately proceeds from term insurance policies;

(g)   direct investment expense;

(h)   general administration expense;

(i)   benefits paid;

(j)   income tax expense; and

   (k)   **by way of note:**

       (i)   **separately, the change during the reporting period in net market values of investments held at the reporting date, other assets held at the reporting date, investments realised during the reporting period and other assets realised during the reporting period; and**

       (ii)   **the rate(s) or other basis of contributions by employers and members during the reporting period, and any change in the rate(s) or other basis of contributions from the corresponding preceding reporting period; and**

   (l)   **changes in net market values of financial liabilities.**

Alternative reporting format

Standards

62   **Defined benefit plans which measure accrued benefits as at the end of each reporting period may elect to adopt a reporting format which includes a statement of financial position, an operating statement, a statement of cash flows and notes thereto. Defined benefit plans which elect to adopt this reporting format shall not comply with the standards set out in paragraphs 60 and 61, but shall prepare financial statements which comply with the standards set out in paragraphs 57(a), (b) and (d); 58(a), (b) and (d) and 59. In addition, such plans shall disclose:**

   (a)   **the amount of benefits expense that has been accrued during the reporting period, measured in accordance with the standards set out in paragraph 55(a); and**

   (b)   **the operating result, measured as the difference between revenues and expenses.**

Actuarial information

Standards

63   **The financial statements of a defined benefit plan shall have appended thereto a copy or summary of the most recent actuarial report prepared for the plan. That copy or summary shall include:**

   (a)   **the effective date of the actuarial report;**

   (b)   **the name and qualifications of the actuary;**

   (c)   **the relationship of the market value of the net assets available to meet accrued benefits to the aggregate vested benefits of the plan at the date of valuation of the plan's assets; and**

   (d)   **the opinion of the actuary as to the financial condition of the plan at the valuation date.**

Commentary

64   While not required by this Standard, it is recommended that the copy or summary of the most recent actuarial report include disclosure of the actuarial assumptions which have had a significant effect on the measurement of accrued benefits, changes in those assumptions since the previous actuarial report and any relevant actuarial ratios.

Vested benefits

Commentary

65   Users of the financial reports of both defined contribution plans and defined benefit plans are likely to be interested in assessing the ability of the plan to meet benefits which have vested as at the reporting date (and which, therefore, members would expect to receive in the event of resignation from membership of the plan at the reporting date) as well as those which have accrued and which may be expected to vest in the future. Therefore, this Standard requires that vested benefits as at the reporting date be separately disclosed by way of note in the financial report.

Plans Whose Only Assets are Endowment, Whole of Life or Other Long-term Insurance Policies which Match and Fully Guarantee the Benefits to be Paid to Individual Members

Standards

66　Superannuation plans whose only assets (other than temporary deposits at call with a bank) are endowment, whole of life or other long-term insurance policies which match and fully guarantee the benefits to be paid to individual members are not required to comply with the standards set out in paragraphs 37, 44, 49, 50, 54, 55, 57, 58, 59, 60, 61, 62 and 63 of this Standard. The general purpose financial report of such plans need only report:

(a)　that such policies are in place;

(b)　whether those policies have been fully maintained as directed by the insurer(s);

(c)　the identity of the insurer(s);

(d)　amounts contributed by employers and members during the reporting period;

(e)　where all amounts contributed by employers and members during the reporting period are not paid as premiums, the premiums paid to insurers during the reporting period; and

(f)　expenses of the plan incurred by the trustees during the reporting period.

Other Information

Standards

67　Where a superannuation plan consists of more than one separate entity, the general purpose financial report for the plan shall include a statement identifying the separate entities which constitute the plan.

Transitional Provisions – General

Initial adjustments

Standards

68　Where application of this Standard results in initial adjustments to the carrying amounts of assets and liabilities the net amount of those adjustments shall be adjusted against the balance of net assets available to pay benefits as at the beginning of the reporting period.

Comparative amounts

Standards

69　On initial application of this Standard, comparative amounts need not be disclosed to the extent that:

(a)　the general purpose financial report has been prepared on a different basis to the report for the preceding corresponding reporting period;

(b)　the Standard requires particular disclosures to be made for the first time; or

(c)　obtaining the information is impracticable.

Transitional Provisions – Defined Contribution Plans

Alternative reporting format

Standards

70　From the operative date of this Standard and for reporting periods ending no later than 30 June 1995, transitional provisions shall apply whereby defined contribution superannuation plans, while encouraged to apply the full provisions of this Standard, may elect to adopt an alternative reporting format comprising a statement of net assets, a statement of changes in net assets and notes thereto. Defined contribution plans which elect to adopt the alternative reporting format shall not comply with the standards set out in paragraphs 57, 58 and 59 but shall prepare financial statements which comply with the standards set out in paragraphs 72 and 73. Once a defined contribution plan elects to apply the full provisions of this Standard it shall no longer have access to the transitional provisions.

Commentary

71   The alternative reporting format for defined contribution plans during the transitional period comprises:

    (a)   a statement of net assets, to highlight assets available to meet accrued benefits;

    (b)   a statement of changes in net assets, to highlight the major factors influencing changes in assets available to pay benefits as a result of investment and other activities of the plan during the reporting period; and

    (c)   notes thereto, which will include a schedule of changes in accrued benefits.

An illustrative example of the alternative reporting format for defined contribution plans is provided in Appendix 2.

Statement of net assets

Standards

72   **The statement of net assets of a defined contribution plan shall disclose:**

    (a)   **the assets of the plan, showing separately investments and other assets by class of assets;**

    (b)   **the liabilities of the plan, showing separately each class of liability but excluding the liability for accrued benefits;**

    (c)   **net assets available to pay benefits; and**

    (d)   **by way of note:**

        (i)   **the liability for accrued benefits, and the benefits accrued during the reporting period measured in accordance with the standards set out in paragraph 54;**

        (ii)   **vested benefits;**

        (iii)   **any benefits which have been guaranteed, the identity of the guarantor(s), the nature of the guarantee(s) and any changes from the corresponding preceding reporting period;**

        (iv)   **the method adopted in determining net market value for each class of asset disclosed; and**

        (v)   **the amount of accrued benefits allocated to members' accounts and the amount not yet so allocated.**

Statement of changes in net assets

Standards

73   **The statement of changes in net assets of a defined contribution plan shall disclose:**

    (a)   **the amount of net assets available to pay benefits as at the beginning and the end of the reporting period;**

    (b)   **amounts contributed by employers;**

    (c)   **amounts contributed by members;**

    (d)   **investment revenue, showing separately its individual components, including changes in net market values for each class of investment;**

    (e)   **changes in net market value of assets other than investments;**

    (f)   **other revenue, showing separately proceeds from term insurance policies;**

    (g)   **direct investment expense;**

    (h)   **general administration expense;**

(i)   benefits paid;

(j)   income tax expense; and

(k)   by way of note:

    (i)   separately, the change during the reporting period in net market values of investments held at the reporting date, other assets held at the reporting date, investments realised during the reporting period and other assets realised during the reporting period; and

    (ii)   the rate(s) or other basis of contributions by employers and members during the reporting period, and any change in the rate(s) or other basis of contributions from the corresponding preceding reporting period.

Transitional Provisions – Defined Benefit Plans

Accrued benefits

Standards

74   From the operative date of this Standard and for reporting periods ending no later than 30 June 1995, transitional provisions shall apply whereby defined benefit superannuation plans are not required to report accrued benefits at an amount measured in accordance with the standards set out in paragraph 50. During this period, when a value for accrued benefits is determined as part of the comprehensive actuarial review, the plan shall report that value.

Commentary

75   For a period of three years from the operative date for application of this Standard, defined benefit plans are encouraged but not required to report accrued benefits measured on the basis outlined in paragraph 50.

Compatibility with International Accounting Standard IAS 26

The accounting standards set out in this Standard are consistent with those set out in IAS 26 "Accounting and Reporting by Retirement Benefit Plans" except that IAS 26 allows changes in net market values to be recognised as an item of revenue only in certain specified circumstances.

The following Appendices form part of the commentary and are provided for illustrative purposes only. Other methods of presentation may equally comply with the accounting standards set out in this Standard.

Appendix 1

Example of a Financial Report for a Defined Contribution Superannuation Plan

(Prepared in Conformity with the Full Provisions of this Standard)

Defined Contribution Plan

Statement of Financial Position
as at 30 June 19X1

	19X1		19X0	
	$'000	$'000	$'000	$'000
Investments				
Government Securities	210		25	
Other Fixed Interest Securities	182		150	
Mortgage Loans	22		22	
Shares in Listed Companies	124		310	
Real Estate Properties	187		97	
Insurance Policies	77	802	65	669
Other Assets				
Cash	113		82	
Contributions Receivable	25		30	
Interest Receivable	72		64	
Fixtures and Fittings	73	283	85	261
Total Assets		1,085		930
Less: Income Tax Payable (Note 7)	13		7	
Provision for Deferred Income Tax (Note 7)	9		6	
Sundry Liabilities Accounts Payable	15	37	17	30
Net Assets Available to Pay Benefits		1,048		900
Represented by:				
Liability for Accrued Benefits (Notes 2, 3, 4)				
Allocated to members' accounts		1,030		875
Not yet allocated		18		25
		1,048		900

Defined Contribution Plan

Operating Statement
for the Reporting Period ended 30 June 19X1

	19X1		19X0	
	$'000	$'000	$'000	$'000
Investment Revenue				
Interest	55		48	
Dividends	12		14	
Property Rentals	22		20	
Changes in Net Market Values (Note 5)	38	127	25	107
Direct Investment Expense		(30)		(25)
Net Investment Revenue		97		82
Contributions Revenue (Note 6)				
Employer Contributions	95		90	
Members' Contributions	80	175	74	164
Other Revenue				
Proceeds from Term Insurance Policies	8		–	
Changes in Net Market Values of Other Assets (Note 5)	(12)	(4)	(10)	(10)
General Administration Expense				
Term Insurance Expense	(16)		(13)	
Other General Administration Expenses	(8)	(24)	(7)	(20)
Income Tax Expense (Note 7)		(16)		(13)
Benefits Accrued as a Result of Operations		228		203

Appendix 1 (continued)

Defined Contribution Plan

Statement of Cash Flows
for the Reporting Period ended 30 June 19X1

	19X1		19X0	
	$'000	$'000	$'000	$'000
	Inflows (Outflows)		Inflows (Outflows)	
Cash Flows from Operating Activities				
Contributions Received				
Employee	98		91	
Member	82	180	77	168
Interest Received	47		28	
Dividends Received	12		14	
Rents Received	22		20	
Proceeds from Term Assurance	8	89	–	62
Benefits Paid		(80)		(74)
Term Insurance Premiums Paid	(16)		(13)	
General Expenses Paid	(10)	(26)	(7)	(20)
Tax Paid		(7)		(5)
Net Cash Flow from Operating Activities (Note 8)		156		131
Cash Flows from Investing Activities				
Proceeds from Sales of Shares	210		–	
Government Securities Purchased	(190)		–	
Other Securities Purchased	(25)		(58)	
Insurance Policies Purchased	(10)		(3)	
Real Estate Purchased	(80)		(40)	
Investment Expenses Paid	(30)		(25)	
Net Cash Used in Investing Activities		(125)		(126)
Net Increase in Cash Held		31		5
Cash at the Beginning of the Reporting Period		82		77
Cash that the end of the reporting period (Note 9)		113		82

Defined Contribution Plan

Notes to the Financial Statements
for the Reporting Period Ended 30 June 19X1

1. **Summary of Significant Accounting Policies**

   The following explains the significant accounting policies which have been adopted in the preparation of the financial statements. Unless otherwise stated, such accounting policies were also adopted in the corresponding preceding reporting period.

   (a) Compliance with Statements of Accounting Concepts, Australian Accounting Standards, the trust deed and legislative requirements

   The financial statements have been drawn up in accordance with Statements of Accounting Concepts, Australian Accounting Standard AAS 25 "Financial Reporting by Superannuation Plans" and with the provisions of the trust deed and relevant legislative requirements.

   (b) Assets

   Assets of the plan are recorded at net market value as at the reporting date and changes in the net market value of assets are recognised in the operating statement in the periods in which they occur. Net market values have been determined as follows: in the case of shares in listed companies and government and other fixed interest securities, by reference to relevant middle-market quotations; in the case of real estate properties and fixtures and fittings, on the basis of Trustees' assessments; in the case of mortgage loans, by reference to the outstanding principal of the loans; and, in the case of insurance policies, by reference to an actuarial assessment of the amount recoverable from the insurer in respect of the policy.

2. **Liability for Accrued Benefits**

   The liability for accrued benefits is the plan's present obligation to pay benefits to members and beneficiaries and has been calculated as the difference between the carrying amounts of the assets and the carrying amounts of the sundry liabilities and income tax liabilities as at reporting date.

   Changes in the Liability for Accrued Benefits

	19X1		19X0	
	$'000	$'000	$'000	$'000
Liability for Accrued Benefits at beginning of period		900		711
Plus: Increase in Accrued Benefits	228		203	
Less: Benefits paid	80	148	74	129
Liability for Accrued benefits at end of period		1,048		900

3. **Vested Benefits**

   Vested benefits are benefits which are not conditional upon continued membership of the plan (or any factor other than resignation from the plan) and include benefits which members were entitled to receive had they terminated their plan membership as at the reporting date.

	19X1	19X0
	$'000	$'000
Vested Benefits	868	652

Defined Contribution Plan

4. Guaranteed Benefits

No guarantees have been made in respect of any part of the liability for accrued benefits.

5. Changes in Net Market Values

(a) Changes in Net Market Value of Investments

	19X1		19X0	
	$'000	$'000	$'000	$'000
Investments Held at the Reporting Date				
Government Securities	(5)		4	
Other Fixed Interest Securities	7		6	
Mortgage Loans	–		–	
Shares in Listed Companies	4		2	
Real Estate Properties	10		12	
Insurance Policies	2	18	1	25
Investments Realised During the Period				
Shares in Listed Companies		20		–
Total		38		25

(b) Changes in Net Market Value of Other Assets

	19X1	19X0
	$'000	$'000
Other Assets Held at the Reporting Date		
Fixtures and Fittings	(12)	(10)
Other Assets Realised during the Period	–	–
Total	(12)	(10)

6. Funding Arrangements

In 19X1 the employer contributed to the plan at a rate of approximately 7.3% (19X0 – 7.3%) of the gross salaries of those employees who were members of the plan. Employees contributed to the plan during 19X1 at the rate of 6% (19X0 – 6%) of gross salary.

7. Income Tax

Income tax expense, assets and liabilities arising from the levying of income tax (including capital gains tax) on superannuation plans have been determined in accordance with the provisions of Australian Accounting Standard AAS 3 "Accounting for Income Tax (Tax-effect Accounting)".

Appendix 1 (continued)

Defined Contribution Plan

8. **Reconciliation of Net Cash provided by Operating Activities to Benefits Accrued from Operations after Income Tax**

	19X1		19X0	
	$'000	$'000	$'000	$'000
Benefits Accrued as a Result of Operations		228		203
Direct Investment Expenses		30		25
Changes in Net Market Values				
Investments	(38)		(25)	
Other assets	12	(26)	10	(15)
Benefits Paid		(80)		(74)
Decrease in Contributions Receivables		5		4
Decrease in Accounts Payable		(2)		–
Increase in Interest Receivable		(8)		(20)
Increase in:				
Income Tax Payable	6		3	
Provision for Deferred Income Tax	3	9	5	8
Net Cash Provided by Operating Activities		156		131

9. **Reconciliation of Cash**

For the purposes of the statement of cash flows, cash includes cash on hand and in banks. Cash at the end of the reporting period as shown in the statement of cash flows is reconciled to the related item in the statement of financial position as follows.

	19X1	19X0
	$'000	$'000
Cash	113	82

Appendix 2

Example of a Financial Report for a Defined Contribution Superannuation Plan

(Prepared in Conformity with the Transitional Provisions set out in Paragraphs 70 to 73)

Defined Contribution Plan

Statement of Net Assets
as at 30 June 19X1

	19X1		19X0	
	$'000	$'000	$'000	$'000
Investments				
Government Securities	210		25	
Other Fixed Interest Securities	182		150	
Mortgage Loans	22		22	
Shares in Listed Companies	124		310	
Real Estate Properties	187		97	
Insurance Policies	77	802	65	669
Other Assets				
Cash	113		82	
Contributions Receivable	25		30	
Interest Receivable	72		64	
Fixtures and Fittings	73	283	85	261
Total Assets		1,085		930
Less: Income Tax Payable (Note 7)		13		7
Provision for Deferred Income Tax (Note 7)		9		6
Sundry Liabilities				
Accounts Payable		15		17
Net Assets Available to Pay Benefits (Notes 2, 3)		1,048		900

Appendix 2 (continued)

Defined Contribution Plan

Statement of Changes in Net Assets
for the Reporting Period ended 30 June 19X1

	19X1		19X0	
	$'000	$'000	$'000	$'000
Net Assets Available to Pay Benefits (beginning of period)		900		771
Investment Revenue				
Interest	55		48	
Dividends	12		14	
Property Rentals	22		20	
Changes in Net Market Values (Note 5)	38		25	
Direct Investment Expense	(30)	97	(25)	82
Changes in Net Market Values of Other Assets (Note 5)		(12)		(10)
General Administration Expense		(24)		(20)
Contributions (Note 6)				
Employer	95		90	
Members	80	175	74	164
Proceeds from Term Insurance Policies		8		–
Benefits Paid		(80)		(74)
Income Tax Expense (Note 7)				
Changes in Tax Assets (Liabilities)				
Income Tax Payable	(13)		(7)	
Provision for Deferred Income Tax	(3)	(16)	(6)	(13)
Net Assets Available to Pay Benefits (end of period)		1,048		900

AAS

Appendix 2 (continued)

Defined Contribution Plan

Notes to the Financial Statements
for the Reporting Period ended 30 June 19X1

1. **Summary of Significant Accounting Policies**

   The following explains the significant accounting policies which have been adopted in the preparation of the financial statements. Unless otherwise stated, such accounting policies were also adopted in the corresponding preceding reporting period.

   (a) Compliance with Statements of Accounting Concepts, Australian Accounting Standards, the trust deed and legislative requirements

   The financial statements have been drawn up in accordance with Statements of Accounting Concepts, the Transitional Provisions set out in Australian Accounting Standard AAS 25 "Financial Reporting by Superannuation Plans" and with the provisions of the trust deed and relevant legislative requirements.

   (b) Assets

   Assets of the plan are recorded at net market value as at the reporting date and changes in the net market value of assets are recognised in the statement of changes in net assets in the periods in which they occur. Net market values have been determined as follows: in the case of shares in listed companies and government and other fixed interest securities, by reference to relevant middle-market quotations; in the case of real estate properties and fixtures and fittings, on the basis of Trustees' assessments; in the case of mortgage loans, by reference to the outstanding principal of the loans; and, in the case of insurance policies, by reference to an actuarial assessment of the amount recoverable from the insurer in respect of the policy.

2. **Liability for Accrued Benefits**

   Accrued benefits represents the plan's present obligation to pay benefits to members and beneficiaries and has been calculated as the difference between the carrying amounts of the assets and the carrying amounts of the sundry liabilities and income tax liabilities as at reporting date.

   (a) Changes in Accrued Benefits

	19X1		19X0	
	$'000	$'000	$'000	$'000
Accrued Benefits at beginning of period		900		771
Plus: Benefits accruing during period	228		203	
Less: Benefits Paid	80	148	74	129
Accrued Benefits at end of peiod		1,048		900

   (b) Allocation of Benefits

	19X1	19X0
	$'000	$'000
Member's accounts	1,030	875
Not yet allocated	18	25
Accrued Benefits	1,048	900

3.   Vested Benefits

Vested benefits are benefits which are not conditional upon continued membership of the plan (or any factor other than resignation from the plan) and include benefits which members were entitled to receive had they terminated their plan membership as at the reporting date.

	19X1 $'000	19X0 $'000
Vested Benefits	868	652

4.   Guaranteed Benefits

No guarantees have been made in respect of any part of accrued benefits.

5.   Changes in Net Market Values

(a)   Changes in Net Market Value of Investments

	19X1		19X0	
	$'000	$'000	$'000	$'000
Investments Held at the Reporting Date				
Government Securities	(5)		4	
Other Fixed Interest Securities	7		6	
Mortgage Loans	–		–	
Shares in Listed Companies	4		2	
Real Estate Properties	10		12	
Insurance Policies	2	18	1	25
Investments Realised During the Period				
Shares in Listed Companies		20		–
Total		38		25

(b)   Changes in Net Market Value of Other Assets

	19X1 $'000	19X0 $'000
Other Assets Held at the Reporting Date		
Fixtures and Fittings	(12)	(10)
Other Assets Realised During the Period	–	–
Total	(12)	(10)

6.   Funding Arrangements

In 19X1 the employer contributed to the plan at a rate of approximately 7.3% (19X0 – 7.3%) of the gross salaries of those employees who were members of the plan. Employees contributed to the plan during 19X1 at the rate of 6% (19X0 – 6%) of gross salary.

7.   Income Tax

Income tax expense, assets and liabilities arising from the levying of income tax (including capital gains tax) on superannuation plans have been determined in accordance with the provisions of Australian Accounting Standard AAS 3 "Accounting for Income Tax (Tax-effect Accounting)".

Income tax paid during 19X1 amounted to $7,000 (19X0 – nil).

Appendix 3

Example of a Financial Report for a Defined Benefit Superannuation Plan which Elects to Prepare a Statement of Net Assets and a Statement of Changes in Net Assets

Defined Benefit Plan

Statement of Net Assets
as at 30 June 19X1

	19X1 $'000	19X1 $'000	19X0 $'000	19X0 $'000
Investments				
Government Securities	210		25	
Other Fixed Interest Securities	182		150	
Mortgage Loans	22		22	
Shares in Listed Companies	124		310	
Real Estate Properties	187		97	
Insurance Policies	77	802	65	669
Other Assets				
Cash	113		82	
Contributions Receivable	25		30	
Interest Receivable	72		64	
Fixtures and Fittings	73	283	85	261
Total Assets		1,085		930
Less: Income Tax Payable (Note 8)		13		7
Provision for Deferred Income Tax (Note 8)		9		6
Sundry Liabilities				
Accounts Payable		15		17
Net Assets Available to Pay Benefits (Notes 2, 3)		1,048		900

Defined Benefit Plan

Statement of Changes in Net Assets
for the Reporting Period Ended 30 June 19X1

	19X1		19X0	
	S'000	S'000	S'000	S'000
Net Assets Available to Pay Benefits (beginning of period)		900		771
Investment Revenue				
Interest	55		48	
Dividends	12		14	
Property Rentals	22		20	
Changes in Net Market Values (Note 6)	38		25	
Direct Investment Expense	(30)	97	(25)	82
Changes in Net Market Values of Other Assets (Note 6)		(12)		(10)
General Administration Expense		(24)		(20)
Contributions (Note 5)				
Employer	95		90	
Members	80	175	74	164
Proceeds from Term Insurance Policies		8		–
Benefits Paid		(80)		(74)
Income Tax Expense (Note 7)				
Changes in Tax Assets (Liabilities)				
Income Tax Payable	(13)		(7)	
Provision for Deferred Income Tax	(3)	(16)	(6)	(13)
Net Assets Available to Pay Benefits (end of period)		1,048		900

Defined Benefit Plan

Notes to the Financial Statements
for the Reporting Period Ended 30 June 19X1

1.   **Summary of Significant Accounting Policies**

The following explains the significant accounting policies which have been adopted in the preparation of the financial statements. Unless otherwise stated, such accounting policies were also adopted in the corresponding preceding reporting period.

(a)   Compliance with Statements of Accounting Concepts, Australian Accounting Standards, the trust deed and legislative requirements

The financial statements have been drawn up in accordance with Statements of Accounting Concepts, Australian Accounting Standard AAS 25 "Financial Reporting by Superannuation Plans" and with the provisions of the trust deed and relevant legislative requirements.

(b)   Assets

Assets of the plan are recorded at net market value as at the reporting date and changes in the net market value of assets are recognised in the statement of changes in net assets in the periods in which they occur. Net market values have been determined as follows: in the case of shares in listed companies and government and other fixed interest securities, by reference to relevant middle-market quotations; in the case of real estate properties and fixtures and fittings, on the basis of Trustees' assessments; in the case of mortgage loans, by reference to the outstanding principal of the loans; and, in the case of insurance policies, by reference to an actuarial assessment of the amount recoverable from the insurer in respect of the policy.

2.   **Liability for Accrued Benefits**

The amount of accrued benefits has been determined on the basis of the present value of expected future payments which arise from membership of the plan up to the measurement date. The figure reported has been determined by reference to expected future salary levels and by application of a market-based, risk-adjusted discount rate and relevant actuarial assumptions. The valuation of accrued benefits was undertaken by the actuary as part of a comprehensive actuarial review undertaken during 19X0. Accrued benefits were previously valued as part of a comprehensive actuarial review undertaken during 19X(–3).

Accrued Benefits

	19X1 $'000	19X(–3) $'000
Accrued Benefits as at the end of 19X0 (19X(–3))	972	600

[If accrued benefits are measured as at each reporting date, the detail set out in Appendix 4, Note 2 should be provided.]

3.   **Vested Benefits**

Vested benefits are benefits which are not conditional upon continued membership of the plan (or any factor other than resignation from the plan) and include benefits which members were entitled to receive had they terminated their plan membership as at the reporting date.

	19X1 $'000	19X0 $'000
Vested benefits	868	652

Defined Benefit Plan

4. **Guaranteed Benefits**

No guarantees have been made in respect of any part of accrued benefits.

5. **Funding Arrangements**

The funding policy adopted in respect of the plan is directed at ensuring that benefits accruing to members and beneficiaries are fully funded as the benefits fall due. As such, in framing employer and member contribution rates, the actuary has considered long-term trends in such factors as plan membership, salary growth and average market value of plan assets.

In the past the employer has contributed to the plan at the rate recommended by the actuary. (In 19X1 that rate was approximately 7.3% (19X0 – 7.3%) of the gross salaries of those employees who were members of the plan. Employees contributed to the plan during 19X1 at the rate of 6% (19X0 – 6%) of gross salary.) Thus, any difference between net assets available to pay benefits and accrued benefits reported by the plan each period has been anticipated, except for the effects of the following factors:

(a) some short-term variations in the experience of the plan from that anticipated when framing contribution rates; and

(b) valuing assets at net market values as at the reporting date (necessary to display the financial position of the plan at that date) rather than adopting average asset values (as is typically done by an actuary when framing contribution rates).

As noted above, the funding policy adopted in respect of the plan will overcome these effects in the long term.

The actuarial report attached to these financial statements includes the actuary's opinion as to the financial condition of the plan as at the last valuation date.

[Where a superannuation plan is only intended to be partly funded, for example, a public sector plan where employee contributions are made on a continuing basis, but the employer contribution is only made as benefits become payable (that is, on a pay-as-you-go basis), the following note may be appropriate:

"It is Government policy that employer contributions to the plan be made only when benefits become payable, that is, on a pay-as-you-go basis. This policy is reflected in the difference between net assets available to pay benefits and the amount of accrued benefits as at the reporting date." (Where appropriate, the following comment could be added: "The Government has, however, given the Trustees an undertaking that it will fund its share of all benefits as they fall due.")]

Defined Benefit Plan

6. Changes in Net Market Values

(a) Changes in Net Market Value of Investments

	19X1		19X0	
	$'000	$'000	$'000	$'000
Investments Held at the Reporting Date				
Government Securities	(5)		4	
Other Fixed Interest Securities	7		6	
Mortgage Loans	–		–	
Shares in Listed Companies	4		2	
Real Estate Properties	10		12	
Insurance Policies	2	18	1	25
Investments Realised During the Period				
Shares in Listed Companies		20		–
Total		38		25

(b) Changes in Net Market Value of Other Assets

	19X1	19X0
	$'000	$'000
Other Assets Held at the Reporting Date		
Fixtures and Fittings	(12)	(10)
Other Assets Realised During the Period	–	–
Total	(12)	(10)

7. Income Tax

Income tax expense, assets and liabilities arising from the levying of income tax (including capital gains tax) on superannuation plans have been determined in accordance with the provisions of Australian Accounting Standard AAS 3 "Accounting for Income Tax (Tax-effect Accounting)".

Income tax paid during 19X1 amounted to $7,000 (19X0 – nil).

Appendix 4

Example of a Financial Report for a Defined Benefit Superannuation Plan which Elects to Prepare an Operating Statement, a Statement of Financial Position and a Statement of Cash Flows

This reporting format is only available to plans which measure accrued benefits as at each reporting date – refer paragraph 62 of this Standard.

Defined Benefit Plan

Statement of Financial Position
as at 30 June 19X1

	19X1 $'000	19X1 $'000	19X0 $'000	19X0 $'000
Investments				
Government Securities	210		25	
Other Fixed Interest Securities	182		150	
Mortgage Loans	22		22	
Shares in Listed Companies	124		310	
Real Estate Properties	187		97	
Insurance Policies	77	802	65	669
Other Assets				
Cash	113		82	
Contributions Receivable	25		30	
Interest Receivable	72		64	
Fixtures and Fittings	73	283	85	261
Total Assets		1,085		930
Less: Income Tax Payable (Note 7)		13		7
Provision for Deferred Income Tax (Note 7)		9		6
Sundry Liabilities				
Accounts Payable		15		17
Net Assets Available to Pay Benefits		1,048		900
*Less: **Liability for Accrued Benefits** (Notes 2, 3, 4)		1,277		972
Excess of Assets over Liabilities (Liabilities over Assets) (Note 5)		(299)		(72)

[* The plan's liability for accrued benefits is set out in Note 2. Note 5 should be read for information concerning the plan's ability to meet benefits accrued to members, and the underlying assumptions concerning future contributions by employers and employees.]

Defined Benefit Plan

Operating Statement
for the Reporting Period Ended 30 June 19X1

	19X1 $'000	19X1 $'000	19X0 $'000	19X0 $'000
Investment Revenue				
Interest	55		48	
Dividends	12		14	
Property Rentals	22		20	
Changes in Net Market Values (Note 6)	38	127	25	107
Direct Invesment Expense		(30)		(25)
Net Investment Revenue		97		82
Contributions Revenue (Note 5)				
Employer Contributions	95		90	
Members' Contributions	80	175	74	164
Other Revenue				
Proceeds from Term Insurance Policies	8		–	
Changes in Net Market Values of Other Assets (Note 6)	(12)	(4)	(10)	(10)
General Administration Expense				
Term Insurance Expense	(16)		(13)	
Other General Administration Expenses	(8)	(24)	(7)	(20)
Benefits Expense		(385)		(200)
Operating Result before Income Tax		(141)		16
Income Tax Expense (Note 7)		(16)		(13)
Operating Result for Period		(157)		3

Appendix 4 (continued)

Defined Benefit Plan

Statement of Cash Flows
for the Reporting Period Ended 30 June 19X1

	19X1		19X0	
	$'000	$'000	$'000	$'000
	Inflows (Outflows)		Inflows (Outflows)	
Cash Flows from Operating Activities				
Contributions Received				
Employee	98		91	
Member	82	180	77	168
Interest Received	47		28	
Dividends Received	12		14	
Rents Received	22		20	
Proceeds from Term Assurance	8	89	–	62
Benefits Paid		(80)		(74)
Term Insurance Premiums Paid	(16)		(13)	
General Expenses Paid	(10)	(26)	(7)	(20)
Tax Paid		(7)		(5)
Net Cash Flow from Operating Activities (Note 8)		156		131
Cash Flows from Investing Activities				
Proceeds from Sales of Shares	210		–	
Government Securities Purchased	(190)		–	
Other Securities Purchased	(25)		(58)	
Insurance Policies Purchased	(10)		(3)	
Real Estate Purchased	(80)		(40)	
Investment Expenses Paid	(30)		(25)	
Net Cash Used in Investing Activities		(125)		(126)
Net Increase in Cash Held		31		5
Cash at the Beginning of the Reporting Period		82		77
Cash at the End of the Reporting Period (Note 9)		113		82

Defined Benefit Plan

Notes to the Financial Statements
for the Reporting Period Ended 30 June 19X1

1. **Summary of Significant Accounting Policies**

    The following explains the significant accounting policies which have been adopted in the preparation of the financial statements. Unless otherwise stated, such accounting policies were also adopted in the corresponding preceding reporting period.

    (a)   Compliance with Statements of Accounting Concepts, Australian Accounting Standards, the trust deed and legislative requirements

          The financial statements have been drawn up in accordance with Statements of Accounting Concepts, Australian Accounting Standard AAS 25 "Financial Reporting by Superannuation Plans" and with the provisions of the trust deed and relevant legislative requirements.

    (b)   Assets

          Assets of the plan are recorded at net market value as at the reporting date and changes in the net market value of assets are recognised in the operating statement in the periods in which they occur. Net market values have been determined as follows: in the case of shares in listed companies and government and other fixed interest securities, by reference to relevant middle-market quotations; in the case of real estate properties and fixtures and fittings, on the basis of Trustees' assessments; in the case of mortgage loans, by reference to the outstanding principal of the loans; and, in the case of insurance policies, by reference to an actuarial assessment of the amount recoverable from the insurer in respect of the policy.

2. **Liability for Accrued Benefits**

    The liability for accrued benefits represents the plan's present obligation to pay benefits to members and beneficiaries and has been determined on the basis of the present value of expected future payments which arise from membership of the plan up to the reporting date. The figure reported has been determined by reference to expected future salary levels and by application of a market-based, risk-adjusted discount rate and relevant actuarial assumptions. The valuation of accrued benefits as at the reporting date was undertaken by the actuary as part of a comprehensive actuarial review undertaken during 19X1.

    Changes in the Liability for Accrued Benefits

	19X1		19X0	
	$'000	$'000	$'000	$'000
Liability for Accrued Benefits at beginning of period		972		846
Plus: Benefits Expense	385		200	
Less: Benefits Paid	80	305	74	126
Liability for Accrued Benefits at end of period		1,277		972

Defined Benefit Plan

Notes to the Financial Statements
for the Reporting Period Ended 30 June 19X1

3. **Vested Benefits**

   Vested benefits are benefits which are not conditional upon continued membership of the plan (or any factor other than resignation from the plan) and include benefits which members were entitled to receive had they terminated their plan membership as at the reporting date.

	19X1 $'000	19X0 $'000
Vested benefits	868	652

4. **Guaranteed Benefits**

   No guarantees have been made in respect of any part of the liability for accrued benefits.

5. **Funding Arrangements**

   The funding policy adopted in respect of the plan is directed at ensuring that benefits accruing to members and beneficiaries are fully funded as the benefits fall due. As such, in framing employer and member contribution rates, the actuary has considered long-term trends in such factors as plan membership, salary growth and average market value of plan assets.

   In the past the employer has contributed to the plan at the rate recommended by the actuary. (In 19X1 that rate was approximately 7.3% (19X0 – 7.3%) of the gross salaries of those employees who were members of the plan. Employees contributed to the plan during 19X1 at the rate of 6% (19X0 – 6%) of gross salary.) Thus, any difference between the assets and liabilities of the plan as reported each period has been anticipated, except for the effects of the following factors:

   (a)   some short-term variations in the experience of the plan from that anticipated when framing contribution rates; and

   (b)   valuing assets at net market values as at the reporting date (necessary to display the financial position of the plan at that date) rather than adopting average asset values (as is typically done by an actuary when framing contribution rates).

   As noted above, the funding policy adopted in respect of the plan has been structured to accommodate any short-term experience variation and to eliminate any difference between the assets and liabilities of the plan over the long term.

   During the period ended 30 June 19X1, members' benefits were significantly improved. That improvement generated a significant increase in the benefits expense for the period and resulted in the excess of liabilities over assets of the plan at the end of the period being significantly greater than at 30 June 19X0.

   A review of the plan's funding policy has been undertaken and the actuary has recommended an increase in the employer contribution rate as necessary to ensure that the plan is fully funded in the long term. The employer has agreed to contribute to the plan at the increased rate as recommended by the actuary. If the employer continues to contribute to the plan at the recommended rate, benefits are not further improved and the plan continues to perform as expected, the funding policy adopted in respect of the plan is such that the difference between the assets and liabilities of the plan will be eliminated in the long term. The actuarial report attached to these financial statements includes the actuary's opinion as to the financial condition of the plan as at the last valuation date.

Defined Benefit Plan

[Where a superannuation plan is only intended to be partly funded, for example, a public sector plan where employee contributions are made on a continuing basis, but the employer contribution is only made as benefits become payable (that is, on a pay-as-you-go basis), the following note may be appropriate:

"It is Government policy that employer contributions to the plan be made only when benefits become payable, that is, on a pay-as-you-go basis. This policy is reflected by the excess of liabilities over assets reported in the statement of financial position and in the current period's operating result, reported in the operating statement." (Where appropriate, the following comment could be added: "The Government has, however, given the Trustees an undertaking that it will fund its share of all benefits as they fall due.")]

6. **Changes in Net Market Values**

   (a) Changes in Net Market Value of Investments

	19X1 $'000	19X1 $'000	19X0 $'000	19X0 $'000
Investments Held at the Reporting Date				
Government Securities	(5)		4	
Other Fixed Interest Securities	7		6	
Mortgage Loans	–		–	
Shares in Listed Companies	4		2	
Real Estate Properties	10		12	
Insurance Policies	2	18	1	25
Investments Realised During the Period				
Shares in Listed Companies		20		–
Total		38		25

   (b) Changes in Net Market Value of Other Assets

	19X1 $'000	19X0 $'000
Other Assets Held at the Reporting Date		
Fixtures and Fittings	(12)	(10)
Other Assets Realised During the Period	–	–
Total	(12)	(10)

7. **Income Tax**

   Income tax expense, assets and liabilities arising from the levying of income tax (including capital gains tax) on superannuation plans have been determined in accordance with the provisions of Australian Accounting Standard AAS 3 "Accounting for Income Tax (Tax-effect Accounting)".

Defined Benefit Plan

8. **Reconciliation of Net Cash provided by Operating Activities to Operating Result after Income Tax**

	19X1		19X0	
	$'000	$'000	$'000	$'000
Operating Result		(157)		3
Benefits Expenses		385		200
Direct Investment Expenses		30		300
Changes in Net Market Values				
Investments	(38)		(25)	
Other assets	12	(26)	10	(15)
Benefits Paid		(80)		(74)
Decrease in Contributions Receivable		5		4
Decrease in Accounts Payable		(2)		–
Increase Interest Receivable		(8)		(20)
Increase in:				
Income Tax Payable	6		3	
Provision for Deferred Income Tax	3	9	5	8
Net Cash Provided by Operating Activities		156		131

9. **Reconciliation of Cash**

For the purposes of the statement of cash flows, cash includes cash on hand and in banks. Cash at the end of the reporting period as shown in the statement of cash flows is reconciled to the related item in the statement of financial position as follows.

	19X1	19X0
	$'000	$'000
Cash	113	82

Interpretation 1
Changes in Existing Decommissioning, Restoration and Similar Liabilities

(Compiled November 2009)

Contents

Compilation Details

Comparison with IFRIC 1

UIG Interpretation 1
Changes in Existing Decommissioning, Restoration and Similar Liabilities

	Paragraphs
Background	1
Scope	2
Issue	3
Consensus	4 – 8
Application	Aus8.1 – Aus8.4

Illustrative Examples

Common facts	IE1
Example 1: Cost model	IE2 – IE5
Example 2: Revaluation model	IE6 – IE12

Basis for Conclusions on IFRIC 1

UIG Interpretation 1 *Changes in Existing Decommissioning, Restoration and Similar Liabilities* (as amended) is set out in paragraphs 1 – Aus8.4. Interpretations are listed in Australian Accounting Standard AASB 1048 *Interpretation and Application of Standards*. In the absence of explicit guidance, AASB 108 *Accounting Policies, Changes in Accounting Estimates and Errors* provides a basis for selecting and applying accounting policies.

Compilation Details

UIG Interpretation 1 *Changes in Existing Decommissioning, Restoration and Similar Liabilities* as amended

This compiled Interpretation applies to annual reporting periods beginning on or after 1 January 2009 that end on or after 30 June 2009. It takes into account amendments up to and including 25 June 2009 and was prepared on 4 November 2009 by the staff of the Australian Accounting Standards Board (AASB).

This compilation is not a separate Interpretation issued by the AASB. Instead, it is a representation of Interpretation 1 (July 2004) as amended by other pronouncements, which are listed in the Table below.

Table of Pronouncements

Pronouncement	Month issued	Application date *(annual reporting periods ... on or after ...)*	Application, saving or transitional provisions
Interpretation 1	Jul 2004	*(beginning)* 1 Jan 2005	
AASB 2007-6	Jun 2007	*(beginning)* 1 Jan 2009	see (a) below
AASB 2007-8	Sep 2007	*(beginning)* 1 Jan 2009	see (b) below
AASB 2009-6	Jun 2009	*(beginning)* 1 Jan 2009 and *(ending)* 30 Jun 2009	see (c) below

(a) Entities may elect to apply this Standard to annual reporting periods beginning on or after 1 January 2005 but before 1 January 2009, provided that AASB 123 *Borrowing Costs* (June 2007) is also applied to such periods.

(b) Entities may elect to apply this Standard to annual reporting periods beginning on or after 1 January 2005 but before 1 January 2009, provided that AASB 101 *Presentation of Financial Statements* (September 2007) is also applied to such periods.

(c) Entities may elect to apply this Standard to annual reporting periods beginning on or after 1 January 2005 but before 1 January 2009, provided that AASB 101 *Presentation of Financial Statements* (September 2007) is also applied to such periods, and to annual reporting periods beginning on or after 1 January 2009 that end before 30 June 2009.

Table of Amendments to Interpretation

Paragraph affected	How affected	By ... [paragraph]
6	amended	AASB 2007-8 [6, 150]
	amended	AASB 2009-6 [103]
8	amended	AASB 2007-6 [16]
Aus8.4	amended	AASB 2007-8 [8]
9A	note added	AASB 2007-8 [151]

Table of Amendments to Illustrative Examples

Paragraph affected	How affected	By ... [paragraph]
IE8	amended	AASB 2007-8 [6]
	amended	AASB 2009-6 [104]
IE10-IE11	amended	AASB 2009-6 [104]
IE12	amended	AASB 2007-8 [6]
	amended	AASB 2009-6 [104]

Comparison with IFRIC 1

Interpretation 1 and IFRIC 1

UIG Interpretation 1 *Changes in Existing Decommissioning, Restoration and Similar Liabilities* as amended is equivalent to International Financial Reporting Interpretations Committee Interpretation IFRIC 1 *Changes in Existing Decommissioning, Restoration and Similar Liabilities* as issued by the International Accounting Standards Board. Paragraphs that have been added to this Interpretation (and do not appear in the text of IFRIC 1) are identified with the prefix "Aus", followed by the number of the preceding IFRIC paragraph and decimal numbering.

For-profit entities that comply with Interpretation 1 as amended will simultaneously be in compliance with IFRIC 1 as amended.

Not-for-profit entities using the added "Aus" paragraphs that specifically apply to not-for-profit entities will be complying with requirements consistent with AASB 116 *Property, Plant and Equipment*, but will not be simultaneously complying with IFRIC 1.

Interpretation 1

UIG Interpretation 1 was issued in July 2004.

This compiled version of Interpretation 1 applies to annual reporting periods beginning on or after 1 January 2009 that end on or after 30 June 2009. It incorporates relevant amendments contained in other AASB pronouncements up to and including 25 June 2009 (see Compilation Details).

Urgent Issues Group

Interpretation 1

Changes in Existing Decommissioning, Restoration and Similar Liabilities

References

Accounting Standard AASB 101 *Presentation of Financial Statements*

Accounting Standard AASB 116 *Property, Plant and Equipment*

Accounting Standard AASB 123 *Borrowing Costs*

Accounting Standard AASB 136 *Impairment of Assets*

Accounting Standard AASB 137 *Provisions, Contingent Liabilities and Contingent Assets*

Background

1   Many entities have obligations to dismantle, remove and restore items of property, plant and equipment. In this Interpretation such obligations are referred to as 'decommissioning, restoration and similar liabilities'. Under Accounting Standard AASB 116 *Property, Plant and Equipment*, the cost of an item of property, plant and equipment includes the initial estimate of the costs of dismantling and removing the item and restoring the site on which it is located, the obligation for which an entity incurs either when the item is acquired or as a consequence of having used the item during a particular period for purposes other than to produce inventories during that period. AASB 137 *Provisions, Contingent Liabilities and Contingent Assets* contains requirements on how to measure decommissioning, restoration and similar liabilities. This Interpretation provides guidance on how to account for the effect of changes in the measurement of existing decommissioning, restoration and similar liabilities.

Scope

2   This Interpretation applies to changes in the measurement of any existing decommissioning, restoration or similar liability that is both:

(a)   recognised as part of the cost of an item of property, plant and equipment in accordance with AASB 116; and

(b)   recognised as a liability in accordance with AASB 137.

For example, a decommissioning, restoration or similar liability may exist for decommissioning a plant, rehabilitating environmental damage in extractive industries, or removing equipment.

Issue

3   This Interpretation addresses how the effect of the following events that change the measurement of an existing decommissioning, restoration or similar liability should be accounted for:

(a)   a change in the estimated outflow of resources embodying economic benefits (e.g. cash flows) required to settle the obligation;

(b)   a change in the current market-based discount rate as defined in paragraph 47 of AASB 137 (this includes changes in the time value of money and the risks specific to the liability); and

(c)   an increase that reflects the passage of time (also referred to as the unwinding of the discount).

Consensus

4   Changes in the measurement of an existing decommissioning, restoration and similar liability that result from changes in the estimated timing or amount of the outflow of resources embodying economic benefits required to settle the obligation, or a change in the discount rate, shall be accounted for in accordance with paragraphs 5-7 below.

5   If the related asset is measured using the cost model:

(a)   subject to paragraph 5(b), changes in the liability shall be added to, or deducted from, the cost of the related asset in the current period;

(b)   the amount deducted from the cost of the asset shall not exceed its carrying amount. If a decrease in the liability exceeds the carrying amount of the asset, the excess shall be recognised immediately in profit or loss; and

(c)   if the adjustment results in an addition to the cost of an asset, the entity shall consider whether this is an indication that the new carrying amount of the asset may not be fully recoverable. If it is such an indication, the entity shall test the asset for impairment by estimating its recoverable amount, and shall account for any impairment loss, in accordance with AASB 136 *Impairment of Assets*.

6   If the related asset is measured using the revaluation model:

(a)   changes in the liability alter the revaluation increase or decrease previously recognised on that asset, so that:

(i)   a decrease in the liability shall (subject to (b)) be recognised in other comprehensive income and increase the revaluation surplus within equity, except that it shall be recognised in profit or loss to the extent that it reverses a revaluation decrease on the asset that was previously recognised in profit or loss; or

(ii)   an increase in the liability shall be recognised in profit or loss, except that it shall be recognised in other comprehensive income and reduce the revaluation surplus within equity to the extent of any credit balance existing in the revaluation surplus in respect of that asset;

(b)   in the event that a decrease in the liability exceeds the carrying amount that would have been recognised had the asset been carried under the cost model, the excess shall be recognised immediately in profit or loss;

(c)   a change in the liability is an indication that the asset may have to be revalued in order to ensure that the carrying amount does not differ materially from that which would be determined using fair value at the end of the reporting period. Any such revaluation shall be taken into account in determining the amounts to be recognised in profit or loss or in other comprehensive income under (a). If a revaluation is necessary, all assets of that class shall be revalued; and

(d)   AASB 101 requires disclosure in the statement of comprehensive income of each component of other comprehensive income or expense. In complying with this requirement, the change in the revaluation surplus arising from a change in the liability shall be separately identified and disclosed as such.

Aus6.1   Notwithstanding paragraph 6, in respect of a not-for-profit entity, the requirements of paragraph 6 shall be applied in relation to a class of assets, consistent with the revaluation model requirements of AASB 116 for not-for-profit entities.

7   The adjusted depreciable amount of the asset is depreciated over its useful life. Therefore, once the related asset has reached the end of its useful life, all subsequent changes in the liability shall be recognised in profit or loss as they occur. This applies under both the cost model and the revaluation model.

8   The periodic unwinding of the discount shall be recognised in profit or loss as a finance cost as it occurs. Capitalisation under AASB 123 *Borrowing Costs* is not permitted.

Interpretations

Application

Aus8.1   This Interpretation applies when AASB 116 applies.

Aus8.2   This Interpretation applies to annual reporting periods beginning on or after 1 January 2005.

[Note: For application dates of paragraphs changed or added by an amending pronouncement, see Compilation Details.]

Aus8.3   This Interpretation shall not be applied to annual reporting periods beginning before 1 January 2005.

Aus8.4   The requirements specified in this Interpretation apply to the financial statements where information resulting from their application is material in accordance with AASB 1031 *Materiality*.

Effective Date of IFRIC 1

9   [Deleted by the UIG]

9A   [Deleted by the AASB]

Transition to IFRIC 1

10   [Deleted by the UIG]

Illustrative Examples

These examples accompany, but are not part of, Interpretation 1. The UIG considers that the examples are an essential feature of the Interpretation.

Common Facts

IE1   An entity has a nuclear power plant and a related decommissioning liability. The nuclear power plant started operating on 1 January 2000. The plant has a useful life of 40 years. Its initial cost was CU120,000[1]; this included an amount for decommissioning costs of CU10,000, which represented CU70,400 in estimated cash flows payable in 40 years discounted at a risk-adjusted rate of 5 per cent. The entity's annual reporting period ends on 31 December.

Example 1: Cost Model

IE2   On 31 December 2009, the plant is 10 years old. Accumulated depreciation is CU30,000 (CU120,000 × 10/40 years). Because of the unwinding of discount (5 per cent) over the 10 years, the decommissioning liability has grown from CU10,000 to CU16,300.

IE3   On 31 December 2009, the discount rate has not changed. However, the entity estimates that, as a result of technological advances, the net present value of the decommissioning liability has decreased by CU8,000. Accordingly, the entity adjusts the decommissioning liability from CU16,300 to CU8,300. On this date, the entity makes the following journal entry to reflect the change:

	CU	CU
Dr decommissioning liability	8,000	
Cr cost of asset		8,000

IE4   Following this adjustment, the carrying amount of the asset is CU82,000 (CU120,000 – CU8,000 – CU30,000), which will be depreciated over the remaining 30 years of the asset's life giving a depreciation expense for the next year of CU2,733 (CU82,000 ÷ 30). The next year's finance cost for the unwinding of the discount will be CU415 (CU8,300 × 5 per cent).

IE5   If the change in the liability had resulted from a change in the discount rate, instead of a change in the estimated cash flows, the accounting for the change would have been the same but the next year's finance cost would have reflected the new discount rate.

---

1   In these examples, monetary amounts are denominated in currency units (CU).

Example 2: Revaluation Model

IE6   An entity has one item of property, plant and equipment.[2] The entity adopts the revaluation model in AASB 116 whereby the plant is revalued with sufficient regularity that the carrying amount does not differ materially from fair value. The entity's policy is to eliminate accumulated depreciation at the revaluation date against the gross carrying amount of the asset.

IE7   When accounting for revalued assets to which decommissioning liabilities attach, it is important to understand the basis of the valuation obtained. For example:

    (a)   if an asset is valued on a discounted cash flow basis, some valuers may value the asset without deducting any allowance for decommissioning costs (a 'gross' valuation), whereas others may value the asset after deducting an allowance for decommissioning costs (a 'net' valuation), because an entity acquiring the asset will generally also assume the decommissioning obligation. For financial reporting purposes, the decommissioning obligation is recognised as a separate liability, and is not deducted from the asset. Accordingly, if the asset is valued on a net basis, it is necessary to adjust the valuation obtained by adding back the allowance for the liability, so that the liability is not counted twice[2]; or

    (b)   if an asset is valued on a depreciated replacement cost basis, the valuation obtained may not include an amount for the decommissioning component of the asset. If it does not, an appropriate amount will need to be added to the valuation to reflect the depreciated replacement cost of that component.

IE8   Assume that a market-based discounted cash flow valuation of CU115,000 is obtained at 31 December 2002. It includes an allowance of CU11,600 for decommissioning costs, which represents no change to the original estimate, after the unwinding of three years' discount. The amounts included in the statement of financial position at 31 December 2002 are therefore:

	CU
Asset at valuation (1)	126,600
Accumulated depreciation	nil
Decommissioning liability	(11,600)
Net assets	115,000
Retained earnings (2)	(10,600)
Revaluation surplus (3)	15,600

Notes:

    (1)   Valuation obtained of CU115,000 plus decommissioning costs of CU11,600, allowed for in the valuation but recognised as a separate liability = CU126,600.

    (2)   Three years' depreciation on original cost CU120,000 × 3/40 = CU9,000 plus cumulative discount on CU10,000 at 5 per cent compound = CU1,600; total CU10,600.

    (3)   Revalued amount CU126,600 less previous net book value of CU111,000 (cost CU120,000 less accumulated depreciation CU9,000).

IE9   The depreciation expense for 2003 is therefore CU3,420 (CU126,600 × 1/37) and the discount expense for 2003 is CU600 (5 per cent of CU11,600). On 31 December 2003, the decommissioning liability (before any adjustment) is CU12,200 and the discount rate has not changed. However, on that date, the entity estimates that, as a result of technological advances, the present value of the decommissioning liability has decreased by CU5,000. Accordingly, the entity adjusts the decommissioning liability from CU12,200 to CU7,200.

IE10   The whole of this adjustment is taken to revaluation surplus. (For a for-profit entity, this is because the adjustment does not exceed the carrying amount that would have been recognised had the asset been carried under the cost model. If it had done, the excess

---

2   For examples of this principle, see AASB 136 and AASB 140 *Investment Property*.

would have been taken to profit or loss in accordance with paragraph 6(b).) The entity makes the following journal entry to reflect the change:

	CU	CU
Dr decommissioning liability	5,000	
Cr revaluation reserve		5,000

IE11   The entity decides that a full valuation of the asset is needed at 31 December 2003, in order to ensure that the carrying amount does not differ materially from fair value. Suppose that the asset is now valued at CU107,000, which is net of an allowance of CU7,200 for the reduced decommissioning obligation that should be recognised as a separate liability. The valuation of the asset for financial reporting purposes, before deducting this allowance, is therefore CU114,200. The following additional journal entry is needed:

	CU	CU
Dr accumulated depreciation (1)	3,420	
Cr asset at valuation		3,420
Dr revaluation surplus (2)	8,980	
Cr asset at valuation (3)		8,980

Notes:

(1)   Eliminating accumulated depreciation of CU3,420 in accordance with the entity's accounting policy.

(2)   The debit is to revaluation surplus because the decrease arising on the revaluation does not exceed the credit balance existing in the revaluation surplus in respect of the asset.

(3)   Previous valuation (before allowance for decommissioning costs) CU126,600, less cumulative depreciation CU3,420, less new valuation (before allowance for decommissioning costs) CU114,200.

IE12   Following this valuation, the amounts included in the statement of financial position are:

	CU
Asset at valuation	114,200
Accumulated depreciation	nil
Decommissioning liability	(7,200)
Net assets	107,000
Retained earnings (1)	(14,620)
Revaluation surplus (2)	11,620

Notes:

(1)   CU10,600 at 31 December 2002 plus 2003's depreciation expense of CU3,420 and discount expense of CU600 = CU14,620.

(2)   CU15,600 at 31 December 2002, plus CU5,000 arising on the decrease in the liability, less CU8,980 decrease on revaluation = CU11,620.

Example 3: Transition

IE13 – IE18 [Deleted by the UIG]

Basis for Conclusions on IFRIC 1

This IFRIC Basis for Conclusions accompanies, but is not part of, UIG Interpretation 1. It is considered that this Basis for Conclusions is an essential feature of the Interpretation. Australian footnotes have been added to the text and are identified with the prefix "Aus". An IFRIC Basis for Conclusions may be amended to reflect the requirements of the UIG Interpretation and AASB Accounting Standards where they differ from the corresponding International pronouncements.

Introduction

BC1   This Basis for Conclusions summarises the IFRIC's considerations in reaching its consensus. Individual IFRIC members gave greater weight to some factors than to others.

Background

BC2   IAS 16 *Property, Plant and Equipment* requires the cost of an item of property, plant and equipment to include the initial estimate of the costs of dismantling and removing an asset and restoring the site on which it is located, the obligation for which an entity incurs either when the item is acquired or as a consequence of having used the item during a particular period for purposes other than to produce inventories during that period.

BC3   IAS 37 *Provisions, Contingent Liabilities and Contingent Assets* requires that the measurement of the liability, both initially and subsequently, should be the estimated expenditure required to settle the present obligation at the end of the reporting period and should reflect a current market-based discount rate. It requires provisions to be reviewed at the end of each reporting period and adjusted to reflect the current best estimate. Hence, when the effect of a change in estimated outflows of resources embodying economic benefits and/or the discount rate is material, that change should be recognised.

BC4   The IFRIC was asked to address how to account for changes in decommissioning, restoration and similar liabilities. The issue is whether changes in the liability should be recognised in current period profit or loss, or added to (or deducted from) the cost of the related asset. IAS 16 contains requirements for the initial capitalisation of decommissioning costs and IAS 37 contains requirements for measuring the resulting liability; neither specifically addresses accounting for the effect of changes in the liability. The IFRIC was informed that differing views exist, resulting in a risk of divergent practices developing.

BC5   Accordingly, the IFRIC decided to develop guidance on accounting for the changes. In so doing, the IFRIC recognised that the estimation of the liability is inherently subjective, since its settlement may be very far in the future and estimating (a) the timing and amount of the outflow of resources embodying economic benefits (e.g. cash flows) required to settle the obligation and (b) the discount rate often involves the exercise of considerable judgement. Hence, it is likely that revisions to the initial estimate will be made.

Scope

BC6   The scope of the Interpretation addresses the accounting for changes in estimates of existing liabilities to dismantle, remove and restore items of property, plant and equipment that fall within the scope of IAS 16 and are recognised as a provision under IAS 37. The Interpretation does not apply to changes in estimated liabilities in respect of costs that fall within the scope of other IFRSs, for example, inventory or production costs that fall within the scope of IAS 2 *Inventories*. The IFRIC noted that decommissioning obligations associated with the extraction of minerals are a cost either of the property, plant and equipment used to extract them, in which case they are within the scope of IAS 16 and the Interpretation, or of the inventory produced, which should be accounted for under IAS 2.

Basis for Consensus

BC7   The IFRIC reached a consensus that changes in an existing decommissioning, restoration or similar liability that result from changes in the estimated timing or amount of the outflow of resources embodying economic benefits required to settle the obligation, or a change in the discount rate, should be added to or deducted from the cost of the related asset and depreciated prospectively over its useful life.

BC8 In developing its consensus, the IFRIC also considered the following three alternative approaches for accounting for changes in the outflow of resources embodying economic benefits and changes in the discount rate:

(a) capitalising only the effect of a change in the outflow of resources embodying economic benefits that relate to future periods, and recognising in current period profit or loss all of the effect of a change in the discount rate.

(b) recognising in current period profit or loss the effect of all changes in both the outflow of resources embodying economic benefits and the discount rate.

(c) treating changes in an estimated decommissioning, restoration and similar liability as revisions to the initial liability and the cost of the asset. Under this approach, amounts relating to the depreciation of the asset that would have been recognised to date would be reflected in current period profit or loss and amounts relating to future depreciation would be capitalised.

BC9 The IFRIC rejected alternative (a), because this approach does not treat changes in the outflow of resources embodying economic benefits and in the discount rate in the same way, which the IFRIC agreed is important, given that matters such as inflation can affect both the outflow of economic benefits and the discount rate.

BC10 In considering alternative (b), the IFRIC observed that recognising all of the change in the discount rate in current period profit or loss correctly treats a change in the discount rate as an event of the present period. However, the IFRIC decided against alternative (b) because recognising changes in the estimated outflow of resources embodying economic benefits in current period profit or loss would be inconsistent with the initial capitalisation of decommissioning costs under IAS 16.

BC11 Alternative (c) was the approach proposed in draft Interpretation D2 *Changes in Decommissioning, Restoration and Similar Liabilities*, published on 4 September 2003. In making that proposal, the IFRIC regarded the asset, from the time the liability for decommissioning is first incurred until the end of the asset's useful life, as the unit of account to which decommissioning costs relate. It therefore took the view that revisions to the estimates of those costs, whether through revisions to estimated outflows of resources embodying economic benefits or revisions to the discount rate, ought to be accounted for in the same manner as the initial estimated cost. The IFRIC still sees merit in this proposal, but concluded on balance that, under current standards, full prospective capitalisation should be required for the reasons set out in paragraphs BC12-BC18.

IAS 8 and a change in accounting estimate

BC12 IAS 8 *Accounting Policies, Changes in Accounting Estimates and Errors* requires an entity to recognise a change in an accounting estimate prospectively by including it in profit or loss in the period of the change, if the change affects that period only, or the period of the change and future periods, if the change affects both. To the extent that a change in an accounting estimate gives rise to changes in assets or liabilities, or relates to an item of equity, it is required to be recognised by adjusting the asset, liability or equity item in the period of change.

BC13 Although the IFRIC took the view that the partly retrospective treatment proposed in D2 is consistent with these requirements of IAS 8, most responses to the draft Interpretation suggested that IAS 8 would usually be interpreted as requiring a fully prospective treatment. The IFRIC agreed that IAS 8 would support a fully prospective treatment also, and this is what the Interpretation requires.

IAS 16 and changes in accounting estimates for property, plant and equipment

BC14 Many responses to the draft Interpretation argued that the proposal in D2 was inconsistent with IAS 16, which requires other kinds of change in estimate for property, plant and equipment to be dealt with prospectively. For example, as IAS 8 also acknowledges, a change in the estimated useful life of, or the expected pattern of consumption of the future economic benefits embodied in, a depreciable asset affects depreciation expense for the current period and for each future period during the asset's remaining useful life. In both cases, the effect of the change relating to the current period is recognised in profit or loss in the current period. The effect, if any, on future periods is recognised in profit or loss in those future periods.

BC15 Some responses to the draft Interpretation noted that a change in the estimate of a residual value is accounted for prospectively and does not require a catch-up adjustment. They observed that liabilities relating to decommissioning costs can be regarded as negative residual values, and suggested that the Interpretation should not introduce inconsistent treatment for similar events. Anomalies could result if two aspects of the same change are dealt with differently—for example, if the useful life of an asset was extended and the present value of the decommissioning liability reduced as a result.

BC16 The IFRIC agreed that it had not made a sufficient case for treating changes in estimates of decommissioning and similar liabilities differently from other changes in estimates for property, plant and equipment. The IFRIC understood that there was no likelihood of the treatment of other changes in estimate for such assets being revisited in the near future.

BC17 The IFRIC also noted that the anomalies that could result from its original proposal, if other changes in estimate were dealt with prospectively, were more serious than it had understood previously, and that a fully prospective treatment would be easier to apply consistently.

BC18 The IFRIC had been concerned that a fully prospective treatment could result in either unrealistically large assets or negative assets, particularly if there are large changes in estimates toward the end of an asset's life. The IFRIC noted that the first concern could be dealt with if the assets were reviewed for impairment in accordance with IAS 36 *Impairment of Assets*, and that a zero asset floor could be applied to ensure that an asset did not become negative if cost estimates reduced significantly towards the end of its life. The credit would first be applied to write the carrying amount of the asset down to nil and then any residual credit adjustment would be recognised in profit or loss. These safeguards are included in the final consensus.

Comparison with US GAAP

BC19 In reaching its consensus, the IFRIC considered the US GAAP approach in Statement of Financial Accounting Standards No. 143, *Accounting for Asset Retirement Obligations* (SFAS 143). Under that standard, changes in estimated cash flows are capitalised as part of the cost of the asset and depreciated prospectively, but the decommissioning obligation is not required to be revised to reflect the effect of a change in the current market-assessed discount rate.

BC20 The treatment of changes in estimated cash flows required by this Interpretation is consistent with US GAAP, which the proposal in D2 was not. However, the IFRIC agreed that because IAS 37 requires a decommissioning obligation to reflect the effect of a change in the current market-based discount rate (see paragraph BC3), it was not possible to disregard changes in the discount rate. Furthermore, SFAS 143 did not treat changes in cash flows and discount rates in the same way, which the IFRIC had agreed was important.

The interaction of the Interpretation and initial recognition under IAS 16

BC21 In developing the Interpretation, the IFRIC considered the improvements that have been made to IAS 16 by the Board and agreed that it would explain the interaction of the two.

BC22 IAS 16 (as revised in 2003) clarifies that the initial measurement of the cost of an item of property, plant and equipment should include the cost of dismantling and removing the item and restoring the site on which it is located, if this obligation is incurred either when the item is acquired or as a consequence of having used the item during a particular period for purposes other than to produce inventories during that period. This is because the Board concluded that whether the obligation is incurred upon acquisition of the item or as a consequence of using it, the underlying nature of the cost and its association with the asset are the same.

BC23 However, in considering the improvements to IAS 16, the Board did not address how an entity would account for (a) changes in the amount of the initial estimate of a recognised obligation, (b) the effects of accretion of, or changes in interest rates on, a recognised obligation or (c) the cost of obligations that did not exist when the entity acquired the item, such as an obligation triggered by a change in a law enacted after the asset is acquired. The Interpretation addresses issues (a) and (b).

The interaction of the Interpretation and the choice of measurement model under IAS 16

BC24 IAS 16 allows an entity to choose either the cost model or the revaluation model for measuring its property, plant and equipment, on a class-by-class basis. The IFRIC's view is that the measurement model that an entity chooses under IAS 16 would not be affected by the Interpretation.

BC25 Several responses to the draft Interpretation sought clarification of how it should be applied to revalued assets. The IFRIC noted that:

(a)   if the entity chooses the revaluation model, IAS 16 requires the valuation to be kept sufficiently up to date that the carrying amount does not differ materially from that which would be determined using fair value at the balance sheet date.[1] This Interpretation requires a change in a recognised decommissioning, restoration or similar liability generally to be added to or deducted from the cost of the asset. However, a change in the liability does not, of itself, affect the valuation of the asset for financial reporting purposes, because (to ensure that it is not counted twice) the separately recognised liability is excluded from its valuation.

(b)   rather than changing the valuation of the asset, a change in the liability affects the difference between what would have been reported for the asset under the cost model, under this Interpretation, and its valuation. In other words, it changes the revaluation surplus or deficit that has previously been recognised for the asset. For example, if the liability increases by CU20, which under the cost model would have been added to the cost of the asset, the revaluation surplus reduces (or the revaluation deficit increases) by CU20. Under the revaluation model set out in IAS 16, cumulative revaluation surpluses for an asset are accounted for in equity,[2] and cumulative revaluation deficits are accounted for in profit or loss. The IFRIC decided that changes in the liability relating to a revalued asset should be accounted for in the same way as other changes in revaluation surpluses and deficits under IAS 16.[3]

(c)   although a change in the liability does not directly affect the value of the asset for financial reporting purposes, many events that change the value of the liability may also affect the value of the asset, by either a greater or lesser amount. The IFRIC therefore decided that, for revalued assets, a change in a decommissioning liability indicates that a revaluation may be required. Any such revaluation should be taken into account in determining the amount taken to profit or loss under (b) above. If a revaluation is done, IAS 16 requires all assets of the same class to be revalued.

(d)   the depreciated cost of an asset (less any impairment) should not be negative, regardless of the valuation model, and the revaluation surplus on an asset should not exceed its value. The IFRIC therefore decided that, if the reduction in a liability exceeds the carrying amount that would have been recognised had the asset been carried under the cost model, the excess reduction should always be taken to profit or loss. For example, if the depreciated cost of an unimpaired asset is CU25, and its revalued amount is CU100, there is a revaluation surplus

---

1   IAS 1 *Presentation of Financial Statements* (revised 2007) replaced the term 'balance sheet date' with 'end of the reporting period'.

2   As a consequence of the revision of IAS 1 *Presentation of Financial Statements* in 2007 the increase is recognised in other comprehensive income and accumulated in equity under the heading of revaluation surplus.

3   [Aus] Under Accounting Standard AASB 116 *Property, Plant and Equipment*, not-for-profit entities account for revaluation increases and decreases in relation to classes of assets.

of CU75. If the decommissioning liability associated with the asset is reduced by CU30, the depreciated cost of the asset should be reduced to nil, the revaluation surplus should be increased to CU100 (which equals the value of the asset), and the remaining CU5 of the reduction in the liability should be taken to profit or loss.[4]

The unwinding of the discount

BC26 The IFRIC considered whether the unwinding of the discount is a borrowing cost for the purposes of IAS 23 *Borrowing Costs*. This question arises because if the unwinding of the discount rate were deemed a borrowing cost for the purposes of IAS 23, in certain circumstances this amount might be capitalised under the allowed alternative treatment of capitalisation.[5] The IFRIC noted that IAS 23 addresses funds borrowed specifically for the purpose of obtaining a particular asset. It agreed that a decommissioning liability does not fall within this description since it does not reflect funds (i.e. cash) borrowed. Hence the IFRIC concluded that the unwinding of the discount is not a borrowing cost as defined in IAS 23.

BC27 The IFRIC agreed that the unwinding of the discount as referred to in paragraph 60 of IAS 37 should be reported in profit or loss in the period it occurs.

Disclosures

BC28 The IFRIC considered whether the Interpretation should include disclosure guidance and agreed that it was largely unnecessary because IAS 16 and IAS 37 contain relevant guidance, for example:

(a)   IAS 16 explains that IAS 8 requires the disclosure of the nature and effect of changes in accounting estimates that have an effect in the current period or are expected to have a material effect in subsequent periods, and that such disclosure may arise from changes in the estimated costs of dismantling, removing or restoring items of property, plant and equipment.

(b)   IAS 37 requires the disclosure of:

    (i)   a reconciliation of the movements in the carrying amount of the provision for the period.

    (ii)   the increase during the period in the discounted amount arising from the passage of time and the effect of any change in the discount rate.

    (iii)   a brief description of the nature of the obligation and the expected timing of any resulting outflows of economic benefits.

    (iv)   an indication of the uncertainties about the amount or timing of those outflows, and where necessary the disclosure of the major assumptions made concerning future events (e.g. future interest rates, future changes in salaries, and future changes in prices).

BC29 However, in respect of assets measured using the revaluation model, the IFRIC noted that changes in the liability would often be taken to the revaluation surplus. These changes reflect an event of significance to users, and the IFRIC agreed that they should be given prominence by being separately disclosed and described as such in the statement of changes in equity.[6]

---

4   [Aus] Not-for-profit entities account for revaluations in relation to classes of assets.

5   In March 2007, IAS 23 was revised to require the previously allowed alternative treatment of capitalisation. Capitalisation of borrowing costs for a qualifying asset becomes the only accounting treatment. That revision does not affect the reasoning set out in this Basis for Conclusions.

6   As a consequence of the revision of IAS 1 *Presentation of Financial Statements* in 2007 such changes are presented in the statement of comprehensive income.

Interpretations

Transition

BC30 The IFRIC agreed that preparers that already apply IFRSs should apply the Interpretation in the manner required by IAS 8, which is usually retrospectively. The IFRIC could not justify another application method, especially when IAS 37 requires retrospective application.

BC31 The IFRIC noted that, in order to apply the Interpretation retrospectively, it is necessary to determine both the timing and amount of any changes that would have been required by the Interpretation. However, IAS 8 specifies that:

(a)   if retrospective application is not practicable for all periods presented, the new accounting policy shall be applied retrospectively from the earliest practicable date; and

(b)   if it is impracticable to determine the cumulative effect of applying the new accounting policy at the start of the current period, the policy shall be applied prospectively from the earliest date practicable.

BC32 The IFRIC noted that IAS 8 defines a requirement as impracticable when an entity cannot apply it after making every reasonable effort to do so, and gives guidance on when this is so.

BC33 However, the provisions of IAS 8 on practicability do not apply to IFRS 1 *First-time Adoption of International Financial Reporting Standards*. Retrospective application of this Interpretation at the date of transition to IFRSs, which is the treatment required by IFRS 1 in the absence of any exemptions, would require first-time adopters to construct a historical record of all such adjustments that would have been made in the past. In many cases this will not be practicable. The IFRIC agreed that, as an alternative to retrospective application, an entity should be permitted to include in the depreciated cost of the asset at the date of transition an amount calculated by discounting the liability at that date back to, and depreciating it from, when it was first incurred. This Interpretation amends IFRS 1 accordingly[7].

---

7   [Aus] This alternative approach is included in AASB 1 *First-time Adoption of Australian Equivalents to International Financial Reporting Standards*.

Interpretation 2
Members' Shares in Co-operative Entities and Similar Instruments

(Compiled September 2011)

Contents

Compilation Details

Comparison with IFRIC 2

UIG Interpretation 2
Members' Shares in Co-operative Entities and Similar Instruments

	Paragraphs
References	
Background	1 – 2
Scope	3
Issue	4
Consensus	5 – 12
Disclosure	13
Application	Aus13.1 – Aus13.4

Appendix:

Examples of Application of the Consensus	A1
Unconditional Right to Refuse Redemption	A2 – A5
Prohibitions against Redemption	A6 – A19

Basis for Conclusions on IFRIC 2

UIG Interpretation 2 *Members' Shares in Co-operative Entities and Similar Instruments* (as amended) is set out in paragraphs 1 – Aus13.4 and the Appendix. Interpretations are listed in Australian Accounting Standard AASB 1048 *Interpretation and Application of Standards*. In the absence of explicit guidance, AASB 108 *Accounting Policies, Changes in Accounting Estimates and Errors* provides a basis for selecting and applying accounting policies.

Compilation Details

UIG Interpretation 2 *Members' Shares in Co-operative Entities and Similar Instruments* as amended

This compiled Interpretation applies to annual reporting periods beginning on or after 1 July 2011 but before 1 January 2013. It takes into account amendments up to and including 11 May 2011 and was prepared on 23 September 2011 by the staff of the Australian Accounting Standards Board (AASB).

This compilation is not a separate Interpretation issued by the AASB. Instead, it is a representation of Interpretation 2 (March 2005) as amended by other pronouncements, which are listed in the Table below.

Table of Pronouncements

Pronouncement	Month issued	Application date *(annual reporting periods ... on or after ...)*	Application, saving or transitional provisions
Interpretation 2	Mar 2005	*(ending)* 31 Dec 2005	see (a) below
AASB 2007-8	Sep 2007	*(beginning)* 1 Jan 2009	see (b) below
AASB 2008-2	Mar 2008	*(beginning)* 1 Jan 2009	see (c) below
AASB 2009-6	Jun 2009	*(beginning)* 1 Jan 2009 and *(ending)* 30 Jun 2009	see (d) below
AASB 2009-12	Dec 2009	*(beginning)* 1 Jan 2011	see (e) below
AASB 2010-2	Jun 2010	*(beginning)* 1 Jul 2013	not compiled*
AASB 2010-7	Dec 2010	*(beginning)* 1 Jan 2013	not compiled*
AASB 2011-1	May 2011	*(beginning)* 1 Jul 2011	see (f) below
AASB 2011-8	Sep 2011	*(beginning)* 1 Jan 2013	not compiled*

*   The amendments made by this Standard are not included in this compilation, which presents the principal Interpretation as applicable to annual reporting periods beginning on or after 1 July 2011 but before 1 January 2013.

(a)   Entities may elect to apply this Interpretation to annual reporting periods beginning on or after 1 January 2005 that end before 31 December 2005.

(b)   Entities may elect to apply this Standard to annual reporting periods beginning on or after 1 January 2005 but before 1 January 2009, provided that AASB 101 *Presentation of Financial Statements* (September 2007) is also applied to such periods.

(c)   Entities may elect to apply this Standard to annual reporting periods beginning on or after 1 January 2005 but before 1 January 2009.

(d)   Entities may elect to apply this Standard to annual reporting periods beginning on or after 1 January 2005 but before 1 January 2009, provided that AASB 101 *Presentation of Financial Statements* (September 2007) is also applied to such periods, and to annual reporting periods beginning on or after 1 January 2009 that end before 30 June 2009.

(e)   Entities may elect to apply this Standard to annual reporting periods beginning on or after 1 January 2005 but before 1 January 2011.

(f)   Entities may elect to apply this Standard, or its amendments to individual pronouncements, to annual reporting periods beginning on or after 1 January 2005 but before 1 July 2011, provided that AASB 1054 *Australian Additional Disclosures* is, or its relevant individual disclosure requirements are, also applied to such periods.

Table of Amendments

Paragraph affected	How affected	By ... [paragraph]
6	amended	AASB 2008-2 [36]
9	amended	AASB 2008-2 [37]
Aus12.1	deleted	AASB 2011-1 [21]
Aus12.2	amended deleted	AASB 2009-6 [105] AASB 2011-1 [21]
Aus13.1	amended	AASB 2007-8 [7, 8]
Aus13.3	amended amended	AASB 2007-8 [6] AASB 2009-12 [21]
Aus13.4	amended	AASB 2007-8 [8]
14A	note added	AASB 2008-2 [38]
A1	amended amended	AASB 2008-2 [39] AASB 2009-6 [106]
A11	amended	AASB 2007-8 [6]
A12	amended	AASB 2008-2 [40]
A14	amended	AASB 2007-8 [6]

Comparison with IFRIC 2

UIG Interpretation 2 *Members' Shares in Co-operative Entities and Similar Instruments* as amended incorporates International Financial Reporting Interpretations Committee Interpretation IFRIC 2 *Members' Shares in Co operative Entities and Similar Instruments*, issued by the International Accounting Standards Board. Paragraphs that have been added to this Interpretation (and do not appear in the text of IFRIC 2) are identified with the prefix "Aus", followed by the number of the preceding IFRIC paragraph and decimal numbering.

Entities that comply with Interpretation 2 as amended will simultaneously be in compliance with IFRIC 2 as amended.

Interpretation 2

UIG Interpretation 2 was issued in March 2005.

This compiled version of Interpretation 2 applies to annual reporting periods beginning on or after 1 July 2011 but before 1 January 2013. It incorporates relevant amendments contained in other AASB pronouncements up to and including 11 May 2011 (see Compilation Details).

Urgent Issues Group

Interpretation 2

Members' Shares in Co-operative Entities and Similar Instruments

References

Accounting Standard AASB 132 *Financial Instruments: Presentation*

Accounting Standard AASB 139 *Financial Instruments: Recognition and Measurement*

Background

1   Co-operatives and other similar entities are formed by groups of persons to meet common economic or social needs. National laws typically define a co-operative as a society endeavouring to promote its members' economic advancement by way of a joint business operation (the principle of self-help). Members' interests in a cooperative are often characterised as members' shares, units or the like, and are referred to below as 'members' shares'.

2   Accounting Standard AASB 132 *Financial Instruments: Presentation* establishes principles for the classification of financial instruments as financial liabilities or equity. In particular, those principles apply to the classification of puttable instruments that allow the holder to put those instruments to the issuer for cash or another financial instrument. The application of those principles to members' shares in co-operative entities and similar instruments is difficult. Constituents have asked for help in understanding how the principles in AASB 132 apply to members' shares and similar instruments that have certain features, and the circumstances in which those features affect the classification as liabilities or equity.

Scope

3   This Interpretation applies to financial instruments within the scope of AASB 132, including financial instruments issued to members of co operative entities that evidence the members' ownership interest in the entity. This Interpretation does not apply to financial instruments that will or may be settled in the entity's own equity instruments.

Issue

4   Many financial instruments, including members' shares, have characteristics of equity, including voting rights and rights to participate in dividend distributions. Some financial

instruments give the holder the right to request redemption for cash or another financial asset, but may include or be subject to limits on whether the financial instruments will be redeemed. How should those redemption terms be evaluated in determining whether the financial instruments should be classified as liabilities or equity?

Consensus

5   The contractual right of the holder of a financial instrument (including members' shares in co-operative entities) to request redemption does not, in itself, require that financial instrument to be classified as a financial liability. Rather, the entity must consider all of the terms and conditions of the financial instrument in determining its classification as a financial liability or equity. Those terms and conditions include relevant local laws, regulations and the entity's governing charter in effect at the date of classification, but not expected future amendments to those laws, regulations or charter.

6   Members' shares that would be classified as equity if the members did not have a right to request redemption are equity if either of the conditions described in paragraphs 7 and 8 is present or the members' shares have all the features and meet the conditions in paragraphs 16A and 16B or paragraphs 16C and 16D of AASB 132. Demand deposits, including current accounts, deposit accounts and similar contracts that arise when members act as customers are financial liabilities of the entity.

7   Members' shares are equity if the entity has an unconditional right to refuse redemption of the members' shares.

8   Local law, regulation or the entity's governing charter can impose various types of prohibitions on the redemption of members' shares, for example unconditional prohibitions or prohibitions based on liquidity criteria. If redemption is unconditionally prohibited by local law, regulation or the entity's governing charter, members' shares are equity. However, provisions in local law, regulation or the entity's governing charter that prohibit redemption only if conditions—such as liquidity constraints—are met (or are not met) do not result in members' shares being equity.

9   An unconditional prohibition may be absolute, in that all redemptions are prohibited. An unconditional prohibition may be partial, in that it prohibits redemption of members' shares if redemption would cause the number of members' shares or amount of paid-in capital from members' shares to fall below a specified level. Members' shares in excess of the prohibition against redemption are liabilities, unless the entity has the unconditional right to refuse redemption as described in paragraph 7 or the members' shares have all the features and meet the conditions in paragraphs 16A and 16B or paragraphs 16C and 16D of AASB 132. In some cases, the number of shares or the amount of paid-in capital subject to a redemption prohibition may change from time to time. Such a change in the redemption prohibition leads to a transfer between financial liabilities and equity.

10   At initial recognition, the entity shall measure its financial liability for redemption at fair value. In the case of members' shares with a redemption feature, the entity measures the fair value of the financial liability for redemption at no less than the maximum amount payable under the redemption provisions of its governing charter or applicable law discounted from the first date that the amount could be required to be paid (see example 3).

11   As required by paragraph 35 of AASB 132, distributions to holders of equity instruments are recognised directly in equity, net of any income tax benefits. Interest, dividends and other returns relating to financial instruments classified as financial liabilities are expenses, regardless of whether those amounts paid are legally characterised as dividends, interest or otherwise.

12   The Appendix, which is an integral part of the consensus, provides examples of the application of this consensus.

Disclosure

13   When a change in the redemption prohibition leads to a transfer between financial liabilities and equity, the entity shall disclose separately the amount, timing and reason for the transfer.

Application

Aus13.1   This Interpretation applies to:

   (a)   each entity that is required to prepare financial reports in accordance with Part 2M.3 of the *Corporations Act 2001* and that is a reporting entity;

   (b)   general purpose financial statements of each other reporting entity; and

   (c)   financial statements that are, or are held out to be, general purpose financial statements.

Aus13.2   This Interpretation applies to annual reporting periods ending on or after 31 December 2005.

   [Note: For application dates of paragraphs changed or added by an amending pronouncement, see Compilation Details.]

Aus13.3   This Interpretation may be applied to annual reporting periods beginning on or after 1 January 2005 that end before 31 December 2005 (due to, for example, a change in end of the reporting period), permitting early application only in the context of adopting all Australian equivalents to International Financial Reporting Standards for such periods. An entity that is required to prepare financial reports in accordance with Part 2M.3 of the Corporations Act may apply this Interpretation to such an annual reporting period when an election has been made in accordance with subsection 334(5) of the Corporations Act in relation to AASB 1048 *Interpretation and Application of Standards*. When an entity applies this Interpretation to such an annual reporting period, it shall disclose that fact.

Aus13.4   The requirements specified in this Interpretation apply to the financial statements where information resulting from their application is material in accordance with AASB 1031 *Materiality*.

Effective Date of IFRIC 2

14   [Deleted by the UIG]

14A   [Deleted by the AASB]

Appendix

Examples of Application of the Consensus

This appendix is an integral part of the Interpretation.

A1   This appendix sets out seven examples of the application of the UIG consensus. The examples do not constitute an exhaustive list; other fact patterns are possible. Each example assumes that there are no conditions other than those set out in the facts of the example that would require the financial instrument to be classified as a financial liability and that the financial instrument does not have all the features or does not meet the conditions in paragraphs 16A and 16B or paragraphs 16C and 16D of AASB 132.

Unconditional Right to Refuse Redemption (paragraph 7)

Example 1

Facts

A2   The entity's charter states that redemptions are made at the sole discretion of the entity. The charter does not provide further elaboration or limitation on that discretion. In its history, the entity has never refused to redeem members' shares, although the governing board has the right to do so.

Classification

A3   The entity has the unconditional right to refuse redemption and the members' shares are equity. AASB 132 establishes principles for classification that are based on the terms of the financial instrument and notes that a history of, or intention to make, discretionary payments does not trigger liability classification. Paragraph AG26 of AASB 132 states:

> When preference shares are non-redeemable, the appropriate classification is determined by the other rights that attach to them. Classification is based on an assessment of the substance of the contractual arrangements and the definitions of a financial liability and an equity instrument. When distributions to holders of the preference shares, whether cumulative or non-cumulative, are at the discretion of the issuer, the shares are equity instruments. The classification of a preference share as an equity instrument or a financial liability is not affected by, for example:
>
> (a)   a history of making distributions;
>
> (b)   an intention to make distributions in the future;
>
> (c)   a possible negative impact on the price of ordinary shares of the issuer if distributions are not made (because of restrictions on paying dividends on the ordinary shares if dividends are not paid on the preference shares);
>
> (d)   the amount of the issuer's reserves;
>
> (e)   an issuer's expectation of a profit or loss for a period; or
>
> (f)   an ability or inability of the issuer to influence the amount of its profit or loss for the period.

Example 2

Facts

A4   The entity's charter states that redemptions are made at the sole discretion of the entity. However, the charter further states that approval of a redemption request is automatic unless the entity is unable to make payments without violating local regulations regarding liquidity or reserves.

Classification

A5   The entity does not have the unconditional right to refuse redemption and the members' shares are a financial liability. The restrictions described above are based on the entity's ability to settle its liability. They restrict redemptions only if the liquidity or reserve requirements are not met and then only until such time as they are met. Hence, they do not, under the principles established in AASB 132, result in the classification of the financial instrument as equity. Paragraph AG25 of AASB 132 states:

> Preference shares may be issued with various rights. In determining whether a preference share is a financial liability or an equity instrument, an issuer assesses the particular rights attaching to the share to determine whether it exhibits the fundamental characteristic of a financial liability. For example, a preference share that provides for redemption on a specific date or at the option of the holder contains a financial liability because the issuer has an obligation to transfer financial assets to the holder of the share. *The potential inability of an issuer to satisfy an obligation to redeem a preference share when contractually required to do so, whether because of a lack of funds, a statutory restriction or insufficient profits or reserves, does not negate the obligation.* [Emphasis added]

Prohibitions against Redemption (paragraphs 8 and 9)

Example 3

Facts

A6   A co-operative entity has issued shares to its members at different dates and for different amounts in the past as follows:

(a)   1 January 20x1 100,000 shares at CU10 each[1] (CU1,000,000);

(b)   1 January 20x2 100,000 shares at CU20 each (a further CU2,000,000, so that the total for shares issued is CU3,000,000).

Shares are redeemable on demand at the amount for which they were issued.

A7   The entity's charter states that cumulative redemptions cannot exceed 20 per cent of the highest number of its members' shares ever outstanding. At 31 December 20x2 the entity has 200,000 of outstanding shares, which is the highest number of members' shares ever outstanding and no shares have been redeemed in the past. On 1 January 20x3 the entity amends its governing charter and increases the permitted level of cumulative redemptions to 25 per cent of the highest number of its members' shares ever outstanding.

Classification

Before the governing charter is amended

A8   Members' shares in excess of the prohibition against redemption are financial liabilities. The co-operative entity measures this financial liability at fair value at initial recognition. Because these shares are redeemable on demand, the co-operative entity determines the fair value of such financial liabilities as required by paragraph 49 of AASB 139 *Financial Instruments: Recognition and Measurement*, which states: 'The fair value of a financial liability with a demand feature (e.g. a demand deposit) is not less than the amount payable on demand …'. Accordingly, the co-operative entity classifies as financial liabilities the maximum amount payable on demand under the redemption provisions.

A9   On 1 January 20x1 the maximum amount payable under the redemption provisions is 20,000 shares at CU10 each and accordingly the entity classifies CU200,000 as financial liability and CU800,000 as equity. However, on 1 January 20x2 because of the new issue of shares at CU20, the maximum amount payable under the redemption provisions increases to 40,000 shares at CU20 each. The issue of additional shares at CU20 creates a new liability that is measured on initial recognition at fair value. The liability after these shares have been issued is 20 per cent of the total shares in issue (200,000), measured at CU20, or CU800,000. This requires recognition of an additional liability of CU600,000. In this example no gain or loss is recognised. Accordingly the entity now classifies CU800,000 as financial liabilities and CU2,200,000 as equity. This example assumes these amounts are not changed between 1 January 20x1 and 31 December 20x2.

---

1   [Aus] In these examples, monetary amounts are denominated in currency units (CU).

After the governing charter is amended

A10   Following the change in its governing charter the co-operative entity can now be required to redeem a maximum of 25 per cent of its outstanding shares or a maximum of 50,000 shares at CU20 each. Accordingly, on 1 January 20x3 the co-operative entity classifies as financial liabilities an amount of CU1,000,000 being the maximum amount payable on demand under the redemption provisions, as determined in accordance with paragraph 49 of AASB 139. It therefore transfers on 1 January 20x3 from equity to financial liabilities an amount of CU200,000, leaving CU2,000,000 classified as equity. In this example the entity does not recognise a gain or loss on the transfer.

Example 4

Facts

A11   Local law governing the operations of co-operatives, or the terms of the entity's governing charter, prohibit an entity from redeeming members' shares if, by redeeming them, it would reduce paid-in capital from members' shares below 75 per cent of the highest amount of paid-in capital from members' shares. The highest amount for a particular co-operative is CU1,000,000. At the end of the reporting period the balance of paid-in capital is CU900,000.

Classification

A12   In this case, CU750,000 would be classified as equity and CU150,000 would be classified as financial liabilities. In addition to the paragraphs already cited, paragraph 18(b) of AASB 132 states in part:

> … a financial instrument that gives the holder the right to put it back to the issuer for cash or another financial asset (a 'puttable instrument') is a financial liability, except for those instruments classified as equity instruments in accordance with paragraphs 16A and 16B or paragraphs 16C and 16D. The financial instrument is a financial liability even when the amount of cash or other financial assets is determined on the basis of an index or other item that has the potential to increase or decrease. The existence of an option for the holder to put the instrument back to the issuer for cash or another financial asset means that the puttable instrument meets the definition of a financial liability, except for those instruments classified as equity instruments in accordance with paragraphs 16A and 16B or paragraphs 16C and 16D.

A13   The redemption prohibition described in this example is different from the restrictions described in paragraphs 19 and AG25 of AASB 132. Those restrictions are limitations on the ability of the entity to pay the amount due on a financial liability, that is they prevent payment of the liability only if specified conditions are met. In contrast, this example describes an unconditional prohibition on redemptions beyond a specified amount, regardless of the entity's ability to redeem members' shares (e.g. given its cash resources, profits or distributable reserves). In effect, the prohibition against redemption prevents the entity from incurring any financial liability to redeem more than a specified amount of paid-in capital. Therefore, the portion of shares subject to the redemption prohibition is not a financial liability. While each member's shares may be redeemable individually, a portion of the total shares outstanding is not redeemable in any circumstances other than liquidation of the entity.

Example 5

Facts

A14   The facts of this example are as stated in example 4. In addition, at the end of the reporting period, liquidity requirements imposed in the local jurisdiction prevent the entity from redeeming any members' shares unless its holdings of cash and short-term investments are greater than a specified amount. The effect of these liquidity requirements at the end of the reporting period is that the entity cannot pay more than CU50,000 to redeem the members' shares.

Classification

A15   As in example 4, the entity classifies CU750,000 as equity and CU150,000 as a financial liability. This is because the amount classified as a liability is based on the entity's unconditional right to refuse redemption and not on conditional restrictions that prevent redemption only if liquidity or other conditions are not met and then only until such time as they are met. The provisions of paragraphs 19 and AG25 of AASB 132 apply in this case.

Example 6

Facts

A16   The entity's governing charter prohibits it from redeeming members' shares, except to the extent of proceeds received from the issue of additional members' shares to new or existing members during the preceding three years. Proceeds from issuing members' shares must be applied to redeem shares for which members have requested redemption. During the three preceding years, the proceeds from issuing members' shares have been CU12,000 and no member's shares have been redeemed.

Classification

A17   The entity classifies CU12,000 of the members' shares as financial liabilities. Consistently with the conclusions described in example 4, members' shares subject to an unconditional prohibition against redemption are not financial liabilities. Such an unconditional prohibition applies to an amount equal to the proceeds of shares issued before the preceding three years, and accordingly, this amount is classified as equity. However, an amount equal to the proceeds from any shares issued in the preceding three years is not subject to an unconditional prohibition on redemption. Accordingly, proceeds from the issue of members' shares in the preceding three years give rise to financial liabilities until they are no longer available for redemption of members' shares. As a result the entity has a financial liability equal to the proceeds of shares issued during the three preceding years, net of any redemptions during that period.

Example 7

Facts

A18   The entity is a co-operative bank. Local law governing the operations of co-operative banks state that at least 50 per cent of the entity's total 'outstanding liabilities' (a term defined in the regulations to include members' share accounts) has to be in the form of members' paid-in capital. The effect of the regulation is that if all of a co-operative's outstanding liabilities are in the form of members' shares, it is able to redeem them all. On 31 December 20x1 the entity has total outstanding liabilities of CU200,000, of which CU125,000 represent members' share accounts. The terms of the members' share accounts permit the holder to redeem them on demand and there are no limitations on redemption in the entity's charter.

Classification

A19   In this example members' shares are classified as financial liabilities. The redemption prohibition is similar to the restrictions described in paragraphs 19 and AG25 of AASB 132. The restriction is a conditional limitation on the ability of the entity to pay the amount due on a financial liability, that is they prevent payment of the liability only if specified conditions are met. More specifically, the entity could be required to redeem the entire amount of members' shares (CU125,000) if it repaid all of its other liabilities (CU75,000). Consequently, the prohibition against redemption does not prevent the entity from incurring a financial liability to redeem more than a specified number of members' shares or amount of paid-in capital. It allows the entity only to defer redemption until a condition is met, that is the repayment of other liabilities. Members' shares in this example are not subject to an unconditional prohibition against redemption and are therefore classified as financial liabilities.

Basis for Conclusions on IFRIC 2

This IFRIC Basis for Conclusions accompanies, but is not part of, UIG Interpretation 2. The UIG considers that this Basis for Conclusions is an essential feature of the Interpretation. An IFRIC Basis for Conclusions may be amended to reflect the requirements of the UIG Interpretation and AASB Accounting Standards where they differ from the corresponding International pronouncements.

Introduction

BC1   This Basis for Conclusions summarises the IFRIC's considerations in reaching its consensus. Individual IFRIC members gave greater weight to some factors than to others.

Background

BC2   In September 2001, the Standing Interpretations Committee instituted by the former International Accounting Standards Committee (IASC) published Draft Interpretation SIC D-34 *Financial Instruments - Instruments or Rights Redeemable by the Holder*. The Draft Interpretation stated: 'The issuer of a Puttable Instrument should classify the entire instrument as a liability.'

BC3   In 2001 the International Accounting Standards Board (IASB) began operations in succession to IASC. The IASB's initial agenda included a project to make limited amendments to the financial instruments standards issued by IASC. The IASB decided to incorporate the consensus from Draft Interpretation D-34 as part of those amendments. In June 2002 the IASB published an exposure draft of amendments to IAS 32 *Financial Instruments: Disclosure and Presentation* that incorporated the proposed consensus from Draft Interpretation D-34.

BC4   In their responses to the Exposure Draft and in their participation in public round-table discussions held in March 2003, representatives of co-operative banks raised questions about the application of the principles in IAS 32 to members' shares. This was followed by a series of meetings between IASB members and staff and representatives of the European Association of Co-operative Banks. After considering questions raised by the bank group, the IASB concluded that the principles articulated in IAS 32 should not be modified, but that there were questions about the application of those principles to co-operative entities that should be considered by the IFRIC.

BC5   In considering the application of IAS 32 to co-operative entities, the IFRIC recognised that a variety of entities operate as co-operatives and these entities have a variety of capital structures. The IFRIC decided that its proposed Interpretation should address some features that exist in a number of co-operatives. However, the IFRIC noted that its conclusions and the examples in the Interpretation are not limited to the specific characteristics of members' shares in European co-operative banks.

Basis for consensus

BC6   Paragraph 15 of IAS 32 states:

> The issuer of a financial instrument shall classify the instrument, or its component parts, on initial recognition as a financial liability, a financial asset or an equity instrument in accordance with the *substance of the contractual arrangement* and the definitions of a financial liability, a financial asset and an equity instrument. [Emphasis added]

BC7   In many jurisdictions, local law or regulations state that members' shares are equity of the entity. However, paragraph 17 of IAS 32 states:

> With the exception of the circumstances described in paragraphs 16A and 16B or paragraphs 16C and 16D, a critical feature in differentiating a financial liability from an equity instrument is *the existence of a contractual obligation of one party to the financial instrument (the issuer) either to deliver cash or another financial asset to the other party (the holder) or to exchange financial assets or financial liabilities with the holder under conditions that are potentially unfavourable to the issuer. Although the holder of an equity instrument may be entitled to receive a pro*

rata share of any dividends or other distributions of equity, the issuer does not have a contractual obligation to make such distributions because it cannot be required to deliver cash or another financial asset to another party. [Emphasis added]

BC8   Paragraphs cited in the examples in the Appendix and in the paragraphs above show that, under IAS 32, the terms of the contractual agreement govern the classification of a financial instrument as a financial liability or equity. If the terms of an instrument create an unconditional obligation to transfer cash or another financial asset, circumstances that might restrict an entity's ability to make the transfer when due do not alter the classification as a financial liability. If the terms of the instrument give the entity an unconditional right to avoid delivering cash or another financial asset, the instrument is classified as equity. This is true even if other factors make it likely that the entity will continue to distribute dividends or make other payments. In view of those principles, the IFRIC decided to focus on circumstances that would indicate that the entity has the unconditional right to avoid making payments to a member who has requested that his or her shares be redeemed.

BC9   The IFRIC identified two situations in which a co-operative entity has an unconditional right to avoid the transfer of cash or another financial asset. The IFRIC acknowledges that there may be other situations that may raise questions about the application of IAS 32 to members' shares. However, it understands that the two situations are often present in the contractual and other conditions surrounding members' shares and that interpretation of those two situations would eliminate many of the questions that may arise in practice.

BC10   The IFRIC also noted that an entity assesses whether it has an unconditional right to avoid the transfer of cash or another financial asset on the basis of local laws, regulations and its governing charter in effect at the date of classification. This is because it is local laws, regulations and the governing charter in effect at the classification date, together with the terms contained in the instrument's documentation that constitute the terms and conditions of the instrument at that date. Accordingly, an entity does not take into account expected future amendments to local law, regulation or its governing charter.

The right to refuse redemption (paragraph 7)

BC11   An entity may have the unconditional right to refuse redemption of a member's shares. If such a right exists, the entity does not have the obligation to transfer cash or another financial asset that IAS 32 identifies as a critical characteristic of a financial liability.

BC12   The IFRIC considered whether the entity's history of making redemptions should be considered in deciding whether the entity's right to refuse requests is, in fact, unconditional. The IFRIC observed that a history of making redemptions may create a reasonable expectation that all future requests will be honoured. However, holders of many equity instruments have a reasonable expectation that an entity will continue a past practice of making payments. For example, an entity may have made dividend payments on preference shares for decades. Failure to make those payments would expose the entity to significant economic costs, including damage to the value of its ordinary shares. Nevertheless, as outlined in IAS 32 paragraph AG26 (cited in paragraph A3), a holder's expectations about dividends do not cause a preferred share to be classified as a financial liability.

Prohibitions against redemption (paragraphs 8 and 9)

BC13   An entity may be prohibited by law or its governing charter from redeeming members' shares if doing so would cause the number of members' shares, or the amount of paid-in capital from members' shares, to fall below a specified level. While each individual share might be puttable, a portion of the total shares outstanding is not.

BC14   The IFRIC concluded that conditions limiting an entity's ability to redeem members' shares must be evaluated sequentially. Unconditional prohibitions like those noted in paragraph 8 of the consensus prevent the entity from *incurring a liability* for redemption of all or some of the members' shares, regardless of whether it would otherwise be able to satisfy that financial liability. This contrasts with conditional prohibitions that prevent payments being made only if specified conditions—such as liquidity constraints—are met. Unconditional prohibitions prevent a liability from coming into existence, whereas the conditional prohibitions may only defer the payment of a liability already incurred.

Following this analysis, an unconditional prohibition affects classification when an instrument subject to the prohibition is issued or when the prohibition is enacted or added to the entity's governing charter. In contrast, conditional restrictions such as those described in paragraphs 19 and AG25 of IAS 32 do not result in equity classification.

BC15 The IFRIC discussed whether the requirements in IAS 32 can be applied to the classification of members' shares as a whole subject to a partial redemption prohibition. IAS 32 refers to 'a financial instrument', 'a financial liability' and 'an equity instrument'. It does not refer to groups or portfolios of instruments. In view of this the IFRIC considered whether it could apply the requirements in IAS 32 to the classification of members' shares subject to partial redemption prohibitions. The application of IAS 32 to a prohibition against redeeming some portion of members' shares (e.g. 500,000 shares of an entity with 1,000,000 shares outstanding) is unclear.

BC16 The IFRIC noted that classifying a group of members' shares using the individual instrument approach could lead to misapplication of the principle of 'substance of the contract' in IAS 32. The IFRIC also noted that paragraph 23 of IAS 32 requires an entity that has entered into an agreement to purchase its own equity instruments to recognise a financial liability for the present value of the redemption amount (e.g. for the present value of the forward repurchase price, option exercise price or other redemption amount) even though the shares subject to the repurchase agreement are not individually identified. Accordingly, the IFRIC decided that for purposes of classification there are instances when IAS 32 does not require the individual instrument approach.

BC17 In many situations, looking at either individual instruments or all of the instruments governed by a particular contract would result in the same classification as financial liability or equity under IAS 32. Thus, if an entity is prohibited from redeeming any of its members' shares, the shares are not puttable and are equity. On the other hand, if there is no prohibition on redemption and no other conditions apply, members' shares are puttable and the shares are financial liabilities. However, in the case of partial prohibitions against redemption, the classification of members' shares governed by the same charter will differ, depending on whether such a classification is based on individual members' shares or the group of members' shares as a whole. For example, consider an entity with a partial prohibition that prevents it from redeeming 99 per cent of the highest number of members' shares ever outstanding. The classification based on individual shares considers each share to be potentially puttable and therefore a financial liability. This is different from the classification based on all of the members' shares. While each member's share may be redeemable individually, 99 per cent of the highest number of shares ever outstanding is not redeemable in any circumstances other than liquidation of the entity and therefore is equity.

Measurement on initial recognition (paragraph 10)

BC18 The IFRIC noted that when the financial liability for the redemption of members' shares that are redeemable on demand is initially recognised, the financial liability is measured at fair value in accordance with paragraph 49 of IAS 39 *Financial Instruments: Recognition and Measurement*. Paragraph 49 states: 'The fair value of a financial liability with a demand feature (e.g. a demand deposit) is not less than the amount payable on demand, discounted from the first date that the amount could be required to be paid'. Accordingly, the IFRIC decided that the fair value of the financial liability for redemption of members' shares redeemable on demand is the maximum amount payable under the redemption provisions of its governing charter or applicable law. The IFRIC also considered situations in which the number of members' shares or the amount of paid-in capital subject to prohibition against redemption may change. The IFRIC concluded that a change in the level of a prohibition against redemption should lead to a transfer between financial liabilities and equity.

Subsequent measurement

BC19 Some respondents requested additional guidance on subsequent measurement of the liability for redemption of members' shares. The IFRIC noted that the focus of this Interpretation was on clarifying the classification of financial instruments rather than their subsequent measurement. Also, the IASB has on its agenda a project to address the accounting for financial instruments (including members' shares) that are redeemable at a pro rata share of the fair value of the residual interest in the entity issuing the financial instrument. The IASB will consider certain measurement issues in this project. The IFRIC was also informed that the majority of members' shares in cooperative entities are not redeemable at a pro rata share of the fair value of the residual interest in the cooperative entity thereby obviating the more complex measurement issues. In view of the above, the IFRIC decided not to provide additional guidance on measurement in the Interpretation.

Presentation

BC20 The IFRIC noted that entities whose members' shares are not equity could use the presentation formats included in paragraphs IE32 and IE33 of the Illustrative Examples with IAS 32.

Alternatives considered

BC21 The IFRIC considered suggestions that:

(a) members' shares should be classified as equity until a member has requested redemption. That member's share would then be classified as a financial liability and this treatment would be consistent with local laws. Some commentators believe this is a more straightforward approach to classification.

(b) the classification of members' shares should incorporate the probability that members will request redemption. Those who suggest this view observe that experience shows this probability to be small, usually within 1-5 per cent, for some types of co-operative. They see no basis for classifying 100 per cent of the members' shares as liabilities on the basis of the behaviour of 1 per cent.

BC22 The IFRIC did not accept those views. Under IAS 32, the classification of an instrument as financial liability or equity is based on the 'substance of the contractual arrangement and the definitions of a financial liability, a financial asset and an equity instrument.' In paragraph BC7 of the Basis for Conclusions on IAS 32, the IASB observed:

Although the legal form of such financial instruments often includes a right to the residual interest in the assets of an entity available to holders of such instruments, the inclusion of an option for the holder to put the instrument back to the entity for cash or another financial asset means that the instrument meets the definition of a financial liability. The classification as a financial liability is independent of considerations such as when the right is exercisable, how the amount payable or receivable upon exercise of the right is determined, and whether the puttable instrument has a fixed maturity.

BC23 The IFRIC also observed that an approach similar to that in paragraph BC21(a) is advocated in the Dissenting Opinion of one Board member on IAS 32. As the IASB did not adopt that approach its adoption here would require an amendment to IAS 32.

Transition and effective date (paragraph 14)

BC24 [Deleted by the UIG]

BC25 [Deleted by the UIG]

Interpretation 4
Determining whether an Arrangement contains a Lease

(Compiled December 2009)

Contents

Compilation Details

Comparison with IFRIC 4

AASB Interpretation 4
Determining whether an Arrangement contains a Lease

Paragraphs

References	
Background	1 – 3
Scope	4
Issues	5
Consensus	
Determining whether an arrangement is, or contains, a lease	6
Fulfilment of the arrangement is dependent on the use of a specific asset	7 – 8
Arrangement conveys a right to use the asset	9
Assessing or reassessing whether an arrangement is, or contains, a lease	10 – 11
Separating payments for the lease from other payments	12 – 15
Application	Aus15.1 – Aus15.5
Transition	17

Illustrative Examples

Example of an arrangement that contains a lease	IE1 – IE2
Example of an arrangement that does not contain a lease	IE3 – IE4

Basis for Conclusions on IFRIC 4

AASB Interpretation 4 *Determining whether an Arrangement contains a Lease* (as amended) is set out in paragraphs 1 – 17. Interpretations are listed in Australian Accounting Standard AASB 1048 *Interpretation and Application of Standards*. In the absence of explicit guidance, AASB 108 *Accounting Policies, Changes in Accounting Estimates and Errors* provides a basis for selecting and applying accounting policies.

Compilation Details

AASB Interpretation 4 *Determining whether an Arrangement contains a Lease* as amended

This compiled Interpretation applies to annual reporting periods beginning on or after 1 January 2011. It takes into account amendments up to and including 15 December 2009 and was prepared on 23 February 2010 by the staff of the Australian Accounting Standards Board (AASB).

This compilation is not a separate Interpretation issued by the AASB. Instead, it is a representation of Interpretation 4 (February 2007) as amended by other pronouncements, which are listed in the Table below.

Table of Pronouncements

Pronouncement	Month issued	Application date (*annual reporting periods … on or after …*)	Application, saving or transitional provisions
Interpretation 4	Feb 2007	(*beginning*) 1 Jan 2008	see (a) below
AASB 2007-8	Sep 2007	(*beginning*) 1 Jan 2009	see (b) below
AASB 2009-6	Jun 2009	(*beginning*) 1 Jan 2009 and (*ending*) 30 Jun 2009	see (c) below
AASB 2009-12	Dec 2009	(*beginning*) 1 Jan 2011	see (d) below

(a) Entities may elect to apply this Interpretation to annual reporting periods beginning on or after 1 January 2005 but before 1 January 2008, provided that AASB Interpretation 12 *Service Concession Arrangements* is also applied to such periods.

(b) Entities may elect to apply this Standard to annual reporting periods beginning on or after 1 January 2005 but before 1 January 2009, provided that AASB 101 *Presentation of Financial Statements* (September 2007) is also applied to such periods.

(c) Entities may elect to apply this Standard to annual reporting periods beginning on or after 1 January 2005 but before 1 January 2009, provided that AASB 101 *Presentation of Financial Statements* (September 2007) is also applied to such periods, and to annual reporting periods beginning on or after 1 January 2009 that end before 30 June 2009.

(d) Entities may elect to apply this Standard to annual reporting periods beginning on or after 1 January 2005 but before 1 January 2011.

Table of Amendments

Paragraph affected	How affected	By … [paragraph]
Aus15.1	amended	AASB 2007-8 [7, 8]
Aus15.4	amended	AASB 2007-8 [8]
16A	note added	AASB 2009-6 [107]
Appendix	deleted	AASB 2009-12 [22]

Comparison with IFRIC 4

AASB Interpretation 4 *Determining whether an Arrangement contains a Lease* as amended incorporates International Financial Reporting Interpretations Committee Interpretation IFRIC 4 *Determining whether an Arrangement contains a Lease*, issued by the International Accounting Standards Board. Paragraphs that have been added to this Interpretation (and do not appear in the text of IFRIC 4) are identified with the prefix "Aus", followed by the number of the preceding IFRIC paragraph and decimal numbering.

Entities that comply with Interpretation 4 as amended will simultaneously be in compliance with IFRIC 4 as amended.

Interpretation 4
AASB Interpretation 4 was issued in February 2007.
This compiled version of Interpretation 4 applies to annual reporting periods beginning on or after 1 January 2011. It incorporates relevant amendments contained in other AASB pronouncements up to and including 15 December 2009 (see Compilation Details).

Australian Accounting Standards Board
Interpretation 4
Determining whether an Arrangement contains a Lease

References

Accounting Standard AASB 108 *Accounting Policies, Changes in Accounting Estimates and Errors*

Accounting Standard AASB 116 *Property, Plant and Equipment*

Accounting Standard AASB 117 *Leases*

Accounting Standard AASB 138 *Intangible Assets*

AASB Interpretation 12 *Service Concession Arrangements*

Background

1   An entity may enter into an arrangement, comprising a transaction or a series of related transactions, that does not take the legal form of a lease but conveys a right to use an asset (e.g. an item of property, plant or equipment) in return for a payment or series of payments. Examples of arrangements in which one entity (the supplier) may convey such a right to use an asset to another entity (the purchaser), often together with related services, include:

- outsourcing arrangements (e.g. the outsourcing of the data processing functions of an entity);

- arrangements in the telecommunications industry, in which suppliers of network capacity enter into contracts to provide purchasers with rights to capacity;

- take-or-pay and similar contracts, in which purchasers must make specified payments regardless of whether they take delivery of the contracted products or services (e.g. a take-or-pay contract to acquire substantially all of the output of a supplier's power generator).

2   This Interpretation provides guidance for determining whether such arrangements are, or contain, leases that should be accounted for in accordance with Accounting Standard AASB 117 *Leases*. It does not provide guidance for determining how such a lease should be classified under that Standard.

3   In some arrangements, the underlying asset that is the subject of the lease is a portion of a larger asset. This Interpretation does not address how to determine when a portion of a larger asset is itself the underlying asset for the purposes of applying AASB 117. Nevertheless, arrangements in which the underlying asset would represent a unit of account in either AASB 116 *Property, Plant and Equipment* or AASB 138 *Intangible Assets* are within the scope of this Interpretation.

Scope

4   This Interpretation does not apply to arrangements that:

(a)   are, or contain, leases excluded from the scope of AASB 117; or

(b)   are public-to-private service concession arrangements within the scope of AASB Interpretation 12 *Service Concession Arrangements*.

Issues

5   The issues addressed in this Interpretation are:

(a)   how to determine whether an arrangement is, or contains, a lease as defined in AASB 117;

(b)   when the assessment or a reassessment of whether an arrangement is, or contains, a lease should be made; and

(c)   if an arrangement is, or contains, a lease, how the payments for the lease should be separated from payments for any other elements in the arrangement.

Consensus

Determining whether an arrangement is, or contains, a lease

6   Determining whether an arrangement is, or contains, a lease shall be based on the substance of the arrangement and requires an assessment of whether:

(a)   fulfilment of the arrangement is dependent on the use of a specific asset or assets (the asset); and

(b)   the arrangement conveys a right to use the asset.

Fulfilment of the arrangement is dependent on the use of a specific asset

7   Although a specific asset may be explicitly identified in an arrangement, it is not the subject of a lease if fulfilment of the arrangement is not dependent on the use of the specified asset. For example, if the supplier is obliged to deliver a specified quantity of goods or services and has the right and ability to provide those goods or services using other assets not specified in the arrangement, then fulfilment of the arrangement is not dependent on the specified asset and the arrangement does not contain a lease. A warranty obligation that permits or requires the substitution of the same or similar assets when the specified asset is not operating properly does not preclude lease treatment. In addition, a contractual provision (contingent or otherwise) permitting or requiring the supplier to substitute other assets for any reason on or after a specified date does not preclude lease treatment before the date of substitution.

8   An asset has been implicitly specified if, for example, the supplier owns or leases only one asset with which to fulfil the obligation and it is not economically feasible or practicable for the supplier to perform its obligation through the use of alternative assets.

Arrangement conveys a right to use the asset

9   An arrangement conveys the right to use the asset if the arrangement conveys to the purchaser (lessee) the right to control the use of the underlying asset. The right to control the use of the underlying asset is conveyed if any one of the following conditions is met.

(a)   The purchaser has the ability or right to operate the asset or direct others to operate the asset in a manner it determines while obtaining or controlling more than an insignificant amount of the output or other utility of the asset.

(b)   The purchaser has the ability or right to control physical access to the underlying asset while obtaining or controlling more than an insignificant amount of the output or other utility of the asset.

(c)   Facts and circumstances indicate that it is remote that one or more parties other than the purchaser will take more than an insignificant amount of the output or other utility that will be produced or generated by the asset during the term of the arrangement, and the price that the purchaser will pay for the output is neither contractually fixed per unit of output nor equal to the current market price per unit of output as of the time of delivery of the output.

Assessing or reassessing whether an arrangement is, or contains, a lease

10   The assessment of whether an arrangement contains a lease shall be made at the inception of the arrangement, being the earlier of the date of the arrangement and the date of commitment by the parties to the principal terms of the arrangement, on the basis of all of the facts and circumstances. A reassessment of whether the arrangement contains a

lease after the inception of the arrangement shall be made only if any one of the following conditions is met.

(a)   There is a change in the contractual terms, unless the change only renews or extends the arrangement.

(b)   A renewal option is exercised or an extension is agreed to by the parties to the arrangement, unless the term of the renewal or extension had initially been included in the lease term in accordance with paragraph 4 of AASB 117. A renewal or extension of the arrangement that does not include modification of any of the terms in the original arrangement before the end of the term of the original arrangement shall be evaluated under paragraphs 6-9 only with respect to the renewal or extension period.

(c)   There is a change in the determination of whether fulfilment is dependent on a specified asset.

(d)   There is a substantial change to the asset, for example a substantial physical change to property, plant or equipment.

11   A reassessment of an arrangement shall be based on the facts and circumstances as of the date of reassessment, including the remaining term of the arrangement. Changes in estimate (for example, the estimated amount of output to be delivered to the purchaser or other potential purchasers) would not trigger a reassessment. If an arrangement is reassessed and is determined to contain a lease (or not to contain a lease), lease accounting shall be applied (or cease to apply) from:

(a)   in the case of (a), (c) or (d) in paragraph 10, when the change in circumstances giving rise to the reassessment occurs;

(b)   in the case of (b) in paragraph 10, the inception of the renewal or extension period.

Separating payments for the lease from other payments

12   If an arrangement contains a lease, the parties to the arrangement shall apply the requirements of AASB 117 to the lease element of the arrangement, unless exempted from those requirements in accordance with paragraph 2 of AASB 117. Accordingly, if an arrangement contains a lease, that lease shall be classified as a finance lease or an operating lease in accordance with paragraphs 7-19 of AASB 117. Other elements of the arrangement not within the scope of AASB 117 shall be accounted for in accordance with other Standards.

13   For the purpose of applying the requirements of AASB 117, payments and other consideration required by the arrangement shall be separated at the inception of the arrangement or upon a reassessment of the arrangement into those for the lease and those for other elements on the basis of their relative fair values. The minimum lease payments as defined in paragraph 4 of AASB 117 include only payments for the lease (i.e. the right to use the asset) and exclude payments for other elements in the arrangement (e.g. for services and the cost of inputs).

14   In some cases, separating the payments for the lease from payments for other elements in the arrangement will require the purchaser to use an estimation technique. For example, a purchaser may estimate the lease payments by reference to a lease agreement for a comparable asset that contains no other elements, or by estimating the payments for the other elements in the arrangement by reference to comparable agreements and then deducting these payments from the total payments under the arrangement.

15   If a purchaser concludes that it is impracticable to separate the payments reliably, it shall:

(a)   in the case of a finance lease, recognise an asset and a liability at an amount equal to the fair value of the underlying asset that was identified in paragraphs 7 and 8 as the subject of the lease. Subsequently the liability shall be reduced as payments are made and an imputed finance charge on the liability recognised using the purchaser's incremental borrowing rate of interest[1]; or

---

1   That is, the lessee's incremental borrowing rate of interest as defined in paragraph 4 of AASB 117.

(b) in the case of an operating lease, treat all payments under the arrangement as lease payments for the purposes of complying with the disclosure requirements of AASB 117, but:

(i) disclose those payments separately from minimum lease payments of other arrangements that do not include payments for non-lease elements; and

(ii) state that the disclosed payments also include payments for non-lease elements in the arrangement.

Application

Aus15.1 This Interpretation applies to:

(a) each entity that is required to prepare financial reports in accordance with Part 2M.3 of the *Corporations Act 2001* and that is a reporting entity;

(b) general purpose financial statements of each other reporting entity; and

(c) financial statements that are, or are held out to be, general purpose financial statements.

Aus15.2 This Interpretation applies to annual reporting periods beginning on or after 1 January 2008.

[Note: For application dates of paragraphs changed or added by an amending pronouncement, see Compilation Details.]

Aus15.3 If an entity applies AASB Interpretation 12 *Service Concession Arrangements* to an annual reporting period beginning on or after 1 January 2005 but before 1 January 2008, this Interpretation shall be applied to that period.

Aus15.4 The requirements specified in this Interpretation apply to the financial statements where information resulting from their application is material in accordance with AASB 1031 *Materiality*.

Aus15.5 When applicable, this Interpretation supersedes UIG Interpretation 4 *Determining whether an Arrangement contains a Lease*, as issued in June 2005.

Effective Date of IFRIC 4

16 [Deleted by the AASB]

16A [Deleted by the AASB]

Transition

17 AASB 108 *Accounting Policies, Changes in Accounting Estimates and Errors* specifies how an entity applies a change in accounting policy resulting from the initial application of an Interpretation. An entity is not required to comply with those requirements[2] when first applying this Interpretation.[3] If an entity uses this exemption, it shall apply paragraphs 6-9 of the Interpretation to arrangements existing at the start of the earliest period for which comparative information under Australian equivalents to IFRSs is presented on the basis of facts and circumstances existing at the start of that period.

---

2 [Aus] That is, the general, fully retrospective application requirements.

3 [Aus] AASB 108 permits an Interpretation to include specific transitional provisions for initial application.

Illustrative Examples

These examples accompany, but are not part of, AASB Interpretation 4.

Example of an arrangement that contains a lease

Facts

IE1   A production company (the purchaser) enters into an arrangement with a third party (the supplier) to supply a minimum quantity of gas needed in its production process for a specified period of time. The supplier designs and builds a facility adjacent to the purchaser's plant to produce the needed gas and maintains ownership and control over all significant aspects of operating the facility. The agreement provides for the following:

- The facility is explicitly identified in the arrangement, and the supplier has the contractual right to supply gas from other sources. However, supplying gas from other sources is not economically feasible or practicable.

- The supplier has the right to provide gas to other customers and to remove and replace the facility's equipment and modify or expand the facility to enable the supplier to do so. However, at inception of the arrangement, the supplier has no plans to modify or expand the facility. The facility is designed to meet only the purchaser's needs.

- The supplier is responsible for repairs, maintenance, and capital expenditures.

- The supplier must stand ready to deliver a minimum quantity of gas each month.

- Each month, the purchaser will pay a fixed capacity charge and a variable charge based on actual production taken. The purchaser must pay the fixed capacity charge irrespective of whether it takes any of the facility's production. The variable charge includes the facility's actual energy costs, which amount to about 90 per cent of the facility's total variable costs. The supplier is subject to increased costs resulting from the facility's inefficient operations.

- If the facility does not produce the stated minimum quantity, the supplier must return all or a portion of the fixed capacity charge.

Assessment

IE2   The arrangement contains a lease within the scope of AASB 117 *Leases*. An asset (the facility) is explicitly identified in the arrangement and fulfilment of the arrangement is dependent on the facility. Although the supplier has the right to supply gas from other sources, its ability to do so is not substantive. The purchaser has obtained the right to use the facility because, on the facts presented—in particular, that the facility is designed to meet only the purchaser's needs and the supplier has no plans to expand or modify the facility—it is remote that one or more parties other than the purchaser will take more than an insignificant amount of the facility's output and the price the purchaser will pay is neither contractually fixed per unit of output nor equal to the current market price per unit of output as of the time of delivery of the output.

Example of an arrangement that does not contain a lease

Facts

IE3   A manufacturing company (the purchaser) enters into an arrangement with a third party (the supplier) to supply a specific component part of its manufactured product for a specified period of time. The supplier designs and constructs a plant adjacent to the purchaser's factory to produce the component part. The designed capacity of the plant exceeds the purchaser's current needs, and the supplier maintains ownership and control over all significant aspects of operating the plant. The arrangement provides for the following:

- The supplier's plant is explicitly identified in the arrangement, but the supplier has the right to fulfil the arrangement by shipping the component parts from another plant owned by the supplier. However, to do so for any extended period of time would be uneconomic.

- The supplier is responsible for repairs, maintenance, and capital expenditures of the plant.

- The supplier must stand ready to deliver a minimum quantity. The purchaser is required to pay a fixed price per unit for the actual quantity taken. Even if the purchaser's needs are such that they do not need the stated minimum quantity, they still pay only for the actual quantity taken.

- The supplier has the right to sell the component parts to other customers and has a history of doing so (by selling in the replacement parts market), so it is expected that parties other than the purchaser will take more than an insignificant amount of the component parts produced at the supplier's plant.

Assessment

IE4   The arrangement does not contain a lease within the scope of AASB 117. An asset (the plant) is explicitly identified in the arrangement and fulfilment of the arrangement is dependent on the facility. Although the supplier has the right to supply component parts from other sources, the supplier would not have the ability to do so because it would be uneconomic. However, the purchaser has not obtained the right to use the plant because the purchaser does not have the ability or right to operate or direct others to operate the plant or control physical access to the plant, and the likelihood that parties other than the purchaser will take more than an insignificant amount of the component parts produced at the plant is more than remote, on the basis of the facts presented. In addition, the price that the purchaser pays is fixed per unit of output taken.

Basis for Conclusions on IFRIC Interpretation 4

This IFRIC Basis for Conclusions accompanies, but is not part of, AASB Interpretation 4. An IFRIC Basis for Conclusions may be amended to reflect the requirements of the AASB Interpretation and AASB Accounting Standards where they differ from the corresponding International pronouncements.

Introduction

BC1   This Basis for Conclusions summarises the IFRIC's considerations in reaching its consensus. Individual IFRIC members gave greater weight to some factors than to others.

Background (paragraphs 1-3)

BC2   The IFRIC noted that arrangements have developed in recent years that do not take the legal form of a lease but convey rights to use items for agreed periods of time in return for a payment or series of payments. Examples of such arrangements are set out in paragraph 1 of the Interpretation. The IFRIC observed that these arrangements share many features of a lease because a lease is defined in paragraph 4 of IAS 17 *Leases* as 'an agreement whereby the lessor conveys to the lessee in return for a payment or series of payments *the right to use an asset* for an agreed period of time' (emphasis added). The IFRIC noted that all arrangements meeting the definition of a lease should be accounted for in accordance with IAS 17 (subject to the scope of that Standard) regardless of whether they take the legal form of a lease. In other words, just as the Standing Interpretations Committee concluded in SIC-27 *Evaluating the Substance of Transactions Involving the Legal Form of a Lease* that an arrangement that is described as a lease is not necessarily accounted for as a lease, the IFRIC concluded that an arrangement can be within the scope of IAS 17 even if it is not described as a lease. The IFRIC therefore decided that it should issue guidance to assist in determining whether an arrangement is, or contains, a lease.

BC3   The IFRIC published Draft Interpretation D3 *Determining whether an Arrangement contains a Lease* for public comment in January 2004 and received 51 comment letters in response to its proposals. In addition, in order to understand better the practical issues that would have arisen on implementing the proposed Interpretation, IASB staff met a number of preparer constituents.

BC4   There was broad support for the IFRIC issuing an Interpretation on this topic (even among those respondents who disagreed with the criteria in D3 for determining whether a lease exists). However, some respondents to D3 questioned whether the proposals were a legitimate *interpretation* of IAS 17. In particular, some suggested that the proposals anticipated the Board's current research project on leasing.

BC5   In considering these comments, the IFRIC concluded that they primarily arose from its observation in the Basis for Conclusions on D3 that 'the lease asset under IAS 17 is the right to use [and] that this asset should not be confused with the underlying item [in the arrangement]' (e.g. an item of property, plant or equipment). As a result, the IFRIC understood that some respondents were concerned that D3 was requiring (or permitting) purchasers (lessees) to recognise an intangible asset for the right of use, even for leases classified as operating leases.

BC6   During redeliberation, the IFRIC affirmed its view that conceptually IAS 17 regards the asset as the right of use (although it acknowledged that in a finance lease, a lessee recognises an asset and accounts for that asset as if it were within the scope of IAS 16 *Property, Plant and Equipment* or IAS 38 *Intangible Assets*). However, the IFRIC decided to emphasise that the objective of the Interpretation is only to identify whether an arrangement contains a lease, not to change the requirements of IAS 17. Accordingly, having identified a lease, an entity accounts for that lease in accordance with IAS 17. This includes following the requirements of paragraphs 7-19 of IAS 17 to determine whether the lease should be classified as an operating lease or as a finance lease. This means, for example, that if a purchaser satisfies the criteria in the Interpretation, it (a) recognises an asset only if substantially all the risks and rewards incidental to ownership are transferred and (b) treats the recognised asset as a leased item, rather than an intangible asset for the right to use that item.

BC7   The IFRIC reconsidered its use of the term 'item' in D3 (as in right to use an item). The IFRIC noted that it had used 'item' rather than 'asset' to refer to the underlying asset in the arrangement (e.g. an item of property, plant or equipment) in order to emphasise that the asset that is the subject of the Interpretation is the right of use and not the underlying item or asset. However, given that many found the use of the term confusing, the IFRIC decided in finalising the Interpretation to revert to the phrase in IAS 17 'right to use an asset'.

Multiple-element arrangements

BC8   The IFRIC observed that many of the arrangements that fall within the scope of the Interpretation are likely to involve services as well as a right to use an asset. In other words, the arrangement is what is sometimes referred to as a multiple-element arrangement. The IFRIC concluded that IAS 17 allows for separate recognition of a lease that is embedded or contained within a multiple-element arrangement because IAS 17 states (paragraph 3) that it applies to 'agreements that transfer the right to use assets even though substantial services by the lessor may be called for in connection with the operation or maintenance of such assets.' In addition, the definition of minimum lease payments in paragraph 4 of IAS 17 clarifies that such payments exclude costs for services. The Interpretation therefore addresses whether a multiple-element arrangement contains a lease and not just whether an *entire* arrangement is a lease.

Portions of an asset (paragraph 3)

BC9   The Interpretation (like D3) does not address what constitutes the underlying asset in the arrangement. In other words, it does not address when a portion of a larger asset can be the subject of a lease.

BC10 Some respondents to D3 suggested that this omission pointed to a flaw in the proposals. They were troubled by the potential inconsistency between the accounting for a take-or-pay arrangement for substantially all of the output from a specific asset (which could have contained a lease) and one for a smaller portion of the output (which would not have been required to be treated as containing a lease). Other respondents argued that D3 would have allowed undue flexibility and that the IFRIC should either explicitly rule out portions or provide additional guidance to clarify which portions should be recognised (for example, those that are physically distinguishable).

BC11 From an early stage in this project, the IFRIC decided that it should not address the issue of portions and should focus on the main question, i.e. what constitutes a lease. The IFRIC noted that the subject of portions was important in itself and had much wider applicability than the Interpretation. The IFRIC affirmed this view during its redeliberations and therefore rejected the suggestion that it also should address portions in the Interpretation. The IFRIC also concluded that it would be inappropriate to specify that the Interpretation should not be applied to an arrangement that contains a right to use a portion of an asset (whether that portion be a physically distinguishable portion of an asset, or defined by reference to the output of the asset or the time the asset is made available) because this would conflict with IAS 17. The IFRIC agreed that the phrase 'right to use an asset' does not preclude the asset being a portion of a larger asset.

BC12 However, in the light of comments from respondents, the IFRIC decided to clarify that the Interpretation should be applied to arrangements in which the underlying asset would represent the unit of account in either IAS 16 or IAS 38.

Scope (paragraph 4)

BC13 The objective of the Interpretation is to determine whether an arrangement contains a lease that falls within the scope of IAS 17. The lease is then accounted for in accordance with that Standard. Because the Interpretation should not be read as overriding any of the requirements of IAS 17, the IFRIC decided that it should clarify that if an arrangement is found to be, or contains, a lease or licensing agreement that is excluded from the scope of IAS 17, an entity need not apply IAS 17 to that lease or licensing agreement.

BC14 The IFRIC considered whether the scope of the Interpretation might overlap with IAS 39 *Financial Instruments: Recognition and Measurement*. In particular it noted the view that an arrangement for output might meet the definition of a derivative under IAS 39 but also be determined to contain a lease under this Interpretation. The IFRIC concluded that there should not be an overlap because an arrangement for output that is a derivative would not meet the criteria in paragraphs 6-9 of the Interpretation. In particular, the IFRIC noted that such an arrangement would be for a product with a quoted market price available in an active market and would therefore be unlikely to depend upon the use of a specifically identified asset.

BC14A The IFRIC considered whether the scope of the Interpretation might overlap with IFRIC 12, which was developed from draft Interpretations D12–D14. In particular it noted the views expressed by some respondents to the proposals that the contractual terms of some public-to-private service concession arrangements would be regarded as leases under IFRIC 4 and would also be regarded as meeting the scope criterion of D12–D14. The IFRIC did not regard the choice between accounting treatments as appropriate because it could lead to different accounting treatments for contracts that have similar economic effects. The IFRIC therefore amended IFRIC 4 to specify that if a public-to-private service concession arrangement met the scope requirements of IFRIC 12 it would not be within the scope of IFRIC 4.

Consensus (paragraphs 6-15)

Criteria for determining whether an arrangement contains a lease (paragraphs 6-9)

BC15 In D3 the IFRIC proposed that three criteria would all need to be satisfied for an arrangement to be, or contain, a lease:

(a) The arrangement depends upon a specific item or items (the item). The item need not be explicitly identified by the contractual provisions of the arrangement. Rather it may be implicitly identified because it is not economically feasible or practical for the supplier to fulfil the arrangement by providing use of alternative items.

	(b)	The arrangement conveys a right to use the item for a specific period of time such that the purchaser is able to exclude others from using the item.
	(c)	Payments under the arrangement are made for the time that the item is made available for use rather than for actual use of the item.
BC16		D3 also proposed that arrangements in which there is only a remote possibility that parties other than the purchaser will take more than an insignificant amount of the output produced by an item would meet the second of the criteria above.
BC17		In its Basis for Conclusions on D3, the IFRIC drew attention to the similarities between its Interpretation and Issue No. 01-8 *Determining Whether an Arrangement Contains a Lease* published by the US Emerging Issues Task Force (EITF) in May 2003. The IFRIC concluded that '[a]lthough the wording of Issue 01-8 and the draft Interpretation differ, ... a similar assessment of whether an arrangement contains a lease is likely under both interpretations.'
BC18		Some respondents disagreed with the IFRIC's conclusion and suggested that the differences between the two interpretations were, in fact, significant. The IFRIC, however, maintained its original conclusion. In particular, it noted that both it and the EITF had concluded that a right of use can be conveyed in arrangements in which purchasers have rights to acquire the output that will be produced by an asset, regardless of any right or ability physically to operate or control access to that asset. Accordingly, many take-or-pay (and similar contracts) would have been similarly assessed under the two interpretations.
BC19		Nonetheless, the IFRIC agreed that some arrangements would be regarded as leases under Issue 01-8 but not under D3. The IFRIC concluded that there were two main reasons for this. First, the effect of the third criterion in D3 ('payments under the arrangement are made for the time that the item is made available for use rather than for actual use of the item') was that a purchaser would always be required to assume some pricing risk in an arrangement for there to be a lease. This is not the case under Issue 01-8. Secondly, the second criterion in D3 ('the arrangement conveys a right to use the item ... such that the purchaser is able to exclude others from using the item') suggested that a right of use is conveyed in an arrangement for the output from an asset only when the purchaser is taking *substantially all* of the output from a specific asset. Under Issue 01-8, a right of use is also conveyed if the purchaser controls or operates the underlying specific asset while taking more than a *minor amount* of the output from an asset.
BC20		The IFRIC noted that the definition of a lease in IAS 17 is similar to its definition in the US standard SFAS 13 *Accounting for Leases*. Given this, the IFRIC concluded that there was no compelling reason for different assessments of whether an arrangement contains a lease under IFRSs and US GAAP. Furthermore, the IFRIC was sympathetic to the practical difficulties highlighted by some respondents that would arise in cases when an agreement would need to be assessed against two similar, but different, sets of criteria. Therefore, the IFRIC decided that it should seek to eliminate the differences between the approach in D3 and Issue 01-8 for determining whether an arrangement contains a lease. The IFRIC concluded that the most effective way of achieving this objective would be to modify its criteria to conform them more fully to the approach in Issue 01-8.
BC21		The IFRIC decided that as far as possible it should adopt the actual words from Issue 01-8, subject to differences between IAS 17 and SFAS 13. It concluded that differences in wording would not promote convergence and would be likely to cause confusion. Therefore, paragraphs 7-9 are virtually identical to Issue 01-8, except that:
	(a)	the Interpretation uses the term 'asset' rather than 'property, plant or equipment' as in Issue 01-8. The IFRIC noted that IAS 17 covers a broader range of leases than SFAS 13 and that there was no reason for restricting this Interpretation only to items of property, plant or equipment.

(b)   the phrase 'more than a minor amount of the output' in Issue 01-8 has been expressed as 'more than an insignificant amount of the output'. This is because the latter is the more customary form of words under IFRSs and is therefore consistent with other Standards. In this context, however, the IFRIC intends 'minor' and 'insignificant' to have the same meaning.

BC22   Apart from small modifications to the wording of the first criterion in D3, the effect of converging fully with the criteria in Issue 01-8 for determining whether an arrangement contains a lease is that the second and third criteria in D3 are replaced by one criterion, requiring the arrangement to convey to the purchaser the right to control the use of the underlying asset.

BC23   Although the requirements for determining whether an arrangement contains a lease are the same under IFRSs and US GAAP, the IFRIC emphasises that any lease identified by the Interpretation may be accounted for differently under IFRSs and US GAAP because of differences between their respective leasing standards.

Fulfilment of the arrangement is dependent on the use of a specific asset (paragraphs 7 and 8)

BC24   The IFRIC agreed that a specific asset needs to be identified in the arrangement for there to be a lease. The IFRIC concluded that this follows from the definition of a lease, which refers to a 'right to use *an* asset' (emphasis added). The IFRIC also observed that dependence on a specifically identified asset is a feature that distinguishes a lease from other arrangements that also convey rights to use assets but are not leases (e.g. some service arrangements).

BC25   However, the IFRIC concluded that the identification of the asset in the arrangement need not be explicit. Rather, the facts and circumstances could implicitly identify an asset because it would not be economically feasible or practical for the supplier to perform its obligation by providing the use of alternative assets. Examples of when an asset may be implicitly identified are when the supplier owns only one suitable asset; the asset used to fulfil the contract needs to be at a particular location or specialised to the purchaser's needs; and the supplier is a special purpose entity formed for a limited purpose.

BC26   Some respondents to D3 noted that the effect of this first criterion is that the *purchaser's* accounting could depend on how the *supplier* chooses to fulfil the arrangement. They noted that the purchaser might have no control over this because (in form) the purchaser has contracted for output. Some respondents were also troubled by the lack of comparability, because similar arrangements for the output of an asset could be accounted for differently according to whether they depend on the use of a specific asset.

BC27   In response to the first of these comments, the IFRIC noted that how an entity chooses to obtain a product normally determines the accounting treatment; for example, an entity requiring power may choose to lease a power plant or connect to the grid and the two options would result in different accounting. Although in the respondents' example the choice is the supplier's (rather than the purchaser's), the IFRIC concluded that the critical matter is the end position of the entity (i.e. is there a lease?) not how it got to that position (i.e. whether it chose that outcome or it was imposed).

BC28   In response to the second comment, the IFRIC observed that it is important to consider the combined effect of the criteria in the Interpretation rather than considering the criteria individually. On reconsidering the proposals in D3 and the requirements of Issue 01-8, the IFRIC concluded that in the context of current IFRSs, in which executory contracts are generally not accounted for, the Interpretation identifies contracts (or an element therein) that for a purchaser warrant recognition (if the definition of a finance lease is satisfied). The IFRIC concluded that identifying and accounting for the lease element would represent an improvement to existing accounting practice.

Arrangement conveys a right to use the asset (paragraph 9)

BC29　　　Following Issue 01-8, the Interpretation specifies that a right of use can be conveyed if any of three criteria is satisfied.

BC30　　　The first two criteria consider the purchaser's ability to control physically the use of the underlying asset, either through operations or access, while obtaining or controlling more than an insignificant amount of the output of the asset. For example, a purchaser's ability to operate the asset may be evidenced by its ability to hire, fire or replace the operator of the asset or its ability to specify significant operating policies and procedures in the arrangement (as opposed to a right to monitor the supplier's activities) with the supplier having no ability to change such policies and procedures.

BC31　　　In D3 the IFRIC explained that it did not regard the ability of a purchaser to operate physically the underlying asset as determinative of whether a right of use has been conveyed. The IFRIC noted that asset managers 'operate' assets, but this does not necessarily convey a right of use. However, the IFRIC noted that under Issue 01-8, in addition to the ability to operate the asset, the purchaser has to be taking more than a minor amount of the output. The IFRIC agreed that in such cases the arrangement would convey a right of use.

BC32　　　The IFRIC agreed with the EITF that a right of use has been conveyed in arrangements in which the purchaser has the ability to control physically the use of the underlying asset through access (while obtaining or controlling more than a minor amount of the output of the asset). The IFRIC noted that in such arrangements the purchaser would have the ability to restrict the access of others to economic benefits of the underlying asset.

BC33　　　The third criterion for determining whether a right of use has been conveyed considers whether the purchaser is taking all or substantially all of the output or other utility of the underlying asset.

BC34　　　As noted above, D3 similarly specified that a right of use could be conveyed in arrangements in which there is only a remote possibility that other parties could take more than an insignificant amount of the output of an asset. Among the respondents who disagreed with the proposals in D3, it was this criterion that was considered most troublesome. They disagreed that, in certain specified circumstances, a purchaser's right to acquire the output from an asset could be equated with a right of use that asset. Among the arguments put to the IFRIC were:

(a)　　A right of use requires the purchaser to have the ability to control the way in which the underlying asset is used during the term of the arrangement: for example, the right for the purchaser's employees to assist or supervise the operation of the asset.

(b)　　In addition to the right to the output, the purchaser needs to have control over the delivery profile of the output; in other words it also needs the ability to determine when the output flows, otherwise it is simply consuming the output of the underlying asset rather than using the asset in its business.

(c)　　In most supply arrangements, the purchaser would not have access to the plant in the event of default by the supplier but would receive damages. The absence of this right points to there not being a lease. If the arrangement did contain a lease, the purchaser would have the ability to receive the output from the plant in the arrangement by replacing the original supplier with another service provider.

(d)　　D3 dismisses 'risks and rewards incidental to ownership' of the asset in determining whether an arrangement contains a lease. Therefore, arrangements in which the supplier retains significantly all of the risks and rewards of operation and ownership of the asset could be deemed to contain leases. However, in such arrangements the supplier's cash flows may have significantly more potential for variability than a 'true' lessor and the supplier may demand a return significantly above the market rate for a lessor.

BC35   In its redeliberations, the IFRIC reaffirmed its view that a purchaser that is taking substantially all of the output from an asset has the ability to restrict the access of others to the output from that asset. The purchaser therefore has a right of use because it controls access to the economic benefits to be derived from the asset. The IFRIC therefore did not agree that the absence of the ability to control physically the way in which the underlying asset is used precludes the existence of a right of use (although, as noted above, such an ability may indicate that a right of use has been conveyed).

BC36   With respect to the other points, the IFRIC noted the following:

(a)   A purchaser that is taking substantially all of the output from an asset in cases when it is remote that others will be taking more than an insignificant amount of the output does in effect determine when the output flows.

(b)   In most straightforward leases, any lessee that terminates the lease because of default by the lessor would no longer have access to the asset. Furthermore, in many leases that contain both a right of use and a service element, the related service contract does not operate independently (e.g. the lessee cannot terminate the service element alone). Indeed, the IFRIC noted that the purchaser's entitlement to damages in the event of default by the supplier indicates that a right of use was originally conveyed, and that the supplier is compensating the purchaser for withdrawing that right.

(c)   Risks and rewards are in general relevant for determining lease classification rather than whether an arrangement is a lease. The IFRIC noted that in many straightforward short-term operating leases, substantially all the risks and rewards are retained by the lessor. Even if it were desirable to specify that a certain level of risks and rewards needed to be transferred for there to be a lease, the IFRIC was doubtful that such a criterion could be made operable. Nonetheless, an arrangement that conveys the right to use an asset will also convey certain risks and rewards incidental to ownership. Therefore, the transfer of risks and rewards of ownership may indicate that the arrangement conveys the right to use an asset. For example, if an arrangement's pricing provides for a fixed capacity charge designed to recover the supplier's capital investment in the underlying asset, the pricing may be persuasive evidence that it is remote that parties other than the purchaser will take more than an insignificant amount of the output or other utility that will be produced or generated by the asset, and the criterion in paragraph 9(c) is satisfied.

BC37   In adopting the approach from Issue 01-8, the IFRIC has specified that an arrangement for all or substantially all of the output from a specific asset does not convey the right to use the asset if the price that the purchaser will pay is contractually fixed per unit of output or equal to the current market price per unit of output as of the time of delivery of the output. This is because in such cases the purchaser is paying for a product or service rather than paying for the right to use the asset. In D3, the IFRIC proposed making a similar distinction by the combination of the second and third criteria (see paragraph BC15(b) and (c) above).

BC38   The IFRIC noted that its Interpretation could result in take-or-pay arrangements, in which purchasers are committed to purchase substantially all of the output from specific assets, being determined to contain leases. This is because in such arrangements the purchaser makes payments for the time that the underlying asset is made available for use rather than on the basis of actual use or output (resulting in the arrangement's pricing being neither fixed per unit of output nor equal to the current market price per unit of output). In many take-or-pay arrangements, the purchaser is contractually committed to pay the supplier regardless of whether the purchaser uses the underlying asset or obtains the output from that asset. Payments are therefore made for the right to use that asset. The IFRIC agreed that the overall effect of such a take-or-pay arrangement is similar to that of a lease plus contracts for related services and supplies (such as contracts for the operation of the asset and the purchase of inputs).

BC39   The IFRIC observed that if an arrangement contains a lease, and the lease is an operating lease, applying the Interpretation is likely to result in the same assets, liabilities and expenses being recognised as if no lease had been identified. However, the IFRIC noted that IAS 17 requires lessors and lessees to recognise operating lease payments on a straight-line basis over the lease term (unless another systematic basis is more representative of the time pattern of the benefit derived from the leased asset), and thus adjustments to the recognition profile of the payments for the lease element might be required in some instances. Also, the IFRIC noted that the Interpretation would often result in additional disclosure, because IAS 17 requires the lessor and lessee to disclose the future minimum lease payments. The IFRIC observed that, for a purchaser, the arrangements discussed in the Interpretation typically represent significant future commitments, and yet these commitments are not specifically required to be disclosed in the financial statements by Standards other than IAS 17. The IFRIC concluded that bringing such arrangements within the scope of IAS 17 would provide users of financial statements with relevant information that is useful for assessing the purchaser's solvency, liquidity and adaptability. The IFRIC acknowledged that the disclosed information might relate only to the lease element of the arrangement; however, it agreed that it would be beyond the scope of this Interpretation to address disclosure of executory contracts more generally.

Assessing or reassessing whether an arrangement contains a lease (paragraphs 10 and 11)

BC40   In D3 the IFRIC proposed that the assessment of whether an arrangement contains a lease should be made at the inception of the arrangement on the basis of the facts and circumstances existing at that time and that, consistently with IAS 17, an arrangement should be reassessed only if there was a change in the terms of the arrangement. Hence, under D3, a supplier that subsequently obtained additional assets with which it could fulfil the arrangement, would not have reassessed the arrangement.

BC41   Some respondents disagreed with this conclusion and argued that the analogy with the requirements for reclassifying a lease in IAS 17 was not relevant because the objective of the Interpretation is to determine whether an arrangement is within the scope of IAS 17. They noted that since this depends on factors such as whether the arrangement depends on a specific asset, it was logical that reassessment should be required if those factors change.

BC42   The IFRIC was persuaded by this argument and concluded that it outweighed the concerns that it had expressed in D3 about it being unduly burdensome to require purchasers to reassess arrangements. The IFRIC also noted that its proposal in D3 was different from Issue 01-8. Given that it had modified its approach to determining whether a lease exists to converge with Issue 01-8, the IFRIC decided that it should also specify the same treatment as Issue 01-8 for reassessments.

BC43   The IFRIC noted that the requirements in paragraphs 10 and 11 relate only to determining when the arrangement should be reassessed and that they do not alter the requirements of IAS 17. Hence if an arrangement that contains a lease is required to be reassessed and found still to contain a lease, the lease is reclassified as a finance lease or operating lease only if so required by paragraph 13 of IAS 17.

Separating payments for the lease from other payments (paragraphs 12-15)

BC44   D3 proposed, and the Interpretation requires, payments in an arrangement containing both a lease and other elements (e.g. services) to be separated into those for the lease and those for other elements on the basis of their relative fair values. The IFRIC concluded that fair value is the most relevant and faithful representation of the underlying economics of the transaction.

BC45   The IFRIC noted that this requirement could be more onerous for purchasers than for suppliers, particularly when a purchaser has no access to the supplier's pricing information. The IFRIC therefore agreed that it should provide some guidance to assist purchasers in separating the lease from other elements in the arrangement. Nonetheless, the IFRIC acknowledged that in rare cases it might be impracticable for the purchaser to separate the payments reliably. The IFRIC noted that if this was the case and the lease was a finance lease, then the requirements of IAS 17 would ensure that the purchaser would not capitalise an amount greater than the fair value of the asset (since paragraph 20 of IAS 17 requires a lessee to recognise a finance lease asset at the fair value of the leased property or, if lower, the present value of the minimum lease payments). Accordingly, the IFRIC decided to specify that in such cases the purchaser should recognise the fair value of the underlying asset as the leased asset. If the lease is an operating lease and it is impracticable to separate the payments reliably, the IFRIC agreed, as a practical accommodation, that the purchaser should disclose all the payments under the arrangement when disclosing the minimum lease payments, and state that these also include payment for other elements in the arrangement.

BC46   Some respondents to D3 noted that if a purchaser with an operating lease does not separate the payments, the usefulness of the disclosures required by IAS 17 would be reduced. The IFRIC agreed that the minimum lease payments are often used by users of financial statements to estimate the value of assets held under operating leases and therefore concluded that lease payments that also include payments for other elements should be disclosed separately.

Transition (paragraph 17)

BC47   D3 proposed, and the Interpretation requires, retrospective application. Some respondents proposed that the Interpretation should be applied only to new arrangements starting after its effective date. Two main arguments were put forward in support of this view:

(a)   convergence with Issue 01-8 (which applies to arrangements starting or modified after the beginning of an entity's next reporting period beginning after 28 May 2003); and

(b)   to ease transition, particularly in the case of longer arrangements that started some years ago and where it might be difficult to make the assessments required by D3 retrospectively.

BC48   The IFRIC noted that EITF Abstracts are usually applied prospectively. In contrast, IFRSs (including Interpretations) are applied retrospectively following the principle articulated in IAS 8 *Accounting Policies, Changes in Accounting Estimates and Errors*. The IFRIC could see no compelling argument for departing from this principle. The IFRIC also noted that unless it were to specify exactly the same effective date as Issue 01-8 (which was before D3 was published), reconciling items with US GAAP would still arise.

BC49   In addition, the IFRIC decided that the continuation of some arrangements for many years emphasised the need for retrospective application. Without retrospective application, an entity could be accounting for similar arrangements differently for many years with a consequent loss of comparability.

BC50   However, the IFRIC was sympathetic to the practical difficulties raised by full retrospective application, in particular the difficulty of going back potentially many years and determining whether the criteria would have been satisfied at that time. Although IAS 8 provides relief from fully retrospective application in cases where such treatment would be impracticable, the IFRIC decided that it should provide transitional relief for existing preparers of IFRSs in the Interpretation itself.[4] The IFRIC emphasises that this relief does not alter the transition requirements of IAS 17 and therefore if an arrangement is determined to contain a lease an entity applies IAS 17 from the inception of the arrangement.

---

4   [Aus] The optional transitional relief in paragraph 17 of the Interpretation would apply to Australian entities where they were not required to apply the Interpretation in the context of adopting all Australian equivalents to IFRSs and they elected not to apply it then.

Interpretation 5

Rights to Interests arising from Decommissioning, Restoration and Environmental Rehabilitation Funds

(Compiled November 2009)

Contents

Compilation Details

Comparison with IFRIC 5

UIG Interpretation 5
Rights to Interests arising from Decommissioning,
Restoration and Environmental Rehabilitation Funds

Paragraphs

References

Background   1 – 3

Scope   4 – 5

Issues   6

Consensus
   Accounting for an interest in a fund   7 – 9
   Accounting for obligations to make additional contributions   10
   Disclosure   11 – 13

Application   Aus 13.1 – Aus 13.4

Appendix:
Amendment to AASB 139 *Financial Instruments: Recognition and Measurement*

Basis for Conclusions on IFRIC 5

UIG Interpretation 5 *Rights to Interests arising from Decommissioning, Restoration and Environmental Rehabilitation Funds* (as amended) is set out in paragraphs 1 – Aus13.4. Interpretations are listed in Australian Accounting Standard AASB 1048 *Interpretation and Application of Standards*. In the absence of explicit guidance, AASB 108 *Accounting Policies, Changes in Accounting Estimates and Errors* provides a basis for selecting and applying accounting policies.

Compilation Details

UIG Interpretation 5 *Rights to Interests arising from Decommissioning, Restoration and Environmental Rehabilitation Funds* as amended

This compiled Interpretation applies to annual reporting periods beginning on or after 1 January 2009. It takes into account amendments up to and including 24 September 2007 and was prepared on 6 November 2009 by the staff of the Australian Accounting Standards Board (AASB).

This compilation is not a separate Interpretation issued by the AASB. Instead, it is a representation of Interpretation 5 (June 2005) as amended by other pronouncements, which are listed in the Table below.

Table of Pronouncements

Pronouncement	Month Issued	Application Date *(annual reporting periods ... on or after ...)*	Application, Saving or Transitional Provisions
Interpretation 5	Jun 2005	*(beginning)* 1 Jan 2006	See (a) below
AASB 2007-8	Sep 2007	*(beginning)* 1 Jan 2009	See (b) below

(a)   Entities may elect to apply this Interpretation to annual reporting periods beginning on or after 1 January 2005 but before 1 January 2006.

(b)   Entities may elect to apply this Standard to annual reporting periods beginning on or after 1 January 2005 but before 1 January 2009, provided that AASB 101 *Presentation of Financial Statements* (September 2007) is also applied to such periods.

Table of Amendments

Paragraph affected	How affected	By ... [paragraph]
Aus13.1	amended	AASB 2007-8 [7, 8]
Aus13.4	amended	AASB 2007-8 [8]

Comparison with IFRIC 5

UIG Interpretation 5 *Rights to Interests arising from Decommissioning, Restoration and Environmental Rehabilitation Funds* as amended incorporates International Financial Reporting Interpretations Committee Interpretation IFRIC 5 *Rights to Interests arising from Decommissioning, Restoration and Environmental Rehabilitation Funds*, issued by the International Accounting Standards Board. Paragraphs that have been added to this Interpretation (and do not appear in the text of IFRIC 5) are identified with the prefix "Aus", followed by the number of the preceding IFRIC paragraph and decimal numbering.

Entities that comply with Interpretation 5 as amended will simultaneously be in compliance with IFRIC 5 as amended.

Interpretation 5

UIG Interpretation 5 was issued in June 2005.

This compiled version of Interpretation 5 applies to annual reporting periods beginning on or after 1 January 2009. It incorporates relevant amendments contained in other AASB pronouncements up to and including 24 September 2007 (see Compilation Details).

Urgent Issues Group

Interpretation 5

Rights to Interests Arising from Decommissioning, Restoration and Environmental Rehabilitation Funds

References

Accounting Standard AASB 108 *Accounting Policies, Changes in Accounting Estimates and Errors*

Accounting Standard AASB 127 *Consolidated and Separate Financial Statements*

Accounting Standard AASB 128 *Investments in Associates*

Accounting Standard AASB 131 *Interests in Joint Ventures*

Accounting Standard AASB 137 *Provisions, Contingent Liabilities and Contingent Assets*

Accounting Standard AASB 139 *Financial Instruments: Recognition and Measurement*

UIG Interpretation 112 *Consolidation – Special Purpose Entities*

Background

1   The purpose of decommissioning, restoration and environmental rehabilitation funds, hereafter referred to as 'decommissioning funds' or 'funds', is to segregate assets to fund some or all of the costs of decommissioning plant (such as a nuclear plant) or certain equipment (such as cars), or in undertaking environmental rehabilitation (such as rectifying pollution of water or restoring mined land), together referred to as 'decommissioning'.

2   Contributions to these funds may be voluntary or required by regulation or law. The funds may have one of the following structures:

(a)   funds that are established by a single contributor to fund its own decommissioning obligations, whether for a particular site, or for a number of geographically dispersed sites;

(b)   funds that are established with multiple contributors to fund their individual or joint decommissioning obligations, when contributors are entitled to reimbursement for decommissioning expenses to the extent of their contributions plus any actual earnings on those contributions less their share of the costs of administering the fund. Contributors may have an obligation to make additional contributions, for example, in the event of the bankruptcy of another contributor;

(c)   funds that are established with multiple contributors to fund their individual or joint decommissioning obligations when the required level of contributions is based on the current activity of a contributor and the benefit obtained by that contributor is based on its past activity. In such cases there is a potential mismatch in the amount of contributions made by a contributor (based on current activity) and the value realisable from the fund (based on past activity).

3   Such funds generally have the following features:

(a)   the fund is separately administered by independent trustees;

(b)   entities (contributors) make contributions to the fund, which are invested in a range of assets that may include both debt and equity investments, and are available to help pay the contributors' decommissioning costs. The trustees determine how contributions are invested, within the constraints set by the fund's governing documents and any applicable legislation or other regulations;

(c)   the contributors retain the obligation to pay decommissioning costs. However, contributors are able to obtain reimbursement of decommissioning costs from the fund up to the lower of the decommissioning costs incurred and the contributor's share of assets of the fund; and

(d)   the contributors may have restricted access or no access to any surplus of assets of the fund over those used to meet eligible decommissioning costs.

Scope

4   This Interpretation applies to accounting in the financial statements of a contributor for interests arising from decommissioning funds that have both of the following features:

     (a)   the assets are administered separately (either by being held in a separate legal entity or as segregated assets within another entity); and

     (b)   a contributor's right to access the assets is restricted.

5   A residual interest in a fund that extends beyond a right to reimbursement, such as a contractual right to distributions once all the decommissioning has been completed or on winding up the fund, may be an equity instrument within the scope of Accounting Standard AASB 139 *Financial Instruments: Recognition and Measurement* and is not within the scope of this Interpretation.

Issues

6   The issues addressed in this Interpretation are:

     (a)   how should a contributor account for its interest in a fund; and

     (b)   when a contributor has an obligation to make additional contributions, for example, in the event of the bankruptcy of another contributor, how should that obligation be accounted for?

Consensus

Accounting for an interest in a fund

7   The contributor shall recognise its obligation to pay decommissioning costs as a liability and recognise its interest in the fund separately unless the contributor is not liable to pay decommissioning costs even if the fund fails to pay.

8   The contributor shall determine whether it has control, joint control or significant influence over the fund by reference to AASB 127 *Consolidated and Separate Financial Statements*, AASB 128 *Investments in Associates*, AASB 131 *Interests in Joint Ventures* and UIG Interpretation 112 *Consolidation – Special Purpose Entities*. If it does, the contributor shall account for its interest in the fund in accordance with those Standards.

9   If a contributor does not have control, joint control or significant influence over the fund, the contributor shall recognise the right to receive reimbursement from the fund as a reimbursement in accordance with AASB 137 *Provisions, Contingent Liabilities and Contingent Assets*. This reimbursement shall be measured at the lower of:

     (a)   the amount of the decommissioning obligation recognised; and

     (b)   the contributor's share of the fair value of the net assets of the fund attributable to contributors.

Changes in the carrying value of the right to receive reimbursement other than contributions to and payments from the fund shall be recognised in profit or loss in the period in which these changes occur.

Accounting for obligations to make additional contributions

10   When a contributor has an obligation to make potential additional contributions, for example, in the event of the bankruptcy of another contributor or if the value of the investment assets held by the fund decreases to an extent that they are insufficient to fulfil the fund's reimbursement obligations, this obligation is a contingent liability that is within the scope of AASB 137. The contributor shall recognise a liability only if it is probable that additional contributions will be made.

Disclosure

11   A contributor shall disclose the nature of its interest in a fund and any restrictions on access to the assets in the fund.

12   When a contributor has an obligation to make potential additional contributions that is not recognised as a liability (see paragraph 10), it shall make the disclosures required by paragraph 86 of AASB 137.

13   When a contributor accounts for its interest in the fund in accordance with paragraph 9, it shall make the disclosures required by paragraph 85(c) of AASB 137.

Application

Aus13.1   This Interpretation applies to:

(a)   each entity that is required to prepare financial reports in accordance with Part 2M.3 of the *Corporations Act 2001* and that is a reporting entity;

(b)   general purpose financial statements of each other reporting entity; and

(c)   financial statements that are, or are held out to be, general purpose financial statements.

Aus13.2   This Interpretation applies to annual reporting periods beginning on or after 1 January 2006.

[Note: For application dates of paragraphs changed or added by an amending pronouncement, see Compilation Details.]

Aus13.3   This Interpretation may be applied to annual reporting periods beginning on or after 1 January 2005 but before 1 January 2006, permitting early application only in the context of adopting all Australian equivalents to International Financial Reporting Standards for such periods. An entity that is required to prepare financial reports in accordance with Part 2M.3 of the Corporations Act may apply this Interpretation to such an annual reporting period when an election has been made in accordance with subsection 334(5) of the Corporations Act in relation to AASB 1048 *Interpretation and Application of Standards*. When an entity applies this Interpretation to such an annual reporting period, it shall disclose that fact.

Aus13.4   The requirements specified in this Interpretation apply to the financial statements where information resulting from their application is material in accordance with AASB 1031 *Materiality*.

Effective Date of IFRIC 5

14   [Deleted by the UIG]

Transition to IFRIC 5

15   [Deleted by the UIG]

Appendix

Amendment to AASB 139 *Financial Instruments: Recognition and Measurement*

AASB 139 is amended by Accounting Standard AASB 2005-5 *Amendments to Australian Accounting Standards*. The amendment applies for annual reporting periods beginning on or after 1 January 2006. If an entity applies this Interpretation for an earlier period, the amendment applies for that earlier period.

A1   In paragraph 2 of AASB 139 *Financial Instruments: Recognition and Measurement*, subparagraph (h) is amended by AASB 2005-5 to delete the word "and" at the end, subparagraph (i) is amended to replace the full stop at the end with "; and", and subparagraph (j) is inserted to read as follows:

2.   **This Standard shall be applied by all entities to all types of financial instruments except:**

      ...

(j)   **rights to payments to reimburse the entity for expenditure it is required to make to settle a liability that it recognises as a provision in accordance with AASB 137** *Provisions, Contingent Liabilities and Contingent Assets*, **or for which, in an earlier period, it recognised a provision in accordance with AASB 137.**

Basis for Conclusions on IFRIC 5

This IFRIC Basis for Conclusions accompanies, but is not part of, UIG Interpretation 5. The UIG considers that this Basis for Conclusions is an essential feature of the Interpretation. An IFRIC Basis for Conclusions may be amended to reflect the requirements of the UIG Interpretation and AASB Accounting Standards where they differ from the corresponding International pronouncements.

Introduction

BC1 This Basis for Conclusions summarises the IFRIC's considerations in reaching its consensus. Individual IFRIC members gave greater weight to some factors than to others.

Background (paragraphs 1-3)

BC2 The IFRIC was informed that an increasing number of entities with decommissioning obligations are contributing to a separate fund established to help fund those obligations. The IFRIC was also informed that questions have arisen in practice over the accounting treatment of interests in such funds and that there is a risk that divergent practices may develop. The IFRIC therefore concluded that it should provide guidance to assist in answering the questions in paragraph 6, in particular on the accounting for the asset of the right to receive reimbursement from a fund. On the issue of whether the fund should be consolidated or equity accounted, the IFRIC concluded that the normal requirements of IAS 27 *Consolidated and Separate Financial Statements*, SIC-12 *Consolidation – Special Purpose Entities*, IAS 28 *Investments in Associates* or IAS 31 *Interests in Joint Ventures* apply and that there is no need for interpretative guidance. The IFRIC published its proposed Interpretation on 15 January 2004 as D4 *Decommissioning, Restoration and Environmental Rehabilitation Funds*.

BC3 Paragraphs 1-3 describe ways in which entities might arrange to fund their decommissioning obligations. Those that are within the scope of the Interpretation are specified in paragraphs 4-6.

Scope (paragraphs 4 and 5)

BC4 D4 did not precisely define the scope because the IFRIC believed that the large variety of schemes in operation would make any definition inappropriate. However, some respondents to D4 disagreed and commented that the absence of any definition made it unclear when the Interpretation should be applied. As a result, the IFRIC has specified the scope by identifying the features that make an arrangement a decommissioning fund. It has also described the different types of fund and the features that may (or may not) be present.

BC5 The IFRIC considered whether it should issue a wider Interpretation that addresses similar forms of reimbursement, or whether it should prohibit the application of the Interpretation to other situations by analogy. The IFRIC rejected any widening of the scope, deciding instead to concentrate on the matter referred to it. The IFRIC also decided that there was no reason to prohibit the application of the Interpretation to other situations by analogy and thus the hierarchy of criteria in paragraphs 7-12 of IAS 8 *Accounting Policies, Changes in Accounting Estimates and Errors* would apply, resulting in similar accounting for reimbursements under arrangements that are not decommissioning funds, but have similar features.

BC6 The IFRIC considered comments from respondents that a contributor may have an interest in the fund that extends beyond its right to reimbursement. In response, the IFRIC added clarification that a residual interest in a fund, such as a contractual right to distributions once all the decommissioning has been completed or on winding up the fund, may be an equity instrument within the scope of IAS 39 *Financial Instruments: Recognition and Measurement*.

Basis for Consensus

Accounting for an interest in a fund (paragraphs 7-9)

BC7   The IFRIC concluded that the contributor should recognise a liability unless the contributor is not liable to pay decommissioning costs even if the fund fails to pay. This is because the contributor remains liable for the decommissioning costs. Additionally, IAS 37 *Provisions, Contingent Liabilities and Contingent Assets* provides that:

(a)   when an entity remains liable for expenditure, a provision should be recognised even where reimbursement is available; and

(b)   if the reimbursement is virtually certain to be received when the obligation is settled, then it should be treated as a separate asset.

BC8   In concluding that the contributor should recognise separately its liability to pay decommissioning costs and its interest in the fund, the IFRIC also noted the following:

(a)   There is no legally enforceable right to set off the rights under the decommissioning fund against the decommissioning liabilities. Also, given that the main objective is reimbursement, it is likely that settlement will not be net or simultaneous. Accordingly, treating these rights and liabilities as analogous to financial assets and financial liabilities would not result in offset because the offset criteria in IAS 32 *Financial Instruments: Disclosure and Presentation* are not met.

(b)   Treating the decommissioning obligation as analogous to a financial liability would not result in derecognition through extinguishment. If the fund does not assume the obligation for decommissioning, the criteria in IAS 39 for derecognition of financial liabilities through extinguishment are not met. At best, the fund acts like an in-substance defeasance that does not qualify for derecognition of the liability.

(c)   It would not be appropriate to treat decommissioning funds as analogous to pension funds, which are presented net of the related liability. This is because, in allowing a net presentation for pension plans in IAS 19 *Employee Benefits*, the International Accounting Standards Board's predecessor organisation, IASC, stated that it believed the situation is 'unique to employee benefit plans and [it did] not intend to permit this net presentation for other liabilities if the conditions in IAS 32 and IAS 39 are not met' (IAS 19, Basis for Conclusions paragraph 68I).

BC9   As to the accounting for the contributor's interest in the fund, the IFRIC noted that some interests in funds would be within the scope of IAS 27, IAS 28, IAS 31 or SIC-12. As noted in paragraph BC2, the IFRIC concluded that, in such cases, the normal requirements of those Standards would apply and there is no need for interpretative guidance.

BC10   Otherwise, the IFRIC concluded that the contributor has an asset for its right to receive amounts from the fund.

The right to receive reimbursement from a fund and amendment to the scope of IAS 39

BC11   The IFRIC noted that under existing IFRSs, there are two forms of rights to reimbursement that would be accounted for differently:

(a)   A contractual right to receive reimbursement in the form of cash. This meets the definition of a financial asset and is within the scope of IAS 39. Such a financial asset would be classified as an available-for-sale financial asset (unless accounted for using the fair value option) because it does not meet the definitions of a financial asset held for trading, a held-to-maturity investment or a loan or receivable.[1]

---

1   An interest in a decommissioning fund would not meet the definition of held for trading because it is not acquired or incurred principally for the purpose of selling or repurchasing it in the near term, nor of a held-to-maturity investment because it does not have fixed or determinable maturity. In addition, an interest in a fund is excluded from the definition of loans and receivables in IAS 39 since it is 'an interest acquired in a pool of assets that are not loans and receivables'.

(b)   A right to reimbursement other than a contractual right to receive cash. This does not meet the definition of a financial asset and is within the scope of IAS 37.

BC12   The IFRIC concluded that both these forms of reimbursement have economically identical effects. Therefore accounting for both forms in the same way would provide relevant and reliable information to a user of the financial statements. However, the IFRIC noted that this did not appear possible under existing IFRSs because some such rights are within the scope of IAS 39, and others are not. Therefore, it asked the Board to amend the scope of IAS 39 to exclude rights to reimbursement for expenditure required to settle:

(a)   a provision that has been recognised in accordance with IAS 37; and

(b)   obligations that had been originally recognised as provisions in accordance with IAS 37, but are no longer provisions because their timing or amount is no longer uncertain. An example of such a liability is one that was originally recognised as a provision because of uncertainty about the timing of the cash outflow, but subsequently becomes another type of liability because the timing is now certain.

BC13   This amendment was approved by the Board and is set out in the Appendix of IFRIC 5.[2] As a result, all such rights to reimbursement are within the scope of IAS 37.

BC14   The IFRIC noted that paragraph 53 of IAS 37 specifies the accounting for rights to receive reimbursement. It requires this right to reimbursement to be separately recognised when it is virtually certain that reimbursement will be received if the contributor settles the obligation. The IFRIC also noted that this paragraph prohibits the recognition of an asset in excess of the recognised liability. For example, rights to receive reimbursement to meet decommissioning liabilities that have yet to be recognised as a provision are not recognised. Accordingly, the IFRIC concluded that when the right to reimbursement is virtually certain to be received if the contributor settles its decommissioning obligation, it should be measured at the lower of the amount of the decommissioning obligation recognised and the reimbursement right.

BC15   The IFRIC discussed whether the reimbursement right should be measured at:

(a)   the contributor's share of the fair value of the net assets of the fund attributable to contributors, taking into account any inability to access any surplus of the assets of the fund over eligible decommissioning costs (with any obligation to make good potential defaults of other contributors being treated separately as a contingent liability); or

(b)   the fair value of the reimbursement right (which would normally be lower than (a) because of the risks involved, such as the possibility that the contributor may be required to make good defaults of other contributors).

BC16   The IFRIC noted that the right to reimbursement relates to a decommissioning obligation for which a provision would be recognised and measured in accordance with IAS 37. Paragraph 36 of IAS 37 requires such provisions to be measured at 'the best estimate of the expenditure required to settle the present obligation at the end of the reporting period'. The IFRIC noted that the amount in paragraph BC15(a)—i.e. the contributor's share of the fair value of the net assets of the fund attributable to contributors, taking into account any inability to access any surplus of the assets of the fund over eligible decommissioning costs—is the best estimate of the amount available to the contributor to reimburse it for expenditure it had incurred to pay for decommissioning. Thus, the amount of the asset recognised would be consistent with the amount of the liability recognised.

BC17   In contrast, the IFRIC noted that the amount in paragraph BC15(b)—i.e. the fair value of the reimbursement right—would take into account the factors such as liquidity that the IFRIC believed to be difficult to measure reliably. Furthermore, this amount would be lower than that in paragraph BC15(a) because it reflects the possibility that the

---

2   [Aus] The scope of AASB 139 *Financial Instruments: Recognition and Measurement* is amended by AASB 2005-5 *Amendments to Australian Accounting Standards* consistent with the amendment of IAS 39 by IFRIC 5.

contributor may be required to make potential additional contributions in the event of default by other contributors. The IFRIC noted that its decision that the obligation to make potential additional contributions should be treated as a contingent liability in accordance with IAS 37 (see paragraphs BC22-BC25) would result in double-counting of the risk of the additional contribution being required if the measure in paragraph BC15(b) were to be used.

BC18 Consequently, the IFRIC concluded that the approach in paragraph BC15(a) would provide the most useful information to users.

The asset cap

BC19 Many respondents to D4 expressed concern about the 'asset cap' that is imposed by the requirement in paragraph 9. This asset cap limits the amount recognised as a reimbursement asset to the amount of the decommissioning obligation recognised. These respondents argued that rights to benefit in excess of this amount give rise to an additional asset, separate from the reimbursement asset. Such an additional asset may arise in a number of ways, for example:

(a) the contributor has the right to benefit from a repayment of any surplus in the fund that exists once all the decommissioning has been completed or on winding up the fund.

(b) the contributor has the right to benefit from reduced contributions to the fund or increased benefits from the fund (e.g. by adding new sites to the fund for no additional contributions) in the future.

(c) the contributor expects to obtain benefit from past contributions in the future, based on the current and planned level of activity. However, because contributions are made before the decommissioning obligation is incurred, IAS 37 prevents recognition of an asset in excess of the obligation.

BC20 The IFRIC concluded that a right to benefit from a repayment of any surplus in the fund that exists once all the decommissioning has been completed or on winding up the fund may be an equity instrument within the scope of IAS 39, in which case IAS 39 would apply. However, the IFRIC agreed that an asset should not be recognised for other rights to receive reimbursement from the fund. Although the IFRIC had sympathy with the concerns expressed by constituents that there may be circumstances in which it would seem appropriate to recognise an asset in excess of the reimbursement right, it concluded that it would be inconsistent with paragraph 53 of IAS 37 (which requires that 'the amount recognised for the reimbursement should not exceed the amount of the provision') to recognise this asset. The IFRIC also noted that the circumstances in which this additional asset exists are likely to be limited, and apply only when a contributor has restricted access to a surplus of fund assets that does not give it control, joint control or significant influence over a fund. The IFRIC expects that most such assets would not meet the recognition criteria in the *Framework* because they are highly uncertain and cannot be measured reliably.

BC21 The IFRIC also considered arguments that there should not be a difference between the treatment of a surplus when a fund is accounted for as a subsidiary, joint venture or associate, and when it is not. However, the IFRIC noted that, under IFRSs, restrictions on assets in subsidiaries, joint ventures or associates do not affect recognition of those assets. Hence it concluded that the difference in treatment between funds accounted for as subsidiaries, joint ventures or associates and those accounted for as a reimbursement right is inherent in IFRSs. The IFRIC also concluded that this is appropriate because, in the former case, the contributor exercises a degree of control not present in the latter case.

Obligations to make additional contributions (paragraph 10)

BC22 In some cases, a contributor has an obligation to make potential additional contributions, for example, in the event of the bankruptcy of another contributor.

BC23 The IFRIC noted that by 'joining' the fund, a contributor may assume the position of guarantor of the contributions of the other contributors, and hence become jointly and severally liable for the obligations of other contributors. Such an obligation is a present obligation of the contributor, but the outflow of resources associated with it may not be probable. The IFRIC noted a parallel with the example in paragraph 29 of IAS 37, which states that 'where an entity is jointly and severally liable for an obligation, the part of the obligation that is expected to be met by other parties is treated as a contingent liability.' Accordingly, the IFRIC concluded that a liability would be recognised by the contributor only if it is probable that it will make additional contributions. The IFRIC noted that such a contingent liability may arise both when the contributor's interest in the fund is accounted for as a reimbursement right and when it is accounted for in accordance with IAS 27, IAS 28, IAS 31 or SIC-12.

BC24 The IFRIC considered the argument that an obligation to make good potential shortfalls of other contributors is a financial instrument (i.e. a financial guarantee) as defined in IAS 32 and hence should be accounted for in accordance with IAS 39. The grounds for this point of view are that the contributor has an obligation to deliver cash to the fund, and the fund has a right to receive cash from the contributor if a shortfall in contributions arises. However, the IFRIC noted that:

(a) a contractual obligation to make good shortfalls of other contributors is a financial guarantee. Financial guarantee contracts that provide for payments to be made if the debtor fails to make payment when due are excluded from the scope of IAS 39.

(b) when the obligation is not contractual, but rather arises as a result of regulation, it is not a financial liability as defined in IAS 32 nor is it within the scope of IAS 39.

BC25 Therefore, the IFRIC concluded that an obligation to make additional contributions in the event of specified circumstances should be treated as a contingent liability in accordance with IAS 37.

Disclosure (paragraphs 11-13)

BC26 The IFRIC noted that the contributor may not be able to access the assets of the fund (including cash or cash equivalents) for many years (e.g. until it undertakes the decommissioning), if ever. Therefore, the IFRIC concluded that the nature of the contributor's interest and the restriction on access should be disclosed. The IFRIC also concluded that this disclosure is equally relevant when a contributor's interest in a fund is accounted for by consolidation, proportional consolidation or using the equity method because the contributor's ability to access the underlying assets may be similarly restricted.

Effective date and transition (paragraphs 14 and 15)

BC27 [Deleted by the UIG]

BC28 [Deleted by the UIG]

Interpretation 6
Liabilities arising from Participating in a Specific Market – Waste Electrical and Electronic Equipment

(Compiled November 2009)

Contents

Compilation Details

Comparison with IFRIC 6

UIG Interpretation 6
Liabilities arising from Participating in a Specific Market
– Waste Electrical and Electronic Equipment

	Paragraphs
References	
Background	1 – 5
Scope	6 – 7
Issues	8
Consensus	9
Application	Aus9.1 – Aus9.4

Basis for Conclusions on IFRIC 6

UIG Interpretation 6 *Liabilities arising from Participating in a Specific Market – Waste Electrical and Electronic Equipment* (as amended) is set out in paragraphs 1 – Aus9.4. Interpretations are listed in Australian Accounting Standard AASB 1048 *Interpretation and Application of Standards*. In the absence of explicit guidance, AASB 108 *Accounting Policies, Changes in Accounting Estimates and Errors* provides a basis for selecting and applying accounting policies.

Compilation Details

UIG Interpretation 6 *Liabilities arising from Participating in a Specific Market – Waste Electrical and Electronic Equipment* as amended

This compiled Interpretation applies to annual reporting periods beginning on or after 1 January 2009. It takes into account amendments up to and including 24 September 2007 and was prepared on 6 November 2009 by the staff of the Australian Accounting Standards Board (AASB).

This compilation is not a separate Interpretation issued by the AASB. Instead, it is a representation of Interpretation 6 (October 2005) as amended by other pronouncements, which are listed in the Table below.

Table of Pronouncements

Pronouncement	Month issued	Application date *(annual reporting periods ... on or after ...)*	Application, saving or transitional provisions
Interpretation 6	Oct 2005	*(beginning)* 1 Dec 2005	see (a) below
AASB 2007-8	Sep 2007	*(beginning)* 1 Jan 2009	see (b) below

(a) Entities may elect to apply this Interpretation to annual reporting periods beginning on or after 1 January 2005 but before 1 December 2005.

(b) Entities may elect to apply this Standard to annual reporting periods beginning on or after 1 January 2005 but before 1 January 2009, provided that AASB 101 *Presentation of Financial Statements* (September 2007) is also applied to such periods.

Table of Amendments

Paragraph affected	How affected	By ... [paragraph]
Aus9.1	amended	AASB 2007-8 [7, 8]
Aus9.4	amended	AASB 2007-8 [8]

Comparison with IFRIC 6

UIG Interpretation 6 *Liabilities arising from Participating in a Specific Market – Waste Electrical and Electronic Equipment* as amended incorporates International Financial Reporting Interpretations Committee Interpretation IFRIC 6 *Liabilities arising from Participating in a Specific Market – Waste Electrical and Electronic Equipment*, issued by the International Accounting Standards Board. Paragraphs that have been added to this Interpretation (and do not appear in the text of IFRIC 6) are identified with the prefix "Aus", followed by the number of the preceding IFRIC paragraph and decimal numbering.

Entities that comply with Interpretation 6 as amended will simultaneously be in compliance with IFRIC 6 as amended.

Interpretation 6

UIG Interpretation 6 was issued in October 2005.

This compiled version of Interpretation 6 applies to annual reporting periods beginning on or after 1 January 2009. It incorporates relevant amendments contained in other AASB pronouncements up to and including 24 September 2007 (see Compilation Details).

Urgent Issues Group
Interpretation 6
Liabilities arising from Participating in a Specific Market – Waste Electrical and Electronic Equipment

References

Accounting Standard AASB 108 *Accounting Policies, Changes in Accounting Estimates and Errors*

Accounting Standard AASB 137 *Provisions, Contingent Liabilities and Contingent Assets*

Background

1   Paragraph 17 of Accounting Standard AASB 137 *Provisions, Contingent Liabilities and Contingent Assets* specifies that an obligating event is a past event that leads to a present obligation that an entity has no realistic alternative to settling.

2   Paragraph 19 of AASB 137 states that provisions are recognised only for 'obligations arising from past events existing independently of an entity's future actions'.

3   The European Union's Directive on Waste Electrical and Electronic Equipment (WE&EE), which regulates the collection, treatment, recovery and environmentally sound disposal of waste equipment, has given rise to questions about when the liability for the decommissioning of WE&EE should be recognised. The Directive distinguishes between 'new' and 'historical' waste and between waste from private households and waste from sources other than private households. New waste relates to products sold after 13 August 2005. All household equipment sold before that date is deemed to give rise to historical waste for the purposes of the Directive.

4   The Directive states that the cost of waste management for historical household equipment should be borne by producers of that type of equipment that are in the market during a period to be specified in the applicable legislation of each Member State (the measurement period). The Directive states that each Member State shall establish a mechanism to have producers contribute to costs proportionately 'e.g. in proportion to their respective share of the market by type of equipment.'

5   Several terms used in the Interpretation such as 'market share' and 'measurement period' may be defined very differently in the applicable legislation of individual Member States. For example, the length of the measurement period might be a year or only one month. Similarly, the measurement of market share and the formulae for computing the obligation may differ in the various national legislations. However, all of these examples affect only the measurement of the liability, which is not within the scope of the Interpretation.

Scope

6   This Interpretation provides guidance on the recognition, in the financial statements of producers, of liabilities for waste management under the EU Directive on WE&EE in respect of sales of historical household equipment.

7   The Interpretation addresses neither new waste nor historical waste from sources other than private households. The liability for such waste management is adequately covered in AASB 137. However, if, in national legislation, new waste from private households is treated in a similar manner to historical waste from private households, the principles of the Interpretation apply by reference to the hierarchy in paragraphs 10–12 of AASB 108 *Accounting Policies, Changes in Accounting Estimates and Errors*. The AASB 108 hierarchy is also relevant for other regulations that impose obligations in a way that is similar to the cost attribution model specified in the EU Directive.

Issue

8   The issue is to determine in the context of the decommissioning of WE&EE what constitutes the obligating event in accordance with paragraph 14(a) of AASB 137 for the recognition of a provision for waste management costs:

- the manufacture or sale of the historical household equipment?
- participation in the market during the measurement period?
- the incurrence of costs in the performance of waste management activities?

Consensus

9   Participation in the market during the measurement period is the obligating event in accordance with paragraph 14(a) of AASB 137. As a consequence, a liability for waste management costs for historical household equipment does not arise as the products are manufactured or sold. Because the obligation for historical household equipment is linked to participation in the market during the measurement period, rather than to production or sale of the items to be disposed of, there is no obligation unless and until a market share exists during the measurement period. The timing of the obligating event may also be independent of the particular period in which the activities to perform the waste management are undertaken and the related costs incurred.

Application

Aus9.1   This Interpretation applies to:

    (a)   each entity that is required to prepare financial reports in accordance with Part 2M.3 of the *Corporations Act 2001* and that is a reporting entity;

    (b)   general purpose financial statements of each other reporting entity; and

    (c)   financial statements that are, or are held out to be, general purpose financial statements.

Aus9.2   This Interpretation applies to annual reporting periods beginning on or after 1 December 2005.

    [Note: For application dates of paragraphs changed or added by an amending pronouncement, see Compilation Details.]

Aus9.3   This Interpretation may be applied to annual reporting periods beginning on or after 1 January 2005 but before 1 December 2005, permitting early application in the context of adopting all Australian equivalents to International Financial Reporting Standards for such periods. An entity that is required to prepare financial reports in accordance with Part 2M.3 of the Corporations Act may apply this Interpretation to such annual reporting periods when an election has been made in accordance with subsection 334(5) of the Corporations Act in relation to AASB 1048 *Interpretation and Application of Standards*. When an entity applies this Interpretation to such an annual reporting period, it shall disclose that fact.

Aus9.4   The requirements specified in this Interpretation apply to the financial statements where information resulting from their application is material in accordance with AASB 1031 *Materiality*.

Effective Date of IFRIC 6

10   [Deleted by the UIG]

Transition to IFRIC 6

11   [Deleted by the UIG]

Basis for Conclusions on IFRIC 6

This IFRIC Basis for Conclusions accompanies, but is not part of, UIG Interpretation 6. The UIG considers that this Basis for Conclusions is an essential feature of the Interpretation. An IFRIC Basis for Conclusions may be amended to reflect the requirements of the UIG Interpretation and AASB Accounting Standards where they differ from the corresponding International pronouncements.

BC1   This Basis for Conclusions summarises the IFRIC's considerations in reaching its consensus. Individual IFRIC members gave greater weight to some factors than to others.

BC2   The IFRIC was informed that the European Union's Directive on Waste Electrical and Electronic Equipment (WE&EE) had given rise to questions about when a liability for the decommissioning of WE&EE for certain goods should be recognised. The IFRIC therefore decided to develop an Interpretation that would provide guidance regarding what constitutes an obligating event in the circumstances created by the Directive.

BC3   The IFRIC's proposals were set out in Draft Interpretation D10 *Liabilities arising from Participating in a Specific Market—Waste Electrical and Electronic Equipment*, which was published in November 2004. The IFRIC received 22 comment letters on the proposals.

BC4   The Directive indicates that it is participation in the market during the measurement period that triggers the obligation to meet the costs of waste management.

BC5   For example, an entity selling electrical equipment in 20X4 has a market share of 4 per cent for that calendar year. It subsequently discontinues operations and is thus no longer in the market when the waste management costs for its products are allocated to those entities with market share in 20X7. With a market share of 0 per cent in 20X7, the entity's obligation is zero. However, if another entity enters the market for electronic products in 20X7 and achieves a market share of 3 per cent in that period, then that entity's obligation for the costs of waste management from earlier periods will be 3 per cent of the total costs of waste management allocated to 20X7, even though the entity was not in the market in those earlier periods and has not produced any of the products for which waste management costs are allocated to 20X7.

BC6   The IFRIC concluded that the effect of the cost attribution model specified in the Directive is that the making of sales during the measurement period is the 'past event' that requires recognition of a provision under IAS 37 *Provisions, Contingent Liabilities and Contingent Assets* over the measurement period. Aggregate sales for the period determine the entity's obligation for a proportion of the costs of waste management allocated to that period. The measurement period is independent of the period when the cost allocation is notified to market participants. The timing of the obligating event may also be independent of the particular period in which the activities to perform the waste management are undertaken and the related costs incurred. Incurring costs in the performance of the waste management activities is a separate matter from incurring the obligation to share in the ultimate cost of those activities.

BC7   Some constituents asked the IFRIC to consider the effect of the following possible national legislation: the waste management costs for which a producer is responsible because of its participation in the market during a specified period (for example 20X6) are not based on the market share of the producer during that period but on the producer's participation in the market during a previous period (for example 20X5). The IFRIC noted that this affects only the measurement of the liability and that the obligating event is still participation in the market during 20X6.

BC8   The IFRIC considered whether its conclusion is undermined by the principle that the entity will continue to operate as a going concern. If the entity will continue to operate in the future, it treats the costs of doing so as future costs. For these future costs, paragraph 18 of IAS 37 emphasises that 'Financial statements deal with the financial position of an entity at the end of its reporting period and not its possible position in the future. Therefore, no provision is recognised for costs that need to be incurred to operate in the future.'

BC9   The IFRIC considered an argument that manufacturing or selling products for use in private households constitutes a past event that gives rise to a constructive obligation. Allocating waste management costs on the basis of market share would then be a matter of measurement rather than recognition. Supporters of this argument emphasise the definition of a constructive obligation in paragraph 10 of IAS 37 and point out that in determining whether past actions of an entity give rise to an obligation it is necessary to consider whether a change in practice is a realistic alternative. These respondents believed that when it would be necessary for an entity to take some unrealistic action in order to avoid the obligation then a constructive obligation exists and should be accounted for.

BC10   The IFRIC rejected this argument, concluding that a stated intention to participate in a market during a future measurement period does not create a constructive obligation for future waste management costs. In accordance with paragraph 19 of IAS 37, a provision can be recognised only in respect of an obligation that arises independently of the entity's future actions. For historical household equipment the obligation is created only by the future actions of the entity. If an entity has no market share in a measurement period, it has no obligation for the waste management costs relating to the products of that type which it had previously manufactured or sold and which otherwise would have created an obligation in that measurement period. This differentiates waste management costs, for example, from warranties (see Example 1 in Appendix C to IAS 37), which represent a legal obligation even if the entity exits the market. Consequently, no obligation exists for the future waste management costs until the entity participates in the market during the measurement period.

Interpretation 7

Applying the Restatement Approach under AASB 129 Financial Reporting in Hyperinflationary Economies

(Compiled November 2009)

Contents

Compilation Details

Comparison with IFRIC 7

UIG Interpretation 7
Applying the Restatement Approach under AASB 129 Financial Reporting
in Hyperinflationary Economies

	Paragraphs
References	
Background	1
Issues	2
Consensus	3 – 5
Application	Aus5.1 – Aus5.4
Illustrative Example	IE1 – IE6

Basis for Conclusions on IFRIC 7

UIG Interpretation 7 *Applying the Restatement Approach under AASB 129* Financial Reporting in Hyperinflationary Economies (as amended) is set out in paragraphs 1 – Aus5.4. Interpretations are listed in Australian Accounting Standard AASB 1048 *Interpretation and Application of Standards*. In the absence of explicit guidance, AASB 108 *Accounting Policies, Changes in Accounting Estimates and Errors* provides a basis for selecting and applying accounting policies.

Compilation Details

UIG Interpretation 7 *Applying the Restatement Approach under AASB 129 Financial Reporting in Hyperinflationary Economies* as amended

This compiled Interpretation applies to annual reporting periods beginning on or after 1 January 2009 that end on or after 30 June 2009. It takes into account amendments up to and including 5 October 2009 and was prepared on 9 November 2009 by the staff of the Australian Accounting Standards Board (AASB).

This compilation is not a separate Interpretation issued by the AASB. Instead, it is a representation of Interpretation 7 (February 2006) as amended by other pronouncements, which are listed in the Table below.

Table of Pronouncements

Pronouncement	Month issued	Application date *(annual reporting periods ... on or after ...)*	Application, saving or transitional provisions
Interpretation 7	Feb 2006	*(beginning)* 1 Mar 2006	see (a) below
AASB 2007-8	Sep 2007	*(beginning)* 1 Jan 2009	see (b) below
AASB 2007-10	Dec 2007	*(beginning)* 1 Jan 2009	see (b) below
AASB 2009-6	Jun 2009	*(beginning)* 1 Jan 2009 and *(ending)* 30 Jun 2009	see (c) below
Erratum	Oct 2009	*(beginning)* 1 Jan 2009 and *(ending)* 30 Jun 2009	see (d) below

(a) Entities may elect to apply this Interpretation to annual reporting periods beginning on or after 1 January 2005 but before 1 March 2006.

(b) Entities may elect to apply this Standard to annual reporting periods beginning on or after 1 January 2005 but before 1 January 2009, provided that AASB 101 *Presentation of Financial Statements* (September 2007) is also applied to such periods.

(c) Entities may elect to apply this Standard to annual reporting periods beginning on or after 1 January 2005 but before 1 January 2009, provided that AASB 101 *Presentation of Financial Statements* (September 2007) is also applied to such periods, and to annual reporting periods beginning on or after 1 January 2009 that end before 30 June 2009.

(d) Entities may elect to apply this Erratum to annual reporting periods beginning on or after 1 January 2005, provided that AASB 2009-6 *Amendments to Australian Accounting Standards* is also applied to such periods.

Table of Amendments to Interpretation

Paragraph affected	How affected	By ... [paragraph]
2	amended	AASB 2007-8 [6]
3	amended amended amended	AASB 2007-8 [6] AASB 2007-10 [101] Erratum, Oct 2009 [9]
4	amended amended	AASB 2007-8 [6] Erratum, Oct 2009 [10]
Aus5.1	amended	AASB 2007-8 [7, 8]
Aus5.4	amended	AASB 2007-8 [8]

Table of Amendments to Illustrative Example

Paragraph affected	How affected	By ... [paragraph]
IE1	amended	AASB 2007-10 [101]
IE2	amended	AASB 2007-8 [6]
IE4-IE5	amended	AASB 2007-8 [6]
IE6	amended amended	AASB 2007-8 [6] AASB 2009-6 [108, 109]

Comparison with IFRIC 7

Interpretation 7 and IFRIC 7

UIG Interpretation 7 *Applying the Restatement Approach under AASB 129* Financial Reporting in Hyperinflationary Economies as amended incorporates International Financial Reporting Interpretations Committee Interpretation IFRIC 7 *Applying the Restatement Approach under IAS 29* Financial Reporting in Hyperinflationary Economies, issued by the International Accounting Standards Board. Paragraphs that have been added to this Interpretation (and do not appear in the text of IFRIC 7) are identified with the prefix "Aus", followed by the number of the preceding IFRIC paragraph and decimal numbering.

Entities that comply with Interpretation 7 as amended will simultaneously be in compliance with IFRIC 7 as amended.

Interpretation 7

UIG Interpretation 7 was issued in February 2006.

This compiled version of Interpretation 7 applies to annual reporting periods beginning on or after 1 January 2009 that end on or after 30 June 2009. It incorporates relevant amendments contained in other AASB pronouncements up to and including 5 October 2009 (see Compilation Details).

Urgent Issues Group

Interpretation 7

Applying the Restatement Approach under AASB 129 Financial Reporting in Hyperinflationary Economies

References

Accounting Standard AASB 112 *Income Taxes*

Accounting Standard AASB 129 *Financial Reporting in Hyperinflationary Economies*

Background

1   This Interpretation provides guidance on how to apply the requirements of AASB 129 *Financial Reporting in Hyperinflationary Economies* in a reporting period in which an entity identifies[1] the existence of hyperinflation in the economy of its functional currency, when that economy was not hyperinflationary in the prior period, and the entity therefore restates its financial statements in accordance with AASB 129.

Issues

2   The questions addressed in this Interpretation are:

(a)   how should the requirement '… stated in terms of the measuring unit current at the end of the reporting period' in paragraph 8 of AASB 129 be interpreted when an entity applies the Standard?

(b)   how should an entity account for opening deferred tax items in its restated financial statements?

Consensus

3   In the reporting period in which an entity identifies the existence of hyperinflation in the economy of its functional currency, not having been hyperinflationary in the prior period, the entity shall apply the requirements of AASB 129 as if the economy had always been hyperinflationary. Therefore, in relation to non-monetary items measured at historical cost, the entity's opening statement of financial position at the beginning of the earliest period presented in the financial statements shall be restated to reflect the effect of inflation from the date the assets were acquired and the liabilities were incurred or assumed until the end of the reporting period. For non-monetary items carried in the opening statement of financial position at amounts current at dates other than those of acquisition or incurrence, that restatement shall reflect instead the effect of inflation from the dates those carrying amounts were determined until the end of the reporting period.

4   At the end of the reporting period, deferred tax items are recognised and measured in accordance with AASB 112 *Income Taxes*. However, the deferred tax figures in the

---

1   The identification of hyperinflation is based on the entity's judgement of the criteria in paragraph 3 of AASB 129.

opening statement of financial position for the reporting period shall be determined as follows:

(a) the entity remeasures the deferred tax items in accordance with AASB 112 after it has restated the nominal carrying amounts of its non-monetary items at the date of the opening statement of financial position of the reporting period by applying the measuring unit at that date; and

(b) the deferred tax items remeasured in accordance with (a) are restated for the change in the measuring unit from the date of the opening statement of financial position of the reporting period to the end of that reporting period.

The entity applies the approach in (a) and (b) in restating the deferred tax items in the opening statement of financial position of any comparative periods presented in the restated financial statements for the reporting period in which the entity applies AASB 129.

5 After an entity has restated its financial statements, all corresponding figures in the financial statements for a subsequent reporting period, including deferred tax items, are restated by applying the change in the measuring unit for that subsequent reporting period only to the restated financial statements for the previous reporting period.

Application

Aus5.1   This Interpretation applies to:

      (a) each entity that is required to prepare financial reports in accordance with Part 2M.3 of the *Corporations Act 2001* and that is a reporting entity;

      (b) general purpose financial statements of each other reporting entity; and

      (c) financial statements that are, or are held out to be, general purpose financial statements.

Aus5.2   This Interpretation applies to annual reporting periods beginning on or after 1 March 2006.

      [Note: For application dates of paragraphs changed or added by an amending pronouncement, see Compilation Details.]

Aus5.3   This Interpretation may be applied to annual reporting periods beginning on or after 1 January 2005 but before 1 March 2006, permitting early application in the context of adopting all Australian equivalents to International Financial Reporting Standards for such periods. Early application is encouraged. An entity that is required to prepare financial reports in accordance with Part 2M.3 of the Corporations Act may apply this Interpretation to such annual reporting periods when an election has been made in accordance with subsection 334(5) of the Corporations Act in relation to AASB 1048 *Interpretation and Application of Standards*. When an entity applies this Interpretation to such an annual reporting period, it shall disclose that fact.

Aus5.4   The requirements specified in this Interpretation apply to the financial statements where information resulting from their application is material in accordance with AASB 1031 *Materiality*.

Effective Date of IFRIC 7

6   [Deleted by the UIG]

Illustrative Example

This example accompanies, but is not part of, UIG Interpretation 7. The UIG considers that the example is an essential feature of the Interpretation.

IE1 This example illustrates the restatement of deferred tax items when an entity restates for the effects of inflation under AASB 129 Financial Reporting in Hyperinflationary Economies. As the example is intended only to illustrate the mechanics of the restatement approach in AASB 129 for deferred tax items, it does not illustrate an entity's complete Australian-equivalents-to-IFRSs financial statements.

Facts

IE2 An entity's Australian-equivalents-to-IFRSs statement of financial position at 31 December 20X4 (before restatement) is as follows:

Note	Statement of financial position	20X4 (a) CU million	20X3 CU million
	ASSETS		
1	Property, plant and equipment	300	400
	Other assets	XXX	XXX
	Total assets	XXX	XXX
	EQUITY AND LIABILITIES		
	Total equity	XXX	XXX
	Liabilities		
2	Deferred tax liability	30	20
	Other liabilities	XXX	XXX
	Total liabilities	XXX	XXX
	Total equity and liabilities	XXX	XXX

Notes

1 *Property, plant and equipment*
All items of property, plant and equipment were acquired in December 20X2. Property, plant and equipment are depreciated over their useful life, which is five years.

2 *Deferred tax liability*
The deferred tax liability at 31 December 20X4 of CU30 million is measured as the taxable temporary difference between the carrying amount of property, plant and equipment of 300 and their tax base of 200. The applicable tax rate is 30 per cent.

Similarly, the deferred tax liability at 31 December 20X3 of CU20 million is measured as the taxable temporary difference between the carrying amount of property, plant and equipment of CU400 and their tax base of CU333.

(a)   In this example, monetary amounts are denominated in currency units (CU).

IE3 Assume that the entity identifies the existence of hyperinflation in, for example, April 20X4 and therefore applies AASB 129 from the beginning of 20X4. The entity restates its financial statements on the basis of the following general price indices and conversion factors:

	General price indices	Conversion factors at 31 Dec 20X4
December 20X2(a)	95	2.347
December 20X3	135	1.652
December 20X4	223	1.000

(a)   For example, the conversion factor for December 20X2 is 2.347 = 223/95.

Restatement

IE4   The restatement of the entity's 20X4 financial statements is based on the following requirements:

- Property, plant and equipment are restated by applying the change in a general price index from the date of acquisition to the end of the reporting period to their historical cost and accumulated depreciation.

- Deferred taxes should be accounted for in accordance with AASB 112 *Income Taxes*.

- Comparative figures for property, plant and equipment for the previous reporting period are presented in terms of the measuring unit current at the end of the reporting period.

- Comparative deferred tax figures should be measured in accordance with paragraph 4 of the Interpretation.

IE5   Therefore the entity restates its statement of financial position at 31 December 20X4 as follows:

Note	Statement of financial position (restated)	20X4 CU million	20X3 CU million
	ASSETS		
1	Property, plant and equipment	704	939
	Other assets	XXX	XXX
	Total assets	XXX	XXX
	EQUITY AND LIABILITIES		
	Total equity	XXX	XXX
	Liabilities		
2	Deferred tax liability	151	117
	Other liabilities	XXX	XXX
	Total liabilities	XXX	XXX
	Total equity and liabilities	XXX	XXX

Notes

1   *Property, plant and equipment*
All items of property, plant and equipment were purchased in December 20X2 and depreciated over a five-year period. The cost of property, plant and equipment is restated to reflect the change in the general price level since acquisition, that is the conversion factor is 2.347 (223/95).

	Historical CU million	Restated CU million
Cost of property, plant and equipment	500	1,174
Depreciation 20X3	(100)	(235)
Carrying amount 31 December 20X3	400	939
Depreciation 20X4	(100)	(235)
Carrying amount 31 December 20X4	(300)	704

2   *Deferred tax liability*
The nominal deferred tax liability at 31 December 20X4 of CU30 million is measured as the taxable temporary difference between the carrying amount of property, plant and equipment of CU300 and their tax base of CU200. Similarly, the deferred tax liability at 31 December 20X3 of CU20 million is measured as the taxable temporary difference between the carrying amount of property, plant and equipment of CU400 and their tax base of CU333. The applicable tax rate is 30 per cent.

continued

In its restated financial statements, at the end of the reporting period the entity remeasures deferred tax items in accordance with the general provisions in AASB 112, that is on the basis of its restated financial statements. However, because deferred tax items are a function of carrying amounts of assets or liabilities and their tax bases, an entity cannot restate its comparative deferred tax items by applying a general price index. Instead, in the reporting period in which an entity applies the restatement approach under AASB 129, it (a) remeasures its comparative deferred tax items in accordance with AASB 112 after it has restated the nominal carrying amounts of its non monetary items at the date of the opening statement of financial position of the current reporting period by applying the measuring unit at that date, and (b) restates the remeasured deferred tax items for the change in the measuring unit from the date of the opening statement of financial position of the current period up to the end of the reporting period.

In the example, the restated deferred tax liability is calculated as follows:

	CU million
At the end of the reporting period:	
Restated carrying amount of property, plant and equipment (see note 1)	704
Tax base	(200)
Temporary difference	504
@ 30 per cent tax rate = Restated deferred tax liability 31 December 20X4	151

	CU million
Comparative deferred tax figures:	
Restated carrying amount of property, plant and equipment [either 400 × 1.421 (conversion factor 1.421 = 135/95), or 939/1.652 (conversion factor 1.652 = 223/135)]	568
Tax base	(333)
Temporary difference	235
@ 30 per cent tax rate = Restated deferred tax liability 31 December 20X3 at the general price level at the end of 20X3	71
Restated deferred tax liability 31 December 20X3 at the general price level at the end of 20X4 (conversion factor 1.652 = 223/135)	117

IE6   In this example, the restated deferred tax liability is increased by CU34 to CU151 from 31 December 20X3 to 31 December 20X4. That increase, which is included in profit or loss in 20X4, reflects (a) the effect of a change in the taxable temporary difference of property, plant and equipment, and (b) a loss of purchasing power on the tax base of property, plant and equipment. The two components can be analysed as follows:

	CU million
Effect on deferred tax liability because of a decrease in the taxable temporary difference of property, plant and equipment (− CU235 + CU133) × 30%	31
Loss on tax base because of inflation in 20X4 (CU333 × 1.652 − CU333) × 30%	(65)
Net increase of deferred tax liability	34
Debit to profit or loss in 20X4	34

The loss on tax base is a monetary loss. Paragraph 28 of AASB 129 explains this as follows:

The gain or loss on the net monetary position is included in net income. The adjustment to those assets and liabilities linked by agreement to changes in prices made in accordance with paragraph 13 is offset against the gain or loss on net monetary position. Other income and expense items, such as interest income and expense, and foreign exchange differences related to invested or borrowed funds, are also associated with the net monetary position. Although such items are separately disclosed, it may be helpful if they are presented together with the gain or loss on net monetary position in the statement of comprehensive income.

Basis for Conclusions on IFRIC 7

This IFRIC Basis for Conclusions accompanies, but is not part of, UIG Interpretation 7. The UIG considers that this Basis for Conclusions is an essential feature of the Interpretation. An IFRIC Basis for Conclusions may be amended to reflect the requirements of the UIG Interpretation and AASB Accounting Standards where they differ from the corresponding International pronouncements.

In this Basis for Conclusions the terminology has not been amended to reflect the changes made by IAS 1 Presentation of Financial Statements *(as revised in 2007).*

Introduction

BC1   This Basis for Conclusions summarises the IFRIC's considerations in reaching its consensus. Individual IFRIC members gave greater weight to some factors than to others.

Background

BC2   The IFRIC was asked for guidance on how an entity should restate its financial statements when it starts to apply IAS 29 *Financial Reporting in Hyperinflationary Economies*. There was uncertainty whether the opening balance sheet at the beginning of the reporting period should be restated to reflect changes in prices before that date.

BC3   In addition, there was uncertainty about the measurement of comparative deferred tax items in the opening balance sheet. IAS 29 states that at the balance sheet date deferred tax items of the restated financial statements should be measured in accordance with IAS 12 *Income Taxes*. However, it was not clear how an entity should account for the corresponding deferred tax figures.

BC4   In response, the IFRIC developed and published Draft Interpretation D5 *Applying IAS 29* Financial Reporting in Hyperinflationary Economies *for the First Time* for public comment in March 2004. It received 30 letters in response to the proposals.

Basis for consensus

The restatement approach

BC5   In developing D5, the IFRIC observed that the purpose of restating financial statements in hyperinflationary economies in accordance with IAS 29 is to reflect the effect on an entity of changes in general purchasing power. Paragraph 2 of IAS 29 states:

> In a hyperinflationary economy, reporting of operating results and financial position in the local currency without restatement is not useful. Money loses purchasing power at such a rate that comparison of amounts from transactions and other events that have occurred at different times, even within the same accounting period, is misleading.

This purpose applies to the financial statements of the first reporting period in which an entity identifies the existence of hyperinflation in the economy of its functional currency as well as to subsequent reporting periods (if the criteria for a hyperinflationary economy are still met).

BC6   The IFRIC considered the meaning of paragraph 4 of IAS 29, which states:

> … this Standard applies to the financial statements of any entity from the beginning of the reporting period in which it identifies the existence of hyperinflation in the country in whose currency it reports.

The IFRIC noted that some may interpret this provision as restricting the restatement of an entity's opening balance sheet in the reporting period in which it identifies the existence of hyperinflation. Consequently, the opening balance sheet should be restated to reflect the change in a general price index for the reporting period only and not for changes in a general price index before the beginning of the reporting period, even though some balance sheet items may have been acquired or assumed before that date. However, the IFRIC also noted that paragraph 34 of IAS 29 requires:

Corresponding figures for the previous reporting period, whether they were based on a historical cost approach or a current cost approach, are restated by applying a general price index so that the comparative financial statements are *presented in terms of the measuring unit current at the end of the reporting period.* Information that is disclosed in respect of earlier periods is also expressed in terms of the measuring unit current at the end of the reporting period ... [emphasis added]

BC7 The IFRIC considered a possible inconsistency between the restriction in paragraph 4 of IAS 29 and the requirement in paragraph 34. The IFRIC noted that paragraph 4 is a scope paragraph, which identifies when an entity has to comply with the Standard. The paragraph clarifies that an entity applies the requirements of the Standard to its financial statements from the beginning of the reporting period to the balance sheet date and not only from the date when it identifies the existence of hyperinflation. However, paragraph 4 does not deal with the restatement and presentation of the financial statements (either at the balance sheet date or in relation to the comparative figures). Hence, paragraph 4 of IAS 29 does not exclude from the restatement of an entity's opening balance sheet changes in the general price level before the beginning of the reporting period in which the entity identifies the existence of hyperinflation.

BC8 The IFRIC concluded that, in the context of the purpose of the Standard, the restatement of the financial statements for the reporting period in which an entity identifies the existence of hyperinflation should be consistent with the restatement approach applied in subsequent reporting periods.

BC9 Some respondents to D5 expressed concerns about whether the restatement approach in IAS 29 was always practicable for preparers and whether it provided decision useful information to users. Though the IFRIC understood those concerns, the IFRIC observed that such concerns reflected broader aspects related to the accounting for hyperinflation in general, rather than how an entity has to apply the current Standard.

BC10 Nevertheless, the IFRIC considered how an entity should apply the Standard if, for example, detailed records of the acquisition dates of items of property, plant and equipment are not available. The IFRIC noted that, in those circumstances, paragraph 16 of IAS 29 states:

... In these rare circumstances, it may be necessary, in the first period of application of this Standard, to use an independent professional assessment of the value of the items as the basis for their restatement.

The IFRIC also noted that a similar exemption exists when a general price index may not be available. Paragraph 17 of IAS 29 states:

... In these circumstances, it may be necessary to use an estimate based, for example, on the movements in the exchange rate between the functional currency and a relatively stable foreign currency.

BC11 The IFRIC observed that, in developing IFRS 1 *First time Adoption of International Financial Reporting Standards*, the International Accounting Standards Board discussed whether IFRS 1 should exempt first time adopters of IFRSs from the effects of restatement in their first IFRS financial statements. Paragraph BC67 of IFRS 1 states:

Some argued that the cost of restating financial statements for the effects of hyperinflation in periods before the date of transition to IFRSs would exceed the benefits, particularly if the currency is no longer hyperinflationary. However, the Board concluded that such restatement should be required, because hyperinflation can make unadjusted financial statements meaningless or misleading.

BC12 However, the IFRIC also observed that first time adopters of IFRSs could use, for example, the fair value at transition date as deemed cost for property, plant and equipment, and, in some instances, also for investment property and intangible assets. Hence, if a first time adopter that would otherwise have to apply IAS 29 at its transition to IFRSs applies the fair value measurement exemption of IFRS 1, it would apply IAS 29 to periods only after the date for which the fair value was determined. Such remeasurements would therefore reduce the need for a first time adopter to restate its financial statements.

BC13 The IFRIC noted that the exemptions from the general restatement approach for preparers that already apply IFRSs, as stated in paragraph BC10 above, apply only in specific circumstances, whereas a first time adopter may always elect to use the fair value remeasurement exemption for property, plant and equipment in IFRS 1. Nevertheless, the IFRIC concluded that the application of the exemptions in the Standards is clear and, therefore, extending the exemptions in IAS 29 to permit preparers that already apply IFRSs to elect fair value remeasurement of property, plant and equipment when applying the restatement approach under IAS 29 would require amendments of the Standard itself, rather than an Interpretation.

BC14 Respondents to D5 also argued that the procedures, as proposed to be clarified, are inconsistent with the accounting for a change in functional currency under IAS 21 *The Effect of Changes in Foreign Exchange Rates*, which in their view is comparable to moving into a state of hyperinflation. Moreover, they noted that retrospective application is also inconsistent with the US GAAP approach, which accounts for a change in hyperinflation status prospectively.

BC15 In relation to the reference to a change in functional currency, the IFRIC observed that the existence of hyperinflation may (but not necessarily should) initiate such a change. The IFRIC noted that a change in functional currency is a change in the currency that is normally used to determine the pricing of an entity's transactions. As clarified in paragraph BC5 above, the purpose of restatement for the effects of hyperinflation is to reflect the effect of changes in purchasing power in the economy of an entity's functional currency. Therefore, the IFRIC did not believe that the application of accounting for hyperinflation should be based on the accounting for the change in an entity's functional currency.

BC16 The IFRIC also observed that respondents' reference to prospective application under US GAAP reflects requirements only for investments in foreign entities in hyperinflationary economies. In this case, paragraph 11 of SFAS 52 *Foreign Currency Translation* states:

> The financial statements of a foreign entity in a highly inflationary economy shall be *remeasured as if the functional currency were the reporting currency*. Accordingly, the financial statements of those entities shall be remeasured into the reporting currency according to the requirements of paragraph 10 ... [emphasis added]

Therefore, under US GAAP a foreign entity's financial statements are remeasured into its investor's functional currency. The IFRIC noted that this approach is different from the restate/translate approach under IFRSs. US GAAP provides different guidance for reporting entities operating with a hyperinflationary functional currency. APB Statement No. 3 *Financial Statements Restated for General Price-Level Changes* is also based on a restatement approach, and would require retrospective application, as under IAS 29. The IFRIC observed that for the purpose of presenting comparative amounts in a different presentation currency under IFRSs paragraphs 42(b) and 43 of IAS 21 apply. In such instances, an entity will have relief from the required restatement of comparatives under IAS 29. Paragraph BC22 of IAS 21 explains the reasoning for this specific exemption as follows:

> ... If exchange rates fully reflect differing price levels between the two economies to which they relate, the SIC 30 approach will result in the same amounts for the comparatives as were reported as current year amounts in the prior year financial statements. Furthermore, the Board noted that in the prior year, the relevant amounts had been already expressed in the non hyperinflationary presentation currency, and there was no reason to change them.

BC17 D5 proposed that applying the restatement approach under IAS 29 should be regarded as a change in circumstances, rather than a change in accounting policy. Some respondents to D5 believed this was inconsistent. This is because IAS 8 *Accounting Policies, Changes in Accounting Estimates and Errors*, paragraph 16, states that a change in circumstances is not a change in accounting policy and an entity would not apply IAS 29 retrospectively. However, the IFRIC observed that IAS 29 contains specific requirements on this point, as noted in paragraphs BC5–BC16 above. The IFRIC concluded that the opening balance sheet for the reporting period in which an entity identifies the existence of hyperinflation ought to be restated as if the entity had always applied the restatement approach under IAS 29. The IFRIC reconfirmed its view that this treatment is similar to the retrospective application of a change in accounting policy described in IAS 8.

Deferred tax items

BC18 The IFRIC was asked for guidance on the accounting for deferred tax items when an entity restates its financial statements according to IAS 29. In particular, the IFRIC was asked for guidance on measuring deferred tax items in the opening balance sheet for the reporting period in which an entity identifies the existence of hyperinflation.

BC19 The IFRIC observed that paragraph 32 of IAS 29 states:

> The restatement of financial statements in accordance with this Standard may give rise to differences between the carrying amount of individual assets and liabilities in the balance sheet and their tax bases. These differences are accounted for in accordance with IAS 12 Income Taxes.

> Therefore, at the closing balance sheet date of the reporting period an entity remeasures its deferred tax items on the basis of the restated financial statements, rather than by applying the general restatement provisions for monetary items or non monetary items. However, the IFRIC noted that it was not clear how an entity should account for its comparative deferred tax items.

BC20 In developing D5, the IFRIC considered the following options:

    (a)   restatement of deferred tax items as monetary items;

    (b)   restatement of deferred tax items as non monetary items; or

    (c)   remeasurement of deferred tax items as if the economy of the entity's functional currency had always been hyperinflationary.

BC21 D5 proposed clarifying that deferred tax items are neither clearly monetary nor non monetary in nature. This was because deferred tax items are determined by the assets' (and liabilities') relative carrying amounts and tax bases. However, some respondents to D5 objected to that view, for various reasons. Some argued that deferred tax items, by nature, are received or paid in a fixed or determinable number of units of currency, and so should be considered as monetary items in accordance with paragraph 8 of IAS 21. Others noted that general practice is to classify deferred taxes as non monetary items.

BC22 When considering respondents' comments the IFRIC confirmed that its conclusion in paragraph BC17 above should also apply to deferred tax items. In other words, the deferred tax items in the opening balance sheet for the reporting period in which an entity identifies the existence of hyperinflation should be calculated as if the environment had always been hyperinflationary, i.e. option (c) in paragraph BC20. Although the IFRIC acknowledged that deferred tax items may meet the definition of monetary items it noted that the purposes of option (c) would not be achieved if opening deferred tax items were restated in the same manner as applied generally for monetary items.

BC23 The IFRIC observed that some respondents to D5 suggested that deferred tax items in the opening balance sheet should be remeasured after restating the opening balance sheet with the measurement unit current at the closing balance sheet date of the reporting period. In the IFRIC's view, that proposal would (in case of a deferred tax liability) overstate the deferred tax item recognised in the opening balance sheet and, accordingly, understate the costs recognised in the reporting period. This is because the loss on the tax base caused by the inflation in the reporting period would be recognised directly in opening equity. The IFRIC illustrated this by the following example:

> At the end of Year 1, a non monetary asset is restated at the measurement unit current at that date. Its restated amount is CU1,000 and its tax base is CU500. If the tax rate is 30 per cent, the entity would remeasure a deferred tax liability of CU150. In Year 2 inflation is 100 per cent. Assuming that nothing has changed the entity would, in its restated financial statements, recognise an asset of CU2,000 (both at the closing balance sheet date of the reporting period and in the comparative figures). At the closing balance sheet date, the deferred tax liability is remeasured at CU450 ((CU2,000 − CU500) × 0.3). However, if the comparative deferred tax liability is remeasured after restating the asset by the measuring unit current at the closing balance sheet date of the reporting period, the entity should recognise

an opening deferred tax liability of CU450, and there would be no impact on profit or loss (CU450 – CU450). On the other hand, if the comparatives are stated as proposed in D5, the restated opening deferred tax liability would be CU300 ((CU1,000 – CU500) × 0.3) × 100% + CU150). Accordingly, the entity should recognise a loss of CU150 (CU450 – CU300), which is the loss of purchasing power on the tax base in the reporting period.

BC24 The IFRIC observed that paragraph 18 of Appendix A to IAS 12 explains:[2]

Non monetary assets are restated in terms of the measuring unit current at the balance sheet date (see IAS 29 *Financial Reporting in Hyperinflationary Economies*) and no equivalent adjustment is made for tax purposes. (notes: (1) *the deferred tax is charged in the income statement;[3] and (2) if, in addition to the restatement, the non monetary assets are also revalued, the deferred tax relating to the revaluation is charged to equity[4] and the deferred tax relating to the restatement is charged in the income statement.)*

BC25 Consequently, the IFRIC confirmed its conclusion that restatement of comparative deferred tax items would require an entity, first, to remeasure its deferred tax items on the basis of the financial statements of the previous reporting period, which have been restated by applying a general price index reflecting the price level at the end of that period. Secondly, the entity should restate those calculated deferred tax items by the change in the general price level for the reporting period.

---

2   Paragraph 18 has been amended as a consequence of the changes made by IAS 1 *Presentation of Financial Statements* (as revised in 2007).

3   IAS 1 (revised 2007) requires an entity to present all income and expense items in one statement of comprehensive income or in two statements (a separate income statement and a statement of comprehensive income).

4   Under IAS 1 (revised 2007), such effect is recognised in other comprehensive income.

Interpretation 9
Reassessment of Embedded Derivatives

(Compiled October 2009)

Contents

Compilation Details

Comparison with IFRIC 9

UIG Interpretation 9
Reassessment of Embedded Derivatives

	Paragraphs
References	
Background	1 – 2
Scope	3 – 5
Issue	6
Consensus	7 – 8
Application	Aus8.1 – Aus8.4
Effective date and transition	10 – 11

Basis for Conclusions on IFRIC 9

UIG Interpretation 9 *Reassessment of Embedded Derivatives* (as amended) is set out in paragraphs 1 – 11. Interpretations are listed in Australian Accounting Standard AASB 1048 *Interpretation and Application of Standards*. In the absence of explicit guidance, AASB 108 *Accounting Policies, Changes in Accounting Estimates and Errors* provides a basis for selecting and applying accounting policies.

Compilation Details

UIG Interpretation 9 *Reassessment of Embedded Derivatives* as amended

This compiled Interpretation applies to annual reporting periods beginning on or after 1 July 2009. It takes into account amendments up to and including 21 May 2009 and was prepared on 8 October 2009 by the staff of the Australian Accounting Standards Board (AASB).

This compilation is not a separate Interpretation issued by the AASB. Instead, it is a representation of Interpretation 9 (April 2006) as amended by other pronouncements, which are listed in the Table below.

Table of Pronouncements

Pronouncement	Month issued	Application date *(annual reporting periods … on or after …)*	Application, saving or transitional provisions
Interpretation 9	Apr 2006	*(beginning)* 1 Jun 2006	
AASB 2007-8	Sep 2007	*(beginning)* 1 Jan 2009	see (a) below
AASB 2008-3	Mar 2008	*(beginning)* 1 Jul 2009	see (b) below
AASB 2009-3	Apr 2009	*(ending)* 30 Jun 2009	see (c) below
AASB 2009-4	May 2009	*(beginning)* 1 Jul 2009	see (d) below

(a) Entities may elect to apply this Standard to annual reporting periods beginning on or after 1 January 2005 but before 1 January 2009 provided that AASB 101 *Presentation of Financial Statements* (September 2007) is also applied to such periods.

(b) Entities may elect to apply this Standard to annual reporting periods beginning on or after 30 June 2007 but before 1 July 2009 provided that AASB 3 *Business Combinations* (March 2008) and AASB 127 *Consolidated and Separate Financial Statements* (March 2008) are also applied to such periods.

(c) Entities are not permitted to apply this Standard to earlier annual reporting periods.

(d) Entities may elect to apply this Standard, or its amendments to individual pronouncements, to annual reporting periods beginning on or after 1 January 2005 but before 1 July 2009.

Table of Amendments

Paragraph affected	How affected	By ... [paragraph]
5	footnote added	AASB 2008-3 [81]
	amended	AASB 2009-4 [12]
7	amended	AASB 2009-3 [7]
7A	added	AASB 2009-3 [7]
Aus8.1	amended	AASB 2007-8 [7, 8]
Aus8.4	amended	AASB 2007-8 [8]
Heading after Aus8.4	amended	AASB 2009-3 [8]
10	added	AASB 2009-3 [8]
11	added	AASB 2009-4 [13]

Comparison with IFRIC 9

Interpretation 9 and IFRIC 9

UIG Interpretation 9 *Reassessment of Embedded Derivatives* as amended incorporates International Financial Reporting Interpretations Committee Interpretation IFRIC 9 *Reassessment of Embedded Derivatives*, issued by the International Accounting Standards Board. Paragraphs that have been added to this Interpretation (and do not appear in the text of IFRIC 9) are identified with the prefix "Aus", followed by the number of the preceding IFRIC paragraph and decimal numbering.

Compliance with IFRIC 9

Entities that comply with Interpretation 9 as amended will simultaneously be in compliance with IFRIC 9 as amended.

Interpretation 9

UIG Interpretation 9 was issued in April 2006.

This compiled version of Interpretation 9 applies to annual reporting periods beginning on or after 1 July 2009. It incorporates relevant amendments contained in other AASB pronouncements up to and including 21 May 2009 (see Compilation Details).

Interpretations

Urgent Issues Group
Interpretation 9
Reassessment of Embedded Derivatives

References

Accounting Standard AASB 1 *First-time Adoption of Australian Equivalents to International Financial Reporting Standards*

Accounting Standard AASB 3 *Business Combinations*

Accounting Standard AASB 139 *Financial Instruments: Recognition and Measurement*

Background

1   Accounting Standard AASB 139 *Financial Instruments: Recognition and Measurement* paragraph 10 describes an embedded derivative as 'a component of a hybrid (combined) instrument that also includes a non-derivative host contract – with the effect that some of the cash flows of the combined instrument vary in a way similar to a stand-alone derivative.'

2   AASB 139 paragraph 11 requires an embedded derivative to be separated from the host contract and accounted for as a derivative if, and only if:

     (a)   the economic characteristics and risks of the embedded derivative are not closely related to the economic characteristics and risks of the host contract;

     (b)   a separate instrument with the same terms as the embedded derivative would meet the definition of a derivative; and

     (c)   the hybrid (combined) instrument is not measured at fair value with changes in fair value recognised in profit or loss (i.e. a derivative that is embedded in a financial asset or financial liability at fair value through profit or loss is not separated).

Scope

3   Subject to paragraphs 4 and 5 below, this Interpretation applies to all embedded derivatives within the scope of AASB 139.

4   This Interpretation does not address remeasurement issues arising from a reassessment of embedded derivatives.

5   This Interpretation does not apply to embedded derivatives in contracts acquired in:

     (a)   a business combination (as defined in AASB 3 *Business Combinations* (as revised in 2008));

     (b)   a combination of entities or businesses under common control as described in paragraphs B1-B4 of AASB 3 (revised 2008); or

     (c)   the formation of a joint venture as defined in AASB 131 *Interests in Joint Ventures* or their possible reassessment at the date of acquisition.[1]

Issue

6   AASB 139 requires an entity, when it first becomes a party to a contract, to assess whether any embedded derivatives contained in the contract are required to be separated from the host contract and accounted for as derivatives under the Standard. This Interpretation addresses the following issues:

     (a)   Does AASB 139 require such an assessment to be made only when the entity first becomes a party to the contract, or should the assessment be reconsidered throughout the life of the contract?

---

1   AASB 3 (as revised in March 2008) addresses the acquisition of contracts with embedded derivatives in a business combination.

(b)   Should a first-time adopter make its assessment on the basis of the conditions that existed when the entity first became a party to the contract, or those prevailing when the entity adopts Australian equivalents to IFRSs for the first time?

Consensus

7   An entity shall assess whether an embedded derivative is required to be separated from the host contract and accounted for as a derivative when the entity first becomes a party to the contract. Subsequent reassessment is prohibited unless there is either (a) a change in the terms of the contract that significantly modifies the cash flows that otherwise would be required under the contract or (b) a reclassification of a financial asset out of the fair value through profit or loss category, in which cases an assessment is required. An entity determines whether a modification to cash flows is significant by considering the extent to which the expected future cash flows associated with the embedded derivative, the host contract or both have changed and whether the change is significant relative to the previously expected cash flows on the contract.

7A   The assessment whether an embedded derivative is required to be separated from the host contract and accounted for as a derivative on reclassification of a financial asset out of the fair value through profit or loss category in accordance with paragraph 7 shall be made on the basis of the circumstances that existed on the later date of:

(a)   when the entity first became a party to the contract; and

(b)   a change in the terms of the contract that significantly modified the cash flows that otherwise would have been required under the contract.

For the purpose of this assessment paragraph 11(c) of AASB 139 shall not be applied (i.e. the hybrid (combined) contract shall be treated as if it had not been measured at fair value with changes in fair value recognised in profit or loss). If an entity is unable to make this assessment the hybrid (combined) contract shall remain classified as at fair value through profit or loss in its entirety.

8   A first-time adopter shall assess whether an embedded derivative is required to be separated from the host contract and accounted for as a derivative on the basis of the conditions that existed at the later of the date it first became a party to the contract and the date a reassessment is required by paragraph 7.

Application

Aus8.1   This Interpretation applies to:

(a)   each entity that is required to prepare financial reports in accordance with Part 2M.3 of the *Corporations Act 2001* and that is a reporting entity;

(b)   general purpose financial statements of each other reporting entity; and

(c)   financial statements that are, or are held out to be, general purpose financial statements.

Aus8.2   This Interpretation applies to annual reporting periods beginning on or after 1 June 2006.

[Note: For application dates of paragraphs changed or added by an amending pronouncement, see Compilation Details.]

Aus8.3   This Interpretation may be applied to annual reporting periods beginning on or after 1 January 2005 but before 1 June 2006, permitting early application in the context of adopting all Australian equivalents to International Financial Reporting Standards for such periods. Early application is encouraged. An entity that is required to prepare financial reports in accordance with Part 2M.3 of the Corporations Act may apply this Interpretation to such annual reporting periods when an election has been made in accordance with subsection 334(5) of the Corporations Act in relation to AASB 1048 *Interpretation and Application of Standards*. When an entity applies this Interpretation to such an annual reporting period, it shall disclose that fact.

Aus8.4   The requirements specified in this Interpretation apply to the financial statements where information resulting from their application is material in accordance with AASB 1031 *Materiality*.

Interpretations

Effective date and transition

9   [Deleted by the UIG]

10   AASB 2009-3 *Amendments to Australian Accounting Standards – Embedded Derivatives* issued in April 2009 amended paragraph 7 and added paragraph 7A. An entity shall apply those amendments for annual reporting periods ending on or after 30 June 2009.

11   Paragraph 5 was amended by AASB 2009-4 *Amendments to Australian Accounting Standards arising from the Annual Improvements Project*, issued in May 2009. An entity shall apply that amendment prospectively for annual reporting periods beginning on or after 1 July 2009. If an entity applies AASB 3 (as revised in 2008) for an earlier period, it shall apply the amendment for that earlier period and disclose that fact.

Basis for Conclusions on IFRIC 9

This IFRIC Basis for Conclusions accompanies, but is not part of, UIG Interpretation 9. The UIG considers that this Basis for Conclusions is an essential feature of the Interpretation. An IFRIC Basis for Conclusions may be amended to reflect the requirements of the UIG Interpretation and AASB Accounting Standards where they differ from the corresponding International pronouncements.

Introduction

BC1   This Basis for Conclusions summarises the IFRIC's considerations in reaching its consensus. Individual IFRIC members gave greater weight to some factors than to others.

BC2   As explained below, the IFRIC was informed that uncertainty existed over certain aspects of the requirements of IAS 39 *Financial Instruments: Recognition and Measurement* relating to the reassessment of embedded derivatives. The IFRIC published proposals on the subject in March 2005 as D15 *Reassessment of Embedded Derivatives* and developed IFRIC 9 after considering the thirty comment letters received.

BC3   IAS 39 requires an entity, when it first becomes a party to a contract, to assess whether any embedded derivative contained in the contract needs to be separated from the host contract and accounted for as a derivative under the Standard. However, the issue arises whether IAS 39 requires an entity to continue to carry out this assessment after it first becomes a party to a contract, and if so, with what frequency. The Standard is silent on this issue and the IFRIC was informed that as a result there was a risk of divergence in practice.

BC4   The question is relevant, for example, when the terms of the embedded derivative do not change but market conditions change and the market was the principal factor in determining whether the host contract and embedded derivative are closely related. Instances when this might arise are given in paragraph AG33(d) of IAS 39. Paragraph AG33(d) states that an embedded foreign currency derivative is closely related to the host contract provided it is not leveraged, does not contain an option feature, and requires payments denominated in one of the following currencies:

(a)   the functional currency of any substantial party to that contract;

(b)   the currency in which the price of the related good or service that is acquired or delivered is routinely denominated in commercial transactions around the world (such as the US dollar for crude oil transactions); or

(c)   a currency that is commonly used in contracts to purchase or sell non-financial items in the economic environment in which the transaction takes place (e.g. a relatively stable and liquid currency that is commonly used in local business transactions or external trade).

BC5   Any of the currencies specified in (a)–(c) above may change. Assume that when an entity first became a party to a contract, it assessed the contract as containing an embedded derivative that was closely related (because it was in one of the three categories in paragraph BC4) and hence not accounted for separately. Assume that subsequently market conditions change and that if the entity were to reassess the contract under the changed circumstances it would conclude that the embedded derivative is not closely related and therefore requires separate accounting. (The converse could also arise.) The issue is whether the entity should make such a reassessment.

BC5A   In 2009 the International Accounting Standards Board observed that the changes to the definition of a business combination in the revisions to IFRS 3 *Business Combinations* (as revised in 2008) caused the accounting for the formation of a joint venture by the venturer to be within the scope of IFRIC 9. Similarly, the Board noted that common control transactions might raise the same issue depending on which level of the group reporting entity is assessing the combination.

BC5B   The Board observed that during the development of the revised IFRS 3, it did not discuss whether it intended IFRIC 9 to apply to those types of transactions. The Board did not intend to change existing practice by including such transactions within the scope of IFRIC 9. Accordingly, in *Improvements* to IFRSs issued in April 2009, the Board amended paragraph 5 of IFRIC 9 to clarify that IFRIC 9 does not apply to embedded derivatives in contracts acquired in a combination between entities or businesses under common control or the formation of a joint venture.

BC5C   Some respondents to the exposure draft *Post-implementation Revisions to IFRIC Interpretations* issued in January 2009 expressed the view that investments in associates should also be excluded from the scope of IFRIC 9. Respondents noted that paragraphs 20–23 of IAS 28 *Investments in Associates* state that the concepts underlying the procedures used in accounting for the acquisition of a subsidiary are also adopted in accounting for the acquisition of an investment in an associate.

BC5D   In its redeliberations, the Board confirmed its previous decision that no scope exemption in IFRIC 9 was needed for investments in associates. However, in response to the comments received, the Board noted that reassessment of embedded derivatives in contracts held by an associate is not required by IFRIC 9 in any event. The investment in the associate is the asset the investor controls and recognises, not the underlying assets and liabilities of the associate.

Reassessment of embedded derivatives

BC6   The IFRIC noted that the rationale for the requirement in IAS 39 to separate embedded derivatives is that an entity should not be able to circumvent the recognition and measurement requirements for derivatives merely by embedding a derivative in a non-derivative financial instrument or other contract (for xample, by embedding a commodity forward in a debt instrument). Changes in external circumstances (such as those set out in paragraph BC5) are not ways to circumvent the Standard. The IFRIC therefore concluded that reassessment was not appropriate for such changes.

BC7   The IFRIC noted that as a practical expedient IAS 39 does not require the separation of embedded derivatives that are closely related. Many financial instruments contain embedded derivatives. Separating all of these embedded derivatives would be burdensome for entities. The IFRIC noted that requiring entities to reassess embedded derivatives in all hybrid instruments could be onerous because frequent monitoring would be required. Market conditions and other factors affecting embedded derivatives would have to be monitored continuously to ensure timely identification of a change in circumstances and amendment of the accounting treatment accordingly. For example, if the functional currency of the counterparty changes during the reporting period so that the contract is no longer denominated in a currency of one of the parties to the contract, then a reassessment of the hybrid instrument would be required at the date of change to ensure the correct accounting treatment in future.

BC8 The IFRIC also recognised that although IAS 39 is silent on the issue of reassessment it gives relevant guidance when it states that for the types of contracts covered by paragraph AG33(b) the assessment of whether an embedded derivative is closely related is required only at inception. Paragraph AG33(b) states:

> An embedded floor or cap on the interest rate on a debt contract or insurance contract is closely related to the host contract, provided the cap is at or above the market rate of interest and the floor is at or below the market rate of interest *when the contract is issued*, and the cap or floor is not leveraged in relation to the host contract. Similarly, provisions included in a contract to purchase or sell an asset (e.g. a commodity) that establish a cap and a floor on the price to be paid or received for the asset are closely related to the host contract if both the cap and floor were out of the money *at inception* and are not leveraged. (Emphasis added)

BC9 The IFRIC also considered the implications of requiring subsequent reassessment. For example, assume that an entity, when it first becomes a party to a contract, separately recognises a host asset and an embedded derivative liability. If the entity were required to reassess whether the embedded derivative was to be accounted for separately and if the entity concluded some time after becoming a party to the contract that the derivative was no longer required to be separated, then questions of recognition and measurement would arise. In the above circumstances, the IFRIC identified the following possibilities:

 (a) the entity could remove the derivative from its balance sheet and recognise in profit or loss a corresponding gain or loss. This would lead to recognition of a gain or loss even though there had been no transaction and no change in the value of the total contract or its components.

 (b) the entity could leave the derivative as a separate item in the balance sheet. The issue would then arise as to when the item was to be removed from the balance sheet. Should it be amortised (and, if so, how would the amortisation affect the effective interest rate of the asset), or should it be derecognised only when the asset is derecognised?

 (c) the entity could combine the derivative (which is recognised at fair value) with the asset (which is recognised at amortised cost). This would alter both the carrying amount of the asset and its effective interest rate even though there had been no change in the economics of the whole contract. In some cases, it could also result in a negative effective interest rate.

  The IFRIC noted that, under its view that subsequent reassessment is appropriate only when there has been a change in the terms of the contract that significantly modifies the cash flows that otherwise would be required by the contract, the above issues do not arise.

BC10 The IFRIC noted that IAS 39 requires an entity to assess whether an embedded derivative needs to be separated from the host contract and accounted for as a derivative when it first becomes a party to a contract. Consequently, if an entity purchases a contract that contains an embedded derivative it assesses whether the embedded derivative needs to be separated and accounted for as a derivative on the basis of conditions at that date.

BC11 The IFRIC considered an alternative approach of making reassessment optional. It decided against this approach because it would reduce comparability of financial information. Also, the IFRIC noted that this approach would be inconsistent with the embedded derivative requirements in IAS 39 that either require or prohibit separation but do not give an option. Accordingly, the IFRIC concluded that reassessment should not be optional.

BC11A Following the issue of *Reclassification of Financial Assets* (Amendments to IAS 39 and IFRS 7) in October 2008 constituents told the International Accounting Standards Board that there was uncertainty about the interaction between those amendments and IFRIC 9 regarding the assessment of embedded derivatives.

Some of those taking part in the public round-table meetings held by the Board and the US Financial Accounting Standards Board in November and December 2008 in response to the global financial crisis also raised that issue. They asked the Board to consider further amendments to IFRSs to prevent any practice developing whereby, following reclassification of a financial asset, embedded derivatives that should be separately accounted for are not.

BC11B   In accordance with paragraph 7 of IFRIC 9, assessment of the separation of an embedded derivative after an entity first became a party to the contract is prohibited unless there is a change in the terms of the contract that significantly modifies the cash flows that otherwise would be required under the contract. Constituents told the Board that some might interpret IFRIC 9 as prohibiting the separation of an embedded derivative on the reclassification of a hybrid (combined) financial asset out of the fair value through profit or loss category unless there is a concurrent change in its contractual terms.

BC11C   The Board noted that when IFRIC 9 was issued, reclassifications out of the fair value through profit or loss category were prohibited and hence IFRIC 9 did not consider the possibility of such reclassifications.

BC11D   The Board was clear that it did not intend the requirements to separate particular embedded derivatives from hybrid (combined) financial instruments to be circumvented as a result of the amendments to IAS 39 issued in October 2008. Therefore, the Board decided to clarify IFRIC 9 by amending paragraph 7.

BC11E   The Board believes that unless assessment and separation of embedded derivatives is done when reclassifying hybrid (combined) financial assets out of the fair value through profit or loss category, structuring opportunities are created that the embedded derivative accounting requirements in IAS 39 were intended to prevent. This is because, by initially classifying a hybrid (combined) financial instrument as at fair value through profit or loss and later reclassifying it into another category, an entity can circumvent requirements for separation of an embedded derivative. The Board also noted that the only appropriate accounting for derivative instruments is to be included in the fair value through profit or loss category.

BC11F   The Board decided also to clarify that an assessment on reclassification should be made on the basis of the circumstances that existed when the entity first became a party to the contract, or, if later, the date of a change in the terms of the contract that significantly modified the cash flows that otherwise would be required under the contract. This date is consistent with one of the stated purposes of embedded derivative accounting (i.e. preventing circumvention of the recognition and measurement requirements for derivatives) and provides some degree of comparability. Furthermore, because the terms of the embedded features in the hybrid (combined) financial instrument have not changed, the Board did not see a reason for arriving at an answer on separation different from what would have been the case at initial recognition of the hybrid (combined) contract (or a later date of a change in the terms of the contract). In addition, the Board clarified that paragraph 11(c) of IAS 39 should not be applied in assessing whether an embedded derivative requires separation. The Board noted that before reclassification the hybrid (combined) financial instrument is necessarily classified at fair value through profit or loss so that for the purpose of the assessment on reclassification this criterion is not relevant but would, if applied for assessments made in accordance with paragraph 7A of the Interpretation, always result in no embedded derivative being separated.

First-time adopters of IFRSs

BC12   In the Implementation Guidance with IFRS 1 *First-time Adoption of International Financial Reporting Standards*, paragraph IG55 states:

> When IAS 39 requires an entity to separate an embedded derivative from a host contract, the initial carrying amounts of the components at the date when the instrument first satisfies the recognition criteria in IAS 39 reflect circumstances at that date (IAS 39, paragraph 11). If the entity cannot determine the initial carrying amounts of the embedded derivative and host contract reliably, it treats the entire combined contract as a financial instrument held for trading (IAS 39, paragraph 12). This results in fair value measurement (except when the entity cannot determine a reliable fair value, see IAS 39, paragraph 46(c)), with changes in fair value recognised in profit or loss.

BC13   This guidance reflects the principle in IFRS 1 that a first-time adopter should apply IFRSs as if they had been in place from initial recognition. This is consistent with the general principle used in IFRSs of full retrospective application of Standards. The IFRIC noted that the date of initial recognition referred to in paragraph IG55 is the date when the entity first became a party to the contract and not the date of first-time adoption of IFRSs. Accordingly, the IFRIC concluded that IFRS 1 requires an entity to assess whether an embedded derivative is required to be separated from the host contract and accounted for as a derivative on the basis of conditions at the date when the entity first became a party to the contract and not those at the date of first-time adoption.

Interpretation 10
Interim Financial Reporting and Impairment

(Compiled November 2009)

Contents

Compilation Details

Comparison with IFRIC 10

AASB Interpretation 10
Interim Financial Reporting and Impairment

Paragraphs

References

Background   1 – 2

Issue   3 – 7

Consensus   8 – 9

Application   Aus9.1 – Aus9.4

Transition   10

Basis for Conclusions on IFRIC 10

AASB Interpretation 10 *Interim Financial Reporting and Impairment* (as amended) is set out in paragraphs 1 – 10. Interpretations are listed in Australian Accounting Standard AASB 1048 *Interpretation and Application of Standards*. In the absence of explicit guidance, AASB 108 *Accounting Policies, Changes in Accounting Estimates and Errors* provides a basis for selecting and applying accounting policies.

Compilation Details

AASB Interpretation 10 *Interim Financial Reporting and Impairment* as amended

This compiled Interpretation applies to annual reporting periods beginning on or after 1 January 2009 that end on or after 30 June 2009. It takes into account amendments up to and including 5 October 2009 and was prepared on 5 November 2009 by the staff of the Australian Accounting Standards Board (AASB).

This compilation is not a separate Interpretation issued by the AASB. Instead, it is a representation of Interpretation 10 (September 2006) as amended by other pronouncements, which are listed in the Table below.

Table of Pronouncements

Pronouncement	Month issued	Application date *(annual reporting periods … on or after …)*	Application, saving or transitional provisions
Interpretation 10	Sep 2006	*(beginning)* 1 Nov 2006	see (a) below
AASB 2007-8	Sep 2007	*(beginning)* 1 Jan 2009	see (b) below
AASB 2007-10	Dec 2007	*(beginning)* 1 Jan 2009	see (b) below
Erratum	Oct 2009	*(beginning)* 1 Jan 2009 and *(ending)* 30 Jun 2009	see (c) below

(a) Entities may elect to apply this Interpretation to annual reporting periods beginning on or after 1 January 2005 but before 1 November 2006.

(b) Entities may elect to apply this Standard to annual reporting periods beginning on or after 1 January 2005 but before 1 January 2009, provided that AASB 101 *Presentation of Financial Statements* (September 2007) is also applied to such periods.

(c) Entities may elect to apply this Erratum to annual reporting periods beginning on or after 1 January 2005 but before 1 January 2009 and to periods beginning on or after 1 January 2009 that end before 30 June 2009, provided that AASB 2009-6 *Amendments to Australian Accounting Standards* is also applied to such periods.

Table of Amendments

Paragraph affected	How affected	By ... [paragraph]
1	amended	AASB 2007-8 [6, 154]
	amended	Erratum, Oct 2009 [11]
2	amended	AASB 2007-10 [102]
3	amended	AASB 2007-10 [103]
7	amended	AASB 2007-8 [6]
	amended	Erratum, Oct 2009 [11]
Aus9.1	amended	AASB 2007-8 [7, 8]
Aus9.4	amended	AASB 2007-8 [8]

Comparison with IFRIC 10

AASB Interpretation 10 *Interim Financial Reporting and Impairment* as amended incorporates International Financial Reporting Interpretations Committee Interpretation IFRIC 10 *Interim Financial Reporting and Impairment*, issued by the International Accounting Standards Board. Paragraphs that have been added to this Interpretation (and do not appear in the text of IFRIC 10) are identified with the prefix "Aus", followed by the number of the preceding IFRIC paragraph and decimal numbering.

Entities that comply with Interpretation 10 as amended will simultaneously be in compliance with IFRIC 10 as amended.

Interpretation 10

AASB Interpretation 10 was issued in September 2006.

This compiled version of Interpretation 10 applies to annual reporting periods beginning on or after 1 January 2009 that end on or after 30 June 2009. It incorporates relevant amendments contained in other AASB pronouncements up to and including 5 October 2009 (see Compilation Details).

Australian Accounting Standards Board

Interpretation 10

Interim Financial Reporting And Impairment

References

Accounting Standard AASB 134 *Interim Financial Reporting*

Accounting Standard AASB 136 *Impairment of Assets*

Accounting Standard AASB 139 *Financial Instruments: Recognition and Measurement*

Background

1   An entity is required to assess goodwill for impairment at the end of each reporting period, to assess investments in equity instruments and in financial assets carried at cost for impairment at the end of each reporting period and, if required, to recognise an impairment loss at that date in accordance with Accounting Standards AASB 136 *Impairment of Assets*

and AASB 139 *Financial Instruments: Recognition and Measurement*. However, at the end of a subsequent reporting period, conditions may have so changed that the impairment loss would have been reduced or avoided had the impairment assessment been made only at that date. This Interpretation provides guidance on whether such impairment losses should ever be reversed.

2   The Interpretation addresses the interaction between the requirements of AASB 134 *Interim Financial Reporting* and the recognition of impairment losses on goodwill in AASB 136 and certain financial assets in AASB 139, and the effect of that interaction on subsequent interim and annual financial statements.

Issue

3   AASB 134 paragraph 28 requires an entity to apply the same accounting policies in its interim financial statements as are applied in its annual financial statements. It also states that 'the frequency of an entity's reporting (annual, half yearly, or quarterly) shall not affect the measurement of its annual results. To achieve that objective, measurements for interim reporting purposes shall be made on an annual reporting period-to-date basis.'

4   AASB 136 paragraph 124 states that 'An impairment loss recognised for goodwill shall not be reversed in a subsequent period.'

5   AASB 139 paragraph 69 states that 'Impairment losses recognised in profit or loss for an investment in an equity instrument classified as available for sale shall not be reversed through profit or loss.'

6   AASB 139 paragraph 66 requires that impairment losses for financial assets carried at cost (such as an impairment loss on an unquoted equity instrument that is not carried at fair value because its fair value cannot be reliably measured) should not be reversed.

7   The Interpretation addresses the following issue:

Should an entity reverse impairment losses recognised in an interim period on goodwill and investments in equity instruments and in financial assets carried at cost if a loss would not have been recognised, or a smaller loss would have been recognised, had an impairment assessment been made only at the end of a subsequent reporting period?

Consensus

8   An entity shall not reverse an impairment loss recognised in a previous interim period in respect of goodwill or an investment in either an equity instrument or a financial asset carried at cost.

9   An entity shall not extend this consensus by analogy to other areas of potential conflict between AASB 134 and other Australian Accounting Standards.

Application

Aus9.1   This Interpretation applies to:

(a)   each entity that is required to prepare financial reports in accordance with Part 2M.3 of the *Corporations Act 2001* and that is a reporting entity;

(b)   general purpose financial statements of each other reporting entity; and

(c)   financial statements that are, or are held out to be, general purpose financial statements.

Aus9.2   This Interpretation applies to annual reporting periods beginning on or after 1 November 2006.

[Note: For application dates of paragraphs changed or added by an amending pronouncement, see Compilation Details.]

Aus9.3   This Interpretation may be applied to annual reporting periods beginning on or after 1 January 2005 but before 1 November 2006, permitting early application in the context of adopting all Australian equivalents to International Financial Reporting Standards for such periods. Early application is encouraged. An entity that is required to prepare financial reports in accordance with Part 2M.3 of the Corporations Act may apply this Interpretation to such annual reporting periods when an election has been made in accordance with subsection 334(5) of the Corporations Act in relation to AASB 1048 *Interpretation and Application of Standards*. When an entity applies this Interpretation to such an annual reporting period, it shall disclose that fact.

Aus9.4   The requirements specified in this Interpretation apply to the financial statements where information resulting from their application is material in accordance with AASB 1031 *Materiality*.

Transition

10   An entity shall apply the Interpretation to goodwill prospectively from the date at which it first applied AASB 136; it shall apply the Interpretation to investments in equity instruments or in financial assets carried at cost prospectively from the date at which it first applied the measurement criteria of AASB 139.

Basis for Conclusions on IFRIC 10

This IFRIC Basis for Conclusions accompanies, but is not part of, AASB Interpretation 10. The AASB considers that this Basis for Conclusions is an essential feature of the Interpretation. An IFRIC Basis for Conclusions may be amended to reflect the requirements of the AASB Interpretation and AASB Accounting Standards where they differ from the corresponding International pronouncements.

BC1   This Basis for Conclusions summarises the IFRIC's considerations in reaching its consensus. Individual IFRIC members gave greater weight to some factors than to others.

BC2   IAS 34 requires an entity to apply the same accounting policies in its interim financial statements as it applies in its annual financial statements. For annual financial statements, IAS 36 prohibits an entity from reversing an impairment loss on goodwill that it recognised in a prior annual period. Similarly, IAS 39 prohibits an entity from reversing in a subsequent annual period an impairment loss on an investment in an equity instrument or in a financial asset carried at cost. These requirements might suggest that an entity should not reverse in a subsequent interim period an impairment loss on goodwill or an investment in an equity instrument or in a financial asset carried at cost that it had recognised in a prior interim period. Such impairment losses would not be reversed even if no loss, or a smaller loss, would have been recognised had the impairment been assessed only at the end of the subsequent interim period.

BC3   However, IAS 34 requires year-to-date measures in interim financial statements. This requirement might suggest that an entity should reverse in a subsequent interim period an impairment loss it recognised in a prior interim period. Such impairment losses would be reversed if no loss, or a smaller loss, would have been recognised had the impairment been assessed only at the end of the subsequent interim period.

BC4   The IFRIC released Draft Interpretation D18 *Interim Financial Reporting and Impairment* for public comment in January 2006. It received more than 50 letters in response.

BC5   The IFRIC noted that many of the respondents believed that in attempting to address contradictions between standards, D18 was beyond the scope of the IFRIC. Some believed that the issue addressed could be better resolved by amending IAS 34. Before finalising its views, the IFRIC asked the International Accounting Standards Board to consider this point. The Board, however, did not wish to amend IAS 34 and asked the IFRIC to continue with its Interpretation.

BC6   Respondents to D18 were divided on whether the proposed Interpretation should prohibit the reversal of impairment losses on goodwill or investments in equity instruments or in financial assets carried at cost that had been recognised in interim periods. The IFRIC considered these responses but maintained its view that such losses should not be reversed in subsequent financial statements. The IFRIC observed that the wide divergence of views evident from respondents' letters underlined the need for additional guidance and it therefore decided to issue the Interpretation with few changes from D18.

BC7 The IFRIC considered the example of Entity A and Entity B, which each hold the same equity investment with the same acquisition cost. Entity A prepares quarterly interim financial statements and Entity B prepares half yearly financial statements. The entities have the same year end. The IFRIC noted that if there was a significant decline in the fair value of the equity instrument below its cost in the first quarter, Entity A would recognise an impairment loss in its first quarter interim financial statements. However, if the fair value of the equity instrument subsequently recovered, so that by the half year date there had not been a significant decline in fair value below cost, Entity B would not recognise an impairment loss in its half yearly financial statements if it tested for impairment only at its half-yearly reporting dates. Therefore, unless Entity A reversed the impairment loss that had been recognised in an earlier interim period, the frequency of reporting would affect the measurement of its annual results when compared with Entity B's approach. The IFRIC also noted that the recognition of an impairment loss could similarly be affected by the timing of the financial year ends of the two entities.

BC8 The IFRIC noted paragraph B36 of Appendix B accompanying IAS 34, which provides examples of applying the general recognition and measurement principles of that standard and states that IAS 34 requires an entity to apply the same impairment testing, recognition, and reversal criteria at an interim date as it would at the end of its financial year.

BC9 The IFRIC concluded that the prohibitions on reversals of recognised impairment losses on goodwill in IAS 36 and on investments in equity instruments and in financial assets carried at cost in IAS 39 should take precedence over the more general statement in IAS 34 regarding the frequency of an entity's reporting not affecting the measurement of its annual results.

BC10 Furthermore, the IFRIC concluded that the rationale for the non reversal of impairment losses relating to goodwill and investments in equity instruments, as set out in paragraph BC189 of IAS 36 and paragraph BC130 of IAS 39, applies at both interim and annual reporting dates.

BC11 The IFRIC considered a concern that this conclusion could be extended to other areas of potential conflict between IAS 34 and other standards. The IFRIC has not studied those areas and therefore has not identified any general principles that might apply both to the Interpretation and to other areas of potential conflict. The IFRIC therefore added a prohibition against extending the consensus by analogy to other areas of potential conflict between IAS 34 and other standards.

BC12 D18 proposed fully retrospective application. A number of comment letters stated that this could be read as being more onerous than the first time adoption requirements of IAS 36. The IFRIC revised the wording of the transition requirements to make clear that the Interpretation should not be applied to periods before an entity's adoption of IAS 36 in the case of goodwill impairments and IAS 39 in the case of impairments of investments in equity instruments or in financial assets carried at cost.

Interpretation 12
Service Concession Arrangements

(Compiled November 2009)

Contents

Compilation details

Comparison with IFRIC 12

AASB Interpretation 12
Service Concession Arrangements

Paragraphs

References

Background   1 – 3

Scope   4 – 9

Issues   10

Consensus

Treatment of the operator's rights over the infrastructure   11

Recognition and measurement of arrangement consideration   12 – 13

Construction or upgrade services   14

Consideration given by the grantor to the operator   15 – 19

Operation services   20

Contractual obligations to restore the infrastructure
to a specified level of serviceability   21

Borrowing costs incurred by the operator   22

Financial asset   23 – 25

Intangible asset   26

Items provided to the operator by the grantor   27

Application   Aus27.1 – Aus27.4

Transition   29 – 30

Appendices

A. Application Guidance   AG1 – AG8

B. Amendments to AASB 1 and to Other Interpretations   B1 – B3

Information notes

1. Accounting Framework for Public-to-Private Service Arrangements

2. References to AASB Pronouncements that Apply to Typical Types
   of Public-to-Private Arrangements

Illustrative Examples

Basis for Conclusions on IFRIC 12

AASB Interpretation 12 *Service Concession Arrangements* (as amended) is set out in paragraphs 1 – 30 and
Appendix A. Interpretations are listed in Australian Accounting Standard AASB 1048 *Interpretation and
Application of Standards*. In the absence of explicit guidance, AASB 108 *Accounting Policies, Changes
in Accounting Estimates and Errors* provides a basis for selecting and applying accounting policies.

Compilation Details

AASB Interpretation 12 *Service Concession Arrangements* as amended

This compiled Interpretation applies to annual reporting periods beginning on or after 1 January 2009 that end on or after 30 June 2009. It takes into account amendments up to and including 25 June 2009 and was prepared on 9 November 2009 by the staff of the Australian Accounting Standards Board (AASB).

This compilation is not a separate Interpretation issued by the AASB. Instead, it is a representation of Interpretation 12 (February 2007) as amended by other pronouncements, which are listed in the Table below.

Table of Pronouncements

Pronouncement	Month issued	Application date *(annual reporting periods ... on or after ...)*	Application, saving or transitional provisions
Interpretation 12	Feb 2007	*(beginning)* 1 Jan 2008	see (a) below
AASB 2007-6	Jun 2007	*(beginning)* 1 Jan 2009	see (b) below
AASB 2007-8	Sep 2007	*(beginning)* 1 Jan 2009	see (c) below
AASB 2009-6	Jun 2009	*(beginning)* 1 Jan 2009 and *(ending)* 30 Jun 2009	see (d) below

(a)   Entities may elect to apply this Interpretation to annual reporting periods beginning on or after 1 January 2005 but before 1 January 2008.

(b)   Entities may elect to apply this Standard to annual reporting periods beginning on or after 1 January 2005 but before 1 January 2009, provided that AASB 123 *Borrowing Costs* (June 2007) is also applied to such periods.

(c)   Entities may elect to apply this Standard to annual reporting periods beginning on or after 1 January 2005 but before 1 January 2009, provided that AASB 101 *Presentation of Financial Statements* (September 2007) is also applied to such periods.

(d)   Entities may elect to apply this Standard to annual reporting periods beginning on or after 1 January 2005 but before 1 January 2009, provided that AASB 101 *Presentation of Financial Statements* (September 2007) is also applied to such periods, and to annual reporting periods beginning on or after 1 January 2009 that end before 30 June 2009.

Table of Amendments to Interpretation

Paragraph affected	How affected	By ... [paragraph]
21	amended	AASB 2007-8 [6]
22	amended	AASB 2007-6 [17]
Aus27.1	amended	AASB 2007-8 [7, 8]
Aus27.4	amended	AASB 2007-8 [8]

Table of Amendments to Additional Material

Paragraph affected	How affected	By ... [paragraph]
Information Note 1	amended	AASB 2009-6 [110]
IE4	amended	AASB 2009-6 [111]
IE6	amended	AASB 2009-6 [111]
IE15	amended	AASB 2007-6 [18]
IE17	amended	AASB 2009-6 [111]
IE19	amended	AASB 2007-8 [6]
IE20	amended	AASB 2009-6 [111]
IE27	amended	AASB 2009-6 [111]
IE31	amended	AASB 2007-6 [18]
	amended	AASB 2009-6 [111]

Paragraph affected	How affected	By ... [paragraph]
IE33	amended	AASB 2009-6 [111]
IE35	amended	AASB 2007-8 [6]
IE36	amended	AASB 2009-6 [111]
IE37	amended	AASB 2009-6 [111]

General Terminology Amendments

References to 'income statement' and 'balance sheet' were amended to 'statement of comprehensive income' and 'statement of financial position' respectively by AASB 2007-8. These amendments are not shown in the above Table of Amendments.

Comparison with IFRIC 12

AASB Interpretation 12 *Service Concession Arrangements* as amended incorporates International Financial Reporting Interpretations Committee Interpretation IFRIC 12 *Service Concession Arrangements*, issued by the International Accounting Standards Board. Paragraphs that have been added to this Interpretation (and do not appear in the text of IFRIC 12) are identified with the prefix "Aus", followed by the number of the preceding IFRIC paragraph and decimal numbering.

Entities that comply with Interpretation 12 as amended will simultaneously be in compliance with IFRIC 12 as amended.

Interpretation 12

AASB Interpretation 12 was issued in February 2007.

This compiled version of Interpretation 12 applies to annual reporting periods beginning on or after 1 January 2009 that end on or after 30 June 2009. It incorporates relevant amendments contained in other AASB documents up to and including 25 June 2009 (see Compilation Details).

Australian Accounting Standards Board

Interpretation 12

Service Concession Arrangements

References

Framework for the Preparation and Presentation of Financial Statements

Accounting Standard AASB 1 *First-time Adoption of Australian Equivalents to International Financial Reporting Standards*

Accounting Standard AASB 7 *Financial Instruments: Disclosures*

Accounting Standard AASB 108 *Accounting Policies, Changes in Accounting Estimates and Errors*

Accounting Standard AASB 111 *Construction Contracts*

Accounting Standard AASB 116 *Property, Plant and Equipment*

Accounting Standard AASB 117 *Leases*

Accounting Standard AASB 118 *Revenue*

Accounting Standard AASB 120 *Accounting for Government Grants and Disclosure of Government Assistance*

Accounting Standard AASB 123 *Borrowing Costs*

Accounting Standard AASB 132 *Financial Instruments: Presentation*

Accounting Standard AASB 136 *Impairment of Assets*

Accounting Standard AASB 137 *Provisions, Contingent Liabilities and Contingent Assets*

Accounting Standard AASB 138 *Intangible Assets*

Accounting Standard AASB 139 *Financial Instruments: Recognition and Measurement*

AASB Interpretation 4 *Determining whether an Arrangement contains a Lease*

AASB Interpretation 129 *Service Concession Arrangements: Disclosures*[1]

Background

1   In many countries, infrastructure for public services – such as roads, bridges, tunnels, prisons, hospitals, airports, water distribution facilities, energy supply and telecommunication networks – has traditionally been constructed, operated and maintained by the public sector and financed through public budget appropriation.

2   In some countries, governments have introduced contractual service arrangements to attract private sector participation in the development, financing, operation and maintenance of such infrastructure. The infrastructure may already exist, or may be constructed during the period of the service arrangement. An arrangement within the scope of this Interpretation typically involves a private sector entity (an operator) constructing the infrastructure used to provide the public service or upgrading it (for example, by increasing its capacity) and operating and maintaining that infrastructure for a specified period of time. The operator is paid for its services over the period of the arrangement. The arrangement is governed by a contract that sets out performance standards, mechanisms for adjusting prices, and arrangements for arbitrating disputes. Such an arrangement is often described as a 'build-operate-transfer', a 'rehabilitate-operate-transfer' or a 'public-to-private' service concession arrangement.

3   A feature of these service arrangements is the public service nature of the obligation undertaken by the operator. Public policy is for the services related to the infrastructure to be provided to the public, irrespective of the identity of the party that operates the services. The service arrangement contractually obliges the operator to provide the services to the public on behalf of the public sector entity. Other common features are:

(a)   the party that grants the service arrangement (the grantor) is a public sector entity, including a governmental body, or a private sector entity to which the responsibility for the service has been devolved;

(b)   the operator is responsible for at least some of the management of the infrastructure and related services and does not merely act as an agent on behalf of the grantor;

(c)   the contract sets the initial prices to be levied by the operator and regulates price revisions over the period of the service arrangement;

(d)   the operator is obliged to hand over the infrastructure to the grantor in a specified condition at the end of the period of the arrangement, for little or no incremental consideration, irrespective of which party initially financed it.

Scope

4   This Interpretation gives guidance on the accounting by operators for public-to-private service concession arrangements.

5   This Interpretation applies to public-to-private service concession arrangements if:

(a)   the grantor controls or regulates what services the operator must provide with the infrastructure, to whom it must provide them, and at what price; and

(b)   the grantor controls – through ownership, beneficial entitlement or otherwise – any significant residual interest in the infrastructure at the end of the term of the arrangement.

6   Infrastructure used in a public-to-private service concession arrangement for its entire useful life (whole of life assets) is within the scope of this Interpretation if the conditions in paragraph 5(a) are met. Paragraphs AG1–AG8 provide guidance on determining

---

1   UIG Interpretation 129 Disclosure – *Service Concession Arrangements* was amended and reissued as AASB Interpretation 129 concurrently with the issue of this Interpretation.

whether, and to what extent, public-to-private service concession arrangements are within the scope of this Interpretation.

7   This Interpretation applies to both:

(a)   infrastructure that the operator constructs or acquires from a third party for the purpose of the service arrangement; and

(b)   existing infrastructure to which the grantor gives the operator access for the purpose of the service arrangement.

8   This Interpretation does not specify the accounting for infrastructure that was held and recognised as property, plant and equipment by the operator before entering the service arrangement. The derecognition requirements of Australian Accounting Standards (set out in AASB 116 *Property, Plant and Equipment*) apply to such infrastructure.

9   This Interpretation does not specify the accounting by grantors.

Issues

10   This Interpretation sets out general principles on recognising and measuring the obligations and related rights in service concession arrangements. Requirements for disclosing information about service concession arrangements are in AASB Interpretation 129 *Service Concession Arrangements: Disclosures*. The issues addressed in this Interpretation are:

(a)   treatment of the operator's rights over the infrastructure;

(b)   recognition and measurement of arrangement consideration;

(c)   construction or upgrade services;

(d)   operation services;

(e)   borrowing costs;

(f)   subsequent accounting treatment of a financial asset and an intangible asset; and

(g)   items provided to the operator by the grantor.

Consensus

Treatment of the operator's rights over the infrastructure

11   Infrastructure within the scope of this Interpretation shall not be recognised as property, plant and equipment of the operator because the contractual service arrangement does not convey the right to control the use of the public service infrastructure to the operator. The operator has access to operate the infrastructure to provide the public service on behalf of the grantor in accordance with the terms specified in the contract.

Recognition and measurement of arrangement consideration

12   Under the terms of contractual arrangements within the scope of this Interpretation, the operator acts as a service provider. The operator constructs or upgrades infrastructure (construction or upgrade services) used to provide a public service and operates and maintains that infrastructure (operation services) for a specified period of time.

13   The operator shall recognise and measure revenue in accordance with AASB 111 *Construction Contracts* and AASB 118 *Revenue* for the services it performs. If the operator performs more than one service (i.e. construction or upgrade services and operation services) under a single contract or arrangement, consideration received or receivable shall be allocated by reference to the relative fair values of the services delivered, when the amounts are separately identifiable. The nature of the consideration determines its subsequent accounting treatment. The subsequent accounting for consideration received as a financial asset and as an intangible asset is detailed in paragraphs 23–26 below.

Construction or upgrade services

14   The operator shall account for revenue and costs relating to construction or upgrade services in accordance with AASB 111.

Consideration given by the grantor to the operator

15   If the operator provides construction or upgrade services the consideration received or receivable by the operator shall be recognised at its fair value. The consideration may be rights to:

(a)   a financial asset; or

(b)   an intangible asset.

16   The operator shall recognise a financial asset to the extent that it has an unconditional contractual right to receive cash or another financial asset from or at the direction of the grantor for the construction services; the grantor has little, if any, discretion to avoid payment, usually because the agreement is enforceable by law. The operator has an unconditional right to receive cash if the grantor contractually guarantees to pay the operator (a) specified or determinable amounts or (b) the shortfall, if any, between amounts received from users of the public service and specified or determinable amounts, even if payment is contingent on the operator ensuring that the infrastructure meets specified quality or efficiency requirements.

17   The operator shall recognise an intangible asset to the extent that it receives a right (a licence) to charge users of the public service. A right to charge users of the public service is not an unconditional right to receive cash because the amounts are contingent on the extent that the public uses the service.

18   If the operator is paid for the construction services partly by a financial asset and partly by an intangible asset it is necessary to account separately for each component of the operator's consideration. The consideration received or receivable for both components shall be recognised initially at the fair value of the consideration received or receivable.

19   The nature of the consideration given by the grantor to the operator shall be determined by reference to the contract terms and, when it exists, relevant contract law.

Operation services

20   The operator shall account for revenue and costs relating to operation services in accordance with AASB 118.

Contractual obligations to restore the infrastructure to a specified level of serviceability

21   The operator may have contractual obligations it must fulfil as a condition of its licence (a) to maintain the infrastructure to a specified level of serviceability or (b) to restore the infrastructure to a specified condition before it is handed over to the grantor at the end of the service arrangement. These contractual obligations to maintain or restore infrastructure, except for any upgrade element (see paragraph 14), shall be recognised and measured in accordance with AASB 137 *Provisions, Contingent Liabilities and Contingent Assets*, that is at the best estimate of the expenditure that would be required to settle the present obligation at the end of the reporting period.

Borrowing costs incurred by the operator

22   In accordance with AASB 123 *Borrowing Costs*, borrowing costs attributable to the arrangement shall be recognised as an expense in the period in which they are incurred unless the operator has a contractual right to receive an intangible asset (a right to charge users of the public service). In this case borrowing costs attributable to the arrangement shall be capitalised during the construction phase of the arrangement in accordance with that Standard.

Financial asset

23   AASB 7 Financial Instruments: Disclosures, AASB 132 *Financial Instruments: Presentation* and AASB 139 *Financial Instruments: Recognition and Measurement* apply to the financial asset recognised under paragraphs 16 and 18.

24   The amount due from or at the direction of the grantor is accounted for in accordance with AASB 139 as:

(a)   a loan or receivable;

(b)   an available-for-sale financial asset; or

(c)   if so designated upon initial recognition, a financial asset at fair value through profit or loss, if the conditions for that classification are met.

25   If the amount due from the grantor is accounted for either as a loan or receivable or as an available-for-sale financial asset, AASB 139 requires interest calculated using the effective interest method to be recognised in profit or loss.

Intangible asset

26   AASB 138 *Intangible Assets* applies to the intangible asset recognised in accordance with paragraphs 17 and 18. Paragraphs 45–47 of AASB 138 provide guidance on measuring intangible assets acquired in exchange for a non-monetary asset or assets or a combination of monetary and non-monetary assets.

Items provided to the operator by the grantor

27   In accordance with paragraph 11, infrastructure items to which the operator is given access by the grantor for the purposes of the service arrangement are not recognised as property, plant and equipment of the operator. The grantor may also provide other items to the operator that the operator can keep or deal with as it wishes. If such assets form part of the consideration payable by the grantor for the services, they are not government grants as defined in AASB 120 *Accounting for Government Grants and Disclosure of Government Assistance*. They are recognised as assets of the operator, measured at fair value on initial recognition. The operator shall recognise a liability in respect of unfulfilled obligations it has assumed in exchange for the assets.

Application

Aus27.1   This Interpretation applies to:

(a)   each entity that is required to prepare financial reports in accordance with Part 2M.3 of the *Corporations Act 2001* and that is a reporting entity;

(b)   general purpose financial statements of each other reporting entity; and

(c)   financial statements that are, or are held out to be, general purpose financial statements.

Aus27.2   This Interpretation applies to annual reporting periods beginning on or after 1 January 2008.

[Note: For application dates of paragraphs changed or added by an amending pronouncement, see Compilation Details.]

Aus27.3   This Interpretation may be applied to annual reporting periods beginning on or after 1 January 2005 but before 1 January 2008. If an entity applies this Interpretation to such an annual reporting period, it shall disclose that fact.

Aus27.4   The requirements specified in this Interpretation apply to the financial statements where information resulting from their application is material in accordance with AASB 1031 *Materiality*.

Effective Date of IFRIC 12

28   [Deleted by the AASB]

Transition

29   Subject to paragraph 30, changes in accounting policies are accounted for in accordance with AASB 108 *Accounting Policies, Changes in Accounting Estimates and Errors*, that is retrospectively.

30 If, for any particular service arrangement, it is impracticable for an operator to apply this Interpretation retrospectively at the start of the earliest period presented, it shall:

(a) recognise financial assets and intangible assets that existed at the start of the earliest period presented;

(b) use the previous carrying amounts of those financial and intangible assets (however previously classified) as their carrying amounts as at that date; and

(c) test financial and intangible assets recognised at that date for impairment, unless this is not practicable, in which case the amounts shall be tested for impairment as at the start of the current period.

Appendix A
Application Guidance

This appendix is an integral part of the Interpretation.

Scope (paragraph 5)

AG1 Paragraph 5 of this Interpretation specifies that infrastructure is within the scope of the Interpretation when the following conditions apply:

(a) the grantor controls or regulates what services the operator must provide with the infrastructure, to whom it must provide them, and at what price; and

(b) the grantor controls – through ownership, beneficial entitlement or otherwise – any significant residual interest in the infrastructure at the end of the term of the arrangement.

AG2 The control or regulation referred to in condition (a) could be by contract or otherwise (such as through a regulator), and includes circumstances in which the grantor buys all of the output as well as those in which some or all of the output is bought by other users. In applying this condition, the grantor and any related parties shall be considered together. If the grantor is a public sector entity, the public sector as a whole, together with any regulators acting in the public interest, shall be regarded as related to the grantor for the purposes of this Interpretation.

AG3 For the purpose of condition (a), the grantor does not need to have complete control of the price: it is sufficient for the price to be regulated by the grantor, contract or regulator, for example by a capping mechanism. However, the condition shall be applied to the substance of the agreement. Non-substantive features, such as a cap that will apply only in remote circumstances, shall be ignored. Conversely, if for example, a contract purports to give the operator freedom to set prices, but any excess profit is returned to the grantor, the operator's return is capped and the price element of the control test is met.

AG4 For the purpose of condition (b), the grantor's control over any significant residual interest should both restrict the operator's practical ability to sell or pledge the infrastructure and give the grantor a continuing right of use throughout the period of the arrangement. The residual interest in the infrastructure is the estimated current value of the infrastructure as if it were already of the age and in the condition expected at the end of the period of the arrangement.

AG5 Control should be distinguished from management. If the grantor retains both the degree of control described in paragraph 5(a) and any significant residual interest in the infrastructure, the operator is only managing the infrastructure on the grantor's behalf – even though, in many cases, it may have wide managerial discretion.

AG6 Conditions (a) and (b) together identify when the infrastructure, including any replacements required (see paragraph 21), is controlled by the grantor for the whole of its economic life. For example, if the operator has to replace part of an item of infrastructure during the period of the arrangement (e.g. the top layer of a road or the roof of a building), the item of infrastructure shall be considered as a whole. Thus condition (b) is met for the whole of the infrastructure, including the part that is replaced, if the grantor controls any significant residual interest in the final replacement of that part.

AG7   Sometimes the use of infrastructure is partly regulated in the manner described in paragraph 5(a) and partly unregulated. However, these arrangements take a variety of forms:

(a)   any infrastructure that is physically separable and capable of being operated independently and meets the definition of a cash-generating unit as defined in AASB 136 *Impairment of Assets* shall be analysed separately if it is used wholly for unregulated purposes. For example, this might apply to a private wing of a hospital, where the remainder of the hospital is used by the grantor to treat public patients;

(b)   when purely ancillary activities (such as a hospital shop) are unregulated, the control tests shall be applied as if those services did not exist, because in cases in which the grantor controls the services in the manner described in paragraph 5, the existence of ancillary activities does not detract from the grantor's control of the infrastructure.

AG8   The operator may have a right to use the separable infrastructure described in paragraph AG7(a), or the facilities used to provide ancillary unregulated services described in paragraph AG7(b). In either case, there may in substance be a lease from the grantor to the operator; if so, it shall be accounted for in accordance with AASB 117 *Leases*.

Appendix B

Amendments to AASB 1 and to Other Interpretations

The amendments noted in this Appendix apply for annual reporting periods beginning on or after 1 January 2008. If an entity applies this Interpretation for an earlier period, these amendments apply for that earlier period.

AASB 1 has been amended by Accounting Standard AASB 2007-2 *Amendments to Australian Accounting Standards* arising from AASB Interpretation 12 (February 2007). Interpretations 4 and 129 have been reissued to incorporate the consequential amendments.

B1   AASB 1 *First-time Adoption of Australian Equivalents to International Financial Reporting Standards* has been amended by AASB 2007-2 as described below.

Paragraph 9 is amended to read as follows:

9   The transitional provisions in other Australian equivalents to IFRSs apply to changes in accounting policies made by an entity that already uses Australian equivalents to IFRSs; they do not apply to a first-time adopter's transition to Australian equivalents to IFRSs, except as specified in paragraphs 25D, 25H, 34A and Aus34B.1.

In paragraph 12(a), the reference to paragraphs 13–25G is changed to 13–25H.

In paragraph 13, subparagraphs (k) and (l) are amended, and subparagraph (m) is inserted, to read as follows:

(k)   leases (paragraph 25F);

(l)   fair value measurement of financial assets or financial liabilities at initial recognition (paragraph 25G); and

(m)   a financial asset or an intangible asset accounted for in accordance with Interpretation 12 *Service Concession Arrangements*, identified in AASB 1048 *Interpretation and Application of Standards* as corresponding to IFRIC 12 (paragraph 25H).

After paragraph 25G, a new heading and paragraph 25H are inserted as follows:

Service Concession Arrangements

25H   A first-time adopter may apply the transitional provisions in Interpretation 12 *Service Concession Arrangements*, identified in AASB 1048 as corresponding to IFRIC 12.

B2   UIG Interpretation 4 *Determining whether an Arrangement contains a Lease* has been amended as described below.

Paragraph 4 is amended to read as follows:

4   This Interpretation does not apply to arrangements that:

         (a)   are, or contain, leases excluded from the scope of AASB 117; or

         (b)   are public-to-private service concession arrangements within the scope of AASB Interpretation 12 *Service Concession Arrangements*.

In the Basis for Conclusions accompanying Interpretation 4, after paragraph BC14 a new paragraph BC14A is inserted as follows:

BC14A   The IFRIC considered whether the scope of the Interpretation might overlap with IFRIC 12, which was developed from draft Interpretations D12–D14. In particular it noted the views expressed by some respondents to the proposals that the contractual terms of some public-to-private service concession arrangements would be regarded as leases under IFRIC 4 and would also be regarded as meeting the scope criterion of D12–D14. The IFRIC did not regard the choice between accounting treatments as appropriate because it could lead to different accounting treatments for contracts that have similar economic effects. The IFRIC therefore amended IFRIC 4 to specify that if a public-to-private service concession arrangement met the scope requirements of IFRIC 12 it would not be within the scope of IFRIC 4.

B3   UIG Interpretation 129 Disclosure – *Service Concession Arrangements* has been amended as described below.

Its title is amended to *Service Concession Arrangements: Disclosures*.

In paragraphs 1–6 references to 'Concession Operator' are changed to 'operator', and references to 'Concession Provider' are changed to 'grantor'.

In paragraph 6, subparagraphs (c)(vi) and (d) are amended, and subparagraph (e) is inserted, to read as follows:

         (c)   …

             (vi)   other rights and obligations (e.g. major overhauls);

         (d)   changes in the arrangement occurring during the period; and

         (e)   how the service arrangement has been classified.

After paragraph 6 a new paragraph 6A is inserted, as follows:

6A   An operator shall disclose the amount of revenue and profits or losses recognised in the period on exchanging construction services for a financial asset or an intangible asset.

In the Basis for Conclusions, the last sentence of paragraph 9 is changed to read as follows:

    … delivering that asset to the grantor at the end of the concession period.

Interpretations

Information Note 1

Accounting Framework for Public-to-Private Service Arrangements

This note accompanies, but is not part of, AASB Interpretation 12.

The diagram below summarises the accounting for service arrangements established by Interpretation 12.

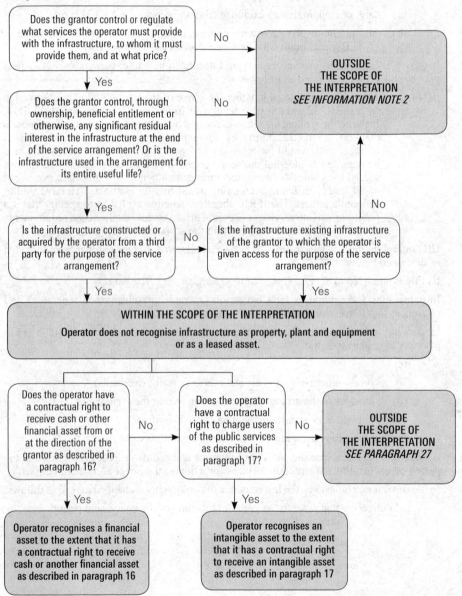

Information Note 2

References to AASB Pronouncements that Apply to Typical Types of Public-to-Private Arrangements

This note accompanies, but is not part of, AASB Interpretation 12.

The table sets out the typical types of arrangements for private sector participation in the provision of public sector services and provides references to Australian equivalents to IFRSs that apply to those arrangements. The list of arrangement types is not exhaustive. The purpose of the table is to highlight the continuum of arrangements. It is not the intention to convey the impression that bright lines exist between the accounting requirements for public-to-private arrangements.

Category	Lessee	Service provider				Owner
Typical arrangement types	Lease (e.g. Operator leases asset from grantor)	Service and/or maintenance contract (specific tasks e.g. debt collection)	Rehabilitate-operate-transfer	Build-operate-transfer	Build-own-operate	100% Divestment/ Privatisation/ Corporation
Asset ownership	Grantor				Operator	
Capital investment	Grantor			Operator		
Demand risk	Shared	Grantor	Operator and/or Grantor		Operator	
Typical duration	8–20 years	1–5 years	25-30 years			Indefinite (or may be limited by licence)
Residual interest	Grantor				Operator	
Relevant pronouncement	AASB 117	AASB 118	AASB Interpretation 12		AASB 116	

Illustrative Examples

These examples accompany, but are not part of, AASB Interpretation 12.

Example 1: The grantor gives the operator a financial asset

Arrangement terms

IE1　The terms of the arrangement require an operator to construct a road – completing construction within two years – and maintain and operate the road to a specified standard for eight years (i.e. years 3–10). The terms of the arrangement also require the operator to resurface the road at the end of year 8 – the resurfacing activity is revenue-generating. At the end of year 10, the arrangement will end. The operator estimates that the costs it will incur to fulfil its obligations will be:

Table 1.1 *Contract costs*

	Year	CU*
Construction services	1	500
	2	500
Operation services (per year)	3–10	10
Road resurfacing	8	100

*　in this example, monetary amounts are denominated in 'currency units' (CU).

IE2　The terms of the arrangement require the grantor to pay the operator 200 currency units (CU200) per year in years 3–10 for making the road available to the public.

IE3   For the purpose of this illustration, it is assumed that all cash flows take place at the end of the year.

Contract revenue

IE4   The operator recognises contract revenue and costs in accordance with AASB 111 *Construction Contracts* and AASB 118 *Revenue*. The costs of each activity – construction, operation and resurfacing – are recognised as expenses by reference to the stage of completion of that activity. Contract revenue – the fair value of the amount due from the grantor for the activity undertaken – is recognised at the same time. Under the terms of the arrangement the operator is obliged to resurface the road at the end of year 8. In year 8 the operator will be reimbursed by the grantor for resurfacing the road. The obligation to resurface the road is measured at zero in the statement of financial position and the revenue and expense are not recognised in profit or loss until the resurfacing work is performed.

IE5   The total consideration (CU200 in each of years 3–8) reflects the fair values for each of the services, which are:

Table 1.2 *Fair values of the consideration received or receivable*

	Fair value
Construction services	Forecast cost + 5%
Operation services	" " + 20%
Road resurfacing	" " + 10%
Effective interest rate	6.18% per year

IE6   In year 1, for example, construction costs of CU500, construction revenue of CU525 (cost plus 5 per cent), and hence construction profit of CU25 are recognised in profit or loss.

Financial asset

IE7   The amounts due from the grantor meet the definition of a receivable in AASB 139 *Financial Instruments: Recognition and Measurement*. The receivable is measured initially at fair value. It is subsequently measured at amortised cost, that is the amount initially recognised plus the cumulative interest on that amount calculated using the effective interest method minus repayments.

IE8   If the cash flows and fair values remain the same as those forecast, the effective interest rate is 6.18 per cent per year and the receivable recognised at the end of years 1–3 will be:

Table 1.3 *Measurement of receivable*

	CU
Amount due for construction in year 1	525
Receivable at end of year 1*	525
Effective interest in year 2 on receivable at the end of year 1 (6.18% × CU525)	32
Amount due for construction in year 2	525
Receivable at end of year 2	1,082
Effective interest in year 3 on receivable at the end of year 2 (6.18% × CU1,082)	67
Amount due for operation in year 3 (CU10 × (1 + 20%))	12
Cash receipts in year 3	(200)
Receivable at end of year 3	961

* No effective interest arises in year 1 because the cash flows are assumed to take place at the end of the year.

Overview of cash flows, statement of comprehensive income and statement of financial position

IE9   For the purpose of this illustration, it is assumed that the operator finances the arrangement wholly with debt and retained earnings. It pays interest at 6.7 per cent per year on outstanding debt. If the cash flows and fair values remain the same as those forecast, the operator's cash flows, statement of comprehensive income and statement of financial position over the duration of the arrangement will be:

Table 1.4 *Cash flows* *(currency units)*

Year	1	2	3	4	5	6	7	8	9	10	Total
Receipts	–	–	200	200	200	200	200	200	200	200	1,600
Contract costs*	(500)	(500)	(10)	(10)	(10)	(10)	(10)	(110)	(10)	(10)	(1,180)
Borrowing costs†	–	(34)	(69)	(61)	(53)	(43)	(33)	(23)	(19)	(7)	(342)
Net inflow/ (outflow)	(500)	(534)	121	129	137	147	157	67	171	183	78

* Table 1.1

† Debt at start of year (table 1.6) × 6.7%

Table 1.5 *Statement of comprehensive income* *(currency units)*

Year	1	2	3	4	5	6	7	8	9	10	Total
Revenue	525	525	12	12	12	12	12	122	12	12	1,256
Contract costs	(500)	(500)	(10)	(10)	(10)	(10)	(10)	(110)	(10)	(10)	(1,180)
Finance income*	–	32	67	59	51	43	34	25	22	11	344
Borrowing costs†	–	(34)	(69)	(61)	(53)	(43)	(33)	(23)	(19)	(7)	(342)
Net profit	25	23	–	–	–	2	3	14	5	6	78

* Amount due from grantor at start of year (table 1.6) × 6.18%

† Cash/(debt) (table 1.6) × 6.7%

Table 1.6 *Statement of financial position* *(currency units)*

End of year	1	2	3	4	5	6	7	8	9	10
Amount due from grantor*	525	1,082	961	832	695	550	396	343	177	–
Cash/(debt)†	(500)	(1,034)	(913)	(784)	(647)	(500)	(343)	(276)	(105)	78
Net assets	25	48	48	48	48	50	53	67	72	78

* Amount due from grantor at start of year, plus revenue and finance income earned in year (table 1.5), less receipts in year (table 1.4).

† Debt at start of year plus net cash flow in year (table 1.4).

IE10 This example deals with only one of many possible types of arrangements. Its purpose is to illustrate the accounting treatment for some features that are commonly found in practice. To make the illustration as clear as possible, it has been assumed that the arrangement period is only ten years and that the operator's annual receipts are constant over that period. In practice, arrangement periods may be much longer and annual revenues may increase with time. In such circumstances, the changes in net profit from year to year could be greater.

Example 2: The grantor gives the operator an intangible asset (a licence to charge users)

Arrangement terms

IE11 The terms of a service arrangement require an operator to construct a road – completing construction within two years – and maintain and operate the road to a specified standard for eight years (i.e. years 3–10). The terms of the arrangement also require the operator to resurface the road when the original surface has deteriorated below a specified condition. The operator estimates that it will have to undertake the resurfacing at the end of the year 8. At the end of year 10, the service arrangement will end. The operator estimates that the costs it will incur to fulfil its obligations will be:

Table 2.1 *Contract costs*

	Year	CU*
Construction services	1	500
	2	500
Operation services (per year)	3–10	10
Road resurfacing	8	100

*   in this example, monetary amounts are denominated in 'currency units' (CU).

IE12   The terms of the arrangement allow the operator to collect tolls from drivers using the road. The operator forecasts that vehicle numbers will remain constant over the duration of the contract and that it will receive tolls of 200 currency units (CU200) in each of years 3–10.

IE13   For the purpose of this illustration, it is assumed that all cash flows take place at the end of the year.

Intangible asset

IE14   The operator provides construction services to the grantor in exchange for an intangible asset, that is a right to collect tolls from road users in years 3–10. In accordance with AASB 138 *Intangible Assets*, the operator recognises the intangible asset at cost, that is the fair value of consideration transferred to acquire the asset, which is the fair value of the consideration received or receivable for the construction services delivered.

IE15   During the construction phase of the arrangement the operator's asset (representing its accumulating right to be paid for providing construction services) is classified as an intangible asset (licence to charge users of the infrastructure). The operator estimates the fair value of its consideration received to be equal to the forecast construction costs plus 5 per cent margin. It is also assumed that, in accordance with AASB 123 *Borrowing Costs*, the operator capitalises the borrowing costs, estimated at 6.7 per cent, during the construction phase of the arrangement:

Table 2.2 *Initial measurement of intangible asset*

	CU
Construction services in year 1 (CU500 × (1 + 5%))	525
Capitalisation of borrowing costs (table 2.4)	34
Construction services in year 2 (CU500 × (1 + 5%))	525
Intangible asset at end of year 2	1,084

IE16   In accordance with AASB 138, the intangible asset is amortised over the period in which it is expected to be available for use by the operator, that is years 3–10. The depreciable amount of the intangible asset (CU1,084) is allocated using a straight-line method. The annual amortisation charge is therefore CU1,084 divided by 8 years, that is CU135 per year.

Construction costs and revenue

IE17   The operator recognises the revenue and costs in accordance with AASB 111 *Construction Contracts*, that is by reference to the stage of completion of the construction. It measures contract revenue at the fair value of the consideration received or receivable. Thus in each of years 1 and 2 it recognises in its profit or loss construction costs of CU500, construction revenue of CU525 (cost plus 5 per cent) and, hence, construction profit of CU25.

Toll revenue

IE18   The road users pay for the public services at the same time as they receive them, that is when they use the road. The operator therefore recognises toll revenue when it collects the tolls.

Resurfacing obligations

IE19 The operator's resurfacing obligation arises as a consequence of use of the road during the operating phase. It is recognised and measured in accordance with AASB 137 *Provisions, Contingent Liabilities and Contingent Assets*, that is at the best estimate of the expenditure required to settle the present obligation at the end of the reporting period.

IE20 For the purpose of this illustration, it is assumed that the terms of the operator's contractual obligation are such that the best estimate of the expenditure required to settle the obligation at any date is proportional to the number of vehicles that have used the road by that date and increases by CU17 (discounted to a current value) each year. The operator discounts the provision to its present value in accordance with AASB 137. The charge recognised each period in profit or loss is:

Table 2.3 *Resurfacing obligation* (currency units)

Year	3	4	5	6	7	8	Total
Obligation arising in year (CU17 discounted at 6%)	12	13	14	15	16	17	87
Increase in earlier years' provision arising from passage of time	0	1	1	2	4	5	13
Total expense recognised in profit or loss	12	14	15	17	20	22	100

Overview of cash flows, statement of comprehensive income and statement of financial position

IE21 For the purposes of this illustration, it is assumed that the operator finances the arrangement wholly with debt and retained earnings. It pays interest at 6.7 per cent per year on outstanding debt. If the cash flows and fair values remain the same as those forecast, the operator's cash flows, statement of comprehensive income and statement of financial position over the duration of the arrangement will be:

Table 2.4 *Cash flows* (currency units)

Year	1	2	3	4	5	6	7	8	9	10	Total
Receipts	–	–	200	200	200	200	200	200	200	200	1,600
Contract costs*	(500)	(500)	(10)	(10)	(10)	(10)	(10)	(110)	(10)	(10)	(1,180)
Borrowing costs†	–	(34)	(69)	(61)	(53)	(43)	(33)	(23)	(19)	(7)	(342)
Net inflow/ (outflow)	(500)	(534)	121	129	137	147	157	67	171	183	78

* Table 2.1

† Debt at start of year (table 2.6) × 6.7%

Table 2.5 *Statement of comprehensive income* (currency units)

Year	1	2	3	4	5	6	7	8	9	10	Total
Revenue	525	525	200	200	200	200	200	200	200	200	2,650
Amortisation	–	–	(135)	(135)	(136)	(136)	(136)	(136)	(135)	(135)	(1,084)
Resurfacing expense	–	–	(12)	(14)	(15)	(17)	(20)	(22)	–	–	(100)
Other contract costs	(500)	(500)	(10)	(10)	(10)	(10)	(10)	(10)	(10)	(10)	(1,080)
Borrowing costs*†	–	–	(69)	(61)	(53)	(43)	(33)	(23)	(19)	(7)	(308)
Net profit	25	25	(26)	(20)	(14)	(6)	1	9	36	48	78

* Borrowing costs are capitalised during the construction phase

† Table 2.4

Table 2.6 *Statement of financial position (currency units)*

End of year	1	2	3	4	5	6	7	8	9	10
Intangible asset	525	1,084	949	814	678	542	406	270	135	–
Cash/(debt)*	(500)	(1,034)	(913)	(784)	(647)	(500)	(343)	(276)	(105)	78
Resurfacing obligation	–	–	(12)	(26)	(41)	(58)	(78)	–	–	–
Net assets	25	50	24	4	(10)	(16)	(15)	(6)	30	78

* Debt at start of year plus net cash flow in year (table 2.4).

IE22   This example deals with only one of many possible types of arrangements. Its purpose is to illustrate the accounting treatment for some features that are commonly found in practice. To make the illustration as clear as possible, it has been assumed that the arrangement period is only ten years and that the operator's annual receipts are constant over that period. In practice, arrangement periods may be much longer and annual revenues may increase with time. In such circumstances, the changes in net profit from year to year could be greater.

Example 3: The grantor gives the operator a financial asset and an intangible asset

Arrangement terms

IE23   The terms of a service arrangement require an operator to construct a road – completing construction within two years – and to operate the road and maintain it to a specified standard for eight years (i.e. years 3–10). The terms of the arrangement also require the operator to resurface the road when the original surface has deteriorated below a specified condition. The operator estimates that it will have to undertake the resurfacing at the end of year 8. At the end of year 10, the arrangement will end. The operator estimates that the costs it will incur to fulfil its obligations will be:

Table 3.1 *Contract costs*

	Year	CU*
Construction services	1	500
	2	500
Operation services (per year)	3–10	10
Road resurfacing	8	100

* in this example, monetary amounts are denominated in 'currency units' (CU).

IE24   The operator estimates the consideration in respect of construction services to be cost plus 5 per cent.

IE25   The terms of the arrangement allow the operator to collect tolls from drivers using the road. In addition, the grantor guarantees the operator a minimum amount of CU700 and interest at a specified rate of 6.18 per cent to reflect the timing of cash receipts. The operator forecasts that vehicle numbers will remain constant over the duration of the contract and that it will receive tolls of CU200 in each of years 3–10.

IE26   For the purpose of this illustration, it is assumed that all cash flows take place at the end of the year.

Dividing the arrangement

IE27   The contractual right to receive cash from the grantor for the services and the right to charge users for the public services should be regarded as two separate assets under Australian Accounting Standards. Therefore in this arrangement it is necessary to divide the operator's consideration into two components – a financial asset component based on the guaranteed amount and an intangible asset for the remainder.

Table 3.2 *Dividing the operator's consideration*

Year	Total	Financial asset	Intangible asset
Construction services in year 1 (CU500 × (1 + 5%))	525	350	175
Construction services in year 2 (CU500 × (1 + 5%))	525	350	175
Total construction services	1,050	700	350
	100%	*67%**	*33%*
Finance income, at specified rate of 6.18% on receivable (see table 3.3)	22	22	–
Borrowing costs capitalised (interest paid in year 1 and 2 × 33%) see table 3.7	11	–	11
Total fair value of the operator's consideration	1,083	722	361

* Amount guaranteed by the grantor as a proportion of the construction services.

Financial asset

IE28   The amount due from or at the direction of the grantor in exchange for the construction services meets the definition of a receivable in AASB 139 *Financial Instruments: Recognition and Measurement*. The receivable is measured initially at fair value. It is subsequently measured at amortised cost, that is the amount initially recognised plus the cumulative interest on that amount minus repayments.

IE29   On this basis the receivable recognised at the end of years 2 and 3 will be:

Table 3.3 *Measurement of receivable*

	CU
Construction services in year 1 allocated to the financial asset	350
Receivable at end of year 1	350
Construction services in year 2 allocated to the financial asset	350
Interest in year 2 on receivable at end of year 1 (6.18% × CU350)	22
Receivable at end of year 2	722
Interest in year 3 on receivable at end of year 2 (6.18% × CU722)	45
Cash receipts in year 3 (see table 3.5)	(117)
Receivable at end of year 3	650

Intangible asset

IE30   In accordance with AASB 138 *Intangible Assets*, the operator recognises the intangible asset at cost, that is the fair value of the consideration received or receivable.

IE31   During the construction phase of the arrangement the operator's asset (representing its accumulating right to be paid for providing construction services) is classified as a right to receive a licence to charge users of the infrastructure. The operator estimates the fair value of its consideration received or receivable as equal to the forecast construction costs plus 5 per cent. It is also assumed that, in accordance with AASB 123 *Borrowing Costs*, the operator capitalises the borrowing costs, estimated at 6.7 per cent, during the construction phase:

Table 3.4 *Initial measurement of intangible asset*

	CU
Construction services in year 1 (CU500 × (1 + 5%) × 33%)	175
Borrowing costs (interest paid in year 1 and 2 × 33%) see table 3.7	11
Construction services in year 2 (CU500 × (1 + 5%) × 33%)	175
Intangible asset at the end of year 2	361

IE32   In accordance with AASB 138, the intangible asset is amortised over the period in which it is expected to be available for use by the operator, that is years 3–10. The depreciable amount of the intangible asset (CU361 including borrowing costs) is allocated using a straight-line method. The annual amortisation charge is therefore CU361 divided by 8 years, that is CU45 per year.

Contract revenue and costs

IE33   The operator provides construction services to the grantor in exchange for a financial asset and an intangible asset. Under both the financial asset model and intangible asset model, the operator recognises contract revenue and costs in accordance with AASB 111 *Construction Contracts*, that is by reference to the stage of completion of the construction. It measures contract revenue at the fair value of the consideration receivable. Thus in each of years 1 and 2 it recognises in profit or loss construction costs of CU500 and construction revenue of CU525 (cost plus 5 per cent).

Toll revenue

IE34   The road users pay for the public services at the same time as they receive them, that is when they use the road. Under the terms of this arrangement the cash flows are allocated to the financial asset and intangible asset in proportion, so the operator allocates the receipts from tolls between repayment of the financial asset and revenue earned from the intangible asset:

Table 3.5 *Allocation of toll receipts*

	CU
Guaranteed receipt from grantor	700
Finance income (see table 3.8)	237
Total	937
Cash allocated to realisation of the financial asset per year (CU937/8 years)	117
Receipts attributable to intangible asset (CU200 × 8 years – CU937)	663
Annual receipt from intangible asset (CU663/8 years)	83

Resurfacing obligations

IE35   The operator's resurfacing obligation arises as a consequence of use of the road during the operation phase. It is recognised and measured in accordance with AASB 137 *Provisions, Contingent Liabilities and Contingent Assets*, that is at the best estimate of the expenditure required to settle the present obligation at the end of the reporting period.

IE36   For the purpose of this illustration, it is assumed that the terms of the operator's contractual obligation are such that the best estimate of the expenditure required to settle the obligation at any date is proportional to the number of vehicles that have used the road by that date and increases by CU17 each year. The operator discounts the provision to its present value in accordance with AASB 137. The charge recognised each period in profit or loss is:

Table 3.6 *Resurfacing obligation (currency units)*

Year	3	4	5	6	7	8	Total
Obligation arising in year (CU17 discounted at 6%)	12	13	14	15	16	17	87
Increase in earlier years' provision arising from passage of time	0	1	1	2	4	5	13
Total expense recognised in profit or loss	12	14	15	17	20	22	100

Overview of cash flows, statement of comprehensive income and statement of financial position

IE37   For the purposes of this illustration, it is assumed that the operator finances the arrangement wholly with debt and retained earnings. It pays interest at 6.7 per cent per year on outstanding debt. If the cash flows and fair values remain the same as those forecast, the operator's cash flows, statement of comprehensive income and statement of financial position over the duration of the arrangement will be:

Table 3.7 *Cash flows* *(currency units)*

Year	1	2	3	4	5	6	7	8	9	10	Total
Receipts	–	–	200	200	200	200	200	200	200	200	1,600
Contract costs*	(500)	(500)	(10)	(10)	(10)	(10)	(10)	(110)	(10)	(10)	(1,180)
Borrowing costs†	–	(34)	(69)	(61)	(53)	(43)	(33)	(23)	(19)	(7)	(342)
Net inflow/ (outflow)	(500)	(534)	121	129	137	147	157	67	171	183	78

* Table 3.1

† Debt at start of year (table 3.9) × 6.7%

Table 3.8 *Statement of comprehensive income* *(currency units)*

Year	1	2	3	4	5	6	7	8	9	10	Total
Revenue on construction	525	525	–	–	–	–	–	–	–	–	1,050
Revenue from intangible asset	–	–	83	83	83	83	83	83	83	83	663
Finance income*	–	22	45	40	35	30	25	19	13	7	237
Amortisation	–	–	(45)	(45)	(45)	(45)	(45)	(45)	(45)	(46)	(361)
Resurfacing expense	–	–	(12)	(14)	(15)	(17)	(20)	(22)	–	–	(100)
Construction costs	(500)	(500)	–	–	–	–	–	–	–	–	(1,000)
Other contract costs†	–	–	(10)	(10)	(10)	(10)	(10)	(10)	(10)	(10)	(80)
Borrowing costs (table 3.7)‡	–	(23)	(69)	(61)	(53)	(43)	(33)	(23)	(19)	(7)	(331)
Net profit	25	24	(8)	(7)	(5)	(2)	0	2	22	27	78

* Interest on receivable

† Table 3.1

‡ In year 2, borrowing costs are stated net of amount capitalised in the intangible (see table 3.4).

Table 3.9 *Statement of financial position* *(currency units)*

End of year	1	2	3	4	5	6	7	8	9	10
Receivable	350	722	650	573	491	404	312	214	110	–
Intangible asset	175	361	316	271	226	181	136	91	46	–
Cash/(debt)*	(500)	(1,034)	(913)	(784)	(647)	(500)	(343)	(276)	(105)	78
Resurfacing obligation	–	–	(12)	(26)	(41)	(58)	(78)	–	–	–
Net assets	25	49	41	34	29	27	27	29	51	78

* Debt at start of year plus net cash flow in year (table 3.7).

IE38 This example deals with only one of many possible types of arrangements. Its purpose is to illustrate the accounting treatment for some features that are commonly found in practice. To make the illustration as clear as possible, it has been assumed that the arrangement period is only ten years and that the operator's annual receipts are constant over that period. In practice, arrangement periods may be much longer and annual revenues may increase with time. In such circumstances, the changes in net profit from year to year could be greater.

Basis for Conclusions on IFRIC Interpretation 12

This IFRIC Basis for Conclusions accompanies, but is not part of, AASB Interpretation 12. An IFRIC Basis for Conclusions may be amended to reflect the requirements of the AASB Interpretation and AASB Accounting Standards where they differ from the corresponding International pronouncements.

Introduction

BC1   This Basis for Conclusions summarises the IFRIC's considerations in reaching its consensus. Individual IFRIC members gave greater weight to some factors than to others.

Background (paragraphs 1–3)

BC2   SIC-29 *Service Concession Arrangements: Disclosures* (formerly *Disclosure – Service Concession Arrangements*) contains disclosure requirements in respect of public-to-private service arrangements, but does not specify how they should be accounted for.

BC3   There was widespread concern about the lack of such guidance. In particular, operators wished to know how to account for infrastructure that they either constructed or acquired for the purpose of a public-to-private service concession arrangement, or were given access to for the purpose of providing the public service. They also wanted to know how to account for other rights and obligations arising from these types of arrangements.

BC4   In response to this concern, the International Accounting Standards Board asked a working group comprising representatives of the standard-setters of Australia, France, Spain and the United Kingdom (four of the countries that had expressed such concern) to carry out initial research on the subject. The working group recommended that the IFRIC should seek to clarify how certain aspects of existing accounting standards were to be applied.

BC5   In March 2005 the IFRIC published for public comment three draft Interpretations: D12 *Service Concession Arrangements – Determining the Accounting Model*, D13 *Service Concession Arrangements – The Financial Asset Model* and D14 *Service Concession Arrangements – The Intangible Asset Model*. In response to the proposals 77 comment letters were received. In addition, in order to understand better the practical issues that would have arisen on implementing the proposed Interpretations, IASB staff met various interested parties, including preparers, auditors and regulators.

BC6   Most respondents to D12–D14 supported the IFRIC's proposal to develop an Interpretation. However, nearly all respondents expressed concern with fundamental aspects of the proposals, some urging that the project be passed to the Board to develop a comprehensive standard.

BC7   In its redeliberation of the proposals the IFRIC acknowledged that the project was a large undertaking but concluded that it should continue its work because, given the limited scope of the project, it was by then better placed than the Board to deal with the issues in a timely way.

Terminology

BC8   SIC-29 used the terms 'Concession Provider' and 'Concession Operator' to describe, respectively, the grantor and operator of the service arrangement. Some commentators, and some members of the IFRIC, found these terms confusingly similar. The IFRIC decided to adopt the terms 'grantor' and 'operator', and amended SIC-29 accordingly.

Scope (paragraphs 4–9)

BC9   The IFRIC observed that public-to-private service arrangements take a variety of forms. The continued involvement of both grantor and operator over the term of the arrangement, accompanied by heavy upfront investment, raises questions over what assets and liabilities should be recognised by the operator.

BC10 The working group recommended that the scope of the IFRIC's project should be restricted to public-to-private service concession arrangements.

BC11 In developing the proposals the IFRIC decided to address only arrangements in which the grantor (a) controlled or regulated the services provided by the operator, and (b) controlled any significant residual interest in the infrastructure at the end of the term of the arrangement. It also decided to specify the accounting treatment only for infrastructure that the operator constructed or acquired from a third party, or to which it was given access by the grantor, for the purpose of the arrangement. The IFRIC concluded that these conditions were likely to be met in most of the public-to-private arrangements for which guidance had been sought.

BC12 Commentators on the draft Interpretations argued that the proposals ignored many arrangements that were found in practice, in particular, when the infrastructure was leased to the operator or, conversely, when it was held as the property, plant and equipment of the operator before the start of the service arrangement.

BC13 In considering these comments, the IFRIC decided that the scope of the project should not be expanded because it already included the arrangements most in need of interpretative guidance and expansion would have significantly delayed the Interpretation. The scope of the project was considered at length during the initial stage, as indicated above. The IFRIC confirmed its view that the proposed Interpretation should address the issues set out in paragraph 10. Nonetheless, during its redeliberation the IFRIC considered the range of typical arrangements for private sector participation in the provision of public services, including some that were outside the scope of the proposed Interpretation. The IFRIC decided that the Interpretation could provide references to relevant standards that apply to arrangements outside the scope of the Interpretation without giving guidance on their application. If experience showed that such guidance was needed, a separate project could be undertaken at a later date. Information Note 2 contains a table of references to relevant standards for the types of arrangements considered by the IFRIC.

Private-to-private arrangements

BC14 Some respondents to the draft Interpretations suggested that the scope of the proposed Interpretation should be extended to include private-to-private service arrangements. The IFRIC noted that addressing the accounting for such arrangements was not the primary purpose of the project because the IFRIC had been asked to provide guidance for public-to-private arrangements that meet the requirements set out in paragraph 5 and have the characteristics described in paragraph 3. The IFRIC noted that application by analogy would be appropriate under the hierarchy set out in paragraphs 7–12 of IAS 8 *Accounting Policies, Changes in Accounting Estimates and Errors*.

Grantor accounting

BC15 The Interpretation does not specify the accounting by grantors, because the IFRIC's objective and priority were to establish guidance for operators. Some commentators asked the IFRIC to establish guidance for the accounting by grantors. The IFRIC discussed these comments but reaffirmed its view. It noted that in many cases the grantor is a government body, and that IFRSs are not designed to apply to not-for-profit activities in the private sector, public sector or government, though entities with such activities may find them appropriate (see *Preface to IFRSs* paragraph 9).

Existing assets of the operator

BC16 The Interpretation does not specify the treatment of existing assets of the operator because the IFRIC decided that it was unnecessary to address the derecognition requirements of existing standards.

BC17 Some respondents asked the IFRIC to provide guidance on the accounting for existing assets of the operator, stating that the scope exclusion would create uncertainty about the treatment of these assets.

BC18 In its redeliberations the IFRIC noted that one objective of the Interpretation is to address whether the operator should recognise as its property, plant and equipment the infrastructure it constructs or to which it is given access. The accounting issue to be addressed for existing assets of the operator is one of derecognition, which is already addressed in IFRSs (IAS 16 *Property, Plant and Equipment*). In the light of the comments

Interpretations

received from respondents, the IFRIC decided to clarify that certain public-to-private service arrangements may convey to the grantor a right to use existing assets of the operator, in which case the operator would apply the derecognition requirements of IFRSs to determine whether it should derecognise its existing assets.

The significant residual interest criterion

BC19 Paragraph 5(b) of D12 proposed that for a service arrangement to be within its scope the residual interest in the infrastructure handed over to the grantor at the end of the arrangement must be significant. Respondents argued, and the IFRIC agreed, that the significant residual interest criterion would limit the usefulness of the guidance because a service arrangement for the entire physical life of the infrastructure would be excluded from the scope of the guidance. That result was not the IFRIC's intention. In its redeliberation of the proposals, the IFRIC decided that it would not retain the proposal that the residual interest in the infrastructure handed over to the grantor at the end of the arrangement must be significant. As a consequence, 'whole of life' infrastructure (i.e. where the infrastructure is used in a public-to-private service arrangement for the entirety of its useful life) is within the scope of the Interpretation.

Treatment of the operator's rights over the infrastructure (paragraph 11)

BC20 The IFRIC considered the nature of the rights conveyed to the operator in a service concession arrangement. It first examined whether the infrastructure used to provide public services could be classified as property, plant and equipment of the operator under IAS 16. It started from the principle that infrastructure used to provide public services should be recognised as property, plant and equipment of the party that controls its use. This principle determines which party should recognise the property, plant and equipment as its own. The reference to control stems from the *Framework*:

   (a)   an asset is defined by the *Framework* as 'a resource controlled by the entity as a result of past events and from which future economic benefits are expected to flow to the entity.'

   (b)   the *Framework* notes that many assets are associated with legal rights, including the right of ownership. It goes on to clarify that the right of ownership is not essential.

   (c)   rights are often unbundled. For example, they may be divided proportionately (undivided interests in land) or by specified cash flows (principal and interest on a bond) or over time (a lease).

BC21 The IFRIC concluded that treatment of infrastructure that the operator constructs or acquires or to which the grantor gives the operator access for the purpose of the service arrangement should be determined by whether it is controlled by the grantor in the manner described in paragraph 5. If it is so controlled (as will be the case for all arrangements within the scope of the Interpretation), then, regardless of which party has legal title to it during the arrangement, the infrastructure should not be recognised as property, plant and equipment of the operator because the operator does not control the use of the public service infrastructure.

BC22 In reaching this conclusion the IFRIC observed that it is control of the right to use an asset that determines recognition under IAS 16 and the creation of a lease under IAS 17 *Leases*. IAS 16 defines property, plant and equipment as tangible items that 'are held for use in the production or supply of goods or services, for rental to others or for administrative purposes …'. It requires items within this definition to be recognised as property, plant and equipment unless another standard requires or permits a different approach. As an example of a different approach, it highlights the requirement in IAS 17 for recognition of leased property, plant and equipment to be evaluated on the basis of the transfer of risks and rewards. That standard defines a lease as 'an agreement whereby the lessor conveys to the lessee in return for a series of payments the right to use an asset' and it sets out the requirements for classification of leases. IFRIC 4 *Determining whether an Arrangement contains a Lease* interprets the meaning of right to use an asset as 'the arrangement conveys the right to control the use of the underlying asset.'

BC23 Accordingly, it is only if an arrangement conveys the right to control the use of the underlying asset that reference is made to IAS 17 to determine how such a lease should be classified. A lease is classified as a finance lease if it transfers substantially all the risks and rewards incidental to ownership. A lease is classified as an operating lease if it does not transfer substantially all the risks and rewards incidental to ownership.

BC24 The IFRIC considered whether arrangements within the scope of IFRIC 12 convey 'the right to control the use of the underlying asset' (the public service infrastructure) to the operator. The IFRIC decided that, if an arrangement met the conditions in paragraph 5, the operator would not have the right to control the use of the underlying asset and should therefore not recognise the infrastructure as a leased asset.

BC25 In arrangements within the scope of the Interpretation the operator acts as a service provider. The operator constructs or upgrades infrastructure used to provide a public service. Under the terms of the contract the operator has access to operate the infrastructure to provide the public service on the grantor's behalf. The asset recognised by the operator is the consideration it receives in exchange for its services, not the public service infrastructure that it constructs or upgrades.

BC26 Respondents to the draft Interpretations disagreed that recognition should be determined solely on the basis of control of use without any assessment of the extent to which the operator or the grantor bears the risks and rewards of ownership. They questioned how the proposed approach could be reconciled to IAS 17, in which the leased asset is recognised by the party that bears substantially all the risks and rewards incidental to ownership.

BC27 During its redeliberation the IFRIC affirmed its decision that if an arrangement met the control conditions in paragraph 5 of the Interpretation the operator would not have the right to control the use of the underlying asset (public service infrastructure) and should therefore not recognise the infrastructure as its property, plant and equipment under IAS 16 or the creation of a lease under IAS 17. The contractual service arrangement between the grantor and operator would not convey the right to use the infrastructure to the operator. The IFRIC concluded that this treatment is also consistent with IAS 18 *Revenue* because, for arrangements within the scope of the Interpretation, the second condition of paragraph 14 of IAS 18 is not satisfied. The grantor retains continuing managerial involvement to the degree usually associated with ownership and control over the infrastructure as described in paragraph 5.

BC28 In service concession arrangements rights are usually conveyed for a limited period, which is similar to a lease. However, for arrangements within the scope of the Interpretation, the operator's right is different from that of a lessee: the grantor retains control over the use to which the infrastructure is put, by controlling or regulating what services the operator must provide, to whom it must provide them, and at what price, as described in paragraph 5(a). The grantor also retains control over any significant residual interest in the infrastructure throughout the period of the arrangement. Unlike a lessee, the operator does not have a right of use of the underlying asset: rather it has access to operate the infrastructure to provide the public service on behalf of the grantor in accordance with the terms specified in the contract.

BC29 The IFRIC considered whether the scope of the Interpretation might overlap with IFRIC 4. In particular, it noted the views expressed by some respondents that the contractual terms of certain service arrangements would be regarded as leases under IFRIC 4 and would also be regarded as meeting the scope criterion set out in paragraph 5 of IFRIC 12. The IFRIC did not regard the choice between accounting treatments as appropriate because it could lead to different accounting treatments for contracts that have similar economic effects. In the light of comments received the IFRIC amended the scope of IFRIC 4 to specify that if a service arrangement met the scope requirements of IFRIC 12 it would not be within the scope of IFRIC 4.

Recognition and measurement of arrangement consideration (paragraphs 12 and 13)

BC30 The accounting requirements for construction and service contracts are addressed in IAS 11 *Construction Contracts* and IAS 18. They require revenue to be recognised by reference to the stage of completion of the contract activity. IAS 18 states the general principle that revenue is measured at the fair value of the consideration received or receivable. However, the IFRIC observed that the fair value of the construction services delivered may in practice be the most appropriate method of establishing the fair value of the consideration received or receivable for the construction services. This will be the case in service concession arrangements, because the consideration attributable to the construction activity often has to be apportioned from a total sum receivable on the contract as a whole and, if it consists of an intangible asset, may also be subject to uncertainty in measurement.

BC31 The IFRIC noted that IAS 18 requires its recognition criteria to be applied separately to identifiable components of a single transaction in order to reflect the substance of the transaction. For example, when the selling price of a product includes an identifiable amount for subsequent servicing, that amount is deferred and is recognised as revenue over the period during which the service is performed. The IFRIC concluded that this requirement was relevant to service arrangements within the scope of the Interpretation. Arrangements within the scope of the Interpretation involve an operator providing more than one service, i.e. construction or upgrade services, and operation services. Although the contract for each service is generally negotiated as a single contract, its terms call for separate phases or elements because each separate phase or element has its own distinct skills, requirements and risks. The IFRIC noted that, in these circumstances, IAS 18 paragraphs 4 and 13 require the contract to be separated into two separate phases or elements, a construction element within the scope of IAS 11 and an operations element within the scope of IAS 18. Thus the operator might report different profit margins on each phase or element. The IFRIC noted that the amount for each service would be identifiable because such services were often provided as a single service. The IFRIC also noted that the combining and segmenting criteria of IAS 11 applied only to the construction element of the arrangement.

BC32 In some circumstances, the grantor makes a non-cash payment for the construction services, i.e. it gives the operator an intangible asset (a right to charge users of the public service) in exchange for the operator providing construction services. The operator then uses the intangible asset to generate further revenues from users of the public service.

BC33 Paragraph 12 of IAS 18 states:

> When goods are sold or services are rendered in exchange for dissimilar goods or services, the exchange is regarded as a transaction which generates revenue. The revenue is measured at the fair value of the goods or services received, adjusted by the amount of any cash or cash equivalents transferred. When the fair value of the goods or services received cannot be measured reliably, the revenue is measured at the fair value of the goods or services given up, adjusted by the amount of any cash or cash equivalents transferred.

BC34 The IFRIC noted that total revenue does not equal total cash inflows. The reason for this outcome is that, when the operator receives an intangible asset in exchange for its construction services, there are two sets of inflows and outflows rather than one. In the first set, the construction services are exchanged for the intangible asset in a barter transaction with the grantor. In the second set, the intangible asset received from the grantor is used up to generate cash flows from users of the public service. This result is not unique to service arrangements within the scope of the Interpretation. Any situation in which an entity provides goods or services in exchange for another dissimilar asset that is subsequently used to generate cash revenues would lead to a similar result.

BC35 Some IFRIC members were uncomfortable with such a result, and would have preferred a method of accounting under which total revenues were limited to the cash inflows. However, they accepted that it is consistent with the treatment accorded to a barter transaction, i.e. an exchange of dissimilar goods or services.

Consideration given by the grantor to the operator (paragraphs 14–19)

BC36 The IFRIC observed that the contractual rights that the operator receives in exchange for providing construction services can take a variety of forms. They are not necessarily rights to receive cash or other financial assets.

BC37 The draft Interpretations proposed that the nature of the operator's asset depended on who had the primary responsibility to pay the operator for the services. The operator should recognise a financial asset when the grantor had the primary responsibility to pay the operator for the services. The operator should recognise an intangible asset in all other cases.

BC38 Respondents to the draft Interpretations argued that determining which accounting model to apply by looking at who has the primary responsibility to pay the operator for the services, irrespective of who bears demand risk (i.e. ability and willingness of users to pay for the service), would result in an accounting treatment that did not reflect the economic substance of the arrangement. Respondents were concerned that the proposal would require operators with essentially identical cash flow streams to adopt different accounting models. This would impair users' understanding of entities involved in providing public-to-private service concession arrangements. Several gave the example of a shadow toll road and a toll road, where the economics (demand risk) of the arrangements would be similar, pointing out that under the proposals the two arrangements would be accounted for differently. In the light of comments received on the proposals, the IFRIC decided to clarify (see paragraphs 15–19) the extent to which an operator should recognise a financial asset and an intangible asset.

BC39 Responses to the draft Interpretations provided only limited information about the impact of the proposals. To obtain additional information, IASB staff arranged for discussions with preparers, auditors and regulators. The consensus of those consulted was that the identity of the payee has no effect on the risks to the operator's cash flow stream. The operator typically relies on the terms of the service arrangement contract to determine the risks to its cash flow stream. The operator's cash flows may be guaranteed by the grantor, in which case the grantor bears demand risk, or the operator's cash flows may be conditional on usage levels, in which case the operator bears demand risk.

BC40 The IFRIC noted that the operator's cash flows are guaranteed when (a) the grantor agrees to pay the operator specified or determinable amounts whether or not the public service is used (sometimes known as take-or-pay arrangements) or (b) the grantor grants a right to the operator to charge users of the public service and the grantor guarantees the operator's cash flows by way of a shortfall guarantee described in paragraph 16. The operator's cash flows are conditional on usage when it has no such guarantee but must obtain its revenue either directly from users of the public service or from the grantor in proportion to public usage of the service (road tolls or shadow tolls for example).

A financial asset (operator's cash flows are guaranteed by the grantor)

BC41 Paragraph 11 of IAS 32 *Financial Instruments: Presentation* defines a financial asset to include 'a contractual right to receive cash or another financial asset from another entity'. Paragraph 13 of that standard clarifies that 'contractual' refers to 'an agreement between two or more parties that has clear economic consequences that the parties have little, if any, discretion to avoid, usually because the agreement is enforceable by law.'

BC42 The IFRIC decided that a financial asset should be recognised to the extent that the operator has an unconditional present right to receive cash from or at the direction of the grantor for the construction services; and the grantor has little, if any, discretion to avoid payment, usually because the agreement is enforceable by law. The operator has a contractual right to receive cash for the construction services if the grantor contractually guarantees the operator's cash flows, in the manner described in paragraph 16. The IFRIC noted that the operator has an unconditional right to receive cash to the extent that the grantor bears the risk (demand risk) that the cash flows generated by the users of the public service will not be sufficient to recover the operator's investment.

BC43 The IFRIC noted that:

(a) An agreement to pay for the shortfall, if any, between amounts received from users of the service and specified or determinable amounts does not meet the definition of a financial guarantee in paragraph 9 of IAS 39 *Financial Instruments: Recognition and Measurement* because the operator has an unconditional contractual right to receive cash from the grantor. Furthermore, the amendments made to IAS 39 in August 2005 by *Financial Guarantee Contracts* do not address the treatment of financial guarantee contracts by the holder. The objective of the amendments was to ensure that issuers of financial guarantee contracts recognise a liability for the obligations the guarantor has undertaken in issuing that guarantee.

(b) Users or the grantor may pay the contractual amount receivable directly to the operator. The method of payment is a matter of form only. In both cases the operator has a present, unconditional, contractual right to receive the specified or determinable cash flows from or at the direction of the grantor. The nature of the operator's asset is not altered solely because the contractual amount receivable may be paid directly by users of the public service. The IFRIC observed that accounting for these contractual cash flows in accordance with IASs 32 and 39 faithfully reflects the economics of the arrangements, which is to provide finance to the grantor for the construction of the infrastructure.

Operator's cash flows are contingent on the operator meeting specified quality or efficiency requirements

BC44 The IFRIC concluded that the definition of a financial asset is met even if the contractual right to receive cash is contingent on the operator meeting specified quality or efficiency requirements or targets. Before the grantor is required to pay the operator for its construction services, the operator may have to ensure that the infrastructure is capable of generating the public services specified by the grantor or that the infrastructure is up to or exceeds operating standards or efficiency targets specified by the grantor to ensure a specified level of service and capacity can be delivered. In this respect the operator's position is the same as that of any other entity in which payment for goods or services is contingent on subsequent performance of the goods or service sold.

BC45 Therefore IFRIC 12 treats the consideration given by the grantor to the operator as giving rise to a financial asset irrespective of whether the contractual amounts receivable are contingent on the operator meeting levels of performance or efficiency targets.

An intangible asset (operator's cash flows are conditional on usage)

BC46 IAS 38 *Intangible Assets* defines an intangible asset as 'an identifiable non-monetary asset without physical substance'. It mentions licences as examples of intangible assets. It describes an asset as being identifiable when it arises from contractual rights.

BC47 The IFRIC concluded that the right of an operator to charge users of the public service meets the definition of an intangible asset, and therefore should be accounted for in accordance with IAS 38. In these circumstances the operator's revenue is conditional on usage and it bears the risk (demand risk) that the cash flows generated by users of the public service will not be sufficient to recover its investment.

BC48 In the absence of contractual arrangements designed to ensure that the operator receives a minimum amount (see paragraphs BC53 and BC54), the operator has no contractual right to receive cash even if receipt of the cash is highly probable. Rather, the operator has an opportunity to charge those who use the public service in the future. The operator bears the demand risk and hence its commercial return is contingent on users using the public service. The operator's asset is a licence, which would be classified as an intangible asset within the scope of IAS 38. And, as clarified in paragraph AG10 of the application guidance in IAS 32:

> Physical assets (such as inventories, property, plant and equipment), leased assets and intangible assets (such as patents and trademarks) are not financial assets. Control of such physical and intangible assets creates an opportunity to generate an inflow of cash or another financial asset, but it does not give rise to a present right to receive cash or another financial asset.

BC49 The IFRIC considered whether a right to charge users unsupported by any shortfall guarantee from the grantor could be regarded as an indirect right to receive cash arising from the contract with the grantor. It concluded that although the operator's asset might have characteristics that are similar to those of a financial asset, it would not meet the definition of a financial asset in IAS 32: the operator would not at the balance sheet date have a contractual right to receive cash from another entity. That other entity (i.e. the user) would still have the ability to avoid any obligation. The grantor would be passing to the operator an opportunity to charge users in future, not a present right to receive cash.

Contractual arrangements that eliminate substantially all variability in the operator's return

BC50 The IFRIC considered whether agreements incorporating contractual arrangements designed to eliminate substantially all variability in the operator's return would meet the definition of a financial asset, for example:

(a)   the price charged by the operator would be varied by regulation designed to ensure that the operator received a substantially fixed return; or

(b)   the operator would be permitted to collect revenues from users or the grantor until it achieved a specified return on its investment, at which point the arrangement would come to an end.

BC51 The IFRIC noted that, as a result of such contractual arrangements, the operator's return would be low risk. Only if usage were extremely low would the contractual mechanisms fail to give the operator the specified return. The likelihood of usage being that low could be remote. Commercially, the operator's return would be regarded as fixed, giving its asset many of the characteristics of a financial asset.

BC52 However, the IFRIC concluded that the fact that the operator's asset was low risk did not influence its classification. IAS 32 does not define financial assets by reference to the amount of risk in the return – it defines them solely by reference to the existence or absence of an unconditional contractual right to receive cash. There are other examples of licences that offer the holders of the rights predictable, low risk returns, but such licences are not regarded as giving the holder a contractual right to cash. And there are other industries in which price regulation is designed to provide the operators with substantially fixed returns – but the rights of operators in these other industries are not classified as financial assets as a result. The operator's asset is a variable term licence, which would be classified as an intangible asset within the scope of IAS 38.

A financial asset and an intangible asset

BC53 The IFRIC concluded that if the operator is paid for its construction services partly by a financial asset and partly by an intangible asset it is necessary to account separately for each component of the operator's consideration. The IFRIC included the requirement to account separately for each component (sometimes known as a bifurcated arrangement) of the operator's consideration in response to a concern raised on the draft Interpretations. The concern was that, in some arrangements, both parties to the contract share the risk (demand risk) that the cash flows generated by users of the public service will not be sufficient to recover the operator's investment. In order to achieve the desired sharing of risk, the parties often agree to arrangements under which the grantor pays the operator for its services partly by a financial asset and partly by granting a right to charge users of the public service (an intangible asset). The IFRIC concluded that in these circumstances it would be necessary to divide the operator's consideration into a financial asset component for any guaranteed amount of cash or other financial asset and an intangible asset for the remainder.

BC54 The IFRIC concluded that the nature of consideration given by the grantor to the operator is determined by reference to the contract terms and when it exists, relevant contract law. The IFRIC noted public-to-private service agreements are rarely if ever the same; technical requirements vary by sector and country. Furthermore, the terms of the contractual agreement may also depend on the specific features of the overall legal framework of the particular country. Public-to-private service contract laws, where they exist, may contain terms that do not have to be repeated in individual contracts.

Contractual obligations to restore the infrastructure to a specified level of serviceability (paragraph 21)

BC55 The IFRIC noted that IAS 37 *Provisions, Contingent Liabilities and Contingent Assets* prohibits an entity from providing for the replacement of parts of its own property, plant and equipment. IAS 16 requires such costs to be recognised in the carrying amount of an item of property, plant and equipment if the recognition criteria in paragraph 7 are met. Each part of an item of property, plant and equipment with a cost that is significant in relation to the total cost of the item is depreciated separately. The IFRIC concluded that this prohibition would not apply to arrangements within the scope of the Interpretation because the operator does not recognise the infrastructure as its own property, plant and equipment. The operator has an unavoidable obligation that it owes to a third party, the grantor, in respect of the infrastructure. The operator should recognise its obligations in accordance with IAS 37.

BC56 The IFRIC considered whether the Interpretation should contain guidance on the timing of recognition of the obligations. It noted that the precise terms and circumstances of the obligations would vary from contract to contract. It concluded that the requirements and guidance in IAS 37 were sufficiently clear to enable an operator to identify the period(s) in which different obligations should be recognised.

Borrowing costs (paragraph 22)

BC57 IAS 23 *Borrowing Costs* permits borrowing costs to be capitalised as part of the cost of a qualifying asset to the extent that they are directly attributable to its acquisition, construction or production until the asset is ready for its intended use or sale[1]. That Standard defines a qualifying asset as 'an asset that necessarily takes a substantial period of time to get ready for its intended use or sale'.

BC58 For arrangements within the scope of the Interpretation, the IFRIC decided that an intangible asset (i.e. the grantor gives the operator a right to charge users of the public service in return for construction services) meets the definition of a qualifying asset of the operator because generally the licence would not be ready for use until the infrastructure was constructed or upgraded. A financial asset (i.e. the grantor gives the operator a contractual right to receive cash or other financial asset in return for construction services) does not meet the definition of a qualifying asset of the operator. The IFRIC observed that interest is generally accreted on the carrying value of financial assets.

BC59 The IFRIC noted that financing arrangements may result in an operator obtaining borrowed funds and incurring associated borrowing costs before some or all of the funds are used for expenditure relating to construction or operation services. In such circumstances the funds are often temporarily invested. Any investment income earned on such funds is recognised in accordance with IAS 39, unless the operator adopts the allowed alternative treatment, in which case investment income earned during the construction phase of the arrangement is accounted for in accordance with paragraph 16 of IAS 23.[2]

Financial asset (paragraphs 23–25)

BC60 Paragraph 9 of IAS 39 identifies and defines four categories of financial asset: (i) those held at fair value through profit or loss; (ii) held-to-maturity investments; (iii) loans and receivables; and (iv) available-for-sale financial assets.

BC61 Paragraph 24 of IFRIC 12 assumes that public-to-private service arrangement financial assets will not be categorised as held-to-maturity investments. Paragraph 9 of IAS 39 states that a financial asset may not be classified as a held-to-maturity investment if it meets the

---

1   In March 2007, IAS 23 was revised to require the previously allowed alternative treatment of capitalisation. Therefore, an entity is required to capitalise borrowing costs as part of the cost of a qualifying asset to the extent that they are directly attributable to its acquisition, construction or production until the asset is ready for its intended use or sale. That revision does not affect the reasoning set out in this Basis for Conclusions.

2   In March 2007, IAS 23 was revised to require the previously allowed alternative treatment of capitalisation. Therefore, an entity is required to capitalise borrowing costs as part of the cost of a qualifying asset to the extent that they are directly attributable to its acquisition, construction or production until the asset is ready for its intended use or sale. That revision does not affect the reasoning set out in this Basis for Conclusions

definition of a loan or receivable. An asset that meets the definition of a held-to-maturity investment will meet the definition of a loan or receivable unless:

(a)   it is quoted in an active market; or

(b)   the holder may not recover substantially all of its initial investment, other than because of credit deterioration.

It is not envisaged that a public-to-private service arrangement financial asset will be quoted in an active market. Hence the circumstances of (a) will not arise. In the circumstances of (b), the asset must be classified as available for sale (if not designated upon initial recognition as at fair value through profit or loss).

BC62   The IFRIC considered whether the contract would include an embedded derivative if the amount to be received by the operator could vary with the quality of subsequent services to be provided by the operator or performance or efficiency targets to be achieved by the operator. The IFRIC concluded that it would not, because the definition of a derivative in IAS 39 requires, among other things, that the variable is not specific to a party to the contract. The consequence is that the contract's provision for variations in payments does not meet the definition of a derivative and, accordingly, the requirements of IAS 39 in relation to embedded derivatives do not apply. The IFRIC observed that if the amount to be received by the operator is conditional on the infrastructure meeting quality or performance or efficiency targets as described in paragraph BC44, this would not prevent the amount from being classified as a loan or receivable. The IFRIC also concluded that during the construction phase of the arrangement the operator's asset (representing its accumulating right to be paid for providing construction services) should be classified as a financial asset when it represents cash or another financial asset due from or at the direction of the grantor.

Intangible asset (paragraph 26)

BC63   The Interpretation requires the operator to account for its intangible asset in accordance with IAS 38. Among other requirements, IAS 38 requires an intangible asset with a finite useful economic life to be amortised over that life. Paragraph 97 states that 'the amortisation method used shall reflect the pattern in which the asset's future economic benefits are expected to be consumed by the entity.'

BC64   The IFRIC considered whether it would be appropriate for intangible assets under paragraph 26 to be amortised using an 'interest' method of amortisation, i.e. one that takes account of the time value of money in addition to the consumption of the intangible asset, treating the asset more like a monetary than a non-monetary asset. However, the IFRIC concluded that there was nothing unique about these intangible assets that would justify use of a method of depreciation different from that used for other intangible assets. The IFRIC noted that paragraph 98 of IAS 38 provides for a number of amortisation methods for intangible assets with finite useful lives. These methods include the straight-line method, the diminishing balance method and the unit of production method. The method used is selected on the basis of the expected pattern of consumption of the expected future economic benefits embodied in the asset and is applied consistently from period to period, unless there is a change in the expected pattern of consumption of those future economic benefits.

BC65   The IFRIC noted that interest methods of amortisation are not permitted under IAS 38. Therefore, IFRIC 12 does not provide exceptions to permit use of interest methods of amortisation.

BC66   The IFRIC considered when the operator should first recognise the intangible asset. The IFRIC concluded that the intangible asset (the licence) received in exchange for construction services should be recognised in accordance with general principles applicable to contracts for the exchange of assets or services.

BC67   The IFRIC noted that it is current practice not to recognise executory contracts to the extent that they are unperformed by both parties (unless the contract is onerous). IAS 37 describes executory contracts as 'contracts under which neither party has performed any of its obligations or both parties have partially performed their obligations to an equal extent'. Paragraph 91 of the *Framework* states:

> In practice, obligations under contracts that are equally proportionately unperformed (for example, liabilities for inventory ordered but not yet received) are generally not recognised as liabilities in the financial statements.

BC68 Therefore, the IFRIC concluded that contracts within the scope of the Interpretation should not be recognised to the extent that they are executory. The IFRIC noted that service concession arrangements within the scope of the Interpretation are generally executory when the contracts are signed. The IFRIC also concluded that during the construction phase of the arrangement the operator's asset (representing its accumulating right to be paid for providing construction services) should be classified as an intangible asset to the extent that it represents a right to receive a right (licence) to charge users of the public service (an intangible asset).

Items provided to the operator by the grantor (paragraph 27)

BC69 For service arrangements within the scope of the Interpretation, pre-existing infrastructure items made available to the operator by the grantor for the purpose of the service arrangement are not recognised as property, plant and equipment of the operator.

BC70 However, different considerations apply to other assets provided to the operator by the grantor if the operator can keep or deal with the assets as it wishes. Such assets become assets of the operator and so should be accounted for in accordance with general recognition and measurement principles, as should the obligations undertaken in exchange for them.

BC71 The IFRIC considered whether such assets would represent government grants, as defined in paragraph 3 of IAS 20 *Accounting for Government Grants and Disclosure of Government Assistance*:

> Government grants are assistance by government in the form of transfers of resources to an entity in return for past or future compliance with certain conditions relating to the operating activities of the entity. They exclude those forms of government assistance which cannot reasonably have a value placed upon them and transactions with government which cannot be distinguished from the normal trading transactions of the entity.

> The IFRIC concluded that if such assets were part of the overall consideration payable by the grantor on an arms' length basis for the operator's services, they would not constitute 'assistance'. Therefore, they would not meet the definition of government grants in IAS 20 and that standard would not apply.

Transition (paragraphs 29 and 30)

BC72 IAS 8 *Accounting Policies, Changes in Accounting Estimates and Errors* states that an entity shall account for a change in accounting policy resulting from initial application of an Interpretation in accordance with any specific transitional provisions in that Interpretation. In the absence of any specific transitional provisions, the general requirements of IAS 8 apply. The general requirement in IAS 8 is that the changes should be accounted for retrospectively, except to the extent that retrospective application would be impracticable.

BC73 The IFRIC noted that there are two aspects to retrospective determination: reclassification and remeasurement. The IFRIC took the view that it will usually be practicable to determine retrospectively the appropriate classification of all amounts previously included in an operator's balance sheet, but that retrospective remeasurement of service arrangement assets might not always be practicable.

BC74 The IFRIC noted that, when retrospective restatement is not practicable, IAS 8 requires prospective application from the earliest practicable date, which could be the start of the current period. Under prospective application, the operator could be applying different accounting models to similar transactions, which the IFRIC decided would be inappropriate. The IFRIC regarded it as important that the correct accounting model should be consistently applied.

BC75 The Interpretation reflects these conclusions.

Amendments to IFRS 1

BC76 The amendments to IFRS 1 *First-time Adoption of International Financial Reporting Standards* are necessary to ensure that the transitional arrangements are available to both existing users and first-time adopters of IFRSs. The IFRIC believes that the requirements will ensure that the balance sheet will exclude any items that would not qualify for recognition as assets and liabilities under IFRSs.

Summary of changes from the draft Interpretations

BC77 The main changes from the IFRIC's proposals are as follows:

(a) The proposals were published in three separate draft Interpretations, D12 *Service Concession Arrangements – Determining the Accounting Model*, D13 *Service Concession Arrangements – The Financial Asset Model* and D14 *Service Concession Arrangements – The Intangible Asset Model*. In finalising IFRIC 12, the IFRIC combined the three draft Interpretations.

(b) By contrast with IFRIC 12 the draft Interpretations did not explain the reasons for the scope limitations and the reasons for the control approach adopted by the IFRIC in paragraph 5. The IFRIC added Information Note 2 to IFRIC 12 to provide references to standards that apply to arrangements outside the scope of the Interpretation.

(c) The scope of the proposals did not include 'whole of life infrastructure' (i.e. infrastructure used in a public-to-private service arrangement for its entire useful life). IFRIC 12 includes 'whole of life infrastructure' within its scope.

(d) Under the approach proposed, an entity determined the appropriate accounting model by reference to whether the grantor or the user had primary responsibility to pay the operator for the services provided. IFRIC 12 requires an entity to recognise a financial asset to the extent that the operator has an unconditional contractual right to receive cash from or at the direction of the grantor. The operator should recognise an intangible asset to the extent that it receives a right to charge users of the public service.

(e) By contrast with IFRIC 12, the draft Interpretations implied that the nature of asset recognised (a financial asset or an intangible asset) by the operator as consideration for providing construction services determined the accounting for the operation phase of the arrangement.

(f) Under the approach proposed in the draft Interpretations, an entity could capitalise borrowing costs under the allowed alternative treatment in IAS 23. IFRIC 12 requires borrowing costs to be recognised as an expense in the period in which they are incurred unless the operator has a contractual right to receive an intangible asset (a right to charge users of the public service), in which case borrowing costs attributable to the arrangement may be capitalised in accordance with the allowed alternative treatment under IAS 23.[3]

(g) In finalising IFRIC 12, the IFRIC decided to amend IFRIC 4.

---

3 In March 2007, IAS 23 was revised to require the previously allowed alternative treatment of capitalisation. Therefore, an entity is required to capitalise borrowing costs as part of the cost of a qualifying asset to the extent that they are directly attributable to its acquisition, construction or production until the asset is ready for its intended use or sale. That revision does not affect the reasoning set out in this Basis for Conclusions.

Interpretation 13
Customer Loyalty Programmes
(Compiled November 2010)

Contents

Compilation Details

Comparison With IFRIC 13

AASB Interpretation 13
Customer Loyalty Programmes

Paragraphs

References

Background   1 – 2

Scope   3

Issues   4

Consensus   5 – 9

Application   Aus9.1 – Aus9.4

Effective Date   10A

Transition   11

Appendix

Application Guidance   AG1 – AG3

Illustrative Examples   IE1 – IE10

Basis for Conclusions on IFRIC 13

Deleted IFRIC 13 Text

> AASB Interpretation 13 *Customer Loyalty Programmes* (as amended) is set out in paragraphs 1 – 11 and the Appendix. Interpretations are listed in Australian Accounting Standard AASB 1048 *Interpretation of Standards*. In the absence of explicit guidance, AASB 108 *Accounting Policies, Changes in Accounting Estimates and Errors* provides a basis for selecting and applying accounting policies.

Compilation Details

AASB Interpretation 13 as amended

This compiled Interpretation applies to annual reporting periods beginning on or after 1 January 2011. It takes into account amendments up to and including 23 June 2010 and was prepared on 26 November 2010 by the staff of the Australian Accounting Standards Board (AASB).

This compilation is not a separate Interpretation issued by the AASB. Instead, it is a representation of Interpretation 13 (August 2007) as amended by other pronouncements, which are listed in the Table below.

Table of Pronouncements

Pronouncement	Month issued	Application date *(annual reporting periods ... on or after ...)*	Application, saving or transitional provisions
Interpretation 13	Aug 2007	*(beginning)* 1 Jul 2008	see (a) below
AASB 2007-8	Sep 2007	*(beginning)* 1 Jan 2009	see (b) below
AASB 2010-4	Jun 2010	*(beginning)* 1 Jan 2011	see (c) below

(a)   Entities may elect to apply this Interpretation to annual reporting periods beginning on or after 1 January 2005 but before 1 July 2008.

(b)   Entities may elect to apply this Standard to annual reporting periods beginning on or after 1 January 2005 but before 1 January 2009, provided that AASB 101 *Presentation of Financial Statements* (September 2007) is also applied to such periods.

(c)   Entities may elect to apply this Standard to annual reporting periods beginning on or after 1 January 2005 but before 1 January 2011.

Table of Amendments

Paragraph affected	How affected	By ... [paragraph]
Aus9.1	amended	AASB 2007-8 [7, 8]
Aus9.4	amended	AASB 2007-8 [8]
10 (preceding heading)	amended	AASB 2010-4 [13]
10A	added	AASB 2010-4 [14]
AG2	amended	AASB 2010-4 [15]
IE1	amended	AASB 2010-4 [16]

Comparison With IFRIC 13

AASB Interpretation 13 *Customer Loyalty Programmes* as amended incorporates International Financial Reporting Interpretations Committee Interpretation IFRIC 13 *Customer Loyalty Programmes* as issued and amended by the International Accounting Standards Board (IASB). Paragraphs that have been added to this Interpretation (and do not appear in the text of IFRIC 13) are identified with the prefix "Aus", followed by the number of the preceding IFRIC paragraph and decimal numbering.

Entities that comply with AASB Interpretation 13 as amended will simultaneously be in compliance with IFRIC 13 as amended.

Interpretation 13

AASB Interpretation 13 was issued in August 2007.

This compiled version of Interpretation 13 applies to annual reporting periods beginning on or after 1 January 2011. It incorporates relevant amendments contained in other AASB pronouncements up to and including 23 June 2010 (see Compilation Details).

Australian Accounting Standards Board
Interpretation 13
Customer Loyalty Programmes

References

Accounting Standard AASB 108 *Accounting Policies, Changes in Accounting Estimates and Errors*

Accounting Standard AASB 118 *Revenue*

Accounting Standard AASB 137 *Provisions, Contingent Liabilities and Contingent Assets*

Background

1   Customer loyalty programmes are used by entities to provide customers with incentives to buy their goods or services. If a customer buys goods or services, the entity grants the customer award credits (often described as 'points'). The customer can redeem the award credits for awards such as free or discounted goods or services.

2   The programmes operate in a variety of ways. Customers may be required to accumulate a specified minimum number or value of award credits before they are able to redeem them. Award credits may be linked to individual purchases or groups of purchases, or to continued custom over a specified period. The entity may operate the customer loyalty programme itself or participate in a programme operated by a third party. The awards offered may include goods or services supplied by the entity itself and/or rights to claim goods or services from a third party.

Scope

3   This Interpretation applies to customer loyalty award credits that:

    (a)   an entity grants to its customers as part of a sales transaction, i.e. a sale of goods, rendering of services or use by a customer of entity assets; and

    (b)   subject to meeting any further qualifying conditions, the customers can redeem in the future for free or discounted goods or services.

The Interpretation addresses accounting by the entity that grants award credits to its customers.

Issues

4   The issues addressed in this Interpretation are:

    (a)   whether the entity's obligation to provide free or discounted goods or services ('awards') in the future should be recognised and measured by:

        (i)   allocating some of the consideration received or receivable from the sales transaction to the award credits and deferring the recognition of revenue (applying paragraph 13 of Accounting Standard AASB 118 *Revenue*); or

        (ii)   providing for the estimated future costs of supplying the awards (applying paragraph 19 of AASB 118); and

    (b)   if consideration is allocated to the award credits:

        (i)   how much should be allocated to them;

        (ii)   when revenue should be recognised; and

        (iii)   if a third party supplies the awards, how revenue should be measured

Consensus

5   An entity shall apply paragraph 13 of AASB 118 and account for award credits as a separately identifiable component of the sales transaction(s) in which they are granted (the 'initial sale'). The fair value of the consideration received or receivable in respect of

the initial sale shall be allocated between the award credits and the other components of the sale.

6   The consideration allocated to the award credits shall be measured by reference to their fair value, i.e. the amount for which the award credits could be sold separately.

7   If the entity supplies the awards itself, it shall recognise the consideration allocated to award credits as revenue when award credits are redeemed and it fulfils its obligations to supply awards. The amount of revenue recognised shall be based on the number of award credits that have been redeemed in exchange for awards, relative to the total number expected to be redeemed.

8   If a third party supplies the awards, the entity shall assess whether it is collecting the consideration allocated to the award credits on its own account (i.e. as the principal in the transaction) or on behalf of the third party (i.e. as an agent for the third party).

   (a)   If the entity is collecting the consideration on behalf of the third party, it shall:

      (i)   measure its revenue as the net amount retained on its own account, i.e. the difference between the consideration allocated to the award credits and the amount payable to the third party for supplying the awards; and

      (ii)   recognise this net amount as revenue when the third party becomes obliged to supply the awards and entitled to receive consideration for doing so. These events may occur as soon as the award credits are granted. Alternatively, if the customer can choose to claim awards from either the entity or a third party, these events may occur only when the customer chooses to claim awards from the third party.

   (b)   If the entity is collecting the consideration on its own account, it shall measure its revenue as the gross consideration allocated to the award credits and recognise the revenue when it fulfils its obligations in respect of the awards.

9   If at any time the unavoidable costs of meeting the obligations to supply the awards are expected to exceed the consideration received and receivable for them (i.e. the consideration allocated to the award credits at the time of the initial sale that has not yet been recognised as revenue plus any further consideration receivable when the customer redeems the award credits), the entity has onerous contracts. A liability shall be recognised for the excess in accordance with AASB 137 *Provisions, Contingent Liabilities and Contingent Assets*. The need to recognise such a liability could arise if the expected costs of supplying awards increase, for example if the entity revises its expectations about the number of award credits that will be redeemed.

Application

Aus9.1   This Interpretation applies to:

   (a)   each entity that is required to prepare financial reports in accordance with Part 2M.3 of the *Corporations Act 2001* and that is a reporting entity;

   (b)   general purpose financial statements of each other reporting entity; and

   (c)   financial statements that are, or are held out to be, general purpose financial statements.

Aus9.2   This Interpretation applies to annual reporting periods beginning on or after 1 July 2008.

   [Note: For application dates of paragraphs changed or added by an amending pronouncement, see Compilation Details.]

Aus9.3   This Interpretation may be applied to annual reporting periods beginning on or after 1 January 2005 but before 1 July 2008. If an entity applies this Interpretation to such an annual reporting period, it shall disclose that fact.

Aus9.4   The requirements specified in this Interpretation apply to the financial statements where information resulting from their application is material in accordance with AASB 1031 *Materiality*.

Effective Date

10   [Deleted by the AASB]

10A   Paragraph AG2 was amended by AASB 2010-4 *Further Amendments to Australian Accounting Standards arising from the Annual Improvements Project* issued in June 2010. An entity shall apply that amendment for annual reporting periods beginning on or after 1 January 2011. Earlier application is permitted. If an entity applies the amendment for an earlier period it shall disclose that fact.

Transition

11   Changes in accounting policy shall be accounted for in accordance with AASB 108 *Accounting Policies, Changes in Accounting Estimates and Errors.*

Appendix — Application Guidance

This appendix is an integral part of AASB Interpretation 13.

Measuring the Fair Value of Award Credits

AG1   Paragraph 6 of the consensus requires the consideration allocated to award credits to be measured by reference to their fair value, i.e. the amount for which the award credits could be sold separately. If the fair value is not directly observable, it must be estimated.

AG2   An entity may estimate the fair value of award credits by reference to the fair value of the awards for which they could be redeemed. The fair value of the award credits takes into account, as appropriate:

    (a)   the amount of the discounts or incentives that would otherwise be offered to customers who have not earned award credits from an initial sale; and

    (b)   the proportion of award credits that are not expected to be redeemed by customers.

    If customers can choose from a range of different awards, the fair value of the award credits will reflect the fair values of the range of available awards, weighted in proportion to the frequency with which each award is expected to be selected.

AG3   In some circumstances, other estimation techniques may be available. For example, if a third party will supply the awards and the entity pays the third party for each award credit it grants, it could estimate the fair value of the award credits by reference to the amount it pays the third party, adding a reasonable profit margin. Judgement is required to select and apply the estimation technique that satisfies the requirements of paragraph 6 of the consensus and is most appropriate in the circumstances.

Illustrative Examples

These examples accompany, but are not part of, AASB Interpretation 13.

Example 1 — Awards supplied by the entity

IE1   A grocery retailer operates a customer loyalty programme. It grants programme members loyalty points when they spend a specified amount on groceries. Programme members can redeem the points for further groceries. The points have no expiry date. In one period, the entity grants 100 points. Management estimates the fair value of groceries for which each loyalty point can be redeemed as 1.25 currency units (CU1.25). This amount takes into account an estimate of the discount that management expects would otherwise be offered to customers who have not earned award credits from an initial sale. In addition, management expects only 80 of these points to be redeemed. Therefore, the fair value of each point is CU1, being the value of each loyalty point granted of CU1.25 reduced to take into account points not expected to be redeemed ((80 points/100 points) × CU1.25 = CU1). Accordingly, management defers recognition of revenue of CU100.

Year 1

IE2   At the end of the first year, 40 of the points have been redeemed in exchange for groceries, i.e. half of those expected to be redeemed. The entity recognises revenue of (40 points / 80* points) × CU100 = CU50.

Year 2

IE3   In the second year, management revises its expectations. It now expects 90 points to be redeemed altogether.

IE4   During the second year, 41 points are redeemed, bringing the total number redeemed to 40† + 41 = 81 points. The cumulative revenue that the entity recognises is (81 points / 90‡ points) × CU100 = CU90. The entity has recognised revenue of CU50 in the first year, so it recognises CU40 in the second year.

Year 3

IE5   In the third year, a further nine points are redeemed, taking the total number of points redeemed to 81 + 9 = 90. Management continues to expect that only 90 points will ever be redeemed, i.e. that no more points will be redeemed after the third year. So the cumulative revenue to date is (90 points / 90§ points) × CU100 = CU100. The entity has already recognised CU90 of revenue (CU50 in the first year and CU40 in the second year). So it recognises the remaining CU10 in the third year. All of the revenue initially deferred has now been recognised.

Example 2 — Awards supplied by a third party

IE6   A retailer of electrical goods participates in a customer loyalty programme operated by an airline. It grants programme members one air travel point with each CU1 they spend on electrical goods. Programme members can redeem the points for air travel with the airline, subject to availability. The retailer pays the airline CU0.009 for each point.

IE7   In one period, the retailer sells electrical goods for consideration totalling CU1 million. It grants 1 million points.

Allocation of consideration to travel points

IE8   The retailer estimates that the fair value of a point is CU0.01. It allocates to the points 1 million × CU0.01 = CU10,000 of the consideration it has received from the sales of its electrical goods.

Revenue recognition

IE9   Having granted the points, the retailer has fulfilled its obligations to the customer. The airline is obliged to supply the awards and entitled to receive consideration for doing so. Therefore the retailer recognises revenue from the points when it sells the electrical goods.

Revenue measurement

IE10   If the retailer has collected the consideration allocated to the points on its own account, it measures its revenue as the gross CU10,000 allocated to them. It separately recognises the CU9,000 paid or payable to the airline as an expense. If the retailer has collected the consideration on behalf of the airline, i.e. as an agent for the airline, it measures its revenue as the net amount it retains on its own account. This amount of revenue is the difference between the CU10,000 consideration allocated to the points and the CU9,000 passed on to the airline.

---

*   total number of points expected to be redeemed

†   number of points redeemed in year 1

‡   revised estimate of total number of points expected to be redeemed

§   total number of points still expected to be redeemed

Interpretations

Basis for Conclusions on IFRIC Interpretation 13

This IFRIC Basis for Conclusions accompanies, but is not part of, AASB Interpretation 13. An IFRIC Basis for Conclusions may be amended to reflect the requirements of the AASB Interpretation and AASB Accounting Standards where they differ from the corresponding International pronouncements.

BC1 This Basis for Conclusions summarises the IFRIC's considerations in reaching its consensus. Individual IFRIC members gave greater weight to some factors than to others.

Scope

BC2 Customer loyalty programmes are widespread, being used by businesses as diverse as supermarkets, airlines, telecommunications operators, hotels and credit card providers. IFRSs lack specific guidance on how entities should account for the awards offered to customers in these programmes. As a result, practices have diverged.

BC3 The main area of diversity concerns award credits that entities grant to their customers as part of a sales transaction, and that the customers can redeem in the future for free or discounted goods or services. The Interpretation applies to such award credits.

BC4 In some sales transactions, the entity receives consideration from an intermediate party, rather than directly from the customer to whom it grants the award credits. For example, credit card providers may provide services and grant award credits to credit card holders but receive consideration for doing so from vendors accepting payment by credit card. Such transactions are within the scope of the Interpretation and the wording of the consensus has been drafted to accommodate them.

Issues

BC5 Different views have emerged about how the entity granting award credits should recognise and measure its obligation to provide free or discounted goods or services if and when customers redeem award credits.

BC6 One view is that the obligation should be recognised as an expense at the time of the initial sale and be measured by reference to the amount required to settle it, in accordance with IAS 37 *Provisions, Contingent Liabilities and Contingent Assets.* In support of this view, it is argued that:

    (a)   customer loyalty programmes are marketing tools designed to enhance sales volumes. Therefore the costs of the programmes are marketing expenses.

    (b)   the value of awards is often insignificant compared with the value of the purchases required to earn them. The obligation to exchange award credits for awards is not a significant element of the sales transaction. Thus, when the initial sale is made, the entity has met the conditions set out in IAS 18 *Revenue* for recognising revenue from that sale. Paragraph 16 of IAS 18 indicates that a selling entity can recognise revenue before it has completed all of the acts required of it under the contract, providing it does not retain the significant risks and rewards of ownership of the goods sold. Paragraph 19 requires expenses relating to the sale, including those for costs still to be incurred, to be recognised at the same time as the revenue.

BC7 A second view is that some of the consideration received in respect of the initial sale should be allocated to the award credits and recognised as a liability until the entity fulfils its obligations to deliver awards to customers. The liability would be measured by reference to the value of the award credits to the customer (not their cost to the entity) and recognised as an allocation of revenue (not an expense). In support of this view, it is argued that:

    (a)   award credits granted to a customer as a result of a sales transaction are an element of the transaction itself, i.e. the market exchange of economic benefits between the entity and the customer. They represent rights granted to the customer, for which the customer is implicitly paying. They can be distinguished from marketing expenses because they are granted to the customer as part of the sales transaction. Marketing expenses, in contrast, are incurred independently of the sales transactions they are designed to secure.

(b)   award credits are separately identifiable from the other goods or services sold as part of the initial sale. Paragraph 13 of IAS 18 states that:

> The recognition criteria in this Standard are usually applied separately to each transaction. However, in certain circumstances, it is necessary to apply the recognition criteria to the separately identifiable components of a single transaction in order to reflect the substance of the transaction. For example, when the selling price of a product includes an identifiable amount for subsequent servicing, that amount is deferred and recognised as revenue over the period during which the service is performed.

Because loyalty awards are not delivered to the customer at the same time as the other goods or services, it is necessary to divide the initial sale into components and apply the recognition criteria separately to each component in order to reflect the substance of the transaction.

BC8   A third view is that the accounting should depend on the nature of the customer loyalty programme. The criteria for determining which accounting treatment should be adopted could refer to the relative value or nature of the awards, or the method of supplying them. Award credits would be regarded as marketing expenses if, say, their value were insignificant and/or they were redeemable for goods or services not supplied by the entity in the course of its ordinary activities. In contrast, award credits would be regarded as a separate component of the initial sales transaction if their value were significant and/ or they were redeemable for goods or services supplied by the entity in the course of its ordinary activities.

Consensus

Attributing revenue to award credits

BC9   The consensus reflects the second view, described in paragraph BC7. In reaching its consensus, the IFRIC noted that:

(a)   the first and second views apply different paragraphs of IAS 18. The first view (paragraph BC6) applies paragraph 19 to recognise the cost of the awards at the time of the initial sale. The second view applies paragraph 13 to identify the award credits as a separate component of the initial sale. The issue is to identify which of the two paragraphs should be applied. IAS 18 does not give explicit guidance. However, the aim of IAS 18 is to recognise revenue when, and to the extent that, goods or services have been delivered to a customer. In the IFRIC's view, paragraph 13 applies if a single transaction requires two or more separate goods or services to be delivered at different times; it ensures that revenue for each item is recognised only when that item is delivered. In contrast, paragraph 19 applies only if the entity has to incur further costs directly related to items already delivered, e.g. to meet warranty claims. In the IFRIC's view, loyalty awards are not costs that directly relate to the goods and services already delivered—rather, they are separate goods or services delivered at a later date.

(b)   the third view, described in paragraph BC8, would be difficult to justify conceptually. It can be argued that the substance of the incentives is the same, whatever their form or value. A dividing line could lead to inconsistencies and accounting arbitrage. Particular difficulties could arise if a programme offered customers a choice of awards, only some of which would be supplied by the entity in the course of its ordinary activities.

BC10 The IFRIC considered an objection that the costs of applying the approach set out in the consensus view in paragraph BC7 would exceed the benefits. Those raising the objection argued that:

- the approach is more complicated to apply than a cost accrual approach;

- it produces information that is less reliable, and no more relevant; and

- the additional costs are not merited because the amounts involved are often relatively insignificant.

BC11 The IFRIC acknowledged that entities might have to incur costs to change systems and procedures to comply with the Interpretation. However, it did not agree that the ongoing costs would exceed the benefits. It noted that most of the variables that have to be estimated to measure the revenue attributable to award credits (such as redemption rates, timing of redemption etc.) also need to be estimated to measure the future cost of fulfilling the obligation. In the IFRIC's view, benefits to users will arise from customer loyalty award obligations being measured on the same basis as other separately identifiable performance obligations to customers.

Allocation method

BC12 IAS 18 requires revenue to be measured at the fair value of the consideration received or receivable. Hence the amount of revenue attributed to award credits should be the fair value of the consideration received for them. The IFRIC noted that this amount is often not directly observable because the award credits are granted as part of a larger sale. In such circumstances, it must be estimated by allocating the total consideration between the award credits and other goods or services sold, using an appropriate allocation method.

BC13 IAS 18 does not prescribe an allocation method for multiple-component sales. However, its overall objective is to determine the amount the customer is paying for each component, which can be estimated by drawing on the entity's experience of transactions with similar customers. Hence, the Interpretation requires the consideration allocated to award credits to be measured by reference to their fair value.

BC14 The Interpretation does not specify whether the amount allocated to the award credits should be:

(a)   equal to their fair value (irrespective of the fair values of the other components); or

(b)   a proportion of the total consideration based on the fair value of the award credits relative to the fair values of the other components of the sale.

The IFRIC noted that IAS 18 does not specify which of these methods should be applied, or in what circumstances. The IFRIC decided that the Interpretation should not be more prescriptive than IAS 18. The selection of one or other method is therefore left to management's judgement.

Measuring the fair value of award credits

BC14A *In Improvements to IFRSs* issued in May 2010, the Board addressed unclear wording that could lead to divergent interpretations of the term 'fair value' in the application guidance for IFRIC 13. The Board was made aware that paragraph AG2 could be interpreted to mean that the fair value of award credits is equal to the fair value of redemption awards because the term 'fair value' is used to refer to both the value of the award credits and the value of the awards for which the credits could be redeemed. To address this, the Board amended paragraph AG2 and Example 1 in the illustrative examples. The amendment clarifies that when the fair value of award credits is measured on the basis of the value of the awards for which they could be redeemed, the fair value of the award credits should take account of expected forfeitures as well as the discounts or incentives that would otherwise be offered to customers who have not earned award credits from an initial sale.

Revenue recognition — awards supplied by the entity

BC15 The consideration allocated to award credits represents the amount that the entity has received for accepting an obligation to supply awards if customers redeem the credits. This amount reflects both the value of the awards and the entity's expectations regarding the proportion of credits that will be redeemed, i.e. the risk of a claim being made. The entity has received the consideration for accepting the risk, whether or not a claim is actually made. Hence, the Interpretation requires revenue to be recognised as the risk expires, i.e. based on the number of award credits that have been redeemed relative to the total number expected to be redeemed.

BC16 After granting award credits, the entity may revise its expectations about the proportion that will be redeemed. The change in expectations does not affect the consideration that the entity has received for supplying awards: this consideration (the revenue) was fixed at the time of the initial sale. Hence the change in expectations does not affect the measurement of the original obligation. Instead, it affects the amount of revenue recognised in respect of award credits that are redeemed in the period. The change in expectations is thus accounted for as a change in estimate in the period of change and future periods, in accordance with paragraph 36 of IAS 8 *Accounting Policies, Changes in Accounting Estimates and Errors*.

BC17 A change in expectations regarding redemption rates may also affect the costs the entity expects to incur to supply awards. If estimated redemption rates increase to the extent that the unavoidable costs of supplying awards are expected to exceed the consideration received and receivable for them, the entity has onerous contracts. The Interpretation therefore highlights the requirement of IAS 37 to recognise a liability for the excess.

Revenue recognition — awards supplied by a third party

BC18 Some customer loyalty programmes offer customers awards in the form of goods and services supplied by a third party. For example, a grocery retailer may offer customers an option to redeem award credits for air travel points or a voucher for free goods from an electrical retailer. The IFRIC noted that, depending on the terms of the arrangement, the reporting entity (the grocery retailer in this example) may retain few, if any, obligations in respect of the supply of the awards. In such circumstances, the customer is still receiving the benefits of — and implicitly paying the entity consideration for — the rights to awards. Hence, consideration should be allocated to the award credits.

BC19 However, the entity may in substance be collecting the consideration on behalf of the third party, i.e. as an agent for the third party. If so, paragraph 8 of IAS 18 would need to be taken into consideration. This paragraph states that:

> Revenue includes only the gross inflows of economic benefits received and receivable by the entity on its own account. ...in an agency relationship, the gross inflows of economic benefits include amounts collected on behalf of the principal and which do not result in increases in equity for the entity. The amounts collected on behalf of the principal are not revenue. Instead, revenue is the amount of commission.

BC20 Depending on the terms of the agreement between the entity, award credit holders and the third party, the gross consideration attributable to the award credits might not represent revenue for the entity. Rather, the entity's revenue might be only the net amount it retains on its own account, i.e. the difference between the consideration allocated to the award credits and the amount paid or payable by the entity to the third party for supplying the awards.

BC21 The IFRIC noted that, if the entity is acting as an agent for a third party, its revenue arises from rendering agency services to that third party, not from supplying awards to the award credit holders. The entity should therefore recognise revenue in accordance with paragraph 20 of IAS 18. As the outcome of the transaction can be estimated reliably (the consideration has been received and the amount payable to the third party agreed), revenue is recognised in the periods in which the entity renders its agency services, i.e. when the third party becomes obliged to supply the awards and entitled to receive consideration for doing so.

Changes from draft Interpretation D20

BC22 A draft of the Interpretation — D20 *Customer Loyalty Programmes* — was published for comment in September 2006. The most significant changes made in the light of comments received relate to:

(a) *allocation of consideration to award credits.* D20 proposed that consideration should be allocated between award credits and other components of the sale by reference to their relative fair values. The IFRIC accepted suggestions that another allocation method — whereby the award credits are allocated an amount equal to their fair value — could also be consistent with IAS 18, and would be simpler to apply. So, as explained in paragraph BC14, the consensus has been revised to avoid precluding this latter method.

(b)   *awards supplied by a third party.* The consensus in D20 did not refer to the possibility that an entity may have collected consideration on behalf of the third party, and hence that its revenue may need to be measured net of amounts passed on to the third party. However, as some commentators pointed out, awards are often supplied by third parties and so this possibility will often need to be considered for transactions within the scope of the Interpretation. The requirements of IAS 18 in this respect have therefore been added to paragraph 8 of the consensus and are explained in paragraphs BC19–BC21.

(c)   *customer relationship intangible assets.* Customer loyalty programmes may create or enhance customer relationship intangible assets. The consensus in D20 had pointed out that such assets should be recognised only if the recognition criteria in IAS 38 *Intangible Assets* had been met. The IFRIC accepted that this comment appeared to suggest that there would be circumstances in which intangible assets were recognised, whereas the requirements of IAS 38 were such that recognition was very unlikely. It also decided that the comment was peripheral to the issues being addressed in the Interpretation. It deleted the comment from the consensus.

(d)   *guidance on measuring the fair value of award credits.* Paragraph AG2 explains that the fair value of award credits may be measured by reference to the fair value of the awards for which they could be redeemed, reduced to take into account various factors. The list of factors in D20 had referred to the time value of money. However, the IFRIC accepted suggestions that the effect of the time value of money will often not be material — especially if awards are specified in non-monetary terms — and that it should not therefore be highlighted as a factor that will routinely need to be measured.

(e)   *location of application guidance.* Two paragraphs of the consensus in D20 comprised guidance on how to apply the paragraphs that preceded them. They have been moved to an appendix, and supplemented by additional explanation that had been located in the Basis for Conclusions in D20.

(f)   *illustrative examples.* These have been added to help readers understand how to apply the revenue recognition requirements, especially in relation to forfeited award credits and changes in estimates of forfeiture rates.

Deleted IFRIC Interpretation 13 Text

Deleted IFRIC Interpretation 13 text is not part of AASB Interpretation 13.

Paragraph 10

An entity shall apply this Interpretation for annual periods beginning on or after 1 July 2008. Earlier application is permitted. If an entity applies the Interpretation for a period beginning before 1 July 2008, it shall disclose that fact.

Interpretation 14
AASB 119 – The Limit on a Defined Benefit Asset, Minimum Funding Requirements and their Interaction

(Compiled February 2010)

Contents

Compilation Details

Comparison with IFRIC 14

AASB Interpretation 14
AASB 119 – The Limit on a Defined Benefit Asset,
Minimum Funding Requirements and their Interaction

Paragraphs

References

Background   1 – 3A

Scope   4 – 5

Issues   6

Consensus

Availability of a refund or reduction in future contributions   7 – 10

    The economic benefit available as a refund   11 – 15

    The economic benefit available as a contribution reduction   16 – 17

The effect of a minimum funding requirement on the economic benefit
available as a reduction in future contributions   18 – 22

When a minimum funding requirement may give rise to a liability   23 – 26

Application   Aus26.1 – Aus 26.4

Transition   28 – 29

Illustrative Examples   IE1 – IE27

Basis for Conclusions on IFRIC 14

Deleted IFRIC 14 Text

AASB Interpretation 14 AASB 119 – *The Limit on a Defined Benefit Asset, Minimum Funding Requirements and their Interaction* (as amended) is set out in paragraphs 1 – 29. Interpretations are listed in Australian Accounting Standard AASB 1048 *Interpretation and Application of Standards*. In the absence of explicit guidance, AASB 108 *Accounting Policies, Changes in Accounting Estimates and Errors* provides a basis for selecting and applying accounting policies.

Compilation Details

AASB Interpretation 14 AASB 119 – *The Limit on a Defined Benefit Asset, Minimum Funding Requirements and their Interaction* as amended

This compiled Interpretation applies to annual reporting periods beginning on or after 1 January 2011. It takes into account amendments up to and including 21 December 2009 and was prepared on 23 February 2010 by the staff of the Australian Accounting Standards Board (AASB).

This compilation is not a separate Interpretation issued by the AASB. Instead, it is a representation of Interpretation 14 (August 2007) as amended by other pronouncements, which are listed in the Table below.

Table of Pronouncements

Pronouncement	Month issued	Application date (*annual reporting periods … on or after …*)	Application, saving or transitional provisions
Interpretation 14	Aug 2007	(*beginning*) 1 Jan 2008	see (a) below
AASB 2007-8	Sep 2007	(*beginning*) 1 Jan 2009	see (b) below
AASB 2009-6	Jun 2009	(*beginning*) 1 Jan 2009 and (*ending*) 30 Jun 2009	see (c) below
AASB 2009-14	Dec 2009	(*beginning*) 1 Jan 2011	see (d) below

(a) Entities may elect to apply this Interpretation to annual reporting periods beginning on or after 1 January 2005 but before 1 January 2008.

(b) Entities may elect to apply this Standard to annual reporting periods beginning on or after 1 January 2005 but before 1 January 2009, provided that AASB 101 *Presentation of Financial Statements* (September 2007) is also applied to such periods.

(c) Entities may elect to apply this Standard to annual reporting periods beginning on or after 1 January 2005 but before 1 January 2009, provided that AASB 101 *Presentation of Financial Statements* (September 2007) is also applied to such periods, and to annual reporting periods beginning on or after 1 January 2009 that end before 30 June 2009.

(d) Entities may elect to apply this Standard to annual reporting periods beginning on or after 1 January 2005 but before 1 January 2011.

Table of Amendments to Interpretation

Paragraph affected	How affected	By ... [paragraph]
3A	added	AASB 2009-14 [6]
10	amended	AASB 2009-6 [112]
16-17	amended	AASB 2009-14 [7]
18	amended	AASB 2009-14 [8]
20-22	amended	AASB 2009-14 [8]
26	amended	AASB 2009-6 [113]
Aus26.1	amended	AASB 2007-8 [7, 8]
Aus26.4	amended	AASB 2007-8 [8]
27A	note added	AASB 2009-6 [114]
27B	note added	AASB 2009-14 [9]
29	added	AASB 2009-14 [10]

Table of Amendments to Illustrative Examples

Paragraph affected	How affected	By ... [paragraph]
IE7	amended	AASB 2009-6 [115]
IE8	amended	AASB 2009-6 [115]
IE9	amended	AASB 2009-14 [11]

Paragraph affected	How affected	By ... [paragraph]
IE11-IE12	amended	AASB 2009-14 [11]
IR16-IE18	amended	AASB 2009-14 [11]
IE20	amended	AASB 2009-6 [115]
IE21	amended	AASB 2009-6 [115]
IE22-IE25 (and preceding heading)	added	AASB 2009-14 [12]
IE26-IE27 (and preceding heading)	added	AASB 2009-14 [12]

General Terminology Amendments

References to 'balance sheet' and 'balance sheet date' were amended to 'statement of financial position' and 'end of the reporting period' respectively by AASB 2007-8. These amendments are not shown in the above Tables of Amendments.

Comparison with IFRIC 14

AASB Interpretation 14 *AASB 119 – The Limit on a Defined Benefit Asset, Minimum Funding Requirements and their Interaction* as amended incorporates International Financial Reporting Interpretations Committee Interpretation IFRIC 14 *IAS 19 – The Limit on a Defined Benefit Asset, Minimum Funding Requirements* and their Interaction as amended, issued by the International Accounting Standards Board. Paragraphs that have been added to this Interpretation (and do not appear in the text of IFRIC 14) are identified with the prefix "Aus", followed by the number of the preceding IFRIC paragraph and decimal numbering.

Entities that comply with AASB Interpretation 14 as amended will simultaneously be in compliance with IFRIC 14 as amended.

Interpretation 14

AASB Interpretation 14 was issued in August 2007.

This compiled version of Interpretation 14 applies to annual reporting periods beginning on or after 1 January 2011. It incorporates relevant amendments contained in other AASB pronouncements up to and including 21 December 2009 (see Compilation Details).

Australian Accounting Standards Board

Interpretation 14

AASB 119 – The Limit on a Defined Benefit Asset, Minimum Funding Requirements and their Interaction

References

Accounting Standard AASB 101 *Presentation of Financial Statements*

Accounting Standard AASB 108 *Accounting Policies, Changes in Accounting Estimates and Errors*

Accounting Standard AASB 119 *Employee Benefits*

Accounting Standard AASB 137 *Provisions, Contingent Liabilities and Contingent Assets*

Background

1   Paragraph 58 of Accounting Standard AASB 119 *Employee Benefits* limits the measurement of a defined benefit asset to 'the present value of economic benefits available in the form of refunds from the plan or reductions in future contributions to the plan' plus unrecognised gains and losses. Questions have arisen about when refunds or reductions in future contributions should be regarded as available, particularly when a minimum funding requirement exists.

Interpretations

2   Minimum funding requirements exist in many countries to improve the security of the post-employment benefit promise made to members of an employee benefit plan. Such requirements normally stipulate a minimum amount or level of contributions that must be made to a plan over a given period. Therefore, a minimum funding requirement may limit the ability of the entity to reduce future contributions.

3   Further, the limit on the measurement of a defined benefit asset may cause a minimum funding requirement to be onerous. Normally, a requirement to make contributions to a plan would not affect the measurement of the defined benefit asset or liability. This is because the contributions, once paid, will become plan assets and so the additional net liability is nil. However, a minimum funding requirement may give rise to a liability if the required contributions will not be available to the entity once they have been paid.

3A   In November 2009 the International Accounting Standards Board amended IFRIC 14 to remove an unintended consequence arising from the treatment of prepayments of future contributions in some circumstances when there is a minimum funding requirement.

Scope

4   This Interpretation applies to all post-employment defined benefits and other long-term employee defined benefits.

5   For the purpose of this Interpretation, minimum funding requirements are any requirements to fund a post-employment or other long-term defined benefit plan.

Issues

6   The issues addressed in this Interpretation are:

     (a)   when refunds or reductions in future contributions should be regarded as available in accordance with paragraph 58 of AASB 119;

     (b)   how a minimum funding requirement might affect the availability of reductions in future contributions; and

     (c)   when a minimum funding requirement might give rise to a liability.

Consensus

Availability of a refund or reduction in future contributions

7   An entity shall determine the availability of a refund or a reduction in future contributions in accordance with the terms and conditions of the plan and any statutory requirements in the jurisdiction of the plan.

8   An economic benefit, in the form of a refund or a reduction in future contributions, is available if the entity can realise it at some point during the life of the plan or when the plan liabilities are settled. In particular, such an economic benefit may be available even if it is not realisable immediately at the end of the reporting period.

9   The economic benefit available does not depend on how the entity intends to use the surplus. An entity shall determine the maximum economic benefit that is available from refunds, reductions in future contributions or a combination of both. An entity shall not recognise economic benefits from a combination of refunds and reductions in future contributions based on assumptions that are mutually exclusive.

10   In accordance with AASB 101 *Presentation of Financial Statements*, the entity shall disclose information about the key sources of estimation uncertainty at the end of the reporting period that have a significant risk of causing a material adjustment to the carrying amount of the net asset or liability recognised in the statement of financial position. This might include disclosure of any restrictions on the current realisability of the surplus or disclosure of the basis used to determine the amount of the economic benefit available.

The economic benefit available as a refund

The right to a refund

11   A refund is available to an entity only if the entity has an unconditional right to a refund:

     (a)   during the life of the plan, without assuming that the plan liabilities must be settled in order to obtain the refund (e.g. in some jurisdictions, the entity may have a right to a refund during the life of the plan, irrespective of whether the plan liabilities are settled); or

(b) assuming the gradual settlement of the plan liabilities over time until all members have left the plan; or

(c) assuming the full settlement of the plan liabilities in a single event (i.e. as a plan wind-up).

An unconditional right to a refund can exist whatever the funding level of a plan at the end of the reporting period.

12 If the entity's right to a refund of a surplus depends on the occurrence or non-occurrence of one or more uncertain future events not wholly within its control, the entity does not have an unconditional right and shall not recognise an asset.

Measurement of the economic benefit

13 An entity shall measure the economic benefit available as a refund as the amount of the surplus at the end of the reporting period (being the fair value of the plan assets less the present value of the defined benefit obligation) that the entity has a right to receive as a refund, less any associated costs. For instance, if a refund would be subject to a tax other than income tax, an entity shall measure the amount of the refund net of the tax.

14 In measuring the amount of a refund available when the plan is wound up (paragraph 11(c)), an entity shall include the costs to the plan of settling the plan liabilities and making the refund. For example, an entity shall deduct professional fees if these are paid by the plan rather than the entity, and the costs of any insurance premiums that may be required to secure the liability on wind-up.

15 If the amount of a refund is determined as the full amount or a proportion of the surplus, rather than a fixed amount, an entity shall make no adjustment for the time value of money, even if the refund is realisable only at a future date.

The economic benefit available as a contribution reduction

16 If there is no minimum funding requirement for contributions relating to future service, the economic benefit available as a reduction in future contributions is the future service cost to the entity for each period over the shorter of the expected life of the plan and the expected life of the entity. The future service cost to the entity excludes amounts that will be borne by employees.

17 An entity shall determine the future service costs using assumptions consistent with those used to determine the defined benefit obligation and with the situation that exists at the end of the reporting period as determined by AASB 119. Therefore, an entity shall assume no change to the benefits to be provided by a plan in the future until the plan is amended and shall assume a stable workforce in the future unless the entity is demonstrably committed at the end of the reporting period to make a reduction in the number of employees covered by the plan. In the latter case, the assumption about the future workforce shall include the reduction.

The effect of a minimum funding requirement on the economic benefit available as a reduction in future contributions

18 An entity shall analyse any minimum funding requirement at a given date into contributions that are required to cover (a) any existing shortfall for past service on the minimum funding basis and (b) future service.

19 Contributions to cover any existing shortfall on the minimum funding basis in respect of services already received do not affect future contributions for future service. They may give rise to a liability in accordance with paragraphs 23-26.

20 If there is a minimum funding requirement for contributions relating to future service, the economic benefit available as a reduction in future contributions is the sum of:

(a) any amount that reduces future minimum funding requirement contributions for future service because the entity made a prepayment (i.e. paid the amount before being required to do so); and

(b) the estimated future service cost in each period in accordance with paragraphs 16 and 17, less the estimated minimum funding requirement contributions that would be required for future service in those periods if there were no prepayment as described in (a).

21 An entity shall estimate the future minimum funding requirement contributions for future service taking into account the effect of any existing surplus determined using the minimum funding basis but excluding the prepayment described in paragraph 20(a). An entity shall use assumptions consistent with the minimum funding basis and, for any factors not specified by that basis, assumptions consistent with those used to determine the defined benefit obligation and with the situation that exists at the end of the reporting period as determined by AASB 119. The estimate shall include any changes expected as a result of the entity paying the minimum contributions when they are due. However, the estimate shall not include the effect of expected changes in the terms and conditions of the minimum funding basis that are not substantively enacted or contractually agreed at the end of the reporting period.

22 When an entity determines the amount described in paragraph 20(b), if the future minimum funding requirement contributions for future service exceed the future AASB 119 service cost in any given period, that excess reduces the amount of the economic benefit available as a reduction in future contributions. However, the amount described in paragraph 20(b) can never be less than zero.

When a minimum funding requirement may give rise to a liability

23 If an entity has an obligation under a minimum funding requirement to pay contributions to cover an existing shortfall on the minimum funding basis in respect of services already received, the entity shall determine whether the contributions payable will be available as a refund or reduction in future contributions after they are paid into the plan.

24 To the extent that the contributions payable will not be available after they are paid into the plan, the entity shall recognise a liability when the obligation arises. The liability shall reduce the defined benefit asset or increase the defined benefit liability so that no gain or loss is expected to result from applying paragraph 58 of AASB 119 when the contributions are paid.

25 An entity shall apply paragraph 58A of AASB 119 before determining the liability in accordance with paragraph 24.

26 The liability in respect of the minimum funding requirement and any subsequent remeasurement of that liability shall be recognised immediately in accordance with the entity's adopted policy for recognising the effect of the limit in paragraph 58 in AASB 119 on the measurement of the defined benefit asset. In particular:

(a) an entity that recognises the effect of the limit in paragraph 58 in profit or loss, in accordance with paragraph 61(g) of AASB 119, shall recognise the adjustment immediately in profit or loss; and

(b) an entity that recognises the effect of the limit in paragraph 58 in other comprehensive income, in accordance with paragraph 93C of AASB 119, shall recognise the adjustment immediately in other comprehensive income.

Application

Aus26.1 This Interpretation applies to:

(a) each entity that is required to prepare financial reports in accordance with Part 2M.3 of the *Corporations Act 2001* and that is a reporting entity;

(b) general purpose financial statements of each other reporting entity; and

(c) financial statements that are, or are held out to be, general purpose financial statements.

Aus26.2 This Interpretation applies to annual reporting periods beginning on or after 1 January 2008.

[Note: For application dates of paragraphs changed or added by an amending pronouncement, see Compilation Details.]

Aus26.3   This Interpretation may be applied to annual reporting periods beginning on or after 1 January 2005 but before 1 January 2008. If an entity applies this Interpretation to such an annual reporting period, it shall disclose that fact.

Aus26.4   The requirements specified in this Interpretation apply to the financial statements where information resulting from their application is material in accordance with AASB 1031 Materiality.

Effective Date of IFRIC 14

27   [Deleted by the AASB]

27A   [Deleted by the AASB]

27B   [Deleted by the AASB]

Transition

28   An entity shall apply this Interpretation from the beginning of the first period presented in the first financial statements to which the Interpretation applies. An entity shall recognise any initial adjustment arising from the application of this Interpretation in retained earnings at the beginning of that period.

29   An entity shall apply the amendments in paragraphs 3A, 16-18 and 20-22 from the beginning of the earliest comparative period presented in the first financial statements in which the entity applies this Interpretation. If the entity had previously applied Interpretation 14 before it applies the amendments, it shall recognise the adjustment resulting from the application of the amendments in retained earnings at the beginning of the earliest comparative period presented.

Illustrative Examples

These examples accompany, but are not part of, AASB Interpretation 14.

Example 1 — Effect of the minimum funding requirement when there is an AASB 119 surplus and the minimum funding contributions payable are fully refundable to the entity

IE1   An entity has a funding level on the minimum funding requirement basis (which is measured on a different basis from that required under AASB 119) of 82 per cent in Plan A. Under the minimum funding requirements, the entity is required to increase the funding level to 95 per cent immediately. As a result, the entity has a statutory obligation at the end of the reporting period to contribute 200 to Plan A immediately. The plan rules permit a full refund of any surplus to the entity at the end of the life of the plan. The year-end valuations for Plan A are set out below.

Market value of assets	1,200
Present value of defined benefit obligation under AASB 119	(1,100)
Surplus	100
Defined benefit asset (before consideration of the minimum funding requirement)[(a)]	100

(a)   For simplicity, it is assumed that there are no unrecognised amounts.

Application of requirements

IE2   Paragraph 24 of AASB Interpretation 14 requires the entity to recognise a liability to the extent that the contributions payable are not fully available. Payment of the contributions of 200 will increase the AASB 119 surplus from 100 to 300. Under the rules of the plan this amount will be fully refundable to the entity with no associated costs. Therefore, no liability is recognised for the obligation to pay the contributions.

Example 2 — Effect of a minimum funding requirement when there is an AASB 119 deficit and the minimum funding contributions payable would not be fully available

IE3   An entity has a funding level on the minimum funding requirement basis (which is measured on a different basis from that required under AASB 119) of 77 per cent in Plan B. Under the minimum funding requirements, the entity is required to increase the funding level to 100 per cent immediately. As a result, the entity has a statutory obligation at the end of the reporting period to pay additional contributions of 300 to Plan B. The plan rules permit a maximum refund of 60 per cent of the AASB 119 surplus to the entity and the entity is not permitted to reduce its contributions below a specified level which happens to equal the AASB 119 service cost. The year-end valuations for Plan B are set out below.

Market value of assets	1,000
Present value of defined benefit obligation under AASB 119	(1,100)
Deficit	(100)
Defined benefit (liability) (before consideration of the minimum funding requirement)[a]	(100)

(a)   For simplicity, it is assumed that there are no unrecognised amounts.

Application of requirements

IE4   The payment of 300 would change the AASB 119 deficit of 100 to a surplus of 200. Of this 200, 60 per cent (120) is refundable.

IE5   Therefore, of the contributions of 300, 100 eliminates the AASB 119 deficit and 120 (60 per cent of 200) is available as an economic benefit. The remaining 80 (40 per cent of 200) of the contributions paid is not available to the entity.

IE6   Paragraph 24 of AASB Interpretation 14 requires the entity to recognise a liability to the extent that the additional contributions payable are not available to it.

IE7   Therefore, the entity increases the defined benefit liability by 80. As required by paragraph 26 of AASB Interpretation 14, 80 is recognised immediately in accordance with the entity's adopted policy for recognising the effect of the limit in paragraph 58 and the entity recognises a net liability of 180 in the statement of financial position. No other liability is recognised in respect of the statutory obligation to pay contributions of 300.

Summary

Market value of assets	1,000
Present value of defined benefit obligation under AASB 119	(1,100)
Deficit	(100)
Defined benefit liability (before consideration of the minimum funding requirement)[a]	(100)
Adjustment in respect of minimum funding requirement	(80)
Net liability recognised in the statement of financial position	(180)

(a)   For simplicity, it is assumed that there are no unrecognised amounts.

IE8   When the contributions of 300 are paid, the net asset recognised in the statement of financial position will be 120.

Example 3 — Effect of a minimum funding requirement when the contributions payable would not be fully available and the effect on the economic benefit available as a future contribution reduction

IE9   An entity has a funding level on the minimum funding basis (which it measures on a different basis from that required by AASB 119) of 95 per cent in Plan C. The minimum funding requirements require the entity to pay contributions to increase the funding level to 100 per cent over the next three years. The contributions are required to make good the deficit on the minimum funding basis (shortfall) and to cover future service.

IE10   Plan C also has an AASB 119 surplus at the end of the reporting period of 50, which cannot be refunded to the entity under any circumstances. There are no unrecognised amounts.

IE11   The nominal amounts of contributions required to satisfy the minimum funding requirements in respect of the shortfall and the future service for the next three years are set out below.

Year	Total contributions for minimum funding requirement	Contributions required to make good the shortfall	Contributions required to cover future service
1	135	120	15
2	125	112	13
3	115	104	11

Application of requirements

IE12   The entity's present obligation in respect of services already received includes the contributions required to make good the shortfall but does not include the contributions required to cover future service.

IE13   The present value of the entity's obligation, assuming a discount rate of 6 per cent per year, is approximately 300, calculated as follows:

$$[120/(1.06) + 112/(1.06)^2 + 104/(1.06)^3].$$

IE14   When these contributions are paid into the plan, the present value of the AASB 119 surplus (i.e. the fair value of assets less the present value of the defined benefit obligation) would, other things being equal, increase from 50 to 350 (300 + 50).

IE15   However, the surplus is not refundable although an asset may be available as a future contribution reduction.

IE16   In accordance with paragraph 20 of Interpretation 14, the economic benefit available as a reduction in future contributions is the sum of:

(a)   any amount that reduces future minimum funding requirement contributions for future service because the entity made a prepayment (i.e. paid the amount before being required to do so); and

(b)   the estimated future service cost in each period in accordance with paragraphs 16 and 17, *less* the estimated minimum funding requirement contributions that would be required for future service in those periods if there were no prepayment as described in (a).

IE17   In this example there is no prepayment as described in paragraph 20(a). The amounts available as a reduction in future contributions when applying paragraph 20(b) are set out below.

Year	AASB 119 service cost	Minimum contributions required to cover future service	Amount available as contribution reduction
1	13	15	(2)
2	13	13	0
3	13	11	2
4+	13	9	4

IE18   Assuming a discount rate of 6 per cent, the present value of the economic benefit available as a future contribution reduction is equal to:

$$(2)/(1.06) + 0/(1.06)^2 + 2/(1.06)^3 + 4/(1.06)^4 + \ldots + 4/(1.06)^{50} + \ldots = 56.$$

Thus in accordance with paragraph 58(b) of AASB 119, the present value of the economic benefit available from future contribution reductions is limited to 56.

IE19   Paragraph 24 of AASB Interpretation 14 requires the entity to recognise a liability to the extent that the additional contributions payable will not be fully available. Therefore, the entity reduces the defined benefit asset by 294 (50 + 300 – 56).

IE20   As required by paragraph 26 of AASB Interpretation 14, the 294 is recognised immediately in accordance with the entity's adopted policy for recognising the effect of the limit in paragraph 58 and the entity recognises a net liability of 244 in the statement of financial position. No other liability is recognised in respect of the obligation to make contributions to fund the minimum funding shortfall.

Summary

Surplus	50
Defined benefit asset (before consideration of the minimum funding requirement)	50
Adjustment in respect of minimum funding requirement	(294)
Net liability recognised in the statement of financial position[a]	(244)

(a)   For simplicity, it is assumed that there are no unrecognised amounts.

IE21   When the contributions of 300 are paid into the plan, the net asset recognised in the statement of financial position will become 56 (300 – 244).

Example 4 — Effect of a prepayment when a minimum funding requirement exceeds the expected future service charge

IE22   An entity is required to fund Plan D so that no deficit arises on the minimum funding basis. The entity is required to pay minimum funding requirement contributions to cover the service cost in each period determined on the minimum funding basis.

IE23   Plan D has an AASB 119 surplus of 35 at the beginning of 20X1. There are no cumulative unrecognised net actuarial losses and past service costs. This example assumes that the discount rate and expected return on assets are 0 per cent, and that the plan cannot refund the surplus to the entity under any circumstances but can use the surplus for reductions of future contributions.

IE24   The minimum contributions required to cover future service are 15 for each of the next five years. The expected AASB 119 service cost is 10 in each year.

IE25   The entity makes a prepayment of 30 at the beginning of 20X1 in respect of years 20X1 and 20X2, increasing its surplus at the beginning of 20X1 to 65. That prepayment reduces the future contributions it expects to make in the following two years, as follows:

Year	AASB 119 service cost	Minimum funding requirement contribution before prepayment	Minimum funding requirement contribution after prepayment
20X1	10	15	0
20X2	10	15	0
20X3	10	15	15
20X4	10	15	15
20X5	10	15	15
Total	50	75	45

Application of requirements

IE26   In accordance with paragraphs 20 and 22 of Interpretation 14, at the beginning of 20X1, the economic benefit available as a reduction in future contributions is the sum of:

(a)   30, being the prepayment of the minimum funding requirement contributions; and

(b)   nil. The estimated minimum funding requirement contributions required for future service would be 75 if there was no prepayment. Those contributions exceed the estimated future service cost (50); therefore the entity cannot use any part of the surplus of 35 noted in paragraph IE23 (see paragraph 22).

IE27   Assuming a discount rate of 0 per cent, the present value of the economic benefit available as a reduction in future contributions is equal to 30. Thus in accordance with paragraph 58 of AASB 119 the entity recognises an asset of 30 (because this is lower than the AASB 119 surplus of 65).

Basis for Conclusions on IFRIC Interpretation 14

This IFRIC Basis for Conclusions accompanies, but is not part of, AASB Interpretation 14. An IFRIC Basis for Conclusions may be amended to reflect the requirements of the AASB Interpretation and AASB Accounting Standards where they differ from the corresponding International pronouncements.

BC1   This Basis for Conclusions summarises the IFRIC's considerations in reaching its consensus. Individual IFRIC members gave greater weight to some factors than to others.

BC2   The IFRIC noted that practice varies significantly with regard to the treatment of the effect of a minimum funding requirement on the limit placed by paragraph 58 of IAS 19 *Employee Benefits* on the amount of a defined benefit asset. The IFRIC therefore decided to include this issue on its agenda. In considering the issue, the IFRIC also became aware of the need for general guidance on determining the limit on the measurement of the defined benefit asset, and for guidance on when that limit makes a minimum funding requirement onerous.

BC3   The IFRIC published D19 *IAS 19 — The Asset Ceiling: Availability of Economic Benefits and Minimum Funding Requirements* in August 2006. In response, the IFRIC received 48 comment letters.

BC3A   In November 2009 the International Accounting Standards Board amended IFRIC 14 to remove an unintended consequence arising from the treatment of prepayments in some circumstances when there is a minimum funding requirement (see paragraphs BC30A-BC30D).

Definition of a minimum funding requirement

BC4   D19 referred to statutory or contractual minimum funding requirements. Respondents to D19 asked for further guidance on what constituted a minimum funding requirement. The IFRIC decided to clarify that for the purpose of the Interpretation a minimum funding requirement is any requirement for the entity to make contributions to fund a post-employment or other long-term defined benefit plan.

Interaction between IAS 19 and minimum funding requirements

BC5   Funding requirements would not normally affect the accounting for a plan under IAS 19. However, paragraph 58 of IAS 19 limits the amount of the defined benefit asset to the available economic benefit plus unrecognised amounts. The interaction of a minimum funding requirement and this limit has two possible effects:

(a)   the minimum funding requirement may restrict the economic benefits available as a reduction in future contributions; and

(b)   the limit may make the minimum funding requirement onerous because contributions payable under the requirement in respect of services already received may not be available once they have been paid, either as a refund or as a reduction in future contributions.

BC6   These effects raised general questions about the availability of economic benefits in the form of a refund or a reduction in future contributions.

Availability of the economic benefit

BC7   One view of 'available' would limit the economic benefit to the amount that is realisable immediately at the end of the reporting period.

BC8   The IFRIC disagreed with this view. The *Framework* defines an asset as a resource 'from which future economic benefits are expected to flow to the entity.' Therefore, it is not necessary for the economic benefit to be realisable immediately. Indeed, a reduction in future contributions cannot be realisable immediately.

BC9   The IFRIC concluded that a refund or reduction in future contributions is available if it could be realisable at some point during the life of the plan or when the plan liability is settled. Respondents to D19 were largely supportive of this conclusion.

BC10   In the responses to D19, some argued that an entity may expect to use the surplus to give improved benefits. Others noted that future actuarial losses might reduce or eliminate the surplus. In either case there would be no refund or reduction in future contributions. The IFRIC noted that the existence of an asset at the end of the reporting period depends on whether the entity has the right to obtain a refund or reduction in future contributions. The existence of the asset at that date is not affected by possible future changes to the amount of the surplus. If future events occur that change the amount of the surplus, their effects are recognised when they occur. Accordingly, if the entity decides to improve benefits, or future losses in the plan reduce the surplus, the consequences are recognised when the decision is made or the losses occur. The IFRIC noted that such events of future periods do not affect the existence or measurement of the asset at the end of the reporting period.

The asset available as a refund of a surplus

BC11   The IFRIC noted that a refund of a surplus could potentially be obtained in three ways:

(a)   during the life of the plan, without assuming that the plan liabilities have to be settled in order to get the refund (e.g. in some jurisdictions, the entity may have a right to a refund during the life of the plan, irrespective of whether the plan liabilities are settled); or

(b)   assuming the gradual settlement of the plan liabilities over time until all members have left the plan; or

(c)   assuming the full settlement of the plan liabilities in a single event (i.e. as a plan wind-up).

BC12   The IFRIC concluded that all three ways should be considered in determining whether an economic benefit was available to the entity. Some respondents to D19 raised the question of when an entity controls an asset that arises from the availability of a refund, in particular if a refund would be available only if a third party (for example the plan trustees) gave its approval. The IFRIC concluded that an entity controlled the asset only if the entity has an unconditional right to the refund. If that right depends on actions by a third party, the entity does not have an unconditional right.

BC13   If the plan liability is settled by an immediate wind-up, the costs associated with the wind-up may be significant. One reason for this may be that the cost of annuities available on the market is expected to be significantly higher than that implied by the IAS 19 basis. Other costs include the legal and other professional fees expected to be incurred during the winding-up process. Accordingly, a plan with an apparent surplus may not be able to recover any of that surplus on wind-up.

BC14   The IFRIC noted that the available surplus should be measured at the amount that the entity could receive from the plan. The IFRIC decided that in determining the amount of the refund available on wind-up of the plan, the amount of the costs associated with the settlement and refund should be deducted if paid by the plan.

BC15   The IFRIC noted that the costs of settling the plan liability would be dependent on the facts and circumstances of the plan and it decided not to issue any specific guidance in this respect.

BC16   The IFRIC also noted that the present value of the defined benefit obligation and the fair value of assets are both measured on a present value basis and therefore take into account the timing of the future cash flows. The IFRIC concluded that no further adjustment for the time value of money needs to be made when measuring the amount of a refund determined as the full amount or a proportion of the surplus that is realisable at a future date.

The asset available in the form of a future contribution reduction

BC17   The IFRIC decided that the amount of the contribution reduction available to the entity should be measured with reference to the amount that the entity would have been required to pay had there been no surplus. The IFRIC concluded that this is represented by the cost to the entity of accruing benefits in the plan, in other words by the future IAS 19 service cost. Respondents to D19 broadly supported this conclusion.

BC18   When the issue of the availability of reductions in future contributions was first raised with the IFRIC, some expressed the view that an entity should recognise an asset only to the extent that there was a formal agreement between the trustees and the entity specifying contributions payable lower than the IAS 19 service cost. The IFRIC disagreed, concluding instead that an entity is entitled to assume that, in general, it will not be required to make contributions to a plan in order to maintain a surplus and hence that it will be able to reduce contributions if the plan has a surplus. (The effects of a minimum funding requirement on this assumption are discussed below.)

BC19   The IFRIC considered the assumptions that underlie the calculation of the future service cost. In respect of the discount rate, IAS 19 requires the measurement of the present value of the future contribution reduction to be based on the same discount rate as that used to determine the present value of the defined benefit obligation.

BC20   The IFRIC considered whether the term over which the contribution reduction should be calculated should be restricted to the expected future working lifetime of the active membership. The IFRIC disagreed with that view. The IFRIC noted that the entity could derive economic benefit from a reduction in contributions beyond that period. The IFRIC also noted that increasing the term of the calculation has a decreasing effect on the incremental changes to the asset because the reductions in contributions are discounted to a present value. Thus, for plans with a large surplus and no possibility of receiving a refund, the available asset will be limited even if the term of the calculation extends beyond the expected future working lifetime of the active membership to the expected life of the plan. This is consistent with paragraph 77 of the Basis for Conclusions on IAS 19, which states that 'the limit [on the measurement of the defined benefit asset] is likely to come into play *only* where ... the plan is very mature and has a very large surplus that is more than large enough to eliminate *all* future contributions and cannot be returned to the entity' (emphasis added). If the contribution reduction were determined by considering only the term of the expected future working lifetime of the active membership, the limit on the measurement of the defined benefit asset would come into play much more frequently.

BC21   Most respondents to D19 were supportive of this view. However, some argued that the term should be the shorter of the expected life of the plan and the expected life of the entity. The IFRIC agreed that the entity could not derive economic benefits from a reduction in contributions beyond its own expected life and has amended the Interpretation accordingly.

BC22   Next, the IFRIC considered what assumptions should be made about a future workforce. D19 proposed that the assumptions for the demographic profile of the future workforce should be consistent with the assumptions underlying the calculation of the present value of the defined benefit obligation at the end of the reporting period. Some respondents noted that the calculation of service costs for future periods requires assumptions that are not required for the calculation of the defined benefit obligation. In particular, the assumptions underlying the present value of the defined benefit obligation calculation do not include an explicit assumption for new entrants.

BC23   The IFRIC agreed that this is the case. The IFRIC noted that assumptions are needed in respect of the size of the future workforce and future benefits provided by the plan. The IFRIC decided that the future service cost should be based on the situation that exists at the end of the reporting period determined in accordance with IAS 19.

Interpretations

Therefore, increases in the size of the workforce or the benefits provided by the plan should not be anticipated. Decreases in the size of the workforce or the benefits should be included in the assumptions for the future service cost at the same time as they are treated as curtailments in accordance with IAS 19.

The effect of a minimum funding requirement on the economic benefit available as a refund

BC24   The IFRIC considered whether a minimum funding requirement to make contributions to a plan in force at the end of the reporting period would restrict the extent to which a refund of surplus is available. The IFRIC noted that there is an implicit assumption in IAS 19 that the specified assumptions represent the best estimate of the eventual outcome of the plan in economic terms, while a requirement to make additional contributions is often a prudent approach designed to build in a risk margin for adverse circumstances. Moreover, when there are no members left in the plan, the minimum funding requirement would have no effect. This would leave the IAS 19 surplus available. To the extent that the entity has a right to this eventual surplus, the IAS 19 surplus would be available to the entity, regardless of the minimum funding restrictions in force at the end of the reporting period. The IFRIC therefore concluded that the existence of a minimum funding requirement may affect the timing of a refund but does not affect whether it is ultimately available to the entity.

The effect of a minimum funding requirement on the economic benefit available as a reduction in future contributions

BC25   The entity's minimum funding requirements at a given date can be analysed into the contributions that are required to cover (a) an existing shortfall for past service on the minimum funding basis and (b) future service.

BC26   Contributions required to cover an existing shortfall may give rise to a liability, as discussed in paragraphs BC31-BC37 below. But they do not affect the availability of a reduction in future contributions for future service.

BC27   In contrast, future contribution requirements in respect of future service do not generate an additional liability at the end of the reporting period because they do not relate to past services received by the entity. However, they may reduce the extent to which the entity can benefit from a reduction in future contributions. Therefore, the IFRIC decided that the available asset from a contribution reduction should be calculated as the present value of the IAS 19 future service cost less the minimum funding contribution requirement in respect of future service in each year.

BC28   If the minimum funding contribution requirement is consistently greater than the IAS 19 future service cost, that calculation may be thought to imply that a liability exists. However, as noted above, an entity has no liability at the end of the reporting period in respect of minimum funding requirements that relate to future service. The economic benefit available from a reduction in future contributions can be nil, but it can never be a negative amount.

BC29   The respondents to D19 were largely supportive of these conclusions.

BC30   The IFRIC noted that future changes to regulations on minimum funding requirements might affect the available surplus. However, the IFRIC decided that, just as the future service cost was determined on the basis of the situation existing at the end of the reporting period, so should the effect of a minimum funding requirement. The IFRIC concluded that when determining the amount of an asset that might be available as a reduction in future contributions, an entity should not consider whether the minimum funding requirement might change in the future. The respondents to D19 were largely supportive of these conclusions.

Prepayments of a minimum funding requirement

BC30A   If an entity has prepaid future minimum funding requirement contributions and that prepayment will reduce future contributions, the prepayment generates economic benefits for the entity. However, to the extent that the future minimum funding requirement contributions exceeded future service costs, the original version of IFRIC 14 did not permit entities to consider those economic benefits in measuring a defined benefit asset. After issuing IFRIC 14, the Board reviewed the treatment of such prepayments. The Board concluded that such a prepayment provides an economic benefit to the entity by relieving the entity of an obligation to pay future minimum funding requirement contributions that exceed future service cost. Therefore, considering those economic benefits in measuring a defined benefit asset would convey more useful information to users of financial statements. In May 2009 the Board published that conclusion in an exposure draft *Prepayments of a Minimum Funding Requirement*. After considering the responses to that exposure draft, the Board amended IFRIC 14 by issuing *Prepayments of a Minimum Funding Requirement* in November 2009.

BC30B   Some respondents noted that the amendments increase the effect of funding considerations on the measurement of a defined benefit asset and liability and questioned whether funding considerations should ever affect the measurement. However, the Board noted that the sole purpose of the amendments was to eliminate an unintended consequence in IFRIC 14. Thus, the Board did not re-debate the fundamental conclusion of IFRIC 14 that funding is relevant to the measurement when an entity cannot recover the additional cost of a minimum funding requirement in excess of the IAS 19 service cost.

BC30C   Many respondents noted that the proposals made the assessment of the economic benefit available from a prepayment different from the assessment for a surplus arising from actuarial gains. Most agreed that a prepayment created an asset, but questioned why the Board did not extend the underlying principle to other surpluses that could be used to reduce future payments of minimum funding requirement contributions.

BC30D   The Board did not extend the scope of the amendments to surpluses arising from actuarial gains because such an approach would need further thought and the Board did not want to delay the amendments for prepayments. However, the Board may consider the matter further in a future comprehensive review of pension cost accounting.

Onerous minimum funding requirements

BC31   Minimum funding requirements for contributions to cover an existing minimum funding shortfall create an obligation for the entity at the end of the reporting period because they relate to past service. Nonetheless, usually minimum funding requirements do not affect the measurement of the defined benefit asset or liability under IAS 19. This is because the contributions, once paid, become plan assets and the additional net liability for the funding requirement is nil. However, the IFRIC noted that the limit on the measurement of the defined benefit asset in paragraph 58 of IAS 19 may make the funding obligation onerous, as follows.

BC32   If an entity is obliged to make contributions and some or all of those contributions will not subsequently be available as an economic benefit, it follows that when the contributions are made the entity will not be able to recognise an asset to that extent. However, the resulting loss to the entity does not arise on the payment of the contributions but earlier, at the point at which the obligation to pay arises.

BC33   Therefore, the IFRIC concluded that when an entity has an obligation under a minimum funding requirement to make additional contributions to a plan in respect of services already received, the entity should reduce the asset or increase the liability recognised in the statement of financial position to the extent that the minimum funding contributions payable to the plan will not be available to the entity either as a refund or a reduction in future contributions.

BC34   Respondents to D19 broadly supported this conclusion. But some questioned
        whether the draft Interpretation extended the application of paragraph 58 of
        IAS 19 too far. They argued that it should apply only when an entity has a defined
        benefit asset. In particular, it should not be used to classify a funding requirement
        as onerous, thereby creating an additional liability to be recognised beyond that
        arising from the other requirements of IAS 19. Others agreed that such a liability
        existed, but questioned whether it fell within the scope of IAS 19 rather than
        IAS 37 *Provisions, Contingent Liabilities and Contingent Assets*.

BC35   The IFRIC did not agree that the Interpretation extends the application of paragraph
        58 of IAS 19. Rather, it applies the principles in IAS 37 relating to onerous contracts
        in the context of the requirements of IAS 19, including paragraph 58. On the
        question whether the liability falls within the scope of IAS 19 or IAS 37, the IFRIC
        noted that employee benefits are excluded from the scope of IAS 37. The IFRIC
        therefore confirmed that the interaction of a minimum funding requirement and the
        limit on the measurement of the defined benefit asset could result in a decrease in
        a defined benefit asset or an increase in a defined benefit liability.

BC36   The IFRIC also discussed whether the liability in respect of the minimum funding
        requirement and the effect of any subsequent remeasurement should be recognised
        immediately in profit or loss or whether they should be eligible for the options
        for deferred recognition or recognition outside profit or loss that IAS 19 specifies
        for actuarial gains and losses. The IFRIC noted that the liability in respect of
        any minimum funding requirements arises only because of the limit on the
        measurement of the asset recognised in the statement of financial position under
        paragraph 58 of IAS 19. Furthermore, all consequences of paragraph 58 should be
        treated consistently.

BC37   Therefore, the IFRIC concluded that any liability in respect of a minimum funding
        requirement and the effect of any subsequent remeasurement should be recognised
        immediately in accordance with paragraph 61(g) or 93C of IAS 19. This is consistent
        with the recognition of other adjustments to the net asset or liability recognised in
        the statement of financial position under paragraph 58 of IAS 19. The respondents
        to D19 broadly agreed with this requirement.

Transitional provisions

BC38   In D19, the IFRIC proposed that the draft Interpretation should be applied
        retrospectively. The draft Interpretation required immediate recognition of all
        adjustments relating to the minimum funding requirements. The IFRIC therefore
        argued that retrospective application would be straightforward.

BC39   Respondents to D19 noted that paragraph 58A of IAS 19 causes the limit on
        the defined benefit asset to affect the deferred recognition of actuarial gains and
        losses. Retrospective application of the Interpretation could change the amount
        of that limit for previous periods, thereby also changing the deferred recognition
        of actuarial gains and losses. Calculating these revised amounts retrospectively
        over the life of the plan would be costly and of little benefit to users of financial
        statements.

BC40   The IFRIC agreed with this view. The IFRIC therefore amended the transitional
        provisions so that IFRIC 14 is to be applied only from the beginning of the first
        period presented in the financial statements for annual periods beginning on or
        after the effective date.

Summary of changes from D19

BC41   The Interpretation has been altered in the following significant respects since it was exposed for comment as D19:

     (a)   the issue of when an entity controls an asset arising from the availability of a refund has been clarified (paragraphs BC10 and BC12);

     (b)   requirements relating to the assumptions underlying the measurement of a reduction in future contributions have been clarified (paragraphs BC22 and BC23);

     (c)   the transitional requirements have been changed from retrospective application to application from the beginning of the first period presented in the first financial statements to which the Interpretation applies (paragraphs BC38-BC40); and

     (d)   in November 2009 the Board amended IFRIC 14 to require entities to recognise as an economic benefit any prepayment of minimum funding requirement contributions. At the same time, the Board removed references to 'present value' from paragraphs 16, 17, 20 and 22 and 'the surplus in the plan' from paragraph 16 because these references duplicated references in paragraph 58 of IAS 19. The Board also amended the term 'future accrual of benefits' to 'future service' for consistency with the rest of IAS 19.

Deleted IFRIC Interpretation 14 Text

Deleted IFRIC Interpretation 14 text is not part of AASB Interpretation 14.

Paragraph 27

An entity shall apply this Interpretation for annual periods beginning on or after 1 January 2008. Earlier application is permitted.

Interpretation 15
Agreements for the Construction of Real Estate

(Issued August 2008)

Contents

Preface

Comparison with IFRIC 15

AASB Interpretation 15
Agreements for the Construction of Real Estate

Paragraphs

References

Background   1 – 3

Scope   4 – 5

Issues   6

Consensus   7 – 21

   Determining whether the agreement is within the scope of AASB 111
    or AASB 118   10 – 12

   Accounting for revenue from the construction of real estate   13 – 19

   Disclosures   20 – 21

Amendment to the Appendix to AASB 118   22 – 23

Application   Aus23.1 – Aus23.4

Transition   25

Information Note
Analysis of a single agreement for the construction of real estate

Illustrative Examples   IE1 – IE11

Basis for Conclusions

Deleted IFRIC 15 Text

AASB Interpretation 15 *Agreements for the Construction of Real Estate* is set out in paragraphs 1–25. Interpretations are listed in Australian Accounting Standard AASB 1048 *Interpretation and Application of Standards*. In the absence of explicit guidance, AASB 108 *Accounting Policies, Changes in Accounting Estimates and Errors* provides a basis for selecting and applying accounting policies.

Preface

Main Features of AASB Interpretation 15

Scope of the Interpretation

This Interpretation applies to the accounting for revenue and associated expenses by entities that enter into agreements for the construction of real estate directly or through subcontractors.

Issues Addressed

This Interpretation addresses two issues:

(a) Is the agreement within the scope of AASB 111 *Construction Contracts* or AASB 118 *Revenue*?

(b) When should revenue from the construction of real estate be recognised?

Main Requirements

This Interpretation specifies that:

(a) within a single agreement, if an entity contracts to deliver goods or services in addition to the construction of real estate (e.g. a sale of land or provision of property management services), in accordance with paragraph 13 of AASB 118, such an agreement may need to be split into separately identifiable components including one for the construction of real estate. If separate components are identified, the entity applies paragraphs 10-12 of this Interpretation (see (b) below) to the component for the construction of real estate in order to determine whether that component is within the scope of AASB 111 or AASB 118;

(b) an agreement for the construction of real estate meets the definition of a 'construction contract' (and therefore falls within the scope of AASB 111) when the buyer is able to specify the major structural elements of the design of the real estate before construction begins and/or specify major structural changes once construction is in progress (whether or not it exercises that ability);

(c) when the agreement is within the scope of AASB 111 and its outcome can be estimated reliably, the entity recognises revenue by reference to the stage of completion of the contract activity in accordance with AASB 111;

(d) if the agreement does not meet the definition of a construction contract and therefore is within the scope of AASB 118, the entity determines whether the agreement is for the rendering of services or for the sale of goods;

(e) if an agreement within the scope of AASB 118 is for the rendering of services, and the criteria in paragraph 20 of AASB 118 are met, revenue is recognised by reference to the stage of completion of the transaction using the percentage of completion method;

(f) if an agreement within the scope of AASB 118 is for the sale of goods:

    (i) the entity recognises revenue by reference to the stage of completion using the percentage of completion method if both of the following occur:

       • the entity transfers to the buyer control and the significant risks and rewards of ownership of the work in progress in its current state as construction progresses; and

       • all the criteria in paragraph 14 of AASB 118 are met continuously as construction progresses; and

    (ii) the entity recognises revenue only when all the criteria in paragraph 14 of AASB 118 are satisfied, if it transfers to the buyer control and the significant risks and rewards of ownership of the real estate in its entirety at a single time (e.g. at completion, upon or after delivery);

(g) when the entity is required to perform further work on real estate already delivered to the buyer, it recognises a liability and an expense in accordance with paragraph 19 of AASB 118; and

Interpretations

(h)   when an entity recognises revenue using the percentage of completion method for agreements that meet all the criteria in paragraph 14 of AASB 118 continuously as construction progresses, it makes various disclosures specified in the Interpretation.

These main requirements are presented as a guide to readers and do not describe all of the requirements of the Interpretation. For a full understanding of the Interpretation, readers should consider the complete text of the Interpretation.

Application Date

This Interpretation is applicable to annual reporting periods beginning on or after 1 January 2009. Early adoption of this Interpretation is permitted for annual reporting periods beginning on or after 1 January 2005 but before 1 January 2009.

Comparison with IFRIC 15

AASB Interpretation 15 is equivalent to International Financial Reporting Interpretations Committee Interpretation IFRIC 15 *Agreements for the Construction of Real Estate*, issued by the International Accounting Standards Board. Paragraphs that have been added to this Interpretation (and do not appear in the text of the equivalent IFRIC Interpretation) are identified with the prefix "Aus", followed by the number of the relevant IFRIC paragraph and decimal numbering.

Entities that comply with AASB Interpretation 15 will simultaneously be in compliance with IFRIC 15.

Australian Accounting Standards Board

Interpretation 15

Agreements for the Construction of Real Estate

References

Accounting Standard AASB 101 *Presentation of Financial Statements* (as revised in 2007)

Accounting Standard AASB 108 *Accounting Policies, Changes in Accounting Estimates and Errors*

Accounting Standard AASB 111 *Construction Contracts*

Accounting Standard AASB 118 *Revenue*

Accounting Standard AASB 137 *Provisions, Contingent Liabilities and Contingent Assets*

AASB Interpretation 12 *Service Concession Arrangements*

AASB Interpretation 13 *Customer Loyalty Programmes*

Background

1   In the real estate industry, entities that undertake the construction of real estate, directly or through subcontractors, may enter into agreements with one or more buyers before construction is complete. Such agreements take diverse forms.

2   For example, entities that undertake the construction of residential real estate may start to market individual units (apartments or houses) 'off plan', ie while construction is still in progress, or even before it has begun. Each buyer enters into an agreement with the entity to acquire a specified unit when it is ready for occupation. Typically, the buyer pays a deposit to the entity that is refundable only if the entity fails to deliver the completed unit in accordance with the contracted terms. The balance of the purchase price is generally paid to the entity only on contractual completion, when the buyer obtains possession of the unit.

3   Entities that undertake the construction of commercial or industrial real estate may enter into an agreement with a single buyer. The buyer may be required to make progress payments between the time of the initial agreement and contractual completion. Construction may take place on land the buyer owns or leases before construction begins.

Scope

4   This Interpretation applies to the accounting for revenue and associated expenses by entities that undertake the construction of real estate directly or through subcontractors.

5   Agreements in the scope of this Interpretation are agreements for the construction of real estate. In addition to the construction of real estate, such agreements may include the delivery of other goods or services.

Issues

6   The Interpretation addresses two issues:

     (a)   Is the agreement within the scope of AASB 111 *Construction Contracts* or AASB 118 *Revenue*?

     (b)   When should revenue from the construction of real estate be recognised?

Consensus

7   The following discussion assumes that the entity has previously analysed the agreement for the construction of real estate and any related agreements and concluded that it will retain neither continuing managerial involvement to the degree usually associated with ownership nor effective control over the constructed real estate to an extent that would preclude recognition of some or all of the consideration as revenue. If recognition of some of the consideration as revenue is precluded, the following discussion applies only to the part of the agreement for which revenue will be recognised.

8   Within a single agreement, an entity may contract to deliver goods or services in addition to the construction of real estate (e.g. a sale of land or provision of property management services). In accordance with paragraph 13 of AASB 118, such an agreement may need to be split into separately identifiable components including one for the construction of real estate. The fair value of the total consideration received or receivable for the agreement shall be allocated to each component. If separate components are identified, the entity applies paragraphs 10-12 of this Interpretation to the component for the construction of real estate in order to determine whether that component is within the scope of AASB 111 or AASB 118. The segmenting criteria of AASB 111 then apply to any component of the agreement that is determined to be a construction contract.

9   The following discussion refers to an agreement for the construction of real estate but it also applies to a component for the construction of real estate identified within an agreement that includes other components.

Determining whether the agreement is within the scope of AASB 111 or AASB 118

10   Determining whether an agreement for the construction of real estate is within the scope of AASB 111 or AASB 118 depends on the terms of the agreement and all the surrounding facts and circumstances. Such a determination requires judgement with respect to each agreement.

11   AASB 111 applies when the agreement meets the definition of a construction contract set out in paragraph 3 of AASB 111: 'a contract specifically negotiated for the construction of an asset or a combination of assets …' An agreement for the construction of real estate meets the definition of a construction contract when the buyer is able to specify the major structural elements of the design of the real estate before construction begins and/ or specify major structural changes once construction is in progress (whether or not it exercises that ability). When AASB 111 applies, the construction contract also includes any contracts or components for the rendering of services that are directly related to the construction of the real estate in accordance with paragraph 5(a) of AASB 111 and paragraph 4 of AASB 118.

12   In contrast, an agreement for the construction of real estate in which buyers have only limited ability to influence the design of the real estate, e.g. to select a design from a range of options specified by the entity, or to specify only minor variations to the basic design, is an agreement for the sale of goods within the scope of AASB 118.

Accounting for revenue from the construction of real estate

The agreement is a construction contract

13   When the agreement is within the scope of AASB 111 and its outcome can be estimated reliably, the entity shall recognise revenue by reference to the stage of completion of the contract activity in accordance with AASB 111.

14   The agreement may not meet the definition of a construction contract and therefore be within the scope of AASB 118. In this case, the entity shall determine whether the agreement is for the rendering of services or for the sale of goods.

The agreement is an agreement for the rendering of services

15   If the entity is not required to acquire and supply construction materials, the agreement may be only an agreement for the rendering of services in accordance with AASB 118. In this case, if the criteria in paragraph 20 of AASB 118 are met, AASB 118 requires revenue to be recognised by reference to the stage of completion of the transaction using the percentage of completion method. The requirements of AASB 111 are generally applicable to the recognition of revenue and the associated expenses for such a transaction (AASB 118 paragraph 21).

The agreement is an agreement for the sale of goods

16   If the entity is required to provide services together with construction materials in order to perform its contractual obligation to deliver the real estate to the buyer, the agreement is an agreement for the sale of goods and the criteria for recognition of revenue set out in paragraph 14 of AASB 118 apply.

17   The entity may transfer to the buyer control and the significant risks and rewards of ownership of the work in progress in its current state as construction progresses. In this case, if all the criteria in paragraph 14 of AASB 118 are met continuously as construction progresses, the entity shall recognise revenue by reference to the stage of completion using the percentage of completion method. The requirements of AASB 111 are generally applicable to the recognition of revenue and the associated expenses for such a transaction.

18   The entity may transfer to the buyer control and the significant risks and rewards of ownership of the real estate in its entirety at a single time (e.g. at completion, upon or after delivery). In this case, the entity shall recognise revenue only when all the criteria in paragraph 14 of AASB 118 are satisfied.

19   When the entity is required to perform further work on real estate already delivered to the buyer, it shall recognise a liability and an expense in accordance with paragraph 19 of AASB 118. The liability shall be measured in accordance with AASB 137. When the entity is required to deliver further goods or services that are separately identifiable from the real estate already delivered to the buyer, it would have identified the remaining goods or services as a separate component of the sale, in accordance with paragraph 8 of this Interpretation.

Disclosures

20   When an entity recognises revenue using the percentage of completion method for agreements that meet all the criteria in paragraph 14 of AASB 118 continuously as construction progresses (see paragraph 17 of the Interpretation), it shall disclose:

   (a)   how it determines which agreements meet all the criteria in paragraph 14 of AASB 118 continuously as construction progresses;

   (b)   the amount of revenue arising from such agreements in the period; and

   (c)   the methods used to determine the stage of completion of agreements in progress.

21 For the agreements described in paragraph 20 that are in progress at the reporting date, the entity shall also disclose:

(a) the aggregate amount of costs incurred and recognised profits (less recognised losses) to date; and

(b) the amount of advances received.

Amendments to the Appendix to AASB 118

22 This Interpretation supersedes the real estate guidance (Example 9) in the appendix to AASB 118.

23 The appendix to AASB 118 is amended as described below.

All of the text under the heading '9 *Real estate sales.*' is deleted.

New text is inserted under the heading as follows:

'This example has been superseded by AASB Interpretation 15 *Agreements for the Construction of Real Estate*'.

Application

Aus23.1 This Interpretation applies to:

(a) each entity that is required to prepare financial reports in accordance with Part 2M.3 of the *Corporations Act 2001* and that is a reporting entity;

(b) general purpose financial reports of each other reporting entity; and

(c) financial reports that are, or are held out to be, general purpose financial reports.

Aus23.2 This Interpretation applies to annual reporting periods beginning on or after 1 January 2009.

Aus23.3 This Interpretation may be applied to annual reporting periods beginning on or after 1 January 2005 but before 1 January 2009. If an entity applies this Interpretation to such an annual reporting period, it shall disclose that fact.

Aus23.4 The requirements specified in this Interpretation apply to the financial report where information resulting from their application is material in accordance with AASB 1031 *Materiality*.

Effective date of IFRIC 15

24 [Deleted by the AASB]

Transition

25 Changes in accounting policy shall be accounted for retrospectively in accordance with AASB 108 *Accounting Policies, Changes in Accounting Estimates and Errors*.

Information Note

Analysis of a single agreement for the construction of real estate

This note accompanies, but is not part of, AASB Interpretation 15.

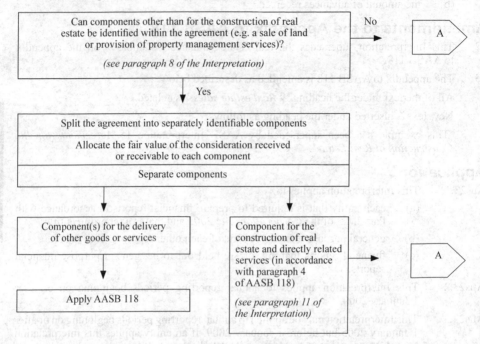

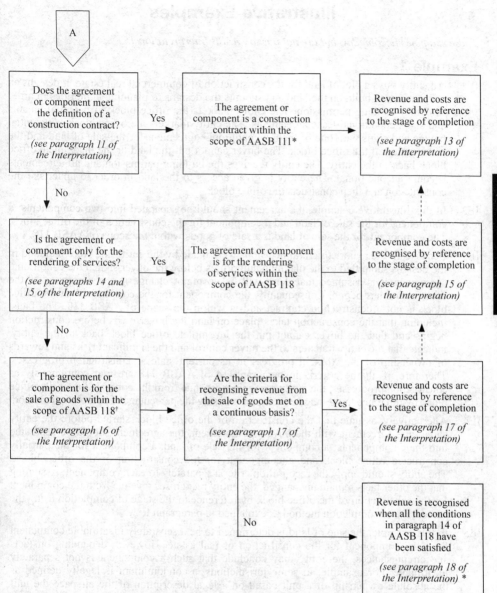

* The construction contract may need to be segmented in accordance with paragraph 8 of AASB 111
† Directly related services may need to be separated in accordance with paragraph 13 of AASB 118

Illustrative Examples

These examples accompany, but are not part of, AASB Interpretation 15.

Example 1

IE1   An entity buys a plot of land for the construction of commercial real estate. It designs an office block to build on the land and submits the designs to planning authorities in order to obtain building permission. The entity markets the office block to potential tenants and signs conditional lease agreements. The entity markets the office block to potential buyers and signs with one of them a conditional agreement for the sale of land and the construction of the office block. The buyer cannot put the land or the incomplete office block back to the entity. The entity receives the building permission and all agreements become unconditional. The entity is given access to the land in order to undertake the construction and then constructs the office block.

IE2   In this illustrative example, the agreement should be separated into two components: a component for the sale of land and a component for the construction of the office block. The component for the sale of land is a sale of goods within the scope of AASB 118.

IE3   Because all the major structural decisions were made by the entity and were included in the designs submitted to the planning authorities before the buyer signed the conditional agreement, it is assumed that there will be no major change in the designs after the construction has begun. Consequently, the component for the construction of the office block is not a construction contract and is within the scope of AASB 118. The facts, including that the construction takes place on land the buyer owns before construction begins and that the buyer cannot put the incomplete office block back to the entity, indicate that the entity transfers to the buyer control and the significant risks and rewards of ownership of the work in progress in its current state as construction progresses. Therefore, if all the criteria in paragraph 14 of AASB 118 are met continuously as construction progresses, the entity recognises revenue from the construction of the office block by reference to the stage of completion using the percentage of completion method.

IE4   Alternatively, assume that the construction of the office block started before the entity signed the agreement with the buyer. In that event, the agreement should be separated into three components: a component for the sale of land, a component for the partially constructed office block and a component for the construction of the office block. The entity should apply the recognition criteria separately to each component. Assuming that the other facts remain unchanged, the entity recognises revenue from the component for the construction of the office block by reference to the stage of completion using the percentage of completion method as explained in paragraph IE3.

IE5   In this example, the sale of land is determined to be a separately identifiable component from the component for the construction of real estate. However, depending on facts and circumstances, the entity may conclude that such a component is not separately identifiable. For example, in some jurisdictions, a condominium is legally defined as the absolute ownership of a unit based on a legal description of the airspace the unit actually occupies, plus an undivided interest in the ownership of the common elements (that includes the land and actual building itself, all the driveways, parking, lifts, outside hallways, recreation and landscaped areas) that are owned jointly with the other condominium unit owners. In this case, the undivided interest in the ownership of the common elements does not give the buyer control and the significant risks and rewards of the land itself. Indeed, the right to the unit itself and the interest in the common elements are not separable.

Example 2

IE6   An entity is developing residential real estate and starts marketing individual units (apartments) while construction is still in progress. Buyers enter into a binding sale agreement that gives them the right to acquire a specified unit when it is ready for occupation. They pay a deposit that is refundable only if the entity fails to deliver the completed unit in accordance with the contracted terms. Buyers are also required to make progress payments between the time of the initial agreement and contractual completion.

The balance of the purchase price is paid only on contractual completion, when buyers obtain possession of their unit. Buyers are able to specify only minor variations to the basic design but they cannot specify or alter major structural elements of the design of their unit. In the jurisdiction, no rights to the underlying real estate asset transfer to the buyer other than through the agreement. Consequently, the construction takes place regardless of whether sale agreements exist.

IE7 In this illustrative example, the terms of the agreement and all the surrounding facts and circumstances indicate that the agreement is not a construction contract. The agreement is a forward contract that gives the buyer an asset in the form of a right to acquire, use and sell the completed real estate at a later date and an obligation to pay the purchase price in accordance with its terms. Although the buyer might be able to transfer its interest in the forward contract to another party, the entity retains control and the significant risks and rewards of ownership of the work in progress in its current state until the completed real estate is transferred. Therefore, revenue should be recognised only when all the criteria in paragraph 14 of AASB 118 are met (at completion in this example).

IE8 Alternatively, assume that, in the jurisdiction, the law requires the entity to transfer immediately to the buyer ownership of the real estate in its current state of completion and that any additional construction becomes the property of the buyer as construction progresses. The entity would need to consider all the terms of the agreement to determine whether this change in the timing of the transfer of ownership means that the entity transfers to the buyer control and the significant risks and rewards of ownership of the work in progress in its current state as construction progresses. For example, the fact that if the agreement is terminated before construction is complete, the buyer retains the work in progress and the entity has the right to be paid for the work performed, might indicate that control is transferred along with ownership. If it does, and if all the criteria in paragraph 14 of AASB 118 are met continuously as construction progresses, the entity recognises revenue by reference to the stage of completion using the percentage of completion method taking into account the stage of completion of the whole building and the agreements signed with individual buyers.

Example 3

IE9 Determining whether the entity will retain neither continuing managerial involvement to the degree usually associated with ownership nor effective control over the constructed real estate to an extent that would preclude recognition of some or all of the consideration as revenue depends on the terms of the agreement and all the surrounding facts and circumstances. Such a determination requires judgement. The Interpretation assumes the entity has reached the conclusion that it is appropriate to recognise revenue from the agreement and discusses how to determine the appropriate pattern of revenue recognition.

IE10 Agreements for the construction of real estate may include such a degree of continuing managerial involvement by the entity undertaking the construction that control and the significant risks and rewards of ownership are not transferred even when construction is complete and the buyer obtains possession. Examples are agreements in which the entity guarantees occupancy of the property for a specified period, or guarantees a return on the buyer's investment for a specified period. In such circumstances, recognition of revenue may be delayed or precluded altogether.

IE11 Agreements for the construction of real estate may give the buyer a right to take over the work in progress (albeit with a penalty) during construction, e.g. to engage a different entity to complete the construction. This fact, along with others, may indicate that the entity transfers to the buyer control of the work in progress in its current state as construction progresses. The entity that undertakes the construction of real estate will have access to the land and the work in progress in order to perform its contractual obligation to deliver to the buyer completed real estate. If control of the work in process is transferred continuously, that access does not necessarily imply that the entity undertaking the construction retains continuing managerial involvement with the real estate to the degree usually associated with ownership to an extent that would preclude recognition of some or all of the consideration as revenue. The entity may have control over the activities related to the performance of its contractual obligation but not over the real estate itself.

Basis for Conclusions on IFRIC Interpretation 15

This IFRIC Basis for Conclusions accompanies, but is not part of, AASB Interpretation 15. An IFRIC Basis for Conclusions may be amended to reflect the requirements of the AASB Interpretation and AASB Accounting Standards where they differ from the corresponding International pronouncements.

Introduction

BC1 This Basis for Conclusions summarises the IFRIC's considerations in reaching its consensus. Individual IFRIC members gave greater weight to some factors than to others.

BC2 The IFRIC released draft Interpretation D21 *Real Estate Sales* for public comment in July 2007 and received 51 comment letters in response.

Scope

BC3 Agreements for the construction of real estate are widespread and may relate to residential, commercial or industrial developments. Construction often spans more than one accounting period, may take place on land the buyer owns or leases before construction begins and agreements may require progress payments.

BC4 The main area of divergence in practice concerns the identification of the applicable accounting standard for agreements for the construction of real estate. In some jurisdictions, the prevailing practice is to apply IAS 11 *Construction Contracts* and to recognise revenue as construction progresses. In others, it is to apply the requirements for the sale of goods in IAS 18 *Revenue* and to recognise revenue only when the completed real estate is delivered to the buyer.

BC5 The IFRIC considered whether the scope of the Interpretation should be confined to agreements for the construction of real estate. It concluded in D21 that the scope should be limited to the request received to clarify the requirements of IAS 18 with respect to 'real estate sales' because that was the area identified as having the most diversity in practice. In redeliberating the issue, the IFRIC took the view that the notion of 'real estate sales' in D21 might create confusion and clarified that this Interpretation applies to 'agreements for the construction of real estate'. The primary issue of whether an agreement is within the scope of IAS 11 or IAS 18 arises only when agreements include construction activities. Such agreements may or may not meet the definition of a construction contract. The IFRIC also clarified that the Interpretation might affect entities that undertake the construction of real estate, directly or through subcontractors.

BC6 The IFRIC noted that respondents to D21 were concerned about the implications of the IFRIC's conclusions for agreements that required manufacture of goods to a customer's specifications in industries other than real estate. The IFRIC reconsidered the scope of the Interpretation after it had redeliberated its conclusions with respect to agreements for the construction of real estate. It concluded that the scope of the Interpretation should remain confined to agreements for the construction of real estate. The IFRIC noted that it might be applied by analogy to industries other than real estate in accordance with IAS 8 *Accounting Policies, Changes in Accounting Estimates and Errors*.

Issue

BC7 The issue is when should revenue from the construction of real estate be recognised? In International Financial Reporting Standards (IFRSs), two standards deal with accounting for revenue: IAS 18 and IAS 11. Because many agreements involve the construction or manufacture of an asset to meet customer's specifications, the IFRIC was asked to clarify how to determine whether an agreement for the construction of real estate is a construction contract within the scope of IAS 11.

Consensus

BC8 The nature and extent of the entity's continuing managerial involvement with the item sold may affect the accounting for the transaction. It may be accounted for as a sale, or as a financing, leasing or some other profit-sharing arrangement. Because the issue addressed in this Interpretation is a revenue recognition issue, the Interpretation assumes that the entity has previously analysed the agreement for the construction of real estate and any related agreements and concluded that it will retain neither continuing managerial involvement to the degree usually associated with ownership nor effective control over the constructed real estate to an extent that would preclude recognition of some or all of the consideration as revenue. This assumption, that the entity would recognise revenue at some point and the issue was one of timing, was implicit in D21 but was not clearly stated. In response to comments received, the IFRIC clarified that an entity must have concluded that the arrangement will result in the recognition of revenue to be within the scope of the Interpretation.

BC9　Some respondents to D21 asked the IFRIC to provide guidance on agreements with multiple components so the Interpretation would cover the more complex transactions that often occur in practice.

BC10　In its redeliberations, the IFRIC noted that, in addition to the construction of real estate, an agreement may include the delivery of other goods or services (e.g. a sale of land or provision of property management services). In accordance with paragraph 13 of IAS 18, such an agreement may need to be split into separately identifiable components, including one for the construction of real estate. Because IAS 18 is the standard that sets out requirements for revenue recognition in general, the IFRIC decided to consider the issue in the context of IAS 18, ie an entity should first determine whether an agreement that includes the construction of real estate also includes other components that do not need further analysis in this Interpretation.

BC11　The IFRIC noted that IFRIC 12 *Service Concession Arrangements* and IFRIC 13 *Customer Loyalty Programmes* already provide guidance on determining whether a single agreement should be divided into components and, if so, how to allocate the fair value of the total consideration received or receivable for the agreement to each component (see paragraph 13 of IFRIC 12 and paragraphs 5–7 of IFRIC 13). Therefore, the IFRIC concluded that this Interpretation should include only a reminder in paragraph 8 that such identification and allocation are required.

BC12　Regarding the issue of whether and when there is a separately identifiable component for the sale of land, the IFRIC concluded from the existing guidance that the identification of a component for the sale of land should be undertaken when first analysing any potential components. Depending on facts and circumstances, the entity may or may not conclude that such a component is separately identifiable from the component for the construction of real estate.

BC13　The IFRIC noted that respondents were uncertain whether an entity applying D21 would follow the guidance on combining and segmenting contracts in IAS 18 or that in IAS 11. The approach adopted in the Interpretation makes it clear that the specific criteria for contract segmentation in IAS 11 are applied only after the entity has concluded that the agreement is within the scope of that standard.

Determining whether the agreement is within the scope of IAS 11 or IAS 18

BC14　One view is that IAS 11 applies to all agreements for the construction of real estate. In support of this view, it is argued that:

(a)　these agreements are in substance construction contracts. The typical features of a construction contract—land development, structural engineering, architectural design and construction—are all present.

(b)　IAS 11 requires a percentage of completion method of revenue recognition for construction contracts. Revenue is recognised progressively as work is performed. Because many real estate development projects span more than one accounting period, the rationale for this method—that it 'provides useful information on the extent of contract activity and performance during a period' (IAS 11 paragraph 25)—applies to real estate development as much as it does to other construction contracts. If revenue is recognised only when the IAS 18 conditions for recognising revenue from the sale of goods are met, the financial statements do not reflect the entity's economic value generation in the period and are susceptible to manipulation.

(c)   US Statement of Financial Accounting Standards No. 66 *Accounting for Sales of Real Estate* requires a percentage of completion method for recognising profit from sales of units in condominium projects or time-sharing interests (provided specified criteria are met). Thus US generally accepted accounting principles (GAAP) acknowledge that such real estate sales have the same economic substance as construction-type contracts. IFRSs can and should be interpreted in the same way to avoid unnecessary differences.

BC15 A second view is that IAS 11 applies only when the agreement meets the definition of a construction contract. When the agreement does not meet the definition of a construction contract, the agreement is within the scope of IAS 18.

BC16 The consensus reflects the second view. In reaching this consensus, the IFRIC noted that:

(a)   the facts that the construction spans more than one accounting period and requires progress payments are not relevant features to consider when determining the applicable standard and the timing of revenue recognition.

(b)   determining whether an agreement for the construction of real estate is within the scope of IAS 11 or IAS 18 depends on the terms of the agreement and all the surrounding facts and circumstances. Such a determination requires judgement with respect to each agreement. It is not an accounting policy choice.

(c)   IAS 11 lacks specific guidance on the definition of a construction contract and further application guidance is needed to help identify construction contracts.

(d)   differences exist between the requirements in IFRSs and US GAAP for revenue recognition in general and for construction contracts in particular. They cannot be eliminated by interpretation. They are being addressed in a general project on revenue recognition conducted jointly by the IASB and the US Financial Accounting Standards Board.

BC17 The IFRIC noted that when IAS 11 applies, for accounting purposes, the construction contract also includes contracts for the rendering of services that are directly related to the construction of the real estate in accordance with paragraph 4 of IAS 18 and paragraph 5(a) of IAS 11.

BC18 In D21 the IFRIC concluded that an agreement for the construction of real estate would be within the scope of IAS 11 in two circumstances—if the agreement met the definition of a construction contract and/or if control and the significant risks and rewards of ownership of the work in progress in its current state transferred to the buyer continuously as construction progresses. Many respondents pointed out that IAS 11 does not require 'continuous transfer' for the use of the percentage of completion method, only that the contract be a 'construction contract'. The IFRIC clarified in the consensus that IAS 11 applies only when the agreement meets the definition of a construction contract and carried forward into the Interpretation the guidance in paragraphs 9(a), 10(a) and BC5(a) of D21.

BC19 In addition, many respondents asked the IFRIC to provide guidance to distinguish between construction contracts that meet the definition included in D21 and other agreements for the manufacture of goods to a customer's specifications. The IFRIC concluded that the most important distinguishing feature is whether the customer is actually specifying the main elements of the structural design. In situations involving the manufacture of goods to a customer's specifications, the customer generally does not have the ability to specify or alter the basic design of the product. Rather, the customer is simply choosing elements from a range of options specified by the seller or specifying only minor variations to the basic design. The IFRIC decided to include guidance to this effect in the Interpretation to help clarify the application of the definition of a construction contract.

Accounting for revenue from the construction of real estate

BC20 When the agreement is within the scope of IAS 11 and its outcome can be estimated reliably, the entity should recognise revenue by reference to the stage of completion in accordance with IAS 11.

BC21 When the agreement does not meet the definition of a construction contract, the agreement is within the scope of IAS 18. The IFRIC identified the following types of agreements for the construction of real estate that are within the scope of IAS 18 and that are distinguishable in substance:

(a)   agreements for the rendering of services only;

(b)   two types of agreements for the sale of goods:

(i)   agreements in which the entity transfers to the buyer control and the significant risks and rewards of ownership of the work in progress in its current state as construction progresses;

(ii)   agreements in which the entity transfers to the buyer control and the significant risks and rewards of ownership of the real estate in its entirety at a single time (e.g. at completion, upon or after delivery).

BC22 The IFRIC noted that a customer may decide to act in essence as its own general contractor and enter into agreements with individual suppliers for specific goods and services. When the entity is responsible only for assembling materials supplied by others (ie it has no inventory risk for the construction materials), the agreement is an agreement for the rendering of services. The IFRIC noted that, if the criteria in paragraph 20 are met, IAS 18 requires revenue to be recognised by reference to the stage of completion using the percentage of completion method. IAS 18 then refers to IAS 11 and states that the requirements of IAS 11 are generally applicable to the recognition of revenue and the associated expenses for such a transaction.

BC23 The IFRIC also noted that construction activities often require an entity that undertakes the construction of real estate, directly or through subcontractors, to provide services together with construction materials. However, the entity delivers to the buyer a real estate asset, either completed or in its current stage of completion. Therefore, the IFRIC concluded that the criteria in paragraph 14 of IAS 18 for recognition of revenue from the sale of goods should apply to such agreements.

BC24 As noted in paragraph BC18, the IFRIC agreed with respondents to D21 that IAS 11 does not require the entity to transfer to the buyer control and the significant risks and rewards of ownership of the work in process in its current state as construction progresses ('continuous transfer') in order to use the percentage of completion method, only that the contract be a 'construction contract'. In its redeliberations, the IFRIC noted that the criterion it included in paragraph 9(b) of D21 was actually one of the criteria in IAS 18 for recognition of revenue from the sale of goods. Although these agreements may not meet the definition of construction contracts, the IFRIC concluded that they may result in the entity meeting all of the criteria for recognising revenue from the sale of goods in IAS 18 (including the transfer of control and the significant risks and rewards of ownership) continuously as construction progresses, as opposed to at a single time (e.g. at completion, upon or after delivery).

BC25 The IFRIC concluded that if all these criteria are met continuously, an entity should recognise revenue on the same basis (by reference to the stage of completion). Like paragraph 21 of IAS 18 for the rendering of services, the Interpretation refers entities to IAS 11 for guidance on applying the percentage of completion method. The IFRIC observed that this conclusion was consistent with the basis for using the percentage of completion method in Statement of Position No. 81–1 *Accounting for Performance of Construction-Type and Certain Production-Type Contracts* issued by the American Institute of Certified Public Accountants, which states:

> ...the business activity taking place supports the concept that in an economic sense performance is, in effect, a continuous sale (transfer of ownership rights) that occurs as the work progresses...

BC26 The IFRIC noted that agreements with 'continuous transfer' might not be encountered frequently. However, the IFRIC decided that the Interpretation should address the accounting for such agreements because some respondents to D21 identified agreements with these characteristics.

BC27 The IFRIC also identified agreements for the construction of real estate in which the entity transfers to the buyer control and the significant risks and rewards of ownership of the real estate in its entirety at a single time (e.g. at completion, upon or after delivery). The IFRIC reaffirmed its conclusion in D21 that these agreements are sales of goods within the scope of IAS 18. Such agreements give the buyer only an asset in the form of a right to acquire, use and sell the completed real estate at a later date. The IFRIC concluded that revenue from such agreements should be recognised only when all the criteria in paragraph 14 of IAS 18 are satisfied.

BC28 The IFRIC noted that this conclusion is consistent with revenue recognition requirements for significant contracts for the delivery of multiple units of goods manufactured to the customer's specifications over more than one accounting period, such as subway cars. In such circumstances, the entity recognises revenue as individual units (or groups of units) are delivered. However, in contrast to the contracts described in paragraph BC24, control and the significant risks and rewards of ownership of the work in process in its current state do not transfer to the buyer as construction/manufacture progresses. This transfer takes place only on delivery of the completed units. In this case, the entity would apply the requirements of paragraph 14 of IAS 18 at that time; use of the percentage of completion method would not be appropriate.

BC29 In some circumstances, an entity has to perform further work on real estate already delivered to the buyer. The IFRIC noted that IFRIC 13 *Customer Loyalty Programmes* already provides guidance on how to apply paragraphs 13 and 19 of IAS 18. Paragraph BC9 of IFRIC 13 states that:

> ... IAS 18 does not give explicit guidance. However, the aim of IAS 18 is to recognise revenue when, and to the extent that, goods or services have been delivered to a customer. In the IFRIC's view, paragraph 13 applies if a single transaction requires two or more separate goods or services to be delivered at different times; it ensures that revenue for each item is recognised only when that item is delivered. In contrast, paragraph 19 applies only if the entity has to incur further costs directly related to items already delivered, e.g. to meet warranty claims. In the IFRIC's view, loyalty awards are not costs that directly relate to the goods and services already delivered—rather, they are separate goods or services delivered at a later date ...

BC30 The IFRIC concluded that the Interpretation should provide similar guidance.

Disclosures

BC31 The IFRIC noted that IAS 1 *Presentation of Financial Statements* (as revised in 2007) requires an entity to provide disclosures about its significant accounting policies (paragraph 117), judgements management has made in applying those policies (paragraph 122) and major sources of estimation uncertainty.

BC32 For greater certainty, the IFRIC concluded that, for agreements with 'continuous transfer', the Interpretation should require specific disclosures similar to those of paragraphs 39 and 40 of IAS 11 to satisfy the general requirements of IAS 1.

BC33 The IFRIC noted that this conclusion was generally consistent with D21 because D21 included such agreements in the scope of IAS 11 and therefore implicitly required the full disclosures of that standard.

Changes from draft Interpretation D21

BC34 Most respondents to D21 supported the IFRIC's conclusion that it should develop an interpretation on this issue. However, nearly all respondents expressed concern with some aspects of the proposals or the possible application by analogy to industries other than real estate.

BC35 The most significant changes made from D21 in the light of comments received relate to:

    (a)   *scope*. D21 referred to 'real estate sales'. The IFRIC clarified that the Interpretation applies to agreements for the construction of real estate.

    (b)   *applicable standard*. D21 listed typical features, including 'continuous transfer', to help determine whether an agreement for the construction of real estate is within the scope of IAS 11 or IAS 18. The IFRIC concluded that only agreements that meet the definition of a construction contract are within the scope of IAS 11 and carried forward into the Interpretation the guidance in paragraphs 9(a), 10(a) and BC5(a) of D21 on when a contract satisfies that definition.

    (c)   *continuous transfer*. Many respondents believed that the indicator of 'continuous transfer' (the entity transfers to the buyer control and the significant risks and rewards of ownership of the work in progress in its current state as construction progresses) set out in paragraph 9(b) of D21 was relevant, although not specifically included in IAS 11. The IFRIC took the view that when the criteria for recognising revenue from the sale of goods set out in paragraph 14 of IAS 18 are met continuously, it is appropriate to recognise revenue as the criteria are met. The IFRIC carried forward the criterion set out in paragraph 9(b) of D21 and concluded that the percentage of completion method appropriately recognises revenue in such circumstances. However, the IFRIC did not carry forward the features set out in paragraph 9(b)(i)–(iii) of D21 on the basis that the criterion was sufficiently clear. Overall, the Interpretation and D21 provide similar revenue recognition conclusions for agreements with 'continuous transfer' but for different reasons.

    (d)   *multiple components*. Some respondents to D21 asked the IFRIC to address the issue of a single agreement with multiple components in order to cover the more complex transactions that often occur in practice. The requirements of IAS 18 in this respect have been included in the consensus and the issue is also addressed in an illustrative example.

    (e)   *disclosures*. D21 did not specify disclosures because agreements with 'continuous transfer' were included in the scope of IAS 11 and its disclosure requirements would have automatically applied. Paragraphs 20 and 21 of the Interpretation have been added to require specific disclosures for such agreements that now fall within the scope of IAS 18.

    (f)   *flow chart and illustrative examples*. The IFRIC decided that a flow chart and illustrative examples should accompany, but not be part of, the Interpretation to help entities apply the Interpretation.

Deleted IFRIC Interpretation 15 Text

Deleted IFRIC Interpretation 15 text is not part of AASB Interpretation 15.

Paragraph 24

An entity shall apply this Interpretation for annual periods beginning on or after 1 January 2009. Earlier application is permitted. If an entity applies the Interpretation for a period beginning before 1 January 2009, it shall disclose that fact.

Interpretation 16
Hedges of a Net Investment in a Foreign Operation

(Compiled February 2010)

Contents

Compilation Details

Comparison with IFRIC 16

AASB Interpretation 16
Hedges of a Net Investment in a Foreign Operation

	Paragraphs
References	
Background	1 – 6
Scope	7 – 8
Issues	9
Consensus	
Nature of the hedged risk and amount of the hedged item for which a hedging relationship may be designated	10 – 13
Where the hedging instrument can be held	14 – 15
Disposal of a hedged foreign operation	16 – 17
Application	Aus17.1 – Aus17.4
Effective Date	18
Transition	19

Appendix

Application Guidance	AG1 – AG15

Illustrative Example	IE1 – IE5

Basis for Conclusions on IFRIC 16

Deleted IFRIC 16 Text

AASB Interpretation 16 *Hedges of a Net Investment in a Foreign Operation* (as amended) is set out in paragraphs 1 – 19 and the Appendix. Interpretations are listed in Australian Accounting Standard AASB 1048 *Interpretation and Application of Standards*. In the absence of explicit guidance, AASB 108 *Accounting Policies, Changes in Accounting Estimates and Errors* provides a basis for selecting and applying accounting policies.

Compilation Details

AASB Interpretation 16 *Hedges of a Net Investment in a Foreign Operation* as amended

This compiled AASB Interpretation applies to annual reporting periods beginning on or after 1 January 2011. It takes into account amendments up to and including 15 December 2009 and was prepared on 23 February 2010 by the staff of the Australian Accounting Standards Board (AASB).

This compilation is not a separate Interpretation issued by the AASB. Instead, it is a representation of Interpretation 16 (August 2008) as amended by other pronouncements, which are listed in the Table below.

Table of Pronouncements

Pronouncement	Month issued	Application date (*annual reporting periods ... on or after ...*)	Application, saving or transitional provisions
Interpretation 16	Aug 2008	(*beginning*) 1 Oct 2008	see (a) below
AASB 2009-4	May 2009	(*beginning*) 1 Jul 2009	see (b) below
AASB 2009-12	Dec 2009	(*beginning*) 1 Jan 2011	see (c) below

(a) Entities may elect to apply this Interpretation to annual reporting periods beginning on or after 1 January 2005 but before 1 October 2008.

(b) Entities may elect to apply this Standard, or its amendments to individual pronouncements, to annual reporting periods beginning on or after 1 January 2005 but before 1 July 2009.

(c) Entities may elect to apply this Standard to annual reporting periods beginning on or after 1 January 2005 but before 1 January 2011.

Table of Amendments

Paragraph affected	How affected	By ... [paragraph]
14	amended	AASB 2009-4 [14]
18 (preceding heading)	amended	AASB 2009-12 [23]
18	added	AASB 2009-4 [15]

Comparison with IFRIC 16

AASB Interpretation 16 *Hedges of a Net Investment in a Foreign Operation* as amended incorporates International Financial Reporting Interpretations Committee Interpretation IFRIC 16 *Hedges of a Net Investment in a Foreign Operation*, issued by the International Accounting Standards Board. Paragraphs that have been added to this Interpretation (and do not appear in the text of IFRIC 16) are identified with the prefix "Aus", followed by the number of the preceding IFRIC paragraph and decimal numbering.

Entities that comply with AASB Interpretation 16 as amended will simultaneously be in compliance with IFRIC 16 as amended.

Interpretation 16

AASB Interpretation 16 was issued in August 2008.

This compiled version of Interpretation 16 applies to annual reporting periods beginning on or after 1 January 2011. It incorporates relevant amendments contained in other AASB pronouncements up to and including 15 December 2009 (see Compilation Details).

Australian Accounting Standards Board

Interpretation 16

Hedges of a Net Investment in a Foreign Operation

References

Accounting Standard AASB 108 *Accounting Policies, Changes in Accounting Estimates and Errors*

Accounting Standard AASB 121 *The Effects of Changes in Foreign Exchange Rates*

Accounting Standard AASB 139 *Financial Instruments: Recognition and Measurement*

Background

1   Many reporting entities have investments in foreign operations (as defined in AASB 121 *The Effects of Changes in Foreign Exchange Rates* paragraph 8). Such foreign operations may be subsidiaries, associates, joint ventures or branches. AASB 121 requires an entity to determine the functional currency of each of its foreign operations as the currency of the primary economic environment of that operation. When translating the results and financial position of a foreign operation into a presentation currency, the entity is required to recognise foreign exchange differences in other comprehensive income until it disposes of the foreign operation.

2   Hedge accounting of the foreign currency risk arising from a net investment in a foreign operation will apply only when the net assets of that foreign operation are included in the financial statements.[1] The item being hedged with respect to the foreign currency risk arising from the net investment in a foreign operation may be an amount of net assets equal to or less than the carrying amount of the net assets of the foreign operation.

3   AASB 139 *Financial Instruments: Recognition and Measurement* requires the designation of an eligible hedged item and eligible hedging instruments in a hedge accounting relationship. If there is a designated hedging relationship, in the case of a net investment hedge, the gain or loss on the hedging instrument that is determined to be an effective hedge of the net investment is recognised in other comprehensive income and is included with the foreign exchange differences arising on translation of the results and financial position of the foreign operation.

4   An entity with many foreign operations may be exposed to a number of foreign currency risks. This Interpretation provides guidance on identifying the foreign currency risks that qualify as a hedged risk in the hedge of a net investment in a foreign operation.

5   AASB 139 allows an entity to designate either a derivative or a non-derivative financial instrument (or a combination of derivative and non-derivative financial instruments) as hedging instruments for foreign currency risk. This Interpretation provides guidance on where, within a group, hedging instruments that are hedges of a net investment in a foreign operation can be held to qualify for hedge accounting.

6   AASB 121 and AASB 139 require cumulative amounts recognised in other comprehensive income relating to both the foreign exchange differences arising on translation of the results and financial position of the foreign operation and the gain or loss on the hedging instrument that is determined to be an effective hedge of the net investment to be reclassified from equity to profit or loss as a reclassification adjustment when the parent disposes of the foreign operation. This Interpretation provides guidance on how an entity should determine the amounts to be reclassified from equity to profit or loss for both the hedging instrument and the hedged item.

---

1   This will be the case for consolidated financial statements, financial statements in which investments are accounted for using the equity method, financial statements in which venturers' interests in joint ventures are proportionately consolidated (subject to change as proposed in ED 157 *Joint Arrangements* published by the Australian Accounting Standards Board, being equivalent to ED 9 *Joint Arrangements* published by the International Accounting Standards Board in September 2007) and financial statements that include a branch.

Scope

7   This Interpretation applies to an entity that hedges the foreign currency risk arising from its net investments in foreign operations and wishes to qualify for hedge accounting in accordance with AASB 139. For convenience this Interpretation refers to such an entity as a parent entity and to the financial statements in which the net assets of foreign operations are included as consolidated financial statements. All references to a parent entity apply equally to an entity that has a net investment in a foreign operation that is a joint venture, an associate or a branch.

8   This Interpretation applies only to hedges of net investments in foreign operations; it should not be applied by analogy to other types of hedge accounting.

Issues

9   Investments in foreign operations may be held directly by a parent entity or indirectly by its subsidiary or subsidiaries. The issues addressed in this Interpretation are:

(a)   the nature of the hedged risk and the amount of the hedged item for which a hedging relationship may be designated:

    (i)   whether the parent entity may designate as a hedged risk only the foreign exchange differences arising from a difference between the functional currencies of the parent entity and its foreign operation, or whether it may also designate as the hedged risk the foreign exchange differences arising from the difference between the presentation currency of the parent entity's consolidated financial statements and the functional currency of the foreign operation;

    (ii)   if the parent entity holds the foreign operation indirectly, whether the hedged risk may include only the foreign exchange differences arising from differences in functional currencies between the foreign operation and its immediate parent entity, or whether the hedged risk may also include any foreign exchange differences between the functional currency of the foreign operation and any intermediate or ultimate parent entity (i.e. whether the fact that the net investment in the foreign operation is held through an intermediate parent affects the economic risk to the ultimate parent).

(b)   where in a group the hedging instrument can be held:

    (i)   whether a qualifying hedge accounting relationship can be established only if the entity hedging its net investment is a party to the hedging instrument or whether any entity in the group, regardless of its functional currency, can hold the hedging instrument;

    (ii)   whether the nature of the hedging instrument (derivative or non-derivative) or the method of consolidation affects the assessment of hedge effectiveness.

(c)   what amounts should be reclassified from equity to profit or loss as reclassification adjustments on disposal of the foreign operation:

    (i)   when a foreign operation that was hedged is disposed of, what amounts from the parent entity's foreign currency translation reserve in respect of the hedging instrument and in respect of that foreign operation should be reclassified from equity to profit or loss in the parent entity's consolidated financial statements;

    (ii)   whether the method of consolidation affects the determination of the amounts to be reclassified from equity to profit or loss.

Consensus

Nature of the hedged risk and amount of the hedged item for which a hedging relationship may be designated

10   Hedge accounting may be applied only to the foreign exchange differences arising between the functional currency of the foreign operation and the parent entity's functional currency.

11   In a hedge of the foreign currency risks arising from a net investment in a foreign operation, the hedged item can be an amount of net assets equal to or less than the carrying amount of the net assets of the foreign operation in the consolidated financial statements of the parent entity. The carrying amount of the net assets of a foreign operation that may be designated as the hedged item in the consolidated financial statements of a parent depends on whether any lower level parent of the foreign operation has applied hedge accounting for all or part of the net assets of that foreign operation and that accounting has been maintained in the parent's consolidated financial statements.

12   The hedged risk may be designated as the foreign currency exposure arising between the functional currency of the foreign operation and the functional currency of any parent entity (the immediate, intermediate or ultimate parent entity) of that foreign operation. The fact that the net investment is held through an intermediate parent does not affect the nature of the economic risk arising from the foreign currency exposure to the ultimate parent entity.

13   An exposure to foreign currency risk arising from a net investment in a foreign operation may qualify for hedge accounting only once in the consolidated financial statements. Therefore, if the same net assets of a foreign operation are hedged by more than one parent entity within the group (for example, both a direct and an indirect parent entity) for the same risk, only one hedging relationship will qualify for hedge accounting in the consolidated financial statements of the ultimate parent. A hedging relationship designated by one parent entity in its consolidated financial statements need not be maintained by another higher level parent entity. However, if it is not maintained by the higher level parent entity, the hedge accounting applied by the lower level parent must be reversed before the higher level parent's hedge accounting is recognised.

Where the hedging instrument can be held

14   A derivative or a non-derivative instrument (or a combination of derivative and non-derivative instruments) may be designated as a hedging instrument in a hedge of a net investment in a foreign operation. The hedging instrument(s) may be held by any entity or entities within the group, as long as the designation, documentation and effectiveness requirements of AASB 139 paragraph 88 that relate to a net investment hedge are satisfied. In particular, the hedging strategy of the group should be clearly documented because of the possibility of different designations at different levels of the group.

15   For the purpose of assessing effectiveness, the change in value of the hedging instrument in respect of foreign exchange risk is computed by reference to the functional currency of the parent entity against whose functional currency the hedged risk is measured, in accordance with the hedge accounting documentation. Depending on where the hedging instrument is held, in the absence of hedge accounting the total change in value might be recognised in profit or loss, in other comprehensive income, or both. However, the assessment of effectiveness is not affected by whether the change in value of the hedging instrument is recognised in profit or loss or in other comprehensive income. As part of the application of hedge accounting, the total effective portion of the change is included in other comprehensive income. The assessment of effectiveness is not affected by whether the hedging instrument is a derivative or a non-derivative instrument or by the method of consolidation.

Disposal of a hedged foreign operation

16   When a foreign operation that was hedged is disposed of, the amount reclassified to profit or loss as a reclassification adjustment from the foreign currency translation reserve in the consolidated financial statements of the parent in respect of the hedging instrument is the amount that AASB 139 paragraph 102 requires to be identified. That amount is the cumulative gain or loss on the hedging instrument that was determined to be an effective hedge.

17   The amount reclassified to profit or loss from the foreign currency translation reserve in the consolidated financial statements of a parent in respect of the net investment in that foreign operation in accordance with AASB 121 paragraph 48 is the amount included in that parent's foreign currency translation reserve in respect of that foreign operation.

In the ultimate parent's consolidated financial statements, the aggregate net amount recognised in the foreign currency translation reserve in respect of all foreign operations is not affected by the consolidation method. However, whether the ultimate parent uses the direct or the step-by-step method of consolidation[2] may affect the amount included in its foreign currency translation reserve in respect of an individual foreign operation. The use of the step-by-step method of consolidation may result in the reclassification to profit or loss of an amount different from that used to determine hedge effectiveness. This difference may be eliminated by determining the amount relating to that foreign operation that would have arisen if the direct method of consolidation had been used. Making this adjustment is not required by AASB 121. However, it is an accounting policy choice that should be followed consistently for all net investments.

Application

Aus17.1   This Interpretation applies to:

(a)   each entity that is required to prepare financial reports in accordance with Part 2M.3 of the *Corporations Act 2001* and that is a reporting entity;

(b)   general purpose financial statements of each other reporting entity; and

(c)   financial statements that are, or are held out to be, general purpose financial statements.

Aus17.2   This Interpretation applies to annual reporting periods beginning on or after 1 October 2008.

[Note: For application dates of paragraphs changed or added by an amending pronouncement, see Compilation Details.]

Aus17.3   This Interpretation may be applied to annual reporting periods beginning on or after 1 January 2005 but before 1 October 2008. If an entity applies this Interpretation to such an annual reporting period, it shall disclose that fact.

Aus17.4   The requirements specified in this Interpretation apply to the financial statements where information resulting from their application is material in accordance with AASB 1031 *Materiality*.

Effective Date

18   An entity shall apply this Interpretation for annual reporting periods beginning on or after 1 October 2008. An entity shall apply the amendment to paragraph 14 made by AASB 2009-4 *Amendments to Australian Accounting Standards arising from the Annual Improvements Project*, issued in May 2009, for annual reporting periods beginning on or after 1 July 2009. Earlier application of both is permitted. If an entity applies this Interpretation for a period beginning before 1 October 2008, or the amendment to paragraph 14 before 1 July 2009, it shall disclose that fact.

Transition

19   AASB 108 *Accounting Policies, Changes in Accounting Estimates and Errors* specifies how an entity applies a change in accounting policy resulting from the initial application of an Interpretation. An entity is not required to comply with those requirements when first applying the Interpretation. If an entity had designated a hedging instrument as a hedge of a net investment but the hedge does not meet the conditions for hedge accounting in this Interpretation, the entity shall apply AASB 139 to discontinue that hedge accounting prospectively.

---

2   The direct method is the method of consolidation in which the financial statements of the foreign operation are translated directly into the functional currency of the ultimate parent. The step-by-step method is the method of consolidation in which the financial statements of the foreign operation are first translated into the functional currency of any intermediate parent(s) and then translated into the functional currency of the ultimate parent (or the presentation currency if different).

Appendix
Application Guidance

This appendix is an integral part of AASB Interpretation 16.

AG1   This appendix illustrates the application of the Interpretation using the corporate structure illustrated below. In all cases the hedging relationships described would be tested for effectiveness in accordance with AASB 139, although this testing is not discussed in this appendix. Parent, being the ultimate parent entity, presents its consolidated financial statements in its functional currency of euro (EUR). Each of the subsidiaries is wholly owned. Parent's £500 million net investment in Subsidiary B (functional currency pounds sterling (GBP)) includes the £159 million equivalent of Subsidiary B's US$300 million net investment in Subsidiary C (functional currency US dollars (USD)). In other words, Subsidiary B's net assets other than its investment in Subsidiary C are £341 million.

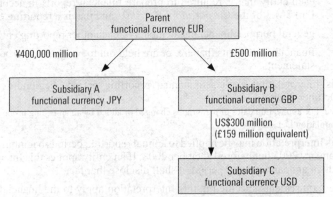

Nature of hedged risk for which a hedging relationship may be designated (paragraphs 10–13)

AG2   Parent can hedge its net investment in each of Subsidiaries A, B and C for the foreign exchange risk between their respective functional currencies (Japanese yen (JPY), pounds sterling and US dollars) and euro. In addition, Parent can hedge the USD/GBP foreign exchange risk between the functional currencies of Subsidiary B and Subsidiary C. In its consolidated financial statements, Subsidiary B can hedge its net investment in Subsidiary C for the foreign exchange risk between their functional currencies of US dollars and pounds sterling. In the following examples the designated risk is the spot foreign exchange risk because the hedging instruments are not derivatives. If the hedging instruments were forward contracts, Parent could designate the forward foreign exchange risk.

Amount of hedged item for which a hedging relationship may be designated (paragraphs 10–13)

AG3   Parent wishes to hedge the foreign exchange risk from its net investment in Subsidiary C. Assume that Subsidiary A has an external borrowing of US$300 million. The net assets of Subsidiary A at the start of the reporting period are ¥400,000 million including the proceeds of the external borrowing of US$300 million.

AG4   The hedged item can be an amount of net assets equal to or less than the carrying amount of Parent's net investment in Subsidiary C (US$300 million) in its consolidated financial statements. In its consolidated financial statements Parent can designate the US$300 million external borrowing in Subsidiary A as a hedge of the EUR/USD spot foreign exchange risk associated with its net investment in the US$300 million net assets of Subsidiary C. In this case, both the EUR/USD foreign exchange difference on the US$300 million external borrowing in Subsidiary A and the EUR/USD foreign exchange difference on the US$300 million net investment in Subsidiary C are included in the foreign currency translation reserve in Parent's consolidated financial statements after the application of hedge accounting.

AG5   In the absence of hedge accounting, the total USD/EUR foreign exchange difference on the US$300 million external borrowing in Subsidiary A would be recognised in Parent's consolidated financial statements as follows:

(a)   USD/JPY spot foreign exchange rate change, translated to euro, in profit or loss, and

(b)   JPY/EUR spot foreign exchange rate change in other comprehensive income.

Instead of the designation in paragraph AG4, in its consolidated financial statements Parent can designate the US$300 million external borrowing in Subsidiary A as a hedge of the GBP/USD spot foreign exchange risk between Subsidiary C and Subsidiary B. In this case, the total USD/EUR foreign exchange difference on the US$300 million external borrowing in Subsidiary A would instead be recognised in Parent's consolidated financial statements as follows:

(a)   the GBP/USD spot foreign exchange rate change in the foreign currency translation reserve relating to Subsidiary C,

(b)   GBP/JPY spot foreign exchange rate change, translated to euro, in profit or loss, and

(c)   JPY/EUR spot foreign exchange rate change in other comprehensive income.

AG6   Parent cannot designate the US$300 million external borrowing in Subsidiary A as a hedge of both the EUR/USD spot foreign exchange risk and the GBP/USD spot foreign exchange risk in its consolidated financial statements. A single hedging instrument can hedge the same designated risk only once. Subsidiary B cannot apply hedge accounting in its consolidated financial statements because the hedging instrument is held outside the group comprising Subsidiary B and Subsidiary C.

Where in a group can the hedging instrument be held (paragraphs 14 and 15)?

AG7   As noted in paragraph AG5, the total change in value in respect of foreign exchange risk of the US$300 million external borrowing in Subsidiary A would be recorded in both profit or loss (USD/JPY spot risk) and other comprehensive income (EUR/JPY spot risk) in Parent's consolidated financial statements in the absence of hedge accounting. Both amounts are included for the purpose of assessing the effectiveness of the hedge designated in paragraph AG4 because the change in value of both the hedging instrument and the hedged item are computed by reference to the euro functional currency of Parent against the US dollar functional currency of Subsidiary C, in accordance with the hedge documentation. The method of consolidation (i.e. direct method or step-by-step method) does not affect the assessment of the effectiveness of the hedge.

Amounts reclassified to profit or loss on disposal of a foreign operation (paragraphs 16 and 17)

AG8   When Subsidiary C is disposed of, the amounts reclassified to profit or loss in Parent's consolidated financial statements from its foreign currency translation reserve (FCTR) are:

(a)   in respect of the US$300 million external borrowing of Subsidiary A, the amount that AASB 139 requires to be identified, i.e. the total change in value in respect of foreign exchange risk that was recognised in other comprehensive income as the effective portion of the hedge; and

(b)   in respect of the US$300 million net investment in Subsidiary C, the amount determined by the entity's consolidation method. If Parent uses the direct method, its FCTR in respect of Subsidiary C will be determined directly by the EUR/USD foreign exchange rate. If Parent uses the step-by-step method, its FCTR in respect of Subsidiary C will be determined by the FCTR recognised by Subsidiary B reflecting the GBP/USD foreign exchange rate, translated to Parent's functional currency using the EUR/GBP foreign exchange rate. Parent's use of the step-by-step method of consolidation in prior periods does not require it to or preclude it from determining the amount of FCTR to be reclassified when it disposes of Subsidiary C to be the amount that it would have recognised if it had always used the direct method, depending on its accounting policy.

Hedging more than one foreign operation (paragraphs 11, 13 and 15)

AG9   The following examples illustrate that in the consolidated financial statements of Parent, the risk that can be hedged is always the risk between its functional currency (euro) and the functional currencies of Subsidiaries B and C. No matter how the hedges are designated, the maximum amounts that can be effective hedges to be included in the foreign currency translation reserve in Parent's consolidated financial statements when both foreign operations are hedged are US$300 million for EUR/USD risk and £341 million for EUR/GBP risk. Other changes in value due to changes in foreign exchange rates are included in Parent's consolidated profit or loss. Of course, it would be possible for Parent to designate US$300 million only for changes in the USD/GBP spot foreign exchange rate or £500 million only for changes in the GBP/EUR spot foreign exchange rate.

Parent holds both USD and GBP hedging instruments

AG10 Parent may wish to hedge the foreign exchange risk in relation to its net investment in Subsidiary B as well as that in relation to Subsidiary C. Assume that Parent holds suitable hedging instruments denominated in US dollars and pounds sterling that it could designate as hedges of its net investments in Subsidiary B and Subsidiary C. The designations Parent can make in its consolidated financial statements include, but are not limited to, the following:

(a)   US$300 million hedging instrument designated as a hedge of the US$300 million of net investment in Subsidiary C with the risk being the spot foreign exchange exposure (EUR/USD) between Parent and Subsidiary C and up to £341 million hedging instrument designated as a hedge of £341 million of the net investment in Subsidiary B with the risk being the spot foreign exchange exposure (EUR/GBP) between Parent and Subsidiary B.

(b)   US$300 million hedging instrument designated as a hedge of the US$300 million of net investment in Subsidiary C with the risk being the spot foreign exchange exposure (GBP/USD) between Subsidiary B and Subsidiary C and up to £500 million hedging instrument designated as a hedge of £500 million of the net investment in Subsidiary B with the risk being the spot foreign exchange exposure (EUR/GBP) between Parent and Subsidiary B.

AG11 The EUR/USD risk from Parent's net investment in Subsidiary C is a different risk from the EUR/GBP risk from Parent's net investment in Subsidiary B. However, in the case described in paragraph AG10(a), by its designation of the USD hedging instrument it holds, Parent has already fully hedged the EUR/USD risk from its net investment in Subsidiary C. If Parent also designated a GBP instrument it holds as a hedge of its £500 million net investment in Subsidiary B, £159 million of that net investment, representing the GBP equivalent of its USD net investment in Subsidiary C, would be hedged twice for GBP/EUR risk in Parent's consolidated financial statements.

AG12 In the case described in paragraph AG10(b), if Parent designates the hedged risk as the spot foreign exchange exposure (GBP/USD) between Subsidiary B and Subsidiary C, only the GBP/USD part of the change in the value of its US$300 million hedging instrument is included in Parent's foreign currency translation reserve relating to Subsidiary C. The remainder of the change (equivalent to the GBP/EUR change on £159 million) is included in Parent's consolidated profit or loss, as in paragraph AG5. Because the designation of the USD/GBP risk between Subsidiaries B and C does not include the GBP/EUR risk, Parent is also able to designate up to £500 million of its net investment in Subsidiary B with the risk being the spot foreign exchange exposure (GBP/EUR) between Parent and Subsidiary B.

Subsidiary B holds the USD hedging instrument

AG13 Assume that Subsidiary B holds US$300 million of external debt, the proceeds of which were transferred to Parent by an inter-company loan denominated in pounds sterling. Because both its assets and liabilities increased by £159 million, Subsidiary B's net assets are unchanged. Subsidiary B could designate the external debt as a hedge of the GBP/USD risk of its net investment in Subsidiary C in its consolidated financial statements.

Parent could maintain Subsidiary B's designation of that hedging instrument as a hedge of its US$300 million net investment in Subsidiary C for the GBP/USD risk (see paragraph 13) and Parent could designate the GBP hedging instrument it holds as a hedge of its entire £500 million net investment in Subsidiary B. The first hedge, designated by Subsidiary B, would be assessed by reference to Subsidiary B's functional currency (pounds sterling) and the second hedge, designated by Parent, would be assessed by reference to Parent's functional currency (euro). In this case, only the GBP/USD risk from Parent's net investment in Subsidiary C has been hedged in Parent's consolidated financial statements by the USD hedging instrument, not the entire EUR/USD risk. Therefore, the entire EUR/GBP risk from Parent's £500 million net investment in Subsidiary B may be hedged in the consolidated financial statements of Parent.

AG14 However, the accounting for Parent's £159 million loan payable to Subsidiary B must also be considered. If Parent's loan payable is not considered part of its net investment in Subsidiary B because it does not satisfy the conditions in AASB 121 paragraph 15, the GBP/EUR foreign exchange difference arising on translating it would be included in Parent's consolidated profit or loss. If the £159 million loan payable to Subsidiary B is considered part of Parent's net investment, that net investment would be only £341 million and the amount Parent could designate as the hedged item for GBP/EUR risk would be reduced from £500 million to £341 million accordingly.

AG15 If Parent reversed the hedging relationship designated by Subsidiary B, Parent could designate the US$300 million external borrowing held by Subsidiary B as a hedge of its US$300 million net investment in Subsidiary C for the EUR/USD risk and designate the GBP hedging instrument it holds itself as a hedge of only up to £341 million of the net investment in Subsidiary B. In this case the effectiveness of both hedges would be computed by reference to Parent's functional currency (euro). Consequently, both the USD/GBP change in value of the external borrowing held by Subsidiary B and the GBP/EUR change in value of Parent's loan payable to Subsidiary B (equivalent to USD/EUR in total) would be included in the foreign currency translation reserve in Parent's consolidated financial statements. Because Parent has already fully hedged the EUR/USD risk from its net investment in Subsidiary C, it can hedge only up to £341 million for the EUR/GBP risk of its net investment in Subsidiary B.

Illustrative Example

This example accompanies, but is not part of, AASB Interpretation 16.

Disposal of a foreign operation (paragraphs 16 and 17)

IE1 This example illustrates the application of paragraphs 16 and 17 in connection with the reclassification adjustment on the disposal of a foreign operation.

Background

IE2 This example assumes the group structure set out in the application guidance and that Parent used a USD borrowing in Subsidiary A to hedge the EUR/USD risk of the net investment in Subsidiary C in Parent's consolidated financial statements. Parent uses the step-by-step method of consolidation. Assume the hedge was fully effective and the full USD/EUR accumulated change in the value of the hedging instrument before disposal of Subsidiary C is €24 million (gain). This is matched exactly by the fall in value of the net investment in Subsidiary C, when measured against the functional currency of Parent (euro).

IE3 If the direct method of consolidation is used, the fall in the value of Parent's net investment in Subsidiary C of €24 million would be reflected totally in the foreign currency translation reserve relating to Subsidiary C in Parent's consolidated financial statements. However, because Parent uses the step-by-step method, this fall in the net investment value in Subsidiary C of €24 million would be reflected both in Subsidiary B's foreign currency translation reserve relating to Subsidiary C and in Parent's foreign currency translation reserve relating to Subsidiary B.

IE4   The aggregate amount recognised in the foreign currency translation reserve in respect of Subsidiaries B and C is not affected by the consolidation method. Assume that using the direct method of consolidation, the foreign currency translation reserves for Subsidiaries B and C in Parent's consolidated financial statements are €62 million gain and €24 million loss respectively; using the step-by-step method of consolidation those amounts are €49 million gain and €11 million loss respectively.

Reclassification

IE5   When the investment in Subsidiary C is disposed of, AASB 139 requires the full €24 million gain on the hedging instrument to be reclassified to profit or loss. Using the step-by-step method, the amount to be reclassified to profit or loss in respect of the net investment in Subsidiary C would be only €11 million loss. Parent could adjust the foreign currency translation reserves of both Subsidiaries B and C by €13 million in order to match the amounts reclassified in respect of the hedging instrument and the net investment as would have been the case if the direct method of consolidation had been used, if that was its accounting policy. An entity that had not hedged its net investment could make the same reclassification.

Basis for Conclusions on IFRIC Interpretation 16

This IFRIC Basis for Conclusions accompanies, but is not part of, AASB Interpretation 16. An IFRIC Basis for Conclusions may be amended to reflect the requirements of the AASB Interpretation and AASB Accounting Standards where they differ from the corresponding International pronouncements.

Introduction

BC1   This Basis for Conclusions summarises the IFRIC's considerations in reaching its consensus. Individual IFRIC members gave greater weight to some factors than to others.

Background

BC2   The IFRIC was asked for guidance on accounting for the hedge of a net investment in a foreign operation in the consolidated financial statements. Interested parties had different views of the risks eligible for hedge accounting purposes. One issue is whether the risk arises from the foreign currency exposure to the functional currencies of the foreign operation and the parent entity, or whether it arises from the foreign currency exposure to the functional currency of the foreign operation and the presentation currency of the parent entity's consolidated financial statements.

BC3   Concern was also raised about which entity within a group could hold a hedging instrument in a hedge of a net investment in a foreign operation and in particular whether the parent entity holding the net investment in a foreign operation must also hold the hedging instrument.

BC4   Accordingly, the IFRIC decided to develop guidance on the accounting for a hedge of the foreign currency risk arising from a net investment in a foreign operation.

BC5   The IFRIC published draft Interpretation D22 *Hedges of a Net Investment in a Foreign Operation* for public comment in July 2007 and received 45 comment letters in response to its proposals.

Consensus

Hedged risk and hedged item

Functional currency versus presentation currency (paragraph 10)

BC6   The IFRIC received a submission suggesting that the method of consolidation can affect the determination of the hedged risk in a hedge of a net investment in a foreign operation. The submission noted that consolidation can be completed by either the direct method or the step-by-step method. In the direct method of consolidation, each entity within a group is consolidated directly into the ultimate parent entity's presentation currency when preparing the consolidated financial statements. In the step-by-step method, each intermediate parent entity prepares consolidated financial statements, which are then consolidated into its parent entity until the ultimate parent entity has prepared consolidated financial statements.

BC7   The submission stated that if the direct method was required, the risk that qualifies for hedge accounting in a hedge of a net investment in a foreign operation would arise only from exposure between the functional currency of the foreign operation and the presentation currency of the group. This is because each foreign operation is translated only once into the presentation currency. In contrast, the submission stated that if the step-by-step method was required, the hedged risk that qualifies for hedge accounting is the risk between the functional currencies of the foreign operation and the immediate parent entity into which the entity was consolidated. This is because each foreign operation is consolidated directly into its immediate parent entity.

BC8   In response to this, the IFRIC noted that IAS 21 *The Effects of Changes in Foreign Exchange Rates* does not specify a method of consolidation for foreign operations. Furthermore, paragraph BC18 of the Basis for Conclusions on IAS 21 states that the method of translating financial statements will result in the same amounts in the presentation currency regardless of whether the direct method or the step-by-step method is used. The IFRIC therefore concluded that the consolidation mechanism should not determine what risk qualifies for hedge accounting in the hedge of a net investment in a foreign operation.

BC9   However, the IFRIC noted that its conclusion would not resolve the divergence of views on the foreign currency risk that may be designated as a hedge relationship in the hedge of a net investment in a foreign operation. The IFRIC therefore decided that an Interpretation was needed.

BC10   The IFRIC considered whether the risk that qualifies for hedge accounting in a hedge of a net investment in a foreign operation arises from the exposure to the functional currency of the foreign operation in relation to the presentation currency of the group or the functional currency of the parent entity, or both.

BC11   The answer to this question is important when the presentation currency of the group is different from an intermediate or ultimate parent entity's functional currency. If the presentation currency of the group and the functional currency of the parent entity are the same, the exchange rate being hedged would be identified as that between the parent entity's functional currency and the foreign operation's functional currency. No further translation adjustment would be required to prepare the consolidated financial statements. However, when the functional currency of the parent entity is different from the presentation currency of the group, a translation adjustment will be included in other comprehensive income to present the consolidated financial statements in a different presentation currency. The issue, therefore, is how to determine which foreign currency risk may be designated as the hedged risk in accordance with IAS 39 *Financial Instruments: Recognition and Measurement* in the hedge of a net investment in a foreign operation.

BC12   The IFRIC noted the following arguments for permitting hedge accounting for a hedge of the presentation currency:

(a)   If the presentation currency of the group is different from the ultimate parent entity's functional currency, a difference arises on translation that is recognised in other comprehensive income. It is argued that a reason for allowing hedge accounting for a net investment in a foreign operation is to remove from the financial statements the fluctuations resulting from the translation to a presentation currency. If an entity is not allowed to use hedge accounting for the exposure to the presentation currency of the group when it is different from the functional currency of the parent entity, there is likely to be an amount included in other comprehensive income that cannot be offset by hedge accounting.

(b)   IAS 21 requires an entity to reclassify from equity to profit or loss as a reclassification adjustment any foreign currency translation gains and losses included in other comprehensive income on disposal of a foreign operation.

An amount in other comprehensive income arising from a different presentation currency is therefore included in the amount reclassified to profit or loss on disposal. The entity should be able to include the amount in a hedging relationship if at some stage it is recognised along with other reclassified translation amounts.

BC13   The IFRIC noted the following arguments for allowing an entity to designate hedging relationships solely on the basis of differences between functional currencies:

(a)   The functional currency of an entity is determined on the basis of the primary economic environment in which that entity operates (i.e. the environment in which it generates and expends cash). However, the presentation currency is an elective currency that can be changed at any time. To present amounts in a presentation currency is merely a numerical convention necessary for the preparation of financial statements that include a foreign operation. The presentation currency will have no economic effect on the parent entity. Indeed, a parent entity may choose to present financial statements in more than one presentation currency, but can have only one functional currency.

(b)   IAS 39 requires a hedging relationship to be effective in offsetting changes in fair values or cash flows attributable to the hedged risk. A net investment in a foreign operation gives rise to an exposure to changes in exchange rate risk for a parent entity. An economic exchange rate risk arises only from an exposure between two or more functional currencies, not from a presentation currency.

BC14   When comparing the arguments in paragraphs BC12 and BC13, the IFRIC concluded that the presentation currency does not create an exposure to which an entity may apply hedge accounting. The functional currency is determined on the basis of the primary economic environment in which the entity operates. Accordingly, functional currencies create an economic exposure to changes in cash flows or fair values; a presentation currency never will. No commentators on the draft Interpretation disagreed with the IFRIC's conclusion.

Eligible risk (paragraph 12)

BC15   The IFRIC considered which entity's (or entities') functional currency may be used as a reference point for the hedged risk in a net investment hedge. Does the risk arise from the functional currency of:

(a)   the immediate parent entity that holds directly the foreign operation;

(b)   the ultimate parent entity that is preparing its financial statements; or

(c)   the immediate, an intermediate or the ultimate parent entity, depending on what risk that entity decides to hedge, as designated at the inception of the hedge?

BC16   The IFRIC concluded that the risk from the exposure to a different functional currency arises for any parent entity whose functional currency is different from that of the identified foreign operation. The immediate parent entity is exposed to changes in the exchange rate of its directly held foreign operation's functional currency. However, indirectly every entity up the chain of entities to the ultimate parent entity is also exposed to changes in the exchange rate of the foreign operation's functional currency.

BC17   Permitting only the ultimate parent entity to hedge its net investments would ignore the exposures arising on net investments in other parts of the entity. Conversely, permitting only the immediate parent entity to undertake a net investment hedge would imply that an indirect investment does not create a foreign currency exposure for that indirect parent entity.

BC18   The IFRIC concluded that a group must identify which risk (i.e. the functional currency of which parent entity and of which net investment in a foreign operation) is being hedged. The specified parent entity, the hedged risk and hedging instrument should all be designated and documented at the inception of the hedge relationship. As a result of comments received on the draft Interpretation, the IFRIC decided to emphasise that this documentation should also include the entity's strategy in undertaking the hedge as required by IAS 39.

Amount of hedged item that may be hedged (paragraphs 11 and 13)

BC19   In the draft Interpretation the IFRIC noted that, in financial statements that include a foreign operation, an entity cannot hedge the same risk more than once. This comment was intended to remind entities that IAS 39 does not permit multiple hedges of the same risk. Some respondents asked the IFRIC to clarify the situations in which the IFRIC considered that the same risk was being hedged more than once. In particular, the IFRIC was asked whether the same risk could be hedged by different entities within a group as long as the amount of risk being hedged was not duplicated.

BC20   In its redeliberations, the IFRIC decided to clarify that the carrying amount of the net assets of a foreign operation that may be hedged in the consolidated financial statements of a parent depends on whether any lower level parent of the foreign operation has hedged all or part of the net assets of that foreign operation and that accounting has been maintained in the parent's consolidated financial statements. An intermediate parent entity can hedge some or all of the risk of its net investment in a foreign operation in its own consolidated financial statements. However, such hedges will not qualify for hedge accounting at the ultimate parent entity level if the ultimate parent entity has also hedged the same risk. Alternatively, if the risk has not been hedged by the ultimate parent entity or another intermediate parent entity, the hedge relationship that qualified in the immediate parent entity's consolidated financial statements will also qualify in the ultimate parent entity's consolidated financial statements.

BC21   In its redeliberations, the IFRIC also decided to add guidance to the Interpretation to illustrate the importance of careful designation of the amount of the risk being hedged by each entity in the group.

Hedging instrument

Location of the hedging instrument (paragraph 14) and assessment of hedge effectiveness (paragraph 15)

BC22   The IFRIC discussed where in a group structure a hedging instrument may be held in a hedge of a net investment in a foreign operation. Guidance on the hedge of a net investment in a foreign operation was originally included in IAS 21. This guidance was moved to IAS 39 to ensure that the hedge accounting guidance included in paragraph 88 of IAS 39 would also apply to the hedges of net investments in foreign operations.

BC23   The IFRIC concluded that any entity within the group, other than the foreign operation being hedged, may hold the hedging instrument, as long as the hedging instrument is effective in offsetting the risk arising from the exposure to the functional currency of the foreign operation and the functional currency of the specified parent entity. The functional currency of the entity holding the instrument is irrelevant in determining effectiveness.

BC24   [Deleted by the IASB][3]

BC24A   Paragraph 14 of IFRIC 16 originally stated that the hedging instrument could not be held by the foreign operation whose net investment was being hedged. The restriction was included in draft Interpretation D22 (from which IFRIC 16 was developed) and attracted little comment from respondents. As originally explained in paragraph BC24, the IFRIC concluded, as part of its redeliberations, that the restriction was appropriate because the foreign exchange differences between the parent's functional currency and both the hedging instrument and the functional currency of the net investment would automatically be included in the group's foreign currency translation reserve as part of the consolidation process.

BC24B   After IFRIC 16 was issued, it was brought to the attention of the International Accounting Standards Board that this conclusion was not correct. Without hedge accounting, part of the foreign exchange difference arising from the hedging instrument would be included in consolidated profit or loss. Therefore, in *Improvements to IFRSs* issued in April 2009, the Board amended paragraph 14 of IFRIC 16 to remove the restriction on the entity that can hold hedging instruments and deleted paragraph BC24.

3   Paragraph BC24 was deleted and paragraphs BC24A-BC24D and paragraph BC40A added as a consequence of *Improvements to IFRSs* issued in April 2009.

BC24C   Some respondents to the exposure draft *Post-implementation Revisions to IFRIC Interpretations* (ED/2009/1) agreed that a parent entity should be able to use a derivative held by the foreign operation being hedged as a hedge of the net investment in that foreign operation. However, those respondents recommended that the amendment should apply only to derivative instruments held by the foreign operation being hedged. They asserted that a non-derivative financial instrument would be an effective hedge of the net investment only if it were issued by the foreign operation in its own functional currency and this would have no foreign currency impact on the profit or loss of the consolidated group. Consequently, they thought that the rationale described in paragraph BC24B to support the amendment did not apply to non-derivative instruments.

BC24D   In its redeliberations, the Board confirmed its previous decision that the amendment should not be restricted to derivative instruments. The Board noted that paragraphs AG13-AG15 of IFRIC 16 illustrate that a non-derivative instrument held by the foreign operation does not need to be considered to be part of the parent's net investment. As a result, even if it is denominated in the foreign operation's functional currency a non-derivative instrument could still affect the profit or loss of the consolidated group. Consequently, although it could be argued that the amendment was not required to permit non-derivative instruments to be designated as hedges, the Board decided that the proposal should not be changed.

BC25   The IFRIC also concluded that to apply the conclusion in paragraph BC23 when determining the effectiveness of a hedging instrument in the hedge of a net investment, an entity computes the gain or loss on the hedging instrument by reference to the functional currency of the parent entity against whose functional currency the hedged risk is measured, in accordance with the hedge documentation. This is the same regardless of the type of hedging instrument used. This ensures that the effectiveness of the instrument is determined on the basis of changes in fair value or cash flows of the hedging instrument, compared with the changes in the net investment as documented. Thus, any effectiveness test is not dependent on the functional currency of the entity holding the instrument. In other words, the fact that some of the change in the hedging instrument is recognised in profit or loss by one entity within the group and some is recognised in other comprehensive income by another does not affect the assessment of hedge effectiveness.

BC26   In the draft Interpretation the IFRIC noted Question F.2.14 in the guidance on implementing IAS 39, on the location of the hedging instrument, and considered whether that guidance could be applied by analogy to a net investment hedge. The answer to Question F.2.14 concludes:

> IAS 39 does not require that the operating unit that is exposed to the risk being hedged be a party to the hedging instrument.

This was the only basis for the IFRIC's conclusion regarding which entity could hold the hedging instrument provided in the draft Interpretation. Some respondents argued that the Interpretation should not refer to implementation guidance as the sole basis for an important conclusion.

BC27   In its redeliberations, the IFRIC considered both the International Accounting Standards Board's amendment to IAS 21 in 2005 and the objective of hedging a net investment described in IAS 39 in addition to the guidance on implementing IAS 39.

BC28   In 2005 the Board was asked to clarify which entity is the reporting entity in IAS 21 and therefore what instruments could be considered part of a reporting entity's net investment in a foreign operation. In particular, constituents questioned whether a monetary item must be transacted between the foreign operation and the reporting entity to be considered part of the net investment in accordance with IAS 21 paragraph 15, or whether it could be transacted between the foreign operation and any member of the consolidated group.

BC29   In response the Board added IAS 21 paragraph 15A to clarify that, 'The entity that has a monetary item receivable from or payable to a foreign operation described in paragraph 15 may be any subsidiary of the group.' The Board explained its reasons for the amendment in paragraph BC25D of the Basis for Conclusions:

> The Board concluded that the accounting treatment in the consolidated financial statements should not be dependent on the currency in which the monetary item is denominated, nor on which entity within the group conducts the transaction with the foreign operation.

In other words, the Board concluded that the relevant reporting entity is the group rather than the individual entity and that the net investment must be viewed from the perspective of the group. It follows, therefore, that the group's net investment in any foreign operation, and its foreign currency exposure, can be determined only at the relevant parent entity level. The IFRIC similarly concluded that the fact that the net investment is held through an intermediate entity does not affect the economic risk.

BC30   Consistently with the Board's conclusion with respect to monetary items that are part of *the net investment*, the IFRIC concluded that monetary items (or derivatives) that are *hedging instruments* in a hedge of a net investment may be held by any entity within the group and the functional currency of the entity holding the monetary items can be different from those of either the parent or the foreign operation. The IFRIC, like the Board, agreed with constituents who noted that a hedging item denominated in a currency that is not the functional currency of the entity holding it does not expose the group to a greater foreign currency exchange difference than arises when the instrument is denominated in that functional currency.

BC31   The IFRIC noted that its conclusions that the hedging instrument can be held by any entity in the group and that the foreign currency is determined at the relevant parent entity level have implications for the designation of hedged risks. As illustrated in paragraph AG5 of the application guidance, these conclusions make it possible for an entity to designate a hedged risk that is not apparent in the currencies of the hedged item or the foreign operation. This possibility is unique to hedges of net investments. Consequently, the IFRIC specified that the conclusions in the Interpretation should not be applied by analogy to other types of hedge accounting.

BC32   The IFRIC also noted that the objective of hedge accounting as set out in IAS 39 is to achieve offsetting changes in the values of the *hedging instrument* and of the *net investment* attributable to the hedged risk. Changes in foreign currency rates affect the value of the entire *net investment* in a foreign operation, not only the portion IAS 21 requires to be recognised in profit or loss in the absence of hedge accounting but also the portion recognised in other comprehensive income in the parent's consolidated financial statements. As noted in paragraph BC25, it is the total change in the hedging instrument as result of a change in the foreign currency rate with respect to the parent entity against whose functional currency the hedged risk is measured that is relevant, not the component of comprehensive income in which it is recognised.

Reclassification from other comprehensive income to profit or loss (paragraphs 16 and 17)

BC33   In response to requests from some respondents for clarification, the IFRIC discussed what amounts from the parent entity's foreign currency translation reserve in respect of both the hedging instrument and the foreign operation should be recognised in profit or loss in the parent entity's consolidated financial statements when the parent disposes of a foreign operation that was hedged. The IFRIC noted that the amounts to be reclassified from equity to profit or loss as reclassification adjustments on the disposition are:

(a)   the cumulative amount of gain or loss on a hedging instrument determined to be an effective hedge that has been reflected in other comprehensive income (IAS 39 paragraph 102), and

(b)   the cumulative amount reflected in the foreign currency translation reserve in respect of that foreign operation (IAS 21 paragraph 48).

BC34   The IFRIC noted that when an entity hedges a net investment in a foreign operation, IAS 39 requires it to identify the cumulative amount included in the group's foreign currency translation reserve as a result of applying hedge accounting, i.e. the amount determined to be an effective hedge. Therefore, the IFRIC concluded that when a foreign operation that was hedged is disposed of, the amount reclassified to profit or loss from the foreign currency translation reserve in respect of the hedging instrument in the consolidated financial statements of the parent should be the amount that IAS 39 requires to be identified.

Effect of consolidation method

BC35   Some respondents to the draft Interpretation argued that the method of consolidation creates a difference in the amounts included in the ultimate parent entity's foreign currency translation reserve for individual foreign operations that are held through intermediate parents. These respondents noted that this difference may become evident only when the ultimate parent entity disposes of a second tier subsidiary (i.e. an indirect subsidiary).

BC36   The difference becomes apparent in the determination of the amount of the foreign currency translation reserve that is subsequently reclassified to profit or loss. An ultimate parent entity using the direct method of consolidation would reclassify the cumulative foreign currency translation reserve that arose between its functional currency and that of the foreign operation. An ultimate parent entity using the step-by-step method of consolidation might reclassify the cumulative foreign currency translation reserve reflected in the financial statements of the intermediate parent, i.e. the amount that arose between the functional currency of the foreign operation and that of the intermediate parent, translated into the functional currency of the ultimate parent.

BC37   In its redeliberations, the IFRIC noted that the use of the step-by-step method of consolidation does create such a difference for an *individual* foreign operation although the aggregate net amount of foreign currency translation reserve for all the foreign operations is the same under either method of consolidation. At the same time, the IFRIC noted that the method of consolidation *should not* create such a difference for an individual foreign operation, on the basis of its conclusion that the economic risk is determined in relation to the ultimate parent's functional currency.

BC38   The IFRIC noted that the amount of foreign currency translation reserve for an individual foreign operation determined by the direct method of consolidation reflects the economic risk between the functional currency of the foreign operation and that of the ultimate parent (if the parent's functional and presentation currencies are the same). However, the IFRIC noted that IAS 21 does not require an entity to use this method or to make adjustments to produce the same result. The IFRIC also noted that a parent entity is not precluded from determining the amount of the foreign currency translation reserve in respect of a foreign operation it has disposed of as if the direct method of consolidation had been used in order to reclassify the appropriate amount to profit or loss. However, it also noted that making such an adjustment on the disposal of a foreign operation is an accounting policy choice and should be followed consistently for the disposal of all net investments.

BC39   The IFRIC noted that this issue arises when the net investment disposed of was not hedged and therefore is not strictly within the scope of the Interpretation. However, because it was a topic of considerable confusion and debate, the IFRIC decided to include a brief example illustrating its conclusions.

Transition (paragraph 19)

BC40   In response to respondents' comments, the IFRIC clarified the Interpretation's transitional requirements. The IFRIC decided that entities should apply the conclusions in this Interpretation to existing hedging relationships on adoption and cease hedge accounting for those that no longer qualify. However, previous hedge accounting is not affected. This is similar to the transition requirements in IFRS 1 *First-time Adoption of International Financial Reporting Standards* paragraph 30, for relationships accounted for as hedges under previous GAAP.

Effective date of amended paragraph 14

BC40A The Board amended paragraph 14 in April 2009. In ED/2009/1 the Board proposed that the amendment should be effective for annual periods beginning on or after 1 October 2008, at the same time as IFRIC 16. Respondents to the exposure draft were concerned that permitting application before the amendment was issued might imply that an entity could designate hedge relationships retrospectively, contrary to the requirements of IAS 39. Consequently, the Board decided that an entity should apply the amendment to paragraph 14 made in April 2009 for annual periods beginning on or after 1 July 2009. The Board also decided to permit early application but noted that early application is possible only if the designation, documentation and effectiveness requirements of paragraph 88 of IAS 39 and of IFRIC 16 are satisfied at the application date.

Summary of main changes from the draft Interpretation

BC41 The main changes from the IFRIC's proposals are as follows:

(a) Paragraph 11 clarifies that the carrying amount of the net assets of a foreign operation that may be hedged in the consolidated financial statements of a parent depends on whether any lower level parent of the foreign operation has hedged all or part of the net assets of that foreign operation and that accounting has been maintained in the parent's consolidated financial statements.

(b) Paragraph 15 clarifies that the assessment of effectiveness is not affected by whether the hedging instrument is a derivative or a non-derivative instrument or by the method of consolidation.

(c) Paragraphs 16 and 17 and the illustrative example clarify what amounts should be reclassified from equity to profit or loss as reclassification adjustments on disposal of the foreign operation.

(d) Paragraph 19 clarifies transitional requirements.

(e) The appendix of application guidance was added to the Interpretation. Illustrative examples accompanying the draft Interpretation were removed.

(f) The Basis for Conclusions was changed to set out more clearly the reasons for the IFRIC's conclusions.

Deleted IFRIC Interpretation 16 Text

Deleted IFRIC Interpretation 16 text is not part of AASB Interpretation 16.

Paragraph 18

An entity shall apply this Interpretation for annual periods beginning on or after 1 October 2008. Earlier application is permitted. If an entity applies the Interpretation for a period beginning before 1 October 2008, it shall disclose that fact.

Interpretations

Interpretation 17
Distributions of Non-cash Assets to Owners

(Compiled November 2009)

Contents

Compilation Details

Comparison with IFRIC 17

AASB Interpretation 17
Distributions of Non-cash Assets to Owners

	Paragraphs
References	
Background	1 – 2
Scope	3 – 8
Issues	9
Consensus	
When to recognise a dividend payable	10
Measurement of a dividend payable	11 – 13
Accounting for any difference between the carrying amount of the assets distributed and the carrying amount of the dividend payable when an entity settles the dividend payable	14
Presentation and disclosures	15 – 17
Application	Aus17.1 – Aus17.4
Illustrative Examples	IE1 – IE4
Basis for Conclusions on IFRIC 17	
Deleted IFRIC 17 Text	

AASB Interpretation 17 *Distributions of Non-cash Assets to Owners* (as amended) is set out in paragraphs 1 – Aus17.4. Interpretations are listed in Australian Accounting Standard AASB 1048 *Interpretation and Application of Standards*. In the absence of explicit guidance, AASB 108 *Accounting Policies, Changes in Accounting Estimates and Errors* provides a basis for selecting and applying accounting policies.

Compilation Details

AASB Interpretation 17 *Distributions of Non-cash Assets to Owners* as amended

This compiled Interpretation applies to annual reporting periods beginning on or after 1 July 2009. It takes into account amendments up to and including 25 June 2009 and was prepared on 10 November 2009 by the staff of the Australian Accounting Standards Board (AASB).

This compilation is not a separate Interpretation issued by the AASB. Instead, it is a representation of Interpretation 17 (December 2008) as amended by other pronouncements, which are listed in the Table below.

Table of Pronouncements

Pronouncement	Month issued	Application date (*annual reporting periods ... on or after ...*)	Application, saving or transitional provisions
Interpretation 17	Dec 2008	(*beginning*) 1 Jul 2009	see (a) below
AASB 2009-7	Jun 2009	(*beginning*) 1 Jul 2009	see (b) below

(a)   Entities may elect to apply this Interpretation to annual reporting periods beginning on or after 1 January 2005 but before 1 July 2009, subject to paragraph Aus17.3 of the Interpretation.

(b)   Entities may elect to apply this Standard to annual reporting periods beginning before 1 July 2009 that end on or after 1 July 2008.

Table of Amendments

Paragraph affected	How affected	By ... [paragraph]
Aus17.3	amended	AASB 2009-7 [16]

Comparison with IFRIC 17

AASB Interpretation 17 *Distributions of Non-cash Assets to Owners* as amended incorporates International Financial Reporting Interpretations Committee Interpretation IFRIC 17 *Distributions of Non-cash Assets to Owners* issued by the International Accounting Standards Board. Paragraphs that have been added to this Interpretation (and do not appear in the text of IFRIC 17) are identified with the prefix "Aus", followed by the number of the preceding IFRIC paragraph and decimal numbering.

Entities that comply with AASB Interpretation 17 as amended will simultaneously be in compliance with IFRIC 17 as amended.

Interpretation 17

AASB Interpretation 17 was issued in December 2008.

This compiled version of Interpretation 17 applies to annual reporting periods beginning on or after 1 July 2009. It incorporates relevant amendments contained in other AASB pronouncements up to and including 25 June 2009 (see Compilation Details).

Australian Accounting Standards Board

Interpretation 17

Distributions of Non-cash Assets to Owners

References

Accounting Standard AASB 3 *Business Combinations*

Accounting Standard AASB 5 *Non-current Assets Held for Sale and Discontinued Operations*

Accounting Standard AASB 7 *Financial Instruments: Disclosures*

Accounting Standard AASB 101 *Presentation of Financial Statements*

Accounting Standard AASB 110 *Events after the Reporting Period*

Accounting Standard AASB 127 *Consolidated and Separate Financial Statements*

Background

1   Sometimes an entity distributes assets other than cash (non-cash assets) as dividends to
         its owners acting in their capacity as owners.[1] In those situations, an entity may also give
         its owners a choice of receiving either non-cash assets or a cash alternative. Constituents
         have requested guidance on how an entity should account for such distributions.

2   Australian Accounting Standards do not provide guidance on how an entity should
         measure distributions to its owners (commonly referred to as dividends). AASB 101
         requires an entity to present details of dividends recognised as distributions to owners
         either in the statement of changes in equity or in the notes to the financial statements.

Scope

3   This Interpretation applies to the following types of non-reciprocal distributions of assets
         by an entity to its owners acting in their capacity as owners:

   (a)   distributions of non-cash assets (e.g. items of property, plant and equipment,
         businesses as defined in AASB 3, ownership interests in another entity or disposal
         groups as defined in AASB 5); and

   (b)   distributions that give owners a choice of receiving either non-cash assets or a cash
         alternative.

4   This Interpretation applies only to distributions in which all owners of the same class
         of equity instruments are treated equally.

5   This Interpretation does not apply to a distribution of a non-cash asset that is ultimately
         controlled by the same party or parties before and after the distribution. This exclusion
         applies to the separate, individual and consolidated financial statements of an entity that
         makes the distribution.

6   In accordance with paragraph 5, this Interpretation does not apply when the non-cash
         asset is ultimately controlled by the same parties both before and after the distribution.
         Paragraph B2 of AASB 3 states that 'A group of individuals shall be regarded as controlling
         an entity when, as a result of contractual arrangements, they collectively have the power
         to govern its financial and operating policies so as to obtain benefits from its activities.'
         Therefore, for a distribution to be outside the scope of this Interpretation on the basis
         that the same parties control the asset both before and after the distribution, a group
         of individual shareholders receiving the distribution must have, as a result of contractual
         arrangements, such ultimate collective power over the entity making the distribution.

7   In accordance with paragraph 5, this Interpretation does not apply when an entity
         distributes some of its ownership interests in a subsidiary but retains control of the
         subsidiary. The entity making a distribution that results in the entity recognising
         a non-controlling interest in its subsidiary accounts for the distribution in accordance
         with AASB 127 (as amended in 2008).

8   This Interpretation addresses only the accounting by an entity that makes a non-cash
         asset distribution. It does not address the accounting by shareholders who receive such
         a distribution.

Issues

9   When an entity declares a distribution and has an obligation to distribute the assets
         concerned to its owners, it must recognise a liability for the dividend payable.
         Consequently, this Interpretation addresses the following issues:

   (a)   When should the entity recognise the dividend payable?

   (b)   How should an entity measure the dividend payable?

   (c)   When an entity settles the dividend payable, how should it account for any
         difference between the carrying amount of the assets distributed and the carrying
         amount of the dividend payable?

---

1   Paragraph 7 of AASB 101 defines owners as holders of instruments classified as equity.

Consensus

When to recognise a dividend payable

10   The liability to pay a dividend shall be recognised when the dividend is appropriately authorised and is no longer at the discretion of the entity, which is the date:

(a)   when declaration of the dividend, e.g. by management or the board of directors, is approved by the relevant authority, e.g. the shareholders, if the jurisdiction requires such approval; or

(b)   when the dividend is declared, e.g. by management or the board of directors, if the jurisdiction does not require further approval.

Measurement of a dividend payable

11   An entity shall measure a liability to distribute non-cash assets as a dividend to its owners at the fair value of the assets to be distributed.

12   If an entity gives its owners a choice of receiving either a non-cash asset or a cash alternative, the entity shall estimate the dividend payable by considering both the fair value of each alternative and the associated probability of owners selecting each alternative.

13   At the end of each reporting period and at the date of settlement, the entity shall review and adjust the carrying amount of the dividend payable, with any changes in the carrying amount of the dividend payable recognised in equity as adjustments to the amount of the distribution.

Accounting for any difference between the carrying amount of the assets distributed and the carrying amount of the dividend payable when an entity settles the dividend payable

14   When an entity settles the dividend payable, it shall recognise the difference, if any, between the carrying amount of the assets distributed and the carrying amount of the dividend payable in profit or loss.

Presentation and disclosures

15   An entity shall present the difference described in paragraph 14 as a separate line item in profit or loss.

16   An entity shall disclose the following information, if applicable:

(a)   the carrying amount of the dividend payable at the beginning and end of the period; and

(b)   the increase or decrease in the carrying amount recognised in the period in accordance with paragraph 13 as result of a change in the fair value of the assets to be distributed.

17   If, after the end of a reporting period but before the financial statements are authorised for issue, an entity declares a dividend to distribute a non-cash asset, it shall disclose:

(a)   the nature of the asset to be distributed;

(b)   the carrying amount of the asset to be distributed as of the end of the reporting period; and

(c)   the estimated fair value of the asset to be distributed as of the end of the reporting period, if it is different from its carrying amount, and the information about the method used to determine that fair value required by AASB 7 paragraph 27(a) and (b).

Application

Aus17.1   This Interpretation applies to:

(a)   each entity that is required to prepare financial reports in accordance with Part 2M.3 of the *Corporations Act 2001* and that is a reporting entity;

(b)   general purpose financial statements of each other reporting entity; and

(c)   financial statements that are, or are held out to be, general purpose financial statements.

Aus17.2   This Interpretation applies prospectively for annual reporting periods beginning on or after 1 July 2009. Retrospective application is not permitted.

[Note: For application dates of paragraphs changed or added by an amending pronouncement, see Compilation Details.]

Aus17.3   Earlier application is permitted. If an entity applies this Interpretation for a period beginning on or after 1 January 2005 but before 1 July 2009, it shall disclose that fact and also apply AASB 3 (March 2008, as amended), AASB 127 (as amended in July 2008) and AASB 5 (as amended by AASB 2008-13 *Amendments to Australian Accounting Standards arising from AASB Interpretation 17 – Distributions of Non-cash Assets to Owners*).

Aus17.4   The requirements specified in this Interpretation apply to the financial statements where information resulting from their application is material in accordance with AASB 1031 *Materiality*.

Effective Date of IFRIC 17

18   [Deleted by the AASB]

Illustrative Examples

These examples accompany, but are not part of, AASB Interpretation 17.

Scope of the Interpretation (paragraphs 3-8)

CHART 1 (distribution of available-for-sale securities)

Before Distribution

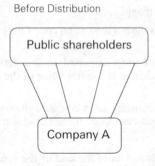

After Distribution

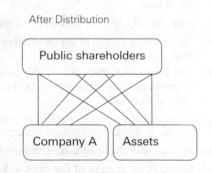

IE1   Assume Company A is owned by public shareholders. No single shareholder controls Company A and no group of shareholders is bound by a contractual agreement to act together to control Company A jointly. Company A distributes certain assets (e.g. available-for-sale securities) pro rata to the shareholders. This transaction is within the scope of the Interpretation.

IE2   However, if one of the shareholders (or a group bound by a contractual agreement to act together) controls Company A both before and after the transaction, the entire transaction (including the distributions to the non-controlling shareholders) is not within the scope of the Interpretation. This is because in a pro rata distribution to all owners of the same class of equity instruments, the controlling shareholder (or group of shareholders) will continue to control the non-cash assets after the distribution.

IE3   Assume Company A is owned by public shareholders. No single shareholder controls Company A and no group of shareholders is bound by a contractual agreement to act together to control Company A jointly. Company A owns all of the shares of Subsidiary B. Company A distributes all of the shares of Subsidiary B pro rata to its shareholders, thereby losing control of Subsidiary B. This transaction is within the scope of the Interpretation.

CHART 2 (distribution of subsidaries)

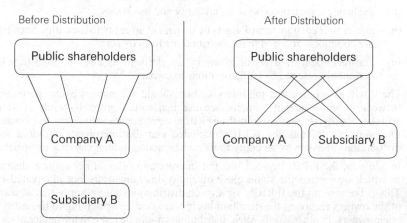

IE3   Assume Company A is owned by public shareholders. No single shareholder controls Company A and no group of shareholders is bound by a contractual agreement to act together to control Company A jointly. Company A owns all of the shares of Subsidiary B. Company A distributes all of the shares of Subsidiary B pro rata to its shareholders, thereby losing control of Subsidiary B. This transaction is within the scope of the Interpretation.

IE4   However, if Company A distributes to its shareholders shares of Subsidiary B representing only a non-controlling interest in Subsidiary B and retains control of Subsidiary B, the transaction is not within the scope of the Interpretation. Company A accounts for the distribution in accordance with AASB 127 *Consolidated and Separate Financial Statements* (as amended in 2008). Company A controls Company B both before and after the transaction.

Basis for Conclusions on IFRIC Interpretation 17

This IFRIC Basis for Conclusions accompanies, but is not part of, AASB Interpretation 17. An IFRIC Basis for Conclusions may be amended to reflect the requirements of the AASB Interpretation and AASB Accounting Standards where they differ from the corresponding International pronouncements.

Introduction

BC1   This Basis for Conclusions summarises the IFRIC's considerations in reaching its consensus. Individual IFRIC members gave greater weight to some factors than to others.

BC2   At present, International Financial Reporting Standards (IFRSs) do not address how an entity should measure distributions to owners acting in their capacity as owners (commonly referred to as dividends). The IFRIC was told that there was significant diversity in practice in how entities measured distributions of non-cash assets.

BC3   The IFRIC published draft Interpretation D23 *Distributions of Non-cash Assets to Owners* for public comment in January 2008 and received 56 comment letters in response to its proposals.

Scope (paragraphs 3-8)

Should the Interpretation address all transactions between an entity and its owners?

BC4   The IFRIC noted that an asset distribution by an entity to its owners is an example of a transaction between an entity and its owners. Transactions between an entity and its owners can generally be categorised into the following three types:

    (a)   exchange transactions between an entity and its owners.

    (b)   non-reciprocal transfers of assets by owners of an entity to the entity. Such transfers are commonly referred to as contributions from owners.

    (c)   non-reciprocal transfers of assets by an entity to its owners. Such transfers are commonly referred to as distributions to owners.

BC5   The IFRIC concluded that the Interpretation should not address exchange transactions between an entity and its owners because that would probably result in addressing all related party transactions. In the IFRIC's view, such a scope was too broad for an Interpretation. Instead, the IFRIC concluded that the Interpretation should focus on distributions of assets by an entity to its owners acting in their capacity as owners.

BC6   In addition, the IFRIC decided that the Interpretation should not address distributions in which owners of the same class of equity instrument are not all treated equally. This is because, in the IFRIC's view, such distributions might imply that at least some of the owners receiving the distributions indeed gave up something to the entity and/or other owners. In other words, such distributions might be more in the nature of exchange transactions.

Should the Interpretation address all types of asset distributions?

BC7   The IFRIC was told that there was significant diversity in the measurement of the following types of non-reciprocal distributions of assets by an entity to its owners acting in their capacity as owners:

    (a)   distributions of non-cash assets (e.g. items of property, plant and equipment, businesses as defined in IFRS 3, ownership interests in another entity or disposal groups as defined in IFRS 5 *Non-current Assets Held for Sale and Discontinued Operations*) to its owners; and

    (b)   distributions that give owners a choice of receiving either non-cash assets or a cash alternative.

BC8   The IFRIC noted that all distributions have the same purpose, i.e. to distribute assets to an entity's owners. It therefore concluded that the Interpretation should address the measurement of all types of asset distributions with one exception set out in paragraph 5 of the Interpretation.

A scope exclusion: a distribution of an asset that is ultimately controlled by the same party or parties before and after the distribution

BC9   In the Interpretation, the IFRIC considered whether it should address how an entity should measure a distribution of an asset (e.g. an ownership interest in a subsidiary) that is ultimately controlled by the same party or parties before and after the distribution. In many instances, such a distribution is for the purpose of group restructuring (e.g. separating two different businesses into two different subgroups). After the distribution, the asset is still controlled by the same party or parties.

BC10   In addition, the IFRIC noted that dealing with the accounting for a distribution of an asset within a group would require consideration of how a transfer of any asset within a group should be accounted for in the separate or individual financial statements of group entities.

BC11   For the reasons described in paragraphs BC9 and BC10, the IFRIC concluded that the Interpretation should not deal with a distribution of an asset that is ultimately controlled by the same party or parties before and after the distribution.

BC12 In response to comments received on the draft Interpretation, the IFRIC redeliberated whether the scope of the Interpretation should be expanded to include a distribution of an asset that is ultimately controlled by the same party or parties before and after the distribution. The IFRIC decided not to expand the scope of the Interpretation in the light of the Board's decision to add a project to its agenda to address common control transactions.

BC13 The IFRIC noted that many commentators believed that most distributions of assets to an entity's owners would be excluded from the scope of the Interpretation by paragraph 5. The IFRIC did not agree with this conclusion. It noted that in paragraph B2 of IFRS 3 *Business Combinations* (as revised in 2008), the Board concluded that a group of individuals would be regarded as controlling an entity only when, as a result of contractual arrangements, they collectively have the power to govern its financial and operating policies so as to obtain benefits from its activities. In addition, in *Cost of an Investment in a Subsidiary, Jointly Controlled Entity or Associate* in May 2008, the Board clarified in the amendments to IAS 27 *Consolidated and Separate Financial Statements* that the distribution of equity interests in a new parent to shareholders in exchange for their interests in the existing parent was not a common control transaction.

BC14 Consequently, the IFRIC decided that the Interpretation should clarify that unless there is a contractual arrangement among shareholders to control the entity making the distribution, transactions in which the shares or the businesses of group entities are distributed to shareholders outside the group (commonly referred to as a spin-off, split-off or demerger) are not transactions between entities or businesses under common control. Therefore they are within the scope of the Interpretation.

BC15 Some commentators on D23 were concerned about situations in which an entity distributes some but not all of its ownership interests in a subsidiary and retains control. They believed that the proposed accounting for the distribution of ownership interests representing a non-controlling interest in accordance with D23 was inconsistent with the requirements of IAS 27 (as amended in 2008). That IFRS requires changes in a parent's ownership interest in a subsidiary that do not result in a loss of control to be accounted for as equity transactions. The IFRIC had not intended the Interpretation to apply to such transactions so did not believe it conflicted with the requirements of IAS 27. As a result of the concerns expressed, the IFRIC amended the Interpretation to make this clear.

BC16 Some commentators on D23 were also concerned about situations in which a subsidiary with a non-controlling interest distributes assets to both the parent and the non-controlling interests. They questioned why only the distribution to the controlling entity is excluded from the scope of the Interpretation. The IFRIC noted that when the parent controls the subsidiary before and after the transaction, the entire transaction (including the distribution to the non-controlling interest) is not within the scope of the Interpretation and is accounted for in accordance with IAS 27.

BC17 Distributions to owners may involve significant portions of an entity's operations. In such circumstances, sometimes referred to as split-off, some commentators on D23 were concerned that it would be difficult to determine which of the surviving entities had made the distribution. They thought that it might be possible for each surviving entity to recognise the distribution of the other. The IFRIC agreed with commentators that identifying the distributing entity might require judgement in some circumstances. However, the IFRIC concluded that the distribution could be recognised in only one entity's financial statements.

When to recognise a dividend payable (paragraph 10) and amendment to IAS 10

BC18 D23 did not address when an entity should recognise a liability for a dividend payable and some respondents asked the IFRIC to clarify this issue. The IFRIC noted that in IAS 10 *Events after the Reporting Period* paragraph 13 states that 'If dividends are declared (i.e. the dividends are appropriately authorised and no longer at the discretion of the entity) after the reporting period but before the financial statements are authorised for issue, the dividends are not recognised as a liability at the end of the reporting period because no obligation exists at that time'.

BC19   Some commentators stated that in many jurisdictions a commonly held view is that the entity has discretion until the shareholders approve the dividend. Therefore, constituents holding this view believe a conflict exists between 'declared' and the explanatory phrase in the brackets in IAS 10 paragraph 13. This is especially true when the sentence is interpreted as 'declared by *management but before the shareholders' approval*'. The IFRIC concluded that the point at which a dividend is appropriately authorised and no longer at the discretion of the entity will vary by jurisdiction.

BC20   Therefore, as a consequence of this Interpretation the IFRIC decided to recommend that the Board amend IAS 10 to remove the perceived conflict in paragraph 13. The IFRIC also noted that the principle on when to recognise a dividend was in the wrong place within the IASB's authoritative documents. The Board agreed with the IFRIC's conclusions and amended IAS 10 as part of its approval of the Interpretation. The Board confirmed that this Interpretation had not changed the principle on when to recognise a dividend payable; however, the principle was moved from IAS 10 into the Interpretation and clarified but without changing the principle.

How should an entity measure a dividend payable? (paragraphs 11-13)

BC21   IFRSs do not provide guidance on how an entity should measure distributions to owners. However, the IFRIC noted that a number of IFRSs address how a liability should be measured. Although IFRSs do not specifically address how an entity should measure a dividend payable, the IFRIC decided that it could identify potentially relevant IFRSs and apply their principles to determine the appropriate measurement basis.

Which IFRSs are relevant to the measurement of a dividend payable?

BC22   The IFRIC considered all IFRSs that prescribe the accounting for a liability. Of those, the IFRIC concluded that IAS 37 *Provisions, Contingent Assets and Contingent Liabilities* and IAS 39 *Financial Instruments: Recognition and Measurement* were the most likely to be relevant. The IFRIC concluded that other IFRSs were not applicable because most of them addressed only liabilities arising from exchange transactions and some of them were clearly not relevant (e.g. IAS 12 *Income Taxes*). As mentioned above, the Interpretation addresses only non-reciprocal distributions of assets by an entity to its owners.

BC23   Given that all types of distributions have the purpose of distributing assets to owners, the IFRIC decided that all dividends payable should be measured the same way, regardless of the types of assets to be distributed. This also ensures that all dividends payable are measured consistently.

BC24   Some believed that IAS 39 was the appropriate IFRS to be used to measure dividends payable. They believed that, once an entity declared a distribution to its owners, it had a contractual obligation to distribute the assets to its owners. However, IAS 39 would not cover dividends payable if they were considered to be non-contractual obligations. In addition, IAS 39 covers some but not all obligations that require an entity to deliver non-cash assets to another entity. It does not cover a liability to distribute non-financial assets to owners. The IFRIC therefore concluded that it was not appropriate to conclude that all dividends payable should be within the scope of IAS 39.

BC25   The IFRIC then considered IAS 37, which is generally applied in practice to determine the accounting for liabilities other than those arising from executory contracts and those addressed by other IFRSs. IAS 37 requires an entity to measure a liability on the basis of the best estimate of the expenditure required to settle the present obligation at the end of the reporting period. Consequently, in D23 the IFRIC decided that it was appropriate to apply the principles in IAS 37 to all dividends payable (regardless of the types of assets to be distributed). The IFRIC decided that to apply IAS 37 to measure a liability for an obligation to distribute non-cash assets to owners, an entity should consider the fair value of the assets to be distributed. The fair value of the assets to be distributed is clearly relevant no matter which approach in IAS 37 is taken to determine the best estimate of the expenditure required to settle the liability.

BC26 However, in response to comments received on D23, the IFRIC reconsidered whether the Interpretation should specify that all dividends payable should be measured in accordance with IAS 37. The IFRIC noted that many respondents were concerned that D23 might imply that the measurement attribute in IAS 37 should always be interpreted to be fair value. This was not the intention of D23 as that question is part of the Board's project to amend IAS 37. In addition, many respondents were not certain whether measuring the dividend payable 'by reference to' the fair value of the assets to be distributed required measurement at their fair value or at some other amount.

BC27 Therefore, the IFRIC decided to modify the proposal in D23 to require the dividend payable to be measured at the fair value of the assets to be distributed, without linking to any individual standard its conclusion that fair value is the most relevant measurement attribute. The IFRIC also noted that if the assets being distributed constituted a business, its fair value could be different from the simple sum of the fair value of the component assets and liabilities (i.e. it includes the value of goodwill or the identified intangible assets).

Should any exception be made to the principle of measuring a dividend payable at the fair value of the assets to be distributed?

BC28 Some are concerned that the fair value of the assets to be distributed might not be reliably measurable in all cases. They believe that exceptions should be made in the following circumstances:

(a) An entity distributes an ownership interest of another entity that is not traded in an active market and the fair value of the ownership interest cannot be measured reliably. The IFRIC noted that IAS 39 does not permit investments in equity instruments that do not have a quoted market price in an active market and whose fair value cannot be measured reliably to be measured at fair value.

(b) An entity distributes an intangible asset that is not traded in an active market and therefore would not be permitted to be carried at a revalued amount in accordance with IAS 38 *Intangible Assets*.

BC29 The IFRIC noted that in accordance with IAS 39 paragraphs AG80 and AG81, the fair value of equity instruments that do not have a quoted price in an active market is reliably measurable if:

(a) the variability in the range of reasonable fair value estimates is not significant for that instrument, or

(b) the probabilities of the various estimates within the range can be reasonably assessed and used in estimating fair value.

BC30 The IFRIC noted that, when the management of an entity recommends a distribution of a non-cash asset to its owners, one or both of the conditions for determining a reliable measure of the fair value of equity instruments that do not have a quoted price in an active market is likely to be satisfied. Management would be expected to know the fair value of the asset because management has to ensure that all owners of the entity are informed of the value of the distribution. For this reason, it would be difficult to argue that the fair value of the assets to be distributed cannot be determined reliably.

BC31 In addition, the IFRIC recognised that in some cases the fair value of an asset must be estimated. As mentioned in paragraph 86 of the *Framework for the Preparation and Presentation of Financial Statements*, the use of reasonable estimates is an essential part of the preparation of financial statements and does not undermine their reliability.

BC32 The IFRIC noted that a reason why IAS 38 and IAS 39 require some assets to be measured using a historical cost basis is cost-benefit considerations. The cost of determining the fair value of an asset not traded in an active market at the end of each reporting period could outweigh the benefits. However, because an entity would be required to determine the fair value of the assets to be distributed only once at the time of distribution, the IFRIC concluded that the benefit (i.e. informing users of the financial statements of the value of the assets distributed) outweighs the cost of determining the fair value of the assets.

BC33   Furthermore, the IFRIC noted that dividend income, regardless of whether it is in the form of cash or non-cash assets, is within the scope of IAS 18 Revenue and is required to be measured at the fair value of the consideration received. Although the Interpretation does not address the accounting by the recipient of the non-cash distribution, the IFRIC concluded that the Interpretation did not impose a more onerous requirement on the entity that makes the distribution than IFRSs have already imposed on the recipient of the distribution.

BC34   For the reasons described in paragraphs BC28-BC33, the IFRIC concluded that no exceptions should be made to the requirement that the fair value of the asset to be distributed should be used in measuring a dividend payable.

Whether an entity should remeasure the dividend payable (paragraph 13)

BC35   The IFRIC noted that paragraph 59 of IAS 37 requires an entity to review the carrying amount of a liability at the end of each reporting period and to adjust the carrying amount to reflect the current best estimate of the liability. Other IFRSs such as IAS 19 *Employee Benefits* similarly require liabilities that are based on estimates to be adjusted each reporting period. The IFRIC therefore decided that the entity should review and adjust the carrying amount of the dividend payable to reflect its current best estimate of the fair value of the assets to be distributed at the end of each reporting period and at the date of settlement.

BC36   The IFRIC concluded that, because any adjustments to the best estimate of the dividend payable reflect changes in the estimated value of the distribution, they should be recognised as adjustments to the amount of the distribution. In accordance with IAS 1 *Presentation of Financial Statements* (as revised in 2007), distributions to owners are required to be recognised directly in the statement of changes in equity. Similarly, adjustments to the amount of the distribution are also recognised directly in the statement of changes in equity.

BC37   Some commentators argued that the changes in the estimated value of the distribution should be recognised in profit or loss because changes in liabilities meet the definition of income or expenses in the *Framework*. However, the IFRIC decided that the gain or loss on the assets to be distributed should be recognised in profit or loss when the dividend payable is settled. This is consistent with other IFRSs (IAS 16, IAS 38, IAS 39) that require an entity to recognise in profit or loss any gain or loss arising from derecognition of an asset. The IFRIC concluded that the changes in the dividend payable before settlement related to changes in the estimate of the distribution and should be accounted for in equity (i.e. adjustments to the amount of the distribution) until settlement of the dividend payable.

When the entity settles the dividend payable, how should it account for any difference between the carrying amount of the assets distributed and the carrying amount of the dividend payable? (paragraph 14)

BC38   When an entity distributes the assets to its owners, it derecognises both the assets distributed and the dividend payable.

BC39   The IFRIC noted that, at the time of settlement, the carrying amount of the assets distributed would not normally be greater than the carrying amount of the dividend payable because of the recognition of impairment losses required by other applicable standards. For example, paragraph 59 of IAS 36 *Impairment of Assets* requires an entity to recognise an impairment loss in profit or loss when the recoverable amount of an asset is less than its carrying amount. The recoverable amount of an asset is the higher of its fair value less costs to sell and its value in use in accordance with paragraph 6 of IAS 36. When an entity has an obligation to distribute the asset to its owners in the near future, it would not seem appropriate to measure an impairment loss using the asset's value in use. Furthermore, IFRS 5 requires an entity to measure an asset held for sale at the lower of its carrying amount and its fair value less costs to sell. Consequently, the IFRIC concluded that when an entity derecognises the dividend payable and the asset distributed, any difference will always be a credit balance (referred to below as the credit balance).

BC40 In determining how the credit balance should be accounted for, the IFRIC first considered whether it should be recognised as an owner change in equity.

BC41 The IFRIC acknowledged that an asset distribution was a transaction between an entity and its owners. The IFRIC also observed that distributions to owners are recognised as owner changes in equity in accordance with IAS 1 (as revised in 2007). However, the IFRIC noted that the credit balance did not arise from the distribution transaction. Rather, it represented the cumulative unrecognised gain associated with the asset. It reflects the performance of the entity during the period the asset was held until it was distributed.

BC42 Some might argue that, since an asset distribution does not result in the owners of an entity losing the future economic benefits of the asset, the credit balance should be recognised directly in equity. This view would be based upon the proprietary perspective in which the reporting entity does not have substance of its own separate from that of its owners. However, the IFRIC noted that the *Framework* requires an entity to consider the effect of a transaction from the perspective of the entity for which the financial statements are prepared. Under the entity perspective, the reporting entity has substance of its own, separate from that of its owners. In addition, when there is more than one class of equity instruments, the argument that all owners of an entity have effectively the same interest in the asset would not be valid.

BC43 For the reasons described in paragraphs BC41 and BC42, the IFRIC concluded that the credit balance should not be recognised as an owner change in equity.

BC44 The IFRIC noted that, as explained in the Basis for Conclusions on IAS 1, the Board explicitly prohibited any income or expenses (i.e. non-owner changes in equity) from being recognised directly in the statement of changes in equity. Any such income or expenses must be recognised as items of comprehensive income first.

BC45 The statement of comprehensive income in accordance with IAS 1 includes two components: items of profit or loss, and items of other comprehensive income. The IFRIC therefore discussed whether the credit balance should be recognised in profit or loss or in other comprehensive income.

BC46 IAS 1 does not provide criteria for when an item should be recognised in profit or loss. However, paragraph 88 of IAS 1 states: 'An entity shall recognise all items of income and expense in a period in profit or loss unless an IFRS requires or permits otherwise.'

BC47 The IFRIC considered the circumstances in which IFRSs require items of income and expense to be recognised as items of other comprehensive income, mainly as follows:

(a) some actuarial gains or losses arising from remeasuring defined benefit liabilities provided that specific criteria set out in IAS 19 are met.

(b) a revaluation surplus arising from revaluation of an item of property, plant and equipment in accordance with IAS 16 or revaluation of an intangible asset in accordance with IAS 38.

(c) an exchange difference arising from the translation of the results and financial positions of an entity from its functional currency into a presentation currency in accordance with IAS 21 *The Effects of Changes in Foreign Exchange Rates*.

(d) an exchange difference arising from the translation of the results and financial position of a foreign operation into a presentation currency of a reporting entity for consolidation purposes in accordance with IAS 21.

(e) a change in the fair value of an available-for-sale investment in accordance with IAS 39.

(f) a change in the fair value of a hedging instrument qualifying for cash flow hedge accounting in accordance with IAS 39.

BC48 The IFRIC concluded that the requirement in IAS 1 prevents any of these items from being applied by analogy to the credit balance. In addition, the IFRIC noted that, with the exception of the items described in paragraph BC47(a)–(c), the applicable IFRSs require the items of income and expenses listed in paragraph BC47 to be reclassified to profit or loss when the related assets or liabilities are derecognised. Those items of income and expenses are recognised as items of other comprehensive income when incurred, deferred in equity until the related assets are disposed of (or the related liabilities are settled), and reclassified to profit or loss at that time.

BC49   The IFRIC noted that, when the dividend payable is settled, the asset distributed is also derecognised. Therefore, given the existing requirements in IFRSs, even if the credit balance were recognised as an item of other comprehensive income, it would have to be reclassified to profit or loss immediately. As a result, the credit balance would appear three times in the statement of comprehensive income – once recognised as an item of other comprehensive income, once reclassified out of other comprehensive income to profit or loss and once recognised as an item of profit or loss as a result of the reclassification. The IFRIC concluded that such a presentation does not faithfully reflect what has occurred. In addition, users of financial statements were likely to be confused by such a presentation.

BC50   Moreover, when an entity distributes its assets to its owners, it loses the future economic benefit associated with the assets distributed and derecognises those assets. Such a consequence is, in general, similar to that of a disposal of an asset. IFRSs (e.g. IAS 16, IAS 38, IAS 39 and IFRS 5) require an entity to recognise in profit or loss any gain or loss arising from the derecognition of an asset. IFRSs also require such a gain or loss to be recognised when the asset is derecognised. As mentioned in paragraph BC42, the *Framework* requires an entity to consider the effect of a transaction from the perspective of an entity for which the financial statements are prepared. For these reasons, the IFRIC concluded that the credit balance and gains or losses on derecognition of an asset should be accounted for in the same way.

BC51   Furthermore, paragraph 92 of the *Framework* states: 'Income is recognised in the income statement when an increase in future economic benefits related to an increase in an asset or *a decrease of a liability* has arisen that can be measured reliably' (emphasis added). At the time of the settlement of a dividend payable, there is clearly a decrease in a liability. Therefore, the credit balance should be recognised in profit or loss in accordance with paragraph 92 of the *Framework*. Some might argue that the entity does not receive any additional economic benefits when it distributes the assets to its owners. As mentioned in paragraph BC41, the credit balance does not represent any additional economic benefits to the entity. Instead, it represents the unrecognised economic benefits that the entity obtained while it held the assets.

BC52   The IFRIC also noted that paragraph 55 of the *Framework* states: 'The future economic benefits embodied in an asset may flow to the entity in a number of ways. For example, an asset may be: (a) used singly or in combination with other assets in the production of goods or services to be sold by the entity; (b) exchanged for other assets; (c) used to settle a liability; or (d) *distributed to the owners of the entity* [emphasis added].'

BC53   In the light of these requirements, in D23 the IFRIC concluded that the credit balance should be recognised in profit or loss. This treatment would give rise to the same accounting results regardless of whether an entity distributes non-cash assets to its owners, or sells the non-cash assets first and distributes the cash received to its owners. Most commentators on D23 supported the IFRIC's conclusion and its basis.

BC54   Some IFRIC members believed that it would be more appropriate to treat the distribution as a single transaction with owners and therefore recognise the credit balance directly in equity. This alternative view was included in D23 and comments were specifically invited. However, this view was not supported by commentators. To be recognised directly in equity, the credit balance must be considered an owner change in equity in accordance with IAS 1. The IFRIC decided that the credit balance does not arise from the distribution transaction. Rather, it represents the increase in value of the assets. The increase in the value of the asset does not meet the definition of an owner change in equity in accordance with IAS 1. Rather, it meets the definition of income and should be recognised in profit and loss.

BC55 The IFRIC recognised respondents' concerns about the potential 'accounting mismatch' in equity resulting from measuring the assets to be distributed at carrying amount and measuring the dividend payable at fair value. Consequently, the IFRIC considered whether it should recommend that the Board amend IFRS 5 to require the assets to be distributed to be measured at fair value.

BC56 In general, IFRSs permit remeasurement of assets only as the result of a transaction or an impairment. The exceptions are situations in which the IFRSs prescribe current measures on an ongoing basis as in IASs 39 and 41 *Agriculture*, or permit them as accounting policy choices as in IASs 16, 38 and 40 *Investment Property*. As a result of its redeliberations, the IFRIC concluded that there was no support in IFRSs for requiring a remeasurement of the assets because of a decision to distribute them. The IFRIC noted that the mismatch concerned arises only with respect to assets that are not carried at fair value already. The IFRIC also noted that the accounting mismatch is the inevitable consequence of IFRSs using different measurement attributes at different times with different triggers for the remeasurement of different assets and liabilities.

BC57 If a business is to be distributed, the fair value means the fair value of the business to be distributed. Therefore, it includes goodwill and intangible assets. However, internally generated goodwill is not permitted to be recognised as an asset (paragraph 48 of IAS 38). Internally generated brands, mastheads, publishing titles, customer lists and items similar in substance are not permitted to be recognised as intangible assets (paragraph 63 of IAS 38). In accordance with IAS 38, the carrying amounts of internally generated intangible assets are generally restricted to the sum of expenditure incurred by an entity. Consequently, a requirement to remeasure an asset that is a business would contradict the relevant requirements in IAS 38.

BC58 Furthermore, in addition to the lack of consistency with other IFRSs, changing IFRS 5 this way (i.e. to require an asset held for distribution to owners to be remeasured at fair value) would create internal inconsistency within IFRS 5. There would be no reasonable rationale to explain why IFRS 5 could require assets that are to be sold to be carried at the lower of fair value less costs to sell and carrying value but assets to be distributed to owners to be carried at fair value. The IFRIC also noted that this 'mismatch' would arise only in the normally short period between when the dividend payable is recognised and when it is settled. The length of this period would often be within the control of management. Therefore, the IFRIC decided not to recommend that the Board amend IFRS 5 to require assets that are to be distributed to be measured at fair value.

Amendment to IFRS 5

BC59 IFRS 5 requires an entity to classify a non-current asset (or disposal group) as held for sale if its carrying amount will be recovered principally through a sale transaction rather than through continuing use. IFRS 5 also sets out presentation and disclosure requirements for a discontinued operation.

BC60 When an entity has an obligation to distribute assets to its owners, the carrying amount of the assets will no longer be recovered principally through continuing use. The IFRIC decided that the information required by IFRS 5 is important to users of financial statements regardless of the form of a transaction. Therefore, the IFRIC concluded that the requirements in IFRS 5 applicable to non-current assets (or disposal groups) classified as held for sale and to discontinued operations should also be applied to assets (or disposal groups) held for distribution to owners.

BC61 However, the IFRIC concluded that requiring an entity to apply IFRS 5 to non-current assets (disposal groups) held for distribution to owners would require amendments to IFRS 5. This is because, in the IFRIC's view, IFRS 5 at present applies only to non-current assets (disposal groups) held for sale.

BC62 The Board discussed the IFRIC's proposal at its meeting in December 2007. The Board agreed with the IFRIC's conclusion that IFRS 5 should be amended to apply to non-current assets held for distribution to owners as well as to assets held for sale. However, the Board noted that IFRS 5 requires an entity to classify a non-current asset as held for sale when the sale is highly probable and the entity is *committed* to a plan to sell (emphasis added). Consequently, the Board directed the IFRIC to invite comments on the following questions:

(a) Should an entity apply IFRS 5 when it is committed to make a distribution or when it has an obligation to distribute the assets concerned?

(b) Is there a difference between those dates?

(c) If respondents believe that there is a difference between the dates and that an entity should apply IFRS 5 at the commitment date, what is the difference? What indicators should be included in IFRS 5 to help an entity to determine that date?

BC63 On the basis of the comments received, the IFRIC noted that, in many jurisdictions, shareholders' approval is required to make a distribution. Therefore, in such jurisdictions there could be a difference between the commitment date (i.e. the date when management is committed to the dividend) and the obligation date (i.e. the date when the dividend is approved by the shareholders). On the other hand, some commentators think that, when a distribution requires shareholders' approval, the entity cannot be committed until that approval is obtained: in that case, there would be no difference between two dates.

BC64 The IFRIC concluded that IFRS 5 should be applied at the commitment date at which time the assets must be available for immediate distribution in their present condition and the distribution must be *highly probable*. For the distribution to be highly probable, it should meet essentially the same conditions required for assets held for sale. Further, the IFRIC concluded that the probability of shareholders' approval (if required in the jurisdiction) should be considered as part of the assessment of whether the distribution is highly probable. The IFRIC noted that shareholder approval is also required for the sale of assets in some jurisdictions and concluded that similar consideration of the probability of such approval should be required for assets held for sale.

BC65 The Board agreed with the IFRIC's conclusions and amended IFRS 5 as part of its approval of the Interpretation.

Summary of main changes from the draft Interpretation

BC66 The main changes from the IFRIC's proposals in D23 are as follows:

(a) Paragraphs 3-8 were modified to clarify the scope of the Interpretation.

(b) Paragraph 10 clarifies when to recognise a dividend payable.

(c) Paragraphs 11-13 were modified to require the dividend payable to be measured at the fair value of the assets to be distributed without linking the IFRIC's conclusion that fair value is the most relevant measurement attribute to any individual standard.

(d) Illustrative examples were expanded to set out clearly the scope of the Interpretation.

(e) The Interpretation includes the amendments to IFRS 5 and IAS 10.

(f) The Basis for Conclusions was changed to set out more clearly the reasons for the IFRIC's conclusions.

Deleted IFRIC Interpretation 17 Text

Deleted IFRIC Interpretation 17 text is not part of AASB Interpretation 17.

Paragraph 18

An entity shall apply this Interpretation prospectively for annual periods beginning on or after 1 July 2009. Retrospective application is not permitted. Earlier application is permitted. If an entity applies this Interpretation for a period beginning before 1 July 2009, it shall disclose that fact and also apply IFRS 3 (as revised in 2008), IAS 27 (as amended in May 2008) and IFRS 5 (as amended by this Interpretation).

Interpretation 18
Transfers of Assets from Customers

(Issued March 2009)

Contents

Preface

Comparison with IFRIC 18

AASB Interpretation 18
Transfers of Assets from Customers

Paragraphs

References

Background   1 – 3

Scope   4 – 7

Issues   8

Consensus

Is the definition of an asset met?   9 – 10

How should the transferred item of property, plant and equipment
    be measured on initial recognition?   11

How should the credit be accounted for?   12 – 13

Identifying the separately identifiable services   14 – 17

Revenue recognition   18 – 20

How should the entity account for a transfer of cash from
    its customer?   21

Application and Transition   Aus21.1 – Aus21.6

Illustrative Examples   IE1 – IE9

Basis for Conclusions on IFRIC 18

Deleted IFRIC 18 text

AASB Interpretation 18 *Transfers of Assets from Customers* is set out in paragraphs 1–Aus21.6.
AASB Interpretation 18 is accompanied by a Basis for Conclusions. Interpretations are listed in Australian
Accounting Standard AASB 1048 *Interpretation and Application of Standards*.

Preface

Introduction

The Australian Accounting Standards Board (AASB) makes Australian
Accounting Standards, including Interpretations, to be applied by:

(a)   entities required by the *Corporations Act 2001* to prepare financial reports;

(b)   governments in preparing financial statements for the whole of government and the
       General Government Sector (GGS); and

(c)   entities in the private or public for-profit or not-for-profit sectors that are reporting entities
       or that prepare general purpose financial statements.

Australian Accounting Standards incorporate International Financial Reporting Standards
(IFRSs), including Interpretations, issued by the International Accounting Standards Board
(IASB), with the addition of paragraphs on the applicability of each Standard in the Australian
environment.

Australian Accounting Standards also include requirements that are specific to Australian entities.
These requirements may be located in Australian Accounting Standards that incorporate IFRSs
or in other Australian Accounting Standards. In most instances, these requirements are either
restricted to the not-for-profit or public sectors or include additional disclosures that address
domestic, regulatory or other issues. In developing requirements for public sector entities,
the AASB considers the requirements of International Public Sector Accounting Standards
(IPSASs), as issued by the International Public Sector Accounting Standards Board (IPSASB)
of the International Federation of Accountants.

Private sector for-profit entities complying with Australian Accounting Standards will
simultaneously comply with IFRSs. Many other entities complying with Australian Accounting
Standards will also simultaneously comply with IFRSs.

AASB Interpretation 1017

AASB Interpretation 1017 *Developer and Customer Contributions for Connection to a Price-
Regulated Network* is superseded by AASB Interpretation 18 *Transfers of Assets from Customers*.

Comparison with IFRIC 18

AASB Interpretation 18 incorporates International Financial Reporting Interpretations Committee
Interpretation IFRIC 18 *Transfers of Assets from Customers*, issued by the International
Accounting Standards Board. Paragraphs that have been added to this Interpretation (and do not
appear in the text of IFRIC 18) are identified with the prefix "Aus", followed by the number of
the preceding IFRIC paragraph and decimal numbering. Paragraphs that apply only to not-for-
profit entities begin by identifying their limited applicability.

Entities that comply with AASB Interpretation 18 will simultaneously be in compliance with
IFRIC 18.

AASB Interpretation 18

Transfers of Assets from Customers

References

*   *Framework for the Preparation and Presentation of Financial Statements*

*   Accounting Standard AASB 1 *First-time Adoption of Australian Equivalents to
     International Financial Reporting Standards*

*   Accounting Standard AASB 108 *Accounting Policies, Changes in Accounting Estimates
     and Errors*

- Accounting Standard AASB 116 *Property, Plant and Equipment*
- Accounting Standard AASB 118 *Revenue*
- Accounting Standard AASB 120 *Accounting for Government Grants and Disclosure of Government Assistance*
- AASB Interpretation 12 *Service Concession Arrangements*

Background

1   In the utilities industry, an entity may receive from its customers items of property, plant and equipment that must be used to connect those customers to a network and provide them with ongoing access to a supply of commodities such as electricity, gas or water. Alternatively, an entity may receive cash from customers for the acquisition or construction of such items of property, plant and equipment. Typically, customers are required to pay additional amounts for the purchase of goods or services based on usage.

2   Transfers of assets from customers may also occur in industries other than utilities. For example, an entity outsourcing its information technology functions may transfer its existing items of property, plant and equipment to the outsourcing provider.

3   In some cases, the transferor of the asset may not be the entity that will eventually have ongoing access to the supply of goods or services and will be the recipient of those goods or services. However, for convenience this Interpretation refers to the entity transferring the asset as the customer.

Scope

4   This Interpretation applies to the accounting for transfers of items of property, plant and equipment by entities that receive such transfers from their customers.

5   Agreements within the scope of this Interpretation are agreements in which an entity receives from a customer an item of property, plant and equipment that the entity must then use either to connect the customer to a network or to provide the customer with ongoing access to a supply of goods or services, or to do both.

6   This Interpretation also applies to agreements in which an entity receives cash from a customer when that amount of cash must be used only to construct or acquire an item of property, plant and equipment and the entity must then use the item of property, plant and equipment either to connect the customer to a network or to provide the customer with ongoing access to a supply of goods or services, or to do both.

7   This Interpretation does not apply to agreements in which the transfer is either a government grant as defined in AASB 120 or infrastructure used in a service concession arrangement that is within the scope of AASB Interpretation 12.

Issues

8   The Interpretation addresses the following issues:

   (a)   Is the definition of an asset met?

   (b)   If the definition of an asset is met, how should the transferred item of property, plant and equipment be measured on initial recognition?

   (c)   If the item of property, plant and equipment is measured at fair value on initial recognition, how should the resulting credit be accounted for?

   (d)   How should the entity account for a transfer of cash from its customer?

Consensus

Is the definition of an asset met?

9   When an entity receives from a customer a transfer of an item of property, plant and equipment, it shall assess whether the transferred item meets the definition of an asset set out in the *Framework*. Paragraph 49(a) of the *Framework* states that 'an asset is a resource controlled by the entity as a result of past events and from which future economic benefits are expected to flow to the entity.' In most circumstances, the entity obtains the

right of ownership of the transferred item of property, plant and equipment. However, in determining whether an asset exists, the right of ownership is not essential. Therefore, if the customer continues to control the transferred item, the asset definition would not be met despite a transfer of ownership.

10   An entity that controls an asset can generally deal with that asset as it pleases. For example, the entity can exchange that asset for other assets, employ it to produce goods or services, charge a price for others to use it, use it to settle liabilities, hold it, or distribute it to owners.

The entity that receives from a customer a transfer of an item of property, plant and equipment shall consider all relevant facts and circumstances when assessing control of the transferred item. For example, although the entity must use the transferred item of property, plant and equipment to provide one or more services to the customer, it may have the ability to decide how the transferred item of property, plant and equipment is operated and maintained and when it is replaced. In this case, the entity would normally conclude that it controls the transferred item of property, plant and equipment.

How should the transferred item of property, plant and equipment be measured on initial recognition?

11   If the entity concludes that the definition of an asset is met, it shall recognise the transferred asset as an item of property, plant and equipment in accordance with paragraph 7 of AASB 116 and measure its cost on initial recognition at its fair value in accordance with paragraph 24 of that Standard.

How should the credit be accounted for?

12   The following discussion assumes that the entity receiving an item of property, plant and equipment has concluded that the transferred item should be recognised and measured in accordance with paragraphs 9–11.

13   Paragraph 12 of AASB 118 states that 'When goods are sold or services are rendered in exchange for dissimilar goods or services, the exchange is regarded as a transaction which generates revenue.' According to the terms of the agreements within the scope of this Interpretation, a transfer of an item of property, plant and equipment would be an exchange for dissimilar goods or services. Consequently, the entity shall recognise revenue in accordance with AASB 118.

Identifying the separately identifiable services

14   An entity may agree to deliver one or more services in exchange for the transferred item of property, plant and equipment, such as connecting the customer to a network, providing the customer with ongoing access to a supply of goods or services, or both. In accordance with paragraph 13 of AASB 118, the entity shall identify the separately identifiable services included in the agreement.

15   Features that indicate that connecting the customer to a network is a separately identifiable service include:

    (a)   a service connection is delivered to the customer and represents stand-alone value for that customer;

    (b)   the fair value of the service connection can be measured reliably.

16   A feature that indicates that providing the customer with ongoing access to a supply of goods or services is a separately identifiable service is that, in the future, the customer making the transfer receives the ongoing access, the goods or services, or both at a price lower than would be charged without the transfer of the item of property, plant and equipment.

17   Conversely, a feature that indicates that the obligation to provide the customer with ongoing access to a supply of goods or services arises from the terms of the entity's operating licence or other regulation rather than from the agreement relating to the transfer of an item of property, plant and equipment is that customers that make a transfer pay the same price as those that do not for the ongoing access, or for the goods or services, or for both.

Revenue recognition

18   If only one service is identified, the entity shall recognise revenue when the service is performed in accordance with paragraph 20 of AASB 118.

19   If more than one separately identifiable service is identified, paragraph 13 of AASB 118 requires the fair value of the total consideration received or receivable for the agreement to be allocated to each service and the recognition criteria of AASB 118 are then applied to each service.

20   If an ongoing service is identified as part of the agreement, the period over which revenue shall be recognised for that service is generally determined by the terms of the agreement with the customer. If the agreement does not specify a period, the revenue shall be recognised over a period no longer than the useful life of the transferred asset used to provide the ongoing service.

How should the entity account for a transfer of cash from its customer?

21   When an entity receives a transfer of cash from a customer, it shall assess whether the agreement is within the scope of this Interpretation in accordance with paragraph 6. If it is, the entity shall assess whether the constructed or acquired item of property, plant and equipment meets the definition of an asset in accordance with paragraphs 9 and 10. If the definition of an asset is met, the entity shall recognise the item of property, plant and equipment at its cost in accordance with AASB 116 and shall recognise revenue in accordance with paragraphs 13–20 at the amount of cash received from the customer.

Application and Transition

Aus21.1   This Interpretation applies to:

    (a)   each entity that is required to prepare financial reports in accordance with Part 2M.3 of the *Corporations Act 2001* and that is a reporting entity;

    (b)   general purpose financial statements of each other reporting entity; and

    (c)   financial statements that are, or are held out to be, general purpose financial statements.

Aus21.2   This Interpretation applies prospectively to transfers of assets from customers received on or after 1 July 2009.

Aus21.3   This Interpretation may be applied to transfers of assets from customers received before 1 July 2009 in financial statements for annual reporting periods beginning on or after 1 January 2005, provided the valuations and other information needed to apply the Interpretation to past transfers were obtained at the time those transfers occurred.

Aus21.4   An entity shall disclose the date from which the Interpretation was applied.

Aus21.5   The requirements specified in this Interpretation apply to the financial statements where information resulting from their application is material in accordance with AASB 1031 *Materiality*.

Aus21.6   When applicable, this Interpretation supersedes AASB Interpretation 1017 *Developer and Customer Contributions for Connection to a Price-Regulated Network*, as issued in November 2004.

Effective date of IFRIC 18

22   [Deleted by the AASB]

Illustrative Examples

These examples accompany, but are not part of, AASB Interpretation 18.

Example 1

IE1   A real estate company is building a residential development in an area that is not connected to the electricity network. In order to have access to the electricity network, the real estate company is required to construct an electricity substation that is then transferred to the network company responsible for the transmission of electricity. It is assumed in this example that the network company concludes that the transferred substation meets the definition of an asset. The network company then uses the substation to connect each house of the residential development to its electricity network. In this case, it is the homeowners that will eventually use the network to access the supply of electricity, although they did not initially transfer the substation. By regulation, the network company has an obligation to provide ongoing access to the network to all users of the network at the same price, regardless of whether they transferred an asset. Therefore, users of the network that transfer an asset to the network company pay the same price for the use of the network as those that do not. Users of the network can choose to purchase their electricity from distributors other than the network company but must use the company's network to access the supply of electricity.

IE2   Alternatively, the network company could have constructed the substation and received a transfer of an amount of cash from the real estate company that had to be used only for the construction of the substation. The amount of cash transferred would not necessarily equal the entire cost of the substation. It is assumed that the substation remains an asset of the network company.

IE3   In this example, the Interpretation applies to the network company that receives the electricity substation from the real estate company. The network company recognises the substation as an item of property, plant and equipment and measures its cost on initial recognition at its fair value (or at its construction cost in the circumstances described in paragraph IE2) in accordance with AASB 116 *Property, Plant and Equipment*. The fact that users of the network that transfer an asset to the network company pay the same price for the use of the electricity network as those that do not indicates that the obligation to provide ongoing access to the network is not a separately identifiable service of the transaction. Rather, connecting the house to the network is the only service to be delivered in exchange for the substation. Therefore, the network company should recognise revenue from the exchange transaction at the fair value of the substation (or at the amount of the cash received from the real estate company in the circumstances described in paragraph IE2) when the houses are connected to the network in accordance with paragraph 20 of AASB 118 *Revenue*.

Example 2

IE4   A house builder constructs a house on a redeveloped site in a major city. As part of constructing the house, the house builder installs a pipe from the house to the water main in front of the house. Because the pipe is on the house's land, the owner of the house can restrict access to the pipe. The owner is also responsible for the maintenance of the pipe. In this example, the facts indicate that the definition of an asset is not met for the water company.

IE5   Alternatively, a house builder constructs multiple houses and installs a pipe on the commonly owned or public land to connect the houses to the water main. The house builder transfers ownership of the pipe to the water company that will be responsible for its maintenance. In this example, the facts indicate that the water company controls the pipe and should recognise it.

Example 3

IE6   An entity enters into an agreement with a customer involving the outsourcing of the customer's information technology (IT) functions. As part of the agreement, the customer transfers ownership of its existing IT equipment to the entity. Initially, the entity must use the equipment to provide the service required by the outsourcing agreement. The entity is responsible for maintaining the equipment and for replacing it when the entity decides to do so. The useful life of the equipment is estimated to be three years. The outsourcing agreement requires service to be provided for ten years for a fixed price that is lower than the price the entity would have charged if the IT equipment had not been transferred.

IE7 In this example, the facts indicate that the IT equipment is an asset of the entity. Therefore, the entity should recognise the equipment and measure its cost on initial recognition at its fair value in accordance with paragraph 24 of AASB 116. The fact that the price charged for the service to be provided under the outsourcing agreement is lower than the price the entity would charge without the transfer of the IT equipment indicates that this service is a separately identifiable service included in the agreement. The facts also indicate that it is the only service to be provided in exchange for the transfer of the IT equipment. Therefore, the entity should recognise revenue arising from the exchange transaction when the service is performed, ie over the ten- year term of the outsourcing agreement.

IE8 Alternatively, assume that after the first three years, the price the entity charges under the outsourcing agreement increases to reflect the fact that it will then be replacing the equipment the customer transferred.

IE9 In this case, the reduced price for the services provided under the outsourcing agreement reflects the useful life of the transferred equipment. For this reason, the entity should recognise revenue from the exchange transaction over the first three years of the agreement.

Basis for Conclusions on IFRIC Interpretation 18

This IFRIC Basis for Conclusions accompanies, but is not part of, AASB Interpretation 18. An IFRIC Basis for Conclusions may be amended to reflect the requirements of the AASB Interpretation and AASB Accounting Standards where they differ from the corresponding International pronouncements.

Introduction

BC1 This Basis for Conclusions summarises the IFRIC's considerations in reaching its consensus. Individual IFRIC members gave greater weight to some factors than to others.

BC2 The IFRIC released draft Interpretation D24 *Customer Contributions* for public comment in January 2008 and received 59 comment letters in response.

Background

BC3 The IFRIC received a request to issue guidance on the accounting for transfers of items of property, plant and equipment by entities that receive such transfers from their customers. Divergence had arisen in practice with some entities recognising the transferred item at fair value and others recognising it at a cost of nil. Among those that recognised the item at fair value, some recognised the resulting credit as revenue immediately, while others recognised it over some longer service period. The IFRIC decided to develop an Interpretation in response to that divergence in practice.

Scope

BC4 This Interpretation applies to the accounting for transfers of items of property, plant and equipment by entities that receive such transfers from their customers. In developing the Interpretation, the IFRIC decided that it would not address how the customers should account for the transfers because the main issue is how the entity receiving the asset should recognise revenue.

BC5 Some respondents questioned whether transfers of assets other than those within the scope of this Interpretation, ie transfers of intangible assets from customers, would lead to the same answer. In its redeliberations, the IFRIC decided not to expand the scope to assets other than those already considered in D24 but did not prohibit application by analogy in accordance with IAS 8 *Accounting Policies, Changes in Accounting Estimates and Errors*.

BC6 In its redeliberations, the IFRIC clarified in paragraph 3 that, for convenience, this Interpretation refers to the entity transferring the item of property, plant and equipment as the customer even though that entity may not be the entity that will eventually have ongoing access to the supply of goods or services and will be the recipient of those goods or services. The IFRIC also added an example to illustrate such a situation.

BC7   Some respondents commented that, in practice, customers often transfer cash instead of transferring an item of property, plant and equipment. The IFRIC reaffirmed its view that transfers of cash should be within the scope of the Interpretation (see also paragraph BC24).

BC8   Many respondents were concerned that D24 could create unintended overlaps with existing IFRSs such as IFRIC 12 *Service Concession Arrangements* and IAS 20 *Accounting for Government Grants and Disclosure of Government Assistance*. In its redeliberations, the IFRIC noted that in a public-to-private service concession arrangement within the scope of IFRIC 12 the grantor controls the infrastructure, not the operator. Therefore, the IFRIC concluded that this Interpretation does not apply to agreements in which the transfer is an item of infrastructure used in a service concession arrangement that is within the scope of IFRIC 12. The IFRIC also clarified that IAS 20 does not apply because transfers of assets from customers do not meet the definition of a government grant in accordance with paragraph 3 of IAS 20.

BC9   Some respondents to D24 questioned the application by analogy to situations other than utility entities providing connection and access to their networks (eg electricity, gas, water or telecommunication networks). In its redeliberations, the IFRIC noted that this Interpretation might also be relevant to industries other than utilities. The IFRIC also clarified the background section of the Interpretation adding an example of an information technology outsourcing agreement.

Issues

BC10 When an entity receives an item of property, plant and equipment from a customer, it should assess whether the transferred item meets the definition of an asset.

BC11 If the entity concludes that the transferred item of property, plant and equipment meets the definition of an asset, it should recognise the transferred item in accordance with paragraph 7 of IAS 16. In that case, the next issues are at what amount it should be recognised on initial recognition and how to account for the resulting credit.

BC12 The last issue the IFRIC considered is how the entity should account for the receipt of cash instead of a transfer of an item of property, plant and equipment.

Consensus

Is the definition of an asset met?

BC13 In its redeliberations, the IFRIC discussed the different steps that D24 required an entity to follow to determine whether an asset should be recognised, including the consideration of IFRIC 4 *Determining whether an Arrangement contains a Lease* and IAS 17 *Leases*. The IFRIC decided to simplify the proposals by focusing on who controls the asset. The Interpretation provides guidance based on the definition of an asset set out in paragraph 49(a) of the Framework and the additional guidance in paragraphs 55 and 57 of the Framework.

How should the transferred item of property, plant and equipment be measured on initial recognition?

BC14 The IFRIC concluded that, in a normal trading transaction, the item of property, plant and equipment is received in exchange for something, ie the provision of services such as connection to a network, provision of ongoing access to a supply of goods or services, or both.

BC15 The IFRIC noted that both paragraph 24 of IAS 16 *Property, Plant and Equipment* and paragraph 12 of IAS 18 *Revenue* lead to the same measurement attribute for such exchange transactions, ie the item received should be measured at fair value on initial recognition. Therefore, if the entity concludes that the definition of an asset is met, it should recognise the transferred asset as an item of property, plant and equipment in accordance with paragraph 7 of IAS 16 and measure it on initial recognition at its fair value in accordance with paragraph 24 of that Standard. The IFRIC also noted that respondents to D24 generally agreed with that conclusion.

How should the credit be accounted for?

BC16 The following discussion assumes that the entity receiving an item of property, plant and equipment from a customer has concluded that the transferred item should be recognised and measured at its fair value on initial recognition. It also assumes that the services to be provided in exchange for the transferred item are part of the ordinary activities of the entity.

Identifying the separately identifiable services

BC17 D24 identified only one service to be delivered in exchange for the transferred item of property, plant and equipment: the provision of ongoing access to a supply of goods or services. Many respondents, including utility entities, questioned whether an entity receiving an asset from a customer always has an obligation to provide ongoing access to a supply of goods or services as a result of the transfer. For example, some respondents argued that when a utility company is required by law or regulation to provide access to a supply of a commodity to all customers at the same price it may have no further obligation once the service connection has been made. They also argued that an obligation to provide ongoing services to the customer who transferred the asset may exist only if the customer obtains in exchange some exclusive right of access to a supply of goods or services, eg a reduced price. Overall, these respondents asked the IFRIC to reconsider the revenue recognition issue on the basis of an IAS 18 approach.

BC18 In its redeliberations, the IFRIC noted that an entity may agree to deliver one or two services in exchange for the transferred item of property, plant and equipment, such as connecting the customer to a network, providing the customer with ongoing access to a supply of goods or services, or both. The IFRIC concluded that identifying the separately identifiable services of a single agreement depends on facts and circumstances and that judgement is required. The IFRIC also acknowledged that a practical weakness of IAS 18 is that it gives insufficient guidance on agreements that deliver more than one good or service to the customer. Therefore, the IFRIC decided to develop guidance based on paragraph 13 of IAS 18 to help identify the services to be delivered in exchange for the transferred asset. This decision resulted in including the indicators in paragraphs 15–17 of the Interpretation and the examples illustrating their application.

Revenue recognition

BC19 In accordance with paragraph 13 of IAS 18, the IFRIC decided that the Interpretation should require that when more than one service is identified the fair value of the total consideration received or receivable for the agreement should be allocated to each service and that the recognition criteria of IAS 18 should be applied to each service. The IFRIC noted that IFRIC 12 *Service Concession Arrangements* and IFRIC 13 *Customer Loyalty Programmes* provide guidance on how to allocate the fair value of the total consideration received or receivable for the agreement to each component (see paragraph 13 of IFRIC 12 and paragraphs 5–7 of IFRIC 13). Therefore, the IFRIC concluded that this Interpretation should include only a reminder in paragraph 19 that such allocation is required if more than one service is identified.

BC20 If a separately identifiable ongoing service is part of the agreement, the entity must identify the period over which revenue should be recognised. Paragraph 20 of D24 stated that 'although the period over which an entity has an obligation to provide access to a supply of goods or services using a contributed asset may be shorter than the useful economic life of the asset, it cannot be longer.' Some respondents asked the IFRIC to clarify whether that period may be determined by the terms of the agreement and why that period cannot be longer than the economic life of the contributed asset.

BC21 The IFRIC clarified that the period over which revenue should be recognised for the ongoing service is generally determined by the terms of the agreement with the customer. If the arrangement does not specify a period, the IFRIC reaffirmed its view that the revenue should be recognised over a period no longer than the useful life of the transferred asset used to provide the ongoing service. This is because the entity can only use the transferred asset to provide ongoing access to a supply of goods or services during its useful life. Any obligation that exists after the asset is replaced does not arise from the original transfer but from the terms of the entity's operating licence or other regulation.

BC22 Almost all respondents disagreed with paragraph BC22 of D24 that the time value of money should be taken into account when measuring revenue. The IFRIC agreed with respondents and noted that paragraph 11 of IAS 18 requires taking the time value of money into account only when payments are deferred.

How should the entity account for a transfer of cash from its customer?

BC23 Respondents were generally supportive of the IFRIC's proposals related to transfers of cash. However, some respondents asked the IFRIC to clarify the circumstances in which a cash transfer would be within the scope of the Interpretation.

BC24 In its redeliberations, the IFRIC discussed the accounting for agreements in which an entity receives a transfer of cash from a customer instead of an item of property, plant and equipment. The IFRIC reaffirmed its view in D24: when that amount of cash must be used only to construct or acquire an item of property, plant and equipment and the entity must then use the item of property, plant and equipment to deliver goods or services to the customer, the economic effect of the transfer of cash is similar to that of a transfer of an item of property, plant and equipment.

Transition

BC25 The IFRIC noted that applying the change in accounting policy retrospectively would require entities to establish a carrying amount for assets that had been transferred in the past. That carrying amount would be based on historical fair values. Those fair values may not be based on an observable price or observable inputs. Therefore, the IFRIC concluded that retrospective application may be impracticable and that the Interpretation should require prospective application to transfers received after its effective date. However, the IFRIC also concluded that earlier application should be permitted provided the valuations and other information needed to apply the Interpretation to past transfers were obtained at the time those transfers occurred.

Changes from draft Interpretation D24

BC26 The most significant changes made from D24 in the light of comments received relate to:

(a)   *Recognition of transferred assets.* As stated in paragraph BC13, the IFRIC decided to simplify the requirements. It addressed the issue of which entity controls the asset by giving guidance based on the definition of an asset set out in the *Framework*.

(b)   *Revenue recognition.* The IFRIC decided that an entity receiving an item of property, plant and equipment from a customer may not always have an obligation to provide ongoing access to a supply of goods or services as a result of the transfer. Therefore, the IFRIC also decided to develop guidance based on paragraph 13 of IAS 18 to help identify the separately identifiable services to be delivered in exchange for the transferred asset.

(c)   *Title of the Interpretation.* The IFRIC noted that in some jurisdictions, the term 'contribution' has the implication of a donation rather than an exchange transaction. In addition, the IFRIC noted that this term might be difficult to translate into some languages. For that reason, the IFRIC decided to use the term 'transfer' and redrafted the Interpretation accordingly.

(d)   *Illustrative examples.* The IFRIC decided that illustrative examples should accompany, but not be part of, the Interpretation to help entities apply the Interpretation.

Deleted IFRIC Interpretation 18 Text

Deleted IFRIC Interpretation 18 text is not part of AASB Interpretation 18.

Paragraph 22

An entity shall apply this Interpretation prospectively to transfers of assets from customers received on or after 1 July 2009. Earlier application is permitted provided the valuations and other information needed to apply the Interpretation to past transfers were obtained at the time those transfers occurred. An entity shall disclose the date from which the Interpretation was applied.

Interpretation 19
Extinguishing Financial Liabilities
with Equity Instruments

(December 2009)

Contents

Preface

Comparison with IFRIC 19

AASB Interpretation 19
Extinguishing Financial Liabilities with Equity Instruments

Paragraphs

References

Background   1

Scope   2 – 3

Issues   4

Consensus   5 – 11

Application   Aus11.1 – Aus11.4

Transition   13

Basis for Conclusions

Deleted IFRIC 19 Text

AASB Interpretation 19 *Extinguishing Financial Liabilities with Equity Instruments* is set out in paragraphs 1–13. AASB Interpretation 19 is accompanied by a Basis for Conclusions. Interpretations are listed in Australian Accounting Standard AASB 1048 *Interpretation and Application of Standards*.

Preface

Introduction

The Australian Accounting Standards Board (AASB) makes Australian Accounting Standards, including Interpretations, to be applied by:

(a)   entities required by the *Corporations Act 2001* to prepare financial reports;

(b)   governments in preparing financial statements for the whole of government and the General Government Sector (GGS); and

(c)   entities in the private or public for-profit or not-for-profit sectors that are reporting entities or that prepare general purpose financial statements.

Australian Accounting Standards incorporate International Financial Reporting Standards (IFRSs), including Interpretations, issued by the International Accounting Standards Board (IASB), with the addition of paragraphs on the applicability of each Standard in the Australian environment.

Australian Accounting Standards also include requirements that are specific to Australian entities. These requirements may be located in Australian Accounting Standards that incorporate IFRSs or in other Australian Accounting Standards. In most instances, these requirements are either restricted to the not-for-profit or public sectors or include additional disclosures that address domestic, regulatory or other issues. In developing requirements for public sector entities, the AASB considers the requirements of International Public Sector Accounting Standards (IPSASs), as issued by the International Public Sector Accounting Standards Board (IPSASB) of the International Federation of Accountants.

Private sector for-profit entities complying with Australian Accounting Standards will simultaneously comply with IFRSs. Many other entities complying with Australian Accounting Standards will also simultaneously comply with IFRSs.

Comparison with IFRIC 19

AASB Interpretation 19 incorporates International Financial Reporting Interpretations Committee Interpretation IFRIC 19 *Extinguishing Financial Liabilities with Equity Instruments*, issued by the International Accounting Standards Board. Paragraphs that have been added to this Interpretation (and do not appear in the text of IFRIC 19) are identified with the prefix "Aus", followed by the number of the preceding IFRIC paragraph and decimal numbering.

Entities that comply with AASB Interpretation 19 will simultaneously be in compliance with IFRIC 19.

AASB Interpretation 19

Extinguishing Financial Liabilities with Equity Instruments

References

- *Framework for the Preparation and Presentation of Financial Statements*
- Accounting Standard AASB 2 *Share-based Payment*
- Accounting Standard AASB 3 *Business Combinations*
- Accounting Standard AASB 101 *Presentation of Financial Statements*
- Accounting Standard AASB 108 *Accounting Policies, Changes in Accounting Estimates and Errors*
- Accounting Standard AASB 132 *Financial Instruments: Presentation*
- Accounting Standard AASB 139 *Financial Instruments: Recognition and Measurement*

Background

1. A debtor and creditor might renegotiate the terms of a financial liability with the result that the debtor extinguishes the liability fully or partially by issuing equity instruments to the creditor. These transactions are sometimes referred to as 'debt for equity swaps'. Constituents have requested guidance on the accounting for such transactions.

Scope

2. This Interpretation addresses the accounting by an entity when the terms of a financial liability are renegotiated and result in the entity issuing equity instruments to a creditor of the entity to extinguish all or part of the financial liability. It does not address the accounting by the creditor.

3. An entity shall not apply this Interpretation to transactions in situations where:

   (a) the creditor is also a direct or indirect shareholder and is acting in its capacity as a direct or indirect existing shareholder.

   (b) the creditor and the entity are controlled by the same party or parties before and after the transaction and the substance of the transaction includes an equity distribution by, or contribution to, the entity.

   (c) extinguishing the financial liability by issuing equity shares is in accordance with the original terms of the financial liability.

Issues

4   This Interpretation addresses the following issues:

(a)   Are an entity's equity instruments issued to extinguish all or part of a financial liability 'consideration paid' in accordance with paragraph 41 of AASB 139?

(b)   How should an entity initially measure the equity instruments issued to extinguish such a financial liability?

(c)   How should an entity account for any difference between the carrying amount of the financial liability extinguished and the initial measurement amount of the equity instruments issued?

Consensus

5   The issue of an entity's equity instruments to a creditor to extinguish all or part of a financial liability is consideration paid in accordance with paragraph 41 of AASB 139. An entity shall remove a financial liability (or part of a financial liability) from its statement of financial position when, and only when, it is extinguished in accordance with paragraph 39 of AASB 139.

6   When equity instruments issued to a creditor to extinguish all or part of a financial liability are recognised initially, an entity shall measure them at the fair value of the equity instruments issued, unless that fair value cannot be reliably measured.

7   If the fair value of the equity instruments issued cannot be reliably measured then the equity instruments shall be measured to reflect the fair value of the financial liability extinguished. In measuring the fair value of a financial liability extinguished that includes a demand feature (e.g. a demand deposit), paragraph 49 of AASB 139 is not applied.

8   If only part of the financial liability is extinguished, the entity shall assess whether some of the consideration paid relates to a modification of the terms of the liability that remains outstanding. If part of the consideration paid does relate to a modification of the terms of the remaining part of the liability, the entity shall allocate the consideration paid between the part of the liability extinguished and the part of the liability that remains outstanding. The entity shall consider all relevant facts and circumstances relating to the transaction in making this allocation.

9   The difference between the carrying amount of the financial liability (or part of a financial liability) extinguished, and the consideration paid, shall be recognised in profit or loss, in accordance with paragraph 41 of AASB 139. The equity instruments issued shall be recognised initially and measured at the date the financial liability (or part of that liability) is extinguished.

10   When only part of the financial liability is extinguished, consideration shall be allocated in accordance with paragraph 8. The consideration allocated to the remaining liability shall form part of the assessment of whether the terms of that remaining liability have been substantially modified. If the remaining liability has been substantially modified, the entity shall account for the modification as the extinguishment of the original liability and the recognition of a new liability as required by paragraph 40 of AASB 139.

11   An entity shall disclose a gain or loss recognised in accordance with paragraphs 9 and 10 as a separate line item in profit or loss or in the notes.

Application

Aus11.1   This Interpretation applies to:

(a)   each entity that is required to prepare financial reports in accordance with Part 2M.3 of the *Corporations Act 2001* and that is a reporting entity;

(b)   general purpose financial statements of each other reporting entity; and

(c)   financial statements that are, or are held out to be, general purpose financial statements.

Aus11.2   This Interpretation applies to annual reporting periods beginning on or after 1 July 2010.

Aus11.3   This Interpretation may be applied to annual reporting periods beginning on or after 1 January 2005 but before 1 July 2010. When an entity applies this Interpretation to an annual reporting period beginning before 1 July 2010 it shall disclose that fact.

Aus11.4   The requirements specified in this Interpretation apply to the financial statements where information resulting from their application is material in accordance with AASB 1031 *Materiality*.

Effective date of IFRIC 19

12   [Deleted by the AASB]

Transition

13   An entity shall apply a change in accounting policy in accordance with AASB 108 from the beginning of the earliest comparative period presented.

Basis for Conclusions on IFRIC Interpretation 19

This IFRIC Basis for Conclusions accompanies, but is not part of, AASB Interpretation 19. An IFRIC Basis for Conclusions may be amended to reflect the requirements of the AASB Interpretation and AASB Accounting Standards where they differ from the corresponding International pronouncements.

Introduction

BC1   This Basis for Conclusions summarises the IFRIC's considerations in reaching its consensus. Individual IFRIC members gave greater weight to some factors than to others.

BC2   The IFRIC received a request for guidance on the application of IAS 39 *Financial Instruments: Recognition and Measurement* and IAS 32 *Financial Instruments: Presentation* when an entity issues its own equity instruments to extinguish all or part of a financial liability. The question is how the entity should recognise the equity instruments issued.

BC3   The IFRIC noted that lenders manage loans to entities in financial difficulty in a variety of ways including one or more of the following:

(a)   selling the loans in the market to other investors/lenders;

(b)   renegotiating the terms of the loan (eg extension of the maturity date or lower interest payments); or

(c)   accepting the creditor's equity instruments in full or partial settlement of the liability (sometimes referred to as a 'debt for equity swap').

BC4   The IFRIC was informed that there was diversity in practice in how entities measure the equity instruments issued in full or partial settlement of a financial liability following renegotiation of the terms of the liability. Some recognise the equity instruments at the carrying amount of the financial liability and do not recognise any gain or loss in profit or loss. Others recognise the equity instruments at the fair value of either the liability extinguished or the equity instruments issued and recognise a difference between that amount and the carrying amount of the financial liability in profit or loss.

BC5   In August 2009 the IFRIC published draft Interpretation D25 *Extinguishing Financial Liabilities with Equity Instruments* for public comment. It received 33 comment letters in response to the proposals.

Scope

BC6   The IFRIC concluded that its Interpretation should address only the accounting by an entity when the terms of a financial liability are renegotiated and result in the entity issuing equity instruments to a creditor of the entity to extinguish part or all of the liability. It does not address the accounting by the creditor because other IFRSs already set out the relevant requirements.

BC7   The IFRIC considered whether to provide guidance on transactions in which the creditor is also a direct or indirect shareholder and is acting in its capacity as an existing direct or indirect shareholder. The IFRIC concluded that the Interpretation should not address such transactions. It noted that determining whether the issue of equity instruments to extinguish a financial liability in such situations is considered a transaction with an owner in its capacity as an owner would be a matter of judgement depending on the facts and circumstances.

BC8   In its redeliberations, the IFRIC clarified that transactions when the creditor and the entity are controlled by the same party or parties before and after the transaction are outside the scope of the Interpretation when the substance of the transaction includes an equity distribution by, or contribution to, the entity. The IFRIC acknowledged that the allocation of consideration between the extinguishment of all or part of a financial liability and the equity distribution or contribution components may not always be reliably measured.

BC9   Some respondents questioned whether the Interpretation should be applied to transactions when the extinguishment of the financial liability by issuing equity shares is in accordance with the original terms of the liability. In its redeliberations the IFRIC decided that these transactions should be excluded from the scope of the Interpretation, noting that IAS 32 includes specific guidance on those financial instruments.

Are an entity's equity instruments 'consideration paid'?

BC10   The IFRIC noted that IFRSs do not contain specific guidance on the measurement of an entity's equity instruments issued to extinguish all or part of a financial liability. Paragraph 41 of IAS 39 requires an entity to recognise in profit or loss the difference between the carrying amount of the financial liability extinguished and the consideration paid. That paragraph describes 'consideration paid' as including non-cash assets transferred, or liabilities assumed, and does not specifically mention equity instruments issued. Consequently, some are of the view that equity instruments are not 'consideration paid'.

BC11   Holders of this view believe that, because IFRSs are generally silent on how to measure equity instruments on initial recognition (see paragraph BC15), a variety of practices has developed. One such practice is to recognise the equity instruments issued at the carrying amount of the financial liability extinguished.

BC12   However, the IFRIC observed that both IFRS 2 *Share-based Payment* and IFRS 3 *Business Combinations* make it clear that equity instruments are used as consideration to acquire goods and services as well as to obtain control of businesses.

BC13   The IFRIC also observed that the issue of equity instruments to extinguish a financial liability could be analysed as consisting of two transactions—first, the issue of new equity instruments to the creditor for cash and second, the creditor accepting payment of that amount of cash to extinguish the financial liability.

BC14   As a result of its analysis, the IFRIC concluded that the equity instruments issued to extinguish a financial liability are 'consideration paid' in accordance with paragraph 41 of IAS 39.

How should the equity instruments be measured?

BC15   The IFRIC observed that although IFRSs do not contain a general principle for the initial recognition and measurement of equity instruments, guidance on specific transactions exists, including:

(a)   *initial recognition of compound instruments* (IAS 32). The amount allocated to the equity component is the residual after deducting the fair value of the financial liability component from the fair value of the entire compound instrument.

(b)   *cost of equity transactions and own equity instruments ('treasury shares') acquired and reissued or cancelled* (IAS 32). No gain or loss is recognised in profit or loss on the purchase, sale, issue or cancellation of an entity's own equity instruments. These are transactions with an entity's owners in their capacity as owners.

(c)   *equity instruments issued in share-based payment transactions* (IFRS 2). For equity-settled share-based payment transactions, the entity measures the goods or services received, and the corresponding increase in equity, directly, at the fair value of the goods or services received, unless that fair value cannot be estimated reliably. If the entity cannot estimate reliably the fair value of the goods or services received (eg transactions with employees), the entity measures their value, and the corresponding increase in equity, indirectly, by reference to the fair value of the equity instruments granted.

(d)   *consideration transferred in business combinations* (IFRS 3). The total consideration transferred in a business combination is measured at fair value. It includes the acquisition-date fair values of any equity interests issued by the acquirer.

BC16   The IFRIC noted that the general principle of IFRSs is that equity is a residual and should be measured initially by reference to changes in assets and liabilities (the *Framework* and IFRS 2). IFRS 2 is clear that when goods or services are received in return for the issue of equity instruments, the increase in equity is measured directly at the fair value of the goods or services received.

BC17   The IFRIC decided that the same principles should apply when equity instruments are issued to extinguish financial liabilities. However, the IFRIC was concerned that entities might encounter practical difficulties in measuring the fair value of both the equity instruments issued and the financial liability, particularly when the entity is in financial difficulty. Therefore, the IFRIC decided in D25 that equity instruments issued to extinguish a financial liability should be measured initially at the fair value of the equity instruments issued or the fair value of the liability extinguished, whichever is more reliably determinable.

BC18   However, in response to comments received on D25, the IFRIC reconsidered whether the entity should initially measure equity instruments issued to a creditor to extinguish all or part of a financial liability at the fair value of the equity instruments issued or the fair value of the liability extinguished. The IFRIC noted that many respondents proposed that a preferred measurement basis should be determined to avoid an 'accounting choice' developing in practice, acknowledging that both measurement approaches would need to be used to identify which was more reliably determinable.

BC19   Therefore the IFRIC decided to modify the proposal in D25 and identify a preferred measurement basis. In identifying this preferred measurement basis, the IFRIC noted that many respondents considered that the principles in IFRS 2 and the *Framework* referred to in paragraph BC16 support a measurement based on the fair value of the liability extinguished.

BC20   However, some respondents argued that the fair value of the equity issued should be the proposed measurement basis. They pointed out that this approach would be consistent with the consensus that the issue of an entity's equity instruments is consideration paid in accordance with paragraph 41 of IAS 39. They also argued that the fair value of the equity issued best reflects the total amount of consideration paid in the transaction, which may include a premium that the creditor requires to renegotiate the terms of the financial liability.

BC21   The IFRIC considered that the fair value of the equity issued should be the proposed measurement basis for the reasons described in paragraph BC20. Consequently the IFRIC concluded that an entity should initially measure equity instruments issued to a creditor to extinguish all or part of a financial liability at the fair value of the equity instruments issued, unless that fair value cannot be reliably measured.

If the fair value of the equity instruments issued cannot be reliably measured then these equity instruments should initially be measured to reflect the fair value of the liability extinguished.

BC22   In redeliberations, the IFRIC noted that these transactions often take place in situations when the terms of the financial liability are breached and the liability becomes repayable on demand. The IFRIC agreed with comments received that paragraph 49 of IAS 39 is not applied in measuring the fair value of all or part of a financial liability extinguished in these situations. This is because the extinguishment transaction suggests that the demand feature is no longer substantive.

BC23   In response to comments, the IFRIC also clarified that the equity instruments issued should be recognised initially and measured at the date the financial liability (or part of that liability) is extinguished. This is consistent with paragraphs BC341 and BC342 of the Basis for Conclusions on IFRS 3, which discuss the views on whether equity instruments issued as consideration in a business combination should be measured at fair value at the agreement date or acquisition date, concluding that measurement should be at the acquisition date.

How should a difference between the carrying amount of the financial liability and the consideration paid be accounted for?

BC24   In accordance with paragraph 41 of IAS 39, the entity should recognise a gain or loss in profit or loss for any difference between the carrying amount of the financial liability extinguished and the consideration paid. This requirement is consistent with the *Framework*'s discussion of income:

(a)   Income is increases in economic benefits during the accounting period in the form of inflows or enhancements of assets or *decreases of liabilities that result in increases in equity*, other than those relating to contributions from equity participants. (paragraph 70(a)) (emphasis added)

(b)   Gains represent other items that meet the definition of income and may, or may not, arise in the course of the ordinary activities of an entity. Gains represent increases in economic benefits ... (paragraph 75)

(c)   Income may also result from the settlement of liabilities. For example, an entity may provide goods and services to a lender in settlement of an obligation to repay an outstanding loan. (paragraph 77)

Full extinguishment

BC25   The IFRIC noted that, as discussed in paragraph BC13, a transaction in which an entity issues equity instruments to extinguish a liability can be analysed as first, the issue of new equity instruments to the creditor for cash and second, the creditor accepting payment of that amount of cash to extinguish the financial liability. Consistently with paragraph BC24, when the creditor accepts cash to extinguish the liability, the entity should recognise a gain or loss in profit or loss.

BC26   Similarly, the IFRIC noted that, in accordance with IAS 32, when an entity amends the terms of a convertible instrument to induce early conversion, the entity recognises in profit or loss the fair value of any additional consideration paid to the holder. Thus, the IFRIC concluded that when an entity settles an instrument by issuing its own equity instruments and that settlement is not in accordance with the original terms of the financial liability, the entity should recognise a gain or loss in profit or loss.

BC27   As a result of its conclusions, the IFRIC decided that the entity should recognise a gain or loss in profit or loss. This gain or loss is equal to the difference between the carrying amount of the financial liability and the fair value of the equity instruments issued, or fair value of the liability extinguished if the fair value of the equity instruments issued cannot be reliably measured.

Partial extinguishment

BC28   The IFRIC also observed that the restructuring of a financial liability can involve both the partial settlement of the liability by the issue of equity instruments to the creditor and the modification of the terms of the liability that remains outstanding. Therefore, the IFRIC decided that the Interpretation should also apply to partial extinguishments. In the case of a partial extinguishment, the discussion in paragraphs BC25–BC27 applies to the part of the liability extinguished.

BC29   Many respondents requested clarification of the guidance on partial extinguishment included in D25. During its redeliberations, the IFRIC acknowledged that the issue of an entity's equity shares may reflect consideration paid for both the extinguishment of part of a financial liability and the modification of the terms of the part of the liability that remains outstanding.

BC30   The IFRIC decided that to reflect this, an entity should allocate the consideration paid between the part of the liability extinguished and the part of the liability that remains outstanding. The entity would consider this allocation in determining the profit or loss to be recognised on the part of the liability extinguished and in its assessment of whether the terms of the remaining liability have been substantially modified.

BC31   The IFRIC concluded that providing additional guidance on determining whether the terms of the part of the financial liability that remains outstanding has been substantially modified in accordance with paragraph 40 of IAS 39 was outside the scope of the Interpretation.

Presentation

BC32   The IFRIC decided that an entity should disclose the gain or loss on the extinguishment of the financial liability by the issue of equity instruments as a separate line item in profit or loss or in the notes. This requirement is consistent with the *Framework* and the requirements in other IFRSs, for example:

     (a)   When gains are recognised in the income statement, they are usually displayed separately because knowledge of them is useful for the purpose of making economic decisions. (paragraph 76 of the *Framework*)

     (b)   An entity shall present additional line items, headings and subtotals in the statement of comprehensive income and the separate income statement (if presented), when such presentation is relevant to an understanding of the entity's financial performance. (paragraph 85 of IAS 1 *Presentation of Financial Statements*)

     (c)   An entity shall disclose net gains or net losses on financial liabilities either in the statement of comprehensive income or in the notes. (paragraph 20 of IFRS 7 *Financial Instruments: Disclosures*)

Transition

BC33   The IFRIC decided that the Interpretation should be applied retrospectively even though it acknowledged that determining fair values retrospectively may be problematic. The IFRIC noted that IAS 8 *Accounting Policies, Changes in Accounting Estimates and Errors* provides guidance on circumstances in which retrospective application might be impracticable. The IFRIC concluded that it was preferable to require entities that could apply the Interpretation retrospectively to do so, rather than requiring all entities to apply it prospectively to future transactions. However, to simplify transition, the IFRIC also concluded that it should require retrospective application only from the beginning of the earliest comparative period presented because application to earlier periods would result only in a reclassification of amounts within equity.

Interpretations

Summary of main changes from the draft Interpretation

BC34   The main changes from the IFRIC's proposals in D25 are as follows:

(a)   Paragraph 3 was added because the IFRIC identified specific transactions that are outside of the scope of the Interpretation.

(b)   Paragraph 6 was modified to state that measurement should be based on the fair value of the equity instruments issued, unless that fair value cannot be reliably measured.

(c)   Paragraph 7 was added to reflect the modification to paragraph 6. It also clarifies the intention of the IFRIC that in measuring the fair value of a financial liability extinguished that includes a demand feature (eg a demand deposit), paragraph 49 of IAS 39 is not applied.

(d)   Paragraph 8 was added, and paragraph 10 was modified, to clarify how the Interpretation should be applied when only part of the financial liability is extinguished by the issue of equity instruments.

(e)   Paragraph 9 was modified to state when the equity instruments issued should be initially measured.

Deleted IFRIC 19 Text

Deleted IFRIC Interpretation 19 text is not part of AASB Interpretation 19.

Paragraph 12

An entity shall apply this Interpretation for annual periods beginning on or after 1 July 2010. Earlier application is permitted. If an entity applies this Interpretation for a period beginning before 1 July 2010, it shall disclose that fact.

Interpretation 20
Stripping Costs in the Production Phase of a Surface Mine

(Issued November 2011)

Contents

Preface

Comparison with IFRIC 20

AASB Interpretation 20
Stripping Costs in the Production Phase of a Surface Mine

Paragraphs

References

Background   1 – 5

Scope   6

Issues   7

Consensus   8 – 16

    Recognition of production stripping costs as an asset   8 – 11

    Initial measurement of the stripping activity asset   12 – 13

    Subsequent measurement of the stripping activity asset   14 – 16

Application   Aus16.1 – Aus16.4

Appendix A: Effective date and transition

Basis for Conclusions on IFRIC Interpretation 20

Deleted IFRIC 20 Text

AASB Interpretation 20 *Stripping Costs in the Production Phase of a Surface Mine* is set out in paragraphs 1-Aus16.4 and Appendix A. Interpretations are listed in Australian Accounting Standard AASB 1048 *Interpretation of Standards*. In the absence of explicit guidance, AASB 108 *Accounting Policies, Changes in Accounting Estimates and Errors* provides a basis for selecting and applying accounting policies.

Interpretations

Preface

Introduction

The Australian Accounting Standards Board (AASB) makes Australian Accounting Standards, including Interpretations, to be applied by:

(a)   entities required by the *Corporations Act 2001* to prepare financial reports;

(b)   governments in preparing financial statements for the whole of government and the General Government Sector (GGS); and

(c)   entities in the private or public for-profit or not-for-profit sectors that are reporting entities or that prepare general purpose financial statements.

AASB 1053 *Application of Tiers of Australian Accounting Standards* establishes a differential reporting framework consisting of two tiers of reporting requirements for preparing general purpose financial statements:

(a)   Tier 1: Australian Accounting Standards; and

(b)   Tier 2: Australian Accounting Standards – Reduced Disclosure Requirements.

Tier 1 requirements incorporate International Financial Reporting Standards (IFRSs), including Interpretations, issued by the International Accounting Standards Board (IASB), with the addition of paragraphs on the applicability of each Standard in the Australian environment.

Publicly accountable for-profit private sector entities are required to adopt Tier 1 requirements, and therefore are required to comply with IFRSs. Furthermore, other for-profit private sector entities complying with Tier 1 requirements will simultaneously comply with IFRSs. Some other entities complying with Tier 1 requirements will also simultaneously comply with IFRSs.

Tier 2 requirements comprise the recognition, measurement and presentation requirements of Tier 1 but substantially reduced disclosure requirements in comparison with Tier 1.

Australian Accounting Standards also include requirements that are specific to Australian entities. These requirements may be located in Australian Accounting Standards that incorporate IFRSs or in other Australian Accounting Standards. In most instances, these requirements are either restricted to the not-for-profit or public sectors or include additional disclosures that address domestic, regulatory or other issues. These requirements do not prevent publicly accountable for-profit private sector entities from complying with IFRSs. In developing requirements for public sector entities, the AASB considers the requirements of International Public Sector Accounting Standards (IPSASs), as issued by the International Public Sector Accounting Standards Board (IPSASB) of the International Federation of Accountants.

Main Features of this Interpretation

Application date

This Interpretation applies to annual reporting periods beginning on or after 1 January 2013. Earlier application is permitted for annual reporting periods beginning on or after 1 January 2005 but before 1 January 2013.

Issues

This Interpretation clarifies when production stripping costs should lead to the recognition of an asset and how that asset should be initially and subsequently measured.

Comparison with IFRIC 20

AASB Interpretation 20 *Stripping Costs in the Production Phase of a Surface Mine* incorporates International Financial Reporting Interpretations Committee IFRIC Interpretation 20 *Stripping Costs in the Production Phase of a Surface Mine*, issued by the International Accounting Standards Board. Paragraphs that have been added to this Interpretation (and do not appear in the text of IFRIC 20) are identified with the prefix "Aus", followed by the number of the preceding IFRIC paragraph and decimal numbering.

Entities that comply with AASB Interpretation 20 will simultaneously be in compliance with IFRIC 20.

AASB Interpretation 20

Stripping Costs in the Production Phase of a Surface Mine

References

* *Conceptual Framework for Financial Reporting*
* Accounting Standard AASB 101 *Presentation of Financial Statements*
* Accounting Standard AASB 102 *Inventories*
* Accounting Standard AASB 116 *Property, Plant and Equipment*
* Accounting Standard AASB 138 *Intangible Assets*

Background

1   In surface mining operations, entities may find it necessary to remove mine waste materials ('overburden') to gain access to mineral ore deposits. This waste removal activity is known as 'stripping'.

2   During the development phase of the mine (before production begins), stripping costs are usually capitalised as part of the depreciable cost of building, developing and constructing the mine. Those capitalised costs are depreciated or amortised on a systematic basis, usually by using the units of production method, once production begins.

3   A mining entity may continue to remove overburden and to incur stripping costs during the production phase of the mine.

4   The material removed when stripping in the production phase will not necessarily be 100 per cent waste; often it will be a combination of ore and waste. The ratio of ore to waste can range from uneconomic low grade to profitable high grade. Removal of material with a low ratio of ore to waste may produce some usable material, which can be used to produce inventory. This removal might also provide access to deeper levels of material that have a higher ratio of ore to waste. There can therefore be two benefits accruing to the entity from the stripping activity: usable ore that can be used to produce inventory and improved access to further quantities of material that will be mined in future periods.

5   This Interpretation considers when and how to account separately for these two benefits arising from the stripping activity, as well as how to measure these benefits both initially and subsequently.

Scope

6   This Interpretation applies to waste removal costs that are incurred in surface mining activity during the production phase of the mine ('production stripping costs').

Issues

7   This Interpretation addresses the following issues:

   (a)   recognition of production stripping costs as an asset;

   (b)   initial measurement of the stripping activity asset; and

   (c)   subsequent measurement of the stripping activity asset.

Consensus

Recognition of production stripping costs as an asset

8   To the extent that the benefit from the stripping activity is realised in the form of inventory produced, the entity shall account for the costs of that stripping activity in accordance with the principles of AASB 102 *Inventories*. To the extent the benefit is improved access to ore, the entity shall recognise these costs as a non-current asset, if the criteria in paragraph 9 below are met. This Interpretation refers to the non-current asset as the 'stripping activity asset'.

9   An entity shall recognise a stripping activity asset if, and only if, all of the following are met:

   (a)   it is probable that the future economic benefit (improved access to the ore body) associated with the stripping activity will flow to the entity;

   (b)   the entity can identify the component of the ore body for which access has been improved; and

   (c)   the costs relating to the stripping activity associated with that component can be measured reliably.

10   The stripping activity asset shall be accounted for as an addition to, or as an enhancement of, an existing asset. In other words, the stripping activity asset will be accounted for as *part* of an existing asset.

11   The stripping activity asset's classification as a tangible or intangible asset is the same as the existing asset. In other words, the nature of this existing asset will determine whether the entity shall classify the stripping activity asset as tangible or intangible.

Initial measurement of the stripping activity asset

12   The entity shall initially measure the stripping activity asset at cost, this being the accumulation of costs directly incurred to perform the stripping activity that improves access to the identified component of ore, plus an allocation of directly attributable overhead costs. Some incidental operations may take place at the same time as the production stripping activity, but which are not necessary for the production stripping activity to continue as planned. The costs associated with these incidental operations shall not be included in the cost of the stripping activity asset.

13   When the costs of the stripping activity asset and the inventory produced are not separately identifiable, the entity shall allocate the production stripping costs between the inventory produced and the stripping activity asset by using an allocation basis that is based on a relevant production measure. This production measure shall be calculated for the identified component of the ore body, and shall be used as a benchmark to identify the extent to which the additional activity of creating a future benefit has taken place. Examples of such measures include:

   (a)   cost of inventory produced compared with expected cost;

   (b)   volume of waste extracted compared with expected volume, for a given volume of ore production; and

   (c)   mineral content of the ore extracted compared with expected mineral content to be extracted, for a given quantity of ore produced.

Subsequent measurement of the stripping activity asset

14　After initial recognition, the stripping activity asset shall be carried at either its cost or its revalued amount less depreciation or amortisation and less impairment losses, in the same way as the existing asset of which it is a part.

15　The stripping activity asset shall be depreciated or amortised on a systematic basis, over the expected useful life of the identified component of the ore body that becomes more accessible as a result of the stripping activity. The units of production method shall be applied unless another method is more appropriate.

16　The expected useful life of the identified component of the ore body that is used to depreciate or amortise the stripping activity asset will differ from the expected useful life that is used to depreciate or amortise the mine itself and the related life-of-mine assets. The exception to this are those limited circumstances when the stripping activity provides improved access to the whole of the remaining ore body. For example, this might occur towards the end of a mine's useful life when the identified component represents the final part of the ore body to be extracted.

Application

Aus16.1　This Interpretation applies to:

(a)　each entity that is required to prepare financial reports in accordance with Part 2M.3 of the *Corporations Act 2001* and that is a reporting entity;

(b)　general purpose financial statements of each other reporting entity; and

(c)　financial statements that are, or are held out to be, general purpose financial statements.

Aus16.2　This Interpretation applies to annual reporting periods beginning on or after 1 January 2013.

Aus16.3　This Interpretation may be applied to annual reporting periods beginning on or after 1 January 2005 but before 1 January 2013. When an entity applies this Interpretation to an annual reporting period beginning before 1 January 2013 it shall disclose that fact.

Aus16.4　The requirements specified in this Interpretation apply to the financial statements where information resulting from their application is material in accordance with AASB 1031 *Materiality*.

Appendix A

Effective date and transition

This appendix is an integral part of AASB Interpretation 20 and has the same authority as the other parts of the Interpretation.

A1　[Deleted by the AASB – see paragraphs Aus16.2 and Aus16.3]]

A2　An entity shall apply this Interpretation to production stripping costs incurred on or after the beginning of the earliest period presented.

A3　As at the beginning of the earliest period presented, any previously recognised asset balance that resulted from stripping activity undertaken during the production phase ('predecessor stripping asset') shall be reclassified as a part of an existing asset to which the stripping activity related, to the extent that there remains an identifiable component of the ore body with which the predecessor stripping asset can be associated. Such balances shall be depreciated or amortised over the remaining expected useful life of the identified component of the ore body to which each predecessor stripping asset balance relates.

A4　If there is no identifiable component of the ore body to which that predecessor stripping asset relates, it shall be recognised in opening retained earnings at the beginning of the earliest period presented.

Basis for Conclusions
on IFRIC Interpretation 20

This IFRIC Basis for Conclusions accompanies, but is not part of, AASB Interpretation 20. An IFRIC Basis for Conclusions may be amended to reflect the requirements of the AASB Interpretation and AASB Accounting Standards where they differ from the corresponding International pronouncements.

Introduction

BC1   This Basis for Conclusions summarises the IFRS Interpretations Committee's considerations in reaching its consensus. Individual Committee members gave greater weight to some factors than to others.

Background

BC2   The Committee received a request to issue guidance on the accounting for waste removal ('stripping') costs incurred in the production phase of a surface mine ('production stripping costs'). Accounting for production stripping costs is challenging, because the costs that are incurred may benefit both future and current period production, and there is no specific guidance in IFRSs that addresses this issue.

BC3   Consequently, there is diversity in practice in accounting for production stripping costs—some entities recognise production stripping costs as an expense (a cost of production), some entities capitalise some or all production stripping costs on the basis of a 'life-of-mine ratio' calculation or some similar basis, and some capitalise the costs associated with specific betterments. The Committee decided to develop an Interpretation in response to this diversity in practice.

Scope

BC4   This Interpretation gives guidance on the accounting for stripping costs incurred in the production phase of a surface mine. In developing the Interpretation, the Committee decided to focus only on surface mining activities and not on underground mining activities. This Interpretation applies to the activity of surface mining and therefore to all types of natural resources that are extracted using this process. Where this Interpretation refers to 'extraction of mineral ore', it applies equally to surface mining activities used to extract other natural resources that may not be embedded in an ore deposit but are nevertheless extracted using a surface mining activity, for example coal. However, the Committee decided not to address oil and natural gas extraction, including the question of whether oil sands extraction was a surface mining activity, when it determined the scope of this Interpretation.

BC5   The Committee decided not to include stripping costs incurred during the development phase of a surface mine because there is no significant diversity in practice in accounting for such costs. During the development phase of a surface mine (before production begins), stripping costs are usually capitalised as part of the depreciable cost of building, developing and constructing the mine if it is probable that these costs will be recovered through future mining activity. These capitalised costs are depreciated or amortised on a systematic basis, usually by using the units of production method, once production begins.

Consensus

Recognition of production stripping costs as an asset

BC6   The Committee decided that an entity may create two benefits by undertaking stripping activity (and incurring stripping costs). These benefits are the extraction of the ore in the current period and improved access to the ore body for a future period. The result of this is that the activity creates an inventory asset and a non-current asset.

BC7   The asset recognition criteria included in paragraph 9 of this Interpretation are those referred to in paragraph 4.44 of the *Conceptual Framework for Financial Reporting*. An additional criterion is, however, also included in this Interpretation for recognising the stripping activity asset—that the entity can specifically identify the 'component' of the ore body for which access is being improved. All three criteria must be met for the costs to qualify for recognition as an asset. If the criteria are not met, a stripping activity asset will not be recognised.

BC8 'Component' refers to the specific volume of the ore body that is made more accessible by the stripping activity. The identified component of the ore body would typically be a subset of the total ore body of the mine. A mine may have several components, which are identified during the mine planning stage. As well as providing a basis for measuring the costs reliably at recognition stage, identification of components of the ore body is necessary for the subsequent depreciation or amortisation of the stripping activity asset, which will take place as that identified component of the ore body is mined.

BC9 Identifying components of the ore body requires judgement. The Committee understands that an entity's mine plan will provide the information required to allow these judgements to be made with reasonable consistency.

BC10 This Interpretation also states that the stripping cost asset should be recognised as 'part' of an existing asset. 'Part' refers to the addition to, or enhancement of, the existing asset that relates to the stripping activity asset. The Committee took the view that the stripping activity asset was more akin to being a part of an existing asset, rather than being an asset in its own right. The stripping activity asset might add to or improve a variety of existing assets, for example the mine property (land), the mineral deposit itself, an intangible right to extract the ore or an asset that originated in the mine development phase.

BC11 The Committee decided that it is not necessary for the Interpretation to define whether the benefit created by the stripping activity is tangible or intangible in nature—this will be determined from the nature of the related underlying existing asset.

Initial measurement of the stripping activity asset

BC12 IAS 16 paragraph 16(b) states that the cost of an item of property, plant and equipment includes 'any costs directly attributable to bringing the asset to the location and condition necessary...'. Examples of the types of costs that the Committee would expect to be included as directly attributable overhead costs (paragraph 12 of the Interpretation) would include an allocation of salary costs of the mine supervisor overseeing that component of the mine, and an allocation of rental costs of any equipment that was hired specifically to perform the stripping activity.

BC13 The Committee thought that it was important to be guided by the principle contained in paragraph 21 of IAS 16 when addressing incidental operations in the Interpretation. The Committee is aware that a number of activities are carried out simultaneously in a mine operation, and it thought that it was important for the entity to be aware of what constitutes production stripping activity, and what does not, when considering the measurement of the stripping activity asset. An example of such an incidental operation would be building an access road in the area in which the stripping campaign is taking place.

BC14 The Committee noted that, when inventory is produced at the same time as the stripping activity asset is created, it may be difficult in practice to measure the separate cost of each benefit directly. The Committee agreed that an allocation basis would be needed in order to differentiate between the cost of the inventory produced and the cost of the stripping activity asset.

BC15 In its discussions of the most appropriate allocation basis, the Committee rejected any basis that was based on sales values. The Committee considered that such a basis in the context of stripping costs would be inappropriate because it was not closely linked to the activity taking place. Furthermore, if the current sales price of the relevant mineral was used in determining the allocation basis, the same current sales price would be applied to the volume of the mineral in both the extracted ore and the identified component. Hence the relevant variable would be the volume of mineral in both the extracted ore and the identified component, ie the current sales price would not change the allocation basis. The Committee understood that applying a future sales price basis would involve practical difficulties and that it would be costly in comparison to the benefit that it would provide. From the outreach performed by the staff, the Committee understood that identifying a future sales price for ore that will be mined in the future can be difficult, given the volatility of market prices for many minerals. Further complexities may arise when more than one mineral is present (whether by-products or joint products) when the ore is extracted.

BC16 The Committee decided to require an allocation approach that was based on a relevant production measure, because a production measure was considered to be a good indicator of the nature of the benefits that are generated for the activity taking place in the mine. The production measure basis requires an entity to identify when a level of activity has taken place beyond what would otherwise be expected for the inventory production in the period, and that may have given rise to a future access benefit.

Subsequent measurement of the stripping activity asset

BC17 The Committee decided that the cost of the stripping activity asset should be depreciated or amortised over the expected useful life of the identified component of the ore body that is made more accessible by the activity, on a basis that best reflects the consumption of economic benefits. The units of production method is commonly used, and would be focused only on the identified component of the ore body, the access to which has been improved by the stripping activity. Because the life of the identified component is expected to be only a part of the entire life of the mine, the stripping activity asset will be depreciated or amortised over a shorter period than the life of the mine, unless the stripping activity provides improved access to the whole of the remaining ore body, for example, towards the end of a mine's useful life when the identified component represents the final part of the ore body to be extracted.

BC18 The Committee decided that the principles of this Interpretation would also be applicable to an entity that subsequently accounts for its mine assets at revaluation, although the Committee noted that this method was seldom used. The Committee decided that the subsequent measurement basis of the stripping activity asset should follow that of the existing asset of which it is a part, that is, if the existing asset is measured using a cost basis, then the stripping activity asset would also be measured using a cost basis. The Committee also decided that there was no need for specific impairment guidance to be given and expects that the principles in IAS 36 *Impairment of Assets* would be applied to the existing asset of which the stripping activity asset is a part, and not at the level of the stripping activity asset itself.

Transition

BC19 Because of the complex and lengthy nature of many mining operations, and the past diversity of practice in respect of this issue, the Committee concluded that the cost of applying the change in accounting policy retrospectively would exceed the benefit that would be gained from doing so. The Committee therefore decided that this Interpretation shall require prospective application to production stripping costs incurred on or after the beginning of the earliest period presented.

BC20 The Committee decided to follow the principles in IAS 8 *Accounting Policies, Changes in Accounting Estimates and Errors* on transition. It decided to require recognition of any predecessor stripping asset balances (see paragraph A3) as at the beginning of the earliest period presented, in opening retained earnings at that date, if such balances could not be identified with a remaining component of the ore body that was made more accessible by the stripping activity.

BC21 The Committee noted that any liability balances resulting from prior production stripping activity that existed at the transition date would not be recognised under the principles described in the Interpretation. The Committee understood from the comments received on the draft Interpretation that such balances were uncommon, and therefore did not think that it needed to provide any guidance on recognition of liability balances, because constituents may find it confusing.

Deleted IFRIC 20 Text

Deleted IFRIC Interpretation 20 text is not part of AASB Interpretation 20.

A1 An entity shall apply this Interpretation for annual periods beginning on or after 1 January 2013. Earlier application is permitted. If an entity applies this Interpretation for an earlier period, it shall disclose that fact.

Interpretation 107
Introduction of the Euro

(Compiled November 2009)

Compilation Details

UIG Interpretation 107 *Introduction of the Euro* as amended

This compiled Interpretation applies to annual reporting periods beginning on or after 1 July 2009. It takes into account amendments up to and including 25 June 2009 and was prepared on 10 November 2009 by the staff of the Australian Accounting Standards Board (AASB).

This compilation is not a separate Interpretation issued by the AASB. Instead, it is a representation of Interpretation 107 (July 2004) as amended by other pronouncements, which are listed in the Table below.

Table of Pronouncements

Pronouncement	Month issued	Application date *(annual reporting periods ... on or after ...)*	Application, saving or transitional provisions
Interpretation 107	Jul 2004	*(beginning)* 1 Jan 2005	
AASB 2007-8	Sep 2007	*(beginning)* 1 Jan 2009	see (a) below
AASB 2007-10	Dec 2007	*(beginning)* 1 Jan 2009	see (a) below
AASB 2008-3	Mar 2008	*(beginning)* 1 Jul 2009	see (b) below
AASB 2009-6	Jun 2009	*(beginning)* 1 Jan 2009 and *(ending)* 30 Jun 2009	see (c) below

(a) Entities may elect to apply this Standard to annual reporting periods beginning on or after 1 January 2005 but before 1 January 2009, provided that AASB 101 *Presentation of Financial Statements* (September 2007) is also applied to such periods.

(b) Entities may elect to apply this Standard to annual reporting periods beginning on or after 30 June 2007 but before 1 July 2009, provided that AASB 3 *Business Combinations* (March 2008) and AASB 127 *Consolidated and Separate Financial Statements* (March 2008) are also applied to such periods.

(c) Entities may elect to apply this Standard to annual reporting periods beginning on or after 1 January 2005 but before 1 January 2009, provided that AASB 101 *Presentation of Financial Statements* (September 2007) is also applied to such periods, and to annual reporting periods beginning on or after 1 January 2009 that end before 30 June 2009.

Table of Amendments

Paragraph affected	How affected	By ... [paragraph]
3	amended	AASB 2007-10 [104]
4	amended	AASB 2007-8 [156]
	amended	AASB 2008-3 [82]
Aus4.4	amended	AASB 2007-8 [8]
5	amended	AASB 2007-8 [6]
	amended	AASB 2009-6 [116]
6	amended	AASB 2009-6 [117]
7	amended	AASB 2009-6 [118]

Comparison with SIC-7

UIG Interpretation 107 *Introduction of the Euro* as amended incorporates Standing Interpretations Committee Interpretation SIC-7 *Introduction of the Euro*, issued by the International Accounting Standards Board. Paragraphs that have been added to this Interpretation (and do not appear in the text of SIC-7) are identified with the prefix "Aus", followed by the number of the preceding SIC paragraph and decimal numbering.

Entities that comply with Interpretation 107 as amended will simultaneously be in compliance with SIC-7 as amended.

Interpretation 107

UIG Interpretation 107 was issued in July 2004.

This compiled version of Interpretation 107 applies to annual reporting periods beginning on or after 1 July 2009. It incorporates relevant amendments contained in other AASB pronouncements up to and including 25 June 2009 (see Compilation Details).

Urgent Issues Group

Interpretation 107

Introduction of the Euro

Issue

1   From 1 January 1999, the effective start of Economic and Monetary Union (EMU), the euro will become a currency in its own right and the conversion rates between the euro and the participating national currencies will be irrevocably fixed, that is the risk of subsequent exchange differences related to these currencies is eliminated from this date on.

2   The issue is the application of Accounting Standard AASB 121 *The Effects of Changes in Foreign Exchange Rates* to the changeover from the national currencies of participating Member States of the European Union to the euro ("the changeover").

Consensus

3   **The requirements of AASB 121 regarding the translation of foreign currency transactions and financial statements of foreign operations shall be strictly applied to the changeover. The same rationale applies to the fixing of exchange rates when countries join EMU at later stages.**

4   **This means that, in particular:**

   (a)   **foreign currency monetary assets and liabilities resulting from transactions shall continue to be translated into the functional currency at the closing rate. Any resultant exchange differences shall be recognised as income or expense immediately, except that an entity shall continue to apply its existing accounting policy for exchange gains and losses related to hedges of the currency risk of a forecast transaction;**

   (b)   **cumulative exchange differences relating to the translation of financial statements of foreign operations, recognised in other comprehensive income, shall be accumulated in equity and shall be reclassified from equity to profit or loss only on the disposal or partial disposal of the net investment in the foreign operation; and**

   (c)   **exchange differences resulting from the translation of liabilities denominated in participating currencies shall not be included in the carrying amount of related assets.**

Application

Aus4.1   This Interpretation applies when AASB 121 applies.

Aus4.2   This Interpretation applies to annual reporting periods beginning on or after 1 January 2005.

[Note: For application dates of paragraphs changed or added by an amending pronouncement, see Compilation Details.]

Aus4.3   This Interpretation shall not be applied to annual reporting periods beginning before 1 January 2005.

Aus4.4   The requirements specified in this Interpretation apply to the financial statements where information resulting from their application is material in accordance with AASB 1031 *Materiality*.

Discussion

5   AASB 121.23(a) requires that foreign currency monetary items (as defined by AASB 121.8) be reported using the closing rate at the end of each reporting period. According to AASB 121.28, exchange differences arising from the translation of monetary items generally should be recognised as income or as expenses in the period in which they arise. The effective start of the EMU after the reporting period does not change the application of these requirements at the end of the reporting period; in accordance with AASB 110 *Events after the Reporting Period*, paragraph 10, it is not relevant whether or not the closing rate can fluctuate after the reporting period.

6   AASB 121.5 states that the Standard does not apply to hedge accounting. Therefore, this Interpretation does not address how foreign currency hedges should be accounted for. AASB 108 *Accounting Policies, Changes in Accounting Estimates and Errors* would allow such a change in accounting policy only if the change would result in a more appropriate presentation of events or transactions. The effective start of EMU, of itself, does not justify a change to an entity's established accounting policy related to hedges of forecast transactions because the changeover does not affect the economic rationale of such hedges.[1] Therefore, the changeover should not alter the accounting policy where gains and losses on financial instruments used as hedges of forecast transactions are initially recognised in other comprehensive income and matched with the related income or expense in a future period.

7   AASB 121.48 requires the cumulative amount of exchange differences relating to the translation of the financial statements of a foreign operation that have been recognised in other comprehensive income and accumulated in a separate component of equity in accordance with AASB 121.32 or 121.39(c) to be reclassified from equity to profit or loss in the same period in which the gain or loss on disposal or partial disposal of the foreign operation is recognised. The fact that the cumulative amount of exchange differences will be fixed under EMU does not justify immediate recognition as income or expenses because the wording and the rationale of AASB 121.48 clearly preclude such a treatment.

Date of SIC's Consensus: [Deleted by the UIG]

Effective Date of SIC-7: [Deleted by the UIG]

---

1   The accounting for hedges is now covered under AASB 139 *Financial Instruments: Recognition and Measurement*.

References

Australia

The Urgent Issues Group discussed Issues Paper UIG/SIC 03/1 "Adoption of Interpretation SIC-7 in Australia" at its meetings on 4 December 2003 and 12 February 2004.

Accounting Standard AASB 108 *Accounting Policies, Changes in Accounting Estimates and Errors*

Accounting Standard AASB 110 *Events after the Reporting Period*

Accounting Standard AASB 121 *The Effects of Changes in Foreign Exchange Rates*

Accounting Standard AASB 139 *Financial Instruments: Recognition and Measurement*

International Accounting Standards Board

International Accounting Standard IAS 21 *The Effects of Changes in Foreign Exchange Rates*

Standing Interpretations Committee Interpretation SIC-7 *Introduction of the Euro*

Interpretation 110
Government Assistance – No Specific Relation to Operating Activities

(Compiled November 2009)

Compilation Details

UIG Interpretation 110 *Government Assistance – No Specific Relation to Operating Activities* as amended

This compiled Interpretation applies to annual reporting periods beginning on or after 1 January 2009. It takes into account amendments up to and including 24 September 2007 and was prepared on 10 November 2009 by the staff of the Australian Accounting Standards Board (AASB).

This compilation is not a separate Interpretation issued by the AASB. Instead, it is a representation of Interpretation 110 (July 2004) as amended by other pronouncements, which are listed in the Table below.

Table of Pronouncements

Pronouncement	Month issued	Application date *(annual reporting periods ... on or after ...)*	Application, saving or transitional provisions
Interpretation 110	Jul 2004	*(beginning)* 1 Jan 2005	
AASB 2007-8	Sep 2007	*(beginning)* 1 Jan 2009	see (a) below

(a) Entities may elect to apply this Standard to annual reporting periods beginning on or after 1 January 2005 but before 1 January 2009, provided that AASB 101 *Presentation of Financial Statements* (September 2007) is also applied to such periods.

Table of Amendments

Paragraph affected	How affected	By ... [paragraph]
3	amended	AASB 2007-8 [157]
Aus3.4	amended	AASB 2007-8 [8]

Comparison with SIC-10

UIG Interpretation 110 *Government Assistance – No Specific Relation to Operating Activities* as amended incorporates Standing Interpretations Committee Interpretation SIC-10 *Government Assistance – No Specific Relation to Operating Activities*, issued by the International Accounting Standards Board. Paragraphs that have been added to this Interpretation (and do not appear in the text of SIC-10) are identified with the prefix "Aus", followed by the number of the preceding SIC paragraph and decimal numbering.

Entities that comply with Interpretation 110 as amended will simultaneously be in compliance with SIC-10 as amended.

Interpretation 110

UIG Interpretation 110 was issued in July 2004.

This compiled version of Interpretation 110 applies to annual reporting periods beginning on or after 1 January 2009. It incorporates relevant amendments contained in other AASB pronouncements up to and including 24 September 2007 (see Compilation Details).

Urgent Issues Group

Interpretation 110

Government Assistance – No Specific Relation to Operating Activities

Issue

1　In some countries government assistance to entities may be aimed at encouragement or long-term support of business activities either in certain regions or industry sectors. Conditions to receive such assistance may not be specifically related to the operating activities of the entity. Examples of such assistance are transfers of resources by governments to entities which:

(a)　operate in a particular industry;

(b)　continue operating in recently privatised industries; or

(c)　start or continue to run their business in underdeveloped areas.

2　The issue is whether such government assistance is a "government grant" within the scope of Accounting Standard AASB 120 *Accounting for Government Grants and Disclosure of Government Assistance* and, therefore, should be accounted for in accordance with this Standard.

Consensus

3　**Government assistance to entities meets the definition of government grants in AASB 120, even if there are no conditions specifically relating to the operating activities of the entity other than the requirement to operate in certain regions or industry sectors. Such grants shall therefore not be credited directly to shareholders' interests.**

Application

Aus3.1　This Interpretation applies when AASB 120 applies. AASB 120 applies only in relation to for-profit entities.

Aus3.2　This Interpretation applies to annual reporting periods beginning on or after 1 January 2005.

[Note: For application dates of paragraphs changed or added by an amending pronouncement, see Compilation Details.]

Aus3.3　This Interpretation shall not be applied to annual reporting periods beginning before 1 January 2005.

Aus3.4　The requirements specified in this Interpretation apply to the financial statements where information resulting from their application is material in accordance with AASB 1031 *Materiality*.

Discussion

4　AASB 120.3 defines government grants as assistance by the government in the form of transfers of resources to an entity in return for past or future compliance with certain conditions relating to the operating activities of the entity. The general requirement to operate in certain regions or industry sectors in order to qualify for the government assistance constitutes such a condition in accordance with AASB 120.3. Therefore, such assistance falls within the definition of government grants and the requirements of AASB 120 apply, in particular paragraphs 12 and 20, which deal with the timing of recognition as income.

Date of SIC's Consensus: [Deleted by the UIG]

Effective Date of SIC-10: [Deleted by the UIG]

References

Australia

The Urgent Issues Group discussed Issues Paper UIG/SIC 04/1 "Adoption of Various SIC Interpretations in Australia" in relation to this Interpretation at its meeting on 18 March 2004.

Accounting Standard AASB 120 *Accounting for Government Grants and Disclosure of Government Assistance*

International Accounting Standards Board

International Accounting Standard IAS 20 *Accounting for Government Grants and Disclosure of Government Assistance*

Standing Interpretations Committee Interpretation SIC-10 *Government Assistance – No Specific Relation to Operating Activities*

Interpretation 112
Consolidation – Special Purpose Entities

(Compiled September 2011)

Compilation Details

UIG Interpretation 112 *Consolidation – Special Purpose Entities* as amended

This compiled Interpretation applies to annual reporting periods beginning on or after 1 July 2011 but before 1 January 2013. It takes into account amendments up to and including 11 May 2011 and was prepared on 23 September 2011 by the staff of the Australian Accounting Standards Board (AASB).

This compilation is not a separate Interpretation issued by the AASB. Instead, it is a representation of Interpretation 112 (December 2004) as amended by other pronouncements, which are listed in the Table below.

Table of Pronouncements

Pronouncement	Month issued	Application date *(annual reporting periods ... on or after ...)*	Application, saving or transitional provisions
Interpretation 112	Dec 2004	*(beginning)* 1 Jan 2005	
AASB 2007-8	Sep 2007	*(beginning)* 1 Jan 2009	see (a) below
AASB 2010-5	Oct 2007	*(beginning)* 1 Jan 2011	see (b) below
AASB 2011-1	May 2011	*(beginning)* 1 Jul 2011	see (c) below

(a) Entities may elect to apply this Standard to annual reporting periods beginning on or after 1 January 2005 but before 1 January 2009, provided that AASB 101 *Presentation of Financial Statements* (September 2007) is also applied to such periods.

(b) Entities may elect to apply this Standard to annual reporting periods beginning on or after 1 January 2005 but before 1 January 2011.

(c) Entities may elect to apply this Standard, or its amendments to individual pronouncements, to annual reporting periods beginning on or after 1 January 2005 but before 1 July 2011, provided that AASB 1054 *Australian Additional Disclosures* is, or its relevant individual disclosure requirements are, also applied to such periods.

Table of Amendments to Interpretation

Paragraph affected	How affected	By ... [paragraph]
10	amended	AASB 2010-5 [67]
Aus11.4	amended	AASB 2007-8 [8]
Aus15C.1	deleted	AASB 2011-1 [22]

Table of Amendments to Guidance

Paragraph affected	How affected	By ... [paragraph]
Title, rubric	renamed and amended	AASB 2010-5 [68]
'Indicators of Control...' first para	amended	AASB 2010-5 [69]

Interpretations

Comparison with SIC-12

UIG Interpretation 112 *Consolidation – Special Purpose Entities* as amended incorporates Standing Interpretations Committee Interpretation SIC-12 *Consolidation – Special Purpose Entities*, issued by the International Accounting Standards Board. Paragraphs that have been added to this Interpretation (and do not appear in the text of SIC-12) are identified with the prefix "Aus", followed by the number of the preceding SIC paragraph and decimal numbering.

Entities that comply with Interpretation 112 as amended will simultaneously be in compliance with SIC-12 as amended.

Interpretation 112

UIG Interpretation 112 was issued in December 2004.

This compiled version of Interpretation 112 applies to annual reporting periods beginning on or after 1 July 2011 but before 1 January 2013. It incorporates relevant amendments contained in other AASB pronouncements up to and including 11 May 2011 (see Compilation Details).

Urgent Issues Group

Interpretation 112

Consolidation – Special Purpose Entities

Issue

1   An entity may be created to accomplish a narrow and well-defined objective (e.g., to effect a lease, research and development activities or a securitisation of financial assets). Such a special purpose entity ('SPE') may take the form of a corporation, trust, partnership or unincorporated entity. SPEs often are created with legal arrangements that impose strict and sometimes permanent limits on the decision-making powers of their governing board, trustee or management over the operations of the SPE. Frequently, these provisions specify that the policy guiding the ongoing activities of the SPE cannot be modified, other than perhaps by its creator or sponsor (i.e., they operate on so-called 'autopilot').

2   The sponsor (or entity on whose behalf the SPE was created) frequently transfers assets to the SPE, obtains the right to use assets held by the SPE or performs services for the SPE, while other parties ('capital providers') may provide the funding to the SPE. An entity that engages in transactions with an SPE (frequently the creator or sponsor) may in substance control the SPE.

3   A beneficial interest in an SPE may, for example, take the form of a debt instrument, an equity instrument, a participation right, a residual interest or a lease. Some beneficial interests may simply provide the holder with a fixed or stated rate of return, while others give the holder rights or access to other future economic benefits of the SPE's activities. In most cases, the creator or sponsor (or the entity on whose behalf the SPE was created) retains a significant beneficial interest in the SPE's activities, even though it may own little or none of the SPE's equity.

4   Accounting Standard AASB 127 *Consolidated and Separate Financial Statements* requires the consolidation of entities that are controlled by the reporting entity. However, the Standard does not provide explicit guidance on the consolidation of SPEs.

5   The issue is under what circumstances an entity should consolidate an SPE.

6   This Interpretation does not apply to post-employment benefit plans or other long-term employee benefit plans to which AASB 119 *Employee Benefits* applies.

7   A transfer of assets from an entity to an SPE may qualify as a sale by that entity. Even if the transfer does qualify as a sale, the provisions of AASB 127 and this Interpretation may mean that the entity should consolidate the SPE. This Interpretation does not address the circumstances in which sale treatment should apply for the entity or the elimination of the consequences of such a sale upon consolidation.

Consensus

8   An SPE shall be consolidated when the substance of the relationship between an entity and the SPE indicates that the SPE is controlled by that entity.

9   In the context of an SPE, control may arise through the predetermination of the activities of the SPE (operating on 'autopilot') or otherwise. AASB 127.13 indicates several circumstances which result in control even in cases where an entity owns one half or less of the voting power of another entity. Similarly, control may exist even in cases where an entity owns little or none of the SPE's equity. The application of the control concept requires, in each case, judgement in the context of all relevant factors.

10   In addition to the situations described in AASB 127.13, the following circumstances, for example, may indicate a relationship in which an entity controls an SPE and consequently shall consolidate the SPE (additional guidance accompanies this Interpretation):

   (a)   in substance, the activities of the SPE are being conducted on behalf of the entity according to its specific business needs so that the entity obtains benefits from the SPE's operation;

   (b)   in substance, the entity has the decision-making powers to obtain the majority of the benefits of the activities of the SPE or, by setting up an 'autopilot' mechanism, the entity has delegated these decision making powers;

   (c)   in substance, the entity has rights to obtain the majority of the benefits of the SPE and therefore may be exposed to risks incident to the activities of the SPE; or

   (d)   in substance, the entity retains the majority of the residual or ownership risks related to the SPE or its assets in order to obtain benefits from its activities.

11   [Deleted by the IASB]

Application

Aus11.1   This Interpretation applies when AASB 127 applies.

Aus11.2   This Interpretation applies to annual reporting periods beginning on or after 1 January 2005.
[Note: For application dates of paragraphs changed or added by an amending pronouncement, see Compilation Details.]

Aus11.3   This Interpretation shall not be applied to annual reporting periods beginning before 1 January 2005.

Aus11.4   The requirements specified in this Interpretation apply to the financial statements where information resulting from their application is material in accordance with AASB 1031 *Materiality*.

Aus11.5   When applicable, this Interpretation supersedes Abstract 28 *Consolidation – Special Purpose Entities*, as issued in July 1999.

Aus11.6   Abstract 28 remains applicable until superseded by this Interpretation.

Discussion

12   AASB 127.12 states that 'Consolidated financial statements shall include all subsidiaries of the parent'. AASB 127.4 defines a parent as 'an entity that has one or more subsidiaries', a subsidiary as 'an entity, including an unincorporated entity such as a partnership, that is controlled by another entity (known as the parent)', and control as 'the power to govern the financial and operating policies of an entity so as to obtain benefits from its activities.' Paragraph 35 of the *Framework for the Preparation and Presentation of Financial Statements* and AASB 108 *Accounting Policies, Changes in Accounting Estimates and Errors*, paragraph 10(b)(ii), require that transactions and other events are accounted for in accordance with their substance and economic reality, and not merely their legal form.

13   Control over another entity requires having the ability to direct or dominate its decision-making, regardless of whether this power is actually exercised. Under the definitions of AASB 127.4, the ability to govern decision-making alone, however, is not sufficient to establish control. The ability to govern decision-making must be accompanied by the objective of obtaining benefits from the entity's activities.

14   SPEs frequently operate in a predetermined way so that no entity has explicit decision-making authority over the SPE's ongoing activities after its formation (i.e., they operate on 'autopilot'). Virtually all rights, obligations, and aspects of activities that could be controlled are predefined and limited by contractual provisions specified or scheduled at inception. In these circumstances, control may exist for the sponsoring party or others with a beneficial interest, even though it may be particularly difficult to assess, because virtually all activities are predetermined. However, the predetermination of the activities of the SPE through an 'autopilot' mechanism often provides evidence that the ability to control has been exercised by the party making the predetermination for its own benefit at the formation of the SPE and is being perpetuated.

15A   In 2004, the UIG amended the scope of Interpretation 112 *Consolidation – Special Purpose Entities*. That amendment is effective for annual periods beginning on or after 1 January 2005. Before that amendment, Interpretation 112 excluded from its scope equity compensation plans and post-employment benefit plans.

15B   Equity compensation plans were excluded from the scope of the superseded UIG Abstract 28 *Consolidation – Special Purpose Entities* because Australian Standards did not specify recognition and measurement requirements for equity compensation benefits. However, AASB 2 *Share-based Payment* specifies recognition and measurement requirements for equity compensation benefits.

15C   AASB 132 *Financial Instruments: Disclosure and Presentation*, paragraphs 33 and 34, which relate to the treatment of treasury shares, should be applied to treasury shares purchased, sold, issued or cancelled in connection with employee share option plans, employee share purchase plans, and all other share-based payment arrangements. However, in some cases, those shares might be held by an employee benefit trust (or similar entity) set up by the entity for the purposes of its share-based payment arrangements. Removing the scope exclusion in Interpretation 112 would require an entity that controls such a trust to consolidate the trust and, in so doing, to apply the requirements of AASB 132 to treasury shares held by the trust.

15D   [Deleted by the UIG]

15E   [Deleted by the UIG]

Date of SIC's Consensus: [Deleted by the UIG]

Effective Date of SIC-12: [Deleted by the UIG]

Guidance on Implementing Interpretation 112

This guidance accompanies, but is not part of, Interpretation 112.

Indicators of Control over an SPE

The examples in paragraph 10 of this Interpretation are intended to indicate types of circumstances that should be considered in evaluating a particular arrangement in light of the substance-over-form principle. The guidance provided in the Interpretation and in this Appendix is not intended to be used as 'a comprehensive checklist' of conditions that must be met cumulatively in order to require consolidation of an SPE.

(a) *Activities*

The activities of the SPE, in substance, are being conducted on behalf of the reporting entity, which directly or indirectly created the SPE according to its specific business needs.

Examples are:

- the SPE is principally engaged in providing a source of long-term capital to an entity or funding to support an entity's ongoing major or central operations; or

- the SPE provides a supply of goods or services that is consistent with an entity's ongoing major or central operations which, without the existence of the SPE, would have to be provided by the entity itself.

Economic dependence of an entity on the reporting entity (such as relations of suppliers to a significant customer) does not, by itself, lead to control.

(b) *Decision-making*

The reporting entity, in substance, has the decision-making powers to control or to obtain control of the SPE or its assets, including certain decision-making powers coming into existence after the formation of the SPE. Such decision-making powers may have been delegated by establishing an 'autopilot' mechanism.

Examples are:

- power to unilaterally dissolve an SPE;

- power to change the SPE's charter or bylaws; or

- power to veto proposed changes of the SPE's charter or bylaws.

(c) *Benefits*

The reporting entity, in substance, has rights to obtain a majority of the benefits of the SPE's activities through a statute, contract, agreement, or trust deed, or any other scheme, arrangement or device. Such rights to benefits in the SPE may be indicators of control when they are specified in favour of an entity that is engaged in transactions with an SPE and that entity stands to gain those benefits from the financial performance of the SPE.

Examples are:

- rights to a majority of any economic benefits distributed by an entity in the form of future net cash flows, earnings, net assets, or other economic benefits; or

- rights to majority residual interests in scheduled residual distributions or in a liquidation of the SPE.

(d) *Risks*

An indication of control may be obtained by evaluating the risks of each party engaging in transactions with an SPE. Frequently, the reporting entity guarantees a return or credit protection directly or indirectly through the SPE to outside investors who provide substantially all of the capital to the SPE. As a result of the guarantee, the entity retains residual or ownership risks and the investors are, in substance, only lenders because their exposure to gains and losses is limited.

Examples are:

*   the capital providers do not have a significant interest in the underlying net assets of the SPE;

*   the capital providers do not have rights to the future economic benefits of the SPE;

*   the capital providers are not substantively exposed to the inherent risks of the underlying net assets or operations of the SPE; or

*   in substance, the capital providers receive mainly consideration equivalent to a lender's return through a debt or equity interest.

References

Australia

The Urgent Issues Group discussed Issues Paper 04/4 "Amendment to Scope of Interpretation on Consolidation of Special Purpose Entities" in relation to this amended Interpretation at meetings on 26 August and 25 November 2004. In developing the superseded Interpretation, the UIG discussed Issues Paper UIG/SIC 04/1 "Adoption of Various SIC Interpretations in Australia" in relation to this Interpretation at its meeting on 18 March 2004.

Accounting Standard AASB 108 *Accounting Policies, Changes in Accounting Estimates and Errors*

Accounting Standard AASB 127 *Consolidated and Separate Financial Statements*

Framework for the Preparation and Presentation of Financial Statements

International Accounting Standards Board

International Accounting Standard IAS 27 *Consolidated and Separate Financial Statements*

Standing Interpretations Committee Interpretation SIC-12 *Consolidation – Special Purpose Entities*

IFRIC Amendment to SIC-12 *Scope of SIC-12 Consolidation – Special Purpose Entities*

IFAC Public Sector Committee

International Public Sector Accounting Standard IPSAS 6 *Consolidated Financial Statements and Accounting for Controlled Entities*

Interpretation 113
Jointly Controlled Entities – Non-Monetary Contributions by Venturers

(Compiled September 2011)

Compilation Details

UIG Interpretation 113 *Jointly Controlled Entities – Non-Monetary Contributions by Venturers* as amended

This compiled Interpretation applies to annual reporting periods beginning on or after 1 July 2011 but before 1 January 2013. It takes into account amendments up to and including 11 May 2011 and was prepared on 23 September 2011 by the staff of the Australian Accounting Standards Board (AASB).

This compilation is not a separate Interpretation issued by the AASB. Instead, it is a representation of Interpretation 113 (July 2004) as amended by other pronouncements, which are listed in the Table below.

Table of Pronouncements

Pronouncement	Month issued	Application date *(annual reporting periods ... on or after ...)*	Application, saving or transitional provisions
Interpretation 113	Jul 2004	*(beginning)* 1 Jan 2005	
Erratum	Jul 2007	*(beginning)* 1 Jul 2007	see (a) below
AASB 2007-8	Sep 2007	*(beginning)* 1 Jan 2009	see (b) below
AASB 2011-1	May 2011	*(beginning)* 1 Jul 2011	see (c) below

(a) Entities may elect to apply this Erratum to annual reporting periods beginning on or after 1 January 2005 but before 1 July 2007.

(b) Entities may elect to apply this Standard to annual reporting periods beginning on or after 1 January 2005 but before 1 January 2009, provided that AASB 101 *Presentation of Financial Statements* (September 2007) is also applied to such periods.

(c) Entities may elect to apply this Standard, or its amendments to individual pronouncements, to annual reporting periods beginning on or after 1 January 2005 but before 1 July 2011, provided that AASB 1054 *Australian Additional Disclosures* is, or its relevant individual disclosure requirements are, also applied to such periods.

Table of Amendments

Paragraph affected	How affected	By ... [paragraph]
3	amended	AASB 2007-8 [158]
4	amended	Erratum, Jul 2007
7	amended	Erratum, Jul 2007
	amended	AASB 2007-8 [6]
Aus7.1	deleted	AASB 2011-1 [23]
Aus7.5	amended	AASB 2007-8 [8]

Comparison with SIC-13

UIG Interpretation 113 *Jointly Controlled Entities – Non-Monetary Contributions by Venturers* as amended incorporates Standing Interpretations Committee Interpretation SIC-13 *Jointly-Controlled Entities – Non-Monetary Contributions by Venturers*, issued by the International Accounting Standards Board. Paragraphs that have been added to this Interpretation (and do not appear in the text of SIC-13) are identified with the prefix "Aus", followed by the number of the preceding SIC paragraph and decimal numbering.

Entities that comply with Interpretation 113 as amended will simultaneously be in compliance with SIC-13 as amended.

Interpretation 113

UIG Interpretation 113 was issued in July 2004.

This compiled version of Interpretation 113 applies to annual reporting periods beginning on or after 1 July 2011 but before 1 January 2013. It incorporates relevant amendments contained in other AASB documents up to and including 11 May 2011 (see Compilation Details).

Urgent Issues Group

Interpretation 113

Jointly Controlled Entities – Non-Monetary Contributions by Venturers

References

Accounting Standard AASB 116 *Property, Plant and Equipment*

Accounting Standard AASB 118 *Revenue*

Accounting Standard AASB 131 *Interests in Joint Ventures*

Issue

1   Accounting Standard AASB 131 *Interests in Joint Ventures*, paragraph 48, refers to both contributions and sales between a venturer and a joint venture as follows: 'When a venturer contributes or sells assets to a joint venture, recognition of any portion of a gain or loss from the transaction shall reflect the substance of the transaction.' In addition, AASB 131.24 says that 'a jointly controlled entity is a joint venture that involves the establishment of a corporation, partnership or other entity in which each venturer has an interest.' There is no explicit guidance on the recognition of gains and losses resulting from contributions of non-monetary assets to jointly controlled entities ('JCEs').

2   Contributions to a JCE are transfers of assets by venturers in exchange for an equity interest in the JCE. Such contributions may take various forms. Contributions may be made simultaneously by the venturers either upon establishing the JCE or subsequently. The consideration received by the venturer(s) in exchange for assets contributed to the JCE may also include cash or other consideration that does not depend on future cash flows of the JCE ('additional consideration').

3   The issues are:

   (a)   when the appropriate portion of gains or losses resulting from a contribution of a non-monetary asset to a JCE in exchange for an equity interest in the JCE should be recognised by the venturer in profit or loss;

   (b)   how additional consideration should be accounted for by the venturer; and

   (c)   how any unrealised gain or loss should be presented in the consolidated financial statements of the venturer.

4　This Interpretation deals with the venturer's accounting for non-monetary contributions to a JCE in exchange for an equity interest in the JCE that is accounted for using either the equity method or proportionate consolidation.

Consensus

5　**In applying AASB 131.48 to non-monetary contributions to a JCE in exchange for an equity interest in the JCE, a venturer shall recognise in profit or loss for the period the portion of a gain or loss attributable to the equity interests of the other venturers except when:**

(a)　**the significant risks and rewards of ownership of the contributed non-monetary asset(s) have not been transferred to the JCE;**

(b)　**the gain or loss on the non-monetary contribution cannot be measured reliably; or**

(c)　**the contribution transaction lacks commercial substance, as that term is described in AASB 116 *Property, Plant and Equipment*.**

If exception (a), (b) or (c) applies, the gain or loss is regarded as unrealised and therefore is not recognised in profit or loss unless paragraph 6 also applies.

6　**If, in addition to receiving an equity interest in the JCE, a venturer receives monetary or non-monetary assets, an appropriate portion of gain or loss on the transaction shall be recognised by the venturer in profit or loss.**

7　**Unrealised gains or losses on non-monetary assets contributed to JCEs shall be eliminated against the underlying assets under the proportionate consolidation method or against the investment under the equity method. Such unrealised gains or losses shall not be presented as deferred gains or losses in the venturer's consolidated statement of financial position.**

Aus7.1　[Deleted by the AASB]

Application

Aus7.2　**This Interpretation applies when AASB 131 applies.**

Aus7.3　**This Interpretation applies to annual reporting periods beginning on or after 1 January 2005.**
[Note: For application dates of paragraphs changed or added by an amending pronouncement, see Compilation Details.]

Aus7.4　**This Interpretation shall not be applied to annual reporting periods beginning before 1 January 2005.**

Aus7.5　**The requirements specified in this Interpretation apply to the financial statements where information resulting from their application is material in accordance with AASB 1031 *Materiality*.**

Aus7.6　**When applicable, this Interpretation supersedes Abstract 36 *Non-Monetary Contributions Establishing a Joint Venture Entity*, as issued in December 2000.**

Aus7.7　**Abstract 36 remains applicable until superseded by this Interpretation.**

Discussion

8　AASB 131.48 requires that, while the assets are retained in the joint venture, the venturer should recognise only that portion of the gain or loss which is attributable to the interests of the other venturers. Additional losses are recognised if required by AASB 131.48.

9　AASB 131.48 refers to the transfer of the 'significant risks and rewards of ownership' as a condition for recognition of gains or losses resulting from transactions between venturers and joint ventures. AASB 118 *Revenue*, paragraphs 16(a) to (d), contain examples of situations where the risks and rewards of ownership are typically not transferred. This guidance also applies by analogy to the recognition of gains or losses resulting from contributions of non-monetary assets to JCEs. Since the venturer participates in joint control of the JCE, it retains some 'continuing managerial involvement' in the asset transferred. However, this does not generally preclude the recognition of gains or losses since joint control does not constitute control to the degree usually associated with ownership (AASB 118.14(b)).

10　　Paragraph 92 of the *Framework for the Preparation and Presentation of Financial Statements* states: 'income is recognised in the income statement when an increase in future economic benefits related to an increase in an asset or a decrease of a liability has arisen that can be measured reliably.' AASB 118.14(c) requires, among other conditions, that revenue from the sale of goods should be recognised when 'the amount of revenue can be measured reliably'. The requirement for reliable measurement also applies to the recognition of gains or losses resulting from a contribution of non-monetary assets to a JCE.

11　　AASB 118.12 explains that 'when goods and services are exchanged or swapped for goods or services which are of similar nature and value, the exchange is not regarded as a transaction which generates revenue.'[1] The same rationale applies to a contribution of non-monetary assets since a contribution to a JCE is, in substance, an exchange of assets with the other venturers at the level of the JCE.

12　　To the extent that the venturer also receives cash or non-monetary assets dissimilar to the assets contributed in addition to equity interests in the JCE, the realisation of which is not dependent on the future cash flows of the JCE, the earnings process is complete. Accordingly, the appropriate portion of the gain on the non-monetary contribution is recognised in profit or loss for the period.

13　　It is not appropriate to present unrealised gains or losses on non-monetary assets contributed to JCEs as deferred items since such items do not meet the recognition criteria for assets or liabilities as defined in the *Framework* (paragraphs 53 to 64 and paragraphs 89 to 91).

Date of SIC's Consensus: [Deleted by the UIG]

Effective Date of SIC-13: [Deleted by the UIG]

14　　[Deleted by the UIG]

15　　[Deleted by the UIG]

1　　AASB 116 requires an entity to measure an item of property, plant and equipment acquired in exchange for a non-monetary asset or assets, or a combination of monetary and non-monetary assets, at fair value unless the exchange transaction lacks commercial substance.

Interpretation 115
Operating Leases – Incentives

(Compiled November 2010)

Compilation Details

UIG Interpretation 115 *Operating Leases – Incentives* as amended

This compiled Interpretation applies to annual reporting periods beginning on or after 1 January 2011. It takes into account amendments up to and including 27 October 2010 and was prepared on 26 November 2010 by the staff of the Australian Accounting Standards Board (AASB).

This compilation is not a separate Interpretation issued by the AASB. Instead, it is a representation of Interpretation 115 (July 2004) as amended by other pronouncements, which are listed in the Table below.

Table of Pronouncements

Pronouncement	Month issued	Application date (*annual reporting periods … on or after …*)	Application, saving or transitional provisions
Interpretation 115	Jul 2004	(*beginning*) 1 Jan 2005	
AASB 2007-8	Sep 2007	(*beginning*) 1 Jan 2009	see (a) below
AASB 2009-6	Jun 2009	(*beginning*) 1 Jan 2009 and (*ending*) 30 Jun 2009	see (b) below
AASB 2010-5	Oct 2010	(*beginning*) 1 Jan 2011	see (c) below

(a) Entities may elect to apply this Standard to annual reporting periods beginning on or after 1 January 2005 but before 1 January 2009, provided that AASB 101 *Presentation of Financial Statements* (September 2007) is also applied to such periods.

(b) Entities may elect to apply this Standard to annual reporting periods beginning on or after 1 January 2005 but before 1 January 2009, provided that AASB 101 *Presentation of Financial Statements* (September 2007) is also applied to such periods, and to annual reporting periods beginning on or after 1 January 2009 that end before 30 June 2009.

(c) Entities may elect to apply this Standard to annual reporting periods beginning on or after 1 January 2005 but before 1 January 2011.

Table of Amendments to Interpretation

Paragraph affected	How affected	By … [paragraph]
Aus6.4	amended	AASB 2007-8 [8]
8	amended	AASB 2009-6 [119]
11	amended	AASB 2007-8 [6]
	amended	AASB 2009-6 [120]

Table of Amendments to Illustrative Examples

Paragraph affected	How affected	By … [paragraph]
Title, rubric, heading	renamed and amended	AASB 2010-5 [70-71]
Example 2	amended	AASB 2009-6 [121]

Comparison With SIC-15

UIG Interpretation 115 *Operating Leases – Incentives* as amended incorporates Standing Interpretations Committee Interpretation SIC-15 *Operating Leases – Incentives*, issued by the International Accounting Standards Board. Paragraphs that have been added to this Interpretation (and do not appear in the text of SIC-15) are identified with the prefix "Aus", followed by the number of the preceding SIC paragraph and decimal numbering.

Entities that comply with Interpretation 115 as amended will simultaneously be in compliance with SIC-15 as amended.

Interpretation 115

UIG Interpretation 115 was issued in July 2004.

This compiled version of Interpretation 115 applies to annual reporting periods beginning on or after 1 January 2011. It incorporates relevant amendments contained in other AASB pronouncements up to and including 27 October 2010 (see Compilation Details).

Urgent Issues Group

Interpretation 115

Operating Leases – Incentives

Issue

1   In negotiating a new or renewed operating lease, the lessor may provide incentives for the lessee to enter into the agreement. Examples of such incentives are an up-front cash payment to the lessee or the reimbursement or assumption by the lessor of costs of the lessee (such as relocation costs, leasehold improvements and costs associated with a pre-existing lease commitment of the lessee). Alternatively, initial periods of the lease term may be agreed to be rent-free or at a reduced rent.

2   The issue is how incentives in an operating lease should be recognised in the financial statements of both the lessee and the lessor.

Consensus

3   **All incentives for the agreement of a new or renewed operating lease shall be recognised as an integral part of the net consideration agreed for the use of the leased asset, irrespective of the incentive's nature or form or the timing of payments.**

4   **The lessor shall recognise the aggregate cost of incentives as a reduction of rental income over the lease term, on a straight-line basis unless another systematic basis is representative of the time pattern over which the benefit of the leased asset is diminished.**

5   **The lessee shall recognise the aggregate benefit of incentives as a reduction of rental expense over the lease term, on a straight-line basis unless another systematic basis is representative of the time pattern of the lessee's benefit from the use of the leased asset.**

6   **Costs incurred by the lessee, including costs in connection with a pre-existing lease (for example costs for termination, relocation or leasehold improvements), shall be accounted for by the lessee in accordance with Australian Accounting Standards applicable to those costs, including costs which are effectively reimbursed through an incentive arrangement.**

Application

Aus6.1   This Interpretation applies when Accounting Standard AASB 117 *Leases* applies.

Aus6.2   This Interpretation applies to annual reporting periods beginning on or after 1 January 2005.

[Note: For application dates of paragraphs changed or added by an amending pronouncement, see Compilation Details.]

Aus6.3   This Interpretation shall not be applied to annual reporting periods beginning before 1 January 2005.

Aus6.4   The requirements specified in this Interpretation apply to the financial statements where information resulting from their application is material in accordance with AASB 1031 *Materiality*.

Aus6.5   When applicable, this Interpretation supersedes Abstract 3 *Lessee Accounting for Lease Incentives Under a Non-Cancellable Operating Lease*, as issued in August 1995.

Aus6.6   Abstract 3 remains applicable until superseded by this Interpretation.

Discussion

7   Paragraph 35 of the *Framework for the Preparation and Presentation of Financial Statements* explains that if information is to represent faithfully the transactions and events that it purports to represent, it is necessary that transactions and events are accounted for and presented in accordance with their substance and economic reality and not merely their legal form. AASB 108 *Accounting Policies, Changes in Accounting Estimates and Errors*, paragraph 10(b)(ii), also requires the application of accounting policies which reflect economic substance.

8   Paragraph 22 of the *Framework* and AASB 101 *Presentation of Financial Statements*, paragraph 27, require the preparation of financial statements under the accrual basis of accounting. AASB 117.33 and 117.50 specify the basis on which lessees and lessors respectively should recognise amounts payable or receivable under operating leases.

9   The underlying substance of operating lease arrangements is that the lessor and lessee exchange the use of an asset for a specified period for the consideration of a net amount of money. The accounting periods in which this net amount is recognised by either the lessor or the lessee is not affected by the form of the agreement or the timing of payments. Payments made by a lessor to or on behalf of a lessee, or allowances in rental cost made by a lessor, as incentives for the agreement of a new or renewed lease are an inseparable part of the net amount receivable or payable under the operating lease.

10   Costs incurred by the lessor as incentives for the agreement of new or renewed operating leases are not considered to be part of those initial costs which are added to the carrying amount of the leased asset and recognised as an expense over the lease term on the same basis as the lease income in accordance with AASB 117.52. Initial costs, such as direct costs for administration, advertising and consulting or legal fees, are incurred by a lessor to arrange a contract, whereas incentives in an operating lease are, in substance, related to the consideration for the use of the leased asset.

11   Costs incurred by the lessee on its own behalf are accounted for using the applicable recognition requirements. For example, relocation costs are recognised as an expense in profit or loss in the period in which they are incurred. The accounting for such costs does not depend on whether or not they are effectively reimbursed through an incentive arrangement as they are not related to the consideration for the use of the leased asset.

Date of SIC's Consensus: [Deleted by the UIG]

Effective Date of SIC-15: [Deleted by the UIG]

Illustrative Examples

These examples accompany, but are not part of, Interpretation 115.

Example Application of Interpretation 115

Example 1

An entity agrees to enter into a new lease arrangement with a new lessor. The lessor agrees to pay the lessee's relocation costs as an incentive to the lessee for entering into the new lease. The lessee's moving costs are 1,000. The new lease has a term of 10 years, at a fixed rate of 2,000 per year.

The accounting is:

The lessee recognises relocation costs of 1,000 as an expense in Year 1. Net consideration of 19,000 consists of 2,000 for each of the 10 years in the lease term, less a 1,000 incentive for relocation costs. Both the lessor and lessee would recognise the net rental consideration of 19,000 over the 10 year lease term using a single amortisation method in accordance with paragraphs 4 and 5 of this Interpretation.

Example 2

An entity agrees to enter into a new lease arrangement with a new lessor. The lessor agrees to a rent-free period for the first three years as incentive to the lessee for entering into the new lease. The new lease has a term of 20 years, at a fixed rate of 5,000 per year for years 4 through 20.

The accounting is:

Net consideration of 85,000 consists of 5,000 for each of 17 years in the lease term. Both the lessor and lessee would recognise the net consideration of 85,000 over the 20 year lease term using a single amortisation method in accordance with paragraphs 4 and 5 of this Interpretation.

References

Australia

The Urgent Issues Group discussed Issues Paper UIG/SIC 04/1 "Adoption of Various SIC Interpretations in Australia" in relation to this Interpretation at its meeting on 4 May 2004.

Accounting Standard AASB 101 *Presentation of Financial Statements*

Accounting Standard AASB 108 *Accounting Policies, Changes in Accounting Estimates and Errors*

Accounting Standard AASB 117 *Leases*

Framework for the Preparation and Presentation of Financial Statements

International Accounting Standards Board

International Accounting Standard IAS 17 *Leases*

Standing Interpretations Committee Interpretation SIC-15 *Operating Leases – Incentives*

IFAC Public Sector Committee

International Public Sector Accounting Standard IPSAS 13 *Leases*

Interpretation 125
Income Taxes – Changes in the Tax Status of an Entity or its Shareholders

(Compiled November 2009)

Compilation Details

UIG Interpretation 125 *Income Taxes – Changes in the Tax Status of an Entity or its Shareholders* as amended

This compiled Interpretation applies to annual reporting periods beginning on or after 1 January 2009 that end on or after 30 June 2009. It takes into account amendments up to and including 25 June 2009 and was prepared on 12 November 2009 by the staff of the Australian Accounting Standards Board (AASB).

This compilation is not a separate Interpretation issued by the AASB. Instead, it is a representation of Interpretation 125 (July 2004) as amended by other pronouncements, which are listed in the Table below.

Table of Pronouncements

Pronouncement	Month issued	Application date *(annual reporting periods … on or after …)*	Application, saving or transitional provisions
Interpretation 125	Jul 2004	*(beginning)* 1 Jan 2005	
AASB 2007-8	Sep 2007	*(beginning)* 1 Jan 2009	see (a) below
AASB 2009-6	Jun 2009	*(beginning)* 1 Jan 2009 and *(ending)* 30 Jun 2009	see (b) below

(a) Entities may elect to apply this Standard to annual reporting periods beginning on or after 1 January 2005 but before 1 January 2009, provided that AASB 101 *Presentation of Financial Statements* (September 2007) is also applied to such periods.

(b) Entities may elect to apply this Standard to annual reporting periods beginning on or after 1 January 2005 but before 1 January 2009, provided that AASB 101 *Presentation of Financial Statements* (September 2007) is also applied to such periods, and to annual reporting periods beginning on or after 1 January 2009 that end before 30 June 2009.

Table of Amendments

Paragraph affected	How affected	By … [paragraph]
4	amended	AASB 2007-8 [159]
Aus4.4	amended	AASB 2007-8 [8]
5	amended	AASB 2009-6 [122]
5A	added	AASB 2009-6 [122]
6-8	amended	AASB 2009-6 [122]

Comparison with SIC-25

UIG Interpretation 125 *Income Taxes – Changes in the Tax Status of an Entity or its Shareholders* as amended incorporates Standing Interpretations Committee Interpretation SIC-25 *Income Taxes – Changes in the Tax Status of an Entity or its Shareholders*, issued by the International Accounting Standards Board. Paragraphs that have been added to this Interpretation (and do not appear in the text of SIC-25) are identified with the prefix "Aus", followed by the number of the preceding SIC paragraph and decimal numbering.

Entities that comply with Interpretation 125 as amended will simultaneously be in compliance with SIC-25 as amended.

Interpretation 125

UIG Interpretation 125 was issued in July 2004.

This compiled version of Interpretation 125 applies to annual reporting periods beginning on or after 1 January 2009 that end on or after 30 June 2009. It incorporates relevant amendments contained in other AASB pronouncements up to and including 25 June 2009 (see Compilation Details).

Urgent Issues Group

Interpretation 125

Income Taxes – Changes in the Tax Status
of an Entity or its Shareholders

Issue

1   A change in the tax status of an entity or of its shareholders may have consequences for an entity by increasing or decreasing its tax liabilities or assets. This may, for example, occur upon the public listing of an entity's equity instruments or upon the restructuring of an entity's equity. It may also occur upon a controlling shareholder's move to a foreign country. As a result of such an event, an entity may be taxed differently; it may for example gain or lose tax incentives or become subject to a different rate of tax in the future.

2   A change in the tax status of an entity or its shareholders may have an immediate effect on the entity's current tax liabilities or assets. The change may also increase or decrease the deferred tax liabilities and assets recognised by the entity, depending on the effect the change in tax status has on the tax consequences that will arise from recovering or settling the carrying amount of the entity's assets and liabilities.

3   The issue is how an entity should account for the tax consequences of a change in its tax status or that of its shareholders.

Consensus

4   **A change in the tax status of an entity or its shareholders does not give rise to increases or decreases in amounts recognised outside profit or loss. The current and deferred tax consequences of a change in tax status shall be included in profit or loss for the period, unless those consequences relate to transactions and events that result, in the same or a different period, in a direct credit or charge to the recognised amount of equity or in amounts recognised in other comprehensive income. Those tax consequences that relate to changes in the recognised amount of equity, in the same or a different period (not included in profit or loss), shall be charged or credited directly to equity. Those tax consequences that relate to amounts recognised in other comprehensive income shall be recognised in other comprehensive income.**

Application

Aus4.1   **This Interpretation applies when Accounting Standard AASB 112 *Income Taxes* applies.**

Aus4.2 This Interpretation applies to annual reporting periods beginning on or after 1 January 2005.

[Note: For application dates of paragraphs changed or added by an amending pronouncement, see Compilation Details.]

Aus4.3 This Interpretation shall not be applied to annual reporting periods beginning before 1 January 2005.

Aus4.4 The requirements specified in this Interpretation apply to the financial statements where information resulting from their application is material in accordance with AASB 1031 *Materiality*.

Discussion

5 AASB 112.58 requires current and deferred tax to be included in profit or loss for the period, except to the extent the tax arises from a transaction or event that is recognised outside profit or loss either in other comprehensive income or directly in equity, in the same or a different period (or arises from a business combination). AASB 112.61A requires current and deferred tax to be recognised outside profit or loss if the tax relates to items that are recognised, in the same or a different period, outside profit or loss.

5A AASB 112.62 identifies examples of circumstances in which a transaction or event is recognised in other comprehensive income as permitted or required by another Australian Accounting Standard. All of these circumstances result in changes in the recognised amount of equity through recognition in other comprehensive income.

6 AASB 112.62A identifies examples of circumstances in which a transaction or event is recognised directly in equity as permitted or required by another Australian Accounting Standard. All of these circumstances result in changes in the recognised amount of equity through recognition of a credit or charge directly to equity.

7 AASB 112.65 explains that where the tax base of a revalued asset changes, any tax consequence is recognised in other comprehensive income only to the extent that a related accounting revaluation was or is expected to be recognised in other comprehensive income (revaluation surplus).

8 Because tax consequences recognised outside profit or loss, whether in other comprehensive income or directly in equity, must relate to a transaction or event recognised outside profit or loss in the same or a different period, the cumulative amount of tax recognised outside profit or loss can be expected to be the same amount that would have been recognised outside profit or loss if the new tax status had applied previously. AASB 112.63(b) acknowledges that determining the tax consequences of a change in the tax rate or other tax rules that affects a deferred tax asset or liability and relates to an item previously recognised outside profit or loss may prove to be difficult. Because of this, AASB 112.63 suggests that an allocation may be necessary.

Date of SIC's Consensus: [Deleted by the UIG]

Effective Date of SIC-25: [Deleted by the UIG]

References

Australia

The Urgent Issues Group discussed Issues Paper UIG/SIC 04/1 "Adoption of Various SIC Interpretations in Australia" in relation to this Interpretation at its meeting on 4 May 2004.

Accounting Standard AASB 112 *Income Taxes*

International Accounting Standards Board

International Accounting Standard IAS 12 *Income Taxes*

Standing Interpretations Committee Interpretation SIC-25 *Income Taxes – Changes in the Tax Status of an Entity or its Shareholders*

Interpretation 127
Evaluating the Substance of Transactions Involving the Legal Form of a Lease

(Compiled November 2010)

Compilation Details

UIG Interpretation 127 *Evaluating the Substance of Transactions Involving the Legal Form of a Lease* as amended

This compiled Interpretation applies to annual reporting periods beginning on or after 1 January 2011 but before 1 July 2013. It takes into account amendments up to and including 27 October 2010 and was prepared on 26 November 2010 by the staff of the Australian Accounting Standards Board (AASB).

This compilation is not a separate Interpretation issued by the AASB. Instead, it is a representation of Interpretation 127 (July 2004) as amended by other pronouncements, which are listed in the Table below.

Table of Pronouncements

Pronouncement	Month issued	Application date (*annual reporting periods … on or after …*)	Application, saving or transitional provisions
Interpretation 127	Jul 2004	(*beginning*) 1 Jan 2005	
AASB 2007-8	Sep 2007	(*beginning*) 1 Jan 2009	see (a) below
AASB 2009-6	Jun 2009	(*beginning*) 1 Jan 2009 and (*ending*) 30 Jun 2009	see (b) below
AASB 2010-2	Jun 2010	(*beginning*) 1 Jul 2013	not compiled*
AASB 2010-5	Oct 2010	(*beginning*) 1 Jan 2011	see (c) below

* The amendments made by this Standard are not included in this compilation, which presents the principal Interpretation as applicable to annual reporting periods beginning on or after 1 January 2011 but before 1 July 2013.

(a) Entities may elect to apply this Standard to annual reporting periods beginning on or after 1 January 2005 but before 1 January 2009, provided that AASB 101 *Presentation of Financial Statements* (September 2007) is also applied to such periods.

(b) Entities may elect to apply this Standard to annual reporting periods beginning on or after 1 January 2005 but before 1 January 2009, provided that AASB 101 *Presentation of Financial Statements* (September 2007) is also applied to such periods, and to annual reporting periods beginning on or after 1 January 2009 that end before 30 June 2009.

(c) Entities may elect to apply this Standard to annual reporting periods beginning on or after 1 January 2005 but before 1 January 2011.

Table of Amendments to Interpretation

Paragraph affected	How affected	By ... [paragraph]
2	amended	AASB 2010-5 [72]
3	amended	AASB 2010-5 [73]
5	amended	AASB 2010-5 [74]
9	amended	AASB 2007-8 [6]
10	amended	AASB 2007-8 [6]
Aus11.1	amended	AASB 2007-8 [7, 8]
Aus11.4	amended	AASB 2007-8 [8]
14	amended	AASB 2009-6 [123]
16	amended	AASB 2010-5 [75]

Table of Amendments to Guidance

Paragraph affected	How affected	By ... [paragraph]
A, title, rubric, heading	renamed and amended	AASB 2010-5 [76-77]
A2	amended	AASB 2010-5 [78]
B, title, rubric, heading	renamed and amended	AASB 2010-5 [79]
B2	amended	AASB 2010-5 [80]

Comparison with SIC-27

UIG Interpretation 127 *Evaluating the Substance of Transactions Involving the Legal Form of a Lease* as amended incorporates Standing Interpretations Committee Interpretation SIC-27 *Evaluating the Substance of Transactions Involving the Legal Form of a Lease*, issued by the International Accounting Standards Board. Paragraphs that have been added to this Interpretation (and do not appear in the text of SIC-27) are identified with the prefix "Aus", followed by the number of the preceding SIC paragraph and decimal numbering.

Entities that comply with Interpretation 127 as amended will simultaneously be in compliance with SIC-27 as amended.

Interpretation 127

UIG Interpretation 127 was issued in July 2004.

This compiled version of Interpretation 127 applies to annual reporting periods beginning on or after 1 January 2011 but before 1 July 2013. It incorporates relevant amendments contained in other AASB pronouncements up to and including 27 October 2010 (see Compilation Details).

Urgent Issues Group

Interpretation 127

Evaluating the Substance of Transactions Involving the Legal Form of a Lease

Issue

1   An entity may enter into a transaction or a series of structured transactions (an arrangement) with an unrelated party or parties (an Investor) that involves the legal form of a lease. For example, an entity may lease assets to an Investor and lease the same assets back, or alternatively, legally sell assets and lease the same assets back. The form of each arrangement and its terms and conditions can vary significantly. In the lease and leaseback example, it may be that the arrangement is designed to achieve a tax advantage for the

Investor that is shared with the entity in the form of a fee, and not to convey the right to use an asset.

2   When an arrangement with an Investor involves the legal form of a lease, the issues are:

(a)   how to determine whether a series of transactions is linked and should be accounted for as one transaction;

(b)   whether the arrangement meets the definition of a lease under Accounting Standard AASB 117 *Leases*; and, if not,

(i)   whether a separate investment account and lease payment obligations that might exist represent assets and liabilities of the entity (e.g., consider the example described in paragraph A2(a) of the guidance accompanying the Interpretation);

(ii)   how the entity should account for other obligations resulting from the arrangement; and

(iii) how the entity should account for a fee it might receive from an Investor.

Consensus

3   **A series of transactions that involve the legal form of a lease is linked and shall be accounted for as one transaction when the overall economic effect cannot be understood without reference to the series of transactions as a whole. This is the case, for example, when the series of transactions are closely interrelated, negotiated as a single transaction, and takes place concurrently or in a continuous sequence. (Part A of the accompanying guidance provides illustrations of application of this Interpretation.)**

4   **The accounting shall reflect the substance of the arrangement. All aspects and implications of an arrangement shall be evaluated to determine its substance, with weight given to those aspects and implications that have an economic effect.**

5   **AASB 117 applies when the substance of an arrangement includes the conveyance of the right to use an asset for an agreed period of time. Indicators that individually demonstrate that an arrangement may not, in substance, involve a lease under AASB 117 include (Part B of the accompanying guidance provides illustrations of application of this Interpretation):**

(a)   **an entity retains all the risks and rewards incident to ownership of an underlying asset and enjoys substantially the same rights to its use as before the arrangement;**

(b)   **the primary reason for the arrangement is to achieve a particular tax result, and not to convey the right to use an asset; and**

(c)   **an option is included on terms that make its exercise almost certain (e.g., a put option that is exercisable at a price sufficiently higher than the expected fair value when it becomes exercisable).**

6   **The definitions and guidance in paragraphs 49-64 of the *Framework for the Preparation and Presentation of Financial Statements* shall be applied in determining whether, in substance, a separate investment account and lease payment obligations represent assets and liabilities of the entity. Indicators that collectively demonstrate that, in substance, a separate investment account and lease payment obligations do not meet the definitions of an asset and a liability and shall not be recognised by the entity include:**

(a)   **the entity is not able to control the investment account in pursuit of its own objectives and is not obligated to pay the lease payments. This occurs when, for example, a prepaid amount is placed in a separate investment account to protect the Investor and may only be used to pay the Investor, the Investor agrees that the lease payment obligations are to be paid from funds in the investment account, and the entity has no ability to withhold payments to the Investor from the investment account;**

(b)   the entity has only a remote risk of reimbursing the entire amount of any fee received from an Investor and possibly paying some additional amount, or, when a fee has not been received, only a remote risk of paying an amount under other obligations (e.g., a guarantee). Only a remote risk of payment exists when, for example, the terms of the arrangement require that a prepaid amount is invested in risk-free assets that are expected to generate sufficient cash flows to satisfy the lease payment obligations; and

(c)   other than the initial cash flows at inception of the arrangement, the only cash flows expected under the arrangement are the lease payments that are satisfied solely from funds withdrawn from the separate investment account established with the initial cash flows.

7   Other obligations of an arrangement, including any guarantees provided and obligations incurred upon early termination, shall be accounted for under AASB 137 *Provisions, Contingent Liabilities and Contingent Assets*, AASB 139 *Financial Instruments: Recognition and Measurement* or AASB 1023 *General Insurance Contracts*, depending on the terms.

8   The criteria in paragraph 20 of AASB 118 *Revenue* shall be applied to the facts and circumstances of each arrangement in determining when to recognise a fee as income that an entity might receive. Factors such as whether there is continuing involvement in the form of significant future performance obligations necessary to earn the fee, whether there are retained risks, the terms of any guarantee arrangements, and the risk of repayment of the fee, shall be considered. Indicators that individually demonstrate that recognition of the entire fee as income when received, if received at the beginning of the arrangement, is inappropriate include:

(a)   obligations either to perform or to refrain from certain significant activities are conditions of earning the fee received, and therefore execution of a legally binding arrangement is not the most significant act required by the arrangement;

(b)   limitations are put on the use of the underlying asset that have the practical effect of restricting and significantly changing the entity's ability to use (e.g., deplete, sell or pledge as collateral) the asset;

(c)   the possibility of reimbursing any amount of the fee and possibly paying some additional amount is not remote. This occurs when, for example;

(i)   the underlying asset is not a specialised asset that is required by the entity to conduct its business, and therefore there is a possibility that the entity may pay an amount to terminate the arrangement early; or

(ii)   the entity is required by the terms of the arrangement, or has some or total discretion, to invest a prepaid amount in assets carrying more than an insignificant amount of risk (e.g., currency, interest rate or credit risk). In this circumstance, the risk of the investment's value being insufficient to satisfy the lease payment obligations is not remote, and therefore there is a possibility that the entity may be required to pay some amount.

9   The fee shall be presented in the statement of comprehensive income based on its economic substance and nature.

Disclosure

10   All aspects of an arrangement that does not, in substance, involve a lease under AASB 117 shall be considered in determining the appropriate disclosures that are necessary to understand the arrangement and the accounting treatment adopted. An entity shall disclose the following in each period that an arrangement exists:

(a)   a description of the arrangement including:

(i)   the underlying asset and any restrictions on its use;

(ii)   the life and other significant terms of the arrangement;

(iii)   the transactions that are linked together, including any options; and

(b)   the accounting treatment applied to any fee received, the amount recognised
       as income in the period, and the line item of the statement of comprehensive
       income in which it is included.

11   The disclosures required in accordance with paragraph 10 of this Interpretation
      shall be provided individually for each arrangement or in aggregate for each class
      of arrangement. A class is a grouping of arrangements with underlying assets of a
      similar nature (e.g., power plants).

Application

Aus11.1   This Interpretation applies to:

(a)   each entity that is required to prepare financial reports in accordance
       with Part 2M.3 of the *Corporations Act 2001* and that is a reporting
       entity;

(b)   general purpose financial statements of each other reporting entity; and

(c)   financial statements that are, or are held out to be, general purpose
       financial statements.

Aus11.2   This Interpretation applies to annual reporting periods beginning on or after
           1 January 2005.
           [Note: For application dates of paragraphs changed or added by an amending pronouncement, see
           Compilation Details.]

Aus11.3   This Interpretation shall not be applied to annual reporting periods beginning
           before 1 January 2005.

Aus11.4   The requirements specified in this Interpretation apply to the financial
           statements where information resulting from their application is material in
           accordance with AASB 1031 *Materiality*.

Aus11.5   When applicable, this Interpretation supersedes Abstract 50 *Evaluating the
           Substance of Transactions involving the Legal Form of a Lease*, as issued in
           September 2002.

Aus11.6   Abstract 50 remains applicable until superseded by this Interpretation.

Discussion

12   Paragraph 9 of AASB 111 *Construction Contracts* requires a group of contracts to be
      treated as a single contract when the group of contracts is negotiated as a single package,
      the contracts are so closely interrelated that they are, in effect, part of a single project with
      an overall profit margin, and the contracts are performed concurrently or in a continuous
      sequence. In such a situation, a series of transactions that involve the legal form of a
      lease are linked and accounted for as one transaction, because the overall economic effect
      cannot be understood without reference to the series of transactions as a whole.

13   An agreement is accounted for as a lease in accordance with AASB 117 when it conveys
      to the lessee in return for a payment or series of payments the right to use an asset for an
      agreed period of time. For information to represent faithfully the transactions it purports
      to represent, paragraph 35 of the *Framework* indicates that it is necessary that transactions
      are accounted for and presented in accordance with their substance and economic reality,
      not merely their legal form.

14   When an entity does not control the assets that will be used to satisfy the lease payment
      obligations, and is not obligated to pay the lease payments, it does not recognise the assets
      and lease payment obligations, because the definitions of an asset and a liability have
      not been met. This is different from the circumstance when an entity controls the assets,
      is obligated to pay the lease payments, and then later transfers assets to a third party
      (including a trust). In that circumstance, the transfer of assets (sometimes called an 'in-
      substance' defeasance) does not by itself relieve the entity of its primary obligation, in the
      absence of legal release. A financial asset and a financial liability, or a portion of either,
      are derecognised only when the requirements of paragraphs 15-37, 39-42, AG36-AG52
      and AG57-AG63 of AASB 139 are met.

15   AASB 1023 provides guidance for recognising and measuring financial guarantees and similar instruments that provide for payments to be made if the debtor fails to make payments when due, if that contract transfers significant insurance risk to the issuer. Financial guarantee contracts that provide for payments to be made in response to changes in relation to a variable (sometimes referred to as an 'underlying') are subject to AASB 139.

16   AASB 118 addresses the accounting treatment of revenue. Paragraph 75 of the *Framework* indicates that gains are no different in nature from revenue. Therefore, the requirements of AASB 118 apply by analogy or otherwise. Example 14(c) in the illustrative examples accompanying AASB 118 states that a fee earned on the execution of a significant act, which is much more significant than any other act, is recognised as income when the significant act has been completed. The example also indicates that it is necessary to distinguish between fees earned on completion of a significant act and fees related to future performance or risks retained.

Date of SIC's Consensus: [Deleted by the UIG]

Effective Date of SIC-27: [Deleted by the UIG]

Guidance on Implementing Interpretation 127

This guidance accompanies, but is not part of, Interpretation 127.

A   Linked Transactions

A1   The Interpretation requires consideration of whether a series of transactions that involve the legal form of a lease are linked to determine whether the transactions are accounted for as one transaction.

A2   Extreme examples of transactions that are viewed as a whole and accounted for as single transactions, include:

    (a)   An entity leases an asset to an Investor (the headlease) and leases the same asset back for a shorter period of time (the sublease). At the end of the sublease period, the entity has the right to buy back the rights of the Investor under a purchase option. If the entity does not exercise its purchase option, the Investor has options available to it under each of which the Investor receives a minimum return on its investment in the headlease – the Investor may put the underlying asset back to the entity, or require the entity to provide a return on the Investor's investment in the headlease.

        The predominant purpose of the arrangement is to achieve a tax advantage for the Investor, which is shared with the entity in the form of a fee, and not to convey the right to use an asset. The Investor pays the fee and prepays the lease payment obligations under the headlease. The agreement requires the amount prepaid to be invested in risk-free assets and, as a requirement of finalising the execution of the legally binding arrangement, placed into a separate investment account held by a Trustee outside of the control of the entity. The fee is retained by the entity.

        Over the term of the sublease, the sublease payment obligations are satisfied with funds of an equal amount withdrawn from the separate investment account. The entity guarantees the sublease payment obligations, and will be required to satisfy the guarantee should the separate investment account have insufficient funds. The entity, but not the Investor, has the right to terminate the sublease early under certain circumstances (e.g., a change in local or international tax law causes the Investor to lose part or all of the tax benefits, or the entity decides to dispose of (e.g., replace, sell or deplete) the underlying asset) and upon payment of a termination value to the Investor. If the entity chooses early termination, then it would pay the termination value from funds withdrawn from the separate investment account, and if the amount remaining in the separate investment account is insufficient, the difference would be paid by the entity. The underlying asset is a specialised asset that the entity requires to conduct its business.

1914
**Evaluating the Substance of Transactions
Involving the Legal Form of a Lease**

(b) An entity leases an asset to another entity for its entire economic life and leases the same asset back under the same terms and conditions as the original lease. The two entities have a legally enforceable right to set off the amounts owing to one another, and an intention to settle these amounts on a net basis.

(c) An entity (Entity A) leases an asset to another entity (Entity B), and obtains a non-recourse loan from a financier (by using the lease rentals and the asset as collateral). Entity A sells the asset subject to the lease and the loan to a trustee, and leases the same asset back. Entity A also concurrently agrees to repurchase the asset at the end of the lease for an amount equal to the sale price. The financier legally releases Entity A from the primary responsibility for the loan, and Entity A guarantees repayment of the non-recourse loan if Entity B defaults on the payments under the original lease. Entity B's credit rating is assessed as AAA and the amounts of the payments under each of the leases are equal. Entity A has a legally enforceable right to set off the amounts owing under each of the leases, and an intention to settle the rights and obligations under the leases on a net basis.

(d) An entity (Entity A) legally sells an asset to another entity (Entity B) and leases the same asset back. Entity B is obligated to put the asset back to Entity A at the end of the lease period at an amount that has the overall practical effect, when also considering the lease payments to be received, of providing Entity B with a yield of LIBOR plus 2 per cent per year on the purchase price.

B   The Substance of an Arrangement

B1   The Interpretation requires consideration of the substance of an arrangement to determine whether it includes the conveyance of the right to use an asset for an agreed period of time.

B2   In each of the examples described in Part A of this guidance, the arrangement does not, in substance, involve a lease under AASB 117 for the following reasons:

(a) in the example described in paragraph A2(a), the arrangement is designed predominantly to generate tax benefits that are shared between the two entities. Even though the periods of the headlease and sublease are different, the options available to each of the entities at the end of the sublease period are structured such that the Investor assumes only an insignificant amount of asset risk during the headlease period. The substance of the arrangement is that the entity receives a fee for executing the agreements, and retains the risks and rewards incident to ownership of the underlying asset.

(b) in the example described in paragraph A2(b), the terms and conditions and period of each of the leases are the same. Therefore, the risks and rewards incident to ownership of the underlying asset are the same as before the arrangement. Further, the amounts owing are offset against one another, and so there is no retained credit risk. The substance of the arrangement is that no transaction has occurred.

(c) in the example described in paragraph A2(c), Entity A retains the risks and rewards incident to ownership of the underlying asset, and the risk of payment under the guarantee is only remote (due to the AAA credit rating). The substance of the arrangement is that Entity A borrows cash, secured by the underlying asset.

(d) in the example described in paragraph A2(d), Entity A's risks and rewards incident to owning the underlying asset do not substantively change. The substance of the arrangement is that Entity A borrows cash, secured by the underlying asset and repayable in instalments over the lease period and in a final lump sum at the end of the lease period. The terms of the option preclude recognition of a sale. Normally, in a sale and leaseback transaction, the risks and rewards incident to owning the underlying asset sold are retained by the seller only during the period of the lease.

References

Australia

The Urgent Issues Group discussed Issues Paper UIG/SIC 04/1 "Adoption of Various SIC Interpretations in Australia" in relation to this Interpretation at its meeting on 4 May 2004.

Accounting Standard AASB 111 *Construction Contracts*

Accounting Standard AASB 117 *Leases*

Accounting Standard AASB 118 *Revenue*

Accounting Standard AASB 137 *Provisions, Contingent Liabilities and Contingent Assets*

Accounting Standard AASB 139 *Financial Instruments: Recognition and Measurement*

Accounting Standard AASB 1023 *General Insurance Contracts*

Framework for the Preparation and Presentation of Financial Statements

International Accounting Standards Board

International Accounting Standard IAS 17 *Leases*

Standing Interpretations Committee Interpretation SIC-27 *Evaluating the Substance of Transactions Involving the Legal Form of a* Lease

IFAC Public Sector Committee

International Public Sector Accounting Standard IPSAS 13 *Leases*

Interpretation 129
Service Concession Arrangements: Disclosures

(Compiled November 2009)

Compilation Details

AASB Interpretation 129 *Service Concession Arrangements: Disclosures* as amended

This compiled Interpretation applies to annual reporting periods beginning on or after 1 January 2009 that end on or after 30 June 2009. It takes into account amendments up to and including 25 June 2009 and was prepared on 12 November 2009 by the staff of the Australian Accounting Standards Board (AASB).

This compilation is not a separate Interpretation issued by the AASB. Instead, it is a representation of Interpretation 129 (February 2007) as amended by other pronouncements, which are listed in the Table below.

Table of Pronouncements

Pronouncement	Month issued	Application date *(annual reporting periods ... on or after ...)*	Application, saving or transitional provisions
Interpretation 129	Feb 2007	*(beginning)* 1 Jan 2008	see (a) below
AASB 2007-8	Sep 2007	*(beginning)* 1 Jan 2009	see (b) below
AASB 2007-10	Dec 2007	*(beginning)* 1 Jan 2009	see (b) below
AASB 2009-6	Jun 2009	*(beginning)* 1 Jan 2009 and *(ending)* 30 Jun 2009	see (c) below

(a) Entities may elect to apply this Interpretation to annual reporting periods beginning on or after 1 January 2005 but before 1 January 2008, provided that AASB Interpretation 12 *Service Concession Arrangements* is also applied to such periods.

(b) Entities may elect to apply this Standard to annual reporting periods beginning on or after 1 January 2005 but before 1 January 2009, provided that AASB 101 *Presentation of Financial Statements* (September 2007) is also applied to such periods.

(c) Entities may elect to apply this Standard to annual reporting periods beginning on or after 1 January 2005 but before 1 January 2009, provided that AASB 101 *Presentation of Financial Statements* (September 2007) is also applied to such periods, and to annual reporting periods beginning on or after 1 January 2009 that end before 30 June 2009.

Table of Amendments

Paragraph affected	How affected	By ... [paragraph]
4	amended	AASB 2007-10 [105]
Aus7.1	amended	AASB 2007-8 [7, 8]
Aus7.4	amended	AASB 2007-8 [8]
8	amended amended	AASB 2007-8 [6] AASB 2007-10 [105]
10	amended amended	AASB 2007-8 [6] AASB 2009-6 [124]

Comparison with SIC-29

AASB Interpretation 129 *Service Concession Arrangements: Disclosures* as amended incorporates Standing Interpretations Committee Interpretation SIC-29 *Service Concession Arrangements: Disclosures*, issued by the International Accounting Standards Board. Paragraphs that have been added to this Interpretation (and do not appear in the text of SIC-29) are identified with the prefix "Aus", followed by the number of the preceding SIC paragraph and decimal numbering.

Entities that comply with Interpretation 129 as amended will simultaneously be in compliance with SIC-29 as amended.

> ### Interpretation 129
> AASB Interpretation 129 was issued in February 2007.
>
> This compiled version of Interpretation 129 applies to annual reporting periods beginning on or after 1 January 2009 that end on or after 30 June 2009. It incorporates relevant amendments contained in other AASB pronouncements up to and including 25 June 2009 (see Compilation Details).

Australian Accounting Standards Board

Interpretation 129

Service Concession Arrangements: Disclosures

References

Accounting Standard AASB 101 *Presentation of Financial Statements*

Accounting Standard AASB 116 *Property, Plant and Equipment*

Accounting Standard AASB 117 *Leases*

Accounting Standard AASB 137 *Provisions, Contingent Liabilities and Contingent Assets*

Accounting Standard AASB 138 *Intangible Assets*

AASB Interpretation 12 *Service Concession Arrangements*

Issue

1   An entity (the operator) may enter into an arrangement with another entity (the grantor) to provide services that give the public access to major economic and social facilities. The grantor may be a public or private sector entity, including a governmental body. Examples of service concession arrangements involve water treatment and supply facilities, motorways, car parks, tunnels, bridges, airports and telecommunication networks. Examples of arrangements that are not service concession arrangements include an entity outsourcing the operation of its internal services (e.g. employee cafeteria, building maintenance, and accounting or information technology functions).

2   A service concession arrangement generally involves the grantor conveying for the period of the concession to the operator:

(a)   the right to provide services that give the public access to major economic and social facilities, and

(b)   in some cases, the right to use specified tangible assets, intangible assets, and/or financial assets,

in exchange for the operator:

(c)   committing to provide the services according to certain terms and conditions during the concession period, and

(d)   when applicable, committing to return at the end of the concession period the rights received at the beginning of the concession period and/or acquired during the concession period.

3   The common characteristic of all service concession arrangements is that the operator both receives a right and incurs an obligation to provide public services.

4   The issue is what information should be disclosed in the notes in the financial statements of an operator and a grantor.

5   Certain aspects and disclosures relating to some service concession arrangements are already addressed by existing Australian Accounting Standards (e.g. Accounting Standard AASB 116 *Property, Plant and Equipment* applies to acquisitions of items of property, plant and equipment, AASB 117 *Leases* applies to leases of assets, and AASB 138 *Intangible Assets* applies to acquisitions of intangible assets). However, a service concession arrangement may involve executory contracts that are not addressed in Australian Accounting Standards, unless the contracts are onerous, in which case AASB 137 *Provisions, Contingent Liabilities and Contingent Assets* applies. Therefore, this Interpretation addresses additional disclosures of service concession arrangements.

Consensus

6   All aspects of a service concession arrangement shall be considered in determining the appropriate disclosures in the notes. An operator and a grantor shall disclose the following in each period:

(a)   a description of the arrangement;

(b)   significant terms of the arrangement that may affect the amount, timing and certainty of future cash flows (e.g. the period of the concession, re-pricing dates and the basis upon which re-pricing or re-negotiation is determined);

(c)   the nature and extent (e.g. quantity, time period or amount as appropriate) of:

(i)   rights to use specified assets;

(ii)   obligations to provide or rights to expect provision of services;

(iii)   obligations to acquire or build items of property, plant and equipment;

(iv)   obligations to deliver or rights to receive specified assets at the end of the concession period;

(v)   renewal and termination options; and

(vi)   other rights and obligations (e.g. major overhauls);

(d)   changes in the arrangement occurring during the period; and

(e)   how the service arrangement has been classified.

6A   An operator shall disclose the amount of revenue and profits or losses recognised in the period on exchanging construction services for a financial asset or an intangible asset.

7   The disclosures required in accordance with paragraph 6 of this Interpretation shall be provided individually for each service concession arrangement or in aggregate for each class of service concession arrangements. A class is a grouping of service concession arrangements involving services of a similar nature (e.g. toll collections, telecommunications and water treatment services).

Application

Aus7.1   This Interpretation applies to:

(a)   each entity that is required to prepare financial reports in accordance with Part 2M.3 of the *Corporations Act 2001* and that is a reporting entity;

(b)   general purpose financial statements of each other reporting entity; and

(c)   financial statements that are, or are held out to be, general purpose financial statements.

Aus7.2   This Interpretation applies to annual reporting periods beginning on or after 1 January 2008.

[Note: For application dates of paragraphs changed or added by an amending pronouncement, see Compilation Details.]

Aus7.3   If an entity applies AASB Interpretation 12 *Service Concession Arrangements* to an annual reporting period beginning on or after 1 January 2005 but before 1 January 2008, this Interpretation shall be applied to that period.

Aus7.4   The requirements specified in this Interpretation apply to the financial statements where information resulting from their application is material in accordance with AASB 1031 *Materiality*.

Aus7.5   When applicable, this Interpretation supersedes UIG Interpretation 129 *Disclosure – Service Concession Arrangements*, as issued in July 2004.

Basis for Conclusions

8   Paragraph 15 of the *Framework for the Preparation and Presentation of Financial Statements* states that the economic decisions taken by users of financial statements require an evaluation of the ability of the entity to generate cash and cash equivalents and of the timing and certainty of their generation. Paragraph 21 of the *Framework* states that financial statements also contain notes and supplementary schedules and other information. For example, they may contain additional information that is relevant to the needs of users about the items in the statement of financial position and statement of comprehensive income. They may also include disclosures about the risks and uncertainties affecting the entity and any resources and obligations not recognised in the statement of financial position.

9   A service concession arrangement often has provisions or significant features that warrant disclosure of information necessary to assist in assessing the amount, timing and certainty of future cash flows, and the nature and extent of the various rights and obligations involved. The rights and obligations associated with the services to be provided usually involve a high level of public involvement (e.g. to provide electricity to a city). Other obligations could include significant acts such as building an infrastructure asset (e.g. power plant) and delivering that asset to the grantor at the end of the concession period.

10   AASB 101 *Presentation of Financial Statements*, paragraph 112(c), requires an entity's notes to provide additional information that is not presented elsewhere in the financial statements, but is relevant to an understanding of any of them. The definition of notes in AASB 101.7 indicates that notes provide narrative descriptions or disaggregations of items disclosed in the statement of financial position, statement of comprehensive income, separate income statement (if presented), statement of changes in equity and statement of cash flows, as well as information about items that do not qualify for recognition in those statements.

Date of SIC's Consensus: [Deleted by the AASB]

Effective Date of SIC-29: [Deleted by the AASB]

Interpretation 131
Revenue – Barter Transactions Involving Advertising Services

(Compiled November 2009)

Compilation Details

UIG Interpretation 131 *Revenue – Barter Transactions Involving Advertising Services* as amended

This compiled Interpretation applies to annual reporting periods beginning on or after 1 January 2009. It takes into account amendments up to and including 24 September 2007 and was prepared on 12 November 2009 by the staff of the Australian Accounting Standards Board (AASB).

This compilation is not a separate Interpretation issued by the AASB. Instead, it is a representation of AASB 131 (July 2004) as amended by other pronouncements, which are listed in the Table below.

Table of Pronouncements

Pronouncement	Month issued	Application date (*annual reporting periods ... on or after ...*)	Application, saving or transitional provisions
Interpretation 131	Jul 2004	(*beginning*) 1 Jan 2005	
AASB 2007-8	Sep 2007	(*beginning*) 1 Jan 2009	see (a) below

(a) Entities may elect to apply this Standard to annual reporting periods beginning on or after 1 January 2005 but before 1 January 2009, provided that AASB 101 *Presentation of Financial Statements* (September 2007) is also applied to such periods.

Table of Amendments

Paragraph affected	How affected	By ... [paragraph]
Aus5.4	amended	AASB 2007-8 [8]

Comparison with SIC-31

UIG Interpretation 131 *Revenue – Barter Transactions Involving Advertising Services* as amended incorporates Standing Interpretations Committee Interpretation SIC-31 *Revenue – Barter Transactions Involving Advertising Services*, issued by the International Accounting Standards Board. Paragraphs that have been added to this Interpretation (and do not appear in the text of SIC-31) are identified with the prefix "Aus", followed by the number of the preceding SIC paragraph and decimal numbering.

Entities that comply with Interpretation 131 as amended will simultaneously be in compliance with SIC-31 as amended.

> ### Interpretation 131
>
> UIG Interpretation 131 was issued in July 2004.
>
> This compiled version of Interpretation 131 applies to annual reporting periods beginning on or after 1 January 2009. It incorporates relevant amendments contained in other AASB pronouncements up to and including 24 September 2007 (see Compilation Details).

Urgent Issues Group

Interpretation 131

Revenue – Barter Transactions Involving Advertising Services

Issue

1. An entity (Seller) may enter into a barter transaction to provide advertising services in exchange for receiving advertising services from its customer (Customer). Advertisements may be displayed on the Internet or poster sites, broadcast on the television or radio, published in magazines or journals, or presented in another medium.

2. In some cases, no cash or other consideration is exchanged between the entities. In some other cases, equal or approximately equal amounts of cash or other consideration are also exchanged.

3. A Seller that provides advertising services in the course of its ordinary activities recognises revenue under Accounting Standard AASB 118 *Revenue* from a barter transaction involving advertising when, amongst other criteria, the services exchanged are dissimilar (AASB 118.12) and the amount of revenue can be measured reliably (AASB 118.20(a)). This Interpretation only applies to an exchange of dissimilar advertising services. An exchange of similar advertising services is not a transaction that generates revenue under AASB 118.

4. The issue is under what circumstances can a Seller reliably measure revenue at the fair value of advertising services received or provided in a barter transaction.

Consensus

5. **Revenue from a barter transaction involving advertising cannot be measured reliably at the fair value of advertising services received. However, a Seller can reliably measure revenue at the fair value of the advertising services it provides in a barter transaction, by reference only to non-barter transactions that:**

    (a) **involve advertising similar to the advertising in the barter transaction;**

    (b) **occur frequently;**

    (c) **represent a predominant number of transactions and amount when compared to all transactions to provide advertising that is similar to the advertising in the barter transaction;**

    (d) **involve cash and/or another form of consideration (e.g., marketable securities, non-monetary assets, and other services) that has a reliably measurable fair value; and**

    (e) **do not involve the same counterparty as in the barter transaction.**

Application

Aus5.1   **This Interpretation applies when AASB 118 applies.**

Aus5.2   **This Interpretation applies to annual reporting periods beginning on or after 1 January 2005.**
[Note: For application dates of paragraphs changed or added by an amending pronouncement, see Compilation Details.]

Aus5.3   **This Interpretation shall not be applied to annual reporting periods beginning before 1 January 2005.**

Aus5.4   **The requirements specified in this Interpretation apply to the financial statements where information resulting from their application is material in accordance with AASB 1031 *Materiality*.**

Aus5.5   **When applicable, this Interpretation supersedes Abstract 49** *Revenue – Barter Transactions involving Advertising Services*, **as issued in August 2002.**

Aus5.6   **Abstract 49 remains applicable until superseded by this Interpretation.**

Discussion

6   AASB 118.9 requires revenue to be measured at the fair value of the consideration received or receivable. When the fair value of the services received cannot be measured reliably, the revenue is measured at the fair value of the services provided, adjusted by the amount of any cash or cash equivalents transferred. AASB 118.26 states that when the outcome of a transaction involving the rendering of services cannot be estimated reliably (e.g., the amount of revenue cannot be measured reliably), revenue should be recognised only to the extent of the expenses recognised that are recoverable. As explained in AASB 118.27, this means that revenue is recognised only to the extent of costs incurred that are expected to be recoverable and, as the outcome of the transactions cannot be estimated reliably, no profit is recognised.

7   Paragraph 31 of the *Framework for the Preparation and Presentation of Financial Statements* states that information has the quality of reliability when it is free from material error and bias and is representationally faithful. Measuring revenue at the fair value of advertising services received from the Customer in a barter transaction is impracticable, because reliable information not available to the Seller is required to support the measurement. Consequently, revenue from a barter transaction involving advertising services is measured at the fair value of the advertising services provided by the Seller to the Customer.

8   AASB 118.7 defines fair value as the amount for which an asset could be exchanged, or a liability settled, between knowledgeable, willing parties in an arm's length transaction. A published price of a service does not constitute reliable evidence of its fair value, unless the price is supported by transactions with knowledgeable and willing parties in an arm's length transaction. For transactions to provide a relevant and reliable basis for support, the services involved are similar, there are many transactions, valuable consideration that can be reliably measured is exchanged, and independent third parties are involved. Consequently, the fair value of advertising services provided in a barter transaction is reliably measurable only when it is supportable by reference to non-barter transactions that have these characteristics.

9   However, a swap of cheques, for example, for equal or substantially equal amounts between the same entities that provide and receive advertising services does not provide reliable evidence of fair value. An exchange of advertising services that also includes only partial cash payment provides reliable evidence of the fair value of the transaction to the extent of the cash component (except when partial cash payments of equal or substantially equal amounts are swapped), but does not provide reliable evidence of the fair value of the entire transaction.

10   Reliable measurement of the fair value of a service also depends on a number of other factors, including the industry, the number of market participants, the nature of the services, and the number of market transactions. In the case of barter transactions involving advertising, the fair value of advertising services is reliably measurable when independent non-barter transactions involving similar advertising provide reliable evidence to substantiate the fair value of the barter exchange.

Date of SIC's Consensus: [Deleted by the UIG]

Effective Date of SIC-31: [Deleted by the UIG]

References

Australia

The Urgent Issues Group discussed Issues Paper UIG/SIC 04/1 "Adoption of Various SIC Interpretations in Australia" in relation to this Interpretation at its meeting on 4 May 2004.

Accounting Standard AASB 118 *Revenue*

Framework for the Preparation and Presentation of Financial Statements

International Accounting Standards Board

International Accounting Standard IAS 18 *Revenue*

Standing Interpretations Committee Interpretation SIC-31 Revenue – *Barter Transactions Involving Advertising Services*

IFAC Public Sector Committee

International Public Sector Accounting Standard IPSAS 9 *Revenue from Exchange Transactions*

Interpretation 132
Intangible Assets – Web Site Costs

(Compiled November 2010)

Compilation Details

UIG Interpretation 132 *Intangible Assets – Web Site Costs* as amended

This compiled Interpretation applies to annual reporting periods beginning on or after 1 January 2011. It takes into account amendments up to and including 27 October 2010 and was prepared on 26 November 2010 by the staff of the Australian Accounting Standards Board (AASB).

This compilation is not a separate Interpretation issued by the AASB. Instead, it is a representation of Interpretation 132 (July 2004) as amended by other pronouncements, which are listed in the Table below.

Table of Pronouncements

Pronouncement	Month issued	Application date (*annual reporting periods ... on or after ...*)	Application, saving or transitional provisions
Interpretation 132	Jul 2004	(*beginning*) 1 Jan 2005	
AASB 2007-8	Sep 2007	(*beginning*) 1 Jan 2009	see (a) below
AASB 2010-5	Oct 2010	(*beginning*) 1 Jan 2011	see (b) below

(a) Entities may elect to apply this Standard to annual reporting periods beginning on or after 1 January 2005 but before 1 January 2009, provided that AASB 101 *Presentation of Financial Statements* (September 2007) is also applied to such periods.

(b) Entities may elect to apply this Standard to annual reporting periods beginning on or after 1 January 2005 but before 1 January 2011.

Table of Amendments to Interpretation

Paragraph affected	How affected	By ... [paragraph]
5	amended	AASB 2007-8 [160]
9	amended	AASB 2010-5 [81]
Aus10.4	amended	AASB 2007-8 [8]

Table of Amendments to Illustrative Example

Paragraph affected	How affected	By ... [paragraph]
Title, rubric	amended	AASB 2010-5 [82]

Comparison with SIC-32

UIG Interpretation 132 *Intangible Assets – Web Site Costs* as amended incorporates Standing Interpretations Committee Interpretation SIC-32 *Intangible Assets – Web Site Costs*, issued by the International Accounting Standards Board. Paragraphs that have been added to this Interpretation (and do not appear in the text of SIC-32) are identified with the prefix "Aus", followed by the number of the preceding SIC paragraph and decimal numbering.

Entities that comply with Interpretation 132 as amended will simultaneously be in compliance with SIC-32 as amended.

Interpretation 132
UIG Interpretation 132 was issued in July 2004.
This compiled version of Interpretation 132 applies to annual reporting periods beginning on or after 1 January 2011. It incorporates relevant amendments contained in other AASB pronouncements up to and including 27 October 2010 (see Compilation Details).

Urgent Issues Group
Interpretation 132
Intangible Assets – Web Site Costs

Issue

1   An entity may incur internal expenditure on the development and operation of its own web site for internal or external access. A web site designed for external access may be used for various purposes such as to promote and advertise an entity's own products and services, provide electronic services, and sell products and services. A web site designed for internal access may be used to store company policies and customer details, and search relevant information.

2   The stages of a web site's development can be described as follows:

(a)   Planning – includes undertaking feasibility studies, defining objectives and specifications, evaluating alternatives and selecting preferences;

(b)   Application and Infrastructure Development – includes obtaining a domain name, purchasing and developing hardware and operating software, installing developed applications and stress testing;

(c)   Graphical Design Development – includes designing the appearance of web pages; and

(d)   Content Development – includes creating, purchasing, preparing and uploading information, either textual or graphical in nature, on the web site before the completion of the web site's development. This information may either be stored in separate databases that are integrated into (or accessed from) the web site or coded directly into the web pages.

3   Once development of a web site has been completed, the Operating stage begins. During this stage, an entity maintains and enhances the applications, infrastructure, graphical design and content of the web site.

4   When accounting for internal expenditure on the development and operation of an entity's own web site for internal or external access, the issues are:

(a)   whether the web site is an internally generated intangible asset that is subject to the requirements of Accounting Standard AASB 138 *Intangible Assets*; and

(b)   the appropriate accounting treatment of such expenditure.

5   This Interpretation does not apply to expenditure on purchasing, developing, and operating hardware (e.g. web servers, staging servers, production servers and Internet connections) of a web site. Such expenditure is accounted for under AASB 116 *Property, Plant and Equipment*. Additionally, when an entity incurs expenditure on an Internet service provider hosting the entity's web site, the expenditure is recognised as an expense under AASB 101.88 and the *Framework* when the services are received.

6   AASB 138 does not apply to intangible assets held by an entity for sale in the ordinary course of business (see AASB 102 *Inventories* and AASB 111 *Construction Contracts*) or leases that fall within the scope of AASB 117 *Leases*. Accordingly, this Interpretation does not apply to expenditure on the development or operation of a web site (or web site software) for sale to another entity. When a web site is leased under an operating lease, the lessor applies this Interpretation. When a web site is leased under a finance lease, the lessee applies this Interpretation after initial recognition of the leased asset.

Consensus

7   An entity's own web site that arises from development and is for internal or external access is an internally generated intangible asset that is subject to the requirements of AASB 138.

8   A web site arising from development shall be recognised as an intangible asset if, and only if, in addition to complying with the general requirements described in AASB 138.21 for recognition and initial measurement, an entity can satisfy the requirements in AASB 138.57. In particular, an entity may be able to satisfy the requirement to demonstrate how its web site will generate probable future economic benefits in accordance with AASB 138.57(d) when, for example, the web site is capable of generating revenues, including direct revenues from enabling orders to be placed. An entity is not able to demonstrate how a web site developed solely or primarily for promoting and advertising its own products and services will generate probable future economic benefits, and consequently all expenditure on developing such a web site shall be recognised as an expense when incurred.

9   Any internal expenditure on the development and operation of an entity's own web site shall be accounted for in accordance with AASB 138. The nature of each activity for which expenditure is incurred (e.g. training employees and maintaining the web site) and the web site's stage of development or post-development shall be evaluated to determine the appropriate accounting treatment (additional guidance is provided in the illustrative example accompanying this Interpretation). For example:

(a) the Planning stage is similar in nature to the research phase in AASB 138.54-.56. Expenditure incurred in this stage shall be recognised as an expense when it is incurred;

(b) the Application and Infrastructure Development stage, the Graphical Design stage and the Content Development stage, to the extent that content is developed for purposes other than to advertise and promote an entity's own products and services, are similar in nature to the development phase in AASB 138.57-.64. Expenditure incurred in these stages shall be included in the cost of a web site recognised as an intangible asset in accordance with paragraph 8 of this Interpretation when the expenditure can be directly attributed and is necessary to creating, producing or preparing the web site for it to be capable of operating in the manner intended by management. For example, expenditure on purchasing or creating content (other than content that advertises and promotes an entity's own products and services) specifically for a web site, or expenditure to enable use of the content (e.g. a fee for acquiring a licence to reproduce) on the web site, shall be included in the cost of development when this condition is met. However, in accordance with AASB 138.71, expenditure on an intangible item that was initially recognised as an expense in previous financial statements shall not be recognised as part of the cost of an intangible asset at a later date (e.g. if the costs of a copyright have been fully amortised, and the content is subsequently provided on a web site);

(c) expenditure incurred in the Content Development stage, to the extent that content is developed to advertise and promote an entity's own products and services (e.g. digital photographs of products), shall be recognised as an expense when incurred in accordance with AASB 138.69(c). For example, when accounting for expenditure on professional services for taking digital photographs of an entity's own products and for enhancing their display, expenditure shall be recognised as an expense as the professional services are received during the process, not when the digital photographs are displayed on the web site; and

(d) the Operating stage begins once development of a web site is complete. Expenditure incurred in this stage shall be recognised as an expense when it is incurred unless it meets the recognition criteria in AASB 138.18.

10   A web site that is recognised as an intangible asset under paragraph 8 of this Interpretation shall be measured after initial recognition by applying the requirements of AASB 138.72-.87. The best estimate of a web site's useful life shall be short.

Application

Aus10.1   This Interpretation applies when AASB 138 applies.

Aus10.2   This Interpretation applies to annual reporting periods beginning on or after 1 January 2005.

[Note: For application dates of paragraphs changed or added by an amending pronouncement, see Compilation Details.]

Aus10.3   This Interpretation shall not be applied to annual reporting periods beginning before 1 January 2005.

Aus10.4   The requirements specified in this Interpretation apply to the financial statements where information resulting from their application is material in accordance with AASB 1031 *Materiality*.

Aus10.5   When applicable, this Interpretation supersedes Abstract 37 *Accounting for Web Site Costs*, as issued in January 2001.

Aus10.6   Abstract 37 remains applicable until superseded by this Interpretation.

Discussion

11   An intangible asset is defined in AASB 138.8 as an identifiable non-monetary asset without physical substance. AASB 138.9 provides computer software as a common example of an intangible asset. By analogy, a web site is another example of an intangible asset.

12   AASB 138.68 requires expenditure on an intangible item to be recognised as an expense when incurred unless it forms part of the cost of an intangible asset that meets the recognition criteria in AASB 138.18-.67. AASB 138.69 requires expenditure on start-up activities to be recognised as an expense when incurred. An entity developing its own web site for internal or external access is not undertaking a start-up activity to the extent that an internally generated intangible asset is created. The requirements and guidance in AASB 138.52-.67, in addition to the general requirements described in AASB 138.21 for recognition and initial measurement of an intangible asset, apply to expenditure incurred on the development of an entity's own web site. As described in AASB 138.65-.67, the cost of a web site recognised as an internally generated intangible asset comprises all expenditure that can be directly attributed and is necessary to creating, producing and preparing the asset for it to be capable of operating in the manner intended by management.

13   AASB 138.54 requires expenditure on research (or on the research phase of an internal project) to be recognised as an expense when incurred. The examples provided in AASB 138.56 are similar to the activities undertaken in the Planning stage of a web site's development. Consequently, expenditure incurred in the Planning stage of a web site's development is recognised as an expense when incurred.

14   AASB 138.57 requires an intangible asset arising from the development phase of an internal project to be recognised only if an entity can demonstrate fulfilment of the six criteria specified. One of the criteria is to demonstrate how a web site will generate probable future economic benefits (AASB 138.57(d)). AASB 138.60 indicates that this criterion is met by assessing the economic benefits to be received from the web site and using the principles in AASB 136 *Impairment of Assets*, which considers the present value of estimated future cash flows from continuing use of the web site. Future economic benefits flowing from an intangible asset, as stated in AASB 138.17, may include revenue from the sale of products or services, cost savings, or other benefits resulting from the use of the asset by the entity. Therefore, future economic benefits from a web site may be assessed when the web site is capable of generating revenues. A web site developed solely or primarily for advertising and promoting an entity's own products and services is not recognised as an intangible asset, because the entity cannot demonstrate the future economic benefits that will flow. Consequently, all expenditure on developing a web site

Interpretations

solely or primarily for promoting and advertising an entity's own products and services is recognised as an expense when incurred.

15   Under AASB 138.21, an intangible asset is recognised if, and only if, it meets specified criteria. AASB 138.65 indicates that the cost of an internally generated intangible asset is the sum of expenditure incurred from the date when the intangible asset first meets the specified recognition criteria. When an entity acquires or creates content for purposes other than to advertise and promote an entity's own products and services, it may be possible to identify an intangible asset (e.g. a licence or a copyright) separate from a web site. However, a separate asset is not recognised when expenditure is directly attributed to creating, producing, and preparing the web site for it to be capable of operating in the manner intended by management – the expenditure is included in the cost of developing the web site.

16   AASB 138.69(c) requires expenditure on advertising and promotional activities to be recognised as an expense when incurred. Expenditure incurred on developing content that advertises and promotes an entity's own products and services (e.g. digital photographs of products) is an advertising and promotional activity, and consequently recognised as an expense when incurred.

17   Once development of a web site is complete, an entity begins the activities described in the Operating stage. Subsequent expenditure to enhance or maintain an entity's own web site is recognised as an expense when incurred unless it meets the recognition criteria in AASB 138.18. AASB 138.20 explains that most subsequent expenditures are likely to maintain the future economic benefits embodied in an existing intangible asset rather than meet the definition of an intangible asset and the recognition criteria set out in AASB 138. In addition, it is often difficult to attribute subsequent expenditure directly to a particular intangible asset rather than to the business as a whole. Therefore, only rarely will subsequent expenditure – expenditure incurred after the initial recognition of a purchased intangible asset or after completion of an internally generated intangible asset – be recognised in the carrying amount of an asset.

18   An intangible asset is measured after initial recognition by applying the requirements of AASB 138.72-.87. The revaluation model in AASB 138.75 is applied only when the fair value of an intangible asset can be determined by reference to an active market. However, as an active market is unlikely to exist for web sites, the cost model applies. Additionally, as indicated in AASB 138.92, many intangible assets are susceptible to technological obsolescence, and given the history of rapid changes in technology, the useful life of web sites will be short.

Date of SIC's Consensus: [Deleted by the UIG]

Effective Date of SIC-32: [Deleted by the UIG]

Illustrative Example

This example accompanies, but is not part of, Interpretation 132. Its purpose is to illustrate examples of expenditure that occur during each of the stages described in paragraphs 2 and 3 of the Interpretation and illustrate application of the Interpretation to assist in clarifying its meaning. It is not intended to be a comprehensive checklist of expenditure that might be incurred.

Example Application of Interpretation 132

Stage / Nature of Expenditure	Accounting treatment
Planning • undertaking feasibility studies • defining hardware and software specifications • evaluating alternative products and suppliers • selecting preferences	Recognise as an expense when incurred in accordance with AASB 138.54
Application and Infrastructure Development • purchasing or developing hardware	Apply the requirements of AASB 116
• obtaining a domain name • developing operating software (e.g. operating system and server software) • developing code for the application • installing developed applications on the web server • stress testing	Recognise as an expense when incurred, unless the expenditure can be directly attributed to preparing the web site to operate in the manner intended by management, and the web site meets the recognition criteria in AASB 138.21 and AASB 138.57*
Graphical Design Development • designing the appearance (e.g. layout and colour) of web pages	Recognise as an expense when incurred, unless the expenditure can be directly attributed to preparing the web site to operate in the manner intended by management, and the web site meets the recognition criteria in AASB 138.21 and AASB 138.57*
Content Development • creating, purchasing, preparing (e.g. creating links and identifying tags), and uploading information, either textual or graphical in nature, on the web site before the completion of the web site's development. Examples of content include information about an entity, products or services offered for sale, and topics that subscribers access	Recognise as an expense when incurred in accordance with AASB 138.69(c) to the extent that content is developed to advertise and promote an entity's own products and services (e.g. digital photographs of products). Otherwise, recognise as an expense when incurred, unless the expenditure can be directly attributed to preparing the web site to operate in the manner intended by management, and the web site meets the recognition criteria in AASB 138.21 and AASB 138.57*
Operating • updating graphics and revising content • adding new functions, features and content • registering the web site with search engines • backing up data • reviewing security access • analysing usage of the web site	Assess whether it meets the definition of an intangible asset and the recognition criteria set out in AASB 138.18, in which case the expenditure is recognised in the carrying amount of the web site asset
Other • selling, administrative and other general overhead expenditure unless it can be directly attributed to preparing the web site for use to operate in the manner intended by management • clearly identified inefficiencies and initial operating losses incurred before the web site achieves planned performance (e.g. false-start testing) • training employees to operate the web site	Recognise as an expense when incurred in accordance with AASB 138.65-.70

* All expenditure on developing a web site solely or primarily for promoting and advertising an entity's own products and services is recognised as an expense when incurred in accordance with AASB 138.68.

References

Australia

The Urgent Issues Group discussed Issues Paper UIG/SIC 04/1 "Adoption of Various SIC Interpretations in Australia" in relation to this Interpretation at its meeting on 4 May 2004.

Accounting Standard AASB 101 *Presentation of Financial Statements*

Accounting Standard AASB 102 *Inventories*

Accounting Standard AASB 111 *Construction Contracts*

Accounting Standard AASB 116 *Property, Plant and Equipment*

Accounting Standard AASB 117 *Leases*

Accounting Standard AASB 136 *Impairment of Assets*

Accounting Standard AASB 138 *Intangible Assets*

Framework for the Preparation and Presentation of Financial Statements

International Accounting Standards Board

International Accounting Standard IAS 38 *Intangible Assets*

Standing Interpretations Committee Interpretation SIC-32 *Intangible Assets – Web Site Costs*

Interpretation 1003
Australian Petroleum Resource Rent Tax

(Issued November 2007)

Contents

Preface

Comparison with International Pronouncements

AASB Interpretation 1003
Australian Petroleum Resource Rent Tax

Paragraphs

References	
Background	1 – 6
Scope	7
Issues	8
Consensus	9
Application	10 – 13
Transition	14

Basis for Conclusion

AASB Interpretation 1003 *Australian Petroleum Resource Rent Tax* is set out in paragraphs 1 – 14. Interpretations are listed in Australian Accounting Standard AASB 1048 *Interpretation and Application of Standards*. In the absence of explicit guidance, AASB 108 *Accounting Policies, Changes in Accounting Estimates and Errors* provides a basis for selecting and applying accounting policies.

Preface

Main Features of AASB Interpretation 1003

Application Date

This Interpretation is applicable to annual reporting periods ending on or after 30 June 2008. Early adoption of this Interpretation is permitted for annual reporting periods beginning on or after 1 January 2005 that end before 30 June 2008.

Issue

This Interpretation specifies that Australian Petroleum Resource Rent Tax falls within the scope of Accounting Standard AASB 112 *Income Taxes*.

Comparison with International Pronouncements

AASB Interpretation 1003 has no corresponding International Financial Reporting Interpretations Committee (IFRIC) Interpretation. Entities that comply with AASB Interpretation 1003 will simultaneously be in compliance with International Financial Reporting Standards, in particular IAS 8 *Accounting Policies, Changes in Accounting Estimates and Errors* and IAS 12 *Income Taxes*.

International Public Sector Accounting Standards (IPSASs) are issued by the International Public Sector Accounting Standards Board of the International Federation of Accountants. There is no specific IPSAS dealing with Australian Petroleum Resource Rent Tax.

Australian Accounting Standards Board
Interpretation 1003
Australian Petroleum Resource Rent Tax

References
Accounting Standard AASB 108 *Accounting Policies, Changes in Accounting Estimates and Errors*

Accounting Standard AASB 112 *Income Taxes*

Background

1 Australian Petroleum Resource Rent Tax (Australian PRRT) is imposed by the *Petroleum Resource Rent Tax Act 1987* at a rate of 40% on the 'taxable profit' of a petroleum project. The calculation of taxable profit is prescribed by the *Petroleum Resource Rent Tax Assessment Act 1987*. Australian PRRT applies to the recovery of all petroleum products from Australian waters other than the North West Shelf and the joint petroleum development area in the Timor Sea.

2 AASB 112 *Income Taxes* deals with accounting for income taxes. AASB 112 provides only limited guidance on what is considered to be an income tax, and divergent interpretations as to whether or not Australian PRRT is an income tax have emerged among Australian reporting entities. Unless AASB 112 specifically applies to Australian PRRT, AASB 108 *Accounting Policies, Changes in Accounting Estimates and Errors* requires that management shall use its judgement in developing and applying an accounting policy that results in information that is relevant to the economic decision-making needs of users and is reliable.

3 In 2005, an Australian constituent requested that the International Financial Reporting Interpretations Committee (IFRIC) clarify the scope of application of IAS 12 *Income Taxes* (AASB 112 is the corresponding Australian Accounting Standard), and identified Australian PRRT (among some other tax and royalty arrangements) as one example of a tax that typically has not been considered to be an income tax.

4 In March 2006, the IFRIC decided not to take a project onto its agenda that would clarify which taxes are within the scope of IAS 12. In its published reasons for not addressing the request for interpretation, the IFRIC explained that its decision was based on "the variety of taxes that exist world-wide and the need for judgement in determining whether some taxes are income taxes" and that, aside from making some general observations about the scope of IAS 12, "guidance ... could not be developed in a reasonable period of time".

5 The general observations made by the IFRIC on the scope of IAS 12 have not curtailed the diversity in practice that has emerged in accounting for Australian PRRT. Some of the different views include accounting for Australian PRRT as:

  (a) a provision, and therefore recognised, measured and presented in accordance with AASB 137 *Provisions, Contingent Liabilities and Contingent Assets*;

  (b) a cost of inventory under AASB 102 Inventories, which is allocated to inventory cost on a units-of-production basis by estimating the total tax expected to be paid over the life of the project;

  (c) a liability that is recognised when an amount becomes payable, measured at the amount payable and presented as an operating expense;

  (d) a liability that is recognised and measured in accordance with deferred tax principles (that is, AASB 112), but presented as an operating expense; and

  (e) an income tax, and therefore recognised, measured and presented in accordance with AASB 112.

6 Concern has been expressed that, in the absence of authoritative guidance, these diverse accounting practices in accounting for Australian PRRT under Australian Accounting Standards will continue. This is considered to undermine the relevance and reliability of general purpose financial statements within Australia.

Scope

7   This Interpretation applies to Australian PRRT.

Issue

8   This Interpretation addresses only the question of whether Australian PRRT falls within the scope of AASB 112 *Income Taxes*.

Consensus

9   Australian PRRT is an income tax within the scope of AASB 112.

Application

10   This Interpretation applies to:

(a)   each entity that is required to prepare financial reports in accordance with Part 2M.3 of the *Corporations Act 2001* and that is a reporting entity;

(b)   general purpose financial statements of each other reporting entity; and

(c)   financial statements that are, or are held out to be, general purpose financial statements.

11   This Interpretation applies to annual reporting periods ending on or after 30 June 2008.

12   This Interpretation may be applied to annual reporting periods beginning on or after 1 January 2005 that end before 30 June 2008. If an entity applies this Interpretation to such an annual reporting period, it shall disclose that fact.

13   The requirements specified in this Interpretation apply to the financial statements where information resulting from their application is material in accordance with AASB 1031 *Materiality*.

Transition

14   Changes in accounting policy shall be accounted for in accordance with AASB 108 *Accounting Policies, Changes in Accounting Estimates and Errors*.

Basis for Conclusions on AASB Interpretation 1003

This AASB Basis for Conclusions accompanies, but is not part of, AASB Interpretation 1003.

BC1   This Basis for Conclusions summarises the Board's considerations in reaching its consensus. Individual Board members gave greater weight to some factors than to others.

Determination of Australian PRRT taxable profit

BC2   Board members noted that Australian PRRT is assessed on a petroleum project basis, and is levied at a rate of 40% on the 'taxable profit' of a project. Taxable profit for Australian PRRT purposes is calculated as the excess of assessable receipts over the sum of:

(a)   eligible expenditures incurred (which include exploration and all project development, operating and decommissioning expenditures);

(b)   undeducted (that is, carried forward) expenditures that are compounded annually at an uplift rate comprising the Australian Government long-term bond rate plus 15% for exploration expenditure or plus 5% for project development and operating expenditure; and

(c)   undeducted exploration expenditures (compounded at the uplift rate) that are transferred from other projects the taxpayer is engaged in or, if the taxpayer is a company in a wholly-owned group, from other projects within the group.

BC3   Other features of the Australian PRRT regime include:

(a)   exploration expenditures in some designated frontier areas are eligible for a 150% uplift;

(b)   some expenditures are not deductible – these include financing costs, private override royalty payments, income tax, goods and services tax, cash bidding arrangements and some indirect administrative costs; and

(c)   Australian PRRT is paid in quarterly instalments, with a final payment (or refund) due following an assessment made by the Commissioner of Taxation on the basis of the Australian PRRT return, which is to be submitted in August each year. Australian PRRT payments are deductible when determining taxable income under the *Income Tax Assessment Act 1997*.

Accounting for income taxes

BC4   The objective of AASB 112 is to prescribe the accounting treatment for income taxes.

BC5   Paragraph 2 of AASB 112 states that "For the purposes of this Standard, income taxes include all domestic and foreign taxes which are based on taxable profits. Income taxes also include taxes, such as withholding taxes, which are payable by a subsidiary, associate or joint venture on distributions to the reporting entity".

BC6   Paragraph 5 of AASB 112 defines a taxable profit as "taxable profit (tax loss) is the profit (loss) for a period, determined in accordance with the rules established by the taxation authorities, upon which income taxes are payable (recoverable)".

BC7   Paragraph 10 of AASB 112 refers to the fundamental principle of AASB 112, that "… an entity shall, with certain limited exceptions, recognise a deferred tax liability (asset) whenever recovery or settlement of the carrying amount of an asset or liability would make future tax payments larger (smaller) than they would be if such recovery or settlement were to have no tax consequences".

Application to Australian PRRT

BC8   In relation to whether Australian PRRT is an income tax, the Board considered whether Australian PRRT is:

(a)   a tax based on taxable profit; and

(b)   based on rules established by a taxation authority.

BC9   Board members noted that the "upon which income taxes are payable (recoverable)" qualification in paragraph 5 of AASB 112 is circular and does not constrain the assessment of whether Australian PRRT is an income tax.

Taxable profit

BC10 Board members noted that AASB 112 does not clearly define the boundaries of what is considered to be 'taxable profit' and therefore an 'income tax'. Board members acknowledged that further, but non-authoritative, guidance has been provided by the International Financial Reporting Interpretations Committee (IFRIC) on the scope of an income tax. This guidance was provided in the March 2006 edition of *IFRIC Update*, which advised that the IFRIC would not add a project to its agenda to provide guidance on the taxes that are within the scope of IAS 12 *Income Taxes* (AASB 112 is the corresponding Australian Accounting Standard).

BC11 Among other things, the reasoning that accompanied the IFRIC agenda decision included that:

(a)   "the term 'taxable profit' implies a notion of a net rather than gross amount"; and

(b)   "because taxable profit is not the same as accounting profit, taxes do not need to be based on a figure that is exactly accounting profit to be within the scope. The latter point is also implied by the requirement in IAS 12 to disclose an explanation of the relationship between tax expense and accounting profit".

BC12 Board members noted that the calculation of Australian PRRT taxable profit (as described at paragraphs BC2 – BC3 above) is a measure of profit that is based on a net amount, whereby the Australian PRRT assessable receipts are reduced by deductible amounts before a taxing rate is levied on the net amount. Board members noted that, under the Australian PRRT regime, deductible amounts can be material in amount in calculating PRRT taxable profit and that material temporary differences can arise between the carrying amounts of assets and liabilities in the balance sheet and their corresponding Australian PRRT tax bases. These factors provide strong supporting evidence that Australian PRRT is a tax based on taxable profit.

BC13 Board members noted that there are differences between the calculation of Australian PRRT taxable profit and accounting profit. These differences can be attributed to specific features of the Australian PRRT regime such as:

(a) the limited extent to which receipts are assessable and expenditures are deductible for Australian PRRT purposes; and

(b) the uplift factor (referred to as 'augmentation') that is applied to undeducted expenditures so that the amount of Australian PRRT payable reflects a tax on what may be considered to be an 'economic return'.

BC14 The existence of such differences was not considered to preclude Australian PRRT from being a tax based on taxable profit. Board members noted that this could be seen to be consistent with the IFRIC's observation that "... because taxable profit is not the same as accounting profit, taxes do not need to be based on a figure that is exactly accounting profit to be within the scope [of IAS 12]. [This] point is also implied by the requirement in IAS 12 to disclose an explanation of the relationship between tax expense and accounting profit".

BC15 Board members noted that it can be difficult to explain the relationship between accounting profit and corporate tax expense in some tax jurisdictions (and given unique tax positions of the taxpaying entity). Regardless, Board members agreed that corporate income tax would be expected to be accounted for as an income tax. Board members therefore expressed the view that although the relationship between Australian PRRT tax expense and accounting profit might not be easily explained, this does not provide sufficient supporting evidence to suggest that Australian PRRT is not an income tax.

Taxation authority

BC16 Board members agreed that Australian PRRT is based on rules established by a taxation authority. They noted that the Parliament of Australia has imposed Australian PRRT through the enactment of the *Petroleum Resource Rent Tax Act 1987* and the *Petroleum Resource Rent Tax Assessment Act 1987*. Australian PRRT is administered by the Australian Taxation Office.

Scope of Interpretation

BC17 The scope of this Interpretation is restricted to the question of whether Australian PRRT is an income tax, given the existence of divergent treatment of Australian PRRT by Australian reporting entities. The Board has not considered whether other tax or royalty regimes that exist in Australia or internationally are income taxes. Instead, Board members noted that AASB 108 must be consulted when determining whether other taxes or royalties are income taxes.

Application of AASB 112

BC18 This Interpretation does not address the application of AASB 112 to the specific features of Australian PRRT. Board members noted that developing application guidance is inconsistent with the objectives of principle-based Standards and Interpretations. Board members contrasted this Interpretation with the provision of application guidance, on the basis that the Interpretation is only clarifying the scope of Australian Accounting Standards, and specifically only in relation to Australian PRRT. However, to avoid doubt regarding the application of AASB 112, Board members emphasised that all the requirements of AASB 112 must be applied to Australian PRRT, including those requirements relating to the definition, recognition, measurement, presentation and disclosure of current and deferred tax relating to Australian PRRT.

Interpretation 1019

The Superannuation Contributions Surcharge

(Compiled November 2009)

Compilation Details

UIG Interpretation 1019 *The Superannuation Contributions Surcharge* as amended

This compiled Interpretation applies to annual reporting periods beginning on or after 1 January 2009. It takes into account amendments up to and including 13 December 2007 and was prepared on 12 November 2009 by the staff of the Australian Accounting Standards Board (AASB).

This compilation is not a separate Interpretation issued by the AASB. Instead, it is a representation of Interpretation 1019 (September 2004) as amended by other pronouncements, which are listed in the Table below.

Table of Pronouncements

Pronouncement	Month issued	Application date *(annual reporting periods ... on or after ...)*	Application, saving or transitional provisions
Interpretation 1019	Sep 2004	*(beginning)* 1 Jan 2005	
AASB 2007-8	Sep 2007	*(beginning)* 1 Jan 2009	see (a) below
AASB 2007-10	Dec 2007	*(beginning)* 1 Jan 2009	see (a) below

(a) Entities may elect to apply this Standard to annual reporting periods beginning on or after 1 January 2005 but before 1 January 2009, provided that AASB 101 *Presentation of Financial Statements* (September 2007) is also applied to such periods.

Table of Amendments

Paragraph affected	How affected	By ... [paragraph]
2	amended	AASB 2007-8 [6]
10	amended	AASB 2007-8 [6]
	amended	AASB 2007-10 [114]
14	amended	AASB 2007-8 [8]
21	amended	AASB 2007-10 [114]
23	amended	AASB 2007-10 [114]

Interpretation 1019

UIG Interpretation 1019 was issued in September 2004.

This compiled version of Interpretation 1019 applies to annual reporting periods beginning on or after 1 January 2009. It incorporates relevant amendments contained in other AASB pronouncements up to and including 13 December 2007 (see Compilation Details).

Urgent Issues Group

Interpretation 1019

The Superannuation Contributions Surcharge

Interpretation 1019 is set out in paragraphs 1 to 23.

Issue

1   The Superannuation Contributions Surcharge (the surcharge) was introduced in the 1996 Federal Budget. The legislation is contained principally in the *Superannuation Contributions Tax (Assessment and Collection) Act 1997* and the related Regulations. It currently applies to surchargeable contributions attributable to a superannuation provider (normally a superannuation plan) for members whose adjusted taxable income exceeds $99,710 for the 2004-05 income year. The threshold is subject to indexation.

2   The surcharge is calculated by the Australian Taxation Office and advised to the superannuation provider via an assessment. Assessments are made in respect of each year ending 30 June, based on members' surchargeable contributions and adjusted taxable income for that year, regardless of the superannuation provider's end of the reporting period.

3   The legislation provides that the superannuation provider holding the surchargeable contributions is liable for the surcharge. The liability may rest with the member or another superannuation provider where benefits have been withdrawn or a pension has begun to be paid before the assessment is made.

4   For years ending on or after 30 June 1998 an advance instalment process was introduced to collect the surcharge. The Australian Taxation Office advises the superannuation provider of the required advance instalment when making the initial assessment. Unfunded schemes may elect not to pay the surcharge until the benefit payment is made, in which case the surcharge amount payable accumulates, accruing interest, until payment is made.

5   Many superannuation providers pass the cost of the surcharge on to members by debiting the cost of the surcharge to each relevant member's account or benefit. However, in some cases the surcharge may be funded from the surplus of a superannuation plan, or an employer may make additional contributions to meet the surcharge.

6   This Interpretation deals with financial reporting by superannuation plans. Superannuation plans are defined in Australian Accounting Standard AAS 25 *Financial Reporting by Superannuation Plans* as arrangements whereby it is agreed between trustees and employers, employees or self-employed persons that benefits be provided upon the retirement of plan members or upon their resignation, death, disablement or other specified event. This Interpretation may also be applicable in analogous circumstances to other entities liable for payment of the superannuation surcharge. As noted in paragraph 3, the legislation places the obligation for payment of the surcharge on superannuation providers. Superannuation providers are defined in the legislation to include trustees of superannuation and approved deposit funds, a provider of retirement savings accounts, a life insurance company or a registered organisation.

7   The issues are:

(a)   is the surcharge a liability and an expense of the superannuation plan; and, if so,

(b)   when should the liability and expense be recognised?

Consensus

8   **The obligation in respect of the superannuation contributions surcharge gives rise to a liability and an expense of a superannuation plan.**

9   **A superannuation plan shall recognise a liability for the superannuation contributions surcharge when the entity has a present obligation (legal or constructive) as a result of a past event, it is probable that an outflow of resources embodying economic**

benefits will be required to settle the obligation and a reliable estimate can be made of the amount of the obligation.

10   The financial statements shall disclose:

(a)   the accounting policy adopted for the recognition of the liability for the superannuation contributions surcharge;

(b)   the amount of the superannuation contributions surcharge recognised as an expense during the reporting period;

(c)   the amount of the liability for the superannuation contributions surcharge recognised as at the end of the reporting period; and

(d)   whether any unrecognised liability for the superannuation contributions surcharge exists as at the end of the reporting period, stating the reasons for not recognising the liability.

Application

11   This Interpretation applies to superannuation plans when Accounting Standard AASB 137 *Provisions, Contingent Liabilities and Contingent Assets* applies.

12   This Interpretation applies to annual reporting periods beginning on or after 1 January 2005.

[Note: For application dates of paragraphs changed or added by an amending pronouncement, see Compilation Details.]

13   This Interpretation shall not be applied to annual reporting periods beginning before 1 January 2005.

14   The requirements specified in this Interpretation apply to the financial statements where information resulting from their application is material in accordance with AASB 1031 *Materiality*.

15   When applicable, this Interpretation supersedes Abstract 19 *The Superannuation Contributions Surcharge*, as issued in July 1998.

16   Abstract 19 remains applicable until superseded by this Interpretation.

Discussion

17   The object of the *Superannuation Contributions Tax (Assessment and Collection) Act 1997* and the related Regulations (the legislation) is to provide for the assessment and collection of the superannuation contributions surcharge payable on surchargeable contributions for individuals whose adjusted taxable income exceeds a certain specified threshold. The legislation provides that the holder of surchargeable contributions for a financial year (usually a superannuation provider) is liable to pay the surcharge. The surcharge is calculated at differential rates, up to a maximum of 12.5%, for adjusted taxable income levels above $99,710 in respect of the income year 2004-05. Threshold amounts for the differential surcharge rates are subject to indexation. Surchargeable contributions are determined as follows:

(a)   for a defined contribution plan, by reference to the tax status of contributions actually paid to superannuation plans. They include taxable contributions, for example, employer contributions, salary sacrifice contributions and contributions by self-employed persons, and may also include a surplus allocated during the year; and

(b)   for a defined benefit plan, by applying an actuarially determined 'notional surchargeable contributions factor' to the member's annual salary.

18   AASB 137 defines a liability as a present obligation of the entity arising from past events, the settlement of which is expected to result in an outflow of resources embodying economic benefits. The *Framework for the Preparation and Presentation of Financial Statements* defines expenses as decreases in economic benefits during the reporting period in the form of outflows or depletions of assets or incurrences of liabilities that result in decreases in equity, other than those relating to distributions to equity participants. Superannuation plans which hold surchargeable contributions are required to make an outflow of resources embodying economic benefits to the Australian Taxation Office.

This Interpretation reflects the view that the obligation to make the outflow is a liability of the plan and gives rise to a corresponding expense.

19 The legislation specifies the basis on which surchargeable contributions for the financial year are to be calculated. Under the legislation, a superannuation plan is liable to pay the superannuation contributions surcharge when it is the holder of surchargeable contributions, or actuarially determined notional surchargeable contributions, in respect of a member. The legislation provides that if a member transfers to another superannuation provider, or is paid a benefit before an assessment is issued, the liability for the surcharge follows the member. Where a superannuation plan has recognised a liability for the surcharge, and the obligation in respect of the surcharge has transferred to another plan or to the member, the plan derecognises the liability.

20 AASB 137 requires a liability to be recognised when an entity has a present obligation as a result of a past event, it is probable that an outflow of resources embodying economic benefits will be required to settle the obligation and the amount can be reliably estimated. This Interpretation requires that a liability for the surcharge be recognised by a plan when these recognition criteria are satisfied. The Interpretation does not require a liability to be recognised where an estimate is not reliable.

21 Whether a reliable estimate of the amount of the superannuation contributions surcharge can be made before the relevant surcharge assessment is received from the Australian Taxation Office will depend on the characteristics of the superannuation plan. For example, differences in the following factors will affect the stage at which a reliable estimate can be made, and therefore a liability recognised in the financial statements of different superannuation plans:

(a) the number and turnover of members;

(b) the size of the plan and the member profile; and

(c) the information available to the trustees on past assessments and the adjusted taxable income of members.

In view of the number of potential factors affecting the estimation process, each superannuation plan makes its own assessment as to when a liability can be reliably measured.

22 This Interpretation deals with the recognition of a liability and an expense of a superannuation plan. It does not deal with the allocation of the surcharge to relevant member's accounts. That is an administrative matter to be determined by the trustees of a plan.

Disclosure

23 This Interpretation requires certain disclosures to be made in respect of the superannuation contributions surcharge. These disclosures will enhance the usefulness and comparability of the financial statements. They are useful input to an assessment of the financial position of a superannuation plan.

References

Australia

The Urgent Issues Group discussed Issues Paper 04/3 "Revision of Various UIG Abstracts for 2005" in relation to this Interpretation at its meeting on 22 July 2004. In developing the superseded Abstract, the UIG discussed Issue Summary 98/1 "The Superannuation Contributions Surcharge" at meetings on 24 March and 18 June 1998.

Accounting Standard AASB 137 *Provisions, Contingent Liabilities and Contingent Assets*

Australian Accounting Standard AAS 25 *Financial Reporting by Superannuation Plans*

Framework for the Preparation and Presentation of Financial Statements

International Accounting Standards Board

International Accounting Standard IAS 37 *Provisions, Contingent Liabilities and Contingent Assets*

Interpretation 1030

Depreciation of Long-Lived Physical Assets: Condition-Based Depreciation and Related Methods

(Compiled November 2009)

Compilation Details

UIG Interpretation 1030 *Depreciation of Long-Lived Physical Assets: Condition-Based Depreciation and Related Methods* as amended

This compiled Interpretation applies to annual reporting periods beginning on or after 1 January 2009. It takes into account amendments up to and including 24 September 2007 and was prepared on 12 November 2009 by the staff of the Australian Accounting Standards Board (AASB).

This compilation is not a separate Interpretation issued by the AASB. Instead, it is a representation of Interpretation 1030 (September 2004) as amended by other pronouncements, which are listed in the Table below.

Table of Pronouncements

Pronouncement	Month issued	Application date *(annual reporting periods ... on or after ...)*	Application, saving or transitional provisions
Interpretation 1030	Sep 2004	*(beginning)* 1 Jan 2005	
AASB 2007-8	Sep 2007	*(beginning)* 1 Jan 2009	see (a) below

(a) Entities may elect to apply this Standard to annual reporting periods beginning on or after 1 January 2005 but before 1 January 2009, provided that AASB 101 *Presentation of Financial Statements* (September 2007) is also applied to such periods.

Table of Amendments

Paragraph affected	How affected	By ... [paragraph]
12	amended	AASB 2007-8 [8]
18	amended	AASB 2007-8 [6]

Interpretation 1030

UIG Interpretation 1030 was issued in September 2004.

This compiled version of Interpretation 1030 applies to annual reporting periods beginning on or after 1 January 2009. It incorporates relevant amendments contained in other AASB pronouncements up to and including 24 September 2007 (see Compilation Details).

Urgent Issues Group

Interpretation 1030

Depreciation of Long-Lived Physical Assets: Condition-Based Depreciation and Related Methods

Interpretation 1030 is set out in paragraphs 1 to 20.

Issue

1   With the adoption of accrual accounting by local, state, territory and Commonwealth governments, there has been increased interest in methods of depreciation of long-lived physical assets, including those assets described as 'infrastructure' assets or an infrastructure system (hereafter, the term 'infrastructure assets' is used to encompass infrastructure assets and infrastructure systems). This interest has intensified with the increased privatisation of public sector activities and the increased application of 'user-pays' and 'purchaser-provider' models of service delivery for public sector entities.

2   Many of the activities of local, state, territory and Commonwealth government entities are capital intensive. For example, there is significant investment in the physical assets that comprise the infrastructure necessary to support the services provided by state, territory and local government road, footpath and sewerage networks; public transport systems; and water storage and distribution systems. Many private sector business entities and public sector trading enterprises also invest heavily in the physical infrastructure necessary to enable them to continue to produce the goods and services they sell. For these public and private sector entities, the depreciation charge is a major expense item, and in some cases the single major expense item.

3   Accounting Standard AASB 116 *Property, Plant and Equipment* requires the depreciable amount of an asset to be allocated on a systematic basis over the asset's useful life. Some commentators argue that depreciation methods that have conventionally been adopted in respect of long-lived physical assets, including infrastructure assets, are not appropriate for such assets, particularly when they are controlled by public sector entities, because, for example:

(a)   these assets have very long useful lives, are often 'complex' assets comprising a number of components and are constantly rehabilitated during the course of their lives, so that it is often not possible to develop a reliable estimate of their useful life;

(b)   variations in estimates of useful life, rate of consumption of future economic benefits (or service potential) or residual value will have a major impact on the operating result of the entity;

(c)   in practice, it is not possible to distinguish between maintenance expenditure and expenditure to enhance the future economic benefits of the asset, so that maintenance and depreciation expenses cannot be reliably determined; and

(d)   the information required to implement these depreciation methods does not 'fit' with the information necessary for asset management purposes.

4   In response to these concerns, some public sector entities have adopted, or are considering the adoption of, alternative approaches to the depreciation of long-lived physical assets. These alternative methods are often described as Condition-Based Depreciation (CBD) methods. While CBD methods may vary in detail, they usually require the condition of the asset to be assessed periodically, often on an annual basis. The cost of restoring the asset from its current condition to a predetermined service level is then estimated and any increase in the restoration cost beyond that estimated in the prior reporting period is recognised as depreciation expense. In addition, all expenditures made in respect of the maintenance and refurbishment of the asset are recognised as an expense in the period in which they are incurred.

5   In many cases, CBD methods are linked to a detailed asset management plan incorporating the estimated maintenance, refurbishment and rehabilitation work required to maintain current or required service levels of the asset over the long term, often 20 years or more. Under some CBD methods, the estimated costs of maintaining the asset over this period are converted to an annual annuity. The annuity is compared with the actual maintenance, refurbishment and rehabilitation expenditures incurred during the reporting period and any shortfall between the amount of the annuity and the expenditure incurred in the period is identified as the depreciation expense because the shortfall represents a deterioration in the service level of the asset. This depreciation expense, together with the maintenance, refurbishment and rehabilitation expenditures incurred during the reporting period, is recognised in profit or loss as an expense.

6   Adoption of CBD or similar methods of depreciation can have a significant impact on the operating results of public and private sector entities. Differing views are held about the extent to which all, or some, CBD methods comply with the requirements of AASB 116. Concern has been expressed that, in the absence of specific authoritative guidance, diverse, and potentially inappropriate, practices may develop and/or become entrenched. Some commentators note that whatever the benefits of CBD and similar methods for asset management, cost projection, cash flow budgeting and pricing purposes, for financial reporting purposes the depreciation method adopted by an entity must comply with the requirements of AASB 116.

7   The issue is what, if any, characteristics of CBD and similar methods of depreciation contravene the requirements of Accounting Standards?

Consensus

8   **Condition-based depreciation and other methods of depreciation of long-lived physical assets, including infrastructure assets, that include any of the following characteristics do not comply with AASB 116, and shall not be adopted:**

     (a)   **the depreciation expense is not determined by reference to the depreciable amount of the asset;**

     (b)   **the depreciation expense is determined without consideration of technical and commercial obsolescence, such as potential changes in consumer demand, and related factors which can influence the consumption or loss of future economic benefits during the reporting period;**

     (c)   **expenditure on maintenance and on enhancement of future economic benefits are not separately identified where reliable measures of these amounts can be determined, and are not recognised as an expense of the reporting period in which the expenditure was incurred in the case of maintenance expenditure or as an asset in respect of asset enhancement expenditure;**

     (d)   **the asset is presumed to be in a steady state and a 'renewals accounting' approach is adopted whereby all expenditure on the asset is recognised as an expense in the period in which it is incurred without consideration of whether that expenditure enhances the future economic benefits of the asset; and**

     (e)   **the major components of complex assets are not identified and are not depreciated separately where this is necessary to reliably determine the depreciation expense of the reporting period.**

Application

9   **This Interpretation applies when AASB 116 applies.**

10   **This Interpretation applies to annual reporting periods beginning on or after 1 January 2005.**

[Note: For application dates of paragraphs changed or added by an amending pronouncement, see Compilation Details.]

11   **This Interpretation shall not be applied to annual reporting periods beginning before 1 January 2005.**

12   The requirements specified in this Interpretation apply to the financial statements where information resulting from their application is material in accordance with AASB 1031 *Materiality*.

13   When applicable, this Interpretation supersedes Abstract 30 *Depreciation of Long-Lived Physical Assets, including Infrastructure Assets: Condition-Based Depreciation and Other Related Methods*, as issued in January 2000.

14   Abstract 30 remains applicable until superseded by this Interpretation.

Discussion

15   AASB 116 requires the depreciable amount of an asset to be allocated over the asset's useful life on a systematic basis that reflects the consumption of the asset's future economic benefits. AASB 116 defines depreciable amount as the cost of an asset, or other amount substituted for cost, less in either case the residual value of the asset. The Standard also requires that expenditure subsequent to the initial recognition of a non-current asset is to be capitalised when, and only when, it is probable that future economic benefits associated with the expenditure will flow to the entity and the cost can be measured reliably.

16   This Interpretation requires the depreciation expense to be determined by reference to the depreciable amount of the asset after consideration of such matters as obsolescence and other factors that might give rise to consumption or loss of the future economic benefits represented by the asset. The Interpretation also requires maintenance and asset enhancement expenditures to be separately identified and recognised in accordance with the requirements of AASB 116 where these amounts can be reliably determined.

17   Condition assessments are used as a mechanism to determine whether, and the extent to which, the future economic benefits of an infrastructure or other long-lived asset have been consumed during the reporting period, and to confirm the pattern of consumption of those future economic benefits. Condition assessments do not involve the pricing of the future economic benefits consumed during a reporting period but can provide input for such purposes. The methodologies adopted for condition assessments will often generate reliable measures of the future economic benefits consumed during the reporting period in accordance with the requirements of AASB 116.

18   Under some CBD and similar methods, the depreciation expense for a reporting period is determined by reference to the current replacement cost, as at the end of the reporting period, of the future economic benefits consumed during that period. Consistent with the requirements of AASB 116, this Interpretation does not allow such an amount to be recognised as a depreciation expense where it would be materially different from that which would be determined by reference to the depreciable amount of the asset. However, where such CBD or similar methods are adopted by public or private sector entities that revalue their assets to current values on a regular basis, the depreciation expense determined under the CBD or similar method may not be materially different from the expense that would have resulted had depreciation expense been determined by reference to the depreciable amount of the asset.

19   This Interpretation prohibits the use of the renewals method of accounting for financial reporting purposes. The renewals method of accounting assumes that the asset is in a steady state and that subsequent expenditure on the asset will not increase future economic benefits of the asset, but will maintain the future economic benefits at existing levels. As such, all expenditure on the asset is treated as maintenance expenditure and recognised as an expense in the period in which it is incurred, and an additional depreciation expense is not recognised. This Interpretation reflects the view that rarely, if ever, will it be possible to reliably determine that an asset is in a steady state. In addition, such a steady state is likely to change at any time as, for example, consumer demand and entity objectives change. Whether an asset is maintained in a steady state as a consequence of expenditure on the asset during the period will be reflected by:

(a)   an analysis of whether the future economic benefits provided by the asset have been consumed during the reporting period and whether expenditure on the asset has restored or increased those future economic benefits; and

Interpretations

(b)   the recognition of maintenance and depreciation expense in accordance with the requirements of AASB 116.

20   Some CBD and similar methods propose that a provision for future maintenance be recognised. However, AASB 137 *Provisions, Contingent Liabilities and Contingent Assets* indicates that a provision for future maintenance cannot be recognised as a liability. Furthermore, AASB 116 states that when each major inspection is performed, its cost is recognised in the carrying amount of the item of property, plant and equipment as a replacement if the recognition criteria are satisfied.

References

Australia

The Urgent Issues Group discussed Issues Paper 04/3 "Revision of Various UIG Abstracts for 2005" in relation to this Interpretation at its meeting on 22 July 2004. In developing the superseded Abstract, the UIG discussed Issue Summary 99/7 "Methods of Depreciation of Long-Lived Physical Assets, including Infrastructure Assets: Condition-Based Depreciation and Other Related Methods" and related papers at meetings on 12 August, 23 September, 4 November and 16 December 1999.

Accounting Standard AASB 116 *Property, Plant and Equipment*

Accounting Standard AASB 137 *Provisions, Contingent Liabilities and Contingent Assets*

Canada

CICA Handbook Section 3061 *Property, Plant and Equipment*

International Accounting Standards Board

International Accounting Standard IAS 16 *Property, Plant and Equipment*

New Zealand

Financial Reporting Standard FRS-3 *Accounting for Property, Plant and Equipment*

United Kingdom

Financial Reporting Standard FRS 15 *Tangible Fixed Assets*

United States of America

Accounting Research Bulletin ARB 43 *Restatement and Revision of Accounting Research Bulletins*, Chapter 9 – Depreciation

Interpretation 1031
Accounting for the Goods and Services Tax (GST)

(Compiled November 2009)

Compilation Details

UIG Interpretation 1031 *Accounting for the Goods and Services Tax (GST)* as amended

This compiled Interpretation applies to annual reporting periods beginning on or after 1 January 2009. It takes into account amendments up to and including 13 December 2007 and was prepared on 12 November 2009 by the staff of the Australian Accounting Standards Board (AASB).

This compilation is not a separate Interpretation issued by the AASB. Instead, it is a representation of Interpretation 1031 (July 2004) as amended by other pronouncements, which are listed in the Table below.

Table of Pronouncements

Pronouncement	Month issued	Application date *(annual reporting periods ... on or after ...)*	Application, saving or transitional provisions
Interpretation 1031	Jul 2004	*(beginning)* 1 Jan 2005	
AASB 2007-8	Sep 2007	*(beginning)* 1 Jan 2009	see (a) below
AASB 2007-10	Dec 2007	*(beginning)* 1 Jan 2009	see (a) below

(a)   Entities may elect to apply this Standard to annual reporting periods beginning on or after 1 January 2005 but before 1 January 2009, provided that AASB 101 *Presentation of Financial Statements* (September 2007) is also applied to such periods.

Table of Amendments

Paragraph affected	How affected	By ... [paragraph]
4	amended	AASB 2007-10 [115]
9-10	amended	AASB 2007-8 [6]
12	amended	AASB 2007-8 [7, 8]
13	amended	AASB 2007-8 [6]
16	amended	AASB 2007-8 [8]
21	amended	AASB 2007-8 [6]
24-25	amended	AASB 2007-8 [6]

Interpretation 1031

UIG Interpretation 1031 was issued in July 2004.

This compiled version of Interpretation 1031 applies to annual reporting periods beginning on or after 1 January 2009. It incorporates relevant amendments contained in other AASB pronouncements up to and including 13 December 2007 (see Compilation Details).

Urgent Issues Group

Interpretation 1031

Accounting for the Goods and Services Tax (GST)

Issue

1   Legislation to introduce the goods and services tax (GST) on 1 July 2000, titled *A New Tax System (Goods and Services Tax) Act 1999*, was assented to on 8 July 1999. The GST replaced the wholesale sales tax regime and a number of other taxes.

2   The GST legislation provides that the price quoted for the supply of goods and services and the price paid by the purchaser must include the amount of the GST where applicable. As such, the gross proceeds collected by the supplier includes the amount of GST. The GST is collected on behalf of the taxation authority. The purchaser of goods and services subject to the GST is, in many circumstances, able to obtain input tax credits for the GST included in the price of the goods and services acquired. Therefore, the price paid by the purchaser includes the GST that will be recovered from the taxation authority where an input tax credit can be claimed.

3   While authoritative requirements in Australia do not deal specifically with accounting for the GST, Accounting Standard AASB 118 *Revenue* defines revenue, specifies revenue recognition criteria and states that amounts collected on behalf of third parties such as goods and services taxes are excluded from revenue. Furthermore, AASB 102 *Inventories* provides that the cost of purchase of inventories does not include taxes that are subsequently recoverable from taxation authorities.

4   Concern has been expressed that, in the absence of authoritative guidance concerning accounting for the GST in general purpose financial statements, diverse or unacceptable practice may occur or develop and that this will undermine the relevance and reliability of general purpose financial statements.

5   The issues are:

    (a)   whether the GST should be recognised as part of the revenue of a supplier and as part of the cost of acquisition of assets and/or part of an item of expense of a purchaser; and

    (b)   whether amounts reported in the statement of cash flows should be reported on a gross basis.

Consensus

6   **Revenues, expenses and assets shall be recognised net of the amount of goods and services tax (GST), except where paragraphs 7 and 8 apply.**

7   **The amount of GST incurred by a purchaser that is not recoverable from the taxation authority shall be recognised as part of the cost of acquisition of an asset or as part of an item of expense.**

8   **Receivables and payables shall be stated with the amount of GST included.**

9   **The net amount of GST recoverable from, or payable to, the taxation authority shall be included as part of receivables or payables in the statement of financial position.**

10   **Cash flows shall be included in the statement of cash flows on a gross basis, subject to paragraph 11 and to AASB 107 *Statement of Cash Flows*.**

11   **The GST component of cash flows arising from investing and financing activities which is recoverable from, or payable to, the taxation authority shall be classified as operating cash flows.**

Application

12   This Interpretation applies to:

(a)   each entity that is required to prepare financial reports in accordance with Part 2M.3 of the *Corporations Act 2001* and that is a reporting entity;

(b)   general purpose financial statements of each other reporting entity; and

(c)   financial statements that are, or are held out to be, general purpose financial statements.

13   The requirements of this Interpretation regarding statements of cash flows also apply to each non-reporting entity that is required to prepare financial reports in accordance with Part 2M.3 of the Corporations Act.

14   This Interpretation applies to annual reporting periods beginning on or after 1 January 2005.
[Note: For application dates of paragraphs changed or added by an amending pronouncement, see Compilation Details.]

15   This Interpretation shall not be applied to annual reporting periods beginning before 1 January 2005.

16   The requirements specified in this Interpretation apply to the financial statements where information resulting from their application is material in accordance with AASB 1031 *Materiality*.

17   When applicable, this Interpretation supersedes Abstract 31 *Accounting for the Goods and Services Tax (GST)*, as issued in January 2000.

18   Abstract 31 remains applicable until superseded by this Interpretation.

Discussion

19   The GST is a tax on the supply of goods and services which is ultimately borne by the final consumer but is collected at each stage of the production and distribution chain. The terms 'taxable supply', 'input taxed', 'input tax credit', 'GST-free' and 'registered entity' have the same meaning as in *A New Tax System (Goods and Services Tax) Act 1999*.

20   AASB 118, paragraph 7, defines revenues as 'inflows of economic benefits during the period arising in the course of the ordinary activities of an entity when those inflows result in increases in equity, other than increases relating to contributions from equity participants.' The GST component of the transaction price does not constitute revenue of the vendor. This is because the transaction gives rise to a present obligation to remit the amounts of the tax collected to the taxation authority. This is reflected in AASB 118, paragraph 8, which states that amounts collected on behalf of third parties such as sales taxes, goods and services taxes and value added taxes are not economic benefits which flow to the entity and do not result in increases in equity.

21   Where an entity undertakes taxable and GST-free activities, it is entitled to claim input tax credits and recover from the taxation authority the GST included in the purchase price of supplies. This Interpretation reflects the view that in these cases the GST is not part of the cost of the asset acquired or the expense incurred. This is consistent with the *Framework for the Preparation and Presentation of Financial Statements*, which states that 'expenses are recognised in the statement of comprehensive income when a decrease in future economic benefits related to a decrease in an asset or an increase of a liability has arisen that can be measured reliably.' It is also consistent with AASB 102, which provides that the cost of purchase of inventories does not include taxes that are subsequently recoverable from the taxing authorities. In addition, AASB 116 *Property, Plant and Equipment* and AASB 138 *Intangible Assets* require assets acquired to be recognised at their cost, being the amount of cash or cash equivalents paid or the fair value of the other consideration given to acquire an asset at the time of its acquisition or construction (production). Therefore, recoverable GST would not be included in the cost of acquisition.

22   Where an entity undertakes input-taxed activities, the amount of the GST incurred comprises part of the cost of acquisition of the related asset or expense item to the extent that it is not recoverable from the taxation authority. This is because, in these cases, the

entity cannot recover the amount of the GST included in a transaction from the taxation authority and, therefore, must sacrifice future economic benefits and suffer a decrease in equity resulting from the amount of the GST included in the price of the supplies.

23   In some cases, an entity carries on a business that comprises a mix of input-taxed activities and taxable activities and GST-free activities. In these circumstances, the entity is not entitled to claim an input tax credit in respect of its input-taxed activities. In these cases, the legislation provides that the related GST is apportioned between input-taxed and other activities in measuring the recognised amount of the acquisition cost. In some cases, periodic adjustments will need to be made in respect of the apportionment. Where the related item is a depreciable asset, consequential adjustments will need to be made to reflect revisions of the acquisition cost and carrying amount of the asset. These adjustments are in the nature of revisions of the depreciable amount and would be accounted for in accordance with the requirements of AASB 108 *Accounting Policies, Changes in Accounting Estimates and Errors*.

24   Receivables and payables are required to be recognised on a gross basis, that is, inclusive of the amount of the GST. This is because the total amount of the transaction as represented by the price is the amount that will be paid or received by the entity. In addition, the net amount of GST receivable from, or payable by the entity to, the taxation authority is also recognised as part of receivables or payables in the statement of financial position.

25   AASB 107 requires cash flows to be classified as arising from operating, investing or financing activities. This Interpretation reflects the principle that all cash flows of the entity, including those relating to the GST component of a receipt or payment, should be reported on a gross basis in the statement of cash flows in accordance with AASB 107. The Interpretation also specifies that the GST component of financing and investing activities which are recoverable from, or payable to, the taxation authority should be classified as part of cash flows from operating activities. This means that investing and financing cash flows are presented net of the GST that is recoverable from, or payable to, the taxation authority and all cash flows relating to GST recoverable from, or payable to, the taxation authority are included in operating cash flows.

References

Australia

The Urgent Issues Group discussed Issues Paper 04/3 "Revision of Various UIG Abstracts for 2005" in relation to this Interpretation at meetings on 4 May and 10 June 2004. In developing the superseded Abstract, the UIG discussed Issue Summary 99/9 "Accounting for the Goods and Services Tax (GST)" at meetings on 4 November and 16 December 1999.

Accounting Standard AASB 102 *Inventories*

Accounting Standard AASB 107 *Statement of Cash Flows*

Accounting Standard AASB 108 *Accounting Policies, Changes in Accounting Estimates and Errors*

Accounting Standard AASB 116 *Property, Plant and Equipment*

Accounting Standard AASB 118 *Revenue*

Accounting Standard AASB 138 *Intangible Assets*

Framework for the Preparation and Presentation of Financial Statements

Canada

Emerging Issues Committee Abstract EIC-18 *Accounting for the Goods and Services Tax*

New Zealand

Financial Reporting Standard FRS-19 *Accounting for Goods and Services Tax*

United Kingdom

Statement of Standard Accounting Practice SSAP 5 *Accounting for Value Added Tax*

Interpretation 1038
Contributions by Owners Made to Wholly-Owned Public Sector Entities

(Reissued December 2007)

Preface

AASB Interpretation

Contributions by Owners Made to Wholly-Owned Public Sector Entities

	Paragraphs
References	
Issue	1 – 5
Consensus	6 – 17
Discussion	18 – 44
Appendix	A1 – A14

> AASB Interpretation 1038 is set out in paragraphs 1 – 44. Interpretations are listed in Australian Accounting Standard AASB 1048 *Interpretation and Application of Standards*. In the absence of explicit guidance, AASB 108 *Accounting Policies, Changes in Accounting Estimates and Errors* provides a basis for selecting and applying accounting policies.

Preface

Main Features of Interpretation 1038

This Interpretation is applicable to annual reporting periods beginning on or after 1 July 2008. This Interpretation may be applied to annual reporting periods beginning on or after 1 January 2005 but before 1 July 2008, provided there is early adoption for the same annual reporting period of the following Australian Accounting Standards being issued at about the same time, as applicable:

(a) AASB 1004 *Contributions*;

(b) AASB 1049 *Whole of Government and General Government Sector Financial Reporting*;

(c) AASB 1050 *Administered Items*;

(d) AASB 1051 *Land Under Roads*;

(e) AASB 1052 *Disaggregated Disclosures*; and

(f) AASB 2007-9 *Amendments to Australian Accounting Standards arising from the Review of AASs 27, 29 and 31*.

This Interpretation is a result of amendments made to the September 2004 version of UIG Interpretation 1038 *Contributions by Owners Made to Wholly-Owned Public Sector Entities*. Those amendments primarily reflect changes resulting from amendments to AASB 1004 in December 2007 that prescribe requirements for accounting for "restructures of administrative arrangements" as defined in that Standard. In particular, this Interpretation does not apply to a government controlled not-for-profit entity or a for-profit government department in respect of a restructure of administrative arrangements. In relation to other circumstances, this Interpretation establishes criteria for determining whether a transfer of assets (or of assets and liabilities) to wholly-owned public sector entities from other entities in the same group of entities satisfies the definition of "contributions by owners" in AASB 1004, based on the rights held directly or indirectly by the controlling government. For example, such a transfer is a contribution by owners where its equity nature is indicated by the issuance of equity instruments or a formal agreement that establishes a financial interest in the net assets of the transferee that can be sold, transferred or redeemed. A transfer may also be designated in advance or concurrently by the transferor as a contribution by owners. This Interpretation prohibits the redesignation of transfers, and requires the consistent classification by transferors and transferees of both contributions by owners and distributions to owners.

The Board intends to undertake a fundamental review of this Interpretation at a later date.

Comparison with Superseded Requirements

This Interpretation supersedes UIG Interpretation 1038. This Interpretation differs from UIG Interpretation 1038 in that it does not apply to a government controlled not-for-profit entity or a for-profit government department in respect of a restructure of administrative arrangements. This Interpretation has also been updated for changes as a result of AASB 2007-8 *Amendments to Australian Accounting Standards arising from AASB 101.*

Australian Accounting Standards Board Interpretation 1038

Contributions by Owners Made to Wholly-Owned , Public Sector Entities

References

Accounting Standard AASB 118 *Revenue*

Accounting Standard AASB 132 *Financial Instruments: Presentation*

Accounting Standard AASB 1004 *Contributions*

Accounting Standard AASB 2007-8 *Amendments to Australian Accounting Standards arising from AASB 101*

Framework for the Preparation and Presentation of Financial Statements

Issue

1.   The treatment of certain transfers of assets (or assets and liabilities) between public sector entities within the same group of entities that occur as a consequence of a government decision to restructure the activities or functions of its controlled entities, or for other purposes, has been the subject of debate. These transfers are transfers other than those made as consideration for the provision by the transferee of assets or services (including the provision of debt finance) at fair value to the transferor.

2.   Australian Accounting Standard AASB 1004 *Contributions* requires contributions by owners and distributions to owners to be recognised directly in equity. The Standard also includes comments concerning whether the transactions of a government department are in the nature of contributions by owners or distributions to owners. Different views have arisen regarding whether, and under which circumstances, the transfers described above should be recognised by the transferees as contributions by owners, and which treatment(s) of these transfers by transferors would be consistent with the treatment by transferees. Concern has been expressed that, in the absence of authoritative guidance, diverse or unacceptable practice may occur or develop and that this will undermine the relevance and reliability of general purpose financial statements. "Contributions by owners" is defined in AASB 1004.

3.   This Interpretation addresses the essential characteristics of contributions by owners and provides indicators of when those characteristics exist. With one significant exception, it applies to parliamentary appropriations and other transfers to statutory authorities, government departments and government-owned corporations from other entities within the same group of entities but only where the transferee is wholly owned by the controlling government. The exception is that this Interpretation does not apply in respect of "restructures of administrative arrangements", as defined in AASB 1004. In such cases the requirements in AASB 1004 apply, which means that government controlled not-

for-profit entities and for-profit government departments account for "restructures of administrative arrangements" as transactions with owners in their capacity as owners.

4.   This Interpretation does not apply to consolidated financial statements of local governments or whole of government or general government sector financial statements of Federal, State or Territory governments. Furthermore, this Interpretation does not address the issue of whether transferees should classify as income or liabilities transfers to them that do not qualify as contributions by owners.

5.   The issues are:

    (a)   What are the primary features of contributions by owners, and are there aspects of public sector entities that affect the determination of whether those features exist?

    (b)   Is it necessary for a contribution by owners to give rise to a financial interest in the net assets of the public sector entity which conveys an entitlement to distributions of a return on investment?

    (c)   Must shares or equivalent instruments be issued if transfers are in the nature of contributions by owners?

    (d)   What is the significance of the form of a transfer for determining whether it qualifies as a contribution by owners?

Consensus

6.   This Interpretation applies to transfers of assets, or assets and liabilities, to wholly-owned public sector entities from other entities within the same group of entities, other than:

    (a)   transfers made as consideration for the provision by the transferee of assets or services (including the provision of debt finance) at fair value to the transferor; and

    (b)   transfers to or from government controlled not-for-profit entities or for-profit government departments arising as a result of a "restructure of administrative arrangements", which is defined in AASB 1004 as:

       "The reallocation or reorganisation of assets, liabilities, activities and responsibilities amongst the entities that the government controls that occurs as a consequence of a rearrangement in the way in which activities and responsibilities as prescribed under legislation or other authority are allocated between the government's controlled entities.

       The scope of the requirements relating to restructures of administrative arrangements is limited to the transfer of a business (as defined in AASB 3 *Business Combinations*). The requirements do not apply to, for example, a transfer of an individual asset or a group of assets that is not a business."

Contributions by Owners

7.   **A transfer to a wholly-owned public sector entity shall be recognised by the transferee as a contribution by owners when and only when it satisfies the definition of "contributions by owners" in AASB 1004. The criteria set out in paragraphs 8 and 9 shall be applied in determining whether a transfer satisfies the definition of contributions by owners.**

8.   **Regardless of the other features or conditions of a transfer, the transfer is a contribution by owners where its equity nature is evidenced by any of the following:**

    (a)   the issuance, in relation to the transfer, of equity instruments which can be sold, transferred or redeemed;

    (b)   a formal agreement, in relation to the transfer, establishing a financial interest in the net assets of the transferee which can be sold, transferred or redeemed; or

    (c)   formal designation of the transfer (or a class of such transfers) by the transferor or a parent of the transferor as forming part of the transferee's contributed equity, either before the transfer occurs or at the time of the transfer.

9.   The classification of a transfer to a wholly-owned public sector entity from the government or another entity controlled by the same government shall be determined by reference to the rights of the government in respect of the transfer held directly by the government or indirectly through any of its controlled entities. Accordingly, for a transfer to a public sector entity to satisfy part (b) of the definition of contributions by owners in AASB 1004, a right to sell, transfer or redeem the financial interest in the net assets of the transferee shall be held directly or indirectly by the government.

10.   Where the original transferor is another entity controlled directly or indirectly by the controlling government of the transferee, a transfer to a wholly-owned public sector entity shall be accounted for by the transferee as a transfer from that government or a government-controlled parent of the transferee. Where the controlling government of the transferee is the original transferor, a transfer to a wholly-owned public sector entity shall be accounted for by the transferee as a transfer from the immediate transferor (which would be the controlling government if there was no interposed parent).

Consistent Classification of Contributions by Owners

11.   If a transfer to a wholly-owned public sector entity is classified by the transferee as a contribution by owners, and the transferor is the transferee's controlling government or another entity controlled directly or indirectly by that government, that transferor shall classify the transfer as:

    (a)   a distribution to owners, if the transferor makes the transfer to all or part of its ownership group; or

    (b)   the acquisition of an ownership interest in the transferee, if the transferor makes the transfer to an investee.

Redesignation of Transfers

12.   A transfer designated as a contribution by owners shall not be redesignated as income. Similarly, a transfer designated as income shall not be redesignated as a contribution by owners.

Consistent Classification of Distributions to Owners as Redemptions of Ownership Interests

13.   A transfer classified by the transferor as a distribution to owners shall be classified by the immediate transferee as a redemption of part or all of its ownership interest in the transferor when and only when its equity nature is evidenced by any of the following:

    (a)   the cancellation, in relation to the transfer, of equity instruments which can be sold, transferred or redeemed;

    (b)   amendment of a formal agreement, in relation to the transfer, to reduce the transferee's financial interest in the net assets of the transferor which can be sold, transferred or redeemed; or

    (c)   formal designation of the transfer (or a class of such transfers) as a redemption of an ownership interest in the transferor, made by the government or a government-controlled parent of the transferee, either before the transfer occurs or at the time of the transfer.

Application

14.   This Interpretation applies to public sector entities as follows:

    (a)   each entity that is required to prepare financial reports in accordance with Part 2M.3 of the *Corporations Act 2001* and that is a reporting entity;

    (b)   general purpose financial statements of each other reporting entity; and

    (c)   financial statements that are, or are held out to be, general purpose financial statements.

15.   This Interpretation applies to annual reporting periods beginning on or after 1 July
        2008. This Interpretation may be applied to annual reporting periods beginning on
        or after 1 January 2005 but before 1 July 2008, provided there is early adoption for
        the same annual reporting period of the following Australian Accounting Standards
        being issued at about the same time, as applicable:

   (a)   AASB 1004 *Contributions*;

   (b)   AASB 1049 *Whole of Government and General Government Sector Financial
           Reporting*;

   (c)   AASB 1050 *Administered Items*;

   (d)   AASB 1051 *Land Under Roads*;

   (e)   AASB 1052 *Disaggregated Disclosures*; and

   (f)   AASB 2007-9 *Amendments to Australian Accounting Standards arising from
           the Review of AASs 27, 29 and 31.*

16.   The requirements specified in this Interpretation apply to the financial statements
        where information resulting from their application is material in accordance with
        AASB 1031 *Materiality*.

17.   When applicable, this Interpretation supersedes UIG Interpretation 1038
        Contributions by Owners Made to Wholly-Owned Public Sector Entities, as issued in
        September 2004.

Discussion

Definition of Contributions by Owners

18.   AASB 1004 defines contributions by owners as "future economic benefits that have been
        contributed to the entity by parties external to the entity, other than those which result in
        liabilities of the entity, that give rise to a financial interest in the net assets of the entity
        which:

   (a)   conveys entitlement both to distributions of future economic benefits by the entity
           during its life, such distributions being at the discretion of the ownership group or
           its representatives, and to distributions of any excess of assets over liabilities in the
           event of the entity being wound up; and/or

   (b)   can be sold, transferred or redeemed."

Classification of Transfers as Contributions by Owners

19.   However, AASB 1004 requirements relating to contributions by and distributions
        to owners, other than in relation to restructures of administrative arrangements by
        government controlled not-for-profit entities or for-profit government departments:

   (a)   do not provide specific guidance on how the definition of contributions by owners
           should be applied to transfers between public sector entities controlled by the same
           government;

   (b)   do not provide guidance on the policies to adopt to achieve consistent classification
           by transferors of transfers recognised by transferees as contributions by owners;
           and

   (c)   do not apply to statutory authorities and government-owned corporations.

20.   This Interpretation adopts the views that the determinant of whether a transfer to a public
        sector entity should be classified as a contribution by owners is whether the transfer meets
        the definition of contributions by owners in paragraph 18, and that such classification
        does not depend:

   (a)   on whether the transfer increases the capacity of the transferee public sector entity
           to provide services;

   (b)   on the composition and extent of the transfer, for example (other than for government
           controlled not-for-profit entities or for-profit government departments involved
           in restructures of administrative arrangements) whether it involves a restructuring; or

     (c)   solely on the nature of the parties to the transfer, for example whether they are for-profit or not-for-profit entities.

21.   In addition, authorisation of a transfer by a legally binding authority (such as a statute or ministerial direction) does not of itself indicate that the transfer should be classified as a contribution by owners unless the instrument authorising the transfer designates that the transfer (or a class of similar transfers) has such a nature.

Evidence that Transfers are Contributions by Owners

Issuance of Equity Instruments, or an Ownership Agreement

22.   One form of evidence that a transfer is a contribution by owners is the issuance of equity instruments in relation to the transfer. Equity instruments may be shares, equivalent ownership instruments (for example, units of contributed equity in a non-corporate entity such as a trust), or debt instruments (or components thereof) that fail the definition of "financial liabilities" and accordingly are classified as equity under AASB 132 *Financial Instruments: Presentation*.

23.   This Interpretation adopts the view that the issuance of equity instruments in relation to a transfer is not essential for the transfer to qualify for recognition as a contribution by owners.

24.   Another form of evidence that a transfer is a contribution by owners as defined in paragraph 18 is an agreement in relation to the transfer setting out the respective ownership interests of equity contributors. In substance, the existence of such an agreement is the same as the issuance of equity instruments, because it specifies the respective interests of the various owners of the transferee's contributed equity.

Designation as Contributions by Owners

25.   Designation of a transfer as a contribution by owners by the original transferor, the government or another entity interposed between the original transferor and the ultimate transferee is sufficient for a wholly-owned public sector transferee to classify the transfer as a contribution by owners, if that transfer is not made as consideration for the provision by the transferee of assets or services at fair value to the transferor. However, designation would be insufficient if the transferee is not wholly owned by the transferor or its controlling government. In these circumstances, either the issuance of equity instruments, or the existence of an agreement setting out the respective ownership interests of equity contributors, in relation to the transfer would be necessary for the transfer to be a contribution by owners. This is because where a minority interest exists, these actions are necessary to specify the respective interests of the various owners of the transferee's contributed equity.

Distributions at the Discretion of the Ownership Group

26.   Part (a) of the definition of contributions by owners in paragraph 18 refers to transfers that "give rise to a financial interest in the net assets of the entity which … conveys entitlement … to distributions of future economic benefits by the entity during its life, such distributions being at the discretion of the ownership group or its representatives …".

27.   For a transfer to a public sector entity to satisfy part (a) of the definition of contributions by owners in paragraph 18, the distributions of future economic benefits to which the owner obtains an entitlement must include returns on investment, as distinct from returns of investment. A consequence of this requirement is that if a transferee public sector entity is a not-for-profit entity, it will be unlikely that the financial interest arising from the transfer will convey an entitlement to discretionary distributions of future economic benefits. Accordingly, it is likely that a transfer to such an entity can only qualify as a contribution by owners if it satisfies part (b) of the definition of contributions by owners – which requires that the financial interest in the net assets arising from the transfer can be sold, transferred or redeemed.

Financial Interest in the Net Assets of the Entity which can be Sold, Transferred or Redeemed

28.   Part (b) of the definition of contributions by owners in paragraph 18 refers to transfers that "give rise to a financial interest in the net assets of the entity which ... can be sold, transferred or redeemed". If the transferee is a wholly-owned subsidiary of the transferor or a parent of the transferor, the transferor or that parent will almost invariably possess rights of redemption.

29.   The requirements of paragraph 10 reflect that a transfer to a public sector entity from another entity controlled directly or indirectly by the same government (other than a transfer made as consideration for the provision by the transferee of assets or services at fair value to the transferor) is, in substance, a transfer from that government. Accordingly, in respect of these rights of redemption:

     (a)   it is irrelevant whether the particular government-controlled transferor is entitled to receive any distribution of future economic benefits comprising a redemption of a financial interest in the net assets of the transferee public sector entity; and

     (b)   the rights of the government, held directly by the government or indirectly through any of its controlled entities, determine the classification of transfers to the public sector entity.

30.   Because any transfer by a parent to its wholly-owned subsidiary (other than a transfer made as consideration for the provision by the transferee of assets or services at fair value to the transferor) has the potential to satisfy the definition of contributions by owners in paragraph 18, this Interpretation adopts the view that it is necessary to refer to the form of the transfer to determine whether it should be classified as a contribution by owners. Accordingly, if the transferee neither issues equity instruments nor is a party to an agreement setting out the respective ownership interests of equity contributors, in relation to the transfer, formal designation that the transfer is to be added to the transferee's contributed equity is necessary to identify contributions by owners (except in relation to government controlled not-for-profit entities or for-profit government departments involved in restructures of administrative arrangements).

Mode and Timing of Designation of Transfers as Contributions by Owners

31.   Designation of transfers as contributions by owners may occur in a variety of ways which include, but are not limited to, a minute of a decision by the governing body of the contributor, correspondence to the transferee, legislation, administrative orders, and allocation statements, directions or bulletins issued by or on behalf of relevant ministers, each of which specifies that the transfer (or a class of such transfers) is to be added to the transferee's contributed equity. In each case, designation of the transfer or class of transfers is made by the transferor (or a parent of the transferor), because the distinction between an entity's contributed equity and its other components of equity (such as retained earnings and certain reserves) is at the discretion of its owners.

32.   This Interpretation adopts the view that for the designation of a transfer (either specifically in respect of that transfer or in respect of the same class of transfers) as a contribution by owners to be effective, it should occur at or before the time of the transfer, because:

     (a)   the character of a transfer does not change after it occurs and therefore the character of a transfer should be evident or determined at or before the time of the transfer; and

     (b)   a contribution by owners changes the formal contributed equity of the recipient of that contribution.

33.   This requirement removes the potential for deferring the classification of a transfer until the entity has more information about the likely profit or loss for the reporting period and the effect of classifying the transfer as a contribution by owners.

Redesignation

34.   This Interpretation does not permit a contribution by owners to be redesignated as income. The definition of income under the *Framework for the Preparation and Presentation of Financial Statements* indicates that an inflow of economic benefits that results in an increase in equity (other than increases relating to contributions from equity participants) has occurred. A transfer to an entity increases its equity only once, and the transferee's equity does not increase at the time of any intended redesignation.

35.   As a consequence of the requirement that, where a transfer is classified as a contribution by owners on the basis of its designation, the designation of the transfer or class of similar transfers must occur at or before the time of the transfer, a transfer designated as income cannot be redesignated as a contribution by owners.

36.   The prohibitions of redesignations in paragraph 12 do not preclude the redesignation of liabilities as contributed equity when converted to equity because:

    (a)   recognition of the liabilities did not involve the recognition of contributions by owners or income; and

    (b)   consistent with AASB 118 and AASB 1004, such redesignations are not recognised as giving rise to income.

Pre-Existing Interest in Net Assets Transferred

37.   A pre-existing interest of the government in all of the net assets transferred to a public sector entity does not preclude a transfer to the public sector entity from being a contribution by owners. The contribution to the transferee public sector entity can give rise to a financial interest in the net assets of that transferee, because that financial interest is in respect of the net assets of the transferee rather than the net assets transferred. That financial interest in the net assets of the transferee public sector entity cannot exist until the transfer is made. Until then, the transferor has a direct interest in the assets it contributes to the transferee.

Consistent Classification by Transferor and Transferee

38.   This Interpretation adopts the view that a transfer recognised by a transferee public sector entity as a contribution by owners should be classified consistently by the transferor(s) in respect of that transfer.

39.   As noted in paragraph 29, a transfer to a public sector entity from another entity controlled directly or indirectly by the same government is, in substance, a transfer from that government. The rights of the government in respect of the transfer, held directly by the government or indirectly through any of its controlled entities, determine the classification of the transfer to the public sector entity. Accordingly, for a transfer to a public sector entity to satisfy part (b) of the definition of contributions by owners in paragraph 18, a right to sell, transfer or redeem the financial interest in the net assets of the transferee must be held by either the government or a government-controlled transferor.

40.   Many transfers are made between public sector entities that are controlled by the same parent. Where the original transferor is another entity controlled directly or indirectly by the same government, the chain of entries that would be recorded by the original transferor, the ultimate transferee and the interposed parent (which will be the government or a subsidiary of the government that controls the transferor and the transferee, if there is only one interposed parent) for transfers classified as contributions by owners by transferee public sector entities are:

    (a)   the government-controlled transferor (the original transferor) would classify the transfer as a distribution to owners;

    (b)   the immediate recipient of the transfer (the interposed parent) would record the transfer received as income or a redemption of part or all of its ownership interest (investment) in the transferor (see paragraph 43);

    (c)   the interposed parent (the immediate transferor) would record the corresponding transfer made as the acquisition of an ownership interest in the ultimate transferee; and

    (d)   the ultimate transferee would classify the transfer as a contribution by owners.

41. However, the entries described in paragraphs 40(b) and 40(c) for the interposed parent (for example, the controlling government) would not be recognised in that entity's whole of government or general government sector financial statements because they concern transfers within the group of entities. They would be recognised in that entity's own financial statements, if prepared.

42. Some transfers between public sector entities controlled by the same government have more than one interposed parent. In these cases, the method of accounting for the transfers by each transferor would follow the general approach underlying the specific case explained in paragraph 40 (where there is only one interposed parent). Under the general approach, which is set out in paragraph 11, if the transfer is classified by the ultimate transferee as a contribution by owners, each transferor must classify the transfer as:

    (a) a distribution to owners, if the transferor makes the transfer to all or part of its ownership group; or

    (b) the acquisition of an ownership interest in the transferee, if the transferor makes the transfer to an investee.

43. Another issue concerning the consistency of treatments by transferors and transferees arises where a transfer between public sector entities within the same group is a distribution to owners in circumstances where the transferee held an equity interest in the transferor. The issue is whether and to what extent the transfer should be accounted for by the transferee (which may be the government) as a redemption of part or all of its ownership interest (investment) in the transferor. The appropriate classification would be clear where, in respect of the transfer, equity instruments are cancelled or a formal ownership agreement is amended. In other circumstances, classification of distributions to owners by the transferee is based on the designation by the government or a government-controlled parent of the transferee of the character of the distribution at or before the time of the transfer. In making this designation, distributions to owners can be classified as redemptions by the transferee of its ownership interest in the transferor only to the extent of the ownership interest recorded by the transferor immediately before the distribution was made.

Application

44. This Interpretation applies to public sector entities in relation to certain transfers to or from other entities within the same group. It applies to transferees in relation to these transfers only where they are wholly owned, and to corresponding transferors whether wholly owned or partly owned by the government or a government-controlled parent.

Appendix

This appendix accompanies, but is not part of, Interpretation 1038.

A1. This appendix discusses five scenarios in a whole of government context to illustrate the classification of certain transfers within a group of entities in which the parent is either a government or a subsidiary of a government, in accordance with the Interpretation. It illustrates the position of interposed parents in a series of such transfers, and the application of paragraphs 10, 11 and 13 of the Interpretation to the classification of such transfers within the group. None of the transfers illustrated in this appendix is made as consideration for the provision by the transferee of assets or services at fair value to the transferor. In addition, none of the transfers involves the issuance or cancellation of equity instruments; and none of the transfers are in relation to a government controlled not-for-profit entity or a for-profit government department in respect of a "restructure of administrative arrangements" as defined in AASB 1004 *Contributions*.

Scenario 1

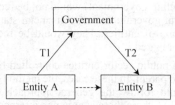

A2.   In this scenario a transfer of assets from Entity A to Entity B (both wholly-owned public sector entities) is denoted by the broken arrow. Under paragraph 10 of the Interpretation, since the transfer is to a wholly-owned public sector entity from another entity controlled by the same government, the transfer is accounted for as two transfers via that government (T1 and T2, denoted by the unbroken arrows). Entity A is the original transferor. The Government is the interposed parent. It is the "immediate transferee" in respect of Transfer 1 (T1) and the "immediate transferor" in respect of Transfer 2 (T2). Entity B is the ultimate transferee.

A3.   Where the transfer to Entity B (T2) is classified as a contribution by owners by the Government to Entity B, as the ultimate transferee, the journal entries that would be recorded by the original transferor (Entity A) and the interposed parent (the Government) are:

(a)   the original transferor would classify Transfer T1 to the Government as a distribution to owners, as required by paragraph 11(a) of the Interpretation, regardless of whether the distribution is a distribution of accumulated surpluses or a return of the transferor's contributed equity to the Government;

(b)   the immediate recipient of Transfer T1 (the interposed parent) would record the transfer received as income or a redemption of part or all of its ownership interest (investment) in the transferor (consistent with paragraph 13); and

(c)   the interposed parent (the immediate transferor) would record the corresponding transfer made (T2) as the acquisition of an ownership interest in the ultimate transferee, as required by paragraph 11(b).

A4.   In Scenario 1, the original transferor and the ultimate transferee are commonly controlled, but neither entity controls the other. Under Scenario 2, the original transferor and the ultimate transferee are commonly controlled, and both of the transfers are from a parent to its subsidiary.

Scenario 2

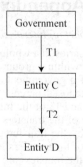

A5.   In this scenario the Government transfers assets to Entity C (a wholly-owned subsidiary) and designates the transfer as a contribution by owners (Transfer 1, indicated as T1). Entity C transfers the assets to Entity D, its wholly-owned subsidiary, and designates the transfer as a contribution by owners (Transfer 2, indicated as T2). Because Entity C controls Entity D, it has the authority to designate the nature of Transfer 2, unless the Government has designated the nature of the transfer in its capacity as the ultimate parent.

A6. For Transfer 1, the Government is the immediate transferor and Entity C is the immediate transferee. For Transfer 2, Entity C is the immediate transferor and Entity D is the immediate transferee. Because Entity C controls Entity D, it is unnecessary to deem Transfer 2 as passing through the Government in order to establish the transferor's financial interest in the transferee's net assets that is essential for a transfer to qualify as a contribution by owners. For both transfers, the transferor accounts for the transfer as the acquisition of an ownership interest in the transferee (as required by paragraph 11(b)), and the transferee accounts for the transfer as a contribution by owners.

Scenario 3

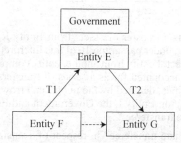

A7. In this scenario the Government controls Entity E, which is the sole owner of Entities F and G. The situation is the same as Scenario 1, except that Entity E (rather than the Government) is the interposed parent. Consistent with paragraph 8(c) of the Interpretation, Entity E has the authority to designate the nature of each transfer, unless the Government has designated the nature of the transfer in its capacity as the ultimate parent. The transfers should be classified by each transferor and transferee in accordance with the classifications outlined in Scenario 1.

Scenario 4

A8. In this scenario, Entity H, which is wholly owned by the Government, makes a distribution to owners to the Government. Entity H is the immediate transferor and the Government is the immediate transferee. The Government would, according to its designation of the transfer, classify the transfer received as income or a redemption of part or all of its ownership interest (investment) in the transferor (see paragraph 43 of this Interpretation).

Scenario 5

A9. Under Scenario 5, transfers occur between public sector entities that are controlled by the same government and have more than one interposed parent. Paragraph 11 of this Interpretation specifies that (regardless of the number of interposed parents involved in the transfer) if the transfer is classified by the ultimate transferee as a contribution by owners, each transferor must classify the transfer as:

(a) a distribution to owners, if the transferor makes the transfer to all or part of its ownership group; or

(b) the acquisition of an ownership interest in the transferee, if the transferor makes the transfer to an investee.

A10. The application of those policies is illustrated in respect of the following entities and transfers. Control relationships are denoted by unbroken lines without arrows. Entities I and J are wholly owned directly by the Government, and Entities K, L, M and N are wholly owned by Entities I or J.

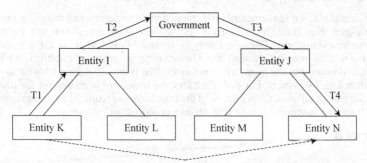

A11. In this scenario there is a transfer of assets from Entity K to Entity N, denoted by the broken arrow. However, under paragraph 10 of this Interpretation, since the transfer is to a wholly-owned public sector entity from another entity controlled by the same government, the transfer instead is accounted for as a series of transfers via that government and its directly-controlled entities, denoted by the unbroken arrows (T1, T2, T3 and T4). Entity K is the original transferor. Entity I, the Government and Entity J are interposed parents. Entity N is the ultimate transferee.

A12. Entity I is the "immediate transferee" in respect of Transfer 1 (T1) and the "immediate transferor" in respect of Transfer 2 (T2). The Government is the "immediate transferee" in respect of Transfer 2 (T2) and the "immediate transferor" in respect of Transfer 3 (T3). Entity J is the "immediate transferee" in respect of Transfer 3 (T3) and the "immediate transferor" in respect of Transfer 4 (T4).

A13. Where Entity N classifies the transfer to it as a contribution by owners, because of the requirements of the Interpretation, the journal entries that would be recorded by the original transferor and the interposed parents are as follows:

(a)   under paragraph 11(a) of the Interpretation, Entities K and I would classify the transfers they make as distributions to owners;

(b)   according to paragraph 13 of the Interpretation, Entity I and the Government would classify the transfers they receive as income or a redemption of part or all of their ownership interest (investment) in the transferor;

(c)   under paragraph 11(b) of the Interpretation, the Government and Entity J would classify the transfers they make as the acquisition of an ownership interest in the transferee; and

(d)   like Entity N, Entity J would classify the transfer made to it as a contribution by owners.

A14. The journal entries described in these scenarios for interposed parents (for example, the controlling government) and for the Government in Scenario 4 would not be recognised in the consolidated financial statements of those entities where they concern transfers within the group. They would be recognised in each entity's own financial statements, if prepared. Similarly, the foregoing references to classification of transfers by the Government concern the Government in its role as the parent, where the Government or a notional entity (such as "the Crown") prepares separate financial statements in that capacity. In such instances, the Government as ultimate transferee would fall outside the scope of the Interpretation, because it is not a wholly-owned public sector entity, although the Interpretation would represent analogous guidance.

Interpretation 1039
Substantive Enactment of Major Tax Bills in Australia

(Compiled February 2010)

Compilation Details

UIG Interpretation 1039 *Substantive Enactment of Major Tax Bills in Australia* as amended

This compiled Interpretation applies to annual reporting periods beginning on or after 1 January 2011. It takes into account amendments up to and including 15 December 2009 and was prepared on 23 February 2010 by the staff of the Australian Accounting Standards Board (AASB).

This compilation is not a separate Interpretation issued by the AASB. Instead, it is a representation of Interpretation 1039 (July 2004) as amended by other pronouncements, which are listed in the Table below.

Table of Pronouncements

Pronouncement	Month issued	Application date (*annual reporting periods ... on or after ...*)	Application, saving or transitional provisions
Interpretation 1039	Jul 2004	(*beginning*) 1 Jan 2005	
AASB 2007-8	Sep 2007	(*beginning*) 1 Jan 2009	see (a) below
AASB 2007-10	Dec 2007	(*beginning*) 1 Jan 2009	see (a) below
AASB 2009-12	Dec 2009	(*beginning*) 1 Jan 2011	see (b) below

(a) Entities may elect to apply this Standard to annual reporting periods beginning on or after 1 January 2005 but before 1 January 2009, provided that AASB 101 *Presentation of Financial Statements* (September 2007) is also applied to such periods.

(b) Entities may elect to apply this Standard to annual reporting periods beginning on or after 1 January 2005 but before 1 January 2011.

Table of Amendments

Paragraph affected	How affected	By ... [paragraph]
2	amended	AASB 2007-8 [6]
	amended	AASB 2009-12 [24]
3	amended	AASB 2007-10 [116]
5	amended	AASB 2007-8 [6]
	amended	AASB 2009-12 [25]
10	amended	AASB 2007-8 [8]
13	amended	AASB 2007-8 [6]
17	amended	AASB 2007-8 [6]
	amended	AASB 2007-10 [116]
	amended	AASB 2009-12 [25, 26]
18	amended	AASB 2007-8 [6]
	amended	AASB 2007-10 [116]
	amended	AASB 2009-12 [26]
References	amended	AASB 2007-8 [6]

Interpretations

Interpretation 1039

UIG Interpretation 1039 was issued in July 2004.

This compiled version of Interpretation 1039 applies to annual reporting periods beginning on or after 1 January 2011. It incorporates relevant amendments contained in other AASB pronouncements up to and including 15 December 2009 (see Compilation Details).

Urgent Issues Group

Interpretation 1039

Substantive Enactment of Major Tax Bills in Australia

Issue

1   The legislation to allow groups comprising a parent and its wholly-owned entities (all being Australian residents for tax purposes) to elect to consolidate and be treated as a single entity for income tax purposes was enacted through a series of Acts. For example, the first Act, the *New Business Tax System (Consolidation) Act (No. 1) 2002*, was passed by Parliament in June 2002. However, its commencement was linked to the day on which the second Act, the *New Business Tax System (Consolidation, Value Shifting, Demergers and Other Measures) Act 2002*, received Royal Assent. The second Act was passed by Parliament and received Royal Assent in October 2002. The third and fourth principal tax consolidation Acts were passed by Parliament in November 2002 and March 2003 respectively. Amendments and additional requirements have been included in other taxation Acts as well. However, the tax consolidation regime or system commenced with effect from 1 July 2002.

2   When the principal tax consolidation legislation was enacted through a series of Acts over a long period, different views arose in relation to whether proposed tax legislation (as individual Bills, linked Bills or a complete package) should be taken into account in determining the carrying amounts of deferred tax assets and liabilities included in statements of financial position at the end of reporting periods prior to the substantive enactment of the proposed legislation.

3   Concern has been expressed that, in the absence of authoritative guidance, diverse or unacceptable practices may occur or develop in determining whether deferred tax balances should be adjusted for any anticipated effects of proposed tax legislation prior to its passage. This will undermine the relevance and reliability of general purpose financial statements.

4   The issue is when the recognition and measurement of deferred tax assets and liabilities should take into account individual tax Bills, linked Bills or a series of Bills.

Consensus

5   **A tax Bill, to the extent that it is relevant to the entity, shall be taken into account in the recognition and measurement of deferred tax assets and liabilities when and only when the Bill has been enacted or substantively enacted prior to the end of the reporting period.**

6   **Substantive enactment of a tax Bill shall be taken to have occurred once the Bill has been tabled in the Parliament and there is majority support for the passage of the Bill through both Houses of Parliament. However, where the commencement of the Bill is linked to the enactment or commencement of another Bill, the first Bill shall not be taken to be enacted or substantively enacted until the second Bill has been enacted or substantively enacted.**

Application

7   This Interpretation applies when Accounting Standard AASB 112 *Income Taxes* applies.

8   This Interpretation applies to annual reporting periods beginning on or after 1 January 2005.

[Note: For application dates of paragraphs changed or added by an amending pronouncement, see Compilation Details.]

9   This Interpretation shall not be applied to annual reporting periods beginning before 1 January 2005.

10   The requirements specified in this Interpretation apply to the financial statements where information resulting from their application is material in accordance with AASB 1031 *Materiality*.

11   When applicable, this Interpretation in part supersedes Abstract 39 *Effect of Proposed Tax Consolidation Legislation on Deferred Tax Balances*, as issued in December 2002.

12   Abstract 39 remains applicable in part until superseded by this Interpretation.

Discussion

13   AASB 112 requires deferred tax assets and liabilities to be measured on the basis of the tax laws and tax rates that have been enacted or substantively enacted by the end of the reporting period.

14   The view adopted in this Interpretation is that an exposure draft of proposed tax legislation does not represent a substantive enactment of changes in tax laws because the content and timing of the actual legislation is too uncertain at that stage. Draft legislation does not indicate the probable specific provisions of the ultimate legislation, as revisions and extensions are expected, even if it were concluded that the enactment of some tax legislation is probable.

15   Under this Interpretation, a tax Bill is taken to be substantively enacted when it has been tabled in the Parliament and there is majority support for its passage through both Houses, provided that the commencement of the Bill is not linked to another Bill that has not been substantively enacted. If the second Bill has not been enacted or substantively enacted, then the first Bill in fact may never commence to operate. Accordingly, it is not appropriate to treat the first Bill as enacted or substantively enacted until the linked second Bill has been enacted or substantively enacted. Furthermore, the second Bill may be linked in a similar way to a third Bill. Linked Bills are taken to be enacted or substantively enacted when the final linked Bill is enacted or substantively enacted.

16   When a Bill has been substantively enacted, it is reasonable to conclude that it is probable that the specific proposals in the Bill will be enacted, and that the proposals will have been specified with sufficient scope and detail to be understood and applied in practice. When tax Bills deal with fundamental changes to taxation arrangements, general statements of support for the legislation prior to the commencement of the legislative process in Parliament are not considered to result in substantive enactment of the proposed legislation.

17   If a tax Bill becomes substantively enacted *prior to* the end of the reporting period, it is taken into account (where relevant) in measuring the deferred tax balances as at that end of the reporting period. However, if a Bill were to become substantively enacted only *after* the reporting period, it is not taken into account in measuring deferred tax balances as at that end of the reporting period. A change in tax laws that occurs after the reporting period, but before the time of completion of the financial statements, does not provide new information relating to conditions existing at the end of the reporting period. This means that if the first and second Bills in a series are substantively enacted prior to the end of the reporting period, but no other related, non-linked tax Bills are, then the first and second Bills are taken into account when appropriate without regard to the published or expected contents of subsequent tax Bills in the series.

Disclosures

18   The subsequent-event disclosure requirements in AASB 110 *Events after the Reporting Period* are applicable where substantive enactment (and enactment) of proposed legislation occurs after the reporting period but before the time of completion of the financial statements. For example, that Standard specifies particular disclosures where events occurring after the reporting period provide new information that does not relate to conditions existing at the end of the reporting period. These disclosures include the nature of the event and the financial effect of the non-adjusting event, if it can be estimated reliably.

References

Australia

The Urgent Issues Group discussed Issues Paper 04/3 "Revision of Various UIG Abstracts for 2005" in relation to this Interpretation at its meeting on 10 June 2004. In developing the superseded Abstract, the UIG discussed Issue Summary 02/1 "Effect of Proposed Tax Consolidation Legislation on Deferred Tax Balances" at meetings on 19 March, 14 May, 14 June, 2 July and 13 August 2002.

Accounting Standard AASB 110 *Events after the Reporting Period*

Accounting Standard AASB 112 *Income Taxes*

Canada

CICA Handbook Section 3465 *Income Taxes*

Emerging Issues Committee Abstract EIC-111 *Determination of Substantively Enacted Tax Rates under CICA 3465*

International Accounting Standards Board

International Accounting Standard IAS 12 *Income Taxes*

United Kingdom

Financial Reporting Standard FRS 19 *Deferred Tax*

United States of America

Statement of Financial Accounting Standards SFAS 109 *Accounting for Income Taxes*

Emerging Issues Task Force EITF Topic D-30 *Adjustment Due to Effect of a Change in Tax Laws or Rates*

Interpretation 1042
Subscriber Acquisition Costs in the Telecommunications Industry

(Compiled November 2010)

Compilation Details

UIG Interpretation 1042 *Subscriber Acquisition Costs in the Telecommunications Industry* as amended

This compiled Interpretation applies to annual reporting periods beginning on or after 1 January 2011. It takes into account amendments up to and including 27 October 2010 and was prepared on 26 November 2010 by the staff of the Australian Accounting Standards Board (AASB).

This compilation is not a separate Interpretation issued by the AASB. Instead, it is a representation of Interpretation 1042 (December 2004) as amended by other pronouncements, which are listed in the Table below.

Table of Pronouncements

Pronouncement	Month issued	Application date (*annual reporting periods ... on or after ...*)	Application, saving or transitional provisions
Interpretation 1042	Dec 2004	(*beginning*) 1 Jan 2005	
AASB 2007-8	Sep 2007	(*beginning*) 1 Jan 2009	see (a) below
AASB 2007-10	Dec 2007	(*beginning*) 1 Jan 2009	see (a) below
AASB 2010-5	Oct 2010	(*beginning*) 1 Jan 2011	see (b) below

(a) Entities may elect to apply this Standard to annual reporting periods beginning on or after 1 January 2005 but before 1 January 2009, provided that AASB 101 *Presentation of Financial Statements* (September 2007) is also applied to such periods.

(b) Entities may elect to apply this Standard to annual reporting periods beginning on or after 1 January 2005 but before 1 January 2011.

Table of Amendments

Paragraph affected	How affected	By ... [paragraph]
2	amended	AASB 2007-10 [117]
8	amended	AASB 2007-8 [7, 8]
11	amended	AASB 2007-8 [8]
14	amended	AASB 2007-8 [6]
15	amended	AASB 2010-5 [83]

Interpretation 1042

UIG Interpretation 1042 was issued in December 2004.

This compiled version of Interpretation 1042 applies to annual reporting periods beginning on or after 1 January 2011. It incorporates relevant amendments contained in other AASB pronouncements up to and including 27 October 2010 (see Compilation Details).

Urgent Issues Group

Interpretation 1042

Subscriber Acquisition Costs in the Telecommunications Industry

Interpretation 1042 is set out in paragraphs 1 to 29.

Issue

1   Entities in the telecommunications industry incur significant expenditures in setting up and establishing business operations that result in the acquisition of various intangible rights rather than tangible assets. Specifically, the expenditures often include subscriber acquisition costs. The entities incur substantial costs in acquiring new customers, including costs relating to advertising, the employment of sales staff, the payment of commissions and the subsidised provision of telephones.

2   Accounting Standards in Australia do not specifically address the accounting for customer acquisition costs in the telecommunications industry. Concern has been expressed that, in the absence of authoritative guidance, diverse or unacceptable accounting practices may occur or develop and that this will undermine the relevance and reliability of general purpose financial statements.

3   The issues are:

(a)   Should subscriber acquisition costs incurred by entities in the telecommunications industry be capitalised, that is, recognised as an asset?

(b)   If so, what costs should be recognised as part of the cost of the asset?

(c)   If subscriber acquisition costs are capitalised, should they be amortised and, if so, on what basis?

Consensus

4   **For the purposes of this Interpretation, subscriber acquisition costs are costs incurred in obtaining and recording telecommunications service contracts with subscribers. Direct subscriber acquisition costs are those incremental subscriber acquisition costs that are directly attributable to establishing specific subscriber contracts and would not have been incurred had those contracts not been entered into. Those costs do not include the cost of telephones provided to subscribers.**

5   **Direct subscriber acquisition costs shall be recognised as expenses as incurred, except that they shall be recognised as an asset when, and only when, the costs can be identified separately and:**

(a)   **the entity controls future economic benefits as a result of the costs incurred;**

(b)   **it is probable that those future economic benefits will flow to the entity; and**

(c)   **the costs can be measured reliably.**

6   **Subscriber acquisition costs other than those dealt with in paragraph 5 shall be recognised as expenses as incurred.**

7   **Subscriber acquisition costs recognised as an asset in accordance with paragraph 5 shall be amortised from the inception of the contract over the lesser of:**

(a)   **the stated period of the contract; and**

(b)   **the period during which the future economic benefits are expected to be obtained.**

Application

8   This Interpretation applies to:

   (a)   each entity that is required to prepare financial reports in accordance with Part 2M.3 of the *Corporations Act 2001* and that is a reporting entity;

   (b)   general purpose financial statements of each other reporting entity; and

   (c)   financial statements that are, or are held out to be, general purpose financial statements.

9   This Interpretation applies to annual reporting periods beginning on or after 1 January 2005.

   [Note: For application dates of paragraphs changed or added by an amending pronouncement, see Compilation Details.]

10   This Interpretation shall not be applied to annual reporting periods beginning before 1 January 2005.

11   The requirements specified in this Interpretation apply to the financial statements where information resulting from their application is material in accordance with AASB 1031 *Materiality*.

12   When applicable, this Interpretation supersedes Abstract 42 *Subscriber Acquisition Costs in the Telecommunications Industry*, as issued in October 2001.

13   Abstract 42 remains applicable until superseded by this Interpretation.

Discussion

14   Accounting Standard AASB 138 *Intangible Assets* defines an asset as a resource controlled by the entity as a result of past events and from which future economic benefits are expected to flow to the entity. AASB 138 also specifies that an intangible asset should be recognised in the statement of financial position only when it is probable that the future economic benefits attributable to the asset will flow to the entity and the asset possesses a cost that can be measured reliably. The Standard defines an intangible asset as an identifiable non-monetary asset without physical substance. The identifiability criterion is satisfied when the asset is separable from the entity or arises from contractual or other legal rights. Subscriber contracts clearly meet this criterion, and are distinguished from internally generated intangible assets such as customer lists since the subscriber contracts involve transactions with external parties.

15   Example 14(b)(iii) in the illustrative examples accompanying AASB 118 *Revenue* illustrates the recognition of an investment management contract as an asset, distinguishing the costs of securing a contract from those relating to providing ongoing services under the contract. Similarly, where an entity has incurred costs to obtain and record telecommunication contracts with subscribers, the characteristics of an asset (and therefore the condition in paragraph 5(a) of this Interpretation) and the asset recognition criteria (paragraphs 5(b) and 5(c)) may or may not be met. Whether these conditions are met in relation to subscriber acquisition costs is considered in the context of the nature of the costs incurred and the types of subscriber contracts, as discussed below.

Nature of Subscriber Acquisition Costs

16   The criteria for the recognition of assets set out in paragraphs 5(b) and (c) are likely to be satisfied only in relation to a limited range of costs incurred in obtaining subscribers. For example, the requirement that it is probable that the costs incurred will result in future economic benefits for the entity is likely to be met only for costs that can be shown to be directly attributable to the obtaining of subscribers to the entity's services and that would not otherwise have been incurred by the entity. These incremental costs can be specifically identified in relation to particular contracts, rather than merely to subscriber contracts in general. Directly attributable costs may include costs incurred prior to the contracts being entered into. Directly attributable costs include costs such as commissions paid for obtaining subscriber contracts, and costs of recording subscriber and contract information in relation to contracts entered into.

17   It is difficult to show a reliable relationship between the incurrence of other costs and the obtaining of subscriber contracts, so that the asset definition or recognition criteria are unlikely to be satisfied in relation to such costs. For example, it may be difficult to reliably measure the portion of the costs related to unsuccessful contract origination efforts or idle time. These costs include wages, salaries and other employee entitlements of the sales force (excluding commissions paid for obtaining subscriber contracts), costs of establishing subscriber credit and operating policies, advertising costs, and other administrative and overhead costs (such as directors' and executives' salaries, rent, depreciation and all other occupancy and equipment costs).

18   An entity may offer prospective subscribers the opportunity to purchase a telephone on a subsidised basis, that is for a discounted amount or for instalment payments over a specified period. The provision of a telephone to subscribers is accounted for as a sale under AASB 118 *Revenue*, as a separately identifiable component of the transaction. Where the payments under a subscriber contract cover both the initial supply of a telephone and the supply of subsequent services, the entity recognises revenue on a basis that reflects the purpose for which the payments are required.

Subscriber Contracts

19   In order for any subscriber acquisition costs to be recognised as assets, it is necessary for the entity incurring the costs to control future economic benefits as a result of the costs incurred. The entity may incur costs in the expectation that they will lead to future revenue streams, however where the expenditure does not give rise to subscriber contracts there is little basis for concluding that future economic benefits are controlled by the entity. Therefore, this Interpretation is based on the view that the characteristics of an asset can be satisfied in relation to subscriber acquisition costs only where subscriber contracts are obtained.

20   There are various types of contracts between subscribers and telecommunications service providers (or carriers). At one end of the spectrum, contracts may commit the subscriber to minimum levels of service or fees. At the other end of the spectrum are 'dial around' facilities, which are contracts that allow the subscriber to dial a special code or prefix to re-route a particular call from the preferred carrier to a second carrier, with whom the subscriber has a contract to pay for the services utilised. In between these types, there are 'exclusive carrier' contracts and 'preferred carrier' contracts. Exclusive-carrier contracts commit the subscriber to use the services of a specific carrier for all or some types of calls for a period of time, to the exclusion of other carriers. Preferred-carrier contracts route calls through the pre-selected carrier, unless a dial-around facility is invoked for a particular call.

21   The type of subscriber contract may affect the degree to which the asset recognition criteria in paragraphs 5(b) and (c) are satisfied. For example, under a minimum service or fee contract it normally would be probable that future economic benefits would eventuate, since at least the minimum revenue would be determinable, especially where the carrier has a policy of enforcing such contracts throughout their term. Where such contracts are not enforced for their full term, an entity may have sufficient historical data on lapse rates that would still enable it to reliably measure the future economic benefits expected to eventuate.

22   This approach does not mean, however, that subscriber acquisition costs should be recognised as an asset only up to the amount of the minimum revenues committed under contract to be paid by subscribers. The recognition criteria refer to the future economic benefits that are probable, which includes the revenues expected from current contracts on the basis of subscriber usage and lapse-rate data. However, the future economic benefits assessed relate to the contract period, and do not include any anticipated subscriber usage beyond the minimum contract period, since the subscriber acquisition costs are recognised as assets (if appropriate) for no longer than the contract period.

23   Similar considerations apply to the other types of subscriber contracts described in paragraph 20. However, it may be more and more difficult to show the probability of future economic benefits arising and to reliably measure them as the type of contract changes from exclusive-carrier contracts through preferred-carrier contracts to dial-

around contracts. In each case it would be necessary to have reliable data for the entity on subscriber usage and lapse rates. For example, under a dial-around contract the revenues from future call charges may reflect the entity's future selling activities. As a result, it would be rare for the recognition criteria to be satisfied for dial-around contracts.

Accounting Requirements Subsequent to Initial Recognition

24   AASB 138 requires the depreciable amount of an intangible asset with a finite useful life to be allocated on a systematic basis over its useful life from the time when the asset is available for use. That Standard also requires the amortisation method applied to an asset to reflect the pattern in which the asset's future economic benefits are expected to be consumed by the entity. This Interpretation reflects the view that subscriber acquisition costs recognised as assets are depreciable assets. As such, this Interpretation requires subscriber acquisition costs recognised as an asset to be amortised from the date of inception of the subscriber contract.

25   The period during which subscriber acquisition costs recognised as assets can be expected to provide future economic benefits to the entity is normally limited, particularly since subscribers may be committed to using the entity's services only for a specified period. Furthermore, subscribers are able to establish relationships with other telecommunications suppliers during or after the period of a non-exclusive contract. Where a subscriber contract terminates at the end of a specified period, the amortisation period is limited to that period. This is consistent with AASB 138 specifying that the useful life of intangible assets that arise from contractual or other legal rights shall not exceed the period of those rights.

26   Where a subscriber contract specifies a minimum contract period, any subscriber acquisition costs recognised as assets are amortised over that period, without extension for any expected continued usage by subscribers beyond that period. This approach is consistent with the requirements in AASB 138 concerning the useful life of intangible assets that arise from contractual or other legal rights: if those rights are conveyed for a limited term that can be renewed, the useful life includes the renewal period(s) only if the term can be renewed by the entity without significant cost. In the case of subscriber contracts, it is the subscriber that may have the option to renew the contract or to continue using the entity's services beyond the minimum period.

27   However, if the period during which future economic benefits are expected to be obtained by the entity is less than the contract period, the subscriber acquisition costs are amortised over that lesser period. The amortisation period therefore is required to reflect expected cancellations of contracts, provided that the terms of the contracts are not enforced by the entity.

28   Where an asset is recognised in accordance with this Interpretation, and measured on the cost basis, it is written down to recoverable amount when its carrying amount is greater than the recoverable amount, in accordance with AASB 136 *Impairment of Assets*. For example, if contracts are terminated during the contract period, unamortised subscriber acquisition costs attributable to terminations in excess of estimated levels already reflected in the amortisation of acquisition costs are written off as an expense.

29   Subsequent costs incurred in relation to subscriber contracts are likely to relate to either the regular servicing of subscribers' requirements or to achieving contract renewals. Servicing costs are expensed as incurred, and costs incurred in relation to contract renewals are expensed unless the criteria specified in paragraph 5 are satisfied.

References

Australia

The Urgent Issues Group discussed Issues Paper 04/3 "Revision of Various UIG Abstracts for 2005" in relation to this Interpretation at meetings on 22 July, 26 August, 5 October and 25 November 2004. In developing the superseded Abstract, the UIG discussed Issue Summary 01/2 "Subscriber Acquisition Costs in the Telecommunications Industry" or a draft Abstract at meetings on 8 February, 15 March, 27 April, 14 June, 26 July, 6 September and 18 October 2001.

Accounting Standard AASB 118 *Revenue*

Accounting Standard AASB 136 *Impairment of Assets*

Accounting Standard AASB 138 *Intangible Assets*

Canada

CICA Accounting Guideline AcG-3 *Financial Reporting by Property and Casualty Insurance Companies*

International Accounting Standards Board

International Accounting Standard IAS 18 *Revenue*

International Accounting Standard IAS 36 *Impairment of Assets*

International Accounting Standard IAS 38 *Intangible Assets*

United Kingdom

Financial Reporting Standard FRS 10 *Goodwill and Intangible Assets*

United States of America

Statement of Financial Accounting Standards SFAS 60 *Accounting and Reporting by Insurance Enterprises*

Statement of Financial Accounting Standards SFAS 91 *Accounting for Nonrefundable Fees and Costs Associated with Originating or Acquiring Loans and Initial Direct Costs of Leases*

FASB Technical Bulletin FTB 90-1 *Accounting for Separately Priced Extended Warranty and Product Maintenance Contracts*

AICPA Statement of Position SOP 93-7 *Reporting on Advertising Costs*

Interpretation 1047
Professional Indemnity Claims Liabilities in Medical Defence Organisations

(Compiled November 2009)

Compilation Details

UIG Interpretation 1047 *Professional Indemnity Claims Liabilities in Medical Defence Organisations* as amended

This compiled Interpretation applies to annual reporting periods beginning on or after 1 January 2009. It takes into account amendments up to and including 13 December 2007 and was prepared on 12 November 2009 by the staff of the Australian Accounting Standards Board (AASB).

This compilation is not a separate Interpretation issued by the AASB. Instead, it is a representation of Interpretation 1047 (November 2004) as amended by other pronouncements, which are listed in the Table below.

Table of Pronouncements

Pronouncement	Month issued	Application date (*annual reporting periods … on or after …*)	Application, saving or transitional provisions
Interpretation 1047	Nov 2004	*(beginning)* 1 Jan 2005	
AASB 2007-8	Sep 2007	*(beginning)* 1 Jan 2009	see (a) below
AASB 2007-10	Dec 2007	*(beginning)* 1 Jan 2009	see (a) below

(a) Entities may elect to apply this Standard to annual reporting periods beginning on or after 1 January 2005 but before 1 January 2009, provided that AASB 101 *Presentation of Financial Statements* (September 2007) is also applied to such periods.

Table of Amendments

Paragraph affected	How affected	By … [paragraph]
5	amended	AASB 2007-10 [118]
6	amended	AASB 2007-10 [118]
10	amended	AASB 2007-8 [7, 8]
13	amended	AASB 2007-8 [8]
22	amended	AASB 2007-8 [6]
25	amended	AASB 2007-8 [6]
28	amended	AASB 2007-8 [6]
	amended	AASB 2007-10 [118]
30	amended	AASB 2007-10 [118]

Interpretation 1047

UIG Interpretation 1047 was issued in November 2004.

This compiled version of Interpretation 1047 applies to annual reporting periods beginning on or after 1 January 2009. It incorporates relevant amendments contained in other AASB pronouncements up to and including 13 December 2007 (see Compilation Details).

Urgent Issues Group

Interpretation 1047

Professional Indemnity Claims Liabilities in Medical Defence Organisations

Interpretation 1047 is set out in paragraphs 1 to 30.

Issue

1   Medical Defence Organisations (MDOs) are mutual organisations that accept subscriptions or premiums from their members for professional indemnity cover. The membership rules of MDOs traditionally have included a discretion for the organisation over whether or not to pay claims made by members, which is a key difference from insurance contracts written by registered general insurers. For this reason, MDOs have been considered by the industry to be outside the scope of Accounting Standards dealing with general insurance. However, under legislative changes applying from 1 July 2003, MDOs (or their subsidiaries) are able to offer new or renewal medical indemnity cover only as general insurers, under contracts of insurance. Such contracts are accounted for in accordance with Accounting Standard AASB 1023 *General Insurance Contracts*. Discretionary indemnity still applies to some arrangements entered into prior to 1 July 2003, depending on any revision of the terms offered by an MDO.

2   Traditionally, MDOs accepted subscriptions on a claims-incurred basis, which requires the member to have been a member of the MDO at the time the incident (event) occurred in order to be able to report a claim for indemnity at any time in the future. However, MDOs generally now accept subscriptions or premiums on a claims-made basis, either in addition to or in place of the claims-incurred basis.

3   Under the claims-made basis, a member normally is required to report claims for indemnity to the MDO whilst they are a member, in respect of events which have occurred during their claims-made membership period, once the member has become aware of the event. Furthermore, MDOs generally require the member to have also been a member since the period in which the event occurred.

4   MDOs may also have offered Extended Reporting Benefits (ERB) indemnity, under which members could pay an exit fee (either upon resignation or over numerous years of membership) and subsequently make claims in relation to incidents that occurred prior to the claimant ceasing to be an active member of the MDO. Similar claims reporting benefits may have been offered by MDOs in relation to the death, disablement or retirement (DDR) of members, with members qualifying for DDR indemnity through death, disablement, purchase upon retirement or satisfying a minimum financial membership period requirement, such as ten or fifteen years' membership. Legislative changes effective 1 July 2004 require MDOs or insurers to provide run-off cover contracts that encompass DDR and similar circumstances, such as not engaging in private medical practice for at least three years and cessation of private medical practice due to maternity. Members' regular premiums include a component to pay for their run-off cover when they become eligible. As the Commonwealth Government will reimburse the claims and costs paid under the run-off cover scheme, a run-off cover support payment is imposed as a tax in relation to the premiums received by the MDO (or insurance subsidiaries) from members.

5   There are different views concerning when MDOs should recognise liabilities for claims by members, for example whether claims liabilities should be recognised prior to any formal exercise of discretion to assist a member with a claim (where discretion continues to be relevant) or prior to notification of the claim by the member, as claims incurred but not reported. Concern has been expressed that, in the absence of authoritative guidance, diverse or unacceptable liability recognition practices may continue in the industry. This will undermine the relevance and reliability of general purpose financial statements.

6   The issues are:

    (a)   should an MDO recognise a liability for a professional indemnity claim reported to the MDO by a member before, or only after, the MDO has exercised its discretion (where relevant) in favour of assisting the member with the claim;

    (b)   should an MDO recognise a liability for a professional indemnity claim incurred but not yet reported to the MDO (IBNRs) by a member, in relation to each of the following:

        (i)   the claims-incurred basis of indemnity;

        (ii)   extended reporting benefit indemnity, death, disablement or retirement arrangements, and other run-off cover; and

        (iii)   the claims-made basis of indemnity; and

    (c)   what disclosures are appropriate in the financial statements?

Consensus

7   **Subject to paragraph 8, liabilities arising for medical defence organisations in respect of outstanding claims shall be recognised in relation to events that have occurred prior to the end of the reporting period that are alleged to be covered by discretionary medical indemnity arrangements of the entity, in the following cases:**

    (a)   unpaid reported claims;

    (b)   incurred but not reported claims arising under claims-incurred indemnity arrangements;

    (c)   incurred but not reported claims arising under extended reporting benefit indemnity arrangements, death, disablement or retirement indemnity arrangements, or other run-off cover, in relation to:

        (i)   members for whom such arrangements are in effect as at the end of the reporting period; and

        (ii)   members expected to qualify in the future for such arrangements as a member of the organisation; and

    (d)   incurred but not reported claims arising under claims-made indemnity arrangements which are, in substance, claims-incurred indemnity arrangements.

8   **Liabilities arising in respect of outstanding claims shall be recognised when the entity has a present obligation (legal or constructive) as a result of a past event, it is probable that an outflow of resources embodying economic benefits will be required to settle the obligation, and a reliable estimate can be made of the amount of the obligation.**

9   **The following information shall be disclosed in relation to the determination of the liability for outstanding claims:**

    (a)   the accounting policies and methods adopted, including the basis of measurement and key assumptions applied; and

    (b)   information about the nature and extent of the underlying indemnity arrangements, including significant terms and conditions that may affect the amount, timing and uncertainty of future cash flows.

Application

10   **This Interpretation applies to entities that are or include medical defence organisations as follows:**

    (a)   each entity that is required to prepare financial reports in accordance with Part 2M.3 of the *Corporations Act 2001* and that is a reporting entity;

    (b)   general purpose financial statements of each other reporting entity; and

    (c)   financial statements that are, or are held out to be, general purpose financial statements.

11   This Interpretation applies to annual reporting periods beginning on or after 1 January 2005.

       [Note: For application dates of paragraphs changed or added by an amending pronouncement, see Compilation Details.]

12   This Interpretation shall not be applied to annual reporting periods beginning before 1 January 2005.

13   The requirements specified in this Interpretation apply to the financial statements where information resulting from their application is material in accordance with AASB 1031 *Materiality*.

14   When applicable, this Interpretation supersedes Abstract 47 *Professional Indemnity Claims Liabilities in Medical Defence Organisations*, as issued in June 2002.

15   Abstract 47 remains applicable until superseded by this Interpretation.

Discussion

16   Medical defence organisations (MDOs) previously offered 'discretionary' professional indemnity cover to their members, whereas general insurers offer professional indemnity 'insurance' cover to policyholders. Both types of entities have issued claims-incurred contracts and claims-made contracts. The view adopted in this Interpretation is that the accounting for these contracts by MDOs and by general insurers should be consistent, since the substance of the contracts is similar. An insurance contract is defined in AASB 1023 as a contract under which one party (the insurer) accepts significant insurance risk from another party (the policyholder) by agreeing to compensate the policyholder if a specified uncertain future event adversely affects the policyholder. Under the indemnity arrangements addressed in this Interpretation, the MDO formally has the discretion to decide whether to compensate a member if a specified uncertain future event adversely affects the member.

17   AASB 1023 addresses the accounting for general insurance contracts, but does not refer in any detail to claims-made insurance policies similar to the claims-made indemnity arrangements of MDOs. AASB 1023 requires the recognition by general insurers of a liability for outstanding claims in relation to unpaid reported claims and claims incurred but not reported. This requirement is reflected in this Interpretation.

18   Liabilities arising in respect of outstanding claims are recognised when it is probable that settlement will be required and the liabilities can be measured reliably. Where there are a number of similar claims, the probability that settlement will be required may be determined by considering the class of claims as a whole. Although the probability for any one claim may be small, or unascertainable, it may be probable that an outflow of resources will be required to settle the class of claims as a whole. In that case, a liability (and expense) is recognised in relation to the class of claims where the amount can be measured reliably.

19   Claims include requests by members to their MDO for discretionary assistance in relation to adverse events involving them. Claims arise from events alleged to be covered by indemnity arrangements that occur during the period of indemnity, whether or not a formal demand has been made by a party on account of an alleged loss. Some events will occur and give rise to claims that are reported to the MDO and settled within the same reporting period. Other reported claims may be unsettled at the end of a particular reporting period. In addition, there may be events which give rise to claims which, at the end of a reporting period, have yet to be reported to the MDO, whether or not the member is aware of the event. These claims are termed claims incurred but not reported (claims IBNR). It is necessary to ensure that claims are recognised as liabilities and expenses in the correct reporting period, as discussed in the following paragraphs.

Unpaid Reported Claims

20   The view adopted in this Interpretation is that a liability should be recognised by an MDO once a claim has been reported to the MDO by a member. MDOs typically have had a discretion to refuse assistance to a member in relation to a claim, but such action is rare.

The members of MDOs have valid expectations that their MDO normally will settle their claims, based either on the terms of the indemnity contracts directly or on the custom or practices of the MDO. Accordingly, any discretion of MDOs to refuse assistance to a member normally is considered not to have substance for financial reporting purposes. Thus, MDOs have at the least a constructive obligation in relation to the claims reported by members. This basis for the identification of liabilities is explained in AASB 137 *Provisions, Contingent Liabilities and Contingent Assets* (paragraph 17). Under this approach, if an MDO subsequently exercises its discretion to reject wholly or partly a reported claim that has been recognised as a liability, then the amount included in the outstanding claims liability for that claim is derecognised to that extent following that decision.

Claims Incurred but not Reported

21   The claims IBNR issue is whether an MDO should recognise liabilities for professional indemnity claims that relate to events that have occurred during a member's period of indemnity and prior to the end of the MDO's reporting period, but which have not yet been reported to the MDO by the member. Some of these events will have been reported by injured parties to the MDO's members, whereas other events may not have been reported to the members or even may not yet be apparent to the injured parties. These claims are all referred to as claims incurred but not reported, or claims IBNR.

Claims IBNR under Claims-Incurred Indemnity

22   This Interpretation requires MDOs to recognise a liability for claims IBNR arising under claims-incurred indemnity arrangements, based on the view that an MDO has a legal or a constructive obligation to meet the claims incurred but not reported. This approach is supported on the grounds that the MDO's discretion to refuse assistance to a member (where still relevant) normally is not substantive for financial reporting purposes, as explained in paragraph 20. Furthermore, the identification of the event by the injured party, their reporting the event to the member, and the member's reporting to the MDO, are all independent of the MDO's future actions or conduct of its operations. Therefore, the MDO is presently obliged as at the end of the reporting period to make future claims payments in respect of these claims IBNR as a result of past events, which is an essential characteristic of liabilities.

Claims IBNR under ERB, DDR and Other Run-off Arrangements

23   Extended reporting benefits (ERB), death, disablement or retirement (DDR) indemnity arrangements and other run-off cover are not relevant to MDO members who have claims-incurred indemnity, since those members are entitled to report claims relating to events that have occurred during their period of indemnity at any time, including after the end of their membership period. Accordingly, ERB, DDR and other run-off cover are sometimes referred to as a type of claims-made indemnity.

24   This Interpretation requires MDOs to recognise a liability for claims IBNR arising under ERB, DDR and other run-off indemnity arrangements where members have qualified for any of those arrangements at some time prior to the end of the reporting period. ERB, DDR and other run-off cover allow a member (or their representative) to report claims arising from events occurring during the indemnity period at any time in the future without further subscription. This is no different from the coverage of claims-incurred indemnity. Accordingly, the same accounting is justified.

25   A liability for outstanding claims is also required to be recognised for claims IBNR in relation to members who are expected to qualify in the future for ERB, DDR and other run-off indemnity arrangements as members of the MDO. This approach is based on the view that the obligation to make future claims payments in these circumstances is independent of the MDO's future actions or conduct of its operations. The death or disablement of members is beyond the control of an MDO, and reliable estimates of their incidence may be able to be made. MDOs may also offer continuing reporting benefits upon the resignation or retirement of a member where the member has been a financial member for the minimum qualifying period specified by the MDO, without further subscription. MDOs may have a discretion not to accept membership renewals, however in practice this discretion has been rarely exercised. Accordingly, that discretion is considered not to have

substance for financial reporting purposes. Thus, MDOs have a constructive obligation in these circumstances. Where reliable estimates can be made of members qualifying for ERB, DDR or other run-off cover, a liability is required to be recognised in relation to that cohort of members for events that have occurred to the end of the reporting period and which are expected to result in future claims payments by the MDO.

Claims IBNR under Claims-Made Indemnity

26   Under claims-made indemnity, members are required to report claims to an MDO during their membership period. If they cease to be a member of the MDO and have no additional claim reporting rights, then any claims that they report to the MDO after that time are not required to be settled by the MDO, and are not liabilities. AASB 1023 notes that an insurer theoretically cannot have claims IBNR under claims-made insurance contracts.

27   However, in some cases, the additional rights of members with claims-made indemnity may be such that the indemnity is effectively the same as claims-incurred indemnity. These additional rights can mean that members are effectively 'locked in' as members of an MDO. This Interpretation requires MDOs to recognise a liability for claims IBNR arising under claims-made indemnity arrangements in such circumstances, because in substance the arrangements represent claims-incurred indemnity. For example, members may have the right to purchase extended reporting benefits upon resignation or retirement (when the member is ineligible for the mandatory run-off cover scheme) for fixed or determinable subscription rates that make it probable that the members will purchase those benefits. However, where a member can only purchase extended reporting benefits upon resignation or retirement from the MDO for fair value at that time, the MDO is not obligated in respect of claims IBNR until the purchase by the member occurs. The determination of fair value would incorporate an assessment of the member's circumstances at that time, including claims history and claims IBNR.

Disclosures

28   The purpose of the disclosures required by this Interpretation is to provide users of an MDO's financial statements with information that will enhance their understanding of the basis upon which claims liabilities have been measured and recognised by the MDO. The disclosure requirements are consistent with those in AASB 1023. Various assumptions are required to be made in estimating the future cash flows arising in relation to claims liabilities, such as the incidence of events occurring to the end of the reporting period, the timing of settlement of claims, inflation and discount rates, member retention rates, and the likelihood of members qualifying for ERB, DDR or other run-off indemnity arrangements. Disclosure of the key assumptions applied by an MDO in measuring its claims liabilities assists users of financial statements in assessing the amount, timing and uncertainty of future cash flows.

29   Future cash flows of an MDO are affected by the different types of claims indemnity arrangements offered by the MDO, such as claims-incurred or claims-made indemnity and ERB, DDR and other run-off arrangements. Accordingly, disclosures are required about the nature of the indemnity arrangements, the extent to which they apply in the MDO's business, and their major terms and conditions. For example, where ERB arrangements are material for an MDO, it discloses any membership period requirements and the basis for determining any exit subscription rates (whether at fair value or otherwise) under which members qualify for those arrangements.

Application

30   This Interpretation applies to reporting entities that are or include medical defence organisations. It also applies to general purpose financial statements that encompass MDOs. The Interpretation applies to an MDO's own financial statements and to the consolidated financial statements where a group of entities includes an MDO. The Interpretation applies to the discretionary medical indemnity arrangements of the MDO.

References

Australia

The Urgent Issues Group discussed Issues Paper 04/3 "Revision of Various UIG Abstracts for 2005" in relation to this Interpretation at meetings on 22 July and 5 October 2004. In developing the superseded Abstract, the UIG discussed Issue Summary 01/11 "Professional Indemnity Claims Liabilities in Medical Defence Organisations" at meetings on 6 December 2001 and 12 February, 19 March, 14 May and 14 June 2002.

Accounting Standard AASB 137 *Provisions, Contingent Liabilities and Contingent Assets*

Accounting Standard AASB 1023 *General Insurance Contracts*

Canada

Accounting Guideline AcG-3 *Financial Reporting by Property and Casualty Insurance Companies*

International Accounting Standards Board

International Financial Reporting Standard IFRS 4 *Insurance Contracts*

United States of America

Statement of Financial Accounting Standards SFAS 60 *Accounting and Reporting by Insurance Enterprises*

Interpretations

Interpretation 1052

Tax Consolidation Accounting

(Compiled February 2010)

Compilation Details

UIG Interpretation 1052 *Tax Consolidation Accounting* as amended

This compiled Interpretation applies to annual reporting periods beginning on or after 1 January 2011. It takes into account amendments up to and including 15 December 2009 and was prepared on 23 February 2010 by the staff of the Australian Accounting Standards Board (AASB).

This compilation is not a separate Interpretation issued by the AASB. Instead, it is a representation of Interpretation 1052 (June 2005) as amended by other pronouncements, which are listed in the Table below.

Table of Pronouncements

Pronouncement	Month issued	Application date (*annual reporting periods ... on or after ...*)	Application, saving or transitional provisions
Interpretation 1052	Jun 2005	(*ending*) 31 Dec 2005	see (a) below
AASB 2007-8	Sep 2007	(*beginning*) 1 Jan 2009	see (b) below
AASB 2007-10	Dec 2007	(*beginning*) 1 Jan 2009	see (b) below
AASB 2009-12	Dec 2009	(*beginning*) 1 Jan 2011	see (c) below

(a)   Entities may elect to apply this Interpretation to annual reporting periods beginning on or after 1 January 2005 that end before 31 December 2005.

(b)   Entities may elect to apply this Standard to annual reporting periods beginning on or after 1 January 2005 but before 1 January 2009, provided that AASB 101 *Presentation of Financial Statements* (September 2007) is also applied to such periods.

(c)   Entities may elect to apply this Standard to annual reporting periods beginning on or after 1 January 2005 but before 1 January 2011.

Table of Amendments

Paragraph affected	How affected	By ... [paragraph]
5	amended	AASB 2007-10 [119]
17	amended	AASB 2007-8 [7, 8]
19	amended amended	AASB 2007-8 [6] AASB 2009-12 [27]
20	amended	AASB 2007-8 [8]
26	amended	AASB 2007-8 [6]
27	amended	AASB 2007-10 [120]
30	amended	AASB 2007-8 [6]
35	amended	AASB 2007-8 [6]
37	amended	AASB 2007-8 [6]
57	amended	AASB 2007-8 [6]
59	amended	AASB 2007-10 [119]
61	amended amended	AASB 2007-8 [6] AASB 2007-10 [119]

Interpretation 1052

UIG Interpretation 1052 was issued in June 2005.

This compiled version of Interpretation 1052 applies to annual reporting periods beginning on or after 1 January 2011. It incorporates relevant amendments contained in other AASB pronouncements up to and including 15 December 2009 (see Compilation Details).

Urgent Issues Group

Interpretation 1052

Tax Consolidation Accounting

Interpretation 1052 is set out in paragraphs 1 to 67.

Issue

1   The tax consolidation legislation includes both mandatory requirements, which are applicable to all entities, and the tax consolidation system provisions, which entities can elect to adopt. The tax consolidation system allows groups comprising a parent entity and its wholly-owned subsidiaries (all being Australian residents for tax purposes) to elect to consolidate and be treated as a single entity for income tax purposes. It also allows Australian-resident wholly-owned subsidiaries of a non-resident company to elect to consolidate for income tax purposes, in various combinations, with an eligible subsidiary being appointed as the head entity of the multiple entry consolidated (MEC) group.

2   The principal tax consolidation legislation was enacted through a series of Acts over a long period. The first Act, the *New Business Tax System (Consolidation) Act (No. 1) 2002*, was passed by Parliament in June 2002. However, its commencement was linked to the second principal tax consolidation Act, which was enacted in October 2002. The third and fourth principal tax consolidation Acts were enacted in November 2002 and March 2003 respectively. Amendments and additional requirements have been included in other taxation Acts as well. However, the tax consolidation regime or system commenced with effect from 1 July 2002.

3   Under the legislation, if a group chooses to be taxed as a consolidated entity, each of the entities in the tax-consolidated group will be taken to be "part" of the head entity for the purposes of the tax consolidation legislation. A single consolidated annual tax return will be required to be prepared for the tax-consolidated group. Transactions between entities in the tax-consolidated group will be ignored for tax purposes. The head entity will be liable for the current income tax liabilities of that group. Each entity in the group will be jointly and severally liable for the current income tax liability of the group where the head entity defaults, subject to the terms of a valid tax sharing agreement between the entities in the group.

4   Accounting Standard AASB 112 *Income Taxes* contains the general requirements for accounting for income taxes. However, there are different views on many issues concerning the recognition of income tax amounts (expense/income, assets and liabilities) under the tax consolidation system which are only relevant to an entity once it is applying the tax consolidation system. For example, the issues raised include whether each entity in a tax-consolidated group should still recognise income tax amounts, whether deferred tax balances previously recognised by subsidiaries in the group should be recognised by the head entity, the accounting for intragroup tax funding (or contribution) arrangements, and potential contingent liability disclosures by subsidiaries in respect of tax liabilities borne by the head entity.

5   Concern has been expressed that, in the absence of authoritative guidance, diverse or unacceptable practices may occur or develop in accounting for the effects of the tax consolidation system. This will undermine the relevance and reliability of general purpose financial statements.

6   The principal issues are:

  (a)   Once tax consolidation is adopted:

    (i)   should current taxes in relation to wholly-owned subsidiaries' transactions be recognised by the subsidiaries and/or the head entity, or only by the group on consolidation?

    (ii)   should the deferred tax effects of the assets and liabilities of wholly-owned subsidiaries be recognised by the subsidiaries or the head entity, or only by the group on consolidation?

  (b)   How should tax funding (or contribution) arrangements be accounted for?

  (c)   What disclosures are appropriate?

Consensus

Income Tax Recognition for the Period

7   **The head entity and each subsidiary in a tax-consolidated group is required by AASB 112 to account for the current and future tax consequences of its assets and liabilities and transactions and other events of the current period.**

8   **The consolidated current and deferred tax amounts for a tax-consolidated group shall be allocated among the entities in the group when they issue separate financial statements. This Interpretation does not require a single allocation method. However, the method adopted shall be systematic, rational and consistent with the broad principles established in AASB 112.**

9   **The following methods are examples of acceptable allocation methods:**

  (a)   **a "stand-alone taxpayer" approach for each entity, as if it continued to be a taxable entity in its own right;**

  (b)   **a "separate taxpayer within group" approach for each entity, on the basis that the entity is subject to tax as part of the tax-consolidated group. This method requires adjustments for transactions and events occurring within the tax-consolidated group that do not give rise to a tax consequence for the group or that have a different tax consequence at the level of the group; and**

  (c)   **subject to paragraph 10, a "group allocation" approach, under which the current and deferred tax amounts for the tax-consolidated group are allocated among each entity in the group.**

10   **The following group allocation methods, for example, are not acceptable:**

  (a)   **a method that allocates only current tax liabilities to an entity in the group that has taxable temporary differences;**

  (b)   **a method that allocates deferred taxes to an entity in the group using a method that is fundamentally different from the temporary difference approach required by AASB 112; and**

  (c)   **a method that allocates no current or deferred tax expense to an entity in the group that has taxable income because the tax-consolidated group has no current or deferred tax expense.**

Tax Consolidation Adjustments

11   **Specific tax consolidation adjustments shall be accounted for by a subsidiary in a tax-consolidated group as follows:**

  (a)   **current tax liabilities (or assets) recognised for the period by the subsidiary shall be accounted for as immediately assumed by the head entity;**

  (b)   **deferred tax assets arising from unused tax losses and unused relevant tax credits recognised for the period by the subsidiary shall be accounted for as immediately assumed by the head entity;**

  (c)   **assets and liabilities (if any) arising for the subsidiary under a tax funding arrangement shall be recognised as amounts receivable from or payable to other entities in the group; and**

    (d)   any difference between the net tax amount derecognised under paragraphs (a) and (b) and the net amount recognised under paragraph (c) shall be recognised as a contribution by (or distribution to) equity participants between the subsidiary and the head entity.

12   In addition to the tax effects of its own transactions, events and balances, the head entity in a tax-consolidated group shall recognise:

    (a)   the current tax liabilities (or assets) and the deferred tax assets arising from unused tax losses and unused relevant tax credits assumed from the subsidiaries in the group;

    (b)   assets and liabilities (if any) arising for the head entity under a tax funding arrangement – as amounts receivable from or payable to other entities in the group; and

    (c)   any difference between the net tax amount recognised under paragraph (a) and the net amount recognised under paragraph (b) – as a contribution by (or distribution to) equity participants between the head entity and its subsidiaries.

13   This Interpretation does not prescribe which account or accounts shall be adjusted for contributions by (or distributions to) equity participants arising under paragraph 11(d) or 12(c).

14   Where a subsidiary in the tax-consolidated group is not a direct subsidiary of the head entity, any contribution by (or distribution to) equity participants shall be accounted for as contributions or distributions through the interposed parents.

15   Where the head entity is in default of its payment obligations under the tax consolidation system, or such default is probable, a subsidiary in the tax-consolidated group shall recognise a liability (if any) arising under the joint and several liability requirements of the tax consolidation system or their tax sharing agreement (if any).

Disclosures

16   The following information shall be disclosed separately by a head entity and by a subsidiary in a tax-consolidated group:

    (a)   the relevance of the tax consolidation system to the entity, including the part of the reporting period for which it applies to the entity where it is not applicable for the whole of the reporting period, and the name of the head entity;

    (b)   the method adopted for measuring the current and deferred tax amounts;

    (c)   information about the nature of any tax funding arrangement and any tax sharing agreement, including significant terms and conditions that may affect the amount, timing and uncertainty of future cash flows; and

    (d)   the net amount recognised for the period as tax-consolidation contributions by (or distributions to) equity participants, its major components and the accounts affected.

Application

17   This Interpretation applies to:

    (a)   each entity that is required to prepare financial reports in accordance with Part 2M.3 of the *Corporations Act 2001* and that is a reporting entity;

    (b)   general purpose financial statements of each other reporting entity; and

    (c)   financial statements that are, or are held out to be, general purpose financial statements.

18   This Interpretation applies to annual reporting periods ending on or after 31 December 2005.

[Note: For application dates of paragraphs changed or added by an amending pronouncement, see Compilation Details.]

19   This Interpretation may be applied to annual reporting periods beginning on or after 1 January 2005 that end before 31 December 2005, permitting early application

only in the context of adopting all Australian equivalents to International Financial Reporting Standards for such periods. An entity that is required to prepare financial reports in accordance with Part 2M.3 of the Corporations Act may apply this Interpretation to such an annual reporting period when an election has been made in accordance with subsection 334(5) of the Corporations Act in relation to AASB 1048 *Interpretation and Application of Standards*. When an entity applies this Interpretation to such an annual reporting period, it shall disclose that fact.

20   The requirements specified in this Interpretation apply to the financial statements where information resulting from their application is material in accordance with AASB 1031 *Materiality*.

21   When applied or operative, this Interpretation supersedes Abstract 52 *Income Tax Accounting under the Tax Consolidation System*, as issued in December 2003. The Interpretation also supersedes, in part, Abstract 39 *Effect of Proposed Tax Consolidation Legislation on Deferred Tax Balances*, as issued in December 2002.

22   Abstract 52 and Abstract 39 have been withdrawn with effect for annual reporting periods beginning on or after 1 January 2005.

23   For the purposes of this Interpretation, references to "tax-consolidated group", "head entity" and "wholly-owned subsidiaries" respectively include a multiple entry consolidated (MEC) group, the head entity of the MEC group, and the other entities that are members of the MEC group.

Discussion

The Tax Consolidation System

24   All mandatory requirements included in enacted or substantively enacted tax consolidation legislation are relevant to an entity, and are taken into account in measuring and recognising income tax amounts. Where an entity is applying the tax consolidation system, the elective tax consolidation requirements are also relevant to the entity. This Interpretation addresses the accounting for income tax amounts where the entity is applying the tax consolidation system during the reporting period (whether for the whole of or a part of the period).

25   Under the tax consolidation system, the head entity in the tax-consolidated group is liable for income taxes arising in relation to the transactions and other events of the wholly-owned subsidiaries in the tax-consolidated group subsequent to the adoption of tax consolidation, with the exception that transactions between entities in the group are ignored for tax purposes. This means that the subsidiaries' transactions, events and balances continue to be subject to income tax.

Implementation of the Tax Consolidation System

26   The implementation date of tax consolidation for an entity is the date from which the tax consolidation system will be applied to the taxation obligations of the entities in the tax-consolidatable group, that is, the date from which a consolidated tax return will be prepared. If the entity (or its head entity) has chosen an implementation date that is *prior to or the same as* the end of the reporting period, then the accounting for income tax amounts is required to reflect the full effects of the tax consolidation system from the implementation date. The implementation date would normally be expected to be specified by the entity or its head entity in a formal resolution of the board of directors or other governing body or of management delegated to determine the implementation date for the entity or group.

27   The implementation date for an entity can be different from the date on which the entity (or its head entity) makes the decision to adopt the tax consolidation system, and from the date on which the decision is formally notified to the Australian Taxation Office. Formal notification can occur up to the date of lodgement of the first consolidated income tax return, which may be after the completion of the financial statements for the reporting period. However, if the implementation date is determined prior to the completion of the financial statements, the appropriate accounting depends on the implementation date, as explained in the preceding paragraph, rather than on the decision date or the date

of formal notification to the taxation authority. Where the implementation date is not determined prior to the completion of the financial statements, the financial statements are not prepared in accordance with the requirements set out in this Interpretation. Those financial statements are not amended and reissued where the implementation date, as subsequently determined, retrospectively falls in that previous reporting period. This Interpretation does not address the accounting prior to the implementation of tax consolidation by a group.

Formation of, or Subsidiary Joins, the Tax-Consolidated Group

28   When a tax-consolidated group is first formed, it comprises the head entity and all the wholly-owned subsidiaries that satisfy the requirements of the tax consolidation legislation at that time. A subsidiary joins an existing tax-consolidated group when it becomes wholly owned by the head entity and satisfies those requirements. The subsidiary may previously have been a partly-owned subsidiary of the head entity, or may be a newly acquired subsidiary. When a subsidiary becomes part of a tax-consolidated group, the subsidiary's transactions, events and balances continue to be subject to income tax, even though it is the head entity in the tax-consolidated group that is then liable for the income taxes.

Income Tax Allocation

29   The view adopted in this Interpretation is that a subsidiary in a tax-consolidated group has taxable profits (or tax losses) as defined in AASB 112, since income taxes are payable or recoverable on the subsidiary's profits or losses as determined in accordance with the rules of the taxation authority – even though the income taxes are payable (recoverable) by the head entity and not the subsidiary itself. Therefore, this Interpretation requires subsidiaries in the tax-consolidated group to recognise current and deferred tax amounts: each entity in the tax-consolidated group in substance remains taxable, and the legal form of the tax-consolidation arrangement should not determine the accounting. Consequently, the head entity does not recognise any initial tax balances relating to the assets and liabilities of subsidiaries when they join the tax-consolidated group (with the possible exception of tax-loss/tax-credit deferred tax assets). The consolidated financial statements covering the tax-consolidated group continue to include income taxes in accordance with AASB 112.

30   Under AASB 112, deferred tax liabilities and assets arise from temporary differences and from unused tax losses and tax credits. Temporary differences are differences between the carrying amount of an asset or a liability in the statement of financial position and its tax base. The tax base of an asset or liability is the amount attributed to that asset or liability for tax purposes.

31   The head entity continues to recognise current and deferred taxes in relation to its own transactions, events and balances. The head entity also recognises, as tax consolidation adjustments, current tax liabilities (or assets) and deferred tax assets relating to tax losses and relevant tax credits that are assumed from the subsidiaries. These deferred tax assets are recognised in accordance with the recognition criteria in paragraph 34 of AASB 112. Relevant tax credits are those assumed by the head entity from the subsidiaries under the tax consolidation system. Subsequent references in this Interpretation to tax credits are only to such tax credits.

32   The subsidiaries in the group are also required to recognise deferred taxes, since amounts are attributed to their assets and liabilities for tax purposes – even though the tax transactions occur (from a legal perspective) in the head entity instead. When a subsidiary joins a tax-consolidated group, the tax bases of its assets and liabilities are determined by reference to the tax values applying under tax consolidation. The tax effects of any change in the tax base are recognised in accordance with paragraph 65 of AASB 112.

33   This Interpretation permits the use of different methods for measuring the current and deferred tax amounts to be recognised initially for each reporting period by the entities in the tax-consolidated group (including the head entity), provided that the method is systematic, rational and consistent with the broad principles in AASB 112. Paragraph 9 indicates that "stand-alone taxpayer", "separate taxpayer within group" and "group allocation" approaches can be acceptable methods. The specific tax consolidation

adjustments required by paragraphs 11 to 15 are recognised only after the application of the chosen method.

Stand-Alone Taxpayer Approach

34   Under this approach, each entity in the tax-consolidated group measures its current and deferred taxes as if it continued to be a separate taxable entity in its own right. This approach means, for example, that an entity recognises tax in relation to its intragroup transactions. The entity also assesses the recovery of its unused tax losses and tax credits only in the period in which they arise, and before assumption by the head entity, in accordance with AASB 112 applied in its own circumstances, without regard to the circumstances of the tax-consolidated group.

35   When recognising deferred taxes in the separate financial statements of each entity in the tax-consolidated group under this approach, temporary differences are measured by reference to the carrying amounts of assets and liabilities in the entity's statement of financial position and their tax bases applying under tax consolidation, as those are the only available tax bases. Therefore, consolidation adjustments to reflect business combinations or other transactions within the group are ignored. As a result, deferred taxes associated with these adjustments are recognised only on consolidation and not in the separate financial statements of an entity in the group under the stand-alone taxpayer approach.

Separate Taxpayer within Group Approach

36   The "separate taxpayer within group" approach involves the calculation of current and deferred taxes for each entity in the tax-consolidated group on the basis that the entity is subject to tax as part of the tax-consolidated group. Therefore, adjustments are made in each entity in relation to its transactions that do not give rise to a tax consequence for the group or that have a different tax consequence at the level of the group. For example, adjustments are required in relation to:

(a)   unrealised profits and losses on the intragroup sale or transfer of inventory or other assets;

(b)   management fees and other charges between entities in the group; and

(c)   tax losses/credits that are not expected to be recoverable by the entity on a stand-alone basis but which are expected to be recoverable in the context of the group.

37   When recognising deferred taxes in the separate financial statements of each entity in the tax-consolidated group under this approach, temporary differences are measured by reference to the carrying amounts of assets and liabilities either in the entity's statement of financial position or at the level of the tax-consolidated group and their tax bases applying under tax consolidation. These alternative approaches illustrate that there are a range of acceptable methods for allocating group current and deferred taxes in accordance with the criteria in paragraph 8.

38   Each entity in the tax-consolidated group assesses the recovery of its unused tax losses and tax credits only in the period in which they arise, and before assumption by the head entity, in accordance with AASB 112 applied in the context of the group. Thus, each entity initially recognises such deferred tax assets arising during a period to the extent that they are recoverable by the group, whether as a reduction of the current tax of other entities in the group or as a deferred tax asset of the head entity. When several entities in a tax-consolidated group derive tax losses/credits in the same period but not all of the aggregate amount of the tax losses/credits is expected to be utilised as a reduction of a current tax liability or recognised as a deferred tax asset by the head entity, the aggregate amount expected to be utilised or recognised is apportioned on a systematic and reasonable basis between those entities for their initial tax-loss/tax-credit deferred tax asset recognition.

Group Allocation Approach

39   A "group allocation" approach may be most appropriate where the tax return for the tax-consolidated group is prepared directly on a consolidated basis. Under this approach, current and deferred taxes are allocated to the entities in the group in a systematic manner that is consistent with the broad principles in AASB 112. Paragraph 10 identifies a number

of potential group allocation methods that do not satisfy this criterion. Other unacceptable allocation methods include:

(a)   a method that allocates current taxes only to entities in the group that have accounting profits, with no allocation to entities that have accounting losses; and

(b)   a method that allocates current taxes to entities in the group on an arbitrary basis, for example on the basis of sales revenue, total assets, net assets or operating profits, without adjustment for material items that are not assessable or deductible for tax purposes.

40   A group allocation approach based on the terms of any tax funding arrangement between the entities in the group would be acceptable only where it satisfies the criteria in paragraph 8.

Tax Consolidation Adjustments

Current Taxes

41   Following the implementation of tax consolidation for the tax-consolidated group, both the head entity and the subsidiaries in the group continue to recognise in each reporting period current tax amounts. However, it is the head entity that normally will settle or recover with the taxation authority current tax liabilities or assets that arise in relation to the subsidiaries. That is, the current tax liability is effectively assumed by the head entity or the current tax asset benefits the head entity. Therefore, a subsidiary's current tax liability or asset needs to be derecognised immediately after its initial recognition in each reporting period.

42   The derecognition of a subsidiary's current tax liability (or asset) is treated under this Interpretation as a contribution by (or distribution to) the head entity, in conjunction with any tax funding arrangement amounts, on the basis that the transaction is with the parent in its capacity as the parent. The definition of "income" (or "expenses") in the *Framework for the Preparation and Presentation of Financial Statements* cannot be satisfied, as the decrease in the subsidiary's current tax liability (or asset) results from a contribution by or distribution to equity participants. This Interpretation does not prescribe which equity accounts are to be adjusted by subsidiaries for tax-consolidation contributions or distributions.

43   The assumption by the head entity of the current tax liability (or asset) arising in a subsidiary in the tax-consolidated group is recognised by the head entity as a contribution to (or distribution from) the subsidiary (not as a component of tax expense or tax income), unless a tax funding arrangement between the entities results in the head entity recognising an inter-entity receivable (payable) equal in amount to the tax liability (asset) assumed. There will be no net contribution (or distribution) where the amounts arising for the period under a tax funding arrangement equate to the amounts initially recognised by the subsidiary for its current taxes and any tax losses/credits assumed by the head entity under the tax consolidation system. Nevertheless, the head entity recognises the assumed current tax amounts as current tax liabilities (assets), adding to its own current tax amounts, since they are also due to or from the same taxation authority.

44   Similarly, the subsidiary recognises the assumption of its current tax liability or asset as a contribution by or distribution to the head entity, in conjunction with any tax funding arrangement amounts. Thus, the subsidiary continues to recognise tax expense (income) even though it derecognises its current tax liability or asset. The subsidiary may choose to classify a tax-consolidation equity contribution from the head entity as contributed equity other than paid-in capital. A transaction that would result in an equity reduction for the subsidiary may be subject to legal restrictions concerning capital distributions.

45   When the tax consolidation adjustments required by this Interpretation result in the recognition of a distribution to an entity, that entity accounts for the distribution in accordance with the requirements of AASB 118 *Revenue* and AASB 127 *Consolidated and Separate Financial Statements* concerning dividends and other distributions. Distributions arising from tax consolidation adjustments may take the form of either a return of capital or a return on capital. The particular circumstances of a distribution need to be considered in determining the appropriate accounting.

Indirect Subsidiaries

46   The head entity's equity investment in subsidiaries relates to the ownership interests it holds directly in subsidiaries. This means that the head entity's assumption of current tax liabilities or assets in relation to indirect subsidiaries needs to be accounted for, in conjunction with any tax funding arrangement amounts, as equity contributions or distributions (if any) via the interposed parents, as each parent in turn holds the investment in the next layer of subsidiaries.

47   In the case of multiple consolidated (MEC) groups, some or all of the subsidiaries in the tax-consolidated group may not be direct or indirect subsidiaries of the head entity in the group. However, in that case, the assumption by the head entity of the other entities' current tax liabilities or assets is treated, in conjunction with any tax funding arrangement between the entities, as equity contributions or distributions via the foreign parent of the head entity, again on the basis that the transactions in substance are transfers via each interposed parent.

48   The entries for interposed parents would not be recognised in the consolidated financial statements for the group, as they concern transactions within the group. However, they would be recognised in each parent's separate financial statements or consolidated financial statements of sub-groups, if prepared. For example, a contribution from an interposed entity's parent would give rise to a contribution by the interposed entity to its subsidiary. Similarly, a distribution from a subsidiary of the interposed entity would give rise to a distribution by the interposed entity to its parent.

Deferred Taxes

49   Following the implementation of tax consolidation for the tax-consolidated group, both the head entity and the subsidiaries in the group continue to recognise deferred tax amounts. The tax consolidation system results in subsidiaries' tax losses/credits being assumed by the head entity, but does not address deferred tax assets and liabilities arising from temporary differences. Therefore, such deferred taxes continue to be recognised by each entity in the tax-consolidated group and are not transferred to the head entity.

Tax Losses/Credits

50   A subsidiary derecognises any tax-loss/tax-credit deferred tax asset that it has initially recognised in a reporting period where the tax losses/credits are transferred to the head entity under tax consolidation. The amount (if any) paid or payable by the head entity for the transferred tax losses/credits is determined in accordance with any tax funding arrangement between the entities. Where the arrangement does not provide for a funding contribution from the head entity to the subsidiary equal to the asset derecognised by the subsidiary (or recognised by the head entity), the assumption of the tax losses/credits results in a contribution to or distribution by the subsidiary in the same manner as with current tax liabilities or assets.

51   Where unutilised and unrecognised tax losses/credits are subsequently recognised by the head entity, the deferred tax income arising is recognised only by the head entity and not treated as an adjustment of the previous accounting by the originating subsidiaries for the tax losses/credits assumed by the head entity. However, if a tax funding arrangement between the entities provides compensation to the subsidiaries in the period in which the tax losses/credits are utilised by the head entity, the compensation is accounted for as contributions by an equity participant.

Tax Funding Arrangements and Tax Sharing Agreements

52   The entities in a tax-consolidated group may choose to enter into a tax funding (or contribution) arrangement in order to fund tax amounts. This Interpretation does not establish any specific requirements for the nature and terms of tax funding arrangements. However, the Interpretation requires an entity subject to any form of tax funding arrangement to account for the inter-entity assets and liabilities (if any) that arise for it under the arrangement. These amounts are treated as arising through equity contributions or distributions, in the same way as the head entity's assumption of subsidiaries' current tax amounts and tax losses/credits, and therefore alter the net amount recognised as tax-consolidation contributions by or distributions to equity participants. As noted in paragraph 43, there will be no net contribution (or distribution) where the amounts arising

for the period under a tax funding arrangement equate to the amounts initially recognised by a subsidiary for its current taxes and any tax losses/credits assumed by the head entity.

53   The entities may also establish a tax sharing agreement to determine the allocation of income tax liabilities between the entities should the head entity default on its tax payment obligations or the treatment of entities leaving the tax-consolidated group. A tax sharing agreement that satisfies the specific tax law requirements has the effect in default circumstances that the liability of subject entities is limited to their contribution as determined in accordance with the agreement. Tax sharing agreements that operate only in the event of default by the head entity normally would not give rise to accounting entries where the possibility of default was remote. A tax sharing agreement may also be used to determine the consequences of a subsidiary leaving the group. Any payments under a tax sharing agreement are accounted for in the same way as tax funding arrangement amounts.

Temporary Differences re Investments in Subsidiaries

54   The head entity may be required to recognise a deferred tax asset or liability in its separate financial statements in relation to temporary differences arising on its investments in subsidiaries in the tax-consolidated group. Differences between the carrying amounts of the investments and the associated tax bases may arise due to the head entity's accounting for tax-consolidation contributions by or distributions to equity participants, whereas the tax bases of the investments may indirectly reflect the aggregate tax values of the subsidiaries' assets and liabilities. Paragraphs 39 and 44 of AASB 112 specify the circumstances in which such deferred taxes are not required to be recognised.

Subsidiary Leaves the Tax-Consolidated Group

55   A wholly-owned subsidiary leaves the tax-consolidated group when it no longer is wholly owned as required by the tax consolidation legislation. This can occur, for example, when the head entity (or another entity in the group) sells the subsidiary or when the subsidiary issues shares to parties outside the group. A subsidiary may leave the tax-consolidated group but remain part of the group of entities where the parent entity continues to control the subsidiary. It may become part of another tax-consolidated group, under a different head entity, or it may become the head entity of its own tax-consolidated group, including its own wholly-owned subsidiaries.

56   Where a subsidiary leaves the tax-consolidated group, the head entity continues to recognise current taxes that arose in relation to the subsidiary as a member of the tax-consolidated group, since the head entity continues to be liable under the tax consolidation system for those taxes. It is only after the subsidiary leaves the group and does not become a subsidiary in another tax-consolidated group that it starts to recognise its own new current tax liabilities or assets without having to derecognise them for their assumption by a head entity.

57   Any tax losses/credits assumed by the head entity from the subsidiary when it joined the group or whilst a member of the group remain with the head entity when the subsidiary leaves the group, and so the head entity continues to recognise deferred tax assets based on those tax losses/credits to the extent that it is probable that they will be recovered by the head entity. However, the subsidiary continues to recognise deferred tax liabilities and assets based on temporary differences. The temporary differences are likely to change where, under the particular allocation method previously adopted, they were not determined by reference to the carrying amounts of the subsidiary's assets and liabilities in its statement of financial position. Furthermore, the tax bases are those applicable to the subsidiary's assets and liabilities under tax law, and may be reset if the subsidiary joins another tax-consolidated group.

58   As noted in paragraph 55, a subsidiary may leave the tax-consolidated group but remain part of the group of entities where the parent continues to control the subsidiary. The change in the structure of the group results from an intragroup transaction which is eliminated in preparing the consolidated financial statements. Therefore, the carrying amounts of the subsidiary's assets and liabilities in those statements would not change. However, the temporary differences at the group level may be different where the subsidiary is now under another head entity in the group, due to its asset tax values being reset upon joining

the second tax-consolidated group. In this case, the group's deferred tax balances would change despite the subsidiary remaining within the group.

Disclosures

59   A number of specific disclosures are required by this Interpretation in addition to those required by AASB 112, to assist users of the financial statements of the head entity or of a wholly-owned subsidiary to understand the impact of tax consolidation upon the entity. Disclosures concerning the relevance of tax consolidation to an entity would normally include, where applicable, a statement that the adoption of the tax consolidation system had not yet been formally notified to the Australian Taxation Office. Other accounting standards may also require disclosures that are relevant to tax consolidation. For example, AASB 124 *Related Party Disclosures* requires disclosure of the identity of certain controlling entities, which may or may not include the head entity in the tax-consolidated group, as well as disclosures concerning transactions and balances with related parties, which includes other entities in the tax-consolidated group.

60   AASB 137 *Provisions, Contingent Liabilities and Contingent Assets* requires the disclosure of contingent liabilities. Wholly-owned subsidiaries in a tax-consolidated group have contingent liabilities as a result of their joint and several liability in default circumstances, which is in effect a guarantee by the subsidiaries. If the probability of default by the head entity or leaving the tax-consolidated group is remote, disclosure of the contingent liability is not required.

Initial Application of this Interpretation

61   Where Abstract 52 was previously applied by an entity in accounting for tax consolidation, the accounting policies adopted under that Abstract can no longer continue to be applied by the entity. When application of this Interpretation begins in the context of adopting all Australian equivalents to International Financial Reporting Standards (IFRSs), AASB 1 *First-time Adoption of Australian Equivalents to International Financial Reporting Standards* requires an entity to use the same accounting policies in its opening Australian-equivalents-to-IFRSs statement of financial position as for all periods presented in its first Australian-equivalents-to-IFRSs financial statements. AASB 1 notes that this may require an entity to apply accounting policies that differ from those used previously. Any adjustments at the date of transition to Australian equivalents to International Financial Reporting Standards are recognised directly in retained earnings or, if appropriate, another category of equity.

62   Initial application of this Interpretation in the context of AASB 1 requires the head entity in the tax-consolidated group to derecognise at the date of transition to Australian equivalents to IFRSs any temporary-difference (or timing-difference) deferred tax balances recognised in relation to subsidiaries in the group. However, the head entity continues to recognise any current tax liability or asset and any tax-loss/tax-credit deferred tax asset (if appropriate) relating to the subsidiaries. Any adjustment is recognised via retained earnings.

63   The head entity (and any interposed parents) also needs to determine whether the application of this Interpretation from the date tax consolidation was implemented to the date of transition would have resulted in carrying amounts for investments in subsidiaries that are materially different from those previously determined at the date of transition. This is particularly likely to be the case where there was no tax funding arrangement and there were no dividends or other distributions from subsidiaries to fund the head entity. Dividends or other distributions used to fund the head entity are likely to offset any equity contributions that would otherwise arise on the retrospective application of this Interpretation. Any adjustment of investment carrying amounts at the date of transition is recognised via retained earnings.

64   At the date of transition, subsidiaries in the tax-consolidated group recognise deferred tax balances measured in accordance with an allocation method that meets the requirements of this Interpretation. Similarly to the head entity, subsidiaries (including interposed parents) may have to account for contributions by or distributions to equity participants in relation to the head entity's assumption of current taxes and tax losses/credits in conjunction with any tax funding arrangement amounts.

65   However, it may be appropriate for subsidiaries to reclassify as deferred tax balances at the date of transition the non-current inter-entity balances that arose under tax funding arrangements, without having to recognise contributions or distributions to the head entity. This would be the case where the pre-date-of-transition tax funding arrangement covered both current and deferred taxes, with the intention of reflecting in a subsidiary the tax amounts relating to its transactions and balances, which it could not recognise directly. Under Abstract 52, the subsidiary would have recognised the amounts as current and deferred tax expense (income) and as current and non-current inter-entity balances, with no contributions by or distributions to equity participants. In substance, this is the same outcome required by this Interpretation, based on the principle that there is no such contribution or distribution where the tax funding arrangement amounts equate to the amounts initially recognised by the subsidiary. For this approach to be justified, it would be expected that the tax funding arrangement would be revised during the reporting period in which Australian equivalents to IFRSs are adopted to address only current tax amounts and tax losses/credits, so that under this Interpretation no contributions or distributions to equity participants would normally arise in the future. The head entity would also need to reverse existing inter-entity balances relating to deferred tax balances arising from subsidiaries' temporary (or timing) differences that were previously recognised by the head entity under Abstract 52, supporting the view that in substance no contribution by or distribution to equity participants had occurred. When this approach is appropriate, the head entity is not required to adjust the carrying amounts of its investments in the relevant subsidiaries at the date of transition.

66   If the tax funding arrangement is not amended as indicated in paragraph 65, this would indicate that the original substance of the arrangement was not to effectively reflect tax balances in the subsidiary, and could result in the recognition of contributions or distributions by affected entities both on transition and on an on-going basis under this Interpretation. Furthermore, in this case the adjustment or writing-off of inter-entity balances arising from the pre-date-of-transition tax funding arrangement is a contribution by or distribution to equity participants in the period in which this occurs, rather than a date-of-transition adjustment, since the application of this Interpretation does not alter the terms of any previous tax funding arrangement.

67   Entities may decide in any case to revise the terms of a tax funding arrangement in response to the requirements of this Interpretation. For example, tax funding arrangements previously may have covered both current and deferred tax amounts since Abstract 52 required the head entity to recognise both current and deferred taxes in relation to subsidiaries. As the head entity no longer recognises subsidiaries' deferred taxes (other than in respect of tax losses/credits) under this Interpretation, entities may prefer tax funding arrangements to address only current tax amounts and deferred tax assets relating to tax losses/credits.

Illustrative Examples

These examples accompany, but are not part of, Interpretation 1052.

IE1   These examples are a simplified illustration of the ongoing tax consolidation accounting required by the Interpretation, both with and without a tax funding arrangement between the entities. Other methods may equally comply with the requirements of the Interpretation. For simplicity, the examples assume that all current and deferred tax amounts are recognised as part of tax expense (income). Paragraph 58 of Accounting Standard AASB 112 *Income Taxes* may require the recognition of tax amounts directly in equity or as part of the initial accounting for a business combination.

IE2   Any contribution by the head entity to a subsidiary upon assuming the subsidiary's current tax liability and tax losses/credits is recognised in the example journal entries by the head entity as "investment in subsidiary" and by the subsidiary as "other contributed equity". This is illustrative only as the Interpretation does not prescribe which accounts are to be adjusted for tax-consolidation contributions by or distributions to equity participants. Similarly, the treatment of a distribution by the subsidiary to the head entity in Example 4 is only illustrative.

Interpretations

IE3   The journal entries shown in the examples include the usual consolidation eliminations, such as inter-entity receivables and payables and equity contributions and investments. The group outcome shown in the examples reflects only tax relating to the subsidiary or subsidiaries. The examples do not illustrate taxes recognised by the head entity in relation to its own transactions, events and balances.

Basic Examples

Example 1 – No Tax Funding Arrangement

IE4   In this example, no tax funding arrangements have been established and there are no transactions between entities in the tax-consolidated group. The subsidiary's initial tax accounting is based on a systematic and rational method consistent with the broad principles of AASB 112, as required by the Interpretation. For the purpose of this simple illustration of specific tax consolidation adjustments, it is not necessary to identify the specific method adopted for the initial recognition of income taxes for the period by the subsidiary.

		$	$
(1) Subsidiary			
Dr Current tax expense		8,000	
Dr Deferred tax expense		2,000	
Cr Current tax liability			8,000
Cr Deferred tax liability			2,000
Initial tax recognition for period in subsidiary			
Dr Current tax liability		8,000	
Cr Other contributed equity			8,000
Current tax derecognised as assumed by the head entity			
(2) Head Entity (Parent)			
Dr Investment in subsidiary		8,000	
Cr Current tax liability			8,000
Assumption of current tax liability re subsidiary			
(3) Consolidation Adjustment			
Dr Other contributed equity – subsidiary		8,000	
Cr Investment in subsidiary			8,000
Elimination of equity contribution			
(4) Group Outcome re subsidiary			
Increase in current tax liability			8,000
Increase in deferred tax liability			2,000
Tax expense			10,000

Example 2 – With Tax Funding Arrangement (Equivalent Charge)

IE5   In this case there are no transactions between entities in the tax-consolidated group, other than those required under a tax funding arrangement. The journal entries illustrate a tax funding arrangement under which the intercompany charge equals the current tax liability of the subsidiary, resulting in neither a contribution by the head entity to the subsidiary nor a distribution by the subsidiary to the head entity.

	$	$
(1) Subsidiary		
Dr Current tax expense	8,000	
Dr Deferred tax expense	2,000	
Cr Current tax liability		8,000
Cr Deferred tax liability		2,000
Initial tax recognition for period in subsidiary		
Dr Current tax liability	8,000	
Cr Intercompany payable		8,000
Current tax derecognised as assumed by the head entity, in return for payment under tax funding arrangement		
(2) Head Entity (Parent)		
Dr Intercompany receivable	8,000	
Cr Current tax liability		8,000
Assumption of current tax liability re subsidiary		
(3) Consolidation Adjustment		
Dr Intercompany payable	8,000	
Cr Intercompany receivable		8,000
Elimination of balances		
(4) Group Outcome re subsidiary		
Increase in current tax liability		8,000
Increase in deferred tax liability		2,000
Tax expense		10,000

Example 3 – With Tax Funding Arrangement (Non-Equivalent Charge)

IE6   In this case there are no transactions between entities in the tax-consolidated group, other than those required under a tax funding arrangement. The journal entries illustrate a tax funding arrangement under which the intercompany charge is less than the current tax liability of the subsidiary, resulting in a contribution by the head entity to the subsidiary.

	$	$
(1) Subsidiary		
Dr Current tax expense	8,000	
Dr Deferred tax expense	2,000	
Cr Current tax liability		8,000
Cr Deferred tax liability		2,000
Initial tax recognition for period in subsidiary		
Dr Current tax liability	8,000	
Cr Intercompany payable		5,000
Cr Other contributed equity		3,000
Current tax derecognised as assumed by the head entity		

	$	$
(2) Head Entity (Parent)		
Dr Intercompany receivable	5,000	
Dr Investment in subsidiary	3,000	
Cr Current tax liability		8,000
Assumption of current tax liability re subsidiary		
(3) Consolidation Adjustments		
Dr Intercompany payable	5,000	
Cr Intercompany receivable		5,000
Elimination of balances		
Dr Other contributed equity – subsidiary	3,000	
Cr Investment in subsidiary		3,000
Elimination of equity contribution		
(4) Group Outcome re subsidiary		
Increase in current tax liability		8,000
Increase in deferred tax liability		2,000
		———
Tax expense		10,000

IE7   If the intercompany charge under the tax funding arrangement instead exceeded the subsidiary's current tax liability, the excess would be a distribution by the subsidiary to the head entity.

Tax Loss Examples

Example 4 – "Stand-Alone Taxpayer" Approach; Assumption of Tax Losses; No Tax Funding Arrangement

IE8   The subsidiary in this example has incurred unused tax losses of $100,000 during the reporting period. The head entity expects to recover the tax losses in full. Based on the "stand-alone taxpayer" income tax recognition method adopted by the subsidiary, it has no current tax liability but initially recognises a deferred tax asset of $18,000 arising from these losses ($60,000 losses × tax rate 30%); that is, only part of the potential tax loss asset can be recognised by the subsidiary in its particular circumstances. There is no tax funding arrangement between the entities, resulting in a distribution by the subsidiary to the head entity.

	$	$
(1) Subsidiary		
Dr Deferred tax asset re losses	18,000	
Cr Current tax income		18,000
Initial tax recognition for period in subsidiary		
Dr Distribution to head entity	18,000	
Cr Deferred tax asset re losses		18,000
Tax loss asset derecognised as assumed by the head entity		
(2) Head Entity (Parent)		
Dr Deferred tax asset re losses	18,000	
Cr Distribution from subsidiary		18,000
Assumption of tax loss asset ex subsidiary		

	$	$
Dr Deferred tax asset re losses	12,000	
Cr Current tax income		12,000
Recognition of additional tax asset		

(3) Consolidation Adjustment

	$	$
Dr Distribution from subsidiary	18,000	
Cr Distribution to head entity		18,000
Elimination of equity distribution		

(4) Group Outcome re subsidiary

		$
Increase in deferred tax asset re losses		30,000
Tax income		30,000

IE9 The consolidation adjustment above is in generic terms, and in practice would reflect the accounts in which the distribution was recognised. For example, if the subsidiary recognised the distribution to the head entity as a reduction in retained earnings, and the head entity recognised the distribution as revenue, then the consolidation adjustment would reverse those entries to give the results from the group's perspective. As another example, the distribution may have been recognised by the subsidiary as a reduction in reserves and by the head entity as a reduction in its investment account. The consolidation adjustment then would reverse those entries. The accounting adopted for the distribution does not affect the group tax outcome.

IE10 In future reporting periods, the subsidiary's measurement of current and deferred taxes does not take into account the $40,000 of unused tax losses remaining from the $100,000 tax loss. As the tax loss is assumed by the head entity at the end of the period, it is then regarded as no longer available to the subsidiary. The subsidiary's accounting is also unaffected if the head entity is required in a later period to derecognise part or all of its tax-loss deferred tax asset due to the recognition requirements in AASB 112 ceasing to be met.

Example 5 – "Stand-Alone Taxpayer" Approach; Assumption of Tax Losses; Tax Funding Arrangement

IE11 The subsidiary in this example has incurred unused tax losses of $100,000 during the reporting period. The head entity expects to recover the tax losses in full. Based on the "stand-alone taxpayer" income tax recognition method adopted by the subsidiary, it has no current tax liability but initially recognises a deferred tax asset of $18,000 arising from these losses ($60,000 losses × tax rate 30%); that is, only part of the potential tax loss asset can be recognised by the subsidiary in its particular circumstances. The tax funding arrangement with the head entity is based on the subsidiary's current tax liability (asset) and the tax losses that the head entity expects to recover.

	$	$
(1) Subsidiary		
Dr Deferred tax asset re losses	18,000	
Cr Current tax income		18,000
Initial tax recognition for period in subsidiary		
Dr Intercompany receivable	30,000	
Cr Deferred tax asset re losses		18,000
Cr Other contributed equity		12,000
Tax loss asset derecognised as assumed by the head entity		

	$	$
(2) Head Entity (Parent)		
Dr Deferred tax asset re losses	18,000	
Dr Investment in subsidiary	12,000	
Cr Intercompany payable		30,000
Assumption of tax loss asset ex subsidiary		
Dr Deferred tax asset re losses	12,000	
Cr Current tax income		12,000
Recognition of additional tax asset		
(3) Consolidation Adjustments		
Dr Intercompany payable	30,000	
Cr Intercompany receivable		30,000
Elimination of balances		
Dr Other contributed equity – subsidiary	12,000	
Cr Investment in subsidiary		12,000
Elimination of equity contribution		
(4) Group Outcome re subsidiary		
Increase in deferred tax asset re losses		30,000
Tax income		30,000

IE12   In this scenario, the head entity recognises a contribution to the subsidiary as it will pay more under the tax funding arrangement for the assumption of tax losses than the subsidiary can recognise initially as a deferred tax asset. The head entity then also recognises the additional deferred tax asset, as appropriate in relation to the tax position of the tax-consolidated group, giving rise to tax income for the head entity. The outcome is that the group recognises tax income of $30,000 arising in relation to the subsidiary. This comprises the tax income of $18,000 initially recognised by the subsidiary, adjusted for the additional $12,000 deferred tax asset relating to the subsidiary's losses that is recognised by the head entity.

IE13   As in Example 4, in future reporting periods the subsidiary's measurement of current and deferred taxes does not take into account the $40,000 of unused tax losses remaining from the $100,000 tax loss. As the tax loss is assumed by the head entity at the end of the period, it is then regarded as no longer available to the subsidiary. The subsidiary's accounting is also unaffected if the head entity is required in a later period to derecognise part or all of its tax-loss deferred tax asset due to the recognition requirements in AASB 112 ceasing to be met.

Example 6 – "Separate Taxpayer within Group" Approach; Assumption of Tax Losses; Tax Funding Arrangement

IE14   The subsidiary in this example has incurred unused tax losses of $100,000 during the reporting period. The head entity expects to recover the tax losses in full. Based on the "separate taxpayer within group" income tax recognition method adopted by the subsidiary, it has no current tax liability and initially recognises a deferred tax asset of $30,000 arising from these losses ($100,000 losses × tax rate 30%); that is, the whole of the potential tax loss asset is recognised by the subsidiary. This is so even if in its own circumstances the subsidiary expected to recover only $60,000 of the tax losses. The tax funding arrangement with the head entity is based on the subsidiary's current tax liability (asset) and the tax-loss deferred tax asset recognised by the subsidiary.

	$	$
(1) Subsidiary		
Dr Deferred tax asset re losses	30,000	
Cr Current tax income		30,000
Initial tax recognition for period in subsidiary		
Dr Intercompany receivable	30,000	
Cr Deferred tax asset re losses		30,000
Tax loss asset derecognised as assumed by the head entity		
(2) Head Entity (Parent)		
Dr Deferred tax asset re losses	30,000	
Cr Intercompany payable		30,000
Assumption of tax loss asset ex subsidiary		
(3) Consolidation Adjustment		
Dr Intercompany payable	30,000	
Cr Intercompany receivable		30,000
Elimination of balances		
(4) Group Outcome re subsidiary		
Increase in deferred tax asset re losses		30,000
Tax income		30,000

IE15   No contribution by or distribution to equity participants is recognised in this case as the tax funding arrangement amount equals the tax amounts recognised by the subsidiary that are assumed by the head entity. Despite the application of a different method for the initial recognition of income tax by the subsidiary, and a different basis for the tax funding arrangement between the entities, the group outcome is the same as in Examples 4 and 5.

IE16   As in Examples 4 and 5, if the subsidiary in this case had not been able to recognise a deferred tax asset in relation to all of its tax losses arising during the reporting period, in future periods the subsidiary's measurement of current and deferred taxes would not take into account the remaining unused tax losses. As the tax loss is assumed by the head entity at the end of the period, it is then regarded as no longer available to the subsidiary. The subsidiary's accounting is also unaffected if the head entity is required in a later period to derecognise part or all of its tax-loss deferred tax asset due to the recognition requirements in AASB 112 ceasing to be met.

Intragroup Sales Examples

Example 7 – "Stand-Alone Taxpayer" Approach; Intragroup Sales; No Tax Funding Arrangement

IE17   In this example the head entity H has two subsidiaries A and B in the tax-consolidated group. The subsidiaries measure tax amounts for their separate financial statements on a "stand-alone taxpayer" basis, as allowed by the Interpretation. There is no tax funding arrangement between the entities. In year 1, subsidiary A sells inventory purchased for $1,000 from an external party to subsidiary B for $1,500 cash. By the end of year 1, subsidiary B has not sold the inventory outside the group. In year 2, subsidiary B sells the inventory to a party outside the group for $1,800 cash.

Year 1

IE18   Subsidiary A recognises tax expense of $150 (profit of $500 × tax rate 30%) in relation to its sale of inventory to subsidiary B, even though the transaction is ignored under the tax consolidation system as it is a transaction between entities in the tax-consolidated group. Subsidiary B recognises no tax as it has not yet sold the inventory purchased from subsidiary A, and the taxable temporary difference for its inventory (carrying amount of $1,500 but tax base of $1,000) is not recognised under the AASB 112 exception concerning the initial recognition of an asset or liability in certain circumstances. The head entity and the group recognise no tax in relation to subsidiary A's profitable sale, since no external sale has occurred. The relevant journal entries:

	$	$
(1) Subsidiary A		
Dr Bank	1,500	
Cr Sales		1,500
Sale of inventory to fellow-subsidiary B		
Dr Cost of sales	1,000	
Cr Inventory		1,000
Recognition of cost of sales		
Dr Current tax expense	150	
Cr Current tax liability		150
Initial tax recognition in selling subsidiary		
Dr Current tax liability	150	
Cr Other contributed equity		150
Current tax derecognised as assumed by the head entity		
(2) Subsidiary B		
Dr Inventory	1,500	
Cr Bank		1,500
Purchase of inventory from fellow-subsidiary A		
(3) Consolidation Adjustments		
Dr Sales	1,500	
Cr Cost of sales		1,000
Cr Inventory		500
Elimination of intragroup sale and unrealised profit in inventory		
Dr Other contributed equity – A	150	
Cr Current tax expense		150
Elimination of asymmetrical equity contribution; reversal of tax on intragroup transaction		
(4) Group Outcome re subsidiaries		
Change in current tax liability		–
Tax expense		–

IE19   The second consolidation adjustment journal entry eliminates the $150 recognised by subsidiary A as a contribution by the head entity via an adjustment of tax expense (income), since the head entity has not recognised any tax-related contribution to the subsidiary. The outcome is that the group does not recognise any tax expense in relation to subsidiary A (or B) or any equity contributions between the subsidiaries and the head entity. (The inventory is recognised at $1,000 by the group.)

Year 2

IE20   Subsidiary B sells the inventory in year 2 for a profit of $300, realising a profit for the group of $800. As an external sale has occurred, this profit is assessable to the head entity in relation to the tax-consolidated group. Subsidiaries A and B continue to recognise their own tax balances based on the stand-alone taxpayer method. There are no entries for subsidiary A in year 2 relating to the inventory. The journal entries for the other entities in the group:

	$	$
(1) Subsidiary B		
Dr Bank	1,800	
Cr Sales		1,800
Sale of inventory outside the group		
Dr Cost of sales	1,500	
Cr Inventory		1,500
Recognition of cost of sales		
Dr Current tax expense	240	
Cr Current tax liability		240
Initial tax recognition in selling subsidiary ($800 × 30%)		
Dr Current tax liability	240	
Cr Other contributed equity		240
Current tax derecognised as assumed by the head entity		
(2) Head Entity (Parent)		
Dr Investment in subsidiary B	240	
Cr Current tax liability		240
Assumption of current tax liability re subsidiary		
(3) Consolidation Adjustments		
Dr Opening retained earnings – A	500	
Cr Inventory		500
Reinstate elimination of unrealised profit in inventory		
Dr Inventory	500	
Cr Cost of sales		500
Unrealised profit in inventory now realised		
Dr Other contributed equity – A	150	
Cr Opening retained earnings		150
Reinstate opening balances re subsidiary A		
Dr Other contributed equity – B	240	
Cr Investment in subsidiary B		240
Elimination of equity contribution		
(4) Group Outcome re subsidiaries		
Increase in current tax liability		240

Tax expense		240

IE21   In this case, subsidiary B recognises a tax expense of $240 even though its accounting profit on the sale of the inventory is only $300. This is because the tax base of the inventory from the perspective of the group is $1,000, being the original cost to subsidiary A when purchased from an external party. Even under the stand-alone taxpayer approach to measuring the subsidiary's taxes, tax values are based on those of the tax-consolidated group, as no other tax values are available. The tax expense of $240 recognised by subsidiary B in year 2 is not divided between the various subsidiaries that held the inventory within the group. Subsidiary A's tax expense of $150 in year 1 (which was eliminated on consolidation) is not revised.

IE22   If there was a tax funding arrangement between the entities, the intercompany amounts arising under the arrangement would affect the amounts recognised as equity contributions or distributions. A tax funding arrangement does not alter the tax expense (income) recognised by an entity.

Example 8 – "Separate Taxpayer within Group" Approach; Intragroup Sales; No Tax Funding Arrangement

IE23   The facts are the same as set out in Example 7 (see paragraph IE17), except that the subsidiaries A and B measure tax amounts for their separate financial statements on a "separate taxpayer within group" basis, as allowed by the Interpretation. Thus, in this example there is no tax funding arrangement between the entities; in year 1, subsidiary A sells inventory costing $1,000 to subsidiary B for $1,500 cash; and in year 2, subsidiary B sells that inventory to a party outside the group for $1,800 cash.

Year 1

IE24   Subsidiary A does not recognise any tax expense in relation to its sale of inventory to subsidiary B, since the transaction is ignored under the tax consolidation system as it is a transaction between entities in the tax-consolidated group. Subsidiary B recognises no tax as it has not yet sold the inventory purchased from subsidiary A, and the taxable temporary difference for its inventory (carrying amount of $1,500 but tax base of $1,000) is not recognised under the AASB 112 exception concerning the initial recognition of an asset or liability in certain circumstances. The head entity and the group recognise no tax in relation to subsidiary A's profitable sale, since no external sale has occurred.

IE25   Thus there are no tax-related journal entries in year 1 concerning the intragroup sale of inventory. The inventory-related journal entries are the same as shown for Example 7 in year 1.

Year 2

IE26   Subsidiary B sells the inventory in year 2 for a profit of $300, realising a profit for the group of $800. As an external sale has occurred, this profit is assessable to the head entity in relation to the tax-consolidated group. The inventory-related journal entries are the same as shown for Example 7 in year 2. The tax-related journal entries:

	$	$
(1) Subsidiary B		
Dr Current tax expense	240	
Cr Current tax liability		240
Initial tax recognition in selling subsidiary ($800 × 30%)		
Dr Current tax liability	240	
Cr Other contributed equity		240
Current tax derecognised as assumed by the head entity		
(2) Head Entity (Parent)		
Dr Investment in subsidiary B	240	
Cr Current tax liability		240
Assumption of current tax liability re subsidiary		

	$	$
(3) Consolidation Adjustment		
Dr Other contributed equity – B	240	
Cr Investment in subsidiary B		240
Elimination of equity contribution		
(4) Group Outcome re subsidiaries		
Increase in current tax liability		240
Tax expense		240

IE27   The group outcomes are the same under both Examples 7 and 8, illustrating that the method adopted for subsidiaries' initial tax recognition for a period does not affect the accounting results for the tax-consolidated group. However, the different income tax allocation methods can result in different reporting in the separate financial statements of the subsidiaries, as indicated for subsidiary A. Subsidiary B has the same result under both Examples because in each case the same tax base applied to the intragroup inventory that it sold during year 2.

References

Australia

The Urgent Issues Group discussed Issues Paper 04/3 "Revision of Various UIG Abstracts for 2005" and/or Issue Summary 04/6 "Tax Consolidation Accounting" in relation to this Interpretation at meetings on 10 June, 5 October and 25 November 2004 and 10 February and 22 March 2005. In developing the superseded revised Abstract 52, the UIG discussed Issue Summary 03/9 "Tax Consolidation Accounting Implementation Guidance" at meetings on 18 September, 30 October and 4 December 2003.

Accounting Standard AASB 1 *First-time Adoption of Australian Equivalents to International Financial Reporting Standards*

Accounting Standard AASB 112 *Income Taxes*

Accounting Standard AASB 118 *Revenue*

Accounting Standard AASB 124 *Related Party Disclosures*

Accounting Standard AASB 127 *Consolidated and Separate Financial Statements*

Accounting Standard AASB 137 *Provisions, Contingent Liabilities and Contingent Assets*

Canada

CICA Handbook Section 3465 *Income Taxes*

International Accounting Standards Board

International Accounting Standard IAS 12 *Income Taxes*

United Kingdom

Financial Reporting Standard FRS 19 *Deferred Tax*

United States of America

Statement of Financial Accounting Standards SFAS 109 *Accounting for Income Taxes*

Interpretations

Interpretation 1055
Accounting for Road Earthworks

(Compiled November 2009)

Compilation Details

UIG Interpretation 1055 *Accounting for Road Earthworks* as amended

This compiled Interpretation applies to annual reporting periods beginning on or after 1 January 2009. It takes into account amendments up to and including 13 December 2007 and was prepared on 12 November 2009 by the staff of the Australian Accounting Standards Board (AASB).

This compilation is not a separate Interpretation issued by the AASB. Instead, it is a representation of Interpretation 1055 (September 2004) as amended by other pronouncements, which are listed in the Table below.

Table of Pronouncements

Pronouncement	Month issued	Application date *(annual reporting periods ... on or after ...)*	Application, saving or transitional provisions
Interpretation 1055	Sep 2004	*(beginning)* 1 Jan 2005	
AASB 2007-8	Sep 2007	*(beginning)* 1 Jan 2009	see (a) below
AASB 2007-10	Dec 2007	*(beginning)* 1 Jan 2009	see (a) below

(a) Entities may elect to apply this Standard to annual reporting periods beginning on or after 1 January 2005 but before 1 January 2009, provided that AASB 101 *Presentation of Financial Statements* (September 2007) is also applied to such periods.

Table of Amendments

Paragraph affected	How affected	By ... [paragraph]
3	amended	AASB 2007-10 [121]
8	amended	AASB 2007-8 [6]
12	amended	AASB 2007-8 [8]

Interpretation 1055

UIG Interpretation 1055 was issued in September 2004.

This compiled version of Interpretation 1055 applies to annual reporting periods beginning on or after 1 January 2009. It incorporates relevant amendments contained in other AASB pronouncements up to and including 13 December 2007 (see Compilation Details).

Urgent Issues Group
Interpretation 1055
Accounting for Road Earthworks

Interpretation 1055 is set out in paragraphs 1 to 23.

Issue

1   Roads are major infrastructure assets for some entities. Road assets comprise a number of components, such as formation or earthworks, drainage, and the road pavement and seal. Earthworks are carried out to prepare the land for the construction of drainage, the road pavement and seal, and other structures. Earthworks typically include clearing the land and reshaping and aligning the land surface through cutting, filling, grading and compacting soil and rock to suit the type of road to be constructed. The amount of construction work involved in building a road depends on many factors, including the nature of the terrain, soil drainage characteristics and weather patterns.

2   Accounting Standard AASB 116 *Property, Plant and Equipment* requires the depreciable amount of an asset to be allocated on a systematic basis over the asset's useful life. The Standard presumes that, with the exception generally of land, a characteristic common to all tangible assets held on a long-term basis is that their useful lives are limited. Land typically has an unlimited useful life, with some exceptions, such as quarries and sites used for landfill.

3   There are different views concerning whether the earthworks component of road assets should be depreciated, with some entities taking the view that it is not feasible to reliably estimate a useful life for earthworks, and other entities determining depreciation on the basis of an estimated average useful life. Concern has been expressed that, in the absence of specific authoritative guidance, diverse or unacceptable practices may occur or develop in accounting for road earthworks. This will undermine the relevance and reliability of general purpose financial statements.

4   The issues are whether particular road earthworks may be assessed as not having a limited useful life, similar to land, and therefore not subject to depreciation, and whether it is possible to reliably estimate a useful life over which particular road earthworks with a limited useful life should be depreciated.

Consensus

5   **Road earthworks shall be recognised as assets only in accordance with the requirements for the recognition of an item of property, plant and equipment in AASB 116.**

6   **The depreciable amount of road earthwork assets that have limited useful lives shall be allocated on a systematic basis over their useful lives, based on best estimates of those useful lives. Difficulty in estimating the useful life of an asset does not justify non-depreciation of the asset.**

7   **Road earthwork assets that are assessed as not having a limited useful life shall not be depreciated. Such an assessment shall be based on engineering reviews of the expected physical wear and tear and technical obsolescence of the particular earthworks and on consideration of commercial obsolescence and legal or other limits on the use of the earthworks.**

8   **The depreciation or non-depreciation of road earthwork assets shall be reviewed at least at the end of each reporting period, to ensure that the accounting policy applied to particular earthwork assets reflects the most recent assessment of the useful lives of the assets, having regard to factors such as asset usage, physical deterioration and technical and commercial obsolescence.**

Application

9   This Interpretation applies when AASB 116 applies.

10   This Interpretation applies to annual reporting periods beginning on or after 1 January 2005.

[Note: For application dates of paragraphs changed or added by an amending pronouncement, see Compilation Details.]

11   This Interpretation shall not be applied to annual reporting periods beginning before 1 January 2005.

12   The requirements specified in this Interpretation apply to the financial statements where information resulting from their application is material in accordance with AASB 1031 *Materiality*.

13   When applicable, this Interpretation supersedes Abstract 55 *Accounting for Road Earthworks*, as issued in May 2004.

14   Abstract 55 remains applicable until superseded by this Interpretation.

Discussion

15   AASB 116 requires the depreciable amount of an asset to be allocated over the asset's useful life on a systematic basis that reflects the consumption of the asset's future economic benefits, with the Standard defining useful life in relation to the availability of the asset to the entity. The depreciation expense is determined by reference to the depreciable amount of the asset after consideration of such matters as obsolescence, changes in demand and other factors that might give rise to consumption or loss of the future economic benefits represented by the asset. AASB 116 states that, with some exceptions, land has an unlimited useful life and therefore is not depreciated. Where land has a limited useful life, it is depreciated.

Some Earthworks Similar to Land

16   This Interpretation adopts the view that road earthworks represent, in some circumstances, another exception to the expectation that all tangible assets have limited useful lives. This view is based on the similarity between land and road earthworks when the service potential of the earthworks is expected to be retained due to the absence of any events that cause physical deterioration, such as excessive usage, flooding or land movement, and the earthworks are not expected to become obsolete in the foreseeable future. Some roads and their earthworks may have limited useful lives because of their connection with an operation or activity that has a limited useful life. For example, roads associated with a particular mine normally would become obsolete when the mine reached the end of its useful life.

17   AASB 116 requires disclosure in relation to each class of property, plant and equipment of the depreciation methods and the useful lives or depreciation rates used. That is, a class of assets can include particular assets that have different lives – a single useful life need not be appropriate for all the assets in a class. Consistent with this, it is necessary under this Interpretation for an entity to assess which of its road earthwork assets do not have limited useful lives and which do have limited useful lives. Application of a single useful-life estimate across all of an entity's road earthwork assets, or even across all depreciable road earthwork assets, is unlikely to result in a reliable depreciation estimate.

Physical Deterioration

18   Road earthworks may not be subject to material physical deterioration. For example, the resealing of roads or the reconstruction of the road pavement that may be required as a result of environmental factors such as the weather and road usage levels may be carried out on top of the existing earthworks. Road improvements, such as increasing the traffic capacity or improving the alignment, can also make use of the existing earthworks. Additional earthworks may be required, but these need not replace the existing earthworks.

19   However, if earthworks are replaced during the reconstruction of a road, the earthworks (or the appropriate portion) are derecognised and the cost of the replacement earthworks is recognised as an asset in its place. This approach is consistent with the requirement in

AASB 116 that an item of property, plant and equipment ceases to be recognised on its disposal.

Obsolescence

20   Earthwork assets are subject to possible technical or commercial obsolescence, regardless of the physical use of the asset. Technical obsolescence occurs as an asset becomes out-of-date due to technological advances, and commercial obsolescence occurs as the asset becomes redundant through a fall in demand for its services. For example, earthworks may become obsolete when a road is realigned for safety or other operating reasons or is replaced by or closed by a new access road or bypass road. In such cases, the particular earthworks affected are derecognised, consistent with the requirements in AASB 116 when no future economic benefits are expected from the use or disposal of an item of property, plant and equipment.

21   When the replacement or redundancy of particular earthworks is planned or expected under a future capital works program, the useful life of those earthworks is assessed on that basis. In such a case, the earthworks would be expected to have a limited useful life, requiring either a reassessment of the rate of depreciation or the commencement of depreciation where the earthworks were previously treated as non-depreciable.

22   Road transport possibly could be replaced in the future by some other means of transport or else road earthworks might require significant reconstruction to remain useful. This Interpretation is based on the view that this possibility should not be reflected in the best estimate of the useful life. Under this approach, the useful lives of earthworks would need to be reassessed should such a technological change become probable.

Transition

23   AASB 116 requires changes in depreciation rates (e.g. due to a reassessment of the estimated useful life) and depreciation methods to be accounted for as a change in an accounting estimate in accordance with AASB 108 *Accounting Policies, Changes in Accounting Estimates and Errors*. AASB 108 specifies that changes in accounting estimates are recognised prospectively by being recognised in the period of the change, if the change affects that period only, or in the period of the change and future periods, if the change affects both. Under the prospective recognition of changes in accounting estimates, depreciation recognised in prior reporting periods is not changed by an adjustment recognised either in profit or loss or in retained earnings. This approach applies to both the initial application of this Interpretation and to its subsequent application by an entity.

References

Australia

The Urgent Issues Group discussed Issues Paper 04/3 "Revision of Various UIG Abstracts for 2005" in relation to this Interpretation at its meeting on 26 August 2004. In developing the superseded Abstract, the UIG discussed Issue Summary 04/1 "Accounting for Earthworks" at meetings on 12 February, 18 March and 4 May 2004.

Accounting Standard AASB 108 *Accounting Policies, Changes in Accounting Estimates and Errors*

Accounting Standard AASB 116 *Property, Plant and Equipment*

Canada

CICA Handbook Section 3061 *Property, Plant and Equipment*

International Accounting Standards Board

International Accounting Standard IAS 16 *Property, Plant and Equipment*

New Zealand

Financial Reporting Standard FRS-3 *Accounting for Property, Plant and Equipment*

United Kingdom

Financial Reporting Standard FRS 15 *Tangible Fixed Assets*

United States of America

Accounting Research Bulletin ARB 43 *Restatement and Revision of Accounting Research Bulletins,* Chapter 9 – Depreciation

Governmental Accounting Standards Board GASB Statement 34 *Basic Financial Statements – and Management's Discussion and Analysis – for State and Local Governments*

APES 110

Code of Ethics for Professional Accountants

(Reissued December 2010: amended and compiled
December 2011)

Issued by the Accounting Professional and Ethical Standards Board.

Note from the Institute of Chartered Accountants Australia

This note, prepared by the technical editor, is not part of APES 110.

Historical development

June 2006: APES 110 issued by the newly constituted Accounting Professional and Ethical Standards Board (APESB) to replace the profession's Code of Professional Conduct (Code). It did not, however, replace Section F.2 of the Code, 'Prospectuses and Reports on Profit Forecasts'. The Code was operative from 1 July 2006, or as otherwise provided within the Code. It was based on the International Federation of Accountants Code of Ethics for Professional Accountants.

December 2007: APES 110 amended to reflect the change to the definition of network firm in the Code issued by the International Ethics Standards Board for Accountants (IESBA) on which APES 110 is based. The change was operative from 1 July 2008.

February 2008: APES 110 amended to include changes to the auditor independence requirements of the *Corporations Act 2001*.

December 2010: APES 110 reissued to bring it into line with the amended Code issued by the IESBA which introduces the concepts of Public Interest Entities and Key Audit Partners. There is now a cooling-off period before Key Audit or Managing Partners can join public interest audit clients in certain positions and the partner rotation requirements are extended to all Key Audit Partners. The APESB has also added specific Australian requirements relating to inadvertent violations and multiple threats to auditor independence. The new Code is operative from 1 July 2011.

December 2011: APESB released an amending Standard that alters the definition of Public Interest Entity (PIE) in APES 110 and adds an Australian paragraph to provide guidance on which entities in Australia are, or are likely to be, Public Interest Entities. The amendmnt is effective from 1 January 2013.

The APESB issued a compiled version of APES 110 incorporating these amendments in December 2011.

Contents

COMPILATION DETAILS

1 SCOPE AND APPLICATION

2 DEFINITIONS

PART A: GENERAL APPLICATION OF THE CODE

100 Introduction and Fundamental Principles

110 Integrity

120 Objectivity

130 Professional Competence and Due Care

140 Confidentiality

150 Professional Behaviour

PART B: MEMBERS IN PUBLIC PRACTICE

200 Introduction

210 Professional Appointment

220 Conflicts of Interest

230 Second Opinions

240 Fees and Other Types of Remuneration

250 Marketing Professional Services

260 Gifts and Hospitality

270 Custody of client Assets

280 Objectivity – All Services

[AUST] PREFACE: SECTIONS 290 AND 291

290 Independence – Audit and Review Engagements

291 Independence – Other Assurance Engagements

PART C: MEMBERS IN BUSINESS

300 Introduction

310 Potential Conflicts

320 Preparation and Reporting of Information

330 Acting with Sufficient Expertise

340 Financial Interests

350 Inducements

TRANSITIONAL PROVISIONS

CONFORMITY WITH INTERNATIONAL PRONOUNCEMENTS

Compilation Details

APES 110 *Code of Ethics for Professional Accountants* as amended

This compilation is not a separate Standard issued by Accounting Professional & Ethical Standards Board Limited (APESB). Instead, it is a compilation of APES 110 (December 2010) as amended or added to by subsequent APESB Standards, which are listed in the tables below.

APES 110 (December 2010) is effective from 1 July 2011 and supersedes the previous APES 110 issued in June 2006 (amended February 2008). The amendments listed in the Tables below and reflected in this compiled Standard are effective from 1 January 2013, with early adoption permitted. The compiled Standard takes into account amendments up to and including December 2011 and was prepared by the Technical Staff of APESB.

Table of Standards

Standard	Month issued	Operative date
Amendment to the Definition of Public Interest Entity in APES 110 *Code of Ethics for Professional Accountants* (issued December 2011)	December 2011	1 January 2013

Table of Amendments

Paragraphs affected	How affected	Amending Standard
290.25 – 290.26	amended	Definition of Public Interest Entity
Transitional Provisions 1 – 6	amended	Definition of Public Interest Entity
Conformity with International Pronouncements	amended	Definition of Public Interest Entity

Table of Additions

Paragraphs added	Amending Standard
AUST 290.26.1	Definition of Public Interest Entity

APES 110 *Code of Ethics for Professional Accountants*

Accounting Professional & Ethical Standards Board Limited (APESB) issued APES 110 *Code of Ethics for Professional Accountants* in December 2010.

This compiled version of APES 110 incorporates amendments contained in subsequent APESB Standards issued by the APESB up to and including December 2011 (see Compilation Details).

---

1 Scope and application

1.1   Accounting Professional & Ethical Standards Board Limited (APESB) issues APES 110 *Code of Ethics for Professional Accountants* (this Code). This Code is operative from 1 July 2011 and supersedes APES 110 *Code of Ethics for Professional Accountants* (issued in June 2006 and subsequently amended in February 2008. Earlier adoption of this Code is permitted. Transitional provisions relating to Public Interest Entities, partner rotation, non-assurance services, Fees – relative size, compensation and evaluation policies apply from the date specified in the respective transitional provisions (refer page 2100).

1.2   All Members in Australia shall comply with APES 110 including when providing Professional Services in an honorary capacity.

1.3   All Members practicing outside of Australia shall comply with APES 110 to the extent to which they are not prevented from so doing by specific requirements of local laws and/or regulations.

1.4   This Code is not intended to detract from any responsibilities which may be imposed by law or regulation. AUASB has issued auditing standards as legislative instruments under the *Corporations Act 2001* (the Act). For audits and reviews under the Act, those standards have legal enforceability. To the extent that those auditing standards make reference to relevant ethical requirements, the requirements of APES 110 have legal enforceability due to Auditing Standard ASA 102 *Compliance with Ethical Requirements when Performing Audits, Reviews and Other Assurance Engagements.*

1.5   All references to Professional Standards, guidance notes and legislation are references to those provisions as amended from time to time.

1.6   In applying the requirements outlined in this Code, Members shall be guided, not merely by the words, but also by the spirit of this Code.

2 Definitions

In this *Code of Ethics for Professional Accountants* the following expressions have the following meanings assigned to them:

[AUST] *AASB* means the Australian statutory body called the Australian Accounting Standards Board that was established under section 226 of the *Australian Securities and Investments Commission Act 1989* and is continued in existence by section 261 of the *Australian Securities and Investments Commission Act 2001.*

Acceptable Level means a level at which a reasonable and informed third party would be likely to conclude, weighing all the specific facts and circumstances available to the Member at that time, that compliance with the fundamental principles is not compromised.

[AUST] *Administration* means an insolvency arrangement arising from an appointment, other than a members' voluntary liquidation, under which an insolvent entity operates.

Advertising means the communication to the public of information as to the services or skills provided by Members in Public Practice with a view to procuring professional business.

Assurance Client means the responsible party that is the person (or persons) who:

(a)   In a direct reporting engagement, is responsible for the subject matter; or

(b)   In an assertion-based engagement, is responsible for the subject matter information and may be responsible for the subject matter.

Assurance Engagement means an engagement in which a Member in Public Practice expresses a conclusion designed to enhance the degree of confidence of the intended users other than the responsible party about the outcome of the evaluation or measurement of a subject matter against criteria.

This includes an engagement in accordance with the *Framework for Assurance Engagements* issued by the AUASB or in accordance with specific relevant standards, such as International Standards on Auditing, for Assurance Engagements.

Assurance Team means:

(a)   All members of the Engagement Team for the Assurance Engagement;

(b)   All others within a Firm who can directly influence the outcome of the Assurance Engagement, including:

   (i)   those who recommend the compensation of, or who provide direct supervisory, management or other oversight of the Assurance Engagement partner in connection with the performance of the Assurance Engagement;

   (ii)   those who provide consultation regarding technical or industry specific issues, transactions or events for the Assurance Engagement; and

   (iii)   those who provide quality control for the Assurance Engagement, including those who perform the Engagement Quality Control Review for the Assurance Engagement.

[AUST] *AuASB* means the Auditing and Assurance Standards Board which issued Australian auditing and assurance standards up to 30 June 2004, under the auspices of the Australian Accounting Research Foundation, a joint venture of CPA Australia and the Institute of Chartered Accountants in Australia.

[AUST] *AUASB* means the Australian statutory body called the Auditing and Assurance Standards Board established under section 227A of the *Australian Securities and Investments Commission Act 2001.*

Audit Client means an entity in respect of which a Firm conducts an Audit Engagement. When the client is a Listed Entity, Audit Client will always include its Related Entities. When the Audit Client is not a Listed Entity, Audit Client includes those Related Entities over which the client has direct or indirect control.

Audit Engagement means a reasonable Assurance Engagement in which a Member in Public Practice expresses an opinion whether Financial Statements are prepared, in all material respects (or give a true and fair view or are presented fairly, in all material respects,), in accordance with an applicable financial reporting framework, such as an engagement conducted in accordance with Auditing and Assurance Standards. This includes a statutory audit, which is an audit required by legislation or other regulation.

Audit Team means:

(a)   All members of the Engagement Team for the Audit Engagement;

(b)   All others within a Firm who can directly influence the outcome of the Audit Engagement, including:

  (i)   those who recommend the compensation of, or who provide direct supervisory, management or other oversight of the Engagement Partner in connection with the performance of the Audit Engagement including those at all successively senior levels above the Engagement Partner through to the individual who is the Firm's senior or managing partner (chief executive or equivalent);

  (ii)   those who provide consultation regarding technical or industry-specific issues, transactions or events for the Audit Engagement; and

  (iii)   those who provide quality control for the engagement, including those who perform the Engagement Quality Control Review for the Audit Engagement; and

(c)   All those within a Network Firm who can directly influence the outcome of the Audit Engagement.

[AUST] *Auditing and Assurance Standards* means:

(a)   the AUASB standards, as described in ASA 100 *Preamble to AUASB Standards,* ASA 101 *Preamble to Australian Auditing Standards* and the *Foreword to AUASB Pronouncements,* issued by the AUASB, and operative from the date specified in each standard; and

(b)   those standards issued by the AuASB which have not been revised and reissued (whether as standards or as guidance) by the AUASB, to the extent that they are not inconsistent with the AUASB standards.

[AUST] *Australian Accounting Standards* means the Accounting Standards (including Australian Accounting Interpretations) promulgated by the AASB.

Close Family means a parent, child or sibling who is not an Immediate Family member.

Contingent Fee means a fee calculated on a predetermined basis relating to the outcome of a transaction or the result of the services performed by the Firm. A fee that is established by a court or other public authority is not a Contingent Fee.

Direct Financial Interest means a Financial Interest:

•   Owned directly by and under the control of an individual or entity (including those managed on a discretionary basis by others); or

•   Beneficially owned through a collective investment vehicle, estate, trust or other intermediary over which the individual or entity has control, or the ability to influence investment decisions.

APES

Director or Officer means those charged with the governance of an entity, or acting in an equivalent capacity, regardless of their title.

Engagement Partner means the partner or other person in the Firm who is responsible for the engagement and its performance, and for the report that is issued on behalf of the Firm, and who, where required, has the appropriate authority from a professional, legal or regulatory body.

Engagement Quality Control Review means a process designed to provide an objective evaluation, on or before the report is issued, of the significant judgments the Engagement Team made and the conclusions it reached in formulating the report.

Engagement Team means all partners and staff performing the engagement, and any individuals engaged by the Firm or a Network Firm who perform procedures on the engagement. This excludes External Experts engaged by the Firm or a Network Firm.

Existing Accountant means a Member in Public Practice currently holding an audit appointment or carrying out accounting, taxation, consulting or similar Professional Services for a client.

External Expert means an individual (who is not a partner or a member of the professional staff, including temporary staff, of the Firm or a Network Firm) or organisation possessing skills, knowledge and experience in a field other than accounting or auditing, whose work in that field is used to assist the Member in obtaining sufficient appropriate evidence.

Financial Interest means an interest in an equity or other security, debenture, loan or other debt instrument of an entity, including rights and obligations to acquire such an interest and derivatives directly related to such interest.

Financial Statements mean a structured representation of Historical Financial Information, including related notes, intended to communicate an entity's economic resources or obligations at a point in time or the changes therein for a period of time in accordance with a financial reporting framework. The related notes ordinarily comprise a summary of significant accounting policies and other explanatory information. The term can relate to a complete set of Financial Statements, but it can also refer to a single Financial Statement, for example, a balance sheet, or a statement of revenues and expenses, and related explanatory note. The requirements of the financial reporting framework determine the form and content of the Financial Statements and what constitutes a complete set of Financial Statement. For the purposes of this Standard financial report is considered to be an equivalent term to Financial Statements.

Financial Statements on which the Firm will express an Opinion means in the case of a single entity, the Financial Statements of that entity. In the case of consolidated Financial Statements, also referred to as group Financial Statements, the consolidated Financial Statements.

Firm means:

(a)   A sole practitioner, partnership, corporation or other entity of professional accountants;

(b)   An entity that controls such parties, through ownership, management or other means;

(c)   An entity controlled by such parties, through ownership, management or other means; or

(d)   An Auditor-General's office or department.

Historical Financial Information means information expressed in financial terms in relation to a particular entity, derived primarily from that entity's accounting system, about economic events occurring in past time periods or about economic conditions or circumstances at points in time in the past.

Immediate Family means a spouse (or equivalent) or dependent.

Independence is:

(a)   Independence of mind – the state of mind that permits the expression of a conclusion without being affected by influences that compromise professional judgment, thereby allowing an individual to act with integrity, and exercise objectivity and professional scepticism.

(b)   Independence in appearance – the avoidance of facts and circumstances that are so significant that a reasonable and informed third party would be likely to conclude, weighing all the specific facts and circumstances, that a Firm's, or a member of the Audit or Assurance Team's, integrity, objectivity or professional scepticism has been compromised.

Indirect Financial Interest means a Financial Interest beneficially owned through a collective investment vehicle, estate, trust or other intermediary over which the individual or entity has no control or ability to influence investment decisions.

Key Audit Partner means the Engagement Partner, the individual responsible for the Engagement Quality Control Review, and other audit partners, if any, on the Engagement Team who make key decisions or judgments on significant matters with respect to the audit of the Financial Statements on which the Firm will express an Opinion. Depending upon the circumstances and the role of the individuals on the audit, "other audit partners" may include, for example, audit partners responsible for significant subsidiaries or divisions.

Listed Entity means an entity whose shares, stock or debt are quoted or listed on a recognised stock exchange, or are marketed under the regulations of a recognised stock exchange or other equivalent body.

[AUST] *Member* means a member of a professional body that has adopted this Code as applicable to their membership, as defined by that professional body.

Member in Business means a Member employed or engaged in an executive or non-executive capacity in such areas as commerce, industry, service, the public sector, education, the not for profit sector, regulatory bodies or professional bodies, or a Member contracted by such entities.

Member in Public Practice means a Member, irrespective of functional classification (e.g., audit, tax or consulting) in a Firm that provides Professional Services. This term is also used to refer to a Firm of Members in Public Practice and means a practice entity and a participant in that practice entity as defined by the applicable professional body.

Network means a larger structure:

(a)   That is aimed at co-operation; and

(b)   That is clearly aimed at profit or cost sharing or shares common ownership, control or management, common quality control policies and procedures, common business strategy, the use of a common brand-name, or a significant part of professional resources.

Network Firm means a Firm or entity that belongs to a Network.

Office means a distinct sub-group, whether organised on geographical or practice lines.

Professional Services means services requiring accountancy or related skills performed by a Member including accounting, auditing, taxation, management consulting and financial management services.

Public Interest Entity means:

(a)   A Listed Entity; and

(b)   An entity (a) defined by regulation or legislation as a public interest entity or (b) for which the audit is required by regulation or legislation to be conducted in compliance with the same Independence requirements that apply to the audit of Listed Entities. Such regulation may be promulgated by any relevant regulator, including an audit regulator.

Related Entity means an entity that has any of the following relationships with the client:

(a)   An entity that has direct or indirect control over the client if the client is material to such entity;

(b)   An entity with a Direct Financial Interest in the client if that entity has significant influence over the client and the interest in the client is material to such entity;

(c)   An entity over which the client has direct or indirect control;

(d)   An entity in which the client, or an entity related to the client under (c) above, has a Direct Financial Interest that gives it significant influence over such entity and the interest is material to the client and its related entity in (c); and

(e)   An entity which is under common control with the client (a "sister entity") if the sister entity and the client are both material to the entity that controls both the client and sister entity.

Review Client means an entity in respect of which a Firm conducts a Review Engagement.

Review Engagement means an Assurance Engagement in which a Member in Public Practice expresses a conclusion whether, on the basis of the procedures which do not provide all the evidence that would be required in an audit, anything has come to the attention of the Member that causes the Member to believe that the Historical Financial Information is not prepared in all material respects in accordance with an applicable financial reporting framework such as an engagement conducted in accordance with Auditing and Assurance Standards on Review Engagements.

Review Team means:

(a)   All members of the Engagement Team for the Review Engagement; and

(b)   All others within a Firm who can directly influence the outcome of the Review Engagement, including:

        (i)   those who recommend the compensation of, or who provide direct supervisory, management or other oversight of the Engagement Partner in connection with the performance of the Review Engagement including those at all successively senior levels above the Engagement Partner through to the individual who is the Firm's senior or managing partner (chief executive or equivalent);

        (ii)   those who provide consultation regarding technical or industry specific issues, transactions or events for the engagement; and

        (iii)   those who provide quality control for the engagement, including those who perform the Engagement Quality Control Review for the engagement; and

(c)   All those within a Network Firm who can directly influence the outcome of the Review Engagement.

Special Purpose Financial Statements means Financial Statements prepared in accordance with a financial reporting framework designed to meet the financial information needs of specified users.

Those Charged with Governance means the persons with responsibility for overseeing the strategic direction of the entity and obligations related to the accountability of the entity. This includes overseeing the financial reporting process.

Part A—General Application of the Code

Section 100 Introduction and Fundamental Principles

Section 110 Integrity

Section 120 Objectivity

Section 130 Professional Competence and Due Care

Section 140 Confidentiality

Section 150 Professional Behaviour

SECTION 100

Introduction and Fundamental Principles

100.1　A distinguishing mark of the accountancy profession is its acceptance of the responsibility to act in the public interest. Therefore, a Member's responsibility is not exclusively to satisfy the needs of an individual client or employer. In acting in the public interest, a Member shall observe and comply with this Code. If a Member is prohibited from complying with certain parts of this Code by law or regulation, the Member shall comply with all other parts of this Code.

100.2　This Code contains three parts. Part A establishes the fundamental principles of professional ethics for Members and provides a conceptual framework that Members shall apply to:

(a)　Identify threats to compliance with the fundamental principles;

(b)　Evaluate the significance of the threats identified; and

(c)　Apply safeguards, when necessary, to eliminate the threats or reduce them to an Acceptable Level. Safeguards are necessary when the Member determines that the threats are not at a level at which a reasonable and informed third party would be likely to conclude, weighing all the specific facts and circumstances available to the Member at that time, that compliance with the fundamental principles is not compromised.

A Member shall use professional judgment in applying this conceptual framework.

100.3　Parts B and C describe how the conceptual framework applies in certain situations. They provide examples of safeguards that may be appropriate to address threats to compliance with the fundamental principles. They also describe situations where safeguards are not available to address the threats, and consequently, the circumstance or relationship creating the threats shall be avoided. Part B applies to Members in Public Practice. Part C applies to Members in Business. Members in Public Practice may also find Part C relevant to their particular circumstances.

100.4　The use of the word "shall" in this Code imposes a requirement on the Member or Firm to comply with the specific provision in which "shall" has been used. Compliance is required unless an exception is permitted by this Code.

Fundamental Principles

100.5　A Member shall comply with the following fundamental principles:

(a)　*Integrity* – to be straightforward and honest in all professional and business relationships.

(b)　*Objectivity* – to not allow bias, conflict of interest or undue influence of others to override professional or business judgments.

(c)　*Professional competence and due care* – to maintain professional knowledge and skill at the level required to ensure that a client or employer receives competent Professional Services based on current developments in practice, legislation and techniques and act diligently and in accordance with applicable technical and professional standards.

(d) *Confidentiality* – to respect the confidentiality of information acquired as a result of professional and business relationships and, therefore, not disclose any such information to third parties without proper and specific authority, unless there is a legal or professional right or duty to disclose, nor use the information for the personal advantage of the Member or third parties.

(e) *Professional behaviour* – to comply with relevant laws and regulations and avoid any action that discredits the profession.

Each of these fundamental principles is discussed in more detail in Sections 110–150.

Conceptual Framework Approach

100.6   The circumstances in which Members operate may create specific threats to compliance with the fundamental principles. It is impossible to define every situation that creates threats to compliance with the fundamental principles and specify the appropriate action. In addition, the nature of engagements and work assignments may differ and, consequently, different threats may be created, requiring the application of different safeguards. Therefore, this Code establishes a conceptual framework that requires a Member to identify, evaluate, and address threats to compliance with the fundamental principles. The conceptual framework approach assists a Member in complying with the ethical requirements of this Code and meeting their responsibility to act in the public interest. It accommodates many variations in circumstances that create threats to compliance with the fundamental principles and can deter a Member from concluding that a situation is permitted if it is not specifically prohibited.

100.7   When a Member identifies threats to compliance with the fundamental principles and, based on an evaluation of those threats, determines that they are not at an Acceptable Level, the Member shall determine whether appropriate safeguards are available and can be applied to eliminate the threats or reduce them to an Acceptable Level. In making that determination, the Member shall exercise professional judgment and take into account whether a reasonable and informed third party, weighing all the specific facts and circumstances available to the Member at the time, would be likely to conclude that the threats would be eliminated or reduced to an Acceptable Level by the application of the safeguards, such that compliance with the fundamental principles is not compromised.

100.8   A Member shall evaluate any threats to compliance with the fundamental principles when the Member knows, or could reasonably be expected to know, of circumstances or relationships that may compromise compliance with the fundamental principles.

100.9   A Member shall take qualitative as well as quantitative factors into account when evaluating the significance of a threat. When applying the conceptual framework, a Member may encounter situations in which threats cannot be eliminated or reduced to an Acceptable Level, either because the threat is too significant or because appropriate safeguards are not available or cannot be applied. In such situations, the Member shall decline or discontinue the specific Professional Service involved or, when necessary, resign from the engagement (in the case of a Member in Public Practice) or the employing organisation (in the case of a Member in Business).

100.10   A Member may inadvertently violate a provision of this Code. Depending on the nature and significance of the matter, such an inadvertent violation may be deemed not to compromise compliance with the fundamental principles provided, once the violation is discovered, the violation is corrected promptly and any necessary safeguards are applied.

100.11   When a Member encounters unusual circumstances in which the application of a specific requirement of the Code would result in a disproportionate outcome or an outcome that may not be in the public interest, it is recommended that the Member consult with a member body or the relevant regulator.

Threats and Safeguards

100.12   Threats may be created by a broad range of relationships and circumstances. When a relationship or circumstance creates a threat, such a threat could compromise, or could be perceived to compromise, a Member's compliance with the fundamental principles. A circumstance or relationship may create more than one threat, and a threat may affect compliance with more than one fundamental principle. Threats fall into one or more of the following categories:

     (a)   Self-interest threat – the threat that a financial or other interest will inappropriately influence the Member's judgment or behaviour;

     (b)   Self-review threat – the threat that a Member will not appropriately evaluate the results of a previous judgment made or service performed by the Member, or by another individual within the Member's Firm or employing organisation, on which the Member will rely when forming a judgment as part of providing a current service;

     (c)   Advocacy threat – the threat that a Member will promote a client's or employer's position to the point that the Member's objectivity is compromised;

     (d)   Familiarity threat – the threat that due to a long or close relationship with a client or employer, a Member will be too sympathetic to their interests or too accepting of their work; and

     (e)   Intimidation threat – the threat that a Member will be deterred from acting objectively because of actual or perceived pressures, including attempts to exercise undue influence over the Member.

     Parts B and C of this Code explain how these categories of threats may be created for Members in Public Practice and Members in Business, respectively. Members in Public Practice may also find Part C relevant to their particular circumstances.

100.13   Safeguards are actions or other measures that may eliminate threats or reduce them to an Acceptable Level. They fall into two broad categories:

     (a)   Safeguards created by the profession, legislation or regulation; and

     (b)   Safeguards in the work environment.

100.14   Safeguards created by the profession, legislation or regulation include:

- Educational, training and experience requirements for entry into the profession.
- Continuing professional development requirements.
- Corporate governance regulations.
- Professional standards.
- Professional or regulatory monitoring and disciplinary procedures.
- External review by a legally empowered third party of the reports, returns, communications or information produced by a Member.

100.15   Parts B and C of this Code discuss safeguards in the work environment for Members in Public Practice and Members in Business, respectively.

100.16   Certain safeguards may increase the likelihood of identifying or deterring unethical behaviour. Such safeguards, which may be created by the accounting profession, legislation, regulation, or an employing organisation, include:

- Effective, well-publicised complaint systems operated by the employing organisation, the profession or a regulator, which enable colleagues, employers and members of the public to draw attention to unprofessional or unethical behaviour.
- An explicitly stated duty to report breaches of ethical requirements.

Ethical Conflict Resolution

100.17   A Member may be required to resolve a conflict in complying with the fundamental principles.

100.18   When initiating either a formal or informal conflict resolution process, the following factors, either individually or together with other factors, may be relevant to the resolution process:

(a) Relevant facts;

(b) Ethical issues involved;

(c) Fundamental principles related to the matter in question;

(d) Established internal procedures; and

(e) Alternative courses of action.

Having considered the relevant factors, a Member shall determine the appropriate course of action, weighing the consequences of each possible course of action. If the matter remains unresolved, the Member may wish to consult with other appropriate persons within the Firm or employing organisation for help in obtaining resolution.

100.19   Where a matter involves a conflict with, or within, an organisation, a Member shall determine whether to consult with Those Charged with Governance of the organisation, such as the board of Directors or the audit committee.

100.20   It may be in the best interests of the Member to document the substance of the issue, the details of any discussions held, and the decisions made concerning that issue.

100.21   If a significant conflict cannot be resolved, a Member may consider obtaining professional advice from the relevant professional body or from legal advisors. The Member generally can obtain guidance on ethical issues without breaching the fundamental principle of confidentiality if the matter is discussed with the relevant professional body on an anonymous basis or with a legal advisor under the protection of legal privilege. Instances in which the Member may consider obtaining legal advice vary. For example, a Member may have encountered a fraud, the reporting of which could breach the Member's responsibility to respect confidentiality. The Member may consider obtaining legal advice in that instance to determine whether there is a requirement to report.

100.22   If, after exhausting all relevant possibilities, the ethical conflict remains unresolved, a Member shall, where possible, refuse to remain associated with the matter creating the conflict. The Member shall determine whether, in the circumstances, it is appropriate to withdraw from the Engagement Team or specific assignment, or to resign altogether from the engagement, the Firm or the employing organisation.

SECTION 110

Integrity

110.1   The principle of integrity imposes an obligation on all Members to be straightforward and honest in all professional and business relationships. Integrity also implies fair dealing and truthfulness.

110.2   A Member shall not knowingly be associated with reports, returns, communications or other information where the Member believes that the information:

(a) Contains a materially false or misleading statement;

(b) Contains statements or information furnished recklessly; or

(c) Omits or obscures information required to be included where such omission or obscurity would be misleading.

When a Member becomes aware that the Member has been associated with such information, the Member shall take steps to be disassociated from that information.

110.3   A Member will be deemed not to be in breach of paragraph 110.2 if the Member provides a modified report in respect of a matter contained in paragraph 110.2.

SECTION 120

Objectivity

120.1   The principle of objectivity imposes an obligation on all Members not to compromise their professional or business judgment because of bias, conflict of interest or the undue influence of others.

120.2   A Member may be exposed to situations that may impair objectivity. It is impracticable to define and prescribe all such situations. A Member shall not perform a Professional Service if a circumstance or relationship biases or unduly influences the Member's professional judgment with respect to that service.

SECTION 130

Professional Competence and Due Care

130.1   The principle of professional competence and due care imposes the following obligations on all Members:

(a) To maintain professional knowledge and skill at the level required to ensure that clients or employers receive competent Professional Service; and

(b) To act diligently in accordance with applicable technical and professional standards when providing Professional Services.

130.2   Competent Professional Service requires the exercise of sound judgment in applying professional knowledge and skill in the performance of such service. Professional competence may be divided into two separate phases:

(a) Attainment of professional competence; and

(b) Maintenance of professional competence.

130.3   The maintenance of professional competence requires a continuing awareness and an understanding of relevant technical, professional and business developments. Continuing professional development enables a Member to develop and maintain the capabilities to perform competently within the professional environment.

130.4   Diligence encompasses the responsibility to act in accordance with the requirements of an assignment, carefully, thoroughly and on a timely basis.

130.5   A Member shall take reasonable steps to ensure that those working under the Member's authority in a professional capacity have appropriate training and supervision.

130.6   Where appropriate, a Member shall make clients, employers or other users of the Member's Professional Services aware of the limitations inherent in the services.

SECTION 140

Confidentiality

140.1   The principle of confidentiality imposes an obligation on all Members to refrain from:

(a) Disclosing outside the Firm or employing organisation confidential information acquired as a result of professional and business relationships without proper and specific authority or unless there is a legal or professional right or duty to disclose; and

(b) Using confidential information acquired as a result of professional and business relationships to their personal advantage or the advantage of third parties.

140.2   A Member shall maintain confidentiality, including in a social environment, being alert to the possibility of inadvertent disclosure, particularly to a close business associate or a Close or Immediate Family member.

140.3   A Member shall maintain confidentiality of information disclosed by a prospective client or employer.

140.4   A Member shall maintain confidentiality of information within the Firm or employing organisation.

APES

140.5   A Member shall take reasonable steps to ensure that staff under the Member's control and persons from whom advice and assistance is obtained respect the Member's duty of confidentiality.

140.6   The need to comply with the principle of confidentiality continues even after the end of relationships between a Member and a client or employer. When a Member changes employment or acquires a new client, the Member is entitled to use prior experience. The Member shall not, however, use or disclose any confidential information either acquired or received as a result of a professional or business relationship.

140.7   The following are circumstances where Members are or may be required to disclose confidential information or when such disclosure may be appropriate:

    (a)   Disclosure is permitted by law and is authorised by the client or the employer;

    (b)   Disclosure is required by law, for example:

       (i)   Production of documents or other provision of evidence in the course of legal proceedings; or

       (ii)   Disclosure to the appropriate public authorities of infringements of the law that come to light; and

    (c)   There is a professional duty or right to disclose, when not prohibited by law:

       (i)   To comply with the quality review of a member body or professional body;

       (ii)   To respond to an inquiry or investigation by a member body or regulatory body;

       (iii)   To protect the professional interests of a Member in legal proceedings; or

       (iv)   To comply with technical standards and ethics requirements.

AUST140.7.1   The circumstances described in paragraph 140.7 do not take into account Australian legal and regulatory requirements. A Member considering disclosing confidential information about a client or employer without their consent is strongly advised to first obtain legal advice.

140.8   In deciding whether to disclose confidential information, relevant factors to consider include:

    (a)   Whether the interests of all parties, including third parties whose interests may be affected, could be harmed if the client or employer consents to the disclosure of information by the Member;

    (b)   Whether all the relevant information is known and substantiated, to the extent it is practicable; when the situation involves unsubstantiated facts, incomplete information or unsubstantiated conclusions, professional judgment shall be used in determining the type of disclosure to be made, if any;

    (c)   The type of communication that is expected and to whom it is addressed; and

    (d)   Whether the parties to whom the communication is addressed are appropriate recipients.

SECTION 150

Professional Behaviour

150.1   The principle of professional behaviour imposes an obligation on all Members to comply with relevant laws and regulations and avoid any action or omission that the Member knows or should know may discredit the profession. This includes actions or omissions that a reasonable and informed third party, weighing all the specific facts and circumstances available to the Member at that time, would be likely to conclude adversely affects the good reputation of the profession.

150.2   In marketing and promoting themselves and their work, Members shall not bring the profession into disrepute. Members shall be honest and truthful and not:

    (a)   Make exaggerated claims for the services they are able to offer, the qualifications they possess, or experience they have gained; or

    (b)   Make disparaging references or unsubstantiated comparisons to the work of others.

Part B—Members in Public Practice

Section 200 Introduction

Section 210 Professional Appointment

Section 220 Conflicts of Interest

Section 230 Second Opinions

Section 240 Fees and Other Types of Remuneration

Section 250 Marketing Professional Services

Section 260 Gifts and Hospitality

Section 270 Custody of client Assets

Section 280 Objectivity – All Services

[AUST] PREFACE: SECTIONS 290 AND 291

Section 290 Independence – Audit and Review Engagements

Section 291 Independence – Other Assurance Engagements

SECTION 200

Introduction

200.1   This Part of the Code describes how the conceptual framework contained in Part A applies in certain situations to Members in Public Practice. This Part does not describe all of the circumstances and relationships that could be encountered by a Member in Public Practice that create or may create threats to compliance with the fundamental principles. Therefore, the Member in Public Practice is encouraged to be alert for such circumstances and relationships.

200.2   A Member in Public Practice shall not knowingly engage in any business, occupation, or activity that impairs or might impair integrity, objectivity or the good reputation of the profession and as a result would be incompatible with the fundamental principles.

Threats and Safeguards

200.3   Compliance with the fundamental principles may potentially be threatened by a broad range of circumstances and relationships. The nature and significance of the threats may differ depending on whether they arise in relation to the provision of services to an Audit Client and whether the Audit Client is a Public Interest Entity, to an Assurance Client that is not an Audit Client, or to a non-assurance client.

Threats fall into one or more of the following categories:

(a) Self-interest;

(b) Self-review;

(c) Advocacy;

(d) Familiarity; and

(e) Intimidation.

These threats are discussed further in Part A of this Code.

200.4   Examples of circumstances that create self-interest threats for a Member in Public Practice include:

- A member of the Assurance Team having a Direct Financial Interest in the Assurance Client.

- A Firm having undue dependence on total fees from a client.

- A member of the Assurance Team having a significant close business relationship with an Assurance Client.

- A Firm being concerned about the possibility of losing a significant client.

APES (side tab)

- A member of the Audit Team entering into employment negotiations with the Audit Client.
- A Firm entering into a Contingent Fee arrangement relating to an Assurance Engagement.
- A Member discovering a significant error when evaluating the results of a previous Professional Service performed by a member of the Member's Firm.

200.5   Examples of circumstances that create self-review threats for a Member in Public Practice include:

- A Firm issuing an assurance report on the effectiveness of the operation of financial systems after designing or implementing the systems.
- A Firm having prepared the original data used to generate records that are the subject matter of the Assurance Engagement.
- A member of the Assurance Team being, or having recently been, a Director or Officer of the client.
- A member of the Assurance Team being, or having recently been, employed by the client in a position to exert significant influence over the subject matter of the engagement.
- The Firm performing a service for an Assurance Client that directly affects the subject matter information of the Assurance Engagement.

200.6   Examples of circumstances that create advocacy threats for a Member in Public Practice include:

- The Firm promoting shares in an Audit Client.
- A Member acting as an advocate on behalf of an Audit Client in litigation or disputes with third parties.

200.7   Examples of circumstances that create familiarity threats for a Member in Public Practice include:

- A member of the Engagement Team having a Close or Immediate Family member who is a Director or Officer of the client.
- A member of the Engagement Team having a Close or Immediate Family member who is an employee of the client who is in a position to exert significant influence over the subject matter of the engagement.
- A Director or Officer of the client or an employee in a position to exert significant influence over the subject matter of the engagement having recently served as the Engagement Partner.
- A Member accepting gifts or preferential treatment from a client, unless the value is trivial or inconsequential.
- Senior personnel having a long association with the Assurance Client.

200.8   Examples of circumstances that create intimidation threats for a Member in Public Practice include:

- A Firm being threatened with dismissal from a Client Engagement.
- An Audit Client indicating that it will not award a planned non-assurance contract to the Firm if the Firm continues to disagree with the client's accounting treatment for a particular transaction.
- A Firm being threatened with litigation by the client.
- A Firm being pressured to reduce inappropriately the extent of work performed in order to reduce fees.
- A Member feeling pressured to agree with the judgment of a client employee because the employee has more expertise on the matter in question.
- A Member being informed by a partner of the Firm that a planned promotion will not occur unless the Member agrees with an Audit Client's inappropriate accounting treatment.

200.9   Safeguards that may eliminate or reduce threats to an Acceptable Level fall into two broad categories:

(a)   Safeguards created by the profession, legislation or regulation; and

(b)   Safeguards in the work environment.

Examples of safeguards created by the profession, legislation or regulation are described in paragraph 100.14 of Part A of this Code.

200.10   A Member in Public Practice shall exercise judgment to determine how best to deal with threats that are not at an Acceptable Level, whether by applying safeguards to eliminate the threat or reduce it to an Acceptable Level or by terminating or declining the relevant engagement. In exercising this judgment, a Member in Public Practice shall consider whether a reasonable and informed third party, weighing all the specific facts and circumstances available to the Member at that time, would be likely to conclude that the threats would be eliminated or reduced to an Acceptable Level by the application of safeguards, such that compliance with the fundamental principles is not compromised. This consideration will be affected by matters such as the significance of the threat, the nature of the engagement and the structure of the Firm.

200.11   In the work environment, the relevant safeguards will vary depending on the circumstances. Work environment safeguards comprise Firm-wide safeguards and engagement-specific safeguards.

200.12   Examples of Firm-wide safeguards in the work environment include:

- Leadership of the Firm that stresses the importance of compliance with the fundamental principles.

- Leadership of the Firm that establishes the expectation that members of an Assurance Team will act in the public interest.

- Policies and procedures to implement and monitor quality control of engagements.

- Documented policies regarding the need to identify threats to compliance with the fundamental principles, evaluate the significance of those threats, and apply safeguards to eliminate or reduce the threats to an Acceptable Level or, when appropriate safeguards are not available or cannot be applied, terminate or decline the relevant engagement.

- Documented internal policies and procedures requiring compliance with the fundamental principles.

- Policies and procedures that will enable the identification of interests or relationships between the Firm or members of Engagement Teams and clients.

- Policies and procedures to monitor and, if necessary, manage the reliance on revenue received from a single client.

- Using different partners and Engagement Teams with separate reporting lines for the provision of non-assurance services to an Assurance Client.

- Policies and procedures to prohibit individuals who are not members of an Engagement Team from inappropriately influencing the outcome of the engagement.

- Timely communication of a Firm's policies and procedures, including any changes to them, to all partners and professional staff, and appropriate training and education on such policies and procedures.

- Designating a member of senior management to be responsible for overseeing the adequate functioning of the Firm's quality control system.

- Advising partners and professional staff of Assurance Clients and Related Entities from which Independence is required.

- A disciplinary mechanism to promote compliance with policies and procedures.

- Published policies and procedures to encourage and empower staff to communicate to senior levels within the Firm any issue relating to compliance with the fundamental principles that concerns them.

APES

200.13   Examples of engagement-specific safeguards in the work environment include:

- Having a Member who was not involved with the non-assurance service review the non-assurance work performed or otherwise advise as necessary.
- Having a Member who was not a member of the Assurance Team review the assurance work performed or otherwise advise as necessary.
- Consulting an independent third party, such as a committee of independent Directors, a professional regulatory body or another Member.
- Discussing ethical issues with Those Charged with Governance of the client.
- Disclosing to Those Charged with Governance of the client the nature of services provided and extent of fees charged.
- Involving another Firm to perform or re-perform part of the engagement.
- Rotating senior Assurance Team personnel.

200.14   Depending on the nature of the engagement, a Member in Public Practice may also be able to rely on safeguards that the client has implemented. However it is not possible to rely solely on such safeguards to reduce threats to an Acceptable Level.

200.15   Examples of safeguards within the client's systems and procedures include:

- The client requires persons other than management to ratify or approve the appointment of a Firm to perform an engagement.
- The client has competent employees with experience and seniority to make managerial decisions.
- The client has implemented internal procedures that ensure objective choices in commissioning non-assurance engagements.
- The client has a corporate governance structure that provides appropriate oversight and communications regarding the Firm's services.

SECTION 210

Professional Appointment

Client Acceptance

210.1   Before accepting a new client relationship, a Member in Public Practice shall determine whether acceptance would create any threats to compliance with the fundamental principles. Potential threats to integrity or professional behaviour may be created from, for example, questionable issues associated with the client (its owners, management or activities).

210.2   Client issues that, if known, could threaten compliance with the fundamental principles include, for example, client involvement in illegal activities (such as money laundering), dishonesty or questionable financial reporting practices.

210.3   A Member in Public Practice shall evaluate the significance of any threats and apply safeguards when necessary to eliminate them or reduce them to an Acceptable Level.

Examples of such safeguards include:

- Obtaining knowledge and understanding of the client, its owners, managers and those responsible for its governance and business activities; or
- Securing the client's commitment to improve corporate governance practices or internal controls.

210.4   Where it is not possible to reduce the threats to an Acceptable Level, the Member in Public Practice shall decline to enter into the client relationship.

210.5   It is recommended that a Member in Public Practice periodically review acceptance decisions for recurring client engagements.

Engagement Acceptance

210.6   The fundamental principle of professional competence and due care imposes an obligation on a Member in Public Practice to provide only those services that the

Member in Public Practice is competent to perform. Before accepting a specific client engagement, a Member in Public Practice shall determine whether acceptance would create any threats to compliance with the fundamental principles. For example, a self-interest threat to professional competence and due care is created if the Engagement Team does not possess, or cannot acquire, the competencies necessary to properly carry out the engagement.

210.7   A Member in Public Practice shall evaluate the significance of threats and apply safeguards, when necessary, to eliminate them or reduce them to an Acceptable Level. Examples of such safeguards include:

- Acquiring an appropriate understanding of the nature of the client's business, the complexity of its operations, the specific requirements of the engagement and the purpose, nature and scope of the work to be performed.

- Acquiring knowledge of relevant industries or subject matters.

- Possessing or obtaining experience with relevant regulatory or reporting requirements.

- Assigning sufficient staff with the necessary competencies.

- Using experts where necessary.

- Agreeing on a realistic time frame for the performance of the engagement.

- Complying with quality control policies and procedures designed to provide reasonable assurance that specific engagements are accepted only when they can be performed competently.

210.8   When a Member in Public Practice intends to rely on the advice or work of an expert, the Member in Public Practice shall determine whether such reliance is warranted. Factors to consider include: reputation, expertise, resources available and applicable professional and ethical standards. Such information may be gained from prior association with the expert or from consulting others.

Changes in a Professional Appointment

210.9   A Member in Public Practice who is asked to replace another Member in Public Practice, or who is considering tendering for an engagement currently held by another Member in Public Practice, shall determine whether there are any reasons, professional or otherwise, for not accepting the engagement, such as circumstances that create threats to compliance with the fundamental principles that cannot be eliminated or reduced to an Acceptable Level by the application of safeguards. For example, there may be a threat to professional competence and due care if a Member in Public Practice accepts the engagement before knowing all the pertinent facts.

210.10   A Member in Public Practice shall evaluate the significance of any threats. Depending on the nature of the Engagement, this may require direct communication with the Existing Accountant to establish the facts and circumstances regarding the proposed change so that the Member in Public Practice can decide whether it would be appropriate to accept the engagement. For example, the apparent reasons for the change in appointment may not fully reflect the facts and may indicate disagreements with the Existing Accountant that may influence the decision to accept the appointment.

210.11   Safeguards shall be applied when necessary to eliminate any threats or reduce them to an Acceptable Level. Examples of such safeguards include:

- When replying to requests to submit tenders, stating in the tender that, before accepting the engagement, contact with the Existing Accountant will be requested so that inquiries may be made as to whether there are any professional or other reasons why the appointment should not be accepted;

- Asking the Existing Accountant to provide known information on any facts or circumstances that, in the Existing Accountant's opinion, the proposed accountant needs to be aware of before deciding whether to accept the engagement; or

- Obtaining necessary information from other sources.

When the threats cannot be eliminated or reduced to an Acceptable Level through the application of safeguards, a Member in Public Practice shall, unless there is satisfaction as to necessary facts by other means, decline the engagement.

AUST210.11.1   A Member in Public Practice who is asked to replace an existing auditor or to accept nomination as a replacement auditor shall:

    (a) Request the prospective client's permission to communicate with the existing auditor. If such permission is refused the Member shall, in the absence of exceptional circumstances, decline the Audit Engagement or the nomination; and

    (b) On receipt of permission, request in writing of the existing auditor all information which ought to be available to enable the Member to make a decision as to whether the Audit Engagement or the nomination should be accepted.

210.12   A Member in Public Practice may be asked to undertake work that is complementary or additional to the work of the Existing Accountant. Such circumstances may create threats to professional competence and due care resulting from, for example, a lack of or incomplete information. The significance of any threats shall be evaluated and safeguards applied when necessary to eliminate the threat or reduce it to an Acceptable Level. An example of such a safeguard is notifying the Existing Accountant of the proposed work, which would give the Existing Accountant the opportunity to provide any relevant information needed for the proper conduct of the work.

210.13   An Existing Accountant is bound by confidentiality. Whether that Member is permitted or required to discuss the affairs of a client with a proposed accountant will depend on the nature of the engagement and on:

    (a) Whether the client's permission to do so has been obtained; or

    (b) The legal or ethical requirements relating to such communications and disclosure, which may vary by jurisdiction.

Circumstances where the Member is or may be required to disclose confidential information or where such disclosure may otherwise be appropriate are set out in Section 140 of Part A of this Code.

210.14   A Member in Public Practice will generally need to obtain the Client's permission, preferably in writing, to initiate discussion with an Existing Accountant. Once that permission is obtained, the Existing Accountant shall comply with relevant legal and other regulations governing such requests. Where the Existing Accountant provides information, it shall be provided honestly and unambiguously. If the proposed accountant is unable to communicate with the Existing Accountant, the proposed accountant shall take reasonable steps to obtain information about any possible threats by other means, such as through inquiries of third parties or background investigations of senior management or Those Charged with Governance of the client.

AUST210.15.1   The requirements of section 210 also apply where a Member in Public Practice is replacing or being replaced by an accountant who is not a Member.

SECTION 220

Conflicts of Interest

220.1   A Member in Public Practice shall take reasonable steps to identify circumstances that could pose a conflict of interest. Such circumstances may create threats to compliance with the fundamental principles. For example, a threat to objectivity may be created when a Member in Public Practice competes directly with a client or has a joint venture or similar arrangement with a major competitor of a client. A threat to objectivity or confidentiality may also be created when a Member in Public Practice performs services for clients whose interests are in conflict or the clients are in dispute with each other in relation to the matter or transaction in question.

220.2   A Member in Public Practice shall evaluate the significance of any threats and apply safeguards when necessary to eliminate the threats or reduce them to an Acceptable Level. Before accepting or continuing a client relationship or specific engagement, the Member in Public Practice shall evaluate the significance of any threats created by business interests or relationships with the client or a third party.

220.3   Depending upon the circumstances giving rise to the conflict, application of one of the following safeguards is generally necessary:

(a) Notifying the client of the Firm's business interest or activities that may represent a conflict of interest and obtaining their consent to act in such circumstances; or

(b) Notifying all known relevant parties that the Member in Public Practice is acting for two or more parties in respect of a matter where their respective interests are in conflict and obtaining their consent to so act; or

(c) Notifying the client that the Member in Public Practice does not act exclusively for any one client in the provision of proposed services (for example, in a particular market sector or with respect to a specific service) and obtaining their consent to so act.

220.4   The Member in Public Practice shall also determine whether to apply one or more of the following additional safeguards:

(a) The use of separate Engagement Teams;

(b) Procedures to prevent access to information (e.g., strict physical separation of such teams, confidential and secure data filing);

(c) Clear guidelines for members of the Engagement Team on issues of security and confidentiality;

(d) The use of confidentiality agreements signed by employees and partners of the Firm; and

(e) Regular review of the application of safeguards by a senior individual not involved with relevant client engagements.

220.5   Where a conflict of interest creates a threat to one or more of the fundamental principles, including objectivity, confidentiality, or professional behaviour, that cannot be eliminated or reduced to an Acceptable Level through the application of safeguards, the Member in Public Practice shall not accept a specific engagement or shall resign from one or more conflicting engagements.

220.6   Where a Member in Public Practice has requested consent from a client to act for another party (which may or may not be an existing client) in respect of a matter where the respective interests are in conflict and that consent has been refused by the client, the Member in Public Practice shall not continue to act for one of the parties in the matter giving rise to the conflict of interest.

SECTION 230

Second Opinions

230.1   Situations where a Member in Public Practice is asked to provide a second opinion on the application of Australian Accounting Standards, Auditing or Assurance Standards, reporting or other standards or principles to specific circumstances or transactions by or on behalf of a company or an entity that is not an existing client may create threats to compliance with the fundamental principles. For example, there may be a threat to professional competence and due care in circumstances where the second opinion is not based on the same set of facts that were made available to the Existing Accountant or is based on inadequate evidence. The existence and significance of any threat will depend on the circumstances of the request and all the other available facts and assumptions relevant to the expression of a professional judgment.

230.2   When asked to provide such an opinion, a Member in Public Practice shall evaluate the significance of any threats and apply safeguards when necessary to eliminate them or reduce them to an Acceptable Level. Examples of such safeguards include seeking client permission to contact the Existing Accountant, describing the limitations surrounding any opinion in communications with the client and providing the Existing Accountant with a copy of the opinion.

230.3   If the company or entity seeking the opinion will not permit communication with the Existing Accountant, a Member in Public Practice shall determine whether, taking all the circumstances into account, it is appropriate to provide the opinion sought.

SECTION 240
Fees and Other Types of Remuneration

240.1   When entering into negotiations regarding services, a Member in Public Practice may quote whatever fee is deemed appropriate. The fact that one Member in Public Practice may quote a fee lower than another is not in itself unethical. Nevertheless, there may be threats to compliance with the fundamental principles arising from the level of fees quoted. For example, a self-interest threat to professional competence and due care is created if the fee quoted is so low that it may be difficult to perform the engagement in accordance with applicable technical and professional standards for that price.

240.2   The existence and significance of any threats created will depend on factors such as the level of fee quoted and the services to which it applies. The significance of any threat shall be evaluated and safeguards applied when necessary to eliminate the threat or reduce it to an Acceptable Level. Examples of such safeguards include:

- Making the client aware of the terms of the engagement and, in particular, the basis on which fees are charged and which services are covered by the quoted fee.
- Assigning appropriate time and qualified staff to the task.

Contingent Fees

240.3   Contingent Fees are widely used for certain types of non-assurance engagements.[1] They may, however, create threats to compliance with the fundamental principles in certain circumstances[2]. They may create a self-interest threat to objectivity. The existence and significance of such threats will depend on factors including:

- The nature of the engagement.
- The range of possible fee amounts.
- The basis for determining the fee.
- Whether the outcome or result of the transaction is to be reviewed by an independent third party.

240.4   The significance of any such threats shall be evaluated and safeguards applied when necessary to eliminate or reduce them to an Acceptable Level. Examples of such safeguards include:

- An advance written agreement with the client as to the basis of remuneration.
- Disclosure to intended users of the work performed by the Member in Public Practice and the basis of remuneration.
- Quality control policies and procedures.
- Review by an independent third party of the work performed by the Member in Public Practice.

---

1   Contingent Fees for non-assurance services provided to Audit Clients and other Assurance Clients are discussed in Sections 290 and 291 of this Code.

2   APESB has prohibited the use of Contingent Fees in certain circumstances. These circumstances are described in the following APESB Standards:

APES 215 *Forensic Accounting Services*;

APES 225 *Valuation Services*;

APES 330 *Insolvency Services*;

APES 345 *Reporting on Prospective Financial Information Prepared in Connection with a Disclosure Document*; and

APES 350 *Participation by Members in Public Practice in Due Diligence Committees in connection with a Public Document*.

Referral fees and commissions

240.5　In certain circumstances, a Member in Public Practice may receive a referral fee or commission relating to a client. For example, where the Member in Public Practice does not provide the specific service required, a fee may be received for referring a continuing client to another Member in Public Practice or other expert. A Member in Public Practice may receive a commission from a third party (e.g., a software vendor) in connection with the sale of goods or services to a client. Accepting such a referral fee or commission creates a self-interest threat to objectivity and professional competence and due care.

240.6　A Member in Public Practice may also pay a referral fee to obtain a client, for example, where the client continues as a client of another Member in Public Practice but requires specialist services not offered by the Existing Accountant. The payment of such a referral fee also creates a self-interest threat to objectivity and professional competence and due care.

240.7　The significance of the threat shall be evaluated and safeguards applied when necessary to eliminate the threat or reduce it to an Acceptable Level. Examples of such safeguards include:

- Disclosing to the client any arrangements to pay a referral fee to another Member in Public Practice for the work referred.

- Disclosing to the client any arrangements to receive a referral fee for referring the client to another Member in Public Practice.

- Obtaining advance agreement from the client for commission arrangements in connection with the sale by a third party of goods or services to the client.

AUST240.7.1　A Member in Public Practice who is undertaking an engagement in Australia and receives a referral fee or commission shall inform the client in writing of:

- the existence of such arrangement;

- the identity of the other party or parties; and

- the method of calculation of the referral fee, commission or other benefit accruing directly or indirectly to the Member.

AUST240.7.2　The receipt of commissions or other similar benefits in connection with an Assurance Engagement creates a threat to Independence that no safeguards could reduce to an Acceptable Level. Accordingly, a Member in Public Practice shall not accept such a fee arrangement in respect of an Assurance Engagement.

240.8　A Member in Public Practice may purchase all or part of another Firm on the basis that payments will be made to individuals formerly owning the Firm or to their heirs or estates. Such payments are not regarded as commissions or referral fees for the purpose of paragraphs 240.5–240.7 above.

SECTION 250

Marketing Professional Services

250.1　When a Member in Public Practice solicits new work through Advertising or other forms of marketing, there may be a threat to compliance with the fundamental principles. For example, a self-interest threat to compliance with the principle of professional behaviour is created if services, achievements, or products are marketed in a way that is inconsistent with that principle.

250.2　A Member in Public Practice shall not bring the profession into disrepute when marketing Professional Services. The Member in Public Practice shall be honest and truthful and not:

(a) Make exaggerated claims for services offered, qualifications possessed, or experience gained; or

(b) Make disparaging references or unsubstantiated comparisons to the work of another.

If the Member in Public Practice is in doubt about whether a proposed form of Advertising or marketing is appropriate, the Member in Public Practice shall consider consulting with the relevant professional body.

SECTION 260

Gifts and Hospitality

260.1   A Member in Public Practice, or an Immediate or Close Family member, may be offered gifts and hospitality from a client. Such an offer may create threats to compliance with the fundamental principles. For example, a self-interest or familiarity threat to objectivity may be created if a gift from a client is accepted; an intimidation threat to objectivity may result from the possibility of such offers being made public.

260.2   The existence and significance of any threat will depend on the nature, value, and intent of the offer. Where gifts or hospitality are offered that a reasonable and informed third party, weighing all the specific facts and circumstances, would consider trivial and inconsequential, a Member in Public Practice may conclude that the offer is made in the normal course of business without the specific intent to influence decision making or to obtain information. In such cases, the Member in Public Practice may generally conclude that any threat to compliance with the fundamental principles is at an Acceptable Level.

260.3   A Member in Public Practice shall evaluate the significance of any threats and apply safeguards when necessary to eliminate the threats or reduce them to an Acceptable Level. When the threats cannot be eliminated or reduced to an Acceptable Level through the application of safeguards, a Member in Public Practice shall not accept such an offer.

SECTION 270

Custody of Client Assets

270.1   A Member in Public Practice shall not assume custody of client monies or other assets unless permitted to do so by law and, if so, in compliance with any additional legal duties imposed on a Member in Public Practice holding such assets.

270.2   The holding of client assets creates threats to compliance with the fundamental principles; for example, there is a self-interest threat to professional behaviour and may be a self-interest threat to objectivity arising from holding client assets. A Member in Public Practice entrusted with money (or other assets) belonging to others shall therefore:

(a)   Keep such assets separately from personal or Firm assets;

(b)   Use such assets only for the purpose for which they are intended;

(c)   At all times be ready to account for those assets and any income, dividends, or gains generated, to any persons entitled to such accounting; and

(d)   Comply with all relevant laws and regulations relevant to the holding of and accounting for such assets.

270.3   As part of client and engagement acceptance procedures for services that may involve the holding of client assets, a Member in Public Practice shall make appropriate inquiries about the source of such assets and consider legal and regulatory obligations. For example, if the assets were derived from illegal activities, such as money laundering, a threat to compliance with the fundamental principles would be created. In such situations, the Member may consider seeking legal advice.

SECTION 280

Objectivity—All Services

280.1   A Member in Public Practice shall determine when providing any Professional Service whether there are threats to compliance with the fundamental principle of objectivity resulting from having interests in, or relationships with, a client or its Directors, Officers or employees. For example, a familiarity threat to objectivity may be created from a family or close personal or business relationship.

280.2   A Member in Public Practice who provides an assurance service shall be independent of the Assurance Client. Independence of mind and in appearance is necessary to enable the Member in Public Practice to express a conclusion, and be seen to express a conclusion, without bias, conflict of interest, or undue influence of others. Sections 290 and 291 provide specific guidance on Independence requirements for Members in Public Practice when performing Assurance Engagements.

280.3   The existence of threats to objectivity when providing any Professional Service will depend upon the particular circumstances of the engagement and the nature of the work that the Member in Public Practice is performing.

280.4   A Member in Public Practice shall evaluate the significance of any threats and apply safeguards when necessary to eliminate them or reduce them to an Acceptable Level. Examples of such safeguards include:

- Withdrawing from the Engagement Team.
- Supervisory procedures.
- Terminating the financial or business relationship giving rise to the threat.
- Discussing the issue with higher levels of management within the Firm.
- Discussing the issue with Those Charged with Governance of the client.

If safeguards cannot eliminate or reduce the threat to an Acceptable Level, the Member shall decline or terminate the relevant engagement.

APES

[AUST] Preface: SECTIONS 290 and 291

SECTION 290 Independence – Audit and Review Engagements and

SECTION 291 Independence – Other Assurance Engagements

Section 290 of this Code addresses Independence requirements for Audit and Review Engagements, which are Assurance Engagements where a Member in Public Practice expresses a conclusion on Historical Financial Information.

Section 291 of this Code addresses Independence requirements for Assurance Engagements that are not Audit or Review Engagements of Historical Financial Information, referred to in this Code as Other Assurance Engagements.

The concept of Independence is fundamental to compliance with the principles of integrity and objectivity. This Code adopts a conceptual framework that requires the identification and evaluation of threats to Independence so that any threats created are eliminated or reduced to an Acceptable Level by the application of safeguards.

This approach contrasts with the rules adopted in legislation, which are often prescriptive in nature. Accordingly, Members and other readers of this Code should be aware that adherence to this Code does not ensure adherence to legislation and they must refer to such legislation to determine their legal obligations.

While this difference in approach makes precise comparisons to specific legislation, such as the *Corporations Act 2001*, difficult, the underlying principles of integrity and objectivity are consistent with objective and impartial judgement, when both approaches are tested in the context of all relevant facts by a reasonable person. Where APESB is aware that there is a more stringent requirement in the *Corporations Act 2001* an appropriate footnote reference has been included for the Members and other readers information. However, please note that not all applicable *Corporations Act 2001* requirements have been addressed and thus Members are referred to the *Corporations Act 2001* to determine their independence obligations when performing Audit and Review Engagements in accordance with the Act.

The statutory Independence of Auditors–General is provided for in legislation by the Parliament of each Australian jurisdiction in a number of ways. This includes defining the scope of an Auditor–General's mandate, the appointment and removal of an Auditor-General and the performance of his or her responsibilities. The requirements within this Code apply to Auditors-General and their senior Officers who are delegated or authorised to sign assurance reports and are Members, to the extent that they do not conflict with applicable legislation.

With regard to the use of the words "material" and "materiality" in Sections 290 and 291, it is not possible to give a definition which covers all circumstances where either word is used. In assessing materiality, a Member in Public Practice or a Firm shall consider both the qualitative and quantitative aspects of the matter under consideration which might have, or be seen to have, an adverse effect on the objectivity of the Member or Firm.

SECTION 290
Independence – Audit and Review Engagements

Contents

Paragraph

Structure of Section 290.1

A Conceptual Framework Approach to Independence 290.4

Networks and Network Firms 290.13

Public Interest Entities 290.25

Related Entities 290.27

Those Charged with Governance 290.28

Documentation 290.29

Engagement Period 290.30

Mergers and Acquisitions 290.33

Other Considerations 290.39

Application of the Conceptual Framework Approach to Independence 290.100

Financial Interests 290.102

Loans and Guarantees 290.118

Business Relationships 290.124

Family and Personal Relationships 290.127

Employment with an Audit Client 290.134

Temporary Staff Assignments 290.142

Recent Service with an Audit Client 290.143

Serving as a Director or Officer of an Audit Client 290.146

Long Association of Senior Personnel (Including partner rotation) with
   an Audit Client 290.150

Provision of Non-assurance Services to Audit Clients 290.156

   Management Responsibilities 209.162

   Preparing Accounting Records and Financial Statements 290.167

   Valuation Services 290.175

   Taxation Services 290.181

   Internal Audit Services 290.195

   IT Systems Services 290.201

   Litigation Support Services 290.207

   Legal Services 290.209

   Recruiting Services 290.214

   Corporate Finance Services 290.216

Fees 290.220

   Fees—Relative Size 290.220

   Fees—Overdue 290.223

   Contingent Fees 290.224

Compensation and Evaluation Policies 290.228

Gifts and Hospitality 290.230

Actual or Threatened Litigation 290.231

Reports that Include a Restriction on Use and Distribution 290.500

APES

Structure of Section

290.1   This section addresses the Independence requirements for Audit Engagements and Review Engagements, which are Assurance Engagements in which a Member in Public Practice expresses a conclusion on Financial Statements. Such engagements comprise Audit and Review Engagements to report on a complete set of Financial Statements and a single Financial Statement. Independence requirements for Assurance Engagements that are not Audit or Review Engagements are addressed in Section 291.

290.2   In certain circumstances involving Audit Engagements where the audit report includes a restriction on use and distribution and provided certain conditions are met, the Independence requirements in this section may be modified as provided in paragraphs 290.500 to 290.514. The modifications are not permitted in the case of an audit of Financial Statements required by law or regulation.

290.3   In this section, the term(s):

- "audit," "Audit Team," "Audit Engagement," "Audit Client" and "audit report" includes review, Review Team, Review Engagement, Review Client and review report; and

- "Firm" includes Network Firm, except where otherwise stated.

A Conceptual Framework Approach to Independence

290.4   In the case of Audit Engagements, it is in the public interest and, therefore, required by this Code of Ethics, that members of Audit Teams, Firms and, Network Firms shall be independent of Audit Clients.

290.5   The objective of this section is to assist Firms and members of Audit Teams in applying the conceptual framework approach described below to achieving and maintaining Independence.

290.6   Independence comprises:

Independence of Mind

The state of mind that permits the expression of a conclusion without being affected by influences that compromise professional judgment, thereby allowing an individual to act with integrity and exercise objectivity and professional scepticism.

Independence in Appearance

The avoidance of facts and circumstances that are so significant that a reasonable and informed third party would be likely to conclude, weighing all the specific facts and circumstances, that a Firm's, or a member of the Audit Team's, integrity, objectivity or professional scepticism has been compromised.

290.7   The conceptual framework approach shall be applied by Members to:

(a) Identify threats to Independence;

(b) Evaluate the significance of the threats identified; and

(c) Apply safeguards, when necessary, to eliminate the threats or reduce them to an Acceptable Level.

When the Member determines that appropriate safeguards are not available or cannot be applied to eliminate the threats or reduce them to an Acceptable Level, the Member shall eliminate the circumstance or relationship creating the threats or decline or terminate the Audit Engagement.

A Member shall use professional judgment in applying this conceptual framework.

290.8   Many different circumstances, or combinations of circumstances, may be relevant in assessing threats to Independence. It is impossible to define every situation that creates threats to Independence and to specify the appropriate action. Therefore, this Code establishes a conceptual framework that requires Firms and members of Audit Teams to identify, evaluate, and address threats to Independence. The conceptual framework approach assists Members in Public Practice in complying with the ethical requirements in this Code. It accommodates many variations in circumstances that create threats to

Independence and can deter a Member from concluding that a situation is permitted if it is not specifically prohibited.

290.9 Paragraphs 290.100 and onwards describe how the conceptual framework approach to Independence is to be applied. These paragraphs do not address all the circumstances and relationships that create or may create threats to Independence.

290.10 In deciding whether to accept or continue an engagement, or whether a particular individual may be a member of the Audit Team, a Firm shall identify and evaluate threats to Independence. If the threats are not at an Acceptable Level, and the decision is whether to accept an engagement or include a particular individual on the Audit Team, the Firm shall determine whether safeguards are available to eliminate the threats or reduce them to an Acceptable Level. If the decision is whether to continue an engagement, the Firm shall determine whether any existing safeguards will continue to be effective to eliminate the threats or reduce them to an Acceptable Level or whether other safeguards will need to be applied or whether the engagement needs to be terminated. Whenever new information about a threat to Independence comes to the attention of the Firm during the engagement, the Firm shall evaluate the significance of the threat in accordance with the conceptual framework approach.

290.11 Throughout this section, reference is made to the significance of threats to Independence. In evaluating the significance of a threat, qualitative as well as quantitative factors shall be taken into account.

AUST290.11.1 Where a Member in Public Practice identifies multiple threats to Independence, which individually may not be significant, the Member shall evaluate the significance of those threats in aggregate and the safeguards applied or in place to eliminate some or all of the threats or reduce them to an Acceptable Level in aggregate.

290.12 This section does not, in most cases, prescribe the specific responsibility of individuals within the Firm for actions related to Independence because responsibility may differ depending on the size, structure and organisation of a Firm. The Firm is required by APES 320 *Quality Control for Firms* to establish policies and procedures designed to provide it with reasonable assurance that Independence is maintained when required by relevant ethical requirements. In addition, Auditing and Assurance Standards require the Engagement Partner to form a conclusion on compliance with the Independence requirements that apply to the engagement.

Networks and Network Firms

290.13 If a Firm is deemed to be a Network Firm, the Firm shall be Independent of the Audit Clients of the other Firms within the Network (unless otherwise stated in this Code). The Independence requirements in this section that apply to a Network Firm apply to any entity, such as a consulting practice or professional law practice, that meets the definition of a Network Firm irrespective of whether the entity itself meets the definition of a Firm.

290.14 To enhance their ability to provide Professional Services, Firms frequently form larger structures with other Firms and entities. Whether these larger structures create a Network depends on the particular facts and circumstances and does not depend on whether the Firms and entities are legally separate and distinct. For example, a larger structure may be aimed only at facilitating the referral of work, which in itself does not meet the criteria necessary to constitute a Network. Alternatively, a larger structure might be such that it is aimed at co-operation and the Firms share a common brand name, a common system of quality control, or significant professional resources and consequently is deemed to be a Network.

290.15 The judgment as to whether the larger structure is a Network shall be made in light of whether a reasonable and informed third party would be likely to conclude, weighing all the specific facts and circumstances, that the entities are associated in such a way that a Network exists. This judgment shall be applied consistently throughout the Network.

290.16   Where the larger structure is aimed at co-operation and it is clearly aimed at profit or cost sharing among the entities within the structure, it is deemed to be a Network. However, the sharing of immaterial costs does not in itself create a Network. In addition, if the sharing of costs is limited only to those costs related to the development of audit methodologies, manuals, or training courses, this would not in itself create a Network. Further, an association between a Firm and an otherwise unrelated entity to jointly provide a service or develop a product does not in itself create a Network.

290.17   Where the larger structure is aimed at cooperation and the entities within the structure share common ownership, control or management, it is deemed to be a Network. This could be achieved by contract or other means.

290.18   Where the larger structure is aimed at co-operation and the entities within the structure share common quality control policies and procedures, it is deemed to be a Network. For this purpose, common quality control policies and procedures are those designed, implemented and monitored across the larger structure.

290.19   Where the larger structure is aimed at co-operation and the entities within the structure share a common business strategy, it is deemed to be a Network. Sharing a common business strategy involves an agreement by the entities to achieve common strategic objectives. An entity is not deemed to be a Network Firm merely because it co-operates with another entity solely to respond jointly to a request for a proposal for the provision of a Professional Service.

290.20   Where the larger structure is aimed at co-operation and the entities within the structure share the use of a common brand name, it is deemed to be a Network. A common brand name includes common initials or a common name. A Firm is deemed to be using a common brand name if it includes, for example, the common brand name as part of, or along with, its Firm name, when a partner of the Firm signs an audit report.

290.21   Even though a Firm does not belong to a Network and does not use a common brand name as part of its Firm name, it may give the appearance that it belongs to a Network if it makes reference in its stationery or promotional materials to being a member of an association of Firms. Accordingly, if care is not taken in how a Firm describes such memberships, a perception may be created that the Firm belongs to a Network.

290.22   If a Firm sells a component of its practice, the sales agreement sometimes provides that, for a limited period of time, the component may continue to use the name of the Firm, or an element of the name, even though it is no longer connected to the Firm. In such circumstances, while the two entities may be practicing under a common name, the facts are such that they do not belong to a larger structure aimed at co-operation and are, therefore, not Network Firms. Those entities shall determine how to disclose that they are not Network Firms when presenting themselves to outside parties.

290.23   Where the larger structure is aimed at co-operation and the entities within the structure share a significant part of professional resources, it is deemed to be a Network. Professional resources include:

- Common systems that enable Firms to exchange information such as client data, billing and time records;
- Partners and staff;
- Technical departments that consult on technical or industry specific issues, transactions or events for Assurance Engagements;
- Audit methodology or audit manuals; and
- Training courses and facilities.

290.24   The determination of whether the professional resources shared are significant, and therefore the Firms are Network Firms, shall be made based on the relevant facts and circumstances. Where the shared resources are limited to common audit methodology or audit manuals, with no exchange of personnel or client or market information, it is unlikely that the shared resources would be significant. The same applies to a common training endeavour. Where, however, the shared resources involve the exchange of people or information, such as where staff are drawn from a shared pool, or a common technical department is created within the larger structure to provide participating Firms with technical advice that the Firms are required to follow, a reasonable and informed third party is more likely to conclude that the shared resources are significant.

Public Interest Entities

290.25　Section 290 contains additional provisions that reflect the extent of public interest in certain entities. For the purpose of this section, a Public Interest Entity is:

(a) A Listed Entity*; or

(b) Any entity (a) defined by regulation or legislation as a public interest entity; or (b) for which the audit is required by regulation or legislation to be conducted in compliance with the same Independence requirements that apply to the audit of Listed Entities. Such regulation may be promulgated by any relevant regulator, including an audit regulator.

290.26　Firms shall determine whether to treat additional entities, or certain categories of entities, as Public Interest Entities because they have a large number and wide range of stakeholders. Factors to be considered include:

- The nature of the business, such as the holding of assets in a fiduciary capacity for a large number of stakeholders. Examples may include financial institutions, such as banks and insurance companies and pension funds;
- Size; and
- Number of employees.

AUST 290.26.1　The following entities in Australia will generally satisfy the conditions in paragraph 290.26 as having a large number and wide range of stakeholders and thus are likely to be classified as Public Interest Entities. In each instance Firms shall consider the nature of the business, its size and the number of its employees:

- Authorised deposit-taking institutions (ADIs) and authorised non-operating holding companies (NOHCs) regulated by the Australian Prudential Regulatory Authority (APRA) under the *Banking Act 1959*;
- Authorised insurers and authorised NOHCs regulated by APRA under Section 122 of the *Insurance Act 1973*;
- Life insurance companies and registered NOHCs regulated by APRA under the *Life Insurance Act 1995*;
- Disclosing entities as defined in Section 111AC of the *Corporations Act 2001*;
- Registrable superannuation entity (RSE) licensees, and RSEs under their trusteeship that have five or more members, regulated by APRA under the *Superannuation Industry (Supervision) Act 1993*; and
- Other issuers of debt and equity instruments to the public.

Related Entities

290.27　In the case of an Audit Client that is a Listed Entity, references to an Audit Client in this section include Related Entities of the client (unless otherwise stated). For all other Audit Clients, references to an Audit Client in this section include Related Entities over which the client has direct or indirect control. When the Audit Team knows or has reason to believe that a relationship or circumstance involving another Related Entity of the client is relevant to the evaluation of the Firm's Independence from the client, the Audit Team shall include that Related Entity when identifying and evaluating threats to Independence and applying appropriate safeguards.

---

* 　*Includes a listed entity as defined in Section 9 of the Corporations Act 2001.*

Those Charged with Governance

290.28   Even when not required by the Code, applicable Auditing and Assurance Standards, law or regulation, regular communication is encouraged between the Firm and Those Charged with Governance of the Audit Client regarding relationships and other matters that might, in the Firm's opinion, reasonably bear on Independence. Such communication enables Those Charged with Governance to (a) consider the Firm's judgments in identifying and evaluating threats to Independence, (b) consider the appropriateness of safeguards applied to eliminate them or reduce them to an Acceptable Level, and (c) take appropriate action. Such an approach can be particularly helpful with respect to intimidation and familiarity threats.

Documentation

290.29   Documentation provides evidence of the Member's judgments in forming conclusions regarding compliance with Independence requirements. The absence of documentation is not a determinant of whether a Firm considered a particular matter nor whether it is Independent.

       The Member shall document conclusions regarding compliance with Independence requirements, and the substance of any relevant discussions that support those conclusions. Accordingly:

(a)   When safeguards are required to reduce a threat to an Acceptable Level, the Member shall document the nature of the threat and the safeguards in place or applied that reduce the threat to an Acceptable Level; and

(b)   When a threat required significant analysis to determine whether safeguards were necessary and the Member concluded that they were not because the threat was already at an Acceptable Level, the Member shall document the nature of the threat and the rationale for the conclusion.

Engagement Period

290.30   Independence from the Audit Client is required both during the engagement period and the period covered by the Financial Statements. The engagement period starts when the Audit Team begins to perform audit services. The engagement period ends when the audit report is issued. When the engagement is of a recurring nature, it ends at the later of the notification by either party that the professional relationship has terminated or the issuance of the final audit report.

290.31   When an entity becomes an Audit Client during or after the period covered by the Financial Statements on which the Firm will express an Opinion, the Firm shall determine whether any threats to Independence are created by:

•   Financial or business relationships with the Audit Client during or after the period covered by the Financial Statements but before accepting the Audit Engagement; or

•   Previous services provided to the Audit Client.

290.32   If a non-assurance service was provided to the Audit Client during or after the period covered by the Financial Statements but before the Audit Team begins to perform audit services and the service would not be permitted during the period of the Audit Engagement, the Firm shall evaluate any threat to Independence created by the service. If a threat is not at an Acceptable Level, the Audit Engagement shall only be accepted if safeguards are applied to eliminate any threats or reduce them to an Acceptable Level. Examples of such safeguards include:

•   Not including personnel who provided the non-assurance service as members of the Audit Team;

•   Having a Member review the audit and non-assurance work as appropriate; or

•   Engaging another Firm to evaluate the results of the non-assurance service or having another Firm re-perform the non-assurance service to the extent necessary to enable it to take responsibility for the service.

Mergers and Acquisitions

290.33　When, as a result of a merger or acquisition, an entity becomes a Related Entity of an Audit Client, the Firm shall identify and evaluate previous and current interests and relationships with the Related Entity that, taking into account available safeguards, could affect its Independence and therefore its ability to continue the Audit Engagement after the effective date of the merger or acquisition.

290.34　The Firm shall take steps necessary to terminate, by the effective date of the merger or acquisition, any current interests or relationships that are not permitted under this Code. However, if such a current interest or relationship cannot reasonably be terminated by the effective date of the merger or acquisition, for example, because the Related Entity is unable by the effective date to effect an orderly transition to another service provider of a non-assurance service provided by the Firm, the Firm shall evaluate the threat that is created by such interest or relationship. The more significant the threat, the more likely the Firm's objectivity will be compromised and it will be unable to continue as auditor. The significance of the threat will depend upon factors such as:

- The nature and significance of the interest or relationship;

- The nature and significance of the Related Entity relationship (for example, whether the Related Entity is a subsidiary or parent); and

- The length of time until the interest or relationship can reasonably be terminated.

The Firm shall discuss with Those Charged with Governance the reasons why the interest or relationship cannot reasonably be terminated by the effective date of the merger or acquisition and the evaluation of the significance of the threat.

290.35　If Those Charged with Governance request the Firm to continue as auditor, the Firm shall do so only if:

(a)　the interest or relationship will be terminated as soon as reasonably possible and in all cases within six months of the effective date of the merger or acquisition;

(b)　any individual who has such an interest or relationship, including one that has arisen through performing a non-assurance service that would not be permitted under this section, will not be a member of the Engagement Team for the audit or the individual responsible for the Engagement Quality Control Review; and

(c)　appropriate transitional measures will be applied, as necessary, and discussed with Those Charged with Governance. Examples of transitional measures include:

- Having a Member review the audit or non-assurance work as appropriate;

- Having a Member, who is not a member of the Firm expressing the opinion on the Financial Statements, perform a review that is equivalent to an Engagement Quality Control Review; or

- Engaging another Firm to evaluate the results of the non-assurance service or having another Firm re-perform the non-assurance service to the extent necessary to enable it to take responsibility for the service.

290.36　The Firm may have completed a significant amount of work on the audit prior to the effective date of the merger or acquisition and may be able to complete the remaining audit procedures within a short period of time. In such circumstances, if Those Charged with Governance request the Firm to complete the audit while continuing with an interest or relationship identified in 290.33, the Firm shall do so only if it:

(a)　Has evaluated the significance of the threat created by such interest or relationship and discussed the evaluation with Those Charged with Governance;

(b)　Complies with the requirements of paragraph 290.35(b) – (c); and

(c)　Ceases to be the auditor no later than the issuance of the audit report.

290.37　When addressing previous and current interests and relationships covered by paragraphs 290.33 to 290.36, the Firm shall determine whether, even if all the requirements could be met, the interests and relationships create threats that would remain so significant that objectivity would be compromised and, if so, the Firm shall cease to be the auditor.

290.38   The Member shall document any interests or relationships covered by paragraphs 290.34 and 36 that will not be terminated by the effective date of the merger or acquisition and the reasons why they will not be terminated, the transitional measures applied, the results of the discussion with Those Charged with Governance, and the rationale as to why the previous and current interests and relationships do not create threats that would remain so significant that objectivity would be compromised.

Other Considerations

290.39   There may be occasions when there is an inadvertent violation of this section. If such an inadvertent violation occurs, it generally will be deemed not to compromise Independence provided the Firm has appropriate quality control policies and procedures in place, equivalent to those required by APES 320 *Quality Control for Firms*, to maintain Independence and, once discovered, the violation is corrected promptly and any necessary safeguards are applied to eliminate any threat or reduce it to an Acceptable Level.

AUST290.39.1   Unless an inadvertent violation of this section is trivial and inconsequential, a Firm shall document and discuss it with Those Charged with Governance.

Paragraphs 290.40 to 290.99 are intentionally left blank.

Application of the Conceptual Framework Approach to Independence

290.100 Paragraphs 290.102 to 290.231 describe specific circumstances and relationships that create or may create threats to Independence. The paragraphs describe the potential threats and the types of safeguards that may be appropriate to eliminate the threats or reduce them to an Acceptable Level and identify certain situations where no safeguards could reduce the threats to an Acceptable Level. The paragraphs do not describe all of the circumstances and relationships that create or may create a threat to Independence. The Firm and the members of the Audit Team shall evaluate the implications of similar, but different, circumstances and relationships and determine whether safeguards, including the safeguards in paragraphs 200.12 to 200.15, can be applied when necessary to eliminate the threats to Independence or reduce them to an Acceptable Level.

290.101 Paragraphs 290.102 to 290.126 contain references to the materiality of a Financial Interest, loan, or guarantee, or the significance of a business relationship. For the purpose of determining whether such an interest is material to an individual, the combined net worth of the individual and the individual's Immediate Family members may be taken into account.

Financial Interests

290.102 Holding a Financial Interest in an Audit Client may create a self-interest threat. The existence and significance of any threat created depends on: (a) the role of the person holding the Financial Interest, (b) whether the Financial Interest is direct or indirect, and (c) the materiality of the Financial Interest.

290.103 Financial Interests may be held through an intermediary (e.g. a collective investment vehicle, estate or trust). The determination of whether such Financial Interests are direct or indirect will depend upon whether the beneficial owner has control over the investment vehicle or the ability to influence its investment decisions. When control over the investment vehicle or the ability to influence investment decisions exists, this Code defines that Financial Interest to be a Direct Financial Interest. Conversely, when the beneficial owner of the Financial Interest has no control over the investment vehicle or ability to influence its investment decisions, this Code defines that Financial Interest to be an Indirect Financial Interest.

290.104 If a member of the Audit Team, a member of that individual's Immediate Family, or a Firm has a Direct Financial Interest or a material Indirect Financial Interest in the Audit Client, the self-interest threat created would be so significant that no safeguards could reduce the threat to an Acceptable Level. Therefore, none of the following shall have a Direct Financial Interest or a material Indirect Financial Interest in the client: a member of the Audit Team; a member of that individual's Immediate Family; or the Firm.

290.105 When a member of the Audit Team has a Close Family member who the Audit Team member knows has a Direct Financial Interest or a material Indirect Financial Interest in the Audit Client, a self-interest threat is created. The significance of the threat will depend on factors such as: The nature of the relationship between the member of the Audit Team and the Close Family member; and The materiality of the Financial Interest to the Close Family member.

The significance of the threat shall be evaluated and safeguards applied when necessary to eliminate the threat or reduce it to an Acceptable Level. Examples of such safeguards include: The Close Family member disposing, as soon as practicable, of all of the Financial Interest or disposing of a sufficient portion of an Indirect Financial Interest so that the remaining interest is no longer material; Having a Member review the work of the member of the Audit Team; or Removing the individual from the Audit Team.

290.106 If a member of the Audit Team, a member of that individual's Immediate Family, or a Firm has a direct or material Indirect Financial Interest in an entity that has a controlling interest in the Audit Client, and the client is material to the entity, the self-interest threat created would be so significant that no safeguards could reduce the threat to an Acceptable Level. Therefore, none of the following shall have such a Financial Interest: a member of the Audit Team; a member of that individual's Immediate Family; and the Firm.

290.107 The holding by a Firm's retirement benefit plan of a direct or material Indirect Financial Interest in an Audit Client creates a self-interest threat. The significance of the threat shall be evaluated and safeguards applied when necessary to eliminate the threat or reduce it to an Acceptable Level[3].

290.108 If other partners in the Office in which the Engagement Partner practices in connection with the Audit Engagement, or their Immediate Family members, hold a Direct Financial Interest or a material Indirect Financial Interest in that Audit Client, the self-interest threat created would be so significant that no safeguards could reduce the threat to an Acceptable Level. Therefore, neither such partners nor their Immediate Family members shall hold any such Financial Interests in such an Audit Client.

290.109 The Office in which the Engagement Partner practices in connection with the Audit Engagement is not necessarily the Office to which that partner is assigned. Accordingly, when the Engagement Partner is located in a different Office from that of the other members of the Audit Team, professional judgment shall be used to determine in which Office the partner practices in connection with that engagement.

290.110 If other partners and managerial employees who provide non-audit services to the Audit Client, except those whose involvement is minimal, or their Immediate Family members, hold a Direct Financial Interest or a material Indirect Financial Interest in the Audit Client, the self-interest threat created would be so significant that no safeguards could reduce the threat to an Acceptable Level. Accordingly, neither such personnel nor their Immediate Family members shall hold any such Financial Interests in such an Audit Client.

290.111 Despite paragraphs 290.108 and 290.110, the holding of a Financial Interest in an Audit Client by an Immediate Family member of (a) a partner located in the Office in which the Engagement Partner practices in connection with the Audit Engagement, or (b) a partner or managerial employee who provides non-audit services to the Audit Client, is deemed not to compromise Independence if the Financial Interest is received as a result of the Immediate Family member's employment rights (e.g., through pension or share option plans) and, when necessary, safeguards are applied to eliminate any threat to Independence or reduce it to an Acceptable Level. However, when the Immediate Family member has or obtains the right to dispose of the Financial Interest or, in the case of a stock option, the right to exercise the option, the Financial Interest shall be disposed of or forfeited as soon as practicable.

290.112 A self-interest threat may be created if the Firm or a member of the Audit Team, or a member of that individual's Immediate Family, has a Financial Interest in an entity and an Audit Client also has a Financial Interest in that entity. However, Independence is deemed not to be compromised if these interests are immaterial and the Audit Client cannot exercise significant influence over the entity. If such interest is material to any party, and the Audit Client can exercise significant influence over the other entity, no safeguards could reduce the threat to an Acceptable Level. Accordingly, the Firm shall not have such an interest and any individual with such an interest shall, before becoming a member of the Audit Team, either:

(a) Dispose of the interest; or

(b) Dispose of a sufficient amount of the interest so that the remaining interest is no longer material.

290.113 A self-interest, familiarity or intimidation threat may be created if a member of the Audit Team, or a member of that individual's Immediate Family, or the Firm, has a Financial Interest in an entity when a Director, Officer or controlling owner of the

---

3   Refer to s 324CH(1) Items 10-12 of the *Corporations Act 2001* which prohibits this arrangement in respect of Audits performed in accordance with the Act.

Audit Client is also known to have a Financial Interest in that entity. The existence and significance of any threat will depend upon factors such as:

- The role of the professional on the Audit Team;

- Whether ownership of the entity is closely or widely held;

- Whether the interest gives the investor the ability to control or significantly influence the entity; and

- The materiality of the Financial Interest.

The significance of any threat shall be evaluated and safeguards applied when necessary to eliminate the threat or reduce it to an Acceptable Level. Examples of such safeguards include:

- Removing the member of the Audit Team with the Financial Interest from the Audit Team; or

- Having a Member review the work of the member of the Audit Team.

290.114 The holding by a Firm, or a member of the Audit Team, or a member of that individual's Immediate Family, of a Direct Financial Interest or a material Indirect Financial Interest in the Audit Client as a trustee creates a self-interest threat. Similarly, a self-interest threat is created when (a) a partner in the Office in which the lead Engagement Partner practices in connection with the audit, (b) other partners and managerial employees who provide non-assurance services to the Audit Client, except those whose involvement is minimal, or (c) their Immediate Family members, hold a Direct Financial Interest or a material Indirect Financial Interest in the Audit Client as trustee. Such an interest shall not be held unless:

(a) Neither the trustee, nor an Immediate Family member of the trustee, nor the Firm are beneficiaries of the trust;

(b) The interest in the Audit Client held by the trust is not material to the trust;

(c) The trust is not able to exercise significant influence over the Audit Client; and

(d) The trustee, an Immediate Family member of the trustee, or the Firm cannot significantly influence any investment decision involving a Financial Interest in the Audit Client.

290.115 Members of the Audit Team shall determine whether a self-interest threat is created by any known Financial Interests in the Audit Client held by other individuals including:

- Partners and professional employees of the Firm, other than those referred to above, or their Immediate Family members; and

- Individuals with a close personal relationship with a member of the Audit Team.

Whether these interests create a self-interest threat will depend on factors such as:

- The Firm's organisational, operating and reporting structure; and

- The nature of the relationship between the individual and the member of the Audit Team.

The significance of any threat shall be evaluated and safeguards applied when necessary to eliminate the threat or reduce it to an Acceptable Level. Examples of such safeguards include:

- Removing the member of the Audit Team with the personal relationship from the Audit Team;

- Excluding the member of the Audit Team from any significant decision-making concerning the Audit Engagement; or

- Having a Member review the work of the member of the Audit Team.

290.116 If a Firm or a partner or employee of the Firm, or a member of that individual's Immediate Family, receives a Direct Financial Interest or a material Indirect Financial Interest in an Audit Client, for example, by way of an inheritance, gift or as a result of a merger and such interest would not be permitted to be held under this section, then:

(a) If the interest is received by the Firm, the Financial Interest shall be disposed of immediately, or a sufficient amount of an Indirect Financial Interest shall be disposed of so that the remaining interest is no longer material;

(b) If the interest is received by a member of the Audit Team, or a member of that individual's Immediate Family, the individual who received the Financial Interest shall immediately dispose of the Financial Interest, or dispose of a sufficient amount of an Indirect Financial Interest so that the remaining interest is no longer material; or

(c) If the interest is received by an individual who is not a member of the Audit Team, or by an Immediate Family member of the individual, the Financial Interest shall be disposed of as soon as possible, or a sufficient amount of an Indirect Financial Interest shall be disposed of so that the remaining interest is no longer material. Pending the disposal of the Financial Interest, a determination shall be made as to whether any safeguards are necessary.

290.117 When an inadvertent violation of this section as it relates to a Financial Interest in an Audit Client occurs, it is deemed not to compromise Independence if:

(a) The Firm has established policies and procedures that require prompt notification to the Firm of any breaches resulting from the purchase, inheritance or other acquisition of a Financial Interest in the Audit Client;

(b) The actions in paragraph 290.116 (a)–(c) are taken as applicable; and

(c) The Firm applies other safeguards when necessary to reduce any remaining threat to an Acceptable Level. Examples of such safeguards include:

• Having a Member review the work of the member of the Audit Team; or

• Excluding the individual from any significant decision-making concerning the Audit Engagement.

The Firm shall determine whether to discuss the matter with Those Charged with Governance.

AUST290.117.1 Unless an inadvertent violation of this section as it relates to a Financial Interest in an Audit Client is trivial and inconsequential, the Firm shall document and discuss it with Those Charged with Governance.

Loans and Guarantees

290.118 A loan, or a guarantee of a loan, to a member of the Audit Team, or a member of that individual's Immediate Family, or the Firm from an Audit Client that is a bank or a similar institution may create a threat to Independence. If the loan or guarantee is not made under normal lending procedures, terms and conditions, a self-interest threat would be created that would be so significant that no safeguards could reduce the threat to an Acceptable Level. Accordingly, neither a member of the Audit Team, a member of that individual's Immediate Family, nor a Firm, or Network Firm, shall accept such a loan or guarantee.

290.119 If a loan to a Firm from an Audit Client that is a bank or similar institution is made under normal lending procedures, terms and conditions and it is material to the Audit Client or Firm receiving the loan, it may be possible to apply safeguards to reduce the self-interest threat to an Acceptable Level. An example of such a safeguard is having the work reviewed by a Member from a Network Firm that is neither involved with the audit nor received the loan.

290.120 A loan, or a guarantee of a loan, from an Audit Client that is a bank or a similar institution to a member of the Audit Team, or a member of that individual's Immediate Family, does not create a threat to Independence if the loan or guarantee is made under normal lending procedures, terms and conditions. Examples of such loans include home mortgages, bank overdrafts, car loans and credit card balances.

290.121 If the Firm or a member of the Audit Team, or a member of that individual's Immediate Family, accepts a loan from, or has a borrowing guaranteed by, an Audit Client that is not a bank or similar institution, the self-interest threat created would be so significant that no safeguards could reduce the threat to an Acceptable Level, unless the loan or guarantee is immaterial to both (a) the Firm or the member of the Audit Team and the Immediate Family member, and (b) the client.

290.122 Similarly, if the Firm or a member of the Audit Team, or a member of that individual's Immediate Family, makes or guarantees a loan to an Audit Client, the self-interest threat created would be so significant that no safeguards could reduce the threat to an Acceptable Level, unless the loan or guarantee is immaterial to both (a) the Firm or the member of the Audit Team and the Immediate Family member, and (b) the client[4].

290.123 If a Firm or a member of the Audit Team, or a member of that individual's Immediate Family, has deposits or a brokerage account with an Audit Client that is a bank, broker or similar institution, a threat to Independence is not created if the deposit or account is held under normal commercial terms.

Business Relationships

290.124 A close business relationship[5] between a Firm, or a member of the Audit Team, or a member of that individual's Immediate Family, and the Audit Client or its management, arises from a commercial relationship or common Financial Interest and may create self-interest or intimidation threats. Examples of such relationships include:

- Having a Financial Interest in a joint venture with either the client or a controlling owner, Director, Officer or other individual who performs senior managerial activities for that client.

- Arrangements to combine one or more services or products of the Firm with one or more services or products of the client and to market the package with reference to both parties.

- Distribution or marketing arrangements under which the Firm distributes or markets the client's products or services, or the client distributes or markets the Firm's products or services.

Unless any Financial Interest is immaterial and the business relationship is insignificant to the Firm and the client or its management, the threat created would be so significant that no safeguards could reduce the threat to an Acceptable Level. Therefore, unless the Financial Interest is immaterial and the business relationship is insignificant, the business relationship shall not be entered into, or it shall be reduced to an insignificant level or terminated.

In the case of a member of the Audit Team, unless any such Financial Interest is immaterial and the relationship is insignificant to that member, the individual shall be removed from the Audit Team.

If the business relationship is between an Immediate Family member of a member of the Audit Team and the Audit Client or its management, the significance of any threat shall be evaluated and safeguards applied when necessary to eliminate the threat or reduce it to an Acceptable Level.

290.125 A business relationship[6] involving the holding of an interest by the Firm, or a member of the Audit Team, or a member of that individual's Immediate Family, in a closely-

---

4 Refer to s 324CH(1) Items 15, 16, 17 & 19 of the *Corporations Act 2001* which prohibits making or guaranteeing loans irrespective of materiality for audits performed in accordance with the Act.

5 Refer to s 324CH(1) of the *Corporations Act 2001* which prohibits certain relationships between a person or the Firm and the corporate Audit Client irrespective of materiality or the significance of the relationship or Financial Interest.

6 Refer to s 324CH(1) of the *Corporations Act 2001* which prohibits certain relationships between a person or the Firm and the corporate Audit Client irrespective of materiality or the significance of the relationship or Financial Interest.

held entity when the Audit Client or a Director or Officer of the client, or any group thereof, also holds an interest in that entity does not create threats to Independence if:

(a) The business relationship is insignificant to the Firm, the member of the Audit Team and the Immediate Family member, and the client;

(b) The Financial Interest is immaterial to the investor or group of investors; and

(c) The Financial Interest does not give the investor, or group of investors, the ability to control the closely-held entity.

290.126 The purchase of goods and services from an Audit Client by the Firm, or a member of the Audit Team, or a member of that individual's Immediate Family, does not generally create a threat to Independence if the transaction is in the normal course of business and at arm's length. However, such transactions may be of such a nature or magnitude that they create a self-interest threat. The significance of any threat shall be evaluated and safeguards applied when necessary to eliminate the threat or reduce it to an Acceptable Level. Examples of such safeguards include:

- Eliminating or reducing the magnitude of the transaction; or

- Removing the individual from the Audit Team.

Family and Personal Relationships

290.127 Family and personal relationships between a member of the Audit Team and a Director or Officer or certain employees (depending on their role) of the Audit Client may create self-interest, familiarity or intimidation threats. The existence and significance of any threats will depend on a number of factors, including the individual's responsibilities on the Audit Team, the role of the family member or other individual within the client and the closeness of the relationship.

290.128 When an Immediate Family member of a member of the Audit Team is:

(a) A Director or Officer of the Audit Client; or

(b) An employee in a position to exert significant influence over the preparation of the client's accounting records or the Financial Statements on which the Firm will express an Opinion,

or was in such a position during any period covered by the engagement or the Financial Statements, the threats to Independence can only be reduced to an Acceptable Level by removing the individual from the Audit Team. The closeness of the relationship is such that no other safeguards could reduce the threat to an Acceptable Level. Accordingly, no individual who has such a relationship shall be a member of the Audit Team.

290.129 Threats to Independence are created when an Immediate Family member of a member of the Audit Team is an employee in a position to exert significant influence over the client's financial position, financial performance or cash flows. The significance of the threats will depend on factors such as:

- The position held by the Immediate Family member; and

- The role of the professional on the Audit Team.

The significance of the threat shall be evaluated and safeguards applied when necessary to eliminate the threat or reduce it to an Acceptable Level. Examples of such safeguards include:

- Removing the individual from the Audit Team; or

- Structuring the responsibilities of the Audit Team so that the professional does not deal with matters that are within the responsibility of the Immediate Family member.

290.130 Threats to Independence are created when a Close Family member of a member of the Audit Team is:

(a) A Director or Officer of the Audit Client; or

(b) An employee in a position to exert significant influence over the preparation of the client's accounting records or the Financial Statements on which the Firm will express an Opinion.

The significance of the threats will depend on factors such as:

- The nature of the relationship between the member of the Audit Team and the Close Family member;
- The position held by the Close Family member; and
- The role of the professional on the Audit Team.

The significance of the threat shall be evaluated and safeguards applied when necessary to eliminate the threat or reduce it to an Acceptable Level. Examples of such safeguards include:

- Removing the individual from the Audit Team; or
- Structuring the responsibilities of the Audit Team so that the professional does not deal with matters that are within the responsibility of the Close Family member.

290.131 Threats to Independence are created when a member of the Audit Team has a close relationship with a person who is not an Immediate or Close Family member, but who is a Director or Officer or an employee in a position to exert significant influence over the preparation of the client's accounting records or the Financial Statements on which the Firm will express an Opinion. A member of the Audit Team who has such a relationship shall consult in accordance with Firm policies and procedures. The significance of the threats will depend on factors such as:

- The nature of the relationship between the individual and the member of the Audit Team;
- The position the individual holds with the client; and
- The role of the professional on the Audit Team.

The significance of the threats shall be evaluated and safeguards applied when necessary to eliminate the threats or reduce them to an Acceptable Level. Examples of such safeguards include:

- Removing the professional from the Audit Team; or
- Structuring the responsibilities of the Audit Team so that the professional does not deal with matters that are within the responsibility of the individual with whom the professional has a close relationship.

290.132 Self-interest, familiarity or intimidation threats may be created by a personal or family relationship between (a) a partner or employee of the Firm who is not a member of the Audit Team and (b) a Director or Officer of the Audit Client or an employee in a position to exert significant influence over the preparation of the client's accounting records or the Financial Statements on which the Firm will express an Opinion. Partners and employees of the Firm who are aware of such relationships shall consult in accordance with Firm policies and procedures. The existence and significance of any threat will depend on factors such as:

- The nature of the relationship between the partner or employee of the Firm and the Director or Officer or employee of the client;
- The interaction of the partner or employee of the Firm with the Audit Team;
- The position of the partner or employee within the Firm; and
- The position the individual holds with the client.

The significance of any threat shall be evaluated and safeguards applied when necessary to eliminate the threat or reduce it to an Acceptable Level. Examples of such safeguards include:

- Structuring the partner's or employee's responsibilities to reduce any potential influence over the Audit Engagement; or
- Having a Member review the relevant audit work performed.

290.133 When an inadvertent violation of this section as it relates to family and personal relationships occurs, it is deemed not to compromise Independence if:

(a) The Firm has established policies and procedures that require prompt notification to the Firm of any breaches resulting from changes in the employment status of their Immediate or Close Family members or other personal relationships that create threats to Independence;

(b) The inadvertent violation relates to an Immediate Family member of a member of the Audit Team becoming a Director or Officer of the Audit Client or being in a position to exert significant influence over the preparation of the client's accounting records or the Financial Statements on which the Firm will express an Opinion, and the relevant professional is removed from the Audit Team; and

(c) The Firm applies other safeguards when necessary to reduce any remaining threat to an Acceptable Level. Examples of such safeguards include:

(i) Having a Member review the work of the member of the Audit Team; or

(ii) Excluding the relevant professional from any significant decision-making concerning the engagement.

The Firm shall determine whether to discuss the matter with Those Charged with Governance.

AUST290.133.1 Unless an inadvertent violation of this section as it relates to family and personal relationships is trivial and inconsequential, the Firm shall document and discuss it with Those Charged with Governance.

Employment with an Audit Client

290.134 Familiarity or intimidation threats may be created if a Director or Officer of the Audit Client, or an employee in a position to exert significant influence over the preparation of the client's accounting records or the Financial Statements on which the Firm will express an Opinion, has been a member of the Audit Team or partner of the Firm.

290.135 If a former member of the Audit Team or partner of the Firm[7] has joined the Audit Client in such a position and a significant connection remains between the Firm and the individual, the threat would be so significant that no safeguards could reduce the threat to an Acceptable Level. Therefore, Independence would be deemed to be compromised if a former member of the Audit Team or partner joins the Audit Client as a Director or Officer, or as an employee in a position to exert significant influence over the preparation of the client's accounting records or the Financial Statements on which the Firm will express an Opinion, unless:

(a) The individual is not entitled to any benefits or payments from the Firm, unless made in accordance with fixed pre-determined arrangements, and any amount owed to the individual is not material to the Firm; and

(b) The individual does not continue to participate or appear to participate in the Firm's business or professional activities.

290.136 If a former member of the Audit Team or partner of the Firm has joined the Audit Client in such a position, and no significant connection remains between the Firm and the individual, the existence and significance of any familiarity or intimidation threats will depend on factors such as:

• The position the individual has taken at the client;

• Any involvement the individual will have with the Audit Team;

• The length of time since the individual was a member of the Audit Team or partner of the Firm; and

---

7   Refer to s 324CK of the *Corporations Act 2001* regarding the 5 year cooling off period before a former Audit partner can be appointed as an Officer or Director of a Corporate Audit Client in circumstances where another former Partner of the Firm is already an Officer or Director of the corporate Audit Client.

- The former position of the individual within the Audit Team or Firm, for example, whether the individual was responsible for maintaining regular contact with the client's management or Those Charged with Governance.

The significance of any threats created shall be evaluated and safeguards applied when necessary to eliminate the threats or reduce them to an Acceptable Level. Examples of such safeguards include:

- Modifying the audit plan;

- Assigning individuals to the Audit Team who have sufficient experience in relation to the individual who has joined the client; or

- Having a Member review the work of the former member of the Audit Team.

290.137 If a former partner of the Firm has previously joined an entity in such a position and the entity subsequently becomes an Audit Client of the Firm, the significance of any threat to Independence shall be evaluated and safeguards applied when necessary to eliminate the threat or reduce it to an Acceptable Level.

290.138 A self-interest threat is created when a member of the Audit Team participates in the Audit Engagement while knowing that the member of the Audit Team will, or may, join the client some time in the future. Firm policies and procedures shall require members of an Audit Team to notify the Firm when entering employment negotiations with the client. On receiving such notification, the significance of the threat shall be evaluated and safeguards applied when necessary to eliminate the threat or reduce it to an Acceptable Level. Examples of such safeguards include:

- Removing the individual from the Audit Team; or

- A review of any significant judgments made by that individual while on the team.

Audit Clients that are Public Interest Entities

290.139 Familiarity or intimidation threats are created when a Key Audit Partner joins the Audit Client that is a Public Interest Entity as:

(a) A Director or Officer of the entity; or

(b) An employee in a position to exert significant influence over the preparation of the client's accounting records or the Financial Statements on which the Firm will express an Opinion.

Independence would be deemed to be compromised unless, subsequent to the partner ceasing to be a Key Audit Partner, the Public Interest Entity had issued audited Financial Statements covering a period of not less than twelve months and the partner was not a member of the Audit Team with respect to the audit of those Financial Statements[8].

290.140 An intimidation threat is created when the individual who was the Firm's Senior or managing partner (chief executive or equivalent) joins an Audit Client that is a Public Interest Entity as (a) an employee in a position to exert significant influence over the preparation of the entity's accounting records or its Financial Statements or (b) a Director or Officer of the entity. Independence would be deemed to be compromised unless twelve months have passed since the individual was the Senior or managing partner (chief executive or equivalent) of the Firm[9].

290.141 Independence is deemed not to be compromised if, as a result of a business combination, a former Key Audit Partner or the individual who was the Firm's former Senior or managing partner is in a position as described in paragraphs 290.139 and 290.140, and:

(a) The position was not taken in contemplation of the business combination;

---

8   Refer to s 324CI of the *Corporation Act 2001* for additional prohibitions on former Audit Partners joining corporate Audit Clients.

9   Refer to s 324CI of the *Corporation Act 2001* for additional prohibitions on former Partners joining corporate Audit Clients.

(b) Any benefits or payments due to the former partner from the Firm have been settled in full, unless made in accordance with fixed pre-determined arrangements and any amount owed to the partner is not material to the Firm;

(c) The former partner does not continue to participate or appear to participate in the Firm's business or professional activities; and

(d) The position held by the former partner with the Audit Client is discussed with Those Charged with Governance.

Temporary Staff Assignments

290.142 The lending of staff by a Firm to an Audit Client may create a self-review threat. Such assistance may be given, but only for a short period of time and the Firm's personnel shall not be involved in:

- Providing non-assurance services that would not be permitted under this section; or

- Assuming management responsibilities.

In all circumstances, the Audit Client shall be responsible for directing and supervising the activities of the loaned staff.

The significance of any threat shall be evaluated and safeguards applied when necessary to eliminate the threat or reduce it to an Acceptable Level. Examples of such safeguards include:

- Conducting an additional review of the work performed by the loaned staff;

- Not giving the loaned staff audit responsibility for any function or activity that the staff performed during the temporary staff assignment; or

- Not including the loaned staff as a member of the Audit Team.

Recent Service with an Audit Client

290.143 Self-interest, self-review or familiarity threats may be created if a member of the Audit Team has recently served as a Director, Officer, or employee of the Audit Client. This would be the case when, for example, a member of the Audit Team has to evaluate elements of the Financial Statements for which the member of the Audit Team had prepared the accounting records while with the client.

290.144 If, during the period covered by the audit report, a member of the Audit Team had served as a Director or Officer of the Audit Client, or was an employee in a position to exert significant influence[10] over the preparation of the client's accounting records or the Financial Statements on which the Firm will express an Opinion, the threat created would be so significant that no safeguards could reduce the threat to an Acceptable Level. Consequently, such individuals shall not be assigned to the Audit Team.

290.145 Self-interest, self-review or familiarity threats may be created if, before the period covered by the audit report, a member of the Audit Team had served as a Director or Officer of the Audit Client, or was an employee in a position to exert significant influence over the preparation of the client's accounting records or Financial Statements on which the Firm will express an Opinion[11]. For example, such threats would be created if a decision made or work performed by the individual in the prior period, while employed by the client, is to be evaluated in the current period as part of the current Audit Engagement. The existence and significance of any threats will depend on factors such as:

- The position the individual held with the client;

- The length of time since the individual left the client; and

- The role of the professional on the Audit Team.

---

10   Refer to s 9 Definition for 'Audit-critical employee' of the *Corporations Act 2001*.

11   Refer to s 324CH(1) Items 8 & 9 and s 324CF(5) Items 3, 4, 5 & 9 of the *Corporations Act 2001* regarding cooling-off period of 12 months immediately preceding the beginning of the audited period for a corporate Audit Client.

The significance of any threat shall be evaluated and safeguards applied when necessary to reduce the threat to an Acceptable Level. An example of such a safeguard is conducting a review of the work performed by the individual as a member of the Audit Team.

Serving as a Director or Officer of an Audit Client

290.146 If a partner or employee of the Firm serves as a Director or Officer of an Audit Client, the self-review and self-interest threats created would be so significant that no safeguards could reduce the threats to an Acceptable Level. Accordingly, no partner or employee shall serve as a Director or Officer of an Audit Client[12].

AUST290.146.1 If a partner or employee of the Firm were to serve as an Officer (including management of an Administration) or as a Director of an Audit Client, or as an employee in a position to exert direct and significant influence over the subject matter of the Audit Engagement, the threats created would be so significant no safeguard could reduce the threats to an Acceptable Level. Consequently, if such an individual were to accept such a position the only course of action is for the Firm to refuse to perform, or to withdraw from, the Audit Engagement.

290.147 The position of company secretary has different implications in different jurisdictions. Duties may range from administrative duties, such as personnel management and the maintenance of company records and registers, to duties as diverse as ensuring that the company complies with regulations or providing advice on corporate governance matters. Generally, this position is seen to imply a close association with the entity.

290.148 If a partner or employee of the Firm serves as company secretary for an Audit Client, self-review and advocacy threats are created that would generally be so significant that no safeguards could reduce the threats to an Acceptable Level. Despite paragraph 290.146, when this practice is specifically permitted under local law, professional rules or practice, and provided management makes all relevant decisions, the duties and activities shall be limited to those of a routine and administrative nature, such as preparing minutes and maintaining statutory returns. In those circumstances, the significance of any threats shall be evaluated and safeguards applied when necessary to eliminate the threats or reduce them to an Acceptable Level.

AUST290.148.1 As the company secretary of a company incorporated in Australia is an Officer under the *Corporations Act 2001*, no Partner or employee of a Firm shall act in the position of the company secretary of an Audit Client. If such an individual were to accept such a position the only course of action is for the Firm to refuse to perform, or withdraw from, the Audit Engagement.

290.149 Performing routine administrative services to support a company secretarial function or providing advice in relation to company secretarial administration matters does not generally create threats to Independence, as long as client management makes all relevant decisions.

Long association of senior personnel (including partner rotation) with an Audit Client

General Provisions

290.150 Familiarity and self-interest threats are created by using the same senior personnel on an Audit Engagement over a long period of time. The significance of the threats will depend on factors such as:

- How long the individual has been a member of the Audit Team;
- The role of the individual on the Audit Team;
- The structure of the Firm;
- The nature of the Audit Engagement;

---

12   Refer to s 324CI of the *Corporations Act 2001* regarding prohibitions on Partners or employees serving as a Director or Officer of a corporate Audit Client.

- Whether the client's management team has changed; and
- Whether the nature or complexity of the client's accounting and reporting issues has changed.

The significance of the threats shall be evaluated and safeguards applied when necessary to eliminate the threats or reduce them to an Acceptable Level. Examples of such safeguards include:

- Rotating the senior personnel off the Audit Team;
- Having a Member who was not a member of the Audit Team review the work of the senior personnel; or
- Regular independent internal or external quality reviews of the engagement.

Audit Clients that are Public Interest Entities

290.151 In respect of an audit of a Public Interest Entity, an individual shall not be a Key Audit Partner for more than seven years[13]. After such time, the individual shall not be a member of the Engagement Team or be a Key Audit Partner for the client for two years. During that period, the individual shall not participate in the audit of the entity, provide quality control for the engagement, consult with the Engagement Team or the client regarding technical or industry-specific issues, transactions or events or otherwise directly influence the outcome of the engagement.

290.152 Despite paragraph 290.151, Key Audit Partners whose continuity is especially important to audit quality may, in rare cases due to unforeseen circumstances outside the Firm's control, be permitted an additional year on the Audit Team as long as the threat to Independence can be eliminated or reduced to an Acceptable Level by applying safeguards. For example, a Key Audit Partner may remain on the Audit Team for up to one additional year in circumstances where, due to unforeseen events, a required rotation was not possible, as might be the case due to serious illness of the intended Engagement Partner.

290.153 The long association of other partners with an Audit Client that is a Public Interest Entity creates familiarity and self-interest threats. The significance of the threats will depend on factors such as:

- How long any such partner has been associated with the Audit Client;
- The role, if any, of the individual on the Audit Team; and
- The nature, frequency and extent of the individual's interactions with the client's management or Those Charged with Governance.

The significance of the threats shall be evaluated and safeguards applied when necessary to eliminate the threats or reduce them to an Acceptable Level. Examples of such safeguards include:

- Rotating the partner off the Audit Team or otherwise ending the partner's association with the Audit Client; or
- Regular independent internal or external quality reviews of the engagement.

290.154 When an Audit Client becomes a Public Interest Entity, the length of time the individual has served the Audit Client as a Key Audit Partner before the client becomes a Public Interest Entity shall be taken into account in determining the timing of the rotation[14]. If the individual has served the Audit Client as a Key Audit Partner for five years or less when the client becomes a Public Interest Entity, the number of years the individual may continue to serve the client in that capacity before rotating off the engagement is seven years less the number of years already served. If the individual has served the Audit Client as a Key Audit Partner for six or more years when the client becomes a Public Interest Entity, the partner may continue to serve in that capacity for a maximum of two additional years before rotating off the engagement.

---

13 Refer to s 324DA of the *Corporations Act 2001* which has more restrictive Audit Partner rotation requirements for Listed Entities in Australia.

14 Refer to s 324DA of the *Corporations Act 2001* which has more restrictive Audit Partner rotation requirements for Listed Entities in Australia.

290.155 When a Firm has only a few people with the necessary knowledge and experience to serve as a Key Audit Partner on the audit of a Public Interest Entity, rotation of Key Audit Partners may not be an available safeguard. If an independent regulator[15] in the relevant jurisdiction has provided an exemption from partner rotation in such circumstances, an individual may remain a Key Audit Partner for more than seven years, in accordance with such regulation, provided that the independent regulator has specified alternative safeguards which are applied, such as a regular independent external review.

Provision of Non-assurance Services to Audit Clients

290.156 Firms have traditionally provided to their Audit Clients a range of non-assurance services that are consistent with their skills and expertise. Providing non-assurance services may, however, create threats to the Independence of the Firm or members of the Audit Team. The threats created are most often self-review, self-interest and advocacy threats.

290.157 New developments in business, the evolution of financial markets and changes in information technology make it impossible to draw up an all-inclusive list of non-assurance services that might be provided to an Audit Client. When specific guidance on a particular non-assurance service is not included in this section, the conceptual framework shall be applied when evaluating the particular circumstances.

290.158 Before the Firm accepts an engagement to provide a non-assurance service to an Audit Client, a determination shall be made as to whether providing such a service would create a threat to Independence. In evaluating the significance of any threat created by a particular non-assurance service, consideration shall be given to any threat that the Audit Team has reason to believe is created by providing other related non-assurance services. If a threat is created that cannot be reduced to an Acceptable Level by the application of safeguards, the non-assurance service shall not be provided.

290.159 Providing certain non-assurance services to an Audit Client may create a threat to Independence so significant that no safeguards could reduce the threat to an Acceptable Level. However, the inadvertent provision of such a service to a Related Entity, division or in respect of a discrete Financial Statement item of such a client will be deemed not to compromise Independence if any threats have been reduced to an Acceptable Level by arrangements for that Related Entity, division or discrete Financial Statement item to be audited by another Firm or when another Firm re-performs the non-assurance service to the extent necessary to enable it to take responsibility for that service.

290.160 A Firm may provide non-assurance services that would otherwise be restricted under this section to the following related entities of the Audit Client:

(a) An entity, which is not an Audit Client, that has direct or indirect control over the Audit Client;

(b) An entity, which is not an Audit Client, with a Direct Financial Interest in the client if that entity has significant influence over the client and the interest in the client is material to such entity; or

(c) An entity, which is not an Audit Client, that is under common control with the Audit Client.

If it is reasonable to conclude that (a) the services do not create a self-review threat because the results of the services will not be subject to audit procedures and (b) any threats that are created by the provision of such services are eliminated or reduced to an Acceptable Level by the application of safeguards.

290.161 A non-assurance service provided to an Audit Client does not compromise the Firm's Independence when the client becomes a Public Interest Entity if:

(a) The previous non-assurance service complies with the provisions of this section that relate to Audit Clients that are not public interest entities;

---

15   Refer to s 342A of the *Corporations Act 2001* which specifies that the Australian Securities and Investments Commission may grant extensions.

(b)   Services that are not permitted under this section for Audit Clients that are public interest entities are terminated before or as soon as practicable after the client becomes a Public Interest Entity; and

(c)   The Firm applies safeguards when necessary to eliminate or reduce to an Acceptable Level any threats to Independence arising from the service.

Management Responsibilities

290.162   Management of an entity performs many activities in managing the entity in the best interests of stakeholders of the entity. It is not possible to specify every activity that is a management responsibility. However, management responsibilities involve leading and directing an entity, including making significant decisions regarding the acquisition, deployment and control of human, financial, physical and intangible resources.

290.163   Whether an activity is a management responsibility depends on the circumstances and requires the exercise of judgment. Examples of activities that would generally be considered a management responsibility include:

- Setting policies and strategic direction;
- Directing and taking responsibility for the actions of the entity's employees;
- Authorising transactions;
- Deciding which recommendations of the Firm or other third parties to implement;
- Taking responsibility for the preparation and fair presentation of the Financial Statements in accordance with the applicable financial reporting framework; and
- Taking responsibility for designing, implementing and maintaining internal control.

290.164   Activities that are routine and administrative, or involve matters that are insignificant, generally are deemed not to be a management responsibility. For example, executing an insignificant transaction that has been authorised by management or monitoring the dates for filing statutory returns and advising an Audit Client of those dates is deemed not to be a management responsibility. Further, providing advice and recommendations to assist management in discharging its responsibilities is not assuming a management responsibility.

290.165   If a Firm were to assume a management responsibility for an Audit Client, the threats created would be so significant that no safeguards could reduce the threats to an Acceptable Level. For example, deciding which recommendations of the Firm to implement will create self-review and self-interest threats. Further, assuming a management responsibility creates a familiarity threat because the Firm becomes too closely aligned with the views and interests of management. Therefore, the Firm shall not assume a management responsibility for an Audit Client.

290.166   To avoid the risk of assuming a management responsibility when providing non-assurance services to an Audit Client, the Firm shall be satisfied that a member of management is responsible for making the significant judgments and decisions that are the proper responsibility of management, evaluating the results of the service and accepting responsibility for the actions to be taken arising from the results of the service. This reduces the risk of the Firm inadvertently making any significant judgments or decisions on behalf of management. The risk is further reduced when the Firm gives the client the opportunity to make judgments and decisions based on an objective and transparent analysis and presentation of the issues.

Preparing Accounting Records and Financial Statements

General Provisions

290.167   Management is responsible for the preparation and fair presentation of the Financial Statements in accordance with the applicable financial reporting framework. These responsibilities include:

- Originating or changing journal entries, or determining the account classifications of transactions; and

- Preparing or changing source documents or originating data, in electronic or other form, evidencing the occurrence of a transaction (for example, purchase orders, payroll time records, and customer orders).

290.168 Providing an Audit Client with accounting and bookkeeping services, such as preparing accounting records or Financial Statements, creates a self-review threat when the Firm subsequently audits the Financial Statements.

290.169 The audit process, however, necessitates dialogue between the Firm and management of the Audit Client, which may involve (a) the application of accounting standards or policies and Financial Statement disclosure requirements, (b) the appropriateness of financial and accounting control and the methods used in determining the stated amounts of assets and liabilities, or (c) proposing adjusting journal entries. These activities are considered to be a normal part of the audit process and do not, generally, create threats to Independence.

290.170 Similarly, the client may request technical assistance from the Firm on matters such as resolving account reconciliation problems or analysing and accumulating information for regulatory reporting. In addition, the client may request technical advice on accounting issues such as the conversion of existing Financial Statements from one financial reporting framework to another (for example, to comply with group accounting policies or to transition to a different financial reporting framework such as International Financial Reporting Standards). Such services do not, generally, create threats to Independence provided the Firm does not assume a management responsibility for the client.

Audit Clients that are Not Public Interest Entities

290.171 The Firm may provide services related to the preparation of accounting records and Financial Statements to an Audit Client that is not a Public Interest Entity where the services are of a routine or mechanical nature, so long as any self-review threat created is reduced to an Acceptable Level. Examples of such services include:

- Providing payroll services based on client-originated data;
- Recording transactions for which the client has determined or approved the appropriate account classification;
- Posting transactions coded by the client to the general ledger;
- Posting client-approved entries to the trial balance; and
- Preparing Financial Statements based on information in the trial balance.

In all cases, the significance of any threat created shall be evaluated and safeguards applied when necessary to eliminate the threat or reduce it to an Acceptable Level. Examples of such safeguards include:

- Arranging for such services to be performed by an individual who is not a member of the Audit Team; or
- If such services are performed by a member of the Audit Team, using a partner or senior staff member with appropriate expertise who is not a member of the Audit Team to review the work performed.

Audit Clients that are Public Interest Entities

290.172 A Firm shall not provide to an Audit Client that is a Public Interest Entity accounting and bookkeeping services, including payroll services, or prepare Financial Statements on which the Firm will express an Opinion or financial information which forms the basis of the Financial Statements.

290.173 Despite paragraph 290.172, a Firm may provide accounting and bookkeeping services, including payroll services and the preparation of Financial Statements or other financial information, of a routine or mechanical nature for divisions or Related Entities of an

Audit Client that is a Public Interest Entity if the personnel providing the services are not members of the Audit Team and:

(a) The divisions or Related Entities for which the service is provided are collectively immaterial to the Financial Statements on which the Firm will express an Opinion; or

(b) The services relate to matters that are collectively immaterial to the Financial Statements of the division or Related Entity.

Emergency Situations – Audit Clients that are not Public Interest Entities

290.174 Accounting and bookkeeping services, which would otherwise not be permitted under this section, may be provided to Audit Clients that are not Public Interest Entities in emergency or other unusual situations when it is impractical for the Audit Client to make other arrangements. This may be the case when (a) only the Firm has the resources and necessary knowledge of the client's systems and procedures to assist the client in the timely preparation of its accounting records and Financial Statements, and (b) a restriction on the Firm's ability to provide the services would result in significant difficulties for the client (for example, as might result from a failure to meet regulatory reporting requirements). In such situations, the following conditions shall be met:

(a) Those who provide the services are not members of the Audit Team;

(b) The services are provided for only a short period of time and are not expected to recur; and

(c) The situation is discussed with Those Charged with Governance.

Valuation Services

General Provisions

290.175 A valuation comprises the making of assumptions with regard to future developments, the application of appropriate methodologies and techniques, and the combination of both to compute a certain value, or range of values, for an asset, a liability or for a business as a whole.

290.176 Performing valuation services for an Audit Client may create a self-review threat. The existence and significance of any threat will depend on factors such as:

- Whether the valuation will have a material effect on the Financial Statements.

- The extent of the client's involvement in determining and approving the valuation methodology and other significant matters of judgment.

- The availability of established methodologies and professional guidelines.

- For valuations involving standard or established methodologies, the degree of subjectivity inherent in the item.

- The reliability and extent of the underlying data.

- The degree of dependence on future events of a nature that could create significant volatility inherent in the amounts involved.

- The extent and clarity of the disclosures in the Financial Statements.

The significance of any threat created shall be evaluated and safeguards applied when necessary to eliminate the threat or reduce it to an Acceptable Level. Examples of such safeguards include:

- Having a Member who was not involved in providing the valuation service review the audit or valuation work performed; or

- Making arrangements so that personnel providing such services do not participate in the Audit Engagement.

290.177 Certain valuations do not involve a significant degree of subjectivity. This is likely the case where the underlying assumptions are either established by law or regulation, or are widely accepted and when the techniques and methodologies to be used are based on generally accepted standards or prescribed by law or regulation. In such circumstances, the results of a valuation performed by two or more parties are not likely to be materially different.

290.178 If a Firm is requested to perform a valuation to assist an Audit Client with its tax reporting obligations or for tax planning purposes and the results of the valuation will not have a direct effect on the Financial Statements, the provisions included in paragraph 290.191 apply.

Audit Clients that are Not Public Interest Entities

290.179 In the case of an Audit Client that is not a Public Interest Entity, if the valuation service has a material effect on the Financial Statements on which the Firm will express an Opinion and the valuation involves a significant degree of subjectivity, no safeguards could reduce the self-review threat to an Acceptable Level. Accordingly a Firm shall not provide such a valuation service to an Audit Client.

Audit Clients that are Public Interest Entities

290.180 A Firm shall not provide valuation services to an Audit Client that is a Public Interest Entity if the valuations would have a material effect, separately or in the aggregate, on the Financial Statements on which the Firm will express an Opinion.

Taxation Services

290.181 Taxation services comprise a broad range of services, including:

- Tax return preparation;
- Tax calculations for the purpose of preparing the accounting entries;
- Tax planning and other tax advisory services; and
- Assistance in the resolution of tax disputes.

While taxation services provided by a Firm to an Audit Client are addressed separately under each of these broad headings; in practice, these activities are often interrelated.

290.182 Performing certain tax services creates self-review and advocacy threats. The existence and significance of any threats will depend on factors such as (a) the system by which the tax authorities assess and administer the tax in question and the role of the Firm in that process, (b) the complexity of the relevant tax regime and the degree of judgment necessary in applying it, (c) the particular characteristics of the engagement, and (d) the level of tax expertise of the client's employees.

Tax Return Preparation

290.183 Tax return preparation services involve assisting clients with their tax reporting obligations by drafting and completing information, including the amount of tax due (usually on standardised forms) required to be submitted to the applicable tax authorities. Such services also include advising on the tax return treatment of past transactions and responding on behalf of the Audit Client to the tax authorities' requests for additional information and analysis (including providing explanations of and technical support for the approach being taken). Tax return preparation services are generally based on historical information and principally involve analysis and presentation of such historical information under existing tax law, including precedents and established practice. Further, the tax returns are subject to whatever review or approval process the tax authority deems appropriate. Accordingly, providing such services does not generally create a threat to Independence if management takes responsibility for the returns including any significant judgments made.

Tax Calculations for the Purpose of Preparing Accounting Entries

Audit Clients that are Not Public Interest Entities

290.184 Preparing calculations of current and deferred tax liabilities (or assets) for an Audit Client for the purpose of preparing accounting entries that will be subsequently audited by the Firm creates a self-review threat. The significance of the threat will depend on (a) the complexity of the relevant tax law and regulation and the degree of judgment necessary in applying them, (b) the level of tax expertise of the client's personnel, and (c) the materiality of the amounts to the Financial Statements. Safeguards shall be applied when necessary to eliminate the threat or reduce it to an Acceptable Level. Examples of such safeguards include:

- Using professionals who are not members of the Audit Team to perform the service;

- If the service is performed by a member of the Audit Team, using a partner or senior staff member with appropriate expertise who is not a member of the Audit Team to review the tax calculations; or

- Obtaining advice on the service from an external tax professional.

Audit Clients that are Public Interest Entities

290.185 In the case of an Audit Client that is a Public Interest Entity, a Firm shall not prepare tax calculations of current and deferred tax liabilities (or assets) for the purpose of preparing accounting entries that are material to the Financial Statements on which the Firm will express an Opinion.

Emergency Situations – Audit Clients that are not Public Interest Entities

290.186 The preparation of calculations of current and deferred tax liabilities (or assets) for an Audit Client that is not a Public Interest Entity for the purpose of the preparation of accounting entries, which would otherwise not be permitted under this section, may be provided to Audit Clients in emergency or other unusual situations when it is impractical for the Audit Client to make other arrangements. This may be the case when (a) only the Firm has the resources and necessary knowledge of the client's business to assist the client in the timely preparation of its calculations of current and deferred tax liabilities (or assets), and (b) a restriction on the Firm's ability to provide the services would result in significant difficulties for the client (for example, as might result from a failure to meet regulatory reporting requirements). In such situations, the following conditions shall be met:

(a) Those who provide the services are not members of the Audit Team;

(b) The services are provided for only a short period of time and are not expected to recur; and

(c) The situation is discussed with Those Charged with Governance.

Tax Planning and Other Tax Advisory Services

290.187 Tax planning or other tax advisory services comprise a broad range of services, such as advising the client how to structure its affairs in a tax efficient manner or advising on the application of a new tax law or regulation.

290.188 A self-review threat may be created where the advice will affect matters to be reflected in the Financial Statements. The existence and significance of any threat will depend on factors such as:

- The degree of subjectivity involved in determining the appropriate treatment for the tax advice in the Financial Statements;

- The extent to which the outcome of the tax advice will have a material effect on the Financial Statements;

- Whether the effectiveness of the tax advice depends on the accounting treatment or presentation in the Financial Statements and there is doubt as to the appropriateness of the accounting treatment or presentation under the relevant financial reporting framework;

- The level of tax expertise of the client's employees;

- The extent to which the advice is supported by tax law or regulation, other precedent or established practice; and

- Whether the tax treatment is supported by a private ruling or has otherwise been cleared by the tax authority before the preparation of the Financial Statements.

For example, providing tax planning and other tax advisory services where the advice is clearly supported by tax authority or other precedent, by established practice or has a basis in tax law that is likely to prevail does not generally create a threat to Independence.

290.189　The significance of any threat shall be evaluated and safeguards applied when necessary to eliminate the threat or reduce it to an Acceptable Level. Examples of such safeguards include:

- Using professionals who are not members of the Audit Team to perform the service;

- Having a tax professional, who was not involved in providing the tax service, advise the Audit Team on the service and review the Financial Statement treatment;

- Obtaining advice on the service from an external tax professional; or

- Obtaining pre-clearance or advice from the tax authorities.

290.190　Where the effectiveness of the tax advice depends on a particular accounting treatment or presentation in the Financial Statements and:

(a)　The Audit Team has reasonable doubt as to the appropriateness of the related accounting treatment or presentation under the relevant financial reporting framework; and

(b)　The outcome or consequences of the tax advice will have a material effect on the Financial Statements on which the Firm will express an Opinion;

The self-review threat would be so significant that no safeguards could reduce the threat to an Acceptable Level. Accordingly, a Firm shall not provide such tax advice to an Audit Client.

290.191　In providing tax services to an Audit Client, a Firm may be requested to perform a valuation to assist the client with its tax reporting obligations or for tax planning purposes. Where the result of the valuation will have a direct effect on the Financial Statements, the provisions included in paragraphs 290.175 to 290.180 relating to valuation services are applicable. Where the valuation is performed for tax purposes only and the result of the valuation will not have a direct effect on the Financial Statements (i.e. the Financial Statements are only affected through accounting entries related to tax), this would not generally create threats to Independence if such effect on the Financial Statements is immaterial or if the valuation is subject to external review by a tax authority or similar regulatory authority. If the valuation is not subject to such an external review and the effect is material to the Financial Statements, the existence and significance of any threat created will depend upon factors such as:

- The extent to which the valuation methodology is supported by tax law or regulation, other precedent or established practice and the degree of subjectivity inherent in the valuation.

- The reliability and extent of the underlying data.

The significance of any threat created shall be evaluated and safeguards applied when necessary to eliminate the threat or reduce it to an Acceptable Level. Examples of such safeguards include:

- Using professionals who are not members of the Audit Team to perform the service;

- Having a professional review the audit work or the result of the tax service; or

- Obtaining pre-clearance or advice from the tax authorities.

Assistance in the Resolution of Tax Disputes

290.192　An advocacy or self-review threat may be created when the Firm represents an Audit Client in the resolution of a tax dispute once the tax authorities have notified the client that they have rejected the client's arguments on a particular issue and either the tax authority or the client is referring the matter for determination in a formal proceeding, for example before a tribunal or court. The existence and significance of any threat will depend on factors such as:

- Whether the Firm has provided the advice which is the subject of the tax dispute;

- The extent to which the outcome of the dispute will have a material effect on the Financial Statements on which the Firm will express an Opinion;

APES

- The extent to which the matter is supported by tax law or regulation, other precedent, or established practice;

- Whether the proceedings are conducted in public; and

- The role management plays in the resolution of the dispute.

The significance of any threat created shall be evaluated and safeguards applied when necessary to eliminate the threat or reduce it to an Acceptable Level.

Examples of such safeguards include:

- Using professionals who are not members of the Audit Team to perform the service;

- Having a tax professional, who was not involved in providing the tax service, advise the Audit Team on the services and review the Financial Statement treatment; or

- Obtaining advice on the service from an external tax professional.

290.193   Where the taxation services involve acting as an advocate for an Audit Client before a public tribunal or court in the resolution of a tax matter and the amounts involved are material to the Financial Statements on which the Firm will express an Opinion, the advocacy threat created would be so significant that no safeguards could eliminate or reduce the threat to an Acceptable Level. Therefore, the Firm shall not perform this type of service for an Audit Client. What constitutes a "public tribunal or court" shall be determined according to how tax proceedings are heard in the particular jurisdiction.

290.194   The Firm is not, however, precluded from having a continuing advisory role (for example, responding to specific requests for information, providing factual accounts or testimony about the work performed or assisting the client in analysing the tax issues) for the Audit Client in relation to the matter that is being heard before a public tribunal or court.

Internal Audit Services

General Provisions

290.195   The scope and objectives of internal audit activities vary widely and depend on the size and structure of the entity and the requirements of management and Those Charged with Governance. Internal audit activities may include:

(a)   Monitoring of internal control – reviewing controls, monitoring their operation and recommending improvements thereto;

(b)   Examination of financial and operating information – reviewing the means used to identify, measure, classify and report financial and operating information, and specific inquiry into individual items including detailed testing of transactions, balances and procedures;

(c)   Review of the economy, efficiency and effectiveness of operating activities including non-financial activities of an entity; and

(d)   Review of compliance with laws, regulations and other external requirements, and with management policies and directives and other internal requirements.

290.196   Internal audit services involve assisting the Audit Client in the performance of its internal audit activities. The provision of internal audit services to an Audit Client creates a self-review threat to Independence if the Firm uses the internal audit work in the course of a subsequent external audit. Performing a significant part of the client's internal audit activities increases the possibility that Firm personnel providing internal audit services will assume a management responsibility. If the Firm's personnel assume a management responsibility when providing internal audit services to an Audit Client, the threat created would be so significant that no safeguards could reduce the threat to an Acceptable Level. Accordingly, a Firm's personnel shall not assume a management responsibility when providing internal audit services to an Audit Client.

290.197   Examples of internal audit services that involve assuming management responsibilities include:

(a)   Setting internal audit policies or the strategic direction of internal audit activities;

(b)   Directing and taking responsibility for the actions of the entity's internal audit employees;

(c)   Deciding which recommendations resulting from internal audit activities shall be implemented;

(d)   Reporting the results of the internal audit activities to Those Charged with Governance on behalf of management;

(e)   Performing procedures that form part of the internal control, such as reviewing and approving changes to employee data access privileges;

(f)   Taking responsibility for designing, implementing and maintaining internal control; and

(g)   Performing outsourced internal audit services, comprising all or a substantial portion of the internal audit function, where the Firm is responsible for determining the scope of the internal audit work and may have responsibility for one or more of the matters noted in (a)–(f).

290.198   To avoid assuming a management responsibility, the Firm shall only provide internal audit services to an Audit Client if it is satisfied that:

(a)   The client designates an appropriate and competent resource, preferably within senior management, to be responsible at all times for internal audit activities and to acknowledge responsibility for designing, implementing, and maintaining internal control;

(b)   The client's management or Those Charged with Governance reviews, assesses and approves the scope, risk and frequency of the internal audit services;

(c)   The client's management evaluates the adequacy of the internal audit services and the findings resulting from their performance;

(d)   The client's management evaluates and determines which recommendations resulting from internal audit services to implement and manages the implementation process; and

(e)   The client's management reports to Those Charged with Governance the significant findings and recommendations resulting from the internal audit services.

290.199   When a Firm uses the work of an internal audit function, Auditing and Assurance Standards require the performance of procedures to evaluate the adequacy of that work. When a Firm accepts an engagement to provide internal audit services to an Audit Client, and the results of those services will be used in conducting the external audit, a self-review threat is created because of the possibility that the Audit Team will use the results of the internal audit service without appropriately evaluating those results or exercising the same level of professional scepticism as would be exercised when the internal audit work is performed by individuals who are not members of the Firm. The significance of the threat will depend on factors such as:

-   The materiality of the related Financial Statement amounts;

-   The risk of misstatement of the assertions related to those Financial Statement amounts; and

-   The degree of reliance that will be placed on the internal audit service.

The significance of the threat shall be evaluated and safeguards applied when necessary to eliminate the threat or reduce it to an Acceptable Level. An example of such a safeguard is using professionals who are not members of the Audit Team to perform the internal audit service.

Audit Clients that are Public Interest Entities

290.200 In the case of an Audit Client that is a Public Interest Entity, a Firm shall not provide internal audit services that relate to:

(a) A significant part of the internal controls over financial reporting;

(b) Financial accounting systems that generate information that is, separately or in the aggregate, significant to the client's accounting records or Financial Statements on which the Firm will express an Opinion; or

(c) Amounts or disclosures that are, separately or in the aggregate, material to the Financial Statements on which the Firm will express an Opinion.

IT Systems Services

General Provisions

290.201 Services related to information technology ("IT") systems include the design or implementation of hardware or software systems. The systems may aggregate source data, form part of the internal control over financial reporting or generate information that affects the accounting records or Financial Statements, or the systems may be unrelated to the Audit Client's accounting records, the internal control over financial reporting or Financial Statements. Providing systems services may create a self-review threat depending on the nature of the services and the IT systems.

290.202 The following IT systems services are deemed not to create a threat to Independence as long as the Firm's personnel do not assume a management responsibility:

(a) Design or implementation of IT systems that are unrelated to internal control over financial reporting;

(b) Design or implementation of IT systems that do not generate information forming a significant part of the accounting records or Financial Statements;

(c) Implementation of "off-the-shelf" accounting or financial information reporting software that was not developed by the Firm if the customisation required to meet the client's needs is not significant; and

(d) Evaluating and making recommendations with respect to a system designed, implemented or operated by another service provider or the client.

Audit Clients that are Not Public Interest Entities

290.203 Providing services to an Audit Client that is not a Public Interest Entity involving the design or implementation of IT systems that (a) form a significant part of the internal control over financial reporting or (b) generate information that is significant to the client's accounting records or Financial Statements on which the Firm will express an Opinion creates a self-review threat.

290.204 The self-review threat is too significant to permit such services unless appropriate safeguards are put in place ensuring that:

(a) The Audit Client acknowledges its responsibility for establishing and monitoring a system of internal controls;

(b) The Audit Client assigns the responsibility to make all management decisions with respect to the design and implementation of the hardware or software system to a competent employee, preferably within senior management;

(c) The Audit Client makes all management decisions with respect to the design and implementation process;

(d) The Audit Client evaluates the adequacy and results of the design and implementation of the system; and

(e) The Audit Client is responsible for operating the system (hardware or software) and for the data it uses or generates.

290.205 Depending on the degree of reliance that will be placed on the particular IT systems as part of the audit, a determination shall be made as to whether to provide such non-assurance services only with personnel who are not members of the Audit Team and who have different reporting lines within the Firm. The significance of any remaining threat shall be evaluated and safeguards applied when necessary to eliminate the threat or reduce it to an Acceptable Level. An example of such a safeguard is having a Member review the audit or non-assurance work.

Audit Clients that are Public Interest Entities

290.206 In the case of an Audit Client that is a Public Interest Entity, a Firm shall not provide services involving the design or implementation of IT systems that (a) form a significant part of the internal control over financial reporting or (b) generate information that is significant to the client's accounting records or Financial Statements on which the Firm will express an Opinion.

Litigation Support Services

290.207 Litigation support services may include activities such as acting as an expert witness, calculating estimated damages or other amounts that might become receivable or payable as the result of litigation or other legal dispute, and assistance with document management and retrieval. These services may create a self-review or advocacy threat.

290.208 If the Firm provides a litigation support service to an Audit Client and the service involves estimating damages or other amounts that affect the Financial Statements on which the Firm will express an Opinion, the valuation service provisions included in paragraphs 290.175 to 290.180 shall be followed. In the case of other litigation support services, the significance of any threat created shall be evaluated and safeguards applied when necessary to eliminate the threat or reduce it to an Acceptable Level.

Legal Services

290.209 For the purpose of this section, legal services are defined as any services for which the person providing the services must either be admitted to practice law before the courts of the jurisdiction in which such services are to be provided or have the required legal training to practice law. Such legal services may include, depending on the jurisdiction, a wide and diversified range of areas including both corporate and commercial services to clients, such as contract support, litigation, mergers and acquisition legal advice and support and assistance to clients' internal legal departments. Providing legal services to an entity that is an Audit Client may create both self-review and advocacy threats.

290.210 Legal services that support an Audit Client in executing a transaction (e.g., contract support, legal advice, legal due diligence and restructuring) may create self-review threats. The existence and significance of any threat will depend on factors such as:

- The nature of the service;
- Whether the service is provided by a member of the Audit Team; and
- The materiality of any matter in relation to the client's Financial Statements.

The significance of any threat created shall be evaluated and safeguards applied when necessary to eliminate the threat or reduce it to an Acceptable Level. Examples of such safeguards include:

- Using professionals who are not members of the Audit Team to perform the service; or
- Having a professional who was not involved in providing the legal services provide advice to the Audit Team on the service and review any Financial Statement treatment.

290.211 Acting in an advocacy role for an Audit Client in resolving a dispute or litigation when the amounts involved are material to the Financial Statements on which the Firm will express an Opinion would create advocacy and self-review threats so significant that no safeguards could reduce the threat to an Acceptable Level. Therefore, the Firm shall not perform this type of service for an Audit Client.

290.212 When a Firm is asked to act in an advocacy role for an Audit Client in resolving a dispute or litigation when the amounts involved are not material to the Financial Statements on which the Firm will express an Opinion, the Firm shall evaluate the significance of any advocacy and self-review threats created and apply safeguards when necessary

APES

to eliminate the threat or reduce it to an Acceptable Level. Examples of such safeguards include:

- Using professionals who are not members of the Audit Team to perform the service; or

- Having a professional who was not involved in providing the legal services advise the Audit Team on the service and review any Financial Statement treatment.

290.213 The appointment of a partner or an employee of the Firm as General Counsel for legal affairs of an Audit Client would create self-review and advocacy threats that are so significant that no safeguards could reduce the threats to an Acceptable Level. The position of General Counsel is generally a senior management position with broad responsibility for the legal affairs of a company, and consequently, no member of the Firm shall accept such an appointment for an Audit Client.

Recruiting Services

General Provisions

290.214 Providing recruiting services to an Audit Client may create self-interest, familiarity or intimidation threats. The existence and significance of any threat will depend on factors such as:

- The nature of the requested assistance; and

- The role of the person to be recruited.

The significance of any threat created shall be evaluated and safeguards applied when necessary to eliminate the threat or reduce it to an Acceptable Level. In all cases, the Firm shall not assume management responsibilities, including acting as a negotiator on the client's behalf, and the hiring decision shall be left to the client.

The Firm may generally provide such services as reviewing the professional qualifications of a number of applicants and providing advice on their suitability for the post. In addition, the Firm may interview candidates and advise on a candidate's competence for financial accounting, administrative or control positions.

Audit Clients that are Public Interest Entities

290.215 A Firm shall not provide the following recruiting services to an Audit Client that is a Public Interest Entity with respect to a Director or Officer of the entity or senior management in a position to exert significant influence over the preparation of the client's accounting records or the Financial Statements on which the Firm will express an Opinion:

- Searching for or seeking out candidates for such positions; and

- Undertaking reference checks of prospective candidates for such positions.

Corporate Finance Services

290.216 Providing corporate finance services such as (a) assisting an Audit Client in developing corporate strategies, (b) identifying possible targets for the Audit Client to acquire, (c) advising on disposal transactions, (d) assisting finance raising transactions, and (e) providing structuring advice may create advocacy and self-review threats. The significance of any threat shall be evaluated and safeguards applied when necessary to eliminate the threat or reduce it to an Acceptable Level. Examples of such safeguards include:

- Using professionals who are not members of the Audit Team to provide the services; or

- Having a professional who was not involved in providing the corporate finance service advise the Audit Team on the service and review the accounting treatment and any Financial Statement treatment.

290.217 Providing a corporate finance service, for example advice on the structuring of a corporate finance transaction or on financing arrangements that will directly affect amounts that will be reported in the Financial Statements on which the Firm will provide an opinion may create a self-review threat. The existence and significance of any threat will depend on factors such as:

- The degree of subjectivity involved in determining the appropriate treatment for the outcome or consequences of the corporate finance advice in the Financial Statements;

- The extent to which the outcome of the corporate finance advice will directly affect amounts recorded in the Financial Statements and the extent to which the amounts are material to the Financial Statements; and

- Whether the effectiveness of the corporate finance advice depends on a particular accounting treatment or presentation in the Financial Statements and there is doubt as to the appropriateness of the related accounting treatment or presentation under the relevant financial reporting framework.

The significance of any threat shall be evaluated and safeguards applied when necessary to eliminate the threat or reduce it to an Acceptable Level. Examples of such safeguards include:

- Using professionals who are not members of the Audit Team to perform the service; or

- Having a professional who was not involved in providing the corporate finance service to the client advise the Audit Team on the service and review the accounting treatment and any Financial Statement treatment.

290.218 Where the effectiveness of corporate finance advice depends on a particular accounting treatment or presentation in the Financial Statements and:

(a) The Audit Team has reasonable doubt as to the appropriateness of the related accounting treatment or presentation under the relevant financial reporting framework; and

(b) The outcome or consequences of the corporate finance advice will have a material effect on the Financial Statements on which the Firm will express an Opinion;

The self-review threat would be so significant that no safeguards could reduce the threat to an Acceptable Level, in which case the corporate finance advice shall not be provided.

290.219 Providing corporate finance services involving promoting, dealing in, or underwriting an Audit Client's shares would create an advocacy or self-review threat that is so significant that no safeguards could reduce the threat to an Acceptable Level. Accordingly, a Firm shall not provide such services to an Audit Client.

Fees

Fees – Relative Size

290.220 When the total fees from an Audit Client represent a large proportion of the total fees of the Firm expressing the audit opinion, the dependence on that client and concern about losing the client creates a self-interest or intimidation threat. The significance of the threat will depend on factors such as:

- The operating structure of the Firm;

- Whether the Firm is well established or new; and

- The significance of the client qualitatively and/or quantitatively to the Firm.

The significance of the threat shall be evaluated and safeguards applied when necessary to eliminate the threat or reduce it to an Acceptable Level. Examples of such safeguards include:

- Reducing the dependency on the client;

- External quality control reviews; or

- Consulting a third party, such as a professional regulatory body or a Member, on key audit judgments.

290.221   A self-interest or intimidation threat is also created when the fees generated from an Audit Client represent a large proportion of the revenue from an individual partner's clients or a large proportion of the revenue of an individual Office of the Firm. The significance of the threat will depend upon factors such as:

- The significance of the client qualitatively and/or quantitatively to the partner or Office; and

- The extent to which the remuneration of the partner, or the partners in the Office, is dependent upon the fees generated from the client.

The significance of the threat shall be evaluated and safeguards applied when necessary to eliminate the threat or reduce it to an Acceptable Level. Examples of such safeguards include:

- Reducing the dependency on the Audit Client;

- Having a Member review the work or otherwise advise as necessary; or

- Regular independent internal or external quality reviews of the engagement.

Audit Clients that are Public Interest Entities

290.222   Where an Audit Client is a Public Interest Entity and, for two consecutive years, the total fees from the client and its related entities (subject to the considerations in paragraph 290.27) represent more than 15% of the total fees received by the Firm expressing the opinion on the Financial Statements of the client, the Firm shall disclose to Those Charged with Governance of the Audit Client the fact that the total of such fees represents more than 15% of the total fees received by the Firm, and discuss which of the safeguards below it will apply to reduce the threat to an Acceptable Level, and apply the selected safeguard:

- Prior to the issuance of the audit opinion on the second year's Financial Statements, a Member, who is not a member of the Firm expressing the opinion on the Financial Statements, performs an Engagement Quality Control Review of that engagement or a professional regulatory body performs a review of that engagement that is equivalent to an Engagement Quality Control Review ("a pre-issuance review"); or

- After the audit opinion on the second year's Financial Statements has been issued, and before the issuance of the audit opinion on the third year's Financial Statements, a Member, who is not a member of the Firm expressing the opinion on the Financial Statements, or a professional regulatory body performs a review of the second year's audit that is equivalent to an Engagement Quality Control Review ("a post-issuance review").

When the total fees significantly exceed 15%, the Firm shall determine whether the significance of the threat is such that a post-issuance review would not reduce the threat to an Acceptable Level and, therefore, a pre-issuance review is required. In such circumstances a pre-issuance review shall be performed.

Thereafter, when the fees continue to exceed 15% each year, the disclosure to and discussion with Those Charged with Governance shall occur and one of the above safeguards shall be applied. If the fees significantly exceed 15%, the Firm shall determine whether the significance of the threat is such that a post-issuance review would not reduce the threat to an Acceptable Level and, therefore, a pre-issuance review is required. In such circumstances a pre-issuance review shall be performed.

Fees – Overdue

290.223   A self-interest threat may be created if fees due from an Audit Client remain unpaid for a long time, especially if a significant part is not paid before the issue of the audit report for the following year. Generally the Firm is expected to require payment of such fees before such audit report is issued. If fees remain unpaid after the report has been issued, the existence and significance of any threat shall be evaluated and safeguards applied when necessary to eliminate the threat or reduce it to an Acceptable Level. An example of such a safeguard is having an additional Member who did not take part in the Audit Engagement provide advice or review the work performed. The Firm shall determine whether the overdue fees might be regarded as being equivalent to a loan to the client and whether, because of the significance of the overdue fees, it is appropriate for the Firm to be re-appointed or continue the Audit Engagement.

Contingent Fees

290.224 Contingent Fees are fees calculated on a predetermined basis relating to the outcome of a transaction or the result of the services performed by the Firm. For the purposes of this section, a fee is not regarded as being contingent if established by a court or other public authority.

290.225 A Contingent Fee charged directly or indirectly, for example through an intermediary, by a Firm in respect of an Audit Engagement creates a self-interest threat that is so significant that no safeguards could reduce the threat to an Acceptable Level. Accordingly, a Firm shall not enter into any such fee arrangement.

290.226 A Contingent Fee charged directly or indirectly, for example through an intermediary, by a Firm in respect of a non-assurance service provided to an Audit Client may also create a self-interest threat. The threat created would be so significant that no safeguards could reduce the threat to an Acceptable Level if:

(a) The fee is charged by the Firm expressing the opinion on the Financial Statements and the fee is material or expected to be material to that Firm;

(b) The fee is charged by a Network Firm that participates in a significant part of the audit and the fee is material or expected to be material to that Firm; or

(c) The outcome of the non-assurance service, and therefore the amount of the fee, is dependent on a future or contemporary judgment related to the audit of a material amount in the Financial Statements.

Accordingly, such arrangements shall not be accepted.

290.227 For other Contingent Fee arrangements charged by a Firm for a non-assurance service to an Audit Client, the existence and significance of any threats will depend on factors such as:

- The range of possible fee amounts;
- Whether an appropriate authority determines the outcome of the matter upon which the Contingent Fee will be determined;
- The nature of the service; and
- The effect of the event or transaction on the Financial Statements.

The significance of any threats shall be evaluated and safeguards applied when necessary to eliminate the threats or reduce them to an Acceptable Level. Examples of such safeguards include:

- Having a Member review the relevant audit work or otherwise advise as necessary; or
- Using professionals who are not members of the Audit Team to perform the non-assurance service.

Compensation and Evaluation Policies

290.228 A self-interest threat is created when a member of the Audit Team is evaluated on or compensated for selling non-assurance services to that Audit Client. The significance of the threat will depend on:

- The proportion of the individual's compensation or performance evaluation that is based on the sale of such services;
- The role of the individual on the Audit Team; and
- Whether promotion decisions are influenced by the sale of such services.

The significance of the threat shall be evaluated and, if the threat is not at an Acceptable Level, the Firm shall either revise the compensation plan or evaluation process for that individual or apply safeguards to eliminate the threat or reduce it to an Acceptable Level. Examples of such safeguards include:

- Removing such members from the Audit Team; or
- Having a Member review the work of the member of the Audit Team.

290.229   A Key Audit Partner shall not be evaluated on or compensated based on that partner's success in selling non-assurance services to the partner's Audit Client. This is not intended to prohibit normal profit-sharing arrangements between partners of a Firm.

Gifts and Hospitality

290.230   Accepting gifts or hospitality from an Audit Client may create self-interest and familiarity threats. If a Firm or a member of the Audit Team accepts gifts or hospitality, unless the value is trivial and inconsequential, the threats created would be so significant that no safeguards could reduce the threats to an Acceptable Level. Consequently, a Firm or a member of the Audit Team shall not accept such gifts or hospitality.

Actual or Threatened Litigation

290.231   When litigation takes place, or appears likely, between the Firm or a member of the Audit Team and the Audit Client, self-interest and intimidation threats are created. The relationship between client management and the members of the Audit Team must be characterised by complete candour and full disclosure regarding all aspects of a client's business operations. When the Firm and the client's management are placed in adversarial positions by actual or threatened litigation, affecting management's willingness to make complete disclosures, self-interest and intimidation threats are created. The significance of the threats created will depend on such factors as:

- The materiality of the litigation; and
- Whether the litigation relates to a prior Audit Engagement.

The significance of the threats shall be evaluated and safeguards applied when necessary to eliminate the threats or reduce them to an Acceptable Level. Examples of such safeguards include:

- If the litigation involves a member of the Audit Team, removing that individual from the Audit Team; or
- Having a professional review the work performed.

If such safeguards do not reduce the threats to an Acceptable Level, the only appropriate action is to withdraw from, or decline, the Audit Engagement.

Paragraphs 290.232 to 290.499 are intentionally left blank.

Reports that Include a Restriction on Use and Distribution

Introduction

290.500 The Independence requirements in Section 290 apply to all Audit Engagements. However, in certain circumstances involving Audit Engagements where the report includes a restriction on use and distribution, and provided the conditions described in 290.501 to 290.502 are met, the Independence requirements in this section may be modified as provided in paragraphs 290.505 to 290.514. These paragraphs are only applicable to an Audit Engagement on Special Purpose Financial Statements (a) that is intended to provide a conclusion in positive or negative form that the Financial Statements are prepared in all material respects, in accordance with the applicable financial reporting framework, including, in the case of a fair presentation framework, that the Financial Statements give a true and fair view or are presented fairly, in all material respects, in accordance with the applicable financial reporting framework, and (b) where the audit report includes a restriction on use and distribution. The modifications are not permitted in the case of an audit of Financial Statements required by law or regulation.

290.501 The modifications to the requirements of Section 290 are permitted if the intended users of the report (a) are knowledgeable as to the purpose and limitations of the report, and (b) explicitly agree to the application of the modified Independence requirements. Knowledge as to the purpose and limitations of the report may be obtained by the intended users through their participation, either directly or indirectly through their representative who has the authority to act for the intended users, in establishing the nature and scope of the engagement. Such participation enhances the ability of the Firm to communicate with intended users about Independence matters, including the circumstances that are relevant to the evaluation of the threats to Independence and the applicable safeguards necessary to eliminate the threats or reduce them to an Acceptable Level, and to obtain their agreement to the modified Independence requirements that are to be applied.

290.502 The Firm shall communicate (for example, in an engagement letter) with the intended users regarding the Independence requirements that are to be applied with respect to the provision of the Audit Engagement. Where the intended users are a class of users (for example, lenders in a syndicated loan arrangement) who are not specifically identifiable by name at the time the engagement terms are established, such users shall subsequently be made aware of the Independence requirements agreed to by the representative (for example, by the representative making the Firm's engagement letter available to all users).

290.503 If the Firm also issues an audit report that does not include a restriction on use and distribution for the same client, the provisions of paragraphs 290.500 to 290.514 do not change the requirement to apply the provisions of paragraphs 290.1 to 290.231 to that Audit Engagement.

290.504 The modifications to the requirements of Section 290 that are permitted in the circumstances set out above are described in paragraphs 290.505 to 290.514. Compliance in all other respects with the provisions of Section 290 is required.

Public Interest Entities

290.505 When the conditions set out in paragraphs 290.500 to 290.502 are met, it is not necessary to apply the additional requirements in paragraphs 290.100 to 290.231 that apply to Audit Engagements for Public Interest Entities.

Related Entities

290.506 When the conditions set out in paragraphs 290.500 to 290.502 are met, references to Audit Client do not include its Related Entities. However, when the Audit Team knows or has reason to believe that a relationship or circumstance involving a Related Entity of the client is relevant to the evaluation of the Firm's Independence of the client, the Audit Team shall include that Related Entity when identifying and evaluating threats to Independence and applying appropriate safeguards.

Networks and Network Firms

290.507 When the conditions set out in paragraphs 290.500 to 290.502 are met, reference to the Firm does not include Network Firms. However, when the Firm knows or has reason to believe that threats are created by any interests and relationships of a Network Firm, they shall be included in the evaluation of threats to Independence.

Financial Interests, Loans and Guarantees, Close Business Relationships and Family and Personal Relationships

290.508 When the conditions set out in paragraphs 290.500 to 290.502 are met, the relevant provisions set out in paragraphs 290.102 to 290.145 apply only to the members of the Engagement Team, their Immediate Family members and Close Family members.

290.509 In addition, a determination shall be made as to whether threats to Independence are created by interests and relationships, as described in paragraphs 290.102 to 290.145, between the Audit Client and the following members of the Audit Team:

(a) Those who provide consultation regarding technical or industry specific issues, transactions or events; and

(b) Those who provide quality control for the engagement, including those who perform the Engagement Quality Control Review.

An evaluation shall be made of the significance of any threats that the Engagement Team has reason to believe are created by interests and relationships between the Audit Client and others within the Firm who can directly influence the outcome of the Audit Engagement, including those who recommend the compensation of, or who provide direct supervisory, management or other oversight of the Audit Engagement Partner in connection with the performance of the Audit Engagement (including those at all successively senior levels above the Engagement Partner through to the individual who is the Firm's senior or managing partner (chief executive or equivalent)).

290.510 An evaluation shall also be made of the significance of any threats that the Engagement Team has reason to believe are created by Financial Interests in the Audit Client held by individuals, as described in paragraphs 290.108 to 290.111 and paragraphs 290.113 to 290.115.

290.511 Where a threat to Independence is not at an Acceptable Level, safeguards shall be applied to eliminate the threat or reduce it to an Acceptable Level.

290.512 In applying the provisions set out in paragraphs 290.106 and 290.115 to interests of the Firm, if the Firm has a material Financial Interest, whether direct or indirect, in the Audit Client, the self-interest threat created would be so significant that no safeguards could reduce the threat to an Acceptable Level. Accordingly, the Firm shall not have such a Financial Interest.

Employment with an Audit Client

290.513 An evaluation shall be made of the significance of any threats from any employment relationships as described in paragraphs 290.134 to 290.138. Where a threat exists that is not at an Acceptable Level, safeguards shall be applied to eliminate the threat or reduce it to an Acceptable Level. Examples of safeguards that might be appropriate include those set out in paragraph 290.136.

Provision of Non-Assurance Services

290.514 If the Firm conducts an engagement to issue a restricted use and distribution report for an Audit Client and provides a non-assurance service to the Audit Client, the provisions of paragraphs 290.156 to 290.231 shall be complied with, subject to paragraphs 290.504 to 290.507.

SECTION 291

Independence – Other Assurance Engagements

Contents

Paragraph

Structure of Section 291.1

A Conceptual Framework Approach to Independence 291.4

Assurance Engagements 291.12

Assertion-based Assurance Engagements 291.17

Direct reporting Assurance Engagements 291.20

Reports that Include a Restriction on Use and Distribution 291.21

Multiple Responsible Parties 291.28

Documentation 291.29

Engagement Period 291.30

Other Considerations 291.33

Application of the Conceptual Framework Approach to Independence 291.100

Financial Interests 291.104

Loans and Guarantees 291.113

Business Relationships 291.119

Family and Personal Relationships 291.121

Employment with Assurance Clients 291.128

Recent Service with an Assurance Client 291.132

Serving as a Director or Officer of an Assurance Client 291.135

Long Association of Senior Personnel with Assurance Clients 291.139

Provision of Non-assurance Services to Assurance Clients 291.140

    Management Responsibilities 291.143

    Other Considerations 291.148

Fees 291.151

    Fees—Relative Size 291.151

    Fees—Overdue 291.153

    Contingent Fees 291.154

Gifts and Hospitality 291.158

Actual or Threatened Litigation 291.159

Structure of Section

291.1   This section addresses Independence requirements for Assurance Engagements that are not Audit Engagements or Review Engagements. Additional Independence requirements for Audit and Review Engagements are addressed in Section 290. If the Assurance Client is also an Audit Client or Review Client, the requirements in Section 290 also apply to the Firm, Network Firms and members of the Audit Team or Review Team. In certain circumstances involving Assurance Engagements where the assurance report includes a restriction on use and distribution and provided certain conditions are met, the Independence requirements in this section may be modified as provided in 291.21 to 291.27.

291.2   Assurance Engagements are designed to enhance intended users' degree of confidence about the outcome of the evaluation or measurement of a subject matter against criteria. *Framework for Assurance Engagements* issued by the AUASB describes the elements and objectives of an Assurance Engagement and identifies engagements to which Auditing and Assurance Standards apply. For a description of the elements and objectives of an Assurance Engagement, refer to the Assurance Framework.

291.3   Compliance with the fundamental principle of objectivity requires being independent of Assurance Clients. In the case of Assurance Engagements, it is in the public interest and, therefore, required by this Code of Ethics, that members of Assurance Teams and Firms be independent of Assurance Clients and that any threats that the Firm has reason to believe are created by a Network Firm's interests and relationships be evaluated. In addition, when the Assurance Team knows or has reason to believe that a relationship or circumstance involving a Related Entity of the Assurance Client is relevant to the evaluation of the Firm's Independence from the client, the Assurance Team shall include that Related Entity when identifying and evaluating threats to Independence and applying appropriate safeguards.

A Conceptual Framework Approach to Independence

291.4   The objective of this section is to assist Firms and members of Assurance Teams in applying the conceptual framework approach described below to achieving and maintaining Independence.

291.5   Independence comprises:

Independence of Mind

The state of mind that permits the expression of a conclusion without being affected by influences that compromise professional judgment, thereby allowing an individual to act with integrity and exercise objectivity and professional scepticism.

Independence in Appearance

The avoidance of facts and circumstances that are so significant that a reasonable and informed third party would be likely to conclude, weighing all the specific facts and circumstances, that a Firm's, or a member of the Assurance Team's, integrity, objectivity or professional scepticism has been compromised.

291.6   The conceptual framework approach shall be applied by Members to:

- Identify threats to Independence;

- Evaluate the significance of the threats identified; and

- Apply safeguards when necessary to eliminate the threats or reduce them to an Acceptable Level.

When the Member determines that appropriate safeguards are not available or cannot be applied to eliminate the threats or reduce them to an Acceptable Level, the Member shall eliminate the circumstance or relationship creating the threats or decline or terminate the Assurance Engagement.

A Member shall use professional judgment in applying this conceptual framework.

291.7   Many different circumstances, or combinations of circumstances, may be relevant in assessing threats to Independence. It is impossible to define every situation that creates threats to Independence and to specify the appropriate action. Therefore, this Code establishes a conceptual framework that requires Firms and members of Assurance Teams to identify, evaluate, and address threats to Independence. The conceptual framework approach assists Members in Public Practice in complying with the ethical requirements in this Code. It accommodates many variations in circumstances that create threats to Independence and can deter a Member from concluding that a situation is permitted if it is not specifically prohibited.

291.8   Paragraphs 291.100 and onwards describe how the conceptual framework approach to Independence is to be applied. These paragraphs do not address all the circumstances and relationships that create or may create threats to Independence.

291.9   In deciding whether to accept or continue an engagement, or whether a particular individual may be a member of the Assurance Team, a Firm shall identify and evaluate any threats to Independence. If the threats are not at an Acceptable Level, and the decision is whether to accept an engagement or include a particular individual on the Assurance Team, the Firm shall determine whether safeguards are available to eliminate the threats or reduce them to an Acceptable Level. If the decision is whether to continue an engagement, the Firm shall determine whether any existing safeguards will continue to be effective to eliminate the threats or reduce them to an Acceptable Level or whether other safeguards will need to be applied or whether the engagement needs to be terminated. Whenever new information about a threat comes to the attention of the Firm during the engagement, the Firm shall evaluate the significance of the threat in accordance with the conceptual framework approach.

291.10   Throughout this section, reference is made to the significance of threats to Independence. In evaluating the significance of a threat, qualitative as well as quantitative factors shall be taken into account.

AUST291.10.1   Where a Member in Public Practice identifies multiple threats to Independence, which individually may not be significant, the Member shall evaluate the significance of those threats in aggregate and the safeguards applied or in place to eliminate some or all of the threats or reduce them to an Acceptable Level in aggregate.

291.11   This section does not, in most cases, prescribe the specific responsibility of individuals within the Firm for actions related to Independence because responsibility may differ depending on the size, structure and organisation of a Firm. The Firm is required by APES 320 *Quality Control for Firms* to establish policies and procedures designed to provide it with reasonable assurance that Independence is maintained when required by relevant ethical standards.

Assurance Engagements

291.12   As further explained in the Assurance Framework, in an Assurance Engagement the Member in Public Practice expresses a conclusion designed to enhance the degree of confidence of the intended users (other than the responsible party) about the outcome of the evaluation or measurement of a subject matter against criteria.

291.13   The outcome of the evaluation or measurement of a subject matter is the information that results from applying the criteria to the subject matter. The term "subject matter information" is used to mean the outcome of the evaluation or measurement of a subject matter. For example, the Framework states that an assertion about the effectiveness of internal control (subject matter information) results from applying a framework for evaluating the effectiveness of internal control, such as COSO[16] or CoCo[17] (criteria), to internal control, a process (subject matter).

---

16   "Internal Control – Integrated Framework" The Committee of Sponsoring Organizations of the Treadway Commission.

17   "Guidance on Assessing Control – The CoCo Principles" Criteria of Control Board, The Canadian Institute of Chartered Accountants.

291.14   Assurance Engagements may be assertion-based or direct reporting. In either case, they involve three separate parties: a Member in Public Practice, a responsible party and intended users.

291.15   In an assertion-based Assurance Engagement, the evaluation or measurement of the subject matter is performed by the responsible party, and the subject matter information is in the form of an assertion by the responsible party that is made available to the intended users.

291.16   In a direct reporting Assurance Engagement, the Member in Public Practice either directly performs the evaluation or measurement of the subject matter, or obtains a representation from the responsible party that has performed the evaluation or measurement that is not available to the intended users. The subject matter information is provided to the intended users in the assurance report.

AUST291.16.1   The AUASB has issued *Framework for Assurance Engagements* which describes the nature of an Assurance Engagement. To obtain a full understanding of the objectives and elements of an Assurance Engagement it is necessary to refer to the full text of that document.

Assertion-based Assurance Engagements

291.17   In an assertion-based Assurance Engagement, the members of the Assurance Team and the Firm shall be independent of the Assurance Client (the party responsible for the subject matter information, and which may be responsible for the subject matter). Such Independence requirements prohibit certain relationships between members of the Assurance Team and (a) Directors or, Officers, and (b) individuals at the client in a position to exert significant influence over the subject matter information. Also, a determination shall be made as to whether threats to Independence are created by relationships with individuals at the client in a position to exert significant influence over the subject matter of the engagement. An evaluation shall be made of the significance of any threats that the Firm has reason to believe are created by Network Firm[18] interests and relationships.

291.18   In the majority of assertion-based Assurance Engagements, the responsible party is responsible for both the subject matter information and the subject matter. However, in some engagements, the responsible party may not be responsible for the subject matter. For example, when a Member in Public Practice is engaged to perform an Assurance Engagement regarding a report that an environmental consultant has prepared about a company's sustainability practices for distribution to intended users, the environmental consultant is the responsible party for the subject matter information but the company is responsible for the subject matter (the sustainability practices).

291.19   In assertion-based Assurance Engagements where the responsible party is responsible for the subject matter information but not the subject matter, the members of the Assurance Team and the Firm shall be independent of the party responsible for the subject matter information (the Assurance Client). In addition, an evaluation shall be made of any threats the Firm has reason to believe are created by interests and relationships between a member of the Assurance Team, the Firm, a Network Firm and the party responsible for the subject matter.

---

18   See paragraphs 290.13 to 290.24 for guidance on what constitutes a Network Firm.

Direct reporting Assurance Engagements

291.20　In a direct reporting Assurance Engagement, the members of the Assurance Team and the Firm shall be independent of the Assurance Client (the party responsible for the subject matter). An evaluation shall also be made of any threats the Firm has reason to believe are created by Network Firm interests and relationships.

Reports that Include a Restriction on Use and Distribution

291.21　In certain circumstances where the assurance report includes a restriction on use and distribution, and provided the conditions in this paragraph and in 291.22 are met, the Independence requirements in this section may be modified. The modifications to the requirements of Section 291 are permitted if the intended users of the report (a) are knowledgeable as to the purpose, subject matter information and limitations of the report and (b) explicitly agree to the application of the modified Independence requirements. Knowledge as to the purpose, subject matter information, and limitations of the report may be obtained by the intended users through their participation, either directly or indirectly through their representative who has the authority to act for the intended users, in establishing the nature and scope of the engagement. Such participation enhances the ability of the Firm to communicate with intended users about Independence matters, including the circumstances that are relevant to the evaluation of the threats to Independence and the applicable safeguards necessary to eliminate the threats or reduce them to an Acceptable Level, and to obtain their agreement to the modified Independence requirements that are to be applied.

291.22　The Firm shall communicate (for example, in an engagement letter) with the intended users regarding the Independence requirements that are to be applied with respect to the provision of the Assurance Engagement. Where the intended users are a class of users (for example, lenders in a syndicated loan arrangement) who are not specifically identifiable by name at the time the engagement terms are established, such users shall subsequently be made aware of the Independence requirements agreed to by the representative (for example, by the representative making the Firm's engagement letter available to all users).

291.23　If the Firm also issues an assurance report that does not include a restriction on use and distribution for the same client, the provisions of paragraphs 291.25 to 291.27 do not change the requirement to apply the provisions of paragraphs 291.1 to 291.159 to that Assurance Engagement. If the Firm also issues an audit report, whether or not it includes a restriction on use and distribution, for the same client, the provisions of Section 290 shall apply to that Audit Engagement.

291.24　The modifications to the requirements of Section 291 that are permitted in the circumstances set out above are described in paragraphs 291.25 to 291.27. Compliance in all other respects with the provisions of Section 291 is required.

291.25　When the conditions set out in paragraphs 291.21 and 291.22 are met, the relevant provisions set out in paragraphs 291.104 to 291.134 apply to all members of the Engagement Team, and their Immediate and Close Family members. In addition, a determination shall be made as to whether threats to Independence are created by interests and relationships between the Assurance Client and the following other members of the Assurance Team:

- Those who provide consultation regarding technical or industry specific issues, transactions or events; and

- Those who provide quality control for the engagement, including those who perform the Engagement Quality Control Review.

An evaluation shall also be made, by reference to the provisions set out in paragraphs 291.104 to 291.134, of any threats that the Engagement Team has reason to believe are created by interests and relationships between the Assurance Client and others within the Firm who can directly influence the outcome of the Assurance Engagement, including those who recommend the compensation, or who provide direct supervisory, management or other oversight, of the Assurance Engagement Partner in connection with the performance of the Assurance Engagement.

291.26   Even though the conditions set out in paragraphs 291.21 to 291.22 are met, if the Firm had a material Financial Interest, whether direct or indirect, in the Assurance Client, the self-interest threat created would be so significant that no safeguards could reduce the threat to an Acceptable Level. Accordingly, the Firm shall not have such a Financial Interest. In addition, the Firm shall comply with the other applicable provisions of this section described in paragraphs 291.113 to 291.159.

291.27   An evaluation shall also be made of any threats that the Firm has reason to believe are created by Network Firm interests and relationships.

Multiple Responsible Parties

291.28   In some Assurance Engagements, whether assertion-based or direct reporting, there might be several responsible parties. In determining whether it is necessary to apply the provisions in this section to each responsible party in such engagements, the Firm may take into account whether an interest or relationship between the Firm, or a member of the Assurance Team, and a particular responsible party would create a threat to Independence that is not trivial and inconsequential in the context of the subject matter information. This will take into account factors such as:

- The materiality of the subject matter information (or of the subject matter) for which the particular responsible party is responsible; and

- The degree of public interest associated with the engagement.

If the Firm determines that the threat to Independence created by any such interest or relationship with a particular responsible party would be trivial and inconsequential, it may not be necessary to apply all of the provisions of this section to that responsible party.

Documentation

291.29   Documentation provides evidence of the Member's judgments in forming conclusions regarding compliance with Independence requirements. The absence of documentation is not a determinant of whether a Firm considered a particular matter nor whether it is independent.

The Member shall document conclusions regarding compliance with Independence requirements, and the substance of any relevant discussions that support those conclusions. Accordingly:

- (a) When safeguards are required to reduce a threat to an Acceptable Level, the Member shall document the nature of the threat and the safeguards in place or applied that reduce the threat to an Acceptable Level; and

- (b) When a threat required significant analysis to determine whether safeguards were necessary and the Member concluded that they were not because the threat was already at an Acceptable Level, the Member shall document the nature of the threat and the rationale for the conclusion.

Engagement Period

291.30   Independence from the Assurance Client is required both during the engagement period and the period covered by the subject matter information. The engagement period starts when the Assurance Team begins to perform assurance services with respect to the particular engagement. The engagement period ends when the assurance report is issued. When the engagement is of a recurring nature, it ends at the later of the notification by either party that the professional relationship has terminated or the issuance of the final assurance report.

291.31   When an entity becomes an Assurance Client during or after the period covered by the subject matter information on which the Firm will express a conclusion, the Firm shall determine whether any threats to Independence are created by:

- Financial or business relationships with the Assurance Client during or after the period covered by the subject matter information but before accepting the Assurance Engagement; or

- Previous services provided to the Assurance Client.

291.32   If a non-assurance service was provided to the Assurance Client during or after the period covered by the subject matter information but before the Assurance Team begins to perform assurance services and the service would not be permitted during the period of the Assurance Engagement, the Firm shall evaluate any threat to Independence created by the service. If any threat is not at an Acceptable Level, the Assurance Engagement shall only be accepted if safeguards are applied to eliminate any threats or reduce them to an Acceptable Level. Examples of such safeguards include:

- Not including personnel who provided the non-assurance service as members of the Assurance Team;

- Having a Member review the assurance and non-assurance work as appropriate; or

- Engaging another Firm to evaluate the results of the non-assurance service or having another Firm re-perform the non-assurance service to the extent necessary to enable it to take responsibility for the service.

However, if the non-assurance service has not been completed and it is not practical to complete or terminate the service before the commencement of Professional Services in connection with the Assurance Engagement, the Firm shall only accept the Assurance Engagement if it is satisfied:

- The non-assurance service will be completed within a short period of time; or

- The client has arrangements in place to transition the service to another provider within a short period of time.

During the service period, safeguards shall be applied when necessary. In addition, the matter shall be discussed with Those Charged with Governance.

Other Considerations

291.33   There may be occasions when there is an inadvertent violation of this section. If such an inadvertent violation occurs, it generally will be deemed not to compromise Independence provided the Firm has appropriate quality control policies and procedures in place equivalent to those required by APES 320 *Quality Control for Firms*, to maintain Independence and, once discovered, the violation is corrected promptly and any necessary safeguards are applied to eliminate any threat or reduce it to an Acceptable Level. The Firm shall determine whether to discuss the matter with Those Charged with Governance.

AUST291.33.1   Unless an inadvertent violation of this section is trivial and inconsequential, the Firm shall document and discuss it with Those Charged with Governance.

Paragraphs 291.34 to 291.99 are intentionally left blank.

Application of the Conceptual Framework Approach to Independence

291.100 Paragraphs 291.104 to 291.159 describe specific circumstances and relationships that create or may create threats to Independence. The paragraphs describe the potential threats and the types of safeguards that may be appropriate to eliminate the threats or reduce them to an Acceptable Level and identify certain situations where no safeguards could reduce the threats to an Acceptable Level. The paragraphs do not describe all of the circumstances and relationships that create or may create a threat to Independence. The Firm and the members of the Assurance Team shall evaluate the implications of similar, but different, circumstances and relationships and determine whether safeguards, including the safeguards in paragraphs 200.11 to 200.15 can be applied when necessary to eliminate the threats to Independence or reduce them to an Acceptable Level.

291.101 The paragraphs demonstrate how the conceptual framework approach applies to Assurance Engagements and are to be read in conjunction with paragraph 291.28 which explains that, in the majority of Assurance Engagements, there is one responsible party and that responsible party is the Assurance Client. However, in some Assurance Engagements there are two or more responsible parties. In such circumstances, an evaluation shall be made of any threats the Firm has reason to believe are created by interests and relationships between a member of the Assurance Team, the Firm, a Network Firm and the party responsible for the subject matter. For assurance reports that include a restriction on use and distribution, the paragraphs are to be read in the context of paragraphs 291.21 to 291.27.

291.102 Interpretation 2005-01 provides further guidance on applying the Independence requirements contained in this section to Assurance Engagements.

291.103 Paragraphs 291.104 to 291.120 contain references to the materiality of a Financial Interest, loan, or guarantee, or the significance of a business relationship. For the purpose of determining whether such an interest is material to an individual, the combined net worth of the individual and the individual's Immediate Family members may be taken into account.

Financial Interests

291.104 Holding a Financial Interest in an Assurance Client may create a self-interest threat. The existence and significance of any threat created depends on: (a) the role of the person holding the Financial Interest, (b) whether the Financial Interest is direct or indirect, and (c) the materiality of the Financial Interest.

291.105 Financial Interests may be held through an intermediary (e.g. a collective investment vehicle, estate or trust). The determination of whether such Financial Interests are direct or indirect will depend upon whether the beneficial owner has control over the investment vehicle or the ability to influence its investment decisions. When control over the investment vehicle or the ability to influence investment decisions exists, this Code defines that Financial Interest to be a Direct Financial Interest. Conversely, when the beneficial owner of the Financial Interest has no control over the investment vehicle or ability to influence its investment decisions, this Code defines that Financial Interest to be an Indirect Financial Interest.

291.106 If a member of the Assurance Team, a member of that individual's Immediate Family, or a Firm has a Direct Financial Interest or a material Indirect Financial Interest in the Assurance Client, the self-interest threat created would be so significant that no safeguards could reduce the threat to an Acceptable Level. Therefore, none of the following shall have a Direct Financial Interest or a material Indirect Financial Interest in the client: a member of the Assurance Team; a member of that individual's Immediate Family member; or the Firm.

291.107 When a member of the Assurance Team has a Close Family member who the Assurance Team member knows has a Direct Financial Interest or a material Indirect Financial

Interest in the Assurance Client, a self-interest threat is created. The significance of the threat will depend on factors such as

- The nature of the relationship between the member of the Assurance Team and the Close Family member; and

- The materiality of the Financial Interest to the Close Family member.

The significance of the threat shall be evaluated and safeguards applied when necessary to eliminate the threat or reduce it to an Acceptable Level. Examples of such safeguards include:

- The Close Family member disposing, as soon as practicable, of all of the Financial Interest or disposing of a sufficient portion of an Indirect Financial Interest so that the remaining interest is no longer material;

- Having a Member review the work of the member of the Assurance Team; or

- Removing the individual from the Assurance Team.

291.108 If a member of the Assurance Team, a member of that individual's Immediate Family, or a Firm has a direct or material Indirect Financial Interest in an entity that has a controlling interest in the Assurance Client, and the client is material to the entity, the self-interest threat created would be so significant that no safeguards could reduce the threat to an Acceptable Level. Therefore, none of the following shall have such a Financial Interest: a member of the Assurance Team; a member of that individual's Immediate Family; and the Firm.

291.109 The holding by a Firm or a member of the Assurance Team, or a member of that individual's Immediate Family, of a Direct Financial Interest or a material Indirect Financial Interest in the Assurance Client as a trustee creates a self-interest threat. Such an interest shall not be held unless:

(a) Neither the trustee, nor an Immediate Family member of the trustee, nor the Firm are beneficiaries of the trust;

(b) The interest in the Assurance Client held by the trust is not material to the trust;

(c) The trust is not able to exercise significant influence over the Assurance Client; and

(d) The trustee, an Immediate Family member of the trustee, or the Firm cannot significantly influence any investment decision involving a Financial Interest in the Assurance Client.

291.110 Members of the Assurance Team shall determine whether a self-interest threat is created by any known Financial Interests in the Assurance Client held by other individuals including:

- Partners and professional employees of the Firm, other than those referred to above, or their Immediate Family members; and

- Individuals with a close personal relationship with a member of the Assurance Team.

Whether these interests create a self-interest threat will depend on factors such as:

- The Firm's organisational, operating and reporting structure; and

- The nature of the relationship between the individual and the member of the Assurance Team.

The significance of any threat shall be evaluated and safeguards applied when necessary to eliminate the threat or reduce it to an Acceptable Level. Examples of such safeguards include:

- Removing the member of the Assurance Team with the personal relationship from the Assurance Team;

- Excluding the member of the Assurance Team from any significant decision-making concerning the Assurance Engagement; or

- Having a Member review the work of the member of the Assurance Team.

291.111 If a Firm, a member of the Assurance Team, or an Immediate Family member of the individual, receives a Direct Financial Interest or a material Indirect Financial Interest in an Assurance Client, for example, by way of an inheritance, gift or as a result of a merger, and such interest would not be permitted to be held under this section, then:

(a) If the interest is received by the Firm, the Financial Interest shall be disposed of immediately, or a sufficient amount of an Indirect Financial Interest shall be disposed of so that the remaining interest is no longer material, or

(b) If the interest is received by a member of the Assurance Team, or a member of that individual's Immediate Family, the individual who received the Financial Interest shall immediately dispose of the Financial Interest, or dispose of a sufficient amount of an Indirect Financial Interest so that the remaining interest is no longer material.

291.112 When an inadvertent violation of this section as it relates to a Financial Interest in an Assurance Client occurs, it is deemed not to compromise Independence if:

(a) The Firm has established policies and procedures that require prompt notification to the Firm of any breaches resulting from the purchase, inheritance or other acquisition of a Financial Interest in the Assurance Client;

(b) The actions taken in paragraph 291.111(a) – (b) are taken as applicable; and

(c) The Firm applies other safeguards when necessary to reduce any remaining threat to an Acceptable Level. Examples of such safeguards include:

(i) Having a Member review the work of the member of the Assurance Team; or

(ii) Excluding the individual from any significant decision-making concerning the Assurance Engagement.

The Firm shall determine whether to discuss the matter with Those Charged with Governance.

AUST291.112.1 Unless an inadvertent violation of this section as it relates to a Financial Interest is trivial and inconsequential, the Firm shall document and discuss it with Those Charged with Governance.

Loans and Guarantees

291.113 A loan, or a guarantee of a loan, to a member of the Assurance Team, or a member of that individual's Immediate Family, or the Firm from an Assurance Client that is a bank or similar institution, may create a threat to Independence. If the loan or guarantee is not made under normal lending procedures, terms and conditions, a self-interest threat would be created that would be so significant that no safeguards could reduce the threat to an Acceptable Level. Accordingly, neither a member of the Assurance Team, a member of that individual's Immediate Family, nor a Firm shall accept such a loan or guarantee.

291.114 If a loan to a Firm from an Assurance Client that is a bank or similar institution is made under normal lending procedures, terms and conditions and it is material to the Assurance Client or Firm receiving the loan, it may be possible to apply safeguards to reduce the self-interest threat to an Acceptable Level. An example of such a safeguard is having the work reviewed by a Member from a Network Firm that is neither involved with the Assurance Engagement nor received the loan.

291.115 A loan, or a guarantee of a loan, from an Assurance Client that is a bank or a similar institution to a member of the Assurance Team, or a member of that individual's Immediate Family, does not create a threat to Independence if the loan or guarantee is made under normal lending procedures, terms and conditions. Examples of such loans include home mortgages, bank overdrafts, car loans and credit card balances.

291.116 If the Firm or a member of the Assurance Team, or a member of that individual's Immediate Family, accepts a loan from, or has a borrowing guaranteed by, an Assurance Client that is not a bank or similar institution, the self-interest threat created would be so significant that no safeguards could reduce the threat to an Acceptable Level, unless the loan or guarantee is immaterial to both the Firm, or the member of the Assurance Team and the Immediate Family member, and the client.

291.117 Similarly, if the Firm, or a member of the Assurance Team, or a member of that individual's Immediate Family, makes or guarantees a loan to an Assurance Client, the self-interest threat created would be so significant that no safeguards could reduce the threat to an Acceptable Level, unless the loan or guarantee is immaterial to both the Firm, or the member of the Assurance Team and the Immediate Family member, and the client.

291.118 If a Firm or a member of the Assurance Team, or a member of that individual's Immediate Family, has deposits or a brokerage account with an Assurance Client that is a bank, broker, or similar institution, a threat to Independence is not created if the deposit or account is held under normal commercial terms.

Business Relationships

291.119 A close business relationship between a Firm, or a member of the Assurance Team, or a member of that individual's Immediate Family, and the Assurance Client or its management arises from a commercial relationship or common Financial Interest and may create self-interest or intimidation threats. Examples of such relationships include:

- Having a Financial Interest in a joint venture with either the client or a controlling owner, Director or Officer or other individual who performs senior managerial activities for that client.

- Arrangements to combine one or more services or products of the Firm with one or more services or products of the client and to market the package with reference to both parties.

- Distribution or marketing arrangements under which the Firm distributes or markets the client's products or services, or the client distributes or markets the Firm's products or services.

Unless any Financial Interest is immaterial and the business relationship is insignificant to the Firm and the client or its management, the threat created would be so significant that no safeguards could reduce the threat to an Acceptable Level. Therefore, unless the Financial Interest is immaterial and the business relationship is insignificant, the business relationship shall not be entered into, or shall be reduced to an insignificant level or terminated.

In the case of a member of the Assurance Team, unless any such Financial Interest is immaterial and the relationship is insignificant to that member, the individual shall be removed from the Assurance Team.

If the business relationship is between an Immediate Family member of a member of the Assurance Team and the Assurance Client or its management, the significance of any threat shall be evaluated and safeguards applied when necessary to eliminate the threat or reduce it to an Acceptable Level.

291.120 The purchase of goods and services from an Assurance Client by the Firm, or a member of the Assurance Team, or a member of that individual's Immediate Family, does not generally create a threat to Independence if the transaction is in the normal course of business and at arm's length. However, such transactions may be of such a nature or magnitude that they create a self-interest threat. The significance of any threat shall be evaluated and safeguards applied when necessary to eliminate the threat or reduce it to an Acceptable Level. Examples of such safeguards include:

- Eliminating or reducing the magnitude of the transaction; or

- Removing the individual from the Assurance Team.

Family and Personal Relationships

291.121 Family and personal relationships between a member of the Assurance Team and a Director or Officer or certain employees (depending on their role) of the Assurance Client, may create self-interest, familiarity or intimidation threats. The existence and significance of any threats will depend on a number of factors, including the individual's responsibilities on the Assurance Team, the role of the family member or other individual within the client, and the closeness of the relationship.

291.122 When an Immediate Family member of a member of the Assurance Team is:

    (a) A Director or Officer of the Assurance Client, or

    (b) An employee in a position to exert significant influence over the subject matter information of the Assurance Engagement,

    or was in such a position during any period covered by the engagement or the subject matter information, the threats to Independence can only be reduced to an Acceptable Level by removing the individual from the Assurance Team. The closeness of the relationship is such that no other safeguards could reduce the threat to an Acceptable Level. Accordingly, no individual who has such a relationship shall be a member of the Assurance Team.

291.123 Threats to Independence are created when an Immediate Family member of a member of the Assurance Team is an employee in a position to exert significant influence over the subject matter of the engagement. The significance of the threats will depend on factors such as:

    • The position held by the Immediate Family member; and

    • The role of the professional on the Assurance Team.

    The significance of the threat shall be evaluated and safeguards applied when necessary to eliminate the threat or reduce it to an Acceptable Level. Examples of such safeguards include:

    • Removing the individual from the Assurance Team; or

    • Structuring the responsibilities of the Assurance Team so that the professional does not deal with matters that are within the responsibility of the Immediate Family member.

291.124 Threats to Independence are created when a Close Family member of a member of the Assurance Team is:

    • A Director or Officer of the Assurance Client; or

    • An employee in a position to exert significant influence over the subject matter information of the Assurance Engagement.

    The significance of the threats will depend on factors such as:

    • The nature of the relationship between the member of the Assurance Team and the Close Family member;

    • The position held by the Close Family member; and

    • The role of the professional on the Assurance Team.

    The significance of the threat shall be evaluated and safeguards applied when necessary to eliminate the threat or reduce it to an Acceptable Level. Examples of such safeguards include:

    • Removing the individual from the Assurance Team; or

    • Structuring the responsibilities of the Assurance Team so that the professional does not deal with matters that are within the responsibility of the Close Family member.

291.125 Threats to Independence are created when a member of the Assurance Team has a close relationship with a person who is not an Immediate or Close Family member, but who is a Director or Officer or an employee in a position to exert significant influence over the subject matter information of the Assurance Engagement. A member of the Assurance Team who has such a relationship shall consult in accordance with Firm policies and procedures. The significance of the threats will depend on factors such as:

    • The nature of the relationship between the individual and the member of the Assurance Team;

    • The position the individual holds with the client; and

    • The role of the professional on the Assurance Team.

The significance of the threats shall be evaluated and safeguards applied when necessary to eliminate the threats or reduce them to an Acceptable Level. Examples of such safeguards include:

- Removing the professional from the Assurance Team; or
- Structuring the responsibilities of the Assurance Team so that the professional does not deal with matters that are within the responsibility of the individual with whom the professional has a close relationship.

291.126 Self-interest, familiarity or intimidation threats may be created by a personal or family relationship between (a) a partner or employee of the Firm who is not a member of the Assurance Team and (b) a Director or Officer of the Assurance Client or an employee in a position to exert significant influence over the subject matter information of the Assurance Engagement. The existence and significance of any threat will depend on factors such as:

- The nature of the relationship between the partner or employee of the Firm and the Director or Officer or employee of the client;
- The interaction of the partner or employee of the Firm with the Assurance Team;
- The position of the partner or employee within the Firm; and
- The role of the individual within the client.

The significance of any threat shall be evaluated and safeguards applied when necessary to eliminate the threat or reduce it to an Acceptable Level. Examples of such safeguards include:

- Structuring the partner's or employee's responsibilities to reduce any potential influence over the Assurance Engagement; or
- Having a Member review the relevant assurance work performed.

291.127 When an inadvertent violation of this section as it relates to family and personal relationships occurs, it is deemed not to compromise Independence if:

(a) The Firm has established policies and procedures that require prompt notification to the Firm of any breaches resulting from changes in the employment status of their Immediate or Close Family members or other personal relationships that create threats to Independence;

(b) The inadvertent violation relates to an Immediate Family member of a member of the Assurance Team becoming a Director or Officer of the Assurance Client or being in a position to exert significant influence over the subject matter information of the Assurance Engagement, and the relevant professional is removed from the Assurance Team; and

(c) The Firm applies other safeguards when necessary to reduce any remaining threat to an Acceptable Level. Examples of such safeguards include:

- Having a Member review the work of the member of the Assurance Team; or
- Excluding the relevant professional from any significant decision-making concerning the engagement.

The Firm shall determine whether to discuss the matter with Those Charged with Governance.

Employment with Assurance Clients

291.128 Familiarity or intimidation threats may be created if a Director or Officer of the Assurance Client, or an employee who is in a position to exert significant influence over the subject matter information of the Assurance Engagement, has been a member of the Assurance Team or partner of the Firm.

291.129 If a former member of the Assurance Team or partner of the Firm has joined the Assurance Client in such a position, the existence and significance of any familiarity or intimidation threats will depend on factors such as:

(a) The position the individual has taken at the client;

(b) Any involvement the individual will have with the Assurance Team;

    (c) The length of time since the individual was a member of the Assurance Team or partner of the Firm; and

    (d) The former position of the individual within the Assurance Team or Firm, for example, whether the individual was responsible for maintaining regular contact with the client's management or Those Charged with Governance.

In all cases the individual shall not continue to participate in the Firm's business or professional activities.

The significance of any threats created shall be evaluated and safeguards applied when necessary to eliminate the threats or reduce them to an Acceptable Level.

Examples of such safeguards include:

- Making arrangements such that the individual is not entitled to any benefits or payments from the Firm, unless made in accordance with fixed pre-determined arrangements.

- Making arrangements such that any amount owed to the individual is not material to the Firm;

- Modifying the plan for the Assurance Engagement;

- Assigning individuals to the Assurance Team who have sufficient experience in relation to the individual who has joined the client; or

- Having a Member review the work of the former member of the Assurance Team.

291.130 If a former partner of the Firm has previously joined an entity in such a position and the entity subsequently becomes an Assurance Client of the Firm, the significance of any threats to Independence shall be evaluated and safeguards applied when necessary, to eliminate the threat or reduce it to an Acceptable Level.

291.131 A self-interest threat is created when a member of the Assurance Team participates in the Assurance Engagement while knowing that the member of the Assurance Team will, or may, join the client some time in the future. Firm policies and procedures shall require members of an Assurance Team to notify the Firm when entering employment negotiations with the client. On receiving such notification, the significance of the threat shall be evaluated and safeguards applied when necessary to eliminate the threat or reduce it to an Acceptable Level. Examples of such safeguards include:

- Removing the individual from the Assurance Team; or

- A review of any significant judgments made by that individual while on the team.

Recent Service with an Assurance Client

291.132 Self-interest, self-review or familiarity threats may be created if a member of the Assurance Team has recently served as a Director, Officer, or employee of the Assurance Client. This would be the case when, for example, a member of the Assurance Team has to evaluate elements of the subject matter information the member of the Assurance Team had prepared while with the client.

291.133 If, during the period covered by the assurance report, a member of the Assurance Team had served as Director or Officer of the Assurance Client, or was an employee in a position to exert significant influence over the subject matter information of the Assurance Engagement, the threat created would be so significant that no safeguards could reduce the threat to an Acceptable Level. Consequently, such individuals shall not be assigned to the Assurance Team.

291.134 Self-interest, self-review or familiarity threats may be created if, before the period covered by the assurance report, a member of the Assurance Team had served as Director or Officer of the Assurance Client, or was an employee in a position to exert significant influence over the subject matter information of the Assurance Engagement. For example, such threats would be created if a decision made or work performed by the individual in the prior period, while employed by the client, is to be evaluated in the current period as part of the current Assurance Engagement. The existence and significance of any threats will depend on factors such as:

- The position the individual held with the client;

- The length of time since the individual left the client; and

- The role of the professional on the Assurance Team.

The significance of any threat shall be evaluated and safeguards applied when necessary to reduce the threat to an Acceptable Level. An example of such a safeguard is conducting a review of the work performed by the individual as part of the Assurance Team.

Serving as a Director or Officer of an Assurance Client

291.135 If a partner or employee of the Firm serves a Director or Officer of an Assurance Client, the self-review and self-interest threats would be so significant that no safeguards could reduce the threats to an Acceptable Level. Accordingly, no partner or employee shall serve as a Director or Officer of an Assurance Client.

291.136 The position of Company Secretary has different implications in different jurisdictions. Duties may range from administrative duties, such as personnel management and the maintenance of company records and registers, to duties as diverse as ensuring that the company complies with regulation or providing advice on corporate governance matters. Generally, this position is seen to imply a close association with the entity.

291.137 If a Partner or employee of the Firm serves as Company Secretary for an Assurance Client, self-review and advocacy threats are created that would generally be so significant that no safeguards could reduce the threats to an Acceptable Level. Despite paragraph 291.135, when this practice is specifically permitted under local law, professional rules or practice, and provided management makes all relevant decisions, the duties and activities shall be limited to those of a routine and administrative nature, such as preparing minutes and maintaining statutory returns. In those circumstances, the significance of any threats shall be evaluated and safeguards applied when necessary to eliminate the threats or reduce them to an Acceptable Level.

291.138 Performing routine administrative services to support a company secretarial function or providing advice in relation to company secretarial administration matters does not generally create threats to Independence, as long as client management makes all relevant decisions.

Long Association of Senior Personnel with Assurance Clients

291.139 Familiarity and self-interest threats are created by using the same senior personnel on an Assurance Engagement over a long period of time. The significance of the threats will depend on factors such as:

- How long the individual has been a member of the Assurance Team;

- The role of the individual on the Assurance Team;

- The structure of the Firm;

- The nature of the Assurance Engagement;

- Whether the client's management team has changed; and

- Whether the nature or complexity of the subject matter information has changed.

The significance of the threats shall be evaluated and safeguards applied when necessary to eliminate the threats or reduce them to an Acceptable Level. Examples of such safeguards include:

- Rotating the senior personnel off the Assurance Team;

- Having a Member who was not a member of the Assurance Team review the work of the senior personnel; or

- Regular independent internal or external quality reviews of the engagement.

Provision of Non-assurance Services to Assurance Clients

291.140 Firms have traditionally provided to their Assurance Clients a range of non-assurance services that are consistent with their skills and expertise. Providing non-assurance services may, however, create threats to the Independence of the Firm or members of the Assurance Team. The threats created are most often self-review, self-interest and advocacy threats.

291.141 When specific guidance on a particular non-assurance service is not included in this section, the conceptual framework shall be applied when evaluating the particular circumstances.

291.142 Before the Firm accepts an engagement to provide a non-assurance service to an Assurance Client, a determination shall be made as to whether providing such a service would create a threat to Independence. In evaluating the significance of any threat created by a particular non-assurance service, consideration shall be given to any threat that the Assurance Team has reason to believe is created by providing other related non-assurance services. If a threat is created that cannot be reduced to an Acceptable Level by the application of safeguards the non-assurance service shall not be provided.

Management Responsibilities

291.143 Management of an entity performs many activities in managing the entity in the best interests of stakeholders of the entity. It is not possible to specify every activity that is a management responsibility. However, management responsibilities involve leading and directing an entity, including making significant decisions regarding the acquisition, deployment and control of human, financial, physical and intangible resources.

291.144 Whether an activity is a management responsibility depends on the circumstances and requires the exercise of judgment. Examples of activities that would generally be considered a management responsibility include:

- Setting policies and strategic direction;
- Directing and taking responsibility for the actions of the entity's employees;
- Authorising transactions;
- Deciding which recommendations of the Firm or other third parties to implement; and
- Taking responsibility for designing, implementing and maintaining internal control.

291.145 Activities that are routine and administrative, or involve matters that are insignificant, generally are deemed not to be a management responsibility. For example, executing an insignificant transaction that has been authorised by management or monitoring the dates for filing statutory returns and advising an Assurance Client of those dates is deemed not to be a management responsibility. Further, providing advice and recommendations to assist management in discharging its responsibilities is not assuming a management responsibility.

291.146 Assuming a management responsibility for an Assurance Client may create threats to Independence. If a Firm were to assume a management responsibility as part of the assurance service, the threats created would be so significant that no safeguards could reduce the threats to an Acceptable Level. Accordingly, in providing assurance services to an Assurance Client, a Firm shall not assume a management responsibility as part of the assurance service. If the Firm assumes a management responsibility as part of any other services provided to the Assurance Client, it shall ensure that the responsibility is not related to the subject matter and subject matter information of an Assurance Engagement provided by the Firm.

291.147 To avoid the risk of assuming a management responsibility related to the subject matter or subject matter information of the Assurance Engagement, the Firm shall be satisfied that a member of management is responsible for making the significant judgments and decisions that are the proper responsibility of management, evaluating the results of the service and accepting responsibility for the actions to be taken arising from the results of the service. This reduces the risk of the Firm inadvertently making any significant judgments or decisions on behalf of management. This risk is further reduced when the Firm gives the client the opportunity to make judgments and decisions based on an objective and transparent analysis and presentation of the issues.

Other Considerations

291.148 Threats to Independence may be created when a Firm provides a non-assurance service related to the subject matter information of an Assurance Engagement. In such cases, an evaluation of the significance of the Firm's involvement with the subject matter information of the engagement shall be made, and a determination shall be made of whether any self-review threats that are not at an Acceptable Level can be reduced to an Acceptable Level by the application of safeguards.

291.149 A self-review threat may be created if the Firm is involved in the preparation of subject matter information which is subsequently the subject matter information of an Assurance Engagement. For example, a self-review threat would be created if the Firm developed and prepared prospective financial information and subsequently provided assurance on this information. Consequently, the Firm shall evaluate the significance of any self-review threat created by the provision of such services and apply safeguards when necessary to eliminate the threat or reduce it to an Acceptable Level.

291.150 When a Firm performs a valuation that forms part of the subject matter information of an Assurance Engagement, the Firm shall evaluate the significance of any self-review threat and apply safeguards when necessary to eliminate the threat or reduce it to an Acceptable Level.

Fees

Fees – Relative Size

291.151 When the total fees from an Assurance Client represent a large proportion of the total fees of the Firm expressing the conclusion, the dependence on that client and concern about losing the client creates a self-interest or intimidation threat. The significance of the threat will depend on factors such as:

- The operating structure of the Firm;
- Whether the Firm is well established or new; and
- The significance of the client qualitatively and/or quantitatively to the Firm.

The significance of the threat shall be evaluated and safeguards applied when necessary to eliminate the threat or reduce it to an Acceptable Level. Examples of such safeguards include:

- Reducing the dependency on the client;
- External quality control reviews; or
- Consulting a third party, such as a professional regulatory body or a Member, on key assurance judgments.

291.152 A self-interest or intimidation threat is also created when the fees generated from an Assurance Client represent a large proportion of the revenue from an individual partner's clients. The significance of the threat shall be evaluated and safeguards applied when necessary to eliminate the threat or reduce it to an Acceptable Level. An example of such a safeguard is having an additional Member who was not a member of the Assurance Team review the work or otherwise advise as necessary.

Fees – Overdue

291.153 A self-interest threat may be created if fees due from an Assurance Client remain unpaid for a long time, especially if a significant part is not paid before the issue of the assurance report, if any, for the following period. Generally the Firm is expected to require payment of such fees before any such report is issued. If fees remain unpaid after the report has been issued, the existence and significance of any threat shall be evaluated and safeguards applied when necessary to eliminate the threat or reduce it to an Acceptable Level. An example of such a safeguard is having another Member who did not take part in the Assurance Engagement provide advice or review the work performed. The Firm shall determine whether the overdue fees might be regarded as being equivalent to a loan to the client and whether, because of the significance of the overdue fees, it is appropriate for the Firm to be re-appointed or continue the Assurance Engagement.

Contingent Fees

291.154 Contingent Fees are fees calculated on a predetermined basis relating to the outcome of a transaction or the result of the services performed by the Firm. For the purposes of this section, fees are not regarded as being contingent if established by a court or other public authority.

291.155 A Contingent Fee charged directly or indirectly, for example through an intermediary, by a Firm in respect of an Assurance Engagement creates a self-interest threat that is so significant that no safeguards could reduce the threat to an Acceptable Level. Accordingly, a Firm shall not enter into any such fee arrangement.

291.156 A Contingent Fee charged directly or indirectly, for example through an intermediary, by a Firm in respect of a non-assurance service provided to an Assurance Client may also create a self-interest threat. If the outcome of the non-assurance service, and therefore, the amount of the fee, is dependent on a future or contemporary judgment related to a matter that is material to the subject matter information of the Assurance Engagement, no safeguards could reduce the threat to an Acceptable Level. Accordingly, such arrangements shall not be accepted.

291.157 For other Contingent Fee arrangements charged by a Firm for a non-assurance service to an Assurance Client, the existence and significance of any threats will depend on factors such as:

- The range of possible fee amounts;
- Whether an appropriate authority determines the outcome of the matter upon which the Contingent Fee will be determined;
- The nature of the service; and
- The effect of the event or transaction on the subject matter information.

The significance of any threats shall be evaluated and safeguards applied when necessary to eliminate the threats or reduce them to an Acceptable Level. Examples of such safeguards include:

- Having a Member review the relevant assurance work or otherwise advise as necessary; or
- Using professionals who are not members of the Assurance Team to perform the non-assurance service.

Gifts and Hospitality

291.158 Accepting gifts or hospitality from an Assurance Client may create self-interest and familiarity threats. If a Firm or a member of the Assurance Team accepts gifts or hospitality, unless the value is trivial and inconsequential, the threats created would be so significant that no safeguards could reduce the threats to an Acceptable Level. Consequently, a Firm or a member of the Assurance Team shall not accept such gifts or hospitality.

Actual or Threatened Litigation

291.159 When litigation takes place, or appears likely, between the Firm or a member of the Assurance Team and the Assurance Client, self-interest and intimidation threats are created. The relationship between client management and the members of the Assurance Team must be characterised by complete candour and full disclosure regarding all aspects of a client's business operations. When the Firm and the client's management are placed in adversarial positions by actual or threatened litigation, affecting management's willingness to make complete disclosures self-interest and intimidation threats are created. The significance of the threats created will depend on such factors as:

- The materiality of the litigation; and
- Whether the litigation relates to a prior Assurance Engagement.

The significance of the threats shall be evaluated and safeguards applied when necessary to eliminate the threats or reduce them to an Acceptable Level. Examples of such safeguards include:

- If the litigation involves a member of the Assurance Team, removing that individual from the Assurance Team; or
- Having a professional review the work performed.

If such safeguards do not reduce the threats to an Acceptable Level, the only appropriate action is to withdraw from, or decline, the Assurance Engagement.

Interpretation 2005-01 (Revised July 2009 to conform to changes resulting from the IESBA's project to improve the clarity of the Code)

Application of Section 291 to Assurance Engagements that are not Financial Statement Audit Engagements

This interpretation provides guidance on the application of the Independence requirements contained in Section 291 to Assurance Engagements that are not Financial Statement Audit Engagements.

This interpretation focuses on the application issues that are particular to Assurance Engagements that are not Financial Statement Audit Engagements. There are other matters noted in Section 291 that are relevant in the consideration of Independence requirements for all Assurance Engagements. For example, paragraph 291.3 states that an evaluation shall be made of any threats the Firm has reason to believe are created by a Network Firm's interests and relationships. It also states that when the Assurance Team has reason to believe that a Related Entity of such an Assurance Client is relevant to the evaluation of the Firm's Independence of the client, the Assurance Team shall include the Related Entity when evaluating threats to Independence and when necessary applying safeguards. These matters are not specifically addressed in this interpretation.

As explained in the International Framework for Assurance Engagements issued by the International Auditing and Assurance Standards Board, in an Assurance Engagement, the Member in Public Practice expresses a conclusion designed to enhance the degree of confidence of the intended users other than the responsible party about the outcome of the evaluation or measurement of a subject matter against criteria.

Assertion-based Assurance Engagements

In an assertion-based Assurance Engagement, the evaluation or measurement of the subject matter is performed by the responsible party, and the subject matter information is in the form of an assertion by the responsible party that is made available to the intended users.

In an assertion-based Assurance Engagement Independence is required from the responsible party, which is responsible for the subject matter information and may be responsible for the subject matter.

In those assertion-based Assurance Engagements where the responsible party is responsible for the subject matter information but not the subject matter, Independence is required from the responsible party. In addition, an evaluation shall be made of any threats the Firm has reason to believe are created by interests and relationships between a member of the Assurance Team, the Firm, a Network Firm and the party responsible for the subject matter.

Direct reporting Assurance Engagements

In a direct reporting Assurance Engagement, the Member in Public Practice either directly performs the evaluation or measurement of the subject matter, or obtains a representation from the responsible party that has performed the evaluation or measurement that is not available to the intended users. The subject matter information is provided to the intended users in the assurance report.

In a direct reporting Assurance Engagement Independence is required from the responsible party, which is responsible for the subject matter.

Multiple Responsible Parties

In both assertion-based Assurance Engagements and direct reporting Assurance Engagements there may be several responsible parties. For example, a public accountant in Public Practice may be asked to provide assurance on the monthly circulation statistics of a number of independently owned newspapers. The assignment could be an assertion based Assurance Engagement where each newspaper measures its circulation and the statistics are presented in an assertion that is available to the intended users. Alternatively, the assignment could be a direct reporting Assurance Engagement, where there is no assertion and there may or may not be a written representation from the newspapers.

In such engagements, when determining whether it is necessary to apply the provisions in Section 291 to each responsible party, the Firm may take into account whether an interest or relationship between the Firm, or a member of the Assurance Team, and a particular responsible party would create a threat to Independence that is not trivial and inconsequential in the context of the subject matter information. This will take into account:

•   The materiality of the subject matter information (or the subject matter) for which the particular responsible party is responsible; and

•   The degree of public interest that is associated with the engagement.

If the Firm determines that the threat to Independence created by any such relationships with a particular responsible party would be trivial and inconsequential it may not be necessary to apply all of the provisions of this section to that responsible party.

Example

The following example has been developed to demonstrate the application of Section 291. It is assumed that the client is not also a Financial Statement Audit Client of the Firm, or a Network Firm.

A Firm is engaged to provide assurance on the total proven oil reserves of 10 independent companies. Each company has conducted geographical and engineering surveys to determine their reserves (subject matter). There are established criteria to determine when a reserve may be considered to be proven which the Member in Public Practice determines to be suitable criteria for the engagement.

The proven reserves for each company as at December 31, 20X0 were as follows:

	Proven oil reserves thousands of barrels
Company 1	5,200
Company 2	725
Company 3	3,260
Company 4	15,000
Company 5	6,700
Company 6	39,126
Company 7	345
Company 8	175
Company 9	24,135
Company 10	9,635
Total	**104,301**

The engagement could be structured in differing ways:

Assertion-based engagements

A1   Each company measures its reserves and provides an assertion to the Firm and to intended users.

A2   An entity other than the companies measures the reserves and provides an assertion to the Firm and to intended users.

Direct reporting engagements

D1   Each company measures the reserves and provides the Firm with a written representation that measures its reserves against the established criteria for measuring proven reserves. The representation is not available to the intended users.

D2   The Firm directly measures the reserves of some of the companies.

Application of Approach

A1   Each company measures its reserves and provides an assertion to the Firm and to intended users.

There are several responsible parties in this engagement (companies 1-10). When determining whether it is necessary to apply the Independence provisions to all of the companies, the Firm may take into account whether an interest or relationship with a particular company would create a threat to Independence that is not at an Acceptable Level. This will take into account factors such as:

- The materiality of the company's proven reserves in relation to the total reserves to be reported on; and
- The degree of public interest associated with the engagement. (Paragraph 291.28.)

For example Company 8 accounts for 0.17% of the total reserves, therefore a business relationship or interest with Company 8 would create less of a threat than a similar relationship with Company 6, which accounts for approximately 37.5% of the reserves.

Having determined those companies to which the Independence requirements apply, the Assurance Team and the Firm are required to be independent of those responsible parties that would be considered to be the Assurance Client (paragraph 291.28).

A2   An entity other than the companies measures the reserves and provides an assertion to the Firm and to intended users.

The Firm shall be independent of the entity that measures the reserves and provides an assertion to the Firm and to intended users (paragraph 291.19). That entity is not responsible for the subject matter and so an evaluation shall be made of any threats the Firm has reason to believe are created by interests/relationships with the party responsible for the subject matter (paragraph 291.19). There are several parties responsible for the subject matter in this engagement (Companies 1-10). As discussed in example A1 above, the Firm may take into account whether an interest or relationship with a particular company would create a threat to Independence that is not at an Acceptable Level.

D1   Each company provides the Firm with a representation that measures its reserves against the established criteria for measuring proven reserves. The representation is not available to the intended users.

There are several responsible parties in this engagement (Companies 1-10). When determining whether it is necessary to apply the Independence provisions to all of the companies, the Firm may take into account whether an interest or relationship with a particular company would create a threat to Independence that is not at an Acceptable Level. This will take into account factors such as:

- The materiality of the company's proven reserves in relation to the total reserves to be reported on; and
- The degree of public interest associated with the engagement. (Paragraph 291.28.)

For example, Company 8 accounts for 0.17% of the reserves, therefore a business relationship or interest with Company 8 would create less of a threat than a similar relationship with Company 6 that accounts for approximately 37.5% of the reserves.

Having determined those companies to which the Independence requirements apply, the Assurance Team and the Firm shall be independent of those responsible parties that would be considered to be the Assurance Client (paragraph 291.28).

D2   The Firm directly measures the reserves of some of the companies.

The application is the same as in example D1.

Part C—Members in Business

Section 300 Introduction

Section 310 Potential Conflicts

Section 320 Preparation and Reporting of Information

Section 330 Acting with Sufficient Expertise

Section 340 Financial Interests

Section 350 Inducements

SECTION 300

Introduction

300.1   This Part of the Code describes how the conceptual framework contained in Part A applies in certain situations to Members in Business. This Part does not describe all of the circumstances and relationships that could be encountered by a Member in Business that create or may create threats to compliance with the fundamental principles. Therefore, the Member in Business is encouraged to be alert for such circumstances and relationships.

300.2   Investors, creditors, employers and other sectors of the business community, as well as governments and the public at large, all may rely on the work of Members in Business. Members in Business may be solely or jointly responsible for the preparation and reporting of financial and other information, which both their employing organisations and third parties may rely on. They may also be responsible for providing effective financial management and competent advice on a variety of business-related matters.

300.3   A Member in Business may be a salaried employee, a partner, Director (whether executive or non-executive), an owner manager, a volunteer or another working for one or more employing organisation. The legal form of the relationship with the employing organisation, if any, has no bearing on the ethical responsibilities incumbent on the Member in Business.

300.4   A Member in Business has a responsibility to further the legitimate aims of the Member's employing organisation. This Code does not seek to hinder a Member in Business from properly fulfilling that responsibility, but addresses circumstances in which compliance with the fundamental principles may be compromised.

300.5   A Member in Business may hold a senior position within an organisation. The more senior the position, the greater will be the ability and opportunity to influence events, practices and attitudes. A Member in Business is expected, therefore, to encourage an ethics-based culture in an employing organisation that emphasises the importance that senior management places on ethical behaviour.

300.6   A Member in Business shall not knowingly engage in any business, occupation, or activity that impairs or might impair integrity, objectivity or the good reputation of the profession and as a result would be incompatible with the fundamental principles.

300.7   Compliance with the fundamental principles may potentially be threatened by a broad range of circumstances and relationships. Threats fall into one or more of the following categories:

(a) Self-interest;

(b) Self-review;

(c) Advocacy;

(d) Familiarity; and

(e) Intimidation.

These threats are discussed further in Part A of this Code.

300.8 Examples of circumstances that may create self-interest threats for a Member in Business include:

- Holding a Financial Interest in, or receiving a loan or guarantee from the employing organisation.

- Participating in incentive compensation arrangements offered by the employing organisation.

- Inappropriate personal use of corporate assets.

- Concern over employment security.

- Commercial pressure from outside the employing organisation.

300.9 An example of a circumstance that creates a self-review threat for a Member in Business is determining the appropriate accounting treatment for a business combination after performing the feasibility study that supported the acquisition decision.

300.10 When furthering the legitimate goals and objectives of their employing organisations, Members in Business may promote the organisation's position, provided any statements made are neither false nor misleading. Such actions generally would not create an advocacy threat.

300.11 Examples of circumstances that may create familiarity threats for a Member in Business include:

- Being responsible for the employing organisation's financial reporting when an Immediate or Close Family member employed by the entity makes decisions that affect the entity's financial reporting.

- Long association with business contacts influencing business decisions.

- Accepting a gift or preferential treatment, unless the value is trivial and inconsequential.

300.12 Examples of circumstances that may create intimidation threats for a Member in Business include:

- Threat of dismissal or replacement of the Member in Business or a Close or Immediate Family member over a disagreement about the application of an accounting principle or the way in which financial information is to be reported.

- A dominant personality attempting to influence the decision making process, for example with regard to the awarding of contracts or the application of an accounting principle.

300.13 Safeguards that may eliminate or reduce threats to an Acceptable Level fall into two broad categories:

(a) Safeguards created by the profession, legislation or regulation; and

(b) Safeguards in the work environment.

Examples of safeguards created by the profession, legislation or regulation are detailed in paragraph 100.14 of Part A of this Code.

300.14 Safeguards in the work environment include:

- The employing organisation's systems of corporate oversight or other oversight structures.

- The employing organisation's ethics and conduct programs.

- Recruitment procedures in the employing organisation emphasising the importance of employing high calibre competent staff.

- Strong internal controls.

- Appropriate disciplinary processes.

- Leadership that stresses the importance of ethical behaviour and the expectation that employees will act in an ethical manner.

- Policies and procedures to implement and monitor the quality of employee performance.

- Timely communication of the employing organisation's policies and procedures, including any changes to them, to all employees and appropriate training and education on such policies and procedures.

- Policies and procedures to empower and encourage employees to communicate to senior levels within the employing organisation any ethical issues that concern them without fear of retribution.

- Consultation with another appropriate Member.

300.15 In circumstances where a Member in Business believes that unethical behaviour or actions by others will continue to occur within the employing organisation, the Member in Business may consider obtaining legal advice. In those extreme situations where all available safeguards have been exhausted and it is not possible to reduce the threat to an Acceptable Level, a Member in Business may conclude that it is appropriate to resign from the employing organisation.

SECTION 310
Potential Conflicts

310.1 A Member in Business shall comply with the fundamental principles. There may be times, however, when a Member's responsibilities to an employing organisation and professional obligations to comply with the fundamental principles are in conflict. A Member in Business is expected to support the legitimate and ethical objectives established by the employer and the rules and procedures drawn up in support of those objectives. Nevertheless, where a relationship or circumstance creates a threat to compliance with the fundamental principles, a Member in Business shall apply the conceptual framework approach described in Section 100 to determine a response to the threat.

310.2 As a consequence of responsibilities to an employing organisation, a Member in Business may be under pressure to act or behave in ways that could create threats to compliance with the fundamental principles. Such pressure may be explicit or implicit; it may come from a supervisor, manager, Director or another individual within the employing organisation. A Member in Business may face pressure to:

- Act contrary to law or regulation.

- Act contrary to technical or professional standards.

- Facilitate unethical or illegal earnings management strategies.

- Lie to others, or otherwise intentionally mislead (including misleading by remaining silent) others, in particular:

  ◦ The auditors of the employing organisation; or

  ◦ Regulators.

- Issue, or otherwise be associated with, a financial or non-financial report that materially misrepresents the facts, including statements in connection with, for example:

  ◦ The Financial Statements;

  ◦ Tax compliance;

  ◦ Legal compliance; or

  ◦ Reports required by securities regulators.

310.3   The significance of any threats arising from such pressures, such as intimidation threats, shall be evaluated and safeguards applied when necessary to eliminate them or reduce them to an Acceptable Level. Examples of such safeguards include:

- Obtaining advice, where appropriate, from within the employing organisation, an independent professional advisor or a relevant professional body.

- Using a formal dispute resolution process within the employing organisation.

- Seeking legal advice.

SECTION 320
Preparation and Reporting of Information

320.1   Members in Business are often involved in the preparation and reporting of information that may either be made public or used by others inside or outside the employing organisation. Such information may include financial or management information, for example, forecasts and budgets, Financial Statements, management's discussion and analysis, and the management letter of representation provided to the auditors during the audit of the entity's Financial Statements. A Member in Business shall prepare or present such information fairly, honestly and in accordance with relevant professional standards so that the information will be understood in its context.

320.2   A Member in Business who has responsibility for the preparation or approval of the general purpose Financial Statements of an employing organisation shall be satisfied that those Financial Statements are presented in accordance with the applicable financial reporting standards.

AUST320.2.1   Where a Member in Business referred to in paragraph 320.2 is not satisfied that the Financial Statements of an employing organisation are presented in accordance with applicable Australian Accounting Standards, the Member shall:

(a)   in all cases, notify Those Charged with Governance and document the communication; and

(b)   qualify any declarations given by the Member in compliance with legislative and regulatory requirements or the organisation's reporting requirements.

320.3   A Member in Business shall take reasonable steps to maintain information for which the Member in Business is responsible in a manner that:

(a)   Describes clearly the true nature of business transactions, assets, or liabilities;

(b)   Classifies and records information in a timely and proper manner; and

(c)   Represents the facts accurately and completely in all material respects.

320.4   Threats to compliance with the fundamental principles, for example, self-interest or intimidation threats to objectivity or professional competence and due care, are created where a Member in Business is pressured (either externally or by the possibility of personal gain) to become associated with misleading information or to become associated with misleading information through the actions of others.

320.5   The significance of such threats will depend on factors such as the source of the pressure and the degree to which the information is, or may be, misleading. The significance of the threats shall be evaluated and safeguards applied when necessary to eliminate them or reduce them to an Acceptable Level. Such safeguards include consultation with superiors within the employing organisation, the audit committee or Those Charged with Governance of the organisation, or with a relevant professional body.

320.6   Where it is not possible to reduce the threat to an Acceptable Level, a Member in Business shall refuse to be or remain associated with information the Member determines is misleading. A Member in Business may have been unknowingly associated with misleading information. Upon becoming aware of this, the Member in Business shall take steps to be disassociated from that information. In determining whether there is a requirement to report, the Member in Business may consider obtaining legal advice. In addition, the Member may consider whether to resign.

SECTION 330
Acting with Sufficient Expertise

330.1   The fundamental principle of professional competence and due care requires that a Member in Business only undertake significant tasks for which the Member in Business has, or can obtain, sufficient specific training or experience. A Member in Business shall not intentionally mislead an employer as to the level of expertise or experience possessed, nor shall a Member in Business fail to seek appropriate expert advice and assistance when required.

330.2   Circumstances that create a threat to a Member in Business performing duties with the appropriate degree of professional competence and due care include having:

- Insufficient time for properly performing or completing the relevant duties.
- Incomplete, restricted or otherwise inadequate information for performing the duties properly.
- Insufficient experience, training and/or education.
- Inadequate resources for the proper performance of the duties.

330.3   The significance of the threat will depend on factors such as the extent to which the Member in Business is working with others, relative seniority in the business, and the level of supervision and review applied to the work. The significance of the threat shall be evaluated and safeguards applied when necessary to eliminate the threat or reduce it to an Acceptable Level. Examples of such safeguards include:

- Obtaining additional advice or training.
- Ensuring that there is adequate time available for performing the relevant duties.
- Obtaining assistance from someone with the necessary expertise.
- Consulting, where appropriate, with:
  - Superiors within the employing organisation;
  - Independent experts; or
  - A relevant professional body.

330.4   When threats cannot be eliminated or reduced to an Acceptable Level, Members in Business shall determine whether to refuse to perform the duties in question. If the Member in Business determines that refusal is appropriate, the reasons for doing so shall be clearly communicated.

SECTION 340
Financial Interests

340.1   Members in Business may have Financial Interests, or may know of Financial Interests of Immediate or Close Family members, that, in certain circumstances, may create threats to compliance with the fundamental principles. For example, self-interest threats to objectivity or confidentiality may be created through the existence of the motive and opportunity to manipulate price sensitive information in order to gain financially. Examples of circumstances that may create self-interest threats include situations where the Member in Business or an Immediate or Close Family member:

- Holds a Direct or Indirect Financial Interest in the employing organisation and the value of that Financial Interest could be directly affected by decisions made by the Member in Business;
- Is eligible for a profit related bonus and the value of that bonus could be directly affected by decisions made by the Member in Business;
- Holds, directly or indirectly, share options in the employing organisation, the value of which could be directly affected by decisions made by the Member in Business;

- Holds, directly or indirectly, share options in the employing organisation which are, or will soon be, eligible for conversion; or

- May qualify for share options in the employing organisation or performance related bonuses if certain targets are achieved.

340.2 The significance of any threat shall be evaluated and safeguards applied when necessary to eliminate the threat or reduce it to an Acceptable Level. In evaluating the significance of any threat, and, when necessary, determining the appropriate safeguards to be applied to eliminate the threat or reduce it to an Acceptable Level, a Member in Business shall evaluate the nature of the Financial Interest. This includes evaluating the significance of the Financial Interest and determining whether it is Direct or Indirect. What constitutes a significant or valuable stake in an organisation will vary from individual to individual, depending on personal circumstances. Examples of such safeguards include:

- Policies and procedures for a committee independent of management to determine the level or form of remuneration of senior management.

- Disclosure of all relevant interests, and of any plans to trade in relevant shares to Those Charged with Governance of the employing organisation, in accordance with any internal policies.

- Consultation, where appropriate, with superiors within the employing organisation.

- Consultation, where appropriate, with Those Charged with Governance of the employing organisation or relevant professional bodies.

- Internal and external audit procedures.

- Up-to-date education on ethical issues and on the legal restrictions and other regulations around potential insider trading.

340.3 A Member in Business shall neither manipulate information nor use confidential information for personal gain.

SECTION 350

Inducements

Receiving Offers

350.1 A Member in Business or an Immediate or Close Family member may be offered an inducement. Inducements may take various forms, including gifts, hospitality, preferential treatment, and inappropriate appeals to friendship or loyalty.

350.2 Offers of inducements may create threats to compliance with the fundamental principles. When a Member in Business or an Immediate or Close Family member is offered an inducement, the situation shall be evaluated. Self-interest threats to objectivity or confidentiality are created when an inducement is made in an attempt to unduly influence actions or decisions, encourage illegal or dishonest behaviour, or obtain confidential information. Intimidation threats to objectivity or confidentiality are created if such an inducement is accepted and it is followed by threats to make that offer public and damage the reputation of either the Member in Business or an Immediate or Close Family member.

350.3 The existence and significance of any threats will depend on the nature, value and intent behind the offer. If a reasonable and informed third party, weighing all the specific facts and circumstances, would consider the inducement insignificant and not intended to encourage unethical behaviour, then a Member in Business may conclude that the offer is made in the normal course of business and may generally conclude that there is no significant threat to compliance with the fundamental principles.

350.4 The significance of any threats shall be evaluated and safeguards applied when necessary to eliminate them or reduce them to an Acceptable Level. When the threats cannot be eliminated or reduced to an Acceptable Level through the application of safeguards, a Member in Business shall not accept the inducement.

As the real or apparent threats to compliance with the fundamental principles do not merely arise from acceptance of an inducement but, sometimes, merely from the fact of the offer having been made, additional safeguards shall be adopted. A Member in Business shall evaluate any threats created by such offers and determine whether to take one or more of the following actions:

(a) Informing higher levels of management or Those Charged with Governance of the employing organisation immediately when such offers have been made;

(b) Informing third parties of the offer – for example, a professional body or the employer of the individual who made the offer; a Member in Business may however, consider seeking legal advice before taking such a step; and

(c) Advising Immediate or Close Family members of relevant threats and safeguards where they are potentially in positions that might result in offers of inducements, for example, as a result of their employment situation; and

(d) Informing higher levels of management or Those Charged with Governance of the employing organisation where Immediate or Close Family members are employed by competitors or potential suppliers of that organisation.

Making Offers

350.5   A Member in Business may be in a situation where the Member in Business is expected, or is under other pressure, to offer inducements to influence the judgment or decision-making process of an individual or organisation, or obtain confidential information.

350.6   Such pressure may come from within the employing organisation, for example, from a colleague or superior. It may also come from an external individual or organisation suggesting actions or business decisions that would be advantageous to the employing organisation, possibly influencing the Member in Business improperly.

350.7   A Member in Business shall not offer an inducement to improperly influence professional judgment of a third party.

350.8   Where the pressure to offer an unethical inducement comes from within the employing organisation, the Member shall follow the principles and guidance regarding ethical conflict resolution set out in Part A of this Code.

Transitional Provisions

The Code is subject to the following transitional provisions:

Public Interest Entities

1.   Section 290 of the Code contains additional Independence provisions when the Audit or Review Client is a Public Interest Entity. The additional provisions that are applicable because of the new definition of a Public Interest Entity and the requirements in paragraph 290.26 are effective on January 1, 2013. For partner rotation requirements, the transitional provisions contained in paragraphs 2 and 3 below apply.

Partner Rotation

2.   For a partner who is subject to the rotation provisions in paragraph 290.151 because the partner meets the definition of the new term "Key Audit Partner," and the partner is neither the Engagement Partner nor the individual responsible for the Engagement Quality Control Review, the rotation provisions are effective for the Audits or Reviews of Financial Statements for years beginning on or after January 1, 2013. For example, in the case of an Audit Client with a calendar year-end, a Key Audit Partner, who is neither the Engagement Partner nor the individual responsible for the Engagement Quality Control Review, who had served as a Key Audit Partner for seven or more years (i.e., the audits of 2005 – 2011), would be required to rotate after serving for one more year as a Key Audit Partner (i.e., after completing the 2012 audit).

3.   For an Engagement Partner or an individual responsible for the Engagement Quality Control Review who immediately prior to assuming either of these roles served in another Key Audit Partner role for the client, and who, at the beginning of the

first fiscal year beginning on or after January 1, 2012, had served as the Engagement Partner or individual responsible for the Engagement Quality Control Review for six or fewer years, the rotation provisions are effective for the audits or reviews of Financial Statements for years beginning on or after January 1, 2013. For example, in the case of an Audit Client with a calendar year-end, a partner who had served the client in another Key Audit Partner role for four years (i.e., the audits of 2003-2006) and subsequently as the Engagement Partner for five years (i.e., the audits of 2007-2011) would be required to rotate after serving for one more year as the Engagement Partner (i.e., after completing the 2012 audit).

Non-assurance services

4. Paragraphs 290.156-290.219 address the provision of non-assurance services to an Audit or Review Client. If, at the effective date of the Code, services are being provided to an Audit or Review Client and the services were permissible under the June 2006 Code (revised February 2008) but are either prohibited or subject to restrictions under the revised Code, the Firm may continue providing such services only if they were contracted for and commenced prior to July 1, 2012, and are completed before January 1, 2013.

Fees – Relative Size

5. Paragraph 290.222 provides that, in respect of an Audit or Review Client that is a Public Interest Entity, when the total fees from that client and its related entities (subject to the considerations in paragraph 290.27) for two consecutive years represent more than 15% of the total fees of the Firm expressing the opinion on the Financial Statements, a pre- or post-issuance review (as described in paragraph 290.222) of the second year's audit shall be performed. This requirement is effective for Audits or Reviews of Financial Statements covering years that begin on or after January 1, 2012. For example, in the case of an Audit Client with a calendar year end, if the total fees from the client exceeded the 15% threshold for 2012 and 2013, the pre- or post-issuance review would be applied with respect to the audit of the 2013 Financial Statements.

Compensation and Evaluation Policies

6. Paragraph 290.229 provides that a Key Audit Partner shall not be evaluated or compensated based on that partner's success in selling non-assurance services to the partner's Audit Client. This requirement is effective on January 1, 2013. A Key Audit Partner may, however, receive compensation after January 1, 2013 based on an evaluation made prior to January 1, 2013 of that partner's success in selling non-assurance services to the Audit Client.

Conformity With International Pronouncements

APES 110 and the IESBA Code

APES 110 incorporates the *Code of Ethics for Professional Accountants* (IESBA Code) issued by the International Ethics Standards Board for Accountants (IESBA) in July 2009.

Compliance with the IESBA Code

The principles and requirements of APES 110 and the IESBA Code are consistent except for the following:

- The addition of a Scope and Application section in APES 110;

- The addition of paragraphs and definitions prefixed as AUST in APES 110. The additional definitions are of AASB, Administration, AuASB, AUASB, Auditing and Assurance Standards, Australian Accounting Standards and Member;

- APES 110 generally refers to Members whereas the IESBA Code refers to professional accountants;

- Defined terms are in title case in APES 110;

- APES 110 tailors the following IESBA defined terms to the Australian environment: Audit Engagement, Engagement Team, Financial Statements, Firm, Member in Public Practice, and Review Engagement;

- Paragraph 290.25 of APES 110 expresses Public Interest Entity in the singular form consistent with its definition in section 2;

- Paragraph 290.26 in APES 110 mandates Firms to determine whether additional entities are Public Interest Entities and the reference to member bodies has been removed ; and

- Unless strict requirements are met, APES 110 prohibits Members in Public Practice from providing accounting and bookkeeping services and preparing tax calculations for Audit Clients which are Public Interest Entities, even in emergency situations (refer paragraphs 290.172 – 290.173 and 290.185).

❖ ❖ ❖

Amendment to the Definition of Public Interest Entity in APES 110 *Code of Ethics for Professional Accountants*

(December 2011)

Contents

Sections

Definitions 2

Independence – Audit and Review Engagements 290

Transitional Provisions

Conformity with International Pronouncements

Section 2 Definitions

Public Interest Entity means:

(a)   A Listed Entity; or

(b)   An entity (a) defined by regulation or legislation as a public interest entity or (b) for which the audit is required by regulation or legislation to be conducted in compliance with the same Independence requirements that apply to the audit of Listed Entities. Such regulation may be promulgated by any relevant regulator, including an audit regulator.

Section 290 Independence – Audit and Review Engagements

[Paragraphs 290.1 – 290.24 of extant Section 290 remain unchanged.]

Public Interest Entities

290.25   Section 290 contains additional provisions that reflect the extent of public interest in certain entities. For the purpose of this section, a Public Interest Entity is:

(a)   A Listed Entity*; or

(b)   An entity (a) defined by regulation or legislation as a public interest entity; or (b) for which the audit is required by regulation or legislation to be conducted in compliance with the same Independence requirements that apply to the audit of Listed Entities. Such regulation may be promulgated by any relevant regulator, including an audit regulator.

290.26   Firms shall determine whether to treat additional entities, or certain categories of entities, as Public Interest Entities because they have a large number and wide range of stakeholders. Factors to be considered include:

- The nature of the business, such as the holding of assets in a fiduciary capacity for a large number of stakeholders. Examples may include financial institutions, such as banks and insurance companies and pension funds;

- Size; and

- Number of employees.

* *Includes a listed entity as defined in Section 9 of the Corporations Act 2001.*

AUST 290.26.1 The following entities in Australia will generally satisfy the conditions in paragraph 290.26 as having a large number and wide range of stakeholders and thus are likely to be classified as Public Interest Entities. In each instance Firms shall consider the nature of the business, its size and the number of its employees:

- Authorised deposit-taking institutions (ADIs) and authorised non-operating holding companies (NOHCs) regulated by the Australian Prudential Regulatory Authority (APRA) under the *Banking Act 1959*;

- Authorised insurers and authorised NOHCs regulated by APRA under Section 122 of the *Insurance Act 1973*;
- Life insurance companies and registered NOHCs regulated by APRA under the *Life Insurance Act 1995*;
- Disclosing Entities as defined in Section 111AC of the *Corporations Act 2001*;
- Registrable superannuation entity (RSE) licensees, and RSEs under their trusteeship that have five or more members, regulated by APRA under the *Superannuation Industry (Supervision) Act 1993*; and
- Other issuers of debt and equity instruments to the public.

[Paragraph 290.27 – 290.514 remain unchanged.]

Effective Date:

The revisions are effective from 1 January 2013 with early adoption permitted.

Transitional Provisions

The Code is subject to the following transitional provisions:

Public Interest Entities

1. Section 290 of the Code contains additional Independence provisions when the Audit or Review Client is a Public Interest Entity. The additional provisions that are applicable because of the new definition of a Public Interest Entity and the requirements in paragraph 290.26 are effective on January 1, 2013. For partner rotation requirements, the transitional provisions contained in paragraphs 2 and 3 below apply.

Partner Rotation

2. For a partner who is subject to the rotation provisions in paragraph 290.151 because the partner meets the definition of the new term "Key Audit Partner," and the partner is neither the Engagement Partner nor the individual responsible for the Engagement Quality Control Review, the rotation provisions are effective for the Audits or Reviews of Financial Statements for years beginning on or after January 1, 2013. For example, in the case of an Audit Client with a calendar year-end, a Key Audit Partner, who is neither the Engagement Partner nor the individual responsible for the Engagement Quality Control Review, who had served as a Key Audit Partner for seven or more years (i.e., the audits of 2005 – 2011), would be required to rotate after serving for one more year as a Key Audit Partner (i.e., after completing the 2012 audit).

3. For an Engagement Partner or an individual responsible for the Engagement Quality Control Review who immediately prior to assuming either of these roles served in another Key Audit Partner role for the client, and who, at the beginning of the first fiscal year beginning on or after January 1, 2012, had served as the Engagement Partner or individual responsible for the Engagement Quality Control Review for six or fewer years, the rotation provisions are effective for the audits or reviews of Financial Statements for years beginning on or after January 1, 2013. For example, in the case of an Audit Client with a calendar year-end, a partner who had served the client in another Key Audit Partner role for four years (i.e., the audits of 2003-2006) and subsequently as the Engagement Partner for five years (i.e., the audits of 2007-2011) would be required to rotate after serving for one more year as the Engagement Partner (i.e., after completing the 2012 audit).

Non-assurance services

4. Paragraphs 290.156-290.219 address the provision of non-assurance services to an Audit or Review Client. If, at the effective date of the Code, services are being provided to an Audit or Review Client and the services were permissible under the June 2006 Code (revised February 2008) but are either prohibited or subject to restrictions under the

revised Code, the Firm may continue providing such services only if they were contracted for and commenced prior to July 1, 2012, and are completed before January 1, 2013.

Fees – Relative Size

5. Paragraph 290.222 provides that, in respect of an Audit or Review Client that is a Public Interest Entity, when the total fees from that client and its related entities (subject to the considerations in paragraph 290.27) for two consecutive years represent more than 15% of the total fees of the Firm expressing the opinion on the Financial Statements, a pre- or post-issuance review (as described in paragraph 290.222) of the second year's audit shall be performed. This requirement is effective for Audits or Reviews of Financial Statements covering years that begin on or after January 1, 2012. For example, in the case of an Audit Client with a calendar year end, if the total fees from the client exceeded the 15% threshold for 2012 and 2013, the pre- or post-issuance review would be applied with respect to the audit of the 2013 Financial Statements.

Compensation and Evaluation Policies

6. Paragraph 290.229 provides that a Key Audit Partner shall not be evaluated or compensated based on that partner's success in selling non-assurance services to the partner's Audit Client. This requirement is effective on January 1, 2013. A Key Audit Partner may, however, receive compensation after January 1, 2013 based on an evaluation made prior to January 1, 2013 of that partner's success in selling non-assurance services to the Audit Client.

Conformity With International Pronouncements

APES 110 and the IESBA Code

APES 110 incorporates the *Code of Ethics for Professional Accountants* (IESBA Code) issued by the International Ethics Standards Board for Accountants (IESBA) in July 2009.

Compliance with the IESBA Code

The principles and requirements of APES 110 and the IESBA Code are consistent except for the following:

* The addition of a Scope and Application section in APES 110;

* The addition of paragraphs and definitions prefixed as AUST in APES 110. The additional definitions are of AASB, Administration, AuASB, AUASB, Auditing and Assurance Standards, Australian Accounting Standards and Member;

* APES 110 generally refers to Members whereas the IESBA Code refers to professional accountants;

* Defined terms are in title case in APES 110;

* APES 110 tailors the following IESBA defined terms to the Australian environment: Audit Engagement, Engagement Team, Financial Statements, Firm, Member in Public Practice, and Review Engagement;

* Paragraph 290.25 of APES 110 expresses Public Interest Entity in the singular form consistent with its definition in section 2;

* Paragraph 290.26 in APES 110 mandates Firms to determine whether additional entities are Public Interest Entities and the reference to Member Bodies has been removed; and

* Unless strict requirements are met, APES 110 prohibits Members in Public Practice from providing accounting and bookkeeping services and preparing tax calculations for Audit Clients which are Public Interest Entities, even in emergency situations (refer paragraphs 290.172 – 290.173 and 290.185).

APES 205

Conformity with Accounting Standards

(Issued December 2007)

Issued by the Accounting Professional and Ethical Standards Board.

Note from the Institute of Chartered Accountants Australia

This note, prepared by the technical editor, is not part of APES 205.

Historical development

December 2007: APES 205 issued. It replaces Miscellaneous Professional Statement APS 1 and has been updated to reflect professional accountant responsibilities with respect to the preparation of general and special purpose financial statements under the current Australian financial reporting framework. It is operative from 1 July 2008.

Contents

Section

Scope and application 1

Definitions 2

Fundamental responsibilities of Members 3
- Public interest
- Professional competence and due care

Responsibilities of Members in respect of the Reporting Entity concept 4

Responsibilities of Members in respect of General Purpose Financial Statements 5

Responsibilities of Members in respect of Special Purpose Financial Statements 6

Conformity with International Pronouncements

1. Scope and application

1.1   Accounting Professional & Ethical Standards Board Limited (APESB) issues professional standard APES 205 *Conformity with Accounting Standards* (**the Standard**), which is effective from 01 July 2008.

1.2   APES 205 sets the standards for Members involved with the preparation, presentation, audit, review or compilation of Financial Statements, which are either General Purpose Financial Statements or Special Purpose Financial Statements, of entities in the private and public sectors. The mandatory requirements of this Standard are in **bold** type, preceded or followed by discussion or explanations in grey type. APES 205 should be read in conjunction with other professional duties of Members, and any legal obligations that may apply.

1.3   **Members in Australia shall follow the mandatory requirements of APES 205 when they prepare, present, audit, review or compile Financial Statements.**

1.4   **Members outside Australia shall comply with the financial reporting framework applicable to the relevant jurisdiction when they prepare, present, audit, review or compile Financial Statements. However, where the Financial Statements are prepared in accordance with the Australian Financial Reporting Framework, Members shall comply with the requirements of this Standard.**

1.5   **Members shall be familiar with relevant professional standards and guidance notes when performing professional work. All Members shall comply with the fundamental principles outlined in the Code.**

1.6   The Standard does not detract from any responsibilities which may be imposed by law.

1.7   All references to accounting, auditing and professional standards are references to those provisions as amended from time to time.

1.8   In applying the requirements outlined in APES 205, Members should be guided not merely by the words but also by the spirit of the Standard and the Code.

2. Definitions

For the purpose of this Standard:

AASB means the Australian statutory body called the Australian Accounting Standards Board that was established under section 226 of the *Australian Securities and Investments Commission Act 1989* and is continued in existence by section 261 of the *Australian Securities and Investments Commission Act 2001*.

Applicable Financial Reporting Framework means the financial reporting framework adopted by those charged with governance in preparing the Financial Statements.

Assurance Engagement means an Engagement in which a conclusion is expressed by a Member in Public Practice designed to enhance the degree of confidence of the intended users other than the responsible party about the outcome of the evaluation or measurement of a subject matter against criteria.

This would include an Engagement in accordance with *Framework for Assurance Engagements* issued by the Auditing and Assurance Standards Board (AUASB) or in accordance with specific relevant standards for Assurance Engagements.

AUASB means the Australian statutory body called the Auditing and Assurance Standards Board established under section 227A of the *Australian Securities and Investments Commission Act 2001*.

Audit Engagement means an Assurance Engagement to provide a reasonable level of assurance that a financial report is free of material misstatement, such as an Engagement in accordance with Australian auditing standards. This includes a statutory audit which is an audit required by legislation or other regulation, and other audits conducted for the purposes of the Corporations Act.

Australian Accounting Standards means the Accounting Standards (including Australian Accounting Interpretations) promulgated by the AASB.

Australian Financial Reporting Framework means the framework that uses Australian Accounting Standards as the Applicable Financial Reporting Framework and is adopted by those charged with governance when preparing Financial Statements.

Client means an individual, firm, entity or organisation to whom or to which Professional Services are provided by a Member in Public Practice in respect of Engagements of either a recurring or demand nature.

Code means APES 110 *Code of Ethics for Professional Accountants.*

Engagement means an agreement, whether written or otherwise, between a Member in Public Practice and a Client relating to the provision of services by a Member in Public Practice. However, consultations with a prospective Client prior to such agreement are not part of an Engagement.

Financial Statements means a structured representation of historical financial information, which ordinarily includes explanatory notes, intended to communicate an entity's economic resources or obligations at a point in time or the changes therein for a period of time in accordance with a financial reporting framework. The term can refer to a complete set of Financial Statements, but it can also refer to a single financial statement, for example, a balance sheet, or a statement of revenues and expenses, and related explanatory notes. The requirements of the financial reporting framework determine the form and content of the Financial Statements and what constitutes a complete set of Financial Statements.

For the purposes of this Standard financial report is considered to be an equivalent term to financial statements.

Firm means   (a)   A sole practitioner, partnership, corporation or other entity of professional accountants;

                      (b)   An entity that controls such parties;

                      (c)   An entity controlled by such parties; or

                      (d)   An Auditor-General's office or department.

Framework means the *Framework for the preparation and presentation of financial statements* issued by the AASB.

General Purpose Financial Statements means those intended to meet the needs of users who are not in a position to require an entity to prepare reports tailored to their particular information needs.

Member means a member of a professional body that has adopted this Standard as applicable to their membership as defined by that professional body.

Member in Public Practice means a Member, irrespective of functional classification (e.g. audit, tax, or consulting) in a Firm that provides Professional Services. The term is also used to refer to a Firm of Members in Public Practice and means a practice entity as defined by the applicable professional body.

Professional Bodies means the Institute of Chartered Accountants in Australia, CPA Australia and the National Institute of Accountants.

Professional Services means services requiring accountancy or related skills performed by a professional accountant including accounting, auditing, taxation, management consulting and financial management services.

Professional Standards mean all standards issued by Accounting Professional & Ethical Standards Board Limited and all professional and ethical requirements of the applicable Professional Body.

Reporting Entity means an entity in respect of which it is reasonable to expect the existence of users who rely on the entity's General Purpose Financial Report for information that will be useful to them for making and evaluating decisions about the allocation of resources. A Reporting Entity can be a single entity or a group comprising a parent entity and all the entities it controls.

Review Engagement means an Assurance Engagement to express a conclusion on whether, on the basis of the procedures which do not provide all the evidence that would be required in an audit, anything has come to the attention of the Member in Public Practice that causes the Member to believe that the historical financial information is not prepared in all material respects in accordance with an Applicable Financial Reporting Framework, which is an Engagement conducted in accordance with applicable assurance standards on Review Engagements.

Special Purpose Financial Statements means financial statements other than General Purpose Financial Statements.

Statements of Accounting Concepts mean SAC 1 *Definition of Reporting Entity* and *SAC 2 Objective of General Purpose Financial Reporting* issued by the AASB.

3. Fundamental responsibilities of Members

Public interest

3.1 **In accordance with Section 100.1 of the Code, Members shall observe and comply with their public interest obligations when they prepare, present, audit, review or compile Financial Statements.**

Professional competence and due care

3.2 **In accordance with Section 130 *Professional Competence and Due Care* of the Code, a Member in Public Practice who is performing professional work based on an Applicable Financial Reporting Framework shall ensure that the Member or the Firm has the requisite professional knowledge and skill or shall engage a suitably qualified external person. If a Member in Public Practice is unable to engage a suitably qualified person when required, the Member shall decline the Engagement.**

4. Responsibilities of Members in respect of the Reporting Entity concept

4.1 Members should take all reasonable steps to apply the principles and guidance provided in the Statements of Accounting Concepts and the Framework when assessing whether an entity is a Reporting Entity .

4.2 Statement of Accounting Concepts SAC 1 "Definition of Reporting Entity" provides guidance on circumstances in which an entity or economic entity should be identified as a Reporting Entity.

4.3 **Members who are involved in, or are responsible for, the preparation and/or presentation of Financial Statements of a Reporting Entity shall take all reasonable steps to ensure that the Reporting Entity prepares General Purpose Financial Statements.**

5. Responsibilities of Members in respect of General Purpose Financial Statements

5.1   Members shall take all reasonable steps to apply Australian Accounting Standards when they prepare and/or present General Purpose Financial Statements that purport to comply with the Australian Financial Reporting Framework.

5.2   Where Members are unable to apply Australian Accounting Standards pursuant to paragraph 5.1, they shall take all reasonable steps to ensure that any departure from Australian Accounting Standards, the reasons for such departure, and its financial effects are properly disclosed and explained in the General Purpose Financial Statements.

5.3   If legislation, ministerial directive or other government authority requires a departure from Australian Accounting Standards, a Member should disclose that fact in the General Purpose Financial Statements as a reason for the departure.

5.4   Where a Member is unable to ensure proper disclosure of a departure from Australian Accounting Standards pursuant to paragraph 5.2, the Member should discuss the matter with the appropriate level of management of the relevant entity and document the results of these discussions.

5.5   Members in Public Practice shall take all reasonable steps to ensure that Clients have complied with Australian Accounting Standards when they perform an Audit or Review Engagement or a compilation Engagement of General Purpose Financial Statements which purport to comply with the Australian Financial Reporting Framework.

5.6   Where a Member in Public Practice is unable to ensure that a Client complies with Australian Accounting Standards pursuant to paragraph 5.5, the Member shall consider Australian auditing standards applicable to Audit or Review Engagements or Professional Standards applicable to compilation Engagements.

6. Responsibilities of Members in respect of Special Purpose Financial Statements

6.1   Members who are involved in, or are responsible for, the preparation, presentation, audit, review or compilation of an entity's Special Purpose Financial Statements (except where the Special Purpose Financial Statements will be used solely for internal purposes) shall take all reasonable steps to ensure that the Special Purpose Financial Statements, and any associated audit report, review report or compilation report clearly identifies:

     (a)   that the Financial Statements are Special Purpose Financial Statements;

     (b)   the purpose for which the Special Purpose Financial Statements have been prepared; and

     (c)   the significant accounting policies adopted in the preparation and presentation of the Special Purpose Financial Statements.

6.2   Where a Member in Public Practice is unable to ensure that a Client complies with an Applicable Financial Reporting Framework pursuant to paragraph 6.1, the Member shall consider Australian auditing standards applicable to Audit or Review Engagements or Professional Standards applicable to compilation Engagements.

6.3   For all other Members, where the Member is unable to ensure that an entity complies with an Applicable Financial Reporting Framework pursuant to paragraph 6.1, the Member should discuss the matter with the appropriate level of management of the relevant entity and document the results of these discussions.

Conformity with International Pronouncements

The International Ethics Standard Board for Accountants (IESBA) has not issued a pronouncement equivalent to APES 205.

APES 315

Compilation of Financial Information

(Issued July 2008, revised 2009)

Issued by the Accounting Professional and Ethical Standards Board.

Note from the Institute of Chartered Accountants Australia

This note, prepared by the technical editor, is not part of APES 315.

Historical development

July 2008: APES 315 'Compilation of Financial Information' replaced the Miscellaneous Professional Statement APS 9 'Statement on Compilation of Financial Reports' and was effective from 1 January 2009. It applies to members in public practice when they compile financial information including financial statements. It is consistent with the International ISRS 4410 'Engagements to Compile Financial Statements'.

APS 9 had been issued in May 1996, operative from 1 January 1997 to replace the old accountants' disclaimer.

November 2009: APES 315 revised and reissued. This revision includes a new paragraph 3.6 on confidentiality and paragraph 3.5 on independence has become a Standard.

Contents

Paragraphs

Scope and application 1

Definitions 2

Fundamental responsibilities of Members in Public Practice 3

- Public interest

- Professional competence and due care

- Professional Independence

- Confidentiality

Objectives of a Compilation Engagement 4

Planning 5

General Purpose or Special Purpose Financial Statements 6

Defining the Terms of Engagement 7

Procedures 8

Misstatements 9

Documentation 10

Responsibility of the Client 11

Reporting on a Compilation Engagement 12

Communication of significant matters 13

Subsequent discovery of facts 14

Conformity with International Pronouncements

Appendix 1 Examples of Compilation Reports

1. Scope and application

1.1   Accounting Professional & Ethical Standards Board Limited (APESB) issues professional standard APES 315 Compilation of Financial Information (the Standard), which is effective for Engagements commencing on or after 01 January 2010. Earlier adoption of this Standard is permitted.

1.2   APES 315 sets the standards for Members in Public Practice who undertake Compilation Engagements in the provision of quality and ethical Professional Services. The mandatory requirements of this Standard are in **bold** type, preceded or followed by discussion or explanation in grey type. APES 315 should be read in conjunction with other professional duties of Members, and any legal obligations that may apply.

1.3   Members in Public Practice in Australia shall follow the mandatory requirements of APES 315 when they undertake Professional Services to Clients that are Compilation Engagements.

1.4   Members in Public Practice practising outside of Australia shall follow the provisions of APES 315 to the extent to which they are not prevented from so doing by specific requirements of local laws and/or regulations.

1.5   Members shall be familiar with relevant Professional Standards and guidance notes when providing Professional Services. All Members shall comply with the fundamental principles outlined in the Code.

1.6   The Standard is not intended to detract from any responsibilities which may be imposed by law or regulation.

1.7   All references to Professional Standards, guidance notes and legislation are references to those provisions as amended from time to time.

1.8   In applying the requirements outlined in APES 315, Members in Public Practice should be guided not merely by the words but also by the spirit of the Standard and the Code.

1.9 This Standard is directed towards Engagements to compile historical or prospective financial information.

1.10 The Standard should be applied to the extent practicable for Engagements to compile non-financial information.

1.11 This Standard is directed towards Members in Public Practice. However, Members in Business should apply this Standard to the extent practicable when they compile information for their employers especially in respect of regulatory reporting requirements and Compilation Reports prepared under ASIC Class Order CO 98/1417 *Audit relief for proprietary companies*.

2. Definitions

For the purpose of this Standard:

Applicable Financial Reporting Framework means in respect of an Engagement to prepare Financial Statements, the financial reporting framework adopted by Those Charged with Governance.

Australian Accounting Standards means the Accounting Standards (including Australian Accounting Interpretations) promulgated by the Australian Accounting Standards Board.

Client means an individual, firm, entity or organisation to whom or to which Professional Services are provided by a Member in Public Practice in respect of Engagements of either a recurring or demand nature.

Code means APES 110 *Code of Ethics for Professional Accountants*.

Compilation Engagement means an Engagement to compile financial information.

Compilation Report means a report prepared in accordance with this Standard.

Compiled Financial Information means a presentation of historical or prospective financial information in a specified form, without undertaking to express any assurance on the information. For the purposes of this Standard Compiled Financial Information includes Financial Statements.

Engagement means an agreement, whether written or otherwise, between a Member in Public Practice and a Client relating to the provision of Professional Services by a Member in Public Practice. However, consultations with a prospective Client prior to such agreement are not part of an Engagement.

Engagement Document means the document (i.e. letter, agreement or any other appropriate means) in which the Terms of Engagement are specified in a written form.

Financial Statements means a structured representation of historical or prospective financial information, which ordinarily includes explanatory notes, intended to communicate an entity's economic resources or obligations at a point in time or the changes therein for a period of time in accordance with a financial reporting framework. The term can refer to a complete set of Financial Statements, but it can also refer to a single financial statement, for example, a statement of financial position, or a statement of comprehensive income, and related explanatory notes. The requirements of the financial reporting framework determine the form and content of the Financial Statements and what constitutes a complete set of Financial Statements.

For the purposes of this Standard, the term financial report is considered to be equivalent to Financial Statements.

Firm means (a) A sole practitioner, partnership, corporation or other entity of professional accountants;

         (b) An entity that controls such parties;

         (c) An entity controlled by such parties; or

         (d) An Auditor-General's office or department.

General Purpose Financial Statements means those intended to meet the needs of users who are not in a position to require an entity to prepare reports tailored to their particular information needs.

APES

Independence means

> (a) Independence of mind - the state of mind that permits the provision of an opinion without being affected by influences that compromise professional judgment, allowing an individual to act with integrity, and exercise objectivity and professional scepticism; and

> (b) Independence in appearance - the avoidance of facts and circumstances that are so significant a reasonable and informed third party, having knowledge of all relevant information, including any safeguards applied, would reasonably conclude a Firm's, or a member of the Engagement team's, integrity, objectivity or professional scepticism had been compromised.

Member means a member of a professional body that has adopted this Standard as applicable to their membership as defined by that professional body.

Member in Business means a Member employed or engaged in an executive or non-executive capacity in such areas as commerce, industry, service, the public sector, education, the not for profit sector, regulatory bodies or professional bodies, or a Member contracted by such entities.

Member in Public Practice means a Member, irrespective of functional classification (e.g. audit, tax, or consulting) in a Firm that provides Professional Services. The term is also used to refer to a Firm of Members in Public Practice and means a practice entity as defined by the applicable professional body.

Professional Services means services requiring accountancy or related skills performed by a Member in Public Practice including accounting, auditing, taxation, management consulting and financial management services.

Professional Standards mean all Standards issued by Accounting Professional & Ethical Standards Board Limited and all professional and ethical requirements of the applicable professional body.

Special Purpose Financial Statements means Financial Statements other than General Purpose Financial Statements.

Terms of Engagement means the terms and conditions that are agreed between the Client and the Member in Public Practice for the Engagement.

Those Charged with Governance include those persons accountable for ensuring that the entity achieves its objectives with regard to reliability of financial reporting, effectiveness and efficiency of operations, compliance with applicable laws, and reporting to interested parties. Those Charged with Governance include management only when it performs such functions.

3. Fundamental responsibilities of Members in Public Practice

3.1   Members in Public Practice undertaking Compilation Engagements shall comply with Section 100 *Introduction and Fundamental Principles* of the Code and relevant legislation.

Public interest

3.2   In accordance with Section 100 *Introduction and Fundamental Principles* of the Code, Members in Public Practice shall observe and comply with their public interest obligations when they undertake Compilation Engagements.

Professional competence and due care

3.3   Members in Public Practice undertaking Compilation Engagements shall maintain professional competence and take due care in the performance of their work in accordance with Section 130 *Professional Competence and Due Care* of the Code.

Professional Independence

3.4   Independence is not a requirement for a Compilation Engagement.

3.5   Where a Member in Public Practice is not independent, the Member shall make a statement to that effect in the Compilation Report.

Confidentiality

3.6   In accordance with Section 140 *Confidentiality* of the Code, a Member in Public Practice who acquires confidential information in the course of a Compilation Engagement for a Client shall not use that information for any purpose other than the proper performance of that Engagement.

4. Objectives of a Compilation Engagement

4.1   The objective of a Compilation Engagement is for the Member in Public Practice to use accounting expertise, as opposed to auditing expertise, to collect, classify and summarise financial information. This will ordinarily entail reducing detailed data to a manageable and understandable form without a requirement to test the assertions underlying that information. The procedures employed are not designed and do not enable the Member to express any assurance on the financial information.

4.2   A Compilation Engagement may involve the preparation of Financial Statements (which may or may not be a complete set of Financial Statements). It may also involve compilation of other financial information without the compilation of Financial Statements.

4.3   Activities which fall outside the scope of APES 315 include:

(a)   preparation of a taxation return and financial information prepared solely for inclusion in the taxation return;

(b)   analysis of figures provided by a Client, in order to report to the Client. For example, providing advice on a Client's proposed purchase of another entity, using the other entity's Financial Statements;

(c)   relaying information to a Client, without collection, classification or summarisation of the information.

5. Planning

5.1   A Member in Public Practice shall plan the Compilation Engagement to ensure that the Engagement is conducted in accordance with this Standard and all applicable Professional Standards, laws and regulations.

6. General Purpose or Special Purpose Financial Statements

6.1   When undertaking a Compilation Engagement in respect of General Purpose Financial Statements or Special Purpose Financial Statements, a Member in Public Practice shall comply with the requirements of APES 205 *Conformity with Accounting Standards*.

7. Defining the Terms of Engagement

7.1   A Member in Public Practice shall document and communicate the Terms of Engagement in accordance with APES 305 *Terms of Engagement*.

7.2   In addition to the *General contents of an Engagement Document of* APES 305 *Terms of Engagement*, a Member in Public Practice should consider the following matters for inclusion in the Engagement Document:

(a)   nature of the Engagement including the fact that neither an audit nor a review will be carried out and that accordingly no assurance will be expressed;

(b)   fact that the Engagement cannot be relied upon to disclose errors, illegal acts or other irregularities, for example, fraud or defalcations that may exist;

(c)   nature of the information to be supplied by the Client;

(d)   in respect of prospective financial information, the basis of forecasting;

(e)   key assumptions relating to prospective financial information provided by the Client;

(f)   in the event that the Member makes assumptions in forecasts these assumptions will be brought to the Client's attention;

   (g)   fact that the Client is responsible for the accuracy and completeness of the information supplied to the Member and that an acknowledgement of such will be required in accordance with paragraph 11;

   (h)   basis of accounting on which the financial information is to be compiled and the fact that it, and any known departures there from, will be disclosed;

   (i)   requirement for General Purpose Financial Statements to be prepared in accordance with Australian Accounting Standards;

   (j)   intended use and distribution of the information, once compiled;

   (k)   form of any Compilation Report to be issued; and

   (l)   nature of any disclaimer or limitation of liability clause between the Member and the Client or the Member and any user of the Compiled Financial Information.

8. Procedures

8.1   A Member in Public Practice should obtain a general knowledge of the business and operations of the Client and should be familiar with the accounting principles and practices of the industry in which the Client operates and with the form and content of the financial information that are appropriate in the circumstances.

8.2   Other than as noted in this Standard, a Member in Public Practice is not ordinarily required to:

   (a)   make any inquiries of management to assess the reliability and completeness of the information provided;

   (b)   assess internal controls;

   (c)   verify any matters; or

   (d)   verify any explanations.

8.3   **A Member in Public Practice who, on reasonable grounds, forms the view that the information supplied by the Client is materially false or misleading or the Client has omitted material information, shall consider performing the procedures noted in paragraph 8.2 and request the Client to provide any additional information required to complete the Engagement.**

8.4   **If the Client refuses to provide the additional information as requested under paragraph 8.3 or, having performed the procedures noted in paragraph 8.2, the Member in Public Practice concludes that the information supplied by the Client is materially false or misleading, the Member shall consider the Firm's policies and procedures established in accordance with *Acceptance and Continuance of Client Relationships and Specific Engagements* of APES 320 *Quality Control for Firms* in determining whether to continue acting for the Client in a professional capacity.**

8.5   **A Member in Public Practice shall perform sufficient reviews of the Compilation Engagement in accordance with Section 130 *Professional Competence and Due Care* of the Code and the Firm's policies and procedures established in accordance with *Engagement Performance* of APES 320 *Quality Control for Firms* prior to issuing the Compilation Report.**

9. Misstatements

9.1   **A Member in Public Practice shall consider whether the Compiled Financial Information is appropriate in form and content and free from obvious material misstatements.**

9.2   In this Standard, material misstatements include the following:

   (a)   material mistakes in the application of the Applicable Financial Reporting Framework or an alternative financial reporting framework;

   (b)   non-disclosure of the financial reporting framework and any material departures there from; and

   (c)   non-disclosure of significant matters.

9.3 For the purpose of paragraph 9.2(a) examples of alternative financial reporting frameworks that may be applied to the presentation of Compiled Financial Information include, but are not limited to:

(a) a tax basis of accounting;

(b) the cash receipts and disbursements basis of accounting for cash flow information;

(c) the financial reporting provisions established by a regulator to meet the requirements of that regulator; and

(d) the financial reporting provisions of a contract, for example a loan agreement or trust deed.

9.4 **If a Member in Public Practice forms the view, on reasonable grounds, that there are material misstatements in the Compiled Financial Information, the Member shall take all reasonable steps to agree appropriate amendments with the Client.**

9.5 **If such amendments are not made as requested under paragraph 9.4 and the Compiled Financial Information is considered to be misleading, the Member in Public Practice shall consider the Firm's policies and procedures established in accordance with** *Acceptance and Continuance of Client Relationships and Specific Engagements* **of APES 320** *Quality Control for Firms* **in determining whether to continue acting for the Client in a professional capacity.**

10. Documentation

10.1 **A Member in Public Practice shall prepare working papers in accordance with this Standard that appropriately document the work performed, including aspects of the Compilation Engagement that have been provided in writing. The documentation prepared by the Member shall:**

(a) **provide a sufficient and appropriate record of the procedures performed for the Engagement;**

(b) **identify the sources of significant information the Member has used in the compilation of financial information; and**

(c) **demonstrate that the Engagement was carried out in accordance with this Standard and all other Professional Standards applicable to the Engagement, including policies and procedures established in accordance with APES 320** *Quality Control for Firms,* **and any applicable ethical, legal and regulatory requirements.**

11. Responsibility of the Client

11.1 **A Member in Public Practice who undertakes a Compilation Engagement in respect of General Purpose or Special Purpose Financial Statements, shall obtain an acknowledgment from the Client of its responsibility for the reliability, accuracy and completeness of the accounting records and disclosure to the Member of all material and relevant information.**

11.2 A Member in Public Practice who undertakes a Compilation Engagement other than those referred to in paragraph 11.1, should obtain an acknowledgement from the Client of its responsibility for the reliability, accuracy and completeness of the financial information and disclosure to the Member of all material and relevant information.

11.3 The acknowledgment referred to in paragraphs 11.1 and 11.2 may be provided by representations from the Client which cover the accuracy and completeness of the underlying accounting data and the complete disclosure of all material and relevant information to the Member in Public Practice.

12. Reporting on a Compilation Engagement

12.1 **When a Member in Public Practice prepares Compiled Financial Information, the Member shall issue a Compilation Report, subject to the requirements of paragraph 12.3, in circumstances where:**

(a) **the Member's name is identified with the Compiled Financial Information;**

(b) **the Compiled Financial Information is for external use; or**

(c) it is more likely than not that the intended user of the Compiled Financial Information may not understand the nature and scope of the Member's involvement with that information.

12.2 Generally when a Member in Public Practice compiles financial information for internal use by the Client, this Standard does not mandate the issue of a Compilation Report. In these circumstances the use of the Compiled Financial Information is restricted. The Member should include a reference that specifies that such Compiled Financial Information is "Restricted for internal use" or similar on each page of the Compiled Financial Information.

12.3 **Where the Client has engaged another Member in Public Practice to audit or review the Compiled Financial Information in accordance with Australian auditing standards applicable to audit or review Engagements, the Member in Public Practice undertaking the Compilation Engagement shall consider the need to issue a Compilation Report. Where the Member decides not to issue a Compilation Report the Member shall document the rationale for that decision.**

12.4 In the circumstances described in paragraph 12.3, if an audit or review report has been issued, this will override the need for the Member in Public Practice to issue a Compilation Report.

12.5 **Where the circumstances described in paragraph 12.3 apply and the scope of the Compilation Engagement extends to significant subject matter not covered under the audit or review Engagement, the Member in Public Practice shall issue a Compilation Report for the subject matter not covered under the audit or review Engagement.**

12.6 **Where a Member in Public Practice issues a Compilation Report in accordance with paragraph 12.1 or 12.5, the Compilation Report shall contain the following:**

(a) a title;

(b) an addressee;

(c) a statement that the Engagement was performed in accordance with this Standard;

(d) when relevant, a statement that the Member is not independent of the Client;

(e) identification of the Compiled Financial Information noting that it is based on the financial information provided by the Client (if applicable);

(f) the basis of any forecast information;

(g) key assumptions (applicable to prospective financial information only);

(h) a statement that the Client is responsible for the financial information compiled by the Member;

(i) a statement that neither an audit nor a review has been carried out and that accordingly no assurance is expressed on the Compiled Financial Information;

(j) if applicable, identification that the Member is reporting on a Special Purpose Financial Statement and the specific purpose for which it has been prepared;

(k) if applicable, a paragraph drawing attention to the disclosure of material departures from the applicable financial reporting framework;

(l) the date of the Compilation Report;

(m) the Member's or Firm's address;

(n) the Member's or Firm's name and signature;

(o) an appropriate disclaimer of liability.

12.7 **Where a Member in Public Practice issues a Compilation Report in accordance with paragraph 12.1 or 12.5, the financial information compiled by the Member shall contain a reference such as "Unaudited", "Compiled without Audit or Review", or "Refer to Compilation Report" on each page of the Compiled Financial Information.**

13. Communication of significant matters

13.1 A Member in Public Practice shall communicate to Those Charged with Governance of the Client any significant matters arising from the Compilation Engagement on a timely basis.

13.2 Communication should ordinarily be in writing. Where the communication occurs orally, a Member in Public Practice should record in the working papers a summary of the significant matters discussed.

13.3 If the Member in Public Practice obtains information that indicates that a material fraud, material misstatement or illegal act has occurred, the Member shall communicate these matters as soon as practicable to Those Charged with Governance of the Client.

13.4 Matters which should be communicated by the Member in Public Practice include:

    (a)   material misstatements identified during the Compilation Engagement and the appropriate amendments agreed with the Client in respect of the misstatements;

    (b)   additional information sought by the Member as a result of information supplied which contained material misstatements or was otherwise unsatisfactory;

    (c)   if additional information sought by the Member is not supplied:

        (i)   the effect that the lack of additional information may have on the Compiled Financial Information;

        (ii) the effect of the lack of additional information on the Member's report; and

        (iii) if appropriate, the fact that the Member proposes to withdraw from the Compilation Engagement as a result of the lack of additional information;

    (d)   any other matters that, in the Member's opinion, are significant in the context of the Compilation Engagement.

13.5 Where the Member in Public Practice obtains information that a material fraud, misstatement or illegal act has occurred and the Member has reason to believe that such an act is the result of actions of Those Charged with Governance of the Client, the Member shall consider the Firm's policies and procedures established in accordance with *Acceptance and Continuance of Client Relationships and Specific Engagements* of APES 320 *Quality Control for Firms* in determining whether to continue acting for the Client in a professional capacity.

14. Subsequent discovery of facts

14.1 Subsequent to the completion of the Compilation Engagement, the Member in Public Practice may become aware of facts that existed at the date of completion of the Compilation Engagement which may have caused the Member to believe that information supplied was materially false or misleading, had the Member been aware of such facts.

14.2 A Member in Public Practice shall consider the impact of subsequent discovery of facts on the Compiled Financial Information, discuss the matter with the Client, and take action appropriate in the circumstances. The Member shall document the reasons for the action taken by the Member.

14.3 If the Member in Public Practice believes that the Compiled Financial Information referred to in paragraph 14.2 needs to be revised, the Member shall take all reasonable steps to ensure that the Client takes the necessary steps to inform anyone who received the previously issued Compiled Financial Information of the situation.

14.4 When determining whether the Compiled Financial Information needs to be revised pursuant to paragraph 14.3, the Member in Public Practice should consider inter alia the duration of time between the issue of the Compiled Financial Information and the subsequent discovery of facts referred to in Paragraph 14.1, and the extent to which important decisions based on the Compiled Financial Information are still to be made.

14.5 If the Member in Public Practice becomes aware that the Client has not taken appropriate action in terms of paragraph 14.3, the Member shall notify Those Charged with Governance of the Client.

14.6 **If appropriate action is not taken by Those Charged with Governance of the Client, the Member in Public Practice shall consider the Firm's policies and procedures established in accordance with *Acceptance and Continuance of Client Relationships and Specific Engagements* of APES 320 *Quality Control for Firms* in determining whether to continue acting for the Client in a professional capacity.**

Examples of suggested Compilation Reports in respect of General Purpose and Special Purpose Financial Statements are contained in Appendix 1

Conformity with international pronouncements

APES 315 and ISRS 4410

The basic principles and essential procedures of APES 315 and of ISRS 4410 *Engagements to Compile Financial Statements* issued by the International Auditing and Assurance Standards Board (IAASB) are consistent in all material respects, except that the scope and application and definitions are unique to APES 315 and except for the matters noted below:

- When undertaking a Compilation Engagement in respect of General Purpose or Special Purpose Financial Statements, APES 315 mandates that the Member in Public Practice needs to comply with APES 205 *Conformity with Accounting Standards*;

- The objectives of the Compilation Engagement (paragraph 4.1) and the requirement for Member to obtain a general knowledge of the business (paragraph 8.1) are included as guidance in APES 315;

- APES 315 requires that the Terms of Engagement be documented in accordance with APES 305 *Terms of Engagement*;

- APES 315 requires that the Compilation Report needs to include, where applicable, identification that the Member in Public Practice is reporting on Special Purpose Financial Statements and the specific purpose for which they have been prepared;

- APES 315 requires the inclusion of an appropriate disclaimer of liability in the Compilation Report;

- APES 315 addresses communication of significant matters to Those Charged with Governance of the Client and procedures to follow when facts are subsequently discovered which indicate that the Compiled Financial Information is materially misstated;

- APES 315 does not include a sample engagement letter; and

- APES 315 includes an example of a Compilation Report for each of General Purpose Financial Statements and Special Purpose Financial Statements. ISRS 4410 only includes an example of a Compilation Report for Financial Statements.

Appendix 1
Examples of Compilation Reports

Example 1

Example Compilation Report on an engagement to compile General Purpose Financial Statements.

COMPILATION REPORT TO [name of entity] ("the Client")

We have compiled the accompanying general purpose financial statements of [name of entity], which comprise the statement of financial position as at [30 June 20XX], the statement of comprehensive income, statement of changes in equity and statement of cash flows for the year then ended, a summary of significant accounting policies and other explanatory notes. These have been prepared in accordance with the *(the financial reporting framework/basis of accounting)* described in Note 1 to the financial statements.

The Responsibility of [Those Charged with Governance]

[Those charged with governance] of [name of entity] are solely responsible for the information contained in the general purpose financial statements and have determined that the *(financial reporting framework/basis of accounting)* used is appropriate to meet their needs and for the purpose that the financial statements were prepared.

Our Responsibility

On the basis of information provided by [Those charged with governance] we have compiled the accompanying general purpose financial statements in accordance with the *(financial reporting framework/basis of accounting)* and APES 315 *Compilation of Financial Information*.

Our procedures use accounting expertise to collect, classify and summarise the financial information, which [those charged with governance] provided, in compiling the financial statements. Our procedures do not include verification or validation procedures. No audit or review has been performed and accordingly no assurance is expressed.

The general purpose financial statements were compiled exclusively for the benefit of [those charged with governance]. We do not accept responsibility to any other person for the contents of the general purpose financial statements.

Independence (if required)

We are not independent of *[name of entity]* because *(reasons why not independent, for example, the member is a close relative of a director or proprietor of the entity)*.

Address   Member or Firm
Date

Example 2

Example Compilation Report on an engagement to compile Special Purpose Financial Statements.

COMPILATION REPORT TO [name of entity] ("the Client")

We have compiled the accompanying special purpose financial statements of [name of entity], which comprise the [statement of financial position] as at [30 June 20XX], the [statement of comprehensive income], [statement of changes in equity] and [statement of cash flows] for the year then ended, a [summary of significant accounting policies] and [other explanatory notes]. The specific purpose for which the special purpose financial statements have been prepared is set out in Note [...].

The Responsibility of [Those Charged with Governance]

[Those charged with governance] of [name of entity] are solely responsible for the information contained in the special purpose financial statements and have determined that the *(financial reporting framework/basis of accounting)* used is appropriate to meet their needs and for the purpose that the financial statements were prepared.

Our Responsibility

On the basis of information provided by [Those charged with governance] we have compiled the accompanying special purpose financial statements in accordance with the *(financial reporting framework/basis of accounting)* and APES 315 *Compilation of Financial Information*.

Our procedures use accounting expertise to collect, classify and summarise the financial information, which [those charged with governance] provided, in compiling the financial statements. Our procedures do not include verification or validation procedures. No audit or review has been performed and accordingly no assurance is expressed.

The special purpose financial statements were compiled exclusively for the benefit of [those charged with governance]. We do not accept responsibility to any other person for the contents of the special purpose financial statements.

Independence (if required)

We are not independent of *[name of entity]* because *(reasons why not independent, for example, the member is a close relative of a director or proprietor of the entity).*

Address   Member or Firm

Date

Example 3

Example Compilation Report on an engagement to compile General Purpose Financial Statements with an additional paragraph that draws attention to a departure from the identified financial reporting framework.

COMPILATION REPORT TO [name of entity] ("the Client")

We have compiled the accompanying general purpose financial statements of [name of entity], which comprise the statement of financial position as at [30 June 20XX], the statement of comprehensive income, statement of changes in equity and statement of cash flows for the year then ended, a summary of significant accounting policies and other explanatory notes. These have been prepared in accordance with the *(the financial reporting framework/basis of accounting)* described in Note 1 to the financial statements.

The Responsibility of [Those Charged with Governance]

[Those charged with governance] of the [name of entity] are solely responsible for the information contained in the general purpose financial statements and have determined that the *(financial reporting framework/basis of accounting)* used is appropriate to meet their needs and for the purpose that the financial statements were prepared.

Our Responsibility

On the basis of information provided by [Those charged with governance] we have compiled the accompanying general purpose financial statements in accordance with the *(financial reporting framework/basis of accounting)* and APES 315 *Compilation of Financial Information*.

Our procedures use accounting expertise to collect, classify and summarise the financial information, which [those charged with governance] provided, in compiling the financial statements. Our procedures do not include verification or validation procedures. No audit or review has been performed and accordingly no assurance is expressed.

The general purpose financial statements were compiled exclusively for the benefit of [those charged with governance]. We do not accept responsibility to any other person for the contents of the general purpose financial statements.

Departure from the financial reporting framework

We draw attention to Note XX to the financial statements. [Those Charged with Governance] of [name of entity] have determined not to ...... (E.g. capitalise leases in accordance with Australian Accounting Standard AASB 117 *Leases*) which is a departure from the applicable financial reporting framework.

Address   Member or Firm

Date